Oxford Dictionary of
National Biography

Volume 16

Oxford Dictionary of National Biography

IN ASSOCIATION WITH
The British Academy

From the earliest times to the year 2000

Edited by
H. C. G. Matthew
and
Brian Harrison

Volume 16
Dewes–Dryland

OXFORD
UNIVERSITY PRESS

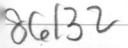

OXFORD
UNIVERSITY PRESS

Great Clarendon Street, Oxford OX2 6DP

Oxford University Press is a department of the University of Oxford.
It furthers the University's objective of excellence in research, scholarship,
and education by publishing worldwide in

Oxford New York

Auckland Bangkok Buenos Aires Cape Town
Chennai Dar es Salaam Delhi Hong Kong Istanbul Karachi
Kolkata Kuala Lumpur Madrid Melbourne Mexico City Mumbai Nairobi
São Paulo Shanghai Taipei Tokyo Toronto

Oxford is a registered trade mark of Oxford University Press
in the UK and in certain other countries

Published in the United States
by Oxford University Press Inc., New York

© Oxford University Press 2004

Illustrations © individual copyright holders as listed in
'Picture credits', and reproduced with permission

Database right Oxford University Press (maker)

First published 2004

British Library Cataloguing in Publication Data
Data available

Library of Congress Cataloging in Publication Data
Data available: for details see volume 1, p. iv

ISBN 0-19-861366-0 (this volume)
ISBN 0-19-861411-X (set of sixty volumes)

Text captured by Alliance Phototypesetters, Pondicherry
Illustrations reproduced and archived by
Alliance Graphics Ltd, UK
Typeset in OUP Swift by Interactive Sciences Limited, Gloucester
Printed in Great Britain on acid-free paper by
Butler and Tanner Ltd,
Frome, Somerset

LIST OF ABBREVIATIONS

1 General abbreviations

AB	bachelor of arts		BCnL	bachelor of canon law
ABC	Australian Broadcasting Corporation		BCom	bachelor of commerce
ABC TV	ABC Television		BD	bachelor of divinity
act.	active		BEd	bachelor of education
A$	Australian dollar		BEng	bachelor of engineering
AD	*anno domini*		bk *pl.* bks	book(s)
AFC	Air Force Cross		BL	bachelor of law / letters / literature
AIDS	acquired immune deficiency syndrome		BLitt	bachelor of letters
AK	Alaska		BM	bachelor of medicine
AL	Alabama		BMus	bachelor of music
A level	advanced level [examination]		BP	before present
ALS	associate of the Linnean Society		BP	British Petroleum
AM	master of arts		Bros.	Brothers
AMICE	associate member of the Institution of Civil Engineers		BS	(1) bachelor of science; (2) bachelor of surgery; (3) British standard
ANZAC	Australian and New Zealand Army Corps		BSc	bachelor of science
appx *pl.* appxs	appendix(es)		BSc (Econ.)	bachelor of science (economics)
AR	Arkansas		BSc (Eng.)	bachelor of science (engineering)
ARA	associate of the Royal Academy		bt	baronet
ARCA	associate of the Royal College of Art		BTh	bachelor of theology
ARCM	associate of the Royal College of Music		*bur.*	buried
ARCO	associate of the Royal College of Organists		C.	command [identifier for published parliamentary papers]
ARIBA	associate of the Royal Institute of British Architects		*c.*	*circa*
ARP	air-raid precautions		c.	*capitulum pl. capitula*: chapter(s)
ARRC	associate of the Royal Red Cross		CA	California
ARSA	associate of the Royal Scottish Academy		Cantab.	Cantabrigiensis
art.	article / item		cap.	*capitulum pl. capitula*: chapter(s)
ASC	Army Service Corps		CB	companion of the Bath
Asch	Austrian Schilling		CBE	commander of the Order of the British Empire
ASDIC	Antisubmarine Detection Investigation Committee		CBS	Columbia Broadcasting System
ATS	Auxiliary Territorial Service		cc	cubic centimetres
ATV	Associated Television		C$	Canadian dollar
Aug	August		CD	compact disc
AZ	Arizona		Cd	command [identifier for published parliamentary papers]
b.	born		CE	Common (*or* Christian) Era
BA	bachelor of arts		cent.	century
BA (Admin.)	bachelor of arts (administration)		cf.	compare
BAFTA	British Academy of Film and Television Arts		CH	Companion of Honour
BAO	bachelor of arts in obstetrics		chap.	chapter
bap.	baptized		ChB	bachelor of surgery
BBC	British Broadcasting Corporation / Company		CI	Imperial Order of the Crown of India
BC	before Christ		CIA	Central Intelligence Agency
BCE	before the common (*or* Christian) era		CID	Criminal Investigation Department
BCE	bachelor of civil engineering		CIE	companion of the Order of the Indian Empire
BCG	bacillus of Calmette and Guérin [inoculation against tuberculosis]		Cie	Compagnie
			CLit	companion of literature
BCh	bachelor of surgery		CM	master of surgery
BChir	bachelor of surgery		cm	centimetre(s)
BCL	bachelor of civil law			

Cmd	command [identifier for published parliamentary papers]	edn	edition
CMG	companion of the Order of St Michael and St George	EEC	European Economic Community
		EFTA	European Free Trade Association
Cmnd	command [identifier for published parliamentary papers]	EICS	East India Company Service
		EMI	Electrical and Musical Industries (Ltd)
CO	Colorado	Eng.	English
Co.	company	enl.	enlarged
co.	county	ENSA	Entertainments National Service Association
col. *pl.* cols.	column(s)	ep. *pl.* epp.	*epistola(e)*
Corp.	corporation	ESP	extra-sensory perception
CSE	certificate of secondary education	esp.	especially
CSI	companion of the Order of the Star of India	esq.	esquire
CT	Connecticut	est.	estimate / estimated
CVO	commander of the Royal Victorian Order	EU	European Union
cwt	hundredweight	ex	sold by (*lit.* out of)
$	(American) dollar	excl.	excludes / excluding
d.	(1) penny (pence); (2) died	exh.	exhibited
DBE	dame commander of the Order of the British Empire	exh. cat.	exhibition catalogue
		f. *pl.* ff.	following [pages]
DCH	diploma in child health	FA	Football Association
DCh	doctor of surgery	FACP	fellow of the American College of Physicians
DCL	doctor of civil law	facs.	facsimile
DCnL	doctor of canon law	FANY	First Aid Nursing Yeomanry
DCVO	dame commander of the Royal Victorian Order	FBA	fellow of the British Academy
DD	doctor of divinity	FBI	Federation of British Industries
DE	Delaware	FCS	fellow of the Chemical Society
Dec	December	Feb	February
dem.	demolished	FEng	fellow of the Fellowship of Engineering
DEng	doctor of engineering	FFCM	fellow of the Faculty of Community Medicine
des.	destroyed	FGS	fellow of the Geological Society
DFC	Distinguished Flying Cross	fig.	figure
DipEd	diploma in education	FIMechE	fellow of the Institution of Mechanical Engineers
DipPsych	diploma in psychiatry		
diss.	dissertation	FL	Florida
DL	deputy lieutenant	*fl.*	*floruit*
DLitt	doctor of letters	FLS	fellow of the Linnean Society
DLittCelt	doctor of Celtic letters	FM	frequency modulation
DM	(1) Deutschmark; (2) doctor of medicine; (3) doctor of musical arts	fol. *pl.* fols.	folio(s)
		Fr	French francs
DMus	doctor of music	Fr.	French
DNA	dioxyribonucleic acid	FRAeS	fellow of the Royal Aeronautical Society
doc.	document	FRAI	fellow of the Royal Anthropological Institute
DOL	doctor of oriental learning	FRAM	fellow of the Royal Academy of Music
DPH	diploma in public health	FRAS	(1) fellow of the Royal Asiatic Society; (2) fellow of the Royal Astronomical Society
DPhil	doctor of philosophy		
DPM	diploma in psychological medicine	FRCM	fellow of the Royal College of Music
DSC	Distinguished Service Cross	FRCO	fellow of the Royal College of Organists
DSc	doctor of science	FRCOG	fellow of the Royal College of Obstetricians and Gynaecologists
DSc (Econ.)	doctor of science (economics)		
DSc (Eng.)	doctor of science (engineering)	FRCP(C)	fellow of the Royal College of Physicians of Canada
DSM	Distinguished Service Medal		
DSO	companion of the Distinguished Service Order	FRCP (Edin.)	fellow of the Royal College of Physicians of Edinburgh
DSocSc	doctor of social science		
DTech	doctor of technology	FRCP (Lond.)	fellow of the Royal College of Physicians of London
DTh	doctor of theology		
DTM	diploma in tropical medicine	FRCPath	fellow of the Royal College of Pathologists
DTMH	diploma in tropical medicine and hygiene	FRCPsych	fellow of the Royal College of Psychiatrists
DU	doctor of the university	FRCS	fellow of the Royal College of Surgeons
DUniv	doctor of the university	FRGS	fellow of the Royal Geographical Society
dwt	pennyweight	FRIBA	fellow of the Royal Institute of British Architects
EC	European Community	FRICS	fellow of the Royal Institute of Chartered Surveyors
ed. *pl.* eds.	edited / edited by / editor(s)		
Edin.	Edinburgh	FRS	fellow of the Royal Society
		FRSA	fellow of the Royal Society of Arts

FRSCM	fellow of the Royal School of Church Music	ISO	companion of the Imperial Service Order
FRSE	fellow of the Royal Society of Edinburgh	It.	Italian
FRSL	fellow of the Royal Society of Literature	ITA	Independent Television Authority
FSA	fellow of the Society of Antiquaries	ITV	Independent Television
ft	foot *pl.* feet	Jan	January
FTCL	fellow of Trinity College of Music, London	JP	justice of the peace
ft-lb per min.	foot-pounds per minute [unit of horsepower]	jun.	junior
FZS	fellow of the Zoological Society	KB	knight of the Order of the Bath
GA	Georgia	KBE	knight commander of the Order of the British Empire
GBE	knight or dame grand cross of the Order of the British Empire	KC	king's counsel
GCB	knight grand cross of the Order of the Bath	kcal	kilocalorie
GCE	general certificate of education	KCB	knight commander of the Order of the Bath
GCH	knight grand cross of the Royal Guelphic Order	KCH	knight commander of the Royal Guelphic Order
GCHQ	government communications headquarters	KCIE	knight commander of the Order of the Indian Empire
GCIE	knight grand commander of the Order of the Indian Empire	KCMG	knight commander of the Order of St Michael and St George
GCMG	knight or dame grand cross of the Order of St Michael and St George	KCSI	knight commander of the Order of the Star of India
GCSE	general certificate of secondary education	KCVO	knight commander of the Royal Victorian Order
GCSI	knight grand commander of the Order of the Star of India	keV	kilo-electron-volt
GCStJ	bailiff or dame grand cross of the order of St John of Jerusalem	KG	knight of the Order of the Garter
		KGB	[Soviet committee of state security]
GCVO	knight or dame grand cross of the Royal Victorian Order	KH	knight of the Royal Guelphic Order
		KLM	Koninklijke Luchtvaart Maatschappij (Royal Dutch Air Lines)
GEC	General Electric Company	km	kilometre(s)
Ger.	German	KP	knight of the Order of St Patrick
GI	government (*or* general) issue	KS	Kansas
GMT	Greenwich mean time	KT	knight of the Order of the Thistle
GP	general practitioner	kt	knight
GPU	[Soviet special police unit]	KY	Kentucky
GSO	general staff officer	£	pound(s) sterling
Heb.	Hebrew	£E	Egyptian pound
HEICS	Honourable East India Company Service	L	lira *pl.* lire
HI	Hawaii	l. *pl.* ll.	line(s)
HIV	human immunodeficiency virus	LA	Lousiana
HK$	Hong Kong dollar	LAA	light anti-aircraft
HM	his / her majesty('s)	LAH	licentiate of the Apothecaries' Hall, Dublin
HMAS	his / her majesty's Australian ship	Lat.	Latin
HMNZS	his / her majesty's New Zealand ship	lb	pound(s), unit of weight
HMS	his / her majesty's ship	LDS	licence in dental surgery
HMSO	His / Her Majesty's Stationery Office	*lit.*	literally
HMV	His Master's Voice	LittB	bachelor of letters
Hon.	Honourable	LittD	doctor of letters
hp	horsepower	LKQCPI	licentiate of the King and Queen's College of Physicians, Ireland
hr	hour(s)	LLA	lady literate in arts
HRH	his / her royal highness	LLB	bachelor of laws
HTV	Harlech Television	LLD	doctor of laws
IA	Iowa	LLM	master of laws
ibid.	*ibidem*: in the same place	LM	licentiate in midwifery
ICI	Imperial Chemical Industries (Ltd)	LP	long-playing record
ID	Idaho	LRAM	licentiate of the Royal Academy of Music
IL	Illinois	LRCP	licentiate of the Royal College of Physicians
illus.	illustration	LRCPS (Glasgow)	licentiate of the Royal College of Physicians and Surgeons of Glasgow
illustr.	illustrated		
IN	Indiana	LRCS	licentiate of the Royal College of Surgeons
in.	inch(es)	LSA	licentiate of the Society of Apothecaries
Inc.	Incorporated	LSD	lysergic acid diethylamide
incl.	includes / including	LVO	lieutenant of the Royal Victorian Order
IOU	I owe you	M. *pl.* MM.	Monsieur *pl.* Messieurs
IQ	intelligence quotient	m	metre(s)
Ir£	Irish pound		
IRA	Irish Republican Army		

m. *pl.* mm.	membrane(s)
MA	(1) Massachusetts; (2) master of arts
MAI	master of engineering
MB	bachelor of medicine
MBA	master of business administration
MBE	member of the Order of the British Empire
MC	Military Cross
MCC	Marylebone Cricket Club
MCh	master of surgery
MChir	master of surgery
MCom	master of commerce
MD	(1) doctor of medicine; (2) Maryland
MDMA	methylenedioxymethamphetamine
ME	Maine
MEd	master of education
MEng	master of engineering
MEP	member of the European parliament
MG	Morris Garages
MGM	Metro-Goldwyn-Mayer
Mgr	Monsignor
MI	(1) Michigan; (2) military intelligence
MI1c	[secret intelligence department]
MI5	[military intelligence department]
MI6	[secret intelligence department]
MI9	[secret escape service]
MICE	member of the Institution of Civil Engineers
MIEE	member of the Institution of Electrical Engineers
min.	minute(s)
Mk	mark
ML	(1) licentiate of medicine; (2) master of laws
MLitt	master of letters
Mlle	Mademoiselle
mm	millimetre(s)
Mme	Madame
MN	Minnesota
MO	Missouri
MOH	medical officer of health
MP	member of parliament
m.p.h.	miles per hour
MPhil	master of philosophy
MRCP	member of the Royal College of Physicians
MRCS	member of the Royal College of Surgeons
MRCVS	member of the Royal College of Veterinary Surgeons
MRIA	member of the Royal Irish Academy
MS	(1) master of science; (2) Mississippi
MS *pl.* MSS	manuscript(s)
MSc	master of science
MSc (Econ.)	master of science (economics)
MT	Montana
MusB	bachelor of music
MusBac	bachelor of music
MusD	doctor of music
MV	motor vessel
MVO	member of the Royal Victorian Order
n. *pl.* nn.	note(s)
NAAFI	Navy, Army, and Air Force Institutes
NASA	National Aeronautics and Space Administration
NATO	North Atlantic Treaty Organization
NBC	National Broadcasting Corporation
NC	North Carolina
NCO	non-commissioned officer
ND	North Dakota
n.d.	no date
NE	Nebraska
nem. con.	*nemine contradicente*: unanimously
new ser.	new series
NH	New Hampshire
NHS	National Health Service
NJ	New Jersey
NKVD	[Soviet people's commissariat for internal affairs]
NM	New Mexico
nm	nanometre(s)
no. *pl.* nos.	number(s)
Nov	November
n.p.	no place [of publication]
NS	new style
NV	Nevada
NY	New York
NZBS	New Zealand Broadcasting Service
OBE	officer of the Order of the British Empire
obit.	obituary
Oct	October
OCTU	officer cadets training unit
OECD	Organization for Economic Co-operation and Development
OEEC	Organization for European Economic Co-operation
OFM	order of Friars Minor [Franciscans]
OFMCap	Ordine Frati Minori Cappucini: member of the Capuchin order
OH	Ohio
OK	Oklahoma
O level	ordinary level [examination]
OM	Order of Merit
OP	order of Preachers [Dominicans]
op. *pl.* opp.	opus *pl.* opera
OPEC	Organization of Petroleum Exporting Countries
OR	Oregon
orig.	original
OS	old style
OSB	Order of St Benedict
OTC	Officers' Training Corps
OWS	Old Watercolour Society
Oxon.	Oxoniensis
p. *pl.* pp.	page(s)
PA	Pennsylvania
p.a.	per annum
para.	paragraph
PAYE	pay as you earn
pbk *pl.* pbks	paperback(s)
per.	[during the] period
PhD	doctor of philosophy
pl.	(1) plate(s); (2) plural
priv. coll.	private collection
pt *pl.* pts	part(s)
pubd	published
PVC	polyvinyl chloride
q. *pl.* qq.	(1) question(s); (2) quire(s)
QC	queen's counsel
R	rand
R.	Rex / Regina
r	recto
r.	reigned / ruled
RA	Royal Academy / Royal Academician

RAC	Royal Automobile Club
RAF	Royal Air Force
RAFVR	Royal Air Force Volunteer Reserve
RAM	[member of the] Royal Academy of Music
RAMC	Royal Army Medical Corps
RCA	Royal College of Art
RCNC	Royal Corps of Naval Constructors
RCOG	Royal College of Obstetricians and Gynaecologists
RDI	royal designer for industry
RE	Royal Engineers
repr. *pl.* reprs.	reprint(s) / reprinted
repro.	reproduced
rev.	revised / revised by / reviser / revision
Revd	Reverend
RHA	Royal Hibernian Academy
RI	(1) Rhode Island; (2) Royal Institute of Painters in Water-Colours
RIBA	Royal Institute of British Architects
RIN	Royal Indian Navy
RM	Reichsmark
RMS	Royal Mail steamer
RN	Royal Navy
RNA	ribonucleic acid
RNAS	Royal Naval Air Service
RNR	Royal Naval Reserve
RNVR	Royal Naval Volunteer Reserve
RO	Record Office
r.p.m.	revolutions per minute
RRS	royal research ship
Rs	rupees
RSA	(1) Royal Scottish Academician; (2) Royal Society of Arts
RSPCA	Royal Society for the Prevention of Cruelty to Animals
Rt Hon.	Right Honourable
Rt Revd	Right Reverend
RUC	Royal Ulster Constabulary
Russ.	Russian
RWS	Royal Watercolour Society
S4C	Sianel Pedwar Cymru
s.	shilling(s)
s.a.	*sub anno*: under the year
SABC	South African Broadcasting Corporation
SAS	Special Air Service
SC	South Carolina
ScD	doctor of science
S$	Singapore dollar
SD	South Dakota
sec.	second(s)
sel.	selected
sen.	senior
Sept	September
ser.	series
SHAPE	supreme headquarters allied powers, Europe
SIDRO	Société Internationale d'Énergie Hydro-Électrique
sig. *pl.* sigs.	signature(s)
sing.	singular
SIS	Secret Intelligence Service
SJ	Society of Jesus
Skr	Swedish krona
Span.	Spanish
SPCK	Society for Promoting Christian Knowledge
SS	(1) Santissimi; (2) Schutzstaffel; (3) steam ship
STB	bachelor of theology
STD	doctor of theology
STM	master of theology
STP	doctor of theology
supp.	supposedly
suppl. *pl.* suppls.	supplement(s)
s.v.	*sub verbo / sub voce*: under the word / heading
SY	steam yacht
TA	Territorial Army
TASS	[Soviet news agency]
TB	tuberculosis (*lit.* tubercle bacillus)
TD	(1) *teachtaí dála* (member of the Dáil); (2) territorial decoration
TN	Tennessee
TNT	trinitrotoluene
trans.	translated / translated by / translation / translator
TT	tourist trophy
TUC	Trades Union Congress
TX	Texas
U-boat	*Unterseeboot*: submarine
Ufa	Universum-Film AG
UMIST	University of Manchester Institute of Science and Technology
UN	United Nations
UNESCO	United Nations Educational, Scientific, and Cultural Organization
UNICEF	United Nations International Children's Emergency Fund
unpubd	unpublished
USS	United States ship
UT	Utah
v	verso
v.	versus
VA	Virginia
VAD	Voluntary Aid Detachment
VC	Victoria Cross
VE-day	victory in Europe day
Ven.	Venerable
VJ-day	victory over Japan day
vol. *pl.* vols.	volume(s)
VT	Vermont
WA	Washington [state]
WAAC	Women's Auxiliary Army Corps
WAAF	Women's Auxiliary Air Force
WEA	Workers' Educational Association
WHO	World Health Organization
WI	Wisconsin
WRAF	Women's Royal Air Force
WRNS	Women's Royal Naval Service
WV	West Virginia
WVS	Women's Voluntary Service
WY	Wyoming
¥	yen
YMCA	Young Men's Christian Association
YWCA	Young Women's Christian Association

2 Institution abbreviations

All Souls Oxf.	All Souls College, Oxford
AM Oxf.	Ashmolean Museum, Oxford
Balliol Oxf.	Balliol College, Oxford
BBC WAC	BBC Written Archives Centre, Reading
Beds. & Luton ARS	Bedfordshire and Luton Archives and Record Service, Bedford
Berks. RO	Berkshire Record Office, Reading
BFI	British Film Institute, London
BFI NFTVA	British Film Institute, London, National Film and Television Archive
BGS	British Geological Survey, Keyworth, Nottingham
Birm. CA	Birmingham Central Library, Birmingham City Archives
Birm. CL	Birmingham Central Library
BL	British Library, London
BL NSA	British Library, London, National Sound Archive
BL OIOC	British Library, London, Oriental and India Office Collections
BLPES	London School of Economics and Political Science, British Library of Political and Economic Science
BM	British Museum, London
Bodl. Oxf.	Bodleian Library, Oxford
Bodl. RH	Bodleian Library of Commonwealth and African Studies at Rhodes House, Oxford
Borth. Inst.	Borthwick Institute of Historical Research, University of York
Boston PL	Boston Public Library, Massachusetts
Bristol RO	Bristol Record Office
Bucks. RLSS	Buckinghamshire Records and Local Studies Service, Aylesbury
CAC Cam.	Churchill College, Cambridge, Churchill Archives Centre
Cambs. AS	Cambridgeshire Archive Service
CCC Cam.	Corpus Christi College, Cambridge
CCC Oxf.	Corpus Christi College, Oxford
Ches. & Chester ALSS	Cheshire and Chester Archives and Local Studies Service
Christ Church Oxf.	Christ Church, Oxford
Christies	Christies, London
City Westm. AC	City of Westminster Archives Centre, London
CKS	Centre for Kentish Studies, Maidstone
CLRO	Corporation of London Records Office
Coll. Arms	College of Arms, London
Col. U.	Columbia University, New York
Cornwall RO	Cornwall Record Office, Truro
Courtauld Inst.	Courtauld Institute of Art, London
CUL	Cambridge University Library
Cumbria AS	Cumbria Archive Service
Derbys. RO	Derbyshire Record Office, Matlock
Devon RO	Devon Record Office, Exeter
Dorset RO	Dorset Record Office, Dorchester
Duke U.	Duke University, Durham, North Carolina
Duke U., Perkins L.	Duke University, Durham, North Carolina, William R. Perkins Library
Durham Cath. CL	Durham Cathedral, chapter library
Durham RO	Durham Record Office
DWL	Dr Williams's Library, London
Essex RO	Essex Record Office
E. Sussex RO	East Sussex Record Office, Lewes
Eton	Eton College, Berkshire
FM Cam.	Fitzwilliam Museum, Cambridge
Folger	Folger Shakespeare Library, Washington, DC
Garr. Club	Garrick Club, London
Girton Cam.	Girton College, Cambridge
GL	Guildhall Library, London
Glos. RO	Gloucestershire Record Office, Gloucester
Gon. & Caius Cam.	Gonville and Caius College, Cambridge
Gov. Art Coll.	Government Art Collection
GS Lond.	Geological Society of London
Hants. RO	Hampshire Record Office, Winchester
Harris Man. Oxf.	Harris Manchester College, Oxford
Harvard TC	Harvard Theatre Collection, Harvard University, Cambridge, Massachusetts, Nathan Marsh Pusey Library
Harvard U.	Harvard University, Cambridge, Massachusetts
Harvard U., Houghton L.	Harvard University, Cambridge, Massachusetts, Houghton Library
Herefs. RO	Herefordshire Record Office, Hereford
Herts. ALS	Hertfordshire Archives and Local Studies, Hertford
Hist. Soc. Penn.	Historical Society of Pennsylvania, Philadelphia
HLRO	House of Lords Record Office, London
Hult. Arch.	Hulton Archive, London and New York
Hunt. L.	Huntington Library, San Marino, California
ICL	Imperial College, London
Inst. CE	Institution of Civil Engineers, London
Inst. EE	Institution of Electrical Engineers, London
IWM	Imperial War Museum, London
IWM FVA	Imperial War Museum, London, Film and Video Archive
IWM SA	Imperial War Museum, London, Sound Archive
JRL	John Rylands University Library of Manchester
King's AC Cam.	King's College Archives Centre, Cambridge
King's Cam.	King's College, Cambridge
King's Lond.	King's College, London
King's Lond., Liddell Hart C.	King's College, London, Liddell Hart Centre for Military Archives
Lancs. RO	Lancashire Record Office, Preston
L. Cong.	Library of Congress, Washington, DC
Leics. RO	Leicestershire, Leicester, and Rutland Record Office, Leicester
Lincs. Arch.	Lincolnshire Archives, Lincoln
Linn. Soc.	Linnean Society of London
LMA	London Metropolitan Archives
LPL	Lambeth Palace, London
Lpool RO	Liverpool Record Office and Local Studies Service
LUL	London University Library
Magd. Cam.	Magdalene College, Cambridge
Magd. Oxf.	Magdalen College, Oxford
Man. City Gall.	Manchester City Galleries
Man. CL	Manchester Central Library
Mass. Hist. Soc.	Massachusetts Historical Society, Boston
Merton Oxf.	Merton College, Oxford
MHS Oxf.	Museum of the History of Science, Oxford
Mitchell L., Glas.	Mitchell Library, Glasgow
Mitchell L., NSW	State Library of New South Wales, Sydney, Mitchell Library
Morgan L.	Pierpont Morgan Library, New York
NA Canada	National Archives of Canada, Ottawa
NA Ire.	National Archives of Ireland, Dublin
NAM	National Army Museum, London
NA Scot.	National Archives of Scotland, Edinburgh
News Int. RO	News International Record Office, London
NG Ire.	National Gallery of Ireland, Dublin

NG Scot.	National Gallery of Scotland, Edinburgh
NHM	Natural History Museum, London
NL Aus.	National Library of Australia, Canberra
NL Ire.	National Library of Ireland, Dublin
NL NZ	National Library of New Zealand, Wellington
NL NZ, Turnbull L.	National Library of New Zealand, Wellington, Alexander Turnbull Library
NL Scot.	National Library of Scotland, Edinburgh
NL Wales	National Library of Wales, Aberystwyth
NMG Wales	National Museum and Gallery of Wales, Cardiff
NMM	National Maritime Museum, London
Norfolk RO	Norfolk Record Office, Norwich
Northants. RO	Northamptonshire Record Office, Northampton
Northumbd RO	Northumberland Record Office
Notts. Arch.	Nottinghamshire Archives, Nottingham
NPG	National Portrait Gallery, London
NRA	National Archives, London, Historical Manuscripts Commission, National Register of Archives
Nuffield Oxf.	Nuffield College, Oxford
N. Yorks. CRO	North Yorkshire County Record Office, Northallerton
NYPL	New York Public Library
Oxf. UA	Oxford University Archives
Oxf. U. Mus. NH	Oxford University Museum of Natural History
Oxon. RO	Oxfordshire Record Office, Oxford
Pembroke Cam.	Pembroke College, Cambridge
PRO	National Archives, London, Public Record Office
PRO NIre.	Public Record Office for Northern Ireland, Belfast
Pusey Oxf.	Pusey House, Oxford
RA	Royal Academy of Arts, London
Ransom HRC	Harry Ransom Humanities Research Center, University of Texas, Austin
RAS	Royal Astronomical Society, London
RBG Kew	Royal Botanic Gardens, Kew, London
RCP Lond.	Royal College of Physicians of London
RCS Eng.	Royal College of Surgeons of England, London
RGS	Royal Geographical Society, London
RIBA	Royal Institute of British Architects, London
RIBA BAL	Royal Institute of British Architects, London, British Architectural Library
Royal Arch.	Royal Archives, Windsor Castle, Berkshire [by gracious permission of her majesty the queen]
Royal Irish Acad.	Royal Irish Academy, Dublin
Royal Scot. Acad.	Royal Scottish Academy, Edinburgh
RS	Royal Society, London
RSA	Royal Society of Arts, London
RS Friends, Lond.	Religious Society of Friends, London
St Ant. Oxf.	St Antony's College, Oxford
St John Cam.	St John's College, Cambridge
S. Antiquaries, Lond.	Society of Antiquaries of London
Sci. Mus.	Science Museum, London
Scot. NPG	Scottish National Portrait Gallery, Edinburgh
Scott Polar RI	University of Cambridge, Scott Polar Research Institute
Sheff. Arch.	Sheffield Archives
Shrops. RRC	Shropshire Records and Research Centre, Shrewsbury
SOAS	School of Oriental and African Studies, London
Som. ARS	Somerset Archive and Record Service, Taunton
Staffs. RO	Staffordshire Record Office, Stafford
Suffolk RO	Suffolk Record Office
Surrey HC	Surrey History Centre, Woking
TCD	Trinity College, Dublin
Trinity Cam.	Trinity College, Cambridge
U. Aberdeen	University of Aberdeen
U. Birm.	University of Birmingham
U. Birm. L.	University of Birmingham Library
U. Cal.	University of California
U. Cam.	University of Cambridge
UCL	University College, London
U. Durham	University of Durham
U. Durham L.	University of Durham Library
U. Edin.	University of Edinburgh
U. Edin., New Coll.	University of Edinburgh, New College
U. Edin., New Coll. L.	University of Edinburgh, New College Library
U. Edin. L.	University of Edinburgh Library
U. Glas.	University of Glasgow
U. Glas. L.	University of Glasgow Library
U. Hull	University of Hull
U. Hull, Brynmor Jones L.	University of Hull, Brynmor Jones Library
U. Leeds	University of Leeds
U. Leeds, Brotherton L.	University of Leeds, Brotherton Library
U. Lond.	University of London
U. Lpool	University of Liverpool
U. Lpool L.	University of Liverpool Library
U. Mich.	University of Michigan, Ann Arbor
U. Mich., Clements L.	University of Michigan, Ann Arbor, William L. Clements Library
U. Newcastle	University of Newcastle upon Tyne
U. Newcastle, Robinson L.	University of Newcastle upon Tyne, Robinson Library
U. Nott.	University of Nottingham
U. Nott. L.	University of Nottingham Library
U. Oxf.	University of Oxford
U. Reading	University of Reading
U. Reading L.	University of Reading Library
U. St Andr.	University of St Andrews
U. St Andr. L.	University of St Andrews Library
U. Southampton	University of Southampton
U. Southampton L.	University of Southampton Library
U. Sussex	University of Sussex, Brighton
U. Texas	University of Texas, Austin
U. Wales	University of Wales
U. Warwick Mod. RC	University of Warwick, Coventry, Modern Records Centre
V&A	Victoria and Albert Museum, London
V&A NAL	Victoria and Albert Museum, London, National Art Library
Warks. CRO	Warwickshire County Record Office, Warwick
Wellcome L.	Wellcome Library for the History and Understanding of Medicine, London
Westm. DA	Westminster Diocesan Archives, London
Wilts. & Swindon RO	Wiltshire and Swindon Record Office, Trowbridge
Worcs. RO	Worcestershire Record Office, Worcester
W. Sussex RO	West Sussex Record Office, Chichester
W. Yorks. AS	West Yorkshire Archive Service
Yale U.	Yale University, New Haven, Connecticut
Yale U., Beinecke L.	Yale University, New Haven, Connecticut, Beinecke Rare Book and Manuscript Library
Yale U. CBA	Yale University, New Haven, Connecticut, Yale Center for British Art

3 Bibliographic abbreviations

Adams, *Drama* — W. D. Adams, *A dictionary of the drama*, 1: *A–G* (1904); 2: *H–Z* (1956) [vol. 2 microfilm only]

AFM — J O'Donovan, ed. and trans., *Annala rioghachta Eireann / Annals of the kingdom of Ireland by the four masters*, 7 vols. (1848–51); 2nd edn (1856); 3rd edn (1990)

Allibone, *Dict.* — S. A. Allibone, *A critical dictionary of English literature and British and American authors*, 3 vols. (1859–71); suppl. by J. F. Kirk, 2 vols. (1891)

ANB — J. A. Garraty and M. C. Carnes, eds., *American national biography*, 24 vols. (1999)

Anderson, *Scot. nat.* — W. Anderson, *The Scottish nation, or, The surnames, families, literature, honours, and biographical history of the people of Scotland*, 3 vols. (1859–63)

Ann. mon. — H. R. Luard, ed., *Annales monastici*, 5 vols., Rolls Series, 36 (1864–9)

Ann. Ulster — S. Mac Airt and G. Mac Niocaill, eds., *Annals of Ulster (to AD 1131)* (1983)

APC — *Acts of the privy council of England*, new ser., 46 vols. (1890–1964)

APS — *The acts of the parliaments of Scotland*, 12 vols. in 13 (1814–75)

Arber, *Regs. Stationers* — F. Arber, ed., *A transcript of the registers of the Company of Stationers of London, 1554–1640 AD*, 5 vols. (1875–94)

ArchR — *Architectural Review*

ASC — D. Whitelock, D. C. Douglas, and S. I. Tucker, ed. and trans., *The Anglo-Saxon Chronicle: a revised translation* (1961)

AS chart. — P. H. Sawyer, *Anglo-Saxon charters: an annotated list and bibliography*, Royal Historical Society Guides and Handbooks (1968)

AusDB — D. Pike and others, eds., *Australian dictionary of biography*, 16 vols. (1966–2002)

Baker, *Serjeants* — J. H. Baker, *The order of serjeants at law*, SeldS, suppl. ser., 5 (1984)

Bale, *Cat.* — J. Bale, *Scriptorum illustrium Maioris Brytannie, quam nunc Angliam et Scotiam vocant: catalogus*, 2 vols. in 1 (Basel, 1557–9); facs. edn (1971)

Bale, *Index* — J. Bale, *Index Britanniae scriptorum*, ed. R. L. Poole and M. Bateson (1902); facs. edn (1990)

BBCS — *Bulletin of the Board of Celtic Studies*

BDMBR — J. O. Baylen and N. J. Gossman, eds., *Biographical dictionary of modern British radicals*, 3 vols. in 4 (1979–88)

Bede, *Hist. eccl.* — *Bede's Ecclesiastical history of the English people*, ed. and trans. B. Colgrave and R. A. B. Mynors, OMT (1969); repr. (1991)

Bénézit, *Dict.* — E. Bénézit, *Dictionnaire critique et documentaire des peintres, sculpteurs, dessinateurs et graveurs*, 3 vols. (Paris, 1911–23); new edn, 8 vols. (1948–66), repr. (1966); 3rd edn, rev. and enl., 10 vols. (1976); 4th edn, 14 vols. (1999)

BIHR — *Bulletin of the Institute of Historical Research*

Birch, *Seals* — W. de Birch, *Catalogue of seals in the department of manuscripts in the British Museum*, 6 vols. (1887–1900)

Bishop Burnet's History — *Bishop Burnet's History of his own time*, ed. M. J. Routh, 2nd edn, 6 vols. (1833)

Blackwood — *Blackwood's [Edinburgh] Magazine*, 328 vols. (1817–1980)

Blain, Clements & Grundy, *Feminist comp.* — V. Blain, P. Clements, and I. Grundy, eds., *The feminist companion to literature in English* (1990)

BL cat. — *The British Library general catalogue of printed books* [in 360 vols. with suppls., also CD-ROM and online]

BMJ — *British Medical Journal*

Boase & Courtney, *Bibl. Corn.* — G. C. Boase and W. P. Courtney, *Bibliotheca Cornubiensis: a catalogue of the writings … of Cornishmen*, 3 vols. (1874–82)

Boase, *Mod. Eng. biog.* — F. Boase, *Modern English biography: containing many thousand concise memoirs of persons who have died since the year 1850*, 6 vols. (privately printed, Truro, 1892–1921); repr. (1965)

Boswell, *Life* — *Boswell's Life of Johnson: together with Journal of a tour to the Hebrides and Johnson's Diary of a journey into north Wales*, ed. G. B. Hill, enl. edn, rev. L. F. Powell, 6 vols. (1934–50); 2nd edn (1964); repr. (1971)

Brown & Stratton, *Brit. mus.* — J. D. Brown and S. S. Stratton, *British musical biography* (1897)

Bryan, *Painters* — M. Bryan, *A biographical and critical dictionary of painters and engravers*, 2 vols. (1816); new edn, ed. G. Stanley (1849); new edn, ed. R. E. Graves and W. Armstrong, 2 vols. (1886–9); [4th edn], ed. G. C. Williamson, 5 vols. (1903–5) [various reprs.]

Burke, *Gen. GB* — J. Burke, *A genealogical and heraldic history of the commoners of Great Britain and Ireland*, 4 vols. (1833–8); new edn as *A genealogical and heraldic dictionary of the landed gentry of Great Britain and Ireland*, 3 vols. [1843–9] [many later edns]

Burke, *Gen. Ire.* — J. B. Burke, *A genealogical and heraldic history of the landed gentry of Ireland* (1899); 2nd edn (1904); 3rd edn (1912); 4th edn (1958); 5th edn as *Burke's Irish family records* (1976)

Burke, *Peerage* — J. Burke, *A general [later edns A genealogical] and heraldic dictionary of the peerage and baronetage of the United Kingdom* [later edns *the British empire*] (1829–)

Burney, *Hist. mus.* — C. Burney, *A general history of music, from the earliest ages to the present period*, 4 vols. (1776–89)

Burtchaell & Sadleir, *Alum. Dubl.* — G. D. Burtchaell and T. U. Sadleir, *Alumni Dublinenses: a register of the students, graduates, and provosts of Trinity College* (1924); [2nd edn], with suppl., in 2 pts (1935)

Calamy rev. — A. G. Matthews, *Calamy revised* (1934); repr. (1988)

CCI — *Calendar of confirmations and inventories granted and given up in the several commissariots of Scotland* (1876–)

CClR — *Calendar of the close rolls preserved in the Public Record Office*, 47 vols. (1892–1963)

CDS — J. Bain, ed., *Calendar of documents relating to Scotland*, 4 vols., PRO (1881–8); suppl. vol. 5, ed. G. G. Simpson and J. D. Galbraith [1986]

CEPR letters — W. H. Bliss, C. Johnson, and J. Twemlow, eds., *Calendar of entries in the papal registers relating to Great Britain and Ireland: papal letters* (1893–)

CGPLA — *Calendars of the grants of probate and letters of administration* [in 4 ser.: *England & Wales, Northern Ireland, Ireland*, and *Éire*]

Chambers, *Scots.* — R. Chambers, ed., *A biographical dictionary of eminent Scotsmen*, 4 vols. (1832–5)

Chancery records — chancery records pubd by the PRO

Chancery records (RC) — chancery records pubd by the Record Commissions

CIPM	Calendar of inquisitions post mortem, [20 vols.], PRO (1904–); also Henry VII, 3 vols. (1898–1955)
Clarendon, Hist. rebellion	E. Hyde, earl of Clarendon, The history of the rebellion and civil wars in England, 6 vols. (1888); repr. (1958) and (1992)
Cobbett, Parl. hist.	W. Cobbett and J. Wright, eds., Cobbett's Parliamentary history of England, 36 vols. (1806–1820)
Colvin, Archs.	H. Colvin, A biographical dictionary of British architects, 1600–1840, 3rd edn (1995)
Cooper, Ath. Cantab.	C. H. Cooper and T. Cooper, Athenae Cantabrigienses, 3 vols. (1858–1913); repr. (1967)
CPR	Calendar of the patent rolls preserved in the Public Record Office (1891–)
Crockford	Crockford's Clerical Directory
CS	Camden Society
CSP	Calendar of state papers [in 11 ser.: domestic, Scotland, Scottish series, Ireland, colonial, Commonwealth, foreign, Spain [at Simancas], Rome, Milan, and Venice]
CYS	Canterbury and York Society
DAB	Dictionary of American biography, 21 vols. (1928–36), repr. in 11 vols. (1964); 10 suppls. (1944–96)
DBB	D. J. Jeremy, ed., Dictionary of business biography, 5 vols. (1984–6)
DCB	G. W. Brown and others, Dictionary of Canadian biography, [14 vols.] (1966–)
Debrett's Peerage	Debrett's Peerage (1803–) [sometimes Debrett's Illustrated peerage]
Desmond, Botanists	R. Desmond, Dictionary of British and Irish botanists and horticulturists (1977); rev. edn (1994)
Dir. Brit. archs.	A. Felstead, J. Franklin, and L. Pinfield, eds., Directory of British architects, 1834–1900 (1993); 2nd edn, ed. A. Brodie and others, 2 vols. (2001)
DLB	J. M. Bellamy and J. Saville, eds., Dictionary of labour biography, [10 vols.] (1972–)
DLitB	Dictionary of Literary Biography
DNB	Dictionary of national biography, 63 vols. (1885–1900), suppl., 3 vols. (1901); repr. in 22 vols. (1908–9); 10 further suppls. (1912–96); Missing persons (1993)
DNZB	W. H. Oliver and C. Orange, eds., The dictionary of New Zealand biography, 5 vols. (1990–2000)
DSAB	W. J. de Kock and others, eds., Dictionary of South African biography, 5 vols. (1968–87)
DSB	C. C. Gillispie and F. L. Holmes, eds., Dictionary of scientific biography, 16 vols. (1970–80); repr. in 8 vols. (1981); 2 vol. suppl. (1990)
DSBB	A. Slaven and S. Checkland, eds., Dictionary of Scottish business biography, 1860–1960, 2 vols. (1986–90)
DSCHT	N. M. de S. Cameron and others, eds., Dictionary of Scottish church history and theology (1993)
Dugdale, Monasticon	W. Dugdale, Monasticon Anglicanum, 3 vols. (1655–72); 2nd edn, 3 vols. (1661–82); new edn, ed. J. Caley, J. Ellis, and B. Bandinel, 6 vols. in 8 pts (1817–30); repr. (1846) and (1970)
DWB	J. E. Lloyd and others, eds., Dictionary of Welsh biography down to 1940 (1959) [Eng. trans. of Y bywgraffiadur Cymreig hyd 1940, 2nd edn (1954)]
EdinR	Edinburgh Review, or, Critical Journal
EETS	Early English Text Society
Emden, Cam.	A. B. Emden, A biographical register of the University of Cambridge to 1500 (1963)
Emden, Oxf.	A. B. Emden, A biographical register of the University of Oxford to AD 1500, 3 vols. (1957–9); also A biographical register of the University of Oxford, AD 1501 to 1540 (1974)
EngHR	English Historical Review
Engraved Brit. ports.	F. M. O'Donoghue and H. M. Hake, Catalogue of engraved British portraits preserved in the department of prints and drawings in the British Museum, 6 vols. (1908–25)
ER	The English Reports, 178 vols. (1900–32)
ESTC	English short title catalogue, 1475–1800 [CD-ROM and online]
Evelyn, Diary	The diary of John Evelyn, ed. E. S. De Beer, 6 vols. (1955); repr. (2000)
Farington, Diary	The diary of Joseph Farington, ed. K. Garlick and others, 17 vols. (1978–98)
Fasti Angl. (Hardy)	J. Le Neve, Fasti ecclesiae Anglicanae, ed. T. D. Hardy, 3 vols. (1854)
Fasti Angl., 1066–1300	[J. Le Neve], Fasti ecclesiae Anglicanae, 1066–1300, ed. D. E. Greenway and J. S. Barrow, [8 vols.] (1968–)
Fasti Angl., 1300–1541	[J. Le Neve], Fasti ecclesiae Anglicanae, 1300–1541, 12 vols. (1962–7)
Fasti Angl., 1541–1857	[J. Le Neve], Fasti ecclesiae Anglicanae, 1541–1857, ed. J. M. Horn, D. M. Smith, and D. S. Bailey, [9 vols.] (1969–)
Fasti Scot.	H. Scott, Fasti ecclesiae Scoticanae, 3 vols. in 6 (1871); new edn, [11 vols.] (1915–)
FO List	Foreign Office List
Fortescue, Brit. army	J. W. Fortescue, A history of the British army, 13 vols. (1899–1930)
Foss, Judges	E. Foss, The judges of England, 9 vols. (1848–64); repr. (1966)
Foster, Alum. Oxon.	J. Foster, ed., Alumni Oxonienses: the members of the University of Oxford, 1715–1886, 4 vols. (1887–8); later edn (1891); also Alumni Oxonienses … 1500–1714, 4 vols. (1891–2); 8 vol. repr. (1968) and (2000)
Fuller, Worthies	T. Fuller, The history of the worthies of England, 4 pts (1662); new edn, 2 vols., ed. J. Nichols (1811); new edn, 3 vols., ed. P. A. Nuttall (1840); repr. (1965)
GEC, Baronetage	G. E. Cokayne, Complete baronetage, 6 vols. (1900–09); repr. (1983) [microprint]
GEC, Peerage	G. E. C. [G. E. Cokayne], The complete peerage of England, Scotland, Ireland, Great Britain, and the United Kingdom, 8 vols. (1887–98); new edn, ed. V. Gibbs and others, 14 vols. in 15 (1910–98); microprint repr. (1982) and (1987)
Genest, Eng. stage	J. Genest, Some account of the English stage from the Restoration in 1660 to 1830, 10 vols. (1832); repr. [New York, 1965]
Gillow, Lit. biog. hist.	J. Gillow, A literary and biographical history or bibliographical dictionary of the English Catholics, from the breach with Rome, in 1534, to the present time, 5 vols. [1885–1902]; repr. (1961); repr. with preface by C. Gillow (1999)
Gir. Camb. opera	Giraldi Cambrensis opera, ed. J. S. Brewer, J. F. Dimock, and G. F. Warner, 8 vols., Rolls Series, 21 (1861–91)
GJ	Geographical Journal

Gladstone, *Diaries* — *The Gladstone diaries: with cabinet minutes and prime-ministerial correspondence*, ed. M. R. D. Foot and H. C. G. Matthew, 14 vols. (1968–94)

GM — *Gentleman's Magazine*

Graves, *Artists* — A. Graves, ed., *A dictionary of artists who have exhibited works in the principal London exhibitions of oil paintings from 1760 to 1880* (1884); new edn (1895); 3rd edn (1901); facs. edn (1969); repr. [1970], (1973), and (1984)

Graves, *Brit. Inst.* — A. Graves, *The British Institution, 1806–1867: a complete dictionary of contributors and their work from the foundation of the institution* (1875); facs. edn (1908); repr. (1969)

Graves, *RA exhibitors* — A. Graves, *The Royal Academy of Arts: a complete dictionary of contributors and their work from its foundation in 1769 to 1904*, 8 vols. (1905–6); repr. in 4 vols. (1970) and (1972)

Graves, *Soc. Artists* — A. Graves, *The Society of Artists of Great Britain, 1760–1791, the Free Society of Artists, 1761–1783: a complete dictionary* (1907); facs. edn (1969)

Greaves & Zaller, *BDBR* — R. L. Greaves and R. Zaller, eds., *Biographical dictionary of British radicals in the seventeenth century*, 3 vols. (1982–4)

Grove, *Dict. mus.* — G. Grove, ed., *A dictionary of music and musicians*, 5 vols. (1878–90); 2nd edn, ed. J. A. Fuller Maitland (1904–10); 3rd edn, ed. H. C. Colles (1927); 4th edn with suppl. (1940); 5th edn, ed. E. Blom, 9 vols. (1954); suppl. (1961) [see also *New Grove*]

Hall, *Dramatic ports.* — L. A. Hall, *Catalogue of dramatic portraits in the theatre collection of the Harvard College library*, 4 vols. (1930–34)

Hansard — *Hansard's parliamentary debates*, ser. 1–5 (1803–)

Highfill, Burnim & Langhans, *BDA* — P. H. Highfill, K. A. Burnim, and E. A. Langhans, *A biographical dictionary of actors, actresses, musicians, dancers, managers, and other stage personnel in London, 1660–1800*, 16 vols. (1973–93)

Hist. U. Oxf. — T. H. Aston, ed., *The history of the University of Oxford*, 8 vols. (1984–2000) [1: *The early Oxford schools*, ed. J. I. Catto (1984); 2: *Late medieval Oxford*, ed. J. I. Catto and R. Evans (1992); 3: *The collegiate university*, ed. J. McConica (1986); 4: *Seventeenth-century Oxford*, ed. N. Tyacke (1997); 5: *The eighteenth century*, ed. L. S. Sutherland and L. G. Mitchell (1986); 6–7: *Nineteenth-century Oxford*, ed. M. G. Brock and M. C. Curthoys (1997–2000); 8: *The twentieth century*, ed. B. Harrison (2000)]

HJ — *Historical Journal*

HMC — Historical Manuscripts Commission

Holdsworth, *Eng. law* — W. S. Holdsworth, *A history of English law*, ed. A. L. Goodhart and H. L. Hanbury, 17 vols. (1903–72)

HoP, *Commons* — *The history of parliament: the House of Commons* [*1386–1421*, ed. J. S. Roskell, L. Clark, and C. Rawcliffe, 4 vols. (1992); *1509–1558*, ed. S. T. Bindoff, 3 vols. (1982); *1558–1603*, ed. P. W. Hasler, 3 vols. (1981); *1660–1690*, ed. B. D. Henning, 3 vols. (1983); *1690–1715*, ed. D. W. Hayton, E. Cruickshanks, and S. Handley, 5 vols. (2002); *1715–1754*, ed. R. Sedgwick, 2 vols. (1970); *1754–1790*, ed. L. Namier and J. Brooke, 3 vols. (1964), repr. (1985); *1790–1820*, ed. R. G. Thorne, 5 vols. (1986); in draft (used with permission): *1422–1504, 1604–1629, 1640–1660, and 1820–1832*]

IGI — *International Genealogical Index*, Church of Jesus Christ of the Latterday Saints

ILN — *Illustrated London News*

IMC — Irish Manuscripts Commission

Irving, *Scots.* — J. Irving, ed., *The book of Scotsmen eminent for achievements in arms and arts, church and state, law, legislation and literature, commerce, science, travel and philanthropy* (1881)

JCS — *Journal of the Chemical Society*

JHC — *Journals of the House of Commons*

JHL — *Journals of the House of Lords*

John of Worcester, *Chron.* — *The chronicle of John of Worcester*, ed. R. R. Darlington and P. McGurk, trans. J. Bray and P. McGurk, 3 vols., OMT (1995–) [vol. 1 forthcoming]

Keeler, *Long Parliament* — M. F. Keeler, *The Long Parliament, 1640–1641: a biographical study of its members* (1954)

Kelly, *Handbk* — *The upper ten thousand: an alphabetical list of all members of noble families*, 2 vols. (1875–7); continued as *Kelly's handbook of the upper ten thousand for 1878* [1879], 2 vols. (1878–9); continued as *Kelly's handbook to the titled, landed and official classes*, 94 vols. (1880–1973)

LondG — *London Gazette*

LP Henry VIII — J. S. Brewer, J. Gairdner, and R. H. Brodie, eds., *Letters and papers, foreign and domestic, of the reign of Henry VIII*, 23 vols. in 38 (1862–1932); repr. (1965)

Mallalieu, *Watercolour artists* — H. L. Mallalieu, *The dictionary of British watercolour artists up to 1820*, 3 vols. (1976–90); vol. 1, 2nd edn (1986)

Memoirs FRS — *Biographical Memoirs of Fellows of the Royal Society*

MGH — Monumenta Germaniae Historica

MT — *Musical Times*

Munk, *Roll* — W. Munk, *The roll of the Royal College of Physicians of London*, 2 vols. (1861); 2nd edn, 3 vols. (1878)

N&Q — *Notes and Queries*

New Grove — S. Sadie, ed., *The new Grove dictionary of music and musicians*, 20 vols. (1980); 2nd edn, 29 vols. (2001) [also online edn; see also Grove, *Dict. mus.*]

Nichols, *Illustrations* — J. Nichols and J. B. Nichols, *Illustrations of the literary history of the eighteenth century*, 8 vols. (1817–58)

Nichols, *Lit. anecdotes* — J. Nichols, *Literary anecdotes of the eighteenth century*, 9 vols. (1812–16); facs. edn (1966)

Obits. FRS — *Obituary Notices of Fellows of the Royal Society*

O'Byrne, *Naval biog. dict.* — W. R. O'Byrne, *A naval biographical dictionary* (1849); repr. (1990); [2nd edn], 2 vols. (1861)

OHS — Oxford Historical Society

Old Westminsters — *The record of Old Westminsters*, 1–2, ed. G. F. R. Barker and A. H. Stenning (1928); suppl. 1, ed. J. B. Whitmore and G. R. Y. Radcliffe [1938]; 3, ed. J. B. Whitmore, G. R. Y. Radcliffe, and D. C. Simpson (1963); suppl. 2, ed. F. E. Pagan (1978); 4, ed. F. E. Pagan and H. E. Pagan (1992)

OMT — Oxford Medieval Texts

Ordericus Vitalis, *Eccl. hist.* — *The ecclesiastical history of Orderic Vitalis*, ed. and trans. M. Chibnall, 6 vols., OMT (1969–80); repr. (1990)

Paris, *Chron.* — *Matthaei Parisiensis, monachi sancti Albani, chronica majora*, ed. H. R. Luard, Rolls Series, 7 vols. (1872–83)

Parl. papers — *Parliamentary papers* (1801–)

PBA — *Proceedings of the British Academy*

Pepys, *Diary*	*The diary of Samuel Pepys*, ed. R. Latham and W. Matthews, 11 vols. (1970–83); repr. (1995) and (2000)
Pevsner	N. Pevsner and others, Buildings of England series
PICE	*Proceedings of the Institution of Civil Engineers*
Pipe rolls	*The great roll of the pipe for . . .*, PRSoc. (1884–)
PRO	Public Record Office
PRS	*Proceedings of the Royal Society of London*
PRSoc.	Pipe Roll Society
PTRS	*Philosophical Transactions of the Royal Society*
QR	*Quarterly Review*
RC	Record Commissions
Redgrave, *Artists*	S. Redgrave, *A dictionary of artists of the English school* (1874); rev. edn (1878); repr. (1970)
Reg. Oxf.	C. W. Boase and A. Clark, eds., *Register of the University of Oxford*, 5 vols., OHS, 1, 10–12, 14 (1885–9)
Reg. PCS	J. H. Burton and others, eds., *The register of the privy council of Scotland*, 1st ser., 14 vols. (1877–98); 2nd ser., 8 vols. (1899–1908); 3rd ser., [16 vols.] (1908–70)
Reg. RAN	H. W. C. Davis and others, eds., *Regesta regum Anglo-Normannorum, 1066–1154*, 4 vols. (1913–69)
RIBA Journal	*Journal of the Royal Institute of British Architects* [later *RIBA Journal*]
RotP	J. Strachey, ed., *Rotuli parliamentorum ut et petitiones, et placita in parliamento*, 6 vols. (1767–77)
RotS	D. Macpherson, J. Caley, and W. Illingworth, eds., *Rotuli Scotiae in Turri Londinensi et in domo capitulari Westmonasteriensi asservati*, 2 vols., RC, 14 (1814–19)
RS	Record(s) Society
Rymer, *Foedera*	T. Rymer and R. Sanderson, eds., *Foedera, conventiones, literae et cuiuscunque generis acta publica inter reges Angliae et alios quosvis imperatores, reges, pontifices, principes, vel communitates*, 20 vols. (1704–35); 2nd edn, 20 vols. (1726–35); 3rd edn, 10 vols. (1739–45); facs. edn (1967); new edn, ed. A. Clarke, J. Caley, and F. Holbrooke, 4 vols., RC, 50 (1816–30)
Sainty, *Judges*	J. Sainty, ed., *The judges of England, 1272–1990*, SeldS, suppl. ser., 10 (1993)
Sainty, *King's counsel*	J. Sainty, ed., *A list of English law officers and king's counsel*, SeldS, suppl. ser., 7 (1987)
SCH	Studies in Church History
Scots peerage	J. B. Paul, ed. *The Scots peerage, founded on Wood's edition of Sir Robert Douglas's Peerage of Scotland, containing an historical and genealogical account of the nobility of that kingdom*, 9 vols. (1904–14)
SeldS	Selden Society
SHR	*Scottish Historical Review*
State trials	T. B. Howell and T. J. Howell, eds., *Cobbett's Complete collection of state trials*, 34 vols. (1809–28)
STC, 1475–1640	A. W. Pollard, G. R. Redgrave, and others, eds., *A short-title catalogue of … English books … 1475–1640* (1926); 2nd edn, ed. W. A. Jackson, F. S. Ferguson, and K. F. Pantzer, 3 vols. (1976–91) [see also Wing, *STC*]
STS	Scottish Text Society
SurtS	Surtees Society
Symeon of Durham, *Opera*	*Symeonis monachi opera omnia*, ed. T. Arnold, 2 vols., Rolls Series, 75 (1882–5); repr. (1965)
Tanner, *Bibl. Brit.-Hib.*	T. Tanner, *Bibliotheca Britannico-Hibernica*, ed. D. Wilkins (1748); repr. (1963)
Thieme & Becker, *Allgemeines Lexikon*	U. Thieme, F. Becker, and H. Vollmer, eds., *Allgemeines Lexikon der bildenden Künstler von der Antike bis zur Gegenwart*, 37 vols. (Leipzig, 1907–50); repr. (1961–5), (1983), and (1992)
Thurloe, *State papers*	*A collection of the state papers of John Thurloe*, ed. T. Birch, 7 vols. (1742)
TLS	*Times Literary Supplement*
Tout, *Admin. hist.*	T. F. Tout, *Chapters in the administrative history of mediaeval England: the wardrobe, the chamber, and the small seals*, 6 vols. (1920–33); repr. (1967)
TRHS	*Transactions of the Royal Historical Society*
VCH	H. A. Doubleday and others, eds., *The Victoria history of the counties of England*, [88 vols.] (1900–)
Venn, *Alum. Cant.*	J. Venn and J. A. Venn, *Alumni Cantabrigienses: a biographical list of all known students, graduates, and holders of office at the University of Cambridge, from the earliest times to 1900*, 10 vols. (1922–54); repr. in 2 vols. (1974–8)
Vertue, *Note books*	[G. Vertue], *Note books*, ed. K. Esdaile, earl of Ilchester, and H. M. Hake, 6 vols., Walpole Society, 18, 20, 22, 24, 26, 30 (1930–55)
VF	*Vanity Fair*
Walford, *County families*	E. Walford, *The county families of the United Kingdom, or, Royal manual of the titled and untitled aristocracy of Great Britain and Ireland* (1860)
Walker rev.	A. G. Matthews, *Walker revised: being a revision of John Walker's Sufferings of the clergy during the grand rebellion, 1642–60* (1948); repr. (1988)
Walpole, *Corr.*	*The Yale edition of Horace Walpole's correspondence*, ed. W. S. Lewis, 48 vols. (1937–83)
Ward, *Men of the reign*	T. H. Ward, ed., *Men of the reign: a biographical dictionary of eminent persons of British and colonial birth who have died during the reign of Queen Victoria* (1885); repr. (Graz, 1968)
Waterhouse, *18c painters*	E. Waterhouse, *The dictionary of 18th century painters in oils and crayons* (1981); repr. as *British 18th century painters in oils and crayons* (1991), vol. 2 of *Dictionary of British art*
Watt, *Bibl. Brit.*	R. Watt, *Bibliotheca Britannica, or, A general index to British and foreign literature*, 4 vols. (1824) [many reprs.]
Wellesley index	W. E. Houghton, ed., *The Wellesley index to Victorian periodicals, 1824–1900*, 5 vols. (1966–89); new edn (1999) [CD-ROM]
Wing, *STC*	D. Wing, ed., *Short-title catalogue of … English books … 1641–1700*, 3 vols. (1945–51); 2nd edn (1972–88); rev. and enl. edn, ed. J. J. Morrison, C. W. Nelson, and M. Seccombe, 4 vols. (1994–8) [see also *STC, 1475–1640*]
Wisden	*John Wisden's Cricketer's Almanack*
Wood, *Ath. Oxon.*	A. Wood, *Athenae Oxonienses … to which are added the Fasti*, 2 vols. (1691–2); 2nd edn (1721); new edn, 4 vols., ed. P. Bliss (1813–20); repr. (1967) and (1969)
Wood, *Vic. painters*	C. Wood, *Dictionary of Victorian painters* (1971); 2nd edn (1978); 3rd edn as *Victorian painters*, 2 vols. (1995), vol. 4 of *Dictionary of British art*
WW	*Who's who* (1849–)
WWBMP	M. Stenton and S. Lees, eds., *Who's who of British members of parliament*, 4 vols. (1976–81)
WWW	*Who was who* (1929–)

Dewes, Garrat (*b*. in or before 1533, *d*. 1591), bookseller and publisher, was the eldest son of Adrian Dewes (*d*. 1551), descended from the ancient lords of Kessel in Guelderland, who during the reign of Henry VIII had moved from the Low Countries to England, where he married Alice Ravenscroft. In his will, Garrat and three other surviving sons are mentioned. Garrat Dewes, who had been apprenticed to London stationer Andrew Hester, was made free of the Stationers' Company on 4 October 1557, when he would have been at least twenty-four years of age. He was taken into the Stationers' Company livery in 1569, served as renter warden in 1572–3 and as under-warden in 1581–2. Between January and September 1568 he received five shipments from Antwerp, each of 20 reams of unbound books, valued at £2. From 1578 to 1587 his bookshop was at the sign of the Swan in Paul's Cross churchyard. His device (McKerrow, nos. 169, 171) was cited by William Camden as a 'most memorable' example of a rebus: 'two in a Garret casting dews at dice' (W. Camden, *Remaines*, 1629, sig. K2*v*). From December 1573 he was one of the 'Assignes of Francis Flower', operating under Flower's lucrative patent as queen's printer for Latin, Greek, and Hebrew, which included the production of Lily's *Grammar*.

Dewes married at some date before 1563 Grace Hynde (*d*. 1583) of Cambridgeshire. They had a daughter, Alice, who married William Lathum of Upminster, Essex, and a son, **Paul Dewes** (1567–1631), government official, was one of the six clerks of the chancery. Born in London, Paul Dewes was twice married. Among the children of his first marriage, to Sissilia (*c*.1581–1618), daughter of Richard Simonds, barrister, of Coxden, Chardstock, Dorset, were Sir Simonds *D'Ewes (1602–1650), diarist and antiquary, and Richard Dewes (*d*. 1643), royalist army officer. Paul Dewes (who lived during the latter part of his life at Stow Hall, Stowlangtoft, Suffolk) died on 14 March 1631.

Probably about 1589, when he was demoted from the governing court of assistants of the Stationers' Company for his 'Contynuall absence' (Greg and Boswell, 33), Garrat Dewes retired to South Ockendon, Essex, where he purchased the manor of Gaines and adopted the life of a country gentleman. He died on 12 April 1591 and was buried at Upminster church, 'very solemnly and decently, with escutcheons of the coat-armour and other accountrements befitting his ancient and noble extraction' (*Autobiography*, 1.9).   H. R. Tedder, *rev*. I. Gadd

Sources *The autobiography and correspondence of Sir Simonds D'Ewes*, ed. J. O. Halliwell, 1 (1845), 6–20 • *STC*, 1475–1640 • Arber, *Regs. Stationers* • J. Weever, *Ancient funerall monuments* (1631), sigs. 3K2v–3v, 3O1r–v • W. W. Greg and E. Boswell, eds., *Records of the court of the Stationers' Company, 1576 to 1602, from register B* (1930) • P. Morant, *The history and antiquities of the county of Essex*, 1 (1768); repr. with introduction by G. H. Martin (1978), 107–8 [Upminster] • R. B. McKerrow, *Printers' and publishers' devices in England and Scotland, 1485–1640* (1949) • J. Ames, *Typographical antiquities, or, An historical account of the origin and progress of printing in Great Britain and Ireland*, ed. W. Herbert, 3 vols. (1785–90), vol. 2, pp. 940–42 • P. W. M. Blayney, *The bookshops in Paul's Cross churchyard* (1990) • B. Dietz, ed., *The port and trade of early Elizabethan London: documents*, London RS, 8 (1972), nos. 304, 361, 490, 634, 828

Likenesses brass monument, Upminster church, Essex; repro. in Weever, *Ancient funerall monuments*, sig. 3K3r

D'Ewes, Gerrard. *See* Dewes, Garrat (*b*. in or before 1533, *d*. 1591).

Dewes, Paul (1567–1631). *See under* Dewes, Garrat (*b*. in or before 1533, *d*. 1591).

D'Ewes, Sir Simonds, first baronet (1602–1650), diarist and antiquary, was the eldest son of Paul *Dewes (1567–1631) [*see under* Dewes, Garrat], barrister and government official, of Wells Hall, Milden, Suffolk, and his first wife, Sissilia (*c*.1581–1618), daughter and heir of another Middle Temple lawyer, Richard Simonds of Coxden, Chardstock, Dorset. Simonds was born at Coxden on 18 December 1602 and baptized in the open gallery there eleven days later. The London printer Garrat *Dewes was his grandfather. From Richard White, vicar of Chardstock, 'the chief thing [he] learnt was the exact spelling and reading of English' (*Autobiography*, 1.29–30). He remained with his grandfather at Coxden until early in 1610, when, having fallen dangerously ill, he was brought to Milden, where the air was considered to be better. In 1607 Paul Dewes spent most of his capital to obtain one of the six clerkships in chancery which tied him to London, so that Simonds saw little of his father. He was at Lavenham School in 1611 when both Simonds grandparents died, leaving him Coxden and a large fortune, to be administered by his father during his minority. The D'Ewes title to Wells Hall was incomplete, and a widow with a life interest had them ejected. They returned to Dorset, where Simonds enjoyed three years under a new tutor, a neighbouring clergyman Christopher Malaker of Wambrook. Malaker was an excellent teacher of Latin, but neglected his pupils' spiritual development. Henry Reynolds of St Mary Axe in London next took him on, but Simonds owed his progress in French and Greek to the remarkable ability of Bathshua, his tutor's eldest daughter. Here he also learned 'to write a moderate good English phrase' (ibid., 1.95). Reynolds taught D'Ewes, still only fourteen, to engage in extemporary prayer in the puritan style, but they fell out in 1616, and as his parents had now acquired Stow Hall at Stowlangtoft in Suffolk, he was sent to Bury grammar school. Here in two years under John Dickinson he learned more than from his other teachers in eight, giving him his twin lifelong enthusiasms: learning and research.

Higher education On 21 May 1618 D'Ewes entered St John's College, Cambridge, as a fellow-commoner under Richard Holdsworth, later professor of theology at Gresham College. The death of his pious and loving mother five weeks later cast a long shadow over his time at Cambridge, making him even more serious than before. Most of his fellows, he alleged, indulged in 'swearing, drinking, rioting & hatred of all vertue and pietie' (*Autobiography*, 1.141). He probably exaggerated, for he certainly found soberly congenial friends, and he worked hard, regularly attending lectures and university exercises. In September 1620 his father, always passionate, obstinate, and avaricious, peremptorily ordered him to leave Cambridge and enter the Middle Temple. As by some means his admission there had been arranged at the age of nine, he now found himself 'ancient' to over two hundred others. His father allowed Simonds only £60 from his own £3000 per annum and made him share his chambers in Chancery Lane; when they burnt down the next year the loss was nearly £6000. When Simonds complained of poverty, his father threatened to marry a young heiress and disinherit him, so he sensibly found his father a 'good and ancient widow' (ibid., 1.227) and saw them safely married at St Faith's Church in March 1623. The following June, Simonds was called to the bar and his father raised his allowance to £100 a year, which he regarded as a 'plentiful annuity' (ibid., 1.232).

Although he had been a conscientious student, D'Ewes had no wish to practise, for he had discovered that 'records, and other exotic monuments of antiquity, were the most ravishing and satisfying part of human knowledge' (Bruce, 'Long Parliament', 81). He therefore devoted himself to the study of historical and legal antiquities. That autumn he began his study of the national archives at the Tower of London, and spent the rest of his days copying and analysing original sources for English history. His stated ambition was to write and publish a definitive history of Britain, but he only appreciated the magnitude of the task as the extent of the evidence available became clear. Sir Robert Cotton befriended and encouraged him, introducing him to Selden, whom D'Ewes (of all people) thought 'a man exceedingly puffed up with the apprehension of his own abilities' (Autobiography, 1.256). Cotton's example, a great stimulus, led him to concentrate on the history of English legal and political institutions. In 1625 he came upon 'an elaborate journal of the parliament held in the thirty-fifth year of Queen Elizabeth' (ibid., 1.280). His analysis laid the foundation of his great work on the parliamentary history of that reign. At that time he recognized that he must also study numismatics. In 1626 he joined Sir Robert Cotton in establishing the claim of Robert Vere to the earldom of Oxford, against Robert Bertie, Lord Willoughby d'Eresby, who had assumed the title; it was granted to Vere by the House of Lords in the next parliament.

The lure of records That August D'Ewes gave up his practice at the bar just as a brilliant career seemed to be opening for him. 'But', he explained high-mindedly:

> when I saw the church of God and the gospel to be almost everywhere ruined abroad, or to be in great peril and danger, and daily feared that things would grow worse at home, I laid by all these aspiring hopes, and I resolved to moderate my desires, and to prepare my way to a better life with the greater serenity of mind and reposedness of spirit, by avoiding these two dangerous rocks of avarice and ambition. (Autobiography, 1.307)

The real cause was probably the arranged marriage with Anne (1613–1641), daughter and heir of Sir William Clopton, late of Lutons Hall at Melford in Suffolk, who, scarcely fourteen, brought him considerable estates bordering his father's property. She was also a cousin of D'Ewes's religious friend and mentor, Sir Nathaniel Barnardiston of Kedington. They were married at St Anne Blackfriars in London on 24 October 1626, and on 6

December D'Ewes was knighted (as an obligation of landholding) at Whitehall. Shortly afterwards he took a house in Islington where he could house his expanding library in the chamber over the hall, add to his collections, and devote himself to his historical and genealogical studies, planning a work called 'Great Britain's strength and weakness' (Watson, 5). Among his close friends at this period was Sir Albertus Joachimi, the ambassador for the Low Countries, for they shared religious and political interests. Alarmed by threats of large fines passed on those who stayed in London during the vacation against the king's proclamation, D'Ewes moved in 1632 to Bury St Edmunds. There he worked on the muniments of the great abbey, then in the possession of Sir Edmund Bacon of Redgrave. His father died on 14 March 1631, but D'Ewes did not move into Stow Hall until June 1633; now at last he enjoyed at least £1300 a year. Here he fell out with the conformist rector, Richard Damport, who disliked D'Ewes's Presbyterian and anti-Episcopalian views, and his studious habits. Small wonder that D'Ewes toyed with the idea of emigrating to New England, encouraged by letters from his friend John Winthrop. Instead he supported a company of thirty-eight while they settled, mostly in Watertown; he also had an interest in the Providence Island Company.

From the elaborate record he had kept from his youth of all he read, wrote, and saw, D'Ewes began in 1637 to prepare an autobiographical summary. He had by then completed his compilation of The Journal of All the Parliaments during the Reign of Queen Elizabeth, which was published in 1682, edited by his nephew Paul Bowes of the Inner Temple, and dedicated to his son Willoughby.

Member of the Long Parliament Having been pricked as high sheriff of Suffolk in 1639, D'Ewes submitted to the 'unwelcome preferment' (BL, Harley MS 379, fol. 60), which carried the heavy responsibility to levy £8000 upon the county for ship money. He reluctantly paid a penny more than rector Damport's 10s., and, having quickly become aware of the widespread public resistance, he petitioned the council with evidence from records to prove the illegality of such taxes. Laud, 'that busy little wheel', urged letters to D'Ewes which were 'terrible, and threatening like thunder and lightning' (Bruce, 'Long Parliament', 83), and the council turned him over to the Star Chamber. Hoping that he could better use his knowledge of records to oppose Arminian innovations and illegal taxation under cover of parliamentary privilege, he looked for an opening there. His attitude to ship money and the support of the Barnardistons brought him the Sudbury seat in November 1640, and he took lodgings in Goats Alley, near Palace Yard, London. He entered the Long Parliament as a reformer both in church and state, and from his first appearance sat near the speaker and took the notes which now fill Harley MSS 162–166. Still largely unpublished, they give an invaluably detailed account of those proceedings and the characters and motives of the men who overturned the monarchy. At first members were fascinated by his grasp of sources and precedents, and the commitment he showed by offering a bond for

£1000, doubled if necessary, towards paying the army in the north. He was voted onto appropriate committees, including the one to which William Prynne's and Burton's petitions were referred. He often spoke with the puritan faction in the house, but 'his demands upon the homage and patience of the House were excessive … He became a glutton, a very horse-leech in his importunity for highly-seasoned compliments to his erudition, and humble submission to the authority of his quoted records' (ibid., 90). As members tired of his wordy interventions and even began to ridicule him, he began to moderate his views, resolving to follow reason and law rather than passion. A sense of humour would have been a great asset to him. The king, always looking for the support of moderates, offered D'Ewes a baronetcy, which was conferred upon him on 15 July 1641. Any pleasure he took from this was short-lived, for about a fortnight later his beloved wife, still under thirty, died of smallpox while he was in London. From Ixworth Abbey, D'Ewes's stepmother sent her gravely sick daughter-in-law home to Stow Hall, and the journey proved fatal. She was presumably buried in Stowlangtoft church that August, but the register is incomplete. Their five sons all died in infancy, but two of five daughters survived: Cecilia, who married Sir Thomas Darcy but had no children, and Isolda, who never married. A year later D'Ewes married another heiress, Elizabeth (d. 1656), daughter of Sir Henry Willoughby, bt, of Risley, Derbyshire.

When the civil war began D'Ewes joined the parliamentary side and took the solemn league and covenant, albeit with reservations, in 1643. It had already caused comment in the house that his brother Richard was a lieutenant-colonel in the royalist army (mortally wounded during the siege of Reading), and D'Ewes's views were too moderate for him to be entirely trusted. He soon tired of taking notes of parliamentary business, not enjoying the stormy debating sessions which took place during the conflict, and his last notes are dated December 1645. That year he was nominated as co-chairman of the tenth (Blackbourn) division of the Suffolk classical presbytery meeting at Ixworth. On 6 December 1648 D'Ewes was excluded from the house with forty others at Pride's Purge. He never returned, perhaps glad to escape duties which had become distasteful to him, and he moved to Great Russell Street, London, cultivated the acquaintance of Archbishop Ussher, and concentrated on his antiquarian and collecting pursuits, planning more great works. On 7 March 1650 a son, Willoughby (1650–1685), was baptized at St Margaret's, Westminster, at last giving Simonds the male heir he so much desired. But on 18 April next Simonds died at Great Russell Street, and was carried off to Suffolk on 29 May to be buried in the chancel at Stowlangtoft on 7 June. Here his widow presumably joined him when she died in 1656. It is strange that they have no memorial there, for D'Ewes had provided a window and a brass commemorating D'Ewes forebears in other churches; he sent John Weever illustrations and descriptions for *Ancient Funerall Monuments* (1631). The infant Willoughby succeeded his father as second baronet and lived quietly on his estates, as, less prosperously, did his son and grandson, and the title became extinct in 1731.

The fate of D'Ewes's collections D'Ewes died without having published anything beyond a few speeches and a dull essay, *The Primitive Practice for Preserving Truth* (1645). He was concerned that his collections should stay in the family and that scholars should always have access to them, but in 1705 his grandson Simonds, third baronet, disposed of the library for £450 through Humphrey Wanley, agent for Sir Robert Harley, later earl of Oxford; the vendor never knew who the buyer was. D'Ewes's books were swallowed up by Harley's, and were dispersed when the earl's books were sold in the 1740s. The manuscripts, which Wanley called 'a rhapsody of indigested notes' (Watson, 13), now account for about one-twelfth of the Harley MSS in the British Library, accessible chiefly through the Harley catalogues and A. G. Watson's *Library of Sir Simonds D'Ewes* (1966). At the heart of the collection D'Ewes's 563 original rolls and 7800 charters form two-thirds of Harley's eventual holdings. The miscellaneous collection embraces everything from D'Ewes's school exercises and letters to his family to voluminous transcripts from cartularies, monastic registers, and early wills and records. The public and private muniments which he so energetically extracted constitute valuable source material for the history of English antiquities and law. His planned Anglo-Saxon dictionary (with Francis Junius) and works on Greek and Roman coinage almost came to fruition, but he always had too many projects in hand at once. His Cambridge journal was last seen in 1859, and unfortunately J. E. B. Mayor's transcript has also disappeared. J. H. Marsden's *College Life in the Time of James the First* (1851) is too loosely based on the original to be an entirely useful substitute. J. O. Halliwell published *The Autobiography and Correspondence of Sir Simonds D'Ewes during the Reign of James I and Charles I* in 1845: it covers his life to 1636, omitting some parts of D'Ewes's lengthy narrative without loss, and adding a few interesting letters. These memoirs give clear and often lively accounts of the periods they cover, and D'Ewes wrote about his relations with insight and compassion. His personal diaries, some in Latin and some in cipher, extend from January 1622 to April 1624, and from January 1643 to March 1647; only the first has been published. He knew all the great antiquaries, but, unlike such men as Selden, Twysden, Dugdale, and Holdsworth, D'Ewes lacked flair and creativity; he was a copyist and collector, conscientious, industrious, and usually accurate. He was not above disparaging the work of others, sneering at Selden and finding fault with Camden. Thomas Fuller, of the *Worthies*, can have the last word:

> He was bred in Cambridge as appeared by his printed speech (made in the Long Parliament) wherein he indeavoured to prove it more Ancient than Oxford. His Genious addicted him to the study of Antiquity. Preferring Rust before Brightness, and more conforming his mind to the Garbe of the former than [the] mode of the moderne times. (Fuller, 75)

J. M. BLATCHLY

Sources *The autobiography and correspondence of Sir Simonds D'Ewes*, ed. J. O. Halliwell, 2 vols. (1845) • J. H. Marsden, *College life in the time of James the First, as illustrated by an unpublished diary of Sir Symonds D'Ewes* (1851) • A. G. Watson, *The library of Sir Simonds D'Ewes* (1966) • J. Bruce, 'The Long Parliament and Sir Simonds D'Ewes', *EdinR*, 84 (1846), 76–102 • J. Bruce, 'Some notes on facts in the biography of Sir Simonds D'Ewes', *Archaeological Journal*, 26 (1869), 323–38 • Keeler, *Long Parliament* • Fuller, *Worthies* (1662), 3.75 • BL, D'Ewes MSS, Harley MSS • will, PRO, PROB 11/212, sig. 90 • *The diary of Sir Simonds D'Ewes, 1622–1624: journal d'un étudiant Londonien*, ed. E. Bourcier (Paris, 1974) • *The journal of Sir Simonds D'Ewes from the first recess of the Long Parliament to the withdrawal of King Charles from London*, ed. W. H. Coates (1942) • parish register, Stowlangtoft [burial], 7 June 1650
Archives BL, corresp., historical collections, parliamentary journals, and papers, Harley MSS • BL, corresp. and library catalogue, Add. MSS 22916, 22918 • BL, list of MSS, Egerton MS 3138 • CUL, MSS • Essex RO, Colchester, historical collections • Harvard U., Houghton L., parliamentary journal • Suffolk RO, MSS • V&A NAL, extracts, parliamentary journal, and miscellanies | BL, Cotton charters • BL, Harley charters • Tower of London, records [transcripts, BL, Egerton MS 3806]
Wealth at death *Autobiography … of Sir Simonds D'Ewes*, ed. Halliwell, vol. 2, pp. 148–59 • income £1500; library sold for £450: will, PRO, PROB 11/212, sig. 90

Dewhurst, Wynford (1864–1941), artist and writer on art, was born in Manchester on 26 January 1864. He was educated by a private tutor and subsequently at Mintholme College. Although originally destined for the legal profession, he showed an early artistic flair, contributing pen drawings and descriptive articles to journals in Lancashire and Cheshire, and to the *Pall Mall Budget* and *St James's Budget*. He spent five years studying art, in Paris, attending the École des Beaux-Arts, where he was a pupil of Jean-Léon Gérome, and the ateliers of Julien and Colarosis, where he worked with William Bouguereau, Ferrier, and Benjamin Constant. Despite this eclectic bunch of teachers, Dewhurst's style was very strongly influenced by the impressionists, especially Monet, whose work he particularly admired and on whom he published an article in the *Pall Mall Magazine* in 1900.

In 1896 Dewhurst exhibited at the Champ-de-Mars salons: over the next decade his work could be seen at a number of international exhibitions (including St Louis in 1904 and New Zealand in 1906), and in shows in Paris, London, and Venice. He exhibited in Buenos Aires in 1910, in Rome in 1911, and at the Royal Academy between 1914 and 1926. He also held two one-man shows in London (at the Walker Galleries in 1923 and at the Fine Art Society in 1925), and a series of solo exhibitions in Germany. Views of the countryside around Dieppe and of the Seine valley became his speciality: examples of his work are owned by Manchester City Galleries and by the National Museum and Gallery of Wales, Cardiff. Dewhurst lectured on modern painting, and published on French landscapists in *The Artist* and *The Studio*, drawing attention to the influence of such artists as Constable, Turner, and Bonington on their work, and thus claiming English origins for the impressionist movement. Dewhurst was not the first to advance this thesis—P. G. Hamerton had presented a similar argument some thirteen years earlier—but his one book-length study, *Impressionist Painting: its Genesis and Development* (1904), dedicated to Monet, was more innovative. It anticipated developments in modern scholarship, looking at American and other continental painters in addition to the French; it also included a whole chapter on women painters, since 'modernity is the note of Impressionism, and that movement was the very first artistic revolt in which women took part' (Dewhurst, *Impressionist Painting*, 77).

In other respects, however, Dewhurst was wary of the new, claiming in 1913 that 'Philistine materialism grips the country as a vice' (Dewhurst, *Wanted*, 26), and singling out both the cinema and advertising hoardings for his disapproval. He was an active campaigner for artistic causes, particularly those with a conservationist bent. Lecturing, pamphleteering, and setting up committees, he argued for the formation of a ministry of art: the result was the establishment in 1913 of a council of royal commissioners for art. In 1922, concerned with the deteriorating condition of royal palaces, he started a press campaign in France to save these buildings. J. D. Rockefeller jun. gave £100,000 towards the maintenance of Versailles, and Dewhurst's efforts also led to the introduction of entrance fees to state-owned palaces.

After a spell in Paris, Dewhurst was living in Leighton Buzzard in 1898, and again in 1907: he sat on Buckinghamshire county council between 1907 and 1910. Subsequently he moved to Tunbridge Wells, and then, in 1917, to Hampstead; he also maintained a house in France, in the department of Creuse. Dewhurst died on 9 July 1941, at 145 Belvedere Road, Burton upon Trent, Staffordshire, and was buried at Repton, in Derbyshire. He was survived by his wife, Antonia, with whom he had had three sons and three daughters. KATE FLINT

Sources *WWW*, 1941–50 • J. Johnson and A. Greutzner, eds., *The dictionary of British artists, 1880–1940* (1976), vol. 5 of *Dictionary of British art*; repr. (1994) • W. Dewhurst, *Impressionist painting: its genesis and development* (1904) • W. Dewhurst, *Wanted: a ministry of fine arts* (1913) • Bénézit, *Dict.*, new edn • *Leighton Buzzard Observer* (15 July 1941), 5 • *The Times* (11 July 1941) • K. McConkey, *British impressionism* (1989) • K. Flint, ed., *Impressionists in England: the critical reception* (1984) • d. cert.

Dewi Môn. *See* Rowlands, David (1836–1907).

Dewi Wyn o Eifion. *See* Owen, David (*bap.* 1784, *d.* 1841).

DeWint, Peter (1784–1849), landscape painter, was born in Hanley, Stoke-on-Trent, Staffordshire, on 21 January 1784, the son of Henry DeWint (1753–1807), physician, and his wife, Elizabeth Watson (*b.* 1754). The DeWint family was of Dutch origin; Henry DeWint, after studying in Europe and America, set up practice as a doctor in the Potteries district in 1781. Peter DeWint himself was originally destined for a medical career but, having shown an interest in art, persuaded his father to allow him to study painting. Accordingly in 1802 he was sent to London to be apprenticed to John Raphael Smith, the mezzotint engraver and painter, who agreed 'to teach … in the best manner that

Peter DeWint
(1784–1849), attrib.
William Hilton

he can, the said Apprentice in the art of Engraving and Portrait Painting' (indentures, Usher Art Gallery). However, it is clear that DeWint's artistic interests lay in directions other than engraving and portrait painting, for when he was released from his indentures three years early, in 1806, it was on condition that he produced for Smith eighteen paintings 'all of which said several pictures are to be Landscapes' (ibid.). This commitment to landscape painting was a bold move in the light of Joseph Farington's advice that 'Portrait painting undoubtedly offers more certain employ than any other branch [of art] … Landscape painting is not so much encouraged' (Farington, *Diary*, 4.1129). Nevertheless, it was as a landscape painter that DeWint was to establish himself as one of the most successful artists of the Romantic period.

After leaving J. R. Smith in 1806, DeWint moved to Broad Street, Golden Square, London, where he was a neighbour of John Varley, probably the most influential teacher of his time, and well known for his generosity to fellow artists. Varley would have introduced DeWint to the principles of Thomas Girtin's art, encouraged him to work *en plein air*, and taken him to Dr Monro's informal 'academy', where he would have been able to study the paintings of Cozens, Gainsborough, Turner, and Girtin.

That his landscape work progressed quickly is confirmed by the fact that in 1807 DeWint exhibited three landscapes at the Royal Academy, and went on to exhibit there a further ten times prior to 1828. In 1809 he was admitted as a student in the Royal Academy Schools. However, he concentrated increasingly on painting in watercolour, then considered an inferior medium, and between 1808 and 1809 he exhibited thirteen works at the Associated Artists in Water-Colours, including in 1808 his *View of Westminster Palace* (V&A). In 1810 he became an associate of the recently formed Society of Painters in Water Colours, and in 1811 a full member. It was at this society, subsequently known as the Old Watercolour Society, that DeWint exhibited over 400 watercolours during the next forty years.

Although his income until 1809 'was very small' (H. DeWint), DeWint was able the following year to invest sums of £150 and £85 in annuities (documents in the Usher Art Gallery). On 16 June 1810 he married Harriet Hilton (*c*.1790–1866), the sister of his close friend William Hilton, and in the same year all three of them set up home together at 10 Percy Street, London. The Hiltons originated in Lincoln, and henceforth DeWint was to have a close association with that city. In 1827, when Hilton was appointed keeper of the Royal Academy, the DeWints moved to 40 Upper Gower Street, London, where they remained until DeWint's death in 1849. During the last years of his life DeWint suffered from bronchitis, and died at his home from resulting complications on 30 June 1849; he was buried on 7 July in the grounds of the Chapel Royal in the Savoy, Strand, London. In the following year the studio sale of DeWint's work was held at Christies and during the five-day sale from 22 to 28 May 493 lots were sold, raising a total of £2364 7s. 6d. Further sales of DeWint's work, mainly from the family collection, took place at Christies on 2 March 1876, 28 June 1904, and 12 September 1941 (Smith, 152–9).

DeWint's artistic reputation was well established by the end of the first decade of the nineteenth century. Despite his Dutch ancestry, DeWint was among the most English of English artists, and no one, with the possible exception of Constable, celebrated with more affection, and less affectation, the simple charm of the English countryside—'they are common scenes made very uncommon' (*The Examiner*, 1827, 325). Although he visited Normandy briefly in 1828, and Wales a few times between 1829 and 1835, his favourite scenes were to be found in the north and east of England, especially the environs of Lincoln.

Early in his career DeWint produced some large and impressive oil paintings such as *The Cornfield* (exh. RA, 1815; V&A). However, it is as a watercolour artist that he is best-known. His watercolours can be divided into large, highly wrought exhibition pieces such as *Lincoln Cathedral* (exh. Old Watercolour Society, 1841; V&A) and his more spontaneous, and generally more admired, sketches such as *Dock Leaves* (*c*.1812; Usher Art Gallery, Lincoln), of which John Clare wrote: 'nothing would appear so valuable to me as one of those rough sketches taken in the fields that breathe the living freshness of open air and sunshine' (J. W. Tibble and A. Tibble, *Life of John Clare*, 136). Technically DeWint developed, more than his contemporaries, the full potential of the more painterly approach to watercolour painting that emerged in the early years of the nineteenth century, and which distinguished the Romantics from the earlier topographers with their preference for tinted drawings. Ruskin quoted DeWint as saying 'never mind your drawing but take plenty of colour on your brush & lay it on thick' (*Works of John Ruskin*, ed. E. T. Cook and A. Wedderburn, 1903–42, 1.426). Working with a fairly limited and subdued palette, DeWint laid in broad, wet washes of colour, which he disturbed as little as possible. In addition, DeWint excelled in the field of still-life painting, and also produced a significant body of work for topographical publications, including George Ormerod's *History of Cheshire* (3 vols., 1819) and Charles Heath's *Views of London* (1825).

It is evident from the sales ledgers that his wife kept that DeWint enjoyed extensive patronage from all strata of society including the Heathcotes of Conington Castle, Huntingdonshire, Richard Ellison of Sudbrooke Holme, Lincolnshire, J. M. W. Turner's friend Walter Fawkes, and the Howards of Castle Rising, Norfolk. He also had a large number of pupils, mostly amateurs, many of whom, such as the Heathcotes, were also patrons. His most notable professional pupil was Samuel Austin.

There are excellent collections of DeWint's work to be found in the Usher Art Gallery, Lincoln; the Victoria and Albert Museum, London (which received a gift from Mrs Tatlock, the artist's daughter, in 1872, and a further bequest in 1921); the Tate collection (which now holds the Henderson bequest of 1879, of twenty-three watercolours, including *Bridge over a Branch of the Witham*), and the British Museum. HAMMOND SMITH

Sources H. Smith, *Peter DeWint* (1982) · H. DeWint, 'A short memoir of Peter DeWint', Usher Art Gallery, Lincoln · W. Armstrong, *Memoir of Peter DeWint* (1888) · J. L. Roget, *A history of the 'Old Water-Colour' Society*, 2 vols. (1891) · M. Hardie, *Water-colour painting in Britain*, ed. D. Snelgrove, J. Mayne, and B. Taylor, 2: *The Romantic period* (1967) · R. Davies, 'Peter DeWint', *Old Water-Colour Society's Club*, 1 (1923–4), 5–13 · *The Studio* [special issue, *Masters of English landscape painting: J. S. Cotman, D. Cox, P. de Wint*, ed. C. Holme] (1903) · D. Scrase, ed., *Peter DeWint* (1979) [exhibition catalogue, FM, Cam.] · J. A. Rennie, ed., *Peter DeWint* [1984] [exhibition catalogue, Stoke-on-Trent Museum and Art Gallery] · Farington, *Diary* · Usher Art Gallery, Lincoln, DeWint MSS, indentures · sale catalogues [Christies, 22–8 May 1850; 2 March 1876; 28 June 1904; 12 Sept 1941] · Staffs. RO · *The exhibition of the Royal Academy* (1807–10) [exhibition catalogues] · records, RA
Archives BM, MSS · Lincoln Castle, MSS · Usher Art Gallery, Lincoln, personal papers · V&A, MSS
Likenesses P. DeWint, self-portrait, pencil, *c.*1816, Usher Art Gallery, Lincoln · attrib. W. Hilton, watercolour miniature, Usher Art Gallery, Lincoln [*see illus.*]
Wealth at death £2364—studio sale: Christies sale catalogues for 22, 23, 24, 27, 28 May 1850

Dewrance, Sir John (1858–1937), mechanical engineer, was born at Peckham, London, on 13 March 1858, the only son of John Dewrance (*d.* 1861), railway pioneer, of Greenhills, Tilford, Surrey, and his wife, Elizabeth, daughter of Joseph Curtis, of Tilford. He was educated at Charterhouse School and King's College, London, where he paid special attention to chemistry, and was a pupil of his stepfather, Colonel John Davis. On coming of age he took control of the engineering business of Dewrance & Co., which had been left him by his father. This business was founded in London in 1835 by Joseph Woods, with the elder Dewrance as a partner. When Woods died in 1842 it became Dewrance & Co., manufacturing engine and boiler accessories. In 1882 Dewrance married Isabella Ann (*d.* 1922), second daughter of Francis Trevithick, of Penzance, and granddaughter of Richard Trevithick, the 'father of the locomotive'; they had a son and a daughter.

Dewrance had a great affection for scientific research,

which he said was implanted in him by the electrometallurgist George Gore, and in 1880 he started a research laboratory, taking over Professor Frederick Barff's assistants and apparatus and working up his process for protecting iron from rust by treatment with superheated steam. In this laboratory he produced, in 1882, an ingot of aluminium by electrolysis, at a time when that metal was too expensive for general use, and he carried out extensive investigations, notably on lubrication and the corrosion of marine boilers, for which the Institution of Civil Engineers awarded him a Telford premium in 1896, and a Watt gold medal and a Telford premium in 1900. Some years before the First World War he gave up this laboratory, which by then had developed into a 2 acre factory with a pier on the Thames, and with it what he called individualistic research. His interest in research, however, continued, and hoping by team work to accomplish more for the benefit of industry than could be done by working alone, he became a member of many research committees, particularly those of the Institution of Mechanical Engineers on alloys and cutting tools, of both of which he was chairman. He encouraged co-ordinated research work, the standardization of engineering measurements, and mass production, believing this would best ensure the future prosperity of British industry.

Dewrance was a prolific inventor who took out more than a hundred patents, mainly relating to steam fittings and boiler mountings. He was also an able administrator and man of business. From 1899 until a few months before his death he was chairman of Babcock and Wilcox Ltd, and from 1914 of Kent Coal Concessions Ltd, and allied companies; aspersions cast by a shareholder on his conduct of these coal companies led him to take legal action, and in 1924 the offender was convicted of defamatory libel. In 1923 he was president of the Institution of Mechanical Engineers and from 1926 to 1928 of the Institute of Metals. He was also president of the Engineering and Allied Employers' National Federation (1920–26), master of the Armourers' and Brasiers' Company (1923), high sheriff of Kent in 1925, and a fellow of King's College, London (1929). He was appointed KBE in 1920 and GBE in 1928. His recreations were riding, shooting, and deerstalking. He died at his home, Wretham Hall, Wayland, Thetford, Norfolk, on 7 October 1937.

H. M. ROSS, rev. ANITA MCCONNELL

Sources *The Engineer* (15 Oct 1937), 424 · *The Times* (8 Oct 1937), 19d · *Engineering* (15 Oct 1937), 435 · *Institution of Mechanical Engineers: Proceedings*, 136 (1937), 396–8 · *Journal of the Institution of Civil Engineers*, 9 (1937–8), 591 · d. cert.
Likenesses W. Stoneman, photograph, 1930, NPG · Elliott & Fry, photograph, repro. in *The Engineer*, 424 · photograph, repro. in *The Times*, 19d
Wealth at death £392,609 4s. 10d.: probate, 15 Dec 1937, CGPLA Eng. & Wales

Dewsbury, William (*c.*1621–1688), Quaker activist, was born and raised in Allerthorpe, in the East Riding of Yorkshire. Of his father and mother nothing is known, beyond the speculation by Smith that William's father died when he was eight years old. Dewsbury's upbringing, working life, and religious experiences are discussed in his *Discovery of the Great Enmity of the Serpent* (1655). His first job as a shepherd afforded him the time to think about God, but he clearly felt isolated. When the time came for him to be apprenticed, therefore, he asked his parents to send him to Leeds so that he could move among 'those that feared the living God' (*Discovery*, 14). He gave up his apprenticeship (to a clothier) in the early 1640s, when he briefly joined the parliamentary army. Failing to find the spiritual satisfaction he had hoped for, and believing that God was telling him to fight no longer with 'carnall' weapons, Dewsbury subsequently drifted between different churches: the presbyterians in Scotland, the Baptists and Independents in his native England (*Discovery*, 17). His first wife, Anne (d. 1659), was a relatively prosperous woman with a history of religious dissent; the couple apparently married at a Baptist meeting in the 1640s. At home again in Yorkshire, but anxious and disillusioned, Dewsbury continued to feel that he was unregenerate, and though Quakerism seems to have given him a sense of purpose, his Calvinistic sense of having been 'conceived in sin and brought forth in iniquity' seems never to have fully left him (*Discovery*, 12). However, he immediately converted to Quakerism in 1651, and he began his ministry in October 1652. Like William, Anne was converted to the Quaker way by George Fox, who remembered her in his contribution to *The Faithful Testimony of … William Dewsbery*, published in 1689. Anne died in October or November 1659, having given birth to at least three children.

Dewsbury was fully committed to advancing the Quaker cause throughout England and Scotland, even though this drew him into dangerous situations. Almost every account seems to confirm that Dewsbury had a natural authority and spirited obduracy, qualities that were antithetical to non-Quakers. Before being imprisoned in York in 1654, Dewsbury had provoked, through his 'plaine & powerful' sermons, many people's conversion to Quakerism (Penney, *First Publishers*, 197). Thomas Thompson's view of Dewsbury's ministry—'I had never heard nor felt the like before' (Thompson, 17)—was perhaps the experience of many Quakers, and it was probably his charisma that made him so dangerous to the authorities, who imprisoned him in York (1654, 1660, 1663), Northamptonshire (1654), Exeter (1657), London (1662), and Warwick (1664, 1679). Indeed, in *The Second Period of Quakerism*, William Braithwaite observed that Dewsbury 'may be described as passing his life in prison with brief intervals of freedom' (p. 221). Inevitably, any account of his life is principally a description of incarceration.

The first charges against Dewsbury show the suspicion in which he was held, with authorities regarding him as an enemy of the social order. In York, accused of 'seducing the people', Dewsbury was criticized for allegedly equating himself with Christ (*The Discovery of the Great Enmity of the Serpent*, 7). In Northampton, the import of Dewsbury's prophecies led to a blasphemy trial and fifteen months' imprisonment. Similarly, in Exeter, Dewsbury was accused of being a Jesuit, though the judge recognized the spuriousness of this charge, and tore up the *mittimus*. In 1661–2 he was barely out of prison (suffering in York and London), and in July 1662 he was taken by the authorities from his home in Durteen, Yorkshire. Dewsbury's early incarcerations, though, were nothing in comparison to his experiences at Warwick. Imprisoned in 1664 for *praemunire*, he was not released until 1672 under the general pardon; during his imprisonment, most probably in 1667, he married a Warwickshire woman called Alice Reads or Meads. When English politics became dominated by fears of a Catholic insurrection from 1678 onwards, Dewsbury was again arrested despite the fact that Titus Oates cleared him of being involved. Dewsbury was probably released under the general pardon of March 1686.

A few months before his death, Dewsbury visited London, where he delivered a final sermon, later published as *A Sermon on the Important Doctrine of Regeneration*. The sense of conflict between the godly and the ungodly, couched in Calvinistic language, emerges in this unrepentant address. Dewsbury then returned to Warwickshire weakened by what John Whiting describes as 'his old Distemper he had contracted in Prison' (Whiting, 182). Clearly, Dewsbury had withstood persecution by still looking towards a new millennium: 'a Dreadful terrible Day is at hand' (*The Faithful Testimony*, sig. a3r). Dewsbury died in Warwick on 17 June 1688, and was buried there the following day: he was aged about sixty-seven. Nothing further is known of his second wife, but William probably predeceased her. He certainly had two children who lived to seniority, one of which was Mary, the wife of John Sam, while Jone [*sic*] Dewsbury was either William's daughter or daughter-in-law. William was not principally a family man, saying: 'live a Married Life as if you were Unmarried' (*Sermon*, 12).

The Faithful Testimony includes the words that are perhaps the best testimony to his life's work: 'I never since played the Coward, but joyfully entered Prisons as Palaces' (sig. a3r).
                                                             CATIE GILL

Sources E. Backhouse and others, *Biographical memoirs*, 1 (1854) · W. C. Braithwaite, *The beginnings of Quakerism*, ed. H. J. Cadbury, 2nd edn (1955); repr. (1981) · W. C. Braithwaite, *The second period of Quakerism*, ed. H. J. Cadbury, 2nd edn (1961); repr. (1979) · J. Besse, *A collections of the sufferings of the people called Quakers*, 2 vols. (1753) · R. Moore, *The lights in their consciences: early Quakers in Britain, 1646–1666* (University Park, PA, 2000) · N. Penney, ed., *Extracts from state papers relating to Friends, 1654–72* (1913) · N. Penney, *The first publishers of truth* (1907) · *The journal of George Fox*, ed. N. Penney, 2 vols. (1911) · Edward Smith, *William Dewsbury, 1621–1688* (1997) · J. Smith, *A descriptive catalogue of Friends' books*, 2 vols. (1867) · J. Tomkins, *Piety promoted* (1812) · J. Whiting, *Persecution expos'd* (1715) · T. Thompson, *An encouragement early to seek the Lord* (1708)
Archives RS Friends, Lond., corresp.

Dexter, John Henry (1925–1990), theatre director, was born on 2 August 1925 in Derby, the only child of Harry Dexter, plumber, and his wife, Rosanne Smith. There were music, painting, and home theatricals in the family, but Dexter's only formal education was at the local elementary school (Reginald Street), which he left at the age of fourteen. He then took a factory job before joining the army as a national serviceman. Not having attended a university was a source of lifelong regret, particularly as his

John Henry Dexter (1925–1990), by unknown photographer

entry into the professional theatre coincided with the rise of the graduate director. For the same reason he developed into a compulsive autodidact, a passionate scholar of stage history who never undertook a classical text without exhaustive research. His career began at the Derby Playhouse, in a company that also included John Osborne. Osborne recommended Dexter to the English Stage Company's artistic director, George Devine, who engaged him in 1957 as an associate director. Dexter had no previous directing experience, but he rapidly gained it at the Royal Court Theatre in London, which he subsequently described as his university; there he forged relationships with working-class writers, notably Michael Hastings and Arnold Wesker. At the same time he formed his long alliance with the designer Jocelyn Herbert, crucially in the 1959 production of Wesker's *The Kitchen*, an elaborately choreographed show on a defiantly undecorated stage, where even the lighting rig was exposed to the audience. This marked the beginning of the text-centred, visually austere style which was to become his trademark.

At the Royal Court, Dexter gained a double reputation: as an electrifying animator of spectacle and crowd movement, and as a 'playwright's director' who could spot not only the defects of a script but also the hidden potential,

and coax the writer into achieving it. The success of his subsequent partnership with Peter Shaffer (*The Royal Hunt of the Sun*, 1964; *Black Comedy*, 1966; *Equus*, 1973) depended as much on pre-rehearsal textual analysis as on the physical staging.

In 1963 Dexter left the Royal Court to become assistant director to Laurence Olivier at the National Theatre when it was in its honeymoon phase. He began widening his range with productions of *Saint Joan* (1963), *Hobson's Choice* (1964), and Olivier's *Othello* (1964), shows that went lastingly into public memory. He also began another fertile partnership with the poet Tony Harrison, whose versions of Molière and Racine (*The Misanthrope*, 1973, and *Phaedra Britannica*, 1975) set a dazzling new standard for creative translation.

By the late 1960s Dexter was building a parallel career as a director of opera—a natural move, given his flair as an animator and his innate musicality (coupled with his temporary withdrawal from the National Theatre following disagreements with Olivier). His first venture, Berlioz's *Benvenuto Cellini* at Covent Garden (1966), was untypically ornate; but with Verdi's *I vespri siciliani* at the Hamburg State Opera three years later he declared himself in a production of characteristically austere magnificence. Staged on Josef Svoboda's gigantic staircase between two vast watch-towers, the production carried his name round the world as a new force on the operatic scene; and although he maintained his connection with Hamburg until 1973 (his production of Verdi's *Un ballo in maschera*), the main focus of his work during the 1970s was at New York's Metropolitan Opera House, where he was appointed director of productions in 1974. Dexter saw the Metropolitan as a Babylonian anachronism, and he made it his mission to drag it into the twentieth century through simplified staging, technical reform, and enlargement of repertory. Against the odds he won over the conservative public with a series of non-standard works, from Meyerbeer's *Le prophète* and Poulenc's *Les dialogues des Carmélites* (both 1977) to *Parade* (1981), a French triptych which he assembled from Satie, Poulenc, and Ravel. By this time, however, his relationship had soured with the Metropolitan's administration and its musical director, James Levine, and during the early 1980s he returned to freelance work.

Dexter continued to direct major productions in London and New York, but he never achieved his ambition of running a house and company of his own; and his final attempt to do so—with a classically based West End troupe—fell apart after its opening production of T. S. Eliot's *The Cocktail Party* (Phoenix Theatre, 1986).

Dexter was a stocky figure of medium height, with chubby features and a domed head that became increasingly prominent as he lost his hair. He had a biting tongue which could wound actors and alienate patrons; he also suffered from declining health, due to diabetes and the aftermath of youthful polio, before his final heart attack. He was a homosexual and suffered a brief term of imprisonment for homosexuality in the 1950s. A collection of his writings, *The Honourable Beast: a Posthumous Autobiography*, was published by his friend Riggs O'Hara in 1993. Dexter died on 23 March 1990 in London, following a heart operation.   Irving Wardle, *rev.*

Sources J. Dexter, *The honourable beast: a posthumous autobiography* (1993) · *The Times* (26 March 1990) · personal knowledge (1996) · private information (1996) · *CGPLA Eng. & Wales* (1991)
Likenesses photograph, News International Syndication, London [*see illus.*]
Wealth at death £26,502: probate, 8 Feb 1991, *CGPLA Eng. & Wales*

D'Eyncourt, Charles Tennyson- (1784–1861), politician, second son and youngest child of George Tennyson (1750–1835) of Bayons Manor, Lincolnshire, MP for Bletchingley, and his wife, Mary (*d.* 1825), daughter of John Turner of Caistor, was born at Market Rasen on 20 July 1784. He was educated at Louth grammar school and at St John's College, Cambridge, where he graduated BA in 1805 and proceeded MA in 1818. From a fairly early stage, he suffered, like many of his family, from epilepsy. He married, on 1 January 1808, Frances (Fanny) Mary, only child of the Revd John Hutton. She was an heiress and brought Tennyson financial security. They had eight children, all in difficult births, and sexual abstinence led to frequent separation between the parents. From 1811 the marriage was in difficulties. Moreover, in April 1816 Tennyson began a long-standing liaison with Mary (Polly) Thornhill, daughter of the squire of Stanton near Bakewell. The eight children were given nicknames by their father ('the Stone', 'the Sot', and so on, except for Eustace, Tennyson's favourite, who was expelled from Sandhurst in 1833).

Tennyson made a promising start to his career as a barrister and entered parliament in 1818 as MP for Great Grimsby. From 1826 until 1831 he represented Bletchingley. He quickly made his mark in the house and seemed likely to have a career in politics on the whig/radical side. He strongly supported Queen Caroline and persuaded the house to pass a Landlord and Tenant Bill; in 1827 he was responsible for a measure prohibiting the setting of spring guns (7 & 8 Geo. IV c.18). Tennyson supported piecemeal parliamentary reform, especially via the redistribution of seats. It was his motion on East Retford which led to the breakup of the tory government. When the whigs took office in 1830 he was, on 30 December, appointed clerk of the ordnance. In May 1831 he was elected as a radical for Stamford, Joseph Parkes being his electoral agent in an intense contest. Lord Thomas Cecil, the other candidate, disparaged his electioneering methods and Tennyson challenged him to a duel, fought at Wormwood Scrubs on 18 June 1831; neither man was injured, both were arrested, but neither was prosecuted. Tennyson joked, 'it is thought a very proper thing that the Clerk of Ordnance should commence the shooting season' (Martin, 144), but the incident led to his ridicule. He retired as clerk in February 1832, ostensibly from ill health. He was sworn of the privy council on 6 February 1832, but the episode ended his official career.

In 1832 Tennyson became MP for the new borough of Lambeth, representing it until 1852. In 1834 and 1835 he

Charles Tennyson-D'Eyncourt (1784–1861), by Charles Picart, pubd 1822 (after Abraham Wivell, *c.*1820)

unsuccessfully attempted to shorten the lifespan of parliaments by amending the Septennial Act. He became increasingly radical in political temper. He supported municipal reform and the repeal of the corn laws and of the Navigation Acts. He also, in line with his earlier proposals, supported various of the Chartists' demands.

In 1835 on the death of his father Tennyson gained further wealth and, in accordance with—as he stressed—his father's wishes, changed his surname to Tennyson-D'Eyncourt, the name deriving from the ancient titles of Scarsdale and D'Eyncourt of Sutton, from the holders of which the family was descended by the female line. He tried to revive the barony of D'Eyncourt, but Melbourne, the prime minister, refused what was generally seen as a grotesque request. Tennyson-D'Eyncourt's father left him that (major) part of his estate which derived from purchase and speculation, with the part derived from entail or inheritance going to the elder brother, George Tennyson, a mentally ill alcoholic who was rector of Somersby and father of the poet Alfred Tennyson; the Somersby branch of the family bitterly resented the disposition of the family wealth, blaming Charles Tennyson-D'Eyncourt for it, and complaining at his change of name.

Tennyson-D'Eyncourt, with his aristocratic patina and antiquarianism, fast became as well as a radical a figure worthy of the wilder fancies of the Young England movement. He at once used his money to plan a new Bayons Manor as a fairy-tale castle, with moat, medieval oratory, and secret passages. His friend Edward Bulwer-Lytton was a frequent visitor. The building became an obsession, 'a monomaniacal pursuit of an elusive past' (Martin, 210), which drove Tennyson-D'Eyncourt almost to madness (and, some thought, into it). This and some of his earlier architectural exploits had some influence on his poetic nephew. He quarrelled with his children, who disliked Bayons, and in the latter part of his life the failure of his once intense political ambition made him bitter. In 1852 he was defeated at Lambeth in the general election, and did not stand again. On 22 June the Lambeth radicals presented him with a testimonial. He was high steward of Louth, a JP, and deputy lord lieutenant of Lincolnshire, but he became something of a recluse, planning further changes at Bayons Manor (the house decayed and was demolished in 1964). He came to be considered something of a bore as well as a snob; he was, in the view of his nephew Alfred Tennyson, 'a considerable humbug' (Martin, 354).

Tennyson-D'Eyncourt's second son, Edward Clayton Tennyson-D'Eyncourt (1813–1903), died an admiral. The third son, Louis Charles Tennyson-D'Eyncourt (1814–1896), was a police magistrate in London from 1851 to 1890, and his son, Edmund Charles Tennyson-D'Eyncourt, filled a like position from 1901. Of his three daughters, Julia Frances (d. 1879) became a Roman Catholic nun in 1852.

Tennyson-D'Eyncourt, who was elected FRS in February 1829, and was also FSA, published a number of his speeches and also *Observations on the Proceedings Against the Queen [Caroline]* (1821) and *Eustace, an Elegy* (1851), composed in memory of his son (1816–1842) who died of yellow fever in Barbados; it was published, somewhat embarrassingly, shortly after *In Memoriam*. Tennyson-D'Eyncourt died at 8A Gloucester Place, Portman Square, London (the house of his son-in-law John Hinde Palmer QC), on 21 July 1861. His wife died on 26 January 1878, though Tennyson-D'Eyncourt lived as a bachelor in his latter years.

G. C. BOASE, rev. H. C. G. MATTHEW

Sources GM, 3rd ser., 11 (1861), 328–30 • Venn, *Alum. Cant.* • *ILN* (25 June 1853), 515 • R. B. Martin, *Tennyson: the unquiet heart* (1980) • W. Thomas, *The philosophical radicals: nine studies in theory and practice, 1817–1841* (1979) • M. B. Baer, 'D'Eyncourt, Charles Tennyson', *BDMBR*, vol. 1 • T. R. Leach and R. Pacey, *Lost Lincolnshire houses: Bayons Manor, Tealby* (1992), vol. 3 • *The letters of Alfred Lord Tennyson*, ed. C. Y. Lang and E. F. Shannon, 1–2 (1982–7)
Archives Lambeth Archives, London, corresp. and papers relating to Lambeth elections • Lincs. Arch., corresp. and papers | Durham RO, corresp. and papers as executor of Matthew Russell MP • Herts. ALS, corresp. with Lord Lytton • Lincs. Arch., corresp. relating to Grimsby politics; letters and papers relating to Grimsby politics • North East Lincolnshire Archives, Grimsby
Likenesses oils, 1810?, repro. in Leach and Pacey, *Lost Lincolnshire houses* • C. Picart, stipple, pubd 1822 (after A. Wivell, c.1820), BM, NPG [see illus.] • F. C. Lewis, aquatint and stipple, pubd 1829 (after J. Harrison), BM, NPG • E. Morton, lithograph, pubd 1838 (after J. Pelham), NPG • G. Hayter, group portrait, oils (*The House of Commons, 1833*), NPG • pencil, repro. in G. Hill, *Electoral history of the borough of Lambeth* (1879)
Wealth at death £7000: probate, 11 Oct 1861, CGPLA Eng. & Wales

D'Eyncourt, Sir Eustace Henry William Tennyson-, first baronet (1868–1951), naval architect, was born on 1 April 1868 at Hadley House, Barnet, Hertfordshire, the sixth and youngest child of Louis Charles Tennyson-D'Eyncourt (1814–1896), metropolitan magistrate, and his wife, Sophia (d. 1900), daughter of John Ashton Yates, of Dinglehead, Lancashire. His father was a cousin of Alfred Tennyson; his grandfather Charles Tennyson [see D'Eyncourt, Charles Tennyson-] added the maternal family name of D'Eyncourt. He was sent to several primary schools, then to Browning's School at Thorpe Mandeville, Northamptonshire, in preparation for Eton, but he failed the scholarship examination and instead went to Charterhouse.

On leaving Charterhouse in 1886, Tennyson-D'Eyncourt was disinclined to follow his brothers to Oxford. The daughter of his father's friend Sir Edward Reed, who had been chief constructor of the navy, suggested that he should take up naval architecture and shipbuilding, an idea which strongly appealed to him. His uncle Admiral Tennyson-D'Eyncourt provided helpful introductions, and so he became an apprentice at the Elswick shipyard of Armstrong, Whitworth & Co. After two years spent in going through the various workshops, he took as a private student the naval architecture course at the Royal Naval College, Greenwich. Returning to Elswick, he was placed in the design office under J. R. Perrett and remained there on the permanent staff at the conclusion of his five years' apprenticeship. Wishing to gain experience in mercantile shipbuilding, in 1898 he obtained a post as naval architect with the Fairfield Shipbuilding and Engineering Company, at Govan, Glasgow, where, in addition to naval vessels, both passenger liners and cargo ships were under construction. Also in 1898 he married Janet, daughter of Matthew Watson Finlay of Langside, near Glasgow. She was a widow and had two children from her marriage to John Burns. She and Tennyson-D'Eyncourt had a son and a daughter.

In 1902, however, Tennyson-D'Eyncourt received what he termed 'an irresistible opportunity to go back to the Tyne' (Tennyson-D'Eyncourt, 48). Philip Watts had left Elswick to become director of naval construction; Perrett had succeeded Watts at Elswick and invited Tennyson-D'Eyncourt to take charge of the design office. This post involved many trips abroad to negotiate naval contracts, on which he sometimes took his wife. In 1904, after handing over the new cruiser *Hamidieh*, he was asked by the Turkish government to report on the condition of its navy. In view of the poor state of many of the ships, this called for very tactful wording and he was awarded the order of the Mejidiye (third class) for his efforts. In 1908 and 1909 he was in Argentina, negotiating for the sale of battleships. Shortly before his return in December 1909 his wife fell ill in Buenos Aires, where she died. His stepdaughter Gwyneth Burns thereafter took over the responsibility for his young family, allowing him to make a long stay in Brazil.

In 1912 Tennyson-D'Eyncourt was appointed director of naval construction in succession to Watts. During his term of office twenty-one capital ships, fifty-three cruisers, 133 submarines of eleven different classes, and numerous other vessels were added to the Royal Navy. The battleships of the Royal Sovereign class were the first capital ship designs for which he was responsible. In lieu of two of the class, the battle cruisers *Renown* and *Repulse* were designed and built in under twenty months. He introduced the 'bulge' form of protection against torpedo attack and no ship so fitted was sunk in the war of 1914–18 by torpedoes.

In 1915 Tennyson-D'Eyncourt was entrusted with the design of rigid airships for the navy and retained this responsibility until it was transferred to an air department. In February of the same year Churchill asked him to undertake the design of a 'landship' which could advance over trenches or wire entanglements. Material for the army was certainly not normally his province, but Tennyson-D'Eyncourt was keenly interested in the project and agreed to head a committee formed to design and produce landships or 'tanks' as they were later termed. The prototype was ready for trials early in 1916 and the first tanks saw action at the battle of the Somme. Although the original Admiralty landship committee was disbanded after the early and successful trials, Tennyson-D'Eyncourt was retained as chief technical adviser.

Among the many naval developments which took place during the war perhaps the most important were those in the design of aircraft-carriers. Under Tennyson-D'Eyncourt's guidance there was rapid progress and a pattern of bridge and superstructure was set which was followed by all other navies. His most impressive design was that of the battle cruiser *Hood*, the first capital ship to be fitted with small tube boilers, a type he had long advocated. In the post-war years he had to contend with the difficult problems consequent on the Washington treaty of 1922, and the *Nelson* and *Rodney* represented his solution for the most powerful battleship of less than 35,000 tons.

Tennyson-D'Eyncourt resigned from the Admiralty in 1924, but remained for some time a special adviser. From 1924 to 1928 he was a director of his old firm, Armstrong, Whitworth & Co. He then joined the board of Parsons Marine Steam Turbine Company until his retirement in 1948. During the inter-war years he designed numerous merchant ships including the very novel heavy lift 'Belships'. He was appointed KCB in 1917 and in 1918 was made a commander of the Légion d'honneur and also awarded the American DSM. He was elected FRS in 1921, and received honorary degrees from Durham and Cambridge. In 1930 he was created a baronet and in 1937 he was elected foreign associate member of the French Académie de Marine in succession to Lord Jellicoe.

Tennyson-D'Eyncourt was chairman of the advisory committee of the William Froude Laboratory for fifteen years and was a prominent and active member of many societies and institutions, including the Shipwrights Company, becoming master in 1927. He read several important papers before the Royal Institution of Naval Architects and was elected a vice-president in 1916 and an honorary vice-president in 1935. He was president of the North-East Coast Institution of Engineers and Shipbuilders from 1925 to 1927. Always preferring rural life, he bought Carters Corner Farm, near Hailsham, Sussex, where he spent his later years. Tennyson-D'Eyncourt died in London at his business premises, 168 Ashley Gardens, Victoria, London, on 1 February 1951 and was succeeded as second baronet by his son, Eustace Gervais (1902–1971).

K. C. BARNABY, *rev.* ANITA MCCONNELL

Sources C. S. Lillicrap, *Obits. FRS*, 7 (1950–51), 341–54 · E. H. W. Tennyson-D'Eyncourt, *A shipbuilder's yarn* [1948] · **Archives** NMM, corresp. and papers · **Likenesses** W. Stoneman, photographs, 1918, NPG · O. Birley, portrait; formerly at Brixton Estate Ltd, 1971 · **Wealth at death** £50,634 8s. 11d.: probate, 11 May 1951, *CGPLA Eng. & Wales*

Deyville [Daiville], **Sir John de** (*c*.1234–1290/91), rebel, was the son of Robert de Deyville and his wife, Denise Fitzwilliam, of Sprotborough. The Deyvilles, who took their name from Déville (Seine-Maritime) in north-east Normandy, were established in Nottinghamshire and north Yorkshire during the twelfth century, above all through their links with the Mowbrays. John de Deyville was probably born *c*.1234, and was still a minor when his father died. His wardship was entrusted to Roger (II) de Mowbray, who may have abused his trust, or at any rate neglected it, since when Deyville attained his majority in 1254 he found it necessary to sell lands at Adlingfleet valued at £400. Resentment at the exploitation of his assets during his minority, perhaps combined with the economic effects of the loss of his family's Norman possessions in 1204, may help to explain the subsequent course of his career. Nevertheless he was made keeper of the forests north of the Trent for three years in 1257 and was summoned for service in Scotland in 1258.

Deyville was among the supporters of Richard de Clare, earl of Gloucester (to whom he had sold his Adlingfleet lands), a member of the baronial regency council, when Gloucester (d. 1262) made an alliance with Henry III in February 1259. He was not then so prominent a supporter of Simon de Montfort to be omitted from the king's summons of his tenants-in-chief and their knights to London in March or April 1260, and he was reappointed keeper of the forests in the north that May. However, he was identified sufficiently closely with the baronial cause to be dismissed in June 1261 in the king's general purge of local officials during his resumption of power at the centre. Thereafter, Deyville became the unofficial baronial keeper (*custos*) for Yorkshire, during a period of largely unco-ordinated local dissent; that November he led disturbances in York. Following Montfort's initial victory and conclusion of peace with the king in July 1263, Deyville was formally appointed keeper and sheriff of Yorkshire. From December 1263, when Henry III regained control of the central government, to April 1264 he held York Castle in defiance of royal edicts, after which he briefly occupied Carlisle Castle. Deyville reaped the benefits of Montfort's victory at the battle of Lewes in May, being made keeper of Yorkshire once more in June, and receiving licence to crenellate his home at Hood, near Kilburn, in August. In September he was reappointed keeper of the forests in the north and in December he was summoned as a baron to the famous parliament that met the following January. He was among those magnates whom Montfort banned from holding a tournament at Dunstable in February 1265, for fear that it would exacerbate tensions with the new earl of Gloucester, Gilbert de Clare (d. 1295). But he remained a firm Montfortian, and in March was deputed to wrest Richmond Castle, Yorkshire, from royalist control.

After Montfort's defeat and death at the battle of Evesham on 4 August 1265 Deyville's lands were confiscated and granted to Queen Eleanor. He led those who continued in rebellion in the Isle of Axholme, Lincolnshire (a Mowbray estate). Although, along with Simon de Montfort the younger, he was forced to submit to the Lord Edward at Bycarr's Dyke, on the border of Nottinghamshire and Yorkshire, in December 1265, he remained one of the leading 'disinherited' rebels. After sacking Sheffield early in 1266, he joined Robert de Ferrers, earl of Derby, and other rebels in May at Chesterfield, where they were surprised and beaten in battle by a royalist force. He was by then heavily in debt to Jewish moneylenders, which may explain why he specifically killed Jews and destroyed charters when he sacked Lincoln after fleeing that defeat. He proceeded to give new heart to the rebel cause by occupying the Isle of Ely, whence he mounted raids on Cambridge and Norwich. Despite negotiations with the committee of twelve magnates who met at Coventry in September and October to agree rules for the redemption of the rebels' lands, Deyville and his men would not accept the dictum of Kenilworth proclaimed on 31 October. According to Robert of Gloucester they replied to the papal legate's overtures with Montfortian demands for the maintenance of the provisions of Oxford and the reversal of their excommunication by the legate. The young and disaffected earl of Gloucester then put himself forward as their champion, and Deyville joined him in his occupation of London in April 1267. 'For two months the city was a rebel camp' (Powicke, *Henry III and the Lord Edward*, 543), and the excommunication of Deyville, who had perhaps been responsible for some pillaging in the city, was renewed at St Paul's at Easter.

Although Deyville was excluded from the treaty made between the king and Gloucester at Stratford in June, his long rebellion came to an end on 1 July 1267 when he was formally pardoned at St Paul's and given immediate seisin of his lands, the redemption fine for which was granted to Queen Eleanor at a lenient four-yearly valuation of £600, to be paid by instalments. Like the other disinherited, he was to benefit from financial aid from the clergy. In 1268 the king granted relief from repayment of his Jewish debts until he had settled his redemption fine, but he incurred other penalties, including one for unlicensed marriage to Maud, the widow of James Audley junior (interestingly, a staunch royalist), in 1275, and still owed 380 of his 900 marks fine in 1272. He finally settled his debt to the queen in September 1276, but sold some pledged lands, and remained in debt until his death. Meanwhile, he was restored to favour, served in Wales in 1277 and the 1280s, was a royal banneret by 1285–6, and attended parliament at Shrewsbury in 1283 and the military council at Gloucester in 1287. At an unknown date he had married Alice, and he died in either 1290 or 1291.

OSCAR DE VILLE

Sources *Chancery records* · PRO · C. H. Knowles, 'The resettlement of England after the barons' war, 1264–67', *TRHS*, 5th ser., 32 (1982), 25–41 · F. M. Powicke, *Henry III and the Lord Edward*, 2 vols. (1947) · F. M. Powicke, *The thirteenth century, 1216–1307*, 2nd edn (1962) · R. F. Treharne and I. J. Sanders, eds., *Documents of the baronial movement of reform and rebellion, 1258–1267* (1973) · M. Altschul, *A baronial family in medieval England: the Clares, 1217–1314* (1965) · H. Summerson, *Medieval Carlisle* (1993) · GEC, *Peerage*, 4.130–32 · O. De Ville, 'Deyville (or de Daiville): origins of an English regional family', *Medieval Prosopography*, 18 (1997), 1–24 · O. De Ville, 'John Deyville: a neglected rebel', *Northern History*, 34 (1998), 17–40 · *Close rolls of the reign of Henry III*, 8, PRO (1929), 88

Dhingra, Madan Lal (1883–1909), Indian nationalist and political assassin, was born on 18 September 1883 in the Dhingra Buildings, Hall Gate, Amritsar, the sixth of the seven children of Dr Sahib Ditta Mal Dhingra, a civil surgeon. The Dhingras were a wealthy, cosmopolitan Hindu family who regarded British rule as a modernizing and stabilizing influence. Dr Dhingra was self-made and all his six sons studied abroad. Dhingra passed his intermediate examination at Municipal College, Amritsar, and then enrolled at Government College, Lahore, for his BA. But his father called him back and induced him to take up a business career. For some time he worked in the Kashmir settlement department and then later in the Kalka Simla Tonga service. Dhingra felt the abrupt termination of his studies keenly. In despair he ran away from home and worked as a stoker on a merchant ship and even tried to emigrate to Australia. He could not because of the colour of his skin. Upon his return home, his elder brothers combined to persuade their father to send him to England to study. In June 1906 he sailed on the SS *Macedonia*, and in November he enrolled at University College, London, to study engineering.

In London, Dhingra was drawn into politics, in particular into the group of revolutionary nationalists at India House set up by Shyamji Krishnaverma, editor of the *Indian Sociologist*. Unlike the moderate nationalists who argued for power-sharing with the British rulers, the India House group advocated complete independence from Britain and was prepared to use force to achieve its aims. Vinayak Damodar Savarkar, one of the leaders of India House, inaugurated the Free India Society, and revered Mazzini and the cult of political assassination. Dhingra had experienced the humiliations of racism at first hand: as a stoker on ship, while working in Kashmir, and not being allowed into Australia. Racist articles in the English press fuelled his indignation. He resonated with India House, was an avid reader of the *Indian Sociologist*, and greatly admired Savarkar.

Dhingra believed in action, that 'mere talk' would get nowhere, and that 'Englishmen understood only violence' (BL OIOC, L/P&J/6/986). At India House he set up a society for teaching martial arts and also tried to establish a shooting range. Having been refused permission for the latter, he enrolled for revolver practice at a shooting gallery in Tottenham Court Road and became quite proficient. He stayed at India House on two occasions, the second in 1908, for six months. At the end of that year he left, having vowed to sacrifice his life for the motherland. He moved to 108 Ledbury Road, Bayswater, and distanced himself from his family and India House to focus on his mission. On 1 July 1909 he shot Sir (William Hutt) Curzon Wyllie at a National Indian Association meeting at the Imperial Institute, South Kensington, as a 'humble revenge for the inhuman hangings and deportations of patriotic Indian youth' (*Daily News*, 18 Aug 1909) and as 'an act of Patriotism and Justice' (PRO, CRIM 10/99). He also shot Dr Cawas Lalcaca, a Parsi physician from Shanghai who had attempted to save Wyllie, though he later insisted that Lalcaca's death was accidental. He remained calm at his arrest, and was found to have a further revolver, a knife, and a handwritten statement. The statement was suppressed.

At his trial Dhingra represented himself, without recognizing the legitimacy of the court. On sentence of death, he thanked the judge, saying: 'I am proud to have the honour of laying down my life for the cause of my motherland' (PRO, CRIM 10/99). His last wish was for a bath and a shave. He was executed at Pentonville prison on 17 August 1909. On the following day his suppressed statement was printed in the *Daily News*, Savarkar having given a copy to his friend David Garnett, who arranged for its publication. In it Dhingra described himself as a patriot working to emancipate his motherland. He ended: 'The only lesson required in India today is to learn how to die and the only way to teach it is by dying ourselves, and so, I die and glory in my Martyrdom. *Bande Mataram*' ('Hail motherland'; *Daily News*, 18 Aug 1909). Fearing the impact in India of the arrival of Dhingra's ashes, the authorities denied him a cremation and buried his body in the grounds of Pentonville prison. In December 1976, however, his remains were exhumed from the prison yard, were returned to India for a hero's welcome, and were cremated at Amritsar.

The impact of the assassination was enormous. Never before had the empire been struck at home, in its own metropolis. Although quickly and loudly condemned both in England and India, Dhingra's actions also drew admiration. Winston Churchill is said to have 'quoted with admiration Dhingra's last words as the finest ever made in the name of Patriotism' (Blunt, 288).

LEENA DHINGRA

Sources V. N. Datta, *Madan Lal Dhingra and the revolutionary movement* (New Delhi, 1978) · R. Visram, *Asians in Britain: 400 years of history* (2002) · I. Yajnik, *Shyamji Krishnaverma: the life and times of an Indian revolutionary* (Bombay, 1950) · D. Garnett, *The golden echo* (1953) · W. S. Blunt, *My diaries (1900–1914)*, 2 (1920) · BL OIOC, L/P&J/6/986 · BL OIOC, POS 5945, POS 8692 · enrolment form for UCL, 12 Nov 1906, UCL, Archives · PRO, CRIM 1/113/1; CRIM 10/99
Archives BL OIOC, L/P&J/6/986; POS 5945; POS 8962 · PRO, CRIM 1/113/1; CRIM 10/99
Likenesses photograph, BL OIOC

Diamond, Hugh Welch (1809–1886), photographer and asylum superintendent, was born in Norwich, the eldest son of William Batchelor Diamond, a surgeon in the East India Company, and his wife, Jane Welch. Diamond was educated at Norwich grammar school and from 1824 studied medicine at the Royal College of Surgeons. In 1828 he became a student at St Bartholomew's Hospital, London, and was appointed pharmacist to the West Kent Infirmary at Maidstone. He married, on 14 June 1831, Jane Warwick,

and opened a private practice near Soho Square in London, where he treated the sick during the cholera outbreak of 1832, the year in which he was elected to the board of health. Two years later he became a fellow of the Royal College of Surgeons, and in 1846 he was elected fellow of the Medical Society of London.

Diamond was active in London antiquarian circles, and built up collections with a particular emphasis on ceramics and prints; in 1834 he was elected a fellow of the Society of Antiquaries where he actively pursued his interest in the printing of images. In 1845 he began meeting with other 'gentleman amateurs' interested in the early art of photography. The group became known as the Calotype Society, later referred to as the Photographic Club.

The period from 1848 to 1858 was crucial to Diamond's involvement with clinical psychiatry and photography. During the 1840s he became interested in the newly reformed treatment of the insane and in 1842 he began studying mental disease at Bethlem Hospital under Sir George Tuthill. In 1848 he was elected the residential superintendent of the female department of the Surrey County Lunatic Asylum at Springfield, where he remained until 1858.

During the 1850s Diamond published more than a dozen essays and notes on photography, including a series in *Notes and Queries* in 1852, 'Photography applied to archaeology and practised in the open air'. His paper delivered to the Photographic Society in 1853, 'The simplicity of the calotype process', popularized the calotype—the earliest means of obtaining a positive image from a negative one—among amateur photographers. He also contributed articles on photography to the *Photographic Journal*, published by the newly formed Photographic Society of London, established in 1853, of which he was a founder member. Within this society Diamond emerged as the dominant figure behind the formation of the Photographic Society Club, a dining club that met five times a year to discuss photographic matters. Between 1855 and 1858 Diamond also belonged to the Photographic Exchange Club, an organization that exchanged prints by post between its twenty-two members twice a year. In addition, he participated in discussions on the recording of antiquities by photography, and in 1854 was elected honorary photographer of the Society of Antiquaries.

It was his portraits of the insane that dominated reviews of Diamond's work throughout the decade, and for which he is best remembered. During the early 1850s he made many photographs of his insane patients using Frederick Scott Archer's collodion process. Archer, inventor of the wet collodion process in photography, communicated the results of his experiments with the collodion process to Diamond in 1850. One of the advantages of the collodion process over the calotype process was its shorter exposure time, which made it easier to photograph human subjects. In 1852 Diamond presented a series, 'The types of insanity', at the first exhibition of photography at the Society of Arts. These portraits were the first systematic use of photography in the history of psychiatry. In a paper read to the Royal Society in 1856, outlining his theories of the use of photography in psychiatry, 'On the application of photography to the physiognomy and mental phenomena of insanity', Diamond argued that photography had three important functions in the treatment of the insane: as a method of recording physiognomies of the mentally ill for study, of treating the mentally ill through the presentation of an accurate self-image, and of documenting the faces of patients to facilitate identification for later readmission and treatment. In 1858 Diamond's photographs of 1852 inspired a major series of essays by John Conolly, professor of medicine at the University of London, 'The physiognomy of insanity', including engravings made from Diamond's photographs. Identified by the noted pictorial photographer H. P. Robinson as the central figure in mid-nineteenth-century photography in Britain, Diamond was credited by his contemporaries with fostering the collection of medical photographs in British medical museums and schools during the nineteenth century.

Following an incident involving the accidental death of a patient in 1856 Diamond resigned his position at the Surrey County Asylum and moved to Twickenham, where he established a private asylum for female patients. During the late 1850s and 1860s Diamond was active in the Photographic Society, editing its journal from 1859 to 1869, serving as its secretary for this period and later as one of its vice-presidents, but he discontinued his practice of photographing inmates around this time. In 1858 he was elected to two Photographic Society committees, one to form a collection of photographs illustrating the progress of photographic science, the other to investigate the subject of copyright. In 1867 he served on the board of jurors for photography during the Paris Exhibition and in that year was awarded the medal for excellence from the Photographic Society. Diamond acquired a reputation as a genial host and a diverse collector. After his wife's death he was cared for by his daughter Terasa. For many years he held weekly gatherings of literary, antiquarian, photographic, and artistic friends at his home and until his death he continued to entertain at his home, Twickenham House, where he died on 21 June 1886.   J. TUCKER

Sources C. Bloore, *Hugh Welch Diamond* (1980) · S. Gilman, *The face of madness: Hugh W. Diamond and the origin of psychiatric photography* (1976) · A. Burrows and I. Schumacker, *Doktor Diamond's Bildnesse von Geisteskranken* (1979) · J. Conolly, 'The physiognomy of insanity', *Medical Times and Gazette* (6 March 1858), 238–41 · H. P. Robinson, *The Practical Photographer* (May 1896), 117 · 'Dr Hugh Welch Diamond', a visual studies workshop research project, 1970 · H. W. Diamond, 'Photography applied to archaeology', *Humphrey's Journal*, 5 (1–15 May 1853) · H. W. Diamond, *On the application of photography to the physiognomic and mental phenomena of insanity* (1856) · IGI · d. cert.
Likenesses woodcut, pubd 1886, NPG
Wealth at death £3346 12s. 2d.: probate, 21 Sept 1886, *CGPLA Eng. & Wales*

Diana [née Lady Diana Frances Spencer], **princess of Wales** (**1961–1997**), was born on 1 July 1961 at Park House, Sandringham, Norfolk, the third daughter of (Edward) John *Spencer, Viscount Althorp, later eighth Earl Spencer (1924–1992), and his first wife, the Hon. Frances Ruth Burke Roche (b. 1936), younger daughter of Edmund Maurice Burke Roche, fourth Baron Fermoy. Her only surviving brother, Charles, was born in 1964. Her parents divorced in 1969 and her mother married Peter Shand Kydd, but in most respects she enjoyed the kind of childhood reserved for the daughters of the British aristocracy for much of the twentieth century. Her early education was at Silfield Nursery School, King's Lynn, Norfolk, and (from 1970) Riddlesworth Hall, a girls' preparatory school at Diss, Norfolk. After her father succeeded to the earldom in 1975, her time was divided between the Spencer family estate at Althorp in Northamptonshire, her mother's London home, and West Heath boarding-school at Sevenoaks, Kent, which she had entered in 1974. A popular, essentially jolly girl with a talent for making friends, she had no academic success (twice failing all her O levels). But, arguably, none was required for girls of her class, who had no need to earn a living; indeed, displays of intellect could be frowned upon by the largely philistine county set. Instead she developed the physical skills of swimming and dancing (although not the quintessential country pursuit of riding) and, like many teenage girls in the 1970s, developed a crush on the prince of Wales (Charles Philip Arthur George; b. 1948). Unlike most of them, however, her family had close connections with the court: both her grandmothers and her father had held court positions; one sister, Jane, married Robert Fellowes, the son of the Sandringham agent and eventually himself private secretary to the queen; the other, Sarah, dated the prince of Wales during 1977. Diana first met the prince that year in November when he visited Althorp to shoot.

Lady Diana left West Heath at the end of 1977 and spent a term at the Institut Alpin Videmanette, a finishing school near Gstaad, Switzerland, where she enjoyed skiing but little else. She returned home in April 1978 and joined the London and county social round of the upper-class wealthy young, soon popularly known as Sloane Rangers. In between the parties and commitments of the season she had a series of jobs working with children. For a few months in 1978 she helped to teach toddlers dancing at Madame Vacani's school. In 1979 she began working three afternoons a week at the Young England Kindergarten in Pimlico, and in the following year she was for two days a week a nanny to the baby son of an American businesswoman. It was not that she needed the money: she had received an inheritance from her great-grandmother, Frances, Lady Fermoy, on her eighteenth birthday, and her parents had bought her a flat at 60 Coleherne Court, Kensington, as a coming-of-age present. It was rather that she needed something to do and that she had a natural talent with children. She had boyfriends but no serious relationship. She clung to the romantic expectation that her ideal man would come along, and that she would marry him and have a crowd of children of her own; she also apparently continued to believe that the ideal man would probably be the prince of Wales.

Engagement and the royal wedding It was not until July 1980 that Lady Diana met the prince again, this time at a house party in Sussex after a polo match. Her directness and sympathy over the death the previous year of his uncle, Lord Mountbatten, caught his attention: she was not afflicted by the usual constraints on people dealing with royalty, and was neither tongue-tied nor overly deferential. Her credentials as a potential royal bride were obvious, and over the next months she was brought into the prince's circle. The prince, at thirty-one, was under great pressure, both from his family and from an expectant press, to marry, and to marry soon. He proposed, and was accepted, on 6 February 1981. The engagement was officially announced on 24 February. At a press conference that day the couple were asked if they were in love. Diana immediately responded 'Of course'; Charles qualified her answer with 'Whatever "in love" means'. Much was later made of this exchange and of the light it shed on the divergent approaches of the couple to their marriage. But the fact that the question could be asked directly by journalists, and an answer expected, was as important: public scrutiny, comment, praise, and criticism were to shape and distort their relationship from the outset in an unprecedented manner.

On the day before the engagement was announced Lady Diana moved into Clarence House, the residence of the queen mother, and a few days later into a suite at Buckingham Palace, where she remained until the wedding. There she was insulated from the press, but also isolated from her friends, and she was left to confront the arcane procedures and practices of life in the royal household virtually alone. The prince of Wales had numerous commitments, including a tour that took him abroad from mid-March to early May. An inevitably difficult period of adjustment was made more so by her discovery of the prince's former attachment to Mrs Camilla Parker Bowles, and by Lady Diana's fear that the relationship was continuing. Dogged by the press whenever she left the palace, largely removed from her network of friends and family, her fiancé often absent, Lady Diana understandably felt some doubt about going through with the wedding. Between the engagement and the wedding she also lost a great deal of weight, possibly marking the beginning of the eating disorders which were to trouble her throughout her life.

The wedding took place on 29 July 1981 at St Paul's Cathedral. That venue was chosen over the more traditional Westminster Abbey at least partly in order to accommodate the huge numbers of people who were expected to pack the route of the procession. Throughout the summer media coverage reached saturation point. The wedding itself was the biggest outside broadcasting venture ever undertaken by the BBC or ITV, and both networks drove themselves into a frenzy over the details of the event. The American networks, too, came out in force, and the BBC broadcast live to an audience of 750 million in seventy-four countries. 'The royal wedding' (as it was universally known, as if there had never been another) was possibly the last true gala occasion of the British monarchy. Of course there were critics, both public and private, and claims that 'the whole of the British people' were enthralled by the event were as exaggerated as such claims always are, but their voices were muted in the clamour of 'wedding fever'. The 'fairy-tale wedding' was a refrain that echoed over and over again: the myth was developed of Lady Diana as a commoner, an ordinary girl, plucked from obscurity to marry the world's most eligible

Diana, princess of Wales (1961–1997), by Mario Testino, 1997

bachelor, to become a princess and eventually a queen, to live happily ever after. Even the archbishop of Canterbury, Robert Runcie, who performed the ceremony, used the metaphor in his sermon: 'This is the stuff of which fairytales are made; the Prince and Princess on their wedding day'. The wedding—complete with glass coach, ivory silk crinoline frock with 25 foot train designed by David and Elizabeth Emanuel, uniformed groom, 2700 distinguished guests, and cheering crowds of thousands—certainly followed the fantasy script. The marriage which followed it did not.

Wife, mother, and media icon No modern princess of Wales has enjoyed an entirely satisfactory marriage: princes of Wales have been serial adulterers, domestic tyrants, even (in the case of George IV) bigamists. But until Diana, all the princesses of Wales went into their marriages with their eyes open. Some, it is true, loved, or came to love, their husbands, but for none was love a prerequisite of the marriage, and none expected its return. Diana, in love with Charles and seeing in her marriage the fulfilment of her youthful fantasies, and, crucially, not bred in the royal tradition of dynastic marriage, was doomed to disappointment.

After a honeymoon on the royal yacht *Britannia*, the prince and princess of Wales paid an extended visit to Balmoral, the queen's residence in Scotland, and the press (tipped off by insiders) began to report cracks in the marriage. Diana, who by the end of September was pregnant, was seen to be bored by the traditional country pursuits of the royal family. It was also evident that she was uncomfortable with the prince's devoted circle of friends, who belonged to an older generation than that of the princess, had known the prince for many years, and shared his interests. But she made an instant sensation when in late October the couple undertook their first tour together, of Wales. She had the gift of empathy with strangers and a talent for repartee which made her accessible to the crowds of well-wishers and contrasted starkly with the normally formal, restrained manners of the royal family when confronted with the ranks of their subjects. She also had the undoubted advantage of youthful good looks, which rapidly matured into well-groomed glamour: blonde, with cornflower blue eyes, and the classic pink-and-white complexion of the 'English rose' to which she was so often compared, it was her dazzling smile and general animation which attracted so many people. The enthusiasm of her reception in Wales was repeated time and again over the years, in Britain and abroad; Princess Diana (as she was universally, and inaccurately, known) soon became a much bigger popular draw than her husband.

The prince and princess of Wales returned to London in November, but they had no home of their own there until May 1983, when their apartments in Kensington Palace were completed. Until then they lived in a suite of rooms in Buckingham Palace, and at the prince's country house, Highgrove, in Gloucestershire. The prince of Wales soon resumed his usual round of public duties. Like all princes

of Wales, he was in the invidious position of having no clearly defined role, and he had worked hard over the years to carve out a meaningful niche for himself in public life without intruding on the prerogatives of the queen or involving himself in party politics. But if his role was poorly scripted, that of his wife hardly existed at all. The position of women in society generally had changed drastically since the days of the last princess of Wales, later Queen Mary, when a royal wife could be expected to smile graciously on the populace, to bear children, to lend her name—and occasionally her presence—to the charitable endeavours of carefully selected good causes, and otherwise to blend gracefully and silently into the background.

Diana had a difficult pregnancy, possibly exacerbated by bulimia, but her unhappiness at discovering the difference between the fairy tales (which end at the altar) and the realities of a royal marriage was not merely hormonal. From a broken home herself, she had, by many accounts, hoped for a 'normal' family life based on a close partnership between husband and wife. Instead she found—as perhaps she should have realized, and as she certainly could have been warned—that her husband, however loving, was frequently required to be absent and had public priorities and obligations which he placed above the needs and wishes of his wife. She had to cope with becoming royal, adapting to her place in the royal family and in the royal household, a process begun during her engagement but only ever fitfully completed. In addition she had to come to terms with the constant presence of the media in her life: even a holiday at a private estate in the Bahamas resulted in the appearance in the papers of long-lens photographs of the couple enjoying themselves on the beach. The birth of a son, Prince William, on 21 June 1982, the day after the ending of the Falklands War, brought the prince and princess together for a time, but the princess suffered badly from postnatal depression, heightening once more the emotional temperature at Kensington Palace. In September 1982 Diana represented the royal family at the funeral of Princess Grace of Monaco. It was the first time she had carried out such a duty by herself, and she performed admirably. She later claimed to have received no congratulations or praise from the royal family for her efforts, despite the favourable press coverage; her desire to impress and support the royal family and their lack of regard for her efforts became a regular refrain.

From 1982 to 1987 Diana captured perfectly something of the *Zeitgeist*. Especially after the birth of her second son, Prince Henry, on 15 September 1984, the princess of Wales became an icon of fashion, her clothes reported and copied slavishly, while changes to her hairstyle became front-page news. With the prince or without him, she drew huge crowds at her public engagements, and the attention given to their international tours, especially those to Australia and New Zealand in 1983 and to the United States in 1985, was unprecedented. Diana was the only member of the British royal family to arouse widespread popular interest outside the old 'white' British colonies:

her face on the cover of a magazine would enhance sales in America, in Europe, and in the Far East.

The deterioration of the Waleses' marriage continued apace. While the popular press generally idolized the princess and mocked her husband, it periodically turned on her, and some publications, notably *Private Eye*, had never stopped their insinuations about the state of her marriage, the fidelity of her husband, and the shallowness of her lifestyle. Diana read the press avidly, deeply concerned about the way she was portrayed. By the summer of 1986 both the prince and princess had taken lovers. The prince returned to his friend Camilla Parker Bowles, and the princess fell in love with a captain in the guards, James Hewitt, with whom she began an affair which lasted until 1989 and which was renewed late in 1990, continuing until the following year. Her craving for romance partially satisfied, the princess sought to redefine her public image with the assistance of her new equerry, Patrick Jephson. She was no longer satisfied to be regarded as the most beautiful woman in the world; her new image was to be invested with moral stature and emotional depth.

Patron of suffering Diana had an affinity with the helpless, the ill, and the suffering which first showed itself in her schooldays, when she regularly visited a home for the handicapped as part of a community project. Like her talent with children, it rested on her ability to communicate in an unaffected way and on her empathy with the individual in front of her. From June 1987, when she visited the first ward for AIDS sufferers in Britain, she associated herself closely with a huge number of causes and organizations devoted to different kinds of sufferers, from large organizations such as the Red Cross to small projects such as the Rainbow House Hospice for sick children, from Relate (the marriage guidance organization) to shelters for battered wives, and for every shade of illness, disease, and injury, from leprosy to AIDS. Her patronage was widely sought and widely bestowed: whatever disadvantages might accrue from having a notoriously temperamental and, as time passed, increasingly unpredictable royal patron, Diana's name—and more especially her presence—were guaranteed to raise the profile of issues and organizations, and to increase revenue significantly. There was nothing novel about the association of a royal woman with good causes of these kinds: charity was the traditional outlet for women of the upper classes. But Diana brought glamour to the work and a degree of publicity which was never available to her less photogenic but no less hard-working sister-in-law, the princess royal, among others.

Much as she intended, her connections with charity provided the princess with a radically different public profile between 1987 and 1992 from that of the preceding five years: where she had previously been portrayed merely as a glamorous woman with an ill-disguisedly unhappy marriage, now she claimed the moral high ground as the royal who cared, who empathized, who suffered with the suffering, and who made lives better by the light of her countenance and sympathy. Hers was not the patronage of the letterhead, the official visit to headquarters, and the charity dinner (although she did those things as well); her preference was to visit the sufferers themselves and the workers in the field, and to chat informally, to hold hands, and to hug the patients. Semi-miraculous healing powers were sometimes attributed to the princess in what has been viewed as a late twentieth-century revival of the ancient practice of 'touching for the king's evil'. (The royal touch was in medieval times said to have curative powers, as evidence of the divine right of kingship.) Diana revelled in the limelight of these occasions, made endless use of the photo opportunities they provided, and deliberately cultivated this new image of caring royalty; and for every press report praising her work there was another accusing her of shameless manipulation, of using the sick, the helpless, the dying, for her own advantage. But whatever her motivations—and they were probably as mixed as those of everyone else—they mattered little or nothing to those whom she met. If her much vaunted caring was an act, it was a thoroughly successful one; if her interest was feigned, for her public the impersonation was good enough to be taken for the real thing. People who met her, from hospital patients and charity workers to hardened journalists, spoke of her charm, her apparently genuine sympathy and interest; men in particular were entranced by a flirtatious manner which made them feel, for the time being, the most important person in the room. While the more cynical dismissed her as irrelevant, the princess built up a huge constituency of admirers among the general public, both in Britain and abroad, a constituency that was to stand her in good stead during the public dissolution of her marriage.

The 'War of the Waleses' In January 1990 an indiscreet telephone conversation between the princess and someone who was apparently a lover (subsequently identified as James Gilbey, a car salesman) was recorded by a radio ham and offered to the press. Although the papers did not at that time make the information public, the princess knew they had the tapes. Knowledge of the damage they could do to her reputation—and her ability to secure her own terms should she separate from the prince of Wales, as she had apparently decided to do—coloured her subsequent actions. There followed what has been termed the 'War of the Waleses', in which the increasingly antagonistic camps of the prince and princess briefed the press against each other. From Diana's side came information about the prince's relationship with Camilla Parker Bowles and, more hurtfully, suggestions eagerly seized upon by an already hostile media that the prince was an absent, uncaring father. From the prince's side came damaging insinuations about the princess's mental health: claims were made that she was unstable, that insane jealousy had driven the couple apart, even that she had a condition known as 'borderline personality disorder'.

This unedifying spectacle of personal misery had kept the tabloids and their readers amused for two full years when in early 1992 Diana seized the initiative by deciding to co-operate with Andrew Morton, a journalist and author, on her biography. Her friends were told they could talk to him, and she herself made a series of tape recordings which were given to Morton. The condition of her assistance was that she have 'total, utter deniability' (Clayton and Craig, 221): if challenged by the royal family or the press she would repudiate any connection with the book. The Waleses made one of their last joint tours in February 1992, to India, where the princess was photographed alone at the Taj Mahal on Valentine's day. *Diana: her True Story* was published and serialized in the *Sunday Times* in June. It caused a sensation: Diana was portrayed as the victim of a callous royal family, the wronged wife of an uncaring and unfaithful husband, a devoted mother betrayed. Claims of serious eating disorders and suicide attempts were made, and the media had another field day. The chairman of the Press Complaints Commission (PCC), Lord McGregor of Durris, condemned the book as 'an odious exhibition of journalists dabbling their fingers in the stuff of other people's souls' (*The Times*, 9 June 1992). He was deeply embarrassed when, despite her assertions to the contrary, it became obvious that Diana must have authorized the book: her relations with the PCC were fatally damaged, and later complaints against media intrusion were treated with scepticism.

In August 1992 the long-withheld tapes of Diana's telephone conversation with James Gilbey were published in full by *The Sun*; but Diana had got her version of events out first, and the damage caused by 'Squidgy-gate' (so called from a term of endearment used on the tape) was limited. In the autumn the prince and princess carried out their final foreign engagement together, a tour to Korea, where a photograph of the unhappy couple looking in different directions encapsulated their collapsing marriage. On 25 November the prince of Wales asked for a formal separation, which was duly announced in the House of Commons on 9 December. There was, according to the prime minister, John Major, no intention of seeking a divorce, and when the prince of Wales succeeded to the throne there would be no constitutional reason why his wife should not be crowned queen.

Diana's popularity reached a peak in 1993. Tapes made of conversations between the prince of Wales and Camilla Parker Bowles in 1989 and published in part in November 1992 and in full in January 1993 proved her assertions that her husband had been unfaithful, and carefully timed excursions (often with her sons) regularly drove more traditional royal activities from the front pages of the papers. She made triumphant official visits abroad, to Nepal and Zimbabwe, and continued her high-profile charitable work. In private a stream of alternative therapists, counsellors, psychics, fitness instructors, and psychologists provided her with reassurance, and a succession of friends were subjected to constant pleas for advice, affirmation, and love. She demanded complete loyalty, and those who did not meet her requirements were ruthlessly excised from her life. In November 1993 she dispensed with her round-the-clock police protection in order to pursue her private life without constant surveillance. But instead of the observation of a few security men she unwittingly exposed herself to the constant harassment of press photographers (or paparazzi), who, unrestrained by the presence of her policemen, followed her everywhere, often shouting abuse and physically intimidating her: photographs of Diana angry, or Diana in tears, Diana at the gym or the corner shop, commanded a far higher price than photographs of Diana carrying out public engagements.

On 3 December 1993, in a speech for the Headway charity, Diana announced her withdrawal from public life. But public interest did not diminish, and was refuelled in June 1994 by a television programme made by Jonathan Dimbleby during 1993 about the prince of Wales, in which the prince admitted his infidelity, and by Dimbleby's fully authorized biography of the prince published later that year. Also James Hewitt discussed his affair with Diana with a journalist: Anna Pasternak's book *Princess in Love* came out in October 1994. Damaging revelations about Diana's relationships with an art dealer and the England rugby captain—both married—excited the Diana-watchers further, but they did not get hold of the story of her affair with Dr Hasnat Khan, a heart surgeon with whom she fell in love in September 1995, for over a year. She had long had the habit of making secret visits to hospital wards to meet patients (which were sometimes strategically leaked to the press); now she used some of these visits as cover for meeting Khan.

Queen of Hearts It was obvious by now that divorce was inevitable, but the revelations of the previous year had been damaging to the princess, and it was probably with the intention of putting herself in the best possible position with regard to the divorce settlement that Diana agreed to give a television interview to Martin Bashir for the BBC programme *Panorama*. It was broadcast on 20 November 1995 to an audience of more than 23 million, and caused yet another furore. She wanted to be 'queen of people's hearts', her husband was not suitable to be king, and she herself would not 'go quietly', she said. Regarded in some circles as a piece of self-serving melodrama, in others the interview consolidated Diana's position as a brave victim, standing up for oppressed women everywhere. It finally prompted the queen to propose that a rapid divorce was now the most desirable outcome for all concerned. On 28 February 1996, after a meeting with the prince of Wales, Diana announced that she had agreed to his request for a divorce, by mutual consent. The decree nisi was granted on 15 July 1996, and the decree absolute on 28 August. In the settlement the princess received something in the order of £17 million, and was deprived of the title 'her royal highness'. Henceforth she was to be known as Diana, princess of Wales. In the immediate aftermath of the divorce Diana announced that she was dropping her work with all but six charities: she said she wanted to make a fresh start, and that the other charities should be able to choose a royal patron, but it looked like petulance.

In conversation with the Conservative prime minister, John Major, Diana had expressed a wish to make use of her celebrity and ability to communicate with people to be a 'roving ambassador' on humanitarian issues for Britain, but no such official role was forthcoming. At the end of 1996 she became interested in the campaign by the Red Cross to ban the use of landmines, which cause terrible injuries long after the conflicts which lead to their planting have ended. In January 1997 she accompanied a Red Cross mission to Angola to see for herself the devastation caused by their extensive use. Although Diana had given up her patronage of the Red Cross on her divorce, the charity agreed to the visit in the hope that her presence would raise the profile of its campaign. It succeeded: pictures of the princess among the injured children of Angola and of the princess walking by a partially cleared minefield made news the world over. Powerful vested interests opposed the landmine ban, and Conservative MPs went on record accusing the princess of being a 'loose cannon', interfering in politics beyond her remit, but her championing of the cause was a significant factor in the promotion of the treaty banning the mines.

1997 was a year of dramatic contrasts. On the one hand, there was Angola; on the other, Diana was firmly establishing herself as one of the international jet set, spending a considerable amount of her time in New York, where in June she gave a large portion of her wardrobe to be auctioned for charity: it raised over $3 million. And in July 1997 she accepted an invitation from the Egyptian businessman Mohamed Al Fayed to take her sons on a holiday on his yacht in the Mediterranean. On the yacht she met Al Fayed's eldest son, Dodi, with whom she began a romance. She visited him in Paris in July, and on 21 August returned to the yacht with him, having spent four days in Bosnia as part of the anti-landmine campaign. On 30 August they returned to Paris, pursued by photographers and journalists. After several changes of plan, at 12.20 on the morning of Sunday 31 August 1997 Diana and Dodi left the Ritz Hotel by a back exit, but they were spotted by photographers. There followed a high-speed chase, and about 12.24 Diana's car crashed into a pillar in the tunnel under the Pont d'Alma. Dodi Al Fayed and the driver of the car, bodyguard Henri Paul, were killed instantly; the other passenger, bodyguard Trevor Rees-Jones, was unconscious for two weeks before eventually recovering. Diana herself was severely injured and had to be cut free from the car. She was taken to La Pitié-Salpêtrière Hospital, where for two hours attempts were made to resuscitate her, until at 4 a.m. she was pronounced dead. The prince of Wales and Diana's sisters flew to Paris to accompany her body home, and at 7 p.m. her coffin arrived at RAF Northolt, west of London. After being taken to a private mortuary her body was taken to the chapel at St James's Palace, where it remained until Friday. That evening it was moved to Kensington Palace, and thence to her funeral in Westminster Abbey on Saturday 6 September. Following the funeral her remains were interred on an island in a lake on the Spencer family estate at Althorp in Northamptonshire.

There were many immediate suggestions for memorials to the princess, including renaming Heathrow airport after her, but it was five years before a national memorial—a water feature in Hyde Park—was commissioned. The Diana, Princess of Wales Memorial Fund, set up

shortly after her death, received public donations in the order of £19 million, considerably enhanced by the proceeds from sales of licensed products: by 1999 it had funds in the order of £100 million. A sister fund set up in the United States received a further $2 million. Both organizations are committed to continuing humanitarian work in Diana's name, working particularly with young people, with prisoners' families, with displaced persons, with palliative care and AIDS/HIV organizations, and on the issue of landmines.

Mourning the 'People's Princess' Diana's death swept every other issue off the news agenda in Britain and much of the rest of the world for the entire week that followed: even the death of Mother Teresa of Calcutta (whom Diana had met several times in India) on 5 September was reduced to a footnote. On the morning of Sunday 31 August Britain woke up to blanket media coverage of the crash in Paris and its aftermath. Most of the Sunday newspapers had been printed before the princess's death, and while some carried the already outdated information of her injury in a car accident, others appeared on the shelves with critical coverage of her relationship with Dodi Al Fayed. In London people began laying flowers outside Kensington Palace and Buckingham Palace, and by the evening crowds had gathered to watch the arrival of the princess's coffin. The royal family remained with Diana's sons at Balmoral, where they attended the usual Sunday morning service at Crathie Kirk. It was left to the recently elected prime minister, Tony Blair, to address the nation, speaking in his Sedgefield constituency of 'a nation in shock', and describing Diana as 'the People's Princess'. Responsibility for the accident was placed initially on the paparazzi who had been pursuing Diana and Dodi, and blame was soon attributed to the media more generally—Diana's brother, Lord Spencer, saying 'I always believed the press would kill her in the end'.

Self-recrimination by the newspapers on Monday gave way to relief on Tuesday, when it was announced that the driver of the car had been under the influence of drugs and alcohol, and self-righteousness on Wednesday, when the paparazzi who pursued Diana into the tunnel were arrested on charges of manslaughter (charges which were dropped two years later). In the meantime the mountain of flowers and other tributes outside the palaces grew by the hour; in towns and cities across the country sites (often statues of Queen Victoria) were found for people who could not make the journey to London to pay homage; florists ran out of flowers. Books of condolence were opened, and in London people queued for up to twelve hours to write their messages of grief, anger, and pain. Soon the crowds of mourners themselves became the dominant story. Foreign observers—who came in droves—were particularly fascinated by the sight of the supposedly repressed British weeping in the streets. The extensive coverage of the events in London brought yet more people to the scene, eager to participate in a historic event.

Genuine anger had been expressed towards press photographers by some of the mourners, but by Wednesday it was redirected towards the royal family. Criticism of their treatment of Diana during her lifetime was mingled with complaints that they remained in seclusion in Scotland while 'the country' grieved; attention soon focused on the empty flagpole at Buckingham Palace, where traditionally only the royal standard was raised when the queen was in residence. Flags elsewhere were brought out to fly at half mast (few flags ever flew at full mast in Britain in the late twentieth century), and the absence of a lowered flag at Buckingham Palace was interpreted in some quarters as a gesture of disrespect to Diana. Demands for the royal family to return to London were directed principally at the queen, who for a week was subjected to a degree of personal public criticism hitherto unknown. Commentators, carried away in the heat of the moment, spoke of the events as a turning point in the history of the monarchy. But it was not republican fervour: few of the mourners wanted to do away with the institution. Some called for the exclusion of the prince of Wales from the succession, seeing in Diana's fifteen-year-old son a more sympathetic heir to the throne; but most were satisfied first by the appearance of the princes at the gates of Balmoral, and then on Friday 5 September by the return of the royal family to London and the live broadcast of a carefully worded address by the queen, paying tribute to 'an exceptional and gifted human being'. Such had been the hostility that for the first time in her reign serious doubts were raised about the reception of the queen by the crowds; in the event her appearance was welcomed with respectful applause.

Diana's funeral, on Saturday 6 September, was broadcast live around the world to an estimated audience of two billion, considerably larger than that of the wedding in 1981. Hundreds of thousands lined the route from Kensington Palace to Westminster Abbey; the service was relayed to huge crowds on screens in Hyde Park. The congregation—friends, political leaders, charity workers, entertainers, and royalty—heard a mixture of popular, traditional, and classical music, including the 'Libera me' from Verdi's Requiem and a hastily rewritten version of 'Candle in the Wind' performed by Elton John, before Lord Spencer delivered a eulogy to his sister that captured a sense of anger and loss which was widely shared. He rounded on the press, and implicitly criticized the royal family for their attitude to Diana in an emotive address which drew applause from the previously silent crowds outside the abbey; it was then taken up by the congregation inside. As the hearse drove along the long route out of London to the motorway to Northamptonshire, the mourners paid their last respects and Diana left London for the last time along a road strewn with flowers.

Legacy The mourning for Diana bore many hallmarks of a popular cult: the sea of flowers at Kensington Palace, the ubiquity of her image, the miniature shrines, the stories told of miraculous cures effected by her visits to the sick, led some to view her as a secular saint. With muddled theology, others saw her as a martyr (though it was not clear in what cause she was martyred), still others as a tragic heroine, destroyed not by any character flaw of her own

but by the flaws in modern society, especially family dysfunction and a free press run wild. Slogans adopted by mourners included 'Born a lady, made a princess, died a saint', and 'Diana, Queen of Hearts', in a reference to her *Panorama* interview. Public mourning for Diana was perhaps unprecedented in scale, enhanced by her international profile and the speed of media communications: memorial services were held in the National Cathedral in Washington, DC, in Central Park in New York, in St Patrick's Cathedral in Dublin, in Paris, and in Rome. Condolence books were opened around the world: in Brussels, Germany, Johannesburg, and Tokyo among others. Much of Britain closed down for the funeral: shops closed, sporting fixtures were cancelled or postponed, and political campaigning prior to the Scottish referendum on devolution on 11 September was suspended. A minute's silence was widely observed at 11 a.m. on the day of the funeral. But for all the hundreds of thousands—even millions—who wept at her passing, placed tributes at impromptu shrines, queued for hours to sign the books of condolence, created memorial websites, or devoured the daily outpourings of the press, there were many more who did not—for whom the death of Diana was a matter of no personal interest, and who regarded the extravagances of the mourners with indifference, incomprehension, amusement, embarrassment, scepticism, or hostility. In the first week of September 1997 these millions had at best a muted voice; as time passed they came to dominate journalistic and academic assessments of Diana, though her popular appeal remained undimmed.

In the wake of 31 August extravagant claims were made for the significance of Diana's death and its impact on institutions from the monarchy to the press, from the church to the national psyche. Committed republicans knew that unhappiness with particular members of the house of Windsor would not translate into a serious threat to the throne because it was not underpinned by any structural alternative: the crowds demanding to see the queen in London wanted the reassurance of her presence and a public affirmation that she shared their feelings, not her removal; those demanding the exclusion of the prince of Wales from the succession did so because they wanted to see Diana's son the heir to the throne, not because they wanted to substitute an elected head of state. But the Windsors did learn from the popular response to Diana's death: the speed of reaction from Buckingham Palace to the attacks on America on 11 September 2001, for example, owed something to the events of four years earlier. The press, threatened with privacy legislation, agreed to a stronger regime of self-regulation, and in particular accepted a self-denying ordinance with regard to coverage of Diana's sons while they remained in education. If no other public figure after Diana received the same degree of intrusive press attention, it was more because nobody achieved the same degree of celebrity than because the press was more restrained. The churches, which had filled on 7 September, soon emptied again, and if—as was often asserted—the demonstrations of public grief represented a longing for a more spiritual dimension to life in an essentially secular society, the longings found little respite in traditional religion.

Where the life and death of Diana had perhaps their greatest impact was on the acceptability of public displays of emotion. It was her willingness to show emotion, to derive strength from admission of weakness, to empathize with victims, that attracted many of her admirers. Her adoption of the language of psychotherapy, her patronage of the culture of alternative therapies and lifestyle gurus, her confessional approach, all reflected and amplified the move of parts of British society away from the traditional culture of stiff upper lips and repressed emotion, exemplified by the royal family, but still shared by many. Diana's place in the feminist pantheon is similarly equivocal. Some regarded her as a symbol of oppressed and unliberated womanhood, destroyed by the patriarchal institutions of marriage and monarchy, while others interpreted her rejection of the double sexual standard and her championship of other victimized women as a triumph for feminist ideals.

A huge publishing industry grew up around Diana: dozens of biographies appeared in the year after her death, and there seemed no end either to the supply of or in the demand for new volumes, many of them portraying the princess in terms of unequivocal admiration which echoed popular sentiments at the time of her death. Friends and employees wrote memoirs (the book by her former private secretary Patrick Jephson struck a particular chord with those who emphasized the erratic, moody, temperamental side of Diana's character); in the United States Diana's life was regularly retold as an exemplary tale for young readers. At least two books were written by mediums claiming to be channelling Diana's thoughts from beyond the grave, and one compiled accounts of dreams about the princess. Conspiracy theories about Diana's death (which began appearing on the internet within hours of the accident), many pointing to a conspiracy between the CIA, MI5, and Mossad (which were supposed to have assassinated her to prevent her from marrying the Muslim Dodi Al Fayed), also flourished and multiplied. Academics wrote about Diana in the language of cultural studies as the iconic figure of the end of the millennium, studied the interconnections between princess and media, and speculated about the significance of the popular demonstrations of grief after her death. Historians, for the most part, wisely left the subject alone until more perspective could be brought to bear.

Parallels between Diana and the American Hollywood icon Marilyn Monroe were frequently drawn: both women were thirty-six at their deaths, both had difficult personal lives, both were adored by huge publics, and both were subjected to intense scrutiny by the media on behalf of those publics. Both received the latterday accolade of celebrity, the use of a single name identifier. The comparison was highlighted by the popular musician Elton John, who rewrote 'Candle in the Wind', originally an elegy for Marilyn, as a tribute to Diana and performed it at her funeral. The recording became the best-selling single of all time and generated large sums for the Diana,

Princess of Wales Memorial Fund. Diana had been the inspiration of photographers and fashion designers, but she did not inspire any visual art comparable in significance to Andy Warhol's pop art images of the actress. A musical about her life toured in Germany for a time, and in 2002 Jonathan Dove's controversial television opera, *When she Died*, was screened.

Adored and vilified, loved and loathed, for almost twenty years Diana personified celebrity. She brought glamour and international prestige to an otherwise grey Britain suffering from economic dislocation and decreasing significance on the world stage. She used the spotlight that followed her everywhere to bring attention to unfashionable causes and to help relieve suffering. Her ready smile found reflections around the world; by her death millions felt diminished.   K. D. REYNOLDS

Sources T. Clayton and P. Craig, *Diana: story of a princess* (2001) • A. Morton, *Diana: her true story—in her own words* (1997) • A. Morton, *Diana: her true story* (1992) • B. Campbell, *Diana princess of Wales: how sexual politics shook the monarchy* (1998) • J. Dimbleby, *The prince of Wales* (1994) • P. D. Jephson, *Shadows of a princess* (2000) • J. King and J. Beveridge, *Princess Diana: the hidden evidence* (2001) • A. Kear and D. L. Steinberg, *Mourning Diana: nation, culture and the performance of grief* (1999) • *The Times* (1–11 Sept 1997) • *The Guardian* (1–11 Sept 1997) • *Daily Telegraph* (1–11 Sept 1997) • *The Independent* (1–11 Sept 1997) • Burke, *Peerage*

Archives FILM BFI NFTVA, *Panorama*, BBC 1, 20 Nov 1995 • BFI NFTVA, *World in action*, ITV, 20 Jan 1997 • BFI NFTVA, 'The private life of Princess Diana', ITV, 25 Feb 1997 • BFI NFTVA, *Heart of the matter*, BBC 1, 11 Feb 1997 • BFI NFTVA, death of Diana, princess of Wales, 31 Aug 1997 • BFI NFTVA, funeral of Diana, princess of Wales, 6 Sept 1997 • BFI NFTVA, 'Memorial of Diana', BBC 1, 21 Dec 1997 • BFI NFTVA, 'Trouble with Diana', Channel 5, 21 Dec 1997 • BFI NFTVA, 'Diana – a tribute', Channel 4, 25 Dec 1997 • BFI NFTVA, *Modern Times*, 30 Dec 1997 • BFI NFTVA, 'Diana – the week the world stood still', ITV, 31 Dec 1997 • BFI NFTVA, *Dispatches*, Channel 4, 4 June 1998 • BFI NFTVA, 'Diana, my sister the princess', BBC 1, 24 June 1998 • BFI NFTVA, *Heart of the matter*, BBC 1, 28 June 1998 • BFI NFTVA, 'The unseen Diana', 30 Aug 1998 • BFI NFTVA, documentary footage • BFI NFTVA, news footage • BFI NFTVA, wedding, 1981 | SOUND BL NSA, wedding, 1981 • BL NSA, documentary recordings • BL NSA, news footage

Likenesses Lord Snowdon, photographs, 1981 • T. Donovan, bromide prints, 1986–90, NPG • T. Donovan, colour prints, 1986–90, NPG • D. Bailey, photograph, 1987, NPG • M. Testino, photographs, 1997, priv. coll. [*see illus.*] • P. Demarchelier, photographs • photographs, Hult. Arch.

Wealth at death £21,468,352—gross

Diaper, William (1685–1717), poet, was born in Bridgwater, Somerset, the son of Joseph Diaper. Nothing else is known of his family or early life. In his poetry he describes himself as 'one bred up in homely Cott'. He matriculated on 3 April 1699 at Oxford, where he studied at Balliol College as 'pauper puer'. He graduated BA in 1702, and remained as a scholar until 1705. His name reappears in the college books in 1710 as a BA commoner.

Diaper was ordained deacon in Wells on 19 June 1709, and served subsequently as curate in Brent in the same diocese. This appointment may not have been entirely happy. His stark but also amusing topographical poem 'Brent' describes the place as 'nature's gaol', where winter flooding leaves its inhabitants isolated with scant food and 'unwholesome ale'. Diaper may have taken another cure in Crick, Northamptonshire, and by March 1714 was serving in Dean, near Basingstoke.

As a poet Diaper made his mark first in 1712 with the publication of *Nereides, or, Sea-Eclogues, Callipaedia*, and *Dryades*. He came to the attention of Jonathan Swift, who wrote:

> I have contrivd to make a Parson of him; for he is half a one already, being in Deacon's Orders, and serves a small Cure in the Country, but has a sword at his A[rse] here in Town. Tis a poor little short Wretch, but will do best in a Gown. (Swift, *Journal*, 586)

Swift introduced Diaper to his circle where he was taken up by Henry St John, first Viscount Bolingbroke, and Sir William Wyndham. On 13 February 1713 Swift speaks of him 'in a nasty Garret, very sick'. On this occasion Swift brought him a gift of £20 from Bolingbroke. Swift was soon appointed dean of St Patrick's in Dublin, though he assured Diaper: 'I will move Heaven and Earth that something may be done for you'. In the same letter he advised Diaper to control his extravagant similes, and write more like a mortal man (*Correspondence of Jonathan Swift*, 346). Swift could do little, however, to relieve Diaper's poverty, and following the death of Queen Anne his other patrons were deprived of influence.

Diaper published *An Imitation of the Seventeenth Epistle of the First Book of Horace* in 1714, and addressed the poem to Swift. His last literary project, *Halieuticks*, was a verse translation of Oppian, of which he completed two books, published posthumously (1722). Diaper's best poetry is contained in *Nereides* and the translation of Oppian, where his descriptions of the ocean and of aquatic life are startling and individual.

There is an unconfirmed suggestion that Diaper was ordained priest in 1715. By May 1716, however, he was again ill. He died some time in 1717, though neither the date nor location is recorded. RICHARD GREENE, rev.

Sources Bodl. Oxf., MS Rawl. J.4⁰, fol. 405 · G. Grigson, 'William Diaper, an unknown poet', *The harp of Aeolus* (1948) · D. Broughton, 'Introduction', *The complete works of William Diaper* (1952), xv–lxxvii · J. Swift, *Journal to Stella*, ed. H. Williams, 2 (1948) · *The correspondence of Jonathan Swift*, ed. H. Williams, 1 (1963)

Diarmait alumnus Daigri (*d.* in or after 831). *See under* Iona, abbots of (*act.* 563–927).

Diarmait mac Cerbaill (*d.* 565), high-king of Ireland, succeeded to the high-kingship, according to the annals, on the death of his kinsman Tuathal Máelgarb in 544. The early years of his reign were overshadowed by the great plague of the 540s which reached Ireland in 549. The first decade of the reign also saw aggressive activity by his kinsmen of the northern Uí Néill within the province of Connacht. The last years, on the other hand, are presented by the annals as a period of defeat for Diarmait himself, initiated by what is called 'the last Feast of Tara', which Diarmait celebrated in 560. In the next year, the northern Uí Néill combined with the Connachta to defeat Diarmait in the battle of Cúl Dreimne; in 562 he was defeated by the king of Tethbae (roughly modern co. Longford), and in 563

the same northern Uí Néill defeated the Cruithni of north-eastern Ireland. Two of them were to succeed Diarmait when he was killed in 565 by a Cruithnian prince, Áed Dub. According to some annals, this took place in Ráith Becc in Mag Line, the kingdom situated in the valley of the Antrim Water on the east side of Lough Neagh. Later accounts suggest that his body was buried at Connor, Antrim, but the head at Clonmacnoise.

The annalists' picture of Diarmait mac Cerbaill seriously underestimates his significance. The reference to the last feast of Tara has been interpreted as the final celebration of a pagan marriage-feast between the king and the goddess of sovereignty. Accordingly it has been suggested that Diarmait may have been the last major king to be a pagan. He belonged to the generation after the concluding dramatic Uí Néill conquests in the midlands, when the Uí Néill must first have formed a distinct lineage, and so reaped the fruits of earlier achievements. He established his own branch of the Uí Néill as the dominant power in the midlands at the expense of Cenél Coirpri, the lineage of his predecessor, Tuathal Máelgarb, and at the expense, also, of Cenél Fiachach, whose ancestor Fiachu mac Néill was still remembered in the annals as having been responsible for the conquest of Mide. The echoes of the removal of Cenél Coirpri from power continued to reverberate in the hagiography both of Patrick and of Brigit written in the second half of the seventh century. The unfavourable portrait in the annals is probably a consequence of their origins in Iona, founded during Diarmait's reign by Columba, a member of Cenél Conaill and thus a close relative of those northern Uí Néill who defeated Diarmait at the battle of Cúl Dreimne. On the other hand, Adomnán, writing more than a century later, judged Diarmait's power to have been exceptionally extensive. He makes Columba warn Diarmait's son *Áed Sláine against the sin of kin slaying, saying that 'if ever you commit that sin, you will enjoy not the whole kingdom of your father, but only some part of it, in your own *gens*, and for but a short time' (*Life of Columba*, 1.14). Adomnán uses *gens* of such groups as the Connachta or the Dál Riata; the implication is that Diarmait's authority was wider than the Connachta, to which all the Uí Néill were still in his time reckoned to belong. In a later chapter Adomnán records Columba's bitter denunciation of Diarmait's killer, Áed Dub: 'This Áed Dub had been a very bloody man, and a slayer of many men; he had also killed Diarmait mac Cerbaill, ordained by the authority of God as ruler of all Ireland' (*Life of Columba*, 1.36). The annals, derived from Iona, and the life, written by an abbot of Iona, present different pictures of Diarmait, perhaps because the annals were earlier and so more involved in the conflicts of the northern Uí Néill against Diarmait.

There is some confusion in the late Middle Irish account of his marital unions, but they suggest that each of his sons was born to a different mother: Mugain, daughter of Conchrad mac Duach of the Connachta, is said to have been the mother of Áed Sláine; Brea (or Breca), daughter of Colmán mac Nemaind, the mother of Colmán Becc;

and Eithne (or Erc), daughter of Brénainn Dall of the Conmaicne Cúile (or the Connachta), the mother of Colmán Mór.   T. M. CHARLES-EDWARDS

Sources Adomnán's Life of Columba, ed. and trans. A. O. Anderson and M. O. Anderson, rev. edn, rev. M. O. Anderson, OMT (1991) · W. Stokes, ed., 'The annals of Tigernach [8 pts]', Revue Celtique, 16 (1895), 374–419; 17 (1896), 6–33, 119–263, 337–420; 18 (1897), 9–59, 150–97, 267–303, 374–91; pubd sep. (1993) · Ann. Ulster · G. Murphy, 'On the dates of two sources used in Thurneysen's Heldensage: 1. Baile Chuind and the date of Cin Dromma Snechtai', Ériu, 16 (1952), 145–56 · M. C. Dobbs, ed. and trans., 'The Ban-shenchus [3 pts]', Revue Celtique, 47 (1930), 283–339; 48 (1931), 163–234; 49 (1932), 437–89 · W. M. Hennessy, ed. and trans., Chronicum Scotorum: a chronicle of Irish affairs, Rolls Series, 46 (1866) · M. A. O'Brien, ed., Corpus genealogiarum Hiberniae (Dublin, 1962) · K. Meyer, ed., 'The Laud genealogies and tribal histories', Zeitschrift für Celtische Philologie, 8 (1910–12), 291–338 · F. J. Byrne, Irish kings and high-kings (1973)

Diarmait mac Máel na mBó (d. 1072), king of Leinster and claimant to the high-kingship of Ireland, was the son of Donnchad mac Diarmata (fl. 1003), and Aife, daughter of Gilla Pátraic mac Donnchada, king of Osraige (Ossory). His customary patronymic máel na mbó (servant of the cattle) had been the usual identification for his father. Diarmait's dynasty was Uí Chennselaig of south-east Leinster and he was king of Leinster between 1042 and 1072; but he was involved not only in Ireland, but also in the Irish Sea and England.

The earliest notices of Diarmait are the blinding of a rival in 1036, a raid on the viking town of Waterford in 1037, and raids on several monasteries in 1040. By 1041 he had begun a feud with Donnchad Ó Briain, the king of Munster and claimant of the Irish high-kingship, who was also the father of Diarmait's wife Derborgaill (d. 1080); their son was Murchad (d. 1070). Donnchad began by burning Ferns (Wexford), in revenge for which Diarmait attacked Killeshin (Laois). By 1048 Donnchad forced Diarmait's submission, which Diarmait promptly disregarded by leading a raid into Munster.

Diarmait became involved in the first of his foreign adventures in 1051 when he provided refuge for two Anglo-Saxon nobles, the brothers Harold and Leofwine Godwineson, during their exile from England. In the summer of 1052 he supplied his guests with a fleet to reinstate themselves in England. Also in 1052 Diarmait captured the important viking town of Dublin after forcing the king Echmarcach Rögnvaldsson to flee. Despite his increasing power, in 1049 and 1053 he was again forced to submit to Donnchad Ó Briain. Using Dublin as a base, Diarmait began to raid northwards and in 1053 his army attacked Meath, which it would raid three more times, in 1059, 1068, and 1072. In 1054 he allied with Gilla Pátraic of Osraige for a raid on Munster, and in 1057 he raided Scattery Island. In 1058 Diarmait made an alliance with Donnchad Ó Briain's nephew Toirdelbach, who hated his uncle for his role in the murder of his father, Tadc. The allies raided Limerick and Diarmait defeated Donnchad at the Galtee Mountains. Diarmait returned the next year and burned Donnchad's forts.

Diarmait again became involved in affairs outside Ireland in 1058, when an attempted conquest of England by the Norwegian heir-apparent Magnus, son of the Norwegian king, Harald Hardrada, used troops from Dublin. This could have encouraged Diarmait in other foreign ventures, and in 1061 his son Murchad led a fleet to the Isle of Man, where he forced his father's old foe Echmarcach Rögnvaldsson to pay tribute. Diarmait busied himself with the destruction of his father-in-law, Donnchad, and in 1062 he and Toirdelbach defeated Donnchad's army at Cleghile (Tipperary); Donnchad submitted to Diarmait. Political assassination was used when Diarmait and Toirdelbach paid one Áed Ó Conchobar 30 ounces of gold to kill a rival prince in 1066.

After his friend Harold Godwineson was defeated and slain in October 1066, Diarmait's court became one of the centres of the Anglo-Saxon resistance. He gave refuge to members of Harold's family, including his sons, Godwine, Edmund, and Magnus, and supplied fleets for their unsuccessful invasions of England in 1068 and 1069. Misfortune would mark Diarmait's final years after the deaths of his sons Glúniairn and Murchad in 1070. Disorder in Leinster that year was put down only with the assistance of Toirdelbach, who was forced to return on the same errand the following year. In 1071 warfare broke out in Diarmait's own family, between his grandson Domnall and nephew Donnchad. The old king made one last expedition, in 1072, into Meath, but in the battle of Odba, 7 February 1072, he was defeated and killed by Conchobar Ó Máil Shechlainn.

BENJAMIN T. HUDSON

Sources W. Stokes, ed., 'The annals of Tigernach [8 pts]', Revue Celtique, 16 (1895), 374–419; 17 (1896), 6–33, 119–263, 337–420; 18 (1897), 9–59, 150–97, 267–303, 374–91; pubd sep. (1993) · M. C. Dobbs, ed. and trans., 'The Ban-shenchus [3 pts]', Revue Celtique, 47 (1930), 283–339; 48 (1931), 163–234; 49 (1932), 437–89 · S. Mac Airt, ed. and trans., The annals of Inisfallen (1951) · B. Hudson, 'The family of Harold Godwinsson and the Irish Sea province', Journal of the Royal Society of Antiquaries of Ireland, 109 (1979), 92–100 · B. T. Hudson, 'The viking and the Irishman', Medium Ævum, 60 (1991), 257–67 · M. A. O'Brien, ed., Corpus genealogiarum Hiberniae (Dublin, 1962) · D. Ó Corráin, 'The career of Diarmait mac Máel na mBó, king of Leinster: pt 1', Old Wexford Society Journal, 3 (1971), 26–35 · D. Ó Corráin, 'The career of Diarmait mac Máel na mBó, king of Leinster: pt 2', Old Wexford Society Journal, 4 (1972–3), 17–24 · E. Hogan, Onomasticon Goedelicum (1910) · D. Ó Corráin, Ireland before the Normans (1972) · AFM · Ann. Ulster · T. W. Moody and others, eds., A new history of Ireland, 9: Maps, genealogies, lists (1984) · S. Duffy, 'Irishmen and Islesmen in the kingdoms of Dublin and Man, 1052–1171', Ériu, 43 (1992), 93–133

Dibben, Thomas (1677/8–1741), Latin poet and Church of England clergyman, was born in London, the son of Richard Dibben. He was admitted to Westminster School on the foundation in 1692, and elected in 1696 aged eighteen to a scholarship at Trinity College, Cambridge, from where he graduated BA (1699), MA (1703), BD (1710), and DD (1721). On 16 July 1701 he was instituted to the rectory of Great Fontmell, Dorset. He was chaplain to John Robinson, bishop of Bristol and lord privy seal, with whom in 1712 he went to the Peace Congress of Utrecht. On Robinson's being translated to the see of London in 1714 Dibben was collated to the precentorship of St Paul's Cathedral.

He represented the diocese of Bristol in the convocations of 1715 and 1727.

Dibben published two sermons, one of which was preached at Utrecht before the plenipotentiaries in March 1712 on the anniversary of Queen Anne's accession. He acquired considerable celebrity as a Latin poet. He wrote one of the poems printed at Cambridge on the return of William III from the continent in 1697, and translated Matthew Prior's *Carmen seculare* for 1700 into Latin verse. Prior later complimented the work of his friend and former schoolfellow, claiming that 'most accurate judges will find the translation exceed the original' (M. Prior, *Poems*, 1733, preface). By this date Dibben was a resident of Poultry Compter in the City of London having, as a result of mental ill health, abandoned his family and fortune. He died there on 5 April 1741.

THOMPSON COOPER, *rev.* PHILIP CARTER

Sources Venn, *Alum. Cant.* · *London Magazine*, 10 (1741), 206 · *Fasti Angl., 1541–1857*, [St Paul's, London] · Watt, *Bibl. Brit.*

Dibbs, Sir George Richard (1834–1904), politician in Australia, born at Flagstaff Hill, Upper Fort Street, Sydney, on 12 October 1834, was the youngest of the three sons of John Dibbs (*b.* 1790), master mariner, and his wife, Sophia Elizabeth Allwright (1809–1891). He was educated in Sydney at St Philip's Church of England School and at J. D. Lang's Australian College. On 18 March 1857 he married Annie Maria Robey (1835–1909), and joined his father-in-law, Ralph Mayer Robey (1809–1864), in a sugar refinery which was bought by the Colonial Sugar Co. two years later. He worked with his brother, John Campbell Dibbs (1830–1899), in a shipping agency, managing in turn the Newcastle and the Sydney offices, and in 1865 started a successful branch at Valparaiso, after running a blockade to enter the city. In 1866 the firm became bankrupt on the failure of the Agra Bank; but by 1875 the creditors had been paid in full, and Dibbs & Co. became one of the foremost firms in Sydney.

At forty years of age Dibbs began his political career with his election as one of the members for West Sydney in the legislative assembly of New South Wales. He was returned as a supporter of local business and as one of the leading members of the Public Schools League, which championed free compulsory and secular education in state primary schools. In 1877 he was defeated, because of working-class opposition to government-assisted immigration, which he supported. In 1880 he won public favour by his coolness in submitting to a year in debtors' prison instead of paying damages in a slander suit. In 1882 he was returned for St Leonards in northern Sydney and in January 1883 became colonial treasurer in the ministry of Sir Alexander Stuart. The government stopped the sale of crown lands on which the colonial revenue had hitherto depended. On 7 October 1885 Dibbs succeeded Stuart as premier. In the elections of October 1885 he lost his seat at St Leonards to Sir Henry Parkes, but was immediately returned by the Murrumbidgee, a country seat he held until 1894. His ministry was defeated on 21 December

1885, owing to a deficit caused by the stoppage of land sales.

From 26 February 1886 to 19 January 1887 Dibbs was colonial secretary in the Jennings ministry, which struggled to restore the revenues through new forms of taxation. In July 1887 Dibbs declared his conversion from free trade to protection, speaking of his road to Damascus. From 17 January to 6 March 1889 he was again premier and colonial secretary in a minority government. In March 1891 he was appointed a delegate to the federation convention held in Sydney, in spite of Parkes's objection on the ground of his ostensible republican sympathies: he preferred unification to federation. On 23 October 1891, on the defeat of Parkes's ministry, Dibbs became, for a third time, premier and colonial secretary in a Protectionist ministry with Labor support. His government introduced a modest protective tariff, electoral reform (one man, one vote), and a labour bureau to assist the unemployed. In June 1892 he visited England on a special mission to reassure London capitalists of the financial stability not only of New South Wales but of Victoria, South Australia, Tasmania, and New Zealand. He was largely successful and was created KCMG on 24 July 1892. In 1893 there was a financial crisis: many banks closed their doors, and the panic was stopped only by the prompt action of Dibbs's government in guaranteeing savings bank deposits, making banknotes legal tender, and providing treasury advances. This made him popular for a time.

In March 1893 Dibbs himself had become bankrupt and resigned his seat, while retaining the premiership. He was at once re-elected. At the elections in July 1894 Protectionist numbers were severely reduced, and Dibbs subsequently resigned office. In further elections a year later he lost his seat and retired from politics in September 1895, but he was managing trustee of the Savings Bank of New South Wales until his death.

Dibbs was very tall and robust physically and temperamentally. In early life he had followed his mother's move from Presbyterianism to the Church of England. He died of heart disease at his home, Passy, Hunter's Hill, Sydney, on 5 August 1904 and was buried on the 6th in St Thomas's Church of England cemetery in North Sydney. His wife, two sons, and nine daughters survived him.

A. B. WHITE, *rev.* BRUCE E. MANSFIELD

Sources B. E. Mansfield, 'Dibbs, George Richard', *AusDB*, vol. 4 · L. F. Crisp, 'George Richard Dibbs, 1834–1904: premier of New South Wales, prophet of unification', *Federation fathers*, ed. J. Hart (1990), 65–9 · T. W. Campbell, *George Richard Dibbs: politician, premier, patriot, paradox* (1999) · *Daily Telegraph* [Sydney] (6 Aug 1904) · *Sydney Morning Herald* (6 Aug 1904) · *New South Wales parliamentary debates*, New South Wales Parliament (1883–95) · T. A. Coghlan, *Labour and industry in Australia, from the first settlement in 1788 to the establishment of the commonwealth in 1901*, 3–4 (1918) · P. Loveday and A. W. Martin, *Parliament, factions and parties: the first thirty years of responsible government in New South Wales, 1856–1889* (1966) · H. Parkes, *Fifty years in the making of Australian history* (1892) · E. W. O'Sullivan, 'From colony to commonwealth: half a century's reminiscences', Mitchell L., NSW · *New South Wales parliamentary record, 1824–1932*, New South Wales Parliament, 11th edn (1932) · parish register (baptism and marriage); T. D. Mutch, Index to St

Philip's register 1815–1958, Mitchell L., NSW · [business directories, Sydney] (1857–83) · [newspapers, Sydney] (8 Aug 1904)

Archives Mitchell L., NSW · State Archives of New South Wales, colonial secretary MSS, special bundles | Mitchell L., NSW, Parkes MSS · NL Aus., Villiers papers

Likenesses P. Spence, portrait, 1893, State Library of New South Wales, Sydney · photograph, repro. in *Daily Telegraph* · photograph, repro. in *Town and Country Journal* (10 Aug 1904) · photograph, repro. in *Bulletin* (11 Aug 1904) · wood-engraving, NPG; repro. in *ILN* (16 July 1892)

Dibdin, Charles (*bap.* 1745, *d.* 1814), actor, composer, and writer, was baptized privately (possibly because he was sickly at birth) on 4 March 1745 at Southampton, and again publicly on 26 March at Holyrood Church, Southampton, where his father, Thomas Dibdin, was parish clerk; his mother's name has been given as Sarah, *née* Wesgarth.

Youth and early career Charles was probably the twelfth of fourteen children, and his father was 'a silversmith, a man of considerable credit' (*Professional Life*, 1.15); nothing is known of his mother's family. His father died when he was young and the family moved to Winchester. When he was nine his fine voice won him a position as chorister at Winchester Cathedral under the organist, Peter Fussell. Dibdin's claim that he was educated at Winchester College is not supported by the school records, although he certainly received substantial schooling from some source in that town. James Kent composed anthems for him, and he and Fussell probably provided Dibdin's earliest musical training. At about the age of eleven he applied for the post of organist at Wathum, Hampshire, but was rejected on account of his youth and probably his lack of musical qualifications; however, anthem parts in his earliest notebook suggest that he had a substantial early grounding in music.

Dibdin next accepted an invitation from his elder brother Thomas (later the father of Thomas Frognall *Dibdin) to move to London. There he quickly learned extempore playing at the organ, and he often played the congregation out at St Bride's, Fleet Street. He also entered into a working relationship (unlikely to have been as an apprentice) with the music and instrument seller John Johnson; later he claimed that all he did at Johnson's shop, the Harp and Crown in Cheapside, was to tune harpsichords. Thomas sailed with the *Hope* in 1757, during the Seven Years' War, and the ship was captured by the French. Charles Dibdin soon discerned a cooling of interest by his brother's friends, and one of them, Richard Berenger, an Irishman, advised him that this was because of his refusal to act as a 'fiddler and a buffoon' while in their company; Berenger advised him to consider the stage as a career. According to Dibdin, at that point he had never been to the theatre or opera:

> I have no power of expression that can give the faintest idea of what I felt when I heard the first crash of an overture. What an immense distinction between this electrical power and the clerical strumming I had been accustomed to in the country! I was music mad; but what astonished me most was that, merely from hearing how the parts were combined and worked together in the band, I completely learnt the secret of composition.   (*Professional Life*, 1.20)

Charles Dibdin (*bap.* 1745, *d.* 1814), by Thomas Phillips, 1799

It is probable that much more was learned from practical experience in the theatres.

By December 1760 Dibdin was occasionally performing with the chorus at Covent Garden, and on 18 April 1761 he shared the benefit with other minor players. John Rich, the licensee, believing that Dibdin would ultimately possess a deep bass voice like Richard Leveridge, encouraged him and made introductions. He gained added experience performing at the 'Histrionic Academy' at the theatre in Richmond in the summer of 1762. The next year he published a few songs and *A Collection of English Songs and Cantatas*. That summer he joined Younger's acting company at Birmingham, sang his own songs at Vauxhall, and acted in other towns. In 1764 his all-sung pastoral *The Shepherd's Artifice* was accepted by John Beard at Covent Garden for performance as the afterpiece at Dibdin's own benefit on 22 May; besides writing both the words and music, Dibdin sang the main role of Strephon. He returned to Birmingham that summer. Although he did not have the appearance necessary to be a leading man, his singing ability and his wide range of dialects ensured a great success in character roles.

Beard thrust Dibdin into the role of Ralph in Isaac Bickerstaff's *The Maid of the Mill* and his performance, beginning on 31 January 1765, was one of the great successes of the decade; every song was encored, and he even set a fashion for 'Ralph-handkerchiefs'. The opera ran for more than fifty performances. Having had his salary increased by 10s. on each of three successive Saturdays, Dibdin was soon offered a three-year set of articles at a salary of £3, £4, and £5 per week.

For the next two years Dibdin spent the summers at

Thomas Lowe's new theatre at Richmond and the winter seasons acting at Covent Garden, all the while continuing to compose songs. His next major success came on 21 February 1767, when he created the role of Watty Cockney in Bickerstaff's *Love in the City*, for which he also composed a substantial portion of the score. On 16 May 1767 Dibdin became the first person to play the pianoforte in public in England, when he accompanied Miss Brickler in a song from *Judith* (written by Bickerstaff and Thomas Arne). That summer, at Richmond, his *The Village Wedding* was produced on 18 July. In the 1767–8 season he composed two-thirds of the music for Bickerstaff's highly successful *Lionel and Clarissa*. At about this time he established a sexual relationship with the dancer and actress Harriet *Pitt (1748?–1814) [*see under* Pitt, Ann]; they had two sons, Charles Isaac Mungo *Dibdin (1768–1833) and Thomas John *Dibdin (1771–1841).

The Drury Lane years When Dibdin was dismissed by the new patentee of Covent Garden, George Colman, at the end of the 1767 season, Bickerstaff came to his defence. David Garrick was able to achieve the double coup of hiring both Bickerstaff and Dibdin for his Drury Lane company, as much to deny their talents to his rivals as for his own use. Their opera *The Padlock* (originally intended for Samuel Foote's Little Theatre in the Haymarket) was a great success. Dibdin not only supplied all the music but, following John Moody's withdrawal, achieved another major success, in the part of the servant Mungo, the first blackface role in British theatre; 'Mungo here, Mungo dere, Mungo ev'ry where', from one of his songs, became a major catchphrase. Dibdin sold the copyright in his music to Bickerstaff, who in 1769 sued two music engravers, Henry Fought and Henry Roberts, for publishing it without his permission. Dibdin had no direct interest in the case, which did not come to court, but the ownership of his work was to become a major concern.

Dibdin's brother Thomas had been imprisoned for debts and, to assist him before he took up an appointment in India, Charles Dibdin had run up a substantial debt to Garrick which he could not repay, and the relationship between the two deteriorated. As a result, Dibdin secured an agreement with Ranelagh Gardens to compose music for the next two summers at £100 per season; the Dibdin/Bickerstaff *Ephesian Matron* was first performed on 12 May 1769. Moreover, the Dibdin/Bickerstaff opera *The Captive* appeared on 21 June at the Haymarket, where Dibdin also sang ballads during the summer.

In the autumn the Stratford jubilee, honouring the 250th anniversary of the death of Shakespeare, used much music composed specially by Dibdin. Severe ructions with Garrick continued and were appeased only by Dibdin's song 'Let beauty with the sun arise', performed by the musicians beneath the window of Garrick's rooms at the inn at daybreak. Virtually none of the newspapers noticed Dibdin's contributions (or, for that matter, those by François-Hippolyte Barthélemon and Theodore Aylward), concentrating instead on the *Ode* composed by Arne.

During the 1769–70 season Dibdin continued to perform at Drury Lane. For Ranelagh he composed the music for Bickerstaff's *The Maid the Mistress* and *The Recruiting Sergeant*, as well as singing the tenor or falsetto roles. In summer 1770 he contributed songs at Sadler's Wells and Marylebone Gardens. The following season Dibdin's dramatic appearances at Drury Lane appear to have been limited to the chorus, although he did compose the music for Garrick's masque *The Institution of the Garter*. He also composed a number of glees and catches as entr'acte pieces, some of which he performed at his benefit on 1 May, for which his profit was £65 12s. Among his compositions in summer 1771 was music for *The Palace of Mirth* at Sadler's Wells, now managed by his friend Tom King.

In May 1772 potentially one of the greatest partnerships of eighteenth-century opera was broken up when an accusation of sodomy forced Bickerstaff to decamp to France. Dibdin subsequently strove to dissociate himself from Bickerstaff, although even as late as the 1790s there were rumours that Bickerstaff wrote Dibdin's lyrics. Dibdin publicly came to Garrick's defence when William Kenrick published his infamous *Roscius's Lamentation for the Loss of his Nyky*; he may have feared the accusations against Bickerstaff would be extended to him and so sought to restore his relationship with Garrick. During the 1772–3 season Dibdin continued to take character roles, and he provided the music for James Messink's pantomime *Harlequin Foundling* (from 26 December). On 1 February his successful comic opera based on Goldoni, *The Wedding Ring*, was produced anonymously. The audience believed that the text was by Bickerstaff and a riot almost erupted, averted only by Dibdin's admission of authorship. Dibdin sang in several benefit performances and that spring and summer provided both text and music for a number of productions at Sadler's Wells, a relationship which continued the following year. His reputation was not all positive, however:

> DIBDIN, alas! we nearly had forgot,
> Perhaps oblivion were the kindest lot;
> How he *composes*, 'tis not fit, we say,
> But grant kind stars that he may never *play*:
> Nor, to enlarge our wish, may never sing;
> MUNGO in this, in that, and ev'ry thing.
> (Nipclose, 53)

In December 1773 he contributed the music to Garrick's extravaganza *A Christmas Tale*. Although he was earning £6 per week plus extras at Drury Lane, as well as additional moneys from publication of his music and commissions for the public gardens, he continued to borrow against wages. His opera *The Waterman* had been rejected by Garrick for the 1773–4 season; Foote produced it to great success at the Haymarket in the summer, and Garrick immediately sent his brother George to charge Dibdin with disloyalty. Relations continued to deteriorate throughout the production of *The Cobbler*, and at the beginning of the 1774–5 season Dibdin was found to be in debt to the theatre for about £200. Despite his claims that he would have been affluent had proper payments for his music been made, he was forced to give up his salary—by then, of £7 per week—until the debt was paid. Dibdin sold his opera

The Quaker for £10 to William Brereton for his benefit (the latter realized £36 15*s.* 6*d.* on the night). Brereton then sold the rights for £100 to Garrick, who suppressed the work; it was not produced until 1777, after Garrick had left Drury Lane.

Freelance years Dibdin was discharged from Drury Lane at the end of the 1775 season. It is impossible to say whether the break with Garrick was due to Dibdin's treatment of his mistress Harriet Pitt (Garrick was godfather to their second son, Thomas), on account of Dibdin's having become undependable regarding rehearsals, or because of Garrick's jealousy. References to an earlier marriage have not been substantiated, and the relationship with Harriet Pitt was probably considered irregular, as she already had two children out of wedlock before she met Dibdin. At about this time Dibdin transferred his affection to Anne Maria Wylde (1757–1835), of Portsea, possibly a relative of the prompter James Wild, and quickly married her. They had at least one daughter, Anne (*bap.* 1776).

Dibdin composed a puppet play, *The Comic Mirror, or, The World as it Wags*, which included a satire on Garrick; it opened at the Grand Saloon at the Exeter Change on 24 June 1775 and ran for four months. In February 1776 it was revived at Marylebone Gardens. However, with no steady employment and hounded by creditors, Dibdin extracted a promise from Samuel Arnold to oversee pieces he might send, and fled to France. Dibdin claimed that his first popular sea song, 'Blow High, Blow Low', was composed during the stormy thirteen-hour channel crossing; it was featured in his opera *The Seraglio*, produced at Covent Garden on 14 November 1776. He spent five months in Calais, avoiding the English locals, and then moved to Nancy, where he continued to learn French and to read—and translate and adapt—French dramas. While in France he sent pieces back to London, of which the most prophetic concerning his future productions was *Yo Yeah, or, The Friendly Tars* (Sadler's Wells, 18 August 1777). *Poor Vulcan*, much altered by Arne and Arnold, was a success at Covent Garden on 4 February 1778.

Forced to return to England in June 1778 by France's involvement in the American War of Independence, Dibdin agreed with the patentee-manager, Thomas Harris, to write three afterpieces for Covent Garden for the 1778–9 season. He also rapidly 'wrote' several plays based on French originals for production at the Haymarket. From 1778 until 1782 he was composer to the Covent Garden theatre at £10 per week, generally producing two pantomimes and a comic opera each year. Dibdin's attempts (1780–81) to publish his songs in monthly anthologies as *The Monthly Lyrist*, later *The Lyrist, or, Family Concert*, proved unsuccessful. Uneasy in his relations with Covent Garden, he began in 1780 to think about joining his elder brother, now a wealthy man, in India; this plan was scuppered when he learned Thomas had died at sea while returning to England. Dibdin returned to Covent Garden and produced three successes—*The Islanders*, the important pantomime *Harlequin Freemason* (29 December

1780), and the burletta *Jupiter and Alcmena* (based on John Dryden's *Amphitryon*, with music by Dibdin and William Shield). Although the last-mentioned was a dramatic success, it was a financial failure, and Dibdin parted company with Covent Garden.

Philip Astley had already demonstrated the popularity of the equestrian theatre, and, in partnership with a Colonel West and some inexperienced amateurs, Dibdin built a theatre for £15,000 on the Surrey shore, outside the jurisdiction of the lord chamberlain. The Royal Circus and Philharmonic Academy opened in November 1782. It appeared to be successful, but Dibdin claimed he was undermined by Charles Hughes, who managed the equestrian business, and the elder Joseph Grimaldi, who oversaw the pantomimes; however, the collapse of the partnership may have been due as much to Dibdin's excessive ambitions. He provided at least twenty-eight works over the 1782–4 seasons and had hoped to develop the Royal Circus into a major theatre and school for young performers; possibly as many as fifty took up residence, but the theatre's finances could not support their board and lessons. When the Surrey magistrates closed the theatre in 1784, Hughes succeeded in obtaining a licence for himself; Dibdin was unsuccessful in going to law for his share of the moveables, but he continued to supply the Royal Circus with works for many years. Other than the success of *Liberty Hall*, for Drury Lane in the 1784–5 season, Dibdin's only other client at this period was Sadler's Wells.

Dibdin was approached by a Clerkenwell architect, Jacob Leroux, about building a theatre, the Helicon, near St Pancras; when the project was abandoned Dibdin had lost about £290. He was also bilked by the Dublin theatre manager Richard Daly, who purchased a number of musical works but paid only about a quarter of what had been agreed. Dibdin retired to the country in 1786, managed to sell a few works to the minor theatres, and published the hebdomadal work *The Devil*, which was discontinued after twenty-one numbers. He again decided to leave England for India, and embarked on a fourteen-month tour of the provinces with a one-man show; the tour was documented in a series of letters which were published as *The musical tour of Mr. Dibdin; in which … previous to his embarkation for India … he finished his career as a public character.* Having sold most of his possessions, including songs such as 'Nothing but Grog', for very little money, Dibdin and his family set sail in the autumn of 1788 but only reached Dunkirk before heavy weather forced the ship back to Torbay. He quarrelled with the captain, and returned to London.

The solo performer years Once again in danger of arrest by his creditors, Dibdin engaged Fischer's (some sources say Hutchin's) Auction Rooms, King Street, Covent Garden, and from 23 January 1789 staged *The Whim of the Moment, or, Nature in Little*, the first of his many 'table entertainments', for which he composed all the lyrics, music, and introductions, and, three times a week, performed as a solo singer to his own accompaniment. The first night's audience numbered only sixteen, but attendance soon increased. Dibdin moved to King and Chapman's Auction Room on 29 April, and the season was a relative success.

From the result of his farewell tour Dibdin had realized that his business was to make his audience laugh rather than to lecture them—and he decided that broad humour and anecdote between songs was the answer. This attitude laid the basis for fifteen years of success in his solo shows. Full entertainments included about thirty songs, or twenty if there was an afterpiece of about ten songs. Dibdin also established a shop for selling his own songs, thereby avoiding losing his copyrights and receiving full value from sales; his songs were extremely popular, and printed and manuscript copies appear in virtually every private English music collection of the late eighteenth century. It was at this point in his career that many of his most popular songs were composed, notably 'Tom Bowling' (1789), 'Poor Jack' (1789), and 'Push the Grog About' (1789)—all sea songs of patriotic sentiment.

From the 1789–90 season onwards Dibdin was at the Lyceum Theatre, performing *The Oddities, or, Dame Nature in a Frolic* from 7 December 1789. He also supplied a number of farces for the Royal Circus and published *The Bystander, or, Universal Weekly Expositor* from 22 August 1789 to 6 February 1790. He was contacted by Harris concerning presenting his songs as *A Divertisement* at Covent Garden and agreed, since this established the precedent of requesting permission to use his songs; because he assisted the theatre with scoring and production he was also entitled to a considerable payment. Dibdin's 1790–91 season included another success, *The Wags, or, The Camp of Pleasure*, from 18 October 1790. The next year he moved to the Polygraphic Rooms, where he produced *Private Theatricals, or, Nature in nubibus* from 31 October 1791.

For the 1792–3 season Dibdin moved to 411 Strand, opposite Beaufort Buildings, calling the room where he presented his entertainments the Sans Souci Theatre; *The Quizes, or, A Trip to Elysium* was the first work produced there (from 13 October 1792). An account of a performance of this piece, made by John O'Keeffe in his *Recollections*, described how Dibdin 'ran on sprightly and with nearly a laughing face, like a friend who enters hastily to impart to you some good news' (O'Keeffe, 2.322), and indicates that Dibdin's customized keyboard (which, besides combining a piano with organ stops including a trumpet, also had a number of pedals for adding drums, cymbals, tambourine, and gong) was already in use by that date. Dibdin's mode of singing was probably in the earlier English ballad-opera tradition rather than the increasingly ornate Italian opera style of the 1790s. By this time he was well established enough to refuse free passes for most reviewers and their friends. Dibdin continued to add new works, at the Sans Souci, circulating them in repertory, though he was also active in other areas, publishing the novel *The Younger Brother* at the beginning of January 1793. In May 1796 he published a further novel, *Hannah Hewit, or, The Female Crusoe*; Tom, his late brother, was said to be the basis for Captain Higgins.

Conditions at the Sans Souci Theatre deteriorated, and during summer 1796 Dibdin erected the 500 seat New Sans Souci Theatre in Leicester Place, Leicester Square, paying £6000 in ready money. The building, a large house with the theatre behind, used the side walls of the two adjoining properties, so that only front and back walls plus roof had to be added. *How Do You Do* (this 'daily paper' was the work of Francis Godolphin Waldron and Dibdin) states:

> When the curtain draws up, the stage presents the interior of an elegant tent, with the front and back parts of it open, so that Mr. DIBDIN appears to stand within it, while the back view presents a perspective of a garden scene, enriched with a temple and a sheet of water. (*How Do You Do*, 7, 22 Oct 1796)

The General Election (from 8 October 1796) was the first entertainment in the theatre, and it was followed by more new short works, including *Datchet Mead, or, The Fairy Court* (from 20 May 1797), written to commemorate the marriage of Charlotte, princess royal. Publication of his five-volume *A Complete History of the English Stage* also began during the 1796–7 season.

At some point during the early 1790s Dibdin had begun to take his table entertainments to a selected area of the provinces during the summer months. The tours could both exploit and enhance the popularity of his songs during the French revolutionary wars, when the public was more sensitive than ever to the sacrifices of the British sailor and soldier, and protective of the national customs Dibdin also celebrated in song. Not only did this provide extra income, but it also allowed him opportunities to compose songs for the next London season, as well as to indulge his hobby of oil painting. He carried on a large correspondence, observing the country, and these letters served as the basis for his two-volume *Observations of a tour through almost the whole of England, and a considerable part of Scotland, in a series of letters, addressed to a large number of intelligent and respectable friends* (published in parts from 5 November 1800 to 10 April 1802), with engravings from his paintings and drawings by his daughter Anne. He continued to present new entertainments at the New Sans Souci, among them in the 1802–03 season *Most Votes* (from 9 October), which was unsuccessful and was withdrawn before Christmas; however, Dibdin had the innovatory idea of publishing a book of the lyrics as well as the individual songs.

Dibdin was approaching his sixtieth year and, intending to retire, completed and published his four volumes of memoirs as *The Professional Life of Mr. Dibdin*. The title clearly states the intent of the work, and accusations of omitting personal details miss this point; however, the work is often inaccurate, biased, and opinionated. From 1789 onwards each chapter includes the lyrics of the songs from that year's entertainment.

Final years As a renewal of war with Napoleonic France loomed in 1803, Addington's government finally recognized the value of Dibdin's songs and commissioned him to publish each month a patriotic song suitable for ships, camp, and home. Following the declaration of war against France in May 1803, Dibdin published monthly eight *British War Songs* (4 June 1803 to 4 January 1804), with accompaniments for piano, small military band, and two flutes or guitars. These songs then formed the backbone of *Britons Strike Home*, which opened on 17 September, adding greatly to patriotic fervour. As a result of his efforts, including abandoning his usual summer tour of the provinces, Dibdin was awarded a pension of £200 by the government.

Dibdin retired at the end of the 1804–05 season and sold the New Sans Souci Theatre and his music stock to Bland and Weller for £1800 and three years' annuities of £100 for any songs he should compose. Whereas for several years he had produced several new entertainments and dozens of new songs, in 1806 he produced only *The Passions, in a Series of Ten Songs* and the ballad opera *The Broken Gold*, and in 1807 only the novel *Henry Hooka*, before the new Grenville government revoked his pension. Financial pressure forced him to leave his country home at Cranford, Middlesex, and return to work. He published *The Musical Mentor, or, St Cecilia at School*, and on 1 March 1808, although his voice was well past its best, he returned to his entertainments with *Professional Volunteers* at the Lyceum. Using his experience as a singing teacher (among his pupils was Rosemund Mountain), he also published several more music pamphlets. He presented *Rent Day, or, The Yeoman's Friend*, from 17 September at the Sans Pareil Theatre (opposite the Adelphi in the Strand) and probably from November *The Melange* at the Assembly Rooms, Cateaton Street, but also at the Sans Pareil; from 16 January 1809 *Commodore Pennant*, a compilation similar to *The Melange*, ran at his Music Rooms, 125 Strand. Dibdin's voice had gone, his songs were not among his finest, and the public were no longer interested; bankruptcy followed.

On 12 April 1810 a public dinner with music raised £640, of which £80 was paid to Dibdin at once and the rest was invested in annuities. Almost certainly some of the money given to him went to pay for a new six-volume edition of his *Professional Life*, of which only the first and second volumes were published; the new volumes exist in manuscript, and are concerned largely with the loss of his pension. He wrote and composed twelve songs for Charles Dignum's entertainment *The Eccentric Travellers* and, in 1811, another twelve 'expressly and exclusively' for William Kitchner's *La Belle Assemblée* magazine. His final play, *The Round Robin*, was produced at the Haymarket on 21 June 1811 but failed after two performances; however, it included his last important sea song, 'A Lass that Loves a Sailor'.

Dibdin was paralysed by an unknown illness in 1813 and lingered at his home in Arlington Street, Camden Town, London, until 25 July 1814. He was survived by his wife and daughter, as well as by his sons from his relationship with Harriet Pitt. He was buried in St Martin's burial-ground, Camden Town, with a stanza of 'Tom Bowling' inscribed on his gravestone.

Assessment Dibdin was undoubtedly unique in British entertainment in the eighteenth century and was arguably the first singer–songwriter, presenting entertainments consisting of songs without any connecting structures. Had it not been for these table entertainments, he would have been remembered only in theatre footnotes. Refusals to provide personal details for biographers can be ascribed to his reluctance to see someone else making money from his endeavours, especially since he could publish his own version of his life. A full list of plays he wrote and/or composed is impossible, and even Dibdin himself was uncertain of the exact number.

Dibdin quarrelled with almost every theatre owner and promoter and was gradually excluded from virtually all outlets for major dramatic works; his career through the 1780s was one of a continuous lowering of musical standards. He was one of the first English composers to attempt to receive an adequate—and copyrighted—return from his compositions, especially those works for the theatre, and he strongly campaigned against composers being merely salaried employees rather than being treated as part of the creative process. At the start of Dibdin's career, even a great composer such as Thomas Arne might receive only £50 for stage music. Arguments also arose over his understanding that song lyrics and poetry, sung and spoken English, were not the same thing, and that disregarding this greatly lowered the dramatic potential of theatre pieces. His own high concept of his abilities as a composer also led to arguments. That said, his early dramatic works show many highly progressive features, and he could have developed into one of the major English composers rather than the first important popular songwriter.

Dibdin's solo table entertainments proved the ideal means of combining all his many talents. His songs greatly expanded the scope of the earlier English ballad, and this—plus the serious, humorous, and dialect songs, introductions, and asides—laid the basis for much of what was to come later in music-halls and other forms of popular music. A substantial number of his songs are well written and composed, despite the rate at which they were produced. Much of their appeal lies in his statement that 'even in my comic songs, I have warmly inculcated morality; and, that I have brought prominently forward those men whose valour has insured, and will perpetuate the glory of their country' (*Professional Life*, 3.42) and in his ability to write simple but memorable melodies. Approximately 100 of his more than 900 songs were sea songs, including important works such as 'Poor Jack', 'Tom Bowling', 'Push the Grog About', 'True Courage' (1798), and 'Every Inch a Sailor' (1789). Many of his sea and army songs concentrate on positive aspects of service rather than the distressing conditions under which men actually served, and much of the popularity of his songs reflected his honest belief in the sailor's and soldier's value to their country. Other songs celebrate the countryside and its pursuits, as well as events and fashions of the day. These songs undoubtedly became an important part of the folk tradition, although they would not have been collected since the composer was known. They generally portray an idealized Britain, especially of the period between 1788 and 1806, and continued to be used two hundred years after Dibdin's time by broadcasters, film-makers, and recording artists seeking to evoke his period. Manuscripts of his songs may be found at the British Library, the National Maritime Museum, Greenwich, and at the University of Leeds.   JON A. GILLASPIE

Sources *The professional life of Mr. Dibdin, written by himself, with the words of six hundred songs*, 4 vols. (1803); enlarged 2nd edn as *The professional life of Mr. Dibdin, written by himself, with the words of eight hundred songs* (1809) [only vols. 1–2 pubd of projected 6] • *Dibdin's own royal circus epitomised* (1784) • *The musical tour of Mr. Dibdin, in which—previous to his embarkation for India—he finished his career as a public character* (1788) • *Observations of a tour through almost the whole of England, and a considerable part of Scotland, in a series of letters, addressed to a large number of intelligent and respectable friends by Mr. Dibdin*, 2 vols. (1800–02) • C. Dibdin, *The public undeceived about his pension* (1807) • C. Dibdin, *The bystander* (1790) • C. Dibdin, *A complete history of the English stage*, 5 vols. (1800) • E. R. Dibdin, *A Charles Dibdin bibliography* (1937) • W. Partington, *Charles Dibdin: the man whose songs helped to win the battle of Trafalgar and who did not allow the nation to forget it, either, being a dissertation by William Partington on a remarkable cache of manuscripts, unpublished material, holograph letters, rare paintings, et cetera, from the pen of Charles Dibdin, the dramatist, songwriter and composer: the collection is offered for sale by Alan Keen, for the Gatehouse, Clifford's Inn, London* (1944) • Highfill, Burnim & Langhans, *BDA* • N. Nipclose [F. Gentleman], *The theatres: a poetical dissection* (1772) • J. O'Keeffe, *Recollections of the life of John O'Keeffe, written by himself*, 2 (1826), 322–3 • R. Fiske, 'Dibdin, Charles', *New Grove* • [J. S. Sainsbury], ed., *A dictionary of musicians*, 2 vols. (1825), 208–9 • G. W. Stone, ed., *The London stage, 1660–1800*, pt 4: *1747–1776* (1962) • *The thespian dictionary, or, Dramatic biography of the present age*, 2nd edn (1805) • C. B. Hogan, ed., *The London stage, 1660–1800*, pt 5: *1776–1800* (1968) • P. A. Tasch, *The dramatic cobbler: the life and works of Isaac Bickerstaff* (1971) • J. Boaden, *The life of Mrs. Dorothy Jordan*, 2 vols. (1831) • L. Hunt, *Critical essays on the performers of the London theatres including general observations on the practice and genius of the stage* (1808) • *Benjamin Crosby's pocket companion to the playhouses* (1796), 99–105 • D. E. Baker, *Biographia dramatica, or, A companion to the playhouse*, rev. I. Reed, new edn, rev. S. Jones, 3 vols. in 4 (1812), vol. 1, p. 187 • *A brief memoir of Charles Dibdin, by William Kitchener, with some documents supplied by his [Dibdin's] granddaughter, Mrs. Lovat Ashe* (1823?) • R. Fiske, *English theatre music in the eighteenth century* (1973) • E. M. Lockwood, 'Charles Dibdin's musical tour', *Music and Letters*, 13 (1932), 207 • E. R. Dibdin, 'Charles Dibdin as a writer', *Music and Letters*, 19 (1938), 149 • H. G. Sear, 'Charles Dibdin: 1745–1814', *Music and Letters*, 26 (1945), 61 • E. P. Holmes, 'Charles Dibdin', PhD diss., U. Southampton, 1974 • P. Van der Merwe, '"Gone aloft": Charles Dibdin's monument', *Theatre Notebook*, 36/2 (1982), 82–5 • N. Mace, 'Music and English copyright before 1773: applications of the act of Anne to music before *Bach v. Longman*', www.wm.edu/CAS/ASP/SHARP/ [abstract of paper read to SHARP conference, 2001], 31 Jan 2001 • W. Roberts, pamphlet (1922)
Archives BL, commonplace book, musical compositions, etc., Add. MSS 30950–30970 • BL, papers, deposit 1995/12 • Harvard TC • Harvard U., Houghton L., personal and family corresp. and papers
Likenesses J. I. Richards, portrait, pubd 1779 • caricature, pubd 1788 • caricature, engraving, pubd 1791 • W. Ridley, engraving, pubd 1794 (after S. De Wilde) • engraving, pubd 1794 (after Dighton) • T. Phillips, oils, 1799, NPG [*see illus.*] • B. Smith, engraving, pubd 1801 (after T. Kearsley) • J. Heath, engraving, pubd 1809 (after T. Kearsley) • R. W. Sievier, bust on monument, 1829, Trinity College of Music, Greenwich • S. J. Arnold, oils, Garr. Club • W. Beechey, oils • B. Clowes, engraving (as Mungo in *The padlock*) • A. Dick, engraving • W. Greatbach, engraving, repro. in G. Hogarth, *Memoirs of the musical drama* (1838) • T. Kearsley, oils, Southampton • H. Meyer, portrait (after drawing by Wageman), repro. in T. J. Dibdin, *Sea songs of Charles Dibdin*, frontispiece • J. Opie, oils; Christies, 29 May 1897 • C. Phillips, engraving, reversed copy (after T. Kearsley) • B. Smith, engraving, repro. in *Thespian dictionary* (1805) • B. Smith, stipple (after A. W. Devis), BM; repro. in *Professional life of Mr. Dibdin* (1803), frontispiece • G. Stodart, engraving • T. Young, engraving (after T. Phillips) • engraving (after S. Drummond), repro. in *European Magazine* (1809) • oils, Royal College of Music, London • photogravure plate (after W. Beechey), BM; repro. in W. Roberts, pamphlet • portrait (as Mungo), repro. in *Dramatic characters … in the days of Garrick* • portrait (as Mungo), repro. in *Political Register* • prints, BM; NPG

Dibdin, Charles Isaac Mungo [*known as* Charles Isaac Pitt; *performing name* Charles Dibdin the younger] (1768–1833), theatre manager and writer, was born on 27 October 1768 in Russell Court, near Drury Lane, London, the eldest son of the actor Charles *Dibdin (*bap.* 1745, *d.* 1814) and the actress Harriet *Pitt (1748?–1814) [*see under* Pitt, Ann]. He was named after his father, his father's writing partner Isaac Bickerstaff, and their famous character Mungo from *The Padlock* (1767), which the elder Dibdin had played to great acclaim, although this last name seems to have been dropped in childhood. He made his theatrical début with his brother Thomas John *Dibdin walking in the procession for the revival of Garrick's *The Jubilee* in 1775. By this time his parents had separated, and young Charles and his mother were known by their mother's surname of Pitt. His mother entrusted her sons to her uncle Cecil Pitt, a household goods broker in the City of London. Charles first attended a school in Hackney, but at the age of nine was sent to a harsh boarding-school at Barnard Castle, co. Durham, where he remained for five years without a holiday. He was joined there after a few years by Thomas.

When he was fourteen Charles Pitt returned to London, where he was apprenticed to a pawnbroker, Mr Cordy, of Snow Hill; after the end of his seven years' apprenticeship he remained there as a shopman. Pitt's tastes were for literature rather than pawnbroking, and in 1792 he published a collection of verse, *Poetical Attempts: by a Young Man*, which was followed by other works. In 1797, with Cordy's support, he left the shop and made his début as an entertainer at the Royalty Theatre in a one-man show called *Sans six sous*, a pun on his poverty and the name of his estranged father's theatre, the Sans Souci. From then on he was known professionally as Charles Dibdin the younger, although when he married an actress, Mary Bates (1781/2–1816), at St George's, Hanover Square, on 13 June 1797, he was entered in the register as Charles Isaac Pitt. The couple had eleven children, nine of whom reached adulthood, including Mary Anne (1799–1886), a harpist, who became the second wife of the controversialist Lewis Hippolytus Joseph *Tonna; Robert William (1805–1887), a clergyman, who was the father of Sir Lewis Tonna *Dibdin (1852–1938); and Henry Edward *Dibdin (1813–1866). Following his marriage Dibdin successfully sold a pantomime to Philip Astley at the Amphitheatre of the Arts, who contracted Dibdin and his wife for a three-year engagement. They toured with the Astley company to Dublin and Liverpool as well as performing in London. For Astley Dibdin wrote a succession of songs, prologues, epilogues, and one-act musical plays, and in the 1798–9 season he was Astley's assistant manager in Dublin. The dismissal of his wife for sewing during rehearsals may have encouraged him to look for other employment, and in autumn 1799 he and his wife joined a touring equestrian company, managed by William Davis and others, visiting Liverpool, Bristol, and Manchester. Ridicule from the audience at Manchester following his inability to perform a song he had composed two hours before led Dibdin to renounce appearing on stage.

Dibdin's existence became less precarious when, in 1800, he successfully applied for the post of manager at Sadler's Wells Theatre, London. His choice of performers, who included (he claimed) the young Edmund Kean among the singers, tightrope-walkers, and pugilists, and seasons that introduced new works by himself and others that met the public taste for spectacle and patriotic sentiment, improved the fortunes of Sadler's Wells. In 1802 he and his brother Thomas became shareholders in the theatre. In 1804 Dibdin installed a water tank that enabled him to advertise Sadler's Wells as an aquatic theatre 'with realistic naval battles and Newfoundland dogs rescuing drowning children' (Highfill, Burnim & Langhans, BDA). According to his doorkeeper, Dibdin's reluctance to spend money meant that the tank was refilled with fresh water only every two months. It was also alleged that he would not provide his performers with a green room, and that his wife's jealousy prevented any woman singer who received an encore for a particular song performing that song again.

Dibdin's management survived the disaster of 15 October 1807, when eighteen people were killed in a stampede to escape a non-existent fire in the theatre. However, the end of the Napoleonic wars also reduced the public's appetite for Dibdin's brand of entertainment. His wife, to whom he expressed devotion—'during the nineteen years we were united she never contravened my wishes' (Memoirs, 118)—died on 16 August 1816. In 1819 he was confined for debt within the rules of the king's bench. In 1821 he sold his shares in Sadler's Wells, and this may have enabled his release at about this time. He continued to write songs and pantomimes, and was stage director for his former colleague William Davis at the Royal Amphitheatre from 1822 to 1823 and manager of the Surrey Theatre from 1825 to 1826. He also continued to publish poetry, including Young Arthur, or, The Child of Mystery: a Metrical Romance (1819). His A History of the London Theatres was published in 1826. His last farce, Nothing Superfluous, was produced at Hull in 1829. In 1830 he completed his memoirs, but they were not published until an abridged version appeared in 1956. He died on 13 January 1833 and may have been buried at St James's Chapel, Pentonville; his last collection of verse, The Physiological Mentor, or, Lessons from Nature, intended as a teaching aid for children, was published after his death. The manuscript of an unfinished novel, Mattias Meddler, is in the British Library; Southampton Central Library has manuscripts of Dibdin's musical scores. Dibdin's work was never as original as that of his father, and he never enjoyed an association with the major theatres as his brother did, but his reign at Sadler's

Wells was for the most part tremendously popular. He was unquestionably an indefatigable showman, deeply obsessed with and devoted to the stage.

MATTHEW KILBURN

Sources Highfill, Burnim & Langhans, BDA · Professional and literary memoirs of Charles Dibdin the younger, ed. G. Speaight (1956) · IGI **Archives** BL, letters as applicant to the Royal Literary Fund, loan no. 96 · Hunt. L., letters **Likenesses** J. Thomson, stipple, pubd 1819 (after R. W. Satchwell), BM, Harvard TC; repro. in Highfill, Burnim & Langhans, BDA

Dibdin, Henry Edward (1813–1866), musician, the youngest son of Charles Isaac Mungo *Dibdin (1768–1833), was born at Sadler's Wells, London, on 8 September 1813, and was taught music by his elder sister, Mary Anne (1799–1886), afterwards Mrs Tonna, who was an excellent harpist, having studied under Neville Challoner and Nicholas Bochsa; she was also the composer of several songs and instrumental pieces. In 1824 she became assistant teacher of the harp at the Royal Academy of Music. Henry Dibdin studied the harp with her and afterwards with Bochsa. He also performed on the viola and organ. His first public appearance took place at Covent Garden Theatre on 3 August 1832, when he played the harp at Paganini's last concert. In 1833 he settled in Edinburgh, where he remained for the rest of his life. He held the honorary post of organist of Trinity Chapel, and occupied himself with private teaching and composition. In 1846 he married Isabella Perkins Palmer, who was born at Southwold, Suffolk, on 19 January 1828, and who later became a good soprano vocalist; she also composed a few hymn tunes.

In 1843 Dibdin published (in collaboration with J. T. Surenne) a collection of church music, a supplement to which appeared in the following year. His best-known work is the Standard Psalm Book (1852), which had a useful historical preface. In 1865 he compiled another collection, The Praise Book. His remaining published works, about forty in number, consist of songs, piano and harp pieces, and a good many hymn tunes. Dibdin was also a skilled painter and illuminator. His death took place at Edinburgh on 6 May 1866.

Dibdin's sons, Edward Rimbault Dibdin, born at Edinburgh on 25 August 1853, and James C. Dibdin, born at Edinburgh on 9 December 1856, both became musicians. The former composed a few songs and partsongs; the latter became best known for his Annals of the Edinburgh Stage (1888).   W. B. SQUIRE, rev. NILANJANA BANERJI

Sources W. H. Hadow, 'Dibdin, Henry Edward', Grove, Dict. mus. (1904–10) · Brown & Stratton, Brit. mus. · G. A. Crawford and J. A. Eberle, Church hymnal: biographical index, [3rd edn] (1878) · private information (1888) **Archives** U. Edin. L., letters to David Laing

Dibdin, Sir Lewis Tonna (1852–1938), ecclesiastical lawyer and administrator, was born in Bloomsbury, London, on 19 July 1852, the third son of the Revd Robert William Dibdin and his wife, Caroline, only child of William Thompson, barrister, of the Temple. He was grandson of Charles Isaac Mungo *Dibdin of Sadler's Wells Theatre, and great-grandson of Charles *Dibdin, the dramatist and songwriter. His uncles included the musician Henry

Edward Dibdin and Lewis Hippolytus Joseph Tonna, author of ultra-protestant religious works. Dibdin's father enjoyed considerable popularity for many years as a preacher at West Street Chapel, Seven Dials, which, as La Tremblade, had been one of the earliest Huguenot churches in London and was later a regular preaching place of John Wesley.

Dibdin was educated at home before going in 1869 to St John's College, Cambridge, where he graduated as a senior optime in the mathematical tripos of 1874 and was awarded an MA in 1878. He was called to the bar by Lincoln's Inn in 1876. In 1881 he married Marianne Aubrey (d. 1927), eldest daughter of Humphrey Senhouse Pinder, rector of Bratton Fleming, Devon; they had five sons and two daughters.

From 1895 to 1901 Dibdin was official counsel to the attorney-general in charity matters. His main interest, however, had from an early date been ecclesiastical law and history, and he was appointed chancellor of the dioceses of Rochester (1886), Exeter (1888), and Durham (1891). In 1899 he was engaged in the Lambeth hearings on the use of incense and the reservation of the sacrament. He took silk in 1901. Next year he appeared for the crown in the proceedings arising out of the appointment of Charles Gore to the see of Worcester; his services had been sought by all four other parties. From 1903 to 1934 he was dean of the arches, master of the faculties, and official principal of the chancery court of York, and from 1925 to 1934 he was vicar-general of the province of Canterbury.

In 1907 the Deceased Wife's Sister's Marriage Act was passed; next year Dibdin had to decide its effect in the memorable litigation known as the 'deceased wife's sister' case, which, in its various phases, lasted from 1908 to 1912. His judgment was upheld in the divisional court, the Court of Appeal, and the House of Lords, and the principle was settled that the Deceased Wife's Sister's Marriage Act of 1907 validates for all purposes a marriage between a man and his deceased wife's sister, wherever and whenever contracted. In view of his evangelical upbringing, several of his decisions in the court of arches came as a welcome surprise to the Anglo-Catholic party and strengthened its position.

Dibdin's main occupation, however, from his appointment as first church estates commissioner in 1905 until his resignation in 1930 was the direction of the business of the ecclesiastical commission. During that time he bore the chief responsibility for its policy and, with Lord Phillimore, for initiating the many schemes for the benefit of the clergy which eventually took statutory shape in the clergy and episcopal pension measures of 1926. To him, too, are largely attributable the numerous measures relating to the Ecclesiastical Commission and to patronage and episcopal endowments. He combined his office of commissioner with that of an active governor and chairman of committees of Queen Anne's Bounty, thus eliminating much of the overlapping of functions and the competition which had formerly existed.

Dibdin had taken a prominent part in the deliberations of the house of laymen of the convocation of Canterbury almost from the formation of the house in 1886 and he was for a time its vice-chairman. Immediately on the establishment of the church assembly in 1920 he took a very active share in its work, both in his personal capacity and as the spokesman of the ecclesiastical commissioners, and he was largely responsible for a great many of its measures. There is probably no one to whom the assembly was more heavily indebted for its procedure and for the spirit in which its business was conducted.

Dibdin served on many royal and other commissions and committees on church affairs. The report of the royal commission on ecclesiastical discipline (1904–6) was mainly his work. As a signatory of the minority report of the royal commission on divorce (1909–12) he, together with the archbishop of York (Cosmo Lang) and Sir William Anson, recommended no alteration in the existing law other than equality of treatment for the sexes. In 1914 he presided over the archbishops' ancient monuments (churches) committee, which led to the formation of the diocesan advisory committees. The historical section of the report of the archbishops' committee on church and state was prepared by Dibdin and A. L. Smith, master of Balliol College, Oxford, and published in 1916; on this report were based the constitution of the church assembly and the proposals which received statutory form in the Church of England (Assembly) Powers Act, commonly called the Enabling Act, of 1919. Between 1923 and 1926 he served on the ecclesiastical courts commission. In 1934 illness compelled his resignation from the commission on the relations between church and state, appointed in 1930 after the rejection by the House of Commons of the 1928 prayer book. At the same time he resigned all his offices, legal and administrative.

Dibdin was knighted in 1903; in 1891 he received the honorary degree of DCL from Durham University; he was elected a bencher of Lincoln's Inn in 1908 and an honorary fellow of St John's College, Cambridge, in 1923. Other honours were offered him and were refused. He died at his home, Nobles, Dormansland, Surrey, on 12 June 1938. His eldest son, Lewis George Dibdin, became secretary of the church assembly in 1939.

Dibdin combined in a rare degree the qualities of lawyer, judge, and administrator, and this, together with his great experience, gave him a unique position for a layman in church affairs. Archbishop Benson relied greatly upon him and Dibdin advised Archbishop Davidson almost daily on many topics. He wrote or edited a number of legal and other works including *The Livery Companies of London* (1886), *Monasticism in England* (1890), and *The Ecclesiastical Commission* (1919). His *Establishment in England* (1932), a collection of essays written over a period of fifty years, emphasizes his strong support of the established church.

WILLIAM CLEVELAND-STEVENS, *rev.* CATHERINE PEASE-WATKIN

Sources *The Times* (13 June 1938) · *The Times* (16 June 1938) · *Church Times* (17 June 1938) · *The Guardian* (3 Aug 1887) · G. K. A. Bell, *Randall Davidson, archbishop of Canterbury*, 2 vols. (1935) · Venn, *Alum. Cant.* · W. P. Baildon, ed., *The records of the Honorable Society of Lincoln's Inn* [incl. *Admissions*, 2 vols. (1896), and *Black books*, 6 vols. (1897–2001)] ·

Reports of Royal Commissions · *Law reports* · private information (1949)
Archives LPL, papers | LPL, corresp. with Edward Benson; letters to Claude Jenkins
Wealth at death £27,808 1s. 1d.: probate, 4 Aug 1938, *CGPLA Eng. & Wales*

Dibdin, Thomas Frognall (1776–1847), bibliographer, was born in Calcutta, India, and baptized there on 31 August 1776, the elder son of Thomas Dibdin (*c*.1731–1780), naval captain and later merchant venturer, and his second wife, Elizabeth Compton (*d. c*.1780). When he was about the age of four both his parents died: his father on his way to England and his mother soon afterwards at Middelburg in the Netherlands. Brought up by his maternal uncle, William Compton, Thomas completed his preparatory studies at Reading, Stockwell, and at a seminary between Isleworth and Brentford. Tutored by Christopher Marlowe, Thomas matriculated at St John's College, Oxford, as a commoner; he passed his examination in 1797, though he did not take his degree until March 1801. He took his degree of MA on 28 April 1825 and was awarded BD and DD degrees on 9 July 1825. As a student he published several anonymous essays in the *European Magazine* along with some juvenile poetry which appeared in 1797.

Upon graduation Dibdin chose the law as his profession. He initially studied under Basil Montagu of Lincoln's Inn and then settled in at Gray's Inn, and became a provincial counsel in Worcester. About 1801 he married Sophia, whom he had apparently met at Oxford, and had two sons (one died in early childhood and the other also predeceased Dibdin) and two daughters, one of whom married. While in Worcester he wrote various pieces, including two tracts on legal subjects (*Blackstone's Rights of Persons* and the *Law of the Poor Rate*) and some tales (including *La Belle Marianne*, privately printed in 1824), as well as contributions to the short-lived weekly on the arts and antiquities, *The Quiz*. Following the advice of his old Reading schoolfriend Thomas Pruen, he abandoned his unsuccessful legal career for the church, and was ordained a deacon in December 1804 and priest shortly thereafter in early 1805 by Bishop North of Winchester.

Dibdin's career as a bibliographer blossomed in 1802 with *An Introduction to the Knowledge of Rare and Valuable Editions of the Greek and Latin Classics*, published in Gloucester, which was well received in contemporary journals and allegedly sold out in six weeks. Although W. A. Jackson considered it 'a paste-pot tabulated compilation from Edward Harwood's *Views*' (1790), this slim volume of sixty-three pages introduced Dibdin to George John, second Earl Spencer, the possessor of one of the most valuable private libraries in the country. One of the great book collectors, Lord Spencer of Althorp became his patron for life, appointed him at one time his librarian, and obtained church patronage for him. Although he was chief cataloguer of the Althorp library, Dibdin could not read the Greek in the books he described, according to H. R. Luard's harsh assessment. In any event, his catalogue entitled *Bibliotheca Spenceriana* (4 vols., 1814–15) is replete with errors,

Thomas Frognall Dibdin (1776–1847), by William Behnes

yet Seymour De Ricci commented that it was 'the handsomest and most elaborate catalogue of a private library yet issued' (De Ricci, 75). Its principal value lay in Dibdin's careful establishment of the principle of first-hand examination of books, an important advance in the study of bibliography.

Dibdin's *Introduction to the … Classics* was reprinted three times, in 1804, 1808, and 1827, each time being greatly enlarged and corrected. Ultimately it contains little of lasting value, but booksellers of his day frequently cited it. Perhaps his most famous book is *Bibliomania, or, Bookmadness, containing some account of the history, symptoms and cure of this fatal disease* (1809); it included biographical sketches of the collectors of his day. It successfully caught the taste of the time among the aristocracy, and the second edition of 1811 had considerable influence in exciting interest in rare books and early editions, which peaked at the duke of Roxburghe sale of May and June 1812. This sale is notable for the fact that a 1471 edition of Giovanni Boccaccio's *Decameron*, printed by Christofer Valdarfer in Venice, sold for the then enormous sum of £2260, paid by the marquess of Blandford. To celebrate its sale Dibdin proposed that the leading bibliophiles dine at St Alban's tavern on 17 June. With Lord Spencer as president and Dibdin as vice-president, this meeting was the beginning of the Roxburghe Club. The club eventually grew to thirty-one members, each expected to produce a reprint of some rare volume of English literature. In certain circles the club became a joke, in part because of the worthless character of some of its early publications—of which it was said by Luard that 'when they were unique there was already one copy too many in existence' (*DNB*)—but in large measure because of Joseph Haslewood's posthumous satire entitled *Roxburghe Revels*, which appeared in

1837. None the less, Dibdin must be credited with being the originator of the English publishing society.

Dibdin was further encouraged in his fine printing and bibliographical efforts by the financial success of *Typographical Antiquities, or, The History of Printing in England, Scotland and Ireland* (1810), which was based upon Joseph Ames's original work of 1749 and William Herbert's extensive revisions of 1785. In 1818, accompanied by artist George Lewis, Dibdin spent nine months in France and Germany visiting various public and private libraries, and eventually published an amusing three-volume account of his travels, full of follies and errors, entitled *A Bibliographical, Antiquarian and Picturesque Tour* (1821). The volumes were published in the spring of that year at £9 9s.; the plates alone were supposed to have cost £5000 and became a sought-after collector's item. This work's inaccuracies upset the French, and when M. Théodore Licquet and Georges A. Crapelet translated the entirety into French in 1825, they added numerous footnotes attacking the original.

In all Dibdin wrote more than forty-six different works including sermons and lectures under at least four different pseudonyms, two of which were Cato Parvus and Mercurius Rusticus. In 1819 he proposed a *History of the University of Oxford* on subscription; fortunately it was never undertaken, because Dibdin's works had become noted for their substantive and typographic errors. By the 1820s he auctioned his drawings and took, as he said, 'a final leave of bibliography' to pursue his clerical career more seriously; however, he still published *The Library Companion* in 1824, which was described as 'a splendidly idiosyncratic, lucky dip of a book [which] abounds with errors, but is remarkably entertaining' (*Dibdin: Selections*, ed. Neuburg, 129). His modest preferments included the preachership of Archbishop Tenison's chapel in Swallow Street, London, the evening lectureship of Brompton Chapel, preacherships at Quebec and Fitzroy chapels, the vicarage at Exning near Newmarket in Suffolk (1823), the rectory of St Mary's, Bryanston Square, in Marylebone, Middlesex (1824), and from 1831 until his death a royal chaplaincy-in-ordinary. This last position apparently saved him from arrest for debt in 1836.

Later in life Dibdin contemplated a *History of Dover* and a *Bibliographical Tour in Belgium*, but although he did some work on them, these never appeared. His two-volume apologia, *Reminiscences of a Literary Life* (1836), focuses on his professional efforts, and barely mentions his children or his long marriage. The end of his life is well documented in numerous letters to Philip Bliss, registrar of Oxford, which contain a sad picture of continuing pecuniary difficulties, leading to poverty and illness. Dibdin suffered a debilitating stroke in late 1845, and he died on 18 November 1847 at 3 Park Road, Kensington, London. He was buried in the churchyard there. Although Lord Spencer had insured his life for £1000, there is some question as to whether Dibdin had in fact borrowed upon it, leaving his widow destitute.

Despite an extravagant and inflated style, Dibdin popularized the word 'bibliomania', a term evocative of that era's antiquarian interests; his main contributions seem to have been his zealous enthusiasm in promoting book collecting generally among the aristocracy, as well as putting forth the principle of first-hand examination of books in the compilation of bibliographies.

JOHN V. RICHARDSON JR.

Sources T. F. Dibdin, *Reminiscences of a literary life*, 2 vols. (1836) • 'Rev. T. F. Dibdin', *GM*, 2nd ser., 29 (1848), 87–92 • S. De Ricci, *The book collector's guide* (1921), 75 • *DNB* • *Thomas Frognall Dibdin: selections*, ed. V. R. Neuburg (1978) • E. J. O'Dwyer, *Thomas Frognall Dibdin, bibliographer and bibliomaniac extraordinary, 1776–1847* (1967) • D. A. Stoker, 'Thomas Frognall Dibdin', *Nineteenth-century British book-collectors and bibliographers*, ed. W. Baker and K. Womack, DLitB, 184 (1997), 69–80 • W. A. Jackson, *An annotated list of the publications of the Reverend Thomas Frognall Dibdin, D. D., based mainly on those in the Harvard College Library* (1965) • A. Lister, 'George John, 2nd Earl Spencer and his "librarian", Thomas Frognall Dibdin', *Bibliophily*, ed. R. Myers and M. Morris (1986) • d. cert. • BL OIOC, N/12, fol. 263 [baptism]
Archives BL, corresp., Egerton MS 2974, C.28.i.13 • Bodl. Oxf., corresp. relating to *Reminiscences of a literary life* • Col. U., Rare Book and Manuscript Library, corresp. • CUL, corresp. • CUL, notes on early printed books • Harvard U., Houghton L., corresp. and papers • Hunt. L., letters • JRL, letters • U. Edin. L., corresp. and papers | BL, letters to Philip Bliss, Add. MSS 34567–34581, *passim* • BL, letters to Lackington & Co., Add. MS 28653 • BL, letters to S. Lahee, Add. MS 45498 • BL, corresp. with Sir Frederick Madden, Egerton MSS 2838–2841, *passim* • BL, letters to Lord Spencer • Bodl. Oxf., letters to Sir Egerton Bridges • Bodl. Oxf., letters to Isaac D'Israeli • Bodl. Oxf., corresp. with Francis Douce • JRL, corresp. and collections • JRL, letters to John Fry • JRL, letters to Nichols family • JRL, corresp. with Lord Spencer • Lpool RO, corresp. with William Roscoe • Magd. Oxf., letters to M. J. Routh • Man. CL, Manchester Archives and Local Studies, letters to John Fry • NL Scot., letters to Blackwoods • NL Scot., letters to Sir Walter Scott • Suffolk RO, Ipswich, account of the parish and church of Exning with MS additions by W. S. Fitch • Trinity Cam., letters to Dawson Turner • U. Edin. L., letters to David Laing
Likenesses oils, c.1800, Royal College of Music, London • Freeman, engraving, 1811, repro. in T. F. Dibdin, *Bibliomania, or, Book madness: a bibliographical romance*, 2nd edn. (1811) • H. Meyer, stipple, pubd 1816 (after H. Edridge), BM, NPG • T. Hodgetts, mezzotint, pubd 1821 (after T. Phillips), BM, NPG • J. Posselwhite, stipple, pubd 1835 (after G. Richmond), BM; repro. in Dibdin, *Reminiscences* • S. T. Arnold, oils, Garr. Club • W. Behnes, chalk drawing, BM [*see illus.*] • T. Phillips, engraving, repro. in *Tour*, 2nd edn • D. Turner, etching (after F. Palgrave), BM, NPG • E. Turner, pencil drawing, V&A • oils, St John's College, Oxford
Wealth at death £1000—life insurance provided by Lord Spencer: Stoker, 'Thomas Frognall Dibdin'; O'Dwyer, *Thomas Frognall Dibdin*

Dibdin, Thomas John (1771–1841), playwright and actor, was born at 5 Peter Street (now Museum Street), Bloomsbury, London, on 21 March 1771, the second of the two illegitimate sons of Charles *Dibdin (*bap.* 1745, *d.* 1814) and the actress and dancer Harriet *Pitt (1748?–1814) [*see under* Pitt, Ann]. He was brother to Charles Isaac Mungo *Dibdin (1768–1833), and half-brother to the musician Cecil Pitt (*c.*1763–1820) and the dancer Harriet Pitt (*b.* *c.*1763).

Early life and the stage As the godson of David Garrick, who befriended the family after Charles abandoned his responsibilities, the four-year-old Dibdin walked on as Cupid in Garrick's revival of his Shakespearian pageant *The Jubilee* (Drury Lane, 1775–6). Mrs Siddons, playing

Thomas John Dibdin (1771–1841), by William Owen

company being full, he was found a niche in the Dover troupe, managed by Richland, playing at Eastbourne, where, in late summer, under the stage name of T. Merchant to avoid detection, he appeared as Captain Valentine in John O'Keeffe's farce *The Farmer* and sang 'Poor Jack', a well-known song of his father's. To supplement his income in this profit-sharing company, he painted scenery (including a smokily realistic armada for *The Critic*) and wrote the first of about 2000 songs. Three months afterwards he joined Mrs Baker's extensive Kent circuit at Deal, a salaried engagement which Dibdin reckoned as 'the next grade to a situation in a theatre royal, the grand aim of my ambition' (*Reminiscences*, 1.92). At Easter 1790 he transferred to Butler's company and visited Beverley and Harrogate, once performing alongside Mrs Jordan.

In 1791, at the jointly managed Liverpool and Manchester theatres, Dibdin achieved his goal of a theatre-royal appointment. With only hours' notice, he played Mungo—'that most favourite of all my father's favourite characters' (*Reminiscences*, 1.111)—in Isaac Bickerstaff's *The Padlock* when the Manchester theatre reopened after a fire. Over three years he established himself as a scene-painter and gained valuable experience in stage-management; he also performed a season at Chester. In summer 1792 he played as far north as Banff and Inverness. After his return to Manchester as 'prompter and *fac-totum*' (ibid., 1.165), his first play, the farce *Sunshine after Rain*, was staged (15 March 1793); it was published pseudonymously in 1795 as *The Mad Guardian* (with 'Fugitive Pieces' of prose and verse). At Manchester collegiate church, as Thomas Pitt, he married, on 23 May 1793, the actress Ann Hilliar (1774?–1828) (familiarly known as Nancy), whom he had met three years before at Beverley.

Following joint engagements at Rochdale and Huddersfield, Dibdin and his now pregnant wife journeyed in deep winter 1793–4 to south-west Wales, where, for Henry Masterman's lively company at Haverfordwest and Carmarthen, Dibdin wrote and performed a new song weekly. Early in 1794 their first child, Maria, was born; and *Comic Songs* (1794), probably Dibdin's first publication, appeared under his Merchant pseudonym. On reading in the newspaper of the staging of *Rival Loyalties*, his recently completed burletta, at Sadler's Wells in May 1794, Dibdin, aspiring to a metropolitan career as a playwright, hurriedly set off for London. Masterman generously kept open his engagement, but Dibdin never returned. His affection for Carmarthen and Haverfordwest audiences, however, inspired the dedication of *St David's Day* (1800) 'to the memory of their liberality' (*Reminiscences*, 1.183).

The Dibdins were engaged at Sadler's Wells from 1794–5, Thomas to act and write burlettas at 5 guineas a week and Ann as a performer. Now safe in his increasing reputation, Dibdin dropped his disguise and for the first time assumed his father's surname, though against the latter's wishes. In 1796 the Dibdins accepted a good offer from Mrs Baker, giving each of them two clear benefits in each town, to return to the Kent circuit. But Dibdin continued to write occasionally for Sadler's Wells, including *The British Raft* (1797), which featured the hugely successful

Venus, assisted in securing one of his wings. Dibdin's mother, as Mrs Davenett, resumed acting at Drury Lane in 1788 for two seasons (and afterwards transferred to Covent Garden) to finance his education at St Paul's Cathedral choir school under Robert Hudson, followed by a year-long interlude boarding at an unexacting establishment in Half-Farthing Lane, Wandsworth, then a rigorous three-year classical training at Barnard's Castle, co. Durham. To keep her son off the stage, Harriet entrusted him at the age of fourteen to his well-to-do great-uncle Cecil Pitt, a retired Dalston upholsterer, who apprenticed him in business to William Rawlins.

Dibdin, however, shared his family's infatuation with the theatre, which stretched back to his maternal grandmother, the Covent Garden actress Ann *Pitt (*c*.1720–1799). At school in co. Durham he had witnessed plays at a local inn, and in young adulthood he benefited from free access by family order to the three patent theatres in London. Through his friendship with John Palmer the Royalty (opened in 1787) became a regular escape hole. When Rawlins discovered and violently destroyed his apprentice's model theatre, Dibdin sought arbitration from John Wilkes, the city chamberlain. Rawlins was admonished and Dibdin agreed to eschew theatricals; but the lure of the stage was irresistible, and two months later he was almost discovered as, unrecognized, he sat adjacent to his master in the Royalty's gallery.

A travelling actor Determined to abandon his apprenticeship, in July 1789, armed with an introduction from Cockran Booth, the prompter at Covent Garden and part owner of the Margate theatre (where his half-brother Cecil was employed), Dibdin absconded by riverboat. The Margate anti-French song 'The Snug Little Island' (bought by Longman for 15 guineas, three times what the theatre paid for the entire burletta). Dibdin's opportunity to break into legitimate theatre arrived in July 1798, when his farce *The Jew and the Doctor* gained such acclaim at Maidstone that it was purchased for performance at Covent Garden. From 19 October 1798 Dibdin appeared on Covent Garden's salary list at £5 weekly, and steadily moved away from acting to concentrate on authorship. (Ann joined on 18 September 1799, at £3, appearing as Aura in *The Farm House*.) In his first season, beginning with *The Mouth of the Nile* (acted twenty-seven times), in celebration of Nelson's naval victory, Dibdin made £466 6s., sufficient to increase his financial support to his mother and grandmother. At the same time his indentures were cancelled when Rawlins, in a spirit of reconciliation, accepted reduced compensation of 50 guineas.

London playwright Dibdin's association with Covent Garden lasted eleven years. A special responsibility was the annual pantomime, regularly occupying six or eight months each year, produced in collaboration with Charles Farley. His outstanding success was *Harlequin and Mother Goose* (1806)—said to have grossed £3000 for Covent Garden in the first three weeks—which reorientated the genre by giving dominance to the clown, played, on Dibdin's personal recommendation, by Jo Grimaldi. In several areas Dibdin was a reliable Covent Garden writer; but there were as many pains as rewards to endure as house author, experiences which later emerged in *Harlequin Hoax, or, A Pantomime Proposed* (1814). In the aptly titled *Family Quarrels* (1802), Dibdin despaired of ever satisfying the vocal requirements of the squabbling principals, and during the performance local Jews' offence at the song 'I Courted Miss Levi' caused uproar over several nights. With *The Cabinet* (1802)—'a very productive stock opera' (*Reminiscences*, 1.309), though plagued, if less severely, by disputes of precedence among performers and staged in nineteen days from conception—Dibdin cleared £700. His most successful season, concluding at the Haymarket with the five-act comedy *Guilty or Not Guilty* (1804), one of several pieces written over the years for George Colman junior, produced a total income of £1515. At the commencement of the 1805–6 season Dibdin negotiated his first salary increase of a pound a week for Ann and himself.

In parallel with his writing and managing career, Dibdin in 1802 joined his brother Charles in acquiring for £1400 a quarter-share in Sadler's Wells, which by 1805 was making good returns. But theatrical speculation was always uncertain, and their involvement in the Dublin theatre about the same time lost the two brothers nearly £2000.

Attempts at management On Thomas Harris's retirement in 1809, Dibdin left Covent Garden—Ann having departed a year earlier—and bought a cottage at Betchworth, in bosky Surrey, intending to write free from London's temptations. Though he kept the cottage until the 1820s, his notion of semi-retirement yielded in October 1810 to R. W.

Elliston's seductive offer of £15 a week as author and manager at the Surrey, where he stayed for two seasons. In October 1812, after deliberating over the seeming drop in professional status, he went to Drury Lane as prompter at £520 per annum, for which he was to write a pantomime and one topical piece on any public or national event. This was not a happy time, since relations with the second proprietor Samuel Whitbread, whose authoritarian style Dibdin abhorred, were often frosty. After Whitbread's death in July 1815 Dibdin was re-engaged at Drury Lane, as joint acting manager with Alexander Rae, an unequal partnership in which Dibdin did most of the work. Although the new management subcommittee as individuals, including Lord Byron, were generally supportive, Dibdin alleged that 'collectively they did not treat me well' (*Reminiscences*, 2.57). His assumption in 1816 of the lease of the Surrey Theatre (then with no intention of managing it personally)—initially not resisted—caused his dismissal on grounds of conflict of interest, though Drury Lane continued his salary until the following October.

Dibdin's management of the Surrey began ambitiously but ended in financial ruin. By the opening night on 1 July, when his wife (resuming her theatrical career) spoke a comic address prefacing a programme comprising the melodrama *Housewarming* and a historical romance, *Chevy Chase*—both 'written on the spur of the moment' (*Reminiscences*, 2.132)—Dibdin had spent £4000 in six weeks on interior refurbishment. Although the productions were highly regarded and Dibdin attracted, at various times, first-rate performers, receipts declined long before the first season was out. Serious competition came not just from Astley's but, unanticipated, from a new rival, the Coburg. Even with a solid repertory of 180 stock pieces and opportunities to change programmes nightly, in six years' management (ending prematurely on 19 March 1822) only two seasons were financially viable: 1817–18 and 1818–19, saved, respectively, by the burlesque *Don Giovanni* (performed over 100 nights and imitated many times in London and elsewhere) and *The Lily of St Leonard's, or, The Heart of Midlothian* (the first of many adaptations of Scott, the copyright of which, exceptionally as a minor theatre piece, realized 60 guineas). Dibdin's debts amounted to a catastrophic £18,000 and he was made bankrupt. His discharge took place on 21 May 1822.

Financial difficulties and declining status At this juncture Dibdin accepted a three-year summer contract as stage-manager at Morris's Haymarket, at £200 with one benefit, while Ann superintended the women's wardrobe for 'a very trifling salary' (*Reminiscences*, 2.215). In October he became stage-manager of Drury Lane, again under Elliston, in whose employ as acting manager was the volatile James Winston. Dibdin clashed with both. Against Elliston, who sought ways to remove him, he resorted in February 1824 to a court order to enforce his contract. Even more unhappy was his experience at the Haymarket, where (in contrast to relations with its former proprietor, Colman) Dibdin complained bitterly of 'daily and nightly degradations' endured in Morris's service (ibid., 2.294).

Continuing financial difficulties forced him to borrow money from extortioners in the winter of 1823–4 and, after *Come if you can* (June 1824) failed, Morris refused him his salary. In July he was arrested for debt and languished until Michaelmas in the king's bench prison. For payment on *The Laplanders*, written—bizarrely—at Morris's request for a piece for a herd of reindeer (which, in the event, died before the performance could take place), Dibdin was again forced into litigation (23 June 1826). Through debt he also lost his library. Such experiences confirmed him in the view that he had led 'a very chequered, and not a very fortunate life' (ibid., 2.405).

Having secured the stage-managership of Sadler's Wells, beginning on 4 April 1825 at £400 per annum, Dibdin moved to the spaciousness of Myddelton Square in the nearby New Town and hoped to start afresh. His contract was renewed at intervals and he continued to write burlettas for Sadler's Wells until mid-1828, shortly before Ann Dibdin's premature death on 29 August. He married Catherine Court at St Pancras on 9 April 1829 and at the age of fifty-eight began a new family.

Overall, however, socially and professionally, the 1830s were even more uncomfortable than the 1820s. Encouraged by Bulwer-Lytton's copyright reform, Dibdin published, under royal patronage and wide theatrical subscription, a collection of 200 songs, the valedictory title of which—*Last Lays of the Last of the Three Dibdins* (1833)—reinforces the sense of his being at the end of a theatrical line. During the reform excitement his new satirical periodical—*Tom Dibdin's Penny Trumpet* (October–November 1832)—foundered after four numbers. While he wrote occasional minor theatre pieces—the last in 1837—his income was extremely small and monetary troubles multiplied. Increasingly desperate applications to the Literary Fund produced grants totalling £175 between 1824 and 1838. In 1834–5 he spent nearly a year, reportedly in a condition of near starvation, in Horsemonger Lane debtors' prison; and in 1838 he wrote despairingly to the fund's managers that 'the situation of my Family and self becomes daily more critically painful' (12 November).

Ironically, Dibdin's last commission, under the patronage of Lord Minto (representing the Admiralty), was to edit the *Songs, Naval and National of the Late Charles Dibdin* (1841), the father who had neglected his hero-worshipping son all his life. While preparing the edition Dibdin received a small weekly stipend in acknowledgement of his financial plight. He died from asthma on 16 September 1841 at his home, 22 Trevor Square, Knightsbridge, and was buried on 21 September at St James's, Pentonville, near his mother and grandmother.

Assessment Open, forthright, but companionable in nature, Dibdin cultivated a wide circle of friends, including George Colman junior, Charles Farley, Benjamin Thompson, Douglas Jerrold, Sam Russell, and Thomas Harris (almost a surrogate father). He was 'poet laureate' of the Covent Garden Beef-Steak Club. However, most of his closest friends (and his brother) predeceased him and, in the last decade of his life, with the responsibilities of a young family, the shocking consequences of his indigence deprived him of much of his spirit.

Outside the drama, several early essays and tales of Dibdin's appeared in the *New Lady's Magazine*, the *Gentleman's and Lady's Pocket Magazine*, and *The Biographic*. He edited briefly the *Monthly Epitome* in 1798; and his *Metrical History*, an eccentric aide-mémoire for schoolchildren of historical events, appeared in 1813. As was the case with many of the period's playwrights, Dibdin's dramatic output was prodigious—about 250 pieces, excluding songs, prologues, and epilogues (which he had a reputation for turning out at the drop of a hat). He wrote at great speed (though never, he claimed, on Sundays), capturing precisely audience tastes. A facility for word play and puns contributed to his substantial success as a pantomimist. His Scott adaptations—for which he established a vogue—were sometimes as spectacular as his pantomimes. About a quarter of his total output was published. Several plays, including popular stock pieces such as *The Birthday* (1799) and *Of Age Tomorrow* (1805), along with *Kenilworth* (1821), were still available in Dicks's series at the end of the century. For Whittingham and Arliss, he compiled *Dibdin's London Theatre* (26 vols., 1815–18), based on prompt books of the theatres royal with original cast lists derived from materials in John Kemble's library. But perhaps his best achievement is his autobiography (2 vols., 1827), a lively and informative theatrical narrative, which, because it ran none of the risks, was 'preferable to writing a play' (*Reminiscences*, 1.7).

Of the numerous children of Dibdin's first marriage, only two survived into adulthood: Thomas Robert Colman Dibdin (1810–1893), a Post Office clerk, who exhibited landscapes at the Royal Academy (1832–74), and Charles Alexander Dibdin (*b.* 1815). His second marriage produced three more children, the eldest of whom was barely eleven at his death, immediately before and after which the family was forced to seek renewed assistance from the Literary Fund.   JOHN RUSSELL STEPHENS

Sources T. Dibdin, *The reminiscences of Thomas Dibdin*, 2 vols. (1827) · *The Times* (20 Sept 1841) · letters, Royal Literary Fund, 144 Temple Chambers, Temple Avenue, London, file 503 · 'Biographical sketch of Mr Thomas Dibdin', *Monthly Mirror* (14 Dec 1802), 363–7 · T. Gilliland, *The dramatic mirror, containing the history of the stage from the earliest period, to the present time*, 1 (1808), 318–21 · *Drury Lane journal: selections from James Winston's diaries, 1819–1827*, ed. A. L. Nelson and G. B. Cross (1974) · C. J. L. Price, *The English theatre in Wales in the eighteenth and early nineteenth centuries* (1948) · *The Times* (30 Dec 1806) · *GM*, 1st ser., 83/2 (1813), 357–9 · A. Nicoll, *Late eighteenth century drama, 1750–1800*, 2nd edn (1952), vol. 3 of *A history of English drama, 1660–1900* (1952–9) [incl. bibliography] · A. Nicoll, *Early nineteenth century drama, 1800–1850*, 2nd edn (1955), vol. 4 of *A history of English drama, 1660–1900* (1952–9) [incl. bibliography] · C. B. Hogan, ed., *The London stage, 1660–1800*, pt 5: *1776–1800* (1968) · Hall, *Dramatic ports.* · parish registers, Pentonville, London, St Pancras and St James · d. cert.

Archives BL, Add. MSS 42867–42941 · BL, letters, as sponsor and applicant, to Royal Literary Fund, loan 96

Likenesses R. Dighton, coloured etching, 1799, BM · J. Young, portrait, 1807 (after W. Owen), repro. in E. Inchbald, *A collection of farces* (1809) · C. Allingham, portrait (now lost?) · A. Crowquill, etching, vignette · S. Freeman, stipple (after W. Owen), repro. in E. Inchbald, *A collection of farces* (1809) · D. Maclise, lithograph, BM,

NPG • H. Meyer, engraving (after drawing by T. Wageman), repro. in Dibdin, *Reminiscences* • H. Meyer, stipple (after S. Drummond), BM, NPG; repro. in *European Magazine* (1817) • W. Owen, oils, Museum of Fine Arts, Boston [*see illus.*] • W. Ridley, stipple (after C. Allingham), BM, NPG; repro. in *Monthly Mirror*

Dicas [*married name* Arstall], **Mary** (*fl.* 1800–1815), maker of scientific instruments, was the elder daughter of John Dicas, a Liverpool wine and brandy merchant, who married Alice Edmonton at Holy Trinity Church, Chester, on 9 July 1777. No record of her birth or baptism has been found, although her brother, Robert, was baptized at St Nicholas's, Liverpool, on 29 May 1787. He does not appear to have survived to maturity.

John Dicas, noted in local directories from 1774, invented an improved hydrometer for measuring the specific gravity of alcoholic liquids, particularly useful in his line of business, as those in use all had a number of disadvantages. He also invented a saccharometer (for measuring sugar content of liquids) and a lactometer (for measuring the strength of milk). He patented the hydrometer in 1780, and ten years later it was adopted by the United States government as their standard instrument for assessing import duty. John Dicas had, however, died by 1802 when the board of inquiry of the Royal Society was advertising in local newspapers throughout the United Kingdom, inviting instrument makers to bring forward hydrometers which could be tested for adoption by the customs and excise for taxation purposes. His name had been replaced in the local directories by that of Mary Dicas from 1800: if she was born in the year after her parents' marriage, she would by then have been in her early twenties. She took examples of her father's instruments and travelled to London, where she was among ten makers who explained their use before the board of inquiry. However, her bid was unsuccessful, and the excise adopted the hydrometer devised by Bartholomew Sikes.

By 1807 Mary Dicas was in partnership with George Arstall, a scale-beam maker who had his own business at Temple Court, while the Dicas manufactory was based on the north side of the Old Dock. At some point they married, and four children were baptized at St Peter's Church, Liverpool, between 1810 and 1815. The eldest, Frederick Dicas Arstall, in due course became a scale maker, working in Manchester from 1838, and returning to Liverpool in 1851. With the redevelopment of the Old Dock from about 1812, the manufacture of the Dicas hydrometer moved to Temple Court, from which most of the instruments (which were illegal for taxation purposes in the United Kingdom) were exported to the United States. It is difficult to estimate the numbers of these that were made, but by the time the firm was being run by Mary's sister Ann, from 1818, and subsequently by Ann's husband, Benjamin Gammage, from 1823, the hydrometers, now marked 'Gammage late Dicas' bore numbers higher than 5599. The date and circumstances of Mary Arstall's death are unknown.

In the 1806 edition of *Directions for using the patent saccharometer for brewing ale and beer … invented by the late J. Dicas*, and made and sold by his successor, M. Dicas, Mary's involvement was not spelt out, but by the 1814 edition, it was clarified as *invented by the late John Dicas, and for upwards of sixteen years, made only by his daughter and successor, Mary Arstall, late Mary Dicas, mathematical instrument maker, Liverpool: the only proprietor of the patent, who, for some time previous to the decease of her father, assisted in making the above instruments*. A manuscript note, added to one copy of this, states 'now made by Ann Dicas, successor to M. Arstall'. Benjamin Gammage appeared in the Liverpool directories as a hydrometer maker until 1851.   A. D. MORRISON-LOW

Sources A. D. Morrison-Low, 'Women in the nineteenth-century scientific instrument trade', *Science and sensibility: gender and scientific enquiry, 1780–1945*, ed. M. Benjamin (1991), 89–117 • G. Clifton, *Directory of British scientific instrument makers, 1550–1851*, ed. G. L'E. Turner (1995), 83–4 • *Gore's Liverpool Directory* (1774–1848) • *Directions for using the patent saccharometer for brewing ale and beer, at all times to the same strength* (1806); later edn (1814)

Dicconson, Edward (1670–1752), vicar apostolic of the northern district, was born on 30 November 1670 at Wrightington Hall, near Wigan, Lancashire, being the third son of Hugh Dicconson (*c.*1621–1691) of Wrightington Hall and his wife, Agnes (*d.* 1719), daughter of Roger Kirkby of Kirkby in that county. His family were Jacobites. His eldest brother, William *Dicconson, followed James II to St Germain and became tutor to the exiled king's son and treasurer to the exiled queen. His elder brother, Roger, joined the 1715 rising. He was educated in the English College at Douai from 1683, and at the end of his course of philosophy, in 1691, returned to England. Subsequently he resumed his studies at Douai, where he took the oath on 8 March 1699. He took priest's orders, became procurator of the college in 1701, and in 1708–9 was professor of syntax and a senior. In 1709–10 he was professor of poetry and in 1711–12 professor of philosophy. He was made vice-president and professor of theology in 1713–14. He assisted Charles Dodd, alias Hugh Tootell, in the preparation of his *Church History of England* (3 vols., 1737–42), copying for him most of the records of the Douai College. In 1719 he went to Paris to deal with the college funds invested there but failed in a bid to profit from the Mississippi Bubble. At some point he was awarded the degree of DD. His career involved him in the struggle between the secular clergy, to which he belonged, and the regulars, including the Benedictines, the Franciscans, and the Jesuits, for control of the English mission. The opponents of the secular clergy sought to brand them as Gallicans, lacking in complete respect for papal authority, and as Jansenists, holding heretical views on moral and dogmatic theology. He defended the English College at Douai against the charge of Jansenism by securing the replacement of their accuser as visitor, and himself accepted the papal condemnation of Jansenism by the papal bull *Unigenitus* of 1713.

Despite a stammer, which made preaching difficult, and his desire for a continental benefice, Dicconson left the college at Douai to serve the English mission on 30 July 1720, having been invited by Peter Giffard to take the ministerial charge at Chillington, Staffordshire. While there he was Bishop Stonor's principal adviser and vicar-general. Afterwards he was sent to Rome as agent-extraordinary of the secular clergy of England. He failed to secure the replacement of the Jesuit superior of the English College at Rome by a secular, but he did succeed in obtaining a ruling that the Franciscans should observe Innocent XII's decree of 1696 requiring the regulars to seek the approbation of the vicars apostolic before accepting appointments on the English mission. On the death of Bishop Thomas Williams he was nominated vicar apostolic of the northern district of England by Benedict XIV in September 1740, and he was consecrated on 19 March 1741 to the see of Mallus *in partibus infidelium* by the bishop of Ghent. Proceeding to his vicariate he fixed his residence at a place belonging to his family called Finch Mill (now demolished), in Appley Bridge, Shevington, near Wrightington. Hence he was sometimes jokingly called the Auditor of the Rota (after the head of a Roman ecclesiastical court, *rota* being the Latin for mill). Together with the other vicars apostolic he obtained from Benedict XIV in 1753 the brief *Apostolicum ministerium*, regulating the English mission along the lines already laid down in 1698 and confirmed by the brief *Emanavit nuper* of 1748: the regulars were required to secure the approbation of the vicars apostolic before accepting appointments on the English mission.

Dicconson died at Finch Mill on 5 May 1752, and was buried in the private chapel attached to St Wilfrid's, the parish church of Standish, near Wigan. His monument, inscribed with his full episcopal style and carved with his arms, crozier, and mitre, is unusual, if not unique, in being on the wall of the chancel. Francis Petre was his successor in the northern vicariate. Dicconson's diary, covering ten years at Douai, has been published. His manuscripts include a detailed account of his agency in Rome, together with reports and other documents relating to the state of his vicariate. These papers provide a useful source for the study of the English Catholic church in the eighteenth century. His library is now at Ushaw College, Durham.   THOMPSON COOPER, *rev.* J. A. HILTON

Sources G. Anstruther, *The seminary priests*, 4 vols. (1969–77) • B. Plumb, *Arundel to Zabi: a biographical dictionary of the Catholic bishops of England and Wales (deceased), 1623–1987* (privately printed, Warrington, [1987]) • B. Hemphill, *The early vicars apostolic of England, 1685–1750* (1954) • P. R. Harris, ed., *Douai College documents, 1639–1794*, Catholic RS, 63 (1972) [incl. diary] • J. Kirk, *Biographies of English Catholics in the eighteenth century*, ed. J. H. Pollen and E. Burton (1909) • Gillow, *Lit. biog. hist.* • W. M. Brady, *Annals of the Catholic hierarchy in England and Scotland* (1877) • G. Scott, *Gothic rage undone: English monks in the age of Enlightenment* (1992) • C. G. Herbermann and others, eds., *The Catholic encyclopedia*, 17 vols. (1907–18)
Archives Diocesan Archives, Leeds, diocesan MSS • Lancs. RO, corresp. and papers • Ushaw College, Durham, corresp. relating to Ushaw College

Dicconson, William (1654/5–1742), Jacobite courtier and biographer, eldest son of Hugh Dicconson (*c*.1621–1691) of Wrightington Hall near Wigan, and his wife, Agnes (*d.* 1719), third daughter of Roger Kirkby of Kirkby, came from a Lancashire Roman Catholic gentry family, which occasionally (as in the 1660s) conformed outwardly. He

had three brothers (including the Catholic bishop Edward *Dicconson) and four sisters; he was probably educated, like his brothers, at the English College at Douai. He married (by contract of 20 July 1681) Juliana (*c*.1661–1751), daughter of Richard Walmesley of Dunkenhalgh, Lancashire.

After the revolution of 1688, William (frequently confused with William Dickenson, a protestant official whom James vainly reappointed as an Irish revenue commissioner in April 1689) took part in the Lancashire Catholics' plotting for a Jacobite rising. They formed themselves from 1689 into cavalry regiments; when Colonel John Parker obtained formal commissions for them in early 1694, William Dicconson was a captain in the regiment of Charles Towneley of Towneley, whose lieutenant-colonel was William's neighbour and cousin William Standish of Standish.

In 1694 a fraudulent attempt to seize the estates of several Lancashire Catholics, including Dicconson's (worth £1000–1100 a year—he also possessed Lincolnshire and London property), as having been given for Catholic 'superstitious uses', collapsed. The false witnesses involved quickly accused these Catholics of a Jacobite plot (based on rumours of the real one), and obtained government authority to make arrests in Lancashire. Among those seized and prosecuted, Dicconson was almost the only active plotter. A renegade witness, John Taaffe, introduced William's younger brother Roger Dicconson (*c*.1666–1742) in disguise to the perjurers as a colleague, and both men's evidence at William's trial at Manchester on 20 October 1694 so discredited the imaginary 'Lancashire plot' that he was acquitted and the prosecutions were dropped.

As protection against future false accusations, Dicconson immediately began a daily journal showing his whereabouts (seldom outside Lancashire) and activities until June 1699, including riot-provoking enclosures of commons. Remaining childless, he in 1697 enabled his brother Roger to marry an heiress to preserve the line. In 1699 William was summoned to the Jacobite court at St Germain, where, after groundless rumours that he would be secretary of state, on 4 August 1700 NS Dominick Sheldon and he were appointed joint under-governors to the prince of Wales, posts renewed after James II's death. In March 1701 Dicconson was outlawed in his absence at the Middlesex assizes, and his estates were (in theory) granted to the bishop of London. However, his 1699 settlement for paying debts allowed Roger Dicconson to hold the estates and pay him an income, and even Roger's forfeiture for joining the 1715 rising did not lose them for the family.

During 1699–1701, a slack period in Jacobite activity, Secretary John Caryll, assisted by under-secretary David Nairne, had begun a large-scale official biography of James II, incorporating his consecutive memoirs of his 1650s campaigns and carrying the narrative to the eve of the Popish Plot. In 1707, when their official duties occupied them, Dicconson was chosen to complete it. Lacking their long personal acquaintance with James and with high politics, he relied more heavily on written sources:

particularly on the fragmentary 'memoirs' James had noted down, usually on contemporary events; on his brother's and his supporters' letters during the exclusion crisis; and on the Jacobite state papers, including reports of top secret negotiations with politicians. For 1660–78 Caryll had absorbed the 'memoirs' into his narrative, leaving uncertain the authority for some important statements. Dicconson directly quoted the 'memoirs' at length—making the *Life* of particular value, since the originals were destroyed in the French Revolution—and gave references when paraphrasing letters. His lack of such primary sources for nearly all James's reign was among the work's weaknesses. Dicconson naturally had few criticisms of James, but did not portray all his betrayers, such as the second earl of Sunderland, as entirely evil, and constitutionally he was not a die-hard. Historians found the *Life*, published in 1816, useful for the extracts it preserved from James's 'memoirs', though they were confused by James Macpherson's deliberate mingling of notes taken from it and from its sources in a publication of 1775. However, the muddled accusation that Dicconson had forged his sources, made by Winston Churchill in his whitewashing 1933 biography of his ancestor Marlborough, caused nearly all historians to ignore it for the next half-century.

From his arrival Dicconson used his financial abilities on the Stuarts' behalf. On 17 May 1708 NS he became one of the commissioners of the royal household, and on 11 March 1709 NS Mary of Modena appointed him her treasurer of the household and receiver-general. His main duties involved paying pensions and charities from the limited funds available. His integrity and plain-spoken insistence on economy made him valuable, and he was trusted in some political matters. After Mary's death in 1718, James employed him informally to pay pensions to the slowly dwindling Jacobite colony at St Germain, from Stuart or French sources; he himself received a French pension. Esteemed to the end, he died of a fever at St Germain on 15 November 1742 NS. Two months later his brother Hugh, one of the under-governors to Prince Henry Benedict, died of influenza at the Stuart court. Juliana Walmesley died at St Germain on 13 August 1751 NS.

PAUL HOPKINS

Sources Royal Arch., Stuart papers [incl. card index] · *The life of James the Second, king of England*, ed. J. S. Clarke, 2 vols. (1816) · P. A. Hopkins, 'Aspects of Jacobite conspiracy in England in the reign of William III', PhD diss., U. Cam., 1981 · *Calendar of the Stuart papers belonging to his majesty the king, preserved at Windsor Castle*, 7 vols., HMC, 56 (1902–23) · Dicconson pedigree, 1810, Wigan Archives Service, Leigh, DDX/EL–230/31 · Lancs. RO, Dicconson of Wrightington family papers, D/D Wr · E. Gregg, 'New light on the authorship of the *Life of James II*', EngHR, 108 (1993), 947–65 · W. Dicconson, 'Diary, 1694–1699', Ampleforth Abbey, Yorkshire, MS 88 · T. C. Porteus, 'New light on the Lancashire Jacobite plot, 1692–4', *Transactions of the Lancashire and Cheshire Antiquarian Society*, 50 (1934–5), 1–64 · *The manuscripts of Lord Kenyon*, HMC, 35 (1894) · W. Dugdale, *The visitation of the county palatine of Lancaster, made in the year 1664–5*, ed. F. R. Raines, 3 vols., Chetham Society, 84–5, 88 (1872–3) · PRO, Papers of the Forfeited Estates Commission, FEC1/537–551 · [E. T. Corp and J. Sanson], eds., *La cour des Stuarts* (Paris, 1992) [exhibition catalogue, Musée des Antiquités Nationales de Saint-Germain-en-Laye, 13 Feb – 27 April 1992] · *VCH Lancashire*, vol. 6 · exchequer commission of enquiry, 1706, PRO, E134/5 Anne/East. 28 · D. Nairne, journal, NL Scot., MS 14266, fols. 159v–160 · E. Corp, 'An inventory of the archives of the Stuart court at Saint-Germain-en-Laye, 1689–1718', *Archives*, 23 (1998), 118–46 · William Dicconson's indictment, March 1701, LMA, MJ/SR/1961 · J. Macpherson, ed., *Original papers: containing the secret history of Great Britain*, 2 vols. (1775)

Archives Ampleforth Abbey, MS 88 · Derbys. RO | Royal Arch., Stuart MSS

Wealth at death probably lived on French pension plus some income sent from the family estate; bequest of 3700 livres a year, to the English College, Paris, and the rest to wife (bequest dated from 1703, almost forty years before his death): N. Genet-Rouffiac, 'Jacobites in Paris and St-Germain-en-Laye', *The Stuart court in exile and the Jacobites*, ed. E. Cruickshanks and E. Corp (1995), 21 · family suspected he had advanced money of his own on Stuart business: Royal Arch., Stuart MSS, vols. 246, 249

Diceto, Ralph de (*d.* 1199/1200), chronicler and ecclesiastic, is of unknown origins. His surname has given rise to much discussion; William Stubbs pronounced it 'an artificial name, adopted by its bearer as the Latin name of a place with which he was associated, but which had no proper Latin name of its own' (*Opera historica*, ed. Stubbs, 1.xvii), and was inclined to connect it with one of three places named Dissai or Dissé in Maine. However, recent scholarship has noted Ralph as occurring in charters under such name forms as Dysci and Dici, which can very plausibly be construed as deriving from Diss. Certainty on the point is not presently to be had, but it is undoubtedly possible that he was a Norfolk man. It would appear that he was born in the 1120s, for his notices of events concerning St Paul's begin in 1136, and 'certainly have the appearance of personal recollections' (*Opera historica*, ed. Stubbs, 1.xx). These recollections imply Ralph's presence there from boyhood, and his nomination as archdeacon of Middlesex by Bishop Richard de Belmeis of London (*d.* 1162), as the latter's first episcopal act after his consecration on 28 September 1152, and the bishop's tenacity in adhering to his choice in the face of competition, alike suggest that Ralph himself belonged to the Belmeis family, which prospered in the diocese under its two Bishop Richards. Diceto's most likely place in the pedigree is as son or nephew of Ralph of Langford (*d. c.*1154?), brother of Bishop Richard de Belmeis, and dean of St Paul's in 1152.

When he was appointed archdeacon in 1152, Diceto was styled 'master'. Twice a student at the Paris schools, Diceto appears to have gone there for the first time in the 1140s. He was back in England in the early 1150s, and was probably present at Henry II's coronation on 19 December 1154, but then seems to have returned to Paris, perhaps to study law. Thereafter evidence for his career is provided both by his own writings and by independent record evidence. By 1164 he had acquired the livings of Aynho, Northamptonshire, and Finchingfield, Essex, and served them both by vicars. In that year he attended the Council of Northampton, and in 1166 was sent as a messenger by the English bishops to Archbishop Thomas Becket, who was then in exile. In the aftermath of Becket's murder, about the end of 1171, he was one of a delegation to the pope, sent to petition for the lifting of the suspension of Gilbert Foliot as bishop of London. He was active as an archdeacon, for instance trying to maintain his own jurisdiction over St

Margaret's, Westminster. In 1180 he was elected dean of St Paul's, and early in the following year conducted a detailed survey of the chapter's property. He also enacted a statute of residence for the cathedral, in which he tried to strike a realistic balance between the needs of St Paul's for residentiary clergy, and the ever-increasing tendency for the canons to be pluralists and absentees. In December 1187 he acted alongside Hubert Walter as a papal judge-delegate, while on 3 September 1189 he acted in place of the bishop of London (the see being vacant) at the coronation of Richard I. The latter's visit to St Paul's in 1194, along with the archbishop of Rouen, was but one of the visits by secular and ecclesiastical rulers in the 1180s and 1190s that Diceto recorded, and presumably attended.

Diceto refers to himself for the last time on 23 May 1199, when he presented William de Ste Mère-Église to Archbishop Walter for consecration. The date of his death, like the place of his birth, is problematic. Although his chronicle continues to 1202, and his obit was commemorated at St Paul's on 22 November, it has been persuasively argued that Diceto died on that day not in 1202 but in either 1199 or 1200, and that the section dealing with events after the coronation of King John, on 27 May 1199, is the work of a continuator. Diceto was fittingly remembered at St Paul's as 'the good dean' (*Opera historica*, ed. Stubbs, 1.lxxxv). He codified the cathedral's customs and statutes, and built a deanery house and chapel within its cathedral precincts, which he bequeathed to his successors, along with relics (which included the staff of St Martin of Tours and the head of St Eugenius), vestments, ornaments, and books.

In this last bequest there was a volume of chronicles. Diceto was the author of two major historical narratives, and also of a collection of shorter pieces, his *opuscula*. Though mainly little more than lists—bishops of various English dioceses, popes, archbishops of Canterbury, emperors, kings, and the like—the latter are nevertheless characteristic of an important side of Diceto's intellectual personality, as both historian and ecclesiastic. For he was a methodical and exact compiler of information of all kinds, and had probably been assembling material for years before he began to compose his chronicles. This can also be seen in his survey of the St Paul's manors, with its list of headings under which the inquest was to be made, the precise timetable under which it was carried out, and the remarkably detailed notice of its date, placing it in time by reference to no less than six different chronological systems, ranging from the year *anno Domini* to Diceto's own deanship.

But in spite of his concern for the minutiae of history, Diceto was a man of wide vision. His epitome of chronicles, the *Abbreviationes chronicorum*, covers the history of the world from the creation to 1147 in a series of brief annals, and represents the most ambitious attempt at a world history made until then by an Englishman. That it contains some original material towards the end, mostly concerning St Paul's, is arguably less significant than the work's terms of reference. In an extended prologue (in which the influence of Hugh of St Victor is apparent), Diceto explains that the *Abbreviationes* are divided into three sections, defined as the very ancient (that is, before Christ), the ancient (the Christian era), and the modern—his own time. He follows this with a list of the important writers on whose work he has drawn, along with notes of the periods covered in their writings, in the process providing evidence for the impressive range of his reading (he was also well read in the classics, elsewhere quoting such authors as Claudian, Lucan, and Sidonius Apollinaris, and making a disparaging reference to the French by way of a neatly adapted line from Virgil's *Aeneid*). And he also makes an important technical innovation (later imitated by Matthew Paris), in the use of a number of marginal *signa*, pictorial devices employed to indicate the presence in the adjacent text of particular subjects, such as councils, royal unction, disputes between king and church.

These signs (along with two new ones, including one for dissension between the king and his sons, represented by two hands grasping a crown from either side) are also used in Diceto's more important historical work, the *Ymagines historiarum*. Starting with the knighting of the future Henry II in 1149, it likewise draws on a wide range of materials, although until 1171, perhaps until 1183, Robert de Torigni is the principal source used. But before, as well as after, 1171 Diceto makes considerable use of documents, as for instance in his account of the Becket dispute, which is largely made up of letters and papal bulls. And he also exploited his personal contacts. Men of the importance of Hubert Walter, William de Longchamp, Walter de Coutances, archbishop of Rouen and justiciar, several of whose letters are quoted verbatim, Richard fitz Nigel, and Richard of Ilchester, who is recorded as asking Diceto for advice in 1166, could provide letters and news. With such sources of information, it is not surprising that Diceto was well informed, not least about events abroad, especially in France, where he often reports on events in Henry II's continental lands. He also followed events in the kingdom of Jerusalem, and sometimes in Constantinople. He made systematic use of Richard I's newsletters.

The *Ymagines historiarum* are not just a valuable source for events in the last half of the twelfth century. Diceto was an intellectual historian, seriously interested in problems arising from the deployment of power, which he saw from the perspective of an ecclesiastic who appreciated the benefits of strong and relatively impartial royal government, and could grasp the concept of public authority. He admired Henry II's concern for good order, and his chronicle is an important source for such acts of government as the peacekeeping measures of 1179; he also condemned acts of rebellion and disorder, like the massacres of Jews in 1190. The dean of St Paul's saw nothing incongruous in bishops' being involved in secular government, arguing rather that they made better officials than did laymen. The Becket dispute inevitably put a severe strain on his loyalties, divided as they were not only between the king and the primate, but also, and perhaps more stressfully, between Becket and Diceto's own bishop, Gilbert Foliot, who remained a determined opponent of the archbishop for as long as the latter lived. To some extent, both in the *Ymagines* and in his abbreviated account of the quarrel, known as the *Series causae*, Diceto used his marginal *signa* simply to draw attention to the issues at stake; but they also acted as a sort of silent commentary on events, and one that had the positive advantage of enabling him to avoid taking up too clear-cut a position on the rights and wrongs of a painful controversy. If in the end Diceto favours Becket, his remarkably even-handed account nevertheless shows that he appreciated the strength of Henry II's position on the issue of criminous clerks.

Diceto's judgement was not always faultless; he was taken in by Geoffrey of Monmouth, and in his account of the events of 1189 shows that he regarded the death of Henry II as fulfilling the prophecies of Merlin. But as a historian he deserves the admiration with which he has been regarded, and the use that has been made of his writings, from the thirteenth century onwards. His chronicles were first printed in 1652, in the *Historiae Anglicanae scriptores X* of Roger Twysden and John Selden, an excellent edition marred only by its failure to reproduce Diceto's *signa*. This deficiency was remedied in Stubbs's edition of 1876, which has remained the basis for the study of Diceto's work.   J. F. A. MASON

Sources *Radulfi de Diceto … opera historica*, ed. W. Stubbs, 2 vols., Rolls Series, 68 (1876) · A. Gransden, *Historical writing in England*, 1 (1974), 230–36, pl. VII · D. E. Greenway, 'The succession to Ralph de Diceto, dean of St Paul's', *BIHR*, 39 (1966), 86–95 · W. H. Hale, ed., *The domesday of St Paul's of the year 1222*, CS, 69 (1858), 109–17 · W. S. Simpson, ed., *Documents illustrating the history of St Paul's Cathedral*, CS, new ser., 26 (1880) · B. Smalley, *Historians in the middle ages* (1974), 114–19 · C. Duggan and A. Duggan, 'Ralph de Diceto, Henry II and Becket', *Authority and power: studies in medieval law and government presented to Walter Ullmann on his seventieth birthday*, ed. B. Tierney and P. Linehan (1980), 59–81 · G. A. Zinn, 'The influence of Hugh of St Victor's *Chronicon* on the *Abbreviationes chronicorum* by Ralph de Diceto', *Speculum*, 52 (1977), 38–61 · J. B. Gillingham, 'Royal newsletters, forgeries, and English historians', *La cour plantagenêt, 1154–1204*, ed. M. Aurell (Poitiers, 2000), 178–9 · B. Smalley, *The Becket conflict and the schools* (1973) · C. R. Cheney, *Hubert Walter* (1967) · F. Barlow, *Thomas Becket* (1986) · *Fasti Angl., 1066–1300*, [St Paul's, London]

Archives St Paul's Cathedral, London

Dicey family (*per. c.*1710–*c.*1800), printers, came to prominence through the marriage of **Elizabeth Dicey** (*fl.* 1713–1731) with **John Cluer** (*d.* 1728), printer, and to the consolidation of their interests with those of her brother William Dicey. John Cluer, apprenticed to Thomas Sowden in 1695 and freed in 1702, was married to Elizabeth Dicey before 6 November 1713 (the date on which their son Dicey Cluer was buried). He enrolled seven apprentices between 1718 and 1726 and was listed by Samuel Negus, who knew him well, among those 'Said to be High Flyers' in 1723 (Harris, 100). This allegation is substantiated by his habit of placing advertisements in the Jacobite *Mist's Weekly Journal* and by the strongly tory flavour of much of the family stock dating from the 1710s and 1720s, which included portraits of the 'glorious Martyr' and 'Queen Anne in glory', for instance. The printing house at the Maiden-Head in Bow Churchyard was equipped with rolling presses as well as letter presses and handled general jobbing work of both kinds, but was already advertising chapbooks as well as cheap woodcuts, engravings, and 'hieroglyphical love letters' in *Mist's Weekly Journal* on 4 January 1718. From about 1720 Cluer moved into music, publishing on a large enough scale to challenge John Walsh, the leading figure in that business. In 1724 and 1725 Cluer and B. Creake launched pocket volumes of opera songs and musical playing cards. According to the *London Journal* of 13 July 1728, Cluer and his foreman Thomas Cobb invented movable types for printing music (which had previously been engraved in intaglio).

Cluer died in 1728, leaving the Bow warehouse to his widow, Elizabeth, who ran it with the help of **Thomas Cobb** (*fl.* 1728–1736), whom she married in 1731. Cobb's publishing continued to be innovative: his sixpenny miniature prints for watch cases were, in 1734, among the earliest to be advertised. The same advertisement described Cobb's general stock of decorative prints: 'great Variety of different Fancies, newly engrav'd for Rooms or Staircases, and ready fram'd' and especially 'royal sheets and Lottery Pictures for Children printed from Copper Plates or Wooden Cuts, both painted and plain'. In 1736 Cobb assigned the business to his brother-in-law William Dicey, who sent his son Cluer Dicey to take charge.

William Dicey (*d.* 1756) now formally united the Bow Printing Office with his own provincial interests, although in reality they had probably been running in harmony for more than a decade. William Dicey was living with his wife, Mary (*d.* 1748?), in St Giles Cripplegate in 1719 but the fact that the birth of their son William was registered at St Mary-le-Bow suggests an association with the printing office in that churchyard. Their eldest son, Cluer, had been born in 1714 or 1715. The name (paired with the naming of John Cluer's son Dicey) is evidently significant, and might indicate that, just as John Cluer had married a Dicey, William Dicey had married a Cluer; at the least, it suggests friendship between the two printers. In 1719, in partnership with Robert Raikes, William Dicey established the *St Ives Mercury*. They then set up in Northampton and on 2 May 1720 printed the first *Northampton Mercury* from a printing office near All Saints' Church. This was followed in 1721 by a periodical, the *Northampton Miscellany*, and in 1722 by the *Gloucester Journal*. From this point Raikes moved to Gloucester to look after the *Journal* while Dicey remained in Northampton, and in 1725 their partnership was dissolved. As well as undertaking jobbing printing, Dicey's printing office sold prints and bound books, and also published chapbooks and cheap woodcut prints. One of the first, a woodcut copy of James Cole's *The Bubbler's Bubbl'd, or, The Devil Take the Hindmost* (1720), was 'cut and printed at Northampton Where Country Shopkeepers and others may be furnish'd with all sorts of Broadsheets, Ballads and Histories, as cheap, and much better done than at any Printing Office in England' (Stephens and George, 1626). From the outset Dicey was also concerned in patent medicines. In 1720 he was selling imported Hungary water for the nerves as well as for 'Scrophulous and Scorbutick Distempers' and 'the most Famous and never-failing Golden Pill for the Gout and Rheumatism' at 3*s.* a box. At his death he left a one-third share in Dr Bateman's Pectoral Drops to his son Cluer, and he was also involved with

> Daffy's Cordial, warm and spicy,
> Sold in Bow-Church-Yard by Dicey
> (Neuberg, 'Diceys and the chapbook trade', 224)

He died in Northampton in 1756 and his business interests were taken over by his sons.

Cluer Dicey (1714/15–1775) was reported, prematurely, to have taken over the *Stamford Mercury* in 1732. It transpired that the *Stamford Mercury* was not for sale and Cluer had to wait four years to be given a much bigger challenge, the printing office in Bow Churchyard. He married another Mary and between 1739 and 1750 they had seven children. In 1754 William and Cluer Dicey issued a printed catalogue of their enormous stock of engraved and woodcut prints, ballads, chapbooks, and other material which establishes them as easily the most important figures of their time in popular publishing. The affection in which the long-established business was held is illustrated by James Boswell's report of a visit in July 1763 to:

> the old printing-office in Bow Church-yard kept by Dicey, whose family have kept it fourscore years. There are ushered into the world of literature *Jack and the Giants*, *The Seven Wise Men of Gotham*, and other story-books which in my dawning years amused me as much as *Rasselas* does now. (*Boswell's London Journal*)

By the next year Cluer Dicey was in partnership with Richard Marshall. Their 1764 catalogue listed 1000 engravings and woodcuts, 150 chapbooks, and 3000 ballads. The numerous smaller prints intended for children were not even listed. He died on 3 October 1775 aged sixty and was buried in Claybrook church, Leicestershire. The epitaph on his monument was written by Hannah More. He had property in Little Claybrook and in Stoke Newington.

Robert Dicey (1721–1757) managed the *Northampton Mercury* for his father, William, from 1747 until his death in 1757. Soon after that **Thomas Dicey** (*b.* 1742, *d.* after 1800), son of Cluer Dicey, took charge. In 1789 Thomas was in possession of Claybrook Hall, Leicestershire, when his son Thomas Edward was born there, but he remained a vestryman of Bow church until about 1800 when he may have retired from business in London. The Dicey family continued to own the *Northampton Mercury* until 1885.

TIMOTHY CLAYTON

Sources V. E. Neuberg, 'The Diceys and the chapbook trade', *The Library*, 24 (1969), 219–31 · G. Duval, 'Littérature de colportage et imaginaire collectif en Angleterre à l'époque des Dicey (1720–vers 1800)', diss., University of Bordeaux, 1991 · *A catalogue of maps, prints, copy-books, drawing books, histories, old ballads, broad-sheet and other patters, garlands, &c. Printed and sold by William and Cluer Dicey, at their warehouse, opposite the south door of Bow-church in Bow-Church-yard* (1754) · *A catalogue of maps, prints, copy-books, drawing books, histories, old ballads, patters, collections, &c. Printed and sold by Cluer Dicey, and Richard Marshall at the printing office, in Aldermary Churchyard, London* (1764) · M. Harris, 'Scratching the surface: engravers, printsellers and the London book trade in the mid-eighteenth century', *The book trade and its customers, 1450–1900: historical essays for Robin Myers*, ed. A. Hunt, G. Mandelbrote, and A. Shell (1997) · V. E. Neuberg, *Popular literature: a history and guide* (1977) · *Northampton Mercury* (1720–55) · J. Burnby, 'Printers ink and patent medicines: the story of the Diceys', *Pharmaceutical Journal*, 14 (Aug 1982), 162–3, 169 · C. Humphries and W. Smith, *Music publishing in the British Isles*

(1970) · *Boswell's London journal, 1762–63*, ed. F. A. Pottle (1950), vol. 1 of *The Yale editions of the private papers of James Boswell*, trade edn (1950–89), 229 · F. G. Stephens and M. D. George, *Political and personal satires* (1870–73), vol. 1 of *Catalogue of prints and drawings in the British Museum* [1935–54] · G. Duval, 'The Diceys revisited', *Factotum*, 35 (1992), 9–11 · G. Duval, 'More facts, afterthoughts and conjectures about the Diceys', *Factotum*, 40 (1995), 13–18 · M. Hobbs, 'The Diceys revisited', *Factotum*, 36 (1993), 27 · will and other documents, Northants. RO, MS Yz 4711–4737 [William Dicey]
Archives Northants. RO

Dicey, Albert Venn (1835–1922), jurist, was the third son of Thomas Edward Dicey (*b.* 1789), proprietor of the *Northampton Mercury*, and his wife, Anne Mary, younger daughter of James Stephen, master in chancery, and was born at the family home, Claybrook Hall, near Lutterworth, Leicestershire, on 4 February 1835. The name Venn was given to him in honour of the leader of the Clapham sect John Venn, whose daughter Jane had married Anne Dicey's brother, Sir James Stephen. Obstetrical error at birth caused a muscular weakness that plagued Dicey throughout life. His handwriting was notoriously difficult to decipher and many of his adult letters were written by an amanuensis. His early education came at home and Dicey recalled in later life his happy memories of lessons taught by his mother. Dicey entered King's College School in London in 1852 and then matriculated at Balliol College, Oxford, in 1854. He obtained a first class in classical moderations in 1856 and in *literae humaniores* in 1858. At Oxford he helped found the Old Mortality society that in a brief existence included a number of individuals who afterwards attained distinction. Among them were Thomas Hill Green, Edward Caird, Algernon Charles Swinburne, James Bryce, and Thomas Erskine Holland. To his Oxford years Dicey owed many of the friendships that he treasured later in life, especially that with Bryce.

In 1860 Dicey was successful in an examination for a fellowship at Trinity College, Oxford, and in the same year he won the Arnold prize for an essay on the privy council, which was published in the same year. Dicey attributed his lifelong interest in constitutional law and history to this work. He moved to London in 1861 and studied for the bar at the Inner Temple, to which he was called in 1863. He enjoyed moderate success at the bar and eventually became queen's counsel in 1890. In 1872 he forfeited his fellowship when he married Elinor Mary Bonham-Carter (*d.* 1923), youngest daughter of John Bonham-Carter (MP for Portsmouth from 1830 to 1841). The marriage, which lasted for fifty years, produced no children; it was a long, happy companionship, marred only by frequent bouts of illness, to which Elinor Dicey was subject.

During his residence in London from 1861 to 1882 Dicey practised at the bar and pursued journalistic and scholarly projects. He contributed to the *Northampton Mercury* (of which he occasionally acted as temporary editor), the *Spectator*, and the New York *Nation*. The articles in the *Nation* provide an excellent record of his political and intellectual maturation. During this period Dicey published *A Treatise on the Rules for the Selection of the Parties to an Action* (1870) and *The Law of Domicil, as a Branch of the Law of England, Stated in the Form of Rules* (1879). Neither book earned

Albert Venn Dicey (1835–1922), by Désiré François Laugée, 1872

an extensive readership but, by virtue of the scholarly reputation of each, Dicey was elected in 1882 to the Vinerian professorship of English law at Oxford. He held this chair, to which a fellowship at All Souls College was attached, for twenty-seven years; he revived its importance after a long period of absentee occupants since the resignation of Sir William Blackstone in 1766.

During his long professorship, Dicey published the three books that gave him a significant place in common-law jurisprudence. His *Introduction to the Study of the Law of the Constitution* (1885), updated by a lengthy introduction to the eighth edition (1915), established his reputation as a major commentator on the British constitution. Focus on three fundamental principles, parliamentary sovereignty, the rule of law, and constitutional conventions, enabled Dicey to provide for the general public an understanding of constitutional law. The clarity of his prose made the work accessible to a wide spectrum of educated opinion, and his ability to reduce the complex topic to three concepts caused him to refer to himself as a prophet of the obvious. His facility for analysis made the work a classic of exposition and ensured its place as a primary influence on the discussion of constitutional law from its first appearance.

Law of the Constitution owed the popularity of its reception as well to polemic features which belied its expository and limited explicit intentions; notably it was a broadly whiggish account of England's history which was implicitly celebratory of English national identity. The centrality of the common law to English history, Dicey held, had produced a tradition of liberty that reached full flower in the individualism so important to Victorian

ideas of self. This legacy separated England from the *droit administratif* institutions in France, where freedom depended upon government licence. His statement of the superiority of England's political heritage placed Dicey squarely in the Burkean tradition and marked out *Law of the Constitution* as a work of political theory, not simply legal analysis. Even the book's modest self-representation as simply a piece of legal analysis had implicit polemical force. Academic legal science was a recently established discipline, the credibility of which was an issue which preoccupied Dicey. A work which so successfully imported England's common law into its population's sense of its heritage and identity, and one which did so not in the language of abstract theory but by the detailed examination of the law, did a great deal to secure the reputation of the discipline. And just as Dicey championed the science of law he championed also the lawyers: in his legalistic overhaul of the whig account, it was judges and not statesmen who emerged as the upholders of liberty.

In 1896 Dicey published *A Digest of the Law of England with Reference to the Conflict of Laws*, his greatest treatise with respect to a mastery of an intricate branch of the law. His ability to consolidate the complex, copious case-law in this area into a limited number of rules exerted a strong influence on the law's development, according to his successor in the Vinerian chair, William Martin Geldart. Successive editions, edited by J. H. C. Morris after Dicey's death, retained the book's place in legal scholarship.

The third book Dicey completed as Vinerian professor was *Lectures on the Relation between Law and Public Opinion in England during the Nineteenth Century* (1905). This work was based on lectures Dicey delivered in 1898 at the Harvard law school. Dicey had visited the United States previously, in 1870, when he befriended such notable Americans as E. L. Godkin, Charles William Eliot, and Justice Oliver Wendell Holmes. In *Law and Opinion* Dicey divided public opinion into the following categories: old toryism (1800–30), Benthamism or individualism (1825–70), and collectivism (1865–1900). As a map of the interaction between law and public opinion Dicey's effort lost the confidence of later historians, and his artificial classifications appeared to sacrifice analysis to symmetry of expression. Of Dicey's three great works, *Law and Opinion* suffered the greatest loss of influence in the twentieth century.

Dicey also possessed a keen interest in contemporary politics, and until the 1880s he embraced orthodox Liberalism with an emphasis on the benefits of free trade. The conversion of William Gladstone to home rule for Ireland turned Dicey into a leading polemicist on Liberal Unionism. Preservation of the union with Ireland became the core of his political creed, and in this cause he published *England's Case Against Home Rule* (1886), *Letters on Unionist Delusions* (1887), *A Leap in the Dark* (1893), and *A Fool's Paradise* (1913). Fears for the Irish union caused him to work tirelessly, by publication and private letter, in opposition to any scheme that would modify Ireland's constitutional status. In part because of his own enunciation of parliamentary sovereignty as a fundamental principle of the constitution, and in part from his reading of federalism in the United States, Dicey rejected federalism in any guise as a solution to the revision of Ireland's constitutional status. Dicey opposed a federal settlement because he believed that it produced an inherently weak form of government that repudiated centuries of historical development. Towards the end of his life his hopes were dashed by the events in Ireland from 1918 to 1921.

Dicey was a gifted conversationalist who sometimes fell prey to the habit of explaining at length any topic with which he was acquainted. Tall and thin, with a splendid white beard in later life, Dicey was for decades a familiar figure in the Oxford University community. Personal generosity of spirit did not extend to politics, where proponents of views contrary to his own drew fierce criticism. He was eighty-five when he published his last book, *Thoughts on the Union between England and Scotland* (1920), with Robert Sangster Rait. Dicey died peacefully of respiratory complications on 7 April 1922, at his home, The Orchard, 80 Banbury Road, Oxford, after a life full of academic distinction and honours. He was buried at St Sepulchre's cemetery, Oxford. His wife, Elinor, died the following year. Dicey was remembered as an individual who sought the national good above all else, and his work continued to influence discussions of constitutional law. His ability to present the complexities of constitutional law to the public has endured since his death, and it will likely remain his greatest achievement.   RICHARD A. COSGROVE

Sources R. A. Cosgrove, *The rule of law: Albert Venn Dicey, Victorian jurist* (1980) • Bodl. Oxf., MSS James Bryce • R. Sangster Rait, ed., *Memorials of Albert Venn Dicey* (1925) • HLRO, J. St Loe Strachey papers • H. G. Hanbury, *The Vinerian chair and legal education* (1958) • F. H. Lawson, *The Oxford law school, 1850–1965* (1968) • C. Harvie, 'Ideology and home rule: James Bryce, A. V. Dicey and Ireland, 1880–1887', *EngHR*, 91 (1976), 298–314 • S. Collini, *Public moralists* (1991) • private information (2004) • *DNB*
Archives LMA, corresp. and papers • U. Edin. L., notebooks • U. Glas. L., corresp. and papers | All Souls Oxf., letters to Sir William Anson • Balliol Oxf., letters to Sir R. B. Morier • BL, corresp. with Arthur James Balfour, Add. MS 49792 • BL, letters to J. H. Bernard, Add. MS 52781 • BL, corresp. with Lord Lang, Add. MS 62406 • BL, corresp. with Macmillans, Add. MSS 55084–55085 • Bodl. Oxf., corresp. with Lord Bryce • CUL, corresp. with Lord Acton • Gon. & Caius Cam., letters to John Venn • HLRO, corresp. with Andrew Bonar Law; corresp. with John St Loe Strachey • JRL, letters to E. A. Freeman • King's Cam., letters to Oscar Browning • NL Scot., Elliot MSS • NRA, priv. coll., letters to Lord Balfour of Burleigh • TCD, letters to W. E. H. Lecky
Likenesses D. F. Laugée, oils, 1872, Trinity College, Oxford [*see illus.*] • R. A. Cosgrove, two photographs, 1886–1907, Tucson, Arizona
Wealth at death £23,068 11s. 0d.: probate, 16 May 1922, *CGPLA Eng. & Wales*

Dicey, Cluer (1714/15–1775). *See under* Dicey family (*per.* c.1710–c.1800).

Dicey, Edward James Stephen (1832–1911), author and journalist, born on 15 May 1832 at Claybrook Hall, Claybrook, near Lutterworth, Leicestershire, was the second son of Thomas Edward Dicey (*b.* 1789), of an old Leicestershire family, who was senior wrangler at Cambridge in 1811, was a pioneer of the Midland Railway, and owned the *Northampton Mercury*. Dicey's mother, Anne Mary, sister of Sir James *Stephen, was aunt of Sir James Fitzjames *Stephen and Sir Leslie *Stephen. His younger brother was Albert Venn *Dicey.

Educated at home and, for about two years, at King's College, London, Dicey went up to Trinity College, Cambridge, in 1850, was president of the Cambridge Union in 1853, and graduated BA in 1854 with a third class in the classical tripos and as a senior optime in mathematics. After leaving Cambridge he went for a short time into business without success, and then took to writing, following in the tradition of many of his relatives. From 1860 he was a regular contributor to *The Spectator*. He travelled abroad and interested himself in foreign politics. In 1861 he published *Rome in 1860* and *Cavour: a Memoir*, thereby establishing his reputation as a political commentator. The following year Dicey visited America and wrote in *Macmillan's Magazine* and *The Spectator* on the American Civil War, in which he supported the Union. There followed in 1863 *Six Months in the Federal States*.

In 1861 Dicey became connected with the *Daily Telegraph*—then a strongly Liberal paper—and his style and knowledge of foreign questions led to his being made a permanent member of the staff in 1862. Among his colleagues were Sir Edwin Arnold (an old schoolfriend), F. C. Lawley, and G. A. Sala. He was a leader writer for the paper, and also acted as special correspondent in the Prussian-Danish War of 1864 and the Austro-Prussian War of 1866. He embodied these experiences in the volumes *The Schleswig-Holstein War* (1864) and *The Battle-Fields of 1866* (1866). He afterwards described other foreign excursions in *A Month in Russia during the Marriage of the Czarevitch* (1867) and in *The Morning Land, being Sketches of Turkey, the Holy Land, and Egypt* (1870), the result of a three-month tour in the Near East.

While in the Near East in 1869 Dicey accepted an offer of the editorship of the *Daily News*, and held this post for three months in 1870. On leaving it he at once became editor of *The Observer*, and filled that office for nineteen years (1870–89), continuing to write for the paper for some time after he ceased to edit it. Under his editorship the paper's tone was scholarly, albeit with a small circulation. Subsequently he was a constant contributor to the *Nineteenth Century*, the *Empire Review*, and other periodicals. His interest in foreign politics remained keen, especially in the affairs of eastern Europe. He was a frequent visitor to Egypt, and formed at first hand well-defined views of England's position there, at one time advocating the annexation of the country by Great Britain. He recorded his views in *England and Egypt* (1881; collected articles), *The Story of the Khedivate* (1902), and *The Egypt of the Future* (1907). He also published *Victor Emmanuel* (1882) and an account of Bulgaria (1894). Dicey, like his better-known brother, was one of those Liberal intellectuals who made their way into Unionism. He strongly attacked Gladstone's Irish and Egyptian policies in the early 1880s and he was an ardent opponent of home rule; but he remained a free-trader. He was a strong supporter of friendly relations between Britain and Germany, and closely studied South African matters in later years.

On 14 August 1867 Dicey married Anne Greene Chapman (*d.* 1878) of Weymouth, Massachusetts, daughter of Henry Grafton Chapman; they had one son, who predeceased his father. During his later life Dicey made his home in chambers in Gray's Inn (he had been called to the bar in 1875, though he never practised). He became a bencher there in 1896 and treasurer in 1903-4. He frequented the Athenaeum and Garrick clubs. C. P. Lucas wrote of him:

> Dicey was by nature a singularly good observer; he had a great store of knowledge, much dry humour, a cool judgment, and a sound and vivid style. Though in a sense reserved and indifferent to outward appearances, he associated easily and genially with men around him, especially with foreigners, while he possessed a rare capacity for easy and clear description of scenes and events which were passing before his eyes. Being neither didactic nor controversial, nor in the ordinary sense professional, he exercised by his writings alike in books and newspapers considerable influence on public opinion. (*DNB*)

Dicey died of cirrhosis of the liver at his chambers, 2 Gray's Inn Square, London, on 7 July 1911 and, after a funeral service in the Inn's chapel, was buried in Brompton cemetery. H. C. G. MATTHEW

Sources *The Times* (8 July 1911) • *Daily Telegraph* (8 July 1911) • *The Observer* (9 July 1899) • L. Stephen, *The life of Sir James Fitzjames Stephen* (1895) • C. L. Graves, *Life and letters of Alexander Macmillan* (1910) • *DNB* • C. Harvie, *The lights of liberalism* (1976) • R. A. Cosgrove, *The rule of law: Albert Venn Dicey, Victorian jurist* (1980) • *Men and women of the time* (1899) • d. cert.
Archives LMA, A. V. Dicey MSS • U. Edin., A. V. Dicey MSS • U. Glas. L., A. V. Dicey MSS
Wealth at death £780 16s. 2d.: probate, 20 Sept 1911, *CGPLA Eng. & Wales*

Dicey, Elizabeth (*fl.* 1713-1731). *See under* Dicey family (*per. c.*1710-*c.*1800).

Dicey, Robert (1721-1757). *See under* Dicey family (*per. c.*1710-*c.*1800).

Dicey, Thomas (*b.* 1742, *d.* after 1800). *See under* Dicey family (*per. c.*1710-*c.*1800).

Dicey, William (*d.* 1756). *See under* Dicey family (*per. c.*1710-*c.*1800).

Díchu mac Trichim (*fl.* 5th cent.). *See under* Ulster, saints of (*act. c.*400-*c.*650).

Dick [*formerly* Cunyngham], **Sir Alexander, third baronet** (1703-1785), physician, born on 22 October 1703, was the third son of Sir William Cunyngham of Caprington, first baronet (*d.* 1740), and Janet (*d.* 1753), only child and heir of Sir James Dick, first baronet (1643-1728), of Prestonfield, near Edinburgh. The family name was changed to Dick because of the mother's inheritance. Not sharing in the large fortune inherited by his elder brother William, Alexander Cunyngham decided to qualify for a profession. He began the study of medicine at the University of Edinburgh, and afterwards went to Leiden University, where he became a pupil of Boerhaave, and graduated MD on 31 August 1725. His inaugural dissertation, 'De epilepsia',

was published the same year. A similar degree was conferred on him two years later by the University of St Andrews. In 1727 he began practising as a physician in Edinburgh, and on 7 November of the same year he became a fellow of the Royal College of Physicians of Edinburgh. Ten years later he travelled on the continent with his friend Allan Ramsay (1713-1784), the painter, son of the well-known Scottish poet, Allan Ramsay (1686-1758). During his travels Cunyngham added to his scientific and cultural acquirements, keeping an extensive journal of his travels, extracts of which appeared in the *Gentleman's Magazine* for 1853. On his return home he settled in Pembrokeshire, where he earned a reputation as a successful practitioner. Meanwhile he maintained a constant correspondence with Allan Ramsay the elder and other friends in Scotland. Cunyngham married first in 1736 his cousin, Janet, daughter of Alexander Dick, merchant in Edinburgh: with her he had three daughters. He married second in 1762 Mary, daughter of David Butler of Pembrokeshire, with whom he had three sons and three daughters.

In 1746, on the death of his brother William, husband of the eccentric Anne, Lady Dick (*d.* 1741), Cunyngham succeeded to the baronetcy as Sir Alexander Dick, and moved to the family mansion of Prestonfield, at the foot of Arthur's Seat, near Edinburgh. While no longer needing to work as a physician, he still practised for scientific purposes, and in 1756 was elected president of the Royal College of Physicians of Edinburgh, an office which he held for seven successive years. He voluntarily resigned in 1763 on the ground 'that it was due to the merits of other gentlemen that there should be some rotation'. Dick continued to devote time to the service of the college; he contributed substantially to the building of the new hall in George Street, and helped to establish the library. His portrait was later placed in the college library as a mark of respect.

Dick helped to obtain a charter for the Royal Society of Edinburgh and was elected a fellow on 3 November 1783. He also promoted the establishment of a medical school in the Royal Infirmary. When James Mounsey of St Petersburg first brought the seeds of the true rhubarb into Britain, Dick, who probably knew the properties of the plant from his old teacher's nephew, A. K. Boerhaave, gave great care to its cultivation and pharmaceutical preparation. The Society of Arts presented him in 1774 with a gold medal 'for the best specimen of rhubarb'. Dick corresponded with Dr Johnson and James Boswell, who paid a visit to Prestonfield during their celebrated journey to Scotland. Boswell apparently wished to marry Dick's daughter. Dick died at the age of eighty-two, on 10 November 1785. ROBERT HARRISON, *rev.* PATRICK WALLIS

Sources Irving, *Scots.* • W. S. Craig, *History of the Royal College of Physicians of Edinburgh* (1976) • Mrs A. Forbes, ed., *Curiosities of a Scots charta chest, 1600-1800* (1897) • Burke, *Peerage* • *GM*, 2nd ser., 39 (1853), 22 • *GM*, 1st ser., 55 (1785), 921 • Chambers, *Scots.* (1855)
Archives NA Scot., corresp. and papers • NL Scot. • Royal College of Physicians of Edinburgh, corresp. | BL, letters to Sir Robert Keith, Add. MSS 35509-35534 • NL Scot., notes taken while attending Boerhaave's lectures • U. Edin. L., letters to James Cumming • Yale U., Beinecke L., corresp. with James Boswell and others

Likenesses J. Brown, pencil drawing, Scot. NPG; on loan from National Museums of Scotland · portrait, Royal College of Physicians of Edinburgh

Dick [*née* Mackenzie], **Anne**, **Lady Dick** (*d*. 1741), eccentric, was the daughter of a Scottish law lord, Sir James Mackenzie, Lord Royston (1671–1744), third son of George *Mackenzie, first earl of Cromarty, and his wife, Elizabeth. Neither the date of Anne's birth nor the date of her marriage to William Cunyngham (*d*. 1746) are known. Cunyngham, who adopted the name of Dick, became Sir William Dick of Prestonfield, bt, on the death of his maternal grandfather in 1728. The marriage did not produce any children. Lady Dick's eccentric behaviour, which included walking through the streets of Edinburgh with her maid, both dressed in boys' clothing, made her notorious in the eyes of her contemporaries. She was also known as a writer of coarse lampoons and epigrams in verse, three specimens of which are reprinted in C. Kirkpatrick Sharpe's *Book of Ballads* (1823). Her verses seem to have earned the disapproval of her friends, who wished her talents could be put to more seemly use. Lady Dick died in 1741. Her husband, who survived her until 1746, was succeeded in his baronetcy by his brother, the physician Sir Alexander Dick.

JENNETT HUMPHREYS, *rev.* DAVID TURNER

Sources Anderson, *Scot. nat.* · *Scots peerage* · J. Todd, ed., *A dictionary of British and American women writers, 1660–1800* (1984)

Dick, George Williamson Auchinvole (1914–1997), pathologist and virologist, was born on 14 August 1914 in Glasgow, the second of three sons of the Revd David Auchinvole Dick (1881–1964) and his wife, Blanche Hay, *née* Spence (*d*. 1945). His younger brother, Sir John Alexander Dick (1920–1994), was sheriff principal of Glasgow and Strathkelvin. Educated at the Royal High School, Edinburgh, and at the University of Edinburgh, he graduated MB ChB in 1938 and followed this with BSc (hons. path.) in 1939, being awarded the Buchanan medal.

Initial ideas of a career in obstetrics were changed by the outbreak of the Second World War and service as a Royal Army Medical Corps pathologist in east Africa command. The challenge of infectious diseases and their control appealed to Dick, and at the end of the war he transferred to the colonial medical research service and was seconded to the Rockefeller Foundation Yellow Fever Research Laboratory at Entebbe, Uganda. In 1941 he married Brenda Marian Cook (*b*. 1916), who joined him at Entebbe, where their first child was born. He spent five productive years there with pioneer American virologists R. M. Taylor, K. C. Smithburn, and others as colleagues. These were exciting times and many new viruses were isolated, mostly by the inoculation of mice. Uganda S and Zika viruses were mosquito borne viruses related to yellow fever virus that caused mild disease in man. Another, Mengo encephalomyelitis virus, proved to be a mouse virus related to poliomyelitis virus which demonstrated its human pathogenicity by infecting Dick, although fortunately the encephalitis was mild and transient.

After his Entebbe period the award of a Rockefeller Foundation Fellowship enabled Dick to visit the Rockefeller Institute, New York, and the Johns Hopkins University, Baltimore, where he enrolled at the School of Hygiene and Public Health and graduated master of public health in 1949. He also received a gold medal for his MD at the University of Edinburgh in the same year. From 1951 to 1954 he joined the division of bacteriology and virology at the National Institute for Medical Research, in Mill Hill, where he published several papers on mouse hepatitis viruses with C. H. Andrewes, J. S. F. Niven, A. W. Gledhill, and F. B. Bang. Colleagues who had the good fortune to be initiated into the mysteries of tropical virology by George Dick during this period were struck by the breadth of his knowledge and his enthusiasm for research.

Dick was now ready to head a department of his own and this he did by becoming professor of microbiology at Queen's University, Belfast, where he remained from 1955 to 1965. His research fields there included poliomyelitis, measles and its variant form, subacute sclerosing panencephalitis, whooping cough, and multiple sclerosis. When live attenuated virus vaccine was first introduced for poliomyelitis it was feared that virus reversion to virulence might occur with consequent spread of the disease. Dick, appreciating the advantages of live attenuated vaccines from his knowledge of poliomyelitis and yellow fever, realized that the risk was very small and had no hesitation in giving live polio vaccine to his four-year-old daughter, causing excited press comment at the time. In Africa he had seen smallpox outbreaks and recognized the need for Jennerian vaccination there but at the annual general meeting of the British Medical Association in 1962 he called for the abandonment of infant vaccination against smallpox in the UK on the grounds that there it caused more sickness and deaths than smallpox itself. The Ministry of Health later accepted this view, the point becoming purely academic following the eradication of smallpox virus.

In 1966 Dick transferred to the Middlesex Hospital, becoming Bland-Sutton professor of pathology in the University of London, and director of the Bland-Sutton Institute, a challenging task with a considerable administrative burden, carried with his customary energy. His research interests at this period included Creutzfeld-Jakob disease and Marburg virus infections, and he was called upon to act as an expert witness in court cases. In 1973 he became assistant director of the British Postgraduate Medical Federation and postgraduate dean, South-West Thames Regional Health Authority. His duties were to see that training kept pace with the new advances in current medical science.

Dick also found time in a busy life to publish *Immunisation* (1978), later reissued as *Practical Immunisation* (1986), *Immunology of Infectious Diseases* (1979), and *Health on Holiday and other Travels* (1982). From 1973 to 1981 he was also emeritus professor of pathology, honorary lecturer, and honorary consultant at the Institute of Child Health, Great Ormond Street. He also served as an examiner at medical schools in the UK, Dublin, Nairobi, Kampala, Riyadh, and Jiddah. These academic appointments did not prevent him from becoming involved with other organizations such as Amnesty International, whose aims and objectives he shared. He was president of the Institute of Medical and Laboratory Technicians, 1966–76, member of Mid-Downs Health Authority, Sussex, 1981–4, and his work on behalf of libraries was recognized by his being made an honorary fellow of the Library Association. Perhaps the recognition that gave him greatest pleasure was to be named outstanding alumnus in public health by Johns Hopkins University in 1986 and hero of public health by Johns Hopkins University School of Hygiene and Public Health in 1992.

Genial and outgoing in nature, Dick was always very good company. He was a founder fellow of the Royal College of Pathologists, a member of council from 1970 to 1973 and its treasurer from 1973 to 1978. As one of the duties of the treasurer was to buy the wine, he attended and passed the examination in a wine appreciation course, with consequent benefit to the college cellar. A son of the manse and of independent spirit, he set up the Rowhook Medical Society which met at his home in Sussex, where matters of moment in medicine and the control of infectious diseases were debated. His personal contributions to this field were considerable, and not fully appreciated during his lifetime. He died from cancer of the prostate at Midhurst, Sussex, on 3 July 1997, and was cremated. He was survived by his wife, Brenda, four children, Bruce, Alison, Caroline, and John-Mark, and nine grandchildren. JAMES S. PORTERFIELD

Sources WWW · *The Times* (1 Aug 1997) · *Daily Telegraph* (24 July 1997) · *The Scotsman* (15 July 1997) · *The Guardian* (8 Aug 1997) · *The Independent* (18 July 1997) · *BMJ* (8 Nov 1997), 1238 · private information (2004) [Mrs Brenda Dick; Librarian, Welch Medical Library, Johns Hopkins School of Hygiene and Public Health, Baltimore, Maryland, USA]
Likenesses photograph, repro. in *The Times* · photograph, repro. in *The Guardian* · photograph, repro. in *The Independent* · photograph, repro. in *Daily Telegraph* · photograph, repro. in *Johns Hopkins University School of Hygiene and Public Health Magazine* (autumn 1991) [special edn, *Heroes of public health*]
Wealth at death under £180,000: probate, 16 Dec 1997, *CGPLA Eng. & Wales*

Dick, James (*bap.* 1743, *d.* 1828), merchant and benefactor, was baptized on 6 February 1743 at Forres, Moray, the son of Alexander Dick (*d.* 1783), shoemaker and town councillor, and his wife, Elizabeth. The house they occupied in Forres High Street still bears their initials on the lintel. As a boy Dick herded cattle in the summer and in the winter attended Rafford grammar school, some 3 miles from Forres, where according to his later testimony he received an excellent education. He was then apprenticed to his father as bookkeeper but, meeting parental objection to his proposed marriage with Jane Anderson, a household servant, at the age of nineteen he left home and sailed for the West Indies. He became clerk in a merchant house in Kingston, Jamaica, entering into partnership with one Milligan to establish a London business for the sale of colonial produce, with his brother John Dick as manager. He traded for twenty years in Jamaica, then transferred his share of the business to his brother and returned a wealthy man, settling in London, where by speculation and investment he added to his holdings. On 8 October 1783 he was admitted a freeman burgess of Forres. When John Dick retired he sold the business and returned to Scotland, but on the return journey he fell ill in Edinburgh, and all his fortune passed to James.

Nothing is known about Dick's wife; they appear to have had one son, who died of consumption aged about twenty, and an elder daughter who married Captain August Keppel Colley of the Royal Marines. Dick lived in a plain, modern house in Finsbury Square, London, with few servants. In old age his hair was silvery white and worked into a queue. He was about 5 feet 7 inches tall, with broad, square shoulders and a pock-marked face with broad, flat nose and high cheekbones. He dressed in a black coat and breeches, white stockings, and neckcloth. Out of doors he wore a cocked hat and carried a gold-headed cane. He died at his home on 24 May 1828 and was buried in Bunhill Fields.

It is not known what charitable donations Dick made before he drew up his will, besides a sum of £500 invested to yield a return for the poor of Forres. When he came to consider how to dispose of his estate, having provided a legacy of £36,000 for his daughter, Dick was left with well over £113,000, and decided to use it 'to elevate the literary character of the parochial schoolmasters and schools' in Aberdeenshire, Banffshire, and Moray, 'it being my wish to form a fund for the benefit of that neglected though useful class of men [the country schoolmasters], and to add to their present trifling salaries' (will, quoted in Douglas, *Annals*, 18). The masters were mostly arts graduates, teaching while they waited for ecclesiastical preferment; Dick hoped to encourage the better among them to make it their career. The endowment was set up as the Dick Bequest, and the money invested in Scottish land securities, yielding £3300 to £5500 per annum, had grown to nearly £200,000 by 1833 when the first grants were made. The trustees were drawn from the Society of Writers to the Signet. Those applying for grants were required to pass examinations in the classics, humanities, mathematics, and science; those who succeeded virtually doubled their salaries. Allan Menzies, writer to the signet, clerk to the bequest, frequently superintended the examinations; he advised teachers and reported back. Through his untiring efforts the bequest became a real force for improvement in these north-eastern counties, until the 1872 Education Act changed its nature by diverting the grants to school boards. According to the third report of the royal commissioners on endowed schools and hospitals (1875), there was not 'any fund [that] has done so much good ... no fund that has produced a shilling's worth for a shilling so fully as the Dick Bequest' ('Royal commission', appx 1, 123). In November 1928, on the centenary of his death, a group of acting and retired Dick Bequest teachers contributed to the erection of a memorial to Dick in his native town of Forres. ANITA MCCONNELL

Sources M. Cruickshank, 'The Dick Bequest: the effect of a famous nineteenth-century endowment on parish schools of north east Scotland', *History of Education Quarterly*, 5/3 (1965), 153–65 · R. D.

Anderson, *Education and opportunity in Victorian Scotland: schools and universities* (1983) • O. Checkland, *Philanthropy in Victorian Scotland* (1980) • R. Douglas, 'James Dick and the Dick Bequest', *Aberdeen University Review*, 13 (1925-6), 97-109 • 'Royal commission to inquire into endowed schools and hospitals: third report', *Parl. papers* (1875), 29.1, C. 1123; 29.257, C. 1123-I; 29.695, C. 1123-II [Scotland] • [F. J. Grant], *A history of the Society of Writers to Her Majesty's Signet* (1890) • R. Douglas, 'James Dick', *Annals of the royal burgh of Forres* (1934), 185-90 • letter, signed 'G', *Elgin Courier and Province of Moray Advertiser* (25 July 1828) [no pagination]

Likenesses oils, Forres town council; repro. in Douglas, 'James Dick and the Dick Bequest'

Wealth at death £150,000-£200,000: Douglas, 'James Dick', 186

Dick, John (1764-1833), United Secession minister and theological writer, was born on 10 October 1764 in Aberdeen, the son of the Revd Alexander Dick, minister of the associate congregation of the Seceder church there, and his wife, Helen Tolmie, who was regarded as a woman of intellect and piety, and the daughter of a Captain Tolmie of Aberdeen. He was educated at Aberdeen grammar school and King's College, Aberdeen. He was accepted as a student for the ministry by the Secession church, studied under the famed John Brown of Haddington, and in 1785 was licensed as a probationer. In the same year he accepted a call from the congregation of Slateford, near Edinburgh, and was ordained there. On 8 August 1789, at Colinton, Edinburghshire, he married Jane or Jeanie, daughter of the Revd G. Coventry, of Stichill, Roxburghshire, and sister of Andrew *Coventry, professor of agriculture in the University of Edinburgh.

After a successful ministry in Slateford, in 1801 Dick accepted a call to the congregation of Shuttle Street, Glasgow (known as Greyfriars from 1821), and he remained minister there until his death. This congregation was one of the oldest and wealthiest of the Secession congregations. Dick's sermons were regarded as models of clarity, conciseness, and simplicity of style. In 1815, he was awarded the degree of DD by Princeton College, USA. In 1820 he was appointed professor of theology to the Associate Synod of the newly formed United Secession church. At first only students belonging to his own synod attended, but his ability and tact soon ensured that those from the other Secession synod (the General Associate Synod) attended also.

In 1788 Dick played a prominent part in the attack mounted by several leading figures in the Secession church on the doctrines of the Revd William McGill of Ayr, who was regarded by many as having espoused Socinian views. When the established church failed effectively to prosecute McGill for heresy, Dick published a sermon entitled *The Conduct and Doom of False Teachers* (1788) and almost certainly was involved in several other contributions to the attack. During the 1790s he joined the debate in the Secession church over adherence to the Westminster confession of faith, especially regarding its doctrine on the relationship of church and state. His sermon, preached at the opening of synod in October 1796, was published as *Confessions of faith shown to be necessary, and the duty of churches with respect to them explained* (1796), and led to a heated pamphlet war with some of those who were of

the 'old light' party in the church and who were opposed to Dick's position. In his sermon, which was argued in a calm and candid spirit, Dick vindicated the use of confessions but supported frequent revision of them and tolerance of minor disagreements. He was also a strong supporter of the foreign missionary movement, then in its infancy.

Dick's reputation as a theological writer was established in his *Essay on the Inspiration of the Holy Scriptures of the Old and New Testaments* (Edinburgh, 1800). This work, which derived from the dispute in the Secession church over continuing adherence to the Scottish covenants, advocated the doctrine of plenary inspiration; that is, that all parts of scripture, including both words and ideas, were written under the movement, direction, and assistance of the Holy Spirit. Dick accepted, however, varying kinds or degrees of inspiration depending on the subject matter or previous states of minds of the authors. His strong commitment to the principles of plenary inspiration explains his being chosen president of the Glasgow auxiliary of the British and Foreign Bible Society at the height of the Apocrypha controversy, which arose largely over Scottish opposition to the society's preparedness to publish bibles containing the Apocrypha for distribution on the continent.

Dick's most influential work, published posthumously by his son, Andrew Coventry Dick, was his four-volume *Lectures on Theology* (1834). This work was reprinted frequently and was also widely used in the Presbyterian churches in the USA. The work commences with fifteen lectures dealing with subjects such as Christian evidences and the doctrine of scripture, before moving on to cover the attributes of God, the Trinity, the divine decrees of creation, providence, and the fall of man and their execution, the covenant of grace, the mediator, the application of redemption, eschatology, and ecclesiology. The section on the mediator is particularly extensive, though it follows the traditional divisions of prophet, priest, and king. The subject of the means of grace receives extended attention, and the ten commandments are considered in the concluding lectures. While Dick held a high position on the doctrine of inspiration, and while as a result his confidence in revelation was absolute and allowed no trust in reason as a guide in religion, outside the area of revelation he was fearless in applying the test of reason to argue for what he termed 'natural theology'. By this he meant 'the knowledge of God which the light of nature teaches, or which is acquired by our unassisted powers, by the exercise of reason, and the suggestions of conscience'. He was careful to limit this, however, to inferring the existence of an invisible creator, and not to innate ideas of God. The leading Reformed theologians in America were well aware of this work and Archibald Alexander, president of Princeton College, rated it as the best systematic theology available in English.

Dick continued actively in the ministry until his death, which occurred suddenly in Glasgow on 25 January 1833.

JOHN R. MCINTOSH

Sources A. C. Dick, 'Memoir', in J. Dick, *Lectures on theology*, 3 (1834), ix–xl · *United Secession Magazine*, 1 (1833), 257–72 · J. M'Kerrow, *History of the Secession church*, rev. edn (1841) · *DSCHT*, 810 · *DNB*

Dick, Quintin (1777–1858), politician and socialite, was born in March 1777 in Dublin, the eldest of four children of Samuel Dick (*d.* 1802), East India proprietor and merchant, and his wife, Charlotte, daughter of Nicholas Forster of Tullaghan, co. Monaghan, Ireland. Educated at Trinity College, Dublin, graduating BA in 1797, he became a barrister of King's Inns, Dublin, in 1800. He began his long parliamentary career as nominee of a relative, sitting in 1800 for Dunleer in the Irish parliament. He opposed the Act of Union. After inheriting his father's wealth in 1802, however, he entered the British parliament by purchase at West Looe, Cornwall, a seat he held from 1803 to 1806.

Dick became celebrated more for his political dinners than his parliamentary activities. He rarely spoke in the Commons, and gained his seats through money and influence, but, although a tory, he liked to maintain his independence. In 1807 he purchased Cashel through the administration, but, when unwilling to vote as they wished in 1809, he resigned. Under current patronage conventions, he was acting honourably, and was surprised when radicals pressed for an inquiry into governmental abuse of power.

There were further charges that he was merely a wealthy cat's-paw for the tories when he unsuccessfully contested Maldon as an anti-Catholic in 1826, and Lord Hertford's interest, Disraeli implied, helped him to win Orford (which he held from 1826 until 1830). He sat for Maldon (1830–47), and in the 1840s was a peripheral (if elderly) Young Englander, figuring as the hospitable millionaire Ormsby in Disraeli's *Coningsby* (1844). His protectionist record (in 1845–6) and money helped him to win Aylesbury (for which he sat 1848–52), but he finally retired after two defeats at Maldon (1852, 1854).

Dick was dandified and stiff, old-fashioned in dress as in politics. He gave opulent Mayfair dinners, so lavishly illuminated that one guest called him 'Jolly Dick, the lamplighter', a nickname, Disraeli sardonically commented, completely unsuited to his habitual expression (Disraeli, 2. 682). Despite his wealth, 'carrotty Quintin' was unpopular and slightly ridiculous (*Harriette Wilson's Memoirs*, 1929, 238). He never married. He died at his house at 20 Curzon Street, Mayfair, London, on 26 March 1858, leaving an estimated £2 million to £3 million in land, stocks, and cash.

MARY S. MILLAR

Sources Boase, *Mod. Eng. biog.* · HoP, *Commons* · *Benjamin Disraeli letters*, ed. J. A. W. Gunn and others (1982–), vols. 2–5 · Bodl. Oxf., Dep. Hughenden B/XXI/D/259–60; B/XXI/H/761; D/III/C/590–96 · *Morning Post* (31 March 1858) · *GM*, 3rd ser., 4 (1858)
Wealth at death approx. £2,000,000–£3,000,000: obituaries *Morning Post*; *Annual Register* (1858) · £813,949—six assets, excl. India stocks: Bodl. Oxf., Dep. Hughenden B/XXI/D/260 · under £300,000—in England: probate, 21 July 1858, *CGPLA Eng. & Wales* · under £600,000: probate, 12 June 1858, *CGPLA Ire.*

Dick, Robert (1722–1782). *See under* Poker Club (*act.* 1762–1784).

Dick, Robert (1810/11–1866), geologist and botanist, was born, probably in January 1811, at Tullibody in Clackmannanshire, the second of four children of Thomas Dick, customs and excise officer at the Cambus Brewery, Tullibody; nothing is known about his mother. When Robert was ten his father married a Miss Knox, and the family moved to Dams Burn. He had begun his schooling at the Barony School, Tullibody, and after the move attended Menstrie parish school. Dick appears to have suffered under a jealous stepmother. He later wrote of these years: 'All my naturally buoyant, youthful spirits were broken. To this day I feel the effects. I cannot shake them off. It is this that still makes me shrink from the world' (Williamson, 6). It was largely through his stepmother's influence that plans for Dick to attend college were abandoned and, at the age of thirteen, he was apprenticed to a Mr Aikman, baker, of Tullibody. In some ways he was glad—it was an escape from his stepmother's cruelty.

Although his working day was long, Dick remained interested in study and read widely, with a particular interest in botany. He spared no expense in obtaining the finest examples of natural science volumes he could obtain. When his library was sold after his death, it consisted of a remarkable 389 volumes, and was sold for £32 12s. Dick completed his apprenticeship in 1828, and worked for three years as a journeyman baker in Leith, Glasgow, and Greenock. He then went to Thurso in Caithness, where his father was customs supervisor, and opened a baker's business in Wilson's Lane. He continued to study and his interests widened to include geology and natural history in general. He began to create collections of rocks, insects, and plants; through collection and exchange he ultimately accumulated a near perfect British flora. He is credited with rediscovering, around 1834, the *Hierochloe borealis*, or northern holy grass, a plant which had been dropped from British flora. He later contributed an account of this to the Botanical Society of Edinburgh (*Ann. Nat. Hist.*, October 1854).

After Hugh Miller (1802–1856) published *Old Red Sandstone* in 1841, Dick wrote to him and there followed a regular correspondence between the two. Dick was able to supply Miller with unique information and fine specimens of fossilized fish. Dick's information ultimately led Miller considerably to modify his *Old Red Sandstone*. He reportedly wrote of Dick, 'He has robbed himself to do me service' (*DNB*). Although Dick himself was never published, this did not prevent him from becoming a recognized authority on the geology and natural history of Caithness. He ably and freely assisted Sir Roderick Murchison and a number of other scientists in their research. In September 1853 he met Charles Peach (1800–1886) and a friendship immediately developed. They would often go for walks together, and in time Peach came to know Dick better than any other; he wrote of his friend that he had a 'cheerful manner', a 'sparkling wit', and a 'frolicsome playfulness' (Williamson, 26).

Dick's life was one of poverty, illness, pain, and extreme fatigue. He would often walk more than 50 miles between one baking and the next, eating nothing but a few pieces of biscuit. Competition and a loss of flour by shipwreck in Aberdeen harbour in March 1863 practically ruined him, and his last years were passed in great privation. He never married but for many years he employed one Annie Mackay, who served him faithfully until he died. She looked after him and his business, especially when he was away collecting flora and fauna. Although he was often solitary, his contemporary biographer wrote of him, that 'To those who knew him best he was cheerful and social. He had a vein of innocent fun and satire about him, and he often turned his thoughts into rhyme' (Smiles). His lifelong passion was the pursuit of knowledge of nature. Even when later in life he was crippled with rheumatism, he would spend hours hunting for fossils. 'I have nearly killed myself several times with over-exertion', he wrote (DNB).

Dick died on 24 December 1866 at his home in Wilson's Lane, Thurso. His great public funeral was testimony to the growing public recognition of his achievements. It was, however, testimony too to the fact that those in Thurso, where he was buried, had never really been aware of the giant in their midst. Robert Dick had always been misunderstood by the community in which he lived. His manner of dress—old and outdated—his introverted nature, and his all-absorbing interest in nature, all contributed to his being seen as a figure of fun. But even though Dick was aware of this he never attempted to set the record straight, for, as he wrote, 'It is surely a strange time we live in when a poor devil cannot gather weeds without being made a nine days' wonder of some and a butt of derision of others' (Williamson, 12).

MICHAEL D. MCMULLEN

Sources J. A. Williamson, *The life of Robert Dick* (1967) · DNB · DSCHT · H. Miller, *My schools and schoolmasters* (1854) · S. Smiles, *Life of Robert Dick* (1878)
Archives Thurso Museum, specimen collection · U. Edin., letters to Charles Peach
Likenesses Rajon, etching, 1878, repro. in Smiles, *Life of Robert Dick*, frontispiece · etching, repro. in Williamson, *Life of Robert Dick*, frontispiece
Wealth at death sale of library settled outstanding debts: Williamson, *Life*

Dick, Sir Robert Henry (*bap.* 1786, *d.* 1846), army officer, was baptized on 6 August 1786 at Calcutta, the son of William Dick, assistant surgeon, and his wife, Charlotte McLaren. According to the *Gentleman's Magazine* (May 1846), when Henry Dundas and Edmund Burke were staying with the duke of Atholl at Dunkeld, while out walking they happened to meet a farmer's daughter, who gave them refreshment. She asked Dundas to help her fiancé, the young Dr Dick, who was too poor to marry. Dundas gave him an East India Company assistant surgeoncy. Dick went to India, married, made a large fortune, and then retired and purchased the estate of Tullimet. Robert Dick, his son, entered the army as an ensign in the 75th regiment on 22 November 1800, and was promoted lieutenant into the 62nd on 27 June 1802 and captain into the 78th (Ross-shire buffs) on 17 April 1804. He accompanied the 2nd battalion to Sicily in 1806, and was wounded at the battle of Maida in the same year. In 1807 his battalion formed part of General Mackenzie Fraser's expedition to

Egypt, and Dick was wounded again at Rosetta. He was appointed major on 24 April 1808, and exchanged into the 42nd highlanders (the Black Watch) on 14 July in that year.

In June 1809 Dick landed in Portugal with the 2nd battalion of his regiment. He was then selected to form a light battalion of detachments from several regiments, which he led successfully in many battles and engagements, including Busaco and Fuentes de Oñoro. After returning to his regiments he was present at Ciudad Rodrigo as senior major in the 2nd battalion, and commanded the 1st battalion at Salamanca and Burgos. For his services he was promoted brevet lieutenant-colonel on 8 October 1812. He then returned to the 2nd battalion as the senior major and remained with it until the end of the Peninsular War, when he was made CB.

The 2nd battalion was disbanded in 1814 and Dick accompanied the 1st battalion of the Black Watch to Flanders in 1815. He was present with it as senior major at Quatre Bras, where his commanding officer was killed and Dick was severely wounded in the hip and left shoulder. He nevertheless brought them out of action and was present next day at the battle of Waterloo.

Dick's commission as lieutenant-colonel of the 42nd was antedated to the day of that great battle, as a reward for his valour. He was promoted colonel on 27 May 1825, and soon after went on half pay and retired to his seat at Tullimet, which he had inherited on his father's death. In 1832 he was made a KCH, on 10 January 1837 was promoted major-general, and in 1838 made a KCB. His wife, Elizabeth Anne Macnabb, died about 1830 leaving a son. Dick applied for re-employment after her death. In December 1838 he was appointed to command the centre division of the Madras army, and as senior general in the presidency he assumed its command-in-chief on the sudden death of Sir S. F. Whittingham in January 1841. This temporary post Dick held until September 1842, when the marquess of Tweeddale was sent as governor and commander-in-chief to Madras. As it was thought undesirable to send Dick back to a divisional command, he was transferred to the Bengal army. He took command of the division on the north-west frontier, but disagreement over an expected mutiny led to his removal by Lord Ellenborough, the governor-general, to the presidency division. He at once sent his resignation to the Horse Guards, but the authorities refused it. His old comrade, Sir Henry Hardinge, went out as governor-general, and the commander-in-chief, Sir Hugh Gough, also a Peninsula veteran, gave him command of the Cawnpore division.

Dick was summoned by Gough in January 1846 to command the 3rd infantry division of the army in the field against the Sikhs, replacing Major-General Sir John M'Caskill, who had been killed at Mudki. Dick had missed the first two important battles of the First Anglo-Sikh War, but he played a leading part in the third and decisive victory of Sobraon. On the morning of 10 February 1846 Gough determined to attack the strong entrenchments of the Khalsa army, and Dick's division was ordered to head the assault. At 4 a.m. his men advanced to a ravine about

1000 yards from the Sikh entrenchments, and lay down while the British artillery bombarded the enemy. At 9 a.m. Dick led his 1st brigade into the Sikh entrenchments. When it had effected a lodgement he returned to lead his 2nd brigade. While leading it from battery to battery, taking them in flank, Dick was struck down by one of the last shots fired that day, and died at 6 p.m. His funeral the next day at Ferozepore was attended by the whole army, and Gough praised Dick highly in his Sobraon dispatch.

H. M. STEPHENS, *rev.* JAMES LUNT

Sources *GM*, 2nd ser., 25 (1846), 539–40 · *Colburn's United Service Magazine*, 2 (1846), 298–300 · *LondG* (1846) · H. C. B. Cook, *The Sikh wars: the British army in the Punjab, 1845–1849* (1975) · Fortescue, *Brit. army*, vols. 7–10, 12 · B. Fergusson, *The black watch and the king's enemies* (1950) · J. Paget, *Wellington's Peninsular War* (1990) · BL OIOC, OIOR, N/1/4, fol. 28
Archives Black Watch Regimental Museum, Balhousie Castle, Perth, corresp. and papers
Likenesses W. Salter, group portrait, oils (*Waterloo banquet at Apsley House*), Wellington Museum, London · W. Salter, oils study (for *Waterloo banquet at Apsley House*), NPG

Dick, Thomas (1774–1857), writer on science and philosopher, was born on 24 November 1774 in the Hilltown of Dundee, the youngest of three children of Mungo Dick and Margaret Stroak. His father was a handloom weaver of moderate means who served as treasurer for the Bell Street church, meeting-house of Anti-Burgher Seceders. His mother taught him to read the Bible before he entered school. By his own account he was a serious minded boy, given to imaginative, and at times disturbing, musings about the heavens and God.

Inspired in 1783 by a spectacularly bright meteor, Dick embarked on a lifelong exploration of the heavens. He begged old spectacle lenses from neighbours, built a lens grinding machine and his own telescopes and microscopes, and resisted his parents' attempts to put him to the loom. Childhood attacks of smallpox and measles, together with his natural temperament, rendered him unfit for physical labour. In 1794 he entered the University of Edinburgh, supporting himself by private tutoring and by taking various teaching positions. He did not take the MA degree since it involved extra fees.

In pursuit of his vocation Dick entered the Theological Hall of the General Associate Synod of the Secession church in 1801. Licensed the same year, he officiated as a probationer before being called to the Viewfield Anti-Burgher congregation of Stirling. Here he was ordained on 30 November 1803. On 26 August 1804 he married Elisabeth Aedie, and soon thereafter became moderator of the Stirling presbytery. In December 1805, however, the presbytery found him guilty of adultery with Betty Ker, his servant. He was deposed and excommunicated. When both his wife's and his servant's babies died soon after birth, he viewed it as God's just punishment for his transgression.

Seeking to rehabilitate himself, Dick endeavoured to become a Christian philosopher in the tradition of Robert Boyle and others who had consecrated their pursuit of natural knowledge to the greater glory of God. He returned to teaching, becoming in 1807 a parish schoolmaster in Methven. During his ten years here, he formed a

Thomas Dick (1774–1857), by unknown artist

rudimentary mechanics' institute. To encourage others in this direction, he penned, in 1814–15, a series of articles for the London *Monthly Magazine* which advocated the establishment of mechanics' institutes for the middle and lower classes. In 1817 he left Methven for Perth and a post as schoolmaster at Stewart's Free Trades' School. Along with teaching he made astronomical observations in the daytime, invented a new telescope which he termed an aërial reflector, and published articles in literary, religious, and scientific periodicals.

The success of his *Christian Philosopher, or, The Connection of Science and Philosophy with Religion* (1823) completed Dick's self-rehabilitation. Defining science as the study of God's revelation in nature, he declared that it had to remain inseparably intertwined with Christianity and that its pursuit was an expression of sincere piety and devout worship of God. Selling his copyright for £120, he retired from teaching in 1827 and had a house built on Fort Hill in Broughty Ferry, which he equipped with a rooftop observatory. His next two works, *Philosophy of Religion* (1826) and *Philosophy of a Future State* (1828), focused on theology. On the basis of his first three works Union College awarded him a doctorate of laws in 1832. Later works included *On the Improvement of Society* (1833), *Mental Illumination and Moral Improvement of Mankind* (1835), *Celestial Scenery* (1837), *Sidereal Heavens* (1840), *Practical Astronomer* (1845), and three works on science and religion for the Religious Tract Society. Nearly all of these sold well, but Dick unwisely sold to his publishers, for comparatively small sums, the copyrights to all but one of his works. Three of his works were translated into Welsh, and one each into German and Chinese. They proved immensely popular in the United States, where collected editions sold in huge numbers into the 1880s.

Viewed collectively, Dick's works, filled with devotional utterances and scriptural citations, espoused a God-praising theology of nature. Citing Christ's two great commandments they promulgated an eirenic protestantism—tinged by evangelicalism—to counter sectarianism, inhibit secularization, and advance the millennium. More radically, they argued that those who properly pursued science acquired heightened conceptions of God and a deeper understanding of his word and works which made them privileged as interpreters of the Bible and as teachers of God's works in the hereafter. Those who possessed such expertise, Dick argued, deserved to be accorded the same respect and status as the most dignified clergymen. Fervidly espousing the plurality of worlds, Dick's works influenced David Livingstone and Edgar Allan Poe, among many others.

Throughout his life Dick pursued numerous philanthropic, educational, and scientific interests. He directed the Watt Institute, Dundee's Mechanics' Institute, in 1830–31, and from 1835 to 1836 edited the *Educational Magazine and Journal of Christian Philanthropy*. Capping his astronomical career was his election to the Royal Astronomical Society in 1853. A Christian pacifist, he wrote forceful articles denouncing slavery and war for American newspapers.

Dick's first wife died some time before 1830. On 25 July 1830 he married Euphemia Young (d. 1840), widow of Alexander Davidson (d. 1826) and on 5 September 1841 he married Elizabeth Glegg (d. 1874). His finances were severely strained partly as a result of his charitable activities, which included supporting a family of five orphans. In 1846 he applied for a government pension but was turned down. A surgical operation on his chest in 1849 left him weakened. Fortunately, the next year a local subscription fund provided him with £30 per year, and his American admirers collected a further £300 for him. Supported by the Royal Literary Fund from 1850 to 1853, he secured a civil-list pension for £50 per year in 1855. This was continued to his widow after his death at home on 29 July 1857. A 14 foot high obelisk in his memory was erected in 1860 at St Aidan's Church in Broughty Ferry, where he was buried.   WILLIAM J. ASTORE

Sources W. J. Astore, *Observing God: Thomas Dick, evangelicalism, and popular science in Victorian Britain and America* (2001) · J. V. Smith, 'Reason, revelation, and reform: Thomas Dick of Methven and the "Improvement of society by the diffusion of knowledge"', *History of Education*, 12 (1983), 255–70 · H. Macpherson, 'Thomas Dick: "The Christian philosopher"', *Records of the Scottish Church History Society*, 11 (1951–3), 41–62 · D. Gavine, 'Thomas Dick LLD, 1774–1857', *Journal of the British Astronomical Association*, 84 (1973–4), 345–50 · J. A. Brashear, 'A visit to the home of Dr. Thomas Dick: the Christian philosopher and astronomer', *Journal of the Royal Astronomical Society of Canada*, 7 (1913), 19–30 · 'Thomas Dick, LL.D.', *Littell's Living Age*, 61 (1859), 131–6 · J. V. Smith, 'Manners, morals, and mentalities: reflections on the popular enlightenment of early nineteenth century Scotland', *Scottish culture and Scottish education, 1800–1980*, ed. W. M. Humes and H. M. Paterson (1983), 25–54 · D. Gavine, 'Thomas Dick (1774–1857) and the plurality of worlds', *Journal of the Astronomical Society of Edinburgh*, 28 (1992), 4–10 · M. J. Crowe, *The extraterrestrial life debate, 1750–1900* (1986) · E. G. Hutcheson, 'Thomas Dick, LL.D., F.R.A.S., astronomer and reformer', *People's Friend* (29 July 1901), 532 · W. Norrie, *Dundee celebrities of the nineteenth century* (1873) · minutes of Stirling Associate presbytery, Stirling Central Regional Archives, 516–35

Archives Dundee Central Library, corresp. and papers; letters · NL Scot., corresp. · U. Glas., letters | Dundee Central Library, Lamb collection · RAS, Vallack collection

Likenesses H. Cook, stipple, 1838 (after portrait), NPG; repro. in R. Burgess, ed., *Portraits of doctors and scientists in the Wellcome Institute of the History of Medicine* (1973), 98, no. 807 · F. Croll, line engraving, 1850, NPG; repro. in *Portrait gallery of Hogg's Weekly Instructor* · portrait (Dick as an old man), repro. in Hutcheson, 'Thomas Dick', 532 · watercolour, Scot. NPG [*see illus.*]

Wealth at death approx. £270–£70 from a local subscription fund; astronomical instruments valued for at least £50; civil-list pension £50 p.a.; house valued at c.£100; left to his son his 3.5 foot achromatic telescope and brass stand, his equatorial instrument, his orrery, and one of his aerial reflectors; wife and daughter to have their choice of the remaining instruments: will, NA Scot., SC 45 (Dundee)

Dick, Sir William, of Braid (*d.* 1655), merchant and financier, was the only son of John Dick, proprietor in Orkney and an Edinburgh town councillor in 1592–3. Nothing is known of his early life. On 15 June 1603 he married Elizabeth, sister of the wealthy Edinburgh merchant Harry Morison; they had at least seven children: John (*b.* 1604x7), Margaret (*bap.* 1608), Elizabeth (*bap.* 1609), Andrew (later Sir Andrew Dick of Craighouse), Alexander, Lewis (*b.* 1619, *d.* before 1650), and William. By right of his father, on 28 March 1604 Dick became a burgess and guild brother. In 1609 he appeared in the records of Edinburgh council as witness to a case of kidnapping. Two years later he was elected for the first time to the town council, where he sat a further fifteen times, including four occasions as bailie, once as both treasurer and dean of guild, and twice as provost.

In the space of thirty years Dick rose from a 'junior player' (Brown, 21) in Edinburgh mercantile circles to a position of 'vast wealth', incomparable to that of the rest of the mercantile population of Scotland (Dingwall, 18). By 1637 Dick alone was responsible for 4 per cent of the burgh's tax burden. His extraordinary wealth was founded on a variety of entrepreneurial activities. These included an investment of 150,000 merks in coal and salt works, herring works at Dunbar worth 60,000 merks, and a soap manufactory valued at 30,000 merks. His business interests were so extensive that by the 1630s Dick operated through a number of factors based in London, Paris, and Dieppe. His son Lewis later seems to have acted for his father in Paris, Bordeaux, and Rouen.

Within Edinburgh, Dick became a proprietor of some significance, renting out five properties with a total annual income of £1122 13s. 4d. Scots in 1635—the highest rental in a town where the average was about £80. Dick's own house in Kintore's Close was certainly one of the most expensive rentals in a town, costing him £500 per annum. His business appears to have been conducted from a forebooth owned by Robert Glen, opposite the custom house at the top of the West Bow. Outside Edinburgh, Dick had interests in Caithness, Aberdeenshire, Moray,

Elginshire, North Berwick, Fife, and Orkney, either by directly holding land or through wadsetting. In 1631 he bought Braid in the sheriffdom of Edinburgh from David McCall and John Cant. It cost him £20,000, but by 1642 the estate was valued at £73,000.

As Dick's fortune increased he became involved in moneylending. When James VI and I visited Scotland in 1617 Dick advanced £15,000 sterling for the king's expenses. He lent James Hamilton, second marquess of Hamilton, funds to facilitate the smooth passage of the king's legislation in the parliament of 1621, and his son and namesake, the third marquess, money for an unsuccessful military campaign in Germany in 1631. In 1624 Dick and a number of other merchants were examined by the Scottish privy council for charging exorbitant rates of interest, but this seems to have been only a temporary setback: his financial services for merchants and landowners alike seem to have placed him at the pinnacle of an increasingly sophisticated system of credit.

Meanwhile Dick's political stature also grew. During the 1630s he sat on a number of committees affiliated to Edinburgh town council. All these positions relied not only on the personal wealth of the individual in office, but also on his business and accounting skills. In time Dick's political influence extended beyond Edinburgh, involving six appearances on the convention of royal burghs. Although in April 1621 he had refused to attend communion tables where recipients were kneeling, he was not among the capital's leading nonconformists, but in December 1637 he was one of three town councillors who met those opposing royal policy, assuring them of the council's support. When the national covenant was signed in February 1638 Dick replaced the royalist Sir John Hay as provost, and he remained in that office in the critical months through to 1640. He met the king's commissioner, the marquess of Hamilton, but refused to publish the king's proclamation which offered to pardon any 'rebels' who renounced the covenant, and according to Archibald Johnston of Wariston he was responsible for collecting voluntary contributions of money, gold, and silver from Edinburgh inhabitants. In March 1639 Dick lent 20,000 merks to the covenanters, with the political community as a whole acting as surety. In May, July, and August he sat on the commissions which co-ordinated Scotland's military action against Charles I and controlled the agenda for the parliament dissolved by John Stewart, earl of Traquair. He also expended £15,000 sterling on unspecified costs of the parliament, as he did again in 1641, when Charles attended in person. It was perhaps as part of the king's efforts to secure both favour and financial resources that Dick, like the current provost John Smith, was knighted, probably in December 1641.

If so, Charles was to be disappointed: through the 1640s Dick continued to devote time and money to the covenanter cause. In 1644 he became a member of the committee of estates instituted to continue the work of parliament during its dissolution and served on the committees for money and for army magazines. In July that year he

was, along with other Edinburgh town councillors, a commissioner for matters pertaining to the solemn league and covenant, signed in 1643 by the parliaments of Scotland and England. He also had local responsibilities as a commissioner for war in the sheriffdoms of Edinburgh, Haddington, and Linlithgow. The result, claimed Hugo Arnot in his *History of Edinburgh* (1779), was that having originally 'flattered his vanity' by making Dick provost, the covenanters 'drained him of large sums, till, in the end, he died a beggar' (121–2). His disbursements during 'the late troubles of Church and State' cannot be accurately calculated, but as certainly resulted in Dick's 'irrevocable ruine' (BL, Add. MS 23116, fols. 49–50). The collapse of the Scottish credit system in the 1640s meant that his loan to the covenanters could not be repaid, while his own debts to the town council amounted to 26,000 merks in 1643. By 1647 he was forced to ask that some of those debts be discharged on account of them being 'ane voluntar died for the good of this Cittie' (Wood, *Edinburgh Records*, 1642–55, 120). Although Dick was granted the tack for the collection of the wine excise (shared with Archibald Campbell, first marquess of Argyll) and part of the 'brotherly assistance' from the English parliament (never fully paid), parliament acknowledged in 1648 that some 'sure and solide course' for Dick's reimbursement had to be found, and in May 1649 he complained that he was still disappointed 'of publict payment in Scotland and England' (*APS*, vol. 6, pt 2, 45, 360).

The degree and effect of Dick's financial difficulties at this point is difficult to gauge. He sat on the committee of estates numerous times between 1649 and 1651 and managed to find £10,000 sterling in response to Charles II's arrival in Scotland in 1650. When Oliver Cromwell occupied Edinburgh in October 1652 Dick led the delegation to greet him. However, this is the last year in which he appears in Edinburgh records, and it seems that within a few months he had departed for England to plead his cause in London. His finances were investigated by a committee at Whitehall in 1653, but a mere £1000 sterling was paid out to him by parliament that September. He apparently continued petitioning until he died in December 1655 at his Westminster lodgings. Contrary to popular belief, he was buried in the plot in Greyfriars churchyard, Edinburgh, which he had purchased fifteen years earlier.

Dick's political prominence and the complexity of his financial dealings ensured that his affairs were not easily wound up. *The Lamentable Estate and Distressed Case of Sir William Dick* (1657) printed correspondence from the mid-1640s illustrating his contribution to the war effort as well as striking woodcuts of Dick as a notable public figure on whom many people of lesser rank relied. The preface suggests that it was circulated in London; the text indicates that sympathetic presbyterians, along with the Scottish community there, were the intended audience. The pamphlet states that Dick was owed over £64,000, but a petition made by his son in 1661 claimed that the crown alone owed him £160,850 sterling. His testament was registered three times, in March 1681, September 1686, and July 1691. Years after Dick's death his heirs were still struggling to gain repayment. In December 1669 his grandson was given immunity from processes against him on account of Dick's debts. In March 1707 William Dick, ensign, petitioned parliament to reclaim the £36,803 5s. 9d. still owed by the public purse. It was William's assertion that various 'noble and worthy persons' collectively owed his grandfather a further 900,000 merks (APS, 11, appx, 136–7), which were now irredeemable.

L. A. M. STEWART

Sources M. Wood, ed., Edinburgh Records, 1589–1603, 1603–26, 1626–41, 1642–55 · APS, vol. 5, 1633–41; vol. 6, pt 1, 1643–51; vol. 6, pt 2, 1648–50; vol. 7, 1661–9 · J. J. Brown, 'The economic, social and political influences on the Edinburgh merchant elite, 1600–38', PhD diss., U. Edin., 1984 · Lauderdale papers, BL, Add. MS 23116 · C. B. B. Watson, ed., Roll of Edinburgh burgesses and guild-brethren, 1406–1700, Scottish RS, 59 (1929) · CSP dom., 1638–40 · John, earl of Rothes, A relation of proceedings concerning the affairs of the Kirk of Scotland, Bannatyne Club, 37 (1830) · J. Gordon, History of Scots affairs from 1637–1641, ed. J. Robertson and G. Grub, 3 vols., Spalding Club, 1, 3, 5 (1841) · Diary of Sir Archibald Johnston of Wariston, 1, ed. G. M. Paul, Scottish History Society, 61 (1911) · 'Fragment of the diary of Sir Archibald Johnston, Lord Wariston, 1639', ed. G. M. Paul, Wariston's diary and other papers, Scottish History Society, 26 (1896), 1–98 · The letters and journals of Robert Baillie, ed. D. Laing, 2 vols. (1841–2) · Reg. PCS, 2nd ser., 1/13; 2/7; 2/8 · F. J. Grant, ed., The commissariot record of Edinburgh: register of testaments, 2, Scottish RS, old ser., 2 (1898) · register of testaments, NA Scot., CC 8/8/76, 78, 79 · H. Arnot, The history of Edinburgh (1779); repr. (1998) · D. Stevenson, 'Financing the cause of the covenants, 1638–51', SHR, 51 (1972), 89–123 · H. Dingwall, 'The importance of social factors in determining the composition of the town councils in Edinburgh', SHR, 65 (1986), 17–33 · J. Gifford, C. McWilliam, and D. Walker, The buildings of Scotland: Edinburgh, 3rd edn (1991), 202
Archives BL, corresp. and MSS, Add. MSS 22878–23138 · BL, corresp. and MSS, Add. MS 24863 · BL, corresp. and MSS, Add. MS 53589 · Bodl. Oxf., papers · NA Scot.
Likenesses G. Jamesone, portrait, repro. in A. Dick, Curiosities of a Scots charta chest, ed. M. A. Forbes (1897) · R. Vaughan, line engraving, BM; repro. in The lamentable estate and distressed case of Sir William Dick (1657)
Wealth at death see Lauderdale papers, BL, Add. MS 23116; NA Scot., register of testaments, CC 8/8/76, 78, 79

Dick, William (1793–1866), veterinary surgeon and founder of the Edinburgh Veterinary College, was born on 6 May 1793 at Whitehorse Close, Canongate, Edinburgh, the second of three children who survived beyond infancy of John Dick (c.1769–1844), and his wife, Jane (Jean) Anderson (c.1765–1837). His parents had moved to Edinburgh some six years before. At the time of the birth his father, a blacksmith and farrier, had his forge and residence at Whitehorse Close at the lower end of the Royal Mile, which runs from Edinburgh Castle to Holyrood Palace. William Dick himself said that he was born 'at the Court end of the Canongate'.

Dick attended two local private schools and afterwards worked with his father in the forge, where he learned about the treatment of diseases of animals that was provided in those days by the farriers. Dick soon formed an ambition to improve the standard of this treatment and to institute some formal training for those offering it. He was 'much inclined to get information on literary matters' and took every opportunity he could to hear lectures by a number of university professors. He attended lectures in

comparative anatomy by John Barclay (1758–1826), one of Scotland's leading anatomists, and Dick admitted after hearing Barclay that 'he had the impudence to think that it was possible that he himself might one day deliver a lecture on veterinary science' (The Veterinarian, 403). He contributed much to the discussions which Barclay held following his lectures and in these put to shame some of the young men attending the classes who were preparing to take their medical degrees. It is reported that Barclay, upon being asked who this young man was, admitted that he did not know; when told that he was a 'common working blacksmith' he replied 'Well, well, all I can say is that, whether he be blacksmith or whitesmith, he's the cleverest chap among you' (Pringle, iv).

There was then no veterinary education in Scotland but in the autumn of 1817 Dick enrolled at the London Veterinary College, founded in 1791. He took up residence in the capital at 27 Middlesex Street, Somer's Town, from where he kept up a correspondence with his father, describing in detail the cases which he saw in the course of his studies and discussing and criticizing the treatments used. He did not stay long in London because, as he said in later years:

finding that it was possible to derive as much knowledge in Edinburgh as would lay the foundation for the successful working out of the scheme which I intently cherished in my mind, I considered it was not necessary to remain longer in the English metropolis. After three months' study there, I had the confidence to apply for a diploma, the time of residence not being then defined, and I obtained it. (The Veterinarian, 403)

After his return to Edinburgh, Dick began to look at how to further his 'scheme' for veterinary education in Scotland. Helped by John Barclay, Dick became involved in providing lectures to the public on veterinary matters. He attracted disappointingly small numbers at first but persevered and made arrangements at his own expense to hold classes in the Calton convening rooms in Edinburgh. Barclay continued to help in the furtherance of Dick's ideas and, following discussions with the university senate, had pursued the suggestion that a veterinary college in Edinburgh might be brought about in conjunction with the Highland Society at Edinburgh (later the Royal Highland and Agricultural Society of Scotland) of which he was a director. As a result of this the society agreed that a lecturer to give instruction in veterinary surgery be appointed under its patronage and that Dick should be that lecturer. It was agreed also that the society would provide a sum of £50 to support this, and arrangements were made for Dick to use his father's forge (which was now situated in Clyde Street in Edinburgh) for practical instruction. For several years Dick continued to lecture in the Calton convening rooms, following the first lecture under the auspices of the Highland Society on 24 November 1823.

Dick built up the college in Clyde Street, and, although it was known as the Highland Society's veterinary school and the society provided a small annual sum in support of the establishment, the buildings and facilities were provided entirely at his own expense. For nearly thirty years he was the sole teacher until in 1840 the first clinical assistant was appointed. By 1847 the number of staff had risen to five, but it remained at that level up to the time of Dick's death.

In 1833 Dick joined the editorial team of *The Veterinarian*, on which he served until 1845. In 1844 he was closely involved in the petition seeking the granting of the royal charter of incorporation which established the Royal College of Veterinary Surgeons on 8 March 1844. In his busy life Dick still found time to be involved in other than veterinary matters in the community. He was a member of the Royal Physical Society of Edinburgh, the oldest scientific society in Scotland, and served as honorary treasurer to that body for fifteen years. As a farrier he belonged to his trade guild and served as deacon of the Hammermen and also, in the period 1835–7, as deacon-convener of trades, in which position he had a seat on the city council. Later, in 1843 and 1844, he was dean of guild and *ex officio* a member of the city council. Dick also owned property in Burntisland in Fife and at one time was a member of the town council there. He was a justice of the peace in the city of Edinburgh and did one term of office as moderator of the high constables of the city of Edinburgh. He worked for the development of Heriot's Hospital (now George Heriot's School), establishing education for the children of 'decayed freemen', and was involved in the charitable purposes of the Morningside Lunatic Asylum.

William Dick was a sturdily built man, 5 feet 7 inches in height, with a habit of running his fingers through his hair as he lectured. He was a strict disciplinarian, showing no mercy to the idle, but bestowing praise and encouragement wherever it was deserved. He was held in high esteem in the profession. His students often sought his advice after they had qualified and he himself followed their progress closely. He was a man of opinions strongly held and defended. 'In political and ecclesiastical matters his views were somewhat extreme, and always expressed with no reserve and some roughness.' He was usually attentive to the opinions of those who differed from him and put forward a 'bold and uncompromising advocacy of the people's rights' (Bradley, 54–5).

William Dick never married. He died from heart disease on 4 April 1866 in his seventy-third year at his home at 15 Clyde Street and was buried on the 11th in the new Calton cemetery within sight of Whitehorse Close, where he was born. He bequeathed his college in trust to the lord provost, magistrates, and council of the city of Edinburgh, and it later formed the faculty of veterinary medicine of the University of Edinburgh. A collection of Dick's writings, entitled *Occasional Papers on Veterinary Subjects*, was published in 1869. Following the incorporation of the veterinary college into the University of Edinburgh in 1951, the university court instituted three new chairs in 1953, named respectively the William Dick chair of veterinary surgery, the William Dick chair of veterinary medicine, and the William Dick chair of veterinary hygiene and preventive medicine.

J. E. Phillips

Sources R. O. Pringle, 'Memoir', in W. Dick, *Occasional papers on veterinary subjects* (1869) · O. C. Bradley, *History of the Edinburgh Veterinary College* (1923) · report of presentation to Professor Dick, *The Veterinarian* (27 Jan 1818), 400–10 · parish register, Edinburgh, Trinity College Church, 25 Nov 1799 [births and baptisms] · *The Scotsman* (6 April 1866) · *The Scotsman* (12 April 1866)

Likenesses W. Shiels, oils, 1850, U. Edin. · T. Knott, oils, 1851, U. Edin. · E. Olden, watercolour, 1853, Scot. NPG · C. Stanton, marble bust, 1857, U. Edin. · J. Rhind, sandstone figure, 1883, U. Edin. · H. Anderson, engraving (after photograph by A. McGlashan), repro. in W. Dick, *Occasional papers on veterinary subjects* (1869) · oils, U. Edin. · photomechanical print?, Wellcome L.

Wealth at death £8709 2*s.* 2*d.*: 1866 · £427 11*s.* 4*d.*: additional inventory, 1867

Dick, Sir William Reid (1879–1961), sculptor, was born on 13 January 1879 in Glasgow, the son of Francis Dick, a journeyman engine fitter, and his wife, Elizabeth Reid (*d. c.*1940). Little is known about the family, but there were at least two other children, Annie and Cathie. Reid Dick was ambitious to sculpt, and at the age of twelve was apprenticed to Scott and Rae, stonemasons, in Glasgow. For five years he learned to carve stone, including granite, and attended drawing and modelling classes at night school. In 1899, as a carver with a firm of stone decorators, he registered at the Glasgow School of Art, studying at night until he received his diploma in 1907. He accepted a post as art master at Bell's Hill Academy in Glasgow (1907–8), but, when first exhibiting at the Royal Academy in 1908 his address was 6 Clifton Hill Studios, St John's Wood, London.

When new to the city, Reid Dick worked as studio assistant to E. Whitney Smith and attended evening classes at the Kennington School of Art. His first noted commission was a portrait of Harry Lauder (marble, exh. RA, 1911). His reputation grew rapidly, and in 1914 he married Catherine Emma, daughter of William John Treadwell of Northampton. They moved to 1 St John's Wood Studios, Queen's Terrace, where they lived until 1924. They had three children, John, Ann, and Mary, at least one of whom was born at their next home, 31 Grove End Road, St John's Wood. In 1938 Reid Dick bought the house and vast studio at 16 Maida Vale (once occupied by the sculptor Alfred Gilbert), where he and his wife lived until his death in 1961.

In September 1914 Reid Dick joined the ranks of the Territorial Army, going on to serve with the Royal Engineers in France and Palestine from 1915 to 1919. While abroad he amused himself carving small figures in trench chalk, some of which were shown and sold at 'several London Galleries' (Reid Dick Archive). He received early recognition for his work, becoming an associate of the Royal Society of British Sculptors in April 1915; he was elected a fellow in August 1923, won the society's silver medal in 1928, and was its president from 1933 to 1938. Following the armistice in 1918, his bronze mask *Androdus* was bought for the Chantrey collection (exh. RA, 1919; Tate collection). In 1921 he was elected an associate of the Royal Academy, and a member in 1928.

Reid Dick's reputation for monumental sculpture was established after the First World War. Memorials at Bushey and Rickmansworth, Hertfordshire (1921), were followed by a major commission, the Kitchener memorial chapel (1922–5) in St Paul's Cathedral, London, the formal clarity of which became his hallmark. The *Pietà* in the

Sir William Reid Dick (1879–1961), by Philippe Ledoux, exh. RA 1934

chapel is one of his finest achievements (sketch model exh. RA, 1922, model 1923, unfinished 1924, marble 1925, original sketch model 1942, study 1953, study 1962). For the architect Sir Reginald Blomfield he made an eagle for the Royal Air Force memorial, Westminster, and the lion for the Menin Gate at Ypres, Belgium (1927). Among his individual memorials are those to David Livingstone at Victoria Falls, Zimbabwe (model exh. RA, 1934), George V in Westminster Abbey (models exh. RA, 1939 and 1941), President Franklin Delano Roosevelt in Grosvenor Square, London (1948; study exh. RA, 1949), and *Lady Godiva* in Coventry (model exh. RA, 1950).

Reid Dick's architectural works include bas-reliefs for Selfridges, Oxford Street, London (1928), where he later supervised elaborate temporary decorations celebrating the coronation of George VI in 1937; *Controlled Energy*, two colossal stone groups for Unilever House, Blackfriars, London (1932); figures for St Andrew's House, Edinburgh (1939); and the bronze *Herald* for the Reuters Building, Fleet Street, London (model exh. RA, 1939). As a portraitist his reputation blossomed after his marble mask of Lady Diana Duff Cooper was shown at the Royal Academy in 1922. A bust of George V (1933) was the first of fourteen royal portraits exhibited at the academy. Other notable sitters included Winston Churchill (bronze, exh. RA, 1943).

Reid Dick was created KCVO in 1935 and subsequently attended many private and public royal gatherings. In 1938 George VI appointed him sculptor-in-ordinary for Scotland (appointment continued 1952–61). He became an honorary Royal Scottish Academician in 1939. He made numerous memorials to George V, Queen Mary, and George VI at the royal residences at Windsor, Balmoral, and Sandringham.

According to *The Times* obituary, Reid Dick was stocky and robust in appearance, with quiet manners and a very soft voice. Alfred Munnings recalled him as 'a simple-minded, short, thick-set raw young Scot' (Munnings, 200). A witty conversationalist at ease in any company, he was liked and admired by his colleagues, and his wide circle of friends included many architects and artists. Straightforward, dynamic, and convivial, he combined a punishing workload with a social life which ranged from grand dinners and parties to the relaxed surroundings of the Chelsea Arts Club. During a bombing raid in 1944 the confident and unflappable Reid Dick, 'a strong tumbler of whisky in his hand, and several inside his body, defied the enemy, scorning to take cover as he leaned against the fireplace in the hall' (ibid., 188).

Reid Dick served in many committees, including the Royal Mint advisory committee (1934–5), the council of the British School at Rome (1930s), and the council of the Royal Academy (1930s). He was also a trustee of the Tate Gallery (1934–41), a royal fine arts commissioner (appointed 1938), and a chairman of the sculpture committee for the London Olympic games in 1948. In 1933 he was made an honorary fellow of the Royal Society of Arts, receiving the society's Albert medal in 1948 for 'National Memorials in Living Stone'.

Reid Dick was a major figure in academic sculpture, a consummate craftsman who combined respect for the past with a passionate search for new conventions. His firm belief that sculpture was at its best when related to architecture informed his entire career. Long dismissed as merely a reactionary monument maker devoid of creativity, critical reassessment by Benedict Read in 1986 revealed his true artistic importance. It lay, ironically, in the innovative stylization of form and material simplicity of his smaller pieces such as *Madonna* (marble, exh. RA, 1922). This vital dash of modernity injected into the traditions of the academy was followed by further figurative experiment by artists such as Charles Sargeant Jagger, Charles Wheeler, and William Macmillan.

William Reid Dick died at his home, 16 Maida Vale, London, on 1 October 1961 and was cremated on 4 October after a memorial service at Golders Green crematorium; his wife survived him. On 17 October 1963 a memorial tablet was unveiled in the crypt of St Paul's Cathedral during a service attended by many artists and architects. The president of the Royal Academy, Sir Charles Wheeler, gave the oration.   SARAH CRELLIN

Sources Tate collection, TGA 8110 · *WWW*, 1961–70 · DNB · K. Parkes, *America, Great Britain, Japan* (1921), vol. 1 of *Sculpture of today* · B. Read and P. Skipwith, *Sculpture in Britain between the wars* (1986) [exhibition catalogue, Fine Art Society, London, 10 June – 12 Aug 1986] · H. G. Fell, *Sir William Reid Dick* (1945) · A. Jarman and others, eds., *Royal Academy exhibitors, 1905–1970: a dictionary of artists and their work in the summer exhibitions of the Royal Academy of Arts*, 6 vols. (1973–82) · A. Munnings, 'An artist's life'; 'The second burst'; 'The finish': the autobiography of Sir Alfred Munnings*, ed. W. G. Luscombe,

abridged edn (1955) • *CGPLA Eng. & Wales* (1962) • records, Glasgow School of Art • *The Times* (2 Oct 1961)
Archives RA, MSS • Tate collection, corresp. and papers
Likenesses W. Stoneman, two photographs, 1930–47, NPG • R. G. Eves, oils, 1933, Scot. NPG • P. Ledoux, oils, exh. RA 1934, NPG [*see illus.*] • H. Coster, photographs, NPG • photographs, Tate collection
Wealth at death £24,265 2s. 5d.: probate, 19 April 1962, *CGPLA Eng. & Wales*

Dickens, Charles Culliford Boz [Charley] (1837–1896), magazine editor and compiler of guidebooks, was born on 6 January 1837 at 15 Furnival's Inn, London, the eldest of the ten children of Charles John Huffam *Dickens (1812–1870), the novelist, and his wife, Catherine, *née* Hogarth (1816–1879). Charley, as he was known, received his string of names as a result of an accident at the baptism—Culliford was the maiden surname of Dickens's grandmother, but Boz was added by his grandfather John Dickens, who shouted it out after the baby's godfather had said the officially chosen names.

Charley Dickens's education was sponsored by Angela Burdett-Coutts, with whom his father worked on several philanthropic projects, and who took an interest in his young son. He was sent to King's College School, and from there to Eton College, where his father reported that 'Charley ... who has already distinguished himself like a Brick, at Eton—got a prize—been declared at the head of his division, and floored all the boys therein' (*Letters*, 6.71). But to Burdett-Coutts he confessed some misgivings about the young boy's character: 'all he wants, is a habit of perseverance. With that, he could do any thing. He wants it as a fixed purpose and habit of his nature' (ibid., 6.467). In 1853 Charley Dickens visited Leipzig to learn German, and in 1854, as he vacillated about his career choices, Dickens's reservations again came to the fore. These were expressed in a letter which also perfectly illustrates the particular burden upon Charley as Dickens's eldest son and namesake: 'I think he has less fixed purpose and energy than I could have supposed possible in my son. He is not aspiring, or imaginative in his own behalf ... he inherits from his mother ... an indescribable lassitude of character—a very serious thing in a man' (ibid., 7.245).

In 1855 Charley Dickens returned to England to a post in Barings Bank, but it was not to his taste. During his four years at the bank he became involved in his parents' messy separation, and in 1859 agreed with his father that, as eldest son, he would live with his mother. In 1860, partly financed by Burdett-Coutts, he embarked upon a trip to China, also visiting Hong Kong, Shanghai, and Japan, aiming to set up as a tea merchant. It is likely that Dickens based *Great Expectations* character Herbert Pocket, in the original manuscript a merchant with interests in China, partially upon his son. 'It is possible too that Herbert's "conquered languor", despite his usually cheerful spirits and briskness, which Pip feels denotes a lack of natural strength, owes something to Dickens's critical assessment of his own son' (Caldwell, xxvii).

On 18 August 1861, having returned to England, Charley Dickens established a paper-making company with his future brother-in-law, Frederick Moule Evans. He married Elizabeth Matilda Moule (Bessie) Evans (d. 1907) on 19 November 1861, at St Mark's, Regent's Park, London. His father, who had had an unresolvable quarrel with Bessie's father, F. M. Evans, did not attend the wedding, and he also warned his son against entering into a business that had Evans as a major shareholder, and Evans's son as a director. One year later Charley and Bessie Dickens had their first of eight children.

After seven years the printing partnership failed, and Charley Dickens was made bankrupt. His father gave him a job working on his periodical *All the Year Round* late in 1868, and in 1869, when W. H. Wills's ill health prevented him from carrying on as sub-editor for the journal, Charley Dickens took over, being installed officially in the post in May 1870. Dickens thought he 'evince[d] considerable aptitude in sub-editing work' (*Letters*, 12.378), although he had earlier stated that Charley had 'no literary bent or taste' (ibid., 8.119). By a codicil to his will on 2 June 1870 his father bequeathed to him his share and interest in *All the Year Round*. Charley argued with Wills about salary and duties, and they agreed in January 1871 to dissolve the partnership, with Charley paying Wills £500 for his interest, leaving Charley Dickens as the sole proprietor and editor of the periodical. Sales of the weekly journal steadily fell during Charley's editorship; he proved unable to attract the same quality of serial novels that his father had commissioned through his literary contacts and influence. The character of the journal also changed, and 'might ... be best expressed as a decline from an important literary force to a "woman's magazine"' (Casey, 91). It remained successful enough, however, for Charley Dickens to continue as editor and proprietor, until he decided to terminate its publication in 1893. In addition to his editorial work Charley Dickens became the chief partner in the printing firm of Dickens and Evans, with whom he had some success as the author of several popular guidebooks. *Dickens's Dictionary of London* (1879) ran into fourteen editions, and was followed by similar guides to Paris (1882), Oxford (1884), Cambridge (1884), and the Thames (1887), all running into multiple editions.

Soon after his father's death Charley Dickens had bought the family home, Gad's Hill Place, in Kent, much to the irritation of his aunt Georgina Hogarth and other members of the Dickens family, who had hoped to purchase it for the estate. He found it impossible to let, however, and so was forced to sell it to another party in 1879. He further angered his formidable aunt through a disagreement over the proposed sale and exhibition of the 'Swiss chalet', a small outbuilding of Gad's Hill in which his father had spent his last day. As a result of the argument Georgina had Charley removed as executor of her will, and reduced her legacies to his daughters.

In 1887 Charley Dickens made a tour of the United States, giving readings from his father's books: 'He was an excellent reader and reciter, and he inherited to the full the gift of the great novelist as an after-dinner orator' (*DNB*). Upon his return to England he left his printing business, and became a reader with Macmillan & Co. He oversaw a new edition of his father's works for the firm (1892–

3), and wrote bio-bibliographical introductions for the volumes. Charley Dickens died of heart disease on 20 July 1896 at his home, 43 Fairholme Road, Fulham, London. He was buried three days later in Mortlake cemetery. He was survived by his wife and seven children.

M. CLARE LOUGHLIN-CHOW

Sources *The letters of Charles Dickens*, ed. M. House, G. Storey, and others, 12 vols. (1965–2002) · m. cert. · d. cert. · *The Times* (22 July 1896); (27 July 1896) · *Daily News* (22 July 1896) · A. Adrian, *Georgina Hogarth and the Dickens circle* (1957) · M. Dickens, *My father as I recall him* (1896) · G. Storey, *Dickens and daughter* (1939) · W. H. Bowen, *Charles Dickens and his family* (1956) · P. Schlicke, ed., *Oxford reader's companion to Dickens* (1999) · E. M. Casey, '"Novels in teaspoonfuls": serial novels in *All the Year Round*, 1859–1895', PhD diss., University of Wisconsin, 1969 · Boase, *Mod. Eng. biog.* · L. C. Staples, *The Dickens ancestry: some new discoveries* (1951) · *DNB* · M. Caldwell, ed., introduction, in C. Dickens, *Great expectations* (1993)
Archives Blackburn Central Library, letters to Percy Fitzgerald
Likenesses portrait, repro. in M. Dickens, *My father as I recall him* (1896)
Wealth at death £17 5s. 3d.: administration with will, 30 Oct 1896, *CGPLA Eng. & Wales*

Dickens, Charles John Huffam (1812–1870), novelist, was born on 7 February 1812 at 13 Mile End Terrace, Portsea, Portsmouth (since 1903 the Dickens Birthplace Museum), the second child and first son of John Dickens (1785/6–1851), an assistant clerk in the navy pay office, stationed since 1808 in Portsmouth as an 'outport' worker, and his wife, Elizabeth, *née* Barrow (1789–1863).

Parents and siblings Dickens's father, John, was the younger son of William Dickens (*d.* 1785) and Elizabeth Ball (*d.* 1824), respectively butler and housekeeper in the Crewe family, who had married in 1781. Old Mrs Dickens was fondly remembered by the Crewe children as 'an inimitable story-teller' (Allen, 12). On 13 June 1809 John married Elizabeth Barrow; her father, Charles Barrow, was a senior official in the navy pay office who shortly afterwards had to flee the country, having been detected embezzling public money. John's genial and convivial personality, his air of gentility, his financial improvidence, and his fondness for grandiloquent phrases are all mirrored in Mr Micawber in *David Copperfield*. Certain of these traits reappear in the character of Mr Dorrit (*Little Dorrit*) where, however, they are presented much less sympathetically. Elizabeth seems to have had, like her husband, a lively and irrepressibly optimistic temperament and aspects of her personality have traditionally been identified in both Mrs Nickleby (*Nicholas Nickleby*) and Mrs Micawber.

The couple's first child, the musically talented Frances Dickens, always known as Fanny, was born in 1810 and was a much loved companion during Dickens's earliest years. In 1837 she married the singer Henry Burnett (1811–1893) and remained very dear to Dickens until her untimely death from consumption in 1848; he commemorated their childhood companionship in his journal *Household Words* (6 April 1850) with a piece entitled 'A Child's Dream of a Star' (*Reprinted Pieces*, 1858). John's and Elizabeth's other children, born after Charles, were: Alfred Allen, who died in infancy in 1814; Letitia Mary

Charles John Huffam Dickens (1812–1870), by Herbert Watkins, 1858

(1816–1893), who married the architect, civil engineer, and active sanitary reformer Henry Austin; Harriet, born in 1819, who died in childhood; Frederick William, always known as Fred (1820–1868); Alfred Lamert (1822–1860); and Augustus Newnham (1827–1866). Alfred Lamert was the only one of Dickens's brothers to make a satisfactory career for himself (as a civil engineer); in adult life the marital problems and generally feckless behaviour of both Fred and Augustus created annoyances for Dickens (as did the continued financial irresponsibility of his father) but he seems always to have retained some brotherly affection for them—even for Augustus, who in 1857 deserted his blind wife and emigrated with another woman to America, living openly with her there as 'Mr and Mrs Dickens'.

Childhood and education After a two-year spell back in London working in Somerset House (1815–16), John Dickens was posted first, briefly, to Sheerness and then to Chatham, where he settled with his growing family at 2 Ordnance Terrace, a six-roomed house, advertised as 'commanding beautiful views ... and fit for the residence of a genteel family' (Allen, 40). His income was rising but so were expenses. Two live-in servants were employed, one of whom, the teenage nursemaid Mary Weller, later gave Robert Langton her reminiscences of Dickens as a child. Dickens recalled his mother teaching him, 'thoroughly well', the alphabet and the rudiments of English and, later, Latin (Forster, 4). He and Fanny attended a nearby dame-school and later (1821?–1822?) he became a promising pupil at a 'classical, mathematical, and commercial school' run by the Revd William Giles, the son of a Baptist minister. By now the family had moved into a slightly smaller house, 18 St Mary's Place, perhaps as a result of John Dickens's increasing financial difficulties. These Chatham years were hugely important for the development of Dickens's imagination. His vivid, astonishingly detailed, memories of everything he experienced there, and of his voracious childhood reading (he was, Mary Weller recalled, 'a terrible boy to read'; Langton, 25), richly fed his later fiction and inspired some of his finest journalistic essays. Being 'a very little and a very sickly boy … subject to attacks of violent spasm' (Forster, 3), he was debarred from sporting activities, though he enjoyed games of make-believe with his friends and getting up magic-lantern shows, also performing (sometimes as duets with Fanny) comic songs and recitations with, according to Mary Weller, '*such* action and *such* attitudes' (Langton, 26). John Dickens was proud of his children's singing talents which were sometimes publicly exhibited at the Mitre tavern in Rochester. This old city, which adjoins Chatham, with its ruined castle, ancient cathedral, and picturesque High Street, fascinated the young Dickens and was indeed 'the birthplace of his fancy' (Forster, 8). He loved dreamily watching the River Medway with 'the great ships standing out to sea or coming home richly laden' and all the other varied shipping described in the 1863 essay 'Chatham Dockyard' (*The Uncommercial Traveller*). Also, it was the little Rochester playhouse that gave him his earliest thrilling experiences of what became one of the master passions of his life, the theatre, as recalled, along with other aspects of the city, in another *Uncommercial Traveller* essay, 'Dullborough Town':

> Richard the Third, in a very uncomfortable cloak, had first appeared to me there, and had made my heart leap with terror by backing up against the stage-box in which I was posted, while struggling for life against the virtuous Richmond.

He constantly read and reread the books in his father's little library—the eighteenth-century essayists, *Robinson Crusoe*, *The Vicar of Wakefield*, *Don Quixote*, the works of Fielding and Smollett, and other novels and stories (most notably *The Arabian Nights* and *The Tales of the Genii*). These books made up that 'glorious host' that, as he wrote in the character of the young David when incorporating this real life material into chapter 4 of *David Copperfield*, 'kept alive my fancy' when life turned suddenly very bleak. Indeed, these books became fundamental to his imaginative world, as is clearly attested by the innumerable quotations from, and allusions to, them in all his writings.

In 1822 John Dickens was recalled to London and the family squeezed itself into a smaller house at 16 Bayham Street in the very lower-middle-class suburb of Camden Town. This was a great shock to the young Dickens, who now began hearing much about his father's increasing financial problems. The abrupt termination of his schooling distressed him greatly. Money was found to send Fanny to the Royal Academy of Music but Dickens was left,

as he once told his friend and biographer John Forster, to brood bitterly on 'all [he] had lost in losing Chatham' and to yearn 'to [be] taught something anywhere!' (Forster, 9). But he began also to be fascinated by the great world of London, transferring to it 'all the dreaminess and all the romance with which he had invested Chatham' and deriving intense pleasure from being taken for walks in the city, especially anywhere near the slum area of Seven Dials which invariably inspired him with 'wild visions of prodigies of wickedness, want and beggary!' (ibid., 11). Forster characterizes the boy's response to Seven Dials as 'a profound attraction of repulsion' (ibid.), a phrase that goes very much to the heart of the later Dickens's attitude towards grim, squalid, or horrific subjects. John's financial situation continuing to deteriorate, and a rather desperate attempt of Elizabeth's to establish a school for young ladies having failed utterly, he was committed to the Marshalsea debtors' prison on 20 February 1824 and was soon joined there by Elizabeth and the younger children. Employment had been found for Dickens by a family friend at Warren's blacking factory at Hungerford Stairs just off the Strand. There he pasted labels on blacking bottles for 6*s*. a week, lodging first in Little College Street with a Mrs Roylance (on whom he modelled Mrs Pipchin in *Dombey and Son*) and later in Lant Street, Borough, closer to the prison. The deep personal and social outrage, and sense of parental betrayal, that Dickens experienced at the time was a profound grief that he never entirely outgrew, and an intense pity (also intense admiration) for his younger self was to be a mainspring of his fiction from *Oliver Twist* to *Little Dorrit*. In the fragmentary autobiography he wrote in the 1840s, and which Forster incorporated into his biography, he wrote:

> No words can express the secret agony of my soul as I sunk into this companionship [of 'common men and boys'] … and felt my early hopes of growing up to be a learned and distinguished man, crushed in my breast. The deep remembrance of the sense I had of being utterly neglected and hopeless; of the shame I felt in my position; of the misery it was to my young heart to believe that, day by day, what I had learned, and thought, and delighted in, and raised my fancy and my emulation up by, was passing away from me, never to be brought back any more; cannot be written. (Forster, 26)

John Dickens left the prison on 28 May, having been through the insolvency court, and having also received a legacy from his mother, but his son seems to have remained working at the blacking factory for another nine or ten months (Allen, 103). He was finally taken away when John for some reason quarrelled with the proprietor. Elizabeth tried to arrange for the boy's return, for which Dickens never forgave her. John, however, had retired from the pay office on health grounds and was now receiving an Admiralty pension, and said that he should go back to school. Dickens then became a day boy at the grandly named Wellington House Classical and Commercial Academy in the Hampstead Road, later depicting it and William Jones, its brutal and ignorant proprietor, in *David Copperfield* ('Salem House') and 'Our School' (*Reprinted Pieces*, 1858). From the day that he entered

Jones's school until the day he died he told no one, his wife and his friend Forster alone excepted, about his time in the blacking factory, or about his father's imprisonment. His parents seem likewise to have maintained a total silence on the subject. The first that anyone, the general public or even his own children, knew about these things was when Forster published passages from his unfinished autobiography in the first volume of his *Life of Charles Dickens* (1876). In March 1827 the Dickens family's finances were again in crisis and Dickens's schooling once more ended suddenly. At fifteen he began work as a solicitor's clerk, a humdrum occupation that he found unappealing, though his experiences at both the firms for which he worked (Charles Molloy of Symond's Inn, and Ellis and Blackmore of Raymond Buildings) provided good material for many passages of legal satire in his later sketches and fiction. During his leisure hours he greatly extended and deepened his knowledge of London, London street life, and London popular entertainments. A fellow clerk, George Lear, later recalled, 'I thought I knew something of the town but after a little talk with Dickens I found I knew nothing. He knew it all from Bow to Brentford' (Kitton, 131).

The young journalist, 1828–1836 By 1828 John Dickens, launched on a new career as a journalist, had established himself as a reporter on his brother-in-law's newly launched paper the *Mirror of Parliament*. Dickens evidently also decided to try for a career in journalism as being— potentially, at least—a good deal more rewarding than drudging on at Ellis and Blackmore's on 15s. a week (exactly Bob Cratchit's wages in *A Christmas Carol*). By fierce application, entertainingly recalled in *David Copperfield*, he taught himself Gurney's system of short-hand, and in November 1828 left the lawyers' office to share a box for freelance reporters in Doctors' Commons rented by Thomas Charlton, a distant family connection. It was probably some time during 1829 that he first met a diminutive beauty called Maria Beadnell (1810–1886) and fell headlong in love with her. This passion was to dominate his emotional life for the next four years, causing him much torment, not so much because of the objections that Maria's prosperous banker father no doubt had about entertaining a struggling young freelance reporter as a prospective son-in-law, but because Maria herself seems to have been of a flirtatious disposition, so that Dickens could never be sure of her real feelings towards him. His steely ambition to make a mark in the world in one way or another was given a keener edge by his passionate desire to make her his wife. He sought to improve himself by reading in the British Museum (Shakespeare and the classics, English and Roman history), having applied for a reader's ticket at the first possible moment, just after his eighteenth birthday. Aware that he had a definite histrionic talent, he also considered the idea of a stage career and obtained (spring 1832) an audition at Covent Garden, but in the event a bad cold prevented him from attending and shortly afterwards came an opportunity to develop his journalistic career. During 1830 or 1831 he had begun to get work, perhaps as a supernumerary, on his uncle's

paper and then in 1832 he was taken on to the regular staff of a new evening paper, the *True Sun*. He rapidly acquired a reputation as an outstanding parliamentary reporter and, having inherited to the full his father's love of convivial occasions, pursued at the same time an energetic social life. In April 1833, anticipating a favourite activity of his later years, he organized some elaborate private theatricals at his parents' home in Bentinck Street. Shortly afterwards came the final cruel collapse of all hopes of winning Maria's heart. The intense pain this caused him left a permanent scar on his emotional life, although he was able to present Maria and his ardent youthful love for her in a comic-sentimental light in the Dora episodes of *David Copperfield*. Many years later he wrote to her that 'the wasted tenderness of those hard years' had bred in him 'a habit of suppression … which I know is no part of my original nature, but which makes me chary of showing my affections, even to my children, except when they are very young' (*Letters*, 7.543).

In December 1833 Dickens's first published literary work appeared in the *Monthly Magazine*; it was a farcical little story of middle-class manners called 'A Dinner at Poplar Walk' (later retitled as 'Mr Minns and his Cousin'). Over the next year it was followed, in the same periodical (the owner of which, a Captain Holland, could not offer any payment) by several other stories in a similar vein, for the sixth of which Dickens first used the pen-name Boz (derived from his little brother Augustus's mispronunciation of Moses, his Goldsmithian family nickname). Dickens's appointment, in August 1834, to the reporting staff of the leading whig newspaper, the *Morning Chronicle*, at a salary of 5 guineas per week, placed his career on a firm footing and he was soon distinguishing himself not only as a brilliant shorthand writer but also as a most effective and efficient special correspondent, reporting provincial elections and other events, and being exhilarated by the keen competition provided by the *Times* correspondent. In September he began to contribute a series of 'Street Sketches', illustrative of everyday London life, to the *Chronicle*. These attracted favourable notice and his offer to write, for extra pay, a similar series, twenty 'Sketches of London', for the newly founded sister paper the *Evening Chronicle*, was welcomed by that paper's editor, George Hogarth. The first, 'Hackney Coach Stands', appeared in January 1835 and the last, 'Our Parish (the Ladies' Societies)', in August 1835. Dickens then began yet another series, twelve 'Scenes and Characters', in *Bell's Life in London*. The last of these, 'The Streets at Night', appeared in January 1836, to be swiftly followed by a collected two-volume edition, *Sketches by Boz*, published by John Macrone and illustrated by the renowned comic artist George Cruikshank. Dickens probably owed his introduction to Macrone and Cruikshank to William Harrison Ainsworth who had become a close friend, providing Dickens with his first entrée into literary circles. The two-volume edition of *Sketches by Boz*, for which Dickens specially wrote two non-comic pieces, 'A Visit to Newgate' and 'The Black Veil', was extremely well received. The sketches were praised for their humour, wit, touches of pathos, and the 'startling fidelity' of their descriptions of London life (Collins, *Critical Heritage*, 30). Meanwhile, he continued with all his routine journalistic work and coped as best he could with his father's recurring financial crises, helped by close friends like his fellow journalist Thomas Beard, who was to remain a lifelong and much loved friend, and the young lawyer Thomas Mitton, who acted as his solicitor for many years. He took lodgings for himself and his fourteen-year-old brother Fred in Furnival's Inn, Holborn. By this time he had become acquainted with George Hogarth's family and had become attracted to the eldest daughter, Catherine (1816–1879), though without the passionate intensity that had characterized his love for Maria Beadnell, and he became engaged to her during the summer of 1835. Catherine was small and pretty like Maria, with blue eyes and brown hair—also gentle, amiable, and proficient in many of the so-called 'accomplishments' expected of young ladies at this time.

Pickwick, marriage, and the coming of fame, 1836 In February 1836, just after the appearance of the two-volume *Sketches by Boz*, two young booksellers who were moving into publishing, Edward Chapman and William Hall, approached Dickens to write the letterpress for a series of steel-engraved plates by the popular comic artist Robert Seymour depicting the misadventures of a group of cockney sportsmen, to be published in twenty monthly numbers, each containing four plates. They offered Dickens £14 a month for the work, an 'emolument' that was, as he wrote to Catherine, 'too tempting to resist' (*Letters*, 1.129). He accepted the commission despite Ainsworth's warning that he would demean himself by participating in such a 'low' form of publication, but stipulated that he should be allowed to widen the scope of the proposed subject 'with a freer range of English scenes and people'. He then, he later recalled, 'thought of Mr Pickwick, and wrote the first number' ('Preface' to the Cheap Edition of *Pickwick*, 1847). This appeared on 31 March 1836 and on 2 April Dickens and Catherine were married at St Luke's, Chelsea. They spent their honeymoon in the Kentish village of Chalk and then set up home in the new and more spacious chambers Dickens had taken in Furnival's Inn where he was already established. On 20 April Seymour committed suicide but the publishers boldly decided to continue the series, despite disappointing initial sales. Seymour was replaced, after the brief trial of R. W. Buss, with a young artist, Hablot Knight Browne (Phiz), who was Dickens's main illustrator for the next twenty-three years. In recognition of the fact that Dickens was now very much the senior partner in the enterprise, the number of plates was halved, the letterpress increased from twenty-eight to thirty-two pages, and his monthly remuneration rose to £21. With the introduction of Sam Weller in the fourth number sales began to increase dramatically and soon *Pickwick* was the greatest publishing sensation since Byron had woken to find himself famous, as a result of the publication of the first two cantos of *Childe Harold*, in 1812. By the end of its run in November 1837 Dickens's monthly serial had a phenomenal circulation of nearly 40,000 and had earned the publishers £14,000, an appreciable

amount of which would have stemmed from the fees paid by advertisers who supplied inserts or took space in the 'Pickwick Advertiser' that eventually occupied twenty-four extra pages each month. The depiction of the benevolent old innocent Mr Pickwick and the streetwise but good-hearted Sam Weller as a sort of latter-day Don Quixote and Sancho Panza, the rich evocation of that pre-railway, pre-Reform Bill England that was so rapidly disappearing, the idyll of Dingley Dell, the sparkling social comedy and hilarious legal satire, the comic and pathetic scenes in the Fleet prison, the astonishing variety of vividly evoked and utterly distinct characters, the bravura wit and, above all, that 'endless fertility in laughter-causing detail' that Walter Bagehot later called 'Mr Dickens's most astonishing peculiarity' (Collins, *Critical Heritage*, 395)—all these things combined to give *The Pickwick Papers* a phenomenal popularity that transcended barriers of class, age, and education. Mary Russell Mitford wrote to an Irish friend, 'All the boys and girls talk [Dickens's] fun—the boys in the street; and yet those who are of the higher taste like it the most. … Lord Denman studies *Pickwick* on the bench while the jury are deliberating' (ibid., 36).

Dickens could hardly have anticipated success on this scale or he would probably not have committed himself to so many other projects such as turning one of his sketches into a two-act 'burletta', *The Strange Gentleman*, as a vehicle for the comedian John Pritt Harley. It was successfully produced at the St James's Theatre (9 September 1836) and ran for fifty nights. He also wrote, under the pseudonym Timothy Sparks, an anti-sabbatarian pamphlet, *Sunday under Three Heads*, the precursor of many later attacks on what he saw as blatantly hypocritical and class-biased legislative proposals. By late October he had clearly decided that he would be able to live by his pen and resigned from his *Morning Chronicle* post. Dickens was, in fact, grotesquely over-committed to publishers who were all eager to sign up the dazzling new literary star. He accepted Richard Bentley's invitation to edit a new monthly magazine, *Bentley's Miscellany*, to begin publication in the new year, being already committed to write two three-volume novels for Bentley, as well as a third novel, *Gabriel Vardon, the Locksmith of London*, for Macrone, and another (as yet unnamed) work of the same length and nature as *Pickwick* for Chapman and Hall. He had been at work, with J. P. Hullah, on a rather vapid operetta, *The Village Coquettes*, which was produced at the St James's on 6 December but had only a short run, and throughout 1836 he had been publishing more sketches in the *Morning Chronicle* and elsewhere, including some of his finest work in this genre, such as 'Meditations in Monmouth Street'. These sketches, together with earlier ones still uncollected, were gathered up in the one-volume *Sketches by Boz: Second Series* published by Macrone on 17 December. This volume ended with an item written specially for it, a Grand Guignol piece called 'The Drunkard's Death'. About this time Dickens first met (probably through Ainsworth) John Forster, a young theatre critic, literary reviewer, and historian, who had moved to London from Newcastle and was already very much in the swim of the metropolitan literary world. Forster became one of Dickens's most intimate friends and his lifelong trusted literary adviser—even to some extent collaborator, since from October 1837 he read everything that Dickens wrote, either in manuscript or proof—as well as his chosen biographer. Forster's legal training and expertise made him an invaluable ally in Dickens's many disputes with publishers, the first of which was with Macrone to whom Dickens had sold the copyright of *Sketches by Boz* as part of a deal to release himself from the promise to write *Gabriel Vardon*. Macrone sought to profit from the success of *Pickwick* by issuing both series of the *Sketches* in twenty monthly parts. Dickens strongly objected and tried through Forster's agency to dissuade Macrone. In the end, Chapman and Hall bought the copyright from Macrone for a substantial sum and themselves issued *Sketches* in monthly parts from November 1837 to June 1839, with additional Cruikshank plates and with pink covers to distinguish the work from *Pickwick* in its green monthly covers. At the conclusion of this serialization, the *Sketches* were published in one volume, described on the title-page as a 'new edition, complete'.

The early novels, 1837–1841 The first number of *Bentley's Miscellany*, edited by 'Boz' and with illustrations by Cruikshank, came out in January 1837 and in February appeared the first instalment of Dickens's new story, *Oliver Twist, or, The Parish Boy's Progress*, which ran in the journal for twenty-four months (during the first ten of which Dickens was also still writing a monthly *Pickwick*). *Oliver Twist* was originally conceived as a satire on the new poor law of 1834 which herded the destitute and the helpless into harshly run union workhouses, and which was perceived by Dickens as a monstrously unjust and inhumane piece of legislation (he was still fiercely attacking it in *Our Mutual Friend* in 1865). Once the scene shifted to London, however, *Oliver Twist* developed into a unique and compelling blend of a 'realistic' tale about thieves and prostitutes and a melodrama with strong metaphysical overtones. The pathos of little Oliver (the first of many such child figures in Dickens), the farcical comedy of the Bumbles, the sinister fascination of Fagin, the horror of Nancy's murder, and the powerful evocation of London's dark and labyrinthine criminal underworld, all helped to drive Dickens's popularity to new heights. But there was mounting tension between himself and Bentley because of the latter's constant interference with Dickens's editorial freedom and his quibbles over the extent of Dickens's own contributions. Bentley also irritated Dickens by pressing for the delivery of a new novel (that is, the *Gabriel Vardon* originally contracted to Macrone, now renamed *Barnaby Rudge*; Dickens, having bought himself out of the arrangement with Macrone, had now signed a contract for the book with Bentley). Sometimes the relationship temporarily improved, as in November 1837, when Dickens agreed to edit for Bentley the memoirs of the great clown Joey Grimaldi (published with an 'Introductory chapter' and a concluding one by Dickens, and wonderful illustrations by Cruikshank, in February 1838), but at last came a complete rupture and Dickens resigned the editorship of

the *Miscellany* in the January 1839 number. By the summer of 1840 he was fully committed to Chapman and Hall as his sole publishers, having gradually disentangled himself—with their help, and that of Forster—from all commitments to Macrone and Bentley, the latter now usually referred to by Dickens in very uncomplimentary terms ('the Vagabond', 'the Burlington Street Brigand', and so on). The promised *Pickwick*-style work for Chapman and Hall, now carrying the very eighteenth-century style title of *The Life and Adventures of Nicholas Nickleby*, had begun its monthly part-issue in March 1838 and was completed in twenty numbers in October 1839. This story, which for thirteen months Dickens wrote alongside *Oliver Twist*, originated in his determination to expose the scandal of unwanted children consigned to remote and brutal Yorkshire schools; accompanied by Browne, he conducted an on-the-spot midwinter investigation just before beginning to write *Nickleby*. In this rambling, episodic, often wildly funny book, written very much in the mode of the Smollett novels Dickens had devoured as a child, the Yorkshire school setting is soon left behind, and the gallant young hero and his pathetic protégé, Smike, wander forth to undergo various adventures, both farcical and melodramatic; they are persecuted by Nicholas's wicked uncle and other villains, who also threaten the virtue of Nicholas's pure young sister Kate, but all is eventually set right by the benevolent Cheeryble brothers, though they cannot save Smike. The story is rich in unforgettable comic characters like the endlessly garrulous Mrs Nickleby and the strolling player Vincent Crummles and his troupe, and in places it resembles *Sketches by Boz* in its vivid evocation of particular London neighbourhoods.

Just before Dickens began *Oliver Twist*, he and Catherine had had their first child, Charles Culliford Boz *Dickens (1837–1896), in January 1837, and had shortly afterwards moved from their Furnival's Inn chambers to a new house, 48 Doughty Street (now the Dickens House Museum); Dickens bought a three-year lease and paid £80 a year in rent. Staying with them was Catherine's younger sister Mary Hogarth, whose sudden death on 7 May, aged only seventeen ('Young, beautiful and Good' according to the epitaph Dickens composed for her headstone in Kensal Green cemetery), was a devastating blow to Dickens—so great, indeed, that he had to suspend the writing of both *Pickwick* and *Oliver Twist* for a month, a unique occurrence in his career. He had lost, he wrote, 'the dearest friend I ever had', one who sympathized 'with all my thoughts and feelings more than any one I knew ever did or will', declaring also, 'I solemnly believe that so perfect a creature never breathed' (*Letters*, 1.263, 629, 259). It was the third great emotional crisis of his life, following the blacking factory experience and the Beadnell affair, and one that profoundly influenced him as an artist as well as a man.

In all other respects Dickens's life, both professional and personal, during the later 1830s became steadily more prosperous. The sales of *Nickleby* 'were satisfactory—highly so' (Patten, 98) and Chapman and Hall were happy to fall in with his plans for editing a weekly miscellany to be called *Master Humphrey's Clock*, for which he would receive a weekly salary of £50 as well as a half-share of net profits. He formed close and lasting friendships with many leading figures in the world of the arts, notably the 'eminent tragedian' William Charles Macready (always a particularly loved and honoured friend), the painters Daniel Maclise and Clarkson Stanfield, the lawyer and dramatist Thomas Noon Talfourd, and Walter Savage Landor; he was elected to both the Garrick and the Athenaeum clubs, invited to Lady Blessington's salon, and lionized generally. He also became acquainted with Thomas Carlyle, whom he greatly revered, and who profoundly influenced his thinking on social matters. He once said, 'I would go at all times farther to see Carlyle than any man alive' (Forster, 839). Carlyle's first impression of Dickens was that he was 'a quiet, shrewd-looking, little fellow, who seems to guess pretty well what he is and what others are' (*Letters*, 2.141). Maclise painted the twenty-eight-year-old Dickens's portrait as an elegant young dandy and the portrait was engraved as the frontispiece to the volume edition of *Nickleby*. At the end of 1839 the growing Dickens family (Mary, always known as Mamie, was born in 1838, Kate Macready in 1839) moved into a much grander house, 1 Devonshire Terrace, Marylebone, near to Regent's Park. Dickens paid £800 for an eleven-year lease and an annual rent of £160. From 1837 onwards the family spent several weeks each summer at the little Kentish resort of Broadstairs, later described in *Household Words* as 'Our Watering Place' ('Our English Watering Place' in *Reprinted Pieces*, 1858). Here Dickens would entertain friends but would also continue working, dashing up to London from time to time for business or social occasions.

Master Humphrey's Clock began publication on 4 April 1840. Initial sales were very large but quickly declined when the public realized the *Clock* was not to be a continuous story. The reclusive old cripple Master Humphrey and his little club of old-fashioned story-tellers did not appeal to the public and even the reintroduction of Mr Pickwick and the Wellers failed to halt the sharp decline in sales. The woodcut illustrations by Cattermole and Browne dropped into the text that were such a feature of the *Clock* made it an expensive product, so some prompt action was needed. Dickens quickly developed one of an intended series of 'Personal Adventures of Master Humphrey' into a full-length story and this, under the title *The Old Curiosity Shop*, soon took over the entire publication. The story of Little Nell's wanderings about England with her helpless old grandfather, fleeing from Quilp, a grotesquely hideous, anarchic, and sexually predatory dwarf, is the most Romantic and fairy tale-like of Dickens's novels, and it also contains, in the story of Dick Swiveller and the Brasses' little slavey, the Marchioness, some of the greatest humorous passages that Dickens ever wrote. By the end of the story's serialization in the *Clock* (6 February 1841) the circulation had reached a phenomenal 100,000 copies. Nell's slow decline and eventual (off-stage) beatified death plunged this vast readership into grief and mourning, Lord Jeffrey famously declaring that there had

been 'nothing so good as Nell since Cordelia' (Forster, 174). For Dickens himself it reopened an old wound: 'Dear Mary died yesterday, when I think of this sad story' (*Letters*, 2.182). The *Shop* was immediately succeeded in the *Clock* by the long projected *Barnaby Rudge*, Dickens's first historical novel, dealing with the anti-Catholic Gordon riots of 1780 and written in conscious emulation of Scott. The Wordsworthian influence, evident in some parts of *The Old Curiosity Shop*, is also seen here in the conception of Barnaby which clearly owes something to Wordsworth's Idiot Boy as well as to Davie Gellatley in Scott's *Waverley*. The completion of *Barnaby* (27 November 1841) 'worked off the last of the commitments so hastily entered into in the heady days of 1836' (Patten, 118), ending five years of intensive labour which saw Dickens established as far and away the most popular writer in Britain, though he was somewhat bitterly aware that he was still making much more money for his publishers than for himself. The triumphal welcome he received in Edinburgh in June 1841, following an invitation to go there from Lord Jeffrey and other distinguished Scottish admirers, was a striking manifestation of the extraordinary public position this young writer now occupied. The dinner in his honour was, he told Forster, 'the most brilliant affair you can conceive' (Forster, 176). He himself spoke, in the two toasts he proposed, with notable effect and eloquence, as he was so often to do in later life as the star turn at other banquets, meetings, charitable dinners, and so on. Four days later he was given the freedom of the city, after which he and Catherine went on a scenic tour that took them as far north as Glencoe; they returned into England via Abbotsford in order to visit Scott's house. The history of Scott's being forced by financial circumstances in his later years to maintain a prolific output was in Dickens's mind when he now proposed to Chapman and Hall that, after the cessation of the *Clock* on 27 November (*Barnaby Rudge* had not gripped the reading public in the way that *The Old Curiosity Shop* had, and the magazine's circulation had fallen to 30,000), he should have a sabbatical year. By continuing to write incessantly he would, he feared, do 'what every other successful man has done' and make himself 'too cheap' (*Letters*, 2.365). Wisely submitting to their hugely lucrative author's wishes, Chapman and Hall agreed to pay Dickens £150 a month for fourteen months as an advance on his profits from his next work (to be published in monthly numbers). He was soon being 'haunted by visions of America, night and day' (Forster, 195) and, Catherine's deep reluctance to leave the children having been overborne, resolved that they should make a six-months' tour there, the children to be left under Macready's care. He would keep a notebook on his travels, and Chapman and Hall should publish it on his return. His eager preparations for the trip, excited as he was by communications like Washington Irving's telling him 'it would be such a triumph from one of the States to the other, as was never known in any Nation' (*Letters*, 2.383), were briefly interrupted by a painful operation for a fistula. He soon recovered, polished off the last numbers of the *Clock* (the final number appeared on 4 December), and engaged in a whirl of pre-embarkation social engagements.

First visit to America and its aftermath, 1842 On 4 January Dickens and Catherine embarked on the steamship *Britannia* which, after a terrifying crossing, reached Halifax, Nova Scotia, on 19 January. Next day Dickens was both fêted by the local dignitaries and cheered by crowds in the streets. He and Catherine then re-embarked and landed (on 22 January) at Boston, where they put up at the Tremont House Hotel. Exhilarated by his initial experience of America, Dickens soon began to find, however, that the surging crowds of admirers who intruded themselves on him and Catherine at all hours were both exhausting and frustrating, and the tremendous flood of correspondence that came pouring in on him was simply overwhelming. To help him cope with the situation he hired a young art student, George Washington Putnam, nicknamed 'Q', as his secretary and travelling companion. He had met Putnam when sitting for his portrait to Francis Alexander (he sat also, but this time for a bust, to another local artist, Henry Dexter). In Boston, Dickens carried out the first of those investigative visits to prisons, asylums, and other public institutions that became such a feature of his American journey, and he met many notables, among them the celebrated poet Henry Wadsworth Longfellow and Cornelius Felton, professor of Greek at Harvard, both of whom became much-loved friends. At a public banquet in his honour (on 1 February) he spoke with passion of having 'dreamed by day and night, for years, of setting foot upon this shore, and breathing this pure air' (*Speeches*, ed. Fielding, 19) but also touched briefly on the vexed question of the absence of any international copyright agreement between Britain and America, allowing the wholesale pirating of his own and other British authors' work by American newspapers. He and Catherine went on to New York via Worcester, Massachusetts, Hartford, Connecticut, and New Haven. Speaking at another banquet in his honour in Hartford (on 8 February), he again referred to the international copyright question. In New York he and Catherine stayed at the Carlton House Hotel (from 12 February to 5 March). The whirlwind of celebrity continued to engulf them, its most spectacular manifestation being the great 'Boz ball' at the Park Theatre (on 14 February) which Dickens called 'a most superb affair' (Forster, 215). Shortly afterwards, however, lying ill in his hotel room, he wrote to Jonathan Chapman, mayor of Boston, 'I am sick to death of the life I have been leading here—worn out in mind and body', and inveighed against the newspapers for attacking him over international copyright 'in such terms of vagabond scurrility as they would denounce no murderer with' (*Letters*, 2.76–7). Press attacks on his 'mercenariness' and bad taste in speaking about money matters at gatherings in his honour were indeed often couched in crudely offensive terms. Dickens's romantic dream of America as a pure, free, 'innocent' land, untrammelled by the corrupt institutions and the pernicious snobberies and class hatreds of the Old World, was rapidly turning sour, and he resolved to decline all future invitations of a public nature. He and Catherine went on to Philadelphia,

where he encountered Edgar Allan Poe, and where, despite his resolve, he found himself duped into holding a 'levee' at his hotel for 600 people. From there they went to Washington where Dickens saw congress in session and had a very low-key meeting with President John Tyler. During an excursion south to Richmond, Virginia, his increasing disillusionment with America was intensified by the shock and disgust he experienced at seeing slavery at first hand. From Baltimore he wrote to Macready, 'This is not the Republic I came to see. This is not the Republic of my imagination. I infinitely prefer a liberal Monarchy—even with its sickening accompaniments of Court Circulars … to such a Government as this' (*Letters*, 3.156).

The travellers proceeded by rail, stagecoach, and (disconcertingly unhygienic) canal boat to Pittsburgh, then by steamboat down the Ohio to Cincinnati, thence to Louisville and Cairo (the horrible 'Eden' of *Martin Chuzzlewit*), and then up the Mississippi (which Dickens thought 'the beastliest river in the world' (Forster, 259) to St Louis. After returning to Cincinnati, Dickens and Catherine headed north via Columbus, Ohio, to Buffalo and Niagara Falls, where they stayed from 26 April to 4 May. The falls impressed Dickens profoundly. He wrote of them, 'It would be hard for a man to stand nearer to God than he does here' and expressed a belief that the spirit of Mary Hogarth had 'been there many times, I doubt not, since her sweet face faded from my earthly sight' (Forster, 270). There followed a four-week tour in Canada, where Dickens felt considerably more at home than in America. He visited both Toronto and Quebec, and in Toronto took great delight in organizing, and participating in, some elaborate amateur theatricals involving the officers of the local garrison. Catherine also took a part and, Dickens wrote to Forster, acted 'devilish well, I assure you!' (ibid., 276). By now, however, both Dickens and Catherine were desperately homesick. She had proved herself, Dickens told Forster, 'a *most admirable* traveller in every respect … has always accommodated herself, well and cheerfully, to everything … and proved herself perfectly game' (ibid., 266), but she could now no longer contain her eagerness to see the children again. The travellers returned to New York and, after a final expedition to see a Shaker village in Lebanon and to West Point, happily embarked on 7 June on a sailing packet (they had had enough of steamships), the *George Washington*. They landed at Liverpool on 29 June and went straight on to London for an ecstatic reunion with the children. Hardly less joyous were Dickens's reunions with his friends Forster, Macready, Maclise, Stanfield, and others but he soon had to buckle down to the writing of his promised American travel book. The furore over international copyright continued, fed by a circular letter Dickens wrote on the topic (on 7 July) which got into American newspapers alongside a forged letter in which he was maliciously represented as branding America a country of gross manners and squalid moneymaking. There was copious and vehement editorializing about this seemingly clear evidence of Dickens's snobbishness and ingratitude. Against this background he wrote his promised travel book for Chapman and Hall,

American Notes, for General Circulation (2 vols.), which appeared on 19 October. In it Dickens praised many of America's public institutions but condemned the national worship of 'smartness' (that is, sharp practice), and attacked particularly the hypocrisy and venality of the American press. He also commented unfavourably on many aspects of American social life, notably the widespread habit of spitting in public, and, predictably, denounced slavery at some length. *American Notes* sold well but attracted little favourable comment in Britain (Macaulay deemed it 'at once frivolous and dull'; Collins, *Critical Heritage*, 124) and, unsurprisingly, it met with a very hostile reception in the American press. Meanwhile, Dickens, having enjoyed the usual summer sojourn with his family in Broadstairs (now included as a permanent member of the family was his fifteen-year-old sister-in-law Georgina Hogarth), began turning his mind to the twenty-monthly-number novel he was contracted to write for Chapman and Hall. Having an idea, in the event not followed up, that he might open the story on the coast of Cornwall, he made what was evidently an exceedingly jolly expedition to that county together with Forster, Maclise, and Stanfield (from 27 October to 4 November).

From *Martin Chuzzlewit* to *David Copperfield*, 1843–1849 *Martin Chuzzlewit* was published in monthly parts from 31 December 1842 to 30 June 1844. Dickens thought it 'in a hundred points immeasurably the best of my stories' (Forster, 305), and declared that he felt his power more than ever before. And, indeed, this is the great transitional novel that leads from the dazzling farce and comedy of humours, the often powerfully effective melodrama and satirical episodes, the sometimes startling grotesquerie and the picaresque pleasures of the early fiction to the complex, resonant, carefully planned and structured masterpieces of Dickens's later years. He had for the first time a conscious overall design, 'to show, more or less by every person introduced, the number and variety of humours and vices that have their root in selfishness' (ibid., 291), and the superb 'humour' characters of Pecksniff and Mrs Gamp as well as the squalid murderer Jonas Chuzzlewit are all very much a part of this design, though they also transcend it. The early 1840s were a bad time for publishing, however, and sales were disappointing. Even Dickens's decision to send his hero to America in the sixth monthly number and his lively satirizing of American manners and institutions failed to push the circulation much above 20,000. Meanwhile, as a man with a highly active social conscience, and mindful always of that desperate time in his own childhood when he 'lounged about the streets, insufficiently and unsatisfactorily fed' and might so easily have become 'for any care that was taken of me, a little robber or a little vagabond' (ibid., 28), Dickens was becoming ever more urgently concerned about the plight of the children of the poor. He was horrified by revelations in a parliamentary commissioners' report about the condition of children employed in mines and factories, and interested himself strongly in the ragged school movement, particularly in persuading the millionaire philanthropist Angela Burdett-Coutts (with whom he had been friendly since 1839) to give financial support to the Field Lane School in the area of London where he had earlier located Fagin's lair in *Oliver Twist*. Disgusted by the squabbles between Anglicans, Catholics, and nonconformists that bedevilled the debate about public education, he joined the Unitarians, remaining a member for three or four years before returning to Anglicanism. In October 1843 he had the sudden inspiration of writing a Christmas story intended to open its readers' hearts towards those struggling to survive on the lower rungs of the economic ladder and to encourage practical benevolence, but also to warn of the terrible danger to society created by the toleration of widespread ignorance and actual want among the poor. The result, written at white heat, was *A Christmas Carol: in Prose*, published by Chapman and Hall on 19 December as a handsomely bound little volume with four hand-coloured illustrations by John Leech, price 5s. This 'Ghost Story of Christmas', as it was subtitled, was a sensational success. The story of the archetypal miser Scrooge's conversion to benevolence by supernatural means, and the resulting preservation of the poor crippled child, Tiny Tim ('who did NOT die'), was greeted with almost universal delight (in the February 1844 number of *Fraser's* Thackeray called it 'a national benefit and to every man or woman who reads it a personal kindness'). But it had been expensive to produce and Dickens's profits from it were very moderate. This so exacerbated the sorry state of his relations with Chapman and Hall (already strained by an unfortunate comment of William Hall's arising from the poor sales of the initial monthly numbers of *Chuzzlewit*) that he determined to break with them completely. He invited his printers, Bradbury and Evans, to become his new publishers and they—somewhat reluctantly on account of their inexperience as publishers—agreed. Dickens was further vexed by the highly unsatisfactory outcome of his prosecution of a cheap publishing concern for blatant piracy of the *Carol* (he had long suffered from gross and widespread exploitation of his work by hack dramatists and gutter publishers). He won his case, but the pirates simply went bankrupt and he was left to pay his own costs. By May 1844 he had agreed with Bradbury and Evans terms by which they were to advance him a total of £3800 in return for a quarter-share in whatever he might write over the next eight years, including a successor to the *Carol* for Christmas 1844.

In July 1844 Dickens moved his entire household (a fifth child, Francis Jeffrey, had been born in January) to Genoa, having decided to live abroad for a year, partly as an economy (it was cheaper to live in the splendid Palazzo Peschiere in Genoa than in Devonshire Terrace), partly to escape the increasing demands on his time at home, and partly for the stimulus of new scenes. He made a midwinter dash back to London, via Venice and Milan, to read the *Carol*'s more overtly political successor, *The Chimes*, to Forster and a group of other friends, including Carlyle and Douglas Jerrold. During 1845 Dickens and Catherine travelled to Rome, Naples, and Florence, Georgina joining them in Naples (where they made a hazardous ascent of Vesuvius). In Genoa and elsewhere he became intensely involved in using, either directly or long-distance, the power of mesmeric healing he discovered in himself to alleviate the condition of Mme de la Rue, an English-woman who suffered great distress from hallucinations. This strange intimacy with Mme de la Rue caused Cather-ine considerable uneasiness, not surprisingly. Dickens's response was righteous indignation (eight years later, when he again met the de la Rues abroad, he wrote home to Catherine admonishing her that he thought it would become her now to write Mme de la Rue a friendly letter, which she obediently did). The Dickens family were back in London in July 1845 and Dickens energetically set about organizing a production of Jonson's *Every Man in his Humour* to be given by a band of his literary and artistic friends, the Amateur Players. This took place on 21 Sep-tember in a private theatre in Dean Street, Dickens's own virtuoso performance as Captain Bobadil winning many plaudits. He had an understanding with Bradbury and Evans that he might start a new weekly magazine jointly with them and he had canvassed Forster with the idea of one to be called *The Cricket* (the title was revived a few months later for his third Christmas book, *The Cricket on the Hearth*). In the event, however, it was Bradbury and Evans's new national newspaper the *Daily News* that he agreed to edit. Liberal in politics and intended specifically to promote the railway interest, the paper first appeared on 21 January 1846. Even Dickens's phenomenal energy proved unequal to editing a national daily on top of all his other commitments, however, and he resigned on 9 Feb-ruary. But he continued to write for the paper, notably a series of 'Travelling Letters' (21 January – 11 March), describing his recent journey through France and sojourn in Italy, and five letters (23 February – 16 March) power-fully arguing against capital punishment. The 'Travelling Letters' formed the basis of his second travel book, *Pictures from Italy* (published in May 1846 with four illustrations by Samuel Palmer), notable for its anti-Catholic bias, which was no doubt the reason for the withdrawal of the artist originally commissioned to illustrate it, Clarkson Stan-field.

In June Dickens once again moved his whole household abroad (a sixth child, Alfred D'Orsay Tennyson, had been born in October 1845). This time he settled in Lausanne, where he quickly formed a congenial circle of Swiss and English friends, finished writing a version of the New Tes-tament intended solely for his children's use and not for publication (it was eventually published in 1934 under the title *The Life of Our Lord*), and began work on his new novel *Dombey and Son*, published in twenty monthly numbers from 30 September 1846 to 31 March 1848. Though ham-pered by not being able to walk London's crowded streets (that great 'magic lantern', as he called it, so necessary to his imagination; Forster, 423), and also by having to write his Christmas book for 1846, *The Battle of Life*, he neverthe-less made excellent progress with the novel. *Dombey* 'was to do with Pride what its predecessor had done with self-ishness' (ibid., 471) but was far more carefully planned and structured than *Chuzzlewit* and is now recognized as one of the greatest of all his works. It is the first novel for which a full set of working notes and number-plans survives (in the Forster collection, Victoria and Albert Museum). It is also the first one to have an explicitly contemporary set-ting. The railway features strongly in the story, which is also much concerned with the fate of women in contem-porary middle-class English society. From the start the sales of *Dombey* were extremely good, outstripping those of *Chuzzlewit* by 10,000 copies, and it is with this novel that Dickens's financial anxieties ceased and he began to be able to build up a solid prosperity. He moved the family to Paris for the winter of 1846-7, then back to London by March for the launch of the first collected edition of his works, the so-called Cheap Edition (published in weekly, monthly, and volume form), the birth of Sydney Smith Haldiman Dickens (18 April), and more activity by the Amateur Players with the object of raising funds for a pen-sion for Leigh Hunt. Dickens repeated his Bobadil tri-umph in performances of *Every Man in his Humour* at Man-chester and Liverpool (26, 28 July), and also took energetic leading roles in the various one-act farces played as after-pieces. As the writing of *Dombey* proceeded Dickens was also devoting tremendous energy to the setting up of a home for homeless women, funded by Miss Burdett-Coutts, and intended for the rehabilitation of women who had fallen into prostitution or petty crime. Urania Cottage (named after Venus Urania) opened at Shepherd's Bush in west London in November 1847 and for the next ten years Dickens was very active in all aspects of its administra-tion, in recruiting suitable inmates and arranging for their training in domestic skills, for maintaining discip-line, and for sending successful 'graduates' of the home to start new lives in Australia (as does the reclaimed prosti-tute Martha in *David Copperfield*). After finishing *Dombey* Dickens once again threw himself into organizing, on behalf of a variety of good causes, many other perform-ances by the Amateur Players (Shakespeare's *Merry Wives of Windsor* with Dickens as Shallow being now added to the repertory) in London, Birmingham, Manchester, Liver-pool, Edinburgh, and Glasgow.

Beneath all the social whirl and charitable activities of Dickens's mid- to late thirties there seems to have lain a growing preoccupation with his earlier years, traces of which may be clearly seen in parts of *Dombey*. He began (probably during 1847–8) writing his autobiography for posthumous publication but, according to his own later account, destroyed it when his narrative reached the epi-sode of his love for Maria Beadnell since that was, he found, still a source of too much pain to him to allow him to describe it. If he did, in fact, burn the whole manuscript as he claimed, he must have begun the projected auto-biography again later since Forster quotes extensively from an (apparently incomplete) manuscript near the beginning of his *Life of Dickens*, a manuscript that he (For-ster) presumably subsequently destroyed. Dickens's fifth and last Christmas book, *The Haunted Man* (1848), is pre-occupied with memory and its relationship to the moral life, especially the negotiation of persisting and debilitat-ing memories of wrongs and sorrows.

Dickens was evidently beginning to think of his next

novel in *Bildungsroman* terms—that is, the story of a young man's life from infancy to maturity—and named his sixth son (*b.* January 1849) after Henry Fielding 'in a kind of homage to the style of work he was now so bent on beginning' (Forster, 524). *David Copperfield*, his next novel (published 30 April 1849 – 31 October 1850), follows on naturally from all the foregoing. It is Dickens's first first-person novel (David as narrator calls it 'my written memory') and in it he draws, much more directly than hitherto, on events and people from his own personal life in 'a very complicated interweaving of truth and fiction' (ibid., 497). The misery of the blacking factory days (his notes for writing the number describing little David labouring in Murdstone and Grinby's bottling factory contain the poignant phrase 'What I know so well'), the details of his career as a journalist, and the raptures of his love for Maria Beadnell are all presented with only the lightest fictional disguise. In depicting the Micawbers and their recurrent crises Dickens draws on the personalities and former financial problems of his parents. Although the novel's initial sales were rather lower than those of *Dombey*, *Copperfield* received considerable critical acclaim and before long was widely held to be his greatest work. Undoubtedly it became for very many readers, then as now, his best-loved novel, an opinion in which Dickens himself coincided, calling it in a preface to the book of 1867 his 'favourite child'.

Household Words and the novels of the 1850s During 1848–9 Dickens wrote frequently and, like all other contributors, anonymously for the distinguished radical weekly *The Examiner*, edited by Forster since 1847. He had earlier written several reviews for the journal but now supplied, besides further reviews, several fiercely polemical pieces on contemporary social issues such as the growth of ritualism in the Anglican church, the temperance movement's campaign, and the Tooting baby farm scandal (on which he wrote no fewer than four scathing articles). On 30 March 1850 appeared the first number of his own long-meditated weekly journal, *Household Words*, which he co-owned with Bradbury and Evans, Wills, and Forster (Dickens owned 50 per cent of the shares, the publishers 25 per cent, Forster 12.5 per cent, and Dickens's sub-editor William Henry Wills another 12.5 per cent). Dickens also received an editorial salary of £500 p.a. and payment for his own contributions. Wills was a highly efficient and resourceful sub-editor and was for the next eighteen years Dickens's trusted right-hand man and confidential man of business. *Household Words* proclaimed itself at every opening as 'Conducted by Charles Dickens'; all non-fictional contributions, however, including his own, were published anonymously. The journal's weekly twenty-four double-columned, unillustrated pages cost 2*d.* and featured a mix of informative and entertaining articles as well as social and political satire, and serialized fiction. Elizabeth Gaskell and Wilkie Collins were notable contributors in the fiction department and Dickens built up a young staff of regular general contributors such as G. A. Sala, Edmund Yates, and Henry Morley. He himself wrote many of his finest essays for *Household Words*, co-wrote

others, and closely monitored all contributions, often revising them extensively, so that the whole journal was stamped with his personality and his views. From the outset the journal was a decided success, achieving in time a stable circulation of 38,500. Particularly popular were the special extra 'Christmas Numbers' (from 1851) which presented multi-authored seasonal stories with a large input from Dickens himself, including each year a different framework for the stories (his own contributions were collected, at first with those of others but later separated out on their own, as *Christmas Stories*). Late in 1850 Dickens embarked on a project (ultimately unsuccessful) with Bulwer to establish a guild of literature and art to assist impoverished authors and artists. To help raise funds Bulwer wrote a drama, *Not so Bad as we Seem*, which was performed, with Dickens in the leading role, before the queen and Prince Albert (May 1851). 1851 was a difficult year in Dickens's domestic life. Catherine was afflicted by some kind of nervous trouble and Dickens settled her in Malvern with Georgina to try the water cure, visiting her there as often as he could; and there were also two deaths in the family. The first was that of John Dickens, after undergoing an agonizing bladder operation. Dickens was deeply moved by his father's death, and some years later told Forster that the longer he lived, the better man he believed John to have been. The second death was a poignant one, that of his ailing eight-month-old daughter Dora, 'our poor little pet' as he called her (*Letters*, 6.355). Dickens sent Forster to fetch Catherine home from Malvern together with a letter seeking to prepare her as gently as possible for being greeted on arrival with news of the baby's death by saying only that little Dora was very seriously ill and that he did not at all expect her to survive ('why should I say I do, to you my dear!'; ibid., 6.353). The letter strangely mingles tender concern for Catherine and strong exhortations to her not to abandon herself to grief.

Dickens's increasing anxieties, and anger, about the social and political condition of England during the 1850s—feelings exacerbated by the débâcle of the Crimean War—are evident from a number of fiercely satirical essays that he wrote for *Household Words*, as well as from his intensely anti-aristocratic and anti-monarchical *Child's History of England* serialized in the journal (25 January 1851 – 10 December 1853). His feelings about public affairs find frequent expression in his letters, for example, when writing to Macready on 4 October 1855:

what with flunkeyism, toadyism, letting the most contemptible Lords come in for all manner of places … reading the Court Circular for the New Testament—and bearing such positively awful slaver in the Papers as I saw the other day about a visit of Lord Palmerston's to Woolwich Arsenal—I do reluctantly believe that the English people are, habitually, consenting parties to the miserable imbecility into which we have fallen, *and never will help themselves out of it.* (*Letters*, 7.715–16)

In his only direct intervention in politics (he always steadily refused the invitations he received to stand for parliament) Dickens joined the newly founded Administrative Reform Association and made a scorchingly scornful antigovernment speech at its third meeting, on 27 June 1855. But it is above all in the three great novels of this decade—*Bleak House* (published in monthly parts, 1852–3), *Hard Times* (serialized in *Household Words*, 1854), and *Little Dorrit* (monthly parts, 1855–7)—that his outrage and deep concern about the condition of England most powerfully manifest themselves. The satire of *Bleak House* focuses on the obfuscations and delays of the court of chancery which result in widespread human misery and suffering, but the novel's complicated plot and centripetal organization bring into the picture a great cross-section of contemporary English society, from the aristocratic Dedlocks down to Poor Jo, a London crossings-sweeper, and reveal social injustice, stupidity, misguided and self-regarding benevolence, charlatanism, and gross irresponsibility pervading all areas of the national life. The court of chancery, 'most pestilent of hoary sinners', serves as the great emblem of this grim state of affairs. Writing at the height of his powers, Dickens adopts a virtuoso form of double narration, and the novel has since the middle of the twentieth century been widely acclaimed as his greatest work. *Hard Times*, set in the northern industrial town of Coketown (usually identified as Preston), is even more urgently topical (the subtitle appended when the book appeared in volume form was 'for these times') and was written, he told Carlyle when asking permission to dedicate the book to him, in the hope that it would 'shake some people in a terrible mistake of these days' (*Letters*, 7.367). 'My satire', he told Charles Knight, 'is against those who see figures and averages, and nothing else—the representatives of the wickedest and most enormous vice of this time' (ibid., 7.492); it is focused on the relentlessly factual, imagination-starving (or warping) educational system favoured by Mr Gradgrind, the embodiment of all that Dickens feared and detested in the theories of political economy and Benthamite utilitarianism. *Little Dorrit*, the saddest of all his novels and also, according to Shaw, 'a more seditious book than *Das Kapital*' (*Shaw on Dickens*, 51), brings together scathing criticism of the country's governing institutions (here represented by the all-powerful and all-pervading 'Circumlocution Office'), a vivid portrayal in the story of Mrs Clennam of the harshly Calvinistic version of Christianity that was so strong in Victorian culture, and a depiction of the public greed and gullibility that produces the frenzy of speculation associated with the activity of the dubious financier Mr Merdle, together with Dickens's deeper personal preoccupations about his childhood sufferings and his father's shaming imprisonment in the Marshalsea. Dickens's attack on the inefficiency and ineptitude of the aristocratic management of the Royal Literary Fund and his repeated but vain attempts, made with Forster and others, to reform it (1854–8) were another manifestation of his fierce exasperation at this time with the state of contemporary public life.

The later 1850s were also a time of markedly growing tension in Dickens's private life. On the surface things seemed to continue as normal—or, at any rate, as normal for Dickens. In November 1851 he had moved into an eighteen-roomed, porticoed mansion, Tavistock House, in Tavistock Square, paying £1524 for a 45-year lease. Catherine bore their tenth and last child, Edward Bulwer Lytton Dickens, in the following year, and the tradition of long family summer holidays was continued, but now across the channel in Boulogne rather than at Broadstairs. The Dickenses first visited Boulogne in 1852 and summered there in 1853, 1854, and 1856 (it is described as 'Our French Watering Place' in *Household Words*, 4 November 1854; *Reprinted Pieces*, 1858). But Dickens's growing restlessness was only partly assuaged by such things as his continued zealous labours for Urania Cottage, an autumn (1853) touring holiday in Switzerland and Italy with two younger friends, Wilkie Collins and Augustus Egg, and several rapturously received public readings of the *Christmas Carol* in various provincial towns and cities for the benefit of local charities. He transferred his whole household to Paris for the winter of 1855–6, and in London busied himself with the organization of amateur performances in the schoolroom at Tavistock House of specially written melodramas by Wilkie Collins: *The Lighthouse* in June 1855 and *The Frozen Deep* in January 1857. In the latter play Dickens created a great sensation with his electrifying performance as the brooding hero Richard Wardour who fights his own murderous jealousy, ultimately sacrificing himself to save the life of his successful rival in love. Beneath all this frenetic activity ran an undercurrent of melancholy and gloom seemingly related, at least in part, to a growing estrangement from Catherine. 'Why is it', he wrote to Forster early in 1855, 'that as with poor David [Copperfield], a sense comes always crushing on me now, when I fall into low spirits, as of one happiness I have missed in life, and one friend and companion I have never made?' Later he remarks, 'I find that the skeleton in my domestic closet is becoming a pretty big one' (Forster, 638–9).

As if responding to a cue, Maria Beadnell, now stout Mrs Henry Winter and unseen by Dickens for at least ten years, chose this moment to get in touch with him again. Her letter affected him very powerfully, releasing a flood of passionate nostalgia for the great love of what he called his 'hobbledehoyhood'. He wrote her a series of ardent letters protesting, 'Believe me, you cannot more tenderly remember our old days and our old friends than I do', and responding to some suggestion from her with 'All that you propose, I accept with my whole heart. Whom can you ever trust if it be not your old lover!' (*Letters*, 7.533, 544). When they actually met, however, Dickens, who had arranged matters so that they should be alone together, was immediately and totally disabused of his wildly romantic idea that the Maria of their 'old days', long cherished so fondly in his imagination, was now to be restored to him, and he quickly retreated into the forms of ordinary social acquaintance. Dickens the artist proceeded to make glorious, if somewhat cruel, novelistic capital out of this serio-comic episode by using the hapless Mrs Winter as a model for the character of the hilariously effusive Flora Finching, the hero's old flame in *Little Dorrit*. For Dickens the man, however, the experience must surely have served to intensify his desolating sense of having always, in his emotional life, missed out on something very major, that now yearned for 'one friendship and companionship' that he felt he had never made (obviously a friendship with a woman, one that combined a sexual charge with intellectual and temperamental compatibility).

The end of the marriage, 1857–1858 In March 1856 at a cost of £1700 Dickens purchased the pleasant but modest Georgian country house Gad's Hill Place, near Rochester, for use as a country home. It was a house he had admired on childhood walks with his father and John Dickens had told him he might come to own it one day if he 'were to be very persevering and were to work hard' (*The Uncommercial Traveller*, 'Travelling Abroad'). This, his 'little Kentish freehold' as he liked to call it, was the first and only home that Dickens ever owned, and it was one in which he took great delight for the rest of his life. He loved to entertain friends there and was always devising 'improvements' to the property. At the time he acquired it, however, his marriage was well into its last, most intensely unhappy phase. The situation between him and Catherine was evidently becoming more and more strained. In a letter of 1854 to Miss Burdett-Coutts, Dickens had referred to a 'certain indescribable lassitude of character' in his eldest son that, along with 'tenderer and better qualities', Charley inherited from his mother (*Letters*, 7.245), and it was about this time that 'an unsettled feeling greatly in excess of what was usual with [him]', which Forster claims to have observed in Dickens since 1852, 'became almost habitual' with him and he failed to find in his home 'the satisfactions which home should have supplied, and which indeed were essential requirements of his nature' (Forster, 635).

It needed only some catalyst to precipitate a catastrophe and such a catalyst soon appeared. Professional actresses were needed to replace Dickens's daughters and sister-in-law Georgina Hogarth for some public performances of *The Frozen Deep* in Manchester in July 1857 (part of the activities organized by Dickens to raise money for the family of the suddenly deceased Douglas Jerrold), and he secured the services of the well-known and highly respected actress Frances Eleanor Ternan (*née* Jarman), and two of her three daughters, Maria and Ellen Lawless *Ternan (1839–1914), who were just beginning in the profession. Ellen, always known as Nelly, was seventeen years old, pretty, fair-haired, and intelligent, and Dickens seems to have fallen headlong in love with her. He began very much to concern himself with her affairs and with the fortunes of the Ternan family generally. That autumn, accompanied by Wilkie Collins, he visited Cumbria and made an excursion to Doncaster, where Nelly and Maria were acting. He smuggled ecstatic but veiled references to Nelly into *The Lazy Tour of Two Idle Apprentices*, the account of their northern tour that he and Collins were jointly writing for serialization in *Household Words*. He also included, in one instalment of the *Tour*, a bizarre short story about a man who, weary of his feeble, doting wife, literally wills her to death. Meanwhile, he was writing to Forster:

> Poor Catherine and I are not made for each other and there is no help for it ... She is exactly what you know, in the way of being amiable and complying; but we are strangely ill-assorted for the bond there is between us.   (Forster, 640)

For all her amiability, Catherine would surely have been much disturbed by her husband's sudden intense friendship with a pretty actress who was the same age as their younger daughter, and no doubt Dickens hotly resented this, much as he had earlier resented Catherine's distrust of his peculiar relationship with Mme de la Rue. According to some reports, matters were brought to a head by some jewels intended by Dickens as a present for Nelly being mistakenly delivered to Catherine instead.

By the following spring Dickens, not content with having moved into a separate bedroom and having had the communicating door between it and his wife's room boarded up, had decided that he must have a legal separation from her and drove the arrangements for this ruthlessly forward. Infuriated by the rumours (no doubt about his relations with Nelly) being spread, apparently by Catherine's mother and her sister Helen, he insisted on their signing a retraction and also took the extraordinary step of publishing a statement about his domestic affairs in *The Times* (7 June 1858) and in other papers, including his own *Household Words* (12 June), imprudently asserting the innocence of a certain young lady unspecified. Scandal had been given further food to chew on when it had become known that Georgina Hogarth had chosen to stay with Dickens while Catherine, with only her eldest son for company and an income of £600 per annum, was resettled in a house in north-west London, and it may well have been his sister-in-law's reputation that Dickens was primarily seeking to protect. There then appeared in the English press, copied from the New York *Tribune* of 16 August 1858, a private letter about the separation written by Dickens to Arthur Smith, manager of his public readings, in which he asserted that Catherine had no real love for her children, nor they for her, and hinted that she suffered from some mental instability. Dickens always strongly protested that this letter had never been intended for publication and referred to it as 'the violated letter', but his continued affectionate friendship for Smith (whom he had commissioned to show the letter 'to anyone who wishes to do him [Dickens] right') suggests that he cannot have been all that sorry that the letter had become public, and may even have connived at this. It was about this time that his attitude to Catherine suddenly changed to one of implacable hostility. She had, he told Miss Burdett-Coutts who was seeking to mediate between him and Catherine, caused him 'unspeakable agony of mind' and he wanted 'to communicate with her no more' (*Letters*, 7.632). During the remaining twelve years of his life he wrote to her only three times, each time merely a terse response to a communication from her.

Before the end of 1859 the pattern of Dickens's domestic and personal life for the remainder of his days was firmly set. Georgina Hogarth, helped by his adoring elder daughter Mary (Mamie), who never married, managed the household at Gad's Hill, to his entire and frequently expressed satisfaction. Georgina devoted herself primarily to the comfort and well-being of her illustrious brother-in-law and secondarily to the welfare of his younger sons, each of whom was early launched into the world, only one of them, Henry, being sent to university (Cambridge). Katey, Dickens's highly spirited and much loved younger daughter, married the artist Charles Collins, brother of Wilkie, in 1860, simply because, according to Gladys Storey, an intimate friend of her later years, she was eager to leave home after her mother's banishment (Katey is quoted as saying 'My father was like a madman when my mother left home. … He did not care a damn what happened to any of us'; Storey, 96).

Mrs Ternan and her daughters settled in a substantial family house in Houghton Place, north-west London. The lease was, almost certainly, purchased for Nelly by Dickens in the name of her sisters Fanny and Maria in 1859; she took over the lease from them when she came of age the following year and retained it until 1901. She and her mother later lived in a cottage in Slough and then a house in Peckham, the rates in both places being paid by a 'Mr Tringham', generally assumed to have been Dickens. After he had sold the lease of Tavistock House in 1860, Gad's Hill was, as far as the public knew, Dickens's only domestic base. There is evidence, however, that he regularly visited Nelly in Houghton Place, as well as in Slough and Peckham, also that he spent time in France with her during the 1860s, staying in a small house in Condette, near Boulogne, that belonged to his former Boulogne landlord, M. Beaucourt-Mutuel (the lovingly portrayed 'M. Loyal Devasseur' of 'Our French Watering Place', *Reprinted Pieces*, 1858). The precise nature and history of their relationship—whether, for example, she—sooner or later—became his mistress, as most biographers now assume, or whether his passion remained, for whatever reason, unconsummated—remains a matter of debate. Storey was apparently told by Sir Henry Dickens in 1928 that Nelly had a son with Dickens but that the child died very young (Slater, 379; Storey, 94); no hard evidence for the existence of this ill-fated putative infant has so far come to light.

One of the non-domestic casualties of Dickens's break with his wife was his friendship with Thackeray. The two men had known each other since 1836, when Thackeray had unsuccessfully proposed himself as a replacement illustrator for *Pickwick Papers* following Seymour's suicide. They had been on friendly and sociable terms but never intimate, and found themselves on opposing sides in the so-called 'dignity of literature debate' (Dickens in his obituary of Thackeray in *The Cornhill*, February 1864, said he thought his fellow novelist 'too much feigned a want of earnestness' in his profession). After the great success of *Vanity Fair* (1847–8) Thackeray was seen by many as challenging Dickens's novelistic pre-eminence, even though his sales never remotely approached those of Dickens's books; injudicious admirers on both sides tended to praise one writer at the expense of the other. When Thackeray was drawn into the welter of clubmen's gossip about the breakup of Dickens's marriage, some well-intentioned comments of his (meant to defend the honour of Georgina Hogarth by mentioning the involvement of an unnamed actress) were reported to Dickens, and Dickens's fury over this no doubt lay behind his energetic championship of one of his 'young men', Edmund Yates, in the celebrated 'Garrick Club affair' of 1858. Thackeray demanded Yates's expulsion from the club for publishing a hostile account of Thackeray's conversational manner which he could have observed only at the Garrick and Yates was duly expelled. Dickens, who had intervened on Yates's behalf, angrily resigned from the club in protest and he and Thackeray ceased to be on speaking terms. There was no reconciliation until they chanced to meet each other at another club, the Athenaeum, late in 1863, just a few weeks before Thackeray's sudden death.

A new career: the public readings, 1858–1867 By 1858 Dickens had many times exploited his considerable histrionic talents in giving enormously successful public readings of the *Carol* and *The Cricket on the Hearth* for charity, and he had long been under pressure to accept invitations to read for money. It was doubtless the combination, in the late 1850s, of his extreme restlessness and his need for increased income after buying Gad's Hill that persuaded him to embark on a series of paid weekly readings during the 1858 London season. This was much against advice from Forster, who considered it undignified for a great writer to present himself to the public as a paid performer, even of his own works. The first series of readings began on 29 April and the tremendous warmth of the audiences' response would certainly have reassured Dickens that he had not been at all damaged, in the eyes of his adoring readers, by the recent upheaval in his domestic life. He went on to tour a number of provincial English cities, as well as Edinburgh, Glasgow, Belfast, and Dublin, with a repertory expanded to include items drawn from *Pickwick* (the Bardell trial), *Chuzzlewit* (a piece centred on Mrs Gamp), and *Dombey* (*The Story of Little Dombey*), as well as from various of the 'Christmas Stories' published in *Household Words*. In Arthur Smith he had an efficient and highly congenial manager, on whom he could rely completely, and he had a full support crew as well. He stood behind a specially designed reading-desk, brilliantly illuminated by gaslights. Each item had been carefully prepared and intensively rehearsed so that he knew the texts by heart, *performed* them rather than read them, and could introduce spontaneous variations in response to the reaction of a particular audience. 'He does not only *read* his story; he *acts* it', wrote one reviewer, 'Each character … is as completely assumed and individualised … as though he was personating it in costume on the stage' (Collins, *Readings*, lix). Everywhere he met with triumphant success and tremendous enthusiasm on the part of his overflowing audiences. The American writer Moncure D. Conway commented that at the end of one of his readings 'it was not mere applause that followed, but a passionate outburst of love for the man' (ibid., xxii). It was striking, and no doubt deeply gratifying, evidence for his belief that his relationship with the British public was a very 'particular' one—

'personally affectionate and like no other man's' (Forster, 646).

Other provincial tours followed in the autumn of 1859 and in the autumn and winter of 1861–2 with more items added to the repertory, including a sensational *Copperfield* reading which became a favourite with both Dickens and his audiences (though the top favourites always remained the Bardell trial from *Pickwick* and the *Carol*). Arthur Smith's untimely death in 1861 was a severe blow and Dickens gave only two short seasons of readings in London in 1862 and 1863 (there were also three very well-received 'charity' readings at the British embassy in Paris in January 1863). He had found it a strain to perform while also continuing to write a novel (*Great Expectations*) so there were no more readings during the time he was writing *Our Mutual Friend* (spring 1864 – winter 1865). But in 1866 he contracted with the music publishers and concert promoters Chappell & Co. for a series of thirty readings in London and elsewhere. Chappell undertook all the business side of the performances and paid Dickens a fee of £50 per night (which by 1870 had risen to £80 per night); the firm also appointed a manager for the readings, George Dolby, who became a trusted friend and confidant of his 'Chief' as he called Dickens. Another tour of England and Ireland took place during January–May 1867, preparatory to taking the readings to America.

All the Year Round, A Tale of Two Cities, and Great Expectations, 1859–1861 When, in 1859, Dickens decided to publish a statement in the press about his personal affairs he expected that Bradbury and Evans would run it in *Punch*, which they also published. He was furious when they, very reasonably, declined to insert 'statements on a domestic and painful subject in the inappropriate columns of a comic miscellany' (Patten, 262). He therefore determined to break with them completely and to return to his old publishers Chapman and Hall. Bradbury and Evans's co-operation was needed, however, for the launch of the elegant Library Edition of Dickens's works (twenty-two volumes published, 1858–9; re-issued with illustrations and eight more volumes, 1861–74). But Dickens forced the dissolution of *Household Words*, owned jointly by himself and Bradbury and Evans, and the last number appeared, despite all the hapless publishers' efforts to prevent the closure, on 28 May 1859. Dickens, meanwhile, had begun publishing, from 30 April, a new weekly periodical with the same format and at the same price as *Household Words* called *All the Year Round*. Wills continued as his sub-editor and he and Dickens were the sole proprietors, Dickens owning 75 per cent of the shares as well as the name and goodwill attached to the magazine. While maintaining the tradition of anonymity for all non-fictional contributions, *All the Year Round* differed from its predecessor in various ways, not least in its greater emphasis on serialized fiction. A new instalment of the current serial stood always first in each weekly number, and Dickens editorially proclaimed 'it is our hope and aim [that the stories so serialized in the journal] may become a part of English literature' (*All the Year Round*, 2.95).

Dickens himself inaugurated the series in spectacularly successful fashion with his second historical novel, *A Tale of Two Cities* (serialized from 30 April to 26 November 1859), the basic plot of which was inspired by the story of the self-sacrificing lover Richard Wardour (Dickens's role) in *The Frozen Deep*. In this novel, the second half of which takes place during the French Revolution, Dickens set himself the task, he told Forster, 'of making *a picturesque story*, rising in every chapter with characters true to nature, but whom the story itself should express, more than they should express themselves, by dialogue', glossed by Forster as meaning that Dickens would be relying 'less upon character than upon incident' (Forster, 730, 731). In its tightly organized and highly romantic melodrama and the near-absence of typical 'Dickensian' humour and humorous characters, *A Tale of Two Cities* certainly stands apart from all his other novels, although—as in his earlier historical novel—one of the great set pieces of the book is the anarchic destruction of a prison, an event to which Dickens's imagination responded with powerful ambiguity. Thanks partly to this new Dickens story, and partly to a vigorous advertising campaign organized by Wills, *All the Year Round* had an initial circulation of 120,000. Wilkie Collins's sensationally popular 'sensation novel' *The Woman in White* followed *A Tale of Two Cities* in the serial slot, contributing not a little to the maintenance of the magazine's impressive circulation figures. These eventually settled down to a steady 100,000 with an occasional dip but soaring always (up as far as 300,000) for the special 'extra Christmas Numbers'. Dickens eventually wearied of this latter feature, however, and killed it off after 1867.

Compared with *Household Words*, *All the Year Round* features far fewer journalistic pieces by Dickens himself, the 'Uncommercial Traveller' essays (see below) notwithstanding, and it has a much greater focus on topics of foreign interest, notably the struggle for Italian unification, and much less concern for the political and social condition of England than the earlier magazine. Nor could it be quite so topical as *Household Words* since every issue had to be finalized a fortnight before its due publication date, Dickens having contracted with the New York publishers J. M. Emerson & Co. to send them stereotype plates of every issue in order to ensure its simultaneous appearance on both sides of the Atlantic (an arrangement later somewhat modified).

On 28 January 1860 Dickens began contributing to his new journal a series of occasional essays in the character of 'the uncommercial traveller'. They were discontinued when he began work in earnest on *Great Expectations* (1 December 1860 – 3 August 1861) and not resumed until 2 May 1863 (carrying on until 24 October 1863). The 'Uncommercial Traveller' essays, which feature some of the finest prose ever written by Dickens, take sometimes a quasi-autobiographical form, with reminiscences of childhood, like 'Nurse's Stories' or 'Dullborough Town' (that is, Rochester), and are sometimes examples of superb investigative reporting, notably of lesser-known aspects of life in London; yet others focus on the process of travel itself, in its many various forms. As for his fictional writing,

Dickens had intended his next novel to be published in the old twenty-monthly-number 'green-leaved' format but changed plans when Charles Lever's *A Day's Ride*, which followed *The Woman in White*, failed to hold readers' interest and caused a perceptible drop in the circulation figures. Dickens assured Forster that 'The property of *All the Year Round*' was 'far too valuable, in every way, to be much endangered' by this development (Forster, 733); nevertheless he was determined to take no risks and so 'struck in' with his new story, *Great Expectations*, the second of his novels to be written wholly in the first person, now replanned as a weekly serial. The circulation figures promptly recovered and in this chance way (at least, as regards its format) there came into being the story that for many critics (and for many 'common readers' too) represents the very highest reach of Dickens's art as a novelist—even with the revised ending that Bulwer Lytton persuaded him to write in order to avoid too starkly sad a conclusion to this masterfully structured and brilliantly written story of money, class, sex, and obsessive mental states with, for the first time ever in Dickens's major fiction, a protagonist who is unambiguously working-class. The novel was published in three volumes unillustrated, Dickens probably recognizing that Browne's style had not really kept pace with the development of his own novelistic art, as was evidenced by the feebleness of the illustrations Browne supplied for the volume edition of *A Tale of Two Cities*.

Our Mutual Friend and the Staplehurst railway disaster, 1861–1865 The gestation of Dickens's last completed novel was 'unusually prolonged and frustrating' (Schlicke, 434). For at least three years before mid-January 1864 when he was at last able to report to Forster that he had actually begun writing, he had been struggling to get started, turning over notions for situations and characters jotted down in a book of memoranda that he had been keeping for some time (ed. Kaplan, published New York Public Library, 1981); many of these notions were used in the novel as it finally took shape. Two family deaths occurred in 1863. The first was that of Dickens's second son, Walter, who died in India, and the second that of his mother. Dickens grieved for his son (but, bleakly, did not communicate with Catherine, who must have been quite as grief-stricken) but it is not difficult to sense a continuing hardness of attitude towards his mother as she sank gradually into increasing senility. He wrote in a grimly comic vein to a woman friend of how

> the impossibility of getting her [his mother] to understand what is the matter, combined with her desire to be got up in sables like a female Hamlet, illumines the dreary scene with a ghastly absurdity that is the chief relief I can find in it. (*Letters*, 9.287)

For *Our Mutual Friend* he reverted to his traditional form of publication in twenty monthly numbers (May 1864 – December 1865) and at first felt 'quite dazed', he told Wilkie Collins, by the return to 'the large canvas and the big brushes' (ibid., 10.346). The illustrator chosen for the work was the orphaned son of an old artist friend, young Marcus Stone, who worked in the sentimental-realist style of 1860s book illustration, quite different from the caricatural style of Cruikshank and Browne. The novel with its panoramic treatment of contemporary society, complex plotting, scathing social satire, and masterly emblematic art recalls both *Bleak House* and *Little Dorrit*, but it differs from these predecessors in a number of important ways, most notably perhaps in that both of the love stories at the heart of the book (the earlier novels each have only one main love story) end on a very positive note, neither involving retreat from the city as in the case of Esther and Alan Woodcourt in *Bleak House*, nor subjection to it as in the case of Little Dorrit and Arthur Clennam in *Dorrit*. Moreover, the powerful evocation of the vast and brooding city of London with its dust heaps and its dark river, so central to the novel's action and so rich in spiritual meaning, is something quite different from the depiction of the city in either of the earlier novels. It had a mixed reception (the young Henry James's harshly dismissive review in *The Nation* is notorious) but its stock has risen dramatically in recent years and it is now generally regarded as one of his very greatest works. While writing it Dickens, travelling back from France with Nelly Ternan and her mother, was involved in a serious railway accident at Staplehurst on 9 June 1865, in which ten people died. Dickens himself was unhurt but very badly shaken, not only by the accident itself but also by the experience of working for hours afterwards among the injured and the dying and trying to alleviate their sufferings, mainly by administering brandy to them from the bottle and a half which 'by an extraordinary chance' he happened to have with him (ibid., 11.61). Nelly seems to have been among those who were only slightly injured and presumably she and her mother were got away to London as quickly as possible. She is often referred to as 'the Patient' in Dickens's letters thereafter.

The second American visit, 1867–1868 From the outset of his public readings career Dickens had been contemplating the possibility of an American tour, but he dreaded the long separation from Nelly and then the outbreak of the civil war put the whole idea out of the question. By May 1867, however, the attractions of America as what he had once called 'a golden campaigning ground' (*Letters*, 5.396) had become very strong indeed in the face of his ever-increasing expenses; he wrote that he began to feel himself 'drawn to America, as Darnay in the Tale of Two Cities was attracted to the Loadstone Rock, Paris' (Forster, 707). Dickens appointed George Dolby as his tour manager and sent him across the Atlantic on a reconnaissance expedition and, after receiving a favourable report and being fêted at a grand farewell banquet, himself left for the States. The tour began in Boston on 2 December 1867 and ended in New York on 20 April 1868, two days before he sailed for home aboard the *Russia*. Harsh weather, a punishing schedule, and the often enormous American auditoria made the tour a severe ordeal for Dickens who was suffering from 'a truly American catarrh' and exhaustion, as well as from lameness resulting from 'a neuralgic affection of the right foot', aggravated by his insistence on walking long distances in deep snow whenever possible.

He seems to have nourished a hope that Nelly might come to America (she had cousins in Newburyport, Massachusetts, and perhaps considered visiting them) but this was soon given up, and he had to content himself with sending her letters via Wills with covering messages such as 'Another letter for my Darling enclosed', for instance (*Letters*, 11.528). He did, however, receive most devoted support and tender care from Dolby, and also from his American publisher James T. Fields and Fields's charming wife, Annie. Dickens and Annie clearly shared a strong bond of mutual affection, and she seems to have been sensitive to the pain and trouble that lay beneath his sparkling public persona ('it is wonderful', she wrote in her journal, 'the fun and flow of spirits C.D. has for he is a sad man'; Curry, 44). Despite constant troubles with ticket touts and continued hostility from some sections of Dickens's old enemy, the American press, the tour was a most triumphant success (neither sickness nor exhaustion ever prevented Dickens from turning in a great performance at the reading-desk) and netted him over £19,000, a sum which might have been much greater if he had not in his distrust of American currency insisted on changing his dollars into gold at a 40 per cent discount.

Last years and *Edwin Drood*, 1868–1870 While in America, Dickens published in the *Atlantic Monthly* (January–March 1868) a hauntingly strange first-person narrative, 'George Silverman's Explanation', which has yielded rich food for biographical criticism, and in *Our Young Folks* (January and March–May 1868) 'Holiday Romance', four stories for children purportedly written by children. All these stories also appeared in *All the Year Round*. Back in England and recuperating from the strenuous tour, he postponed starting a new novel and concentrated on planning a long farewell tour partly in London and partly in the provinces. This began in London on 6 October 1868. Now included in Dickens's repertory was a highly sensational new reading derived from *Oliver Twist* (the murder of Nancy), the performance of which became almost an obsession with him despite warnings by doctors and friends that it was adversely affecting his health. In fact, by late April 1869 he had become so unwell that his doctors ordered him to abandon the tour. Anxious to compensate Chappells for the loss they had sustained, he prevailed on his doctor to allow him to present a final series of twelve readings in London (January–March 1870). He famously ended the last of these by saying, 'From these garish lights I vanish now for evermore with a heartfelt, grateful, respectful and affectionate farewell' (*Speeches*, ed. Fielding, 413). On 9 March he was received in audience by Queen Victoria, who recorded that he 'talked of the division of classes in England which he hoped would get better in time. He felt sure it would come gradually' (*Letters of Queen Victoria*, ed. G. E. Buckle, 2nd ser., 1926–8, 2). On 5 April Dickens presided in sparkling form, as he had done many times before, at the annual dinner of the Newsvendors' Benevolent Institution and on 30 April replied to the toast to 'literature' at the Royal Academy banquet, paying an eloquent and heartfelt tribute to his old friend Maclise whose

sudden death just a few days before had greatly shaken him.

In April also there appeared the first instalment of Dickens's new novel, *The Mystery of Edwin Drood*, set mainly in Rochester ('Cloisterham') and planned for publication in eleven monthly instalments, the last one to be a double number. It was to be a murder story, 'the originality of which was to consist in the review of the murderer's career by himself at the close, when its temptations were to be dwelt upon as if, not he the culprit, but some other man were the tempted' (Forster, 808). It was the culmination of Dickens's lifelong fascination with the demeanour and psychology of murderers and he was, his daughter Katey remembered, 'quite as deeply fascinated and absorbed in the study of the criminal Jasper as in the dark and sinister crime that has given the book its title' ('"Edwin Drood" and the last days of Charles Dickens', *Pall Mall Magazine*, June 1906, 644). *Drood* was very favourably received, selling 10,000 more copies than *Our Mutual Friend* and showing in its descriptive passages, Forster believed, that Dickens's 'imaginative power was at its best' (Forster, 808). The story was to have been illustrated by Katey's husband, Charles Collins, but ill health compelled him to withdraw after designing the monthly-part cover and he was replaced by Luke Fildes. Dickens lived long enough to complete only six numbers of the novel, and soon a whole *Drood* 'industry' (which still flourishes today) grew up, concerned with providing a plausible solution to the mystery. Dickens was working on *Drood* in his little Swiss chalet (the gift of his actor friend Charles Fechter) in the garden at Gad's Hill on the morning of 8 June 1870, the day on which he later suffered a stroke from which he died the following day. His wish to be buried 'in the small graveyard under Rochester Castle wall' (ibid., 855) was overridden by a national demand that he should rest in Westminster Abbey where he was accordingly buried on 14 June, in the strictly private ceremony that he had so forcefully enjoined in his will.

Descendants Dickens was survived by his estranged wife for nine years, during which time Catherine preserved, in public at least, a dignified silence about their marital history, though she did when dying ask her younger daughter to give her collection of letters from Dickens to the British Museum, 'that the world may know he loved me once' (Storey, 164). Dickens was also survived by eight of his children. His eldest son, Charley, died leaving seven children in 1896, the same year as Mamie who died unmarried. Katey, who had some success as a painter, exhibiting regularly at the Royal Academy, had one son with her second husband, another artist, Carlo Perugini, but the child died in infancy and Katey herself died in 1929. Francis died childless in America in 1886, after serving for twelve years in Canada with the North-West Mounted Police. Alfred emigrated to Australia, married twice, and in 1910 returned to England to begin a successful career lecturing on his father and his books, dying suddenly in New York in 1912, survived by two daughters from his first marriage (both of whom died unmarried). Sydney, a naval cadet, died at sea in 1872, leaving no children;

Henry became a High Court judge and a knight of the realm and died, leaving children, in 1933; and Edward (always known as Plorn), who married and became a member of the parliament of New South Wales, died in Australia childless in 1902. The numerous direct descendants of Dickens alive today all trace their descent from their illustrious ancestor either through Charley's line or through Henry's.

Dickens's after-fame: general From a very early period of Dickens's career many of his great comic and/or grotesque characters took on a life of their own in the culture (both high and low) of the English-speaking world and have ever since been recognized and referred to by people who may well have never read a single Dickens novel. This resulted from his extraordinary ability to create, and give unforgettably expressive names to, figures who are highly individualized by their physical appearance, dress, and mannerisms, and who are also powerfully allegorical, being brilliant incarnations of various aspects of perennial human nature. Mr Pickwick and Sam Weller, Oliver Twist asking for more, the Artful Dodger, Fagin, Sikes and the murder of Nancy, the death of Little Nell, Scrooge and Tiny Tim, Mr Pecksniff, Mrs Gamp, Uriah Heep, Mr Micawber hourly expecting something to turn up and Mrs Micawber refusing to desert him—these are some of the main Dickens characters and scenes that have been, and continue to be, drawn on over and over again by advertisers, illustrators, cartoonists, journalists, politicians, and public speakers generally throughout the English-speaking world to point a moral or adorn a tale, to satirize or to celebrate some contemporary figure or state of affairs. After Shakespeare, Dickens is probably the most quoted writer in English and, indeed, the names of certain characters, Bumble and Scrooge, for instance, have become part of the language itself. The same is true of the adjective 'Dickensian' which, depending on the context, is used to mean one of three things: festive or jolly (a Dickensian Christmas, for example); squalid or antiquated (as in 'a Dickensian slum' or 'to work in positively Dickensian conditions'); characters so idiosyncratic and improbable as to seem to belong in a Dickens novel ('a truly Dickensian waiter').

The general concept of Victorian London derives in great measure from Dickens's elaborate, haunting descriptions of labyrinthine courts and alleyways, quaint old buildings, fogs, gaslight, and teeming street life; and tourists still come to the capital from all over the world eager to discover and experience 'Dickens's London'. Nor is such topographical enthusiasm confined to the capital. 'Dickens's England' in general has also always been attractive to tourists, strongly drawn as they are to places closely associated with either his life or his books; an early classic of this kind of tourism was William Hughes's *A Week's Tramp in Dickens-Land* (1891). Pre-eminent in this respect are the Kentish towns of Broadstairs and Rochester, both of which have for many years held an annual 'Dickens festival', Rochester having the additional advantage of proximity to Gad's Hill Place and to 'the *Great Expectations* country' of the Kentish marshes.

At his death Dickens was regarded by the great mass of his contemporaries not simply as a great writer but also as a great and good man, a champion of the poor and downtrodden, who had striven hard throughout his whole career for greater social justice and a better, kinder world. It was this perception of him as much as relish for his literary art that inspired the founding of the international Dickens Fellowship in 1902, intended, according to its stated aims and objects, to 'knit together in a common bond of friendship lovers of the great master of humour and pathos, Charles Dickens', to spread the love of humanity ('the keynote of all his work'), to campaign against those 'social evils' which would most have concerned him, and to help preserve buildings and objects associated with him. This organization still flourishes today and still engages in charitable work, though it now approximates more closely to a conventional literary society. It has over forty autonomous branches throughout the English-speaking world (with, currently, others in Boulogne, Holland, and Japan), it elects the majority of the board of trustees governing the Dickens House Museum, London (which it saved from threatened demolition in 1923 and opened to the public two years later), and since 1905 it has published a journal called *The Dickensian*, devoted to the study and discussion of all aspects of Dickens's life, work, and reputation and the monitoring of his public image.

The perception of Dickens as a great good man underwent a marked change after 1934 when the first revelations about his relationship with Nelly Ternan were published in the *Daily Express* by the biographer and literary antiquary Thomas Wright (Nelly herself had quietly married six years after Dickens's death, had become the mother of two children, and had died in 1914). The continuing fascination with Dickens's connection with her (every twenty or thirty years a new book about it appears, and it is constantly being excitedly rediscovered by the media) attests to the unique position occupied by Dickens in contemporary Anglo-American culture. Despite his broken marriage and the periodic re-investigations of the Ternan affair, he is still very much an icon of those traditional domestic and social virtues often assumed to have been part of 'Victorian values', his universally recognizable image as a bearded great Victorian having appeared for several years on British £10 notes; and he is forever inextricably associated with Christmas cheer and seasonal charitable feelings.

For some seventy years following Dickens's death there was a marked gap between his enormous and unfailing popularity with ordinary readers and the attitude towards him of the highly cultured, including members of the academic world. As George Ford showed in his *Dickens and his Readers* (1955), admirers of George Eliot and Meredith tended to dismiss Dickens as 'vulgar' and lacking in artistic merit, an attitude that persisted into the Bloomsbury-dominated criticism of the 1920s and 1930s. Writing on Dickens in the *Dictionary of National Biography* (1888), Sir Leslie Stephen commented: 'If literary fame could safely be measured by popularity with the half-educated, Dickens must claim the highest position among English novelists', and Aldous Huxley made Dickens and the death of Little Nell his prime example in his *Vulgarity in Literature* (1930). Dickens and his art did, however, have a magnificent champion during the early decades of the last century in the bulky shape of G. K. Chesterton, now generally acknowledged to be the greatest Dickens critic of all time, but it was not until the American cultural critic Edmund Wilson, responding to the Ternan revelations and invoking Freudian theory, argued for a much more complex interpretation of Dickens's personality and art in his seminal essay 'Dickens: the two Scrooges' (in *The Wound and the Bow: Seven Studies in Literature*, 1941), that a truly seismic shift began in high-cultural and academic attitudes towards Dickens. Where Chesterton had celebrated above all the comic splendours of the earlier Dickens novels, Wilson directed readers' attention towards the later, 'darker' works. Important studies by George Orwell (in his *Inside the Whale*, 1940) and Humphry House (*The Dickens World*, 1941) further encouraged a total and wide-ranging revaluation of Dickens by literary critics and academic professionals, as did the first full-scale scholarly biography by Edgar Johnson (1952), the pioneering textual work of John Butt and Kathleen Tillotson (*Dickens at Work*, 1957), and the American literary scholar J. Hillis Miller's hugely influential *Charles Dickens: the World of his Novels* (1958), a rereading of many of the novels in the light of the phenomenological theory of Georges Poulet. Even F. R. Leavis, who in 1948 had, very magisterially and influentially, excluded all Dickens, apart from *Hard Times*, from 'the great tradition' of the English novel, underwent a conversion and in *Dickens the Novelist* (1970) joined forces with his wife, Q. D. Leavis, to praise him as one of the greatest writers of all time. From the second half of the twentieth century Dickens has been, and continues to be, the subject of innumerable academic treatises and conferences (including an annual week-long gathering at the Dickens Project in the University of California at Santa Cruz). A never-ending stream of editions of his novels has poured from the press, alongside books and scholarly articles investigating and variously interpreting all aspects of his life and work, and major scholarly editions of his speeches, letters, and journalism. The Dickens Society of America (founded 1970) publishes the *Dickens Quarterly*, originally the *Dickens Studies Newsletter*. Once again, the only comparison is with the great proliferation of all branches of Shakespeare studies in recent decades. Meanwhile, Dickens continues to be widely read by non-academic readers, many of them nowadays perhaps turning to his books for the first time as a result of seeing film or television adaptations.

Dickens on stage, screen, and air   From the time of *The Pickwick Papers* onwards, Dickens found his phenomenal popularity being extensively exploited, with complete immunity under the law, by theatrical hack writers such as William Moncrieff and Edward Stirling who produced (often very crude) dramatized versions of his books for the London theatres. Such versions were frequently staged with clumsily inept endings even before Dickens had finished writing his novel. They provided splendid roles for star actors, like W. J. Hammond whose Sam Weller in Moncrieff's *The Pickwickians* (1837) was hugely popular, or O. Smith who played Scrooge in Stirling's *A Christmas Carol* (1844), and they generally drew large audiences so were popular with both actors and managers. No fewer than seventeen different adaptations of *The Cricket on the Hearth* appeared on the London stage within a month of the book's publication (December 1845). Although, as Philip Bolton shows in his *Dickens Dramatised*, the spate of Dickens dramatizations diminished somewhat after the mid-century, Bolton, writing in 1987, is nevertheless able to list some 3000 dramatic adaptations of the novelist's work for stage, screen, and radio, at the same time acknowledging that this must be a very incomplete reckoning. For there has never been a period when Dickens's work has ceased to interest dramatizers and actors. Jennie Lee, a Victorian actress, made a whole career out of playing the title-role in her husband J. P. Burnett's *Jo, or, Bleak House* (first produced in 1876), and Sir John Martin-Harvey played Sidney Carton for over forty years in a hugely successful adaptation of *A Tale of Two Cities* called *The Only Way* (first produced 1899). The music-hall artist Bransby Williams, who was celebrated from 1896 onwards for his impersonations of Dickens characters, lived long enough to perform them on radio and even television. In 1951 Emlyn Williams impersonated Dickens himself in a one-man show based on Dickens's public readings. This proved enormously popular all over the world and he continued to present it until he died nearly forty years later. More recent successes in this line have been Patrick Stewart's one-man performance of *A Christmas Carol* in London during the 1993–4 Christmas season, and Simon Callow's *The Mystery of Charles Dickens*, scripted by Dickens's greatest modern biographer, Peter Ackroyd, at the Albery Theatre, London, in 2000–01. Both these productions were indebted to Dickens's public readings style. Stewart actually used a reading-desk similar to that used by Dickens himself, and Callow had earlier performed several of Dickens's reading texts on BBC television before a studio audience. Highly successful also was Miriam Margolyes's one-woman show *Dickens's Women* (1991, Duke of York's Theatre, London) in which Margolyes introduced and performed a remarkable range of Dickens's female characters. At the other end of the theatrical spectrum from one-man shows, Lionel Bart's *Oliver!*, first produced in 1960 and very frequently revived, must be regarded as one of the most successful musicals of all time, and the Royal Shakespeare Company's tremendously popular epic production in 1982 of an eight-hour version of *Nicholas Nickleby*, scripted by David Edgar and with thirty-nine people in the cast, was another landmark in the history of Dickens on stage.

Dickens was a great standby of the early film industry and a profound influence on the legendary Hollywood director D. W. Griffith, as famously discussed in Sergei Eisenstein's 'Dickens, Griffith and the film today' (in *Film Form: Essays in Film Theory*, 1949). A number of silent films were made of Dickens's novels, notably by the British film-maker Thomas Bentley in the second decade of the twentieth century. The arrival of the talkies reproduced the situation created by the nineteenth-century theatre with many cinematic versions of Dickens's novels built around star actors: MGM's *David Copperfield* (1934), for example, starring W. C. Fields as Micawber, and the same studio's *A Tale of Two Cities* (1935) starring Ronald Colman as Sydney Carton; Paramount's *A Christmas Carol* (1935) starring Sir Seymour Hicks as Scrooge; and, in Britain, Renown's *A Christmas Carol* (1951) starring Alastair Sim as Scrooge and J. Arthur Rank's *A Tale of Two Cities* (1958) starring Dirk Bogarde as Sydney Carton. Since the Second World War dozens of Dickens films have been made in Britain and America; one, directed by David Lean, stands out as a real masterpiece: *Oliver Twist* (1948). This is not simply a vehicle for star actors (though it has a superb cast), but a totally successful, highly imaginative translation of Dickens's novel into another medium, as is also the Portuguese director João Botelho's striking screen version of *Hard Times* (*Tempos difíceis, este tempo*, 1988), set in contemporary Portugal and filmed in black and white. Compared with the rarity of successful stage or film versions of Dickens's novels, there have been, since the 1940s, scores of very good radio and television serializations of the books, mainly on the BBC, something that should come as no surprise given that the stories were themselves originally conceived of as serials and published in this form. Outstanding among more recent adaptations have been *Bleak House* (1985), *Martin Chuzzlewit* (1994), scripted by David Lodge, and *Our Mutual Friend* (1998).

Dickens's impact on world literature There can be few other English writers—apart, of course, from Shakespeare—with such widespread influence as Dickens, not only on their successors in the national literature, but also on major foreign writers, and few have been the subject of so many outstanding treatises by foreign critics. Gissing, Shaw, Wells, Conrad, Joyce—these are among the most distinguished of late nineteenth-century and early twentieth-century writers whose work shows clear signs of Dickens's influence without any of the slavish imitativeness shown by the great tribe of avowedly 'Dickensian' writers like William De Morgan. Gissing also wrote some outstandingly good criticism of Dickens. The most celebrated examples of great foreign writers profoundly influenced by Dickens are Dostoyevsky (in his 'Two Scrooges' essay Edmund Wilson noted the irony that 'The Bloomsbury that talked about Dostoevsky ignored Dostoevsky's master, Dickens') and Franz Kafka. The intense and abiding admiration felt for Dickens by Turgenev and Tolstoy is also well documented. And, as Ada Nisbet amply demonstrated in her Dickens chapter in Lionel Stevenson's *Victorian Fiction: a Guide to Research* (1964), the presence of Dickens has been clearly traced in writers as various, and from as varied backgrounds, as Hans Christian Andersen, William Faulkner, Proust, Fontane, Benito Galdos, and Strindberg, and a number of communist Chinese authors. The great Japanese novelist Soseki Natsume (1867–1916) is another outstanding example she might have cited. Nisbet also surveys the wealth of foreign (non-

English-speaking) critical response to Dickens, with important and substantial studies by critics as distinguished as Hippolyte Taine, Wilhelm Dibelius, Stefan Zweig, and Mario Praz. And today there exists, as has been indicated above, a mighty international academic industry centred on Dickens, demonstrating, in a way that the gasman who accompanied Dickens on his readings tours could hardly have imagined, the truth of his fervent praise of his great 'Chief': 'The more you want out of the Master, the more you will get out of him.'

MICHAEL SLATER

Sources J. Forster, *The life of Charles Dickens*, ed. J. W. T. Ley (1928) · *The letters of Charles Dickens*, ed. M. House, G. Storey, and others, 12 vols. (1965–2002), 1–12 · R. Langton, *The childhood and youth of Charles Dickens* (1891) · *The speeches of Charles Dickens*, ed. K. J. Fielding (1960) · *Dickens's journalism*, ed. M. Slater and J. Drew, Dent Uniform Edition, 1–4 (1994–2000) · M. Allen, *Charles Dickens's childhood* (1988) · F. G. Kitton, ed., *Charles Dickens by pen and pencil* (1890) · R. L. Patten, *Dickens and his publishers* (1978) · E. Johnson, *Charles Dickens: his tragedy and triumph*, 2 vols. (1952) · P. Ackroyd, *Dickens* (1990) · P. Schlicke, ed., *Oxford reader's companion to Dickens* (1999) · M. Slater, *Dickens and women* (1983) · P. Collins, ed., *Dickens: the critical heritage* (1971) · P. Collins, ed., *Dickens: interviews and recollections*, 2 vols. (1981) · K. Perugini, '"Edwin Drood" and the last days of Charles Dickens', *Pall Mall Magazine*, 37 (June 1906), 643–52 · G. Storey, *Dickens and daughter* (1939) · M. Dickens, *My father as I recall him* (1896) · G. Dolby, *Charles Dickens as I knew him* (1885) · G. Curry, *Dickens and Annie Fields* (1988) · P. Collins, ed., *Charles Dickens: the public readings* (1975) · C. Tomalin, *The invisible woman: the story of Nelly Ternan and Charles Dickens*, new edn (1991) · *Shaw on Dickens*, ed. D. Laurence and M. Quinn (1985) · G. Ford, *Dickens and his readers* (1955) · P. Bolton, *Dickens dramatised* (1987) · J. Cohen, *Charles Dickens and his original illustrators* (1980) · K. Chittick, *Dickens in the 1830s* (1990) · D. Walder, *Dickens and religion* (1981) · N. Pope, *Dickens and charity* (1978)

Archives BL, literary MSS, corresp., and papers · BL, publishing agreements, legal and financial papers, Dep 9964 · BL, letters, RP 2554(i) [copies] · Boston PL, corresp. and papers · Central Library, Blackburn, papers · Dickens House Museum and Library, London, MSS of him and his circle, collections relating to him; papers · Free Library of Philadelphia, papers incl. literary MSS and corresp. · Harvard U., Houghton L., letters and literary MSS · Hunt. L., corresp., papers and literary MSS · JRL, letters, literary MSS, etc. · Keat's House, Hampstead, London, manuscripts · Morgan L., corresp., literary MSS, and papers · Northants. RO, papers relating to him · Princeton University Library, letters and literary MSS · Ransom HRC, letters · Ransom HRC, corresp. · V&A NAL, Forster collection, literary MSS, corresp., and papers | BL, Dexter collection · BL, corresp., mainly with Richard Bentley, Add. MSS 46612–46649 · BL, letters to his wife, Catherine, Add. MS 43689 · BL, corresp. with Lord Holland, Add. MS 51641 · BL, letters to Richard Henry Horne, RP 797(1) · BL, letters to Sir A. H. Layard, Add. MS 38947 · BL, letters to Macvey Napier, Add. MSS 34622–34625 · BL, letters, as sponsor to the Royal Literary Fund, loan no. 96 · Bodl. Oxf., letters to J. Ellis · Chatsworth House, Derbyshire, letters, mostly to sixth duke of Devonshire · Herts. ALS, corresp. with Lord and Lady Lytton · JRL, letters to William Gaskell and Elizabeth Gaskell · LUL, corresp. with Mrs Davis · Morgan L., letters to Baroness Burdett-Coutts · NL Scot., letters to Thomas Carlyle · NYPL, Berg collection, letters · Trinity Cam., letters to Lord Houghton · Trinity Cam., letters and cards, mostly to Mr and Mrs Milner Gibson · UCL, letters to Lord Brougham · UCL, corresp. with Mrs Eliza Davis · V&A NAL, letters, mainly to John Forster · V&A NAL, letters to W. P. Frith · Wilts. & Swindon RO, corresp. with Sidney Herbert and Elizabeth Herbert · Yale U., Beinecke L., letters to John Pyke Hullah | FILM BFI NFTVA

Likenesses J. Barrow, miniature, 1830, Dickens House, London • G. Cruikshank, pencil drawing, 1836–7, V&A • S. Laurence, chalk drawing, 1838, NPG • A. Fletcher, marble bust, 1839, Dickens House, London • D. Maclise, oils, 1839, NPG • R. J. Lane, pencil drawing, c.1840, Royal Collection • A. D'Orsay, drawings, 1841–2, Dickens House, London • H. Dexter, bust, 1842, Dickens House, London • C. Stanfield, group portrait, 1842, V&A • D. Maclise, group portrait, drawing, 1843, V&A • J. C. Armytage, stipple, pubd 1844 (after M. Gillier, c.1843), NPG • D. Maclise, group portrait, pencil drawing, 1844, V&A • A. Egg, oils, 1850, Dickens House, London • Scheffer, oils, 1855–6, NPG • H. Watkins, photographs, 1858, NPG [see illus.] • W. P. Frith, oils, 1859, V&A; related oil sketch, The Free Library of Philadelphia, Pennsylvania • R. Lehmann, pencil drawing, 1861, BM • W. W. Gallimore, Parian ware bust, 1870, Lady Lever Art Gallery, Port Sunlight • G. G. Fontana, marble bust, 1872, Walker Art Gallery, Liverpool • F. Alexander, oils, Museum of Fine Arts, Boston • R. Doyle, double portraits, caricatures, pen sketches (with John Forster), BM • H. Edwin, silhouette, drawing, NPG • W. P. Frith, portrait, V&A • H. Furniss, caricatures, pen-and-ink sketches (posthumous), NPG • S. Laurence, portrait, Dickens House, London • T. H. Maguire, lithograph (as Captain Bobadil in Jonson's *Every man in his humour*; after C. P. Leslie, c.1846), BM • Phiz [H. K. Browne], etching, BM; repro. in *Court Magazine* (1837) • J. Stephenson, wood-engraving (after unknown artist), NPG • group portrait, photograph (after Mason), NPG • photographs, Dickens House, London • prints, BM, NPG

Wealth at death under £80,000: probate, 19 July 1870, *CGPLA Eng. & Wales*

Dickens, Frank (1899–1986), biochemist, was born on 15 December 1899 in Northampton, the youngest in the family of five sons and one daughter of (William) John Dickens, master currier and leather merchant, and his wife, Elizabeth Ann Pebody. His father, who had built up a leather factory in Northampton, died when Frank was four years old. He had been an active member of the Baptist church at Walgrave, near Northampton, but his wife belonged to the Church of England. Frank's four brothers joined the family leather firm, Dickens Brothers Ltd, situated in Kettering Road, Northampton. He was educated at Northampton grammar school from 1910 to 1918. From the age of sixteen he became seriously interested in science and was always grateful that his science masters were good teachers. In January 1918 he won an open scholarship to Magdalene College, Cambridge, but because of the war he could not take it up until January 1919. He enlisted in the army (Artists' Rifles, and then, as a second lieutenant, the Northamptonshire regiment) but did not see active service. At Cambridge he took the shortened post-war course of eight terms and graduated second class in both part one (1920) and part two (1921) of the natural sciences tripos (physics and chemistry). He then went on to Imperial College, London, to study for a PhD in organic chemistry, which profoundly influenced his later work in biochemistry.

In October 1923 Dickens took his first appointment, at the Middlesex Hospital, London, to work with a newly qualified medical graduate, E. Charles Dodds. Two years before, Frederick Banting and Charles H. Best in Canada had isolated insulin. Dickens set out to simplify the method of isolation and make the substance available for patients. He was thus precipitated into biochemistry, from 1924 to 1930 assisting Dodds in his work on the isolation of a female sex hormone. With Dodds he wrote The

Chemical and Physiological Properties of the Internal Secretions (1925). He also developed a lasting interest in carbohydrate metabolism. In 1929 he spent a year with Otto Warburg in Berlin, which greatly influenced him. He translated into English Warburg's book *Über den Stoffwechsel der Tumoren* (as *The Metabolism of Tumours*, 1930). On his return home he worked in the newly opened Courtauld Institute of Biochemistry at the Middlesex Hospital, searching for differences between the metabolism of tumour and normal tissue. In the meanwhile he had married, in 1925, Molly, daughter of Arthur William Jelleyman, the owner of a rope-walk and tenting factory in Northampton, which among other items made special ropes for the local hangman. They had two daughters.

In 1933 Dickens moved to Newcastle upon Tyne to be the director of the cancer research laboratory at the Royal Victoria Infirmary. Apart from a year in London on war work (for the royal naval personnel committee of the Medical Research Council in 1943–4) he remained in Newcastle until 1946, when Dodds invited him back to the Courtauld Institute and he became the Philip Hill professor of experimental biochemistry. His research work on the mechanism whereby living tissues derive energy from the breakdown of carbohydrates culminated in the description of what is known as the 'pentose phosphate pathway', for which he is best-known. He was a major contributor to the discovery of this important route of glucose metabolism, a significant marker of the rate of tumour growth. Dickens's happy relationship with Dodds was crucial: although Dickens had a more academic intellect, Dodds was the leader, being imaginative, ambitious, and a superb tactician in committee. Dickens admired Dodds even if he would not have wanted to be in his shoes. Dickens's last appointment was as director of the Tobacco Research Council's research laboratories at Harrogate, Yorkshire, where he spent two years (1967–9) and was influential in advising the tobacco industry about a 'safer' cigarette. In addition to his research, he played a full part in the wider development of biochemistry and a decisive role in the organization of the first international congress of biochemistry in Cambridge in 1949. For eight years (1938–46) he was one of the editors of the *Biochemical Journal*. Throughout his career he was fortunate in the circumstances in which he worked, being supported first by the Medical Research Council and then by the Cancer Research Campaign. He was thus able to choose his research activities and never had to resort to self-promotion. He was an honorary member of the Biochemical Society (1967), of which he was chairman in 1950–51, and was elected a fellow of the Royal Society in 1946. In 1972 he received an honorary DSc from the University of Newcastle upon Tyne. He was also a fellow of the Institute of Biology (1968).

Dickens was a kind and gentle man, of medium height, spruce in appearance, and with a healthy complexion and a welcoming air. He was an attentive host. He enjoyed good food and was very put out when as external examiner at the University of Leeds he was accommodated in a temperance hotel. Frank Dickens died of throat cancer at his home, 15 Thakeham Drive, Ferring, near Worthing, Sussex, on 25 June 1986. PETER N. CAMPBELL, *rev.*

Sources R. H. S. Thompson and P. N. Campbell, *Memoirs FRS*, 33 (1987), 189–210 · personal knowledge (1996) · private information (1996) · *CGPLA Eng. & Wales* (1986)
Archives CUL, corresp. with Joseph Needham · Wellcome L., corresp. with Henry McIlwain
Wealth at death £17,256: probate, 18 Sept 1986, *CGPLA Eng. & Wales*

Dickens, Monica Enid (1915–1992), author, was born on 10 May 1915 at 52 Chepstow Villas, Bayswater, London, the fifth of the five children of Henry Charles Dickens (1878–1966), barrister, and his wife, Fanny (1876–1966), daughter of Herman and Emma Runge. Monica Dickens was a great-granddaughter of the novelist Charles Dickens. Her father was the eldest son of Dickens's eighth child, Sir Henry Fielding Dickens, common serjeant of London. She herself became one of the two or three best-selling women novelists of her generation, with the publication of forty-three books between 1939 and 1993.

Monica Dickens was educated at St Paul's Girls' School, on a double scholarship, but was expelled for throwing her school uniform over Hammersmith Bridge. A lively, attractive girl, with glamorous blonde hair, she joined the Central School of Speech Training and Dramatic Art but was asked to leave, she claimed, for not being able to act. Although she was presented at court in 1935, she was not a success as a débutante. With no career training, she took jobs as a cook-general in a variety of London houses. Then, at a chance meeting with a young publisher in 1937, she was encouraged to write about her experiences below stairs. Within three weeks she completed her first book, *One Pair of Hands*, which was an immediate success and earned the approbation of such influential figures as Compton Mackenzie and Malcolm Muggeridge. A humorous yet pointed depiction of the relationship between the upper classes and the servants, it revealed her keen eye for detail and her sense of the absurd.

Monica Dickens's first novel, *Mariana*, followed in 1940, and then in 1942, after she had taken up nursing as her war work, she wrote *One Pair of Feet*, based on her time at the Edward VII Hospital in Windsor. Before this was published, she moved to a factory as a fitter, making spare parts for Spitfires. Her novels *The Fancy* (1943) and *Thursday Afternoons* (1945) increased her reputation.

Praise came with every book, Monica Dickens's admirers at this time including J. B. Priestley, Rebecca West, and John Betjeman. She was becoming well established on the literary scene, and her novels were appearing at regular intervals. They included *The Happy Prisoner* (1946), *Joy and Josephine* (1948), and *Flowers on the Grass* (1949). *My Turn to Make the Tea* (1951) was inspired by her experiences as a junior reporter on a local newspaper. She was by now living in a thatched cottage called Bury End in the village of Hinxworth, Hertfordshire, where she kept horses and ponies and entertained her many friends from the Royal Ballet. For twenty years she wrote a weekly column for *Woman's Own*, and this brought her in touch with

Monica Enid Dickens (1915–1992), by Mark Gerson, 1964

a readership of 9 million. Her articles were noted for their originality and common-sense approach.

On 7 December 1951 Monica Dickens married Commander Roy Olin Stratton (1900–1985), US Navy, and went to live in Washington before settling into a large family house in the village of North Falmouth, on Cape Cod, Massachusetts. The house, which could sleep at least fourteen, was often full. As well as their two adopted daughters, Pamela and Prudence, there were countless friends and family members who came to visit, including Monica Dickens's parents and her sister Doady. She was very close to her family, who called her by her childhood nickname, Monty.

Monica Dickens's books continued with, among others, *The Winds of Heaven* (1955) and *The Heart of London* (1961). *Cobbler's Dream* (1963) indulged her lifelong love of horses and was later made into a thirty-part television serial—*Follyfoot*—while *Kate and Emma* (1964) was arguably her most accomplished novel. Monica Dickens's popularity was explained not so much by her skills as a story-teller as by her ability to sketch characters that were instantly recognizable. A book signing session in Sydney in 1965 was the birth of the language known as Strine, when Monica Dickens asked, 'Shall I write someone's name in it?' and the reply came, 'Emma Chisit'. 'To Emma Chisit, with best wishes'. 'No, Emma Chisit?' 'Twenty-three shillings'.

Between 1970 and 1971 Monica Dickens wrote a number of books for children, including the World's End series. These were followed by *Last Year when I was Young* (1974) and her autobiography, *An Open Book* (1978). In 1985 Roy Stratton died and Monica went back to her roots. In the village of Brightwalton, on the Berkshire downs, she found a thatched cottage that closely resembled her beloved Bury End. Here she entered her 'third age', surrounded by friends, family, dogs, and a garden overlooking a glorious valley. Novels written at this time included *Dear Doctor Lily* (1988), *Scarred* (1991), and her last book, *One of the Family*, which was published in 1993.

Her curiosity about people and her ability to empathize with their problems, combined with her deep understanding of human behaviour, led Monica Dickens, in the early 1970s, to become a Samaritan. She had great admiration for the Samaritans' founder, the Revd Chad Varah, and in 1974 she opened a branch in Boston, Massachusetts. Other branches followed, and, owing to her inspiration and persistence, the Samaritans eventually became a thriving organization throughout the United States. Her novel *The Listeners* (1970) was based on her experiences with the Samaritans in London. She said becoming a Samaritan was simply the most important thing she had ever done (Grove, 122). In 1981 she was appointed MBE.

Monica Dickens was modest enough to put much of her success down to 'unbelievable luck', but all her life she was determined to succeed. When things went wrong, her attitude was a brisk 'What's next?' She was warm, wise, and strong, sometimes stubborn, but always witty. When operated on for bowel cancer, she wrote to a friend, 'It's not a full stop—just a semi-colon' (Grove, 128). For Monica Dickens, a worthy descendant of her famous great-grandfather, not only on account of her literary skills, but also because of her strong sense of humanity, the full stop came two years later, in 1992, at the BUPA Dunedin Hospital, Reading. It was Christmas day. She was cremated and her ashes scattered a week later, on 1 January 1993.

CHARLES PICK

Sources personal knowledge (2004) · private information (2004) · M. Dickens, *An open book* (1978) · V. Grove, 'Unforgettable Monica Dickens', *Reader's Digest* (Dec 1993), 122–8
Archives priv. coll., MSS
Likenesses M. Gerson, photograph, 1964, NPG [*see illus.*] · photographs, Hult. Arch.
Wealth at death £458,971: *The Independent* (21 Aug 1993)

Dickenson, John (*c*.1570–1635/6), author and government official, began and ended his career in London but spent much of his adult life in the Low Countries and Germany. Nothing is known of his early life. He probably studied at Cambridge and may be identified with a pensioner at Clare College who matriculated in Easter term 1586.

In 1591 Dickenson published his first work, *Deorum concessus* ('The Assembly of the Gods'), a scholastic satire in Latin hexameters. This was followed by three English works, of which the most rewarding is *Arisbas: Euphues amongst his Slumbers* (1594). Although the title points to John Lyly, the erudite dedication to Sir Edward Dyer and the epistle to the reader tout the work's more substantial Sidneian lineage. The work itself mingles Sir Philip Sidney and dashes of Heliodorus, Apuleius, and Ovid in an Arcadian dreamscape. Interspersed are elegant lyrics which include avant-garde trochaic and classical metres:

poetically Dickenson is fluent and up to date. *Arisbas* manages a compendious breadth of contemporary and classical literary reference, often by avowed digression.

A similar pastoral dream vision frames Dickenson's *The Shepheardes Complaint: a Passionate Eclogue, Written in English Hexameters*. The work's date is unknown; it is usually given as 1596, but references to recent publications at the work's start, and allusions to this work in *Arisbas*, suggest 1592–3. Three of its lyrics were reprinted in *Englands Helicon* (1600).

Greene in Conceipt (1598) is now remembered for its title-page depiction of Robert Greene scribbling in his winding-sheet. The work raises Greene 'from his grave to write the tragique historie of faire *Valeria* of London' and owes as much again to Geoffrey Chaucer and Boccaccio, managing a calculatedly absurd density of similes, proverbs, and adduced exempla per page. Five more lyrics, one in classical hexameters, enliven the racy exemplary narrative of an old man and his young wife. Other works may be lost—the author mentions 'some sleight translations of generall novelties' in the epistle to *Greene in Conceipt*.

In 1598 Dickenson was hired by the bookseller Adam Islip to translate Louis Leroy's French version of Aristotle's *Politics* (1568; 1576), complete with Leroy's discursive introduction and massive commentary (based primarily on comparison to Plato and to classical and recent history). Dickenson dedicated the work to Sir Robert Sidney, and allowed his own name to be printed only in the presentation copy, now at Shrewsbury School (in all other copies the dedicatory epistle is signed only 'I.D.', the initials which the self-effacing Dickenson liked all his title-pages to bear). *Aristotles Politiques, or, Discourses of Government* advertises not only Dickenson's mastery of Latin, Greek, and French (the diplomatic language of the Low Countries), but also his familiarity with political theory and history. Dickenson may have already been employed as a spy in the Low Countries (*Salisbury MSS*, 5.254). But Aristotle seems to have been the passport to the next stage of his career.

As governor of Flushing, Robert Sidney may have been responsible for Dickenson's employment as secretary to George Gilpin, the queen's agent at The Hague. Dickenson later called Gilpin his Maecenas, for the post afforded him time to write his *Speculum tragicum*, printed at Delft in 1601. Dedicated to Gilpin, the *Speculum* offers Latin prose accounts of the most spectacular downfalls of kings and princes in the previous century, and includes a full account of the last days of the earl of Essex. When Gilpin died on 4 September 1602 Dickenson first wrote to Cecil and then hastened to London to learn his fate. By November, Ralph Winwood had been appointed Gilpin's successor, and Dudley Carleton had spoken to him to secure Dickenson's position. Ever-expanding editions of the *Speculum* were published in 1602, 1603, 1605, and 1611, adding an epitaph for Gilpin, verses to friends, and a set of 'Parallela tragica' (for instance Xerxes and Tamburlaine, Ariadne and Rosamund). At Leiden in 1606, Elzevier, who had taken over the publication of *Speculum* in 1602, printed Dickenson's *Miscellanea ex historiis Anglicanis concinnata*, a work of imaginary letters and orations of figures from English history in Latin verse; those between lovers have a marked affinity to Drayton's *England's Heroical Epistles*. According to an autograph note in a gift copy of the *Miscellanea* (Bodl. Oxf., MS Wood 332), a French translation of the *Speculum* was printed but subsequently called in; it does not appear to have survived.

After this period Dickenson's literary activities ceased and his political experience started to prove more useful to England. Through correspondence and travel he had acquired a grasp of the complexities of the Low Countries and the Holy Roman empire which few could match. The focus of England's diplomatic efforts was shifting from the now independent Dutch United Provinces (for his efforts the states presented Dickenson with a chain and medal worth £60) to the German protestant states. And in November 1610 Dickenson was appointed to act as the English agent to the princes possessioners of the disputed and strategically important Jülich–Cleves territories, Ernest, marquess of Brandenburg and Wolfgang William of Palatinate–Neuberg, arriving in Düsseldorf in mid-December. A long letter to Winwood records his first meeting with the two princes, and the Latin address he prepared for them. Despite his ability to negotiate with them in French and Italian, his 'credence', he admitted to the marquess, was in Latin (Sawyer, 3.243). Many of his letters from these years survive, most notably in the collection of his diplomatic colleague William Trumbull.

In 1613 Dickenson attended Princess Elizabeth from Arnhem to Cologne, meeting and then corresponding with Robert Sidney, and received the dedication of John Stephens's play *Cinthias Revenge*. Henry Wotton was sent to The Hague in 1614 to negotiate the Jülich–Cleves succession, and, soon discouraged, he asked to be joined by Dickenson, 'who through his long experience in these countries (where men's minds are not very transparent) will be of great use to me'. The treaty of Xanten concluded, Dickenson returned to London at the end of the year, with a covering note from Wotton to Secretary Winwood: 'This bearer is a full dispatch of himself, in whose conversation and erudition we have all taken singular contentment.' Without Dickenson, Wotton admitted, 'I had been very naked' (Smith, 2.53, 67).

On 28 July 1615 James sent Dickenson on a mission to Poland to persuade Sigismund III to suppress the *Alloquiorum Osiecensium … libri quinque* of the Jesuit apologist Gaspar Cichocki, with its inflammatory account of James's career and family history. On 20 October Dickenson delivered his customary Latin address to the king; he may have had further instructions to contribute to a Polish–Swedish conference over Pomerania. It is likely that he married some time after his return, for he now settled in London, being sworn a clerk of the privy council extraordinary on 10 May 1618. The first rumblings of the Thirty Years' War disturbed his domestication: with each vain mission to Brussels to protect the Palatinate and preserve peace (Conway and Weston in 1620; Digby in 1621; Weston in 1622) Dickenson went along as secretary. In

June 1626, as Christian IV prepared to invade the empire for the second time, Dickenson was readied for a mission to Denmark via the Netherlands; one rumour was that he was taking a million florins, although the trip may have been overtaken by events. On 7 November 1622 he had been granted one of the four ordinary clerkships of the privy council, a post he kept to his death and which allowed time for business ventures with his friend John More, in part directed to paying off the debts of their late master, Secretary Winwood. The letters to the Trumbulls from this period show a warmer, wittier, and happier man than is previously apparent. He had four children, all of whom survived him: Joanna (b. 1618); John (b. 1622); George; and Elizabeth (b. 1627). His wife, Elizabeth, died after giving birth to her namesake, and was buried in the church of St Martin-in-the-Fields on 1 June 1627. Dickenson was buried beside her on 11 January 1636. The council acted to sort the papers in his study in the Strand; administration of his estate was granted to the surveyor-general, Charles Harbord, on 7 March.

Learned and analytical, Dickenson is in his literary writings as in his political letters a master of the small details. His polyglot talents sometimes lead to verbosity, and those of his often colourful letters not in Latin are peppered with Latin tags. But his ability to unpick the wording of treaties, where ambiguous syntax and confusions of translation were rife, and his insightful analyses of people and politics, were valued. The veteran French diplomat Jean Hotman feared diverting Dickenson from his studies when the two lodged together in Düsseldorf. Dickenson himself complained about only one kind of diplomatic duty, as he wrote to his colleague Trumbull: 'for what have we to doe with Germane complements and daily drinking?' (BL, Add. MS 72283, fol. 11r). His Latinity and circumspection have hindered his reputation as an author: only recently has it become clear that the English author Dickenson was identical with the Latin poet Dickensonus, and *Aristotles Politiques* has not previously been identified as his. His role in the movement for English verses in classical metres has been largely ignored. In the broad view his literary achievements show a deep talent and facility, and their function as preparation for a career of state service is notable.   GAVIN ALEXANDER

Sources BL, Add. MSS 72283, 72399 • Edmondes papers, BL, Stowe MSS, 171, 172, 174, 175 • CSP dom., 1602–36 • CSP Venice, 1620–26 • *Report on the manuscripts of the marquis of Downshire*, 6 vols. in 7, HMC, 75 (1924–95) • *Report on the manuscripts of his grace the duke of Buccleuch and Queensberry … preserved at Montagu House*, 3 vols. in 4, HMC, 45 (1899–1926), vol. 1 [Winwood papers] • *Calendar of the manuscripts of the most hon. the marquis of Salisbury*, 24 vols., HMC, 9 (1883–1976) • *The manuscripts of the Earl Cowper*, 3 vols., HMC, 23 (1888–9) • J. V. Kitto, ed., *The register of St Martin-in-the-Fields, London, 1619–1636*, Harleian Society, register section, 66 (1936) • M. Fitch, ed., *Index to administrations in the prerogative court of Canterbury*, 6: 1631–1648, British RS, 100 (1986) • PRO, PROB 6/15, fol. 157v • E. Sawyer, ed., *Memorials of affairs of state … from the original papers of … Sir Ralph Winwood*, 3 vols. (1725) • *The life and letters of Sir Henry Wotton*, ed. L. P. Smith, 2 vols. (1907) • A. Kraushar, ed., *Poselstwo Dickensona do Zygmunta III w sprawie książki awtaczającej domowi Stuartów (r. 1615)*, 32 (Warsaw, 1909) • W. Hendricks, 'John Dickenson: the man and his works', PhD diss., Northwestern University, 1941 • M. J. Svob,

'The scholar's *Aliquid* of John Dickenson', PhD diss., University of Illinois, 1966 · *Prose and verse by John Dickenson*, ed. A. B. Grosart (privately printed, Blackburn, 1878) · *Dudley Carleton to John Chamberlain, 1603–1624: Jacobean letters*, ed. M. Lee (1972) · *APC, 1623–36* · Venn, *Alum. Cant.* · BL, Hardwicke papers, Add. MS 35832
Archives BL, Trumbull MSS, esp. Add. MS 72283 · BL, Edmondes papers, Stowe MSS 171, 172, 174, 175 · Northants. RO, Winwood papers

Dickenson [*née* Welsh], **Sarah** (1868–1954), trade unionist and suffragist, was born on 28 March 1868 in Borsall Road, Hulme, Manchester, the second of five children of Scot John Welsh, enameller and coach-painter, and his wife, Jane Ferguson. From 1879, when she was eleven years old, until 1895, Sarah Welsh worked in Howarth's mill, a cotton mill in Salford. During these years she became involved in the efforts of the Manchester and Salford Trades Council to organize women workers and by 1889 had become secretary of the small Manchester and Salford Association of Machine, Electrical, and Other Women Workers. When the Manchester and Salford Women's Trade Union Council was set up in 1895, as one of the few working women involved in its launch, Sarah Welsh was appointed one of two full-time organizers. The aims of the council were to work for improved wages and working conditions by encouraging women to join unions which would be able to negotiate on their behalf. In 1896 Sarah married William Roger Dickenson, an iron enameller who had his own bicycle workshop; they had no children.

Sarah Dickenson firmly believed that no improvement in women's working conditions would take place until women, as voters, could influence legislation. This belief was shared by other women textile workers who related their commitment to the extension of the franchise to women to the situation of working women and the wider labour movement. Accordingly she resigned from the Women's Trade Union Council in 1904, when the council decided that support of women's suffrage was outside its remit. As an alternative, Sarah Dickenson and Eva Gore Booth set up the Manchester and Salford Women's Trade and Labour Council with a clear commitment to women's suffrage.

Sarah Dickenson's involvement in the issue of women's suffrage dates from the late 1890s when she became a member of the North of England Society for Women's Suffrage (NESWS), an organization modelled closely on the National Union of Women's Suffrage Societies (NUWSS) set up in 1897 with Millicent Fawcett as its president. Sarah Dickenson took a leading part in its activities, and was closely involved in the 1900–01 campaign to petition women factory workers in support of women's suffrage. When this petition, with almost 30,000 signatures, was presented to the Lancashire MPs at the House of Commons on 8 March 1901, Sarah Dickenson was among the speakers. In 1903 she was a founder member of the Lancashire and Cheshire Women Textile and Other Workers Representation Committee, formed to select and support a parliamentary candidate who would campaign for women's suffrage. The NESWS split in 1905 over the issue of targeting factory workers and a number of the executive committee members, including Sarah Dickenson, resigned to set up an alternative society, the National Industrial and Professional Women's Suffrage Society.

Sarah Dickenson worked for women's suffrage at a national as well as a local level. She was employed periodically as a salaried organizer for the NUWSS and took part in several major demonstrations on behalf of women's suffrage. In 1906 she spoke during a large deputation to the prime minister, Sir Henry Campbell-Bannerman, on the right of women wage-earners to political enfranchisement.

In 1918 when a limited number of women were granted the vote, the Women's Trade Union Council and the Women's Trade and Labour Council merged to form the women's group of the Manchester and Salford Trades Council. Sarah Dickenson continued to play an active role in the work of the trades council: from 1920 to 1925 she was a member of the council's executive committee, and secretary of the women's group; in 1925 and 1926 she served on the employment exchange committee and the women's housing advisory committee; and she was a member of the war pensions committee and the children's subcommittee. She remained a delegate to the council until 1930, representing the small union of the Machine, Electrical, and other Women Workers.

Sarah Dickenson lived throughout her life in and around Manchester, and in 1931 she was appointed MBE for her services to the city. In 1923 she was appointed a JP, a post she held until 1939. She died on 26 December 1954 at her home, 107 Birch Hall Lane, Rusholme, Manchester, and was cremated at Manchester southern cemetery.

SERENA KELLY

Sources J. Liddington and J. Norris, *One hand tied behind us: the rise of the women's suffrage movement* (1978) · *DLB*, vol. 6 · O. Banks, *The biographical dictionary of British feminists*, 1 (1985) · *CGPLA Eng. & Wales* (1955)
Archives People's History Museum, Manchester, labour party archives
Wealth at death £1854 7s. 7d.: probate, 2 March 1955, *CGPLA Eng. & Wales*

Dickenson, Thomas (*bap.* 1717, *d.* 1751), grocer, was baptized in the parish of St Mary's, Stafford, in November 1717, the younger of two sons of Thomas and Elizabeth Dickenson. Little is known of his early life, but in May 1741 Dickenson became a freeman of Worcester having been apprenticed to grocer Timothy Edwards, probably for the usual seven years. In the March of that year he was elected to the annual office of overseer of the poor for the parish of St Nicholas, where he was churchwarden in 1743 and 1744, attending parish meetings there until 1751.

On 9 August 1748 Dickenson married Jane Bearcroft of Evesham, who had been left £600 by her father, with £200 to come after her mother's death. According to a certificate signed in 1764, the Dickensons' daughter Frances was christened on 5 March 1750; strangely, despite the rector's claim that it was a 'true copy of the Register Book of the Parish of St Nicholas' (Worcester Borough RO, Bearcroft deeds 3964/25), there is no corresponding entry in the actual book.

Dickenson left detailed records of his Foregate Street shop: the bought ledger, 1744–51, contains names and addresses of his suppliers; his account book, 1740–49, shows method and dates of payment; while in his day-books for the years 1740–51 Dickenson recorded 252 named customers. Approximately half the customer entries include their occupation, address, method of payment, and details of their purchases. Some, perhaps as many as 18 per cent, were themselves retailers. Just over half his customers came from Worcester, but he also supplied people from Droitwich, Evesham, and Bromyard, and as far afield as Shrewsbury, Wolverhampton, Stafford, and Bridgnorth.

Dickenson had a good number of middle-class customers, among whom were apothecaries, clergy, and attorneys. There were also skilled craftspeople, including several who would rank quite high within the hierarchy of working people, such as a tailor and a mantua maker. Their systems of payment varied considerably: cash, credit, bills or notes for other goods or services, or a combination of these methods. Some, such as a gardener, paid for goods by 'work done', others paid in kind; the carpenter settled his account with a pig!

Dickenson mainly obtained his basic supplies from thirty-three Bristol firms, including sugar imported from the colonies, soap, and flour. More sophisticated produce came from twenty-one London companies: candied fruit and ginger, tea, Turkey coffee, 'pistache nutts', Durham mustard. Gloucester supplied snuff and twine; starch, hardware, and hops came from Worcester, clay pipes from Broseley, and anchovies from Chester. Many of his suppliers were on or near the transport system of the River Severn or its coastal links; goods from London combined River Thames shipping with road haulage. Best-selling items were tea, followed closely by sugar and sugar products. Dickenson stocked such ready-made goods as several varieties of biscuit, including 'Savoy biscakes', and a range of confectionery—orange chips, round drops, barley sugar, and Bristol chocolates. He also sold alcohol, some hardwares, and tobacco. His wares clearly define him as a grocer in the mid-eighteenth-century interpretation of that term; unlike the mercers, he had little in the way of cloth, clothes, haberdashery, or apothecary wares.

The account books Dickenson kept are of special interest, being those of a young man just setting up in the retail trade. They illustrate the eighteenth-century system of delayed payment of bills by both customer and retailer; Dickenson generally paid his smaller suppliers within four weeks, but larger companies had to wait for several months. He allowed customer discounts for cash and short-term credit, yet his daybooks indicate an income of only two or three sales per day and the expected extended credit must have made considerable demands on the finances of a new shopkeeper.

Dickenson was buried in Worcester on 23 August 1751; his wife had died twelve days earlier. Although Dickenson was probably not regarded as an influential man by his contemporaries, his up-to-date selection of goods and the range of his suppliers were doubtless important in helping to promote in Worcester and its environs the rapid expansion of wares in the mid-1700s. Dickenson's records are helpful in illuminating an area which suffers from a paucity of documentary evidence—that of the eighteenth-century county-town retailer, his wares, and his customers.

POLLY HAMILTON

Sources S. A. Stone, 'Grocers and groceries: the distribution of groceries in four contiguous English counties, c.1660–1750', MPhil diss., University of Wolverhampton, 1994 · C. Shammas, *The pre-industrial consumer in England and America* (1990) · account book, 1740–49, Staffs. RO, Hand Morgan collection, HM29/1 · daybooks, 1740–51, Staffs. RO, Hand Morgan collection, HM29/2–29/4 · bought ledger, 1744–51, Staffs. RO, Hand Morgan collection, HM29/5 · IGI · parish records, 9 Aug 1748, Worcs. RO [marriage] · parish records, 23 Aug 1751, Worcs. RO [burial]
Archives Worcs. RO, parish records [microfilm] | Staffs. RO, Hand Morgan MSS, HM 29/1–5 · Worcs. RO, Bearcroft deeds · Worcs. RO, churchwarden's account book · Worcs. RO, freemen book

Dickenson, William (1584/5–1642/3), Church of England clergyman, was the son of Thomas Dickenson, cook at Eton College. He was educated at the college, then matriculated on 15 April 1603, aged eighteen, from St Alban Hall, Oxford, where he graduated BA in 1606. He moved to Merton and proceeded MA in 1612 and BD in 1619, having become chaplain to the earl of Pembroke, chancellor of the university. That year he preached at the midsummer assizes at Reading. The sermon was a highly political one on the nature of royal authority, perhaps prompted by the recent death of Bishop Overall, whose extreme views on divine right it espoused. In transparent allusions to current political debate Dickenson managed to compliment personalities—notably Bacon—at that time in royal favour, while attacking others—the Howards, Coke—who were in disgrace. Its publication, as *The King's Right* (1619), followed rapidly: the impression is that this was part of a positioning exercise on behalf of his patron.

Soon afterwards, and perhaps as a reward, Dickenson was presented to the two contiguous and lucrative parishes of Appleton and Besselsleigh, close to Oxford on the Berkshire side of the Thames. There was another claimant to Appleton, Thomas Drope, chaplain of Magdalen College and well known locally. The archbishop's court ruled in Dickenson's favour, but he was never accepted by his parishioners. One reason may have been that it was 1625 before he received from the moderately Calvinistic Bishop Davenant his licence to preach. In an explicit effort to influence his parishioners individually he dedicated to them a catechism, *Milk for Babes* (1628). The work was decidedly Arminian in tone and its impact seems to have been disappointing, for he took over the small local manor of Tinteyn and began to concentrate on farming. In or before 1624 Dickenson had married Marie, daughter of Edmund Culpeper, probably a Berkshire clergyman; they had four sons and two daughters, the eldest of whom was Edmund (*bap.* February 1625).

In 1642 Dickenson, like all adult males, was expected to sign the protestation, a parliamentary loyalty oath. His answer was evasive, showing that he maintained his earlier royalist opinions. The manors of Appleton and Besselsleigh had been acquired during the 1630s by William Lenthall, now speaker of the Commons. As the civil war began with campaigning in the midlands, it became clear that the Thames-side parishes around Oxford would be vulnerable to a royalist advance and Dickenson may have seemed a threat. In October 1642, representatives from both his parishes were received at the bar of the House of Commons with a petition against him; he was declared a delinquent and deprived. The serjeant-at-arms was directed to take him into custody, but there is no evidence that he did so. Dickenson had ceased to keep his parish registers in April 1641 and was unwell when he made his will on 7 November. He was dead by the time James Marten replaced him as rector of Besselsleigh in 1643. His will, which was proved on 28 September 1650, left property both in Appleton and around Marlow. His eldest son, Edmund, became a fashionable physician after the Restoration; Marie Dickenson continued farming at Tinteyn until her death in 1685.   MANFRED BROD

Sources *JHC*, 2 (1640–42), 823 · Wood, *Ath. Oxon.*, new edn, 4.477 · *The life and times of Anthony Wood*, ed. A. Clark, 2, OHS, 21 (1892), 134 · J. Gibson, ed., *Oxfordshire and north Berkshire protestation returns and tax assessments, 1641–1642*, Oxfordshire RS, 59 (1994), 177, 181 · Berks. RO, D/A2 d4, fol. 46 · will, Berks. RO, D/A1/62/185 · Foster, *Alum. Oxon.* · W. Sterry, ed., *The Eton College register, 1441–1698* (1943), 103 · Berks. RO, D/A2 C.4, fol. 180

Dickie, Edgar Primrose (1897–1991), theologian and Church of Scotland minister, was born on 12 August 1897 in Dumfries, the younger son of William Dickie (1856–1916), editor of the *Dumfries and Galloway Standard*, and his wife, Jane Paterson (1859–1917). After attending Dumfries Academy, he was commissioned in the King's Own Scottish Borderers in 1914 (reportedly having added a year to his age, and later subtracted one to participate in the Second World War). He served in France, Flanders, and Palestine, was wounded, and was awarded the Military Cross.

On demobilization in 1918 Dickie took a first in classics at Edinburgh University (1921), followed by a first in *literae humaniores* at Christ Church, Oxford (1923), a brilliant BD degree at Edinburgh (1926), and a year's study at Marburg and Tübingen. In 1927 he married Ishbel Holmes Johnston (1899–1985), daughter of Andrew Freer Johnson and his wife, Magdalen Ross Holmes, of Edinburgh. That year he was ordained, and ministered at St Cuthbert's, Lockerbie (1927–33), and at St Anne's, Edinburgh (1933–5). His reputation enhanced by various examinerships at Edinburgh University and the publication of *The Obedience of a Christian Man* (1934), Dickie was appointed to Scotland's oldest chair of divinity, at St Andrews (1935–67), where, said a colleague recklessly, he 'brought Scottish wit and commonsense to bear on continental theological non-sense' (Black).

As general superintendent of the kirk's huts and canteens work, Dickie accompanied the British expeditionary forces in 1940, and landed on the Normandy beaches with the liberation army in 1944, when he was mentioned in dispatches. He recounted his experiences vividly in *Normandy to Nijmegen* (1946). His many other publications included *Revelation and Response* (1937), *God is Light* (1953), *The Unchanging Gospel* (1960), and translations of Karl Heim. His whimsical humour went into three delightful volumes for children; one review incensed a scholarly friend by beginning 'This is pure nonsense' (personal knowledge). *Punch* approved by carrying a lengthy series from the pen of this professor who was once pictured on the front page of a Scottish daily, skiing from home to college. Ishbel, an amused abetter of such idiosyncrasies, was herself known for her work in the kirk at large, and for tongue-in-cheek letters to newspapers.

With no children of their own, the Dickies had a special concern for the welfare of students, particularly ex-servicemen finding it hard to readjust from war to Wellhausen. Edgar was a favourite event-opener, after-dinner speaker, and preacher in churches throughout Scotland. He received a royal chaplaincy (1956) and honorary doctorates from Edinburgh (1946) and St Andrews (1969), but he valued equally the rare bestowal of an honorary blue from the St Andrews athletics association, and life membership of the union.

Edgar Dickie was above all a gentle man, who walked uneasily in the knockabout world of controversial divinity. His department dealt with apologetics rather than dogmatics, but it seemed bewildering that a gallant soldier should not be moved occasionally to send a critical word to war. That his solid, entertaining, doctrinally liberal works sparked off no debate perhaps detracts from their lasting significance. If the acid test of any theology asks 'What does it deny?', one might find a difficulty in assessing Dickie's importance. He tended to sidestep M. Arnold's 'long contention', and might inhibit robust discussion by facing even some preposterous statement with the disarming rejoinder that two men might think differently without one of them being wicked. Such a surfeit (dare one say misuse?) of Christian charity dismayed his friends and gave rise to cheerful mimicry among his students. There was no malice about it, however, and it took away not at all from the affectionate regard in which he was held throughout the university.

The Dickies had each lost a brother in the First World War, and they dedicated themselves to doing their own work plus that which their brothers had been deprived of accomplishing. Edgar died at Craigmount, The Scores, St Andrews, on 28 June 1991 and, in the same humanitarian spirit as Ishbel six years before, bequeathed his body for purposes of medical research.   J. D. DOUGLAS

Sources personal knowledge (2004) · private information (2004) · *WWW* · M. Black, *St Mary's College Bulletin* [U. St Andr.], 10 (1968) · 'Rev. Prof. Edgar Dickie: 32 years at St Andrews', *The Scotsman* (3 July 1991) · *St Andrews Citizen* (5 July 1991) · senate minutes, U. St Andr., FUFCS 99, FESIX, 10, 135, 769–70, X, 430
Wealth at death £294,454.68: resworn confirmation, 28 Aug 1991, NA Scot., SC/CO 533/65 & 533/126 · £17,767.47: further grant, 15 Oct 1991, NA Scot., SC/CO 533/65 & 533/126

Dickie, George (*bap.* 1812, *d.* 1882), botanist, was baptized at Old Machar, Aberdeen on 23 November 1812, the son of

John Dickie, purser in the Royal Navy, and his wife, Isabella Fowler. Born in the house in which he was to spend most of his life, he was educated at the grammar school and Marischal College in Aberdeen, graduating AM from the latter in 1830. He then went on to study medicine at the universities of Aberdeen and Edinburgh, qualifying as MRCS in 1834. His ambition of becoming a naval surgeon having had to be abandoned for domestic reasons, he then reluctantly entered into medical practice locally while devoting every spare moment to his real passion, field botany.

Already Dickie had explored the local countryside sufficiently to supply a list for the area to H. C. Watson's *New Botanist's Guide* (1832), and further work led to a slim *Flora Aberdonensis* (1838) and eventually to the rich store of information on which William Macgillivray was able to draw in 1855 for his pathmaking ecological essay, *The Natural History of Deeside and Braemar*. A fern found in a local cave was named *Cystopteris dickieana* in his honour; it was later found in several other parts of Scotland and widely in the Arctic, but its claims to be a separate species were disproved by allozyme study over a century and a half later. Dickie studied and collected extensively lichens and fungi, but it was seaweeds that from 1844 increasingly engaged his attention. These were at that period the subject of intensive investigation in which Dickie played a major part. In later years they would become his exclusive interest, and his expertise was such that collections received from around the world at Kew were regularly referred to him for determination and description. Though primarily a taxonomist, he was nevertheless also deeply interested in plant morphology and physiology.

In 1839 Dickie's botanical abilities were at last drawn on professionally with his appointment as lecturer in that subject, and the next year in materia medica as well, by King's College, Aberdeen, which conferred an honorary MD on him in 1842. In 1844 he was further appointed college librarian. From that strong foothold he moved in 1849 to the more substantial one of professor of natural history in the newly established Queen's College in Belfast, where his teaching responsibilities extended beyond botany and zoology to geology and physical geography. This Irish interlude was no less productive, considerably increasing knowledge of plant distribution in the northern half of the country and culminating in an excellent little *Flora of Ulster* (1864), which somewhat belied its name by taking in the botanically interesting area of Sligo and Leitrim as well. Most of the records in this were of his own making.

From Belfast Dickie returned to Aberdeen in 1860 on the creation of a separate botanical chair in the newly-merged university, and that same year his long-delayed *Botanist's Guide to the Counties of Aberdeen, Banff, and Kincardine* was finally published. That very first teaching session, however, he had the misfortune to develop pneumonia while leading a group of his students in the Cairngorms. This left him with chronic bronchitis and increasing deafness, removing him from active fieldwork and, by 1876, from any further teaching. Dickie was known for his intensely earnest manner and a deep piety, which did not prevent him early accepting Darwin's evolutionary theory. Retiring in 1877, Dickie died in Aberdeen on 15 July 1882, a year after the crowning of his career with election as a fellow of the Royal Society. He was survived by his wife, Agnes Williamson Low.   B. D. JACKSON, *rev.* D. E. ALLEN

Sources P. J. A. [P. J. Anderson], ed., *Aurora borealis academica: Aberdeen University appreciations, 1860–1889* (1899), 326–35 · *Transactions of the Botanical Society* [Edinburgh], 16 (1886), 3–6 · *Proceedings of the Linnean Society of London* (1882–3), 40 · *Journal of Botany, British and Foreign*, 21 (1883), 80 · P. J. Anderson, ed., *Officers and graduates of University and King's College, Aberdeen, MVD–MDCCCLX*, New Spalding Club, 11 (1893) · J. W. H. Trail, 'Natural science in the universities', *Studies in the history and development of the University of Aberdeen*, ed. P. J. Anderson (1906), 157 ff. · R. L. Praeger and W. R. Megaw, *A flora of the north-east of Ireland*, 2nd edn (1938), xiv · *PRS*, 34 (1882–3), xii-xiii · *Scottish Naturalist*, new ser., 1 (1883–4), 3–8 · parish register (births and baptisms), Aberdeen, Old Machar, 23 Nov 1812 · *CCI* (1882)
Archives U. Aberdeen, herbarium
Likenesses engraved portrait, repro. in Anderson, *Aurora borealis*, facing p. 326 · photograph, Carnegie Mellon University, Pittsburgh, Hunt Botanical Library
Wealth at death £8117 12s.: confirmation, 11 Aug 1882, *CCI*

Dickin, Maria Elisabeth (1870–1951), founder of the People's Dispensary for Sick Animals (PDSA), known by her friends as Mia, was born at 1 Farrington Terrace, South Hackney, Middlesex, on 22 September 1870, daughter of William George Dickin (*d.* in or before 1899), Wesleyan minister, and his wife, Ellen Maria, *née* Exell. Maria was the eldest of their eight children, and to supplement the family's slender income she established a voice production studio in Wimpole Street. On 1 September 1899 she married—at the parish church of St John the Evangelist, Westminster—her first cousin Arnold Francis Dickin (*b.* 1874/5), son of Henry Dickin. Her husband was an accountant living at 4 Orlando Road, Clapham. The 1901 census found the couple living at 12 Mount Nod Road, Streatham, with one servant, and described Arnold Dickin as 'accountants' articled clerk' and Mia as 'professor of singing'. She later gave up her studio to keep house in Hampstead Heath; they had no children.

Maria Dickin collected short 'thoughts and sayings' on religious subjects of Reginald John Campbell (1867–1956)—then Congregational minister of City Temple, London—and published them without commentary as *Suggestive Thoughts from the Temple* (1905). She was a practising spiritualist and became active in the revived movement for religious healing. For many years she collaborated with James Moore Hickson, editor and publisher of *The Healer*, in promoting 'Sunday evenings with the sick', in the course of which she too was healed. Her preoccupation with pain shifted from human beings to animals when she began visiting the poor in the East End. In 1917 the sight of the injured animals there was, she later recalled, 'a revelation to me' and 'made me indescribably miserable' (Dickin, 1). At about this time she went through the 'heartrending' experience of nursing her sick dog, which eventually had to be put down, and in describing what followed she momentarily set aside her customary reticence about herself. A 'deep and sacred experience' (ibid., 2) united her own suffering with a semi-obsessive concern about the sufferings of others in the powerful combination often found in reforming pioneers at their moment of creative vision. The mystery of human pain had long troubled her and now became haunting, engulfing her in 'an agony of spirit' (ibid.) and temporarily threatening her religious faith. Sitting alone on holiday in a hotel garden, with her golfing friends elsewhere, she felt the eyes of millions of animals focused imploringly upon her. It was 'a command I dare not refuse' (ibid.).

Dickin's hunt for East End premises led her to a sympathetic clergyman who lent her a cellar in Whitechapel, and there she opened the first People's Dispensary for Sick Animals of the Poor on 17 November 1917. In the PDSA's early documents Baroness de Teissier was listed as co-founder but this shadowy figure soon faded from the scene. By 1922 Dickin had become 'honorary director', chairing the PDSA's committee of management—roles that she retained until shortly before she died. No large donations from her were publicized and at no stage did she use the PDSA's literature for self-advertisement; not until 1949 did an annual report publish her photograph. The PDSA aimed to provide free treatment in dispensaries for animals whose owners could not afford a vet. Non-political and non-sectarian, it focused entirely on remedial work and on the educational effort flowing from that, leaving others to prosecute cruelty. Understandably, prominent registered vets were at first discouraging, although Dickin persuaded an experienced and well-known unregistered one, named Hartshorn, to work with her. For the rest of her life vets' hostility threatened her movement, with the Royal Society for the Prevention of Cruelty to Animals and the PDSA on one occasion aligned on opposite sides in a lawsuit.

The new movement prospered by drawing together two humanitarian strands: the individualist preoccupation with pain, often emphasized in the analogy that the PDSA drew between human and animal suffering; and the collectivist environmentalism involved in recognizing that working-class cruelty flowed ineluctably from economic necessity and required a co-ordinated remedy. In its first decade the PDSA grew very fast, at first within London but after Dickin's caravan tour of 1923—its mare provided by her husband—within many parts of England. As with other pioneering causes the evil under attack seemed far more prevalent than had been at first supposed, and in the same year the first of several overseas branches was founded, in Tangier. Also in 1923 the PDSA was incorporated, and within seven years its annual income had grown five-fold, more than doubling again during the 1930s. In her will, however, Dickin referred to 'the strain ... endured' by herself and by the PDSA's staff during its early years and especially in the national crisis of 1930–32. She published The Cry of the Animal and other humanitarian works, edited PDSA periodicals, and—combining energy with firmness—ran the organization almost as a family gathering, with its annual staff dinner and its annual church parade and service. She also instituted the Dickin medal (the 'animals' VC'), awarded to any animal displaying conspicuous gallantry and devotion to duty

associated with the armed forces or civil defence in the Second World War; the first was awarded in 1943, and the 53 beneficiaries included 31 pigeons, 18 dogs, 3 horses, and one cat. Her OBE of 1929 was raised in 1948 to a CBE.

All too little is known about Maria Dickin's private life, although she listed 'music, literary work and philanthropic' as her recreations in Who's Who. She died of influenzal broncho-pneumonia at her home, 4 Lansdowne House, Lansdowne Road, Kensington, London, on 1 March 1951, her husband having predeceased her. In her last will, made in 1947, there were two executors: Maurice Cole of Radlett, an accountant; and Albert Webb of Knightsbridge, deputy chairman of the PDSA. In this will Dickin left many bequests to her sisters and to PDSA officers, but she drew special attention to Albert Webb, noting her gratitude to him 'for the many acts of kindness readily given to me' and 'for his untiring efforts' in helping her to establish the PDSA, and expressing the hope that he would take her place as its chairman. She asked the trustees to employ her residuary estate to set up a foundation in her name.

By 1950 the PDSA was providing in Britain a regular service in 207 communities, not to mention its animal ambulances and hospitals and its five homes for stray dogs. By the 1960s, according to the PDSA's annual reports, many of its early dispensaries were disappearing in slum-clearance schemes: mass affluence and suburbanization were carrying away the Whitechapel world where Dickin's movement had begun, and were opening up new opportunities and structures. The PetAid hospital and PetAid practice gradually replaced the dispensary, and a network of retail shops reinforced more traditional ways of raising funds. Yet the PDSA retained its name and its objective remained the same: the protection of sick animals whose owners could not pay for the necessary treatment.   BRIAN HARRISON

Sources M. E. Dickin, The cry of the animal (PDSA, [n.d.]) • People's Dispensary for Sick Animals, annual reports, PDSA head office, Telford, Shropshire • F. Montague, Let the good work go on [n.d.] • The Times (3 March 1951), 8; (6 March 1951), 6 • Mia Dickin: the story of Maria Dickin, founder of the PDSA and pioneer in the field of animal welfare (PDSA, [n.d.]) • WW (1951) • b. cert. • m. cert. • d. cert. • will, 1 Dec 1947, principal registry of the family division, London, probate department • census returns, 1901

Likenesses photograph, repro. in PDSA 36th Annual Report • photographs, PDSA head office, Telford, Shropshire

Wealth at death £8970 19s. 10d.: probate, 20 July 1951, CGPLA Eng. & Wales

Dickins, Frederick Victor (1838–1915), Japanologist, was born on 24 May 1838, the eldest son of Thomas Dickins JP, of Edgemoor House, Broughton, Manchester. He was educated at private schools and then at the Lycée Buonaparte in Paris. In 1855 he became an apprentice at Manchester Royal Infirmary, and he subsequently took his medical degrees at London University, qualifying in 1859 as a member of the Royal College of Surgeons. On 13 May 1862 he joined the navy as an acting assistant surgeon, and he served in east Asia on HMS Euryalus and HMS Coromandel, first setting foot in Japan in 1863. On 10 October 1864 he

Frederick Victor Dickins (1838–1915), by unknown artist, c.1900–10

was detached from his ship and appointed surgeon in charge of the naval sick-quarters at Yokohama; he remained there until 1 February 1866, when he brought his naval career to an end. By this time he had already been much impressed by Japan and had made considerable progress with the language, sufficient to be able to refer to a number of Japanese books in 'Hints to students of the Japanese language' (1864) and to translate the 100 poems of the *Hyakunin isshu*, producing one of the first translations ever made from Japanese literature into English.

On returning to England, Dickins was admitted to the Middle Temple on 21 November 1867, and on 10 June 1870 he was called to the bar. On 13 May 1869 he married Mary Jane Wilkinson (d. 1920), daughter of William Massingale Wilkinson of Manchester. While in England he mixed with some Japanese students in London and continued to translate Japanese literature. He returned to Japan with his wife in 1871 and practised in the consular courts there until 1878, when his health broke down. On 1 January 1879 he, his wife, and their three children (a fourth child was born subsequently) left Japan. The most celebrated case in which he was involved during those years in Japan concerned some indentured Chinese coolies who were being taken to Peru on the Peruvian ship *Maria Luz* and who were seized by Japanese officials when the ship put in to Japan. Dickins was retained by the captain and argued not only that Japan had no right to detain a foreign vessel but that similar work contracts were enforceable in Japan in the case of indentured prostitutes. Although the presiding judge refused to accept this argument, it had the effect of

embarrassing the government into partially abolishing the indenture system for prostitutes.

After his return to England, Dickins began to establish himself in legal practice, including a spell at the bar in Egypt, but in 1882 he became assistant registrar of the University of London; he was appointed registrar in 1896. Upon his retirement in 1901 he was made CB and moved to Seend, Wiltshire. In 1909–10 he was given the honorary title of reader by the University of Bristol, and he gave three lectures entitled 'Old Japan' in 1911.

Although Dickins was, along with his friend Ernest Satow, a founder member of the Asiatic Society of Japan and made some contributions to its *Transactions*, it was after his return to England that he did his most important work on Japan. In 1880 he published the first scholarly study of the art of Hokusai in any language, and he regularly reviewed books on Japan for *The Athenaeum*. He firmly believed in the value of transliteration, and was convinced that roman script would eventually replace Japanese script; he published several texts in this form, each with the Japanese script and a translation, such as *Taketori monogatari* (1888) and *Primitive and Medieval Japanese Texts* (1906). Like many of his generation he made much use of Japanese informants, in particular the learned folklorist Kumagusu Minakata (1867–1941), who resided in London during the 1890s and who seems to have assisted Dickins without due acknowledgement ever being made. Dickins never overcame the feeling that Japanese literature did not measure up to the Greek and Latin classics, and in 1905 he went so far as to write that 'my falling in love with things Japanese in the early '60s was a terrible misfortune for me' (Dickins to Satow, 30 Aug 1905, PRO, 30/33/11/4), but he continued to apply the highest standards of classical philology to his work on Japanese literature and to believe that it was worth studying. He died of cancer at his home, Seend Lodge, Seend, Wiltshire, on 16 August 1915.

P. F. KORNICKI

Sources *Collected works of Frederick Victor Dickins*, 7 vols. (1999) [incl. introduction by P. F. Kornicki] · *The Lancet* (4 Sept 1915) · *Wiltshire Archaeological and Natural History Magazine*, 39 (1915–17), 273–7 · F. V. Dickins, 'Medical and surgical journal of HMS *Coromandel*', 1864, PRO, ADM 101/178 · P. F. Kornicki, 'The Japanese collection in the Bibliotheca Lindesiana', *Bulletin of the John Rylands University Library*, 75 (1993), 209–300 · Hatsue Kawamura, *F. V. Dikkinzu: nihon bungaku eiyaku no senkusha* (1997) · CGPLA Eng. & Wales (1915) · m. cert. · d. cert.

Archives Minakata Kumagusu Kinenkan, Shirahama, Japan · Oxf. U. Mus. NH, letters to Sir. E. B. Poulton · PRO, corresp. of Dickins, his wife, and daughter with Sir Ernest Satow, PRO 30/33 · UCL, letters to Karl Pearson

Likenesses portrait, c.1900–1910, priv. coll. [see illus.] · photograph, repro. in M. Paske-Smith, *Western barbarians in Japan and Formosa in Tokugawa days, 1603–1868*, 2nd edn (1968)

Wealth at death £20,854 13s. 9d.: probate, 19 Oct 1915, CGPLA Eng. & Wales

Dickinson, Sir Arthur Lowes (1859–1935), accountant, was born on 8 August 1859 at Langham Chambers, Marylebone, London, the elder son of Lowes Cato *Dickinson (1819–1908), a portrait painter, and his wife, Margaret Ellen, *née* Williams (d. 1882). Arthur's younger brother was the historian and fellow of King's College, Cambridge,

Goldsworthy Lowes *Dickinson (1862–1932). Arthur was educated at Charterhouse School and at King's College, Cambridge, where he obtained a first in mathematics in 1882. He then served his articles with the chartered accountants William Edwards, Jackson, and Browning, which was based in the City of London. In 1883 Dickinson won the first prize in the intermediate examination of the Institute of Chartered Accountants in England and Wales (ICAEW) and joint first place in the final examinations (1886). He married in 1888 Mary Kathleen, daughter of William Jennings, manager of a finance company and actuary. They had two daughters.

Dickinson joined with another City-based firm, in 1888, to form Lovelock, Whiffin, and Dickinson. Three years later he accepted the invitation from Edwin Waterhouse to take charge of Price Waterhouse's recently established American operations. Together with a number of other British accountants working in the United States, Dickinson helped to organize the newly developing American accountancy profession. Although the first professional association was established in 1886, progress had been slow. Dickinson served as president of the Federation of Societies of Public Accountants in 1904, and as secretary of the American Association of Public Accountants in 1905 helped to bring about the merger of those two bodies. Following his return to Britain in 1913, as partner in Price Waterhouse's London office, he continued his professional involvement, serving as a member of the ICAEW's council between 1914 and 1928.

While in the United States, Dickinson also made his mark in the development of financial reporting practices. One of Price Waterhouse's largest clients—possibly the largest—was the United States Steel Corporation. Dickinson collaborated with the company's controller, William J. Filbert, to produce solutions to financial reporting problems associated with the newly emerging conglomerate form of business organization. The company's accounts for 1902 attracted widespread recognition as representing major progress towards fuller and more meaningful financial disclosure, and of particular interest is the fact that they contained an early example of a group consolidated statement.

Substantial contributions were made by Dickinson to the accounting literature on both sides of the Atlantic. Presentations to the International Congress on Accounting at St Louis in 1904, and to the school of commerce, accounts, and finance, New York University, in 1905, are notable for their thoughtful analyses of the theory and practice of consolidated statement preparation. Together with two American professional colleagues, William M. Lybrand and Robert H. Montgomery, Dickinson did much to encourage the early widespread adoption of group financial reporting procedures in the United States. Curiously, he was not a prominent public advocate of these procedures following his return to Great Britain, and it is an interesting question whether he exerted any influence on his partner at Price Waterhouse, Gilbert Garnsey, who caused such a stir with his lecture 'Holding

companies and their published accounts', presented to the London members of the ICAEW in 1922.

Dickinson was, however, an outspoken critic of a number of aspects of contemporary accounting practice. A widely published paper presented to the Royal Statistical Society in 1924 (Dickinson had become a fellow of the Institute of Actuaries as early as 1886) drew attention to the lack of business statistics published either for public consumption or for corporate shareholders. The importance of full publicity was also the subject of a paper published in 1926 which, in a climate of industrial unrest, argued the need to recognize the interests of the various partners in business as part of an endeavour to achieve a greater degree of co-operation between representatives of capital and labour.

Professional accounting examinations were thought by Dickinson to be narrow and technical in their content. *Accounting Practice and Procedure*, published in 1913, was designed to help rectify this situation by supplying a text which would provide accounting students and practitioners with a deeper understanding of the nature, scope, and limitations of accountancy. Dickinson's experience as a company director (directorships included the Ebbw Vale Steel, Iron and Coal Company Ltd, the Alvis Car and Engineering Company Ltd, and the Goodyear Tyre and Rubber Company Ltd) and as partner in an accounting practice, together with the possession of a high intellect, enabled him to combine theory with practice, so as to produce effective solutions to pressing accounting problems.

Dickinson was active in public service during the First World War as financial adviser, first to the controlled establishments division of the Ministry of Munitions, and later to the controller of coal mines. Other public appointments included membership of the Miners' Welfare Committee, the commerce degree committee of the University of London, and the board of governors of the London School of Economics. He was knighted in 1919 for government service during the war. He lived, towards the end of his life, at Alding, Grayswood, near Haslemere, in Surrey. He died at Queen Anne's Mansions, St James's Park, London, on 28 February 1935, and was survived by his wife.

JOHN RICHARD EDWARDS

Sources J. R. Edwards, 'Dickinson, Sir Arthur Lowes', *DBB* · M. E. Murphy, 'An accountant in the 1880s', *The Accountant* (26 July–9 Aug 1947) · M. E. Murphy, 'Arthur Lowes Dickinson, pioneer in American professional accountancy', *Bulletin of the Business Historical Review*, 21 (1947), 27–38 · *The Accountant* (9 March 1935) · G. J. Previts, 'Foreword to reissue', in A. L. Dickinson, *Accounting practice and procedure* (1975) · d. cert. · E. M. Forster, *Goldsworthy Lowes Dickinson* (1934) · *WWW* · b. cert. · *CGPLA Eng. & Wales* (1935)

Wealth at death £27,168—gross: Edwards, 'Dickinson, Sir Arthur Lowes' · £21,840 4s. 4d.: probate, 10 May 1935, *CGPLA Eng. & Wales*

Dickinson, Charles (1792–1842), Church of Ireland clergyman, was born in Cork in August 1792, the youngest son of sixteen children of Charles Dickinson, an Englishman originally from Cumberland, and his wife, whose maiden name was Austen, of an old Cork family. He was a precocious child, and his aptitude for mathematics was already apparent when he was only five or six years old. He entered Trinity College, Dublin, in 1810, under the tutorship of the Revd Dr Meredith. He was elected a scholar in 1813 and took a leading part in the College Historical Society. He graduated BA in 1815, and was awarded the gold medal for distinguished answering at every examination during his undergraduate course. He became MA in 1820, and BD and DD in 1834. In 1817 he stood for a fellowship but was unsuccessful; as he became engaged to be married shortly afterwards and celibacy was a condition of fellowships, he did not compete again.

In 1818 Dickinson entered holy orders, and became curate of Castleknock, near Dublin. In 1819 he was appointed assistant chaplain of the Magdalen Asylum, Dublin. In April 1820 he married Elizabeth, the daughter of Abraham Russell of Limerick, and sister of his friend and classmate, the late Archdeacon Russell. They had four daughters and at least three sons, including Hercules Henry *Dickinson (1827–1905). In the same year he became chaplain of the Magdalen Asylum, but resigned from the post after only a few months. In 1822 he accepted the offer of the chaplaincy of the Female Orphan House, Dublin. In 1832, while he still held this chaplaincy, he was singled out by Richard Whately, the archbishop of Dublin, and was soon appointed one of the archbishop's chaplains, as assistant to Samuel Hinds. In early 1833, on Hinds's retirement, Dickinson became the archbishop's domestic chaplain and secretary. In July 1833 the archbishop collated him to the vicarage of St Anne's, Dublin, which he held with the chaplaincy. He remained a close associate of Whately's until 1840, when he was promoted to the bishopric of Meath. After being consecrated bishop on 27 December in Christ Church, Dublin, he began work but soon fell ill of typhus fever. He died at the palace, Ardbraccan, co. Meath, on 12 July 1842 and was buried in Ardbraccan churchyard on 16 July. An inscription was left to his memory at St Anne's Church, Dublin, and his son-in-law John West published a memoir of his life, *Remains of Bishop Dickinson, with a Biographical Sketch* (1845), which includes selections from his sermons and tracts, several of which were also published independently.

B. H. BLACKER, rev. DAVID HUDDLESTON

Sources J. West, *Remains of Bishop Dickinson, with a biographical sketch* (1845) · J. Willis, *Lives of illustrious Irish men* (1847), vol. 3 · H. Cotton, *Fasti ecclesiae Hibernicae*, 3 (1849), 125 · *GM*, 2nd ser., 18 (1842), 318–19 · J. Healy, *History of the diocese of Meath* (1908), vol. 2 · D. Bowen, *The protestant crusade in Ireland, 1800–70* (1978)
Archives TCD

Dickinson, Desmond Evelyn Otho Cockburn (1902–1986),

cinematographer, was born on 25 May 1902 at 9 Clifton Road, Kingston, Surrey, the son of Edgell Antonio Fitzgerald Albert Dickinson, a glove merchant's clerk, and his wife, Ethel Lily Emily Bennett. Nothing is known about his early life and education, but in 1919 he joined the Clarendon film studio near Croydon, Surrey. After a short spell at the American-owned Famous Players' Lasky studio in Islington (later to become Gainsborough studios) he joined the Stoll Company as a camera assistant and was to remain there for sixteen years. In 1927 he was given his

first film to light, *Carry on*, by Dinah Schury, the first woman film director in Britain. Dickinson earned a reputation as an innovative and economical technician who specialized in low-budget production. In 1939 he photographed the quirky whodunit *The Arsenal Stadium Mystery* for Thorold Dickinson, which was to lead to a break into a higher league of production.

Men of Two Worlds (1946) was a major propaganda feature made at the behest of the Colonial Office. Set in Tanganyika, it was intended to counter German propaganda against Britain's role as an imperial power. Thorold Dickinson, by now a leading figure in the Army Kinematograph Service, suggested that the film be shot in Technicolor by Desmond Dickinson, and in October 1943 a crew set off to film the location scenes and back projection plates in Africa. Unfortunately the film stock used proved to be faulty and the majority of the 'locations' had to be recreated from scratch in the studio at Denham, using glass shots for backgrounds. Drawing on his considerable experience, Dickinson made a major contribution to salvaging the film. Some of his most interesting and dramatic work was in the low-key night-time scenes, where the simulated orange firelight and deep black shadows ran counter to the orthodox tendency in Technicolor productions of the time to use high-key, flat lighting to show off the colours.

Dickinson's other major contribution to his craft was his work on Laurence Olivier's film version of *Hamlet*, shot at Denham in 1948 on big open sets. Olivier wanted a visual style that would convey an appropriately brooding atmosphere—hence the use of black and white—but also to allow flexibility in the staging of the action. This required sufficient depth of field for characters in the foreground and the background of a shot to remain simultaneously in focus. However, deep focus, such as that achieved by Gregg Toland in Hollywood films such as *Citizen Kane* (1941) and *The Best Years of our Lives* (1946), was practically unknown in Britain. Toland achieved the effect by means of a combination of wide-angle lenses and a very small aperture. Dickinson was restricted to a normal lens, as Olivier wanted a certain naturalism in the image, with no distortion, but depth was created by shooting the film using very small apertures, which required as much as sixteen times the normal amount of lighting on the set. The results, however, enabled Olivier to use long takes, with actors free to move around the set. The soliloquies in particular were planned with a great deal of movement, with the camera constantly panning, tracking, and craning. As the first British film to make full use of deep focus, *Hamlet* proved to be the crowning achievement of Dickinson's career.

Dickinson continued to be a prolific technician until his retirement in the early 1970s, but failed to follow younger contemporaries such as Jack Cardiff or Robert Krasker into the international arena as the British domestic film industry went into decline. Among his more notable films during the 1950s and 1960s were collaborations with Anthony Asquith, including *The Browning Version* (1951) and *The Importance of being Earnest* (1952), a handful of features

using new widescreen technologies—such as *The Black Tent* (1956), in VistaVision, and the low-budget horror *City of the Dead* (1960), photographed in atmospheric black and white. In addition to his work as cinematographer, Dickinson was a founder member of the Association of Cine Technicians, the film technicians' union, and the British Society of Cinematographers. He died on 1 March 1986 at home at Hundred Acres, Banstead, Surrey.

DUNCAN PETRIE

Sources R. Sturges, 'There is a divinity that shapes', *Eyepiece* (Oct 1989), 17–18 · R. Sturges, 'The film business: a tribute to the late Desmond Dickinson', *Eyepiece* (July–Aug 1986), 148–150 · D. Petrie, *The British cinematographer* (1996) · J. Huntley, 'Men of two worlds', *British technicolor films* (1949), 89–102 · D. Dickinson, 'Camera and lighting', *The film 'Hamlet': a record of its production*, ed. B. Cross (1948), 29–35 · J. Richards, 'Filming emergent Africa: "Men of two worlds"', *Thorold Dickinson: the man and his films* (1986), 109–36 · D. Elley, 'Desmond Dickinson', *Focus on Film*, 13 (1973), 24–5 · *CGPLA Eng. & Wales* (1986) · b. cert. · d. cert.
Wealth at death £13,720: administration with will, 3 Nov 1986, *CGPLA Eng. & Wales*

Dickinson, Edmund (1624–1707), physician and alchemist, was born at Appleton, Berkshire, on 26 September 1624, the son of the Revd William Dickinson (*d.* before 1649), rector of Appleton, and his wife, Mary, daughter of Edmund Colepepper. He was educated at Eton College, after which he entered Merton College, Oxford, in 1642, being admitted as one of the Eton postmasters. He became BA on 22 June 1647, and was elected probationer-fellow of Merton. He received the MA on 27 November 1649, after which he applied himself to medicine, and earned the MD on 3 July 1656. Soon after he was made the senior Linacre lecturer in medicine, and about 1663 began to practise medicine from a house in the High Street, Oxford.

About 1654 Dickinson had become involved with the Experimental Philosophy Club, a group of Oxford virtuosi which included Robert Boyle, Thomas Willis, Seth Ward, Jonathan Goddard, and many others with whom Dickinson continued to associate. His early interests centred on anatomy and physiology, but by the early 1660s he had turned towards chemistry, set up a laboratory, and employed an operator. The Danish polyhistor Olaus Borrichius visited Dickinson's laboratory during June or July 1663. Dickinson was elected an honorary fellow of the College of Physicians in December 1664, but was not formally admitted a fellow until 9 April 1677. He was also elected fellow of the Royal Society on 31 January 1678, but was completely inactive in that body and never formally admitted.

At Oxford Dickinson became proficient in many languages, including Greek, Hebrew, and Arabic—languages which occur in all his major publications. These languages were the key to his first book, *Delphi Phoenicizantes* (1655), a philological and etymological attempt to show that Greek stories of Delphos and Apollo's battle with the Python were derived from Hebrew accounts of Joshua, and that Bacchus and Hercules were based on Moses and Joshua. The volume also contains notions about Noah's arrival in Italy, and the origin of the druids. This work

made Dickinson widely known both at home and abroad. Wood (*Ath. Oxon.*, 2.90–91) claims that the true author of this work was Henry Jacob, a Mertonian ejected at the 1648 visitation. According to Wood, Jacob left the completed manuscript in a locked book-chest, but his quarters were later given to Dickinson, who took possession of the chest and published the manuscript under his own name. There is no clear evidence for this assertion, and Wood was ill-disposed towards Dickinson, owing to a £70 fine for the renewal of the lease on his family house, the imposition of which he blamed on Dickinson, then (1664) bursar of Merton.

In 1669 Dickinson married Elizabeth Luddington, who died giving birth to their only child, Elizabeth. She was buried in St Peter's Church, Oxford. Dickinson then married Helena Mole, who died soon after, without issue. Following the death of Thomas Willis in 1675, Dickinson acquired Willis's house in St Martin's Lane in London. Although Dickinson lived in that house until his death, it is not clear when he actually moved to London; various authorities suggest dates between 1675 and 1684, the latter date probably stemming from an erroneous date for Willis's death (*Biographia Britannica*, 5.176).

Among Dickinson's many patients was Henry Bennet, earl of Arlington, lord chamberlain, whom he cured of a serious tumour. Upon his recovery, Bennet recommended Dickinson to Charles II, who about 1677 appointed him physician-in-ordinary and physician to the royal household. The alchemist Johann Joachim Becher claims in the dedication of his *Tripus hermeticus fatidicus* that in 1680 Dickinson, as a court physician, helped Becher and introduced him to the court. Dickinson managed an alchemical laboratory, built under the royal bedchamber and accessible by a private staircase, where he performed experiments in the company of the king and George Villiers, duke of Buckingham. On the accession of James II in 1685, Dickinson was confirmed in his royal appointments, continuing there until James's deposition in 1688, whereupon he retired from practice.

Dickinson's long-term interest in transmutational alchemy began in Oxford, where he was visited about 1662 by a French adept known only as Theodore Mundanus. In 1678 or 1679 Mundanus visited Dickinson again and performed two transmutations before him. Dickinson's subsequent enquiries about alchemy addressed to Mundanus (dated London, 31 July 1683) were published in Oxford as *Epistola ad Mundanum de quintessentia philosophorum* (1686), together with Mundanus's response (dated Paris, 10 October 1684), translated from French into Latin. The French text survives in the British Library (Sloane MS 3629, fols. 202–229v). This volume achieved much popularity, appearing in three editions. Dickinson afterwards reiterated to John Evelyn his belief in the philosophers' stone and metallic transmutation. Robert Boyle chose Dickinson as one of the three executors of his chemical and alchemical papers, a task he attempted in 1692 after Boyle's death.

In his retirement Dickinson wrote his last work, *Physica vetus et vera*, which asserted the literal truth of the six days of creation, and presented a broad system of natural philosophy drawn from the Pentateuch and contemporary corpuscularian theories. This lengthy work, some of which had to be rewritten after parts of the manuscript were accidentally burnt, was published in 1702. After suffering from bladder stones for over twenty years, Dickinson died at his house in St Martin's Lane on 3 April 1707. He was buried in St Martin-in-the-Fields, where a large black marble monument with an elaborate inscription was erected on the east wall, following the dictates of his will, made on 11 September 1705.

Dickinson was survived by his daughter, Elizabeth, then wife of Charles John, Baron Blomberg, and his four grandsons. His youngest grandson, William Nicholas Blomberg (1702?–1750), wrote a rambling biography of Dickinson; and, being in possession of his grandfather's papers, published in 1739 a manuscript by Dickinson on the Grecian games as an appendix to the biography's second edition.

LAWRENCE M. PRINCIPE

Sources W. N. Blomberg, *Life and writings of Edmund Dickinson*, 2nd edn (1739) · Wood, *Ath. Oxon.* · A. Kippis and others, eds., *Biographia Britannica, or, The lives of the most eminent persons who have flourished in Great Britain and Ireland*, 2nd edn, 5 (1793), 175–9 · H. Rolleston, 'Edmund Dickinson', *Annals of Medical History*, 3rd ser., 4 (1942), 175–80 · Munk, *Roll* · R. G. Frank, *Harvey and the Oxford physiologists* (1980) · L. M. Principe, *The aspiring adept: Robert Boyle and his alchemical quest* (1998) · M. Hunter, *The Royal Society and its fellows, 1660–1700: the morphology of an early scientific institution*, 2nd edn (1994) · G. C. Brodrick, *Memorials of Merton College*, OHS, 4 (1885) · *Diary and correspondence of John Evelyn*, ed. W. Bray, new edn, ed. [J. Forster], 4 vols. (1850–52), vol. 2, p. 354 · *Olai Borrichii itinerarium, 1660–1665: the journal of the Danish polyhistor Ole Borch*, ed. H. D. Schepelern, 4 vols. (Copenhagen, 1983) · J. J. Becher, *Tripus hermeticus fatidicus* (1689) [dedication] · will, 11 Sept 1705, PRO, PROB 11/494, sig. 105
Wealth at death see will, 11 Sept 1705, PRO, PROB 11/494, sig. 105

Dickinson, Goldsworthy Lowes (1862–1932),

scholar and advocate of a league of nations, was born on 6 August 1862 at Langham Chambers, near Oxford Circus, London, the third of the five children of Lowes Cato *Dickinson (1819–1908) and his wife, Margaret Ellen (d. 1882), daughter of William Smith Williams. The accountant Sir Arthur Lowes *Dickinson (1859–1935) was his elder brother. His father, the portrait painter, was a Christian socialist who taught at the Working Men's College; his mother was related to the inventor Sir Goldsworthy Gurney, after whom her son was named, though in his circle it was always shortened to Goldie. Dickinson's career was in keeping with these intellectual and high-minded associations, especially from 1881 when, after several unhappy years at a preparatory school and Charterhouse School, he entered King's College, Cambridge, as an exhibitioner. At Cambridge he was elected to the Society of Apostles and fell under the influence of Oscar Browning (he later wrote on him for the *Dictionary of National Biography*). He also became devoted to Shelley's poetry, the route by which he first approached politics. The visit to Cambridge of Henry George led him to read *Progress and Poverty*, and imbued by these ideas he spent the summer of 1885 working on a co-operative farm in Surrey. He had graduated in 1884

with first-class honours in classics, but returned to Cambridge in order, from idealistic motives, to study medicine—an idea he gave up after a dissertation on Plotinus, on which he had been working at the same time, had secured for him a fellowship at King's College in 1887. He also lectured, from 1896 to 1920, at the London School of Economics, offering the same courses on political science that he taught at Cambridge.

Among Dickinson's early books were *Revolution and Reaction in Modern France* (1892) and *The Development of Parliament during the Nineteenth Century* (1895), but he also wrote *The Greek View of Life* (1896) as well as some works of imagination. His *Letters from John Chinaman* (1901), which was widely noticed, might be included among the latter; purporting to be from a Chinese official (though Dickinson denied any attempt at deception), the letters were a means of criticizing Western society. Another form he used to explore ideas was the imaginary dialogue, most notably *A Modern Symposium* (1905) in which thirteen men discussed from different standpoints the ideas of the time. He also wrote for the progressive journals of the period, including the *Independent Review* which he had helped to set up in 1903. His academic standing led to two lecture tours in the United States, in 1901 and 1909. An Albert Kahn travelling fellowship enabled him to visit India (he was accompanied on this part of the journey by E. M. Forster), China, and Japan in 1912. With like-minded companions, he spent various holidays in several European countries.

The advent of war affected Dickinson's outlook and activities profoundly. Before 1914 his espousal of progressive causes had not drawn him far into the public sphere, for which he had little liking. Thereafter most of his writings were intended to influence opinion and, although not by nature a political activist, he began to work against what he regarded as the international anarchy that had led to war. In the first weeks of the war he called for the establishment of a league of nations (a term he is believed to have coined). He was prominent in the Bryce Group, known as such from the involvement of Lord Bryce, although his friend Forster considered it would more justly have been called the Lowes Dickinson Group. His involvement in the Union of Democratic Control, a body more critical of the government, brought some obloquy, although not to the extent experienced by his friend Bertrand Russell. When Russell was stripped of his lectureship at Trinity College, Cambridge, Dickinson wrote in his defence. He also travelled to The Hague in 1915 and the United States in 1916 to promote his proposals. Inevitably, he was dissatisfied with the terms of the peace and in common with other critics of the war with whom he had been associated (such as J. A. Hobson, Arthur Ponsonby, and E. D. Morel) he moved towards the Labour Party; for a time he was a member of the party's advisory committee on international affairs. The war also resulted in his most substantial book, on which he worked for several years, *The International Anarchy, 1904–1914* (1926).

Dickinson retired from lecturing in 1920, but retained his fellowship of King's College and continued to live in rooms there. Until the end of his life he wrote prolifically, especially on Goethe and Plato, both the subjects of several radio broadcasts in 1930–31. In 1931 he published a memoir of an old friend, the philosopher J. M. E. McTaggart. In the same year 'Edward Carpenter as a friend' appeared, an essay that throws some light on his own socialism in the 1880s.

Like his mentor Oscar Browning, Dickinson believed that fellows of colleges should encourage close friendships with undergraduates, and many were drawn by his charm and humour. Those who knew him well noticed a melancholy side to his outlook, in part a consequence of disappointed hopes for a higher diplomacy but also the result of personal circumstances. He candidly discussed the latter in some recollections, drawn on by E. M. Forster, his biographer, but not published until 1973. It was his intention in these, he noted, 'to tell what is usually not told', though he did so 'with the feeling that those who read, if they are what is called normal men, will not understand, and if they are homosexual, likely enough will find it absurd' (Autobiography, 43, 89). Not only was Dickinson drawn to young heterosexual men, but his friendships were also coloured by a boot fetish. It was a side of his nature he expressed in verse form:

> We're alone,
> I and the youth I dream of as my own.
> He sits and at his feet I take my place,
> He plants them firmly on my neck and face,
> Both pleasing me and pleased himself at heart,
> Because he loves the domineering part.
> I snuff the scent of leather at my nose
> And squirm and wriggle as the pressure grows,
> While he, more masterful the more I gulp,
> Cries 'Quiet! or I'll tread you into pulp!'
> (ibid., 273)

Roger Fry was the first of five young men to whom Dickinson was particularly drawn. The last was Dennis Proctor, the editor of his recollections and the author of the Dictionary of National Biography article on Dickinson, who wrote that each of the five 'did his best in his own way to assuage his physical desires' (ibid., 7).

Most who knew Dickinson admired his passionate desire for the improvement of mankind and the sense of service that impelled him into the public sphere. Friends of all ages found him lovable, for the unhappiness brought by personal and political disappointments did not sour his gaiety and compassion. Even his foibles, such as his complaints that he always felt cold and what Kingsley Martin called 'the spite of "so-called inanimate objects" which pestered him from the moment in the morning when he could not find his collar stud until the final discomfort of undressing at night' (Martin, 121), endeared him to others. Occasionally he exasperated, as when Virginia Woolf recalled Dickinson as 'Always alone on a mountain top asking himself how to live, theorising about life; never living … always Shelley and Goethe, and then he loses his hot water bottle'. In quoting these remarks, Leonard Woolf suggested Dickinson's 'thin vapour of gentle high-mindedness sometimes irritated her' (L. Woolf, Beginning Again: an Autobiography of the Years

1911–1918, 1964, 190–91). However, such strictures were untypical of his associates who saw in his thinking a wish to deal fairly with all points of view. This approach characterized too his religious beliefs: he was neither a Christian nor an atheist, but has been compared to a pilgrim who passed through phases of mysticism and religion. His short book The Magic Flute: a Fantasia (1920) explored in allegorical form an idea that always attracted him, how to combine reason and faith.

When in 1956 Forster gave a radio talk on Dickinson he suggested he was no longer much read or talked about even in King's College. This he regretted, 'not for his sake but because he has so much to offer'—challenges and correctives that were still relevant (Forster, 212). Though gradually his reputation as a scholar lessened, a few of his books remained in print, including The Greek View of Life, issued as a University Paperback in 1962, and A Modern Symposium. His ability to gain the friendship of the young meant he was remembered for many years after his death. Those who were drawn to his personality acknowledged that his appearance was unprepossessing—bald, thin-featured, and rather shabby, as Roger Fry showed him in a portrait of 1925. His lasting importance perhaps lies in his position as a member of the liberal-socialist intelligentsia of the late nineteenth and early twentieth centuries, not least for his response to, and desire to learn from, the First World War. Dickinson died in Guy's Hospital, London, on 3 August 1932, following a prostate operation, and was cremated at Golders Green on 8 August.   D. E. MARTIN

Sources E. M. Forster, Goldsworthy Lowes Dickinson and related writings (1973) · The autobiography of G. Lowes Dickinson and other unpublished writings, ed. D. Proctor (1973) · The Times (4 Aug 1932) · The Times (9 Aug 1932) · K. Martin, Father figures: a first volume of autobiography, 1897–1931 (1966) · G. W. Egerton, Great Britain and the creation of the League of Nations: strategy, politics, and international organisation, 1914–1919 (1979) · H. R. Winkler, The League of Nations movement in Great Britain, 1914–1919 (1952) · K. Robbins, The abolition of war: the 'peace movement' in Britain, 1914–1919 (1976) · M. Swartz, The Union of Democratic Control in British politics during the First World War (1971)
Archives King's Cam., corresp. and papers | Bodl. Oxf., corresp. with Robert Bridges · CUL, letters to C. K. Ogden · JRL, letters to Manchester Guardian · King's Cam., corresp. with C. R. Ashbee · King's Cam., letters to Oscar Browning · King's Cam., letters to E. F. Bulmer · King's Cam., corresp. with A. E. Felkin · King's Cam., corresp. with Roger Fry and MS poems · King's Cam., letters to G. H. W. Rylands · King's Cam., letters to W. J. H. Sprott · King's Cam., letters to Nathaniel Wedd and Rachel Wedd · McMaster University, Hamilton, Ontario, corresp. with Bertrand Russell · Sheff. Arch., corresp. with Edward Carpenter · U. Sussex, letters to Leonard Woolf · U. Sussex, corresp. with Virginia Woolf
Likenesses L. C. Dickinson, oils, c.1868, NPG · Dickinson Bros., photograph, 1868 · Thorpe of Hastings, photograph, 1876 · photograph, 1884 · F. Hollyer, photograph, 1885 · R. Fry, chalk drawing, 1893, NPG · A. Boughton, photograph, c.1916, NPG · photograph, 1922 · R. Fry, oils, 1925, King's Cam.; repro. in Forster, Goldsworthy Lowes Dickinson, frontispiece · W. Stoneman, photograph, 1931, NPG · photograph, 1931 · two photographs, c.1932, NPG
Wealth at death £9286 13s. 6d.: probate, 4 Oct 1932, CGPLA Eng. & Wales

Dickinson, Henry Douglas (1899–1969), economist, was born at 31 Parma Crescent, Battersea, London, on 25 March 1899, the only son of Henry Winram *Dickinson

(1870–1952), historian of engineering and technology, who was at that time assistant keeper at the Department of Science and Art, South Kensington, and his wife, Edith Emerson (d. 1937). From King's College School, Wimbledon, he went to Emmanuel College, Cambridge, where he took the part two tripos in economics (1921) and history (1922). In 1924, after two years' research at the London School of Economics, he was appointed to an assistant lectureship in economics at Leeds University. On 27 March 1925 he married Sylvia Sworn (1899/1900–1965), a medical student, the daughter of Henry George Sworn, a doctor of medicine; they had two daughters.

Dickinson taught economics and economic history at Leeds until 1947. He was an enthusiastic teacher for the Workers' Educational Association, and the book for which he was best known, *The Economics of Socialism* (1939), was based on his extension lectures to a WEA class in north Yorkshire. As an intellectual of the left he argued, in the 1930s, that rational socialism could be implemented using actual market mechanisms. He and his writings were well known to other left-wing intellectuals, including G. D. H. Cole, Hugh Dalton, Evan Durbin, and Harold Laski. He played an important part in the discussions of 'market socialism' that arose from Ludwig von Mises's view that rational allocation under socialism was impossible; socialist planners could not, von Mises had argued, make the huge number of ever-changing computations required to calculate prices scientifically. In two key articles, 'The economic basis of socialism' (*Political Quarterly*, 1, 1930) and 'Price formation in a socialist community' (*Economic Journal*, 43, 1933), Dickinson asserted, paradoxically, that planners would not need to make such calculations since socialism could best be effected via the market mechanism itself. 'The beautiful systems of economic equilibrium described by Böhm-Bawerk, Wieser, Marshall and Cassel are not descriptions of society as it is but prophetic visions of a socialist economy of the future' (*Economic Journal*, 1933, 247). It was not necessary for the planner to compute prices; this could be left to the market once the distribution of income had been settled. Most importantly for Dickinson, in this system consumers and workers would retain their freedom of choice. But would not market wage and interest rates reintroduce capitalist inequalities? To minimize inequality essential services would be provided free under a system of progressive taxation.

It can now be seen that Dickinson had prepared his ground well in his book *Institutional Revenue* (1932), which had been developed while he was researching at the London School of Economics under Cannan. That book, whose preface acknowledged help from Dalton and Dobb, showed how a theory of surplus value could be restated in modern marginalist terms. Dickinson had also argued that, since incomes under capitalism were largely a matter of capturing 'rents', the distribution of income was an institutional matter, that is, factor prices played a less decisive role in resource allocation than had been thought. Dickinson had thereby tried to block an obvious line of attack on his version of market socialism.

In 1947 Dickinson was appointed senior lecturer in economics at the University of Bristol, where he was promoted to professor in 1951, holding the chair until his retirement in 1964. His article in the *Review of Economic Studies* (22, 1954–5), 'A note on economic dynamics', pioneered the constant elasticity of substitution (CES) production function and anticipated some of the neo-classical growth results of Robert Solow and Trevor Swan. The elasticity of substitution measures the degree to which capital is substituted for labour as the real wage rises relative to the price of capital. The assumption of a constant elasticity simplified complex technical problems in growth theory while avoiding over-simplification, and is still widely used. Dickinson also worked out at the time, but never published, 'a simple way of fitting the [CES] equation … statistically, to the time series, by using evidence on factor shares' (Whitaker, 166–7). In this paper he accepted that technical progress was a more powerful tool than redistribution for raising living standards: 'Technical progress is a necessary condition for a permanent and continuous increase in real wages. Even if we assume that the State has an unlimited power to redistribute real income, we cannot escape the conclusions reached here' (ibid., 179).

Dick, as Dickinson was almost universally known, was an impressively versatile economist, being an accomplished theorist and historian of economic ideas as well as an expert numismatist. His colleagues regarded this unworldly, eccentric figure with great affection. He died at Southmead Hospital, Bristol, on 11 July 1969 and was cremated at Canford crematorium, Bristol.

DAVID COLLARD

Sources *Economic Journal*, 79 (1969), 681–2 • M. H. Dobb, *History of Economic Thought Newsletter*, 3 (1968) • *The Times* (14 July 1969) • *WWW* • J. K. Whitaker, 'A note on the CES production function', *Review of Economic Studies*, 31 (1964), 166–7, 179 • b. cert. • m. cert. • d. cert. • *CGPLA Eng. & Wales* (1969) • personal knowledge (2004)
Wealth at death £21,391: probate, 17 Oct 1969, *CGPLA Eng. & Wales*

Dickinson, Henry Winram (1870–1952), historian of engineering and technology, was born at Ulverston, Lancashire, on 28 August 1870, the eldest son of John Dickinson, general manager and secretary of the North Lonsdale Iron and Steel Company Ltd, and his wife, Margaret Anne, *née* Winram. From Victoria Grammar School at Ulverston he went to Manchester grammar school with a foundation scholarship. After a two-year engineering course at the University of Manchester, and four years' apprenticeship (1888–92) at the Parkhead steel works of William Beardmore & Co. Ltd, Glasgow, he became a draughtsman at the Glasgow Iron and Steel Company's Wishaw works and then assistant engineer at the Frodingham Iron and Steel Company.

Dickinson's career was settled when he was twenty-five: in 1895 he was appointed by open competition junior assistant in the science department, South Kensington Museum, London, which became the Science Museum in 1909. On 15 June 1897 he married Edith (d. 1937), youngest daughter of Richard Emerson, schoolmaster, of Low Dunsforth, Yorkshire. Their only son, Henry Douglas

*Dickinson (1899–1969), was later professor of economics at Bristol, 1951–64. Promoted assistant keeper in the machinery division in 1900, Dickinson was, in addition, made secretary to the advisory council in 1914. From 1915 to 1918 he was secretary of the munitions inventions panel at the Ministry of Munitions. On his return to the Science Museum he was promoted in 1924 keeper of mechanical engineering, taking charge of numerous industrial collections, including motive power. He supervised the erection of the original Newcomen type and Watt beam engines and many other historical exhibits in the museum's new eastern block, opened by George V in 1928, and was responsible for the transfer from Handsworth and the arrangement as a museum exhibit of the contents of James Watt's garret workshop.

Dickinson represented the Board of Education in 1919 on the memorial committee to commemorate at Birmingham the centenary of the death of Watt. Resulting from this, Dickinson and other engineers founded in 1920 the Newcomen Society for the Study of the History of Engineering and Technology, named after Thomas Newcomen (d. 1729) of Dartmouth, maker of the first successful steam engine using a piston in a cylinder. Dickinson was honorary secretary until 1951, except for two years (1932–4) when he was president. As sole editor of the *Transactions* until 1950, he set a very high standard and the first twenty-five volumes are a lasting memorial of his devoted work. He was made secretary emeritus in 1951 for his very distinguished services in guiding the society for over thirty years, including the critical war period. After he retired from the Science Museum in 1930, his main interest was the Newcomen Society. During his career he presented twenty-three papers to it, and two to the Institution of Mechanical Engineers, of which he was a member for over fifty years.

Dickinson was the British government's representative at the opening of the Deutsches Museum, Munich, in 1925; he served as president of the Croydon and Purley natural history and scientific societies, besides being a vice-president of the Cornish Engines Preservation Society. He made two lecture tours in the United States, in 1923 and 1938, and received the honorary degree of EngD from Lehigh University, Pennsylvania. On 31 May 1939 he married his second wife, Elsa Lees, eldest daughter of Frank Walker Burgan, railway traffic agent, of Saltburn by Sea, Yorkshire. He died at his home, 20 St James Road, Purley, Surrey, on 21 February 1952, survived by his wife.

Dickinson was the author of definitive books on his favourite subjects: the biographies *Robert Fulton* (1913), *John Wilkinson* (1914), *James Watt* (1936), and *Matthew Boulton* (1937); the two memorial volumes *James Watt and the Steam Engine* (with Rhys Jenkins, 1927) and *Richard Trevithick* (with Arthur Titley, 1934); also *A Short History of the Steam Engine* (1939). His series of articles in *The Engineer* during 1948 was republished after his death as a memorial volume entitled *Water Supply of Greater London* (1954).

By his industrious researches and enthusiasm, tempered with sound judgement, Dickinson made a valuable contribution to establishing the history of technology on a firm basis and was one of the leading authorities on the evolution and application of steam power in the industrial revolution. He inspired others by his example and advice to undertake similar research. He lived modestly and was a lucid author and speaker, his knowledge being based on observation, systematic reading, travel, and the material in the Science Museum, for which he wrote several official catalogues. To perpetuate his memory, the Newcomen Society founded in 1954 the Dickinson biennial memorial lecture; the series was inaugurated by Charles Singer, who received the first Dickinson memorial medal. In 1956 the Newcomen Society in North America, inspired by Dr Charles Penrose, senior vice-president, erected a memorial tablet to Dickinson at the Thomas Newcomen Library, West Chester, Pennsylvania.

ARTHUR STOWERS, *rev.*

Sources *Transactions* [Newcomen Society], 28 (1951–3), 286–8 · C. Singer, 'The happy scholar: the first Dickinson memorial lecture', *Transactions* [Newcomen Society], 29 (1953–5), 125–35 · *The Times* (1 March 1952), 8e · *The Engineer* (29 Feb 1952) · *Engineering* (29 Feb 1952) · m. certs. · d. cert.
Archives Sci. Mus., research and working notes
Likenesses photograph, repro. in *Transactions of the Newcomen Society*, frontispiece
Wealth at death £8845 18s. 9d.: probate, 26 April 1952, *CGPLA Eng. & Wales*

Dickinson, Hercules Henry (1827–1905), Church of Ireland clergyman, was the youngest son of Charles *Dickinson (1792–1842), afterwards bishop of Meath, and his wife, Elizabeth, daughter of Abraham Russell, of Limerick. He was born at Dublin on 14 September 1827. Two brothers, Charles and John Abraham, were in holy orders, and the eldest of his four sisters, Elizabeth, married John West, afterwards dean of St Patrick's Cathedral. Dickinson was educated at Dr Flynn's school, Harcourt Street, Dublin, and, from October 1845, at Trinity College, Dublin, where he obtained a classical scholarship in 1848, graduated BA in 1850, and proceeded MA in 1856. He was ordained deacon by Archbishop Richard Whately, who was an old friend of his father's, became BD in 1852, and proceeded DD in 1866. In 1852 he became curate of St Ann's, Dublin, considered an important parish, and was appointed vicar there in 1855. He continued to minister St Ann's for forty-seven years. On 2 October 1867 he married Mary Mabel, the daughter of Dr Evory Kennedy of Belgard, co. Dublin. They had nine children.

In 1868 Dickinson was appointed dean of the Chapel Royal, Dublin, in 1869 treasurer of St Patrick's Cathedral, and in 1876 precentor. In 1894 the Irish bishops elected him to the chair of pastoral theology at Dublin University. For many years Dickinson was a prominent figure in Dublin clerical life: he was examining chaplain to successive archbishops, an active supporter of the Association for Promoting Christian Knowledge, chairman of the Dublin Clerical Association, a member of the Representative Church Body, and a frequent speaker at the annual meetings of the general synod, where his humour enlivened debates. He was an ardent advocate of temperance, and he served on the royal commission for licensing reform from

1896 to 1899. He was also an advocate of the higher education of women, and he helped Archbishop Richard Trench in the foundation in 1866 of Alexandra College, Dublin, of which he was warden for thirty-six years.

Like his ecclesiastical patron, Dickinson was opposed to Tractarianism and was a strong supporter of the Society for the Propagation of the Gospel at a time when it was not popular in Ireland. He was the author of *Lectures on the Book of Common Prayer* (1859) and *Scripture and Science* (1879), as well as occasional sermons and papers. He resigned his offices because of poor health in 1902, and died at his home, Baldonnel, Clondalkin, co. Dublin, on 17 May 1905. He was buried in Mount Jerome cemetery. Three decorated panels to his memory were placed in the chancel of St Ann's Church, Dublin.

J. H. BERNARD, *rev.* DAVID HUDDLESTON

Sources WW · Crockford (1901) · *The Times* (18 May 1905), 9 · private information (1912) · *Annual Register* (1905) · H. Cotton, *Fasti ecclesiae Hibernicae*, 6 (1878), 57 · [J. H. Todd], ed., *A catalogue of graduates who have proceeded to degrees in the University of Dublin, from the earliest recorded commencements to … December 16, 1868* (1869), 155 · Burtchaell & Sadleir, *Alum. Dubl.* · H. E. Patton, *Fifty years of disestablishment* (1922) · *CGPLA Ire.* (1905)
Likenesses photograph, repro. in Patton, *Fifty years*
Wealth at death £1896 8s. 0d.: probate, 2 June 1905, *CGPLA Ire.*

Dickinson, James (1659–1741), Quaker preacher, was born in April 1659 at Lowmoor House in the parish of Dean, Cumberland, the son of Matthew Dickinson (d. c.1669) and his wife, Jane (d. c.1666). Before his parents died—his mother when he was about seven and his father when he was ten—they taught him Quaker principles, but for a time he engaged in worldly pursuits before embracing Quakerism in 1678. A dealer in animal skins (and later a glover), he spent much of the rest of his life travelling on behalf of the Friends. He began with his witness to a presbyterian congregation at Tallentire, near Cockermouth, and a Baptist church at nearby Broughton, and after preaching in Westmorland, the Yorkshire dales, Durham, and Northumberland, in 1680–81, he went in 1682 to Ireland, where he travelled with Thomas Wilson. He made his initial foray into Scotland in 1683 and then traversed Westmorland, Lancashire, the West Riding, Cheshire, and Wales, before returning to Ireland by 1685, this time with Thomas Trafford.

Dickinson made his first trip to southern England in 1686, going from Cornwall and Devon, where he was briefly arrested at Kirton, to Kent, London, Essex, and East Anglia. With Peter Fearon he went to the Netherlands, where they arrived safely after their vessel was chased by a Turkish ship. He journeyed throughout much of the country, engaging in a disputation in the Jewish synagogue at Amsterdam, and went as far as the German city of Emden. He returned again to Ireland, where he met John Burnyeat and was once again accompanied by Wilson. By 1688 he visited south-western England before going to London and York for the yearly meetings. As he criss-crossed England in 1689, he preached in Berkshire, Wiltshire, and Bristol with John Tiffin. In deciding where and when to travel, he followed what he believed to be the Holy Spirit's

leading, as in 1690, when he 'had a Concern upon me to visit Friends in *Scotland*' (Dickinson, 44); on this trip he met Robert Barclay.

After a journey to the eastern counties in early 1691, Dickinson and Wilson voyaged to Barbados; they left on 9 July and escaped a French fleet *en route*, under cover of fog and darkness. In Barbados they participated in large meetings before sailing to New York, where they arrived on 23 November. On their American peregrination, which extended from Carolina to New England, their pacifist message enjoyed some success because the colonists were apprehensive of war. They sailed from Boston on 17 August 1692, and stopped at Barbados, Antigua, and Nevis, before reaching Britain on 15 April 1693. Dickinson was now engaged to a member of the Quaker meeting at Pardshaw, Cumberland, though they delayed marriage while he continued his itinerant preaching. On another visit to southern England, he had a confrontation at Reading with a follower of the Quaker schismatic John Story. Dickinson then went to Ireland again, where he 'travell'd hard, and had good Service' (Dickinson, 67–8). He married in late 1694, though within weeks he was on his way to London where, following the queen's death, he walked through the streets exhorting the people to repent.

After further trips through northern and central England, Dickinson returned to America, landing in Virginia on 23 July 1696. While awaiting passage he had written *A Salutation of Love to the Seed of God* (18 February 1696), urging Friends to remain humble and feel divine power within them. In America he was accused of being a Jesuit, defended mainstream Quakerism against George Keith's disciples, and enjoyed some success witnessing to Welsh immigrants at Haverford. After leaving the colonies on 7 May 1697, he reached Plymouth on 22 June and briefly met with William Penn. During the ensuing years he not only continued to preach throughout much of England but twice returned to Ireland and Scotland (in 1698–9 and 1701). With Wilson he sailed a third time to America, stopping on the way at Dublin and leaving there on 8 December 1713. After trekking up and down the seaboard, they departed on 17 February 1715 and reached Cork on 30 March. By the time Dickinson was back in Cumberland, he reckoned he had travelled 12,000 miles. In the spring of 1717 he apparently played a role in healing the long-standing breach among the Friends at Reading.

Periodically Dickinson pursued his trade: 'When I was at Liberty I laboured diligently in my outward Business, not only because of the Benefit I received there-from, but that I might be exemplary among my Neighbours' (Dickinson, 162). According to his fellow Friends he made a total of twelve trips to Ireland, the last of which, in 1727, took place during his campaign to persuade Friends in England and Ireland to compile a catalogue of Quaker sufferings; the eventual result was the collection published by Joseph Besse in 1753. Dickinson's wife died in 1726, and in the ensuing years his own health began to fail. About 1740 he and Jane Fearon related their narrow escape from murderers on a visit to Scotland, a tale published as *A Memorable*

Instance of Divine Guidance (1793). Dickinson apparently suffered a stroke in 1740 that paralysed one side of his body and impaired his speech. Following his death at Moorside on 6 May 1741, he was interred on 8 May in the Quaker burial-ground at Eaglesfield, Cumberland.

RICHARD L. GREAVES

Sources J. Dickinson, *A journal of the life, travels, and labour of love in the work of the ministry* (1745) • 'Record of Friends travelling in Ireland, 1656–1765 [pt 1]', *Journal of the Friends' Historical Society*, 10 (1913), 157–80 • 'Dictionary of Quaker biography', RS Friends, Lond. [card index] • W. C. Braithwaite, *The second period of Quakerism*, ed. H. J. Cadbury, 2nd edn (1961), 285, 492, 551 • R. L. Greaves, *Dublin's merchant-Quaker: Anthony Sharp and the community of Friends, 1643–1707* (1998), 276 • *The papers of William Penn*, ed. R. S. Dunn and M. M. Dunn, 3 (1986), 361, 363, 468; 4 (1987), 172, 175

Archives RS Friends, Lond., letters and treatises

Dickinson, John (1732–1808), revolutionary politician and writer in America, was born on 2 November 1732 at Croisadore plantation, Talbot county, Maryland, the first of two children of Samuel *Dickinson (1690–1760), planter and judge, and his second wife, Mary Cadwalader (1700–1776), daughter of John Cadwalader. His father's family were English Quakers who settled in Maryland's Eastern Shore about 1660; his mother's were Welsh Quakers who emigrated to Pennsylvania. In 1741 the family moved to Kent county, Delaware, to be closer to Philadelphia. The Dickinsons employed private tutors for their children. In 1750 John went to Philadelphia to read law with John Moland, and in 1754 he crossed the Atlantic to enrol at the Middle Temple, where he was a diligent student and avid reader. He obtained his degree in 1757, and returned to open his practice in Philadelphia.

Politics and religion Dickinson's political career began with his election to the Delaware assembly in 1759. The next year, after re-election, he became speaker of the assembly. Because he regarded Philadelphia as his home, he did not stand again for his prominent post in Delaware in October 1761, but ran unsuccessfully for an assembly seat from Philadelphia county in the Pennsylvania assembly. The Philadelphia county assembly delegation was a phalanx of adherents to the anti-proprietary and pro-Quaker political leaders of the colony, Benjamin Franklin and Joseph Galloway. In 1762 one of this political contingent died, and Dickinson, possessing the credentials of a Quaker background, won the by-election. Dickinson did not, however, consider himself a Quaker. His father stopped attending meetings in 1739 because he was upbraided for allowing his daughter to marry an Anglican in a church. For the next forty-two years John avoided all aspects of organized religion. When he married Mary Norris (1740–1803), daughter of the late Speaker Isaac Norris, on 19 July 1770, he insisted on a civil ceremony. In 1781, perhaps because of a revived Quaker conviction which his wife urged on him, he refused an oath of office, taking an affirmation instead, and also freed his slaves. By the 1790s he was attending Quaker meetings, though not as a member. He believed that Christianity mainly concerned doing one's duty to others, and was noted in his later years for many charitable donations.

John Dickinson (1732–1808), by Charles Willson Peale, 1770

Before March 1764 Dickinson sided with the Pennsylvania assembly leaders, contesting against the proprietary governor over taxation. Dickinson believed that the Penn proprietors, using their executive authority, were attempting to shirk their financial obligations. But he parted with the leadership in 1764 because he viewed Franklin's solution to the executive–legislative conflict—royal government for Pennsylvania—a threat to charter liberties. He attacked it in the house and in print. His opposition led to a fight with Joseph Galloway on the state house steps and a fierce election battle in October 1764. Although Dickinson was re-elected, while Franklin and Galloway temporarily lost their seats, the petition for royal government went forward, only to fail in London. Intense rivalry between Dickinson and Galloway continued, and cool collaboration marked later relations with Franklin.

Revolutionary leader In 1765 Dickinson began his career as a publicist for American rights within the empire and an advocate for peaceful means to get Britain to acknowledge these rights. At the Stamp Act Congress in October 1765, he drafted its declarations and resolves, asserting that while the colonies had the obligation to obey imperial legislation, taxation without representation was an infringement on colonial rights. Dickinson's writings advised that to persuade Britain to repeal the tax the colonies should ignore it. He endorsed demands that stamp officers resign and supported the merchant boycott of British trade. In his most famous work, the *Letters from a Farmer in Pennsylvania* (1767–8), he challenged the Townshend duties on legal and constitutional bases. The *Letters* were designed to prove that, while Britain had rightful authority to regulate colonial trade, the Townshend duties were taxation for revenue, no different from the Stamp Act or the impositions of the Mutiny Act of 1765, and equally unconstitutional. They should be resisted by non-importation of goods from Britain, as had been the Stamp Act. Dickinson strongly advised against any violent resistance. Mob action against the Stamp Act had antagonized Britain, while peaceful efforts won repeal. Published throughout the colonies, the *Letters* established Dickinson's reputation as America's foremost defender against British taxation. Outside Pennsylvania he was toasted and honoured, and his 'Liberty Song' of 1768 widely published and sung; in his home colony Joseph Galloway and his political allies, hesitant to resist British authority, kept Dickinson out of political office most years until 1774.

When parliament passed the Tea Act in 1773 Dickinson condemned it not only as an underhand device to get colonials to pay the unconstitutional tea tax, but also as unlawfully establishing a monopoly to aid only one merchant enterprise. Dickinson had heretofore always restricted his condemnation of British policy to the taxes and duties imposed for revenue, and the misuse of those funds. In his address to the merchants of Philadelphia in April 1768 he had noted that some of the acts of trade and the manufacturing restrictions bore hard on the colonists, but that they had accepted these out of 'filial respect'. Dickinson's condemnation of the tea monopoly signalled that he was now ready to broaden his attack to include other British legislation. He warned against violent resistance and advocated peaceful boycott of the tea, and Philadelphia's threats turned the tea ships back. When peace was not preserved in Boston, and parliament adopted the punitive Coercive Acts, Dickinson's imperial views changed quickly: he now opposed parliamentary legislation that intervened in internal colonial matters. He still believed, however, that parliament could legislate concerning imperial trade.

Under Dickinson's direction Philadelphia reacted carefully and sensibly to Boston's plea for assistance. City leaders rejected precipitate action and called for a continental congress. Dickinson's political enemies in the assembly prevented his appointment as congressional delegate, but in October 1774 the Pennsylvania voters repudiated the cautious majority in the legislature and elected Dickinson and his allies. The assembly added Dickinson to the continental congress delegation. Even before he became a member he drafted for the congress its declaration and resolves. He was also the principal author of congress's address to the king. Dickinson's thinking influenced every action of the first continental congress: rejecting British impositions but not advocating independence, imposing a comprehensive economic boycott, and making a reasoned appeal to Britain to change course.

The British government was bent on repressing what it saw as rebellion, and Dickinson's hopes for conciliation became unrealistic with Lexington and Concord. In May 1775 he accepted appointment as colonel of a Philadelphia battalion. In the second continental congress in June he edited Thomas Jefferson's draft of the 'Declaration of the causes of taking up arms', embellishing some pointed passages about American determination to fight until free. To this time Dickinson had been regarded as the chief spokesman of the principles of colonial resistance. However, in June he lost credibility with many members, particularly John Adams, by insisting on an 'olive branch' petition to the king, which the congress approved in July probably on the expectation that its rejection would settle the issue of independence. Later in July Dickinson successfully led opposition to the independence faction's motion to open American ports in six months and to Franklin's plan for confederation. However, the British government in successive hostile steps evinced no desire to conciliate, and by February 1776 its intransigence converted a bare majority of colonies to independence.

Dickinson refused to alter his views, though he had great difficulty making up his mind. He told Charles Thomson that if the British hired foreign troops he would join the pro-independence advocates. Yet when news of British contracts to hire mercenaries from several German states reached Philadelphia in late May, he did not change his stance. Dickinson feared that colonial Pennsylvania's charter liberties and legislative privileges, the political dominance of the Philadelphia élite, and his own political influence would be overthrown: he chose reconciliation with a unified, liberalized empire rather than vote to create independent states that would probably quarrel endlessly and seek intervention by various European nations. By mid-June 1776 even Pennsylvania no longer opposed independence, by July congress was almost unified in favour of it, and Dickinson could only argue unpersuasively that independence was premature, and that both firm union of the colonies and alliance with France should precede it. In January 1777 he was still hoping for reconciliation.

Military and public offices Independence or not, defence was imperative. In mid-July 1776 Dickinson led his militia battalion to northern New Jersey to counter the large British force invading the New York harbour area. His unit saw no action. When he returned to Philadelphia in September 1776, he got into a series of clashes with Pennsylvania's new government. It removed him from its continental congress delegation and reduced his military stature, whereupon he resigned his commission. He obtained election to the new government's legislature but quit when the majority refused to revise the new Pennsylvania constitution. Dickinson's opponents censured him for advising his brother not to take continental currency while the American army was in retreat across New Jersey in late 1776. He never satisfactorily explained his advice, but did not himself refuse the paper money of the revolutionary government.

In early 1777 Dickinson quit Philadelphia for his Delaware estate. He volunteered for the Delaware militia and served as a private at the battle of the Brandywine, but took no part in the fighting. He refused the offers of both command of the militia and election to congress from Delaware in 1778, pleading ill health. However, in April

1779 he returned to congress and was very active until about September, when he ceased to attend. Although he was re-elected in December 1779, he never served in congress again. In October 1781 Delaware's leaders persuaded Dickinson to go into the legislature, and then in November to take the presidency of the state. In this office he was active, energetic, and committed, borrowing money for the state on his own credit. His Philadelphia friends, fellow opponents of the Pennsylvania constitution, gave his administration favourable publicity. In October 1782 Philadelphia elected him to Pennsylvania's supreme executive council, and in November he became council president. Dickinson was chief executive of the two states until he resigned from the Delaware post, at that state's request, in January 1783. His major achievement in Pennsylvania, in June of that year, was to disperse mutinous unpaid troops and to agree to a hearing of their grievances, without calling out the militia and risking bloodshed. Dickinson served the constitutionally permissible three annual terms. Although successive elections vindicated his honour among most Pennsylvanians, he resented his opponents' continued press attacks, and after his final term he retired to Wilmington, Delaware. The Delaware assembly called on him, as a private citizen, to attend the Annapolis convention on interstate commerce in September 1786, and again to attend the Philadelphia convention in May 1787 to revise the articles of confederation.

Constitution making Dickinson's involvement in forming a central government dated back to June 1776, when he chaired a continental congress committee that prepared what eventually became the articles of confederation. The committee report gave the federal government few powers and little vigour. National majorities could not frame policy, because each state had one congressional vote, important actions required supermajorities of states, and the confederation government could not tax. Dickinson was not responsible for all weaknesses of the articles, but he evidently concurred with most provisions that guaranteed feeble central government. During the early 1780s, as various leaders criticized the restrictive character of the articles, Dickinson realized that congress needed the power to control commerce and levy port duties. However, one or two states twice vetoed import duties by refusing to grant the unanimous consent necessary to amend the articles, a provision that Dickinson had included in his draft. He also came to oppose unicameralism.

When Dickinson and the other delegates assembled for the Philadelphia convention, he was well prepared by experience to advocate particular governmental measures. His most important contributions related to checks and balances, and to the separation of powers. He was chief advocate of the election of the upper house by the state legislatures, so that it would be a check on the popularly elected lower house. He believed that indirect election of the executive originating in the people, for a short term, rather than election by the national legislature or by state governments voting as equals, would make the

president the agent of the people and would separate the executive from both the national legislature and the state governments. He also favoured judicial independence. He was too conservative in his unsuccessful opposition to a broad suffrage, believing that only freehold landowners should vote in federal elections and not mere taxpayers, who in Pennsylvania probably supported his opponents, the constitutionalists. He unsuccessfully advocated a tripartite, sectionally based executive committee and a judiciary unable to overrule the legislature.

Dickinson was very willing to get agreement by compromise. He endorsed the eventual solution of two houses with differing representation schemes, and also recommended the compromise of permitting foreign slave importation for twenty years. He represented his own small state well, asserting the need for equality of the states in one house of the legislature and, unsuccessfully, for basing representation on state tax revenues rather than on population. His ideas of separation and balance showed his moderation. He wanted a constitution slightly more restrictive on national power, and with a weaker executive and judiciary than those that the convention approved. None the less Dickinson strongly supported the ratification of the constitution as presented by the convention. Pseudonymously he wrote nine Fabius letters in 1788. These argued that Americans would greatly benefit from this balanced government, which could easily be contrasted with that under the deficient articles.

Retirement Ill health kept Dickinson inactive for much of the time after 1788. He had suffered lung problems since his youth, and by 1774 was added that of gout. Undoubtedly he would have been elected senator from Delaware, but he refused to run. He presided over Delaware's constitutional convention of 1791–2, and accepted election as state senator. He left that position in 1793, never to hold office again.

Dickinson continued to comment on diplomatic issues because he sympathized with the principles of the French Revolution. In 1795 he denounced the Jay treaty at a public meeting. In 1797 he published fifteen more Fabius letters, championing friendship with France, and in 1798 his pamphlet warned John Adams's administration to avoid antagonizing France. By 1803 Napoleon's territorial ambitions, particularly regarding Louisiana, turned Dickinson against France, and he wrote a pamphlet suggesting naval co-operation with Britain. Dickinson died on 14 February 1808, at Wilmington, and was buried in the Quaker burial-ground there. He left a large estate, including over 6000 acres in Delaware and almost 1300 in Pennsylvania, to his two daughters. Historians have seen Dickinson as both radical (Bernard Bailyn) and conservative (Milton Flower), but he seems best described as a moderate, contributing to the mainstream of American political thought, except at the critical time of independence.

BENJAMIN H. NEWCOMB

Sources M. E. Flower, *John Dickinson: conservative revolutionary* (1983) · D. L. Jacobson, *John Dickinson and the revolution in Pennsylvania* (1965) · *Political writings of John Dickinson*, ed. P. L. Ford (1895) · C. J.

Stille, *Life and times of John Dickinson* (1891) · E. K. Ginsburg, 'Dickinson, John', *ANB* · J. N. Rakove, *The beginnings of national politics: an interpretive history of the continental congress* (1979) · J. H. Hutson, 'John Dickinson at the federal constitutional convention', *William and Mary Quarterly*, 40 (1983), 256–82 · P. H. Smith and others, eds., *Letters of delegates to congress, 1774–1789*, 26 vols. (1976–2000) · M. Jensen, *The founding of a nation: a history of the American Revolution, 1763–1776* (1968) · G. Mackinney and C. F. Hoban, eds., *Votes and proceedings of the house of representatives of the province of Pennsylvania*, 8 vols. (1754–76), vols. 5–6 [Oct 1758 – June 1776] · B. Bailyn, *Pamphlets of the American revolution, 1750–1776*, 1 (1965) · M. P. Zuckert, 'Federalism and the founding: toward a reinterpretation of the constitutional convention', *Review of Politics*, 48 (1986), 166–210 · J. H. Powell, *The house on Jones Neck: the Dickinson mansion* (1954)

Archives Hist. Soc. Penn., MSS; commonplace book; memorandum book | Hist. Soc. Penn., Dreer collection · Hist. Soc. Penn., Gratz collection · Hist. Soc. Penn., Loudon collection · Hist. Soc. Penn., McKean collection · Historical Society of Delaware, Wilmington, R. S. Rodney collection

Likenesses C. W. Peale, oils, 1770, Hist. Soc. Penn. [*see illus.*] · C. W. Peale, oils, Independence National Historical Park, Philadelphia

Wealth at death over 7300 acres: Flower, *John Dickinson*

Dickinson, John (1815–1876), writer on India, was the only surviving son of John Dickinson (1782–1869), an eminent paper maker of Nash Mills, Abbots Langley, Hertfordshire—who with Henry Fourdrinier first patented a process for manufacturing paper of an indefinite length, and so met the increasing demands of the newspaper press—and his wife, Ann, *née* Grover (1789–1870). He was born on 28 December 1815 at Nash House, Apsley, Hemel Hempstead, Hertfordshire. He was educated at Eton College, and afterwards briefly worked in his father's business. He had, however, no taste either for accounts or for mechanical processes. Being in delicate health, he left England in 1839 to travel on the continent, where, with occasional visits to his friends at home, he spent several years studying languages, art, and foreign politics. His sympathies were entirely given to the struggling liberal party on the continent, on whose behalf he wrote desultory essays in periodicals of no great note. He was in Paris during the revolution of 1848, and wrote a series of letters to *The Times* describing his experiences and analysing the events.

It was not until 1850 that Dickinson found his vocation as an independent Indian reformer. His uncle Colonel (later General) Thomas Dickinson, of the Bombay Engineers, and his cousin Sebastian Stewart Dickinson encouraged and assisted him in this enterprise. Dickinson criticized the Indian government's apathy in improving communications, thereby inhibiting the growth of commerce, and its excessive zeal under the administration of Lord Dalhousie in expanding British political control at the expense of the princely states. In these areas, he believed, reforms were needed. In 1850 and 1851 a series of letters appeared in *The Times* on the best means of increasing the produce and promoting the supply to English manufacturing towns of Indian cotton. These were from Dickinson's pen, and were afterwards published as *Letters on the Cotton and Roads of Western India* (1851). A public works commission was appointed by Lord Dalhousie the next year to inquire into the deficiencies of administration pointed out by Dickinson and his friends.

John Dickinson (1815–1876), by unknown photographer, *c.*1875

On 12 March 1853 a meeting was held in Dickinson's rooms in Charles Street, St James's Square, London, and a society was formed under the name of the India Reform Society. The debate in parliament that year on the renewal of the East India Company's charter gave the society and Dickinson, as its honorary secretary, constant occupation. Already in 1852 the publication of Dickinson's *India, its Government under a Bureaucracy*—a small volume of 209 pages—had produced a marked effect. It was reprinted in 1853 as one of a series of India Reform Tracts, and had a very large circulation. The maintenance of good faith and goodwill to the princely states was the substance of all these writings. Public attention was diverted from the subject for a time by the Crimean War, but was roused again in 1857 by the Indian mutiny. Dickinson worked incessantly throughout the two years of the uprising and pacification, and afterwards, when the transfer of the Indian government from the company to the crown was carried into effect. He attempted to moderate public excitement, and to prevent exclusive attention to penal and repressive measures. To this end he organized a series of well-attended public meetings. After 1859 the India Reform Society began to languish, and at a meeting in 1861 John Bright resigned the chairmanship, which he had assumed in 1855; a unanimous vote appointed Dickinson his successor. Dickinson married Alicia Martha Bicknell (*d.* 1875) in 1859 and family affairs occupied more of his time. In 1863 he began to study law and was called to the bar. But he retained his interest in the princely states.

The publication in 1864–5 of two pamphlets entitled *Dhar not Restored* roused in Calcutta a feeling of great indignation against the writer, Dickinson, who was stigmatized as a 'needy adventurer'.

On the death of his father in 1869 Dickinson inherited a large fortune and was much occupied in the management of his property. By then the India Reform Society had become inactive. Still, despite being in weak health from heart disease, he kept alive to the last his interest in India, corresponding with Holkar, maharaja of Indore, with great regularity. He indignantly repelled the accusation made against Holkar, in the affair of Colonel Durand, namely, that the maharaja had acted equivocally towards the British during the uprising in 1857, when his troops mutinied, attacked the residency, and forced the resident, H. M. Durand, to retreat from Indore.

In 1872 Dickinson was deeply grieved by the death of his youngest son, and in 1875 felt still more deeply the loss of his wife, whom he did not long survive. On 23 November 1876 he was found dead in his study, at 1 Upper Grosvenor Street, London. From the papers lying on the table it was evident that he had been engaged in writing a reply to Holkar's assailants; this was afterwards completed and published by his friend Major Evans Bell under the title of *Last Counsels of an Unknown Counsellor* (1877). He was buried at Kings Langley, Hertfordshire. Dickinson was survived by two sons, John Ehret (1860–1896) and Thomas Gordon (1862–1908), and by the elder of his two sisters, Frances Elizabeth Pratt Barlow (1814–1881).

ROBERT HARRISON, *rev.* PETER HARNETTY

Sources E. Bell, 'Memoir', in J. Dickinson, *Last counsels of an unknown counsellor*, ed. E. Bell (1877), 3–60 · J. Evans, *The endless web: John Dickinson and Co. Ltd., 1804–1954* (1955) · J. L. Sturgis, *John Bright and the empire* (1969) · C. S. Srinivasachari, 'The India Reform Society and its impact on India administration (1853–62)', *Indian Journal of Political Science*, 8 (1946), 648–61
Likenesses photograph, *c*.1875, NPG [*see illus.*] · portrait, repro. in Bell, 'Memoir'
Wealth at death under £40,000: probate, 26 Jan 1877, CGPLA Eng. & Wales

Dickinson, Joseph (*c*.1805–1865), physician and botanist, the son of Joseph Dickinson, was born at Lampleigh, Whitehaven, Cumberland. He graduated MB in 1837 from Trinity College, Dublin, and proceeded MA and MD in 1843; he was granted an *ad eundem* degree at Cambridge in 1844. Dickinson was appointed physician to the Liverpool Royal Infirmary in 1839, and subsequently also to the Fever Hospital, the Liverpool workhouse, and the South Dispensary. Although ill health forced him to retire he remained as consulting physician until his death. In addition to his clinical appointments Dickinson enjoyed a successful private practice in Liverpool and was renowned for his professional attitude among both his patients and his colleagues. Dickinson lectured on medicine and on botany at the Liverpool school of medicine. His book, *The Flora of Liverpool*, was published in 1851, and a supplement appeared in 1855. In recognition of this work he was elected FRS in 1854. He served as president of the Liverpool Literary and Philosophical Society, and was a fellow of the Linnean Society and of the Royal College of Physicians. He also served as president of the Lancashire and Cheshire branch of the British Medical Association.

Dickinson was twice married. His first wife died during a visit by the couple to Egypt, when Dickinson was attempting to recover his own health. His second wife outlived him. Dickinson died at Waterloo, near Liverpool, on 21 July 1865.   HELEN J. POWER

Sources *BMJ* (29 July 1865), 124 · T. H. Bickerton and R. M. B. MacKenna, *A medical history of Liverpool from the earliest days to the year 1920*, ed. H. R. Bickerton (1936) · *Liverpool Daily Post* (24 July 1865) · Desmond, *Botanists*, rev. edn · Munk, *Roll* · CGPLA Eng. & Wales (1865) · Venn, *Alum. Cant.* · Boase, *Mod. Eng. biog.*
Archives Merseyside Museums, herbarium · Wellcome L., diary
Wealth at death under £12,000: probate, 19 Sept 1865, CGPLA Eng. & Wales

Dickinson, Lowes Cato (1819–1908), portrait painter, was born on 27 November 1819 at Kilburn, London, one of seven sons and four daughters of Joseph Dickinson, stationer and lithograph publisher, and his wife, Anne Carter of Topsham, Devon. He was educated at Topsham School and Dr Lord's school, Tooting, Surrey, and began earning a living working for his father's Bond Street business from the age of sixteen. In later correspondence Dickinson alludes to 'circumstances' that 'prevented [him] from following the bent of [his] inclination in early life' (letter to John Thompson, 10 March 1851, Dickinson, 62). One such circumstance may have been the administration of a drawing academy Dickinson had established with his brother Robert, which was attended by Ford Madox Brown in 1848.

With the help of Captain (later General) Robert Michael Laffan, Dickinson travelled to Italy where he lived from November 1850 to June 1853. His desire to be a practising artist was often quelled by a 'morning's reflection … that I have begun to paint too late in life' (Dickinson, 40). However, Dickinson remained optimistic, filling his correspondence with vivid descriptions of Rome and Genoa, anecdotes of the more interesting people he encountered, and reflections on Italian culture. The more rigorous practice of Catholicism in Rome led him to 'quite respect, esteem and honor' Roman Catholicism in England as the 'essence of purity and good sense' (ibid.).

On returning to London in 1853 Dickinson took a studio in Langham Chambers. According to Dante Gabriel Rossetti, his rooms were more handsome than those later acquired by John Everett Millais. When not working in his studio, Dickinson visited at Weybridge, Surrey, the early Christian socialist Archibald Campbell, whom he had met and befriended in Italy. In 1851 Campbell acquainted Dickinson with F. D. Maurice's plans to establish a college for working men. The Christian socialist ideals espoused by Maurice changed Dickinson's 'ideal of life': 'the life of pleasure was not a noble, and might be a very useless one' (Davies, 26). He joined the lawyer Tom Hughes, the writer Charles Kingsley, Maurice, and others as founding members of the London Working Men's College. Together with Ruskin, Dickinson conducted the first art classes, which met on Thursday evenings, from seven to nine o'clock.

Lowes Cato Dickinson (1819–1908), by Frederick Hollyer, pubd 1904

These classes were subdivided into three sections shortly after Rossetti began teaching at the college in 1855; Dickinson and Ruskin taught elementary and landscape classes, while Rossetti taught figure and colour drawing. Dickinson was characterized by J. P. Emslie as 'an influence for good in the midst of a somewhat disturbed atmosphere' (ibid., 46). He 'never indulged in the profuse praise of which his two colleagues were so liberal, but would point out to a student the very spot in his drawing which was weak, and then show him how to amend it' (ibid., 47).

On 15 October 1857 Dickinson married Margaret Ellen Williams (d. 1882) at All Souls Church, St Marylebone, London, and enjoyed a happy and active family life. In 1864 they took a cottage at Hanwell, Essex, where they lived until 1879. Dickinson continued teaching for some eleven or twelve years after Ruskin retired, during which time Madox Brown, Stacy Marks, Cave Thomas, Edward Burne-Jones, V. Prinsep, and Arthur Hughes also came to teach.

Despite his experience as a teacher, Dickinson often doubted his competence, and struggled with his own limitations as a painter which he felt imposed limits on his teaching. Emslie noted, however, that while in the classroom 'in a couple of hours he would have painted a picture some eighteen inches square … a picture full of colour, light and texture' (ibid., 47–8). He also possessed a 'gift for posthumous portraiture in crayons' (Dickinson, vi). He painted many portraits of writers including George Eliot (1872; NPG), the politician Richard Cobden (NPG), lawyers, divines, and men of letters and science. He is perhaps best-known for his portraits of Maurice (1862; London Working Men's College), Charles Kingsley (1862; NPG), and Tom Hughes (1862; London Working Men's College), painted for the college. His first portraits of these close friends and colleagues were completed in 1858 at the request of the publisher Alexander Macmillan, who also sat to Dickinson for a portrait in crayons. His portrait of General Gordon at Khartoum hung in the Gordon Boys' Home, Worthing; that of George Peabody, merchant and founder of the Peabody Institute, is now in the Peabody Institute, Schapiro House, Johns Hopkins University, Maryland. Dickinson regularly exhibited portraits at the Royal Academy from 1848 to 1891. Through his friend Augustus Vansittart he established a connection with Cambridge, where many of his portraits hung in college halls.

In 1860 Dickinson took an active part in the formation of the Artists' volunteer rifle corps, of which he was treasurer. In 1879 he built a house, 1 All Souls Place, off Portland Place, St Marylebone, London, where he lived until his death there on 15 December 1908. He was buried at Kensal Green cemetery. His children and colleagues remembered the 'tender expression of his eyes and tones of his gentle voice', his 'beautiful face, white hair and beard' (Dickinson, vi). C. P. Lucas wrote that 'If ever a man had and kept to the end, the heart of a little child, it was Mr. Lowes Dickinson … He saw beauty and goodness in everything' (Lucas, 27–8). In 1909 his two sons and five daughters founded the Lowes Dickinson memorial studentship at the London Working Men's College for the study of art abroad. His portrait of his son Goldsworthy Lowes *Dickinson (1862–1932), scholar, is in the National Portrait Gallery. His other son was the accountant Sir Arthur Lowes *Dickinson (1859–1935).   SHANNON R. MCBRIAR

Sources L. Dickinson, Letters from Italy, 1850–1853 (privately printed, [1914]) • J. Llewelyn Davies, ed., The Working Men's College, 1854–1904 (1904) • C. P. Lucas, 'Friends who have gone before', Working Men's College Journal, 11/189 (Jan 1909), 1–4, and 11/190 (Feb 1909), 27–8 • J. F. C. Harrison, A history of the Working Men's College 1854–1954 (1954) • Letters of Dante Gabriel Rossetti, ed. O. Doughty and J. R. Wahl, 4 vols. (1965–7) • The Athenaeum (2 Jan 1909) • The Times (21 Dec 1908) • DNB • m. cert. • d. cert. • CGPLA Eng. & Wales (1909) • will, probate department of the principal registry of the family division, London

Archives NPG, Heinz Archive and Library, general corresp. • Princeton University Library, New Jersey, corresp. | King's AC Cam., letters to Oscar Browning • NPG, Heinz Archive and Library, corresp. relating to portraits at the NPG • V&A NAL, letters to Emma Brown and Ford Madox Brown

Likenesses F. Hollyer, photograph, repro. in Llewelyn Davies, ed., The Working Men's College, facing p. 26 [see illus.]

Wealth at death £4002 17s. 4d.: probate, 20 Jan 1909, CGPLA Eng. & Wales

Dickinson, Robert Eric (1905–1981), geographer, was born on 9 February 1905 at 10 Chalfont Street, Salford, the son of William Dickinson, a commercial traveller, and Mary Millichump Jones.

Educated at Upholland grammar school, Dickinson

went in 1922 to the fledgeling department of geography at the University of Leeds, gaining first-class honours in 1925: a diploma in education in 1926 from the University of Leeds was followed by his first academic post, as assistant lecturer in geography at University College, Exeter. His interests were strongly influenced by C. B. Fawcett at Leeds, and his undergraduate dissertation, 'Leeds as a regional capital', initiated the focus on regional delimitation and planning that characterized his entire career. Fawcett moved to University College, London, in 1928, and Dickinson joined him as an assistant lecturer, being promoted to lecturer in 1932 and reader in 1941. He married Mary Winwood (b. 1911/12), who had nursed his mother during her final illness, on 6 November 1940: there were no children. He returned to University College in 1945 after war service (1941–5) in the Royal Air Force (in cartographic intelligence), moving to Syracuse University in 1947. He was appointed professor of geography at Leeds in 1958, but his time there was marred by controversy and he transferred to a research professorship there in 1963 before moving to the University of Arizona in 1967. He travelled widely throughout his career (with Rockefeller fellowships in the USA and France and Germany during the 1930s), invariably accompanied by his wife after 1945, and was multilingual; his main outside interests were in theatre and music, and he took lessons in the 'cello after moving to Arizona.

The spatial organization of settlements ('the inherent geographical structure of society upon which planning must be based'; *City and Region*, 1964, xv) was the constant core of Dickinson's research programme. From pioneer studies of Leeds and Bradford and the hierarchical ordering of settlements in East Anglia, he expanded his interests through wide reading of American, French, and German sources. His key concept was the region, both the nodal region focused on a central place, and the social region, such as a homogeneous urban neighbourhood: he argued that both were key elements for the emerging practice of urban and regional planning. His major texts—*City Region and Regionalism* (1947; revised and expanded as *City and Region*, 1964) and *The West European City* (1951, 1961)—synthesized large literatures, several years before their topics became popular areas of geographic study. He was one of the pioneers in geography's shift of emphasis from society–environment interactions towards what became known as locational analysis; in London he stimulated others to work in the area and to realize the practical potential of their knowledge, notably in the new field of town and country planning. (He argued for the practical value of regional study in *Sociological Review* and the *Architects Journal* in 1943.)

The large volumes of material amassed during Dickinson's travels (almost as voracious as his reading) were employed in major texts on *The Regions of Germany* (1945), *Germany: a General and Regional Geography* (1953) and *Environments of America* (1974). He also published a Penguin Special, *The German Lebensraum* (1943). The idea of *Lebensraum* ('living space') originated in biology, but was adapted by a Swedish geographer, Rudolf Kjellen, to refer to competition between states (conceived as organisms), introduced to Germany by the founder of *Geopolitik*, Karl Haushofer, and used by the Nazi regime to justify German expansionism. From his deep knowledge of Germany and German writing (exemplified by articles in the *New Commonwealth Quarterly* in 1941), as well as of geography, Dickinson wrote both what he termed a 'debunking' of the concept and an analysis of the geography of Germany and adjacent lands as a basis for post-war political restructuring.

Dickinson's wider ideas about the nature of geography were reflected in a seminal and widely used early book with O. J. R. Howarth (*The Making of Modern Geography*, 1933: revised edition, 1969). They were later crystallized in books promoting the regional concept as the core of geography's field of study (*The Regional Concept*, 1976, *Regional Ecology*, 1970), as well as in his inaugural lecture at Leeds (published as *Some Problems of Human Geography*, 1960), but by then regional geography was in decline.

At Arizona Dickinson taught undergraduate courses on urban and political geography and on western Europe, plus a graduate course on the history of geographic thought, until his retirement in 1975. But he published no new research during that last period, concentrating on books which were mainly compilations of his own writings, plus extracts from the writings of others: he was opposed to contemporary developments in his discipline, and sought to counter them by reproducing classic statements reiterating his views of what geography was and should be.

Dickinson died on 1 September 1981 in Arizona. Gordon East's obituary (East, 123) claimed that 'a proper estimation of the place of Robert Dickinson in the world of geographers has yet to be made', and this is still the case. Certainly Dickinson did not have the impact that the breadth of his reading and writing might suggest, especially after his move to the USA, perhaps because he could be a difficult colleague and was rather a loner who lacked a school of graduate students. What he referred to as a 'serious error' in returning to the UK in the 1950s possibly added to this, as his period at Leeds was clearly unhappy (immediately before his move to Leeds an operation to remove a tumour from behind his left eye led to the loss of the eye and subsequent difficulties in reading). He was a scholar much more than either a teacher or an administrator. He was early in recognizing the importance of German and American studies of urban areas, but later generations successfully imported these into Anglo-American geography during what was known as the discipline's 'quantitative and theoretical revolution', which he found bewildering and in which he played no part.

RON JOHNSTON

Sources L. R. Pederson, 'Robert Eric Dickinson', *Geographers: biobibliographical studies*, 8, ed. T. W. Freeman (1984), 17–25 · G. East, *Transactions of the Institute of British Geographers*, new ser., 8 (1983), 122–4 · [W. Freeman], *GJ*, 148 (1982), 147–8 · Syracuse University, New York, department of geography, MSS · personnel department papers, U. Leeds · private information (2004) [L. R. Pederson, M. J. Wise] · personal knowledge (2004) · b. cert. · m. cert. · *WWW* · R. Johnston, 'City regions and a federal Europe: Robert Dickinson and post-World War II reconstruction', *Geopolitics*, 5 (2000), 153–76 · R. Johnston, 'Robert E. Dickinson and the growth of urban geography: an evaluation', *Urban Geography*, 22 (2002), 702–36 **Archives** RGS, field notes · U. Cal., Berkeley, field notes **Likenesses** portrait, repro. in Pederson, 'Robert Eric Dickinson', 17

Dickinson, Samuel (1690–1760), planter and jurist in America, was born on 9 March 1690 at Croisadore plantation, Talbot county, on the eastern shore of Maryland, the third and only surviving child of William Dickinson (1658–1717), planter, and his wife, Elizabeth Powell. His father, the son of an immigrant from London who converted to Quakerism, owned at his death five tobacco plantations totalling 2500 acres. His mother was a daughter of a locally prominent Quaker family. Samuel was educated at home and apprenticed for a year to Quaker tobacco merchants in London, the Hanburys and the Barclays. He married Judith (d. 1729), daughter of Andrew Troth, planter of Talbot county, on 4 January 1711 at the quarterly meeting, and took up residence at Croisadore. He and his wife were leaders of a nearby Friends' meeting.

Dickinson rapidly expanded the land holdings inherited from his father. By 1727 he had to provide for four sons and three daughters, and had acquired three more plantations in Maryland, as well as several hundred acres in Delaware. Numerous tenants and slaves worked his land. He purchased farms when tobacco prices were low and struggling smaller landholders were willing to sell out. He also studied law on his own, and probably gave his neighbours legal advice.

Dickinson married his second wife, Mary (1700–1776), daughter of John Cadwalader and Martha Jones, at the Philadelphia meeting on 4 November 1731. Mary's parents were Welsh Quakers; her father was a Philadelphia merchant. Dickinson and Mary had two surviving children; the elder was John *Dickinson (1732–1808), American statesman. When John was born in November 1732 only two of Dickinson's older children were alive. His only surviving daughter, Elizabeth, in 1739 married Charles Goldsborough, son of a wealthy Talbot county planter, in a Church of England ceremony. Dickinson consented to the wedding arrangements over the objections of the Friends' quarterly meeting; consequently, the meeting disowned his daughter for marrying out of the meeting and blamed him. Dickinson did not continue his relationship with the Society of Friends, though his wife remained in good standing.

By 1732 Dickinson was buying large tracts to set up another group of plantations in Delaware, to provide for the children that he and Mary would have. He bought about 1000 acres from his cousin, and by 1735 about 2000 acres more. This involved him in many legal disputes, and perhaps to occupy a position of influence he obtained appointment in 1738 as a judge of the Kent county court of common pleas. He successfully petitioned the Delaware legislature to dock the entail on lands formerly held by his cousin, to enable his younger sons to inherit it; his eldest son managed and would inherit the entailed Maryland

plantations. Dickinson built an elegant mansion, named Poplar Hall, on the St Jones River, 5 miles south-east of Dover, Kent county, Delaware, to which he moved in early 1741. His wife was now closer to her Philadelphia relatives, and he was further from the censorious Talbot county Friends. He could also supervise the growing and harvesting of his wheat crop, to which he had converted his Delaware plantations in the face of falling tobacco prices.

Dickinson was successful as a planter and in his public service. His total holdings amounted to about 9000 acres in Maryland and over 3000 acres in Delaware. Dickinson expanded his judicial responsibilities in 1744 to those of justice of the peace as well as first judge of the common pleas court. In the 1750s he suffered severe attacks of gout. He died at Poplar Hall of a sudden illness on 6 July 1760 and was buried three days later in the family plot near his home.   BENJAMIN H. NEWCOMB

Sources J. H. Powell, *The house on Jones Neck: the Dickinson mansion* (1954) · M. E. Flower, *John Dickinson: conservative revolutionary* (1983) · D. L. Jacobson, *John Dickinson and the revolution in Pennsylvania* (1965) · *Pennsylvania Gazette* (24 July 1760) · J. A. Monroe, *Colonial Delaware: a history* (1979) · W. W. Hinshaw, *Encyclopedia of American Quaker genealogy*, ed. [T. W. Marshall and others], 7 vols. (1936–50), vol. 2 · C. J. Stille, 'Life and times of John Dickinson', *Life and writings of John Dickinson* (1895) · H. T. Colbourn, 'A Pennsylvania farmer at the court of King George: John Dickinson's London letters', *Pennsylvania Magazine of History and Biography*, 86 (1962), 241–86, 417–53 **Archives** Hist. Soc. Penn., Logan collection **Likenesses** G. Hesselius, oils, Division of Historical and Cultural Affairs, Dover, Delaware **Wealth at death** over 12,000 acres: Flower, *John Dickinson*

Dickinson, Thorold Barron (1903–1984), film director and teacher, was born on 16 November 1903 in Bristol, the son of the Ven. Charles Henry Dickinson (1871–1930), archdeacon of Bristol, and his wife, Beatrice Vindhya. He was educated at Clifton College, Bristol, and at Keble College, Oxford (1923–7), where he studied history, but he devoted more time to college theatricals and a burgeoning interest in films than to his academic studies. Through his friendship with Malcolm Pearson he got a job as general assistant in 1926 with Pearson's father, George, then one of Britain's most respected film-makers, who taught him the rudiments of film-making. In 1929 Dickinson went to New York to study the new techniques of sound film and on his return to Britain began work as a film editor, first at British and Dominions Studios, Elstree, then at the Stoll Studios, Cricklewood, and from 1932 to 1936 at Ealing Studios. Many of the films Dickinson worked on as editor were dull and stagey but they enabled him to master the technical side of film-making and sometimes to experiment in order to enliven the films visually.

The technical training of the cutting rooms was complemented by the creative and aesthetic influence of the Film Society. This had been founded in 1925 to promote a serious interest in the art of film and it showed uncut imported prints of German, Russian, French, and experimental films. Throughout the 1930s Dickinson was in charge of technical presentation of the programmes and from 1932 to 1939 he was a member of the governing council of the society. He was strongly influenced by French

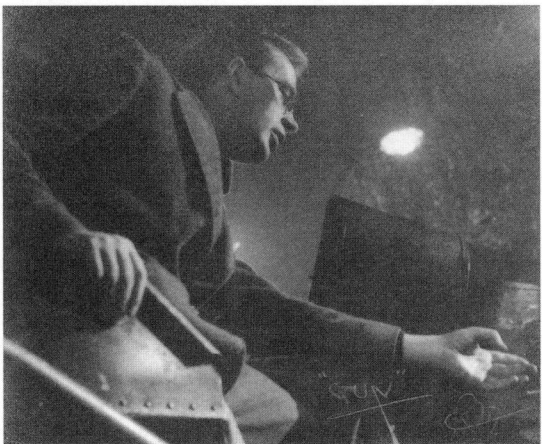

Thorold Barron Dickinson (1903–1984), by Russell Westwood, 1930s

cinema, particularly the films of Marcel Carné. He later recounted with pride that Patrick Hamilton had described his film *Gaslight* as 'a French film made in English' (Richards, 3).

Many of the people Dickinson worked with at the Film Society became involved in setting up and running the cinema technicians' union the Association of Cinematograph Technicians, and having himself experienced intolerable working conditions, Dickinson became a union activist, strongly committed to improving conditions for his fellow technicians. He was vice-president of the union from 1936 to 1953. One of the most significant influences on his life was his wife, (Irene) Joanna MacFadyen. An architect by training, she shared Dickinson's intellectual interests, his sense of humour, his forthrightness, and his hatred of snobbery and injustice. She was fiercely protective, some said excessively so, of Dickinson and his career. They married in 1929 and remained lifelong companions and collaborators until her death in 1979. She was credited as co-writer and co-editor on his last feature film, *Hill 24 doesn't Answer* (1954).

Dickinson's ultimate aim had always been to direct and he got the chance in 1936, when he was engaged by a small independent company (Fanfare) to direct a crime thriller, *The High Command* (1936), set in a British colony in west Africa. He persuaded the producers to sanction location-shooting in the Gold Coast Colony. The trip resulted in footage which enhanced the authenticity of the film and Graham Greene, then a film critic, commented admiringly on the film: 'British West Africa comes alive as it never did in Mr. Korda's lavish and unimaginative *Sanders of the River*' (*Night and Day*).

In 1938 Dickinson joined a unit assembled by Ivor Montagu to go to Spain to make three documentary films for use in fund-raising for the Spanish republican cause. Dickinson was chiefly responsible for *Spanish ABC*, a forceful and well-argued affirmation of the educational programme of the republican government. The film was put together in difficult circumstances in Barcelona during repeated air raids by the Franco forces. Back in Britain

Dickinson directed another crime thriller, the lively *Arsenal Stadium Mystery* (1939), which was uniformly liked by the critics. But his reputation was decisively made with his film of the psychological thriller *Gaslight* (1940), starring Anton Walbrook and Diana Wynyard, in which he applied his love of French style and Russian montage to a very English story which contained a critique of nineteenth-century patriarchal tyranny. It received rave reviews from the critics and an invitation from producer David O. Selznick to go to Hollywood. But Dickinson refused to leave Britain while the war was on. *Gaslight* became a *cause célèbre* when Metro-Goldwyn-Mayer bought the rights to the film with the intention of remaking it in Hollywood and a plan to destroy all prints of the Dickinson version. There was a press furore in Britain. Dickinson and his editor, Sidney Cole, secretly struck a print from the original negative and subsequently deposited it at the British Film Institute. But the film remained unseen for years.

For much of the war Dickinson's film-making activities were part of Britain's propaganda offensive, and he worked closely with the Ministry of Information. He directed two short documentaries for the ministry, *Westward Ho—1940* and *Yesterday is over your Shoulder*, and a morale-building biopic of the life of Disraeli, *The Prime Minister* (1940), which he later disowned as a piece of hackwork. But his principal cinematic achievement of the war years was a superb dramatized documentary feature, *The Next of Kin* (1941), made for the War Office and illustrating the truth of the wartime slogan 'Careless talk costs lives'. Released to cinemas, it was both a box office and a critical success.

While he was editing *The Next of Kin*, Dickinson was asked to organize a production unit for the Army Kinematograph Service and was commissioned as a second lieutenant, from which he rose rapidly to the rank of major. He assembled an expert team of film-makers and they produced seventeen military training films in their first year. But in December 1942 Dickinson was released from the Army Kinematograph Service to make a feature film commissioned by the Colonial Office to dramatize the government's new policy of colonial partnership. Dickinson worked with the novelist Joyce Cary on the script for *Men of Two Worlds* (1946), in which an African concert pianist and a British district officer in Tanganyika co-operate in the battle against sleeping sickness. The project involved lengthy location shooting under very difficult conditions in Tanganyika, but the Technicolor film stock that was used had decayed so badly by the time it reached Hollywood for processing that 90 per cent of the footage was unusable and most of the film was eventually shot at Denham Studios. The film took three years to make, cost £600,000, and was greeted by critics on its release in 1946 as a well-meaning bore. Dickinson ruefully declared: 'The whole thing was a misery' (Richards, 118).

A plan to film Somerset Maugham's novel *Then and Now* fell foul of the censors. But Dickinson was called on to take over the direction of *The Queen of Spades* (1949), which starred Anton Walbrook and Edith Evans. The result was an assured Romantic masterpiece in which extravagant style, exuberantly fluid camerawork, expressionist lighting, and a mastery of the mechanics of suspense combined to create one of the great achievements of British film-making. A prestige project for Festival of Britain year, *The Mayor of Casterbridge*, was cancelled by Associated British Pictures on grounds of cost, and Dickinson returned to Ealing to fulfil his dream of making a British 'art house' film. *Secret People* (1952) was a drama that explored the ethics of terrorism. But the film fell between the two stools of thriller and ethical drama, the reviews were damning, and communists demonstrated during performances, believing the film to be an attack on them.

On the basis of his wartime experience, Dickinson was invited to Israel to make a short propaganda film about the army, *The Red Ground* (1953), and then to make the first ever Israeli feature film, *Hill 24 doesn't Answer* (1954), a powerful and emotional account of three volunteers in the 1948 Arab–Israeli war. It received respectful notices in Britain but was little shown. However, *Hill 24* was seen and liked at the United Nations and in 1956, despairing of the commercial film industry, Dickinson accepted an appointment as chief of film services in the radio and visual services division of the UN department of public information. During his four years in New York he put together a multinational team of film-makers who produced a stream of short documentaries on aspects of UN work. But his main achievement during these years was a feature-length documentary, which he produced and co-edited, *Power among Men* (1958–9), which described the successful co-operation between men and women of different nationalities on development projects. It won prizes at the Venice and Moscow film festivals and the Selznick golden laurel award in 1959.

In 1960, frustrated by the inability to do more with the UN documentary programme, Dickinson returned to Britain to take up a newly established senior lectureship in film at the Slade School of Fine Art in University College, London. The aim of the department, which Dickinson set up, was to turn out film students who would go into production, teaching, and criticism. In 1967 he became the first professor of film in Britain; a postgraduate diploma course was set up and Dickinson pioneered film studies teaching in the United Kingdom.

Dickinson had always been deeply committed to the cause of film education. Involved in the British Film Institute from the first, from 1950 to 1956 he served on the national film archive committee. He was involved in the creation of the British Film Academy, set up in 1946 to confer intellectual respectability on the cinema, and was its chairman in 1952–3. He was a long-standing supporter of the film society movement, and saw film societies as a crucial means of educating people cinematically. He was a member of the council of the Film Society from 1932 to 1939 and president of the International Federation of Film Societies from 1958 to 1966. In his later years he was a regular member of prestigious film festival juries, and chaired those at Venice, Berlin, and Guadalajara. He wrote many articles setting out his ideas about film as an art form, and in 1971 published a grand synthesis of these, *A Discovery of Cinema*, in which he rejected the dream-factory, conveyor-belt Hollywood system in favour of the continental tradition of art cinema, making films of ideas for discriminating audiences.

Dickinson retired from teaching in 1971 and was made professor emeritus and awarded a PhD of London University. His dedication to the promotion of a film culture was recognized in the honours and awards showered on him in his retirement. He was appointed CBE in 1973 and was visiting professor of film at the University of Surrey, Guildford, from 1975 to 1977: he received that university's honorary doctorate in 1976. He received honorary life membership of the Association of Cinematograph and Television Technicians, the British Universities' Film and Video Council, and the International Association of Audio-Visual Media in Historical Research and Education. He was made a fellow of the British Film Institute and his eightieth birthday was commemorated by a season of his films at the National Film Theatre.

Dickinson lived in retirement in Lambourn, Berkshire, but his last years were darkened by failing eyesight, increasing ill health, and (in 1979) the death of his wife, Joanna, to whom he was devoted. He was wholly out of sympathy with the new critical orthodoxies and felt anger and frustration at what he saw as the undermining of the new discipline of film studies by militant young theorists. He died at Oxford on 14 April 1984.

Although his body of work as a director was slim, Dickinson was undoubtedly a cinematic *auteur*, whose primary concern was with the working of his characters' minds and their psychological development. He was drawn in particular to 'secret people', divided beings whose inner selves emerged at moments of crisis. This reflected his own divided allegiance, the desire for both art and education, both to entertain and to enlighten. His visual style, influenced by German expressionism, Eisensteinian montage, Marcel Carné's poetic realism, and latterly Italian neo-realism, was also distinctive: long takes, mobile camera, sparing use of close-ups, musical form. Intellectually, he was a product of the left-wing inter-war intelligentsia; but basically he was an old-fashioned liberal with a characteristic paternalism that made him in many ways a natural teacher. He retained a romantic faith in education and in the creation of an intelligent, cultured, and articulate film audience. It was this didactic side which made him a natural and effective propagandist for causes in which he believed such as Spanish republicanism, the allied cause in the Second World War, Israel, and the United Nations. His commitment to all these causes stemmed from a basic belief in justice, truth, and humanity. As a romantic and an idealist, he threw himself successively into commercial cinema, sponsored cinema, and full-time education in pursuit of his dream of a British 'art house' cinema. He ended up disillusioned with all of them. Perhaps the most fulfilled period of his creative life was during the war when, under the benign patronage of the Ministry of Information, he was able to commit himself to work that would simultaneously entertain, educate, and enlighten, while raising the qualitative level of British cinema.   JEFFREY RICHARDS

Sources J. Richards, *Thorold Dickinson and the British cinema* (1997) • T. Dickinson, *A discovery of cinema* (1971) • R. Durgnat, *A mirror for England: British movies from austerity to affluence* (1970) • L. Anderson, *Making a film: the story of 'Secret People'* (1952) • G. Greene, *The pleasure dome* (1972) • M. Foster, *Joyce Cary* (1968) • J. Huntley, *British technicolor films* (1949) • *WWW* • *Night and Day* (29 July 1937) • *CGPLA Eng. & Wales* (1984)
Archives BFI, MSS | FILM BFI NFTVA, 'Thorold Dickinson interview', 1979
Likenesses R. Westwood, photograph, 1930–39, NPG [*see illus.*] • photographs, 1931–45, Hult. Arch.
Wealth at death £423,399: probate, 8 June 1984, *CGPLA Eng. & Wales*

Dickinson, William (1746/7?–1823), engraver and printseller, is said to have been born in London; he might possibly have been the son of Joseph and Grace Dickinson, baptized at St Mary, Whitechapel, Stepney, on 6 May 1747. It is not known who taught Dickinson to engrave, but in 1767 he was awarded a premium for mezzotint by the Society for the Encouragement of Arts, Manufactures, and Commerce. His later training was almost certainly given by the painter Robert Edge Pine, at whose house in St Martin's Lane he lodged between 1768 and 1771. His first eight exhibited drawings and prints (1768–73) were after paintings by Pine; his portrait of Sir Joseph Banks (1774) was the first of twenty-two mezzotints after Reynolds. Dickinson produced in all some hundred portraits, judged 'well drawn and finely scraped … their brilliance often enhanced by the use of warm brown inks' (Alexander, 863).

In 1773 Dickinson began to publish his own prints, and in 1778 he took under his wing the engraver Johann Jacobe, who was on a state-sponsored visit from Vienna to perfect his mezzotint technique. It has been suggested that Reynolds arranged for Jacobe to lodge with Dickinson; Reynolds was a major supplier of work to Dickinson, who published a number of his paintings in mezzotint and in stipple. By 1778 Dickinson had entered into partnership with Thomas Watson (1743–1781), another engraver in stipple and mezzotint. About Christmas they took over the established print shop of Walter Shropshire in fashionable New Bond Street, insuring their joint stock for about £2400—a sizeable sum. Their stock of plates was based on modern artists, with Reynolds, Kauffman, Bunbury, Peters, and Gardner featuring prominently. Watson died in 1781 but Dickinson continued to run the business alone. At first he was very successful, and he built up a large and distinguished stock of modern plates. In 1791 he took a new shop at 20 Old Bond Street and was appointed engraver and printseller to the prince of Wales. His bankruptcy in 1793 was presumably attributable principally to the war in Europe rather than to the notoriously unreliable patronage of Prince George, but he was obliged to auction his stock at Christies in 1794, and there was a further sale in 1797. Soon after this he emigrated to France, where he worked as a mezzotint engraver. In Paris he

engraved portraits of the king of Saxony in 1811 and of the emperor Napoleon in 1815. He seems to have returned to London after Waterloo and was living at Twickenham from 1817 to 1820, but he is said to have died in Paris in 1823.   TIMOTHY CLAYTON and ANITA McCONNELL

Sources D. Alexander, 'Dickinson, William', *The dictionary of art*, ed. J. Turner (1996) • G. Meissner, ed., *Allgemeines Künstlerlexikon: die bildenden Künstler aller Zeiten und Völker*, [new edn, 34 vols.] (Leipzig and Munich, 1983–) • Redgrave, *Artists* • *LondG* (9–13 April 1793); (4–8 June 1793), 295, 476 • *LondG* (12–15 April 1794), 331 • C. Le Blanc, *Manuel de l'amateur d'estampes*, 2 (Paris, 1855–6), 125–6 • T. Clayton, *The English print, 1688–1802* (1997) • Royal Exchange Insurance, policy no. 74950, GL, MS 7253 • *A catalogue of the extensive and valuable stock of copper plates … the property of Mr William Dickinson* (1794) [sale catalogue, Christies, 14 Feb 1794] • *A catalogue of a collection of modern prints … of Mr William Dickinson … a bankrupt* [sale catalogue, Christie, Sharp, and Harper, London, 22 May 1797]

Dickinson, William (*bap.* 1756, *d.* 1822), antiquary and political manager, was baptized William Dickinson Rastall at St Mary's, Newark-on-Trent, Nottinghamshire, on 15 June 1756, the only son of the Revd Dr William Rastall (1724–1788) and his wife, Mary Allgood of Branton, Northumberland. His father, who in 1774 became vicar-general of the chapter of Southwell, Nottinghamshire, suffered from some debilitating physical infirmity, which may be the reason for his son's statement that he 'was induced early in life, by concurrence of circumstances somewhat out of the ordinary course, to embark on a tempestuous ocean' (Dickinson, i). He followed his father to Jesus College, Cambridge, graduating BA in 1777 and MA in 1780. He studied law and by 1787/8 was described as 'of Lincoln's Inn'. On 6 December 1787 he married Harriot (*b.* 1767), daughter of John Kenrick, lord of the manor and MP for the pocket borough of Bletchingley, Surrey, with whom he had six surviving children. He became a JP for Nottinghamshire in 1786 and at various dates also for Lincolnshire, Middlesex, Surrey, and Sussex. He published three treatises on the work of a JP in 1815, 1818, and 1822. In 1795 he was bequeathed property in 'the north' by a very distant collateral relation, Mrs Henrietta Dickinson of 'Eastwood Hoo' in Yorkshire, on the condition of his adoption of the Dickinson surname alone; the bequest was subsequently the subject of litigation. He expanded his Nottinghamshire estates by purchases at North Muskham and Sutton-on-Trent, including the mansion called Muskham Grange in 1789, which he subsequently enlarged and embellished.

Having over a hundred, tenants of his own within the town of Newark, Dickinson was drawn into the bitter political struggles between the ruling 'red' party, mainly tenants of the two largest landlords, the dukes of Newcastle and of Rutland, and the independent opposition 'blue' party, loosely affiliated to the duke of Portland. By 1790 Dickinson was leader of the blues, although he declined to stand as a parliamentary candidate for either of the two Newark seats in that year on the grounds of ill health. As a moderate he accepted 'that if great property united with great rank had a claim to the compliment of *one* member and bringing up a family of two legitimate children alongside a second family of nine illegitimate offspring by his housekeeper.

Joseph Wright of Derby's portrait of Dickinson as a young boy shows him with his hand resting on a book of topographical drawings, and his antiquarian interests formed an escape from his personal problems throughout his life. At the age of thirty-one he published his *History of the Antiquities of the Town and Church of Southwell* (1787, with later editions to 1819). A companion *History and Antiquities of the Town of Newark* followed in 1805–6 (also with later editions until 1819). The 1816 edition was prefaced with the apology for the delay in publication as he had been 'overwhelmed with calamities of unusual magnitude' (Dickinson, *History of Newark*, preface). Dickinson died on 13 October 1822 at 10 Cumberland Place, New Road, Middlesex, and was buried ten days later in the family vault in North Muskham church. An obituary appeared in the *Annual Register*. Because of the complications with his financial affairs his will was not proved in the province of York until 1843.   ADRIAN HENSTOCK

Sources M. J. Smith, 'Politics in Newark in the 1790s', *Transactions of the Thoroton Society*, 84 (1980), 59–67 · A. Henstock, 'The Halls of Whatton: the faltering rise of a Victorian landed family', *Transactions of the Thoroton Society*, 86 (1982), 97–105 · W. Dickinson, *Interrogatories and answers in a commission of bankruptcy against messrs. Pocklington, Dickinson & Co.* (1810) · J. Britton, E. W. Brayley, and others, *The beauties of England and Wales, or, Delineations topographical, historical, and descriptive, of each county*, [18 vols.] (1801–16), vol. 12, pt 1 · *Thoroton's history of Nottinghamshire*, ed. J. Throsby, 3 vols. (1797), vol. 3 · *A complete collection of papers … on the … election for the borough of Newark … in 1790* (1791) · M. Dobbin, *Notts history and topography: a select descriptive bibliography to 1980* (1983) · T. M. Blagg, *Newark as a publishing town* (1898) · *GM*, 1st ser., 57 (1787), 424–7 · *GM*, 1st ser., 71 (1801), 925–8 · *GM*, 1st ser., 73 (1803), 1045–7 · *GM*, 1st ser., 76 (1806), 1034–6 · *GM*, 1st ser., 92/2 (1822), 376 · C. Brown, *A history of Newark on Trent*, 2 (1907) · G. Y. Hemingway, *Some notes on Newark banks* (1977) · F. C. Laird, *A topographical and historical description of the county of Nottingham* (1812?) · U. Nott. L., Portland MSS, esp. letter of William Dickinson to duke of Portland, 18 May 1795 (PWF 3348) · Notts. Arch., esp. DD985, DD.BM, DD.H, DD.LK, DD.TB, QDE · *IGI*
Archives Notts. Arch., various solicitors' and family collections, title deeds, legal papers, etc., esp. DD985, DD.BM, DD.H, DD.LK, DD.TB, QDE, *passim* | U. Nott., Portland MSS
Likenesses J. Wright, portrait, *c*.1765, priv. coll. · W. Holl, stipple (after miniature by W. P. Sherlock), BM, NPG; repro. in W. Dickinson, *Antiquities historical, architectural, chorographical, and itinerary, in Nottinghamshire … comprising the histories of Southwell … and of Newark*, 4 vols. (1801–19) [*see illus.*]
Wealth at death under £600: will, proved 28 Jan 1823 (London); 2 Nov 1843 (York)

William Dickinson (*bap.* 1756, *d.* 1822), by William Holl, pubd 1801 (after William P. Sherlock)

for the Borough of Newark', then it was only fair 'to prevent the further incroachment on the liberty of the inhabitants' and to oppose the election of a *second* representative of 'those great families who have of late years represented the town' (*Complete Collection*, 40–41). He published two political pamphlets in Newark in 1798 under the guise of 'a Nottinghamshire Magistrate'. F. C. Laird, writing in 1812, believed that Dickinson's 'liberal character and conduct' had 'prevented an overflow of party spirit on more occasions than one' (Laird, 244).

In 1788–9 Dickinson entered into partnership with a distant cousin, Roger Pocklington, and others as bankers in Newark. However, the partnership was declared bankrupt in 1809. Most of Dickinson's property, including his family home, had to be sold for the benefit of over 3000 creditors; in 1810 he published in his defence a transcript of the proceedings of the commission of bankruptcy. In this he remarked that 'storms wholly unlooked for, and from a quarter in which all appeared perfect sunshine, have overtaken me, in which fame, fortune, health … have been wrecked' (Dickinson, i).

An additional cause of Dickinson's personal problems was the elopement to Gretna Green in 1807 of his sixteen-year-old daughter Harriot with the nineteen-year-old son of a wealthy Nottingham merchant hosier. The marriage was re-celebrated a month later in Balderton church at Dickinson's instigation 'in order to place the couple in the eyes of the world in a respectable situation' (Nottinghamshire Archives, DD. TB 1/20/3), but his firm's bankruptcy led to protracted legal suits over the marriage settlement. In addition his son-in-law proved a profligate rake, frequently moving around the country to avoid his creditors,

Dickons [*née* Poole], **Martha Frances Caroline** [Maria; *known as* Caroline Poole] (*c*.1774–1833), singer, is said to have been born in London about 1774—perhaps a few years earlier—the daughter of William Poole (1737/8–1812). A precocious musician, she sang and played the harpsichord at an Oxford concert in 1785 and studied at Bath with Venanzio Rauzzini, in whose opera *La vestale* she made her London stage début at the King's Theatre on 1 May 1787. She was known professionally as Caroline Poole in her early career. In the summer of 1787 she began a series of engagements at Vauxhall, and in Lent 1790 sang in the Covent Garden oratorios, as she was to do almost annually through the 1790s. In the same year she started appearing in the Salomon concerts, for one of which (1792) Haydn wrote an aria for her (now lost). A new departure was her engagement at Covent Garden as an actress and singer at £8 a week; her début as Ophelia on 9 October 1793 was noted more for her singing in the mad scenes than for her acting, though her Polly in *The Beggar's Opera*, three days later, was said to be delightful. In 1793–5 she appeared in many comic operas and patriotic plays; after an unexplained hiatus she again acted and sang at Covent Garden in 1798–9. In the summers she performed in Edinburgh (1794) and Ireland (1795–6). She retired to marry, on 7 August 1800, a Liverpool merchant, Peter Dickons, but his trading losses led her to resume her professional career in 1807. The marriage ended in separation in 1810.

As Mrs Dickons she reappeared at Covent Garden on 20 October 1807 in Arne's *Artaxerxes*. Between then and 1815 she also performed at the Lyceum, in Drury Lane oratorios, and at the Italian Opera (as the Countess in the first London performance of Mozart's *Le nozze di Figaro*, 18 June 1812). A foray to the Théâtre Italien in Paris in Peter Winter's *Il ratto di Proserpina* (7 December 1816) failed. Engagements in Italy in 1816–17, later described in England as successful, remain undocumented. She is said to have been elected to the Istituto Filarmonico at Venice—a short-lived academy that ended in 1816. If she was the Maria Castiglioni who sang at La Fenice, Venice, in 1816 and 1817, she was demoted in the latter year to secondary parts. She returned to London and reappeared at Covent Garden in Henry Bishop's perversions of Rossini's *Il barbiere di Siviglia* (13 October 1818) and of *Le nozze di Figaro* (6 March 1819, again as the Countess). She then retired. She died of cancer at her house in Regent Street on 4 May 1833. Her voice at its best was 'powerful and mellifluous', and she possessed 'a sensible and impressive intonation and a highly polished taste'. W. B. SQUIRE, rev. JOHN ROSSELLI

Sources C. B. Hogan, ed., *The London stage, 1660–1800*, pt 5: 1776–1800 (1968), 1479, 1484–5, 1533, 1573, 1579, 1605, 1680, 1784, 1889, 1893, 1897, 2105–6, 2109 · G. W. Stone, ed., *The London stage, 1660–1800*, pt 4: 1747–1776 (1962), 1479, 1576, 1683, 1684, 1999, 2003 · Highfill, Burnim & Langhans, *BDA* · T. J. Walsh, *Opera in Dublin, 1705–1797: the social scene* (1973), 299–300 · H. C. Robbins Landon, *Haydn in England: 1791–1795* (1976), vol. 3 of *Haydn: chronicle and works* · [Clarke], *The Georgian era: memoirs of the most eminent persons*, 4 (1834), 302 · Castil-Blaze [F. H.-J. Blaze], *L'opéra-italien de 1548 à 1856* (Paris, 1856), 368 · M. Girardi and F. Rossi, eds., *Il Teatro la Fenice: cronologia degli spettacoli*, 2 vols. (1989–91) · *Il conservatorio di musica 'Benedetto Marcello' di Venezia, 1876–1976* (1977), 186 · *GM*, 1st ser., 77 (1807), 263 · *GM*, 1st ser., 82/1 (1812), 93 · *GM*, 1st ser., 103/1 (1833), 649

Likenesses G. K. Ralph, portrait, 1795, RA · MacKenzie, engraving, 1805 · Alais, engraving, pubd 1811 · Alais, engraving, pubd 1813 · A. E. Chalon, pen and watercolour sketch, 1815, NPG · C. Penry, engraving, 1819 (after Bradley) · M. A. Bourlier, stipple, BM, NPG; repro. in *La Belle Assemblée* (1812) · W. Bradley, pencil and watercolour drawing (as Rosina in *The barber of Seville*), Garr. Club · S. De Wilde, watercolour, Harvard TC · S. Freeman, engraving, repro. in *Monthly Mirror* (1808) · Kennerley, engraving, repro. in *Theatrical Inquisitor* (1819) · J. Martyn, engraving · W. Ridley, engraving, repro. in Parson, *Minor Theatre* (1794) · Woodman junior, engraving, repro. in *The Cabinet* (1808) · engraving, repro. in *Hibernian Magazine* (Aug 1796) · pencil, ink, and watercolour drawing, NPG

Dicks, John Thomas (*bap.* 1818, *d.* 1881), publisher, was born in London and baptized on 20 September 1818 at the church of St Dunstan, Stepney, the son of John Dicks and his wife, Sibyl. Not much is known of his early life, but he appears to have had at least three sisters, Elizabeth, Sibyl Rebecca, and Jane, as well as one brother, Walter George. John Thomas Dicks himself later married, and he and his wife, Maria Louisa, had ten children, including the two sons named in his will as executors, Henry and John Thomas, and a daughter, Kate Alice Taylor, whose husband William and children he excluded from his will by codicil.

Dicks began in the printing trade in 1832, being employed in the Stationery Office by the queen's printer, as well as in other offices. In 1841 he became the chief assistant of P. P. Thomas, a scholar of Chinese, who was at that time in the business of publishing, printing, and stereotyping in Warwick Square. Dicks's subsequent career and the expansion of his publishing business were intricately tied up with the fortunes of G. W. M. Reynolds, a radical, and purveyor of popular and often sensational fiction; he was the 'most popular writer in England' in the nineteenth century according to *The Bookseller* (July 1868, 447). Early in his career Reynolds had several bankruptcies, but his association with Dicks turned him into a wealthy man. In turn, Reynolds's popular novels and periodicals, which provided a good portion of Dicks's list throughout most of the mid-nineteenth century, made a fortune for Dicks.

Their connection began in 1848 when Dicks, still employed by Thomas, took over as publisher of *Reynolds's Miscellany*, establishing an office at Wellington Street North, Strand, London. For a decade after 1848 Dicks published Reynolds's novels and periodicals including a very successful Sunday paper, *Reynolds's Weekly Newspaper*, which started in 1850. He was also the publisher of Reynolds's massive multi-novel series, *Mysteries of the Court of London* (1849–56). In 1852 Dicks, 'the managing and confidential clerk' of Reynolds's publications, had 'all the details of the business placed under his supervision' (*Reynolds's Weekly*, 18 July 1852, 3). In 1863 the two men formed a partnership, and eventually (probably at Reynolds's death in 1879) Dicks purchased for a large sum the name and copyrights of G. W. M. Reynolds.

In the 1860s Dicks's publishing house had begun to expand dramatically by reprinting novels, plays, 'classics', and miscellaneous material rather than originating new works. According to Montague Summers, during the latter half of the century the firm was 'one of the largest and busiest printing and publishing offices in England' (Summers, 552). In 1866 Dicks began his first and one of his most popular series of cheap reprints, Dicks's Shakespeare (individual plays for a penny, thirty-seven plays in one volume for a shilling); in 1868 Reynolds announced at the annual dinner of the firm that 150,000 copies of the penny Shakespeare had been sold (*Reynolds's Weekly*, 12 July

1868, 1). In 1864 Dicks began to issue Dicks's Standard Plays, at 1d. each. For over twenty years he published a play a week and from 1882 two a week. Over 1000 were published altogether, and include such titles as Dion Boucicault's *The Shaughraun: an Original Drama in Three Acts, Illustrative of Irish Life and Character*, numbered 390 in the Standard Plays series; Henry Hersee's *All's Fair in Love: an Original Charade Written Expressly for Drawing-Room Acting*, billed as number 490 of Dicks's Standard Charades and Comedies; and F. F. Cooper's *The Spare Bed, or, The Shower Bath: a Farce in Two Acts*, number 786 in the Standard Plays. Dicks's dramatic series also included adaptations of popular novels, with dramatizations of Charles Dickens's proving especially popular. At least one catalogue of Dicks's publications was printed, as the *List of Dicks' Standard Plays and Free Acting Drama* (1884). Many of the popular melodramas, farces, and comedies of the nineteenth century exist only in a Dicks imprint.

In 1869 Dicks merged *Reynolds's Miscellany* with *Bow Bells*, the latter being a popular family magazine that he had begun in 1864, designed 'to cultivate a taste for beauty and goodness in humanity'. One historian has suggested that as Dicks prospered, his increasing respectability contrasted sharply with the nature of the earlier publications on which he had collaborated with Reynolds, and that the title change of *Bow Bells* was perhaps a tactic used 'to conceal the way by which he had come to his wealth' (James, 47). Also in 1869 he began the series Dicks's English Novels (6d. a volume), which eventually included 243 titles, by authors such as Dickens and Thackeray, but also by lesser-known novelists of the period. The wide variety of other publications that were issued at one time or another under the Dicks imprint included various albums of songs (such as *Gems from the Great Composers*); illustrations and prints (Hogarth's various works and Francis Wheatley's *London Cries*); and chromolithographs (at 6d.) 'for framing', including works by Landseer and portraits of various politicians. In 1884, three years after his death, the firm began a new series in his name, Dicks's English Library of Standard Works.

Dicks retired from the firm in the late 1870s. His two sons, Henry and John Thomas, continued to manage the firm for him, and he moved to the villa St Valentine in Menton, France. Apparently he maintained some connection with the business: writing long after the fact, George Augustus Sala gives the only known personal account of Dicks, recalling that:

> at a pretty little villa at Menton there resided a very old business friend of mine, the Late Mr. John Dicks ... [whose] appetite for novelettes was insatiable, and whenever I wanted cash I had only to scribble for a few hours, take the copy over to Menton and receive from the hands of my friendly publisher a crisp ten-pound note and two louis and a half in gold. (*Life and Adventures*, 2.367)

Dicks died at Menton on 4 February 1881. After this the firm bearing his name published from several different London locations, including Effingham House, Arundel Street, Strand (beginning 1905), and finally in 1909 as John Dicks Press Ltd, at 8 Temple Avenue. In 1929 *Reynolds's*

Newspaper (which continued until 1963) ceased to be published by John Dicks Press Ltd. No further publication was issued under this imprint.

The survival in libraries of books that bear the Dicks imprint is haphazard and his several series of cheap reprints of English classics are almost everywhere incomplete. Because of his policy of issuing and reissuing publications and series almost constantly, the initial publication dates of many of his series are uncertain. But his achievement is clear: he was one of the most important forces in the increase of cheap reading material for the masses. As his obituary indicated, his publishing concern was 'a marvel in cheap and good literature' (*Bow Bells*, 2 March 1881). ANNE HUMPHERYS

Sources M. Summers, 'John Dicks, publisher', *TLS* (7 Nov 1942), 552 · J. T. Dicks, will, 5 March 1881 · 'Death of Mr. John Thomas Dicks', *Bow Bells* (2 March 1881) · V. E. Neuburg, *Popular literature: a history and guide* (1977) · *Reynolds's Weekly Newspaper* (18 July 1852), 3 · *Reynolds's Weekly Newspaper* (12 July 1868), 1 · *The life and adventures of George Augustus Sala*, 2 vols. (1895) · L. James, *Fiction for the working man, 1830–1850* (1963) · d. cert. · *The Bookseller* (3 March 1881), 231 · IGI · CGPLA Eng. & Wales (1881)

Wealth at death under £50,000: probate, 5 March 1881, *CGPLA Eng. & Wales*

Dicksee, Sir Francis Bernard (1853–1928), historical genre and portrait painter, was born in London on 27 November 1853. He was the elder son of the painter and illustrator Thomas Francis Dicksee (1819–1895) and his wife, Eliza, the daughter of John Bernard, of Church Place, Piccadilly, London; his uncle John Robert Dicksee (1817–1905) was also a painter. Dicksee was educated at the Revd George Henslow's school, Bloomsbury. He studied art with his father and from 1870 to 1875, at the Royal Academy Schools where he showed early promise, winning gold and silver medals. While still a student, Dicksee exhibited at the Society (later Royal Society) of British Artists in Suffolk Street in 1872; he began to exhibit regularly at the Royal Academy from 1876, when he showed *Elijah confronting Ahab and Jezebel in Naboth's Vineyard*, for which he had been awarded the Royal Academy's gold medal the previous year.

Dicksee's art was firmly rooted in Pre-Raphaelite concepts. Along with the illustrator and designer Walter Crane, the painter and designer Henry Holiday, and the painter J. W. Waterhouse, he was influenced by Edward Burne-Jones and William Morris. The romantic, dreamlike visions that they espoused are epitomized by Dicksee's best-known work, *La Belle Dame sans Merci* (Bristol Art Gallery). Dicksee worked for some time under Holiday, who is perhaps best-known for his stained glass designs. He learned much from Holiday's interpretation of Pre-Raphaelitism and incorporated into his allegorical painting *Harmony* (exh. RA, 1877; Tate collection) a stained-glass window that could have been designed by Holiday. Equally, the organ case, seen on the left of the painting, might have been designed by William Morris's firm—as Graham Reynolds points out, the scene is more akin to a St John's Wood studio than a medieval home. Dicksee was only twenty-four when this painting, which depicts a young woman in medieval costume playing an organ while a young man listens in rapt attention, met with great success at the Royal Academy exhibition. It was hailed as 'picture of the year' and was purchased by the Chantrey trustees for 350 guineas. *The House Builders* (1880; priv. coll.), a large painting showing Sir William and Lady Welby-Gregory examining the plans and model of Denton Manor (dem.) built for them by A. W. Blomfield between 1879 and 1884, has itself been interpreted as a model of Victorian architectural patronage (see Physick and Derby, 152).

Early in his career Dicksee also illustrated books and magazines. The best-known of these are probably those for Longfellow's *Evangeline* (1882) and for Cassell's 'royal' editions of Shakespeare: *Romeo and Juliet* (1884) and *Othello* (1889). Several of his woodcut illustrations for the *Cornhill Magazine* are in the Victoria and Albert Museum.

In 1881 Dicksee was elected an associate of the Royal Academy, and in 1891 he became a full academician. His diploma work, *Startled*, was deposited in 1892. It depicts two nude girls—one a child, the other an adolescent—rushing from their bathing place, covered only by loosely held diaphanous robes, as a boat approaches. Dicksee had found a profitable niche, and continued to paint similarly titillating and ephemeral subjects for many years to come. He was not an innovative artist and frequently borrowed compositions from artists he knew and admired. Thus in a portrait of Lady Inverclyde of 1910 (Glasgow Museum and Art Gallery) he utilized a pose (albeit in reverse) derived from D. G. Rossetti's painting of Jane Morris, *Mariana* (Aberdeen Art Gallery), of forty years earlier. The exotically sensual women depicted in *The Magic Crystal* (1894; Lady Lever Art Gallery, Port Sunlight) and *Passion* (or *Leila*) owe much to the powerful, almost masculine women who populate the paintings of Frederic Leighton. The ghostly figure in *A Reverie* (1895; Walker Art Gallery, Liverpool) was clearly inspired by Millais's earlier *Speak Speak* (1895; Tate collection).

Dicksee did not restrict himself to an imagined past but repeated his favoured composition, the interaction of two romantically paired figures, in modern moralizing scenes, such as *The Crisis* (1891; Melbourne Art Gallery) and *The Confession*, in which a young woman dressed in white is seen awaiting the reaction of her husband to whom she has confessed. Occasionally, however, he moved away from this format to paint large, intricate compositions, such as the dramatic *Funeral of a Viking* (1893; Manchester City Galleries).

Dicksee was a strident opponent of modern art. His retrogressive stance, however, did not adversely affect his popularity. In his own lifetime his paintings achieved high prices at auction—the record for his work being set by *Too Late* (1883), bought for £997 10s. at the A. Shuttleworth sale at Christies on 3 May 1890. In 1900 he won a gold medal at the Universal Exhibition, and the same year his painting entitled *The Two Crowns* (Tate collection) was purchased by the Chantrey trustees for £2000. Even into the 1920s he continued to exhibit and sell sentimental, melodramatic paintings that had not changed significantly from his much earlier work, such as *The End of the*

Quest (1921; Leighton House, London) and *This for Remembrance* (1924; Walker Art Gallery, Liverpool). Dicksee's romantic scenes found favour with his female audience and for a time he was also a fashionable portrait painter, especially for women, though towards the end of the century his melancholy style was eclipsed by John Singer Sargent's 'swagger' school of portrait painting.

In 1924 Dicksee was elected president of the Royal Academy. He was knighted in 1925 and in the following year was nominated by the newly elected chancellor of Oxford University, Viscount Cave, for the honorary degree of DCL. He was created KCVO in 1927. He was a trustee of the British Museum and the National Portrait Gallery and president of the Artists' General Benevolent Association. He died, unmarried, on 17 October 1928, at the Cambridge Nursing Home, 4 Dorset Square, London. A retrospective selection of his works was included in the Royal Academy winter exhibition of 1933.   JENNIFER MELVILLE

Sources *DNB* · J. Treuherz, *Victorian painting* (1993) · W. Gaunt, *Painting in Britain, 1800–1900* (1972) · G. Reynolds, *Victorian painting* (1966) · R. Strong, *The British portrait, 1600–1960* (1991) · Wood, *Vic. painters*, 3rd edn · d. cert. · Graves, *RA exhibitors* · J. Physick and M. Derby, eds., *Marble halls: drawings and models for Victorian secular buildings* (1973) [exhibition catalogue, V&A, London]
Archives JRL, letters to Manchester Art Gallery · U. Leeds, Brotherton L., letters to Sir Edmund Gosse
Likenesses F. Dicksee, self-portrait, oils, 1883, Aberdeen Art Gallery · W. Stoneman, photograph, 1917, NPG · W. & D. Downey, woodburytype photograph, NPG; repro. in W. Downey and D. Downey, *The cabinet portrait gallery*, 4 (1893) · Lock & Whitfield, woodburytype photograph, NPG; repro. in T. Cooper, *Men of mark: a gallery of contemporary portraits* (1883) · R. W. Robinson, photograph, NPG; repro. in *Members and associates of the Royal Academy of Arts* (1891)
Wealth at death £37,905 7s. 8d.: probate, 29 Nov 1928, CGPLA Eng. & Wales

Dicksee, Lawrence Robert (1864–1932), chartered accountant and writer on accounting, was born on 1 May 1864 at 27 Howland Street, London, the youngest of five children of John Robert Dicksee (1817–1905), artist, and his wife, Mary Ann, *née* Barnard. He grew up in a family with strong artistic associations, and was the cousin of the painter Francis Bernard *Dicksee (1853–1928). Dicksee was educated at the City of London School (c.1867–1881), where his father taught between 1852 and 1897, holding the position of head drawing-master. He was articled in 1881 to the chartered accountant George Norton Read, whose office was at 31 Queen Victoria Street, in the City of London. This was just one year after the formation of the Institute of Chartered Accountants in England and Wales, and in November 1886 Dicksee was one of the earliest to qualify for membership by examination. He then set up in practice in London, three years later joining Peter Price in Cardiff to form Price and Dicksee. Dicksee returned to London in 1894 as partner (from 1898 senior partner) in Sellars, Dicksee & Co. in the City of London. Dicksee married in 1894 Nora Beatrice, daughter of Rowland Plumbe FRIBA. The couple lived at a number of addresses in north London before settling at Hampstead, about 1908. They had one son who was a casualty of the 1914–18 war.

It has been said that fraud was endemic in Victorian

business, and it is widely believed that the young accountancy profession did much to establish its reputation by the ability of accountants to discover and disentangle the financial implications of fraudulent schemes. Dicksee, together with Peter Price's son, discovered one such fraud at the Cardiff Building Society in 1890, £8500 (at that time a substantial sum) having been stolen by the society's bookkeeper. Dicksee also demonstrated an early interest in education. He took evening classes at the University of South Wales and Monmouthshire, and in 1892 published *Auditing: a Practical Manual for Auditors*. Dicksee's *Auditing* was a major landmark in the development of an accounting literature. It was the second major textbook on auditing (the first was F. W. Pixley's *Auditors, their Duties and Responsibilities*, 1881), but contained a much broader coverage of accounting matters than did its predecessor. It was phenomenally influential, being read both by students preparing for professional examinations and by practising accountants. It ran to fourteen British editions during Dicksee's lifetime. The impact of Dicksee's *Auditing* was not merely local: Robert H. Montgomery, founder of the firm which became the American segment of Coopers and Lybrand, published, with permission, an American version of Dicksee's *Auditing* in 1905. Indeed, it has been said that Montgomery's adaptation of Dicksee's text to American needs marked the beginning of an American literature in accounting.

Dicksee's experience with the Cardiff Building Society may well have been responsible for the famous text's emphasis (possibly overemphasis) on the detection of error and fraud as audit objectives. The weight given to these matters by Dicksee has been interpreted as evidence of a late nineteenth-century preoccupation with error and fraud detection to the exclusion of the informational content of published accounts. There is growing evidence to suggest that the nineteenth-century audit was rather more broadly based, and it is possible that Dicksee's influential text may have contributed to a narrowing in the scope of the audit in the years that followed.

A second major textbook, entitled *Advanced Accounting*, appeared in 1903, and many other books and articles by Dicksee were published. Not all his writing carried his name and he is thought to have been responsible for a great deal of editorial comment in *The Accountant*—the highly influential and authoritative journal first published in 1874. The conclusion that Dicksee 'provided a literature for accounting single-handed' (Kitchen and Parker, 218) is ambitious but not without foundation.

Dicksee's two major texts were principally directed towards the identification of best practice and encouraging its more widespread adoption. Concerns with the need for conservatism and the strict application of the realization principle (the recognition of profit at the time a sale takes place) feature prominently in his writings. Dicksee's later work grew increasingly critical of contemporary practice. The period after the First World War was marked by the growing use of secret reserves, a device for smoothing reported profits and dividend payments, based on the conviction that a significant upturn in profits

gives rise to demands for larger dividends and disappointment on the part of the capital market and shareholders generally when the rate must be cut. Secret reserves, viewed favourably by many of the profession's leaders until the revelations in the case of *R. v. Lord Kyslant and another* in 1931, were the subject of swingeing criticism by Dicksee in a public lecture delivered at the London School of Economics (LSE) on 7 October 1920, as was the practice of using omnibus headings to encapsulate most of the assets belonging to a company in a single financial total.

The development of accounting as an academic discipline was slower in Britain than in the USA and Europe. Dicksee's appointment to the first British chair of accounting within the faculty of commerce at the University of Birmingham in 1902 was an early encouraging development, however. He combined this part-time appointment with a lectureship at the LSE. He was awarded an honorary MCom by Birmingham in 1903, but resigned his appointment there three years later in order to give more time to his work at the LSE, where he became professor of accounting in business organization in 1914, reflecting the commercial orientation of his commitments. In 1919 he was appointed Sir Ernest Cassel professor of accounting when the London commerce degree was introduced, and served as dean of the faculty of economics at the University of London for the 1925–6 session, at the end of which he retired. Dicksee died of cancer at his home, Hazeboro Lodge, 153 Haverstock Hill, Belsize Park, London, on 14 February 1932. His wife survived him.

JOHN RICHARD EDWARDS

Sources J. Kitchen and R. H. Parker, 'Lawrence Robert Dicksee, 1864–1932', *Twentieth-century accounting thinkers*, ed. J. R. Edwards (1994), 206–44 · S. W. Rowland, *The Accountant* (27 Feb 1931), 283–4 · *The Accountant* (20 Feb 1932), 236 · P. L. Defliese, 'British standards in a world setting', *British accounting standards: the first ten years*, ed. R. Leach and E. Stamp (1981), 105–18 · R. P. Brief, *Dicksee's contribution to accounting theory and practice* (1980) · WWW · d. cert.

Wealth at death £18,607 16s. 8d.: resworn probate, 8 April 1932, CGPLA Eng. & Wales

Dickson, Adam (*bap.* **1721**, *d.* **1776**), agricultural writer, was baptized on 5 October 1721 at Aberlady, Haddingtonshire, the son of the Revd Andrew Dickson, minister of Aberlady, and his wife, Agnes Burnside. He studied at Edinburgh University, and took the degree of MA in 1744. In 1742 he married Anne Haldane. They had one son and one daughter. From his childhood his father had intended him to go into the church, and Dickson was presented in 1748 as minister of Duns in Berwickshire, though he did not take up the post until 1750, after a long lawsuit on the subject of the presentation, which went to the House of Lords. He soon lived down the opposition which this raised in his parish. After twenty years at Duns, he was transferred in 1769 to Whittingham in Haddingtonshire.

Dickson became interested in farming at an early age, and after moving to Duns he decided to write *A Treatise on Agriculture*. The first volume of this appeared in 1762, and was followed by a second in 1769. A new edition was published in 1785. Concerned with farming in Scotland, the first four books of this work dealt with soils, tillage, and manures in general; the other four concentrated on problems of farm management. One section, an essay on manures, was reprinted in Alexander Hunter's *Georgical Essays* (1770); it attacked Jethro Tull, who held that careful ploughing alone provided adequate fertilization for the soil. Dickson also wrote *Small Farms Destructive to the Country in its Present Situation* (1764), and *An Essay on the Causes of the Present High Prices of Provisions etc.* (1773).

Dickson died on 25 March 1776 at Whittingham, after falling from his horse. Twelve years after his death the work by which he was best known was printed, with a dedication to the duke of Buccleuch. Entitled *The Husbandry of the Ancients* (1788), this had been written at the end of Dickson's life, after many years devoted to studying ancient writers on agriculture. He compared ancient agricultural practice with the practice of his day. The first volume discussed the Roman villa, and crops, manures, and ploughs; the second dealt with the different ancient crops and the times of sowing. He translated freely from Latin sources, and his scholarship was often faulty. The book was translated into French in 1802.

M. G. WATKINS, *rev.* ANNE PIMLOTT BAKER

Sources *Fasti Scot.* · *Cottage Gardener*, 7 (1851–2), 157 · A. Dickson, 'Some account of the author', *The husbandry of the ancients*, 1 (1788) · IGI

Sir Alexander Dickson (1777–1840), by William Salter, 1838

Dickson, Sir Alexander (1777–1840), army officer, was born on 3 June 1777 at Sydenham House, Roxburghshire, the third son of Admiral William Dickson and his first wife, daughter of William Collingwood of Unthank, Northumberland. His brother was Admiral Sir Collingwood Dickson, second baronet. He was educated presumably at a private school. He entered the Royal Military Academy, Woolwich, as a cadet on 5 April 1793 and became second lieutenant Royal Artillery on 6 November 1794. His subsequent commissions in the British artillery were first lieutenant (6 March 1795), captain-lieutenant (14 October 1801), captain (10 April 1805), major (26 June 1823), lieutenant-colonel (2 April 1825), and colonel (1 July 1836). As a subaltern he served at the capture of Minorca in 1798, and at the blockade of Malta and siege of Valletta in 1800, where he was employed as acting engineer. As captain he commanded the artillery of the reinforcements sent out to South America under Sir Samuel Auchmuty, which arrived at the River Plate on 5 April 1807 and captured Montevideo, and which was afterwards present at, but not engaged in, the disastrous attempt to take Buenos Aires. For a time Dickson commanded the artillery of the army, in which he was succeeded by Augustus Frazer.

When Colonel Howorth arrived in Portugal to assume command of the artillery of the army of Arthur Wellesley (the duke of Wellington) in April 1809, Dickson, who hoped to obtain employment in a higher grade in the Portuguese artillery under Marshal W. C. Beresford, accompanied Howorth and served as his brigade major in the operations before Oporto and the subsequent expulsion of Maréchal Soult's army from Portugal. Soon afterwards he was appointed to a company in the Portuguese artillery when Captain John May returned home. He subsequently became major and lieutenant-colonel in the Portuguese

service, which gave him precedence over officers who were his seniors in the British artillery. In command of the Portuguese artillery he took part in the battle of Busaco in 1810, the action at Campo Mayor, the siege and capture of Olivenza, and the battle of Albuera in 1811. His abilities were recognized by Wellington, and the artillery details at the various sieges were chiefly entrusted to him. He superintended the artillery operations in the first and second sieges of Badajoz under the immediate orders of Wellington in 1811, as well as the siege and capture of Ciudad Rodrigo and the siege and capture of Badajoz in 1812. He joined the force assembled by Rowland Hill to march secretly against the forts at Almaraz. His feints and the planting of false information effectively screened his movements from the French, and the operation ended in a close-run but brilliant capture of the forts and bridge on the River Tagus. In 1812 he also contributed to the siege and capture of the forts of Salamanca, and the siege of Burgos. He commanded the reserve artillery at the battle of Salamanca and the capture of Madrid. He was a lieutenant-colonel in the Portuguese artillery, and brevet major and first captain of a company of British artillery (no. 5 of the Old 10th battalion Royal Artillery, which under its second captain, Cairns, did good service in the Peninsula and was afterwards disbanded). On 27 April 1812 he became brevet lieutenant-colonel in the British service. An earnest and active officer, he suffered recurring attacks of fever.

In May 1813 Wellington, whose relations with the commanding officers of the Royal Artillery in Spain for some time past had been very unsatisfactory, invited Dickson to take command of the allied artillery, his brevet rank giving him the necessary seniority. Dickson, still a captain of artillery, thus succeeded to what properly was a lieutenant-general's command, having 8000 men and between 3000 and 4000 horses under him. He commanded the allied artillery at Vitoria, and by virtue of his brevet rank was senior to Augustus Frazer (under whom he had served in South America) at the siege of San Sebastian, who wrote of his 'manly simplicity'. Dickson commanded the allied artillery at the passage of the River Bidassoa, in the battles of the Nivelle and the Nive, at the passage of the River Adour, and in the battle of Toulouse. After the war the officers of the field train department who had served under him presented him with a splendid piece of plate, and the officers of the Royal Artillery who served under him in the campaigns of 1813–14 presented him with a sword of honour.

In the Anglo-American War of 1812–14 Dickson commanded the artillery in the expedition to New Orleans and at the capture of Fort Bowyer at Mobile, Alabama. He returned from the United States in time to take part in the Waterloo campaign. At this time he was first captain of G (afterwards F) troop, Royal Horse Artillery. He was present at the battles of Quatre-Bras and Waterloo in 1815, with Sir George Wood, commanding the artillery. He subsequently commanded the battering train sent to aid the Prussian army at the sieges of Maubeuge, Landrecies, Philipville, Marienburg, and Rocroy, in July and August of 1815, but which Wellington, disapproving of the acts of Prince Augustus of Prussia, directed later to withdraw to Mons. In all his campaigns Dickson was never once wounded.

In 1822 Dickson was appointed inspector of artillery, and he succeeded Lieutenant-General Sir John Macleod as deputy adjutant-general Royal Artillery on Macleod's removal to the office of director-general in 1827. On William Millar's death in 1838 Dickson succeeded him in the office of director-general of the field train department, combining this duty with that of deputy adjutant-general of Royal Artillery until his death in 1840; during this period artillery progress was stifled by parliamentary retrenchment. He became a major-general on 10 January 1837. In 1838 Dickson, who had been made KCH in 1817 and KCB in 1825, was made GCB, the only Royal Artillery officer then holding the grand cross of the military division. He was royal aide-de-camp (1825–37), a commissioner of the Royal Military College at Sandhurst, and was one of the original fellows of the Royal Geographical Society and a fellow of other learned societies.

Dickson was not only a great artilleryman but also a most industrious and methodical collector of data. During the Peninsula sieges he kept diaries, in which he mentioned even the most trifling facts, and on his return to England he obtained from General Macleod the letters he had written to him between 1811 and 1814. All this became the property of his son General Sir Collingwood *Dickson (1817–1904), Royal Artillery, who lent it to Colonel Francis Duncan who used it in preparing his *History of the Royal Regiment of Artillery*.

Dickson was twice married, first, on 19 September 1802, to Eulalia Brionès (d. 24 July 1830), daughter of Don Stefano Brionès of Minorca, with whom he had a large family; and second, on 18 December 1830, to Harriet Maria, widow of Eustace Meadows of Conholt Park, Hampshire, who after Dickson's death married Major-General Sir John Campbell of the Portuguese service. He died at his residence in Charles Street, Berkeley Square, London, on 22 April 1840, at the age of sixty-two, and was buried on 28 April in Plumstead old churchyard, Plumstead, Middlesex. In 1847 a monument was erected by regimental subscription in the grounds of the Royal Military Repository, Woolwich. Sir Collingwood Dickson, Dickson's third son with his first wife, presented his father's papers to the Royal Regiment of Artillery: an edition of them, edited by J. H. Leslie, was published as *The Dickson Manuscripts* in 1908.   H. M. CHICHESTER, rev. GORDON L. TEFFETELLER

Sources *Annual Register* (1840) · F. Duncan, ed., *History of the royal regiment of artillery*, 3rd edn, 2 vols. (1879) · *GM*, 2nd ser., 13 (1840) · Fortescue, *Brit. army* · J. T. Jones, *Journals of the sieges undertaken by the allies in Spain*, 2 vols. in 1 (1814) · *The Dickson manuscripts*, ed. J. H. Leslie (1908) · J. H. Leslie, *The services of the royal regiment of artillery in the Peninsular War, 1808 to 1814*, 3 vols. (1908–12) · A. C. Mercer, *Journal of the Waterloo campaign*, 2 vols. (1870) · W. F. P. Napier, *History of the war in the Peninsula and in the south of France*, rev. edn, 6 vols. (1876) · C. W. C. Oman, *A history of the Peninsular War*, 7 vols. (1902–30) · G. L. Teffeteller, *The surpriser: the life of Rowland, Lord Hill* (1983) · *The dispatches of … the duke of Wellington … from 1799 to 1818*, ed. J. Gurwood, 13 vols. in 12 (1834–9)
Archives Royal Artillery Institution, Woolwich, London, papers | BL, corresp. with C. C. Dansey, Add. MS 41581
Likenesses W. Salter, oils, 1838 (study for *Waterloo banquet at Apsley House*), NPG [*see illus.*] · Quenedy, aquatint (after a physionotrace, pubd 1815), NPG · W. Salter, group portrait, oils (*Waterloo banquet at Apsley House*), Wellington Museum, London · photograph, repro. in Duncan, *History*, frontispiece

Dickson, Alexander (1836–1887), botanist,

was born on 21 February 1836 at 6 Fettes Row, Edinburgh, second son among the eight children of David Dickson (1793–1866), advocate and landowner, and his wife, Jemima, daughter of the Revd David Pyper. His father's family had long held estates at Kilbucho in Lanarkshire and Hartree in Peeblesshire. He was educated privately and at the University of Edinburgh, whence he graduated MD in 1860 with a thesis on the development of the seed vessel of *Caropyllacae*. In 1862, having already written a number of papers for the *Transactions of the Edinburgh Botanical Society*, Dickson lectured in botany at the University of Aberdeen during the illness of professor George Dickie (1812–1882). In 1866 he was appointed to the chair of botany at Dublin University and, for a brief period in 1868, he was concurrently professor of botany at Dublin's Royal College of Science. In the latter year he returned to Scotland as professor of botany at Glasgow, where he remained until 1879. He was then appointed professor of botany at Edinburgh, and regius keeper of the Royal Botanic Garden.

Dickson, whose early researches were into reproductive organs of the Coniferae (conifers), was regarded by contemporaries as an excellent field botanist. His later studies included work on phyllotaxis (arrangement of leaves on a stem), flower and embryo development, and the morphology and structure of pitchers in carnivorous plants. The results of his researches were published in a number of journals including the proceedings and transactions of the Royal and Botanical societies of Edinburgh and the *Journal of Botany, British and Foreign*; the Royal Society catalogue lists a total of some fifty papers. However, he was essentially a cautious botanist, and believed that if the latest botanical publications were left for a year or two, those worth reading would sort themselves. He was a fellow of the Linnean Society and of the Royal Society of Edinburgh, was twice president of the Botanical Society of Edinburgh, and was awarded an honorary MD from Dublin and an LLD from Glasgow.

In 1866 Dickson succeeded to the family estates, where he was considered a generous and improving landlord. It was said of him that he would 'spend everything on his tenants, on his gates, on his trees—as little as possible on himself' (Hole, 201). Of a quiet and retiring nature, he was a skilled draughtsman and accomplished musician, and in later years collected many Gaelic airs. During the winters he was fond of curling on the ponds near Hartree House, his Peeblesshire home. It was while playing a game on 30 December 1887 at Thriepland Pond, Peeblesshire, that he 'dropped dead in the act of making a shot' (*Nature*). He was widely mourned by students and tenants; a contemporary wrote of him that 'He could never lose a friend, for he could never say an unkind word or omit to do a kind action' (*Nature*).   PETER OSBORNE

Sources DNB · *Nature*, 37 (1887–8), 229–30 · W. B. Hole, *Quasi cursores: portraits of the high officers and professors of the University of Edinburgh at its tercentenary festival* (1884) · Boase, *Mod. Eng. biog.* · Burke, *Gen. GB* · Desmond, *Botanists*, rev. edn · b. cert. · d. cert.
Likenesses W. B. Hole, etching, NPG; repro. in Hole, *Quasi cursores*
Wealth at death £5042: confirmation, 1891, Scotland

Dickson, Alexander Graeme [Alec] (1914–1994), community educationist, was born on 23 May 1914 at Duxhill Lodge, Ruislip, the youngest child and third son of Norman Bonnington Dickson (1868–1944), civil engineer, and his wife, (Agnes) Anne Edith Higgins (*c*.1875–1953). His father worked on railway construction in South America, Thailand, and Nyasaland, and was involved in building the Victoria Falls Bridge. As he spent so much time away from his family, his wife's role in their children's upbringing was pivotal, and the relationship with her youngest child remained especially close. Known to his family as Sandy, to colleagues and the wider community he was Alec Dickson. He was educated at Rugby School—an experience he claimed to find cold in every sense—and at New College, Oxford, from which he graduated in 1935 with a second in modern history. His first career was in journalism, initially with the *Yorkshire Post* (1936–7) and then with the *Daily Telegraph* (1937–8), as a correspondent from Czechoslovakia, but he gave up journalism for relief work after the German invasion in 1938.

Commissioned into the Cameron Highlanders during the Second World War, Dickson was seconded to the King's African rifles, and fought in the Abyssinian campaign. He was then posted to Nairobi, where he found the culture of the officers' mess uncongenial and grew restless. He began considering how the African population might respond to a Japanese attack on east Africa, and how to prepare them for that possibility. East African command headquarters was willing to let him try, and thus was born the mobile propaganda unit with Dickson at its head. For his work he was appointed MBE in 1945. In 1946 he returned to refugee relief work in Berlin.

Between 1948 and 1954 Dickson (who had independent means) was in west Africa, first in the Gold Coast and then in the trust territory of the British Cameroons (administered by Nigeria at that time). There he introduced a number of innovative mass education and community development training schemes. In the Cameroons, Dickson and a colleague who had worked at the Outward Bound Sea School developed the idea of the Man O' War Bay Training Centre. Influenced by the programmes of the Outward Bound schools, the centre provided one-month courses for potential community leaders (originally men, but courses were later also provided for women and young people). Challenges from the local sea and mountain environment were incorporated in the courses, but their focus was on community development, leading up to a week spent in a village in the Cameroons or Nigeria, where participants worked with the villagers on a current project, such as improving the water supply or building a bridge or a school. On 30 August 1951 Dickson married Mora Agnes Hope Robertson (1918–2001), artist and writer. It was a singularly happy union, Mora Dickson sharing fully in her husband's interests and labours. There were no children.

After leaving west Africa in 1954, Dickson spent some months in the United Kingdom, writing and developing his ideas on mass education, before spending a couple of largely sterile years as head of the UNESCO fundamental education mission in Iraq. The Iraqi authorities expected his team to restrict themselves to advising in Baghdad, while the team wanted to be out in the villages working with communities. The winter of 1956–7 found the Dicksons back in central Europe, assisting refugees from the Soviet occupation of Hungary. They worked with an international group of students who were helping refugees to escape at night across a canal into Austria. This experience prompted Dickson to set up Voluntary Service Overseas (VSO) in 1958, to tap the energy of young people in education for community service. VSO was originally intended to provide formal openings for service abroad for the increasing numbers of school leavers who wanted to take a year off from formal education before going to university. (Over the years, and at the request of the governments hosting the volunteers, recruitment shifted to young professionally qualified candidates, and to other experienced personnel.) VSO was the inspiration for the American Peace Corps, and Dickson was invited to the

United States in 1961 to advise President Kennedy on setting it up. In 1962, after a disagreement with senior colleagues over the direction of the organization, he left VSO.

VSO was an élite concept and organization: it enrolled in social service the relatively privileged, and had high expectations of their performance. The next venture undertaken by the Dicksons—Community Service Volunteers (CSV), which they founded in 1962—had the same purpose, the involvement of young people in community service, but it differed in two important respects. First, the service was to be in Britain, not abroad. And second, to be accepted by CSV, a young person had only to be prepared to serve. None was rejected, and a young offender was as likely as a boy or girl from a public school to be found a place in social work in Britain. Nor did the Dicksons see why people with disabilities should be only the recipients of help: seeing them as an undervalued community resource, they recruited them too. The Dicksons travelled widely at the invitation of overseas governments seeking new ways to cope with the youth culture of the 1960s and 1970s.

By the early 1980s prostate cancer was beginning to have its effect on Dickson, and the pressures of work and long-distance travel took their toll. In 1982 he was persuaded to give up directing CSV and become its president—a form of retirement he accepted with great reluctance. He had been appointed CBE in 1967, and received honorary doctorates from Leeds and Bristol universities. He died from cancer on 23 September 1994 at his home, 19 Blenheim Road, Chiswick, London, and his ashes were scattered in the rose garden at Mortlake crematorium.

Deeply embedded in Dickson's Christian, but non-denominational, faith were two beliefs. One was that everybody had a capacity for service, a need to be needed, and that service benefited both provider and recipient. The other was that emphasis should be placed on responsibilities rather than rights. His volunteers at Man O'War Bay, in VSO, and in CSV responded positively to his challenge, because they felt he trusted them to do a good job: it was rare for a volunteer to feel anything but admiration for and gratitude to him. Colleagues could be, and often were, more critical. He was an inspiring person to work with, but not an easy one. Most decidedly not a bureaucrat, he operated essentially as a one-man show: he found it difficult to let things out of his own hands, and frustrated colleagues could find that matters for which they were responsible had been dealt with by Dickson, sometimes with wasteful duplication of effort. Only too often it led to a parting of the ways. Professional educators, too, felt threatened by his unorthodoxy, and were often dismissive of his ideas. He had a great sense of adventure, not only in devising appropriate responses to social problems, but also in physical activity. He was brave in both; indeed, in the latter he could be foolhardy, even irresponsible. Alec Dickson was a great social innovator, a restless genius who needed constantly to be moving on, to experiment, to challenge. Maintenance and repetition bored him. It was

fortunate that in his three main ventures there were successors at hand who shared his beliefs, but with different temperament and skills, to consolidate and continue his pioneering work.   H. C. SWAISLAND

Sources A. Dickson, *A chance to serve* (1976) · personal knowledge (2004) · private information (2004) [Mora Dickson, widow] · *The Times* (26 Sept 1994) · *The Independent* (10 Oct 1994) · *WW* · b. cert. · d. cert.

Archives Bodl. RH, papers · Community Service Volunteers, London, corresp. and papers, mainly relating to Community Service Volunteers

Likenesses photograph, repro. in *The Times*

Wealth at death £858,260: probate, 27 Feb 1995, CGPLA Eng. & Wales

Dickson, Sir Collingwood (1817–1904), army officer, born at Valenciennes, France, on 20 November 1817, was the third son of Major-General Sir Alexander *Dickson (1777–1840) and Eulalia (d. 1830), daughter of Don Stefano Brionès of Minorca. Educated at the Royal Military Academy, Woolwich, he was commissioned second lieutenant in the Royal Artillery on 18 December 1835, and promoted first lieutenant on 29 November 1837. In February 1837 he went to Spain with the artillery detachment of the British Legion under Sir George De Lacy Evans. He served with the legion and the Christinist army until after the defeat of the Carlists near Berga in 1840, and was made a knight of Charles III, of San Fernando (first class), and of Isabella the Catholic.

In March 1841 Dickson went to Constantinople to instruct the Turkish artillery, and remained there until June 1845, employed under the British Foreign Office. He was promoted second captain on 1 April 1846, and brevet major on 22 May. He married on 14 January 1847 Harriet, daughter of Thomas Burnaby, vicar of Blakesley, Northamptonshire. They had three sons, two of whom predeceased him. He became first captain on 2 September 1851, and was inspector of gunpowder at Waltham Abbey from 1 July 1852 to 14 February 1854.

Dickson served in the Crimea from June 1854 to July 1855. At the battle of the Alma he was on Lord Raglan's staff; when Raglan rode forward to a knoll on the Russian flank and asked for guns there, Dickson brought up two 9-pounders and helped to serve them. Their fire forced the Russian batteries guarding the post-road to retire. He was promoted brevet lieutenant-colonel from that date, 20 June 1854. He commanded the siege-train of the right attack during the siege of Sevastopol up to 21 July 1855. In the first bombardment on 17 October 1854 the siege batteries ran short of powder, and Dickson directed several field-battery wagons to be brought up under a heavy fire and helped unload them; for this action he received the Victoria Cross on 23 June 1855.

At the battle of Inkerman, Dickson, after Colonel Gambier was wounded, brought up the two 18-pounders which dominated the Russian guns. He chose the site for them, and maintained them there, though he was urged by French officers to withdraw. When the Russians retreated, Lord Raglan said to him: 'You have covered yourself with glory' (Kinglake, 5.439). He was wounded on 4 February, but took part in the bombardments of 9 April and 17 June and in the expedition to Kerch. He was mentioned in dispatches, made aide-de-camp to the queen on 29 June 1855, and received the CB, the Légion d'honneur, and the Mejidiye (second class).

From September 1855 until the end of the war Dickson was employed with the Turkish contingent, first as brigadier-general and latterly with the temporary rank of major-general (15 February 1856). After the war he was assistant adjutant-general for artillery in Ireland for six years from 4 November 1856, and was then at Leith Fort for five years in command of the Royal Artillery. He was promoted regimental lieutenant-colonel on 23 February 1856, and regimental colonel on 5 April 1866. Four months later he became major-general. In 1868–9 he served on the fortifications committee, which investigated the work carried out under the Palmerston loan for defences, and enlivened its proceedings by his anecdotes and humour.

From April 1870 to 1875 Dickson was inspector-general of artillery. The adoption of rifled guns had caused great changes in artillery, and he therefore went through courses at Woolwich arsenal and at Shoeburyness. His inspections were thorough, but everyone felt the charm of his personality. He was made KCB on 20 May 1871, and he became colonel-commandant on 17 November 1875, lieutenant-general on 8 June 1876, and general on 1 October 1877. In May 1877 he went as military attaché to Constantinople, where his old friend Sir Austen Henry Layard was ambassador. Collingwood remained in Turkey throughout the Russo-Turkish War, until 9 September 1879. He was president of the ordnance committee (1881–5), though he was retired on 20 November 1884. On 24 May 1884 he received the GCB. He was master gunner from 1891 until his death.

Collingwood's wife died in February 1894, and thereafter he lived a retired life at 79 Claverton Street, London. He died there on 28 November 1904 and was buried at Kensal Green. He was a good linguist, fluent in French, Spanish, and Turkish, and a man of 'downright commonsense'. He closely and affectionately studied the traditions of his regiment.　　　E. M. LLOYD, rev. JAMES FALKNER

Sources The Times (30 Nov 1904) • Army List • Hart's Army List • A. W. Kinglake, The invasion of the Crimea, 8 vols. (1863–87) • LondG (2 Dec 1854) • LondG (20 Feb 1855) • LondG (15 Feb 1856) • F. Duncan, The English in Spain (1877)
Archives Royal Artillery, Woolwich, London, papers | BL, letters to Sir Austen Layard, Add. MSS 38978–39039, 39138, passim
Likenesses W. Truscott, oils, 1886, Royal Artillery Institution, Woolwich, London • photograph, c.1890, repro. in Toomey, Heroes of the VC (1895), 45
Wealth at death £9472 19s. 9d.: probate, 19 Dec 1904, CGPLA Eng. & Wales

Dickson [Dick], **David** (c.1583–1662), Church of Scotland minister and theologian, was born in Glasgow, the only son of John Dick or Dickson, a wealthy and devout Glaswegian merchant. He was educated at the University of Glasgow and, after graduating MA, served an eight-year term as a regent of the university. On 23 September 1617 he married Margaret Roberton (d. in or before 1662) and on 31 March 1618 was ordained minister of Irvine, Ayrshire. After publicly testifying against the five articles of Perth

he was summoned to appear before the court of high commission at Edinburgh on 9 January 1622. He declined the jurisdiction of the court in what he maintained was a purely ecclesiastical matter, was deprived the following day, and was confined to Turriff, Aberdeenshire. He was permitted to return to Irvine at the end of July 1623, where he remained, relatively unmolested, until 1640.

During the 1620s and 1630s Dickson became one of the leading members of what David Stevenson has termed the kirk's 'radical party' (Stevenson, 24). This band of zealous presbyterians opposed the religious policies of James VI and Charles I and reacted against them by holding conventicles, private prayer meetings where the godly could assemble for religious instruction and mutual edification. By all accounts Dickson was a powerful preacher of 'experimental Calvinism'. His method and style of preaching were considered by many of his contemporaries to be second only to those of William Guthrie, minister of Fenwick. Serious Christians from all over Scotland converged on Irvine to hear his sermons, particularly during communion seasons, the kirk's twice yearly celebration of the Lord's supper. It was during one such season, under Dickson's preaching, that the famous revival of religion known as the 'Stewarton sickness' broke out in Irvine and its environs (Tweedie, 8).

In the early years of his ministry Dickson's expository sermons on various books of the Bible were transcribed by his auditors and widely circulated in manuscript form among the godly. In response to the demand for his sermons Dickson developed a plan, with the approval of his radical colleagues, to produce a series of brief popular biblical commentaries, the first instalment of which was A Short Explanation of the Epistle of Paul to the Hebrews (Aberdeen, 1635).

During the tumultuous period leading up to and following the signing of the national covenant in 1638 Dickson emerged as one of the natural leaders of the presbyterian party. Together with Alexander Henderson he was instrumental in organizing the infamous prayer book riots which occurred at Edinburgh on 23 July 1637. He also influenced the presbytery of Irvine to denounce the prayer book and petition the Scottish council to suspend letters of horning issued against ministers who refused to purchase copies. In 1638 he was one of the ministers who engaged in a polemical war with the 'Aberdeen doctors', a group of six Arminian ministers holding the degree of doctor of divinity who supported the religious policies of Charles I. In response to the doctors' anti-covenanting pamphlet, Generall Demands Concerning the Late Covenant (Aberdeen, 1638) Dickson and Henderson wrote Ansueris of Sum Bretheren of the Ministrie (Aberdeen, 1638). He was a member of the 1638 Glasgow general assembly and, according to Robert Wodrow, 'made a great figure there', giving a learned discourse against Arminianism, and delivering an influential speech when the king's commissioner threatened to leave the assembly (Tweedie, 10). The following year he was elected moderator of the general assembly which met at Edinburgh, and distinguished himself by his 'wise management' of the assembly's business at 'so critical a juncture' (Tweedie, 10).

Throughout the 1640s Dickson continued to be very active in the affairs of the national kirk. In 1640 he was translated to the newly created professorship of divinity at the University of Glasgow, and was admitted to the collegiate charge of St Mungo's. He appears to have relinquished his ministerial charge after attending one session meeting, but continued to preach frequently at the kirk. During the 1640 general assembly Dickson staunchly defended the radicals' practice of conventicling against the attacks of Henry Guthry, and for his pains was verbally abused by the assembly's conservative members. From 1642 onwards, as a regular member of the general assembly's powerful standing committee, the commission for the public affairs of the kirk, he continued to defend the radicals' use of conventicles and support their calls for the further reformation of the national kirk. In 1643 he was appointed by the general assembly, along with Alexander Henderson and David Calderwood, to draw up a directory for public worship. Two years later he published a learned commentary on St Paul's epistles, *Expositio analytica omnium apostolicarum epistolarum* (1645), and subsequently a second popular commentary, *A Brief Exposition of the Gospel According to Matthew* (1647).

In early 1650 Dickson was translated to the chair of divinity at Edinburgh and appointed to the second charge of St Giles. The same year he and James Durham produced their famous *Sum of Saving Knowledge*, an important work espousing federal theology which, while never officially sanctioned by the kirk, was traditionally bound with the Westminster confession of faith and catechisms. In February 1650 Dickson abandoned his allegiance to the kirk regime's radical party and joined with the forces of the 'new moderatism' in calling for the return of Charles II from exile. Following the Cromwellian invasion of Scotland in the summer of 1650 he resisted the radicals' demands for a severe purge of the covenanting army in accordance with the 1646 and 1649 acts of classes, and supported the moderate controlled commission's public resolution to allow royalist malignants and former engagers back into the military. In early 1651 he wrote a number of papers vindicating the commission's role in this matter, including 'No separation of the weill affected from the army of the covenanters'. In May 1651 he supported the commission's second public resolution, which paved the way for parliament's full repeal of the acts of classes. During the ensuing schism at the 1651 general assembly he sided with the 'resolutioners' against his former radical colleagues, the 'protesters'. He was elected moderator of the equally controversial 1652 general assembly, and as outgoing moderator the following year, saw the assembly dissolved by English troops before it could be constituted. Throughout the remainder of the 1650s Dickson remained a zealous resolutioner and, together with his colleagues 'the Ministers of Edinburgh', led the national party during the assembly's suspension. During 1655 and 1656 he was instrumental in the resolutioners reaching an accord with Lord Broghill and the Scottish council, and in 1657 and 1659 he and his colleague Robert Douglas helped to direct the activities of the party's agent, James Sharp, in his sojourns at London.

At the height of the protester–resolutioner controversy Dickson found time to return to his plan for a series of popular commentaries and published his three-volume *Brief Explication of the Psalms* (London, 1653-4). He also returned to his academic writings, and, two years later, produced his most important theological work, an exposition of federal theology entitled, *Therapeutica sacra* (London, 1656).

After the Restoration, Dickson refused to take the oath of supremacy and in October 1662 was ejected from his university chair and ministerial charge. The hardships which resulted from this loss broke his health, and in December of the same year he fell extremely ill and died in Edinburgh before the month was out. He was buried on 31 December. Among his last spoken words are those recorded by his friend and former radical colleague John Livingstone:

> I have taken all my good deeds, and all my bad deeds, and cast them through each other in a heap before the Lord, and fled from both, and have betaken me to the Lord Jesus Christ, and in him I have sweet peace.   (Tweedie, 12)

K. D. HOLFELDER

Sources W. K. Tweedie, ed., *Select biographies*, 2, Wodrow Society, 7/2 (1847), 2.5-28 · R. Wodrow, *Analecta, or, Materials for a history of remarkable providences, mostly relating to Scotch ministers and Christians*, ed. [M. Leishman], 3, Maitland Club, 60 (1843), 2-12 · *Fasti Scot.*, new edn, 1.64-5; 3. 98 · A. F. Mitchell and J. Christie, eds., *The records of the commissions of the general assemblies of the Church of Scotland*, 3 vols., Scottish History Society, 11, 25, 58 (1892–1909) · W. Stephen, ed., *Register of the consultations of the ministers of Edinburgh*, 2 vols., Scottish History Society, 3rd ser., 1, 16 (1921–30) · A. Peterkin, ed., *Records of the Kirk of Scotland* (1838) · D. Stevenson, *The Scottish revolution, 1637-44: the triumph of the covenanters* (1973) · *The letters and journals of Robert Baillie*, ed. D. Laing, 3 vols. (1841–2) · D. Calderwood, *The history of the Kirk of Scotland*, ed. T. Thomson and D. Laing, 8 vols., Wodrow Society, 7 (1842–9) · *The historical works of Sir James Balfour*, ed. J. Haig, 4 vols. (1824–5)

Archives NL Scot., Wodrow collection, letters and MSS

Dickson, David (1754-1820), Church of Scotland minister and theologian, was born in the parish of Newlands, Peeblesshire, on 30 March 1754, the son of David Dickson (1709-1780), minister of Newlands, and his wife, Ann Gillon (d. 1756). After attending school at West Linton and Peebles grammar school, he studied at Glasgow University from 1766 to 1774 or 1775, and then at Divinity Hall, Edinburgh University. He became assistant to his uncle John Noble, minister of Libberton, and, on Noble's death replaced him in that parish, being ordained on 1 May 1777. On 10 December 1777 he married Christiana Wardrobe (1754/5-1832); they had eight children, including David *Dickson (1780-1842), Church of Scotland minister. In 1783 Dickson was translated to Bothkennar in Stirlingshire. In 1795 he was transferred to the chapel in New Street, Edinburgh; in 1799 to Trinity Church; and in 1801 to the New North Church in the same city, where he remained until his death.

Dickson was a popular minister in all his parishes; his appointments to Libberton and Bothkennar were both the results of petition by parishioners to the parish patrons. He was always conscientious about visiting his parishioners, and was involved in all of Edinburgh's charitable institutions.

Dickson was a supporter of the popular party in the Church of Scotland. He voted in the general assembly of 1789 against receiving the explanation of the Revd William McGill of Ayr as a satisfactory answer to the heresy with which he was charged. This case was satirized in Robert Burns's poem 'The kirk's alarm'. Dickson was outspoken in his championship of popular party principles and was prepared to face censure by the ecclesiastical courts, as he did in the cases of the settlements of Biggar and Larbert, rather than act against his conscience. During his life he published several separate sermons, as well as a collection in 1818. He also wrote the account of Bothkennar parish for John Sinclair's *Statistical Account*. He died in Edinburgh on 2 August 1820. He was survived by his wife, who died on 14 March 1832, aged seventy-seven.

ALEXANDER DU TOIT

Sources *Fasti Scot.*, new edn · J. Kay, *A series of original portraits and caricature etchings … with biographical sketches and illustrative anecdotes*, ed. [H. Paton and others], new edn [3rd edn], 2 (1877), 310–13 · W. Hunter, *Biggar and the house of Fleming* (1867), 73–4 · D. Dickson, preface, *Sermons preached on different occasions* (1818), v–viii · L. R. Timperley, ed., *A directory of landownership in Scotland, c.1770*, Scottish RS, new ser., 5 (1976), 208, 253

Archives NL Scot., Airth MSS · NL Scot., Watson collection · U. Edin. L., signature, Dc.3.87

Likenesses J. Kay, etching, 1797, BM, NPG; repro. in J. Kay, *Edinburgh portraits*, 2 (1877), facing p. 310 · W. Ridley, stipple, BM, NPG; repro. in *Evangelical Magazine* (1805)

Wealth at death £146 14s. value of estate of Persilands: valuation roll, 1771 · proprietor of estate of Kilbucho: Kay, *Series of original portraits*, 2.310

Dickson, David (1780–1842), Church of Scotland minister, was born on 23 February 1780 at Libberton, Lanarkshire, the son of David *Dickson (1754–1820), minister of Libberton, and his wife, Christiana, *née* Wardrobe (1754/5–1832). He was educated at the parish school of Bothkennar and then at Edinburgh University. In December 1801 he was licensed as a preacher in the Church of Scotland; early in 1802 he was appointed to a chapel at Kilmarnock. In 1803 he was chosen as junior minister of St Cuthbert's Church, Edinburgh. After the death of the Revd Sir Henry Moncrieff in 1827 he became senior minister, a position he held until his death. On 27 August 1808 he married Janet, daughter of James Jobson of Dundee; they had four sons and five daughters between 1810 and 1825.

Dickson had a contemporary reputation as a Hebrew scholar, and in 1824 the University of Edinburgh conferred a DD on him. He wrote several articles in the *Edinburgh Encyclopaedia* and in the *Christian Instructor* and other magazines, and published *The Influence of Learning on Religion* in 1814. He edited the *Memoir of Miss Woodbury* (1826), the sermons of W. F. Ireland (1829), and the lectures and sermons of G. B. Brand (1841).

Dickson's sermons were plain and straightforward; besides publishing several separate sermons, he also published a volume of sermons in 1818; *Discourses, Doctrinal and*

Practical appeared posthumously in 1857. Dickson served as secretary for the Scottish Missionary Society for many years. Stout and bespectacled, he was a kindly and peaceable man: although one of the leading figures in the whig evangelical wing of the Church of Scotland, originally associated with Henry Wellwood Moncrieff and Andrew Thomson, he avoided prominence in the controversies preceding the Disruption. He is perhaps better remembered for officiating at the Church of Scotland funeral service for Sir Walter Scott in the house at Abbotsford. Dickson died on 28 July 1842 in Edinburgh, and was buried in St Cuthbert's Church, where a monument by Handyside Ritchie was erected to his memory.

A. C. BICKLEY, *rev.* ROSEMARY MITCHELL

Sources *Fasti Scot.* · B. W. Crombie and W. S. Douglas, *Modern Athenians: a series of original portraits of memorable citizens of Edinburgh* (1882), 5–6 · J. Grant, *Cassell's old and new Edinburgh*, 3 vols. [1880–83]; repr. (1884–7), vol. 2, p. 134 · S. J. Brown, *Thomas Chalmers and the godly commonwealth in Scotland* (1982), 259

Archives U. Edin., New Coll. L., letters to Thomas Chalmers, CHA4

Likenesses J. Kay, caricature, etching, 1812, NPG · B. W. Crombie, coloured lithograph, c.1840, repro. in Crombie and Douglas, *Modern Athenians*, 5 · H. Ritchie, monument, 1840–49, St Cuthbert's Church, Edinburgh · W. Holl, stipple (after J. Wildman), BM, NPG; repro. in *Evangelical Magazine* (1829)

Wealth at death £2020 17s. 5d.: 1842

Dickson [*née* Dalzel], **Elizabeth** (c.1793–1862), philanthropist, was the daughter of Archibald Dalzel, a surgeon and slave merchant, who for many years was employed by the Company of Merchants Trading to Africa, first at Ouidah and later (c.1791) at Cape Coast Castle, and eventually became governor-in-chief of the company's establishments on the west coast of Africa. In 1788 he was one of five delegates chosen by Liverpool common council and the African Merchants of Liverpool to give evidence against Sir William Dolben's Slave Limitation Bill, then going through parliament. Dalzel was also the author of *The History of Dahomy* (1793), a book which again reflected his strong anti-abolitionist sentiments.

It seems likely that Elizabeth Dalzel was born on the west coast of Africa. Little is known about her early education, but while she was still a teenager she visited Algiers, where her brother, Edward, was a merchant and, from 1812, agent and vice-consul for the Portuguese government. It was here that she witnessed the terrible plight of white Christians who had been captured and enslaved by Barbary pirates. In Algiers alone in 1816 there were more than 1500 of these slaves, including men, women, and children from France, Spain, Portugal, and Britain. Others were held in captivity in Tunis and Tripoli.

Elizabeth was so incensed by what she saw in Algiers that she furnished reports to the British press. These, in turn, attracted the attention of the Knights Liberators and Anti-Piratical Society, founded in 1814 by Admiral Sir William Sidney Smith to agitate for the abolition of the Barbary slave trade. As a result Elizabeth was made a member of the society, 'with the honours and privileges of a lady Foundress' (*GM*, new ser., 13, 1862, 112), and presented with a gold medal and a unanimous vote of thanks.

Through these and other efforts the plight of the Christian slaves in Barbary was brought to the attention of the wider public. Henry Brougham took up the issue in the House of Commons in June 1816, and in August Lord Exmouth led a naval expedition to Algiers that crushed the Algerian slave trade and resulted in the release of 3000 Christian slaves.

Elizabeth Dalzel was married to John Dickson, who was a surgeon in the Royal Navy. Dickson was declared unfit for active service in 1839, but in May 1845 he was reported to be surgeon to the bashaw of Tripoli, where he and Elizabeth had made their home. Elizabeth died a widow at Tripoli on 30 April 1862, aged about seventy. Her will, executed in February of the previous year, mentions four sons and two daughters.   J. R. OLDFIELD

Sources GM, 3rd ser., 13 (1862), 112 · F. E. Sanderson, 'The Liverpool delegates and Sir William Dolben's bill', *Transactions of the Historic Society of Lancashire and Cheshire*, 124 (1972), 57–84 · BL, Liverpool MSS · BL, Heytesbury MSS · *Hansard 1* (1816), 34.1148 · *Navy List* (1804–48) · C. Lloyd, *English corsairs on the Barbary coast* (1981) · *The cruelties of the Algerine pirates* (1816) · J. A. Rawley, 'London's defence of the slave trade', *Slavery and Abolition*, 14 (1993), 48–69 · D. Richardson, 'The British empire and the Atlantic slave trade, 1660–1807', *The Oxford history of the British empire*, ed. P. J. Marshall, 2: *The eighteenth century* (1998), 440–64 · J. Barrow, *Sir William Sidney Smith* (1848) · *DNB* · *CGPLA Eng. & Wales* (1862)
Wealth at death under £800: resworn probate, March 1868, *CGPLA Eng. & Wales*

Dickson, James (1738?–1822), botanist, was born at Kirke House, Traquair, Peeblesshire, allegedly of humble parentage, and began work as an apprentice in the gardens of the earl of Traquair. He then went to London and worked as an improver at the famous nurseries of Jeffrey & Co. in Brompton. He held several posts as a gardener before opening his own shop in Covent Garden in 1772 and establishing a business as nurseryman and seedsman. Dickson could now count among his friends William Forsyth, the king's gardener, Sir Francis Drake, master of the household, and Sir Joseph Banks. With Banks's support he secured in 1781 the contract to maintain the British Museum's garden. Several of Banks's overseas correspondents enclosed with their letters plant material for Dickson.

The identity of Dickson's first wife is unknown, but after her death he married, on 24 October 1786 at Selkirk, Margaret (1762–1837), sister to his friend the then medical student and later explorer, Mungo Park (1771–1806). Their son, James (b. 1800), and daughters Isabella (b. 1796) and Jean (b. 1805) were baptized at the Scottish presbyterian church in Covent Garden. Before leaving for Africa, Park gave Dickson power of attorney, and in 1806 and 1807, when Park had been missing for some time, Dickson reminded the Treasury of the government's promise to support Park's family.

In February 1788 Dickson was one of seven who formed the first 'fellows' meeting' of the Linnean Society at Marlborough Coffee House. Sixteen years later, on 7 March 1804, he was one of seven who gathered in the house of bookseller John Hatchard to found 'a society for the improvement of horticulture'. This body developed into the Royal Horticultural Society, with Dickson as one of its vice-presidents.

Although his daily work concerned cultivated plants and vegetables, Dickson's reputation as a botanist rested on his studies of mosses, begun in 1781, and on grasses and fungi, much of his material being gathered in visits to Scotland between 1793 and 1802. In 1785 he began publication of *Fasciculus plantarum cryptogamicarum Britanniae*, a quarto work in four parts with 400 descriptions. However, Dickson himself was ill-educated, as his correspondence shows, and the Latin texts were prepared by John Zier, a Polish-born London apothecary. Zier died in 1796, before the last volume was completed, and Dickson was then assisted by Robert Brown. Neither man was credited in the work, and Zier's role only came to light in the 1880s with the discovery of some of his manuscripts. Dickson also published *A Collection of Dried Plants, Named on the Authority of the Linnaean Herbarium* (1789–92), consisting of 425 species, followed by *Hortus siccus Britannicus* (1793–1802). Few copies of this work survive as many purchasers extracted the specimens to add to their own dried collections.

From the 1790s Dickson also had a nursery garden at Croydon, Surrey. He lived at Bedford Street, Covent Garden, from 1795 to 1799, thereafter at Broad Green, Croydon, where he died on 14 August 1822. On 22 August he was buried, at his own request, in the churchyard of All Saints, Sanderstead, among the Surrey hills where he was accustomed to gather mosses. The Covent Garden nursery passed to Dickson's nephew, James Anderson (1800–1830), and Margaret Dickson inherited the Croydon house and garden; she was buried at Sanderstead on 17 June 1837, passing the property to their unmarried daughter Jean. Dickson's memory is preserved in the genus *Dicksonia*, consisting chiefly of tree ferns.   ANITA McCONNELL

Sources introduction, J. Dickson, *Plantarum cryptogamicarum Britanniae* (1976) · A. Simmonds, 'James Dickson', *Journal of the Royal Horticultural Society*, 68 (1943), 66–72 · H. R. Fletcher, *The story of the Royal Horticultural Society, 1804–1968* (1969) · A. T. Gage and W. T. Stearn, *A bicentenary history of the Linnean Society of London* (1988) · *The Banks letters*, ed. W. R. Dawson (1958) · J. Britten, 'John Zier FLS', *Journal of Botany, British and Foreign*, 24 (1886), 101–4 · parish register, All Saints, Sanderstead, Surrey, 22 Aug 1822 [burial] · PRO, PROB 11/1661, sig. 469 · B. Henrey, *British botanical and horticultural literature before 1800*, 3 vols. (1975) · *The parish of St Paul, Covent Garden*, Survey of London, 36 (1970), 254 · *GM*, 1st ser., 92/2 (1822), 376
Archives Bodl. Oxf. · Bodl. Oxf., catalogue of dried plants · Linn. Soc., herbarium · Linn. Soc. | Linn. Soc., corresp. with Sir James Smith · NHM, Sowerby collection
Likenesses H. P. Briggs, oils, 1820, Royal Horticultural Society, London · Wagemann, portrait, Linn. Soc. · portrait, Hunt. L.
Wealth at death several thousand pounds in bequests: will, PRO, PROB 11/1661, sig. 469

Dickson, James Douglas Hamilton (1849–1931), mathematician, was born on 1 May 1849 at 144 Bath Street, Glasgow, the son of John Robert Dickson, physician; he was the elder brother of Lord Scott Dickson. Dickson attended Hale School. He was fifteen when he matriculated at Glasgow University, where he studied from 1864 to 1869 and graduated in 1870. During his time there, he studied Latin, Greek, logic, mathematics, natural philosophy, and ethics. After taking the degree of master of arts, with second-class honours in mathematics and natural philosophy from Glasgow, he was awarded the Eglington fellowship of Glasgow University from 1870 to 1871. At Glasgow he was under the tutelage of William Thomson. In 1867 Thomson employed Dickson in his laboratory for mathematical work on electricity to determine the relation between electromagnetic and electrostatic units of electricity. Together with W. F. King of Edinburgh and C. Cuttriss of Boston, Massachusetts, Dickson devised the apparatus and made the preliminary experimentation for Thomson's determination of 'V' (the ratio of the electromagnetic to the electrostatic unit of electricity). Dickson also assisted Thomson with his work on deep-sea cables. Thomson made the first attempt to lay the French transatlantic cable in 1857, and until its completion in 1866 Dickson was engineer-in-charge, during which time he assisted Thomson to develop the siphon recorder for telegraph signals.

In 1870 Thomson urged Dickson to resign his appointment and go up to Peterhouse, Cambridge, to read mathematics. During much of the nineteenth century Peterhouse was a popular college for Scottish students and also had the reputation of being mathematical; Dickson was admitted as a pensioner on 4 July 1870, was coached for the mathematical tripos by Cambridge's chief mathematical coach, Edward John Routh (who was also at the college), and was bracketed fifth wrangler in 1874. Dickson rowed in the college boats and played in the cricket eleven. On 29 October 1874 he was elected to a fellowship which he held for life. When James Porter became master of Peterhouse in 1876, Dickson succeeded him as tutor and held this office from 1877 to 1897; he became senior fellow when Lord Kelvin died in 1907. Probably about 1878, he married Isabella Catherine, daughter of James Banks, an Edinburgh printer; they had a son and a daughter. (Dickson's brother and the chemist James Dewar married Banks's other two daughters.)

Dickson was also able to assist the statistician and eugenicist Francis Galton when the latter was working on his index of correlation and his regression coefficient. After Galton plotted the regression line from his midparental data, he discovered that the data took on the shape of two ellipses; he then wanted to find a single formula to express the results of this table from the ellipses. As he could not remember all the formulae of conic sections, he went up to Cambridge to meet Dickson who examined mathematically the system of concentric ellipses that would correspond to the ellipses described by Galton in his 1885 paper, 'Regression towards mediocrity in heredity stature'. Dickson's calculations confirmed Galton's theory that the value of the mid-parental regression was very nearly one-third.

Dickson published occasional papers, principally on thermodynamics and thermoelectricity, which appeared in the *Transactions of the Royal Society of Edinburgh*, *Philosophical Magazine*, and the *Proceedings of the London Mathematical Society*. He was also one of the three literary executors to whom was entrusted the publication of the collected papers of Sir James Dewar. He was a fellow of the Royal Society of Edinburgh, and a member of the London Mathematical Society and of the Royal Institution.

Dickson's interests were varied. He became involved in a special study of Japan and the Japanese and assisted Genjiro Yamazaki (who was a student at Peterhouse) in the preparation of catalogues of the Japanese sword-hilts contained in Cambridge and Edinburgh. He contributed biographies of E. J. Routh, P. G. Tait, J. Hamblin Smith, and James Porter (all of whom were mathematicians and fellows at Peterhouse) to the *Dictionary of National Biography*. He was an enthusiastic musician who was for many years president of the Peterhouse Musical Society. Dickson died on 6 February 1931 at his home, 6 Cranmer Road, Cambridge, and was buried three days later in the chapel at Peterhouse. He was survived by his wife.

M. EILEEN MAGNELLO

Sources *The Times* (7 Feb 1931) · T. A. Walker, ed., *Admissions to Peterhouse or St Peter's College in the University of Cambridge* (1912) · M. M'C. F., *Proceedings of the Royal Society of Edinburgh*, 51 (1930–31), 205–6 · F. Galton, *Memories of my life* (1908) · F. Galton, 'Family likeness in stature, with appendix by J. D. Hamilton Dickson', *PRS*, 40 (1886), 42–73
Archives NL Scot., papers · Sci. Mus., corresp. relating to experiments concerning the vacuum flask
Wealth at death £5257 13s. 2d.: probate, 24 March 1931, *CGPLA Eng. & Wales*

Dickson, Sir James Robert (1832–1901), politician in Australia, was born at Plymouth, England, on 30 November 1832, the only son of James Dickson and his wife, Mary Maria, *née* Palmer. He was educated at the Glasgow high school, then worked as a clerk in the City of Glasgow Bank. In 1854 he emigrated to Victoria, entering the Bank of Australasia, and on 8 November 1855 he married Annie Ely (1838–1880); his second wife was Mary MacKinlay (1841–1900), whom he married on 5 January 1882. About 1859 he joined his merchant cousin's firm, Rae Dickson & Co. In 1862 he moved to Queensland, working with an estate agent; in the early 1870s Dickson opened his own firm which actively participated in the subdivision and building boom that characterized the development of Brisbane, especially in the early 1880s. As a leading auctioneer he held executive positions in four financial and property institutions.

Dickson was elected to the legislative assembly in 1873, winning the seat of Enoggera. He was appointed secretary for public works and mines in 1876, then treasurer, until 1879. After a trip to England, on 31 December 1883 he was chosen (for his commercial experience and as a friend) as colonial treasurer in the Griffith ministry. Here he was involved in obtaining large overseas loans, especially for railways and immigration. He resigned in 1887 in protest against Griffith's proposed land tax, which, since it was to be levied on freehold only, Dickson considered to be a 'class tax with a vengeance'. Standing for re-election he won handsomely, but at the general elections of 1888 he was defeated for the seat of Toombul.

After a stay in Europe between 1889 and 1891, Dickson returned to political life in Queensland. Aligned with the ministerialist cause, he promoted the issue of resuming the importation of Melanesian indentured labourers to work the sugar fields. In a by-election in 1892 he won the seat of Bulimba. He resumed ministerial rank in 1897 as secretary for railways; later postmaster-general was added. In 1898 he was appointed home secretary. When premier Byrnes died suddenly, Dickson, as a stopgap measure, was chosen as premier, chief secretary, and home secretary on 1 December 1898.

In 1899 Dickson played a most influential role in bringing Queensland into the federation of the Australian colonies. Although he had been a Queensland representative at meetings of the federal council of Australasia in 1886, 1888, and 1897, from the mid-1890s there had been a general waning of interest in federation on the part of Queenslanders. While attending the premiers' conference on federation held at Melbourne in January 1899, Dickson secured two amendments in Queensland's favour. At the elections held in 1899 his manifesto proclaimed that federation should be accepted by the people on the 'broad basis of national will'. Through strenuous electioneering and political promises he helped considerably to obtain a 'yes' vote at the referendum held in September. He was chosen in 1900 as Queensland's representative among the Australian delegates attending the London meeting where the final details of the new commonwealth were worked out. Here Dickson stood apart from senior Australian colleagues in his desire to retain some form of appeal to the privy council.

Although generally a staunch supporter of Griffith's liberal approach, much of Dickson's political thinking was governed by considerations of expediency. He was also a keen advocate of the imperial cause; accordingly, in 1899 he readily committed Queensland troops to the Second South African War. Described as 'rather sententious in manner', as 'stiff and punctilious', and a 'tedious and monotonous' speaker with a 'complaining or querulous' tone, Dickson was also noted as being capable and courteous, and wisely attentive to the press. He enjoyed a full life, residing most of his time in Toorak House, 16 Anne Street, Hamilton, Brisbane; and he was a very staunch high-church Anglican. He was appointed CMG in 1897 and KCMG in 1901, and he was chosen to be the first minister of defence in Barton's new federal administration. He travelled to Sydney for the inauguration celebrations, became ill, and died on 10 January 1901 at the Australian Club, Sydney, after attending the first cabinet meeting. He was buried in the Nundah cemetery, Brisbane, and was survived by six sons and seven daughters of his first marriage.   W. Ross Johnston

Sources AusDB · R. Lawson, *Brisbane in the 1890s* (1973) · R. B. Joyce, *Samuel Walker Griffith* (1984) · A. Deakin, *The federal story: the inner history of the federal cause*, ed. J. A. La Nauze, 2nd edn (1963) · J. A. La Nauze, *The making of the Australian constitution* (1972) · A. Jenkins, 'Attitudes towards federation in Queensland', MA diss., University of Queensland, 1979 · R. S. Browne, *A journalist's memoirs* (1927) · D. H. Johnson, *Volunteers at heart* (1975) · *Brisbane Courier* (10 Jan 1901) · C. A. Bernays, *Queensland politics during sixty years, 1859–1919* [1919] · D. B. Waterson, *A biographical register of the Queensland parliament, 1860–1929* (1972) · J. McCormack, 'The politics of expediency: Queensland government in 1890s', MA diss., University of Queensland, 1974

Archives State Library of Queensland, Brisbane, John Oxley Library

Likenesses portrait, Canberra, Australia, Parliament House

Dickson, Margaret [*called* Half Hanged Maggy Dickson] (*d.* in or after **1753**), survivor of execution, is of unknown parentage. She lived in Musselburgh, about 6 miles from Edinburgh, with her fisherman husband, a Mr Dickson, with whom she had several children, and made a living in the town's salt-making industry. After her husband was press-ganged into the navy Margaret had a liaison with a local man, which resulted in pregnancy. All accounts suggest that she feared the humiliation of the punishment, laid down in Scottish law, by which unchaste women were seated in a special place in church on three successive Sundays and rebuked by the minister. Margaret hid her pregnancy and it is unclear whether her child was stillborn or not.

Contesting her innocence to the very end Margaret Dickson was none the less found guilty, under the act of 1690, for concealment of pregnancy. She was sentenced in 1728 to be hanged in the Grassmarket, near Edinburgh Castle. Chambers quotes from an unnamed broadside, printed within days of her execution, which gives minute detail of the proceedings. According to this account Margaret was hanged for the usual length of time, and the public executioner 'did his usual office' of pulling down her legs in order to hasten death. She was then placed in her coffin and the coffin lid nailed down at the gibbet foot. The family had already gained permission for Margaret's body to be removed to her birthplace and interred in the churchyard of Inveresk, near Musselburgh. As the cart carrying Margaret's coffin set off a scuffle broke out between her family and some surgeon-apprentices, the latter presumably wanting the body for dissection. During the affray the coffin lid was damaged, which allowed air to circulate within the coffin, and it was this, combined with the jolting movement of the cart, that was believed to have revived Margaret. For when those entrusted with transporting her body stopped for refreshment about 2 miles into their journey at a small village called Peffer Mill two passing joiners heard noises from within the coffin. When the lid was removed Margaret sat up in a somewhat befuddled state. A phlebotomist, Peter Purdie, was on hand to let blood, which revived Margaret sufficiently for her to be driven to Musselburgh, at the direction of the local magistrate, where she spent the night recovering. The next day she was visited by Robert Bonally, a minister, before being transferred to the house of her brother James, a weaver. The broadside suggests that Margaret was delirious for a couple of days, crying out that she was to be executed on Wednesday, but that she eventually recovered to complain only of a painful neck. The following Sunday she attended church where 'a multitude' of people gathered to see her. Another unnamed account, mentioned by Chambers, suggests that Margaret devoted the following Wednesday, a week to the day of her execution, to solemn fasting and prayer and vowed to do the same every Wednesday for the rest of her life.

Scottish law accepts that once the judgment of the court has been carried out the condemned is exculpated, since the executed person, even if surviving execution, is regarded as dead in law and his or her marriage dissolved. In English law the judgment was to be hanged until dead and so those who survived execution were required by law to be re-hanged. Margaret was therefore at liberty, although the *Newgate Calendar* claims that the king's advocate 'filed a bill in the High Court of Justiciary against the Sheriff' for not seeing the judgment carried out properly. Margaret's husband remarried her in a public ceremony a few days later. The date of her death is unknown but the *Newgate Calendar* reports that she was still living in 1753 and that she was a familiar figure around Edinburgh, where she sold salt and was known as 'Half Hanged Maggy Dickson'.   BARBARA WHITE

Sources R. Chambers, *Domestic annals of Scotland from the revolution to the rebellion of 1745* (1861) · J. L. Rayner and G. T. Crook, eds., *The complete Newgate calendar*, 3 (privately printed, London, 1926), 44–6 · J. Atholl, *Shadow of the gallows* (1954) · *N&Q*, 2nd ser., 11 (1861), 395

Dickson, Robert (1804–1875), physician, was born in Dumfries. Educated at the Royal High School, Edinburgh, and Edinburgh University he graduated MD in 1826 with a thesis on pulmonary consumption. His love of botany began at Edinburgh, leading him to an extensive knowledge and use of vegetable remedies in his medical practice. He became licentiate of the Royal College of Physicians in 1830 and fellow in 1855. In 1834 Dickson married Mary Ann Coope, daughter of a member of the celebrated brewing firm of Ind Coope & Co. In London he looked for a post at a teaching hospital and began by lecturing on botany at St George's Hospital medical school and also at the private medical school in Webb Street, Southwark, established by Edward Grainger in 1819. In 1848 Dickson was disappointed not to receive the support of the medical staff and governors at St George's in his application to be elected physician there and this failure he felt coloured his future practice in London. As a result his clinical appointments were varied and widespread. He was visiting physician to the Camberwell House Lunatic Asylum, physician to the Scottish Hospital, 7 Crane Court, Fleet Street, the British Orphan Asylum in St Mary Axe, and the London branch of the Edinburgh Life Assurance Office (established 1823). In 1855 he assisted his friend Major the Hon. Henry Littleton Powys Keck in founding the Soldiers' Daughters' Home in Rosslyn Hill, Hampstead. Originally intended for destitute war orphans, it later took the daughters of serving officers or retired soldiers. They were admitted from infancy to thirteen and left at the age of sixteen, the able ones being trained to become teachers. Dickson also selected all the shrubs and flowers for the garden. In 1841 he sat on the founding committee of the Brompton Hospital for Consumption and Diseases of the Chest.

Dickson was a fellow of the Royal Medical and Chirurgical Society, and of the Linnean Society, and was a member of the Microscopical Society. In 1837 he gave a lecture to the Institute of British Architects, 'Dry rot and the most effectual means of preventing it'. He wrote popular articles on science in the weekly *Church of England Magazine* under the heading: 'Sacred philosophy: contributions to the natural theology of the vegetable kingdom', and also many of the articles on materia medica and therapeutics in the *Penny Cyclopaedia* (1833–43) including one on wine, of which his knowledge was extensive and his cellar well stocked. In the *Gardeners' Magazine*, 1839, it is said that Dickson gave the botanical descriptions in the first volume and part of the second of Maund's *Botanist* which included a collection of fifty articles, each devoted to one plant with a full description of genus, species, character of genus, where grown, derivation of name, and reference in other journals. Dickson had been stimulated to involve himself in this work by Mr Bentham, the secretary to the Horticultural Society. Dickson was also a patron of popular music and art, and was an early subscriber to the Art Union of London, established in 1837.

Dickson was also an early and earnest advocate of sanitary reform. When the cholera epidemic broke out in London in 1831 he offered his house for a cholera hospital to show his contempt of others for their fear of contagion. He was one of the original promoters and guarantors of the public baths and wash houses in Goulston Street, Whitechapel. Dickson was an honest, active, learned, and well cultivated gentleman, a friend to any deserving person. In spite of this his practice was small and select, mainly as a result of his failure to be appointed to the clinical staff of St George's Hospital or any other teaching hospital in London.

Dickson and his wife lived for a time at 14 Finsbury Square but soon moved west to 16 Hertford Street, Mayfair. In 1868, with his retirement from active practice, they moved to Cambridge Lodge, Harmondsworth, Middlesex, where Dickson enjoyed gardening. His wife died shortly before him in July 1875. On the evening of 9 October 1875 he took a hot bath and badly scalded his right hand and both legs. Shock and collapse followed and although he seemed to recover he died on 13 October. Of their six children, Frederick John joined the civil service in Ceylon; Robert Bruce entered the church; Charlotte married C. Major, and three daughters, Frances Barton, Anna Maria Emily, and another whose name is unknown, were unmarried at his death.   SUE WEIR

Sources *Proceedings of the Royal Medical and Chirurgical Society*, 8 (1875–80), 73–4 · *Medical Times and Gazette* (30 Oct 1875), 509–10 · *London and Provincial Medical Directory* (1845–68) · Munk, *Roll* · *Burdett's Hospital Annual* (1893), 473, 488 · *Gardeners' Magazine*, 15 (1839), 91 · *Church of England Magazine*, 5 (1837), 222–5 · *Homeopathy: British Annals*, tracts 1–10 · *Dissertatio medica inauguralis*, U. Edin., 1826 · *N&Q*, 9th ser., 12 (1903), 149, 194, 236 · *VCH Middlesex*, vol. 9 · Desmond, *Botanists*, rev. edn · J. Britten and G. S. Boulger, eds., *A biographical index of deceased British and Irish botanists*, 2nd edn, ed. A. B. Rendle (1931), 91 · J. Reynolds Green, *A history of botany in the United Kingdom* (1914), 434 · *CGPLA Eng. & Wales* (1875)

Wealth at death under £4000: probate, 4 Nov 1875, *CGPLA Eng. & Wales*

Dickson, Samuel (1802–1869), physician, studied medicine at Edinburgh (where he attached himself to Robert Liston in anatomy and surgery), and at Paris, qualifying at the Edinburgh College of Surgeons in 1825. Having obtained a commission as assistant surgeon in the army, he went to India to join the 30th regiment of foot at Madras. During five years' service in India he acquired a large surgical experience. When cholera broke out there, he bled his patients, and most of them died. After this he began to express doubts about the value of bloodletting. In 1829 he published his *Report on the Endemic Cholera of his Majesty's 30th Regiment, 1828–29*. On his return home he graduated MD at Glasgow University in 1833, and began private practice, first at Cheltenham, and afterwards in Mayfair, Westminster.

In 1836 Dickson published *The Fallacy of the Art of Physic*, in which he gave an unqualified condemnation of bloodletting. Arguing both theoretically and from clinical experience, he believed that all remedies acted solely by altering temperature, and that other measures were more effective than bloodletting at doing this. He later called his alternative system 'chrono-thermalism'. Dickson's two main themes, opposition to antiphlogistic measures and the value of chrono-thermalism, were embellished but largely unrevised in most of his subsequent writings. Although he wished his opposition to bloodletting to be his main message, this was largely overlooked by the medical profession. Instead, they condemned Dickson's books for their fiery polemics against organized medicine.

In Dickson's later works, such as *Fallacies of the Faculty, with the Principles of the Chrono-Thermal System* (1839), his tirades against the profession became more extreme and more personal. This led to scathing reviews by the medical press. Some of Dickson's other books that cover similar ground include *The unity of disease analytically and synthetically proved, with facts subversive of the received practice of physic* (1838); *The Destructive Art of Healing, or, Facts for Families* (1853); *London Medical Practice and its Shortcomings* (1860); and *Memorable Events in the Life of a London Physician* (1863). In 1850 Dickson started a monthly journal, *The Chrono-Thermalist, or, People's Medical Inquirer*, which was written by him alone. This ran for twenty-two months. He also produced a poem, *Physic and its Phases, or, The Rule of Night and the Reign of Wrong* (1857).

Dickson's *What Killed Mr Drummond—the Lead or the Lancet?* (1843) used the accidental shooting of Sir Robert Peel's private secretary, Edward Drummond, as a platform to air Dickson's views against bloodletting. Dickson (calling himself 'an old army surgeon') claimed that 'every successive bleeding brought the unfortunate gentleman nearer the grave' (Bryan, 25). Again, the medical press largely ignored these views, apart from alluding to 'clamours and boastings by ignorant and discreditable charlatans' (ibid.).

Despite such criticism, Dickson's books did find a definite market: *The Fallacies* went through five London editions by 1845. Dickson's chief following was in the United States, where the Penn Medical College of Philadelphia was founded to teach Dickson's doctrines. There a staff of ten professors spoke of 'the system for which we are indebted to that mastermind, Samuel Dickson of London' (Abrahams, 176). That Dickson's attacks on the profession were resented is reflected in his career. By 1850 he had practised in London for twelve years, but belonged to no medical society, faculty, or hospital.

By the early 1850s most patients were being treated with stimulants, rather than antiphlogistic measures. In his later works Dickson claimed that these changes were a direct result of his calls for reform. These claims were ignored. As the practice of bloodletting disappeared, so Dickson's arguments became irrelevant. Later works reflect Dickson's feeling that he had become a victim of a professional conspiracy. Among those he attacked were the queen's attendants and Sir Benjamin Brodie. He also began to argue that other leaders of medicine, such as Paget, were plagiarizing his ideas.

Dickson was perhaps the first and surely the most vehement British physician of his generation to condemn bloodletting openly and completely. However, his arguments relied too heavily on personal opinion and sweeping generalizations to be the driving force behind changes in therapeutics. Dickson died at his home, 12 Bolton Street, Mayfair, on 12 October 1869, leaving a widow, Eliza. His obituaries reflect the bitterness felt towards him within the medical profession. The *Medical Times and Gazette* described him as a man of 'moderate ability' with a 'talent for abuse which he exercised to an unlimited extent' (*Medical Times and Gazette*, 23 Oct 1869, 502).

The character of Dr Sampson in Charles Reade's 1863 novel, *Hard Cash*, was based on Dickson.

TIM O'NEILL

Sources C. S. Bryan, 'Dr Samuel Dickson and the spirit of chrono-thermalism', *Bulletin of the History of Medicine*, 42 (1968), 24–42 · S. Dickson, *Memorable events in the life of a London physician* (1863) · *London and Provincial Medical Directory* (1869–70) · H. Abrahams, *Extinct medical schools of nineteenth-century Philadelphia* (1966), 176 · *Medical Times and Gazette* (23 Oct 1869), 502 · *CGPLA Eng. & Wales* (1869)

Wealth at death under £3000: probate, 22 Nov 1869, *CGPLA Eng. & Wales*

Dickson, William (1744/5–1804), Church of Ireland bishop of Down and Connor, was the son of James Dickson, dean of Down from 1768 until 1787. He was educated at Eton College, where he formed a lifelong friendship with Charles James Fox and several of Fox's nearest friends, one of whom, Lord Robert Spencer, became his executor. Dickson matriculated at Hertford College, Oxford, aged eighteen, on 28 September 1763, graduating BA (1767), MA (1770), and DD by diploma (1784). He was first chaplain to Lord Northington, who became lord lieutenant of Ireland on 3 June 1783, and was promoted to the bishopric of Down and Connor by patent dated 12 December 1784. He was indebted for this rapid promotion to Fox, who informed him that: 'I have ceased to be minister, and you are bishop of Down' (Mant, 2.686). Dickson's appointment made him the official superior of his father, who was still dean of Down. He married a Miss Symmes, and the couple had six children, of whom one son, John, was archdeacon of Down (1796–1814); another, William, was prebendary of Rathsarkan or Rasharkin, in the diocese of Connor (1800–50); and a third, Stephen, held the position of prebendary of Carncastle, in the same diocese (1802–49). A man of notable kindness and politeness, Dickson was admired by churchmen from different parties and faiths. He died at Charles James Fox's house in Arlington Street, London, on 19 September 1804, and was buried in the cemetery of St James's Chapel, Hampstead Road, London, where a monument was erected to his memory.

B. H. BLACKER, rev. PHILIP CARTER

Sources GM, 1st ser., 74 (1804), 890–91 · Annual Register (1804), 501 · Foster, Alum. Oxon. · H. Cotton, Fasti ecclesiae Hibernicae, 1–5 (1845–60) · R. Mant, History of the Church of Ireland, 2 vols. (1840)
Likenesses W. Daniell, soft-ground etching, pubd 1808 (after G. Dance, 1794), BM, NPG · J. Heath, stipple, pubd 1810, BM, NPG; repro. in J. Barrington, Historic memoirs of Ireland, 2 vols. (1809–10)

Dickson, Sir William Forster (1898–1987), air force officer, was born in Northwood, Middlesex, on 24 September 1898, the only child of Campbell Cameron Forster Dickson, solicitor, and his wife, Agnes Nelson-Ward, a direct descendant of Lord Nelson. He was educated at Haileybury College, Hertfordshire, and joined the Royal Naval Air Service in 1916. After training as a pilot he served with the Grand Fleet aboard the aircraft-carrier *Furious*, where he pioneered deck landings and participated in the first carrier-based bombing raid, earning appointment to the DSO (1918). After the war he became a flying instructor in the newly independent Royal Air Force and flew as a test pilot, being awarded the AFC (1922). Then, after working in the Air Ministry (1923–6) as the expert on naval/air operations for Sir Hugh Trenchard, he flew with 56 squadron (1926–7), attended the Royal Air Force Staff College, Andover (1927–8), spent several years in India, commanded 25 squadron (1935–6), and thoroughly enjoyed three years on the directing staff at Andover (1936–8), where he proved a fine instructor. In 1932 he had married Patricia Marguerite, sister of Sir George (Gubby) Allen, cricketer, and daughter of Sir Walter Macarthur Allen, commandant-in-chief of the metropolitan special constabulary. They had two daughters, one of whom died in childhood in 1952.

On the outbreak of war, having attended the Imperial Defence College (1939), Dickson was called upon to use his exceptional staff skills in the joint planning staff, first as group captain (1940) and then as air commodore (1941). He contributed greatly to the forward planning in the early years of the war, working directly for Winston Churchill and the chiefs of staff, joining in meetings with the Soviet ambassador to discuss military aid, and attending the Arcadia conference, where the future Anglo-American strategy was decided. After a year (1942–3) in Fighter Command (as air vice-marshal) he spent another year (1943–4) preparing 83 group for the Normandy invasion, whereupon General Montgomery insisted that the group be handed over to Harry Broadhurst, the commander whom he knew. Dickson, accepting the inevitable disappointment with good grace, departed for Italy to command the desert air force, and for most of 1944 ably directed its intensive interdiction and close army support operations.

At the end of the year Dickson returned to London as assistant chief of air staff (policy); in June 1946 he was promoted air marshal and joined the Air Council as vice-chief of air staff, working under Lord Tedder and devoting much of his attention to the RAF's post-war re-equipment programme; and in March 1948 he became commander-in-chief in the Middle East. A year later he was criticized in parliament after four reconnaissance Spitfires had been shot down by the Israelis, but Clement Attlee, the prime minister, firmly defended him over what had been essentially a political air operation. Dickson returned to the Air Ministry in March 1950, as air member for supply and organization. Central to his work was the expansion programme necessitated by the Korean War, and he also negotiated an agreement with his American counterpart to cover the deployment of a large American air force contingent in the United Kingdom.

Dickson became chief of air staff on 1 January 1953. Churchill, again prime minister, remembered him well from wartime and fully supported him in his prime task: the planning and preparation for the RAF's nuclear deterrent. Recognizing the increasing importance of cold war operations Dickson also pressed forward the development of the air transport force, but was ever mindful of the growing economic pressures on the RAF's budget. He became marshal of the Royal Air Force in 1954. Then, on 1 January 1956, Sir Anthony Eden, now prime minister, appointed him to the new position of separate chairman of the chiefs of staff. Dickson, convinced of the need for a stronger 'centre' in the Ministry of Defence, readily accepted the post, which he held throughout the Suez crisis of 1956 and the subsequent defence review by Duncan Sandys; unable to exercise much influence during this controversial debate he supported the proposal by Harold Macmillan in 1958 to convert his post to chief of defence staff. On 1 January 1959 he became the first incumbent, handing over to Lord Mountbatten of Burma six months later.

Dickson had served at the top of the defence hierarchy for six and a half years, at a time of turmoil, defence cuts, and post-Suez reforms in the armed services. While short of stature, he always commanded attention, combining a razor-sharp brain with a great sense of fun. His sense of humour often defused awkward situations. His love of flying had enamoured him of the RAF, but he retained deep respect for the other services and was seen as an ideal choice for Britain's first chief of defence staff. In retirement at Cold Ash, near Newbury, Berkshire, his interests included the Royal Central Asian Society, the Ex-Services Mental Welfare Society, and the Forces Help Society and Lord Roberts Workshops; he also loved to play golf. He was appointed OBE (1934), CB (1942), CBE (1945), KBE (1946),

KCB (1952), and GCB (1953). William Dickson died on 12 September 1987 at the Royal Air Force Hospital, Wroughton, Wiltshire.   HENRY A. PROBERT, *rev.*

Sources official records, Ministry of Defence, London, air historical branch • *The Times* (15 Sept 1987) • personal knowledge (1996) • private information (1996) • *CGPLA Eng. & Wales* (1987)
Archives CAC Cam., corresp. and papers
Wealth at death £398,434: probate, 8 Dec 1987, *CGPLA Eng. & Wales*

Dickson, William Gillespie (1823–1876), advocate and legal writer, was born on 9 April 1823, the second son of Henry Gordon Dickson, writer to the signet in Edinburgh. He was educated at the Edinburgh Academy and at Edinburgh University, and destined for the legal profession. On 9 March 1847 he was admitted a member of the Faculty of Advocates. He practised at the bar of the supreme court of Scotland in Edinburgh for some years. His success as an advocate was moderate, leaving him time, during his first years of practice, to prepare *A Treatise on the Law of Evidence in Scotland*, the first edition of which was published in July 1855. The work had immediate success. A second edition was published in 1864.

In July 1856 Dickson accepted the office of procureur and advocate-general of Mauritius, where he remained for the next ten years and was greatly liked. In 1867, on account of the failing health of his wife, he obtained leave of absence, and while in Britain in 1868 he was offered by Sheriff Glassford Bell, then sheriff-principal of Lanarkshire, the office of sheriff-substitute in Glasgow. Dickson accepted the post, and on Sheriff Bell's death in 1874 he succeeded him as sheriff-depute (or principal sheriff) of the county. He was installed on 21 January 1874, and in April 1874 he received the honorary degree of LLD from Edinburgh University.

In Glasgow as in Mauritius Dickson made himself a general favourite, with a reputation for diligence. His reputation rested, however, on his *Treatise on the Law of Evidence*, which was republished by John Skelton (2 vols., 1864) and P. J. Hamilton Gierson (2 vols., 1887); it was for long the standard work. Dickson's amiability and geniality made him popular in private life. He died suddenly on 19 October 1876, and was survived by his wife, Mary Clementina Dickson, formerly Tytler.

G. W. BURNET, *rev.* ERIC METCALFE

Sources *The Scotsman* (20 Oct 1876) • *Glasgow Herald* (20 Oct 1876) • *Journal of Jurisprudence*, 20 (1876) • D. Laing, ed., *A catalogue of the graduates … of the University of Edinburgh*, Bannatyne Club, 106 (1858) • *CCI* (1877)
Wealth at death £5353 12s. 2d.: confirmation, 2 Feb 1877, *CCI*

Dickson, William Kennedy Laurie (1860–1935), electrical engineer and film-maker, was born on 3 August 1860 at Château St Buc, Le Minihic-sur-Rance, Brittany, France, the second of three children of James Waite Dickson (d. 1870s), an artist, and his second wife, Elizabeth Kennedy-Laurie (1823?–1879). His father had three daughters by his previous marriage. Dickson apparently spent much of his youth in Brittany, except for a short stay in Germany while his older sister, Antonia, a child-prodigy pianist, studied in conservatories in Leipzig and Stuttgart. He may have been able to claim US citizenship since there was an unverified report that his mother was born in Virginia. His multinational background, combined with an education based on the arts and classics and a strong interest in science, provided Dickson with unusual resources for his future career as an inventor and as the producer of some of the first motion pictures exhibited to audiences throughout the world.

In 1879 Dickson, his mother, and two sisters moved from Britain to Virginia in the United States. His mother died very shortly after they arrived. In 1883 he moved to New York city, where he was employed in the testing-room of the Edison Electric Light Co., Thomas Edison's prototype for urban electrification. By 1884 Dickson was designated as Edison's photographer and in 1887, when Edison opened a state-of-the-art laboratory in Orange, New Jersey, he was on the staff as an experimenter and photographer. In 1888 Edison designated Dickson as leading experimenter for the Kinetoscope, 'an instrument to do for the Eye what the phonograph does for the Ear' (Dickson and Dickson, *Century Magazine*, May 1894). Simultaneously, Dickson was also a principal experimenter on Edison's favourite project, a costly and ultimately unsuccessful experiment to separate low-grade ores magnetically—a project that took priority over the effort to make images move. Dickson was co-patentee with Edison on the ore separation process.

Experimental work on the Kinetoscope (a peep-show viewing device) and Kinetograph (camera) was completed late in 1893 and the Kinetoscope, showing a small image which ran for about thirty seconds, was introduced on 14 April 1894 and was a short-lived sensation. There were immediate demands for projection but Edison was sceptical about the future of moving pictures and reluctant to develop a 'screen machine'. Within two years a number of rival 'scope' and 'graph' projection machines appeared, stimulated by a worldwide demand for new, novel film subjects. Although many of these machines were directly influenced by the Kinetoscope, the rapid acceptance of projection pushed Edison's innovative peep-show machine aside and Dickson's contribution to the development of the newly popular form of communication was obscured.

Most of the parts used in the Kinetoscope had been used in earlier inventions. Edison's and Dickson's achievement was the innovative assembly of these components and Edison, whose name alone was marketable, was the first successfully to commercialize a cinema device. Although he had solved a number of design problems, Dickson's most tangible and enduring contribution was the creation of the standard film gauge known today as 35 mm film. At the end of 1891 he increased the size of his image to a width of one inch and placed four rectangular sprocket holes, slightly rounded at the corners, on either side of the image or frame. His film was designed to record a sequence of successive images on a single strip which moved perpendicularly through the camera and the viewing device. Following the introduction of the Kinetoscope,

86132

Robert Paul, Birt Acres, C. Francis Jenkins, and Thomas Armat each produced machines designed to use 'Edison standard film' and the format gained immediate international acceptance. Although the size of the sprocket holes and the frame ratio have altered slightly, the film used today is essentially identical with the film Dickson began using in 1892. Dickson's 35 mm 'standard' was the common substructure that made it possible for films to be produced and shown throughout the world—the common denominator that sustained the rapid spread of one of the earliest, most pervasive, and most popular forms of international communication.

Dickson also pioneered the production of movies and during his career, from 1891 through to 1903, he produced more than 500 films. In 1893 he designed the first operational motion picture studio, Edison's 'Black Maria', and a laboratory to develop and copy the films shot in the studio. He trained camera operators and initiated the first regular production of motion pictures. During 1894 and 1895 he produced about 125 films which were exhibited before any competing films were produced. He is one of the few film-makers who also designed cameras, production facilities, and viewing machines.

In April 1895 Dickson resigned from Edison's laboratory. Edison's manager, William Gilmore, learned that Dickson was visiting the Lathams, who were making a rival camera and projector, and he accused Dickson of disloyalty. The exact nature of Dickson's relations with the Lathams was, and still is, controversial. Some historians assumed that Dickson designed the Lathams' Eidoloscope, but the Lathams denied this and Dickson never claimed that he invented their machines, even though he considered joining their company. Instead, Dickson and three long-time friends—Elias B. Koopman, Henry Marvin, and Herman Casler—formed the KMCD syndicate to market the Mutoscope, a flip-card peep-show machine built by Casler with unspecified help from Dickson. At the beginning of 1896, after making a camera and projector, the syndicate established the American Mutoscope Company (later the American Mutoscope and Biograph Co., then Biograph Co.), a well-financed challenge to Edison's domination of the American motion picture business. After designing some equipment for the company, Dickson organized film production. He designed a roof-top studio in New York city, a laboratory to develop and print film, and he trained several projectionists and camera operators, among them G. W. 'Billy' Bitzer, later famous as D. W. Griffith's cameraman. Regular production began in the summer of 1896 and the Biograph projector, showing film about the size of today's Imax, premièred in New York in October 1896.

In May 1897, after the American operation was established, Dickson and Koopman moved to London to create a multinational production–exhibition company. A semi-autonomous British company was established, distribution offices for Belgium, Italy, South Africa, and India were set up, and production branches were created in France, the Netherlands, and Germany. Once again Dickson designed studios and technical facilities, and trained camera operators. He travelled throughout England and Europe making films that were popular features on the programmes of the most important variety theatres in several countries. During the last years of the Victorian era the Biograph was a prominent and regular feature on the programs of Keith's Union Square in New York, the Palace in London, the *Folies Bergère* in Paris, and the Winter Garden in Berlin.

Although often thought of as a cameraman, Dickson actually functioned as a producer–director and rarely operated the bulky Biograph camera. He chose subjects, negotiated the arrangements for filming, planned and timed the shots, and supervised the set-up of the camera. His films were carefully composed, with the subjects clearly defined in the frame. Since most of the films were less than one minute long, the camera was placed to make maximum use of the short lengths of film, and subjects were chosen to appeal to the varied tastes of a multinational audience. He developed or improved a number of film genres which sustained the popularity of the Biograph: 'phantom' train rides, spectacular military manoeuvres, and vividly pictured scenes of newsworthy current events and prominent world figures. Several topical films, including one of the return of the sirdar from the Sudan, were premièred on the day they were filmed. In May and June 1898, after several weeks of negotiations, Dickson made news by filming Pope Leo XIII, one of the most sensational and longest-running spectacles of the early cinema. His pioneering films of troop movements and some actual combat during the Second South African War were a remarkable accomplishment, considering that the immense Biograph camera weighed more than 1000 lb. On his return to Britain he published his diary notes of the campaign as *The Biograph in Battle: its Story in the South African War Related with Personal Experiences* (1901).

While Dickson was still experimenting on the Kinetoscope, he began selling still photographs made from his films to newspapers and the illustrated press, a practice he continued throughout his career. These photographs were used both as publicity for the films and as illustrations for newsworthy stories. Beginning in 1892, and with Edison's permission, Dickson's photographs of Edison, the laboratory, and projects at the laboratory were offered for sale by *The Phonogram* magazine and he continued the practice when he began producing films. The half-tone process that made the publication of photographs possible was a recent development, and Dickson's practice created an early link between motion pictures and the emerging illustrated press at a time when the public was still curious about distant lands and anxious to learn what public figures really looked like. It also established precedence for publicity photographs of film productions.

In 1893, independent of his work for Edison, Dickson and his friend Herman Casler designed the Photoret, a 'detective' camera the size and shape of a pocket watch. It was one of the smallest cameras ever made and it attracted international attention. Dickson also patented a lamp for bicycles and another for use by miners. He had brown, wavy hair and frequently had a moustache and/or a short goatee beard. Slender until late in life, he was a stylish dresser. He was a skilled rifle marksman, a talented amateur musician, and was made a fellow of the Royal Geographical Society for the discovery of three caves in Virginia. Although he had no professional degree, he was made an associate of the Institution of Electrical Engineers in 1909 and an honorary member of the Society of Motion Picture Engineers in 1933. Dickson was twice married. He married Lucie Agnes, daughter of Allen L. Archer, of Petersburg, Virginia, on 21 April 1886. She died early in 1908. There were no children. He secondly married Margaret Helen Gordon (*d.* 1938), daughter of James Urquhart Mosse, in 1913. It was her second marriage, and they had one son.

In addition to his remembrances of the Second South African War, Dickson and his sister Antonia Dickson wrote a series of articles, *The Life and Inventions of Thomas A. Edison*, which appeared in *Cassier's Magazine* (November 1892–December 1893). These articles, supplemented by two articles they wrote about the Kinetoscope, were compiled in book form as *The Life and Inventions of Thomas A. Edison* (1894). The Kinetoscope articles were also adapted by the two Dicksons as *History of the Kinetograph, Kinetoscope and Kineto-Phonograph* (1895), a publicity brochure distributed to Kinetoscope dealers by Raff and Gammon's Kinetoscope Co. All of these publications had photographs taken by Dickson as well as some original decoration created by him. In 1933, at the request of the Society of Motion Picture Engineers, he described his experiences in an article for their journal: *A Brief History of the Kinetograph, the Kinetoscope and the Kineto-Phonograph.*

Shortly after returning from South Africa Dickson retired from motion picture work and opened a testing and experimental laboratory and machine works at 64 Strand, London. Modelled on Edison's laboratory, but on a more modest scale, Dickson worked on a variety of projects, a number of them related to the amusement industry. Among these were an automatic piano, an amusement park ride, and a portable dining facility for carnivals. He was joined in the laboratory by his friend Eugene Lauste, whose pioneering experiments to record sound on film were begun in Dickson's laboratory. Dickson operated this laboratory until about 1920, when he retired. During his retirement Dickson lived in Richmond upon Thames, Twickenham, and Jersey. He died of carcinoma of the prostate at Montpelier House, 29 Montpelier Row, Twickenham, on 28 September 1935, and was buried in Twickenham cemetery on 2 October.   PAUL C. SPEHR

Sources W. K. L. Dickson, 'A brief history of the Kinetograph, the Kinetoscope and the Kineto-Phonograph', *Journal of the Society of Motion Picture Engineers*, 21 (Dec 1933), 9–17 • W. K. L. Dickson and A. Dickson, *History of the Kinetograph, Kinetoscope and Kineto-Phonograph* (1895) • G. Hendricks, *Origins of the American film* (1972) • C. Musser, *The emergence of cinema: the American screen to 1907* (1990) • R. Conot, *Thomas A. Edison: a streak of luck* (1979) • T. Ramsaye, *A million and one nights: a history of the motion picture*, new edn (1964) • E. Brayer, *George Eastman: a biography* (1996) • W. K. L. Dickson and A. Dickson, *Century Magazine* (May 1894) • C. Musser, *Edison motion pictures, 1890–1900: an annotated filmography* (1997) • G. W. Bitzer, *Billy Bitzer: his story* (1973) • A. Millard, *Edison and the business of innovation* (1990) • W. K. L. Dickson, *The Biograph in battle: its story in the South African War* (1901) • *The Post Office London directory* (1898–1920) • *Journal of the Institution of Electrical Engineers*, 40 (1907–8) • *Electrical trades directory* (1900–22) • *Jersey directory and express almanac*, 1928, 1929, 1930 • d. cert. • *Richmond and Twickenham Times* (5 Oct 1935)

Archives Edison National Historic Site, West Orange, New Jersey, archives | Georgetown University, Washington, DC, Terry Ramsaye MSS and Thomas Armat MSS • Harvard U., Baker Library, Raff and Gammon collection • Museum of Modern Art, New York, Merritt Crawford MSS and records of the Biograph Company • Smithsonian Institution, Washington, DC, National Museum of American History, Gordon Hendricks collection | FILM BFI NFTVA, actuality footage • L. Cong., motion picture, broadcasting and recorded sound division • Museum of Modern Art, New York • Nederlands Filmmuseum, Amsterdam

Likenesses photograph, *c.*1889, Smithsonian Institution, Washington, DC, National Museum of American History, photographic history collection, Eugene Lauste collection • group portrait, 1895, Museum of Modern Art, New York • group photograph, *c.*1898, Smithsonian Institution, Washington, DC, Eugene Lauste collection • group photograph, 1898, Edison National Historic Site, West Orange, New Jersey • photograph, *c.*1898, Smithsonian Institution, Washington, DC, National Museum of American History, Gordon Hendricks collection • group photograph, 1900, Smithsonian Institution, Washington, DC, Gordon Hendricks collection

Dickson, William Kirk (1860–1949), librarian, was born at 20 George Square, Edinburgh, on 24 November 1860, the son of William Dickson, a wholesale stationer of Mauricewood, Glencorse, Linlithgowshire, and his wife, Anne Kirk. He was educated at Merchiston Castle School, Edinburgh, and at the University of Edinburgh, where he graduated MA in 1880. He passed advocate on 3 November 1887. He was not in strong practice at the bar—his interests were mainly literary and historical—but in 1897 he was appropriately elected a curator of the library of the Faculty of Advocates. He married in 1897 Kathleen, daughter of Sir Robert Murdoch Smith, whose biography he wrote in 1901. They had two sons, one of whom was killed at the battle of Jutland.

As a curator Dickson joined a managing committee that was trying to solve the many problems of maintaining a working library for the Scots bar while fulfilling, with inadequate funding and increasingly constricted premises, the obligation to retain and make available the general books that came to it through provisions of the copyright acts. The Treasury had proved markedly unsympathetic to the faculty's requests for government financial support of its under-funded library.

In 1906 the resignation of the Advocates' librarian J. T. Clark, after nearly thirty years of lax administration, opened the way to the appointment of Dickson, the first member of the faculty for well over a century to have held the office. Having served as clerk of faculty he was well known, and much liked, by his colleagues, and on library matters formed an effective partnership with his brother advocate H. P. Macmillan. He was skilled at suggesting, though subordinating, his own views to those of the curatorial body.

The question of eventual nationalization was a pressing one, in which there was growing interest in Scotland as a whole, and notably in the higher echelons of the Scottish Office. Within the faculty there remained a residual opposition very defensive of members' rights. Dickson was initially inclined to take a similarly protective view but was gradually converted to the inevitability of full nationalization. Before this important question could be considered there were many housekeeping problems to be solved, in acquisitions policy, cataloguing, and accommodation. The last at least was temporarily alleviated by government when improvements to the court buildings allowed for some extensions in the library.

The desirability of a national library (not least following recent developments in Wales) was in 1911 again voiced by Lord Rosebery, the former prime minister, himself a considerable bibliophile and a patriotic Scot. Persuaded by internal reports written by Dickson, the faculty approached government with a national take-over in mind. The First World War intervened to make a postponement inevitable, and also severely to deplete the faculty's financial reserves. After the war government proved sympathetic and proposed an annual grant, but it was constrained by national financial stringency from immediately re-establishing the library on a national basis. An appeal to distinguished Scots advanced the cause, and was followed by a *Proposal to Establish a Scottish National Library*, drafted by Dickson and Macmillan (and tellingly revised by John Buchan), which led to an endowment trust being set up in 1923. An arduous fund-raising campaign was expected, but the philanthropic biscuit-maker Alexander Grant, head of the Edinburgh firm of McVitie and Price, offered £100,000: this was decisive in ensuring that the new foundation could proceed.

Much remained to be done, and Dickson consulted widely to design a sound administrative structure with direct Treasury funding. He devised means of ensuring that the Advocates' Library continued to receive the law books statutorily claimed by the new institution, and that existing advocates' borrowing rights were protected. The constitutional and legislative channel was navigated by Macmillan, but Dickson (as a contemporary put it) was 'the steersman [who] does not show himself'.

On 26 October 1925, the vesting day specified in the National Library of Scotland Act, Dickson became a civil servant, the former keeper being designated librarian of the new institution. He served as such for six years, with an enlarged senior staff, and devoted much of his time to negotiations for the George IV Bridge site, adjacent to the Parliament House, to be eventually a new building. It was far from ideal as a location, but on balance he saw it as an admissible solution, especially in the library's proximity to its historic roots.

Dickson retired in October 1931 but remained active in historical and administrative work, for example by chairing Edinburgh University's library committee. He edited texts for the Scottish History Society and was a prominent member of the Society of Antiquaries of Scotland, of which he was secretary for some years. He wrote on Napoleonic subjects and edited texts in Jacobite history, and was prominent in the Franco-Scottish Society; he was

awarded the grand cross of the Légion d'honneur in 1939. Dickson died at Chalmers Hospital, Edinburgh, on 14 July 1949.   ALAN BELL

Sources I. F. Maciver, 'The making of a national library', *For the encouragement of learning: Scotland's national library, 1689–1989*, ed. P. Cadell and A. Matheson (1989), 215–65 · I. G. Brown, *Building for books* (1989) · *WWW*, 1941–50 · *University of Edinburgh Journal*, 15 (1949–51), 36 · b. cert. · d. cert.
Archives NL Scot., autograph collection · NL Scot., memoirs, lectures, and corresp. · NL Scot., corresp. with his son Robert and papers

Dickson, William Purdie (1823–1901), theologian and translator, was the third son of George Dickson, Church of Scotland minister of Pettinain, and afterwards of Kilrenny, Fife, and his first wife, Mary Lockhart; he was born at Pettinain manse, Lanarkshire, on 22 October 1823. After attending Pettinain parish school and the grammar school at Lanark, he studied at St Andrews (1837–44) for the ministry of the Church of Scotland. A high prizeman in Greek, at the Divinity Hall he gained in 1843 the Gray prize for an English essay. On 5 May 1845 he was licensed as a preacher by St Andrews presbytery, and he retained his first charge at Grangemouth, Stirlingshire, from 1846 to 1851. On 9 September 1851 Dickson was ordained minister of Cameron parish, St Andrews, where he remained until 1863. During this time Dickson lectured at the university, helped to reorganize the library, and was examiner for classics in 1861–2. He was a lifelong friend of the principal John Tulloch. On 7 December 1853 Dickson married Tassie Wardlaw, daughter of John *Small, the Edinburgh University librarian; they had two daughters and a son.

From 1863 to 1873 Dickson held the new chair of biblical criticism in Glasgow University, and from 1873 until his retirement in 1895 he was professor of divinity, having succeeded John Caird. His theology was unoriginal and he was critical of the new 'higher criticism' influencing biblical scholarship. From 1866 to his death he was curator of Glasgow University Library, the post having been created for him; in this capacity he was responsible for the printing of a new catalogue, the rearrangement of the library according to subject, and the introduction of an alphabetic catalogue. He was president of the Library Association in 1888. From 1875 to 1888 he was the convener of the education committee of the Church of Scotland, but he twice declined nomination as moderator of the general assembly. He was made DD by both St Andrews (in 1864) and Glasgow University (in 1896) and honorary LLD by Edinburgh (in 1885). He was Church of Scotland Baird lecturer in 1883. While minister of Cameron, Dickson began the translation of Mommsen's *History of Rome* (1862–6), with the author's permission. Mommsen reviewed the translation and added comments which are not in his original work. A second and revised edition appeared in 1895. Dickson's translation of Mommsen's *Provinces of the Roman Empire* followed in 1887. He also edited the translation of Meyer's *Critical and Exegetical Commentary on the New Testament* (10 vols., 1873–80). In 1889 he published a pamphlet arguing against the proposals for universal free education, and he wrote other articles on the subjects of education and theology.

Dickson died at 16 Victoria Crescent, Glasgow, on 9 March 1901, and was buried in the Glasgow necropolis.

T. W. BAYNE, rev. MYFANWY LLOYD

Sources Irving, *Scots.* · *Fasti Scot.* · P. Schaff and S. M. Jackson, *Encyclopedia of living divines and Christian workers of all denominations in Europe and America: being a supplement to Schaff-Herzog encyclopedia of religious knowledge* (1887) · W. P. Dickson, *The Glasgow University library* (1888) · *Glasgow Herald* (11 March 1901) · *The Scotsman* (11 March 1901) · T. Mommsen, *The history of Rome*, trans. W. P. Dickson, 4 vols. (1862–6) [some additions by W. P. Dickson] · J. L. Galbraith, *The curator of the Glasgow University library* (1909) · Mrs Oliphant, *A memoir of the life of John Tulloch* (1888) · A. L. Drummond and J. Bulloch, *The church in late Victorian Scotland* (1978) · Allibone, *Dict.* · W. A. Munford, *A history of the Library Association, 1877–1977* (1976)

Wealth at death £8079 4*s.* 8*d.*: confirmation, 30 April 1901, *CCI*

Dickson, William Steel (1744–1824), minister of the Presbyterian General Synod of Ulster and political radical, was born William Dickson on Christmas day 1744, the eldest son of John Dickson, farmer, and his wife, Jane Steel, at Ballycraigy, in the parish of Carnmoney, co. Antrim. Following the death, on 13 May 1747, of his uncle William Steel he was given the additional name of Steel. Having received a grounding in classics, logic, metaphysics, morals, and natural theology from the Revd Robert White of Templepatrick he matriculated from Glasgow University in 1763. He was received on 'trial' by Templepatrick presbytery on 20 January 1766 and licensed on 8 April 1767. This presbytery had abolished subscription to the Westminster confession and so Dickson was not required to subscribe. Four years later, on 6 March 1771, he was ordained by Killyleagh presbytery at Ballyhalbert and, as this presbytery was also non-subscription, he was not required to sign the confession. Soon after his ordination he 'became an husband and a farmer' (Dickson, *A Narrative*, 7). His wife, Isabella McMinn (*d.* 1819), whom he married on 21 August 1771, came from a 'genteel family, brought up in affluence and liberally educated' (ibid., 7). They had four sons and two daughters.

Dickson first entered the political arena when he denounced the war with the American colonies as 'unnatural, impolitic and unprincipled' (Dickson, *A Narrative*, 7). During the conflict the government appointed two general fast days. On 13 December 1776 Dickson spoke to his congregation on 'The advantages of national repentance', and on 27 February 1778 on 'The ruinous effects of civil war'; both sermons were published later that year and caused considerable offence to those who sympathized with the British government. For his part Dickson defended his stance: 'If we have, in any instance censured the principle or conduct of the war … [it] has been justified by the general feelings of humanity, and a zealous concern for the common interests of Britain and America' (W. S. Dickson, *Sermons*, 1778, 58). Alexander Gordon has suggested that it was Dickson's radical politics that caused a portion of his congregation to secede and build a new church at Kircubbin in 1777. But a remonstrance presented to the synod of Ulster by commissioners from neighbouring congregations of Greyabbey and Portaferry maintained that the Kircubbin seceders had not separated 'on account of any religious concern, matter of or objection against the conduct or ministry of Mr Dixon' (*Records of the General Synod of Ulster*, 2.588).

When the volunteers were raised with government approval in 1778 to meet a possible French invasion Dickson was an enthusiastic supporter. On 28 March 1779 he delivered a sermon to the Echlinville Company, entitled 'The propriety and advantages of acquiring the knowledge and use of arms in times of public danger'. In his address he deplored the exclusion of Catholics from the movement. The effect of his remarks was 'to offend all the Protestant and Presbyterian bigots in the country' (Dickson, *A Narrative*, 10), but the general tenor of the sermon was approved as promoting the volunteer cause.

Dickson preached at Portaferry on 14 November 1779 on the occasion of the death of its pastor, the Revd James Armstrong. His address so impressed his hearers that he was invited to fill the vacant pulpit. He accepted, resigned his charge at Ballyhalbert on 1 February 1780, and was installed at Portaferry by Killyleagh presbytery on 6 March. There he opened an academy from which he derived about £100 per annum. In 1781 he was appointed to preach the annual sermon at synod. In 1784 Glasgow University conferred on him a doctorate in divinity.

When Robert Stewart, later first marquess of Londonderry, stood for re-election to parliament as MP for County Down in 1783 Dickson devoted a considerable amount of time, labour, and purse to further Stewart's cause against the marquess of Downshire's interest, but in vain. However, at the 1790 parliamentary election Stewart's son Robert, the future Lord Castlereagh, was successful, and again Dickson was prominent in the election campaign. His political commitment to the Stewarts, who were independent whigs, stemmed from their championing of the dissenting interest in the county.

The Society of United Irishmen was founded at Belfast in October 1791. Dickson took the 'test' early in December but apparently did not attend any further meetings, although he later admitted that he was often in their company. He was present at the volunteer rally in Belfast on 14 July 1792 to mark the third anniversary of the storming of the Bastille. Aided by two ministerial colleagues, Thomas Ledlie Birch of Saintfield and Sinclaire Kelburn of Belfast, he strongly challenged a proposal calling for the gradual emancipation of Catholics; consequently a proposal for total and immediate emancipation was overwhelmingly adopted. In the same year he published a small pamphlet, *Psalmody an Address to the Presbyterian Congregations of the Synod of Ulster*, issued with the approbation of nine presbyteries.

At a volunteer convention at Dungannon, co. Tyrone, on 15 and 16 February 1793 Dickson supported radical resolutions such as that calling for Catholic emancipation. So impressive was his oratory that he was invited to preach in the local meeting-house on the Sunday afterwards. A crowded church heard him expound Joseph's advice to his brethren: 'See that ye fall not out by the way' (Genesis 45:

24). A few weeks later he published his celebrated *Three Sermons on the Subject of Scripture Politics*, in which he argued forcibly for the need and enforcement of reform and emancipation on biblical grounds. In June he was elected moderator of synod, which congratulated their Roman Catholic countrymen on their regaining of the franchise under the Catholic Relief Act of April 1793. His stance on reform, however, caused many families in the Portaferry congregation to withdraw from his ministry. Spurred on by the dissension Dickson used every effort to regain the confidence of the disaffected; the church committee marked his success with a presentation 'for the services he had rendered to the congregation' (Portaferry congregation MSS, 24 Oct 1793).

Little is known about Dickson's activities during 1794 and 1795 and most of 1796. There was some civil unrest among the Presbyterians and Catholics in the upper Ards district which he sought to resolve, only to find that charges of sedition were directed against him for his pains. His detractors contended that he occupied these years preaching inflammable and seditious sermons. In the autumn of 1796 the government, alarmed by rumours that the French were about to invade Ireland, arrested a number of leading northern United Irishmen. Several members of Dickson's congregation were detained and efforts were made to obtain evidence of his involvement in the United Irishmen's plot to overthrow the government. One of those arrested, a man named Carr, was offered £1000 to provide information leading to Dickson's conviction, but his testimony was judged unreliable.

In the spring of 1797 Dickson was summoned by the defence to attend the co. Antrim assizes at Carrickfergus to impeach the character of the chief prosecution witness, Bell (or Belle) Martin (originally from Portaferry), at the trial of a United Irishman. He attended a meeting of co. Down magistrates and gentlemen at Ballynahinch in May and endorsed the resolution 'not to relax in our exertions by any legal and constitutional means to obtain a full and adequate representation of the people of Ireland without regard to differences of religious opinions' (*Belfast News-Letter*, 15 May 1797). At the summer assizes in Downpatrick, Dickson—along with J. Philpot Curran—persuaded the attorney-general to release the Portaferry prisoners. In the latter part of the year illness confined him to the manse.

In March–April 1798, the year of the Irish rising, Dickson visited Scotland, and on return his baggage was searched at Portaferry but no incriminating documents were found. In May he was active, attending to sacramental duties in parts of co. Down and visiting friends in Belfast. It has been alleged that he agreed to accept the post of adjutant-general for the United Irishmen of co. Down around this time. He was arrested, on the orders of Lord Annesley, at Ballynahinch on 5 June, some days before the outbreak of the rising in co. Down, and was taken to Lisburn before being transferred to Belfast, where he was detained in various prisons until 25 March 1799. Having been put on board a ship he and other important United Irish prisoners sailed for Scotland and were conveyed overland to Fort George, near Inverness, where they arrived on 9 April. During Dickson's incarceration government officials in Belfast made strenuous efforts to obtain sufficient evidence to indict him. Two United Irishmen-turned-informers were offered inducements to confirm that he was appointed adjutant-general by the co. Down colonels in May 1798 but they refused to testify in open court. Later Dickson was offered his liberty on condition of his emigrating to a foreign country. He insisted on being brought to court and tried, but to no avail. Having been confined for over three years he was taken back to Belfast and released on 13 January 1802.

At first Dickson contemplated emigrating to America but, aware that this would be taken as evidence of his guilt, he decided to remain. Efforts to have him installed as minister at Donegore, co. Antrim, failed, as it was implied that payment of the *regium donum* would not be granted in his case because of his alleged connection to the rising. He attended the meetings of synod in 1802 and, as he did not have a congregation, he was received as an honorary member. He was installed in the newly formed congregation of Second Keady, co. Armagh, on 24 March 1803. As his installation service did not involve signing the confession some members of Tyrone presbytery moved that he should not be admitted unless he subscribed. Since this was not the majority view of presbytery he was accordingly received. His stipend was fixed at £50 without the *regium donum* and so his congregation petitioned synod for a share of the *regium donum* but this was rejected in 1804 and again in 1805. In response Dickson submitted a memorial requiring synod to state explicitly whether or not it had been referred to in a minute of 1799 that he was 'implicated in treasonable or seditious practices' in 1798 (*Records of the General Synod of Ulster*, 3.302). His memorial was summarily dismissed, at which he 'entreated the Moderator to hear him one word, [and] laying his hand upon his breast, he pronounced with great emphasis, "Farewell for ever"!, and left the house' (Black, 8). He absented himself from synod in 1806 but returned in 1807 and remained until 1810, without making any reference to his complaint.

At synod in 1811 Dickson obtained permission to use synodical documents for the forthcoming publication of his narrative of his life. He took part in the speeches at a Catholic dinner in Dublin on 9 May and was probably the first Presbyterian parson ever to address a wholly Catholic gathering. He also spoke at a Catholic meeting in Armagh on 9 September; on his way home to Keady he was waylaid and assaulted. His *Narrative*, published in May 1812, caused a major storm at synod. The members, led by the Revd Dr Robert Black, declared that the work 'contained a number of gross misstatements and misrepresentations, highly injurious to the reputation of the ministers of this body' and demanded a public retraction (*Records of the General Synod of Ulster*, 3.383). Dickson refused to put his signature to an apology prepared by synod. The immediate reaction was to suspend him *ab officio*, which was later amended to postponement for a year to allow him to retract. Dickson used the time to publish what he facetiously termed

Retractations, which was an attack on Black's criticism of him. This led to a reappraisal of Dickson's situation by synod in 1813. The Revd William Porter and the Revd Henry Montgomery questioned whether the minute of 1799 had been accurate, and it was agreed that the words as applied to Dickson had been inaccurately used. However, an apology from him regarding certain statements made in his *Narrative* relative to the synod was demanded. Dickson later handed in a paper purporting to be an apology but this was refused as inadequate and synod decided to dismiss the whole subject. His last political appearance was at a meeting of Catholics at Newry on 19 October 1813. He did not intend to address the gathering but responded to a 'general cry from every quarter' to speak. He did so 'amidst expressions of the most unbounded applause' ('Proceedings at public meetings', 400, 403).

Increasing infirmity caused Dickson to resign from Second Keady on 27 June 1815. He retired to Belfast and was forced to depend on the support of friends to provide him with accommodation and a weekly allowance. In 1817 he published a book of fifteen sermons, which did not alleviate his financial situation. His wife died on 15 July 1819, and a small annuity ceased with her death. As a member of the synod's committee Dickson attended the public examinations of theological students from 1821 to 1824. He died in Belfast on 27 December 1824 and was buried in a pauper's grave in Clifton Street cemetery, at which the Revd W. D. H. McEwen delivered a panegyric to a small group of mourners.   W. D. BAILIE

Sources W. S. Dickson, *A narrative of the confinement and exile of W. S. Dickson, D.D.* (1812) · *Records of the General Synod of Ulster, from 1691 to 1820*, 3 vols. (1890–98) · minutes of the General Synod of Ulster, 1821–4, Presbyterian Historical Society, Belfast · W. D. Bailie, 'William Steel Dickson', *Protestant, Catholic, and dissenter*, ed. L. Swords (Dublin, 1997), 45–80 · 'Proceedings at public meetings', *Belfast Monthly Magazine*, 11 (1813), 396–403 · Portaferry congregation, MS minutes, Portaferry, co. Down · *Belfast News-Letter* (15 May 1797) · *Belfast News-Letter* (30 July 1819) · *Belfast News-Letter* (31 Dec 1824) · W. S. Dickson, *Retractations, or, A review of, and reply to a pamphlet, entitled 'Substance of two speeches'* (1813) · R. Black, *Substance of two speeches, delivered in the General Synod of Ulster at its annual meeting in 1812* (1812) · *DNB* · baptismal record, Carnmoney Presbyterian Church, Presbyterian Historical Society, Church House, Belfast, 30 Dec 1744 · marriage record, Carnmoney Presbyterian Church, Presbyterian Historical Society, Church House, Belfast [John Dickson and Jane Steel], 6 Dec 1743 · Ballyhalbert church marriage records, session book, Glastry Congregation, Ballyhalbert, co. Down

Likenesses oils, repro. in M. Hill, B. Turner, and K. Dawson, eds., *1798 rebellion in county Down* (1998)

Dicsone [Dickson], **Alexander** (*bap.* 1558, *d.* 1603/4), philosophical writer and political agent, was baptized at Kirkton, Errol, Scotland, in December 1558, as the son of Alexander Dickson and Margaret Hay. He was educated at St Leonard's College, St Andrews (graduating 1577). He may have spent part of the next few years on the continent (perhaps in Paris as one of Queen Mary's scholars) before he is heard of again, in 1583, when 'Alexander Dixson / Scott / Gentleman' is listed among alien inhabitants of the Tower ward, London. By this time he was a disciple of the Italian hermetic philosopher and cosmologist Giordano

Bruno (1548?–1600), who came to stay in England from March 1583 to November 1585. Bruno inscribed to Dicsone a copy of his *De umbris idearum* (Paris, 1582) in token of their friendship, and in his dialogue *De la causa, principio et uno* (1584) Bruno introduces Dicsone as one of his four speakers, describing him as 'that learned, honest, affectionate, cultured, and very faithful friend, Alexander Dixon, whom the Nolan [Bruno] loves as his own eyes, and who has made it possible for this thesis to be planned' (Bruno, *Concerning the Cause*, 103).

For his part Dicsone published in London in '1583' (actually 1584) his own *De umbra rationis & judicii, sive, De memoriae virtute prosopopæia*, a philosophical tract based on the mnemonic theories of Bruno, the title of whose *De umbris idearum* ('On the shadows of ideas') is echoed in Dicsone's title ('On the shadow of reason and judgement'). This book became well known in intellectual circles, and Dicsone was cited for years afterwards as he 'Of the Art of Memory'. It also became extremely controversial, sparking what Frances Yates has described as one of the most extraordinary controversies of the age relating to the art of memory and its connections with a hermetic religious cult. It was vehemently attacked, most especially in 1584 by the Cambridge puritan theologian William Perkins (1558–1602) in his *Antidicsonus* and *Libellus de memoria*. Besides implying that Dicsone's views were impious and redolent of old barbarism and popery, Perkins chafed at his denigration of Ramism, the influential teaching on logic of the Huguenot philosopher Petrus Ramus (1515–1572), which was espoused by Cambridge academics. Dicsone retaliated against Perkins's attacks later in 1584 in his *Heii Scepsii defensio pro Alexandro Dicsono*, adopting for his sobriquet the term 'Scepsian' which Perkins had hurled at him as an insult (implying one who uses the zodiac in his impious artificial memory).

It was also in 1583–4 that Dicsone (as well as his mentor Bruno) came into the circle of the earl of Leicester (to whom Dicsone's two published works are dedicated) and his nephew, Sir Philip Sidney. When Dicsone later gave a 'casket' of state papers and tracts to the French ambassador Guillaume de L'Aubespine, it included copies of three prose works by Sidney. These included Sidney's *Defence* of the earl of Leicester against the Catholic libel published in 1584 generally known as *Leicester's Commonwealth*. Not only was Dicsone allowed personal access to a 'Defence' which was restrained from general circulation, but, by his account, he wrote his 'own answer' to the libel as well, 'done by the advice and order of my Lord [Leicester] and his nephew Sir Philip' (Dicsone to Robert Bowes, 9 Aug 1595).

By 1588, if not earlier, Dicsone seems to have been in the service of the Scottish Catholic rebel Francis Hay, ninth earl of Erroll, and his family (with whom his mother, Margaret Hay, was perhaps related). He was bequeathed £110 'for taxation' by Dame Margaret Stewart, countess of Erroll, in her will of 12 April 1588. From other evidence it is clear that *c.*1590 Alexander Dicsone was acting as Lord Erroll's emissary to ministers of the kirk and that in 1591 he was caught conveying letters from the Catholic exile earl of Westmorland, for which he was 'sharply checked & warned' by James VI himself (Robert Bowes to Lord Burghley, 3 April 1591). Nevertheless, despite his exasperation with him, the king had Dicsone released when the general assembly of the kirk angrily consigned him to the Tolbooth prison in Edinburgh for admitting he was a Catholic. In 1592, after attending the Scottish court for a 'long time' and behaving 'very humbly with the King' (Bowes to Burghley, 6 June 1592), he was described as 'servant to the Earl of Errol', and in 1594 as 'now secretary to Errol' (Francis Tennant to Archibald Douglas, 4 June 1592; John Colville to Henry Lock, 17 July 1594).

It was presumably his early 'service' to Erroll and his allies which launched Dicsone on his career not only as an agent and emissary, sent on repeated missions in England, France, and the Low Countries, but also as a spy. While ostensibly a moderate Scottish Catholic, who professedly loved Mary, queen of Scots, but hated those extremist counsellors who drove her to her death, Dicsone—described by both French and English agents as early as 1586 as a man not to be trusted and subsequently as 'a false knave'—effectively offered allegiance not only to the Catholic earls but also to the episcopalian James VI, to the French government, and to the English crown. Whether a self-serving opportunist or a double agent, Dicsone offered in 1593 to draw the rebel earls of Angus, Huntly, and Erroll into the service of Queen Elizabeth and also personally 'to discover the practices [plots] in this realm [Scotland], Spain or Low Countries' in return for an annual pension (Bowes to Burghley, 10 June 1593). Though the offer was cautiously welcomed, the English continued throughout the 1590s to regard Dicsone with suspicion as they monitored his various missions. Their annoyance with his gift of papers to 'his dear friend' L'Aubespine in 1595 prompted a lengthy letter by him of self-vindication, in which he argued (somewhat disingenuously) for the harmlessness of the gift, which he offered to try and retrieve (with the help of his uncle Robert) if someone would give him the means. As if to confirm his good faith, only weeks later he wrote to inform the English ambassador of the arrival in Scotland of the Jesuit priest Alexander McQuhirrie (a contemporary of Dicsone's at St Andrews).

Nevertheless, despite the king's view that Dicsone had 'become their [the earls'] enemy, and is over privy with the ministers [of the kirk]' (Dr Macartney to Bowes, 23 May 1595), Dicsone continued to be reported over the years as engaged on continental missions involving Catholic interests and 'practisers', employing as his 'servant', at least in 1595, the surgeon Peter Lowe (1550?–1612?), who later founded the Faculty of Physicians and Surgeons in Glasgow. Yet although the English government was assured by one agent in 1598 that Dicsone was 'an enemy of your state' (Andrew Hunter to Sir Robert Cecil, 12/22 Nov 1598), James VI found use for him in Scotland. At least from 1598 onwards, Dicsone served the king as an unofficial propagandist, writing (if not publishing) tracts both to support James's claim to the English succession and to justify particular actions by him. Dicsone's last recorded

act seems to have been in April 1603 when, as the king's 'servitour', he strongly urged the recalcitrant minister of the kirk John Davidson (1549?–1603) to submit totally to the royal will, only about four months before Davidson's death (Dicsone to Davidson, April 1603; copy in BL, Add. MS 4739, fols. 128v–129r).

Dicsone himself was dead by 1604, when a laudatory elegy on him appeared in Thomas Murray's *Naupactiados, sive, Lepantiados Jacobi magni*. The Scottish court poet Murray (1564–1623) celebrated an intimate friendship with Dicsone also in his epigram 'In verissimam Alexandri Dicsoni & authoris amicitiam'.

Besides the Latin treatises published in 1584 (reprinted at Leiden in 1597) and his defences of Leicester (1584) and of the king's execution of the Catholic laird of Bonnington (1601), Dicsone wrote at least one more philosophical essay (now BL, Harley MS 6866) and two treatises defending James VI's title to the English crown (one is now NL Scot, MS Adv. 31. 4. 8). Apart from the two early Latin treatises, none of these works is known to have been published.   PETER BEAL

Sources P. Beal, 'Alexander Dicsone, Elizabethan philosopher, propagandist, spy: a checklist of his writings', *The Library*, 7th ser., 2 (2001), 116–26, see also 394 [addenda] · P. Beal, 'Philip Sidney's *Letter to Queen Elizabeth* and that "False Knave", Alexander Dicsone', *English Manuscript Studies, 1100–1700*, 11 (2002), 1–51 · J. Durkan, 'Alexander Dickson and STC 6823', *The Bibliothek*, 3 (1962), 183–90 · F. A. Yates, *The art of memory* (1966); repr. (1978), 260–78, 406–9 · *CSP Scot.*, 1585–6; 1588–1603 · *Calendar of the manuscripts of the most hon. the marquis of Salisbury*, 24 vols., HMC, 9 (1883–1976), vol. 4, pp. 205–6; vol. 6, p. 427 · *Aliens in London*, Publications of the Huguenot Society of London, 10/2 (1902), 324 · T. Murray, *Naupactiados, sive, Lepantiados Jacobi magni: metaphrasis poetica authore T. Moravio* (1604) · R. Sturlese, 'Un nuovo autografo del Bruno', *Rinascimento*, 27 (1987), 387–91 · J. Bossy, *Giordano Bruno and the embassy affair* (1991) · G. Bruno, *De la causa, principio et uno*, ed. G. Aquilecchia (Turin, 1973), xliii–xlvi · G. Bruno, 'Concerning the cause, principle, and one', *The infinite in Giordano Bruno: with a translation of his dialogue, Concerning the cause, principle, and one*, ed. and trans. S. Greenberg (1950) · J. M. Anderson, ed., *Early records of the University of St Andrews*, Scottish History Society, 3rd ser., 8 (1926), 177, 287 · register of baptisms, Errol, 1553–1691, General Register Office for Scotland, Edinburgh, fol. 2r

Archives BL, letters, Add. MS 4739, fols. 128v–129r · BL, writings, Harley MS 6866, fols. 52r–72v · NL Scot., volumes owned, Adv. MS 33.3.11 · NL Scot., writings, Adv. MS 31.4.8 · PRO, letters, SP 52/56/84, SP 52/27/20 · UCL, volumes owned, Ogden A 50 | NA Scot., 'Inventory of Errol charters', item 1211

Dícuil (*fl. c.*795–825), scholar and teacher, of Irish descent, went to the continent some time between 795 and 814 as one of an international constellation of Anglo-Saxon, Visigothic, Italian, and Irish scholars attracted to the court of Charlemagne (*r.* 768–814). The palatine scholars provided impetus and direction to the Carolingian reform of education and learning.

Dícuil wrote in prose and in poetry for an emperor and for schoolboys. His talents ranged over Latin grammar, astronomy, calendar reckoning, and geography. A careful schoolmaster, he often outlined the contents of his works, recorded the dates of their composition, and noted his own literary output. While his works lack style and polish, they are remarkable for their originality and keen critical sense.

In 814, probably while teaching at the palace school, Dícuil began work on his *Liber de astronomia et computo*, which he dedicated in four yearly instalments to the emperor Louis the Pious (r. 814–40). The work, which alternates prose with poetry, enabled Dícuil to display his erudition and virtuosity in two fields, metrics and time reckoning (computus). The extensive use of poetry served to honour the emperor and to encourage his continued patronage. Dícuil's verses also served a mnemonic function when they conveyed difficult computistical rules. Verse could also be used to entertain. 'In these verses I playfully spin puzzles' ('Astronomical treatise', ed. Esposito, 392), Dícuil announced when he showed the emperor how the four verse endings of four hexameters could be manipulated to produce seventy-two hexameters. He repeated the ingenious exercise in the second book of his treatise where he worked the permutation to produce 166 verses based on the same limited vocabulary. His model was Optatianus Porfyrius, court poet to Constantine the Great. Porfyrian verse, especially acrostic and figure poems, enjoyed great vogue among Carolingian court poets.

Computus, one of the few disciplines specifically emphasized in Carolingian educational reform legislation, also attracted considerable attention among scholars and royal patrons. Proper observance of the liturgical cycle required delicate calculations between solar and lunar calendar systems and knowledge of astronomical phenomena. The variety of calculations and rules inherited from earlier centuries and cultures proved difficult for Carolingian computists when they tried to devise an efficient and uniform method of time reckoning. Charlemagne was deeply interested in calendar and astronomical problems and in 809 charged a committee of computus experts to resolve disagreements. In 811, Dúngal, another Irish scholar, replied with a wide-ranging letter to Charlemagne's request for information on solar eclipses. Dícuil's *Liber de astronomia et computo* is a product of this intense interest in astronomical and calendar issues.

Dícuil's treatise had no impact in the ninth century. The author himself acknowledged that even Louis the Pious turned a deaf ear to its metrical passages and did not reward the scholar for his efforts. Dícuil's misfortune was to write on computus for the wrong emperor; Louis did not share his father's enthusiasm for the subject. Nevertheless, Dícuil's treatise remains significant on its own merits. Unlike the more widely copied *De computo* of Hrabanus Maurus (c.780–856), Dícuil's work is that of an experienced computist thinking through the theoretical problems that vexed his colleagues. Hrabanus Maurus's compilation provided a polished, general overview of its subject, better fitted for non-specialists than Dícuil's technical and terse, but more critical and innovative, treatise. Dícuil's computus opens with a set of calculations for determining that if one begins the year in April, April will be the first month of the year 814. Modern commentators

have not appreciated the force of Dícuil's example. Medieval calendars were lunisolar. Since the lunar year is approximately eleven days shorter than the solar year, the lunar and solar months diverge after three years. To correct this discrepancy, computists inserted a periodic *saltus lunae* ('moon's leap') into their calculations. Dícuil's formula, based on the pedagogically astute strategy of proceeding from the familiar and the particular (the example of the current year) to general principles, attempted to provide a simple calculation to reconcile easily the lunar and solar cycles. Although Dícuil drew on Pliny and Isidore of Seville, he critically appraised his sources. He refrained from discussing the effect of the moon on the ocean since, writing far from the ocean's shores, he could not verify the sources. He challenged received tradition regarding the south polar star and planetary orbits. When his own ingenuity failed him, he encouraged his readers to improve upon the unsatisfactory explanations found in his sources and expressed his readiness to follow his colleagues' solutions to obscure questions rather than those of earlier authorities.

Dícuil's critical spirit also animated his second major work, the *De mensura orbis terrae*, completed in 825. Its nine chapters treat in order Europe, Asia, Africa, Egypt, and Ethiopia, the longitude and latitude of the earth, rivers, islands, the latitude and longitude of the Tyrrhenian Sea, and the six principal mountains. Dícuil began his book, the first medieval geography, with an evaluation of the merits of his authorities. He preferred the Theodosian *Divisio orbis* to Pliny the Elder's more ancient and authoritative *Naturalis historia* because he believed that the envoys of the Roman emperor Theodosius II (r. 408–50) actually measured the distances they recorded. Dícuil also noted that scribal mistakes sometimes falsified the distances reported in manuscripts of Pliny's work. In these cases, he left spaces blank which readers with access to better manuscripts could complete with correct numbers. Dícuil's attitude toward texts prefigures that of the noted bibliophile, Abbot Lupus of Ferrières (c.805–c.862). Although much of Dícuil's text derives from his sources, he approached these not as a mere compiler, but as a scholar. He challenged Solinus's statement that elephants could not lie down on the basis of the evidence provided by Abul Abaz, the elephant Caliph Harun-al-Rashid presented to Charlemagne. He reported at length the experiences of Irish monks who had visited remote islands in the north Atlantic and used their information again to challenge Solinus. He described his own voyages among the islands north of Britain: 'I have never found these islands mentioned in the authorities' (vii, 15, ed. Tierney and Bieler). The sources likewise were silent on the canal that joined the Nile to the Red Sea. Young Dícuil, however, had overheard Fidelis (a pilgrim and presumably a fellow Irishman) report on the canal and other Egyptian wonders to Suibne, Dícuil's teacher. In addition to preferring the authority of contemporaries over traditional textual sources, Dícuil maintained a healthy scepticism towards claims made for exotic places. He doubted Solinus's account of the eating habits of the people who dwell on the Ganges, as well as his description of the crocodile. He questioned Isidore of Seville's figures for the circumference of Sicily. He again took Solinus to task for describing Mount Atlas both as snow-covered and as rising above the clouds. Experience indicates that snow falls from clouds, thus the mountain's snow-covered peaks cannot rise above the clouds.

Dícuil noted in the preface to the *De mensura orbis terrae* that he had just completed an *Epistula de quaestionibus decem artis grammaticae*. This work is lost, but three other minor works emanating from Dícuil's teaching survive: the *De prima syllaba* was also written in 825, as a guide to Latin prosody for 'little boys'; his *Epistula censuum* (unpublished), composed in 818, begins with 225 verses on weights and measures and includes a glossary of homonyms and synonyms; and the twenty-seven hexameters he wrote to accompany the text of Priscian's *Partitiones duodecim versuum Aeneidos principalium*, a fundamental Carolingian schoolbook, summarized the contents of Priscian's work for Dícuil's pupils. It is not known when Dícuil died.   JOHN J. CONTRENI

Sources Dicuil, 'Micons von St. Riquier De primis syllabis', ed. M. Manitius, *Münchener Museum für Philologie des Mittelalters und der Renaissance*, 1 (1912) [*De prima syllaba*], 124–6, 154–77 · Dicuil, 'An unpublished astronomical treatise by the Irish monk Dicuil', ed. M. Esposito, *Proceedings of the Royal Irish Academy*, 26C (1906–7), 378–446; repr. in M. Esposito, *Irish books and learning in mediaeval Europe*, ed. M. Lapidge (1990) [on *Liber de astronomia et computo*] · M. Esposito, 'A ninth-century astronomical treatise', *Modern Philology*, 18 (1920–21), 177–88; repr. in M. Esposito, *Irish books and learning in mediaeval Europe*, ed. M. Lapidge (1990) · A. Cordoliani, 'Le comput de Dicuil', *Cahiers de Civilisation Médiévale*, 3 (1960), 325–37 · *Dicuili 'Liber de mensura orbis terrae'*, ed. J. J. Tierney and L. Bieler, Scriptores Latini Hiberniae, 6 (1967) · Dicuil, 'Versus in Prisciani Partitiones duodecim versuum Aeneidos principalium', *Poetae Latini aevi Carolini*, ed. E. Dümmler, MGH Poetae Latini Medii Aevi, 2 (Berlin, 1884), 667–8 · W. Bergmann, 'Dicuil's *De mensura orbis terrae*', *Science in western and eastern civilization in Carolingian times*, ed. P. L. Butzer and D. Lohrmann (1993), 525–37 · M. Lapidge and R. Sharpe, *A bibliography of Celtic-Latin literature, 400–1200* (1985), 174–5

Diefenbaker, John George (1895–1979), prime minister of Canada, was born in Neustadt, Ontario, on 18 September 1895, the older of the two sons of William Thomas Diefenbaker (1868–1945), a schoolteacher, and his wife, Mary Florence Bannerman (1872–1951). William Diefenbaker moved to Saskatchewan in 1903 and began homesteading in 1906. Although the family relocated to Saskatoon in 1910 when William joined the provincial civil service, the homesteading experience provided John Diefenbaker with the classic North American success story. His grandfather had emigrated from Baden but William Anglicized his name and brought up his son to be a fervent admirer of the British crown and British parliamentary institutions. In later life Diefenbaker repeatedly claimed that his parental grandfather had been born in Canada rather than Germany and he reacted angrily when anyone gave his name a German pronunciation. He was more proud of his mother's highland Scottish forebears, tracking down the graves of his Bannerman great-grandparents in Toronto and entering political rallies escorted by kilted bagpipers.

John George Diefenbaker (1895–1979), by Elliott & Fry, 1961

His mother remained a powerful (it seemed to his first wife, Edna, an all-powerful) force in his life until her death in 1951. From her he derived his Baptist faith, his ascetic lifestyle, and his driving ambition.

Although the family had modest means and Diefenbaker had to work as a newspaper boy, a supply teacher, and a door-to-door salesman (of Bible lessons), he entered the University of Saskatchewan in 1912, receiving the degrees of BA in 1915 and MA in political science and economics in 1916. In 1916 he enlisted in the Canadian army and was commissioned as a lieutenant. Although briefly stationed overseas, he never saw action but was invalided home.

After receiving his law degree from the University of Saskatchewan in 1919 Diefenbaker opened a practice in Wakaw, Saskatchewan, and in 1924 moved to Prince Albert. Specializing in criminal law, Diefenbaker excelled before a jury, developing the aggressive and confrontational debating style which he would later use to good effect on the hustings and in the House of Commons. Like any great defence attorney, Diefenbaker was a master in the art of destruction. An accomplished mimic, he left many a prosecution attorney and later many a political opponent writhing in agony as he ridiculed their arguments. A brilliant campaigner and one of the most feared debaters in the House of Commons, he rarely spoke from a prepared text. He interacted with his audience, at one point hectoring them with his finger jabbing into the air as he drove home his point, at the next inviting them to join with him in a great crusade for good against evil. He never tired of delivering the same speech, continuously honing and improving it. In later life he developed a nervous habit of shaking his jowls which led to rumours that he was suffering from Parkinson's disease and provided a boon for caricaturists. Increasingly frequently during a long speech—he rarely gave short ones—he also lost the thread of his own argument. But in his prime he had few equals as a public speaker.

The years in opposition Even as a youth (since the age of eight if one can believe his memoirs) Diefenbaker saw himself as a future prime minister. Yet his political affiliation remained unclear until the federal election of 1925 when he unsuccessfully contested Prince Albert for the Conservatives. Although he claimed to have been motivated by his commitment to the imperial connection, he may have chosen the minority party in western Canada simply because it offered more rapid advancement. But he remained an outsider in a party dominated by Ontario politicians of a wealthier and more patrician background than his own and his inability to win office increased his sense of frustration. He was defeated again in the federal election of 1926 and the Saskatchewan provincial election of 1929, defeated when he ran to become mayor of Prince Albert in 1933, and defeated as leader of the provincial Conservatives (along with every member of his party) in the 1938 Saskatchewan election. In 1940 he finally won a seat in the federal House of Commons for Lake Centre, Saskatchewan. Re-elected in 1945 and 1949, he transferred in 1953 to Prince Albert, which he held until his death. But in 1942 and again in 1948 he was unsuccessful when he sought to become national leader of the Conservative Party. Personal tragedy struck when Edna Mae Brower (b. 1899), a schoolteacher whom he had married on 29 June 1929, died of leukaemia on 7 February 1951.

Diefenbaker required constant female support and reassurance and on 8 December 1953 he married a widow, Olive Evangeline Palmer (1902?–1976), daughter of the Revd D. B. Freeman; she worked for the Ontario department of education. Olive would prove the perfect partner, completely devoting her life to his advancement and serving as his closest confidante. Fortune also smiled on Diefenbaker when George Drew resigned as leader of the Progressive Conservative Party in 1956. By this time Diefenbaker had created an elaborate persona for himself as the perpetual outsider fighting against the establishment, the defender of the weak and disadvantaged. Like all good political personae, it contained an element of truth. As a western Canadian Diefenbaker was an outsider in the Conservative Party. His origins were comparatively humble and he did show more concern for the poor and underprivileged than his colleagues. One of the leading progressives in the party (which in 1942 had renamed itself the Progressive Conservative Party), in 1945 he forced the leadership to support the Liberals' Family Allowances Act. Yet Diefenbaker's radicalism had distinct limits. He strongly believed in individual initiative and the free enterprise system. While sympathetic to government support for the poor and the aged, he was generally opposed to universal social programmes, denouncing medicare and compulsory pension plans as socialistic. But there can be no doubt about his commitment to civil rights, to ending discrimination against ethnic minorities (from which he had suffered because of his German name), and to 'an unhyphenated Canadianism'. He supported the Canadian Citizenship Act of 1946 and was an early advocate of a Canadian Bill of Rights to prevent abuses of power by the state. He was not entirely consistent. Although he later claimed that he opposed the treatment of Japanese Canadians during the war, there is no evidence that he spoke out on this issue until after 1945.

Diefenbaker's outsider status was a useful political asset but it could easily become a handicap. He was a loner with few close friends, even fewer relaxations, and very limited intellectual and cultural interests. Although an amusing raconteur, he disliked social events he did not dominate. Diefenbaker demanded adulation and he viewed disagreement as disloyalty. He was a poor loser and an even worse winner for he held grudges. At the 1956 convention he was supported by 80 per cent of the caucus and easily won the leadership of the Progressive Conservative Party, but he continued to refer to those who had opposed his nomination as his 'enemies'.

In 1957 the Conservatives campaigned on the slogan 'It's time for a Diefenbaker government'. Merril W. Menzies, a young economist from western Canada who believed in the need for a programme of national development to stimulate growth in the hinterlands of Canada, was recruited to give focus to Diefenbaker's criticism of the lack of national vision of the Liberals. Diefenbaker crisscrossed the country in an exhausting campaign, visiting every province and appealing to the 'common people' to vote for one of their own. The result was a stunning upset. The Conservatives won 112 seats and Diefenbaker formed a minority government, the first Conservative government in twenty-two years.

Diefenbaker in power Diefenbaker was just three months short of sixty-two when he became prime minister. He had never administered anything larger than a small and somewhat disorganized law firm. After forming his cabinet, he triumphantly represented Canada at the Commonwealth conference in London, where he met his greatest political hero, Winston Churchill, and was invited to Windsor Castle to see the queen. The *Daily Mail* hailed him as the new strongman of the Commonwealth. Upon his return Diefenbaker announced that he hoped to divert 15 per cent of Canada's imports from the United States to the United Kingdom, a promise he was never able to fulfil. Although Diefenbaker was a dedicated Canadian nationalist, occasionally apprehensive about American policies and resentful of the American practice of taking Canada for granted, he was not anti-American. A dedicated cold warrior, he was prepared to accept American leadership of the 'free world' and in 1957 he endorsed the creation of the North American defence command (NORAD). His relationship with President Dwight D. Eisenhower was unusually close and based on mutual respect.

Diefenbaker's priority was to turn his minority government into a majority government and his legislative programme included increases in pensions for the aged and for veterans, more funds for public housing and for the provinces, and even tax cuts. At the first available opportunity he dissolved parliament. In 1957 he had been the beneficiary of the disillusionment with the Liberals. The sweeping victory of 1958 was more clearly due to his personal charisma and his successful appeal to 'my fellow Canadians' (a phrase which became his trade mark) to join in an idealistic crusade to create a powerful and autonomous northern nation, linked to the Commonwealth. Diefenbaker was returned to power with 208 out of 265 seats, the largest majority up to that time in Canadian history.

Ironically, the sheer scale of the Diefenbaker victory proved a mixed blessing. The majority was an unwieldy one and Diefenbaker had raised public expectations which were difficult to fulfil. He had promised to strengthen the Commonwealth but his courageous decision to uphold the principle of a multi-racial Commonwealth led to South Africa's withdrawal and he engaged in a bitter public debate with the British government over the terms of Britain's proposed entry into the EEC. Yet the government's accomplishments were far from negligible. Diefenbaker viewed as his greatest achievement the 1960 Canadian Bill of Rights, even though it was a very limited measure. He extended to Canada's native peoples the right to full citizenship and appointed the first Indian to the senate. He appointed the first woman to the cabinet. He was concerned about rural poverty, which he had seen at first hand, and his government introduced the Agricultural Rehabilitation and Development Act, which improved the lot of many rural people. Favouring a fairer distribution of the national wealth among the regions, Diefenbaker opened the federal government purse strings to the provinces and introduced the first programmes of regional economic development. His government invested in regional infrastructures, such as the South Saskatchewan Dam, which incidentally created Lake Diefenbaker, and negotiated the first wheat sales to China. Diefenbaker's appeal was to those individuals and regions which had not benefited equally from the post-war boom and he turned the Conservative Party into the dominant party in the west and in rural English Canada.

Diefenbaker had declared during the 1958 election that no Canadian need fear unemployment under his administration, but unfortunately unemployment rates had already begun to rise. Although he favoured responding with a programme of economic expansion, this was not the view of the majority of the cabinet and Diefenbaker deferred to his Conservative minister of finance, Donald Fleming. Even the mildly interventionist policies in the areas of rural and regional development had to be curtailed because of the growing deficit and the government made the controversial (but entirely justified) decision to cancel a multi-million dollar contract for the Avro Arrow, a Canadian-designed military aircraft. This decision proved unpopular in Ontario and Diefenbaker became a target of bitter public criticism. From this point on he showed an increasing unwillingness to make unpopular decisions. Cabinet meetings became more frequent and longer but increasingly unproductive. His reluctance to act partly explains the clumsy way in which the government finally removed the governor of the Bank of Canada, James Coyne, who opposed the moderately Keynesian thrust of their policies.

More serious politically was Diefenbaker's failure to strengthen the party's weak base in Quebec. Diefenbaker was not anti-French Canadian. He desperately sought to learn French, even though he found it agonizing to give speeches in the language and he was cruelly mocked for his efforts. But his prairie roots led him to espouse a vision of 'One Canada' in which there was no place for hyphenated Canadians nor special status for any province. In 1956 Diefenbaker antagonized French-Canadian Conservatives by not having his nomination seconded by a French-speaking delegate. In 1957 he won only nine seats in Quebec and he appointed Leon Balcer, the senior French-Canadian Conservative, to a relatively minor post. In 1958, although the party won fifty seats in Quebec, he refused to allow Balcer to hold a provincial caucus so that the Quebec members could discuss issues in their own language. The introduction of simultaneous translation in parliament and bilingual cheques and the appointment of the first French-Canadian governor-general did not alter the image of a government unconcerned with the winds of change sweeping across Quebec in the 1960s. Diefenbaker paid a heavy price in the election of 1962 when his Quebec representation was reduced from fifty to fourteen. The timing of the election was unfortunate. During the spring of 1962 there was a run on the Canadian dollar which, on 2 May, the government pegged at 92.5 cents American. In the long run devaluation was a sensible policy, but the Liberals immediately dubbed the devalued Canadian currency as a 'Diefendollar' and the exchange crisis haunted the Conservatives during the June election. The prairies and rural Ontario prevented the government's defeat, but the party lost ninety-two seats and Diefenbaker returned as the head of a minority government.

Under pressure from the International Monetary Fund, the revamped Diefenbaker cabinet began to prepare a much more fiscally conservative budget. It was never presented, for the Cuban missile crisis in October 1962 brought to the centre of Canadian politics the issue of whether to arm the Bomarc missiles acquired from the Americans when the Avro Arrow was cancelled. The minister of defence, Douglas Harkness, had been pushing for the acquisition of nuclear warheads since 1960 but the minister of external affairs, Howard Green, was equally determined that Canada should remain free of nuclear weapons. Although instinctively in favour of whatever measures were necessary to deter a Soviet attack on North America, Diefenbaker was increasingly influenced by the mail flowing into his office against the acquisition of nuclear weapons and by the arguments of those in the cabinet and in the civil service who opposed arming the Bomarcs.

Moreover, his relationship with the new American president, John F. Kennedy, began badly and quickly deteriorated. Diefenbaker loyally supported the Americans during the Berlin crisis. He also reluctantly accepted the necessity of placing Canadian armed forces on alert during the Cuban missile crisis, even though the president had engaged in no real consultation with Canada and was engaged in what Diefenbaker and many others regarded as dangerous brinkmanship. But he dithered over whether to arm the Bomarcs and whether to equip Canada's forces in NATO with tactical nuclear weapons. As it became clear that the Social Credit Party in the House of Commons was unwilling to sustain the minority government, several ministers tried to persuade Diefenbaker to step aside, but with the solid support of the caucus Diefenbaker refused. When he continued to vacillate over arming the Bomarcs, Harkness resigned, and the government was defeated in the House of Commons.

For Diefenbaker the cabinet revolt was further evidence of a plot to unseat him. During the years of waiting in the wings he had come to see himself as the classic outsider, the prairie populist opposed by the forces of big business and the eastern establishment. In 1957 he overcame his natural paranoia and appointed a cabinet which he himself described as composed of his enemies, but even after the unprecedented victory of 1958 he remained suspicious of their loyalty. He was also suspicious of the loyalty of the federal bureaucracy and angry at criticism in the press. While in opposition Diefenbaker had been a popular figure with the parliamentary press gallery, but after 1958 the press became increasingly critical. Diefenbaker reacted badly, cutting himself off from all but a handful of loyal reporters and frequently lashing out against the press (and the Canadian Broadcasting Corporation) for distorting his government's accomplishments. He blamed the press for the crushing loss of seats in 1962. By 1963 he saw himself as the victim of an even broader conspiracy with the Liberals, the press, Toronto, Quebec, and the Americans ganging up on him. In all of this there was an element of truth. The Liberal opposition had targeted Diefenbaker and was obstructionist, the press was largely unsympathetic, urban Ontario and French-speaking Quebec had lost confidence in him, and Kennedy wanted to see the election of a more sympathetic administration in Canada and allowed his frustration with Diefenbaker to become public knowledge. In the election of 1963 Diefenbaker conducted an energetic and highly charged whistle-stop campaign, travelling across the country by train and briefly stopping at as many little towns as possible. His message was overtly (but only moderately) anti-American, as he denounced the Kennedy administration for interfering in Canadian politics. The crowds were large and enthusiastic and Diefenbaker was confident that the little people, the average Canadians, were on his side. At least in the west and in rural Ontario and parts of the maritimes they were and the Liberals, although they won the election, did not win a majority. On 22 April 1963 Lester B. Pearson replaced Diefenbaker as head of another minority government.

Back in opposition Over the next two years Diefenbaker subjected the Pearson government to the same unrelenting hostility to which it had subjected him. But he refused to co-operate with the other opposition parties, thus ensuring the survival of Pearson's minority government. He was persuaded to appoint Balcer as his Quebec lieutenant but refused to give him any real power. In 1964–5 he led a prolonged and futile campaign against the adoption of the Canadian flag, destroying any hope of a reconciliation with Balcer and the other Quebec members, who broke party ranks and voted for the new flag. In 1965 Pearson attempted once again to get a majority and once again the seventy-year-old Diefenbaker entered the fray. Pearson gained only two seats and outside of Quebec Diefenbaker held a lead of fourteen seats over the Liberals. But if the election demonstrated that Diefenbaker could prevent a Liberal majority, it made equally clear that he could not deliver an election victory. The pressure for a leadership review now became irresistible. Diefenbaker refused to go quietly. At the convention in 1966 he placed his name in nomination and faced the humiliation of coming fifth. The convention turned to Robert Stanfield. Stanfield had loyally supported Diefenbaker in the election of 1965 but Diefenbaker did not return the favour, continually denouncing Stanfield's efforts to rebuild the party in Quebec as dangerous to the unity of Canada.

In the election of 1968 Diefenbaker won his own seat and gloated at the poor showing of the Conservative Party. He remained in parliament until his death, occasionally embarrassing the government but more frequently embarrassing his own party. In 1976 he was named a Companion of Honour by Queen Elizabeth, but he refused to believe that the honour had been bestowed at the request of Pierre Elliott Trudeau, whom he loathed. On 22 December 1976 the death of Olive Diefenbaker filled him with despair and led him to begin planning his own state funeral, which he wished modelled upon that of Winston Churchill. On 16 August 1979 he died in Ottawa. His body was carried across the country in a state train, with frequent stops along the way, to Prince Albert. He was buried on 22 August on a hilltop above the South Saskatchewan River, just outside Saskatoon.

An assessment Books assessing the Diefenbaker legacy began to appear even before his death. In 1963 Peter C. Newman's critical study of Diefenbaker, *Renegade in Power: the Diefenbaker Years*, became an immediate bestseller and in 1965 George Grant in *Lament for a Nation: the Defeat of Canadian Nationalism* mythologized Diefenbaker as a tragic and flawed hero in the struggle against American dominance in Canada. Diefenbaker sought to put the historical record straight by writing a three-volume memoir and leaving money in his will for copies to be distributed to schools across Canada. He also left an extensive collection of private papers which Denis Smith used to produce *Rogue Tory: the Life and Legend of John G. Diefenbaker* (1995), the most balanced study of Diefenbaker, although Smith clearly prefers Diefenbaker the legend to Diefenbaker the man. Perhaps that is as it should be. Diefenbaker was a larger than life figure who aroused great hatred and fanatical loyalty. His legacy remains ambiguous. He led the Conservative Party out of the wilderness and back into it, but he left it a stronger party than he found it. In every election between 1958 to 1988 (except 1968) the Conservatives were the dominant party outside of Quebec. His sweeping 1958 victory forced the Liberals to swing to the left and the New Democratic Party to the centre. His policies made the Canadian union a more equitable one. Indeed, by increasing federal grants to the provinces, he made possible a number of social programmes, including the hitherto moribund hospital insurance scheme, ironically paving the way for medicare, a national programme of which he thoroughly disapproved. He aroused a latent sense of Canadian nationalism in 1957 and 1958 and many Canadians shared his fears of American dominance in 1963. Yet his nationalism was based upon a vision of Canada as a British nation which no longer held much imaginative appeal to a new generation to whom the red ensign, the monarchy, and even the Commonwealth had less and less emotional meaning. His cry for 'One Canada' in which all Canadians and all provinces would be treated equally did have lasting imaginative appeal to English Canadians, but it hindered Conservative efforts to rebuild the party in Quebec and ultimately provided an insufficient basis for unity in a country as ethnically diverse as Canada. Even Diefenbaker's Bill of Rights has been all but forgotten, overshadowed by Trudeau's 'Charter of rights and freedoms'. In retrospect, Diefenbaker was a better prime minister than his critics claimed. But he contributed to the destruction of his own reputation by his intense egotism and paranoid style and by the tenacity with which he clung to power after 1965.

PHILLIP BUCKNER

Sources D. Smith, *Rogue tory: the life and legend of John G. Diefenbaker* (1995) · D. C. Storey and R. B. Shepard, eds., *The Diefenbaker legacy: Canadian politics, law and society since 1957* (1998) · J. G. Diefenbaker, *One Canada: memoirs of the Right Honourable John G. Diefenbaker*, 3 vols. (1975–7) · T. McIlroy, ed., *Personal letters of a public man: the family letters of John G. Diefenbaker* (1985) · P. Stursberg, *Diefenbaker*, 1: *Leadership gained, 1956–62* (Toronto, 1975) · P. Stursberg, *Diefenbaker*, 2: *Leadership lost, 1962–67* (Toronto, 1976) · H. B. Robinson, *Diefenbaker's world: a populist in foreign affairs* (1989) · P. C. Newman, *Renegade in power: the Diefenbaker years* (1963) · P. C. Newman, *The distemper of our times* (1978) · M. Bliss, *Right honourable men: the descent of Canadian politics from Macdonald to Mulroney* (1994) · J. Johnston, *The party's over* (1971) · P. Nicholson, *Vision and indecision: Diefenbaker and Pearson* (1968) · D. Spencer, *Trumpets and drums: John Diefenbaker on the campaign trail* (1994) · E. L. Fairclough, *Saturday's child: memoirs of Canada's first female cabinet minister* (1995) · D. Camp, *Gentlemen, players and politicians* (1970) · M. Conrad, *George Nowlan: maritime conservative in national politics* (1986) · D. Fleming, *So very near: the political memoirs of the Honourable Donald M. Fleming*, 2 vols. (1985) · K. Nash, *Kennedy and Diefenbaker: fear and loathing across the undefended border* (1990) · G. Wilson and K. Wilson, *Diefenbaker for the defence* (1988) · G. Grant, *Lament for a nation: the defeat of Canadian nationalism* (1965)
Archives University of Saskatchewan, Saskatoon, Diefenbaker Center, archives | U. Leeds, Brotherton L., corresp. with Henry Drummond-Wolff | FILM BFI NFTVA, current affairs footage · BFI NFTVA, documentary footage
Likenesses Elliott & Fry, photograph, 1961, NPG [*see illus.*] · group portrait, photograph, 1962, Hult. Arch. · portraits, University of Saskatchewan, Saskatoon, Canada, Diefenbaker Center · portraits, NA Canada
Wealth at death C$475,000—trust fund and various properties: Smith, *Rogue tory*, 578–80

Dieren, Bernard Hélène Joseph van (1887–1936), composer and writer, was born on 27 December 1887 at 51a Coolsingel, Rotterdam, of Dutch/French ancestry, the last of five children of Bernard Joseph van Dieren (*d.* 1904), wine merchant, and his second wife, Julie Françoise Adelle Labbé (*b.* 1852), a dressmaker. Although details of his education are shrouded in mystery, it would seem that his initial training was as a scientist, since his first post was that of a research assistant in a laboratory. Highly intelligent and with a phenomenal memory, he was also talented not only in the scientific and literary fields but also at drawing and at playing the violin, which he learned as a boy at school. He began to compose at the age of twenty, and some of his early works (a number of songs and a violin piece) were published locally. By this time he had made up his mind to study composition and music history seriously.

At the end of 1909 van Dieren moved to London together with Frida Kindler (1879–1964), one of a talented musical family, whom he married on 1 January 1910. A son, Hans Jean Jules Maximilian Navarre Benvenuto Bernard van Dieren (1910–1974), was born later that year. In Britain van Dieren carried on composing and, although largely self-taught, spent a year travelling about Europe in 1912, studying for a time in Germany and having contact with composers such as Ferruccio Busoni and Arnold Schoenberg. Strongly influenced by these early twentieth-century atonal composers, his music is highly complex, with counterpoint one of its most important components: the often unexpected resultant harmonic effect gives his work its very distinctive flavour.

Apart from six string quartets and a large corpus of songs, van Dieren's works do not fall easily into any specific categories. Rather, his output encompasses a wide variety of highly complex and often enigmatic compositions that make very considerable demands on the performers and listeners alike. His influence was restricted to a comparatively small band of loyal admirers, of whom Philip Heseltine (Peter Warlock) was the most vociferous, though composers of the stature of William Walton moved briefly into his orbit. Despite various attempts to resuscitate his music, he has not received any notable acclaim or widespread recognition. Finding it difficult to earn a living and to devote time to composing, van Dieren acted for some years as musical correspondent for a number of European newspapers and periodicals, including the *Nieuwe Rotterdamsche Courant*. For a brief part of the First World War he was involved in secret service in the Netherlands, employed as a cipher expert by the intelligence department.

Van Dieren spent most of his life troubled by ill health as a result of an operation in 1912 which left him a chronic sufferer from a kidney complaint; this plagued him for the rest of his life, and necessitated numerous operations in Britain, Germany, and the Netherlands. Because of often constant pain he had recourse to morphine, to which he is believed later to have become addicted. These frequent bouts of ill health forced him to spend a great deal of time as an invalid; his wife, Frida, a fine pianist and one-time pupil of Busoni, supported the family by teaching and performing. For much of his life the couple had often to rely on the support and goodwill of their friends. Van Dieren's charismatic, powerful personality and strong intellect drew around him a number of devoted and loyal admirers which included the Sitwell brothers (Osbert and Sacheverell), the sculptor Jacob Epstein (who used him as a model for one of his bronzes, *The Risen Christ*, now in the Scottish National Gallery of Modern Art), the painter Augustus John, the composer Philip Heseltine, and the critic Cecil Gray. He was fortunate in having this duo of musical supporters, who not only assisted him materially, but also did their utmost to promote performances of his works and to secure for him the place they felt he deserved in English music. In February 1917 Heseltine (aided financially by Gray) organized a concert of his music in the Wigmore Hall in London. The occasion was, in almost every respect, a disaster. Heseltine's and Gray's overblown pre-concert publicity made wild claims about van Dieren's genius, and the critics, finding the music largely inaccessible, were extremely hostile in their reviews. In many ways this occasion did more harm than good, and for a long time a veil of suspicion hung over both the man and his music.

At the end of the war the van Dierens returned to the Netherlands, where they lived in The Hague until March 1921, when the need for further medical treatment necessitated a return to London. Limited and brief success followed: the six *Sketches* for piano were published by Universal Edition in 1921, some of van Dieren's works were performed in London, and, in July 1922, the Donaueschingen festival programmed his second string quartet. In 1925 the Oxford University Press published a dozen of his songs, and in the same year a number of his works were performed in a concert conducted by the young John Barbirolli. In 1925 van Dieren briefly went into the world of business, working for the Philips Electrical Company; a return of his illness, however, forced him to resign the post the following year. More works were published in 1927, and in the same year his fourth string quartet was performed at the Frankfurt festival. Although 1929 found him recuperating in Paris from yet another bout of illness, the following year he completed his opera *The Tailor* (begun in 1916 with the encouragement of Heseltine and Gray). In addition he wrote the first book on Epstein (1920) as well as a collection of wide-ranging and fascinating essays entitled *Down among the Dead Men* (1935). More of his music was heard when the BBC programmed performances of his works: *Diaphony* in 1934 and the *Chinese Symphony* in 1935. Van Dieren eventually succumbed to the illness that had dogged him for so long and died on 24 April 1936, at home at 68 Clifton Hill, St John's Wood, London. He was buried on the edge of the graveyard of St Laurence's Church, West Wycombe.   BARRY SMITH

Sources A. Chisholm, *Bernard Van Dieren: an introduction* (1984) • F. Tomlinson, *Warlock and Van Dieren: with a Van Dieren catalogue* (1978) • C. Gray, *A survey of contemporary music* (1924) • K. S. S. Sorabji, *Mi contra fa: the immoralisings of a Machiavellian musician* (1947) • H. Davies, 'Bernard Van Dieren, Philip Heseltine and Cecil Gray: a significant affiliation', *Music and Letters*, 69 (1988), 30–48 • L. Foreman, ed., *From Parry to Britten: British music in letters, 1900–1945* (1987) • d. cert.
Archives BL, corresp. with Philip Heseltine, Add. MS 65187
Likenesses J. Epstein, bust • J. Epstein, sculpture (*The risen Christ*), Scottish National Gallery of Modern Art, Edinburgh

Diest, Adriaen van (1655–1704), painter, was born in The Hague and baptized there on 12 December 1655, the son of Jeronimus van Diest (b. 1634, d. after 1675) and Catharina van der Hegge, and grandson of Willem van Diest (b. before 1610, d. after 1663). Both his father and his grandfather were well-known painters of marine subjects. He received his principal instruction from his father, and came to England with him when he was about seventeen. After the Restoration there was an expanding market for paintings, especially portraits and marine subjects—but increasingly also for landscapes in the Italianate or northern styles—that could not be satisfied by English artists. In 1672 Charles II invited Dutch artists to emigrate to England, even though the two countries were then at war. The French invasion of the Netherlands in that year and the concomitant difficulties in finding work must have made the invitation particularly welcome to artists such as the van Diests and the two Willem van de Veldes, sea painters who also came to England about this time. E. H. H. Archibald suggests that the younger van Diest might have become part of the van de Velde studio, working under the younger Willem. His marine paintings at the National Maritime Museum, London (two of the battle of La Hogue on 23 May 1692 and one of the battle of Bantry Bay, 1 May 1689), show a similarity of style.

In 1677 van Diest appeared before the Painter–Stainers' Company and 'promised to give his proofe piece he lives with Vaubert in Durham Yard' (Croft-Murray and Hulton, 534). He married Huberta, the daughter of the painter Adam Isaackson de Colonia (1634–1701). Four children were baptized at the Dutch Reformed church of Austin Friars, London, between 1686 and 1691; their first daughter, Catharina, probably died in infancy, as a second daughter was baptized Catharina three years later.

It has generally been assumed that van Diest had a connection with Sir Peter Lely or had even been employed by him, because the latter was said to own seven van Diest landscapes. However, when the catalogue of Lely's collection was retranscribed in 1943 for the *Burlington Magazine* it was noted that in the transcription published in 1758 'Van Diest' was an error and, according to the original, the artist was actually Dankers, presumably Hendrik Danckerts. Van Diest was patronized by various members of the nobility, particularly John Grenville, earl of Bath, and gained some repute for his landscapes, both topological and ideal. According to Bainbrigg Buckeridge:

> that which contributed most to make the son a master, as he often owned, was drawing after those noble views of England in the western parts, and along our coasts. He also

drew many of the ruined castles in Devonshire and Cornwall. (Buckeridge, 428)

Of the country seats that he painted the best known today is Dunham Massey, Cheshire (1696). Three of his landscapes are at Kedleston Hall, Derbyshire, and two with figures are at Chatsworth, Derbyshire.

Van Diest's landscapes were chiefly in the Italian manner, suitable for mantelpieces or to be placed over doors. Six of the seven landscapes by or attributed to him in the Royal Collection were probably painted *c*.1690 for use over doors. That he visited Italy at one time is evident from a statement by Vertue that he had seen a portrait of van Diest:

> done (from a drawing done at Rome. when he was there.) by a painter in England. he is represented with a sort of Rayed stuff about his head. & a drawing in his hand partly unrold. representing part of a Landskip. (Vertue, *Note books*, 1.88)

He also painted animals (his *Mountainous Landscape with a Bull* is at the Ashmolean Museum, Oxford) and engraved his landscapes (*Italian Scene*, 1 and 2, etchings, Harvard U., Fogg Art Museum; *Study for a Landscape, with a Fisherman*, drawing, British Museum). His best works were 'highly finisht and with great spirit & freedom in a masterly manner' (ibid., 86), but 'gout, and the low prices for which he painted afterwards, checked his fancy and made him less careful in his designs' (Buckeridge, 428). Buckeridge says he was working on a set of prints after his own drawings of landscapes, but before he could finish them he died, of gout, in London in 1704, aged forty-eight. He was buried in St Martin-in-the-Fields. Johan van Diest, a portrait painter whose work has been engraved, was his son.

L. H. CUST, rev. ARIANNE BURNETTE

Sources [B. Buckeridge], 'An essay towards an English school of painting', in R. de Piles, *The art of painting, with the lives and characters of above 300 of the most eminent painters*, 3rd edn (1754), 354–439 · Vertue, *Note books*, vols. 1–2 · E. H. H. Archibald, *Dictionary of sea painters* (1980) · H. V. S. Ogden and M. S. Ogden, *English taste in landscape in the seventeenth century* (1955) · 'Sir Peter Lely's collection', *Burlington Magazine*, 83 (1943), 185–91 · C. Wright, *Dutch painting in the seventeenth century: images of a golden age in British collections* (1989) · O. Millar, *The Tudor, Stuart and early Georgian pictures in the collection of her majesty the queen*, 2 vols. (1963) · D. Dethloff, 'The executors' account book and the dispersal of Sir Peter Lely's collection', *Journal of the History of Collections*, 8 (1996), 15–51 · H. Walpole, *Anecdotes of painting in England: with some account of the principal artists*, ed. R. N. Wornum, new edn, 2 (1849); repr. (1862) · E. Croft-Murray and P. H. Hulton, eds., *Catalogue of British drawings*, 1 (1960) · *Allgemeines Künstler-Lexikon*, 27 (Munich, 2000) · W. J. C. Moens, *The marriage, baptismal and burial registers, 1571 to 1874 and monumental inscriptions of the Dutch Reformed church, Austin Friars, London* (1884) · E. K. Waterhouse, *The dictionary of British 16th and 17th century painters* (1988) · W. Bernt, *The Netherlandish painters of the seventeenth century*, 2 (1970) · *DNB* · artists' boxes, Courtauld Inst., Witt Library
Archives BL, executors' account-book of P. Lely, Add. MS 16174 · BL, Vertue catalogue of Lely sale, Add. MSS 23081, 71–8
Likenesses A. Bannerman, line engraving, 1762 (after A. van Diest), BM; repro. in Walpole and others, *Anecdotes of painting* · A. van Diest, painting, priv. coll.; photograph, NPG · portrait (after drawing done at Rome)

Dietz, Diana. *See* Hill, Diana (d. 1844).

Digby, Everard (d. **1605**), Church of England clergyman and author, was a scion of the Digby family of Stoke Dry,

Rutland, although not of its main branch as historians once believed. In later life he described his county of origin as Rutland, but he was possibly a son of John Digby (d. 1556) of Welby, Leicestershire, brought up by his cousins of Stoke Dry after his father's death. He first appears for certain in 1567 when he matriculated as a sizar (poor scholar) of St John's College, Cambridge, gaining a college scholarship in 1570 and a fellowship in 1574. He graduated BA in 1571, MA in 1574, and BD in 1581, was appointed as principal lecturer in the college in 1584, and was elected a senior fellow in 1585. After ordination as deacon in 1576, and probably as priest, he acquired parochial benefices which he held, until 1588, with his college post. These included the rectories of Lyndon, Rutland (1581–2), Glaston, Rutland (1582–1605), Hamstall Ridware, Staffordshire (1583–6 and 1590–1601), and Orton Longueville, Huntingdonshire (1593–1605).

In 1579 Digby published in Latin *Theoria analytica*, an outline of knowledge and proposals for a method of research drawn from ancient philosophers, notably Aristotle, and from continental scholars of the sixteenth century, including Jacques Charpentier, Jacob Degen, and Nicolas de Grouchy. In it Digby attacked the methodology of Peter Ramus, the French protestant logician who had recently been killed in the St Bartholomew's day massacre. This provoked William Temple, fellow of King's College, Cambridge, to publish a defence of Ramus under the pseudonym *Francisci Mildapetti—Navarrensi ad Everardum Digbeium Anglum* (1580)—to which Digby replied with *Admonitioni F. Mildapetti responsio* (1580), dedicated to Sir Christopher Hatton. A rejoinder was published by Temple under his own name, *Pro Mildapetti de unica methodo* (1580). The controversy had a religious as well as a philosophical significance: Ramus was a hero to protestants, and Temple represented Digby as a follower of medieval Catholic scholasticism.

Digby's next and most original publication was *De arte natandi* (1587), a Latin treatise on swimming. The Swiss writer Nicholas Wynman had written a dialogue on the subject, *Colymbetes* (1538), which Digby's treatise resembled in discussing the history and value of the art, but he surpassed Wynman by systematically describing a large number of strokes, feats, and manoeuvres. The text was illustrated by forty-three detailed woodcuts, making the treatise also a landmark in the use of pictures to convey techniques. An abridgement in English by Christopher Middleton, entitled *A Short Introduction for to Learne to Swimme*, appeared in 1595 with the same woodcuts, and Digby's work was copied by other writers on swimming in the seventeenth century, notably Melchisedech Thevenot, whose *L'art de nager* (Paris, 1696) drew extensively on *De arte natandi* and reissued its illustrations in updated form. Since Thevenot's work circulated in both France and England until the late eighteenth century, Digby may be said to have influenced the understanding and teaching of swimming for the next 200 years.

In the autumn of 1587 Digby became involved in a disagreement about the payment of college dues. He refused to pay in the manner demanded, and was declared to have forfeited his fellowship by the master of St John's, William Whitaker, in January 1588. This dispute, too, involved religious prejudices. Whitaker was a strong protestant and suspected Digby of Roman Catholic sympathies, alleging that he had 'inveighed against Calvinists', 'never preach[ed] any sermons more than of necessity he must', and 'delivered nothing almost but magical, suspicious and popish conceits of angels' (Lake, 172). He also accused him of being insubordinate, coarse, and overindulgent in outdoor pursuits. Contemptuously refuting the charges, and affirming his support for the oath of supremacy, the articles of religion, and the Book of Common Prayer, Digby appealed to the college visitors, Lord Burghley and Archbishop Whitgift, who restored him in May 1588, but Whitaker enlisted the help of the earl of Leicester and Digby vacated his fellowship on 29 September (it is not clear whether voluntarily or by compulsion). He left Cambridge and finally lived at Orton Longueville. In 1590 he published his last book, *Everard Digbie his Dissuasive* 'from taking away the livings and goods of the Church', a work in English lamenting the ruin of religious buildings, the misappropriation of church endowments, and the avarice to acquire what remained in the hands of bishops and cathedrals. The work emits a sense of bitterness and exile. Digby died in 1605, at about the time of the Gunpowder Plot, which involved his namesake and kinsman Sir Everard Digby of Stoke Dry, but the cause and place of his death and burial are not known.

NICHOLAS ORME

Sources N. Orme, *Early British swimming, 55 BC–AD 1719: with the first swimming treatise in English, 1595* (1983) · J. Venn, ed., *Grace book Δ* (1910) · R. F. Scott, *Notes from the records of St John's College, Cambridge*, 3 (1913) · J. Heywood and T. Wright, eds., *Cambridge University transactions during the puritan controversies of the 16th and 17th centuries*, 2 vols. (1854) · N. W. Gilbert, *Renaissance concepts of method* (1960) · register of officers, fellows and scholars, St John Cam., vol. 1 · P. Lake, *Moderate puritans and the Elizabethan church* (1982), 171–80 · IGI
Archives St John Cam., archives

Digby, Sir Everard (*c*.1578–1606), conspirator, was the son of Everard Digby (*d*. 1592) and Maria Digby (*née* Neale) of Stoke Dry, Rutland. Maria Digby was daughter and coheir of Francis Neale of Keythorpe, Leicestershire. John Gerard the Jesuit says in his account of the Gunpowder Plot that Digby, upon the early death of his Catholic father, was brought up 'at the University by his guardians, as other young gentlemen use to be', but his name does not appear in any surviving record for Oxford or Cambridge (*Catholics under James I*, 88). Gerard, in a glowing portrait, also describes Digby as handsome, 6 feet tall, a complete sportsman and gentleman, skilled at riding and at arms, an accomplished musician and generous patron (ibid., 87–90). In 1596 he married Mary (*c*.1581–1653), only daughter of William Mulsho of Gayhurst or Gotehurst, Buckinghamshire. He was appointed to a household office at the court of Queen Elizabeth, and by his own admission 'was a pencioner to Quene Elizabeth aboute six yeres, and tooke the othe belonging to the place of a pencioner and no

other' (PRO, SP 14/216/135). The historian of the Elizabethan gentleman pensioners, however, explains that although Digby was associated with the band he was never formally a pensioner (Tighe, 358). Towards the end of the century he made the acquaintance of Father Gerard, who effected the conversion of both husband and wife. Nevertheless Digby was knighted by the new king, James I, at Belvoir Castle on 24 April 1603, during his journey south to London. Four days afterwards he appears as a gentleman pensioner extraordinary at the queen's funeral.

Little more than two years later, however, Digby's friendship for Robert Catesby, and the latter's need of money to underpin his enterprise, resulted in the admission of Digby to the Gunpowder Plot, early in October 1605, as the two men rode together from Harrowden to Gothurst. He was one of the last to be recruited, and the motive was clearly financial. Sworn to secrecy before, as he insisted, he was told the details of Catesby's secret, he scrupled against the sweeping nature of the design, but took his friend's bland guarantees at face value. 'Assure your selfe', said Catesby, 'that such of the nobilitie as are worth the saving shalbe preserved and yet knowe not of the matter'. No one they regarded as a friend, he went on, would suffer in the explosion (PRO, SP 14/216/135).

That was sufficient. There can be no doubt that Digby entered into the conspiracy heart and soul. On 4 November he travelled to Dunchurch, the planned rendezvous in Northamptonshire, sending his hounds on ahead—the lure of a day's hunting drew together many of the local Catholic gentry. After supper, however, the arrival of Catesby, Thomas Percy, and other confederates brought news of Guy Fawkes's arrest, and the frustration of all their hopes. Catesby tried a final, desperate lie—the king, he said, had indeed died, now was the time to rise on behalf of the Catholic cause. But no one believed him, and the panic-stricken majority, wishing no part in treason, fled into the night. Digby's brother George was among those at Dunchurch on 5 November, and like so many others he declined to join in an open rebellion against the crown.

Buoyed by desperation, Sir Everard still felt that there was a chance of success; he remained with Catesby, Percy, and their associates, some eighty in number, all told. At eleven that same night the rebels raided Warwick Castle, seizing fresh horses from the stables. But thereafter the tale is a dismal succession of desertions and ultimate disillusion. At Hewell Grange, plundering weapons, the conspirators tried to recruit curious bystanders, announcing that they were 'for God and the countrie'. The response underlined the futility of their cause. 'One of the countrimen sett his backe to the wall and sett his staff before him saying he was for King James for whome he would live and die and would not goe against him' (PRO, SP 14/216/119). Digby afterwards recalled how the hopelessness of their predicament gradually dawned on the rebel band. At his examination on 2 December he said 'that they in the whole when they had most were not above fiftie horse. And that not one man cam in to take there parte thoughe they expected for verie many' (PRO, SP 14/216/135).

Perhaps the keenest blow, so far as Digby himself was concerned, was the denunciation of their actions by senior Jesuits. He wrote to the superior, Henry Garnett, on 6 November, asking his pardon for these rash actions and, optimistically, seeking Garnett's support. But Garnett wrote back from Coughton saying that he 'marvelled they would enter into so wicked actions, and not be ruled by the advice of frends' (Nicholls, 63). Digby's wife was also at Coughton at the time, and she came into the room while Garnett and his fellow Jesuit Oswald Tesimond were discussing Digby's letter with the messenger, Thomas Bate. Her reaction is recorded simply and movingly in a letter from Garnett, smuggled out of the Tower of London the following year: 'what did shee? Alas what but cry' (PRO, SP 14/216/241). Some of Garnett's colleagues were slower to condemn the rebels. Tesimond visited the plotters at Huddington that day, with Garnett's knowledge, while another priest, Father Hammond, comforted his co-religionists in their extremity, saying mass at Huddington on 7 November.

At daybreak on Friday 8 November, shortly before his colleagues made their final stand against the sheriff of Worcestershire's men at Holbeach House, Digby rode off with two servants, by his own account to find further reinforcements. Reading between the lines this amounted to desertion, or common sense woefully delayed. No one now truly believed that new recruits were to be found. After trying to outrun the hue and cry he was eventually arrested near Halesowen, at about nine in the morning. Gerard tells how Digby tried to hide in a wood, waiting for nightfall, and how he was tracked to a dry ditch by the pursuing forces, following his horse's hoofmarks. 'Here he is, here he is', cried the excited posse. Digby rode out to meet them. 'Here he is indeed, what then?' he answered. At first he hoped to break through them, drawing on superior horsemanship, but recognizing at last the overwhelming odds he surrendered, in order, says Gerard:

> to have some time before his death for his better
> preparation, and withal out of a desire (as it afterwards
> appeared) to have done some service to the Catholic cause by
> word, sith he saw he could not do it by the sword.   (*Catholics
> under James I*, 111)

He was taken to London and lodged in the Tower, where to begin with he tried to insist that he had first heard of the plot on 5 November. But the investigators had Guy Fawkes's and Thomas Winter's evidence to hand, and confronted with this Digby admitted prior knowledge.

Digby remained a prisoner while all the evidence was sifted carefully by the privy council and its agents. A series of letters to his family was smuggled out of the Tower, preserved by his sons as precious relics, and rediscovered among the papers of his eldest child only in 1675. Written over the two and a half months between arrest and trial they prove that he was never, despite many lurid stories spread down the years, subjected to torture, although in one letter he fancied that torture had been 'in a fashion,

offered' to him (Barlow, 248). The truth is that after the initial panic and confusion in the days immediately after 5 November the prisoners were well looked after in the Tower, to the extent that they wondered at the motives behind their treatment. Digby's letters make painful reading, for they show an idealistic, poetic, faithful young man distracted by the dreadful fate he has brought upon himself and his family. He tries to defend Gerard and other Jesuits, attempts to excuse the savagery of Catesby's design, but also offers in one bizarre letter to secure the services of a priest who might visit Rome and obtain from the pope guarantees that any Catholic setting out 'to disturbe the kinges quiet and hapie raygne' will be excommunicated. He mixes the offer with threats, warning that Catholics will not stand quietly by and let James treat them as Elizabeth had done. Not surprisingly the earl of Salisbury rejected the proposal out of hand (PRO, SP 14/17/10; Barlow, 245).

Meanwhile, Digby's wife was facing up to the vindictiveness of local authorities in Buckinghamshire. She petitioned Salisbury for relief from the depredations of the sheriff, who had permitted her house to be ransacked. The lord chief baron of the exchequer, Sir Thomas Fleming, supported her, censuring the sheriff's actions in uncompromising terms, and the council ordered measures for her relief, somewhat ineffectively implemented.

Digby was arraigned with seven others in Westminster Hall on 27 January 1606. Because his treason was first committed in Northamptonshire he was tried upon a separate indictment at the end of the day. Alone among the eight accused he pleaded guilty. At the same time he insisted that the king had reneged upon promises of toleration for Catholics, and mitigated his offence by maintaining that affection for Catesby and love of the Catholic cause had prompted his actions. The earls of Northampton and Salisbury refuted these statements at some length. His arguments entirely failed to sway the court, but Digby's gallantry nevertheless impressed many in the packed hall. He sought a gentleman's death by the axe, begged mercy from the king for his young family, and left the court with a grand flourish, bowing to the lords commissioners and asking their forgiveness. 'God forgive you,' they replied, 'and we do' (*State trials*, 2.194).

No place of execution was specified at the trial, and the matter may have been given further consideration over the next forty-eight hours. However, on 30 January Digby and his co-conspirators Robert Winter, John Grant, and Thomas Bate were drawn on traitors' hurdles through streets lined with guards recruited from among the householders of London. Their destination was St Paul's Churchyard, where a gallows had been erected. All four were hanged, drawn, and quartered. The first to suffer, Digby met his death bravely.

Everard and Mary Digby had two sons. Digby took an affecting farewell of his children in his last surviving letter, dated 23 January. Sir Kenelm *Digby was the elder. The younger boy, John *Digby, knighted in 1635, died while fighting for his king in 1645.   MARK NICHOLLS

Sources PRO, SP 14/16, 17, and 216; LC 2/4/(4) · Hatfield House, Hertfordshire, Salisbury–Cecil MSS · M. Nicholls, *Investigating Gunpowder Plot* (1991) · T. Barlow, ed., *The gunpowder-treason, with a discourse of the manner of its discovery* (1679) · [T. Longueville], *The life of a conspirator, being a biography of Sir Everard Digby by one of his descendants* (1895) · W. J. Tighe, 'The gentleman pensioners in Elizabethan politics and government', PhD diss., U. Cam., 1984 · *The condition of Catholics under James I: Father Gerard's narrative of the Gunpowder Plot*, ed. J. Morris (1871) · *The Gunpowder Plot: the narrative of Oswald Tesimond alias Greenway*, ed. and trans. F. Edwards (1973) · journals, CLRO, court of common council · W. Oldys and T. Park, eds., *The Harleian miscellany*, 10 vols. (1808–13) · BL, Add. MS 5839
Archives PRO, state MSS
Likenesses portrait, priv. coll.; repro. in Longueville, *Life of a conspirator*

Digby, George, second earl of Bristol (1612–1677), politician, was the eldest known son of John *Digby, first earl of Bristol (1580–1653), and his wife, Beatrice or Beatrix (1574?–1658), daughter of Charles Walcot of Walcot, Shropshire, and widow of Sir John Dyve of Bromham, Bedfordshire. He was baptized at Madrid, where his father was ambassador to the Spanish court, on 5 November 1612; his birth may therefore be presumed to have taken place there shortly before.

Early life Spain remained Digby's home for eleven years, and he grew up fluent in its language. His first public appearance was at the age of twelve, when he presented a petition to the House of Commons on behalf of his father, who had been recalled from his embassy in disgrace and committed to the Tower. His bearing and eloquence much impressed the members, and the elder Digby was released soon after. George Digby matriculated at Magdalen College, Oxford, on 15 August 1626, and proceeded MA on 31 August 1636. The delay was not due to any lack of aptitude for learning, for he gained a reputation at Oxford, and in the cultivated circle which his father gathered at his country seat of Sherborne in Dorset, as an assiduous scholar. His two greatest enthusiasms in this period were for astrology and theology, and in 1638–9 he exchanged a series of letters with his Roman Catholic kinsman Sir Kenelm Digby (son of the executed gunpowder plotter Everard Digby), advancing the claims of the Church of England against that of Rome; these were to be published in 1651. After achieving his degree he travelled in France, and completed his learning of that language in turn. Observers thought him a youth of unusual brilliance as well as cherubic blond good looks.

During a visit to London in 1634 Digby was slighted by a court favourite, William Crofts, and challenged him to a duel with swords, which he won. The action was technically treasonable, having taken place within the precincts of Whitehall, and Digby took the blame for it and underwent a term in the Fleet prison. This was recognized at the time as compounding an alienation from the government which had been natural in his family since his father's disgrace, and it cannot be accidental that when he married, in 1635 or 1636, it was into a noble house associated with sustained opposition to the royal policies of the decade. His bride was Lady Anne Russell (d. 1697), second daughter

George Digby, second earl of Bristol (1612–1677), by Sir Anthony Van Dyck, c.1638–9

of Francis, fourth earl of Bedford, and they produced two sons and two daughters.

Politics and the civil war With these experiences and associations it is hardly surprising that Digby was in the forefront of the attacks which brought down the personnel and measures of Charles I's personal rule. He was elected to represent Dorset in both the Short and the Long parliaments of 1640, and distinguished himself near the opening of the latter, on 10 November, by presenting to the Commons a petition from his county against royal misgovernment and proposing that a remonstrance against it should be made by the house to the king. The following day he became one of the managers of the impeachment of the earl of Strafford, describing him as 'that grand Apostate to the Commonwealth' (*Journal*, ed. Notestein, 25–9). By February 1641 he had also become one of the foremost proponents of the bill for triennial parliaments. It is true that on the 8th of that month he was also one of the most determined opponents of the proposals for root and branch reform of the church and showed dislike of the Scots who were encouraging it, but this stance was still consistent with that of his erstwhile allies.

Digby parted company with the latter spectacularly on 21 April, when he became the most celebrated opponent of Strafford's attainder in the Commons. The move probably reflected the inclinations of his father and father-in-law, and was intended to prevent the complete estrangement of the king from the reform party, but it left him in a small minority. On 1 June his speech was published in an attempt to rally support for Charles during another period of tension. Whether or not he countenanced this action it infuriated most of the Commons, and on 9 June the king rescued him from probable committal by elevating him to the Lords as Baron Digby of Sherborne. The MPs were left to order the public burning of his speech on 13 July and to request the king not to give him any office thereafter; Charles promptly appointed him ambassador to France. In this manner the partnership between the two men, to their mutual political disadvantage, was formed.

Digby did not proceed to France but became one of the most extreme of the king's defenders in the Lords. He encouraged Charles to bring moderate MPs into the government but was also almost certainly his principal adviser in the rash courses which finally lost the king control of London and the Commons: the appointment of the notorious Thomas Lunsford to govern the Tower in December and the attempted arrest of the five members on 4 January 1642. Following the latter débâcle Digby and Lunsford went to meet disbanded officers at Kingston upon Thames, and the Commons assumed (with what truth will never be known) that they were planning a military coup. Parliament ordered the Surrey militia to disperse their men and Digby was summoned to explain himself to the Lords. Instead, using a pass from the king, he sailed on 16 January from Deal to Middleburg in the Dutch Netherlands. There he wrote letters to his friends and the queen encouraging Charles to avoid compromise in his now open breach with parliament. It was the interception of these that caused the Commons to decree his impeachment on 26 February. He had become the stereotypical evil royal counsellor.

All that can be said with any certainty about Digby's activities in the summer of 1642, as civil war commenced, is that at some point he rejoined the king. There are tales of secret journeys between the Netherlands and the royal court, on one of which he was captured by a parliamentarian warship and only escaped by first pretending to be a seasick Frenchman and then talking the governor of Hull, Sir John Hotham, into assisting him. Whatever the truth of these he was with the royal army by the time that it went on campaign, and commanding a horse regiment which he had raised for it. As such he displayed exemplary courage, charging with his regiment at Edgehill on 23 October, proposing and participating in the taking of Marlborough on 5 December, and being wounded in the thigh at the attempted storming of Lichfield on 20 April 1643. In this initial period of the war the king carefully failed to give him any employment as a minister or adviser, doubtless as a gesture of reassurance to moderate and hostile opinion. By the autumn, however, parliament's continued refusal to make peace had hardened the king's mood. The death of Lord Falkland at the battle of Newbury on 20 September left vacant one of the two posts of secretary of state and a seat on the privy council, and eight days later Digby was appointed to both. This promotion of one of the men in the kingdom least acceptable to parliament was a sign of the hardening of Charles's attitude towards his enemies.

Digby proved to be an industrious and conscientious administrator, and the clarity of his thought and handwriting remains a boon to the historian as it was to contemporaries. Nor did he immediately become part of any ultra-royalist bloc among Charles's counsellors. His main allies in the winter of 1643–4 were two civilians, Sir Edward Hyde and Lord Culpeper, moderates whom he had helped to bring into government in 1641, and two soldiers, lords Wilmot and Percy, who had been associated with plots to use armed force against parliament in that year. He and Culpeper became Charles's most trusted civilian advisers and accompanied him on campaign in 1644. There they fell out with Wilmot and Percy, as the former became jealous of them, and were obliged in self-defence to work upon the king's own growing suspicion of Wilmot, and achieve the dismissal of both him and Percy in August.

Digby now badly needed an ally in the royal army and found one in Prince Rupert, with whom he had formerly been at enmity, but whom he now wooed by supporting the appointment of the prince to command the army in November. In February Culpeper and Hyde were removed to duties in the west, with Digby's connivance, leaving the latter the main civilian adviser of the king. His position, however, depended upon his partnership with Rupert, and this broke down as the prince turned against him just as Wilmot had done. There was clearly something about Digby which soldiers found instinctually unpleasant and untrustworthy. It may have been simply that he had become the courtier-politician *par excellence*, whose mode of dealing with opponents was to behave impeccably to their faces while undermining their credit with the king. It was of a piece with this behaviour that he repeatedly attempted to win over enemy garrisons by suborning their officers—a tactic employed, with total lack of success, at Gloucester, Aylesbury, and Abingdon.

The breach with Rupert proved catastrophic for their cause. First it encouraged Digby to urge Charles into committing the royal army to battle at Naseby on 14 June 1645, an action undertaken against the advice of Rupert and which resulted in its destruction. This turned the prince into his implacable enemy, a feud which took on ideological dimensions as Rupert advised the king to make peace while Digby counselled continued resistance. On 14 September he convinced Charles that his nephew had become untrustworthy and caused the dismissal of Rupert and his supporters from their commands. The furious prince set out to plead his case to the king in person, at Newark. Digby, desperate to avoid the encounter, persuaded Charles on 13 October to commission him as lieutenant-general in England north of the Trent and give him his remaining cavalry, with which he proposed to break through to Scotland. The odds against this expedition were probably too great from the start, and Digby's force was defeated at Sherburn, Yorkshire, on the 15th and disintegrated on the banks of the Solway six days later. Its commander's only achievement was to evade death or capture himself and reach safety in Ireland.

Exile and Restoration Digby now formed the new project of persuading the prince of Wales to become the figurehead for a royalist counter-attack to be launched from Ireland, and in April 1646 followed the track of the prince's own flight into exile, to Jersey. Finding the boy's councillors, who included Hyde and Culpeper, opposed to the venture, he went on to France and concocted a plan with Cardinal Mazarin to bring the prince to the French court and persuade Charles to make concessions to the Scots which would turn them against parliament on his behalf. This scheme got further than the last, only to backfire. The king joined the Scots but would not make the intended concessions, and so became their prisoner. The prince crossed to France and became stranded there, at the court of his mother, together with Digby and other exiles. The latter included Rupert, who would have duelled with Digby had not the queen prevented it, and Wilmot, who did cross swords with him and was wounded and disarmed as effectively as Crofts had been long before.

By 1648 Digby had managed to lose the confidence of the queen in turn, and entered the French royal army as a volunteer, serving with such courage and energy that by 1651 he had become commander of the French forces in Normandy, with the rank of lieutenant-general. In that year the exiled Charles II reappeared in France and Digby somehow talked his way back into his favour and that of Hyde, being awarded the Garter in January 1653 and a place on the new privy council in April; on 6 January he had succeeded his father as earl of Bristol. He remained in the French service until the summer of 1656, when he somehow managed to make a mortal enemy of Mazarin and had to leave the country. Most opportunely Charles II had just settled in the Southern Netherlands as an ally of Spain, and Bristol moved straight to Brussels and used all his charm and linguistic ability to befriend the governor of the province. He then did good service to Charles by pleading his case, being rewarded on 1 January 1657 with his old posts of secretary of state and privy councillor. In March he delighted the Spanish by talking the French garrison of St Ghislain into defecting, and was given the soldiers as his own regiment. He remained one of the inner ring of the exiled court, though subordinate to Hyde, until January 1659, when he committed political suicide by making a personal conversion to Roman Catholicism. As he never reversed it when its political disadvantages became obvious and lasting it must have been wholly sincere, but it represented an acute embarrassment for Charles at a time when he was trying to distance himself from identification with Catholicism. Bristol was dismissed from all his offices. At the same time he ruined his credit with the Spanish by a piece of indiscretion which leaked military secrets to the French, and lost his regiment. In the autumn he accompanied Charles on a mission to Spain as an interpreter, but was abandoned as his master hurried back north on the first lap of the journey which was to end in his restoration.

Bristol followed him, and was restored to his own lands and titles along with other former royalists, but remained barred from office because of his religion and his track record. He became instead one of the ornaments of the court, noted for the recklessness of his gambling and the extravagance of his entertainments. He specially became identified with the interests of his fellow Catholics and of Spain, and with the enemies of his old colleague Hyde, who was still chief royal minister and had become earl of Clarendon; in particular, he was associated with the king's mistress, the countess of Castlemaine. Doubtless jealousy would have propelled these moves in any case, but he had a particular reason to dislike Clarendon. On 31 October 1643, when he was a new royal minister, he had been appointed to the honorary post of high steward of Oxford University, which had been left to him, in theory, upon his dismissal from office in 1659. After the Restoration he claimed it in earnest, only to be dispossessed of it by Clarendon, in the latter's new dignity of chancellor of the university, upon the grounds of Bristol's Catholicism. It must have rankled also that in 1661 Bristol had almost persuaded Charles to marry the daughter of an Italian client of Spain, and actually set out to negotiate the match, only for Clarendon to lead the lobby which persuaded the king into a Portuguese marriage alliance instead.

By 1663 Bristol's fortunes again seemed in the ascendant; the king was disappointed with his Portuguese wife and devoted to Castlemaine, while Bristol had acquired a potent ally in the new secretary of state, Lord Arlington. Clarendon seemed to be increasingly isolated and out of favour. Once again, however, Bristol spoiled his chances, with a risky agreement with an ambitious MP, Sir Richard Temple, to manage the House of Commons in the king's interest. When news of it leaked, and the Commons reacted with fury, Bristol was abandoned by all his friends, and had to protest his innocence to the MPs on 1 July. Humiliated, he turned on Clarendon and accused him of high treason before the House of Lords on the 10th. The hearing lasted four days, and represented the final disaster of Bristol's political career. His charges were soon revealed to be so baseless that they wasted the time of the house, and a furious Charles ordered his arrest as a troublemaker. Bristol went into hiding and had to remain there for years. He was able to emerge only in October 1667, when Clarendon finally fell out with the king, and his enemy was able to obtain both forgiveness and revenge by helping to draw up a fresh impeachment of the earl, this time with royal support. This restored him to public life but not to favour. In 1673 he courted popularity by supporting the Test Act, which formally disabled Catholics like himself from office, but this was his last notable appearance. He died at his house in Chelsea on 20 March 1677, and his wife had him buried in the Russell family chapel at Chenies, Buckinghamshire, four days later.

Character George Digby remains one of the foremost English examples of irresponsible brilliance. He possessed apparent exceptional talent as a politician, administrator, courtier, soldier, and scholar, and failed as all of those, a pattern which may be related to three defects. One was an inability to keep friends: during the civil war he already saw himself as 'single against all the world' (PRO, SP 16/510/74). Another was his constant tendency to choose the most flamboyant, sensational, and risky course out of every political and military problem, without the skills needed to steer such courses to success. The third was an ingrained carelessness in planning actions and observing discretion. He was and remained remorselessly self-destructive, with a proportionate tendency to destroy all those, including monarchs, whom he carried along with him. In this sense, he was one of English history's most dangerous men.

RONALD HUTTON

Sources Lord George Digbie's apologie for himselfe (4 Jan 1643) · Bodl. Oxf., MSS Clarendon 24, 25, 45–67 · J. Rushworth, Historical collections, 2nd edn, 3/1 (1692) · The journal of Sir Symonds D'Ewes: from the beginning of the Long Parliament to the opening of the trial of the earl of Strafford, ed. W. Notestein (1923) · BL, Add. MS 18980–18982 · Bodl. Oxf., MSS Carte 12–14 · Bodl. Oxf., MS Firth C7 · Wilts. & Swindon RO, 413/444 MS 'A' · E. Walker, Historical discourses upon several occasions (1705) · JHL, 4–5 (1628–43) · JHL, 11–12 (1660–75) · JHC, 2 (1640–42) · PRO, SP 16/510 · GEC, Peerage · Report on the manuscripts of the marquis of Downshire, 6 vols. in 7, HMC, 75 (1924–95), vol. 3, p. 400
Archives BL, Sloane MSS, papers and speeches · BL, letters, Add. MSS 18980–18982 | Worcester College, Oxford, corresp. with Sir Kenelm Digby [copies]
Likenesses A. Van Dyck, oils, 1637–9, Spencer Collection, Althorp; version, Sherborne Old Castle, Dorset · A. Van Dyck, portrait, c.1638–1639, Dulwich Picture Gallery [see illus.] · line engraving, pubd 1663, BM, NPG; repro. in J. Heath, A chronicle of the late intestine war, 2nd edn (1676) · W. Hollar, etching (after H. van der Borcht), BM · A. Van Dyck, sketch (after his earlier portrait), Sherborne Old Castle, Dorset

Digby, Jane Elizabeth (1807–1881), adventuress, who was known successively as countess of Ellenborough, Baroness von Venningen Üllner, Countess Theotoky, and the Honourable Mrs Digby el Mesreb, was born on 3 April 1807, the eldest child of Captain, later Admiral, Sir Henry Digby (1763?–1842) and his wife, Jane Elizabeth, Viscountess Andover (1777–1863), at the family home of Holkham Hall, Norfolk, where Jane spent her childhood. On 15 September *1824 she became the second wife of Edward *Law, earl of Ellenborough (1790–1871), later governor-general of India and lord privy seal, who was nearly twice her age and whom she did not love. She occupied herself with the pleasures of the London season, where she attracted much attention for her youth and beauty, particularly her fine complexion, blonde hair, and blue eyes. In 1827 she fell in love with Frederick Madden, then librarian at Holkham, but returned to London, where her affair with her cousin Colonel George Anson provoked much comment. Two months after the birth on 15 February 1828 of her first child, Arthur Dudley, who died on 1 February 1830, she became the lover of Prince Felix Ludwig Johann von Nepomuk Friedrich zu Schwarzenberg (1800–52), Austrian attaché. The liaison led to scandal and, after sensational legal proceedings, to divorce from Ellenborough on 8 April 1830. Rumours that Ellenborough fought a duel with Schwarzenberg and received £25,000 from him (see GEC) appear groundless. With a generous allowance from Ellenborough, Jane left for Basel to await Schwarzenberg and the birth of their child, a daughter, Mathilde Selden, born on 12 November 1829 and after early childhood brought up by the Schwarzenberg family. Jane moved to Paris in 1830 where she lived with Schwarzenberg, enjoying those circles of Parisian society which would admit her. A son, Felix, was born to them in December 1830, but

Jane Elizabeth Digby (1807–1881), by Sir George Hayter, c.1825

lived only a few weeks. Schwarzenberg, with his eye to his career and to please his Roman Catholic family, left Jane early in 1831. She moved with her daughter to Munich that summer, where she became the close friend and reputedly the lover of Ludwig I, king of Bavaria, and certainly the lover of Baron Karl Theodore Herbert von Venningen Üllner (d. 1874). While Jane was in Palermo on an extended visit, a son, Filippo Antonio Herberto, was born to her on 27 January 1833. Venningen assumed paternity, but Jane's reluctance to tell Ludwig of the birth lends credence to the king's having been her lover.

Leaving her son in Palermo, Jane left Italy in the summer of 1833, arriving in Germany that autumn. On 16 November 1833 she married Venningen in a civil ceremony in Darmstadt, followed shortly by a Roman Catholic service in Sinsheim. Venningen was devoted to Jane, though she clung to hopes of a reconciliation with Schwarzenberg. In August 1834 she and Venningen had a daughter, Berthe, whose mental weakness led to suggestions that Ludwig was her father. Jane and Venningen retired that summer to Schloss Weinheim, near Heidelberg, where in 1835 she met Honoré de Balzac; she probably provided the model for Lady Arabella Dudley in his Le lys dans la vallée. Suggestions that she was the lover of both Balzac and his companion Prince Alfred von Schönburg are unsubstantiated. On a visit to Munich in 1835 Jane met Count Spiridion Theotoky, one of many Greeks in the city after Ludwig's son Otto had become king of Greece in 1832. Late in 1835 their affair came to the notice of Venningen who pursued the fleeing couple and wounded Theotoky in an ensuing duel.

Theotoky was nursed back to health at Schloss Venningen and the spouses were temporarily reconciled but, in the spring of 1839, Jane abandoned her husband and children to go to Paris with Theotoky. Here, on 21 March 1840, a son, Jean Henry, Comte Theotoky, called Leonidas, was born to them. Venningen entreated Jane to return, but eventually granted her a divorce and remained a faithful friend until his death. In 1841, the year before her divorce was finalized, Jane had her marriage annulled by the Greek Orthodox church, into which she was accepted and according to whose rites she reputedly married Theotoky in Marseilles in 1841 before sailing for Greece and settling in 1842 in Dukades, Corfu, Theotoky's estate. She enjoyed her life furnishing the house, laying out the grounds, and entertaining.

Jane's rumoured affair with King Otto in 1844–5 and the death in 1846 of Leonidas, Jane's favourite child, who fell before his mother's eyes from a Tuscan balcony, hastened her separation from Theotoky in 1846. The course of her life immediately after this is unclear, but by 1852 she had fallen in love with Cristodoulos (Cristos) Hadji-Petros, one of King Otto's aides-de-camp and sometime Albanian brigand, whom she followed to join his mountain band. Her marriage with Theotoky was annulled in 1853 by the Greek Orthodox church, but her expected marriage to Hadji-Petros never took place and in April 1853 she left the sycophantic and uncouth brigand to travel east.

Jane landed in Syria, and in May 1853, while making preparations for further travel, fell in love with the Bedouin Saleh whose household she briefly joined before setting off for Damascus. Here she sought the protection of the Mesreb tribe, with whom she made the dangerous journey to and from Palmyra, meeting *en route* Abdul Medjuel al-Mesreb, a cultured and intelligent man who later became the head of the Mesreb tribe. On returning to Damascus in November 1853 after a brief visit to Greece to settle her affairs, Jane discovered that Saleh had married. She sought consolation in an abortive liaison with Sheikh al-Barrak in 1854, before falling in love with Medjuel, who had meanwhile divorced his wife. Despite the opposition of his family, Medjuel married Jane at Hims in 1854 according to Muslim rites. Styling herself the Hon. Mrs Digby el Mesreb, Jane adopted Arab dress, learned Arabic, and was gradually accepted by Medjuel's family. They lived partly in Damascus—where Jane laid out an English garden, fitted out a library, and spent much time with her horses—and partly in the desert with the Mesreb, whom Jane supplied with arms and ammunition to help them fight rival tribes and levy ransom on travellers seeking passage to Palmyra. In 1859 Jane's help to Christians in Damascus, then under attack by Druses, caused a rift with her husband which later healed, despite her continued support for Christian missionaries. When peace returned her house was open to European visitors to the country, notably Sir Richard and Lady Burton. On 11 August 1881 she died of dysentery in Damascus and was buried in the protestant section of the Jewish cemetery there. Allegations that at the time of her death she was preparing to elope with her dragoman (see GEC) are unproven.

Jane Digby was admired for her beauty, for her artistic gifts (she painted and sculpted and was musical), and for her intellect (she was proficient in nine languages and a witty conversationalist). Her way of life, sustained by personal charm and a comfortable private income, made her the object of sensational contemporary cartoons, fiction, and press reports, acid comment from the establishment and, latterly, romantic popular biography.

ELIZABETH BAIGENT

Sources M. F. Schmidt, *Passion's child* (1977) · A. Allen, *Travelling ladies* (1980) · L. Blanch, *The wilder shores of love* (1954) · M. S. Lovell, *A scandalous life: the biography of Jane Digby el Mezrab* (1995) · *Gothaischer Genealogischer Hof-Kalender* · GEC, *Peerage* · E. W. Oddie, *The odyssey of a loving woman* (1936)
Archives Mirtirne House, Dorset · priv. coll. | Geheimes Hausarchiv, Munich, Wittelsbach MSS
Likenesses G. Hayter, drawing, c.1825, NPG [*see illus.*] · J. Stieler, portrait, 1831, Nymphenburg Palace, near Munich, Germany · Lawrence, portrait, repro. in GEC, *Peerage*
Wealth at death £6022 2s. 6d.: probate, 13 April 1882, CGPLA Eng. & Wales

Digby, John, first earl of Bristol

Digby, John, first earl of Bristol (1580–1653), diplomat and politician, was born in February 1580, the fourth and youngest son of Sir George Digby (d. 1586), of Coleshill, Warwickshire, and of Abigail Heveningham of Ketteringham, Norfolk. He became a fellow-commoner of Magdalen College, Oxford, in 1595, and was created an MA on 30 August 1605. He was also admitted to the Inner Temple in 1598. In November 1605 Lord Harrington, who had charge of Princess Elizabeth, sent Digby to inform the king that the gunpowder plotters' plan to seize Elizabeth had failed. James took a liking to Digby and made him a gentleman of the privy chamber and a carver. Digby was knighted on 16 March 1607, and on 31 May 1609 he married Beatrice or Beatrix (1574?–1658), daughter of Charles Walcot of Walcot in Shropshire, and widow of Sir John Dyve of Bromham in Bedfordshire.

Ambassador to Spain, 1610–1618 In October 1610 Digby was appointed resident ambassador in Madrid, and arrived there in June 1611. He succeeded in obtaining concessions for English merchants trading with Spain, but James I's hopes of a marriage alliance between Prince Henry and the infanta Anne, daughter of Philip III, were dashed when Digby learned that she was already engaged to Louis XIII of France. Then, in November 1612, Prince Henry died. In 1613 Digby uncovered details of the pensions that the Spanish court had paid to prominent figures in England, and early the following year he returned to London to present this information to James.

Later in 1614 James decided to propose a match between Prince Charles and Philip III's younger sister, the infanta Maria, and Digby was sent back to Madrid to pursue the negotiations. Despite his private conviction that the prince should marry a protestant, Digby wished to see a good understanding between the protestant and Catholic powers of Europe, and was determined to promote the negotiations to the best of his ability. However, early in 1616 he was again summoned home, following the fall of the earl of Somerset, to give evidence of the disgraced

John Digby, first earl of Bristol (1580–1653), by Cornelius Johnson, 1628

favourite's links with Spain. He arrived in March, and candidly informed James that he thought it unwise to proceed further in the marriage negotiations given that the king of Spain could not dispose of his daughter's hand without papal consent. It is likely that James appreciated Digby's frankness, and further preferment quickly followed: on 3 April he was made vice-chamberlain of the royal household and was sworn of the privy council.

In May 1617 James nevertheless dispatched Digby back to Madrid to open formal marriage negotiations, and he left in August. Digby once again threw himself into the task and tried to obtain the best terms possible, especially with regard to the bride's portion, which James wished to fix at not less than £500,000. Matters such as the arrangements for the infanta's future household were successfully resolved, but the issue of liberty of conscience for English Catholics was reserved for James's own decision. In April 1618 Digby was able to return to England with the news that the infanta's portion would be £600,000. He was rewarded on 25 November 1618 by being created Baron Digby of Sherborne. However, James refused to sanction liberty of conscience for English Catholics, and the marriage negotiation was suspended.

Diplomacy, 1620–1622 Early in 1620 James asked Digby for advice concerning the crisis that had arisen on the continent following the election of the king's son-in-law, Frederick, elector palatine, to the Bohemian throne. Digby apparently advocated the search for an understanding with Spain while also making preparations for the defence of the palatinate. In June 1620 he accompanied Buckingham on a visit to the Spanish ambassador, Gondomar, at which the possible partition of the Dutch republic

between England and Spain was discussed. Digby's hostility towards the Dutch did not, however, imply subservience to Spain, and in March 1621, following Frederick's expulsion from Bohemia, Digby was sent to Brussels to urge the Archduke Albert to mediate a cessation of arms. On 23 May, shortly after his return to England, Digby was instructed to embark on a mission to the emperor, Ferdinand II. He was authorized to make peace on the basis that Frederick would abandon his claims to Bohemia while in return Ferdinand would not seek to punish him. Digby reached Vienna on 4 July and initially the talks appeared to go well. However, by the end of September the duke of Bavaria had occupied the upper palatinate in the emperor's name, and Frederick's forces were obliged to retreat to the lower palatinate. Digby left Vienna soon afterwards, and on his way home visited Frederick at Heidelberg in mid-October. By the end of the month he was back in England, and his return prompted James to reconvene parliament on 20 November. The next day Digby addressed both houses: he 'narrated his embassage and the state of the Lower Palatinate' (*Buccleuch MSS*, 222) and urged parliament to prepare forces for the relief of the lower palatinate, costing £900,000. However, before this proposal could be fully debated, James quarrelled with the House of Commons over the issue of free speech and promptly dissolved the parliament. This seriously weakened England's bargaining position by ensuring that threats of military force could not be backed up in practice.

Ambassador to Spain, 1622–1624 In February 1622 Digby was again instructed to return to Spain, where Philip IV had succeeded his father the previous year. Digby resumed the marriage negotiations that had been in abeyance since 1618, and on 15 September was rewarded with the earldom of Bristol. By January 1623 the marriage articles were sufficiently far advanced, except the one relating to toleration for English Catholics, for James to feel able to accept them. Bristol was unable to secure a Spanish promise that the palatinate would be restored, and he was convinced that the goodwill of Spain afforded the best chance of restitution.

On 7 March 1623 Prince Charles and the marquess of Buckingham arrived at Bristol's residence at Madrid, thereby taking negotiations out of Bristol's hands. He appears to have deeply offended the prince by believing a rumour that Charles had come with the purpose of declaring himself a Catholic, and by expressing his willingness to collude in this. During the course of the visit Bristol persisted in his attempts to maintain good relations with Spain, and he further alienated Charles by supporting a scheme for educating the elector palatine's eldest son in Vienna. He also incurred Buckingham's lasting enmity when, on 29 August, he wrote to James describing the 'high … dislike' that Philip IV and his ministers felt towards the newly created duke (*Miscellaneous State Papers, 1501–1726*, 1.477). By the time they left for home in September Buckingham and Charles were thoroughly hostile to Spain, and believed that Bristol had been far too easily taken in by vague assurances from Philip and his chief minister, Olivares.

When Charles departed from Madrid he left Bristol with a proxy authorizing him to appear in the marriage ceremony on his behalf, but shortly afterwards he ordered him not to use this without further instructions. Bristol continued to try to avert the breach with Spain on which Charles and Buckingham were now set. In October James insisted that the marriage would have to be postponed until satisfactory assurances were received regarding the restitution of the palatinate, and Bristol only conveyed this ultimatum to Olivares with great reluctance. By this time Bristol's wish to preserve relations with Spain diverged so strongly from the prevailing mood at the English court that on 30 December he was recalled. He formally took his leave of Philip IV on 29 January 1624. Before he left Olivares offered him a blank piece of paper on which he invited Bristol to write down anything that he wished in the way of favours or protection as a mark of the king's gratitude. Bristol courteously declined, saying that he had acted out of loyalty to the English crown and 'would rather offer himself to the slaughter in England than be duke of Infantado in Spain' (S. R. Gardiner, *History of England from the Accession of James I to the Outbreak of the Civil War, 1603–1642*, 10 vols., 1883–4, 5.165).

Political troubles, 1624–1628 Meanwhile Buckingham was deeply fearful that if Bristol had an audience with James he would reveal damaging information about the duke's conduct in Madrid. He therefore ensured that when Bristol landed at Dover he received instructions to 'retyer yourselfe to your house or lodgeing' ('Defence', v). Bristol went, under virtual house arrest, to his home in St Giles' Fields, but he refused to admit any error on his part and declared his willingness to stand trial before parliament. Buckingham successfully resisted this request. Instead, Bristol was sent a list of twenty interrogatories relating to his conduct to which he replied in detail, demonstrating that he had at no time acted without James's prior knowledge or subsequent approval. However, though Bristol was granted permission to return to Sherborne in July, he was neither brought to trial nor set at liberty, despite his repeated pleas to the king and to Buckingham.

On the accession of Charles I in March 1625 Bristol was removed from the privy council, and in June Charles instructed him not to attend parliament, his writ of summons notwithstanding. In January 1626 Bristol asked to attend Charles's coronation. The king retaliated by accusing Bristol of trying to make him convert to Catholicism while in Madrid. Bristol reiterated his willingness to stand trial, but Charles then denied him a writ of summons to the parliament that assembled in February 1626. On 22 March Bristol submitted a petition to the House of Lords, requesting either to be summoned to parliament or to be placed on trial. The Lords' committee on privileges upheld his right to take his seat, whereupon Charles grudgingly issued a writ of summons but intimated, via a letter from Lord Keeper Coventry, that 'your Lordship's personal attendance is to be forborn' ('Defence', xxxv). Bristol replied, sardonically, that the monarch's writ of summons must take precedence over the lord keeper's letter, and promptly journeyed to Westminster.

Having taken his seat in the Lords, Bristol indicated his wish to bring charges against Buckingham. Charles immediately instructed the attorney-general to charge Bristol with high treason, and on 1 May he was brought to the bar of the House of Lords. Bristol at once presented twelve specific charges against Buckingham, including that of bringing Prince Charles to Spain with the purpose of converting him to Catholicism, and of conspiring with the Spanish ambassador, Gondomar, to this end. The Lords ordered that consideration of the king's charges against Bristol and of Bristol's charges against Buckingham should proceed simultaneously. However, these proceedings were brought to an abrupt halt by the king's dissolution of parliament in June. Bristol was then sent to the Tower, pending prosecution before the Star Chamber. Shortly afterwards he fell ill and Charles and Buckingham, fearing the damaging revelations that a trial was likely to bring, used the earl's illness as an excuse to postpone the case indefinitely. In September 1626, probably through the earl of Pembroke's intervention, Bristol was allowed to return to his home at Sherborne, but he remained under house arrest.

When Charles's third parliament met in March 1628 the Lords insisted that Bristol be set at liberty and restored to his place in the upper house. In the debates over the king's powers of imprisonment without cause shown, which ultimately gave rise to the petition of right, Bristol attempted to secure a compromise and argued that certain royal discretionary powers were necessary for use in emergencies. As he reportedly put it on 22 April: 'As Christ upon the Sabbath healed' (thus breaking Jewish law for the greater good), 'so the prerogative is to be preserved for the preservation of the whole' (*Proceedings in Parliament, 1628*, 5.327). The Lords accepted this proposal, but it was rejected by the Commons. When the Commons sent the petition to the Lords, Bristol again sought a compromise. However, on 20 May he came out against the idea of incorporating a clause saving the royal prerogative, and suggested instead that such a saving should be verbal (ibid., 483–4). He allegedly regarded the king's first answer (2 June) as 'rather a waiving of the petition than any way satisfactory to it' (ibid., 598), and demanded a fuller and better answer.

Political rehabilitation Following the end of the 1628 session Bristol regained a certain amount of favour, and payment of his ambassador's pension, which had fallen into arrears, was resumed. However, for most of Charles I's personal rule he seems to have lived quietly at Sherborne, and a fuller rehabilitation—for which he gave the credit to the earl of Holland—did not occur until August 1637. He apparently played no further part in public affairs until the spring of 1639, when Charles summoned the peers to assist his expedition against the Scots. In May Bristol vainly tried to dissuade the king from advancing against Berwick with such a poorly prepared army. The following month he warned Charles that most peers wished to see parliament recalled, and was influential in persuading the king to pursue the talks with the Scots that led to the pacification of Berwick. After the dissolution of the Short Parliament he advocated the calling of another parliament, though he refused to have anything to do with the twelve peers who in August 1640 petitioned the king to recall parliament. He played a prominent part in the great council of peers which Charles summoned to meet at York on 24 September. In particular, he moved for—and was appointed to—a committee of sixteen peers to conduct negotiations with the Scots, and these talks occupied most of his time over the next few months.

Unsympathetic towards the Scots, and deeply resentful of their interference in English affairs, Bristol's main hope seems to have been that Charles would cut his losses by reaching a settlement with them as rapidly as possible. In a speech on 12 January 1641 he attached particular blame to 'the improvidence and evill counsells of certaine badd instruments, who had reduced his roiall Majestie and this kingdome to these straits', a veiled reference to Strafford (*The Journal of Sir Simonds D'Ewes from the Beginning of the Long Parliament to the Opening of the Trial of the Earl of Strafford*, ed. W. Notestein, 1923, 247).

Bristol's rehabilitation was finally complete when, on 19 February 1641, he was again appointed a privy councillor, apparently in recognition of his services in the negotiations with the Scots. The following spring, despite his earlier implied criticism of Strafford, he attempted to reach a compromise whereby the earl would be deprived of his offices but his life spared. This stance incurred the wrath of the anti-Straffordian crowds outside the palace of Westminster, and on 3 May some members of the mob denounced Bristol as 'an apostate from the cause of Christ, and our mortall enemie' (*A Briefe and Perfect Relation, of the Answeres and Replies of Thomas Earle of Strafford*, 1647, 85). He was excused from voting on Strafford's attainder on the grounds that he had been a witness in the earl's trial. Charles clearly approved of his conduct, and when the king departed for Scotland the following August he made Bristol a gentleman of the bedchamber.

Royalism Bristol's identification with the emerging royalist party became even clearer after parliament reassembled after the autumn recess. On 17 December he was responsible for an amendment to a Commons declaration against any toleration for Catholics, to the effect that 'no religion shall be tolerated in His Majesty's dominions but what is or shall be established by laws of this kingdom' (*JHL*, 4.480). Like many other royalists he combined anti-Scottish sentiments with an attachment to episcopacy and the prayer book. By this time he had increasingly become a target for the more radical members of the Commons. On 27 December Walter Long named him an 'evill counsellor' in the Commons, and the house ordered that Charles's letter of 1626 accusing Bristol of trying to lure him away from protestantism be produced (*The Journal of Sir Simonds D'Ewes from the Final Recess of the Long Parliament to the Withdrawal of King Charles from London*, ed. W. H. Coates, 1942, 352–3). The following day Oliver Cromwell

moved that the Commons join with the Lords in requesting the king that Bristol 'bee removed from his Counsell' on the grounds that he had 'perswaded his Majestie to putt' the northern army 'into a posture' against parliament the previous spring (ibid., 358). There appears to be no surviving evidence either to support or to refute this statement and several other members, including Bristol's close friend Sir John Strangways, succeeded in thwarting the motion.

On 28 March 1642 the Lords committed Bristol to the Tower of London for his failure to disclose that he had been given a copy of the Kentish petition, which the house regarded as 'scandalous, dangerous and tending to sedition' (*JHL*, 4.678). He was released on 19 April, and spoke twice in the Lords advocating an accommodation, though on 27 May he disowned the printing of a speech bearing his name. He joined the king shortly afterwards, and he became widely perceived among parliamentarians as a hardliner who wished to perpetuate the conflict, a perception that may have been fuelled by his earlier association with Spain. In October 1642 the houses exempted Bristol from a general amnesty and stopped his pension. The Oxford propositions of February 1643 demanded that he be removed from the king's counsels, and that he and Lord Herbert of Raglan be 'restrained from coming within the verge of the Court, and that they may not bear any office, or have any employments concerning the State or commonwealth' (S. R. Gardiner, ed., *Constitutional Documents of the Puritan Revolution, 1625–1660*, 3rd edn, 1906, 264).

Between November 1643 and January 1644 Bristol became involved in secret talks with Thomas Ogle, a prisoner in Winchester House. The aim appears to have been to develop an anti-presbyterian coalition between royalists and Independents, and the terms that Ogle devised included a plan for a modified episcopacy that bore some resemblance to that later embodied in *The Heads of Proposals* in 1647 (Gardiner). However, Ogle indicated that the parliamentarian garrison of Aylesbury would be betrayed as proof of the serious intentions behind the proposals, and this intelligence quickly reached the committee of safety. The 'plot' collapsed and Ogle fled abroad early in January 1644.

Bristol's involvement in these secret talks appears only to have reinforced the houses' negative perception of him, and in the Uxbridge propositions (November 1644) he was listed among fifty-eight royalists who could 'expect no pardon' (S. R. Gardiner, ed., *Constitutional Documents of the Puritan Revolution, 1625–1660*, 3rd edn, 1906, 278). This image of him was probably reinforced by the fact that his eldest son, George *Digby, Lord Digby, who was also listed among those exempted from pardon, was known to be one of the more hardline royalists. Although father and son do not appear to have been closely politically aligned during the civil war, Digby's association with Henrietta Maria and his swashbuckling military career may well have coloured views of his father. However, Bristol's reputation among those at Westminster as a hardline advocate of the prolongation of the war appears to have been mis-placed. Following the Oxford propositions he withdrew from the king's court at Oxford in order to remove a cause of difference between the two sides, and he went first to his house at Sherborne and then in the spring of 1644 to Exeter, where he remained until that city capitulated to Fairfax on 13 April 1646. The following month he submitted a petition to the Lords asking to be allowed to compound for his estate by paying a composition fine, and to remain in England. The houses rejected this request, and on 11 July ordered that he receive a pass to go overseas. He left for France shortly afterwards and spent the rest of his life there. He died in Paris on 21 January 1653 and was buried in the protestant cemetery in the city. His widow lived on until 12 September 1658, and was buried at Sherborne.

Reputation In 1647, at Caen, Bristol published *An Apologie of John Lord Digby Earl of Bristoll* in which he repudiated the 'many most unjust and untrue calumnies and aspersions which have been cast upon me both in print and otherwise' (*Apologie*, 5). Bristol then robustly defended his reasons for adhering to the king, insisting that he was bound to do so

> by the law of God, by the doctrine and practice of all Christian Churches, and in all times, by many oathes, by the laws of the kingdome, by my natural allegiance as a subject, and by gratitude and fidelity, as a sworn servant, both to his father and himself. (ibid., 12)

Using both common law arguments and scriptural texts, he denied the lawfulness of resistance and argued that to take up arms against the king was contrary to all 'duties of religion, of oaths, of loyalty, of laws, of gratitude, and moral honesty' (ibid., 61–2). This *Apologie* was reprinted in London in 1660.

The overall impression of Bristol's career is of a man who gave much important public service and did not always gain the rewards or recognition that he merited. He surely did not deserve the intense hostility he received from Buckingham in the 1620s, or the parliamentarians in the 1640s. Yet his own temperament may have been partly to blame for his fate. His integrity and high principles at times verged on self-righteousness and prickliness, and helped to make him something of a loner, both politically and personally. His character was well summed up by Clarendon, who wrote that

> though he was a man of great parts, and a wise man, yet he had been for the most part single, and by himself, in business, which he managed with good sufficiency, and had lived little in consort; so that in Council he was passionate and supercilious, and did not bear contradictions without much passion, and was too voluminous a discourser; so that he was not considered there with much respect. (Clarendon, *Hist. rebellion*, 2.532)

Sir Philip Warwick offered a similar assessment:

> Well accomplished, and of great parts natural and acquired, … but he had likewise so much of a romantick spirit, and of such superfined politics … so as these eminences made him never prosperous either to himself or his master. (P. Warwick, *Memoires of the Reigne of King Charles*, 1701, 1.279)

DAVID L. SMITH

Sources PRO, SP 14; 16; 94 · BL, Aston MSS, Add. MSS 36444–36446 · Bristol's letter-book, 1622–3, BL, Add. MS 48166 · BL, Trumbull MSS, Add. MSS 72284–72285 · 'The earl of Bristol's defence of his negotiations in Spain', ed. S. R. Gardiner, *Camden miscellany, VI*, CS, 104 (1871) · *An apologie of John Lord Digby earl of Bristoll* (1660) · *Cabala, sive, Scrinia sacra: mysteries of state and government in letters of illustrious persons*, 3rd edn (1691) · *JHL*, 3–9 (1620–47) · W. B. Bidwell and M. Jansson, eds., *Proceedings in parliament, 1626*, 1: *House of Lords* (1991) · R. C. Johnson and others, eds., *Proceedings in parliament, 1628*, 5 (1983) · P. Yorke [earl of Hardwicke], ed., *Miscellaneous state papers, 1501–1726*, 2 vols. (1778) · B. M. Gardiner, ed., 'A secret negociation with Charles the First, 1643–4', *Camden miscellany, VIII*, CS, new ser., 31 (1883) · GEC, *Peerage*, new edn · Clarendon, *Hist. rebellion* · *DNB* · Foster, *Alum. Oxon.* · *Report on the manuscripts of his grace the duke of Buccleuch and Queensberry … preserved at Montagu House*, 3 vols. in 4, HMC, 45 (1899–1926), vol. 3, p. 222
Archives BL, letter-book as ambassador to Spain, Add. MS 48166 · Bodl. Oxf., copy of articles against, alleging high treason, with answers · HLRO, petitions about his conduct while ambassador to Spain · PRO, private and diplomatic corresp., HMC 7, *8th report* [transcripts] · PRO, state papers, foreign, Spanish, SP 94 · Sherborne Castle estates, corresp. and papers | BL, corresp. with Sir William Aston, Add. MSS 36444–36446 · BL, parliamentary speeches and papers, Harley MSS · BL, Sloane MSS, papers · BL, letters and papers, Stowe MSS, *passim* · BL, letters to William Trumbull, Add. MSS 72284–72285
Likenesses C. Johnson, oils, 1628, NG Ire. [*see illus.*] · R. Elstrack, line engraving, BM, NPG, V&A · portrait (after Van Dyck), repro. in J. E. Doyle, *The official baronage of England*, 3 vols. (1886)
Wealth at death value not certain; estate sequestered as royalist delinquent: *Calendar of the committee for compounding*, 2168–70

Digby, Sir John [*alias* John Salisbury] (1605–1645), soldier, was born a few months before the Gunpowder Plot, the younger son of Sir Everard *Digby (c.1578–1606), executed for involvement in that plot, and his wife, Mary, *née* Mulsho (c.1581–1653). The main source for his life is a manuscript biography, 'Hector Britannicus', by Edward Walsingham, who knew him well. Unlike his brother Kenelm *Digby (1603–1665) he seems not to have been especially tall or handsome, but he was immensely strong. John Digby was initially brought up with his brother at his parents' home, Gayhurst (or Gotehurst), Buckinghamshire. At thirteen he was sent to the English College at St Omer in Flanders under the alias John Salisbury. In 1624 he went on to the English College at Rome, which accepted a proportion of students with no vocation to the priesthood. John Salisbury of the English College at Rome is associated with the Latin poem 'Panacrides apes musicis concentibus advocandae ad philosophicas theses', published at Rome in 1627 with three other poems by members of the college. Digby may not have been the author, but may have been the student who delivered the poem on the occasion when Francesco Barberini, cardinal protector of England, presided over philosophical disputations at the college. He completed his studies on 21 December 1627, and then spent a further period abroad.

In the summer of 1632 Digby was one of fifteen courtiers, with sixty servants, accompanying Jerome Weston, son of Richard, earl of Portland, as ambassador-extraordinary to the courts of France, Savoy, Venice, and Florence. When the party recrossed the channel in March 1633 Digby distinguished himself by his confidence under fire during an engagement with ten Dutch East Indiamen.

Subsequently he pursued the life of a courtier and country gentleman; according to Walsingham, his skill as a swordsman became famous, and John Aubrey said that he was 'a proper person of great strength and courage ... and yielded to be the best swordsman of his time' (*Brief Lives*, 2.241). In 1634 he was the rival of Sir John Suckling, the poet and rake, in courting Anne, daughter of Sir Henry Willoughby of Riseley, Derbyshire. Anne was terrified of Suckling's advances and Digby tried unsuccessfully to provoke a duel. In return Suckling with a party of sixteen ambushed Digby and two friends outside the Blackfriars Theatre but was beaten off.

In 1635 Digby was commissioned as a naval officer and was knighted on 23 September. In Charles I's first campaign against the Scottish covenanters in 1639 Digby served as a cornet and then adjutant of the personal troop of the commander-in-chief, the earl of Arundel. In the second campaign of 1640 he raised his own troop as a captain and was one of three officers who were generally thought to have distinguished themselves in the defeat at Newburn, Northumberland. After capture, when threatened with death as a papist, he replied: 'I am a Roman Catholic and so am resolved to live and die' (Walsingham, 76–8). His Scottish captors were later ambushed near Richmond, Yorkshire, and Digby was released, but he was among sixty Catholic officers cashiered when the Long Parliament assembled in November 1640. The same year, when Queen Henrietta Maria was trying to secure a cardinal for England, Digby was the favoured lay candidate of the papal envoy, Count Rossetti.

After the civil war began Digby was detained in the Fleet prison by order of the Commons on 23 November 1642, but he escaped to the royalist headquarters at Oxford in June 1643. At General Wilmot's instance he became a colonel of horse. He fought in the royalist victory of Roundway Down near Bath on 13 July and was wounded at the indecisive battle of Newbury in September. In October he was ordered by Prince Rupert to fortify Grafton House near Buckingham, where he was besieged and bombarded by Major-General Skippon and forced to surrender on Christmas eve. Imprisoned in the Tower of London, he was exchanged for a parliamentarian prisoner in October 1644 and was soon back in Buckinghamshire with 8000–9000 horse and foot; by December he and his cavalry were astride the Great North Road. Early the following year he was promoted brigadier and then major-general in Lord Goring's army in the west. Over three weeks he used his cavalry to disperse parts of General Waller's army marching to relieve Taunton. After further successes against parliamentary cavalry at Faringdon and Radcot Bridge he joined Sir Richard Grenville and Lord Goring in attacking Taunton. On 14 June, the day of the king's crowning defeat at Naseby, Digby was shot in his right upper arm in an engagement with enemy cavalry. The wound was dressed but never properly searched to extract the bullet. Digby spent thirty-one days in agony and died on 16 July 1645 at Bridgwater; he was buried in St Mary's Church there. He was unmarried.   MICHAEL FOSTER

Sources [E. Walsingham], 'Life of Sir John Digby, 1605–1645', ed. G. Bernard, *Camden miscellany, XII*, CS, 3rd ser., 18 (1910), 67–114 • M. Foster, *Major-General Sir John Digby, 1605–45*, in Royal Stuart Society, Royal Stuart Papers, 20 (1982) • *Brief lives, chiefly of contemporaries, set down by John Aubrey, between the years 1669 and 1696*, ed. A. Clark, 2 (1898), 241, 244 • *CSP Venice, 1629–36* • Count Rossetti's correspondence, 14 Sept–5 Oct 1640, PRO, Roman Transcripts, 31/9/19, fols. 20–21 • *CSP dom., 1631–3; 1639–41; 1644–7* • 'List of popish officers of horse and foot', Dec 1640, PRO, SP 16/473 • K. Digby to T. Mathew, BL, Add. MS 41846, fol. 57b [undated] • J. Nalson, *An impartial collection of the great affairs of state*, 1 (1682), 426 • *JHC*, 2 (1640–42), 859–60 [23 Nov 1642] • W. B. [William Barclay], *A true relation of the taking of Grafton House* (1643) • J. Digby to George, Lord Digby, 18 May 1645, PRO, SP 16/507 • parish register (burial), Bridgwater, St Mary, 16 July 1645 • G. Holt, *St Omers and Bruges colleges, 1593–1773: a biographical dictionary*, Catholic RS, 69 (1979) • private information (2004) [Bucks. RLSS] • BL, Add. MS 5839

Digby, Sir Kenelm

Digby, Sir Kenelm (1603–1665), natural philosopher and courtier, was born on 11 July 1603 at Gayhurst, Buckinghamshire, the elder son of Sir Everard *Digby (c.1578–1606), later executed for involvement in the Gunpowder Plot, and his wife, Mary (c.1581–1653), only daughter and heir of William Mulsho. The Digbys were an ancient gentry family. They had held the manor of Tilton, Leicestershire, since the thirteenth century and the manor of Stoke Dry, Rutland, since the fifteenth. However, Sir Everard's bride brought him the richer manor of Gayhurst and there Kenelm and his brother, Sir John *Digby (1605–1645), spent their childhood.

Early years and education Mary Digby did not remarry after her husband's execution. She remained a steadfast Roman Catholic and lived at Gayhurst with a companion, Dorothy Habington, devoting herself to religion and good works. Wisely, Sir Everard had entailed his manors of Stoke Dry and Tilton-on-Kenelm while Gayhurst was in the hands of trustees, so all were secure from permanent appropriation. Under the Recusancy Act of 1606 Mary's two children were required to be brought up by relatives who conformed to the established church but the act was seldom enforced with full rigour. The boys were mainly taught by Jesuits, probably including John Percy, though Kenelm, as the heir, is likely to have had instruction from Richard Napier (known to Kenelm as Parson Sandy), rector of Great Linford near by and a learned medical man and astrologer. Napier remained a good friend and probably started Kenelm's interest in medicine and astrology.

Digby had as a childhood playmate the beautiful Venetia (1600–1633), daughter of Sir Edward Stanley and his wife, Lady Lucy Percy, daughter of the Roman Catholic Thomas Percy, seventh earl of Northumberland [see Digby, Venetia, Lady Digby]. When his wife died young, Sir Edward left Venetia and her sister Frances to be brought up by a devout Roman Catholic not far from Gayhurst. Later, when he inherited Eynsham Abbey, near Oxford, the girls went to live with their father and the relationship was broken off. In 1617–18 Digby visited Spain with his distant Anglican cousin, Sir John Digby, who had been appointed ambassador. When he was fifteen, then not an unusual age for entry, he entered Gloucester Hall, Oxford, to the care of a humanist don with Roman Catholic sympathies,

Sir Kenelm Digby (1603–1665), by Sir Anthony Van Dyck, *c*.1640

Thomas Allen, a well-known manuscript collector, mathematician, and astrologer and one of Sir Thomas Bodley's main collaborators in founding the Bodleian Library. Allen had been a friend of Sir Everard's stepfather, Sampson Erdeswicke, the Roman Catholic antiquary, and at Gloucester Hall a Roman Catholic might attend the university without damaging his faith because there was no chapel and conformity in religion was not enforced. The tall, handsome, and precocious Digby impressed Allen: he was to call him, according to John Aubrey, 'the Mirandola of his age' after the Renaissance prince and philosopher Pico della Mirandola (*Brief Lives*, 1.225).

The grand tour, embassy to Spain, and marriage Digby left Gloucester Hall in 1619 for the grand tour: his mother hoped in this way to end the infatuation he already felt for Venetia, a girl of high birth but small fortune. They had met again and fallen in love at a house party held by a friend of Mary Digby; later Kenelm gave Venetia a diamond ring in exchange for a long lock of her chestnut hair. Before he left London for Paris on 31 May 1620 Digby sent a manuscript of elections (horoscopes) to Parson Sandy for safe keeping. An outbreak of plague drove him from Paris to Angers where the queen mother, Marie de' Medici, was living with her court. Here, according to 'Loose Fantasies' (his early private memoirs), he attended a court masque, where a lady-in-waiting whom he had met in Paris invited him to dance and he caught the eye of the middle-aged queen. The next day a messenger brought him to the lady's lodgings and escorted him to a bedchamber where to his amazement the queen declared herself desperately in love and implored him to go to bed with

her. Appalled, Digby made his politest excuses, said his heart was committed elsewhere, and contrived nimbly to escape. The queen at the time was at war with her young son, Louis XIII; there was fighting around Angers and many were killed. Digby gave out that he was dead and fled south, taking ship to Leghorn; he was established at Florence by November 1620. Digby wrote to Venetia to reassure her but his first letter miscarried and the rest were suppressed by his mother. During two years in Florence he survived an attack of smallpox, became fluent in Italian, and collected books and manuscripts. He also gave three addresses to the Accademia dei Filomati in Siena; a master-of-arms dedicated a military textbook to him; and an aged Carmelite gave him the recipe for his famous 'powder of sympathy'.

Digby's cousin John Digby, now earl of Bristol, hearing that he was alive after all, summoned him to Spain to join the negotiations for the marriage of Charles, prince of Wales, to the Spanish infanta. Digby arrived in Madrid in the spring of 1623. Here he and his kinsman Lewis Dvye were involved in a dangerous affray and, at the suggestion of Henry Rich, Lord Kensington, he paid court to Donna Anna Maria Manrique, sister of the duke of Maqueda. He also found time to collect books and make some lifelong acquaintances, including the courtiers Toby Matthew and Walter Montagu and the letter-writer James Howell. More important, he made an excellent impression not only on the earl of Bristol but also on Prince Charles. The marriage negotiations failed but on returning to England, Digby was knighted on 28 October 1623 and became a gentleman of the privy chamber to the prince.

Living alone in London, grief-stricken by the news of Digby's death, and unaware of his survival, Venetia had embarked on a disordered life of pleasure. According to John Aubrey, she became the mistress of Sir Edmund Wyld and Richard, third earl of Dorset, who had one or more children with her and settled on her an annuity of £500. But Wyild was dead by April 1620 and Dorset's will of 1624 shows no sign of a settlement or children. 'Loose Fantasies' suggests that both Dorset and his brother Edward Sackville pursued Venetia, the latter imploring her to 'marry' him, but since Sackville had been married since 1612 Digby here as elsewhere retouched the true picture. In any event Sackville began pursuing another beauty and Venetia broke off the 'engagement'. The lovers made contact on Digby's return to court but only gradually became reconciled. Venetia had been overjoyed to hear that he was alive but the lack of letters had convinced her that she had lost his affection, while gossip about Venetia's relations with Sackville, who had succeeded his brother as the fourth earl in March 1624, made Digby chary of marrying her. However, in the summer of 1624, while Mary Digby was abroad, Venetia arranged to stay with her sister Frances, who had married John Fortescue and lived at Linslade, near Gayhurst. Digby and Venetia went riding together and became deeply enamoured. In December Digby accompanied the duke of Buckingham to Paris to make arrangements for the marriage of Prince Charles to Princess Henrietta Maria and Venetia sacrificed most of her jewellery and plate to pay for his expenses. This so moved Digby that he determined to overrule his mother's objections. Probably in January 1625 the lovers were secretly married. Digby had come of age, and into a rich patrimony, in July 1624, but Venetia's father was disposing of some estates to Venetia and since he was quarrelling with Mary Digby it seemed prudent not to reveal the marriage until the will was made. The couple's eldest son, Kenelm, was born on 6 October 1625.

The voyage to Iskenderun Charles had ascended the throne the previous March and Lord Bristol advised Digby to advance himself in the king's service. Since England was at war with France and Spain he now determined on a privateering voyage to the Mediterranean to attack and plunder French and Spanish ships and eventually to seize French ships in the rich Venetian port of Iskenderun (Scanderoon) at the junction of Asia Minor and Syria. Despite his wife's tearful protests and the duke of Buckingham's opposition, Digby finally obtained letters of marque on 13 December 1627. He commissioned two ships, the *Eagle* (400 tons) and the *George and Elizabeth* (250 tons), with as principal officers Captain Milborne, an experienced seaman, and Sir Edward Stradling, a Glamorgan gentleman. Before Digby set sail on 6 January Venetia gave birth to a second son, John, and Digby told her to make their marriage public.

Digby kept a day-to-day log of the voyage. He passed Gibraltar on the night of 19 January but his crews sickened in a severe epidemic. After an action with seven Spanish ships, on 15 February he reached Algiers, where he stayed six weeks, buying the freedom of forty to fifty captive English sailors to replace his dead crewmen. He took several prizes before passing the Strait of Messina. Digby suppressed a mutiny in April and visited Zante to buy provisions in May, arriving off Iskenderun on 10 June. He attacked the following day, cannonading the Venetian galleasses guarding the port because they fired on him. After a three-hour battle, according to Digby, the Venetian admiral asked for a ceasefire. This he agreed provided he could take the French vessels in port. In the event there was no plunder since the French crews had taken their goods ashore and, at the English vice-consul's plea, he did not damage the ships for fear of a heavy fine on the English merchants. Digby lost no men killed, according to his account, while the Venetians, according to theirs, lost one man killed and two wounded. On 16 June Digby left, exchanging salutes with the Venetians. Subsequently the English merchants in the Levant complained to the privy council and the Venetian ambassador lodged a protest in London.

On the return journey, on 16 August 1628 Digby reached the island of Milos, where he stayed a week and wrote out 'Loose Fantasies'. Elsewhere in the Cyclades he collected antiquities and then careened his ships and bought provisions at Zante. He captured two prizes off Sardinia on 10 December but allowed the crews, with two ships, to go to Leghorn. He passed Gibraltar on 1 January and anchored at Woolwich on 2 February 1629. The court of admiralty then had to consider claims brought by foreign merchants

against him. There was little trouble over his French and Spanish prizes (he had already disposed of most of the ships) but all Italian captures, including a ship, were returned to their owners. Meanwhile the English merchants of Aleppo were severely fined. Nevertheless the audacious voyage, with its booty and the battle at Iskenderun, made Digby a hero at court.

The Navy Board, family life, and the 'tribe of Ben' Digby could now launch his career on a favourable tide, just as Lord Bristol had recommended. As Edward, earl of Clarendon, was later to recall:

> he was a man of a very extraordinary person and presence, which drew the eyes of all men upon him, which were more fixed by a wonderful graceful behaviour, a flowing courtesy and civility, and such a volubility of language that surprised and delighted.   (G. D. Boyle, *Characters of the Great Rebellion*, 1889, 294)

In 1630 Digby found employment with the Navy Board and in October was made a junior principal officer of the navy. The Venetian ambassador reported on 27 December that 'moved by ambition, he has recently abandoned the Catholic Faith and become a Protestant' (*CSP Venice, 1629–32*). John Aubrey said more accurately that he 'received the sacrament in the chapel at Whitehall and professed the Protestant religion' (*Brief Lives*, 1.227). Appointment to office made the oaths of supremacy and allegiance virtually inescapable and Digby was following the example of other crypto-Catholic courtiers. He became friendly with Sir John Coke, one of the secretaries of state, and various further appointments came his way, including membership of the Council for New England in 1632.

At this time the Digby family lived in Charterhouse Yard in fashionable Clerkenwell while a new home was built in Aldwych Close, Holborn, from the profits of privateering. Digby commissioned his friend Van Dyck to paint a portrait of Venetia, his two sons, Kenelm and John, and himself in 1632; other portraits followed and Peter Oliver painted miniatures. Meanwhile Venetia lost another son, Everard, after childbirth and twins in a miscarriage; a fourth son, George, was born in 1633. Digby was deeply uxorious. To preserve Venetia's health and beauty he introduced edible snails into the grounds of Gayhurst and concocted 'viper wine'. Ben Jonson, the court poet, celebrated the Digbys' domestic bliss in a collection of verses and called Venetia his muse. Digby was Jonson's patron and one of the 'tribe of Ben' who dined in the 'Apollo room' of the Devil tavern in the City. Digby himself was a competent lyric poet and it was he who later prepared the manuscript material of the 1640 folio of Jonson's poems for printing. But the 'tribe of Ben' included several rakes, and Digby was not above temptation. Letters acknowledge several extra-marital 'escapes' and one prolonged liaison which made him later wonder 'what devil reigned in my blood' ('Letter book', 9.146, 448). Venetia, on the other hand, given the security of matrimony, became a model wife and mother. Careful and vigilant in managing her household, she joined a group of court ladies who were Franciscan 'tertiaries'. But Digby was becoming disillusioned with official life: he dreamed of retreating to the library of his new house in Holborn. Late in 1632 his Oxford friend Thomas Allen died and left him a huge collection of manuscripts—some of immense value and antiquity—and all the printed books he fancied, apart from special bequests. Digby therefore added to his new home a library wing.

Death of Venetia, reconversion, and life in France Suddenly everything was utterly changed. On the night of 30 April / 1 May 1633 Venetia had a cerebral haemorrhage. As Digby was sitting in his drawing-room after breakfast, discussing literature with a recusant friend, Sir Thomas Hawkins, she was found dead in bed. It was a thunderbolt from heaven: God had taken her to punish his sins. Digby was grief-stricken. On 2 May he had Van Dyck make a death-mask for a deathbed portrait and on 3 May Venetia was buried in Christ Church, Newgate. To his brother John, Digby wrote, 'This torment must never have an end while I live … I can have no physician but death' ('Letter book', 9.137). But gradually the frenzy burned out: the wife so suddenly snatched away by providence he now idealized. He had been fortunate to possess this angelic creature: having reached perfection she was ripe for heaven. In a long letter addressed to his children when they were older, he recorded all Venetia's virtues and urged them to emulate her. After receiving a cluster of funeral verses from Ben Jonson, Aurelian Townshend, William Habington, and others from the 'tribe of Ben', Digby gathered the drafts of forty-five letters he had written to relatives and friends after her death and added five memoranda, entitling the whole collection, copied on vellum, 'In Praise of Venetia'. Despite the advice of a friend to remarry and the entreaties of a youthful maid of honour with whom he had had a long liaison and who was herself resisting the importunity of the earl of Dorset, he resolved to remain faithful to Venetia's memory. In a memorandum of 23 June 1634 he concluded that Venetia was 'either in glory or in the way to it'. He would offer up 'masses, prayers, penances and other devotions … to expiate … any human infirmity in her'. 'I ought to … make an entire renunciation … and pass the remnant of my sad days … where I may be free from all worldly cares' (ibid., 10.96–102). He never remarried.

Late in 1633, having handed over his two older sons to their grandmother and put the youngest to nurse, Digby, as Aubrey noted:

> retired into Gresham College at London, where he diverted himself with his chemistry and the professors' good conversation. He wore there a long mourning cloak, a high-crowned hat, his head unshorn—looked like a hermit—as signs of sorrow for his beloved wife. (*Brief Lives*, 1.226–7)

He had Van Dyck paint him in black, bearded and bare-headed, with his right hand touching his breast in plaintive repentance. The college had become an important research centre and Digby had had scientific interests for many years. He had dabbled in experiments since 1624 and his earliest medical recipe dates from 1625. In making his 'viper wine' he bred vipers from the egg, dissected them, and made observations about the movements and fibres of their hearts. When Venetia died he took detailed notes of the results of the post-mortem dissection and examination.

Digby had a large laboratory at the college and engaged a Hungarian alchemist, Johannes Hunyades, as his instructor. Among his experiments Digby investigated the theory, revived by Paracelsus, that a bird could be reconstituted from its own ashes. Henri IV's court physician, Joseph Duchesne, had claimed success for such experiments in 'palingenesis'. Digby's failed, but he reckoned that he succeeded with baked crayfishes. He also produced a recipe for making silver into apparent gold through mercury, nitric acid, heating, and a powdering process: the result was yellow but could not have passed a goldsmith's assay. It was from Gresham that he negotiated with Archbishop Laud his famous donation in 1634 to the Bodleian Library, Oxford, of more than 200 manuscripts inherited from Thomas Allen, together with about 100 of his own, all magnificently bound in 233 books. They were to be followed by thirty-six Arabic manuscripts in 1640–42.

However, Paris, the capital of northern European culture, became Digby's objective. Here Gallican Roman Catholicism allowed scientists and natural philosophers to exchange ideas in freedom. On 29 September 1635 he informed Sir Francis Windebank of his arrival. Digby took rooms in the Collège de Boncourt, a hostel in the Quartier du Jardin du Roi, near the University of the Sorbonne and the royal chemistry laboratory. He collected books for a second library and obtained rare volumes for friends like Sir Edward Conway and John Selden. On the bindings of his books that survive is embroidered the loving monogram 'KDV'.

Digby had confessed to Archbishop Laud in March 1634 his doubts of the validity of Anglican claims to catholicity, and now thought it time to make his reconversion public. On 22 October 1635 his friend James Howell disclosed his defection in a letter to Thomas Wentworth. On 15 February 1636 Digby wrote to his old patron, Sir John Coke, to thank him for his sympathy, saying that he had written to Laud. The archbishop replied on 27 March, deeply pained by Digby's decision 'to enter again the communion of the Church of Rome, in which you had been born and bred, against that semblance of good reason which … made you adhere to the Church of England'. Nevertheless he praised Digby's letter as 'full of discretion and temper and so like yourself … Most sorry I am that a man whose discourse did so much content me should thus slide away'. But he said he retained 'all the love and friendliness' which Digby had won from him (Wharton, 610–16).

Late in 1636 Walter Montagu, a recent convert to Rome, took Digby to an Ursuline convent at Loudun where an outbreak of diabolical possession was believed to have occurred among the nuns. Digby acquired a manuscript describing the events but considered them of psychological, not spiritual, significance. What fascinated him, unlike Montagu, were the phenomena of collective hysteria and *folie à deux*. At a time when witches were put to death he denied the possibility of possession by evil spirits. (He was later prepared to participate in séances with

John Dee's medium, John Evans.) After many months of theological study, Digby's last intellectual difficulties were resolved by a Carmelite lecturer in theology, Father Hilary, whom he visited with Montagu for ten days in January 1637. Two controversial works on religion announced unequivocally his return to Rome. One was a letter to an intending convert, Lady Purbeck, the other a treatise in French on the question of which faith was the true one. The preface to a little book on 'infallibility in religion', published fourteen years later and addressed to Lord George Digby (son of the earl of Bristol), related how in the summer of 1638 they enjoyed a 'long discourse' about religion. The ensuing correspondence was published in 1651.

Digby now formed a lifelong association with Thomas White, a philosopher and former professor of theology at the English College at Douai. Owing to unorthodox ideas, White had fallen from favour at Rome but he confirmed the Aristotelian cast of Digby's thinking. An introduction to Marin Mersenne, a Minim friar who corresponded with all the leading scientific thinkers and whose convent was a scientific and philosophical rendezvous, linked Digby to the new philosophical world of the continent. He became friendly with Thomas Hobbes, who was in Paris in 1635–6, and they corresponded during 1636–7. Digby adopted the 'atomist' and 'mechanical' ideas of the new philosophers but, like Gassendi in France, sought to integrate them with the Aristotelianism that was currently reviving in the universities. Mersenne introduced him to the works of Descartes and in 1637 he read the newly published *Discours sur le méthode*, of which he sent a copy to Hobbes, greatly praising it. In 1638 Digby wrote to Descartes, enclosing a refutation of the philosopher's proof of the existence of God, almost certainly written by White. In 1640 he went to the Netherlands to meet Descartes and they enjoyed a week's conversation. The philosopher evidently took to him because after the publication of Digby's *Two Treatises* in Paris in 1644 they met again at the Collège de Boncourt. According to Descartes's seventeenth-century biographer, Baillet, their conversations were concluded in mutual esteem. Descartes became the main influence on Digby among the new philosophers, though he never accepted Descartes's basic principle that everything must be rejected unless it could be proved beyond doubt. Digby accepted the substantial validity of Thomist metaphysics and his citing of authorities, ancient and modern, was precisely what Descartes most objected to; nor did he question so carefully the foundation of his own knowledge.

Civil war and the *Two Treatises* Digby returned to England late in 1638 and was soon involved in a scheme of the queen to raise money from Roman Catholics to aid her husband's campaign against the Scottish covenanters. On 17 April 1639 she issued an appeal, covered by a letter from Digby and Walter Montagu. The response was meagre. Digby himself seems unlikely to have contributed materially since on 6 December 1639 he had to mortgage his estates at Stoke Dry and Tilton to pay a debt of £10,000 to

Eliab and Daniel Harvey of London. But the Long Parliament, which opposed the Scottish war, called Digby and Montagu to account on 28 January 1641. On 16 March the Commons resolved to petition the king to remove all 'Popish recusants' from court, including Digby, Montagu, and Sir Toby Matthew. Removed they were, but Digby was called before the Commons again on 22 June. He spoke at length with great eloquence, making no secret of his loyalty both to his faith and to the king and the laws. The Commons were mollified but he thought it prudent to leave for France. Later that year he challenged a Baron Mont le Ros to a duel for calling Charles I 'the arrantest coward in the world' at a dinner party, and killed him. Duelling incurred the death penalty in France but Louis XIII excused him, provided he left the country. The Commons, however, were offended by a tract recounting the affair, *Sir Kenelm Digby's Honour Maintained* (1641), which concluded, 'May more such Noble Digbies increase … Then shall the enemies of our gracious King be scattered'. Now a suspect character, having returned to England, Digby was arrested on 7 August 1642 but was released after a week at the instance of the House of Lords.

The civil war broke out in August 1642 and Digby was rearrested on 12 November. He was detained by parliament at Winchester House, a former episcopal palace in Southwark, for almost a year, but took to imprisonment with zest. At the earl of Dorset's request he wrote in twenty-four hours a critical commentary on Sir Thomas Browne's recently published *Religio medici* (and after a courteous exchange of letters with the author, later editions were often printed with Digby's commentary annexed). He also wrote out the first draft of his treatise 'On bodies' (as early as 24 February 1640 he had told Mersenne that he had fully thought out a work 'On the soul').

Digby's combined work, the *Two treatises, in the one of which the nature of bodies, in the other the nature of man's soul is looked into: in way of discovery of the immortality of reasonable souls*, is on a massive scale. The essential design was to trace the course of nature and to demonstrate immortality from the basic facts of physical existence. 'On bodies' was much the larger and more significant treatise, much of its thought derived, as Digby confessed, from White. In thirty-eight chapters he took all natural phenomena for his subject and onto an Aristotelian framework built concepts selected from current thinkers. Digby adopted the two dominant ideas of the time—the atomist theory, that everything in nature consists of atoms, and mechanical explanations, that every physical effect has a physical cause. Digby's own experiments provided part of the evidence leading to his conclusions. In three chapters on the embryology of animals, for example, his experiments upheld Aristotle's theory of epigenesis against the prevailing theory of pre-formation and led him to the modern conception of embryonic development. Medical historians are agreed that Digby deserves a very high place among seventeenth-century biologists: indeed he has been called the father of modern embryology. The much briefer second treatise, 'On the soul', contains no explicit reference to Christian revelation or even the existence of

God. Digby sought to prove immortality from ordinary experience: only the life of the body could be proved to end at death. But despite complex argument, how and where the soul subsists after death seems unsatisfactorily explained.

'On bodies' for a time made Digby's reputation as a natural philosopher. It was the first comprehensive synthesis of the new philosophy with the Aristotelian thought then current in the universities and one of the first fully developed atomist systems of the seventeenth century. Thus Isaac Barrow of Cambridge in 1652 picked out Digby among those, like Descartes, Bacon, and Gassendi, who had renewed ancient thought and struck out new paths in natural philosophy. When John Webster recommended reform of the university curriculum in his *Academiarum examen* (1653) he took for granted the importance of Digby and White, as well as Descartes. John Wallis, the Oxford mathematician, dedicated his *Commercium epistolicum* (1658) to Digby and included in it a letter praising Digby and White. Thomas Barlow, a friend of Robert Boyle and later bishop of Lincoln, in his *Library for Younger Scholars* (*c*.1655) cited Digby and White, along with Descartes, Gassendi, and Bacon, as modern natural philosophers. The first edition of the *Two Treatises* was published in Paris in 1644. Four further English and two Latin editions were printed by 1669, though none since.

Embassies at Rome and dealings with the protectorate Publication had become possible when Digby's imprisonment ended. Having undertaken to do nothing directly or indirectly prejudicial to parliament, he was released on 30 July 1643 and left for France. There in the following year, after the defeat at Marston Moor, Queen Henrietta Maria set up her household and made Digby her chancellor. She had him in mind for a further, more desperate, exercise in raising cash, this time from the pope. By the end of February 1645 Digby left Paris with his two older sons, Kenelm and John; George was left at school. Evidently, like his royal master, Digby attached little weight to a promise to a rebel parliament. White accompanied them to help press the case for two additional bishops for England and formal recognition of the status of the dean and chapter of the secular clergy. When Digby left Rome at the end of 1645 he had obtained an advance of 20,000 crowns. He was back in Rome in October 1646, offering to lead a fleet against the Turks in return for greater financial support but the curia prevaricated, knowing the weakness of Charles's cause after the crowning defeat of Naseby the previous June. Digby had no more luck even in persuading the curia to recognize the dean and chapter. After a year's frustration Digby addressed a long memorandum to Pope Innocent and in an audience on 30 November 1647 'he grew high and hectored with His Holiness' (*Brief Lives*, 1.225–6). He left Rome in February 1648 never to return. His only consolation was the friendships formed with Luke Holstenius, the Vatican librarian, and Cassiano dal Pozzo, a fellow art patron and book collector.

In the summer of 1647 Digby had joined an abortive scheme to persuade the puritans, now in power in England, to rescind the penal laws against Roman Catholics in return for a guarantee of obedience to the state. The plan, mainly devised by Henry Holden, a professor at the Sorbonne and vicar-general of the Paris diocese, was to have English bishops ordained in France who would be independent of the pope except as 'chief pastor' and to provide an oath of allegiance omitting any reference to the pope. The scheme collapsed because neither the English chapter nor the French authorities would support it.

From then on Digby's main concerns were to return to England and to raise money from his estates. These had been confiscated and all or most were mortgaged and burdened by further debts. He petitioned the central committee for compounding, appealed to the barons of the exchequer, petitioned both houses of parliament, and in 1653 even appealed to the protector, Cromwell, himself. In November 1653 and January 1654 orders in council finally permitted Digby to return to England and freed his estates from sequestration, and he seems to have been granted a pension. He acted as intermediary between Cromwell and the ruler of France, Cardinal Mazarin, in 1654–6 and was occasionally keeping company with high officials—even the protector. But he was a middle-man, not an informer. During 1654–5 he lived for a while at Gayhurst with his surviving son John, who had inherited the use of the estate (the younger Kenelm had been killed in action on 7 July 1648 and George had died at school the same year). In 1654 Digby published a translation of Albert the Great's mystical treatise, *Of Adhering to God*, and he sent a gift of about forty, mainly theological, books to Harvard University the following year.

Chemistry and the Royal Society After *Two Treatises* was published Digby set himself the task of examining on mechanical principles the concepts of current Paracelsian chemistry, especially alchemy and the 'universal spirit' giving life to all things. In Paris he studied chemistry under the Scottish royal physician, William Davidson. John Evelyn visited Digby at his laboratory on 7 November 1651 and was given his 'powder with which he affirmed that he had fixed mercury before the late King' and 'a dissolvent of calx of gold' (Evelyn, *Diary*, 3.20, 48). Digby's experiments often involved faulty observation and conclusions that went further than the facts allowed. A prime example was the celebrated 'sympathetic powder'. Made from dried green vitriol, this was a variant of the well-known Paracelsian 'weapon salve' which cured wounds by being applied, not to the patient, but to the offending weapon. He offered a complex mechanical explanation in a lecture to a congress of French virtuosi (*A Late Discourse Made … at Montpellier*, 1658). Digby had cured his friend James Howell, then the duke of Buckingham's secretary, of a sword-cut in the hand by dissolving some powdered vitriol crystals in water and plunging into the mixture a cloth stained with blood from the wound. The pain in Howell's hand, some yards away, immediately ceased. Many were convinced by Digby's evidence, including Joseph Glanvill, later a Royal Society fellow, and Nathaniel Highmore, a distinguished anatomist and friend of William Harvey. In fact the cure lay in washing and bandaging the wound. There were four editions in English of Digby's oration, three in German, and at least seven in French.

On the restoration of Charles II in 1660 Digby returned to England. He remained the queen mother's chancellor, continued to support Thomas White, and unsuccessfully petitioned the king for toleration for Roman Catholics. On 14 June 1661 a warrant for payment to him of £1325 was issued in respect of his ransoming captives in Algiers in 1628; on 6 December bonds for £12,000, £2000, and £300 were diverted to him for the same purpose. He lived 'in the last fair house westward in the north portico of Covent Garden … He had a laboratory there' (*Brief Lives*, 1.227). His operator, George Hartmann, collected Digby's records of experiments and after his death published them as *A Choice Collection of Rare Secrets* (1682). The first section of 143 pages is devoted mainly to alchemical recipes and processes: virtually all are presented in practical laboratory terminology. A second section of 125 pages lists medical and cosmetic recipes.

Digby was not among the ten men who held the initial meeting of the Royal Society on 28 November 1660 but was among the twelve additional members elected a fortnight later. He became a member of the chemical committee. His personal distinction added lustre to the new body, whose patron, Charles II, was himself a chemist in the Paracelsian tradition. Digby's paper on the vegetation of plants, read on 23 January 1661, was the first formal publication authorized by the society, entitled *A Discourse Concerning the Vegetation of Plants* (1661). It described Digby's detailed observation and experiments and attempted to draw wider conclusions, among them that a nitrous salt in earth 'attracteth a like salt that fecundateth the air … a hidden food of life' (p. 64), echoing Paracelsus, Duchesne, Seton, and Sendivogius. Never one of the central core of members, Digby's attendance at the society's meetings decreased with time, perhaps owing to ill health and the increasingly obvious divergence of his thinking from that of Robert Boyle and his associates. Digby's paper was his last publication. Increasingly he turned to medicine and collecting recipes for cookery and wine-making.

Burdened by debts and suffering from gout and the stone, Digby prepared a will in January 1665. He expressed the wish to have his 'dust lie by hers who was my greatest worldly blessing' (PRO, PROB 11/325, fol. 130). He succumbed to a violent fever and died at home in Covent Garden on 11 June of the same year, aged almost sixty-two. He was buried in the elaborate tomb of black marble and copper which he had prepared for Venetia in the crypt of Christ Church, Newgate. By his direction no inscription was added.

Assessment The extraordinary intelligence, courage, and ambition that carried Sir Kenelm Digby through so many adventures in his youth and made such an impression at court inspired him to take part in the philosophical and scientific revolution of the seventeenth century. His pioneering work in integrating mechanical philosophy with traditional Aristotelianism was soon superseded. Credulity mingled with precise observation in his wide-ranging,

receptive mind but some of his research, especially in embryology, made positive contributions to scientific progress. All in all, Digby was one of the most remarkable thinkers and scientific enquirers of his day.

MICHAEL FOSTER

Sources K. Digby, *Loose fantasies*, ed. V. Gabrieli (1968) · M. Foster, 'Sir Kenelm Digby as man of religion and thinker', *Downside Review*, 106 (1988), 35–58, 101–25 · 'A new Digby letter book', ed. V. Gabrieli, *National Library of Wales Journal*, 9 (1955–6), 113–48, 440–62; 10 (1957–8), 81–105 · *CSP dom.*, 1629–33; 1635–7; 1641; 1644–7; 1649–50; 1653–6; 1661–4 · *CSP Venice*, 1628–32; 1643–52; 1655–6 · *Brief lives, chiefly of contemporaries, set down by John Aubrey, between the years 1669 and 1696*, ed. A. Clark, 1 (1898), 224–32 · G. J. Armytage, ed., *The visitation of the county of Rutland in the year 1618–19*, Harleian Society, 3 (1870) · W. H. Rylands, ed., *The visitation of the county of Buckingham made in 1634*, Harleian Society, 58 (1909) · K. Digby, *Journal of a voyage into the Mediterranean*, ed. J. Bruce, CS, 96 (1868) · R. H. Kargon, *Atomism in England from Hariot to Newton* (1966), 70–73, 77–9, 95–6 · J. Needham, *History of embryology* (1959), 121–7, 130, 235 · B. J. Dobbs, 'Studies in the natural philosophy of Sir Kenelm Digby', *Ambix*, 18 (1971), 1–25; 20 (1973), 143–63; 21 (1974), 1–28 · H. Wharton, *The troubles and trial of Archbishop Laud* (1695), 610–16 · A. G. Watson, 'Thomas Allen of Oxford and his manuscripts', *Mediaeval scribes, manuscripts and libraries*, ed. M. B. Parkes and A. G. Watson (1978), 279–314 · will, PRO, PROB 11/325, fol. 130 · L. Thorndike, *A history of magic and experimental science*, 8 vols. (1958), vol. 7, pp. 498–503 · J. R. Partington, *A history of chemistry*, 4 vols. (1961), vol. 2, pp. 423–6 · R. T. Petersson, *Sir Kenelm Digby, ornament of England* (1956) · *A letter sent by the queen's majesty concerning the collection of the recusants' money* (1641) · *JHC*, 2 (1640–42), 182 · Wood, *Ath. Oxon.*, new edn, 3.688–96 · *DNB* · M. A. E. Green, ed., *Calendar of the proceedings of the committee for compounding … 1643–1660*, 5 vols., PRO (1889–92), 2173 · R. Pugh, *Blacklo's cabal* (1680) · M. Foster, 'Thomas Allen (1540–1632), Gloucester Hall and the survival of Catholicism in post-Reformation Oxford', *Oxoniensia*, 46 (1982), 99–128 · K. T. Hoppen, 'The nature of the early Royal Society', *British Journal for the History of Science*, 9 (1976), 243–67, esp. 252–6, 264 · *Ben Jonson*, ed. C. H. Herford, P. Simpson, and E. M. Simpson, 11 vols. (1925–52), vol. 2, p. 337; vol. 8, pp. 272–89 · 'Horoscope', Bodl. Oxf., MS Ashmole 174, fol. 75 · W. A. Shaw, *The knights of England*, 2 vols. (1906) · BL, Add. MS 5839, fol. 86a · M. Foster, 'Major General Sir John Digby', *Royal Stuart Papers*, 20 (1982) · BL, Add. MS 41846, fols. 114a, 115a · Foster, *Alum. Oxon.*

Archives BL, corresp. and papers, Add. MSS 38175, 41846 · Bodl. Oxf., letters and papers · Hunt. L., journal · NL Wales, journal · NYPL, corresp. and papers [copies] · NYPL, letters and memoranda · Sherborne Castle estates, Sherborne, journal and letters · Wellcome L., chemical papers | Worcester College, Oxford, journal, corresp. with Lord Digby [corresp.: copies]

Likenesses P. Oliver, watercolour miniature on vellum, 1627, NPG · A. Van Dyck, group portrait, oils, 1630?, priv. coll. · A. Van Dyck, double portrait, watercolour miniatures on vellum, 1632 (with Venetia), Sherborne Castle, Dorset · A. Van Dyck, oils, 1632, Royal Collection · group portrait, oils, 1632 (after A. Van Dyck), Sherborne Castle, Dorset · A. Van Dyck, oils, 1633–5, Euston Hall, Suffolk · C. Johnson, oils, 1634, Pen-y-lan, Oswestry · A. Van Dyck, oils, c.1640, NPG [see illus.] · line engraving, pubd 1645, BM · R. Gaywood, etching, 1654, BM, NPG · T. Cross, line engraving, BM, NPG; repro. in K. Digby, *Choice and experimented receipts in physick and chirurgery* (1668) · C. Johnson, oils (after A. Van Dyck, c.1640), Althorp House, Northamptonshire · oils (after A. Van Dyck, after type, c.1636), Antony, Cornwall; version, oils, Weston Park, Shropshire

Wealth at death apart from small annuity to Thomas White and other small bequests, Charles Cornwallis was sole beneficiary; Digby's sole surviving son, John, received nothing: will, PRO, PROB 11/325, fol. 130; Aubrey, *Brief lives*, 1.228–9

Digby, Sir **Kenelm Edward** (1836–1916), lawyer and civil servant, was born on 9 September 1836 at The Ridge, Wotton under Edge, Gloucestershire, the eldest of six sons of the Hon. and Revd Kenelm Henry Digby (1811–1891), honorary canon of Norwich and rector of Tittleshall, Norfolk, and his wife, Caroline (d. 1866), daughter of Edward Sheppard of Firgrove, Shropshire. The Digbys were an old-established county family from Dorset, with a strong tradition of public service. His father's elder brother became the ninth Baron Digby in 1856.

Digby attended a school in Blakeney, Norfolk, and from Harrow School (1849–55) gained a closed scholarship to Corpus Christi College, Oxford (where he matriculated in 1855). As an undergraduate he played cricket for the university (1857–9), became president of the union, and took firsts in classical honour moderations and Greats (BA 1859, MA 1861). He was elected a fellow and tutor of Corpus (1864), where he threw himself into the teaching and study of law, continued to excel at cricket and rowing for his college, and became a leading and seemingly universally popular figure of his generation. He was called to the bar as a member of Lincoln's Inn in 1865.

From 1868 to 1874 Digby was Vinerian reader in English and civil law at Oxford and in 1875 was a university examiner for the new school of jurisprudence. Concerned about the lacuna in law textbooks for undergraduates, he published *An Introduction to the History of the Law of Real Property* (1875), which became a standard text and ran to five editions. At Oxford, Digby moved in the same circles as a group of young reformers associated with the positivist movement, and became a close friend of Frederic Harrison. As a young barrister in London he shared chambers with his lifelong friend and contemporary James Bryce, who was also a member of Lincoln's Inn. He was a strong supporter of Gladstonian Liberalism and believed in 'the greater importance of giving substantial power to the working classes'. Later in his life he was involved in working out fair and effective means of compensating workmen for industrial injuries.

Digby married on 30 August 1870 Caroline (1848–1926), second daughter of Edward *Strutt, first Baron Belper, the Liberal politician. They settled in Kensington in their early married life, when he left Oxford to make his career as a young barrister, and had four children—two sons and two daughters. Always an enthusiast for physical activity and travel, Digby was a keen sportsman, a good shot, and an experienced fisherman, and in London regularly rode before breakfast. A mountaineer and member of the Alpine Club (from 1867), he recorded many climbs with friends such as Harrison, Bryce, and Courtenay Ilbert. He enjoyed regular holidays with his family, during which they frequently walked and climbed in Scotland, Austria, Switzerland, and Italy.

Digby was a sound, learned, and painstaking lawyer with a strong practical sense. In 1892 he was appointed county court judge in Derbyshire and the family moved to Aston Hall just outside Derby. In 1891 he became a bencher of Lincoln's Inn and in 1904 took silk. He enjoyed his Derbyshire life and was hesitant about abandoning it

when in 1894 he was unexpectedly approached on behalf of the Liberal home secretary, H. H. Asquith, about an appointment as permanent under-secretary at the Home Office. However, a strong devotion to public duty weighed in the balance against his fears about his inexperience in administration and public office. Digby was appointed permanent under-secretary at the Home Office in January 1895, succeeding Sir Godfrey Lushington (whom he must have known as another Oxford positivist).

Digby's personal fears about becoming a senior civil servant late in life proved unfounded. Edward Troup, subsequently to fill the same post, later commented that 'no one could have been quicker in leaving behind the ways of a lawyer and adapting himself to administrative work on broad and vigorous lines' (Bryce, 248). In fact, Digby's very lack of detailed personal knowledge about the work of the Home Office may have been an advantage. He arrived at a time when senior civil servants in the department were for the first time forced, through the growth of legislation and the complexity of new responsibilities, to devolve responsibility. Digby recognized that the new breed of open competitive entry officials was now reaching maturity and must shoulder a greater amount of the workload. Part of this derived from new industrial legislation, such as the 1897 Workmen's Compensation Act, much of which involved delegated powers and the need for analysis of statistics. On the criminal side of the office's work, the sheer increase in the volume of papers, together with a lack of the necessary legal expertise, led to the departmental scandal of the Beck case in 1904. Digby and his subordinates were blamed for their failure to spot a case of mistaken identity which led to wrongful imprisonment. (The case eventually led to the establishment in 1907 of the court of criminal appeal.)

Immigration was another area of increased activity as England was affected by the great influx of eastern European refugees migrating westwards. Digby was appointed to the royal commission on alien immigration, which reported in 1903. He wrote an influential minority memorandum, which did much to discredit the majority report. He was strongly opposed to the idea of an inquisitorial immigration sub-department with wide powers of investigation and referral of cases to the courts, partly because it involved the reversal of long-established policies on the right of asylum and the law of extradition. Digby's doubts about the practicality of implementing the recommendations of the report were fully justified in the years following the Aliens Act, 1905.

Digby retired from the Home Office on 9 September 1903, having had a two-year extension of the normal retirement age. He was created KCB in 1898 and GCB in 1906. He was one of the last of a type of Victorian head of department: socially highly placed, a brilliant 'all-rounder' who was appointed to the highest ranks of the civil service from outside. Over the subsequent ten years he sat as a member of numerous departmental committees of inquiry, chairing the Home Office departmental committee on workmen's compensation (1904), and acted as an arbitrator in labour disputes. In 1914 he was appointed a member of the commission chaired by Bryce to investigate alleged German war atrocities in Belgium. He died peacefully, after two days' illness, on 21 April 1916 at the Bankes Arms Hotel, Studland, Swanage, Dorset.

JILL PELLEW

Sources L. Digby, *My ancestors* (1928) · J. Bryce, 'Sir Kenelm Digby', *Law Quarterly Review*, 32 (1916), 245–8 · J. Pellew, *The home office, 1848–1914* (1982) · J. Pellew, 'The home office and the Aliens Act', *HJ*, 32 (1989), 369–85, esp. 371–2 · H. A. Strong, 'Corpus in the early sixties', *Pelican Record*, 7 (1903–5), 179–82 · *The Times* (24 April 1916) · *Manchester Guardian* (24 April 1916) · PRO, Home Office MSS, HO 45 series · letters to James Bryce, 1865–1907, Bodl. Oxf., MS Bryce 56, fols. 77–117 · Burke, *Peerage*
Archives Bodl. Oxf., Asquith MSS, vol. 9, fol. 44 · Bodl. Oxf., Bryce MSS, corresp. from Digby · PRO, Home Office MSS, HO 45 series
Likenesses P. F. S. Spence, engraving, repro. in *ILN*, 125 (1904), 613
Wealth at death £32,703 8s. 2d.: probate, 12 Aug 1916, *CGPLA Eng. & Wales*

Digby, Kenelm Henry (1795/6–1880), writer, was born at Geashill, King's county, Ireland, the younger of the two sons of the Very Revd William Digby (c.1735–1812), dean of Clonfert, and his third wife, Mary, née Wood, of Devon descent, widow of William Cooper. The Irish branch of the Digby family had provided a baron in the seventeenth century, bishops of Dromore and Elphin in the eighteenth, and had originated from a Leicestershire branch of the same name. Kenelm Henry Digby inherited his powerful physique from his father, who had been a considerable athlete, was over 6 feet tall, had a swarthy complexion, and dark hair and eyes. The deaths of his father in 1812, of his mother shortly after, and of his elder brother, Richard Edward, in 1820, provided him with ample independent means and the ability to finance the publication of his works.

Digby was educated at Petersham, near Richmond, Surrey, and entered Trinity College, Cambridge, on 22 October 1814 at the age of eighteen. Having taken his degree in mathematics in 1819, he continued to keep his rooms at Trinity as a base until 1829. In 1820 he won a Norrisian prize for an essay on the evidences of the Christian religion, regarded as displaying a wide range of reading, although not closely reasoned. The rest of his considerable literary output showed precisely these characteristics; his creativity was derivative rather than imaginative. During travel in France, Germany, Switzerland, and Italy, he researched the culture of the middle ages and the concept of chivalry, resulting in his first published work, *The Broadstone of Honour, or, Rules for the Gentlemen of England*, in 1822, and his reception into the Roman Catholic church in 1825 by Father Edward Scott SJ. With Ambrose Phillipps De Lisle, an undergraduate at Trinity with whom he had a long friendship, he rode each Sunday to mass at the nearest Roman Catholic chapel, at the seminary of Old Hall, St Edmund's, Ware, a journey of 26 miles each way. His relationship with De Lisle endured, but a coolness developed when Digby did not share enthusiasm for the members of the Oxford Movement and De Lisle's

attitude towards corporate reunion of the churches. Some of their correspondence is preserved by the De Lisle family. Over a hundred letters to another close friend and fellow Roman Catholic, Squire Richard Huddleston of Sawston Hall, are held in the Cambridgeshire Record Office.

Digby rewrote *The Broadstone of Honour* after his conversion, with the subtitle *The True Sense and Practice of Chivalry*, in four lengthy parts between 1826 and 1829. It and the eleven long volumes of *Mores Catholici, or, Ages of Faith* (1831–42), and seven volumes of *Compitum, or, The Meeting of the Ways at the Catholic Church*, written between 1848 and 1854, were his major works. The remainder, five books of prose and eleven books of verse, were of less consequence, though two of the latter, *Ouranogaia, or, Heaven on Earth* (1872) and *The Temple of Memory* (1874), are of interest for their descriptions of his contemporaries at Trinity. All his work showed an uncritical and élitist view of the past, particularly of the medieval period; his style was laboured, his sentences long, and punctuation sparse; there were few paragraphs. His saving grace was the enthusiasm he was able to transmit. This undoubtedly conveyed itself to those who were open to fresh interest in the middle ages, a large number in the first half of the nineteenth century. Since Digby was, however, one of several contemporary or near contemporary writers in this vein, his particular influence is not easy to gauge. Some of his friends wrote approvingly of his works in his lifetime, but sales were slow and the fact that subsequent editions were paid for by their author makes calculation of appreciation difficult. Modern readers, used to more succinct modes of expression, would undoubtedly find his works hard going; but it is likely that they would find evidence of his character and outlook more interesting than his writing.

In 1833, in Dover, Digby had married Jane Mary Dillon (1816/17–1860), daughter and coheir of Thomas Dillon of Mount Dillon, co. Dublin, and this had brought him further financial provision at the time. Although Irish, she had been educated in France and was sixteen when married. The couple had seven children: Thomas, Marcella, Kenelm Thomas, Mary-Ann Letitia, John Gerard, and Mary; a fourth daughter died in infancy. The only children who survived their father were Kenelm Thomas, who became an Irish MP, Marcella, a nun, and Mary, who married the Hon. Hubert Dormer.

Digby lived in Paris and various towns in France until 1857 when he and his family settled in England, his literary energy still matched by physical strength. He was credited with having plunged into the Rhine, despite the current, and reaching the further shore with difficulty 3 miles downstream; also with riding a tiger from a travelling zoo. Daily swimming in the Serpentine in London was his practice in old age. He died at his home, Shaftesbury House, Hammersmith, London, on 22 March 1880, and was buried in Kensal Green Roman Catholic cemetery, London.

MARGARET PAWLEY

Sources B. Holland, *Memoir of Kenelm Henry Digby* (1919) · M. Pawley, *Faith and family: the life and circle of Ambrose Phillipps de Lisle*

(1993) • M. Girouard, *The return to Camelot: chivalry and the English gentleman* (1981) • private information (2004) [family, friends]
Archives BL, anonymous diary of travels in Italy and Switzerland with Digby, Add. MS 64096 • NRA, priv. coll., family MSS | Cambs. AS, letters to Richard Huddleston • Quenby Hall, Hungarton, Leicestershire, De Lisle archives, corresp. with Ambrose De Lisle • Trinity Cam., letters to W. Whewell
Likenesses Lawrence, portrait, priv. coll. • photograph, priv. coll.
Wealth at death under £4000: probate, 28 May 1880, *CGPLA Eng. & Wales*

Digby [née Fitzgerald], **Lettice, Lady Digby and *suo jure* Baroness Offaly** (*c.*1580–1658), landowner, was the only surviving child of Gerald Fitzgerald (1559–1580), Lord Gerald, and his wife, Catherine (*d.* 1632), daughter of Sir Francis *Knollys (1511/12–1596). She may have lived first on her mother's Irish jointure lands at Portlester, Woodstock, and Athy, but these were forfeited on Catherine's remarriage to Sir Philip Boteler of Walton Woodhall, Hertfordshire. Shortly after a pre-nuptial settlement on 19 April 1598 Lettice married Sir Robert Digby (*bap.* 1575, *d.* 1618) of Coleshill, Warwickshire, a client of the earl of Essex; they had seven sons and three daughters. Following the successive deaths of her paternal grandfather, Gerald *Fitzgerald, eleventh earl of Kildare and first Baron Offaly (*d.* 1585), and uncles Henry Fitzgerald (*d.* 1597) and William Fitzgerald (*d.* 1599), respectively twelfth and thirteenth earls, Lady Digby (as heir general) assumed the style of Baroness Offaly and claimed the title and certain lands, while the earldom went to the heir male, another Gerald Fitzgerald (*d.* 1612). Although Sir Robert Digby represented his native county as an MP in 1601, thereafter the couple spent most of their time in Ireland.

Over the next two decades the Digbys made concerted efforts to consolidate their position. Making common cause with Mabel Fitzgerald, widow of the eleventh earl of Kildare, they pressured the fourteenth earl for restitution of jointure rights and concession of the Offaly title. Digby became a justice of the peace in co. Kildare and a member of the Irish privy council. He was an active supporter of the government in the Irish parliament of 1613 and in 1615 became a member of the council of Munster. With powerful friends at the English court, including Lady Digby's uncle William Knollys (1547–1632), Villiers connections of her stepfather, and Digby's younger brother Sir John Digby, ambassador to Spain, the Digbys continued to press their case through the minority of Gerald Fitzgerald, fifteenth earl of Kildare (1611–1620). The cost of the dispute meant that, when Sir Robert died on 24 May 1618, he left his estate, and Dame Lettice as his executor, in financial difficulties, but on 11 July 1619 James I awarded her and her heirs the manor and parsonage of Geashill, comprising considerable lands near Philipstown in King's county. Although the king dismissed her claim to be heir general of her grandfather, on 26 June 1620 he confirmed her as Baroness Offaly for life, stipulating that the barony was then to revert to the earls of Kildare. The baroness's eldest son, Robert Digby, was in compensation created on 29 July Baron Digby of Geashill.

Anticipating by several months the final formal transfer of Geashill into her hands, Lady Offaly took up residence at Geashill Castle and lost no time in placing an English clergyman, John Meall, in the local living. She regarded the estates as traditionally a nest of rebels, and energetically collaborated in setting up English plantations with successive guardians of the sixteenth earl of Kildare. From 1629 this was Richard Boyle, first earl of Cork, whose daughter Sarah had married Robert Digby in 1626. Following Sarah's death in 1633 her children lived with Lady Offaly at Geashill, provided for by their grandfather Cork. The plantations came in for fierce local resistance, and in 1642 Lady Offaly was closely besieged. She resisted with spirit, though the rebels sent four messages to remind her that the castle was garrisoned only by women and boys. In reply to their first summons to surrender she avowed her loyalty to the king, proclaiming 'I will live and die innocently and will do my best to defend my own, leaving the issue to God' (GEC, *Peerage*, 10.19*n*). The besiegers' guns burst upon themselves, and she was at last rescued, in October that year, by Sir Richard Grenville. She then retired to Coleshill, in which her husband had left her a life interest and where she died on 1 December 1658, and was buried with her husband. A portrait of her at Sherborne Castle represents her with a book inscribed Job 19:20 ('I am escaped with the skin of my teeth').

SEAN KELSEY

Sources *CSP Ire., 1615–25*, 587 • J. Lodge, *The peerage of Ireland*, rev. M. Archdall, rev. edn, 6 (1789), 280–83 • GEC, *Peerage*, 7.239; 10.18–19 • V. Treadwell, *Buckingham and Ireland, 1616–1628: a study in Anglo-Irish politics* (1998) • A. Hughes, *Politics, society and civil war in Warwickshire, 1620–1660* (1987) • L. Digby, *My ancestors. Being the history of the Digby and Strutt families* (1928) • PRO, PROB 11/131, sig. 65 [will of Sir Robert Digby, 1618]
Archives PRO, corresp., transcripts II, 198, pp. 233, 241, etc.
Likenesses oils, Sherborne Old Castle, Dorset

Digby, Mabel Mary Josephine (1835–1911), Roman Catholic nun, was born at Ashford House, Staines, Middlesex, on 7 April 1835, the fourth of the six children of Simon Digby (*d.* 1858) and Elizabeth Anne Morse (*d.* 1890), heir of Baron Haversham. When Mabel Digby was five the family moved to Aranhill House, Bath, where she was educated under the supervision of her mother. Digby was, however, a much keener hunter than scholar, an enthusiasm she shared with her adored father. On account of her mother's health a further move was made to France in 1849. In September 1852 both her mother and her sister Geraldine were received into the Roman Catholic church. This caused a rift in the family: Mabel Digby at once avowed her intent of remaining a protestant and returned to England with her equally staunch father. The following winter her health broke down and she rejoined her mother at Montpellier. On 17 February 1853 Mabel Digby was coaxed into the church of Notre-Dame des Tables by some Catholic friends on the pretext of attending a concert of sacred music. The performance concluded with benediction of the blessed sacrament, during which she underwent a profound spiritual experience which led to her reception into the Roman church a month later, when she took the additional names Mary Josephine.

At Marmoutier-lès-Tours, where her younger sister Eva was at school, Mabel Digby became acquainted with the sisters of the Sacred Heart. Her application to enter the society was initially rejected by the assistant-general. After the personal intervention of the founder Madeleine-Sophie Barat, who recognized Digby's qualities of leadership, she was accepted and received the habit at the noviceship of Conflans-Saint-Honorine on 20 March 1857. A year later she returned to teach at Marmoutier, becoming superior of the house in 1865. Her term of office saw the terrible floods of 1866, and the Franco-Prussian War and occupation of 1870–71. During this time the convent became a hospital, and Mother Digby herself assisted the surgeons. In August 1872 she was appointed vicaress of the English house at Roehampton. Within the year she had established a teachers' training college at Wandsworth, with further houses following at Hove, Carlisle, and Hammersmith. The new English vicariate also made foundations in Dublin, Sydney, and Melbourne.

During the thirteenth General Congregation of the society in August 1894 Mother Digby was elected assistant-general of the Society of Sacred Heart. Within a year, upon the sudden death of Mother von Satorius, she was elected to succeed her as superior-general of the society. Mother Digby's generalate was a period of enormous difficulty but great hope. It saw the celebration of the centennial of the society in 1900 and the beatification of the founder in 1908, both of which served as focal points for the renewal of its spirit and vigour. Soon after her election Mother Digby began the visitation of the houses in Europe and north Africa, and in 1898–9 those of Mexico, the United States, and Canada.

On the other hand, in France, the anti-association legislation of the Combes government in 1903 effectively closed all religious teaching establishments in the country. Beginning with Moulins in March 1903 and ending with Conflans in 1909, forty-seven Sacred Heart houses were closed, their furnishings disposed of, and more than 2000 religious sent to existing and newly established houses across the globe. The general administration moved to Ixelles, near Brussels. Mother Digby conducted the business of the society under such difficult conditions with diplomacy and efficiency, displaying great clarity of mind and strength of will. However, some in the society considered her style of government too independent: complaints were made to the cardinal protector in Rome, and Archbishop Richard of Paris was sent as apostolic delegate to the fifteenth General Congregation which met in 1904. Nevertheless, despite her outward reserve Digby had gained the affection of many of her sisters in religion; she possessed a quick wit and the ability to express herself in a powerfully succinct manner. Richard expressed his satisfaction with both the government of the society and its general direction.

In 1895 Mother Digby had suffered a severe heart attack. The heavy administrative burdens arising from the situation in France further undermined her health. On 15 May 1911 she suffered a stroke and died on the 21st at the Convent of the Sacred Heart, Ixelles. Because the society possessed no cemetery in Belgium the decision was made to take Digby's body to Roehampton, where she was buried after a requiem mass celebrated on 26 May.

ANSELM NYE

Sources A. Pollen, *Mother Mabel Digby* (1914) • M. H. Quinlan, *Mabel Digby, Janet Erskine Stuart: superiors general of the Society of the Sacred Heart, 1895–1914*, rev. edn (1984) • M. Williams, *The Society of the Sacred Heart: history of a spirit, 1800–1975* (1978) • M. K. Richardson, *Mabel Digby* (1956)
Archives Casa Generalizia, Via Adolfo Gandiglio 27, Rome, Italy, general archives of the Society of the Sacred Heart • Convent of the Sacred Heart, Roehampton Lane, London, provincial archives of the Society of the Sacred Heart

Digby, Robert (1732–1814), naval officer, was born on 20 December 1732, the son of Edward Digby (*c.*1693–1746), MP for Warwickshire, and Charlotte, daughter of Sir Stephen Fox and sister of Stephen, first earl of Ilchester, and Henry, first Baron Holland. Robert's grandfather was William *Digby, fifth Baron Digby of Geashill, and his elder brother was Henry, first Earl Digby. Robert Digby first went to sea in 1744 in the *Edinburgh* (74 guns), and was promoted lieutenant in October 1752. On 5 August 1755 he was promoted captain of the frigate *Solebay* and in the following year he was advanced to command the *Dunkirk* (60 guns), in which he continued until the peace, serving for the most part on the home station, and being present in the abortive expedition against Rochefort in 1757. In 1758 he took part in the successful attack by Commodore Augustus Keppel on Goree and in 1759 in Sir Edward Hawke's victory in Quiberon Bay. In 1760 he was ordered to join the Mediterranean Fleet and served under Captain Hugh Palliser in the pursuit of the Toulon fleet. Following the peace of Paris in 1762 he retired from active service, though he was appointed colonel of marines on 4 April 1775.

In 1778, with the outbreak of war, Digby was appointed to the *Ramillies* (74 guns), which he commanded in the indecisive battle of Ushant (27 July 1778) under the immediate command of his friend Palliser (now an admiral). This led to his being summoned by Palliser as a witness for the prosecution at Keppel's court martial. However, Digby's evidence tended distinctly to Keppel's advantage, as indicated in Edmund Burke's letter to Frances Pelham of 12 January 1779 (*The Correspondence of Edmund Burke*, vol. 4, 1778–82, ed. J. A. Woods, 1963, 37).

Upon promotion to rear-admiral of the blue (19 March 1779), Digby was ordered at once to hoist his flag on the *Prince George*, so that he might—as was affirmed by the opposition—sit on Palliser's court martial. During the summer of 1779 he was second in command of the Channel Fleet under Sir Charles Hardy, and in December he was second in command of the fleet which sailed under Sir George Rodney for the relief of Gibraltar. It was at this time that he was first appointed the governor of Prince William Henry, who began his naval career on the *Prince George*. Digby had previously received warm praise from George III, who in November 1778 described him as 'a most excellent officer, sensible, prudent, and discreet' (*Correspondence*, ed. Fortescue, 4.225). When, after relieving Gibraltar, Rodney, with one division of the fleet, went on to the West Indies, Digby, with the other, returned to England, having the good fortune on the way to disperse a French convoy laden with military stores for the Île de France. Three merchant ships and the *Prothée* (64 guns) were captured. After being advanced to rear-admiral of the red he continued as second in command of the Channel Fleet during the summers of 1780 and 1781, and in the second relief of Gibraltar by Vice-Admiral George Darby. In August 1781 Digby was sent as commander-in-chief to North America. He arrived just as his predecessor, Thomas, Lord Graves, was preparing to sail for the Chesapeake in hopes, in a second attempt, of effecting the relief of Cornwallis; and, courteously refusing to take on himself the command at this critical juncture, Digby remained at New York while Graves sailed on his vain errand. Afterwards, when he had assumed the command, he removed into the *Lion*, a smaller ship, in order to allow the *Prince George*, as well as most of his other ships, to accompany Sir Samuel Hood to the West Indies. The tide of the war rolled away from North America, and in any case Digby had no force to undertake any active operations. His command was therefore uneventful, and he returned home at the peace in 1783. He held no further appointment, though duly promoted vice-admiral four years later and admiral in 1794, and living to see the end of the French Revolutionary Wars.

Digby married in 1784 Mrs Jauncy, the daughter of Andrew Elliot, brother of Sir Gilbert Elliot, third baronet, and Admiral John Elliot. Digby died on 25 February 1814; his wife died on 28 July 1830, leaving no children.

J. K. LAUGHTON, *rev.* NICHOLAS TRACY

Sources *Naval Chronicle*, 2 (1804), 98 · letters from North American squadron, PRO, ADM 1/490 · J. Charnock, ed., *Biographia navalis*, 6 (1798), 119 · J. Ralfe, *The naval biography of Great Britain*, 4 vols. (1828), 1.189 · R. Bentson, *Naval and military memoirs of Great Britain*, 6 vols. (1804) · S. Matthews, 'Digby, Edward', HoP, *Commons, 1715–54*, 1.612 · GEC, *Peerage* · *The correspondence of King George the Third from 1760 to December 1783*, ed. J. Fortescue, 6 vols. (1927–8)
Archives PRO, corresp., PRO 30/55 | NMM, letters to Lord Sandwich · Staffs. RO, letters to Lord Dartmouth
Likenesses J. Chapman, stipple, pubd 1802, NPG

Digby [née Stanley], **Venetia, Lady Digby** (1600–1633), gentlewoman and celebrated beauty, was born on 19 December 1600 at Tong Castle, Shropshire, the daughter of Sir Edward Stanley (*d.* 1629?), from a younger branch of the family of the earls of Derby, and his wife, Lady Lucy Percy (*b.* before 1572, *d.* 1601?), daughter and coheir of Thomas *Percy, seventh earl of Northumberland (1528–1572). Venetia's mother died a few months after her birth and she was brought up in the Roman Catholic faith of her family by Francis and Grace Fortescue, of Salden, Buckinghamshire. At nearby Gayhurst lived another Catholic family, the Digbys, and Sir Kenelm *Digby (1603–1665) later recorded in his *Loose Fantasies*, that he and Venetia were childhood friends and sweethearts, despite the fact that he was two and a half years younger.

Growing up to be a very beautiful young woman, Venetia was presented at the court of James I, where she was pursued by many aristocratic admirers, among them Edward Sackville, later fourth earl of Dorset. According to contemporary gossip recounted in Aubrey's *Brief Lives*, Venetia had affairs with several young men, including Sir Edmund Wyld and the earl of Dorset; the latter allegedly had 'one if not more children by her' (*Brief Lives*, 260). There is no evidence to support these allegations, however, and the rumours of Venetia's promiscuity as a young unmarried woman were hotly denied by Sir Kenelm in his memoirs and letters. After a period of separation during which Digby was abroad the couple were married about May or June 1624 (though some sources suggest January 1625). As Sir Kenelm later explained to his sons, the marriage was kept secret for years, mainly because of strong disapproval of the match by both Sir Kenelm's mother and Venetia's father, from whom Venetia was hoping for a financial settlement. While Sir Kenelm was away at sea, on 6 October 1625, Venetia had her first child, Kenelm, in secret, with no help except that of a single servant. In all she had five more pregnancies: she had a son, Everard, who died as an infant, two more sons, John and George, and twins whom she lost in a miscarriage. All her labours were 'exceeding painefull and dangerous', as her husband recalled, but she suffered with stoic patience, with her husband at her side holding her hand, which she said 'did abate a great part of her paines' (Digby, *Letter-Book*, 126).

All contemporary sources agree that Venetia was the perfect companion to Sir Kenelm: a loyal, chaste, and obedient wife, a loving and careful mother, a frugal and efficient housewife, and a fervent Roman Catholic like her husband. She gave large sums to the poor, earning the money through gambling, in which pursuit she was both skilful and lucky. Toward the end of her short life she became increasingly pious, mortifying herself with fasts, penances, and the wearing of a hair shirt, partly because of her premonition that she would die young like her mother. In the event her premonition was fulfilled: she died suddenly in her sleep on 1 May 1633 at the Digby London residence at Charterhouse Yard, and was buried three days later. An autopsy performed by several eminent physicians found that her brain tissue was 'much putrifyed and corrupted: all the cerebellum was rotten, and retained not the forme of the braine but was meere pus and corrupted matter' (Digby, *Letter-Book*, 134).

Venetia Digby was painted by Anthony Van Dyck both in her lifetime (as the allegorical figure Prudence) and on her deathbed. Sir Kenelm also had a death mask made. A number of contemporary poets including Ben Jonson dedicated elegies to her memory (a manuscript volume of elegies is now Add. MS 30259 in the British Library). Although Venetia herself composed devotional meditations and other works, none of her own writings has survived. Virtually all the information on her life and death comes from Sir Kenelm's autobiographical romance, *Loose Fantasies*, and his memorial letters to his sons and other relations written after Venetia's death. SARA H. MENDELSON

Sources K. Digby, *Loose fantasies*, ed. V. Gabrieli (Rome, 1968) · K. Digby, *A new Digby letter-book 'In praise of Venetia'*, ed. V. Gabrieli (1955) [off-printed from *The National Library of Wales Journal*, vols. 9 and 10] · A. Sumner, ed., *Death, passion and politics: Van Dyck's portraits of Venetia Stanley and George Digby* (1995) [exhibition catalogue, Dulwich Picture Gallery, London] · H. A. Bright, *Poems from Sir Kenelm Digby's papers in the possession of Henry A. Bright*, Roxburghe Club (1877) · J. R. [Joseph Rutter], *The shepheards holy-day: a pastorall tragicomaedie. Acted before both their majesties at White-Hall, by the queenes servants. With an elegie on the death of the most noble lady, the Lady Venetia Digby* (1635) · elegies on Venetia Digby's death, BL, Add. MS 30259 · *Aubrey's Brief lives*, ed. O. L. Dick (1949); repr. (1972), 259–61 · A. Sumner, 'Venetia Digby on her deathbed', *History Today*, 5/45 (Oct 1995), 20–25 · E. W. Bligh, *Sir Kenelm Digby and his Venetia* (1932) · R. T. Petersson, *Sir Kenelm Digby* (1956) · R. C. Evans, 'Jonson, Weston, and the Digbys: patronage relations in some later poems', *Renaissance and Reformation*, 16/1 (1992), 5–37

Likenesses double portrait, miniature, 1632 (with husband; after A. Van Dyck), Sherborne Old Castle, Dorset · group portrait, oils, 1632 (after A. Van Dyck), Sherborne Old Castle, Dorset · A. Van Dyck, oils, 1633, Dulwich Picture Gallery, London · A. Van Dyck, oils, *c*.1633, Palazzo Reale, Milan; version, Royal Collection · A. Van Dyck, oils, *c*.1633–1634, NPG · J. Basire, line engraving, BM, NPG; repro. in Pennant, *Tour from Chester to London* (1786) · P. Oliver, miniature, Burghley House, Northamptonshire

Digby, William, fifth Baron Digby of Geashill (*bap.* 1661/2, *d.* 1752), politician and philanthropist, was baptized on 20 February 1661 or 1662 at Coleshill, Warwickshire, the third (and perhaps the posthumous) son of Kildare Digby, second Baron Digby of Geashill (*c*.1631–1661), governor of King's county, Ireland, and his wife, Mary (*d.* 1692), the daughter of Robert Gardiner of London. He was educated privately before entering Winchester College in 1677. He matriculated at Magdalen College, Oxford, on 16 May 1679, graduated BA on 5 July 1681, and then travelled on the continent. Following the deaths of his elder brothers, Robert, third baron, and Simon, fourth baron, he succeeded to the peerage, an Irish barony, on 19 January 1686, as well as substantial estates in Warwickshire and King's county. On 22 May 1686 a licence was issued for his marriage to Lady Jane Noel (1666/7–1733), the second daughter of Edward, first earl of Gainsborough. The couple had four sons and eight daughters.

Appointed deputy lieutenant of Warwickshire by James II, Digby sat in the Convention Parliament for Warwick, and was re-elected to the Commons in 1689, 1690, and 1695. He was a follower of John Kettlewell, vicar of Coleshill from 1682 until he was deprived as a nonjuror in 1690. A sincere and devout believer in passive obedience, Digby voted against making William and Mary king and queen, but none the less sat on the committees which drafted the coronation oath and the oaths of allegiance and supremacy in 1689. His concern for the doctrinal integrity of the Church of England led him to sympathize with the nonjurors. While he remained in communion with the established church he financially supported nonjuring clergymen, including Kettlewell, and Coleshill itself became a renowned retreat for nonjurors. In the Commons, Digby spoke against the Abjuration Bill of 1690, arguing that it would make enemies of those who could live under the government of William III while in principle acknowledging the rights of James II. The support of Digby and others like him was important to the broadly based ministries of the early part of William III's reign, but they were marginalized as the reign progressed. Digby was an active legislator during this period, and was involved in drafting the Game Bill of 1693 and redrafting the Place Bill of 1694. In December 1694 and January 1695 he managed the bill for the rebuilding of Warwick, which had been devastated by fire, through the Commons, and served on the commission which oversaw the reconstruction of the town. In February 1696 he was one of the most prominent non-signatories of the Association, as he and other tory members could not permanently renounce the possibility of the restoration of James II or his heirs, and in November he opposed the attainder of Sir John Fenwick.

Digby retired from parliament in 1698, as he disagreed with the direction the revolution settlement had taken and could no longer sit in the parliament of a king he could not wholeheartedly affirm. His stance probably offended the borough patron at Warwick, Fulke Greville, fifth Baron Brooke of Beauchamps Court. However, that year Digby inherited the Sherborne estate in Dorset on the death of his kinsman John Digby, third earl of Bristol. This was a grander estate than Coleshill, including the mansion built for Sir Walter Ralegh. Although Digby's existing estates made him wealthier than Lord Bristol, Sherborne allowed him more scope for exercising the responsibilities of an independent country gentleman. He retained his political connections, principally through his friend Edward Nicholas, MP for Shaftesbury, and later through his sons John (*d.* 1717), Robert (*d.* 1726), and Edward (*d.* 1746), all of whom were at different times members of parliament. However, extra-parliamentary expression for his priorities became more important. He was a patron of Thomas Bray, supported the goals of the SPCK, and in 1701 was one of the founding members of the Society for the Propagation of the Gospel. In 1703 he resisted pressure to stand again for the Commons at Oxford University. At Sherborne, Digby showed his continued attachment to the Church of England by designing and building a new chapel and adding new features to the cathedral. He is said to have made regular visits to the Fleet prison to pay the debts of the inmates. His theological conservatism did not prevent him developing friendships with those of differing views, including the anti-trinitarian clergyman William Whiston, who hailed him as 'the best Christian Nobleman whom I ever knew, the good Lord Digby' (Erskine-Hill, 165), although in 1712 Digby had refused to support Whiston's plan for an anti-trinitarian society.

Digby demonstrated his attachment to the Stuarts by maintaining the ruins of old Sherborne Castle, destroyed by parliament during the civil war. He refused to take the oaths to George I in 1714, and it is possible that he was at least aware of the Atterbury plot to place James Stuart on the throne in 1721. Alexander Pope knew many of those connected to the scheme, but it was probably through Digby's niece Frances, Viscountess Scudamore, who lived in Twickenham, that Pope was introduced to the Digby family. Pope visited Digby at Sherborne in 1724. When composing the epitaph which appears on the monument at Sherborne to Digby's son Robert and daughter Mary (d. 1729), Pope wrote to Digby (8 September 1729) that 'your whole family is an example of what is almost now lost in this Nation, the Integrity of ancient Nobility' (*Correspondence of Alexander Pope*, 3.52). He had already expressed these sentiments to others and alluded to them in the *Essay on man* and *Epilogue to the Satires*.

Following the death of his wife, Jane, on 10 September 1733, Digby took over the school that she had founded in Sherborne, and in 1743 he endowed it with provision for a mistress and thirteen poor girls as scholars. This school was the basis for the Lord Digby's School, which survived in Sherborne past the end of the twentieth century. He also became a member of the common council of the society for the establishment of Georgia in 1733, and his third son, Edward, MP for Warwickshire, was the first chairman of the trustees.

Digby outlived most of his children; aside from those mentioned above, his second daughter, Elizabeth, who had married the clergyman Sir John *Dolben in 1720, died in 1730. His youngest son, Wriothesley, became a barrister and died in 1767. Digby himself died at Sherborne on 29 November 1752, leaving an estate of approximately £23,000 with a further £14,000 to clear debts and support his younger grandsons. He was succeeded by his grandson Edward (1730–1757), the son of the Georgia trustee, who may have confounded the expectations of his grandfather and Pope by compromising with the whig ascendancy and sitting in parliament as a follower of his maternal uncle Henry Fox.   MATTHEW KILBURN

Sources H. Erskine-Hill, *The social milieu of Alexander Pope: lives, example, and the poetic response* (1975) · A. M. Mimardière, 'Digby, William', HoP, *Commons, 1660–90* · A. A. Hanham, 'Digby, William', HoP, *Commons, 1690–1715* · Cobbett, *Parl. hist.*, 5.595, 1101 · *The correspondence of Alexander Pope*, ed. G. Sherburn, 2–3 (1956) · M. Mack, *Alexander Pope: a life* (1985) · J. H. P. Gibb, *The book of Sherborne* (1984) · A. Browning, *Thomas Osborne, earl of Danby and duke of Leeds, 1632–1712*, 3 (1951) · L. Digby, *My ancestors* (1928) · S. R. Matthews, 'Digby, Hon. Robert', HoP, *Commons, 1715–54* · S. R. Matthews, 'Digby, Hon. Edward', HoP, *Commons, 1715–54* · G. S. Holmes, *British politics in the age of Anne*, rev. edn (1987) · GEC, *Peerage*, new edn · R. March, *Sherborne Castle* (1979) · Foster, *Alum. Oxon.* · IGI
Archives priv. coll., corresp. with sons | Birm. CL, MSS · BL, Egmont MSS, corresp. with Edward Nicholas · Warks. CRO, letters to Sir John Mordaunt
Likenesses G. Kneller, oils, before 1686, Sherborne Old Castle, Dorset; repro. in Erskine-Hill, *Social milieu*, 185 · F. Hayman, group portrait, Sherborne Old Castle, Dorset · F. Hayman, group portrait, Sherborne Old Castle, Dorset · W. Wissing, portrait, Sherborne Old Castle, Dorset
Wealth at death approx. £37,000: Erskine-Hill, *Social milieu*, 185; will, PRO, PROB 11/799, sig. 9

Digby, William (1849–1904), journalist and social campaigner, the third son of William Digby and his wife, Ann Drake, was born on 1 May 1849 at Walsoken, Wisbech, Cambridgeshire. Mostly self-taught, Digby became an apprentice in the office of the *Isle of Ely and Wisbech Advertiser* at the age of fifteen in 1864. He subsequently became chief reporter of the *Sussex Advertiser*, before leaving England in 1871 for Colombo to take up the post of sub-editor of the *Ceylon Observer*. There he advocated temperance and successfully campaigned for the abolition of revenue farming. Digby also advocated free trade, publishing *The Food Taxes of Ceylon* (1875), and was made an honorary member of the Cobden Club in 1878. As official shorthand writer for the legislative council, he prepared six volumes of the Ceylon *Hansard* (1871–6). He also published *Forty Years of Official and Unofficial Life in a Crown Colony* (2 vols., 1879), a biography of Sir Richard F. Morgan, acting chief justice in Ceylon. In 1874 Digby married Ellen Amelia, only daughter of Captain Little of Wisbech; she died in June 1878. The couple had one son, William Pollard, who became an electrical engineer.

In 1877 Digby moved to India and assumed the editorship of the *Madras Times*. He used his influence to call for the alleviation of the great famine in south India. Largely owing to his representations a relief fund was opened at the Mansion House in London, and £820,000 was subscribed. Digby was active as honorary secretary in India of the executive committee, which distributed relief through 120 local committees. He was made CIE on 1 January 1878. His *Famine Campaign in Southern India* (2 vols., 1878) is a graphic portrayal of the hunger and distress suffered by the local population. On returning to England in 1879, Digby married, in December, Sarah Maria (d. 1899), eldest daughter of William Hutchinson, a former mayor of Wisbech. He edited the *Liverpool and Southport Daily News* for a few months in 1880 before becoming, until 1882, editor of the *Western Daily Mercury* at Plymouth. From November 1882 until 1887 he was secretary of the newly founded National Liberal Club in London. He stood unsuccessfully as a Liberal for North Paddington in 1885 and South Islington in 1892.

In 1887 Digby became senior partner of William Hutchinson & Co., East India agents and merchants, a firm he established in conjunction with his wife's family. Meanwhile he pursued in the press and on the platform the campaign for extending self-government to Indians. In 1885 he published *India for the Indians—and for England*, setting out his ideas chiefly on Indian reform. In 1888 he founded, and until 1892 also directed, an Indian political agency in London, which distributed information on behalf of Indian interest groups in Britain. Digby also became, in 1889, secretary to the newly constituted British committee of the Indian National Congress, and edited the committee's journal, *India* (1890–92). In *Prosperous British India* (1901) he attacked the economic consequences of the empire, claiming to prove a steady growth of poverty among the majority of Indians under British rule. Digby died from nervous exhaustion at 50 Weymouth Street, London, on 24 September 1904, and was buried at Bromley Hill cemetery by the side of his second wife; they had a daughter and three sons, the eldest of whom, Everard, became editor of the *Indian Daily News* in Calcutta.   F. H. BROWN, *rev.* CHANDRIKA KAUL

Sources E. C. Moulton, 'Digby, William', BDMBR, vol. 3, pt 1 · *The Times* (26 Sept 1904) · *Biographical Magazine* (July 1885) · *Isle of Ely and Wisbech Advertiser* (24 Sept 1904) · *Isle of Ely and Wisbech Advertiser* (27 Sept 1904) · *Isle of Ely and Wisbech Advertiser* (20 Dec 1905) · WWW · personal knowledge (1912) · m. cert.

Archives BL OIOC, corresp. and papers, MS Eur. D 767 | Bodl. Oxf., corresp. with Lord Kimberley
Likenesses J. C. Forbes, oils; presented 19 Dec 1905, National Liberal Club, London
Wealth at death £472 13s. 4d.: probate, 6 Oct 1904, CGPLA Eng. & Wales

Digges, Sir Dudley (1582/3–1639), politician and diplomat, was the elder surviving son of the mathematician Thomas *Digges (c.1546–1595) of Digges Court, Barham, Kent, and his wife, Anne or Agnes (d. in or after 1595), daughter of Sir Warham St Leger of Leeds Castle, Kent. The poet and translator Leonard *Digges (1588–1635) was his younger brother. Dudley's godfather was Robert *Dudley, earl of Leicester, under whom his father had served in the Netherlands. On 18 July 1600 Digges matriculated from University College, Oxford, aged seventeen. He graduated BA in 1601. In 1602 the master of his college, George Abbot (later archbishop of Canterbury), introduced Digges to Sir Robert Cecil, who may have provided him with his introduction to political life. In 1604 Digges published his father's tract on military discipline, entitled *Four Paradoxes*. In 1605 he married Mary (*bap*. 1590, *d*. 1631), daughter and coheir of Sir Thomas Kempe of Olantigh, near Wye, Kent. He then went on his first trip to the continent. After he returned he was knighted at Whitehall on 29 April 1607. In 1610 he was elected to parliament to represent the newly enfranchised borough of Tewkesbury, Gloucestershire. Following the death of his wife's father that year, Mary's three sisters conveyed their shares in Chilham Castle and manor (Kent) to her and Sir Dudley, who became possessed of the entire fee of it. Digges proceeded to demolish the ancient mansion and built a magnificent new house, finally taking up residence there about 1616.

In 1611 Digges contributed a few lines to the collection of 'panegyrick verses' which prefaced Thomas Coryats's *Coryats Crudities*. Much preoccupied with overseas trade, he was a shareholder in the Virginia Company and the East India Company. He also took a keen interest in the search for the much vaunted north-west passage. One of the founders of a company incorporated in 1612 for the purpose of trading by that route, he published an account of the ensuing exploration. In 1613 Digges was appointed to the high commission, a prerogative court with jurisdiction in church matters, and his appointment was renewed periodically thereafter. The following year he was candidate for the governorship of the East India Company. Also in 1614 he sat at Westminster for Tewkesbury again, taking an active role as a committee member and speaking out against papists and the impositions which he believed were responsible for putting English merchants out of business. His papers on the subject of impositions were requisitioned and burnt by order of the privy council at the dissolution of that assembly. It is said that he himself was even imprisoned for a short time. In 1615, in connection with investigations into the murder of Sir Thomas Overbury, Digges gave testimony which has been interpreted as having helped to incriminate the earl of Somerset. In the same year he published the treatise *The Defense of East India Trade*, an apology for the East India Company's monopoly.

In 1618 the tsar of Russia, who was then engaged in a war with Poland, approached James I for a loan. The king ordered the Muscovy and East India companies to furnish £20,000, and Digges was dispatched to convey the money to Moscow. Years later, Digges claimed that he had been honoured by appointment to the service of the king's bedchamber in respect of this diplomatic mission. He left England in April, and on reaching Russia he sent his secretary, Finch, to Moscow, with half of the cash and letters from the king. Refusing the terms of the loan, the tsar extorted the money from the hapless Finch, and Digges returned to England with the balance in October. An account of this journey, written by John Tradescant, who accompanied Digges in the capacity of naturalist, is preserved in manuscript in the Ashmolean Museum, Oxford. In 1620 Digges and the president of the East India Company, Maurice Abbot, brother of Archbishop George Abbot, went to the United Provinces to negotiate a settlement of the company's disputes with its Dutch counterpart, but returned unsuccessful.

In 1621 Digges was returned for a third time by the electors of Tewkesbury. He spoke against monopolists and Catholics, and was a keen advocate of war with Spain. Initially popular in the lower house for his stance during the stand-off with the king at the end of the first session, later, in the dispute regarding privilege, he was hesitant in supporting the Commons and as a result lost his reputation with his fellow MPs. Digges's quest for favour at court had become all the more urgent as his financial position deteriorated. The cost of rebuilding Chilham forced him to request the withdrawal of his stock from the East India Company, but he was turned down, despite the grant of royal warrants in support of his request. In 1622 he was appointed to the commission sent to Ireland to investigate the kingdom's financial straits, a development which has been described inaccurately as a punishment for his behaviour in parliament. The commission had been conceived by Lord Treasurer Cranfield as a weapon against the marquess of Buckingham, whose exploitation of Irish resources was notorious. But having marked Digges as a potential client, Buckingham secured his appointment as a counterweight to those commissioners who might seek to damage his interests. Digges certainly saw his posting as a 'probation for promotion' made honourable by his appointment as commission vice-president and Irish privy councillor (Treadwell, 189).

By the autumn of 1622 Digges was back in England, trailing the court to Royston and Newmarket in the hope of pressing the case for his preferment. But as far as his intended patron was concerned, Digges mishandled his responsibilities by making a preliminary report on the commission's work which led to a moratorium on grants of royal bounty in Ireland, and his hopes of catching a ride on Buckingham's bandwagon were disappointed. His only appointment was to attend a welcoming ceremony for the Spanish ambassador in June 1623, which can hardly have been to his taste, given his publicly stated views on relations with Spain. Naturally it was these views which eventually made him useful once the tide of foreign policy turned, and there are suggestions that Digges was courted by the duke of Buckingham and the prince of Wales prior to the parliamentary elections of 1624. Certainly his rival for one of the county seats in Kent, Sir Edwin Sandys, was able to triumph over him by portraying him as a courtier, while colleagues in the house appear to have regarded Digges, the member for Tewkesbury once more, as a would-be 'undertaker'.

But Digges, like many contemporaries, was always caught between his desire for a war with Spain and a reluctance to pay for it. When his hopes of reward once again came to nothing, his support for court policy began to wane. After the accession of Charles I he composed a long letter of advice to the new king in which he added his own voice to the calls for an 'advised council' which were increasingly becoming the staple of the anti-Buckingham opposition. In the parliament of 1625 he was hesitant in his defence of the duke. By 1626 he had apparently become positively 'disgusted at the failure of his attempt to become a Buckingham man' (Russell, 33). Henceforth he was a leader of the attack on the king's favourite.

Digges was not motivated solely by the frustration of his quest for preferment. He argued that the duke should be held to account for the detention of the French merchant vessel the *St Peter*, and for the deleterious consequences for English merchants trading in France. These concerns doubtless reflected the nature of his constituency among the merchants of the London exchange, and probably indicate that he co-operated with the French ambassador, who was vehement in his prosecution of the same business. Digges may even have been involved in co-ordinating the attack on Buckingham with supporters of the king's new French wife, Henrietta Maria. Sir James Bagg wrote to the duke that Digges, 'being privately more dangerous than publicly, is thought to be wholly my Lord of Canterbury's', also indicating the strength of Digges's continuing association with George Abbot (*CSP dom.*, addenda, 1625–49, 113).

Pressing for the foundation of a West Indies Company, Digges clearly also continued to hanker after a freebooting war with Spain in the Caribbean which would avoid burdening the country with direct taxation, clearly setting him at odds with Buckingham's preferred strategy. He got into trouble for his introduction and preamble to the charges of impeachment against the duke, in which he compared him to a comet which, having appeared suddenly amid a firmament of fixed stars, demanded closer examination. Following Digges's speech, Sir John Eliot compared the duke to Sejanus, and by implication likened the king to the tyrant Tiberius. On 11 May both men were thrown into prison. Amid uproar over the implications for parliamentary privilege, Digges's release was secured four days later, and he kissed hands with the king. But whatever the hopes for a reconciliation, the slight in parliament to the king's favourite was evidently not forgotten.

In September 1626 Digges's appointment to the commission for the collection of the privy seal loan in Kent was rescinded by the privy council. He appears to have lost his place on the county bench about the same time. Summoned before the board in December, apparently for insisting that he be allowed to pay the forced loan in London rather than at home in Kent, he spoke out of place and was imprisoned for sharp words against Lord Tufton, and for showing disrespect to the council. He spent two months in gaol. Relations apparently improved by the time of his appointment to the Kent recusancy commission in November 1627, increasing the likelihood that, for fear of any further punishment, Digges had eventually complied with the demands that he offer the king a loan.

In 1628 Digges won the parliamentary seat to represent his home county. He was appointed chair of the committee of trade and consequently was in a position to forward legislation supporting the chartered companies, particularly the East India Company. He also sat on committees for drafting the petition of right and gave the introduction, subsequently printed, at the first major conference with the Lords on 7 April. In the first session of this parliament Digges spoke more than ninety times; in the second he addressed the matter of tonnage and poundage, called for an inquiry regarding the increase of Catholics in England, and vigorously supported parliamentary privilege for John Rolle, a merchant whose goods had been seized on his refusal to pay tonnage and poundage. He also spoke up against the burdens which military preparations were placing on his county. It has been said that he strongly disapproved of the violent scenes which preceded the dissolution of 1629. In 1630 hard cash finally obtained that which fortune had denied him hitherto when he obtained the reversion of the office of master of the rolls for a down payment of £5000 and the promise of the same amount at the death of Sir Julius Caesar, the incumbent. Having obtained honorific admission to Gray's Inn by right of the house's lord of misrule, the prince of Purpoole, in 1618, Digges now had himself readmitted and was called to the bench with full voting rights five days later. He served as master of chancery from 1631 to 1637. In 1636 he assumed the mastership of the rolls. The judge Sir Richard Hutton wrote that Digges was 'an able and sufficient man of great understanding, very affable and courteous and gives good orders' (*Diary of Sir Richard Hutton*, 107).

Digges retained his interest in the trading companies until the end of his life. In 1631 he was named as a commissioner for advancing the Virginia plantation, and in 1637 he was called upon to advise regarding the formation of a new company for the West Indies. He died on 18 March 1639 and was buried in the family mausoleum at Chilham, which he began constructing in 1620. In his will he charged his estate near Faversham, where he had much increased his water courts, with an annuity of £20 to provide prizes for a foot-race, open to competitors of both sexes, to be run in the neighbourhood every 19 May. The annual competition was kept up until the end of the eighteenth century. Digges was survived by four sons. The eldest, Thomas, married a daughter of Sir Maurice Abbot and had one son, Maurice, who was created a baronet on 6 March 1666, but died childless. His third son, Dudley *Digges (1613–1643), achieved some distinction as a royalist pamphleteer, publishing The Unlawfulnesse of Subjects Taking up Armes against their Soveraigne in what Case soever in 1643, the year of his death of camp fever at Oxford. Digges also had three daughters, of whom one, Anne, married William Hammond of St Alban's Court, near Canterbury, and was an ancestor of James *Hammond, the elegiac poet. A memorial in the Chilham mausoleum records the eventual success of Digges's judicial career, but draws a veil over his earlier days as a parliamentarian. In 1643 the Long Parliament ordered publication of his speech at the opening of the prosecution of the duke of Buckingham. In 1655 a tract was published entitled The Compleat Ambassador, compiled from Digges's copies of the correspondence of Queen Elizabeth with Leicester, Burghley, Walsingham, and Sir Thomas Smith regarding the negotiations for a treaty of alliance with France.

SEAN KELSEY

Sources DNB · J. M. Lipscomb, 'The Chilham mausolea', Archaeologia Cantiana, 102 (1985), 135–47 · W. R. Prest, The inns of court under Elizabeth I and the early Stuarts (1972) · C. Russell, Parliament and English politics, 1621–1629 (1979) · R. P. Cust, The forced loan and English politics, 1626–1628 (1987) · V. Treadwell, Buckingham and Ireland, 1616–1628: a study in Anglo-Irish politics (1998) · The diary of Sir Richard Hutton, 1614–1639, ed. W. R. Prest, SeldS, suppl. ser., 9 (1991)
Archives Northants. RO, speech to the Lords | BL, Harley MSS, parliamentary speeches and papers
Likenesses C. Johnson, oils, 1636, Gray's Inn, London · H. R. Cook, stipple, pubd 1810 (after J. Harding), BM, NPG · C. Turner, mezzotint, pubd 1813 (after C. Johnson), NPG

Digges, Dudley (1613–1643), royalist political writer, was born in Chilham, Kent, the third son of Sir Dudley *Digges (1582/3–1639), diplomat and judge, and Mary, daughter of Sir Thomas Kempe of Olantigh, Kent, and a grandson of Thomas *Digges, mathematician. He entered University College, Oxford, in 1629, proceeding BA on 17 January 1632 and MA on 15 October 1635. He was elected fellow of All Souls College in 1632, and in 1637 was incorporated into the University of Cambridge. In 1641 he was entered at Gray's Inn, but before September 1642 was back in Oxford, as one of the delegacy appointed to provide means for defending the town against parliament during the civil war. Digges contributed loyal poems to collections published by the university, including Musarum Oxoniensium and Solis Britannici perigaeum coronæ Carolinæ, both in 1633, and Flos Britannicis versis novissimi filiola Carolæ et Mariæ, in 1637. A poem by him on the great frost of 1634 also survives in the Bodleian Library. In the same year Digges published an edition of his grandfather's mathematical work Nova corpora regularia, but he is remembered as a royalist pamphleteer and political philosopher.

In July 1642 Henry Parker, secretary to the parliamentary army, argued in an anonymous pamphlet that the parliament had a 'special function of "umpirage" between king and kingdom in rare cases of conflict' (Burgess, 204). Digges replied with An Answer to a Printed Book, Intituled, Observations upon some of His Majesties Late Answers and Expresses, printed at Oxford in November 1642, by his

majesty's command. It was one of several royalist responses to Parker, but is regarded as the most detailed and persuasive. Two counterfeit editions of this work were printed in London, one in 1642, and another in 1647. A Reply to the 'Answer' … by 'J. M.' (previously ascribed to John Milton by the first edition of Wing's Short-Title Catalogue) was also published in November 1642. An Appendix to the Late 'Answer' followed, but this was both written and printed in a different style from the original, and Falconer Madan questioned whether it was the work of Digges or published in Oxford (Madan, 2.181). Madan also contradicts the otherwise widely accepted attribution to Digges of yet another answer to Parker's Observations entitled A Review of the 'Observations' upon some of His Majesties Late Answers. This 'ponderous' work was issued in April 1643, and Digges is named as the author in Philip Bliss's edition of Wood's Athenae Oxonienses, in the Dictionary of National Biography, and in the British Museum Catalogue of the Thomason Tracts. Madan suspected this may have been due to confusion with An Answer to a Printed Book by a previous owner of a copy of A Review, and regarded the attribution as 'unlikely' (ibid., 2.249–50).

Digges's most substantial work, and his contribution to contemporary political philosophy, was The Unlawfulnesse of Subjects Taking up Armes against their Soveraigne, which appeared in late 1643, after his death. This was a detailed and closely reasoned debate over the respective authorities of the king and parliament, described as 'a sort of compendium of royalist argumentation' (Allen, 494). It is based mainly on natural rights arguments, and 'closer to Hobbesian than to James I and Filmer's school of royalist thought' (Burns, 670–71). Digges argued that people were originally in a condition of complete liberty, but that it was rational for them to covenant to establish a civil sovereign. The renunciation of original rights was irreversible, and to suggest their continuance in civil society was subversive. He did not argue for absolute royal authority, but 'the right of the monarchy not to be accomptable to any inferior jurisdiction' (Burgess, 210). This work enjoyed continuing popularity among royalists and was reprinted in London in 1644, and on three occasions after the Restoration (in 1662, 1664, and 1679).

Digges died at Oxford from a malignant camp fever (presumably typhus) on 1 October 1643 and was buried in the antechapel of All Souls. He left over 1000 volumes to the college. Anthony Wood described him as 'advantaged by a great memory, and excellent natural parts, which he improved by close studying, he became a general scholar and a good poet and linguist' (Biographia Britannica, 3.1717–18).

DAVID STOKER

Sources F. Madan, Oxford books: a bibliography of printed works, 3 vols. (1895–1931); repr. (1964) · Wood, Ath. Oxon., new edn, 3.63–4 · J. H. Burns, ed., The Cambridge history of political thought, 1450–1700 (1991) · J. Allen, English political thought, 1603–1660 (1938) · G. Burgess, 'Repacifying the polity: the responses of Hobbes and Harrington to the "crisis of the common law"', Soldiers, writers and statesmen of the English revolution, ed. I. Gentles and others (1998), 202–28 · Biographia Britannica, or, The lives of the most eminent persons who have flourished in Great Britain and Ireland, 3 (1750), 1717–18 · G. K. Fortescue and others, eds., Catalogue of the pamphlets, books, newspapers, *and manuscripts relating to the civil war, the Commonwealth, and Restoration, collected by George Thomason, 1640–1661*, 2 vols. (1908) • *ESTC* • R. Tuck, *Natural rights theories: their origin and development* (1979) • A. Wood, *The history and antiquities of the University of Oxford*, ed. J. Gutch, 2 vols. in 3 pts (1792–6) • J. Foster, *The register of admissions to Gray's Inn, 1521–1889, together with the register of marriages in Gray's Inn chapel, 1695–1754* (privately printed, London, 1889), 230 • *Hist. U. Oxf. 4: 17th-cent. Oxf.*

Digges, Leonard (*c*.1515–*c*.1559), mathematician, was the son of James Digges (*d*. 1535), of Digges Court, Barham, Kent, and his second wife, Phillippa, daughter of John Engham of Chart, Kent. Little is known of Digges's upbringing, though he appears to have been educated at Oxford. A letter written by his father in 1531 refers to the maintenance of his son at Oxford and his grandchildren at school. The grandchildren are presumably the children of Digges's elder brother John, son of James Digges's first marriage, so Digges must therefore be the student, though no university evidence survives to prove the point. This letter of 1531 is also the best evidence from which his year of birth can be inferred. His subsequent education is known more securely: he entered Lincoln's Inn in 1537.

The Digges family was substantial and long established, with a record of holding county office, but Digges held no major office. He was named as one of those charged with defending the Kent coast from Dover to Folkestone in 1545 and was also listed as a supporter of Sir Thomas Wyatt the younger's 1549 scheme for a militia. He took part in Wyatt's revolt against the marriage of Queen Mary in January 1554 and, after its failure, was charged with high treason and sentenced to death. He was pardoned on 1 April 1554 but his lands and goods, which had been seized after his attainder, continued to be held subject to payment of recognizances to the crown. Digges's major fine of 400 marks was imposed in February 1555 and paid off in instalments, being finally discharged on 7 May 1558. Digges married Bridget, daughter of Thomas Wilford of Hartridge, Kent, and they had at least three sons and four daughters, of whom the best known is his eldest son, Thomas *Digges (*d*. 1595), who edited and republished several of his father's mathematical works. Leonard Digges was left the manor of Brome, Kent, by his father but sold this and established himself near by at Wootton in 1546 or 1547. The record of lands seized by the crown in 1554 reveals the extent of his landholdings in Kent.

Digges was an important member of the first generation of English mathematical authors to publish in the vernacular. Only two of his works were printed during his lifetime, a popular almanac and a short treatise on mensuration, both of which appeared in the 1550s. However, his interest in practical mathematics had been established much earlier. In 1542 he and three other gentlemen visited the English castle of Guînes near Calais where they impressed their host through debate and demonstration of their skills in geometry, navigation, measurement, and artillery.

The earliest surviving edition of Digges's almanac is *A Prognostication of Right Good Effect, Fructfully Augmented*. This was published in 1555 and dedicated to Sir Edward Fiennes, Lord Clinton and Saye, who was thanked for his help in preserving Digges during his 'troubles', evidently a reference to the consequences of Digges's participation in the Wyatt uprising. Digges described the 1555 text as a revision and expansion of a now lost earlier version, referred to as his 'general prognostication', printed in 1553. After 1555 there were at least thirteen subsequent editions into the early seventeenth century, usually under the title *A Prognostication Euerlasting*. From 1576, the work became the vehicle for an addition by his son Thomas, which included a presentation of Copernicus's heliocentric world system.

Digges's almanac deliberately departed from the usual form of such texts, which were typically printed for a single year and required annual renewal. The material he included was intended to be more generally valid; surviving fragments of a single sheet almanac for Kent dated 1556 show that he also contributed to the more standard genre. The *Prognostication* has calendrical tables and explanations of meteorological phenomena, with basic astrological information and rules for predicting the weather as well as times for planting, grafting, and bloodletting. Digges discussed the use of instruments such as the quadrant and square for time-telling, and provided tide tables for mariners. To satisfy readers who doubted the possibility of the astronomical statements in his early editions he included diagrams of the geocentric world system and of the relative sizes of the planets. This collection of miscellaneous material was prefaced by an apology for astronomy and the mathematical sciences, citing Melanchthon and Guido Bonatus to defend these against charges of impiety and vanity. Digges here recommended the mathematical sciences for their pleasure as well as their utility: 'the ingenious learned and well experienced circumspect student mathematical receiveth daily in his witty practices more pleasant joy of mind than all thy goods (how rich soever thou be) can at any time purchase' (*Prognostication*, 1555, sig. [*iiij]r*).

Digges's *Tectonicon* appeared in 1556, advertised on its title-page as a book for surveyors, 'landmeters', joiners, carpenters, and masons. It taught the measurement of land, the calculation of quantities, and the use of various instruments such as the carpenter's rule, the square, and a version of the cross-staff ('the profitable staff'). Digges was at pains to correct common errors practised by those without an adequate grounding in mathematics; this theme of 'vulgar errors' became standard in many subsequent mathematical texts. The success of *Tectonicon* is evident from its subsequent history: at least twenty editions were printed, the last in 1692. The work also marks the public début of the commercial trade in mathematical ('scientific') instruments in England: the text's publisher, the Flemish immigrant Thomas Gemini, used the title-page to advertise the availability of the instruments described in the volume.

In the *Prognostication* and *Tectonicon*, Digges promised several other volumes: a larger work on the use of the square to expand on the brief treatment in *Tectonicon*, a treatise on the construction of the letters of the alphabet, a volume devoted to astrology, and a more substantial text on practical mathematics. Only the latter appeared, in the form of *Pantometria*, published posthumously by his son Thomas in 1571, with a second edition in 1591. The three books of *Pantometria* covered the measurement of length, area, and volume and show Digges's familiarity with the latest continental sources. The work extended and complemented *Tectonicon* through its focus on surveying, and offered accounts of new and important devices such as the 'topographical instrument', the first appearance in England of the altazimuth theodolite. Thomas Digges added a work of his own on geometrical solids to the volume but his role in *Pantometria* was limited to revising the text for the press. He dedicated the work to Sir Nicholas Bacon, doing so in fulfilment of the wishes of his father, who had both discussed mathematics with Bacon and planned to present him with this particular treatise.

Leonard Digges also wrote on arithmetic, and some surviving papers became the basis for the first book of Thomas Digges's *Stratioticos* of 1579, a work on military mathematics whose second edition appeared in 1590. Other investigations by Digges senior never reached print. On the basis of comments by his son, occasional claims have been made that Digges devised a reflecting telescope; there is no evidence that his reported optical experimentation led to a working instrument for astronomical observation, but it seems likely that he did indeed use a rather unwieldy lens–mirror combination for terrestrial viewing. He was interested in the closely related topic of burning mirrors and in the seventeenth century he was also credited with skill in fortification and architecture.

Digges's other major research was on artillery and ballistics. The most important text in this area was Niccolò Tartaglia's *Nova scientia* of 1537, which had inaugurated the mathematical study of ballistics. Although his published works of the 1550s were elementary and popular, Digges's artillery investigations were pursued as a self-conscious combination of theory and practice. After a programme of mathematical work and experimental trials, Digges concluded that a number of the most important results announced by Tartaglia were incorrect. Some of his artillery conclusions were published by his son in *Stratioticos*, but in a form which makes the respective contributions of father and son impossible to distinguish.

Thomas Digges, who actively publicized the life and work of his father, is also the only source for his death. From Thomas's autobiographical comments in a legal dispute of the 1590s it can be inferred that Leonard died about 1559, shortly after he had resumed possession of his confiscated lands and when he had only just begun the mathematical education of his eldest son. The close ties between the published work of father and son have obscured the marked differences in their careers—historians have often simply referred to the Diggeses as if the two were indistinguishable. Leonard was an able popularizer who had enormous success in writing for a large audience, but he was more than just a talented compiler with a flair for instrumental innovation and exposition. Through his promotion of the mathematical arts and his claims for the civic utility of practical geometry, he was a key figure in the establishment of the role of the mathematical practitioner. STEPHEN JOHNSTON

Sources J. B. Easton, 'Digges, Leonard', *DSB* · A. R. Hall, *Ballistics in the seventeenth century* (1952) · A. W. Richeson, *English land measuring to 1800: instruments and practices* (1966) · A. J. Turner, 'The prehistory, origins and development of the reflecting telescope', *Bollettino del Centro Internazionale A. Beltrame di Storia dello Spazio e del Tempo*, 3–4 (Sept 1984), 11–22 · *LP Henry VIII*, 5, no. 639 (p. 291); 17, no. 405 (p. 234); 20/1, no. 672(2) (p. 350) · D. M. Loades, *Two Tudor conspiracies* (1965) · *CPR, 1553–7* · E. Hasted, *The history and topographical survey of the county of Kent*, 2nd edn, 9 (1800), 354, 366 · *Calendar of the manuscripts of the most hon. the marquis of Salisbury*, 4, HMC, 9 (1892), 396–9 · Emden, *Oxf.* · T. Benolt and R. Cooke, *The visitation of Kent taken in the years 1530–1 … and 1574*, ed. W. B. Bannerman, 1, Harleian Society, 74 (1923), 9, 73 · R. Hovenden, ed., *The visitation of Kent, taken in the years 1619–1621*, Harleian Society, 42 (1898), 64–5 · *STC, 1475–1640* · Wing, *STC* · E. G. R. Taylor, *The mathematical practitioners of Tudor and Stuart England* (1954) · W. P. Baildon, ed., *The records of the Honorable Society of Lincoln's Inn: admissions*, 1 (1896), 50

Digges, Leonard (1588–1635), poet and translator, was born in London, the son of Thomas *Digges (c.1546–1595), mathematician, and Anne (or Agnes), daughter of Sir Warham St Leger. Sir Dudley *Digges (1582/3–1639) was his brother. He went to University College, Oxford, in 1603, aged fifteen, and graduated BA on 31 October 1606. Having left Oxford, he returned briefly to London before embarking on a period of study in foreign universities. In consideration of the accomplishments he acquired in classical and modern languages he was created MA at Oxford on 20 November 1626, and allowed to reside at University College, where he died on 7 April 1635 and was buried in the chapel.

Digges has been lauded as an 'eminent-poet' (Hunter) and his earliest text, a verse translation from Claudius Claudianus's *The Rape of Proserpine*, was published in 1617, with further editions appearing in 1628. It is dedicated to Digges's sister (1587–1619), wife of Sir Anthony Palmer KB (1566–1630), who had recently nursed Digges through a 'desperate sicknesse' (L. Digges, *Rape of Proserpine*, 1617, sig. A2r) and whose devotion was similarly recorded on her funerary monument in Chitham church, Kent. In 1622 he issued a translation of a Spanish novel by the former prisoner G. de Cespedes y Meneses, entitled *Gerardo, the Unfortunate Spaniard*, and dedicated it, admitting that he was a 'stranger rather than an intruder', to the brothers William, earl of Pembroke, and Philip, earl of Montgomery.

In addition Digges composed short verses prefixing a number of texts. The first of these, praising the accuracy and originality of the succeeding narrative, was printed in Matheo Aleman's *The Rogue, or, The Life of Guzman de Alfarache* (1623). This work, a highly moral depiction of a linguistically gifted cleric's refusal to heed good counsel, and the subsequent calamities he suffered, was followed in 1639 by Giovanni Sorriano's *The Italian Tutor, or, A New and most Compleat Italian Grammar*. Digges again celebrated the author's skills:

What reader but will say thy paines are such,
No tongue nor pen can praise too much

For what although thou mortall quickly die? Thy fame shall
    live eternally.
(L. Digges, *Italian Tutor*, 1639, sig. [a2v])

Consolidating his association with the stationer Edward
Blount, Digges produced commendatory verses prefacing
Shakespeare's first folio (1623)—

> This Booke,
> When Brasse and Marble fade, shall make thee looke
> Fresh to all Ages
> (sig. A7r)

—and the 1640 edition of his *Poems*. The latter verses
reveal Digges's admiration for the poet's inventive creativity and fame:

> Briefe, there is nothing in his wit fraught Booke,
> Whose sound we would not heare; on whose worth looke
> Like old coynd gold, whose lines in every page,
> Shall passe true currant to succeeding age.

SIDNEY LEE, *rev.* ELIZABETH HARESNAPE

Sources *STC, 1475–1640* • J. Hunter, *Chorus vatum Anglicanorum: collections concerning the poets and verse-writers of the English nation*, 6 vols.
(1838–54), BL, Add. MS 24488, fols. 181–2 • Wood, *Ath. Oxon.*, new
edn, 2.592–3 • Wood, *Ath. Oxon.: Fasti* (1815), 316, 428 • M. Brennan,
Literary patronage in the English Renaissance: the Pembroke family (1988),
118–19, 140–41 • L. Digges, *Gerardo, the unfortunate Spaniard* (1622)

Digges, Thomas (*c.*1546–1595), mathematician and member of parliament, was the eldest son of Leonard *Digges
(*c.*1515–*c.*1559), practical mathematician, and his wife,
Bridget, daughter of Thomas Wilford of Hartridge, Kent.
Digges was presumably brought up on his father's estate
at Wootton, Kent, but Leonard's land and property were
seized after his involvement in the Wyatt uprising of 1554.
Condemned to death for high treason, Leonard was pardoned and subsequently recovered his lands, but his sons
lost their right of inheritance. Thomas Digges and his
younger brother James were restored in blood by act of
parliament only in 1563. In the interim their father had
died and Thomas Digges's education was taken over by
John Dee; Digges would later refer to Dee as his 'revered
second mathematical father' (*Alae seu scalae mathematicae*,
1573, sig. A2r) and Dee considered Digges as 'my most
worthy mathematical heir' (Dee, sig. A2v).

The combination of filial duty and the unusually mathematical nature of Digges's upbringing helps to explain
the character of much of his published work. His first publication was *Pantometria* (1571), an edition of a manuscript
on surveying and practical geometry by his father.
Appended to this text was Digges's own contribution, *A
Mathematicall Discourse of Geometricall Solids*. This was the
most self-consciously advanced and novel work on geometry published in sixteenth-century England. Digges provided several hundred theorems on the properties,
dimensions, and interrelations of the five regular (Platonic) polyhedra, and the final section of his text extended
the enquiry to an investigation of five 'transformed' bodies—semi-regular (Archimedean) solids generated by the
metamorphosis of each of the five Platonic solids.

The elevated level of Digges's work was confirmed by
Alae seu scalae mathematicae (1573), a text prompted by the
appearance of the new star of 1572. Addressed to a European audience of astronomers, *Alae* was Digges's only
Latin publication and offered an analysis and improvement of the mathematical and instrumental techniques
available for the study of the nova. Recent radio astronomy has shown that Digges's observations were the most
accurate then made. Moreover, he concluded that the new
star was indeed a celestial body rather than a meteorological phenomenon, thus challenging the interpretations offered by contemporary Aristotelian natural
philosophy.

Digges's cosmological ambitions went beyond his
claims concerning the new star. In *Alae* he condemned the
'monstrous' planetary astronomy of Ptolemy and wrote
approvingly of Copernicus (*Alae*, sigs. A4v, 2A3r, 2A4v, L2v).
But he did not wholeheartedly endorse the Copernican
heliocentric system, in which the sun rather than the
earth is stationed at the centre of the universe. Writing
only shortly after the appearance of the new star, Digges
initially hoped that its changing brightness might provide
concrete observational evidence to support or modify the
Copernican doctrine.

Digges's hopes were frustrated, as the star simply faded
from view. But he nevertheless became the first English
author publicly to declare his support for Copernicus's
cosmological scheme, in the 1576 edition of his father's *A
Prognostication Everlasting*. As an appendix to this popular
almanac, Digges included his 'Perfit description of the
caelestiall orbes', which made Copernicus's general
claims accessible to an English audience by providing a
free translation of the cosmological sections of book one
of *De revolutionibus orbium caelestium* (1543). Digges also
added his own touches, particularly in a famous diagram
which went beyond Copernicus's own scheme, by showing an infinite universe in which the stars extended indefinitely outwards from the solar system.

In parallel with his innovative mathematical work of
the early 1570s Digges also began a gentlemanly career of
service. He was selected as MP for Wallingford in 1572 and
sat at this parliament's subsequent sessions in 1576 and
1581. For the next parliament in 1584, he was returned as
MP for Southampton. Over this period Digges was increasingly active, whether making speeches, sitting on committees, or consulting with the privy council. He has been
identified as one of the House of Commons' 'men of business' and he earned a reputation for speaking 'for the
common wealth of all England, and for no private cause'
(Hitchcock, last page).

Digges's parliamentary work reached a peak in 1584–5
when he drafted memoranda on such topics as the provision of a standing army, the oath of association, a bill on
Jesuits, and the question of the succession to Queen Elizabeth. He was by then a prominent and respected figure:
'Digges commonly doth speak last, and therefore saith,
every matter must have an end, and therefore to draw this
to a conclusion' (HoP, *Commons*, 38). Outside parliament he
took on other public duties. He promoted plans for a new
harbour at Dover in the early 1580s and involved himself
in the detailed design of this major Elizabethan technical

project. He was appointed a commissioner for the harbour in 1582 and made surveyor, but delegated his responsibilities to a local deputy. His mathematical skills were also called on in 1582 when he was asked to review John Dee's proposal for reform of the calendar, prepared after the introduction of the Gregorian calendar.

Rather than keep them in separate spheres, Digges sought to integrate his twin commitments to civic service and to mathematics. As early as 1576 he had included a programmatic call for the mathematical reformation of navigation along with the Copernican appendix to his father's *Prognostication Everlasting*. He subsequently spent fifteen weeks at sea, both to satisfy himself and to overcome the scepticism of experienced mariners. Digges not only proclaimed his criticisms of navigational errors to be triumphantly vindicated, but demonstrated that he could not be dismissed as merely a study-bound scholar.

Digges developed his vision of the identity of the mathematician most explicitly in *Stratioticos* (1579), a text on military mathematics. He confessed that he had once been delighted with the elevated subtlety of mathematical demonstration but that, with more mature judgement, he had spent his time 'in reducing the Sciences Mathematical from Demonstrative Contemplations to Experimental Actions, for the Service of my Prince and Country' (*Stratioticos*, 1579, sig. A2r). *Stratioticos* exemplifies this self-conscious choice of role and agenda. Its first book is on arithmetic and was based on surviving manuscript material of Leonard Digges. The remaining two books are Thomas Digges's own, adapting elementary algebra for use by soldiers and providing a lengthy treatment of the qualities and roles of all the ranks of men in an army. The volume was dedicated to the earl of Leicester, and had been composed in response to hopes over the winter of 1577–8 that he would lead an English force against the Spanish in the Netherlands. The last book of *Stratioticos* was evidently intended as a blueprint for a model army and, although Leicester's expedition came to nothing at the time, Digges himself visited the Low Countries in the autumn of 1578, touring and reporting on fortifications, and observing the troops.

When the Netherlands crisis came to a head in the mid-1580s Digges was again exhorting Leicester to active intervention. He was appointed as both trench-master and muster-master in the expeditionary force sent over in late 1585 and, after initially busying himself surveying fortifications, concentrated wholly on the office of muster-master. Although praised for his unswerving rectitude, his attempts to check abuses in the distribution of soldiers' pay led to increasing hostility and dispute. Far removed from the textbook military prescriptions of *Stratioticos*, Digges already complained of intolerable malice in September 1586 and, when he finally received his official discharge in early 1588, he considered that the disorders and abuses plaguing the army were above his power to remedy.

Digges's last years were dogged by continued and bitter wrangling over his army accounts and his position was weakened by the loss of his principal patron. While he appears to have been most closely linked with Lord Burghley in the early 1570s, by the end of the decade Digges had aligned himself with the activist and interventionist policy associated with Leicester. As well as the dedication of *Stratioticos* and the contacts leading to Digges's military service, Digges was nominated to his parliamentary seat in 1584 by Leicester; in addition, he named his eldest son Dudley after his patron. Digges also served Leicester in print, defending his reputation and military honour in both *A Briefe Report of the Militarie Services done in the Low Countries, by the Erle of Leicester* (1587) and *A Briefe and True Report of the Proceedings of the Earle of Leycester for the Reliefe of the Towne of Sluce* (1590).

Despite promising books on a wide range of mathematical subjects, *Stratioticos* was Digges's last major composition. His military concerns were reflected in new editions of *Stratioticos* (1590) and *Pantometria* (1591), which both contained additions on artillery, and particularly ballistics. Digges had built once again on prior work of his father by publishing a series of questions on artillery in the first edition of *Stratioticos*. His subsequent answers and notes of 1590 and 1591 foreshadowed his projected treatise on the subject and also demonstrated how advanced mathematics could be brought to bear on urgent military matters.

Despite the disappointments of his own military service, Digges still upheld the ideal of joining theory and practice in the service of the commonwealth. In presenting himself as a gentleman mathematician he became probably the most important Elizabethan promoter of mathematics as an engaged and effective worldly practice. His significance lay not only in his advocacy of novel geometry and cosmology but in shaping the tradition of practical mathematics.

Digges established his country residence at Chevening in Kent and also maintained a house in London. He married Anne (or Agnes), daughter of Sir Warham St Leger, and his will lists their surviving children as Dudley *Digges (1582/3–1639), Margaret, Ursula, and Leonard *Digges. Digges died on 24 August 1595 and his will was proved on 1 September, being opposed by his brother James and by William Digges, who were excluded by codicil. He was buried in the chancel of St Mary Aldermanbury, London, where his wife erected a monument to his memory.

STEPHEN JOHNSTON

Sources J. B. Easton, 'Digges, Thomas', *DSB* • T. Digges, *Pantometria* (1571) • F. R. Johnson, *Astronomical thought in Renaissance England* (1937) • *HoP, Commons* • A. R. Hall, *Ballistics in the seventeenth century* (1952) • J. Summerson, 'Dover harbour', *The history of the king's works*, 4 (1982), 755–64 • S. Johnston, 'Making mathematical practice: gentlemen, practitioners and artisans in Elizabethan England', PhD diss., U. Cam., 1994 • S. Johnston, 'Like father, like son? John Dee, Thomas Digges and the identity of the mathematician', *John Dee: interdisciplinary studies*, ed. S. Clucas (1999) • M. Graves, 'The management of the Elizabethan House of Commons: the council's men-of-business', *Parliamentary History*, 2 (1983), 11–38 • P. Collinson, 'The monarchical republic of Queen Elizabeth I', *Bulletin of the John Rylands University Library*, 69 (1986–7), 394–424 • D. H. Clark and F. R. Stephenson, *The historical supernovae* (1977), 185–6 • J. Dee, *Parallaticae commentationis praxeosque nucleus quidam* (1573) • R. Hitchcock, *A pollitique platt* (1580) • *JHC*, 1 (1547–1628), 66–7, 69 • Baron Kervyn de Lettenhove [J. M. B. C. Kervyn de

Lettenhove] and L. Gilliodts-van Severen, eds., *Relations politiques des Pays-Bas et de l'Angleterre sous le règne de Philippe II*, 10 (Brussels, 1892), 794–6 • *CSP for.*, 1586–8 • J. Stow, *A survey of the cities of London and Westminster*, ed. J. Strype, 2 vols. (1720), 1, bk 3, 71–2 • PRO, PROB 11/86, fols. 164r–166v

Archives BL, plan of Dover town, castle, and harbour • PRO, state papers, Elizabeth I

Digges, West (1725?–1786), actor and theatre manager, was probably born in 1725, the elder of the two sons (there was no daughter) of Thomas Digges, gentleman, of Chilham Castle, Kent, and his wife, Elizabeth West (*bap.* 1695, *d.* 1762), who were married on 18 August 1724. George Colman the younger claimed in his *Random Records* that Digges was the illegitimate son of Elizabeth's brother John *West, seventh baron and later first Earl De La Warr (1693–1766), but as Elizabeth clearly identifies West Digges as the elder son of her marriage to Thomas Digges this can be discounted.

Thomas Digges's income had since 1727 been administered by trustees, possibly connected to failed investments in the South Sea Company, and the young West Digges was expected to be guided in his career by his uncle Lord De La Warr. According to his mother's will, with De La Warr's help Digges obtained a commission in the army, but 'by his Extravagance suffered a Commission of Bankruptcy to be issued against him' and 'instead of applying himself to any Profession or Calling worthy of his Birth has betaken himself to the publick Stage to the great Disgrace of himself and Family' (PRO, PROB 11/875, sig 192). The first public notice of West Digges as an actor occurred when he appeared on stage at the Smock Alley Theatre in Dublin on 29 November 1749, playing Jaffeir in Thomas Otway's *Venice Preserv'd*. His success was immediate, and he soon added Hamlet, Lear, Antony, Romeo, George Barnwell, and Macheath to his repertory, attaining overwhelming popularity for six seasons and attracting the attention of David Garrick. However, in November 1754 Digges was unwittingly party to a political riot at Smock Alley for refusing to repeat a volatile political passage in James Miller's *Mahomet the Impostor*.

In spring 1756 Digges performed major roles at the Canongate Theatre in Edinburgh; by autumn he had become manager there. His flamboyant style led him to puff his first production, John Home's tragedy *Douglas*; the success of the play created a national furore, fuelled by a clergy apprehensive of secular entertainment. Although it was condemned by the Edinburgh presbytery, the tragedy enjoyed unprecedented success. Digges remained at Canongate for three years as manager, but in 1758 a quarrel with his musicians over salary precipitated a strike and a series of six pamphlets airing the dispute. When his partner, Sarah *Ward (1726/7–1771), with whom he had been living since 1752, left him, thus breaking the contract both had with the theatre, the Canongate's owners dismissed Digges.

Digges's personal life consistently impinged upon his prospects for success; he was damaged both by unsatisfactory relationships with women and by his consistent extravagance, which kept him in debt throughout his life.

His marriage to Mary Wakeling, on 3 March 1746 at All Hallows, London Wall, though short-lived, coloured his future relationships with women. His liaison between 1752 and 1759 with the actress Sarah Ward, which produced at least six children, ended with mutual recriminations, revealed in *Letters which Passed between Mr. West Digges, Comedian, and Mrs. Sarah Ward, 1752–1759*. A later stormy relationship with the actress George Anne *Bellamy (1731?–1788) lasted several years, during which the couple lived on Newhaven Road in Bonington, near Edinburgh. Digges's impecuniousness placed him in situations both embarrassing and criminal; he was forced to flee his creditors (1753, 1759), suffer arrest (1772), and endure imprisonment (1777).

Despite these distractions, Digges pursued his career energetically, especially in Edinburgh, where he was always warmly welcomed. He performed in Edinburgh in 1759 and 1762 and in Dublin in 1760 and 1761. His apparent inactivity for a few years after 1762 may be related to his inheritance from his mother, whose will stipulated that he was entitled to a half-share of her South Sea stock, worth £7312 7s., if he could assure his younger brother, Dudley, that he would give up the stage and discharge his debts. If he did retire, that retirement was brief; he was acting at Limerick in 1767, and in August 1771 he resumed managing at the Canongate. Extant stage bills indicate that he acted at Limerick again in 1774, at Cork in 1774, at York in 1775, and at Liverpool in 1776. Digges made his London début in the title role of Joseph Addison's *Cato* at the Haymarket on 14 August 1777. During that season he performed a number of his celebrated roles, including Wolsey in *Henry VIII*, Sir John Brute in John Vanbrugh's *The Provoked Wife*, and Macheath in John Gay's *The Beggar's Opera*; the next season he performed Caratach in George Colman's version of Beaumont and Fletcher's *Bonduca*, called 'an excellent piece of acting' (Colman, 1.255). The critic from the *London Chronicle* of 14 August 1777, although noting his antiquated style of acting and citing 'the extreme difference between the stile of the old school … and the modern', could not deny the power of Digges's performance, admitting that he 'awed us into esteem and admiration'. Digges performed in London until 1781, and from 1781 to 1783 he acted in Edinburgh, Cork, and Limerick. From 1782 to 1784 he was a member of Daly's company in Dublin, where he suffered a stroke on 2 July 1784 during a rehearsal of *Venice Preserv'd*.

Digges was a commanding figure on stage. John O'Keeffe remembered that 'he had a noble presence, a fine figure, large and manly; a full expressive and pleasing face, and ruddy complexion' (*Recollections of the Life of John O'Keeffe*, 1826, 1.290). Victor remarked that 'almost all the Requisites to form a great Actor seemed to unite [in him]; every Advantage of Art and Nature, except an harmonious Voice' (Victor, 1.147). James Boswell wrote to Garrick that Digges 'threw open to me the portals of Theatrical Enchantment' (Yale MS L 569), while Colman mentions that, as Wolsey, he drew tears 'even from the eyes of flinty-hearted critics' (Colman, 1.255).

Digges died on 11 November 1786 at his home on the Coal Quay in Cork and was buried the following day in the cathedral of St Fin Barre in Cork. PHYLLIS T. DIRCKS

Sources *Letters which passed between Mr. West Digges, comedian, and Mrs. Sarah Ward, 1752–1759* (1833) · R. Hitchcock, *An historical view of the Irish stage from the earliest period down to the close of the season 1788*, 2 vols. (1788–94) · J. Jackson, *The history of the Scottish stage* (1793) · J. C. Dibdin, *The annals of the Edinburgh stage* (1888) · Highfill, Burnim & Langhans, *BDA* · B. Victor, *The history of the theatres of London and Dublin*, 3 vols. (1761–71) · G. Colman, *Random records*, 2 vols. (1830) · R. B. Peake, *Memoirs of the Colman family*, 2 vols. (1841) · *The letters of David Garrick*, ed. D. M. Little and G. M. Kahrl, 3 vols. (1963) · T. Davies, *Dramatic miscellanies*, 3 vols. (1784) · G. A. Bellamy, *An apology for the life of George Anne Bellamy*, ed. [A. Bicknell], 3rd edn, 6 vols. (1785) · T. Tobin, *Plays by Scots, 1660–1800* (1974) · *Hibernian Chronicle* [n.d., 1786?] [of Cork]
Likenesses print, pubd 1778, BM · J. Roberts, coloured drawing (as Cato), BL · sepia drawing, Harvard U.

Diggle, Joseph Robert (1849–1917), educational administrator, was born at Canal Bank, Pendleton, Lancashire, on 12 May 1849, the youngest son of William Diggle, a warehouseman, and his wife, Nancy Ann, daughter of John Chadderton. His elder brother, John William Diggle (1847–1920), became bishop of Carlisle. He was educated at Manchester grammar school and Wadham College, Oxford, where he gained first-class honours in modern history. Ordained in 1874, he was curate of St Matthew's, Liverpool, before becoming in 1876 curate of St Mary's, Bryanston Square, London, whose rector was William Henry Fremantle (1831–1916). In 1878 he married Jane Wilkinson Macrae, daughter of John Wrigley Macrae of Aigburth, Liverpool; they had a family of two sons and two daughters.

Resigning his curacy, Diggle was elected in 1879 to the London school board (LSB) as member for the Marylebone division. He dominated the proceedings of the board between 1885 and 1894 when he was its chairman and leader of the Moderate (that is, Conservative) party. His oratorical skills evinced a strong and abrasive manner, while he was adroit in the management of committees. He was opposed by the Progressive Party on the board, and its leader Edward Lyulph Stanley, whom Diggle accused of extravagance in the running of the board's schools. During the period of Diggle's ascendancy, the progressives coined the term 'Diggleism' to denote his alleged parsimonious approach to educational expenditure, a critique set out in a booklet, *The Case Against Diggleism* (1894). It was claimed that in order to help Anglican schools compete against secular board schools, he had deliberately neglected school accommodation, equipment, and teachers' welfare. Differences between the parties became particularly acrimonious during the early 1890s as a result of allegations about the state of religious education in board schools by the Revd J. J. Coxhead and a young Anglican lawyer, Athelstan Riley. The resulting storm led to the breakdown of the W. H. Smith compromise of 1871 concerning the teaching of scripture in LSB schools and the eventual unseating of Diggle as leader of the Moderates after their defeat in the 1894 school board election. He lost his seat on the board in 1897.

Joseph Robert Diggle (1849–1917), by W. & D. Downey, pubd 1892

Diggle attempted to enter national politics, standing as an independent candidate for West Marylebone in November 1885 so as to test the eligibility of clergy to enter parliament; he polled 101 votes. Having relinquished his orders in 1889 under the Clerical Disabilities Act, he stood as a Conservative for Camberwell North in October 1900 but was defeated by the Liberal T. J. Macnamara, a former bitter opponent from the LSB. His wider interests in education and social issues connected with it were expressed in ninety-three letters to *The Times*. From 1906 to 1908 he was chairman of the council of the Ragged School Union and of the Shaftesbury Society.

Diggle left London to live in Tenterden, Kent, where he was mayor, 1896–8, and chairman of the Kent elementary schools education committee in 1908. An inveterate committee man, he was chairman of the council of the Royal Botanic Society in 1907, an honorary fellow of the British Institution of Public Health, a corresponding member of the Society of Public Medicine of Belgium in 1891, and a section president at the international congresses of hygiene and demography held at London (1892) and Budapest (1894). His last seven years were spent in Oxford where he died at 24 Merton Street on 16 January 1917. His wife survived him. DONALD P. LEINSTER-MACKAY

Sources *WWW* · *The Times* (18 Jan 1917) · T. Gautrey, *Lux mihi laus: school board memories* (1937) · D. Leinster-Mackay, 'The continuing religious difficulty in late-Victorian and Edwardian England: a case of gratuitous advice from the antipodes?', *History of Education*, 19 (1990), 123–37 · D. Leinster-Mackay and E. Sarfaty, eds., *Education and* The Times: *an index of letters to 1910* (1994), 333 · *CGPLA Eng. & Wales* (1917)

Likenesses W. & D. Downey, photograph, pubd 1892, NPG [*see illus.*]

Wealth at death £3619 2s. 7d.: probate, 10 March 1917, *CGPLA Eng. & Wales*

Dighton, Denis (1791–1827), military painter, was born in London on 16 October 1791, the son of Robert *Dighton sen. (1751–1814), actor, caricaturist, and printseller, and Catherine Caroline. Although baptized Mark James Dennis Dighton (at St Martin-in-the-Fields, Westminster, on 24 November 1791), he seems to have used only the last forename, spelt Denis, during his adult life. His half-brother, Robert Dighton jun. (*c.*1786–1865), and his younger brother, Richard (1795/6–1880), were also known as watercolourists and printmakers. In 1807 Denis became a student at the Royal Academy Schools. Then, having come to the attention of the prince of Wales early in his career, he was commissioned in the 90th regiment (Perthshire volunteers) on 11 July 1811, through royal patronage. However, he resigned not long afterwards, on 17 March 1812, in order to marry Phoebe Earl (*b. c.*1790), flower painter and daughter of the portraitist, James Earl (1761–1796). They were married on 22 June 1812 at St Pancras church, and settled in London, initially at Denis's father's address, 4 Spring Gardens, Westminster, London.

In 1813 Dighton may have visited the British army on campaign in the Peninsular War, where his brother Robert was serving with the 38th (1st Staffordshire) regiment. He produced a number of fine watercolours depicting Spanish patriot leaders and their men, signed and dated that year and apparently drawn from life, one of which is inscribed 'from a sketch from life at Cadiz' (Royal Collection). Robert was also wounded at the sortie from Bayonne, France, on 14 April 1814 and there is a watercolour portrait of General Thouvenot, governor of Bayonne, signed by Dighton and dated 1814 (Royal Collection). In 1814 he exhibited at the Royal Academy *The Storming of San Sebastian, 31st August* [*1813*] (Leith Hall, Aberdeenshire).

Appointed military draughtsman to the prince regent in 1815, Dighton painted the dramatic *Battle of Orthez* (exh. RA, 1815; Plas Newydd, Anglesey) which the prince sent as a present to the marquess of Anglesey on 27 July. Anglesey also acquired Dighton's large canvas celebrating Napoleon's final defeat on 18 June 1815, *The Battle of Waterloo; the General Advance of the British Lines* (exh. RA, 1816; Plas Newydd, Anglesey), based on the artist's own studies of the topography. Dighton had visited the battlefield only days after the event and made nine studies in watercolour (Royal Collection), from which he also produced two battle paintings in watercolour (NAM). On 7 November 1816 the prince paid Dighton £50 for a smaller version of Lord Anglesey's Waterloo painting (Royal Collection), and in the following year he purchased *The Battle of Waterloo; the Charge of the Second Brigade of Cavalry*, depicting Sergeant Ewart of the Scots Greys capturing the eagle of the French 45th regiment (exh. RA, 1817; Royal Collection).

Between 1811 and 1825 Dighton exhibited seventeen pictures at the Royal Academy, the first of which was *The Lace Maker*. Thereafter, his work was mainly military, either battle paintings or detailed uniform studies, although he also painted the notable naval work, *The Battle of Trafalgar, 21 October 1805, Fall of Nelson* (NMM). When the prince regent succeeded to the throne, Dighton painted a large watercolour, *The Coronation Banquet Champion* (1821), and in 1822 he accompanied the king on his visit to Scotland, where he made drawings of the ceremonies (all Royal Collection). However, according to Redgrave, 'he lost his access to his royal patron, and … the chief source of his income was stopped' (Redgrave, *Artists*, 126). This is said to have affected his health and eventually his sanity. Dighton's wife took him to Brittany, where he died at St Servan, on 8 August 1827. Phoebe Dighton painted fruit and flower pieces influenced by Dutch masters, and was appointed flower painter to Queen Adelaide. Between 1820 and 1835 she exhibited sixteen pictures at the Academy, and eight at the British Institution. In 1835 Ackermann published *Relics of Shakespeare, from Drawings by Mrs Denis Dighton*. Following this, she married Peter McIntyre and, between 1841 and 1854, exhibited a further three pictures under her second married name.

Dighton was an accomplished watercolourist and graphic artist, and the Royal Collection holds some 243 watercolours and sixty-seven preliminary pencil drawings by him, all depicting European military uniform between about 1811 and 1822, which are generally very accurate. There are also four indian-ink drawings in the British Museum's department of prints and drawings, which were engraved to illustrate Maria, Lady Callcott's, works on Chile and Brazil. He also etched and lithographed several plates of military subjects and portraits of Russian leaders, among which is *Denis Davidoff, the Black Captain* (1814).
           JENNY SPENCER-SMITH

Sources Redgrave, *Artists* · Graves, *RA exhibitors* · A. E. H. Miller and N. P. Dawnay, *Military drawings and paintings in the collection of her majesty the queen*, 2 vols. (1966–70) · O. Millar, *The later Georgian pictures in the collection of her majesty the queen*, 2 vols. (1969) · D. Rose, *Life, times and recorded works of Robert Dighton (1752–1814), actor, artist and printseller and three of his artist sons* (1981) · A. Wilson, *A dictionary of British military painters* (1972) · IGI · H. M. Hake, 'Dighton caricatures', *The Print Collectors' Quarterly*, 13/1 and 2 (April 1926), 137 ff., 237–47 · administration of Robert Dighton's estate, PRO, IR 26/445, fols. 99–199 · statement of service of Robert Dighton, jun., 1829, PRO, WO 25/756, fol. 92 · *Journal of the Society for Army Historical Research* · L. Lambourne and J. Hamilton, eds., *British watercolours in the Victoria and Albert Museum* (1980) · parish register, St Martin-in-the-Fields, Westminster, 24 Nov 1791, City Westm. AC [baptism]

Dighton, (Ellen) Margaret. *See* Torrie, (Ellen) Margaret (1912–1999).

Dighton, Robert (1751–1814), draughtsman and singer, was baptized at St Andrew's, Holborn, on 5 December 1751, the son of John Dighton, a print seller, and his wife, Hannah. Both were portrayed in a mezzotint by Robert Laurie after Robert Dighton, *Court of Equity, or, A Convivial City Meeting* (1778), which shows a gathering of friends at the Belle Savage on Ludgate Hill, London. Robert Dighton entered the Academy Schools in 1772 and afterwards set

Robert Dighton (1751–1814), self-portrait, *c.*1787

up as a drawing-master and miniature portrait painter. The first prints that he designed were of actors in character for John Bell's edition of Shakespeare's works (1775–6) and for Thomas Lowndes's *New English Theatre* (1776–7). In 1779 sets of his portraits of actors and actresses in mezzotint were published by William Richardson and a *Book of Heads*, with a self-portrait as title-plate, was engraved for Carington Bowles. Dighton exhibited seventeen miniature portraits and comic drawings with the Free Society (1769–74), and he also occasionally exhibited at the Royal Academy (1775–99).

Dighton's career developed in two distinct directions. He achieved considerable popularity as a singer. On 27 August 1776 the *Morning Post* identified him as the gentleman who had performed at the Haymarket the night before, and in 1777 he probably appeared at Brighton during the summer season. Quite soon he was in demand for benefit nights at Covent Garden, playing such leading roles as Mungo in *The Padlock* (1781), Hawthorn in *Love in a Village* (1784), and, for his own benefit, Macheath in *The Beggar's Opera* (1784). Since he had no regular place in the Covent Garden company it is likely that this celebrity status was acquired by singing at the pleasure gardens. By 1792 he was certainly also appearing at Sadler's Wells, but it is impossible to establish how frequent his performances were owing to the fragmentary nature of the evidence. He was principal tenor in 1794 and appeared regularly until 1800.

As an artist Dighton is most interesting as the foremost designer of droll mezzotints and engravings after the death in 1780 of the previous master of the field, John Collett. Dighton worked chiefly for Carington Bowles, and also designed comic literary series such as *Twelve prints illustrating the most interesting, sentimental and humorous scenes in Tristram Shandy* (1785) and, around 1800, sporting prints. Most of these were published anonymously but can be assigned to Dighton, as his original drawings, 128 signed watercolours, and twenty-one Indian ink wash drawings were preserved in an album by the Bowles family. The album surfaced at auction in 1953 but was broken up and dispersed at a second auction in 1978. Dighton's earliest comic designs date from 1781, and their flavour is indicated by such titles as *Mr Deputy Dumpling and Family Enjoying a Summer Afternoon* (1781), *The Return from a Masquerade—a Morning Scene* (*c.*1784), or *The Frenchman in Distress* (1797). Much of his work is enduringly funny.

On 22 September 1771 Dighton was married to a Latitia Clark and they had two children, Latitia Sarah (*b.* 1775) and Robert (*b.* 1777). By the late 1780s Dighton was involved with the Vauxhall Gardens soprano Catherine Caroline Bertles (*fl.* 1787–1794), who in 1792 appeared on stage with him at Sadler's Wells. Together they had four sons and two daughters. With the help of his offspring he drew, etched, and published lightly caricatured portraits from his house at Charing Cross. But times were hard in the art world on account of the war. In 1806 it was discovered that since 1798 Dighton had been regularly stealing prints from the British Museum. In 1812 he tried to put one of his daughters on the stage 'by which she might obtain the favour of assisting me in my present pecuniary embarasment [*sic*]' (Rose, 27). He died in 1814 at his home, 4 Spring Gardens, Charing Cross. His prints and drawings are held by the British Museum, London, the Royal Library, Windsor, the Sadler's Wells Library, and several private collectors.

After his death Latitia Sarah, by then married to Thomas Burnell, was, as 'the natural and lawful daughter and only next of kin of the said deceased' (Rose, 26), granted administration of her father's estate. This implies that Dighton's three (or possibly four) surviving sons were conceived out of wedlock. Of these, Robert Dighton (*c.*1786–1865) worked as a caricature portrait etcher from 1800 until 1809, when he was commissioned in the army; he served as a regular soldier until 1847. Denis *Dighton (1791–1827) painted battle scenes, while Richard Dighton (1795/6–1880) continued his father's business as an etcher of mildly caricatured portraits. A Joshua Dighton produced sporting caricatures between 1820 and 1840.

TIMOTHY CLAYTON

Sources *Catalogue of watercolours by Robert Dighton, 1752–1814, the property of the late Mr Jeffrey Rose* (Christies, 1978) · D. Rose, *Life, times and recorded works of Robert Dighton (1752–1814)* (1981) · S. House, 'Some letters of Robert Dighton', *Print Quarterly*, 19/1 (March 2002), 45–9 · Highfill, Burnim & Langhans, *BDA*, 4.412–16 · H. Hake, 'Dighton caricatures', *Print Collector's Quarterly*, 13 (1926), 136–55, 237–47 · R. Edwards, 'The watercolour drawings of Robert Dighton', *Apollo*, 14 (1931), 98–102 · M. D. George, *Hogarth to Cruikshank: social change in graphic satire* (1967) · A. E. H. Miller and N. P. Dawnay, *Military drawings and paintings in the collection of her majesty the queen*, 2 vols. (1966–70) · D. Donald, *The age of caricature: satirical*

prints in the reign of George III (1996) • T. Clayton, *The English print, 1688–1802* (1997) • Redgrave, *Artists*
Likenesses R. Dighton, self-portrait, pen-and-wash drawing, *c*.1787, NPG [*see illus.*] • R. Dighton, self-portrait, pen and watercolour, *c*.1800; Sothebys 1978, lot 75 • R. Dighton, self-portrait, repro. in *A book of hands* (1779), frontispiece • R. Dighton, self-portrait, etching (as the Muffin man), Sadler's Wells Library • R. Laurie, portrait, probably BM • engraving, Sadler's Wells Library
Wealth at death not great: consistory court of London case of 1814; Rose, *Life, times and recorded works*, 26

Dignan, David Brown (*b.* **1754/5**, *d.* in or after **1780**), author and fraudster, was the second son of an Irish physician who served in the Austrian army and rose to the rank of colonel before retiring to an estate in co. Clare. Dignan was said to have been educated at the Jesuit Missionary College at Douai in France.

Dignan's time in France provided the background for the two books which became his principal claim to any favour or regard. The *Monthly Review* declared his *Essai sur les principes politiques de l'économie publique* (1776) to be the work of 'a very promising writer', and further observed (ironically, given Dignan's subsequent activities) that 'the principles it inculcates would open, upon the young susceptible mind, an idea of public virtue, which might happily expand and grow into practice, in the mature stages of manhood' (*Monthly Review*, 55.444). The *Essai* is now believed to have been a translation—by someone else!—of an uncredited Italian original. If so, it was only the first of Dignan's deceptions. A second work, *Anecdotes of French Literature* (*c*.1777), like the *Essai*, was excerpted extensively in the *Morning Chronicle* after he had become far better known for other, non-literary enterprises.

In February 1777 Dignan stood for the borough of Hindon, Wiltshire, but he polled only eleven votes and withdrew from the contest after half an hour. On 12 March 1777 he was charged with two counts of obtaining money under false pretences. Since June 1776 he had bilked John Clark of £1000 on the promise of using his 'connections' among government officials to obtain a sinecure for Clark in the Dublin customs house. He claimed to be a member of the Irish parliament and supported that claim by printing a list of Irish MPs that included his own name. He had also received £850 from Josiah Brown in return for a promise to secure for Brown the lucrative writership of the *London Gazette*. In both instances, Dignan supported his pretences by forging the signature and seal of Viscount Weymouth, one of the secretaries of state in Lord North's government.

In addition to the crimes with which he was charged—and in part, perhaps, to lend credence to his claims of high connections—Dignan had also told North's other secretary of state, the earl of Suffolk, of a plot to assassinate the king, the principal instigators of which included such prominent members of the opposition as the duke of Richmond, the earl of Shelburne, and the Wilkite aldermen John Sawbridge and William Lee. But Dignan was also foolish enough to specify times and places at which the conspirators were supposed to meet and act, and the utter speciousness of his claims was soon discovered by spies, who were reported subsequently to have discovered

Dignan himself in a brothel, 'revelling with strumpets in the plunder of the innocent' (*Morning Chronicle*, 8 April 1777, 4c). The seriousness with which it had first treated Dignan's tales was a source of profound embarrassment to North's government, which was accused in the Commons of having employed Dignan in order to discredit its opponents, and this may help to explain the severity of Dignan's sentence after his conviction on the charge brought by Clark.

On 5 April 1777 the Westminster quarter sessions sentenced Dignan to five years' hard labour on board the prison hulks at Woolwich, a penal option which had been devised the year before, when the outbreak of the American War of Independence ended the transportation of convicts from Britain. The prospect of so harsh and degrading a punishment terrified the effete young criminal, who pleaded for his sentence to be altered to banishment in consideration of 'the weakness of my constitution and the disorders that I understand reign there' (BL, Add. MS 34413, fols. 392–3). Legal difficulties held up Dignan's prosecution for the charges concerning Brown, and he was detained in the Tothill Fields bridewell for nearly three weeks (during which time he reportedly attempted suicide by pistol, poison, and self-strangulation) before being removed to Woolwich.

From his first day on board, when a servant who had rowed over with a full-course meal for him was turned away, Dignan's experience of life on the hulks was one of unadulterated misery. As one of several famous 'gentlemen convicts', his presence drew attention to the new system of punishment. He often complained of the deprivations that he suffered, although the report of a fellow convict being given 150 lashes for stealing sundry articles from him—not to mention the quantities of paper and ink that Dignan expended in his many appeals—suggest that he enjoyed privileges which must surely have been unavailable to most of his fellow convicts (*Morning Chronicle*, 5 Sept 1777, 3b).

The contrast of Dignan's apparent gentility and intellectual gifts with the extreme degradation of his punishment inspired sympathy in some observers. A similar 'injustice' of a far more dramatic character—the execution for forgery of the popular clergyman and author William Dodd—had taken place in June 1777 following intense public debate, and Dignan may have sought to benefit by the association when, that same month, he petitioned (unsuccessfully) to have his sentence changed to imprisonment for seven years. His desire for some mitigation of his punishment was intensified the following year when his father died and left him an estate worth £200 per annum. In July 1779 Dignan wrote an appeal to William Eden, a former under-secretary of state and advocate of penal reform who had been instrumental in the creation of the hulks. Invoking Eden's own reformist tract, *Principles of Penal Law* (1771), Dignan claimed that his punishment was disproportionate: his crime had been a misdemeanour only, and far more serious offenders had already been released from the hulks on conditional pardons. But the clearest sentiment in Dignan's long and self-pitying missives was a conviction that his punishment was particularly disproportionate for a man of his supposed character, and it was on these grounds that Edmund Burke felt compelled to intercede on his behalf. 'Is it not shocking', wrote Burke to Eden, invoking Dignan's supposed literary accomplishments, 'that a man capable of such things should Spend his Youth wheeling a barrow of Gravel at Woolwich amidst the outcasts of Society?' (*Correspondence*, 10.5-6).

On 1 January 1780 an order was issued for Dignan to be removed from the hulks on account of his health being 'much impaired by that situation'; he was now allowed to serve the remainder of his sentence in Newgate prison (PRO, SP 44/93, pp. 337-8). Almost immediately he began issuing new letters of complaint, particularly concerning the threats of a still unsatisfied Josiah Brown to lodge an action against him for debt. But Dignan's fears and complaints alike were soon terminated in a completely unexpected fashion; he was among the many convicts to escape when Newgate was gutted during the Gordon riots in June 1780 (PRO, PCOM 2/170, entry for 5 June 1780). Although his name does not appear on the official list of escapees, four months later the *Morning Chronicle* reported that 'A certain distinguished convict ... is now living with great elegance and ease upon his paternal estate in Ireland' (PRO, PC 1/3097; *Morning Chronicle*, 3 Oct 1780, 2c). And that appears to have been the last to be heard by anyone in England of the outrageously deceitful, incessantly self-pitying, and, finally, uncommonly lucky David Brown Dignan.   SIMON DEVEREAUX

Sources *Morning Chronicle* (13 March 1777-3 Oct 1780) · *Monthly Review*, 55 (1776), 442-4 · *Monthly Review*, 62 (1780), 409 · *London Magazine*, 46 (1777), 227-8 · *The correspondence of Edmund Burke*, ed. T. W. Copeland and others, 10 vols. (1958-78) · HoP, *Commons, 1754-90*, 1.415-16 · A. Knapp and W. Baldwin, *The Newgate calendar, comprising interesting memoirs of the most notorious characters*, 4 vols. (1824-6) · Fitzwilliam-Burke papers, Northants. RO, A.viii.81-2 · BL, Add. MS 34413, fols. 392-3 · pardon for David Brown Dignan, PRO, SP 44/93, pp. 337-8 · M. D. Browne Dignan, *Essai sur les principes politiques de l'économie publique* (1776) · [D. Brown Dignan?], *Anecdotes of French literature and of the most celebrated French literati* (c.1777)
Archives PRO, pardon for David Brown Dignan, SP 44/93, pp. 337-8 · PRO, return of prisoners released from Newgate during the Gordon riots, PC 1/3097 | BL, Auckland MSS, Add. MSS 34413, 34416-34417 · Northants. RO, Fitzwilliam-Burke MSS · PRO, Sir John Fielding to William Eden enclosing three other letters, SP 37/12, fols. 63-4
Likenesses portrait, repro. in *London Magazine*, facing p. 227

Dignum, Charles (1765?-1827), singer, was born at Rotherhithe, London, probably in 1765. His father, a master tailor and a Roman Catholic, moved to Wild Street, Lincoln's Inn Fields, London, and young Dignum became a chorister at the Sardinian chapel; there his fine voice attracted the attention of Samuel Webbe, the organist, who taught him music. Dignum, however, wished to become a priest, and was prevented only by his father being too poor to pay for his training. A proposed apprenticeship to a carver and gilder was cut short after nine months. He was then articled for seven years to the composer Thomas Linley. For the first two years Linley would not let him sing in public,

so as to allow his voice to mature. He made his début at Drury Lane, as young Meadows in *Love in a Village*, on 14 October 1784; according to the advertisements he was received by a packed house with unbounded applause. He appeared in Michael Arne's *Cymon* on 26 November and as Damon in Boyce's *The Chaplet* on 18 December. Dignum remained associated with Drury Lane during the greater part of his life, but for an interval at Covent Garden in 1792-4. At both theatres his salary, where known, was £4 a week. He had a fine tenor voice, but his build was clumsy, ultimately fat, and he seems to have been good-natured but somewhat stupid. He sang both leading and supporting parts, chiefly in ballad opera, pantomime, and musical romance; his speciality was patriotic, sailor, and sentimental songs, some of which he composed himself. He was particularly successful as Tom Tug in *The Waterman* and as Crop in *No Song, No Supper*. He also sang oratorio, and on 28 March 1800 took part at Covent Garden in the first London performance of Haydn's *The Creation*. During the summers Dignum sang at Vauxhall, where he was a great favourite. In 1786 he married the heiress daughter of Charles Rennett, an attorney of the Middle Temple; she died at 23 New North Street, Red Lion Square, in 1799, and of their children only one daughter survived. Dignum's name disappears from the theatre bills after 1812. He died of inflammation of the lungs at his home, 47 Gloucester Street, Queen Square, on 29 March 1827. He is said to have accumulated, together with his wife's property, a fortune of some £30,000.   W. B. SQUIRE, *rev.* JOHN ROSSELLI

Sources W. T. Parke, *Musical memoirs*, 2 vols. (1830), vol. 1, pp. 176-7; vol. 2, p. 63 · *European Magazine and London Review*, 34 (1798), 363-4 · C. B. Hogan, ed., *The London stage, 1660-1800*, pt 5: *1776-1800* (1968) · Highfill, Burnim & Langhans, *BDA* · R. Fiske, *English theatre music in the eighteenth century*, 2nd edn (1986) · *GM*, 1st ser., 69 (1799), 258 · *Boyle's Court Guide*
Likenesses W. Ridley, stipple, 1799 (after S. Drummond), BM, NPG · S. De Wilde, watercolour drawing, 1801, Garr. Club · Bond, engraving (after a drawing by S. De Wilde), BM · S. De Wilde, sketch, Harvard TC · K. Mackenzie, stipple (after R. Dighton), BM · miniature (after A. W. Calcott), Garr. Club
Wealth at death approx. £30,000: Parke, *Musical memoirs*, 1.176-7 · married coheir to very considerable Hampshire property: *European Magazine*

Dilhorne. For this title name *see* Buller, Reginald Edward Manningham-, first Viscount Dilhorne (1905-1980).

Dilke, Ashton Wentworth (1850-1883), traveller and politician, was born on 11 August 1850 in London, the younger son of Sir (Charles) Wentworth *Dilke, first baronet (1810-1869), and Mary (d. 1853), the only daughter of Captain William Chatfield, Madras cavalry; his elder brother was Sir Charles Wentworth *Dilke, second baronet, the Liberal cabinet minister. Dilke was educated privately before matriculating at Trinity Hall, Cambridge, in 1869. He was made a scholar in 1870, but left without taking his degree, being anxious to travel in and discover more about Russia. He spent some two years visiting much of Russia and central Asia, living for some months in a Russian village, studying the language, and examining the condition of the peasantry. He returned showing symptoms of the consumption which later killed him, but began a book on Russia, one or two chapters of which appeared in the *Fortnightly Review*, although it was never published complete. His energies were absorbed by the *Weekly Dispatch*, which he bought for £14,000 in January 1875 and edited until his death. He published a translation of Turgenev's *Virgin Soil* in 1878.

On 10 April 1876 Dilke married Margaret Mary [*see below*], the eldest daughter of Thomas Eustace Smith MP. They had two sons. In 1880 he was returned to parliament for Newcastle upon Tyne. Variously described as an advanced Liberal and a radical, he seemed set for an active career but his health, never robust, gradually gave way and he resigned his seat at the beginning of the session of 1883. He spent the last few months of his life at Algiers where he died on 12 March 1883.

Margaret Mary [Maye] **Dilke** (1857–1903), campaigner for women's rights, was brought up in Newcastle upon Tyne. She was educated at Orléans and passed the public examination for French schoolmistresses. From 1878 she was an active member of the Woman's Suffrage Society. She lectured extensively on the subject and in 1885 published *Women's Suffrage*. After her husband's death she became a trustee of the *Weekly Dispatch*, from which position she effectively controlled the paper. She took an active interest in education, the position of women in general, and in working men's and radical clubs. On 19 September 1891 she married William Russell Cooke, solicitor, at Kensington parish church. She died in 1903.

NORMAN MACCOLL, rev. ELIZABETH BAIGENT

Sources *The Athenaeum* (17 March 1883), 344 · *CGPLA Eng. & Wales* (1883) · Venn, *Alum. Cant.* · S. Gwynn and G. M. Tuckwell, *The life of the Rt. Hon. Sir Charles W. Dilke*, 2 vols. (1917) · R. Jenkins, *Sir Charles Dilke: a Victorian tragedy* (1958) · *Dod's Parliamentary Companion* · Ward, *Men of the reign* · Burke, *Peerage* · Boase, *Mod. Eng. biog.* · Allibone, *Dict.* · *Men and women of the time* (1899)
Archives CAC Cam., corresp. and papers | BL, corresp. with Sir Charles Dilke, Add. MS 43902
Likenesses portrait, repro. in *The Graphic*, 27 (1883), 469
Wealth at death £26,689 10s. 10d.: probate, 26 May 1883, *CGPLA Eng. & Wales*

Dilke, Charles Wentworth (1789–1864), newspaper editor and writer, was born on 8 December 1789 at Bedhampton, Hampshire, the third of four children and elder son of Sarah Blewford (1765/6–1825) and Charles Wentworth Dilke (1742/3–1826), a chief clerk in the paymaster branch of the Admiralty. Although he attended schools in Portsea and London, his education was primarily by private tutoring. In April 1805 he entered the navy pay office of the Admiralty as a clerk, and in London, on 10 October 1806, he married Maria Walker (1790–1850), daughter of an official in the East India Company. They had one child, (Charles) Wentworth *Dilke (1810–1869), who served as leading commissioner of the Great Exhibition of 1851, and later became first baronet; he, in turn, was the father of Charles Wentworth *Dilke (1843–1911), politician and cabinet minister. In 1816 the family settled in Wentworth House, Hampstead, which they built with Charles Armitage Brown, an old school friend, and it was here, probably early in 1817, that Dilke made the acquaintance of members of the 'cockney school' such as Leigh Hunt, John

Hamilton Reynolds, Thomas Hood, and John Keats, all of whom became close friends. He also knew Shelley. In April 1819 when the Dilkes moved to Westminster, where Dilke was to remain until the early 1850s, Mrs Brawne occupied the Dilkes' portion of the Hampstead house. Long after Keats's death, Dilke was active in the affairs of the Keats family and served as a trustee for Fanny Brawne. Dilke's friendship with Charles Brown ended in 1830 in a disagreement over the probity of George Keats, which Dilke defended robustly and Brown denounced. Later commentators endorsed Brown's view, noting Dilke's inflexibility once he formed an opinion, and citing Lamb's phrase 'a Dilkish blockhead' and Keats's opinion that Dilke was 'a Godwin-Methodist' who lacked the gift of negative capability (Richardson, 119–20).

Dilke's leisure hours were devoted to reading and, sharing the enthusiasm for the Elizabethan dramatists which was fostered by the publication of Lamb's *Specimens of the English Dramatic Poets*, he began to edit Renaissance play texts. William Gifford, editor of Massinger and Jonson as well as the *Quarterly Review*, encouraged him, and between 1814 and 1815 Dilke published the first of his antiquarian works, a continuation of Robert Dodsley's *Old English Plays, being a Selection from the Early Dramatic Writers*.

From about 1818 Dilke began to contribute anonymously to the crop of new periodicals, and when Henry Southern's distinctively antiquarian *Retrospective Review* started in 1820, Dilke became one of its contributors. His anonymous pieces in *The Champion* (1818) edited by John Scott, *The Retrospective*, the Benthamite *Westminster Review* (1830), also edited by Southern, and probably other magazines of the period, were mainly literary. In 1821 he produced a political pamphlet addressed to Lord John Russell, which was characteristically radical in tone, and pleaded for the repeal of the corn laws. This caught the attention of John Taylor, by then editor of the *London Magazine*, who invited both antiquarian and political contributions from Dilke, the latter of which, in 1823, became a dominant political voice of the journal's monthly 'View of public affairs'. In January 1824, in the first of his editing stints, Dilke became editor of the *London Magazine*, with 'its passion for anciency' (Bauer, 246), and probably served a year until Southern took over in 1825. Dilke's lifelong radical politics are clearly visible here, before he took on the mantle of neutrality that characterized his association with *The Athenaeum*. So closely was Dilke associated with the *London Magazine*, its circle, and the ethos of honest journalism promulgated by its first editor, John Scott, that Dilke's conduct of *The Athenaeum* has been seen by Bauer (ibid., 335) as a continuation of the cultural work of the *London Magazine*.

The Athenaeum (1828–) was a London arts and science weekly which eschewed politics and religion; in its earliest years it was closely associated with the Cambridge Apostles. It was purchased first by John Sterling and eventually in 1830 by a group which included Dilke, the latter becoming editor in that year. The effect of his firm hand on the management of the paper was speedily seen. In 1831 he reduced the price by half to 4*d*., a measure which resulted in a marked increase in its sales and a corresponding reduction in the circulation of its rival, the *Literary Gazette* at the then customary price of 8*d*. Alarmed by the change, the majority of his co-proprietors gave up their shares while continuing to write for it, leaving the financial responsibility to Dilke and the printer, James Holmes. Gathering support from a group which included Lamb, Barry Cornwall, H. F. Chorley, George Darley, and other friends, Dilke also enlisted the aid of Sainte-Beuve, Jules Janin, and other continental writers of repute, an unusual move for a British journalist at the time. Although the circulation of the paper responded quickly and dramatically to the reduction in price, the heavy tax on advertisements prohibited their growth in the paper, and for several years there was no surplus profit; throughout his tenure as editor Dilke worked without a salary, putting profits back into the business.

The main principle of Dilke's editorship was to preserve a complete independence from the trade, and to criticize a book without concern for the writer or the publisher; promulgated most concertedly between 1830 and 1832, this antipathy to puffing was singular at the time. To maintain it Dilke withdrew from general society, confining his social life to entertaining at home, and thus avoiding as far as possible personal contact with authors or publishers who might seek to influence the reviews in *The Athenaeum*. In 1836 the navy pay office was abolished and Dilke, retired on a pension, was able to devote all his energies to the improvement of the paper. By the 1840s *The Athenaeum*'s success was established, and Dilke handed over the editorship to T. K. Hervey in 1846. In that year too W. J. Thoms's monthly columns of material on folklore began appearing in *The Athenaeum* with Dilke's encouragement, and so popular did they become that in 1849 Thoms founded *Notes and Queries* to accommodate the burgeoning material.

Called in to aid the infant *Daily News*—by this time abandoned by Dickens and edited by John Forster—Dilke became its manager in April 1846; he reduced the price of the daily by half from 5*d*. to 2½*d*., halved the number of pages from eight to four, and increased the amount of copy. Although the circulation rose from 4000 to 22,000 per day, the paper lost money, and the old price was eventually restored in February 1849. Closure was avoided, despite a massive drop in sales, and in April 1849 Dilke completed his contract and retired. *The Bookseller* in 1864 commended Dilke's *Daily News* prospectus for its strong endorsement of the importance of the newspaper press and praised his foresight in creating a cheap daily before the removal of the stamp duty, lamenting that 'had this policy been persevered in there can be little doubt that the *Daily News* would have occupied a foremost position in the cheap issue of the present day' (31 Aug 1864, 526). In 1850 his wife died, and by 1853 Dilke had moved from Lower Grosvenor Street to the house of his son in Sloane Street, where he acted as companion and mentor to his grandson.

A third period in Dilke's career began with his retirement from newspaper management, and all the articles on which his literary reputation rests are subsequent to 1847. While editing *The Athenaeum* he had on principle avoided writing in it; having ceased to edit it he became a contributor. The mystery attaching to the authorship of the highly political 'Letters of Junius', which appeared from 1768 to 1772 in the *Public Advertiser*, especially fascinated him, and he acquired a knowledge of everything bearing on the problem that has remained unsurpassed (Ellegard, 10). Unlike others, he was not so anxious to identify the author of the articles as to show who he was not. He commenced in *The Athenaeum* of July 1848 by demolishing John Britton's theory that Colonel Barre was Junius, and over the next five years he wrote a series of reviews which form the most weighty contribution of his day to the controversy. The Junius pieces led to the study of Edmund Burke and John Wilkes MP, founder in 1762 of the *North Briton*. Dilke was the first to rescue Wilkes from the obloquy that attached to his name for allegedly libelling the king in 1745 and for publishing the obscene 'Essay on women'. He also became the apologist for the satires of Peter Pindar, the pseudonym of John Wolcot.

Articles on Pope followed, informed by Dilke's purchase of the Caryll papers in 1854. In a series of contributions to *The Athenaeum* and *Notes and Queries* Dilke was able to explain the mystery of the publication of the letters by Edmund Curll, to make clear the poet's parentage, to settle several matters in his early life, to identify the 'Unfortunate lady', and in various other points to throw fresh light on Pope's career and his poetry. These articles brought the writer into controversy with various Pope scholars, but his conclusions remained unshaken and were adopted by Whitwell Elwin in his edition of Pope (1871–89). One of his last articles in *The Athenaeum* was devoted to Lady Mary Wortley Montagu and her quarrel with Pope, an article prompted by the appearance of Moy Thomas's edition of her work in 1861. Other issues to which Dilke turned in his retirement included the systemization of the British Museum catalogue and establishing the corpus of work by Jonathan Swift which involved the attribution of work by 'William Wagstaffe' to Swift.

In his later life the reform of the Literary Fund occupied a large part of Dilke's attention. As early as 1836 he had begun to scrutinize its management from within its general committee; but it was not until 1849 that the controversy, which had been regularly reported in *The Athenaeum*, became open and heated. In 1858 he joined with Dickens and John Forster in the pamphlet called 'The case of the reformers of the Literary Fund', part of which appeared in *The Athenaeum* (6 March 1858, 304–6). The reformers, although they had the best of the argument, had the worst of the voting, and finding it impossible to convert their minority into a majority, they attempted, with the aid of Lord Lytton, to found the Guild of Art and Literature, a scheme which did not meet with the success anticipated.

In 1862 Dilke withdrew altogether from London, and settled at Alice Holt near Farnham in Hampshire where he died from kidney disease on 10 August 1864. He was buried privately on 16 August in Kensal Green cemetery, London.

The best contemporary comments on his character and work were those of his old friend W. J. Thoms, in *Notes and Queries*:

> The distinguishing feature of his character was his singular love of truth, and his sense of its value and importance, even in the minutest points and questions of literary history. What the independence of English literary journalism owes to his spirited exertions, clear judgment, and unflinching honesty of purpose will, we trust, be told hereafter.   (13 Aug 1864, 140)

LAUREL BRAKE

Sources W. Garrett, *Charles Wentworth Dilke* (1982) · L. A. Marchand, *The Athenaeum: a mirror of Victorian culture* (1941) · C. W. Dilke, 'Memoir', *The papers of a critic: selected from the papers of Charles Wentworth Dilke*, ed. C. W. Dilke, 1 (1875), 1–91 · J. Bauer, *London Magazine* [Anglistica] (1953) · J. Richardson, *The everlasting spell: a study of Keats and his friends* (1963) · *DNB* · A. Sullivan, ed., *British literary magazines*, [2]: *The Romantic age, 1789–1836* (1984) · A. Sullivan, ed., *British literary magazines*, [3]: *The Victorian and Edwardian age, 1837–1913* (1984) · *The Bookseller* (31 Aug 1864), 525–6 · A. Ellegard, *Who was Junius?* (1962) · C. W. Dilke, C. Dickens, and J. Forster, 'The case of the reformers of the Literary Fund' (1858) [pamphlet] · *The Athenaeum* (1829–46) · *London Magazine*, 1–new ser., 3 (1820–25) · *Retrospective Review* (1820–25)

Archives BL, corresp. and literary MSS, Add. MS 43899 · CAC Cam., corresp. · LUL, *Athanaeum* 1830 [marked file] · University of Chicago Library, department of special collections, corresp. relating to the *Athenaeum* | BL, Dilke, Sir Charles W., 2nd baronet, Add. MSS 43910–43913 · BL, Dilke, Sir Charles W., 3rd baronet, Add. MSS 43910–43913 · BL, letters to William Hepworth Dixon, Add. MS 38794

Likenesses T. Hood, cartoon, repro. in T. Wood, *Up the Rhine* (1840) · A. Hughes, portrait (in later life), repro. in Richardson, *Everlasting spell* · miniature (in youth), repro. in Richardson, *Everlasting spell* · oils, London, Keats House; repro. in Richardson, *Everlasting spell*

Wealth at death under £5000: probate, 22 Feb 1865, *CGPLA Eng. & Wales*

Dilke, Sir Charles Wentworth, second baronet (1843–1911)

Dilke, Sir Charles Wentworth, second baronet (1843–1911), writer and politician, was born in London on 4 September 1843 at 76 Sloane Street, on the edge of Belgravia and Chelsea, which house he was to inherit from his father, (Charles) Wentworth *Dilke, first baronet (1810–1869), in 1869, and in which he was to live until his own death forty-two years later. He also inherited enough property, much of it in the form of two literary publications, *The Athenaeum* and *Notes and Queries*, as well as more specialized publications, including the *Gardeners' Chronicle* and the *Agricultural Gazette*, to bring him an income of £6000–8000 of mid-Victorian money. The first baronet (created 1862) was one of the commissioners for the Great Exhibition of 1851, and was subsequently regarded, in an age of exhibitions, as an exhibition expert. He was in St Petersburg as British commissioner for a horticultural exhibition when he died. He was also briefly MP for Wallingford. But despite these attributes he was not greatly esteemed by his elder son (who subsequently wrote of him: 'brain-power wasted and heart misunderstood'), and as a result exercised comparatively little influence upon him. Nor did the second baronet's mother have much obvious formative effect. She was Mary, daughter of William Chatfield, a captain in the Madras cavalry. She

Sir Charles Wentworth Dilke, second baronet (1843–1911), by George Frederic Watts, 1873

entered a decline when her second son, Ashton Wentworth *Dilke (the explorer), was born, and died when her elder son was ten.

Youth and education The family figure who was most influential in the upbringing of the second baronet was his grandfather, yet another Charles Wentworth *Dilke (1789–1864), a prominent literary figure; together, for instance, they visited every English cathedral, as well as a great number of other English and French sights. The boy's health (although it was perfectly good from the age of eighteen onwards) was judged too delicate for him to go normally to school; he was taught mainly at home by a variety of tutors and relatives.

To compensate for any deficiencies Dilke was open to a wide range of cosmopolitan culture and fashion. He heard and saw all the great mid-century actors and singers, both in London and in Paris. At the age of eleven and in the first flush of display of the Second Empire he was taken to Paris for four months, and managed to observe everything from the great balls to military tattoos and gala performances at the Opéra and the Théâtre Français. He became strongly francophone and francophile, and in subsequent summers in Normandy mingled with the fringes of the imperial family. In England he was also exposed to a remarkable range of acquaintanceship for a boy, but here it was more to men of solid achievement—literary, scientific, or commercial—than to the beau monde. Thackeray, Browning, Joseph Paxton, Robert Stephenson the engineer, Joseph Martin the painter, and John Forster the historian, all made an imprint upon him. When he said near the end of his life: 'I have known everyone worth knowing from 1850 until my death', he was not being modest, which was not in his nature, but nor was he exaggerating foolishly. When he arrived at Trinity Hall, Cambridge, his first and only educational institution, in the autumn of 1862, he had absorbed only a patchy academic instruction but a remarkable knowledge of the world.

At Cambridge, Dilke devoted himself with almost excessive dedication to three interests: the tripos, the river, and the union (debating society), and achieved considerable success in all three. In Trinity Hall the dominant influence was Leslie Stephen, and Dilke attuned easily to his anti-emotional, muscular, competitive approach to work and games. Switching from mathematics to law after his first year, Dilke became senior legalist, the highest distinction in the university open to a law student. At rowing, which he had never done before, he stroked the Trinity Hall boat and saw it go head of the river; he recorded that he was offered a place in the university boat, but was made by his doctor to decline because of the long course on the London tideway. In the union he was not only president for two terms (his re-election was unusual) but left a more permanent mark by being mainly responsible for building the gabled Gothic premises which have since been its home.

Travel, writing, and early political career Dilke remained at Cambridge until the spring of 1866, when he was twenty-two, and then paused only to be called to the bar as a member of the Middle Temple (though he never practised) before leaving in June for a North American tour which extended itself into a year-long excursion around the world, taking in New Zealand, Australia, India, and Egypt. One result of this tour was by far the most successful of the eight books which he wrote in the course of his life. *Greater Britain* was published in the early autumn of 1868, quickly ran through four editions, and remained in print and widely read for nearly half a century. Its title was chosen to encapsulate not only his itinerary but a large part of his political philosophy. He had 'followed England round the world', and the conclusions he drew from his journey were at once radical and racialist. He was for what he regarded as British energy and superiority, but against such archaic British institutions as the monarchy and an oligarchic parliament. The United States, although he maintained a sharp edge of criticism during his four months there, greatly excited him. 'America offers the English race the moral directorship of the globe', he wrote, 'by ruling mankind through Saxon institutions and the English tongue. Through America, England is speaking to the world.' He carried his views to the logical conclusion that Canada should sever the London connection.

Yet (in relation to the American Indians) he could express with pride the brutally harsh view that 'the Anglo-Saxon is the only extirpating race on earth'; he believed in 'the defeat of the cheaper by the dearer peoples', and he constructed an elaborate theory that the banana was the most dangerous crop—you could live on it, raw or fried, but do nothing constructive with it. Thus it offered the fatal prospect of a soft life in a soft climate. Despite such occasional excursions into fantasy his picture of America in the immediate lee of the civil war was a brilliant and memorable one, whether he was writing about Washington, with the unfinished dome of the Capitol rising above the swamp town along the Potomac, or of mammon-ridden New York, whose drawing rooms were already the most exclusive (but not the most distinguished) in the world, or of Boston (much superior), where Emerson, Longfellow, and Agassiz held sway, or of Cincinnati, where the cholera was killing 200 a day, or of the great hardships and dangers of a transcontinental journey three years before the railway link was completed. It was much the best part of the book.

Greater Britain brought Dilke much attention. Gladstone read and carefully annotated his copy (though referring to it in his diary as Dilke's *Greater World*). J. S. Mill, hitherto a stranger, was captivated by it, and for the remaining four years of his life was Dilke's principal mentor. Within a few weeks of publication Dilke was elected to parliament as a radical Liberal at the top of the poll for the two-member constituency of Chelsea. He was part of a Liberal majority of 112 which made Gladstone prime minister for the first time. He was only just twenty-five and his prospects seemed dazzling.

A future of climbing smoothly and gradually up the ladder of conventional political success did not, however, fit in with Dilke's predilections, which were at once generous and arrogant. He took one small step up the ladder when, in February 1870, he was chosen by Gladstone to second the address, but for the most part he preferred to criticize the government for being too cautious, to work with a semi-detached group of more or less rebellious radicals, and to promote his own pet (and worthy) measures of reform. Thus in 1869 he played a leading part both in restoring to women ratepayers the right to vote in municipal elections, which they had lost in 1835, and in securing the abolition of hanging, drawing, and quartering in New Zealand. In 1870 he was one of the sharpest critics of W. E. Forster's Elementary Education Bill. On this he came into conflict not only with the high-Anglican approach of the prime minister but also with the nonconformist simple 'Bible-teaching' approach of his normal provincial radical allies. He was more a secularist than he was a protestant, and he was the only Liberal member to vote against the Cowper-Temple compromise. Dilke was much more in the radical mainstream when he moved a crucial amendment providing that the new school boards should be directly elected rather than committees of the existing boards of guardians. The beginning of his close partnership and friendship with Joseph Chamberlain sprang out of his work on this bill and Chamberlain's first political foray as the animator of the National Education League.

Republicanism and first marriage In the autumn of 1871 Dilke's good fortune for almost the first, but by no means the last, time in his life deserted him. He had long been a theoretical republican, although not a very actively pros-elytizing one. In that year, however, provoked by the continued invisibility of the queen ten years into her widow-hood, the lack of respect commanded by the prince of

Wales, and the frequent applications to parliament for allowances or dowries for royal children, he decided to use a series of constitutional addresses in provincial cities for the deployment of a somewhat tentative republican case. He began at Newcastle in early November, and made enough impact to provoke a heavily rebuking *Times* leader. Much more damaging to him than this, however, was the dramatic recovery of the prince of Wales from typhoid. The prince accomplished more for the popularity of the monarchy in 1871 than during the whole of his previous thirty years of life.

Meanwhile Dilke had to continue with his speaking programme, from Bristol to Leeds to Bolton and Birmingham, in an increasingly hostile climate. He also felt that he could not abandon the issue without repeating in the House of Commons what he had said outside. It took him some months to get a day, then on 19 March 1872 he went down to defeat by 276 votes to 2, and abandoned the subject with relief. It cost him a year or two of semi-ostracism in parliament and society, and the hostility of the queen for the remaining thirty years of her reign.

In the early 1870s there were two other disparate ingredients in his life which showed that Dilke was not exactly as other men were. During the Franco-Prussian War he demonstrated the cosmopolitan adventurer side of his character. In late July and August 1870 he travelled with the Prussian army and was present on most of the battlefields of their victorious campaign. Then he switched sides, or at least location, and was in Paris on 4 September for the fall of the empire and the proclamation of the republic. During the subsequent nine months of siege and commune he was in and out of Paris and the trajectories of the shells of different nations and ideologies.

Then, between January 1872 and September 1874, there was the brief interlude of Dilke's first marriage. His wife was Katherine Mary Eliza Sheil, the daughter of a long-dead Captain Arthur Gore Sheil of the 89th foot; from her mother, also dead, a member of an old Devon family, the Wises, she had acquired property and connection in Devon. She possessed, according to Dilke, an unusual combination of attributes: extreme attractiveness of appearance, vivacity, intimidating violence of temper, and debilitating ill health. She sang and she played croquet to professional standards. They were married suddenly and semi-secretly on 30 January 1872. In December 1873 the Dilkes went to Monte Carlo, with Kate recovering from the death of a stillborn son; there Dilke wrote *The Fall of Prince Florestan* (1874), a picaresque novel. At the time of the marriage there was little suggestion that they were seriously in love with each other; yet when Kate died in childbirth on 20 September 1874 Dilke became deranged—'When I was mad', he later wrote of the period.

Dilke fled to Paris, shaved off his beard, and lived in secret isolation for six weeks, until he was recognized in the street by Léon Gambetta. Gambetta was a genuine friend who brought him back to sanity. But it was typical of Dilke that, even in such a condition of disarray, it should be the most famous Frenchman of the day who found him. He spent most of December and January in north Africa, became a teetotaller (which he remained for eleven years) and a vegetarian, and returned to London, though remaining in an enfeebled condition until Easter, for the beginning of the parliamentary session in 1875. During his four and a half months' absence he had left everything in London, including the naming and baptism of his new-born son, to be settled by his grandmother. At least the name caused her little problem: he became the fourth Charles Wentworth Dilke, but added no lustre to the name before his early death in 1918.

A rising politician   Dilke himself had a successful summer in the House of Commons, initiating four debates, each of which paved the way for future reforms. He also renewed an interrupted friendship with the notable historian of French art who, ten years later, was to become his second wife [*see* Dilke, Emilia Francis (1840–1904)]. She had been born Emilia Francis Strong, the daughter of Major Henry Strong of the Indian army, was three years older than Dilke, and was currently unhappily married to Mark Pattison, rector of Lincoln College, Oxford. Having thus re-established both his parliamentary and his emotional bearings, Dilke left for a second world trip, taking in America, Japan, China, and Singapore between August 1875 and January 1876.

During the four years that intervened between his return and the Liberal victory in the spring of 1880, Dilke's most important activity was the forging of an alliance between himself and Joseph Chamberlain. Chamberlain, after his not altogether successful foray with the National Education League, had been a brilliantly constructive mayor of Birmingham in 1873–6. Then, with his fortieth birthday approaching, he decided that, if he was to make a comparable impact on the national scene, he must quickly enter parliament. One of the three members for Birmingham had hinted that he might retire. Thereupon he was ejected from the seat with all the certainty and expedition with which the mechanism works in a modern fighter aircraft. It was a tribute to the effectiveness of the Birmingham machine that Chamberlain had built up, and to the ruthlessness with which he was prepared to use it. In 1877 he also used this Birmingham caucus as the nucleus around which he built the National Liberal Federation, which brought together most of the radically inclined constituency organizations in the other big towns.

Chamberlain was thus a most valuable ally for Dilke, who as a metropolitan parliamentarian, most of whose outside contacts were across the channel and even the oceans, lacked lines of communication with provincial radicalism. Chamberlain was a much better speaker than Dilke, and in the last resort a more formidable, if not more attractive, personality. But he lacked Dilke's parliamentary experience, his knowledge of the fashionable world, and his foreign affairs expertise. They therefore each had balancing advantages to bring to the partnership, and Dilke deliberately set about exploiting his by acting as Chamberlain's sponsor in metropolitan life, putting him up at 76 Sloane Street and giving frequent dinner parties to introduce him to a wider world. They were very useful to each other, and there was probably also a genuine degree of emotional attachment, although stronger on Dilke's side than on Chamberlain's.

These four years saw Gladstone's re-entry into political leadership after his brief retirement. It began with his pamphlet *The Bulgarian Atrocities* (1876) and it ended with the Midlothian campaign (1879–80). Neither Chamberlain nor Dilke was dazzled by Gladstone, who was too moralizing for their taste. Chamberlain, however, tried to make use of him for the launch of the National Liberal Federation and as a counterweight to Hartington. Dilke found his sentimental generalities offensive to the *realpolitik* based on detailed knowledge which was always his own approach to foreign policy, and mostly preferred the cool whiggery of Hartington. This was not because he agreed with Hartington's domestic conservatism, but because he thought it would have to be compensated for within the Liberal Party by giving great positions, even the Foreign Office and the exchequer, to himself and Chamberlain. Such a triumvirate, leading after an interval to the emergence of one or the other radical as leader of a Lib–Lab party, dedicated to social reform and unfrightened by collectivism, became the strategic aim of Dilke (and less clearly of Chamberlain) from the late 1870s onwards. The significance of Dilke's fall in 1885–6 was that, by allowing Chamberlain to block the early achievement of home rule (which an unweakened Dilke might well have prevented him from doing), it kept Gladstone in politics for nearly another decade, drove the Liberal Party along the worthy but sterile axis of an Irish-dominated policy, and opened the way for the emergence of an Independent Labour Party, which eventually ended the Liberal governing tradition.

In office, 1880–1885 Before these developments there were the five years of Gladstone's second government and of Dilke's only experience of office, as opposed to previous promise and subsequent contemplation of what might have been. After the 1880 election but before the formation of the government, Chamberlain proposed to Dilke, who was thought of as the better placed of the two, that neither should accept office unless they were both in the cabinet. Dilke thought this might be over-bidding on Chamberlain's part, which was ironical as the eventual outcome was that Dilke, the first to be approached, by holding out for one cabinet post between them, forced Chamberlain into the presidency of the Board of Trade over his head, and had himself to settle for under-secretary at the Foreign Office, though with the advantage that his chief, Granville, was in the Lords. He began his official duties on 27 April 1880.

Dilke then had to wait nearly three years for promotion, in spite of his being a notably effective minister, especially in the complex matter of the renegotiation of the trade treaty with France. Delay in promotion was partly due to a combination of the queen's determination not to have him in any office 'close to the sovereign' and of his own taste for high-stake play. The latter attribute showed

itself in May 1882, when the assassination of Lord Frederick Cavendish dramatically created a vacancy in the office of chief secretary for Ireland. Dilke was offered it, without membership of the cabinet. A lesser man would have felt it necessary to accept to avoid a charge of cowardice. Dilke coolly held out. He would not accept responsibility without power. Eventually, in December 1882, he entered the cabinet as president of the Local Government Board. It was perhaps the least glamorous of all departments, and one which certainly met the queen's demand that he should not be close to her person. But it was also one suited to Dilke's talents, and which he made more constructively central to the government than were the great traditional departments. He set up, and himself presided over, a royal commission on the housing of the working classes in 1884, which had perhaps the most remarkable membership of any royal commission ever assembled. There sat under him the trio of the prince of Wales, Cardinal Manning, and Lord Salisbury. Octavia Hill was vetoed (as a woman) by a combination of Harcourt and Hartington, but he none the less secured three other former or future cabinet ministers among the dozen members. He was also a member of the quintet of ministers which fatefully took all the decisions in relation to the dispatch of General Gordon to evacuate the Sudan.

Dilke's best work was, however, done on the Redistribution of Seats Bill in 1885, which was of repercussive as well as inherent importance because it unblocked the passage into law of the Franchise Bill of 1884, which extended household suffrage from the towns to the counties, and was the most important reform carried through by that somewhat sterile government of 1880–85. The Lords would not pass it without a redistribution bill. Chamberlain responded with a violent denunciation of the peers, Dilke by being (with Gladstone) the key figure in negotiating with Salisbury in November 1885 a settlement that seemed acceptable from a Liberal point of view, and piloting the resultant bill through the House of Commons with skill and authority. In both the negotiations and the parliamentary process he had the decisive (and for him typical) advantage of knowing twice as much about the subject as anyone else.

It was not therefore fanciful by the spring of 1885 to see Dilke, perhaps after a Hartington interlude, as Gladstone's most likely successor. His radical credentials were secure, but he was also a man who could work the system and get things done. The government was admittedly on the brink of disintegration. Nearly half its members, including Dilke and Chamberlain, had submitted their resignations. Nevertheless few doubted there would be a bright medium-term Liberal future, underpinned by the extension of the franchise, and that Dilke would have a major part in it. He was also about to be married again, having announced his engagement to the recently widowed Mrs Pattison in the autumn of 1884.

The Crawford divorce In June 1885 the government—further weakened by a row about a central board for Ireland promoted by Chamberlain and Dilke—was defeated on the Finance Bill and resigned. This was a blow which, with his prospects as they appeared to be, Dilke was easily able to survive. In the following month there fell a very different sort of blow and one that was wholly fatal to his career in high politics. Virginia Crawford, the 22-year-old wife of Donald Crawford, a dour Scottish Liberal lawyer, and also the sister of Mrs Ashton Dilke, his brother's wife, made first a confession to her husband and then a public accusation that Dilke had seduced her in 1882 (the first year of her marriage) and had then conducted an intermittent affair with her for two and a half years. Dilke resolutely denied the charges, although his position was complicated from the beginning by the fact that he had, both before and after his first marriage, been the lover of her mother, Ellen, Mrs Eustace Smith. The case followed a tortuous legal course, during which period Dilke was excluded from any effective political action, despite its being the most seismic year in late nineteenth-century politics. He did manage to get narrowly returned for a new and smaller Chelsea constituency in November 1885 (although he lost it in a second general election eight months later). This apart, everything went from bad to worse for him, each act of the tragedy plumbing new depths.

The Crawford divorce action was heard and decided in one day on 12 February 1886. Donald Crawford took the court through the details of the confession and one or two vaguely corroborating servants were called. Mrs Crawford was not in court. Dilke's lawyers, aided by the lay advice of Chamberlain, took the view that he should not give evidence. No evidence had been adduced against him ('I cannot see any case whatsoever against Sir Charles Dilke', the judge was later to say), and they feared his being cross-examined about the whole of his past life. The result was that Crawford got his divorce but that Dilke was dismissed from the suit as having no case to answer. It might have been satisfactory for a private individual, but not for a public figure. The verdict appeared to be the perverse one that Mrs Crawford had committed adultery with Dilke, but that he had not done so with her.

A public campaign, greatly fostered by the early investigative journalist W. T. Stead, was then mounted against Dilke's failure to go into the witness box. By April this had persuaded him that he should seek to reopen the case by getting the queen's proctor to intervene. He did so under a grave misapprehension. He falsely assumed that his counsel would be able to submit Mrs Crawford to a devastating cross-examination. But he had been dismissed from the case and his counsel had no *locus*. Furthermore the queen's proctor had to try to prove a negative, that Dilke had not committed adultery, before Mrs Crawford was exposed in the witness box. It was he and not she who was subjected to a most stringent and damaging cross-examination. The result was a disaster. He proved a very bad witness, she a very good one. The summing up by the president of the Probate, Divorce, and Admiralty Division was highly unfavourable to Dilke. The verdict of the jury—in form that the divorce should stand, in fact that Mrs Crawford was a witness of the truth and that Dilke was not—was reached quickly and unanimously.

Dilke's career and reputation were shattered. Indeed the question for a time was whether he was to be subject to a criminal prosecution for perjury, carrying the risk of a long sentence of penal servitude and the sequestration of his property. When this threat was removed he and his wife (they had been married on 3 October 1885, after the scandal had broken) devoted themselves to his case for several years, with the help of a few devoted 'believers' and the expenditure of a good deal of money on enquiry agents. Much helpful evidence was accumulated, certainly enough to prove the central thesis that, contrary to the view of the court, Mrs Crawford lied in the witness box, and that her activities which she described as having taken place with Dilke were either figments of her imagination or, more probably, had taken place with others.

Elements of highly charged mystery remained. Dilke, although almost certainly not guilty as charged, obviously had things to hide in his life. But what prompted Mrs Crawford's false story? Cardinal Manning, who instructed her for her reception into the Roman Catholic church in 1889 and was amiably disposed towards Dilke, was said to know the whole truth, but never revealed it. There were conspiracy theories, some involving figures as eminent as Rosebery (no evidence worth speaking of) and Chamberlain (some considerable circumstantial evidence but an absence of convincing motive), and others involving several ladies who had grievances against Dilke. These enigmas have remained unresolved for over a hundred years, and are unlikely now ever to be fully explained.

Later career and death Dilke re-entered the House of Commons, and sat for the Forest of Dean, still as an advanced radical, from 1892 until his death nineteen years later. He achieved great local popularity, particularly with the miners of what was then a detached but significant small coalfield. He vigorously pursued their interests and those of labour generally, as well as being an independent parliamentary expert on military, colonial, and foreign questions, and was an important link with Labour members and trade unionists. He was a vital influence in the founding of the committee of imperial defence in 1904, a subject he had discussed in works such as *Problems of Greater Britain* (2 vols., 1890) and *Imperial Defence* (1892, written with Spenser Wilkinson). His reputation abroad held up rather better than at home, though in the Commons he became a respected independent back-bencher. But he never again came near to political office. The last third of his life was a sad anticlimax. He spent part of it preparing his large collection of manuscript papers for posterity by mutilating them with a pair of scissors. The death in 1904 of his second wife (whose memoir he wrote as a preface to *The Book of the Spiritual Life*, 1905) and the mental illness and subsequent incarceration of his son and heir greatly disturbed him. Dilke died of heart failure at his house, 76

Sloane Street, London, on 26 January 1911, and was cremated at Golders Green on 30 January after a funeral service at Holy Trinity Church, Sloane Square, London. During his son's illness, Dilke altered his will, largely in favour of May Tennant and Gertrude Tuckwell, his second wife's niece and, with Stephen Gwynn, his biographer.

ROY JENKINS

Sources *DNB* · S. Gwynn and G. M. Tuckwell, *The life of the Rt. Hon. Sir Charles W. Dilke*, 2 vols. (1917) · R. Jenkins, *Sir Charles Dilke: a Victorian tragedy* (1958) · D. Nicholls, *The lost prime minister: a life of Sir Charles Dilke* (1995) [with bibliography of Dilke's works] · Gladstone, *Diaries* · S. Leslie, 'Virginia Crawford, Sir Charles Dilke, and Cardinal Manning', *Dublin Review*, 241 (1967), 177–205

Archives BL, corresp., Add. MSS 47911, 48215, 48937–48939, 48607, 48614 · BL, corresp. and papers, Add. MSS 43874–43967, 49385–49455, 49610–49612 · BL, papers relating to the two divorce cases, loan MS 119 · Boston PL, letters · CAC Cam., corresp. and notes · Duke U., Perkins L., letters · NL Scot., corresp., MSS 10075–10145, 10249–10291 · U. Birm. L., diaries | Balliol Oxf., corresp. with Sir Robert Morier · BL, corresp. with Sir Francis Adams, Add. MS 64796 · BL, letters to W. H. Dixon, Add. MS 38794 · BL, letters to Lord Gladstone, Add. MSS 46048–46068 · BL, letters to W. E. Gladstone, Add. MS 44149 · BL, corresp. with Sir Edward Walter Hamilton, Add. MS 48614 · BL, corresp. with W. C. Hazlitt, Add. MSS 38904–38907 · BL, corresp. with Macmillans, Add. MS 55242 · BLPES, corresp. with E. D. Morel · BLPES, corresp. with the Independent Labour Party · Bodl. Oxf., corresp. with Sir William Harcourt · Bodl. Oxf., letters to F. G. Stephens · Bodl. Oxf., letters to Sir James Thursfield · CAC Cam., corresp. with Lord Randolph Churchill · CAC Cam., corresp. with W. T. Stead · CKS, letters to Edward Stanhope · Co-operative Union, Holyoake House, Manchester, letters to George Holyoake · HLRO, letters to Herbert Samuel · King's AC Cam., letters to Oscar Browning · NA Scot., corresp. with A. J. Balfour · NAM, letters to Lord Roberts · NAM, letters to Spenser Wilkinson · NL Aus., corresp. with Alfred Deakin · NL Ire., letters to John Redmond · NL Wales, letters to T. E. Ellis · PRO, corresp. with Lord Granville, PRO 30/29 · PRO, letters to Sir William White, FO 364/1–11 · St Deiniol's Library, Hawarden, letters to W. E. Gladstone · U. Birm. L., corresp. with Joseph Chamberlain · UCL, corresp. with Sir Edwin Chadwick

Likenesses G. F. Watts, oils, 1873, NPG [*see illus.*] · B. Stone, photograph, 1897, NPG · O. Roty, bronze plaque, 1900, NPG · E. T. Reed, pencil drawing, *c.*1902, NPG · H. Speed, chalk drawing, 1908, NPG · W. Strang, pencil drawing, 1908, NPG · Dalziel, woodcut, BM · W. & D. Downey, woodburytype photograph, NPG; repro. in W. Downey and D. Downey, *The cabinet portrait gallery*, 5 (1894) · H. Furniss, caricature, pen-and-ink sketch, NPG · H. Lenthall, oils, National Liberal Club, London · Lock & Whitfield, woodburytype photograph, NPG; repro. in T. Cooper, *Men of mark: a gallery of contemporary portraits* (1881) · London Stereoscopic Co., cabinet photograph, NPG · London Stereoscopic Co., carte-de-visite, NPG · H. Speed, chalk drawing, National Liberal Club, London · Spy [L. Ward], drawing, NPG · caricature, chromolithograph, NPG; repro. in *VF* (25 Nov 1871) · prints, NPG

Wealth at death £130,878 8s.: probate, 29 March 1911, CGPLA Eng. & Wales

Dilke [*née* Strong; *other married name* Pattison], **Emilia Francis**, Lady Dilke (1840–1904), art historian and trade unionist, was born on 2 September 1840 in Ilfracombe, Devon, the fourth of the six children of Henry Strong (1794–1876) and his wife, Emily Weedon (*d.* 1879?). Little is known of her mother, who was from Oxford, but her paternal family, of which she wrote proudly in 'Samuel Strong and the Georgian loyalists' (1899), were American colonists, and her father was a retired Indian army officer

Emilia Francis Dilke, Lady Dilke (1840–1904), by Sir Hubert von Herkomer, 1887

and amateur artist, who became manager of the London and County Bank in Oxford in 1841. The young Francis Strong (who preferred to go by her second, masculine name) was educated at home in Iffley by Miss Bowdich, who gave her an excellent grounding in languages, including French, German, Latin, and Greek. She grew up in a household in which cultural pursuits were highly valued, and her father was active in local art circles at a time when Oxford was an important centre of intellectual and artistic life. In her youth, through her family's friendship with Henry and Sarah Acland and Thomas and Martha Combe, she came into contact with leading figures in the Victorian art world, such as John Ruskin, John Everett Millais, and William Holman Hunt (who proposed to her in 1859, but was rejected).

It was Ruskin who, having seen some of her drawings, encouraged Francis Strong to go to London in 1858 and study at the Government School of Design in South Kensington, where she became a regular attendant in March 1859 and was a student for two years. As a public institution which offered training in art, design, and industrial application to an inclusive body of students, and raised consciousness about the relations between art, government, political and economic institutions, and the public sphere, the South Kensington school had a formative influence on her later scholarship as an art historian. She was a good student, with a special interest in anatomical drawing. As a woman, she was denied access to formal life-drawing classes at South Kensington, but in 1859, defying convention, she took private tuition from William Mulready in drawing from the nude. Like a number of other female artists of the day, she protested against the exclusion of women from what was considered to be the most prestigious area of art education. She later withdrew an offer to found a scholarship for female art students at the Royal Academy Schools when the authorities refused to concede to her condition that the women's education include drawing from the nude.

After completing her art education, Strong returned to Oxford, where she became engaged to the 48-year-old scholar Mark *Pattison (1813–1884), rector of Lincoln College, in June 1861, and married him at Iffley church on 10 September 1861. Despite her intellectual marginalization as a woman in Oxford, Francis Pattison entered upon a life of serious scholarship, focusing upon the study of French cultural history and art. At the same time she cut a striking figure socially, developing an artistic and intellectual circle more in keeping with the salons of seventeenth-century France—upon which she was establishing herself as an authority—than with the stuffy masculine culture of Oxford college life. According to contemporary accounts, and on the evidence of the early portrait of Mrs Pattison painted by her friend Pauline, Lady Trevelyan, in 1864, her dress and general demeanour were particularly stylish and picturesque. The Pattisons' marriage was famously unhappy, allegedly the model for the mésalliances of Dorothea Brooke and Edward Casaubon in George Eliot's Middlemarch (1871–2) and of Belinda and Professor Forth in Rhoda Broughton's Belinda (1883), and a possible source for Robert Browning's poem 'Bad Dreams' in Asolando (1889). Its miseries, and her own ill health, led Pattison to spend increasing periods of time in France, where she was able to pursue her research interests with greater resources and more independence.

Pattison began writing reviews, articles, and notes on art for the periodical press from the mid-1860s, and became the salaried art editor of The Academy from 1873 to 1883. It was in this context that she began to carve out her own scholarly and critical principles, differentiating her approach to art equally from the moral aesthetic of her former mentor, Ruskin, and the ahistorical impressionism of Walter Pater. She offered a critique of the former in her article 'Art and morality' (Westminster Review, 35, January 1869) and in her signed review of his Lectures on Art and Catalogue of Examples (The Academy, 1870), and reviewed the latter's Studies in the History of the Renaissance in the Westminster Review in April 1873. Throughout her marriage to Mark Pattison, when not following the widespread convention of journalistic anonymity, she published under the signature E. F. S. Pattison. Her second husband attributed her insertion of the initial 'S.', standing for her family name Strong, to 'her wish for some recognition of the independent existence of the woman, and in some resistance to the old English doctrine of complete merger in the husband' (Dilke, 19).

It was under this name that Pattison published her first book, The Renaissance of Art in France (1879), in which the hallmarks of her scholarship are already evident: her meticulous archival research into primary and unpublished sources; her interest in the institutional organization of the arts, and in the political, economic, and social conditions under which they were produced; and her deep conviction of the profound connectedness of the works of decoration, furniture, painting, engraving, sculpture, and architecture of a period. This was followed in 1882 by a short biography of Sir Frederic Leighton, in the Dumas series Illustrated Biographies of Modern Artists, and in 1884 by another major study, Claude Lorrain: sa vie et ses œuvres, published in French.

At the same time as she was building a formidable reputation as a historian and critic of art, Pattison was active in a quite different field. Her commitment to social reform, and in particular to improving the working conditions of women, led to her involvement, from its inception, in the Women's Trade Union League, founded as the Women's Protective and Provident League by Emma Smith Paterson in 1874. In 1886, on Paterson's death, she herself became president until her death, when she was mourned in the league's journal as 'one … fitted, as few human beings … to fill the post of leader in a crusade against the tyranny of social tradition and the callousness of social indifference' (Women's Trade Union Review, Jan 1905, 1). In 1878 she was elected to membership of the Radical Club, one of only five women; there she presented a paper entitled 'The conditions which should determine the wages of female labour' (Dilke, 54). The management and expansion of women's trade unions, and in particular her championing of the cause of unskilled workers in dangerous trades, became lifelong concerns.

In the 1870s Francis Pattison renewed her friendship with the liberal politician and periodical proprietor Sir Charles Wentworth *Dilke, second baronet (1843–1911), whom she had first met in 1858 as a fellow student at South Kensington. They shared interests in radical politics and in France and its art, and from mid-1875 they were in close correspondence. Their marriage, which took place in Chelsea on 3 October 1885, a year after Mark Pattison's death, although initially shadowed by the scandal surrounding the naming of Charles Dilke as co-respondent in a divorce case, appears to have been happy. Thenceforward she was known by and published under the name Emilia Dilke. Portraits of her from this period—as Francis Strong Pattison in 1882 by Charles Camino, and as Emilia Dilke in 1887 by Hubert von Herkomer—depict a poised and elegant woman with a forthright gaze. At the same time she extended her activities for the women's trade union movement, speaking at public meetings across the country, regularly attending and addressing the annual Trades Union Congress as part of her promotion of male–female working-class co-operation, and writing for the league's papers and the general press. She also published a further series of important studies of French art. In Art in the Modern State (1888), on seventeenth-century French art, and in her encyclopaedic four-volume study of eighteenth-century French art (1899–1902) she sought 'to trace the action of those social laws under the pressure of which the arts take shape' (*French Engravers and Draughtsmen of the Eighteenth Century* 1902, v), drawing attention to the political determinants of art and the economics of production and of the modern art market. In these volumes she is concerned with the role of women in the arts as both producers and subjects, drawing parallels between the social and institutional constraints upon earlier and contemporary female artists. She also published two volumes of allegorical stories, *The Shrine of Death and Other Stories* (1886) and *The Shrine of Love and Other Stories* (1891), and a collection entitled *The Book of the Spiritual Life* was published posthumously in 1905.

Dilke died following a brief illness on 24 October 1904 at her Surrey house, Pyrford Rough near Woking. Her remains were cremated at Golders Green after a funeral service at Holy Trinity Church, Sloane Square, London. She had no children. Despite recurring ill health, she had been a woman of prodigious energy which she had directed into a number of channels in the belief that

> Ordinary life widens the horizon for men. Women are walled in behind social conventions. If they climb over, they lose more than they gain. It is therefore necessary to accept the situation as nature and society have made it, and to try to create for one's self a position from which on peut dominer ce qu'on ne peut pas franchir. (Dilke, 55)

HILARY FRASER

Sources K. Israel, *Names and stories: Emilia Dilke and Victorian culture* (1999) • C. W. Dilke, 'Memoir', in Lady Dilke, *The book of the spiritual life* (1905), 1–128 • *DNB* • B. Askwith, *Lady Dilke: a biography* (1969) • C. Eisler, 'Lady Dilke (1840–1904): the six lives of an art historian', *Women as interpreters of the visual arts, 1820–1979*, ed. C. R. Sherman and A. M. Holcomb (1981), 147–80 • M. Demoor, 'An honourable gentleman revisited: Emilia Strong Pattison's noted entry into the world of Sir Charles Wentworth Dilke and the *Athenaeum*', *Women's writing: the Elizabethan to Victorian period*, 2 (1995), 201–20 • M. Demoor, *Their fair share: women, power and criticism in the Athenaeum, from Millicent Garrett Fawcett to Katherine Mansfield, 1870–1920* (2000) • D. Mermin, 'Some sources for Browning's "Bad dreams"', *Studies in Browning and his Circle*, 9 (1981), 81–6

Archives BL, corresp. and papers, Add. MSS 42570, 42575, 43903–43908, 43913, 43934, 43946, 45655, 49455, 49611 • CAC Cam., Roskill-Enthoven-Dilke papers | Bodl. Oxf., Acland papers, papers of Ingram Bywater, Max Müller deposit • Bodl. Oxf., Pattison papers • HLRO, corresp. with Herbert Samuel • U. Newcastle, Trevelyan papers

Likenesses photograph, 1861, repro. in Dilke, 'Memoir' • Pauline, Lady Trevelyan, oils, 1864, NPG • C. Camino, miniature on ivory, 1882, NPG • H. von Herkomer, oils, 1887, NPG [*see illus.*] • W. & D. Downey, woodburytype, 1894, NPG; repro. in W. Downey and D. Downey, *The cabinet portrait gallery* (1894), vol. 5 • Thomson, photograph, 1904, repro. in Dilke, 'Memoir'

Wealth at death £28,955 19s. 11d.: probate, 2 Dec 1904, *CGPLA Eng. & Wales*

Dilke, Margaret Mary (1857–1903). *See under* Dilke, Ashton Wentworth (1850–1883).

Dilke, Sir (Charles) Wentworth, first baronet (1810–1869), art patron, was born in London on 18 February 1810, the only son of the civil servant, art critic, and *Daily News* editor Charles Wentworth *Dilke (1789–1864) and his wife, Maria Walker (1790–1850). He was known as Wentworth Dilke in order to distinguish him from his father. His eminent family included ancestors who had sat in the parliament of Elizabeth I and in the Long Parliament. By the seventeenth century they were known as 'sturdy reformers of the Puritan type' (Pearce, 8), and the family seat was Maxstoke Castle, in Warwickshire. Dilke was educated at Westminster School, and at sixteen, following his father's educational principles, he was sent to Florence to live with the painter Seymour Kirkup; thereafter he studied at Trinity Hall, Cambridge, and graduated LLB in 1834. In his early years in London, Dilke 'was principally known to his friends for never missing a night at the Opera' (Gwynn and Tuckwell, 6). After his marriage, on 30 March 1840 to Mary (d. 1853), daughter of William Chatfield, a captain in the Madras cavalry, Dilke began to follow his father's editorial and entrepreneurial example by founding the *Gardeners' Chronicle*, with John Lindley and Sir Joseph Paxton, and the *Agricultural Gazette*. His wide cultural and aesthetic interests, coupled with his horticultural and editorial work, led to his involvement in efforts to improve national education in design and technology.

From 1845 Dilke was party to the Society of Arts's discussions regarding the Great Exhibition; this brought him into close personal contact with John Scott Russell, Henry Cole, and Prince Albert. He served as both council member and chairman of the society. As one of the society's group who promoted the Great Exhibition, and then a member of the royal commission's executive committee for the exhibition from 1849 to 1851, he proved himself one of its most assiduous, organized, and hard-working members; he was one of the representatives appointed by Prince Albert to travel the country and sound out the public's views on the proposed exhibition. The executive committee, which also included Henry Cole, William Reid, Matthew Digby Wyatt, and Francis Fuller, co-ordinated and corresponded with local and international commissions formed to organize the exhibition, and oversaw the setting up and layout of the event. The exhibition itself would prove to be highly complex, vast in scale, and hugely successful. Dilke's role included investigating the best means of producing an exhibition catalogue; dealing with the press and publicity; strategically managing the often fractious local and international commissions; and overseeing the arrival and installation of exhibits. He also acted as Queen Victoria's trusted purchaser of goods at the exhibition. His deep involvement in the project is demonstrated by his massive bequest of exhibition material now held at the Victoria and Albert Museum. A reliable executor of the royal commission's directives, he was afterwards called on repeatedly to report on other such exhibitions (Dublin, 1852; New York, 1853; Paris, 1855; St Petersburg, 1868); he was also one of the five royal commissioners for the 1862 International Exhibition in London. Dilke was created baronet on 22 January 1862.

The Great Exhibition brought Dilke into contact with influential people, notably Lord Granville, who worked to bring him into parliament. In 1865 he was elected Liberal MP for Wallingford, although he lost his seat at the general election of 1868. The absorbing nature of his work in promoting and reporting on exhibitions, together with his meticulous, unostentatious nature, set him apart from his family. They lived at 76 Sloane Street, London, and at Alice Holt, a small country property near Farnham, Surrey. Mary Dilke, having given birth to two sons, was 'almost certainly unhappy in her marriage' (Jenkins, 13), and died in 1853. The first son, Sir Charles Wentworth *Dilke, second baronet (1843–1911), formed a close temperamental bond with his grandfather and disparaged his father's work on exhibitions as pen-pushing. Charles eventually overshadowed his father as a well-known travel writer and Liberal MP. The younger son was Ashton Wentworth *Dilke, traveller and politician.

Dilke died at the Hotel de France, St Petersburg, on 10 May 1869, while reporting there on the horticultural exhibition. The importance of mid-nineteenth-century exhibitions as agents of modernization and opportunities for the formation of complex economic and commercial links is only now being recognized. Dilke's role in this development was significant; Prince Albert awarded him a commemorative medal for his work on the Great Exhibition 'as one of those who stood by its cradle, helped in its education and served it truly and zealously after it had been brought to maturity' (Prince Albert to Dilke, 15 Oct 1851, F25, the Great Exhibition of 1851, 1851–3, Royal Archives, Windsor).　　　　　　JOHN R. DAVIS

Sources C. W. Dilke, corresp. and papers, 1837–69, BL, Add. MS 43901 · C. W. Dilke, corresp. with his father, 1853–64, BL, Add. MS 43899 · C. W. Dilke, corresp. with his son, Charles, 1853–69, BL, Add. MSS 43900, 43901 · R. Jenkins, *Sir Charles Dilke: a Victorian tragedy* (1958) · S. Gwynn and G. Tuckwell, *The life of the Rt. Hon. Sir Charles Dilke, bart., M.P.* (1917) · J. Pearce, *Sir Charles Dilke, bart, M.P.* (1880) · *The Right Hon. Sir Charles Wentworth Dilke* (1903) [Biographical Press Agency] · Boase, *Mod. Eng. biog.* · Y. Ffrench, *The Great Exhibition, 1851* (1951) · D. A. Robertson, *Sir Charles Eastlake and the Victorian art world* (1978) · CGPLA Eng. & Wales (1869)
Archives BL, corresp., Add. MSS 43900–43901 · Boston PL, corresp. · CAC Cam., corresp. | Bodl. Oxf., corresp. with Lord Kimberley
Likenesses photograph, 1867, BL, Add. MS 49612 · Dalziel, woodcut (after J. Scott), BM · H. W. Phillips, group portrait, oils (*The royal commissioners for the Great Exhibition, 1851*), V&A
Wealth at death under £35,000: probate, 20 July 1869, CGPLA Eng. & Wales

Dilkes, Sir Thomas (c.1667–1707), naval officer, was described in 1687 as a relative of Sir William *Coventry, and later as a protégé of Lord Carbery. He served as a king's letter boy between 1683 and 1686, became a lieutenant in 1687, and took command of the fireship *Charles* in April 1689. In 1692 he was appointed to the *Adventure* (50 guns), in which he shared in the victories of Barfleur and La Hogue. In different ships he remained actively employed in the channel, on the coast of Ireland, in the Bay of Biscay, or on the coast of Portugal until, in 1696, commanding the *Rupert* (60 guns) he went to the West Indies in the squadron under Vice-Admiral John Nevell. Following the deaths of Nevell, Rear-Admiral George Mees, and nearly all the other captains, Dilkes succeeded to the command, and brought the squadron home in October 1697. He held a series of short-lived commands in the years of peace that followed, and was seriously injured when his ship was wrecked on the Irish coast in 1699. In 1702 he commanded

the *Somerset* (70 guns) in the fleet under Sir George Rooke, who hoisted his flag in that ship for the attack on the combined fleets in Vigo harbour.

In March 1703 Dilkes was promoted rear-admiral of the white, and during the summer, with his flag in the *Kent*, he commanded a squadron on the coast of France. On 26–7 July he drove onshore near Granville and Avranches, and captured or destroyed almost all the fleet of forty-five merchant ships and three frigates which formed their escort—a service for which the queen ordered gold medals to be struck and presented to the admirals and captains. Dilkes was then employed cruising in the channel, and he returned to Spithead just in time to escape the fury of the great storm on 26 November 1703. In the same year he was elected MP for Castle Martyr in the Irish House of Commons, a seat he held until 1707.

In 1704 Dilkes sailed with Sir Cloudesley Shovell to join Rooke at Lisbon; afterwards he took a prominent part in the battle of Malaga as rear-admiral of the White squadron, in acknowledgement of which he was knighted by the queen on 22 October 1704. In February 1705 he sailed again for the straits, with his flag in the *Revenge*, and on 10 March, after joining Sir John Leake, he played a major role in capturing and destroying the French squadron that was blockading Gibraltar. He remained with the Mediterranean Fleet under the earl of Peterborough before returning to England with Shovell in November. During 1706 he was employed chiefly in the blockade of Dunkirk but in January 1707 he sailed in company with Shovell for the Mediterranean, where he took part in the operations, including the siege of Toulon. On the siege being lifted Dilkes remained commander-in-chief and, after conferring with Archduke Charles at Barcelona, he sailed for Leghorn where he anchored on 19 November. On his arrival Dilkes became involved in a dispute over salutes with the fort. He claimed the right to be saluted first, but it was contended that the fort never saluted any flag first, except those of admirals or vice-admirals. Dilkes had to be content with this. To show that there was nothing personal in this refusal, he was invited to a public dinner on shore on 1 December. In going back to his ship from the heated room he got a chill, followed by a fever, of which he died on 12 December 1707; his death, so soon after his dispute with the grand-ducal court, led to a groundless rumour that he had been poisoned. He was survived by his wife, Mary, daughter of Murrough *O'Brien, first earl of Inchiquin, and widow of Henry Boyle of Castle Martyr; they had at least one child, Michael O'Brien Dilkes, army officer. Mary Dilkes later married Colonel John Irwin.

J. K. LAUGHTON, rev. J. D. DAVIES

Sources J. Charnock, ed., *Biographia navalis*, 2 (1795), 242–52 · W. L. Clowes, *The Royal Navy: a history from the earliest times to the present*, 7 vols. (1897–1903); repr. (1996–7), vol. 2, pp. 382, 399, 412, 469, 479, 494, 504–6 · NMM, Sergison MSS, SER/136 · J. H. Owen, *War at sea under Queen Anne, 1702–1708* (1938) · S. Martin-Leake, *The life of Sir John Leake*, ed. G. Callender, 2 vols., Navy RS, 52, 53 (1920) [orig. pubd 1750] · list of services, PRO, ADM/6/424 · list of recommendations, 1692, PRO, ADM/8/2 · J. Thynne to S. Pepys, Bodl. Oxf., MS

Rawl. A. 189, fol. 146 · J. Burchett, *Memoirs of transactions at sea during the war with France* (1703)

Likenesses G. Kneller, oils, *c*.1704–1705, NMM

Dill, Sir John Greer (1881–1944), army officer, was born on 25 December 1881 at Lurgan, co. Armagh, the second child of John Dill (*d*. 1894), bank manager, and his wife, Jane Greer (*d*. 1894), daughter of a prominent Lurgan JP. The perfect English gentleman was, like so many successful soldiers, an Ulsterman. 'In my youth', he recalled half a century later for the Pennsylvania Scotch–Irish Society, 'I have seen Orangemen on side-cars driving down what they called Papish streets spoiling for a fight, and getting it' (Danchev, 'The early years', 28). Dill's was a lonely youth, uncomfortably foreshadowing later developments. He came from a long line of Dill worthies—scholars and ministers all—an oppressive inheritance. He did not make friends easily. Having been orphaned at twelve, he and his elder sister Nina (who also died prematurely, in 1921) were taken on by an aunt and uncle, Joseph Grundy Burton, a well-known campaigner against home rule, a teller of tales, and a diligent parish priest. Dr Burton and his nephew were never close, and in 1895 Dill was swiftly dispatched across the water to Cheltenham College. One Ulster friendship alone survived, transplanted to America from the dismal afternoons spent playing in Belfast's botanical gardens: that with his cousin Foster Kennedy, the future neurologist, who emigrated to New York a few years before Dill found his way to Washington, to whom he would ultimately entrust his life.

Education and early career At Cheltenham he rose laboriously from the bottom form to upper fifth military more by the effluxion of time in each form than by any sign of intellectual distinction. His science teacher followed his subsequent career with all the more interest because he found young Dill one of the slowest pupils he ever taught in the military class, no mean feat. In 1900 he passed into the Royal Military College, Sandhurst, 154th out of 210, greatly relieved to have so much to spare. At Sandhurst his conduct was exemplary, his marks uniformly mediocre. Worthiness outbid distinction.

In 1901 Dill was commissioned into the 1st battalion (100th foot), the Prince of Wales's Leinster regiment—a Southern Irish regiment, there being no other vacancies at the time of the Second South African War. 'It was a serious thing for a Black Northerner like me to be thrown among a lot of gossoons [boys] from Kings County, but we mixed, we got to love each other' (Danchev, 'The early years', 28). He read Dickens and Thackeray and was periodically concerned to acquire what he euphemistically called 'curios', or more straightforwardly 'loot', but was disappointed to find nothing better than a bed, a jug, a basin, and some other items of furniture, which served to alleviate the hardships of the campaign.

Marriages and private life Second South African War service was followed by his only period of regimental duty, as assistant adjutant and then adjutant of the 1st Leinsters, 1902–9. It was during this period (in 1907) that he married Ada Maud, daughter of Colonel William Albert le Mottée

Sir John Greer Dill (1881–1944), by Yousuf Karsh, 1944

(late of 18th foot), in Fermoy, co. Cork, the bride's home town. The marriage was precipitate and unsuitable. Though an accomplished tennis player and rider, Maud was a woman of nervous disposition, painfully shy, given to headaches, depression, and excessive self-medication. She died in 1940, after a long series of paralytic strokes, while Dill was chief of the Imperial General Staff (CIGS). As to how deeply he was affected by all this, testimony is conflicting. Foster Kennedy 'never knew how close they were', but thought 'not very'. Their son, John (1916–71), who lived very much in his father's shadow, wrote ambiguously that Dill's family life 'was not always as happy as it could have been'. Brooke, his protégé, ally, and successor, left a harrowing vignette of Maud's paralysis:

> Every visit home to his wife in Windsor was a desperate ordeal; she could not make herself understood, he kept guessing at what she could mean, usually unsuccessfully, and finally with a disappointed look in her eyes she used to throw her head back on the pillow. (Danchev, 'The early years', 33)

Yet Dill's immediate reaction to her death betrays a certain stoicism, even relief, and he seems quickly to have recovered his equilibrium. A year later, moreover, on 8 October 1941, he married a much younger woman: Nancy Isabelle Cecil Furlong (*née* Charrington), daughter of a brewery magnate, and widow of a former member of Dill's staff. This time he made a very happy marriage, in more than one sense. 'I don't think Nancy dislikes Washington and Washington certainly likes her', he wrote with feeling in 1942. 'She makes a great difference to my life and keeps me young' (ibid., 34).

First World War and Staff College Meanwhile another sea change had taken place. In 1913 Dill became a student at the Staff College, Camberley, under Sir William Robertson, who told the intake that they were all very lucky as they had a definite war to train for. This was the determining experience of Dill's life. It was the impress and ambience of the Staff College, coupled with the immediate praxis of the First World War, that really launched his career. A captain in 1914, by the end of the war he was a temporary brigadier, Haig's brigadier-general, general staff operations, and on the evidence of the official historian 'the real operations brain in GHQ' (Danchev, 'The early years', 35). Staff work was meat and drink to him. At the same time he began truly to master his profession. Between the wars he regularly attracted the epithet 'intellectual'—an equivocal judgement—and a pattern of postings to give it currency. He preached what he practised. He was senior instructor at the Staff College (1919–22), army instructor at the Imperial Defence College (IDC) (1926–8), and commandant of the Staff College (1931–4). These postings tended to confirm his inspiration or his insipidity, according to taste. For some there could be no argument. Colonels Auchinleck and Brooke were among the students on the inaugural course at the tri-service IDC in 1927. For Auchinleck, 'perhaps the most valuable and best remembered gain was the association with and the friendship of Sir John Dill, whose character, modesty and power of imparting knowledge left a lasting impression on me and, I think, on many others'. For Brooke, 'Dill's genius shone throughout the course; with no precedent to work from he built up studies of all the important factors, and carried everyone with him owing to his unbounded enthusiasm and immense capacity for work' (ibid., 35–6).

The myth of Dill's failure All accounts agree on Dill's vigour and 'drive' before the early 1930s. In the previous decade he was said to have been bitten by a mad soldier, so energetically did he work. Thereafter, however, any assessment of his achievement is bedevilled by questions about his health. He died of aplastic anaemia, the onset of which is usually insidious, the prognosis grim. The conventional wisdom tends to be retrospective: later knowledge of his anaemia is used to underpin an analysis of a decline in vigour dating from 1931–2, coincident with the assumption of increasingly onerous responsibilities: director of military operations and intelligence (1934–6), general officer commanding Palestine and Trans-Jordan (1936–7), and general officer commanding-in-chief home command (1937–9). On this analysis he had already 'gone off', as Liddell Hart put it, by the time he was first considered for the position of CIGS in 1937. When he was eventually appointed, in April 1940, he was in no condition to do what was both necessary and desirable; that is, stand up to Churchill at home and Hitler abroad. He is held to have been an ineffective CIGS because he allowed himself to be worn down, if not worn out, by the prime minister, who called him 'Dilly-Dally' and framed the charge for posterity. 'I do not think that we are having the help from General Dill which we hoped for at the time of his appointment', complained the prime minister, eight short weeks later. 'He

strikes me as being very tired, disheartened, and over-impressed with the might of Germany' (Danchev, 'Dilly-Dally', 25). Spent, Dill was expelled from the inner sanctum in 1941, at the very moment when the USA entered the war. He rose again, phoenix-like, as head of the British joint staff mission in Washington (1942–4), but he was never a well man. His death in harness at the age of sixty-two was remarkable only for being so long postponed. An extraordinary public outpouring of grief in Washington found no echo in London. The equestrian statue subsequently erected in Arlington national cemetery (a unique tribute to a foreigner) has no counterpart in his own country. On a Churchillian reading Dill's American apotheosis was uncovenanted, expedient, and fundamentally mysterious.

In this fable of failure—Dilly-Dally in decline—the root cause is held to be congenital defects of character and personality, encapsulated in Lord Moran's feline observation that he lacked 'the he-man stuff' (Danchev, 'Strange case', 353) and exposed in working with Winston; personal misfortune incarnate in his invalid wife; and above all deterioration in his own health consequent on the early onset of the anaemia, exacerbated by a series of riding accidents, in 1931, 1939, and 1943. But the fable is just that. None of it will withstand close scrutiny. In his last years Dill had his own Moran, Foster Kennedy, who monitored the field marshal with cousinly thoroughness. Kennedy's evidence is unimpeachable. The anaemia did not take hold until 1944; it was detected almost immediately. The first break in his health was occasioned by the riding accident of 1943. The picture of life with Maud as a marriage of maladies has been grossly exaggerated. If Dill appeared weak or lethargic as CIGS, or even before, the explanation must be sought elsewhere—often in the eye of the beholder. In Washington he was not seriously impaired until mid-1944. For Dill, D-day had a more sinister connotation. After that he never really recovered. But he did return to work, and worked on until he died, literally bone-weary.

Dill and Churchill As for Dilly-Dally, he did stand up to Churchill—on strategic priorities, on particular operations, on the competence of individual commanders—but not on the prime minister's terms. What he failed to do was adapt to Churchill's parliamentary manners.

> The prime minister lost his temper with me. I could see the blood come up in his great neck and his eyes began to flash. He said: 'What you need out there [the Middle East] is a court martial and a firing squad'. I should have said, whom do you want to shoot exactly; but I did not think it till afterwards. (Danchev, 'Dilly-Dally', 21)

Dill was by no means inarticulate, as Wavell could be impenetrably inarticulate. Rather, it was a matter of temperament. He refused to pander. Instead he addressed to the prime minister a stream of closely argued minutes and explanatory notes. These efforts left Churchill unmoved and Dill unrequited. They were poorly calculated to achieve their purpose, not only because Churchill so rarely found a written case convincing, but also because Dill's style entirely left out of account the necessity to enthrall. As Wavell said, 'Winston is always expecting rabbits to come out of empty hats' (Danchev, 'Dilly-Dally', 27). It was not for want of comprehension on Dill's part; he understood the requirements well enough. 'Finest hours' were beyond the army's means in 1940–41; and Dill was not the man for conjuring tricks. It was his misfortune to join the chiefs of staff at a time when acquiescent colleagues, scarce resources, and impetuous ministers combined to make the cautionary advice of the CIGS at once vital and unpalatable. Caution was anathema to Churchill. In cabinet, he called Dill 'the dead hand of inanition' (ibid., 25). Dill did not answer back. Waltzing with Winston was not his style. He could advise others, but in more than one sense he could not help himself.

Dill's achievements as CIGS Dill's achievement as CIGS from May 1940 to December 1941 was fundamental nevertheless. It was he, above all, who responded to the imperative of the moment and established the wearying but constructive adversarial relationship between Churchill and the chiefs of staff on which Brooke built so successfully for the duration of the war. In 1940 no one knew, and many doubted, whether such a relationship could be made to work. The need and pain of definition are often forgotten. Yet the essential forerunner of the matchless combination of Churchill and Brooke was the ill-matched combination of Churchill and Dill. The prerequisite for Brooke's acceptability was Dill's purgatory. Dill accustomed Churchill to the trammelling of professional advice. 'I live a very hectic life', he wrote. 'Most of it is spent trying to prevent stupid things being done rather than in doing clever things! However, that is rather the normal life of a Chief of Staff' (Danchev, 'Dilly-Dally', 28–9).

Apotheosis in Washington Dill's 'retirement' was announced for 25 December 1941, his sixtieth birthday. Churchill intended that he become governor of Bombay, 'a position of great honour, followed by a bodyguard with lances' (Danchev, 'Dill', 52). But excommunication in Bombay was not to be Dill's fate. When the prime minister embarked post-haste for Washington to confer with the president after Pearl Harbor he felt compelled to take Dill with him. When the British contingent returned home Dill stayed on, in an unprecedented if indeterminate position of enormous influence at the epicentre of allied decision-making. He became not only head of the joint staff mission and senior British member of the combined chiefs of staff, but also, ironically, personal representative of the minister of defence, an office claimed by Winston Churchill himself. So began his life's greatest work. Dill's very presence in Washington became crucial to the operation and consolidation of an extra-special relationship. His highest service to the alliance was to contain its tremendous fissile potential. Dill is perhaps best seen as an amateur ambassador, complementing and in some measure supplanting Lord Halifax. His unarguable success in this role is the more striking for the absence of what has always been considered essential for a British ambassador in Washington—the confidence of the prime minister. So far from enjoying that confidence, Dill was retired as CIGS precisely because he had forfeited it. The change wrought by his removal to the USA was that the tension became creative. To official America, to one American in particular, Dill quickly came to be seen as a guarantor: a guarantor of the British, against their notorious and incorrigible duplicities; a guarantor of Brooke, against his overbearing advocacy; a guarantor of Churchill himself, against the fatal lullaby of his imperial pretensions and eccentric strategies.

With General George C. Marshall, the US army chief of staff and organizer of victory, Dill discovered an empathy unparalleled in Anglo-American military relations. To this American he was *sans peur et sans reproche*. When his statue was unveiled in 1950 it was Marshall's simple eloquence which set the tone of the occasion:

> Here before us in Arlington, among our hallowed dead, lies a great hero, Field Marshal Sir John Dill. He was my friend, I am proud to say, and he was my intimate associate through most of the war years. … I have never known a man whose high character showed so clearly in the honest directness of his every action. He was an inspiration to all of us. (Danchev, *Very Special Relationship*, 1)

Such a man was an ideal guarantor and mediator, fixer and broker, in the Anglo-American market place. Dill could be trusted: trusted to deliver. He was efficacious—for Brooke and Marshall, uniquely efficacious—and ambidextrous. He was able to comprehend both sides. In effect he interpreted each to the other. Hence his exhortations to mutual frankness: to reveal as much as possible of 'how minds are working', as he was fond of saying, in order to allay suspicion and promote understanding. 'Without him', ran the War Office epitaph, 'Britain could not have understood America so thoroughly and quickly, nor America Britain'. It was Dill, in tandem with Marshall, who made the combined chiefs of staff work, in Henry Stimson's words, 'not as a mere collecting point for individual rivalries between services and nations, but as an executive committee for the prosecution of global war' (Danchev, *Very Special Relationship*, 133).

Dill, who had been made KCB in 1937 and GCB in 1942, died in the Walter Reed Hospital, Washington, DC, on 4 November 1944. Four days later a memorial service was held at Washington Cathedral. Afterwards a motorized cortège proceeded along a route lined by thousands of troops to Arlington national cemetery. The coffin, folded in a Union Jack, with an unsheathed sword and a field marshal's cocked hat on top, was transferred to a gun carriage drawn by six grey horses. The US joint chiefs of staff acted as honorary pall bearers. A simple service was held at the graveside. Salutes were fired, the last post and reveille sounded. 'I have never seen so many men so visibly shaken by sadness', wrote Foster Kennedy afterwards. 'It was a remarkable and noble affair.' The joint chiefs sent as a message of condolence to their British counterparts an extraordinary tribute:

> [We] feel [we] share equally with you the loss to our combined war effort from the death of Field Marshal Sir John Dill. … We have looked to him with complete confidence as a leader in our combined deliberations. He has been a personal

friend of all of us. ... We mourn with you the passing of a great and wise soldier, and a great gentleman. His task in this war has been well done.   (ibid., 1 and 3)

ALEX DANCHEV

Sources A. Danchev, *Very special relationship* (1986) • A. Danchev, 'Dilly-Dally, or, Having the last word', *Journal of Contemporary History*, 22 (1987), 21–44 • A. Danchev, 'Field Marshal Sir John Dill: the early years', *Journal of the Society for Army Historical Research*, 67 (1989), 28–39 • A. Danchev, 'Dill', *Churchill's generals*, ed. J. Keegan (1991), 51–69 • A. Danchev, ed., *Establishing the Anglo-American alliance* (1990) • A. Danchev, 'Waltzing with Winston', *War in history*, 2 (1995), 202–30 • A. Bryant, *The turn of the tide, 1939–1943: a study based on the diaries and autobiographical notes of Field Marshal the Viscount Alanbrooke* (1957) • A. Bryant, *Triumph in the West, 1943–1946* (1959) • J. Kennedy, *The business of war: the war narrative of Major-General Sir John Kennedy*, ed. B. Fergusson (1957) • A. Danchev, 'The strange case of Field Marshal Sir John Dill', *Medical History*, 35 (1991), 353–7 • m. cert. • d. cert. • *CGPLA Eng. & Wales* (1945)
Archives King's Lond., Liddell Hart C., papers mainly relating to First World War; additional papers, incl. corresp. and speeches • PRO, corresp. and papers, WO 282 • PRO, British joint staff mission MSS, CAB 122 | CAC Cam., corresp. with Sir E. L. Spears • IWM, papers of military assistant, R. H. Winn • JRL, corresp. with Sir Claude Auchinleck • King's Lond., Liddell Hart C., corresp. with Lord Alanbrooke • King's Lond., Liddell Hart C., corresp. with Sir B. H. Liddell Hart • Marshall Research Library, Lexington, Virginia, Marshall MSS • NAM, Winn MSS | FILM BFI NFTVA, documentary footage • BFI NFTVA, news footage • BFI NFTVA, propaganda film footage (British Council) • IWM FVA, news footage | SOUND BL NSA, news recordings • IWM SA, recorded talk
Likenesses W. Stoneman, three photographs, 1920–41, NPG • Banano, photograph, 1936, NPG • E. Murray, oils, 1942?, Cheltenham College • group portrait, photograph, 18 Aug 1943, Hult. Arch. • Y. Karsh, bromide print photograph, 1944, NPG [*see illus.*] • Karsh of Ottawa, photographs, 1944, Camera Press Agency; repro. in Danchev, *Very special relationship* • H. Haseltine, bronze statue, Staff college, Camberley, Surrey • H. Haseltine, statue, Arlington national cemetery, Virginia
Wealth at death £21,384 4s. 11d.: administration with will, 13 June 1945, *CGPLA Eng. & Wales*

Dill, Sir Samuel (1844–1924), classical scholar and educationist, was born on 26 March 1844 at Hillsborough, co. Down, the eldest son of the Revd Samuel Marcus Dill (*d.* 1870), DD, Presbyterian minister of Hillsborough, later professor of systematic theology and first president of Magee College, Londonderry, and his wife, Anna Harrison, daughter of James Cowan Moreland, of Hillsborough. The family of which he came was founded by a soldier of Dutch descent in William III's army, and gave noted ministers, writers, and controversialists to Irish Presbyterianism. One of his brothers became headmaster of Foyle College, Londonderry.

Dill was educated in Belfast at the Royal Academical Institution and the Queen's College, where he took his degree in arts in 1864. He then went, as a scholar, to Lincoln College, Oxford, and obtained first classes in classical moderations (1867) and in *literae humaniores* (1869). In 1869 he was elected fellow and tutor of Corpus Christi College, Oxford. Later he became librarian and dean of the college, and was made an honorary fellow in 1903. In 1877 Dill was appointed high master of Manchester grammar school— this being the last appointment to that post made by a president of Corpus. During his headmastership the school was reorganized; new buildings were erected and

school societies developed. Dill was equally effective as administrator and teacher. His liberal conception of education is illustrated by his development of the teaching of modern subjects, and by the connection that he established between the school and working boys' clubs. He attached particular importance to developing the corporate life of the school outside the classroom. A former pupil, Gordon Hewart, described him as 'one of the very few men who appear to the boy to be heroes, and throughout life never lose that character' (*The Times*, 27 May 1924). In 1884 Dill married Fanny Elizabeth, daughter of Richard Cadwallader Morgan of Shrewsbury. They had three daughters.

Dill resigned his headmastership in 1888 and devoted himself to the preparation of his first book. In 1890 he returned to the Queen's College as professor of Greek. As a member of the Belfast University Commission, he took a large share in transforming the college into a university in 1909. He was chairman of the viceregal committee of inquiry into primary education (1913–14), whose unanimous report he drafted. A supporter of the claims of teachers for decent salaries and security of tenure, he influenced Irish education by his work as a member, and later as chairman, of the intermediate Board of Education. He was a man of strong religious feeling. A Presbyterian by birth, in his later years he became more identified with the Church of Ireland. His views were unionist, but he took no part in politics, being on friendly terms with H. H. Asquith and receiving a knighthood from the Liberal government in 1909 for his services to education.

Dill was best known as a writer. His literary power and productiveness gave him a high rank among the ancient historians of his day and country. In 1898 he published *Roman Society in the Last Century of the Western Empire*, which was followed in 1904 by *Roman Society from Nero to Marcus Aurelius*. Then at the age of sixty he turned to a wide and ill-mapped field. His *Roman Society in Gaul in the Merovingian Age*, edited and published posthumously in 1926 by his son-in-law, the Revd C. B. Armstrong, showed much of his old gift but also the lack of his finishing touch. Although not research in the technical sense, Dill's works were founded on a thorough study both of the primary and secondary sources. Less histories of a period than studies of the life of societies in dissolution or in spiritual crisis or decay, they reveal his moral and religious sympathies. Their interest, combined with the lucidity and charm of their style, attracted the general reader as well as the scholar.

Dill received the honorary degrees of LittD from the University of Dublin, and of LLD from Edinburgh and St Andrews. He resigned his professorship in 1924, and died at Montpelier, Malone Road, Belfast, on 26 May of that year.   R. W. LIVINGSTONE, rev. M. C. CURTHOYS

Sources *The Times* (27 May 1924) • *The Times* (29 May 1924) • J. R. Dill, *The Dill worthies*, 2nd edn (1892) • J. Bentley, *Dare to be wise: a history of the Manchester grammar school* (1990) • T. W. Moody and J. C. Beckett, *Queen's, Belfast, 1845–1949: the history of a university*, 2 vols. (1959) • J. Foster, *Oxford men and their colleges* (1893) • *CGPLA Eng. & Wales* (1925)

Archives BL, corresp. with Macmillans, Add. MS 55126 · Suffolk RO, Bury St Edmunds, corresp. with William Starkie
Wealth at death £4966 1s. 1d.: Northern Irish probate sealed in England, 27 Feb 1925, *CGPLA Eng. & Wales*

Dillenius, Johann Jakob (1687–1747), botanist, was born at Darmstadt where his family, formerly Dill and later Dillen, civil servants in the state of Hesse, had settled at the end of the sixteenth century; his mother was the daughter of Danile Funk, clergyman. His father was professor of medicine at the University of Giessen, where he latinized his name to Dillenius. The young Dillenius practised medicine in Grünberg, Hesse, and qualified in 1713, being appointed town doctor (*Poliater*) in Giessen. His botanical interests led to his being elected to the Caesare Leopoldina-Carolina Academia Naturae-Curiosorum under the name of 'Glaucias', and he contributed several papers, mostly botanical, especially on cryptogams and their sexual organs. In 1718 (with another edition in 1719), he published *Catalogus plantarum circa Gissam sponte nascentium*, enumerating 980 species of vascular plants, 200 of 'mosses' and 160 fungi from the Giessen area, with many new genera and sixteen plates (now preserved in the Natural History Museum, London), drawn and engraved by the author. Although the work attracted much attention, Dillenius made little progress in Germany, probably because in it he criticized the classificatory system, based on the number and regularity of petals, of Augustus Bachmann (Rivinus), rightly preferring the system of the Englishman John Ray.

The British consul at Smyrna, the wealthy William Sherard, who was interested in the sexuality of cryptogams, persuaded Dillenius to move to England, which he did by August 1721. Dillenius stayed with Sherard at Oxford and afterwards in London, and with Sherard's brother James at Eltham, Kent, but also had lodgings in London, which in 1728 were in Barking Alley. He was the first president of the Botanical Society (London), being appointed in 1721. With John Martyn as its first secretary, the society met in the Rainbow Coffee House, Watling Street.

Sherard wanted Dillenius to arrange his herbarium and compile an encyclopaedia (*Pinax*) of all names given to plants, according to a 1623 plan originally conceived by Gaspard Bauhin (1560–1624). He also wanted to endow the existing chair of botany at Oxford and appoint Dillenius to the post, but the unendowed chair was occupied by Gilbert Trowe (*c*.1685–1737). Dillenius's first published work in England, however, was the third edition of Ray's *Synopsis stirpium Britannicarum* (July 1724), to which he added many species and twenty-four plates of rare plants; the basis for this work, which was effectively the textbook of British botany until the publication of Hudson's *Flora Anglica* (1762), was his *Synopsis* herbarium, which is preserved at Oxford. In 1726, perhaps in preparation for a fourth edition, Dillenius made a botanical tour of Wales and the west of England with Littleton Brown (1699–1749) and Samuel Brewer; plants, including the first British collection of a grass (*Koeleria vallesiana*) are preserved in Sloane's herbarium at the Natural History Museum.

About 1724 Dillenius, at James Sherard's suggestion, had

Johann Jakob Dillenius (1687–1747), by James Heath

begun illustrating and engraving plates for 'the most important book to be published in England during the eighteenth century on the plants growing in a private garden' (Henrey, 2.265), the *Hortus Elthamensis sua plantarum rariorum quas in horto suo Elthami … Jacobus Sherard* (two large folio volumes, 1732), illustrated by 417 drawings (a Leiden edition of 1774 comprising merely the plates), some also coloured by himself, with the pertinent specimens preserved at Oxford. It is important because of the new genera described and later taken up by Linnaeus and because of the accuracy of the plates, especially of succulent plants, which make bad specimens. James Sherard wanted a sumptuous tribute to his own glory but Dillenius resented neglecting his other work for a project on which he personally lost some £200.

Dillenius was elected FRS in 1724 and was foreign secretary of the Royal Society in 1728–47. In 1728 William Sherard died, bequeathing his herbarium and library and £3000 to Oxford University to provide a salary for the professor of botany, on condition that the university pledge greater financial support for the botanic garden and that Dillenius should be the first professor, which post he finally gained, on Trowe's resignation, and after six years' wrangling between Sherard's executors and the university, in 1734, the same year he was admitted MD from St John's College. He had already visited Oxford to supervise plantings and construction of new conservatories in which the herbarium was temporarily housed. By 1735 he found that Sherard's legacy had been invested unwisely and his stipend was both in arrears and reduced.

Before August 1724 he had begun research on his greatest work, the *Historia muscorum* (1742), illustrated by eighty-five plates of which the drawings for the first seventy-nine are preserved in the Natural History Museum; the *Historia* is one of the first English botanical books to include references to the work of Linnaeus, who in the summer of 1736 spent a month with Dillenius at Oxford after which the Swedish naturalist dedicated his *Critica botanica* to him. Subscribers paid a guinea for a copy but sales were poor and Dillenius decided on an abridged edition; this, however, was never published, though there were 1763 and 1768 (London) and 1822 (Edinburgh) editions of the complete work. He prepared in Oxford a catalogue of Thomas Shaw's plants collected in north Africa and the Levant and at least 250 unpublished coloured drawings of fungi, a subject which he studied with his friend, the German George Deering.

Dillenius was somewhat corpulent and, in March 1747, was seized with apoplexy, from which he died in Oxford on 2 April; he was buried at St Peter-in-the-East, Oxford, leaving the *Pinax* unfinished. His pupil, Humphrey Sibthorp, succeeded him as professor.

Dillenius was contemporaneous with both Ray and Linnaeus: adhering to the 'natural system' of Ray, which philosophy is acceptable today, he was wise to appreciate the pragmatic approach of Linnaeus. He was central to British botany in academic as opposed to virtuoso circles, advancing basic knowledge besides cataloguing the world's flora. Linnaeus, who sent him specimens of Old World tropical trees, commemorated him in a genus *Dillenia*: 'of all plants [it] has the showiest flower and fruit, even as Dillenius made a brilliant show among botanists'.

G. S. BOULGER, rev. D. J. MABBERLEY

Sources R. Olby, 'Dillenius, Johann Jacob', *DSB* • B. Henrey, *British botanical and horticultural literature before 1800*, 3 vols. (1975) • G. C. Druce, *The Dillenian herbaria* (1907) • S. K. Marner, 'IDC and Oxford University herbaria', *Oxford Plant Systematics*, 3 (1995), 10–12 • C. Webster, 'The medical faculty and the physic garden', *Hist. U. Oxf. 5: 18th-cent. Oxf.*, 683–723
Archives NHM, corresp., drawings and papers • NMG Wales, notes on plants • U. Oxf., department of plant sciences, corresp. and papers; Dillenian herbaria; herbaria, also on IDC microfiche, 1995 | Linn. Soc., letters to Carolus Linnaeus • NHM, Sloane herbarium, specimens • NHM, letters to Samuel Brewer
Likenesses J. Heath, stipple, BM, NPG [*see illus.*] • oils, Radcliffe Science Library, Oxford; repro. in Druce, *Dillenian herbaria*, frontispiece; copies, Linn. Soc. and department of plant sciences, U. Oxf.

Dillingham, Francis (*d.* 1625), Church of England clergyman and author, was born at Deane, Bedfordshire. He matriculated as a pensioner at Christ's College, Cambridge, in June 1583, graduating BA early in 1587 and proceeding MA in 1590. From 1594 he was a fellow of the college, resigning in 1599, the year of his admission to the degree of BD. Fuller reports his father's testimony that Dillingham was:

> an excellent linguist and subtle disputant … a Greek act was kept, between him and William Alabaster of Trinity College, to their mutual commendation; a disputation so famous that it served for an era or epoch for the scholars in that age thence to date their seniority.   (Fuller, *Worthies*, 1.170–71)

Ordained priest by Bishop Wickham of Lincoln, Dillingham was instituted in 1601, on the presentation of a gentleman, John Roult, to the rectory of Wilden, Bedfordshire, which had been rated in the *valor ecclesiasticus* at the large annual sum of £18 7s. 4d.

Dillingham was a prolific writer on religious themes. The frequency of his publications, and the dedications to prominent men and women which so often preface them, suggest that he was well connected as well as prosperous. In *A Disswasive from Poperie* (1599) the author recalls, in his dedication to Oliver Lord St John, his 'honourable and singular favour towards me and all my friends'. By 1617, in *Enchiridion Chrisianae* [sic], the even greater eminence of Archbishop Abbot appears as the object of Dillingham's prefatory obsequies. He was chosen to work on the translation of the King James Bible published in 1611. It is clear, however, that Dillingham was acutely aware that few clergymen were as comfortably placed as himself, and that he hoped for reforms. Dedicating *A Silver Locke* (1611) to Lady Sara Hastings he laments the times, with their 'deluge and flood of iniquity … a great and main cause thereof no doubt, is the example of great men', and asks whether they are 'to be laughed at, or rather to be pitied, who are puffed up with their greatness, and have no religion in them, which is the greatest jewel in the world' (Dillingham). A second epistle directs to William Barlow, bishop of Lincoln, some outspoken criticism of the meanness of lay patrons, a chief cause of clerical impoverishment; also included in the book is a long attack on simoniacal practices in the church.

It has been plausibly suggested that Dillingham remained unmarried, and his will (dated 14 January 1625 and proved at the Bedford archdeaconry court on 21 May) mentions neither wife nor children. But he left substantial sums to various members of the Selby family, much larger than the bequests to his own four sisters, and this may hint at an earlier marital link with that family. Dillingham named as executor and residual legatee his brother Thomas, probably the man of Jesus College, Cambridge, who was rector of Deane, Bedfordshire, between 1603 and 1632, who died there on 10 December 1647, and who was father of Theophilus *Dillingham (1613–1678). Francis Dillingham himself died at Wilden and was buried in the parish on 24 February 1625.

STEPHEN WRIGHT

Sources Venn, *Alum. Cant.* • H. I. Longden, *Northamptonshire and Rutland clergy from 1500*, ed. P. I. King and others, 16 vols. in 6, Northamptonshire RS (1938–52), vol. 4 • C. W. Foster, ed., *The state of the church in the reigns of Elizabeth and James I*, Lincoln RS, 23 (1926) • Fuller, *Worthies* (1840) • F. Dillingham, *A silver locke* (1611) • *Bedfordshire Notes and Queries*, 1 (1886)

Dillingham, John (*fl.* 1639–1649), journalist, of unknown parentage and geographical origin, was originally a tailor who supplemented his income by writing newsletters. During the first bishops' war he was detected sheltering a Scot and retreated to Paris, whence he wrote news to Edward Montagu, earl of Manchester. By June 1643 he was in London, and was the first newswriter licensed after the 1643 parliamentary printing ordinance had briefly stopped the production of all periodical newsbooks. Dillingham's the *Parliament Scout*, which appeared weekly until January 1645, combined news and editorial opinion. In 1639 he had written to Manchester claiming that one of the ways his script newsletters differed from the printed versions was that 'they print all, and ours seldome proues false', and accordingly he tried to offer in *Parliament Scout* a moderate and accurate version of events (Cotton, 'London newsbooks', 83). In an editorial in a subsequent newsbook he promised to 'represent an extract weekly of such things as come to knowledge, and are fit for publike view … which shall ever be according to intelligence, and without invectives' (*Moderate Intelligencer*, 1, 6 March 1645, 1). His newswriting and editing generally fitted this description.

Believing that news had a role in a political cause and in finding a political settlement, Dillingham did not hide his allegiances. He was politically allied with Manchester, Oliver St John, and the 'middle group' in parliament; the royalist newsbook *Mercurius Aulicus* accused Dillingham of having been the earl's 'pensioner' (23, 8 June 1644, 1009). At first the *Parliament Scout* promoted unity, denying the significance of opposition between presbyterians and Independents, but Dillingham gradually fell out with Manchester and developed sympathy for Cromwell. In January 1645 Dillingham and Robert White, the bookseller responsible for the *Parliament Scout*, were apprehended for defaming the lord-general. This involved an odd reading of the offending newsbook, and it was probably Dillingham's opposition to peace talks that had caused actual offence. Dillingham was soon released and, with White, founded his second newsbook, the pro-army *Moderate Intelligencer*. This second newsbook received the doubtful tribute of an ironic treatment by John Cleveland: 'An Intelligencer is a State-spie, he pries into each mans breast, and would faine know all mens crimes but his owne … He is the Countrimans Chronicler, and he sings JO PEANS to his Muse, as to the Rusticke Dieties' (Cleveland, 1).

During this period Dillingham seems to have continued working as a tailor: in 1648 he was required to inspect the uniforms of the army, a subject on which he discoursed in his newsbook editorials. By 1648 his opinions had turned again, and he expressed sympathy, privately in correspondence and publicly in the *Moderate Intelligencer* (164, 11 May 1648), with the king's cause and with the Leveller leader John Lilburne. This was hardly opportunism, though Dillingham may properly be called a trimmer, as he leaned against the prevailing wind. In June White produced an alternative *Moderate Intelligencer*, presumably because he found his political sympathies or interests no longer lay with his editor. Dillingham petitioned the House of Lords, claiming that Gilbert Mabbott, the licenser, had refused to pass his own copy and had instead approved another man's. The Lords upheld his complaint and Dillingham kept the title of his journal, working instead with another publisher. Later that year the Lords sought recompense by asking for Dillingham's assistance in identifying the editor of the radical newsbook *The Moderate*.

Strangest of all of Dillingham's shifts was his support for Cromwell during 1649, particularly in the Irish campaign. This was not enough to preserve his employment, however, and the *Moderate Intelligencer* disappeared a month after the September 1649 Act Against Unlicensed and Scandalous Books. Dillingham may have been the editor of two brief revivals of a newsbook of the same title in 1652 and 1653, and may have had a hand in other newsbooks during the 1640s and 1650s. In all cases his role is founded on indirect evidence, and his shifting allegiances make internal evidence inconclusive. Dillingham disappeared from the public stage between 1649 and 1653, presumably returning to tailoring.

One theme repeatedly picked up in Dillingham's editorials was education; he often advocated more vocational, practical modes of schooling. This suggests that the tailor and newsletter writer may have been the John Dillingham who in 1672 bequeathed money to the city of Leicester for the foundation of a young men's school for riding, fencing, vaulting, and other accomplishments.

JOAD RAYMOND

Sources A. N. B. Cotton, 'John Dillingham, journalist of the middle group', EngHR, 93 (1978), 817–34 · A. N. B. Cotton, 'London newsbooks in the civil war: their political attitudes and sources of information', DPhil diss., U. Oxf., 1972 · J. Raymond, *The invention of the newspaper: English newsbooks, 1641–1649* (1996) · G. E. Manwaring, 'Journalism in the days of the Commonwealth', EdinR, 244 (1926), 105–20 · *Report on the manuscripts of Lord Montagu of Beaulieu*, HMC, 53 (1900) · *CSP dom.*, 1648–9 · JHL, 10 (1647–8) · *Parliament Scout* (June 1643–Jan 1645) · *Moderate Intelligencer* (Feb 1645–Oct 1649) · *Mercurius Aulicus* (Jan 1643–Sept 1645) · J. Cleveland, *The character of a moderate intelligencer* (1647) · C. Nelson and M. Seccombe, eds., *British newspapers and periodicals, 1641–1700: a short-title catalogue of serials printed in England, Scotland, Ireland, and British America* (1987)

Dillingham, Theophilus (1613–1678), college head, was born on 18 October 1613 at Over Deane, Bedfordshire, the elder son of Thomas Dillingham (d. 1647), rector of that parish. He was educated at the school at Over Deane and then matriculated at Emmanuel College, Cambridge, on 13 September 1629. From that college he graduated BA in 1634 and proceeded MA in 1637. The following year he moved to Sidney Sussex College as a fellow, taking his BD there in 1644.

In 1654 Dillingham was elected master of Clare and proceeded DD from that college the following year. At the Restoration he was ejected from the mastership, but the successful claimant, Thomas Paske (d. 1662), who had been master from 1620 to 1645, became his father-in-law on 30 March 1661 on Dillingham's marriage to Elisabeth Paske at St Edward's, Cambridge. With the assent of the fellows Paske resigned his mastership to Dillingham. His popularity within the university both before and after the Restoration is evident in the fact that he served as vice-chancellor in 1655–6, 1656–7, and 1662. Evidently, too, he was not out of favour with the restored regime, since he became prebendary of Ulleskelf, in the church of York, on 29 January 1661 (a position he again owed to the fact that his father-in-law resigned in his favour) and archdeacon of Bedford on 3 September 1667, as well as retaining the rectory of Offord Cluny, Huntingdonshire (to which he was appointed in 1654), until 1678.

Dillingham died at Cambridge on 22 November 1678 and was buried at St Edward's Church, Cambridge. He was survived by his wife, three sons (Thomas (*d.* 1722), John, and Theophilus), and three daughters (Elizabeth, Dorothy, and Ann).   JOHN GASCOIGNE

Sources Venn, *Alum. Cant.* · J. Le Neve, *Monumenta Anglicana*, 2: 1650–1679 (1718), 190 · W. Kennett, *A register and chronicle ecclesiastical and civil* (1728), 222, 615, 646 · will, CUL, Mm.1.37, 251–7 · IGI
Archives CUL, letters and papers, Mm.1.47
Wealth at death probably substantial; estate of Deane, Bedfordshire, Wilburton, Isle of Ely, manor of Camay, freehold estate in Cambridge, lease of parsonage impropriate of Witcham in Isle of Ely, lease of tenement of land called Chapman in Isle of Ely; £500 of lawful money; large scholarly library: will, CUL, Mm.1.37, 251–7

Dillingham, William (*c.*1617–1689), Latin poet and anthologist, was the eldest of the three sons of Thomas Dillingham (*d.* 1647), rector of Barnwell All Saints, Northamptonshire, and his wife, Dorothy. On 22 April 1636 he was admitted sizar of the puritan foundation of Emmanuel College, Cambridge, where he roomed with William (later Archbishop) Sancroft, who had gone up in 1633. They shared a taste for poetry, and despite differing political and religious perspectives remained close friends throughout life. Dillingham proceeded BA in 1639, was elected fellow of his college in 1642, and incepted MA in the following year. In 1646 he wrote commendatory English verses for the *Poems* of John Hall of St John's, and in 1649 was one of three fellows who bore witness to some feats of engineering carried out by Captain John Bulmer. He took the degrees of BD in 1650 and DD in 1655.

As a moderate presbyterian Calvinist who voluntarily subscribed the solemn league and covenant (1643), Dillingham remained untouched by the ejections carried out by Edward Montagu, second earl of Manchester. While Sancroft was deprived in 1651 for refusing the engagement, Dillingham's own acquiescence in the new order was rewarded two years later with the mastership of Emmanuel. In September 1654 he was appointed by Cromwell one of the thirty visitors of the university. Although puritanism had passed its zenith, religious observances in the college remained much as described by John Cosin in 1636; the chapel, built on a north–south axis, was still unconsecrated. Dillingham's rule coincided with a decline in the numbers and social standing of entrants, though in April 1658 he supported Matthew Poole's initiative for funding students who showed a vocation for the ministry.

Emmanuel's position at the heart of the Cambridge Platonist movement occasioned Dillingham's début as an entrepreneur of letters, when he put into print Nathaniel Culverwell's *Spiritual Opticks* (1651) and *The Light of Nature* (1652). In 1653 he edited from manuscript Theodore Bathurst's Latin verse-translation of Spenser's *The Shepheardes Calender*, and in the next year wrote Latin verses on the death of the puritan controversialist Thomas Gataker. Between 1656, when he issued two of his own sermons on the biblical maxim *Prove all things, hold fast to that which is good*, and his departure from Cambridge in 1662 his name appeared as a syndic of the university press on licences for sixteen works (CUL, UA, Pr.P.4(8)). These included his own Latin translation (1656) of the Westminster assembly's confession of faith and his edition of Sir Francis Vere's military *Commentaries* (1657). He was also involved in editing Ferrarius's *Lexicon geographicum* (1657), and published John Arrowsmith's *Armilla catechetica* (1659) with his friend Thomas Horton, whose *Forty Six Sermons* and *Choice … Expositions on Four Select Psalms* he was to bring out in 1674 and 1675 respectively. Besides contributing Latin verses to the various congratulatory volumes (1659–62) issued by the university, he helped to draft new regulations for its library.

About this time Dillingham married, and with his wife, Elizabeth, had a daughter and three sons, the eldest of whom, Thomas, was born on the eve of the Restoration, while Dillingham was serving as vice-chancellor. In this capacity he drafted a letter to Monck on his election as MP for the university in April 1660 (*N&Q*, 1st ser., 7, 1853, 427 and 486) and introduced *Musarum Cantabrigiensium* [*SOSTRA*] on the king's restoration. When the Act of Uniformity was passed his refusal to reject his obligations to the solemn league prevented him from taking the new oath, and he automatically forfeited his posts in August 1662. To Sancroft, who was unanimously elected master in his place, he addressed a generous letter (Waters, 2.639) from Oundle, where his brother Benjamin (*d.* 1679) was vicar. There Dillingham lived in retirement for the next ten years, amusing himself by writing verses in English and Latin which he shared with neighbours (ibid., 2.642; *Diary of Thomas Isham*, 82 n. 11 and 84 n. 19). He was briefly joined by another ejected presbyterian poet, Robert Wild, the Ferus of his poem 'Campanae undelenses'. Following the death of Elizabeth Dillingham he was persuaded to conform, and in May 1672 was presented to the rectory of Woodhill (now Odell) in Bedfordshire, by Sir Thomas Alston, over whose wife he read the funeral sermon in September 1677 (published 1678). On 30 October 1673 he married Mary Toller (1622/3–1690) at Horbling in Lincolnshire. Mary was fifty years old, three times a widow, and mother to seven children.

In 1678 Dillingham published *Poemata varii argumenti*, the first English anthology of neo-Latin verse. The anthology included many poems by Dillingham himself; his translations from George Herbert take up nearly a quarter of the whole. The translations of Herbert's 'The Church Porch' and 'The Sacrifice' had been discussed in detail with Sancroft, whose appointment as primate he had celebrated in verse (Waters, 2.641) and who now contributed anonymously a Latin version of an epigram by Thomas Bastard (BL, Sloane MS 1710, fol. 210). Besides 'Campanae undelenses' Dillingham's own compositions include 'Sphaeristerium Suleianum', inspired by the earl of Westmorland's bowling green at Sullehay Lodge, and 'Sepes hortensis', some lines 'on a garden clipt hedge' that he had sent to Sir Justinian Isham of Lamport in February 1672 (*Diary of Thomas Isham*, 85). The prescriptive hexameters

'De moribus puerorum' were written for his son Thomas, whose ownership inscription appears in a copy of the work that bears his father's autograph notes and corrections (BL, 1213.g.30). An earlier anthology entitled 'Wilhelmi Dillinghami poemata ab eo vel inventa, vel versa' (BL, Sloane MS 1815, fols. 54–61) had been abandoned, and a later one, 'Poemata selecta ex auctoribus qua veteribus, qua neotericis', comprising forty-six poems in manuscript or printed texts, remained unpublished (BL, Sloane MS 1766).

Until the year of his death Dillingham continued to consult Sancroft on various schemes for publication (BL, Sloane MS 1710, fols. 206–15; Waters, 2.643–7). These included an enlarged edition of Richard Parker's historical register 'Skeletos Cantabrigiensis' (now BL, Sloane MS 1765), a 'collection of academical orations and epistles which I had made 30 yeares since' (listed in Bodl. Oxf., MS Tanner 461, fols. 1–2, 174–6), an ambitious compendium of Greek poets with their commentators (Waters, 2.643–4), and William Bedell's pastoral dialogue on the Gunpowder Plot, *A Protestant Memorial*. Only the last of these was published, from Dillingham's papers, in 1713. His Latin lives of Laurence Chaderton, first master of Emmanuel, and of Archbishop Usher, together with his exercises for the degrees of BD and DD, all of which survive in autograph (BL, Harley MS 7052), were published posthumously by his son Thomas at Cambridge in 1700.

Dillingham's last published poem, *Aegyptus triumphata* (1680), was a brief epic in hexameters on the plagues of Egypt. His version of the essay 'Concerning the cure of anger' appeared in a collaborative translation of Plutarch's *Morals* (1684, 1.48–82). The British Library (Sloane MS 1818) holds an autograph manuscript of this and of *Protestant certainty, or, A short treatise showing how a protestant may be well assured of the articles of his faith* that was issued in the summer of 1689. He followed this in the autumn with *The Mystery of Iniquity Anatomized*, alleging the erosion of primitive Christianity by the Catholic church. He was buried at Odell on 28 November 1689, and his wife at Horbling on 21 June 1690. His son Thomas died in 1704 as rector of his grandfather's old parish.

W. H. KELLIHER

Sources R. E. C. Waters, *Genealogical memoirs of the extinct family of Chester of Chicheley*, 2 vols. (1878) [an annotated copy, BL, 09915.tt.10] · J. B. Mullinger, *The University of Cambridge from the earliest times to the decline of the Platonist movement*, 3 vols. (1873–1911) · C. H. Cooper and J. W. Cooper, *Annals of Cambridge*, 5 vols. (1842–1908), vol. 3 · E. S. Shuckburgh, *Emmanuel College* (1904) · J. C. T. Oates, *Cambridge University Library: a history from the beginnings to the Copyright Act of Queen Anne* (1986) · D. McKitterick, *A history of Cambridge University Press*, 1 (1992) · J. Twigg, *The University of Cambridge and the English Revolution, 1625–1688* (1990) · *The diary of Thomas Isham of Lamport (1658–81)*, ed. G. Isham, trans. N. Marlow (1971) · M. Poole, *A model for the maintainance of students of choice at the university* (1658) · W. Beloe, *Anecdotes of literature and scarce books*, 6 vols. (1807–12) · S. W. Carruthers, *The Westminster confession of faith* (1937) · D. K. Money, *The English Horace: Anthony Alsop and the tradition of British Latin verse* (1998)
Archives BL, corresp., etc., Add. MS 1710 | BL, autograph works, Harley MS 7052, Sloane MSS 1710, 1765, 1766, 1815, 1818 · BL, corresp., etc., Harley MS 3783, 3784 · Bodl. Oxf., corresp., etc, MSS Tanner 20–89, *passim*, 147, 306, 461

Dillon. For this title name *see* individual entries under Dillon; *see also* Lee, Henry Augustus Dillon-, thirteenth Viscount Dillon (1777–1832).

Dillon, Agnes Joseph Madeline [Una] (1903–1993), bookseller, was born on 8 January 1903 at 4 Westcroft Villas, Cricklewood, London, the third of the four daughters and fifth of the six children of Joseph Thomas Dillon, company secretary, and his wife, Teresa Joseph, *née* McNale, schoolteacher. Her younger sister was Carmen *Dillon (1908–2000), film art director. Their parents defied Edwardian convention by ensuring that all their children, boys and girls, had a good education—an expensive business. There was little money to spare, but the children were encouraged to be adventurous high achievers, and to 'plough their own furrow'. After the older brother was killed in the First World War and the second left for India, followed by the oldest sister, who became a Carmelite nun, the three youngest Dillon children—Tess, Una, as she was always called, and Carmen—became the focus of their parents' ambition. Una, dazzled by Tess's first-class degree in physics, mistakenly followed her sister to Bedford College, London, but scraping through her science examinations 'by the skin of my teeth' (Grove) convinced her that she was no academic. She accepted a post with the Central Association for Mental Welfare (later MIND); she was soon organizing successful bookstalls on its behalf, and found herself drawn to the pleasurable world of publishing and publishers. Convinced that she had found her niche she left her job, determined to buy a Bloomsbury bookshop, 9 Store Street. Unfortunately the owner, Ronald Burns, did not wish to sell. A year later her persistence paid off and Burns accepted her offer of £800. Now in her middle thirties, with no retail experience, and with loans of £600 from her father and £200 from a friend, Dillon found herself the owner of a run-down bookshop with little stock and few customers.

Dillon quickly established herself as a formidable businesswoman, becoming a familiar sight flying round London on an old bicycle—a tweed-suited Valkyrie determined to fulfil a customer's order within eight hours. Her philosophy, that 'trade follows the book' (*Independent*), proved sound, as did her insistence on stocking academic books alongside general subjects. She disliked specialization, believing that it stifled curiosity. Her instinct, as always, was impeccable. The small shop proved a magnet for bibliophiles and writers such as C. Day Lewis and the poet John Betjeman, who became friends as well as customers.

In 1939 Dillon ignored advice to close her business. The total evacuation of London University and Froebel Training College was, like her bomb-shattered shop, seen as no more than a slight inconvenience. Hundreds of packing-cases were used to transport books to customers who had moved out to Cardiff, Leicester, and Knebworth House, while university library trolleys transferred her stock to an empty shop opposite in a seemingly never-ending wagon-train of books, old and new. Despite paper shortages and bombing raids, Dillon's Bookshop continued to serve the needs of London readers.

The war over, Dillon reached a watershed in her life. She needed to expand her business if it was to survive and if she was to emulate her sisters' success in their chosen fields; Tess was now head of physics at Queen Elizabeth College, London, and Carmen had left the Architectural Association to become one of Britain's first women film directors. Una Dillon set her sights on the newly instituted teacher-training courses, and her shop soon became an educational Mecca for Commonwealth students. Further expansion seemed impossible when a proposed partnership, with London University, Dillon, and another bookseller, fell through; the row of shops in Torrington Place, next to Gower Street, acquired by the university after the war, remained tantalizingly empty. Then in 1956, quite unexpectedly, the principal of the university, Dillon's friend Sir Douglas Logan, urged the university to approach Dillon again. She used her stock and goodwill to purchase a minority share on the understanding that the shop bore her name. By the time she retired eleven years later, Dillon's University Bookshops Ltd had an annual turnover of over £1 million and an enviable worldwide reputation.

Even in retirement Dillon's enthusiasm and commitment to the work of booksellers never waned. She remained on the board of Dillon's until 1977, when the university sold to Pentos. One of the founders of the Charter Group of the Booksellers' Association, she campaigned to keep the 'protective' net book agreement, and assisted the British Council with the low-priced book scheme for British overseas books. A Roman Catholic, art lover, inveterate traveller, and gifted musician, for many years she was organist at St James's, Spanish Place. She was awarded an honorary MA in 1965 by London University, and three years later was appointed CBE for her services to bookselling. Although remarkably sanguine about her achievements, she found comparisons with Miss Christina Foyle, who 'inherited' her empire, odious. She also loathed the modern title Ms, which seemed to encapsulate for her an alien and impersonal London far removed from the halcyon days of childhood and pre-war Britain.

None of the sisters married, and in 1985 Una and Carmen Dillon left their Kensington High Street mansion flat, after forty-four years, for a Victorian villa and the respectability of Hove; they were preceded by twenty packing-cases of books. Una Dillon died at the Victoria Nursing Home, 96 The Drive, Hove, Sussex, on 4 April 1993, of generalized atherosclerosis and terminal bronchopneumonia; her body was cremated. Her sister Carmen survived her.   JEAN H. COOK

Sources F. Newman, 'Before and after', *Publishing News* (10 Oct 1986) · U. Dillon, 'Looking back and forward', *The Bookseller* (16 Sept 1967) · V. Grove, 'A last dash for the Dillons', *The Standard* (29 April 1985) · *The Times* (20 April 1993) · *The Guardian* (23 April 1993) · *The Independent* (17 April 1993) · b. cert. · d. cert.
Archives St Bride Institute, London, St Bride Printing Library, MSS · Women's Library, London, MSS

Wealth at death under £125,000: probate, 15 July 1993, *CGPLA Eng. & Wales*

Dillon, Arthur, Jacobite Earl Dillon (1670–1733), Jacobite army officer and politician, was born in co. Roscommon, the third, but second surviving, of six sons of Theobald, seventh Viscount Dillon of Costello-Gallen (d. 1691), of Loughglinn, co. Roscommon, and Mary (d. 1691), daughter of Sir Henry Talbot of Mount Talbot, co. Roscommon. His mother was a niece of the duke of Tyrconnell, and during the Williamite wars both his father and elder brother, Henry, served in the Irish army, the latter in command of an infantry regiment. His father was killed at the battle of Aughrim (1691), and his mother soon afterwards by an exploding bomb during the siege of Limerick. With his father and brothers, Arthur Dillon, a lifelong Roman Catholic, was outlawed by the Williamites; however Henry, eighth Viscount Dillon of Costello-Gallen, was pardoned and remained on the family estate in Ireland after the war.

In 1690 Arthur Dillon was chosen to go to France as colonel of a second Dillon regiment. This unit was newly raised to form part of Lord Mountcashel's brigade, a body of Irish troops exchanged for a French brigade sent by Louis XIV to Ireland. On disembarkation at Brest in May the Irish soldiers were reorganized into three infantry regiments and incorporated into the French army. Dillon's regiment, numerically weak on arrival, was brought up to two-battalion strength with reinforcements from two regiments which were disbanded, and he was confirmed as colonel on 1 June 1690. He served until 1697 in Catalonia under the duc de Noailles, participating in a number of engagements, including the taking of Roses (1693); the crossing of the River Ter and the capture of Palamos, Girona, and Hostalric (1694); the relief of Hostalric, during which he commanded the rearguard with great distinction (1695); and the capture of Barcelona by the duc de Vendôme (1697). In the War of the Spanish Succession he served under Vendôme in Italy in 1702–6, where he participated in the battle of Luzzara (1702); the invasion of the Trentino, during which he won distinction at Riva, the victory of San Sebastiano, and the capture of Asti (1703); the capture of Vercelli and Ivrea (1704); the capture of Mirandola, the defence of Moscalino, and the victory at Cassano (1705); and the victories of Calcinato and Castiglione (1706). He was promoted brigadier on 1 October 1702, *maréchal de camp* on 26 October 1704, and lieutenant-general on 24 September 1706. In 1707, under Marshal de Tessé, he played a role in the manoeuvres that compelled Prince Eugene to abandon the siege of Toulon. In 1709, while posted near Briançon under the duke of Berwick, he defeated two considerable bodies of the enemy in quick succession. Having transferred to the army of the Rhine, under Marshal de Villars, in 1713, he took Kaiserslautern and Verastein Castle, and was prominent in the reduction of Landau and Fribourg. His last campaign was in 1714, when he played a prominent role, under Berwick, in the capture of Barcelona. He was created *comte* in 1711 and received into the order of St Louis.

Although widely respected as a soldier of courage and

ability, and popular with his troops, Dillon was given no further military appointment after 1715, evidently because the French regency government disapproved of his pro-Jacobite activities. The tension between the French government and the Jacobite exiles (during a rare period of Anglo-French harmony) is well illustrated by the collapse in 1722 of the Atterbury plot which, before Mar betrayed its aims, Dillon had helped to plan. He resigned the command of the Dillon regiment in favour of his eldest son in 1730. Throughout his long military career, although often in the thick of action, he was fortunate never to have received a serious wound, and was regarded as handsome in his appearance. Some time before 1701 he had married Christiana (Catherine) Sheldon (1684–1757), a lady-in-waiting to Queen Mary of Modena. Described as 'a very good woman and much esteemed by everybody' (Fagan, 2.132), she was the daughter of Ralph Sheldon, equerry to James II, and the niece of the Jacobite general Dominic Sheldon. Dillon was rumoured to have been an early lover of Claudine de Tencin, who later, as the lover of Viscount Bolingbroke, betrayed the Jacobite plans in 1715 to the French. Otherwise, apart from occasional amours while on campaign, he was considered a fond husband and an attached father to his family of ten children.

Dillon played a leading role in Jacobite politics. He was active in the preparations for the attempted rising in Scotland in 1715 and was mentioned as a suitable leader of a parallel expedition to Ireland, which was also under consideration at the time. From 1717 to 1725 he acted as ambassador in Paris for James III (James Francis Edward Stuart). He was given the title of Viscount Dillon by James in 1717, and of earl on 24 June 1721. He recommended Charles Wogan to James to assist in his search for a bride, an introduction which ultimately resulted in the Pretender's marriage to Clementina Sobieska. In 1717 he negotiated with Sweden to raise troops and, as part of the Atterbury plot, was charged with leading forces from France to assist in the proposed London rising. He died on 5 February 1733 at the château of St Germain-en-Laye, where he had an apartment. Soon after his death, at the request of James III, his widow lodged his papers in the Scots College at Paris, where they were destroyed during the French Revolution. His widow entered a Paris convent in 1750, where she died and was buried in 1757. Four of his sons, Charles (1701–1741), Henry (d. 1787), James, and Edward, commanded the Dillon regiment in succession. Charles and Henry succeeded as tenth and eleventh viscounts Dillon of Costello-Gallen following the death of the ninth viscount, Arthur Dillon's nephew. Both Charles and Henry returned to live in Ireland. A fifth son, Arthur Richard *Dillon (1721–1806), was ordained a priest and became archbishop of Narbonne and president of the states of Languedoc. Two of Dillon's daughters, Catherine (d. 1758) and Frances, entered the Carmelite convent at Pontoise. A third, Marie-Elizabeth, did not marry. Brigitte married Baron Blaisel, a French general, and Laure (1708–1741) married the Jacobite exile Lucius Cary, sixth Viscount Falkland. A grandson, Lieutenant-General Arthur *Dillon

(1750–1794), the last colonel-proprietor of the Dillon regiment in France, was guillotined in 1794 during the revolution.   HARMAN MURTAGH

Sources R. d'Amat and R. Limouzin-Lamothe, *Dictionnaire de biographie française*, ed. J. Balteau and others, 11 (Paris, 1967), 354 · J. C. O'Callaghan, *History of the Irish brigades in the service of France*, [new edn] (1870), 46–52 · GEC, *Peerage*, new edn, 4.359–64 · J. Lodge, *The peerage of Ireland*, rev. M. Archdall, rev. edn, 4 (1789), 194–200 · R. Hayes, *Biographical dictionary of Irishmen in France* (1949), 59–60 · J. G. Simms, ed., 'Irish Jacobites: lists from Trinity College Dublin MS N.1.3', *Analecta Hibernica*, 22 (1960), 11–230, esp. 77 · S. Mulloy, ed., *Franco-Irish correspondence, December 1688 – February 1692*, IMC, 1 (1983), 296, 367–9 · P. Fagan, ed., *Ireland in the Stuart papers*, 1: *1719–42* (1995), 31–2, 36, 48–9, 65; 2: *1743–65* (1995), 132–4 · C. Petrie, *The marshal duke of Berwick: the picture of an age* (1953), 242, 251, 255–7 · P. Miller, *James* (1971), 212, 223, 232, 235, 257
Archives Royal Arch., corresp. and papers | NA Scot., corresp. with T. Gordon

Dillon, Arthur, Count Dillon in the French nobility (1750–1794), army officer in the French service, the second son of Henry Dillon, eleventh Viscount Dillon (1705–1787), also an army officer in the French service and a French count, and his wife, Lady Charlotte Lee, and the nephew of Arthur Richard Dillon, archbishop of Narbonne, was born on 3 September 1750 at Braywick, Berkshire. In 1768 he married Lucy de Rothe (1751–1782), the daughter of General Édouard de Rothe (1710–1766) and Lucie Cary (1728–1804). She became lady-in-waiting to Marie Antoinette. The couple had one surviving child, Henriette Lucy (1770–1853), who in 1787 married the marquis de La Tour du Pin; she later wrote her memoirs, *Journal d'une femme de cinquante ans*. In 1785 Dillon married, secondly, Marie de Girardin de Montgirald, comtesse de La Touche, a widow; they had one daughter, Elisabeth Frances (Fanny), who married General Bertrand in 1808. As the younger son of a French count, he was known in France as Count Dillon.

A junior officer in the family regiment, Dillon became its proprietary colonel on 25 August 1767, but did not take command until five years later, on 1 May 1772. During the American War of Independence he participated in combat at Grenada, St Eustatius, Savannah, Tobago, and St Kitts, of which he served as governor (1782–3). He was named brigadier on 1 March 1780 and major-general on 1 January 1784, and was governor of Tobago from 1786 to 1789. As deputy for Martinique in the national assembly of 1789 he defended colonial interests but generally voted with the liberals. He was promoted lieutenant-general on 13 January 1792 and served under the command of Lafayette and of Dumouriez during the fighting of July to October. Because of his ambivalent response to the overthrow of the monarchy on 10 August and his correspondence with the landgrave of Hesse, he was recalled to Paris to explain his conduct on 13 October and suspended from his duties five weeks later. He was reinstated on 23 February 1793 and associated with Camille Desmoulins, but was again suspended on 1 June; on 13 July he was arrested and imprisoned in the Luxembourg. He was accused of being a leader of an alleged royalist conspiracy and was condemned to death by the revolutionary tribunal on 13 April

1794. The following day he was executed in Paris, together with Lucille Desmoulins, who met her death nine days after her husband.   SAMUEL F. SCOTT

Sources R. F. Hayes, *Irish swordsmen of France* (1934) · G. Bodinier, *Dictionnaire des officiers de l'armée royale qui ont combattu aux États-Unis pendant la guerre d'indépendance, 1776–1783* (Vincennes, 1982) · R. F. Hayes, *Ireland and Irishmen in the French Revolution* (1932) · G. Six, *Dictionnaire biographique des généraux et amiraux français de la Révolution et de l'Empire, 1792–1814*, 2 vols. (1934) · H. L. Dillon, *Memoirs of Madame de la Tour du Pin*, ed. and trans. F. Harcourt (1971) · J. C. O'Callaghan, *History of the Irish brigades in the service of France*, [new edn] (1870) · *DNB*
Likenesses portrait, repro. in Dillon, *Memoirs*

Dillon, Arthur Richard (1721–1806), archbishop of Narbonne and émigré leader, was born on 1 September 1721 at St Germain-en-Laye, Paris, the fifth and youngest son of Arthur *Dillon, Jacobite Earl Dillon (1670–1733), *maréchal de camp* and head of the Dillon regiment in the French service, and Christiana (1684–1757), daughter of Ralph Sheldon, first equerry to James II of England. Arthur Dillon was intended for the church, and from 1740 was educated at St Sulpice in Paris, the seminary invariably attended by young men destined for leadership positions in the Gallican church, taking his master's degree on 26 October 1743.

After ordination Dillon benefited from Louis XV's particular regard following his (fourth) brother Edward's death leading the Dillon regiment at the battle of Lauffelt in 1747. In the same year Dillon became vicar-general of Pontoise, a post which was usually a springboard to the episcopate. In 1753 he was appointed bishop of Évreux; in 1758 he was translated to the archdiocese of Toulouse, and in 1763 became archbishop of Narbonne and primate of the Gauls, a valuable diocese with an income of 250,000 livres annually. In 1766 he additionally received the abbey of St Jean-des-Vignes (diocese of Soissons) *in commendam*. Dillon also held the titular headship of the abbey of St Étienne de Caen (worth 110,000 livres), which he exchanged in 1787 for the equally lucrative religious house of Cigny in the diocese of Rheims. These revenues enhanced his existing fortune, albeit one burdened by his own debts, his efforts to relieve those incurred by other members of the Dillon family, and his personal charity. He spent large sums on his Paris town house and on his estate at Hautefontaine, near Soissons, where he maintained his own pack of staghounds.

An eloquent orator and capable administrator, Dillon was a man who combined intellectual capacity with style and physical presence which went to make up what his niece called 'an air of elegant assurance' (*Memoirs of Madame de la Tour du Pin*, 38). Before the revolution he served as president of the general assembly of the clergy of France in 1775 and 1785, and was a member of both the first and second Assemblies of Notables in 1787 and 1788. Though ready to abandon clerical fiscal privileges and to advocate the doubling of the third estate, Dillon defended the hierarchical principle in the Gallican church at the moment it was coming under intensive criticism from the lower clergy. As *président* of the Languedoc estates, the archbishop had a leading influence in the government of the province, and established a reputation as one of the leading *prélats administratifs* of the pre-revolutionary generation, one who also supported civil rights for members of the reformed faith. He visited the province annually and promoted the building of roads, bridges, canals, harbours, and other improvements in Languedoc, but paid less attention to the spiritual direction of his diocese beyond the immediate vicinity of Narbonne. Dillon was not popular with his neglected parish clergy, and his standing fell generally in 1788–9 through his association with what was increasingly seen as the antiquated constitution of the Languedoc estates.

Dillon was unsympathetic to the changes brought about by the French Revolution, especially the reorganization of the Gallican church by the civil constitution of the clergy, passed by the national assembly in July 1790. Dillon refused to take the oath to the civil constitution and thereby forfeited his possession of the see of Narbonne, which was anyway one of those abolished under this legislation. Until September 1791 he remained on his estates at Hautefontaine, then emigrated to England via the émigré centre of Koblenz, and Prussia. He had debts of 1,800,000 livres when he left France, and the loss of all his offices ensured they were never repaid. In London, Dillon lived modestly, supported by his nephew Viscount Dillon, but his house was still large enough for six other bishops to join him. As the most senior of the prelates exiled in London he resisted efforts by Louis XVIII in 1796–7 to reduce episcopal independence in the interests of a more streamlined organization for the church. He subsequently refused to accept the concordat of 1801, and concerted the opposition of those in London to Pius VII's request for resignation of their sees without reference to a conciliar ruling on the question. Archbishop Dillon died in George Street, Portman Square, London, on 5 July 1806, and was buried in St Pancras old churchyard. Some of his speeches to the general assembly of the clergy were published, as was his uncompromising *Lettre de Monseigneur l'archevêque de Narbonne au très-saint père, en envoyant à sa sainteté la lettre des évêques réfugiés à Londres* (1802).   NIGEL ASTON

Sources *Memoirs of Madame de la Tour du Pin*, ed. and trans. F. Harcourt (1969) · *GM*, 1st ser., 76 (1806) · F.-A. A. De La Chenaye-Desbois, *Dictionnaire de la noblesse: contenant les généalogies, l'histoire et la chronologie des familles nobles de la France*, 3rd edn, 6 (Paris, 1865), 893 · [J. C. F. Hoefer], ed., *Nouvelle biographie générale*, 14 (1855), col. 181 · M. Péronnet, *Les évêques de l'ancienne France*, 2 vols. (1977) · N. Aston, *The end of an elite: the French bishops and the coming of the revolution, 1786–90* (1992) · L. Audibert, *Le dernier président des états de Languedoc* (1868) · C. Viguier, 'Notes sur le dernier archevêque de Narbonne (1763–1806)', *Bulletin de la Commission Archeologique et Littéraire de l'Arrondissement de Narbonne*, 38 (1964–5), 83–97 · L. Dutil, 'Un prélat d'ancien régime: A. -R. Dillon', *Annales du Midi*, 53 (1941), 51–77 · A. Sabarthès, *Arthur-Richard Dillon, dernier archevêque de Narbonne* (1943) · C. -J. Trouvé, *Essai historique sur les états-généreux de la province de Languedoc*, 2 vols. (1818) · C. -F. de Lubersac, *Journal historique et réligieux de l'émigration et déportation du clergé de France en Angleterre* (1802) · A. Theiner, *Documents inédits relatifs aux affaires religieuses de la France, 1790 à 1800*, 2 vols. (1857) · A. Sicard, *Les évêques pendant … concordat* (1903), vol. 3 of *L'ancien clergé de France*, 250–51, 344–6 · D. A. Bellenger, *The French exiled clergy in the British Isles after 1789* (1986) · Y. Fauchois, 'Les évêques émigrés et le royalisme pendant la révolution française', *Les résistances à la révolution*, ed.

R. Dupuy and F. Lebrun (1987), 386–93 • F. T. Cansick, *A collection of curious and interesting epitaphs*, 1 (1869), 80
Archives Archives du Ministère des Affaires Étrangères, Paris, Fonds Borbons 589 (France et divers états), documents relatifs à l'émigration • BL, Add. MS 37064, fols. 10, 12, 14, 15 • Recusant Studies Centre, Bellenger card index of exiled clergy | BL, letters to William Windham, Add. MS 37856, fol. 382 ff.
Likenesses J. Hoppner, portrait, 1800; Dillon sale, lot 56, 1933, formerly in possession of Viscount Dillon • portrait, repro. in Bellenger, *French exiled clergy*

Dillon, Carmen Joseph (1908–2000), film art director, was born on 25 October 1908 at 149 Walm Lane, Hendon, Middlesex, the fourth daughter and youngest of the six children of Irish-born Joseph Thomas Dillon, company secretary for a British firm with railway interests in South America, and his wife, Teresa Joseph McNale, schoolteacher. The third daughter was Agnes Joseph Madeline (Una) *Dillon (1903–1993), bookseller. Born into a strict Catholic family, Carmen Dillon was educated at New Hall Convent School, Chelmsford. She developed two passions there. The first was for the theatre; she designed (and performed in) several amateur productions. Second, she discovered a talent for drawing. Her precocious artistic skills earned her the offer, in 1924, of a scholarship from the Architectural Association School. Being too young—at sixteen—she opted to further her artistic studies for one year at the North London Collegiate School. Dillon subsequently studied at the Architectural Association School for six years. Her classmates included several figures who were to make a particular impact upon British film art direction, including Lawrence P. (Bill) Williams and Ralph Brinton. The film art director (or production designer) designs and builds sets. The Architectural Association School graduates of the early 1930s were instrumental in the movement towards architectural standards in British art direction. However, following her graduation, Dillon initially chose a more traditional career path, working as an architect in London and Dublin.

Dillon's entry into films came in 1934, when Brinton invited her to join him at the Wembley studios. This entailed certain sacrifices for her. Her pay declined from £8 to £3 a week. Moreover, she had to accept poor conditions. The studios made lowly 'quota quickie' films on derisory budgets: the sets rarely cost more than £100 overall. She also had to endure sexual discrimination. She was not allowed to issue orders to men or to step onto the studio floor. In addition, she suffered male taunts, such as the complaint that she was 'keeping a man out of a job'. These prejudices remained even after she was made chief art director in 1937 (following Brinton's illness). The director of *The Five Pound Man* maintained that her overspending of £3 on a prison cell set proved that women could not work to budgets. Dillon none the less maintained that she learned much via the Wembley treadmill.

Dillon applied the lessons through the next decade, when she art-directed twenty-three films, either in her own right or as assistant to Paul Sheriff or Roger Furse. Two films stood out during this period, *Henry V* (1944) and *Hamlet* (1948), both directed by Olivier. Dillon made vital contributions to each. In the case of *Henry V* (her favourite

film) it was she who suggested the radical use of 'false perspectives' based on Froissart's fifteenth-century engravings. For *Hamlet*, she supervised Furse's massive interlocking set sections and camera towers. She also introduced minor innovations, such as the studio weeds which disguised the camera tracks for the drowning of Ophelia. These achievements earned her an Academy award (for best set decoration of a black and white film).

Dillon saw the 1940s as a high point for British film design. Although by nature a realist, she disliked the mundane location-led aesthetic which subsequently prevailed. Her own assignments often lacked flavour after 1950. *The Importance of being Earnest* (1952), *The Prince and the Showgirl* (1957), and a last collaboration with Olivier, *Richard III* (1955), offered the 'arty side' which she desired in a film project. But her talents were lent increasingly to visually unprepossessing comedies, such as *Doctor in the House* (1954) and *Carry on Cruising* (1962). Of her later projects, two stood out, both of them directed by Joseph Losey: *Accident* (1967) and *The Go-Between* (1970). Losey was notoriously demanding, but Dillon worked well with him. On *Accident* she achieved seamless matches between the Oxford locations and the studio sets. She also used key props to suggest the characters' self-absorbed psychologies. For *The Go-Between*, she completely renovated a country house at Melton Hall near Norwich, and made spare use of mainly authentic props. This, taken together with the consistent colour sense, helped to make *The Go-Between* a quiet yet pungent costume film.

Dillon's energy, combined with her discipline and acute organizational skills, led to her being in continuous employment for thirty-five years: for twenty-five of these she was Britain's sole named female art director. These facts paid their own tribute, given the perennially brittle financing of British films. She never married, and for most of her life shared a large Kensington flat with her sisters Una and Tess before moving with Una to Hove. She died at the Victoria Nursing Home, 96 The Drive, Hove, Sussex, on 12 April 2000, of bronchopneumonia and acute bronchitis.   LAURIE N. EDE

Sources C. de la Roche, 'The stars behind the camera', *Picturegoer* (16 July 1949) • J. Stockwood, 'Feminine art in films', *Sunday Times* (21 June 1959) • S. Cole and C. Dillon, interview for the BECTU Oral History Project, 23 June 1993, BFI • C. O'Brien, 'Carmen overcame prejudice … and put on her slacks', *Cinema Studio* (Nov 1951) • R. Miller, 'She puts reality into film sets', *Daily Telegraph* (2 Sept 1957) • C. Dillon and E. Ronay, interview for *Fifties features*, 1968 [BBC Television] • publicity materials for *Hamlet*, 1948, BFI • B. Cross, ed., *The film 'Hamlet': a record of its production* (1948) • publicity materials for *The go-between*, 1970, BFI • 'Woman in a man's world', BFI fiche on Carmen Dillon, *c.*1965 • *Daily Telegraph* (20 April 2000) • *The Guardian* (21 April 2000) • *The Times* (26 April 2000) • b. cert. • d. cert.
Archives FILM BFI NFTVA | SOUND BFI, S. Cole interview with Carmen Dillon for the BECTU Oral History Project, 23 June 1993
Likenesses photograph, 1960–69, repro. in *Daily Telegraph* (20 April 2000) • photograph, repro. in *The Guardian* • photograph, repro. in *The Times*

Dillon, Cecily (*c.*1603–1653), Poor Clare abbess, was born in Ireland, the daughter of Theobald Dillon, first Viscount Dillon of Costello-Gallen, co. Mayo (*d.* 1624), and Eleanor, *née* Tuite (d. 1638), of Tuitestown, co. Westmeath. Her father, made viscount in 1621, was a prominent Catholic landowner with extensive properties in co. Mayo and co. Westmeath. Like her elder sister Eleanor (1598–1629), Cecily travelled to the continent to make her noviciate with the exiled English Poor Clare house at Gravelines (now in France), a community renowned for the severity of its rule. Both women were professed there on 8 September 1622, she receiving the name Sister Cecily of St Francis. She left Gravelines in May 1625, being among a group of five Irish nuns, directed by her sister, who founded a new convent in Dunkirk. Their stay there proved brief as rents were high, and in November 1626 they moved to Nieuwpoort, where they re-established themselves as a community in early 1627.

With a view to capitalizing on increasing religious toleration in Ireland, both women agreed to suggestions from their two brothers, both priests in the Irish province of Franciscans, that they should consider returning home to found a convent in Ireland. Having arrived in Dublin on 13 June 1629, they established themselves in Merchant's Quay. As her sister Eleanor died soon after her return to Ireland, it was Cecily Dillon who was elected abbess, while her brother Father Bonaventure was appointed confessor to the new foundation. The convent initially enjoyed a period of calm and prosperity. Within their first year they accepted twelve postulants, and for a time were free from the harassment experienced by other religious houses in Dublin. This may have been the result of the support from her brother Sir Lucas (Luke) Dillon, then a privy councillor. However the convent's fortunes went into decline in October 1630 following a visit from the wife of a prominent government official. Although the annalist Bonaventure Browne incorrectly described the visitor as the lady deputy, it is thought to have been either Lady Cork, wife of the lord justice, who refers to the nuns in her diary, or Eleanor Loftus, wife of the lord chancellor, Adam Loftus. The convent was subsequently sacked, after which Dillon, with four other nuns, was brought before the lord deputy. According to Browne she proved herself adept in handling the situation, and so moved the deputy that he abandoned his initial intention of ordering them from the country, commanding them instead to leave Dublin. Having been given a month to leave, they stayed in the home of sympathetic nobles before moving to a new convent on her father's estate in 1631. Located on the shore of Lough Ree the new convent, known as Bethlehem, proved extremely successful and attracted numerous postulants from gentry families, among them six of Dillon's nieces. It also engaged the curiosity of Elizabeth Rhodes, wife of Thomas Wentworth, and Katherine Villiers, duchess of Buckingham, later wife of Randal MacDonnell, earl of Antrim.

Following the outbreak of conflict in 1641 the community was once again thrown into crisis. Acting on the advice of Sir James Dillon they evacuated their convent in 1642, after which it was sacked and set alight. Cecily Dillon and her nuns found themselves scattered throughout the area in homes of local Catholic nobles before they managed to regroup in Athlone, where they again re-established themselves as a religious community. Their position remained precarious, and in 1647 Dillon was forced to petition the supreme council of the confederate Catholics for assistance. Her letter to the council, dated 5 May, states that 'Petitioners being unable to subsist by reason of people crowding into the town, the Superior issued orders of dispersion. They can however no longer live on their friends and pray for relief' (Concannon, *Poor Clares*, 36). Nevertheless, they remained in Athlone until 1653, when as a result of Cromwell's edict of 6 January they were commanded to marry or leave the country. Like many of the Irish Poor Clares, Dillon chose exile in Spain, and as the most senior member of her order took charge of the group that fled there. However she died on board ship while it was held in quarantine off the coast of Galicia in 1653. Browne, in her annals, makes a brief reference to her death, describing Dillon as a 'woman endowed with such prudence, rare virtues and discretion, that she was elected Abbess five times' (*Recollections*, 12).

FRANCES CLARKE

Sources Mrs T. Concannon [H. Concannon], *The Poor Clares in Ireland* (A.D.1629–A.D.1929) (1929) • *Recollections of an Irish Poor Clare in the seventeenth century, Mother Mary Bonaventure Browne third abbess of Galway, 1647–1650*, ed. C. O'Brien (1993) • S. O'Brien, 'Daughters of St Clare, being the story of some Irish Poor Clares', *Poor Clares Tercentenary Record, 1629–1929* (1929), 22–5 • Mrs T. Concannon, *Daughters of Banba* (1922) • GEC, *Peerage*, new edn, vol. 4 • J. Lodge, *The peerage of Ireland*, rev. M. Archdall, rev. edn, 4 (1789)

Dillon, Charles (1819–1881), actor, was born in Diss, Norfolk, probably the illegitimate son of Charles James Church, an itinerant actor, and Eliza, who married Arthur Dillon, a minor London actor and theatrical agent, whose name he adopted.

Until 1856 Dillon played small roles in London's minor theatres, writing plays on demand while at the Marylebone Theatre, and toured provincial towns, including Hull, Sheffield, Wolverhampton, Manchester, and Dublin. During this period he established himself as a Shakespearian actor in roles such as Macbeth, Othello, and Hamlet, roles which he retained for the rest of his career. He married Clara (1824/5–1888), the daughter of a London theatre manager, Benjamin Conquest, and their daughter, also Clara, was born in 1845. With the financial assistance of his father-in-law, Dillon managed the Theatre Royal and, subsequently, the Adelphi, Sheffield, between 1850 and 1856.

The period 1856 to 1860 was the most successful of Dillon's career. His performance as Belphegor in *Belphegor the Mountebank, or, Woman's Constancy*, adapted by Charles Webb from *Le Paillasse* by Dennery and Fournier, brought him to the attention of London theatre critics. The play opened at Sadler's Wells on 21 April 1856, and John Oxenford's review in *The Times* two days later, in which he stated that 'it was not often that we see such rare effects of pathos produced with such a thorough absence of stage trick', made Dillon's reputation. On the strength of his success, and again with Conquest's assistance, he took a lease of the Lyceum Theatre in September 1856, which he retained for two seasons, until March 1858. During this time his performances as D'Artagnan in his own version of *The Three Musqueteers* (16 October 1856), Claude Melnotte in Bulwer-Lytton's *The Lady of Lyons* (10 November 1856), Othello (1 December 1856), and Macbeth, opposite Helen Faucit as Lady Macbeth (25 February 1858), were particularly commended for their geniality, tenderness, and understatement, characteristics which, at his best, became hallmarks of Dillon's acting. His relationship, however, with Eliza Webb, the daughter of Charles Webb, contributed to the breakup of his marriage after the closing of the second Lyceum season. Following a further tour of the provinces he sailed for New York on 22 December 1860.

The third period in Dillon's career, from 1861 to 1867, was taken up by a tour which included North America, Australia, New Zealand, Peru, and Chile. He began by playing a range of his repertory in New York, Boston, Baltimore, and Philadelphia, including Belphegor and Virginius (in Sheridan Knowles's play of the same name) and also Boucicault's *Louis XI*. Accompanied by Eliza Webb, he then toured Canada, including Toronto, Quebec, and Montreal. They left for San Francisco and opened there at the Metropolitan Theatre on 21 October 1861. Critical assessment mirrored that of the London critics, but financially the tour was proving disastrous. Dillon left for Australia from Vancouver and arrived in Melbourne, Victoria, in November 1862.

From 1862 to 1864 Dillon and Eliza Webb (now billed as Mrs Charles Dillon, although there is no evidence that they married) remained in Australia, touring the Victorian country towns of Bendigo and Ballarat, and Adelaide and Sydney, where they spent the greater part of their time. Dillon found himself occasionally in direct competition with Barry Sullivan as well as Charles and Ellen Kean, who were also in Australia in 1863–4. Following a short stay in Tasmania that began in August 1864, the Dillons sailed for New Zealand. Dillon opened as Virginius in Auckland (5 January 1865) and once again included Othello, Macbeth, and Belphegor in his season. After playing in Christchurch and Dunedin, the Dillons left for Peru in July 1865. Although he intended an extensive tour of South America, political instability forced the Dillons to leave Chile hurriedly, and in December 1865 they returned to New York, where Eliza died of typhoid fever. Dillon remained in the United States until the end of 1866, and left for England in early 1867 after a final season in New York.

Throughout his extended tour Dillon had relied heavily on a repertory that he had developed in London, the British provinces, and on tour in North America, augmented by versions of *King Lear* and *Timon of Athens*, Byron's *Manfred*, Taylor's *The Ticket-of-Leave Man*, and John Brougham's adaptation of *The Duke's Motto*. However, there were ominous signs of deterioration in Dillon's performances, which had been noticed by Australasian and, subsequently, American critics. He was increasingly unable to sustain his roles vocally and was losing the ability to play the emotional nuances that earlier critics had applauded.

The last phase of Dillon's career was marked by an increasing personal sense of disappointment and, critically, by one of irrelevance to contemporary theatre practice. He opened in Manchester as Lear on 7 March 1867. Although he repeated his performance as Lear at Sadler's Wells (17 February 1868) and as Manfred at the Princess's (16 August 1873), he spent his final years in the provinces. He married Bella Mentrup, an actress, in Cardiff in June 1874. His last appearances in London were at Drury Lane, as Leontes in *The Winter's Tale* (28 September 1878) and as Shylock (7 December 1878). He died suddenly of a stroke in Hawick, Roxburghshire, on 24 June 1881 and was buried in Brompton cemetery on 26 June.

Although physically unattractive, Dillon embodied a seedy flamboyance perhaps best captured in Mrs Sam Cowell's memory of him at the beginning of his American tour: 'in a threadbare suit, big, dirty boots, and a large, Theatrical [*sic*] cloak (which was braided profusely, and lined with red silk), so ragged, as to hang down on all sides in festoons' (Disher, 325). As an actor, Dillon's lack of technique and his reliance on momentary inspiration rather than on consistency in characterization made his deficiencies more apparent when his vocal abilities deteriorated. Westland Marston described him as 'an actor of great emotional gifts, but very deficient in intellectual ones' (Marston, 308).   VICTOR EMELJANOW

Sources *The Era* (25 June 1881), 5 • *The Era* (9 July 1881), 14 • J. W. Marston, *Our recent actors*, new edn (1890) • F. Fleetwood, *Conquest* (1953) • K. Barker, 'A provincial tragedian abroad', *TRI*, 11/1 (1986), 31 • J. Coleman, *Players and playwrights I have known*, 2 (1888) • M. W. Disher, ed., *The Cowells in America* (1934) • C. E. Pascoe, ed., *The dramatic list*, 2nd edn (1880) • K. Barker, 'Charles Dillon: a provincial tragedian', *Shakespeare and the Victorian stage*, ed. R. Foulkes (1992) • G. T. Harris, 'Charles Dillon: a provincial tragedian in the former colonies', *Scenes from provincial stages*, ed. R. Foulkes (1994) • m. cert. (1874)
Archives University of Bristol, Theatre Collection, Kathleen Barker MSS
Likenesses nine prints, Harvard TC • portrait (as Othello), repro. in Fleetwood, *Conquest* • portrait (as Belphegor), repro. in A. Jackson, *The Standard Theatre of Victorian England* (1993)

Dillon, Edouard (1750–1839), army officer and diplomatist in the French service, was born at Wrightington, Lancashire, on 20 June 1750, the second son of Robert Dillon (1710–1764), formerly a banker at Dublin, and his second wife, Marie Dicconson. His father settled in Bordeaux, where he became a shipowner and outfitter. On 19 June 1777 Dillon married Fanny Harland (*bap.* 1749, *d.* 1777), the daughter of Sir Robert Harland at Hautefontaine, but she died six months later. He remarried in London on 20 October 1796; his new wife was Emilie Pocquet de Puilhery; they had a daughter, Georgine. During the American War of Independence he fought in the West Indies and was wounded at Grenada. Known as *le beau* Dillon, he became a favourite at the court of Louis XVI, where he was closely associated with the Polignac family and Queen Marie Antoinette. He was appointed colonel of the regiment of Provence and gentleman-in-waiting to the king's younger brother, the comte d'Artois.

Shortly after the outbreak of the French Revolution, Dillon emigrated from France, joined Artois, and, together with some of his brothers, raised counter-revolutionary forces to attack France. After the failure of the invasion of 1792 he continued his exile and served in the Irish brigade sponsored by England. At the restoration of Louis XVIII in 1814 he was named lieutenant-general and later served as ambassador to Saxony (1816–18) and to Tuscany (1819). He died in Paris in 1839.

SAMUEL F. SCOTT

Sources J. Balteau and others, eds., *Dictionnaire de biographie française*, [19 vols.] (Paris, 1933–) · R. F. Hayes, *Ireland and Irishmen in the French Revolution* (1932) · R. F. Hayes, *Irish swordsmen of France* (1934) · G. Bodinier, *Dictionnaire des officiers de l'armée royale qui ont combattu aux États-Unis pendant la guerre d'indépendance, 1776–1783* (Vincennes, 1982) · DNB

Dillon [*née* Mathew], **Elizabeth** (1865–1907), Irish nationalist, born at 6 Pembroke Villas, Richmond, Surrey, on 2 March 1865, was the eldest daughter and second child of Sir James Charles *Mathew (1830–1908), judge, and his wife, Elizabeth Blackmore, *née* Biron. The Mathews were a Cork family, but lived at 46 Queen's Gate Gardens, Kensington, and Elizabeth Mathew was educated in London at a small day school before studying literature and Old English at King's College, London, from 1882 to about 1884. She was well-versed in the arts and several modern languages and had travelled in Europe. She was a devout Roman Catholic, and she engaged in philanthropic ventures, especially workhouse visiting.

Always interested in politics, Elizabeth Mathew met many leading Liberal and Irish MPs through her father; in 1887 she wrote an essay (unpublished) on the home rule question, which clearly displayed her powerful intellect. Her sympathy for Irish nationalism was fostered by her family's home rule sympathies, and by witnessing the poverty of tenant farmers in Galway which caused her to declare her opposition to landlordism. Her political education was advanced in the Ladies' Gallery of the House of Commons, which she attended regularly from the mid-1880s; her visits were increasingly motivated by her admiration for John *Dillon (1851–1927), who came to embody her ideal of patriotism. She followed his activities and those of his fellow nationalists, and was alarmed by his imprisonments over the Plan of Campaign; she prided herself on using her influence at the dinner table to effect the transfer of Dillon and William O'Brien to a more congenial prison.

On 21 November 1895, nine years after their first meeting, Elizabeth Mathew married Dillon. It was a happy marriage and they were a devoted couple. Their fourth son, and fifth among their six children, was James Mathew *Dillon (1902–1986). A woman of definite opinions, Elizabeth Dillon usually deferred to her husband, though she certainly influenced him in his growing estrangement from his former friend and colleague in the 'land war', William O'Brien, whom she profoundly distrusted. The retired domesticity expected of married women was not easy for her to accept: she adored her children, but her papers reflect a sense of frustration in her exclusion from Dillon's political work, and a fear that she would lose touch with his life. Her own commitment to Ireland intensified with motherhood. Making her home in Dublin, she came to view England as alien; she referred to her children by their Irish names, and encouraged them to learn Irish. However, her marriage was a short one. On 14 May 1907, at the age of forty-two and suffering from probable pneumonia, she died, at her home, 2 North Great George's Street, Dublin, giving birth to her seventh child, a still-born daughter. She was buried in the family vault in Glasnevin cemetery.

The nationalist press noted her death, describing Elizabeth Dillon as the perfect helpmate for her husband, who had radiated happiness since their marriage, but barely acknowledged her own independent interests and qualities, subsuming her into her husband's identity. Elizabeth Dillon's own papers reveal her to have been a woman of considerable ability, who accepted, albeit with a sense of loss, a secondary role.

SALLY WARWICK-HALLER

Sources E. Dillon, diary, 1879–1906, TCD, Dillon MSS, 6667–6702 · E. Dillon, essays, TCD, Dillon MSS, 6882, 6882a · F. S. L. Lyons, *John Dillon* (1968), chap. 9 · 'Mathew, Sir James Charles', DNB · *Weekly Freeman, National Press and Irish Agriculturist* (30 Nov 1895) · *Freeman's Journal* [Dublin] (15 May 1907) · E. Dillon, correspondence (esp. with J. Dillon), TCD, Dillon MSS · private information (2004) · b. cert.

Archives TCD

Likenesses portraits, 1890–1900, repro. in F. S. L. Lyons, *John Dillon* · L. Boyle, drawing, priv. coll.

Dillon, Emile Joseph [*pseud.* E. B. Lanin] (1854–1933), journalist and philologist, was born in Dublin on 21 March 1854, the second son of Michael Dillon, a foundry and hardware merchant, and his wife, Mary Byrne. In accord with his father's wishes, Dillon studied for the priesthood in the Carmelite school and Holy Cross College in Dublin; he spent a further three years in St David's Monastery, Pentasaph, Wales, at the Grande Chartreuse, at the seminary of St Sulpice in Paris, and at the college of the Paulist Fathers in New York. At the age of twenty-one, he effectively abandoned theology to pursue his interest in oriental languages and returned to Paris; he worked briefly as assistant librarian in the Bibliothèque Nationale and began his philological studies under Ernest Renan at the Collège de France. Encouraged by Renan, Dillon completed his study of Sanskrit, Arabic, and Hebrew at the University of Innsbruck. In 1875 he finally left the priesthood and moved to the University of Leipzig (where he was awarded a doctorate of philosophy).

During the late 1870s Dillon travelled in Europe and studied briefly at the universities of Tübingen, Louvain, St Petersburg, and Kharkov. He first visited Russia in 1877, when he was temporarily employed in Kiev as tutor in German to the sons of a Russian nobleman. From Kiev, he went to the University of St Petersburg to continue his studies of oriental languages and to obtain a teaching position, but he was denied a post because of his criticism of influential faculty members. He left for the University of

Emile Joseph Dillon (1854–1933), by Sir William Orpen

Louvain, where he achieved a doctorate in oriental languages and literature and helped to found the literary review, *Le Muséon*. Returning to St Petersburg in 1880, Dillon was briefly employed by a Russian newspaper; in 1881 he married a widow, Yelena Maksimovna Bogachova, who bore him four sons during the 1880s. By the early part of this decade Dillon possessed an excellent command of Latin, Greek, French, German, and Russian, and had mastered, among other languages, Sanskrit and Armenian; he claimed to speak twenty-six languages, and to be completely fluent in ten. With these qualifications he was appointed professor of comparative philology, Sanskrit, and ancient Armenian, at the University of Kharkov in 1884. He had already achieved renown for his translations of ancient Armenian manuscripts into Russian (which merited his election to the Armenian Academy in Venice) and studies on ancient Bactrian and Iranian languages, and the university awarded him a doctorate in comparative philology in 1884. But his promising academic career ended abruptly when he resigned in protest against the bureaucratic administration of the university.

In 1886 Dillon migrated to Odessa, where he became foreign editor of the liberal *Odessky Vestnik*, and later editor of the *Odesskiye Novosti*. After a year of conflicts with the censor, he moved to St Petersburg, where he began to contribute articles on Russia to the London press, and by the late 1880s had become well established as a journalist. During 1887 he was recruited by the proprietor of the *Daily Telegraph*, Harry Lawson (later Lord Burnham), as the paper's correspondent in Russia, and in this capacity, and later as roving foreign correspondent, served the *Telegraph* for almost three decades (until 1914). Soon after this arrangement was established, Dillon began to contribute

monthly articles on Russia and foreign affairs to the *Contemporary Review*, *Fortnightly Review*, *National Review*, *Review of Reviews*, and some American periodicals. His 'Russian Characteristics' series in the *Fortnightly Review* and the *National Review* (1889–92), under the pseudonym E. B. Lanin, firmly established him as an authority on Russian affairs; his keen reporting and his subsequent exploits as a special correspondent inspired journalists such as W. T. Stead to acclaim him as Britain's premier foreign correspondent.

Dillon's most spectacular coup was his first-hand reporting for the *Daily Telegraph* of the Turkish massacres of Armenians during 1894–5. Barred from Armenia by the Turkish authorities, he slipped into the beleaguered region in various disguises and rendered harrowing descriptions of Turkish genocide, which aroused British public opinion and provided Gladstone with the evidence to indict the Turks for the Armenian 'horrors'. Dillon's success in Armenia and his development of close contacts with statesmen and diplomats greatly enhanced his reputation as an innovative foreign correspondent, and persuaded the *Telegraph* to permit him to undertake, on his own initiative, missions in Europe and Asia. Thus, in 1897, disguised as an Orthodox priest living with Cretan insurgents, Dillon reported the revolt in Crete against Turkish rule and, abetted by his close friend, the Greek patriot Eleutherios Venizelos, he served as an intermediary between the insurgents and the allied fleet coercing the Turks. During the following year Dillon reported the Spanish-American War from Madrid, and a year later (1899) was in France covering the second court martial of Captain Alfred Dreyfus. From France he went to the Netherlands, where he reported the first Hague peace conference in 1899, and during 1900 was in China describing the Western powers' suppression of the Boxer uprising in Peking (Beijing).

Returning to his home in St Petersburg, Dillon became a firm friend and ardent advocate of the Russian finance minister and later (1905–6) chief minister, Sergey Witte. In August 1905 Dillon accompanied Witte as publicity adviser to the Portsmouth peace conference, which ended the Russo-Japanese War, and contributed to influencing American public opinion on behalf of Russia. During the Russian Revolution of 1905, Dillon sedulously reported what was occurring, and warned that, without such a progressive leader as Witte, Russia would be consumed by a bloody peasant upheaval; he subsequently bitterly assailed Tsar Nicholas II for dismissing Witte in 1906. Henceforth, Dillon was pessimistic about orderly reform in Russia and became increasingly concerned with the deteriorating international situation. In the Bosnian crisis of 1908–9, his defence of his friend, the Austro-Hungarian foreign minister, Count Alois L. von Aehrenthal, against the charges of the Russian foreign minister, Aleksandr Izvolsky, caused considerable embarrassment to the British Foreign Office. From 1909 to 1913 Dillon, accompanied by a bevy of pretty female secretaries, traversed the European capitals and covered the Balkan wars of 1912–13. In 1913 he terminated his residence in Russia and divorced his wife, and in the following year married his long-time companion and secretary, Kathleen Mary Ireland of Belfast.

By this time Dillon had become overly opinionated and discursive and had outlived his value for the *Daily Telegraph*, which gradually ceased publishing his dispatches. Now the ageing 'greyish little man with a stubby beard and soft voice' could no longer indulge his 'cloak and dagger' complex and pose as a 'mystery man' (Burnham, 44, 47). Even so, many journalists and diplomats still respected his skill in getting everywhere and learning everything, his intimacy with prominent statesmen, his multilingual facility, and his realism. During 1915 he predicted the imminent collapse of Russia, and throughout the war and the ensuing peace conference (which he attended) was very pessimistic about Europe's prospects. Despairing of the future of Europe, he left for Mexico after the conference, hoping that the Mexican Revolution might provide some 'helpful hints and fruitful parallels' for post-war Europe. On a brief visit to the United States and Mexico in 1920–21, he found in President Alvaro Obregón another Witte; his view of the Mexican situation was set out in *Mexico on the Verge* (1921). Returning to Mexico in 1922, Dillon became a confidant of Obregón and served him as a contact with foreign oil corporations.

Plagued by ill health, Dillon returned to Europe in 1924 and settled at Barcelona. In 1928 he visited the Soviet Union and, although he admired some Bolshevik achievements, left lamenting that the old Russia he had known was now only a vague memory. By the time of his death on 9 June 1933, at 49 Calle Salud, Barcelona, Dillon had completed the book *Count Leo Tolstoy: a New Portrait* (1934), a lively account of his experiences and difficulties with Tolstoy, whose works he helped to translate and popularize in Britain. On his death, Dillon was remembered in Fleet Street as 'a man of mystery … whose business in life it was to know and understand foreign affairs in a way peculiar to himself' (Bentley, 318).   JOSEPH O. BAYLEN

Sources P. W. Johnson and J. O. Baylen, 'Dillon, Dr. Emile Joseph, 1854–1933', *The modern encyclopedia of Russian and Soviet history*, ed. J. L. Wieczynski, 7 (1978) • P. W. Johnson, 'The journalist as diplomat: E. J. Dillon and the Portsmouth peace conference', *Journalism Quarterly*, 53 (1976), 689–93 • J. E. Courtney and W. L. Courtney, 'Dr. Dillon', *Fortnightly Review*, 140 (1933), 22–8 • *Daily Telegraph* (10 June 1933), 13 • *The Times* (10 June 1933), 14 • '"The semi-official ambassador". The exploits of Dr. E. J. Dillon', *Irish Times* (20 March 1954), 10 • Lord Burnham [E. F. L. Burnham], *Peterborough Court: the story of the Daily Telegraph* (1955) • E. C. Bentley, *Those days* (1940) • H. Baerlien, *All roads lead to people* (1952) • S. J. Witte, *Vospominania*, 2 (1960) • H. Nicolson, *Some people* (1927) • personal information (2004) • E. B. Lanin, *Russian characteristics* (1892) • E. J. Dillon, *The eclipse of Russia* (1918) • E. J. Dillon, *The inside story of the peace conference* (1920) • E. J. Dillon, *Mexico on the verge* (1921) • d. cert.
Archives Stanford University, California, Hoover Institution • University of Dublin, MSS | CAC Cam., Spring-Rice MSS • Central State Archives, Moscow, Count Sergius Ju. Witte MSS • L. N. Tolstoy State Museum, Moscow, Count L. N. Tolstoy MSS • London School of Economics, Courtney MSS • National Archives of Mexico, Mexico City, President Alvaro Obregón MSS • News Int. RO • PRO, Spring-Rice MSS • TCD, corresp. with John Dillon
Likenesses F Cuairan, bust, 1930?, NG Ire. • J. O. Baylen, photographs • P. May, caricature (after J. O. Baylen) • W. Orpen, oils, NG Ire. [*see illus.*] • Owl, caricature, mechanical reproduction, NPG; repro. in *VF* (5 Nov 1913), 518 • J. Russell & Sons, photograph, NPG
Wealth at death £14,855 10s. 9d.: probate, 14 Sept 1933, *CGPLA Eng. & Wales*

Dillon, Francis [Frank] (1823–1909), landscape painter, was born in London on 24 February 1823, the younger son of John Dillon (d. 1868), of Morrison, Dillon & Co., a successful firm of silk mercers, of Fore Street, London, and the owner of a fine collection of watercolour drawings, including several by J. M. W. Turner; only the forename of his mother, Mary (d. 1856), is known. Following Mary's death, John Dillon remarried and with his second wife had three more children. Francis was educated at Bruce Castle School, Tottenham. In 1846 he joined the Royal Academy Schools, and subsequently became a pupil of James Holland. On 27 March 1847 he married Emma Josephine Case (1822–1860), and in the following year he took her and their daughter to Madeira for several months, also visiting Lisbon. This trip, the first of many, resulted in Dillon's first exhibits in oil, *On the Tagus, Lisbon* (ex P. Polak, 1966) at the Royal Academy, and *Ribeiro Brava, Madeira* at the British Institution, both in 1850, and also in the publication of *Sketches in the Island of Madeira* (1850), a volume of thirteen lithographs.

Dillon continued to exhibit frequently at the Royal Academy until 1903 and at the British Institution until its close in 1867. He was a founder member of the Dudley Gallery in 1865, and exhibited there until, in 1882, it was assimilated into the Institute of Painters in Water Colours, of which he then became a member, exhibiting there until 1908. He exhibited elsewhere in London, including the Society of British Artists, the Grosvenor Gallery, and the New Gallery, and also in Manchester and Paris. Much of the subject matter for his paintings was drawn from the scenery and buildings he encountered during his extensive travels abroad. He visited several parts of Europe, including France, Italy, Switzerland, Austria, and Norway, and, in 1881–2, he travelled to Portugal, Spain, and Morocco; but two countries further afield, Egypt and Japan, made the greatest impact on his career.

Dillon visited Egypt on at least four occasions. In 1854–5 he ascended the Nile as far as Aswan, making many fine watercolour sketches (examples ex Christies, 9 June 1970, 9 November 1971). He returned in 1861–2 when he shared a studio in Cairo with George Price Boyce and the Swedish artist Egron Lundgren. They lived in an oriental manner and were befriended by Iskender Bey, son of Süleyman Pasha, formerly a French officer. Several drawings from this trip were published in the *Illustrated London News* (April 1862). Subsequent visits were in 1869–70, 1873–4, and possibly later in the 1870s. Several of Dillon's exhibited paintings reflect his interest in the antiquities of Egypt, including *The Colossal Pair, Thebes* (exh. British Institution, 1857; ex Christies, 30 November 1984) and *The Pyramids from the Island of Roda* (exh. Royal Academy, 1863; ex Maas Gallery, 1983–4). These were highly acclaimed at the time, the *Art Journal* judging *The Colossal Pair* 'among the most admirable of modern works' (1857, 69), but, while the best deserve recognition for their atmospheric treatment of orientalist subjects, others that have survived are variable in quality.

In the 1870s Dillon became concerned for the Islamic monuments of Cairo, especially its domestic houses, which were then suffering wholesale destruction from the modernization of the city; he joined others, such as J. D. Crace, R. P. Spiers, and Stanley Lane-Poole, in efforts to study and preserve this heritage. The watercolour and gouache sketches that he made in Cairo, particularly those that depict specific and identified domestic interiors—to which few other European artists had access—are his most individual and distinctive works. They are now considered his most significant contribution to the British orientalist tradition; examples are held in the Victoria and Albert Museum. Several of these interiors were later worked up for exhibition and were well received by the critics: such, for example, were *The Harem of a Wealthy Arab, Cairo* (exh. Dudley Gallery, 1875) and *Hareem of Sheikh Sadât* (exh. Dudley Gallery, 1876; probably related to *Ka'ah in the Harem of Sheykh Sadat*, Searight collection, V&A). Seven were reproduced in G. Ebers's *Egypt: Descriptive, Historical and Picturesque* (1878–9). Dillon brought several Islamic artefacts back to London, and created an Arab studio in his house in Upper Phillimore Gardens.

Dillon was one of the first Western artists to visit Japan, travelling there in 1875 via North America. He spent a year based in Osaka with his son, but also sketched the scenery in other parts of the country. On his return he exhibited Japanese subjects, such as *The Stray Shuttlecock* (V&A), at the Royal Academy and the Dudley Gallery. He brought home several Japanese curios and his appreciation of the arts of Japan enabled him to write an introduction to the catalogue for an exhibition of Japanese and Chinese art works held at the Burlington Fine Arts Club in 1878; two years later he published *Sketches by Japanese Artists*. He also became a member of the council of the Japan Society.

Dillon's interest in conservation was not confined to Egypt: in 1880 he joined an international committee to assist the progress of the restoration of St Mark's Basilica in Venice, and six years later he participated in the controversy over the effects of light and environmental conditions on watercolours. In the 1890s he opposed the construction of the Nile dam at Aswan which would result in the submergence of the temples at Philae.

As a young man Dillon was sympathetic to the ideas behind the revolutions of 1848. He knew Giuseppe Mazzini during his exile in England—almost certainly as a result of his connections with the Ashurst family, notable for their liberal tendencies—and also assisted some of the leaders of the Hungarian revolution. His marriage produced two daughters, Georgina and Mary, and a son, Edward, but his wife died in 1860—which possibly contributed to his frequent travelling—and his elder daughter also predeceased him. He died at 13 Upper Phillimore Gardens, Kensington, on 2 May 1909.

BRIONY LLEWELLYN

Sources *Art Journal*, new ser., 29 (1909), 223 • *The Athenaeum* (8 May 1909), 567 • *The Times* (5 May 1909) • *The Times* (8 May 1909) • private information (2004) • B. Llewellyn, 'Frank Dillon and Victorian pictures of old Cairo houses', *Ur*, 3 (1984), 2–10 • Graves, *RA exhibitors* • Graves, *Brit. Inst.* • B. Llewellyn, 'Two interpretations of Islamic domestic interiors in Cairo: J. F. Lewis and Frank Dillon', *Travellers in Egypt*, ed. P. Starkey and J. Starkey (1998), 148–56 • *DNB* • registry papers, V&A, P.6-1916; 852-862-1900 • *A portion of the remaining works of Frank Dillon* (1911) [sale catalogue, Christies, 21 Jan 1911] • J. L. Roget, *A history of the 'Old Water-Colour' Society*, 2 (1891), 405 • C. E. Clement and L. Hutton, *Artists of the nineteenth century and their works: a handbook containing two thousand and fifty biographical sketches*, 1 (1879), 208–9 • BL, Dillon MSS, Add. MSS 28511; 38831, fol. 40; 42575, fol. 215 • E. W. Cooke, journal, Jan 1874, priv. coll., Cooke MSS [by permission] • m. cert. • will • *Mazzini's letters to an English family*, ed. E. F. Richards, 3 vols. (1920–22) • T. Sato and T. Watanabe, eds., *Japan and Britain: an aesthetic dialogue, 1850–1930* (1991) [exhibition catalogue, Barbican Art Gallery, London, and Setagaya Art Museum, Tokyo, 1991]

Likenesses pastel, before 1843, priv. coll. • C. E. Watkins, photograph, repro. in *The Year's Art* (1892), facing p. 94 • carte-de-visite (standing at his easel), priv. coll. • photograph (standing by a window), priv. coll.

Wealth at death £14,240 7s. 8d.: resworn probate, 26 June 1909, *CGPLA Eng. & Wales*

Dillon, Francis Edward Juan [Jack] (1899–1982), radio producer, was born on 9 December 1899 at 16 Lewis Street, Walsall, son of Francis Herbert Dillon, a gymnastics instructor, and his wife, Monica Gannon. He spent his early years abroad with his parents in Halifax, Nova Scotia, and Kingston, Jamaica, where he was educated by a private tutor. In 1907 the family returned to Surrey, where he attended Frimley School, Norwood Polytechnic, and Bromley high school. At the age of fourteen he went to Dr Stephenson's academy in Yorkshire to train for the army. In 1915 he went on to Ayr Academy before active service in Flanders. He is reported to have fought with the White Army in Russia, but escaped via the Far East and ended his military career with the Black and Tans in Ireland.

Dillon's next employment was as a tax inspector in Manchester, where he remained until 1936. At the time Manchester was the centre of exciting experimental work in the new medium of the radio feature. Now better known as Jack, Dillon joined producers Archie Harding and D. G. Bridson as a scriptwriter. He married and he and his wife, (Hilda) Tania (b. 1901), had at least one daughter. By 1938 he had moved to Bristol as west regional features producer and in 1941 he joined London features and drama department to contribute to the BBC's war effort. His impact on the department was recalled by Bridson:

> He was a man of infinite and strident wit, whose croaky voice had been raised to its unusual pitch by a dose of mustard gas in Flanders. The parties that he threw with his wife Tania were focal points for the brighter part of local Bohemia. Jack himself was one of the liveliest minds I knew at the time … He was a witty and thoroughly competent radio craftsman … He had a peculiar knack for the handling of actuality programmes, and a true devotion to the chronicling of country life. (Bridson, 32, 82)

In 1941 Dillon joined another features writer and producer, the poet Louis MacNeice, on an infamous recording trip on board the destroyer HMS *Chelsea*. They spent nine days patrolling the northern Atlantic and indulging in late night drinking sessions that kept the crew awake. The trip resulted in a programme, *Freedom's Ferry*, and began a life-time friendship between the two men, with Dillon's character immortalized as Devlin in MacNeice's poem 'The Autumn Sequel'.

In 1942 Dillon began the Sunday radio series *Country Magazine* which ran for twelve years with the professed intention 'to create a better team spirit between people working in factories and people working in fields' (Dillon, 1). The idea for the series originated from the Ministry of Agriculture which felt such a programme would be helpful in wartime when travel between town and country was so restricted. On the third anniversary of the series the *Sunday Pictorial* ran an article on the producer:

> Francis Dillon, the man who has gathered the farmers, basket makers, cowherds and glovemakers together is ... a homespun type, wears corduroys and a fisherman's hand knitted guernsey in Portland Place bars, drinks beer, and doesn't like the idea of getting publicity in the Press.

Dillon's other wartime programmes included *Know your Enemies* written by William Empson and Igor Vinogradoff and concerning the Japanese people. In 1947 he accompanied Louis MacNeice and Wynford Vaughan Thomas on a three-month trip to India to record the events leading up to independence. In later years Dillon made a number of imaginative adaptations of fairy tales. He won second prize and £500 at the first Prix Italia award in 1949 for *The Old and True Story of Rumpelstiltskin*. His factual series such as *I Like my Job* made good use of new recording technologies in the field. While researching the career of the probation officer he was attacked by three men with razors in Covent Garden and he received eighteen stitches to his hands. Francis Dillon retired from the BBC in 1959, but continued as a freelance writer and producer from his home in Arundel. He died of pneumonia on 9 December 1982, his eighty-third birthday, at Arundel Hospital, Arundel.   KATE WHITEHEAD

Sources BBC WAC · D. G. Bridson, *Prospero and Ariel: the rise and fall of radio* (1971) · J. Stallworthy, *Louis MacNeice* (1995) · A. Briggs, *The history of broadcasting in the United Kingdom*, 4 (1979) · F. Dillon, ed., *'Country magazine': book of the BBC programme* (1950) · b. cert. · d. cert. · staff files, BBC WAC
Archives BBC WAC | SOUND BBC WAC · BL NSA, current affairs recording
Wealth at death under £25,000: probate, 18 Jan 1983, *CGPLA Eng. & Wales*

Dillon, Harold Arthur Lee-, seventeenth Viscount Dillon (1844–1932), antiquary, born on 24 January 1844 at 1 Albert Street, Victoria Square, London, was the elder son of Arthur Edmund Dillon-Lee or Lee-Dillon, sixteenth Viscount Dillon (1812–1892), and his wife, Ellen (1809–1896), daughter of James Adderley of King's county, Leinster. The eleventh viscount had married, in 1744, the heiress of the Lees of Ditchley, Oxfordshire, collateral heirs of Sir Henry Lee, champion to Elizabeth I: through them Dillon was descended from Charles II and Barbara Villiers. He was educated at a private school at Eltham, Kent (1855–60), and at Bonn University. He passed out fourth in the army examination of 1862, was gazetted ensign in the rifle brigade on 8 November of that year, and promoted lieutenant in 1866. He saw service in India and Canada, and, on leaving the regular army in 1874, was promoted captain in the Oxfordshire light infantry (militia battalion), retiring with the rank of major in 1891.

After leaving the rifle brigade Lee-Dillon developed the antiquarian interests which eventually led to his becoming one of Britain's leading authorities on the history of arms and armour, medieval costume, and kindred subjects. His first major publication was a new and completely revised edition in 1885 of *Costume in England*, by F. W. Fairholt. This was followed by over fifty others, mostly articles in learned journals, notably *Archaeologia*, the *Archaeological Journal*, and the *Journal of the Society of Army Historical Research*, a few under his pen-name Armadillo. The majority are on some aspect of the history of arms and armour, but others include an important study of Calais and the Pale (*Archaeologia*, 53, 1893), and a catalogue of the paintings, and accounts of various historical manuscripts, at Ditchley.

In 1888 Lee-Dillon had published a seminal paper on the sections of the great 1547 inventory of Henry VIII's possessions covering arms and armour at Westminster, the Tower of London, and Greenwich (*Archaeologia*, 51, 1888), and in 1892, the year in which he succeeded his father as Viscount Dillon, he was appointed as the first curator of the Tower of London armouries, where the residue of these collections had ended up. At this date the armouries still included arms for current use and were administered by the War Office. Their historic contents were under the charge of army storekeepers, who mistreated them and whose lack of historical knowledge led to the eventual nullification of attempts to arrange and label them correctly by, successively, S. R. Meyrick, J. Hewitt, and J. R. Planché. This scandalous state of affairs led to the creation of the official, but semi-honorary, post of curator of the armouries, with responsibility for the study and care of the historic pieces. Dillon was not only the first curator, but he was also the first person to be involved with the armouries to have made a serious study of arms and armour 'in the metal' and not only from early documents and illustrations. He carried out a complete reorganization of the collection, during which he made a detailed examination of all the major pieces, identifying for the first time a number of those with important historical associations and correcting many inaccurate attributions. In 1910 he published an *Illustrated Guide to the Armouries*, which was, in fact, a summary catalogue of pieces exhibited. He retired from the armouries in 1913, having laid the foundation for their eventual conversion into a modern museum.

Dillon was assisted in identifying the original owners of some of the Tower armours by the reappearance of a folio album of captioned designs of armours produced in the English Royal Almain Armoury at Greenwich for Marian and Elizabethan courtiers. The album had resurfaced in the catalogue of the collection of Frédéric Spitzer in 1892; the South Kensington (now Victoria and Albert) Museum failed to purchase it at the Spitzer sale in 1893, but, thanks to Dillon's intervention and support, managed to acquire it privately in 1894. In 1895 Dillon published an article on it (*Archaeological Journal*, 52, 1895) followed in 1905 by a volume of facsimile reproductions of a selection of the plates under the title *An Almain Armourer's Album*. Both, although now out of date, were milestones in the study of English armour.

Dillon was chairman of the trustees of the National Portrait Gallery (1894–1928), to which he presented and bequeathed various portraits from Ditchley, among them likenesses of Elizabeth I, Archbishop William Wareham, Sir Philip Sidney, and Sir Henry Lee (by Antonio Moro). He was also president of the Royal Archaeological Institute (1892–8) and of the Society of Antiquaries (1897–1904), a trustee of the British Museum (1905–12) and of the Wallace Collection (1918–31), and antiquary to the Royal Academy. He was elected a fellow of the British Academy on its foundation in 1902, appointed CH in 1921, and was also an honorary freeman of the Armourers' and Brasiers' Company of London.

Dillon married twice: first, on 3 November 1870, in Ottawa, Julia (d. 1925), eldest daughter of Isaac Brock Stanton of Ottawa and his wife, Maria, daughter of James Wilson of Scarr, co. Wexford, with whom he had one son who predeceased him; second, on 15 June 1926, Margaret Louisa Everard (d. 1954), daughter of the Revd Henry Edward Browne ffolkes, and widow of the Revd John Erasmus Philipps.

A true aristocrat, with a fine head and figure, Lord Dillon was equally at home in a royal palace and in the third-class carriage of the Great Western Railway, by which for many years he travelled from Charlbury to London and back several times a week. He had two maxims, one that 'Duty is doing more than you are paid for', and the other, in connection with enquiries relating to his expertise, 'Never say you do not know, but find out and then reply'. He died at Ditchley on 18 December 1932, and was buried in Enstone church, Oxfordshire. He was succeeded as eighteenth viscount by his nephew Arthur Henry (1875–1934), who sold Ditchley in 1933, when nearly all the remaining pictures in the collection were dispersed.

C. FFOULKES, rev. CLAUDE BLAIR

Sources J. G. Mann, 'Lord Dillon', *Zeitschrift für historische Waffen- und Kostümkunde*, 13 (1932–4), 141–2 · *The Times* (20 Dec 1932) · C. J. Ffoulkes, 'Viscount Dillon, 1844–1932', *PBA*, 18 (1932), 335–44 · Burke, *Peerage* · C. J. Ffoulkes, *Arms and the tower* (1939) · personal knowledge (1949, 2004) · GEC, *Peerage* · S. B. Bailey, 'Lord Dillon: curator of the armoury, 1895–1912', *Royal Armouries Yearbook*, 7 (2002), 108–29

Archives BL, corresp. and papers relating to a manuscript collection of ordinances of chivalry, Add. MS 42725 · Oxon. RO, Oxfordshire Archives · Royal Armouries Museum, Leeds, papers

Likenesses G. Brackenburg, oils, 1894, NPG · S. W. Carlin, lead medallion, 1913, NPG · M. Codner, drawing, S. Antiquaries, Lond. · J. Russell & Sons, photograph, NPG · G. Scharf, watercolour, NPG · W. Stoneman, photograph, NPG · photograph, repro. in Ffoulkes, *Arms and the tower*, frontispiece · sculpture, Tower of London · window, St Kenelm's Church, Enstone, Oxfordshire

Wealth at death £226,672 6s. 4d.: probate, 27 Feb 1933, CGPLA Eng. & Wales

Dillon, Sir James (b. c.1600, d. in or after 1669), army officer, was probably born at Kilfaughny, co. Westmeath, the eighth and youngest son of nineteen children of Theobald, first Viscount Dillon of Costello-Gallen (d. 1624), an extensive landowner in Connaught and co. Westmeath, and his wife, Eleanor (d. 1638), daughter of William Tuite of Tuitestown, co. Westmeath. Nothing is known of his education or youth. He was twice married. His first wife was Elizabeth (d. before 1653), daughter of Thomas Plunkett of Rathmore, co. Meath. They had two sons, Ulick and James, both of whom predeceased him. His second marriage, to Mary (d. before January 1665), daughter of Roger Jones of Sligo and widow of Major John Ridge of co. Roscommon, was childless.

Dillon had an estate of 2500 acres in Mayo and Roscommon, but he seems to have lived near Athlone. He was the senior member of his family resident in co. Westmeath, which he represented in parliament in 1634–5 and from 1640 until his expulsion as a rebel in 1642. In 1641, after the disbandment of Wentworth's 'new army' in which he was a captain, he was authorized to recruit a regiment for service in the Spanish army from the soldiers affected. His investment of £1000 in this project was lost when the scheme became a casualty of the growing conflict between King Charles I and parliament. This setback, possibly coupled with the belief that he was acting in accordance with the king's wishes, involved him with Lord Maguire and others in the conspiracy that preceded the 1641 rebellion. He made the radical proposal to seize Dublin Castle, but then withdrew from the plot, probably on the insistence of the commander-in-chief of the army, the earl of Ormond, that it was unhelpful to the king's cause.

After the outbreak of the 1641 rising Dillon was sent to the midlands as governor of Longford and Westmeath. Initially he exercised a restraining hand on the rebels, many of whom were his kinsmen, before reluctantly following his fellow Old English Catholics into revolt. He remained very much on the moderate wing of the confederacy. He was appointed colonel of an infantry regiment in the Leinster army. The prestige and wealth of his family made him the dominant military leader in west Leinster, where he recruited and provided sustenance for more than 1000 men. Throughout 1642 he invested Athlone, the key midland fortress on the Shannon. His forces twice broke into the east town but failed to dislodge the Connaught president, Viscount Ranelagh, from his stronghold in the castle west of the river. Dillon did not oppose Ormond's relief of the town in the summer, but in January 1643 he took part in an unsuccessful attack on a second relief force at Rathconnell, near Mullingar, as it retired to Dublin having evacuated Ranelagh and the remnants of his garrison. He then occupied east Athlone, and eventually gained the castle after his royalist nephew, Viscount Dillon, to whom he was closely allied, became president of Connaught in 1644. Smaller strongholds in the midlands were also brought under his control. In 1643 he helped negotiate a truce with Ormond, who recommended him as 'person of honour and good affection' (*Irish Confederation*, ed. Gilbert, 4.355). His regiment took part in Castlehaven's fruitless offensive in Ulster (1644). He joined Taaffe in reducing pro-parliament strongholds in co. Roscommon in 1645, and was present the following year with his regiment when Preston took Roscommon and Jamestown. Competition for quarters and ideological differences embittered his relations with Owen Roe O'Neill, who responded to his lethargic military performance with the sarcastic suggestion that he 'forego a military career, as not suiting to his humours, and at ease at home court ladies for which he was a fit instrument' (Gilbert, *Contemporary history*, 2.72). In 1646 the seizure of Athlone by O'Neill's supporters briefly drove him to side with Ormond, but he soon reverted to the confederacy, recovering the town and eventually the castle with Preston's help. He escaped from the battle of Dungan's Hill (1647), leaving his regiment to be destroyed with the rest of the Leinster army. His efforts to re-form it made slow progress, and by 1649 he could only muster 100 men in addition to two companies supplied to the Drogheda garrison. He served under Ormond in 1649–50. In 1651 he was much criticized by other royalist leaders for his hasty surrender of Athlone to the parliamentarians. His own surrender followed in 1652. He forfeited his estate, but was permitted to take a regiment to Spain, from which he was sent to France to support the Bordeaux Fronde. His Franciscan brother, Father George Dillon, persuaded him to surrender the château of Lormont to the duc de Vendôme in 1653. His regiment then entered the French army, and he was promoted to brigadier-general. His change of allegiance met with the approval of the exiled Charles II, who later acknowledged his loyalty. He served in the army of Flanders and fought with distinction at the battle of the Dunes (1658). His regiment was disbanded in 1664. He returned to the British Isles, where Charles II granted him a pension of £500. In 1664 he sought a licence for the distribution of a new artificial fuel in Ireland. In 1666 he obtained a pass for Flanders, from where he corresponded with Ormond in Irish, evidently performing an intelligence-related role during the war with France and Holland.

The date and place of Dillon's death are unknown, but he was still in receipt of his pension in 1669. Much of his estate seems eventually to have reverted to his nephew, Thomas, fourth Viscount Dillon, who was presumably his heir.   HARMAN MURTAGH

Sources J. T. Gilbert, ed., *A contemporary history of affairs in Ireland from 1641 to 1652*, 3 vols. (1879–80) · *History of the Irish confederation and the war in Ireland … by Richard Bellings*, ed. J. T. Gilbert, 7 vols. (1882–91) · P. Gouhier, 'Mercenaires irlandais au service de la France (1635–1664)', *Irish Sword*, 7 (1965–6), 58–75 · B. O'Ferrall and D. O'Connell, *Commentarius Rinuccinianus de sedis apostolicae legatione ad foederatos Hiberniae Catholicos per annos 1645–1649*, ed. J. Kavanagh, 6 vols., IMC (1932–49) · *CSP Ire.*, 1633–69 · J. Lodge, *The peerage of Ireland*, 4 (1754), 182–4 · A. Clarke, *The Old English in Ireland, 1625–1642* (1966) · B. Jennings, ed., *Wild geese in Spanish Flanders, 1582–1700*, IMC (1964) · H. Murtagh, *Athlone: history and settlement to 1800* (2000) · [E. Borlase], *The history of the execrable Irish rebellion*, new edn (1743) · J. I. Casway, *Owen Roe O'Neill and the struggle for Catholic Ireland* (1984) · P. Lenihan, 'The Leinster army and the battle of Dungan's Hill, 1647', *Irish Sword*, 18 (1990–92), 139–53 · R. C. Simington, ed., *Books of survey and distribution: being abstracts of various surveys and instruments of title, 1636–1703*, 1–2 (1949–56) · P. Lenihan, *Confederate Catholics at war, 1641–49* (2001)

Dillon, James Mathew (1902–1986), politician, was born on 26 September 1902 in Dublin, the fourth son and fifth among the six children of John *Dillon (1851–1927), politician, and his first wife, Elizabeth (1865–1907) [see Dillon, Elizabeth], daughter of the Anglo-Irish High Court judge Sir James Charles *Mathew and his wife, Elizabeth. His childhood years were spent between his parents' Dublin home in North Great George's Street and Ballaghaderreen, co. Roscommon, where the family's mercantile business was located.

Dillon was first educated at home by a governess, before being sent to Mount St Benedict in Gorey, co. Wexford, founded by the Benedictine monk Father John Sweetman (1913–19). He matriculated at University College, Dublin, in 1919. Despite beginning a course in commerce and being active in a range of student societies and politics, Dillon failed to engage with his studies and left the university in June 1921. He travelled to London to learn about the wholesale and retail trade, aiming at an eventual return to the family business. While in London, Dillon worked for Selfridges, and in February 1923 he left for America to continue his business education. He spent eighteen months in Chicago working in the city's major department stores, first at the Fair, and later at Marshall Field's. In the autumn of 1924 he returned to Ballaghaderreen to run the family business. In his absence the fledgeling Irish Free State had suffered civil war; his family home had been occupied by troops and many of his friends from university had been killed, while those that remained were divided over the Anglo-Irish treaty. Dillon, given his father's political career at the head of the home rule Irish Parliamentary Party, was a political animal by upbringing, yet could not bring himself to support either the pro-treaty Cumann na nGaedheal Party or the rejectionist Sinn Féin.

Using the skills he had acquired in Britain and America, Dillon ran the family firm successfully. His approach was deeply conservative, but he managed to produce steady profits year after year. His great skill was reorganizing the whole scope of the business and reinvigorating areas that had been neglected during the upheavals of war, such as the family's farm. As a result of his independent outlook on politics, and the esteem in which the family name was generally held, Dillon was approached by the national league to stand as a parliamentary candidate at the election of 1927. He declined, but took an active part as a campaigner, and his effective political style was widely noted. Shortly after his father's death in 1927 he decided to return to education, and studied law in Dublin. He was called to the bar in 1931.

At the election of February 1932 Dillon was invited to contest Donegal, as an independent, by John D. Nugent of the Ancient Order of Hibernians. His campaign was successful, and he was elected in second place, beating the Fianna Fáil candidate by several hundred votes. Dillon was a truly independent member of the Dáil, at times supporting the Fianna Fáil government, on others vehemently opposing them. With other independent members of the

Dáil he discussed the concept of forming a new party. The major figure in such moves was Frank MacDermot, and on 5 January 1933, with Dillon's support, the National Centre Party came into being. Despite outlining a broad programme that included the revision of the treaty by consent, the new party was understood by many observers as essentially one based on the interests of the nation's farmers. The party put in a credible performance in the 1933 election, gaining eleven seats, although Dillon's own first preference vote in Donegal was reduced by over 2000. Fianna Fáil won a majority, however, and despite Dillon's prediction that it would hold the balance of power the National Centre Party was forced to join Cumann na nGaedheal on the opposition benches.

In office Fianna Fáil continued to prosecute a tariff war with Britain, and the economy began to suffer. In opposition, both Dillon's party and Cumann na nGaedheal were impotent. Negotiations began towards a merger, in which Dillon was a key player. The most dynamic opposition organization at the time, however, was outside parliament: the uniformed and fascist-style Army Comrades Association, or Blueshirts, led by General Eoin O'Duffy. The two parliamentary parties realized that their hand would be strengthened by inviting the Blueshirts to join them. This they did, and the new party, Fine Gael, came into being in September 1933, with O'Duffy, despite his not holding a Dáil seat, as its leader. Dillon, despite his short service in active politics, was chosen as one of the party's vice-presidents. He was now at the heart of national politics.

The former Blueshirts, and O'Duffy in particular, pursued a chaotic course that offered violent resistance to the policies of Fianna Fáil, while at the same time flirting with ideas inspired by European fascism. Dillon became aware that the success of the new party was compromised by O'Duffy's leadership, and sought to control him throughout the summer of 1934. In August matters came to a head, and Dillon manoeuvred O'Duffy into resigning from the party. This period enhanced Dillon's political reputation, while also convincing him of the dangers inherent in the political agenda of Fianna Fáil. In the post-O'Duffy period W. T. Cosgrave became leader of Fine Gael, while Dillon, now central to the party hierarchy, continued as vice-president. The remainder of the 1930s, although providing many challenges, saw Dillon working tirelessly within the party, and helped to stabilize the structures of—and support for—Fine Gael.

During the Second World War, the Fianna Fáil government's policy of neutrality was widely supported in the country and by opposition parties. Almost the lone voice in political life raised against this stance was Dillon's: on 16 July 1941 he argued in the Dáil that Ireland should drop its neutrality and join the allies in fighting Germany. He followed this with a similar address at the Fine Gael árd fheis (conference) in February 1942, arguing that Ireland had to join the war to show support for the Irish-American relationship. This view was a singular one, even in his own party, and on 20 February 1942 he resigned from Fine Gael

and resumed an independent status. He thereby consigned himself to the political wilderness, yet raised his national profile considerably.

On 30 September 1942 Dillon married Maura Phelan (1920–1991), the daughter of a Clonmel draper. They had one child, John Blake (b. July 1945). Dillon's years as an independent were hard, but the downturn in Fianna Fáil fortunes at the elections of 1948 offered him the chance of resurrection. He was offered, and accepted, the post of minister of agriculture in the first inter-party government, in which office he was successful and well respected. Among his achievements were the Anglo-Irish trade agreement of 1948 and the land rehabilitation scheme of the following year. The inter-party government fell in 1951, and amid the subsequent political realignments Dillon rejoined Fine Gael in 1953. From 1954 to 1957 he served once more as minister of agriculture in the second inter-party government.

Despite its role in these coalitions Fine Gael could not challenge the electoral dominance of Fianna Fáil. In search of a new direction, the party chose Dillon as leader in 1959. He claimed not to enjoy his six years in the post, all of which were spent in opposition, arguing that he would rather be an effective minister of agriculture than a taoiseach (he regarded agriculture as the fount of Ireland's future prosperity). Although he never guided the party into power, he was, in electoral terms at least, very successful, guiding Fine Gael from a low point of 26 per cent of the vote in 1959 to 34 per cent in 1965—its highest level of support since the early 1930s. He committed the party to the abolition of compulsory Irish in schools and offered strong opposition to De Valera's attempt to end proportional representation in elections. After his departure from the leadership Dillon spent four more years on the back benches before finally leaving the Dáil in 1969. In his retirement he returned to Ballaghaderreen, where he played an informal role in the family business and an active one in the Ancient Order of Hibernians, eventually being elected as national president.

Dillon died of emphysema on 10 February 1986 at the family home—Monica Duff's, Ballaghaderreen—and was buried on 16th in the family's plot in the local churchyard. Garret Fitzgerald, a successor as leader of Fine Gael, rated him 'Ireland's foremost parliamentarian'; his oratory was renowned, and Maurice Manning, his biographer, observed that Dillon 'never trimmed, he had this great belief in telling the truth, which was often very uncomfortable for those all around him' (Manning, UCD News, November 1999).   MIKE CRONIN

Sources M. Manning, *James Dillon: a biography* (Dublin, 1999) · B. Maye, *Fine Gael, 1923–87* (Dublin, 1993) · F. S. L. Lyons, *John Dillon: a biography* (1968) · G. FitzGerald, review of M. Manning's *James Dillon: a biography*, www.ucd.ie/~ucdnews/nov99/james.htm [UCD News, Nov 1999], April 2002 · H. Boylan, *A dictionary of Irish biography*, 3rd edn (1998) · www.finegael.com/history/leaders/leaders-of-fine-gael.htm [biographies of party leaders, Fine Gael website], April 2002

Archives priv. coll. · TCD

Likenesses photographs, priv. coll. · portraits, priv. coll.

Dillon, John (1851–1927), Irish nationalist, was born into the Catholic bourgeoisie in Blackrock, co. Dublin, on 4 September 1851, second son among eight children of the Young Irelander John Blake *Dillon (1814–1866) and Adelaide (1828–1872), daughter of William Hart, a Dublin solicitor.

Early life and career summary John Dillon was educated privately (one of his tutors was the Fenian James Stephens) and at the age of thirteen was sent to Dr Quinn's school in Harcourt Street. From 1865 to 1870 he studied in the arts faculty of the Catholic University, where he won several prizes and was auditor of the Literary and Historical Society. A voracious reader, he devoured works on literature, history, philosophy, medicine, and science, among many topics. In 1870 Dillon briefly was apprenticed to a Manchester cotton broker but he returned to Dublin and began studies at the Catholic University medical school, before becoming a licentiate of the Royal College of Surgeons in 1875. Dillon then was a demonstrator in anatomy at the Cecilia Street medical school, but ceased active involvement in medicine when he entered political life. Family financial means enabled him to devote his energies exclusively to politics. A romantic revolutionary aura hung over this tall (6 feet 2 inches), thin man, who was plagued by chronic bouts of illness, including dyspepsia (a condition that affected him in every political crisis), varicose veins, a degree of heart trouble, and eye problems—although he was also prone to hypochondria.

Dillon's liberal, independent Irish Catholic notion of an inclusive political nation based on civic rights was in consonance with his father's vision. He articulated radical–Liberal opinions: C. P. Scott observed, 'on social subjects and in foreign politics he is a keen and active Liberal' (*Political Diaries of C. P. Scott*, 202), though in later years he was essentially conservative on labour questions and women's suffrage. Dillon—solitary, aloof, fastidious, and lacking in bonhomie—was respected in Ireland and by the House of Commons. At the height of the land war, when he was locked in political combat with the government, the Irish chief secretary's adopted daughter none the less recorded, 'there is always something impressive in Mr Dillon's tragical face and manner, and belief in his undoubted honesty and political unselfishness never fail to get him a respectful hearing from the House' (*Florence Arnold-Forster's Irish Journal*, 494). Yet he also had a vindictive streak that manifested itself later in his attitude to Sir Horace Plunkett, Sir Antony MacDonnell, James Larkin, and James Connolly. Possibly he had more of a Catholic concept of the 'nation' than he would have wished to acknowledge; Dillon was unwilling to accommodate the Irish landlord class. His public career falls into three phases: radical and agrarian up to 1891; party and parliamentary leader from 1891 to 1914; and an increasingly critical though constitutional opponent of Britain and its Irish policy from 1914 to 1918.

Radical and agrarian: the Home Rule League and the Land League Dillon joined the Home Rule League when it was

John Dillon (1851–1927), by Sir Benjamin Stone, 1898

founded in November 1873. He surfaced in the parliamentary by-election campaign of John Mitchel, his father's old associate, for Tipperary in 1875, when he first met William O'Brien, for many years his closest colleague and later an unrelenting critic. Dillon became ill in 1876 and remained largely outside the political arena until the next year, when he was elected to the council of the Home Rule League and began working with Charles Stewart Parnell. He also joined the council of the Society for the Preservation of the Irish Language and later the Gaelic League, though he never succeeded in learning Irish himself. A political rather than a cultural nationalist, he was a foremost opponent of making Irish a compulsory subject in the new National University in February 1909. From the time he entered politics until the early 1890s he was seen as a radical with an affinity for Fenianism, though he never joined the movement. By attacking the supposedly anaemic parliamentary approach of Isaac Butt in January 1878 Dillon won public notice; on 4 February 1879 he famously condemned the ailing Butt on the leader's last appearance at the Home Rule League council in Dublin.

In 1879 Dillon made his first speech on the land question and on 5 October he advocated what would become known as 'boycotting'. When the Irish National Land League was formed in October 1879, he was a member of the original committee and accompanied Parnell on a mission to North America to raise funds for the new body; he remained there until July. In April 1880 he joined the executive of the league. Though Dillon admired Parnell, the two were never intimate colleagues. In his absence Dillon was returned to the House of Commons for Tipperary at the general election in April. But his principal forum was Land League meetings; on 5 November he was among those unsuccessfully prosecuted for conspiracy to prevent the payment of rent. Dillon was a close ally and friend of Michael Davitt, the spearhead of the land agitation. In January he was elected to the committee of the party and, after Davitt's imprisonment, he was appointed Land League head of organization on 13 February. A stern critic of Gladstone's Land Bill introduced in April 1881, which he believed would do nothing for small farmers, Dillon stole a march on Parnell by calling for its rejection (12 April). No other member of the Irish party ever took the initiative away from Parnell in that period. Dillon was detained under the Protection of Person and Property Act (1881) on 2 May (ultimately he was imprisoned six times) but his health quickly deteriorated and he was released on 6 August. At that time he declined to be associated with Parnell's newly launched newspaper, *United Ireland*. On 15 October he was incarcerated again, with Parnell and others, in Kilmainham prison. Although opposed to the 'No rent manifesto' issued on 18 October, as a gesture of solidarity Dillon signed it. Shortly after his release from prison on 2 May he (and Parnell) received the freedom of Dublin (16 August). As part of the 'Kilmainham treaty', Parnell sought to end the land war; unhappy with this change of direction, on 25 September Dillon announced his withdrawal from politics 'for the next few years' (Moody, 539); he left Ireland in November and in the summer of 1883 departed for Colorado, where his elder brother, William, lived. There he avoided politics and did not mix with Irish-Americans.

In the summer of 1885 Dillon re-emerged tentatively in politics, after returning home to find the political climate altered. Though he had differed from Parnell over cessation of the land war, he now believed that the Irish leader's strategy on home rule had borne fruit. Persuaded to contest the Ulster seat of North Tyrone, where he was narrowly defeated in the autumn general election, Dillon also was selected to fight the safe constituency of East Mayo, which he held until 1918. When Parnell, at the risk of undermining party unity, insisted on the selection of Captain William O'Shea for the parliamentary vacancy at Galway borough in February 1886, Dillon remained neutral. Gladstone's adoption of home rule in 1886 confirmed Dillon's acceptance of Parnell's strategy and convinced him of the utility of the Liberal alliance. But the Conservatives' return to office in July 1886 heralded renewal of the land agitation and the following years were dominated by the second phase of the land struggle, the Plan of Campaign, which Dillon authored with O'Brien and T. C. Harrington; it was published on 23 October in *United Ireland*. He and

O'Brien were the most visible leaders of the agitation. During 1887 he first met his future wife, Elizabeth Mathew [see Dillon, Elizabeth (1865–1907)], daughter of Sir James Mathew, at her parents' home in London, where he became a frequent guest. In the most notorious incident of the struggle on 9 September 1887 at Mitchelstown, Cork, where Dillon was speaking, the constabulary opened fire, killing three and wounding two. Although an earnest Catholic, Dillon always opposed clerical interference in secular politics; following the papal rescript condemning the Plan of Campaign, Dillon on 4 May 1888 retorted, 'that document is not binding on the conscience of any Irishman at all' (C. C. O'Brien, 221). From this period he faced a stream of criticism from some ecclesiastics, and notably engaged in a long-running dispute with the bishop of Limerick. Confined to Dundalk prison on 20 June, Dillon was released on 15 September because of weakening health. The Plan of Campaign was chronically bereft of funds and Parnell was not prepared to lend more than token aid. On 6 March 1889 Dillon sailed for Australia to solicit contributions; he also toured New Zealand, and returned to Ireland via the United States in late April 1890. His mission raised about £33,000, but the financial woes of the plan persisted and the movement was nearly bankrupt by mid-1890. Dillon was arrested again on 18 September 1890, but received bail, and he and O'Brien disappeared on 9 October and travelled to America. He was thus abroad and unable to re-enter the United Kingdom during the crucial stages of the Parnell divorce crisis. After initial hesitation he declared against Parnell's continued leadership. He reached France on 18 January 1891 to join O'Brien in the 'Boulogne negotiations' with Parnell over the leadership of the party. When these broke down, Dillon and O'Brien travelled on 12 February to Folkestone, where they were immediately arrested. They were detained in Galway gaol until 30 July, in what proved to be his final spell in prison. While interned, Dillon and O'Brien became increasingly disgusted with the tenor of Irish politics, especially by T. M. Healy's venomous attacks on Parnell. On their release they sided with the anti-Parnellites.

Parliamentary manoeuvrings, 1891–1914 Parnell's death marked the emergence of the second phase of Dillon's career. Although he never lost sight of the land question, especially the fate of evicted tenants, he increasingly focused on the management of the anti-Parnellites and the home rule question, though his active participation was limited by illness during later 1891 and early 1892. On his recovery he took the lead in resisting Healy's influence. As deputy to the aged Justin McCarthy, Dillon was effectively the anti-Parnellite chairman, and consolidated his pre-eminence by 1894. He worked to reconstruct Parnell's authority, with its emphases on united control, strong leadership, vigorous discipline, the reassertion of the party in the national movement, and on placing the constituencies in a subordinate position to the parliamentarians. When the Liberals reclaimed office in August 1892 Dillon was one of the Irish leaders routinely consulted about policy. He urged John Morley, the chief secretary, to treat the case of the evicted tenants and was party to the negotiations over the Government of Ireland Bill in 1893. Gladstone's retirement created a political vacuum in the Liberal alliance, presenting problems for Dillon's direction of the national agenda. Following the general election of 1895 the Conservatives returned to office, which limited nationalist influence, but the outcome of the election also provided Dillon with the ammunition to expel Healy from positions of influence in the movement. His personal circumstances changed when he married Elizabeth Mathew on 21 November at the Brompton Oratory. They had six children, five sons (born in 1896, 1898, 1900, 1902, and 1905) and a daughter (born in 1897). Their fourth son was James Mathew *Dillon (1902–1986).

On McCarthy's resignation, Dillon was elected chairman of the anti-Parnellites by thirty-eight votes to twenty-one on 18 February 1896. He immediately abolished the troublesome party committee but never enjoyed uncontested allegiance; the Healy faction and the *Irish Catholic* constantly snapped at his heels. At this point there were in reality three Irish national parties, though Dillon led much the largest. Dillon announced at the Irish Race Convention in September that he was ready to stand aside if this would abet reunion. However, he was less accommodating towards Sir Horace Plunkett's attempts to bring Unionists and nationalists together. Although he attended the All-Ireland Committee conference in 1896, Dillon never shed mistrust of dialogue with Irish Unionists, and displayed an animus against Plunkett, the co-operative movement, and Unionist reformism generally. Similarly, though he supported the Irish Local Government Bill (1898) sponsored by the tory government, he was uneasy about plums proffered from that quarter. In 1898 O'Brien initiated the United Irish League on an agrarian platform. Dillon was ambivalent about this new association, believing that it could lead to confrontation with the government and endanger the alliance with the Liberals. This time marked the first significant strains in the O'Brien–Dillon relationship. In February 1899 Dillon resigned the party chairmanship in order to facilitate party reunion.

Freed from the constraints of leadership, Dillon felt able to take a more forthright political stance. He was a key critic of the Second South African War. Although faithfully supporting John Redmond after his selection for the chairmanship of the unified Irish party in February 1900, Dillon during late 1901 and early 1902 made a series of speeches on the land question. He went on a fund-raising tour of America in 1902 but became ill and was sidelined from politics from October until April 1903. During the interlude the land conference in December 1902 agreed a formula for tenant land purchase which became the backbone of the Wyndham Act (1903), the single largest measure of its type. Whereas O'Brien was a keen promoter of the accord and thereafter became the chief nationalist proponent of 'conference plus business', as the way to unite all classes and creeds for Ireland, Dillon's instinctive dislike of negotiations with landlords soon surfaced. While some of his objections to the act were well founded, at Swinford on 23 August he attacked the legislation and

also the 'doctrine of conciliation' (Bew, *Conflict and Conciliation*, 102–3), believing that the right approach was to put unrelenting pressure on the landlords and government. An ensuing breach with O'Brien was never healed; O'Brien's later published accounts severely tarnished Dillon's reputation. Dillon successfully urged Redmond to resist the conference approach to deal with the vexed question of universities in Ireland. Similarly, the devolution proposals promoted by the under-secretary, MacDonnell, were seen by Dillon as insidious. For much of 1904 he was once more afflicted by illness, and only resumed regular attendance in the House of Commons the next year.

When the Liberals returned to office in January 1906 Dillon again was regularly consulted. In 1906 he laboured assiduously to defend Catholic interests in the abortive Education Bill (for England and Wales) and was deeply involved in negotiations over the local government proposal of the chief secretary, James Bryce, which, however, he always disliked. A much modified scheme incorporating Dillon's major objections was proposed by Bryce's successor, Augustine Birrell, the next year. The nationalist response was uncertain; a national conference was called; this rejected the measure and it was withdrawn by the government. Dillon's part in the conference was curtailed abruptly when his wife died on 14 May; effectively he was inactive for some months afterwards. Subsequently, he spent most of his time in Dublin and raised a young family. The passage of the Evicted Tenants Act (1907), the Irish University Act (1908), and the Irish Land Act (1909) were more satisfying outcomes for Dillon. During the budget crisis of 1909 he spoke frequently in Ireland, incurring unpopularity for his stance on a measure which would increase the Irish tax burden.

Between 1910 and 1914 the home rule question re-emerged. Dillon twice suffered debilitating injuries during this period. From 4 June until October 1911 he was incapacitated and then in October 1912 he was thrown from a pony trap, which caused him to be inactive. During 1913 he was mostly in Ireland, casting an unsympathetic eye on the 'malignant enemy', James Larkin, during the Dublin 'lock-out' (Carroll, 208). Dillon was at the hub of negotiations over home rule in 1914, and was present at the abortive Buckingham Palace conference (21–24 June). Opposed to 'partition', he was prepared to support local autonomy for northern protestant areas so long as the formal unity of the country was not compromised. During 1914 Dillon was frustrated by the government's handling of the 'Curragh mutiny' (20–25 March) and the fatal consequences of the use of troops at Bachelors Walk on 26 July.

The First World War: reputation With the opening of the First World War, Dillon entered a final phase of his public career. At the outbreak of war in August 1914, Dillon accepted Redmond's support of the British decision to enter the conflict, though he never shared his leader's enthusiasm and he abstained from the military recruiting campaign. Between the Easter rising, April 1916, and the general election of 1918 Dillon's political statesmanship was severely tested. When the rebellion broke out he was in Dublin and able to estimate its effect. On 11 May he made an impassioned speech in the House of Commons against further executions. Thereafter Dillon, a natural pessimist, was plunged into constant gloom about the situation. He was immersed in David Lloyd George's abortive attempt to resolve the home rule question (May–July 1916) and offered important criticisms of the government's actions in Ireland during the autumn. His reservations about the war accelerated, and he was 'deeply concerned … from the point of view especially of the protection of the smaller nationalities, and now of Rumania' (*Political Diaries of C. P. Scott*, 239). In 1917 he declined nomination to the Irish Convention. On 12 March 1918 Dillon was elected party chairman in succession to the recently deceased Redmond. He joined forces with Sinn Féin and the Catholic bishops in resisting the government's plan to introduce conscription to Ireland which, in the event, was never imposed. He made a further vain effort to persuade the government to introduce Irish self-government, introducing a motion for self-determination on 29 July 1918. After the failure to reach an electoral pact with Sinn Féin, the Irish party was overwhelmed by it in the December general election; Dillon himself was defeated in East Mayo by Eamon de Valera by 8975 votes to 4514.

Afterwards Dillon played little active part in Irish affairs, though he corresponded with old colleagues about public events. Between 1919 and 1922 he came to a rapprochement with his old antagonist Plunkett. Had Dillon left politics in 1882 or 1892, he would have been remembered as one of the foremost figures of the land struggle. As it is, his reputation was scarred by the long years of parliamentary manoeuvres after Parnell's fall and the failure to achieve home rule. Furthermore, his Young Ireland brand of nationalism seemed outmoded in the years after 1916, while his conservative views on labour and women did not endear him to a rising generation. His standing was also harmed in unflattering memoirs by several old colleagues. Following surgery, he died in a nursing home at Portland Place, London, on 4 August 1927, and was buried four days later in Glasnevin cemetery, Dublin.

ALAN O'DAY

Sources F. S. L. Lyons, *John Dillon* (1968) · T. W. Moody, *Davitt and Irish revolution* (1982) · *Florence Arnold-Forster's Irish journal*, ed. T. W. Moody and others (1988) · P. Bew, *Conflict and conciliation in Ireland, 1880–1910* (1987) · P. Bew, *Ideology and the Irish question* (1994) · F. M. Carroll, *American opinion and the Irish question* (1978) · M. Davitt, *The fall of feudalism in Ireland* (1904) · *The political diaries of C. P. Scott, 1911–1928*, ed. T. Wilson (1970) · C. C. O'Brien, *Parnell and his party, 1880–90* (1957) · H. W. Lucy, *Peeps at parliament* (1903) · M. O'Callaghan, *British high politics and a nationalist Ireland* (1994) · S. Warwick-Haller, *William O'Brien and the Irish land war* (1990) · F. Callanan, *The Parnell split* (1992) · F. Callanan, *T. M. Healy* (1996) · L. M. Geary, *The plan of campaign, 1886–1891* (1986) · P. Bull, *Land, politics and nationalism* (1996) · E. Larkin, *The Roman Catholic church and the Plan of Campaign in Ireland, 1886–1888* (1978) · J. Loughlin, *Gladstone, home rule and the Ulster question, 1882–1893* (1986); repr. (1987) · W. S. Blunt, *My diaries: being a personal narrative of events, 1888–1914*, 2 vols. (1919–20); repr. (New York, 1932) · J. McCarthy and Mrs Campbell Praed, *Our book of memories* (1912) · T. M. Healy, *Letters and leaders of my day* (1928) · W. O'Brien, *Recollections* (1905) · W. O'Brien, *Evening memories* (1920) · W. O'Brien, *An olive branch in Ireland* (1910) · F. H. O'Donnell, *A history of the Irish parliamentary party*, 2 vols. (1910) · T. P. O'Connor, *Memoirs of an old parliamentarian*, 2 vols. (1929) · M. A. Banks, *Edward Blake, Irish nationalist* (1957) · T. West, *Horace Plunkett: co-operation and politics* (1986) · D. Gwynn, *John Redmond* (1932) · D. Thornley, *Isaac Butt and home rule* (1964) · M. Tierney, *Croke of Cashel: the life of Archbishop Thomas William Croke, 1823–1902* (1976) · J. Hutchinson, *The dynamics of cultural nationalism* (1987) · *Irish Times* (8 Aug 1927) · *The Times* (5 Aug 1927) · CGPLA *Éire* (1927) · TCD, John Dillon MSS · TCD, Michael Davitt MSS · NL Ire., John Redmond MSS · NL Ire., T. C. Harrington MSS · NL Ire., Justin McCarthy MSS · NL Ire., J. F. X. O'Brien MSS · NL Ire., William O'Brien MSS · University College, Cork, William O'Brien MSS

Archives TCD, corresp. and papers · TCD, diary · University of Kansas, Kenneth Spencer Research Library, notes on Irish politics | Bodl. Oxf., corresp. with Herbert Asquith · CAC Cam., letters to W. T. Stead · HLRO, letters to David Lloyd George · HLRO, letters to Herbert Samuel · NL Ire., letters to John Hagan · NL Ire., T. C. Harrington MSS · NL Ire., letters to John Horgan · NL Ire., Justin McCarthy MSS · NL Ire., letters to J. F. X. O'Brien · NL Ire., letters to William O'Brien · NL Ire., letters to John Redmond · TCD, letters to Shane Leslie · TCD, corresp. relating to Francis Sheehy-Skeffington and Hannah Sheehy-Skeffington · TCD, letters to William Starkie, memorandum · University College, Dublin, letters to D. J. O'Donoghue · University College, Dublin, letters to John Greene · University College, Cork, William O'Brien MSS

Likenesses S. P. Hall, group portrait, pencil, 1885/6, NG Ire. · H. Holiday, pencil drawing, 1887, NG Ire. · H. Holiday, pencil drawing, 1888, NG Ire. · S. P. Hall, pencil, 1889 (with M. Davitt), NG Ire. · S. P. Hall, pencil drawings, 1889–96, NG Ire. · B. Stone, photograph, 1898, NPG [*see illus.*] · Ape [C. Pellegrini], caricature, chromolithograph, NPG; repro. in *VF* (7 May 1887) · H. Furniss, double portrait, caricature, chromolithograph (with Parnell), NPG; repro. in *VF* (7 Dec 1881) · F. C. Gould, two sketches, NPG · S. P. Hall, double portrait, pencil (John Dillon; with Justin McCarthy), NG Ire. · S. P. Hall, group portraits, pencil, NG Ire. · S. P. Hall, pencil and wash on card, NG Ire. · S. P. Hall, two double portraits, pencil (with C. S. Parnell), NG Ire.

Wealth at death £780 0s. 7d.: probate, 13 Feb 1928, CGPLA Eng. & Wales · £17,439 16s. 7d.: probate, 16 Nov 1927, CGPLA Éire

Dillon, John Blake (1814–1866), Irish nationalist and journalist, was born on 5 May 1814 in Ballaghaderreen, on the borders of Mayo and Roscommon, the fourth of seven children of Luke Dillon (d. 1825), farmer and shopkeeper, and his wife, Anne Blake, of Dunmacrina, co. Mayo. Dillon was educated at St Patrick's College, Maynooth (1830–32), and Trinity College, Dublin (1834–41). A prizewinner in political economy, he gained a BA in logic and ethics, and was called to the Irish bar. At Trinity College he made the most important friendship of his political career, with Thomas Davis, whom he succeeded as president of the Historical Society, the student debating forum. In 1842, Dillon, Davis, and Charles Gavan Duffy launched *Nation*, one of the most notable journalistic ventures in Irish history. Initially, the *Nation*, or Young Ireland, group supported O'Connell's repeal agitation, but as its hopes were not realized, they turned increasingly towards the romantic nationalism then sweeping through Europe.

Dillon married Adelaide Hart (1828–1872), the daughter of a Dublin solicitor, in October 1847. In an unpublished memoir she described him as tall, 'dark as a Spaniard in complexion, with regular noble features and great melancholy eyes'. He associated 'nearly all the sweet memories' of his life with Druid Lodge, her home in Killiney, co. Dublin (Dillon MSS, TCD: 26 June 1849); it became their home after 1856. It was a happy marriage but troubled by ill

John Blake Dillon
(1814–1866), by
Henry MacManus

Sources B. Ó Cathaoir, *John Blake Dillon: Young Irelander* (1990) • *The Nation* (22 Sept 1866) • *Freeman's Journal* [Dublin] (17 Sept 1866) • *The Times* (18 Sept 1866) • *The Times* (20 Sept 1866) • C. G. Duffy, *Young Ireland: a fragment of Irish history, 1840–1845*, rev. edn, 2 vols. (1896) • C. G. Duffy, *Four years of Irish history, 1845–1849: a sequel to 'Young Ireland'* (1883) • A. M. Sullivan, *New Ireland* (1877) • K. B. Nowlan, *The politics of repeal: a study in the relations between Great Britain and Ireland, 1841–50* (1965) • F. S. L. Lyons, *John Dillon: a biography* (1968) • R. V. Comerford, 'Representation at Westminster, 1801–1918', *Tipperary: history and society* (1986) • TCD, Dillon MSS • A. Dillon, memoir, TCD

Archives TCD, corresp. and papers | Dublin Diocesan Archives, Paul Cullen MSS • NL Ire., Thomas Davis MSS • NL Ire., Charles Gavan Duffy MSS • NL Ire., William Smith O'Brien MSS • Royal Irish Acad., Charles Gavan Duffy MSS

Likenesses M. Brady, daguerreotype, *c.*1850, priv. coll. • H. MacManus, oils on panel, NG Ire. [*see illus.*]

health, especially Adelaide's. They had eight children: five boys and three girls.

The Paris revolution of February 1848 raised unrealistic expectations in famine-stricken Ireland. With the suspension of habeas corpus on 22 July, Dillon and Thomas Francis Meagher persuaded William Smith O'Brien to lead an insurrection, which ended in failure one week later in co. Tipperary. In spite of a £300 reward for his capture, Dillon escaped with the assistance of clerical friends to the United States. During his exile in New York he prospered as a lawyer. In the era of reaction which succeeded the year of revolutions in Europe, he went through a period of disillusionment with Irish politics and the Roman Catholic church. His perspective changed, however, after his wife induced him to return to Ireland in 1856, following an amnesty offered in the previous year.

Dillon was a liberal Catholic (among his papers in Trinity College is his translation of part of *Words of a Believer*, by Félicité Lamennais). But in the last phase of his political career he formed the anti-Fenian National Association with the ultramontane archbishop of Dublin, Paul Cullen. The best explanation for this paradox is perhaps that they were both deeply religious men and, essentially, constitutional nationalists.

Dillon was elected MP for Tipperary in July 1865. He died suddenly of cholera in Killiney on 15 September 1866, and was buried in Glasnevin cemetery, Dublin. According to Gavan Duffy, John Blake Dillon's 'generous nature made him more a philanthropist than a politician' (Duffy, *Young Ireland*, 1.38). During his brief parliamentary career, none the less, he made a decisive contribution to the Irish–Liberal understanding which ushered in the great era of Gladstonian reform. Together with his wife, Adelaide, he founded a political dynasty: their son John *Dillon was a leading figure at Westminster for nearly forty years, and a grandson, James Mathew Dillon (1902–1986), was a tribune of democracy in independent Ireland.

BRENDAN Ó CATHAOIR

Dillon, John Talbot (1734–1806), traveller and historian, was the elder son of Francis Dillon (*d.* 1767), whose father was William Dillon of Proudstown, Ireland, and Mary, daughter of Sir Mervyn Wingfield, sixth and last baronet, of Letheringham in Suffolk (the Wingfield baronetcy, granted by Charles I, could not pass through the female line). He was educated at Westminster School from about 1742 to 1747. In the latter year, at the age of thirteen, he joined the Royal Navy under the protection of Captain Dennis of the 28-gun frigate the *Mermaid*. He is not to be confused with Sir John Talbot Dillon [*see below*] of Lismullen, co. Meath, Ireland. The confusion, perpetuated by the *Dictionary of National Biography*, arose not only from the two men having the same names and their each having a son named William, but also from the curious coincidence of their both being barons of the Holy Roman empire. The two men knew each other and their branches of the Dillon family were certainly related, but distantly. Clarification of their separate identities came in 1953–6 when the Navy Records Society published *A Narrative of my Professional Adventures* (1790–1839) (2 vols.) by Sir William Henry Dillon, illegitimate son of John Talbot Dillon: the introduction and notes by M. A. Lewis provide essential information.

Only two years after entering the navy Dillon seems to have peremptorily engineered his own discharge following a perceived insult in Portsmouth when he was evicted from the Parade Coffee House, an establishment reserved for naval captains. Thereafter, he seems to have spent much of his life abroad, particularly in Spain where he travelled extensively and learned the language and literature. His son's *Narrative* records that Dillon married first into a noble family from Namur, that his first wife died in childbirth, and that he had a network of friends and relatives in France. Sir William Henry *Dillon (1780–1857) was born to Dillon and Elizabeth, daughter of Henry Collins, but the couple do not seem to have married.

Dillon was clearly proud to be a baron of the Holy Roman empire—a title conferred on his father, Francis, and passed down on his death in 1767—since it is emblazoned on the title-page of his first publication, *Travels through Spain, with a view to illustrate the natural history and physical geography of that kingdom, in a series of letters* (1780). The preface makes clear that the *Travels* are the fruit of three separate visits to Spain. Much of the text is lifted (and acknowledged as such) from the *Introduction to the Natural History and Physical Geography of Spain* by William Bowles, published in Spanish at Madrid in 1775. Dillon weaves his own commentary and itinerary into Bowles's account and he also incorporates some of the observations of Don Antonio Ponz, secretary of the Royal Academy of San Fernando. The resulting work offered one of the most complete pictures of Spain then available to the British reading public and it was favourably reviewed, although its focus on natural history and antiquity made it old-fashioned at a time when travelogues were increasingly concerned with politics and cultural anthropology. In 1781 Dillon published *Letters from an English traveller in Spain, in 1778, on the origin and progress of poetry in that kingdom.* This text integrates personal anecdote with a comprehensive literary history that can be related to other mid-eighteenth-century explorations of the origins of national poetry (by, for example, Thomas Percy and Thomas Warton).

Dillon was soon regarded as an authority on the Spanish language. In 1781 John Bowles published an edition of *Don Quixote* in which he acknowledged Dillon's expertise. In 1786 Joseph Baretti published *Tolondron*, a ferocious attack on the inaccuracies of Bowles's edition; he related a meeting in a Holborn tavern with Dillon and Bowles in which Bowles had boasted that 'he could not utter a syllable of Spanish, nor understand a word of it, when spoken' (p. 6), Baretti wonders why Bowles had not consulted 'Baron Dillon' for advice on his edition, since 'he speaks Spanish fluently' (ibid., 231). In the summer of 1781 Dillon corresponded briefly with Thomas Percy (the letters are reprinted in Nichols's *Illustrations*), who had read Dillon's account of Spanish poetry. Clearly emboldened by Percy's interest, Dillon wrote to ask for his help in requesting permission from the duke of Northumberland to be the dedicatee for his forthcoming history of the Holy Roman empire. Despite Percy's efforts this request was not granted. Dillon seems at this time to have been living on the proceeds of his literary labours: he writes to Percy that 'Though in my commercial occupations I have very limited prospects, very much so at present, I endeavour to occupy my mind and time with literary pursuits' (Nichols, *Illustrations*, 8.194). His literary output in the following years was substantial, if miscellaneous, and seems to reflect both his need to generate income and his genuine interest in European culture, liberty, and toleration. In 1782 he published *Sketches on the Art of Painting*, a translation from the Spanish of Anthony Raphael Mengs, painter to the Spanish king, and in 1783 *A Political Survey of the Roman Empire*. In 1788 appeared *The History of the Reign of Peter the Cruel, King of Castile and Leon*, in which Dillon attempted to acquit that ruler from charges of tyranny, somewhat to the scepticism of contemporary reviewers. A similar, though more romanticized work appeared in 1800, *Alphonso and Eleonora, or, The Triumphs of Valour and Virtue*, in which Dillon attempted to redeem the reputation of Alfonso VIII of Castile: the book's novelistic title seems

calculated to attract a wide readership. In 1790 Dillon published a rather rushed compilation entitled *Historical and Critical Memoirs of the General Revolution in France in the Year 1789*, which is condemned for its opportunism, but praised for its editor's 'rational attachment to the cause of liberty' (*Monthly Review*, new ser., 10, Jan 1793, 84–7). Perhaps surprisingly, Dillon speaks out against extending the right of liberty to slaves in the West-Indian plantations, maintaining that freedom would not improve their condition. Overall Dillon's works project a mixture of enlightened cosmopolitanism and aristocratic paternalism.

In later years Dillon resided in different parts of London with Mary Barbara, whom he had married in 1797 when he was sixty-three. Dillon's son describes her as his father's 'third wife', though she was probably only his second if, as seems likely, he never married his son's mother. Dillon was engaged in a protracted lawsuit over a property in Suffolk, which he eventually lost, and he seems to have had some connection with Manchester since he left to the Manchester Literary and Philosophical Society some of his works on agriculture. He encouraged his son's active and successful naval career, and was acquainted with such diverse persons as Lord George Gordon, William Wilberforce, and the travel writer and agriculturist Arthur Young (Dillon was under-secretary to the board of agriculture when Young was secretary). His son describes his visits to Dillon's London residences as 'one continued round of dinners and entertainments' (W. H. Dillon, 1.157).

Dillon died at Brompton on 19 March 1806. In his will, he bequeathed to his 'beloved wife' the:

> two Imperial Diplomas of Nobility granted by the most serene Emperors of Germany, Francis I and Joseph II to my Father and family … for her to keep and preserve in memory of her affection for me and to be disposed of by her according to her own discretion. (M. A. Lewis, 'Introduction' to W. H. Dillon, *Narrative*, 1.x)

This suggests that he had no legitimate issue. Although the *Gentleman's Magazine* obituary notice refers to him as 'Bart' and his son's *Narrative* as 'Sir', he seems to have had no legitimate title save that of baron of the Holy Roman empire.

Dillon's namesake, **Sir John Talbot Dillon**, first baronet (1740?–1805), of Lismullen, co. Meath, Ireland, was the son of Arthur Dillon (whose own father was Sir John Dillon of Lismullen, MP for County Meath) and his wife, Elizabeth, daughter of Dr Ralph Lambert, bishop of Meath. In 1767 he married Millicent (d. 1788), daughter of George Drake of Fernhill, Berkshire, and they had six sons and three daughters. Dillon sat in the Irish parliament representing co. Wicklow from 1771 and then Blessington, 1776–83. He seems to have resided for some time at Vienna, and in 1782 Emperor Joseph II created Dillon and his heirs free barons of the Holy Roman empire in recognition of his 'exertions in Parliament to serve his country, by granting liberty to Roman Catholics to realize property in their native land' (*GM*, 75, 1805, 878). He was a member of the Royal Irish Academy and was created a baronet on 31 July 1801. He died in Dublin in August 1805, 'much lamented by his acquaintance and numerous tenantry' (ibid.). He was succeeded as baronet by his eldest son, Sir Charles Drake Dillon (1770–1840).

KATHERINE TURNER

Sources GM, 1st ser., 76 (1806), 294 • W. H. Dillon, *A narrative of my professional adventures (1790–1839)*, ed. M. A. Lewis, 2 vols., Navy RS, 93, 97 (1953–6) • Nichols, *Illustrations*, 8.193–5 • J. Baretti, *Tolondron: speeches to John Bowles about his edition of Don Quixote; together with some account of Spanish literature* (1786) • J. T. Dillon, *Travels through Spain, with a view to illustrate the natural history and physical geography of that kingdom, in a series of letters* (1780) • J. T. Dillon, *Letters from an English traveller in Spain, in 1778, on the origin and progress of poetry in that kingdom* (1781) • W. Betham, *The baronetage of England*, 3 (1803), 55 • *List of the members of the board of agriculture* (1796), 27 • 'review', *Analytical Review*, 7 (1790), appx, 502–5 • review of *Travels*, *Monthly Review*, 64 (1781), 45–9 • review, *Monthly Review*, new ser., 1 (1790), 185–93 • review, *Monthly Review*, new ser., 10 (1793), 84–7 • review, *Critical Review*, 50 (1780), 42–7 • review, *Critical Review*, 50 (1780), 110–19
Archives Birm. CA, letters to Matthew Boulton
Likenesses W. Bond, stipple, 1798 (John Talbot Dillon), NPG
Wealth at death see will, 26 March 1806, Principal Registry of the Family Division, London

Dillon, Sir John Talbot, first baronet (1740?–1805). *See under* Dillon, John Talbot (1734–1806).

Dillon, Sir Lucas (d. 1592), judge, was the eldest son and heir of Sir Robert *Dillon (d. 1579?), of Newtown Trim, co. Meath, chief justice of common pleas, and his wife, Elizabeth, daughter of Edward Barnewall of Crickstown. He was probably born after 1530 and entered the Middle Temple in 1551. On his return to Ireland he resided at Moymet Castle, which he built 3 miles north-west of Trim. His first wife was Jane, daughter of James Bathe, chief baron of the exchequer from 1535 to 1570.

Dillon took office as the queen's principal solicitor in 1565 and in 1566 became, like his father, attorney-general. In 1566 he was a commissioner to hear civil causes in Kilkenny, and he commended the lord deputy, Sir Henry Sidney, to Sir William Cecil in 1568 for expanding the judicial presence in Ireland beyond the pale, citing the 'marvellous' resort of litigants to the council (PRO, SP 63/26/68). He was sent to London in 1569 with bills for the parliament, and the following year he explained to the queen the need for a university in Dublin. Dillon returned to Ireland as the new chief baron of the exchequer in 1570 on the nomination of Sidney, succeeding his father-in-law. He was a constitutional moderate and maintained a long correspondence with Cecil, noting in 1570 'that it stode better with good polecy to procede by degrees (as wherein stode safetie) then to take in hande so moche as we should not be hable to welde' (PRO, SP 63/30/130).

Dillon was the most loyal of the Old English privy councillors and Sidney knighted him in 1575 at Drogheda, calling him 'meus fidelis Lucas' (Ball, 212). Sir Lucas was a commissioner of the court of wards and his merit as a councillor was acknowledged in 1572 by Fitzwilliam, who recommended him to replace his father on the junior bench. Sidney sought the chief justiceship for him, whereas the lord chancellor, Gerard, proclaimed his honesty, 'though he dealeth and conveyeth conninglye' (LPL, Carew MS 628, fol. 312), and employed him in the hotly contested cess controversy in 1577 to examine legal precedents for purveyance. Dillon argued before the privy council in 1578 that the cess was traditionally authorized by the grand council and thus required the sanction of the leading palesmen. Yet he was lauded in 1577 by Sir Nicholas Malby for his support of the cess on a badly divided council, and by Sir Edward Waterhouse for his service to the crown and his willingness to afford 'a good table in town and campe' (PRO, SP 63/72/147). He attended Sidney on numerous expeditions to apprehend and punish Irish rebels, such as those who aided Rory Oge O'More in 1578.

Dillon joined Lord Justice Pelham in Philipstown in 1579 at the outset of the Desmond rebellion of 1579–83, and in 1580 journeyed with him to Munster. In May 1581 he was proposed as a candidate for the vacant lord chancellorship, but his rival for the post, Archbishop Adam Loftus, denounced him as corrupt in 1582 and won the post for himself. Dillon was nominated chief justice of queen's bench in 1583, but his reputation was compromised by an Irish exile who informed that he kept a Catholic priest named Charles, and was 'catholick at hart' (PRO, SP 63/88/60). During the multiple crises of the Desmond rebellion the new chief justice of common pleas, Nicholas Nugent, was accused of supporting his cousin's insurrection in the pale, conspiring to take Dublin Castle, and planning to ambush Dillon on his way to hold sessions at Mullingar. At a special tribunal on 4 April 1582, convened out of term and held at Trim, Dillon and other councillors, including his cousin Sir Robert *Dillon (c.1540–1597) of Riverston, sat as judges when the chief justice was tried for treason before a Meath jury. Nugent protested both the exceptional venue and the intervention of his adversaries, complaining that only one, tainted, witness gave testimony. Dillon was accused of bullying the jurors into reversing their verdict, and Nugent was hanged at Trim two days later.

After the departure of Lord Deputy Grey in 1582 Dillon helped to arrange the trial by battle in the yard of Dublin Castle between two O'Connor chieftains in 1583, a cynical attempt to kill off the leaders of a prominent Gaelic family. The appointment of Sir John Perrot as lord deputy on 4 January 1584 signalled a return to reform, and Dillon became one of Perrot's leading supporters on the faction-ridden Irish council. He joined Perrot on progresses to Ulster and Munster, and was sent to England for the required sanctioning of an Irish parliament, returning at the head of 400 troops on 6 March 1585 and bringing the parliamentary robes for the viceroy. Dillon and Nicholas White, master of the rolls, attempted to steer Perrot's ambitious reform of the cess through parliament, but the queen rebuked her intemperate chief governor for toleration of recusancy and she encouraged Loftus and his allies to exclude Old English councillors from most confidential business after 1586. Although named a commissioner for the plantation of Munster on 26 April 1587, Dillon was later implicated in the charges of coddling recusants brought against Perrot by the new lord deputy, Sir William Fitzwilliam, in 1590. In 1592 Sir Lucas and Sir

Robert Dillon were accused of instigating Sir Brian O'Rourke's rebellion in Connaught, charges probably inspired by the Nugents. The crucial involvement of moderate voices in Irish government was effectively silenced on the departure of Perrot, and after Dillon's death, which took place in Dublin in 1592, he was replaced by Sir Robert Napier of Dorset, completing the practical exclusion of the Old English.

As a loyal privy councillor and a key member of its inner circle, Dillon enjoyed the patronage of several chief governors. He became steward of the royal manors near Dublin in 1574. After the death of his first wife, Jane, he married Marion (*née* Sharl), widow of Sir Christopher Barnewall of Turvey, in 1575. He succeeded his father as steward of Kilkenny West in 1578, and in 1580 inherited the profitable estates at Newtown, joining them with the dissolved priory of St Mary in Trim. He resided in St Nicholas Street when in Dublin, and he was buried in 1592 in the parish church at Newtown Trim, where his fine Renaissance altar tomb, with effigies of Lucas and Jane, may still be seen. In 1589 Dillon had also erected a marble monument at Lusk in honour of his second wife's first husband. He and his first wife had seven sons and five daughters, including their eldest son, James (*d.* 1642), who was granted livery of his father's lands on 8 April 1594. James was created Baron Dillon on 24 January 1620 and earl of Roscommon on 5 April 1622. Another son, John, married the daughter of Sir William Sarsfield of Lucan, co. Dublin.

JON G. CRAWFORD

Sources F. E. Ball, *The judges in Ireland, 1221–1921*, 2 (1926) · J. G. Crawford, *Anglicizing the government of Ireland: the Irish privy council and the expansion of Tudor rule, 1556–1578* (1993) · C. Brady, *The chief governors: the rise and fall of reform government in Tudor Ireland, 1536–1588* (1994) · C. Brady, 'Court, castle and country: the framework of government in Tudor Ireland', *Natives and newcomers: essays on the making of Irish colonial society, 1534–1641*, ed. C. Brady and R. Gillespie (1986), 22–49, 217–19 · J. L. J. Hughes, ed., *Patentee officers in Ireland, 1173–1826, including high sheriffs, 1661–1684 and 1761–1816*, IMC (1960) · PRO, SP 63/25/115; 63/50/4; 63/59/59; 63/67/24–25; 63/72/147; 63/26/68 · Lord Chancellor Gerard's report, 1576, LPL, Carew MS 628, fol. 312 · council book of the Irish privy council, 1556–71, Royal Irish Acad., MS 24 F. 17 · A. Vicars, ed., *Index to the prerogative wills of Ireland, 1536–1810* (1897), 134, 487 · C. Kenny, 'The exclusion of Catholics from the legal profession in Ireland, 1537–1829', *Irish Historical Studies*, 25 (1986–7), 337–57 · N. P. Canny, *The Elizabethan conquest of Ireland: a pattern established, 1565–76* (1976) · S. G. Ellis, *Tudor Ireland: crown, community, and the conflict of cultures, 1470–1603* (1985) · tombstone, Ireland, co. Meath, Newtown Trim parish church

Likenesses stone monument on altar tomb, parish church, Newtown Trim, co. Meath, Ireland

Dillon, (Laurence) Michael (1915–1962), transsexual and Buddhist monk, was born Laura Maud Dillon on 1 May 1915 at 20 Ladbroke Gardens, London, the only daughter and second child of Robert Arthur Dillon (1865–1925) and his Australian wife, Laura Maud McCliver, *née* Reese (*d.* 1915), who died just after giving birth to Laura. Robert Dillon, heir to the baronetcy of Lismullen, was a lieutenant in the Royal Navy, but a drinking problem did not allow him to continue his career. Devastated by the death

of his wife, and resenting his daughter, Laura's father dispatched his children to his sisters in Folkestone, and saw them only once a year. Laura had a stifling existence with her strict and parsimonious aunts, leading 'a dog's life' (Hodgkinson, 22). Often in ill health, she was educated at home and then at Brampton Down school, before triumphantly proceeding to St Anne's College, Oxford, in 1934 where she graduated with a third in Greats in 1938. A rowing blue, and president of the Oxford University Women's Boat Club, she had some success in furthering the acceptance of women's rowing as a recognized university sport.

It was at Oxford that Laura Dillon, who had always inclined towards male pursuits and cultivated a boyish appearance—she was attractive and serious-looking, with short hair—felt for the first time that she was 'in the wrong body … People thought I was a woman. But I wasn't. I was just me' (Hodgkinson, 37). On graduation she secured a post dissecting brains in a laboratory near Bristol. This work fuelled her interest in the relationship between mind and body (which she thought was closer and more complex than had been supposed).

In 1939 Dillon joined the WAAF territorials, becoming a dispatch rider, but was told that she was unsuited to the women's corps. She returned to the laboratory, and began making tentative enquiries about her condition, persuading a doctor to prescribe testosterone, which deepened her voice, halted menstruation, and triggered the growth of facial hair. When the signs became obvious she resigned from the laboratory and joined the First Aid Nursing Yeomanry, but eager to take on 'real' war work she left after a month. Unable to fit in anywhere, she became a petrol pump attendant in a garage near Bristol and stayed there for 'four miserable years' (Hodgkinson, 56).

During this time Laura Dillon consolidated her identity as a man, and started calling herself Michael. Hospitalized for hypoglaecemia, she confided her secret to a house surgeon, who performed a double mastectomy on her in 1942. She officially became Laurence Michael Dillon in 1944 when she had her birth certificate amended. This meant that 'he' was now heir presumptive to the baronetcy. Dillon was one of the few transsexuals able legally to change his identity at this time. In 1969 the marriage of the transsexual April Ashley was declared null, and thenceforth change of sex could not be legally recognized. In December 2002 the Labour government proposed that transsexuals in Britain (one of the few European countries not to uphold the rights of transsexuals) would be able once again to change their birth certificates (and therefore legally marry).

In 1946 Michael Dillon published *Self: a Study in Ethics and Endocrinology*, the first book about sex change. It was part scientific and part philosophical, arguing for greater tolerance for those who experienced sexual anomalies (the term 'transsexual' had not yet been coined). It preempted later research into the biological root of transsexualism and the idea that the body must be reconstructed in accord with the mind.

Having attended Merchant Venturers' technical college, Bristol, Dillon entered medical school at Trinity College, Dublin, in 1945. He lived entirely in the male role and grew a beard. Vacations were spent undergoing ground-breaking operations for the construction of a penis at Rooksdown House, near Basingstoke, performed by Sir Harold Gillies, who had pioneered advances in plastic surgery during the Second World War. Michael Dillon became the first person to change sex from female to male. He wanted people to accept him in his new identity, and tried to keep his transformation a secret. His medical treatment complete by 1949, the following year he fell in love with Roberta (born Robert) Cowell, a well-known racing driver who was undergoing sex reassignment; she had read *Self*, and wished to meet the author. Dillon wanted to marry her, and he considered himself engaged, but Cowell did not return his feelings.

Dillon qualified as a doctor in 1951 and worked as a medical officer in a Dublin hospital. He gave a portion of his salary to help disadvantaged students finish university. After a year he became a naval doctor for P&O, and then the China Navigation Company, and spent the next six years at sea. On board ship he wrote unoriginal verse, published as *Poems of Truth* (1957): they are brooding works with titles such as 'Adversity', 'Knowing and Being', and 'Karma', but they reveal the spiritual turn that his mind had taken after reading the Russian mystics G. I. Gurdjieff and P. D. Ouspensky. Between voyages he worked on radionics (a controversial diagnostic and healing therapy) at the De La Warr Laboratories in Oxford.

During his time as a naval doctor Dillon had requested that his entry in Debrett's and Burke's Peerage be changed to Laurence Michael. Debrett's concurred, but Burke's at first did not. This discrepancy, reported by the *Sunday Express* on 11 May 1958, to his horror led to his public exposure and determined the final course of his life. While on a voyage Dillon visited Calcutta and made enquiries about learning Buddhist meditation, with a view to retreating from the world. Within a few months he was living in India, where he spent the rest of his life, first at an English Buddhist monastery in Kalimpong, then at Sarnath, near Varanasi, where he attended the Sanskrit University in 1959, and at Rizong monastery in Ladakh (he wrote an account of Rizong in *Imji Getsul*, 1962). He was first ordained as a Sramenera, or novice monk, of the Theravadin order of the Hinayana school, took the name of Jivaka (doctor), and was the first westerner to be ordained in the Tibetan order. He became interested in Mahayan Buddhism, but was denied ordination when the secret about his sex change became known. He lived solely by writing books on Buddhism, giving away all his possessions, and asking a lawyer to dispose of his estate. His most notable work of this period was an adapted popular version of *The Life of Milarepa* (1962), originally translated by W. Y. Evans-Wentz.

Dillon was generous and kind, but could be snobbish and humourless. There is scant evidence in his writings that he ever achieved spiritual enlightenment. He found it difficult to adjust to the Tibetan Buddhist diet, and could not always afford to feed himself. He became emaciated and was often starving. He courted controversy one last time when he was denied a permit to revisit Ladakh. He was suspected of being a spy hired by Nehru to observe the Chinese in the area, before Nehru intervened to quell the rumours. Michael Dillon died on 15 May 1962 in the Civil Hospital in Dalhousie, India, possibly on his way to Kashmir to join his guru, Kushok Bakula. He was cremated according to Mahayana rites. A few months after Dillon's death his agent, John Johnson, received the manuscript of his autobiography, completed on 1 May 1962, his forty-seventh birthday. It indicated that he wished all the facts of his remarkable life to be known. It remains unpublished.   CLARE L. TAYLOR

Sources L. Hodgkinson, *Michael, née Laura* (1989) · H. Devor, *FTM: female-to-male transsexuals in society* (1997) · J. Prosser, 'Transsexuals and the transsexologists: inversion and the emergence of transsexual subjectivity', *Sexology in culture: labelling bodies and desires*, ed. L. Bland and L. Doan (1998), 116–31 · J. Prosser, *Second skins: the body narratives of transsexuality* (1998) · b. cert. · Burke, *Peerage* (1959)
Likenesses photographs, repro. in Hodgkinson, *Michael née Laura*

Dillon, Peter (1788–1847), adventurer in the south seas, was born on 15 June 1788 on Martinique, the son of an Irishman, Peter Dillon, probably a soldier stationed on the island. About 1806 Dillon appears to have sailed for Calcutta and he later traded sandalwood between the west Pacific islands and China. In 1809 he spent four months in Fiji, mixing with Fijians and learning their language. He lived on Bora-Bora, in the Society Islands, from 1810 to 1812 and claimed to have become the adopted son of Tapoa, a powerful chief; he took as his mistress a daughter of another chief.

In 1812 and 1813 Dillon was third mate on the *Hunter*. In September 1813 men from the *Hunter*, when on shore at Vilear, were attacked by Fijians, who killed twelve Europeans and about forty others, later eating many of them. Dillon's coolness and knowledge of the Fijians allowed him and two others to escape. Those who had fled the fighting were taken by Dillon on the *Hunter*'s sister ship *Elizabeth* to Tikopia (lat. 12°10′ S, long. 168°50′ E), an island never before visited by Europeans, where the Prussian Martin Buchert, his Fijian wife, and a Lascar known as Joe were landed. After his return to Sydney, Dillon achieved some fame by recounting the affair. In 1814 he was commissioned by the Church Missionary Society to take missionaries to New Zealand. On 22 September 1814 he married Mary Moore in Sydney and she and their children often accompanied him on his voyages. From 1819 to 1825 he shipped criminals, mail, and merchandise between India and Australia in his own ships, two of which wrecked.

On a trip to South America, Dillon met the widow of Máximo Rodríguez, the Spanish explorer to Tahiti, whose diary she gave to Dillon and a summary of which he published in the Bengal *Government Gazette*. This fostered his interest in early Pacific exploration, an interest which gained impetus in May 1826, when, on a visit to Tikopia, Dillon obtained from Buchert and Joe a silver sword-guard and spoon, which he rightly guessed were relics of the lost expedition of J. F. G. de la Pérouse. The artefacts had come from Vanikoro, in the Santa Cruz Islands; Dillon made for the islands, but when his supplies ran short and the ship began to leak he was forced to divert to Calcutta.

Keen to investigate the discovery further, the East India Company fitted out the *Research* which, under Dillon's command, sailed from Calcutta in January 1827. The voyage was marred by illness and a quarrel between Dillon and Robert Tytler, the ship's doctor. Dillon thought Tytler mutinous: Tytler thought Dillon mad. Although Tytler was the more reprehensible, it was Dillon who was tried and imprisoned in Hobart for assault and false imprisonment. Dillon's sentence was remitted and the *Research* sailed on, reaching New Zealand, where he learned that Dumont D'Urville was also looking for the remains of Pérouse's expedition. In September Dillon reached Tikopia, where, through Buchert's influence, he bought further artefacts; he sailed on to Vanikoro, where he found the remains of Pérouse's two wrecked ships, and numerous artefacts unquestionably from Pérouse's expedition, which he carried off. D'Urville, hearing of Dillon's discovery, landed at Tikopia, gathered further relics and erected a memorial. On reaching Calcutta in April 1828, Dillon was warmly received by the governor, but found that the failure of his agents had left him penniless. He and his family sailed to England where, despite acclaim from the press, he got a mixed reaction from the East India Company. They left, after only three days, for Paris, where Dillon gave his finds to Charles X, who placed them in the Louvre; the king awarded Dillon the Légion d'honneur, an annual pension of 4000 francs, and a grant towards his expenses. Through the *Narrative* (1829) of his voyage, Dillon tried to secure public acclaim, a scientific reputation, and financial security; its valuable descriptions of the peoples of the south seas won it some fame, and French and Dutch editions were published, but it is marred by diatribes against Tytler.

After this Dillon never found occupation which made use of his knowledge of the south seas or which relieved his poverty. His plans for French Roman Catholic missions in the Pacific, his employment in 1834 as a flax trader to New Zealand, and his repeated petitions to the British, French, and other governments for a pension in recognition of his services to exploration all came to nothing. After the death of his wife in 1840 Dillon went to Paris, where he died, at 23 rue des Postes, on 9 February 1847. Dillon was 6 feet 4 inches tall, heavily built with a mop of red hair. He was courageous, and understood and liked the peoples of the Pacific. He could be brutal to his wife and subordinates, but in general commanded the respect even of those who disliked him. His knowledge of the Pacific and its exploration was impressive in one who lacked formal education.   ELIZABETH BAIGENT

Sources J. W. Davidson, *Peter Dillon of Vanikoro: chevalier of the south seas*, ed. O. H. K. Spate (1975)

Dillon, Sir Robert (*d.* 1579?), judge, was the third son of James Dillon of Riverston, co. Meath, and his wife, Elizabeth, daughter of Bartholomew Bathe of Dollardstown. His father was chief remembrancer and second baron of the exchequer about 1499. Robert probably received legal training at the inns of court, since nearly all of his contemporaries were in residence there prior to commencing their legal careers in Ireland. His eldest brother, Sir Bartholomew Dillon (*d.* 1534), became an important ally of the earl of Kildare, to whom Bartholomew owed promotion as chief baron of the exchequer and under-treasurer (1514–20), second justice of king's bench (1520–33), and chief justice of king's bench (1533–4). Another brother, Thomas, was prior of the cathedral canons of Sts Peter and Paul in Trim, co. Meath, in 1511.

Dillon married Elizabeth, daughter of Edward Barnewall of Crickstown and granddaughter of Sir Thomas Plunket (*d.* 1471), chief justice of common pleas. As a well-connected member of a distinguished family of jurists, Robert was named attorney-general of Ireland on 9 June 1534, at the outset of the Kildare rebellion. Though undoubtedly Catholic, he assisted in the dissolution of the Irish monasteries, receiving on 22 December 1538 the site of St Peter's Priory at Newtown, near Trim. Dillon made Newtown his principal seat, and he acquired the Carmelite monastery at Athnecarne, co. Meath, on 20 March 1546. He resided in Dublin, near St Patrick's Cathedral, from 1547, and in 1548 he acted as civil governor of Athlone. He became second justice of queen's bench on 17 January 1554, and was commended for his discretion and learning. On 9 November 1556 Dillon travelled with John Plunket on a commission to Munster to take depositions in a controversy between the lord of Upper Ossory and the earl of Ormond. A witness to constant political intrigue, Dillon was a survivor who established the family's fortune without risking his investment in partisan alignments at court.

Elizabeth renewed Dillon's appointment in January 1559, and on 3 September 1559 he was made chief justice of common pleas with a fee of £67 10s. He attended the Irish privy council regularly, served as commissioner for ecclesiastical causes on 6 October 1564, and was knighted by Sir Henry Sidney in 1567. He was frequently commissioner for martial law and for collection of the cess in co. Meath and won additional lands, including estates in Connaught worth £30 in April 1568, and the monastery of Kilkenny West in co. Westmeath in 1569. Nevertheless, he was described by Sidney on 20 April 1567 as 'a man muche spent in yeares and decayed both in sence and bodie' (PRO, SP 63/20/142). After 1571 he was notably absent from meetings of the privy council, and on 8 March 1575 Elizabeth declared her intention of sending an Englishman to replace him on the bench. Lord Chancellor Sir William Gerard in 1576 cited Dillon's incapacity to serve on regular assize courts as part of the rationale for judicial reform, and on 5 July 1579 he wrote to Walsingham that Dillon had died. A famous quarrel over his succession in office ended with the trial and execution of his successor, Nicholas Nugent, and his replacement by Dillon's great-nephew,

Robert *Dillon of Riverston. Dillon and his wife had four sons and three daughters, including his eldest son, Sir Lucas *Dillon, who joined his father on the privy council in 1570 as chief baron of the exchequer.

JON G. CRAWFORD

Sources F. E. Ball, *The judges in Ireland, 1221–1921*, 2 (1926) · J. L. J. Hughes, ed., *Patentee officers in Ireland, 1173–1826, including high sheriffs, 1661–1684 and 1761–1816*, IMC (1960) · J. G. Crawford, *Anglicizing the government of Ireland: the Irish privy council and the expansion of Tudor rule, 1556–1578* (1993) · B. Bradshaw, *The dissolution of the religious orders in Ireland under Henry VIII* (1974) · B. Bradshaw, *The Irish constitutional revolution of the sixteenth century* (1979) · C. Brady, *The chief governors: the rise and fall of reform government in Tudor Ireland, 1536–1588* (1994) · C. Brady, 'Court, castle and country: the framework of government in Tudor Ireland', *Natives and newcomers: essays on the making of Irish colonial society, 1534–1641*, ed. C. Brady and R. Gillespie (1986), 22–49, 217–19 · S. G. Ellis, *Reform and revival: English government in Ireland, 1470–1534*, Royal Historical Society Studies in History, 47 (1986) · S. G. Ellis, *Tudor Ireland: crown, community, and the conflict of cultures, 1470–1603* (1985) · C. Kenny, 'The exclusion of Catholics from the legal profession in Ireland, 1537–1829', *Irish Historical Studies*, 25 (1986–7), 337–57 · council book of the Irish privy council, 1556–71, Royal Irish Acad., MS 24 F. 17 · Lord Chancellor Gerard's report, 1576, LPL, Carew MS 628, fol. 312 · PRO, state papers, Ireland, SP 63

Dillon, Sir Robert (*c.*1540–1597), judge, was the eldest son of Thomas Dillon of Riverston, co. Meath, and his wife, Anne, daughter of Sir Thomas Luttrell (*d.* 1554), former chief justice of common pleas. His grandfather Sir Bartholomew Dillon (*d.* 1534) had been an important ally of the earl of Kildare and served briefly as chief justice of king's bench in 1533–4. Sir Robert *Dillon (*d.* 1579?), of Newtown Trim, his great-uncle, was chief justice of common pleas from 1559 to 1579, and Sir Lucas *Dillon (*d.* 1592), his cousin, was chief baron of the exchequer from 1570 to 1592. Robert Dillon of Riverston was probably born about 1540 and studied law at Lincoln's Inn where he was escheator in 1560. After a quarrel with Nicholas Nugent in that year he was bound to keep the peace. In 1562 he signed the book of twenty-four articles, a critique of the Dublin government's use of purveyance. He was called to the bar in England in 1567 and on 1 June 1569 was named second justice of the newly installed presidency and council of Connaught as 'a suitable man of this country, learned in the laws and with the knowledge of the Irish tongue' (Morrin, 533–4).

Dillon was an ambitious and exceedingly well-connected member of a distinguished judicial family. In his first post, however, he exhibited the combative temper which marked his subsequent career. Allied with the first president of Connaught, the wily Sir Edward Fitton, Dillon defended his ruthless campaigns against the criticism of the cautious lord deputy, Sir William Fitzwilliam. When the truculent Fitton won higher office as vice-treasurer, after retreating from his precarious role in Athlone, Dillon was appointed chancellor of the exchequer in Ireland on 5 June 1572. Though aligned with his moderate older cousin Sir Lucas Dillon, who was made chief baron in 1570, Robert the younger made an enemy of Fitzwilliam. The viceroy attacked Fitton in council for refusing to sign a warrant and imprisoned the unruly vice-treasurer

in June 1573. Fitzwilliam urged Elizabeth to commit Dillon to the Fleet when he arrived in London as agent for the closeted Fitton. However, the queen took the side of Dillon and Fitton, reprimanding Fitzwilliam, who was soon to be replaced.

When Sir Henry Sidney succeeded as chief governor in 1575 he regarded the Dillons as loyal allies and Robert was appointed second justice of common pleas, under his aged great-uncle, on 26 November 1577. Lord Chancellor Gerard commended him for his learning in 1576, and in 1580 the vice-treasurer, Wallop, sought the chief justiceship for him, noting that he had executed both offices during the past four years while the senior Dillon was too enfeebled to serve. During the constitutional crisis of the cess (1577–9) Dillon was apparently an interested bystander, while his nemesis and rival Nicholas Nugent was summarily expelled as second baron of the exchequer for his challenge to the legality of purveyance. None the less, on the death of the ancient chief justice, Nugent was preferred as his successor on the nomination of the lord chancellor, frustrating the expectations of Dillon. Wallop claimed that Nugent had purchased the reversion of office for a mere £100 and that he was a covert papist. The recommendation of Dillon by Edward Waterhouse on 20 April 1580 declared 'he is reported one of the most sufficient in knowledge and Judgment and he is of very good ability to beare out the Countenace of a Consaillor, being born to fair living as the chief of that surname' (PRO, SP 63/72/147).

Denied his chance in 1580, another opportunity came quickly for Dillon in the form of the Nugent rebellion in the pale in 1581. The new lord chancellor, Archbishop Adam Loftus, had written in April 1581 to Cecil that the chief justiceship had been promised by Sidney to Dillon, that Nugent was less skilful, and that Dillon's loyalty to the queen was not inferior to those of English birth. Dillon was appointed chief justice of common pleas on 14 July 1581 and the dismissed Nugent was accused of supporting his cousin's insurrection, conspiring to take Dublin Castle, and planning to ambush Sir Lucas and Sir Robert on their way to hold sessions at Mullingar. At a special tribunal at Trim on 4 April 1582 Nugent was tried for treason. He complained that only one tainted witness gave testimony, and Sir Robert was accused of soliciting witnesses and bullying jurors into reversing their verdict; but Nugent was hanged at Trim two days later.

Despite the political scandal Dillon was knighted in 1581 and raised to the honour of privy councillor. He was reputed the wealthiest commoner in the pale in 1586, and received a lease of land in Oxmantown in 1588 as token of gratitude from Dublin corporation. Like his cousin, Dillon was a supporter of Lord Deputy Perrot in council. In 1588 he was named a commissioner for the new composition of Connaught, but after Perrot's dismissal he faced his old enemy Sir William Fitzwilliam as the new chief governor. Dillon had quarrelled with Sir Richard Bingham over the management of the Connaught presidency and was excluded from the council during the inquiry into Bingham's government in 1589. In 1591 Dillon was accused by the former rebel William Nugent of encouraging Sir Brian O'Rourke in rebellion. His trial was managed by the English privy council in June 1593, seeking proofs from Dublin and requiring a speedy conclusion out of respect of the office of chief justice. On the evidence, Dillon was removed from office and imprisoned in October 1593, yet his supporter, Lord Chancellor Loftus, declared him innocent of the charges on 22 November. Five days later he was named a commissioner of ecclesiastical causes, and he was restored to the council in the following year. On the death of his replacement, Sir William Weston, on 23 September 1594, Secretary Fenton wrote to Burghley that Dillon should be restored to office. He regained the chief justiceship by patent on 15 March 1595, a notable exception to the elimination of loyal Old English councillors after 1592.

Dillon's first wife was Eleanor, daughter of Thomas Allen of Kilteel, co. Kildare, with whom he had one son who predeceased him. After the death of Eleanor he married Katherine (d. 1615), daughter of the wealthy Dublin alderman Sir William Sarsfield of Lucan; with his second wife he had five sons and nine daughters. Dillon died in office while at Riverston on 15 July 1597, and was buried at the parish church in Tara where a memorial was placed in his honour. His brother Gerald was clerk of the crown and third justice of queen's bench, though he was imprisoned as part of the anti-Dillon inquisition of 1591-3. His kinsman Thomas Dillon of Proudstown was chief justice of Connaught and third justice of common pleas, though he also was briefly imprisoned in the Bingham conflict of the 1590s. JON G. CRAWFORD

Sources F. E. Ball, *The judges in Ireland, 1221-1921*, 2 (1926) · C. Brady, *The chief governors: the rise and fall of reform government in Tudor Ireland, 1536-1588* (1994) · J. G. Crawford, *Anglicizing the government of Ireland: the Irish privy council and the expansion of Tudor rule, 1556-1578* (1993) · S. G. Ellis, *Tudor Ireland: crown, community, and the conflict of cultures, 1470-1603* (1985) · J. L. J. Hughes, ed., *Patentee officers in Ireland, 1173-1826, including high sheriffs, 1661-1684 and 1761-1816*, IMC (1960) · C. Kenny, *King's Inns and the kingdom of Ireland* (1992) · C. Lennon, *The lords of Dublin in the age of the Reformation* (1989) · PRO, SP 63/81/106; 63/72/147; 63/82/26 · Lord Chancellor Gerard's report, 1576, LPL, Carew MS 628, fol. 312 · J. Morrin, ed., *Calendar of the patent and close rolls of chancery in Ireland for the reigns of Henry VIII, Edward VI, Mary, and Elizabeth*, 2 vols. (1861-2) · entry book of the court of castle chamber, BL, Add. MS 47172 · 'Trial of Nicholas Nugent', TCD, MS 842

Likenesses memorial, Tara parish church, Ireland

Dillon, Robert Crawford (1795-1847), author and rebel Church of England clergyman, was born in the rectory house of St Margaret's, Lothbury, in the City of London, on 22 May 1795. His parents' names are unknown, but his father is said to have died when Robert was young; his mother then had him privately educated by John Cawood. He entered St Edmund Hall, Oxford, in the Michaelmas term of 1813. He took his BA on 16 May 1817 and his MA on 3 February 1820, and proceeded BD and DD 27 October 1836. He was ordained on 20 December 1818 to the curacy of West Milton, Dorset. Having received priest's orders, in 1819 he was appointed assistant minister of St John's Chapel, Bedford Row, London, the recognized centre of evangelical teaching, of which Daniel Wilson, later

bishop of Calcutta, was at that time the incumbent. There he became a popular preacher, and was much sought after, especially by the female members of the congregation. Dillon moved in 1824 to the curacy of Willesden and Kingsbury, Middlesex, and the next year to that of St James's, Clerkenwell; the following year, 1826, he obtained an appointment at St Matthew's Chapel, Denmark Hill, London. In 1822 Dillon was chaplain to Alderman Venables when sheriff and remained so when Venables was lord mayor of London in 1826-7. In the latter year he accompanied the lord mayor and corporation on an official visit to Oxford, of which, on Venables's request, he wrote an account, published in 1826, which quickly became notorious. Its preface acknowledges that 'it is a species of writing not altogether in accordance with the sacred profession of which the writer is the unworthiest member' (R. C. Dillon, *The Lord Mayor's Visit to Oxford*, 1826). Its style is hyperbolic and it was felt that the mayorial party had been held up to ridicule. Dillon tried to buy up copies—which were 'rigorously suppressed', as the bookseller's advertisement, tipped into the copy in the Bodleian, reads—and the book became a collector's item.

In 1828 Dillon was elected by a large majority to be morning preacher of the Female Orphan Asylum, a post which he resigned the next year for a proprietary chapel in Charlotte Street, Pimlico, to which he was licensed on 24 July 1829. From 1829 to 1837 he was early-morning lecturer at St Swithin's, London Stone, where he attracted large congregations. During this period Dillon continued his evening lectureship at St James's, Clerkenwell, and in 1839, on the vacancy of the rectory, which was in the gift of the parishioners, he became candidate for the benefice. The consequent election was marked by bribery and the publication of broadsheets. Dillon's private life was closely enquired into, and various sexual scandals were brought to light; despite the support of a vocal group of female parishioners (organized as a 'ladies' committee'), Dillon was not elected. The charges of immorality having been proved, C. J. Blomfield, bishop of London, revoked Dillon's licence, and suspended him from his ministry in Charlotte Street on 29 February 1840. In defiance of the inhibition, Dillon continued to officiate in the chapel, and a suit was brought against him in the consistory court in April of the same year, when he was condemned with costs.

Dillon then left the Church of England, and, helped by his female followers, set up a 'reformed English church' in Friar Street, Blackfriars, with a new system of discipline and a reformed liturgy. His congregation increased, and Dillon moved to a large building in White's Row, Spitalfields, where he appointed himself 'first presbyter' or 'bishop' of his new church, and ordained ministers to serve branch churches in various parts of London. On 26 November 1839, Dillon married Frances Charlotte, daughter of John Rumball, from whom he soon separated. In 1842 Dillon was involved in an unsavoury case in the consistory court, brought against him by his wife, for the restitution of conjugal rights. His defence was that his wife had committed adultery with James Nicholls, a barrister.

In his evidence he claimed that his wife was the illegitimate daughter of John Rumball and the wife of Captain Augustus Vere Drury. Despite this, Dillon continued to be a popular preacher, and at the time of his sudden death on 8 November 1847, in the vestry of his chapel in Spitalfields, he had received large promises of money for expanding his church outside London. He was buried in the churchyard of his native parish, St Margaret's, Lothbury, in which church a mural slab was erected to his memory.   H. C. G. MATTHEW

Sources GM, 2nd ser., 29 (1848), 669 · Church Magazine, 1 (1839), 289–95 · R. C. Dillon, Speech … in the consistorial and episcopal court of London on Tuesday, May 31, 1842 (1842) · DNB
Likenesses E. Dixon, portrait · R. Smith, stipple (after E. Dixon), NPG · mezzotint (after T. Bridgeford), NPG

Dillon, Théobald Hyacinthe [*known as* Chevalier Dillon] (1745–1792), army officer in the French service, the son of Thomas Dillon and his wife, Marie Hussey, the daughter of Edward Hussey of Donore, co. Kildare, and a distant relative of General Arthur Dillon, was born in Dublin on 22 July 1745. The following year his father moved his family to France and settled near Orléans. Dillon never married, but he and Josephine de Viefville lived together for nine years and had three children, all of whom took his name.

On 1 September 1761 or 1762 Dillon entered the family regiment as a cadet, and was a captain in 1779 when it participated in the attack on Grenada and the siege of Savannah, after which he fell ill and returned to France. He was promoted colonel in second on 13 April 1780, received the cross of St Louis on 29 July 1781, and was admitted to the order of Cincinnatus on 15 March 1785. Three years later he assumed command of the regiment, and on 25 August 1791 was promoted general. After commanding the garrison at Valenciennes and at Lille he was given command of a detachment of the army of the north with orders to feign an attack on Tournai in order to divert the enemy from the real objective, Mons. But upon encountering an advancing Austrian force, Dillon ordered a retreat; the retreat turned into a rout, with the French troops claiming they had been betrayed, and Dillon, having failed to rally his command, was first wounded and then conveyed back to Lille and brutally murdered by his own men. His body was burnt in the main square of the city on 29 April 1792, and his remains were probably buried in the communal cemetery in the faubourg St Maurice in Lille.
                                    SAMUEL F. SCOTT

Sources R. F. Hayes, Irish swordsmen of France (1934) · G. Bodinier, Dictionnaire des officiers de l'armée royale qui ont combattu aux États-Unis pendant la guerre d'indépendance, 1776–1783 (Vincennes, 1982) · R. F. Hayes, Ireland and Irishmen in the French Revolution (1932) · G. Six, Dictionnaire biographique des généraux et amiraux français de la Révolution et de l'Empire, 1792–1814, 2 vols. (1934) · DNB
Likenesses line engraving, July 1792, NG Ire.; repro. in Walker's Hibernian Magazine (July 1792)

Dillon [de León], **Thomas** (1613–1690), Jesuit and scholar, was born in Ireland and was educated in Spain, where he entered the Society of Jesus at Seville in 1627. He was a teacher of the humanities at the Jesuit college of Cadiz, and later taught philosophy at Seville before becoming professor of theology at the College of St Paul, Granada. Also known as Thomas de León, he enjoyed a reputation among his contemporaries as a polymath and a linguist, with a knowledge of Hebrew and Arabic, but he left behind no learned work of any substance other than a manuscript commentary on Maccabees. He died at Granada on 7 February 1690.
            THOMPSON COOPER, rev. G. MARTIN MURPHY

Sources A. de Backer and others, Bibliothèque de la Compagnie de Jésus, new edn, 3, ed. C. Sommervogel (Brussels, 1892) · J. S. Díaz, Bibliografía de la literatura Hispánica, 13 (1984), 169–70

Dillon, Thomas, **fourth Viscount Dillon** (1614/15–1673x5), royalist army officer, was the second son of Sir Christopher Dillon (d. 1624), Irish administrator, and Lady Jane, daughter of James Dillon, first earl of Roscommon. His father, of Ballylagham, co. Mayo, was president of Connaught. Thomas converted from Roman Catholicism to protestantism at the age of fifteen when he succeeded his nephew as Viscount Dillon in May 1630. Before 1636 he married Frances (d. 1674), daughter of Sir Nicholas White of Leixlip and Ursula, daughter of Garret, first Viscount Moore of Drogheda. Frances brought him a portion of £3000; the couple had seven sons.

In November 1640 the Irish House of Lords appointed Dillon as one of four delegates to Charles I. While in England and Scotland during the autumn of 1641 he may also have acted as an intermediary in a plan to bring an Irish army to Charles's assistance against the Scottish covenanters. This allegation rests primarily on a contemporaneous Scottish pamphlet of 1643 and the fact that Sir James *Dillon, his uncle, one of the colonels licensed to recruit from Strafford's disbanded Irish army, became tangentially involved in a plot to seize Dublin Castle.

On his return from Edinburgh in October 1641 Dillon was appointed to the Irish council and made governor of Roscommon. He was part of a moderate party that tried unavailingly to keep the Irish parliament in session and to defuse the recent rebellion. He left for England in late November 1641 on a secret mission to Charles I on behalf of the Catholic lords. Arrested by the English parliament, he and his brother-in-law Theobald, Viscount Taaffe, made their escape after four months, joined the emergent royalist party, and fought in the early part of the first civil war.

Dillon returned to Ireland after the cessation of hostilities in September 1643 'to sit quiet tippling, gaming and working division and rent in his majesties subjects' (Gilbert, 1.76), according to a jaundiced confederate Catholic source. He was appointed governor of Athlone town and castle in February 1643 and joint president of Connaught in 1644. He accompanied Ormond, the king's lord lieutenant in Ireland, in August 1646 when he marched on Kilkenny and Cashel, in order to secure support for a treaty between the confederate Catholics and Charles I. When Ormond was forced to turn back, Dillon fled to Connaught. Meanwhile, in September 1643, his uncles George Dillon, a Franciscan friar, and Sir James Dillon, by then a colonel in the Leinster confederate Catholic army, captured Athlone Castle by a ruse. According to the hostile author of the *Aphorismical Discovery* Dillon's subsequent public conversion to Roman Catholicism on 6 December 1646 was a gambit to secure the aid of Rinuccini, the papal nuncio, in regaining possession of Athlone Castle. Following his conversion and pledge of loyalty to the confederate Catholic cause, the confederate supreme council ordered that Athlone Castle be restored to him. However, the occupant defied the order and, early in the following year, Dillon rejoined Ormond. When the latter subsequently surrendered Dublin to parliament, Dillon joined the Leinster confederate Catholic army and led the cavalry contingent at the catastrophic defeat of Dungan's Hill in August 1647. Dillon personally commanded the reserve, which fled in the opening stages of the battle, 'never giving the least notice of such a base cowardly act' (Gilbert, 1.156). Following the split in the confederate Catholics between clericalist and Ormondist factions Dillon fought for the latter and was captured in an ambush but escaped soon afterwards.

In 1649 Ormond returned to Ireland and secured a definitive alliance between the confederate Catholics and the royalist party. In July that year Dillon was reinstated as governor of Athlone. During the royalist siege of Dublin Dillon was left with a force of 2500 men to cut off the northern approaches while the bulk of the army encamped at Rathmines to the south of the city. On 2 August a surprise attack overran Ormond's camp; at some point in the battle Ormond sent a message ordering Dillon to march south and attack the rear of the parliamentary army. Dillon refused, probably because it seemed to him that it was too late to prevent a rout.

In 1650 Dillon was tasked with the command of royalist forces in Offaly. In March that year Kilkenny was threatened by parliamentary thrusts from the south under Cromwell and from Dublin. Dillon's failure to hinder the thrust from Dublin was 'astonishing' (Wheeler, 13), and he refused Lord Castlehaven's appeal to help save Kilkenny from capture. In August 1650 he tricked Henry Ireton (who had replaced Cromwell as parliamentary commander-in-chief in Ireland) into believing that he would surrender Athlone in exchange for money and an assurance of personal safety, thereby causing Ireton to waste a crucial fortnight waiting for the expected betrayal. On the other hand, the following year in June he surrendered the castle without a fight because, he said, 'he desired to submit to the government of England, as being of English descent and extract' (Murtagh, 106). Charles Coote, parliamentary president of Connaught, received the surrender, promising to 'mediate with the parliament', for a pardon and a 'competency of land' (ibid.) for the support of Dillon's family but nothing came of this promise. Dillon retired to Hare Island on Lough Ree where he lived in relative poverty. In 1651 his wife was implicated in a failed attempt to recapture Athlone; this told against Dillon when he unsuccessfully sought relief from the government in 1652. Later petitions suggest that he may then have travelled abroad.

Dillon's estates were confiscated by the protectorate but he recovered them following the Restoration. In 1661 he was one of those who stood bail for the marquess of Antrim, to whom he was related by marriage and who was then in the Tower on a charge of treason. In 1663 he signed the remonstrance of Irish Catholic nobles and gentry professing their loyalty in the hope of some measure of toleration of their religion. He died between 23 May 1673 when he wrote his will and 1675 when the will was proved in Ireland. His wife died on 20 December 1674.

PÁDRAIG LENIHAN

Sources J. T. Gilbert, ed., *A contemporary history of affairs in Ireland from 1641 to 1652*, 3 vols. (1879–80), vol. 1, pp. 124–7, 136, 155–6, 265–7; vol. 2, pp. 107–8, 111; vol. 3, p. 171 • B. O'Ferrall and D. O'Connell, *Commentarius Rinuccinianus de sedis apostolicae legatione ad foederatos Hiberniae Catholicos per annos 1645–1649*, ed. J. Kavanagh, IMC, 2 (1936), 467–9 • J. S. Wheeler, *Cromwell in Ireland* (Dublin, 1999), 74, 134, 135 • M. Archdall, *The peerage of Ireland* (1779), vol. 4, pp. 185–6 • M. Perceval-Maxwell, *The outbreak of the Irish rebellion of 1641* (1994), 90, 138, 198–9 • GEC, *Peerage*, new edn • H. Murtagh, *Athlone history and settlements to 1800* (2000) • J. H. Ohlmeyer, *Civil war and Restoration in the three Stuart kingdoms: the career of Randal MacDonnell, marquis of Antrim, 1609–1683* (1993) • *CSP Ire.*, 1660–63

Dillon, Wentworth, fourth earl of Roscommon (1637–1685), poet, was born in Dublin, probably in St George's Lane, in October 1637. Thomas Wentworth, earl of Strafford, then lord deputy, was his uncle, his father, James Dillon, third earl of Roscommon (c.1605–1649), having married Elizabeth, daughter of Sir William Wentworth of Wentworth Woodhouse, Yorkshire, and sister to the earl of Strafford. He was educated in the protestant faith, as his father had been 'reclaimed from the superstition of the Romish church' by James Ussher, primate of Ireland (Wood, *Ath. Oxon.: Fasti*, 2.389). For his early years we have only the doubtfully reliable information of Elijah Fenton, who in his memoir of 1730 says that when Dillon was very young, Strafford sent him to study under a Dr Hall at his own seat in Yorkshire. Upon the impeachment of Strafford, Fenton goes on, he was by Archbishop Ussher's advice sent to the learned Samuel Bochart at Caen in Normandy, where there was a long-established protestant university. During his residence there his father died at Limerick in November 1649. Aubrey states that Dillon, possessed by an 'extravagant fit', exclaimed 'My father is dead!' and that the news of the death arrived from Ireland a fortnight later (Aubrey, 162).

After leaving Caen, Roscommon made a tour of France and Germany, accompanied by Lord Cavendish (afterwards duke of Devonshire), later a member of Roscommon's literary circle. This was in the late 1650s, when ardent royalists were unwelcome in England and Ireland. They also stayed a considerable time at Rome, and Roscommon was reputed to have learned the language so well as to be taken for an Italian. In Rome he also acquired great skill as a numismatist.

Soon after the Restoration Roscommon returned to England, and had a favourable reception at the court of Charles II. An act of parliament restoring to him all the honours, castles, lordships, lands, and property in the possession of his great-grandfather, grandfather, or father on 23 October 1641 was read a first time in the English House of Lords on 18 August 1660, and received the royal assent on 29 December. By virtue of this statute he became seised of several estates in co. Meath, co. Westmeath, King's county, and counties Mayo, Galway, Sligo, Roscommon, and Tipperary. He took his seat in the Irish parliament by proxy on 10 July 1661 and began to re-establish his position. On 16 October 1661 he had a grant of the first troop of horse that should become vacant, pursuant to privy seal dated 23 September. In the same year he addressed to the king a petition in which he said that his father and grandfather being protestants, and having from the beginning of the rebellion constantly adhered to the royal cause, lost at least £50,000 or £60,000 for their loyalty to Charles I. Partly owing to the good offices of the duke of Ormond, the king promptly ordered a part payment of arrears. In April 1662 Roscommon married Lady Frances, eldest daughter of Richard *Boyle, second earl of Cork (later also first earl of Burlington), widow of Colonel Francis Courtenay, and niece to Roger Boyle, first earl of Orrery, the well-known statesman and dramatist and thereafter a loyal friend to Roscommon. Shortly after the Restoration Roscommon had made friends who led him into gambling, then popular at court. His gaming led to duels, and he became famous as a duellist though he used to say that he was more fearful of killing others than of losing his own life.

In 1662 Roscommon returned to Ireland, partly to pursue his land interests. To the ensuing years in Ireland belong the first substantial indications of his literary interests, though he had written accomplished verse in both English and Latin as a youth. Katherine Philips praised his early, as yet unpublished translations in a letter of 19 October 1662; Roscommon returned the compliment in more than one of his works and wrote the prologue for Philips's *Pompey* of 1663 (his first published poem). There is evidence of the existence of a Dublin literary circle including both these figures in the years 1662–5.

By 1665 Roscommon had recovered all the Irish lands to which he had a title, though he had still received only a fraction of the money promised him by the king in 1661. Through the late 1660s his military duties continued. He received a formal commission for a troop of horse in 1666. He was also involved in local and national government matters, until eventually, in the early 1670s, there was talk of his becoming a lord treasurer of Ireland. Instead, he raised an infantry regiment in Ireland in 1671 to serve the French against the Dutch. He accompanied the regiment, but it was disbanded by the French in Lorraine in 1672. He then returned to Ireland, but became a widower in 1673 or 1674, at which date he seems to have 'determined to leave his native country and join himself to the English court' (Niemeyer, 'Life and works', 73). He soon married again, in London, where on 9 November 1674 he wed Isabella (d. 1721), youngest daughter and coheir of Sir Matthew Boynton of Barmston, Yorkshire.

In 1676 Roscommon became a captain of the band of gentlemen pensioners, a small troop with largely ceremonial duties paid directly by the king; by 1679 he was on the continent again. This may or may not have been on state business, but he was still concerned with political matters. He is recorded as a companion of James, duke of York, later in 1679, and travelled with him during the duke's 'exile' to Scotland in 1679–80. Two political poems doubtfully attributed to Roscommon can be dated to 1679–81: 'Tom Ross's Ghost' and 'The Ghost of the Late Parliament'.

In 1679 (though the title page gives 1680) appeared one of Roscommon's two most substantial literary works, *Horace's Art of Poetry*, a translation of Horace's *Ars poetica*. The first English version of this famous poem to be published since Jonson's, its blank verse treatment of its original is freer and in several ways more attractive than its predecessors'. The following few years are Roscommon's most productive as a poet. Many of his productions have clear connections with the informal 'academy' he established about 1682 in conjunction with George Savile, marquess of Halifax, Richard Maitland (later earl of Lauderdale), the earl of Dorset, Lord Cavendish (later duke of Devonshire), Sir Charles Scarborough, Heneage Finch, John Dryden, and others. These names, as well as the term 'academy', are supplied by Roscommon's friend Knightley Chetwood, whose memoir also shows the circle's interests to have been extensively literary, with a special emphasis on translation from the classics, and not narrowly lexicographical as suggested by Fenton and some other later writers. Hence the clear relationship between the 'academy' and Roscommon's *Essay on Translated Verse*, published in 1684, in which specific allusion is made to works of verse translation from the Latin and Greek classics recently published by members of the circle. Three of Roscommon's own translations, from Virgil and Horace, appeared in Dryden's miscellany of 1684, and he contributed a commendatory poem to the 1683 issue of Dryden's *Religio laici* (Dryden responding with one on Roscommon's *Essay on Translated Verse*). The *Essay*, probably Roscommon's best-known poem and certainly his most distinguished, is in several ways his most unusual. It helped to usher in the great age of Augustan translation from the classics, drawing on the ideas of Dryden and influencing Pope, two of its greatest exponents. Yet it may also be said to be designed to promote the work of a small clique, Roscommon's translating 'academy'. The second edition of 1685, 'corrected and enlarged', includes a new ending in praise of *Paradise Lost* which may well constitute the first printed commendation of the poem.

Of the twenty to twenty-five works attributed to Roscommon, the most extensive of those not yet mentioned is his translation into French of Bishop William Sherlock's treatise *The Case of Resistance of the Supreme Powers*. This was undertaken in 1684 at the request of Roscommon's friend the duke of Ormond, and its purpose was evidently to show the French that the Church of England would no longer tolerate such defiance of the notion of divine right as was reflected in recent English history. Its anti-republican stance conforms with Roscommon's own conservative sympathies.

During the 1680s Roscommon must have spent part of his time in Ireland. He was given a new troop of horse there in 1682, and sought the post of master of the ordnance in Ireland in 1684. But he had apparently also been master of the horse to the duchess of York for some years before his death; evidently he had duties in both London and Ireland. A few days before his death, which occurred at his home at St James's Park, St Martin-in-the-Fields, London, on 17 January 1685, he requested a friend, probably Chetwood, who recounts the story in his memoir of Roscommon, to preach a sermon to him at St James's Chapel. He went in spite of warnings, saying that, like Charles V, he would hear his own funeral oration. Returning home he wrote, Chetwood says (Chetwood, fol. 44), 'an excellent divine poem', which, however, the physicians would not allow him to finish. Fenton's less plausible account, in which Roscommon's death is brought about suddenly by a quack remedy for gout, has the dying earl pronounce with fervour two lines of his own version of the 'Dies irae':

My God, my Father, and my Friend,
Do not forsake me at my end.

He was buried with great pomp in Westminster Abbey, 'neare the Shrine staires', on 21 January 1685 (Chester, 212). STUART GILLESPIE

Sources C. A. Niemeyer, 'The life and works of the earl of Roscommon', PhD diss., Harvard U., 1933 · *The works of Edmund Waller*, ed. E. Fenton (1730) · K. Chetwood [Chetwode], 'A short account of…Wentworth earle of Roscommon', CUL, MS Mm.1.47 · C. Niemeyer, 'The earl of Roscommon's academy', *Modern Language Notes*, 49 (1934), 432–7 · C. Niemeyer, 'A Roscommon canon', *Studies in Philology*, 36 (1939), 622–36 · J. Aubrey, *Miscellanies*, new edn (1784) · Wood, *Ath. Oxon.: Fasti*, new edn · GEC, *Peerage*, new edn · J. L. Chester, ed., *The marriage, baptismal, and burial registers of the collegiate church or abbey of St Peter, Westminster*, Harleian Society, 10 (1876) · *CSP Ire.*, 1663–5 · J. Childs, *The army of Charles II* (1976)
Archives LMA, corresp. | BL, letters, Stowe MSS
Likenesses C. Maratti, oils, *c*.1658, priv. coll.

Dillon, Sir William Henry (1780–1857), naval officer, the illegitimate son of John Talbot *Dillon (1734–1806) and Elizabeth, daughter of Henry Collins, was born in Birmingham on 8 August 1780. He claimed paternal descent from Logon Delome, son of O'Neill, monarch of Ireland. Entering the navy in May 1790, he served as a midshipman under Captain Gambier in the *Defence*, and was stunned by a splinter in Lord Howe's battle of 1 June 1794 in the north Atlantic. He was present in Lord Bridport's action off the Île de Groix on 23 June 1795, and at the capture of St Lucia in May 1796, when he carried a flag of truce to take possession of Pigeon Island. Promoted lieutenant on 29 April 1797, he was serving in the *Glenmore* in 1798 when he co-operated with the army at Wexford during the rebellion. Here he arrested the Irish chief Skallian. As senior lieutenant of the *Africaine*, he was sent with a flag of truce from Lord Keith to the Dutch commodore Valterbach, at Helvoetsluys, where he was made prisoner in breach of the truce, on 20 July 1803. He was then handed over to the French, and detained in captivity until September 1807. In the meantime (8 April 1805) he had been made a commander, and after his release he took command of an old, worn-out sloop, the *Childers*, carrying only fourteen 12-pounder carronades and sixty-five men. On 14 March 1808, on the coast of Norway, the *Childers* drove off a Danish brig of twenty guns and one hundred and sixty men after a long action. Dillon was severely wounded, and his bravery was acknowledged by the Patriotic Fund at Lloyd's by the presentation of a sword valued at 100 guineas. After obtaining his post commission (21 March 1808) he served at Walcheren, on the coasts of Portugal and Spain, at Newfoundland, in China and India, and finally, between 1835 and 1838, in the Mediterranean, in command of the *Russell* (74 guns), when he rendered great service to the Spanish legitimist cause. He was made naval equerry to the duke of Sussex, and obtained flag rank on 9 November 1846. He was nominated KCH on 13 January 1835, was knighted by his long-time friend William IV at St James's Palace, on 24 June of the same year, and in 1839 received the good-service pension. He became vice-admiral of the blue on 5 March 1853, and of the red in 1857. Dillon was a short, lightly built man, an accomplished linguist and a pronounced tory in politics. He was married three times, but had no children. His first wife, *née* Roberts, the widow of a man named Voller, he married on 22 September 1808; they separated in November 1813. In September 1832 he married Isabella (d. 2 Nov 1842), daughter of John Willan of Hatton Garden, London, and on 6 June 1843 Elizabeth (d. 1887), eldest daughter of J. T. Pettigrew of Savile Row, London. Dillon died at Monaco on 9 September 1857, leaving in manuscript an account of his professional career, with a description of the many scenes in which he had been engaged. This was subsequently (1953–6) published by the Navy Records Society.

G. C. BOASE, *rev.* ANDREW LAMBERT

Sources W. H. Dillon, *A narrative of my professional adventures (1790–1839)*, ed. M. A. Lewis, 2 vols., Navy RS, 93, 97 (1953–6) · *GM*, 3rd ser., 3 (1857), 460 · Boase, *Mod. Eng. biog.* · O'Byrne, *Naval biog. dict.* · *The Times* (22 Sept 1857), 12
Archives Duke U., Perkins L., corresp.
Likenesses Baugniet, lithograph, 1852, NMM

Dillwyn, (Elizabeth) Amy (1845–1935), novelist and businesswoman, was born at Parc Wern, Sketty, Swansea, on 16 May 1845, the second daughter and third child in the family of three daughters and one son of Lewis Llewelyn *Dillwyn (1814–1892), an industrialist and Liberal MP for Swansea (1855–92), and his wife, Elizabeth (Bessie) De la Beche (1819–1866), the only legitimate daughter of the geologist Sir Henry Thomas De la *Beche. She was the granddaughter of Lewis Weston *Dillwyn, owner of the famous Cambrian pottery, and great-granddaughter of William Dillwyn, the American Quaker abolitionist. Educated privately at home by tutors and governesses, first at Parc Wern and later at Hendrefoilan, her father's new mansion at Sketty, she inherited a long family tradition of unorthodox and innovative ideas. Shortly after her début in London society in 1863 she became engaged to Llewellyn Thomas of Llwynmadog, the heir to a large coal fortune, but his early death from smallpox in 1864 on the eve of their wedding left her to face a lifetime of spinsterhood and good works, divided between Swansea and her London home in fashionable Knightsbridge.

Bored with the formalities of mid-Victorian high society, scornfully documented in her private diaries, Amy Dillwyn sought refuge in a form of neurasthenia and turned her hand to writing popular fiction, producing half a dozen still very readable novels which reflected her rebellious discontent with women's role as second-class citizens in a world often dominated by relatively untalented men. *Chloe Arguelle* (1881) and *Jill and Jack* (1887) are typical examples of her ability to combine trenchant social criticism with a positive affirmation of women's rights. Having thus resigned herself to the passive lifestyle of a semi-invalid literary lady, she became a regular contributor to *The Spectator*, then edited by her father's close friend Richard Holt Hutton, and between 1880 and 1893 published over fifty articles in it. But when her father, the widely respected leader of the Welsh radicals in parliament, died suddenly in 1892 she found to her horror that he had left a crippling burden of debt and that his principal business enterprise, the Dillwyn spelterworks at Llansamlet, Swansea, was on the verge of financial ruin and was now her personal responsibility as his residuary legatee.

Determined to honour the family tradition of social concern, Amy Dillwyn forgot her various ailments, put aside her unfinished literary manuscripts, and took on the onerous commitment of managing one of the most important zinc factories in the United Kingdom at a time when women were virtually excluded from the boardrooms of industry and commerce. After several years of sheer hard work and dedicated self-sacrifice, which involved giving up her fine home, Hendrefoilan House, and living in cheap lodgings, she finally turned the ailing enterprise around and by 1904 was able to sell her shares in Dillwyn & Co. at a very substantial profit to Metallgesellschaft of Frankfurt, the German industrial giant then striving to create an international monopoly of zinc manufacture.

By 1902 Amy Dillwyn's fame as a hard-headed businesswoman, capable of holding her own with the shrewdest of her male rivals in the intensely competitive world of industry, had already won her recognition (from the *Pall Mall Gazette*) as 'one of the most remarkable women in Great Britain', famous enough to be caricatured by the *Punch* cartoonist Bert Thomas in the comic journal *Ally Sloper* in 1904. For a brief period she became a national celebrity, often portrayed by her contemporaries as a spare, bespectacled woman wearing the plainest of short serge skirts with a pocket on each side in which she buried her hands when talking, a short, rather mannish jacket, a trilby hat, and a simple bunch of violets at her throat, and carrying a stick or umbrella and striding out in a thoroughly businesslike manner. Staunchly Liberal like her father and an ardent but always non-violent feminist, she campaigned vigorously for women's rights, fought hard to improve rudimentary state education and medical services, and was one of the first women to stand for election to a borough council after the passing of the Qualification of Women Act in 1907. By this time she was consciously beginning to play the role that most appealed to her ironic sense of self-awareness: the rather eccentric and certainly unorthodox grand old lady of her native Swansea, whose celebrated love of a good cigar, smoked in public, masked a deep attachment to the humanitarian principles instilled into her by her Quaker family background. Yet for all her passionate dedication to public service she also knew how to enjoy herself, and as an elderly lady she was often seen at the gaming tables of Monte Carlo in the late 1920s, savouring to the full the social pleasures made possible by her unique commercial success.

Amy Dillwyn died in her ninety-first year at her home, Tŷ-Glyn, West Cross, Swansea, on 13 December 1935, leaving a personal fortune of £114,500—striking testimony to her rare achievement as a businesswoman in a man's world. She was cremated without ceremony at Pontypridd, and her ashes were laid to rest in the Dillwyn family grave at St Paul's Church, Sketty, Swansea.

DAVID PAINTING

Sources D. Painting, *Amy Dillwyn* (1987) · private information (2004) · L. W. Dillwyn, diaries, NL Wales · L. L. Dillwyn, diaries, U. Wales, Swansea · contributors' file, 1880–93, *The Spectator* · *The Times* (14 Dec 1935) · *Daily Telegraph* (14 Dec 1935) · *Daily Express* (14 Dec 1935) · *Daily Mirror* (14 Dec 1935) · *Western Mail* [Cardiff] (14 Dec 1935)
Archives priv. coll. · priv. coll., family MSS
Likenesses B. Thomas, cartoon, repro. in *Ally Sloper* (July 1904) · photographs, priv. coll.
Wealth at death £114,513 7s. 9d.: resworn probate, 27 Jan 1936, CGPLA Eng. & Wales

Dillwyn, Lewis Llewelyn (1814–1892), industrialist and politician, was born on 19 May 1814 at The Willows, Swansea, the fourth of the six children of Lewis Weston *Dillwyn (1778–1855), botanist and MP, and his wife, Mary Adams (1776–1865), natural daughter of John Llewelyn of Penlle'r-gaer, Glamorgan (she retained her mother's surname). He had two brothers and three sisters: his elder brother was John Dillwyn *Llewelyn, a pioneer photographer. His grandfather was the American Quaker William Dillwyn, who had worked closely with Clarkson and Wilberforce for the abolition of the slave trade.

Lewis Dillwyn was educated at Kilvert's academy, Bath, and was intended for Oriel College, Oxford, but when his father became one of Glamorgan's MPs in the Reform parliament of 1832 he was obliged to take over the family business as manager of the Cambrian pottery at Swansea. On 16 August 1838 he married Elizabeth (1819–1866), only legitimate daughter of the eminent geologist Henry De la *Beche, and with her artistic help the pottery produced the beautiful Etruscan ware which is now a collector's item. They had four children, the best-known of whom was Amy *Dillwyn, and the family made their home at a newly built neo-Gothic mansion called Hendrefoilan.

As mayor of Swansea, Dillwyn acted as host to the British Association meeting of 1848 and used the opportunity to initiate a scheme of urban improvement which secured the town's supply of pure water and the paving and naming of its streets. In February 1855 he was elected

Lewis Llewelyn Dillwyn (1814–1892), by James Andrews

Liberal MP for Swansea District, a seat he held until his death. He began to expand his extensive industrial interests to include silver refining and later entered into partnership with William Siemens to establish the Landore Siemens Steel Co., which by 1874 had become one of the four largest producers in the world, employing some 2000 workers. When the steel industry slumped in the 1880s, he concentrated his principal manufacturing activities on his Dillwyn spelter works at Llansamlet, Swansea, and soon became one of the major zinc producers in the country. He was an assiduous director of the Great Western Railway Co., chairman of the Glamorganshire Banking Co., and owner of several collieries. His leisure was devoted to shooting, watercolour painting, and playing chess at the Athenaeum with his close friend R. H. Hutton.

As a parliamentarian Dillwyn achieved a solid reputation as an advanced radical who led the Welsh Liberal Party for many years from his regular corner seat below the gangway. He was a poor speaker but a dogged and universally respected critic of clerical privilege. Although an Anglican, he supported the campaigns of the Liberation Society to remove the privileges of the established church. He introduced bills in 1860 and 1863 to enable dissenters to be elected as trustees of endowed schools. His famous motion on the Church of Ireland (28 March 1865)

influenced Gladstone's gradual move towards disestablishment. From 1883 he moved annual resolutions in favour of disestablishment of the Anglican church in Wales, and he supported the Denbighshire tenantry in their resistance to tithes during 1886–7. During the passage of the second Reform Bill Dillwyn's intervention as a leading member of the 'Tea Room' cabal of disaffected Liberals in April 1867 helped to bring about household suffrage, a measure that was to have far-reaching consequences for democracy in Great Britain. Like other Welsh radicals, after 1886 he was a firm supporter of Irish home rule.

Caricatured by *Vanity Fair* as a 'Wet Quaker' (although his father had married out of the Society of Friends in 1807), Dillwyn embodied many of the moral values espoused by his Quaker forebears and well deserved the accolade of Rugged Honesty bestowed on him by his parliamentary colleagues. Dillwyn was still campaigning vigorously when he collapsed and died of a heart attack on 19 June 1892 at the Royal Hotel, Swansea, during the general election of that year. He was buried in the family grave in St Paul's churchyard, Sketty, Swansea. His only son, Henry, a hard-drinking barrister on the South Wales circuit, had died unmarried two years earlier and the Hendrefoilan estate passed to Dillwyn's grandson John, son of his eldest daughter, Mary Nicholl of Merthyr Mawr, near Bridgend. DAVID PAINTING

Sources Boase, *Mod. Eng. biog.* · *DWB* · J. Morley, *The life of William Ewart Gladstone*, 3 vols. (1903) · M. Cowling, *1867: Disraeli, Gladstone and revolution* (1967) · D. Painting, *Amy Dillwyn* (1987) · H. W. Lucy, *A diary of two parliaments*, 2 vols. (1885–6) · F. B. Smith, *The making of the second Reform Bill* (1966) · *The Cambrian* (24 June 1892) · *CGPLA Eng. & Wales* (1892) · private information (1987, 2004)

Archives NL Wales, catalogue and notes relating to fauna of Swansea · NL Wales, papers · U. Wales, Swansea, corresp., travel journals, and papers

Likenesses J. Andrews, photograph, NPG [*see illus.*] · J. D. Llewelyn, photographs, Swansea city council, photographic archives · Spy [L. Ward], cartoon, NPG; repro. in *VF* (13 May 1882) · portrait, repro. in *ILN* (25 June 1892), 782

Wealth at death £7819 19s. 11d.: probate, 22 July 1892, *CGPLA Eng. & Wales*

Dillwyn, Lewis Weston (1778–1855), naturalist and porcelain manufacturer, was born on 21 August 1778 at St Thomas's Square, Hackney, the son of William Dillwyn (1743?–1824), merchant, of Higham Lodge, Walthamstow, and his wife, Sarah, daughter of Lewis Weston of Highall, Essex. He was descended from a Welsh Quaker family who had emigrated to Pennsylvania at the end of the seventeenth century. His father, who was born and lived much of his life in America, was a prominent campaigner against slavery. He received his early education at a Friends' school at Tottenham, where he became acquainted with his lifelong friend, Joseph Woods (1776–1864), with whom he was sent to Folkestone on account of his then weak health. In 1798 he went to Dover and there began his study of plants. He became a fellow of the Linnean Society in 1800 and subsequently reported to it on his observations.

In 1802 Dillwyn's father bought the Cambrian pottery at

Swansea, placing him at its head, and in 1803 he moved there from Walthamstow. He began publishing his principal botanical work, the *Natural History of British Confervae* in 1802, and in 1805 he and Dawson Turner published the *Botanist's Guide through England and Wales*. His interest in natural history was turned to good account in business, and his porcelain became celebrated for the true and spirited paintings on it of butterflies, flowers, birds, and shells, besides the beauty of the material itself. It attained its greatest renown about 1814, after which its production was abandoned for ordinary earthenware, the staple product of the works.

In 1807 Dillwyn married Mary Adams (1776–1865), the natural daughter of John Llewelyn of Penlle'r-gaer, Llangyfelach, Glamorgan; she retained her mother's surname. They had three sons and three daughters. Their son John Dillwyn *Llewelyn (1810–1882) was a photographer and experimental scientist, who worked with Sir Charles Wheatstone on the experiments on the submarine electric telegraph made in Swansea Bay in 1844. Their son Lewis Llewelyn *Dillwyn MP (1814–1892) was a prominent Welsh Liberal. Amy *Dillwyn, successful businesswoman and colourful feminist, was one of their grandchildren. Although Dillwyn obliged to leave the Society of Friends for marrying a non-Quaker, his younger son was seen as continuing in the tradition of Quaker political radicalism.

Dillwyn was elected a fellow of the Royal Society in 1804. In 1809 he toured Killarney, Ireland. He kept a diary of his observations on natural history there. In the same year he completed his *British Confervae*. Eight years later in 1817, he brought out *A Descriptive Catalogue of British Shells*. He was a good friend of Sir Joseph Banks, whose library he used to prepare his book on shells. In 1823 his *Index to the Historia conchyliorum of Lister* was printed at the Oxford Clarendon Press at the cost of the university, which on this occasion offered him the honorary degree of DCL, which he declined. In 1823 and 1824 he sent Sir Humphrey Davy, president of the Royal Society, his observations on fossil shells and his ideas about the 'relative periods at which the different families of testaceous animals appear to have been created' (Royal Society Archives, PT 17. 12). These were subsequently published in the *Philosophical Transactions*.

Dillwyn was returned in 1832 to the first parliament to sit after the Reform Act as member for Glamorgan, of which he had been a magistrate for some years, and high sheriff in 1818. He supported the whigs and was not sympathetic to calls for further constitutional reform. The freedom of the borough of Swansea was presented to him in 1834, and from 1835 to 1840 he served as alderman and mayor. He gave up parliamentary duties in 1837.

As a prominent local manufacturer and MP Dillwyn supported local causes, donating some of the profits from his *Contributions towards a History of Swansea* (1840) to Swansea Infirmary. He cordially welcomed the British Association to Swansea in 1848, was one of the vice-presidents of that meeting, and produced for the occasion his *Flora and Fauna of Swansea*. This was his last literary production; his health

gradually declined, and for some years before his death he withdrew from outside pursuits. He died at his home, Sketty Hall, Glamorgan, on 31 August 1855.

B. D. JACKSON, *rev.* ALEXANDER GOLDBLOOM

Sources *Proceedings of the Linnean Society of London* (1855–6), xxxvi–xxxix · *Biographical catalogue: being an account of the lives of Friends and others whose portraits are in the London Friends' Institute*, Society of Friends (1888) · *DWB* · RS · *WWBMP* · Desmond, *Botanists*, rev. edn · R. B. Mosse, *The parliamentary circle* (1836) · private information (2004)
Archives Linn. Soc., catalogue of insects · NL Wales, corresp. and papers; diaries relating to estate, local bench, and political affairs · RBG Kew · RS Friends, Lond. · TCD, travel journal · V&A NAL, receipt book for glazes | BL, corresp. with Sir Joseph Banks · NL Wales, letters to J. M. Traherne · NRA, corresp. with Sir Joseph Banks
Likenesses E. U. Eddis, engraving, 1833, RS · T. G. Davies, group portrait (*Lewis Weston Dillwyn and his doctors*), repro. in *Morganawg*, 32 (1988), 70–89 · G. Hayter, group portrait, oils (*The House of Commons, 1833*), NPG · lithograph (after E. U. Eddis), BM · portrait, Royal Institution of Great Britain, London · portrait, Carnegie Mellon University, Pittsburgh, Hunt Botanical Library · portrait, NMG Wales; repro. in *Guide to the collection of Welsh porcelain* (1931)

Dilly, Charles (1739–1807), bookseller, was born on 22 May 1739 at Southill, Bedfordshire, the third son of Thomas Dilly, a substantial yeoman farmer. The family had been based in Southill for at least two centuries, according to James Boswell. On 1 June 1756 he was bound as an apprentice to his elder brother Edward *Dilly (1732–1779), a bookseller established at the sign of Rose and Crown at 22 Poultry, London, and was freed on 7 June 1763; he became a liveryman of the Stationers' Company on the same day. He made a short trip to America, visiting Philadelphia in 1764, but was back in London by spring that year when he became a junior partner in his brother's successful bookselling business.

During the years of their partnership the Dillys produced a great number and range of titles, with a particular specialism in dissenting and 'American' literature, reflecting the brothers' whig and patriot political sympathies. The brothers were well known for their support of their authors—they practically adopted James Boswell, who said they made him feel 'like blood relations'—and Charles in particular was described as 'a kind and faithful adviser' to 'young and inexperienced authors' (*Boswell in Search of a Wife*, 151; Nichols, *Lit. anecdotes*, 3.191). Their premises in the Poultry, in which they both lived and worked, became an important nexus for social, political, and literary figures; Benjamin Rush described their shop as a 'kind of Coffee house for authors' (Rush, *Autobiography*, 62–3). In particular, the brothers threw legendary dinner parties, which attracted high praise from Nichols and Richard Cumberland among others. The company was varied—Samuel Johnson was a frequent guest—and was by no means limited to those who shared the brothers' religious or political beliefs.

Charles Dilly remained very much the junior partner until Edward's death in 1779, after which he carried on the business in his own name. However, the character and volume of the firm's output did not significantly change. Nichols noted that, on his brother's death, Charles 'became the sole proprietor of a very valuable trading concern, which he continued to cultivate with that industry and application which ... leads to opulence' (Nichols, *Lit. anecdotes*, 3.191). Charles also had interests in the *London Magazine* until its demise in 1787, and by 1792 had become a partner in the *London Packet, or, New Lloyd's Evening Post*. Politically more moderate than his brother, he was a member of John Cartwright's Society for Constitutional Information, and was also one of the controversial 'pro-Americans' who supported the colonies during their campaign and eventual war for independence. This did not prevent him from being approached to serve as an alderman and as a sheriff of London, both offers he declined, the latter on grounds of his religious nonconformity. He did, however, accept promotion within the Stationers' Company during the 1790s, eventually serving as the company's master for 1802–3.

At the end of January 1800 Dilly sold the firm to Joseph Mawman of York and retired to Clophill, Bedfordshire. However, he did not take well to his retirement, and returned to London life about 1802, living in Brunswick Row, Queen Square, in Holborn. A sudden 'oppression of breath' afflicted him on 3 May 1807 while visiting his friend Richard Cumberland at Ramsgate, at whose house he died the following day (*GM*, 1807, 480). He was buried on 12 May in St George the Martyr, Queen Square, London. Like his brother—and indeed like his two other siblings—he was unmarried, and his substantial estate (estimated at nearly £60,000) passed primarily to maternal relations. Mawman succeeded to the business although the exact timing and terms of the handover are unclear.

The third Dilly brother, **John Dilly** (1731–1806), gentleman, was born at Southill, Bedfordshire, in 1731, the eldest son of Thomas Dilly. He was known almost entirely on account of kinship to his bookselling brothers—Boswell nicknamed him Squire Dilly (Tinker, 2.285). He 'cultivated the paternal inheritance' at Southill, and maintained the family image as 'of some consequence in the higher ranks of old English yeomen' (Bingham, 1–2). He was elected high sheriff of the county in 1783, and died a bachelor on 18 March 1806 at Clophill, Bedfordshire, while visiting Charles. J. J. CAUDLE

Sources S. H. Bingham, 'Publishing in the eighteenth century with special reference to the firm of Edward and Charles Dilly', PhD diss., Yale U., 1937 • D. W. Hollis, 'Edward and Charles Dilly', *The British literary book trade, 1700–1820*, ed. J. K. Bracken and J. Silver, DLitB, 154 (1995), 97–102 • Nichols, *Lit. anecdotes*, esp. 3.190–93 • *Boswell in search of a wife, 1766–1769*, ed. F. Brady and F. A. Pottle (1957), vol. 6 of *The Yale editions of the private papers of James Boswell*, trade edn (1950–89) • *A catalogue of books printed for, and sold by Charles Dilly, in London* (1787) • R. Cumberland, *Memoirs of Richard Cumberland written by himself*, 2 vols. (1806–7), esp. vol. 2, pp. 199–200, 226–9 • L. H. Butterfield, 'The American interests of the firm E. and C. Dilly, with their letters to Benjamin Rush, 1770–1795', *Papers of the Bibliographical Society of America*, 45 (1951), 283–332 • J. Boswell, *The life of Samuel Johnson*, 3rd edn, 4 vols. (1799) • H. R. Plomer and others, *A dictionary of the printers and booksellers who were at work in England, Scotland, and Ireland from 1726 to 1775* (1932), 74–5, 186–7 • I. Maxted, *The London book trades, 1775–1800: a preliminary checklist of members* (1977) • *Letters of James Boswell*, ed. C. B. Tinker, 2 (1924), 285 • *GM*, 1st ser., 49 (1779), 271; 76 (1806), 874; 77 (1807), 478–80 •

Annual Register (1783), 235 • *London Chronicle*, 45.454 • B. Rush, *Letters*, ed. L. H. Butterfield, 2 vols. (1951) • *The general correspondence of James Boswell, 1766–1769*, ed. R. C. Cole and others, 1 (1993), vol. 5 of *The Yale editions of the private papers of James Boswell*, research edn • *The correspondence and other papers of James Boswell relating to the making of the 'Life of Johnson'*, ed. M. Waingrow, rev. edn (2001) • *The letters of Samuel Johnson*, ed. B. Redford, 3–4 (1992–4) • K. A. Esdaile, 'A footnote to Boswell', *TLS* (23 Oct 1937), 783 • *The autobiography of Benjamin Rush: his 'Travels through life' together with his commonplace book for 1789–1813*, ed. G. W. Corner (1948) • C. Bonwick, *English radicals and the American revolution* (1977) • F. G. Emmison, ed., *Bedfordshire parish registers* (1931–53)

Archives BL, assignment of share in *Nugent's French Dictionary*, Add. MS 38730 • Library Company of Philadelphia, Benjamin Rush papers and John Dickinson papers, letters • Mass. Hist. Soc., Josiah Quincy jun. and Jeremy Belknap papers, letters • New York Historical Society, New York, Jedediah Morse papers, letters • Yale U., Morse papers, letters • Yale U., Beinecke L., corresp. with James Boswell

Wealth at death £60,000; incl. various bequests totalling £4400; Charles Dilly: Bingham, 'Publishing', 29–32

Dilly, Edward (1732–1779), bookseller, was born on 25 July 1732 at Southill, Bedfordshire, the second son of Thomas Dilly, a substantial yeoman farmer. According to James Boswell, the Dilly family had lived there for at least two centuries. He was the brother of John *Dilly (1731–1806) [*see under* Dilly, Charles] and Charles *Dilly (1739–1807). Bound as an apprentice to the London bookseller John Oswald on 6 December 1748, he was freed by redemption on 11 June 1754. In the following year he succeeded to Oswald's shop at the sign of Rose and Crown at 22 Poultry near the Mansion House, which remained with the family until the 1800s. In 1756 he took on his younger brother Charles as an apprentice; in 1764 Charles joined him as a junior partner in the business. The firm's output was prodigious and varied, including religious, historical, medical, legal, philosophical, mathematical, and literary works; the Dillys also gained a notable reputation for promoting dissenting and 'American' material. Nichols described Edward as 'a Bookseller of great eminence ... particularly in the line of American exportation; and in the Writings of the good old School of Presbyterians' (Nichols, *Lit. anecdotes*, 3.190). He maintained commercial interests in a number of newspapers including both the *Public Advertiser* and the *London Magazine*. He also was a generous and effective literary patron, supporting James Beattie and Elizabeth Montagu among others.

Edward was described by Charles as 'a good-natured and well-disposed man ... the useful man in business', but lamented that he was 'dreadfully contaminated with false ideas in politics': 'to a stranger he must and does appear in a disagreeable point of view' ('Letters to Josiah Quincy', 492). This obsession was underlined in an account of him by Elizabeth Fothergill: 'Politics is his constant theme, and he will force one's attention whether one will give it or not' (J. J. Abraham, *Lettsom; his Life, Times, Friends and Descendants*, 1933, 94). He was a loyal supporter of John Wilkes and fiercely pro-American, and even proved himself to be a fairly competent political writer. None the less, the brothers were famed for their wide and remarkably diverse social circle, which included many 'patriots', 'true whigs', and crypto-republicans as well as a number of their political opponents. Notable friends included John Wilkes, Catharine Macaulay, Benjamin Rush, Benjamin Franklin, Samuel Johnson (who first met Wilkes at a dinner party hosted by Edward), and James Oglethorpe, as well as clergymen and ministers from a wide variety of religious persuasions. Nichols underlined the brothers' trait of cheerful sociability when he famously observed that Edward was 'a man of great pleasantry of manners; and so fond of conversation, that he almost literally *talked himself to death*' (Nichols, *Lit. anecdotes*, 3.191). Fothergill went further: Edward was 'one of the greatest talkers I ever met with, tongue, hands, and head all moving at a time with so much rapidity that I wonder how his lungs sustain it' (Abraham, *Lettsom*, 94).

The brothers, neither of whom married, lived upstairs from their shop in the Poultry; they also inhabited a country house near Hemel Hempstead, and were regular visitors to their native Southill. Edward's health declined from March 1778 and he died from consumption on 11 May 1779 at Southill, in whose churchyard he was buried. His will, dated 8 February 1779 and proved on 13 May 1780, named Charles as administrator and residuary legatee, and Charles continued the business until his own retirement.   J. J. CAUDLE

Sources S. H. Bingham, 'Publishing in the eighteenth century with special reference to the firm of Edward and Charles Dilly', PhD diss., Yale U., 1937 · D. W. Hollis, 'Edward and Charles Dilly', *The British literary book trade, 1700–1820*, ed. J. K. Bracken and J. Silver, DLitB, 154 (1995), 97–102 · Nichols, *Lit. anecdotes*, esp. 3.190–93 · *Boswell in search of a wife, 1766–1769*, ed. F. Brady and F. A. Pottle (1957) · *A catalogue of books printed for, and sold by Charles Dilly, in London* (1787) · R. Cumberland, *Memoirs of Richard Cumberland written by himself*, 2 vols. (1806–7), esp. vol. 2, pp. 199–200, 226–9 · L. H. Butterfield, 'The American interests of the firm of E. and C. Dilly, with their letters to Benjamin Rush, 1770–1795', *Papers of the Bibliographical Society of America*, 45 (1951), 283–332 · J. Boswell, *The life of Samuel Johnson*, 3rd edn, 4 vols. (1799) · H. R. Plomer and others, *A dictionary of the printers and booksellers who were at work in England, Scotland, and Ireland from 1726 to 1775* (1932), 74–5, 186–7 · I. Maxted, *The London book trades, 1775–1800: a preliminary checklist of members* (1977) · D. F. McKenzie, ed., *Stationers' Company apprentices*, [3]: *1701–1800* (1978) · *Letters of James Boswell*, ed. C. B. Tinker, 2 (1924), 285 · *GM*, 1st ser., 49 (1779), 271; 76 (1806), 874; 77 (1807), 478–80 · *Annual Register* (1783), 235 · *London Chronicle*, 45, 454 · B. Rush, *Letters*, ed. L. H. Butterfield, 2 vols. (1951) · *The general correspondence of James Boswell, 1766–1769*, ed. R. C. Cole and others, 1 (1993), vol. 5 of *The Yale editions of the private papers of James Boswell*, research edn · *The correspondence and other papers of James Boswell relating to the making of the 'Life of Johnson'*, ed. M. Waingrow, rev. edn (2001) · *The letters of Samuel Johnson*, ed. B. Redford, 3–4 (1992–4) · K. A. Esdaile, 'A footnote to Boswell', *TLS* (23 Oct 1937), 783 · 'Letters to Josiah Quincy, Jr.', *Massachusetts Historical Society: Proceedings*, 50 (1917), 492 · 'Journal of Josiah Quincy, jun., during his voyage and residence in England from September 28th, 1774, to March 3d, 1775', *Massachusetts Historical Society: Proceedings*, 50 (1917), 433–70 · F. G. Emmison, ed., *Bedfordshire parish registers* (1931–53)

Archives Library Company of Philadelphia, Benjamin Rush papers and John Dickinson papers, letters · Mass. Hist. Soc., Josiah Quincy jun., and Jeremy Belknap papers · Yale U., Morse papers, letters · Yale U., Beinecke L., corresp. with James Boswell

Dilly, John (1731–1806). *See under* Dilly, Charles (1739–1807).

Dimbleby, Richard Frederick (1913–1965), radio and television broadcaster, was born on 25 May 1913 at Richmond, Surrey, the elder child and only son of Frederick Jabez George Dimbleby (1876–1943), journalist and local newspaper proprietor, and Gwendoline Bolwell (b. 1886), daughter of a Bath surveyor. The families of both parents were low-church, committed to temperance, and supporters of the Liberal Party. Dimbleby's mother—as a girl she had wanted to go on the stage—was a pillar of the Richmond Operatic and Dramatic societies. His father combined a succession of jobs in Fleet Street with editorial control of the family newspaper, the *Richmond and Twickenham Times*; during the First World War he worked in Whitehall as a government public relations officer. Dimbleby went to a preparatory school near Battle in Sussex and in 1927 to Mill Hill School, then on the northern outskirts of London. He was an amiable, idle boy; broad and heavy even in his teens, he disliked organized games and was happiest when messing about in boats. He excelled only at music; having passed matriculation at the third attempt he left school at eighteen and started work on the family paper.

After brief spells as a reporter in Hampshire and on the staff of the *Advertiser's Weekly*, Dimbleby was taken on by the BBC. In 1936 Britain's 'national instrument of broadcasting' relied for its news reports on the agencies. Dimbleby had suggested to the BBC's chief news editor that there were ways in which the *News* might be enlivened without robbing it of authority and boldly proposed recruiting to the staff a number of reporters or correspondents. This revolutionary idea was not immediately adopted, but Dimbleby soon attracted attention by his enthusiasm for eyewitness reports and authentic sound effects; when covering the story of a record-breaking new train, he spent much of the journey recording the sound of the wheels by dangling a microphone down a lavatory pan.

Dimbleby reported the royal tour of Canada in the spring of 1939—the first to include a BBC correspondent—and on the day war was declared he put on uniform as the BBC's first war correspondent (although he had been briefly in Spain as an 'observer' earlier in the year). He experienced the frustrations of the phoney war in France (and of explaining his expense claims to BBC administrators—after recording a Christmas programme in a casualty clearing station, he thought it fitting that the corporation should foot the bill for the turkey and plum pudding). Before disaster overtook the British expeditionary force he was sent to the Middle East, and over the next two years he witnessed the campaigns in Libya and Eritrea, saw fighting in Albania and Greece, and was ambushed by guerrillas in Iran.

In 1942 Dimbleby was recalled to London, a victim of the internecine warfare that was being waged between the war cabinet in Whitehall and Middle East command, and between a romantic and stubborn prime minister at home and his cool-headed but equally obdurate commander in the field. 'I found', General Wavell noted drily, 'that Winston's tactical ideas had to some extent crystallised at

Richard Frederick Dimbleby (1913–1965), by John Gay, 1949

the South African war' (Dimbleby, 106). Dimbleby, carefully briefed by Wavell's general headquarters, had been sending back dispatches which did nothing to ease the strained relations between the BBC and Whitehall. When he left Cairo, he was fêted by ministers, ambassadors, and army commanders. Godfrey Talbot, the BBC colleague sent out to replace him, said: 'I was a journalist succeeding a personality' (Dimbleby, 159).

Early in 1943 Dimbleby became the BBC's air correspondent; his first mission took him on a raid on Berlin in a Lancaster bomber. Shortly after D-day in 1944 he was appointed director of the war reporting unit. He himself reported the crossing of the Rhine. He was the first correspondent to enter Belsen, and he broadcast from there what his son Jonathan later described as 'an unforgettable, definitive statement about human atrocity' (Dimbleby, 190). Shortly afterwards, he was in Berlin. 'As a clean, solid, efficient city, it has ceased to exist', he reported. He broadcast one of his dispatches from the filth and rubble that had been Hitler's study in the chancellery, sitting in the Führer's chair.

When Dimbleby returned from Germany in the summer of 1945, his BBC salary was £1000. When the BBC refused to raise it by £100, he decided to resign and take his chance as a freelance. On 26 June 1937 he had married Dilys Violet Constance Thomas (b. 1913), who had been his father's personal assistant on the family paper. They already had two sons (both David and Jonathan were to follow their father into broadcasting), and they would later have a third son and a daughter.

Work came slowly, and Dimbleby was grateful when his uncle, none too willingly, offered him the editorship-in-chief of the family papers. (His father had died three years previously.) From television, which had been under wraps during the war, he earned less than £150 in his first two years as a freelance, but his versatility and professionalism soon attracted the attention of radio producers. He joined the new panel game *Twenty Questions* (the idea was imported from American radio). He also travelled the length and breadth of the country to interview people for *Down your Way*, a programme devised to get round the stringent restrictions imposed on the broadcasting of recorded music by the industrial muscle of the Musicians' Union.

By the early 1950s Dimbleby was in demand as a commentator for outside broadcasts. He described the lying-in-state of George VI, and at the coronation of Queen Elizabeth in 1953 it was Dimbleby's happy choice of words which added colour to the black and white images on the small screen. Dimbleby was also influential in the shaping of current affairs broadcasting—what he described as 'the big and vital field of topical but non-immediate news' (Dimbleby, 267). By the time the *Panorama* programme was launched in 1955 he was seen as the only possible presenter, and he remained as its anchorman for the rest of his life. Leonard Miall, who worked closely with him in those years, wrote that he 'almost acted as a national Ombudsman' (Miall, *Inside the BBC* 58). His bulk and his unflappability were hugely reassuring. During a programme on the Cuban missile crisis in 1962, a viewer telephoned to say she would send her children to school only if Richard Dimbleby said it was safe to do so.

Dimbleby's mastery of television techniques and the meticulous attention he paid to his 'homework' made him a natural choice for presenting the exhausting marathons screened at general election time. He also continued into the 1960s as the voice of the BBC on state and other important occasions—the first televised opening of parliament, Princess Margaret's wedding, the funeral of President Kennedy. To critics who complained that his tone was reverential, he would point out that a commentator at a solemn occasion who did not lower his voice to a hushed whisper might quickly be hustled off the premises.

The politics of broadcasting being what they are, Dimbleby had to contend with more than one attempt to dislodge him. As he moved into his fifties, however, he knew he was being stalked by an enemy more formidable than any of the BBC's young turks. By the time he delivered his moving commentary on the pageantry of Churchill's funeral in January 1965 Dimbleby had already been suffering from cancer for five years.

When he went into hospital and the nature of his illness was made known, he received 7000 letters. A woman travelled from the country to London with a basket of eggs; the queen sent six bottles of champagne to his bedside. He died on 22 December 1965, and his passing was marked by a memorial service in Westminster Abbey—the place he had sometimes called his 'workshop'. A quarter of a century later, a memorial plaque, sculpted by his third son,

Nicholas, was unveiled in Poets' Corner, an honour never previously accorded to a broadcaster.

Dimbleby's family life was richly contented. It had been his ambition as a young man to escape from suburbia into the English countryside, a dream he realized in 1952 with the purchase of a farm with 25 acres of grassland in Sussex. In his later years he was the proud owner of a succession of Rolls Royces; the honorary doctorate of laws conferred on him by the University of Sheffield was also a source of great pride. He was an enthusiastic pianist favouring, according to his son Jonathan, 'loud ringing chords and long ralentandos' (Dimbleby, 294). He was never happier than when on the water; when he covered the coronation in 1953, he operated from his Dutch sailing barge, *Vabel*, which he brought round from Chichester and moored in the Thames.

Dimbleby's broadcasting career spanned almost thirty years. In the last ten years of his life he was widely regarded as 'the voice of the BBC'. His personal and professional qualities were well summed up in Westminster Abbey by his old friend and colleague Wynford Vaughan-Thomas: 'We knew him as a simple man, a good man, and in the end a very brave man. Richard brought a sense of permanence to our impermanent profession' (Miall, 61).

IAN McINTYRE

Sources J. Dimbleby, *Richard Dimbleby: a biography* (1975) · A. Briggs, *The history of broadcasting in the United Kingdom*, rev. edn, 5 vols. (1995), vols. 2–5 · P. Scannell and D. Cardiff, *A social history of British broadcasting*, [1] (1991) · L. Miall, 'Richard Dimbleby', *Inside the BBC: British broadcasting characters* (1994), 53–61 · L. Miall, ed., *Richard Dimbleby, broadcaster* (1966) · DNB · CGPLA Eng. & Wales (1966)
Archives BBC WAC | FILM BBC WAC · BFI NFTVA, current affairs footage · BFI NFTVA, documentary footage · BFI NFTVA, performance footage · IWM FVA, *Panorama*, BBC2, 9 Jan 1995, 3023 · IWM FVA, performance footage | SOUND BBC WAC · BL NSA, 'Richard Dimbleby — voice of a nation', BBC, 1991, V6 951/01 · BL NSA, oral history interview · IWM SA, 'British broadcaster struggles to remain objective as he describes the scenes on the liberation of Bergen Belsen', BBC, 19 April 1945, 17714 · IWM SA, oral history interview · IWM SA, performance recording
Likenesses photographs, 1947–65, Hult. Arch. · J. Gay, photograph, 1949, NPG [*see illus.*] · photographs, repro. in Dimbleby, *Richard Dimbleby*, facing pp. 118, 246
Wealth at death £21,982: probate, 18 March 1966, CGPLA Eng. & Wales

Dimock, James Francis (1810–1876), Church of England clergyman and historian, second son in the family of three sons and five daughters of John Giles Dimock (1773–1858), rector of Uppingham, Rutland, and his wife, Sarah (1781/2–1851), daughter of William Humphries of Baldock, Hertfordshire, was born at Stonehouse, Gloucestershire, where his father owned land, on 22 November 1810. He was educated at Uppingham School under Dr Josiah Buckland, was admitted pensioner of St John's College, Cambridge, in 1829, and was elected Bell's scholar in 1830. He graduated BA as twenty-eighth wrangler in 1833, and MA in 1837. Having been ordained deacon (1836) and priest (1837) by the bishop of Lincoln, he published a commentary on the Thirty-Nine Articles (1843) and a sermon on the holy communion (1844). In 1846 he was appointed minor

canon of Southwell; he gave up the canonry in 1863 on his appointment as rector of Barnborough, near Doncaster, a living in the gift of Southwell collegiate church. In 1869 he was made prebendary of Lincoln, and he held the prebend with his rectory until his death. Dimock married in 1841 Caroline (d. 1890), daughter of John Tatam of Moulton, Lincolnshire, with whom he had eight sons and six daughters. He died at Barnborough on 22 April 1876, and was buried there on 26 April.

Dimock was deeply interested in ecclesiastical and medieval history; his earliest work was *Illustrations of the Collegiate Church of Southwell* (1854). In 1860 he published at Lincoln an edition of the *Metrical Life of St Hugh*, and in 1864 he edited for the Rolls Series the *Magna vita S. Hugonis, episcopi Lincolniensis* (1864). This was the first complete text of the life of St Hugh to be published and, although later superseded, Dimock's work received favourable notice from the editors of a subsequent standard edition (2 vols., 1985; eds D. L. Douie and D. H. Farmer). His most important work remains his edition of part of the works of Giraldus Cambrensis (Gerald of Wales) for the Rolls Series; the first four volumes were edited by J. S. Brewer, and volumes 5–8, which appeared between 1867 and 1877, by Dimock. The edition was completed with an eighth volume by Sir G. F. Warner.

A. F. POLLARD, rev. M. C. CURTHOYS

Sources Boase, *Mod. Eng. biog.* · Venn, *Alum. Cant.* · *The Guardian* (26 April 1876), 544 · W. G. D. Fletcher, 'The family of Dimock, of Randwick and Stonehouse', *Gloucestershire Notes and Queries*, 5 (1894), 240–49; pubd separately as *The family of Dimock, of Randwick, Stonehouse and Gloucester* (1892)
Wealth at death under £1500: administration, 11 May 1876, CGPLA Eng. & Wales

Dimock, Nathaniel (1825–1909), liturgical scholar and theologian, was born on 8 July 1825 at Stonehouse, Gloucestershire, son of John Dimock of Bridge-end, Stonehouse, and his wife, Emma Rook, daughter of Dr James Parkinson of Hoxton. He was educated at two private schools before matriculating at Oxford in 1843. He graduated BA from St John's College in 1847, proceeding MA in 1850. He was ordained deacon by Dr Edward Stanley, the bishop of Norwich, on behalf of the archbishop of Canterbury in 1848, and ordained priest by Archbishop Sumner in 1850. He married on 31 March 1853 Georgiana, daughter of John Alfred Wigan of Clare House, Kent, and sister of Sir Frederick Wigan, bt. She died three months after the marriage on 14 July 1853. Dimock was curate of East Malling, Kent, from 1848 to 1872. He was then vicar of Womenswold, Kent, from 1872 to 1876, and vicar of St Paul's, Maidstone, from 1876 to 1887. Owing to ill health he went abroad and became English chaplain at Sanremo from 1887 to 1888.

Dimock was a fine liturgical scholar. He approached questions from an evangelical standpoint, responding creatively and with great learning to the ferment of new thinking on sacramental questions occasioned by the Oxford Movement, in particular in its second, ritualistic phase. Evangelicals like Dimock argued against the ritualist teaching on the priestly office, on the real presence of the body and blood of Christ, and on the sacrifice of the mass. Dimock also sought to prove that this teaching was without warrant from most of the church fathers or from Anglican divines, including those of the Jacobean and Caroline period, whom high-church clerics particularly esteemed. In *The Christian Doctrine of Sacerdotium* (1897) Dimock maintained that there was a true priesthood within the Church of England, but that it was located not within its ministers but entirely in Christ and in his finished work. In his books *On Eucharistic Worship in the English Church* (1876) and *Papers on the Doctrine of the English Church Concerning the Eucharistic Presence* (2 vols., mem. edn 1911) he argued that the 'real presence' was not local but spiritual, like the presence of the Lord in baptism. He maintained that Christ was present in the worthy recipient of communion only, and claimed an Anglican pedigree for this reformed, rather than Lutheran, view in Lancelot Andrewes, Jeremy Taylor, William Wake, and Daniel Waterland. Dimock followed on from William Goode, a mid-nineteenth-century evangelical theologian, and ultimately from Cranmer, developing the objection that the dogma of the real presence has deleterious consequences on the doctrine of the incarnation, denying the full humanity of Christ through the presence of a non-natural body on many altars following the ascension. Other important books by Dimock include *The Doctrine of the Death of Christ* (1890), *Missarum sacrificia* (1890), *Dangerous Deceits* (1895), *Vox liturgiae Anglicanae* (1897), and *Light from History on Christian Ritual* (1900). Dimock's greatest weakness was stylistic: his prose can be turgid, but his argument is clear and his sources exhaustively cited.

Dimock retired in 1888 and lived at Eastbourne. He passed a quiet life, uninvolved in public debate and controversy, until in 1900 he was invited to take part in Bishop Mandell Creighton's Fulham round-table conference on the holy communion and ritual. Dimock substantially influenced many of the conference's conclusions. From 1896 he lived at Redhill, and died there on 3 March 1909 at his home, Hemstede, Station Road. He was buried at Reigate cemetery on 8 March.

Dimock was recognized for his liturgical scholarship by those of other churchmanships, such as the high-church bishop of Edinburgh, John Dowden, who respected his work on the eucharist. From his own evangelical party Bishop Handley Moule of Durham acknowledged Dimock's standing, stating that 'in him the grace of God combined in perfect harmony a noble force and range of mental power, an unshaken fidelity to conscience and Revelation, and a spirit beautiful with humility, peace and love' (N. Dimock, *On Eucharistic Worship in the English Church*, mem. edn 1911, x).   ERIC M. CULBERTSON

Sources DNB · Crockford (1888) · Crockford (1902) · *The Times* (4 March 1909) · N. Dimock, *Papers on the doctrine of the English church concerning the eucharistic presence*, mem. edn, 2 vols. (1911)
Wealth at death £18,193 10s. 10d.: probate, 25 May 1909, CGPLA Eng. & Wales

Dimond, William (*c.*1784–1837?), playwright, the eldest surviving son of William Wyatt *Dimond (*c.*1750–1812), actor and theatrical manager, and his wife, Matilda Martha, *née* Baker (*d.* 1823), was born at Bath, where Dimond

senior managed the Theatre Royal jointly with the theatre at Bristol. He was educated by the Revd Dr Morgan; the title-page of *Adrian and Orrila* (1807) describes him as 'of the Honourable Society of the Inner Temple'. But he had already entered on a literary career by contributing Della Cruscan poems to the *Morning Herald* under the signature Castalio. *Petrarchal Sonnets, and Miscellaneous Poems* was published in 1800 by subscription and dedicated to the duchess of York; the volume was criticized for its immature extravagances of diction. In the following year, however, Dimond had a comic opera, *The Sea-Side Story*, produced as a benefit piece, with some success. In all he wrote about thirty pieces for the stage, including operas, musical entertainments, and melodramas. Despite his rejection of 'scenic shew' in the prologue to *The Sea-Side Story*, his dramas evinced a strong tendency towards the striking tableau, the exotic setting, and the picturesque pose; his adaptation of Byron's *Bride of Abydos* (1819) offers a series of frenzied encounters and explosive scenic effects. The *British Critic* found *Adrian and Orrila* interesting, but criticized the dialogue for being 'generally too florid, bordering frequently upon affectation, and occasionally ... not far removed from nonsense' (*British Critic*, 29, 431–2). Six years later the same journal, reviewing Dimond's patriotic extravaganza *The Royal Oak* (1811), commented:

> We have often met with Mr. Dimond, and have always found something to praise and something to censure in him. It will never be better. The talents he received from nature have wanted the cultivation of good taste; and the offences against propriety which wild genius commits, will never be corrected by ill-judging audiences.   (ibid., 41, 302–3)

Hazlitt found in Dimond's plays

> so strong a family likeness that, from having seen any one of them, we may form a tolerable correct idea of the rest ... The author does not profess to provide a public entertainment at his own entire expense, and from his own proper funds, but contracts with the manager to get up a striking and impressive exhibition in conjunction with the scene-painter, the scene-shifter, the musical composer, the orchestra, the chorusses on the stage, and the *lungs* of the actors!   (*Complete Works*, 5.366)

In a late play, however (*Stage Struck*, 1835), Dimond burlesques melodramatic styles of acting.

Dimond's father died in 1812, leaving him a joint share of the estate. He took over the management of the Bath and Bristol theatres. In 1817 he was living in what was his father's house in Norfolk Crescent, Bath. He relinquished control of the Bath theatre in 1823, according to Alfred Bunn, who added that since that time, Dimond had been

> in many jails (in Horsemonger Lane, under the name of James Bryant,) and tried in many courts, (he was tried at Croydon assizes under the name of *William Driver*,) under many names, for heinous crimes—out of all of which he escaped by more miracles; his deeds at Bath, the early and great scene of his profligacy, would fit a volume in the narration.   (Bunn, 10–11)

Bunn was not, however, a disinterested witness, having been hoaxed by Dimond in 1834 by some forged letters purportedly from Mrs Mardyn, a lover of Byron, volunteering to come and perform Byron's work as he had taught her in Bunn's production. Bunn announced the coup, 'Mrs Mardyn' pulled out at the last minute, and Bunn investigated to find that Dimond (writing from Paris) had been the author of the letters. Bunn reports that Dimond died in Paris in late 1837.   PAUL BAINES

Sources *A new biographical dictionary of 3000 cotemporary [sic] public characters, British and foreign, of all ranks and professions*, 2nd edn, 3 vols. in 6 pts (1825) · *The thespian dictionary, or, Dramatic biography of the present age*, 2nd edn (1805) · D. E. Baker, *Biographia dramatica, or, A companion to the playhouse*, rev. I. Reed, new edn, rev. S. Jones, 3 vols. in 4 (1812) · A. Nicoll, *A history of early nineteenth century drama*, 2 vols. (1930) · Highfill, Burnim & Langhans, *BDA*, vol. 4 · A. Bunn, *The stage: both before and behind the curtain*, 3 vols. (1840) · W. S. Ward, *Literary reviews in British periodicals, 1798–1820: a bibliography*, 2 vols. (1972) · W. S. Ward, *Literary reviews in British periodicals, 1821–1826: a bibliography* (1977) · *The complete works of William Hazlitt*, ed. P. P. Howe, 21 vols. (1930–34), 5.366–8; 18.209–10, 406 · *Monthly Review*, new ser., 33 (1800), 318–19 · *British Critic*, 29 (1807), 431–2 · *British Critic*, 41 (1813), 302–3
Archives Bath Central Library, letters

Dimond, William Wyatt (*c.*1750–1812), actor and theatre manager, was, according to James Winston, apprenticed as a chaser (an engraver of precious metals) (Winston, section 1). Since Dimond was still alive when Winston's book was published, and likely to be interested in the author's record of his tour of provincial theatres, and did not contradict the claim, it can be accepted. Dimond's gentlemanliness and easy civility were widely acknowledged, fulsomely by Tate Wilkinson (Wilkinson, 3.111, 197), and this is consistent with apprenticeship in so specialized a craft. Hogarth had served a similar apprenticeship some fifty years earlier, but Dimond, unlike Hogarth, was not content to observe actors. He was ambitious to be one. He made his first known appearance, anonymously as a 'Young Gentleman', at Drury Lane on 1 October 1772, in the part of Romeo. The prompter William Hopkins noted in his diary, 'He is very younge a Smart Figure good Voice and made a very tolerable first appearance he met with great applause' (Stone, 1660). In attendance at Drury Lane throughout that season, though, he acted on only five further nights. In Canterbury for the summer season, he took a share in managerial responsibilities, but he returned to a subsidiary role in Garrick's Drury Lane company for the 1773–4 season. His best opportunities came as Rovewell in Shadwell's *The Fair Quaker* and the Dauphin in *King John*. For his benefit on 7 May 1774 he shrewdly chose to play Florizel in Garrick's reduction of *The Winter's Tale* to *Florizel and Perdita*.

It may have been at Garrick's prompting that Dimond included the Theatre Royal, Bath, in his theatrical perambulations during the summer of 1774. He made his first appearance in the city with which he would be associated for over thirty years on 20 October 1774, inconspicuous in a minor role against John Henderson's towering Richard III. Bath's fashionable reputation was at its height, and the Orchard Street theatre was too small to profit from the crowds of visitors. By the time Dimond returned for the 1775–6 season the managers had contrived to double its capacity. In Bath, moreover, he was able to play the leading roles he hankered for, particularly after Henderson's

departure for London in 1777. For three important seasons, from 1779 to 1782, he played opposite Sarah Siddons: Jaffier to her Belvidera in Otway's *Venice Preserv'd*, Posthumus to her Imogen in *Cymbeline*, Bassanio to her Portia in *The Merchant of Venice*, and Lord Townly to her Lady Townly in Vanbrugh's *The Provoked Husband*. Dimond excelled in society comedies such as *The Provoked Husband*. They allowed him to indulge his extravagant taste in costume and to parade his graceful body before his indulgent patrons. Sheridan thought his Joseph Surface 'more consonant to his own ideas when he wrote the part, than anybody else' (Genest, 8.527). But Dimond was unwilling to abandon his tragic roles. He was still playing Romeo in 1790, when Wilkinson featured him during the week of the York races on 23 August, and his Hamlet was admired in both Bath and Bristol. In a measured review of his career, at a time when his retirement from acting was imminent, the *Bristol Journal* commended his good ear, sound judgement, and unmatched skill in genteel comedy, but feared that his performances in tragedy were too smooth, orderly, and correct: 'nothing is irregular, nothing is left to chance. … Hence it is, that if you have little to excite astonishment, you have a great deal to admire' (*Bristol Journal*, 28 June 1800).

By that time Dimond had long been settled in Bath, initially in Devonshire Buildings and later in Norfolk Crescent. He married Matilda Martha Baker (*d.* 1823), a Norfolk woman of independent wealth, on 2 December 1779, and their three known children were brought up and educated in Bath. The elder son, William *Dimond, became a prolific playwright of little quality and a theatrical manager of little more. Dimond's own opportunity to manage the Bath theatre arrived in 1786. John Palmer's interest in the postal service had caused him to relinquish the management to William Keasberry in 1785, and Dimond was sufficiently prosperous, perhaps with his wife's help, to purchase a share when, in the following year, he was invited to do so by Keasberry. Since 1779 the theatres royal in Bristol and Bath had been run jointly as a compact and self-sufficient 'circuit', already established as the most prolific producer of future London stars. As a manager Dimond proved uncommonly popular, not only with the directors, but also with the public and the company of players. Keasberry retired in 1795, and Charles Charlton was appointed assistant manager, with specific responsibilities to Bristol.

It was in Bristol that Dimond made his farewell performance, on 1 July 1801, as Edgar in Nahum Tate's version of *King Lear*, but continued in management until his death, having been granted a seventeen-year lease in 1799. His most visible achievement was the building of Bath's new Theatre Royal in Beaufort Square, the exterior of which remained largely unaltered two centuries later. It opened on 12 October 1805 with an undistinguished production of *Richard III*, but Dimond found no difficulty in attracting the stars of the London stage to appear in the magnificent playhouse. Mrs Siddons performed there on her final tour in 1811, following such luminaries as Mrs Jordan, G. F. Cooke, R. W. Elliston, Joseph Munden, Charles Kemble, and John Bannister. In the full promise of prosperity, Dimond suffered a stroke on 24 December 1811, and died at his home in Norfolk Crescent on 2 January 1812. He was buried in Bath Abbey on 10 January. His will bequeathed his property and theatrical interests to his widow, and it was through her that their son inherited the management of the Bath Theatre Royal. According to Belville Penley, the younger Dimond relinquished the management on his mother's death in June 1823 (Penley, 122).

PETER THOMSON

Sources B. S. Penley, *The Bath stage: a history of dramatic representations in Bath* (1892) · K. Barker, *The Theatre Royal, Bristol, 1766–1966* (1974) · A. Hare, 'William Wyatt Dimond: provincial actor-manager', *Scenes from provincial stages*, ed. R. Foulkes (1994) · H. Bryant, A. Hare, and K. Barker, eds., *Theatre Royal, Bath: a calendar of performances at the Orchard Street Theatre, 1750–1805* (1977) · T. Wilkinson, *The wandering patentee, or, A history of the Yorkshire theatres from 1770 to the present time*, 4 vols. (1795) · J. Winston, *The theatric tourist* (1805) · G. W. Stone, ed., *The London stage, 1660–1800*, pt 4: *1747–1776* (1962) · Genest, *Eng. stage* · *Bath Herald* (11 Jan 1812)
Likenesses F. Bartolozzi, engraving, 1796 (as Romeo; after painting by E. Shirreff), BM · S. De Wilde, oils (as Don Felix), Garr. Club · S. De Wilde, watercolour drawing (as Philaster), Harvard TC · nine paper silhouettes, Garr. Club

Dimsdale, Thomas (1712–1800), physician, was born on 29 May 1712 in Theydon Garnon, Essex, the fourth son and one of the eight children of John Dimsdale, of Theydon Garnon, a surgeon and a member of the Religious Society of Friends. The family held property in Essex for many years. Dimsdale's mother was Susan, daughter of Thomas Bowyer, of Albury Hall, near Hertford. His grandfather, Robert Dimsdale, accompanied William Penn to America in 1684. Dimsdale was trained first by his father, and later at St Thomas's Hospital, London, under Joshua Symons and John Girle; he began to practise medicine at Hertford in 1734. He married in 1739 Mary (d. 1744), only daughter of Nathaniel Brassey MP. There were no children. In 1745 Dimsdale offered his services to the duke of Cumberland, and accompanied the English army as far north as Carlisle, on the surrender of which he returned home. In 1746 he married Anne Iles (d. 1779), daughter of John Iles, and a relative of his first wife; they had seven sons and two daughters.

Dimsdale retired from practice on inheriting a fortune, but having a large family, he resumed practice and took the MD degree from King's College, Aberdeen, in 1761. In 1767 he published, *The Present Method of Inoculating for the Small-Pox*, which enjoyed great popularity, going through six large editions in five years. It was also translated into several foreign languages. In this work, Dimsdale described a safer, less invasive inoculation procedure, which had first been pioneered by Daniel Sutton. In 1768 he was invited to St Petersburg by the Empress Catherine the Great to inoculate herself and her son, the Grand Duke Paul. The empress seems to have been confident of Dimsdale's good faith, but she could not answer for her subjects, and therefore had relays of post-horses prepared for him so that his escape might be instant and rapid in case of disaster. Fortunately both patients did well, and

Thomas Dimsdale (1712–1800), attrib. Nathaniel Plimer, 1780s

Dimsdale was created a councillor of state, with the hereditary title of baron. He received a sum of £10,000, with an annuity of £500, and £2000 for his expenses. The empress presented him with miniatures set in diamonds of herself and her son, and granted him an addition to his family arms in the shape of a wing of the black eagle of Russia. The patent, embellished with the imperial portrait and other ornaments, was preserved at Essendon, the family seat in Hertfordshire. Dimsdale was admitted a fellow of the Royal Society in 1769. In 1779 he married Elizabeth, daughter of Joseph Dimsdale, of Bishop's Stortford.

In 1784 Dimsdale returned to Russia to inoculate the Grand Duke Alexander and his brother Constantine, and the empress presented him with her own muff, made of the fur of the black fox, which only the royal family were allowed to wear. On his first return journey he paid a visit to Frederick the Great at Sans Souci, and on his second, to the emperor Joseph at Vienna. When Prince Omai came to England with Captain Cook in 1775, he was inoculated by Dimsdale.

Dimsdale wrote several additional works on inoculation, including: *Thoughts on General and Partial Inoculation* (1776); *Observations on the Plan of a Dispensary and General Inoculation* (1780); and *Tracts on Inoculation*, written and published at St Petersburg in 1768 and 1781. At Hertford he opened an inoculating house, and, about the same time, entered banking, eventually retiring from the business in 1776. Dimsdale was an independent whig and served as MP for Hertford between 1780 and 1790. Of his one speech to parliament it was said that he 'spoke for some time, but in so low a tone, that we could not distinctly hear him' (HoP, *Commons*). He died at Hertford on 30 December 1800 and was buried in the Quakers' burial-ground at Bishop's Stortford, Hertfordshire. He was survived by his wife.

T. E. KEBBEL, rev. ANDREA RUSNOCK

Sources Munk, *Roll* · P. H. Clendenning, 'Dr Thomas Dimsdale and smallpox inoculation in Russia', *Journal of the History of Medicine and Allied Sciences*, 28 (1973), 109–25 · P. Razzell, *The conquest of smallpox: the impact of inoculation on smallpox mortality in eighteenth century Britain* (1977) · private information (1888) · HoP, *Commons* · *GM*, 1st

ser., 71 (1801), 88, 209, 669 · 'Memoirs of the Hon. Baron Dimsdale', *European Magazine and London Review*, 42 (1802), 83–7
Archives Herts. ALS, papers · priv. coll.
Likenesses attrib. N. Plimer, watercolour, 1780–89, NPG [*see illus.*] · H. Bone, pencil, 1800, NPG · W. Ridley, stipple, 1802, BM, NPG; repro. in *European Magazine* (1802) · H. R. Cook, stipple, 1820, Wellcome L. · T. Burke, mezzotint (after T. Burke), Wellcome L. · Ridley, portrait, repro. in Munk, *Roll* · Tulley, engraving · line engraving (after C. L. Christeneke), Russian Museum, Leningrad · oils, Hertford county hall

Dineley [*formerly* Dineley-Goodere], **Sir John**, **fifth baronet** (*c.*1729–1809), eccentric, was born at Burhope, Herefordshire, the second of three sons of Samuel *Goodere (1687–1741), landowner and naval officer, of Burhope, and his second wife, a widow, Elizabeth, *née* Watts (d. 1742). The claim that Dineley-Goodere once practised physic is unsubstantiated and probably derived from his regular purchases of medical books. Dineley-Goodere's father, Samuel, lived on bad terms with his elder brother, Sir John Goodere, third baronet, who adopted the name Dineley-Goodere as heir to his maternal ancestors. He married Mary Lawford but their only son died young and unmarried. Because of this bad feeling Sir John threatened to disinherit Samuel in favour of his niece's husband, John Foote of Truro. To prevent this threat being carried out Samuel, then in command of the naval vessel *Ruby*, caused his brother to be kidnapped at Bristol, and then to be strangled by two sailors on board his vessel. The murder took place on the night of Sunday 18 January 1741, and on 15 April following the fratricide Samuel was hanged with his two accomplices at Bristol. The precise status of the baronetcy thereafter is unclear. It is possible that Samuel's eldest son, Edward, succeeded as baronet, or was merely granted a courtesy title. On Edward's death in March 1761, aged thirty-two, the title of fifth baronet passed to his brother John, assuming that his father never inherited the title. What little remained of the family estates he soon wasted; about 1770 he was obliged to part with Burhope to Sir James Peachey and he lived for a time in a state bordering on destitution. At length his friendship with the Pelhams, coupled with the interest of Lord North, procured for him the pension and free residence of a poor knight of Windsor. From then on he seems to have used the surname of Dineley only.

By the oddity of his dress, demeanour, and mode of life Dineley became one of the chief sights of Windsor. Each morning he locked up his house in the castle, which no one entered but himself, and went forth to purchase provisions. According to the *Penny Magazine*:

> He then wore a large cloak called a roquelaure, beneath which appeared a pair of thin legs encased in dirty silk stockings. He had a formidable umbrella, and he stalked along upon pattens. All luxuries, whether of meat, or tea, or sugar, or butter, were renounced ... Wherever crowds were assembled—wherever royalty was to be looked upon—there was Sir John Dineley. He then wore a costume of the days of George II—the embroidered coat, the silk-flowered waistcoat, the nether garments of faded velvet carefully meeting the dirty silk stocking, which terminated in the half-polished shoe surmounted by the dingy silver buckle. The old wig, on great occasions, was newly powdered, and the best cocked hat was brought forth, with a tarnished lace

Sir John Dineley, fifth baronet (*c.*1729–1809), by W. Hopkins, 1809

edging. He had dreams of ancient genealogies, and of alliances still subsisting between himself and the first families of the land.

Dineley's second preoccupation was his search for a wife whose wealth he hoped would allow him to establish his lineage:

> To secure for himself a wife was the business of his existence; to display himself properly where women most do congregate was the object of his savings. The man had not a particle of levity in these proceedings; his deportment was staid and dignified. He had a wonderful discrimination in avoiding the tittering girls, with whose faces he was familiar. But perchance some buxom matron or timid maiden who had seen him for the first time gazed upon the apparition with surprise and curiosity. He approached. With the air of one bred in courts he made his most profound bow; and taking a printed paper from his pocket, reverently presented it and withdrew. (*Penny Magazine*)

More than once he paid court to some lad dressed up as a fine lady. His marriage proposals were crudely printed by himself. Occasionally he advertised in the newspapers. He also printed some extraordinary rhymes under the title of 'Methods to get husbands ... with the advertised marriage offer of Sir John Dineley, bart., of Charleton, near Worcester, extending to 375,000*l.*, to the reader of this epistle, if a single lady, and has above one hundred guineas fortune'.

Although obsessed by his search for a wife and for his lost inheritance, in other matters Dineley was both sane and shrewd. Twice or thrice a year he visited Vauxhall Gardens and the London theatres, taking care to apprise the public of his intention through the medium of the most fashionable daily papers. Wherever he went the place was invariably well attended, especially by women. Dineley persevered in his addresses to the ladies until the very close of his life, but without success. When he failed to appear at chapel one morning his door was broken open. His passage was filled with coals, his sitting room with his printing materials; there was little furniture. Dineley was found in bed. He died a few days later, in November 1809, aged about eighty. On his death the baronetcy became extinct. GORDON GOODWIN, rev. ANITA McCONNELL

Sources J. Burke and J. B. Burke, *A genealogical and heraldic history of the extinct and dormant baronetcies of England, Ireland, and Scotland* (1838), 220–21 · S. Foote, *The genuine memoirs of Sir J. D. Goodere, who was murder'd by the contrivance of his own brother on board the Ruby … Jan. 19, 1740-1* [1741] · B. Burke, *Romance of the aristocracy*, 3 vols. (1855), 2.19–25 · W. Granger and others, *The new wonderful museum, and extraordinary magazine*, 1 (1803), 422–8 · GM, 1st ser., 79 (1809), 1084, 1171 · GM, 1st ser., 95/2 (1825), 136 · C. J. Robinson, *A history of the mansions and manors of Herefordshire* (1873) · VCH *Worcestershire*, vol. 3 · 'Sir John Dinely', *The Penny Magazine of the Society for the Diffusion of Useful Knowledge*, new ser., 10 (1841), 356–7 · L. Stone, *Broken lives: separation and divorce in England, 1660–1857* (1993)
Likenesses etching, pubd 1799, BM · J. Mills, line engraving, pubd 1803, NPG · line engraving, pubd 1803, BM; repro. in Granger and others, *New wonderful museum*, vol. 1, facing p. 422 · W. Hopkins, etching, 1809, BM, NPG [*see illus.*] · engraving, repro. in H. Lemoine and J. Caulfield, *The eccentric magazine, or, Lives and portraits of remarkable persons*, 2 vols. (1812–13) · etching, NPG

Dineley [Dingley], **Thomas** (*d.* 1695), antiquary, was the son of Thomas Dineley or Dingley, controller of customs at Southampton. Having attended the school kept by the dramatist James Shirley in Whitefriars, London, in August 1670 he became a student at Gray's Inn, but in the following year joined the household of Sir George Downing, on his appointment as ambassador to the states general of the United Provinces.

Thereafter Dineley travelled extensively in the British Isles and on the continent, recording his trips in manuscript journals illustrated by vigorous pen-and-ink drawings, such as *Travails through the Low Countreys, 1674* and *Observations in a Voyage in the Kingdom of France, 1675*. His work is typical of that of many antiquaries of the late seventeenth century, not only in that none of it was published during his lifetime, but also in its shift over time in perspective and choice of subject matter. His journey to Ireland in 1680, possibly undertaken in a military capacity, provided a very detailed description (written the following year) of what he saw there, which also records what Dineley clearly considered to be the outlandish customs and behaviour of its people. Less prone to his personal prejudices and more 'archaeological' in approach—and thus more reliable from an antiquarian perspective—is the account he wrote of Wales as he accompanied Henry Somerset, first duke of Beaufort, in his 1684 progress through the principality as lord president of the council in Wales and the marches. The information and drawings of churches, castles, country houses, and other historic sites contained in this diary formed the basis for Theophilus Jones's *A History of the County of Brecknock*, published in two volumes in 1805 and 1809, while a substantial part of Dineley's own journal was privately printed as *Notitia Cambro-Britannica* for the eighth duke of Beaufort in 1864.

Of equal antiquarian interest is Dineley's manuscript 'History from marble', the last observation in which is dated 30 April 1684, containing many fine drawings and short accounts of country houses as well as church monuments and inscriptions. In geographical spread it concentrates on Bath, Oxford, and the counties of Herefordshire and Worcestershire, providing much of the material used in Richard Rawlinson's *History and Antiquities of the City and Cathedral Church of Hereford* (1717) and Treadway Russell Nash's *Collections for the History of Worcestershire* (2 vols., 1781–2).

Virtually nothing is known of Dineley's personal life, other than that when not travelling he lived at Dilwyn, Herefordshire, and that he died at Louvain, Flanders, in May 1695. At this time he seems to have been unmarried: his heir was his niece, the daughter of his sister, Eliza, wife of William Melling.

C. J. ROBINSON, rev. NICHOLAS DOGGETT

Sources *History from marble, compiled in the reign of Charles II by Thomas Dingley*, ed. J. G. Nichols, 1, CS, 94 (1867) · *History from marble, compiled in the reign of Charles II by Thomas Dingley*, ed. J. G. Nichols, 2, CS, 97 (1868) · T. Dineley, 'Observations in a voyage through the kingdom of Ireland, 1680', *Journal of the Kilkenny and South-East of Ireland Archaeological Society*, new ser., 1 (1856–7), 143–6, 170–88; new ser., 2 (1858–9), 22–32, 55–6; new ser., 4 (1862–3), 38–52, 103–9, 320–38; new ser., 5 (1864–6), 40–48, 268–90, 425–46; new ser., 6 (1867), 73–91, 176–204 · C. Baker, ed., *Notitia Cambro-Britannica* (1864) · *The account of the official progress of His Grace Henry first duke of Beaufort … through Wales in 1684*, ed. R. W. Banks (1888) · J. Foster, *The register of admissions to Gray's Inn, 1521–1889, together with the register of marriages in Gray's Inn chapel, 1695–1754* (privately printed, London, 1889), 310 · *First report*, HMC, 1/1 (1870); repr. (1874), 53–4 · GM, 2nd ser., 43 (1855), 45 · PRO, PROB 6/71, fol. 68v · PRO, PROB 6/79, fol. 5r · M. Hunter, *Science and the shape of orthodoxy: intellectual change in late seventeenth-century Britain* (1995) · G. Parry, *The trophies of time: English antiquaries of the seventeenth century* (1995)
Archives Bodl. Oxf., descriptions of monuments in churches, MS Top. gen. d. 19

Dines, William Henry (1855–1927), meteorologist, was born on 5 August 1855 at 74 Charlwood Street, Pimlico, London, the only surviving son (two daughters also reached adulthood) of George Dines (1812–1887), builder and meteorologist, and his wife, Louisa Sara Coke of Norfolk. George Dines's father, Charles, gamekeeper to the Whitbread family, had been murdered by a poacher and the Whitbreads retained an interest in the welfare of the Dines family. George Dines was apprenticed to the building firm of Thomas Cubitt, rising to become foreman of works at Osborne. His meteorological interests probably arose out of his building work, and may have encouraged similar interest in his son.

Dines was educated at Woodcote House School, Windlesham, Surrey, then articled as an engineering pupil at the Nine Elms Works of the London and South Western Railway. After completing his articles in 1877 he went to Corpus Christi College, Cambridge, where he passed the mathematical tripos in 1881 as twentieth wrangler. He remained in residence as a mathematical coach for a year after graduation, but his retiring nature and spare constitution did not fit him for a teaching career, though he continued to offer mathematical tuition by correspondence.

He married, on 3 January 1882, Catharine Emma (b. 1856/7), daughter of Frederick Tugwell, a clergyman. Two of their sons later became notable meteorologists. As he had private means Dines was able to devote himself to the study of dynamical and physical meteorology. He became the leading exponent of experimental meteorology in England at the turn of the century, and his work in anemometry, the upper air, solar and terrestrial radiation, and the structure of the atmosphere was particularly notable.

The collapse of the Tay Bridge in 1879 led engineers and builders to raise questions about the maximum wind pressure tolerance of structures, and meteorologists to face the problem of how to relate wind velocity and force to the corresponding pressures. The Royal Meteorological Society commissioned a wind force committee in June 1885 to examine the matter. Dines was one of the most active members, his colleagues being William Marcet, the society's president, the instrument makers William Ford Stanley and R. W. Munro, and, from the Meteorological Office, R. H. Scott, secretary, and Captain Toynbee, superintendent.

Dines used his engineering skills to devise an anemometer that would be independent of friction, and to compare alongside each other various types of anemometer. On this latter task he collaborated with G. M. Whipple, superintendent of Kew observatory. Having failed to persuade any railway company to allow instruments to be fixed to a speeding locomotive, they set up their experiments on a steam powered whirligig in the Dines's family garden. Their results were jointly published in the *Proceedings* and in the *Philosophical Transactions* of the Royal Society in 1888. After several years of development with Munro's instrument engineering firm, Dines produced the pressure tube anemometer. This robust instrument achieved widespread and international popularity, the type having more than eighty years of active life after its original conception.

Although of independent means Dines was far from isolated. Interest in his work was sustained through his reports to the annual meetings of the British Association for the Advancement of Science, his membership of meteorological committees, and his circle of friends from university days. For a study of the effect of exposure on the readings of wind pressure recorders Dines collaborated with Captain D. Wilson-Barker, who took the observations over a two-year period on HMS *Worcester* for their 1899 paper. Six years later he devised a micro-barograph in association with William Napier Shaw. Another long-time friend was Lewis Fry Richardson, the father of analytical forecasting.

Elected president of the Royal Meteorological Society for 1901 and 1902, Dines encouraged the society and the British Association for the Advancement of Science to support upper air investigations. He himself began to develop lightweight instruments that could be suspended from large box kites. These required a considerable expanse of open countryside for safe operation, as they were attached to steel wire that could be several miles long. Firstly at Pyrton Hill, then from Benson Observatory in Oxfordshire, he took copious measurements of the upper air and coupled them with the results from balloon experiments to investigate the newly discovered stratosphere. His ideas formed the basis for theories concerning variations in atmospheric pressure on account of processes in the upper troposphere and lower stratosphere. The effects of this linkage are known to this day as the Dines compensation.

Dines applied the same mix of experimental skill and theoretical grasp to the problem of the heat balance of the earth and the atmosphere. During the early years of the First World War he had attempted to establish a balance sheet for solar radiation; the outcome was the development of an instrument for measuring night-time radiation.

His home at Benson became one of five weather stations to submit daily weather reports to the Meteorological Office in London. It also remained a focus for family life, one of his two meteorologist sons being married there in 1915, and one of his grandchildren in 1937. In his later years he succumbed to Parkinson's disease, leaving the running of the observatory to his son Lewen. He died at Benson on 24 December 1927. He was survived by his wife.   JANE INSLEY

Sources J. Insley, ed., *The Dines dynasty: a family of meteorologists* (1995) · b. cert. · m. cert.
Archives National Museum of Science and Industry, London · RS, corresp. and papers | CUL, letters to Sir George Stokes
Likenesses photograph, 1903, repro. in *Quarterly Journal of the Royal Meteorological Society of London*, 29 (1903)
Wealth at death £21,570 0s. 5d.: resworn probate, 10 March 1928, CGPLA Eng. & Wales

Dinesen, Isak. *See* Blixen, Karen Christenze (1885–1962).

Dingane ka Senzangakhona (c.1798–1840), king of the Zulu, born in the south-eastern corner of emaKhosini, Babanango district, Natal, was the son of Senzangakhona (c.1757–1816), Zulu chief, and a junior wife, Mpikase. He spent his early manhood under his half-brother *Shaka's reign. He served in the amaWombe butho ('age-mate military unit') and accompanied Shaka on campaigns. In September 1828, he and his brother Mhlangana, in league with the induna Mbopha, assassinated Shaka. Dingane then had Mhlangana killed and dismissed Mbopha. Insecure and suspicious, he also killed some of Shaka's favourites and most of his own surviving brothers, but spared Mpande as ineffectual. Dingane was slothful and cunning but not astute. He lacked Shaka's urge to conquest, and loved pageantry and dancing. He had many concubines but never produced an heir. Under him the quality of the Zulu army declined, and although he apparently realized the importance of firearms he failed both to obtain them in sufficient numbers and to use them effectively.

Dingane initially halted campaigns and dissolved some amabutho. His kingdom was shaken, however, by the secession of the Qwabe chiefdom. Dingane then restored military discipline and resumed campaigning. His forces raided the Npondo and the Swazi, attacked Mzilikazi's

Ndebele (Matabele) in the central Transvaal, and in September 1833 stormed the Portuguese fort at Delagoa Bay, Mozambique, and killed its governor.

Dingane was uneasy with the white traders at Port Natal (Durban) who harboured refugees from his kingdom. In 1835 they agreed to send refugees back in return for peace. Dingane also admitted missionaries to his kingdom. The agreement soon failed, however, and tense relations resumed.

From 1837 the Zulu kingdom was threatened by land-hungry Boers, with Old Testament attitudes and nineteenth-century firearms, on their great trek away from British ruled Cape Colony, who wanted to take Natal. On 6 November 1837 the trekker leader Pieter Retief arrived at Dingane's capital, Mgungundhlovu, to ask for Natal south of the Thukela (Tugela) for their republic, which the Port Natal traders had decided to join. Dingane knew that in January a trekker force had defeated Mzilikazi. He himself had then sent a second expedition against the Ndebele. To buy time Dingane promised the concession if Retief would recapture cattle taken by Chief Sekonyela. Retief first reported to the trekkers, who immediately began crossing the Drakensberg and settling in numerous camps, and then tricked Sekonyela into trying on a pair of handcuffs and ransomed him for Dingane's cattle. Before Retief returned to claim his reward Dingane learned that the trekkers had decisively defeated the Ndebele, driving them north towards modern Zimbabwe. Dingane apparently believed that only by destroying the trekkers while they were unprepared could he save his people from expropriation and massed his forces in preparation. On Retief's arrival Dingane reportedly signed a document assigning land in Natal. He tricked the Boers into attending a farewell dance without their arms, during which Retief and his companions were seized and killed. Dingane then sent his forces to destroy the trekkers in their camps. His masterstroke miscarried. The Zulu massacred the occupants of the first camps they encountered but gunfire gave the alarm to others, who drove them off. A large part of the trekkers' stock had been taken, however. They were confined to defensive laagers and short of a decisive victory would be forced to return over the Drakensberg. Dingane's position was further improved when the first trekker counter-attack was halted and routed by his army on 11 April 1838. An invasion by the Natal traders was also defeated and their settlement dispersed.

With the arrival of Andries Pretorius and his commandos from the Cape, the trekkers invaded the Zulu kingdom in December 1838. Dingane's army attacked their laager by the Ncome River, at the battle of Blood River, on 16 December. The Zulu were routed by Boer firepower and tactics, and sustained massive losses. Dingane then negotiated an agreement granting the Boers land south of the Tongati River. His half-brother Mpande rebelled and in September 1839, with his followers, crossed the Thukela and took refuge with the trekkers. In January 1840 Mpande's army, shadowed by a Boer force, marched into Zululand. The two Zulu armies fought at the Maqonqo hills (near Magudu in the far north of Zululand) on 29 January. Dingane's army, commanded by Ndlela, was defeated. Mpande then claimed the Zulu kingship. Ndlela, wounded, fled back to Dingane, who had him strangled. Dingane and his followers fled across the Pongola, north-east into the territory of Silevana of the Nyawo. Helped by a force of Dingane's enemies—the Swazi, led by Sonyezane Dlamini—Silevana attacked Dingane at night and mortally wounded him. Dingane died on 15 March 1840 at Esankoleni (near Golela on the Natal–Swaziland border) and was buried there.

In Afrikaner mythology Dingane was the treacherous, murderous, savage villain; the anniversary of Blood River was long celebrated as Dingane's day. He was portrayed in three South African films, *De Voortrekker* (1916), *They Built a Nation* (1938), and *Die Voortrekkers* (1973), and sculpted on the frieze in the Voortrekker monument (1949) at Pretoria. Zulu also reviled his memory, both for his failure and for his treatment of the Cele and Qadi. Magema ka Magwaza, the Zulu historian, wrote, 'he had the heart of a dog and the nature of a witch. Dingane was truly like a poisonous snake' (Fuze, 17). Nevertheless, for all his cruelty and duplicity, arguably he had done the best he knew to save his kingdom and people.

JOHN D. OMER-COOPER

Sources *The James Stuart archive of recorded oral evidence relating to the history of the Zulu and neighbouring peoples*, ed. and trans. C. de B. Webb and J. B. Wright, [5 vols.] (1976–) · J. Laband, *Rope of sand: the rise and fall of the Zulu kingdom in the nineteenth century* (1995) · E. Walker, *The great trek* (1960) · *DSAB* · D. R. Morris, *The washing of the spears* (1966) · P. Bonner, *Kings, commoners and concessionaries* (1982) · N. Isaacs, *Travels and adventures in eastern Africa*, ed. L. Herrman, 2 vols. (1936) · P. R. Kirby, ed., *Andrew Smith and Natal: documents relating to the early history of that province* (1955) · A. F. Gardiner, *Narrative of a journey to the Zoolu country* (1836) · *Diary of Rev Francis Owen*, ed. C. Cory (1926) · S. Taylor, *Shaka's children: a history of the Zulu people* (1994) · M. Wilson and L. Thompson, eds., *The Oxford history of South Africa*, 2 vols. (1971), vol. 1 · I. Knight and I. Castle, *The Zulu War: then and now* (1993) · M. M. Fuze, *The black people and whence they came* (1986)

Likenesses sculpture, 1949 (in frieze in Voortrekker monument), Pretoria · A. Gardiner, drawing, repro. in Taylor, *Shaka's children*, facing p. 114

Dingley, Robert (1618/19–1660), clergyman, was born in Surrey, possibly in Chertsey, the second son of Sir John Dingley (*d.* 1679) of London and his wife, Jane, daughter of John Hammond of Chertsey Abbey. He matriculated from Magdalen College, Oxford, on 10 October 1634 aged fifteen, graduating BA on 27 January 1638 and proceeding MA on 3 November 1640; he held a fellowship at the college from 1638 to 1644. If Wood is to be credited, he was at first 'a great observer of church ceremonies, and a remarkable bower to the altar when he came into the chapel' but cynically turned presbyterian (Wood, *Ath. Oxon.*, 3.487). He was admitted by the House of Lords on 17 June 1643 to the rectory of Barnes in Surrey, in place of John Cutts, then absent at Oxford, on the petition of the leading parishioners. A Thomas Rutton is listed as having been appointed to the benefice three days later; the reasons are unclear, but Dingley did indeed serve as a minister at Barnes. In *The Spirituall Taste Described* (1649) there appears a preface to Elizabeth, daughter of Daniel Oxenbridge, third wife of Oliver St John (d. 1673), and her sister Mary, wife of William Langhorn (possibly father of the East India Company merchant of the same name), signed 4 November 1648, in which Dingley reveals that they had been 'members of my congregation' there, 'the fairest flowers in my garden'. The book also contains a portrait of the author.

In 1648 Dingley was presented to the rectory of Brighstone near Newport on the Isle of Wight, close to Wolverton House, where his father Sir John, deputy to the earl of Pembroke, then had his chief residence. There he published three works, notably *The Deputation of Angels, or, The Angell-Guardian* (1654). This contained an epistle to Colonel William Sydenham, councillor of state and governor of the Isle of Wight, Major Bowerman, the deputy governor, Lord Commissioner Lisle, and Colonel Robert Hammond thanking them for their 'many favours', and urging them to 'do worthily for sion; to undermine atheism, profaneness, and heresy'. Dingley attacks those who 'condemn the ministry and cannot endure sound doctrine' as also 'despisers of all superiority and government political'. In furtherance of these views he acted as an assistant to the Hampshire commissioners for ejection of insufficient or scandalous ministers and schoolmasters. In the preface to his *Vox coeli* (1658) Dingley observed that Edward III, Henry VIII, and Sir Walter Ralegh were among the many who 'could equally handle both the sword and pen' and hoped to 'provoke our military worthies to the love of the muses'; he notes that the dedicatee, Captain Samuel Bull JP, captain of Cowes Castle, has been 'instrumental in carrying the gospel to a town [West Cowes] that never before enjoyed it; consisting of about a thousand souls; and have helped them to build a synagogue'. He died, possibly in Brighstone, on 12 January 1660 and was buried in the chancel of Brighstone church.   STEPHEN WRIGHT

Sources Foster, *Alum. Oxon.* • G. D. Squibb, ed., *The visitation of Hampshire and the Isle of Wight, 1686*, Harleian Society, new ser., 10 (1991) • *VCH Hampshire and the Isle of Wight*, vol. 5 • Wood, *Ath. Oxon.*, new edn • R. Dingley, *The spirituall taste described* (1649) • W. A. Shaw, *A history of the English church during the civil wars and under the Commonwealth, 1640–1660*, 2 vols. (1900) • *JHL*, 6 (1643–4) • *JHL*, 10 (1647–8) • R. Dingley, *Vox coeli, or, Philosphical, historical and theological observations of thunder* (1658) • A. MacLachlan, *The civil war in Hampshire* (2000) • R. Dingley, *The deputation of angels, or, The angell-guardian* (1654) • *Fifth report*, HMC, 4 (1876)
Likenesses T. Cross, line engraving, BM • portrait, repro. in Dingley, *The spirituall taste described*

Dingley, Robert (*bap.* 1710, *d.* 1781), philanthropist, was baptized on 12 September 1710 at St Helen's, Bishopsgate, London, the eldest in the family of two surviving sons and four daughters (there were nineteen children in all) of Robert Dingley (1678–1741), a Bishopsgate jeweller and goldsmith, and his wife, Susanna, daughter of Henry Elkin. In August 1726 Robert Dingley senior, together with Sir Randolph Knipe, shipped exceptionally fine silver table services to Empress Catherine I of Russia and for her favourite, the statesman Prince Menshikov FRS. Made freemen of the Russia Company in August 1731, Robert and his brother Charles traded as partners, with an agency

in St Petersburg, where, with other merchants, they financed two sugar refineries. Robert represented the company's interests at the Commons and the Admiralty, becoming its consul and auditor in 1759. He was a director of the Bank of England (1757–67) and of the Equitable Life Assurance Society, the earliest of its kind, when it was founded in 1762. A member of the Society of Dilettanti from its foundation (*c.*1736) he devised an influential plan in February 1749 for a public Academy of Arts, and was also an active fellow of the Society of Antiquaries (1734–48). Elected FRS in 1748, he contributed useful items to the *Philosophical Transactions* on gemstones (44, 1747)—though harshly criticized by John Hill in 1751—and irregular Thames tides (49, 1756).

As a philanthropist, Dingley served on a committee of the Merchant Seamen's Corporation (established in 1747), and was a governor and an innovative inspector (1758–62) of the London Foundling Hospital. He pioneered the Magdalen Hospital for Penitent Prostitutes, the first English charity of its kind, founded at Prescot Street, Whitechapel, in 1758, and largely designed its second building, which opened at Southwark in 1772. Its treasurer and then, from 1768, vice-president, he is commemorated by Dingley Lane, SW16. Several of his talented architectural designs exist, including engravings of those for rebuilding the king's and queen's baths at Bath (published by I. and J. Taylor, *c.*1787). His proposals of 1757 as a fellow of the Society of Arts resulted in premiums being awarded for modelling in various media. His exceptional collection of gemstones, engraved gems, drawings, prints, and natural-history specimens was auctioned by White's on 23 June 1785. His brother Charles Dingley (1711–1769), who projected London's New Road and New City Road (1756–61), received the Society of Arts gold medal in 1768 for building a large sawmill at Limehouse.

Dingley owned a house at Little St Helen's, Bishopsgate. From 1753, when he sold two Sussex farms, until the death in 1759 of his wife, Elizabeth (daughter of Henry Thompson, of Kirby Hall, Yorkshire), whom he had married in 1744, his country home was in Charlton, Kent; he moved to Lamorbey, at Bexley, when he married Esther Spencer (*d.* 1784) in March 1760. He had a son and two daughters (one of whom died very young) by his first marriage. Dingley died at Lamorbey on 8 August 1781, according to the monumental inscription in Charlton parish church, where he and his wives are buried. His portrait, painted and presented in 1762 by William Hoare to the Magdalen Hospital, was engraved in mezzotint by John Dixon and is in a private collection.   JOHN H. APPLEBY, *rev.*

Sources H. F. B. Compston, *The Magdalen Hospital* (1917) • S. P. B. Pearce, *An ideal in the working: the story of the Magdalen Hospital, 1758–1958* (1958) • J. H. Appleby, 'Robert Dingley … merchant, architect, and pioneering philanthropist', *Notes and Records of the Royal Society*, 45 (1991), 139–54 • J. H. Appleby, 'Mills, models and magdalens: the Dingley brothers and the Society of Arts', *RSA Journal*, 140 (1991–2), 267–73 • J. H. Appleby, 'Charles Dingley, projector, and his Limehouse sawmill', *London Topographical Record*, 27 (1995), 179–93 • M. Lopato, 'English silver in St Petersburg', *British art treasures from the Russian imperial collections in the Hermitage*, ed. B. Allen and L. Dukelskaya (1996), 124–37 [exhibition catalogue, Yale U. CBA, 5

Oct 1996 – 5 Jan 1997] · M. E. Ogborn, *Equitable assurances … the Equitable Life Assurance Society, 1762–1962* (1962) · J. Hill, 'A precious treatise upon precious stones', *A review of the works of the Royal Society of London* (1751), 242–52

Likenesses W. Hoare, portrait, 1762, priv. coll. · J. Dixon, engraving (after W. Hoare)

Dingley, Sir Thomas (1506x8–1539), knight of the hospital of St John of Jerusalem, was the son of John Dingley of the Isle of Wight and Mabel, or Mabell, Weston of Rozel, Jersey. His mother was the sister of Sir William *Weston, a prominent hospitaller who became prior of the order of St John in England in 1527. Weston granted Dingley a pension of 125 écus on his reception into the order in 1526, when he would have been at least eighteen, and continued to favour him throughout his career. Although licensed to return home almost immediately, between 1528 and 1532 the young knight remained with the order's convent as it migrated between Italy, southern France, and Malta. In 1531 he was rewarded with the preceptory of North Baddesley, Hampshire, and was retained in the service of the grand master, a sign that further advancement was likely. Shortly after this he returned to England, where Weston granted him the prioral estate of Stansgate, and secured royal letters asking the grand master that he should receive further preferment. In 1535–6 he shuttled back and forth between England and Malta, and passing through southern France during one of these journeys he managed to persuade the grand master elect, Didier de Sainct-Jailhe, to collate him to another preceptory, Shingay (Cambridgeshire). Sainct-Jailhe, however, had no right to confer any benefices until he should reach the convent, and died before he could make the journey. In the meantime Ambrose Cave had been appointed to Shingay from Malta. A bitter row developed, with the prior taking Dingley's side, refusing to obey conventual mandates to put Cave in possession, and securing royal confirmation of his nephew's appointment.

The situation was completely transformed in September 1537, when an envoy of the order and three English brethren gained access to court. On 18 September, probably as a result of accusations advanced by his brethren, Dingley was committed to the Tower under suspicion of treason. It was alleged that at Richard Pate's house in Genoa he had openly discussed the possibility of Henry VIII losing his throne, had accused the king of bloodthirstiness before a prominent French hospitaller, and had committed youthful misdemeanours of which Henry was reminded by Clement West, the head of the English brethren in Malta. Soon after Dingley's arrest Baddesley and Shingay were granted to Thomas Seymour and Richard Longe. On 18 May 1539 Dingley was attainted, on the grounds that he had 'moved divers outward princes to levy war' against the king (*LP Henry VIII*, 14/1, 867(15)), and on 9 July he was beheaded on Tower Hill, along with Sir Adrian Fortescue.   G. J. O'MALLEY

Sources H. P. Scicluna, ed., *The book of deliberations of the venerable tongue of England, 1523–1567* (1949) · *LP Henry VIII* · archives of the knights, National Library of Malta, vols. 85, 86, 286, 415–17, 54 · W. B. Bannerman, ed., *The visitations of the county of Surrey … 1530 … 1572 … 1623*, Harleian Society, 43 (1899), 7 · R. Rex, 'Blessed Adrian

Fortescue: a martyr without a cause?', *Analecta Bollandiana*, 115 (1997), 307–53 · M. Elvins, *Bl. Adrian Fortescue: Englishman, knight of Malta, martyr* (1993) · J. Caley and J. Hunter, eds., *Valor ecclesiasticus temp. Henrici VIII*, 6 vols., RC (1810–34), vol. 2, p. 26; vol. 3, p. 503

Dingley, Thomas. *See* Dineley, Thomas (*d.* 1695).

Dingwall. For this title name *see* Butler, Elizabeth, duchess of Ormond and *suo jure* Lady Dingwall (1615–1684); Herbert, Auberon Thomas, eighth Baron Lucas of Crudwell and fifth Lord Dingwall (1876–1916).

Dingwall, Eric John (1891?–1986), anthropologist and librarian, was born in Nuwara Eliya, Ceylon, the only son of Alexander Harvey Dingwall (1860–1936), a tea planter, and his wife, Catherine Emily, formerly Marson (1863?–1932). He seems not to have known his date of birth, but for official purposes would put down 21 April 1891. His death certificate gives his year of birth as 1890. He was educated at Fairleigh School, Weston-super-Mare (his father had retired there), then privately, and at Pembroke College, Cambridge, where he read modern languages, taking his BA in 1915 and his MA in 1918. From 1915 to 1918 he worked in Cambridge University Library, becoming an assistant librarian. In 1918 he married Doris Dunn, daughter of S. P. Dunn JP, of Bradfield, Berkshire.

Dingwall came from an affluent family and was astute in financial matters (he left an estate valued at £678,246). This enabled him to engage freely in his many unusual interests, of which the earliest was perhaps conjuring—he joined the Magic Circle in 1909 and ultimately became an honorary vice-president. Related was his interest in the performances of mediums and clairvoyants. In 1920 he joined the Society for Psychical Research (SPR) and in 1921 he went to New York as director of the department of physical phenomena in the American SPR. From 1922 to 1927 he was research officer of the SPR in London. In these two capacities he sat with many notable American and European mediums (mainly physical mediums). His most important reports (all of them negative or noncommittal) are to be found in the *Proceedings* of the SPR. In 1922 with Harry Price he republished, with an added bibliography, *Revelations of a Spirit Medium* (1891), a classic exposé of the methods of fraudulent mediums, and in 1927 he brought out a brief handbook, *How to Go to a Medium*.

Dingwall's interests and outlook were very different from those of the SPR's ruling body, and disagreements mounted over apparently successful experiments on telepathy for which the classical scholar, Gilbert Murray, had been the subject. Dingwall felt that essential control conditions had been neglected because of Murray's great eminence. In 1927 his tenure as research officer was allowed to lapse. Meanwhile Dingwall had become increasingly interested in anthropology and the study of aberrant human customs, particularly sexual ones. In 1925 and 1927–9 he registered as a research student at the University of London, where his anthropological work, published as *Male Infibulation* (1925), *The Girdle of Chastity* (1931), and *Artificial Cranial Deformation* (1931), obtained him a PhD (1929) and a DSc (1932). He was the 'editor' (really the translator and reviser) of the work by H. H. Ploss, M. Bartels, and

P. Bartels, *Woman: an Historical, Gynaecological and Anthropological Compendium* (3 vols., 1935). All these works, like most of Dingwall's writings, are permeated with great quantities of bibliographical information. During this period he also published two highly characteristic short books, *Ghosts and Spirits in the Ancient World* (1930) and *How to Use a Large Library* (1933).

From 1935 (by which time his marriage had ended) to 1937 Dingwall travelled extensively in Europe, North and South America, and the West Indies, studying 'rare and queer customs', and 'abnormal mental phenomena'. From 1941 to 1945 he was attached to the Ministry of Information and to a department of the Foreign Office, but always remained very secretive about this work.

In 1946 Dingwall offered his services to the department of printed books of the British Museum, and was appointed an honorary assistant keeper. He worked principally on the 'private case' of erotic material, to which he added many rarities, often at his own expense. In addition he dealt by post and telephone with numerous enquiries on out of the way subjects, and went on doing so from his home when age made it harder for him to travel. He remained closely in touch with the scientific and medical literature on sexual behaviour, normal, abnormal, and criminal, and would occasionally give lectures on the last to groups of police officers.

Psychical research, which Dingwall saw as a key area in an ongoing struggle between rationality and superstition, continued to intrigue and exasperate him. He was strongly but not undeviatingly sceptical about psychic phenomena. His post-war publications included *Some Human Oddities* (1947) and *Very Peculiar People* (1950), which contain, *inter alia*, sympathetic essays, with extensive bibliographies, on such psychic enigmas as St Joseph of Copertino, D. D. Home, and Eusapia Palladino. His trenchant scepticism found expression in *The Haunting of Borley Rectory* (with K. M. Goldney and T. H. Hall, 1956) and *Four Modern Ghosts* (with T. H. Hall, 1958). *Abnormal Hypnotic Phenomena: a Survey of Nineteenth-Century Cases* (4 vols., 1967–8), which he edited and in considerable part wrote, raised the scholarly history of mesmerism and hypnosis to a new level. In 1956 came his most commercially successful book, *The American Woman*, an unflattering social and historical analysis which was much resented by its targets, but sold well (no doubt to American men).

On 13 December 1954 Dingwall married a psychologist, Dr Norah Margaret Davis (*d.* 1976), daughter of Edgar William Davis, clergyman, and a year or two later left Cambridge (where he had lived for over twenty years) to set up home in a pleasant small estate at Crowhurst in Sussex. He had become rather well known. Few people could claim to be an authority on so many different subjects, and few were so ready to pass on information and references. He had, however, certain eccentricities. He was an avid and enterprising collector not just of books, but of photographs, clocks, automata, porcelain, workshop tools, and all sorts of oddments. It was typical of him that he once bought the wreck of a magnificent cage of automaton singing birds from a passing rag-and-bone man, restored

it, and ultimately presented it to the British Museum. He tended to see persons and issues in black or white, and would scent plots, deception, and double-dealing rather readily. He did not hesitate to make these opinions known, but beneath his edgy and combative exterior lay a real vein of generosity and kindness.

Dingwall was blue-eyed, of middle height, and spare build, and he possessed a restless energy. Though short-sighted, he was keenly observant. He had a sharp and incisive voice, and was an excellent public speaker and a highly entertaining conversationalist. The death of his wife on Christmas eve 1976, soon after they had moved into a flat in St Leonards, Sussex, was a crippling blow, but with great fortitude Dingwall stayed on alone, working steadily until his own death from heart disease in St Helen's Hospital, Hastings, on 7 August 1986. He arranged to have his carotid artery severed prior to cremation in Hastings.

Dingwall's massive card indexes, his notebooks, and newspaper cuttings, were left to the University of London Library. The bulk of his remaining estate was divided between the British Library and the horological section of the British Museum's department of medieval and later antiquities.   ALAN GAULD

Sources A. Gauld, 'Recollections of E. J. Dingwall', *Journal of the Society for Psychical Research*, 54 (1987), 230–37 · E. J. Dingwall, 'The early world of psychical research', *Parapsychology Review*, 6 (1975), 6–9 · P. R. Harris, ed., *The library of the British Museum: retrospective essays on the department of printed books* (1993), 213–17 · *The Times* (14 Aug 1986) · *Daily Telegraph* (12 Aug 1986) · *Journal of the Society for Psychical Research*, 54 (1987), 92–5 · *British Library News*, no. 119 (Sept 1986) · *Parapsychology Review*, 18 (Jan–Feb 1987), 14 · *The Magic Circular*, 80 (1986), 183 · personal knowledge (2004) · private information (2004) · *WW* · d. cert. · m. cert. [Norah Margaret Davis]
Archives LUL, Harry Price Library, corresp. and papers | CUL, Society for Psychical Research archives · CUL, corresp. with Charles Ogden
Likenesses double portrait, photograph (with Dr Kinsey), BL; repro. in Harris, ed., *The library*, 215
Wealth at death £678,246: probate, 5 Nov 1986, *CGPLA Eng. & Wales*

Dinham [de Dinham] **family** (*per. c.*1200–*c.*1500), gentry, was in origin a branch of the Breton family of Dinan, named from the seigneurie of Dinan. The Breton Dinans formed part of a group of baronial families whose seats were located in north-east Brittany, bordering on western Normandy, and whose allegiances were consequently courted by the rulers of Normandy and post-conquest England. The Norman chronicler Wace, probably writing early in Henry II's reign, lists the Dinans among those who participated in the Norman conquest of England; but the first evidence for the family's presence in England is provided by a charter of 1122 of the Breton lord Geoffroi de Dinan, recording his grant of two manors in Devon (Harpford and Nutwell, previously granted to Geoffroi by Henry I) to the Norman monastery of Marmoutier, for the support of its Breton priory of St Malo at Dinan. Although there would later be claims for a greater antiquity for the Dinans in Britain, it is clear that they arrived among the 'new men' promoted by Henry I.

Geoffroi de Dinan had three sons, Olivier, Alain, and Josselin, all of whom had significant interests in both England and Brittany. The pipe roll of 1130 shows that the English lands of Olivier, the eldest, were located exclusively in Devon, and it was in south-west England that his descendants were to be increasingly ensconced. Their main seat was to be the large manor of Hartland, on Devon's north coast, and it was there that an earlier college of secular canons was to be refounded as an Augustinian abbey some time before 1169. The refoundation was largely the responsibility of Geoffroi's grandson, another Olivier de Dinan, and his son Geoffrey, but they also had the co-operation of another Geoffroi de Dinan, whose interests lay principally in Brittany. However, by the late twelfth century the Breton and English lines of the family had decisively diverged, and in the following century the Dinhams of Hartland, as they came to be called, start to become prominent in English national life.

The process is to be associated above all with **Oliver de Dinham**, Lord Dinham (c.1234–1299), the great-great-grandson of Olivier, the founder of Hartland. Like several of his descendants he was active as a soldier. In March 1264 he was summoned to Oxford for operations against Simon de Montfort, and continued to support the king during the civil war, notably as constable of Exeter Castle later in 1264. A knight by 1271, he had the custody of Lundy island between 1272 and 1275. Under Edward I he campaigned in Wales in 1277 and 1282, and only ill health prevented his serving there again in 1295. He was frequently appointed to commissions in Devon. It was probably a determination to safeguard his interests which led Dinham into a dispute with Hartland Abbey. In 1272, following the death of the abbot, Dinham occupied the abbey, and was only persuaded to withdraw by the bishop of Exeter. He was also active in augmenting his estates. He repurchased the two manors once given to Marmoutier, and between 1268 and 1272 bought several Cornish manors from Isolda of Cardinham, including Cardinham itself. But he made his greatest contribution to his family's standing through his marriage, apparently his second, to Isabel, widow of Sir John Courtenay of Okehampton, and daughter of Hugh de Vere, earl of Oxford. Their union, which had taken place by 1277, cost Dinham £100. Royal service and aristocratic connections no doubt account for the personal summonses to parliament which Dinham received in 1295 and 1296, in consequence of which he is regarded as having become Lord Dinham. When Oliver de Dinham died, on 26 February 1299, he held four manors in Devon, three in Cornwall, and one in Somerset.

Oliver was succeeded by his son **Joce de Dinham** (1273×5–1301), who was probably the child of his father's first marriage, born between 1273 and 1275 according to different accounts of his age at his father's death. He was summoned to serve in Scotland in 1300, but his death on 30 March 1301 ruled out any possibility of a summons to parliament. He followed his father, however, in making an advantageous marriage, to Margaret, daughter and heir of Sir Richard de Hydon of Clayhidon and Hemyock, though the benefits to his descendants were slow to

become apparent. Joce had two sons with Margaret, John and Oliver, and it was the latter who succeeded to Clayhidon and Hemyock, which only reverted to John's descendants at the end of the fourteenth century. A minor until 1316, **John** [i] **Dinham** (1295–1331/2), was also a soldier, receiving several summonses to campaigns in Scotland, and also to service in Aquitaine in 1325. He was a commissioner of the peace in Devon in 1327 and 1331. But public service was overshadowed by the scandal of his private life. Although married to Margaret, possibly the daughter of Sir William Grandson, John was by 1329 involved in a liaison with Matilda Moleton, said to be his kinswoman. For this he was excommunicated by Bishop Grandison. Dinham appealed, and proceedings were only brought to an end in October 1331, when he was absolved by the archbishop of Canterbury, and went on pilgrimage by way of penance. He did not return, having died some time before 15 April 1332.

His affair with Matilda Moleton notwithstanding, John [i] Dinham left a legitimate heir, **Sir John** [ii] **Dinham** (1317/18–1383), who was a minor at his father's death. Although he had been knighted by 1346, he does not appear to have served in Edward III's French campaigns, and he played relatively little part in local government, in 1359 obtaining exemption from jury service and office-holding. Instead he appears to have concentrated on the consolidation and extension of his estates, long reduced by the dowers of his grandmother and mother, who lived until 1357 and 1361 respectively. He made a particularly advantageous marriage, to Muriel, daughter of Sir Thomas Courtenay of Woodhuish, which renewed his own family's links with that of the earls of Devon, and brought him a number of manors, above all that of Kingskerswell; she died in 1374. In 1379 Dinham was said to hold twenty-six knights' fees in Devon and Cornwall.

John [ii] Dinham died on 7 January 1383, killed by two 'notorious' thieves, probably in Somerset. His death was speedily avenged by his son, **Sir John** [iii] **Dinham** (1358/9–1428), who, then aged twenty-four, slew one of his father's killers and captured the other in Exeter Cathedral, shedding blood in the process. This violent act was one of many in which John [iii] was to be involved. Following a dispute with the abbot of Hartland, in 1397 he was bound in the sum of 1000 marks to keep the peace, only to commit assaults in 1402 and 1404 which cost him 700 marks for a royal pardon. He quarrelled again with the abbey at the end of his life, over his rights as patron in times of vacancy, but the dispute was resolved in 1428. Unlike his immediate forebears, John [iii] had links with the court, perhaps through the Courtenays. Already a knight at his father's death, in 1382 he attended Richard II's wedding, giving a party for his friends before he left for Westminster. Under Henry IV he was appointed to the escort accompanying the king's daughter Blanche to Germany for her marriage, though in the end he did not go, and he came to be styled 'king's knight'. A taste for luxury, deducible from his use of hunting arrows bound with gold, may bespeak the courtier. But Dinham was also a useful royal servant in his homeland, being several times appointed to commissions in Devon. In 1401 he obtained exemption from jury service and office-holding, but was still a commissioner of the peace in 1402 and a commissioner of array in 1418 and 1421.

Sir John [iii] married three times: his first wife was Eleanor (surname unknown), who died between 1387 and 1396; his second was Maud Mautravers, widow of Sir Peter de la *Mare, who brought half the Dorset manor of Hooke to the Dinhams, and who died in 1402; and the third was Philippa, daughter of Sir John *Lovell. Philippa was the mother of John Dinham's son and heir, but her husband had earlier shown himself concerned for the descent of his estates. In 1398 he had the manors of Kingskerswell and Nutwell conveyed jointly to his wife Maud and himself, and in 1401 he conveyed what seem to have been all his lands to feoffees, who still held them at his death. His evident concern for his family's possessions makes John [iii] the likeliest compiler of the Dinham cartulary (BL, Add. MS 34792A).

In 1400 John [iii] was reported to be suffering from 'a bloody flux', but he clearly rallied, dying only on Christmas day 1428. His son and heir, **Sir John** [iv] **Dinham** (1405/6–1458), was then twenty-two. The fact that his mother lived until 1465, in occupation of her dower lands, may have been one reason why John [iv] took a more active part in public life than his father had done. A knight by 1 May 1430, he attended the young Henry VI to France in that year, and in 1436 was retained to serve at the relief of Calais with eleven men-at-arms and seventy-two archers. Regularly a JP in Devon from 1440, he frequently acted in the same capacity in Cornwall, and received numerous other commissions in both counties. Many of these were for military or peace-keeping purposes, but he was also appointed to assess a subsidy in 1436, to raise a loan to the crown in 1446, and to raise money for the defence of Calais in 1455. During the 1450s he seems to have remained loyal to Henry VI, a fact which makes his son's eventual Yorkism the more surprising. John [iv] married Joan, daughter of Sir Richard Arches, a match which brought him lands in Oxfordshire. He died on 25 January 1458, and was long outlived by his widow, who died early in 1497. Their son, John *Dynham (c.1433–1501), would enter the peerage as Lord Dynham, though his title, like that of Oliver two centuries earlier, endured only for a single generation.   KAREN JANKULAK

Sources GEC, *Peerage*, 4.369–82 • M. Jones, *The family of Dinan in England in the middle ages / La famille de Dinan en Angleterre au moyen âge*, trans. J. Métayer (1987) • R. P. Chope, *The book of Hartland* (1940) • R. Wace, *Le 'Roman de Rou' et des ducs de Normandie*, ed. F. Pluquet (Rouen, 1827) • M. Jones, 'Les branches anglaises des seigneurs de Dinan', *Dinan au moyen age*, ed. X. Barral i Altet and others (1986), 221–35 • M. Jones, 'Notes sur quelques familles bretonnes en Angleterre après la conquête normande', *The creation of Brittany: a late medieval state* (1988), 69–93 • R. P. Chope, 'The early history of the manor of Hartland', *Report and Transactions of the Devonshire Association*, 34 (1902), 418–54 • R. P. Chope, 'The last of the Dynhams', *Report and Transactions of the Devonshire Association*, 50 (1918), 431–92 • Chancery records • CIPM, vols. 6–7, 12, 15 • BL, Add. MS 34792A • CEPR letters, vol. 5 • N. H. Nicolas, ed., *Proceedings and ordinances of the privy council of England*, 7 vols., RC, 26 (1834–7), vols.

4, 6 • F. Palgrave, ed., *The parliamentary writs and writs of military summons*, 2 vols. in 4 (1827–34), vols. 1/2, 2/3 • F. C. Hingeston-Randolph, ed., *The register of Edmund Lacy, bishop of Exeter, 1: The register of institutions, with some account of the episcopate of John Catrik*, AD 1419 (1909) • *The register of Edmund Lacy, bishop of Exeter*, ed. G. R. Dunstan, 5 vols., CYS, 60–63, 66 (1963–72), vol. 3 • F. C. Hingeston-Randolph, ed., *The register of John de Grandisson, bishop of Exeter*, 3 vols. (1894–9) • G. Oliver, *Monasticon dioecesis Exoniensis* (1846) • O. J. Reichel and others, eds., *Devon feet of fines*, 2, Devon and Cornwall RS, old ser., 6 (1939) • K. B. McFarlane, *The nobility of later medieval England* (1973) • W. Dugdale, *The baronage of England*, 2 vols. (1675–6), vol. 1, p. 514
Archives BL, Add. MS 34792A | Cornwall RO, Arundell collection, charters
Likenesses monuments, c.1400 (probably John [ii] Dinham), Kingskerswell parish church, Devon

Dinham, Joce de (1273x5–1301). *See under* Dinham family (*per.* c.1200–c.1500).

Dinham, John (1295–1331/2). *See under* Dinham family (*per.* c.1200–c.1500).

Dinham, Sir John (1317/18–1383). *See under* Dinham family (*per.* c.1200–c.1500).

Dinham, Sir John (1358/9–1428). *See under* Dinham family (*per.* c.1200–c.1500).

Dinham, Sir John (1405/6–1458). *See under* Dinham family (*per.* c.1200–c.1500).

Dinham, Oliver de, Lord Dinham (c.1234–1299). *See under* Dinham family (*per.* c.1200–c.1500).

Dinizulu [Dinuzulu] **ka Cetshwayo** (1868–1913), Zulu king, was the eldest son of *Cetshwayo kaMpande (c.1826–1884) and his senior wife, Novimbi Msweli, and thus the heir apparent to the Zulu kingship. Aged five, in 1873 he witnessed his father's coronation by Theophilus Shepstone. In 1879 British forces invaded and conquered the Zulu kingdom, defeating Cetshwayo's forces. Cetshwayo was exiled, and the kingdom was divided into thirteen kingdoms. Dinizulu was left in the area assigned to the Mandhlakazi chief, Zibhebu, who had quarrelled with Cetshwayo and was hostile to his Usuthu faction. Dinizulu was briefly reunited with his father when in 1883 Cetshwayo was restored to a truncated kingdom shorn of a large reserve on the Natal border and another area in the north set aside for the renegade Zibhebu. The ensuing civil war (a direct consequence of the British policy of causing dissension among the Zulu), Zibhebu's victory over the Usuthu, and Cetshwayo's flight and death in 1884 left Dinizulu in mortal danger. As Zibhebu's forces ravaged the kingdom's heartland, Dinizulu was hidden by Ndabuko in the fastnesses of the Nkandla Forest.

The Usuthu petitioned the British to install Dinizulu as king and to restore order, but there was official reluctance to reinstate the Zulu kingdom. As many of the Usuthu were reduced to starvation by Zibhebu's raiding, Usuthu leaders negotiated with a committee of Transvaal Boers, who offered to install Dinizulu as paramount chief in return for land on which to establish a so-called New Republic. On 22 May 1884 the Boers proclaimed Dinizulu king. They then supported the Usuthu forces in attacking and routing Zibhebu; in return, however, they claimed almost the entire Zulu heartland, right down to the coast. In response to Zulu pleas, growing anarchy, and their own hostility to Boer expansionism, the British intervened, acknowledging the New Republic within greatly restricted boundaries; it was shortly afterwards amalgamated with Transvaal. The rest of the Zulu territory was annexed and placed under direct crown rule on 14 May 1887.

Informed that his kingship was abolished, and enraged by the reinstatement of Zibhebu as a chief by the British, Dinizulu put himself at the head of an uprising. His forces successfully attacked Zibhebu, but were broken up by British troops on 2 July 1888. Dinizulu then fled to Transvaal, but was persuaded by the missionary and Zulu sympathizer Harriet Colenso to travel to Bishopstowe, the Colenso family home in Natal, where he surrendered to the British. He was convicted of treason, and was exiled to the island of St Helena. There, allowed considerable freedom, he learned to read and write, and to play the American organ. In 1898 he was freed and allowed to return to Zululand, no longer as king but as 'government Induna' (local headman), a role which recognized the authority he still held in the eyes of many Zulu. He was also installed as chief of the core of the Usuthu faction, which was now constituted by the British administration as a tribe with a defined territory. Before his return, however, Zululand had been handed over to Natal; the authorities in the territory were thus responsible to a legislature elected exclusively by white men, who had a direct interest in exploiting its resources of land and labour. Dinizulu found his central role deeply frustrating. He had little opportunity to influence legislation or administrative policy in the interests of his people. His function was rather to justify government policy to his tribe, a role which threatened to destroy the widespread loyalty and respect he still enjoyed. He thus spent most of his time in his local chiefdom at Osuthu, using it as a base to maintain and extend his personal authority and links among the Zulu at large. He married wives from the leading lineage groups of the previous kingdom, dispatched messengers to the headquarters of its constituent chiefdoms, and received visits from their leading men.

By the early years of the twentieth century, changes in the South African economy and policies of the Natal government conspired to raise tensions in Natal and Zululand, which made Dinizulu's position increasingly difficult. The crown, absentee landlords, and land companies could now more profitably sell or lease land to white capitalist farmers than to African tenants. Many African tenants were forced off the land and the rents of those who remained were raised. Their struggle to maintain economic independence became increasingly difficult. In 1902 the Natal government tightened the squeeze by making substantial areas of Zululand available to white farmers, confining the Zulu to defined reserves in the heartland of their old kingdom. Finally, in 1906, taxes on Africans in Natal and Zululand were substantially raised by the introduction of a poll tax. Attempts to collect the tax met with a number of instances of resistance. Bambatha, chief of the Zondi in Natal, was involuntarily involved in one of these attempts, and, accompanied by a wife and two children, sought asylum at Osuthu. Anxious not to offend the government, or to undermine his standing with his own people, Dinizulu sent Bambatha back to Natal but allowed his wife and children to stay. On his return, Bambatha found that he had been deposed in favour of an uncle, and at once attacked him, initiating a rebellion. To strengthen his support, he claimed that Dinizulu had authorized his attack, and given him charms which would turn bullets into water. The rebellion spread, and proved difficult and costly to suppress. To prove his own loyalty to the government, Dinizulu offered to send all his forces to assist against Bambatha; but in the later stages of the rebellion he allowed some of the rebels who fled to Osuthu to remain there, rather than hand them over to the authorities.

On these grounds, and on suspicion of his involvement in the murder of some pro-government chiefs, Dinizulu's arrest was ordered. Once again on the advice of Harriet Colenso he surrendered himself. Through the efforts of the Colensos and their friends, his defence was undertaken by the former liberal premier of Cape Colony W. P. Schreiner. Although the presiding judge remarked that his actions had not been motivated by any hostile intention against the state, Dinizulu was convicted of treason for harbouring rebels, and sentenced to four years' imprisonment. On the inauguration of the South African Union in 1910, however, its first prime minister, Louis Botha (who had been involved in the Boer expedition to put Dinizulu on the throne in 1884), released him. Dinizulu settled on a farm in Transvaal, but his health had long been poor, and he died there on 18 October 1913.

Dinizulu's lifelong commitment to maintaining the Zulu kingship had tragic consequences for his people as well as for himself. It facilitated the annexation by Transvaal of a large part of the Zulu kingdom, precipitated direct British rule, and assisted the formal extinction of the kingdom and its incorporation into white settler-ruled Natal. It did, however, keep the idea of the kingdom alive in the minds of the Zulu people and of white administrators and politicians, with profound consequences for the future. JOHN D. OMER-COOPER

Sources C. T. Binns, Dinizulu: the death of the house of Shaka (1968) · S. Marks, Reluctant rebellion (1970) · J. Guy, The destruction of the Zulu kingdom (1979) · C. T. Binns, The last Zulu king: the life and death of Cetshwayo (1963) · E. H. Brookes and C. de B. Webb, A history of Natal (1965) · C. Bundy, The rise and fall of the South African peasantry (1979) · R. H. Palmer and N. Parsons, eds., The roots of rural poverty in central and southern Africa (1977) · S. Marks, 'Harriette Colenso and the Zulus, 1874–1913', Journal of African History, 4 (1963), 403–11

Dinnie, Donald (1837–1916), athlete, was born on 8 July 1837 at Balnacraig, near Aboyne, Aberdeenshire, the eldest of ten children of Robert Dinnie (1808–1892), a stonemason, and Christine Hay. He left school at fifteen and won his first prize for wrestling one year later in 1853, when he turned professional. During the Victorian period the issue of professionalism was handled in a variety of ways by different sports, and Dinnie was earning money from athletics several years before the matter had been resolved in rugby, cricket, or football. By 1867 he had decided to make athletics his full-time employment. That same year he recorded nine firsts and one second at the inaugural Aboyne highland games. He was the undefeated highland games heavyweight champion from 1856 to 1869 and then again from 1871 to 1876. During his first year as a full-time professional athlete Dinnie's records included throwing the heavy hammer 81 feet 6 inches, throwing the heavy stone 35 feet 5 inches, throwing the light stone 45 feet 7 inches, and clearing 5 feet 1 inch in the high jump. By 1868 he had also advanced the records at the Braemar Royal Highland Gathering to: 92 feet 4 inches for the 16 lb hammer, 84 feet 9 inches for the 22 lb hammer, and 5 feet 4 inches for the high jump. Promoters were prepared to pay him between £25 and £100 to appear at Scottish highland games events.

In 1870 Dinnie was invited by the Caledonia Clubs to tour America, and the New York Caledonian Club paid $130 towards his passage. He acted as a judge at the New York Caledonian games of 1872 where his attendance helped to attract a crowd of 25,000 spectators, and by 1877 he was able to earn as much as $700 a day. At Plainfield, New Jersey, he won the mixed styles wrestling championship of America in 1882. At one San Francisco highland games his winnings totalled £350 plus half of the gate money. Dinnie moved to Australia in 1844 and then on to New Zealand. Still reluctant to perform without payment he earned £85 for defeating the Maori wrestling champion of fifteen consecutive years. In 1888 he toured South Africa, returning home a year later.

As an athlete, Dinnie was an all-rounder, equally proficient at putting the stone, tossing the caber, leaping, jumping, or running. Proud and independent of character, he stood 6 feet 1 inch high, and weighed 15 stone; his chest measured 48 inches, his biceps 15 inches, and his thighs 26½ inches. During his professional career (1853–c.1912) he won more than 11,000 contests: these included 2000 prizes for throwing the hammer, 1800 prizes for putting the stone, more than 2000 prizes for wrestling, 300 prizes for throwing weights, 1400 prizes for tossing the caber, 1800 prizes for jumping, and about 500 prizes for running and hurdles races. Dinnie sincerely believed that the athlete, like the labourer, should be paid for his work, and his estimated cash winnings from athletics, excluding displays from strength promotions and displays, were in excess of £25,000.

Dinnie's first wife died in the 1870s while he was on tour. His son Edwin Dinnie was born in June 1877, and won over a hundred prizes in light and field events. Dinnie married for a second time, in 1885, in Melbourne, where his daughter Eva was born.

Dinnie continued to compete as a professional athlete until well into his seventies. In 1907 he asked the Aboyne highland games committee to arrange two events for veterans of over sixty years. At the age of seventy-five he competed in a health and strength show in London. Best

remembered as one of Scotland's chief professional athletes, Dinnie died at his home, 144 Portland Road, Kensington, London, on 2 April 1916. His second wife, Eleanor, survived him. The Donald Dinnie trophy remains one of the most sought-after Scottish athletic awards.

GRANT JARVIE

Sources *Aboyne highland games, centenary programme* (1967) • I. Colquhoun and H. Machell, *Highland gatherings* (1927) • A. G. Cumming, 'In the green arena: athletes and records at the Braemar gathering', *Book of the Braemar gathering* (1926), 113–19 • E. A. Donaldson, *The Scottish highland games in America* (1986) • R. Holt, *Sport and the British: a modern history* (1989) • G. Jarvie, *Highland games: the making of the myth* (1991) • G. Redmond, *The Caledonian games in nineteenth century America* (1971) • D. Webster, *Scottish highland games* (1959) • d. cert. • private information (2004)
Likenesses photograph, repro. in Colquhoun and Machell, *Highland gatherings*

Dinwiddie, James (1746–1815), scientist, was born on 8 December 1746 on a farm in Kirkland, Dumfriesshire, the youngest child of three sons and two daughters of John Dinwoody (d. 1746), farmer, and his wife, Catharine Riddick. James's father died six months before he was born and left his family in very difficult circumstances. James, who seems to have changed his name to Dinwiddie at a very early age, disliked farmwork, and relatives, hoping he would become a Presbyterian minister, paid his fees at Dumfries Academy and Edinburgh University. At the end of his studies, even after he had given his maiden sermon before the presbytery, he decided against the ministry; he had been 'irrecoverably rivetted by science' (Proudfoot, 2).

In 1771 Dinwiddie became a mathematics teacher at Dumfries Academy, where he introduced scientific experiments and outdoor practical surveying lessons. He graduated MA from Edinburgh in 1778 and was granted leave to go on a lecture tour to settle debts, incurred when he spent the enormous sum of £150 on scientific equipment. He lectured successfully in Scotland, and after July 1779 throughout Ireland. His courses on chemistry and mechanics were supplemented by lectures on gunnery, fortification and pyrotechnics, aerostatics, and the diving bell. His apparatus included a 16 foot long model illustrating the siege of Gibraltar, and specially cast miniature brass cannons; he recreated ancient war engines using animal sinews, and exhibited steam-powered model boats and, in May 1785 in Dublin, what seems to have been a very early form of velocipede. He experimented with large hot-air balloons, but, despite ambitious plans, rivalry with Richard Crosbie, and public announcements in 1783 in Dublin and Belfast, was unable to make a manned ascent, and Crosbie became the first Irish aeronaut. Dinwiddie's impressive, expensive apparatus often became a millstone round his neck. It was difficult to store or transport and he was often careless about money; he purchased equipment rather than life's necessities, and was cheated by his nephew and by acquaintances.

Off the Dublin coast in May 1783 Dinwiddie descended in the diving bell of Charles Spalding, a pioneer submariner, to make scientific observations; on 2 June, Spalding and an assistant died of asphyxiation. Dinwiddie did not proceed with Spalding's attempt to recover bullion from the shipwreck of the *Belgioso*; his investigations probably suggested that it was too risky. He declined the offer of a professorship in Manchester, and left Ireland in 1786 to lecture with ever greater success in Scotland and England; it is said that a member of the royal family attended his lectures in the summer of 1790. In 1792 he was made LLD by Edinburgh University.

Prince Potyomkin, a Russian landowner, and the marqués del Campo, the Spanish ambassador in London, tried to persuade Dinwiddie to visit their respective countries to popularize the study of science, but in September 1792 Dinwiddie accompanied the embassy of George, Lord Macartney, to China. It is not quite clear why he was chosen for this task, though he may have met Macartney previously and was certainly well known by this date. On the journey he tested a set of chronometers for suitability in determining longitude. During the stay in China, Dinwiddie was responsible for setting up a planetarium, a gift to the Chinese emperor, collected botanical specimens, and made scientific observations. His copious and perceptive journal records the impressions made by China on a European scientist, and provides valuable information about their ultimately unproductive and somewhat humiliating mission. After its abrupt end in September 1794 Dinwiddie, at Macartney's request, successfully transported Chinese tea plants, assorted seeds, and silkworms to Calcutta. The Indian tea industry may be partly derived from Dinwiddie's carefully nurtured plants. Dinwiddie also brought Malayan rubber trees to India, but details of his alleged discovery of a process to make the rubber completely watertight have not been preserved. He made a fortune lecturing in Calcutta, and was asked by the Indian board of trade to assess the economic importance of India's raw materials and native technologies. In 1800 Dinwiddie became a professor in Fort William College in Calcutta. He investigated galvanism, finding that it cured St Vitus's dance in an Indian patient, and noted the efficacy of coal oil on cutaneous disorders.

In India, as throughout his life, Dinwiddie enthusiastically supported investigation and experiment in every branch of science, supplying advice and apparatus. He also manufactured and supplied sulphuric acid and lightning conductors. Dinwiddie was said to be the 'centre or focus of philosophy in the East' (Proudfoot, 102); he advised Brahman priests on astronomical questions and worked with Indians on mathematics. He had an extensive correspondence with savants and technologists throughout India and Europe, which was maintained even after he retired and returned to London in 1807. There he was elected a member of the Royal Institution on 6 July 1810 and, despite deafness, served on two of its committees. He spent a year in Dumfries with his daughter's family, and died on 19 March 1815 in Pentonville, London. He was buried in St James's, Pentonville. His will mentions Ann Muir, the mother of his daughter Ann Proudfoot; it appears that they were never married and that Ann Muir and her daughter had remained in Dumfries.

LINDE LUNNEY

Sources W. J. Proudfoot, *Biographical memoir of James Dinwiddie, LLD* (1868) · L. Lunney, 'The celebrated Mr Dinwiddie: an eighteenth-century scientist in Ireland', *Eighteenth-Century Ireland*, 3 (1988), 69–83 · *Public Register, or, Freeman's Journal* (3–5 May 1785) · A. Peyrefitte, *The collision of two civilisations: the British expedition to China in 1792–4*, trans. J. Rothschild (1993) · PRO, PROB 11/1573, fols. 218v–219r
Archives Dalhousie University, Halifax, Nova Scotia, archives, corresp., journals, lecture notes, scientific observations, etc.
Likenesses bust, repro. in Proudfoot, *Biographical memoir*
Wealth at death £2200 bequests: will, PRO, PROB 11/1573, fols. 218v–219r · came from India with £10,000 in 1806; some of his money remained in India earning interest: Proudfoot, *Biographical memoir*

Dinwiddie, Lawrence (1696/7–1764), merchant and civic leader, was born in Glasgow, the eighth child of Robert Dinwiddie (d. 1708/9), laird of Germiston, a trader who had prospered after moving from Dumfriesshire in 1691, and Elizabeth Cumming (fl. 1685–1696). He attended Glasgow University and became a burgess of the town in 1723. On 11 June of the following year he married the daughter of a Glasgow merchant, Janet Coulter (d. 1744), with whom he had fifteen children.

Dinwiddie became a successful Glasgow merchant, a 'tobacco lord' of the second rank who was one of the first to diversify into ancillary manufactures. He owned shares in several ships in the Virginia trade as well as a sloop, the *Butterfly*, that sailed to the Mediterranean in 1737. He invested in Port Glasgow Ropeworks and in the Delftfield Pottery Company, both of which proved profitable and had home and colonial markets. With his partner, Archibald Cochran, and several other leading tobacco merchants, he built Bell's Tanneries on the banks of the Molendar burn, and took an active part in its management; he later became a partner in the adjacent Glasgow tan works. Bell's grew into the largest leather works in Britain during the second half of the eighteenth century, eventually employing 300 shoemakers and generating complaints about pollution of the burn. It was described as 'a prodigious large building consisting of bark and lime pits, storage houses … with all other conveniences' (Robertson, 1.466). As a result of its success, the tannery began to engage in private banking activities, taking large deposits in bills or personal bonds at 4–5 per cent interest. The bond business may have led to Dinwiddie's participation in the founding of the Glasgow Arms Bank, one of the first provincial Scottish banks to contest the supremacy of the Royal Bank of Scotland and the Bank of Scotland in Edinburgh. Dinwiddie was among twenty-six prominent Glasgow merchants who advertised the opening of the Arms Bank as partners on 6 November 1750. In spite of the antagonism of the Edinburgh banks, the Arms Bank did satisfactory business, fulfilling the requirements of the growing mercantile community.

Unlike the Presbyterian majority, Dinwiddie worshipped with the small Episcopalian congregation at St Andrew's at what later became St Andrew's Square. He played an active part in Glasgow civic affairs throughout his career, serving many years on the town council and two terms as lord provost in 1742–3 and 1743–4. After the death of his first wife, on 9 June 1745 he married another daughter of a respected Glasgow merchant, Elizabeth Kennedy (d. 1787), with whom he had six more children. In 1748 he purchased his father's lands of Germiston and Balornock from his bankrupt elder brother, Matthew. Dinwiddie died on 3 May 1764, in or near Glasgow, leaving his lands and business commitments to his son Lawrence, one of the few of his twenty-one children who survived childhood.   MONICA CLOUGH

Sources J. R. Anderson, ed., *The provosts of Glasgow from 1609 to 1832* (1942) · T. M. Devine, *The tobacco lords: a study of the tobacco merchants of Glasgow and their trading activities, c.1740–1790* (1975) · D. R. [D. Robertson], rev., *Glasgow, past and present: illustrated in dean of guild court reports and in the reminiscences and communications of Senex, Aliquis, J.B., &c*, 3 vols. (1884) · J. O. Mitchell, *Old Glasgow essays* (1905) · C. W. Munn, *The Scottish provincial banking companies* (1981) · J. Gibson, *The history of Glasgow* (1778)

Dinwiddie, Robert (1692–1770), merchant and colonial administrator, was born in Germiston, outside Glasgow, on 3 October 1692, one of nine children of Robert Dinwiddie (d. 1712), merchant in Glasgow, and his wife, Elizabeth, daughter of Glasgow bailie Mathew Cumming of Carderock. Robert entered the transatlantic trade immediately following graduation in 1710/11 from the University of Glasgow, where he studied under John Law, professor of moral philosophy. The university later awarded him two honorary degrees.

In 1718 Dinwiddie settled in St George's parish, Bermuda, where he became one of the island's most substantial men. Like many industrious and enterprising eighteenth-century Scots, Dinwiddie sought his fortune in the service of the British crown. He began his public career in 1727 with his appointment by Horatio Walpole, brother of the prime minister, Sir Robert Walpole, as the collector of customs in Bermuda, at an annual salary of £30.

Some time in the mid-1730s Dinwiddie married Rebecca (d. 1793), only daughter of the Revd Andrew Auchinleck, member of the council of Bermuda, who also served three times as chief executive of the colony in the absence of a governor. Rebecca's mother came from the Tucker family, one of the most influential families in Bermuda. They had two daughters: Elizabeth, born in 1738, and Rebecca, born in 1742.

Dinwiddie corresponded frequently with the Board of Trade in London, commenting and advising on economic and political problems in the West Indies and America. In 1736 he suggested to the board that a special agent inspect and report on the American colonies. On 11 April 1738 Walpole appointed him 'Surveyor General of the Southern Part of the Continent of North America. Viz. South and North Carolina, Virginia, Maryland, Pennsylvania, Bahama Islands and Jamaica'. In effect this post made him overseer of the British customs service for most of the British possessions in North America and the West Indies. The appointment was for life and carried an annual salary of more than £300. As a result of this new post, Dinwiddie moved with his family in 1741 to Norfolk, Virginia, where he remained for five years before moving to London. He

consigned his post of surveyor-general to the Virginian Peter Randolph in 1749. But Dinwiddie was not content with remaining outside of government service, and sought the lieutenant-governorship of Virginia. On 4 July 1751 his appointment was confirmed and he returned to the Old Dominion.

An ardent defender of British interests, Dinwiddie soon came into conflict with colonial Virginians. In 1752 controversy arose over the selection of a president for the College of William and Mary, the use of executive power, and Dinwiddie's plan to charge a fee of 1 pistole for every land grant he signed. Viewed by the lieutenant-governor as a legitimate and lucrative source of income for the Treasury, the fee was seen as a sign of Dinwiddie's greed by members of Virginia's house of burgesses. The conflict between royal authority and colonists' interests culminated during the threat of French occupation of the Ohio district in 1753. As lieutenant-governor Dinwiddie struggled to defend and expand the British empire against the French, and to strengthen the authority of the crown over Britain's colonies in North America. It was his decision to send a young Major George Washington to confront the French in the Ohio valley, and to demand their removal from land claimed by the British. The French refusal prompted the outbreak of the French and Indian War. Although he urged intercolonial support for common defence in the face of the French threat, Dinwiddie was constantly frustrated by the lack of co-operation. In response he called for parliamentary action for the royalization and the confederation of the American colonies for their common protection. To reassert the authority of the mother country he strongly advocated the levying of British taxes on the Americans to pay for their own defence but found his efforts limited by restrictions imposed by members of the general assembly.

Dinwiddie's efforts in the colonies affected his health, and he left Virginia on 12 January 1758 to return to England. He died at Hotwells at Clifton, near Bristol, on 27 July 1770, and was buried at the parish church of Clifton. Dinwiddie was a hard-working and talented colonial politician. His confrontations over revenue prompted early questions to be raised over the relationship between lieutenant-governors and colonial legislatures, and over the treatment of the colonies by the British government that eventually led to the American War of Independence.   A. W. PARKER

Sources J. R. Alden, *Robert Dinwiddie, servant of the crown* (1973) · L. K. Koontz, *Robert Dinwiddie: his career in American colonial government and westward expansion* (1941) · R. A. Brock, ed., *The official records of Robert Dinwiddie, lieutenant-governor of the colony of Virginia, 1751–58*, 2 vols. (1883–4) · L. K. Koontz, ed., *Robert Dinwiddie: correspondence illustrative of his career in American colonial government and westward expansion*, 2 vols. (1951) · P. R. Shrock, 'Maintaining the prerogative: three royal governors in Virginia as a case study, 1710–1758', PhD diss., University of North Carolina, 1980 · R. W. Bailey, *Robert Dinwiddie: grandfather of the United States* (1956) · C. Innes, ed., *Munimenta alme Universitatis Glasguensis / Records of the University of Glasgow from its foundation till 1727*, 4 vols., Maitland Club, 72 (1854) · B. Tarter, 'Dinwiddie, Robert', *ANB*

Archives BL, letters · New Brunswick Museum, survey of British colonies · PRO, corresp. with British government, Colonial Office

5: 6, 17, 1325–1338, 1344; 324: 38, and Treasury I: 348, 358, 360, 372, 1324, 3818 · Virginia Historical Society, corresp. | Colonial Williamsburg Foundation, Richard Corbin letter-book · Colonial Williamsburg Foundation, Lockhart family papers · LPL, corresp., mainly with Bishop Sherlock · Virginia State Library, James Abercromby letter-book

Likenesses C. Dixon, miniature, c.1750, Colonial Williamsburg · portrait, NPG

Wealth at death £100 to University of Glasgow for book purchase; £50 to Glasgow relief; to each daughter £10,000; to widow, an annuity of £350 p.a., plus all his household goods, and the income from £1000 held in trust and from house and lot in Bermuda; plus various bequests to friends and relatives: Alden, *Robert Dinwiddie*

Diodati, Charles (1609/10–1638), friend of John Milton, was born in Middlesex, probably in Brentford, the son of Theodore *Diodati (1573–1651), a physician of Tuscan descent; his mother was an Englishwoman whose name is not known. By September 1618 he was living in London with his family (including his sister Philadelphia and his brother John) in the Castle Baynard ward of the parish of St Mary Magdalen, near St Paul's Cathedral and the home of Milton on Bread Street. Diodati was educated at St Paul's School and at Trinity College, Oxford. He was admitted to Trinity in late 1621 or early 1622, and matriculated on 7 February 1623, aged thirteen. He proceeded BA on 10 December 1625 and MA on 8 July 1628; his MA was incorporated at Cambridge on 7 July 1629.

By 1630 Diodati was living in Geneva, the birthplace of his father and the residence of his uncle Jean Diodati, a distinguished protestant theologian. He matriculated as a student of theology at the Academy of Geneva on 16 April 1630; a later record shows that he was still at the academy on 15 September 1631 but it is not known how long he remained in residence. He subsequently decided not to enter the church, and instead followed his father into medicine. There is no record of Diodati having studied medicine at a university so he may have been apprenticed to his father. He practised medicine with his father in Chester and in the London parish of St Ann Blackfriars, where he lived with his sister Philadelphia in the house of a Mr Dollam. The evidence for his intermittent residence in Chester is contained in Milton's poetry, but the name of Theodore Diodati also occurs in the churchwardens' accounts of St Peter's, Chester. In the middle of 1638 Diodati's family buried three of its members in St Ann Blackfriars: Isabel, his brother John's wife since 28 July 1635, was buried on 29 June; his sister Philadelphia was buried on 10 August; and Diodati himself was buried on 27 August, having died at Mr Dollam's house in Blackfriars while his friend Milton was in Italy. The causes of these youthful deaths are not recorded but plague must be a possibility.

Diodati's sole published work was an elegy in Latin alcaics on the death of William Camden, which was published in *Camdeni insignia* (1624). Diodati's only other writings known to have survived are two light-hearted letters to Milton, now in the British Library (BL, Add. MS 5016, fols. 5, 71); the letters, which are undated, are written in Greek prose. The friendship between Milton and Diodati

dated from childhood (*a pueritia*, as Milton says in the headnote to *Epitaphium Damonis*). Diodati wrote to Milton from Chester early in April 1626; the letter is lost but Milton's reply, in Latin elegiacs, was later printed as *Elegia I*; similarly, *Elegia VI* is Milton's response to a lost verse-letter by Diodati written on 13 December 1629. Milton also addressed an exuberant sonnet (Sonnet 4) in Italian to Diodati, probably in late 1629. In 1637 he twice wrote to Diodati in Latin prose (*Epistolarum familiarium*, 6 and 7); these letters allude to Diodati's nascent medical career, and the second letter glances at the fraught issue of Theodore Diodati's remarriage after the death of his first wife.

After Diodati's death Milton wrote a commemorative poem, *Epitaphium Damonis*, which survives in a single printed copy in the British Library. The poem is a pastoral elegy which movingly conveys Milton's sense of loss; because it is in Latin it is less well known than 'Lycidas' but it is one of the greatest poems in the final flowering of Latin literature.

The exchanges between Milton and Diodati depict Milton as a serious and austere student with a passion for learning, and Diodati as his light-hearted and playful friend with a great appetite for conviviality and the life of the countryside; the literary persona is not a reliable guide to temperament, but the portrait of Milton can be verified from other sources, so it is not unlikely that the literary image of Diodati was a faithful reflection of his character.   GORDON CAMPBELL

Sources D. C. Dorian, *The English Diodatis* (1950) · Oxford University matriculation register, Bodl. Oxf., 126 · 'Matricula studiosorum', Bibliothèque Publique et Universitaire de Genève, MS fr 141c (Inv. 345), fol. 9v · churchwardens' accounts, St Peter's, Chester, Ches. & Chester ALSS, P63/7/1, 81, 82, 89 · Munk, *Roll*, 1.169 · *Return of aliens in London*, Huguenot Society of London, 3.195 · BL, Add. MS 5884 · parish register, St Ann Blackfriars, 27 Aug 1638 [burial]

Archives BL, Add. MS 5016, fols. 5, 71

Diodati, Theodore (1573–1651), physician, was born in Geneva on 23 August 1573, the eldest of ten children of Carlo Diodati (1541–1625), a merchant banker, and his second wife, Maria Mei. The family was from the northern Italian town of Lucca, where they had been prominent in public life. Family tradition identifies Carlo's godfather and namesake as the emperor Charles V. Despite this tie Carlo Diodati was converted to protestantism and was settled in Calvinist Geneva by 1567. He prospered there in banking and silk manufacture, was a leader in the Italian reformed church, and a member of the Genevan town council from 1584 to 1619.

Among other accomplishments some Diodatis had pursued the practice of medicine in Lucca. This tradition was carried on by Theodore Diodati who matriculated in medicine at Leiden, on 3 August 1594. He did not take a degree at this time but a 1596 thesis of his, on smallpox and measles, survives and was dedicated to his medical professor Peter Paaw, and to Marc Offredi, a Genevan physician who had encouraged his medical studies. Diodati remained at Leiden until 1598, at which time he accepted employment in England as a tutor to John Harington, the six-year-old son of Sir John Harington of Exton. Diodati was mentioned in this capacity in 1603 in John Florio's classic English translation of Montaigne's *Essais*, on which Diodati had assisted.

Attendance on the Haringtons brought Diodati into the orbit of the court of James I. The care and education of Princess Elizabeth eventually became the responsibility of Sir John Harington, while his son became the boon companion of Prince Henry. Diodati was both tutor and physician to the royal children in 1609, although by this time he had his own house in Brentford, Middlesex. He was now also practising more widely and gained great fame by curing a 76-year-old neighbour with a heroic phlebotomy, taking 60 ounces of blood over a three-day period, without any ill effect to the aged patient.

About this time, if not earlier, Diodati married an Englishwoman 'of good birth and fortune' (Dorian, 51). Their first child, Charles *Diodati, was born in 1609 or 1610. The younger Diodati achieved eternal fame as the best and most intimate friend of John Milton, from their schooldays together in London until Charles Diodati's early death in 1638. It has been suggested that Milton found aristocratic patrons for his earliest poetry through the medium and connections of the elder Diodati. A son, John, and a daughter, Philadelphia, followed the birth of Charles.

Diodati's medical practice continued to prosper and by 1612 he was well known enough as a physician to earn an epigram in print from the famous epigrammatist, John Owen, who played on the uniqueness of Diodati's Greek Christian name and his Latinate surname, both of which can be roughly translated as 'God's gift', and linking that meaning with the injunction in Ecclesiasticus to honour the physician because he has been given to men as a gift from God.

In the same year that Diodati received his epigram he was also reported to the College of Physicians for his unlicensed medical practice in London, suggesting that Diodati had moved that practice to the City of London proper. To strengthen his credentials Diodati returned to Leiden where, on 19 September 1615, he took his long delayed MD. He appeared before the London college, degree in hand, in 1616 and was eventually licensed by the college on 24 January 1617. Even then his relationship with the college was often less than cordial: on one occasion he flung French curses at a Huguenot physician and college fellow, Paul Delaune, who had questioned Diodati's use of a vomit in a case they both attended. In 1622 the college censors vindicated Diodati's medical judgement and practice, but severely reprimanded him for his disrespectful behaviour towards other fellows and the officers of the college. Differences with other fellows seemed to be over matters of professional judgement rather than medical philosophy. Many of Diodati's conflicts at the college were personal in origin and seemed to stem from his own aristocratic bearing, pride, and a temperament that was quick to anger at even the slightest criticism. Despite these occasional differences Diodati

remained a college licentiate in good standing for the remainder of his life.

Through all Diodati's tempests at the college he was always supported by the chief royal physician Theodore Turquet de Mayerne. Born in Geneva in 1573 within a month of each other, they were both descended from Italian protestant families of intellectual distinction. In 1622, during a typically nasty interchange at the College of Physicians, Diodati requested that Mayerne be present at the meeting. In 1628 Mayerne recommended Diodati in what turned out to be an unsuccessful petition for the office of physician to the Tower of London. Seventy of Diodati's bills or prescriptions can still be found among the Mayerne papers at the British Library.

Diodati's movements are fairly easy to track after his licensing by the college in 1617. A census of strangers residing in London found him and his family in the parish of St Mary Magdalen, in September 1618. A similar census placed him in Christchurch and St Faith's under St Paul's parishes in 1625. He was naturalized as an English subject on 9 January 1628, just prior to his application for the physicianship to the Tower. On the evidence of the annals of the College of Physicians, he was still in London in 1630. Gradually Diodati had built up his patient list among the English gentry and aristocracy, treating the families of Sir Thomas Egerton, Sir Richard Anderson, the earl of Bridgewater, and the countess of Derby.

Diodati's movements after 1630 remain something of a mystery. No longer in London, he seems to have been a travelling physician, serving the counties of England between Herefordshire and Lancashire, perhaps relocating his household to Chester, where his son Charles Diodati seems also to have practised medicine. During these years the elder Diodati added yet another prestigious family to his patient list, that of Sir Robert and Lady Brilliana Harley. By 1637 Diodati's first wife had died and he married a woman known only as Abigail. The marriage estranged Diodati from his children who, by 1638, had returned to London. In the summer of that year both Charles Diodati and his sister, Philadelphia, died and were buried in the parish church of St Ann Blackfriars.

Diodati continued his provincial practice until at least 1641, at which time he too had returned to London where he took up residency in the parish of St Bartholomew by the Exchange. In 1643 Diodati was assessed for £100 by the parliamentary committee for the advance of money. Like most of those assessed, he settled for a lesser sum in 1644. He remained estranged from his surviving son, John Diodati, who had his own business in London. At least two of Diodati's nephews, Charles and Theodore Diodati, followed their uncle into the medical profession. The younger Theodore Diodati, along with the physician's wife, Abigail, were the principal legatees of Diodati's will, written in 1649. There was no mention in his will of his son, John Diodati.

Diodati died in the parish of St Bartholomew by the Exchange and was buried in the body of the church on 12 February 1651. His loan of £1008 to the earl of Cleveland

and his son was eventually repaid to his nephew Theodore in 1654 through the action of a parliamentary committee for confiscated estates.   WILLIAM BIRKEN

Sources D. C. Dorian, *The English Diodatis* (1950) · annals, RCP Lond. · J. K. Franson, 'The Diodatis in Chester', *N&Q*, 234 (1989), 435 · R. W. Innes Smith, *English-speaking students of medicine at the University of Leyden* (1932)
Archives BL, Mayerne MSS · BL, Sloane MSS

Diplock, (William John) Kenneth, Baron Diplock (1907–1985), judge, was born on 8 December 1907 at 8 Barclay Road, South Croydon, the only child of William John Hubert Diplock, solicitor, and his wife, Christine Joan Brooke. He was educated at Whitgift School and University College, Oxford, of which in 1958 he became an honorary fellow. He passed chemistry (part one) in 1928 and took a second class in chemistry in 1929. He was called to the bar in 1932 by the Middle Temple, where he swiftly made his mark, spending two years in the chambers of Sir Valentine Holmes and then transferring to those of Sir Leslie Scott. But in 1939 he left his practice for war service, joining the Royal Air Force two years later and reaching the rank of squadron leader. He returned to the bar in 1945. In 1939 he had been appointed secretary to the master of the rolls, Lord Greene, a position which he held until 1948. He took silk in 1948 at the early age of forty-one and acquired an extensive practice in commercial work and as adviser to Commonwealth governments. He was recorder of Oxford from 1951 to 1956, when he was appointed a judge of the Queen's Bench Division, with the customary knighthood (January 1956). Promotion to the Court of Appeal and privy council followed in October 1961 and to the House of Lords, as Baron Diplock, in September 1968. The universities of Alberta (1972), Oxford (1977), and London (1979) conferred honorary degrees on him.

Diplock's colossal learning and intellectual power were apparent to everyone. At the bar they made him a formidable advocate, methodical, quietly spoken, meticulous, and deadly. On the bench they made him an equally formidable tribunal, but his consciousness of his own ability made him dismissive of ideas at which his own fast brain had not arrived first. Those who were able to pick up his *sotto voce* comments in court (smoker's emphysema made his voice weak) would hear a well-known textbook greeted as 'The boy's book of income tax'. Anticipating the weak points of an argument, he would mine the advocate's path with Socratic questions the answers to which would in due course, as he knew, destroy the case.

Light moments in the court of a judge whose leisure reading was the works of Sir William Holdsworth were not numerous, but he was able in one of his later judgments to admit wryly that his use in an earlier case of the word 'synallagmatic' had been regarded as 'a typical example of gratuitous philological exhibitionism' (*United Dominions* v. *Eagle Aircraft*, 1968). Moments of bonhomie tended to be characterized on his long and boyish face by what a colleague later described as a 'smile that would have done credit to any shark' (personal knowledge). But it was not only advocates who feared Diplock. The disdain

he found increasingly difficult to conceal for judicial views contrary to his own sometimes stifled discussion and dissent. It was to this, as much as to policy, that the tendency of the house when he was in the chair to limit decisions to a single speech may have been due; but that the single speech was as often as not Diplock's was more of a tribute to his phenomenal industry than to his personal dominance.

It was not, however, simply intellectual arrogance which drove Diplock. He had both a panoptic knowledge and comprehension of the law and a scientist's desire to rationalize it. His most conspicuous contribution was to constitutional and public law. The constitutions created in the post-war years for former British colonies and protectorates included chapters defining and protecting fundamental rights and freedoms. Appeals arising from these chapters soon reached the judicial committee of the privy council, which thus became involved in constitutional interpretation and enforcement forty years before the United Kingdom itself had any statutory source of equivalent rights. Diplock and his contemporaries Lord Wilberforce and Lord Scarman were the leading figures in this process.

Diplock gave an extensive interpretation to constitutional definitions of individual rights, following the principle, originally proclaimed by Lord Wilberforce, that such measures should receive 'a generous interpretation avoiding what has been called "the austerity of tabulated legalism", suitable to give to individuals the full measure of the fundamental rights and freedoms referred to' (*Minister of Home Affairs* v. *Fisher*, 1980). At the same time Diplock held that these definitions, thus widely interpreted, had to be observed, and constitutional rights were not to be pressed beyond them.

The same balance is displayed by Diplock's judgments on constitutional remedies. The special jurisdiction, created by a number of constitutions, to apply to the court for redress when invasion of a fundamental right occurred or was likely was, Diplock said in one case, 'an important safeguard of those rights and freedoms' (*Harrikissoon* v. *Attorney-General for Trinidad and Tobago*, 1980). On the other hand, the ordinary law was not superseded. If it provided an appropriate remedy for an unlawful administrative act, resort to the special constitutional procedure was not justified. These principles have had lasting importance in guiding the courts of a number of countries, particularly in the Caribbean, from which came most of the constitutional cases in which Diplock sat.

Diplock's decisions on appeals in capital cases were sometimes said to show that he was a hard man. His judgments do not necessarily support this view. What characterizes them is their intellectual integrity. He held that the task of a judge faced with a written constitution was to reach the proper interpretation of the constitutional language (the concept of 'a' proper interpretation was not within his mindset) and apply it. With the desirability of the result he was not concerned; that was the responsibility of the legislative arm of government, not the judicial. To this he adhered with complete consistency, even in a case in which a statute of Singapore imposed a mandatory sentence of death for trafficking in very small quantities of heroin. Diplock emphasized in his judgment that:

> in their judicial capacity [judges] are in no way concerned with arguments for or against capital punishment or its efficacy as a deterrent to so evil and profitable a crime as trafficking in addictive drugs. Whether there should be capital punishment in Singapore and, if so, for what offences, are questions for the legislature of Singapore.
> (*Ong Ah Chuan v. Public Prosecutor*, 1981)

Other approaches to such matters, deriving more from humanitarian than from juristic concerns, gained currency after Diplock's death, and his reputation suffered, some would have said unfairly, in consequence.

In parallel with his pioneering work in the privy council, Diplock—alongside Lord Denning—had the acumen and the learning to anticipate and encourage the post-war regrowth of English public and constitutional law. As early as 1967, as a puisne judge, observing that the royal prerogative was the last unclaimed prize of the constitutional conflict of the seventeenth century, he held that how ministers deployed it was now subject to judicial review for consistency and fairness. Almost two decades later as a law lord he was able to describe the modern development of public law as perhaps the greatest achievement of his judicial lifetime.

It was a development to which Diplock contributed probably more than any other judge. In 1982, however, he used the occasion of an undeserving attempt to exploit public law in lieu of private law remedies to set up by judicial decision a rigidly binary system of recourse, much criticized from the start by academics and finally abandoned by his successors. But it played the part that he had intended of announcing that, from a post-war base of almost zero, a coherent and comprehensive system of remedies against the abuse of state power had grown to maturity. When in 1985 the challenge to the government's ban on trade union membership at the government communications headquarters came before the house, Diplock—ever the scientist—took the opportunity to classify the principles of public law as they had so far developed and to sketch the lines of further growth. It says something for his sense of history that, as the century ended, the patriation of the European convention on human rights had finally brought into Britain's public law the concept of proportionality to which he had looked forward in the early 1980s.

Diplock himself was clear that it was the changes in the contemporary state which had prompted and necessitated the growth of English public law. The rules of standing, he said:

> were made by judges, by judges they can be changed; and so they have been over the years to meet the need to preserve the integrity of the rule of law despite changes in the social structure, methods of government and the extent to which the activities of private citizens are controlled by governmental authorities, that have been taking place continuously, sometimes slowly, sometimes swiftly, since the rules were originally propounded. Those changes have been particularly rapid since World War II. (*R. v. IRC, ex parte National Federation of Self-Employed*, 1982)

His espousal of public-law rights and remedies was in this sense a judicial response to long-term political and social changes at home, much as his decisions on Commonwealth cases were in part a response to the handing over of political power in the former empire.

Public and constitutional law were no more than a segment of Diplock's judicial work. His incursions into some specialized fields, equity for example, were not always well received; but in field after field of law—crime, contempt of court, intellectual property, restraint of trade, defamation, commercial and maritime law—his judgments became benchmarks of organized and logical jurisprudence, rationalizing concepts that were or had become historically and intellectually confused. His decisions on the interpretation of statutes creating criminal offences were morally rigorous, tending always to hold individuals answerable for the consequences of their actions. These attracted academic criticism and have not always stood the test of time; they also contributed to his reputation as a hard man. But his rigour shut out intellectual dishonesty, and he accorded considerably more importance to the body of precedent than his more populist contemporary Lord Denning. Diplock would never 'cheat' in order to reach a desired conclusion.

Nevertheless, where precedent went one way and reason the other, Diplock would say so. As early as 1965 he had urged that the notorious discrepancy between libel damages and personal injury damages, though entrenched, was indefensible; but it was not until thirty years later, a decade after his death, that the courts finally broke the mould and set out to bring libel damages into a proportionate relationship with damages for physical or mental pain and suffering. It was not untypical to find a speech of his which began: 'I understand your Lordships to be at one in holding that both of these appeals must be dismissed. I am of the same opinion—reluctantly, because I do not think that this outcome is either sensible or just' (*Gammell v. Wilson*, 1982). Thus his chosen role as a jurist was to consolidate and to rationalize the law. It fell to others, albeit in his wake, to reform it.

Diplock's second main role, and the one to which his name became permanently attached, was as a safe pair of hands for governmental inquiries. The Diplock courts of Northern Ireland were set up on the advice of a three-man commission which was set up under his chairmanship in October 1972 to consider the problem of jury intimidation in cases involving terrorism. By December in the same year he had recommended the introduction of trial by judge alone in specified classes of case. Not only was the system adopted in the Republic of Ireland as well as in the north, but by replacing jury verdicts with reasoned judgments open to scrutiny on appeal it resulted in more acquittals. While the outcome might not have been what he envisaged, it would not have induced him to go back on his scheme.

From 1971 to 1982 Diplock was chairman of the permanent security commission, charged with inquiring into failures of state security, among them the Sir Roger Hollis affair. He was also called upon in 1976 to report on whether the Foreign Enlistment Act of 1870 was of continuing use. The context of the inquiry was the recruitment of British personnel as mercenaries for the civil war in Angola, and Diplock's advice that the act was ineffectual and obsolete, though both contested at the time and called in question by later events, was welcome to government at the time. For some years he led a British team, very successfully, in exchanges with senior American judges and lawyers.

Diplock was a passionate and surprisingly reckless horseman and fox-hunter. The guest list for the Middle Temple's 'grand day' in 1974, the year of his treasurership, included the duke of Beaufort and seven masters of hounds. It was said that when he was a puisne judge of the Queen's Bench he had a horse which he named Circuit, so that his clerk could truthfully tell enquirers that Mr Diplock was unavailable because he was out on circuit. He attended at least one sitting of his commission adorned with a black eye, the result of a fall from his horse, and went on riding until later in life than lord chancellors would have liked.

In 1938 Diplock married Margaret Sarah Atcheson, a nurse, the daughter of George Atcheson who had set up and owned a shirt factory in Londonderry. They had no children. She survived him, but before his death she had begun to suffer from senile dementia. He visited her daily in hospital, and her deterioration was a source of grief to him in the last months of his life.

Diplock's final attendance at the privy council must be unique in judicial history. A special sitting was held during the long vacation of 1985, to deal with an urgent civil case from Trinidad and Tobago (not, as legend has recreated the story, a capital punishment case). Diplock, who was suffering from complications of severe and longstanding emphysema, came from hospital and took part in the hearing, in a wheelchair and sustained by a cylinder of oxygen. He died a month later in King Edward VII's Hospital for Officers, London, on 14 October 1985.

STEPHEN SEDLEY and GODFRAY LE QUESNE

Sources personal knowledge (2004) · *DNB* · *The Times* (16 Oct 1985); (26 Oct 1985) · Sainty, *Judges* · b. cert. · *WWW* · *CGPLA Eng. & Wales* (1985)

Likenesses M. Noakes, group portrait, 1972, Middle Temple, London

Wealth at death £359,989: probate, 18 Dec 1985, *CGPLA Eng. & Wales*

Dirac, Paul Adrien Maurice (1902–1984), theoretical physicist, was born at 15 Monk Road, Bishopston, Bristol, on 8 August 1902, the son of Charles Adrien Ladislas Dirac (1866–1936), a native of Monthey in the canton of Valais, Switzerland, and a teacher of French in the Merchant Venturers' Technical College at Bristol, and his wife, Florence Hannah (1878–1941), daughter of Richard Holten, master mariner in a Bristol ship. Paul had an older brother, Reginald Charles Felix (b. 1900), and a younger sister, Beatrice Isabelle Marguerite (b. 1906). He was registered as Swiss by birth, and only in 1919 did he acquire British nationality. As a result of his father's domineering nature and dislike

Paul Adrien Maurice Dirac (1902–1984), by Ramsey & Muspratt, 1934

of social contacts, he developed early on into an introvert, without friends or a social life, and later described his childhood as unhappy.

Quantum mechanics From 1914 Dirac attended the Merchant Venturers' Technical College, where he received a good education in science and modern languages. In 1918 he entered the University of Bristol, graduating as an electrical engineer in 1921. Having no employment, he accepted the Bristol mathematics department's proposal that he stay on and take its course, from which he graduated in 1923. During this period he specialized in electrodynamics and became acquainted with the theory of relativity, which profoundly influenced his later thinking about problems in physics. In the autumn of 1923 he went up to Cambridge, to become a research student in mathematics at St John's College under the supervision of the theoretical physicist Ralph Fowler. Dirac had originally wanted to do graduate work in relativity, but under the impact of Fowler he changed to statistical physics and quantum theory. Totally absorbing himself in studies and research, he quickly transformed himself into a promising physicist and before the summer of 1925 he had published six scientific papers. These were interesting, but not of striking originality, and it was only after Werner Heisenberg's introduction of quantum mechanics that Dirac turned into a pioneer of theoretical physics.

In August 1925 Fowler received a proof copy of Heisenberg's seminal paper 'Über quantentheoretischer

Umdeutung' and passed it on to Dirac for study. It contained a mysterious law of multiplication according to which the product of two physical quantities 'P' and 'Q' (an electron's momentum and position, for example) does not commute; that is, PQ differs from QP. Dirac realized that this feature of the theory, not fully understood by Heisenberg, was essential and tried to make it the basis of a more satisfactory formulation of quantum mechanics that would conform with the theory of relativity. In October he found the solution—'the idea first came in a flash', he recalled—namely that the Heisenberg commutator PQ–QP could be related to the Poisson bracket expression used in classical dynamics. His paper on the fundamental equations of quantum mechanics led him to an independent formulation of the new theory, which enabled him to find the energy levels of the hydrogen atom. In 1926 Dirac developed his theory into an algebraic formulation in which physical quantities can be divided into two classes, being either c-numbers or q-numbers. Whereas c-numbers are classical quantities (ordinary numbers), q-numbers are dynamical variables representing observable quantities such as position, momentum, or energy. Contrary to c-numbers, q-numbers do not satisfy the commutative law, and Dirac showed that his q-number theory gave the same results as Heisenberg's theory but in a logically more satisfactory way.

In one of the classics of quantum mechanics ('On the theory of quantum mechanics') Dirac in August 1926 incorporated Erwin Schrödinger's new wave mechanics into his own theory and thereby created a more general and powerful formalism which he immediately applied to develop what subsequently became known as Fermi-Dirac quantum statistics. Particles obeying this form of statistics are today known as fermions, while those obeying Bose-Einstein statistics are called bosons. These names were invented by Dirac in 1945.

A still more general version of quantum mechanics was developed by Dirac during a stay at Bohr's institute in Copenhagen in the autumn of 1926. This 'extraordinarily grandiose generalization', as Heisenberg called it in a letter of November 1926, comprised Max Born's probabilistic interpretation of quantum mechanics within the more general framework of transformation functions. Dirac introduced in this paper the 'δ-function', which soon became a standard tool in physics. While at Copenhagen, Dirac was also occupied with the interaction between matter and electromagnetic fields, and in 1927 he published 'The quantum theory of the emission and absorption of radiation', which is recognized as the pioneering paper of quantum electrodynamics. It was in this work that the idea of 'second quantization'—according to which the wave function is treated as an operator—was first introduced. Following this work, Dirac applied his theory to dispersion and resonance, and he continued throughout his life to make important contributions to the theory of quantum electrodynamics.

Dirac's outstandingly significant achievement was his relativistic wave equation for the electron. Earlier attempts to formulate a relativistic Schrödinger wave equation had failed, but in early 1928, Dirac found a new wave equation of the same formal structure as Schrödinger's ($H\Psi = E\Psi$), but with a Hamilton function (H) that made the equation fit the requirements of relativity. The new equation was of the first order in both the time and space derivatives and included a new type of matrix with four rows and columns (Dirac matrices). The Dirac equation led to many empirically correct predictions and was immediately hailed as a great theoretical progress. The Dirac matrices are related to the Pauli spin matrices and Dirac proved that the correct value of the electron's spin appeared as a consequence of his theory. He also proved that it was possible to give an exact explanation of the hydrogen spectrum, including the so-called fine structure. 'The quantum theory of the electron' marked a turning-point in modern physics and the Dirac equation was received enthusiastically and created a minor industry in mathematical physics. However, some of the consequences appeared strange, especially that the theory seemed to predict the existence of electrons with positive charge and negative energy. The difficulty was solved by Dirac in 1930–31 by a brilliant and imaginative interpretation of the negative energies formally occurring in the theory. He suggested the existence of positively charged 'antielectrons' that would annihilate in collision with ordinary electrons, and at first believed that antielectrons were identical with protons. In a remarkable paper of 1931, 'Quantised singularities in the electromagnetic field', he realized that the idea did not work and instead predicted that the antielectron was a new kind of particle, with the same mass as the electron but opposite charge. The daring speculation was unexpectedly confirmed in 1932 when positive electrons (positrons) were discovered in the cosmic radiation. In his 1931 paper Dirac also suggested the existence of antiprotons—negatively charged protons—and isolated magnetic poles. Whereas the antiproton was eventually discovered (in 1955), the magnetic monopole has escaped discovery in spite of many attempts and some discovery claims.

Honours and awards On 2 January 1937 Dirac married Margit Balazs (b. 1905), daughter of Antal Wigner, manager of a leather factory at Budapest, and sister of the physicist Eugene Wigner. His wife had a son and a daughter, Gabriel and Judith, from her previous marriage; the Diracs had two daughters, Mary Elizabeth and Florence Monica. Until his marriage Dirac had lodged at St John's College, but the family then moved to a house at 7 Cavendish Avenue, Cambridge. Dirac had taken his PhD degree at Cambridge in 1926 and was the following year invited to the Solvay Congress in Brussels, a sign of his rising international reputation. He was frequently invited to the continental centres of physics and also to the USSR and America. For example, he visited the USSR in 1928 and in 1929 he was in the United States from where he returned via Japan, China, and the Soviet Union. In 1930 he was elected a fellow of the Royal Society and in 1932 Lucasian professor of mathematics at Cambridge University. The following year he received, jointly with Schrödinger, the Nobel prize, primarily for his wave equation of the electron. Much to his dismay, this made him a public figure. A London newspaper portrayed him under the headline 'The genius who fears all women' and described him—not inaccurately—to be 'as shy as a gazelle and modest as a Victorian maid' (*Sunday Dispatch*, 19 Nov 1933). In his Nobel lecture he speculated about antimatter made up of positrons and antiprotons and suggested that entire stars might be built up in this way. From the autumn of 1927 onwards Dirac lectured on quantum mechanics at Cambridge and in 1930 he published his authoritative textbook *The Principles of Quantum Mechanics*, which became translated into many languages and deeply influenced a generation of physicists. A second edition appeared in 1935, a third in 1947, and a fourth edition in 1958.

New directions in physics Although Dirac continued to do important work in physics, his main contributions dated from the period 1925-33. He spent the war years in England, where he did consultancy work on the uranium bomb project, especially dealing with the separation of isotopes and the calculation of neutron multiplication in atomic bomb models. When the bomb project was taken over by the Manhattan Project in the United States, Dirac was asked to join the project, but he refused. After about 1950 he turned away from mainstream physics and became increasingly heterodox in his views and areas of research. In particular, he objected strongly to the new renormalization quantum electrodynamics that was developed by Julian Schwinger, Richard Feynman, and others and which soon obtained a paradigmatic status. According to Dirac, the theory was illogical and could not possibly be correct, in spite of its empirical success. He never came to peace with the direction quantum theory took after the Second World War and preferred to stay away from what he called the rat race of mainstream physics. Deeply distressed by the mathematical and conceptual problems of quantum electrodynamics, he suggested alternatives to the theory until the end of his life. For example, in 1965 he published a theory of quantum electrodynamics without making use of renormalization ideas; however, the theory did not lead to new results and failed to win acceptance. Other post-war work—on magnetic monopoles, classical electron theory, quantization of constrained dynamical systems, and Hamiltonian formulations of general relativity—were important, but not of the same revolutionary nature as his early work in quantum theory. He summarized much of his later work in the semi-popular *Directions in Physics* (1978).

In 1937-8 Dirac suggested a new cosmological model based on the hypothesis that the dimensionless large numbers constructed from fundamental constants of nature are inter-related. Based on the 'large number hypothesis' he suggested a non-relativistic version of Big Bang cosmology which he only developed much later, in the 1970s. According to Dirac's theory the gravitational constant decreases with time and he sought to avoid the conclusion from experimental evidence that this is not the case. In spite of the failure of Dirac's cosmological theory, the large number hypothesis has been a source of inspiration for many cosmologists.

Dirac produced more than 200 publications, the first in 1924 and the last in 1984. Of these, his 1928 paper on the relativistic wave equation was the most important and the one most often cited. After retirement in 1969 he was invited to the University of Miami and in 1971 he took up a research professorship at Florida State University, Tallahassee, where he stayed for the rest of his life. He received many honours apart from the Nobel prize, among them the James Scott prize (1939), the Copley medal (1952), the Max Planck medal (1952), the Helmholtz medal (1964), and the Oppenheimer prize (1969); he was an honorary member of many scientific societies and in 1973 he was admitted to the Order of Merit.

Dirac was a legendary figure, not only because of his exceptional contributions to physics but also because of his personality. He was taciturn and seldom spoke spontaneously. As a rationalist who insisted on logic and intellectual economy in both science and life, he had little appreciation for emotions and what most people would call the human aspects of life. He was not a religious man and in his younger days he favoured an atheistic view. Neither was he interested in politics, although in the 1930s he had a brief flirtation with Marxism and expressed some sympathy with the new economic order of the Soviet Union. This, and his many travels to the country, was probably the reason why he was denied a visa to the United States in 1954 (the decision was later retracted). He was never a member of any church or political party. Dirac was fascinated by the concept of mathematical beauty, which he made his lodestar for most of his work after the early 1930s. He believed that there is a deep connection between the fundamental laws of nature and the theoretical formulations that can be expressed in mathematically beautiful ways and that physicists should strive for mathematical beauty rather than experimentally verified theories. 'A theory with mathematical beauty is more likely to be correct than an ugly one that fits some experimental data' he declared in 1970 (Dirac, 'Equations', 29). Dirac kept to this philosophy until his death in Tallahassee, Florida, on 20 October 1984. He was buried in Tallahassee cemetery. In 1995 Cambridge University Press began publication of his collected works, edited by R. H. Dalitz.

H. KRAGH

Sources P. A. M. Dirac, 'Recollections of an exciting era', *History of twentieth century physics*, ed. C. Weiner (1977), 109–46 • *The collected works of P. A. M. Dirac, 1924–1948*, ed. R. H. Dalitz (1995) • R. H. Dalitz and R. E. Peierls, *Memoirs FRS*, 32 (1986), 139–85 • H. Kragh, *Dirac: a scientific biography* (1990) • J. G. Taylor, ed., *Tributes to Paul Dirac* (1985) • B. Kursunoglu and E. P. Wigner, eds., *Paul Adrien Maurice Dirac: reminiscences about a great physicist* (1987) • J. Mehra and H. Rechenberg, *The historical development of quantum theory*, 4 (1982) • H. Kragh, 'Cosmonumerology and empiricism: the Dirac–Gamow dialogue', *Astronomy Quarterly*, 8 (1991), 109–26 • R. C. Hovis and H. Kragh, 'P. A. M. Dirac and the beauty of physics', *Scientific American*, 268 (May 1993), 104–9 • O. Darrigol, *From c-numbers to q-numbers* (1992) • J. W. McAlister, 'Dirac and the aesthetic evaluation of theories', *Methodology and Science*, 23 (1990), 87–102 •

P. A. M. Dirac, 'Can equations of motion be used in high-energy physics?', *Physics Today*, 23 (April 1970), 29–31
Archives Archive for History of Quantum Physics, Cambridge · CAC Cam., corresp. and papers · Florida State University, Tallahassee · L. Cong. | Royal Swedish Academy of Science, Stockholm, Nobel archive · U. Sussex, letters to J. G. Crowther · University of Copenhagen, Copenhagen, Denmark, Niels Bohr Institute for Astronomy, Physics and Geophysics, corresp. with Niels Bohr
Likenesses Ramsey & Muspratt, photograph, 1934, NPG [*see illus.*] · R. Tollast, pencil sketch, 1963, St John Cam. · G. Bollobás, cold cast bronze sculpture, 1973, RS · M. Noakes, oils, 1978, St John Cam. · photographs, Hult. Arch.
Wealth at death £75,548: probate, 3 May 1985, *CGPLA Eng. & Wales*

Dircks, Henry (1806–1873), historian of technology, was born at Liverpool on 26 August 1806, the eldest son of Egbert Dircks, a bookkeeper, of 14 Burnswick Road, and his wife, Maria, *née* Nightingale. As a boy Henry was apprenticed to a mercantile company in Liverpool. He educated himself in practical mechanics, chemical science, and general literature. Before the age of twenty-one he was lecturing on chemistry and electricity, and publishing articles in the *Mechanics Magazine* and other journals. During the 1830s he was involved in the Liverpool Mechanics' Institute (established 1825), and urged such institutes to co-operate with literary institutions. Dircks was a friend of the instrument maker John Benjamin Dancer. In 1837 he became a life member of the British Association, and regularly contributed to its proceedings. He and his wife, Mary, who were married in the early 1830s, had at least one child. Their son William Egbert was baptized on 24 July 1835 at St Nicholas, Liverpool.

Dircks left the mercantile company to become a practical engineer supervising railway, canal, and mining works, but by the early 1840s was settled in London, describing himself as a consulting engineer. Between 1840 and 1857 he took out patents for several inventions, but no engineering works of any significance are credited to him.

Dircks is best-known for publications in the history of technology. In Liverpool he had disputed the claims of Thomas Spencer, a carver and gilder, to have invented electrotyping, which Dircks claimed had been plagiarized from a London printer, C. J. Jordan. Dircks used increasingly abusive letters in the *Mechanics Magazine* to pursue his attack. He summarized his crusade in two books, *Jordantype, Otherwise Called Electrotype* (1852) and *Contributions towards a History of Electro-Metallurgy* (1863). Dircks's two-volume history of attempts to construct perpetual motion machines (1861 and 1870) is still useful. This interest in investigating the reality of invention was continued in three works on the inventions of the marquess of Worcester (Edward Somerset, 1601–1667), which were well received. Dircks invented his own optical delusion, intended as an illustration of Dickens's 'haunted man', which was exhibited at the London Polytechnic under the name of 'Pepper's ghost'; he described this in a notice to the British Association in 1858. Dircks sought to develop what he called nature study as a literary technique for improving poetry and sacred songs (1869, 1871, 1872).

Dircks joined the Royal Society of Literature, and was elected a fellow of the Royal Society of Edinburgh (1867). In 1868 he procured the title of LLD from the so-called college of Tusculum in Tennessee, USA. Styled a gentleman on his death certificate, and leaving several thousand pounds, Dircks died in the New Ship Hotel, Ship Street, Brighton, on 17 September 1873.   ROGER HUTCHINS

Sources *Men of the time* (1875), 579 · *N&Q*, 6th ser., 12 (1885), 309 · *Report of the Royal Society of Literature* (1874), 31 · *Mechanics Magazine*, 40 (1839), 73–9 · private information (2004) · d. cert.
Likenesses J. Cochran, stipple (after photograph by Negretti and Zambra), NPG · portrait, repro. in H. Dircks, *Nature-study, or, The art of attaining those excellencies in poetry … (1869)*
Wealth at death under £5000: probate, 4 Oct 1873, *CGPLA Eng. & Wales*

Dirleton. For this title name *see* Nisbet, Sir John, Lord Dirleton (1610–1688).

Dirom, Alexander (1757–1830), army officer, was born on 21 May 1757 at Banff, Banffshire, the son of Alexander Dirom of Muiresk, Banffshire, and his wife, Ann Fotheringham. His name occurs in the *Army List* for the first time as a lieutenant in the 88th foot on 13 October 1779. He was promoted captain on 8 December 1780.

From 1780 to 1784 Dirom served in the West Indies, first with the 88th foot, then with the 60th (Royal American), to which he transferred as captain on 10 August 1781. After a period on half pay, Dirom obtained a commission with the 52nd (Oxfordshire) foot, stationed in Madras. From 1790 to 1792 he served as deputy adjutant-general of the forces engaged in the Third Anglo-Mysore War. He was made brevet major on 12 February 1791. During the voyage home he drew up *A Narrative of the Campaign in India*, which was published in London in 1794.

After his return from India, Dirom served on the staff in England. On 7 August 1793 he married Magdalen, daughter of Robert Pasley of Mount Annan, Dumfriesshire, and they had five sons and two daughters. He became brevet lieutenant-colonel on 13 April 1795, full lieutenant-colonel on 6 June 1799, brevet colonel on 29 April 1802, major-general on 25 October 1809, and lieutenant-general on 4 June 1814. He was elected FRS on 10 July 1794. He died at Mount Annan, Dumfriesshire, on 6 October 1830.
    GORDON GOODWIN, *rev.* ALEX MAY

Sources *Army List* · Burke, *Gen. GB* · W. S. Moorsom, ed., *Historical record of the fifty-second regiment (Oxfordshire light infantry), from the year 1755 to the year 1858* (1860) · D. Forrest, *Tiger of Mysore: the life and death of Tipu Sultan* (1970) · IGI
Archives BL, corresp. and papers, MS Eur f. 76 · Coutts & Co., London, corresp., journals, letter-books, and papers · NL Scot., memoir of the military state of north Britain | BL, corresp. with Sir C. W. Pasley, Add. MSS 42961–42963

D'Irumberry de Salaberry, Charles-Michel (1778–1829), army officer, born on 19 November 1778 at the manor house of Beauport, near Quebec, Canada, was the eldest son of Ignace-Michel-Louis-Antoine d'Irumberry de Salaberry and his wife, Françoise-Catherine, *née* Hertel de Saint-François. Charles-Michel's grandfather, Michel de Salaberry, who settled in Canada in 1735, was descended from the noble family of Irumberry de Salaberry in the Pays Basques. At fourteen Charles-Michel enlisted as a volunteer in the 44th regiment. In 1794, through Prince Edward (later duke of Kent and father of Queen Victoria), a family friend, he was commissioned ensign in the 60th foot. He served for eleven years in the West Indies under General Robert Prescott, and in 1794 was at the conquest of Martinique. In late 1799, following a recommendation by his patron, the prince, he was promoted captain-lieutenant. In 1805 he went to England, and in 1806 transferred to the 5th battalion of the 60th. In 1808–9 he was stationed in Ireland, then took part in the disastrous Walcheren expedition, suffering from fever. In 1811 he returned to Canada, promoted brevet major (2 July 1811) as aide-de-camp of Major-General Rottenberg.

In 1812, on the declaration of war by the United States, Salaberry was promoted lieutenant-colonel, and entrusted with the organization and command of the voltigeurs Canadiens. In November 1812, at the head of them, he encountered General Dearborn's vanguard of the United States invasion, numbering 1400 men, near Lacolle, and drove them back. In 1813 the Americans renewed the invasion with larger forces. Two armies, each numbering 7000 or 8000 men, invaded Canada, intending to converge on Montreal. One, under Major-General Wade Hampton, took the route by Lake Champlain; the other, under Dearborn and Wilkinson, advanced by Kingston. In October, Salaberry, at the head of 400 voltigeurs militia and Indians, encountered Hampton's outposts at Odelltown. He repulsed them, and succeeded in striking terror into the whole force. After several days' indecision, Hampton marched westward to unite his forces with Wilkinson's. To prevent the junction, Salaberry posted himself at Allan's Corners on the Châteauguay on Hampton's route in a strong position, which he fortified, amid swamps and woods. Although he had little more than 300 men at his disposal and was heavily outnumbered, on 26 October he repulsed the American attack and forced Hampton to retreat from Canada, saving Montreal. The battle of Châteauguay became a source of Canadian pride and gained for Salaberry the name of the 'Canadian Leonidas'. On learning of the battle, Wilkinson decided to abandon offensive operations, and Lower Canada was secured from further invasion. Salaberry was made a CB in 1817.

After the war Salaberry turned to politics, and in 1818 was appointed to the legislative chamber. He married on 13 May 1812 Marie-Anne-Julie Hertel de Rouville, daughter of Jean-Baptiste-Melchior Hertel de Rouville; they had four sons and three daughters. Their sons were: Alphonse Melchior, deputy adjutant-general of militia for Lower Canada; Louis Michel, Maurice, and Charles René. He and his wife owned much land, and he also lent money. Salaberry died following an attack of apoplexy, on 26 February 1829 at his residence at Chambly, near Montreal.

E. I. CARLYLE, rev. ROGER T. STEARN

Sources M. Guitard, 'Irumberry de Salaberry, Charles Michel d'', DCB, vol. 6 · GM, 1st ser., 83/2 (1813) · GM, 1st ser., 84/1 (1814) · R. Christie, *The military and naval operations in the Canadas during the*

late war (1818) · W. James, *A full and correct account of the military occurrences of the late war …*, 2 vols. (1818) · H. J. Morgan, ed., *The Canadian men and women of the time* (1898)

Disbrowe, Sir Edward Cromwell (1790–1851), diplomatist, was the eldest son of Colonel Edward Disbrowe (d. 1818), MP and vice-chamberlain to Queen Charlotte, and his wife, Lady Charlotte Hobart (d. 1798). He was named in memory of his ancestor Major-General John Disbrowe, the Commonwealth general who married Oliver Cromwell's sister. He was educated at Eton College and Christ Church, Oxford, where he matriculated on 21 October 1808, and in 1810 he entered the diplomatic service as attaché to his cousin Sir Charles Stuart at Lisbon. After service at the headquarters of the Russian army and at St Petersburg (May 1813 – April 1814), he was appointed secretary of legation first at Copenhagen, where he remained until June 1820, and then at Bern until April 1823. On his way to Bern, Disbrowe undertook a mysterious trip to Milan 'on the affairs of Queen Caroline' shortly before parliament began proceedings to dissolve her sad and unfortunate marriage to George IV. Disbrowe himself married Anne Kennedy (d. 1855), the eldest daughter of the Hon. Robert Kennedy, on 24 October 1821. The Disbrowes had two sons and three daughters; both sons died on military service, Edward at the battle of Inkerman (5 November 1854) during the Crimean War and William while in Canada. Disbrowe served briefly as MP for New Windsor (February 1823 – June 1826) and was as a consequence able to live in the family home, Walton Hall, Walton-on-Trent, Derbyshire, for the only time in his life.

After another tour of duty at St Petersburg (March 1825–April 1828), Disbrowe received his first independent appointment, as minister to Württemberg, a *mission de famille* as Charlotte, the princess royal, had married the king of Württemberg. In 1831 he was made a KCG. In 1833 he went to Stockholm as minister to Sweden, and in January 1836 he went to The Hague, where he remained minister until his sudden death there on 29 October 1851. He was buried in the family vault at Walton Hall.

A representative example of the unreformed diplomatic service, and according to Lord Palmerston a man of only moderate ability, Disbrowe nevertheless served with distinction at The Hague. He successfully negotiated a commercial treaty with the Netherlands in 1837 and manoeuvred the irate Dutch towards the recognition of an independent and neutral Belgium.   R. A. JONES

Sources C. A. A. Disbrowe, *Old days in diplomacy* (1903) · S. T. Bindoff and others, eds., *British diplomatic representatives, 1789–1852*, CS, 3rd ser., 50 (1934) · R. A. Jones, *The British diplomatic service, 1815–1914* (1983) · K. Bourne, *Palmerston: the early years, 1784–1841* (1982) · C. R. Middleton, *The administration of British foreign policy, 1782–1846* (1977) · *The Times* (4 Nov 1851) · Burke, *Peerage*

Archives BL, corresp. with Lord Aberdeen, Add. MSS 43143, 43167–43168 · LPL, corresp. with Bishop Howley and others · PRO, corresp. with Stratford Canning, FO 352 · U. Southampton L., corresp. with Palmerston

Likenesses engraving (after a portrait; in youth), repro. in Disbrowe, *Old days in diplomacy*

Disbrowe [Desborough], **John** (*bap.* 1608, *d.* 1680), parliamentarian army officer and politician, was baptized at

Eltisley, Cambridgeshire, on 13 November 1608, the second son of James Disbrowe (1582–1638) and his wife, Elizabeth Marshall (d. 1628/9). James was a gentleman and owner of the advowson of Eltisley, where the family had lived for at least three generations, and at the time of John's birth was living in the parsonage house.

Although he did not attend either English university or any of the London inns of court, Disbrowe is said to have practised as an attorney, and combined this with farming an estate worth £70 per annum settled on him by his father. On 23 June 1636 he married Jane Cromwell (bap. 1606, d. 1656). She was the sister of Oliver *Cromwell, who at that time enjoyed no more than local importance, but on the outbreak of the civil war Disbrowe was among the earliest members of his brother-in-law's troop of horse, a unit of the parliamentarian army of the earl of Essex. Disbrowe was quartermaster or adjutant, receiving from as early as September 1642 sums from the treasurer-at-war to pay the soldiers.

Army officer From April 1643 Disbrowe captained his own troop of horse in Cromwell's regiment. An ordinance of 2 May 1643 named Disbrowe among prominent soldiers of the eastern association empowered to sequester the goods of royalists. It is likely that the high reputation of the regiment for military efficiency and godly commitment attracted recruits from beyond the immediate confines of East Anglia: the minister and commentator Richard Baxter noted that to his knowledge Disbrowe and his men never once fell back before the enemy. After the New Model Army was established Disbrowe became major of the first horse regiment, that of Sir Thomas Fairfax, when Edward Whalley was promoted to command a regiment of his own. On 14 June 1645 Disbrowe saw action at Naseby, where his regiment led the final charge, and his troop was prominent at the battle of Langport on 10 July. On 8 August, Disbrowe was dispatched by Fairfax to quell troublesome 'clubmen' at Shaftesbury: leading a charge at Hambledon Hill with spectacular success, he captured their ringleader and took 300 prisoners. From December 1645 he was quartered in Oxfordshire, first taking part in the siege of Oxford, and negotiating the surrender of Woodstock House to parliament on 26 April 1646.

During May 1647 Disbrowe acted as an intermediary between parliament and his regiment, when parliament had resolved on plans to reduce the size of the army and ship certain units to Ireland. He was among the officers chosen to present the grievances of the whole army to parliamentary commissioners. At Saffron Walden church on 16 May, Disbrowe reported to the council of officers that six days earlier, after representing the parliamentary plans to the troops of his regiment, they had convinced him that some of their grievances were 'very sober things' (Works, 1.50). He pressed the council of officers to ask the regiment to confirm that these discontents were widespread, evidently in the conviction that they were, and a paper emanating from the regiment confirmed his view. On 2 July, Disbrowe was one of the army officers that met

with commissioners of parliament at High Wycombe; at the council of war at Reading the following week he was clearly pressing for the army not to delay in its march on London. Fairfax appointed him to meet with the agitators, representatives of the rank and file, to complete proposals for settling a peace. During the army's advance to the capital Disbrowe was involved in a surprise raid on troops of the presbyterian Robert Pye, at Deptford, and in August he drilled a thousand cavalry in Hyde Park. There is no doubt that he was an Independent in politics, sharing the impatience of many in the New Model with repeated attempts at a compromise settlement with the king. In May 1648 he suppressed a royalist insurrection at Bury St Edmunds, and was among the besieging party at the protracted siege of Colchester. On 15 September, Fairfax appointed Disbrowe governor of Yarmouth, a commission which took him from the centre of events during the political crisis of the winter of 1648–9, and removed him temporarily from a field regiment.

First tour of the western counties In September 1649, during the first year of the new republic, Disbrowe was given command of what had been the horse regiment of Oliver Cromwell, assigned to guard the western counties of England. This marked the beginning of Disbrowe's association with the west of England, which persisted for most of the 1650s, and confirmed his closeness to his brother-in-law, the lord general. Disbrowe wrote to Cromwell in September 1650, reminding him of the need for those in public life to heed the voice of God: 'Sir, high places are slippery, except God establisheth our goings; he hath been very faithful to us, and I trust will still do us good himself, help us to trust in him, and then, I am sure, we shall not be ashamed' (Firth and Davies, 1.205). Late in 1649 he quelled a mutiny at Plymouth garrison, but he also gave the charge to the grand jury at the Devon quarter sessions, an indication that he would not confine himself to the military sphere. Disbrowe attempted a reform of public life in the counties of his charge from his first tour, and demonstrated a willingness to work closely and in detail with the justices of the peace and other agents of the traditional structure of local government. By August 1650 he had been given the title major-general. His regiment marched north to participate in the battle of Worcester in September 1651, but moved quickly back to the south-west, in time for the escaping Charles Stuart to pass close to him incognito at Shaftesbury in October. His appointment to the Hale commission on law reform in January 1652 acknowledged the range of his interests in public affairs as well as his original calling, though he himself was no radical reformer. He supported a policy of leniency towards former royalists, enshrined in the Rump's act of oblivion (February 1652), and that summer supported Cromwell in cautioning the army officers against precipitate action against parliament when the pace of reform seemed to have grown slack. After the Rump Parliament was expelled in exasperation by Cromwell in April 1653, Disbrowe defended his own volte-face.

His comment on his earlier support for the Rump against the army officers was 'if ever he drolled [i.e. jested] in his life, he had drolled then' (*Memoirs of Edmund Ludlow*, 1.356).

High civil and military office Further civil and military commissions now fell to Disbrowe. He was among the appointees to Cromwell's first council of state (29 April 1653), having apparently rejected offers to become general of the army in Scotland. On 5 July he was co-opted to sit in the nominated assembly, and he played an active role in its proceedings. On 28 July he was made a commissioner for the admiralty and navy, and by September he had replaced Edmund Prideaux, attorney-general, as *custos rotulorum* of Devon. He retained this distinction until 1660. He sat on a parliamentary committee charged with reforming the law, but was no more radical in his outlook there than on the Hale commission, and became identified with the socially conservative element in the house. Nevertheless he continued in office as a judge of probate during this administration, having been appointed in the last month of the Rump's sitting. He came third in the ballot for sixteen places on the new council of state on 1 November; on 3 December was approved by the house as one of the generals-at-sea, and retained his place as an admiralty commissioner. The growing gulf between the radicals and their critics had become unbridgeable, however, and on 12 December he used his prominence in the house on behalf of the conservative majority to play a leading part in the dissolution of the nominated assembly. He was among those who signed the warrant to the lord mayor of London to proclaim Cromwell lord protector. Nearly a year later, on 10 November 1654, he reminded MPs in the first protectorate parliament that the lord protector could have kept all power to himself, and that they should reflect on that before tampering with the 'Instrument of government'.

As a relative and close associate of Cromwell's, Disbrowe rose even further in standing during the protectorate, and by 1658 it was reported that public office brought him an annual income of over £6000. On 24 April 1654 he was granted the office of constable of St Briavel's hundred, in the Forest of Dean, which confirmed his policing authority there: during the time of the nominated assembly he had tried to advance the interests of Gloucestershire tobacco planters on the other side of the Severn from the forest. In elections to the first protectorate parliament, which met in September 1654, he was returned for Cambridgeshire, and for two seats in the west country, Somerset and Totnes: he chose to sit for his native county. In October he and William Penn quelled unrest among seamen at Portsmouth, Disbrowe having kept the naval offices bestowed upon him before the protectorate was established. He never served at sea, however, and his contribution to the navy lay in the areas of discipline and logistics. He was the principal organizer of supply to the ill-fated western design, a naval expedition to the West Indies which sailed in December 1654. Even before it left

England its leader, Robert Venables, quarrelled with Disbrowe over inadequate supplies, and when it failed disastrously Venables ensured that the general-at-sea received his share of the blame.

A major-general In January 1655 Disbrowe's interventions in parliament were all strongly in support of the lord protector and his executive, and he kept a close eye on home intelligence matters. When, in March, the rebellion in the west country known as Penruddock's rising broke out, Disbrowe was the natural choice to be commissioned to suppress it. A few days later he was also given wide powers of policing in the Isle of Ely in his home region. During this tour of the west he again worked closely with local government. These developments, and Disbrowe's interest in compiling lists of those disaffected to the government, provided a blueprint for what in the summer of that year became the expedient of rule by major-generals. Disbrowe received the first commission of its type on 28 May 1655, gaining the widest civil and military authority in the counties of Gloucester, Somerset, Wiltshire, Dorset, Devon, and Cornwall. He reformed the militia, galvanized justices of the peace into implementing legislation on offences that were abominable to the godly, and did what he could to reform juries. He intervened in the affairs of the corporations of Bristol, Tewkesbury, Gloucester, and Tiverton to remove councillors considered hostile.

Despite his purges of boroughs Disbrowe's style was, overall, not particularly confrontational; he preferred to work with sympathetic figures among the gentry, the 'honest people in every county' (Thurloe, 5.303). He was able to intervene to settle disputes among the clergy, and to support congregations—notably that of the Baptists in Exeter. His sympathies towards protestant minorities seem to have been generally recognized. Although he was expected by some to release the Quakers imprisoned at Launceston he found himself unable to comply because their demeanour, and particularly that of George Fox, convinced him that they would not live peaceably. His reports to John Thurloe reveal his concern to receive the proper authorization for his actions. Nevertheless, despite his sometimes tentative approach to his task, a measure of his achievement is the surviving volume, preserved in the British Library, of names of about 5000 individuals who came to his attention for a variety of negative reasons during his tour of duty.

Like the other major-generals, Disbrowe worked hard to ensure that candidates sympathetic to the government were successful in the parliamentary elections of 1656. He himself was returned for Somerset, Gloucester, King's Lynn, and Bridgwater, choosing to sit for the county. During the protracted debates on the Quaker James Nayler he took a consistent, moderate line, agreeing that his offence was blasphemy, but aware of the constitutional implications for the secular authority of entering the hazardous territory of theological nuances. He opposed the death penalty for Nayler, 'for life is precious' (*Diary of Thomas Burton*, 1.39). There is little doubt that Disbrowe was voicing the views of the lord protector on Nayler, but the brothers-in-law by no means spoke with one voice. It was fitting that on Christmas day 1656 Disbrowe, as the pioneer of the major-generals' regime, should promote the continuation of the decimation tax on royalists: 'I have a short bill to offer you, for continuance of a tax upon some people, for the maintenance of the militia' (ibid., 1.230). But to Cromwell's scorn, the bill was rejected and the expedient fell. This was an indication that Disbrowe still kept open channels to the leading army officers, as well as to the Cromwellian household.

A frequent speaker in the second Cromwellian parliament, Disbrowe remained silent in the house during the debates on the *Humble Petition and Advice* that would have bestowed the crown on the protector. It is clear that he opposed this development. He and Charles Fleetwood, his fellow grandee in the army, confronted Cromwell, who was attracted to the kingship, with their view that its promoters were royalist fellow-travellers. In one account of this exchange Disbrowe is reported to have viewed it as a watershed in his relations with Cromwell: 'though he was resolved never to act against him, yet he would not act for him after that time' (*Memoirs of Edmund Ludlow*, 2.24). It seems likely that Disbrowe's intervention contributed significantly to Cromwell's eventual rejection of the crown, but his loyalties to the protector and to the basic principles of the protectorate ran deep, and he accepted a place in the new second chamber on 11 December 1657 without demur. At the opening of the second session of the parliament on 18 January 1658 Disbrowe carried the sword ahead of the protector in the solemn procession. On 25 March 1658 he married Anne Everard, his first wife, Jane Cromwell, having died in 1656.

The fall of the protectorate and the restoration of monarchy There were a number of reports that Disbrowe was discussing future constitutional options with army colleagues during 1658, but, on the death of Oliver Cromwell, Disbrowe was at least superficially an enthusiast for the rule of his nephew Richard *Cromwell. But his feud with Edward Montagu was ominous. Disbrowe and Montagu, a naval administrator and devotee of the protectorate, had been on opposing sides during the kingship debates, and now openly clashed in council, when Disbrowe alleged a plot by Montagu to have him kidnapped. By 6 April 1659 the officers had grown impatient of the lack of attention in parliament to issues regarding army pay, and, on 18 April, Disbrowe rather brutally told his nephew to step down or be removed from power. On 7 May, Disbrowe was named to the committee of safety, and on 13 May, when the Rump Parliament was recalled, he secured a place on the new council of state. In July his military commission was confirmed in parliament, but only after he had expressed scepticism about its supposed superiority to one bestowed by the army itself, and by 5 October strains between the leading army officers and parliament were evident. Disbrowe had been proposed as lieutenant-general of horse by the regiment of John Lambert, and

remained of the view that the Rump Parliament had nothing more to offer. On 8 November he sought finance for an army-run regime from the City of London. Before parliament was restored again on 26 December 1659 he proposed a new select senate of sixty to exercise a veto on a new assembly. He nevertheless preferred the Rump to a restored monarchy, and on 29 December wrote a letter of apology to the speaker for his disobedience.

The tide now began to run strongly against the Wallingford House group of disaffected senior officers, and on 9 January 1660 Disbrowe and other leading officers were confined to their country houses. By March he and Charles Fleetwood were objects of popular derision. He accepted the order of the council of state to remain quiescent, but that summer it was inconceivable that prominent republicans would simply be left alone by the restored monarchy, and in May he was arrested and brought to London while making his way through Essex to take ship. Humiliated by the jeers of youths on his way to be interrogated, he was nevertheless treated relatively well because of his critical attitude towards the restored Rump. In the Act of Indemnity and Oblivion of 13 June 1660 he was disqualified from public office for life. He was imprisoned briefly in the Tower of London for allegedly plotting the death of the king and the queen mother, and escaped to Holland. Thereafter he was never absent from the nervous government's list of alleged plotters, though it is unlikely there was any determined purpose in his meetings with old comrades-in-arms. On 9 April 1665 a proclamation was issued demanding his return to England on pain of being declared a traitor, and on his return, by 13 July, he was imprisoned in Dover Castle, and then in the Tower. Released on 23 February 1667, he was seen walking in London on 17 April by Samuel Pepys, who observed that Disbrowe 'looks well, and just as he used to do heretofore' (Pepys, 8.169). He lived afterwards quietly at Hackney, where he and other former army officers attended the Independent conventicle of John Owen. He died, probably at Hackney, in 1680. By his will, made on 26 March 1678 and proved on 20 September 1680, he left lands in Cambridgeshire (including the manor of Eltisley), Essex, and Lincolnshire.

Conclusion There is a contrast between Disbrowe's conscientious, effective, and generally conciliatory style as a police officer in the provinces and his demeanour during the crisis of 1659–60 when he was pugnacious, perhaps quarrelsome, and seemed reluctant to consider the drift of political events, even when warned by subtler colleagues, such as Bulstrode Whitelocke. He was a soldier with the soldier's simple belief in military strength and security. Attacks on him in the popular press as 'a perfect clown' (*The Mystery of the Good Old Cause Briefly Unfolded*, 8) had begun as early as 1654, intensified on the eve of the Restoration, and persisted both in cheap lampoons and more sophisticated literary works such as Samuel Butler's *Hudibras*. But though he could certainly be blunt in his manner, his royalist critics, in social and political sneers, exaggerated his supposed rusticity, and doubtless dwelt on his shortcomings because of his kinship ties and personal affinity with Oliver Cromwell. His many cogent letters to John Thurloe during 1655–6 reveal a man convinced of the importance of completing not only reforms but simple administrative tasks; his speeches in parliament, one who appreciated the virtues of strong government tempered by reconciliation for those willing to conform. STEPHEN K. ROBERTS

Sources B. Whitelocke, *Memorials of English affairs*, new edn, 4 vols. (1853) · *The memoirs of Edmund Ludlow*, ed. C. H. Firth, 2 vols. (1894) · *CSP dom.*, 1649–60 · C. H. Firth and R. S. Rait, eds., *Acts and ordinances of the interregnum, 1642–1660*, 3 vols. (1911) · *Diary of Thomas Burton*, ed. J. T. Rutt, 4 vols. (1828), vols. 1–2 · *The Clarke papers*, ed. C. H. Firth, 1–3, CS, new ser., 49, 54, 61 (1891–9), vols. 1–3 · Thurloe, *State papers*, esp. vols. 3–4 · I. Gentles, *The New Model Army in England, Ireland, and Scotland, 1645–1653* (1992) · *The journal of George Fox*, rev. edn, ed. J. L. Nickalls (1952) · *The writings and speeches of Oliver Cromwell*, ed. W. C. Abbott and C. D. Crane, 4 vols. (1937–47) · S. K. Roberts, *Recovery and restoration in an English county: Devon local administration, 1649–1670* (1985) · C. H. Firth and G. Davies, *The regimental history of Cromwell's army*, 2 vols. (1940) · A. Woolrych, *Commonwealth to protectorate* (1982) · A. H. Woolrych, *Soldiers and statesmen* (1987) · Pepys, *Diary*, vol. 8 · will, PRO, PROB 11/363, fol. 439v · pay warrants, 1642, PRO, SP 28/2a/232; 2b/391; 3a/223; 3b/378; 4/161 · Disbrowe's book of suspects, 1655–66, BL, Add. MS 34012 · G. E. Aylmer, *The state's servants: the civil service of the English republic, 1649–1660* (1973) · *A narrative of the late parliament, Harleian miscellany*, 8 vols. (1745), vol. 3 · *A second narrative of the late parliament, Harleian miscellany*, 8 vols. (1745), vol. 3 · Clarendon, *Hist. rebellion* · B. Capp, *Cromwell's navy: the fleet and the English revolution, 1648–1660* (1989) · M. Noble, *Memoirs of the protectoral-house of Cromwell* (1787) · *Reliquiae Baxterianae, or, Mr Richard Baxter's narrative of the most memorable passages of his life and times*, ed. M. Sylvester, 1 vol. in 3 pts (1696) · *The manuscripts of the corporations of Southampton and King's Lynn*, HMC, 18 (1887) · *Report on the manuscripts of F. W. Leyborne-Popham*, HMC, 51 (1899) · *Calendar of the manuscripts of the marquis of Bath preserved at Longleat, Wiltshire*, 5 vols., HMC, 58 (1904–80), vol. 2 · H. F. Waters, *Genealogical gleanings in England*, 2 vols. (Boston, MA, 1886–9) · R. L. Greaves, *Enemies under his feet: radicals and nonconformists in Britain, 1664–1677* (Stanford, CA, 1990) · C. Holmes, *The eastern association in the English civil war* (1974) · R. K. G. Temple, ed., 'The original officer list of the New Model Army', *BIHR*, 59 (1986), 50–77 · *IGI* · *The mystery of the good old cause briefly unfolded* (1660) · *The devil's cabinet discovered* (1660) · M. Noble, *Lives of the English regicides*, 2 vols. (1798) · C. Durston, *Cromwell's major-general: godly government during the English revolution* (2001) · A. Woolrych, introduction, in *Complete prose works of John Milton*, ed. D. M. Wolfe, 7, ed. R. W. Ayers (1980), 1–228

Archives BL, Add. MSS, letters · BL, Stowe MSS, letters · Bodl. Oxf., Thurloe state papers, letters · Bodl. Oxf., MSS Rawl. A

Likenesses line engraving, NPG · portrait, AM Oxf., Sutherland collection; repro. in M. Ashley, *Cromwell's generals* (1954) · silver medal, BM

Wealth at death lands in Cambridgeshire, Essex, and Lincolnshire: will, 20 Sept 1680, PRO, PROB 11/363, fol. 439v

Disibod [St Disibod] (*supp. d.* 674), holy man, is the subject of a life written *c.*1170 by the abbess and visionary Hildegard von Bingen (1098–1179), which is the sole witness for his Irish origin. The judgement of Thomas Olden, who summarized its content for the *Dictionary of National Biography*, that Hildegard's work has no historical value, is sound. The life of Disibod is, rather, a visionary text, reflecting the significance of the mystical experience in medieval society; it does not justify Olden's characterization of Hildegard as 'scarcely sane'.

Hildegard did not invent Disibod, however. At the age of seven, she herself had entered the community of nuns at Disibodenberg (now Disenberg, Rhenish palatinate, Germany). This had then been established recently as an adjunct of the male monastery at the same place, where the bones of the saint were said to be buried and which was founded *c.*1000 by Archbishop Willigis of Mainz. By that time the cult of Disibod had already been current in the region for a century and a half, for his birth is recorded under 8 September in the martyrology of Hrabanus Maurus, archbishop of Mainz from 847 to 856. No historical evidence, therefore, indicates Disibod's Irish origin, though such claims were made of other continental saints whose cults first appear at this time (for instance Gall and Dympna). Reliable sources offer no description of his status, beyond Hrabanus Maurus's statement that he was a 'confessor', nor any indication of the date at which he lived. The notion that he died in 674 is highly unreliable, deriving from an entry in a set of annals, partly based on the chronicle of Marianus Scotus (*d.* 1082), but partly also on many other works, which was compiled in the later twelfth century by a monk at Disibodenberg, where there was an obvious incentive to create biographical data for its patron. In the face of such uncertainty over his historical existence, Disibod is probably best regarded as a figure ultimately inextricably entangled with the place with which he shared a name. MARIOS COSTAMBEYS

Sources Hildegard, 'Vita Sancti Disibodi', *Patrologia Latina*, 197 (1855), 1095–1116 · Rabanus Maurus, 'Martyrologium', *Patrologia Latina*, 110 (1852) · F. Beer, *Women and mystical experience in the middle ages* (1992) · 'Annales sancti Disibodi', ed. G. Waitz, [*Annales aevi Suevici*], ed. G. H. Pertz, MGH Scriptores [folio], 17 (Stuttgart, 1861), 4–30 · D. G. Waitz, ed., 'Mariani Scotti chronicon', [*Annales et chronica aevi Salici*], ed. G. H. Pertz, MGH Scriptores [folio], 5 (Stuttgart, 1844), 481–568 · 'Disibodenberg', *Lexikon des Mittelalters*, 10 vols. (1980–99)

Dismorr, Jessica Stewart (1885–1939). *See under* Vorticists (*act.* 1914–1919).

Disney, John (1677–1730), Church of England clergyman and moral reformer, was born at Lincoln on 26 December 1677, the son of Daniel Disney (1656–1734) of Swinderbury and his wife, Catherine Fynes (*d.* 1690). None of his four brothers and four sisters survived childhood. He was educated at grammar school and at a dissenting academy in Lincoln. On 20 May 1698 he married Mary Woodhouse (1677–1763), daughter and heir of William Woodhouse. They had nine children, including John Disney (1700–1771), father of the Unitarian minister, John *Disney (1746–1816).

On 19 November 1702 Disney entered the Middle Temple but, according to his biography by his grandson John Disney, published in Kippis's *Biographia Britannica*, his legal training was intended only to equip him for service as a JP. He served effectively on the commission of the peace for Lindsey, Lincolnshire, but was removed from the bench at least twice during tory purges in 1711–12. Active as a layman and as a clergyman in the work of the SPCK and the societies for the reformation of manners, he

John Disney (1677–1730), by Robert White, pubd 1710

helped establish charity schools in Lincoln and wrote extensively in defence of reform. He published two essays exhorting JPs to enforce the laws against immorality and profaneness; he wrote *A View of Ancient Laws Against Immorality and Profaneness* (1729) and planned a 'Corpus legum de moribus reformandis'. He also published several sermons, a genealogy of the house of Hanover, and devotional works in both prose and verse.

Disney, who was brought up a dissenter, explained to Archbishop Wake in 1718 that, 'as soon as I came of age, I betook myself to the Church of England, and that upon principle and conviction' (Kippis, 5.257). He was ordained deacon on 15 March 1719 and priest on 20 September 1719 by the bishop of Lincoln, Edmund Gibson, and was immediately afterwards presented to the Lincolnshire livings of Croft and Kirkby-on-Bain. In 1720 he was admitted as a fellow commoner of Magdalene College, Cambridge, and became MA in 1722. In the same year he resigned his country benefices, and was appointed to the important living of St Mary's, Nottingham. He died at Nottingham on 3 February 1730 and was buried near the altar in St Mary's.

J. H. OVERTON, rev. JOHN SPURR

Sources A. Kippis and others, eds., *Biographia Britannica, or, The lives of the most eminent persons who have flourished in Great Britain and Ireland*, 2nd edn, 5 vols. (1778–93) · J. Hutchins, *The history and antiquities of the county of Dorset*, 3rd edn, ed. W. Shipp and J. W. Hodson, 4 vols. (1861–74) · H. A. C. Sturgess, ed., *Register of admissions to the Honourable Society of the Middle Temple, from the fifteenth century to the year 1944*, 3 vols. (1949) · E. McClure, ed., *A chapter in English church history: being the minutes of the Society for Promoting Christian Knowledge for … 1698–1704* (1888) · L. J. G. Glassey, *Politics and appointment of the justices of the peace, 1675–1720* (1979)
Archives S. Antiquaries, Lond., papers relating to laws against immorality · U. Nott. L., prayers | BL, letters to J. W. Imhoff, Add. MS 24929 · N. Yorks. CRO, corresp. with Christopher Wyvill
Likenesses R. White, line engraving, BM, NPG; repro. in J. Disney, *Essay upon the execution of the laws against immorality and prophaneness* (1710) [*see illus.*]

Disney, John (1746–1816), Unitarian minister, the third son of John Disney of Lincoln and his wife, Frances Cartwright of Ossington, Nottinghamshire, was born on 28 September 1746 at Swinderby in Lincolnshire. His grandfather John *Disney (1677–1730) was rector of St Mary's, Nottingham, but his ancestors were zealous nonconformists. Disney was educated at Wakefield grammar school under John Clark, and then at Lincoln grammar school. He was intended for the bar, but his health broke down under preliminary studies and he turned to the church. He entered Peterhouse, Cambridge, in 1764, and after graduation was ordained in 1768; in 1770 he proceeded LLB. His sympathies with the latitudinarians within the Church of England quickly became evident; he appeared as a writer in April 1768 in defence of Archdeacon Francis Blackburne's *The Confessional* (1766). Immediately after his ordination he was appointed honorary chaplain to Edmund Law, master of Peterhouse, bishop of Carlisle, and a latitudinarian whig. In 1769 he was presented to the vicarage of Swinderby, Lincolnshire, and soon afterwards to the rectory of Panton, in another part of the same county; he held both livings, residing at Swinderby. On 17 November 1774 he married Jane (d. 1809), the eldest daughter of Archdeacon Francis *Blackburne.

Disney became an active member of the Feathers Tavern Association formed on 17 July 1771 to promote a petition to parliament for relief of the clergy from subscription to the Thirty-Nine Articles of the Church of England. The petition was rejected by the House of Commons on 6 February 1772. Disney did not immediately follow the example of his friend Theophilus Lindsey, who resigned his benefice in the following year (on his way to London in December 1773, Lindsey stayed for more than a week at Swinderby). Like some others, Disney chose to accommodate the public service to suit his special views. The Athanasian creed he had always ignored; he now omitted the Nicene creed and the litany, and made other changes in reading the common prayer. On 5 June 1775 the University of Edinburgh made him DD, through the influence of Bishop Law with the principal, William Robertson; in 1778 he was admitted a fellow of the Society of Antiquaries.

Temporarily Disney found in secular duties and political action a sedative for his religious scruples. He was an energetic magistrate, and while staying at Flintham Hall, near Newark, the seat of his eldest brother, he joined in 1780 the Nottingham county committee for retrenchment and

John Disney (1746–1816), by James Basire, 1810 (after Guy Head, 1800)

Holy Trinity from certain penalties'. He continued to support political reform: in 1806 he declined to advise his Dorset tenants as to how they should vote in the county election, commenting only 'I know of no recommendation more important or pressing, or more constitutional than that of the candidate's being well disposed towards a legal reform in the constitution of that parliament of which they solicit to become members' (Disney to E. Patten, 29 Oct 1806, Wyvill of Constable Burton MSS).

Disney was a prolific author, with some forty-five separate works to his credit; they included memoirs of latitudinarians such as Arthur Ashley (1785) and Edmund Law (1800) and Unitarians such as John Jebb (1787) and Michael Dodson (1800). Two volumes of his sermons were published in 1793 and two more in 1816: Socinian in their theology, they show his extreme anti-trinitarianism, which went as far as the denial of even the pre-existence of Christ.

In his later years Disney lived for some time in Bath, attempting to recover his declining health and withdrawing from political involvements. He died at The Hyde on 26 December 1816, and was buried in the churchyard of Fryerning, Essex. He left three children, John *Disney, Algernon, who entered the army, and Frances Mary, wife of Thomas *Jervis. A collection of literature related to *The Confessional* controversy, which had been arranged by Disney in fourteen volumes, was deposited at Dr Williams's Library, of which he had been a trustee from 1796 to 1806. As a minister, memoirist, and a religious and political writer Disney was an important, if secondary, figure in the development of English Unitarianism.

ALEXANDER GORDON, *rev.* G. M. DITCHFIELD

Sources BL, Disney MSS, Add. MS 36527, fol. 79 · T. Jervis, *The memorial of the just* (1817) · *Monthly Repository*, 12 (1817), 55–6 · *GM*, 1st ser., 86/1 (1816), 627 · W. Turner, *Lives of eminent Unitarians*, 2 (1843), 178–213 · T. Belsham, *Memoirs of the late Reverend Theophilus Lindsey* (1812) · G. M. Ditchfield, 'Some aspects of Unitarianism and radicalism, 1760–1810', PhD diss., U. Cam., 1968, chap. 3 · *Life and correspondence of Joseph Priestley*, ed. J. T. Rutt, 2 vols. (1831–2) · W. Wilson, *The history and antiquities of the dissenting churches and meeting houses in London, Westminster and Southwark*, 4 vols. (1808–14), vol. 3, pp. 488–90 · R. E. Richey, 'Disney, John', *BDMBR*, vol. 1 · N. Yorks. CRO, Wyvill of Constable Burton papers · will of John Disney, PRO, PROB 11/1589, fols. 90–94

Archives BL, Add. MSS 24, 867, 36527 · DWL, corresp. and papers | Bodl. Oxf., corresp. with J. C. Brooke · Lincs. Arch., corresp. with his son John Disney and others · N. Yorks. CRO, corresp. with Christopher Wyvill · William Salt Library, Stafford, Samuel Pipe-Wolferstan MSS

Likenesses J. Basire, line engraving, 1810 (after G. Head, 1800), NPG [*see illus.*] · P. MacDowell, plaster bust (posthumous), DWL · C. Picart, stipple (after G. Head), BM, NPG

Wealth at death over £20,000: will, PRO, PROB 11/1589, fols. 90–94

parliamentary reform. But in November 1782 he resigned his preferments, and offered his services as colleague to his friend Lindsey at the Unitarian chapel in Essex Street, London. At the end of December he moved to London with his family, having been engaged at a stipend of £150. He justified his decision in *Reasons for resigning the rectory of Panton and vicarage of Swinderby, in Lincolnshire, and quitting the Church of England* (1782). In 1783 Disney became the first secretary of a Unitarian Society for Promoting the Knowledge of the Scriptures. On the retirement of Lindsey from active duty in July 1793, Disney became sole minister. The services at Essex Street had been conducted by means of a modified common prayer book, on the basis of a revision made by Samuel Clarke (1675–1729). In 1802 Disney introduced a new form of his own composition, but the congregation, on his retirement, immediately reverted to the old version.

Disney's resignation of office was occasioned by a large bequest of property, which reached him in a curious way. Thomas Hollis (d. 1774) had left his estates in Dorset to his friend Thomas Brand of The Hyde, near Ingatestone, Essex, who took the name of Hollis. Brand Hollis (d. 1804), by a will dated 1792, left both estates, worth about £5000 a year, to Disney, who resigned his ministry on 25 March 1805 on the grounds of ill health, and in the following June left London and took up his residence at The Hyde. He was succeeded at Essex Street by Thomas Belsham. The rest of his life was spent in the literary and agricultural pursuits of a country gentleman. He took part in various representations to parliament which resulted in the act of 1813 'to relieve persons who impugn the doctrine of the

Disney, John (1779–1857), barrister and art collector, born at Flintham Hall, Nottinghamshire, the home of his paternal uncle Lewis Disney, on 29 May 1779, was the eldest son of seven children of the Revd John *Disney DD (1746–1816), a Church of England, and later Unitarian, clergyman, and his wife, Jane (1745/6–1809), eldest daughter of the Ven. Francis *Blackburne (1705–1787), rector of Richmond, Yorkshire, and archdeacon of Cleveland. The Disney family could trace its descent back to the Normans. The focus for the family was Norton D'Isney (Norton Disney) and Swinderby, both between Newark-on-Trent and Lincoln; Disney's father was vicar of Swinderby until he resigned his living in 1782.

In December 1782 the Disney family moved to London, when the Revd Disney became the first secretary of the Unitarian Society for Promoting the Knowledge of the Scriptures. In 1783 he became minister of the Essex Street Chapel with the Revd Theophilus Lindsey. By 1785 the family had moved to Sloane Street in Chelsea, and Disney received his education at home. In April 1796 he was admitted, aged sixteen, as pensioner to Peterhouse, his father's Cambridge college; his younger brother Algernon (1780–1848) followed him to Peterhouse in October of the same year. Two years later, in April 1798, Disney was admitted to the Inner Temple, following a legal career which his father had been forced to abandon through ill health. In May 1803 he was called to the bar. On 22 September 1802 he married, at St George's, Hanover Square, his first cousin Sophia (1777–1856), youngest daughter of Lewis Disney-Ffytche (1738–1822) of Swinderby, Lincolnshire, and Danbury Place, Essex, and Elizabeth, daughter of William Ffytche, governor of Bengal; there were three children of the marriage, John (1808–1829), Edgar (1810–1881), his successor, and Sophia.

Disney's family stayed in London until March 1805 when his father retired to The Hyde, near Ingatestone, Essex. The Hyde, designed by Sir William Chambers, had been bequeathed (in a will of 2 November 1792), along with land in Dorset at Corscombe, Halstock, and Netherstoke, by Thomas Brand Hollis (d. 1804), the friend of the 'republican' Thomas Hollis (1720–1774). In this way the Disney family acquired a significant income from both estates (estimated at about £5000 a year) as well as the substantial collection of classical sculptures displayed at The Hyde which had been largely acquired, often through Thomas Jenkins in Rome, by Hollis and Brand during the grand tour in a series of journeys made from 1748 to 1753. The display included a portrait of Marcus Aurelius once in the Palazzo Barberini at Rome. Other pieces were acquired on their return to England, such as from the sale of Dr Richard Mead's antiquities. This Dorset interest may have influenced Disney's appointment in September 1807 as recorder of Bridport, a position he held until 1823; in 1818 he was appointed sheriff of Dorset. During this period he resided at Corscombe.

On the death of his father, on 26 December 1816, Disney inherited The Hyde and its contents, as well as land in Dorset. One of his first actions was to dispose of the libraries of his father, Thomas Hollis, and Thomas Brand Hollis at Sothebys, on 22 April 1817. He also seems to have taken more interest in affairs in Essex and about 1820 sold part of his Halstock estate; in 1822 his wife inherited part of the estate of her father (and Disney's uncle).

In 1818 Disney started work on a major catalogue of the collection of antiquities at The Hyde; an earlier catalogue of the collection, A Catalogue of some Marbles, Bronzes, Pictures and Gems, at The Hyde, Near Ingatestone, Essex (1807), had been prepared by his father. A study by the Revd James Tate of the inscriptions in the collection was added to the second impression (1809) after a visit to The Hyde in August 1809. The collection itself was supplemented by small antiquities from Pompeii and Herculaneum acquired by a relative during a visit to Italy between 1795 and 1798. Disney's research was interrupted by a visit to Italy and in particular Rome in 1826 and 1827, during which time he made a number of purchases. He found Italy disappointing, writing to C. Rankin, his agent, from Rome, 'the country round the Eternal City is … as dreary and desolate as Hounslow heath was 30 years ago' (Disney to Rankin, 17 Dec 1826, Chelmsford, Essex RO, MSD/DQC 211). He also received gifts of antiquities from Charles Callis Western and James Christie. Among his acquisitions was a Latin inscription said to have been found in March 1821 on the site of the County Hospital at Colchester, but almost certainly purchased abroad. Disney was active in local societies. He was president of the Chelmsford Philosophical Society and instrumental in the creation of the Chelmsford and Essex Museum, which moved to new premises in 1843. He was the first president of the Essex Archaeological Society, founded in 1852.

After relinquishing his position in Dorset, Disney continued to pursue his legal interests and published *Outlines of a Penal Code* (1826). By 1832 he was chairman of the quarter sessions of the justices of the peace for the county of Essex. He seems to have had a long-standing desire to become a member of parliament. He edited a work entitled *A collection of acts of parliament, relative to county and borough elections, with reference to several reported cases, containing the determinations of the House of Commons* (1811), and contested the constituencies of Harwich (1832) and North Essex as a Liberal candidate, but without success. During the 1835 campaign he had to defend himself against the accusation that he supported whipping as 'a fit punishment for females' (*The Times*, 9 May 1835) as well as to suffer the re-airing of the celebrated 1815 scandal between his brother Algernon and Lady Cranstoun (*The Times*, 1 May 1835). The expenses for these elections, as well as the upkeep of The Hyde, may have led Disney to dispose of the Corscombe estate in 1836.

The catalogue of The Hyde, illustrated with engravings, appeared in 1846 as *Museum Disneianum, being a description of a collection of ancient marbles, in the possession of John Disney, esq., F.R.S. F.S.A., at The Hyde, near Ingatestone*. A second edition followed in 1849 with supplements entitled, 'Specimens of ancient art' (dated on a separate title page, 1848) and 'Various ancient fictile vases' (dated on a separate title page, 1849). The volume subsequently appeared under a new title, *Fitzwilliam Museum*, reflecting Disney's donation of most of his collection of sculptures to the fledgeling Fitzwilliam Museum at Cambridge in 1850, initiating the Greek and Roman collection. Along with E. D. Clarke's collection of marbles, presented to the University of Cambridge in 1803, the Disney marbles continue to form the core of the Fitzwilliam's ancient sculpture collection. The remaining antiquities were left at The Hyde, and were subsequently dispersed at auction by Christies on 1 May 1884 and 28 January 1886 after the death of his son Edgar; in 1885 the Fitzwilliam acquired the marble *Apollo of Miletus*, restored under John Flaxman and Antonio d'Este. Adolf Michaelis commented that Disney showed 'more zeal than knowledge or criticism' and that the collection itself was 'trash rather than treasure' (A. Michaelis, *Ancient Marbles in Great Britain*, 1882, 159). Disney's generosity to the University of Cambridge continued when in 1851 he gave an endowment of £1000 to create a chair of archaeology, the first in Great Britain. The endowment was augmented to £3500 by bequest. Disney specified in a deed of trust of 28 May 1851 that the Disney professor should lecture 'on the subject of Classical Mediaeval and other Antiquities the Fine Arts and all matters and things connected therewith' (Clark, 224). Disney reserved the right in his lifetime to make the appointment, and J. H. Marsden of St John's College was the first holder.

Disney was elected a fellow of the Royal Society on 9 June 1832; his nomination was supported by the traveller W. M. Leake, whose collection of Greek pottery and cabinet of coins and gems were also to find their way to the Fitzwilliam Museum. This was followed on 20 June 1839 by Disney's election as a fellow of the Society of Antiquaries; he served on its council in 1845 and 1850, and acted as one of the auditors in 1850. He was awarded the honorary degree of DCL at the University of Oxford in 1854, and was incorporated with the degree of LLD at the University of Cambridge in the same year, an honour which he marked with the presentation of a bust of himself to the Fitzwilliam Museum. Disney died at The Hyde on 6 May 1857 and was buried with his wife in Fryerning churchyard, Essex.

DAVID GILL

Sources GM, 3rd ser., 2 (1857), 741 · *Proceedings of the Society of Antiquaries of London*, 4 (1857–9), 194–5 · J. Hutchins, *The history and antiquities of the county of Dorset*, 3rd edn, ed. W. Shipp and J. W. Hodson, 4 vols. (1861–74); facs. edn (1973) · T. A. Walker, ed., *Admissions to Peterhouse or St Peter's College in the University of Cambridge* (1912) · J. W. Clark, *Endowments of the University of Cambridge* (1904) · D. W. J. Gill, 'Antiquities from the grand tour: the Disney collection at the Fitzwilliam Museum', *Cambridge*, 26 (1990), 34–7 · D. W. J. Gill, '"Ancient fictile vases" from the Disney collection', *Journal of the History of Collections*, 2 (1990), 227–31 · L. Budde and R. V. Nicholls, *A catalogue of Greek and Roman sculpture in the Fitzwilliam Museum, Cambridge* (1967) · *Cambridge University Calendar* (1885), 328–9 · A. R. Maddison, ed., *Lincolnshire pedigrees*, 1, Harleian Society, 50 (1902) · *DNB* · private information (2004) [J. D. Brown]
Archives Essex RO, Chelmsford, corresp. with family and with C. Rankin of Gray's Inn · Lincs. Arch., corresp. with his father, John Disney
Likenesses R. Westmacott?, marble bust, 1854, FM Cam.; repro. in J. W. Goodison, *Catalogue of Cambridge portraits*, 1: *The university collection* (1955) · Maull & Polyblank, photograph, FM Cam.

Disney, Sir Moore (1765/6–1846), army officer, eldest son of Moore Disney of Churchtown, co. Waterford, one of the Irish descendants of the family of Disney of Norton Disney in Northamptonshire, entered the army as an ensign in the 1st Grenadier guards on 17 April 1783. He served in America for the last few months of the American War of Independence, and was promoted lieutenant and

captain on 3 June 1791. He was with the guards throughout the campaign in the Netherlands under the duke of York from 1793 to May 1795, and was promoted captain and lieutenant-colonel on 12 June 1795. He was promoted colonel on 29 April 1802, and served for a short time as a brigadier-general in the home district in 1805, but he resigned that appointment in July 1806, in order to go to Sicily in command of the 3rd battalion of the 1st guards.

Disney was made a brigadier-general in Sicily in August 1807, and was commandant of Messina from January to July 1808, when he started home to take command of a brigade in England. On 6 October, however, his ship touched at Lisbon, and he was at once begged by General Cradock to land and take command of a brigade consisting of the 2nd, 3rd, 6th, and 50th regiments, which Cradock wished to send to join the army of Sir John Moore in Spain. Disney led the brigade safely through Abrantes before halting at Castelo Branco on 27 November, when he was ordered to hand over command to Major-General Alan Cameron, and to join the main army under Sir John Moore.

Disney reached Toro in safety, and was at once put in command of a brigade of Edward Paget's reserve, consisting of the 28th and 91st regiments. The reserve had to cover the famous retreat of Sir John Moore, and Disney greatly distinguished himself both at the action at Betanzos on 11 January 1809, and in the battle of Corunna. For his services at that battle he received a gold medal, and was promoted major-general on 25 April. Later in 1809 he commanded the 1st brigade of guards, attached to Hope's division, in the Walcheren expedition, and on his return to England was given the command of the home district.

In 1810 Disney went to Cadiz to act as second in command to General Graham (afterwards Lord Lynedoch), and in June 1811 he succeeded him in the chief command there. He handed over the command at Cadiz to Major-General George Cooke in November 1811, returned to England, and never again went on active service. He was promoted lieutenant-general on 4 June 1814, became colonel of the 15th regiment on 23 July 1814, was made a KCB in 1815, and was promoted general on 10 January 1837.

Disney had married Mary (d. 26 Jan 1831), widow of Ralph Sneyd of Belmont, and daughter of George Cooke Yarborough of Streetthorpe, Yorkshire. He died at his house in Upper Brook Street, London, on 19 April 1846, at the age of eighty.

H. M. STEPHENS, *rev.* ROGER T. STEARN

Sources GM, 2nd ser., 26 (1846) · F. W. Hamilton, *The origin and history of the first or grenadier guards*, 3 vols. (1874) · *Hart's Army List* · Fortescue, *Brit. army*, vols. 6–7 · A. J. Guy, ed., *The road to Waterloo: the British army and the struggle against revolutionary and Napoleonic France, 1793–1815* (1990) · D. Gates, *The Spanish ulcer: a history of the Peninsular War* (1986) · R. Muir, *Britain and the defeat of Napoleon, 1807–1815* (1996) · T. C. W. Blanning, *The French revolutionary wars, 1787–1802* (1996)

Disney, William (*b.* in or after 1633, *d.* 1685), conspirator, was the eldest son of Molyneux Disney (1614–1694), army officer, and his wife, Mary (*bap.* 1616, *d.* 1669), youngest daughter of Sir Robert Monson of North Carlton. The family had been well-known puritan landowners at Norton

Disney, Lincolnshire, for many generations. Molyneux Disney married Mary Monson on 14 January 1633. He raised a troop of horse for parliament in 1642–3 and was active in local government in 1645–6, but appears to have become somewhat disillusioned with the parliamentary side and in 1649 was fined for having corresponded with the royalists. In 1673 he was commissioned as an officer in the duke of Albemarle's regiment of foot.

Disney was admitted to the Middle Temple on 12 November 1654 but was apparently never called to the bar, although a contemporary later claimed he was a barrister. Disney's activities in the 1660s and 1670s remain a mystery. In the 1680s, when he became active in whig politics, he can once again be traced. In 1680 Disney confessed to Secretary of State Leoline Jenkins and the earl of Essex that he had been investigating the issue of the duke of Monmouth's possible legitimacy, trying to discover whether Charles II had indeed married Monmouth's mother, Lucy Walters. In 1681 he published a pro-parliament treatise entitled *Nil dictum quod non dictum prius, or, A transcript of government considered as it is in the state of nature or religion*. Disney set out to prove that the 'Saxon constitution', with its emphasis on the great council of the kingdom, survived the conquest of 1066 intact. He next asserted that the power of parliament remained

> unlimited and universal … it hath power above the Law it self, having power to alter the common law of England, to declare meaning of any doubtful law, to repeal old patents, grants, or charters and Judgements whatsoever of the king, or any court of justice, if erroneous or illegal, not without, but against the king's personal consent. (W. D., 135)

Disney was reportedly related to the Rye House plotter Major John Wildman. While there is no evidence directly linking Disney to the plot to assassinate Charles II and the duke of York at Rye House in 1683 it seems highly likely that he was involved or at least knew about the conspiracy. Following the suspicious death of the earl of Essex in the Tower in July 1683 while awaiting trial for involvement in the plot, Disney was also active in whig efforts to prove that Essex was murdered and had not committed suicide. In the months preceding Monmouth's rebellion in June 1685, Disney acted as a contact between whigs and dissenters in the Netherlands and England. He apprised Wildman and former Fifth Monarchist Henry Danvers of Monmouth's plans, but both were reluctant to give support. At one point, Disney told a Monmouth envoy in London that he had consulted with some unnamed gentlemen (probably lords Delamere and Macclesfield) and that they had suggested that the duke join the earl of Argyll's invasion of Scotland, believing that the people of England were not inclined to help Monmouth. With the help of the Quaker bookseller John Brickhurst and a Rye House conspirator, Thomas Weeks, Disney printed advance copies of Monmouth's notorious *Declaration* (penned by 'the Plotter', Robert Ferguson).

Disney was arrested at Lambeth on 15 June 1685 with 750 partially printed copies of Monmouth's *Declaration* and five perfect copies. According to *A true and full account given by the minister of St. George, concerning the behaviour and last dying speech of William Disney, esq.* (1685) he was caught with just 'his shirt on and his maid in his bed'. On 16 June he was committed by Judge Jeffreys for conspiring the death of the king and exciting persons to rebellion. He was tried on 25 June in Southwark by special commission and the lord chief justice and found guilty of treason. Disney was hanged, drawn, and quartered on 29 June 1685 at Kennington Common in Surrey. His quarters were ordered to be fixed to the city gates. In his final moments he refused to make any discovery, begged God's pardon, and told the Anglican minister with him that 'he lived in and did now die in the communion of the Church of England which he repeated again in these words, "the Protestant Church of England"' (*A True and Full Account*). The name of Disney's wife is unknown, but they had at least three children, who in 1692 petitioned for and were granted pensions in compensation for the 'services and sufferings' of their father (*CSP dom.*, 1691–2, 157).   MELINDA ZOOK

Sources *A true and full account given by the minister of St. George, concerning the behaviour and last dying speech of William Disney, esq.* (1685) · *A warning to traytors, or, A brief account of apprehending, tryal, condemnation … and execution of William Disnie late esq.* (1685) · W. D., esq. [W. Disney], *Nil dictum quod non dictum prius* (1681) · *The autobiography of Sir John Bramston*, ed. [Lord Braybrooke], CS, 32 (1845), 193 · P. R. Newman, *Royalist officers in England and Wales, 1642–1660: a biographical dictionary* (1981), 111 · G. Roberts, *The life, progresses and rebellion of James duke of Monmouth*, 1 (1844), 233 · J. C. Jeaffreson, ed., *Middlesex county records*, 4 vols. (1886–92), vol. 4, p. 293 · *Calamy rev.*, 165 · Venn, *Alum. Cant.* · *Report on the manuscripts of the late Reginald Rawdon Hastings*, 4 vols., HMC, 78 (1928–47), vol. 4, p. 308 · J. Greenberg, *The radical face of the ancient constitution* [forthcoming] · M. Zook, *Radical whigs and conspiratorial politics* (Penn State, 1999), 29, 35, 141, 197 · R. L. Greaves, *Secrets of the kingdom: British radicals from the Popish Plot to the revolution of 1688–89* (1992) · *The manuscripts of the House of Lords*, 4 vols., HMC, 17 (1887–94), vol. 2, pp. 393–4 · W. Disney, *The forgetfulness of God* (1681) · A. R. Maddison, ed., *Lincolnshire pedigrees*, 1, Harleian Society, 50 (1902), 306–8 · H. A. C. Sturgess, ed., *Register of admissions to the Honourable Society of the Middle Temple, from the fifteenth century to the year 1944*, 1 (1949) · *CSP dom.*, 1679–80; 1686–7; 1691–2 · M. A. E. Green, ed., *Calendar of the proceedings of the committee for compounding … 1643–1660*, 5 vols., PRO (1889–92) · J. Hutchins, *The history and antiquities of the county of Dorset*, 3rd edn, 4 vols. (1861–70), vol. 2, pp. 99–100 · C. Holmes, *Seventeenth-century Lincolnshire* (1980) · J. W. F. Hill, *Tudor and Stuart Lincoln* (1956) · L. Spring, *The regiments of the Eastern Association*, 2 vols. (1998) · W. A. Shaw, ed., *Calendar of treasury books*, 9–10, PRO (1931–5)

Archives BL, Add. MS 28094, fols. 71r–72v · BL, Add. MS 32095, fols. 198r–198v, 200r | BL, Lansdowne MS, 115A, fol. 266 · BL, Middleton collection, Add. MSS 41812, fol. 226; 41819, fol. 15

Disney, William (1731–1807), university professor and Church of England clergyman, was born on 29 September 1731, probably at Cranbrook in Kent; he was the second son of the Revd Joseph Disney MA (1695–1777), vicar of Cranbrook and Appledore, and his wife, Ann Ross (d. 1782), of Biddenden. He was descended from Lincolnshire stock, through whom he is almost certainly related to the twentieth-century American animator Walt Disney.

William Disney was educated in London at Merchant Taylors' School under Dr Creech, and from there went on to Trinity College, Cambridge, where he was admitted pensioner on 26 January 1749. He matriculated and was admitted as a scholar on the Newman foundation in that year; he obtained his BA in 1753 and his MA in 1756. In 1754 he had been named a fellow of his college, and on 22 December had been ordained deacon in the Church of England by Matthias Mawson, bishop of Ely. He was ordained priest by Mawson on 19 February 1758. From 1757 to 1771 he held the post of regius professor of Hebrew in the University of Cambridge.

Disney gained his BD in 1768 and in 1777 became rector of Pluckley in Kent, where he was to spend the rest of his life. He married Anna Maria Smyth (*bap.* 1736, *d.* 1820), youngest daughter of John and Elizabeth Smyth of Chart Sutton, Kent, but there appear to have been no children of the marriage.

Disney was made DD of Cambridge University in 1789 and on the occasion preached a sermon that was printed in Cambridge in the same year under the title *A sermon preached before the University of Cambridge … with some strictures on the licentious notions avowed or insinuated in the three last volumes of Mr Gibbon's Roman history*. Disney shared the discomfort felt by many readers concerning Gibbon's account of the early Christian church and its effect on the Roman empire, which was widely interpreted as irreligious.

Having left the academic world Disney devoted the last thirty years of his life to the duties of a clergyman. His brief correspondence with Edward Hasted, historian of Kent, shows him to have been the caring incumbent of a well-run parish, and Hasted, who outlived his near-contemporary, noted Disney's death in his commonplace book with the words 'rich in good works' (Canterbury Cathedral Archives, U11/5). Disney's obituary in the *Gentleman's Magazine* was therefore stating no more than the truth in saying 'his death will be sincerely regretted by all who had the happiness of being numbered among his friends, but more particularly by the neighbouring poor, who in him have lost a kindly friend, and a most liberal benefactor' (*GM*, 77, 385). Mourned by his wife as a 'truly good man' (ibid.), William Disney died at Pluckley on 28 March 1807 and was buried in the family vault at Cranbrook on 4 April. SHIRLEY BURGOYNE BLACK

Sources *GM*, 1st ser., 47 (1777), 404 · *GM*, 1st ser., 52 (1782), 94 · *GM*, 1st ser., 77 (1807), 385 · Venn, *Alum. Cant.* · W. W. Rouse Ball and J. A. Venn, eds., *Admissions to Trinity College, Cambridge*, 3 (1911), 159 · CKS, P83/1/1 (Chart Sutton); P100/1/13; P100/1/14 (Cranbrook) · W. Disney, *A sermon preached before the University of Cambridge, on Sunday June 28, 1789, with some strictures on the licentious notions, avowed or insinuated in the three last volumes of Mr Gibbon's Roman history* (1789) · *Index to archbishop's act books, 1663–1859*, LPL · J. M. Cowper and A. J. Willis, eds., *Canterbury marriage licences*, 6 vols. (1892–1906); with suppl. A. J. Willis, ed., 3 vols. (1967–71), vol. 6, p. 122; vol. 7 · Canterbury Cathedral Archives, U11/5; U11/6/3 (Hasted MS) · W. Hustler, ed., *Graduati Cantabrigienses* (1823), 140 · *Archaeologia Cantiana*, 22 (1897), 94

Disraeli, Benjamin, earl of Beaconsfield (1804–1881), prime minister and novelist, was born on 21 December 1804 at 6 King's Road, Bedford Row, London, the eldest son and second of five children of Isaac *D'Israeli (1766–1848) and his wife, Maria (1775–1847), daughter of Naphtali and Ricca Basevi. From 1810 or 1811 he attended a school at Islington kept by a Miss Roper, and then, probably from

Benjamin Disraeli, earl of Beaconsfield (1804–1881), by Sir John Everett Millais, 1881

1813, one at Blackheath belonging to the Revd John Potticary, where he was given separate instruction in Judaism. However, he was baptized into the Christian faith (as an Anglican) on 31 July 1817 and thereafter attended a different school, Higham Hall in Epping Forest, run by the Unitarian minister Eli Cogan, until 1819 or 1820, after which he was taught at home. The family had moved to 6 Bloomsbury Square after the death of Benjamin's grandfather in 1816 had increased Isaac D'Israeli's means. That death also removed the family's last tie with the Jewish religion and led to the baptism of the children. Isaac was an easy-going Voltairean sceptic whose interests were those of a reclusive literary dilettante and whose friends tended to be London publishers and antiquaries. From an early age Benjamin was introduced to this circle and to his father's extensive and eclectic library, which left a much clearer stamp on his mind and tastes than the more disciplined classical training offered at Higham Hall. Benjamin had dropped the apostrophe in his surname by December 1822, though it was still widely used (for example, in *Hansard*) until the 1840s.

Disraeli in the 1820s In November 1821 Disraeli was articled at his father's arrangement to a solicitor's firm in the Old Jewry, and spent three years there. Subsequently (in April 1827) his name was entered at Lincoln's Inn, but though he ate dinners for a time, he had rejected the idea of a career at the bar some years before he withdrew his name in November 1831. He had, and retained, a strong dislike of the mundane lifestyle of the English middle classes: for them, marriage was 'often the only adventure of life' (Smith, *Disraeli*, 69). 'To be a great lawyer, I must give up my chance of being a great man' (*Vivian Grey*, bk 1, chap. 9). An ardent admirer of Byron (whom his father knew), he dreamed instead of literary fame. The example of Byron—and of Canning in politics—showed him how men of unusual charisma and insight could win international admiration with the aid of the burgeoning media. Disraeli fell heavily under the influence of Romanticism. From the early 1820s he had adopted an appropriately eye-catching and narcissistic style of dress, with ruffled shirts, velvet trousers, coloured waistcoats, and jewellery, and he wore his hair in cascades of ringlets. It was on his first continental travels, to Germany in 1824 with his father, that he decided to try to escape from a legal career. The latter parts of his first published novel, *Vivian Grey*, were set in Germany—the home of Goethe, whose *Wilhelm Meister*, translated into English in 1824, clearly influenced his early literary style. A longer tour of the continent in August 1826 included a stay at Geneva, where Disraeli engaged Byron's former boatman to row him on the lake. He reflected self-consciously, in Romantic fashion, on the sublime natural creations that he observed on his travels, and concluded that he loved 'trees better than men' (*Letters*, 1.92).

In May 1824 Disraeli submitted a manuscript to his father's friend John Murray, but it was not published. His attempt over the next year to establish the financial independence necessary for a literary career was a catastrophic failure. With a friend he sought to capitalize on the speculative bubble in South American mining companies. Disraeli also wrote pamphlets puffing the operations. By June 1825 they had lost £7000. A third partner took on much of this debt; Disraeli could not finally settle with him until 1849. Later in 1825 he urged a willing Murray to establish a new morning paper, *The Representative*, to compete with *The Times*. He worked hard on this venture, impressing Murray with his energy and insight, but failed to persuade J. G. Lockhart to take up a major editorial role, and the journal collapsed after six months. Disraeli used this episode in *Vivian Grey*, the first part of which was published anonymously in two volumes in April 1826. It was publicized by the publisher Henry Colburn as a sensational *roman-à-clef* in the then fashionable silver-fork style. It portrayed with intensity the desperate, unscrupulous ambition of a clever young man, and his come-uppance. It also set out a highly irreverent view of London society, exposing the egotism, superficiality, and charlatanism of its members. This combination of unmistakable self-exposure and reckless satire did Disraeli's reputation great and lasting damage—for the identity of the author was soon revealed. The book also earned some damning reviews, which dwelt on its solecisms and general immaturity. Moreover, Murray and Lockhart, men of great influence in literary circles, were deeply offended by the sneering treatment of characters based on them.

The financial disaster and literary abuse to which Disraeli was subjected in 1825–6 almost certainly contributed to the onset of a major nervous crisis that affected him for much of the next four years. He had always been moody, sensitive, and solitary by nature, but now became seriously depressed and lethargic. The 'cold, dull world', he later wrote, could not remotely conceive the 'despondency' of 'youthful genius' that was conscious of 'the strong necessity for fame', yet had 'no simultaneous faith in [its] own power' (*Contarini Fleming*, pt 1, chap. 11).

Widening horizons, 1830–1832 It was not until a lengthier journey, to the East in 1830–31 (financed partly by a fashionable but light novel, *The Young Duke*, written in 1829–30), that Disraeli finally acquired a strong enough sense of identity to sustain him in his search for fame. Between June and September 1830 he travelled with William Meredith in Gibraltar, Spain, and Malta, where they joined up with James Clay, an Oxford friend of Meredith. Clay's buccaneering temperament, raffish habits, and sexual experience fascinated Disraeli and made the rest of the journey more adventurous. Joined by Byron's former servant Tita, the three men toured the Ottoman empire experiencing Eastern lifestyles. Disraeli spent a week at the court of the grand vizier Redschid Ali in Albania, and, after visiting Athens, a further six weeks in Constantinople. The exotic, colourful splendour of Turkish courts appealed immensely to his imagination; he felt that the 'calm and luxurious' existence of the people accorded with his 'indolent and melancholy' tastes (Monypenny and Buckle, 1.159, 170). He loved the duplicitous intrigue of court politics and its distance from the puritanical moralism of the Western bourgeoisie; staying with Redschid, Disraeli wrote of the 'delight of being made much of by a man who was daily decapitating half the province' (ibid., 158). The travellers then proceeded to Jerusalem, where Disraeli spent a seminal week, before staying five months in Egypt. The tour was cut short dramatically by Meredith's death from smallpox in Cairo in July 1831. Disraeli had to be treated for venereal disease on his return to London.

Like other nineteenth-century travellers to the East, Disraeli felt enriched by his experiences, becoming aware of values that seemed denied to his insular countrymen. The journey encouraged his self-consciousness, his moral relativism, and his interest in Eastern racial and religious attitudes. On his return he could strike others as insufferably affected: according to one account, he was much given to sticking his fingers in his lapels and drawling, 'Allah is great' (Bradford, 51). There is a malicious contemporary portrait of him in dandy mode, as Jericho Jabber in Rosina Bulwer's *Very Successful* (1856). In 1833 he published a novel, *The Wondrous Tale of Alroy*, which concerned the dilemma faced by a twelfth-century Middle Eastern Jew who sought fame, but who faced conflicting ideals: between establishing a purely Jewish regime and a larger empire assimilating other religions. The moral of his failure was that a taste for action and the power of imagination were both needed in a leader. Though neither meritorious nor commercially successful, *Alroy* shows Disraeli thinking about problems that were to concern him a great deal in the future; it portrayed 'my ideal ambition' (Monypenny and Buckle, 1.236).

The other literary product of Disraeli's travels was *Contarini Fleming* (1832). Subtitled 'a psychological autobiography', *Contarini*, like *Vivian Grey*, was a *Bildungsroman* exploring the development of the artistic consciousness and containing much tortured reflection on Disraeli's destiny. It presents the dual nature of the eponymous hero, a man of mixed Mediterranean and northern background, a brooding artist but aspiring man of action, deeply imaginative yet energetic and courageous. Disraeli was very aware of these two sides of his personality. *Contarini* ends on a new theme, the transition of Europe from feudal to federal principles (pt 7, chap. 2). In a diary of 1833 Disraeli claimed that his insights were 'continental' and 'revolutionary' (Monypenny and Buckle, 1.236), by which he presumably meant broad and original enough to encompass the intellectual and social forces that were shaping Europe. In 1834 he finished a heroic poem, on the scale of Homer and apparently conceived when standing on the plain of Troy; its object was to evoke the clash of feudal and democratic principles in Europe since the French Revolution. Entitled *The Revolutionary Epick*, it was not remotely a success, but it testified to Disraeli's enthusiasm for the fashionable continental conception that the progress of human affairs was realized through the interaction of individual will, ideas, and great social forces. Disraeli was fascinated by the creativity with which the greatest statesmen, such as Napoleon, moulded social change and thus won worldwide renown.

It was in the early 1830s that Disraeli decided to begin a political career. In 1833 he recorded that he would 'write no more about myself' (Monypenny and Buckle, 1.236); certainly there seemed little prospect of fame through literature. His pride sought an existence independent of the literary pundits and titled and frivolous patrons who seemed to dictate fortunes in letters. Politics, he later wrote, offered the chance of 'power o'er the powerful' (*Letters*, 4.250). It also offered therapeutic excitement: 'action may not always be happiness, but there is no happiness without action' (*Lothair*, chap. 79). The reform crisis of 1830–32 opened the prospect of political realignments and quick fame for men of resource and vision. The Disraelite hero of *A Year at Hartlebury*, the novel he wrote with his sister and published anonymously in 1834 (and whose authorship was established in 1983 by Ellen Henderson and John P. Matthews), turned, 'at the prospect of insurrection … with more affection towards a country he had hitherto condemned as too uneventful for a man of genius' (p. 58). More mundanely, the cost of attempting to cut a dash in society, on top of his incompetent management of his previous debts, ensured that a long queue of creditors hounded him. A seat in parliament offered immunity from imprisonment for debt.

Towards parliament and marriage Disraeli's first parliamentary candidature was at High Wycombe, the nearest borough to the house at Bradenham that his father rented from 1829. The two sitting MPs were whigs, and one was the son of the local landowner Lord Carrington. It was both necessary and congenial for Disraeli to declare himself an independent radical, opposed to whiggism and oligarchy, at a by-election in June 1832 and then at the general election held on the new franchise in December 1832. On both occasions he was defeated. His friend Edward Lytton Bulwer secured him letters of support from leading radicals O'Connell and Burdett. As the only opposition candidate, Disraeli naturally courted tory voters, and in 1833, excited by accusations that in doing so he was inconsistent, he published *What is He?*, in which he argued for a tory–radical coalition against the whigs. His background, ostentatious manner, and verbal pyrotechnics ensured that opponents would charge him with lack of principle, but in fact few politicians of the 1830s were more interested than he was in fashioning a coherent individual perspective on politics. Disraeli sought independence from faction and from condescension, and to be noticed; his rise would surely have been more rapid had he made more compromises with the system.

Disraeli's political path began to clear when in 1834 he met one of the few leading tories colourful, indiscreet, and clever enough to appreciate his talents: Lord Lyndhurst. Disraeli was introduced to him by Henrietta Sykes, an older married lady with whom Lyndhurst had been having an increasingly public affair since the summer of 1833. She seems to have cured Disraeli of some immature affectations. It was suspected that he was happy to share Henrietta's affections with Lyndhurst. Certainly the triangular friendship expanded his political circle and lowered her social reputation. Disraeli loved Lyndhurst's gossip and taste for intrigue, and became his secretary and go-between. When he stood again at Wycombe at the 1835 election, once more unsuccessfully, and still as an independent radical, it was with the assistance of £500 from tory funds. The events of this period made it clear that the future lay with a two-party system, and in the spring of 1835 he fought the Taunton by-election as a tory. In March 1836 he was elected to the Carlton Club. Encouraged by Lyndhurst, and invoking Bolingbroke as an exemplar, he wrote some vigorous tory propaganda. The most important, his *Vindication of the English Constitution*, was published in December 1835. It used a historical perspective to claim the tories' sympathy with the people, to attack whig, Irish, and utilitarian views, and to assert the legitimacy of the House of Lords' opposition to government policy. More scurrilous were *The Letters of Runnymede*, nineteen anonymous pieces of satire on politicians of the day, which he published in *The Times* in 1836. They included some abuse of the Irish. Disraeli used the whigs' increasingly pro-Catholic Irish policy to justify his toryism, as did the famous former radical Sir Francis Burdett, for whom he canvassed at the Westminster election of 1837. At Taunton in 1835 Disraeli had compared the proposal of Irish church appropriation to the spoliation of the monasteries by the whigs' ancestors. His misreported remarks about O'Connell led the latter to charge him with being a Jew 'of the lowest and most disgusting grade of moral turpitude' (Monypenny and Buckle, 1.288). As on other occasions,

Disraeli's pride flared up at such language, and he provoked a public row with O'Connell and his son Morgan, whom he challenged to a duel.

Disraeli was also taken up by Lady Londonderry in the 1836 season, a sign of his increasing reputation in tory circles. He was given a winnable seat at the 1837 election, when he became MP for Maidstone with the other tory candidate, Wyndham Lewis, who lent him money to pay part of the election expenses. Disraeli's debts had grown into a serious problem, and Henrietta's husband's solicitor had helped him to manage them. However, in late 1836 he terminated the affair with her; she was very demanding emotionally, and began a passionate romance with the painter Daniel Maclise (whose drawing of Disraeli in 1828 effectively recorded his dandyism). Shortly afterwards Disraeli published *Henrietta Temple*, a love story and social comedy, and followed it by *Venetia* (1837), a portrayal of Byronic existence in the late eighteenth century, which was written quickly in order to raise money.

When Wyndham Lewis died suddenly in March 1838, Disraeli consoled his widow, who had been left with an income of about £5000 per year, together with their house in London, 1 Grosvenor Gate. Mary Anne Lewis [see Disraeli, Mary Anne (1792–1872)] was the daughter of a naval lieutenant and farmer, John Evans, of Brampford Speke, near Exeter, and his wife, Eleanor. She was coquettish, impulsive, not well educated, and extremely talkative, but also warm, loyal, and sensible. She shared something of Disraeli's love of striking clothes and social glitter while feeling, like him, an outsider in very high social circles. Her money, house, and solid position were undoubtedly attractive to him (though she had only a life interest in her husband's estate). But so also were her vivacity and her childless motherliness. All his life older women appealed to Disraeli, apparently in search of a mother-substitute more appreciative of his genius than his own stolid parent had been. Their courtship lasted most of a year, for much of which time she seems to have been unsure of his motives. In the end he convinced her of his genuine emotional attachment; he certainly pursued her ardently. As before when he was absorbed in passion, he wrote a poetic work, the blank verse play *The Tragedy of Count Alarcos*, which was only performed as a curiosity after Disraeli became prime minister. They were married at St George's, Hanover Square, on 28 August 1839. Their union thereafter presented a picture of remarkable mutual devotion and respect. She provided the domestic stability and constant admiration that he sorely needed. She also paid off many of his debts: she had spent £13,000 on these and his elections by 1842 alone. Like his father's, her payments would have been more effective had Disraeli straightened out his affairs, approached his debts rationally, and been straightforward with her about the sums owing; instead, his tendency was to renew his obligations at ruinous interest rates. At the 1841 election his opponent printed posters listing judgments in the courts against Disraeli to the extent of over £22,000, and alleged that he owed at least £6800 more than that.

Political career, 1837–1846 Disraeli made his maiden speech in parliament on 7 December 1837, in a debate on MPs' privileges. It was another challenge to O'Connell, the previous speaker, and was hooted down by jeering O'Connellite Irishmen, though not before its extraordinarily elaborate and affected language had caused much hilarity. After that unpropitious beginning Disraeli avoided publicity for most of the rest of the parliament, generally supporting Peel and attacking the free trade agitators. However, he did urge respect for the Chartist movement. Feeling unable to satisfy the financial expectations of the electors of Maidstone, he sought a cheaper seat for the 1841 election; his friend Lord Forester secured him the nomination at Shrewsbury. At this election his crest made its first appearance, with the motto *forti nihil difficile* ('nothing is difficult to the brave').

When Peel became prime minister after the 1841 election, Disraeli sought office from him; unsurprisingly, he did not get it. He continued his support for Peel in 1842 and 1843, seeking fame by attacking the foreign policy of the late government. He blamed the economic depression partly on the whigs' warmongering extravagance and failure to sign a commercial treaty with France. He projected himself as an authority on the needs of British international trade, urging a reversion to the historical policy of commercial diplomacy and reciprocity. He went to France in late 1842 in order to make connections at the court there which would assist his claim to be promoting a new entente with that country. His contacts there—supplied through Bulwer, Count d'Orsay, and Lyndhurst—gained him an audience with Louis Philippe.

In a memorandum to the French king, Disraeli talked of organizing a party of youthful, energetic tory backbenchers in pursuit of a policy sympathetic to France. Though nothing came of this notion as such, it showed his susceptibility to the excitement of high intrigue with a group of youthful men of independence and vision. A small group of such men was in fact forming on the tory benches, inspired by George Smythe, Lord John Manners, and Alexander Baillie-Cochrane. This trio had been at Eton and Cambridge together and had a romantic attachment to the ideals of chivalry, paternalism, and religious orthodoxy which had become fashionable in some landed and university circles in reaction to reform, utilitarianism, and political economy. Disraeli did not adopt all of the specific enthusiasms of Young England, as the group came to be known in 1843. But by the end of the session he was accepted as a fertile contributor to its activities in the house, and some of the group's enthusiasms rubbed off on him, especially a respect for historic religious ideals evident in *Sybil*. Over the winter of 1843–4 Disraeli wrote *Coningsby*, his most effective and successful novel to date, a vibrant commentary on the political and social worlds of the 1830s. Featuring the three friends, it gave considerable publicity to the idea of Young England, contrasting its ideals with Peel's lack of principle. Published in May 1844, it quickly sold 3000 copies, for which Disraeli received about £1000.

In 1843 Disraeli offended the Conservative leadership by

his vote against the Canada Corn Bill and his speech against Irish coercion. Early in 1844 Peel rebuked him by omitting him from the list of MPs to be summoned to the official party meeting at the start of the session. Over the coming months Disraeli made three speeches containing pointed and sarcastic criticism of the party leadership, such as his attack on its inability to tolerate dissent over the sugar issue.

In October 1844 Disraeli, Manners, and Smythe made successful addresses to young artisans at the Manchester Athenaeum, testifying to the impact made by Young England. While in the north, Disraeli also collected observations about industrial life which he used in *Sybil*, the novel which he wrote over the winter of 1844–5 and published in May 1845, again to considerable interest; it too sold 3000 copies. But Young England broke up in 1845, partly owing to a difference of opinion on the government's proposals for the Maynooth seminary, and partly because of parental pressure on Smythe and Manners not to be disloyal to the party. Meanwhile, Disraeli's abuse of Peel was mounting. In late February he made a celebrated, extended, and neatly vindictive assault on Peel's shiftiness, described by one onlooker as 'aimed with deadly precision', yet delivered with Disraeli's normal 'extreme coolness and impassibility' (Monypenny and Buckle, 2.316). On 17 March he declared that a 'Conservative government is an organised hypocrisy' (*Selected Speeches*, 1.80). His opposition to the Maynooth grant (11 April) was similarly based on the argument that Peel cared nothing for tory principles and sought to extend the 'police surveillance' of Downing Street to entrap Irish Catholics, when they required independence and respect (ibid., 88). By the end of the 1845 session Disraeli had become a celebrated orator. He undoubtedly helped to stimulate the questioning of Peel's trustworthiness on the back benches. Yet he stood essentially alone, without allies, and in such circumstances his capacity to tolerate abuse and short-term political injury is testimony to his remarkable self-confidence and self-reliance.

Disraeli's position was transformed by the events of late 1845, which brought Peel to the Commons in January 1846 as an advocate of repealing the corn laws, in defence of which the vast majority of tory MPs had been elected in 1841. Disraeli seized the initiative against him with a stinging attack (22 January), accusing him of betraying 'the independence of party' and thus 'the integrity of public men, and the power and influence of Parliament itself' (*Selected Speeches*, 1.110). Now, suddenly, he was no longer alone, as Lord George Bentinck and Lord Stanley took the lead in organizing party opposition to the repeal, while in the constituencies there was an active protectionist campaign. In his speeches on the subject in 1846 Disraeli reiterated his earlier arguments in favour of the historic policy of multilateral tariff reductions through treaty diplomacy. But his greatest contribution to the movement against Peel continued to be his scathing attacks on the latter's inability to uphold the principles of the territorial constitution on which toryism must rest. This was expressed most devastatingly in his famous denunciation

of Peel's career as a 'great Appropriation Clause' in his speech on the second reading of the repeal bill on 15 May, which roused the back benches to extraordinary fervour (ibid., 170). Later in the month he lied to the Commons in denying Peel's charge that he had sought office from him in 1841, but Peel was unable or unwilling to capitalize on this, a mark of his powerlessness to deal with Disraeli's invective. As the session continued, Disraeli had hopes of a coalition between protectionist tories and some whigs and Irish MPs in defence of a compromise tariff. But corn law repeal passed the Lords in late June. On the same night the leading protectionists, including Disraeli, voted with the opposition to defeat Peel's Irish Coercion Bill, on the grounds that the lack of necessity for it had been demonstrated by the long delay in promoting it. Peel resigned, and Disraeli's fame—for good and ill—was assured.

The background to Disraeli's political views In the 1840s Disraeli wrote three major novels (*Coningsby*, *Sybil*, and *Tancred*, 1847), worked on his biography of Lord George Bentinck (1852), and delivered many ambitious speeches. This output, together with his earlier political comment, helps to chart the progress of his ideas.

Disraeli had begun political life as a proud romantic individualist with radical leanings, standing 'for myself' rather than any party (Ridley, 112). This was a sign of his youthful arrogance, but also a typical declaration against what radicals saw as whig factionalism and falseness. Gifted with an ability to expose the selfish and hypocritical underbelly of the glittering social and political world, he shared the views of those who saw the whigs as frauds who had arrogated the title of the popular party when they were in fact a 'Venetian' oligarchy. After he had adopted tory colours, Disraeli continued—especially in *Sybil*—to portray the whigs as a rapacious clique of great families, who had secured their hold on power by their canting claim to be protecting the civil and religious liberties of the people from attack in 1688–9. He asserted that popular liberties in fact rested on the territorial constitution—on the land, the church, and other interests whose vitality prevented central government despotism. The Venetian instincts of eighteenth-century whigs had crippled the country with heavy indirect taxes levied in order to fight unnecessary wars and to siphon off rewards for themselves. The one man who might have moralized whig misrule—the outsider–prophet Burke—was refused a cabinet place by these snobs, and in his vengeance turned his eloquence against them, thereby helping to keep them out of power for forty-five years. It was only the blunders of Pitt's heirs that gave the whigs the opportunity to mount an audacious *coup d'état* in 1830 and once again to restrict power to an aristocratic clique by claiming to follow libertarian sentiments. Their true intentions were seen in their centralizing initiatives of the 1830s with regard to the poor law, education, and policing, all of which Disraeli criticized. They also had to be opposed for their exclusiveness, their incapacity, and their willingness to consort with destructive allies, particularly O'Connell.

Here and on other subjects Disraeli derived his arguments from books—mainly from Burke and tory historians, and Carlyle and Germanic writers—and from the literary and religious interests of his father. But he assembled and developed his ideas in an inimitable confection, and with a degree of purpose rare among parliamentarians. He thought of himself as a prophet of deep insights who had arrived at his opinions by 'reading and thought' rather than having 'had hereditary opinions carved out' for him (Monypenny and Buckle, 2.371). As he commented with respect to Christ, all the great minds were formed in seclusion (*Disraeli's Reminiscences*, ed. H. M. Swartz and M. Swartz, 1975, 8).

Views on Jewishness and Englishness For Disraeli historical and sociological awareness was necessary in order to govern men. In particular, 'all is race' (Disraeli, *Bentinck*, 331); the values of each race determined its past and prospects. Some races were superior; others were degraded (by interbreeding or luxury) and would be conquered. Conquest was a natural objective of races such as the Slavs. But Disraeli was most concerned with two other races: the Semites (especially the Jews) and the English. These were races that understood the essence of civilization: the Jewish values of 'religion, property, and natural aristocracy' (ibid., 497). 'A civilised community must rest on a large realised capital of thought and sentiment; there must be a reserved fund of public morality to draw upon. ... Society has a soul as well as a body' (Disraeli, *Inaugural Address*, 15). The alternative to government in tune with indigenous traditions was a resort to a 'philosophic' or 'cosmopolitan' basis—to abstract theories, such as 'cosmopolitan fraternity' and the equality of man, 'pernicious' doctrines that would 'deteriorate the great races and destroy all the genius of the world' (Disraeli, *Bentinck*, 496). Republicanism and socialism involved a relapse into 'primitive ... savagery' (ibid., 509), though their vitality and appeal were all too comprehensible. One reason for their attraction was that men, who were 'made to adore and obey', had been failed by their political and religious leaders and left to 'find a chieftain in [their] own passions' (*Coningsby*, bk 4, chap. 13). A nation that had 'lost its faith in religion is in a state of decadence' (*Selection from the Diaries of ... Derby*, 97). Modern Europe had fallen victim to materialism: it had mistaken comfort for civilization (*Tancred*, bk 3, chap. 7). Disraeli drew two conclusions. A properly run society was necessarily élitist: 'the Spirit of the Age is the very thing that a great man changes' (*Coningsby*, bk 3, chap. 1). And it must rest on the national, not the cosmopolitan, principle.

It followed that England should venerate the Jews, who understood all this. They represented the 'Semitic principle—all that is spiritual in our nature' (Disraeli, *Bentinck*, 496), being descended from the Arabian peoples to whom divine truth had been revealed and who had founded the great religions. The Christian church in particular was completed Judaism, a 'sacred corporation for the promulgation and maintenance in Europe of certain Asian principles ... of divine origin and of universal and eternal application' (*Coningsby*, preface to 5th edn, 1849). Jesus and

the Virgin Mary were Jews. 'Half Christendom worships a Jewess and the other half a Jew. ... Which do you think should be the superior race; the worshipped or the worshippers?' (*Tancred*, bk 3, chap. 4). The Roman church had been founded by a Hebrew when the English were 'tattooed savages' (ibid., bk 2, chap. 11), and the crusades, by bringing medieval Westerners to Jerusalem, had renewed Asia's spiritual hold on Europe. The Arabs, 'Jews on horseback', retained much of the spiritual sense, social cohesion, and harmony with nature that the West so badly needed to rediscover. The hero of *Tancred* goes to Jerusalem in an attempt to penetrate and draw spiritual sustenance from 'the great Asian mystery' (bk 2, chap. 11; bk 4, chap. 3). Disraeli convinced himself (wrongly) that he derived from the Sephardi aristocracy of Iberian Jews driven from Spain at the end of the fifteenth century. The English aristocracy, he pointed out, were descended merely from 'a horde of Baltic pirates' (Blake, 203).

Presenting himself as Jewish symbolized Disraeli's uniqueness when he was fighting for respect, and explained his set-backs. Presenting Jewishness as aristocratic and religious legitimized his claim to understand the perils facing modern England and to offer 'national' solutions to them. English toryism was 'copied from the mighty [Jewish] prototype' (*Coningsby*, bk 4, chap. 15). Disraeli was thus able to square his Jewishness with his equally deep attachment to England and her history. Hardly any nineteenth-century politician was more deeply enthused by the English past; he almost never made a significant speech without invoking it, and talked at length about local history to visitors to his house at Hughenden. Remodelling the house in 1862–3 'realised a romance' to restore its pre-civil war appearance, including a garden of terraces 'in which cavaliers might roam' (Monypenny and Buckle, 3.472). On leaving office in 1852 he disobeyed the custom of passing on the chancellor of the exchequer's gown to his successor (Gladstone); instead, he kept it until the end of his life because it had been worn by his hero Pitt.

Disraeli believed that England's history explained her greatness, and that her future greatness depended on the maintenance of her constitutional traditions. In the aftermath of the 1848 revolutions England was the 'only important European community that is still governed by traditionary influences' (Disraeli, *Bentinck*, 555). These influences were 'bulwarks of the multitude' against the destructive despotism of an over-mighty central government (*Lothair*, general preface to 1870 edn); they included the Church of England, the ancient universities, the principles of historic parties, and the 'noble system of self-government' (*Selected Speeches*, 2.455). Local self-government and parliamentary government were essential aspects of England's strength; her uniqueness was that 'society has always been more powerful than the State', thus guaranteeing order and liberty (*The Times*, 18 June 1868, 9).

Views on the crisis of the 1840s and the need for leadership At times in the 1840s Disraeli argued that these constitutional and social traditions were collapsing, and with them the character of England as a community. In *Tancred* he wrote that 'the people of this country have ceased to be a nation' (bk 2, chap. 1). Parliament no longer represented a 'disciplined array of traditionary influences' but a bundle of crotchets and ambitions, incapable of reaching agreement on an organic, spiritual, or elevating artistic policy (*Selected Speeches*, 2.455). *Tancred* in particular is very critical of the decay of the historic parliamentary ideal, reflecting the shortcomings, successively, of Peel's autocracy and Russell's minority government. (At this juncture Disraeli even played with the possibility that the monarchy, buttressed by a free press, might represent the national will better, a view raked up and used against him by his opponents at the 1880 election.) But the fundamental problem was social disorganization, with materialism and religious sectarianism following in its wake. The church is portrayed, in *Sybil* and *Tancred*, as riddled with small-minded compromisers incapable of touching the heart of nations. *Sybil* dwells on the immoral brutality of working-class life in manufacturing and inner-city areas untouched by upper-class guidance; this was the abnegation of civilization. He attacked the exploitation of labour, whether by selfish industrialists or by squires imbued with the doctrine of political economy; both reduced human relations to the cash nexus. Yet Disraeli was equally critical of the sybaritic and insular English aristocracy, ignorant, pampered, obsessed with trivialities, and instinctively exclusive and oppressive in their political responses. A return to the old feudalism was not possible. Manchester, he wrote in *Coningsby*, was the Athens of the scientific age (bk 4, chap. 1). It represented ideas which would not go away; politicians had to deal with them.

The 1840s presented a further danger, an international one. Disraeli appropriated Burkean anti-Jacobin polemic in arguing that the difference between tory and whig/Liberal government was the difference between government on the national and on the cosmopolitan principle—a view that he reiterated throughout his career. This analysis relied mainly on the fact that the whigs were allied to O'Connellite Catholics, dissenters, Cobdenite internationalists, and, later, a handful of republicans and atheists. In the 1840s the main 'cosmopolitan' threat presented by the Liberal forces in parliament came from the Cobdenite free-traders who naïvely claimed that their principles would promote 'peace and plenty' when the world was 'in arms' (Monypenny and Buckle, 3.97). Disraeli was profoundly alarmed by the insularity of commercial opinion in England, because it would prevent an intelligent European policy counteracting corrosive democratic principles. In 1848–9 he repeated the view of the *Revolutionary Epick*, that Europe was declining from feudal into federal, republican American-style politics (ibid., 166, 178). But he thought that the transatlantic model would not work there because of the debris left behind by traditional influences, and that the resulting disturbances would have to be suppressed by military power, by vast standing armies (Disraeli, *Bentinck*, 554–5). Europe faced a future alternating between revolution and

Russian-influenced militarism, unless Britain co-operated with France and/or Austria to defend traditional values. (He admired Metternich, with whom he had several conversations after 1848.) 'Once destroy the English aristocracy, and enthrone the commercial principle as omnipotent in this island', and nothing can stop 'the Slavonians conquering the whole of the South of Europe' (Monypenny and Buckle, 3.195). Paradoxically but crucially, Disraeli interpreted British isolationism as cosmopolitanism, and believed that a vigorous continental policy was necessary to prevent the triumph in Britain and Europe of cosmopolitan principles.

There is no reason to doubt Disraeli's pessimism about the state of England in this crisis-ridden decade; many shared it. However, the crisis was also convenient, because it pointed up the need for leadership capable of making England a nation again. Ideally, such a man would have the insight and imagination of Sidonia, the Jewish sphinx of the novels, who could solve 'with a phrase some deep problem that men muse over for years' (*Coningsby*, bk 3, chap. 1). He need not be personally religious, as long as he understood the importance of religion to the English. Many passages in *Sybil* admire the medieval spirit—of mutual obligation within a powerful religious framework. But these passages sought to make a point about the English character rather than to prescribe a particular religious solution. Disraeli himself, though interested in theological subjects and a practising Anglican, told the fifteenth earl of Derby in 1872 that he was 'personally incapable of religious belief' (*Selection from the Diaries of … Derby*, 97). In *Tancred* he defined faith as 'inward and personal energy in man' (bk 2, chap. 14). But though the novels were in one sense a personal manifesto of an ambitious man, this view gains from retrospect. Disraeli, a very marginal figure when he wrote *Coningsby* and *Sybil*, believed that the natural leaders of society were 'the gentlemen of England' (Monypenny and Buckle, 3.101). The novels urged young men of property, energy, and vision to enter politics to defend their heritage. Disraeli always idealized such men, and *Sybil* ends with a rallying cry to the nation's youth, 'the trustees of Posterity'.

Disraeli's principles were general and intended to apply in a variety of circumstances; that is why they may appear insubstantial. He never diverged from his broad assumptions about tradition, leadership, cosmopolitanism, and national dissolution, or from his belief that politics involved applying the first two concepts to defeat the second two. But the form in which challenges to national harmony and greatness arose necessarily changed over time; and for Disraeli the art of politics was the settlement of specific problems as they emerged. In the 1840s the overwhelming difficulty was the unrest of the Chartists and the Anti-Corn Law League. In the 1860s and 1870s the greatest threat was to religion at home and abroad, from atheism and church factionalism. In the 1870s and 1880s the major danger was the international challenge to property. In foreign affairs there was a constant problem about British commercial isolationism and an intermittent one about the destabilizing effect on Europe of Palmerstonian

Liberal interventionism. For most of his life, also, Disraeli was out of power, and confined to the luxury of criticizing the inadequate leadership skills of others. *Coningsby* contains no definite solutions to the crisis of the 1840s, merely a demand for firm, responsive government to reduce social tension. None the less, in his attack on Peel can be discerned Disraeli's general conception of toryism—which, he wrote in the *Vindication*, should embody 'the national will and character' (p. 193).

Views on toryism, protection, empire, and practical politics
To Disraeli historic toryism involved a defence of the territorial constitution and local independence against centralization; a hostility to Venetian borough-mongering (and therefore a Pittite willingness to contemplate parliamentary reform); a reliance on direct as well as indirect taxation; the pursuit of international commercial advantage by traditional tariff diplomacy; a peaceful but shrewd foreign policy; and the firm but inclusive government of Ireland, rescuing its Catholics from the Cromwellian/whig puritanical yoke. But the mistake of the long conflict with France had overtaxed the country and forced farmers into expensive mortgages; Liverpool, the 'Arch-Mediocrity', had rejected Pitt's youthful sympathy with the people and his support for Catholic emancipation, and had fallen back on repression; Wellington had fashioned an absurdly exclusive and arrogant image of government which had alienated the aristocracy and middle classes and had allowed the whigs to mount their *coup d'état* in 1830. His successor Peel had failed to demonstrate an understanding of history, a loyalty to party tradition, or any power of imagination. Lacking historical insight or intellectual independence, he had swallowed fashionable cosmopolitan ideas, which he disguised with displays of urbane plausibility and empty rhetoric. In assuming that men could be governed by adjusting tables of import duties and other expedients, he was a symbol of the artificiality and rootlessness of politics in a materialistic age. And, lacking real leadership skills, he had resorted to the 'intolerable yoke of official despotism' to retain power (*Selected Speeches*, 1.97). This attempt to check dissent betrayed back-benchers' honour and party principle, the 'realised experience of our ancient society' (ibid., 2.455). The job of the tory party was to uphold the aristocratic settlement of the country in the impending struggle with the democratic principle (Monypenny and Buckle, 3.125, 134).

Disraeli was equally definite in defending the idea of protection. But for him it was a great historic concept, a crucial aspect of constitutional, imperial, and foreign policy. He had consistently argued in favour of a policy of regulating tariffs by treaties of reciprocity; these also reduced foreign tension and allowed lower defence expenditure. As for the empire, relations with the white settler colonies were in flux in the 1840s as the idea of responsible government developed. Disraeli wanted them to be regularized on a coherent basis, with an imperial tariff, a code for colonial defence, and representatives

attending a council in the metropolis. He spoke repeatedly in later years of his sadness that this had not happened. In December 1851 he proposed that in any scheme of parliamentary reform at Westminster the colonial chambers should elect their own representatives, on the lines of the United States senate; this might revive their affection for Britain. The failure to bring about that outcome led Disraeli to lament the collapse of real power over the self-governing colonies—especially when he was chancellor of the exchequer, dealing with the consequences of the whigs' failure to get them to accept the burden of their own defence. He even remarked, impatiently, 'what is the use of these colonial deadweights which *we do not govern*?' (Monypenny and Buckle, 4.476). (This remark has been misinterpreted by many critical commentators to indicate a general lack of commitment to empire.) It was crucial that India and Ireland did not go the same way; Britain must exercise firm but inclusive government over them. In 1844 Disraeli urged that Ireland needed a stronger, more comprehensive executive, just administration, and equality of treatment for all religions. In both places an amicable treatment of the diverse religious groups was the only way to prevent them from developing grievances that might lead them to coalesce against the governing power.

Disraeli was obviously motivated by personal ambition in moving to the tories and in attacking Peel over the corn laws and Irish policy. Equally, he was no unprincipled charlatan. For him the fascination of politics was the simultaneous opportunity that it offered for intrigue as well as the formulation of high policy. The basis of his admiration for Burke was his ability to combine the two goals, to inspire men with ideals while manoeuvring for the advantage of his party connection. Disraeli's élitist conception of politics attached great importance to the role of individuals in making initiatives, patiently constructing alliances, holding parties together, and dividing opponents. The tension between intrigue and idealism is a major theme in *Tancred*, which is in part a dialogue between Tancred, an imaginative young English aristocrat, and Fakredeen, an emir of Lebanon. Tancred is an ingenuous idealist disgusted with the sordidness of British parliamentary life. Fakredeen has a deep understanding of human nature, honed by years of manoeuvre to evade his creditors. He is vain, reckless, and desperate for all Europe to talk of him. He uses his imaginative understanding in reckless intrigue. Tancred says that only faith, not intrigue, will conquer the imagination of public opinion; but he is too ingenuous for the modern world. Fakredeen argues that 'England won India by intrigue … intrigue has gained half the thrones of Europe' (bk 3, chap. 5); but he can also see the attraction of ideals. The ideal statesman would be a combination of both.

The resolution of the crisis of 1845–6 left Disraeli a leading figure in the Conservative Party, whose role as the defender of aristocratic ideals in British politics he henceforth upheld vigorously. Unfortunately, the protectionists were in a minority, needing to make alliances in order to exercise power, with the danger that those coalitions might swamp them or cause them to betray their principles. In September 1846 Disraeli wrote that an alliance between the protectionists and the 'real whigs' in defence of the territorial constitution and strong, inclusive government was the natural solution to the problems of Britain and Ireland (*Letters*, 4.258). He was equally aware of the enormous obstacles to this solution, among them the instinctive protectionism and No Popery of the tory back benches. Could Conservatives—could he—manoeuvre towards power without damaging the party's independence and ideals? The rest of this essay charts Disraeli's attempt to reconcile intrigue with imagination and ideas in that objective. It would be an absorbing task for a man of action. After 1846 Disraeli would not need to retreat into fictional worlds in order to find something to manipulate.

Hughenden and protectionism, 1846–1852 The Conservative Party split elevated Disraeli to the front opposition bench in 1847. This completed a change of parliamentary image: colourful attire had by now given way to the black frock coat (sometimes blue in summer), grey trousers, plush waistcoat, and sober neckerchief which was to be his Commons uniform for the next thirty years. He worked hard on his oratory, mugging up blue books and spending all day memorizing figures so that his mastery of them in debate could seem as spontaneous as Peel's. He capitalized on his clear voice, great command of language, and extraordinarily retentive memory, and now began to learn the art of managing parliamentary debates tactically. Bentinck, the protectionists' leader in the Commons, regarded him as an indispensable lieutenant. And his new eminence in a landed party allowed him to abandon the vexations of a borough seat to become MP for Buckinghamshire at the 1847 election; he retained the seat, usually unopposed, until he became a peer in 1876. He had been a justice of the peace in Buckinghamshire since 1836 and a deputy lieutenant since 1845.

Most significantly for his lifestyle, Disraeli acquired the small country house of Hughenden Manor, outside High Wycombe, in late 1848. The purchase was negotiated by Philip Rose, a lawyer and Buckinghamshire neighbour, whom Disraeli had placed in charge of his financial affairs in 1846. Hughenden was not a large house, and the estate ran only to 750 acres (later increased to 1400 by enclosures and purchases). None the less, it was way beyond his means when he agreed to buy it for £35,000 in March 1847; his wife's income was already heavily burdened by his debt repayments. The money was to come from his father and from Bentinck and his two brothers, who were anxious to establish Disraeli as a landowner MP. The purchase was delayed for over a year while the financial details were sorted out; in the event Disraeli's father and Bentinck both died before it was completed. Despite a small legacy from Isaac, the transaction ended with Disraeli owing Bentinck's brothers £25,000. In 1857 the outstanding money was called in by the elder brother, now duke of Portland, who disliked Disraeli's politics; he had to resort once more to moneylenders. Hughenden was an essential

status symbol for Disraeli, but he also gained spiritual succour in this adopted homeland. His was not a typical *arrivisme*; it was an affair of the inward imagination rather than one of outward snobbery. Though he liked to wear the clothes of a country sportsman (initially with excessive zeal), he neither shot nor hunted and disliked country-house visiting with its conventions, its 'constant dressing & indigestion' (*Letters*, 5.210), and its masculine conversations. Mary Anne and he did not entertain very much at Hughenden, at least in the early years (though their Buckinghamshire neighbours the Rothschilds were frequent visitors). The house's attraction was that it gave him roots in England, allowing him to place himself in a tradition of defenders of property and civilization, and thus focusing his Burkean sentiments. Hence his love of his woods, a symbol of permanence; he prided himself on the number of trees he planted, persuaded visitors to add specimens, and carried a small hatchet on his estate inspections with which to strip ivy from the bark. His homely estate—with its terrace of peacocks and its little pond presided over by the swans Hero and Leander—and his spacious library (greatly enhanced by his father's death in January 1848) were appropriate settings for self-conscious reflection on the long continuum of English history and his own place in it. For all that, Disraeli frequently found the isolation of Hughenden stifling, especially at times of marital tension or political frustration. He needed the bustle and excitement of London public life in order to raise his spirits.

Fervent protectionism and protestantism made the party difficult to lead. An early test of protestant feeling came with a Commons motion in December 1847 for the removal of Jewish civil and political disabilities. Disraeli took this opportunity to articulate his defence of the Jews as proto-Christians. This argument, met by silence and private anger on the protectionist benches, did his prospects little good. However, Bentinck's support for the same motion led to a rebellion against his leadership and his resignation in December 1847, which created a vacuum. Since it was impossible to find an alternative with the fervour and talent of Bentinck and Disraeli, the two men remained informally in charge of strategy throughout the 1848 session. When Bentinck died suddenly in September 1848, Disraeli was bereft of his strongest supporter; he showed the debt he owed to Bentinck by writing an eloquent and reverential biography, published in December 1851 (1852 on the title page). Yet Bentinck's death also left Disraeli unchallenged as the party's most vigorous debater. However, his status, reputation, and opinions prevented the protectionists from formally nominating him to replace Bentinck. Moreover, Lord Stanley in the Lords, the unquestioned leader of the whole party because of his great social position, ability, and experience, knew that Disraeli's behaviour to Peel had made him unacceptable to the Peelites, whose allegiance Stanley was trying to win. On the other hand, Disraeli refused to serve under any other protectionist, even had any been suitable. The upshot, in January 1849, was the proposal by Stanley of a committee of three: Disraeli,

Granby, and Herries. Disraeli was too proud to declare his acceptance of this situation, but Stanley pointed out that he would in practice be leader, and this was generally recognized well before the end of the 1849 session; the committee maintained a shadowy existence until Granby resigned from it at the beginning of 1852.

Disraeli recognized that a return to the corn laws was politically impossible, since too many mainstream politicians feared the radical social and political reaction that would follow their revival. Upholding protection would confirm the Conservatives' minority status in the country and scare off potential parliamentary allies. He sought a difficult balancing act, trying to find a broader fiscal strategy that would compensate the economic, social, and colonial interests that protection had benefited, yet which would also settle the fiscal question on a 'national' basis, terminating 'the unhappy quarrel between town and country' (Selected Speeches, 1.323). He was also worried that, in the agricultural depression of the late 1840s, farmers were being wooed away from the landed interest by the appeals of financial reformers. Restlessly and experimentally, he proposed various fiscal remedies, principally rate relief for agriculture, but also malt tax reduction and income tax differentiation in favour of tenant farmers. He unsuccessfully opposed the repeal of the navigation laws in 1849—with the result that a grateful shipowner named a 400 ton vessel after him in the following year. He angrily attacked the 'thoughtless societies out of doors' which were agitating for the return of protection (ibid., 322). But Stanley rebuked him and declared uncompromisingly for protection, deeming it to be essential for the honour of himself and his party. In the short term Stanley's strategy was the only feasible one, on tactical and principled grounds, and Disraeli was forced to be more equivocal in his public statements. When the Liberal government was defeated in February 1851, no public man outside protectionist ranks would join Stanley, who felt that he must reject the queen's request to form a government—to Disraeli's great annoyance. The following February the Liberals fell more conclusively, and Stanley, now fourteenth earl of Derby, formed a government on the basis that protectionist legislation would not be attempted unless a majority was secured at an election to be held in the summer. At that election (at which Disraeli made only the vaguest reference to protection) no majority was forthcoming, and protection was finally laid to rest in a debate in November 1852, marked by taunts and a crude antisemitic jibe levelled at Disraeli by the Peelite Sidney Herbert.

The 1852 government Disraeli was leader of the House of Commons and chancellor of the exchequer in the 1852 government. Derby had little choice but to give him high office, though his view of him remained equivocal. He appreciated Disraeli's hard work and oratorical ability, but lamented his restlessness as a tactician, and did not invite him to Knowsley until late 1853—and then for a dressing-down. Disraeli waived his claim to the leadership in the hope of securing Palmerston's allegiance, but the latter refused to join the cabinet. Disraeli also professed

unease that his first government post should be at the Treasury despite his financial ignorance, but Derby told him: 'You know as much as Mr. Canning did. They give you the figures' (Monypenny and Buckle, 3.344). He introduced a provisional budget in April 1852 which extended the income tax for a year; he hoped that a consensus would meanwhile emerge in favour of a more permanent settlement. There was little enthusiasm on the government benches for his speech, which made few concessions to protectionist ideas.

Disraeli's major test came in December, when he was forced (by Peelite pressure) to introduce another budget in the light of the abandonment of protection. This placed him in an almost impossible position. He had to enthuse his back-benchers while not alienating the Liberal majority in the Commons. He made his task harder by opting for an ambitious budget which might give the government momentum for the session. Politically, he could not afford to give landowners rate relief, since this would open him to the charge of class favouritism. But this abandonment of proposals made in opposition, which he justified by pointing to the 20 per cent fall in the cost of poor relief since 1848, was unpopular with his back-benchers. Instead, he offered them a halving of the malt tax, which would also please the urban beer drinker, and coupled this with a staged reduction of the tea duty. In order to pay for this and what he hoped would be a popular reduction of the income tax, he extended the house tax (which had been reintroduced the previous year). This move, unattractive to urban voters, might have been mitigated by a reduction in income tax, but the war scare resulting from Louis Napoleon's imperial pretensions forced the government to increase defence estimates in the autumn and so prevented this. He fell back on the expedient of differentiating between categories of income, proposing to tax farmers and salary-earners at a lower rate, while at the same time bringing more people into the tax net and extending it to Ireland. This complex scheme offended too many interest groups. Opposition MPs had no difficulty in finding enough criticisms of it to justify combining in a negative vote. The government was defeated and resigned.

Disraeli's ten-month spell in office was very important in his career. His ability had been widely recognized and he had become a national figure: he even earned a place at Madame Tussaud's shortly afterwards. (Gladstone did not appear until 1870.) In 1853 he took advantage of this fame to bring out a shilling edition of his novels (including a drastically revised Vivian Grey); this sold 300,000 copies in a year. His leading position in the Conservative Party was more secure, now that protection had been abandoned and the Peelites had offended many Conservatives by their behaviour. Nominated by the new chancellor, Derby, he was made DCL at Oxford University in 1853, and his appearance was much cheered by tory undergraduates. However, this eminence had been achieved at a considerable cost to his reputation. Die-hard protectionists blamed the chancellor of the exchequer above all for the abandonment of their creed, while the Jewish issue prevented him from pleasing ultra-protestants even had he sought to do so. He told Lord Henry Lennox that both these old tory principles were 'exclusive and limited … clearly unfitted for a great and expanding country' (Monypenny and Buckle, 3.383). Yet he was also demonized by the Peelites and their allies in the press as a man of low birth who had goaded the squirearchy against the martyred Peel only to surrender to the wisdom of his policy. In 1854 a member of what Disraeli called 'the Peel school' (in fact, Thomas Macknight) anonymously published a long and venomous *Literary and Political Biography* of him, which capitalized on the awkward incidents in his past (ibid., 3.531). Conservatives who sought reunion regarded him as the symbol of party disunity. Disraeli's reputation never recovered from opponents' interpretations of his political behaviour between 1846 and 1852, though his most visible political trait in these years was, arguably, excitable naïvety rather than fiendish cunning.

Strategies in the 1850s The Conservative Party was now to be in opposition for over five years, to Disraeli's frustration. He was furious when, on the fall of the Aberdeen coalition in early 1855, Derby gave up the queen's commission to form a government once Palmerston had declined to serve under him. Disraeli had concluded that, by taking office at that point, the party might get the credit for a satisfactory conclusion to the war and force the other conservative influences in politics—principally Palmerston and Gladstone—to accept its dominance. However, Derby thought that public opinion would demand Palmerston as minister, if only until disillusioned, and he was only too aware how opposed the leading Peelites would be to serving with Disraeli.

Throughout these years Disraeli also encountered a lot of distrust from Conservative MPs, despite purging the old protectionist influence in the whips' office and appointing Sir William Jolliffe as chief whip. Derby—hardly a sociable leader himself—criticized his aloofness and unwillingness to court back-benchers. A good part of the unrest was due to Disraeli's insatiable enthusiasm for planning parliamentary sorties against the governments of Aberdeen and Palmerston in the company of other amenable factions, whether Irishmen, radicals, or opposition Liberals. Such tactics were temperamentally irresistible to him, but they were hardly unusual for an opposition leader, and were indeed inevitable in this decade of ideological confusion and ego-ridden intra-party factionalism. Disraeli bewildered his more unimaginatively stolid back-benchers by his sudden parliamentary attacks, which gave further ammunition to his party critics, for whom he remained 'the Jew' (Monypenny and Buckle, 4.44). He appeared to them to be consorting with dangerous radical opinion, at a time of widespread fear in propertied circles of the growing power of 'middle-class' 'Manchester' sentiment, which might undermine the social as well as the political position of the aristocracy.

However, Disraeli was not just a tactical opportunist; his air of mystery helped to obscure his motives. On the four issues which most preoccupied him, he was working out a more or less coherent Conservative creed. His policies had the great merit to him of appealing beyond the party, but also of upholding a historically coherent position that was viable for a modern empire. Those four issues—finance, foreign policy, India, and parliamentary reform—need to be examined in turn. Though they added to disquiet about him, they also formed the basis of his position over the next fifteen years, especially during the minority government of 1858–9, when he was again chancellor of the exchequer and leader of the Commons.

On finance and foreign policy Disraeli fell foul of the 'John Bull' wing of the party. He saw the political attraction of reducing taxation and appreciated that, if the Conservatives returned to office, a bold and popular budget would be the best way of strengthening their position in the Commons. Many MPs disliked the income tax, and after 1855 Disraeli sought, more assiduously than Gladstone, to uphold the latter's plans of 1853 for its progressive reduction and eventual abolition. Disraeli's own budget of April 1858 reduced income tax to 5*d*., while he postponed the reduction of the national debt. As a result, in the winter of 1858–9 he was a critic of the renewed war scare and of those Conservatives who advocated a large reconstruction of the navy. Unluckily, his plans for a tax-cutting budget in 1859, repealing the paper duties as well as lowering income tax, were scuppered by Derby's insistence on naval expansion but also, in the event, by the fall of the government before the budget could be presented.

Disraeli's hostility to defence panics was in line with his dislike of emotional popular Francophobia (though he was flexible enough to be able to justify his vote against Palmerston on the Orsini affair in 1858, which brought the Conservatives into government). He made frequent attempts to ingratiate himself and his party with Napoleon III, as he had with Louis Philippe before 1848. To this end he used Ralph Earle, a young and unscrupulous employee of the British embassy at Paris who became Disraeli's private secretary (1858–66), and whom he sent for confidential negotiations of a highly impractical kind. Advocating a cordial relationship with France secured common ground with Peelites and radicals who criticized Palmerston's chauvinism (though Palmerston himself also upheld cordiality when it suited him). But Disraeli also defended the French entente on historical grounds. He adhered to it almost unvaryingly throughout his life, as a way of keeping defence expenditure low while allowing Britain influence in Europe and preventing a damaging general war, which threatened to undermine the balance of power and to unleash revolutionary influences on continental states. Disraeli had innate respect for Palmerston's active involvement in Europe in the teeth of commercial isolationism, and took a Palmerstonian line on the Russian danger in 1853. But he criticized Palmerston for his populist Liberalism, which had alienated continental leaders from Britain and encouraged disruptive nationalist sentiment in Italy. And after the spring of 1855 he became as critical of Palmerston's Crimean War policy as was politically sensible, by tentatively advocating an honourable peace and opposing the notion of an ideologically inspired extension to the war aimed at reshaping Europe in a liberal direction. As a result, in 1855–6, as at other times in the 1850s, many Conservatives felt that he was too ineffective against Palmerston, out of touch with popular patriotic sentiment, and too closely associated with some radicals.

Disraeli's third sphere of concern was the inadequacy of British rule in India. In 1853 he opposed the renewal of the East India Company's charter on the grounds that its government was weak and careless; it had failed to provide effective finance, justice, public works, or education. 'Clear and complete responsibility' was needed and was badly lacking; if the Commons failed to insist on a searching inquiry in preparation for firm and just rule, it would lose India (*Hansard 3*, 128, 1853, 1032). These arguments were too close to those of radical India reformers for the taste of many Conservatives, who wished to uphold the traditional ties between the East India Company and the party. Disraeli further alarmed party opinion by his response to the 1857 revolt, when he disparaged the vindictiveness, racism, and misrepresentations of the British media. (He was particularly amused by the consequences of the report that thirteen British ladies had had their noses cut off by the rebels, which had generated outraged cant from Lord Shaftesbury and an offer by a surgeon to supply artificial noses if the taxpayer would foot the bill.) Rather than meeting 'atrocities by atrocities', he called for a more philosophical approach by British rulers (Monypenny and Buckle, 4.99). Since 1848 British policy had taken a new and foolish path, alienating Hindu and Muslim alike by a lack of respect for native religions, a contempt for traditional property rights, and an ignorance of other laws and customs. The Indians had been goaded to do what in 1853 he had thought impossible: to sink their differences against the British. Disraeli urged, among other things, a greater symbolic role for the queen as a comprehensible, god-like embodiment of British interest and authority capable of engaging the oriental imagination. She should pledge to respect 'their laws, their usages, their customs, and above all their religion' (*Hansard 3*, 147, 479). He attacked Palmerston's proposals of 1858 for Indian government on the ground that they involved another quick fix, in this case an entirely nominated council, selected by the home government, to advise the governor-general. A nominated body, reminiscent of Foxite corruption, would be unaccountable to parliament and unable to check the governor-general's despotism. A royal commission, sent out to India, was needed to investigate the practical failings of government and maximize its revenues. Palmerston fell and the new minority Conservative government had to settle the immediate question and to accept the principle of a council. Disraeli proposed 'a real Council', with half its members directly elected, five by the electors of major British towns, but the Liberal majority in parliament forced the government to remodel the bill on more conventional lines. The India issue demonstrated how Disraeli could be a committed

supporter of empire, yet be distrusted for both his radical reformism and his distaste for populist chauvinism.

The fourth issue was parliamentary reform. Disraeli's quixotic proposals for colonial representation demonstrated a willingness to experiment with the electoral system in order to consolidate the empire. In 1848 he had criticized the whig reformers of 1832 for their narrowness and ahistoricism in introducing a rigid property qualification for the borough franchise, while disparaging the factitious reopening of the question until there was a prospect of settling it (*Hansard 3*, 99, 1848, 952). Once Russell had placed parliamentary reform on the agenda again, Disraeli saw that a blustering Conservative response risked uniting their opponents in favour of a bill, and leaving themselves typecast, as in 1832, as unthinking opponents of reform. Equally, the longer the issue remained unsettled, the more scope there would be for dangerous agitation in support of radical ends such as a major redistribution of seats, diminishing the number of MPs who would represent the 'realised experience of a nation' (ibid., 956). So it was sensible for the government of 1858–9 to attempt to settle the question, especially given the scope for party advantage in the detailed terms, and the momentum that a minority government would gain by carrying a prestigious bill. However, the proposals could not afford to upset Conservative MPs in case they formed an anti-reform cave in alliance with Palmerston. So the 1859 Reform Bill concentrated on equalizing the county and borough franchise. This conceded the principle of a lower county franchise to radicals who had campaigned for it, while crucially allowing the government to propose the exclusion of (largely Liberal) borough freeholders from the county constituencies, thus preserving their historic identity. But the government's failure to agree on any safe and definitive reduction of the borough franchise ensured the bill's defeat by Liberal MPs. Ministers dissolved parliament after the defeat, and gained seats at the 1859 election.

In the 1850s Disraeli also spent much energy on disseminating these and other Conservative ideas in *The Press*, a weekly journal founded in 1853 on his initiative and that of Derby's son Lord Stanley, his close ally in these years. Disraeli conceived of this as a modern *Anti-Jacobin*, engaged in an urgent war of ideas with an overwhelmingly and previously unchallenged Liberal press. It was tolerably successful, with a circulation of over 3000 at its best. Disraeli and Stanley wrote many articles for it, as did some able young journalists; in the case of the second editor, D. T. Coulton (1854–7), it is known that Disraeli dictated a policy to him at the Commons each week (Kebbel, 3–4). Many Conservatives were annoyed at the way in which Disraeli used the journal to expound his opinions, and he severed his connection with it on taking office in 1858.

The Press was merely one of the ways in which Disraeli sought to enhance the standing of the party in the 1850s. He took an active interest in the overhaul of party organization, and appointed his solicitor Philip *Rose to handle it in 1853; Markham *Spofforth, a member of Rose's firm, succeeded him as agent between 1859 and 1870. Yet the party could not break through to gain a majority, even in 1859. Nor could the government win supporters from outside Conservative ranks, though Gladstone and Graham were approached to join the cabinet in 1858. (Disraeli was willing to surrender the leadership of the Commons to the latter but not the former.) Disraeli also made various attempts to woo independent whig, radical, and Irish MPs in the last desperate days of the ministry in 1859. These failed, as did the attempt to persuade Palmerston to join the government. As a result, it was defeated in parliament on the question of Italy in June 1859. Disraeli was out of office once again. He had a pension of £2000 p.a.—and praise from Bagehot, who argued that he alone had kept the government in power for sixteen months and that he had learned (unlike in 1852) to 'lead with dignity, and fail with dignity' (*Historical Essays*, 485).

Opposition, 1859–1866; the religious problem in Britain and elsewhere Disraeli knew that it would be impossible to persuade enough Conservative MPs to mount a full-scale opposition to a reassuringly quietist Palmerston government. By manoeuvring against it, he would be forced into alliances that they found distasteful, which would further weaken his own position. His 'shameless' past tendencies in this direction were bitterly criticized in an anonymous article in the *Quarterly Review* in April 1860 (written, as was quickly well known, by Lord Robert Cecil, the future marquess of Salisbury). Depressed, he offered to resign the Commons leadership in a letter to an influential senior back-bencher, Sir William Miles, written in June. This had the predictable effect of rallying support to him. But Disraeli learned his lesson and made few controversial initiatives during the next five sessions. Parliamentary reform was a dormant issue, while there was little scope to unite the party in criticism of government finance.

Disraeli's main activity between 1861 and 1865 was on an issue on which he could develop his ideas while satisfying most Conservative prejudices and (potentially) one other parliamentary group: church defence. The abolition of church rates was one of the few principles on which Palmerston was willing to court advanced Liberal opinion, and in reaction the Conservatives were able to defend the rate successfully in divisions in 1861, 1862, and 1863. Disraeli, not previously a clerical politician, identified a 'real Church party in the House of Commons' for the first time in twenty years (Monypenny and Buckle, 4.291), and became interested in the wider potential of the issue. He held discussions with Bishop Wilberforce and addressed gatherings in the cause outside parliament. The most famous took place at Oxford in November 1864, when he asserted that the root question between the evolutionists and the church was, 'Is man an ape or an angel?', and declared himself 'on the side of the angels' (ibid., 374). Disraeli's epigrammatic and idiosyncratic language on religious matters was mocked by opponents and offensive to grave churchmen. He in turn criticized the factionalism of the high-church ritualists, a 'finical and fastidious crew' who

were as corrosively subversive of church power as the radical dissenters (ibid., 358) and whose ceremonial symbolized doctrines that the church had been established in order to repudiate (*Letters … to Lady Bradford and Lady Chesterfield*, 1.156). He made some serious proposals for greater lay involvement in church life and politics, maintaining that exclusive clericalism was damaging the church's ability to engage on a broad basis with the national imagination and to regain its position as the natural, safe, and patriotic depository of man's age-old religious instincts.

Arguably that position was occupied by the Catholic church in most of Ireland, and by the papacy in its own dominions, hence Disraeli's fascination with the power of Catholicism. In the 1860s he sought to court Irish Catholic MPs at the same time as he upheld the Church of England. Indeed the successful Commons defence of church rates was assisted by the abstention of some Irish Catholic MPs, while a significant number of Irishmen supported the opposition's censure motion on Palmerston's foreign policy in 1864. Disraeli claimed to defend religion on an international basis against the modern decaying principles of republicanism and atheism. He upheld the temporal power of the pope—'an old man on a Semitic throne' (Disraeli, *Bentinck*, 509)—against its circling opponents. At one stage he was alarmed that Napoleon III, mishandled by the British government, might incite nationalist and revolutionary movements against the papacy. Almost alone of major British politicians, Disraeli refused to meet Garibaldi on his visit of 1864. He thought that the religious principles of Irish Catholics should make them natural Conservatives. A shared defence of religion was also the only way of forming an alliance with the numerous group of Irish MPs without surrendering to separatist or anti-landlord principles.

By the time of the 1865 election Disraeli had gained in position. The Conservatives, though still in a minority, won 290 seats at that election, and would doubtless have won more but for the popularity of Palmerston. Disraeli had become a more familiar figure in establishment circles, especially at court, where his ability to pay lavish public respect to the memory of Prince Albert won the queen's affection even more than his willingness to refrain from attempting to unseat her government. He was excited beyond measure by his reception there, particularly by a much coveted invitation to the wedding of the prince of Wales in 1863 (shrewdly arranged by Palmerston). In 1865 he was at last made a member of Grillion's, a socially select political dining club, and in 1866 of the Athenaeum, from which he had been blackballed in 1832. It was also now that he could finally put his debts behind him, owing to two strokes of financial good fortune. In 1862 Andrew Montagu, a landed Yorkshire bachelor who wished to assist the party, bought up Disraeli's debts in return for offering him a £57,000 mortgage on Hughenden, charging a rate of interest only 30 per cent of that asked by his previous creditors. In 1863 Disraeli inherited over £30,000 from Mrs Sarah Brydges *Willyams, an aged Jewish lady of Torquay with whom he had struck up a close friendship in the early 1850s. He and she were united in the belief that they were descended from aristocratic Jewish Iberian houses, and Mrs Brydges Willyams's legacy—given in 'approbation and admiration of his efforts to vindicate the race of Israel' (Monypenny and Buckle, 3.466)—was accompanied by the hope that he would adopt the names and arms of the two families concerned, though fortunately this was not a condition of the bequest. She was buried at Hughenden (which she never visited), with the Disraelis beside her.

Despite these advances, Disraeli was not much nearer power, and was frequently lethargic and depressed at this time. He was over sixty, still widely distrusted personally, and a leading member of a party that could neither win elections on its own nor attract parliamentary support from other potentially sympathetic factions. In this situation the death of Palmerston in October 1865 was both an opportunity and a danger. It made the radical forces in the Liberal coalition more undisciplined; it encouraged Russell and Gladstone to court them by resuscitating the issue of parliamentary reform. It was fairly clear that this initiative would restore a vigorous two-party system and allow a proper battle between conservatism and radicalism. It was far less clear that the Conservative Party would be able to control the former tendency. This was evident from the events generated by the 1866 Reform Bill, which was staunchly opposed by a faction of anti-democratic Liberals, the Adullamites, who eventually defeated it in alliance with the Conservatives in June 1866 and forced Russell's Liberal government out of office. The Adullamites then demanded a coalition with the Conservatives in which Derby and Disraeli should surrender the leading places to more centrist figures. Derby and Disraeli rejected this offer and formed a purely Conservative government, with Disraeli once again chancellor of the exchequer and leader of the Commons. In doing so, they were attempting to keep alive not only their own careers but also the Conservative Party. That remained their first objective throughout the following eighteen turbulent months, and does much to explain the history of the second Reform Act.

The 1867 Reform Act The history of the reform question, and of previous minority Conservative governments, held a number of crucial lessons for the new ministers. First, they had to consolidate their reputation as reformers by bringing in a bill—a fact that became all the clearer as extra-parliamentary agitation, exploited by radicals, developed during the months after the Liberal defeat. Second, they had to satisfy urban agitators by lowering the borough franchise, which they had been condemned for not doing in 1859; they might mitigate the radical effects of this by establishing a principle broad enough to settle the question for a generation. Third, their proposals had to benefit the Conservatives electorally and uphold the territorial element within the constitution, by ridding the county constituencies of as many Liberal urban and suburban voters as possible. Fourth, they needed to establish a definite parliamentary identity which could keep the party in charge of the political situation and avoid an enforced subordination to Liberals and Adullamites that

might last for years. Fifth, they could do this only by exploiting splits in the Liberal Party that would prevent it from asserting its natural majority. None of this need involve a breach of principle.

The events that resulted in the 1867 Reform Act followed naturally from those points. Disraeli hoped originally to avoid introducing a bill in the 1867 session, and to proceed by resolutions instead, with the aim of establishing some sort of consensus; however, that was too unpopular in the Commons. It was decided to base the government proposal on the principle of household suffrage in the boroughs for those who paid rates personally (accompanied by qualifications such as a two-year residence requirement and various 'fancy franchises'). This was popular among Conservative MPs, politically attractive, and potentially capable of providing a defensible long-term resting place. When a minority in cabinet dissented, and forced the government to propose a more limited bill, large numbers of MPs on both sides disliked that idea and, in March, forced the ministry back on household suffrage, a decision that Derby and Disraeli welcomed (though it led to the resignation of three cabinet ministers, led by Cecil, who had become Lord Cranborne). A bill constructed on this basis, with the threat of a dissolution if it was defeated, placed the Liberal leadership in an awkward position. Disraeli exploited this effectively throughout the 1867 session, dividing Gladstone from radical MPs and showing up many Liberals as much less wholehearted reformers than their self-presentation as champions of 'the people' had suggested. A crucial influence on the outcome was that the main qualifications to household suffrage in the original bill did not survive the process of amendment in committee, because they were inconsistent with existing electoral practice or politically unattractive to a majority of the Commons. Disraeli accepted amendments when he considered them necessary to get the bill through, including, most importantly, the amendment proposed by Grosvenor *Hodgkinson in mid-May, abolishing compounding. This increased substantially the numbers paying rates personally, with consequent effects for the size of the borough electorate (though it was generally assumed that many of those affected would not register). He refused to accept amendments proposed by Gladstone, in order to underline his loss of control over both wings of his party. Liberal discomfiture assisted Conservative support for Disraeli throughout the session, indeed made him generally popular on the back benches. Most Conservatives, including Disraeli, had no precise sense of the consequences of the bill for the borough electorate, but these were in any case almost impossible to predict. The essence of the matter was that the Liberals would continue to dominate in the large boroughs most affected by the bill, while the lack of large-scale redistribution prevented the destruction of traditional interest representation. The redistribution arrangements also altered some county boundaries so as to reinforce their rural and Conservative nature. One estimate suggests that the Liberal majority was reduced by twenty-five seats at the 1868 election as a result (Cowling, *1867*, 344–5).

The passage of the 1867 Reform Act added to the distrust of Disraeli felt by his critics in the party, most vehement among them Lord Cranborne (later Lord Salisbury). Elsewhere, however, it increased his reputation. The act had strengthened the government's hold over the Commons, given it a legislative success in the country, settled a difficult question quickly (to the pleasure, among others, of the queen), and made it impossible for Liberals to sustain their claim to a monopoly of electoral progressivism. It introduced a more democratic political era in which the most fundamental division would clearly be between conservatism and radicalism, but it destroyed the schemes of political reconstruction that might have prevented the Conservative Party from reaping the benefit of any Conservative reaction. Disraeli's tactical skill and courage in steering a bill through the Commons with a majority of seventy against him was remarkable, though he was by no means master of the situation, and his broad strategy was similar to that of many shrewd Conservatives. None the less the drama contributed to the myth of him as a mysterious, aloof manipulator, and consolidated both positive and negative sides of his public image. It made it even easier than before for his enemies to question his principles, but it also ensured that, when Derby's gout became so bad that he was forced to resign the premiership in February 1868, the queen turned to Disraeli to continue the government. He kissed hands at Osborne on 27 February, declaring 'In loving loyalty & faith' (Blake, 491).

Disraeli's first premiership, 1868   Little opposition to Disraeli's appointment was expressed within the party. However, he was hardly in a position to develop a new line of policy, even had he wanted to do so. He made little change to the cabinet. Having long been Derby's Commons manager, he seemed very anxious to continue to seek his protection; he consulted him frequently and in his election address of October 1868 wrote that he had carried out Derby's policy 'without deviation' (Monypenny and Buckle, 5.88). It was ironic that on expenditure, the issue on which he and Derby had most frequently failed to see eye to eye, Disraeli was not able to implement tax reductions: income tax, 4*d*. in 1866, had to rise from 5*d*. to 6*d*. in 1868. Disraeli had finally succeeded in checking Conservative tendencies to increase defence expenditure, only to have to meet the bill for the Abyssinian expedition of 1867–8. The expedition was forced on the government, and certainly not undertaken for electoral popularity, but Disraeli none the less used its successful conclusion to make a point to commercial public opinion, the isolationism of which was beginning to irritate him. In two speeches he suggested that in an age accused, 'perhaps not unjustly, of selfishness, and a too great regard for material interests', it was a legitimate source of pride to have 'elevated the military' and 'moral … character of England throughout the world' (*Selected Speeches*, 2.132; *The Times*, 18 June 1868, 9).

Disraeli's first premiership was dominated by Ireland,

but this was not his doing. Derby had controlled the government's Irish policy, together with the Irish secretary, Lord Mayo. They aimed to conciliate moderate Catholics without alienating protestant feeling by any major concession on the status of the Church of Ireland. Negotiations had taken place with the Irish hierarchy and Archbishop Manning about the possible grant of a charter to a Catholic university. On 10 March, Mayo announced this policy, which met with a lukewarm response from the Catholic bishops, who sought amendments. He proposed a small endowment for university expenses, and left open the larger issue of endowment for the denominational teaching colleges. Six days later Gladstone declared that an endowed university was a political impossibility and soon proposed the disestablishment and disendowment of the Irish church. This initiative united whig and radical wings of the Liberal Party, attracted Irish Catholic MPs away from the government, played to evangelical British protestants' visceral hatred of Catholic endowment, and placed the Conservative Party in the position of having to defend an institution which few British voters admired. Whatever other motives Gladstone had for this move, the desire to remove Disraeli from the highest office was widely assumed to be one of them. The future of the Irish church became the major question at the general election of November 1868. In speech after speech Gladstone ruthlessly charged Disraeli with favouring a policy of Catholic endowment, which he had not been able to persuade his party to support. Conservatives were indeed divided on an Irish church policy, and scarcely able to counter-attack.

The election was delayed until fresh registers, including the new electors, were ready. This allowed Disraeli to cling to office, despite the indignity of several crucial defeats on the Irish church issue in April and May. He had little knowledge of electoral opinion nationwide, but county agents' reports suggested hostility to Catholic and high Anglican practices, and this confirmed his decision to base his campaign around the church defence policy that he had been maturing earlier in the decade. He accused Romanists and ritualists of forming an open confederacy in favour of disestablishment, from which each hoped to benefit. However, Disraeli's campaign was low-key; he made only one speech, on re-election to his seat, after most of the contests had been decided. Instead, he sought to use the church patronage that fell to him to rally evangelical protestant sentiment, by making the fiery Liverpool preacher Hugh McNeile dean of Ripon in an obvious bid for their votes. He also rejected the leading high-church candidate for the bishopric of London, Samuel Wilberforce. Disraeli did not seek to alienate traditional high-churchmen, and in fact made several low-key appointments from that party. Moreover, he was not sufficiently well informed about candidates for promotion to be able to dominate church patronage (he had to give way to the queen, for example, over the appointment of the new archbishop of Canterbury, A. C. Tait). His strategy of rallying churchmen to the party achieved little, partly because of the tension between church factions and between representatives of those factions in his own party. In any case, more important in explaining the election result was the attraction of Gladstone's policy to many evangelical dissenters and Celtic voters. The Liberals nearly doubled their majority, to 110 seats, and Disraeli resigned on 1 December 1868, without meeting parliament: a constitutional innovation that was generally approved in the circumstances. The queen granted his request to confer the title of Viscountess Beaconsfield on his wife.

In opposition, 1868–1874 The defection of the Irish Catholics ended Disraeli's dream of combining them with Anglicans in defence of the Semitic religious legacy. He reflected on this in the light of stirring contemporary events outside Britain: the unification of Italy (and in particular the struggle for control of Rome), the papal declarations that culminated in the Vatican Council, the resurgence of the American republic in 1865, the emergence of the First International, and developments in biblical criticism and scientific materialism. To him all seemed evidence of an immense conflict between faith and ecclesiastical organization on the one hand, and free thought, republicanism, and secular nationalism on the other. This 'death struggle' was the theme of *Lothair*, the novel that—to general astonishment—Disraeli produced secretly for publication in May 1870. Lothair—another Tancred—is a young English aristocrat, heir to fabulous wealth, whose affections are engaged alternately by three charismatic young women, representing respectively his own caste, the Catholic church, and the secret societies (which Disraeli, true to his Romantic individualism, persisted in seeing as the fount of international radical agitation). Disraeli portrays the appeal of each value system with unmistakable affection; a part of him could see how each could appeal to a noble youth of ambition, and indeed the title-page quotation suggested that it was salutary for young men to experiment with them all. Catholicism offers tradition, a mother figure, imposing ceremonial, and an unshakeable faith with which to combat modern doubts and luxury. The various secular ideals described in the book are similarly hostile to contemporary selfish materialism and celebrate freedom of conscience, humanity, and the beauty of nature. The English landowning ideal reverences order, hierarchy, patriotism, and public service. None the less, Disraeli's intention is to show that the continent's two warring principles are flawed owing to their infidelity to the Semitic legacy. The Roman church is based on too narrow and conciliar a conception of religion, discourages mental liberty, locks beautiful young women in nunneries, and seeks power for itself by unscrupulous, casuistical deception. Secular ideals will end in the collapse of monarchies, law, and order and in an orgy of body-worship. Fortified by a meeting with a wise Christian in Jerusalem, Lothair chooses Anglicanism. The suggestion is that this is the best way because of its inherent capacity to unite the Semite and Aryan inheritance, the understanding of the spiritual nature of man with a reverence for human and natural beauty. As a symbol of the Anglican aristocracy, Lothair's duty is to supply

leadership in this direction. But the more sober implication running through the book is that the English propertied world that he describes is too mundane, too uncultured, and too luxurious to succeed in this goal, because it is too much in thrall to the commercial spirit and to pagan leisure pursuits. It cannot compete with the intense ideals of its two external assailants, one of which will soon destroy it. Disraeli's satire was never finer than in *Lothair*, where he revealed with superb lightness of touch his persistent ambivalence about English political and social life, and, beneath his controlled urbanity, his sense of superiority to it—which was his consolation on experiencing yet another rejection by it.

The novel, the first ever published by a former prime minister, was a great success, and led Longmans to produce a collected edition of Disraeli's novels (including a 'General preface' in which he claimed that the attempt to reconstruct a national church had been undone by the behaviour of high-churchmen, one of whom, Manning, was satirized in *Lothair*). Disraeli received over £10,000 from sales of the novel and collected edition. But at this point he may well have believed that he would never hold office again. The general political situation seemed as unpromising as ever, and his opposition to the government bills of 1869–70 was perfunctory. His wife was increasingly ill during these years, and by early 1872 it was evident that she was dying of cancer; Disraeli tended her devotedly, but she died on 15 December, leaving him desolate with grief—and without a house. During the session of 1873 he had to operate from lonely quarters in Edwards's Hotel. For most of Gladstone's government there was also muted internal party criticism of Disraeli's leadership, though as before he was saved by the lack of alternatives. The most obvious successor, Stanley, who succeeded as fifteenth earl of Derby on his father's death in 1869, even refused the leadership in the Lords in 1870, because he did not like to handle such a clerical party and preferred to be an *éminence grise* steering it towards the middle ground.

However, a change of political climate in the early 1870s went some way to justifying the forebodings expressed in *Lothair*. The Vatican Council and the *Kulturkampf* on the one hand, the fall of Rome and the Paris commune on the other, imparted a new intensity to the struggle between the papacy and secular nationalism, and brought home to Englishmen the disturbing foreignness of both ideals. Meanwhile the rapid outcome of the Franco-Prussian War, the unification of Germany, the Russian abrogation of the neutralization of the Black Sea, and the indignity of the Alabama claims settlement alarmed a domestic public opinion nurtured on Palmerstonian and free-trading confidence in Britain's global position. In such circumstances, the self-effacement of British foreign policy seemed weak and dangerous, while the government's concessionary Irish policy, the Liberal Party's republican fringe, and the radical demands for disestablishment and secular education could be presented as indications of Gladstonian unsoundness in the impending battle for the maintenance of the nation's institutions, religious establishments, property, and world influence. These themes badly damaged Gladstone's government. Conservatives needed no leading to press these points home, and Disraeli's contribution to the collapse of Liberal popularity was small. However, a major theme of the two extra-parliamentary speeches that he made in 1872, at Manchester and the Crystal Palace, was that England faced a crucial choice: whether to play a responsible world role befitting her imperial status, or to decay under the spell of cosmopolitan principles. The most important decision he took in these years was a strategic parliamentary one, not to take office in a minority when Gladstone's Irish University Bill was defeated in March 1873, but to wait for an enfeebled Liberal Party to dissolve parliament.

Disraeli's second premiership: domestic affairs, 1874–1876
Even so, at the beginning of 1874 there was little reason to expect a rapid return to power. In fact, Disraeli was prime minister again before the beginning of the session, owing to Gladstone's unexpected dissolution and decisive defeat at the election. The Conservatives had over 350 seats. Disraeli took office on 18 February. At last he had achieved his great ambition, power with a majority—something that had seemed impossible for most of his life. He certainly took pleasure in the position. He enjoyed the process of dispensing patronage, especially to deserving old connections, and was amused by the number of beseeching letters that he received. Patronage was very valuable for a party so long in opposition, and he asserted his right to appoint to a number of posts that the Treasury had tried to depoliticize. From now until his death he enjoyed a close proximity to the queen, to whom he reported political and social news with irreverent gusto; in 1868, for example, he had commented to her of his colleague Ward Hunt that, 'like St. Peter's no one is aware of his dimensions. But he has the sagacity of an elephant as well as the form' (Blake, 488–9). She responded with obvious marks of favour to him (including allowing him to sit during audiences), though he found her excessively demanding—and sometimes 'very mad' (*Selection from the Diaries of … Derby*, 290)—and he needed all his tact to deal with her and especially with the affairs of the prince of Wales.

Disraeli was a ceremonious, slightly remote, but patient and unassertive chairman of cabinet, which conducted its business with laxity. Its priorities were broadly agreed. On the one hand, it stood for the principle of 'not harassing the country' (Mitchell, 61), and was dominated by landowners and high-churchmen anxious to prevent assaults on property and religious institutions. Most formidable of these was Salisbury, who now returned to office. On the other, it reflected the great opportunity that the party had to become a centrist force, offering competent, sober government as uncontroversially as possible, leaving undisturbed the fiscal basis of mid-Victorian England, and offering the Liberals little chance of recovering the middle ground. This was the strategy associated particularly with Derby, and with R. A. Cross, the 'middle-class' Lancashire man brought in as home secretary at Derby's prompting,

despite Disraeli's 'odd dislike' of men of that class (*Selection from the Diaries of … Derby*, 416). Fiscal rectitude was signalled by the appointment as chancellor of the exchequer of Northcote, Disraeli's protégé but also Gladstone's. The cabinet was reduced to twelve members, the smallest since 1832, to indicate the importance of efficiency, economy, and individual responsibility in government.

Disraeli's election address had reverted to the theme of *Lothair*, the need to maintain England's influence as the defender of civil and religious liberty against the threat from Catholicism and atheism. In the 1874 session he capitalized on this protestant cry in such a way as to ensure that the Liberals remained split and listless. (He unsuccessfully offered one whig dissident, the duke of Somerset, cabinet office in 1874 and again in 1878.) 'I detest and disagree' with the Irish MPs, he told Henry Ponsonby, the queen's private secretary (Monypenny and Buckle, 5.211). But especially now that so many had declared for home rule, he needed to do little in that direction except to oppose the home rule idea staunchly. He exploited divisions in the Liberals most effectively by his handling of the Public Worship Regulation Bill, urged on the government by Archbishop Tait in order to provide the bishops with a way of disciplining ritualist excesses in parishes. Protestant feeling for such a measure was very strong, and some action was politically necessary. The government improved Tait's bill behind the scenes, but by delaying official support for it Disraeli kept the clerical factions in his cabinet united. When Gladstone opposed it, opening a rift with most of his party, he finally supported it and was influential in the subsequent compromise which carried the bill. He thus achieved the dual objective of damaging Gladstone (who subsequently retired as Liberal leader) and of settling a question that had the potential to antagonize all church parties. The church, he wrote, 'will be immensely strengthened' by the disciplining of such a controversial minority (ibid., 5.322), though the act itself was to cause tension inside the Anglican body. Another government act of 1874 abolished patronage in the Church of Scotland, in the hope of reducing the threat of a disestablishment agitation there. This terminated Disraeli's active involvement with church issues. Though they were very contentious in the 1870s, producing further squabbles between clerical factions within the party, these were kept in check.

The strategy of concentrating on bipartisan social issues was developed by Cross and Derby in association with Disraeli in 1874 and matured in the six substantial bills passed in the 1875 session, which were intended to make an effective contrast with the Liberals' destructive hyperactivity. This was a strategy particularly attractive to the hard-headed practical Conservatism of northern MPs, and Disraeli was well advised to insert two paragraphs on sanitary reform in the long speech that he had been persuaded to make at Manchester in 1872. They bestowed extravagant praise on the 'practical' scheme to consolidate sanitary legislation then being proposed by his colleague Sir Charles Adderley. He accompanied this praise with a conventional warning against abstractions, against dreamily trusting too much to the state in social affairs rather than to private effort (*Selected Speeches*, 2.510–11). That these paragraphs later spawned the exceptionally long-lived myth of Disraeli as social reformer is a great historical curiosity. In government Disraeli left his departmental heads to produce their own legislation and was no man for detail; indeed Derby felt that one of his shortcomings as cabinet chairman was that he 'detests the class of business which he is apt to call parochial' (*Selection from the Diaries of … Derby*, 448). He did not mention his government's social measures in his only intervention at the 1880 election. What he especially valued in the legislation of 1875 was that by settling difficult questions it reduced the 'materials for social agitation' (Mitchell, 89). This was so particularly of the labour laws legislation and the Agricultural Holdings Act, which he saw as checking ill feeling between employers and employees and between landlords and farmers. In the financial sphere the large surplus inherited in 1874 made it easy to agree a policy for the first budget. Northcote pleased all the major interest groups by relieving the three categories of direct, indirect, and local taxation; income tax fell to 2*d*.

In the 1874 session and the first half of the next Disraeli was widely agreed to be in command of the Commons, demonstrating an 'easy confidence', a 'polite consideration' for MPs, and a refusal to cajole or hurry them (Lucy, 39, 46, 68, 82). However, his powers then seemed to wane. He was often ill—with gout, asthma, and bronchitis—and tired: he once fell asleep in cabinet in 1875. In 1876 he had to encounter persistent Liberal factionalism over the Royal Titles Bill, and the beginnings of obstruction from the home-rulers. The Conservative back-benchers were restive at the lack of achievement in the session. Despite having the 'most numerous and obedient majority since Pitt', he seemed unable to dispatch routine matters at ordinary times. That he lacked facility for business became apparent: 'an incessant and almost avowed inaccuracy pervades him' (*Historical Essays*, 503). He perceived that his physical powers were not sufficient to continue to lead the Commons effectively. Though he volunteered to resign the premiership, neither he nor his colleagues seriously considered this step. In August 1876 the queen made him earl of Beaconsfield and from the session of 1877 he led the ministry from the Lords.

The problem of Europe, 1874–1876 In 1877 Derby, the sceptical and peace-loving foreign secretary, noted that one reason for the unbusinesslike habits of the cabinet was that Beaconsfield 'takes peculiar pleasure in turning over & discussing all sorts of foreign questions, on which action is not necessary, & often not possible' (*Selection from the Diaries of … Derby*, 448). International issues excited the premier in a way that most others did not: 'these are politics worth managing', he wrote in 1876 (Monypenny and Buckle, 6.32). This was not just because of the attractions of continental intrigue. In 1871 he had hoped that public interest in foreign affairs might divert attention from the 'morbid spirit of domestic change and criticism' (ibid., 5.132). In 1875 he wondered whether the spirit of

patriotism was dead or whether it could be rekindled. The attempt to do so became a—perhaps the—major goal of his government.

However, an additional obstacle facing a spirited British policy was that German unification and the fall of France in 1870 had destroyed the European balance and forced Russia, Austria, and Germany to try to settle international questions by mutual agreement for fear of the alternative. Disraeli did not set much store by the French in their enfeebled state, and sought a good understanding with Bismarck, in accordance with his protestant declarations at the 1874 election. However, the war scare of May 1875 showed the impossibility of relying on Bismarck's goodwill, and the British participation in the protest against his threatening behaviour reassured the French. This paid important dividends in November, when news came of the wish of the khedive of Egypt to sell his large minority stake in the Suez Canal Company to French businessmen, thus making it entirely French-owned. The cabinet agreed on the importance of the British securing some stake, and the shares were bought without diplomatic awkwardness, with the assistance of a loan from the Rothschilds arranged by Disraeli (on extravagantly generous terms). Though the company had no control over the canal, and the shares were mortgaged and so had no voting rights, the impression was given that Britain had bought a controlling stake in the canal itself. The general public enthusiasm for this step was an encouraging sign of the popularity of an active international policy.

When, in 1875, revolts began in the Balkans against Turkish rule, Disraeli suggested that the need of Russia, Austria, and Germany to work together to settle the Balkan question threatened to 'drive the Turk from Europe' (Monypenny and Buckle, 6.13). Always susceptible to racial interpretations of history, he feared that Russia would incite pan-Slav sentiment in what he later called a war of 'extermination directed equally against a religion and a race' (*Selection from the Diaries of … Derby*, 442). Secret societies, he claimed, were operating in Serbia and elsewhere to stir up pan-Slav spirit, and this would end in a war that might have revolutionary implications. European Turkey would be partitioned into Russian and Austrian spheres, and Germany would seek compensation elsewhere, perhaps to the west, which would leave France, Belgium, and Britain in a disastrously weakened state. These sweeping notions made Disraeli suspicious of the early attempts by the three eastern powers to seek a limited settlement of the Balkan question; he feared that popular pressure would force the Russian and Austro-Hungarian governments into a partition of European Turkey. As a result, he wished to reject the Andrassy note (which demanded that the Ottoman empire should reform its European administration), which the three powers agreed and sent to Britain for support in December 1875.

It was not easy for the British government to find an alternative to this policy, and Derby secured the acceptance of the note. However, when war between Serbia and

Turkey seemed likely in May 1876, Disraeli and Derby agreed to reject a further communication from the three powers, the Berlin memorandum, which sought to pre-empt war by warning of great-power intervention in the Ottoman empire if reforms were not carried out. The British asserted instead the importance of the powers upholding the old treaty policy of guaranteeing the integrity and independence of the Ottoman empire. This was essentially an attempt to buy time for a better policy. Indeed, the government tried unsuccessfully to reach a settlement with Russia in June 1876 that would not only assert British influence in the region but, while revising Ottoman frontiers, would also avert a general partition.

At this point news reached Britain of Turkish massacres of Bulgarian Christians in response to an uprising. This prompted a prolonged and virtuous agitation at home, into which Gladstone entered with relish. The Bulgarian agitation had three effects on the prime minister. First, he believed that it made Russia more likely to go to war against Turkey, with pan-Slavism aroused and sympathy for the Balkan Christians so strong in the British public that the British government could not object. Second, it delivered another and perhaps the greatest blow to his reputation with Liberal opinion, because he proclaimed his suspicion that many of the sensational details published in the newspapers were inventions of Slavonic intriguers. His remarks were seen as callous and flippant. Indeed in September 1876 he was famously and disastrously misunderstood when he described Gladstone's pamphlet on the atrocities as likely to cause 'general havoc and ruin' in the Balkans (by encouraging war) and thus 'worse than any of those Bulgarian atrocities which now occupy attention' (*The Times*, 21 Sept 1876, 6). Third, it added to internal Conservative Party pressure for a change of policy, particularly from the section of high-churchmen led by Salisbury who sympathized with the persecuted Orthodox Christians.

Neither Beaconsfield nor Derby believed it very likely that Russia could be stopped from declaring war on Turkey. However, Derby proposed an international conference at Constantinople in an attempt to reach agreement on increased self-government for parts of European Turkey, and the government sent Salisbury as its representative in an effort to show British and continental opinion that it was amenable to reform. The Turks resisted the conference proposals, as expected, and despite further attempts at a settlement, the Russians prepared for war in the spring of 1877; they declared it in late April.

An assertive Eastern policy, 1877–1878 Until this point Beaconsfield had generally followed the policy laid down by Derby, though he embellished it with a few characteristically restless but fruitless initiatives and a general desire to make an impression in Europe. The Russian invasion of European Turkey changed the situation because the ultimate threat was now to Constantinople and thus to British interests in the eastern Mediterranean, Egypt, and Asia. The immediate consequence was a deeply damaging

split in the Liberal opposition, which benefited the government temporarily. However, Beaconsfield was extremely aware of the disaster that would strike any government that appeared lax in safeguarding British interests. He was haunted by the experience of 1853 and the obloquy earned by Aberdeen's government for failing to prevent the Crimean War. Old and ill as he was, this was not how he wished to be remembered by posterity. From now until January 1878 cabinet politics were dominated by various attempts made by him to counter the Russian advance, all of which were frustrated by Derby and (usually) a majority of the cabinet. The situation was worsened by the Turkish resistance at Plevna from July to December 1877, which delayed the dénouement. At various times Beaconsfield proposed to occupy the Gallipoli peninsula, with or without the sultan's permission (which was not given). However, this required money from parliament, for which he shrank from asking. It was also likely to offend the powers on whose goodwill Derby thought Britain depended in order to achieve a settlement of the crisis. Derby and some other ministers believed that the Russians' goals were moderate, that they would not occupy Constantinople permanently even if they entered it, and that the weight of European pressure on them would then ensure a fair solution. Derby (who was seen in cabinet as at least as plausible an interpreter of middle-class sentiment as Beaconsfield) also argued that, with trade worsening, there was little pro-war feeling in the country. Salisbury at this stage was similarly averse to strong measures. In an attempt to explain the absence of action Beaconsfield, continually harassed by the belligerent Victoria, traduced both these colleagues in letters to her. For many years these letters provided the main version of cabinet discussions and still influence many accounts, but it is now clear, from Derby's diary, that the cabinet as a whole was in charge of policy and able to rationalize it.

However, the situation was altered in December 1877 by the fall of Plevna and the impending return of parliament. The first of these excited both the Conservative press, with which Beaconsfield's private secretary Montagu Corry was in daily contact, and the queen, who visited Hughenden on 15 December in order to show her support for her prime minister against his critics. Political society and the press became aware of splits in the cabinet. The balance within the cabinet was affected by the threat to British interests and by the imminence of the parliamentary session; Salisbury in particular became much more sympathetic to Beaconsfield's position. On 23 January 1878, with Russia menacing Constantinople, the cabinet supported Beaconsfield's proposal to send the fleet through the Dardanelles and to ask parliament for a vote of credit. Carnarvon and Derby resigned. The fleet was recalled almost immediately, because of reports that the sultan had agreed to peace, together with alarm in the City at the evidence of victory by the war faction in cabinet, and panic within the Conservative Party at the prospect of losing Derby's influence in Lancashire. Derby (but not Carnarvon) thus remained in the cabinet. This crisis lowered respect for the government outside Westminster, generating hostility to further vacillation and a widespread and often bellicose anti-Russian sentiment, christened 'jingoism' after a popular music-hall song. This was accompanied by the spread of ugly rumours about Derby in political society, including the allegation that he or his wife was telling the (surely unsurprised) Russian ambassador of cabinet divisions. These rumours, which Beaconsfield helped to publicize, conveniently disguised the extent of his own covert operations with secret agents and the Rothschilds. The combined effect of these developments was to create a strong climate of opinion within the party in favour of a policy of resistance to Russia.

Part of the fleet was sent through the Dardanelles in early February, in response to exaggerated rumours of further Russian advances. This was a popular move at home, though of doubtful strategic value. Had it led to a Russian occupation of Gallipoli and Constantinople, as well it might have, the British were in a vulnerable position. Instead the Russians forced the Turks to sign an objectionable treaty at San Stefano, which at first they seemed unwilling to submit for ratification by the European powers at the congress that Austria now proposed. In response, on 27 March, Beaconsfield persuaded the cabinet to agree to call out the reserves, to bring Indian troops to Malta, and, if Russia was not sufficiently amenable at the congress, to seize the Turkish territory of Cyprus and Iskenderun as British naval bases. (Only the first of these measures was then announced and the third was not necessarily definitely adopted.) This policy had several advantages for him: it satisfied an expectant party, it met the desire of a majority of cabinet that Britain should increase her claim to influence in Asiatic Turkey, and it led to the final resignation of Derby and his replacement as foreign secretary by Salisbury. It also involved little risk, since Germany, Austria, and most Balkan politicians were similarly aggrieved at the treaty of San Stefano and were insistent that Russia must come to the conference table, at Berlin.

Accordingly, Beaconsfield's policy of firmness appeared to lead to a triumphant diplomatic victory almost as soon as it was adopted. Salisbury negotiated a settlement with Russia in advance of the congress at Berlin. This settlement forced her to abandon the idea of a Mediterranean coast for the new Bulgarian state. However, it accepted most of her demands in the Near East; in compensation, Salisbury increased Britain's commitment to the region markedly. He gave the Turks a military alliance, in return for which he forced them to accept British control of Cyprus and the installation of British military consuls in Turkey's Asia Minor territories to guarantee administrative stability and British influence. In cabinet Beaconsfield envisaged that infiltration by British state servants would produce a steady growth of influence in Turkey and Egypt and argued that 'the virtual administration of the East by England was the only hope for the prosperity of those Countries and Peoples' (Howard and Gordon, 19). The public affirmation of Britain's increased weight in Europe

came at the Congress of Berlin itself, in June and July, at which Beaconsfield was the most prominent British representative. Despite frequent illness, he revelled in its great set pieces and social events, and the feeling that men of power like himself had assembled to remake the map of Europe. He was fascinated by Bismarck, with whom he enjoyed discussions about the preservation of the aristocratic system with which they both identified so strongly; Bismarck told him that there was no danger of socialism in England as long as upper and working classes were united by a love of horse-racing. On returning from Berlin, Beaconsfield and Salisbury encountered cheering crowds at Dover and Charing Cross, and Beaconsfield made a telling comparison with the failure of 1853 by remarking that he hoped he had brought back peace with honour. The queen offered him a marquessate or dukedom, which he refused; he and Salisbury accepted the KG.

Beaconsfield believed that the events of 1878 had restored the prestige of England, both abroad and in the eyes of her own people. This was only one aspect of the story. What had started as a tentative and awkward reaction to isolation, and developed into a desperate avoidance of parliamentary humiliation, had ended in a controversial new line of policy, the occupation of Cyprus and the military alliance with Turkey, and a significant heightening of tension with Russia. This new policy instinctively appealed to Beaconsfield and Salisbury, by asserting Britain's power. But her position in the Near East was arguably unsustainable, at least without major extra military commitments at which a subsequent government would probably cavil. Meanwhile, the crisis of 1876–8 had divided opinion at home and had made Beaconsfield a demonic figure to many Liberals, exciting a lot of antisemitic and anti-alien sentiment. He knew only too well that public opinion was fickle and deeply unreliable, and it is unlikely that his policy in the Eastern crisis was driven largely by a search for electoral gain. The cabinet rejected the idea of a premature dissolution in the summer of 1878, as unconstitutional and unpredictable in its consequences, given the state of the economy, which would determine more votes than a foreign triumph. As far as elections were concerned, the major significance of the Eastern crisis was that its divisiveness gave an enormous fillip to party organization on both sides. Though in the long run the association of the Conservatives with the national cause was to benefit the party greatly, in the context of 1878–80 it ended their best chance at an election by undermining the bipartisan tone with which they had been wooing 'moderate' opinion. The crisis destroyed not only Derby's career in the party but also the centrist strategy for it that he had been promoting for thirty years.

'Imperialism', 1876–1880 From 1878 until the election of 1880 Gladstone attacked Beaconsfield for pursuing a vainglorious policy of territorial aggrandizement, military display, imperial symbolism, and contempt for parliament, which was inappropriate for a modern commercial and Christian people. Though much exaggerated, these charges were effective because of the variety of evidence that appeared to support them.

The word 'imperialism' was first applied to British politics by hostile newspapers during the debates about the government bill of 1876 to confer on the queen the title of empress of India. The title was said to be un-English and particularly resonant of the tawdry glitter of the regime of Napoleon III. The proposal of the measure also seemed to suggest an unhealthily close political relationship between Disraeli and the queen. The pressure for the bill did indeed stem from her. However, there was no obligation on Disraeli to accept it, and no reason to think that it did not appeal to him as a natural corollary of the suggestions that he had made in 1857 for a more direct, imposing, imaginative, and sympathetic tone to British rule in India. But it was more controversial than he had anticipated; from February to May 1876 it generated strong opposition from Liberal MPs, forcing him to make several parliamentary speeches in its defence.

Disraeli had no strategy for imperial development, and most of the territorial expansion that took place during his ministry was minor and done in order to facilitate the maintenance of order by local British troops. However, he was extremely concerned about the threat to India apparently posed by the Russian advance in central Asia. Even before the outbreak of tension with Russia over the Balkans, he was anxious to secure the north-west frontier. When that tension arose, he and Salisbury toyed with a plan that the Indian army should occupy Afghanistan and rouse the Muslims of central Asia against the Russians. This was extremely impractical, and the only result was to increase the suspicion of Britain entertained by the emir of Afghanistan, Sher Ali. When the Russians sent a mission to Afghanistan in 1878, Bulwer-Lytton, the Indian viceroy, considered it essential to demand a similar privilege for Britain. Bulwer-Lytton, an appointee and admirer of Beaconsfield, sought to emulate his international achievements. Unfortunately, his headstrong and hectoring approach to Sher Ali met with a rebuff, in response to which Britain declared war against him in November 1878. Beaconsfield sought no war: Bulwer-Lytton ignored one set of cabinet instructions, while the cabinet's decision for war was dictated primarily by Cranbrook, the Indian secretary, after Beaconsfield had proposed a more moderate course, the temporary occupation of some territory. None the less, throughout the crisis Beaconsfield regarded the issue of war or peace as secondary to the maintenance of British honour. He consistently urged firmness to assert Britain's ascendancy, and to avoid the impression of vulnerability before the Muslims of Asia, the powers of Europe, and the Conservative opinion of Britain. In November he justified the war in public as facilitating the creation of a more 'scientific' frontier for India against Russia, and reminded his audience that the future of the empire would depend on whether the people of England had 'the courage and determination of their forefathers' (Monypenny and Buckle, 6.393). By early 1879 the war was won, Sher Ali had fled to die, and his son seemed willing to meet all the British demands, including the acceptance of a mission at Kabul. However, the mission was slaughtered in an uprising six weeks after arriving there. To Beaconsfield this was an opportunity to establish the scientific frontier beyond doubt. Kabul was occupied while a longer-term policy was worked out. Before the government's downfall in 1880 the only decision that had been taken was that to create a British sphere of influence in southern Afghanistan by installing a chieftain at Kandahar.

When in February 1879 news reached London of a defeat for British forces in southern Africa at Isandlwana at the hands of the Zulu, Beaconsfield's main concern was that it will 'reduce our Continental influence, and embarrass our finances' (Monypenny and Buckle, 6.424). He had all but ignored southern African affairs since 1874, and had left them in the hands of successive colonial secretaries; they, in turn, were forced by the poor state of communications to cede much initiative to local British officials. Sir Bartle Frere, the new high commissioner, unwisely provoked a clash with the Zulu as part of his plan to consolidate British power in the region. Once this had happened, Beaconsfield's concern was with British prestige. The cabinet had already agreed to send out reinforcements in order to prevent domestic criticism. Beaconsfield, fearing the loss of face, prevented the recall of Frere, for which a majority of the cabinet wished. But he also showed his displeasure with Frere and the commander of the British forces, Lord Chelmsford, by sending out Sir Garnet Wolseley to exercise supreme power in the troubled area—to the great annoyance of the queen. Beaconsfield later told her that without the fiasco in southern Africa Britain would have had the international respect necessary to settle her problems in the eastern Mediterranean more easily. In particular, he saw a connection between the African embarrassment and the protest made by the khedive of Egypt in March 1879 against British and French interference in his financial policy. Britain and France were forced to secure the khedive's abdication and to assume a dual control over Egyptian finance. As this shows, Beaconsfield and Salisbury were determined to assert Britain's influence abroad, which Beaconsfield proclaimed in November 1879 was a guarantee of continental peace. Shortly beforehand the government had reached an understanding with Austria and Germany to prevent British (and, it was also intended, French or Italian) assistance to Russia in the event of her attacking the central powers. The British thus hoped to prevent reconciliation between the three Eastern powers—which would diminish British influence at Constantinople—while maintaining good relations with France. It was in defence of an active European policy of this sort, and the search for a scientific frontier in India, that Beaconsfield sought to impress a spirit of patriotism on the British people in his Guildhall speech of November 1879, in which he proclaimed as his ministry's creed 'Imperium et Libertas' (ibid., 6.495).

The 1880 election defeat If continental influence was restored, financial health was not, and this became the government's major problem up to and at the election called in the spring of 1880. Beaconsfield later complained that it had been his misfortune to govern the country during six consecutive bad harvests, while farmers were not even compensated by high prices, because of cheap food imports. Already in the summer of 1879 he feared that agricultural bankruptcy would 'finish' the government (Monypenny and Buckle, 6.477), while by early 1880 there was considerable landlord–farmer tension, which was damaging Conservative prospects and morale. Industry was also depressed in the late 1870s, which increased urban unemployment and forced the government to look for extra revenue. The state of the economy is generally held to have been the prime cause of the Conservative defeat in 1880, a belief shared by Beaconsfield himself: 'like Napoleon, I have been beaten by the elements' (Gower, 349). Gladstone alleged that the government's costly foreign adventures and its lack of fiscal rectitude were worsening the economic climate. Income tax, 2*d*. in 1874, had been increased to 5*d*. in 1878, and in a desperate attempt to avoid defeat Beaconsfield refused to consider new taxes thereafter. Much of the money for the south African expedition was borrowed, while swingeing economies in defence were undertaken.

Beaconsfield had little choice but to base the Conservative campaign on his record as defender of national interests. However, there was no clearly visible Liberal threat to those interests, and so he chose to make his point by focusing on the Irish issue. Ireland had been a marginal question for most of the parliament, though Beaconsfield claimed to have settled the Irish university question, which had upset two governments. However, Irish MPs were now obstructing business, with some prospect of encouragement from Liberal MPs. Beaconsfield launched the campaign with a letter to the lord lieutenant of Ireland, the duke of Marlborough, in which he claimed that influential Irishmen were attempting to sever the constitutional tie with Britain and that some Liberals might exploit this to 'challenge the expediency of the imperial character of the realm'. This prospect warranted a reminder that 'the power of England and the peace of Europe will largely depend on the verdict of the country' (Monypenny and Buckle, 6.515). His strategy was ineffective: the official leaders of the opposition were moderates whose presence reassured potential defectors; the Liberal Party remained united and the Conservatives lost the election conclusively, collecting only 238 seats. Beaconsfield resigned office on 21 April 1880 and had a farewell audience with the queen six days later, though he visited Windsor three more times that year and continued a confidential correspondence with her, which was more personal than political but by no means exclusively so.

The last year Beaconsfield was inevitably cast down by another rejection and by the new political climate. He was gloomy about the future of the landed interest and, consequently, the grand social world that had been sustained by its wealth: in 1879 he predicted the end of London seasons and of racing, that antidote to socialism (Monypenny and Buckle, 6.500). He disliked the tension between landlords and farmers and interpreted the new government's budget and Ground Game Bill as an attempt to widen it. As

Conservative leader in the Lords, he worked with whig dissidents to defeat the government's Compensation for Disturbance Bill, which he saw as 'not merely an Irish measure but as the opening of a great attack on the land' (ibid., 6.582). He foresaw a 'falling empire' (ibid., 6.596), and the absence of any will in foreign policy to keep 'the democrats of Europe in check' (Gower, 350).

As after the rejection of 1868, he returned to fiction. *Endymion*, published in November 1880, had largely been written in the early 1870s; Longmans paid £10,000 for the rights, said to be the largest sum then paid for a fictional work. (This was the final step in Beaconsfield's financial rehabilitation; at his death he left a personal estate of just over £84,000, so that Andrew Montagu's mortgage could be paid off without embarrassing the estate.) It was a survey of British politics between 1827 and 1855, lovingly recreated and emphasizing the importance of aristocratic—especially female—social influence on political fortunes. That influence helps a colourless, conventional, well-mannered man to rise to the premiership; he is also assisted by not offending the insular prejudices of a commercial country. Beaconsfield then began what may have become a more direct commentary on his election defeat, a sequel to *Lothair* that was unfinished at his death. It is known to posterity as *Falconet*, after its anti-hero, the devout, humourless, self-serving, self-righteous, ill-tempered politician of that name, who is manifestly a young Gladstone. One theme is Falconet's ability to exploit the religious sentiment of the constituencies to assist his political ascent. The other is the emergence of a powerful nihilist movement in Europe, fomented by secret organization, devoted to the overthrow of civilization, but aware that it can only achieve its ends by enlisting 'some religious faith in [its] resources' (Monypenny and Buckle, 5.556). It is irresistible to speculate that these two themes were to be brought together by Falconet's becoming, for career reasons, an unconscious promoter of the revolutionary cause who vainly justifies his actions on religious grounds.

For most of 1880 after losing office, Beaconsfield was at Hughenden, writing either novels or a flood of letters, especially to the sisters Selina, countess of Bradford, and Anne, countess of Chesterfield. He had enjoyed an ardent friendship and remarkably revealing correspondence with both since 1873, and had often seemed to be completely dependent on their affection. He once proposed to marry the widowed Lady Chesterfield in order, as they well knew, to be nearer her younger sister, with whom he was clearly infatuated, but who was married to the master of the horse in his own government. He had not had a permanent house in London since giving up the residence in Whitehall Gardens (rented since 1874) in order to move into Downing Street during the Eastern crisis. In November 1880 he took a nine-year lease on 19 Curzon Street. Though he claimed to be searching for a leader to replace him in the Lords, he showed no sign of giving way to the obvious successor, Salisbury. In March 1881, having taken a drug to fortify him, he made his last significant speech in the Lords, in which he argued for the retention of Kandahar and reverted to the fundamental theme of his later years, that the prospects for India, as for Britain's world standing generally, would be determined by 'the spirit and vigour of your Parliament' (*Selected Speeches*, 2.270). Later that month he caught a chill which, playing on his existing chest weakness, developed into severe bronchitis. He took to his bed in Curzon Street, became progressively weaker, and died there on 19 April 1881, having declined a visit from the queen; he is said to have remarked: 'No it is better not. She would only ask me to take a message to Albert' (Blake, 747). In his will he refused a public funeral and was buried at Hughenden on 26 April, with his wife and Mrs Brydges Willyams. Three royal princes, Derby, Hartington, and other leading Liberals (but not Gladstone) attended his funeral. The queen sent two wreaths, one of fresh primroses, which she claimed were his favourite flowers (she had sent him spring blooms regularly since 1868). She visited the grave four days later and subsequently had a monument erected to him above his seat in Hughenden church, a rare compliment from a British sovereign to a subject. The inscription was bowdlerized from Proverbs: 'Kings love him that speaketh right'.

Papers and editions Disraeli's letters are to be found in most Victorian political collections. He was quite an assiduous preserver of his incoming mail and left a substantial archive. It was initially in the care of Monty Corry and later in that of the Beaconsfield trustees. It was then preserved at Hughenden and was not easily available for research. After the cataloguing of the manuscripts by Robert Stewart and the publication of Blake's biography in 1966, the papers were deposited in the Bodleian Library, Oxford, by the National Trust, which had acquired them when it took over Hughenden in 1947 through the generosity of the family of W. H. Abbey, who bought the estate in 1937, and the Disraelian Society.

There have been several publications of Disraeli materials, notably Lord Zetland's edition of *The Letters of Disraeli to Lady Bradford and Lady Chesterfield* (2 vols., 1929), Lady Londonderry's edition of *Letters from Benjamin Disraeli to Frances Anne, Marchioness of Londonderry* (1938), *Disraeli's Reminiscences*, comprising autobiographical memoranda and edited by H. M. Swartz and M. Swartz (1975), and the comprehensive edition published from Queen's University, Ontario, *Benjamin Disraeli Letters* (1982 onwards).

Disraeli has always been of interest to foreign authors; of particular interest are the lives by Georg Brandes, the Danish literary critic (1879), and André Maurois (1927). The latter encouraged Alfred Green's American film *Disraeli* (1929), starring George Arliss, appropriately one of the first talking films; it was based on a New York play by Louis Parker (1911), and was an extravagantly fanciful rendering of the Suez Canal affair. Arliss had earlier starred in a silent version directed by Henry Kolker (1921). Collected editions of Disraeli's novels were published in 1853 by David Bryce, in 1870–71 and 1881 by Longmans, in 1888 by Routledge, in 1904–5 (for subscribers only) by M. W. Donne, in 1905–6 and 1927–8 by the Bodley Head, and in 1926–7 by Peter Davies, with introductions by Philip Guedalla.

Portraiture Disraeli was an attractive subject for artists. Daniel Maclise's drawing (1828; Hughenden) depicts the young aesthete, but most portraits were designed to emphasize the gravity of the statesman rather than the wit of the author. The principal oils are those by Sir Francis Grant (1852; Hughenden), Heinrich von Angeli (1877; Royal Collection), and, much the best, Sir John Millais (1881; NPG). Von Angeli's portrait was commissioned by the queen, and was painted in her private dining-room, fitted up with the pagoda furniture from the Brighton Pavilion. Millais's was painted at the artist's request as Beaconsfield was dying, as a pair with Millais's 1879 portrait of Gladstone. The sittings were arranged by Lord Ronald Leveson-Gower at a meeting of the trustees of the National Portrait Gallery (both Leveson-Gower and Disraeli were active trustees). As a precaution, Millais used the same pose as the excellent carte-de-visite by Downie (1868; NPG). The portrait was finished posthumously and shown at the Royal Academy exhibition of 1881. It had several owners, including W. H. Smith, before it was acquired by the National Portrait Gallery. Millais painted a smaller replica for the queen. Cartoons of Disraeli often emphasized his Jewish ancestry, and especially during the Eastern crisis in the 1870s. *Judy*, the tory antidote to *Punch*, had a fine series, published later as a separate volume (1880). There are many photographs of Disraeli in the National Portrait Gallery archive, often of fine quality. The earliest bust is that by S. Frugoni (1827; Hughenden), followed by William Behnes's bust of 1847 (Hughenden), Lord Ronald Leveson-Gower's bronzed plaster bust and statuette (1878–9; NPG and Hughenden), and Count Gleichen's marble bust for the queen (1880; Royal Collection). Following his death, recorded by R. Glassby's death mask, statues in London were erected in Westminster Abbey (Sir Edgar Boehm, 1883), the Palace of Westminster (Count Gleichen, 1883), and Parliament Square (M. Raggi, 1883); there were also some in provincial towns, though on nothing like the scale of the memorials to Peel and Gladstone, and none in the other national capitals. Hughenden has a fine collection of Disraeliana.

Disraeli in history In a letter to *The Times* just before the anniversary of Disraeli's death, the Anglo-Indian Sir George Birdwood suggested that those who admired his achievements and ideals should celebrate it by wearing a primrose. The gesture was repeated in 1883, by which time it had become popular—especially among those who disapproved of the external and Irish policies of the Gladstone government. Accordingly, Drummond Wolff, an independently minded Conservative MP, suggested capitalizing on Disraeli's popularity by setting up a Primrose League, a cross-class institution celebrating monarchy, social hierarchy, chivalric values, and the volunteer spirit. This became a bulwark of local Conservative electoral organization and marked the beginning of Disraeli's extraordinary posthumous life as a Conservative icon. As both parties developed a professional organization, they needed attractive figureheads, which the burgeoning mass media assisted in projecting. A new Disraeli and Gladstone were invented, competing for commemoration on ashtrays and dishcloths. Disraeli has remained a Conservative Party hero ever since. His career had been colourful, while his sonorous, inclusive, but unspecific rhetoric was ambiguous enough to make him a useful symbol of a remarkable variety of policies. Accordingly, his name has often been invoked in support of ends that would have alarmed him, such as state welfare.

The league's aim to attract middle- and lower-class members was part of a broader strategy of 'tory democracy' within the party, to reach out to the expanded electorate of the 1880s. Disraeli's achievement in 1867 could help in this, and an article in *The Times* on 18 April 1883 suggested that he had been the first to discern 'the Conservative working man, as the sculptor perceives the angel prisoned in a block of marble'. Even more stress was placed on Disraeli's record as a social reformer, as the party realized the rhetorical attractiveness of a practical interventionist image. The interpretation of him as a man of the people, who had the insight to appreciate the merits of a policy of imperial consolidation and social reform, became widely held by Conservatives in the 1890s. It was underpinned by the conclusion to the six-volume biography of him begun by W. F. Monypenny and finished after Monypenny's death by G. E. Buckle in 1920. (However, buried in the rest of the work is a great deal of material about other aspects of Disraeli's ideas. It remains the only biography to treat those ideas with anything like the importance they deserve, in a conscious effort to answer Liberal and other criticisms of his lack of convictions.) This tory democrat myth did not survive detailed scrutiny by professional historical writing of the 1960s. Specific works by Paul Smith (1967) and Maurice Cowling (1967) demonstrated that Disraeli had little interest in a programme of social legislation and was very flexible in handling parliamentary reform in 1867. Meanwhile, Robert Blake's biography of 1966, written with enviable elegance and shrewdness, replaced the old interpretations with an insistent pragmatism. Blake paid little attention to Disraeli's ideas, and belittled his philosophy as 'romantic but basically unrealistic'. He described his views on foreign policy as 'out of touch with the realities of the day', his imperial notions of 1872 as 'casual'—though he had been articulating them for four decades—and the arguments of Young England as 'gothic rubbish' (Blake, 758, 570–71, 523, 172). Instead, he pointed up Disraeli's inconsistency, oddly suggesting that his willingness to take office under Peel in 1841 cast doubt on his sincerity in later attacking him, and that his later practice was 'essentially Peelite' (ibid., 759). This argument articulated an anachronistic but then fashionable view of nineteenth-century politics that saw Peel rather than Disraeli as the founder of the Conservative Party by basing its electoral fortunes on a 'constructive' appeal to the middle classes.

More recent work on the changing electoral and ideological contexts of Victorian politics has underlined the pre-modernity of Disraeli's political world, while undermining facile comparisons of him with Peel. There has been comparatively little interest in Disraeli's political practice, but a great deal in his fiction, his ideas, his psychological orientation, and his Jewishness. These studies have revealed problems in Blake's interpretation, and drawn attention to Disraeli's uniqueness. Some scholars have begun the attempt to integrate his ideas with his practice, but in general scepticism still abounds about the latter. There has also been considerable speculation about Disraeli's private life, which was sanitized by Monypenny and Buckle (in whose biography there is not even any coherent reference to Henrietta Sykes). One biography of 1993 suggested that Disraeli had not just extramarital affairs (which seems likely) but also two illegitimate children in the mid-1860s: a boy, Ralph, with Lady Dorothy Nevill, and a girl, Catherine Donovan (Weintraub, 427–36). It is unlikely that such allegations will ever be proved, not least because Rose and later his son, as executors, deliberately destroyed many of Disraeli's letters.

Throughout the twentieth century, then, interpretations of Disraeli revolved around two issues: the extent of his sympathy for democracy, and his assumed lack of principle. The decline of the 'tory democrat' interpretation, combined with the vitality of the notion that Disraeli sat loose to convictions, has had the effect of diminishing respect for his political achievement. Yet the suggestion that he was an unscrupulous charlatan was originally just as politically motivated as the heroic tory democrat interpretation (though assisted by his youthful self-exposure). It was first associated with his Peelite opponents and later with Liberals and with Disraeli's high tory enemies, who used his conduct over protection and parliamentary reform as their major examples. It also has to be said that Victorian snobbery and antisemitism, and Liberal moralism then and since, have played a large part in entrenching it.

Concluding assessment It is arguable not only that both these dominant interpretations are misconceived in themselves but that they have positively hindered the attempt to understand Disraeli by leading enquirers down side-tracks. There is surely no need to cast the career of such an egotist, élitist, and parliamentary intriguer in a populist light in order to understand it. Disraeli had fixed notions about the attractiveness of a few electoral cries, such as anti-Catholicism. But he had little detailed electoral knowledge, at any rate outside the home counties and Lancashire, and though on occasion he positioned himself in accordance with these fixed notions, on many others he did not do so. In any case, all his instincts were attuned to an era before that in which elections were won by national policy initiatives. He always talked of the tories as the national and popular party, but this was in contrast to whig exclusiveness and factionalism. He believed that leadership required imaginative insight into the popular psychology, and that historically inspired patriotic and monarchical language had the potential to appeal to the British public. But his rhetoric in these areas arguably aimed not so much to exploit existing prejudices for electoral gain as to tease out a rarely articulated patriotism from beneath a dominant complacency about continental affairs; this, he believed, was the job of leadership. As for his supposed inconsistency, to say that he had to abandon his original position on protection and parliamentary reform is to say little more than that he lived in the nineteenth century. Altered perspectives were imposed on all politicians of his generation; Gladstone made a virtue of them. He retained a studied flexibility on some difficult issues (such as Catholic endowment). He also habitually romanticized and exaggerated potentially humdrum affairs. However, that was because he viewed politics not as a legislative draftsman but as an artist and sociologist. He was exceptionally anxious to develop and adhere to an individual interpretation of social and political movements. He was a first-rate politician because he upheld that individual interpretation while demonstrating a necessary expediency in parliamentary manoeuvre.

Disraeli's was not a trained university mind, and it is not surprising that more fastidious intellects have criticized his 'fatal facility in suggesting hazy theories' and his lack of 'the kind of practical sagacity which most easily inspires Englishmen with confidence' (*Historical Essays*, 492, 486). But his haziness can be exaggerated. He had coherent ideas on the importance of the land, the church, and historic tory ideals in maintaining civilization and social cohesion, and about the threat posed to nineteenth-century society by the (in fact very gradual) decay of these 'traditionary influences'. This pessimistic analysis, natural in a romantic historian, was mitigated by a fascination with the interplay of social forces and with the human comedy of which he was an acutely ironic observer. His love of life and nature, his constant sense of wonder at new experiences, and his sanguine temperament ensured that—when not affected by a self-obsessive melancholy—he was in a good humour with the world. In any case, he had very limited power to arrest the development of Victorian political society: he could do nothing about the triumph of free trade, the decline of the old colonial relationships, and the waning of paternalism. For much of his life he had to accept the broad policy assumptions laid down by Liberal politicians.

Notwithstanding all this, Disraeli's objective was clearly conservative: to frustrate radical initiatives which he saw as challenging national institutions and traditions. He disparaged the raising of contentious issues (and therefore premature declarations of opinion on them) unless there was a chance of solving them. All his major political moves were designed to settle questions, to take them out of the political sphere, to prevent destructive social or parliamentary agitation. When confronted with specific problems, he sought to reduce tension between town and country, landlords and farmers, capital and labour, and warring religious sects in Britain and Ireland—in other words, to create a unifying synthesis. 'Practical' social legislation was useful to the extent that it reduced the threat of government on abstract 'socialist' and centralizing principles. Had he not made possible the 1867 Reform

Act, something similar would have been enacted, but it might well not have been as conservative in its social instincts and would certainly not have been as beneficial to the Conservative Party.

It must also be remembered that one objective of the struggle of 1867 was to put the party on a better footing so that it might escape having to endure another minority government, in which there was always the danger of being forced to accept radical proposals. Before 1868 Disraeli believed that he had no choice but to work with radicals; he also believed, rightly, that he was skilful enough to do so on honourably Conservative terms. This is not to deny that he was addicted to conspiracy. Moreover, he was not an infallibly expert parliamentary operator: despite the mask of aloof imperturbability that he wore in the Commons, he was impulsive and sometimes short-sighted tactically, and his colleague Northcote remarked that he always spoiled his hand by 'overdoing something or other' (Monypenny and Buckle, 4.297). None the less, his long-term aim for the party was a position of independence. He believed that the only way in which strong government and Conservative ideas could be upheld, while constitutional and local liberties were secured, was by the maintenance of a two-party system in which parties were faithful to their ideals. The Conservative Party might easily have been swallowed in coalitions headed by whig grandees. Instead he sought Conservative leadership of a strong party that defended Burkean traditional influences against abstractions, novelties, and democratic enthusiasms. However, his theory that there should be a natural aristocratic and a natural democratic party was only partly realized in his lifetime, since propertied Liberals succeeded in keeping radicals on a tight rein.

Disraeli certainly did not offer electors a programme of legislation, or even speak in public to any significant extent. In 1879–80 he was contemptuous of Gladstone's 'spouting all over the country, like an irresponsible demagogue', which was 'wholly inexcusable in a man who was a statesman' (Monypenny and Buckle, 6.524). After the 1880 election he asserted the right of politicians to challenge the spirit of the age, which was 'generally public sentiment' and 'frequently … public passion' (*Hansard 3*, 255, 107–8). From the time of the Bulgarian agitation Disraeli believed that Gladstone had abandoned the politics of gentlemanliness: 'posterity will do justice to that unprincipled maniac Gladstone … with one commanding characteristic—… whether preaching, praying, speechifying, or scribbling—never a gentleman!' (Monypenny and Buckle, 6.67). Disraeli's beliefs and political position required him to maintain that parliament was at the centre of public life and that the guiding principle of parliament was that it was a free assembly of gentlemen. He attached immense significance to its traditions and dignity, which he upheld with studious ceremony. He attached equal importance to his image in parliament: he dyed his hair, which he carefully arranged (with increasing difficulty) to preserve the trademark curl on his forehead; he resorted only to an inadequate eye-glass to remedy chronic short-sightedness; his figure was assisted by stays, of which a glimpse could occasionally be seen protruding from his frock coat (fortunately, he had a small appetite). The basis of his power was his parliamentary influence. His performance in the Commons was never without its critics; some detected a tendency to 'false melodramatic taste' (*Historical Essays*, 486). His success there was due to his devastating capacity to discern his opponents' weak (and strong) points: his epigrammatic sarcasm increasingly intimidated them from attacking him, and dissuaded rivals from seeking to supplant him and banish him to a dangerous exile below the gangway. Disraeli held tenaciously to the party leadership in the Commons for twenty-eight years; but he did so by dint of rhetorical bravado and dextrous party management, not by exploiting his position outside parliament even to the extent that Palmerston did, let alone Gladstone. As late as 1876 Bagehot claimed that 'ten miles from London … there is scarcely any real conception of him' (ibid., 504).

Disraeli had little time for demagogic politics because of his intensely individualistic conception of political leadership. Whatever the crisis, his letters were full of boasts that he was the man who had arranged affairs, that no one else was on hand to share the responsibility, or that no one else was competent (though in public he was nearly always very supportive of his disciples, earning their loyalty). His astonishing egotism sustained him through all the rejections of his career. It was all the more effective for being tempered by adversity, preventing the bumptious flamboyance of his youth from hardening into an inflexible arrogance. He had a remarkable capacity to learn from his mistakes. His tenacity and will-power allowed him to conquer his youthful lethargy and periodic depressions; they gave him courage when isolated and defiance in defeat. The conviction of his superiority to the fools and drones whom he observed occupying high positions in society and politics never left him. He disliked the company of intellectual equals: he preferred to be surrounded by idealistic young men and, especially, by sympathetic women who could caress his ego. He was never vindictive except when he thought his honour had been impugned; that he regarded as a heinous offence.

As he despised the parochialism of little men, commercial opinions, and ecclesiastical factionalism, only his ardour for the political game saved Disraeli from being bored by most of what counted for politics in Britain. He sought a stage fit for a great man: he loved to philosophize about the fate of races, nations, and empires. Sometimes he fantasized; sometimes he stuck to outdated ideas; usually there was a kernel of real insight. He reflected at length on the conflicts and consequential radical dangers facing Europe in a way that distanced him from insular contemporaries. He believed it essential to alter blinkered and comfortable domestic views of the continent; he hoped that a more patriotic public voice would increase Britain's European clout while keeping defence expenditure low. He was helped by the alarms generated by the expansion of Germany and Russia and their emergence as rival 'empires', which encouraged acceptance of the word

in British debate. When Disraeli talked of empire, he meant the historic and symbolic greatness of England, exemplified by its power in Europe and its global prestige. This certainly did not necessitate territorial acquisition, especially if that illuminated military weakness. It did require an active European policy and an attitude of resistance to Russia. Disraeli was innately attracted by the merits of an assertive international stance, but, true to character, he also saw the specifics of the Eastern crisis in terms of short-term parliamentary necessity on the one hand, and the long-term aim of sustaining the aristocratic European order against militarism or revolution on the other.

Disraeli's grandiose ideas, cynicism about human motives, and his ability to marry high rhetoric with low intrigue, make him a difficult figure to read. Many of his enthusiasms and objectives would have been more familiar to continental politicians, or to those of an earlier period, than to his British contemporaries. Bright took exception to his candid declaration that the search for fame brought him to parliament, though this was an eighteenth-century commonplace. His egocentricity can be seen as that of an eternally maladjusted social-climbing adolescent, or that of an unprivileged outsider forced to endure watching the social and political prizes go to lesser men with better connections. His foreign policy can be seen as a gigantic castle in the air (as it was by Gladstone), or as an overdue attempt to force the British commercial classes to awaken to the realities of European politics. With Gladstone, Disraeli was one of the two most fascinating and complex politicians of the nineteenth century. He was hardly understood at the time, and it would be presumptuous to claim that he is fully understandable now. Neither Gladstone nor Disraeli communicated very clearly what he really felt; certainly neither understood the other. But they shared a rebelliousness against the complacency and materialism of mid-Victorian Britain. Disraeli used un-English insights to urge on England a world role befitting her power and traditional values. Given the weight of commercial, sectional, and isolationist opinion in the country, this was a task that was bound to involve more failure than victory. After his last election defeat he told the Social Democratic Federation leader H. M. Hyndman that England was 'a very difficult country to move … and one in which there is more disappointment to be looked for than success' (Blake, 764). Disraeli certainly suffered many disappointments and rejections in his courting of the British political classes. He wanted to play both the roles that he idealized in his novels, the artist–prophet and the man of action; political circumstances conspired to ensure that he had few chances to put his insights into practice. Even so, the conclusion must be that, though only intermittently, Disraeli still succeeded, infinitely more than anyone could have imagined, in realizing the object of political life that he set out in the poem he wrote for his wife's birthday in 1846: 'to sway the race that sways the world' (*Letters*, 4.250).

JONATHAN PARRY

Sources W. F. Monypenny and G. E. Buckle, *The life of Benjamin Disraeli*, 6 vols. (1910–20) • R. Blake, *Disraeli* (1966) • *Disraeli's reminiscences*, ed. H. M. Swartz and M. Swartz (1975) • *Benjamin Disraeli letters*, ed. J. A. W. Gunn and others (1982–) • *Letters of Disraeli to Lady Chesterfield and Lady Bradford*, ed. marquis of Zetland, 2 vols. (1929) • *Selected speeches of the late earl of Beaconsfield*, ed. T. E. Kebbel, 2 vols. (1882) • B. Disraeli, *Vindication of the English constitution in a letter to a noble and learned lord* (1835) • B. Disraeli, *Lord George Bentinck: a political biography* (1852) • *Disraeli, Derby and the conservative party: journals and memoirs of Edward Henry, Lord Stanley, 1849–1869*, ed. J. R. Vincent (1978) • *A selection from the diaries of Edward Henry Stanley, 15th earl of Derby (1826–93), between March 1869 and September 1878*, ed. J. R. Vincent, CS, 5th ser., 4 (1994) • S. Bradford, *Disraeli* (1982) • J. R. Vincent, *Disraeli* (1990) • S. Weintraub, *Disraeli: a biography* (1993) • J. Ridley, *The young Disraeli* (1995) • P. Smith, *Disraeli: a brief life* (1996) • D. R. Schwarz, *Disraeli's fiction* (1979) • B. Disraeli, *Inaugural address delivered to the University of Glasgow* (1873) • *Hansard 3* • C. Howard and P. Gordon, eds., 'The cabinet journal of Dudley Ryder, Viscount Sandon', *BIHR*, special suppl., 10 (1974) [whole issue] • *The historical essays*, ed. N. St John-Stevas (1968), vol. 3 of *The collected works of Walter Bagehot* • H. Lucy, *A diary of two parliaments: the Disraeli parliament, 1874–1880* (1885) • J. Bryce, *Studies in contemporary biography* (1903) • R. S. Gower, *Records and reminiscences* (1903) • T. E. Kebbel, *Lord Beaconsfield and other tory memories* (1907) • *The diary of Gathorne Hardy, later Lord Cranbrook, 1866–1892: political selections*, ed. N. E. Johnson (1981) • A. Lang, *Life, letters and diaries of Sir Stafford Northcote*, 2 vols. (1890) • G. Cecil, *Life of Robert, marquis of Salisbury*, 4 vols. (1921–32) • D. J. Mitchell, *Cross and tory democracy: a political biography of Richard Assheton Cross* (1991) • J. Ogden, *Isaac D'Israeli* (1969) • M. Cowling, *1867: Disraeli, Gladstone and revolution* (1967) • P. Smith, *Disraelian Conservatism and social reform* (1967) • E. J. Feuchtwanger, *Disraeli, democracy and the tory party: conservative leadership and organization after the second Reform Bill* (1968) • R. Millman, *Britain and the Eastern question, 1875–1878* (1979) • M. Swartz, *The politics of British foreign policy in the era of Disraeli and Gladstone* (1985) • R. Stewart, *The foundation of the conservative party, 1830–1867* (1978) • R. Shannon, *The age of Disraeli, 1868–1881: the rise of tory democracy* (1992) • H. C. G. Matthew, 'Disraeli, Gladstone, and the politics of mid-Victorian budgets', *HJ*, 22 (1979), 615–43 • P. R. Ghosh, 'Disraelian conservatism: a financial approach', *EngHR*, 99 (1984), 268–96 • P. R. Ghosh, 'Style and substance in Disraelian social reform, c.1860–80', *Politics and social change in modern Britain*, ed. P. J. Waller (1987) • M. Cowling, 'Lytton, the cabinet and the Russians, August to November 1878', *EngHR*, 76 (1961), 59–79 • A. Warren, 'Disraeli, the conservatives and the government of Ireland', *Parliamentary History*, 18 (1999), 45–64, 145–67 • A. Warren, 'Disraeli, the conservatives and the national church', *Parliamentary History*, 19 (2000), 96–117 • J. P. Parry, 'Disraeli and England', *HJ*, 43 (2000), 699–728 • GEC, *Peerage*

Archives BL, corresp., RP 134 [photocopies of exported MSS] • BL, corresp. with secretary, Add. MS 58210 • BL, letters and papers, Add. MS 59887 • Bodl. Oxf., corresp., diaries, literary MSS, papers • Bodl. Oxf., household accounts • Bodl. Oxf., Hughenden MSS • Col. U., Rare Book and Manuscript Library, letters and papers • Hunt. L., letters • Jewish Museum, Finchley, London, MSS • NA Scot., letters • NL Wales, letters • NRA, priv. coll., corresp. and MSS • Queen's University, Kingston, Ontario, corresp. • University of Illinois, Chicago, letters and papers | Alnwick Castle, Northumberland, letters to Sir Henry Drummond; corresp. with duke of Northumberland • BL, corresp. with Benjamin Austen, Add. MS 45908 • BL, corresp. with fifth Earl Beauchamp and sixth Earl Beauchamp, Add. MS 61892 • BL, corresp. with Lord Carnarvon, Add. MSS 60763–60764 • BL, corresp. with Lord Cross, Add. MS 51265 • BL, corresp. with W. E. Gladstone, Add. MSS 44374–44652 • BL, corresp. with John Charles Herries, Add. MS 57409 • BL, Iddesleigh MSS • BL, corresp. with Sir Austen Layard, Add. MSS 39130–39137 • BL, corresp. with Sir Stafford Northcote, Add. MSS 50015–50018 • BL, corresp. with Sir Robert Peel, Add. MSS 40421–40539 • BL, letters, as sponsor, to Royal Literary Fund, loan 96 • BL, letters to his sister Sarah, Add. MS 74793 • BL, letters to his sister Sarah and others, Add. MS 37502 • BL OIOC, corresp. with Lord Napier, MS Eur. F 114 • Bodl. Oxf., corresp., mainly with William Beckford • Bodl. Oxf., corresp. with Sir William Harcourt • Bodl. Oxf., corresp. with Sir Thomas Phillipps • Bodl. Oxf., letters to Bernard Quaritch • Bodl. Oxf., letters to Samuel Wilberforce • Bucks. RLSS, corresp. with Lord Cottesloe • CKS, corresp. with duke of Cleveland and duchess of Cleveland • CKS, corresp. with Lord Stanhope • CKS, letters to Edward Stanhope • CUL, letters to duke of Marlborough • Durham RO, corresp. with Frances Anne, marchioness of Londonderry; letters to third marquis of Londonderry • FM Cam., letters to William Pyne; literary papers and family corresp. • Glos. RO, corresp. with Sir Michael Hicks Beach • Harrowby Manuscript Trust, Sandon Hall, Staffordshire, letters to Lord Harrowby • Herts. ALS, corresp. with first Baron Lytton • Herts. ALS, corresp. with first earl of Lytton • HLRO, corresp. with Sir Henry Brand • HLRO, letters to Lord Cadogan and Lady Cadogan • Hunt. L., letters to Grenville family • ING Barings, London, letters to Thomas Baring • Jewish Museum, Finchley, London, letters to Sir Charles Fremantle • Jewish Museum, Finchley, London, letters to Lady Dorothy Nevill • Jewish Museum, Finchley, London, letters to his sister Sarah and others • Jewish Museum, Finchley, London, letters to Spencer Walpole • LMA, letters relating to Francis Villiers • LPL, letters to A. C. Tait • Lpool RO, letters to fourteenth earl of Derby • Lpool RO, corresp. with fifteenth earl of Derby • Mitchell L., Glas., Glasgow City Archives, letters to Sir William Stirling-Maxwell • NA Scot., letters to Lord Rosslyn and Lady Rosslyn • News Int. RO, letters to John Thadeus Delane • NRA, priv. coll., letters to Lady Dorothy Nevill • NRA, priv. coll., letters to earl of Rosebery • NRA, priv. coll., letters to John Swinton • NRA, priv. coll., letters to S. H. Walpole • NRA, priv. coll., corresp. with Lord Wemyss • PRO, corresp. with Lord Ampthill, FO 918/5/1–10 • PRO, letters to Lord Cairns, PRO 30/51 • PRO NIre., letters to Lord Abercorn • PRO NIre., letters to Lady Londonderry • Royal Arch., corresp. with Queen Victoria • Som. ARS, letters to Sir William Jolliffe • St Deiniol's Library, Hawarden, corresp. with Sir Thomas Gladstone • Staffs. RO, corresp. with earls of Bradford and countess of Chesterfield • Staffs. RO, corresp. with duchess of Sutherland • Suff. RO, Ipswich, letters to Lord Cranbrook • Trinity Cam., letters to Lord Houghton • U. Durham L., corresp. with third Earl Grey • U. Durham L., corresp. with Charles Grey • U. Durham L., letters to John, Viscount Ponsonby • U. Nott. L., letters to John Evelyn Denison • U. Nott. L., letters to Viscount Galway • U. Nott. L., corresp. with Lord John Manners • U. Nott. L., letters to Lord Portland • U. Reading L., corresp. with Longmans • U. Southampton L., corresp. with Lord Palmerston • UCL, corresp. with Sir Edwin Chadwick • W. H. Smith and Son Ltd, Abingdon, letters to W. H. Smith • W. Sussex RO, letters to Lady Caroline Maxse • W. Sussex RO, letters to William Townley Mitford • W. Sussex RO, letters to fifth duke of Richmond • W. Sussex RO, letters to sixth duke of Richmond • W. Yorks. AS, Calderdale, letters to Sir Henry Edwards • Watts Gallery, Compton, Surrey, letters to G. F. Watts • Worcs. RO, letters to Sir John Pakington

Likenesses drawing, 1812, Hughenden Manor, Buckinghamshire • S. Frugoni, marble bust, 1827, Hughenden Manor, Buckinghamshire • D. Maclise, drawing, 1828, Hughenden Manor, Buckinghamshire • D. Maclise, drawing, 1833, repro. in *Fraser's Magazine* • by or after D. Maclise, pen-and-ink cartoon, c.1833, NPG; repro. in *Fraser's Magazine*, 7 (1833) • A. E. Chalon, pencil drawing, 1840, Hughenden Manor, Buckinghamshire • W. Behnes, marble bust, 1847, Hughenden Manor, Buckinghamshire • F. Grant, oils, 1852, Hughenden Manor, Buckinghamshire • Mayall, cartes-de-visite, 1860–69, NPG • T. J. Barker, oils, 1862, Hughenden Manor, Buckinghamshire • W. P. Frith, group portrait, oils, 1863 (*The marriage of the prince of Wales*), Royal Collection • Downie, carte-de-visite, 1868, NPG • C. Lucy, oils, c.1869, V&A • J. Blackburn, drawing, 1873 (*Disraeli attending chapel at Glasgow University*), Hughenden Manor, Buckinghamshire • J. Blackburn, drawing, 1873 (*Being sworn in as rector*), Hughenden Manor, Buckinghamshire • C. Mercier, group portrait, 1874 (*The Disraeli cabinet, 1874*), Junior Carlton

Club, London • H. von Angeli, oils, 1877, Royal Collection • T. Blake Wirgman, oils, 1877, Weston Park, Shropshire • J. Hughes, photographs, 1878, repro. in Blake, *Disraeli*, facing p. 741 • J. Hughes, photographs, 1878 • R. Leveson-Gower, bronzed plaster bust, 1878–9, NPG • Count Gleichen, marble bust, 1880, Royal Collection • F. Sargent, group portrait, wash drawing, *c.*1880 (*Disraeli addressing the House of Lords*), Palace of Westminster, London • H. Weigall, oils, 1880, Burghley House, Northamptonshire • R. C. Belt, bronze bust, 1881, Wallace Collection, London • R. C. Belt, medallion on memorial, *c.*1881, Hughenden church, Buckinghamshire • R. Glassby, wax death mask, 1881, NPG • J. E. Millais, oils, 1881, NPG [*see illus.*] • W. H. Thornycroft, plaster statuette, 1881, NPG • C. B. Birch, bronze statue, 1883, St George's Hall, Liverpool • J. E. Boehm, marble statue, 1883, Westminster Abbey • Count Gleichen, marble statue, 1883, Palace of Westminster, London • M. Raggi, bronze statue, 1883, Parliament Square, London • H. T. Margetson, statue, 1884, Moorgate, Ormskirk • T. Rawcliffe, statue, 1887, Queen's Park, Bolton • J. Adams-Acton, bust, Gov. Art Coll. • H. Barraud, group portrait, oils (*The lobby of the House of Commons, 1872–3*), Palace of Westminster, London • R. Caldecott, chalk caricature, NPG • attrib. R. Cosway, drawing (as a child), Hughenden Manor, Buckinghamshire • W. & D. Downey, photographs, NPG • J. Doyle, several caricatures, NPG • R. Doyle, caricature, pen-and-ink drawing (*Lord Derby conferring the DCL on Disraeli*), BM • R. Doyle, double portrait, caricature, pen-and-ink drawing (with Lord John Russell), BM • H. Furniss, caricatures, several pen-and-ink sketches, NPG • H. Gales, group portrait, watercolour (*The Derby cabinet, 1867*), NPG • R. Leveson-Gower, statuette, Hughenden Manor, Buckinghamshire • Lock & Whitfield, photographs, NPG • London Stereoscopic Co., photographs, NPG • Mayall, photographs, NPG • C. Pellegrini, chromolithograph caricature, NPG; repro. in *VF* (30 Jan 1869) • C. Pellegrini, chromolithograph caricature, NPG; repro. in *VF* (2 July 1878) • J. Phillip, group portrait (*The House of Commons in 1860*), Palace of Westminster, London • Spy [L. Ward], chromolithograph caricature, NPG; repro. in *VF* (16 Dec 1879) • Henry Taunt & Co., photographs, NPG • H. Weigall, oils, Royal Commonwealth Society, London • cartoons, repro. in Blake, *Disraeli*, facing p. 708 • engraving (after photograph by Mayall), repro. in Blake, *Disraeli*, frontispiece • photographs (one as a young man), Hughenden Manor, Buckinghamshire • portraits, repro. in Monypenny and Buckle, *Life* • various caricatures, BM, NPG

Wealth at death £84,019 18s. 7d.: resworn probate, April 1882, *CGPLA Eng. & Wales* (1881)

D'Israeli, Isaac (1766–1848), writer, was born on 11 May 1766 at 5 Great St Helen's, London, the only child of Benjamin D'Israeli (1730–1816), merchant, and his second wife, Sarah Syprut de Gabay Villa Real (1742/3–1825). D'Israeli's father was born at Cento, Ferrara, emigrated to London in 1748, and began business on his own there in 1757 as an importer of Italian goods, especially the fashionable Leghorn straw hats. From 1776 he was also in business as a stockbroker, and in 1801 he became an English denizen and a founder member of the London stock exchange. On his death his estate was valued at £35,000. D'Israeli's mother was the daughter of one of her husband's business associates. His father seems to have been sociable and generous, and his mother withdrawn and difficult.

Isaac was 'a pale, pensive child, with large brown eyes, and flowing hair … timid, susceptible, lost in reverie, fond of solitude, or seeking no better company than a book' (Disraeli, 'Life and writings', xi). He was sent to a school kept by a Scotsman named Morison, near Enfield, Middlesex, where his father had a country house. The elder D'Israeli hoped his son would go into business, and in 1780–81

Isaac D'Israeli (1766–1848), by Daniel Maclise, 1828

sent him to stay with his agent in Amsterdam; but he showed no aptitude for business, began to acquire a wide knowledge of modern languages and literatures, and came home determined to be a poet and man of letters. His mother ridiculed his ambition, and his father urged him to join a commercial house at Bordeaux, so he wrote a satire on commerce, which he left at Bolt Court hoping for Dr Johnson's approval, but Johnson was ill and the manuscript was returned unread. D'Israeli's first critical article was a vindication of Johnson's character in the *Gentleman's Magazine* for December 1786. His first published poem was a panegyric on Richard Gough the topographer, an Enfield neighbour, in the *St James's Chronicle* for 20 November 1787, to which Gough wrote a sarcastic reply. His father's patience was exhausted, and in 1788–9 D'Israeli was sent abroad again, to travel in France, Germany, and Italy. He became an enthusiast for French philosophy and, for a time, the French Revolution. In July 1789 he achieved some notoriety by publishing an anonymous satire on the popular satirist Peter Pindar (Dr John Wolcot) in the *Gentleman's Magazine*. Wolcot attributed the satire to the poet William Hayley and published a counterblast, whereupon D'Israeli acknowledged the authorship and was befriended not only by some of Wolcot's earlier victims but also by Wolcot himself. The friendly intervention of Henry James Pye, the poet laureate, may have persuaded the elder D'Israeli to acquiesce in his son's adoption of a literary career; D'Israeli's first volume of verse, *A Defence of Poetry* (1790), was dedicated to Pye. As a poet his most ambitious work was *Narrative Poems* (1803). His neo-classical manner was by then hopelessly outmoded, but being a poet of sorts himself he had a sympathetic understanding of the poetical temperament.

In 1791 D'Israeli inherited the whole fortune of his maternal grandmother Esther Syprut, and so became financially independent. He took rooms in James Street, Adelphi, then a haunt of literary men, and began to frequent the British Museum, where he met Francis Douce and other scholars. In the same year he published anonymously the first volume of *Curiosities of literature, consisting of anecdotes, characters, sketches, and observations, literary, critical, and historical*. This compilation followed the fashion for biographical anecdotes, and was an immediate success. A second volume, with the author's name on the title-page, was added in 1793; a third in 1817; and a *Second Series*, in three more volumes, in 1823. The work was often revised (13th edn, 1843) and gradually became more like a collection of essays. Between 1794 and 1796 D'Israeli apparently suffered a nervous breakdown, certainly enjoyed a convalescence at Exeter, and wrote *An Essay on the Literary Character* (1795), and *Miscellanies, or, Literary Recreations* (1796), which he dedicated to his medical adviser Dr Hugh Downman. By now his books had made a name for him in London, and in 1796 he was the subject of a highly respectful 'Biographical sketch' in the *Monthly Mirror*. Expanded versions of the *Essay*, under the title *The Literary Character*, appeared in 1818, 1822 (2 vols.), and 1828 (2 vols.). It developed into an influential study of the characteristics of men of genius, and a romantic assertion of their importance to society. Offshoots were *Calamities of Authors* (2 vols., 1812) and *Quarrels of Authors* (3 vols., 1814).

D'Israeli for a time fancied himself as a writer of prose fiction. His *Romances* ('Mejnoun and Leila: a Persian Romance', 'Love and Humility: a Roman Romance', and 'The Lovers, or, The Birth of the Pleasing Arts: an Arcadian Romance') were published in 1797 (3rd edn, 1807). 'Mejnoun and Leila' was the most elaborate of these, and its flowery orientalism had some influence on Benjamin Disraeli. D'Israeli's first novel, *Vaurien, or, Sketches of the Times*, also appeared in 1797. *Flim-Flams! or, The Life and Errors of my Uncle* followed in 1805 (2nd edn, 1806) and *Despotism, or, The Fall of the Jesuits* in 1811. *Vaurien* was a satire on William Godwin and other English Jacobins; *Flim-Flams!* in a more frivolous vein satirized various contemporary literary men, scientists, and inventors; *Despotism* was a melodramatic historical novel comparing the despotisms of the Jesuits and Napoleon. D'Israeli pioneered types of subject-matter and modes of presentation which were more effectively used by Thomas Love Peacock, Benjamin Disraeli, and others, but his novels lacked interesting characterization and artistic unity.

On 10 February 1802 D'Israeli entered 'the matrimonial state of literature' (a chapter heading in *The Literary Character*). His wife, Maria Basevi (1774/5–1847), belonged to another Italian-Jewish family living in London, and was the aunt of the architect George Basevi (1794–1845). The marriage was a happy one. The D'Israelis went to live at 6 King's Road, Bedford Row, where their five children were born: Sarah (1802–1859); Benjamin *Disraeli (1804–1881), the statesman and novelist; Naphtali (b. 1807, died in infancy); Ralph (1809–1898); and James (1813–1868). The children were named according to Jewish naming customs, and the boys were circumcised. D'Israeli was a member of the Bevis Marks Synagogue, and an annual contributor to its funds, but not a regular attender at its services. In 1813 the elders elected him warden, anticipating that he would refuse to serve and pay a fine. D'Israeli told them the office was 'repulsive to his feelings'; he could 'never unite in your public worship because, as now conducted, it disturbs, instead of exciting, religious emotions' (Picciotto, 297–8). He refused to pay a fine, and after a long quarrel withdrew from the synagogue in 1821. In a chapter in *Vaurien*, an essay on Moses Mendelssohn (*Monthly Magazine*, 6, July 1798, 38–44), and especially in *The Genius of Judaism* (1833), D'Israeli argued for the emancipation of the Jews rather than their conversion to Christianity, and for the Jews themselves to educate their children as 'the youth of Europe, and not of Palestine' (D'Israeli, *The Genius of Judaism*, 1833, 265). On the advice of his friend the historian Sharon Turner, all his children were baptized at St Andrew's, Holborn, in 1817, but apparently membership of the Church of England was valued for its social advantages. In the same year the family moved to a larger house in Bloomsbury Square near the British Museum, and in 1829 they moved to Bradenham House near High Wycombe. This part of Buckinghamshire attracted D'Israeli by its many literary and historical associations.

D'Israeli was well known in several literary circles. Pye introduced him to the poet Samuel Rogers, who enviously remarked, 'There is a man with only half an intellect; and yet he makes books that can't help living' (*Selections from the Letters of Robert Southey*, 4.265). He was for a while on the fringe of the Jacobin group associated with the publisher Richard Phillips and the bookseller Joseph Johnson, and was one of the early customers for William Blake's illuminated books. But D'Israeli's own books were mostly published by John Murray II, and through him he met Murray's other authors and contributors to the tory *Quarterly Review*. Among these was Sir Walter Scott, who at their first meeting is said to have repeated one of D'Israeli's poems, adding 'if the writer of these lines had gone on, he would have been an English poet' (Disraeli, 'Life and writings', xxv). Lord Byron greatly admired *The Literary Character* and told Murray 'I don't know a living man's book I take up so often or lay down more reluctantly' (Smiles, 152). When a defence of the poetry of Pope appeared in the *Quarterly* in 1820 Byron was delighted and recognized D'Israeli as the author by the style. Robert Southey thought D'Israeli 'thoroughly good-natured, the strangest mixture of information and ignorance, cleverness and folly' (*Selections from the Letters of Robert Southey*, 3.352). D'Israeli dedicated the fourth edition of *The Literary Character* to him, remarking that knowing each other primarily through their books they had long enjoyed 'an intimacy, without the inconvenience, often resulting from a personal acquaintance' (Ogden, 126). D'Israeli also met through Murray the poet Thomas Moore, the critic John Wilson Croker, and the antiquary Thomas Crofton Croker. Moore he also met at the Athenaeum, and Crofton Croker at the Society of Antiquaries. Murray quarrelled with the D'Israeli family in 1826 when with some reason the publisher thought himself caricatured in Benjamin's novel *Vivian Grey*. But Benjamin introduced his father to another admirer, Edward Bulwer-Lytton, who dedicated to D'Israeli the fourth book, *View of the Intellectual Spirit of the Time*, of his *England and the English* (1833). When he was in his seventies his son introduced him into Lady Blessington's circle, where he met Walter Savage Landor. D'Israeli, then, was a more sociable and forceful character than his son's memoir suggests.

In his own time D'Israeli had a considerable reputation as a historian. In 1816 he published *An Inquiry into the Literary and Political Character of James I*, and between 1828 and 1830 the five volumes of *Commentaries on the Life and Reign of Charles I*. *Commentaries* marked an advance in historical research, as D'Israeli consulted many unpublished manuscripts, but his claims to objectivity were exaggerated. Both works defend the Stuart kings against the whig historians; he concedes that they had their faults, but argues that James was no fool and Charles was a man more sinned against than sinning. The effect was to support a tory view of history, and so to influence the ideas of Benjamin Disraeli and the 'Young England' group. *Commentaries* was attacked for its implicit toryism by Lord Nugent in his *Memorials of Hampden* (1832), and D'Israeli immediately replied with the pamphlet *Eliot, Hampden, and Pym*. All three of these were reviewed by Robert Southey, who described *Commentaries* as 'by far the most important work' on its subject in recent times (*Quarterly Review*, 47, 1832, 470). It was as the defender of Charles I that D'Israeli was created honorary doctor of civil law by Oxford University later in the same year.

Commentaries distracted D'Israeli from his ultimate project, a history of English literature. In 1833 he returned to work on it, but by January 1835 he feared the deterioration of his eyesight would prevent its completion. Another problem was a controversy with the antiquarian Bolton Corney, who in *Curiosities of Literature Illustrated* (1837) exposed many of D'Israeli's mistakes in the original *Curiosities*. D'Israeli replied with *The Illustrator Illustrated* (1838), but Corney's attacks continued in further publications, and D'Israeli admitted that 'a voluminous miscellany, composed at various periods, cannot be exempted from slight inadvertencies' (*Curiosities*, 11th edn, 1839, 'Preface'). Towards the end of that year he suffered 'a paralysis of the optic nerve' (Disraeli, 'Life and writings', xxxv), or acute retinal degeneration, and became almost blind. But with the help of his daughter he was able to publish *Amenities of Literature* (3 vols., 1841), which he originally intended to call 'A fragment of a history of English literature'. In an unsystematic way *Amenities* carries the subject down to the early seventeenth century. It includes much curious information, appreciative essays on Chaucer, Skelton, and Spenser, and in the essay on Shakespeare an early protest against bardolatry. D'Israeli's enthusiasm saves him from the pedantry and dogmatism of some later authorities. *Amenities* was his last book, but he lived long enough

to see his son's first successes in literature and politics. He found Disraeli's *Tancred* (1847), a novel about the reconciliation of Judaism and Christianity, 'faultless in composition, profound in philosophy' (Monypenny and Buckle, 1.865). Isaac D'Israeli died at his home, Bradenham House, High Wycombe, Buckinghamshire, on 19 January 1848, a victim of influenza, and was buried in the churchyard at Bradenham.

D'Israeli's reputation in the nineteenth century was founded on his talent for popularizing literary and historical research. He read widely and in some fields deeply, and Bulwer-Lytton remarked that often what looked like gossip was really philosophy, especially in *The Literary Character*. Benjamin Disraeli edited new editions of *Curiosities* in 1849, of *Commentaries* in 1851, and of the complete literary and historical *Works* (other than *Commentaries*) in 1858–9. *Curiosities* and the *Works* were frequently reissued in popular editions both here and in the United States. Before the development of secondary and higher education, these books were for many readers exciting introductions to new areas of knowledge and speculation.

JAMES OGDEN

Sources J. Ogden, *Isaac D'Israeli* (1969) [incl. bibliography] • B. Disraeli, 'On the life and writings of Mr Disraeli', in I. D'Israeli, *Curiosities of literature*, 14th edn, 3 vols. (1849) • W. F. Monypenny and G. E. Buckle, *The life of Benjamin Disraeli*, rev. G. E. Buckle, 2nd edn, 2 vols. (1929) • S. Smiles, *A publisher and his friends: memoir and correspondence of the late John Murray*, 2 vols. (1891) • J. Picciotto, *Sketches of Anglo-Jewish history* (1875) • *Selections from the letters of Robert Southey*, ed. J. W. Warter, 4 vols. (1856) • H. F. Chorley, *Autobiography, memoir and letters*, ed. H. G. Hewlett (1873) • P. H. Emden, *Jews of Britain: a series of biographies* (1944) • L. Wolf, 'The Disraeli family', *The Times* (20–21 Dec 1904); repr. in *Transactions of the Jewish Historical Society of England*, 5 (1902–5), 202–18 • S. Kopstein, *Isaac D'Israeli* (1939) • *Benjamin Disraeli letters*, ed. J. A. W. Gunn and others (1982–), vols. 1–5 • d. cert. [M. D'Israeli]

Archives Bodl. Oxf., corresp., literary MSS, and papers • Hughenden Manor, High Wycombe, Buckinghamshire, Hughenden MSS, corresp. and MSS • Jewish Museum, London, MSS | BL, letters to Philip Bliss and others • Bodl. Oxf., corresp. with Francis Douce • John Murray, London, archives • Reform Congregation Keneseth Israel, Philadelphia, collection of Bertram Korn

Likenesses oils, c.1777, Hughenden Manor, Buckinghamshire • S. Drummond, oils, before 1797, repro. in *Monthly Mirror* (Jan 1797) • J. Downman, pencil drawing, 1804, NPG • J. Downman, watercolour drawing, 1805, Hughenden Manor, Buckinghamshire; repro. in R. Blake, *Disraeli* (1966) • D. Maclise, drawing, 1828 (half-length), Hughenden Manor [*see illus.*] • B. Norris, sketch, c.1832, priv. coll.; repro. in *Disraeli Newsletter*, 2 (1977) • pen-and-ink drawing, c.1832 (after D. Maclise), NPG; repro. in Ogden, *Isaac Disraeli* • S. P. Denning, drawing, 1834, Coningsby Disraeli collection; repro. in Monypenny and Buckle, *Life of Benjamin Disraeli* • Count D'Orsay, pencil drawing, 1839, NPG • J. B. Hunt, mezzotint (after S. Drummond), Cecil Roth collection; repro. in C. Roth, ed., *Encyclopaedia Judaica*, 16 vols. (1971–2) • H. Robinson, engraving (after portrait, c.1777), repro. in Disraeli, 'On the life and writings of Mr Disraeli', vol. 1 • H. Robinson, engraving (after Denning), repro. in Disraeli, 'On the life and writings of Mr Disraeli', vol. 3 • W. Ross, pencil and chalk drawing, BM

Wealth at death £10,803: Monypenny and Buckle, *Life of Benjamin Disraeli*, 1.961

Disraeli [*née* Evans; *other married name* Lewis], **Mary Anne**, **Viscountess Beaconsfield** (1792–1872), political wife,

Mary Anne Disraeli, Viscountess Beaconsfield (1792–1872), by James Godsell Middleton

was born in Exeter on 11 November 1792, the second surviving child and only daughter of John Evans (1760–1794), naval lieutenant, and his wife, Eleanor Viney (d. 1842), daughter of James Viney, vicar of Bishopstrow, Wiltshire. After her father's premature death in the West Indies, Mary Anne Evans and her elder brother, John, were brought up by their mother at Brampford Speke, near Exeter, the home of her Evans grandparents, a family of Devon farmers. In 1807 Mary Anne and her mother moved to Gloucester to live with her uncle, Sir James Viney of College Green. She was poorly educated, even by early nineteenth-century standards (according to Benjamin Disraeli, she never could remember which came first, the Greeks or the Romans), and her handwriting was execrable; but she early on acquired the habit of keeping accounts and compiling albums. In 1810 she moved to Bristol, where her mother married a second husband, the shadowy and unsatisfactory Thomas Yate. Mary Anne's life at this stage is clouded by myths, some of them invented by her; Augustus Hare's story that she walked barefoot to work in a factory each morning is untrue, though she may have worked in a milliner's shop. Small and birdlike—her feet were size four, her rings the size of a child's—she was a vivacious flirt in Bristol society. In 1815 she married Wyndham Lewis (1778–1838), fourteen years her senior and a wealthy ironmaster (he owned a one-fifth share in the Dowlais ironworks), and she went to live at Greenmeadow, near Cardiff, a small plain house, nestling under green hills and surrounded by dripping trees. She soon tired of the country, and as Wyndham Lewis grew rich on Dowlais profits, becoming MP for Cardiff (1820–26), Mary Anne propelled herself into London society. In 1827 they moved into 1 Grosvenor Gate (now 93 Park Lane), a smart white stucco house belonging to the Grosvenor estate overlooking Hyde Park, and here she flourished in a whirl of parties, one foot in the marquess of Worcester's disreputable set (she had several affairs), another in the literati: she was a friend of Rosina, wife of Edward Bulwer Lytton, and it was through her that she

met Benjamin Disraeli in 1832. 'A pretty little woman, a flirt and a rattle', was his verdict; but he made sufficient impression for Lewis to invite him at the last minute to come in as second tory member for Maidstone at the 1837 election.

In March 1838 Wyndham Lewis suddenly died. On 28 August 1839 Mary Anne married Benjamin *Disraeli (1804–1881). Initially, at least, it was a match of expediency. Disraeli, desperately in debt, needed the wealthy widow's money; Mary Anne, who at forty-seven was twelve years older than Disraeli, was in no position to tarry. A thin, scrawny figure, outlandishly dressed in girlish pink satin and ringlets, she was mocked by the smart young men who revolved around Disraeli. Sir William Gregory found her repulsive—'flat, angular, under-bred, with a harsh, grating voice'—and her embarrassing remarks provided copy for countless unkind stories. She once announced, after learning that Lord Hardinge was sleeping in the room next to hers at a country house party, that she had slept between the greatest orator and the greatest soldier. 'You should see my Dizzy in his bath', she declared, when someone mentioned the beauty of white skin. Then there was the story of her remark about a picture of Venus and Adonis in her bedroom at a country house: 'I have been awake half the night trying to prevent Dizzy from looking at it.'

But Mary Anne was not wholly ridiculous. That Disraeli's ascent of the greasy pole only began in earnest after his marriage was no coincidence. Her role was crucial. At elections she campaigned tirelessly and tactfully, winning over the shopkeepers estranged by Disraeli's offhand manner. She entertained, as the rising politician's wife must, but her real strength was less as hostess than as manager. Unstintingly generous in paying off Disraeli's debts, she advanced his creditors about £4000 each year out of her income of approximately £6500, running a very tightly budgeted domestic establishment in order to do so—every expenditure, down to the very last cup of tea or spoonful of sugar, was costed in her account book. Each morning early while Disraeli slept Mary Anne digested *The Times*, scanned the reviews for references to her husband, and sorted through his post (this had its disadvantages). She cut his hair and paid his tailor. Above all, Mary Anne's earthy wit and native shrewdness enabled her to give the practical advice and support Disraeli most needed, and her unshakeable belief in his genius gave him the emotional anchor he lacked.

Nervous and prone to bouts of acute anxiety, when she became near-hysterical, Mary Anne was jealous of other women. She quarrelled with Disraeli's sister Sarah and with his brothers. As she grew older, she grew odder. Her stinginess was legendary. She once ordered a quarter pound of cheese from the shop at Hughenden (where their country house was), only to send it back next day when Disraeli returned unexpectedly to London; when the prince and princess of Teck came to stay, she ordered six rolls for breakfast. Despite the strains, and probably the occasional infidelity on Disraeli's part, they were a devoted couple. Driving down to the house one day in 1852 when Disraeli was to make an important speech, she slammed her hand painfully in the carriage door, but remained silent in order not to upset him. Disraeli never forgot how much he owed her. 'Why, my dear, you are more like a mistress than a wife', he famously remarked when he returned home late from the Carlton Club, after celebrating his triumph over the 1867 Reform Bill, to find the 75-year-old Mary Anne waiting up with a Fortnum and Mason's pie and a bottle of champagne.

On his resignation as prime minister in 1868, Disraeli persuaded Queen Victoria to create his wife Viscountess Beaconsfield in her own right. Cynics sneered; they little knew that Mary Anne was already gravely ill with stomach cancer. She battled bravely on, her face garishly painted, her body shrunken and swollen; she died at Hughenden on 15 December 1872, a heartbroken Dizzy by her side, and was buried at Hughenden church on 20 December. After her death he discovered that she had squirrelled away packets of his hair, as well as every scrap of paper he ever wrote—the latter a devotion for which historians must be truly grateful.   JANE RIDLEY

Sources M. Hardwick, *Mrs Dizzy* (1972) · J. Sykes, *Mary Anne Disraeli* (1928) · W. F. Monypenny and G. E. Buckle, *The life of Benjamin Disraeli*, 6 vols. (1910–20) · J. Ridley, *The young Disraeli* (1995) · *National Trust guide to Hughenden Manor* (1988) · *Benjamin Disraeli letters*, ed. J. A. W. Gunn and others (1982–), vols. 1–5 · S. Weintraub, *Disraeli* (1993) · R. Blake, *Disraeli* (1966) · *Sir William Gregory, KCMG, formerly member of parliament and sometime governor of Ceylon: an autobiography*, ed. Lady Gregory (1894)

Archives Bodl. Oxf., corresp., papers, and related material · Hughenden Manor · Queen's University, Kingston, Ontario, Disraeli project

Likenesses Rochard, miniature, 1829, Hughenden Manor, Buckinghamshire · A. E. Chalon, portrait, 1840, Hughenden Manor, Buckinghamshire · W. C. Ross, miniature, c.1868, NPG · J. G. Middleton, oils, 1873, Hughenden Manor, Buckinghamshire · J. G. Middleton, miniature, Hughenden Manor, Buckinghamshire [*see illus.*]

Wealth at death under £600: administration, 8 May 1874, CGPLA Eng. & Wales

Diss, Walter (c.1330–1403/4), prior of Norwich and theologian, as his name indicates, came from Diss in Norfolk. When he was ordained deacon at Ely, on 16 February 1353, he had already entered the Carmelite house in Norwich, and was appointed its prior in 1376. According to Leland he studied at Paris and Rome, but it is known for certain only that he was in the Cambridge house and became DTh there. By the 1370s Diss had already established himself as a scholar with a considerable reputation as a preacher. Bale credits him with several theological and philosophical works—*Ex Augustino et Anselmo*, *Lectura theologiae*, *Quaestiones theologiae*, and *Determinationes variae*—and he is said to have published a commentary on the Psalms and two volumes of sermons. He also wrote a tract *Contra Lolhardos*, and seems to have been one of the compilers of the material that eventually appeared as the *Fasciculi zizaniorum*. The great schism stimulated a number of writings: *Epistolae ad Urbanum et Bonifacium*, *Ad ecclesiarum praesides*, and a poem, *Carmen de schismate ecclesiae*, of which some fragments were printed in the works of Nicholas de Clemangiis (*Opera*, 31–4). He always strongly supported the English government in its recognition of the Roman papacy against that of Avignon.

Diss was appointed confessor to Edward III's son John of Gaunt, duke of Lancaster (d. 1399), and his duchess, Constanza of Castile (d. 1394), in succession to William Badby, another Carmelite, and was instrumental in encouraging the duke's piety and his veneration for the Virgin Mary. On 12 January 1375 Gaunt granted *nostre confessour* Walter Diss an annual payment of £10 while he remained in the duke's service (this annuity was doubled in 1380) to be drawn from the income of Gaunt's Norfolk manor of Gimingham, and a further payment was made on 12 October for administering mass at the Garter ceremony. Gaunt's register records similar payments regularly until the spring of 1382, and shows that Diss normally travelled with the duke. He was also a beneficiary in 1379 under the terms of the will of the Lancastrian retainer Sir Roger Trumpington. When Gaunt was obliged to sort out the complex case of the Lathom inheritance in Lancashire, in which one of the issues was the legality of the marriage of another retainer, Sir John Dalton, it was Diss who remarried the couple after the pope had sanctioned a divorce. Diss was replaced as confessor by yet another Carmelite, John Kenningham of Ipswich, in 1386, but remained closely connected with Gaunt.

Diss was one of the group of friars who appealed to Gaunt on 18 February 1382 and persuaded him that it was dangerous for him to continue to support John Wyclif, and when Archbishop Courtenay summoned a council to the London Blackfriars in May of that year to condemn Wyclif's teachings, Diss was an obvious choice to be one of the distinguished panel of judges, and represented the University of Cambridge. He was subsequently a member of the smaller group that assembled to continue the process against Nicholas Hereford and Philip Repyndon in June and July.

In the years that followed, Diss's fortunes continued to be linked with those of his patron. Prominent among the factors shaping English foreign policy in the 1380s were the competition of Rome and Avignon for the spiritual loyalties of western Europe, and the ambition of John of Gaunt to be king of Castile in the right of his wife, at the expense of Juan I, who was supported by both the French monarchy and the Avignon papacy. Diss was one of a group of papal nuncios for England, Gascony, and the Spanish kingdoms empowered by Urban VI in 1386 to raise money by the sale of indulgences and authorized to award fifty papal chaplaincies—an act that considerably irritated the chronicler Thomas Walsingham, a long-standing adversary of Gaunt, who lamented that even the Benedictines of St Albans were being seduced by this opportunity to secure honour and preferment. Gaunt eventually led an army to Galicia in July 1386 in alliance with João of Portugal, but the campaign had virtually petered out by May 1387, although it took until the summer of the following year to arrange a general truce. Although he was appointed Carmelite prior provincial for Spain in 1387, there is no evidence that Diss accompanied the expedition. Walsingham suggests that he was detained in England by the scandal caused by the grant of one of the chaplaincies to the Lollard Peter Pateshull, a dubious story, although Diss may well have been involved in dealings with this renegade friar during 1387–8. He subsequently remained in contact with Gaunt, whom he is known to have visited in 1396, but he seems to have spent most of the last decade of his life in quiet retirement in Norwich, where he died in 1404 or possibly towards the end of the previous year.   MICHAEL WILKS

Sources Emden, *Cam.*, 188 · [T. Netter], *Fasciculi zizaniorum magistri Johannis Wyclif cum tritico*, ed. W. W. Shirley, Rolls Series, 5 (1858) · *John of Gaunt's register*, ed. S. Armitage-Smith, 1, CS, 3rd ser., 20 (1911), xx–xxi · *John of Gaunt's register, 1379–1383*, ed. E. C. Lodge and R. Somerville, 1, CS, 3rd ser., 56 (1937), lvi–lvii · *Thomae Walsingham, quondam monachi S. Albani, historia Anglicana*, ed. H. T. Riley, 2 vols., pt 1 of *Chronica monasterii S. Albani*, Rolls Series, 28 (1863–4) · *Gesta abbatum monasterii Sancti Albani, a Thoma Walsingham*, ed. H. T. Riley, 3 vols., pt 4 of *Chronica monasterii S. Albani*, Rolls Series, 28 (1867–9) · [T. Walsingham], *Chronicon Angliae, ab anno Domini 1328 usque ad annum 1388*, ed. E. M. Thompson, Rolls Series, 64 (1874) · Bale, *Cat.* · *Commentarii de scriptoribus Britannicis, auctore Joanne Lelando*, ed. A. Hall, 2 (1709), 385, 393f. · H. B. Workman, *John Wyclif*, 2 vols. (1926) · S. Armitage-Smith, *John of Gaunt* (1904) · A. Goodman, *John of Gaunt: the exercise of princely power in fourteenth-century Europe* (1992) · S. Walker, *The Lancastrian affinity, 1361–1399* (1990) · F. Blomefield and C. Parkin, *An essay towards a topographical history of the county of Norfolk*, [2nd edn], 11 vols. (1805–10), vol. 4, p. 416 · G. Wessels, ed., *Acta capitulorum generalium ordinis fratrum B. V. Mariae de Monte Carmelo*, 1 (Rome, 1912), 100 · *Nicolai de Clemangiis … opera*, ed. J. M. Lydius (Leiden, 1613)

Ditchfield, John Edwin Watts- (1861–1923), bishop of Chelmsford, was born on 17 September 1861 at Green Lane, Patricroft, Manchester, the fifth child and only surviving son of John Ditchfield (b. 1814) and his wife, Mary Ann Watts (b. c.1823). His father had started work in a cotton mill at the age of eight, but had risen to become headmaster of Patricroft higher grade school.

The family was strongly Methodist and concerned with social questions and temperance. From an early age the younger John Ditchfield was taken on pastoral visits by his father, and during adolescence had a profound religious experience which left him determined to enter the ministry. He preached his first sermon in 1877, and gradually worked through the Wesleyan hierarchy until in 1887 he was accepted for the ministry and entered Headingley College, Leeds. But the Methodist ministry was overcrowded and Ditchfield was advised that he could not make it his profession, either in Britain or overseas. He converted and in 1888 was confirmed in the Church of England at Manchester Cathedral. About the same time he changed his name to Watts-Ditchfield. He studied at St John's Hall in Highbury (north London), was ordained in 1891, and became curate at St Peter's, Upper Holloway. On 3 September 1892 he made a happy and successful marriage to Jane Wardell (b. 1864/5), daughter of Thomas Lax Wardell of Bow, a commercial clerk. A daughter was born in 1895.

Many churchmen of the time saw the Sunday school as the chief means of evangelism, on the assumption that the child, once captured, would remain in the church. Watts-Ditchfield disagreed: he believed that the church was seen as something fit only for women and children,

and argued that if the church got the man, it got the whole family. He instituted a men's service at St Peter's, and, by adroit publicity, eye-catching and provocative titles for his sermons, and careful attention to pastoral work, built up a regular attendance of several hundred. He also instituted several thrift and benefit societies, besides clubs for ramblers and sportsmen, and a reading-room.

In 1897 Watts-Ditchfield was offered the living of St James-the-Less, Bethnal Green, a parish of some 11,000 people. The several parishes in the borough presented the churches with a recognized challenge. The area was poor; its housing was dilapidated, insanitary, and overcrowded; there was little provision for any recreation, and the population was largely employed in low-paid and insecure casual labour or in 'sweated' industries. These cumulative distresses found their outlet in heavy drinking, domestic violence, and attitudes to the church which ranged from contemptuous dismissal to a cringing hope of charity. If the church could succeed in evangelizing Bethnal Green, it could succeed anywhere.

Watts-Ditchfield applied the same methods as at Upper Holloway: the institution of separate men's and women's services, active evangelism, and the provision of facilities for recreation. As vicar he showed a remarkable talent for fund-raising, and so was able to provide his parishioners with a parish centre, a recreation ground, hostels for single working men, and a medical service. He insisted that if people would not come to church, the church must go to them, and held open-air services in Green Street Market and Victoria Park, besides instituting a brass band which toured the area on Sunday afternoons. Watts-Ditchfield was also active on the side of social justice: in 1902 and 1904 he held exhibitions of goods produced by 'sweated' labour, and these activities led to the *Daily News* exhibition of 1906 and eventually to the Trades Boards Act of 1909.

Bethnal Green was a make-or-break job, and it made Watts-Ditchfield. There were twenty-six Easter communicants in 1897, but 597 in 1903, and 915 in 1914. According to the *Daily News* religious census of 1903, 1699 people attended at St James-the-Less, more than double the number at any other Anglican church in the borough. The diocese of Chelmsford was created out of that of St Albans in 1914, and as it was to include the large suburban area of 'London over the border', Watts-Ditchfield was an excellent if surprising choice as its first bishop. He had the urban mission experience, but the bench was full of men from Anglican families, educated at public schools and the ancient universities. Watts-Ditchfield was a convert; he was not a graduate, and his experience had been in parish work rather than administration. He was consecrated on 24 February and enthroned on 23 April 1914.

Almost immediately Watts-Ditchfield had to face the challenges presented by the First World War. His was not an unthinking patriotism and he continued to insist on social justice and on Christian conduct, not only on Britain's part but on that of its allies, particularly Belgium and Russia. Perhaps for this reason, he was an enthusiastic supporter of the 'national mission of repentance and hope' of 1916. After the war Watts-Ditchfield's main difficulties were clerical discipline and organization. Perhaps because he was a convert to Anglicanism, he appeared to have an exaggerated view of his episcopal powers and the degree of conformity he could expect from his clergy, and some of his subordinates resented the rigid and even menacing tone of his doctrinal pronouncements. A particular thorn in Watts-Ditchfield's side was Conrad Noel, vicar of Thaxted, who combined extreme Anglo-Catholicism with revolutionary socialism. The problems of diocesan organization included an underpaid workforce and inadequate buildings. In Chelmsford itself, the parish church had been chosen as the cathedral without any provision being made for its new function.

A favourite saying of Watts-Ditchfield's father was that it was 'better to wear out than to rust out'. His son lived and died by that precept. Watts-Ditchfield added to his burdens without thought for his health, and he was exhausted when obliged to have an operation for appendicitis. He never recovered from the anaesthetic, and died on 14 July 1923 at 41 Beaumont Street, St Marylebone, London. He was buried in the churchyard of Chelmsford Cathedral five days later.   C. J. BEARMAN

Sources E. N. Gowing, *John Edwin Watts-Ditchfield, first bishop of Chelmsford* (1926) · *The Times* (16 July 1923) · G. Hewitt, *A history of the diocese of Chelmsford* (1984) · H. McLeod, *Class and religion in the late Victorian city* (1974) · R. Groves, *Conrad Noel and the Thaxted movement: an adventure in Christian socialism* (1967) · census returns for Barton upon Irwell, 1881, PRO, RG 11/3881/120/59 · b. cert. · m. cert. · d. cert. · CGPLA Eng. & Wales (1923)
Likenesses H. Neale, portraits, Chelmsford Cathedral, chapter house
Wealth at death £31,998 7s. 5d.: probate, 3 Oct 1923, CGPLA Eng. & Wales

Ditton, Humphry [Humphrey] (1675–1714), mathematician, was born on 29 May 1675, in Salisbury, the only son of Humphry Ditton, gentleman, and Miss Luttrell of Dunster Castle, near Taunton, Somerset. He did not receive a university education; although his father was an ardent nonconformist Ditton was educated under a Dr Olive, a clergyman of the established church. Afterwards, and at his father's wish, he became a dissenting preacher at Tunbridge Wells, Kent, where he married a Miss Ball. After his father's death and in poor health he gave up the ministry. In 1706 he was appointed, through Isaac Newton's influence, as the first mathematics teacher at the New Mathematical School established in that year at Christ's Hospital, London. The school was discontinued as a failure after his death.

Ditton's original mathematical work appeared mainly in two articles in the *Philosophical Transactions of the Royal Society*. The first was on tangents of curves deduced from the theory of maxima and minima (vol. 23, 1703). The second was on optics, and dealt with the reflection of light (vol. 24, 1705); this was republished in the *Acta Eruditorum* of Leipzig and in the *Memoirs* of the Academy of Science at Paris. However, Ditton's main work in mathematics was not in original research but in producing textbooks and expository articles. Newton had recommended him for the post at Christ's Hospital after being impressed with his contributions to John Harris's *Lexicon technicum* (1704) and with his textbooks, *The General Laws of Nature and Motion … being a Part of the Great Mr Newton's Principles* (1705) and *An Institution of Fluxions … According to the Incomparable Sir Isaac Newton* (1706). In 1709 Ditton corrected and added to Joannes Alexander's *A Synopsis of Algebra*, which was intended for the use of the students at Christ's Hospital. His main remaining mathematical works were on perspective and on the shape assumed by a fluid between two contiguous glass plates. As well as teaching his students he also lectured publicly on mathematics in London at the Marine Coffee House in 1710, and in 1712 assisted at courses in experimental philosophy which were organized by the Hauksbees.

Ditton's most important theological work was *A Discourse Concerning the Resurrection of Jesus Christ*, an event which he attempted to prove by taking a mathematical, deductive approach. The first of its four editions appeared in 1712 and it was also translated into French and German. It contained an appendix about the nature of thought, where he argued that thought could not be produced from matter and motion. He was, however, unable to complete his response to the various criticisms that this work received before his death. A diary of his religious meditations was published in the *Gospel Magazine* (September 1777, 393–403; December 1777, 437–41).

Ditton is best remembered for his pamphlet *A New Method for the Discovery of Longitude at Sea* (1714), on which he collaborated with William Whiston. With the rapid expansion of British overseas trade the problem of determining a ship's longitude at sea was becoming acute. In May 1714 a number of sea captains and London merchants petitioned parliament to establish a prize for the discovery of a suitable method. A committee was set up to consider proposals and to consult technical experts including Newton, Halley, Cotes, and Samuel Clarke. A prize was offered varying from £10,000 to £20,000 depending on the degree of accuracy that a workable method achieved. The solution proposed by Whiston and Ditton was to establish a network of ships at known positions from which a rocket or cannon would be fired. From the difference in time between seeing the flash and hearing the sound of its explosion a seafarer could calculate the meridian distance from the signalling ship and (if the latitude of the passing ship were known) would be able to calculate its longitude. Newton was unenthusiastic about the proposal although he recognized that it had some merit in limited circumstances. The idea was submitted to the board of longitude but was subsequently rejected; indeed, it was widely ridiculed as useless for practical purposes, by Jonathan Swift among others. The preface to the German translation of his *Discourse Concerning the Resurrection* suggests that Ditton developed a further method for determining longitude. Raphael Levi, a student of Leibniz, maintained that Ditton had corresponded with Leibniz about his invention of a clockwork mechanism which Leibniz had apparently approved of for use on land, although he doubted its usefulness at sea because of the motion of the ship. Ditton died on 15 October 1714, and was buried two days later at Christchurch Newgate. RAYMOND FLOOD

Sources DNB · A. Kippis and others, eds., *Biographia Britannica, or, The lives of the most eminent persons who have flourished in Great Britain and Ireland*, 2nd edn, 5 (1793) · W. Trollope, *A history of the royal foundation of Christ's Hospital* (1834) · E. G. R. Taylor, *The mathematical practitioners of Tudor and Stuart England* (1954); repr. (1967) · R. S. Westfall, *Never at rest: a biography of Isaac Newton* (1980) · W. Whiston, *Memoirs of the life and writings of Mr William Whiston: containing memoirs of several of his friends also*, 2nd edn, 2 vols. (1753) · parish register, London, Christchurch Newgate, 17 Oct 1714, GL [burial]

Dive, de, family (*per. c.*1100–1310), gentry, took its name from Dives-sur-Mer near Caen in Normandy and became established in England in the late eleventh century. The family is first represented in the historical record by a William de Dive, who had probably died before 1100, and who was most likely the father of **Buselin de Dive** (*d.* before 1130?) and **Hugh de Dive** (*d.* before 1130). Buselin, who was probably a knight of Archbishop Lanfranc of Canterbury, is recorded as holding land at Cholington in Eastbourne in a charter dated between 1076 and 1081 and he may also have been the Boselinus who held land in Pevensey from the count of Mortain in 1086. Buselin and Hugh were benefactors of the abbey of St Étienne at Caen, and Hugh was also a benefactor of Lewes Priory and witnessed charters of the counts of Mortain between *c.*1095 and 1106. The family is also said to have become established at Horsted Keynes in Sussex and at East Haddon in Northamptonshire, both part of the estate of the count of Mortain in 1086. However, the first specific reference to the family in Northamptonshire is not made until 1130.

The early genealogy of the family is unclear but a William de Dive (*d.* before 1130), the son of Buselin de Dive, witnessed a charter of Henry I in 1103–4. In 1130 William's son and heir, Hugh de Dive (*d.* before 1155?) was in the custody of Geoffrey de Clinton. Hugh and his son **William de Dive** (*d.* before 1185) made grants to Lewes Priory, including land at Broadhurst in Horsted Keynes and at Eastbourne, given for the soul of William's mother, Cecily. William was also a patron of Sulby Abbey in Northamptonshire, his gifts including the church of East Haddon. He was a constable of Robert de Breteuil, earl of Leicester, and supported Robert against Henry II in the rebellion of 1173, being put under pledge as a result. William married Matilda, the daughter and coheir of Geoffrey de Waterville, and was dead by 1185 when he left two sons and two daughters. In 1185 William's son Hugh de Dive (*d.* after 1202) was only ten or twelve, and another William de Dive was acting as his guardian. Hugh died childless, and his younger brother Ranulf de Dive (*d.* after 1202?) succeeded him.

The connection between William, Hugh, and Ranulf de Dive, and the Dive family which held lands in Northamptonshire, Sussex, and Oxfordshire in the late twelfth and thirteenth century, is not easy to establish. However, it is possible that **Guy de Dive** (*d.* 1214) inherited the Dive lands in Northamptonshire, and possibly Sussex, after the death of Ranulf de Dive in the early thirteenth century, and that therefore there was a continuity between the families. Guy witnessed at least ten charters of King Richard I between 1189 and 1194, over half describing him as marshal. He acted as bailiff of Gavray in 1195 and was constable of Chinon in 1201–5. He married Lucy, the daughter and heir of Ralph de Chesney, and through his marriage he gained possession of lands in Oxfordshire which evidently included a third part of land at Deddington, for which he owed one mark in 1190. In 1204 Guy had possession of the Deddington land with the exception of the castle, which was retained in the king's hand. When Guy died his widow was given in marriage to Robert de Harcourt, and in 1224 the custody of his lands and children was given to John of Bassingbourn, whose daughter Margaret married Guy's eldest son, **William de Dive** (*d.* 1261). Bassingbourn became liable for Guy's debts to the crown which amounted to over £370, and in 1229 he was granted permission to levy an aid from the Dive tenants' lands to pay the debt.

In 1241 William de Dive claimed against Ralph Hareng and his wife, Alice, two parts of one third of two knights' fees in Deddington, and against Ralph and Alice and Alice's sister Beatrice one third of two parts of one third of two knights' fees in Deddington (both claims excluded the advowson of the church, a messuage, a fishery, three mills, and three yardlands). William claimed right from William de Chesney, his great-grandfather's brother, in the time of King Henry II. In addition to the Oxfordshire lands, the thirteenth-century Dives continued to hold land in Sussex and Northamptonshire. In 1243 William was recorded as holding one fee in Graffham and 'Merlirs' in Sussex, and in 1248 there is a reference to his court at Wonworth in Graffham. The Graffham lands had belonged to the Chesney family in the twelfth century and presumably passed to the Dives as a result of the marriage between Guy de Dive and Lucy de Chesney. By 1243 William was also in possession of one fee in Wyke Dive, Northamptonshire, held from the heirs of the earl of Warwick, and on his death in 1261 William was recorded as holding the manor there.

William was succeeded by his son **John de Dive** (*d.* 1265), who did homage to King Henry III in February 1261 and had livery of lands in Northamptonshire and Sussex. However, he evidently fell out with Henry and probably died of wounds incurred fighting against the king at the battle of Evesham in 1265. In January 1266 by the king's clemency John's widow, Sibyl, received the manor and park of Ducklington, Oxfordshire, for herself and her children for life. The rest of John's lands had been committed to Osbert Giffard. An extent taken in 1272 revealed that these comprised the manors of Wonworth, Wyke Dive, Deddington, and Ducklington. In 1276 John's son **Henry de Dive** (*d.* 1277) granted all his lands in Northamptonshire, including the manor of Wyke Dive, to Lady Edelina Corbet for the term of her life, and at his death he was recorded as holding an old castle at Deddington from the crown. Henry's son, **John de Dive** (1272/3–1310) was only four at his father's death, and the wardship of the lands and heir were granted first to Queen Eleanor of Provence, and then to Henry's widow, Alice, who died in 1282. John gained livery of his father's lands in 1295, having already obtained a charter of free warren in Deddington, Ducklington, and Graffham. Between 1297 and 1305 he was active in the king's service overseas, he was a commissioner of the peace in Oxfordshire in 1308, and in 1309 he was given protection for going on pilgrimage to Jerusalem. In 1310 he died holding a third part of the manor of Deddington for a third of two fees from the crown, and the manor of Ducklington for two fees. He was succeeded by his son, Henry Dive, who died in 1327. Thereafter the family declined into obscurity.   JOHN WALKER

Sources W. Farrer, *Honors and knights' fees ... from the eleventh to the fourteenth century*, 3 (1925) • D. C. Douglas, *Domesday monachorum of Christ Church, Canterbury* (1944) • *VCH Sussex*, vol. 4 • *CIPM* • *Chancery records* • J. Cooper, ed., *The Oxfordshire eyre, 1241*, Oxfordshire RS, 56 (1989) • L. C. Loyd, *The origins of some Anglo-Norman families*, ed. C. T. Clay and D. C. Douglas, Harleian Society, 103 (1951) • I. J. Sanders, *English baronies: a study of their origin and descent, 1086–1327* (1960) • L. Landon, *The itinerary of King Richard I*, PRSoc., new ser., 13 (1935) • C. Moor, ed., *Knights of Edward I*, 1, Harleian Society, 80 (1929)

Dive, Buselin de (*d.* before 1130?). *See under* Dive, de, family (*per. c.*1100–1310).

Dive, Guy de (*d.* 1214). *See under* Dive, de, family (*per. c.*1100–1310).

Dive, Henry de (*d.* 1277). *See under* Dive, de, family (*per. c.*1100–1310).

Dive, Hugh de (*d.* before 1130). *See under* Dive, de, family (*per. c.*1100–1310).

Dive, John de (*d.* 1265). *See under* Dive, de, family (*per. c.*1100–1310).

Dive, John de (1272/3–1310). *See under* Dive, de, family (*per. c.*1100–1310).

Dive, William de (*d.* before 1185). *See under* Dive, de, family (*per. c.*1100–1310).

Dive, William de (*d.* 1261). *See under* Dive, de, family (*per. c.*1100–1310).

Divers, Edward (1837–1912), chemist, was born in London on 27 November 1837 of unrecorded parents. His early education was at the City of London School where his interest in chemistry was stimulated by Thomas Hall. At the age of fifteen he came under the influence of A. W. Hofmann and W. Crookes at the Royal College of Chemistry in Oxford Street. After one year's study (1852–3) Divers was briefly at the School of Mines and at John Stenhouse's laboratory in St Bartholomew's Hospital, where he came into contact with F. August Kekulé and Heinrich Buff, both products of Liebig's Giessen laboratory. In 1854 he was appointed as teaching assistant and demonstrator at the newly created Queen's College, Galway, where he studied medicine, one of the few scientific degrees then available in Ireland; he was awarded the MD degree in 1860. For the next six years he engaged in a limited medical practice, also giving public lectures on chemistry in the Galway region. He started to investigate

the chemistry of oxy-salts and acids; his first paper on magnesium ammonium carbonate appeared in the *Journal of the Chemical Society* in 1862. In 1865 he married Margaret Theresa (*d.* 1897), daughter of D. G. Fitzgerald of Mayfield, co. Cork, with whom he had a son and two daughters.

Realizing that the scope for undertaking investigations in chemistry was seriously restricted in Galway, Divers returned to England in 1866. He did not abandon medicine completely: in the following seven years he was successively lecturer in materia medica at Queen's College, Birmingham, in medical jurisprudence at Middlesex Hospital, and in physics at Charing Cross Hospital, as well as lecturing on chemistry at the Albert Veterinary College. These institutions provided him with the facilities to accelerate his research on inorganic chemistry and papers describing his work began to flow from his pen. The most significant, 'The existence and formation of salts of nitrous oxide', describing the first synthesis of hyponitrites, was published in 1871.

In July 1873, on the recommendation of A. W. Williamson, Divers went to Tokyo as lecturer in general and applied chemistry at the new Imperial Engineering College at Toranomon. In the previous decade a great transformation of Japan had taken place with the overthrow of the isolationist and xenophobic Togugawa regime and the establishment of the Meiji (Enlightenment) government. A crash programme of education was put in place to bring Japan, still largely feudal in its institutions, into line with occidental countries. The new government saw the way forward by the importation of foreign experts. Divers was one of some forty-five scientists and engineers from England, Scotland, America, and Germany recruited to achieve this aim.

Divers was the first British chemist to go to Japan, where he immediately set about building laboratories on the Liebig and Hofmann models. On Henry Dyer's retirement from the Engineering College in 1882 Divers became its principal, and when the college was incorporated into the Imperial University in 1886 he was appointed professor of inorganic chemistry. His dedication to research now became paramount, even after a test-tube explosion in 1885 robbed him of sight in his right eye. Together with Japanese co-workers he published extensively in international journals on the compounds of selenium and tellurium, and many other subjects. He was elected FRS in June 1885.

In recognition of his role as founder of modern chemical studies in Japan, Divers was appointed to the order of the Rising Sun, third class, in 1886, and to the order of the Sacred Treasure, second class, in 1898. On retirement in 1899 he was made emeritus professor of the University of Japan, and a bronze bust was erected on the university campus. He returned to London in 1899, but continued his chemical activity, becoming president of the chemical section of the British Association in 1902, president of the Society of Chemical Industry in 1905, and vice-president of both the Chemical Society (1900–02) and the Institute of Chemistry (1905). He died, following an operation, at his home, 3 Canning Place, Palace Gate, Kensington, on 8 April 1912 and was buried at Brookwood, Surrey, on 11 April.   WILLIAM J. DAVIS

Sources A. S. [A. Scott] and J. Sakurai, *JCS*, 103 (1913), 746–55 · *PRS*, 88A (1912–13), viii–x · *Nature*, 89 (1911–12), 170 · *Journal of the Society of Chemical Industry* (July 1931), 73 [jubilee number] · T. Tezuka, *Twenty-five tales in memory of Tokyo's foreigners* (1989) · H. Tuge, ed., *Historical development of science and technology in Japan* (1961) · O. Checkland, *Britain's encounter with Meiji Japan, 1868–1912* (1989) · 'Inauguration of memorial bust of Dr E. Divers', *Chemical News* (28 Dec 1900), 310–11
Likenesses M. Naganuma, bronze bust, 17 Nov 1900, University of Tokyo, Japan, department of chemistry · photographs, RS
Wealth at death £2121 8s. 6d.: probate, 1 May 1912, CGPLA Eng. & Wales

Dix, George Eglinton Alston [*name in religion* Gregory Dix] (**1901–1952**), Benedictine monk and liturgical scholar, was born at Woolwich on 4 October 1901, the elder son of George Henry Dix (1872–1932), a schoolmaster of partly French descent who afterwards took orders and became the first principal of the College of St Mark and St John, Chelsea, and his wife, Mary Jane Walker (1872/3–1939). Little information survives about his early years, apart from his education at Temple Grove, Eastbourne (1908–15) and Westminster School (1915–20), where he was a king's scholar and discovered a marked talent for acting (a significant element in his developed personality). After proceeding as an exhibitioner to Merton College, Oxford, in 1920, he took a lively part in the activities of the turbulent post-war undergraduate generation. His second-class honours in the school of modern history in 1923 reflected this, though they did less than justice to the proficiency in medieval studies that he acquired under the tuition of Arthur Johnson of All Souls. This was evidently recognized in his immediate appointment as lecturer in church history at Keble College. In his first year in this post he attended Wells Theological College, and was ordained deacon to the title of his college in 1924 and priest in 1925.

In 1926 he left Keble, and joined the small Anglican Benedictine community which was shortly to move from Pershore to Nashdom Abbey, Burnham, in Buckinghamshire. Though the timing for this was unexpectedly abrupt, the project had been forming in his mind for some while, and in time it was to give him the identity and stability he needed. His progress towards this goal, however, was far from smooth. Having been sent as a novice to the abbey's house in the Gold Coast Colony, he had to be invalided home in 1929; and his health played a part in his decision not to be professed in the following year, but to assume instead the status of an 'intern oblate'. In the seven years for which this continued he laid the foundations of his patristic and liturgical scholarship. In 1936 he re-entered the novitiate and in 1940 he was solemnly professed.

From this time onwards Dix's activity was increasingly in the public arena. He shared the papalist stance with which his monastery was associated; but he also saw it as his vocation to reclaim for the church of his baptism—as a whole—a Catholic character which Rome could recognize

as such, and to prevent it from travelling down paths which would preclude this. Among the latter, in his eyes, were current proposals for church union in south India (and the possibility of their being used as a model for England). He masterminded a public campaign against these, with repeated lobbying of Archbishop William Temple (who remained nevertheless a revered friend); in the time of Temple's successor the resistance was conducted from the lower house of convocation after his election in 1945. There he skilfully exploited the inferior clergy's traditional suspicion of the motives of their bishops, and won a substantial measure of confidence. But the bitterness of the campaign soured the spirits of lesser men, and the time and energy that Dix devoted to ecclesiastical politics was ultimately to the detriment of his writing, and probably also his health. A by-product of the campaign, and one that well illustrates both the strengths and the weaknesses of his scholarship, was his essay on the ministry in the early church in the collection *The Apostolic Ministry* (1946), which he persuaded his close friend and ally K. E. Kirk, bishop of Oxford, to edit.

Dix's attraction to liturgical studies had begun long before this time, though the course it took did not remain unaffected. His first major publication in this field was his critical text (1937) of the *Apostolic Tradition* of Hippolytus of Rome, which had come to light through the researches of Dom R. H. Connolly some twenty years earlier. Dix was a pioneer in his emphasis (some would now say overemphasis) on the importance of this document for the early history of the liturgy, and his edition was a milestone towards a definitive reconstruction, though the final result is likely to look rather different. His text was to have been followed by a commentary, but that was shelved in favour of the more ambitious project for which he is most widely known, *The Shape of the Liturgy* (1945). Written with verve, imagination, and often mischievous humour, and in places with real eloquence, this is an outstanding piece of *haute vulgarisation*, liturgy made accessible to the general reader. Yet it could only have been produced by a master of his subject. Its breadth of insight decisively altered the scope and the course of liturgical reform both within and beyond the Church of England. And despite the haste of its composition under wartime conditions, and the proportion of bold solutions to individual questions which have not stood the test of time, it is still unreplaced as a unified vision of what Christian liturgy is really about.

Dix is remembered as a wit and lover of paradox, as a superb (and irrepressible) raconteur, and as a deliverer of devastating put-downs to tendentious scholarship or episcopal self-importance. Beneath the surface there was genuine spiritual conviction and a rare capacity for friendship. Little of substance came from his pen after 1946. Besides his convocation work he was increasingly concerned with the affairs of his abbey (of which he became prior in 1948), particularly the demands of its daughter foundation in the United States, to which he paid two extended visits. On the second of these, after he had committed himself to raising funds for a new chapel by an extensive programme of lecturing, and with building already in progress, an intestinal cancer was diagnosed. Seeing no other alternative to bankruptcy for the daughter house, he postponed surgery for eight months while the money was raised. The treatment was initially successful, but secondaries developed before his convalescence was complete, and he died at Grovefield House, Burnham, on 12 May 1952. He was buried on 16 May in the cemetery of Nashdom Abbey.   H. BENEDICT GREEN

Sources S. Bailey, *A tactful God* (1995); see also review [H.] B. Green, 'Dom Gregory Dix revisited', *CR Quarterly*, 372 (1996), 8–15; 373 (1996), 12–21 • P.-M. Gy, 'Re-visiting Dom Gregory Dix after fifty years', *Worship*, 70 (1996), 2–15 • P. Bradshaw, 'Gregory Dix', *They shaped our worship*, ed. C. Irvine (1998), 111–17 • E. L. Mascall, *Sarabande* (1992), 151–66 • *DNB* • personal knowledge (2004) • private information (2004) • Crockford (1924–5)
Archives LPL, papers collected for a biography • NRA, papers relating to his edition of *Apostolic tradition* • Order of St Benedict, Elmore House, Speen, corresp. and papers | Heythrop College, London, corresp. with Maurice Bévenot SJ
Likenesses photographs, Elmore Abbey, Newbury, Berkshire

Dix, John (*fl.* 1829–1864), writer, was born in Bristol of partly Scottish descent. His mother, he claimed, was taught by Mary Newton, the sister of Thomas Chatterton. Dix attended medical school and practised in Bristol as a physician and surgeon, and married a local woman named Susanna. He also wrote poetry about Bristol sites, first published in the *Bristol Mirror* and later collected in *Lays of Home* (1829).

In 1837 Dix published *The Life of Thomas Chatterton*, praised by Leigh Hunt as 'heart-touching' (*DNB*). Chatterton pervades much of Dix's writing, but despite being the first to attribute and print some of Chatterton's early poems and political journalism, his biography displays a hopeless credulity towards anecdotes, and also misrepresents aspects of Chatterton's life and works—ironically enough through forged documents and a suppositious portrait. Dix's work was later condemned by Moy Thomas, Buxton Forman, and Walter Thornbury, the last concluding Dix had 'muddied so many subjects with his wilful untruths' (Thornbury, 295).

Dix's medical practice failed because of his alcoholism, which perhaps inspired him to write the poems that accompanied E. V. Rippingville's engravings, *Progress of Intemperance* (1839). He also gathered his verse for *Local Legends and Rambling Rhymes* (1839), and was rashly ranked alongside Wordsworth for 'The Church-Wreck' (1842). He illustrated his own poems and perhaps worked as an itinerant artist during the 1840s; later he claimed to have been a journalist, an 'esquire and body guard' (*Pen and Ink Sketches*, 70), and a European traveller. Possibly he also worked as a ship's surgeon for the East India Company. This would explain *Jack Ariel* (1847), a novel of life on board an Indiaman. The attribution is, however, dubious: none of Dix's other publications is written with the same verve, and he makes no use of India and China elsewhere.

About 1845 Dix went to New York as a ship's surgeon. A Boston edition of his *Chatterton* appeared in 1845, and he wrote a handbook for Lake Memphremagog (1845) and *Local Loiterings* (1846). Dix also took the temperance pledge but resumed drinking on his return to London. He was apparently drunk for five years, during which time he was arrested for intoxication, but discharged. His adventures during this period, which include writing ballads and verses for St Valentine cards, are described in *Passages from the History of a Wasted Life* (1853)—although here, as elsewhere, everything Dix says must be treated with extreme scepticism. *Pen and Ink Sketches* had appeared in 1846, in which Dix reminisced about his encounters with Hannah More, Feargus O'Connor, Felicia Hemans, Robert Southey, Joseph Cottle, and Ebeneezer Elliott, among others. Although most of these memoirs were drunken fantasies, he nevertheless followed it up in 1852 with the equally imaginary *Lions: Living and Dead*, which includes his accounts of Wordsworth, Coleridge, Lamb, Shelley, Hazlitt, and various other luminaries.

Dix abandoned his family in Bristol, returned to America, took the name John Ross Dix, and lived in Newport, publishing *Loiterings in America* in 1850. He continued to write poetry, and contributed the text to J. Wesley Jones's *Amusing and Thrilling Adventures of a Californian Artist* (1854). He rejoined the temperance movement, publishing *The Worth of the Worthless* (with illustrations by Hammatt Billings) under the Shakespeare Division of the Sons of Temperance in 1854, and his religious faith was also restored: between 1851 and 1854 he published three accounts of popular preachers. *The New Apostles* (1860), an attack on the Catholic Apostolic church, has also been attributed to Dix; if so, it involved him in a theological dispute with Edward Wilton Eddis and John George Francis. John Dix's last works appear to be unionist civil war ballads, published in 1864; more than a dozen survive.

A review of *Wasted Life* described the author as 'rather slender—of a nervous bilious temperament—has black curly hair … a nose that would have suited Napoleon—and his pale classic face is lit up with a pair of black eyes' (Dix, *Wasted Life*, preface). He was twitchy, and given to blinking rapidly when excited. Dix had at least one son, William Chatterton Dix (*b.* 14 June 1837), who wrote a number of hymns, including 'As with gladness, men of old'.   NICK GROOM

Sources C. Rogers, *N&Q*, 4th ser., 10 (1872), 55 • W. Thornbury, *N&Q*, 4th ser., 9 (1872), 294–6 • M. Thomas, *The Athenaeum* (5 Dec 1857) • M. Thomas, *The Athenaeum* (23 Jan 1858) • J. Dix, *Passages from the history of a wasted life* (1853) • J. Dix, *Pen and ink sketches of poets, preachers, and politicians* (1846) • America singing: nineteenth-century song sheets, memory.loc.gov/ammem//amsshtml/amsshome.html, 1999 • E. H. W. Meyerstein, *A life of Thomas Chatterton* (1930) • *DNB*

Dixey, Sir Frank (1892–1982), geologist, was born on 7 April 1892 at Bedminster, Bristol, the third of three children of George Dixey, journeyman boilermaker and riveter in the ship repair yards of Barry, Glamorgan, and his wife, Mary Nippress. The family moved to Barry when Dixey was two, and he grew up, with a father whose favourite recreation was walking, within easy reach of the rocky coast. His elder brother died when Dixey was fourteen.

From Barry grammar school he entered University College, Cardiff, to read chemistry and physics with the intention of becoming a teacher, but he changed to geology and gained a first-class degree in 1914.

After a short academic spell Dixey became a gunner in the Royal Garrison Artillery, serving on the western front from 1915 to 1918. He was gazetted out to go to Sierra Leone and make a reconnaissance survey of the territory. By foot traverse, using compass and barometer, he produced single-handed a geological and topographic map, and he recognized the importance of erosion surfaces in the physiography of Africa. On 23 June 1919 Dixey married (Henrietta Frederika Alexandra) Helen (d. 1961), daughter of Henry Golding, engineer, of Cardiff.

Dixey was appointed government geologist to Nyasaland in 1921 (being later made director) and the striking landscape seen from the headquarters at Zomba stimulated his interest in landscape evolution which became such an important element in his scientific work. He investigated the coal deposits and described the dinosaur beds of Lake Nyasa. He prospected the bauxite deposits of Mlanje Mountain, and described the carbonatites, making the first record of these remarkable rocks in Africa, with W. Campbell Smith.

Owing to the economic depression the geological survey in the early 1930s turned its attention to matters immediately productive, and especially to the provision of groundwater supplies from boreholes. This initiated one of Dixey's major and continuing interests. The influence of his work spread throughout Africa, with hand-pumped boreholes, often drilled in crystalline rocks, contributing greatly to the supply of pure water for rural populations. Dixey set down the knowledge and experience he gained in his *Practical Handbook of Water Supply* (1931; 2nd edn, 1950).

Dixey served in Northern Rhodesia as director of water development (1939–44), and travelled widely in north-east Africa on advisory services, which further enlarged his experience of African landscape. He then became director of the geological survey in Nigeria (1944–7).

The interplay of tectonics, erosion cycles, and sedimentation was the theme explored by Dixey in a series of papers. He recognized, classified, and dated the major planation surfaces and showed that they were developed throughout Africa; also that they were deformed and disrupted by the Rift Valley movements, and that they could be used to elucidate the history of rifting and the geomorphic development of the continent.

After the Second World War, to meet the demands for increased mineral exploration and mapping, geological surveys were initiated or expanded in many British colonies. A headquarters was set up in the Imperial Institute building in London with Dixey as director of Colonial (later Overseas) Geological Surveys. This provided (both before and after the territories reached independence) co-ordinated recruiting and specialist services, such as geophysics, geochemistry, and notably photogeology, in which training was provided for the many young geologists on their way from the universities to overseas posts.

Dixey's practical experience and scientific prestige, as well as his diplomatic personality, contributed to the strength of the organization and to its *esprit de corps*.

Dixey officially retired in 1959 but thirteen more years of activity lay ahead, much of it serving the United Nations in a consultative capacity, especially in hydrology. He was joint founder of the *Journal of Hydrogeology* and was one of its editors almost until his death. As consultant geologist to the Cyprus government (1967–73) he undertook active fieldwork in his seventies. Dixey's first wife died in 1961 and on 14 March 1962 he married Cicely Mary Hepworth, daughter of Herbert Milner, bank manager.

In appearance Dixey was slightly stooping, with heavy shoulders. He was reserved, almost diffident in manner, and invariably courteous. He was not an easy man to know, had few interests apart from his work, and was kind and thoughtful to his staff. His steady determination, meticulous observation, interest in his subject, and ability to write at length, established him as an important figure in African geology. He was honoured by many learned societies and he served on their councils. He received the Murchison medal (1953) and was elected FRS (1958). He was appointed OBE in 1929, CMG in 1949, and KCMG in 1972. Dixey died at his home, Woodpecker Cottage, in Bramber, Steyning, Sussex, on 1 November 1982.

J. V. HEPWORTH, rev.

Sources K. C. Dunham, *Memoirs FRS*, 29 (1983), 159–76 · J. W. Pallister, 'Sir Frank Dixey', *Annual Report* [Geological Society of London] (1983), 22–4 · *The Times* (8 Nov 1982) · personal knowledge (1990) · *CGPLA Eng. & Wales* (1983)
Archives BGS, corresp. and papers relating to geology of central Africa | NHM, corresp. with W. Campbell Smith · Wellcome L., corresp. with Sir Edward Sharpey-Schafer and Maud Sharpey-Schafer
Likenesses W. Bird, photograph, 1959, RS
Wealth at death £97,978: probate, 7 Feb 1983, *CGPLA Eng. & Wales*

Dixey, John (1763–1820), sculptor and modeller, was born on 19 August 1763 in Dublin but spent the vast majority of his life outside Ireland. Of his parents, nothing is known. As a young man he moved to London in order to study at the Royal Academy Schools, which he entered as a painter on 29 October 1784 at the age of twenty-one. His industry and talent earned him a Royal Academy visiting scholarship to Italy, where he was intended to finish his aesthetic education. In 1789, however, when he was about to leave for Italy, he was offered a position in the United States, which was sufficient to induce him to emigrate immediately, and he abandoned his prestigious scholarship.

On arrival in the United States, Dixey settled first in New York city, where he worked as a carver and gilder, and then in Pennsylvania, where he became a leading light on the American aesthetic scene, devoting himself assiduously to the promotion and resurrection of the arts. He exhibited at both the American and Pennsylvania academies. In the early 1810s his manifold efforts were rewarded when he was elected vice-president of the Pennsylvania Academy of the Fine Arts. Alongside his administrative endeavours he also worked prolifically as an architectural sculptor, principally employed in the ornamental and decorative embellishment of various important civic and private buildings, including New York city hall and the state house at Albany, New York, for both of which he executed a statue of Justice. While in the United States he also executed some free-standing sculptural groups. His copy of Giuseppe Ceracchi's bust of Alexander Hamilton, the secretary of the treasury, is in the collection of the New York Historical Society. Although scarcely known in England, Dixey had a quiet yet good reputation in both Ireland and the United States until the early decades of the twentieth century. His name was kept alive after his death in New York city in 1820 by his son George Dixey, who adopted his father's profession as a modeller, and his second son, John V. Dixey, who was both a modeller and a proficient landscape painter.

L. H. CUST, rev. JASON EDWARDS

Sources Redgrave, *Artists* · W. Dunlap, *History of the rise and progress of the arts of design in the United States*, 2 vols. (New York, 1834) · M. H. Grant, *A dictionary of British sculptors from the XIIIth century to the XXth century* (1953) · W. G. Strickland, *A dictionary of Irish artists*, 2 vols. (1913); repr. with introduction by T. J. Snoddy (1989) · *Who was who in America: historical volume, 1607–1896*, rev. edn (1967) · S. C. Hutchison, 'The Royal Academy Schools, 1768–1830', *Walpole Society*, 38 (1960–62), 123–91

Dixie [*née* Douglas], **Florence Caroline**, **Lady Dixie** (1857–1905), author and traveller, was born in London on 24 May 1857, one of a pair of twins, the youngest of the six children of Archibald William Douglas, eighth marquess of Queensberry (1818–1858), and his wife, Caroline Margaret (*d.* 1904), younger daughter of General Sir William Robert Clayton, bt.

The Douglases were an ancient Scottish family, vigorous and combative, and in Florence's generation they were haunted by disaster, dissension, and scandal: in 1858 Florence's father died from an accidental shot while cleaning a gun; her brother Francis was killed in 1865 on the first ascent of the Matterhorn; James, Florence's twin, was to commit suicide in middle age in 1891; and their eldest brother, the ninth marquess of Queensberry (John Sholto *Douglas), was the defendant in the notorious Oscar Wilde case. Dissension affected the twins when they were seven years old and their mother alarmed their guardians by becoming a Roman Catholic and converting the children; she was threatened with the loss of her children, a real danger in an age which allowed a woman no rights over her own progeny, and an injustice against which Florence was to campaign in later life and which was the subject of her novel *The Story of Ijarn* (1903).

Their mother took the children abroad for two years and on their return Florence was sent to a convent school where she hated the repressive regime and the dogmatism of the religious teaching. She found relief in poetry, writing *Songs of a Child* under the pseudonym Darling—verses which were not, however, published until 1902. Early in life she developed a passion for sport and travel. She was a first rate horsewoman and a keen hunter of big game, one of the first women to take up this activity. She learned to swim and was a rapid walker. On 3 April 1875

Florence Caroline Dixie, Lady Dixie (1857–1905), by Andrew Maclure, pubd 1877

she married Sir Alexander Beaumont Churchill Dixie, eleventh baronet (1851–1924), a strikingly handsome man, nicknamed Beau. They shared a taste for adventure and outdoor life, and the one flaw in an otherwise equal partnership seems to have been Beau's love of gambling, which was to prove a constant threat to the family property at Bosworth Park in Leicestershire, eventually sold to pay his debts. They had two sons, George Douglas (1876–1948) and Albert Edward Wolston (1878–1940), godson of the then prince of Wales.

Neither domestic nor social life appealed to Lady Dixie, and, having accomplished the duty of motherhood, she determined to escape 'the monotony of society's so-called pleasures' (Dixie, 2). In December 1878 she set off for South America where 'scenes of infinite beauty and grandeur' might be lying hidden in the solitude of the mountains which bound the barren plains of the Pampas, into whose mysterious recesses no one had yet ventured. 'And I was to be the first to behold them: an egotistical pleasure, it is true; but the idea had a great charm for me' (Dixie, 3). She was accompanied by her husband, her eldest and her twin brothers, and a friend, J. Beerbohm, a naturalist with some knowledge of the country. Although she was the only woman in the party she took the lead throughout their six months abroad, not only in the pursuit of the big game with which they stocked their larder but also in coping with emergencies varying from the entertainment of unexpected visitors to the devastating shock of an earthquake.

The publication of *Across Patagonia* (1880) established Lady Dixie's reputation as a bold and resourceful traveller with a pen as ready as her gun. It was also partly the reason for her appointment as the *Morning Post*'s war correspondent in South Africa where the Anglo-Zulu War was raging; she was the first woman to be officially appointed by a British newspaper to cover a war. Her husband accompanied her and, although on arriving in Cape Town in March 1881 they found to her chagrin that hostilities were over, they spent the next six months in southern Africa. They toured the country, visiting the battlefields and learning something of the causes and the course of the late conflict, while Lady Dixie contributed articles to the *Morning Post* in which she championed the cause of Cetewayo and his Zulu people. These provided material for *A Defence of Zululand and its King* (1882). The same views were expressed in her account of the South African adventure, *In the Land of Misfortune* (1882), a more serious work than *Across Patagonia* though it has its lighter moments. In some of these Beau is made to cut a less than heroic figure, as when he sleeps through the invasion of their tent by errant mules which his wife is left to drive out—or so she alleges (*In the Land of Misfortune*, 372).

On her return to England, home politics engaged Lady Dixie's attention, particularly those affecting Ireland which she saw as another 'land of misfortune' in need of her support. She was strongly in favour of home rule (as also for Scotland) but opposed measures advocated by the Land League during the agitations of 1880–83, thereby incurring the enmity of the extremist Fenians. On 17 March 1883, when Fenian outrages were exciting London, she announced that, while she was walking by the Thames near Windsor, two men disguised as women, whom she inferred to be Fenian emissaries, vainly attempted her assassination. Her statement attracted worldwide attention, but Sir William Harcourt, the home secretary, declared in the House of Commons that the story was unconfirmed, and nothing further followed.

Lady Dixie's political interests were thenceforth concentrated on the advocacy of complete sex equality. Her aims ranged from the reform of female attire to that of the royal succession law, which, she held, should prescribe the accession of the eldest child, of whichever sex, to the throne. She desired the emendation of the marriage service and of the divorce laws so as to place man and woman on the same level. She formulated such views in *Gloriana, or, The Revolution of 1900* (1890); her stories for children, *The Young Castaways, or, The Child Hunters of Patagonia* (1890) and *Aniwee, or, The Warrior Queen* (1890) had a like purpose. In later life she became convinced of the cruelty of blood sports, which she denounced in *Horrors of Sport* (1891) and the *Mercilessness of Sport* (1901). Lady Dixie died at Glen Stuart, Annan, Dumfriesshire, on 7 November 1905, and was buried in the family grave at Kinmount. **DOROTHY MIDDLETON**

Sources F. C. Dixie, *Across Patagonia* (1880) · C. Stevenson, *Victorian women travel writers in Africa* (1982) · *The Times* (8 Nov 1905) · Burke, *Peerage* · A. Sebba, *Battling for news: the rise of the woman reporter* (1994) · B. Roberts, *Ladies in the Veldt* (1965) · *DNB*
Archives Bodl. Oxf., corresp. with Lord Kimberley
Likenesses A. Maclure, lithograph, 1877, BM, NPG [*see illus.*] · T [T. Chartran], chromolithograph caricature, NPG; repro. in *VF* (24 March 1883) · cartoon, repro. in *VF* (1884) · engraving, repro. in Sebba, *Battling for news*, facing p. 114
Wealth at death £257 2s. 1d.: administration, 12 Dec 1905, *CGPLA Eng. & Wales*

Dixie, Sir Wolstan (1524/5–1594), merchant and administrator, mayor of London, was the fourth son of Thomas Dixie, a husbandman of Catworth in Huntingdonshire, and of Anne Jephson. In 1547 he was apprenticed to a leading merchant adventurer and freeman of the Skinners' Company, Geoffrey Walkeden (whose daughter he subsequently married), and he secured his freedom in 1555. His own trading interests seem to have concentrated on northern France and the Low Countries, and he showed little interest in developing new trades (he did not follow his master's interests in the Russia trade). His subsidy assessments (£50 in 1559, £150 in 1564, £250 in 1577, £300 in 1582, and £400 in 1589) are an indication of his steady accumulation of wealth. He invested in property in London and the provinces, owning the manors of Southwick, Wiltshire, and Market Bosworth, Leicestershire. But he was a Londoner at heart, residing successively in the parishes of St Lawrence Jewry, St Christopher-le-Stocks, St Mary Woolchurch, and St Michael Bassishaw, while maintaining a suburban retreat at Ealing.

Dixie was an assiduous member of his livery company, serving as master on no fewer than seven occasions. After service on the court of common council for Cheap ward (c.1559–c.1570) and Cordwainer Street ward (1572–4), he was elected to the court of aldermen on 4 February 1574, serving for Broad Street ward (1574–93) and briefly for Bassishaw (1593–4). He was a committed alderman, attending 60 per cent of the court's twice-weekly meetings during his tenure. He was sheriff of London in 1575–6 and lord mayor in 1585–6. On 6 February 1586 he was knighted. Dixie assumed the mayoral dignity against the shadows cast by the outbreak of war with Spain and escalating prices. There were rumours of anti-alien disturbances in the spring of 1586, and the tension among the ruling group is evident in Dixie's reaction to a personal attack upon him made at a Paul's Cross sermon on 6 March. George Closse, the minister of St Magnus, had criticized the lord mayor for some act of injustice (unfortunately unspecified in the sources). Although Closse submitted at a well-publicized sermon at Paul's Cross on Palm Sunday as ordered by the court of high commission, Dixie remained dissatisfied and complained to the privy council. Refusing to accept the proffered private reconciliation, he was forced to content himself with the matter being put in suspension during his term of office, a compromise which may well have tainted his reputation for the rest of his term. It was fortunate for Dixie that the attention of Londoners was diverted by the horrific revelation of the Babington plot, the news of the capture of the conspirators in July being greeted with scenes of extraordinary jubilation in the capital.

Dixie married twice. His first wife was Agnes (d. 1567), daughter of his master, Geoffrey Walkeden. In 1569 he married Agnes (d. 1600), daughter of Sir Christopher Draper (d. 1581), lord mayor of London. It was a marriage which connected him with other leading members of the aldermanic bench, for Agnes's sisters married William Webb and Henry Billingsley, who became close friends and colleagues of Dixie. Dixie died on 8 January 1594 in the parish of St Michael Bassishaw in London and was buried there the following day. Dying without children, he left half of his goods to his wife, and the bulk of his estates to his great-nephew, Wolstan, later a prominent Leicestershire gentleman. His widow (who had custody of young Wolstan) remarried shortly after his death, taking as her husband William Hickman, a gentleman and a longstanding family friend.

Dixie's childless state helps to explain the extent of his charitable bequests totalling £4484 13s. 0d., but his religious sympathies, which lay with the godly, also played a role. He left bequests to the strangers' churches in London and provided £600 for the establishment of two fellowships and two scholarships at Sir Walter Mildmay's godly seminary, Emmanuel College, Cambridge. He provided for an annuity of £10 to the support of a lecturer in the church of St Michael Bassishaw. Dixie counted among his friends William Ashbold, the conformist parson of St Peter Cornhill and chaplain to Archbishop Whitgift, Henry Holland, then lecturer at St Martin Orgar, and Thomas Crooke, the presbyterian-inclined lecturer at Gray's Inn and brother-in-law to Laurence Chaderton, master of Emmanuel. To Christ's Hospital, of which he had been president since 1590, he left the manor of Southwick. Other charitable activities were focused upon the manor of Market Bosworth which he had purchased from Henry Hastings, third earl of Huntingdon, in 1589. He left the Skinners a total of £700 to establish a school for fifty to sixty poor scholars in the town, from which also one of the Emmanuel scholarships was to be drawn. There were, however, difficulties in getting the school properly established. The executors delayed the handover of money to the Skinners' Company and withheld the interest which had accrued. As the company declined to take on the charity without full funding, the lord keeper decreed in 1605 that Wolstan Dixie junior should enjoy the nomination of the schoolmaster and scholars.   IAN W. ARCHER

Sources M. Benbow, 'Index of London citizens involved in city government, 1558–1603', U. Lond., Institute of Historical Research, Centre for Metropolitan History · subsidy assessments; customs accounts; will, PRO, PROB 11/83, sig. 1 · wardens' accounts, court minutes, and apprentice bindings/freedom records of Skinners' Company, GL · repertories of court of aldermen; journals of court of common council, CLRO · W. Camden, *The visitation of the county of Leicester in the year 1619*, ed. J. Fetherston, Harleian Society, 2 (1870) · P. J. Foss, *The history of Market Bosworth* (1983) · A. B. Beaven, ed., *The aldermen of the city of London, temp. Henry III–[1912]*, 2 vols. (1908–13) · J. Stow, *The survey of London*, ed. A. M. [A. Munday] and others, rev. edn (1633) · G. Peele, *The device of the pageant borne before Woolstone Dixi lord maior of the citie of London an 1585* (1585) · G. S. Fry and S. J. Madge, eds., *Abstract of inquisitiones post mortem relating to the City of London*, 3 vols., British RS, 15, 26, 36 (1896–1908) · A. W. Hughes Clarke, ed., *The registers of St Mary Magdalen, Milk Street, 1558–1666, and St Michael Bassishaw, London, 1538–1625*, Harleian Society, register section, 72 (1942) · A. W. Hughes Clarke, ed., *The register of St Lawrence Jewry, London*, 1, Harleian Society, registers, 70 (1940) · *Holinshed's chronicles of England, Scotland and Ireland*, ed. H. Ellis, 6 vols. (1807–8) · J. S. Ibish, 'Emmanuel College: the founding generation', PhD diss., Harvard U., 1985, 111–15

Likenesses portrait, 1593, Christ's Hospital, Horsham · engraving, 1600–40, repro. in A. M. Hind, *Engraving in England in the sixteenth and seventeenth centuries*, part 2: *The reign of James I* (1955), p. 370, pl. 278 · T. Trotter, engraving, 1795 (after portrait at Christ's Hospital), repro. in Nichols, *History of Leicestershire*, 4, pt 2, pl. 78, p. 497 · portrait (after portrait at Christ's Hospital), Emmanuel College, Cambridge

Dixon family (*per.* 1770s–1880), iron and coal masters, were for three generations deeply involved in the coal and iron industries of western Scotland. They came to prominence with **William** [i] **Dixon** (1753–1824), iron and coal master, whose origins are obscure but who is reputed to have come to Scotland from Northumberland in 1770 or 1771; during the 1770s he was engaged as manager of the Govan colliery, indicating that he had probably trained as a mining engineer in the north-east of England. This appointment commenced an association of the names Dixon and Govan that was to last almost 200 years until the Govan ironworks, or 'Dixon's blazes', so named for its furnaces' lighting up the night sky, was dismantled in 1958.

The first William Dixon was ambitious and hardworking, and while manager at Govan set up the Calder ironworks in Lanarkshire in 1795 in partnership with David Mushet, the discoverer of the local blackband iron ore which was intermixed with the coal-seams, and James Creelman, a local pottery manufacturer. The partnership lasted until 1802, when Dixon bought out the concern for £19,000; he followed this in 1803 with the purchase of the estate of Palacecraig, lying centrally in the rich coal and ore seams of north Lanarkshire. All of this was undertaken while Dixon still managed the Govan collieries, and when these were put up for sale in 1813 at a price of £30,000 he acquired four-ninths of the stock. He worked with the other members of the purchasing combine for six years, and finally acquired sole control of the Govan colliery in 1819. To this he added further mineral estates at Govanhill and Faskine, also in 1819, and the mineral lands and ironworks at Wilsontown in 1824, the year of his death. In a long working life he had created an extensive coal and iron empire with collieries at Govan, Faskine, Palacecraig, Wilsontown, and Legbrannock, together with ironworks at Calder and Wilsontown.

On William Dixon's death in 1824 his considerable empire passed to his two sons John and William. There was property but little liquid capital, and the elder son John, unwilling to take on the business, sold out to the younger **William** [ii] **Dixon** (1788–1859), iron and coal master. To buy out his brother, William like his father before him had to resort to a partnership with three other investors. This arrangement lasted eleven years until 1835, when Dixon regained control of the family business.

He married Elizabeth Strang, and they had at least one son, who was born at Gallowknow, Gorbals, in Lanarkshire.

The second William Dixon shared his father's drive and ambition. Some time between 1835 and 1840 he sold the lands of Palacecraig to the Bairds of Gartsherrie, purchased another estate at Carfin, near Wishaw, and began smelting and puddling at his newly established Govan Bar Iron Works. He was active in experimenting with the substitution of raw coal for coke in the furnace, and also with J. B. Neilson's idea of heating the blast. He managed to reach a temperature of 600°F in tests and was reported to have made three times as much iron with the same quantity of coal as before. Satisfied with this he blew in the first blast furnace at Govan in 1837. He then closed the Wilsontown ironworks in 1842, and concentrated his iron interests at Govan and Calder.

By the late 1840s Dixon was among the leading coal and iron masters in Scotland, his collieries then providing around 150,000 tons of coal per year. He was a man of great energy and drive, and one who exercised close and detailed control over all his business operations. He was also a citizen of some standing, a trustee of the savings bank of Glasgow and a town councillor. Unfortunately, he was a man of inflexible opinion. He constantly engaged in litigation, notably over Neilson's hot blast patent and with the trustees of the Clyde Navigation, and the Monkland Canal Authority. In the early 1850s this brought him close to bankruptcy, and he was rescued only by loans from friends to meet his debts; these were not repaid until after his death in 1859.

Control of the Dixon empire passed over to his son **William Smith Dixon** (1824–1880), iron and coal master, who had been assistant to his father for some years. Unlike his father and grandfather, William S. Dixon was a cautious manager rather than a risk taker. Under his control the colliery side expanded in the 1860s with new mines at Cockerhill, Titwood, and Ibrox. In the early 1870s, when the new deeper coalfield around Blantyre, 10 miles southeast of Glasgow, was being developed, Dixon chose to convert his company to limited liability status. In 1872 Dixon issued 465 shares of £1000 each, and with the capital extended mining into the Blantyre district. After this it seems that William S. Dixon withdrew from active management and spent much of his time in London or at his estate at Belleisle, Ayr. He served as deputy lieutenant for Lanarkshire and Ayrshire, and was also a major in the 2nd Lanarkshire militia. The community where his works were situated benefited from his generosity, including his funding of the town halls of the joint burghs of Crosshill and Govanhill. Dixon married Catherine Ann, daughter of David Napier, a Singapore merchant, on 21 August 1851.

William S. Dixon died on 16 June 1880 at his home, 14 Grosvenor Place, London, at the early age of fifty-six. He and his wife (who survived him) did not have any children, and thereafter the company was carried on by trustees, becoming a publicly limited company in 1906. The Govan colliery finally closed in 1926. ANTHONY SLAVEN

Sources A. Slaven, 'Dixon, William Smith', *DSBB* · d. cert. [W. S. Dixon] · *Glasgow Herald* (17 June 1880) · parish register (births), Gorbals, Lanarkshire [William Smith Dixon], 7 Sept 1824 · parish register (marriage), Gorbals, Lanarkshire [William Smith Dixon], 21 Aug 1851 · parish register (births), Gorbals, Lanarkshire [William [ii] Dixon], 9 Aug 1788
Likenesses A. Edouart, paper silhouette (William Dixon, 1788–1859), Scot. NPG
Wealth at death £597 1s. 3d.—William Dixon: confirmation, 1863, CCI · £353,706 1s. 8d.—William Smith Dixon: confirmation, 30 Sept 1880, CCI

Dixon, Sir Alfred Herbert, baronet (1857–1920), cotton spinner, was born at 14 St George's Terrace, Kensington, London, on 22 February 1857, the sixth son of Henry Hall *Dixon (1822–1870), barrister and racing journalist, and Caroline, daughter of Thomas Lynes of Hackleton House, Northamptonshire. Educated at Kensington grammar school and Brighton School, Dixon followed his grandfather, Peter Dixon of Carlisle, in entering the cotton industry. He served his apprenticeship with William Houldsworth at the Reddish Spinning Company, Stockport. In 1876 he joined A. & G. Murray, a well-established but by then declining Manchester firm of fine cotton spinners, which, under his youthful but astute management, re-emerged in the forefront of the industry. On 7 April 1880 he married Caroline (d. 1941), daughter of Henry Sandford, cotton manufacturer of Cringle Hall, Manchester.

In 1898 Dixon rejoined Houldsworth in establishing the Fine Spinners' and Doublers' Association, a pioneering amalgamation of thirty-one firms in the cotton industry, which sought to achieve economies of scale in a form of corporate enterprise appropriate to the early twentieth century. The Fine Spinners, with Dixon as its managing director, developed a strong central organization, able to co-ordinate its component firms into a successful vertically integrated whole, avoiding the problems of continuing family autonomy, which bedevilled other early amalgamations. The Fine Spinners was to be the most successful of the early textile mergers in England, with an effective dominance, but never a monopoly, of the fine-spinning sector. By 1909 it had grown to comprise fifty firms, 4 million spindles, and over 30,000 employees, forming Edwardian Britain's largest firm. Under Dixon's guidance, it also set a lead in scientific research, employee welfare, and direct investment in cotton plantations in America and cotton merchanting in Egypt. Dixon remained managing director until 1917, when he became chairman until his death. He cautiously but decisively held back the Fine Spinners from overcapitalization at the end of the war, thus putting the firm in a relatively strong position during the 1920s, and earning his reputation as 'perhaps the wisest as well as the most courageous of cotton men' (B. Bowker, *Lancashire under the Hammer*, 1928, 40).

Dixon also played a pre-eminent part in the business politics of cotton. He was active within the Federation of Master Cotton Spinners, particularly in its labour and conciliation work, was a director of the Manchester Royal Exchange, president of the Textile Institute (1919), and a leading advocate of the empire cotton-growing movement. His strong belief in the collective organization of industry led to his participation in the Federation of British Industry in 1916, serving on several of its early committees and chairing its Manchester branch. Dixon was also one of the growing breed of internationally minded pre-war men of business, an ardent supporter of the International Cotton Federation before 1914 and, as its president in 1919, ready to promote it as a 'businessman's League of Nations'. He led the British delegation to the World Cotton Congress in New Orleans in 1919, and but for his untimely death, he would have presided at the Manchester congress of 1921.

Dixon's standing with masters and men made him an excellent choice as chairman of the Cotton Control Board set up by the government in June 1917 in order to keep the industry working with a minimum supply of raw cotton. It successfully provided a form of collective regulation, a buffer between the government, the unions, and the employers. The board's schemes avoided redundancies in cotton, allaying the government's fears of the social and political unrest which a second cotton famine might have brought. The wisdom of retaining labour in cotton has been questioned, but there is no doubt that Dixon skilfully achieved the board's objectives, combining, in Hubert Henderson's words, 'in a high measure the devotion to duty, the resourceful vigour, the shrewdness, the tenacity of purpose, even obstinacy of a Lancashire businessman' with 'the graces of a singularly gentle and winning personality' (Henderson, 10). Dixon's work was rewarded with a baronetcy on 7 February 1918. He was also a valued contributor to the post-war Board of Trade advisory committee.

Dixon was an enthusiastic actor and cricketer in his youth, but his later activities were hampered by ill health, though in 1915 he chaired the committee which raised the Manchester Pals volunteer battalions. He died at his home, The Moss, Great Warford, Cheshire, on 10 December 1920, of the bronchial asthma from which he had long suffered. He was buried on 13 December at Chelford parish church, where he had served as churchwarden. He was survived by his wife and daughter.   A. C. Howe

Sources A. C. Howe, 'Dixon, Sir Alfred Herbert', *DBB* • H. D. Henderson, *The cotton control board* (1922) • *The jubilee distaff, 1898–1948* (privately published, 1948) • *Manchester Guardian* (11 Dec 1920) • *Manchester Guardian* (13 Dec 1920) • *Manchester City News* (11 Dec 1920) • *Alderley Edge and Wilmslow Advertiser* (17 Dec 1920) • *The Times* (11 Dec 1920) • *The Times* (15 Dec 1920) • F. Kempster and H. C. E. Westropp, eds., *Manchester city battalions of the 90th and 91st infantry brigades*, 2nd edn (1917) • J. Singleton, 'The cotton industry and the British war effort, 1914–1918', *Economic History Review*, 2nd ser., 47 (1994), 601–18 • Burke, *Peerage*
Archives priv. coll., family MSS | Courtaulds, Fine Spinners' records • PRO, BT7, BT197/1, RECO 1/798, SUPP 14/457 • U. Warwick Mod. RC, CBI predecessor archive
Likenesses photograph, repro. in W. B. Tracy and W. T. Pike, *Manchester and Salford at the close of the nineteenth century* (1899) • photograph, repro. in Kempster and Westropp, eds., *Manchester city battalions* • photograph, repro. in *Textile Recorder* (15 Dec 1920), 60
Wealth at death £233,157 4s. 6d.: probate, 30 March 1921, *CGPLA Eng. & Wales*

Dixon, Sir Arthur Lewis (1881–1969), civil servant, was born in Swindon on 30 January 1881, the only son of Seth Dixon, a Wesleyan minister, and his wife, Caroline Lewis. He was educated at Kingswood School, Bath, of which for many years he was later a governor, and entered Sidney Sussex College, Cambridge, where he became ninth wrangler (1902). In 1903 he passed fourth in the open competitive examination for class 1 clerkships in the home civil service and joined the Home Office. In 1909 Dixon married Marie (1863/4–1949), daughter of Alfred Talbot Price, architect; she was seventeen years older than he and there were no children.

It was Dixon's achievement at the Home Office to refashion two great public institutions—the police and fire services—from disparate elements which had scarcely changed since Victorian times. In both he helped to enlarge the powers and responsibilities of the Home Office, imposing his own strong ideals on later development. On the outbreak of war in 1914 he was put in charge of a 'war measures' division. From there he could assess the handicaps suffered by police forces and fire brigades alike, given the absence of any effective system for co-ordination and control. Following Zeppelin raids he drew up a successful mutual assistance scheme between fire brigades, an experience valuable in preparing for the war of 1939–45.

At the end of the First World War the troubles of the police, which had led them to strike, demanded attention. In 1919 the government set up a review committee under Lord Desborough, and Dixon became its secretary. The subsequent reports (1919 and 1920) marked a watershed between old and new police services: as Dixon himself put it later, the changes proposed by Desborough offered 'what amounted to a new conception of the police as a service, an integrated system, rather than a collection of separate forces each concerned with its merely local requirements and personnel' (Critchley, 190).

The 'new conception' had to be worked out in practical terms and Dixon was consequently placed in charge of a newly formed police division in the Home Office. From there he rapidly gained the confidence, and frequently the affection, of those concerned with police administration: chief constables, members of police authorities, and the new Police Federation. By temperament a brilliant planner and organizer rather than an administrator, Dixon maintained his unique authority, virtually unchallenged, for more than twenty years. His reward came with the realization, when war broke out in 1939, that 183 separate police forces, under his guidance, were already acknowledging not only a local loyalty but also a loyalty to the idea of a single police service dedicated to promoting the wider national interest. Meanwhile, his fertile and ingenious mind always fascinated by scientific discovery, Dixon also cast about for ways of harnessing science to detective work. The development of early radio links within forces, the systematic training of detectives, and the establishment of forensic science laboratories stemmed largely from his enthusiasm and drive.

Dixon was promoted to assistant under-secretary of

state in 1932, and four years later he took over the fire brigades division of the Home Office. Convinced that in a future war the real menace would be incendiary rather than high-explosive bombs, he set about developing and equipping the fire brigades with the same drive with which he had modernized the police. Hence he made sure that, on the outbreak of war, ample fire-fighting equipment was available. However, it soon became clear that the service's fragmented organization was dangerous, and when the first heavy air raids came in 1940–41 the government decided on an immediate and radical restructuring of the whole service. The task of creating the National Fire Service during wartime fell naturally to Dixon. The basic plan—the unification of all fire-fighting arrangements, with standard conditions of service—was characteristically drawn up within weeks. It was, said the home secretary, Herbert Morrison, 'one of the quickest administrative revolutions that ever took place'—and it was brilliantly successful. In thus modernizing both the fire service and the police, Dixon made a large personal contribution towards ensuring the stability of the home front during the war. Recognition came with a knighthood in 1941 and promotion to a special rank of principal assistant undersecretary of state in the same year.

Dixon was shy, and to many colleagues seemed aloof and gluttonous for work. He had little social life: he lived, recluse-like, in a succession of private hotels. He inherited from his father abstemious attitudes: he did not smoke, and was a strict teetotaller. He was an active Christian, and gave great help to the British and Foreign Bible Society, of which he was vice-president. He was also a generous benefactor of the Methodist church, of his old school, and of the Police College. While reserved, however, Dixon was not cold; those who penetrated the reserve were devoted to him. Listening to music, walking, and keeping abreast of scientific discoveries were Dixon's chief delights, but his interests were wide-ranging, encompassing geology, for example, as well as palaeontology, astronomy, and nuclear fission—about which he published a book, *Atomic Energy for the Layman* (1950). He was welcomed in many of the observatories and atomic stations of Europe and America, and was a visiting lecturer at Berkeley, California.

Dixon retired from the Home Office on 30 January 1946, but he continued to keep in touch with the two services which he had refashioned. From official papers he compiled three (unpublished) administrative histories which record his work. He died at the Bourne Hall Hotel, Bournemouth, on 14 September 1969.   T. A. CRITCHLEY, rev.

Sources *The Times* (16 Sept 1969) · T. A. Critchley, *A history of police in England and Wales, 900–1966* (1967) · *WWW* · *CGPLA Eng. & Wales* (1969)
Likenesses W. Rothenstein, oils, 1941, Man. City Gall.
Wealth at death £50,045: probate, 15 Dec 1969, *CGPLA Eng; & Wales*

Dixon, Ella Nora Hepworth [*pseud.* Margaret Wynman] (1857–1932), novelist and journalist, was born on 27 March 1857 at Essex Villa, Queens Road, Marylebone, London, the seventh of the eight children (two of whom died young) of William Hepworth *Dixon (1821–1879), author and traveller, who came from Yorkshire, and his wife, Mary Ann MacMahon, a forward-looking Irishwoman. Hepworth Dixon's reminiscences, *As I Knew Them: Sketches of People I have Met on the Way* (1930), portray some of the people she met at her parents' parties. Privately tutored, she went briefly to school in Heidelberg and studied painting in Paris. After her father died she began a career as a journalist, writing for *The World*, the *Daily Telegraph*, and the *Daily Mail*. She was the *Westminster Gazette*'s art critic and published short stories in *Lady's Pictorial*, *Woman's World*, the *St James's Gazette*, and *Woman*. Her first book, published under the pseudonym Margaret Wynman, was *My Flirtations* (1892), light-hearted pieces about contemporary life.

In 1894 Hepworth Dixon published *The Story of a Modern Woman*, a realistic novel which explores (by implication) the difficulties women have in writing truthfully about their lives. Partly autobiographical, it is about Mary Earle, who attends art school while living with her eminent scientist father; after his early death she is close only to Alison Ives and Vincent Hemming. The former dies after visiting her fiancé's abandoned mistress; on her deathbed she exhorts Mary: 'If women ... were only united we could lead the world' (Dixon, *Modern Woman*, 213). Vincent rejects Mary and marries for money, unhappily; she becomes an illustrator and journalist. In the end she refuses to become her lover's mistress but chooses instead a life that is fulfilled, if lonely. Her motive is solidarity with Vincent's wife: 'All we modern women mean to help each other now' (ibid., 255). This phrase, Hepworth Dixon said, was the keynote of the book: 'It is a plea for a kind of moral and social trades-unionism among women' (*Review of Reviews*, 71). An additional theme is a satire on Grub Street, as Mary is shown trying to earn her living despite the prejudices of male editors who tell her that, unlike newspapers, fiction has to be written for 'healthy English homes' (*Modern Woman*, 181). Published to huge acclaim by William Heinemann, 'a lifelong friend', the novel 'led to many literary friendships' (Dixon, *As I Knew Them*, 187) in England, America, and Europe—it was translated into French—and also led to the nickname the 'New Woman' for its author.

Hepworth Dixon never published another novel but led an extremely sociable life, describing in her reminiscences people such as Oscar Wilde, H. G. Wells, Max Beerbohm, Yeats, Osbert Sitwell, and Somerset Maugham. Her life is an example of the seductive rewards of literary success leaving little time for further serious literary work; also an example, perhaps, of someone whose emotional life was blighted by the death of an adored parent. Hepworth Dixon edited *The Englishwoman* from March 1895 to December 1899 (and increasingly came to champion women's rights); in 1904 she published *One Doubtful Hour, and other Side-Lights on the Feminine Temperament*, a collection of short stories. In 1908 her one-act play *The Toy-Shop of the Heart* was produced in London. She continued in her 'pleasant, easy style' (*The Times*) to write numerous articles for magazines on subjects such as 'Is marriage a failure?'

or 'Wardrobes'. She was vice-president of the committee of the Femina Vie Heureuse and Northcliffe prizes for literature. A charming-looking woman with curly brown hair and a pert nose, Ella Hepworth Dixon died unmarried, of respiratory disease, on 12 January 1932 at the Savoy Court Hotel, 23 Granville Place, London, and was cremated three days later at Golders Green.

NICOLA BEAUMAN

Sources E. H. Dixon, *As I knew them: sketches of people I have met on the way* (1930) · K. Flint, introduction, in E. H. Dixon, *The story of a modern woman* (1990) · *Review of Reviews*, 10 (1894), 70–71 · *The Times* (13 Jan 1932), 14 · *WWW* · b. cert. · d. cert.
Likenesses engraving, repro. in *Review of Reviews*, 70 · photographs, repro. in Dixon, *As I knew them*, frontispiece and facing p. 136

Dixon, Frederick William [Freddie] (1892–1956), racing motorist, was born on 21 April 1892 at 31 Alliance Street, Stockton-on-Tees, one of the eight children of John Dixon, a general labourer, and his wife, Martha, *née* Agar. After leaving school at the age of thirteen he began work in a garage in Stockton, before transferring to the Middlesbrough branch of the firm. He first owned a motor cycle in 1909 and began racing with the Middlesbrough motor club. Within a year he was winning local speed trials and hill-climbing events.

In 1912 Dixon made his début in an Isle of Man tourist trophy (TT) race, riding a Cleveland Precision manufactured in Middlesbrough by Egerton Price. Known as F. W. or Freddie, Dixon was one of a band of riders who raced both before and after the First World War, during which he served in the Army Service Corps and rose to the rank of staff sergeant. In 1920 he made a return to TT racing with the team run by the manufacturers of the Indian motor cycle and came twelfth in the senior race. In 1921 he came second, his best ever placing, and that year made his Brooklands début, in which he came second in the 500 mile race on a Harley Davidson. He also raced at the Belgian grand prix, on an Indian, and in 1922 recorded the fastest time at the Clipstone speed trials, by reaching 130 m.p.h. on a Harley Davidson.

In 1923 Dixon began a close association with the Douglas factory, and gained his first TT victory that year on one of its machines when he won the inaugural race for sidecars. Dixon himself designed the famous 'banking sidecar' in which his passenger, Walter Denny, rode to victory. By means of a lever Denny was able to raise or lower the sidecar to suit the bends, thereby increasing the safe cornering speed and giving a significant advantage over the traditional rigid-frame designs. 'This was typical of Dixon's ingenuity ... he was a gifted engineer, albeit of the type that could be described as an inspired mechanic rather than an academic theorist, and his services were much in demand by Douglas, Brough Superior and others' (Setright, 50). Dixon also came third in the senior TT race in 1923 and won the Belgian grand prix on a 500 cc Indian. He crowned an impressive year by setting a new world motor cycle speed record of 106.5 m.p.h. on a course in the Bois de Boulogne on 9 September, though this was soon broken by his compatriot Claude Temple, who reached 108.48 m.p.h. at Brooklands in November 1923.

On 20 January 1926 Dixon married Margaret (Dolly) Thew. They had one daughter, Jean, who often accompanied her father to races. He secured his first and only solo win in a TT race in 1927, when he won the junior event on an H.R.D.; he also came sixth in the senior race that year. But after a poor showing in 1928 he retired from the sport, judging that he no longer had the stamina or the physique for it. He stayed with Douglas for another two years, working with the design and racing department, and after experimenting with his own motor cycle designs he launched a new career racing Riley motor cars. His first major race was at the Ulster TT at Ards in August 1932, when he crashed out at Quarry Corner, 'probably due to a lack of concentration after spending the previous night re-building the engine' (Herbert, 48). The Riley company had supplied Dixon with a fully race-prepared 1100 cc four-cylinder engine, but he always preferred to 'fettle' his machines, as he put it, tuning them for optimum performance. In September 1932 he built his own single-seat racing special with Riley parts, which he dubbed the 'red mongrel', and at Brooklands in October he broke six international speed records, driving 120 miles in torrential rain at an average of over 110 m.p.h. In 1933 he won the March sprint handicap at Brooklands and helped Rita Don to victory in the ladies' race, when he took the passenger seat in his own Riley: he reputedly spurred her on by keeping the hand throttle open and prodding her with a pin if she braked too early. She won by a large margin.

In June 1934, after further victories at Brooklands, Dixon came third in the Le Mans 24-hour race, with Cyril Paul. He enjoyed continued success with Riley, winning the British Racing Drivers' Club 500 mile race in September, and leading the Riley team to a first, second, and third in the British empire trophy race at Brooklands in July 1935. In September 1935 he won the Ulster TT in a 1.5 litre factory-built Riley, thereby becoming the only man to win TT races on two, three, and four wheels. He repeated his success in the Ulster TT in 1936 and again won the Brooklands 500 mile race. The British Racing Drivers' Club awarded Dixon its gold star for track racing in 1934, and its gold star for road racing in 1935. About this time ambitious plans for an attempt on the world land-speed record were scrapped when problems developed with the car, a Sunbeam Silver Bullet. Towards the end of his racing career Dixon helped to develop a four-wheel-drive racing car. The project was resumed after the Second World War but Dixon left following a disagreement with Harry Ferguson, the tractor manufacturer, who became involved in financing the work.

Freddie Dixon came to prominence during the era when Britain emerged as a dominant force in world motor cycle racing. A colourful character of medium height and solid build, he was 'very much a hard man, whether it were a matter of taking knocks or taking drink' (Setright, 50). His drinking attracted comment, and he made it a rule never to indulge before a race. A 'complex character not averse to practical joking', he was 'especially fond of getting his own way with officialdom', and when obliged to wear goggles in his motor cycle racing days he complied only after first taking out the lenses (Herbert, 7). He also had his road cars fitted with the same controls as his racing cars, so that he could practise continuously: a driving offence led to a brief spell in Durham prison in 1935.

Dixon died suddenly at his home at Ardverness, Wray Common Road, Reigate, Surrey, on 5 November 1956. His wife survived him. The F. W. Dixon challenge trophy was instituted by the British Automobile Racing Club in his memory. MARK POTTLE

Sources J. Herbert, ed., *F. W. Dixon: Flying Freddie, 1892–1956* [1986] · *The Times* (2 Nov 1925), 4c · *The Times* (31 Oct 1932), 5e · *The Times* (6 Nov 1956), 13c · *The Times* (22 Feb 1963), 4d · P. Carrick, *Encyclopedia of motor-cycle sport* (1982) · L. J. K. Setright, *The Guinness book of motor-cycling facts and feats* (1982) · *The Autocar* (9 Nov 1956), 733 · 'The Brooklands Society', www.brooklands.org.uk/ · d. cert.
Likenesses photograph, 1923, repro. in Setright, *Guinness book of motor-cycling facts*, 113 · photographs, repro. in Herbert, ed., *F. W. Dixon*
Wealth at death £29,604 8s. 6d.: probate, 18 Nov 1956, CGPLA Eng. & Wales

Dixon, George (*fl.* 1776–1791), naval officer and fur trader, details of whose parents and upbringing are unknown, served as a petty officer in the *Discovery* during James Cook's last voyage in 1776 and appears later to have had the command of a merchant ship. Dixon, always interested in the search for the north-west passage, wrote to Sir Joseph Banks in August 1784, urging the overland exploration of Canada from Quebec to the north-west coast of North America. In May 1785 he was engaged by the King George's Sound Company (headed by Richard Cadman Etches) for the development and prosecution of the fur trade of the north-west coast. Dixon was appointed to command the *Queen Charlotte* and sailed from Gravesend on 29 August 1785 in company with the *King George*, whose captain, Nathaniel Portlock, had been his shipmate in the *Resolution* and was now the commander of the expedition. Having doubled Cape Horn and touched at the Sandwich (Hawaiian) Islands, they sailed from there on 13 June 1786; on 18 July they reached the coast of North America, near the mouth of Cook Inlet, in latitude 59° N. They remained there for several weeks and then worked their way south towards King George's Sound (Nootka Sound), off which they were on 24 September. Prevented from entering the sound by baffling winds and calms they returned to the Sandwich Islands, where they wintered.

On 13 March 1787 the *Queen Charlotte* and the *King George* again sailed for the north-west coast of North America, and on 24 April they anchored off Montague Island. Here on 14 May Dixon's ship separated from the *King George*, it being considered more likely to lead to profitable results if the two worked independently. During the next three months Dixon was employed as far south as Nootka Sound (in mid-August), purchasing sea otter pelts from the Haida, taking eager note of Native American manners and customs, as well as of the trade facilities, and making a careful survey of the several points which came within his reach. James Cook had already denoted the general outline of the coast but the detail was still wanting, much of

which Dixon now provided. Of these additions the most important was the large archipelago that he named Queen Charlotte Islands and later described as having surpassed 'our most sanguine expectations, and afforded a greater quantity of furs than perhaps any place hitherto known' (*Voyage Round the World*, 235). Though he sighted and named Queen Charlotte Sound, Dixon failed to discover that it was a southward passage. Since the first object of the voyage was trade, and as the Queen Charlotte Islands seemed to more than answer immediate wants, Dixon was perhaps careless of further discoveries and, 'while claiming to have made considerable additions to the geography of this coast', he contented himself with the remark that:

> so imperfectly do we still know it that it is in some measure
> to be doubted whether we have yet seen the mainland.
> Certain it is that the coast abounds with islands, but whether
> any land we have been near is really the continent remains
> to be determined by future navigators. (ibid., 235–6)

An examination of Dixon's chart shows in fact that most of his work lay among the islands.

On leaving Nootka Sound the *Queen Charlotte* returned to the Sandwich Islands, whence she sailed on 18 September for China, where it had been agreed that she was to meet her consort. On 9 November she anchored at Macao, and at Whampoa (Huangpu) on 25 November she was joined by the *King George*. There they sold their furs, of which the *Queen Charlotte* had a particularly good cargo. Having taken on board a shipment of tea they dropped down to Macao, and on 9 February 1788 they sailed for England. In bad weather off the Cape of Good Hope the ships parted company and, though they met again at St Helena, they then sailed independently. The *Queen Charlotte* arrived off Dover on 17 September, having been preceded by the *King George* by about a fortnight.

When a rival trader and explorer, John Meares, published an account of his voyages of 1788 and 1789 Dixon wrote a pamphlet criticizing its many inaccuracies and false claims to priority of discovery. There followed a brief pamphlet exchange, from which Dixon emerged victorious. Thereafter he continued to advise politicians and promoters of British discoveries on the possibility of finding a north-west passage. Of his later life little more is known. He may have taught navigation at Gosport and he may be the author of *The Navigator's Assistant* (1791). Previously, in 1789, Dixon had published, with Portlock, *A Voyage Round the World; but More Particularly to the North-West Coast of America*; aside from the introduction and appendix the text was actually written by the supercargo of the *Queen Charlotte*, William Beresford. Regardless of his actions after returning to England, Dixon had established himself as a man of ability and attainments, a keen observer, and a good navigator. Details of his death are unknown.

J. K. LAUGHTON, *rev.* BARRY M. GOUGH

Sources F. W. Howay, ed., *The Dixon–Meares controversy* (1929); repr. (1969) · B. M. Gough, *The northwest coast* (1992) · B. M. Gough, 'Dixon, George', *DCB*, vol. 4 · W. B. [W. Beresford], *A voyage round the world*, ed. G. Dixon, 2nd edn (1789) · 'Letters of Captain George

Dixon in the Banks collection', ed. R. H. Dillon, *British Columbia Historical Quarterly*, 14 (1950), 167–71

Dixon, George (1820–1898), educational reformer and politician, was born on 1 July 1820 at Gomersal, Yorkshire, the fourth son in the family of five sons and three daughters of Abraham Dixon (*d.* 1850), merchant, of Whitehaven in Cumberland, and his wife, Letitia (*d.* 1842), daughter of John Taylor of Gomersal. He was educated at Leeds grammar school (1829–37) and travelled to France to learn the language in 1837–8. He then followed his brother Abraham into employment with Rabone Bros. & Co., foreign merchants of Birmingham. After spending three years in Australia in connection with the business, he became a partner in 1844 and succeeded his brother as head of the firm, which manufactured measuring instruments. On 11 September 1855 he married Mary (1832/3–1855), youngest daughter of Judge James Stansfeld of the Halifax county court, and sister of James Stansfeld.

Dixon came to public attention as an active member of the Birmingham and Edgbaston Debating Society, in which local politicians learned and practised the art of public speaking. He was known for his donations to the poor, his promotion of the rifle volunteer movement in Birmingham (December 1859), and his generous lead in securing Aston Hall for the town in September 1866. He became president of the Birmingham chamber of commerce and a magistrate (1864), town councillor for the Edgbaston ward (1863), and, in November 1866, mayor. In June 1867 his decisive action averted sectarian disorder during Catholic riots against the protestant demagogue William Murphy.

Dixon detested religious bigotry of all kinds. Early in 1867 he began a series of Birmingham conferences to represent various religious and political opinions on the state of education. It was resolved that the municipal corporation should levy a rate for education and curb the employment of uninstructed young children. Dixon, supported by Joseph Chamberlain, advocated a compulsory education system, but this was controversial in view of its proposed non-sectarian, and indeed secular, aspects. The Birmingham Education Aid Society was founded by Dixon and others, using their own resources, to extend school provision and pay the fees of the poorer children. In 1869 Dixon was elected president of the National Education League, founded by himself, Chamberlain, John Sandford, George Dawson, and R. W. Dale, to press for a national education system in England and Wales.

Dixon's educational interests assisted his election as Liberal MP for Birmingham in July 1867. In a maiden speech to the Commons (*Hansard 3*, 12 March 1868) he asserted that three causes were uppermost in the minds of the working-class electorate which he represented: justice for Ireland through the disestablishment of the Irish church; justice for themselves through abolition of the rate-paying clauses relating to the recent Reform Act; justice for their children through the extension and improvement of national education. Dixon supported a Married Women's Property Act (10 June 1868) and was concerned about the adulteration of food and drink, the powers of

George Dixon (1820–1898), by Henry John Whitlock

the board of guardians, election expenses, the provision of rifles for India, and the bankruptcy laws. He wished the Licensing Act to be impartially administered, which would have increased political patronage in the localities (*Birmingham Biographia*, 1872–5). He argued the case for representative government with radical working men (*Diplomatic Review*, April 1872).

Dixon's arguments for the improvement of national education were based on the need for a skilled workforce to meet overseas competition (*Hansard 3*, 24 March 1868). On the introduction of W. E. Forster's bill in 1870, Dixon dropped his own proposals and generally voted in support, but, prompted by Chamberlain, he moved a hostile amendment to the second reading, opposing the provision that religious instruction should be determined by local authorities. On 5 March 1872 he pressed for the establishment of school boards in rural as well as urban areas. In 1874 he failed in an attempt to make school attendance compulsory, which he repeated with the support of the Agricultural Labourers' Union during 1875–6.

Suffering from pressure of work and anxious about his wife's health, in June 1876 Dixon admitted his intention to resign his parliamentary seat knowing that it would pass to Chamberlain, whom he greatly admired, though his decision was forced by an announcement in the *Birmingham Post*. He had served on the Birmingham school board since 1870 and now replaced Chamberlain as its chairman (1876), though the latter tried to maintain his influence over the board in favour of secularism. This caused a temporary estrangement between the two men, to Dixon's great regret. Himself a moderate Anglican, he came to support Bible reading without comment in board schools, with religious teaching and prayer on a voluntary basis. He advocated compulsory attendance, better provision for basic literacy, and the growth of technical education in the upper standards VI and VII. In 1884 he equipped at his own expense the Bridge Street seventh grade school, which later perpetuated his name, and which served as a model of its type. He advocated a trained and fully qualified teaching profession through queen's scholarships, day training colleges, and rewards to certificated teachers. His speeches to the Birmingham school board were published as policy documents in 1881 and 1889.

When the parliamentary boundaries of Birmingham were extended in 1885 Dixon returned to the Commons as MP for the Edgbaston division in November of that year. Although he expressed anti-imperialist views during the Suez Canal crisis of 1883, he separated from Gladstone on the issue of home rule for Ireland, which he opposed in 1885–6, falling silent on all but educational issues in parliament. He took a prominent part in the round-table conference of 1887, which unsuccessfully attempted to achieve Liberal reunion, and later pressed for Conservative concessions in return for Unionist support. His voyage to Cape Town and New Zealand in 1888 increased his concern for imperial trade, but he threatened resignation over rating reform and subsidy to the agricultural interest in his later years (*Birmingham Daily Post*, 25 January 1898). He strongly opposed Sir John Gorst's Education Bill on the grounds that it tilted financial provision towards voluntary agencies and away from school boards (*Hansard 4*, 1 Feb 1897), and revived the National Education League to campaign against it.

Dixon died of heart and kidney failure at his residence, The Dales, 42 Augustus Road, Edgbaston, Birmingham, on 24 January 1898. He received no public honours apart from the freedom of the city of Birmingham on 4 January, shortly before his death. He protested that he wanted recognition only from those with whom he had worked for so long (*Birmingham Biographia*, 941–2). His obituary in *The Times* stressed his achievement as an educational reformer, his conscientious public work, and kindness of heart, while noting his lack of humour and limited power of oratory. Joseph Chamberlain's tribute to him as a vice-president of the Unionist Party in Birmingham referred to his services to education and strenuous opposition to home rule: 'a tower of strength to us' (*The Times*, 26, 27 Jan 1898). Chamberlain's late colleague may, however, have been less 'simple-minded' than he supposed. Dixon's funeral on the 28th matched his importance, and its interdenominational character, Jewish as well as Christian, was noted (*Birmingham Daily Post*, 30 Jan 1898). He was buried in Witton cemetery.   V. E. CHANCELLOR

Sources *Birmingham Daily Post* (25 Jan 1898) · *Birmingham Daily Post* (27 Jan 1898) · *Birmingham Daily Post* (28 Jan 1898) · *Birmingham Daily Post* (29 Jan 1898) · *The Times* (25 Jan 1898) · *The Times* (29 Jan 1898) · *Birmingham Biographia*, Birm. CL · J. M. Jones, *George Dixon, the man and the schools* (1980) [pamphlet, privately circulated] · Burke, *Gen. GB* · D. Fraser, *Urban politics in Victorian England* (1976) · P. T. Marsh, *Joseph Chamberlain, entrepreneur in politics* (1994) · J. P. Parry, *Democracy and religion* (1986) · J. Murphy, *Church, state and schools in Britain, 1800–1970* (1971) · Gladstone, *Diaries* · T. W. Reid, *Life of the Right Honourable William Edward Forster*, new edn, 2 vols. (1888); repr. in 1 vol. (1970) · *CGPLA Eng. & Wales* (1898) · m. cert. · d. cert. · IGI · DNB · Hansard

Archives Birm. CL, town council minutes · U. Birm. L., special collections department, corresp. | BL, Dilke MSS · BL, Gladstone MSS · BL, Alfred Russell Wallace MSS · Lpool RO, Melly MSS · U. Birm. L., special collections department, corresp. with Joseph Chamberlain · W. Yorks. AS, Leeds, corresp. relating to travels in Great Britain; journal relating to travels in Spain and Portugal; papers relating to his life

Likenesses H. J. Whitlock, photograph, NPG [*see illus.*] · lithographs, Birm. CL · photograph, George Dixon School, Birmingham · photographs, Birm. CL

Wealth at death £184,766 5*s.* 11*d.*: probate, 23 March 1898, *CGPLA Eng. & Wales*

Dixon, Henry Hall [*pseuds.* the Druid, General Chasse] (1822–1870), sporting writer, was born on 16 May 1822 in Carlisle, Cumberland, the second son of Peter Dixon (1789–1866), a cotton manufacturer, and his wife, Sarah Rebecca, daughter of General Tredway Clarke. He was educated at Rugby School (1838–40) under Thomas Arnold and at Trinity College, Cambridge (1841–6), where he graduated BA in 1846. He would have obtained high honours in classics had he not had an attack of ophthalmia, a disease from which he suffered for over twenty-five years. In 1847 he moved to Doncaster, where his father had arranged for him to be articled to a firm of solicitors headed by Robert Baxter.

No greater mistake could have been made, for Baxter detested horse-racing and campaigned for the abolition of Doncaster races, whereas Dixon had already become a lifelong devotee of the sport. At Rugby he saw Lottery, the greatest steeplechaser of the time, win the 1840 Dunchurch steeplechase, and reported this famous race to his form master as 'Lottery primus erat; Nonna secunda fuit' (Lawley, 79). While still at school, and later at Cambridge, he wrote on sporting subjects for *Bell's Life in London and Sporting Chronicle*, so it was natural that after he moved to Doncaster he should spend more time writing on the same subjects for the *Doncaster Gazette* than studying for the law. In a short time he became editor of the paper, and from it was introduced to Vincent Dowling, editor of *Bell's Life*; on Dowling's death in November 1852 he was offered, but refused, the editorship of *Bell's Life*. He also declined the offer of a government post from Sir James Graham.

Dixon married on 12 May 1847 Caroline (*b.* 1824), daughter of Thomas Lynes; they had thirteen children, many of whom died in infancy. Among those who survived into adulthood was Sir Alfred Herbert *Dixon, cotton spinner. In 1850 they moved from Doncaster to London, where Dixon was reading for the bar, living first at St George's Terrace, Gloucester Road, and then at Kensington Square. The same year he began writing regularly for the *Sporting*

Magazine, first under the pseudonym of General Chasse, and then as the Druid. Much of the material that first appeared in his articles in this and other sporting journals was later incorporated into his books *The Post and the Paddock* (1856), *Silk and Scarlet* (1859), and *Scott and Sebright* (1862). These books are important sources for turf history; they rapidly became best-sellers, and have retained their position as classics of sporting literature to this day. He was also a regular contributor to reviews and magazines. For many years he wrote the columns 'National sports' and 'The farm' for the *Illustrated London News*; he did biographies and leaders for the *Sporting Life*, wrote political verse for *Punch* and *The Examiner*, and contributed articles to the *Gentleman's Magazine* and the *Daily News*. Perhaps the two best articles he wrote were 'Cub-hunting' in the *Daily News* and a memoir of the marquess of Hastings in the *Sporting Life*.

The Druid rarely hunted or betted on a horse-race, but he was an enthusiastic spectator of many kinds of sport, including coursing, cricket, and billiards as well as horse-racing; prize-fighting and rowing, however, had little appeal to him. He wrote 'rather for the amusement than the conviction of mankind' (*Baily's Magazine*, 18, 1870, 119) and his style was regarded as 'quaint almost to oddity' (*Field Quarterly Magazine and Review*, 1, 1870, 179). He collected an immense amount of information, to which he then gave a somewhat rose-coloured hue. Perhaps betraying their origins as magazine articles, and suffering from a lack of revision (which the Druid never cared to do), his books have a certain formlessness, and they contain a number of obscure allusions, but there is also a strong vein of poetry in many of his sporting recollections and landscape descriptions. Although many sporting journalists have tried to emulate him since, few have succeeded.

Dixon was called to the bar by the Middle Temple in 1853 and practised for a time on the midland circuit. While writing *Silk and Scarlet*, he was also, to placate his father, compiling *A Treatise on the Law of the Farm* (1858), which remained a standard work for over forty years. This awakened his interest in farming matters, and, following its publication, he began a series of articles on 'The flocks and herds of Great Britain' for the *Mark Lane Express*. He visited over eighty herds, and towards the end of his life he became more interested in cattle and farming matters than the turf. *Saddle and Sirloin* (1870) is his principal work on the herds and cattle of England. In 1865 he published *Field and Fern*, which brought together the results of a tour he made of all the principal Scottish herds. At the end of this tour he rode from the Orkney Islands back to his house in London on a half-broken mare to arrive home utterly exhausted in the middle of a snowstorm with the words 'Thank God for bringing me home to die with wife and children around me' (Lawley, 330).

The Druid had a reputation for eccentricity, arising for the most part from absent-mindedness and introspection. He never kept regular meal times, and displayed a marked indifference to money. Perhaps as a result of his numerous tramps, he suffered from a succession of severe colds, which led to asthma and then to bronchitis, and his health deteriorated. Towards the end of his life he was in considerable pain, aggravated by a polyp in the nose, and he confided to his eldest son that he would be the happiest man at his own funeral. He died of heart disease and dropsy on 16 March 1870 at his home, 59 Warwick Gardens, Kensington, London. His wife survived him. Few of the journals for which he wrote paid him, and he died a relatively poor man. His eldest son, Henry Sydenham Dixon (1848–1931), became a noted writer on sporting topics.

JOHN PINFOLD

Sources F. Lawley, *Life and times of 'The Druid'* (1895) · *Sporting Magazine*, 3rd ser., 55 (1870), 294–7 · *Field Quarterly Magazine and Review*, 1 (1870), 179 · *Baily's Magazine*, 18 (1870), 119–20 · J. B. Booth, *Bits of character: a life of Henry Hall Dixon, 'The Druid'* (1936) · Venn, *Alum. Cant.* · DNB · d. cert.

Likenesses W. J. Alais, engraving, repro. in Lawley, *Life and times* · engraving, repro. in *Illustrated Sporting and Dramatic News*, 1 (1874), 64 · two photographs, repro. in Booth, *Bits of character*, facing p. 28

Wealth at death under £3000: resworn probate, July 1879, *CGPLA Eng. & Wales* (1870)

Dixon, Henry Horatio (1869–1953), botanist, was born in Dublin on 19 May 1869, the son of George Dixon (*d.* 1871), the owner of a soap works who had scientific interests, and his wife, Rebecca, daughter of George Yeates of Dublin, whose family were scientific instrument makers. Following his father's death, Henry, his six brothers, and two sisters were raised by his mother. He was educated at Rathmines School and entered Trinity College in 1887 with an exhibition. He obtained a classical scholarship in 1890 but changed to natural science, in which he obtained a senior moderatorship in 1891. After working in Bonn under Eduard Strasburger he returned in 1894 to Trinity College as assistant to E. P. Wright, whom he succeeded in the university chair of botany in 1904. In 1906 he became director of the botanic garden; in 1910 keeper of the herbarium; and in 1922 professor of plant biology in Trinity College. In 1907 Dixon married Dorothea Mary, daughter of Sir John Franks, secretary of the Irish land commission. They had three sons, all of whom maintained the tradition of academic distinction, one as a neurologist, and two as biochemists and fellows of King's College, Cambridge.

Two of the major fields of work at Bonn were the studies of nuclear division and of transpiration and ascent of sap. The significance of reduction division (meiosis) was just being recognized in the Strasburger school where a great part of the cytological studies was based on hand sections. In a paper to the Royal Irish Academy in 1895 Dixon expressed the view that bivalents owed their appearance to the joining of chromosomes rather than the splitting of some structure. In the school of botany he maintained his interests in cytology and kept a collection of his sections of endosperm made in Bonn until 1926. From these sections he had developed the idea of a mitotic hormone, as the sections appeared to show waves of nuclear division. They showed a zone of prophases, followed by zones of metaphases, anaphases, and telophases. This must have been one of the first demonstrations of synchronous cell divisions. Photographs of the sections, made about 1892, were published by the Royal Dublin Society in 1946.

Dixon's most important work was on transpiration and water relations of plants. This also stemmed from his association with Strasburger who in 1890–93 published work on channels of transport of sap. Dixon's observations of Strasburger's experiments demonstrating that the ascent of sap killed sections of trees posed the problem of possible physical mechanisms. Dixon, together with his great friend John Joly (1857–1933), provided the solution in their classic paper published by the Royal Society of London in 1895, in which they established the role of cohesion of water as an essential factor in plant water relations. Dixon followed this paper with many studies on tensile strength of water and of sap containing gases in solution. Then followed a series of studies with W. R. G. Atkins on osmotic pressures in plant cells. Further studies concerned the resistance to flow of sap presented by the channels of transport and its relation to the detailed structure of wood.

In his presidential address to the botany section of the British Association (1922) Dixon put forward the view that rates of transport of sugar were such that the channel of transport could not possibly be the phloem but must be the xylem. (Later Dixon's former student T. G. Mason, working on the subject of transport of sugar in yams and later in cotton, showed that the phloem was responsible for the transport and that what Dixon regarded as an impossibly fast rate of movement did occur. The mechanism remained to be elucidated.)

Dixon was full of ideas, some of them with terrifying consequences, as when he measured hydrostatic pressures in leaf cells by compressing leafy shoots in glass containers which occasionally blew up. He grew seedlings in sterile culture in 1892, some thirty years before this became a fashionable research procedure. In 1902 he published the compensated manometric technique for study of respiration and photosynthesis in plants, which was subsequently much extended by others. In the very different field of taxonomy, he developed keys for the recognition of timbers, especially mahogany, and worked on the experimental taxonomy of some of the saxifrages of co. Kerry. His publications included *Transpiration and the Ascent of Sap in Plants* (1914) and *Practical Plant Biology* (1922).

The school of botany in Trinity College, Dublin, was Dixon's creation. The building and laboratory, opened in 1907, were Dixon's design and the school and the activities within it were an expression of his orderly and very active nature. His critical and at the same time cordial personality pervaded it. Visitors travelled there from all over the world.

Dixon, who retired from his chair in 1949, served in many public capacities. He was a commissioner of Irish Lights, a trustee of the National Library of Ireland, and a member of the council of the International Institute of Agriculture. He was elected FRS in 1908 and was Croonian lecturer in 1937; he was awarded the Boyle medal (1916) of the Royal Dublin Society, over which he later presided, and was an honorary fellow of Trinity College. He was an honorary life member of the American Society of Plant Physiologists. He died at his home, Somerset House, Temple Road, Dublin, on 20 December 1953; he was survived by his wife. T. A. BENNET-CLARK, *rev.* V. M. QUIRKE

Sources W. R. G. Atkins, *Obits. FRS*, 9 (1954), 79–97 · personal knowledge (1971) · *WWW*, 1951–60
Archives TCD, corresp., notebooks | TCD, corresp. with John Joly · U. Glas., Archives and Business Records Centre, letters to F. O. Bower
Likenesses W. Stoneman, photograph, 1922, NPG
Wealth at death £6633 4*s.* 11*d.* in England: probate, 27 Sept 1954, *CGPLA Eng. & Wales*

Dixon, James (1788–1871), Wesleyan Methodist minister, was born on 29 October 1788 at King's Mills, a hamlet near Castle Donington in Leicestershire. After his conversion in 1807 and a period in local preaching, he became a Wesleyan minister in 1812. For some years he attracted no particular notice in the circuits in which he served. It was after his return from Gibraltar in 1825 that his remarkable gifts began to be observed, and he was soon regarded as among the leading preachers of the Wesleyan body. He was elected president of the conference in 1841, when he preached the sermon 'Methodism in its origin, economy, and present position' (subsequently published). In 1847 he was elected representative of the English conference to the conference of the Methodist Episcopal church in the United States, and also president of the conference of Canada. While in North America he preached and addressed meetings in many of the chief cities. His well-known work *Methodism in America* (1849) was the fruit of this visit.

Dixon remained in the itinerant Wesleyan ministry for fifty years, travelling in London, Liverpool, Manchester, Birmingham, Sheffield, and other large towns. His preaching was entirely original, and was marked by grandeur, thought, and impassioned feeling. His reputation as a platform speaker was equally high. His speeches at the great Wesleyan missionary anniversaries, and on the slave trade, popery, and other such questions as then stirred the evangelical party in England, were celebrated. He was selected several times to represent the Methodist church at mass meetings connected with these issues. Dixon belonged to the middle period of Methodism, the period with which are associated the names of Jabez Bunting, Richard Watson (whose daughter Mary he married), and Thomas Jackson. Dixon was author of a *Memoir of the Rev. W. Edward Miller*, the organist and tune writer, and of several published sermons, charges, and lectures. He also wrote occasionally in the *London Quarterly Review*, which he had helped to establish. But the great work of his life was preaching, and his sermons were among the most ennobling and beautiful examples of the modern evangelical pulpit. Because of his failing sight Dixon retired from the full-time ministry in 1862, spending his closing years in Bradford, where he died on 28 December 1871. Among his surviving children was the ecclesiastical historian and poet Richard Watson *Dixon.

R. W. DIXON, *rev.* TIM MACQUIBAN

Sources Minutes of the Methodist Conference, 1872 · W. Hill, *An alphabetical arrangement of all the Wesleyan-Methodist ministers and preachers*, rev. M. C. Osborn, 11th edn (1869) · R. W. Dixon, *Life of James Dixon* (1874) · 'Watson, Richard (1781–1833)', *DNB*

Wealth at death under £2000: probate, 5 July 1872, *CGPLA Eng. & Wales*

Dixon, Jeremiah (1733–1779), surveyor and astronomer, was born in Bishop Auckland, co. Durham, on 27 July 1733, the fifth of the seven children of George Dixon, a well-to-do Quaker coalmine owner, and his wife, Mary Hunter of Newcastle. He was educated at John Kipling's school in Barnard Castle, where he acquired an interest in mathematics and astronomy. While still a young man in south Durham, he made the acquaintance of the mathematician William Emerson, the instrument maker John Bird, and the natural philosopher Thomas Wright. The Quaker minute book of Raby, co. Durham, has the following entry under 28 October 1760: 'Jery Dixon, son of George and Mary of Cockfield, disowned for drinking to excess'. This weakness was apparently inherited from his father, but there is no evidence that it affected his career.

In 1760 the Royal Society chose Charles Mason to go to Sumatra to observe the 1761 transit of Venus, and, probably on Bird's recommendation, Mason suggested Dixon should go as his assistant. An encounter with a French frigate delayed their final sailing so that they could not reach Sumatra in time. They therefore landed at the Cape of Good Hope, where the transit was successfully observed on 6 June 1761. On the passage home they stopped at St Helena in October and, after discussion with Nevil Maskelyne, who had observed the transit there, Dixon returned temporarily to the Cape with Maskelyne's clock to carry out gravity experiments. Mason and Dixon eventually reached England early in 1762.

In August 1763 Mason and Dixon signed an agreement with Thomas Penn and Frederick Calvert, seventh Baron Baltimore, the hereditary proprietors of the provinces of Pennsylvania and Maryland respectively, to go to North America to help local surveyors define the disputed boundary between the two provinces. After arriving in Philadelphia with their instruments in November, they began operations before Christmas 1763. When work for the proprietors on what was to become the famous Mason–Dixon line was complete late in 1766, they began on the Royal Society's behalf, at Dixon's suggestion, to measure a degree of the meridian on the Delmarva peninsula in Maryland and to make gravity measurements with a clock sent out by the society—the same one that Maskelyne had had in St Helena and Dixon took to the Cape in 1761. They reported their task complete on 21 June 1768 and sailed for England on 11 September. Before leaving, they were both admitted as corresponding members of the American Society for Promoting Useful Knowledge.

On 13 April 1769 Dixon sailed to Norway with William Bayly in HMS *Emerald* to make observations of the transit of Venus on 3 June on the Royal Society's behalf. Dixon observed on Hammerfest Island, Bayly at Nordkapp, about 60 miles apart. However, Dixon's observation of the transit was frustrated by cloud. They reached England again on 30 July.

Dixon returned to Durham and resumed his work as a surveyor. Among places he surveyed at this time were the park of Auckland Castle and Lanchester Common. He died unmarried in Cockfield, near Staindrop, co. Durham, on 22 January 1779. He should not be confused with a contemporary, Jeremiah Dixon FRS (1726–1782), of Gledhow, near Leeds, the son-in-law of John Smeaton.

DEREK HOWSE

Sources H. W. Robinson, 'Jeremiah Dixon (1733–1779)—a biographical note', *Proceedings of the American Philosophical Society*, 94 (1950), 272–4 · T. D. Cope and H. W. Robinson, 'Charles Mason, Jeremiah Dixon and the Royal Society', *Notes and Records of the Royal Society*, 9 (1951–2), 55–78 · *The journal of Charles Mason and Jeremiah Dixon … 1763–1768*, ed. A. H. Mason (1969) · C. Mason and J. Dixon, 'Observations made at the Cape of Good Hope', *PTRS*, 52 (1761–2), 378–94 · C. Mason and J. Dixon, 'Observations for determining the length of a degree of latitude in the provinces of Maryland and Pennsylvania', *PTRS*, 58 (1768), 274–328 · C. Mason and J. Dixon, 'Astronomical observations, made in the forks of the River Brandiwine', *PTRS*, 58 (1768), 329–35 · J. Dixon, 'Observations made on the island of Hammerfost [sic]', *PTRS*, 59 (1769), 253–61 · council minutes, 1768, RS

Dixon, John (*fl.* 1574–1597), annotator of *Faerie Queene*, was the eldest of the three sons of Humphry Dixon (*fl.* 1538–1555) of Hilden Manor, near Tonbridge, Kent, and his wife, Elizabeth (*fl.* 1540–1555), a daughter of the Stace family of Hallenden. Dixon was born into a landowning family, originating in Scotland but established at least since his grandfather's time in Kent. He may, like his younger brother William, have attended Tonbridge School and gone on to university (it is just possible that he is the same 'John Dixon' who matriculated at Jesus College, Cambridge, in 1573). He married Joan Launce of Stanstead, Kent, and had two sons, Henry and William—the first born about 1574. John Dixon inherited Hilden Manor from his father and was able to pass it on to his elder son.

Dixon is of significance today solely as the presumed author of the copious annotations to be found in a copy of Edmund Spenser's *Faerie Queene* (1590) now in the possession of the Stansted Park Foundation in Hampshire. The volume has the name 'John Dixon' written on its title-page, but the specific connection to the resident of Hilden can be established only through the book's provenance. The annotations show John Dixon to have been of nationalist and puritan sympathies—a man very familiar with the Bible but not, apparently, with Spenser's Latin or Italian models. Dixon interprets Book I in the context of the prophecies of Revelation. In addition, he links episodes in the poem to recent history (sometimes making use of a basic letter-substitution code). The Redcrosse Knight is, for example, identified as the earl of Leicester, while his betrothal to Una is (with no apparent sense of contradiction) later paralleled with the accession of Elizabeth. Although Dixon displays a sound grasp of Spenser's didactic intentions (for instance glossing the reconciliation of Guyon and Britomart as 'unitie between Temperance and Chastitie'; III.i.12) his understanding of plot is often less secure. In this, as in other ways, his priorities sometimes appear the reverse of those of modern readers. The annotations are the only trace which remains of Dixon's character. It is possible to determine that he wrote them in 1597. We do not know his date of death, but a document showing that his son had inherited Hilden Manor by 1642 does give a late date by which that event had occurred (Almack).   BART VAN ES

Sources G. Hough, ed., *The first commentary on the 'The faerie queene'* (1964) • B. van Es, 'The life of John Dixon, *The faerie queene*'s first annotator', *N&Q*, 246 (2001) • R. Hovenden, ed., *The visitation of Kent, taken in the years 1619–1621*, Harleian Society, 42 (1898) • E. Hasted, *The history and topographical survey of the county of Kent*, 2nd edn, 12 vols. (1797–1801); facs. edn (1972) • W. Berry, *Pedigrees of the families in the county of Kent* (1830) • W. G. Hart, ed., *The register of Tonbridge School from 1553 to 1820* (1935) • Foster, *Alum. Oxon.*, *1500–1714* • Venn, *Alum. Cant.*, 1/1–4 • G. Hough, 'First commentary on *The faerie queene*: annotations in Lord Bessborough's copy of the first edition of *The faerie queene*', *TLS* (9 April 1964), 294 • will of Humphry Dixon, Rochester consistory court registers, DRb/PWr, fols. 187–92 • M. O'Connell, 'John Dixon', *The Spenser encyclopedia* (1990) • R. Almack, ed., 'Papers relating to proceedings in the county of Kent, AD 1642–AD 1646', *Camden miscellany*, III, CS, 61 (1855)
Archives Stansted Park, Rowland's Castle, Hampshire, annotated copy of *The faerie queene*

Dixon, John (*c*.1740–1811), engraver, the fourth son of Thomas Dixon (*d*. 1758), a hosier, of Cork Hill, Dublin, was born about 1740, probably in Dublin. He trained at the drawing school of the Dublin Society and possibly then worked for his brother Samuel and on plates for the linen-printing works at Leixlip. In 1760 he engraved John Rocque's four-sheet map of co. Dublin and in 1761 he produced portraits of admirals Boscawen and Granby for the *Dublin Annual Register*. In 1763, from Cork Hill, he published his first mezzotint, a portrait of Nicholas, Viscount Taafe, after Robert Hunter. This won him a premium of 5 guineas from the Dublin Society and also inspired admiring verses in *Sleator's Public Gazetter*.

Dixon arrived in London about 1765 and was proposed for a fellowship of the Society of Artists in May 1766, when he first exhibited there. This exhibited work (1766–75) was dominated by large portraits after Joshua Reynolds, but Dixon also showed subjects from old masters and after other contemporary painters. In 1769 he was one of those appointed to arrange models at the society's teaching academy in Maiden Lane. He was a director in 1770–71, and again from 1772 to 1775, and regularly attended meetings. His sympathy with the Wilkite cause was signalled by prints of its leading spokesmen: he engraved his own portrait of William Beckford and Robert Edge Pine's portraits of Wilkes and Sir Joseph Mawbey.

Most of Dixon's early plates were published by William Wynne Ryland, among them five of the seven Reynolds mezzotints that he exhibited. His work was distinguished and included several of the most highly rated plates of the day, notably *A Tigress*, after George Stubbs (1772), *An Incantation*, after John Hamilton Mortimer (1773), Reynolds's most celebrated history painting, *Ugolino* (1774), and two plates of David Garrick—as Abel Drugger, after Johann Zoffany (1771), and as Richard III, after Nathaniel Dance (1772). When he published another political design, *The Oracle*, in 1774, Dixon was at the height of his powers and his fame. His style was distinctive—featuring dramatic contrasts with marked use of etching and of drypoint burr to create rich blacks. Unusually, he signed his plates in the

image, a self-conscious assertion of his prowess as an artist. He also designed and etched a few landscapes and such droll mezzotints as *The Dentist, or, Teeth Drawn with a Touch* (1768).

Dixon moved, in 1771, to Kempe's Row, Chelsea, and then, if not before, he must have made the acquaintance of his neighbour and landlord Nicholas Kempe, a bullion porter to the Royal Mint and one of the original proprietors of Ranelagh Gardens, and of his beautiful wife, Ann, the daughter of Henry Meriton of Chelsea. Kempe died in 1774, and on 15 July 1775 the tall, handsome artist married his widow at St George's, Hanover Square. He now enjoyed a life of leisure: in 1776 Johann Georg Wille, a celebrated German engraver living in Paris, noted in his journal that 'M. Dixon, formerly an engraver in London, but having become very rich through his marriage and having abandoned his art, came to see me while travelling for pleasure' (*Mémoires et journal*, 2.52). Dixon was on friendly terms with Edmund Burke and Garrick. In 1801 he joined the Society of Arts and wrote a series of pamphlets advocating the improvement of the fisheries in Ireland. He died in December 1811 at Phillimore Place, Kensington, and his will was proved in January 1812. His prints may be found in the British Museum and the Bibliothèque Nationale in Paris.   TIMOTHY CLAYTON

Sources W. G. Strickland, *A dictionary of Irish artists*, 1 (1913), 280–85 • T. Clayton, *The English print, 1688–1802* (1997) • Society of Artists, minute books, RA • J. C. Smith, *British mezzotinto portraits*, 4 vols. in 5 (1878–84) • C. E. Russell, *English mezzotint portraits and their states*, 2 vols. (1926) • Graves, *Soc. Artists* • *Mémoires et journal de Jean-Georges Wille*, ed. G. Duplessis, 2 vols. (1857)

Dixon, Joseph (1806–1866), Roman Catholic archbishop of Armagh, born at Coalisland, co. Tyrone, on 2 February 1806, entered St Patrick's College, Maynooth, in 1822. He was ordained priest in 1829, and after holding the office of dean in the college for five years was promoted to the professorship of sacred scripture and Hebrew. As a native of Armagh diocese, he was chosen as *dignissimus* by the clergy of that diocese to succeed the primate, Archbishop Crolly, who died in 1849. As Dixon supported the policies of Archbishop Murray, the opponents of the Queen's Colleges sought to prevent his appointment by the pope. Accordingly they proposed Dr Paul Cullen, a stranger to the diocese, as more suitable. Cullen was appointed and steered the resolutions condemning the colleges through the Synod of Thurles. On the translation of Cullen to Dublin, Dixon was chosen to succeed him as archbishop of Armagh and primate of all Ireland. His appointment by propaganda, on 28 September 1852, was confirmed by the pope on 3 October, and he was consecrated on 21 November. He was an excellent diocesan bishop but failed to live up to expectations that he might assume leadership of Murray's conciliatory party in the hierarchy. As a result, episcopal politics became polarized between the ultramontane Cullen and the ultranationalist archbishop John MacHale of Tuam.

Dixon wrote *A General Introduction to the Sacred Scriptures* (2 vols., 1852). This was a scholarly summary of the subject, but the implications of the new 'higher criticism' were dismissed. In 1855 he published *The Blessed Cornelius, or, Some tidings of an archbishop of Armagh who went to Rome in the twelfth century and did not return*, an interesting devotional work.

Dixon died at Armagh after a short illness on 29 April 1866, and was buried in the grounds of the Sacred Heart Convent, Armagh.

THOMPSON COOPER, *rev.* DESMOND KEENAN

Sources [M. F. C. Cusack and others], *The life of … Joseph Dixon* [1878] · *Freeman's Journal* [Dublin] (30 April 1866) · *Freeman's Journal* [Dublin] (3 May 1866) · W. M. Brady, *The episcopal succession in England, Scotland, and Ireland, AD 1400 to 1875*, 3 vols. (1876–7) · *Catholic Directory* (1867) · McNally MSS, PRO NIre., Clogher Diocesan Records, DIO(RC) 1/10 · E. R. Norman, *The Catholic church and Ireland in the age of rebellion, 1859–1873* (1965) **Archives** NL Ire., corresp. · NRA, corresp. and papers · Roman Catholic diocesan archives, Armagh, episcopal corresp. and papers · University College, Dublin, notebooks relating to scriptural exegesis **Wealth at death** under £1500: resworn probate, May 1869, *CGPLA Ire.* (1866)

Dixon, Joshua (*bap.* 1743, *d.* 1825), physician and biographer, was baptized at St Nicholas's Church, Whitehaven, Cumberland, on 12 August 1743, the son of Joshua and Elizabeth Dixon. He graduated MD from the University of Edinburgh in 1768, and thereafter practised medicine in Whitehaven. In 1775 Dixon married Ann Fletcher; they had three sons and a daughter. Dixon was instrumental in the establishment of the dispensary at Whitehaven in 1783, and acted as its physician and chief administrator. His medical career was characterized as 'one continued scene of usefulness and benevolence' (*GM*, 185). Dixon died on 7 January 1825 in Lowther Street, Whitehaven, and was buried at St Nicholas's Church on the 14th.

Dixon was the author of *The Literary Life of William Brownrigg, M.D., F.R.S.* (1801). Brownrigg, of whom Dixon was a former pupil, was a Whitehaven medical practitioner and chemist who conducted important scientific research on salt making, mineral waters, and the effects of fire-damp. Brownrigg was noted for his diffidence in publishing, and Dixon wrote his biography to help publicize Brownrigg's findings, and also to idealize Brownrigg's character.

THOMPSON COOPER, *rev.* MARTEN HUTT

Sources *GM*, 1st ser., 95/1 (1825), 185 · J. Russell-Wood, 'A biographical note on William Brownrigg', *Annals of Science*, 6 (1948–50), 186–96 · Watt, *Bibl. Brit.* · parish registers (births and deaths), Whitehaven · C. R. Hudleston and R. S. Boumphrey, *Cumberland families and heraldry*, Cumberland and Westmorland Antiquarian and Archaeological Society, extra ser., 23 (1978) **Archives** Wellcome L., letter-book **Likenesses** S. Crosthwaite, engraving, pubd 1830 (after G. Sheffield the elder), The Beacon, Whitehaven [*see illus.*] · photograph (after portrait), repro. in D. Hay, *Whitehaven: an illustrated history* (1966), 46

Dixon, Matthew (*d.* 1710), portrait painter, was a pupil of Sir Peter Lely. In her article 'Nicholas Dixon, limner, and Matthew Dixon, painter, died 1710', Mary Edmond noted that 'Vertue's "Mr John Dixon" was … non-existent', and that 'Walpole added to the confusion by combining details given by Vertue about Nicholas Dixon the limner with those about "John" Dixon, and attributing them to

Joshua Dixon (*bap.* 1743, *d.* 1825), by Samuel Crosthwaite, pubd 1830 (after George Sheffield the elder)

the latter' (Edmond, 611). Matthew Dixon 'drew in Crayons from the life … with great excellence. … There are several peices of Art of his performance in Crayons. the Dutches Cleveland, Portsmouth … after Lilly. & his own picture excellently well done in a fine manner' (Vertue, *Note books*, 4.50). Vertue noted further that 'he left London & the practice of painting & retir'd to a Small estate in the Country. at Thwaite near Bungay in Suffolk' (ibid.). Mary Edmond established that Dixon bought the 'farm at Thwaite after 1666 and by Feb 1691/2 was one of the principal inhabitants of the village. One month later he had married Mary, daughter of John and Alice Gosling, members of a fairly prominent Norfolk family'; Mary was described in the register as 'the last of the Goslings' and was married on her eighteenth birthday. She was born on 22 March 1674 and baptized five days later. Matthew and Mary had six children: Catherine (*b.* 1692), Mary (*b.* 1694), John Gosling (*bap.* 28 Jan 1696), Alice (*bap.* March 1698), and Anne (*bap.* 1708); there was also a younger son, Matthew. Matthew Dixon was buried at Thwaite on 2 November 1710. His will records that he bequeathed his own picture to his wife; Sir Peter Lely's picture to his elder son, John; and to his daughters pictures including those of the duchesses of Portsmouth and Cleveland (Edmond, 612). Whinney and Millar noted that Matthew Dixon was among the 'more shadowy figures in Lely's *atelier* … of whose wooden imitations of the later Lely a good example was at Ecton in the portrait of James Sotheby (1679)' (Edmond, 612). ANNETTE PEACH

Sources M. Edmond, 'Nicholas Dixon, limner, and Matthew Dixon, painter, died 1710', *Burlington Magazine*, 125 (1983), 611–12 · Vertue, *Note books*, 2.59; 4.50 · E. K. Waterhouse, *The dictionary of British 16th and 17th century painters* (1988) · M. Whinney and O. Millar, *English art, 1625–1714* (1957), 181 **Likenesses** M. Dixon, self-portrait, crayon

Wealth at death property at Thwaite: Edmond, 'Nicholas Dixon' · portraits bequeathed to family

Dixon, Nicholas (*c*.1645–1708×20), miniature painter, remains the most obscure of the leading figures in the tradition of seventeenth-century miniaturists. Neither his dates nor his parentage are known; his date of birth remains a matter of conjecture based on the dating of his earliest signed work in the 1660s, and his last documented act is of February 1708. Even to George Vertue, who might have known him but evidently did not, he was already a shadowy figure. His emergence into recognition, at least as the artist of a distinguished body of work for the court in the 1670s, is due to R. W. Goulding, the librarian of Welbeck Abbey, who showed in 1911 that the ND monogram was his and that it was distinct from others, such as DM, possibly the monogram of a Daniel Myers, with which it had been confused (Goulding, 'Nicholas Dixon').

Dixon is recorded as paying poor rate from his house on the south side of Long Acre in the painters' parish of St Martin-in-the-Fields, London, in the 1670s, the decade of his principal activity. By 1691 he had moved to St Martin's Lane. Vertue says that at his death he was living 'at last in the King's Bench Walk, Temple, at that time to prevent prosecutions' (Vertue, *Note books*, 4.193). This would probably have been between about 1708 and 1720.

Dixon would have been a relatively young man when he succeeded Richard Gibson as the king's limner. The payment of the salary of £200 per annum was ordered under the privy seal on 16 September 1673 (Goulding, 'Welbeck Abbey miniatures', 25; private information). There must have been considerable lobbying for the post. Richard Gibson had been a senior and well-known figure among artists, well connected in the royal household, and at the summit of his powers; of the younger generation Peter Cross was already established and producing impressive work. Dixon's appointment may have been due to some extraneous influence but it was more probably due to his being seen as the natural successor to Cooper's courtly manner of painting. For Dixon's technique, which is based on red-brown hatching carefully and subtly blended with gouache into the carnation ground, is close to that of Cooper in the 1660s, and it is a reasonable assumption that he learnt the art directly from the master (Murdoch, *English Miniature*, 151–2). Dixon had not only a thorough mastery of the technical mystery of limning, by which he could produce a miniature with far more satisfying surface qualities than could Gibson, but he also had the visual flair to produce an image instantly recognizable as by him. As a court painter Dixon had the esoteric ability to endow his sitters, particularly the young women, with the appearance of belonging at court. The famously languorous almond eyes, as in the portrait possibly of Anne, duchess of Buccleuch (*c*.1675), in the Victoria and Albert Museum, London, which have the upper part of the pupil covered by the eyelid, are the miniaturist's answer to the sensual elaborations of pose and accoutrement in late works by Sir Peter Lely, Willem Wissing, and Henri Gascars.

Dixon was duly succeeded in the king's limnership by Peter Cross, on 23 July 1678. By this time he seems to have formed other interests, and it seems that he was not content to continue to produce smooth repetitions of the successful basic formula. Vertue refers to the change in Dixon's style as a deterioration, and so it must have seemed to many of his previous clients. His later portraits have a harshly graphic quality, produced by elongated hatching lines combined with shorter, disordered strokes that are allowed to remain visible and unblended into the overall complexion of the sitter. Similar developments are evident in the work of Thomas Flatman and other practitioners of the later 1670s and the 1680s, and they relate partly to the increasing interest among artists and connoisseurs in the general aesthetic of the sketch and partly to the particular influence of Cooper's unfinished work, recently sold off by his widow.

Apart from his role as king's limner Dixon was keeper of the king's picture closet. He was evidently, like his predecessors Isaac and Peter Oliver, also active in the art market. Vertue records that he 'bought once a picture at a broker's at a very small price, & sold it to the Duke of Devonshire for £500' (Vertue, *Note books*, 4.193). During 1684–5, according to 'documents found in Florence' (Foskett, 1.247) he organized a lottery of 'excellent miniature paintings', which may have encouraged him to float the later 'hopeful adventure' of 1698. This was a lottery of miniature copies after the old masters, painted by himself:

> a collection of Pictures in limning not to be equalled anywhere if this collection falls into the hands of any person that don't understand them or will part with them they shall receive for them £2000 in money of the Proposer. (Vertue, *Note books*, 4.144)

The lottery failed, and seventy of the limnings were mortgaged on 23 November 1700 and subsequently, on 14 February 1708, transferred under a bill of sale to John Holles, duke of Newcastle (creation of 1694), for the sum of £430. Thirty of them remain at Welbeck Abbey. It may have been about this time that Dixon was commissioned by the duke to paint the portrait of Lady Henrietta Cavendish (1693–1755), his only daughter. Vertue's comment on this miniature was: 'done by Dixon whose feeble work shows him aged then' (Goulding, 'Welbeck Abbey miniatures', 202, no. 362). JOHN MURDOCH

Sources R. W. Goulding, 'Nicholas Dixon, the limner', *Burlington Magazine*, 20 (1911–12), 24–5 · R. W. Goulding, 'The Welbeck Abbey miniatures', *Walpole Society*, 4 (1914–15) [whole issue] · Vertue, *Note books*, 1–6 · M. Edmond, 'Limners and picturemakers', *Walpole Society*, 47 (1978–80), 60–242 · D. Foskett, *A dictionary of British miniature painters*, 2 vols. (1972) · K. Gibson, '"Best belov'd of kings": the iconography of King Charles II', PhD diss., Courtauld Inst., 1997 · PRO, Lord Chamberlain's papers, LC5/140, fol. 308 · J. Murdoch and others, *The English miniature* (1981) · J. Murdoch, *Seventeenth-century English miniatures in the collection of the Victoria and Albert Museum* (1997) · private information (2004)

Dixon, Sir Owen (1886–1972), judge in Australia, was born on 28 April 1886 at Glenferrie Road, Hawthorn, Victoria, Australia, the only child of Joseph William Dixon (1859–1929), a Melbourne lawyer, and his wife, Edith Annie (1859–1934), daughter of Edward Owen. Both parents came from Morley in Yorkshire, emigrating separately

Sir Owen Dixon (1886–1972), by Walter Stoneman, 1950

with their parents in the 1860s. He was educated at Hawthorn College and the University of Melbourne where he graduated as bachelor of arts in 1906 and bachelor of laws in 1908.

Dixon read classics and law. He was much influenced by T. G. Tucker, professor of classical philology, from whom he acquired a love of classical literature and thought that nourished his naturally sceptical mind, and by Sir William Harrison Moore, professor of law, in whom he observed the detachment of the scholar's judgement on modern problems, particularly in public law. He began practice at the Victorian bar in 1910. Dixon soon acquired a reputation for knowledge and skill as a barrister, obtaining an enormous practice and achieving a dominance not seen before or since. 'His quiet and friendly personality, his high standards of professional probity and his powerful mind dominated the Bar' (Dean, 219).

On 8 January 1920 at St Paul's Anglican Cathedral, Dixon married Alice Crossland Brooksbank (1893–1971), daughter of the Revd H. A. Brooksbank. He was greatly attached to his wife and kept in constant contact with her whenever they were separated. They had two sons and two daughters, all of whom survived them. He took silk in 1922 and in that year made the first of several appearances before the privy council. He made a profound impression on many English lawyers. Sir John Simon suggested that he should take chambers in London and practise at the English bar, but for professional and personal reasons he decided not to do so. In 1926 Dixon agreed to sit for some

months as an acting judge of the supreme court of Victoria. In that period he delivered some important judgments but declined permanent appointment at the end of the year.

In 1929 Dixon was persuaded to accept appointment to the high court, the highest court in Australia with both constitutional and appellate jurisdiction. It was there that his greatness became permanently recognized. He at once began to make a profound contribution to the law which can only be fully appreciated by a close study of his judgments. He believed deeply in Maitland's dictum that the common law was a reflection of 'strict logic, and high technique, rooted in the Inns of Court, rooted in the Year Books, rooted in the centuries' (SeldS year book series, 1.xviii).

When war broke out in 1939 Dixon offered his services to the government and while continuing to discharge judicial duties undertook the chairmanship of various government boards. In 1942 he accepted appointment as Australian minister to Washington and was relieved of judicial duties. His tasks were considerable and exacting. He worked closely with the heads of the administration and formed friendships that lasted throughout his life, in particular with Justice Frankfurter. He returned to Australia in 1944. Later he formed a close friendship with Lord Simonds with whom he corresponded regularly.

Dixon was once again absent from judicial duties when, in 1950, he was asked by the Security Council of the United Nations to act as mediator between India and Pakistan in Kashmir. He was received with respect by the disputants, who appreciated his judicial approach, but he failed to devise an acceptable solution for the region's intractable problems.

On 21 April 1952 Dixon was appointed chief justice of the high court of Australia and there began a period during which the court was regarded as the finest in the English-speaking world. He found judicial work hard and unrewarding but through the work of the court he had a profound influence on the standards of all courts in Australia. The intellectual penetration and meticulous legal scholarship of his judgments set standards for all and his insistence that the court should sit in all state capitals and avoid permanent residence in Canberra kept them to the fore.

Dixon firmly believed that the judicial task required the application by strict logic and high technique of external standards to ascertained facts. He strove to maintain the unity of the common law but continually faced the dilemma of whether to eradicate error or maintain legal and judicial authority. Some of his most interesting judgments are those concerned with that dilemma, *Mayfair Trading Co. Pty Ltd* v. *Dreyer* (1958), for example. He regretted that he had to make the pronouncement he did in *Parker* v. *R.* (1963). Many of his judgments have had a profound effect on legal thought in the common-law world: for example, in the field of estoppels see *Thompson* v. *Palmer* (1933); *Newbon* v. *City Mutual Life Assurance* (1935); and *Grundt* v. *Great Boulder Pty Gold Mines Ltd* (1937). His address,

'Concerning judicial method' (delivered at Yale in 1955 and published with other papers and addresses under the title *Jesting Pilate*, 1965), was written in response to what he considered the unsatisfactory reasoning in recent English cases. That address is a masterly exposition of the judicial technique and shows his convictions and his humility. No understanding of his work can be complete without a study of it. In revenue cases *Sun Newspapers Ltd* (1938), *Hallstroms Pty Ltd* (1946), and *Ronpibon Tin NL* (1949), Dixon analysed the concepts of capital and income in the context of deductible outgoings in a way not previously attempted. His judgment in *National Research Development Corporation* (1959) developed the principles applicable in determining patentable processes. His judgment in *McDonald v. Dennys Lascelles Ltd* (1933) concerning the right of an innocent party to a sale of land to recover damages on the contract being terminated by an accepted repudiation was followed by the House of Lords in *Johnson v. Agnew* (1980). His judgment in *Birmingham v. Renfrew* (1937) concerning the position of the survivor of persons who make mutual wills has also been much referred to in English courts.

In public and in court Dixon was reserved and circumspect: in private he was irreverent and sometimes indiscreet. Tall, slightly stooped, loose-limbed, with an unusual physiognomy, he led a frugal life and was a teetotaller. He was excellent company. He trusted his friends to treat his conversation as it was intended. He frequently discussed a most serious subject with an extraordinary lightness of touch, almost with flippancy, but generally because he was confident of his own capacity to deal with it. Typical of his sardonic wit was his comment that the Australian constitution had contrived to combine the most difficult features of both the British and the American systems: in Britain there was a totally flexible constitution and utterly rigid judges; in America there was a rigid constitution and totally flexible judges; but unhappily in Australia both the constitution and the judges were equally strict. Similarly he observed that the principal reason for having trial by jury is the experience of what happens when there is a trial by judge alone and the principal reason for having trial by a judge alone is the experience of what happens when there is a trial by jury. Above all he was amused by evidence of human foibles in any form. Although shy by nature he had a great interest in people and enjoyed conversation, especially with those of a younger generation to whom he was particularly kind and generous.

Dixon retired on 13 April 1964 and took no part in public life thereafter. At his farewell Sir Robert Menzies said that two lord chancellors and a distinguished justice of the supreme court of the United States had described him as the greatest judicial lawyer in the English-speaking world. Dixon received many appointments and honours: KCMG in 1941, privy councillor in 1951, GCMG in 1954, the Howland memorial prize of Yale University in 1955, an honorary DCL from Oxford and an honorary LLD from Harvard in 1958, an honorary LLD from Melbourne in 1959, in 1963 the Order of Merit, an honorary LLD from the Australian

National University in 1964, and in 1970 he became a corresponding fellow of the British Academy. Lady Dixon died in September 1971 and thereafter as Dixon's own health further declined, he declined in spirit also and died at his home, Yallambee, 4 Higham Road, Hawthorn, Victoria, Australia, on 7 July 1972. He was buried in Boroondara cemetery, Kew, Victoria, on 11 July.

JOHN McI. YOUNG

Sources J. D. Merralls, *Australian Law Journal*, 46 (Sept 1972), 429–35 · K. O. Shatwell, *Australian Bar Gazette*, 1/3 (1964), 3–4 · 'Sir Owen Dixon: a commemoration', *Melbourne University Law Review*, 15/4 (Dec 1986), 543–90 · D. Dawson and M. Nicholls, 'Sir Owen Dixon and judicial method', *Melbourne University Law Review*, 15/4 (Dec 1986), 543–52 · C. Saunders, 'Owen Dixon: evidence to the royal commission on the constitution, 1927–29', *Melbourne University Law Review*, 15/4 (Dec 1986), 553–74 · C. Howard, 'Sir Owen Dixon: giant who enriched the law', *Melbourne University Law Review*, 15/4 (Dec 1986), 575–6 · F. Kitto, 'Some recollections of Sir Owen Dixon', *Melbourne University Law Review*, 15/4 (Dec 1986), 577–8 · P. Ryan, 'Sir Owen Dixon: an intellectual man of passion', *Melbourne University Law Review*, 15/4 (Dec 1986), 579–81 · H. A. J. Ford, 'Sir Owen Dixon: his judgments in private law', *Melbourne University Law Review*, 15/4 (Dec 1986), 582–90 · G. Anderson, 'Sir Owen Dixon', monograph, 1993, Library of High Court of Australia · A. Dean, *A multitude of counsellors: a history of the bar of Victoria* (1968), 218–20 · R. G. Menzies, *Afternoon light: some memories of men and events* (1967) · R. G. Menzies, *The measure of the years* (1970), 229–44 · N. Stephen, *Sir Owen Dixon* (1986) · *Commonwealth Law Reports* [CLR], 41–114 (1928–66); 126 (1971) · *Mayfair Trading Co. Pty Ltd v. Dreyer* (1958), 101 CLR 428 · *Parker v. R.* (1963), 111 CLR 610, 632 · *Thompson v. Palmer* (1933), 49 CLR 507 · *Newbon v. City Mutual Life Assurance* (1935), 52 CLR 723 · *Grundt v. Great Boulder Pty Gold Mines Ltd* (1937), 59 CLR 641 · *Sun Newspapers Ltd* (1938), 61 CLR 337 · *Hallstroms Pty Ltd* (1946), 72 CLR 634 · *Ronpibon Tin NL* (1949), 78 CLR 47 · *National Research Development Corporation* (1959), 102 CLR · *McDonald v. Dennys Lascelles Ltd* (1933), 48 CLR 457 · *Johnson v. Agnew* [1980], AC 367 · *Birmingham v. Renfrew* (1937), 57 CLR 666 · A. Watt, *Australian diplomat* (1972) · custody of J. D. Merralls QC, Melbourne, Dixon MSS · personal knowledge (2004) · private information (2004) · b. cert. · m. cert. · d. cert.

Archives priv. coll.

Likenesses W. Stoneman, photograph, 1950, NPG [*see illus.*] · A. D. Colquhoun, oils, 1955, high court of Australia, Canberra · A. D. Colquhoun, oils, 1960, Owen Dixon Chambers, 205 William Street, Melbourne · photograph, repro. in *Melbourne University Law Review*, frontispiece · photographs, priv. coll., Melbourne

Wealth at death $80,000—realty · $256,602—personalty: inventory filed in Registry of Supreme Court of Victoria on application for probate

Dixon, Sir Pierson John [Bob] (1904–1965), diplomatist, was born on 13 November 1904 at Englefield Green, Surrey, the elder son and eldest of the four children of Pierson John Dixon (1868–1934), estate agent, and his wife, Helen Barbara (Nellie), daughter of James Ownby Beales, a royal caterer. His forenames reflected a long-standing family tradition, and he was in practice always known as Bob. His childhood was not particularly happy—his father had persistent financial difficulties, was often absent from home, and had an increasingly strained marriage. The children were badly off and undernourished. Dixon's intellectual ability became his escape from these unhappy circumstances. He was educated at Bedford School and there began consistently to win academic prizes. This run

Sir Pierson John Dixon (1904–1965), by Dorothy Wilding, 1954

of success culminated in 1922 when he won two scholarships allowing him to go up to Pembroke College, Cambridge, in the following year to read classics. Further prizes, notably the prestigious Craven scholarship (1926), enabled him to live a reasonably comfortable and active life as a student. In 1927 he followed his double first-class degree by being awarded a junior research fellowship at Pembroke. A life as a classical scholar appeared to beckon. He had moreover fallen passionately in love not only with Greece, where he had travelled in 1927, but also with (Alexandra) Ismene Melas, an Englishwoman who had been brought up largely in Greece. She was the widow of Michael Melas and daughter of Shirley Clifford Atchley, first secretary at the British embassy in Athens. They married on 4 July 1928 and had two daughters, Jennifer (*b.* 1930) and Ann (*b.* 1941), and a son, Piers (*b.* 1928), who was Conservative MP for Truro from 1970 to 1974.

In 1929 Dixon's career switched from academia to diplomacy. He passed the Foreign Office examination comfortably, emerging second out of a distinguished intake which included Harold Caccia, later permanent secretary of the Foreign Office, and was appointed a third secretary in October 1929. Postings in Spain (1932–6), Turkey (1936–8), and Italy (1938–40) followed in close succession, providing Dixon with a solid grounding in the workings of the diplomatic corps. His spell in the Italian capital also allowed him to observe at first hand British efforts to appease Mussolini. He was, meanwhile, promoted second secretary in October 1934 and first secretary in December

1939. It was not until the outbreak of the Second World War, however, that his career really took off.

Dixon's wartime years were mainly spent in close proximity to Anthony Eden. In 1941 he accompanied the foreign secretary on a lengthy mission to the Middle East and the Balkans, and two years later, in November 1943, he was appointed Eden's principal private secretary, with the rank of counsellor. In this capacity he was present at many of the crucial allied encounters in the course of which both the shape of wartime strategy and the post-war settlement were determined. At the Yalta summit in February 1945 he was responsible for co-ordinating the work of the British delegation and was deeply involved in the frantic attempts to draft a satisfactory communiqué before Roosevelt's earlier than expected departure.

Midway through the Potsdam conference the general election result in 1945 prompted a change in the British government. Labour's victory, however, had no professional impact on Dixon, since he was immediately appointed principal private secretary to Ernest Bevin, Eden's successor. His position at the heart of British foreign policy making thus remained secure. Indeed in many ways the spell as Bevin's right-hand man must rank as the most impressive of Dixon's career. The foreign secretary's schedule was arduous, dominated by the increasingly fraught conferences of foreign ministers at which the wartime allies struggled to contain their growing mistrust of each other and to reconcile their highly divergent priorities for the post-war world. Against this gloomy backdrop Dixon had not merely to act as companion, counsellor, speech-writer, and administrator for Bevin, but also to join the foreign secretary in the late-night singsongs which marked the end of at least some of the foreign ministers' meetings. He was appointed CMG in 1945 and CB in 1948.

In January 1948 Dixon received his first ambassadorial posting, to Prague. According to Bevin's biographer this was the direct result of Dixon's relationship with the foreign secretary, since Bevin had identified Czechoslovakia as a likely flashpoint of East–West tension and wanted a British representative there upon whom he could rely. This proved all too prescient. Within a month of his arrival, Dixon could only watch powerlessly as the non-Communist ministers resigned *en masse* from the Czech government, and Klement Gottwald and the Czech communists used the opportunity to declare a state of emergency and seize total power. Few British diplomats could have had a clearer illustration both of how tense East–West relations had become and of Britain's incapacity to exercise a decisive influence over the downward spiral of events in central and eastern Europe. Dixon was appointed KCMG in January 1950, and in June of that year returned to London as deputy under-secretary of state, with responsibility first for political and then for economic affairs. He also served as UK representative on the Brussels Treaty Permanent Commission, with the personal rank of ambassador, until November 1952.

Dixon's next foreign posting gave him an even more graphic demonstration of the slippage of Britain's power:

he was posted to New York as Britain's permanent representative to the United Nations in March 1954. Within two years of arrival he was swept up by the growing crisis caused by Nasser's nationalization of the Suez Canal. As a result it fell to him to justify the heavily criticized build-up of British military power in the region, to exercise for the first time ever the British veto in the Security Council in an effort to prevent a resolution being passed which would require members to refrain from the use of force, and to represent Britain at the emotional general assembly debate of 1–2 November at which the British, French, and Israeli military action was condemned by sixty-four votes to five. The emotional strain of defending a policy about which he had serious personal misgivings was considerable; looking back on the episode he later wrote:

> It really was an extraordinary situation in which we were quite incompetent to influence the course of events. Flanked by our faithful Australians and New Zealanders, we wandered about the UN halls like lost spirits. Our best friends averted their gaze or burst into tears as we passed. (Dixon, 277)

Despite the harm done to Britain's international standing, Dixon's own reputation was only enhanced by the Suez episode. Thus he was promoted GCMG in 1957 and rewarded with the highly sought-after Paris embassy as his next posting, in October 1960, in succession to Sir Gladwyn Jebb. In 1961 this already demanding role was made still more important when he was asked also to act as leader at official level of the British delegation seeking to negotiate entry into the EEC. After his stints at the shoulders of Eden and Bevin, he was now to act as principal lieutenant to Edward Heath, lord privy seal and the minister responsible for the Brussels negotiations.

Dixon's diplomatic swansong revealed both his strengths and his limitations. As ambassador in Paris he did succeed in establishing a reasonable, if necessarily distant, rapport with General de Gaulle. This allowed him to forewarn Whitehall that the French president harboured strong misgivings about the enlargement of the EEC. In October 1962 he sent a dispatch to the prime minister predicting that de Gaulle would veto Britain's entry. Macmillan is said to have read the report and scribbled in the margin 'interesting but not convincing' (Beloff, 155). But the negotiations in Brussels also highlighted the discomfort felt by a generalist such as Dixon in dealing with the highly technical and economic nature of the multilateral negotiations between Britain and the six EEC member states. On most of the substantive issues which dominated the Brussels agenda, his grasp was much less sure than that of his deputy, Eric Roll (formerly an official in the Ministry of Agriculture, Fisheries and Food). Moreover Dixon never seemed entirely at home in the Brussels of the early EEC. Obliged to move constantly between Paris and the Belgian capital, not to mention trips back to London for consultations, he never built up the network of contacts and the feel for Community matters which would have greatly facilitated his task. He could thus do little to bridge the significant gap in attitude and understanding which developed between those members of the British team who were posted in Brussels for the duration of the talks and those more senior figures who flew in on the eve of each major meeting. How costly this inexperience in Community affairs proved is hard to determine; it is nevertheless significant that Britain's later, successful, negotiations to enter the EEC in 1970–72 were masterminded by Sir Con O'Neill, a man who was as much a Brussels 'insider' as Dixon had been an inexperienced 'outsider'.

Paris, where Dixon remained until February 1965, proved his final posting. Having experienced a couple of years of poor Anglo-French relations in the aftermath of de Gaulle's veto, he then left the diplomatic service. His plan was to return in his retirement to the classical studies which he had left nearly forty years earlier. (He had, meanwhile, published a study of *The Iberians of Spain and their Relations with the Aegean World*, 1939, as well as two works of fiction set in antiquity, *Farewell, Catullus*, 1953, and *The Glittering Horn*, 1958, and a biography, *Pauline: Napoleon's Favourite Sister*, 1964.) Such plans were cut short by his death from a heart attack in Egham, Surrey, on 22 April 1965. He was survived by his wife and their three children.

Dixon's career was at one and the same time exceptionally distinguished and highly emblematic of a generation of British diplomats. He was catapulted by the Second World War into a position of remarkable influence and was privileged to be present when many of the crucial decisions about both wartime strategy and the post-war world were made. But the years which followed, although not without professional satisfaction, underlined how changed were the circumstances of the country which he represented. His experiences in New York and Brussels in particular could only emphasize how dramatically Britain's influence had dwindled since its wartime position as one of the 'big three'. N. PIERS LUDLOW

Sources DNB · P. Dixon, *Double diploma: the life of Sir Pierson Dixon, don and diplomat* (1968) · D. Dutton, *Anthony Eden, a life and reputation* (1997) · A. Bullock, *The life and times of Ernest Bevin*, 3 (1983) · N. P. Ludlow, *Dealing with Britain: the six and the first UK application to the EEC* (1997) · N. Beloff, *The general says no* (1963) · E. Johnson, 'The diplomat's diplomat: Sir Pierson Dixon, ambassador to the United Nations', *Contemporary British History*, 13/2 (1999) · *The Times* (23 April 1965) · WWW · Burke, *Peerage* · FO List (–1965) · CGPLA Eng. & Wales (1965)
Archives NRA, papers | Bodl. Oxf., corresp. with Clement Attlee · Bodl. Oxf., corresp. with William Clark · PRO, letters to Sir Perry Loraine, FO 1011/284 · U. Birm. L., corresp. with Lord Avon [photocopies]
Likenesses J. Chillingworth, photograph, 1953, Hult. Arch. · D. Wilding, photograph, 1954, NPG [*see illus.*] · photograph, repro. in *The Times*
Wealth at death £67,932: probate, 25 Aug 1965, CGPLA Eng. & Wales

Dixon, Sir Raylton (1838–1901), shipbuilder, was born on 8 July 1838 at Westgate, Newcastle upon Tyne, the second of at least three sons of Jeremiah Dixon of Balla Wray, Ambleside, Westmorland, a bank employee, and his wife,

Mary, *née* Frank. His elder brother, John Dixon, an engineer, was involved in the transfer of Cleopatra's Needle from Egypt to the Thames Embankment in 1879. Dixon was privately educated before being apprenticed to Coutts and Parkinson, shipbuilders, of Willington quay on Tyneside. From there he moved in 1856 to work for Charles Mitchell & Co., iron shipbuilders, at Walker, on the Tyne.

Dixon moved to Teesside in 1859 as manager of the former Rake Kimber shipyard in Middlesbrough, which Richardson, Duck & Co. had just taken over, and three years later, with a partner, Thomas Backhouse, he bought the yard. They later added the former Candlish Fox and David Jays yards to establish the Cleveland Dockyard, which they ran with the help of Dixon's younger brother Waynman. Dixon married Elizabeth (*b. c.*1842), *née* Walker, of Glasgow in 1863; they had two sons and six daughters, one of whom married a member of the Bolckow family. By the time Backhouse retired in 1873, and Dixon became sole owner, they had built more than eighty ships. Although they built mainly passenger and cargo steamers, the yard launched its first warship, HMS *Tourmaline*, in 1875, and went on to build many more naval vessels, especially gunboats and cruisers, for the Royal Navy and several foreign governments, in association with Harroway, the naval architect. Between 1873 and 1882 output grew from 5000 tons a year to 27,000 tons. When Dixon launched his first steel ship in 1883 his workforce had grown to 2300. Despite the depression of 1884 to 1887, when production at the yard shrank to 24 per cent of the 1883 output and many workers were laid off, the yard survived, and in 1886 the SS *Santiago*, the largest ship ever built on the Tees, was launched to be used on the north Atlantic route of the Wilson Line. In 1887 Dixon took over a yard on the site of the old Teesside Iron and Engine Works, and by 1889 had increased his tonnage to over 40,000 tons. In 1889 Dixon was the largest shipbuilder on the Tees, launching 48 per cent of the total output that year, and seven of the ten largest ships built on the Tees between 1889 and 1914 were made at the Cleveland Dockyard, including the SS *Montrose* (1897), the first Teesside ship over 5000 tons, and the SS *Manchester City* (1898), which was 7696 tons. The firm became a limited liability company, Sir Raylton Dixon & Co. Ltd, in 1897, and by the time of Dixon's death over 500 ships had been built at the yard, which had expanded to 7 berths. The company built steamers for all the leading passenger lines, including P. & O., and Union Castle, and for mercantile marines all over the world.

Dixon had other business concerns. He was a director of Sadler & Co. Ltd, chemical manufacturers of Middlesbrough, Robert Stephenson & Co., the Newcastle engineering company, and the Elder, Dempster Shipping Company, Liverpool. He joined the Institution of Naval Architects in 1868, serving twice on the council, and was a member of the North East Coast Institution of Engineers and Shipbuilders. A man with very wide interests, Dixon enjoyed drawing caricatures and photography, and was first president of the Tees Amateur Boating Club. A good shot, he was a major in the 1st North Yorkshire artillery

volunteers for eighteen years. He was also a churchwarden of St Hilda's parish church in Middlesbrough. In the 1880s, Dixon moved into Gunnergate Hall, Marton, built by the ironmaster John Vaughan, partner of Henry Bolckow, who had lived nearby in Marton Hall.

A member of Middlesbrough town council from 1868 to 1874, and from 1878 to 1884, Dixon served as mayor of Middlesbrough from 1888 to 1889, when the prince and princess of Wales opened the new town hall and municipal buildings. His yard was given the contract for a ferry steamer when his proposal for a transporter bridge linking the two sides of the Tees was turned down. He contested Middlesbrough as a Conservative in the general election of 1885, but was defeated by the sitting member, Isaac Wilson, a Cleveland ironmaster. A JP for Middlesbrough from 1872 and on the commission of the peace for the North Riding of Yorkshire from 1885, Dixon served as deputy lieutenant of the county in 1889. He was knighted for public services in 1890, and was appointed a freeman of the borough of Middlesbrough.

Sir Raylton Dixon died at his home, Gunnergate Hall, on 28 July 1901 after a long illness; he was survived by his wife. He had been one of the leading shipbuilders in the north-east. The yard was taken over by Lambert Bros. Ltd during the First World War, although members of the Dixon family retained their influence, and was closed in 1921.   ANNE PIMLOTT BAKER

Sources J. F. Clarke, *Building ships on the north east coast*, 1: *c.*1640–1914 (1997) · W. Lillie, *The history of Middlesbrough* (1968), 299, 308 · J. F. Clarke, 'Dixon, Sir Raylton', *DBB* · *The Engineer* (2 Aug 1901) · census returns, 1881 · *WWW* · A. Briggs, 'Middlesbrough', *Victorian cities* (1963), chap. 6, 245–82 · *CGPLA Eng. & Wales* (1901) · b. cert. · d. cert.

Likenesses photograph, repro. in Clarke, 'Sir Raylton Dixon', 1.112

Wealth at death £131,844 17*s.* 8*d.*: probate, 13 Nov 1901, *CGPLA Eng. & Wales*

Dixon, Richard Watson (1833–1900), ecclesiastical historian and poet, was born on 5 May 1833 at Islington, London, the eldest of the six surviving children of James *Dixon (1788–1871) and his third wife, Mary Watson (*d.* 1856), the only daughter of Richard *Watson (1781–1833). In the biography he wrote of his father, Dixon described his mother as 'an excellent Latin and Greek scholar, a perfect French and a sufficient Italian linguist, and an exquisite musician' (Dixon, 169). His father was a famous Wesleyan preacher, leader of his church, and president of the Methodist conference, who, said his son, 'lived upon a vast height of holiness' (ibid., 476). With such a father it is perhaps not surprising that Dixon was a diffident, solitary, reserved, and impressionable child.

As his father was obliged by Methodist practice to change the circuit of his ministry every three years, Dixon's childhood was spent successively in Islington, Liverpool, Sheffield, Manchester, and Poplar, London, and he received his early education at home. In 1847 the family moved to Birmingham and he entered King Edward VI School, where his schoolfriends included Edwin Hatch and Edward Burne-Jones. On 3 June 1852 he matriculated at Pembroke College, Oxford, and in his time there was

Richard Watson Dixon (1833–1900), by unknown photographer

founder of and a contributor to the *Oxford and Cambridge Magazine* (1856), modelled in part upon the Pre-Raphaelite journal *The Germ* (1848). For a few months in 1857 Dixon joined William Morris, Burne-Jones, and Dante Gabriel Rossetti at their bohemian lodgings in Red Lion Square in London to study painting, but, lacking means, confidence, and ability, he soon returned to his first intention of preparing for Anglican orders. (As both his parents were conservative Methodists who did not renounce membership in the Church of England, they did not see their son's vocation as disloyal to their own communion.)

Dixon was ordained in 1858, the year in which, redeeming his inglorious third class in greats (1856), he won the Arnold historical prize at Oxford for his essay 'The close of the tenth century of the Christian era'. The three years following his ordination he spent as a curate in the populous working-class London parishes of St Mary-the-Less, Lambeth (1858–61), and St Mary, Newington Butts (1861). On 9 April 1861 he married a widow with three daughters— Maria Thomson (1821–1876), daughter of Charles Sturgeon and the former wife of William Thomson of East Lothian. Later that year he became assistant master at Highgate School, Middlesex, where he talked of John Keats by the hour to his pupils, one of whom was Gerard Manley Hopkins.

Dixon's first publication was a colourful Keatsian narrative, *The Sicilian Vespers* (1852). His *St. John in Patmos* (1863), another long narrative–descriptive prize poem, is more restrained. New Testament or historical subjects are also prominent in his collections, *Christ's Company* (1861) and *Historical Odes* (1864), but the collections' most remarkable verse is found in dream lyrics exploring the psyche in terms of a private symbolism, or in brooding nature poems. This early verse was ignored or dismissed by reviewers and found so few readers that the print runs of the 1861 and 1864 volumes were not sold out until after 1935.

Dixon moved from London for the sake of his health and became, in turn, second master at Carlisle high school (1862–8); minor canon and honorary librarian of Carlisle Cathedral (1868–75) and honorary canon from 1874; vicar of Hayton, near Carlisle (1875–83); and rural dean of Brampton, Cumberland (1879–83). He continued to write poetry and he published essays on ecclesiastical history. His piously eulogistic biography of his father appeared in 1874, and in that year he also embarked on his major scholarly undertaking: the *History of the Church of England from the Abolition of the Roman Jurisdiction* (6 vols., 1879–1902). His wife died in 1876 and he had long been separated from his Oxford friends, but he was reinvigorated when, unexpectedly, in 1878, Gerard Manley Hopkins wrote in praise of his neglected poetry. Hopkins valued it so much, in fact, that he copied out three of Dixon's long poems ('St. Paul', 'St. John', and 'Love's Consolation') to keep when, as a Jesuit, he no longer owned books of his own. Hopkins introduced Dixon to Robert Bridges and the three friends formed, mostly by correspondence, a close, mutually comforting circle united by poetry. Dixon was a less skilled poet and critic than Bridges, but he perceived and appreciated the quality and power of Hopkins's innovative poetry more than Bridges could. On 9 February 1882 he married Matilda Elizabeth Routledge (1840–1922), daughter of the publisher George *Routledge. Two grownup daughters of his first wife continued to live at home, but he had no children of his own from either marriage. On 30 November 1883 he was inducted as vicar of Warkworth in Northumberland, and in 1884 he was appointed rural dean of Alnwick.

Stimulated by Hopkins and Bridges, Dixon revised and completed *Mano, a Poetical History of the Time of the Close of the Tenth Century*, a long poem begun in 1875 and published by Routledge in 1883. A work of epic scale, more than 5000 lines long, it is written in well-controlled *terza rima*: its fictional action, a vain struggle of faith against fate, is placed within the historical setting of a savage and pious age when people lived in daily expectation of the end of the world (the age Dixon had first studied in his Arnold prize essay). Two slim volumes, *Odes and Eclogues* (1884) and *Lyrical Poems* (1887), handsomely printed by Bridges' friend C. H. O. Daniel on his private press at Worcester College, Oxford, contain Dixon's finest lyrics on nature and mutability. His verse was much clearer than in the early volumes: youthful themes of supernatural terror were replaced by more human concerns of advancing age. His third Daniel Press book, *The Story of Eudocia and her Brothers* (1888), is a competent narrative poem in heroic couplets.

Mano was admired by Algernon Charles Swinburne, who

recommended Dixon for the poet laureateship after Tennyson's death in 1892; Bridges and Hopkins praised highly the imaginative penetration and freshness of *Lyrical Poems*; and reviewers were kinder to Dixon in the 1880s than they had been in the 1860s. Dixon himself, however, suffered a mental depression in 1891–2 (following bouts of influenza, bronchitis, and pneumonia), which caused him to destroy his verse manuscripts and resolve to write no more poetry except on religious subjects. The only poem he subsequently sent to the press was a funeral elegy in Latin on his boyhood friend Edwin Hatch (1892). Bridges kept some manuscripts and, over the years, edited three selections of Dixon's published and unpublished poetry: *Songs and Odes* (1896); *Last Poems* (1905), with a preface by Mary Coleridge; and *Poems: a Selection* (1909), with a fine, affectionate memoir by Bridges himself.

Dixon's work on the *History of the Church of England* continued, much interrupted by ill health. As the four volumes published by 1891 were well reviewed and his worth as an ecclesiastical historian was widely accepted, his friends were angry that he received no church preferment. He was proposed for two lay academic appointments, the Oxford chair of poetry in 1885 and the Dixie chair of ecclesiastical history at Cambridge in 1891, but in both cases, overcome with diffidence, he withdrew before the election. However, his historical labours received overdue recognition when in October 1899 he was admitted to an honorary fellowship at Pembroke College, Oxford, and when in December the university conferred upon him the honorary degree of DD. Soon afterwards he again contracted influenza: he died of influenza and heart disease on 23 January 1900 at the vicarage at Warkworth and was interred four days later in Warkworth burial-ground. He was survived by his second wife.

The last two volumes (5 and 6) of the *History of the Church of England*, which brought the narrative to 1570, were published in 1902, bringing to completion a work planned on a massive scale and, in view of Dixon's parochial and decanal duties and his remoteness from good libraries, one executed with great determination and intellectual stamina. Although superseded by later scholarship, the *History* remains highly readable. Dixon writes as if from the viewpoint of a fair-minded contemporary, observing a process without any view of an end which could distort the facts or excuse injustice in the light of ultimate benefit. His narrative is continually enlivened by an unobtrusive dry humour; his frequent character studies are serious but witty, charitable but acute. Some trace of these qualities appears also in the dozen articles he wrote for the *Dictionary of National Biography* between 1886 and 1890.

Dixon was fairly tall and was left-handed; he was dark-complexioned and full-bearded with a good head of hair which turned white in middle age; his voice was deep, slow, and melancholy; he was an inveterate pipe-smoker (a habit that may have contributed to frequent bronchial complaints in the last decade of his life). According to H. C. Beeching, 'it was often remarked that Dixon had a great look of Chaucer as he appears in Hoccleve's portrait, and the resemblance was more than external, reaching to a

characteristic and humorous interest in all sorts and conditions of people' (*DNB*). Bridges was struck by Dixon's humility, which with strangers passed for shyness and gaucherie, thus disguising his eager, ingenuous temper. Hopkins found something of this temper in Dixon's best verse: 'an extreme purity, a directness of human nature, and absence of affectation which is most rare' (*Hopkins to Robert Bridges*, 139).   JAMES SAMBROOK

Sources J. Sambrook, *A poet hidden: the life of Richard Watson Dixon, 1833–1900* (1962) • R. Bridges, 'Memoir', in R. Bridges, *Poems by the late Rev. Dr. Richard Watson Dixon: a selection* (1909) • *The correspondence of Gerard Manley Hopkins and Richard Watson Dixon*, ed. C. C. Abbott, rev. 2nd edn (1955) • R. W. Dixon, *The life of James Dixon, D. D., Wesleyan minister* (1874) • *The letters of Gerard Manley Hopkins to Robert Bridges*, ed. C. C. Abbott, rev. 2nd edn (1955) • *The selected letters of Robert Bridges*, ed. D. E. Stanford, 2 vols. (1983) • H. Gee, preface, in R. W. Dixon, *History of the Church of England*, ed. H. Gee, 5 (1902) • G. Burne-Jones, *Memorials of Edward Burne-Jones*, 2 vols. (1904) • J. W. Mackail, *Life of William Morris*, new edn, 2 vols. (1901) • M. Coleridge, 'The last hermit of Warkworth', *Non sequitur* (1900) • H. Newbolt, *My world as in my time* (1932) • S. Nowell-Smith, 'Some uncollected authors XXIX: Richard Watson Dixon', *Book Collector*, 10 (1961), 322–8 • H. Summerfield, 'The lyric poetry of R. W. Dixon', *Trivium*, 5 (1970), 57–71 • G. Rupp, 'The Victorian churchman as historian: a reconsideration of R. W. Dixon's *History of the Church of England*', *Essays in modern English church history: in memory of Norman Sykes*, ed. G. V. Bennett and J. D. Walsh (1966), 206–16 • P. Turner, *Victorian poetry, drama and miscellaneous prose, 1832–1900* (1990), vol. 14 of *The Oxford history of English literature* (1945–) • m. certs. • *DNB* • Warkworth church service book

Archives Bodl. Oxf. • U. Leeds, Brotherton L. • William Morris Gallery, Walthamstow • Worcester College, Oxford

Likenesses W. Rothenstein, lithograph, 1898, NPG; repro. in *Northern Counties Magazine*, 6 (1901) • J. Russell, photograph, repro. in Sambrook, *A poet hidden* • photograph, repro. in *The last poems of Richard Watson Dixon: a selection* (1905) • photograph, repro. in *Poems by the late Rev. Dr. Richard Watson Dixon* (1909) • photograph, NPG [see illus.]

Wealth at death £973 3s. 4d.: probate, 24 Feb 1900, CGPLA Eng. & Wales

Dixon, Robert (1614/15–1688), Church of England clergyman, was the son of James Dixon of Aldersgate, London, a member of the Cutlers' Company, and his wife, Joan, daughter of Walter Betson of Cambridge. He attended the Perse School in Cambridge and matriculated at St John's College, Cambridge, on 22 March 1631, aged sixteen, by which time his father had died. He graduated BA in 1635 and proceeded MA in 1638. He was ordained on 21 September 1639 and afterwards seems to have obtained a benefice in Kent. He married Sarah Mabb of Bearsted; by 1663 they had three children, of whom the eldest was then aged seventeen.

In 1644, returning from preaching a funeral sermon in Gravesend, he was arrested in the yard of The Crown inn, Rochester, apparently for his royalism and his refusal to take the covenant. According to his son James he spent fourteen months in close confinement in Knole House, near Sevenoaks, and, later, at Leeds Castle in Kent. In 1647 he was presented to the rectory of Tunstall in Kent, from which he was soon sequestrated for royalism. He was incorporated at Oxford on 12 July 1653. He was restored to the parish of Tunstall in 1660 and was made vicar of St

Robert Dixon (1614/15–1688), by John Collins (after William Reader)

Nicholas, Rochester, and a prebendary of Rochester Cathedral in the same year. In June 1661 his son Robert (b. 1646) entered St John's, Cambridge, as did his other son, James (b. 1648), in March of the following year. In March 1668 he dedicated *The Doctrine of Faith, Justification and Assurance* to the royalist Sir Edward Hales of Tunstall Place, his 'first Benefactor and most liberal Patron of my Studies' (sig. A2v). Later in the same year he was created DD after the king wrote to the University of Cambridge on his behalf. In 1670 he became vicar of Stockbury in Kent. In 1674 he published *The Degrees of Consanguinity, and Affinity*. This work was intended to inform readers as to which relationships were prohibited by God and which were not: the first page contains a quotation from Leviticus 18: 6, 'None of you shall approach to any that is near of Kin to him.' In *The Nature of the Two Testaments* (1676) he attacked presbyterians and Catholics alike, and argued: 'I take them to be the best Divines … that preach the New Testament and not the Old'. This work also contains a particularly striking eulogy of 'the most Excellent' Hugo Grotius (sig. B2r). In 1681 he published *A Short Essay of Modern Divinity*, and two years later a certain R. D. published *Candida, or, The Witches*, a 'crazy' and 'eccentric' (*DNB*) verse satire on existing society. The *Dictionary of National Biography* doubted the traditional attribution of this title to Robert Dixon, but it was printed and published by Samuel Roycroft and Robert Clavell, both of whom produced two titles for Dixon in

1681. In addition Samuel Roycroft's father, Thomas, had printed two pamphlets for Dixon in the 1670s. The likelihood is, therefore, that *Candida* was indeed written by Robert Dixon. He died in May 1688, and was survived by his wife.   JASON M^c ELLIGOTT

Sources Walker rev. · Venn, *Alum. Cant.* · *CSP dom.*, 1667–8, 393 · Foster, *Alum. Oxon.* · R. Dixon, *The doctrine of faith, justification and assurance* (1668) · R. Dixon, *The degrees of consanguinity, and affinity* (1674) · R. Dixon, *The nature of the two testaments* (1676) · R. Dixon, *A sermon preached* (1681) · R. Dixon, *A short essay of modern divinity* (1681) · R. Dixon, *Candida, or, The witches* (1683) · J. Walker, *An attempt towards recovering an account of the numbers and sufferings of the clergy of the Church of England*, 2 pts in 1 (1714) · G. J. Armytage, ed., *A visitation of the county of Kent, begun … 1663, finished … 1668*, Harleian Society, 54 (1906), 49 · administration, PRO, PROB 6/64, fol. 119v
Archives BL, Add. MS 5867, fol. 27b
Likenesses J. Collins, line engraving (after W. Reader), BM, NPG [*see illus.*]

Dixon, Sir Robert Bland (1867–1939), engineer and naval officer, was born on 30 March 1867 at Darlington, the elder son of Robert Bland Dixon, architect and surveyor, and his wife, Mary Ann Whitecomb (*née* Parr). He was the elder brother of Walter Ernest *Dixon, a pharmacologist. He was educated at Queen Elizabeth Grammar School, Darlington, and at the Royal Naval Engineering College at Keyham, then recently established, and was in fact the first student of the college to reach the head of his profession. In 1888 he passed for further training to the Royal Naval College, Greenwich, with the rank of assistant engineer (the equivalent of sub-lieutenant). His first year's progress qualified him for an additional two years' study and for specialization in machinery design and the more scientific side of his profession, with only sea service required to qualify him for successive steps of promotion.

On leaving Greenwich in 1891 Dixon joined the *Hecla*, one of the earliest repair ships, in the Mediterranean. A special feature of her equipment was the carriage of a flotilla of 'second-class torpedo boats' which were hoisted out and exercised together, and provided the initial experience in the evolution of destroyers and destroyer tactics. On promotion to engineer in 1892 he was sent to the battleship *Trafalgar*, and in 1893 to the Royal Naval College, Greenwich, as instructor in applied mechanics to assist J. H. Cotterill. Dixon married in 1896 Hettie Alice (d. 1936), daughter of Dr Frank Sextus Tuck, of Aylesford, Kent. There were no children.

After two years' service on the China station in the *Centurion* (1896–8) Dixon went home and was posted successively to Chatham Dockyard as assistant to the chief engineer (1899), to the Admiralty, to Portsmouth as first assistant to the engineer manager (1902), and, in 1904, soon after his promotion to chief engineer, he joined the staff of the director of dockyards.

In that same year, owing to the change in naval titles then introduced, Dixon became engineer commander, and as such he spent his last spell of sea service in the battleship *Dominion* during 1907 and 1908. By then he was recognized by both his seniors and juniors as an exceptionally capable and popular officer, and after three years at Haulbowline yard as chief engineer he was appointed engineer manager of Portsmouth yard in 1912.

Dixon held this post until 1917, having been promoted engineer captain in 1915, a period which gave his powers of organization and technical judgement a full test on account of the great increase in both men and machinery demanded by first the threat and second the outbreak of war. He left Portsmouth in order to become assistant director of dockyards, and he remained at Whitehall until his retirement in 1928, being successively assistant engineer (1919), deputy engineer (1920), and, in succession to Sir George Goodwin, engineer-in-chief of the fleet in 1922, receiving then the usual promotion from engineer rear-admiral (1919) to engineer vice-admiral on appointment.

On retirement in 1928, Dixon became chairman and director of several engineering firms, notably of Messrs Babcock and Wilcox. He was an active member of several technical societies and was president in 1926 of the Junior Institute of Engineers, and in 1929 of the Institute of Marine Engineers. He served on the privy council committee of scientific and industrial research. He took a keen and continuous interest in engineering education, and served on the committee on the training of naval cadets under the chairmanship of Sir Reginald Custance in 1912, and on the education committee of the Mechanical Engineers.

Although no spectacular advance marked Dixon's tenure of high office comparable with the introduction of the water tube boiler and the steam turbine, the British lead in Admiralty engineering was fully maintained. In the *Kent* class, designed to embody the experience of the First World War and to meet the growing menace from the air, the 'unit' system, whereby each propeller can have, as required, its own independent supply of steam, with high pressures and temperatures, was, after long opposition, introduced in the *Nelson* and the *Rodney* and later became almost universal in all important vessels. The cure of 'condenseritis' was achieved after prolonged tests by the use of cupro-nickel tubes, while the introduction of corrugated steam-pipes to provide for expansion successfully met a difficulty in spite of opposition from competent opinion. Another development was the use of electric drive at cruising speeds for auxiliary machinery, but of steam drive with independence of the vulnerable 'ringmain' when in action.

At a time when the German navy had adopted the diesel engine—notably in the *Deutschland* and *Graf von Spee*—and the United States had done the same in the *Maryland* and others, it was largely owing to the representations of Dixon that despite persistent and repeated pressure the Royal Navy retained its faith in the steam turbine, a faith fully justified, since both countries reverted to British practice. Further, during Dixon's term of office there largely disappeared the lack of understanding and contact between seagoing engineer officers and the higher engineer officers at the Admiralty of which the former had long been conscious.

Dixon was a man of quiet and retiring disposition, with great tenacity of character. He rarely thrust his views forward, but was always ready, when called upon, with a well weighed and considered opinion. He was appointed CB on leaving Portsmouth in 1918 and KCB in 1924. The University of Sheffield conferred upon him the honorary degree of DEng in 1926. He died at St Luke's Hospital, Sydney, New South Wales, while on a business visit for Messrs Babcock and Wilcox, on 28 July 1939.   W. S. HILL, *rev.*

Sources *The Times* (29 July 1939) · personal knowledge (1949) · *WWW* · M. E. Day, ed., *The engineers' who's who* (1939) · *CGPLA Eng. & Wales* (1939)

Wealth at death £4346 6s. 1d.: resworn probate, 16 Sept 1939, *CGPLA Eng. & Wales*

Dixon, Sarah (1671/2–1765), poet, was born in Kent, the daughter of James Dixon, a barrister originally of Rochester, Kent, who was admitted to the Middle Temple as a clerk on 20 May 1663 and called to the bar on 13 May 1670, and his wife, Elizabeth Soulhouse. Her only known brother, James Dixon, matriculated at University College, Oxford, on 17 February 1694, aged seventeen, but seems to have died soon afterwards; he was not awarded a degree. Details of Dixon's life are sparse and sometimes contradictory. She may have been born in Newnham, though much of her life seems to have been spent in or near St Stephen's parish, near Canterbury.

Dixon is known from her single volume of *Poems on Several Occasions*, published anonymously in Canterbury in 1740 but attributed to her in inscriptions in the Bodleian and British Library copies of the book. The 500 subscribers to this volume were chiefly local, but some members of the nobility, as well as better-known poets, including Elizabeth Carter and Alexander Pope, also appear on the list. Additional poems bearing individual dates were transcribed onto the endpapers of the British Library copy from a manuscript owned by Dixon's niece, a Mrs Eliza Bunce (*née* De Langle), possibly the child of an unidentified sister. Eliza Bunce was the widow of the Revd John Bunce (*d.* 1786), vicar of St Stephen's, who encouraged Dixon's writing and corrected it for publication. This volume also has appended a poem 'On the Ruins of St Austin's, Canterbury'; it was published in the *Kentish Gazette* of 9 July 1774, and was said to have been written some time after Dixon was seventy-three years old.

An inscription in the Bodleian copy of Dixon's *Poems* describes her as a widow. However, a memorial stone in the chancel floor of St Stephen's identifies her as the daughter of James Dixon, barrister. Her writings contain references to members of her family: one, from 1739, is addressed to John and Eliza Bunce on the death of their young daughter; another, among those published in her *Poems* in 1740, is entitled 'On the Death of my Dear Brother, Late of University College, Oxford'. There are, conspicuously, no references or dedications to a husband or child.

Dixon's verse is chiefly pastoral; her preface suggests a source for her poetic impulse in the peaceful solitude of her youth in the country. Individual poems range from light but pointed satire on the follies and failings of women, through romantic, ballad-like lyrics, to earnest, mature, religious verse. She characteristically underplays her education, intellect, and talent as a 'weaker Woman', but her religious rationalization of women's intellectual and social position in relation to men has a rather bitter tone:

Eve's Theft serv'd but to dignify Man's Soul,
Her Sex denied the Knowledge which she stole.

The only other recorded detail of Sarah Dixon's life also comes from the memorial stone at St Stephen's. She died on 23 April 1765 at the age of ninety-three.

RICHARD GREENE, rev.

Sources Foster, *Alum. Oxon.* · H. A. C. Sturgess, ed., *Register of admissions to the Honourable Society of the Middle Temple, from the fifteenth century to the year 1944*, 1 (1949) · J. Todd, ed., *A dictionary of British and American women writers, 1660–1800* (1984) · R. Lonsdale, ed., *Eighteenth-century women poets: an Oxford anthology* (1989)

Dixon, Thomas (1679/80–1729), Presbyterian minister and college teacher, was probably the son of an episcopalian, but not, as formerly believed, of Thomas Dixon (*d.* 1704), who was ejected from the vicarage of Kelloe, co. Durham, as a nonconformist. Dixon studied at Manchester dissenting academy under John Chorlton and James Coningham, probably from 1700 to 1704. While a student, he wrote to Edmund Calamy 'in a state of suspense between conformity and nonconformity' (McLachlan, 133). His first ministerial appointment was at Colchester in 1704.

Before October 1705 Dixon had succeeded Roger Anderton as minister of a congregation at Whitehaven, founded by presbyterians from the north of Ireland and meeting in a 'chapel for the use of protestant presbyterian or congregational dissenters in the worship of God in their way, so long as the law alloweth thereof'. Having obtained a bond on 21 September 1708, he married Eleanor Stanger, daughter of the ruling elder at Cockermouth Independent Church, who no doubt subsequently acted as matron of the boarding establishment of his academy. In a trust deed of March 1711 he is described as 'Thomas Dixon, clerk'. The academy Dixon established at Whitehaven was for the education mainly of students for the ministry. He probably acted under the advice of Calamy, whom he accompanied on his journey to Scotland in April 1709. During his visit to Edinburgh, Dixon received (21 April 1709) the honorary degree of MA, with Calamy receiving a DD at the same time. Dixon took with him two students, including Jeremiah Sawrey of Broughton Tower, near Coniston, a grandson of Dr Richard Gilpin. The academy was in operation in 1710, and on the removal of Coningham from the Manchester academy in 1712, it became the leading nonconformist academy in the north of England. Mathematics was taught by John Barclay until 1714, when there may have been a partial suspension of activities due to the Schism Act. Among Dixon's pupils were John Taylor, of the Hebrew concordance, George Benson, the biblical critic, Caleb Rotheram, who became head of the Kendal academy, and Henry Winder, author of the *History of Knowledge*. In 1712 Dixon provided particulars of Cumberland and Westmorland congregations to John Evans, who recorded them in his manuscripts. During his residence at Whitehaven he was the leading nonconformist in the county, and secured aid from the Presbyterian Fund for many of his brethren.

In 1722 or 1723 Dixon moved to Bank Street Chapel, Bolton, Lancashire, as successor to the minister Samuel Bourn (1648–1719). He still continued his academy, and educated several ministers, including Thomas Butterworth. On 20 May 1718 he had been awarded an MD by King's College, Aberdeen, and he is said to have attained a considerable medical practice in Bolton. Probably this accumulation of duties in a steadily growing town shortened his life. His congregation exceeded 1000, and was second only to Manchester in the county. He died at the manse, Bank Street, Bolton, on 14 August 1729, in his fiftieth year, and was buried in his meeting-house. There, a mural tablet erected to his memory by his elder son, Richard Dixon, also a medical practitioner, characterizes him as 'facile medicorum et theologorum princeps' ('easily chief amongst physicians and theologians').

Dixon's younger son, **Thomas Dixon** (1721–1754), Presbyterian minister, was born on 16 July 1721 and educated for the ministry in Caleb Rotheram's academy at Kendal, which he entered in 1738, having received a student grant from the Presbyterian Fund. His first settlement was at Thame, Oxfordshire, from 1743, on a salary of £25 a year. On 13 May 1750 he became assistant to Dr John Taylor at Norwich. Here, at Taylor's suggestion, he began a Greek concordance, on the plan of Taylor's Hebrew one, but the manuscript fragments of the work show that not much was done. He found it difficult to satisfy the demands of a fastidious congregation, and gladly accepted, in August 1752, a call to his father's former flock at Bolton. He was not ordained until 26 April 1753. With John Seddon of Cross Street Chapel, Manchester, then the only Socinian preacher in the district, he maintained a warm friendship, and is believed to have shared his views, though his publications are silent in regard to the person of Christ. According to Nightingale, his heterodox views led to a secession which assisted in the formation of the Duke's Alley Congregational Church. Dixon was also tolerant towards Methodism: Nightingale quotes a letter from Dixon, stating 'I think the Methodists behaving peaceably should not be molested' (Nightingale, *Lancashire Nonconformity*, 11–12).

Dixon died on 23 February 1754 and was buried beside his father. Joshua Dobson of Cockey Moor preached his funeral sermon. His friend Seddon edited from his papers a posthumous tract, *The sovereignty of the divine administration … a rational account of our blessed Saviour's temptation*, which was published in a second edition in 1766. In 1810 William Turner of Newcastle had two quarto volumes, in shorthand, containing Dixon's notes on the New Testament.

ALEXANDER GORDON, rev. AIDAN C. J. JONES and
B. ANNE M. DICK

Sources H. McLachlan, *Essays and addresses* (1950), 131–46 · F. Baker, *The rise and progress of nonconformity in Bolton* (1854), 43–4, 105–6 · *Calamy rev.*, 165 · B. Nightingale, *Lancashire nonconformity*, 6 vols. [1890–93], vol. 3, pp. 8–12 · F. Nicholson and E. Axon, *The older* nonconformity in Kendal (1915) • J. Evans, 'List of dissenting congregations and ministers in England and Wales, 1715–1729', DWL, MS 38.4 • B. Nightingale, *The ejected of 1662 in Cumberland and Westmorland*, 2 vols. (1901), vol. 2, pp. 1281–2 • Trust deeds, Whitehaven United Reformed Church, Cumbria AS, Whitehaven • P. J. Anderson, ed., *Officers and graduates of University and King's College, Aberdeen, MVD–MDCCCLX*, New Spalding Club, 11 (1893), 125 • senate minutes, U. Aberdeen, MS K 41 • D. Laing, ed., *A catalogue of the graduates … of the University of Edinburgh*, Bannatyne Club, 106 (1858), 185, 239 • R. S. Robson, '1662 and some of its survivals', *Whitehaven News* (27 June 1912) • F. J. G. Robinson and P. J. Wallis, 'Some early mathematical schools in Whitehaven', *Transactions of the Cumberland and Westmorland Antiquarian and Archaeological Society*, new ser., 75 (1975), 262–74 • J. Brownbill and others, eds., *Marriage bonds for … part of the archdeaconry of Richmond now preserved at Lancaster*, Lancashire and Cheshire RS, 74 (1920)

Archives Cumbria AS, Whitehaven, Whitehaven United Reformed Church deeds, YDFC P 3

Dixon, Thomas (1721–1754). *See under* Dixon, Thomas (1679/80–1729).

Dixon, Walter Ernest (1870–1931), pharmacologist, was born at Fern Bank, Darlington, on 2 June 1870, the younger son of Robert Bland Dixon, architect and surveyor, and his wife, Mary Ann Whitecomb (*née* Parr). He was the younger brother of Sir Robert Bland *Dixon. Dixon was educated at Queen Elizabeth Grammar School, Darlington, and entered St Thomas's Hospital in 1890, graduating BSc in 1891 and MD (London) in 1898. In 1899 he was appointed assistant to the Downing professor of medicine at Cambridge. On 25 September 1907 he married Hope (*b.* 1874/5), only daughter of Francis Glen Allan, banker, of Dulwich; they had no children. In 1909 Dixon was made lecturer and in 1919 first reader in pharmacology at Cambridge, a post he held until his death. He also held concurrently, until 1919, the chair of materia medica at King's College, London. For his services in the intelligence department of the Royal Navy during the First World War he was appointed OBE in 1919.

When Dixon began to devote himself to pharmacology in 1899, there was no university chair in this subject in England, and the science received little attention from the point of view of teaching or research. By the time of Dixon's death, chairs of pharmacology had been established in many English universities and the subject was achieving something like the recognition it deserved. Dixon played a dominant part in fostering this development. He taught pharmacology as an experimental science and as the scientific basis of therapeutics. As a writer, teacher, lecturer, and investigator, he became one of the foremost pharmacologists in the world. H. H. Dale said that, under Dixon, pharmacology became 'a lively adventure in experimental science, offered with an inimitable racy humour' (*BMJ*). Dixon was author of *A Manual of Pharmacology* (1905; 7th edn, 1929) and *Practical Pharmacology* (1920).

Dixon's original researches, of which only a few can be mentioned, covered a wide field. With the help of various collaborators he investigated the physiology and pharmacology of the bronchial muscles, the pulmonary circulation, and the cerebro-spinal fluid. He was greatly interested in the subjects of addiction and tolerance to drugs

and in various papers dealt with the pharmacology of hallucinogens and the physiology of addiction. His work on Indian hemp in the 1890s concluded that it was a 'useful and refreshing stimulant and food accessory' ('The pharmacology of cannabis indica', *BMJ*, 11 Nov 1899, 1357). In other papers he dealt with tobacco, morphine, alcohol, cocaine, and heroin. Dixon was a member of the departmental committee on morphine and heroin addiction (1924–6), chaired by Sir Humphry Rolleston, the report of which confirmed a medical basis for drug control in Great Britain. Dixon's public pronouncements strongly favoured this policy and opposed attempts to bring Britain into line with the prohibitionist drug control policy of the United States. He was subsequently a member of the League of Nations expert committee on drug addiction.

In 1907 Dixon suggested that when a nerve is excited the resultant effect may be due to the liberation of some chemical substance. The subsequent corroboration of this hypothesis revolutionized concepts of the nature of transmission of nerve impulses, and constituted one of the most far-reaching advances in physiology of the twentieth century. Dixon's suggestion was, however, based on somewhat slender experimental data, and gained little credence at the time.

Dixon's impact on his generation rested not only on his own contributions to science: he also took a wide and participating interest in medical affairs. His witty and persuasive lectures and dogmatic writing had a potent influence in moulding medical thought within and beyond his own university. His buoyant and resolute spirit was a stimulus and example to his fellows. He was 'the leader, life, and soul of the party. His wit was sprightly and never cruel' (*The Lancet*).

Dixon was elected FRS in 1911 and FRCP in 1930. The University of Manitoba conferred upon him the honorary degree of LLD in 1930. He died suddenly at his home, The Grove, at Whittlesford, near Cambridge, on 16 August 1931. He was survived by his wife.

J. A. GUNN, *rev.* VIRGINIA BERRIDGE

Sources H. H. Dale, *BMJ* (22 Aug 1931), 361–3 • *The Times* (17 Aug 1931) • *The Lancet* (22 Aug 1931), 429–30 • *Journal of Pharmacology*, 44 (1932), 3–21 [bibliography] • *PRS*, 110B (1932), xxix–xxxi • V. Berridge, '"Stamping out addiction": the work of the Rolleston committee, 1924–1926', *150 years of British psychiatry*, ed. H. Freeman and G. E. Berrios, 2: *The aftermath* (1996), 44–60 • personal knowledge (1949) • b. cert. • m. cert. • d. cert. • *CGPLA Eng. & Wales* (1931)

Likenesses portrait, repro. in *PRS*

Wealth at death £7228 6s. 9d.: probate, 25 Sept 1931, *CGPLA Eng. & Wales*

Dixon, William (1753–1824). *See under* Dixon family (*per.* 1770s–1880).

Dixon, William (1788–1859). *See under* Dixon family (*per.* 1770s–1880).

Dixon, William Henry (1783–1854), Church of England clergyman and antiquary, was born at the vicarage house, Wadworth, Yorkshire, on 2 November 1783, son of the Revd Henry Dixon (1750–1820), vicar of Wadworth, and his first wife, Ann, daughter of the Revd William Mason and half-sister to the poet William *Mason. Dixon later inherited Mason's estates in the East Riding, together with various manuscripts by Mason and Thomas Gray. He attended the grammar schools of Worsborough and Houghton-le-Spring, and in 1801 matriculated at Pembroke College, Cambridge, where he studied music under Charles Hague. In January 1805 he graduated BA, proceeding MA in 1809, and in 1807 entered into orders. His first curacy was at Tickhill, Yorkshire. On 9 January 1809 he married Mary Ann (d. 1830), daughter of James Fenton of Loversall, Doncaster.

Dixon's first preferment was a canonry of Ripon, to which he was appointed in 1815 by the dean, Robert Waddilove. Thereafter he amassed Yorkshire benefices, mainly in the gift of the York chapter, including Mapleton (1821–4), Wistow and Cawood (1821–4), Topcliffe, and Sutton on the Forest, also holding the prebend of Weighton from 1825. In 1828 Edward Harcourt, archbishop of York, appointed him domestic chaplain, a position he also held under Harcourt's successor, Thomas Musgrave. He became a residentiary canon of York in 1831 and held the livings of Etton and Bishopthorpe, both in the gift of the archbishop, from 1837 until his death. He was considered an able steward of the church's temporalities, improving vicarage houses and rebuilding chancels, and was a supporter of public charities and church schools. As rural dean of York from 1842 he made a personal visitation of every church in his jurisdiction, and maintained good relations with dissenters. His role in the efforts to revive the convocation of York was controversial. Having attended the first such clergy meeting in November 1837, he was president of the next gathering in November 1847 as representative of the dean and chapter of York. In fulfilment of what he considered the wishes of the recently deceased Harcourt, who resisted a revival of convocation's powers, he prorogued the assembly, defending his actions in Synodus Eboracensis (1848), a reply to criticisms by Robert Wilberforce, archdeacon of the East Riding. Dixon's stand was said to have brought him into conflict with many of his friends.

Dixon was married a second time, on 2 February 1832, to Mary Anne, daughter of Rear-Admiral Hugh Robinson. An accomplished scholar, he devoted his leisure to antiquarian researches, mainly into church history. He was elected FSA in 1821. For several years he worked on extending James Torre's manuscript annals of the members of the cathedral of York. After Dixon's death it was proposed to publish these materials as a memorial to their collator and, after spending a further ten years working on the materials, James Raine (the younger) published a first volume of Fasti Eboracenses (1863), including the lives of the first forty-three primates of the northern province, ending with John de Thoresby (1373). Dixon died at Minster Yard, York, on 17 February 1854, and was buried in the public cemetery at York, which he had helped to found.

C. W. SUTTON, rev. M. C. CURTHOYS

Sources [C. B. Norcliffe], *A memoir of the Rev W. H. Dixon, MA, FSA* (1860) · W. H. Dixon, *Fasti Eboracenses: lives of the archbishops of York*, ed. J. Raine (1863) [preface] · Venn, *Alum. Cant.* · Boase, *Mod. Eng.*

biog. · D. A. Jennings, *The revival of the Convocation of York, 1837–1861*, Borthwick Papers, 47 (1975)
Archives York City Archives, commonplace books and notebooks

Dixon, William Hepworth (1821–1879), journalist and writer, was born on 30 June 1821 at Newton Street, Great Ancoats, in Manchester, the son of Abner Dixon and his wife, Mary, *née* Cryer, of whom little is known. He grew up in Over Darwen, where he was tutored by his great-uncle, Michael Beswick. He later became clerk to a merchant named Thompson at Manchester. He married, on 16 September 1844, Mary Ann McMahon. Dixon began writing at an early age, beginning with a play called *The Azamoglan*, which was printed privately. Between 1842 and 1846 he wrote for both the *North of England Magazine* and the *Illuminated Magazine*. In 1846 he became editor of the *Cheltenham Journal*. During his two months as editor he won two principal essay prizes in Madden's *Prize Essay Magazine*. Later in the same year he moved to London, where he entered the Inner Temple. He was not called to the bar until 1 May 1854 and never practised law.

After abandoning the law, Dixon began contributing to *The Athenaeum* and the *Daily News*, in which he published two series of bold articles, 'The literature of the lower orders' and 'London prisons'; the latter led to his first serious works, *John Howard and the Prison World of Europe* (1849, three editions) and *The London Prisons* (1850). At about the same time he was appointed a deputy commissioner of the Great Exhibition of 1851, held at the Crystal Palace in London, and helped to start more than one third of the committees then formed. His *Life of William Penn* was published in 1851, and this included answers to Macaulay's charges against Penn. Although Macaulay never responded to this work in print, a copy of Dixon's *Life* was found in his possession at his death.

In the same year, during a panic over fears of a French invasion, Dixon published an anonymous pamphlet, *The French in England, or, Both Sides of the Question on both Sides of the Channel*, which dismissed the possibility. In 1852 he also published a life, *Robert Blake, Admiral and General at Sea, Based on Family and State Papers*, which won popular acclaim but was not taken seriously by historians. After a long tour in Europe, in January 1853 he became editor of *The Athenaeum*.

In 1854 Dixon began researching the life of Francis Bacon, Lord Verulam. He published articles in *The Athenaeum* in 1860 and these were republished as *The Personal History of Lord Bacon from Unpublished Papers* in 1861. He also published *A Statement of the Facts in Regard to Lord Bacon's Confession* (1861) and the *Story of Lord Bacon's Life* (1862).

In 1861 Dixon travelled in Portugal, Spain, and Morocco, and edited the *Memoirs of Lady Morgan*, who had appointed him her literary executor. In 1863 he travelled in the Middle East, and on his return helped to found the Palestine Exploration Fund, of which he eventually became chairman. In 1865 he published *The Holy Land*, a guide to the region then known as Palestine. In 1866 he travelled in the United States. During his trip he discovered in the public library at Philadelphia a collection of Irish state papers belonging to the English national archives, which had been missing since the time of James II and included the original manuscript of the memoirs of Ulick Bourke, fifth earl and marquess of Clanricarde, covering 23 October 1641 to 30 August 1643. At his suggestion, they were returned to the British government.

In 1867 Dixon published his *New America*, which went through many editions, not only in England, but also in France, Russia, Holland, Italy, and Germany. He also travelled through the Baltic provinces. In 1868 Dixon's controversial work *Spiritual Wives* brought accusations of indecency. He brought a libel action against the *Pall Mall Gazette*, which had made the charge, and obtained nominal damages of 1 farthing on 29 November 1872.

At the general election of 1868 Dixon declined an invitation to stand for Marylebone. Although he spoke at many political meetings, he was not prepared to give up his career as a writer to go into politics. In 1869 he brought out the first two volumes of *Her Majesty's Tower* (vols. 3 and 4, 1871). In August 1869 he resigned as editor of *The Athenaeum* and soon afterwards was appointed justice of the peace for Middlesex and Westminster. In 1869 Dixon travelled for some months in the north, and wrote about his journey in *Free Russia* (1870). During that year he was elected a member of the London school board. In direct opposition to Dudley Francis Stuart Ryder, Viscount Sandon, he succeeded in carrying a resolution which established drill in all rate-paid schools in London. He worked hard as a member of the school board during its first three years. He spent most of 1871 in Switzerland, and then published *The Switzers* (1872). Shortly afterwards he was sent to Spain on a financial mission by a council of foreign bondholders.

On 4 October 1872 Dixon was created a knight commander of the Crown by the Kaiser Wilhelm. While in Spain he wrote most of his *History of Two Queens* (Katherine of Aragon and Anne Boleyn) (1873, 1874). Before starting upon his next journey he began a campaign to open the Tower of London to the public free of charge. He obtained the support of then prime minister, Benjamin Disraeli, and on public holidays Dixon personally conducted tours through the buildings. In September 1874 he travelled through Canada and the United States, which he described in *The White Conquest* (1875). Later that year he returned to visit Italy and Germany. In the following year he wrote 'The way to Egypt' for the *Gentleman's Magazine*, as well as two other articles in which he suggested that the government should purchase from Turkey its Egyptian suzerainty. In 1877 he published his first romance, *Diana, Lady Lyle*. The following year he published *Ruby Grey* and the first two volumes of his four-volume work *Royal Windsor*. A fall from his horse while in Cyprus in 1878 broke his shoulder bone; from then on his health deteriorated. *British Cyprus* was published in 1879; he subsequently lost most of his savings, which he had unwisely invested in Turkish stock.

On 2 October 1874 Dixon's house near Regent's Park, 6 St James's Terrace, was completely wrecked by an explosion of gunpowder on the Regent's Canal. He suffered more distress at the death of his eldest daughter and the sudden death at Dublin, on 20 October 1879, of his eldest son, William Jerrold Dixon. He was revising the proof sheets of the concluding volumes of *Royal Windsor*, and on Friday 26 December 1879 made a great effort to finish the work. He died in his bed on the following morning from a seizure. On 2 January 1880 he was buried in Highgate cemetery.

Dixon took a leading part in improving accommodation for the poor and labouring classes. He was a popular writer, but his work was sometimes questioned for its accuracy. He was a fellow of the Royal Geographical Society, the Society of Antiquaries, and the Pennsylvania Society. His wife survived him. Among their children was Ella Nora Hepworth *Dixon, novelist and journalist.

CHARLES KENT, rev. SINÉAD AGNEW

Sources *The Times* (29 Dec 1879), 4 • *The Times* (31 Dec 1879), 4 • Boase, *Mod. Eng. biog.* • *Portraits of distinguished London men* [1878], pt 1, no. 4 • *Men of the time* (1879), 321–2 • *Illustrated Review* (11 Sept 1873), 226–8 • *Annual Register* (1879), 236 • Allibone, *Dict.* • *Men of the time* (1856), 224–5 • *Daily Telegraph* (29 Dec 1879), 5 • *Daily Telegraph* (31 Dec 1879), 6 • [T. T. Shore], ed., *Cassell's biographical dictionary* (1867–9), 589 • *A dictionary of contemporary biography* (1861), 131–2 • *The Athenaeum* (1879), 236 • *CGPLA Eng. & Wales* (1880) • C. Knight, ed., *The English cyclopaedia: biography*, 2 (1856), 611–12 • F. Espinasse, 'Dixon, William Hepworth', *The imperial dictionary of universal biography*, ed. J. F. Waller (1857–63); repr. (1865) • W. D. Adams, *Dictionary of English literature*, rev. edn [1879–80], 180–81 • Ward, *Men of the reign*, 268 • L. C. Sanders, *Celebrities of the century: being a dictionary of men and women of the nineteenth century* (1887), 343

Archives BL, letters to William Baker, Add. MS 35058 • BL, corresp. with M. Ommaney, Add. MS 41340 • U. Edin. L., corresp. with James Halliwell-Phillipps, LOA

Likenesses Lock & Whitfield, woodburytype photograph, 1881, NPG; repro. in T. Cooper, *Men of mark: a gallery of contemporary portraits* (1881) • A. Claudet, carte-de-visite, NPG • Elliott & Fry, two cartes-de-visite, NPG • F. Joubert, carte-de-visite, NPG • Maclure & Macdonald, lithograph, NPG • chromolithograph, NPG; repro. in *VF* (27 April 1872) • portrait, repro. in *The Graphic*, 21 (1880), 69 • stipple, NPG • woodcut, NPG; repro. in *Illustrated Review* (11 Sept 1873), 227–38

Wealth at death under £5000: probate, 2 Feb 1880, *CGPLA Eng. & Wales*

Dixon, William Smith (1824–1880). *See under* Dixon family (*per.* 1770s–1880).

Dixwell, John [alias James Davids] (c.1607–1689), politician and regicide, was the younger son of Edward Dixwell of Coton, Warwickshire, and his wife, Mary (née Hawksworth), although he may have been brought up by an uncle, Sir Basil Dixwell of Brome in Kent. Dixwell was living at Folkestone when he was admitted to Lincoln's Inn in 1631. He was called to the bar on 30 January 1638. His elder brother, Mark Dixwell, was an active parliamentarian during the early part of the civil war, and upon his death in February 1644 Dixwell succeeded to the sizeable estate which Mark had inherited from their uncle and became guardian of his brother's children. Having been active in promoting godly reformation during the early 1640s, and as a captain of the Kentish militia, Dixwell assumed a prominent role in organizing the parliamentarian war effort in the county and received numerous commissions from parliament. He was appointed to the committee for sequestrations in Kent and made a commissioner for the New Model Army. More importantly, he served on both the county committee and the commission of the peace. Such zeal for the parliamentarian cause resulted in his being elected to parliament as MP for Dover in 1646. His appearances at Westminster were probably rare, however, since he remained preoccupied with Kentish business, not least during the royalist rising of 1648. By the summer of 1647 it had become clear that he was aligned with the political independents and the army at Westminster, although it was only after Pride's Purge in December 1648 that he assumed a position of prominence in the House of Commons, where he was appointed to the committee for plundered ministers and the navy committee. Nominated as one of the commissioners for the trial of Charles I, he attended the majority of their meetings, as well as every day of the trial in Westminster Hall, and signed the death warrant on 29 January 1649 [see also Regicides].

During the Commonwealth, Dixwell's political allies were committed republicans such as Edmund Ludlow, although he also remained active in the county as a militia officer and, after January 1652, as governor of Dover Castle. In November 1651 he was elected to the council of state, on which he served until November 1652, being particularly active in relation to admiralty business. Although he may have been opposed to the dissolution of the Rump and the establishment of the protectorate, he was not an active opponent of Oliver Cromwell, and remained willing to serve in parliament. He was returned as a knight of the shire for Kent in both 1654 and 1656, and member for Dover during the parliament of Richard Cromwell in 1659. He did not resume an active role in political events, however, until the recall of the Rump in May 1659, when he was elected to the council of state and confirmed as governor of Dover Castle. His allegiance was to civilian rather than military rule, and after the interruption of the Rump by the army in the autumn of 1659 Dixwell's control of Dover was important to the campaign against John Lambert and the Wallingford House party.

Having recognized the drift towards a restoration of the Stuart dynasty in early 1660, Dixwell sold at least part of his estate and fled to the continent to escape arrest and execution for his role in the trial of Charles I. He travelled to Hanau with other regicides, but subsequently sought greater safety in New England, where he was recorded as having arrived by 1665. He eventually settled in New Haven, where he lived until his death under the assumed name of James Davids. Upon settling in New Haven, Dixwell married Joanna, widow of a Mr Ling, in November 1673, although she died almost immediately. In 1677 he married Bathsheba How (d. 1729), with whom he had a son and two daughters. He made a settlement of his estate in 1682, although the deeds were not made public until after his death, in the interest of preserving his anonymity. A portion of his lands in England had successfully been concealed from the crown and had evaded confiscation by the government of Charles II. One of Dixwell's papers contained a comment which displayed his continued support

for the policies and ideas which had forced him to flee England. He expressed his confidence that 'the Lord will appear for his people, and the good old cause for which I suffer, and that there will be those in power again who will relieve the injured and oppressed' (N&Q, 5th ser., 9, 1878, 466).

Although Dixwell's friends, including the old republican John Wildman, saw the revolution of 1688 as an opportunity for him to return to England, they were unaware that he had died on 18 March 1689 at New Haven, where he was buried, before the news of William III's arrival reached New England. In New Haven Dixwell and his fellow regicides Edward Whalley and William Goffe (whom he is known to have visited at their refuge in Hadley, Massachusetts, in February 1665) are commemorated in the names of streets which branch off from a common intersection.   J. T. PEACEY

Sources E. Stiles, *A history of three of the judges of King Charles I* (1794) · *JHC*, 5–7 (1646–59) · *CSP dom.*, 1649–60 · C. H. Firth and R. S. Rait, eds., *Acts and ordinances of the interregnum, 1642–1660*, 3 vols. (1911) · F. B. Dexter, 'Dixwell papers', *Papers of the New Haven Colony Historical Society*, 6 (1900), 337–74 · BL, Add. MS 40717, fols. 160–99 · D. Gardiner, *The Oxinden and Peyton letters, 1642–1670* (1937) · *The memoirs of Edmund Ludlow*, ed. C. H. Firth, 2 vols. (1894) · CKS, 4270/T264, 267 · J. G. Muddiman, *The trial of King Charles the First* (1928) · G. J. Armytage, ed., *A visitation of the county of Kent, begun … 1663, finished … 1668*, Harleian Society, 54 (1906)
Archives BL, letters and papers · New Haven Colony Historical Society, Connecticut, corresp. and family papers

Do Biu mac Comgaill (*fl.* 5th cent.?). *See under* Ulster, saints of (*act. c.*400–*c.*650).

Dobb, Maurice Herbert (1900–1976), economist, was born in London on 24 July 1900, the only child of Walter Herbert Dobb, merchant, and his wife, Elsie Annie Moir. He was educated at Charterhouse School, and in 1919 went up to Pembroke College, Cambridge (where other Dobbs had been before him), as an exhibitioner, saved from military service by the armistice of 1918. There he switched from history to economics, then a somewhat unusual choice of subject, and gained a double first (1921 and 1922). After two years of research under Edwin Cannan at the London School of Economics, from which he acquired a London PhD degree, he returned to Cambridge as a university lecturer in 1924. There, apart from visiting lectureships and professorships, he remained for the rest of his life. He became a reader in economics in 1959.

In 1923 Dobb married Phyllis, daughter of Carleton Grant, artist. This marriage ended in divorce and in 1931 he married Barbara Marian Nixon, stage manager and author, daughter of Christopher Nixon, a Gloucestershire merchant; he had made her acquaintance some time after she had come up to Newnham as an undergraduate in 1926. Her professional activities in London (including as an air-raid warden and instructor during the war) prevented them from setting up a permanent joint domestic establishment until 1951, when they moved to the village of Fulbourn, Cambridgeshire. There were no children.

The somewhat unusual pattern of his earlier marital life

suggests that Dobb's career was less conventional and tranquil than might be supposed from this outline. He had become a socialist through opposition to the First World War, before leaving school. He joined the small band of Cambridge socialists as soon as he went up and, in 1922, the Communist Party. Neither body was then used to such notably well-dressed recruits of such impeccably bourgeois comportment. He remained quietly loyal to his cause and party for the remainder of his life, pursuing a course, at times rather lonely, as a communist academic. From the 1930s on he was increasingly recognized, in Britain and outside, as an exceptionally distinguished Marxian economist, and indeed the founder of this field of academic study in this country. He published much, especially during the last fifteen years of his life. While his learned output contains relatively little that does not repay rereading, his reputation as a scholar is likely to rest above all on the closely argued *Political Economy and Capitalism* (1937) and the modestly titled *Studies in the Development of Capitalism* (1946), which form a landmark in the Marxist, and indeed the wider, historiography of European economic development, and on his association with his close friend Piero Sraffa in the monumental edition of the *Works of David Ricardo* (11 vols., 1951–73), which bears his name as well as Sraffa's. It recalls both his erudition in the history of economic thought and a collaboration whose roots may go back to a common visit to the USSR in 1930.

The relations between even so gentlemanly and quiet a revolutionary as Dobb and the conventional academic world were far from easy. Nor were they smoothed by the dangers apprehended from a communist presence in a university that might educate royalty, or by a divorce which some in the Cambridge of those days found difficult to distinguish from other varieties of subversive behaviour. Pembroke withdrew its undergraduates and dining rights, and though he taught there from 1926 it was not until 1948 that Dobb obtained a college fellowship at Trinity. He himself, isolated in Cambridge, found political encouragement in the 1920s in work for the (London) Labour Research Department and the National Council of Labour Colleges, of whose journal *Plebs* he was, for some years, the *de facto* editor. After 1930 Marxism became less uncommon, and Dobb increasingly made his mark as a writer and an unofficial as well as official teacher of students. After a renewed period of relative isolation in the 1950s, his intellectual merits and achievements finally won the wider recognition they undoubtedly deserved.

Dobb received honorary doctorates from the universities of Prague (1964) and Leicester (1972), and upon his retirement a Festschrift from a distinguished international company of pupils and colleagues (*Socialism, Capitalism and Economic Growth*, edited by C. H. Feinstein, 1967). To his considerable satisfaction he was elected a fellow of the British Academy in 1971. He received his distinctions with his habitual, unjustified, but perfectly genuine diffidence.

Dobb's life was that of the scholar and teacher rather than the political activist, though he took the duties of his party membership seriously. R. P. Dutt almost certainly had him in mind when he complained, at one moment, about certain 'incurably professorial' communist intellectuals. His lifetime of devotion to his cause—which was by no means always uncritical—never had the slightest effect on the natural courtesy that once led a visiting foreigner to say that he had always heard about English gentlemen, but had never met any until he encountered Maurice Dobb. A slight touch of unconventionality in his toilette and domestic arrangements, which was not discouraged by his marriage to Barbara Nixon, did not disturb this impression. As a teacher, he took endless trouble. As a friend, he was uneffusively loyal. Perhaps he is best remembered, rosy-faced and ageing well—he had been a very handsome young man—in the many settings of the Cambridge that finally accepted him as one of its own. He died at Cambridge on 17 August 1976, and was survived by his wife.   E. J. E. HOBSBAWM, *rev.*

Sources *The Times* (19 Aug 1976) • E. J. Hobsbawm, 'Maurice Dobb', *Socialism, capitalism and economic growth*, ed. C. Feinstein (1967) • R. L. Meek, 'Maurice Herbert Dobb, 1900–1976', *PBA*, 63 (1977), 333–44 • 'Maurice Dobb, random biographical notes', *Cambridge Journal of Economics*, 2 (1978) • Trinity Cam., Dobb MSS [by permission of Mrs B. Nixon Dobb and Mr B. Pollitt] • personal knowledge (2004)
Archives People's History Museum, Manchester, papers • Trinity Cam., papers | BLPES, corresp. with editors of *Economic Journal* • BLPES, corresp. with J. E. Meade • King's AC Cam., letters to Joan Violet Robinson • People's History Museum, Manchester, corresp. with R. Palme Dutt • Trinity Cam., corresp. with Piero Sraffa • U. Hull, Brynmor Jones L., corresp. with R. Page Arnot
Likenesses photograph, repro. in Meek, *PBA*
Wealth at death £17,564: probate, 4 Oct 1976, *CGPLA Eng. & Wales*

Dobbie, Sir William George Shedden (1879–1964), army officer and colonial governor, was born on 12 July 1879 in Madras, the younger child and only son of William Herbert Dobbie, of the Indian Civil Service, and his wife and first cousin, (Agatha) Margaret, only child of Colonel Robert Shedden Dobbie, of the Madras staff corps. He was a classical scholar at Charterhouse School, and was commissioned into the Royal Engineers in August 1899 from the Royal Military Academy, Woolwich.

At Woolwich, Dobbie joined the Plymouth Brethren and devoted much of his time to Sunday school and soldiers' welfare work. In 1904 he married Sybil (*d.* 1962), daughter of Captain Charles Orde-Browne of the Royal Artillery, a leading army evangelical. Her sister Mary was the mother of Major-General Orde Wingate. On marriage the Dobbies agreed to dedicate a tenth of their income to 'the Lord's work'. Christian faith was the mainspring of Dobbie's life, and he personified the ideal of the officer as missionary propagated by Charles Kingsley. Dobbie and his wife had two sons, one of whom died on active service in 1944, and one daughter.

After training at the School of Military Engineering, Chatham, Dobbie served in the Second South African War (1901–2) and then in Chatham (1904), Bermuda (1904–7), Harwich (1907–9), and Ireland (1909–12), before passing top into the staff college at Camberley in 1912. At the outbreak of war in 1914 he went to France and took part in the

Sir William George Shedden Dobbie (1879–1964), by Walter Stoneman, 1942

campaigns of the Marne and Aisne. Thereafter his war service was entirely as a staff officer. Promoted lieutenant-colonel in 1916, he signed the order to the British expeditionary force ending hostilities on 11 November 1918.

The war had proved Dobbie's exceptional ability as a staff officer, and for nine of the ten following years he served in staff appointments in the Rhine army, Aldershot, the War Office, and western command. Promoted to command the Cairo brigade in 1928, he put down disturbances between Arabs and Jews in Palestine in 1929. From 1933 to 1935, as major-general, he commanded the Chatham area and the School of Military Engineering and was inspector, Royal Engineers. His last appointment before retiring in August 1939 was as general officer commanding Malaya and Singapore.

On the outbreak of the Second World War, Dobbie sought re-employment without success until in April 1940 he was asked by General W. E. Ironside to go to Malta as governor and commander-in-chief, in the rank of lieutenant-general. He arrived two months before the siege began in June. For two years the Italians and Germans launched air raids, blockaded the island to the verge of starvation, and kept it under constant threat of invasion. Dobbie shared the islanders' hardships and broadcast to and visited the people constantly. His belief in divine aid was evident to all.

By May 1942 Dobbie was worn out and was relieved by Viscount Gort, who brought with him the George Cross awarded to Malta by George VI. Dobbie was colonel-commandant, Royal Engineers, from 1940 to 1947, but was not actively re-employed and dedicated the remainder of his life to missionary work, serving on a number of Christian committees. In 1945 he published *A Very Present Help* and in 1948 *Active Service with Christ*.

Dobbie was appointed to the DSO in 1916, and was appointed CMG (1919), CB (1930), KCB (1941), and GCMG (1942). He received an LLD from the Royal University of Malta in 1942 and from Leeds University in 1944. Sir William Dobbie died at his home, 89 Coleherne Court, Kensington, on 3 October 1964. JOHN KEEGAN, rev.

Sources S. Dobbie, *Faith and fortitude* (1979) • private information (1993) [family] • *The Times* (5 Oct 1964) • *WWW* • *CGPLA Eng. & Wales* (1965)

Archives NRA, papers | FILM BFI NFTVA, news footage • IWM FVA, actuality footage • IWM FVA, new footage

Likenesses W. Stoneman, photograph, 1933, NPG • W. Stoneman, photograph, 1942, NPG [*see illus.*] • D. Gilbert, plaster bust, 1943, IWM • H. Lamb, oils, 1943, IWM • J. Gunn, oils, Royal Engineers, Brompton barracks, Chatham, Kent

Wealth at death £30,955: probate, 15 Jan 1965, *CGPLA Eng. & Wales*

Dobbs, Arthur (1689–1765), colonial governor and writer on trade, was born at Girvan in Ayrshire on 2 April 1689, the son of Richard Dobbs, army officer and future high sheriff of Antrim, and his first wife, Mary (d. before 1711), daughter of Archibald Stewart of Ballintoy. Richard Dobbs, a supporter of the protestant interest in Ireland, had sent his pregnant wife to Scotland to avoid the fighting which followed the revolution of 1688–9. Mary and her child returned to Ireland at the peace and settled in the family's residence, Castle Dobbs in co. Antrim. Prior to his father's death in 1711 Arthur Dobbs served in the British dragoons in Scotland. In 1719 he married Anne (d. 1747), daughter of John Osburn, a London silk dyer, and the widow of Captain Norbury; the couple had three children. After inheriting his father's property, he became sheriff of Antrim in 1720, represented Carrickfergus in the Irish parliament in 1727–30, and in 1728 became deputy governor of Carrickfergus. In 1730 the archbishop of Armagh introduced Dobbs to Robert Walpole, who in 1733 appointed him engineer-in-chief and surveyor-general in Ireland. Although Walpole's fall from power in 1742 was a set-back, Dobbs secured other patrons, notably lords Hertford, Holdernesse, and Halifax, who helped secure his appointment as governor of North Carolina in 1754, a colony in which he was already a substantial landowner thanks to his association with Henry McCulloh.

The quarter-century that Dobbs spent seeking preferment was uniquely creative. He made himself useful to Lord Halifax, president of the Board of Trade from 1748 to 1761, and Lord Holdernesse, a privy councillor and trusted protégé of the duke of Newcastle, by drafting lengthy proposals about Irish and colonial affairs which combined scrupulous research with bold and candid advocacy of policies for strengthening and reforming the empire. His two-part *Essay on the Trade and Improvement of Ireland* (1728, 1730) advocated relaxation of restrictions on Catholics and the benefits of free trade between England and Ireland. His unpublished 'Scheme to enlarge the colonies

Arthur Dobbs (1689–1765), by James Macardell (after William Hoare)

and increase commerce and trade' (*c*.1730) fused imperial energy with Anglican piety. Historically, Dobbs argued, empires had arisen from either 'thirst for dominion' or a more mature appetite for trade and commerce. Domineering imperialism tended to become self-destructive, and even commercial empire needed a mature metropolitan economy to absorb colonial wealth and free institutions (especially churches) to discipline and channel the energies and desires of the colonial populace. The British empire of the Augustan age, Dobbs warned, was in danger of degenerating from a commercial to a domineering regime because African slavery institutionalized human exploitation, and the dispossession of the Indians from their ancestral lands perverted Britain's civilizing mission and threatened a whirlwind of retaliation. In the long run both Africans and Indians would have to be incorporated into the colonial populace, but for the immediate future Britain should invest massive sums in Anglican missionary work so that both minorities could be converted to Christianity and brought under the protection and blessing of the Church of England:

> Shall we, who by the precepts of our Lord and Saviour, ought to love our neighbours as ourselves … instead … pride our selves by our superior knowledge in arts and sciences and despise them as an inferior race, not worthy of reclaiming? (Calhoon, 59–60)

Dobbs's Irish sensitivities, his personal stake in colonial development in the prosperity and development of North Carolina, and his career ambitions as a crown official were a volatile and potentially creative compound of attitudes,

temperament, and ideology. His friend and early patron, Lord Hertford (who had introduced him to Holdernesse), frankly warned both Dobbs and Holdernesse that his visionary proposals for reforming English–Irish relations could wreck his career. The rebuke only spurred Dobbs to bolder advocacy for the reform of Irish policy. Dobbs's experience in Scotland, moreover, convinced him that free trade could effect the same social miracle in Ireland that it had in Scotland. Dobbs's encyclopaedic knowledge of Irish economic problems, especially the wool trade, were of a piece with his candour, eloquence, and sense of imperial urgency. He argued cogently for a strengthening of the North American colonies as the best preparation for the inevitable next war with France, and the implication that a distressed Ireland threatened Britain's national security lay just below the surface of his policy recommendations. Dobbs's ability to incorporate a radical indictment of exploitation and injustice into writings on Irish and colonial policy administration was typical of Anglican–Irish political discourse in the age of Swift and Burke, and he was one of the foremost Irish protestant 'commonwealth men' of the eighteenth century (Robbins, 149–51).

Dobbs's governorship in North Carolina (1754–65) was one of the most significant in the colony's proprietary or royal history. No governor in any of the southern royal colonies worked as hard or manoeuvred as adroitly as Dobbs to curb legislative autonomy and maintain his own and the Board of Trade's influence over appointments and fiscal policy. He recognized that the assembly's control of the colony's accounts undermined imperial administration, and he waged a persistent and fruitless campaign to curb this crucial means of legislative supremacy. He regained royal control over the way the assembly spent the money reimbursed by the crown for provincial military expenditures during the Seven Years' War. He worked closely with the Board of Trade to influence the extension of legislative representation to new towns. He sought to limit the power of John Starkey, the colony's treasurer, a creature of the legislature whom Dobbs considered a 'professed violent Republican', and he resisted assembly efforts to make the office of colonial printer a legislative prerogative. But Dobbs also recognized that, by respecting custom and practice in the administration of the court system, he could most effectively serve the crown's long-term interests, and he risked censure in London for concurring with the legislature on issues of the independence of the judiciary.

Dobbs's skill and patience in dealing with the assembly and his tenacity in seeking to curb legislative power set the stage for the pre-uprising struggle, between 1765 and 1775, over the ultimate location of authority. Neither a high-handed villain nor an ambitious careerist, Dobbs exemplified British administration at its best. His character and conduct taught North Carolina leaders that they would have to become more than a legislative opposition; they would need to become arbiters of the public good and defenders of both liberty and order. Dobbs died at his home in Brunswick, North Carolina, while packing to return to England, on 28 March 1765, and was buried in the town's St Philip's Church.   ROBERT M. CALHOON

Sources *DNB* · D. Clarke, *Arthur Dobbs, esquire, 1689–1765* (1957) · J. McKay, '"To begin the world anew": Arthur Dobbs, eighteenth-century speculator', MA diss., Western Carolina University, 1998 · R. M. Calhoon, *Evangelicals and conservatives in the early south* (1988) · J. P. Greene, *The quest for power: the lower houses of assembly in the southern royal colonies, 1689–1776* (1963) · C. Robbins, *The eighteenth-century commonwealthman* (1961) · J. Russell Snap, 'Dobbs, Arthur', *ANB*
Archives PRO NIre., corresp. and papers
Likenesses J. Macardell, engraving (after W. Hoare), AM Oxf., Hope collection [*see illus.*]

Dobbs, Francis (1750–1811), politician and barrister, was born on 27 April 1750, the third son of Richard Dobbs, Church of Ireland clergyman, of Lisburn, co. Antrim, and Mary (*d.* 1775), daughter of William Young and widow of Cornet McManus; he was the nephew of Arthur Dobbs, sometime governor of North Carolina. As a young man he devoted himself to literary pursuits but soon became engrossed in military affairs. He purchased an ensigncy at the age of eighteen in the 63rd regiment and subsequently became lieutenant and adjutant. In 1773 he left the army and entered the Middle Temple, London. In the same year he married Jane Stewart, daughter of Alexander Stewart of Ballintoy, co. Antrim, and Acton, co. Armagh, and later settled on the Acton property as its agent. They had six sons and one daughter. In 1774 he wrote a play called *The Patriot King, or, The Irish Chief*, which was published in London and performed in the Smock Alley Theatre, Dublin, in Rathfarnham, co. Dublin, and Belfast.

After being called to the Irish bar in 1775 Dobbs took a keen interest in the political life of Ireland and published a number of political pamphlets during the agitation for Irish legislative independence and parliamentary reform. He also kept a close eye on the activities of the reform movement in England and was in regular contact with leading English radical figures such as Major John Cartwright. He was an influential member of the volunteer movement in Ulster and was captain of the Tyrone's Ditches and Acton Volunteers. He believed that the extra-parliamentary pressure which the volunteers had brought to bear on the British government to grant a 'free trade' to Ireland in 1779 should be applied again to win legislative independence for Ireland. He was also a member of the 'Monks of the Order of St Patrick', sometimes known as the 'Monks of the Screw', a political and convivial society founded in September 1779, whose primary object was to win a constitution for Ireland. Dobbs pursued this goal with vigour and his activities soon came to the attention of British as well as Irish politicians. Indeed, his radical views on Ireland's legal right to make her own laws were commented upon by Lord George Gordon in the British parliament in January 1780.

Dobbs later became a major in the southern battalion of the 1st Ulster regiment, which, in December 1781, called on every volunteer company in Ulster to send elected delegates to Dungannon on 15 February 1782 to propose and discuss resolutions in support of Irish legislative independence. The resolutions to be considered by the volunteer convention were drawn up in advance by Lord Charlemont, with the assistance of a few other patriots. However, parliamentary duties, or a wish not to influence proceedings unduly, led to the absence of the patriot parliamentarians, and it was Charlemont's close friend and political ally Dobbs who was the main spokesman at the convention.

Dobbs's involvement with the volunteers continued after 'the constitution of 1782' had been achieved. He was one of a carefully selected group of volunteer delegates who met as a national committee in Dublin on 18 June 1782 and declared their support for Henry Grattan's view that the 'simple repeal' of the Declaratory Act (6 Geo. I c. 5) was a sufficient guarantee of Ireland's constitutional security. But cracks were beginning to appear in the façade of volunteer unity. The Belfast volunteer companies took umbrage at this stage-management and declared that they would make up their own minds about the sufficiency of 'simple repeal'. Dobbs took this as an affront, and in a series of angry clashes with the Belfast volunteer companies brought the constitutional dispute down to the level of a personal confrontation. Henceforth the Belfast volunteers allied themselves with Grattan's rival, Henry Flood, who argued that Ireland would never be free until the British parliament renounced all rights to interfere in Irish legislation. Worse was to follow for Dobbs. He was refused admission to the third Dungannon convention, which met on 8 September 1783, because he had accepted a commission in the fencibles—regiments of soldiers raised locally for home service that were commanded by local landowners and armed and paid for by the government.

After the 'renunciation' dispute Dobbs turned for a time from politics and became consumed with a belief in the millennium. In 1787 he published four large volumes of a *Universal history, commencing at the creation and ending at the death of Christ, in letters from a father to his son*, in which he exerted himself to prove historically the exact fulfilment of the Messianic prophecies. He also published in 1788 a volume of poems, most of which had appeared in various periodicals. His interest in politics was renewed briefly in 1793 when he joined the Association of the Friends of the People, a political club founded by the second duke of Leinster, which sought to promote the cause of parliamentary reform. He also continued to pursue his career as a practising barrister with some success. His services were engaged regularly and he dealt with a wide range of cases. In 1798 he acted as a negotiator for some of the captured United Irishmen because, as Leslie Hale states, he was 'a barrister respected by both sides, whose political activities were always honourable' (Hale, 189).

Dobbs made a decisive political comeback in 1797 when he was returned to the Irish House of Commons for Lord Charlemont's borough of Charlemont in co. Armagh. He delivered an important speech and submitted five propositions for tranquillizing the country which were published in 1799. However, the success of that speech was quite overshadowed by the enormous popularity of his great speech delivered against the bill for a legislative union with Great Britain on 7 June 1800, of which, it is said, 30,000 copies were immediately sold. The popularity of this speech was due as much to the eccentric nature of his arguments against the union as to its eloquence, for he devoted himself to proving that the union was forbidden by scripture, by quoting texts from Daniel and the Revelation. He took advantage of the attention he had attracted to publish in the same year his *Concise View of the Great Predictions in the Sacred Writings* and nine volumes of his *Universal History*, under the title *A Summary of Universal History*. With the passing of the union Dobbs sank into obscurity; he could not get any more of his books published, he became encumbered with debts, his eccentricities increased to madness, and he died in great pecuniary difficulties on 11 April 1811.   DAVID LAMMEY

Sources P. D. H. Smyth, 'The volunteers and parliament, 1779–84', *Penal era and golden age: essays in Irish history, 1690–1800*, ed. T. Bartlett and D. W. Hayton (1979), 113–36 • *The Volunteers, 1778–84* (PRO NIre., 1974) [education facs. pack] • A. T. Q. Stewart, *A deeper silence: the hidden roots of the United Irished movement* (1993); repr. as *A deeper silence: the hidden origins of the United Irishmen* (1998) • *The Drennan–McTier letters*, ed. J. Agnew, 3 vols. (1998–9) • *DNB* • PRO NIre., McClintock family MSS, D 3000/129/1 • E. Keane, P. Beryl Phair, and T. U. Sadleir, eds., *King's Inns admission papers, 1607–1867*, IMC (1982) • L. Hale, *John Philpot Curran: his life and times* (1958) • D. Lammey, 'A study of Anglo-Irish relations between 1772 and 1782, with particular reference to the " Free Trade" movement', PhD diss., Queen's University of Belfast, 1984 • letters to Francis Dobbs, 1779–83, NL Ire., MS 2251 • H. Grattan, *Memoirs of the life and times of the Rt Hon. Henry Grattan*, 5 vols. (1839–46) • R. B. McDowell, *Irish public opinion, 1750–1800* (1944) • T. G. F. Paterson, 'The county Armagh volunteers of 1778–1793', *Ulster Journal of Archaeology*, 3rd ser., 4–7 (1941–4) • I. R. McBride, *Scripture politics: Ulster Presbyterians and Irish radicalism in the late eighteenth century* (1998)
Likenesses engraving, *c.*1780, repro. in Paterson, 'The county Armagh volunteers of 1778–93', *Ulster Journal of Archaeology*, 3rd ser., 6 (1943) • engraving (after painting by Wilson, 1780), repro. in *Memoirs of Francis Dobbs* (1800)

Dobbs, Sir Henry Robert Conway (1871–1934), administrator in India, was born in London on 26 August 1871, the second son of Robert Conway Dobbs (1842–1915) of Camphire House, Cappoquin, co. Waterford, Ireland, and his wife, Edith Juliana, *née* Broadwood (d. 1932). He was a scholar of Winchester College and of Brasenose College, Oxford, although he left Oxford after two years without taking a degree. He entered the Indian Civil Service in 1892, and was transferred to the political department in 1899. His first 'political' post was in the state of Mysore, but it was not long before he found his way to the north-west frontier, an area with which much of his later career was to be associated. On 4 March 1907 he married Esmé Agnes, eldest daughter of George Wilmot Rivaz of Canterbury, formerly of the Indian Civil Service; they had two sons and two daughters.

Dobbs carried out some adventurous journeys in his earlier years in the political department. In 1902–3 he travelled across Persia from Baghdad to Sistan; in 1904 he explored the then little-known tract of Hazarajat between Herat and Kabul. In 1904–5 he was attached as secretary to Sir Louis Dane's mission to Kabul, whose outcome was the

treaty with Britain by which the Amir Habibullah renewed the engagements entered into by his father, Amir ʿAbd al-Rahman, in 1880. Since it stipulated that the amir should hold 'relations with no foreign power except the British government', the treaty aroused some criticism at the time. However, it stood the test of the First World War, during which Habibullah remained neutral.

Between 1907 and 1914 Dobbs served in Baluchistan under Sir Arthur McMahon, and was particularly influenced by the 'Sandeman system', a method of administration devised for tribal areas by Sir Robert Sandeman, governor of Kaharistan in the latter part of the nineteenth century. This gave official governmental recognition to tribal chiefs and tribal law, and set up the chiefs, under the overlordship of the raj, to police their own districts. As revenue commissioner in the civil administration formed in the wake of Indian expeditionary force D's invasion of Mesopotamia, where he served between January 1915 and October 1916, Dobbs translated these principles into the tribal criminal and civil disputes regulation (February 1916), and collected information on revenue and land tenure that was to form the basis of the taxation system of the future state of Iraq.

Dobbs returned to India at the end of 1916 and served successively as revenue and judicial commissioner (April 1917) and chief commissioner (December 1917) in Baluchistan, and subsequently (1919) as foreign secretary to the government of India. In 1920–21 Dobbs headed a mission to Kabul where—in very difficult circumstances—he negotiated a revision of the treaty of 1905 with Amir Habibullah's successor, Amir Amanullah. At this stage the Soviet government was eagerly courting the Afghans, largely in order to consolidate and expand its influence in central Asia. Eventually Amanullah signed treaties with both the Soviet Union and Britain in 1921. The Anglo-Afghan treaty marked something of a rapprochement with Britain, setting up full diplomatic relations between the two states. In his report on his mission to Kabul, Dobbs's description of his difficulties with Amanullah and of the latter's highly mercurial character shows its author's talent for shrewd judgement and nuanced observation.

In February 1923 Dobbs succeeded Sir Percy Cox as high commissioner for Iraq. It was not an easy post to fill; at the time of Dobbs's arrival no agreement had been reached at Lausanne on the frontier between Iraq and Turkey, and calls were still being made in the British press for Britain to evacuate Iraq. Eventually negotiations for the Anglo-Iraqi treaty were completed in 1924, although Dobbs had gambled heavily by deporting a number of anti-treaty Shiʿi religious leaders to Persia in 1923, and had also crossed swords with King Faisal I. After 1924, and particularly after the settlement of the Mosul boundary question in Iraq's favour, Dobbs encouraged the Colonial Office in London not to 'make it appear to the Iraqi public that H. B. M.'s Government is desirous of binding them hand and foot', on the grounds that Britain would ultimately find it easier and cheaper to administer the mandate for Iraq if it did not make excessive and unpopular demands, a policy which was eventually adopted.

During the six years Dobbs was high commissioner the political horizon was seldom clear for many weeks in succession. The election of the constituent assembly, and subsequently of the Iraqi parliament; the ratification of the Anglo-Iraqi treaty in 1924; the control of the Kurdish districts, and the difficulty of persuading the Kurdish tribal leaders to accept the political framework of the Iraqi state; the Mosul frontier question; the financial viability of the new state; these and other issues demanded constant attention. By the end of Dobbs's time in Iraq it was clear that Britain's goal of maintaining strong indirect control over the country had been achieved enough to make Iraq's entry to the League of Nations only a matter of time. As a diplomat and administrator Dobbs played a crucial role in securing this objective.

Dobbs was appointed CIE in 1905, CSI in 1916, KCIE and KCSI in 1921, KCMG in 1925, and GBE on his retirement from Iraq in 1929. The last years of his life were spent at his family home at Cappoquin, where he died after a long illness on 30 May 1934.

J. E. SHUCKBURGH, rev. PETER SLUGLETT

Sources *The Times* (1 June 1934) · W. K. Fraser-Tytler, *Afghanistan: a study of political developments in central and southern Asia* (1967) · P. W. Ireland, *Iraq: a study in political development* (1937) · L. B. Poullada, *Reform and rebellion in Afghanistan, 1919–1929* (1973) · P. Sluglett, *Britain in Iraq, 1914–1932* (1976) · A. T. Wilson, *Loyalties: Mesopotamia, 1914–1917* (1930) · Colonial Office records · Burke, *Gen. Ire.* (1958)
Likenesses W. Stoneman, photograph, 1930, NPG · G. F. Kelly, portrait, Gov. Art Coll. · portrait, repro. in Wilson, *Loyalties*
Wealth at death £7627 11s. 3d.—in England: probate, 7 Sept 1934, *CGPLA Eng. & Wales* · £644: probate, 6 March 1935, *CGPLA Eire*

Dobbs, William Cary (1806–1869), barrister and politician, was born in Belfast, the eldest of five children and only son of the Revd Robert Conway Dobbs and his wife, Wilhelmena Josepha, daughter of the Revd William Bristow, rector of Belfast. A scholar of Trinity College, Cambridge, he took a wrangler's degree in 1827, and an MA in 1830. He was called to the bar in 1833, and married Elinor Jones, daughter of Henry Sheares Westropp of co. Limerick, in 1834. They had five children: Robert Conway, Henry Sheares, Elinor, Whilhelmena Josepha, and Charity Frances. He became crown prosecutor for Drogheda and Dundalk, in the Irish north-eastern circuit, in 1851, and a queen's counsel in 1858.

In 1857 Dobbs had sought and obtained the Conservative nomination for the constituency of Carrickfergus, for which his grandfather had been returned to the Irish parliament, and his cousin, Conway Richard Dobbs, to Westminster (1832). Successful in the election over his Liberal opponent, Francis Macdonogh QC, he espoused free trade as a practical necessity, having been previously a protectionist, and promised his constituents to uphold the protestant interest and protect the constitution. A committed Anglican, he supported all protestant denominations at a time of anti-Catholic feeling in England and of perceived Catholic threat in Ireland. On the issue of landlord–tenant relations he sought clarification of the law and contracts

acceptable to both parties, while on the thorny issue of the Maynooth grant he favoured its cessation, believing public money should not go to support a despotic church. Committed to the extension of education and of the franchise, he was cautious on the Irish national school system, believing that religion should be a central feature of education and fearing that the system gave Catholic priests too much power in Ireland in general; his preference for Lord Derby's Reform Bill of March 1859 was not realized owing to the defeat of the government.

Dobbs's own career did not suffer, however, as he was appointed to a judgeship in the landed estates court, in Dublin, in succession to Judge Martley, in April 1859, an appointment which rendered him ineligible to stand at the general election of the same month. By the time of his death ten years later he had become senior judge of the court, where, according to his obituary in the *Irish Law Times and Solicitors Journal*, his 'amiable character ... intelligent and cultivated mind ... [and] the consistency and uprightness of his conduct' had gained the appreciation of the public. Although the Dobbs family were living at Ashurst, Dalkey, co. Dublin, Dobbs died at 93 Wimpole Street, London, on 17 April 1869, while seeking medical attention. His body was returned to Dublin, and subsequently interred in the family burying-ground near Carrickfergus. He had been a member of the Carlton Club.

DAVID HARKNESS

Sources WWBMP · *Hansard 3* (1857–9) · *Belfast News-Letter* (1857–9) · *Northern Whig* (1857–9) · *Irish Times* (19 April 1869) · *Irish Times* (29 April 1869) · *Irish Law Times and Solicitors' Journal* (1869), 283 · Burke, *Gen. Ire.* · register of wills, 1869, PRO NIre. · genealogy, PRO NIre., Dobbs MSS, T 1190/1
Wealth at death under £14,000: probate, 21 May 1869, *CGPLA Ire.*

Dobell, Bertram (1842–1914), bookseller and literary scholar, was born on 9 January 1842 at Battle, Sussex, the eldest son of Edward Dobell, a journeyman tailor, and his wife, Elizabeth, *née* Eldridge (*d.* 1899). The family moved to London, where Edward Dobell was stricken with paralysis. In the Dobell MSS Bertram Dobell has recorded that life was in consequence 'very hard' and that he himself was compelled 'to work at the most laborious and uncongenial tasks'. Apart from that comment he was quite secretive about his early years. Nothing is known of his education. His first job was as a grocer's errand boy and he went on to serve as an assistant in the grocer's shop. He showed an early interest in old books, buying from the penny boxes on bookstalls.

When Dobell was nearly thirty he used his scanty savings to open a shop at 62 Queen's Crescent, Haverstock Hill, selling newspapers and stationery as well as books. He was aided by an advance of £10 from a loan society, which was used to buy stock, £3 being spent on books. From these humble beginnings, aided by a love of literature and a flair for recognizing a rare book when he saw one, and by dint of much hard work, he rose to become the proprietor of two bookshops in Charing Cross Road,

Bertram Dobell (1842–1914), by unknown photographer

held in high esteem by the leading bibliophiles of his day.

The diaries that Dobell kept meticulously throughout his bookselling years show that until a month before his death he attended auction sales assiduously, not infrequently taking in three or even four sales in a week. Dobell was, in modern terms, a workaholic, and family relationships may have suffered in consequence. Even when business was good money seemed always to be in short supply, and this may have led him to excessive restraint where personal expenditure was concerned. As an exception to this rule he regularly indulged his taste for opera. By 1901 he had accumulated stocks and shares worth £2000. On 24 July 1869 Dobell married Eleanor Wymer (d. 1910), daughter of Henry Wymer, a timber merchant. They had five children, three boys and two girls, but in a letter (now in the Bodleian Library) to the New Zealand poet Dora Wilcox he confessed that there was 'little sympathy' between himself and his wife, and that they 'did not live happily together, though [they] managed to endure the matrimonial yoke to the end'.

As a bookseller Dobell published some 250 catalogues of books and manuscripts, his footnotes giving the catalogues their special flavour. His various catalogues devoted to books printed for private circulation remain useful bibliographical tools because of his annotations. Dobell was the author of *Sidelights on Charles Lamb* (1903), *The Laureate of Pessimism: a Sketch of the Life of James Thomson*

(1910), and various books of verse, notably *Rosemary and Pansies* (1901), and *A Century of Sonnets* (1910). Other collections of his verse were published posthumously. He contributed articles on various literary topics to such periodicals as *The Athenaeum*, *Notes and Queries*, and the *Quarterly Review*.

As an editor Dobell was responsible for editions of James Thomson, Shelley, Goldsmith, Strode, and others, but he is chiefly remembered for correctly identifying Thomas Traherne as the author of *Poetical Works* and *Centuries of Meditation* when their anonymous manuscripts were wrongly attributed to Henry Vaughan. A number of these edited works appeared over Dobell's own imprint. Closest to Dobell's heart were the works of Thomson, who, writing under the pseudonym B. V., first came to his notice in the columns of the *National Reformer* in 1868. Six years later, when that journal began serialization of 'The City of Dreadful Night', Dobell wrote to Thomson, urging him to have his poems published in book form, and later offered to bring out such an edition himself. When a business setback prevented him from doing so, he was able to persuade Reeves and Turner to take up the project. Dobell's first letter began a friendship that lasted until Thomson's death. Family legend has it that on occasion Thomson slept on the floor of Dobell's shop.

At seventy-two, although complaining of failing powers, Dobell was regularly going to Charing Cross Road and putting in a few hours' work each day until very shortly before his death. He eschewed the spectacles that had been prescribed for him and likewise found that he managed better without his dentures than with them. At his death from liver cancer at his home, 21 Queen's Crescent, Haverstock Hill, London, on 14 December 1914, his business passed to his sons Percy and Arthur.

ANTHONY ROTA

Sources Bodl. Oxf., MSS Dobell · private information (1927) · *DNB* · S. Bradbury, *Bertram Dobell: bookseller and man of letters* (1909) · A. Rota, 'Bertram Dobell', *Nineteenth-century British book-collectors and bibliographers*, ed. W. Baker and K. Womack, DLitB, 184 (1997) · Bertram Dobell's catalogues, 1876–1914, Bodl. Oxf., MSS Dobell · *The Times* (15 Dec 1914)
Archives Bodl. Oxf., corresp., journals, diaries, literary MSS, and other papers | Bodl. Oxf., corresp. with L. I. Guiney relating to William Alabaster · Bodl. Oxf., letters to T. B. Mosher · Bodl. Oxf., notes on Thomas Traherne · JRL, letters to W. E. A. Axon · TCD, letters to Edward Dowden · U. Lpool, letters to John Fraser
Likenesses M. Landseer, drawing, c.1900–1908, Bodl. Oxf., MSS Dobell; repro. in Bradbury, *Bertram Dobell* · E. J. W., portrait, repro. in Bradbury, *Bertram Dobell* · drawing, Bodl. Oxf., MSS Dobell · photogravure, BM, NPG [*see illus.*] · process print, NPG
Wealth at death £9045 15s. 7d.: probate, 22 Feb 1915, CGPLA Eng. & Wales

Dobell, Sydney Thompson (1824–1874), poet and literary scholar, was born on 5 April 1824 at Cranbrook in Kent, the eldest son in the family of ten children of John Dobell, wine merchant and author, and Julietta Thompson, daughter of Samuel *Thompson (1766–1837), a religious reformer, who founded the Freethinking Christians, a church based on primitive Christianity. He was also a descendant of Daniel Dobell (b. 1700), a Quaker of Cranbrook. Dobell's father, who had published a pamphlet entitled

Sydney Thompson Dobell (1824–1874), by Briton Riviere

Man Unfit to Govern Man, moved from Kent to Cheltenham in 1836. Sydney inherited from both parents strong religious convictions, such as Judaic exclusiveness, with its insistence on separation from the world, which accounted for Sydney's extreme individualism. He was educated entirely at home, where he was given a sense of his uniqueness and brilliance. Schooling might have weakened his precocity, but lack of it might also have deprived him of effective external criticism.

By the time Sydney Dobell reached adolescence he was already caught up in a sensitive analysis of individual experience and feeling. An ardent admirer of *Manfred*, Byron's exploration of the tyranny of reason, Dobell memorized whole sections of the poem which, his biographer claimed, he knew 'by heart' (Jolly, 1.37). Dobell is perhaps one of the most representative figures of the transition between Romantic and Victorian sensibilities. He seems to have had a deeper psychological grasp of the conflicting demands of Romantic self-consciousness and Victorian social earnestness than his contemporaries.

As a dissenter, Dobell was well aware that religion was beginning to lose its hold. He felt that God designed each soul to find its own creed out of an individual experience of scripture (*Thoughts*, 153). Dobell's was a deliberate attempt to concretize religious abstractions like love, purity, and freedom, and to enable poetry to embody states of mind like guilt, fear, national pride, and ambition. By means of the confessional mode he tried to dramatize in his poetry how divisions between people and nations, and especially divisions between the sexes (he was a believer in rights for women), could be assimilated into a new creation.

Dobell became engaged to Emily Fordham in 1839 and married her on 18 July 1844. They had no children. Emily

seems to have rescued Sydney from the burden of perfectionism, a harsh asceticism, and a rigorous work ethic that had been imposed on him by loving but stern parents. At some time after 1847 John Dobell gave his son the management of the Gloucester branch of his wine business, and the young Dobells lived at Lark Hay in the village of Hucclecote, where Sydney began work on his first major poem, *The Roman*. In 1848 Dobell and his wife moved to Coxhorne House, near Cheltenham, where he met two avid enthusiasts for the Italian nationalist movement, Sir James Stansfeld and George Davis, who introduced Dobell to the Society of the Friends of Italy (Jolly, 1.195–8). In April 1850, under the pseudonym Sydney Yendys, *The Roman* was published by Bentley. It revealed the interpretative power of the poet, the superiority of the intuition of the imagination over reason, and especially the use of associative metaphors to achieve epical unity. Particularly because the cause of Italian nationalism was such a stirring event of the time, the poem was enormously successful.

In 1853 Dobell published *Balder*. The poem was intended to be his master work in which he would demythologize a male-dominated culture, dramatize a divided consciousness, and invigorate epical poetry by metaphoric language which followed the untrammelled path of free association (Westwater, 65). Instead, he infuriated critics. William Edmondstoune Aytoun lampooned the hero in his uproarious drama *Firmilian* (1854). Dobell was branded a 'Spasmodic' poet, a title Aytoun coined to satirize poetry which he considered to be extravagant and formless. He objected to the lack of plot, the exploration of profane subjects, the sensationalism, and the unintelligibility of Dobell's *Balder, Part the First*. Aytoun effectively buried both the poem and Sydney Dobell's poetic reputation, and the poem has lain neglected. But despite all its problems, particularly that of its length, *Balder* has unusual modern merit in its treatment of nature (perhaps Dobell's greatest gift), in its mythopoeic emphasis, and in its psychological realism. For instance, where Balder, the extreme individualist, the arrogant, chauvinistic intellectual, has to confront his own darkness, his neglected, deranged wife cries:

> Oh yes, thy glory! Yes—he must have glory,
> Yes, he must have his glory; he can stand
> All day in the sun, but he must have his glory!
> He has walked up in the sunshine world,
> He has been in the wind and the sweet rain,
> And none cried 'Upset the cup o' the honey-time,
> Upset the cup o' the honey-time'. And I am empty and dry.

Dobell intended to redeem Balder in subsequent parts of the poem, but nothing was ever published. In 1854, seeking medical treatment for his wife, Dobell moved to Edinburgh. Here he befriended Alexander Smith, and in 1855 he collaborated with Smith, another victim of Aytoun's 'Spasmodic' label, in a collection of poems on the Crimean War entitled *Sonnets on the War*. The book was not a success. Dobell recognized that he could never confine himself to the sonnet form which 'forbids anything like adequacy' (Jolly, 1.385). He wrote about seventeen of the thirty-five sonnets and showed how he could still master the startling image. In 'The Army Surgeon', for instance, the doctor goes about his duties on the battlefield where there 'bubbles a cauldron vast of many-coloured pain'. In 'Austrian Alliance' the speaker warns England of the Habsburg 'Vampyre' who was wrenched

> from the breathing throat
> Of living Man, and he leaps up and flings
> Thy rotten carcase at the heads of Kings.

In the summer of 1856 Dobell published *England in Time of War*, a collection of his short lyrics on the Crimean War. Because critics had condemned him for obscurity, in this new book Dobell laboured for simplicity. He did not write on the extraordinary hero, but on people in every segment of society. He maintained that the book was 'a collection of about forty ballads, exponent of the Home feelings of England on the subject of the War' (Jolly, 2.15). The favourable reviews far outweighed the unfavourable ones, and 'Grass from the Battlefield' was singled out as a poem 'which will be enshrined in memory along with the acknowledged masterpieces' of modern poets (*GM*, 227). Certainly in this poem Dobell revealed an acute perception of the mind's ability to concentrate on something quite trivial when under unbearable pressure. The ballad 'Keith of Ravelston' was another much praised poem.

On 8 April 1857 Dobell lectured before the Edinburgh Philosophical Society on 'The nature of poetry'. Although his theory of poetry revealed an extraordinary knowledge of scripture, nevertheless the poet relied not so much on God and the future life in heaven, but on life itself and a spiritual presence in that life. In Dobell's view truth belonged to the individual and could be wrested only from the shadowy depths of one's own psyche. (The intensity of his struggle to face up to the demands of the distinctive self can be seen in his depiction both of the disillusioned Monk in *The Roman* and in the solipsistic hero of *Balder*.) Scriptural events, Dobell argued, should be reinterpreted on an individual basis; they were metaphors for survival tactics in an increasingly complex world. For Dobell metaphors were the symbolic 'equivalents' of feelings; they reconcile the mind with the external world, the seen with the unseen; the metaphor was 'something more than a phenomenal similarity'. His ideas anticipate those of I. A. Richards, who called on critics to discover what a poem 'expresses' as well as what it states, and also T. S. Eliot's 'objective correlative'. However, these ideas were entirely neglected at the time. Even John Nichol, Dobell's contemporary critic and friend, when preparing the lecture for publication, did little to elucidate the 'clearly conceived theory', or to give an 'honest study' to the 'extraordinary view of poetry' taken by 'this singularly thoughtful man' (*Thoughts*, viin.). Modern critics however have found the lecture to be 'an impressive and significant document for the literary historian and theorist' (Preyer, 163), and 'one of the most sophisticated accounts of metaphor' (Armstrong, 11).

Dobell delivered his three-hour lecture on poetry while suffering from bronchitis. His already fragile constitution had been weakened by the strain placed on an overtaxed nervous system and the harsh climate of an Edinburgh winter. The Dobells returned to England and by 1858 settled at Detmore, where Sydney resumed the management of his father's wine business in Gloucestershire. Despite chronic illness Dobell did manage to publish some poetry in 1860, 'The Youth of England to Garibaldi's Legion' and 'The Magyars' New Year's Eve', but neither created any sensation. In 1862 he began a series of nomadic wanderings, in search of better health, to France until 1863, Spain until 1864, and Italy until 1866. In April 1865, while stopping at Puteoli, Italy, where St Paul had landed, he fell into an old open drain and injured his spine and brain (Jolly, 2.203); he was later treated for epilepsy. Although there was another trip to Italy in the following year, Sydney Dobell's health was broken. The next ten years were passed mostly in the pain and boredom of the sick-room in his homes in Gloucestershire. He died peacefully on 22 August 1874 at his last home, Barton End House, Horsley, near Nailsworth, and was buried in Painswick cemetery. His wife survived him.   MARTHA WESTWATER

Sources *The poetical works of Sydney Dobell*, ed. J. Nichol, 2 vols. (1875) · *Thoughts on art, philosophy and religion*, ed. J. Nichol (1876) · E. Jolly, *The life and letters of Sydney Dobell* (1878) · M. Westwater, *The spasmodic career of Sydney Dobell* (1992) · R. Preyer, 'Sydney Dobell and the Victorian epic', *University of Toronto Quarterly*, 30 (Jan 1961), 163–78 · I. Armstrong, *Victorian scrutinies: review of poetry, 1830–1870* (1972) · *GM*, 3rd ser., 2 (1857), 227 · *CGPLA Eng. & Wales* (1874) · *DNB*
Archives Indiana University, Bloomington, Lilly Library, personal corresp. | NL Scot., poems and letters to J. S. Blackie · NL Scot., corresp. with Samuel Brown · NL Scot., corresp. with David Gray
Likenesses B. Riviere, pencil drawing, NPG [*see illus.*] · wood-engraving (after photograph by C. R. Pottinger of Cheltenham), NPG; repro. in *ILN* (3 Oct 1874)
Wealth at death under £600: probate, 26 Oct 1874, *CGPLA Eng. & Wales*

Dobie, William Jardine (1892–1956), lawyer, judge, and author, was born on 21 March 1892 at 133 Dalkeith Road, Edinburgh, the elder son of John Dobie, an Edinburgh solicitor, and his wife, Agnes Ballantyne. Even as a young schoolboy it seems that Dobie was intent on following his father's profession and, after his schooling at George Watson's College, Edinburgh, he went on to Edinburgh University to study law. As was the custom of the time he entered the university solely to take those classes which were required for professional purposes, and without any thought of proceeding to a degree. However, he proved to be a distinguished scholar, and he was awarded the Thow scholarship as the best student of his year in Scots law. In the following year he obtained the same distinction in conveyancing. After acquiring the necessary professional qualifications he underwent an apprenticeship, and from 1920 to 1939 he was a solicitor and a partner in the Edinburgh legal firm Inglis, Orr, and Bruce, writers to the signet. In 1932 Dobie was admitted as a member of the Society of Solicitors in the Supreme Courts of Scotland.

Despite the rigours and distractions of practice as a solicitor, Dobie found time for other things. On 15 April 1922 he married Agnes Ferguson Ross (1886–1951) of Edinburgh, and they remained happily married until she predeceased him on 11 August 1951. They had no children.

Dobie also retained the academic interest in Scots law which he had displayed with such distinction while at Edinburgh University, and in 1936 he contributed articles on Udal law and Allodial law for the first volume published by the newly created Stair Society. That was but the beginning of a long series of writings on aspects of Scots law and practice which were to enrich Scottish legal literature for many years to come. As a well-established solicitor, Dobie in due course became solicitor in Scotland to the British Medical Association. He was also a practising member of the Church of Scotland, and for some time he was the session clerk of Newington and St Leonard's Church in Edinburgh.

Dobie's career as a solicitor did not, however, continue as he might at first have expected because, on 4 March 1939, he was appointed as sheriff-substitute at Campbeltown in Argyll. At that time most judicial appointments came from the bar, and it was very rare for a solicitor to be so honoured. As a result he spent the rest of his life working as a judge in both criminal and civil matters in the local courts of Scotland. It is clear that from the beginning he brought a mixture of learning, good humour, and common sense to his work as a judge, and he soon earned the respect and affection of all who appeared before him. In 1942 his abilities and reputation resulted in a transfer to the much larger court at Hamilton, and finally, in 1946, he moved to the sheriff court at Glasgow, where he remained in office until his death ten years later.

After taking up judicial office Dobie continued with his writing. In 1941 his *Manual of the Law of Liferent and Fee in Scotland* was published, and that was followed by *The Law and Practice of the Sheriff Courts in Scotland* (1948) and *Sheriff Court Styles* (1951). During the Second World War he edited the *Juridical Review* and, at the time of his death he was well advanced in preparing a new edition of *Dickson on Evidence*, a classical work of the mid-nineteenth century which had never hitherto been revised or updated. In a more lighthearted vein he also found the time to write notes of his experiences in the sheriff courts. These notes were edited posthumously by his colleague S. G. Kermack and were published in 1957 as *Plain Tales from the Courts*. Of all Dobie's writings the most influential was undoubtedly his work on *The Law and Practice of the Sheriff Courts in Scotland*. From the time of its publication it became an indispensable guide to practice and procedure in the sheriff courts, and it continued to be relied on by sheriffs and by court practitioners for close on forty years until superseded by a new work on that subject in 1988.

Dobie's work as a sheriff, and in particular his singular contribution to Scottish legal literature, eventually gained formal recognition when, on 2 July 1948, Edinburgh University, where he had not taken a degree as an undergraduate, conferred on him the honorary degree of doctor of laws. The commendation which preceded the award of that degree stated that 'the taste for scholarship was strong in him and his pen was seldom idle', and it went on to describe his recently published work on *The Law and Practice of the Sheriff Courts in Scotland* as 'a new and

original creation, reflecting the wide experience, the diligent and accurate scholarship, and the great legal knowledge of its author' (Edinburgh University minutes). For an essentially modest man a commendation in such terms must have been immensely satisfying.

Apart from his judicial work and his legal writing, Dobie's other interests were wide, and included the church, support of youth organizations, painting, fishing, and gardening. On 31 January 1956 he died at his home at Davaar, Glasgow Road, Uddingston, near Glasgow, aged sixty-three. Throughout most of his sixty-three years Dobie was, in the truest Scottish sense, 'a lad o' pairts'.

GORDON NICHOLSON

Sources WW (1956) · *Scots Law Times: News* (4–11 March 1939), 53, 54, 63 · *Scots Law Times: News* (11 Feb 1956), 31 · *Scottish Law Review*, 72 (1956), 44 · minutes of the senatus academicus, 2 July 1948, U. Edin. · private information (2004) [keeper of the library, Society of Solicitors in the Supreme Courts of Scotland] · b. cert. · CGPLA Eng. & Wales (1956)

Likenesses photograph, repro. in W. J. Dobie, *Plain tales from the courts* (1957)

Wealth at death £5747 6s. 3d.: confirmation, 28 June 1956, CCI

Dobrée, Bonamy (1891–1974), literary scholar and university teacher, was born at 4 Queen's Gate Place, London, on 2 February 1891, the youngest child and only son of the three children of Bonamy Dobrée and his wife, Violet Chase. The Dobrées were a well-known Guernsey family, originally armament manufacturers; Dobrée's father was a banker, and his grandfather, also Bonamy Dobrée (1794–1863), was governor of the Bank of England. He was educated at Haileybury College and at the Royal Military Academy, Woolwich; he was commissioned in the Royal Field Artillery in 1910. He resigned, as a subaltern, in 1913 and on 21 November of that year married the artist and poet (Valentine) Gladys May Pechell (1893/4–1974), daughter of Sir (Augustus) Alexander Brooke-Pechell, seventh baronet, a colonel in the Royal Army Medical Corps. The young married couple toured France in a horse-drawn caravan until April 1914, then stayed in Florence until the outbreak of war, when Dobrée rejoined the army, serving with the Royal Horse Artillery and Royal Field Artillery in France, Egypt, and Palestine. He was twice mentioned in dispatches and attained the rank of major. After the war he went to Christ's College, Cambridge (1920–21), and was captain of the university fencing team.

From 1921 to 1925 the Dobrées lived mainly at Larrau, a village in the Pyrenees. Here he wrote *Restoration Comedy* (1924), *Essays in Biography* (1925), and edited Congreve's *Comedies* (1925). His editions of Vanbrugh's plays (1928) and of Congreve's *The Mourning Bride: Poems and Miscellanies* (1928) were followed by *Restoration Tragedy, 1660–1720* (1929). In 1925–6 Dobrée was a lecturer at East London College (London University); from 1926 to 1929 he was professor of English at the Egyptian University, Cairo.

From 1929 to 1935 the Dobrées lived at Meadham Priory, Harleston, Norfolk; their daughter Georgina was born in 1930. This was a period of intense literary activity. In addition to being a drama critic and contributing essays on many diverse topics to various journals, Dobrée wrote several books; he also started to compile the *London Book of English Verse* with his friend Herbert Read, edited the *Letters of Philip Dormer Stanhope, earl of Chesterfield* (6 vols., 1932), and collected his earlier biographical conversations in *As their Friends Saw them* (1933).

The Dobrées moved to Earls Colne, Essex, in 1936; in that year he was appointed to the chair of English literature at the University of Leeds, a post he held until his retirement in 1955. He rejoined his regiment in 1939, worked in the War Office, and was appointed officer commanding the Leeds University Senior Training Corps with the rank of lieutenant-colonel; he resumed his university post in 1945. Dobrée lectured widely, in France, Canada, and the United States as well as in the United Kingdom; gave the Clark lectures (1952–3); and was Lord Northcliffe memorial lecturer (1963). He was Gresham professor in rhetoric at the City University, London (1955–61).

Dobrée's distinction was recognized by his appointment as OBE in 1929, and by honorary degrees from Dijon (1960) and Kent at Canterbury (1968), where the library has a Dobrée collection. There is a Dobrée Hall at the University of Leeds, a tribute not only to his work in the department of English literature (handsomely described by Richard Hoggart in *Of Books and Humankind*, essays and poems presented to Dobrée in 1964) but also in the university, where he promoted a department of fine art and where he persuaded his friend Peter Gregory to establish the pioneering Gregory fellowships in poetry, painting, sculpture, and music. Dobrée's broad humanity informed his teaching of literature; he brought to Leeds a connoisseur's attitude to the arts. Also the author of a play, a novel, and much poetry, through his scholarship and criticism he had an inspiring effect upon his colleagues and pupils. His own publications continued, with essays, editions, and such stimulating books as *Alexander Pope* (1951) and *Rudyard Kipling* (1965) reflecting an impressive intellectual energy. In 1949 he and Herbert Read completed *The London Book of English Verse*; in 1959 his volume in the *Oxford History of English Literature* (of which he was co-editor with F. P. Wilson) showed his liking for the liveliness of early eighteenth-century literature.

Like Swift, Dobrée enjoyed the bagatelle; and like him he enjoyed it in good company. His many friends included T. S. Eliot, Leonard and Virginia Woolf, Wyndham Lewis, and Henry Moore. Dobrée's appreciation of literature was wide; he was a man of letters who wore his learning lightly. Witty, yet profoundly serious, he disliked solemnity in others. His military training had given him a briskness that enabled him to execute his business, whether teaching, writing, or administering, with prompt efficiency. This left him time for the civilities of life, for innumerable kindnesses, and for the hospitality he and his wife always dispensed generously. He conveyed his enjoyment of the creative arts convincingly, was patron as well as critic. He died at his home, 15 Pond Road, Blackheath, London, on 3 September 1974.   A. NORMAN JEFFARES

Sources personal knowledge (2004) · private information (1986) · *WW* · *WWW* · G. W. Knight, 'Emeritus professor Bonamy Dobrée OBE', *University of Leeds Review* (1955) · M. Britton, 'A selected list of the published writings of Bonamy Dobrée', *Of books and humankind*, ed. J. Butt (1964) · *The Times* (4 Sept 1974) · b. cert. · m. cert. · d. cert.

Archives PRO, MSS relating to visits to Holland and France with British Council · U. Leeds, Brotherton L., corresp., literary MSS, and papers | BBC WAC, corresp. with BBC · BL, letters to Alida Monro, Add. MS 57752 · BL, letters to James Strachey, Add. MS 60665 · U. Leeds, Brotherton L., papers relating to Social Credit · U. Reading, Hogarth Press archives, corresp.

Likenesses H. Coster, photographs, NPG · E. Hutton, photograph, repro. in Britton, 'A selected list', frontispiece · M. de Sausmarez, oils, U. Leeds

Wealth at death £69,036: administration with will, 3 Jan 1975, *CGPLA Eng. & Wales*

Dobree, Peter Paul (1782–1825), classical scholar, was born in Guernsey, the son of William Dobree of Guernsey. He was educated under Dr Richard Valpy at Reading School before matriculating in 1800 at Trinity College, Cambridge, where he graduated BA as fourth senior optime in 1804. Elected a fellow of Trinity in 1806, he lived there for the rest of his life, graduating MA in 1807, and being ordained deacon in 1812 and priest in 1813. Charles Burney gave him an introduction in London in 1805 to Richard Porson; so began an acquaintance which, although it lasted only three years until Porson's death, led to Dobree's becoming perhaps his most illustrious and devoted pupil.

Dobree's first appearance as an author was in the *Monthly Review* (52, 1807, appendix) to which he contributed an important review of Bothe's *Aeschylus* in which he attacked its freedom of textual conjecture, while displaying the more conservative, informed, but penetratingly sharp style of criticism which he never abandoned. He contributed a few other reviews to the same journal, but these were less significant. On Porson's death in 1808 Dobree came forward as a candidate for the regius professorship of Greek at Cambridge, and was to have read his probationary lecture on Aristophanes; finding the electors unanimous, or nearly so, in favour of James Henry Monk, he withdrew from the contest. On Monk's resignation in 1823, Dobree was the only candidate, and was elected after a praelection on the funeral oration ascribed to Lysias (published in volume 1 of his *Adversaria*, 1831–3, repr. 1874). His health gave way almost immediately afterwards, and he died, unmarried, in his rooms at Trinity on 24 September 1825. He was buried close to Porson in the chapel, where at his sister's provision a bust and tablet to his memory were erected. The inscription emphasizes his candid but equable temper, affability, and moral concern, before extolling his scholarship; it is printed in the preface to the *Adversaria*.

Though a man of varied acquirements, Dobree spent his life on classical, chiefly Greek, literature. He laid up vast stores for future years: besides a large body of notes on the Greek dramatists and Athenaeus, he left very extensive collections on the historians and orators, and probably meditated an edition of Demosthenes. He gave a great deal of attention to Greek inscriptions, writing over the years a number of papers signed usually 'O.' (significance unknown) or 'Stelocopas' (stonecutter); he appears to

Peter Paul Dobree (1782–1825), by Edward Hodges Baily, exh. RA 1828

have been one of the first editors of inscriptions to have used sublinear dots to indicate letters imperfectly read (*Miscellaneous Notes on Inscriptions*, ed. J. Scholefield, 1835, 84). When the annotated portion of Porson's library was bought by Trinity College, he was selected, with two of his brother fellows, Monk and Charles James Blomfield, to edit the manuscripts. He was at first prevented by illness from taking a share in the work, and shortly after his recovery set out on a journey to Spain; thus the volume of Porson's *Adversaria* was edited by his two colleagues. But all of the papers on Aristophanes were entrusted to his care, and in 1820 he produced *Notae in Aristophanem*, with the *Plutus* prefixed, chiefly from Porson's autograph. In 1822 he edited the *Lexicon* of Photius from Porson's transcript of the Gale MS in Trinity College Library, which Porson had twice copied out, the first transcript having perished in the fire at the premises of Perry the bookseller; to this volume he added a fragment of a rhetorical lexicon edited from the margin of a Cambridge manuscript, and corrections and supplementary indexes to Porson's work. He had a share in the founding of his teacher Edward Valpy's *Classical Journal* in 1810, and occasionally wrote in it, chiefly on inscriptions. To Thomas Kidd's *Tracts and Criticisms of Porson* (1815) he added the brief *Auctarium*, and to Hugh James Rose's *Inscriptiones Graecae* (1825) the letter on the Greek marbles in Trinity

College Library. With the exception of the notes on inscriptions, everything he published in his lifetime sprang from his reverence for Porson (not least his perpetuating of Porson's own suspicion that Peter Elmsley had purloined some of Porson's conjectures).

Dobree bequeathed 1000 volumes to the library of his college, but his books with manuscript notes to that of the university. From these his successor in the regius chair, James Scholefield, published his *Adversaria* and *Miscellaneous Notes on Inscriptions, with Addenda to the Adversaria* (1835), and he reissued the *Lexicon rhetoricum Cantabrigiense* (1834) which Dobree had appended to Porson's *Photius*. These amply justify Dobree's being classed in the first rank of English textual scholars. Julius Hare set Dobree on a par with his master, Porson, observing:

> his mind seems to have been of kindred character; [with] the same unwieariable accuracy, the same promptness in coming to the point, the same aversion to all roundabout discussions, the same felicity in hitting on the very passage by which a question is to be settled … both [were] preserved by their wary good sense from ever committing a blunder; both … equally fearful of going beyond their warrant, equally distrustful of all theoretical speculations, equally convinced that in language usage is all in all. (Hare, 1.205–6)

Modern assessments agree in finding much of the master's 'spirit and something of the genius' (Brink, 112) in the pupil, but praise Dobree for his deliberate extension of the Porsonian method and tradition to Greek prose writers. A. E. Housman distinguishes between Porson's followers and characterizes Dobree as 'the shrewder emendator' and Elmsley as 'the subtler grammarian' (Housman, *Classical Papers*, 1972, 1006). CHRISTOPHER COLLARD

Sources R. Dawes, *Miscellanea critica*, ed. T. Kidd (1827), xxxvii–xxxviii · J. Scholefield, 'Praefatio', in P. P. Dobree, *Adversaria*, 1 (1831) · J. C. H. [J. C. Hare], 'Dobree's *Adversaria*', *Philological Museum*, 1 (1832), 204–8 · C. O. Brink, *English classical scholarship: historical reflections on Bentley, Porson, and Housman* (1986), 112 · Venn, *Alum. Cant.* · *DNB*
Archives CUL, notebooks on classical scholars
Likenesses E. H. Baily, marble bust, exh. RA 1828, Trinity Cam. [*see illus.*]

Dobson, (Henry) Austin (1840–1921), poet and author, born at Plymouth, Devon, on 18 January 1840, was the eldest son of George Clarisse Dobson, civil engineer, and his wife, Augusta Harris. He was educated at Beaumaris grammar school and at a private school in Coventry before being sent to the *gymnase* at Strasbourg, then a city belonging to France. At the age of sixteen he came home and entered the Board of Trade, in which he served from 1856 to 1901. His service was chiefly in the marine department, of which he was a principal clerk from 1884 until his retirement. William Cosmo Monkhouse and Samuel Waddington were in the same branch with him, and Edmund Gosse was attached to the commercial department as translator, so that the Board of Trade of those days was lyrically described by an American observer as 'a nest of singing birds'. Lord Farrer, one of the official heads, propounded an alternative view when he wrote of 'certain civil servants who would have been excellent administrators if they had not been indifferent poets'.

(Henry) Austin Dobson (1840–1921), by Sylvia Gosse, 1908

Dobson's first publication, the poem 'A City Flower', appeared in *Temple Bar* for December 1864—an immature work, as is also 'Incognita' dated 1866. But 'Une marquise', written in 1868, and 'The Story of Rosina', in 1869, showed the perfection of his talents. These appeared in *St Paul's*, and to its editor, Anthony Trollope, Dobson dedicated his first volume, *Vignettes in Rhyme* (1873). It contained some of his most characteristic pieces, mixed with inferior stuff. *Proverbs in Porcelain*, published in 1877, was almost all in his best vein. These two works, blended in one volume with certain additions and omissions, appeared in the United States in 1880 as *Vignettes in Rhyme*. In 1883 this selection, again somewhat altered, was published in London as *Old World Idylls* and achieved immense popularity. Two years later a companion book, *At the Sign of the Lyre*, was equally successful. The latter contained some of his best compositions—'The Ladies of St James's', 'The Old Sedan Chair', and the enchanting verses 'My Books', written as late as 1883–4. But though he continued to write verse intermittently for the rest of his life, and at least a quarter of his collected *Poetical Works* is dated after 1885, none of this later verse has much importance.

Dobson's first prose volume, *The Civil Service Handbook of English Literature*, published in 1874, was probably written as a piece of hack work. But in 1879, when he was at his best in verse writing, his *William Hogarth*, part of the Great Artists series, appeared. By this time his acquaintance with the eighteenth century was becoming well known, and in 1883 John Morley persuaded him to write *Fielding* for the English Men of Letters series. He next wrote *Thomas*

Bewick and his Pupils (1884) and biographies of Richard Steele (1886) and Oliver Goldsmith (1888). In 1890 he reprinted, under the title *Four Frenchwomen*, essays on Charlotte Corday, Madame Roland, the Princesse de Lamballe, and Madame de Genlis, which had appeared as early as 1866 in the *Domestic Magazine*. This was followed by a memoir of Horace Walpole (1890) with an appendix listing the books printed at Strawberry Hill, Walpole's home, an extended memoir of Hogarth (1891), and a series of *Eighteenth Century Vignettes* (1892–6). In 1902 he published *Samuel Richardson* and in the following year *Fanny Burney*, both for the English Men of Letters series. From this time any publisher intending to reissue an eighteenth-century work went to Dobson for an introduction. Altogether, some fifty such volumes with his editorial superintendence have been catalogued. Of his complete prose works, over and above *The Civil Service Handbook of English Literature*, there are eight biographies and ten volumes of collected essays to his credit.

Dobson's immense knowledge of eighteenth-century literature and art should have made the past live again in his biographies, but his achievement varied. His style, though simple, serviceable, and pleasant, never for an instant suggested a poet's prose. His mastery of artificial rhythms was excellent, but at his lightest he lacked gaiety; at his gravest he lacked weight; as a poet he lacked personality. Yet nobody could read the best of his verses—and at least fifty pieces were of his best—without delight in the witty invention, the ease of movement, and the exquisite finish in the style of Restoration poetry that had his verses likened to 'Dresden china'.

In 1868 Dobson married Frances Mary, the daughter of Nathaniel *Beardmore, civil engineer, of Broxbourne, Hertfordshire. They had five sons and five daughters, all of whom survived their father when he died at his home, 75 Eaton Rise, Ealing, London, on 2 September 1921. His funeral was held on 6 September at St Peter's Church, Ealing, and his remains were interred at the Kensington Hanwell cemetery, Ealing.

S. L. GWYNN, *rev.* NILANJANA BANERJI

Sources A. Dobson, 'Biographical note', in *Austin Dobson: an anthology of prose & verse* (1922) · *The Times* (3 Sept 1921) · A. H. Miles, ed., *The poets and poetry of the nineteenth century*, 6 (1905) · private information (1927) · *CGPLA Eng. & Wales* (1921)

Archives Bodl. Oxf., verses and letters · Hunt. L., letters, literary MSS; MSS and letters · LUL, corresp. and papers | BL, corresp. with Macmillans, Add. MS 55010 · BL, corresp. with Society of Authors, Add. MS 56694 · Ealing Local History Centre, letters relating to illustrations for edition of Boswell's *Johnson* · Harvard U., Houghton L., letters to Frederick Locker-Lampson · U. Leeds, Brotherton L., letters to Sir Edmund Gosse · UCL, letters to David Hannay · W. Sussex RO, letters to L. J. Maxse · Yale U., Farmington, Lewis Walpole Library, notebook and papers relating to Horace Walpole

Likenesses A. N. Fairfield, chalk caricature, 1874, NPG · Barraud, photograph, 1891, NPG; repro. in *Men and Women of the Day*, 4 (1891) · J. Russell & Sons, photogravure, *c*.1897, NPG · S. Gosse, oils, 1908, NPG [*see illus.*] · F. Brooks, oils, 1911, NPG · J. Russell & Sons, photograph, NPG · W. Strang, three etchings, BM · three photographs, NPG

Wealth at death £7150 7*s.* 11*d.*: probate, 4 Nov 1921, *CGPLA Eng. & Wales*

Dobson, Sir Benjamin Alfred (1847–1898), textile machinery manufacturer, was born on 27 October 1847 at Douglas, Isle of Man, the eldest son of Arthur Dobson (1825–*c*.1876) and Henrietta Elizabeth, *née* Harrison. He was a direct descendant of the Dobsons of Westmorland, holders of land near Patterdale at the head of Ullswater since at least the fifteenth century. From 1864 he was employed as a mechanical engineer on the Belfast and Northern Counties Railway. In 1869 he moved from Belfast to Bolton in order to begin work at the firm of Dobson and Barlow, manufacturers of spinning machinery, which was then managed by his uncle. The firm had been founded in 1790 by the cabinet maker Isaac Dobson (1767–1833), and the timber merchant Peter Rothwell (*d.* 1816). It was carried on by the nephew of the founder, Benjamin Dobson (1787–1839), and then by his son, Benjamin Dobson (1823–1874), who took Edward Barlow (1821–1868) into partnership in 1851. After Barlow's death it continued to trade as Dobson and Barlow. As the great-grandson of Isaac Dobson's brother, Benjamin Alfred was the fourth generation of the family in the business. On the retirement of his uncle in 1871 he became a partner, together with Thomas Henry Rushton (1845–1903), the son of Thomas Lever Rushton (1810–1883), a banker and erstwhile ironfounder. At that time the firm faced a harsh dilemma, having almost exhausted the range of its market opportunities. It had specialized in the manufacture of spinning machinery and especially of the mule, as was most fitting for a Bolton engineer. Its operations had expanded in harmony with the expansion of the spinning trade of Bolton, Preston, and Manchester, which spun medium and fine counts of yarn. The demand for its machines remained, however, limited because the medium and fine trade was a relatively small sector of the industry. Thus between 1811 and 1870 Oldham, the seat of the coarse trade, had expanded its spindleage half as fast again as had Bolton. During the 1840s Platts of Oldham had surpassed Dobsons in size, and by the 1870s employed a workforce four times that of Dobsons, manufacturing five times the mule spindleage of the Bolton firm. Above all, customers demanded machinery designed to spin coarse counts. Sales of replacements remained insignificant since Lancashire machinery was built to last. It was the achievement of the two new partners to realize the full potential of the firm's resources, to escape from the restraints imposed by the Bolton-type trade, and to expand into more promising markets.

New machinery and business expansion Benjamin Alfred Dobson began the task of creative innovation by improving the performance of the Heilmann comber, which the firm had manufactured since 1871: he succeeded in enhancing its productivity by one half. Between 1878 and 1886 local mills replaced their hand mules with the perfected self-acting mule, so generating orders for the firm. Bolton however enjoyed no joint-stock boom comparable to that which made Oldham in 1873–5 the spinning centre of the cotton universe, although Dobson did invest £500 in 1874 in the borough's first limited company, the Bolton Union Spinning Co. Ltd. The firm supplied a large market in France with its machines after the Franco-Prussian War which had transferred Alsace, with its flourishing textile trade, to Germany. Those machines won a gold medal at the Paris Exhibition of 1878 and earned for B. A. Dobson enrolment in the Légion d'honneur. When France introduced a protective tariff in 1891, Dobsons equipped a mill in Lille, financed by Lancashire, to supply fine yarns to the French market. Dobsons then undertook the systematic extension of its operations into the markets of its Oldham rival, improving the mule for spinning coarse counts, and bringing out, in 1887, a mule designed for the high-speed spinning of Oldham counts, and more significantly, investing in the manufacture of ring spinning frames, the spinning machine of the future, invented in the USA. From 1874 Dobsons manufactured ring frames, using the American Rabbeth spindle from 1879, the Dobson–Marsh cork-cushioned spindle patented in 1880, and William Dobson's improved flexible spindle patented in 1884. From 1887 it supplied ring frames to the new mills of Japan in direct competition with Platts. In 1896 B. A. Dobson, while on a round-the-world trip, lectured on the subject of the cotton industry in Japan, and was presented by the Japan Cotton Spinners' Association with a magnificent lacquered cabinet as a memento of his visit. From 1891 the firm equipped the new mills of China and there achieved a success denied to Platts: by 1895 it had supplied 77 per cent of the 180,000 spindles operating in Shanghai. It further equipped the first spinning mills to be established in Ceylon in 1889, in Turkey in 1890, and in Peru in 1897. It also realized the full potential capacity of the ring frame. By 1888 it was supplying to Bolton firms frames capable of spinning up to counts of 160. From 1891 it introduced the technique of electric welding in order to impart a perfect finish to its ring spindles. By 1898, 38 per cent of the firm's production of spindles were designed for ring frames, or almost as much as the proportion of 42 per cent of Platts', while its production of ring frames amounted to four-fifths of the total made by Platts.

Capturing overseas markets Dobson gave a marked impetus to technical innovation: he established an experiment room, and presented in 1886 Crompton's original mule to the Bolton Museum. Between 1869 and 1898 the firm took out 128 patents in England and 50 abroad, in the USA and Germany from 1878, in Belgium and France from 1880, in Austria from 1886 and in Switzerland from 1889. Dobson himself patented twenty-two inventions between 1877 and 1897. The patent machines were promoted by all the means available. An extensive network of foreign agents was employed. Dobson, an accomplished linguist, travelled widely in order to meet potential customers. He toured the continent, the USA and Canada, Egypt and India, as well as Japan. Foreign-language catalogues were published from 1883. Awards were won at four international exhibitions (1878–88). The new textile trade press spoke well of his machines, as did the textbooks on spinning written by R. Marsden in 1883, H. E. Walmsley in 1883, and J. Nasmith in 1890.

From 1884 the firm embarked on an era of sustained innovation. It devised the Simplex Revolving Flat Card in

1886, and further improved it in 1890, raising its productivity some 35 per cent above that of any rival. Dobson also elucidated the theory of carding, and lectured upon it in Massachusetts in 1888, devoting his first two books to the subject. Thereby he opened a large market for the products of the firm because the preparatory processes played a vital role in determining the quality of the yarn spun. In 1890 the firm celebrated its centenary by financing a trip to the seaside for its 3700 hands, who filled six trains. In return they presented the partners with an illuminated address testifying to the 'excellent relations' between principals and employees. Since at least 1820 Dobsons had accepted loans from its own workfolk: in 1890 it introduced a profit-sharing scheme whereby loanholders secured a share in profits as well as interest. In 1891 it became a limited company, with a capital of £750,000 or one-fifth the capital of Platts in 1898. Under the regime of the two partners the workforce had doubled in size, from 2000 in 1873 to 4000 in 1897, while the proportion of the population of Bolton supported by the firm had risen from 14 per cent in 1871 to 20 per cent in 1898. 'Its success since 1871 has been conspicuous and its development phenomenal' reported the *Textile Mercury* (12 March 1898, 210). The range of products had been enlarged to include machinery for wool, worsted, silk, vigogne (vicuña), and waste yarns, and a pattern of continuous innovation had been established.

Professional and political achievements In 1876 Benjamin Dobson married Coralie Palin (1853–1904), daughter of William Thomas Palin, a railway engineer serving in India. They had six sons and three daughters. In 1886 Dobson bought the Doffcockers estate, and later another estate at Haverthwaite in Westmorland. His talents were widely recognized within his own profession. He became a member of the Institution of Mechanical Engineers in 1872: he served as a member of its council from 1885 to 1891 and again from 1893 to 1894. The firm overcame opposition from its workmen to the introduction of improved methods of working. It emerged victorious from local strikes in 1875 and 1887 as well as from a national strike in 1897–8. Dobson was elected chairman of the Bolton Engineering Employers' Association, and president of the Bolton Iron Trades Employers' Association as well as, in 1893, an honorary member of the Manchester Association of Engineers. He was chosen by the Engineering Employers' Federation as a representative at the conferences which ended the strike of 1897–8. He entered the Bolton town council in 1874 as a Conservative, and was elected an alderman and borough magistrate in 1880. He took a prominent part in the formation of Bolton Conservative council in 1884, and became the leader of the local Conservative Party. He was an enthusiastic churchman as well as a freemason. He was especially proud of his service as a rifle volunteer with the Loyal North Lancashire regiment, wherein he rose to the rank of lieutenant-colonel and earned the Volunteer Decoration for twenty years of service. As a town councillor he worked steadily from 1887 for the improvement in the facilities available for technical education, endowing

scholarships for his workmen, but always viewing education as a lifelong process. As chairman of the council's Technical Instruction committee, he helped to transform the mechanics' institute into a new technical school, which was opened in 1892 and was equipped free of charge with machinery from his firm's own workshops.

In 1894 a new phase in his life began when Dobson was elected mayor of Bolton, having earlier declined the honour. The appointment was an inspired one, for Dobson had become the borough's senior magistrate as well as its leading businessman, and had been elected president of Bolton's chamber of commerce in 1893. Dobson proved to be an outstanding success as mayor and more popular than any of his predecessors. His personal qualities served him as well in public life as they had in the conduct of business. He was a born leader of men, with a commanding presence, and a pronounced capacity for persuasive speech. Those qualities were reinforced by his keen insight, his sure grasp of detail, his immense tact, and his great determination. He succeeded where two previous mayors had failed, in conciliating the opposition of the out-townships to incorporation in a 'Greater Bolton'. As mayor he accepted office in a dozen associations established for charitable purposes. He had been a governor of Bolton School since 1882. He became vice-president of Bolton Infirmary and president of Bolton Humane Society. As the first citizen of the borough he held official functions for his fellow Boltonians, a ball for children in the town hall, a garden party at Doffcockers, and an autumn conversazione and a Christmas party for the aged poor. Three times he was re-elected to office, in 1895, in 1896, and in 1897, becoming the first mayor of Bolton to hold office for a fourth term. In recognition of his civic services he was knighted in the Queen's Diamond Jubilee honours of 1897, a dignity never conferred upon any member of the Platt family.

In his fifty-first year, and apparently still in the prime of life, Dobson died at Doffcockers on 4 March 1898. The military funeral was attended by some 20,000 people, by mourners occupying 300 carriages, and by 33 clergymen: it became the occasion for an unprecedented display of public sympathy, and for heart-felt allusions from some 31 pulpits. Dobson was buried on 7 March at St Peter's Church, Smithills, Bolton. He left an estate of £240,134 where his uncle had left one of £140,000 in 1874. His eldest son, Benjamin Palin Dobson (1878–1936) left only £37,646. The profits generated by the firm were apparently reaped by the Rushton family. Dobson's death preceded the year of peak demand for the firm's machines in 1906. Dobson and Barlow had, however, continued to look to the future and manufactured in 1901–3 the first rayon spinning machine, for a Zürich firm. The works lost the name of its founders in 1975 and were closed in 1984. Bolton retained however a permanent memorial of Benjamin Alfred Dobson in the form of a 20 feet tall statue in Victoria Square, outside the town's magnificent town hall. The statue was sculpted by John Cassidy (1860–1939) and was unveiled on 17 February 1900 in the presence of 20,000 spectators. It bore the inscription 'erected by public subscription to commemorate a useful life and service to the town of Bolton'. The statue was never moved from its site, unlike the statue of John Platt erected in Oldham in 1878.

D. A. FARNIE

Sources Lancs. RO, Platt–Saco–Lowell papers · 'The rise and progress of leading Bolton firms: Messrs. Dobson and Barlow', *Bolton Weekly Journal and District News* (19 July–9 Aug 1879) · *Lancashire, the premier county of the kingdom* (1888), 1.68 · *Textile Manufacturer* (Nov 1891), 551–3 · 'The mayor elect of Bolton', *Textile Recorder* (15 Oct 1894), 191 · *Men of the period: Lancashire, the records of a great county; portraits and pen pictures of leading men* [1897], 204–6 · [E. Gaskell], ed., *Lancashire leaders, social and political* (1897), 1.66–8 · *Bolton Review*, 3 (1897), 66–9 · A. Sparke, *Bibliographia Boltoniensis* (1913), 59 · *Bolton Chronicle* (5 March 1898) · *Transactions of the Manchester Association of Engineers* (1898), 217–18 · *Institution of Mechanical Engineers: Proceedings* (1898), 136–7 · *The Engineer* (11 March 1898), 238 · *Textile Mercury* (12 March 1898), 209–12 · *Textile Recorder* (15 March 1898), 343–4 · b. cert.
Archives priv. coll., diaries
Likenesses portrait, 1897, Bolton Town Council, Lancashire · J. Cassidy, statue, 1900, Victoria Square, Bolton, Lancashire · F. Baum, photograph (in mayoral robes), repro. in *Bolton Review*, 66 · N. S. Kay, photograph (in robes of a knight), Bolton Town Hall, Lancashire · photograph, repro. in *The Engineer*, 238 · portrait (in mayoral robes), repro. in *Textile Recorder*, 343
Wealth at death £240,134 9s. 10d.: probate, 9 Aug 1898, *CGPLA Eng. & Wales*

Dobson, Sir Denis William (1908–1995), lawyer and civil servant, was born at Shortlands, Graham Park Road, Gosforth, Northumberland, on 17 October 1908, the son of William Gordon Dobson, shipbuilder, and his wife, Laura Janet, *née* Muskett. He was educated at Charterhouse School (1922–6) and at Trinity College, Cambridge (1926–30), where he took a first class in part one of the law tripos and in the LLB examination. He was admitted a solicitor in 1933 after being articled in Newcastle upon Tyne. He then moved to London and joined a firm in the City, but after what he was later to call 'a mutually disenchanting year' (*The Times*, 16 Dec 1995) joined a firm of parliamentary agents, where he laid the foundations of his skill as a draftsman. On 4 December 1934 he married Thelma (b. 1906/7), daughter of Charles Curry Swinburne, engineer and brassfounder, of Newcastle upon Tyne. They had a son and a daughter.

During the Second World War, Dobson served in the Royal Air Force, including three years with the desert air force (1942–5), first with the Eighth Army in north Africa and later in Malta and Italy. His drive and energy were already recognizable and by the end of his service he was senior personnel staff officer. He was appointed OBE in 1945. Following demobilization he had hoped to join the legal branch of the Foreign Office but he was excluded on medical grounds, having contracted tuberculosis. Instead he joined the statutory publications office, which came under the Treasury. His skills there were recognized by Sir Thomas Barnes, the Treasury solicitor, who introduced him to Sir Albert Napier, who wished to strengthen the small legal staff of the Lord Chancellor's Office. Dobson joined the office in 1947. In the same year his first marriage was dissolved and on 29 December 1948 he married Mary Elizabeth, daughter of Captain Joseph Alexander

Allen, RAF officer, of Haywards Heath, Sussex; they had two sons and a daughter.

Dobson was soon recognized as a future contender for the post of permanent secretary of the Lord Chancellor's Office, and was advised to qualify as a barrister. He was called to the bar by the Middle Temple in 1951. In 1954 Napier was succeeded by Sir George Coldstream as permanent secretary, and Dobson became deputy clerk of the crown in Chancery and assistant permanent secretary to the lord chancellor. Coldstream retired in 1968 and, at the relatively late age of sixty, Dobson succeeded him as clerk of the crown in Chancery and permanent secretary. In the same year he was made a bencher of the Middle Temple. He took silk as a QC in 1971. He was promoted KCB in 1969, having been made CB in 1959.

On joining the Lord Chancellor's Office, Dobson had at first a keen interest in both law reform and legislation, and became a master of every detail of bills with which the lord chancellor was concerned. His earlier experience with parliamentary agents and the statutory publications office gave him extra confidence to challenge parliamentary counsel and departmental lawyers on aspects of bills for which other ministers were responsible. There were many expert and acrimonious exchanges, and his opening form of address to opponents, 'Now look here, X', became legendary across Whitehall.

By 1969 Dobson's outlook had become conservative. It was in that year that the royal commission chaired by Lord Beeching on assizes and quarter sessions reported. Both the Labour and the subsequent Conservative government adopted its radical conclusions. These included the establishment of a single crown court with jurisdiction to sit wherever it was needed, and the creation under the lord chancellor of a unified, full-time court service to run the new system. The effect was to transform the small Lord Chancellor's Office, largely concerned with advising the lord chancellor, into a major government department. Dobson had reservations about these reforms, and was generally believed to have held back several lord chancellors from making desirable changes in other areas.

Dobson retired as permanent secretary of the Lord Chancellor's Office in 1977. He served as a member of the Advisory Council on Public Records from then until 1983. As a civil servant he had been memorable for his forceful vigour, the speed of his intelligence, and his command of the law, but also for his quick temper, and his distrust of change. Policy issues were less attractive to him than the law itself, and there were those who felt that the best outlet for his talents would have been as an outstanding parliamentary draftsman. He died of heart failure on 15 December 1995 at the Charing Cross Hospital, Fulham, London; he was survived by his wife Mary and their three children, and by the two children of his first marriage.

ARTHUR GREEN

Sources *The Independent* (20 Dec 1995) · *The Times* (16 Dec 1995) · *WWW, 1991–5* · private information (2004) · b. cert. · m. certs. · d. cert.
Likenesses photograph, repro. in *The Times* · photograph, repro. in *The Independent*

Wealth at death under £145,000: probate, 13 June 1996, *CGPLA Eng. & Wales*

Dobson, Frank Owen (1886–1963), sculptor, was born at Queen Charlotte's Hospital, Marylebone Road, London, on 18 November 1886, the son of Frank Dobson (1857–1900), artist, and his wife, Alice Mary Owen. His parents lived at 7 Acton Street, Clerkenwell, London. His father specialized in bird and flower studies, most of which were sold as greetings cards. He attended school first in Forest Gate and then in Harrow Green. At the age of eleven he won an art scholarship to Leyton Technical School, which he attended part-time. His father died when he was fourteen and he went to live with an aunt in Hastings, Sussex, and attended evening classes at Hastings School of Art. After a few months he left to take up a position with the sculptor William Reynolds-Stephens as a studio assistant, and stayed for a year and a half. He then travelled to Devon and afterwards to Cornwall, where he shared a studio with Cedric L. Morris and managed to make a living by selling his paintings. In 1906 he was granted a scholarship to the Hospitalfield Art Institute in Arbroath, Scotland.

In 1910 Dobson moved to London, where he attended the City and Guilds Art School, Kennington. He then returned to Cornwall, settled in Newlyn, and made the acquaintance of Augustus John through whom he was offered a one-man exhibition of paintings and drawings at the Chenil Galleries in London in 1914. Early in 1915 he enlisted in the Artists' Rifles and in October 1916 was posted to France, where he was a lieutenant in the 5th Border regiment. In January 1917 he was diagnosed as suffering from a duodenal ulcer and sent back to England. On 27 April 1918, while at a military convalescent centre in London, he married, at Christ Church, Marylebone, Cordelia Clara Tregurtha (*b.* 1888/9), daughter of Thomas Tregurtha, a fitter, whom he had met in Newlyn before the war. He was invalided out of the army in November 1918. In August of that year he was commissioned by the Ministry of Information to paint the balloon apron at Canvey Island, Essex (Imperial War Museum, London), for which purpose he took a studio in Trafalgar Studios, Manresa Road, Chelsea, London, where he lived until 1939.

In March 1920, at the invitation of Wyndham Lewis, Dobson took part in the Group X exhibition at Ambrose Heal's Mansard Gallery, London. He showed *Pigeon Boy* (Portland stone, 1920, Courtauld Inst.), *Concertina Man* (Portland stone, 1920), and two studies of the artist Ben Nicholson—a plaster cast (now lost) and a drawing (priv. coll.). In November 1921 he exhibited sculpture and drawings at the Leicester Galleries, London, including *The Man Child* (Portland stone, 1921, Tate collection), *Two Heads* (Red Mansfield sandstone, 1921, Courtauld Inst.), and *The Rt. Hon H. H. Asquith, M.P.* (bronze, 1921, Tate collection).

In 1922 Dobson spent three months working on a portrait of the writer Osbert Sitwell (polished bronze, 1922, Tate collection). Sitwell invited him to design the curtain for *Façade*, a theatrical entertainment written by his sister, the poet Edith Sitwell, with music by William Walton, which had its first performance in his house in Carlyle Square, Chelsea. During the 1920s Dobson made portraits

of the ballerina Lydia Lopokova (bronze, 1924, University of Hull Art Gallery), the American actress Tallulah Bankhead (bronze, 1924–5), the composer and conductor Eugene Goossens (bronze, 1924 or 1925), the American writer Robert Menzies McAlmon (bronze, 1923, priv. coll.), and Sidney Bernstein, founder of the Granada group (bronze, 1929, priv. coll.).

In 1923 Dobson first exhibited *Seated Torso* (Ham Hill stone, 1923, Aberdeen Art Gallery) and *Robert McAlmon* with the avant-garde London Group, of which he was president from 1924 to 1927. He exhibited at the 14th Venice Biennale in 1924, showing *Concertina Man* and *Male Head*, and again in 1926 at the 15th Biennale, when he showed *Susanna* (bronze, 1922–4, Tate collection). In 1925 he showed in the Tri-National Exhibition in Paris, London, and New York, and in 1926 he was included in the European artists' exhibition that toured Canada and the United States. During the winter of 1925 he travelled with the writer Leo H. Myers to Ceylon. On returning to England he started one of his most important works, a large stone carving of a wading female figure, *Cornucopia* (Ham Hill stone, 1925–7, University of Hull Art Gallery). In 1925 the Contemporary Art Society purchased his *Head of a Girl* (*Study for 'Cornucopia I'*) (bronze, 1925) and presented it to the Tate Gallery.

Dobson's view of sculpture as essentially a composition of abstract forms led to his creating simplified, harmonious figures and groups which excluded extraneous detail and narrative content and respected the intrinsic qualities of the materials of which they were made. Roger Fry and Clive Bell, the leading critics of the day, welcomed the appearance of a British sculptor whose work they considered exemplified their fundamental artistic philosophy. Fry wrote that:

> Perhaps Mr. Dobson did not know at the start what he was in for when he set out as a sculptor, and a sculptor who would confine himself to sculptural plasticity. Whether he knew it or not, his having pulled through to some kind of recognition is one of the happiest omens for English art of today. For whether we like his work or not, we must admit that it is true sculpture and pure sculpture, and that this is almost the first time that such a thing has even been attempted in England. (Fry, 172)

By 1926 Dobson had separated from his wife and embarked on a new relationship with (Caroline) Mary Bussell (1904–1989), daughter of the art dealer William Charles Bussell. On 29 March 1928 their daughter was born, and on 6 August 1931, following his divorce, Dobson married Mary in Chelsea, London.

In March 1927 Dobson's first major exhibition in London opened at the Leicester Galleries. He showed twenty-three sculptures, including *Cornucopia*, *Susanna*, and *Marble Woman* (also known as *Reclining Nude*; white marble, 1924–5, Courtauld Inst.), together with portraits of Lydia Lopokova, Tallulah Bankhead, Eugene Goossens, and Leo Myers (bronze, 1927, priv. coll.). He also showed with the London Artists' Association (of which he was a founder member) in November of that year. In 1930 he designed a series of gilded faience panels, *The Chain of Commerce*, for the Hay's Wharf Company's new headquarters on the

Thames at London Bridge. In the same year his larger-than-life bronze figure *Truth* was purchased by public subscription and erected outside the Tate Gallery. During the 1930s he continued to receive commissions for portraits; two of the most notable are the bronze busts of the actress Margaret Rawlings (Lady Barlow) (1936, versions in Manchester City Galleries, Leeds City Art Gallery, and the Tate collection) and the patron and collector Sir Edward Marsh (1938, Museum and Art Gallery, Doncaster). He also produced designs for textiles (Victoria and Albert Museum, London). In 1937 he was commissioned to design a silver-gilt cup, *Calix majestatis* (Royal Collection), in honour of the coronation of George VI and Queen Elizabeth.

Dobson fractured his left arm in 1933, an injury which severely restricted his ability to carve. His last large stone carving was *Pax* (1934, priv. coll.) which was shown in the London Group exhibition in April and May 1935, in 'Two hundred years of British art', at The Hague in 1936, and at the New York World Fair in 1939. At the outbreak of the Second World War, Dobson and his family moved to Bristol and in March 1940 the Bristol Art Gallery held the largest retrospective exhibition accorded to him in his lifetime. Following a series of air raids the Dobsons moved to Kingsley in Hampshire. During the war he received official commissions for drawings and for two portrait busts, *Admiral Sir William Melbourne James KCB* and *Chief Petty Officer Harris John Whitehorne DSM* (both bronze, 1941, Imperial War Museum, London).

Having first shown work in the Royal Academy's annual summer exhibition in 1933, Dobson was elected an associate in 1942 and Royal Academician in 1951. At the suggestion of Henry Moore he was appointed head of sculpture at the Royal College of Art, London, in 1946, and remained until his retirement in 1953. He was appointed CBE in 1947. During the 1951 Festival of Britain, Dobson's *London Pride* was displayed on the south bank of the Thames. Originally shown in plaster, it was cast posthumously in bronze and placed in front of the Royal National Theatre in 1987.

Among Dobson's last commissions were a portrait of Sir Thomas Lipton (bronze, 1954), an engraved glass goblet entitled *The Wave* (1954, Steuben glass collection, Corning, New York), the statuette for the *Evening Standard* drama awards (1955), and a zodiac clock (1959) for the façade of Sir Albert Richardson's Bracken House in Cannon Street, London. His declining health led to his being admitted to the Princess Beatrice Hospital in Kensington, London, where he died on 22 July 1963. His wife and daughter survived him. He was cremated and his ashes were scattered in the River Thames.

Dobson's early experiments with angular forms influenced by cubism soon gave way to a softer, more sensual style. His subject was the female body, and his treatment of it was undoubtedly influenced by his admiration for the French sculptor Aristide Maillol. At their best his figures have a monumental dignity and repose. Although during the 1920s he was seen as one of the adventurous spirits of the British modern movement, his reputation began to be eclipsed during the 1930s and 1940s by the emerging talents of Henry Moore and Barbara Hepworth. He is seen as a transitional figure in the development of British sculpture, linking the previous school of traditional academic or Romantic sculptors with the generation which followed him. While he may be said to share his position as a pioneer with two other sculptors, Henri Gaudier-Brzeska and Jacob Epstein, Dobson was the only one of these three to have been born in England.   NEVILLE JASON

Sources N. Jason and L. Thompson-Pharoah, *The sculpture of Frank Dobson* (1994) · F. Dobson, autobiographical notes, unpublished MS, *c.*1951, priv. coll. · R. Fry, 'Mr Frank Dobson's sculpture', *Burlington Magazine*, 46 (1925), 171–7; repr. in R. Fry, *Transformations: critical and speculative essays on art* (1926) · R. Mortimer, *Frank Dobson, sculptor* (1926) · C. Bell, *Vogue* (March 1927), 64–5 · F. Dobson, 'The quest', *Ark* [journal of the Royal College of Art] (1951), 24–32 · C. Tennyson, *Stars and markets* (1957) · C. E. Vulliamy, *Calico pie* (1940) · N. Lewis, *Studio encounters* (1963) · E. Marsh, correspondence, NYPL · F. Dobson, correspondence, IWM · A. Gibson, *Postscript to adventure* (1930) · *H. H. A.: letters of the earl of Oxford and Asquith to a friend*, ed. D. MacCarthy, 2 vols. (1933–4) · O. Sitwell, *Laughter in the next room* (1949) · *Selected letters of T. E. Lawrence*, ed. D. Garnett (1938) · K. Hare, *London's Latin quarter* (1926) · S. Casson, *XXth century sculptors* (1930) · K. Parkes, *The art of carved sculpture*, 2 vols. (1931) · b. cert. · m. certs. · d. cert. · [R. Hopper], *True and pure sculpture: Frank Dobson, 1886–1963* (1981) [exhibition catalogue, Kettle's Yard Gallery, Cambridge]

Archives Henry Moore Institute, Leeds, Centre for the Study of Sculpture, corresp., papers, photographs, sketchbooks · V&A NAL, questionnaire completed for Kineton Parkes

Likenesses B. Abbott, Man Ray studio, photograph, *c.*1922 · B. Abbott, gelatine silver print, *c.*1926, NPG · H. Coster, photographs, 1929, NPG · photographs, *c.*1930–1940, Hult. Arch. · R. Buhler, oils, 1952, priv. coll.

Wealth at death £2532 3*s.* 11*d.*: probate, 5 Dec 1963, *CGPLA Eng. & Wales*

Dobson, George Edward (1848–1895), zoologist, was born on 4 September 1848 at Edgeworthstown, co. Longford, the son of Parke Dobson of Killinagh in co. Westmeath. He was educated at the Royal School of Enniskillen and at Trinity College, Dublin, where he graduated BA in 1866, MB and MCh in 1867, and MA in 1875. He was first senior moderator and first gold medallist in experimental and natural science, and was also awarded the gold medal of the Dublin Pathological Society for his 'Essay on the diagnosis and pathology of the injuries and diseases of the shoulder-joint'. He entered the army medical department in 1868, and retired in 1888 with the rank of surgeon-major. He was elected a fellow of the Linnean Society on 16 April 1874 and of the Royal Society on 7 June 1883. He was also a fellow of the Zoological Society and a corresponding member of the Academy of Natural Sciences of Philadelphia and of the Biological Society of Washington.

Dobson will be remembered chiefly for his investigation over a period of twenty years into the structure and classification of two groups of mammals, the Chiroptera and Insectivora, on both of which he became the chief authority of his time. While stationed in India (*c.*1868–*c.*1875) he made a careful study of the bats of that country and published papers on the subject in the *Proceedings of the Asiatic Society of Bengal*, the *Proceedings of the Zoological Society*, and the *Annals and Magazine of Natural History*. In 1876 the trustees of the Indian Museum brought out his *Monograph of the Asiatic Chiroptera*, which led, on his return to England, to his being employed by the trustees of the British Museum to prepare the *Catalogue of the Chiroptera in the Collection of the British Museum* (1878). It became a standard work on the anatomy, nomenclature, and classification of bats.

Dobson was soon afterwards placed in charge of the museum of the Royal Victoria Hospital at Netley, where he extended his researches to other groups of mammals. His *Monograph of the Insectivora, Systematic and Anatomical* (1882–90) was not completed at the time of his death. His important paper 'On the homologies of the long flexor muscles of the feet of Mammalia' was published in the *Journal of Anatomy and Physiology* in 1883, and he wrote numerous papers on zoology and comparative anatomy for British and foreign scientific journals.

Dobson died on 25 November 1895 at his home, Malling Place, West Malling, Kent, and was buried on 29 November at West Malling. Besides the works already mentioned he wrote *Medical Hints to Travellers*, published by the Royal Geographical Society, which reached a seventh edition in 1893, and contributed several sections to the ninth edition of the *Encyclopaedia Britannica*. These articles were afterwards used by William Henry Flower and Richard Lydekker in their *Introduction to the Study of Mammals* (1891).

E. I. CARLYLE, *rev.* P. E. KELL

Sources *PRS*, 59 (1895–6), xv–xvii · *Nature*, 53 (1895–6), 86–7 · *Men and women of the time* (1895), 244–5 · d. cert.
Archives NHM, corresp. with Albert Gunther and R. W. T. Gunther
Wealth at death £463 2s. 0d.: probate, 29 Feb 1896, *CGPLA Eng. & Wales*

Dobson, Gordon Miller Bourne (1889–1976), physicist and meteorologist, was born at Knott End, Windermere, on 25 February 1889, the youngest child in the family of two sons and two daughters of Thomas Dobson, a general practitioner in Windermere, and his wife, Marianne Bourne. He was educated at Sedbergh School and entered Gonville and Caius College, Cambridge, in 1907, obtaining a first class in part one of the natural sciences tripos in 1910.

From an early age Dobson showed an interest in practical things. When a young boy he set up a field telephone between the house and the stable, and at school spent much of his spare time in the physics laboratory. While an undergraduate he devised a simple apparatus he set up at his father's boathouse for recording the seiches on Windermere. The results were published in *Nature* in 1911. Following this work Dobson came to the notice of W. Napier Shaw, director of the Meteorological Office, who offered him a post at Kew observatory under Charles Chree. In 1913 Dobson was appointed meteorological adviser to the newly formed Military Flying School on Salisbury Plain where, using pilot balloons, he made the first measurements of the variation of wind with height. In 1914 Dobson married Winifred Duncome Rimer (d. 1952), the sister of one of his friends at Sedbergh School and the

daughter of Henry Rimer, a solicitor. Their three children were a daughter and two sons.

In 1916 Dobson was appointed director of the experimental department at the Royal Aircraft Establishment, Farnborough, and he worked closely with F. A. Lindemann. After the war Lindemann moved to Oxford as Dr Lee's professor of experimental philosophy. Dobson followed him in 1920 as university lecturer in meteorology at the Clarendon Laboratory. With Lindemann he immediately began research on meteors. Lindemann concentrated on the theory of their burn-up in the upper atmosphere; Dobson analysed the observations. In 1922 they published in the *Proceedings of the Royal Society* a paper clearly demonstrating the presence of a warm layer at a height of about 50 km in contrast to the expected result of a steady fall of temperature with height throughout the atmosphere. Dobson was made DSc of Oxford in 1924.

Realizing that the source of heating for the warm layer was likely to be the absorption of ultraviolet radiation by ozone, Dobson embarked on the study of atmospheric ozone, a subject which he pursued with unrelenting vigour for the rest of his life. Ozone measurements were made by means of ultraviolet solar spectroscopy. In building his spectrograph, a task which he carried out personally in the laboratory of his home on Boars Hill near Oxford, Dobson showed a great deal of ingenuity and practical skill. For the measurement of the photographic plates he built the first photoelectric microphotometer using a potassium photocell, the current from which was measured by a Lindemann–Keeley electrometer; both photocell and electrometer were made in the Clarendon Laboratory, and the new techniques were published in 1926.

During 1925 and 1926 five spectrographs were built and deployed at various locations in Europe, the photographic plates being returned to Oxford for measurement. More extensive measurements of atmospheric ozone were organized during 1928 and 1929 by redistributing the instruments to locations widely scattered over the world including one as far afield as Christchurch, New Zealand. By 1929 Dobson had established the main features of the variations of total ozone with synoptic conditions and with latitude and season. In 1927 his work was recognized by his election to a new university readership in meteorology, to a fellowship at Merton College, and to fellowship of the Royal Society.

Dobson continued with instrument development. He designed and built, about 1927 or 1928, a photoelectric spectrophotometer which enabled the relative intensity at two wavelengths and hence the ozone amount to be measured directly. Remarkably advanced for its day, this became the standard instrument for measuring atmospheric ozone and its basic design was little changed for many decades. For the International Geophysical Year in 1956, 144 were distributed throughout the world, the organization and much of the calibration of the instruments still being carried out from Dobson's home in Oxford.

In the 1930s Dobson became concerned with the study

of atmospheric pollution. From 1934 to 1950 he served as chairman of the atmospheric pollution committee of the Department of Scientific and Industrial Research. Under his guidance reliable methods were developed for the measurement of smoke, deposited matter, and sulphur dioxide.

During the Second World War, Dobson became involved with the Meteorological Office in the forecasting of conditions under which aircraft form condensation trails. This led him to a further piece of ingenious instrument design, the Dobson–Brewer hygrometer for measuring the very low humidities found in the stratosphere. The first water vapour measurements in the stratosphere together with a summary of the ozone work were described in the Bakerian lecture of the Royal Society which Dobson gave in 1945. To explain the results from these measurements together with the seasonal and latitudinal variations of ozone, a simple arrangement of the mean motions of air in the stratosphere was proposed which became known as the Dobson–Brewer circulation. In 1942 Dobson was awarded the Royal Society Rumford medal and in 1945 Oxford University conferred on him the title of professor. In 1947–9 he was president of the Royal Meteorological Society. In 1951 he was appointed CBE. He retired from his readership in 1950 and from his demonstratorship in 1956.

Dobson's wife died in 1952 and in 1954 he married Olive Mary Bacon, who survived him. She was the daughter of Ernest Arthur Bacon, assistant registrar for the diocese of Oxford. In 1937 Dobson had moved his home and private laboratory to Shotover on the east side of Oxford where 10 acres of ground allowed him to pursue his interests in farming, especially in fruit growing. He was a keenly religious man, being a churchwarden at St Aldates Church, Oxford, for many years. Throughout his retirement years Dobson continued with work on ozone, helping considerably with its international organization through the International Ozone Commission. Observations were made from Shotover Hill on all possible occasions, the last being made on 30 January 1976, the day before he had the stroke from which he died on 10 March 1976 at Thames Bank Nursing Home, Goring, Oxfordshire.

J. T. HOUGHTON, rev.

Sources C. D. Walshaw, 'G. M. B. Dobson: the man and his work', *Planetary and Space Science*, 37/12 (1989), 1485–507 · J. T. Houghton and C. D. Walshaw, *Memoirs FRS*, 23 (1977), 41–57 · d. cert. · personal knowledge (1986) · private information (1986)
Archives Bodl. Oxf. · Sci. Mus., ozonometers, other apparatus
Likenesses photograph, repro. in Houghton and Walshaw, *Memoirs FRS*
Wealth at death £72,384: probate, 30 July 1976, *CGPLA Eng. & Wales*

Dobson, John (1633–1681), Church of England clergyman, was born in Warwickshire, in which county his father, whose name is unknown, was a minister. He matriculated from Magdalen College, Oxford, on 9 December 1653, graduating BA in October 1656 and proceeding MA in 1659. Admitted as a fellow of Magdalen in 1661, he was ordained as deacon in the diocese of Lincoln on 21 December of that year. He soon became known as an eloquent preacher and the possessor of a remarkable memory, repeating at Easter 1663 four Latin sermons in St Mary's Church, Oxford 'to the wonder of the auditory' (Wood, *Ath. Oxon.*, 4.2).

At this time the president of Magdalen was Thomas Pierce (1622–1691), 'a resolute maintainer of the ancient establishment of the Church of England' against 'specious and plausible pamphleteers', but also a domineering and vindictive character, who several times discommuned, and eventually expelled, one of the fellows, Dr Henry Yerbury, 'for which action most people cried shame' (Bloxam, 1.42, 46). A protest, in manuscript, provoked Pierce into print, and in August 1663 there appeared two lampoons, *Dr Pierce his Preaching Confuted by his Practise*, and *Dr Pierce his Preaching Exemplified in his Practise*. These were purportedly directed against Pierce, but as it later emerged, had been issued anonymously by Dobson with Pierce's connivance, apparently with the objective of getting his opponents into trouble. The Magdalen register refers to Dobson as 'one of Pierce's creatures' (ibid., 46). For breaching the regulations, on 10 September 1663 Dobson was expelled from the university, but rapidly restored. In the same year he was incorporated MA at Cambridge, and in December 1667 obtained the degree of BD from Oxford. He had, on 24 September 1665, been ordained as a priest in the diocese of Peterborough, and on 20 May 1668 he was instituted to the rectory of Easton Neston, Northamptonshire; on the presentation of Sir William Farmor (his former pupil at Magdalen) of that parish, he was admitted on 13 July 1674 to the rectory of Cold Higham in the same county. From 1670 Dobson was also rector of Corscombe, Dorset, and seems to have divided his time between there and his Northamptonshire living. He died on 9 June 1681 at Corscombe and was buried there, where a monument was erected to his memory. In his will, signed on 22 May 1679, Dobson left money to a brother, Samuel, and sisters, Dorothy and Elizabeth; he seems never to have married. To Sir William Farmor he left 'several volumes of pamphlets published in the late troublesome times' (will).

A. C. BICKLEY, rev. STEPHEN WRIGHT

Sources J. R. Bloxam, *A register of the presidents, fellows ... of Saint Mary Magdalen College*, 8 vols. (1853–85), vols. 1–2 · Wood, *Ath. Oxon.*, new edn, vol. 4 · H. I. Longden, *Northamptonshire and Rutland clergy from 1500*, ed. P. I. King and others, 16 vols. in 6, Northamptonshire RS (1938–52) · will, PRO, PROB 11/367, fols. 180–81 · Foster, *Alum. Oxon.* · Venn, *Alum. Cant.*
Wealth at death see will, PRO, PROB 11/367, fols. 180–81

Dobson, John (1787–1865), architect, was born on 9 December 1787 at The Pineapple inn, Chirton, North Shields, Northumberland, the only son of John Dobson (d. c.1827), a native of Stamfordham in Northumberland, and his wife, Margaret (d. 1828). His father combined innkeeping with a substantial business as a market and landscape gardener, and his extensive fruit gardens at

John Dobson (1787–1865), by unknown artist

Chirton were ornamentally laid out with walks and arbours for the enjoyment of fashionable visitors.

Dobson was the most eminent architect to be born and have worked in the north-east of England. He produced over 400 works of virtually every building type, most of them in Northumberland and co. Durham, some in Yorkshire and Cumberland, and a few further afield. He is especially linked with the city of Newcastle upon Tyne, where he practised for over fifty years and designed many public buildings; the majority of these have been demolished, but many of his numerous villas and country houses in the region survive. Perhaps most highly regarded as a classicist, Dobson was also, like most leading architects of his period, a highly competent exponent of what he regarded as the adaptable and picturesque Tudor Gothic style, and in the ecclesiastical field was a pioneer of the Gothic revival in the north-east. He also undertook a great deal of restoration work.

Early training and studies Dobson's precocious talent for design led to occasional employment while still in his early teens as draughtsman to Mr J. McGlashan, a damask and linen weaver in the neighbouring village of Preston, and later to other local businesses. Although he had evidently been intended to follow his father's main profession, about 1802 he was allowed to begin artistic studies in Newcastle under Boniface Muss, an Italian émigré (the painter John Martin was a fellow pupil), and then to be instructed in architectural and mechanical drawing, and surveying, by Mr Hall of Stamfordham, bridge surveyor for Northumberland. About 1804 Dobson further confirmed his commitment to the architectural profession by entering into an apprenticeship, perhaps with Hall's recommendation, with David Stephenson of Newcastle,

shortly to be appointed architect to the duke of Northumberland and at that time the leading practitioner in the north-east.

After completing his clerkship with Stephenson in 1809 Dobson travelled to London, where he studied watercolour painting with John Varley, presumably in order to acquire the necessary facility in producing the kind of colour perspective with which architects were then presenting their designs. He had probably already met Varley during the latter's sketching and teaching tour of the north-east a year before, and Varley's painting *Dobson's Dream*, a landscape with buildings, wood, and water, appears to be the product of Dobson's early morning lessons; further evidence that their relationship matured into friendship is provided by another watercolour by Varley, in the Victoria and Albert Museum, London, inscribed with Dobson's name. Other valuable friendships were with the painters W. H. Hunt, Mulready (both also studied under Varley), Turner, West, and, significantly, Robert Smirke. Smirke's architect sons Robert and Sydney were also important to Dobson; Robert Smirke the elder was one of the leading exponents of the newly fashionable Greek revival style, while Sydney was later to become his son-in-law. Indeed, useful though Varley's instruction was, it was the opportunity to become immersed in the London architectural scene that was crucial to Dobson's development and Sir John Soane, then commencing his Royal Academy lectures on architecture, may have been a further indirect influence. Contrary to the advice of his London friends, Dobson returned to the north-east in 1810. He set up practice in North Shields and soon afterwards in Newcastle, where he immediately introduced a more authentic Greek revival neo-classicism with his first building, the Royal Jubilee School in City Road (1810; dem.); this, however, had to be built with pilasters instead of the intended portico.

Establishment of independent practice and marriage From the outset Dobson insisted on his status as a professional architect in the modern sense. Following the precepts of Soane, he was careful to distance himself from the earlier generation of builder–architects in Newcastle and elsewhere, including Stephenson, and was at first a comparatively isolated figure who, in spite of some early commissions, had to work hard to create a demand for his services. In the intervals between employment he undertook study tours of England, Wales, and France, which reinforced his growing interest in medieval architecture, although unlike many of his contemporaries he never visited Italy or Greece. By 1815, however, Dobson was becoming involved in planning several residential developments in Newcastle and was able to take on as a pupil Thomas Oliver (who worked for him until 1821). He also had the beginnings of a useful villa and country house practice for the local gentry, designing, for example, the neo-classical Prestwick Lodge (1815), Doxford Hall (1817–18), both in Northumberland, and the Villa Reale, Newcastle (1817); at about this time he also produced, for Sir Jacob Astley, an elaborate though unexecuted scheme for the enlargement of Seaton Delaval Hall.

In the mid-1820s Dobson married Isabella (1794–1846), daughter of Alexander Rutherford, a master mariner, and his wife, Isabella, of Gateshead. His wife was a talented amateur artist. Of their eight children (three sons and five daughters) the two eldest sons and two eldest daughters survived to adulthood. Isabella married the architect Sydney Smirke; Margaret Jane (1830–1905) is best known for her useful, if not entirely reliable, biography of her father, published in 1885. The Dobsons' second son, Alexander Ralph (b. 1828), showed considerable architectural talent, working for his father before and after a pupillage (1849–52) with Sydney Smirke, and being elected an associate of the Royal Institute of British Architects in 1850. He was clearly intended to take over the practice, but was killed in the Newcastle quayside fire of 1854. After this his elder brother John (b. 1827) was employed, but probably only in an administrative capacity since he had begun his career as a master mariner; possible hopes of an architectural dynasty were not to be.

Major commissions: domestic and public Major country house designs in Northumberland, both for established county families and for industrialists setting up as landed proprietors, followed during the next two decades. Mitford Hall (begun 1823), Longhirst Hall (1824–5), and Meldon Park (1832), beautifully sited and built with superb ashlar masonry, were influenced by two recent examples of Greek revival architecture in the county, namely Belsay Hall (1807–17), where its Graecophil owner, Sir Charles Monck, was his own architect, and John Shaw's Cresswell Hall (1821–4; dem. 1938). From the latter Dobson derived what became on both aesthetic and functional grounds his preferred country house and villa plan: L-shaped, having the principal rooms on the south (sometimes with a bay) and east, the entrance to the west, and a service wing running north, often linked at right-angles to a conservatory on the eastern side. This plan was also used in some of his Tudor Gothic houses, such as Lilburn Tower, near Wooler, Northumberland (1828–9). However, a later work in the same style, Beaufront Castle, near Hexham, also in Northumberland (1837–41), incorporating an earlier house, is a looser, more picturesque design.

Dobson also undertook a small amount of landscape gardening. His work for Ralph Riddell at Cheeseburn Grange, Northumberland, of c.1813 included not only the Tudor Gothic reconstruction of the house itself but also a scheme (partially implemented) for replanning the park, with ha-ha, serpentine paths, a 'primitive' cottage set deep in trees, and irregular areas of woodland coming right up to the house, reminiscent of Repton's picturesque style. His most important landscape commission was probably that for the Hon. W. H. Beresford at Bolam Hall, Northumberland, where in 1816 he laid out extensive areas of carefully variegated woodland and a substantial artificial lake. Dobson also revived, again in the manner of Repton, the use of formal elements such as borders, paths, and lawns in the immediate vicinity of a house. Meldon, in its elevated position with terrace overlooking and shading into the surrounding landscape, is a good example of this.

Meanwhile, in Newcastle, Dobson had become sufficiently established and well connected to win the competition for the design of the gaol and house of correction in Carliol Square (1822–8; dem. c.1929), which he planned according to the radiating principle (a year earlier he also designed the rather similar Northumberland county gaol at Morpeth, of which the gigantic, castellated gatehouse still survives). In 1827 he won a limited competition to build for the Newcastle corporation his first major church, that of St Thomas the Martyr, Barras Bridge, then on the northern extremity of the town and replacing a medieval chapel of the same name demolished in order to widen the entrance from the old Tyne Bridge. It is a typically late Georgian lancet-style design (completed 1830) without chancel, reminiscent of the 'commissioners' Gothic' of that time; its interior, however, is particularly spacious and elegant, having slender columns and vaulted roof, although slightly marred by the later insertion of galleries.

Also in Newcastle, for the speculative builder Richard Grainger, Dobson laid out Blackett Street (1824; subsequently almost entirely redeveloped), Eldon Square (1825–31; largely dem., somewhat controversially, c.1972), and the Royal Arcade (1831–2; dem. 1963–9), all of which reinforced the air of fashionable elegance Grainger was bringing to the town. But Dobson's plan for the redevelopment of Newcastle of c.1824, involving the construction of a classical square and 'civic palace' on the site of the historic manor of Anderson Place (which, curiously, still occupied an almost vacant central site), was superseded by the more pragmatic, commercially viable scheme evolved by Grainger himself. This was largely carried out between 1834 and 1839, Dobson being responsible at this time only for the design of the 'Grainger' market and the lower east side of Grey Street. Another of Dobson's planning schemes which unfortunately remained largely unexecuted, although actually begun in 1828, was that for a new town at Seaham, co. Durham; this had been intended by the third marquess of Londonderry to complement the harbour he was building for the export of coal, but the original classical layout was soon abandoned because of financial constraints.

Later, in Newcastle, Dobson added a substantial new wing to the old infirmary in the Forth (1852–5; dem. 1954) and in 1854 drew up plans for the rebuilding of the quayside, which had been devastated by a fire caused by an explosion over the river in Gateshead in October of that year; these were partially implemented a few years later, but with street elevations by different architects. Dobson's scheme, illustrated in a drawing in the Laing Art Gallery, Newcastle upon Tyne, proposed a series of picturesque frontages in the more eclectic manner of his later years. His greatest public building was the Central Station, Newcastle, designed 1847–8 and opened by Queen Victoria and Prince Albert on 29 August 1850, albeit in an unfinished state. It has a fine, curving train shed of iron and glass, a model of which was exhibited at the Great Exhibition of 1851 and which won Dobson an honourable mention, and a façade in the grand style of Vanbrugh, even in the altered and reduced form in which it was finally completed in 1863. Much of the last five years of Dobson's career was taken up with the remarkable feat of underpinning and reconstructing Lambton Castle, co. Durham, an enormous building dating mainly from the early nineteenth century which was threatened with serious mining subsidence; his extensive additions to the house, begun in 1857 and completed after 1862 by Sydney Smirke, are, however, now largely demolished.

Church commissions Dobson also built up a substantial ecclesiastical practice, for all denominations, especially in the second half of his career, although this aspect of his work has been less admired in the twentieth century. However, it should be noted that in this context many of his designs were built to a limited budget in the growing urban and industrial areas of the north-east and as such had to be fairly plain and functional. Most of his churches after about 1825 are in the Gothic revival style, for which he had become an enthusiast and in which he steadily developed, under the influence of Pugin and the Ecclesiologists, a more archaeologically and liturgically 'correct' approach (also adopted in his restoration work). This can be seen in such late works as St John's, Otterburn, Northumberland (1855–7), a rather delicate Decorated design, and Jesmond parish church, Newcastle (1858–61). His occasional excursions into the briefly fashionable neo-Norman style are exemplified by St James's, Benwell, Newcastle (1831–2; subsequently much altered and enlarged), and St Cuthbert's, Bensham, co. Durham (1845–8; north aisle added 1875).

By the 1850s and 1860s the spread of Ruskinian ideas meant that Dobson's rather thoroughgoing church restorations, admittedly usually encouraged if not demanded by incumbent clergymen, were becoming increasingly controversial. Nowhere was this more evident than at Hexham Abbey, Northumberland, where between 1858 and 1860 he replaced most of the late Gothic east end, including the Perpendicular lady chapel, with a rather over-academic lancet design based on that of Whitby Abbey, which he deemed to be contemporary with the building's basic form. Yet Dobson was also capable of sensitively reconstructing (for the duke of Northumberland) the Percy chapel at the east end of Tynemouth Priory, Northumberland, a highly decorative example of Perpendicular work; that this was no routine task is indicated by the fact that in the same year (1852) he gave a scholarly paper on the subject to a meeting in Newcastle of the Archaeological Institute of Great Britain and Ireland, illustrated with large-scale drawings of the elaborately carved heraldic bosses of the chapel's roof.

Later years Dobson was elected FRIBA on 28 June 1845, proposed by W. Burn, T. L. Donaldson, A. Salvin, and S. Smirke, and was president of the newly formed Northern Architectural Association from 1859. His practice, possibly one of the last great provincial ones, was substantial, with clerks, draughtsmen, and pupils. Among his later assistants were Johnson Hogg; Gibson Kyle; George Ridley,

later chief clerk to Sydney Smirke; E. R. Robson, a nationally known school board architect; and Thomas Prosser, who as architect to the North Eastern Railway Company completed the Newcastle Central Station after Dobson's career was terminated by an incapacitating stroke in 1862. Thomas Austin completed some of Dobson's works and, in partnership with his fellow Gothic revivalist R. J. Johnson, purchased his practice after his death. Dobson himself was a fine draughtsman but large numbers of his drawings—and office records—have disappeared. Of the drawings and watercolours that do survive, the largest collection is in the Laing Art Gallery, Newcastle upon Tyne; a few other drawings are to be found in, for example, the RIBA drawings collection, London, and in the libraries of the Society of Antiquaries of London and of the University of Newcastle.

Dobson was of middle height, with dark hair. A bust of him is reproduced in his daughter's *Memoir of John Dobson* (1885). There are also two portraits of Dobson in the Laing Art Gallery, Newcastle upon Tyne, one painted by J. Dixon (c.1820), in which the architect is seated at a desk, and the other, unattributed, showing him in late middle age. Of these the former is by far the better likeness. Although dedicated, determined, and industrious, and robust and vigorous in physique—he enjoyed boxing and fencing in his youth—Dobson had 'the fastidiousness of a retiring nature' (Dobson, 65) and may have lacked the ultimate degree of ambition necessary to promote himself fully; hence, possibly, his decision to set up in Newcastle rather than the metropolis. He published no treatises, although his 'Presidential address to the Northern Architectural Association' of 1859 (repr. in Wilkes, 99–110) does give some account of his career and approach. Nor did he enter any of the great national architectural competitions or, except on rare occasions, exhibit his work nationally.

Dobson achieved a remarkable level of professional integrity and competence throughout his long career. He was noted for his technical and constructional expertise, and unusual sensitivity in the siting of his designs. He was not a stylistic innovator and avoided doctrinaire commitment to any single mode. However, his architecture almost invariably has a distinctive solidity and strength; this found its most appropriate expression in the Greek revival and neo-classical styles. After Dobson's enforced retirement through ill health he moved to Ryton, co. Durham, but returned to his Newcastle home at 15 New Bridge Street shortly before his death there on 8 January 1865. Dobson was buried in Jesmond cemetery, which he himself had laid out thirty years before and of which the monumental chapels and gates are among his finest works.

T. E. FAULKNER

Sources T. E. Faulkner and A. Greg, *John Dobson: architect of the north east* (2001) · M. J. Dobson, *Memoir of John Dobson* (1885) · L. Wilkes, *John Dobson: architect and landscape gardener* (1980) · *Newcastle Daily Journal* (9 Jan 1865) · *CGPLA Eng. & Wales* (1865) · parish register (marriage)
Archives Durham RO, corresp. with Lord Londonderry
Likenesses J. Dixon, oils, c.1820, Laing Art Gallery, Newcastle upon Tyne · photograph, c.1850, repro. in Faulkner and Greg, *John Dobson* · T. H. Carrick, pencil drawing, Laing Art Gallery and

Museum, Newcastle upon Tyne · marble bust, repro. in Dobson, *Memoir of John Dobson* · oils, Laing Art Gallery, Newcastle upon Tyne [*see illus.*]

Wealth at death under £16,000: probate, 24 Feb 1865, *CGPLA Eng. & Wales*

Dobson, Matthew (1732–1784), physician and natural philosopher, was the son of Joshua Dobson (*c*.1692–1767), minister of New Mill, Lydgate, near Todmorden, Yorkshire, from 1715 to 1720 and of Cockey Moor Chapel, Ainsworth, near Bolton, Lancashire, from 1732 to 1767, and Elizabeth Smith (*d*. 1767), daughter of the Revd Matthew Smith, Independent minister of Mixenden, Yorkshire. Matthew Dobson matriculated at Glasgow in 1750. Among his fellow students were George Walker and Nicholas Clayton. He is said to have assisted William Cullen with his experiments on evaporation; this was probably at Glasgow, as Cullen published the work in 1755 before moving to Edinburgh in 1756. Cullen encouraged several of his best students to investigate the effects of temperature, and the subject continued to intrigue Dobson for the rest of his life. Cullen also appears to have inspired in Dobson a lifelong interest in chemistry.

After graduating MA in 1753, Dobson attended the Edinburgh medical school; he became a member of the Medical Society (later the Royal Medical Society of Edinburgh) and graduated MD in 1756 with a thesis, *De menstruis* ('On menstruation'). In 1759 Dobson married Susannah [*see* Dobson, Susannah (*d*. 1795)], writer and translator, daughter of John Dawson of the parish of St Dunstan, London. There are records for the birth and baptism of two children, Susannah Dobson, born on 22 January 1764, and Dawson Dobson, born on 22 March 1766; both were baptized at the Octagon Chapel in Liverpool. A third child, Elisa Dobson, died at the age of seventeen in 1778; Dobson placed a monument to her memory in the Ancient Chapel of Toxteth.

It appears that Dobson settled in Liverpool shortly after his marriage. At this time Liverpool contained a lively community of radical nonconformists and medical researchers who formed part of a network extending throughout the north-west, and Dobson seems to have found a comfortable niche in this society. About 1760 he joined a committee of dissenters led by Thomas Bentley, who later became Josiah Wedgwood's partner. After three years of prolonged negotiations, the committee established the Octagon Chapel and persuaded Nicholas Clayton to become the senior minister. The chapel used a written liturgy, edited by the Arian divine John Seddon, who was then the librarian of the Warrington Academy. His participation caused great dissension in the academy, being strongly opposed by the divinity tutor, John Taylor. It is possible that Dobson knew Seddon personally, as Joshua Dobson had corresponded with him concerning the establishment of the academy. On the dissolution of the chapel in 1776, Clayton and many of the congregation moved to Benn's Garden, a Presbyterian chapel, which in turn was succeeded by the Unitarian chapel in Renshaw Street in 1811. Although a few Anglicans are reported to have attended the Octagon Chapel, Dobson's history and associations make it clear that he was a rational dissenter of the sort that would soon become a unitarian.

In 1770 Dobson became physician to the Liverpool Infirmary, succeeding John Kennion. Another Edinburgh graduate, John Bostock the elder, was also appointed physician that year. They joined a group of physicians in the north-west who agreed to meet each quarter at Warrington for the discussion of medical subjects and for the exchange of views; other members of the circle included John Haygarth of Chester, Thomas Percival of Manchester, and John Aikin the younger, then of Chester and Warrington.

In 1769 Dobson helped Matthew Turner, the freethinking Liverpool surgeon, to establish the Liverpool Academy of Art. Dobson became a fellow of the Royal Society in 1778, the first Liverpool physician to achieve that honour. He also served as first president of the Liverpool Medical Library in 1779 and was a member of the Manchester Literary and Philosophical Society. In 1780 he retired to Bath because of ill health, and there he became a member of the Bath Philosophical Society. He died on 25 July 1784 in Bladud Buildings, Bath, and was buried at Walcot church nearby.

Dobson's major medical achievement was his discovery that the urine of diabetic patients contained sugar. This was reported in an article, 'Experiments and observations on the urine in diabetes', in *Medical Observations and Inquiries* (vol. 5, 1774). Thomas Willis had mentioned the sweet taste of diabetics' urine in 1674 but had not investigated the cause. In 1772, when a patient with diabetes was admitted to the Liverpool Infirmary, Dobson was able to study his urine and blood. He found that the urine did not coagulate but, when two quarts were evaporated, the 'white cake' that remained smelled and tasted like sugar. Dobson also found that the blood serum was sweet, though not as sweet as the urine. At the time of his report he had seen a total of nine patients with the disease. Dobson concluded that diabetes was a form of imperfect digestion or assimilation that affected the entire body and that it was not, as others had claimed, a disease of the liver or kidneys. His work was cited by John Rollo, who established the dietary management of diabetes at the end of the century. Dobson also published other articles on medical topics in *Medical Observations*.

In addition Dobson carried out experiments on the physiological effects of external heat; these were reported in *Philosophical Transactions* (vol. 61, 1775). A 'sweating room' of 9 cubic feet was created at the infirmary and was heated to various temperatures, while Dobson recorded the effect on the pulse rate and body temperature of those who entered it. One adventurous colleague, Henry Park, remained in the room while three eggs cooked in the heat and then ate them. Following this ordeal, he walked to Everton in a hard frost and reported no ill effects. Dobson's interest in temperature extended to meteorology. In addition to observations and comments on the subject published in *Philosophical Transactions*, he contributed two chapters on the temperature of the air and the sea around

Liverpool to William Enfield's *Essay towards the History of Liverpool* (1773).

Dobson was also interested in chemistry. His *Medical Commentary on Fixed Air* was published in Chester in 1779. Dobson recommended the use of fixed air (carbon dioxide) as an internal stimulant and an external disinfectant. He argued that kidney stones were probably caused by metabolic disorders and were not the result of eating some sort of stony matter that collected in the kidneys. Joseph Priestley included four of Dobson's cases as an appendix to the second volume of his *Experiments and Observations on Different Kinds of Air*.

MARGARET DELACY

Sources O. T. Williams, 'Matthew Dobson, physician to the Liverpool Infirmary, 1770–1780: one who extended the confines of knowledge', *Liverpool Medico-Chirurgical Journal* (1912), 245–54 · J. Dobson, 'Matthew Dobson', *Collected papers concerning Liverpool medical history* [Liverpool 1971], ed. J. A. Ross (1977), pt 2, 1–13 · [W. Gomer], 'Historical notes on medicine, surgery and quackery, no. 3', *The Lancet* (10 April 1897), 1049 · T. H. Bickerton and R. M. B. MacKenna, *A medical history of Liverpool from the earliest days to the year 1920*, ed. H. R. Bickerton (1936), 39, 43–4, 51, 166, 278, 286 · A. Holt, 'An experiment with a liturgy', *Walking together: a study in Liverpool nonconformity, 1688–1938* (1938), 126–49 · IGI · F. W. Lowndes, 'The life of Matthew Dobson', *Liverpool Medico-Chirurgical Journal*, 36 (1916), 127–9 · private information (2004) · *Jubilee memorial of Canning Street Presbyterian Church, Liverpool, 1846–96* (1896), 102–4 · J. A. Shepherd, *A history of the Liverpool Medical Institution* (1979), 10–11, 22–3 · J. B. Blake, ed., *A short title catalogue of eighteenth century printed books in the National Library of Medicine* (1979) · locatorplus. gov/ [National Library of Medicine online catalogue; lists Dobson's two theses, which the printed STC catalogue did not] · P. J. Wallis and R. V. Wallis, *Eighteenth century medics*, 2nd edn (1988), 168 · *List of the graduates in medicine in the University of Edinburgh from MDCCV to MDCCCLXVI* (1867), 6 [1705–1866] · 'Index Librorum Societatis Medicae Edensis 1766', Bodl. Oxf. [printed pamphlet] · will, PRO, PROB 11/1128, fols. 212r–213v · 'Ancient Chapel', memorial to Elisa Dobson, died 1778, erected by her father Matthew Dobson, Toxteth, Liverpool · memorial to Joshua and Elizabeth Dobson, transcript by the Rev J. D. Allerton, Ainsworth Unitarian chapel, near Bolton, Lancashire · B. Nightingale, *Lancashire nonconformity*, 6 vols. [1890–93], vol. 3, p. 124; vol. 6, pp. 66–118, 128–39 · *DNB*

Wealth at death estate divided equally between wife and daughter: will, PRO, PROB 11/1128, fols. 212r–213v

Dobson, Sir Richard Portway (1914–1993), businessman, was born on 11 February 1914, at 64 Coldharbour Road, Bristol, in a family of four sons and one daughter of John Frederic Dobson (1875–1947), professor of Greek at Bristol University, and his wife, Dina, elder daughter of Harry Harvey Portway, gentleman, of Bois Hall, Halstead, Essex. Dobson was educated at Clifton College and at King's College, Cambridge. On graduating he joined the British–American Tobacco Company (BAT), in which he was to spend the greater part of his life as a businessman. He went almost immediately to China, which was at that time the most lucrative market for the company, and he remained there until late 1940.

BAT had been formed in 1902, to achieve a division of world markets between Imperial Tobacco and American Tobacco. The American James Buchanan Duke was chairman of BAT from its formation to 1923, when he was succeeded by Sir Hugo Cunliffe-Owen, who remained in that

Sir Richard Portway Dobson (1914–1993), by unknown photographer

post until 1945, when he became titular president. A Supreme Court judgment in 1911 had forced American Tobacco to sell its interest in BAT and by 1915 British interests held a majority of BAT shares. Cunliffe-Owen visited China in 1923 and created autonomous regional units of BAT (China) Ltd, designed to isolate the effects of localized difficulties from the business as a whole. He also negotiated at ministerial level on taxation and trading matters. After the communist takeover in 1949 BAT's Chinese interests were nationalized, having incurred strong nationalist criticism.

Dobson gave a breathless and at times rather jejune account of his time in China in *China Cycle*, published in 1946 by Macmillan in their Centenary Books series and awarded a supplementary prize of £100 in the non-fiction category. The dust-wrapper referred to Dobson's 'robust, cheerful and friendly personality' and these qualities would have been essential to endure the hardships and dangers of 'getting out in the field' in a territory as vast and diverse as China, with an infrastructure at that time so incomplete as to render travel over long distances a dangerous as well as unpredictable activity. To these inherent problems were added those created by the Sino-Japanese War, but even in that context BAT's target was always 'business as usual' (Dobson, 56). Dobson described the cigarette trade in China as very active and complex (ibid., 14), highly competitive, and only marginally profitable for its participants, from the supplying company down to the street-hawker, selling single cigarettes. Something of Dobson's boisterousness, which led to the famous gaffe which marked his later departure from British Leyland, will be found in *China Cycle*, although it has to be read in the context of its times: 1930s attitudes expressed in the subsequent wartime situation. Strongly critical of what he called the Asiatic 'disease of resignation' (ibid., 50), he advised the foreigner 'never [to] go further [towards the Chinese] than a bow and a smile and a shake of the hand' (ibid., 49), although his own account shows him to have been less remote than his advice suggests. Dobson considered that such Eurasians as those of Portuguese origin 'drift with the stream', although he was sufficiently fair to mention a few exceptions.

At the end of October 1940 Dobson prevailed on BAT to allow him to enlist, and after a voyage of eleven weeks he reached the United Kingdom. The process of acceptance as a trainee pilot in the RAF was lengthy, but in November 1941 Dobson departed for South Africa, for the training overseas for which he had opted. While there, he was critical of the treatment of the African population by the white community, but came to consider that 'the South African native in general cannot be compared, for intelligence, industry and virility, with the Chinese' (Dobson, 214). Active service finally came for Dobson as a Spitfire pilot with the rank of flight lieutenant, in the Italian campaign and then in the Far East. After the war, he rejected the idea of joining the Indian Civil Service and returned to BAT in 1946. On 3 May the same year, at Holy Trinity Church, Kensington, he married Emily Margaret (Betty) Carver, widow, the daughter of James Russell Herridge, chartered accountant; there was one daughter from her previous marriage.

Dobson worked for BAT in China and Rhodesia, and then at its London head office, where he rose to board level in 1955. He became deputy chairman in 1962, vice-chairman in 1968, and chairman in 1970, completing his life's work with BAT as president from 1976 to 1979. During these three decades, as Dobson rose to, and wielded, power, BAT prospered, often in a difficult economic and political climate. Not only was it necessary to adjust to such a major loss as that of the company's China business, but diversification of activity had to be embraced. BAT was over-dependent on a single product, especially as opposition to smoking on health grounds became a force to be reckoned with. Dobson himself made a point of posing for the camera with cigarette or pipe prominently in view and he had little time for medical or other criticism of BAT's activity. His management style as board chairman has been described as 'essentially that of a team leader, practising an "open-door" policy' (*The Times*, 27 Oct 1993). Criticism of BAT's activity, however, would not be tolerated by Dobson, whose reaction could be 'testy' (ibid.), and he firmly adhered to any course of action he had decided on. As Dobson had risen in the BAT hierarchy, the company took steps to reduce its heavy reliance on tobacco. In the 1960s and 1970s it acquired paper and packaging companies, such as Wiggins Teape, perfume and fragrance houses, such as Lentheric, and department stores. This diversity of interests led to a change of name to BAT Industries in 1976.

In February 1976, following the death of Sir Ronald Edwards, the non-executive chairman of the ailing vehicle manufacturer British Leyland (BL), Dobson, who had been awarded a knighthood in the new year's honours, accepted an invitation to take on the post. His eventual successor at BL, Michael Edwardes, chairman of Chloride, warned him at the time that the post as constituted was unlikely to work, and so it proved. Dobson's resignation eighteen months later appeared to be the result of some injudicious remarks of a racist nature made by him, which received unexpected publicity. At a businessmen's supper club at the Dorchester Hotel his speech was secretly recorded, and appeared in the International Marxist Group's *Socialist Challenge*. The adverse publicity for Dobson was, however, the pretext rather than the cause of his replacement by Michael Edwardes, for Edwardes had already been offered the post of chief executive at BL and had insisted on the combined role of chairman and chief executive. The robustness of character and bluntness of expression, marked already in the *China Cycle* and necessary for the head of a major international company in an era of change, was a precipitant of this unfortunate episode, which clouded the final stage of Dobson's business life. In the event Dobson resigned on 21 October 1977, the reputation of his long and successful career at BAT tarnished at least for a time by his unwise and unsuccessful venture into a very difficult industry at a time of crisis, and by an indiscretion which did less than justice to an articulate and capable businessman. However, Dobson continued to hold other directorships, including those of the American oil company Exxon and Lloyds Bank International. He also continued his interest in writing; at his memorial service readings were given from his poems. He died of respiratory failure and pneumonia, on 24 October 1993, at 20 Devonshire Place, Westminster. RICHARD A. STOREY

Sources *The Times* (27 Oct 1993) • R. P. Dobson, *China cycle* (1946) • M. Edwardes, *Back from the brink* (1983) • T. Derdak, ed., *International directory of company histories* (1988), vol. 1 • R. P. T. Davenport-Hines, 'Cunliffe-Owen, Sir Hugo Reitzenstein', *DBB* • H. Cox, 'Learning to do business in China: the evolution of B.A.T.'s cigarette distribution network, 1902–41', *Business History*, 39/3 (1997), 30–64

Likenesses photograph, 1 April 1976, Hult. Arch. • photograph, News International Syndicate, London [*see illus.*]

Wealth at death £1,102,325: probate, 16 March 1994, *CGPLA Eng. & Wales*

Dobson, Sir Roy Hardy (1891–1968), aircraft manufacturer, was born at Horsforth, Yorkshire, on 27 September 1891, the eldest child of Horace Dobson, farmer, and his wife, Mary Ann Hardy. He became an engineering apprentice with T. and R. Lees, a firm then operating in Hollinwood, near Manchester. He joined the company of A. V. Roe, aeroplane manufacturer, in 1914, becoming its works manager in 1919 and general manager in 1934. He was elected to the board of the company in 1936 and became

Sir Roy Hardy Dobson (1891–1968), by Walter Stoneman, 1949

managing director in 1941, retaining that position until he became in 1958 managing director of the Hawker Siddeley Group Ltd, a company of which A. V. Roe had become a subsidiary in 1935, and to which Dobson was appointed a director in 1944.

The increasing possibility of war in the late thirties gave Dobson an opportunity to develop his talents to the full. During the 1930s A. V. Roe had been engaged in the design of a twin-engined bomber aircraft, the Manchester, which suffered from underpowered and unreliable engines and seemed bound to fail. At the time, the Merlin engine, developed by Rolls-Royce, was designed to be used in fighter aircraft. Roy Chadwick, then chief designer at A. V. Roe, felt that if he could redesign the twin-engined Manchester using four of the Merlins, he might overcome the problems. This was a proposal which the authorities were loath to accept, if only because they felt that the need for fighters would absorb as many Merlins as could be provided. Dobson faced this problem with characteristic vigour. Somehow four Merlins were obtained and speedily fitted into the Manchester prototype. From this work emerged the Lancaster, which was undoubtedly the most successful bomber developed by either side in the war. Dobson's ability to procure such a new and vital weapon displayed to the full his energy, determination, and imagination.

With similar vigour Dobson initiated and supervised the provision of resources to manufacture this aeroplane in quantity for Hawker Siddeley in Canada, as he was also doing in English factories. In Canada, however, he was starting from the beginning, and he created a factory which produced an excellent product in large numbers. An aero-engine factory was set up at the same time. At the end of the war Dobson arranged the purchase by Hawker Siddeley of both the aeroplane and engine units. At this time he set up A. V. Roe Canada Ltd, and Orenda Engines Ltd, as design and manufacturing organizations. He was the first president of these companies and later, in 1951, became their chairman. Their first product was a successful military aircraft, the Avro CF100, powered by an engine (the Orenda) designed and built by Orenda Engines. The Canadian company also built a prototype jet-propelled civil aircraft which was almost certainly the first jet civil machine to fly. It was slightly ahead of the Comet, designed by De Havilland in England, although it did not enter passenger service, as did the Comet, which therefore became the first jet-propelled aircraft to carry commercial passengers.

Under Dobson's chairmanship, A. V. Roe Canada proceeded from these successes to design and build, in conjunction with the Canadian government, prototypes of a very advanced fighting aircraft which became known as the Arrow. In retrospect it can be seen that this very costly venture was probably beyond the financial resources of a country with the small population then possessed by Canada, and the Arrow, although technically successful, was cancelled in a storm of controversy. Dobson, perhaps sensing that there were limits to the investment which Canada could make alone in military development, had already extended the business of A. V. Roe Canada into other areas, particularly railway engineering in which he made a series of company acquisitions. He had many associates in Canada, a country for which he had great affection, and was a director of the Canadian Imperial Bank of Commerce (1955–66).

Despite his heavy responsibilities in Canada, Dobson continued to develop his interests in England. After the war A. V. Roe designed and built the revolutionary delta-winged Vulcan bomber and entered the civil aviation field with the Avro 748, which enjoyed a long production run. As a director and managing director of the Hawker Siddeley Group, and subsequently its chairman (1963–7), Dobson did much to widen the company's aeronautical interests, particularly in the early 1960s, when he initiated the acquisition of the De Havilland, Blackburn, and Folland companies, so forming, with the existing Hawker Siddeley aviation interests, a strong aeronautical unit which eventually became Hawker Siddeley Aviation Ltd. Simultaneously he initiated early moves to bring the company into areas of engineering other than aeronautics. He retired from his chairmanship in 1967 at the age of seventy-five.

Dobson—known the world over as Dobbie—was a man of great vigour and imagination, with a drive and determination which enabled him to make a definitive impact on the development of industry and particularly the aeronautical industry. He was warm-hearted and enthusiastic, if sometimes a little hard on others in his outbursts of anger when things went wrong, but always immediately contrite if he had been too harsh. He was apt, from time to time, to address people in somewhat heightened language, but never to an extent greater than he would readily apply to himself if he concluded that the fault was really his own. He was a colourful man with a tremendous capacity for hard work and for overcoming difficulties. He gathered around him others whose devotion to him increased the more he drove them, although not without the occasional casualty.

Dobson was created CBE in 1942, was knighted in 1945, and was awarded an honorary fellowship of the Royal Aeronautical Society in 1956. In 1916 he married Annie Smith (d. 1954). They had two sons, one of whom was killed in a flying accident in 1946, and a daughter. He died at King Edward VII Hospital, Midhurst, Sussex, on 7 July 1968.   ARNOLD HALL, rev.

Sources Hawker Siddeley Group Ltd records · private information (1981) · personal knowledge (1981) · *The Times* (9 July 1968), 10f · *The Times* (26 July 1968), 10d · R. Higham, 'Dobson, Sir Roy Hardy', *DBB* · *New York Times* (9 July 1968), 35
Likenesses W. Stoneman, photograph, 1949, NPG [*see illus.*] · photograph, 1957, Hult. Arch. · T. Peruis, pastels, British Aerospace Corporation Club House, Manchester · photograph, repro. in *The Times* (9 July 1968), 10f · photograph, repro. in *New York Times*
Wealth at death £121,794: probate, 21 Aug 1968, *CGPLA Eng. & Wales*

Dobson [*née* Dawson], **Susannah** (*d.* 1795), translator, was the daughter of John Dawson of the parish of St Dunstan, London. In 1759 she married Matthew *Dobson (1732–1784), a physician and natural philosopher. They had three children: Susannah (*b.* 1764), Dawson (*b.* 1766), and Elisa (1760/61–1778).

Susannah Dobson's first published work, in 1775, was an abridged translation in two volumes of *Mémoires pour la vie de François Pétrarque*, by Jacques François Paul Aldonce, abbé de Sade. According to Samuel Johnson, 'Mrs Dobson, the Directress of rational conversation, did not translate Petrarch; but epitomised a very bulky French life of Petrarch' (*Letters of Samuel Johnson*, 249). De Sade's work was extremely controversial: he claimed to prove the true identity of Petrarch's Laura and identified her with the Laura de Noves, wife of Hugues de Sade, on the basis of a sonnet found in her tomb in the De la Croix Chapel in Avignon. His work attracted the attention of Horace Walpole and Alexander Fraser Tytler, Lord Woodhouselee. The latter rejected de Sade's theory in his *Essay on the Life and Character of Petrarch*.

Susannah Dobson might have become interested in the work through Baretti's praise of it in his *Manners and Customs of Italy* (1768). Her reviewer in the *Gentleman's Magazine* praised Dobson's translation for maintaining 'that pathos and spirit of the original' and for a preface by Dobson intended, now that Laura was revealed to have been a married woman, 'to guard against the impression which such an attachment might otherwise make on susceptible

hearts' (*GM*, 45, 1775, 186). Dobson's translation enjoyed long-lasting popularity, and by 1805 there had been one Irish and six English editions, many of which were illustrated with appropriate engravings. In 1780 she claimed to have earned £400 from it (*Diary and Letters*, 1.369). According to Roderick Marshall, 'this book restored Petrarch, after a hundred and fifty years of banishment, to an active part in English literature' (Marshall, 124).

In 1777 Susannah Dobson published a *Dialogue on Friendship and Society*. She then translated two works by the French Academician Jean-Baptiste de la Curne de Sainte-Palaye (1697–1781): *Literary History of the Troubadours* (1779) and *Memoirs of Ancient Chivalry* (1784). In 1791 she published a translation of Petrarch's *De remediis utriusque fortunae* as *Petrarch's View of Human Life*. In the last year of her life she published *Historical Anecdotes of Heraldry and Chivalry* (1795).

In 1780 Susannah Dobson followed her husband to Bath, where he had retired on the grounds of ill health. The novelist Fanny Burney mentions her in her diary for the same year. According to Burney, Susannah Dobson had 'long been trying to make acquaintance with Mrs Thrale, but Mrs Thrale, not liking her advances, has always shrunk from them' (*Diary and Letters*, 1.360). Eventually Susannah Dobson was introduced to Mrs Thrale, but does not seem to have succeeded in winning her friendship. While Fanny Burney admitted that, 'though coarse, low-bred, forward, self-sufficient, and flaunting, she seems to have a strong masculine understanding' (ibid., 1.370), Mrs Thrale wrote that 'Mrs Dobson ... persecutes me strangely as if with violent & undesired Friendship; yet Mrs Lewis says She is jealous' (*Thraliana*, 1.595). By this time Susannah's husband had become Mrs Thrale's practitioner. Susannah Dobson died in London on 30 September 1795 and was buried at St Paul's, Covent Garden.   ANTONELLA BRAIDA

Sources *GM*, 1st ser., 54 (1784), 42, 636–7 · *GM*, 1st ser., 44 (1774), 468n., 477 · *GM*, 1st ser., 45 (1775), 187 · *GM*, 1st ser., 49 (1779), 259 · *GM*, 1st ser., 65 (1795), 881 · Walpole, *Corr.*, 4.22n., 24, 33, 37n., 46, 56; 32.95n.; 40.377; 43.87 · R. Marshall, *Italy in English literature, 1755–1855* (1934), 123–41 · H. Smithers, *Liverpool, its commerce and institutions, with a history of the cotton trade* (1825), 418 · *Thraliana: the diary of Mrs. Hester Lynch Thrale (later Mrs. Piozzi), 1776–1809*, ed. K. C. Balderston, 2nd edn, 1 (1951), 580, 584, 587, 588n., 589, 595n. · *Diary and letters of Madame D'Arblay (1778–1840)*, ed. C. Barrett and A. Dobson, 6 vols. (1904–5), vol. 1, pp. 360, 365–7, 369–70; vol. 2, p. 210 · *The letters of Samuel Johnson*, ed. B. Redford, 5 vols. (1992–4), vol. 4, pp. 147, 249–50 · *A medical history of Liverpool from the earliest days to the year 1920* (1936), 43–4 · *Gore's Liverpool Directory* (1766), 11 · *Gore's Liverpool Directory* (1775), 13 · *Gore's Liverpool Directory* (1781) · *DNB* · will, PRO, PROB 11/1128, 183 [Matthew Dobson, husband]

Dobson, William (*bap.* 1611, *d.* 1646), portrait painter, was baptized at St Andrew's, Holborn, London, on 24 February 1611 (City of London Guildhall MS 6667/1). His father was also called William Dobson (*d.* 1626), and was probably the painter–stainer mentioned in the corporation of London court of common council records on 5 February 1622 (journal 31, fol. 393). John Aubrey described the artist's father as a gentleman who was assistant to the lord chancellor, Francis Bacon, helping him in the building and decoration of Verulam House, near St Albans (*Brief Lives*, 1.78).

William Dobson (*bap.* 1611, *d.* 1646), self-portrait, *c.*1642–6

In 1607 a William Dobson was paying taxes at 'The Villa, Albani'. Whether he was the same William Dobson who was master of the alienation office and 'clerk of recognizances for recovery of debts in the Courts of the Chief Justices of King's Bench and Common Pleas' (Spencer, xiv) remains speculative. William Dobson senior married Alice Barnes (*d.* 1642x4?), a prosperous mercer's daughter, on 8 April 1605 at All Hallows, Honey Lane, London, and they had eight children. At her death in 1642, the artist's grandmother Katherine Barnes owned a number of pictures, including *Judith and Holofernes* and two royal portraits (PROB 11/191/20).

Facts about Dobson's life are few. He was married twice: in the first instance to Elizabeth (surname unknown, date of marriage unknown), who was buried at St Martin-in-the-Fields on 26 September 1634, and secondly to Judith Sander on 18 December 1637 at St Bride's, Fleet Street, London (Guildhall MS 6537). After his death, Judith may have been married again, to one Henry Boulton in 1648, but, although according to Aubrey (2.318) she lived to see the Restoration, her death has not been traced.

Dobson senior lived beyond his means, and when he died intestate in February 1626, the young Dobson was forced to think of earning a living. According to Buckeridge, Dobson spent his apprenticeship under William Peake, the Holborn picture dealer, printseller, and stationer (Buckeridge, 369). Elizabeth's death in St Martin-in-the-Fields suggests the young Dobsons had set up house there. Abraham van der Doort, surveyor of the king's pictures, would have been their neighbour in St Martin's

Lane, which was close to the court in Whitehall. A haunting portrait, possibly by Dobson and traditionally said to be van der Doort, who committed suicide in 1640, now hangs in the Hermitage Museum, St Petersburg. Richard Symonds noted that Dobson then took further training under Francis Cleyn, the German engraver, decorative painter, and designer of Mortlake tapestries, whose work survives at Ham House, Middlesex (Symonds, fol. 89v). Cleyn's influence can be seen in Dobson's curious painting at Rousham, Oxfordshire, entitled *The Civil Wars of France*, made in preparation for the engraved frontispiece to the translation by Sir Charles Cotterell and William Aylesbury of D'Avila's *Istoria delle guerre civili di Francia* published in 1647.

During his formative years Dobson is said to have had 'the advantage of copying many excellent Pictures, especially some of Titian and Van Dyck' (Buckeridge, 369). Anthony Van Dyck had arrived in London in 1632, and later imported his private collection of paintings known as his Cabinet du Titien. According to Graham, Dobson's first biographer, it was through Van Dyck's encouragement that Dobson received royal favour (Graham, 340). Dobson plainly benefited from this contact with the king's principal painter, and with van der Doort's help, too, he would have been able to view the exceptional pictures (many Venetian) in the Royal Collection. *The Four Ages of Man*, now at Hardwick Hall, Derbyshire, and thought to be one of Dobson's rare subject paintings, is indebted to both Van Dyck and Titian. Copying may have provided him with a meagre living, but a paucity of surviving works from the 1630s shows that Dobson did not easily build a reputation. Rogers estimated that he set up independently by about 1640, not the most auspicious moment to start a career (Rogers, 12).

The metropolis was seething with unrest, and the king and his supporters abandoned London in January 1642. Civil war skirmishing began in early summer, and in October the court settled in Oxford. The Dobsons moved to Oxford early in 1643, where in April 1644 William was listed as a parishioner of All Saints in the High Street. Here, in 1645, another Elizabeth Dobson was buried (perhaps a child of William's first wife). The Dobsons presumably remained there until the court left the city in June 1646. William found a workshop assistant, a priest called Hesketh, who also painted landscapes. There is a puzzling reference in Symonds's notebook (fol. 102) to a Mr Vaughan of the exchequer office releasing Dobson from prison by paying his debts, but this incident cannot be placed or dated. It proves only that Dobson received few financial rewards either in London or in Oxford.

Van Dyck died in December 1641 and, without his towering shadow, Dobson could make more headway. He was called upon to paint not only the king (priv. coll.), the prince of Wales, the duke of York (both Royal Collection), and the palatine princes Rupert and Maurice (both priv. coll.), but many of the cavaliers who had flocked to Oxford. A fine *ad vivum* study (NMM) of the elderly Inigo Jones dates from this period (second version, Chiswick House, Department of the Environment). Dobson built up a busy practice, and possibly took profile drawings of the king and the prince of Wales for the military award medals produced by Thomas Rawlins in Oxford. Rawlins wrote a collection of poems called 'Calanthe' (now lost) which contained a eulogy to Dobson. The title referred to Dobson's royal appointment as serjeant painter to the king and groom of the privy chamber, and the artist was hailed as 'the very Soul of Art, the Prince and Prime of Painters' (Vertue, BL, Add. MS 19027, fol. 43v).

Apart from one drawing attributed to Dobson (see Brown, 70–71; Rogers, 11) there are no preparatory drawings by his hand. He usually worked *alla prima*, painting directly onto the canvas. His earlier Oxford portraits are rich in pigment, but towards the end of 1645 the paint begins to be brushed thinly onto visibly unprimed canvases, revealing the difficulty of getting materials during wartime. As royal hopes sank, his portraits took on a 'ghostly insubstantiality' (Rogers, 19). Three of Dobson's paintings were engraved by William Faithorne (another of Peake's trainees) and sold in London, but surprisingly few were copied by miniaturists.

Dobson's portraits are distinguished by their directness. They glow with brightly coloured silks and rose-red royalist sashes, and often carry symbolic allusions to the sitter's role in life. Lacking the spaciousness of Van Dyck's portraits, Dobson's portraits fill the canvas, and he conveyed their individuality with force. He painted intimate head and shoulders compositions, such as the portrait of his wife, Judith (priv. coll.), or his good friend and patron Sir Charles Cotterell, master of ceremonies to Charles I (priv. coll.), which is counted among his finest personal tributes. His unfinished painting of the king is equally sensitive (priv. coll.).

Dobson attempted full-length portraits but these are less successful. He also experimented with double and triple portraits, and whole families, though his skill at bringing individual studies together into one composition is doubtful. His group portraits have been described as 'inelegant', but some can be applauded for their vigour and novelty. His triple portrait of Prince Rupert and Colonel John Russell, with Colonel William Murray dipping his cockade into a glass of wine (priv. coll.), commemorated a particular historical moment. There is a mock-heroic analogy in the choice of Hercules behind another painting of himself with Sir Charles Cotterell, who appears to be shielding him from the pleasurable temptation offered by a third figure, almost certainly Nicholas Lanier (priv. coll.).

By far Dobson's most successful portrayals are half and three-quarter lengths. Those painted between 1640 and 1644, such as *Endymion Porter* (Tate collection), *The Prince of Wales* (Scottish National Portrait Gallery, Edinburgh), and *John, first Lord Byron* (University of Manchester), brim with resplendent colour and rich impasto, as well as defiant confidence in the royal cause. Lord Byron's portrait, which is painted in flamboyant gold, scarlet, and crimson, was chosen to represent the visual richness of this era in the 'Treasure houses' exhibition at the National Gallery, Washington, DC, in 1985. The portraits of Sir Thomas Chicheley (priv. coll.) and Sir Richard Fanshaw (Valence House Museum, Dagenham, Essex) are perhaps the most Van Dyckian and confident of his works. Other likenesses, such as those of Colonel Richard Neville (NPG), the earl of Northampton (priv. coll.), the earl of Macclesfield (Dunedin Art Gallery, New Zealand), Lord Rockingham (priv. coll.), and Sir Charles Lucas (priv. coll.), reflect the anxieties of wartime and the sitters' fears for the future. The last two particularly show the raw weave of the canvas beneath the thin paint. Another late picture, signed and dated 1645, of an unknown girl from the Annesley or Hanbury families (Birmingham Museums and Art Gallery), demonstrates his sympathetic touch when painting women.

Dobson painted several self-portraits. Buckeridge described him as:

> a fair middle-sized man, of ready wit, and a pleasing conversation, yet being somewhat loose and irregular in his way of living, he, notwithstanding the many opportunities he had of making his fortune, died poor at his house in St. Martin's Lane … (Buckeridge, 369)

His burial took place on 28 October 1646 at St Martin-in-the-Fields (Westminster city archives, St Martin's register, no. 3). His death was plainly unexpected for he had been nominated as a steward of the Painter–Stainers' Company on 5 August (Guildhall MS 5667/1, fol. 209).

Considering that artists of standing at the English court until then (and indeed for the following seventy years) were, with the exceptions of the miniaturists Hilliard and Cooper, imported from abroad, it was astonishing that there should emerge such a striking home-bred talent, able to convey with penetrating sensitivity such psychological depths. As a gentleman, Dobson would have brought a personal insight into the values of the aristocracy when many were under threat. A very promising career, with only some sixty known paintings to his credit, was cut short at the age of thirty-five. His influence can be detected in the paintings of Sir Peter Lely, John Michael Wright (who also trained with Cleyn), Isaac Fuller, and John Hayls. For many years he was overlooked, but two exhibitions in the twentieth century (the exhibitions at the Tate Gallery in 1951 and at the National Portrait Gallery in 1983–4) established his reputation among the first rank of English painters. Other examples of Dobson's works are in the National Gallery, London; the Scottish National Gallery, Edinburgh; the Tate collection; the National Maritime Museum, Greenwich; the Walker Art Gallery, Liverpool; and the Courtauld Institute.

KATHARINE GIBSON

Sources M. Rogers, *William Dobson 1611–46* (1983) [exhibition catalogue, NPG, 21 Oct 1983–8 Jan 1984] · private information (2004) [Mary Edmond] · B. M. Spencer, 'William Dobson', MA diss., U. Lond., 1937 · *Brief lives, chiefly of contemporaries, set down by John Aubrey, between the years 1669 and 1696*, ed. A. Clark, 1 (1898), 38, 78; 2 (1898), 318 · [R. Graham], 'A short account of the most eminent painters, both ancient and modern', in C. A. Du Fresnoy, *De arte graphica / The art of painting*, trans. J. Dryden (1695), 227–355 [appended] · [B. Buckeridge], 'An essay towards an English school', in R. de Piles, *The art of painting, with the lives and characters of 300 of the most eminent painters*, 3rd edn (1754), 354–439; facs. edn (1969), esp. 368–70 · Richard Symonds, notebook, BL, Egerton MS

1636, fols. 89v, 102v • exchequer, king's remembrancer, certificates of residence, PRO, E115/115/139, E115/115/140, E115/117/128 • G. Vertue, collection of notes, BL, Add. MS 19027, fol. 43v, from William Oldys • O. Millar, *William Dobson* (1951) [exhibition catalogue, Tate Gallery, London] • D. B. Brown, *Catalogue of the collection of drawings in the Ashmolean Museum*, 4 (1982), 70–71 • H. Walpole, *Anecdotes of painting in England: with some account of the principal artists*, ed. R. N. Wornum, new edn, 2 (1849); repr. (1862), 351–4 • parish register, Holborn, St Andrew's, GL, MS 6667/1, 24 Feb 1611 [baptism] • PROB 11/191/20 • J. Hunter, *Hunter's pedigrees: a continuation of Familiae minorum gentium*, ed. J. W. Walker, Harleian Society, 88 (1936), 289 • parish register, St Martin-in-the-Fields, City Westm. AC, register 3 [burial]

Likenesses W. Dobson, self-portrait, oils, 1636–9, priv. coll. • W. Dobson, self-portrait, oils, 1640–44, priv. coll. • W. Dobson, self-portrait, oils, 1642–6, NPG • W. Dobson, self-portrait, oils, c.1642–1646, priv. coll. [*see illus.*] • J. English, etching, c.1650 (after W. Dobson), BM, NPG

Dobson, William (*bap.* 1820, *d.* 1884), journalist and antiquary, was the eldest son of Lawrence Dobson and his wife, Mary Bowe. His father was a stationer and part proprietor with Isaac Wilcockson of the *Preston Chronicle*. William Dobson was baptized at Preston on 26 January 1820, and educated at the grammar school of that town. He afterwards pursued a career in journalism. On the retirement of Wilcockson his father purchased the remaining interest in the *Chronicle*, and took William into partnership with him. William was for some years the editor, until March 1868, when the proprietorship of the *Chronicle* was transferred to Anthony Hewitson. Dobson's career as a journalist was at an end, but he continued, along with his brother James, to carry on the family stationery business at 23 Fishergate.

Dobson was a Liberal in politics and in August 1866 he first sat on the town council, with the expressed intention of opening Dr Shepherd's library more fully to the public. He remained on the council until November 1872, and subsequently sat for a further term from 1874 to November 1883. On 18 June 1867 he married Esther, daughter of Job Hallmark, a hop merchant, and sister of Alderman Hallmark of Preston; they had no children.

A member of the Chetham Society, Dobson had an extensive knowledge of local history and antiquities, especially the Preston area, and published nine books relating to the town. His keen interest in politics is evident from his writings, which include *The Preston Municipal Elections from 1835 to 1862* (1862) and *A History of Parliamentary Representation of Preston during the Last Hundred Years* (1856). Preston Guild was a subject which naturally drew his attention: he wrote an account of the 1862 celebrations and was the co-author with John Harland (1806–1868) of a history of the guild published in 1862. His other work of note is *Rambles by the Ribble* (1864–83), originally published as a serial in the *Chronicle*.

Dobson belonged to the Independent Order of Oddfellows, Manchester Union, and served as provincial grand master to the Pleasant Retreat Lodge, Preston, in 1882. He was also on the council of the Avenham Institute in the town. At one time he was a large shareholder of various local and district companies, but lost money when some of them failed. A Unitarian initially, in later years he became a member of the Church of England. In 1882 he moved to Churton Road, Chester, where he died on 8 August 1884, aged sixty-four. He was buried on 11 August in Chester cemetery.

ZOË LAWSON

Sources *Preston Guardian* (13 Aug 1884) • *Preston Chronicle* (16 Aug 1884) • *Palative note-book*, 1882–5, 4, 180 • *The Athenaeum* (16 Aug 1884), 210 • H. Fishwick, *The Lancashire library* (1875), 164–6, 170, 237 • C. W. Sutton, *A list of Lancashire authors* (1876), 31 • m. cert. • *DNB*

Wealth at death £180: probate, 4 Nov 1884, *CGPLA Eng. & Wales*

Dobson, William Charles Thomas (1817–1898), painter, was born in Hamburg, Germany, on 8 December 1817, the son of John Dobson, an English merchant, and a German mother. While Dobson's early years are obscure, it appears that financial concerns necessitated the family's move to London in 1826. Dobson's artistic training began under Edward Opie, the nephew of the portrait painter John Opie, and included diligent study in the gallery of antiquities at the British Museum by the age of fourteen. In 1836 Dobson entered the Royal Academy Schools and made sufficient progress to attract the attention and active encouragement of the academician and future president Charles Lock Eastlake. Dobson exhibited his work at the Royal Academy for the first time in 1842 and was soon appointed to a prominent position in the School of Design, recently established at Somerset House.

In 1843 Dobson was appointed headmaster of the Government School of Design in Birmingham, a post which he resigned after two years in order to further his artistic training in Italy, particularly in Rome. In 1846 Dobson sent a genre piece entitled *The Young Italian Goatherd* to the Royal Academy exhibition to advertise his Italianate training. He then made a less conventional choice and travelled to his native Germany, where he acquainted himself with the Nazarene school of painting, which may have given him the confidence to enter the 1847 Westminster Hall competition with two cartoons, *Lamentation* and *Boadicea*. While the precise length and timing of his continental sojourn is uncertain, Dobson exhibited a number of fanciful subjects such as *Saul with the Witch of Endor* in the 1848 Royal Academy exhibition, and *The Knight Huldbrand Relating his Adventures in the Enchanted Forest* in 1849, which sought to capitalize on his German experience.

Possibly recognizing the limited appeal of such works, Dobson began to focus on religious subjects, which firmly established his reputation in the Victorian art world. One of his greatest successes was *The Almsdeeds of Dorcas* (1855; Royal Collection) which was purchased by Queen Victoria as a present for Prince Albert on his birthday. Dobson's religious paintings combined the Raphaelesque roundness and finish of William Dyce and Charles Lock Eastlake with the 'primitive' backgrounds of the Nazarenes. About 1854 Dobson had at least one painting student, Edward Poynter, who would become a highly celebrated neoclassical painter. Dobson returned to Germany, residing from approximately 1858 to 1860 in Dresden, where he

William Charles Thomas Dobson (1817–1898), by Elliott & Fry

Petworth, Sussex. He died at Undercliff House, Ventnor, Isle of Wight, on 30 January 1898. He left a widow, Caroline, and a son, Edmund Arthur Dobson.

DOUGLAS FORDHAM

Sources J. Dafforne, 'William Charles Thomas Dobson, ARA', *Art Journal*, 22 (1860), 137–9 · W. Sandby, *The history of the Royal Academy of Arts*, 2 (1862), 344–6 · Graves, *RA exhibitors*, 2 (1905), 342–4 · 'Mr William Charles Thomas Dobson, Royal Academician, retired: obituary', *The Athenaeum* (5 Feb 1898), 190 · J. Oldcastle, 'Our living artists: William C. T. Dobson, RA', *Magazine of Art*, 1 (1877–8), 183–6 · d. cert. · will, proved, 28 April 1898, Principal Registry of the Family Division, London · *CGPLA Eng. & Wales* (1898) · Bénézit, *Dict.* · S. W. Fisher, *A dictionary of watercolour painters, 1750–1900* (1972) · 'Technical notes', *The Portfolio*, 7 (1876), 116–17 · Thieme & Becker, *Allgemeines Lexikon*, 9.354 · C. Wood, *Olympian dreamers: Victorian classical painters, 1860–1914* (1983), 132–3 · M. Warner, 'Victorian paintings at the Tate Gallery: recent acquisitions', *Apollo*, 123 (1986), 259–60 · D. Millar, *The Victorian watercolours and drawings in the collection of her majesty the queen*, 2 vols. (1995), 60 · C. Wood, 'William Charles Thomas Dobson', Wood, *Vic. painters*, 2nd edn · C. E. C. Waters [C. E. Clement] and L. Hutton, *Artists of the nineteenth century and their works*, [new edn], 2 vols. in 1 (1969), 209 · Mallalieu, *Watercolour artists*, 2nd edn, 1.109 · H. M. Cundall, *A history of British water colour painting*, 2nd edn (1929), 92 · Bryan, *Painters* (1930), 2.77 · *Art Journal*, 17 (1855), 177 · *Art Journal*, 35 (1873), 170 · *Art Journal*, new ser., 18 (1898), 94 · 'The almsdeeds of Dorcas', *Art Journal*, 21 (1859), 212–13

Likenesses woodcut, 1878 (after photograph), repro. in Oldcastle, 'Our living artists' · W. C. T. Dobson, self-portrait, oils, 1884, Aberdeen Art Gallery · Elliott & Fry, photograph, NPG [*see illus.*] · Lock & Whitfield, woodburytype photograph, NPG; repro. in T. Cooper, *Men of mark: a gallery of contemporary portraits* (1881) · Maull & Polyblank, carte-de-visite, NPG · woodcuts, NPG

Wealth at death £19,634 3s. 0d.: probate, 28 April 1898, *CGPLA Eng. & Wales*

again sought to master the techniques and styles of German painting. In 1860 one critic wrote,

> We cannot afford to see such a painter spending even a portion of his time upon the heads of little children, beautiful as these pictures are; nor can we desire to find, as some of his latest pictures have shown, the influence of the German school pervading his works. Mr Dobson has been passing several months recently in Dresden; we shall look with some anxiety to see what effect has been produced by his residence there. (Dafforne, 139)

In 1878 Dobson served as a juror for the fine art department of the Paris Universal Exhibition, where he exhibited watercolour drawings. Throughout his career Dobson helped to bridge British and continental art.

Dobson did not entirely give up secular subjects, and, as the above critic notes, was well known for his idealized depictions of children. From his sentimental genre subjects to his most ambitious religious paintings, children were prevalent in Dobson's work, and they were central to his moral message of purity and innocence.

Dobson turned relatively late to watercolour, motivated by the desire to preserve it from the corrupting influences of body colour. Dobson attempted to preserve David Cox's transparent wash tradition, and this technical conservatism again allied him with the Nazarenes. This conservative tendency also applied to his oil painting technique where he used a restricted palette of ten pigments which went back to Sir Joshua Reynolds's working method. Dobson was elected an associate of the Society of Painters in Water Colours in 1870 and a full member in 1875. Dobson was also a member of the Etching Club, founded in 1842.

Based on his success as a painter of religious art, Dobson was elected an associate of the Royal Academy in 1860 and a full academician in 1872. Exhibiting 117 pictures at the Royal Academy over the course of a fifty-two-year career, Dobson retired from the academy in 1895; he was apparently well liked by his colleagues. A resident of Langham Chambers, Oxford Street, London, by 1858, Dobson had by 1884 acquired a country house, Gentils, Lodsworth, near

Docharty, James (1829–1878), landscape painter, was born at Bonhill, Dunbartonshire, the son of James Docharty, a journeyman calico printer, and his wife, Catherine. He was trained as a pattern designer at the School of Design in Glasgow, and thereafter he continued his design studies for some years in France where he may have seen the paintings of Gustave Courbet. On his return to Glasgow he began to practise on his own account, and was so successful that, in his early thirties, he was able to give up designing patterns and become a full-time landscape painter.

Docharty's earliest works were views of the village of Ardenadam on the lower Clyde and scenes of the lochs of the western highlands, which he exhibited at the Glasgow (later Royal Glasgow) Institute of the Fine Arts. Afterwards he extended his range of subjects on the Clyde, working also in Perthshire and painting in the more remote highland areas, such as in western Ross-shire and the Hebrides. He treated his landscapes with vigour and a direct naturalism achieved without artifice. His mature works are distinguished by the quiet harmony of their colour. Most of his paintings were exhibited in Glasgow, but he was also a regular exhibitor at the Royal Scottish Academy between 1864 and 1878, and also at the Royal Academy in London between 1865 and 1877. Among the most popular were *The Haunt of the Red Deer on the Dee, Braemar* (exh. RA, 1869) and *The Head of Loch Lomond* (exh. RA, 1873). His last exhibited works were *The Trossachs*, in the Royal Scottish Academy show of 1878, and *A Salmon Stream* in the Glasgow Institute of the Fine Arts exhibition in the same year.

In 1876, owing to his failing health, Docharty went abroad, making a lengthy tour through France, Italy, and Egypt, but without much benefit. Late in 1877 he was elected an associate of the Royal Scottish Academy. He died of consumption at 7 Berlin Terrace, Pollokshields, Glasgow, on 5 April 1878 and was buried in Cathcart cemetery in that city. He was survived by his wife, Robina Bruce Lang. Most of his paintings entered private collections but he is represented in public collections in, for example, Aberdeen, Dundee, Glasgow, and Paisley.

R. E. GRAVES, rev. JOANNA SODEN

Sources *The Scotsman* (6 April 1878) · *Edinburgh Courant* (6 April 1878) · *Glasgow Herald* (6 April 1878) · *Art Journal*, 40 (1878), 155 · *Annual Report of the Council of the Royal Scottish Academy of Painting, Sculpture, and Architecture*, 51 (1878), 11–12 · C. B. de Laperriere, ed., *The Royal Scottish Academy exhibitors, 1826–1990*, 4 vols. (1991), vol. 1, pp. 421–2 · R. Billcliffe, ed., *The Royal Glasgow Institute of the Fine Arts, 1861–1989: a dictionary of exhibitors at the annual exhibitions*, 4 vols. (1990–92), vol. 1, pp. 362–4 · Graves, *RA exhibitors*, 2 (1905), 344–5 · J. L. Caw, *Scottish painting past and present, 1620–1908* (1908), 193–4 · R. Brydall, *Art in Scotland, its origin and progress* (1889), 389–90 · P. J. M. McEwan, *Dictionary of Scottish art and architecture* (1994), 172 · Wood, *Vic. painters*, 2nd edn · d. cert. · exhibition records; letters collection, Royal Scot. Acad. · *CCI* (1878)

Archives Royal Scot. Acad., archives, corresp.

Likenesses two photographs, Royal Scot. Acad.

Wealth at death £13,058 12s. 3d.: confirmation, 22 May 1878, *CCI*

Docker, Sir Bernard Dudley Frank (1896–1978), industrialist, was born at Rotton Park Lodge, Edgbaston, on 9 August 1896, only child of Frank Dudley *Docker (1862–1944) and Lucy Constance (d. 1947), daughter of John Benbow Hebbert. His father was protective, arbitrary, and ambitious for him. He was educated at Harrow School (1911–13) and by private tutors before being successfully crammed for the Oxford University entrance by A. L. Smith. However, in 1915, probably to forestall his conscription, he was put to work by his father in munitions production at the Metropolitan Carriage, Wagon, and Finance Company. In 1918 he was appointed to its board, serving as deputy chairman in 1924–7.

Despite an immaturity of character that lasted beyond adolescence, Docker was pushed by his father into other positions of responsibility and learned a certain business capacity. He was a member of the Birmingham advisory committee of the Midland Bank from 1925, and later a full board director (until obliged to resign in 1953 on account of his non-attendance at meetings and bad publicity surrounding him). He similarly graduated from the industrial management board to the board of directors of Vickers Ltd, and after his father's rupture with that company, was chairman of one of its competitors, the Birmingham Railway Carriage and Wagon Company (1930–60). He held other important directorships in industrial, financial, electrical, and railway companies operating in Britain and abroad. He joined the board of the Birmingham Small Arms Company (BSA) in 1939.

In 1944, with his father's deathbed support, Docker consolidated his position by becoming both chairman and managing director of BSA. Its subsidiaries included a motorcycle company and Daimler Motors, manufacturers of limousines. Though the company enjoyed a burst of post-war prosperity, it had been riven by board factionalism for many years and had major difficulties of strategy and structure. A Warwickshire magistrate from 1924, in 1936 Docker became both chairman of Westminster Hospital and president of King Edward VII Memorial Hospital in Birmingham. He was created KBE in 1939, and encouraged political friends to press his claims for a baronetcy in 1941–2.

Docker in April 1933 married an actress, Jeanne Stuart (who had taken that name by deed poll), daughter of William John Sweet. This marriage was broken up by his father after a few months and was dissolved in 1934. In 1949 Docker married his second wife, Norah (1905–1983), widow of Sir William Collins, previously widow of Clement Callingham, and daughter of Sidney Turner, an unsuccessful Birmingham car salesman. Norah was a glamorous, excitable adventuress, and she shared Docker's dependence on alcohol. They had no children. Docker and his father had detested publicity, but his second wife courted cheap celebrity and together they were ruined by it. Her ostentation and interference in the Daimler business resulted in a notoriously protracted board-room struggle which culminated in Docker's dismissal from BSA in 1956. Hale and amiable within his own social set, in business he had the obstinacy of a weak man. Though puritanism and envy had a part in his downfall at BSA, he and his wife proved themselves to be foolhardy. This impression was confirmed when the Dockers were excluded from Monaco by Prince Rainier after a drunken night-club row in 1958. His yacht *Shemara* (built to his specifications at a cost of £100,000 in 1938) was later sold. His family power and fortune were thereafter dissipated.

Docker was physically imposing, with a sleek, opulent, and self-confident manner; in the 1950s he looked at the world with a glassy-eyed bonhomie, and showed many signs of soft living. Having sold his estate at Stockbridge in Hampshire for £400,000 in 1966, he retired to Jersey. He died at Branksome Park, Dorset, following a stroke, on 22 May 1978. His father's hopes of an industrial dynasty died with him.

RICHARD DAVENPORT-HINES

Sources private information (2004) · N. Docker, *Norah* (1969) · R. P. T. Davenport-Hines, *Dudley Docker: the life and times of a trade warrior* (1984) · M. J. Benkovitz, ed., *A passionate prodigality: letters to Alan Baird from Richard Aldington, 1949–62* (1975), 147, 239 · b. cert. · m. certs.

Archives Bodl. Oxf., Woolton MSS · HLRO, Hannon MSS · Staffs. RO, corresp. · U. Warwick Mod. RC

Likenesses photograph, c.1900, repro. in *DBB* · four photographs, 1950–59, repro. in Docker, *Norah* · two photographs, 1954, Hult. Arch.

Docker, (Frank) Dudley (1862–1944), industrialist and financier, was born at Paxton House, South Street, Smethwick, on 26 August 1862, youngest son of Ralph Docker (1809–1887), a solicitor who was for many years coroner for East Worcestershire and clerk of Smethwick's board of health, and Sarah Maria (1830–1900), daughter of Richard Sankey, horse dealer, and sister of Ralph Docker's deceased first wife. Dudley Docker, as he was known, had

(Frank) **Dudley Docker** (1862–1944), by unknown photographer, c.1916

four brothers, four sisters, and three half-sisters. He was educated privately and at King Edward VI's Grammar School, Birmingham (where he was bottom of his class), before joining his father's law firm. Legal work proved to be uncongenial, and he often subsequently expressed contempt for lawyers.

In 1881 Docker joined in forming Docker Brothers, dealers in varnish for blacking stoves. After a few years the company began making its own varnish and it prospered in the 1890s. It was through the firm's connections that in 1902 Docker masterminded the merger of five of the largest British rolling-stock companies to form the Metropolitan Amalgamated Carriage and Wagon Company. The name of the business was changed in 1912 to the Metropolitan Carriage, Wagon and Finance Company (MCWF). Docker became chairman of this new combine, which was the second largest employer in the midlands. He was resourceful and effective in all its operations, but his financial dexterity was specially notable. Through MCWF he became interested in electrical engineering trusts, and he led the wartime merger movement by negotiating in 1918 the joint purchase for £1.2 million by MCWF and Vickers of the British Westinghouse Electrical Company, subsequently known as Metropolitan-Vickers.

In 1919 Docker persuaded Vickers to buy MCWF at the inflated price of £12.1 million. He was a director of Vickers in 1919–20, and through warehoused shareholdings and nominee directors exercised a critical influence on its fortunes in the 1920s. His role as intermediary in the transfer of control of Metropolitan-Vickers to the General Electric

Company of America in 1928 was regarded as unforgivable by some colleagues.

Docker also had a prodigious range of other business interests. In 1906 he became a director of Birmingham Small Arms (BSA), and as deputy chairman in 1909–12 he masterminded its purchase of Daimler Motors in 1910. Though he had left the board, he made crucial interventions in BSA in the early 1930s and rejoined its board in 1943. As a director of the Midland Bank from 1912 until his death he had a powerful influence on banking policy both inside the bank and nationally; his internal influence was pervasive and from 1923 he dominated the bank's Birmingham advisory committee. He was a director of several railway companies, notably the Metropolitan Railway (1915–34) and the Southern Railway (1922–38). He was one of the promoters of the British Trade Corporation, formed under royal charter in 1917, but he resigned from its board in 1920. The following year he formed the Electric and Railway Finance Corporation which acted as his private financial house until his death. Through it he exerted considerable power in two Belgian-based trusts, Sofina, which had worldwide interests in public utilities and electrical engineering, and the International Sleeping Car Syndicate associated with Davison Dalziel.

From 1906 Docker was keenly interested in midlands constituency politics and had contacts with Unionist, Liberal, and Labour candidates. He also had confidential financial arrangements with the *Midland Advertiser* and possibly the *Birmingham Gazette*. Believing in the superiority of businessmen over professional politicians and administrators he launched in 1910 the Business League Movement in the midlands working for a 'business government' of businessmen. He was a founder of the Midlands Employers Federation in 1913, and in 1914 bought a London evening newspaper, *The Globe*, to agitate for a business policy. This brought him into conflict with the government and the paper was briefly suppressed in 1915 under the Defence of the Realm Act. It also led Docker into association with right-wing publicists such as Leo Maxse, to whose *National Review* he contributed.

Docker was founder president in 1916 of the Federation of British Industries, which he intended to act as a 'business parliament' supplanting the responsibilities of the Westminster parliament in commercial, fiscal, and labour matters. In 1922–5 he was president of the British Commonwealth Union, which confidentially funded the parliamentary candidatures of business-minded acquaintances. Some of the details of his dealings with politicians would have embarrassed them if published: Philip Cunliffe-Lister and Arthur Steel-Maitland were perhaps his most important contacts.

Docker was a Warwickshire magistrate from 1909 and became a companion of the Bath in 1911 after donating a heavy artillery battery for the use of his factory workers in the Territorial Army. He hated Germans and was a zealot in trying to destroy German prosperity and establish a British business hegemony. He was first chairman of the Birmingham Munitions Output Organization in 1915, and his rolling-stock company was the chief manufacturer of tanks in the First World War. His advice was solicited by government departments, and he served on several government committees, including those chaired by Alexander *Henderson, first Baron Faringdon, on financial facilities for trade (1916) and the reorganization of commercial intelligence (1916–17). The offer of a barony by the Baldwin government in 1929 was withdrawn after protests from the City of London.

Docker married in 1895 Lucy Constance (d. 1947), daughter of John Benbow Hebbert (1809–1887), clerk to the Birmingham justices. Their only child, Bernard *Docker, usually referred to his father as 'the chief'. Dudley Docker served on the committee of Warwickshire County Cricket Club until 1892, having been the highest scoring batsman at the inaugural match of the Edgbaston ground in 1886 and playing for his county against Australia in 1887. He was a keen shot, and usually spent time in Scotland each year, and a member of the Royal Thames Yacht Squadron.

Docker was tall and well built, with a big nose. As a young man he seemed jovial and frank, although he could be intimidating: his small, intense, unblinking eyes quelled dissidence. He was always mercenary, and had an unbeatable understanding of other mercenary men. He disliked others being in authority over him, and resented politicians or officials whom he could not bribe or browbeat. In business he was always bold, flexible, persuasive, ruthless, and opportunistic; from 1918 onwards he might be judged unscrupulous. At committee meetings Docker was taciturn and even inarticulate, but he was so shrewd and calculating that he was often able to direct deliberations by informal pressure. Increasingly he liked to operate through nominees, and was usually a good delegator. He had a retentive memory, and an acuity in financial affairs that was hard to surpass. The least gullible of men, some of his political enthusiasms were nevertheless unrealistic. Apparently he suffered from nervous strains which made him increasingly pessimistic and aggressive; he may have developed claustrophobia, and about 1916 came to dislike crowded meetings or public attention. Latterly he was secretive.

Docker died of Ludwig's angina and tonsillitis on 8 July 1944, at his home, Coleshill House, near Amersham, Buckinghamshire, and was buried at Coleshill.

RICHARD DAVENPORT-HINES

Sources R. P. T. Davenport-Hines, *Dudley Docker: the life and times of a trade warrior* (1984) · S. Chapman, *Labour and capital after the war* (1918) · D. Docker, 'The labour unrest', *Daily Mail* (8 June 1912) · D. Docker, 'Letter to Sir Algernon Firth', *Midland Advertiser* (17 Aug 1912) · D. Docker, 'Foreign loans and British industries', *The Economist* (7 Feb 1914) · D. Docker, 'The port of finance', *The Globe* (26 Oct 1914) · D. Docker, 'Causes of industrial unrest', *Sunday Times* (2 Sept 1917) · D. Docker, 'The industrial problem', *National Review*, 72 (1918–19) · D. Docker, 'The large view in business', *Ways and Means* (27 Sept 1919) · J. Dale, *Warwickshire: historical, descriptive and biographical in the reign of King Edward VII* (1910) · b. cert. · m. cert. · d. cert.

Archives CAC Cam., Lord Swinton MSS · CUL, Vickers archives · HLRO, Sir Patrick Hannon MSS · NA Scot., Sir Arthur Steel-Maitland MSS · W. Sussex RO, Leo Maxse MSS

Likenesses photograph, c.1908, repro. in Dale, *Warwickshire*, 105 · S. Forbes, oils, 1913 · photograph, c.1916, University of Warwick, Confederation of British Industry archives · photograph, c.1916, repro. in Davenport-Hines, *Dudley Docker* [see illus.] · photograph, c.1925, HSBC Group Archives, Midland Bank archives

Wealth at death £887,962 5s. 8d.: probate, 2 Nov 1944, CGPLA Eng. & Wales

Docking, Thomas of (d. c.1270), Franciscan friar and ecclesiastical writer, was born at Docking, Norfolk, and may have entered the Franciscan order at Norwich. He had certainly become a Franciscan by 1252–3, when Adam Marsh (d. 1259) wrote a letter asking the provincial minister to assign Docking the Bible of a deceased friar. In this letter Marsh described Docking as 'distinguished by good morals and pleasant manners, a clear hand, great learning and eloquence' (Brewer, 359–60). Docking was at various times among the pupils of Robert Grosseteste (d. 1253), Adam Marsh, and Roger Bacon (d. 1294), and went on to fulfil his earlier promise by becoming seventh lector to the Oxford Franciscans (c.1262–5), succeeding John of Wales (d. 1285). Like John, he was not a philosopher, but rather a moralist and theologian. He remained in Oxford after his time as lector, and was among the speakers during the controversy between the Friars Preacher and the Friars Minor at Oxford in 1269. He was later warden of Norwich, and died c.1270.

Docking was a prolific writer, his works being both lengthy and numerous. Although enthusiasm for his works waned in the fourteenth century, being given rather to the Paris theologian Nicholas de Lyre, interest in Docking did revive in the fifteenth century. His commentary on the *Sentences* (now lost) was well known in the middle ages, as was his 'Biblical grammar', also now lost. His commentary on Deuteronomy survives in five manuscripts, his commentary on Isaiah in two. He also left commentaries on nine of the Pauline epistles, and parts of commentaries on Corinthians, Luke, and Job.

Docking has been described as having a mania for encyclopaedic lore: this was an enthusiasm shared by a number of Oxford friars of his period. His lengthy commentaries show a wide range of interests. He commented extensively on social conditions, children, young people, physical sciences including optics, law, the beauties of natural scenery, and many other topics, quite apart from his theological interests. In many ways he tended to accept the social conditions of his time, but he did make some political comments that can seem pointed, considering that he was lecturing at Oxford in the 1260s, at the time of the barons' wars. When he wrote that 'it seems to me … that if some man who is prudent and well-fitted for the business of rule … should aspire to the dignity of ruling for … the benefit of the subjects, his aim is good' (Little, *Grey Friars*, 278 n.4), he may have been referring to Simon de Montfort.

Docking showed himself acquainted with a wide range of sources. He quotes a number of classical writers—mainly poets apart from Cicero—many anonymous medieval verses, and Bernard Sylvestris. Philosophy was represented by Plato, Aristotle, Seneca, Boethius, Ptolemy, Pliny, and Pseudo-Dionysius. Docking refers to very many ecclesiastical writers, together with John of Salisbury,

Alexander Neckham, and, most unusually, the *De prescientia Dei* of Bartholomew, bishop of Exeter (*d.* 1184). Guillaume d'Auxerre and Robert Grosseteste are mentioned infrequently, and Adam Marsh not at all.

Docking was first quoted by the Franciscan John Russel, who cited the 'Biblical grammar' in 1292. Later Franciscans who also quoted his works included William of Nottingham (*c.*1312), John Lathbury (*c.*1350), and William Woodford (*c.*1373), while William Gray, bishop of Ely (*d.* 1478), had copies of Docking's works made for his library in the mid-fifteenth century.   JENNY SWANSON

Sources A. G. Little, *Franciscan papers, lists, and documents* (1943), 6, 69, 91, 98–121 · A. G. Little, *The Grey friars in Oxford*, OHS, 20 (1892), 36–7, 56, 324–6 · J. Catto, 'New light on Thomas Docking OFM', *Mediaeval and Renaissance Studies*, 6 (1968) · B. Smalley, *The Bible in the middle ages* (1952), 278ff., 323ff. · B. Smalley, *English friars and antiquity in the early fourteenth century* (1960), 49 · J. S. Brewer, ed., *Monumenta Franciscana*, 1, Rolls Series, 4 (1858)

Dockwra [Dockwray], **William** (*c.*1635–1716), promoter of the penny post and copper and brass manufacturer, was the son of John Dockwra, an armourer. Williams was apprenticed in 1651 to Anthony Hatch of the Armourers' Company. He was married and had nine children. The marriage of his niece, Mary Davies, to Sir Thomas Grosvenor of Eaton in Cheshire provided an influential contact with that family.

In the 1660s Dockwra was able to secure an official position at the London custom house. His involvement in the African slave trade was later challenged by the Royal African Company in defence of its monopoly. As a consequence he suffered losses in 1676 when the *Ann*, a merchant ship in which he had the major share, was seized. On bringing an action against those responsible and petitioning for redress, Dockwra further alienated the company and its supporters. He suffered additional losses in other aspects of his African trade.

In 1683, at a time when no adequate provision existed for the carriage of letters and parcels between different parts of London, Dockwra improved upon an idea suggested and partly implemented by Robert *Murray (*bap.* 1633, *d.* 1725?) to establish a penny postal system in the city. He secured a patent allowing letters and parcels taken in at the receiving houses in principal streets to be carried by messengers at hourly intervals to six large 'grand offices'. When the letters and parcels were sorted and registered, other messengers delivered them six or eight times a day in central streets near the exchange. Within the city 1*d.* was charged for delivery of letters and parcels not exceeding 1 lb in weight, or any sum of money, or parcels of not more than £10 in value. In the suburbs there were four deliveries daily at a charge of 2*d.* for delivery within a given 10 mile radius.

For Dockwra there was little benefit from this enterprise. Complaints resulted from city porters, who felt their interests were threatened, and legal action ensued from the duke of York, to whom revenue had been granted from the Post Office monopoly. This lawsuit resulted in losses of £2000 to Dockwra and the surrender of his patent. In 1690, in recompense for this treatment, parliament granted him a pension of £500 a year for seven years, which was continued on a new patent until 1700. In 1697 he was appointed as comptroller of the penny post, and in that year a poem on his 'invention of the penny post' is recorded in a volume entitled *State Poems*. He later complained of the transfer of a number of his destinations in favour of the general post. He was then accused of removing the Post Office from Cornhill to a less central station, of detaining and opening letters, and of refusing to take parcels of more than 1 lb in weight, thereby injuring the trade of the Post Office porters. After an investigation by Sir Thomas Frankland and Sir Robert Cotton, postmasters-general, Dockwra was eventually dismissed from his post as a comptroller of the penny post in June 1700.

Meanwhile, Dockwra had involved himself in the Armourers' Company, in 1688 becoming a member of the courts of assistants and master between 1692 and 1694. During the 1680s Dockwra had acquired other interests through association with the Grosvenors, owners of lead mines in Flintshire. Acting as London agent for sales of lead from these mines, he learned of new lead-smelting methods being developed at Bristol. The practical application of this work was largely due to John Coster, who was later responsible for extending similar coal-fired techniques to the smelting of copper. The old monopolies, whose failure to establish a lasting production in copper and brass had left the country dependent on expensive imported goods, were restricted by the Mines Royal Act of 1689. This act, legalizing the formation of new enterprise in this industry, enabled the adoption of the new smelting methods under development.

In 1689 Dockwra led a new partnership, formed to smelt copper ore. Cornish ore was carried by water to Redbrook on the Wye in Gloucestershire to be processed there by Coster. From Redbrook refined copper ingot was transported by Severn and Thames to Esher in Surrey, mainly for the production of brass and for manufacture to finished goods. The Esher works, established in 1690 under a separate partnership led by Dockwra, was convenient to supply the lucrative London market. Formerly the premises had been the brass works of Jacob Momma, who earlier in the century had struggled for survival against the old privileged monopolies and the price manipulation of imports. Under Dockwra brass was now produced in the traditional manner from refined copper and crushed calamine (the carbonate ore of zinc) from Mendip in Somerset. Brass and copper sheet was manufactured by water-powered rolling mills, believed to have been quite new to England. The resulting brass sheet was beaten under water-powered hammers to form pots, pans, and industrial vessels. Brass rod drawn to wire was used for pin manufacture in the first comprehensive works of its kind. By 1696 it was found that such advances in technical expertise provided only small profit margins. A newly introduced manager was dismissed after two years by a leading co-partner when Dockwra himself, now elderly, was withdrawing from practical involvement. The action precipitated a lawsuit, and compensation, culminating in a decline of the Esher works until, in 1709, it came under the control of the brass works at Bristol.

Dockwra's fortune, reduced by his dismissal as comptroller of the penny post, was further depleted by diminishing profit from Esher and by litigation expenses. In 1702 he petitioned Queen Anne for compensation, stating that six of his seven surviving children were unprovided for. Dockwra died on 25 September 1716, aged about eighty-four according to his will, although recorded elsewhere as 'aged near 100' (*Historical Register*, 544).

JOAN DAY

Sources J. Houghton, *Husbandry and trade improv'd*, 3 (1697), 190, 192–4 • BL, Add. MS 22675, vol. 3, fol. 37 • J. Day, *Bristol brass: a history of the industry* (1973) • R. Jenkins, 'Copper works of Redbrook and Bristol', *Transactions of the Bristol and Gloucestershire Archaeological Society*, 62 (1940), 145–67 • H. Hamilton, *The English brass and copper industries to 1800* (1926) • J. Day, 'The Costers, copper-smelters and manufacturers', *Transactions* [Newcomen Society], 47 (1974–6), 47–58 • J. Morton, 'The rise of the modern copper and brass industry, 1690–1750', PhD diss., U. Birm., 1985 • J. Day and R. F. Tylecote, eds., *The industrial revolution in metals* (1991) • *DNB* • *The historical register*, 1 (1716), 544 • *Poems on affairs of state ... by the greatest wits of the age* (1697) • Wood, *Ath. Oxon.* • William Dockwra's will, 26 Oct 1712, PRO, PROB 11/554, fols. 250–52 • GL, Armourers and Brasiers Company MSS • private information (2004) [Claude Blair]

Archives BL, Add. MS 22675, vol. 3, fol. 37

Dockwray [Docwra], **Thomas** (*d.* 1559), master of the Stationers' Company and ecclesiastical lawyer, about whose origins and parentage nothing is known, does not seem to have been related to his namesake and near contemporary Sir Thomas *Docwra (*d.* 1527), prior of the knights of St John of Jerusalem at Clerkenwell. Although a member of the Stationers' Company from at least 1519, Dockwray's name appears in no surviving book imprints. However, he was associated with both the printer and bookseller Henry Pepwell and the bookseller John Reynes. In 1533 Dockwray was in Antwerp on behalf of the bishop of London, John Stokesley, on unknown business, to the nature of which Pepwell was said to be privy. Dockwray's early relationship with the Stationers' Company is difficult to assess as no company records survive before 1554; however, he served as master from 1554 to 1558—a crucial period that saw the company incorporated by Queen Mary in 1557.

Dockwray had a lifelong association with the London parish of St Faith which included the main bookselling areas of St Paul's Churchyard and Paternoster Row, both as a resident—he occupied premises on the north side of the churchyard—and as a property developer. He seems, at least for a time, to have been a wealthy man, and in 1536 he and Pepwell, another St Faith's resident, were described as substantial inhabitants of the parish in their appointment as petty collectors of the king's subsidy. However, in 1539 Dockwray was listed as one of many churchyard tenants in arrears. In 1552 he built tenements in Paternoster Row, and at his death he held property in both Paternoster Row and Warwick Lane.

Dockwray also had a long legal career. From at least 1527 he was a proctor in the court of arches—that is, one of a dozen or so lawyers in the highest ecclesiastical court in

the Canterbury province based in St Mary-le-Bow Church, London. At some point between 1542 and 1550 he was suspended, as in the latter year he was reinstated by the archbishop; eight months later Dockwray was one of the defending lawyers at the trial of Stephen Gardiner, bishop of Winchester.

In 1532, despite having been successfully sued two months earlier for armed assault, Dockwray was appointed the city's proctor for 'speciall matters & Causes' (CLRO, repertory, 8, fol. 242r); he was still drawing a fee for this in 1536, and in 1541 he was consulted by the city recorder, Roger Cholmley, regarding a conflict of rights between the lord admiral and the Thames conservators. Earlier in 1541, he seems to have been a common councilman as he was among a list of 'Commoners' appointed by the court of aldermen to view the former London friaries.

Dockwray died on 23 June 1559 and was buried in the church of St Faith's under St Paul's two days later, attended by 'mony morners' (*Diary of Henry Machyn*, 201). An epitaph was recorded by William Dugdale. He was survived by a widow, Anne, and had held property in London, Middlesex, and Hertfordshire.

Dockwray did not mention the Stationers' Company in his will, although a bequest of 20s. and a gilt-silver spoon was made on his behalf by his widow; however, he left a tenement in Paternoster Row to the Jesus Guild, a religious fraternity re-established in St Faith's in 1556 but dissolved very early in Elizabeth's reign.

Of Anne, nothing is known although she may have been the 'mistress Dockwra' buried in April 1561 (*Diary of Henry Machyn*, 254).

I. GADD

Sources Arber, *Regs. Stationers*, 1.xxviii–xxxvi, 33, 49, 61, 66, 69, 86, 90, 102, 103 • will, PRO, PROB 11/42B, sig. 34, fols. 272r–272v [partially transcribed in Arber, *Stationers' reg.*, 1.xxxiv–xxxv] • repertories of court of aldermen; journals of court of common council, CLRO • *LP Henry VIII* • P. W. M. Blayney, *The bookshops in Paul's Cross churchyard* (1990), 19, 33, 34–5, 51 n. 1, 75 • *The diary of Henry Machyn, citizen and merchant-taylor of London, from AD 1550 to AD 1563*, ed. J. G. Nichols, CS, 42 (1848), 201, 254, 373 • W. Dugdale, *The history of St Paul's Cathedral in London* (1658), sigs. Gg1v, Hh2v • B. R. Masters, ed., *Chamber accounts of the sixteenth century* (1984), no. 295e, p. 115 • lay subsidy, *c.*1523, PRO, E179/251/15B • King's bench, 24 Hen. VIII Trinity, PRO, KB27/1084 r.27d • King's bench, 24 Hen. VIII Michaelmas, PRO, KB27/1085 r.29 • *Thomas Dockeray v. Francis Clark, c.*1583, PRO, C2/Eliz/D12/44 • *The acts and monuments of John Foxe*, ed. J. Pratt, [new edn], 6 (1877), 99, 120, 125, 134 • R. G. Lang, ed., *Two Tudor subsidy assessment rolls for the city of London, 1541 and 1581*, London RS, 29 (1993), 72 • H. R. Plomer, *Abstracts from the wills of English printers and stationers from 1492 to 1630* (1903), 6–7 • archiepiscopal register, Cranmer, LPL, fol. 60 • private information (2004) [P. W. M. Blayney] • J. Stow, *A survey of London*, rev. edn (1603); repr. with introduction by C. L. Kingsford as *A survey of London*, 2 vols. (1908), 337 • S. Brigden, *London and the Reformation* (1989), 582–3

Dockwray, William. *See* Dockwra, William (*c.*1635–1716).

Docwra [née Waldegrave], **Anne** (*c.*1624–1710), religious writer, was the eldest daughter of Sir William Waldegrave of Bures, Suffolk, of a leading gentry family and a justice under Charles I. When she was about fifteen her father stimulated what became her considerable study of the law by directing her to read the statutes of the realm, since women 'must live under [the laws] as well as men'

(Mack, 316). Her antecedents were Anglican and her political views remained basically royalist; the date of her Quaker 'convincement' is not known, but she married a member of a well-established landed family, James Docwra (1617–1672), who became a Quaker before 1655, in which year he left lands in trust for the benefit of Friends. Following her husband's death in 1672 she moved into Cambridge, where she made her home available for Friends' meetings and the accommodation of travelling ministers.

Because, as she claimed, Christ died 'to end shadows and typical forms' (Mack, 317), she regretted the growing formalism of the Friends' post-Restoration administrative and disciplinary structures, and opposed separate women's meetings on the grounds that St Paul had debarred women from having authority over men; women, however, could prophesy and guide men Friends in the administration of charity funds. Her first published work, partly in verse, *A looking-glass for the recorder and justices of the peace and grand juries for the town and county of Cambridge* (1682) forms an eloquent plea for toleration—'Force makes Hypocrites' (Phillipson, 'Quakerism in Cambridge before the Act of Toleration', 23). In the following year she visited George Fox (1626–1691) and other Quaker leaders in London to discuss disagreements over Friends' church government, and, invoking her royalist credentials, wrote a defence of women's ministry, *An epistle of love and good advice to my old friends and fellow-sufferers in the late times, the old royalists*. In the same year her *A Brief Discovery of the Work of the Enemy of Sion's Peace* commented on expulsions of dissidents from the society. *True Intelligence to be Read and Considered in the Light* (1683) opposed administrative 'Formalities and Directories' (ibid., 22).

Anne Docwra was, apparently, immune from persecution throughout the post-Restoration period, perhaps, as she claimed, as a result of her knowledge of the law and also, probably, because of her rank and background, and maybe in return for the clear royalist standpoint she and some local Friends professed in 1680. In 1687 her *Spiritual Community Vindicated amongst People of Different Perswasions in some Things* fully supported James II's pursuit of toleration. In 1699, in *An Apostate Conscience Exposed*, she attacked her nephew, the Quaker renegade Francis *Bugg (1640–1727): the work also contains a vivid defence of Fox's simplicity of life against Bugg's charges of luxury against the Quaker leader. In the following year, in *The Second Part of an Apostate Conscience Exposed*, Docwra countered Bugg's riposte, *Jezebel Withstood*.

Docwra's enduring gift to Cambridge Friends came in a two-part legacy in 1700 and 1710, in which she gave an estate in Jesus Lane to the society with a 1000 year lease; in her will, dated 4 and 6 May 1710, by now living in reduced circumstances, she made further bequests to several Friends, confirmed her husband's earlier gifts of lands, and added a gift of £20 for a graveyard. She died the same year in Cambridge, where she was buried.

Criticized both by Bugg and by voices of mainstream Quakerism in her day, an individualist difficult to contain within an organization acquiring structural coherence,

Anne Docwra was a spirited, intelligent, articulate, educated, and wise lady, one who preferred 'rational argument to visionary insight' (Mack, 316) and who yet held to a deep spiritual sense of the Quaker 'glad tidings of the Light' (ibid., 318).   MICHAEL MULLETT

Sources P. Mack, *Visionary women: ecstatic prophecy in seventeenth-century England* (1992) · E. Backhouse, T. J. Backhouse, and T. Mounsey, 'Ann Docwra of Cambridge', RS Friends, Lond., MS Cc.1845-501 · L. Phillipson, 'Quakerism in Cambridge before the Act of Toleration', *Proceedings of the Cambridge Antiquarian Society*, 76 (1987) · L. Phillipson, 'Quakerism in Cambridge from the Act of Toleration to the end of the nineteenth century', *Proceedings of the Cambridge Antiquarian Society*, 77 (1988) · H. Smith and S. Cardinale, eds., *Women and literature of the seventeenth century: an annotated bibliography based on Wing's 'Short-title catalogue'* (1990) · R. Foxton, 'Hear the word of the Lord': a critical and bibliographical study of Quaker women's writings, 1650–1700 (1994) · J. Smith, ed., *A descriptive catalogue of Friends' books*, 1 (1867) · W. C. Braithwaite, *The second period of Quakerism* (1919) · *The short journal and itinerary journals of George Fox*, ed. N. Penney (1925) · C. Trevett, *Women and Quakerism in the 17th century* (1991) · R. Barclay, *The inner life of the religious societies of the Commonwealth* (1876) · catalogue [Friends' House] · *VCH Cambridgeshire and the Isle of Ely*, vol. 3 · 'Dictionary of Quaker biography', RS Friends, Lond. [card index]

Wealth at death £35 17s.—goods and chattels: Phillipson, 'Quaker in Cambridge from the Act of Toleration', 6

Docwra, Henry, first Baron Docwra of Culmore (*bap.* 1564, *d.* 1631), army officer, was baptized on 30 April 1564 at Thatcham parish church, Berkshire, the second son of Edmund Docwra (*d.* in or after 1590), politician and landowner, and his wife, Dorothy. Docwra's family owned the manor of Chamberhouse, Berkshire, but his father, an undistinguished MP for Aylesbury and New Windsor, fell into financial difficulties and was forced to sell. This situation may have influenced Docwra's decision to go into the army: he became a professional soldier serving under Sir Richard Bingham in the west of Ireland in 1585 and soon captained his own company. For the next decade he was actively engaged in warfare in Ireland.

Warfare in Ireland, 1586–1600 On 1 March 1586 Docwra was prominent in Bingham's siege of Cloonoan Castle in Thomond, one of the strongest fortresses in the present co. Clare, then held by Mathghamhain or Mahon O'Brien; on O'Brien's surrender all the warders were put to the sword without mercy. After this victory against the O'Briens Bingham turned his forces against the Mayo Burkes, besieging their castle of Annagh near Ballinrobe, sometimes called Annis, as well as their other stronghold on an ancient crannog towards the middle of Lough Mask known as Caislean-na-Caillighe (the 'hag's castle'). On refusing a parley to surrender, Bingham's men including Docwra's company burnt the boats which the Burkes had in dock at Castle Hag to prevent their escape but the first attack failed in a storm on the Mask, some soldiers were drowned, and the Burkes secured a number of boats to escape to the woods of Kilbride. Bingham also then abandoned the attack on Annagh Castle. In July 1586 Docwra's headquarters was at Ballinrobe whence he made sorties against the Burkes, and their allies the O'Malleys, Gibbons, Joyces, Philbins, and MacDonnells.

Meanwhile a force of hired Scottish mercenaries was on

the Erne waterways, advancing to ally with the Burkes; Docwra, under Bingham, marched north to Sligo to prevent their advance. Some of the O'Rourkes of Leitrim, the McGuires and supporters of Art O'Neill of Tyrone, who was later an ally of Docwra, joined the Scots on the Curlew Mountains. At first the invaders into Connaught were successful; Bingham and Docwra had to retreat, many men were drowned at the confluence of the Owenmore and Owenboy rivers near Colooney, and some of the enemy Scots escaped into the Ox Mountains. The decisive engagements, however, took place at Aclare, near modern Tobercurry, in co. Sligo, and on the River Moy outside Ballina at Ardnarea on 23 September 1586, where over 1000 fighting men and an equal number of attendants, women, and children, were slaughtered. Little was accomplished by severity and many of the Mayo Burkes continued in rebellion. In recognition of his distinguished military services Docwra was made constable of Dungarvan Castle, the chief administrative centre of co. Waterford, in 1594, which post he relinquished to Sir George Carey, treasurer at war, on 23 August 1599. On the decline of Bingham's fortunes Docwra transferred his allegiance to Robert Devereux, second earl of Essex; Docwra gained his own command under the earl and fought with him at Cadiz, where he was knighted in 1596. When Essex was given the supreme command in Ireland he employed Docwra in the preparation and conduct of the seasoned troops who were to be transported from the Netherlands to Ireland in the winter of 1598–9. George Gilpin told Essex in a letter from The Hague that Docwra had 'fine prospects of advancement, being well thought of; but the importance of the war in Ireland, and his devotion to the queen and to you [Essex] have made him resolve to return' (*Salisbury MSS*, 9.21), while Docwra himself assured Essex on 12 January 1599 of his 'unspeakable contentment' that he had been given this particular service (ibid., 22–3). Docwra's company, with that of Sir Charles Percy, was employed in reducing the rebellion in the Wicklow Mountains, where Docwra distinguished himself at Arklow in June 1599.

In the winter of 1600–01, following Essex's disgrace, the government earmarked Docwra for 'the most desperate assignement', as he would later describe his task under Lord Deputy Mountjoy, Essex's replacement, of planting garrisons along the Foyle to divide the forces of O'Neill from those of O'Donnell. Over the winter and spring months of 1600 he gathered an army of about 4000 foot and 200 horse at Chester, and he landed the bulk of them at Carrickfergus on 25 April 1600; there they were reinforced by a further 1000 troops, before reaching the Foyle on 14 May. A landing was made at Culmore, where they dug in with earthworks and refurbished the remains of a castle abandoned by Colonel Edward Randolph in 1566. A detachment under Captain Lloyd fortified the ancient fort of Ellaugh, which commanded the southern approach to Innishowen, co. Donegal, and on 22 May Docwra's forces possessed the 'iland and the fort of the Derry' (McGurk, plate facing p. 222). In the building up of his forts, ramparts, houses, and the beginnings of the celebrated 'walls of Derry' as well as a military hospital—a process which

destroyed many ancient monastic and ecclesiastical buildings—Docwra may be considered the founder of the modern city of Derry. He had accomplished his first major objective.

Concluding the war, 1600–1602 Docwra's second project, and the wish of the government—that he accomplish similar works at Ballyshannon, the key crossing point between Ulster and Connaught and much used by O'Donnell—was greatly delayed for lack of resources. His forces in Derry were decimated by sickness and desertions, and he could not establish Ballyshannon by sea for lack of men and ships. His final strategy, slow yet certain (though subsequent events in the war rendered its completion unnecessary), was to continue his chain of forts connecting the Foyle and the Erne to reach Enniskillen, whence he could embark a force to Belleek, a mere 3 miles overland march to Ballyshannon. On 1 June 1600 he received the submission of Sir Art O'Neill, and on 28 June, with a force of 500 foot and 40 horse, Docwra fought a major battle against O'Dogherty and his allies at Ellaugh, Innishowen. His lieutenant Sir John Chamberlain was unhorsed and Docwra's own horse shot under him in rescuing Sir John. In these engagements the Irish captured horses and prisoners, and generally had the immediate advantage. Irish chroniclers lauded Docwra's personal courage in battle, calling him 'an illustrious knight of wisdom and prudence, a pillar of battle and conflict' (*AFM*, 6.2193).

At the end of July, O'Donnell, the McSwineys, and Scottish mercenaries made a major attack in which Docwra was wounded by Hugh Dubh (the Black) O'Donnell, son of Hugh Roe (Red Hugh). Docwra graphically described the incident:

> At the first encounter I was stricken with a horseman's staff in the forehead, in so much as I fell for dead, and was a good while deprived of my senses … but the captains and gentlemen that were about me enforced the enemy to give ground … by means whereof I recovered myself was set up on my horse and so safely brought of and conducted home … I kept my bed of this wound by the space of a fortnight, my chamber a week after, and then I came abroad to take view and muster of all the companies.   (*Narration*, 242)

Outbreaks of camp diseases reduced his soldiers to about one third of their complement, but they managed to repulse night attacks by the Irish.

Docwra had some talent in weaning local support from his enemies, and he managed to bring over to his side Niall Garbh (the Rough) O'Donnell and his three brothers. Niall probably joined Docwra on the assumption that he would be given the whole of Tyrconnell, modern co. Donegal, as hereditary chief on the cessation of hostilities and by October 1600 he had secured the fortress of the Lifford, opposite Strabane on the Donegal side of the Foyle, for Docwra.

During 1601 Docwra became convinced that the Spanish would invade in the north of Ireland, but few shared his fears; his letters and detailed reports with 'shopping lists' of requisite supplies greatly irritated the authorities. However, all was not inactivity, or 'dullness and difficulty' (Brewer and Bullen, 4.153), at Lough Foyle as Cecil claimed. In 1601 incursions were made into O'Cahan's lands around the present Coleraine and as far east as the Bann. The Innishowen peninsula was taken, providing Docwra with a granary as well as cutting off communication between O'Donnell and O'Neill and O'Cahan, a major objective of the expedition which allowed Mountjoy to attack south Ulster. And, from the Lifford, attacks were conducted by Docwra into Newtown and towards Omagh which he was able to fortify by July 1602. In that year too Dungiven in the Sperrin Mountains bordering north Tyrone and the present co. Londonderry was taken and fortified. In the final phase after Mountjoy's victory at Kinsale, Docwra commanded forces in the famous three-pronged pincer movement of Sir Arthur Chichester from the east, Mountjoy from the south, and Docwra from the west to hem in O'Neill in his final resistance in his homelands around Dungannon.

Post-war career and death, 1603–1631 On the conclusion of the war in 1603 Docwra's accustomed prudence and fair dealings with his Irish allies helped to prevent a rising when news of Elizabeth's death reached Ulster. He remained governor of Derry and devoted himself to the general improvement of the city. On 12 September 1603 he received a grant to hold markets on Wednesdays and Saturdays and monthly fairs, and on 11 July 1604 he was appointed provost of Derry for life, with a pension of 20s. a day. In 1606 Docwra applied unsuccessfully for the presidency of Ulster. In 1606 in disgust at the government's treatment of his Irish allies he sold his house, appointed George Pawlett as vice-governor of Derry, and returned to England. By 1607 he had married Anne (d. 1648), daughter of Francis Vaughan of Sutton upon Derwent, Yorkshire. They had at least three sons and two daughters. Two of their children, named Henry and Anne, were baptized at Bradfield, Berkshire, on 16 August 1607 and 2 May 1609, and Docwra bought the manor of Bradfield in 1610. While in England Docwra wrote up his 'Relation of the service done in Ireland', an account of his time with Sir Richard Bingham in the west, and in 1614 he wrote 'A narration of the services done by the army ymployed to Lough-Foyle, under the leadinge of mee Sir Henry Docwra knight … together with a declaration of the true cause and manner of my coming away and leaving that place'. Both were published in the nineteenth century. The majority of his Irish letters are printed in extenso throughout the Irish state papers. Robert Pentland Mahaffy, the editor, commented: 'Sir Henry Docwra writes in a style of verbose magniloquence which is remarkable even for this period … [and] makes the task of abstracting difficult and unsatisfactory' (CSP Ire., 1601–3, 53). Contemporaries objected to the verbosity and frequency of Docwra's letters.

In 1616 Docwra sold Bradfield and returned to Ireland, where he was appointed treasurer-at-war, and created Lord Docwra, baron of Culmore, co. Derry, on 15 May 1621. On 15 July 1624 he became keeper of the peace in the provinces of Leinster and Ulster and on 30 May 1627 joint keeper of the great seal of Ireland in the absence in England of the chancellor, Viscount Loftus. At the trial of Lord Dunboyne for manslaughter Docwra was appointed one of the fifteen peers on 4 June 1628 and was the only one who voted for a conviction. Docwra died in Dublin on 18 April 1631 and was buried in Christ Church Cathedral, Dublin. His eldest son, Theodore, succeeded him in the title but died without issue, whereupon the barony became extinct.

Assessment Docwra was a respected soldier whose personal valour and generally honourable conduct won the admiration of his men and of the enemy. He resorted to battle only when negotiations failed and was consistent in his tactic of dividing the Irish, winning over Niall Garbh O'Donnell for the crucial years of the fighting, Donal O'Cahan, who disputed Coleraine (later Londonderry) with Hugh O'Neill, and Sir Cahir O'Doherty, who occasionally went over to the government side. Docwra was publicly minded and less greedy for advancement and emolument than was usual among Elizabethan officers in Ireland, and as treasurer-at-war he was solicitous for the welfare of the soldiers in Ireland.   J. J. N. McGURK

Sources Docwra's relation of service done in Ireland, ed. J. O'Donovan, Celtic Miscellany (1849), 187–229 • A narration of the services done by the army ymployed to Lough-Foyle, under the leadinge of mee Sir Henry Docwra, ed. J. O'Donovan, Celtic Miscellany (1849), 233–325 • CSP Ire., 1599–1610 • J. C. Erck, ed., Repertory of the inrollments on the patent rolls of Chancery in Ireland, 1 (1846) • The Irish fiants of the Tudor sovereigns, 4 vols. (1994), vol. 3 • AFM, 2nd edn, vols. 5–6 • Calendar of the manuscripts of the most hon. the marquis of Salisbury, 24 vols., HMC, 9 (1883–1976), vols. 9–10 • J. S. Brewer and W. Bullen, eds., Calendar of the Carew manuscripts, 6 vols., PRO (1867–73), vols. 3–4 • APC, 1597–1601 • G. Hill, Plantation in Ulster, 1608–1620 (1877); facs. (1970) • T. W. Moody, The Londonderry plantation, 1609–1641 (1939) • J. Stevens Curl, The Londonderry plantation (1986) • J. McGurk, The Elizabethan conquest of Ireland: the 1590s crisis (1997) • VCH Berkshire, vols. 3–4 • W. J. Jones, 'Docwra, Edmund', HoP, Commons, 1558–1603 • S. Barfield, Thatcham, Berks, and its manors, ed. J. Parker, 2 vols. (1901) • GEC, Peerage, new edn • T. W. Moody and others, eds., A new history of Ireland, 9: Maps, genealogies, lists (1984) • J. Lodge, The peerage of Ireland, rev. M. Archdall, rev. edn, 7 vols. (1789), vols. 1, 6 • official Irish papers, 1618–20, CKS, Cranfield papers, U269/1 Hi • IGI

Archives BL, extracts, notes of the Relation and the Narration, Add. MS 21993 • BL, letters, Stowe MS 145 • NL Ire., original of the Narration, etc., MS 12095 • Royal Irish Acad., MS 14B.11 | CKS, Cranfield papers, U269/1 Hi • PRO, State Papers, Ireland, SP 63/207/pt VI, no. 84 (I) (II) (III) • TCD, letters to Secretary Davidson, MS 845

Docwra, Mary Elizabeth (1847–1914), temperance activist, was born at Kelvedon, Essex, on 20 January 1847, the third of seven children of George Docwra and his wife, Mary Jesup, née Knight. Members of the Society of Friends, her parents were from old Essex stock, tracing their family back more than 180 years. They were originally moderate drinkers, but early in their marriage embraced total abstinence and became active in temperance circles. Their seven children were all abstainers and workers for temperance reform. The mother organized the local children's temperance organization, the Band of Hope, in 1862, in which she enrolled her children, including Mary Elizabeth.

When the Independent Order of Good Templars, a teetotal fraternal organization, was established in England in the following decade, the Docwra family joined and Mary Elizabeth became one of its early leaders. From 1876 to 1886 she was the district secretary for the local Good Templars lodge, and in 1881 she was elected to the national office of grand worthy vice-templar of the English grand lodge, being re-elected the following year.

The two Marys, mother and daughter, both joined the British Women's Temperance Association when it was founded in 1876. Mary Jesup Docwra was to be a long-time leader in the local Kelvedon branch; her daughter, in 1879, became Kelvedon's representative to the national organization. Four years later she became a member of its London-based national executive committee. When the president of the association, Margaret Bright Lucas, fell fatally ill in late 1889, Mary Elizabeth Docwra took over the ailing president's work and virtually ran the association headquarters. Upon the death of Lucas the following year the association was reorganized, with its ultimate authority divided between a socially prominent president and working executive committee with its own president. Under this new arrangement the first appointment as president of the association was a wealthy nationally known social reformer, Lady Henry Somerset, and the head of the national executive committee was Docwra, unanimously elected to its presidency.

The early 1890s was a stormy time for the association. Lady Henry Somerset spent a good deal of her time abroad, especially in the United States, where she forged close ties with the American Frances Willard and her Woman's Christian Temperance Union (WCTU). While the president was absent, Docwra conducted most of the association business. Trouble quickly emerged over the association's journal, the British Women's Temperance Journal, which was owned and edited by a male publisher who had no official position in the women's association. In 1891, while the association president was in the United States, the executive committee under the leadership of Docwra took control of the Journal, organizing a limited liability company to run it and selling shares to members of the association only. Most of these shares were bought up by members of the executive committee, who appointed a new editor. All this was done without the authorization or any consultation with the association president. This was the beginning of a split in the association between Lady Henry Somerset and her supporters, including the American WCTU and the international World's Woman's Christian Temperance Union, and the executive committee led by Mary Elizabeth Docwra, who received much support from the local association branches.

The final break came when Lady Henry Somerset wanted to expand the association's mission from a traditional narrow temperance focus to the more recent 'do everything' policy that had been developed by Willard and her organization in the United States. This policy promoted all women's issues, including women's suffrage and women's 'purity' and public action groups. At the annual council meeting in 1892, after a long and bitter fight between the two sides, with Lady Henry Somerset and Mary Docwra speaking for many hours in support of their respective positions, Docwra and her supporters walked out of the meeting and left the association.

Docwra claimed that she supported women's suffrage and many of the political, social, and philanthropic reforms in the American 'do everything' policy, but she believed that they were not appropriate goals for a temperance organization—there were other organizations devoted to these causes. She and her supporters believed that a temperance organization should focus solely on the issue of drink and closely related matters. She was a leader in organizing the Women's Total Abstinence Union which embodied this philosophy, and was chairwoman of its executive committee from 1893 to 1914, except during the years 1898–1900, when she was its president. Docwra supported many activities for women that would help the family to eliminate the use of alcoholic beverages. She proposed that the local temperance organizations should meet in church rooms and set up cooking lessons for the local women. She also supported seaside temperance meetings and other public open-air temperance meetings.

In her later years Docwra focused her efforts on the women's movement. She supported the women's suffrage cause but her main work was with women and temperance. She gave many public talks on this subject, a number of which were published as pamphlets by the women's temperance organization. The best known was Women's Work in the Victorian Era, originally a paper presented to a Women's Total Abstinence Union conference in 1893 and later reprinted as a tract. In 1897 it was expanded, brought up to date, and renamed A Glimpse at Woman's Work for Temperance during the Victorian Era, and read at a Women's Total Abstinence Union meeting. It was again printed as a pamphlet. Docwra also wrote BWTA: What it Is, What it has Done, What it has Still to Do, which was also published, as well as 'How women can assist local and imperial legislation', a paper read to a British Women's Temperance Association conference in May 1888. Docwra was also the author of the very successful Non Alcoholic Cookery Book, published in November 1879, sold out, and reissued in 1882 by the association.

A lifelong resident at The Greys in Kelvedon, Mary Elizabeth Docwra never married. After a very brief illness she died there on 26 February 1914, and was buried in the Quaker burial-ground, Kelvedon, on 3 March 1914. Representatives from local and national temperance groups, as well as local political and religious organizations, attended.

LILIAN LEWIS SHIMAN

Sources The Good Templars' Watchword (14 March 1914) · P. T. Winskill, The temperance movement and its workers, 4 vols. (1891–2), vol. 3, pp. 259–60 · Annual Report of the British Women's Temperance Association (1885–95) · Reports of Women's Total Abstinence Union (1894–5) · E. H. Cherrington and others, eds., Standard encyclopedia of the alcohol problem, 6 vols. (1924–30), vol. 2, p. 825 · M. E. Docwra, Women's work for temperance in the Victorian era (1897) · British Women's Temperance Association, minute books, 1879–1904, Rosalind Carlisle House, London, National British Women's Total Abstinence Union · b. cert. · d. cert.

Archives Rosalind Carlisle House, London, National British Women's Total Abstinence Union, minute books

Likenesses photograph, repro. in Cherrington, ed., Standard encyclopedia, 825 · photograph, repro. in The Good Templars' Watchword

Wealth at death £10,530 7s. 9d.: probate, 9 April 1914, CGPLA Eng. & Wales

Docwra, Sir Thomas (*d.* 1527), prior of the hospital of St John of Jerusalem in England and diplomat, was descended from the Westmorland family of Docwra of Docwra Hall, Kendal, belonging to a cadet branch which had settled in Hertfordshire. His father, Richard Docwra, had married Alice, daughter of Thomas Green of Gressingham, Lancashire. Nothing certain is known of Thomas Docwra's education, or of his early career until 1 May 1502, when he succeeded Sir John Kendal as prior of the knights of St John of Clerkenwell; he remained the head of the hospitallers in England until his death. Four years later, in 1506, he began his career in the king's service as one of the envoys used by Henry VII to negotiate with Philip of Castile. Philip's ships had been driven by storm onto the English coast, and his enforced stay in England was put to some use. An economic and trade treaty with the Netherlands was negotiated by Docwra and other English commissioners with representatives of the Dutch merchants. Docwra's success here led to his appointment to negotiate Henry VII's proposed marriage to Philip's sister, Margaret of Savoy, and he soon became an indispensable diplomatic journeyman. In September 1507 he was one of a body of commissioners sent to Calais on a peace embassy, their purpose being to settle the terms of an alliance with Philip and a treaty for the marriage of Charles, prince of Castile (later the emperor Charles V) with the Princess Mary. Although Philip died on 25 September, these treaties were successfully concluded on 21 December.

Docwra's career did not suffer as a result of the accession of Henry VIII, and he continued to be employed as a diplomat. Between 29 May and 23 July 1510 he and Nicholas West (later bishop of Ely) were dispatched as ambassadors to France in order to receive from Louis XII a formal acknowledgement of the sums he owed to the English crown for arrears of tribute. At about the same time Docwra's services were requested by the grand master of the knights of St John at their headquarters in Rhodes, as a result of Turkish military manoeuvres, but Henry would not spare him. As prior of St John's, Docwra was also employed on a number of more mundane domestic commissions by the king. These included gaol deliveries for Newgate and a commission of inquiry into alleged extortion by masters of the mint, and he was also appointed to inspect both the sewers of Lincolnshire (hospitaller interests were involved here) and of the River Thames between Greenwich and Lambeth. Then, on 4 February 1512, he was nominated as an ambassador to the Lateran council, set to start on 19 April. But these orders were subsequently revoked, and instead Docwra became caught up in the war with France of 1512. On 2 May of that year he was appointed to review and report upon the troops which were to be sent to Spain, under the marquess of Dorset, for an Anglo-Spanish attack upon Aquitaine, and further to this, on 22 February 1513, he was summoned to be ready by April to attend the king with 300 men at his own expense. His forces were incorporated into the army, under the command of the earl of Shrewsbury, which crossed into Calais in May and into France on 6 June. His

order's contribution to the effort is noteworthy—it included a ship of 'two hundred tons burden', placed under the command of Lord Edmund Howard. Among the badges borne in the standards of the expedition was that of 'the lord of St John's' (BL, Cotton MS Cleo. C.v, fol. 59).

When the fighting ceased in the autumn Docwra soon resumed his usual diplomatic duties. He was sent to France again in August 1514, with the earl of Worcester and Nicholas West, to obtain Louis XII's ratification of a peace treaty and to witness his marriage to the Princess Mary. The envoys remained there to witness her subsequent coronation at St Denis, on 5 November. In February 1515 Docwra attended parliament, the prior of the hospitallers being *ex officio* a peer of the realm. He was appointed a trier of petitions from Gascony, and the government clearly counted on his support against ecclesiastical attempts to prevent the renewal of the 1512 statute denying benefit of clergy to men in minor orders. But Docwra was equivocal on this issue, perhaps in consequence of his dual status as a churchman and an important baron, while he voted with the clergy on later bills relating to the *cause célèbre* of Richard Hunne. On 10 March it was decided that he should be sent to Rome, along with John Fisher (bishop of Rochester), Sir Edward Poynings, and Dr John Taylor. But although very large sums of money had been devoted to this embassy (£800 apiece to Fisher, Docwra, and Poynings and £266 13s. 4d. to Taylor), it was halted by Wolsey (as Polydore Vergil expected that it would be). Docwra is next recorded the following November, when he was among those present in Westminster Abbey when Wolsey received his cardinal's hat. Perhaps it was due to the king's, or Wolsey's, favour that on 21 February 1516 he obtained for himself and the hospital there a licence to hold the prebend of Blewbury, Berkshire, in mortmain. In May 1516 he was recorded once again in a diplomatic context, attending on Scottish ambassadors and acting as interpreter in an interview between the Venetian ambassador and the duke of Suffolk.

It would seem that there were only short periods when Docwra was not engaged in diplomacy, and these tended to be times of emergency. In late April 1517, for instance, he was in Thérouanne on a commission concerning trade, but was almost immediately back in London during the May day riots; with Thomas Howard, George Talbot, and George Neville he drove off the rowdy apprentices through a timely appearance at St Martin's parish. Their troops blocked the surrounding roads and many arrests were made. This was a brief interlude, however. In September 1518, when French ambassadors arrived in England, Docwra was one of the lords appointed to meet with them, and in the following month he was a member of the return embassy sent to France to take the oath of François I to the new treaty of alliance, by which he was to marry Princess Mary. The embassy crossed from Dover to Calais in twenty-six ships in November, and received François's oath at Notre Dame on 14 December following. Docwra was also one of the commissioners who returned Tournai to the French in February 1519, for a payment of 50,000 francs.

Another break in Docwra's usual diplomatic routine came about on 8 July 1519, when a search for suspicious characters was ordered for London and its suburbs, the districts in and about the city being parcelled out among different commissioners appointed to conduct it. As the prior of St John's, Docwra was made responsible for this investigation in Islington, Holloway, St John Street, Cowcross, Trille Mylle Street (Turnmill Street), and Charterhouse Lane, conducting it on Sunday night, 17 July, when two persons were apprehended in Islington and eleven in places nearer the city. Docwra's name also occurs about this time on a list of councillors appointed by Wolsey to sit at Whitehall and hear the causes of poor men who had suits in the Star Chamber. In 1520 he crossed with the king to the Field of Cloth of Gold, and accompanied Henry at his initial meeting with François I on 7 June. Later, he accompanied the king to Gravelines for his meeting with the emperor. In 1521 he was one of the peers who sat in judgment when the duke of Buckingham was condemned for treason.

Later that year Docwra resumed his diplomatic career. In August he went with Wolsey to Calais, where the cardinal sat as umpire between the French and the imperialists, and afterwards he was sent with Sir Thomas Boleyn to the emperor at Oudenarde. But their efforts to arrange a truce were unsuccessful, and they returned to England in November. In 1522 Docwra accompanied the king to meet Charles V again, on his visit to England between Dover and Calais and, shortly thereafter, he was appointed one of the commissioners for raising a forced loan in the county of Middlesex; this was a regular assessment upon property, in which Docwra himself was assessed at £1000. In the parliament which convened in April of that year he was once again appointed a trier of petitions, while on 2 November 1523 he was appointed one of the commissioners for Middlesex to collect the subsidy granted in that same parliament. On 25 May 1524, following a commission from the king, he and the imperial ambassador, Louis De Praet, drew up a treaty for a joint invasion of France. Later, on 12 February 1525, he was again appointed to conduct a search for suspicious characters in the north of London. So much activity may well have been too much for him, as in early April 1527 it was reported that he had fallen ill, and he probably died within the month, in London, and was possibly buried at St John's, Clerkenwell.

Docwra appears to have owned property in Hertfordshire, on the evidence of a sculptured stone, preserved in buildings of a later date at Highdown, the old family seat near Hitchin, bearing the arms of his family with the inscription 'Thomas Docwra, miles, 1504' (*VCH Hertfordshire*, 3.46). This and his seal, appended to the receipt (preserved in the French archives) given to François I for the money agreed on in 1518 for the surrender of Tournai, is all that remains of him. The seal is in the form of a shield bearing the device of a lion issuant holding a pomegranate, with the initials T. D..   ANDREW A. CHIBI

Sources J. D. Mackie, *The earlier Tudors, 1485–1558* (1952); pbk edn (1994) · *LP Henry VIII*, vols. 1–4 · *State papers published under … Henry VIII*, 11 vols. (1830–52) · *CSP Spain, 1509–25* · *CSP Venice, 1509–26* · *The Anglica historia of Polydore Vergil, AD 1485–1537*, ed. and trans. D. Hay, CS, 3rd ser., 74 (1950) · A. F. Pollard, *Wolsey* (1929) · Dugdale, *Monasticon*, new edn · Rymer, *Foedera*, 1st edn · *VCH Hertfordshire* · DNB

Likenesses W. Rogers, line engraving, BM, NPG; repro. in W. Segar, *Honor military and civil* (1602)

Wealth at death limited property in Hertfordshire

Dod [Dodd], **Charles Roger Phipps** (1793–1855), political journalist and author of reference works, was born on 8 May 1793 in Drumlease, co. Leitrim, the son of the Revd Roger Dod, vicar of Drumlease, and his second wife, Margaret, *née* Phipps. Dod's father's family came from Cloverley in Shropshire, his mother's from Spurrtown, co. Leitrim. For most of his life, until 1847, he preferred to spell his name Dodd. On 30 July 1816 he entered King's Inns, Dublin, with the intention of studying law, but he soon gave it up for literature and journalism. Between 1816 and 1818 he was part-owner and editor of a provincial journal. On 24 October 1814 Dod married Jane Eliza Baldwin, the daughter of John Baldwin of Cork; they had one son, Robert Phipps Dod [*see below*].

Dod settled in London in 1818 and joined *The Times* parliamentary reporting staff. He worked initially for John Tyas, the head of the press gallery staff, whom he eventually succeeded. Horace Twiss and Tyas had established a tradition of providing summaries of parliamentary debates for readers of *The Times*, a tradition that Dod continued. His summaries were generally regarded as highly accurate and clear, and soon became more widely read than the complete transcriptions of debates. Dod's other duty at *The Times* was writing obituary notices and memoirs. An oft-repeated story was that he was so skilled at this, and so knowledgeable about the lives of public figures, that he was able to write *The Times* obituary of Lord George Bentinck during a railway trip to London from Ramsgate (where he had been informed of Bentinck's death), without the aid of reference books or notes.

Dod is best known for his own publications, most notably the *Parliamentary Companion* and *Dod's Peerage, Baronetage and Knightage*. The *Parliamentary Companion* was founded in 1832 as an annual biographical guide to MPs and peers, and included a short description of parliamentary procedure and other aspects of political life in London. The first edition appeared in 1833. It was originally entitled the *Parliamentary Pocket Companion*, and was a small and thin volume, as its name suggests. It immediately became an essential tool for parliamentary journalists and editors, but politicians and the politically active also found it a useful reference book. Dod changed its name to the *Parliamentary Companion* in 1841, and the series continued as *Dod's Parliamentary Companion*. The *Peerage, Baronetage and Knightage* began life in 1841 as a guide to the titled classes, and continued as a competitor to *Debrett's Peerage* until 1960 when the peerage information was incorporated into the *Parliamentary Companion*. Dod's other publications include *A Manual of Dignities, Privileges and Precedence* (1852) and *Electoral Facts from 1832 to 1852 Impartially Stated* (1852, 1853). Dod died at 5 Foxley Road, Brixton, London, on 21 February 1855.

Robert Phipps Dod (*d.* 1865), political editor, was educated at King's College, London. Afterwards he entered the 54th Shropshire regiment and became a captain, a title he held until his death. He worked on the *Parliamentary Companion* and *Peerage* until his father's death in 1855, when he took over the editorship of both. He also wrote *Birth and Worth, an Enquiry into the Practical Uses of a Pedigree*, which was privately published in 1844. On 9 February 1859 he married Catherine Emma Kinchant, the daughter of the Revd John Kinchant. Dod died at his residence, Nant Isa Hall, Selattyn, near Oswestry, Shropshire, on 9 January 1865 from the effects of a shotgun wound to his foot, an accident which occurred while hunting in December 1864.
JOSEPH COOHILL

Sources *The Times* (24 Feb 1855) · *The Times* (12 Jan 1865) [Robert Phipps Dod] · *GM*, 3rd ser., 18 (1865), 123 [Robert Phipps Dod] · *WWBMP* · *Dod's Parliamentary Companion* (1966) · private information (2004) · [S. Morison and others], *The history of The Times*, 1 (1935) · [S. Morison and others], *The history of The Times*, 2 (1939) · Boase, *Mod. Eng. biog.* · Ward, *Men of the reign* · *CGPLA Eng. & Wales* (1865) [Robert Phipps Dod] · m. cert. [Robert Phipps Dod]
Archives Yale U., Beinecke L., papers
Wealth at death under £2000; Robert Phipps Dod: probate, 4 Sept 1865, *CGPLA Eng. & Wales*

Dod, Charlotte [Lottie] (**1871–1960**), sportswoman, was born on 24 September 1871 at Lower Bebington, Cheshire, the fourth and youngest child of the two sons and two daughters of Joseph Dod (*d.* 1879), a Liverpool cotton broker and banker, and his wife, Margaret Aspinall (*d.* 1901). By the time of Lottie's birth, her father was wealthy enough to retire from business, and on his death in November 1879 he left his family well provided for, so that Lottie enjoyed an independent income throughout her life. Like her brothers and sister, she was educated by governesses and private tutors at the family home, Edgeworth at Bebington. The Dods were an engaging band of enthusiasts for the types of sports which were gaining favour in late Victorian country houses: croquet, archery, golf, bowls, billiards, and skating. Her elder sister, Ann, an accomplished skater, was considered one of the best woman billiards players in England; her eldest brother, William Dod (1867–1954), won a gold medal for archery at the 1908 Olympic games in London; and her second brother, Anthony, was chess champion of Cheshire and Lancashire.

At the age of nine Lottie Dod was introduced to the recently invented game of lawn tennis on the grass court at Edgeworth. In 1883 she won a consolation doubles competition with her sister, Ann, at the northern championships, held at Manchester Lawn Tennis Club, impressing many judges with the consistency of her ground strokes. When she was still only thirteen, in 1885, she won all three open events at the Waterloo tournament and gave the Wimbledon champion Maude Watson a close contest in the finals of the northern championships, exploits which gained her the title Little Wonder. She entered the United Kingdom championships at Wimbledon for the first time in July 1887, aged fifteen years and ten months. After beating two opponents in the opening rounds, she

Charlotte [Lottie] Dod (1871–1960), by unknown photographer, 1886 [at the West of England Championships, Bath]

met Blanche Bingley in the challenge round. The match became a rout, as Lottie Dod took the title for the loss of only two games; the second set was completed in ten minutes. Easy victories in the Irish, north of England, and west of England championships in the same year confirmed her position as the unrivalled women's champion.

Dod was less dominant in 1888 but again defeated Bingley at Wimbledon (6–3, 6–3) in a match which lasted under half an hour. Unwilling to disrupt a yachting holiday, she declined to defend her title in 1889 and played no championship tennis in 1890. But she returned to win Wimbledon in 1891 and 1892. By then her powerful volleying and overheads were untouchable. In the 1893 competition she was hard pushed by Bingley's tireless retrieving, and she lost the first set, but recovered to win her fifth Wimbledon title by exposing a weakness in her opponent's backhand. She retired from competition tennis in 1893 partly, it was said, through boredom and partly through a desire to try her hand at other sports.

Lottie Dod hit the ball fiercely but with little spin. She was not particularly tall—at 5 foot 6½ inches, she was slightly above medium height—nor obviously muscular, though she had powerful biceps, but her groundstrokes had the pace and authority of her male contemporaries. Her game was based on superb anticipation and footwork. To allow her greater mobility around the court, she wore shorter skirts than were fashionable. These, worn with black stockings and black shoes, and a white cricket cap, which emphasized her jet black hair and oval face, gave the initial impression of a tomboy, but off the court she dressed with elegance. Her main 'heresies' were adamant counselling that ground strokes should be taken just before the top of the bounce and that players should switch from a 'western' forehand grip to a pronounced backhand grip when switching wings. Six decades later her techniques became the norm. As a doubles player, she and her sister were among the first players to attack the net in tandem. In eleven years of tournament tennis she was defeated only five times in singles matches played on level terms.

Lottie Dod's interests widened in the early 1890s and she received much press attention as a cyclist. She began playing golf and entered the 1894 British ladies' championship but was defeated in an early round. It was one of the few sports for which she did not possess prodigious talent; her swing was mechanical and often involved contortions to avoid a slice. In the winter of 1895–6 she participated in a variety of winter sports at St Moritz. She negotiated the Cresta run and showed ability as a mountaineer, making an ascent of Piz Zupo (13,130 ft) in February 1896 with Elizabeth Main and a Swiss guide. Extending her European tour to Italy, she and some friends covered considerable distances by bicycle in a trip which took in Genoa, Florence, and Rome.

In 1898 Lottie Dod was defeated in the semi-final of the British ladies' golf championship at Great Yarmouth. While her play was immaculate from tee to green, erratic putting resulted in defeat by one hole. In the following year she lost again at the semi-final stage but recovered a few days later to defeat the leading Irish player, Elaine Magill, in an international match between England and Ireland. In 1904, at Troon, she won the ladies' championship, defeating May Hezlet on the final green before a raucous crowd of 5000, including hundreds of dock workers who had deserted the Clyde. She became an unofficial ambassador for British golf and competed in the American championship of the same year but lost in the first round. However, she succeeded in persuading many of the top American players, including the Curtis sisters, to visit Britain in 1905. In so doing she laid the foundations for what became the Curtis cup.

At the turn of the century Lottie Dod had underlined her versatility by making two appearances for the England hockey team. In March 1899 she played at inside right against Ireland on the Richmond athletic ground, where her adroit dribbling contributed to a 3–1 victory for the home side. In March 1900 at Ballsbridge she scored twice and impressed many with her reverse stickwork during an England victory by two goals to one.

In 1906 Dod began to concentrate on archery, and competed at the White City for the women's Olympic archery title in July 1908. She won a silver medal, losing narrowly to Sybil (Queenie) Newall. The event was debased by the absence of Alice Legh, and Lottie Dod can be counted as only the third strongest archer of her time.

At the outbreak of the First World War, Dod gained nursing qualifications and made repeated applications to be stationed in France, but was rejected for such duties because of her sciatica. However, her work at a military hospital near Newbury resulted in a Red Cross gold medal. In 1921 she settled in London, where she was active in musical circles. As a contralto she sang for many years with the London Oriana Madrigal Society and became its honorary secretary. In the late 1920s she became a member of the Bach Cantata Club under the baton of her close friend Charles Kennedy Scott.

In the mid-1930s Lottie Dod did much youth work. She taught piano and part singing to a group of Girl Guides in Whitechapel and assisted at many youth clubs in the East End. She was reluctant to leave London during the blitz but eventually settled at Westward Ho! with her unmarried brother William and served as lady president of the Royal North Devon Golf Club in 1949. She returned to live in Earls Court, London, in 1950. As her health declined she spent much time in nursing homes on the south coast of England. She died (unmarried), following a fall, at Birch Hill Nursing Home, Sway, Hampshire, on 27 June 1960. Her attendant reported that she was listening to radio commentary from Wimbledon at the time. She must be counted as one of the most remarkable female athletes of all time.   JEREMY MALIES

Sources Lottie Dod scrapbook, All England Lawn Tennis and Croquet Club, Wimbledon, London, Kenneth Ritchie Library • J. Pearson, *Lottie Dod: champion of champions* (1988) • A. Little, *Lottie Dod: Wimbledon champion and all-rounder extraordinary* (1983) • b. cert. • d. cert. • *DNB* • *The Times* (28 June 1960) • *CGPLA Eng. & Wales* (1960)
Archives All England Lawn Tennis and Croquet Club, Wimbledon, London, Kenneth Ritchie Library, scrapbook
Likenesses photograph, 1886, Wimbledon Lawn Tennis Museum [*see illus.*] • W. & D. Downey, photograph, repro. in W. Downey, *The cabinet portrait gallery*, 3 (1892), facing p. 92 • photograph, Hult. Arch. • photographs, repro. in Pearson, *Lottie Dod*
Wealth at death £24,013 3s. 6d.: probate, 10 Aug 1960, *CGPLA Eng. & Wales*

Dod, Henry (*fl.* **1583?–1620**), poet and merchant, was of the old family of Dod, or Doddes, the son of Peter Dod of Smithes Pentrey, Broxton, in Cheshire, and Anne, daughter of Hugh Carrington of Over, in Cheshire. He versified nine psalms 'into English meter fitting the common tunes', and at the request of certain friends, as he writes, he published them in 1603 as *Certaine Psalmes of David in Meter*. The undertaking was sanctioned by James I, and the impression was quickly sold. Afterwards, at the request of some of the puritan clergy, Dod undertook a metrical recast of the entire psalter, published as *Al the Psalmes of David, with Certaine Songes and Canticles*. It is dedicated to John Brewen (Bruen), John Dod of Tussingham, and John Dod of Broxon, all of Cheshire. It has no name of author, printer, or place. It is dated 1620, and the initials H. D. are appended to its 'Address to the Christian Reader'. It was perhaps printed abroad, and Wither, who is scornful of the quality of the verse, was possibly right when he said it was condemned in England by authority to the fire. With it Dod printed his metrical version of the act of parliament for ordering a Gunpowder Plot thanksgiving service.

Dod is described as a 'mercer' (*Pedigrees*) and Wither calls him 'Dod the silkman'. He is unlikely to have been the Henry Dod who was incumbent of Felpham, Sussex, in 1630: the record of matriculation of this particular Dod into Corpus Christi College, Oxford, gives his year of birth as approximately 1592. He may very likely be the 'H. D.' for whom Gregory Seaton printed *A Treatise of Faith and Workes* in 1583. Nothing is known of his death; he had four sons.

JENNETT HUMPHREYS, *rev.* CHRISTOPHER BURLINSON

Sources STC, 1475–1640 · G. J. Armytage and J. P. Rylands, eds., *Pedigrees made at the visitation of Cheshire, 1623*, Lancashire and Cheshire RS, 58 (1909) · T. Corser, *Collectanea Anglo-poetica, or, A ... catalogue of a ... collection of early English poetry*, 5, Chetham Society, 91 (1873) · G. Wither, *The schollers purgatory* [n.d., 1625?] · Foster, *Alum. Oxon.*

Dod, John (1550–1645), Church of England clergyman, was born in March 1550 at Shocklach, Cheshire, and baptized there on 15 March 1550, the youngest of seventeen children. He was educated at Chester School and Jesus College, Cambridge, graduating BA in 1576. In 1578 he was appointed a fellow; in 1579 he proceeded MA and in 1580 he was ordained priest at Ely. While under suspicion of fraud at college he fell ill and converted to godly religion—or puritanism as his opponents would have described it. Calvinist predestinarianism was the prevailing norm, but puritans claimed to be able to achieve a degree of assurance of elect status. As Dod's contemporary hagiographer Samuel Clarke explained 'the Lord sealed to him that his sins were washed away' (Clarke, *Generall Martyrologie*, 404). He befriended the Elizabethan reformer Thomas Cartwright, who was later to make him and Arthur Hildersham his literary executors; Dod preached Cartwright's funeral sermon. He joined a conference of Cambridge academics dedicated to scriptural study—William Fulke, Laurence Chaderton, and William Whitaker—and commenced his preaching career first as university lecturer then as lecturer to a godly congregation at Ely.

Dod was one of a handful of seventeenth-century puritan leaders with national standing. Cartwright described him as 'the fittest man in England for a pastoral office' (Clarke, *Lives of Thirty-Two English Divines*, 319), and Chaderton duly recommended him to Anthony Cope for his living of Hanwell, Oxfordshire. He resigned his fellowship in 1585, but always stayed in touch with his alma mater. At Hanwell, Dod practised a piety which treated parochial observances merely as the starting point for an entire evangelical puritan way of life. Preaching twice every sabbath was insufficient; he also read a lecture on Wednesdays, conducted catechism classes, and led a combination of ministers—including Robert Cleaver, Robert Harris, William Scudder, and William Whately—who preached at Banbury, ordered public fasts, and acted as a seminary. He enjoyed much godly kudos as a spiritual physician to assuage deathbed doubts about election—performing this service for Thomas Peacock in 1611. Godly dynasticism is seen at work in Dod's choice of a bride, Ann

Bownd, sister of the sabbatarian controversialist Nicholas Bownd, and stepdaughter of Richard Greenham. They had twelve children, two of whom, Timothy *Dod and John, became divines. In 1604 puritan aspirations to national reformation under a new, Calvinist monarch suffered a serious set-back. James I placated moderate puritans, but Dod and other hardliners rejected the proffered compromise—subscription to Whitgift's three articles as the price of latitude on the observation of ceremonial conformity—and as a result Bishop Bridges of Oxford suspended him from Hanwell about 1604 and ejected him by March 1607. The tight collegiality of his following is shown by the seamless transition that was made to the ministry of his pupil Harris.

On the run Dod tried to eke out a living at Fenny Compton, Warwickshire, before being invited to Northamptonshire by Sir Erasmus Dryden (the grandfather of the poet), who shielded him at Canons Ashby, which was little more than a private chapel. From here Dod and Cleaver evangelized the surrounding parishes between 1606 and 1611. Archbishop Abbot of Canterbury, who respected Dod, at first took no action, and this facilitated the production between 1605 and 1615 of Dod's and Cleaver's phenomenal *œuvre*, although their most enduring work on the ten commandments (*A Plaine and Familiar Exposition of the Ten Commandements*, which had nineteen editions between 1603 and 1635, and which led to Dod's being nicknamed Decalogue Dod) had been produced at Hanwell. Three of the works were dedicated to Dryden and a further one to Lord John Harrington of Rutland; several were edited by John Winston of Ashby. Their work constitutes the most cogent explication not only of the religious observances of the community of the saints but of a distinctly godly code of ethics pervading every aspect of life: marriage, the household, the calling, dealings with the unregenerate mass. The convert was to reject his previous values and rely on the godly: 'Vicinitie and neighbourhood will faile, and alliance will fail, but grace and religion will never faile' (Dod and Cleaver, 119). Their sabbatarianism was particularly uncompromising. In an age when the book trade was crucial to disseminating ideas, this output explains the great scope of Dod's influence: both John Bunyan and Nehemiah Wallington possessed a copy of his work on the decalogue.

James I shattered this peaceful existence by requiring a reluctant Archbishop Abbot to interrogate Bishop Dove of Peterborough concerning Dod's unlicensed preaching in Northamptonshire and, under the wing of Lord Harrington, in Rutland. It was not until James's reiteration of the demand in 1614 that Dove took action and Dod was forced into hiding: the sympathy he aroused in Abbot and other moderates such as James Ussher was inadequate protection. (Dod, Ussher, and Ezechiel Culverwell had held a fast in 1612 on the day of Prince Henry's funeral, who was thought to be more sympathetic to the godly.) Dod was closely linked with London puritanism. On Ann's death he married a Miss Cleiton of Stratford-le-Bow at some date between 1607 and 1621. Before so doing he consulted the puritan minister Stephen Egerton of Blackfriars; and the ceremony was conducted by another godly friend, William Gouge. Dod also established contact with the Cambridge puritan leaders Richard Sibbes and John Preston, and in 1616 he approved Henry Jacob's formation of a semi-separatist church at Southwark. By the 1620s he was participating (with Preston and Thomas Hooker) in the quasi-exorcism of Joan Drake of Surrey. This backfired, initially at least, as the patient collapsed in gales of laughter comparing the heavily bearded Dod to Ananias, the fanatical puritan of Ben Jonson's *Alchemist*. This was strangely appropriate, as the playwright had heard of Dod and had previously told a joke about a gentlewoman who longed for sexual intercourse with the preacher 'for the procreation of an Angel or Saint' but it proved 'an ordinary birth' (Collinson, 'Ben Jonson', 158). On James I's death in 1625 Abbot lifted Dod's suspension from preaching, but he was probably never required to subscribe, a singular favour. He now began to enjoy the patronage of the Drydens' godly neighbours, the Knightleys of Fawsley. Richard Knightley in 1625 installed him as the *de facto* vicar while another minister was titular incumbent. Dod remained at this essentially private chapel for the rest of his life, free to practise his own brand of semi-separatism as the patriarch of a godly enclave.

Through Preston and Knightley, Dod was now linked with a puritan network in the midlands centred on William Fiennes, first Viscount Saye and Sele, which led opposition to crown policies from the 1620s onwards. Dod demonstrated his opposition to prerogative taxation by preaching a sermon at London's Fleet prison to stiffen the resolve of Sir Francis Barrington, the first to refuse to pay the forced loan of 1626. Preston retired to Fawsley to die in 1628; Dod received a special mention in his will and preached at the funeral. In the same year Dod again served as spiritual physician—this time for a dying minister called Throgmorton at Ashby. In 1630 Knightley set up a trust to support his protégé; trustees included Fiennes, Christopher Sherland, John Hampden, John Pym, John Crewe, Sir Nathaniel Rich, Edward Bagshaw, and Sir Arthur Hesilrige. In 1630–31 Dod operated as an intermediary between Sir Erasmus Dryden and Sir John Isham during their attempted negotiation of a marriage settlement for Dryden's grandson John (not the poet) and Isham's daughter Elizabeth. The breakdown was chiefly the result of disagreements over finance, but Isham perhaps also baulked at Dryden's insistence that he employ a godly household chaplain approved by Knightley and 'worthely beloved Mr Dodd' (Northants. RO, Isham correspondence, 184). Dod's own response to the Caroline emphasis on ceremonial conformity was predictably resolute: in 1633 Bishop Lindsell of Peterborough reported that he was preaching heresy, and at Archbishop Laud's visitation of 1635 he was described as having refused to conform since 1607. He must also have supported Knightley's failure to set up an east-end railed altar at Fawsley in 1637. However, a variety of godly responses were tolerated: when John Cotton was harassed by the courts in 1632

Dod condoned the young man's emigration. Growing disillusionment with several bishops was balanced by concerns at the sectarianism of the New England churches, which was deemed to pose a threat to ministerial authority. In 1637 Dod led a gathering of midlands clergy including his son Timothy, Cleaver, and Winston, Julines Herring, Simeon Ashe, Ephraim Huitt, and John Ball which controverted several points of colonial ecclesiology.

In 1637 Knightley appointed first John Wilkins, who was Dod's grandson by marriage, and then Dod himself as titular incumbent of Fawsley. Knightley, to whom Dod dedicated a grateful printed work in 1634, died in the same year, but his son and namesake continued to harbour the ageing evangelist, as he confirmed to another patron, Sir Robert Harley, in 1639. He also received the support of Lady Mary de Vere of London. Dod was harassed by royalist forces during the civil war, but continued to comfort his fellow professors; at the last he longed to be 'dissolved and to be with Christ' (Clarke, *Generall Martyrologie*, 416) and died at Fawsley, where he was buried on 19 August 1645. J. FIELDING

Sources A. J. Fielding, 'Conformists, puritans and the church courts: the diocese of Peterborough, 1603–1642', PhD diss., U. Birm., 1989, 15–17, 50, 67, 110, 114, 153–4 • T. Webster, *Godly clergy in early Stuart England: the Caroline puritan movement, c.1620–1643* (1997), 25, 28, 53, 66–8, 157, 234, 277, 284, 295, 301 • S. Clarke, *A generall martyrologie … whereunto are added, The lives of sundry modern divines* (1651), 404–16 • H. I. Longden, *Northamptonshire and Rutland clergy from 1500*, ed. P. I. King and others, 16 vols. in 6, Northamptonshire RS (1938–52), vol. 4, p. 107 • W. Haller, *The rise of puritanism: … the New Jerusalem as set forth in pulpit and press from Thomas Cartwright to John Lilburne and John Milton, 1570–1643* (1938); repr. (1947), 25, 74, 121, 131, 132, 54, 56–8, 61, 105, 119–20 • P. Collinson, *The religion of protestants* (1982), 111, 140–41, 268 • P. S. Seaver, *Wallington's world: a puritan artisan in seventeenth-century London* (1985), 5 • C. Hill, *A turbulent, seditious, and factious people: John Bunyan and his church* (1988), 142 • C. Hill, *The English Bible and the seventeenth-century revolution* (1993), 73, 158–61, 169, 257, 259, 292 • K. Fincham, ed., *The early Stuart church, 1603–1642* (1993), 7 • R. P. Cust, *The forced loan and English politics, 1626–1628* (1987), 232, 300–01 • K. Fincham, *Prelate as pastor: the episcopate of James I* (1990), 226 • R. Bolton, *The last conflicts and death of Mr Thomas Peacock, batchelour of divinity, and fellow of Brasennose Colledge in Oxford, published by E[dward] B[agshaw] from the copy of that famous divine, Mr. Robert Bolton, late minister of Broughton in Northampton-shire* (1646), 6, 30–44, 46 • S. Clarke, *The lives of thirty two English divines*, in *A general martyrologie*, 3rd edn (1677), 319 • J. Dod and R. Cleaver, *A plain and familiar exposition of the thirteenth and fourteenth chapters of the Proverbs of Salomon* (1609), 119 • parish register, Shocklach, Ches. & Chester ALSS • state papers domestic, Charles I, PRO, SP 16/251/25; 308/52 • 'Bownde or Bound, Nicholas', *DNB* • 'Egerton, Stephen', *DNB* • 'Gouge, William', *DNB* • P. Collinson, 'Ben Jonson's Bartholomew fair', *The theatrical city: culture, theatre, and politics in London, 1576–1649*, ed. D. L. Smith, R. Strier, and D. M. Bevington (1995), 157–8 • Northants. RO, Isham correspondence, 182–4, 186–8, 191, 193, 196–200 • *DNB*

Archives Jesus College, Cambridge, collection of divine aphorisms

Likenesses print, *c*.1661, repro. in J. Dod, *Ten sermons tending chiefly to the fitting of men for the worthy receiving of the Lord's supper*, ed. (1661) • T. Cross, line engraving, BM, NPG • print, repro. in S. Clarke, *A general martyrologie, containing a collection of all the greatest persecutions which have befallen the Church of Christ*, 3rd edn (1677)

Dod, Peirce (1683–1754), physician, was born probably at Hackney, Middlesex, the fourth of the five sons of John

Dod, citizen and mercer of London, and of his wife, Mary, daughter of Richard Thorowgood, alderman of London (Bodl. Oxf., MS Rawl., 4, fol. 276; D. Lysons, *The Environs of London*, 4 vols., 1792–6, 2.471). Dod matriculated at Brasenose College, Oxford, on 19 March 1697, and graduated BA on 14 October 1701. He was elected a fellow of All Souls in 1703, and graduated MA on 6 June 1705, MB on 22 March 1710, and MD on 29 October 1714. He was admitted a candidate of the Royal College of Physicians on 30 September 1719, and a fellow on 30 September 1720; he was Goulstonian lecturer in 1720, Harveian orator in 1729 (his oration was published at London in the same year), and censor in 1724, 1732, 1736, and 1739. He was appointed physician to St Bartholomew's Hospital on 22 July 1725, and continued in that office until his death. He became a fellow of the Royal Society on 19 March 1730, and contributed two papers to the *Philosophical Transactions*.

Dod and his wife, Elizabeth, had four children, Peirce (d. 1797), Jacky, Elizabeth (d. 1802), and another daughter, who died in Dod's lifetime. The eldest son, Peirce, was vicar of Godmersham, Kent, from 1772 to 1778.

Dod was a steady opponent of smallpox inoculation, and sought to discredit the new practice in a little work entitled *Several cases in physick, and one in particular, giving an account of a person who was inoculated for the small-pox … and yet had it again* (1746). This pamphlet presents nine case histories, only one of which addresses inoculation. In that particular case, a boy of three was inoculated and two years later, at the age of five, he contracted natural smallpox. Dod concluded from this single incident that inoculation did not provide effective protection against smallpox. Dod did not witness this case personally; it was reported to him in a letter from a Dr Brodrepp, a name which came to be satirized in *A letter to the real and genuine Pierce Dod, MD, exposing the low absurdity of a late spurious pamphlet falsely ascrib'd to that learned physician: with a full answer to the mistaken case of a natural small-pox, after taking it by inoculation, by Dod Pierce, MS* (1746). According to Munk, the authors of this letter—which is said to have done considerable damage to Dod's professional reputation and practice—were Dr J. Kirkpatrick, author of *The Analysis of Inoculation*, Dr W. Barrowby, and Dr I. Schomberg. They dismissed Dod's narrative first by pointing out that occasionally an individual succumbed to natural smallpox twice, and by contending that the boy's illness at the age of five was probably not smallpox. They implied that Dod opposed inoculation because it cost him business, and described Dod as 'This delirious Scribbler … violently infected with the itch of Authorism' (Lawrence, 223).

Dod died at his house in Red Lion Square, London, on 6 August 1754 (Munk wrongly gives the date as 18 August). He was buried in the ground of St George the Martyr, Queen Square. In the church is an altar tomb to his memory.   GORDON GOODWIN, *rev.* ANDREA RUSNOCK

Sources Munk, *Roll* · Foster, *Alum. Oxon.* · will, PRO, PROB 11/810, sig. 225 [affidavit appended to will] · *GM*, 1st ser., 24 (1754), 387 · S. C. Lawrence, *Charitable knowledge: hospital pupils and practitioners in eighteenth-century London* (1996), 223

Dod, Robert Phipps (d. 1865). *See under* Dod, Charles Roger Phipps (1793–1855).

Dod, Timothy (d. 1665), clergyman and ejected minister, was a son of John *Dod (1550–1645), clergyman, and his first wife, Ann Bownd. He matriculated in 1612 from Emmanuel College, Cambridge, where he graduated BA in 1616 and proceeded MA in 1619. He, or a namesake, was admitted to the University of Leiden on 3 June 1620. He was married to Jane Combes, widow of the London haberdasher Richard Combes, some time before 1642. It is likely that he was a lecturer in Daventry, Northamptonshire, in the 1630s as Mr Samuel Sutton of the town, who died in 1636, left him 10s. in his will to preach his funeral sermon. In mid-1637 Timothy was one of the signatories of a document containing nine questions to the clergy of New England concerning church government. It is reported that Dod was publicly ordained in Daventry some time after 1640. He became the afternoon lecturer and because he was a very popular preacher the residents of the town contributed £40 per annum to his income.

Some time in 1644 Dod went to London. On 25 July 1644 he was admitted interim rector of St Peter Westcheap and in October was appointed by the Westminster assembly to the examining body of twenty-three City presbyterian ministers responsible for approving and ordaining candidates for the ministry, set up in response to a parliamentary ordinance and the perceived lack of properly educated and competent ministers. On 20 March 1645 he became vicar of Daventry, but was removed in 1646, when in January he was confirmed as rector of St Peter Westcheap, where one John Dod was among the ruling elders. His stay in London proved to be short because he informed his congregation in June 1646 that he was returning to Daventry, although he remained at St Peter's until Easter 1647. During the years of the protectorate Dod remained active in Northamptonshire and in August 1654 became an assistant to the commissioners responsible for ejecting 'Scandalous, Ignorant and Insufficient Ministers and Schoolmasters' (Firth and Rait, 2.982). The famous and much-repeated story told about Dod is that he was so corpulent in his later years that he could not mount the pulpit, so had to preach either from a pew or sitting behind a desk.

In 1662 Dod seems again to have been officiating as lecturer in Daventry. His wife died there that summer and was buried on 26 August. Simultaneously, as the Act of Uniformity was enforced, Dod was ejected from his place. He became very ill with gout and other ailments. He eventually moved to Everdon, where he died on 12 December 1665 and was buried. His son John, a clergyman of Hinton, was granted administration of his estate the following month.   KENNETH GIBSON

Sources *Calamy rev.*, 166 · A. Argent, 'Aspects of the ecclesiastical history of the parishes of the City of London, 1640–49, with special reference to the parish clergy', PhD diss., U. Lond., 1983 · C. H. Firth and R. S. Rait, eds., *Acts and ordinances of the interregnum, 1642–1660*, 3 vols. (1911) · H. I. Longden, *Northamptonshire and Rutland clergy from 1500*, ed. P. I. King and others, 16 vols. in 6, Northamptonshire RS (1938–52) · J. Bridges, *The history and antiquities of Northamptonshire,* ed. P. Whalley, 2 vols. (1791) · *Walker rev.*, 61 · Tai Liu, *Puritan London: a study of religion and society in the City parishes* (1986), 71

Dodd [*née* Barnes], **Anne** (*c*.1685–1739), pamphlet shop keeper, was born Anne Barnes, but nothing is known of her before her marriage, on 18 March 1708, to the stationer Nathaniel Dodd, the licence allegation describing her merely as a spinster of St Bride's parish, London, aged upwards of twenty-two years. The couple were married in St Bride's and apparently lived in the parish for the next four years, two of their children being baptized there.

In February 1708, just before his marriage, Nathaniel Dodd had purchased the freedom of the Stationers' Company, but what trade he or his wife carried on during these early years is not known. Some time in late 1711 or early 1712, however, the Dodds moved to the sign of the Peacock without Temple Bar in St Clement Danes parish where they established what quickly became, and for forty years remained, the best-known pamphlet shop in London.

By law any wife's business was then legally her husband's, and this makes it difficult to determine whose business the shop really was. Nathaniel Dodd, testifying in 1718 after one of the many arrests which such a business involved, speaks of himself taking the offending newspaper, Mist's *Weekly Journal*, from the printer and supplying copies to a subsidiary distributor, while others later describe being his servant, or taking receipts from him. However, the shop itself is generally referred to as kept by Mrs Dodd, and even the witness who claimed to serve Mr Dodd testified that it was Dodd's wife who was the 'retailler of newspapers and pamphlets commonly called a Mercury' (PRO, SP 35/28/18, 12 Aug 1721).

Whatever her husband's role, it was always Anne Dodd's name which appeared on the imprints of the hundreds of newspapers and pamphlets advertised as for sale at the Peacock. And even if for the first decade Anne Dodd was merely the nominal proprietor, all that changed with Nathaniel's early death in October 1723. Thereafter Anne had sole charge of the business, and the fact that it continued to prosper for three more decades strongly suggests that she had always been perfectly capable of running things on her own.

Anne Dodd's success and renown should not, however, be confused with real importance in the publishing world, for she owned no copyrights and merely distributed those papers on which her name appeared, buying them in bulk from the actual publishers and supplying them wholesale to the hawkers or retail to the public. Pope's use of her imprint on the early editions of *The Dunciad* (almost certainly without her consent) was thus mere parodic obfuscation.

This subsidiary role did not, however, save Mrs Dodd from government harassment or even, in 1728, from imprisonment, though she pleaded in 1731 that:

> the business sometimes compels me to sell Papers that give Offense, but I must beg leave to Declare Sincerely that what Papers I sell in just Praise of our Happy Government, far exceed the other in Number. Hard Case! that I must either offend where I am shure I would not, or else starve my Poor Babes. (PRO, SP 36/23/134, 26 May 1731)

This was pure hyperbole for the youngest of Dodd's surviving 'Babes' was then at least seven and the eldest twenty-two. Nor were they near to starving, for when Anne Dodd died she left £500 to the children of her eldest daughter, Elizabeth, wife of the London surgeon Mileson Hingeston, and £600 each, besides jewellery and personal effects, to her two younger daughters, Anne and Sarah, who were also left the lease of the shop. They were strongly encouraged to carry on the business which continued, apparently unchanged, until the mid-1750s. Fielding's description in the *Covent Garden Journal* of 21 January 1752 of 'Mrs. Dodd's shop' with 'all that vast and formidable Host of Papers and Pamphlets arranged on her Shelves' might have portrayed any moment over the previous forty years, though Fielding's 'Mrs. Dodd' was the younger Anne Dodd (*fl.* 1739–1756), in whose name the business was carried on, and who is thus often confused with her more famous mother. The older Anne Dodd died in April 1739 and was buried on the 22nd at Enfield in Middlesex. MICHAEL TREADWELL

Sources H. R. Plomer and others, *A dictionary of the printers and booksellers who were at work in England, Scotland, and Ireland from 1726 to 1775* (1932) · H. R. Plomer and others, *A dictionary of the printers and booksellers who were at work in England, Scotland, and Ireland from 1668 to 1725* (1922) · M. Treadwell, 'London trade publishers, 1675–1750', *The Library*, 6th ser., 4 (1982), 99–134 · M. Harris, *London newspapers in the age of Walpole* (1987) · D. F. McKenzie, ed., *Stationers' Company apprentices*, [3]: 1701–1800 (1978) · Faculty Office marriage licence allegations, 16 March 1708, LPL · parish register, London, St Bride's, Fleet Street, 18 March 1708, GL [marriage] · parish register, London, St Bride's, Fleet Street, 19 Dec 1708, GL [baptism] · parish register, London, St Bride's, Fleet Street, 30 Sept 1711, GL [baptism] · parish register, London, St Clement Dane, City Westm. AC, 13 Sept 1716 [baptism] · parish register, London, St Clement Dane, City Westm. AC, 30 April 1718 [baptism] · parish register, Enfield, Middlesex, 25 Oct 1723, GL [burial] · parish register, Enfield, Middlesex, 22 April 1739, GL [burial] · Court books, 9 Feb 1708, Stationers' Hall, Stationers' Company Archives · PRO, state papers, domestic, SP35, 36 · will, PRO, PROB 11/695, sig. 76

Archives PRO, state papers, domestic, SP35/1/96,98; SP35/13/57,79,83; SP35/28/18; SP35/30/193; SP35/55/56; SP36/8/238; SP36/23/134; SP36/48/32; SP36/50/19

Wealth at death bequests of £1760 10*s*.; incl. plate, jewellery, household goods, lease of shop, and goodwill of business: will, PRO, PROB 11/695, sig. 76

Dodd, Catherine Isabella (1860–1932), educationist and author, was born on 8 April 1860 at Hyrwicks Lane, Aston, Birmingham, one of four children of Thomas Milner Dodd, a factor's clerk and commercial traveller in the hardware trade, and his wife, Christian Kelly of the Isle of Man. Encouraged by her father she aspired to university education, but financial problems diverted her to teaching through a pupil-teachership and a queen's scholarship to Swansea Training College. In addition she attended lectures at Mason's College, Birmingham, and Oxford summer schools, and gained the LLA of St Andrews University. After teaching experience in Wales, the midlands, and Hull she was appointed head of a board school in Reading. In 1892 she became the first mistress of method in the women's training department at Owens College in the Victoria University of Manchester, the first woman to become a member of the academic staff in the university,

Catherine Isabella Dodd (1860–1932), by Dorothy Stanton Wise, c.1911

subsequently gaining her MA degree and becoming lecturer in education.

Catherine Dodd's reputation as innovator rests on this Manchester period. She was determined to induct an early generation of young women undergraduates into the challenges and opportunities of university life through immersion in intellectual and social activity. Her colleague and admirer, Professor Samuel Alexander, described how she 'swept her students into the whirlwind of her own energy and enthusiasm and faith in the value of pedagogy' (*Manchester Guardian*, 17 Nov 1932). Students recalled how she 'made us enthusiastic about our profession, giving us ideals to strive for, and above all others, deserves the title of pioneer' (Wilson, 42). Dodd's judgement of an effective teacher is summed up in her observation, 'a teacher is a person who learns', and she valued above all else the stimulation of creativity and self-expression. She had a strong, even overpowering, personality, with a capacity for devoted friendship and deeply held resentments. Her great self-confidence, creative energy, and ability impressed her male colleagues, and with her friend, the like-minded Edith Wilson, tutor to women students, led initiatives to create debating, study, and drama societies, access to medical degrees, and a union for women students, and to develop heightened political and social awareness. She attended the 1896 International Women's Conference in Berlin and her radical, independent outlook is also seen in her Fabianism and extensive travels in central and eastern Europe exploring educational developments. Her profound belief in the movement for enlarged opportunities for women permeated her professional work and writing, but she does not seem to have been an activist in the suffrage movement.

Catherine Dodd's great contribution lies in an understanding of the nature and needs of childhood. The philosophy associated with the Froebelians had permeated English education slowly, but Dodd exploited the new position of authority provided by a university. She gained a national reputation for her training methods, particularly in encouraging teacher resourcefulness, self-evaluation, and experimentation. In 1903 she founded privately the experimental College House School at 223 Brunswick Street, Manchester, in which students played a key part and stimulated three influential books, *Introduction to the Herbartian Principles of Teaching* (1898), *Fairy Tales for Infant Schools and Infant Classes* (1904), and *The Child and the Curriculum* (1906). The school gained prestige when publicized by Michael Sadler in his *Visit to a School with a New Work* (1904). It was opened by Wilhelm Rein of Jena University who inspired Dodd to adopt the principles of J. F. Herbart (1776–1841) during her annual visits to Rein's internationally famous pedagogical seminar. Here the three elements of her educational credo came together—the centrality of the child, the need for a scientific approach to the process of learning and teaching, and a curriculum developed on rational principles. At Manchester she worked with W. H. Herford, of the influential Ladybarn School, and was a founder member of the Child Study and Teachers' Guild movements. Her beliefs were disseminated at conferences, in official reports, articles in such professional journals as the *Practical Teacher*, and in literary journals, notably the *National Review*, in which appeared her well-researched articles on children: twins, urban and rural differences, attitudes to gender, and role models. From Germany the influential idea of the 'school journey' evolved, an educational experience combining environmental, historical, and social components, and given official recognition in Sadler's *Special Reports on Educational Subjects* (1896), as was her major study, *Hungarian Education* (1902). Also inspired by continental experiences was *A Vagrant Englishwoman* (1905), in typically unpretentious, conversational style which disguised sharp observation and an underlying melancholy as it wove together attitudes to feminism and education and demonstrated her love of social interaction and mental stimulation. Her intense sensitivity to the natural world was also a link with those educators who saw in nature a metaphor for growth and development in the young.

The appointment of J. J. Findlay as professor of education in 1903 brought to Manchester a kindred spirit. Findlay studied at Jena and was the leading teacher trainer and advocate of child-centred methods. He aimed to reform the education department through a holistic process of training, derived from Rein and John Dewey and identical to that in Dodd's school. Unfortunately, their personalities clashed and Dodd moved in 1905 to the principalship of Cherwell Hall Training College at Oxford, where she had greater independence. The college was founded in 1902 and incorporated Milham Ford secondary and preparatory schools. This permitted Dodd to develop her work with young children and to extend it to the challenging field of training secondary school teachers. Her achievement was marked by visits in 1906 and 1911 by the president of the Board of Education, who praised 'the remarkable success' of the college. But it is noticeable that during this period less was heard of Dodd in the forum of educational ideas, and she became gradually conservative in politics and even lost confidence in education as a means of improving society, a tendency intensified by the First World War, to which she responded with great pessimism.

Catherine Dodd, who was unmarried, retired in 1920 and became immersed in literary activities in London. Her deeply personal novel *Apples and Quinces* (1929) charts the bitter-sweet lives of three women, and, while ending positively, is pessimistic about many aspects of social change. In a similar vein *Bells of Thyme* (1930) reworked the themes of *A Vagrant Englishwoman*. In contrast, *The Farthing Spinster* (1925), *Clad in Purple Mist* (1926), and *The Feildings of Startforth* (1932) grew from family connections and her love of historical episodes. The posthumously published *Eagle Feather* (1933) was her homage to Shelley and symbolizes her lifelong hatred of formalism and routine.

Catherine Dodd died at the Hospital of St John and St Elizabeth, Marylebone, London, on 13 November 1932 and was buried in Marylebone cemetery four days later. In 1931 she had endowed a fellowship in literature or philosophy at the University of Manchester and in her will gave bequests to a number of literary organizations.

A. B. ROBERTSON

Sources E. C. Wilson, *Catherine Isabella Dodd, 1860–1932: a memorial sketch* (1936) [incl. bibliography] · *The Times* (18 Nov 1932) · S. Alexander, *Manchester Guardian* (17 Nov 1932) · *Oxford Times* (25 Nov 1932) · A. B. Robertson, 'Catherine I. Dodd and innovation in teacher training, 1892–1905', *History of Education Society Bulletin*, 47 (1991), 32–41 · A. B. Robertson, *A century of change: the study of education in the University of Manchester* (1990), chaps. 1–3 · *The department of education in the University of Manchester, 1890–1911* (1911) [incl. bibliography] · R. J. W. Selleck, *The new education: the English background, 1870–1914* (1968) · b. cert. · d. cert.
Archives St Hilda's College, Oxford | JRL, archive of the council, senate and general administration · JRL, archive of Professor Samuel Alexander · University of Manchester, faculty of education, archive
Likenesses D. S. Wise, medallion, c.1911, repro. in Wilson, *Catherine Isabella Todd*, frontispiece [see illus.] · photograph, repro. in *The department of education in the University of Manchester*, 32
Wealth at death £16,463 11s. 1d.: probate, 28 Dec 1932, CGPLA Eng. & Wales

Dodd, Charles [*formerly* Hugh Tootel] (1672–1743), Roman Catholic priest and historian, was born Hugh Tootel at Durton in Broughton, near Preston, Lancashire. He was confirmed in the Roman Catholic church at Euxton Burgh Chapel, the property of the Dalton family, on 13 September 1687, by Bishop John Leyburn, vicar apostolic of the London district. After studying with his uncle, the Revd Christopher Tootel of Ladywell Chapel at Fernyhalgh, Lancashire, he was sent to the English College at Douai, where he arrived on 23 July 1688, and studied philosophy. On 16 July 1690 he was matriculated and took the college oath. While a student in France he adopted the name

Charles Dodd to protect his father from a fine levied on Catholic families who sent their sons to continental schools and colleges. On 22 September 1690 he received minor orders at Cambrai from James Theodore de Bayes. Dodd then studied divinity under Dr Hawarden at Douai for three years until 1693, when he was admitted into the English seminary of St Gregory at Paris, where after four additional years of theological study he took the degree of BD. He then returned to Douai, where he stayed until May 1698, when he came upon the English mission, and had the charge of a congregation at Fernyhalgh, Lancashire. Before 1718 Dodd had decided to write a church history of England, presenting a view more favourable to the Catholic case as an antidote to the protestant history of Bishop Burnet. He left for Douai in 1718 to begin his researches, and spent the next four years travelling in Europe visiting various Catholic institutions in search of material. He was assisted by the Revd Edward Dicconson, vice-president of the college of Douai, and Dr Ingleton of the Paris seminary.

On his return to England, John Talbot Stonor, vicar apostolic of the midland district, recommended Dodd in August 1722 to Sir Robert Throckmorton, bt, as a suitable assistant to Mr Bennett, in the charge of the congregation at Harvington, Worcestershire, to which Dodd succeeded on Bennett's death in September 1726. While living at Harvington, Dodd arranged his materials, and finished his great work, *The Church History of England from 1500 to 1688* (1737–42). The cost of its publication was in a great measure met by Edward, duke of Norfolk, Sir Robert Throckmorton, Cuthbert Constable, and bishops Stonor and Hornyold. This history bears the imprint of Brussels, but was believed to have been printed in England, as both type and paper are English made. The attribution to Brussels may have been motivated by the prohibition against the printing of Catholic material which operated in Britain at the time. The work was favourable to English Catholics, but hostile to the regular clergy, and it involved Dodd in controversy with both the Jesuits and the Church of England.

Dodd died on 27 February 1743 at Harvington and on 1 March was buried at Chaddesley Corbett, Worcestershire. The Revd James Brown, who attended him in his last illness, made a solemn protestation in writing to the effect that Dodd on his deathbed expressed an earnest desire to die in charity with all mankind, and particularly with the Society of Jesus, of whom he had been critical. Dodd is said to have left some sixty-four written works both published and in manuscript. In the late eighteenth and early nineteenth centuries plans for continuation of his history were made by the Revd Thomas Eyre, the Revd John Kirk, and the Revd Mark Tierney, but none of these projects was completed.

THOMPSON COOPER, *rev.* ALEXANDER DU TOIT

Sources C. Butler, *Historical memoirs of the English, Irish, and Scottish Catholics since the Reformation*, 3rd edn, 4 (1822), 451–3 · C. Butler, *Reminiscences*, 4th edn, 1 (1824), 319–22 · J. Chambers, *Biographical illustrations of Worcestershire* (1820), 591–7 · C. Hardwick, *History of the borough of Preston and its environs* (1857), 664 · *Catholicon*, 3 (1816),

120–23 • *Catholicon*, 4 (1817), 120–22 • *Catholicon*, 5 (1817–18), 60–61 • P. Whittle, *The history of the borough of Preston*, 2 (1837), 207–8 • *Dublin Review*, 6 (1839), 395–415 • *Catholic Miscellany*, 6 (1826), 250–63, 328–33, 405–7 • H. Foley, ed., *Records of the English province of the Society of Jesus*, 2 (1875), 57–9 • H. Foley, ed., *Records of the English province of the Society of Jesus*, 4 (1878), 714 • H. Foley, ed., *Records of the English province of the Society of Jesus*, 7/1 (1882), 384–5 • *N&Q*, 2 (1850), 347, 451 • *N&Q*, 3 (1851), 476 • *N&Q*, 4 (1851), 11 • W. T. Lowndes, *The bibliographer's manual of English literature*, ed. H. G. Bohn, [new edn], 2 (1864), 654–5 • *The miscellaneous works of the Rt Hon. Sir James Mackintosh* (1851), 304–5

Archives Bodl. Oxf., copy of *Certramen utriusque ecclesiae* (1724) with MS notes, MS 29220

Dodd, Charles Harold (1884–1973), biblical scholar, was born on 7 April 1884 at Wrexham, Denbighshire, the eldest of a family of four sons of Charles Dodd, headmaster of Brookside School, and his wife, Sarah, daughter of Edward Parsonage of Wrexham. The family's love of learning and its deep involvement in the life of the local Congregational chapel were strong formative influences on Dodd as a boy, although it was on his own initiative that he learned Welsh. He was educated in Wrexham (of which in 1963 he became an honorary freeman), first at his father's school and then at Grove Park secondary school. In 1902 he went to University College, Oxford, with an open scholarship in classics; he achieved a first in honour moderations (1904) and in *literae humaniores* (1906). Later the college made him an honorary fellow (1950).

In 1907 Dodd was elected a senior demy of Magdalen College, Oxford, and started research in early Christian epigraphy, but in less than a year he put his academic future at risk by entering Mansfield College, Oxford, to be trained for the ministry of the Congregational church. After being ordained in 1912 he served for three years as the minister of Brook Street Church, Warwick, before being recalled to Oxford to succeed James Moffatt at Mansfield College, as Yates lecturer (and subsequently professor) in New Testament Greek and exegesis. This appointment in 1915 launched him on a life of scholarship so free of major crises that his bibliography is virtually his biography.

The years 1915–30 were Dodd's great Oxford period, during which the first of his twenty books were published (*The Meaning of Paul for Today*, 1920, *The Authority of the Bible*, 1928) and many of the themes of his later writings adumbrated. As Grinfield lecturer on the Septuagint (1927–31), he developed the consuming interest in the background of early Christianity and the meticulous handling of language which characterized all his work. Two papers in this period (1923 and 1927) contained the germ of his most influential contribution to the interpretation of the New Testament. His revolutionary affirmation that the kingdom of God is a present reality in the ministry of Jesus came to be known as 'realized eschatology' and won wide acceptance, more popularly through his *The Parables of the Kingdom* (1935). Aberdeen University crowned this phase of Dodd's career with its honorary DD, the first of no less than eleven honorary degrees: from Oxford (DD and DLitt), Cambridge, London, Manchester, Glasgow, Wales,

Harvard, Oslo, and Strasbourg. Curiously, the British Academy failed to make him a fellow until 1946.

In 1930 Dodd moved to Manchester to succeed A. S. Peake in the Rylands chair of biblical criticism and exegesis and his new professorial duties gave him more time for his own books. These included the classic Moffatt Commentary, *The Epistle to the Romans* (1932), *The Bible and the Greeks* (1935), and *The Apostolic Preaching and its Developments* (1936), a little masterpiece culled in haste from his Manchester lectures, which for the first time demonstrated an oral tradition behind the New Testament epistles.

In 1935 Dodd succeeded F. C. Burkitt as the Norris–Hulse professor of divinity in Cambridge and so became the first non-Anglican since the Restoration to hold a chair of divinity at either of the ancient universities. In 1936 he was elected a fellow (and in 1949 an honorary fellow) of Jesus College and immensely enjoyed the company at high table. During his fourteen years in Cambridge, Dodd turned his attention to the enigmatic character of the fourth gospel, although the magisterial scale of his investigations delayed the publication of the results until after his retirement. In *The Interpretation of the Fourth Gospel* (1953) he analysed the evangelist's relationship to his complex cultural milieu and in *Historical Tradition in the Fourth Gospel* (1963) he argued that the evangelist was independent of the other gospels and had access to unique historical material about the ministry of Jesus. The latter work was perhaps the greatest of his writings.

Dodd was always too enthusiastic a teacher and churchman to accept the view (especially prevalent in Cambridge) that popular lectures and broadcast talks were beneath the dignity of a scholar; since he nearly always wrote his lectures and published almost everything he wrote, a large number of small books (rarely equalled for their clarity) extended his influence far beyond the universities. It was this rapport with the wider public, as well as his formidable learning, which led to the most sustained enterprise of his whole career. No sooner had he retired from his Cambridge chair in 1949 than he was appointed the general director of the *New English Bible*. Those who considered this undertaking a misguided dissipation of Dodd's time and energy were quite mistaken. To observe him at work with the translation panels over a period of twenty years was to know beyond a doubt that it engaged all his gifts and fulfilled all his deepest aspirations. In 1961, the year when the New Testament was published, he was created CH, and in Westminster Abbey on 16 March 1970, less than a month from his eighty-sixth birthday and only four years before his own memorial service there, he had the immense satisfaction of presenting the completed translation to the queen mother and the representatives of the sponsoring churches. In the same year he published *The Founder of Christianity* (1970). This last book summed up his lifelong conviction that the quest for the historic Jesus lies at the core of New Testament scholarship.

Dodd was a tiny man (once the cox of his college boat), neat in dress, rapid in speech, and physically immensely energetic. Despite his strict puritan upbringing, he was tolerant and catholic in his sympathies and a leading figure in the ecumenical movement. In 1925 he married Phyllis Mary (d. 1963), the widow of John Elliott Terry and the daughter of George Stockings of Norwich. They had a son and a daughter. In his youth he had enjoyed organizing camps for boys and in his later years he took great pleasure in the company of his seven grandsons and two granddaughters. He spent his years of retirement in Oxford and died on 21 September 1973 in a nursing home at Goring-on-Thames.   E. W. HEATON, rev.

Sources F. W. Dillistone, C. H. Dodd (1977) · G. B. Caird, 'Charles Harold Dodd, 1884–1973', PBA, 60 (1974), 497–510 · R. W. Graham, Charles Harold Dodd, 1884–1973: a bibliography of his published writings, Lexington Theological Library Occasional Studies (1974) · CGPLA Eng. & Wales (1973)
Likenesses W. Stoneman, photograph, 1946, NPG · W. Bird, photograph, 1962, NPG · E. H. Nelson, oils, Jesus College, Cambridge
Wealth at death £7930: probate, 13 Dec 1973, CGPLA Eng. & Wales

Dodd, Daniel (fl. 1752–c.1780), painter, principally of portraits and fashionable scenes, also produced subject and flower paintings. He is first mentioned in the Daily Advertiser of 28 November 1752, as having etched a portrait of Mr Leveridge in the style of Rembrandt.

Dodd was a member of the Free Society of Artists, first exhibiting there in 1761. He continued to contribute many works to the same exhibition up to 1780 from various London addresses. His works were mainly portraits in crayon or oils on a small scale. Among them may be mentioned a portrait in crayon of Garrick between Tragedy and Comedy, portraits of Mr. Darley, Mr. Fielding, and of Buckhorse, the pugilist, 'the notorious bruiser' ('Anstey, Christopher', DNB), of whom he exhibited both a crayon and a mezzotint portrait in 1769.

Dodd was also known for his large scenes of fashionable life, crowded with figures, such as A View of the Ball at St. James's on Her Majesty's Birthnight (engraved by Tukey), A View of the Exhibition of the Royal Academy at Somerset House (engraved by William Angus), and The Royal Procession to St. Paul's, among others. He also provided grey wash illustrations for the Bible, the Novelist's Magazine, published by J. Harrison & Co., G. F. Raymond's A new, universal and impartial history of England … embellished with upwards of 120 beautiful copper-plate engravings, taken from the original drawings of Messrs. Metz, Stothard, and Samuel Wale esq. (c.1786), and other similar publications.

A pastel portrait by Dodd of Sir Watkin Lewes is in the National Portrait Gallery, London. The Victoria and Albert Museum possesses a wash drawing of Joseph George Holman, the actor. D. P. Dodd and Miss Dodd, who both exhibited with the Free Society of Artists, were his son and daughter. A 'Master Smart' exhibited as his pupil at the Free Society of Artists in 1780 and the miniaturist Thomas Day exhibited from 'Mr Dodds, Great Portland St' from 1768 to 1771 (Foskett, Miniatures, 525). Both are believed to have been his pupils.

L. H. CUST, rev. JILL SPRINGALL

Sources Graves, Soc. Artists · D. Foskett, A dictionary of British miniature painters, 2 vols. (1972) · H. Hammelmann, Book illustrators in eighteenth-century England, ed. T. S. R. Boase (1975) · Engraved Brit. ports. · B. Stewart and M. Cutten, The dictionary of portrait painters in Britain up to 1920 (1997) · Redgrave, Artists · Novelist's Magazine (1780), facing 16, 70, 157 [illustrations after engravings by D. Dodd] · D. Foskett, Miniatures: dictionary and guide (1987) · Daily Advertiser [London] (28 Nov 1752)

Dodd, Edward (1704/5?–1810), musical instrument maker, was probably born in Northumberland in 1704 or 1705 (although Sheffield has also been suggested) and was probably either the son of John Dodd baptized at Simonburn, Northumberland, on 19 November 1704, or the son of Edward Dodd, baptized at Chollerton, Northumberland, on 19 April 1705. Considering his longevity, there are surprisingly few surviving details of his life. The first record of him in city directories, as a bow maker, is from 1802 to 1807, when he was at 11 Paradise Road, Lambeth, although he was probably resident in London by the early 1780s. From Lambeth he moved to the parish of St Bride, Fleet Street, 'whose archives record his death at the age of 105' (Beare and Kass). He died in London on 1 April 1810 and was apparently buried at St Bride's. Edward has been credited with many of the unmarked 'transitional' bows from the eighteenth century that bridge the gap between the baroque and the modern bow developed in late eighteenth-century France by François Xavier Tourte. However, it is possible that he did not make bows before his arrival in London and probable that his output has been vastly over-estimated.

Dodd's son **John Dodd** [called Kew Dodd] (1752–1839), often referred to as the English Tourte, continued the family tradition and remains historically important for his contributions to the evolution of the bow, which may or may not have occurred independently of French advancements. John was baptized at Simonburn, Northumberland, on 28 December 1752 (which may also have been the day of his birth), and became a gunlock fitter and a money scale maker before turning to bow making with his father, probably from the 1780s. Active in the London area, he apparently lived in Southwark, Lambeth, Kew (during the early nineteenth century), and then Richmond, Surrey. His intemperate tendencies are said to have brought financial difficulties, often forcing him to place productivity over quality and ultimately, despite generous friends, landing him in Richmond workhouse. He died in Richmond on 4 October 1839.

Although his craftsmanship was not as consistent as that of Tourte, John Dodd is still considered 'the greatest English bowmaker before Tubbs' (Beare and Kass). His bows 'often have ivory frogs with "DODD" stamped on the frog or stick' (Harvey, 333), although there are also many unauthentic examples with these characteristics. Dodd's later bows made use of all the continental innovations, and his cello bows in particular were favoured among late twentieth-century players. Bows by Edward and John Dodd are in the Hill collection of musical instruments at the Ashmolean Museum, Oxford, and bows by Edward Dodd in the Smithsonian Institution, Washington, DC.

Thomas *Dodd (d. 1834), an instrument dealer who ran successful businesses in Covent Garden, Charing Cross, and Berners Street, London, and James Dodd (c.1761–1833) were also sons of Edward. James worked as a bow maker with his father in Lambeth and had two sons, James *Dodd (1792–1865) and Edward (1797–1851), both of whom continued to work in the family business.

DAVID J. GOLBY

Sources C. Beare and P. J. Kass, 'Dodd (i)', *New Grove*, 2nd edn · B. W. Harvey, *The violin family and its makers in the British Isles: an illustrated history and directory* (1995), 333–4 · R. Stowell, *Violin technique and performance practice in the late eighteenth and early nineteenth centuries* (1985) · V. Walden, *One hundred years of violoncello* (1998) · W. Sandys and S. A. Forster, *The history of the violin* (1864) · W. C. Retford, *Bows and bowmakers* (1964) · E. H. Fellowes, 'Dodd', Grove, *Dict. mus.* (1940) · *IGI*
Wealth at death in debt; John Dodd

Dodd, Francis Edgar (1874–1949), painter and etcher, was born in Upper Park Street, Holyhead, Anglesey, on 29 November 1874, the third son of the Revd Benjamin Dodd, a Wesleyan Methodist minister who had once been a blacksmith, and his wife, Jane Frances, daughter of Jonathan Shaw, cotton broker, of Liverpool. After his family had moved to Glasgow, Dodd attended Garnett Hill School. There in 1889 he began to learn painting. There he also met his future brother-in-law and lifelong friend the painter and etcher Muirhead Bone. While he worked as a china decorator with Messrs MacDougal he began to study at the Glasgow School of Art, winning the Haldane travelling scholarship of £100 per annum, which he eked out for eighteen months, in 1893. He went to Aman-Jean's academy in Paris but on the advice of J. A. M. Whistler he spent some time in Venice, studying Tintoretto, and visited Florence, Milan, and Antwerp.

In 1895 Dodd settled with his family at Manchester. His circle of acquaintance included the newspaper editor C. P. Scott and the literary scholar Oliver Elton, whose portraits he etched in 1916. He was closely associated with the artist Susan Isabel Dacre (1844–1933), who posed for his painting *Signora Lotto* (1906), now in Manchester City Galleries. She was also the model for some of his first drypoints as in *Looking at a Picture* (1907). He had absorbed something of the Glasgow school's impressionism and something of the style of the painter Alfred Stevens. At Manchester he began to explore the possibilities of painting suburban scenes. Works in various media were exhibited by him in the Manchester Academy, and in 1898 Bernhard Sickert invited him to exhibit with the New English Art Club. He became an active member of both institutions; the latter owed much to his skilful handling of its finances.

In 1901 Dodd went on the first of three visits to Spain, and in 1904 he settled in London. His friends at this period included Charles March Gere, Henry Lamb, and Henry Rushbury; all four later became Royal Academicians. Dodd began to exhibit at the Royal Academy in 1923, and was elected an associate in 1927 and Royal Academician in 1935. He was also a member of the Royal Society of Painters in Water Colours and of the Royal Society of Portrait Painters, and a trustee of the Tate Gallery (1929–35). As official artist to the Ministry of Information during the

Francis Edgar Dodd (1874–1949), self-portrait

First World War, Dodd made portraits of British naval and military commanders, and was afterwards attached to the Admiralty to carry out drawings of submarines. These are now in the Imperial War Museum. Portraits by him are in the National Portrait Gallery, London, at the Ashmolean Museum, Oxford, and at the Fitzwilliam Museum, Cambridge.

It was in his portraits that Dodd excelled as an etcher, above all in those of his brother artists. Direct, relaxed, and highly competent, the portraits reveal him as a master of his craft. Dodd got off to a flying start producing thirty-six plates in 1907 and 1908, among them the forceful image of his fellow etcher, *Bone at the Press*. In 1909 Dodd executed the drypoint which Bone considered 'a masterpiece', of the young sculptor Jacob Epstein. In 1915 he made twenty-three plates, the most he ever produced in a year, including David Muirhead seated at his easel, and the Lancastrian architect Charles Holden. Charles Cundall, in his studio (1926), was another of his best subjects. He did only eighteen plates after 1929, but he produced a total of 210. He gave a complete collection of his prints to the Ashmolean Museum in Oxford in 1948.

On 8 April 1911 Dodd married Mary Arabella (1871/2–1948), daughter of John Brouncker Ingle, a solicitor, of London. On 27 January 1949 he married, as his second wife, Ellen (Nell) Margaret (b. 1908/9), daughter of Charles Tanner, builder's assistant, of London. She had been his model for many years. There were no children by either marriage. Dodd gassed himself at his home at 51 Blackheath Park, Blackheath, Greenwich, and died on 7 March

1949. Examples of Dodd's work are in the Tate collection, the Victoria and Albert Museum, London, Manchester City Galleries, and the Hunterian Art Gallery, Glasgow.

BRIAN READE, *rev.* IAN LOWE

Sources K. Clements, *Henry Lamb the artist and his friends* (1985), 19–26 · K. Clements, MS account of Dodd, Man. City Gall. · *Manchester Guardian* (9 March 1949) · *The Times* (10 March 1949) · M. Bone, 'Francis Dodd RA', 1951, V&A, L.2401 11.IX. 1951 · R. Schwabe, 'Francis Dodd', *Print Collectors' Quarterly*, 13/3 (1926), 248–72 · R. Schwabe, 'Francis Dodd', *Print Collectors' Quarterly*, 13/4 (1926), 369–75 · F. Dodd, list of prints, AM Oxf. · F. Rutter, review of solo exhibition at James Connell & Sons gallery, *Sunday Times* (27 Feb 1927) · *Gloucestershire Echo* (3 Oct 1944) [review of retrospective exhibition at Cheltenham Art Gallery] · 'Francis Dodd centenary exhibition', (typescript), 1974–5, AM Oxf. · b. cert. · m. certs. · d. cert. · *CGPLA Eng. & Wales* (1949)
Archives AM Oxf., departmental files relating to accession of collection in 1948 and artist's MS handlist · Man. City Gall., departmental files and catalogue notes · Tate collection, departmental files and catalogue notes | BL, corresp. with C. E. Montague, Add. MS 45910 · U. Glas., letters to D. S. MacColl
Likenesses R. Schwabe, etching, 1916, NPG · S. Bone, oils, *c*.1936, Man. City Gall. · A. C. Cooper, photograph, *c*.1936, NPG · W. Stoneman, photograph, 1936, NPG · D. S. MacColl, pencil drawing, 1939, Athenaeum, London · F. Dodd, self-portrait, drawing, FM Cam. [*see illus.*] · F. Dodd, self-portrait, oils, FM Cam.
Wealth at death £11,984 6s. 3d.: probate, 28 May 1949, *CGPLA Eng. & Wales*

Dodd, George (*bap.* 1782, *d.* 1827), civil engineer, was baptized in Stepney, London, on 4 September 1782, the son of Ralph *Dodd, civil engineer, and his wife, Fanny, *née* Lambert. His father trained the boy in his own profession, and George served as his assistant on his Thames and Medway and Grand Surrey Canal schemes. George Dodd invented a form of gun lock in 1802, which he patented in 1805 and which was adopted by the Board of Ordnance.

About 1806 he began to promote a new crossing of the Thames, which was to become Waterloo Bridge. His design was exhibited at the Royal Academy in 1810. He was for a short time employed by John Rennie, but seems to have withdrawn from the project before the foundation stone was laid in 1811, the design and engineering work being handled thereafter by Rennie himself. From 1814 Dodd became involved with steamboats on the Thames, but after some initial success the fierce competition drove him out of the business.

Much depressed by this disappointment, and by the lack of interest in his patent for a means of extinguishing fires at sea, he took to drink and by September 1827 he was destitute. At his own request he was committed to the Giltspur Street compter and he died there on 25 September 1827. Nothing is known of his marriage, but he left a son and a daughter. ROBERT HUNT, *rev.* MIKE CHRIMES

Sources GM, 1st ser., 97/2 (1827), 468–9 · J. G. James, 'Ralph Dodd, the very ingenious schemer', *Transactions* [Newcomen Society], 47 (1974–6), 161–78 · R. Stuart [R. S. Meikleham], *Historical and descriptive anecdotes of steam-engines, and of their inventors and improvers*, 2 (1829), 534–6 · S. Snell, *A story of railway pioneers, being an account of the inventions of Isaac Dodds and his son Thomas Weatherburn Dodds* (1921) · G. W. Younger, 'Robert and Ralph Dodd, marine painters, and others of the name [pts 1–2]', *The Connoisseur*, 71 (1925), 73–80; 73 (1925), 87–94 · G. W. Younger, 'Robert and Ralph Dodd, marine

painters, and others of the name [pt 3]', *The Connoisseur*, 74 (1926), 35
Archives Inst. CE, J. G. James MSS
Wealth at death destitute: *GM*

Dodd, George (1808–1881), writer, was a journeyman author employed in supplying Victorian publications with the type of factual article for which there was a vast demand. Nothing is known of his parentage and education. During nearly half a century he was known as an industrious and painstaking writer. An aptitude for presenting statistics in an attractive form made him a useful assistant to the publisher Charles Knight. He wrote numerous articles on industrial art in the *Penny Cyclopaedia*, the *English Cyclopaedia*, and supplements. He edited and wrote much of the *Cyclopaedia of the Industry of All Nations* (1851). He contributed to the *Penny Magazine*, to *London*, to *The Land we Live in*, and to several other of Knight's serial publications. Some of his papers were collected and published in volumes, under the titles of *Days at the Factories, or, The Manufacturing Industry of Great Britain Described* (1843; repr. 1967) and *Curiosities of Industry* (1852). For Knight's *Weekly Volumes* he provided an account of *The Textile Manufactures of Great Britain* (6 vols., 1844–6). The work by which he was probably best known was an elaborate volume on *The food of London: a sketch of the chief varieties, sources of supply … and machinery of distribution, of the food for a community of two millions and a half* (1856). On Knight's retirement as a general publisher, Dodd joined Messrs Chambers, contributing to their serial publications. He also compiled *Chambers's Handy Guide to London* (1862) and *Chambers's Handy Guide to the Kent and Sussex Coasts* (1863). For over thirty years he contributed one or more papers annually to the *Companion to the* [British] *Almanac*. He also wrote on locks (1853), the Crimean War (1856), and the Indian 'revolt' (as he unusually called it) (1859), and he published two useful summaries of economic progress: *Railways, Steamers, and Telegraphs: a Glance at their Recent Progress and Present State* (1867) and *Dictionary of Manufactures, Mining, Machinery, and the Industrial Arts* (1871). Dodd was found dead at his home, 133 Torriano Avenue, Kentish Town, London, on 20 or 21 January 1881; his death was, the coroner noted, 'accelerated by cold weather'.

GORDON GOODWIN, *rev.* H. C. G. MATTHEW

Sources *The Athenaeum* (29 Jan 1881), 167 · *The Bookseller* (2 Feb 1881), 103 · Boase, *Mod. Eng. biog.* · d. cert. · *CGPLA Eng. & Wales* (1881)
Wealth at death under £800: probate, 4 Feb 1881, *CGPLA Eng. & Wales*

Dodd, Henry (1801–1881), refuse collector and philanthropist, was born in Hackney, Middlesex, on 27 October 1801, the son of William Dodd (*c*.1761–1846) and his wife, Mary. Little is known of his early years, but he claimed to have worked in his youth as a ploughboy. By the 1820s, however, Dodd had set up as a dust contractor, with premises at 14 Pump Row, Hoxton, London, from about 1826 to 1838, then at City Wharf, New North Road, Hoxton, from 1838 to his death. In this capacity he held cleaning contracts for the parishes of St Luke and St James's, Clerkenwell, and St Leonard, Shoreditch, in the 1850s. He became a major operator employing hundreds of men and horses, and gave evidence on London traffic to the select committee on metropolitan communications in 1854.

Dodd attributed his initial success to his satisfactorily clearing the streets after a heavy fall of snow had brought the city to a standstill. He invested his profits in brickfields in Islington and by the canal at Yeading, near Uxbridge, Middlesex, and he bought a number of canal boats and Thames barges in which he transported both bricks and rubbish. His interest in water transport led him in 1863 to initiate races for sailing barges as an inducement to owners to improve the build and equipment of their boats, and these became popular events. He ensured their continuation after his death by providing a trust fund in his will. He also funded ploughing matches in recognition of his agricultural origins.

A member of the Tylers' and Bricklayers' Company and a liveryman of the City of London, Dodd amassed a considerable fortune and used it for a variety of charitable causes. One of these projects brought him some notoriety rather than satisfaction, when in 1858 he offered 5 acres of land and 100 guineas to a committee which wished to build a home for retired and destitute actors. Because of a misunderstanding about the conditions of the offer, it was finally rejected at a meeting held at the Adelphi Theatre on 12 January 1859, and a somewhat acrimonious debate arose in the periodical press. Dodd was prompted to put his case in a pamphlet reproducing all the relevant correspondence. The idea of a retirement home came to fruition, but without Dodd's involvement, with the formation of the Royal Dramatic College at Maybury, near Woking, in 1860, but it had only a short life. Despite his unhappy experience, the incident brought Dodd immortality. It was during the negotiations that Dodd became known to Charles Dickens, a trustee of his proposed gift, who later used him as a model for Nicodemus Boffin, the Golden Dustman, in *Our Mutual Friend* (1865). It is not known what Dodd thought of the portrait.

In 1868 Dodd retired from the business, which was continued by his son William Henry Dodd. He lived quietly at The Hall, Rotherfield, near Crowborough, Sussex, until his death, devoting himself to the improvement of the house and grounds. He also spent time in Farnham Royal, Buckinghamshire, where his father had lived, and paid for a new organ for the rebuilt parish church and for a tower to be added. It was here that he chose to be buried in an elaborate mausoleum erected in his lifetime, which contained bas-reliefs of the ploughing and the sailing matches that he had promoted, and an inscription that attributed his successful career to 'his industry, integrity and perseverance'.

Dodd died on 27 April 1881 and was buried in the churchyard at St Mary's, Farnham Royal. He left a personal estate valued at more than £113,000, and in his will he made a number of bequests to charitable causes including orphanages both in England and on the continent, schools, and to the National Life Boat Society for a boat to be named after him. He left money to two sons and a daughter, but as he is not known to have been married, these children may have been adopted.   PETER HOUNSELL

Sources *Royal Dramatic College: correspondence respecting gift of land at Langley, Bucks by Mr Henry Dodd*, 2nd edn with additions (1859) · Boase, *Mod. Eng. biog.* · *The Builder*, 40 (1881), 567 · *ILN* (15 Oct 1881) [report of will] · C. R. Smith, *Retrospectives, social and archaeological*, 2 (1886) · F. C. Carr-Gomm, *Records of the parish of Farnham Royal, Bucks* (1901) · E. J. March, *Spritsil barges of the Thames and Medway* (1970) · 'Mr Dodd's dustyard', *Illustrated Times* (23 March 1861) [reprinted in J. Greenwood, *Unsentimental journeys* (1867)] · parish register, bishop's transcript, LMA [microfilm]
Wealth at death £113,267 5s. 5d.: resworn probate, June 1882, CGPLA Eng. & Wales (1881)

Dodd, James (1792–1865), bow maker, was born on 7 May 1792 in London, the eldest son of James Dodd (c.1761–1833) and grandson of Edward Dodd (1704/5?–1810), both of whom were bow makers. Details about his life are sparse, but he worked for a long period as a bow maker with his brother Edward Dodd (1797–1851), who made only violin strings after 1833. James, however, continued to make bows, mainly for the trade, until the year before his death. Those from the early part of his career, particularly the cello bows, are perhaps the finest examples of his work. John Dodd (1752–1839), his uncle, must have been an early influence, and James used the brand 'J. DODD' for many of his bows. He was probably also associated with early members of the Tubbs family. James won awards for his bows (and Edward for his strings) at the London exhibitions of 1851 and 1862. A photograph of a viola bow with gold and tortoiseshell mounts by Dodd, presented at the 1851 exhibition, is included in W. C. Retford's *Bows and Bow Makers* (1964, pl. X and XI).

Dodd died at Image Cottage, Holloway Road, Islington, on 19 December 1865, leaving a son, the Revd James Dodd.   DAVID J. GOLBY

Sources C. Beare and P. J. Kass, 'James Dodd', *The new Grove dictionary of musical instruments*, ed. S. Sadie (1984) · B. W. Harvey, *The violin family and its makers in the British Isles: an illustrated history and directory* (1995) · W. C. Retford, *Bows and bow makers* (1964) · W. Henley, *Universal dictionary of violin and bow makers*, 5 vols. (1959–60) · d. cert. · CGPLA Eng. & Wales (1866) · W. Sandys and S. A. Forster, *The history of the violin* (1864), 160
Wealth at death under £450: probate, 20 Feb 1866, CGPLA Eng. & Wales

Dodd, James Solas (1720/21–1805), surgeon and actor, was born in London, the son of Jago Mendozo Vasconcellos de Solis, and his wife, Rebecca, daughter of John Dodd. John Dodd was in 1719 commander of the *St Quintin*, a merchantman trading from London to Barcelona. At Barcelona he became acquainted with Don Jago, who, having had a duel with the son of the governor of Barcelona and left him for dead, took refuge in Dodd's ship, and sailed in it for London the same evening. Don Jago lodged at Captain Dodd's house and in 1720 married his host's daughter. On his marriage Don Jago took the name of Dodd in order to bequeath to his children a small estate near Newcastle upon Tyne. In 1727 Don Jago died in London, having failed to reconcile his father, Don Gaspard de Solis, to his marriage with a protestant, by which he lost his patrimony and commission.

Young Dodd received a good education, as it was his mother's wish that he should enter the church, but, in 1742, 'on some family reasons' he was apprenticed to John Hills, a surgeon practising in the Minories, London. In 1745 Dodd entered the navy as surgeon's mate of the hospital ship *Blenheim* and served until the end of the war in the *Devonshire* and the *St Albans*. He continued for some months after the peace in the *St Albans*, then stationed at Plymouth. Dodd took up his diploma as a member of the Company of Surgeons, London, in 1751, and practised in Gough Square, Fleet Street, and afterwards in Suffolk Street, Haymarket. In 1752 he published *An Essay towards a Natural History of the Herring*, written to promote the industry on the behalf of the Society of the Free British Fishery. He was indebted to Dr Thomas Birch for assistance in his literary projects (Dodd, his letter to Birch, 14 April 1752, BL, Add. MS 4305, fol. 2). The next year he took part in the great Canning controversy by publishing *A physical account of the case of Elizabeth Canning, with an enquiry into the probability of her subsisting in the manner therein asserted* (1753), in which he argues strongly for the truth of the girl's story. Towards the close of January 1754, 'on account of some deaths in his family', Dodd set out for the continent, returning in the following May. In 1759 he again entered the navy: 'came as supernumerary in the *Sheerness* from Leghorn to Gibraltar'; there he went on board the *Prince*, and served on her until June 1762. In the same year he qualified at Surgeons' Hall as master surgeon of any ship of the first rate, and was warranted for the *Hawke*, in which he served until she was paid off at the peace in February 1763. He then settled once more in London, 'chiefly', as he says, 'in the literary line'.

One of Dodd's literary undertakings was a series of lectures first delivered in 1766 in the great room of Exeter Exchange, and afterwards published with the title *A Satyrical Lecture on Hearts, to which is Added a Critical Dissertation on Noses* (1767). The reviewer of the book in the *Gentleman's Magazine* (37, 1767, 73–4) attributes to Dodd the authorship of a periodical essay published some years before under the title of 'The scourge'. On 7 February 1767 the house in which he lodged, adjoining the gateway of the Saracen's Head inn on Snow Hill, suddenly collapsed, but he and his family escaped with the loss only of their belongings. His wife's health being affected by this accident, Dodd left London and went to Bath and Bristol in order to hasten her recovery; from there he wandered to Ireland, where he 'followed his business and literary employments' in Dublin. In Ireland, Dodd published his *Essays and Poems* (1770) which claimed to contain 'A collection of all the Airs, Catches, Glees, Cantatas, and Roundelays … performed at Stratford upon Avon, on occasion of the Jubilee … in honour of Shakespeare' in 1769. The book also contains a first-hand account of the jubilee. On 9 October 1769 Dodd was engaged by William Parsons, manager of the Birmingham Theatre, to re-read Garrick's *Jubilee Ode to Shakespeare* (Highfill, Burnim & Langhans, *BDA*). In

March 1779 Dodd was invited to return to London. He brought with him a play, *The Funeral Pile* (originally entitled *Gallic Gratitude*), based largely on *Le naufrage* of Joseph de Lafont, which had just two performances at Covent Garden (30 April and 19 May 1779).

In 1781 Dodd became friendly with a Major John Savage, who styled himself Baron Weildmester, and had, he alleged, a number of claims on Lord North. Savage, on promising to defray all expenses, persuaded Dodd and his family to travel with him to Russia, where, he said, he had a plan to propose to the empress from a foreign power to enter into a treaty of alliance, and that he and Dodd were to act as ambassadors; Savage also proposed 'that Mrs. Dodd, &c. should remain under the czarina's protection, and that on their return they would be decorated with the order of St. Catherine & have 1,000*l*. a year pension'. Charmed with this proposal Dodd cheerfully bore the expense until Riga was reached, where he learned Savage's true character. Dodd soon joined a ship bound for Bowness on the Firth of Forth. He landed at Leith in December 1781 almost penniless. In the following year he appeared at Edinburgh as actor and lecturer. David Stewart Erskine, eleventh earl of Buchan, was interested in him, and among Buchan's manuscripts is a paper in Dodd's handwriting relating the story of his career from his earliest years. A verbatim transcript is given in *Notes and Queries*, 6th series, 7, 1883, 483–4. In 1786 a marriage licence was granted to Dodd and Ann Hurley Mason. Dodd died in Mecklenburgh Street, Dublin, in the spring of 1805, aged eighty-four. John O'Keeffe wrote in his *Recollections* that Dodd's 'learning and general knowledge were great; and though he had but small wit himself, [he] delighted to find it in another. He turned actor but was indifferent at that trade. He was a lively smart little man, with a cheerful laughing face' (Highfill, Burnim & Langhans, *BDA*). GORDON GOODWIN, *rev.* MICHAEL BEVAN

Sources *Walker's Hibernian Magazine* (1805), 256 • A. Fergusson, 'The story of James Solas Dodd, actor and surgeon', *N&Q*, 6th ser., 7 (1883), 483–4, 495 • *European Magazine and London Review*, 47 (1805), 402 • Highfill, Burnim & Langhans, *BDA* • *IGI* • P. J. Wallis and R. V. Wallis, *Eighteenth century medics*, 2nd edn (1988) • *GM*, 1st ser., 75 (1805), 388 • J. S. Dodd, letter, BL, Add. MS 4305

Dodd, James William (*c*.1740–1796), actor, was born in London, reportedly the son of a hairdresser. A successful appearance in a school play turned him towards the theatre, and at the age of sixteen he became a strolling player. His first part was said to be Roderigo in *Othello*, at Sheffield. There is firm evidence of his being a member of the Norwich Company of Comedians early in 1759, when he was already married and living in Bury St Edmunds, one of the towns on the company's circuit. He and his wife, Martha (*d.* 1769), also in the company, had four children before 1765.

In Norfolk, Dodd played a wide range of parts, from George Barnwell to Hamlet, and was also a singer and dancer. Tate Wilkinson, who appeared there in 1763, described him as 'the reigning favourite' of Norwich (Wilkinson, *Memoirs*, 3.114). But it was in comedy that he came to excel. He began to specialize when in 1764 he and his wife moved to the Bath theatre and came under the influence of John Arthur. A year later Garrick recruited them both for Drury Lane.

Garrick needed an urgent replacement for William O'Brien, whose secret marriage to Lady Susan Strangways had forced him to quit the stage, but with his usual caution he first sought opinions from various talent scouts. The letter from his friend John Hoadly is a model of what such a report should be (Thomas, 255). In spite of his distaste for 'Strolers', Garrick engaged them. Dodd was to remain at Drury Lane for over thirty years. His forte was the fop, in the tradition created by Cibber and Vanbrugh; he was 'the prince of pink heels, and the soul of empty eminence' (Jenkins, 81) and he chiefly excelled in those roles where the fop is sinister as well as comic.

The insect tribe Dodd paints with nicest art
And gives a double edge to satire's dart.
(*The Drama: a Poem*, 1775)

After Sheridan had succeeded Garrick at Drury Lane, Dodd created a number of important roles for him: Sir Benjamin Backbite in *The School for Scandal* (1777), Lord Foppington in *A Trip to Scarborough* (1777), and Dangle in *The Critic* (1778). He also played many other types of part in his long and successful career. In the 1780s he was regularly the Drury Lane Caliban; he played Richard III, once; and he was one of a notable trio of witches in *Macbeth*. Charles Lamb praised his Sir Andrew Aguecheek especially: 'Dodd was *it*, as it came out of nature's hands … In expressing slowness of apprehension the actor surpassed all others' (Lamb, 159).

In the long summer closures of the patent theatres, London actors worked in the provinces and occasionally undertook provincial managements. In his second year at Drury Lane, Dodd helped to open the new theatre in Bristol. He appeared there again in 1767, with his wife, and in 1768, without her. In 1769 he lost the favour of Bristol audiences through his notorious association with Mary *Bulkley (1747/8?–1792), of Covent Garden, who was also spending the summer in Bristol. His marriage had long been stormy, and in that year Martha, after a quarrel, took an engagement at Richmond rather than in Bristol. Dodd's angry attempts to retrieve her cost him two nights in gaol. Martha died in September of that year, and Dodd found it wiser to stay away from Bristol for a year or two.

In summer 1772 Dodd returned to Bristol as manager, succeeding Tom King. While recruiting his company in London he tried to seduce the young Elizabeth Simpson (later Inchbald), who was seeking a first engagement, but she threw hot water over him and escaped. The season itself went badly. Dodd changed the playbills too late and too often, while the local actresses complained of his public rudeness and resented the best parts' going to Londoners. He never tried management again.

In summer 1774 Dodd went on tour with Mary Bulkley to York (where a quarrel with John Moody disturbed Garrick when he heard of it) and to Dublin, where their season ended disastrously through public disapproval of their behaviour. Dodd was stranded in Ireland and had to be rescued by Garrick, and Bulkley returned temporarily to her husband. The couple had a far more successful season in York four years later, by which time they had set up house together. But after a year or two the relationship collapsed again.

Physically, Dodd was very small, with 'a white, calf-like stupid face' (Thomas, 255), on which he could register all the comic emotions. He was sprightly when young, but grew slow and portly. He was respected by audiences and by colleagues who acknowledged his professional skill, but he never challenged King as the principal Drury Lane comedian. In his last season, 1795–6, he was criticized for a poor Roderigo; his Mercutio was too fat, too old, and too slow; and he was made a scapegoat for the fiasco of *The Iron Chest*, a play by George Colman the younger with music by Stephen Storace. Colman himself attached greater blame to the leading player, John Philip Kemble, but Dodd bore the brunt of audience hostility. He retired at the end of the season, and during his last summer would take the air in Gray's Inn garden, where Lamb once met him. He died at his home, 8 Southampton Row, Bloomsbury, on 17 September 1796. He left an extensive library, which was auctioned by Sothebys in 2435 lots over nine days. He was survived by his son the Revd James Dodd (d. 1818), fellow of King's College, Cambridge, rector of North Runcton, and for many years an usher at Westminster School.

JOHN LEVITT

Sources G. W. Stone, ed., *The London stage, 1660–1800*, pt 4: 1747–1776 (1962) · C. B. Hogan, ed., *The London stage, 1660–1800*, pt 5: 1776–1800 (1968) · Highfill, Burnim & Langhans, *BDA* · *The letters of David Garrick*, ed. D. M. Little and G. M. Kahrl, 3 vols. (1963) · [J. Haslewood], *The secret history of the green rooms: containing authentic and entertaining memoirs of the actors and actresses in the three theatres royal*, 2 vols. (1790) · D. Thomas, ed., *Restoration and Georgian England, 1660–1788* (1989) · T. Wilkinson, *Memoirs of his own life*, 4 vols. (1790) · T. Wilkinson, *The wandering patentee, or, A history of the Yorkshire theatres from 1770 to the present time*, 4 vols. (1795) · K. Barker, *The Theatre Royal, Bristol: the first seventy years* (1961) · R. Jenkins, *Memoirs of the Bristol stage* (1826) · C. Lamb, 'On some of the old actors', *The essays of Elia*, [another edn] (1906) · *Memoirs of Mrs Inchbald*, ed. J. Boaden, 2 vols. (1833) · *IGI* · *Norfolk Mercury* (1759–65)
Likenesses J. Roberts, drawing, c.1766, Garr. Club · F. Wheatley, oils, c.1771–1772, Man. City Gall. · R. Laurie, mezzotint, 1779 (after F. Wheatley), NPG · R. Dighton, watercolour drawing, 1793?, Garr. Club · H. Spicer, watercolour drawing, c.1799, Garr. Club · S. De Wilde, watercolour drawing, Garr. Club · R. Dighton, watercolour drawing, Garr. Club · gouache drawing, Garr. Club
Wealth at death see administration, PRO, PROB 6/172, fol. 368r

Dodd, John [*called* Kew Dodd] (**1752–1839**). *See under* Dodd, Edward (1704/5?–1810).

Dodd, Philip Stanhope (1775–1852), Church of England clergyman, was the son of the Revd Richard Dodd (1735/6–1811), rector of Cowley, Middlesex, author of a translation of Formey's *Ecclesiastical History*, and his wife (*née* Wynant; d. 1802). He was educated at Tonbridge School, and, having entered Magdalene College, Cambridge, in 1792, was elected a fellow, and proceeded BA in 1796 and MA in 1799. In 1796 he published anonymously *Hints to Fresh-Men, from a Member of the University of Cambridge*, of which the third edition was printed in 1807. He was ordained by the bishop of London in 1797 and was for some years curate of Camberwell, Surrey, which he exchanged in 1803 for the ministry of Lambeth Chapel, retaining the afternoon lecture at Camberwell.

In 1806 Dodd was chaplain to the lord mayor, Sir William Leighton, and published five sermons preached in that capacity. The fourth of these, *The Lawfulness of Judicial Oaths and on Perjury*, preached at St Paul's Cathedral on 31 May 1807, produced a reply by Joseph Gurney Bevan. He was rewarded for his civic services by the valuable rectory of St Mary-at-Hill in the City of London in 1807, where he was one of the most popular clergymen of the metropolis.

In 1812 Dodd was presented by his college to the sinecure rectory of Aldrington in Sussex, the church of which had been destroyed. Sir J. S. Sidney, bt, in 1819 gave him the rectory of Penshurst, Kent, worth £766 per annum, and he became rural dean of Malling in 1846. He married on 4 August 1814 Martha, second daughter of the late Lieutenant-Colonel Wilson, deputy treasurer of Chelsea Hospital. In 1837 Dodd wrote *A View of the Evidence afforded by the Life and Ministry of St Paul to the Truth of the Christian Revelation*. He died at Penshurst rectory on 22 March 1852.

G. C. BOASE, *rev.* M. C. CURTHOYS

Sources Boase, *Mod. Eng. biog.* · Venn, *Alum. Cant.* · *GM*, 2nd ser., 37 (1852), 626–7 · [J. Watkins and F. Shoberl], *A biographical dictionary of the living authors of Great Britain and Ireland* (1816) · *GM*, 1st ser., 84/2 (1814), 186
Archives LPL, corresp. with Charles Golightly
Likenesses J. T. Linnell, lithograph (after Corton), NPG

Dodd, Ralph (1756?–1822), civil engineer, was probably born in 1756 in South or North Shields, one of three known sons of Alexander Dodd. After some education in practical mechanics he studied at the Royal Academy for about five years, and in the 1780s, like his brother Robert *Dodd, attempted to make a living from painting. He married Fanny Lambert on 16 February 1778; she and their three sons and a daughter survived him. His earliest connection with engineering was the trial of an excavating machine on the Grand Junction Canal near Hayes in 1794. The same year he carried out a survey of the River Wear, and a succession of reports followed relating to canals and harbours in the north-east. His short historical *Account of the Principal Canals in the Known World* (1795) was largely plagiarized from J. Phillips's *General History of Inland Navigation* (1792). He then promoted tunnels beneath the Tyne and the Thames from Gravesend to Tilbury. Work began on the latter in 1799 but was abandoned in 1802. In 1798 he proposed to construct the Thames and Medway Canal, from near Gravesend to Strood, which was eventually completed by W. T. Clark. In 1799 he published *Letters on the Improvement of the Port of London without Making Wet Docks*, and became involved with proposals for a new London bridge. In 1804 he turned his attention to the water supply of London, and became involved in the establishment of the South London, West Middlesex, East London, and Kent waterworks companies. As with almost all of his proposals, Dodd's active involvement with these schemes was short-lived.

Dodd's sons George *Dodd and Barrodall Robert assisted him in many of his schemes, including the Grand Surrey Canal, from which they were all dismissed in 1802. They all became heavily involved in the development of steam navigation. Dodd was involved in the initial plans for Vauxhall Bridge, and almost certainly assisted George in his proposals for Waterloo Bridge.

In 1815 Dodd issued his *Practical Observations on the Dry Rot in Timber*. The same year he took out a patent with George Stephenson for a steam locomotive. He then began advocating iron bridges 'of tenacity', and built one over the Chelmer at Springfield (1819–20). In April 1822 Dodd was injured by the bursting of a steam vessel at Gloucester. He was advised to go to Cheltenham for his health and, with virtually no money, had to walk there. He died there on 11 April 1822.

MIKE CHRIMES

Sources J. G. James, 'Ralph Dodd, the very ingenious schemer', *Transactions* [Newcomen Society], 47 (1974–6), 161–78 · *GM*, 1st ser., 92/1 (1822), 474 · R. Stuart [R. S. Meikleham], *Historical and descriptive anecdotes of steam-engines, and of their inventors and improvers*, 2 (1829), 534–6 · S. Snell, *A story of railway pioneers, being an account of the inventions of Isaac Dodds and his son Thomas Weatherburn Dodds* (1921) · G. W. Younger, 'Robert and Ralph Dodd, marine painters, and others of the name [pts 1–2]', *The Connoisseur*, 71 (1925), 73–80; 73 (1925), 87–94 · G. W. Younger, 'Robert and Ralph Dodd, marine painters, and others of the name [pt 3]', *The Connoisseur*, 74 (1926), 35 · A. W. Skempton, *British civil engineering, 1640–1840: a bibliography of contemporary printed reports, plans, and books* (1987) · Inst. CE, J. G. James papers · parish register (marriage), St Andrew by the Wardrobe, London · evidence on Camberwell Waterworks Bill, 1805, LMA, papers of various waterworks companies
Archives Inst. CE, J. G. James MSS
Likenesses engraving, repro. in Stuart, *Historical and descriptive anecdotes* · portrait, repro. in Snell, *A story of railway pioneers*
Wealth at death £2 5s.: *GM*

Dodd, Robert (1748–1815), marine painter and engraver, was one of the three known sons of Alexander Dodd; Ralph *Dodd (1756?–1822) was his younger brother. He began his career as a landscape painter, achieving some recognition by the age of twenty-three. He soon developed as a painter of marine scenes, having ample opportunity to study the busy shipping life of London. On 1 November 1772, when he was living in the parish of St John-at-Wapping, London, he married Mary Fulton (b. 1748), a spinster of the parish of St Marylebone. He first exhibited at the Society of Artists in 1780. In 1782 he exhibited three paintings at the Royal Academy and continued to exhibit there regularly until 1809.

Much of Dodd's work records specific battles and actions of the French Revolutionary Wars and the American War of Independence. He painted a large canvas of the battle of the First of June, 1794 (1795; NMM). In 1797, during a trip to Sheerness to 'get a plan of the action' of the battle of Camperdown, he was described as 'the nice Mr Dodd' for his diplomatic behaviour (Edwards). A painting of HMS *Victory* sailing from Spithead (1791; NMM) illustrates his skill at ship portraits. His work also includes scenes of the River Thames and naval dockyards. Many of his paintings were reproduced in line or aquatint by engravers such as Robert Pollard, Frances Jukes, and Robert Laurie.

From about 1783 Dodd himself engraved and published over 100 aquatints of his work. Of interest are his views of the naval dockyards, including those at Chatham, Woolwich, and Deptford, and sets of engravings of the battles of the Nile, 1798 (1799), and Trafalgar, 1805 (1806). In his engravings as in his paintings his strength lies in the depiction of water and in accuracy of the details of ships' rigging, masts, and sails in different conditions. In particular he depicted storm scenes and rough seas with great realism, including a set of five paintings showing the loss of the *Ramillies*, September 1782 (1783; NMM). His prolific work is significant as a historical record, along with that of several contemporary marine painters working on the same subjects. He is sometimes confused with his brother, the painter Ralph Dodd (c.1756–1822), who also lived and worked in London. Towards the end of his life Robert Dodd was living at Lucas Place, Commercial Road, east London. He died in 1815 and was buried on 20 February at St Dunstan and All Saints, Stepney.

LINDSEY MACFARLANE

Sources G. W. Younger, 'Robert and Ralph Dodd, marine painters', *Mariner's Mirror*, 10 (1924), 243–51, 327 • H. S. V., 'R. Dodd', *Mariner's Mirror*, 11 (1925), 91 • G. W. Younger, 'Robert and Ralph Dodd, marine painters, and others of the name [pts 1–2]', *The Connoisseur*, 71 (1925), 73–80; 73 (1925), 87–94 • *DNB* • *Concise catalogue of oil paintings in the National Maritime Museum* (1988) • Graves, *RA exhibitors* • J. Turner, ed., *The dictionary of art*, 34 vols. (1996) • E. H. H. Archibald, *Dictionary of sea painters*, 2nd edn (1989) • Redgrave, *Artists*, 2nd edn • Bryan, *Painters* (1930) • C. N. Edwards, 'An account of an expedition to Sheerness', 1797, NMM, MID/11/3 • A. Wilson, *A dictionary of British marine painters* (1967) • parish register, London, St Marylebone, 1 Nov 1772 [marriage]
Archives NMM
Likenesses R. Bull, miniature, 1805

Dodd, Sir Samuel (1652–1716), judge, the son of Ralph Dodd, was from a Cheshire family settled at Little Budworth, but was born in London. He was probably the 'Samuel Dod' who entered Merchant Taylors' School, London, on 11 September 1664. He entered the Inner Temple in 1670, was called to the bar in 1679, and became a bencher in 1700. On 11 March 1686 he married Isabel (d. 1722), daughter and coheir of Sir Robert Croke of Chequers, Buckinghamshire. They had two sons, only one of whom survived his father. Dodd was employed in 1693 and 1700 for the bankers against the government over the long-drawn-out case of the crown's liability for interest on loans made to Charles II. Commercial cases seem to have been something of a speciality, for Dodd was one of the lawyers chosen in 1694 to prepare the by-laws for the Bank of England and he played an important role in matters appertaining to the East India trade. In February 1700 he was counsel for the new company against a bill to incorporate the old company, and counsel for the new company again in June 1700. In October 1701 he acted for the new company in negotiations for uniting the two East India companies. He also appeared as counsel in cases before the House of Lords, such as representing the duchess of Norfolk against the divorce bill promoted by her husband.

In February 1710 Dodd was assigned as counsel for Dr Henry Sacheverell in his impeachment before the Lords.

His speech on the first article of the impeachment followed that of Sir Simon Harcourt and was notable only for its length. Once Harcourt had been removed from the defence team following his return to parliament, Dodd usually took the lead in the defence team. However, his part in the trial did not damage his relations with the whigs. Indeed, he reached the apogee of his career shortly after the Hanoverian succession. When Lord Cowper advised George I on the appointment of the judges at the start of his reign he remarked that for the exchequer 'Mr Dodd, an ancient practiser of this court, is the fittest person to supply the place of Chief Baron, now void, and I must confess experience is requisite for this post above all others' (Holmes and Speck, 65). Dodd was knighted on 11 October 1714, appointed a serjeant-at-law on 26 October, his patrons on the latter occasion being lords Wharton and Somers, two of the leading whigs of the day, and created chief baron of the exchequer on 20 November. Dodd died on 14 April 1716 'after a long indisposition, leaving behind him the reputation of a learned and eminent lawyer, and a plentiful fortune to his only son' (Boyer, 11.505). He was buried in the Temple Church on 20 April. There is a volume of his manuscript reports in the British Library's Hargrave collection. STUART HANDLEY

Sources Sainty, *Judges*, 97 • Baker, *Serjeants*, 453, 509 • A. Boyer, *The political state of Great Britain*, 11 (1716), 505; 24 (1722), 101 • G. Holmes and W. Speck, eds., *The divided society: parties and politics in England, 1694–1716* (1967), 65 • G. Holmes, *The trial of Dr Sacheverell* (1973), 118, 187–8, 195 • N. Luttrell, *A brief historical relation of state affairs from September 1678 to April 1714*, 3 (1857), 126, 357; 4 (1857), 605, 609, 641, 658; 5 (1857), 96; 6 (1857), 545 • J. E. Martin, ed., *Masters of the bench of the Hon. Society of the Inner Temple, 1450–1883, and masters of the Temple, 1540–1883* (1883), 57 • Mrs E. P. Hart, ed., *Merchant Taylors' School register, 1561–1934*, 2 vols. (1936) • G. Lipscomb, *The history and antiquities of the county of Buckingham*, 4 vols. (1831–47), vol. 2, p. 189 • IGI

Dodd, Thomas (1771–1850), printseller and author, was born in Spitalfields on 11 July 1771, the eldest child of Elizabeth Tooley, tailor, and her husband, Thomas Dodd, also a tailor. At the age of five he moved with his family across London, to settle in Paradise Row, Chelsea, where he attended a local dame-school. Although his family were humble, this must have been a period of prosperity, as shortly afterwards the young Dodd was transferred to a private academy at Shooters Hill to study under a tutor named Dufour. He remained there until his father, who had habitually absented himself for lengthy periods, finally abandoned the family in 1781, leaving Dodd's mother to provide them with a meagre living. In such straitened circumstances, Dodd was sent to work with the flamboyant American impresario Colonel de Vaux, who planned to establish a juvenile band and taught the boy the clarinet. Under the protection of Vaux, this ensemble travelled through England, stopping to perform in various town squares; the experience must have encouraged Dodd's willingness to travel in later life.

Within a year Vaux had given up this enterprise, leaving Dodd to lodge with a butcher named Chapman where he was ill-treated; within another year the boy ran away to

Liverpool in pursuit of his charismatic master. After wandering, penniless, he eventually found Vaux and travelled with him to Llanrwst where he was again abandoned; this time, however, he was left in the care of an itinerant harp player who, although he neglected Dodd's well-being, did teach him to play the harp. Ever resourceful and seemingly hardened to such set-backs, Dodd earned his board by performing for a local Welsh innkeeper and then for the Revd John Royle. These teenage exploits were later recorded, though probably in a romanticized form, in an autobiographical manuscript (now lost) entitled 'A narrative of incidents and adventures in my progress of life', which Dodd eventually presented to his friend Joseph Mayer.

By 1788 Dodd had returned to London, where he accepted a menial post in the house of an uncle before taking up service as a footman, first for 'Mrs Stuart [of] 48, Weymouth Street, Portland Place' (GM, 481), and then for Timothy Mangles of Suffolk Lane. Finally, these domestic positions afforded Dodd sufficient security to pursue his new desire for self-education. Between 1790 and 1793, with access to Mangles's library, he read voraciously, particularly favouring treatises on drawing; he also taught himself to copy engravings. In 1794 he married Miss Mangles's maid and then took up employment as a clerk at the chancery court. This position exploited his draughtsmanship and writing skills and allowed him further time to indulge his passion for prints and to frequent auctions where he would buy miscellaneous lots of prints and cheap books.

On the basis of these activities, in 1796 Dodd opened his first print shop, in Lambeth Marsh, where he came under the influence of William Henry Ireland, the infamous forger of Shakespeare, who encouraged him to excise flyleaves from the many old books in his stock; this was to supply Ireland with suitably aged paper for his own counterfeiting activities. Dodd apparently remained unaware of Ireland's ulterior motives and his own comments on this period describe his intense and devoted study of the history of engraving. After such a chequered start, Dodd had finally fixed on his vocation and by 1798 he had moved his print shop to the more fashionable and competitive location of Tavistock Street, Covent Garden.

With his charismatic personality and his remarkable knowledge of prints, Dodd's shop soon became a resort for many of the leading printmakers, collectors, and connoisseurs of the day. By 1806 his stock had grown so large that he moved to premises in St Martin's Lane, where he also began to hold auctions; by 1809 he had established his reputation with the auction of General Dowdeswell's celebrated engraved portrait collection, which raised sums far in advance of those paid by their original collector. He also held successful auctions in Portsmouth, Liverpool, and Manchester but by 1817, in the aftermath of Waterloo, Dodd lost his London business and so relocated to Manchester where the competition was not so great. Between 1817 and 1825 he continued to hold auctions; he also played an active part in the northern intellectual and art worlds and was influential in the formation of the Royal Manchester Institution in 1823.

During a prolonged illness in 1818–19 the largely self-taught Dodd started to write pieces on the history of engraving and the lives of engravers. The first was his 'Dissertation on the origin of the art of engraving', a lecture delivered in Liverpool in 1819. This was followed by a long-term project to compile a biographical history of the arts; it began publication in 1824 under the title The Connoisseurs Repertory, and it was in the interest of research that Dodd returned to London in 1825. The book, however, was quickly discontinued as its publisher went bankrupt. Consequently, although he continued to conduct some independent sales, Dodd was forced to take up the position of foreman for his former rival, the auctioneer Martin Colnaghi, for only £4 per week. This job was not without benefits: after he had catalogued Lord Yarborough's collection for sale by Colnaghi, the Bodleian Library invited Dodd, as a now renowned authority, to catalogue the 50,000 prints left to them on the death of Francis Douce; however, the catalogue was found inadequate and was never printed. In 1842 he was invited to catalogue Horace Walpole's collections at Strawberry Hill for the auctioneer George Robins.

Undeterred by this change in fortunes, during his final years Dodd continued to compile notes on the history of engraving and his most important contribution to the history of art is his extensive manuscript 'Memoirs of English engravers, 1550–1800' (now in the British Library, London), which he is said to have completed two days before his death. He died at the home of Joseph Mayer, in Lord Street, Liverpool, on 17 August 1850 and was buried in St James's cemetery in Liverpool.   LUCY PELTZ

Sources J. Mayer, *Memoirs of Thomas Dodd, William Upcott and George Stubbs* (1879) · *Regulations of the Royal Manchester Institution, with a list of the governors and annual subscribers* (1839) · J. L. Roget, *A history of the 'Old Water-Colour' Society*, 2 vols. (1891) · *GM*, 2nd ser., 34 (1850), 480–85 · [S. G. Gillam], ed., *The Douce legacy: an exhibition to commemorate the 150th anniversary of the bequest of Francis Douce, 1757–1834* (1984), 17 [exhibition catalogue]
Archives BL, collections relating to British engravers, etc., Add. MSS 33394–33408, 34411, 34664–34667 · JRL, catalogues of engravers and engravings, Eng. MSS 1115–1116
Likenesses W. Holl, stipple, pubd 1828 (after A. Wivell), BM, NPG; repro. in *GM*, p. 480 · etching, BM

Dodd, Thomas (d. 1834), musical instrument maker and music-seller, was the third son of Edward *Dodd (d. 1810), bow maker. His family moved from Sheffield to London and he was originally apprenticed to a firm of brewers. From 1786 to 1789 he worked as a bow maker in Blue Bell Alley, Mint Street, Southwark, and from 1794 he appears in city directories as a music-seller. He maintained a shop at 11 New Street, Covent Garden, from 1798 and became a successful dealer in instruments and music. Publications that bear his name as printer and vendor and quote this address include a treatise from around 1800 (which uses material originally by Francesco Geminiani) entitled *Compleat Instructions for the Violin*. The shop was at 92 St Martin's Lane, Charing Cross, from 1809 to 1826, and another branch producing harps and pianos was located at 3 Berner's Street from around 1819 until 1843. In that year Thomas's son Edward was drowned. Both he and his brother Thomas, who died while his father was residing in St Martin's Lane, were pupils of Bernhard Fendt and were involved with the instrument business, but neither managed to emulate their father's success.

Dodd's business produced violins, violas, cellos, and basses of excellent quality, using Stradivari, Guarneri, Amati, and Stainer models, but the construction of the instruments appears to have been the work of Fendt and John Frederick Lott. Dodd was responsible for what he described on his label as 'the original Cremona oil varnish', the formula for which was a closely guarded secret. It is therefore often the name of the dealer and not the maker that appears on the instrument labels and bows. Dodd almost certainly sold bows made by his brother John Dodd (1752–1839), and Thomas Tubbs's bows are frequently found with the Dodd brand, as are thousands of inferior German bows from the end of the nineteenth century.

Dodd died in London on 8 February 1834, and, according to a nephew, was buried at St Giles-in-the-Fields.

DAVID J. GOLBY

Sources W. M. Morris, *British violin makers: classical and modern, being a biographical and critical dictionary* (1904) · C. Beare and P. J. Kass, 'Thomas Dodd', *The new Grove dictionary of musical instruments*, ed. S. Sadie (1984) · B. W. Harvey, *The violin family and its makers in the British Isles: an illustrated history and directory* (1995) · W. Sandys and S. A. Forster, *The history of the violin* (1864) · W. Henley, *Universal dictionary of violin and bow makers*, 5 vols. (1959–60), vol. 2, pp. 65–7 · A. Pougin, ed., *Biographie universelle des musiciens, et bibliographie générale de la musique: supplément et complément*, 1 (Paris, 1878), 274 · C. Humphries and W. C. Smith, *Music publishing in the British Isles, from the beginning until the middle of the nineteenth century: a dictionary of engravers, printers, publishers, and music sellers*, 2nd edn (1970), 134
Archives Bodl. Oxf.

Dodd, William [*nicknamed* the Macaroni Parson] (1729–1777), Church of England clergyman and forger, was born in Bourne, Lincolnshire, the eldest of the six children of the Revd William Dodd (1703?–1757), vicar of Bourne. He was probably born on 29 May 1729 (Howson), though the parish register for Bourne shows that a William Dodd, son of William Dodd, was baptized at Bourne on 23 May 1728 (*IGI*). His mother was possibly Elizabeth Dickson or Dixon, who married a William Dodd on 3 April 1726, perhaps at Bourne (or at Norton Disney or Surfleet in the same county).

Dodd entered Clare College, Cambridge, in 1746 as a sizar, and in 1749 he was entered in the first tripos list as a wrangler. He was made MA in 1759. On leaving Cambridge in 1749 he went to London, where he lived for the rest of his life. There he sought to pursue a literary career which had begun at Cambridge with *Diggon Davy's Resolution on the Death of his Last Cow* (1747), a poem on foot-and-mouth disease. In London he rapidly produced a co-authored student crammer of philosophical texts and wrote both a farce on Sir Roger de Coverley, which was apparently

William Dodd (1729–1777), by John Russell, 1769

never staged, and *A New Book of the Dunciad*. In 1751 he married Mary Perkins (*d.* 1784), the daughter of a verger of Durham Cathedral, and his initial literary success encouraged him to lease an expensive house in Wardour Street. The fatal pattern was thus established of over-extending his limited financial resources in pursuit of advancement. It quickly became clear that his writings would not support him so he returned to Cambridge, he was ordained at Gonville and Caius College on 19 October 1752, and he became curate at All Saints', West Ham. He continued to write and, while his talent for originality was limited, he did have a facility for extracting from the work of others, most successfully in *The Beauties of Shakespeare* (1752), a collection of quotations which stayed in print well into the twentieth century. This book proved a boon to those who wished to demonstrate erudition without the inconvenience of actually having to read the plays, although it did provide Goethe with his first exposure to Shakespeare. Dodd also tried his hand at fiction and published *The Sisters* (1754), a novel whose dullness at least conceals its limp eroticism. During the 1760s he concentrated on theological writing; he published a *Commentary of the Bible* in monthly parts from 1764 and became almost solely responsible for the *Christian Magazine* (1760–67), some articles from which were collected in *Dodd on Death*.

Meanwhile Dodd's reputation as a preacher was growing. He was appointed to a lectureship at All Saints' in 1752; this was followed by lectureships in the City of London at St James Garlickhythe, in May 1753, and St Olave, Hart Street, in April 1754. He also delivered the Lady Moyer lectures at St Paul's Cathedral from 1754. In 1764 he attacked John Wesley for allegedly claiming that Methodists were perfect and for failing to control his followers. Wesley at first ignored the attack but then silenced his opponent with a fierce response in *Lloyd's Evening Post* (3 April 1767). In 1765 Dodd became tutor to the heir of Philip Dormer Stanhope, earl of Chesterfield, so he reluctantly turned schoolmaster and opened a small private school; he also graduated LLD in 1766 in the hope of attracting other wealthy pupils. His precarious finances received a boost when his wife received an inheritance and a lottery prize. With the money he opened Charlotte (or Pimlico) Chapel in Charlotte Street, behind Buckingham House, in July 1767. The aim was to attract royalty and thereby the cream of London society through his reputation as a preacher. Initially aristocracy joined his congregation and newspapers printed his sermons but the chapel struggled to attract members of the royal family. Dodd failed to obtain the vacant livings of either All Saints', in 1762, or St Olave, in 1769, although in 1772 he was preferred to the rectory of Hockliffe, Bedfordshire, to which was joined the vicarage of Chalgrove. His debts continued to mount as his lifestyle outstripped his income and he was forced to assign some of his literary works to the publisher of the *Christian Magazine*, to whom he owed money. Then, in 1767, he was sacked as its editor, and in 1771 his school, which had never been a financial success, collapsed when Philip Stanhope departed on the grand tour. Another attempt to rescue his finances, by leasing Bedford Chapel, Bloomsbury, in 1770, failed and he gave up the venture the following year.

In spite of all these difficulties Dodd supported a number of charities. While such endeavours were undoubtedly a means of mixing with influential people the fact that he was often the initiator of several successful schemes suggests a generous nature. He was instrumental in the establishment of the Society for the Relief and Discharge of Persons Imprisoned for Small Debts (later the Discharged Prisoners' Society) and of the Society for the Resuscitation of Persons Apparently Drowned (later the Royal Humane Society), and he was connected to the Magdalen Hospital for the reformation of penitent prostitutes. In 1767 he preached in favour of inoculation against smallpox and he wrote in support of the campaign against the death penalty in 1772. However, when in that year he and his wife were passengers in a coach that was robbed they were the only ones who appeared as witnesses against William Griffiths, who subsequently was convicted and hanged. It is worth remarking, however, that Dodd was equivocal in his evidence and interceded on Griffiths's behalf after his conviction.

There can be no doubting that Dodd worked hard, both as a writer and as a clergyman. Horace Walpole described his preaching style as 'haranguing entirely in the French style, and very eloquently and touchingly', by which he seems to have meant that he spoke rapidly, with emotion and in a high-pitched tone (letter to George Montagu, 28 Jan 1760, Walpole, *Corr.*, 9.274). Walpole noted that some of the congregation were moved to tears, and this effect was presumably the result of Dodd's method of delivery since his printed sermons were similar in content to those preached by less popular colleagues. Dodd was certainly careful to cultivate the aristocrats among his congregation, even to the extent of sending them 'odes', the sycophantic tone of which says as much about their expectations as about his character. He enjoyed a degree of success both as a writer and a preacher but, while his income was not small, it was never adequate to maintain the impression of a successful clergyman, which he needed to promote in order to advance his career and to satisfy his own vanity. He kept a carriage, and his fashionable dress earned him the less than complimentary sobriquet the Macaroni Parson: 'In the streets he walked with his head erect and with a lofty gait, like a man conscious of his own importance, and, perhaps, the dignity of his sacred calling' (Taylor, 2.250–52). Yet, according to the accounts of those who knew him, while he might have been vain he was not as pompous as this description suggests; Sir Philip Thicknesse said that he was 'one of the best-tempered men I ever knew', good company, generous, although, significantly, 'void of all prudence' (Thicknesse, 1.220–30). This popularity among fashionable society, however, brought little financial reward and even that was subject to the vagaries of fashion.

By the early 1770s Dodd's popularity had begun to wane as the fashion in preaching styles changed. His creditors became more pressing and this may have led him to live for a time near Hounslow Heath. But he needed to maintain his connection with wealthy society and so he took a house in Queen Street, Mayfair, about 1774. This made him more accessible to creditors, who besieged the house. To make matters worse his wife tried to bribe Lady Apsley so that her husband might present Dodd to the living of St George's, Hanover Square. Although Dodd seems to have been ignorant of his wife's efforts Lord Apsley was furious and had him removed from the list of royal chaplains. All hope of preferment in the church had gone and such reputation as Dodd had enjoyed went with it. Ridiculed in newspapers and satirized by Samuel Foote in *The Cozeners*, he fled to Geneva to join his old pupil Philip Stanhope, now earl of Chesterfield. On his return to England Chesterfield gave him the living of Wing in Berkshire and some money to pay off his most pressing creditors. Dodd continued to write and became editor of the *New Morning Post*. Unfortunately his absence abroad gave the governors of Magdalen Hospital the excuse to sack him, and in 1776 he relinquished the Charlotte Chapel, which had failed to bring the expected preferment and wealth.

By 1777 Dodd was living in Argyle Buildings, Argyle Street. Then came the final incident of his life. On 1 February he discounted a bill of exchange allegedly drawn by the earl of Chesterfield through Lewis Robertson, a broker. Dodd obtained £4200 but the bill was a forgery and he was arrested on 5 February. He immediately confessed, exonerated Robertson, and arranged for repayment. Promises that the matter would not be pressed further were not honoured and he was taken before Sir Thomas

Halifax, the lord mayor, at Guildhall, London. Both Halifax and Chesterfield's solicitor pressed forward the prosecution with enthusiasm, arguing that such offences threatened financial stability and deserved the severest punishment. Dodd was remanded to the Wood Street compter, where, at his request, he was visited by John Wesley, who also saw him when he was moved to Newgate prison. He was convicted of a capital forgery at the Old Bailey on 22 February 1777 but the jury recommended mercy. The passing of the death sentence was delayed while the judges decided that it had been correct to admit Robertson as a witness for the prosecution. Meanwhile a popular campaign began with the aim of obtaining mercy for Dodd. Newspaper coverage suddenly became sympathetic to him: no longer the Macaroni Parson he was now the 'unfortunate divine'. Dodd approached Dr Johnson to assist him in seeking mercy, and, while Johnson disliked Dodd's lifestyle, he thought the penalty harsh and agreed to help him. The two men did not meet at this time, although they may have done so briefly some years previously. Johnson devoted a considerable amount of time to writing the speeches and prayers that were published under Dodd's name, including the one that he delivered to the court when he was eventually sentenced to death in May 1777 and a speech he was to have given, but did not, at the gallows. A large number of petitions were presented, including one with 23,000 signatures and others from Oxford and Cambridge universities, the trial jurors, and the common council of the corporation of the City of London. This support seemed to lead Dodd to believe that he would not be executed but it may have had the opposite effect by moving the lord chief justice, Lord Mansfield, to speak against mercy in the privy council from a belief that it might be dangerous to give in to such pressure. On 27 June 1777 Dodd was taken to be hanged at Tyburn. The crowds lining the streets along which he passed were said to have stood in silence. Efforts by the physician John Hunter to revive him failed and he was interred at St Lawrence's Church, Cowley, Middlesex, where his brother was vicar. A plaque on the church wall commemorates him, and according to local legend he is buried in the grounds of the modern rectory. Dodd, in his work, life, and death, exemplified some of the main concerns of the period: the fickleness and extravagance of London society, the decline of literary patronage, the dependence of individuals on wealthy patrons for their advancement, and the excesses and controversy surrounding capital punishment.   PHILIP RAWLINGS

Sources G. Howson, *The Macaroni Parson* (1973) • J. Villette, *A genuine account of the behaviour and dying words of William Dodd, LL.D.* (1777) • *The trial of the Reverend Doctor William Dodd* (1777) • P. Fitzgerald, *A famous forgery, being the story of the unfortunate Dr Dodd* (1865) • J. Taylor, *Records of my life*, 2 vols. (1832) • P. Thicknesse, *Memoirs and anecdotes of Philip Thicknesse*, 3 vols. (privately printed, London, 1788–91) • *Lloyds Evening Post* (3 April 1767)
Archives Boston PL • PRO, SP 37.12 | BL, Add. MS 24419, fol. 6 • BL, Egerton MSS 2182, fol. 44; 3085, fol. 111; 32887, fol. 90r; 35639, fol. 188; 38198, fol. 78; 45359, fol. 23 • Somerville, New Jersey, Hyde collection

Likenesses J. Russell, oils, 1769, NPG [*see illus.*] • line engraving, pubd 1777, BM, NPG • line engraving, pubd 1777, NPG • mezzotint, pubd 1777, BM, NPG • T. L. Atkinson, mezzotint (after T. Gainsborough), BM • T. Gainsborough, portrait • engraving, repro. in *The Newgate calendar*

Dodderidge [Doddridge], **Sir John** (1555–1628), judge, was the eldest of eight children of Richard Dodderidge, a merchant of South Molton in Devon, and his wife, Joan Badcock (*née* Horder). Although seemingly not born to wealth, his father took advantage of the economic growth of north Devon in the second half of the sixteenth century and became a prosperous shipowner, trader, and privateer. He established himself in Barnstaple, where he was alderman in 1583 and mayor in 1589. His wife having died in 1604, he survived until 1619. Tradition has it that John Dodderidge attended the grammar school at Barnstaple; he matriculated at Exeter College, Oxford, in 1572, graduating BA in 1577. After a period at New Inn he was admitted to the Middle Temple in 1577 and called to the bar in 1585. In 1593 and 1602 he was appointed reader at New Inn, where he lectured on the law of advowsons. One year later, in 1603, he delivered his first reading at the Middle Temple and was created bencher. In 1604 he was created serjeant-at-law, having been proposed one year earlier. Only nine months afterwards, however, he was discharged from his serjeanty in order to take up the office of solicitor-general. He occupied this office for three years, resigning in 1607 to allow the promotion of Francis Bacon, whereupon Dodderidge resumed the coif and was immediately appointed king's serjeant and, later the same year, knighted. In 1612 he was appointed judge of the court of king's bench, retaining his place on the bench until his death in 1628.

Dodderidge retained his connections with Devon. He represented Barnstaple in the parliament of 1589, acted as counsel for the borough in 1611, and in his later life took an active interest in local administration in Barnstaple and South Molton. Perhaps because of his Devon antecedents he took an interest in the early settling of the American colonies, serving as a member of the king's council for Virginia in 1606. His family continued to live in the vicinity of Barnstaple, and all three of his wives were from Devon. First of these was Joan, daughter of Michael Jermyn, who was mayor of Exeter in 1591. On her death Dodderidge married, probably in 1604, Dorothy Hancock (*née* Bampfield) (1582–1614), the widow of Edward Hancock, the member of parliament for Barnstaple who had committed suicide in 1603 after the fall of Walter Ralegh. Three years after her death Dodderidge married Anne (*d.* 1630), daughter of Nicholas Culme of Canon's Leigh in Devon and widow of Giles Newman of London. Although he is said to have preferred to live near London, and in his later years had a substantial mansion near Egham in Surrey, Dodderidge's main properties were in Devon. He kept up his family home at Bremridge, South Molton, causing it to be rebuilt in 1622, and through his second wife came into possession of Mount Radford, near Exeter. His second wife was buried in Exeter Cathedral and in his

Sir John Dodderidge (1555–1628), by unknown artist, in or after 1612

will (written one month before his death) he expressed the wish that he too should be buried there.

Dodderidge played a full part in public affairs. He was one of the more active members in the parliament of 1604–11, where he represented Horsham. He spoke with great learning and sense in the debate on the lawfulness of royal impositions, though his lack of rhetorical flourish meant that his speech was less effective than it might otherwise have been. In the debate on the naturalization of the Scots, where the House of Commons was in danger of clashing both with the king and with the judges, he spoke with considerable wisdom in favour of a workable compromise consistent with common-law principles. He was a faithful servant of the crown, more royalist in his leanings than were many contemporary common lawyers, though his primary concern was with legal propriety. In Peacham's case, when the judges were asked to give their opinions in secret to the king, Dodderidge was said to be perfectly willing to oblige: as a judge he had taken an oath to give counsel to the king, and there was therefore no constitutional impediment to his obeying the royal demand. On the other hand, when directed by royal warrant not to enforce the statutes against recusancy in 1623, he is reported to have said that some lawful means should be discovered whereby the statutes could be dispensed with: the strong inference is that he did not believe that an instruction from the king was sufficient.

As a lawyer Dodderidge was—rightly—immensely well respected. He was known as the Sleeping Judge, not because of any shortcoming on his part, but because of his habit of concentrating on legal argument with eyes firmly closed. Recommending him for appointment as a serjeant-at-law in 1603, Cecil described him as 'a very great learned man' (*CSP dom.*, *1601–3*, 285), and about the same time Francis Bacon is said to have described him as 'shooting a fair arrow' (*Diary of John Manningham*, 100). Dodderidge got to the heart of matters very quickly, and his arguments—as advocate, as judge, and as parliamentarian—had a compelling lucidity. His writings show the same quality: his reading on advowsons, published in 1630 as *The Compleat Parson*, is marked by its clarity of structure; and his *The English Lawyer* (1631; earlier printed from an imperfect copy as *The Lawyers Light* in 1629) was a creditable attempt to impose some order on the depressingly haphazard common law of his day. Other legal works plausibly attributed to him are *The Lawes Resolution of Womens Rights* (1632), and perhaps *The Office and Duty of Executors* (1641, also ascribed to Thomas Wentworth). Long tradition has associated Dodderidge with the *Touchstone of Common Assurances*, published by William Sheppard in 1648, but this cannot withstand serious scrutiny. Nor is it likely that he wrote the *Treatise on Estates*, printed with later editions of William Noy's *Maxims*, which was once attributed to him.

Dodderidge's scholarship reached far beyond that of most contemporary lawyers. His knowledge of the civil law, though not profound by continental standards, extended into the modern commentaries on the *Digest* of Justinian: his manuscript commonplace book, now in the British Library, and his *English Lawyer* have many references to civilian works, and a paper discussing the question whether a nation had the right to appropriate parts of the high seas to its own exclusive use displays a familiarity with continental lawyers' discussions of the prescriptibility of rights over the sea. Nor was his learning limited to the law. He was a member of the fledgeling Society of Antiquaries—tradition has him as one of its founders—and he is known to have given papers to it on a variety of subjects, including one on the antiquity of parliament, published by his nephew in 1658. He wrote a history of Wales, Cornwall, and Chester, published in 1630, and a work on the degrees of nobility published in 1642 as *The Magazine of Honour*. As well as being renowned for his learning, Dodderidge had a reputation for integrity, for loyalty, and for ample hospitality. He died at his home at Forsters, Egham, Surrey on 13 September 1628 and his remains were transported to Exeter and interred in the cathedral there on 14 October beneath a fine effigy of him in his judicial robes. He is said to have died with great cheerfulness. His nephew John Dodderidge (*bap.* 1610, *d.* 1658) practised as a barrister, represented Barnstaple in the Long Parliament, founded a free library in Barnstaple, and left money in his will to Harvard University.

DAVID IBBETSON

Sources C. Stebbings, *A man of great knowledge: the life of Sir John Dodderidge* (c.1989) • S. E. Dodderidge and H. G. H. Shaddock, *The Dodderidges of Devon* (1909), 12–22 • J. Prince, *Danmonii orientales illustres, or, The worthies of Devon* (1701) • HoP, *Commons*, 1558–1603 • Fuller, *Worthies* (1811) • *The parliamentary diary of Robert Bowyer, 1606–*

1607, ed. D. H. Willson (1931) • *Diary of Walter Yonge*, ed. G. Roberts, CS, 41 (1848), 69 • *The diary of John Manningham of the Middle Temple, 1602–1603*, ed. R. P. Sorlien (Hanover, NH, 1976), 100 • BL, Sloane MS 3479 • BL, Harg MS 407, 408 • N. Matthews, *William Sheppard* (1984), 79–84 • T. Gray, ed., *The lost chronicle of Barnstaple, 1586–1611* (1998) • K. R. Andrews, *Elizabethan privateering: English privateering during the Spanish war, 1585–1603* (1964) • Baker, *Serjeants*, 509 • Sainty, *Judges*, 31 • J. R. Chanter, *Sketches of the literary history of Barnstaple* [1866] • E. D. Wheeler, *Sir John Dodderidge* (c.1992) • private information (1913) [Sidney E. Dodderidge] • BL, Harley MS 5053, fol. 32

Archives BL, discourses, observations, etc., Add. MSS 22580, 25253, 28842 • BL, Harley MSS, tracts, legal papers, lectures **Likenesses** oils, in or after 1612, S. Antiquaries, Lond. [*see illus.*] • oils, NPG; repro. in *The Ancestor*, 3. 40 • oils, Exeter College, Oxford

Doddridge, Sir John. *See* Dodderidge, Sir John (1555–1628).

Doddridge [*née* Maris], **Mercy** (1709–1790), dissenting lay-woman and letter-writer, was born on 4 September 1709 at The Friary, Worcester, the daughter of Richard Maris (*bap.* 1672, *d.* in or before 1730), a well-established baker and maltster, and his wife, Elizabeth Brindley (*d.* in or before 1730). She had three brothers, Richard, George, and Samuel. Both sides of the family appear to have been people of substance, the Brindleys having provided the city of Worcester with a mayor, Richard Brindley, in 1668–9. By 1730 Mercy was orphaned and living under the guardianship of a maternal uncle, Ebenezer Hankins, at his home, Soley's Orchard, Upton upon Severn. A relation, William Hankins (*d.* 1723), had been appointed the first Baptist minister at Upton, so it would appear that she was brought up in the atmosphere of religious dissent which by now was widely tolerated in the British Isles.

Mercy Maris first met the young dissenting minister Philip *Doddridge (1702–1751) in July 1730, at the home of her great-aunt Mrs Edward Owen, in Coventry, and they fell in love at first sight. Within a week he wrote to Mrs Owen saying that he felt 'the Impulse of a rising Passion' and sought permission to woo her (P. Doddridge to Mrs E. Owen, 6 Aug 1730, Castle Hill church, Northampton). After a short courtship, during which he wrote to her weekly, Mercy accepted him and they were married at Upton on 22 December 1730. Her dowry of £400 was relatively small. They took up residence at 34 Marefair, Northampton, where Doddridge had his home and had established what became the leading dissenting academy of the day. In 1740 they moved with the academy to a large town house in Sheep Street rented from Lord Halifax of Horton. Their marriage was 'a superb relationship' (Deacon, *The Church on Castle Hill*, 7), and they had nine children, five of whom died in infancy.

Their eldest child, Elizabeth (nicknamed Tetsy or Tetsey), was born on 8 October 1731 and died on 1 October 1736 of consumption, a disease from which her father suffered and which terminated his relatively short life. The four children who survived infancy were Mary, always known as Polly (1733–1799), who became the second wife of John Humphreys, a Tewkesbury lawyer; Mercy (1734–1809) and Anna Cecilia (1737–1811), who were both unmarried; and Philip (1735–1785), who neither married nor outlived his mother. After the premature birth and death

within a year of another son, Samuel (1739–1740), Mercy suffered a succession of miscarriages and the birth of three further children each of whom lived for only a few days. In 1742 she was so seriously ill that she went to Bath to recuperate, accompanied by her companion Elizabeth Rappitt. She stayed there for seven months under the medical supervision of William Oliver FRS, the celebrated physician.

Mercy Doddridge's chief claim to recollection is as the wife of Philip Doddridge. Throughout their married life they were often parted, he on pastoral journeys and she on visits to relations or taking the waters at Bath for her health. They corresponded very frequently, their correspondence facilitated by improving road communication in the mid-eighteenth century, and a large number of their letters survive. It is clear from these that they were very much in love, a love that endured throughout their marriage. They addressed each other in terms of great endearment, and Mercy's letters were always sealed with wax bearing the impression of her personal seal inscribed with the motto *Fidelle en absence*. The letters also reveal that she was an educated woman, able to discuss both theological and secular matters with her scholarly husband. She was modest, apologizing for her poor grammar and spelling, and on one occasion requested that he send her a 'spelling book' (dictionary) (Doddridge MS 14). She claimed to be no businesswoman: she wrote, 'Your absence has convinced me how little capable I am of doing business whatever my will may be' (Doddridge MS 26). But she appears nevertheless to have been much involved in the running of the domestic affairs of the academy, which had sixty-three students and a staff of seven servants at its height. In her husband's absence Mercy controlled the finances, on one occasion dismissed an employee, and was greatly concerned with the health and welfare of the students. She was a caring woman, but her paramount care was for the well-being of her beloved husband, whose health throughout was far from robust. He was her 'greatest earthly joy and treasure', and she urged him to take care of his life, 'far dearer to me than my own' (Doddridge MS 57).

Mercy Doddridge was a devout woman sustained by her unswerving faith and religious convictions. She was assured that 'infinite wisdom and goodness cannot err'; that the outcomes of events are 'all known to our Heavenly Father' who will determine them 'in mercy to them and us' (Doddridge MS 12). On one occasion, when their son was recovering from serious illness, she wrote, 'My first business will be to thank God', and shortly after her husband's death she added a postscript to a letter to Nathaniel Neal, their lawyer: 'My heart as yet is pained when I think of this bad world, yet not without hope. What cannot God do?' (Doddridge MSS 59, 61).

The Doddridges moved in high society both near home and further afield; noblemen and noblewomen were among their acquaintances, and the prince of Wales himself presented Mercy with a ball dress. Though not affluent Mercy kept up with current fashion in the home, in one letter requesting her husband to bring items of blue-

and-white china, fashionable brass candlesticks, and silver spoons back with him from London (Doddridge MS 50).

By 1751, when he was only forty-nine, Philip Doddridge's ill health was incapacitating him. It was eventually decided to send him to recuperate in a warmer climate and on 13 October he arrived in Lisbon accompanied by Mercy. He died there thirteen days later and is buried there. Mercy returned to Northampton. The *Northampton Mercury* reported on 13 November 1751: 'His disconsolate Widow (whose chief Dowry is that she inherits the Spirit of this excellent Man) is returning to England'. She set about settling her husband's affairs 'with great composure', taking a great interest in the posthumous publication of his written works and corresponding with his associates and past students.

Philip Doddridge had made provision for 'a considerable annuity' to be paid to Mercy 'in case of widowhood', but because he died abroad the arrangements became invalid. When she returned to Northampton a subscription was opened for her by the church, chiefly in London; it amounted to more than the lost annuity. She remained in Northampton until the mid-1770s, when she and her two unmarried daughters, Mercy and Anna Cecilia, went to live in Tewkesbury. Her correspondence of this period was largely concerned with raising subscriptions towards the posthumous publication of Philip Doddridge's works and urging Job Orton to finish the work of editing them. She died in Tewkesbury on 4 April 1790, in her eighty-first year.   W. N. TERRY

Sources Northamptonshire libraries, Northampton, Doddridge MSS · *Calendar of the correspondence of Philip Doddridge*, ed. G. F. Nuttall, HMC, JP 26 (1979) · M. Deacon, *Philip Doddridge of Northampton, 1702–1751* (1980) · G. F. Nuttall, ed., *Philip Doddridge, 1702–1751: his contribution to English religion* (1951) · M. Deacon, *The church on Castle Hill: the history of Castle Hill United Reformed Church, Northampton* (1995) · W. N. Terry, *Philip Doddridge of Northampton: an exhibition to celebrate the 250th anniversary of the ordination of Philip Doddridge* (1980) · J. Orton, *Memoirs of the life, character and writings of the late Rev. Philip Doddridge of Northampton*, new edn (1819) · G. F. Nuttall, *Handlist of the correspondence of Mercy Doddridge, 1751–1790* (1984)
Archives BL, Add. MSS · DWL, MSS · JRL, MSS · Northampton Library, MSS · U. Aberdeen L., MSS | Castle Hill United Reformed Church, Northampton, MSS and artefacts · DWL, Congregational library, Reed MSS

Doddridge, Philip (1702–1751), Independent minister and writer, was born on 26 June 1702 in London, the last of the twenty children of Daniel Doddridge (*d.* 1715), an oilman or dealer in oils and pickles, and his wife, Monica Bauman (*d.* 1711). His father was a son of John Doddridge (1621–1689), rector of Shepperton, Middlesex, who resigned his living after the Act of Uniformity and became a nonconformist minister, and a great-nephew of the judge and MP Sir John Doddridge (1555–1628). His mother was the daughter of John Bauman (*d. c.*1668), a protestant refugee who fled from Prague in 1626; after spending twenty years in Germany he moved to London in 1646 and set up a school at Kingston, Surrey. Doddridge inherited his grandfather's German Bible, and recorded in it his flight from

Philip Doddridge (1702–1751), by George Vertue, 1751 (after Andrea Soldi)

persecution (Deacon, 29). Only one of Doddridge's siblings survived infancy, his elder sister, Elizabeth (*d.* 1735), who married John Nettleton, a schoolmaster at Hampstead and then a dissenting minister at Ongar, Essex. On both sides of his family Doddridge was descended from men who had suffered for their religion, and he was obviously proud of this inheritance, but he was also conscious of the social position of his Doddridge forebears. His lawyer uncle Philip Doddridge (*d.* 1715), some of whose books he inherited, was steward to the first duke of Bedford. The place of evangelical religion in polite society was a question that was to concern his nephew greatly.

Education When very young, Doddridge was taught Bible stories by his mother from the Dutch tiles in the fireplace. He was sent first to a private tutor, Mr Stott, and then in 1712 he was put under the Presbyterian minister Daniel Mayo at the school in Kingston founded by his grandfather. He spent his holidays on the Bedford estates with his uncle, and kept up his friendship with the Russell family in later life. At the age of eight he lost his mother; at the age of thirteen, after the deaths of his father and uncle, he was made ward to a Mr Downes, who moved him to a school at St Albans run by another dissenter, Dr Nathaniel

Wood. In St Albans he boarded in the same house as the Presbyterian minister Samuel Clark, who was to become one of the three most important influences on his intellectual and religious development. Though not a master, Clark took charge of his education. In the dedication of his funeral sermon for Clark, *Meditations on the Tears of Jesus*, preached at St Albans on 16 December 1750, Doddridge described him as 'my ever honoured friend and father' (*Works*, 3.382). Downes, on the other hand, proved to be an utterly unsuitable guardian: in 1718 he lost his ward's inheritance through speculation. Many years later Doddridge described himself as 'an Orphan quite defrauded & stripd of all by those that should have been my Guardians' (Nuttall, *Calendar*, no. 1016). As a result he left St Albans to stay with his sister and brother-in-law in Hampstead while he made up his mind about his future. The duchess of Bedford offered to provide for him at Oxford or Cambridge so that he could take orders in the Church of England, but he was already, at sixteen, considering the dissenting ministry. The dissenting historian and spokesman Edmund Calamy, from whom he sought advice, told him to think of another profession. He was offered the opportunity to train as a lawyer, but instead Clark undertook to give him a temporary home in St Albans and find him a place at a dissenting academy. In October 1719, at seventeen, he became a student at the academy of the Independent minister John Jennings, first at Kibworth Harcourt, south-east of Leicester, and then from July 1722 at Hinckley, about 10 miles west of Kibworth. On 24 January 1723 he was satisfactorily examined by three neighbouring ministers; he left Hinckley on 1 June, having completed the four-year course shortly before his twenty-first birthday. Jennings died of smallpox on 8 July 1723, and the academy closed.

After Clark, Jennings was the second person decisively to shape Doddridge's way of thinking and his future career. Invaluable information survives about his studies and Jennings's methods, in the form of his letters to Clark (who paid most of his bills), Nettleton, and others, books he owned while a student, and Jennings's manuscript notebooks. He told Clark on 22 September 1722 that Jennings encouraged 'the greatest freedom of inquiry' and did not follow 'the doctrines or phrases of any particular party' (Nuttall, *Calendar*, no. 35); he told Nettleton on 27 February 1723 that Jennings 'furnishes us with all kinds of authors upon every subject, without advising us to skip over the heretical passages for fear of infection' (*Correspondence*, 1.198). On 16 November 1725 he wrote a long letter to Thomas Saunders, minister at Kettering, with a detailed account of the range of topics covered in the eight halves of the course; in October 1728 he completed the 64-page manuscript 'Account of Mr Jennings's method of academical education with some reflections upon it in a letter to a friend'. During his period at the academy he read very widely, in divinity, philosophy, classical and French literature, and history (he read sixty books in one half-year in addition to the parts of books to which Jennings referred in his lectures). He told Nettleton in February 1722 that Tillotson was his particular favourite. He

also developed the habits of intense self-discipline and husbandry of time that were to prove essential for the demands of his later career. The 'Rules for the direction of my conduct while a student' written in his copy of the New Testament include the warning, 'Never let me trifle with a book with which I may have no present concern … [L]et me continually endeavour to make all my studies subservient to practical religion and Ministerial usefulness' (ibid., 1.97).

Minister at Kibworth Harcourt Doddridge preached his first sermon at Nuneaton on 30 July 1722, while still a student. In April 1723 he was invited to Kibworth, which had been without a minister since Jennings's removal to Hinckley; the congregation, consisting mostly of farmers and graziers, numbered fewer than 250, and the salary was only £35 p.a. Advised by Clark to accept, in the meantime Doddridge was tempted by the prospect of an invitation to Coventry, with a very large congregation of 1200 members. By May he had accepted Kibworth, as support for him at Coventry was not unanimous. On 1 June he moved to a village near Kibworth called Little Stretton, where he boarded with a farmer called Thomas Perkins; later he moved to Burton Overy, another nearby village, to the house of William Freeman, whose daughter Kitty rejected him after a long courtship. As his situation with the Freemans had become difficult he moved in September 1725 to Market Harborough (inconveniently further from Kibworth), where he boarded with John Jennings's widow and turned his attentions, again unsuccessfully, to her daughter Jenny. He remained with Mrs Jennings until December 1729.

The work at Kibworth was not onerous: Doddridge was required to preach twice a week in winter and once in summer, though after moving to Harborough he also preached there for the minister, David Some, who had been one of his examiners. He described himself in December 1723 as 'moderately inclined' to the Congregational form, 'our method of discipline at Kibworth, as it was in the time of Mr Jennings' (Nuttall, *Calendar*, no. 91). He told Clark on 17 February 1725 that he liked the Kibworth ministry because 'I may have an Opportenity of dealing very plainly in the pulpit, wch perhaps amongst a nicer People I might not at these years have ye Confidence to do' (DWL, LNC MS L1/10/5). His biographer Andrew Kippis, who heard Doddridge read these carefully prepared Kibworth sermons in later years to his students, thought them 'far superior' to those he then had time for (Kippis, 271). In his rural solitude, in which he lived 'buried alive' or 'like a tortoise shut up in its shell' (Nuttall, *Calendar*, nos. 129, 144), Doddridge spent most of his time continuing his programme of study. He received money for books from both the Presbyterian and the Congregational funds—he told Nettleton on 5 August 1725 that he had bought £20 worth of books in two years (*Correspondence*, 2.57); he also belonged to a book society, had access to the libraries of neighbouring ministers, and borrowed from his Kibworth congregation the books they had in their houses, chiefly seventeenth-century works of practical religion. His great love was Richard Baxter: he received a set of his *Practical Works* (1707) in 1724 (now in Dr Williams's Library), and observations in his letters and resolutions in his diaries indicate how carefully he read them. Reading Baxter's *Gildas Salvianus: the Reformed Pastor* made him think he should spend more time among his people and less on his studies. He was not ordained at Kibworth (which meant that he could not administer the Lord's supper), though there are several references in his letters from 1724 to 1728 to his intention to be so. His reputation was obviously increasing, and he received several further invitations during his Kibworth years from other congregations: Coventry again; Pershore, Worcestershire—'a very rigid set of people' (Nuttall, *Calendar*, no. 84); Girdlers' Hall, London, which Clark was keen for him to accept (ibid., no. 89); Bradfield, Norfolk; New Court, Carey Street, Lincoln's Inn Fields, London; and two separate Nottingham congregations, Independent at Castle Gate and Presbyterian at High Pavement. He refused partly because of emotional ties, partly because the Kibworth congregation would be in difficulty without him, and partly because, having been taught by Jennings 'that latitude of expression which the Scriptures indulge and recommend', he could not accept the obligation 'to talk in the phrases of the [Westminster] assembly's catechism' at Girdlers' Hall or the high orthodoxy of some members of Castle Gate (ibid., nos. 108, 315).

Meanwhile a new career was opening up. According to Job Orton, his biographer and close friend, Jennings had asked Doddridge when he left Hinckley to add to and improve his course of lectures, and Doddridge later learned that Jennings thought him 'the most likely of any of his Pupils, to pursue the Schemes which he had formed' (Orton, *Memoirs*, 48). He was fully responsible for bringing up Jennings's son John. In November 1726 he began going through some of Jennings's course with a pupil who had started it just before his tutor's death, and in December 1727 Thomas Saunders asked him to take his brother Joseph as a pupil, boarding with Mrs Jennings, to which Doddridge agreed in early 1729. Late in 1728 Doddridge's 'Account of Mr Jennings's method' (originally written for Thomas Benyon, who died just as Doddridge was finishing it) was shown to Isaac Watts, the leading educational theorist among the dissenters. Watts, who was to become the third key influence on Doddridge's development after Clark and Jennings, was impressed by the account and thought him a suitable person to continue the academy. On 10 April 1729 at a meeting of ministers in Lutterworth, Some proposed the establishment of the new academy at Market Harborough under Doddridge. Though he had initially refused Saunders's request, after seeking advice from Calamy among others Doddridge began teaching a small group of students at Whitsuntide 1729. This was the beginning of what was to become the most influential of eighteenth-century dissenting academies.

Minister at Northampton Not long after he had established himself as a tutor at Market Harborough, Doddridge received an invitation from a local congregation. Castle Hill Church, Northampton, had been without a minister since Thomas Tingey's departure for Fetter Lane, London,

at the end of 1728. On 28 September 1729 the congregation, having heard Doddridge preach to them occasionally, formally invited him to preach among them as a candidate for a month, 'in order for whole Satisfaction' (Deacon, 59). Clark, Some, and Doddridge all hesitated because of the double burden of a new academy and a large church on a young man, but the congregation were persuasive. On 21 October they applied to Clark, earnestly asking for Doddridge to settle among them, and agreeing to facilitate the transfer of the academy and recompense Mrs Jennings. Doddridge, having twice in November sought the advice of Watts and other London ministers, finally accepted the invitation on 6 December, and despite his distress at leaving the Jennings household moved to Northampton on Christmas eve 1729. His salary was £70 p.a. On 19 March 1730 he was ordained, with Clark giving the charge. He was to remain based in Northampton as pastor and tutor for the rest of his working life.

The meeting-house at Castle Hill was built in 1695, but the church, Presbyterian in origin, was in existence in some form by 1674. The Independent Samuel Blower, ejected from Woodstock, Oxfordshire, after the Act of Uniformity in 1662, became its first minister. He was succeeded in 1694 by Thomas Shepherd or Shepard, under whom the church building was erected, and then in 1699, after a three-year gap, by John Hunt (like Shepard a hymn writer), and in 1709 by Doddridge's predecessor, Tingey. In the 1690s Castle Hill had an uneasy relationship with what was to become in 1697 College Lane Church (later College Street), the Baptist church in Northampton associated with the Congregationalist Richard Davis of Rothwell. Under Doddridge these denominational differences, which had been the cause of much bitterness, ceased to be significant. His ministry became the source of a new and eclectic kind of dissent in which seventeenth-century puritanism and eighteenth-century freedom of thought fed into the evangelical revival.

Soon after moving to Northampton, Doddridge set out his views on what the distinctive character of modern dissent should be in the anonymous pamphlet *Free Thoughts on the most Probable Means of Reviving the Dissenting Interest* (1730), his first important publication, written in answer to Strickland Gough's *Enquiry into the Causes of the Decay of the Dissenting Interest* (1730), also anonymous. Gough blamed the falling membership of dissenting congregations on neglect of the fundamental dissenting principle of liberty of conscience, and attacked dissenting ministers for their anachronistic adherence to the manners of their puritan forebears. Doddridge agreed with Gough on the damage caused by 'unscriptural impositions' (it was for this reason that he had turned down invitations from several congregations), but he insisted that the crucial issue was the revival of practical religion. The minister should be in the fullest sense popular: 'he who would be generally agreeable to dissenters, must be an evangelical, an experimental, a plain and an affectionate preacher'. Where Gough emphasized liberty and politeness, Doddridge's key terms were 'piety and catholicism'. He claimed that these methods, as practised by his 'fathers and brethren', had brought about an increase in membership in the Northampton region in the last twenty years (*Works*, 4.202, 204, 213, 219, 220).

Information about Doddridge's activities as a minister in Northampton and beyond can be gained from his diaries, letters, and published sermons, the church book still held at Castle Hill (drawn on by Deacon), and the biographies by his former pupils Orton and Kippis. In his diaries (transcribed by Thomas Stedman from shorthand) he habitually considered himself 'in the treble view, of a Pastor, a Tutor, and a Student'; as pastor he devoted every afternoon from 2 to 6 to visiting members of the congregation, especially 'servants, young people, children, and those under serious impressions', and to catechizing (*Correspondence*, 5.273, 281). He encouraged the young men to form religious associations. He preached twice on Sundays and administered the Lord's supper once a month, reviewing his activities in his diary each sacrament day. He also preached in surrounding villages to outlying members of his congregation. From 1741 he had four elders (including Orton) and six deacons to help him with administration and pastoral visits. He kept a close eye on the numbers at Castle Hill: on 13 May 1741 he told Watts that the congregation (or church attenders) totalled about 800, and the church members about 240, of whom about 180 had been admitted since he came; in December 1742 and December 1743 he reported a further increase in church membership, but in 1749 the congregation had fallen by 500 since 1741, partly through defection to the Moravians, though he was hopeful of new members. He was also active outside his own church, preaching for ministers in nearby towns and often taking part in ordinations. Early in 1741 he helped form an association of Northamptonshire ministers. Every summer he travelled to visit ministerial and other friends and former pupils, often to London, but also in different years to East Anglia and the south-west, and on these journeys he was much in demand as a preacher, however exhausted he found himself. At the beginning of 1744 he recorded having preached over 140 sermons the previous year, more than ever before. He continued to refuse invitations from prominent churches to be their minister, for example Princes Street, Westminster (Calamy's church), in 1733.

Doddridge's sermons (usually extempore) were often followed by his own hymns, based on specific biblical texts, which epitomized what the congregation had just heard. In his lectures on preaching (first published 1804) for his ministerial students in the academy he emphasized that the preacher should avoid topics such as the doctrines of natural religion and the evidences of Christianity, and concentrate on the covenant of grace, the operations of the Spirit, and the love of Christ. This emphasis is apparent in his published collections of sermons preached at Northampton, which include *Sermons on the Religious Education of Children* (1732), *Sermons to Young Persons* (1735), *Ten Sermons on the Power and Grace of Christ* (1736), and *Practical Discourses on Regeneration* (1741). He also published several separate sermons for ordinations, funerals, and public occasions.

Doddridge was brought up by Clark and Jennings to deplore the movement among orthodox dissenters to demand subscription to the doctrine of the Trinity, and he frequently spoke disparagingly in his letters of orthodoxy and bigotry. Clark was therefore surprised and disappointed when Doddridge denied his pulpit to the Arian James Foster in 1737: 'we cant be too careful not to give any Countenance to that narrow Spirit, which has done so much Mischief in the Christian Church' (Nuttall, *Calendar*, no. 480). Doddridge's usual spirit was anything but narrow; his ecumenical evangelicalism caused concern and embarrassment to many dissenters, including Watts and the trustees who administered William Coward's fund. In the late 1730s he took a keen interest in the activities of the Moravians, corresponding with James Hutton, though after meeting their leader, Count Zinzendorf, in 1741 he began to have doubts. He was welcoming to the Methodists: in July 1743 he preached at George Whitefield's London Tabernacle, and in October Whitefield reciprocated at Northampton; John Wesley visited him in September 1745, and at his request took his place in expounding scripture to his students; he dedicated *Christ's Invitation to Thirsty Souls* to James Hervey (1748), with a preface stressing that though they disagreed about conformity and nonconformity, they preached the same doctrine; and his sermon entitled *Christian Candour and Unanimity* (1750) was inscribed in adulatory terms to the countess of Huntingdon.

Marriage and family As a young minister Doddridge had for some time been looking for a wife. In the summer of 1730 he found her. She was Mercy [see Doddridge, Mercy (1709–1790)], daughter of Richard Maris, a baker and maltster of Worcester, and his wife, Elizabeth Brindley. When her parents died she moved to Upton-on-Severn, the home of her uncle and guardian, Ebenezer Hankins. Doddridge met her at the house of her great-aunt in Coventry in July 1730, and they were married at Upton on 22 December. Their income at first consisted of about £120 p.a. (£70 from the church, £30 from the academy, and £20 from the dissenting funds), but Doddridge had hopes of an income of £56 p.a. from land in Hounslow and ground rent in London, which he inherited in 1743. A full and delightful picture of their married life emerges from the playful and passionate letters they exchanged when he was on his regular tours or she was away at Bath for her health (September 1742 to April 1743). They had nine children. The first, Elizabeth or Tetsey (1731–1736), died just before her fifth birthday; Doddridge preached her funeral sermon under the title *Submission to Divine Providence* (1737), but he found such submission very hard, and rebuked himself in his diary for doting on her. Their four children who survived to adulthood were Mary or Polly (1733–1799), who married John Humphreys of Tewkesbury; Mercy (1734–1809); Philip (1735–1785); and Anna Cecilia or Caelia (1737–1811). Mercy Doddridge had several miscarriages and gave birth to four other children who died as infants: Samuel (1739–1740), named after Clark; Sarah and Jane, twins who lived for two days (1746); and William (1748), who lived for six.

Academy tutor In January 1730 Doddridge set up his academy in his house in Marefair, Northampton; in 1740, in order to accommodate increasing numbers, he moved it to a substantial house in Sheep Street, rented from the earl of Halifax. A great deal of information about the academy survives in various forms: letters about principles and organization and the problems of individual students, and diary entries about teaching preparation; his description of his teaching methods in 'Some account of the life and character of the Rev. Thomas Steffe', prefixed in 1742 to the *Sermons* of Steffe, a former student who died in 1740; 'Constitutions orders & rules relating to the academy at Northampton', agreed between tutors and students in 1743 (Deacon, appx 9); the idealized portrait of the academy of Euphranor in *Dialogues Concerning Education* (1745–8) by his friend David Fordyce, the Aberdeen moral philosopher; his posthumously published *Course of Lectures on the Principal Subjects in Pneumatology, Ethics, and Divinity* (1763) and *Lectures on Preaching* (1804); and the biographies of Orton and Kippis. Doddridge originally wanted to take students for the ministry only, but he was roundly rebuked for this in a letter of 9 December 1732 by his ministerial friend David Jennings, his former tutor's younger brother: 'The Support of our Interest comes from the Layity, and they will not be obliged to bring up all their sons ministers or Dunces' (Nuttall, *Calendar*, no. 382). In November 1733 he was prosecuted at the instigation of the chancellor of the diocese of Lincoln, George Reynolds, son of the bishop of Lincoln, Richard Reynolds, for teaching without an episcopal licence. He sought legal advice with the help of his Northampton patron Lord Halifax and prominent London dissenters, and was supported in his refusal to take out a licence by Sir Robert Walpole and the attorney-general. He told his wife on 31 January 1734, 'The Judges [in Westminster Hall] order'd a prohibition to be issued which secures me from all further Trouble' (Nuttall, *Calendar*, no. 400), and Reynolds failed in his attempt to challenge the prohibition in June. This case, of great importance for the cause of dissenting education, may have helped recruitment to the academy.

According to Orton, in his twenty-two years as tutor Doddridge educated over 200 students, of whom 120 became ministers (Orton, *Memoirs*, 120). At a high point in July 1737 he had forty-four students; the numbers dropped in later years, but he was confident of their quality: he told the Connecticut minister Daniel Wadsworth in an important letter of 6 March 1741, 'I have at present a greater proportion of pious & ingenious Youths under my care than I ever before had' (Nuttall, *Calendar*, no. 663). The students paid £16 p.a. for board (£14 if they were assisted by one of the dissenting funds), and £4 for tuition; they also paid a guinea (£1 1s.) for a closet (or small study), another for the library, and another towards the cost of the scientific apparatus, and they brought their own sheets and paid for their own candles and laundry.

As a tutor Doddridge owed the basic framework of his course to Jennings, but he considerably enlarged its content. Among his surviving books and manuscripts in Dr Williams's Library are his annotated copies of Jennings's text books, *Logica* (1721) and *Miscellanea* (1721), and Jennings's interleaved divinity lectures, 'THEOLOGIA'. His own lectures were in continuous process of revision and expansion. He provided an invaluable summary for Wadsworth: 'Most of the Lectures I read are such as I myself draw up, specially in Algebra; Jewish Antiquities; Pneumatology, Ethicks, Divinity, & the Manner of Preaching, & the Pastoral care in its Several branches.' He also lectured on texts such as Watts's *Logick*, Keill's *Anatomy*, Desaguliers's *Philosophy*, Buddeus's *Compendium historiae philosophicae*, and Lampe's *Ecclesiastical History*,

> besides Severall Miscellaneous Lectures on other Subjects the Number of which I shall be continually increasing. I have also every Morning an Exposition of a Chapter of the Old Testament and in the Evening in the New they are reading the Chapter from the Original. I also give them once a week critical notes on the N: T which they transcribe as they do my other MSS Lectures generally in short hand, which I teach them as soon as they come under my care. (Nuttall, *Calendar*, no. 663)

The course lasted four years, with a fifth year for ministerial students. All students were required to have a reasonable standard of Latin and Greek on arrival, and they continued the study of classical literature for the first two years. They began Hebrew in the first year. Kippis queried Orton's statements that they were taught natural and civil history, civil law, mythology, and English history, but they were in agreement that the lectures on pneumatology, ethics, and divinity formed the most important part of the course (manuscript copies survive at Dr Williams's Library, Harris Manchester College, Oxford, and Doddridge and Commercial Street United Reform Church, Northampton). The 230 lectures in ten parts begin with the faculties of the human mind, continue with natural religion (the being of God, the nature of moral virtue, and the immortality of the soul), then turn to the evidences for revelation, and conclude with Christian doctrine. Doddridge used an idiosyncratic structure derived from Jennings: 'axioms, definitions, propositions, lemmata, demonstrations, corollaries, and scholia, just in the method which mathematicians use' ('Account of Steffe', *Works*, 4.253n.). Watts had criticized this aspect of Jennings's course when he read Doddridge's 'Account of Mr Jennings's Method', but Doddridge was certain of its value: 'It is with the humblest Deference to the vastly superior judgement of Dr Watts that I still think Mr Jennings's Method of Treating Logical & Ethical subjects of all others the most proper for Academical Lectures' (DWL, MS 24.180.3).

In practice the lectures must have been much more exciting than they at first appear on paper. Doddridge's method clearly illustrated his principle of free enquiry: he assembled from various authors arguments for and against a particular position, discussed their merits, and indicated his own position; the students followed up the references in the library, and at the next lecture were questioned on their reading and conclusions. He introduced them to a very wide and heterogeneous group of philosophical and theological authors, ranging from dissenters and churchmen to deists and freethinkers. In his treatment of Christian doctrine, according to Kippis,

> though he stated and maintained his own opinions, which in a considerable degree were Calvinistical, he never assumed the character of a dogmatist. … The students were left to judge for themselves; and they did judge for themselves, with his perfect concurrence and approbation. (Kippis, 280)

The remarkable library which made this wide reading possible contained several thousand volumes, many presented to the library by Doddridge's friends, some bought by him with the guinea of each new student, and inscribed 'In Usum Academiae' with the date and the donor's name. They also had access to his own collection. Kippis warmly remembered Doddridge lecturing on the use of the library, going over the shelves in order and giving the character of each book and author. (About 200 of the academy books and about 500 of his own survive in Dr Williams's Library, brought together by G. F. Nuttall.)

Doddridge could not sustain unaided the burden of the academy and church, his writing, his correspondence, and his engagements outside Northampton, so he employed a succession of assistants from among his former students to help him with teaching: Orton, Thomas Brabant, James Robertson, and Samuel Clark, the son of his early mentor. Students who went on to make their mark as ministers, educators, or men of letters included, in addition to these, Risdon Darracott, Benjamin Fawcett, Fordyce, Kippis, John Aikin, and William Rose. The academy attracted not only English dissenters but Scottish Presbyterians, members of the Church of England (Steffe, the son of a clergyman, became a dissenting minister), and some students from the Netherlands.

Doddridge's status as one of the foremost educators in England was widely recognized: he received the degree of DD from Marischal College, Aberdeen, in 1736 with the support of Fordyce and Thomas Blackwell, and from King's College, Aberdeen, the following year; he was consulted in January 1744 by Richard Newton, principal of Hertford College, Oxford, who was grateful for his summary of his methods in the life of Steffe; he was asked by John Wesley for help with *A Christian Library*, and on 18 June 1746 he sent Wesley a long and important letter of suggestions (based on his *Lectures on Preaching*), characteristically emphasizing that 'a young minister should know the chief strength of error' (*Correspondence*, 4.484–95).

Principal publications Doddridge's publishing career began in February 1728, when he was asked to review books for the *Present State of the Republick of Letters*; he offered to review Isaac Newton's *Chronology of Ancient Kingdoms Amended* and Francis Hutcheson's *Essay on the Nature and Conduct of the Passions and Affections*. A lengthy abstract of Newton appeared in the journal in April 1728 (pp. 253–352). It is not possible to determine which reviews he wrote (they were all anonymous), but Kippis refers to 'papers' in the plural (Kippis, 292). In 1742–3 he published *An Answer to a Late Pamphlet, Intitled, Christianity not Founded on Argument*, in the form of three letters to the anonymous author Henry Dodwell, a freethinker masquerading as a

Methodist. Doddridge had long been interested in the attacks by freethinking writers on natural and revealed religion and in the importance of mounting a rational defence of Christianity. His copies of several freethinking works survive in Dr Williams's Library, notably Toland's *Letters to Serena* (1704) and *A Collection of Several Pieces* (2 vols., 1726, with a record of the names of students among whom these circulated in 1733–5, including Aikin and Orton), Collins's *The Scheme of Literal Prophecy Considered* (1727), and Tindal's *Christianity as Old as the Creation* (1732, annotated in shorthand). He recommended in his *Answer* to Dodwell his own sermons on the evidences of Christianity (the last three of *Ten Sermons*, 1736), and pointed out that in several dissenting academies, 'to my certain knowledge, the rational evidences of natural and revealed religion, with such a view of the objections against both, are as regularly, and as methodically taught, as logic or geometry' (*Works*, 1.490, 499). This material forms parts 5 and 6 of *A Course of Lectures*.

Doddridge's most influential publications in his lifetime were *The Rise and Progress of Religion in the Soul* (1745), *Some Remarkable Passages in the Life of the Honourable Col. James Gardiner* (1747), and *The Family Expositor* (1739–56). The subtitle of *The Rise and Progress* indicates that it is 'a Course of Serious and Practical Addresses, suited to Persons of every Character and Circumstance: with a Devout Meditation or Prayer added to each Chapter'. The dedication to Watts describes it as 'a book, which owes its existence to your request, its copiousness to your plan, and much of its perspicuity to your review' (*Works*, 1.211). Watts had originally envisaged 'a small Book for the Poor, like Baxters *Call to the Unconverted*', and he did his best, after trying out the manuscript on his servants, to make Doddridge 'reduce the Language into easier Words and plainer Periods' (10 April 1744, Nuttall, *Calendar*, no. 963). Nevertheless Watts was certain of its usefulness: 'I am not ashamed, by what I have read, to recommend it as the best treatise on practical religion which is to be found in our language' (13 Sept 1744, *Correspondence*, 4.356–7). Doddridge partly attributed Dr James Stonhouse's conversion to it. Both this work and the next were widely distributed and translated into Dutch, French, and German. The *Life of Gardiner*, an exemplary biography and conversion narrative of the close friend whom Doddridge regarded as a 'Christian hero' (*Works*, 4.104), had the dual aim of persuading the doubting reader that Gardiner's experiences were not the product of enthusiasm and the devout reader that religious rapture must have a rational basis, and as a result it had a mixed reception from his friends. He was attacked in an anonymous *Letter to the Reverend Dr. Doddridge* (1747, possibly by William Wishart) for suggesting, after criticizing Gardiner's excessive doctrinal zeal, that ministers of the established churches of England and Scotland subscribed to formularies that they did not believe. Orton thought he did not reply because of the delicacy of the issue of subscription.

The Family Expositor, or, A Paraphrase and Version of the New Testament, the longest of Doddridge's works and the one to which he attached most importance, had its origin in his habit of expounding the New Testament in the evening to his students, though he had told Samuel Clark as early as 1724 that he was drawing up 'but only for my own use, a sort of analytical scheme of the contents of the epistles' (Nuttall, *Calendar*, no. 149). The *Expositor* was arranged in four parts: the Authorized Version in the margin; his own version, in italics, interwoven with his paraphrase; notes to the text; and the improvement (suggested prayer and meditation) at the end of each section (usually part of a chapter). The paraphrase and improvements unfortunately illustrate his reluctance to check his own fluency. He wrote the work in shorthand and then transcribed it for the press, the process taking much longer than he intended even though he worked on it daily. Volumes 1 to 3 (1739–48) appeared in his lifetime; volumes 4 to 6 (1753–6) were edited by Orton, who transcribed part of the sixth volume with help from some of Doddridge's students. According to a letter in the *Monthly Repository*, much of the introductory material in the fifth volume was written by Sir Philip Furneaux and others (*Monthly Repository*, 13, 1818, 734–5). In the preface to volume 1, dedicated to the princess of Wales, Doddridge explained that his aim was 'chiefly to promote *family religion*' and that he wrote for those without a learned education who did not have access to commentators (*Works*, 6.9). The lengthy lists of subscribers prefacing volumes 1, 4, and 5, about 2800 in all, indicate a very wide readership, among members of the established church as well as dissenters, and among the aristocracy (many of them women) as well as academics and ministers. It had reached its eighth English edition by 1799.

Doddridge also edited the works of others and gave literary help to his friends. For example, he made an abstract of the second volume of Warburton's *Divine Legation* and corrected Whitefield's *Journals* and Fordyce's *Dialogues* at their authors' request, wrote a prefatory letter to Joseph Williams's *Abridgment of Mr. David Brainerd's Journal* (1748), edited Robert Leighton's *Expository Works* (1748), and as Watts's literary executor together with David Jennings edited Watts's posthumous *The Improvement of the Mind*, part 2 (1751) and his *Works* (6 vols., 1753).

Last years and reputation Until a few months before his death Doddridge continued to do all he could to further the cause of protestant dissent and evangelical Christianity at home and abroad. Anxious letters from his friends urged him to slow down; after his recovery from a serious illness in early 1745, his friend the London minister John Barker warned him, 'may not a Man be intemperate in Labour as well as in liquors?' (Nuttall, *Calendar*, no. 1048). His additional labours in Northampton included starting a charity school in 1738, founding the county infirmary together with Stonhouse in 1743–4, and raising a volunteer force, together with Halifax, during the Jacobite rising of 1745. He was an active member of the Northampton Philosophical Society, founded in 1743, and supported inoculation against smallpox.

Outside Northampton, Doddridge became widely regarded as Watts's heir as the leading representative of the dissenting interest. Watts wrote a recommendation

for him to David Longueville, minister of the English church at Amsterdam, as a preface to the Dutch translation (1746) of *Practical Discourses on Regeneration*, in which he stated: 'if there were any Man, to whom Providence would permit me to commit a second Part of my Life and Usefulness in the Church of *Christ*, Dr. *Doddridge* should be the Man' (Orton, *Memoirs*, 150). Doddridge had friendly meetings with the archbishop of Canterbury, Thomas Herring, in the summers of 1748, 1749, and 1751, at the first of which he discussed the possibility of comprehending dissenters in the Church of England. In the spring of 1751 he intervened unsuccessfully with the bishop of London, Thomas Sherlock, over the case of the harassment of the Presbyterian minister Samuel Davies in Virginia. He took a keen interest in the development of New Jersey College, later Princeton, evident in letters to him from the president, Aaron Burr, from 1748 to 1750. In a sermon preached at a meeting of ministers in Kettering in 1741, *The Evil and Danger of Neglecting the Souls of Men*, he had asked 'Whether something might not be done, in most of our congregations, towards assisting in the propagation of christianity abroad, and spreading it in some of the darker parts of our own land?' (*Works*, 2.232), and in April 1751 he was still trying to promote missionary activity among the American Indians. Unsurprisingly, his correspondence became increasingly demanding, and though he sometimes coped by dictating his letters to his students, Kippis among them, he had to leave many unanswered.

From August 1750 Doddridge suffered from a violent cough, which became worse when he went to St Albans to preach Clark's funeral sermon in December, and badly affected him on his annual travels in June 1751. In July he set out with his wife from Northampton for the last time, leaving the younger Clark in charge of the congregation and academy, and staying for a month with Orton in Shrewsbury. In August it became apparent that he was dying. His doctors sent him to the Hot Wells at Bristol, and then advised that if he were to have any chance of survival he should go to Lisbon for the winter. His many friends, including the countess of Huntingdon, his congregation, and the Coward trustees, raised £300 for the fruitless journey. The Doddridges sailed from Falmouth on 30 September, reaching Lisbon on 13 October; he died just outside the city on 26 October, aged forty-nine. When his body was opened his lungs were found to be heavily ulcerated. He was buried in the cemetery of the British Factory. A monument with an inscription by Gilbert West was erected in Castle Hill church, but with an error in his age at death.

According to Kippis Doddridge was tall and thin, though his portraits show him plump-faced; in character he was sociable, open, and affectionate. He had an extraordinary capacity for work and for dividing his time between his ministerial, educational, and literary activities—as can be seen from the detailed 'schemes of business', meditations, and reflections recorded in his diaries from 1729 to 1751 (*Correspondence*, vol. 5). Kippis, who admired him greatly and inscribed his biography 'to the memory of my benefactor, my tutor, my friend, and my father', thought him ostentatious in describing his many commitments and too fond of applause (Kippis, 308). Doddridge was vain of his standing in the intellectual and social worlds, seen in his haughty reaction when the University of Glasgow would not award Clark the degree of DD on his testimony alone. More significant was the charge that he was a trimmer, made by those who were unsympathetic to his lifelong attempt as a moderate Baxterian Calvinist and opponent of subscription to steer between the extremes of old Calvinist orthodoxy and new rational dissent. Both Orton and Kippis strongly defended him against the charge. According to Orton: 'He used to take Comfort in this, that he was no worse treated, than those four excellent *Divines*, whose Writings, above all others, he admired, the Arch-bishops *Leighton* and *Tillotson*, Mr. *Baxter* and Dr. *Watts*' (Orton, *Memoirs*, 257). Kippis acutely pointed out that the rational dissenters 'could not easily persuade themselves that a man of such abilities, and general liberality of mind, could entertain very different opinions from their own; and they wished to have him rank more explicitly among them' (Kippis, 307).

In his will Doddridge left his manuscripts to Orton, and his library (except for 100 books) to the Coward trustees in perpetuity for the use of the academy; he hoped that Caleb Ashworth, minister at Daventry, would take on the academy (in place of his original choice of Orton, who had left to become minister at Shrewsbury). His most important posthumous publications, in addition to volumes 4 to 6 of *The Family Expositor*, were his *Hymns*, his *Course of Lectures*, and his *Lectures on Preaching*. He had awkwardly drawn attention to his unpublished hymns by describing Gardiner's delight in them (*Works*, 4.68, 92–4). Orton edited *Hymns Founded on Various Texts in the Holy Scriptures* (1755, corrected 1776); a few have long been popular, notably 'O God of Jacob', 'O happy day', 'Hark the glad sound!', and 'Ye servants of the Lord' (nos. 4, 23, 203, 210). There were several editions of *A Course of Lectures*: by Clark (1763; repr. 1776), Kippis (1794; repr. 1799), and Edward Williams in volumes 4 and 5 (1803–4) of his and Edward Parsons's edition of the *Works*; the editions of Kippis and Williams have a large number of updated references. The lectures, used as textbooks in several academies, were described by Williams as 'the most complete syllabus of controversial theology, in the largest sense of the term, ever published in the English language' (*Works*, 4.282). The *Lectures on Preaching*, to which Doddridge attached great importance, were published in volume 5 of the *Works* following the divinity lectures (as he had requested in his will) and separately in 1821. In addition to the *Works* (10 vols., 1802–5), the most important addition to the corpus was *The Correspondence and Diary* edited by his descendant John Doddridge Humphreys (5 vols., 1829–31), though Humphreys was a very cavalier editor, even by nineteenth-century standards. His scholarly fortunes have been transformed following the bicentenary of his death in 1951 thanks to the important work of G. F. Nuttall.   ISABEL RIVERS

Sources *Calendar of the correspondence of Philip Doddridge*, ed. G. F. Nuttall, HMC, JP 26 (1979) · *The correspondence and diary of Philip Doddridge*, ed. J. D. Humphreys, 5 vols. (1829–31) · *The works of the Rev. P. Doddridge, D.D.*, ed. E. Williams and E. Parsons, 10 vols. (1802–5) · J. Orton, *Memoirs of the life, character and writings of the late Reverend Philip Doddridge, D.D. of Northampton* (1766) · A. Kippis, 'Doddridge (Philip)', *Biographica Britannica, or, The lives of the most eminent persons who have flourished in Great Britain and Ireland*, 2nd edn, ed. A. Kippis, 5 (1793), 266–315 · G. F. Nuttall, ed., *Philip Doddridge, 1702–1751: his contribution to English religion* (1951) · G. F. Nuttall, *Richard Baxter and Philip Doddridge: a study in a tradition* (1951) · G. F. Nuttall, *New College, London, and its library* (1977) · M. Deacon, *Philip Doddridge of Northampton, 1702–51* (1980) · I. Rivers, 'Affectionate religion: Watts, Doddridge, and the tradition of old dissent', *Reason, grace, and sentiment: a study of the language of religion and ethics in England, 1660–1780*, 1 (1991), 164–204 · I. Rivers, *The defence of truth through the knowledge of error: Philip Doddridge's academy lectures* (2003) · I. Rivers, 'Dissenting and Methodist books of practical divinity', *Books and their readers in eighteenth-century England*, ed. I. Rivers (1982), 127–64 · J. van den Berg and G. F. Nuttall, *Philip Doddridge (1702–1751) and the Netherlands* (1987) · P. Doddridge, *The family expositor*, 6 vols. (1739–56) [subscription lists in vols. 1, 4, 5, not in *Works*] · A. Everitt, 'Springs of sensibility: Philip Doddridge of Northampton and the evangelical tradition', *Landscape and community in England* (1985) [includes analysis of subscription lists in *Family expositor*] · G. F. Nuttall, *Philip Doddridge: additional letters* (2001) · P. Jones, 'The polite academy and the Presbyterians, 1720–1770', *New perspectives on the politics and culture of early modern Scotland*, ed. J. Dwyer, R. A. Mason, and A. Murdoch (1982) [on the relation between Doddridge and Fordyce] · H. McLachlan, *English education under the Test Acts: being the history of the nonconformist academies, 1662–1820* (1931) · I. Parker, *Dissenting academies in England* (1914) · T. Gasquoine, J. J. Cooper, and others, *A history of Northampton Castle Hill church, now Doddridge, and its pastorate, 1674–1895* (1896) · J. Orton, *The Christian's triumph over death: a sermon occasioned by the much-lamented death of the Reverend Philip Doddridge, D.D.* (1752)

Archives Doddridge and Commercial Street United Reformed Church, Northampton, corresp. and papers · DWL, New College MSS, corresp., lecture notes, sermon notes, diary · DWL, Congregational Library MSS, lectures, letters · Harris Man. Oxf., lecture notes · JRL, transcript by T. Stedman of early shorthand letters · Northampton Library, family corresp. · Senate House Library, corresp. · UCL, lecture notes | BL, corresp. with Lord Lyttelton, RP1778 [copies] · Devon RO, letters to his daughter Mercy · JRL, letters to his wife, Mercy Maris · Yale U., Beinecke L., corresp. with Lord Lyttelton

Likenesses G. Vertue, line engraving, 1751 (after A. Soldi), NPG [*see illus.*] · oils, DWL; repro. in Nuttall, *Calendar* · prints, repro. in Deacon, *Philip Doddridge*, facing pp. 34 and 72

Wealth at death property in Hounslow and ground rent in London: will, 11 June 1741; codicil, 4 July 1749

Dodds, Sir (Edward) Charles, first baronet (1899–1973), medical scientist, was born on 13 October 1899 in Liverpool, the only child of Ralph Edward Dodds, businessman, of West Derby, Liverpool, and his wife, Jane, daughter of Charles Pack, businessman, of London. He was educated at Harrow County School for Boys, and entered the Middlesex Hospital medical school in 1916.

At the Middlesex Dodds very quickly showed his abilities as a scientist: he won the class prize for chemistry in his first year. A period of military service ended after he had a bout of pneumonia; soon after returning to the medical school, he became a demonstrator in chemistry to Dr A. M. Kellas. This helped him to meet the costs of his medical education, and he obtained further income by coaching students. In 1919, after achieving distinction in the second MB examination, he became assistant in physiology to Professor Swale Vincent, and in 1920 he succeeded E. L. Kennaway as first assistant in chemical pathology to the

Middlesex Hospital. Dodds was appointed lecturer in biochemistry in 1921, the year in which he qualified MRCS, LRCP. The following year he graduated MB, BS (Lond.) with honours. He had been an exemplary student, and had already proved his abilities as an excellent teacher, especially of the emerging subject of biochemistry.

Dodds's early researches were concerned principally with gastric and upper intestinal secretions, and their relationship to changes in alveolar carbon dioxide tensions. However, from 1923 onwards he became increasingly involved in endocrinological research, where his early interests included improving the methods then available for the purification of insulin, and studies that sought to identify the 'female sex hormone'. In 1923 Dodds married Constance Elizabeth (d. 1969), only daughter of John Thomas Jordan; they had one son. Dodds graduated PhD in 1924 and MD (Lond.) in 1926.

In 1925 Samuel Augustine Courtauld endowed the Courtauld chair of biochemistry for Dodds, who at the age of twenty-five became the youngest professor in the University of London. Courtauld also financed the building of an Institute of Biochemistry for the Middlesex, whose first director Dodds became in 1927. He continued to hold both these posts until he retired in 1965.

In 1928 Dodds undertook some investigations required during the illness of George V; for this he was appointed MVO the following year. However, his greatest fame derived from his work on the synthetic oestrogens; this began in 1932 and led to the discovery of diethylstilboestrol in 1938. In carrying out this research Dodds demonstrated his ability to recognize and to attract to the Courtauld highly talented research workers, of whom Wilfrid Lawson deserves special mention for the part he played in the synthesis of the artificial oestrogens.

Diethylstilboestrol had the great advantage of being active when taken by mouth. It proved valuable for the control of menopausal symptoms, but its major therapeutic application was in the control of metastatic carcinoma of the prostate. It was also used in veterinary practice, for caponizing, and for the tenderizing of meat. In recognition of this work, Dodds was elected FRSE in 1941 and FRS the following year. He had become FRCP in 1933.

Dodds's scholarship was recognized in many ways. At various times he held office as chairman of the Biochemical Society, chairman of the biological chemistry section of the International Union of Pure and Applied Chemistry, master of the Worshipful Society of the Apothecaries of London, and Harveian librarian of the Royal College of Physicians, London. He became FRIC in 1968. He was knighted in 1954 and created baronet in 1964. He was awarded numerous prizes and medals and was invited to deliver many named lectures. He received honorary degrees from the universities of Birmingham, Bologna, Cambridge, Chicago, Glasgow, and Melbourne, and honorary fellowships from several colleges worldwide. The recognition that gave him most pleasure was his election as president of the Royal College of Physicians, the first

time this distinction had been accorded to a laboratory-based physician; he held the post from 1962 to 1966.

Dodds served on many important committees, including Research Council committees, the National Research Development Corporation, the Food Standards committee, the scientific advisory committee of the British Empire Cancer Campaign, and the council of the Royal Society. He was chief consultant to the Beecham Group, and was to a large extent responsible for the development of facilities that enabled it later to produce and market successfully several semi-synthetic penicillins.

As a young man Dodds had greatly enjoyed motor racing, and for some years drove as an amateur at Brooklands. Thereafter he retained his love of Bentleys, latterly chauffeur-driven because (he said) he always speeded if he drove himself. Dodds liked to entertain, and his taste in food and wine was of the highest order. For twenty-three years he was custodian of the cellar of the Society of Apothecaries.

Dodds died at his home at 49 Sussex Square, Paddington, London, on 16 December 1973.

GORDON WHITBY, rev.

Sources F. Dickens, *Memoirs FRS*, 21 (1975), 227–67 · *Munk, Roll* · *The Times* (18 Dec 1973) · *The Times* (28 Dec 1973) · private information (1986)
Archives RCP Lond., corresp. and papers | RS, letters to Sir Robert Robinson · Wellcome L., corresp. with Sir Ernst Chain
Likenesses W. Stoneman, photograph, 1943, NPG · G. Argent, photograph, 1970, NPG · G. Argent, photograph, RS · A. C. Cooper Ltd, photograph, RS · R. Piper, oils, RCP Lond. · W. Stoneman, photograph, RS · photograph, repro. in Dickens, *Memoirs FRS*
Wealth at death £274,604: probate, 25 April 1974, *CGPLA Eng. & Wales*

Dodds, Eric Robertson (1893–1979), classical scholar, was born on 26 July 1893 at Church Street, Banbridge, co. Down in Ireland, the son of Robert Dodds (d. 1900) and his wife, Anne Fleming, née Allen. His father's family were northern Presbyterians, descended from Scottish immigrants; his mother's were Anglo-Irish, who had a dubious claim to aristocratic connections, but had intermarried with the natives. His father was the headmaster of Banbridge Academy, a small grammar school, who came to grief because of drink and died when his son was seven years of age. Dodds thus became wholly dependent on his mother, who supported him by teaching, first at Bangor on Belfast Lough and later, from 1902 or 1903, in Dublin. She was a conscientious but possessive and unsympathetic parent, and though Dodds escaped religious indoctrination his childhood was by no means altogether happy. But from an early age he was able to read widely; an author who made a specially deep impression was Sir Walter Scott, which is an interesting indication of the vein of romanticism which—though it stayed beneath the surface—never left him.

Education in Dublin and Oxford At St Andrew's College, Dublin, where his mother taught, and later at Campbell College, Belfast, Dodds obtained a good grounding in the classics and in modern literature, particularly from the sixth-form master at the latter school, Roby Davis, besides playing football well enough to be tolerated by the herd.

Eric Robertson Dodds (1893–1979), by Walter Stoneman, 1945

At an early age he thought independently about serious problems, without fear of questioning authority, and found that he did not believe in Christianity. Finally he was provoked by the tyrannical behaviour of a pompous headmaster into writing him an angry letter, and was expelled from Campbell College for 'gross, studied and sustained insolence'; a later headmaster apologized, and expunged this statement from the official records.

In 1912 Dodds entered University College, Oxford, with a scholarship in classics. Coming from a different country and holding radical opinions, he did not find life in pre-war Oxford altogether easy; but he made good friends among his contemporaries, and was successful in his studies. While working for classical moderations, the literary and linguistic part of the course, he had an excellent tutor in A. B. Poynton, who published little but later impressed Eduard Fraenkel as a learned man; and he was deeply influenced by the teaching of Gilbert Murray, who since 1908 had held the regius chair of Greek and who at this time lectured on the *Bacchae* of Euripides and held his famous class on the art of translation. In 1914 Dodds obtained a first class in classical moderations and won the Ireland scholarship.

During that summer Dodds spent a holiday in Germany, and only just got back in time. The university rapidly emptied, and for a time Dodds worked at an army hospital in Serbia, but after a few months the hospital ceased to exist and he returned to Oxford. He was a member of a small group of undergraduates, including Aldous Huxley and the future art critic T. W. Earp, who met weekly to read each other their poems. At a class on Plotinus given by J. A. Stewart, he found no other student present except T. S. Eliot, then a graduate student, who when Dodds had invited him to address this group read them 'The Love Song of J. Alfred Prufrock', which he had just written.

As an undergraduate Dodds continued to read widely in several languages. His interest in the occult, which had begun while he was still at Campbell College, continued. In 1911 he had discovered Ibsen and Yeats, and in 1912 he read Nietzsche, who taught him to reject not only Christian theology but Christian ethics. His discovery of Freud, which had even more important consequences for him, came rather later, after he had left Oxford.

In 1916 the head of Dodds's college objected to his support of the Easter rising, and though not formally sent down he was asked to leave Oxford. Many years afterwards, when it was put to him that in a year when England was fighting for her life and sustaining appalling casualties on the Somme, this was hardly surprising, he did not dissent. But he continued to work for Greats, and came back to Oxford to take the examination in 1917, obtaining a first class.

Lectureship at Reading and chair at Birmingham Returning to Dublin, he spent two years teaching in three different schools. He much enjoyed the literary life of the city, getting to know W. B. Yeats, George William Russell (AE), Lennox Robinson, and Stephen MacKenna, the translator of Plotinus, whose journals he later (1936) edited. But, as he once remarked, he had the wrong religion for one part of Ireland and the wrong politics for the other, and from 1919 he lived in England.

In that year Dodds was appointed to a lecturership in classics at the University of Reading, where he had several interesting colleagues and a congenial head of the department in P. N. Ure. He studied Neoplatonism, at that time by no means a fashionable subject, with the enthusiasm of a believer in its doctrines; later, after the belief had left him, the interest would remain. In 1922 he published valuable notes on Plotinus, and followed them with two small volumes, *Select Passages Illustrative of Neoplatonism*, the first (1923) containing texts and the second (1923) translations. On 11 August 1923 he married Annie Edwards Powell (1886/7–1973), the daughter of Canon Astell Drayner Powell. She was then a lecturer in English at Reading University, a highly cultivated and intelligent woman whose somewhat formidable manner and appearance concealed a sensitive and understanding nature. Despite the not entirely easy temperaments of both partners, the marriage was entirely happy, down to the time of her death in 1973.

In 1924 Dodds was appointed to a chair of Greek in the University of Birmingham. After a few years he and his wife managed to obtain a delightful house, with vegetable and flower gardens and a lake, in which they spent what was probably the happiest time of their lives. They were at the centre of a lively circle of congenial friends. Dodds appointed to a lecturership the poet Louis MacNeice, and became intimate with him and with his fellow poet W. H. Auden, whose family lived in Birmingham. Dodds later helped MacNeice with his fine translation of Aeschylus' *Agamemnon*, and after his death in 1963 acted as his literary executor. In 1929 Dodds himself published *Thirty-Two Poems*, some of which have found a place in various anthologies. He had a genuine poetic gift, as those who heard him lecture might easily guess; but he came to feel that his kind of poetry was old-fashioned, and ceased to write it.

In 1928 Dodds published in the *Hibbert Journal* a penetrating article on the *Confessions* of St Augustine, which he called 'a study of spiritual maladjustment'. In the following year he brought out an article called 'Euripides the irrationalist', later reprinted in his book *The Ancient Concept of Progress*. No author had suffered more than Euripides from the perennial tendency of scholars to read modern tendencies into ancient writings, and this paper, reversing the title of a then popular book by A. W. Verrall, supplied a valuable corrective. In 1933 appeared his edition with commentary of the *Elements of Theology* of Proclus, the most useful summary of Neoplatonic metaphysics which has survived from antiquity; A. D. Nock, later a valued friend of Dodds, in a review drew attention to the book's high quality.

Oxford chair In 1936 the regius chair of Greek at Oxford was due to be vacated by the retirement of Gilbert Murray, an incumbent of unique prestige. The prime minister, Stanley Baldwin, was content to leave the choice of a successor to Murray himself, thus presenting him with an awkward problem. The Oxford Hellenist who had the most distinguished work to show was J. D. Denniston, who had brought out in 1934 his authoritative study of *The Greek Particles*, and who was greatly liked and admired by both his colleagues and his pupils. But Murray felt that particles were too technical a subject, and did not think Denniston sufficiently 'original', an important word in his vocabulary. An energetic and colourful candidate for the chair, eleven years younger than Denniston, was C. M. Bowra, but though Murray liked him he did not altogether approve of him, and doubted whether his scholarship was sound enough. So Murray compromised by recommending Dodds, who was by no means eager to leave Birmingham, but found it difficult to refuse.

For many years both Dodds and his wife greatly regretted this decision. Virtually all members of the Oxford faculty had wanted either Denniston or Bowra, and few of them knew enough of Neoplatonism to appreciate the high quality of the main publications of Dodds up to that time. Unlike Denniston and Bowra, Dodds had not fought in the First World War, and his rumoured support of Irish republicanism and socialism did not add to his popularity, particularly in Christ Church, the college to which the regius professor of Greek automatically belongs. In his inaugural lecture, 'Humanism and technique in Greek studies', Dodds suggested that as there now existed texts of most ancient authors adequate for understanding scholars would do well to devote less energy to textual criticism and more to general interpretation. Though

there was much to be said for this view, Oxford was not a place in which it needed to be put forward, as Dodds afterwards became aware, and the lecture was not a success. A more outgoing character might have dealt more successfully with the awkward situation in which Dodds found himself. If one could find a way through his defences he had an unusual charm, together with a highly individual wit and humour, but he did not easily get on terms with new acquaintances, and his experiences intensified a natural tendency to be suspicious. It was many years before he really settled down among his Oxford colleagues.

Undergraduates, however, from the first greatly appreciated Dodds's teaching. A deep and impressive voice, in which he read poetry superbly, enhanced the appeal of lectures which combined scholarly exactitude with literary sensitivity to a remarkable degree. He was now working on his edition of Euripides' *Bacchae* and at the same time compiling the notes that were later to take shape as *The Greeks and the Irrational*; he delivered a memorable course of lectures on the *Oresteia* of Aeschylus, whose main connecting argument was later set out in his article 'Morals and politics in the *Oresteia*'.

On the outbreak of the Second World War, Dodds had no hesitation about supporting the war effort, and at once volunteered for service. He was active in preparations for dealing with the problems of German education, and in 1942–3 travelled to China on a cultural mission, vividly described in his autobiography. Later he visited the United States, and after the war travelled to Germany to help with the rehabilitation of the educational system.

In 1944 Dodds published his edition of the *Bacchae*, with introduction and commentary, later revised and appreciably improved in the second edition of 1960. Despite the preference given to humanism over technique in his inaugural lecture, the constitution of the text and other technical matters are dealt with in masterly fashion; but an even more notable feature of the book is the imaginative sympathy, matching in quality its exact scholarship and deep learning, with which the Dionysiac religion and its antagonist are treated.

The Greeks and the Irrational In 1949 Dodds travelled to Berkeley, California, to deliver the Sather lectures, and this resulted in the publication two years later of *The Greeks and the Irrational*. Interest in the problems discussed went back to Nietzsche and Rohde, if not to Creuzer, and the application of modern anthropology and psychology to their treatment was not new; Gilbert Murray and Jane Harrison had been pioneers in this respect. But now these disciplines had acquired a new assurance and stability, and Dodds was able to employ them with an impressive mastery of the material, ancient and modern. He was influenced by the social psychology of such neo-Freudians as Erich Fromm and Abram Kardiner, and by the new school of American anthropologists founded by Franz Boas.

In the first two chapters Dodds discusses the apology for his mistake in quarrelling with Achilles which Agamemnon offers in the nineteenth book of the *Iliad*. Agamemnon says that Zeus and the Erinys have placed in his mind

Ate, who has for the moment taken away his wits. Dodds finds parallels in other cultures for this kind of belief in divine interventions in human behaviour. Seeking a psychological explanation for it, he derives one first from the theory that Homer lacked a unified concept of the self and second from the Greek belief that wrongdoing was the consequence of ignorance, which made it imperative for anyone who had made a mistake to save face by attributing it to a divine intervention. It was necessary to save face because the Greek culture was at this stage a 'shame culture', though Greek culture would later become a 'guilt culture'.

This part of Dodds's book now seems open to criticism. First, the theory of Hermann Fränkel and Bruno Snell that Homer lacked a unified notion of the self is not now generally believed. Second, most people now hold that both guilt and shame figure in most cultures, and in any case, the attribution of the action to a god never causes the human agent to abdicate responsibility, so that no real belief in a supernatural interference with the course of nature is found here. But Dodds goes on to give a valuable account of Greek beliefs about madness and an analysis of the distinctive patterns of Greek dreams. The theory of the shamanistic origin of dualistic beliefs about the soul which he espoused has been refuted; more important is his account of the rise of these beliefs and their effect on Plato.

Dodds's account of the rationalism of the fifth century and the reaction against it is somewhat conditioned by an unconscious equation of the ancient with the modern 'enlightenment'. Much fifth-century rationalizing was only a working-out of what had been implicit in earlier thought, and in any case was the product of a limited number of intellectuals; the irrational forces thought to have been set in motion by the reaction to it had been at work much earlier, and even in the fifth century prevailed among ordinary men. But Dodds, building on a notable article of 1947, gives an admirable account of Plato's dealings with the problems of the irrational. The factor in the decline of Greek rationalism to which he gives most weight is what he called, echoing Fromm, 'the fear of freedom—the unconscious flight from the heavy burden of choice which an open society lays on its members'. Not everyone can share the cautious hope which Dodds expresses in the final pages that psychoanalysis will prove to be a remedy for this trouble. The book is written with great literary skill and much persuasive power, and throughout uses consummate erudition to illuminate many problems. Many of its contentions are open to dispute; it may be argued that Dodds was not sufficiently aware that the early religion was not dogmatic, like that of Jews and Christians, and so did not seriously impede rational argument. But the book set in motion a highly interesting discussion which has continued ever since.

Later life and work After the war Dodds's life in Oxford became much easier. He and his wife moved from their lodgings in the High Street to a pleasant house at Old Marston, at which Cromwell is believed to have received the surrender of the city, where Dodds was able to indulge his love of gardening. Younger men who owed much to his teaching and writing took their places on the faculty; the great value of his work gradually came to be understood, and he now exercised considerable influence. In 1959 he brought out a new text, with introduction and commentary, of Plato's *Gorgias*. Like his *Bacchae*, his *Gorgias* is excellent from the technical as well as from the interpretative point of view; but he chose this dialogue for its relevance to the modern situation, and the book fulfils a humanistic purpose.

So does the book *Pagan and Christian in an Age of Anxiety*, which resulted from the Wiles lectures delivered at Belfast in 1963 and published two years later. This work deals mainly with the period between the accession of Marcus Aurelius and the conversion of Constantine, sketching first the grim picture of the cosmos common to pagans and Christians at that time, second the equally common belief in daemons and other supernatural agencies, third the mysticism of the period, and fourth the dialogue between pagan and Christian, clearly bringing out their distressing resemblance to each other. This learned book has much value, though it has been objected that the picture of an 'age of anxiety' (a phrase borrowed from its author's friend Auden) is obtained by the selection of a limited portion of the evidence.

In 1973 Dodds reprinted six of his articles, adding four that had not been published, in a book called *The Ancient Concept of Progress*. In the same year his eightieth birthday was marked by the dedication to him of a special number of the *Journal of Hellenic Studies*, containing a 'Nocturne' by Auden, who died soon afterwards.

From his early youth Dodds was interested, like his predecessor Gilbert Murray, in psychical research; he served on the council of the Society for Psychical Research from 1927, and was its president from 1961 to 1963. He found the evidence for telepathy convincing, but though retaining an open mind upon the subject he was never persuaded by the alleged evidence for survival after death.

In 1977 Dodds brought out his autobiography, *Missing Persons*. It is beautifully written, and describes with modesty and candour a life more varied and eventful than most lives of scholars; it was awarded the Duff Cooper prize. Dodds died at his home, Cromwell's House, 17 Mill Lane, Old Marston, Oxford, on 8 April 1979.

Dodds became a fellow of the British Academy in 1942, and received its Kenyon medal in 1971. He was a corresponding member of the Academia Sinica, the Bavarian Academy, the American Academy of Arts and Sciences, and the Institut de France; he had honorary degrees from Manchester, Dublin, Edinburgh, Birmingham, and Belfast. He was an honorary fellow of University College, Oxford, and an honorary student of Christ Church.

HUGH LLOYD-JONES

Sources E. R. Dodds, *Missing persons: an autobiography* (1977) • D. A. Russell, 'Eric Robertson Dodds, 1893–1979', *PBA*, 67 (1981), 357–70 • H. Lloyd-Jones, *Gnomon*, 52 (1980), 78–83; repr. in *Blood for the ghosts: classical influences in the nineteenth and twentieth centuries* (1982), 287–94 • H. Lloyd-Jones, *Freud and the humanities*, ed. P. Horden (1985), 172–80 [repr. in H. Lloyd-Jones, *Academic papers* (1990), 297–305] •

B. Williams, *Shame and necessity* (1993) · personal knowledge (2004) · b. cert. · m. cert. · d. cert.
Archives Bodl. Oxf., corresp. and papers | Bodl. Oxf., corresp. with Clement Attlee, MS Eng. lett. c 469 · Bodl. Oxf., corresp. with Gilbert Murray · TCD, corresp. with Thomas McGreevy
Likenesses W. Stoneman, photograph, 1945, NPG [*see illus.*] · C. MacNeice, portrait, AM Oxf. · photograph, repro. in Lloyd-Jones, *Gnomon*, facing p. 80 · portraits, repro. in Dodds, *Missing persons*, facing p. 139
Wealth at death £74,400: probate, 10 Aug 1979, CGPLA Eng. & Wales

Dodds, James (1812–1885), Free Church of Scotland minister and author, was born at Hitchell Yett, Cummertrees, near Annan, Dumfriesshire, on 13 August 1812, the eldest son of William Dodds and his wife, Helen Irving, a relative of Edward Irving. He was educated at parish schools in Annan and Ruthwell, before attending the University of Edinburgh, where he gained the highest distinction in the class of Professor John Wilson. For a brief time he was tutor in the family of Henry Duncan, the well-known minister of Ruthwell. After studying for the ministry in the Church of Scotland, Dodds was licensed to preach in 1839 and assisted at Inveresk, Musselburgh, before his appointment to Humbie, East Lothian, in 1841. In 1843, after he had joined the Free Church, he was called to Dunbar, where he remained for the rest of his life. On 3 February 1843 he married Duncan's only daughter, Barbara Anne.

Dodds devoted his leisure time to literary pursuits: he was a frequent contributor to various periodicals, including the *Christian Treasury*, *Sunday at Home*, and *Leisure Hour*, and was an early editor of the *Dumfries and Galloway Courier*, which belonged to his father-in-law. In 1846 he published *A Century of Scottish Church History*, an outline of Scottish religious history from the Secession of 1733 until the Disruption in 1843. He wrote a biographical sketch of his friend Patrick Fairbairn, which was published in the latter's *Pastoral Theology* in 1875, as well as a memoir of the Revd Thomas Rosie, entitled *Coast Missions* (1862). His taste for biography was further indulged in *Famous Men of Dumfriesshire* (n.d.), a collection of sketches of well-known figures from his native region. He also wrote a memoir of his cousin James Dodds, which was published with the latter's *Lays of the Covenanters* in 1880, and a novel about the Disruption, *Jeannie Wilson, the Lily of Lammermoor* (1876). The *Dictionary of National Biography* claimed that Dodds was a regular correspondent of Thomas Carlyle, another native of Dumfriesshire, but this contention is not borne out by the sole letter addressed to him in Carlyle's collected letters. Dodds died on 3 September 1885 at Dunbar.

ROSEMARY MITCHELL

Sources Fasti Scot. · *Haddingtonshire Advertiser* (11 Sept 1885) · B. Dodds, 'Memoir', in J. Dodds, *Personal reminiscences and biographical sketches* (1887) · *The collected letters of Thomas and Jane Welsh Carlyle*, ed. C. R. Sanders and K. J. Fielding, 12 (1985), 29–31 · CCI (1885)
Wealth at death £3884 11s. 3d.: confirmation, 19 Oct 1885, CCI

Dodds, James (1813–1874), public lecturer and poet, was born on 6 February 1813 at Softlaw, near Kelso, Roxburghshire, the illegitimate son of Christian Dodds. James was brought up by his grandfather, a member of the Secession church, for whose humble, pious, and proselytizing character he had a lifelong admiration. From his earliest years he showed great abilities, a very impulsive and imaginative nature, and a daring, and sometimes adventurous, spirit. He was enabled through the sponsorship of friends to attend the University of Edinburgh, where he became well known among his companions for his remarkable powers of speech. He was, in succession, an actor in an itinerant theatrical company; schoolmaster at Sandyknowe; apprentice for five years to a Melrose lawyer, who seems to have experimented how to extract from a clerk the largest amount of work for the smallest amount of pay; then, in 1841, a lawyer's clerk in Edinburgh.

In Edinburgh Dodds served in the office of a firm of which John Hunter, writer to the signet, a connection of Lord Jeffrey, and well known in the literary circles of Edinburgh, was a member. Mr Hunter treated Dodds as a friend, and introduced him to many literary men. Thomas Carlyle, to whom he wrote regularly, gave him advice about his professional and artistic decisions. This friendship continued for many years, and when, in 1846, Dodds moved to London to become a parliamentary solicitor, he regularly visited Carlyle. From 1845 to 1847 he wrote the 'Lays of the covenanters'. These historical and biographical sketches of the victims of seventeenth-century religious persecutions appeared in different journals in Edinburgh, and were gathered into a volume in 1880. Dodds was also very close to Leigh Hunt whom he met in London. Hunt being constantly in pecuniary and other difficulties found in Dodds a most valuable friend. 'More than once he took the management of his affairs, giving him legal advice, conferring with his creditors, and arranging about the payment or partial payment of his debts' (Dodds, 80).

In the 1850s Dodds delivered many lectures on the subject of the Scottish covenanters; usually these were given in Scottish towns, but occasionally to metropolitan audiences; one of his lectures, in which he combined prose and poetry, lays and lecture, was given to an enthusiastic London assemblage of 3000 people. These lectures were composed with scrupulous historical care. When they came to be published in 1861 as *The Fifty Years' Struggle of the Covenanters, 1638–1688*, renewed pains were taken to make sure of accuracy. During this period, he also helped to secure the erection of the Wallace monument in Stirling. It was his intention to give another series of lectures on the Scottish Reformation, but of these only two were written. His natural eloquence, and his way of throwing his soul into the delivery, gave him great popularity and power as a lecturer. A lecture on Thomas Chalmers, for whom he had an intense admiration, developed into a volume of great interest. Dodds died of heart disease at Gordon Street, Lochee, Dundee, on 12 September 1874, and was survived by his widow, Janet, *née* Pringle.

W. G. BLAIKIE, *rev.* S. R. J. BAUDRY

Sources J. Dodds, *'Lays of the covenanters' with a memoir of the author* (1880) · W. A. Knight, *Some 19th century Scotsmen* (1903) · *The Scotsman* (Sept 1874) · CGPLA Eng. & Wales (1874) · d. cert.
Wealth at death under £600: administration, 8 Oct 1874, CGPLA Eng. & Wales

Dodds, Madeleine Hope (1885–1972), historian, was born on 2 January 1885. She was the second of the five children (four daughters and one son) of Edwin Dodds (*d.* 1929) of Home House, Kells Lane, Low Fell, Gateshead, co. Durham, and his wife, Emily (*d.* 1896), daughter of John Mawson of Low Fell. Edwin ran a printing and stationery business on Quayside, Newcastle upon Tyne, which had been founded by his father, M. S. Dodds, in 1834. Hope attended Gateshead High School for Girls and went to Newnham College, Cambridge, in 1904. She was awarded second-class honours in each part of the history tripos in 1906 and 1907. She spent a further year at Newnham researching for a thesis on the boroughs of the bishops of Durham which won the Creighton memorial prize in 1909. Women were not allowed to graduate at Cambridge until 1948, and in 1949 Hope took her MA. She was an associate of Newnham from 1945 until 1958.

Dodds's thesis derived from work which she began in 1907 for the Durham volumes in the Victoria History of the Counties of England. Newnham had established a link for its students with the Victoria history. Anxious to secure a fourth year at Cambridge, Hope wrote in June 1907 to the general editor of the Victoria history, William Page, asking whether he could provide her with a research project relating to Northumberland or co. Durham. Her tutor backed her request, and Page offered her paid work on his staff in London for as long as she wanted in order that she could gain some experience. She may have taken up the offer for a few weeks during the autumn. By October she was back at Newnham with a commission from Page to write the article on Darlington as an outside contributor at the rate of 1 guinea for every 1000 words, with a limit of around 5000 words. She submitted the article in August 1908. She went on to write several more articles, including those on Gateshead and Easington. Finally, in February 1913 Page commissioned her to write the article on Hartlepool and three shorter articles. The Victoria history was suspended nationally in 1916 because of the war but was revived in the early 1920s. Three of Hope's articles were at last published when volume 3 of the Durham Victoria history appeared in 1928. Work on the Durham history then ceased until the 1990s, but her unpublished articles remain part of its archives. Hope also found time to write, in collaboration with her younger sister Ruth, *The Pilgrimage of Grace, 1536–7, and the Exeter Conspiracy, 1538*, a two-volume history begun by 1909 and published in 1915 (reprinted in 1971).

In October 1915 Hope joined Ruth in weekend work at the munitions factory at Elswick, near Newcastle. With labour short because of the war, they next worked in the family business: Ruth started that October and Hope and the youngest sister, Sylvia, by the following February. By July 1916 Hope was helping her father transcribe the register of All Saints', Newcastle, for the Durham and Northumberland Parish Register Society, which he was instrumental in founding, but she found the work dull. In 1920 she published extracts from the Newcastle corporation minute book 1639–56 as the first volume of the publications of the Newcastle upon Tyne Records Committee. She

followed it in 1923 with a further volume relating to the freemen of Newcastle. In 1922 the Northumberland County History Committee appointed her editor of the multi-volume history of Northumberland which had been in progress since the early 1890s. Between 1926 and 1940 she produced the final four volumes (12–15), not only editing them but writing much of the contents. Other publications included contributions to various historical journals, notably *Archaeologia Aeliana*, published by the Newcastle Society of Antiquaries. She was a member of that society from 1908 and its librarian from 1941 until eye trouble forced her to resign in 1946. The society made her an honorary member in 1947.

Hope also had strong literary interests, including the history of English drama, and she published on literary as well as historical topics. She was an active member of the Progressive Players of Gateshead from the time of their foundation in 1920, and she provided much of the money for building the Gateshead Little Theatre, opened in 1943. When her eyesight failed towards the end of her life, she learned braille so as to be able still to read. In 1918 Hope and her sister Ruth started to attend Quaker meetings, and Hope had become a member of the Newcastle Society of Friends by the end of 1919. She was also a socialist and contributed to the monthly *Gateshead Labour News* (later the *Gateshead Herald*), of which the more politically active Ruth became editor in 1925.

Hope continued to live at Home House after her father's death in 1929, sharing it with Ruth and Sylvia. From 1940 to 1942 she also had a flat on the Isle of Wight, where her married sister Molly lived. Remembered as a quiet and retiring person but one who was full of gaiety and generosity, Hope died at Home House, 231 Kells Lane, Low Fell, Gateshead, on 13 May 1972. M. W. GREENSLADE

Sources *Archaeologia Aeliana*, 5th ser., 1 (1973), 223–4 · *The Times* (28 June 1972) · M. Callcott, ed., *A pilgrimage of grace: the diaries of Ruth Dodds, 1905–1974* (1995) · VCH records, U. Lond., Institute of Historical Research · E. Dodds and M. S. Dodds, letter book, 1915–20, Northumbd RO, ZMD 171/9 · [A. B. White and others], eds., *Newnham College register, 1871–1971*, 2nd edn, 1 (1979) · *Archaeologia Aeliana*, 3rd ser., 10 (1913), 84 · *Archaeologia Aeliana*, 4th ser., 19 (1941), xv · *Archaeologia Aeliana*, 4th ser., 24 (1946), xiii
Likenesses photograph (in old age), repro. in Callcott, ed., *A pilgrimage of grace*
Wealth at death £97,843: probate, 13 July 1972, *CGPLA Eng. & Wales*

Dodgson, Campbell (1867–1948), museum curator and art historian, was born at Oakwood, Crayford, Kent, on 13 August 1867, the youngest child in the family of one daughter and seven sons of William Oliver Dodgson, stockbroker, and his wife, Lucy Elizabeth Smith. He was educated at Winchester College (1880–86), before going up to New College, Oxford, where he took a first-class honours degree in Greats in 1890 and a second in theology in 1891. He abandoned his initial intention to take holy orders, and in 1893 was appointed to the department of prints and drawings at the British Museum; he succeeded Sir Sidney Colvin as keeper in 1912, a post he held until his retirement in 1932.

Although he came with no prior expertise in the field,

Dodgson swiftly established himself as a formidable print scholar of international repute, specializing in the early German school after the British Museum's acquisition in 1895 of William Mitchell's collection of woodcuts of the fifteenth and sixteenth centuries. Dodgson's *Catalogue of Early German and Flemish Woodcuts in the British Museum* (2 vols., 1903–11) immediately became the standard work on the subject. He was co-editor of the Dürer Society publications (1898–1911), and a tireless contributor on many aspects of print connoisseurship to all the major scholarly journals in his field, including the Viennese periodical *Die graphischen Künste*, the *Burlington Magazine*—he was a member of its advisory board from 1903, the date of its inception—and the *Print Collectors' Quarterly*, which he helped to found in 1911 and edited single-handed from 1921 to 1936. Apart from his work on the German school he was actively engaged in the acquisition of important French eighteenth-century prints for the British Museum, publishing a book entitled *Old French Colour Prints* in 1924, and in 1933, after his retirement, the Roxburghe Club catalogue of the proof states for Goya's *Desastres de la guerra*.

Dodgson's importance was not confined to the field of old master prints. Using the income derived from the family firm of Hope, Dodgson, and Cobbold, he built an extensive private collection which ranged from fine examples of the work of Manet, Degas, Pissarro, Toulouse-Lautrec, Odilon Redon, Käthe Kollwitz, and Carl Larsson to comprehensive holdings of many contemporary French and British printmakers. Muirhead Bone, Charles Conder, and Augustus John were among many artists working in Britain of whose prints he published *catalogues raisonnés*. From the outset, Dodgson developed his collection to complement the holdings of the prints and drawings department, ultimately bequeathing more than 5000 items to the British Museum, together with the sum of £3000 to be administered by the National Art Collections Fund for the department's benefit. In 1919 he was a prime mover in establishing a special prints and drawings fund under the auspices of the Contemporary Art Society, from which the British Museum had first refusal on all purchases until 1945.

Dodgson was an outstanding public servant in the integrity and mental discipline he brought to bear on all that he did. After supervising the move of the British Museum's prints and drawings collection to new quarters in the Edward VIIth Wing shortly before the outbreak of the First World War, he ran the department virtually single-handed from 1916 to 1918; at the same time he was working in intelligence for the War Office, a service for which he was made a CBE in 1918. After his retirement the pattern of Dodgson's existence remained much the same; he frequented the Burlington Fine Arts Club (of which he became a member in 1902), travelled extensively until the Second World War, and continued to both collect and publish to the very end of his life, as well as serving as honorary keeper of prints at the Fitzwilliam Museum in Cambridge from 1939 to 1946. He received the German government's Goethe medal for services to the history of German art in July 1933, honorary degrees from Oxford

and Cambridge in 1934 and 1936, and decorations from France and Belgium.

As a personality, Dodgson appeared an austere man of retiring manner whose iron-clad sense of duty—'Diligentia' was the Dodgson family motto which appeared on Dodgson's own book-plate designed by Thomas Sturge Moore in 1909—did not always endear him to more gregarious colleagues such as Sidney Colvin and Laurence Binyon; to the young John Pope-Hennessy he appeared in the latter part of his life to be 'like an old tortoise' (Pope-Hennessy to Antony Griffiths, 23 April 1978, BM), an impression aptly conveyed by the portrait of him etched by Andrew Freeth in 1938. Behind this reserve a more passionate nature was glimpsed by Oscar Wilde, who met him in February 1893 when Dodgson was engaged as a tutor to Lord Alfred Douglas. The engagement lasted no more than a few days, but Dodgson confessed to their mutual friend the poet Lionel Johnson to being quite spellbound by Wilde.

On 24 September 1913 Dodgson married (Frances) Catharine Spooner (1883–1954) [*see* Dodgson, (Frances) Catharine], daughter of William Archibald *Spooner, warden of New College, Oxford, and his wife, Frances; she was a practising artist who had studied at the Ruskin School of Drawing in Oxford and at the Royal Academy Schools and the Slade School of Fine Art in London. They set up house at 22 Montagu Square, Marylebone, London, where they maintained a comfortable existence devoted to serious cultural pursuits, holding regular exhibitions of Dodgson's own collection and the work acquired for the Contemporary Art Society after 1919. Although they had no children, the Dodgsons were notably kind to Campbell's many nieces and nephews, among whom they were particularly close to John Dodgson, who became a professional artist, and to Eveline Dodgson, who also studied at the Slade. She was briefly married to James Byam Shaw of Colnaghis, who remained a close friend until Dodgson's death, which occurred on 11 July 1948 at Chapel House, Mattock Lane, Ealing, London.   FRANCES CAREY

Sources F. A. Carey, *Campbell Dodgson: scholar and collector, 1867–1948* (1998) · F. Carey, 'Campbell Dodgson (1867–1948)', *Landmarks in print collecting: connoisseurs and donors at the British Museum since 1753*, ed. A. Griffiths (British Museum Press, 1996), 211–35 [exhibition catalogue, Museum of Fine Arts, Houston, TX, 1996, and elsewhere] · BM, department of prints and drawings, Campbell Dodgson MSS · A. E. Popham, 'Campbell Dodgson, 1867–1948', *PBA*, 36 (1950), 290–97 · *DNB* · J. B. Shaw, 'Campbell Dodgson, 1867–1948', in J. B. Shaw, *J. B. S.: selected writings* (1968), 133–5 · J. Pery, 'Painting a dream world from life', *John Dodgson: paintings and drawings* (1995), 6–25 [exhibition catalogue, Fine Art Society, London, 25 April – 19 May 1995; Gainsborough's House, Sudbury, Suffolk, 27 May – 23 July 1995; Royal West of England Academy, 30 July – 19 Aug 1995] · m. cert. · d. cert. · J. Pope-Hennessy, letter to Antony Griffiths, 23 April 1978, BM

Archives BM, department of prints and drawings | BL, corresp. with L. P. Johnson, Add. MS 46363 · LUL, corresp. with T. S. Moore · TCD, corresp. with Thomas Bodkin · U. Glas. L., letters to D. S. MacColl

Likenesses W. Strang, drawing, 1904, Dresden Print Room; photograph, BM · F. Dodd, etching, 1908, NPG · C. Dodgson, chalk drawing, 1934, BM · W. Born, pencil drawing, 1936, FM Cam. · H. A. Freeth, etching, 1938, BM, NPG, V&A · H. A. Freeth, drawing, 1939,

BM · W. Stoneman, photograph, 1939, NPG · F. Dodd, chalk drawing, BM · W. Strang, etching, NPG

Wealth at death £78,532 7s.: probate, 3 Dec 1948, *CGPLA Eng. & Wales*

Dodgson [*née* Spooner], **(Frances) Catharine** (1883–1954), portrait painter, was born on 15 December 1883 at Oxford, the eldest daughter of the Revd William Archibald *Spooner (1844–1930), afterwards warden of New College, Oxford, and his wife, Frances Wycliffe, daughter of Harvey *Goodwin, bishop of Carlisle. At the age of fifteen she studied drawing at the Ruskin School of Drawing at Oxford, and later attended the Royal Academy Schools and (for a short period) the Slade School of Fine Art. In 1913 she married Campbell *Dodgson (1867–1948), keeper of prints and drawings in the British Museum, and from that time until her husband's retirement in 1932 she was chiefly occupied with social and domestic responsibilities in her house in Montagu Square, and found little time for drawing or painting. An oil painting by her, a portrait of Dean Inge (whose wife was her first cousin), was exhibited at the Royal Academy in 1923; but it was not until the middle of the 1930s that Catharine Dodgson began again to indulge her artistic inclinations, and it was from that time onwards that most of her surviving work was produced. She then abandoned painting in oils, and her favourite medium, in which she achieved considerable success, was drawing in pen or black or red chalk, with transparent washes of pale brown, often on coloured paper and heightened with white.

Between 1933 and 1945 Catharine Dodgson exhibited about a dozen portrait drawings at the Royal Academy, including those of her husband (1933; British Museum), of Dean Inge (1934; priv. coll.), and of Sir Thomas Barlow (1936; priv. coll.). She had a real flair for catching a likeness, her portrait drawings were in great demand, and she could have had many more commissions than she had time or inclination to carry out. She remained in the best sense an amateur; she was too conscientious to enjoy a commission for its own sake, and she lacked the self-confidence that enables a professional portrait painter to impose his personality on a subject in which he is not particularly interested. Her best portraits, therefore, were those of her own family, of intimate friends, or of children.

A visit with her husband to Würzburg, and the charming gardens of Veitshöchheim, provided Dodgson with a new source of inspiration, with equally successful results; and excellent examples of her elegant drawings of German rococo sculpture, made on this occasion, are now in the Ashmolean Museum at Oxford and in various private collections. In the same vein she drew the busts of Sir Christopher Wren by Edward Pierce (Ashmolean Museum) and Charles II by Honoré Pelle in the Victoria and Albert Museum. She also produced some drawings of dancers in the Covent Garden Opera in the same medium, and, towards the end of the war of 1939–45, some sketches of Regent's Park, rather more elaborate in colour, and remarkable for their lightness and deftness of touch.

Her husband's illness a year or two before his death in 1948 affected Catharine Dodgson's own health very seriously, and she hardly drew again; she died in London on 30 April 1954. Two exhibitions of her drawings were held at Colnaghi's in Bond Street, in the autumn of 1936 and in the spring of 1939, and both were warmly praised by the critics. She was modest to a fault, and was inclined to attribute this success to the writers' friendship with her husband, who was of course widely known and respected in artistic circles. But few seemed to share this view, least of all Campbell Dodgson himself, who was genuinely proud of her achievements. A loan exhibition in her memory was held in the same gallery after her death, October–November 1954. JAMES BYAM SHAW, *rev.*

Sources private information (1971) · personal knowledge (1971)
Archives Wellcome L., letters to Helen Barlow

Dodgson, Charles Lutwidge [*pseud.* Lewis Carroll] (1832–1898), author, mathematician, and photographer, was born at Daresbury parsonage, Cheshire, on 27 January 1832, the eldest son and third of eleven children of Charles Dodgson (1800–1868), curate of the parish, later rector of Croft-on-Tees, Yorkshire, examining chaplain to the bishop of Ripon, archdeacon of Richmond, and canon of Ripon Cathedral, and his wife and first cousin, Frances Jane, *née* Lutwidge (1803–1851).

Early years and education For eleven years the Dodgsons lived in 'complete seclusion from the world', during which time Charles's precocity and uncommon nature emerged: he 'invented strange diversions for himself', made pets of 'odd and unlikely animals', and implored his father to explain the meaning of logarithms (Collingwood, 11). In later years Dodgson reminisced about:

An island-farm—broad seas of corn …
The happy spot where I was born.
('Faces in the Fire')

In 1843 Peel, the prime minister, appointed the elder Dodgson to the more lucrative living at Croft-on-Tees, and at this bustling spa and hunting centre the young Dodgson grew and blossomed. At thirteen he inaugurated a series of family magazines and produced single-handedly the first one, *Useful and Instructive Poetry*, containing fifteen verses, a prose piece, and numerous drawings, altogether a remarkably gifted performance, adumbrating the infectious wit and literary ingenuity that would later bring him fame. He went on to edit and compose most of the seven later family magazines. He wrote plays for a marionette theatre that the family and a local carpenter built; he dressed up in a brown wig and white gown and as Aladdin nimbly performed conjuring tricks.

Dodgson was educated at home by his parents until he was twelve; then he entered Richmond School, 10 miles from home, and two years later, Rugby, where he spent almost four unhappy years. At both schools he distinguished himself and took numerous prizes. In 1851 he matriculated at Christ Church, Oxford, where his father had taken a double first. His mother's death, a few days after he arrived at university, affected Dodgson deeply and is thought by some to have inhibited his emotional

Charles Lutwidge Dodgson [Lewis Carroll] (1832–1898), by unknown photographer, c.1856–60

growth. He none the less did well in his studies, won a Boulter scholarship, and with his BA (1854) took first-class honours in mathematics and a second class in classics.

Oxford don and cleric In 1852 E. B. Pusey nominated Dodgson for a studentship (life fellowship) of Christ Church and in 1855 he became mathematical lecturer there. Christ Church dons were at that time required to take clerical orders and remain unmarried. Dodgson was ordained deacon on 22 December 1861, but never took priest's orders. His lifelong stammer and a deaf right ear may have contributed to that decision, but it is more likely that he did not see eye to eye with church doctrine. Influenced by the works of S. T. Coleridge and F. D. Maurice, whom he knew and admired, Dodgson veered from his father's high-church and ritualist faith to embrace the less pretentious broad church. He was genuinely devout, relying on inner instinct perhaps more than external teachings as a basis for divine truth; he rejected eternal punishment as a doctrinal certainty; with an ecumenical outlook, he embraced the whole of humanity, even those who had never heard of Christ, as children of God; and he was convinced that all sinners could find salvation through repentance.

In spite of his infirmities, Dodgson preached from various pulpits, impressing congregations with his religious fervour. He also lectured away from his college, to children and older students, particularly at girls' schools and colleges, on mathematics and logic. He often gave private tuition to youngsters as well, and observers could not help noticing the stream of young females arriving at Christ Church and mounting Tom Quad staircase 7 to be taught and photographed by Mr Dodgson. Remarkably, Christ Church actually allowed him to break through the roof above his rooms and build a glasshouse where he could photograph his protégées in daylight.

Early publications Dodgson wrote and published voluminously, mathematical and literary works and a good deal else. From his early days as lecturer he brought out mathematical broadsheets to help students meet Oxford's requirements. Opinions of him as a lecturer were divided: '"unwilling men" found him a very uninspiring lecturer', a niece of his wrote, 'dull as ditchwater' (V. Dodgson). One of his students recalled, however, that 'his methods of explaining the elements of Euclid … [were] extremely lucid, so that the least intelligent of us could grasp at any rate "the Pons Asinorum"' (Pearson). A sixth-form student at the Oxford High School for Girls remembered that he:

> compelled me to that independence of thought I had never before tried to exercise. … gradually under his stimulating tuition I felt myself able … to judge for myself, to select, and … to reject. … Mr Dodgson at the same time bestowed on me another gift. … He gave me a sense of my own personal dignity. He was so punctilious, so courteous, so considerate, so scrupulous not to embarrass or offend, that he made me feel that I counted.   (Rowell)

Dodgson worked assiduously at his mathematics. His first book appeared in 1860, when he was twenty-eight: *A syllabus of plane algebraical geometry, systematically arranged, with formal definitions, postulates, and axioms*, a 154-page effort to translate some of Euclid into algebraical terms and to claim for analytical geometry a greater role in developing reason and logical thinking than was generally conceded. He went on to publish major works which have earned fresh analysis and new appreciation a century and more after he died. Dodgson revered Euclid. Euclid dominated his professional work, and he devised fresh approaches to the master, refusing to tamper with his texts, since he insisted that Euclid had to be seen plain. Instead, he sought to clarify difficulties and to make Euclid more accessible to modern minds. In *Euclid and his Modern Rivals* (1879), engagingly built as a four-act comedy and a Platonic dialogue enhanced by Dodgson's trump card, his whimsy, he presented a forceful argument against all who had meddled with Euclid's text. From that point on esoteric work followed esoteric work, virtually always embellished by his hallmark, that characteristic Dodgsonian wit; even a century later, when professional mathematicians see a reference to some of the examples that Dodgson used to illustrate his arguments—for instance 'What the tortoise said to Achilles' or 'The barber-shop paradox'—they chuckle. Some try to imitate his method of leavening serious labours with lively jests, but they invariably lack his remarkable inspiration. In *Condensation of Determinants* (1866), according to one specialist, it 'is possible that Dodgson produced the first proof in print of … [a] fundamental theorem on rank' (F. Abeles, 'Determinants and linear systems: Charles L. Dodgson's view', *British Journal for the History of Science*, 19, 1986, 331–5); another writes of 'Dodgson's startling contribution to linear algebra and to the theory of determinants' (Seneta). Other important works included *The Fifth Book of Euclid Treated Algebraically* (1868), *Euclid, Book V* (1874), *Euclid, Books I, II* (1875), and *Curiosa mathematica* (3 pts, 1888–99).

From 1854 onwards, when two of his poems appeared in the *Oxonian Advertiser*, Dodgson produced a steady flow of creative works. Poems and prose pieces, games, and puzzles appeared in the *Whitby Gazette*, the *Comic Times*, *The Train*, *College Rhymes*, *Temple Bar*, Dickens's *All the Year Round*, *Punch*, *Fun*, *Vanity Fair*, the *Educational Times*, the *Monthly Packet*, *Aunt Judy's Magazine*, and *The Lady*. For his poem 'Solitude' (*The Train*, March 1856), he created his famous pseudonym by inverting 'Charles' and his metronymic, 'Lutwidge', translating them first into Latin and then back into English.

Alice Liddell and *Alice's Adventures in Wonderland* Dodgson's elevation from undergraduate to don coincided with the arrival at Christ Church of a new dean, Henry George Liddell, and his family, an event that only briefly preceded Dodgson's purchase, on 18 March 1856, of a camera and lens to allow him to take up photography. It was through photography that, on 25 April 1856, he first became acquainted with the Liddells' three daughters, including the middle one, Alice Liddell [*see* Hargreaves, Alice Pleasance], not quite four years old, when he and a friend went over to the deanery to photograph Christ Church Cathedral. 'The three little girls were in the garden most of the time, and we became excellent friends,' Dodgson wrote; 'we tried to group them in the foreground of the picture, but they were not patient sitters' (*Diaries*, 83). Thus began one of the most exceptional friendships, indeed love affairs, of all time.

We can only imagine the exhilaration that Dodgson experienced at the coalescence of these events, all three occurring within a mere six-month period, but surely they worked together to help generate the instantaneous fulguration that we know as *Alice's Adventures in Wonderland*. The tale flashed into Dodgson's mind on 4 July 1862, on that memorable river picnic when he responded to the girls' eager plea for 'a story'.

Dodgson's visits to the deanery became frequent, his emotional attachment to Alice grew and ripened, and for some seven years he lived the charmed life of a cherished friend and sometimes consort to the beautiful, impetuous child. In late June 1863, however, some event that he recorded on a page in his diary, but which a Dodgson heir later razored out, caused a breach in the relationship, and Dodgson was 'sent to Coventry'. Although he and the Liddells managed again to be civil to one another, the romance was over. Dodgson kept a formal distance from his 'ideal child friend' (*Letters*, 561), and Alice went on to

marry a suitor her parents judged more acceptable, Reginald Hargreaves. She lived out her life in a large, dull country house in the New Forest, where she sought to emulate her mother's social success at the Christ Church deanery. She named her third son Caryl.

Child friends For his part, Dodgson had other strings to his bow. As a don, cleric, and successful photographer in the age when everyone sought to be photographed, he had access to the best homes and to troops of attractive children, particularly the female of the species. He doted on them, took them on outings, bought them gifts, fed them, clothed them, carried them off on railway journeys, gave them inscribed copies of his books, wrote poems for and to them, told them stories, paid for their French and art lessons, took them to the theatre and to the seaside, sat them on his knees, hugged them, kissed them, and, of course, photographed them, in all manner of poses, in a variety of dress and costume, and even 'sans habillement', as he put it (unpublished diary, 21 May 1867, BL, Add. MSS 54340–54348)—all this with their parents' approval in that unsuspicious pre-Freudian heyday of Victorian innocence. Only after Dodgson's death, when psychoanalysts began to pry into what they imagined to have been Dodgson's subconscious, did serious suspicions arise about his motives. But if Dodgson did harbour deep unconventional desires he certainly reined them in, severely, never violating Victorian propriety, because, as a deeply, genuinely religious man, he knew that he could not endure any transgressions. Unremitting self-recriminations and dire pleas to God for help in self-improvement and control appear frequently in his diaries, signifying a troubled conscience, particularly when they occur in conjunction with his meetings with child friends. One of his poems in particular, 'Stolen Waters' (1862), an allegory written in the first person, tells the tale of a sinning youth who, in the end, manages through repentance to find salvation.

Dodgson's repressed nature took its toll; matched with his quick mind and his genius, it made him sharp and fractious at times. But many who knew him attested to his magnanimity and to his winning, spontaneous wit. Even in carrying out the humdrum tasks of curator of senior common room (which tedious job he held for almost ten years), he introduced wit into his frequent memoranda and three reports (*Twelve Months in a Curatorship*, 1884: 'at once financial, carbonaceous, aesthetic, chalybeate, literary and alcoholic'; *Three Years in a Curatorship*, 1886: 'Airs, glares and chairs'; and *Curiosissima curatoria*, 1892: 'A curatorial parting gift').

Artist and photographer Dodgson harboured artistic aspirations from his youth; he enjoyed drawing, later from live models, particularly nudes. The Dodgson family magazines contain a varied sampling of his early efforts. He illustrated the story of *Alice's Adventures under Ground*, the original version of *Alice's Adventures*, which he gave Alice Liddell as a Christmas gift in 1864. Many of his letters contain sketches, and a number of stray drawings survive. The art critic John Ruskin told him, however, that his talents as an artist were severely limited (Collingwood, 102), and he knew enough to seek out professionals to illustrate his books. Still, he continued to enjoy sketching sessions, and he moved freely among artists. He was acquainted with many, including Arthur Hughes, Holman Hunt, J. E. Millais, Alexander Munro, V. Princep, D. G. Rossetti, J. Sant, C. A. Swinburne, Mrs E. M. Ward, and G. F. Watts. He lionized them and got most of them to sit for his camera. Others who sat for him included Frederick, crown prince of Denmark; Prince Leopold, youngest son of Queen Victoria; George MacDonald and his family; F. D. Maurice; Tom Taylor, the editor of *Punch*; Tennyson and his family; Henry Taylor and his family; the famous Terry family; Charlotte M. Yonge and her mother; and Mrs Humphry Ward as bride with her sister bridesmaids.

What Dodgson could not achieve in sketching, he did achieve in photography in those early days of the art, when sittings had to last some 45 seconds and the process of taking and developing the glass negatives was extremely difficult. He had an eye for the beauty around him and a good sense of composition, qualities amply evident in his photographs, many of which he proudly inscribed 'from the Artist'. When he first began to experiment with photography he took pictures of adults (his family, friends, and Oxford colleagues), and tried some architectural photographs, some landscapes, and still life. But in time he focused on his child friends, dressing them up in costumes—often genuine stage costumes that he had collected and kept in a wardrobe, and sometimes costumes he borrowed from Oxford museums, including the Ashmolean. His greatest achievement with his camera was in photographing the young. Helmut Gernsheim, the historian, called his 'photographic achievements … truly astonishing' and proclaimed him 'the most outstanding photographer of children in the nineteenth century' (Gernsheim, 28). Edmund Wilson wrote in the *New Yorker* that 'in the posing, the arrangement of background, and the instinct for facial expression … [Dodgson's photographs] show a strong sense of personality'. He finds 'a liveliness and humor in these pictures that sometimes suggest Max Beerbohm' and says that they anticipate Beerbohm's volume of drawings *Rossetti and his Circle*. 'As for the pictures of children,' Wilson continues, 'they, too, are extremely varied and provide a … revelation of Lewis Carroll's special genius for depicting little English girls that is as brilliant in its way as *Alice*' (E. Wilson, *New Yorker*, 13 May 1950).

Dodgson as author Dodgson's writing meant a great deal to him; writing was the main course by which he could do something for others, to fulfil a deep religious desire to contribute something to humanity—it was his offering to God. After resigning his mathematical lectureship in 1881, at the age of forty-nine (he retained his studentship and resident privileges at Christ Church to the end), he devoted himself primarily to his writing. Often standing at his upright desk (he calculated that he could stand and write for ten hours a day), he turned out a myriad of works. *Alice's Adventures in Wonderland* was followed in late 1871 by its sequel, *Through the Looking-Glass and What Alice Found There*, and in 1876 by that longest and most revered

nonsense poem in English, *The Hunting of the Snark*. While these are the works that have made Lewis Carroll a household name, his bibliography contains over 300 varied items, many of them highly specialized, even arcane, the mass characterized by facility and punctilious care.

Dodgson sought always to provide his readers with books of the finest quality, and because of an unusual relationship with his publisher, Macmillan, he achieved exceptional results. Macmillan arranged for printing and distribution of his books in exchange for a 10 per cent commission, but Dodgson paid all costs of printing, illustrating, and advertising, retaining control and making all decisions. He was, consequently, able to suppress the first edition of *Alice's Adventures in Wonderland* in 1865 because his artist, John *Tenniel, was not satisfied with the printing of the illustrations; and, dissatisfied himself for one reason or another, he disposed of an inferior edition of *The Game of Logic* in 1886; in 1889 he condemned the entire first run of 10,000 copies of *The Nursery 'Alice'*, and in 1893 scuttled the sixtieth thousand run of *Looking-Glass*.

Dodgson collected his poems in three anthologies: *Phantasmagoria and other Poems* (1869), *Rhyme? and Reason?* (1883), and *Three Sunsets and other Poems* (1898). His verse falls into one of three categories: the nonsense poetry for which he is world famous; his narrative verse, which is undervalued; and, least memorable, his serious poems. These last were strongly influenced by Romantic conventions and Victorian sentimentality, but are none the less important for an understanding of him because here, in fact and in symbol, he reveals his emotional travails.

Dodgson invented and published a cascade of puzzles and games, some in verse, for what he imagined to be a world of child friends, even though many of these high-spirited exercises elude solution by mature and experienced minds. Among these efforts are: *Castle-Croquet* (1866), *Doublets* (1879), *Lanrick* (1880), *Mischmasch* (1881), *A Tangled Tale* (1885), *The Game of Logic* (1886), *Circular Billiards* (1890), *Syzygies* (1891), and *Arithmetical Croquet* (first published 1953).

As gadgeteer and inventor Dodgson was an inveterate gadgeteer, collecting all manner of contrivances and trinkets, and he invented a good many himself. His own inventions included an *'in statu quo* chessboard' (*Diaries*, 249) with holes into which the chess pieces could be secured when travelling; any number of card games; an early form of what was later to be known as Scrabble; a rule for finding the day of the week for any date; a means of justifying the right margins on the typewriter; a steering device for a tricycle; a new sort of postal money order; rules for reckoning postage; rules for a win in betting; rules for dividing numbers by various divisors; a cardboard scale for Christ Church common room, which, held next to a glass, insured the right amount of liquor for the price paid; a substitute for gum, 'for fastening envelopes …, mounting small things in books, etc.—viz: paper with gum on both sides' (*Diaries*, 526); a device for helping a bedridden invalid to read from a book placed sideways; and at least two ciphers.

Three other inventions are remarkable. In 1877 Dodgson produced his *Memoria technica*, a significant improvement on Dr Richard Grey's system (1730) for memorizing dates and events, with which Dodgson must have struggled as a schoolboy. Dodgson's method assigns two consonants to each number from 0 to 9, fills in vowels to make words, and sets the words in rhymed couplets that help one remember not just dates but other facts as well. The rhymes turn the process into a game. Here is how he prods the reader to remember 1492:

Columbus sailed the world around
Until America was **FOUND**.

The consonants **F N D** represent 492; the prefix 1 is always assumed.

In 1888 he designed, and later published, *The Wonderland Postage-Stamp Case*, with slots for different denominations of postage stamps and containing a miniature pamphlet, *Eight or Nine Wise Words about Letter-Writing*, an entertaining, tongue-in-cheek set of prescriptions and proscriptions for how to write letters.

In 1891 he invented the 'nyctograph', a description of which he published in *The Lady* (29 October), offering it freely to the general public. It is a small device that he used for composing and recording in the dark, while lying awake, 'a few lines, or even a few pages, without even putting the hands outside the bed-clothes'.

Proportional representation and lawn tennis Dodgson's concern with fair voting practices at a time when the franchise was being extended more and more drove him to contribute significantly to the theory of parliamentary elections. In 1873 he published his first pamphlet, *Discussion of Procedure in Elections*, intended to alter voting methods at Christ Church. He sought to replace majority principles by a system of awarding marks or points. Always keenly interested in British politics, he took his arguments beyond the university into the public forum with a number of other publications, including his pamphlet *The Principles of Parliamentary Representation* (1884). His work on voting theory and redistribution remained significant throughout the twentieth century. It 'presents the longest connected chain of reasoning in Political Science', wrote the mathematician F. Abeles in 1970. 'Dodgson showed a grasp of ideas on the intuitive level that were not formalized until 1928'. In 1996 it was noted that 'few ... [voting theorists were] capable of expressing their principles clearly and only two [succeed]—G. C. Andrae, a Danish mathematician ... and C. L. Dodgson—trained in axiomatic reasoning' (McLean and Urken, introduction). Another twentieth-century critic deeply regretted that:

Dodgson never completed the book that he planned to write [on voting theory]. ... Such were his lucidity of exposition and his mastery of the topic that it seems possible that, had he ever published it, the political history of Britain would have been significantly different. (Dummett, 5)

Dodgson devised a new system for conducting lawn tennis competitions to improve upon the rules in use, which he deemed inherently unjust: he did not think it fair that players should be knocked out of competition after only one loss. In 1883 he published four letters on the subject in the *St James's Gazette* and a pamphlet, *Lawn Tennis Tournaments: the True Method of Assigning Prizes*. His system, while complex, is still considered more equitable to players than current practice.

Dodgson: the man Contrary to some myths, Dodgson was anything but a shy recluse sequestered behind college walls. He travelled frequently throughout Britain, sometimes with his cumbersome camera in tow; he was often to be seen in London theatres and art galleries, and even in corridors of power; and he hobnobbed with artists, writers, and actors. He left Britain once, accompanying his friend H. P. Liddon across Europe on a mission to Russia, where Liddon explored the possibilities of *rapprochement* between the Eastern church and the West. He went regularly to Guildford in Surrey, where his unmarried sisters and brothers lived after their father's death in 1868, and he spent summers at the seaside, usually Eastbourne, on writing holidays.

Dodgson was about 6 feet tall, slender, had either grey or blue eyes, wore his hair long, and 'carried himself upright, almost more than upright, as if he had swallowed a poker'. He dressed customarily in clerical black and wore a tall silk hat, but when he took Alice and her sisters out on the river, he wore white flannel trousers and a hard white straw hat (A. and C. Hargreaves, 'Alice's recollections'). He ate frugally when he ate at all, disliked tea but enjoyed a glass of wine. He had a pleasant speaking voice, but left no recording of it, and a tolerably good singing voice which he did not mind using. He sometimes talked to himself.

Dodgson was interested in many branches of science, particularly medicine, and was a member of the Society for Psychical Research. Art and music were two of his delights; he was fond of quotations. He disliked physical sports but was known to play croquet. He went on long walks, sometimes covering 23 miles in a day. He was orderly in all things and kept extensive records. While many attested to his kind, considerate, courteous nature, he could be rude and was known suddenly to walk out of tea parties. Certainly he stomped out of theatres when he found anything on the stage irreligious or otherwise offensive. He once reprimanded the bishop of Ripon for including in a Bampton lecture an anecdote that elicited laughter. He planned but never completed a volume of Shakespeare plays especially for girls, out-Bowdlerizing Bowdler. He so resented Shakespeare's lines at the end of *The Merchant of Venice* requiring Shylock to abandon his faith and become a Christian that he wrote to Ellen Terry, after seeing her and Henry Irving perform the play, asking her to delete the lines from future performances: 'it is ... entirely horrible and revolting to ... all who believe in the Gospel of Love' (*Letters*, 365). He was an anti-vivisectionist and denounced blood sports. He valued his privacy and hated the limelight, jealously concealing the true identity of Lewis Carroll from strangers. He was by many accounts unselfish and generous. He helped to support his sisters and brothers, other relatives, friends, and even strangers. He was always willing to take on new students, and he was ready, though in all humility, to try to help young and old with spiritual problems. He claimed generally to be happy, but at least one observer guessed that he was a 'lonely spirit and prone to sadness' (Rowell). When he realized that his children's books would yield a modest income for the rest of his life, he asked his dean to reduce his lecturing responsibilities and his salary accordingly.

Dodgson was constantly involved in extramural (if not worldly) affairs. Essentially conservative—and in politics definitely so—he none the less fought for reforms that won for him and his fellow Christ Church dons a voice in college matters. He inundated members of his college and university with frequent broadsheets and pamphlets, in prose and verse, on a multiplicity of subjects that ranged from opposing cricket pitches in University Parks to a spoof, dripping with irony, of the wooden cube that Dean Liddell had erected atop Tom Quad's Great Hall staircase to house bells removed from the cathedral. He also sent off, from his Christ Church eyrie, letters and articles to a string of periodicals, including *The Times*, the *Pall Mall Gazette*, *Aunt Judy's Magazine*, the *Fortnightly Review*, the *St James's Gazette*, *The Observer*, and *Mind*, on widely varying subjects ranging from Gladstone and cloture to vivisection and hydrophobia, and from education for the stage and an Oxford scandal to a logical paradox and the spirit of reverence on the stage.

As letter writer Dodgson's private letters, usually written in purple ink, were more than occasionally works of art; when addressed to his young friends, they were fanciful creations, self-contained microcosms of Wonderlands. In them he created puzzles, puns, and pranks; he teased, feigned, fantasized. He sent letters in verse, sometimes set down as prose to see if his correspondent would detect the hidden metres and rhymes; letters written backwards so that one has to hold them up to a looking-glass; acrostic letters, rebus letters, letters written from back to front. By his own confession, he wrote 'wheelbarrows full almost' (*Letters*, 355); 'one third of my life seems to go in receiving letters', he wrote, 'and the other two-thirds in answering them' (ibid., 336); and 'I'm beginning to think that the proper definition of "Man" is "an animal that writes letters"' (ibid., 663). A letter register he kept for the last thirty-seven years of his life recorded that he sent and received 98,721 letters over that period.

Late works Late in life Dodgson published *Sylvie and Bruno* (1889) and *Sylvie and Bruno Concluded* (1893), two long, complicated novels depicting three realms of being. Essentially love stories, they contain some imaginative flights that sparkle, but, where Dodgson in the *Alice* books eschewed any moral lesson, here he set himself a mission to edify and instruct, suggesting 'some thoughts that may prove … not wholly out of harmony with the graver cadences of Life' (L. Carroll, 'Preface', *Sylvie and Bruno*, 1889, xiii); his Victorian sentimentality and heavy messages become burdens.

Dodgson's most exacting efforts of the 1890s went into a three-layered work on symbolic logic, beginning with elementary concepts and reaching ethereal, theoretical heights. He published *Symbolic Logic: Part I, Elementary* in 1896, and when he died in 1898 he had much of the other two volumes fleshed out and almost all of the second volume set in type. His family, compelled to clear his Christ Church rooms soon after his death, disposed as best they could of the enormous quantity of his possessions, burning many seemingly unimportant papers. No doubt parts of the two advanced logic books went up in flames. But, miraculously, much of the second volume survived, along with bits of the third, and in the mid-1960s a proof of the second volume was found at All Souls, Oxford, Dodgson having sent it to another don for comment. Its publication brought Dodgson fresh professional attention and regard.

Dodgson in retrospect Had Dodgson never written the *Alice* books, he would have earned a nod or a paragraph in various specialized histories: mathematics and logic, photography, parliamentary voting systems, and games and puzzles. But the *Alice* books have earned him a place in the firmament of the great, for they are not only acts of imaginative genius but they also revolutionized writing for children. Children's books after Carroll grew less serious, more entertaining, and sounded less like sermons and more like the voices of friends than earlier prototypes. It follows that the influence of the *Alice* books upon children as they mature has been considerable, and it is difficult to think of a great writer in recent times who has not declared or demonstrated that influence.

Although the wheels of an *Alice* 'industry' did not begin to whirr fiercely until well into the twentieth century, Dodgson reaped some satisfaction at their modest record in his lifetime. Six years before he died, he was able to write to Alice herself that 'your adventures have had a marvellous success. I have now sold well over 100,000 copies' (*Letters*, 561). Translations into foreign languages had already proliferated, and the *Alice* characters were even then inspiring art and commercial enterprises. Imitations and parodies burgeoned, sequels appeared, and Dodgson gave his blessing to the manufacture of a *Looking-Glass* biscuit tin. Poems that he never wrote were attributed to him. He did not garner a fortune by any means, and left under £5000, but he must have gleaned considerable satisfaction from the popularity of these books.

The *Alice* books and *The Hunting of the Snark* have had an impact upon the English language as well, and after Shakespeare and the Bible are the most frequently quoted round the world. These works grow more popular with time even as the fascination with the life of their begetter increases. Dodgson died, unmarried and celibate, on 14 January 1898, of pneumonia, in his family home, The Chestnuts, Guildford, and was buried in Guildford old cemetery, The Mount, on 19 January.

MORTON N. COHEN

Sources *The works of Lewis Carroll*, ed. R. L. Green (1965) · *The diaries of Lewis Carroll*, ed. R. L. Green, 2 vols. (1953) · C. L. Dodgson, diaries, 9 vols., BL · *The letters of Lewis Carroll*, ed. M. N. Cohen and R. L. Green, 2 vols. (1979) · S. D. Collingwood, *The life and letters of Lewis Carroll (Rev. C. L. Dodgson)* (1898) · S. H. Williams and F. Madan, *A handbook of the literature of the Rev. C. L. Dodgson*, ed. D. Crutch, rev. edn (1979) · *Jabberwocky* (1969) [journal of the Lewis Carroll Society] · M. N. Cohen, *Lewis Carroll: a biography* (1995) · M. N. Cohen, ed., *Lewis Carroll: interviews and recollections* (1989) • M. N. Cohen and A. Gandolfo, eds., *Lewis Carroll and the house of Macmillan* (1987) • A. Clark, *The real Alice* (1981) • H. Gernsheim, *Lewis Carroll: photographer*, 2nd edn (1969) • M. N. Cohen, *Reflections in a looking glass* (1998) • M. Gardner, *The annotated Alice* (1960) • M. Gardner, *More annotated Alice* (1990) • [A. Hargreaves and C. Hargreaves], 'The Lewis Carroll that Alice recalls', *New York Times* (1 May 1932) • C. Hargreaves, 'Alice's recollections of Carrollian days, as told to her son', *Cornhill Magazine*, [3rd] ser., 73 (1932), 1–12 • V. Dodgson, 'Lewis Carroll—as I knew him', *London Calling* (28 June 1951) • J. H. Pearson, letter, *The Times* (22 Dec 1931) • E. M. Rowell, 'To me he was Mr Dodgson', *Harper's Magazine*, 186 (1943), 320–23 • E. Wilson, *New Yorker* (13 May 1950) • F. Abeles, 'Evaluating Lewis Carroll's theory of parliamentary representation', *Jabberwocky* (summer 1970) • I. McLean and A. B. Urken, eds., *Classics of social choice* (1996) • M. Dummett, *Voting procedures* (1984) • E. Seneta, 'Lewis Carroll's "Pillow problems": on the 1993 centenary', *Statistical Science*, 8 (1993), 180–86 • private information (2004)

Archives BL, diaries, Add. MSS 54340–54348 • Castle Arch Museum, Guildford • Christ Church Oxf., corresp. and literary papers • Harvard U., Houghton L., letters and drawings • Hunt. L., letters and literary MSS • Indiana University, Bloomington, Lilly Library, corresp. and writings • National Museum of Photography, Film, and TV, Bradford • New York University, Fales Library • NPG • Princeton University Library, corresp. and mathematical papers • Ransom HRC • Rosenbach Museum, Philadelphia • Surrey HC, corresp. and papers • University of British Columbia Library | Birm. CA, letters to Miss Cooper of Edgbaston High School • Bodl. Oxf., letters to C. S. Erskine • Bodl. Oxf., letters to Ella Monier-Williams • Keble College, Oxford, letters to H. P. Liddon • Man. CL, Manchester Archives and Local Studies, letters to Alice Crompton • Morgan L., letters to Harry Furniss • NYPL, Berg collection • Toronto, Osborne Collection

Likenesses photograph, c.1856–1860, NPG [*see illus.*] • O. G. Rejlander, photograph, 1863, U. Texas, Gernsheim collection • C. L. Dodgson, self-portraits, photographs • H. Furniss, double portrait, pen-and-ink caricature sketch (with Harry Furniss), NPG • H. Furniss, pen-and-ink caricatures, NPG • H. von Herkomer, oils, Christ Church Oxf. • Hills & Saunders, photograph, NPG • S. Lutwidge, photograph, NPG • E. G. Thomson, sketch, Rosenbach Museum, Philadelphia • photographs, Castle Arch Museum, Guildford, Surrey

Wealth at death £4596 7s. 7d.: resworn probate, Dec 1898, CGPLA Eng. & Wales

Dodgson, George Haydock (1811–1880), watercolour painter and illustrator, was born on 16 August 1811 in Liverpool, son of Pearson Dodgson, a hosier. After receiving what an obituarist referred to as a 'middle class education' (*The Athenaeum*, 831)—including drawing lessons from the father of Alfred W. Hunt—from 1827 until 1835 he was apprenticed to the engineer George Stevenson who employed him to survey land, make specifications, and calculate the expenses of railway construction for the Board of Trade. George Dodgson was extremely conscientious; the same obituarist recalled that, to complete the plans for the Whitby and Pickering Railway in time, Dodgson and three others did not remove their clothes for two weeks 'and kept themselves awake through many nights by eating opium and drinking strong black coffee' (ibid.). His health suffered and in 1835 he abandoned engineering for art.

After a sketching tour of Wales, Cumberland, and Yorkshire, Dodgson moved to London, living at first in Lambeth (1835–6) and subsequently Gower Street (1837–9). Later, following his marriage on 30 September 1839 to Jane Sims (*b.* c.1818, *d.* in or after 1880), daughter of George Sims, clerk of the Mercers' Company, he settled near Regent's Park, occupying 21 Mornington Place (1841–9), 18 Mornington Road (1850–58), and 18 St Mark's Crescent (1861–late 1870s). Dodgson embarked on his new career immediately. He executed picturesque drawings of many public buildings in and around London—St Paul's, Westminster Abbey, and Greenwich Hospital were among his subjects—and soon found employment making drawings for eminent architects. One of these, *Tribute to the Memory of Sir Christopher Wren*, a group of Wren's principal works arranged by C. R. Cockerell, was exhibited at the Royal Academy in 1838 and afterwards engraved. Plates from drawings by George Dodgson depicted the 'highly romantic and beautiful scenery' of north-eastern Yorkshire in the *Illustrations of the Scenery on the Line of the Whitby and Pickering Railway*, published in 1836 with text by Henry Belcher (p. iv). His work was also engraved on steel and wood for the *Cambridge Almanack* (1840–47); the *Art Union* (1851); the *Illustrated London News* (1853–6); *The Book of Celebrated Poems* (1854); *The Poets of the Nineteenth Century*, edited by R. E. Willmott (1857); *Lays of the Holy Land*, edited by H. Bonar (1858); and *The Home Affections*, edited by C. Mackay (1858). *Summer Time* (exh. Society of Painters in Water Colours, 1855) was chromolithographed by George Rowney.

From 1835 onwards Dodgson exhibited watercolour drawings of buildings, landscapes (including garden scenes, *fêtes-champêtres*, and, later, coastal scenes), and some interiors and subject pictures (a few of them literary) at the Society of British Artists (1835–9), the Royal Academy (1841–50), the British Institution (1841), and the Liverpool Academy (and Liverpool Society of Fine Arts), where he showed thirty-five pictures between 1841 and 1861. Most of his exhibited work, however, appeared at the watercolour societies. Forty-eight paintings were shown at the New Society of Painters in Water Colours (1842–7), of which he was elected an associate in 1842 and then a member in 1844. Having resigned from this position in 1847, he was elected an associate (1848) and subsequently a member (1852) of the Society of Painters in Water Colours where he was represented by 353 exhibits (1848–80). In addition, Dodgson contributed to the Royal Manchester Institution (1849–62) and the Royal Hibernian Academy (1852).

George Dodgson's works attracted increasing patronage; his popularity was founded on a repertory of landscapes and coastal scenes, many of which were executed during recurrent visits to favourite locations in Yorkshire (Richmond and Whitby), Cumberland (Cockermouth), Westmorland (the Lake District), south Wales (Gower, Swansea, and the Mumbles), and Haddon Hall in Derbyshire, Knole Park in Kent, and along the Thames. He was very fond of beech trees, a favoured specimen at Knole being known as Dodgson's Beech. In all his travels, he never left Britain. Dodgson was described by a contemporary as one of a small group of 'searchers after idealized truth' (*Art Journal*, 300). He exaggerated the chiaroscuro in sun and moonlit scenes (and artificially lit interiors), introduced small figures in historical costume, and often appended poetical descriptions—from Walter Scott, Coleridge, and Longfellow, among others—to his titles. Dodgson's atmospheric and at times visionary effects owed much to an unusual technique: he was one of the first watercolour painters to exploit a wet method, dropping spots of colour (including vermilion and emerald green) on very damp paper and then blending them together. This practice may have resulted partly from a nervous condition affecting control of the hands.

George Dodgson died of congestion of the lungs at 28 Clifton Hill, St John's Wood, London—to which address he had recently moved—on 4 June 1880. The following winter the Society of Painters in Water Colours exhibited a loan collection of fifty-two of his works. His remaining pictures were sold at Christies on 25 March 1881. Two of his three children, George Peter and Jessie, were also artists. Examples of his works can be found in the Victoria and Albert Museum and the British Museum in London, as well as provincial public collections, including the Laing Art Gallery in Newcastle upon Tyne and the Walker Art Gallery, Liverpool.   CHARLOTTE YELDHAM

Sources J. L. Roget, *A history of the 'Old Water-Colour' Society*, 2 vols. (1891) · *The Athenaeum* (26 June 1880), 831 · *ILN* (26 June 1880), 612 · *Art Journal*, 42 (1880), 300 · *The Times* (9 June 1880) · E. Morris and E. Roberts, *The Liverpool Academy and other exhibitions of contemporary art in Liverpool, 1774–1867* (1998) · *The Royal Watercolour Society: the first fifty years, 1805–1855* (1992) · Graves, *RA exhibitors* · Graves, *Brit. Inst.* · Graves, *Artists*, 3rd edn · J. Johnson, ed., *Works exhibited at the Royal Society of British Artists, 1824–1893, and the New English Art Club, 1888–1917*, 2 vols. (1975) · M. Hardie, *Water-colour painting in Britain*, ed. D. Snelgrove, J. Mayne, and B. Taylor, 2nd edn, 3 vols. [1967–8] · Mallalieu, *Watercolour artists* · L. Lambourne and J. Hamilton, eds., *British watercolours in the Victoria and Albert Museum* (1980) · S. Fenwick and G. Smith, eds., *The business of watercolour: a guide to the archives of the Royal Watercolour Society* (1997) · exhibition catalogue (1852) [Royal Hibernian Academy, Dublin] · exhibition catalogues (1849); (1861–2) [Royal Manchester Institution] · m. cert. · d. cert.
Archives Bankside Gallery, London, archives of Royal Watercolour Society
Likenesses wood-engraving (after photograph by J. Waller), NPG; repro. in *ILN* (26 June 1880), 612
Wealth at death under £5000: administration, 24 June 1880, *CGPLA Eng. & Wales*

Dodington, Bartholomew (1535/6–1595), Greek scholar, was born in Middlesex of unknown parentage. He was admitted a scholar at St John's College, Cambridge, on the Lady Margaret Beaufort foundation on 11 November 1547 and proceeded BA in 1551–2. In 1552 he was admitted a fellow of the college, on the same foundation, and in 1555 proceeded MA and signed the Marian articles imposed on the university. He was senior proctor from 1559 to 1560 and was elected a fellow of Trinity College, Cambridge, at about the time he left office. In 1561 he unsuccessfully solicited the interest of Sir William Cecil, principal secretary, for the vacant oratorship at Cambridge, but was in the following year elected regius professor of Greek.

As a Johnian and a regius professor Dodington was well placed to attract the friendship of Cecil, himself a Johnian and one-time brother-in-law of Sir John Cheke, regius professor of Greek from 1540 to 1547, and surviving correspondence demonstrates that this was the case. His

nephew leased a house in Westminster from Cecil, and it is likely that it was in this house that Dodington spent his last years. That he was a conscientious professor is witnessed by a copy of Hermogenes' *Rhetorica*, interleaved and copiously annotated by him, apparently as a source of lectures, with references to Demosthenes, Dionysius Halicarnassus, Isocrates, Iamblichus, Plato's *Gorgias*, Lysias, and, of course, Aristotle. On Elizabeth I's visit to Cambridge in 1564 Dodington made Greek and Latin orations before her and before Robert Dudley, earl of Leicester, and his Greek contribution to the verses presented to her by the university opened the volume with thirty-three lines of Greek hexameters in his own hand—fittingly, both because of his status as regius professor and fellow of Trinity and because his calligraphy in Latin and Greek has long been recognized as the finest example of Cambridge humanist italic.

In 1571 Dodington published an edition of the translation of Demosthenes by his predecessor in the regius chair, Nicholas Carr, prefaced by not only Greek verses but also a sensitive and revealing life of Carr. In later years he contributed verses to Edward Grant's *Graecae linguae spicilegium* (1575), William Whitaker's translation of John Jewel's reply to Thomas Harding (1578), Peter Baro's *Praelectiones in Jonam* (1579), Everard Digby's *Theoria analytica* (1579), Edward Grant's edition of Crispinus's *Lexicon* (1581), and William Camden's *Britannia* (1586), as well as verses on the death of Cecil's daughter, Anne de Vere, countess of Oxford, in 1588. Dodington's friendship with Baro, a fellow Calvinist, is attested to by his having acted as godson to Baro's son, Andrew, in 1574, and he was one of those who signed the petitions in favour of Thomas Cartwright in 1570. From Westminster in 1581 he wrote for John Whitgift, bishop of Worcester, a learned disquisition in connection with some matter of controversy on the distinction between the terms 'eidolon' and 'simulachrum'.

In 1585 Dodington resigned from his chair, but was allowed to retain the emoluments of his fellowship. He never married. He died on 22 August 1595 aged fifty-nine and was buried in the north transept of Westminster Abbey. His arms were: sable, three bugle horns azure, stringed gules.

ELISABETH LEEDHAM-GREEN and N. G. WILSON

Sources BL, Add. MS 5867 · CUL, MS Dd.4.56 · CUL, Add. MS 8915 · CUL, Adv.d.44 · N. Carr, *Demosthenis Graecorum oratorum principis, Olynthiacae orationes tres & Philippicae quatuor* (1571) · A. Fairbank and B. Dickins, *The italic hand in Tudor Cambridge*, Cambridge Bibliographic Society, monograph no. 5 (1962) · J. Lamb, ed., *A collection of letters, statutes and other documents … illustrative of the history of the University of Cambridge during the Reformation* (1838) · T. Baker, *History of the college of St John the Evangelist, Cambridge*, ed. J. E. B. Mayor, 2 vols. (1869) · J. Strype, *Annals of the Reformation and establishment of religion … during Queen Elizabeth's happy reign*, new edn, 1/1 (1824) · H. Keepe, *Monumenta Westmonasteriensia* (1682)

Dodington, George Bubb, Baron Melcombe (1690/91–1762), politician and diarist, was the only son of Jeremiah Bubb (d. 1692) of Foy, Herefordshire, and his second wife, Alicia (d. 1721), daughter of John Dodington of Dodington in Somerset. Nothing is known of Jeremiah Bubb's origins, but he made his way as a minor courtier in the 1670s, probably through the offices of Lord Scudamore, and at the time of the duke of Monmouth's invasion in 1685 he was commissioned into the army as a captain. He later became acting commander of the Carlisle garrison, and in 1689 governor of the castle and one of the town's MPs.

Education and early political career After his father's death in 1692 young George Bubb's upbringing was supervised by his maternal uncle George Dodington (c.1658–1720), a highly successful financier and contractor in the service of William III's armies who went on to a minor career in politics as an MP and office-holder, and latterly adopted Bubb as his heir. In 1703 Bubb was sent to Winchester College and in July 1707 he matriculated at Exeter College, Oxford, his age then being given as sixteen. At Lincoln's Inn, where he was enrolled in 1711, his studies had hardly begun when he was packed off later that year on a grand tour that lasted until 1713, taking him to France, the Low Countries, Switzerland, and Italy. In 1715 his uncle brought him into parliament for his own former seat of Winchelsea, and in May Bubb—again presumably through his uncle's contacts among the new whig ministers—was appointed envoy at Madrid where for the next two years he ably represented Britain's commercial interests and renegotiated several vital agreements with the Spanish court. He was replaced, however, in the summer of 1717, shortly after the beginning of the whig split, having already identified himself with the faction of Robert Walpole and Charles, second Viscount Townshend.

His uncle's death in March 1720 put Bubb in possession of a fine estate at Eastbury, Dorset, where a magnificent mansion designed by Sir John Vanbrugh was in the process of construction, an income of £4000 per annum, and a fortune of £100,000. He had already in 1718 taken the name Dodington. He quickly set about overturning his uncle's will and brought the Eastbury trust under his own direct control. In doing so, he set himself permanently at odds with one of the executors, his kinsman Richard Temple, Viscount Cobham (a cousin through his maternal grandfather's marriage into the Temple family), who stood next in line to the estate after another childless Dodington relation. Temple initiated a chancery suit against Dodington which kept him on tenterhooks well into the 1740s. The Eastbury 'palace' was to cost Dodington more than £140,000 to complete and was a drain on his pocket throughout most of his career. Its purpose was to fulfil Dodington's soaring, if buffoonish, aspirations to rank among the foremost whig grandees, and though loving nothing better than to ridicule and snipe at his colleagues in power, his pressing financial needs required the cushioning of salaried office. This weakness in his position, coupled with his naturally orotund personality, portly appearance, and sententious humour, ensured that he remained a political lightweight, a slightly ridiculous larger than life character, blinkered, vain, and with little principle.

In the early 1720s, however, everything seemed possible. Recognition of Dodington's elevated social status and his potential usefulness came almost as soon as his uncle was laid to rest with his appointment as lord lieutenant of Somerset, followed in the same year by the clerkship of the pells in Ireland, a life sinecure which yielded some £2000 annually. At the 1722 election he fought a successful campaign at Bridgwater and continued to sit for that borough until 1754. In April 1724 Walpole selected Dodington to join him at the Treasury board as a lord commissioner. Walpole, of course, was at least partially mindful of Dodington's useful influence in several parliamentary boroughs—Weymouth and Melcombe Regis (returning four MPs), Winchelsea, and Bridgwater—which set him above most rank-and-file whigs. It was probably in 1725 that Dodington married Katherine (d. 1756), daughter of Edmund Beaghan of Sissinghurst, Kent, though for reasons most likely connected with the chancery dispute concerning his estate, the union was concealed from the world until 1742. Dodington, however, was hardly the philandering type, a characteristic which only enhanced his absurd and old-fashioned bearing. The story was told that on one occasion he had urged himself upon a female acquaintance declaring 'Oh that I had you, but in a wood!', only to incur the lady's astonished, rather than shocked, response: 'In a wood, Dodington! What would you do—*rob* me?' (Carswell, 169).

Middle years Dodington was always much more intent on wooing politicians. In 1726, mortified by Walpole's recent failure to nominate him to the newly revived knighthood of the Bath, he published an epistle to the minister which, though complimentary, conveyed the pointed message that loyalty outshone merit as a qualification for advancement, an unmistakable hint of his growing discontent. At the accession of George II in 1727 he made an ill-judged bid to swing behind the new king's favourite Sir Spencer Compton, who it was generally believed would supplant Walpole. However, Walpole remained in office but in future was circumspect towards Dodington. Though remaining a member of Walpole's administration, Dodington aligned himself thereafter with its discontented elements, notably Lord Wilmington, as Compton had become, and Wilmington's kinsman the duke of Dorset. By 1732 Dodington was deeply in the confidence of Frederick, prince of Wales. Ministerial insiders felt that the prince used him more as a court jester off whom he could scrounge than as a serious political adviser. At all events, Dodington was too careful to allow the prince's headstrong feelings against the king's premier to run to extremes, and during the excise crisis in 1733 gave his royal protégé no encouragement to patronize the opposition. However, Dodington himself gave the government scant support for the measure in parliament, and in the aftermath recriminations were flung in his direction. Sir Robert Walpole's brother Horatio described him as 'the vilest man, vain, ambitious, loose, and never to be satisfied. He wants now to be a lord and when he is that he will want to be a duke' (*Egmont Diary*, 1.427).

From the middle of 1734 the prince began to spurn Dodington's moderating influence and turned his attention to the young and certainly more provocative patriot 'cubs'. For the next five years Dodington appears to have avoided any form of conduct which might be badly construed by his ministerial colleagues, and doggedly continued to fulfil his responsibilities at the Treasury board. He resisted the prince's strong overtures in February 1737 to support the opposition motion for an increase of his allowance from the king's civil list, but kept Walpole in suspense over the voting intentions of his five followers in the Commons until almost the last minute, savouring the moment when, on finally assuring the minister of his full support, he strode off before Walpole could finish uttering ungenuine promises of 'future expectations'.

Dodington finally broke with Walpole in the spring of 1740, and in May was dismissed from his well-paid Treasury position. In the preceding months he had importuned relentlessly for a peerage which Walpole refused to sanction. Walpole told one colleague that 'there had been no cordiality between them ever since this King's reign … [he] thinks he is not considered enough' (HoP, *Commons, 1715–54*, 1.501). With the approach of the next general election, Walpole went to endless lengths to usurp Dodington's hold over the four Weymouth and Melcombe seats, but this unseemly struggle only resulted in the election of three new MPs beholden neither to Dodington nor to Walpole. Failure in his other constituencies in 1741 meant an overall reduction in Dodington's Commons following from five to one. At some point before the election Dodington had established a rapport with the duke of Argyll, who had also lately taken himself and his Scottish followers into opposition. He soon found, however, that Argyll could not be animated into taking the initiative to co-ordinate the opposition forces in such a way that Walpole's entire administration might be replaced by a new one constructed on 'broad-bottom' lines. In the debate on 21 January 1742 on the opposition motion calling for a secret committee on the war, Dodington described the minister's whole administration as 'infamous'. Walpole thrust back in his reply, pointing out that Dodington was 'a person of great self-mortification, who for sixteen years had condescended to bear part of the odium' (Walpole, *Corr.*, 17.297). Dodington did not profit from Walpole's fall at the beginning of the following month despite much expectation that he would become secretary at war in the new administration. For the next few years he languished discontentedly in opposition, dabbling in various journalistic ventures among which was his *Comparison of the Old and New Ministry*. In 1744 he collaborated with Henry Fielding's assistant, the historian James Ralph, on a more searching piece of polemic, *The Use and Abuse of Parliaments*, a work which argued that the Walpole administration had unravelled rather than safeguarded the achievements of the 1688 revolution.

In December 1744 Dodington's political fortunes took a turn for the better when Henry Pelham brought him back into government in the lucrative post of treasurer of the navy. Participation in office offered him interim contentment, but his ultimate goal, a peerage, still eluded him. By 1749 he was therefore prepared to accept an invitation from the prince of Wales to join his household in the senior position of treasurer of the chamber, with a salary of £2000. Encouragement to sever once more his ties with the government lay in the apparent certainty that the prince's accession could not be many years away. He was duly promised not only a peerage but also a secretaryship of state upon George II's demise, while in the meantime he was to have 'principal direction' over the prince's affairs. There were also promises 'in reversion' for a number of Dodington's friends such as Sir Francis Dashwood and Lord Talbot. Although Dodington's seniority—he was now not far off sixty—and experience were essential to a group largely of younger political aspirants, he was variously disliked, viewed with suspicion, and regarded as a coxcomb by other leading figures at Leicester House, the centre of the prince's court. The chief of these was the second earl of Egmont, who wrote that Dodington 'presumes a great deal—and hints at measures quite contrary to our system' (HoP, *Commons, 1715–54*, 1.502). In a memorial to the prince, Dodington condemned the aggressive style of opposition pursued by Egmont and his colleagues and warned that its factional overtones would affect its credibility. However, his attempts to discipline the behaviour of the prince's followers and urge them to play a dignified and patient 'waiting game' only alienated him further from Egmont and his associates, and they refused to consult with him on parliamentary business and tactics. Dodington thereafter quickly tired of his master's meagre understanding of political affairs, and after one of his gibes reached the prince's ears, communication between them all but ceased. The prince accordingly relegated him from future high office to the less exalted household position of master of the wardrobe. Frederick's sudden death, however, on 20 March 1751, after a brief illness, brought this phase of Dodington's career to an abrupt and unexpected end.

Later years Dodington was once more in the political wilderness and left to his own resources. He at first thought of retirement, and indeed his parliamentary attendance slackened considerably. His health now somewhat impaired by a hernia, he spent an increasing amount of time at La Trappe, the villa on the riverbank at Hammersmith which he had acquired in 1749 and where he loved to play the consummate host to an odd coterie of friends, retainers, and minor literati. At Eastbury, Hammersmith, and his town house in Pall Mall he surrounded himself in tasteless splendour. His own literary endeavours were nondescript occasional pieces couched in his usual highflown, lapidary prose. A far more significant though private venture, however, was the diary which he had begun to keep in 1749. Recording day to day the intrigues of an apparently compulsive, self-seeking place-hunter who seemed equally attached to the sentiments of virtue and poetry, Dodington's diary, first published in 1784, has subsequently anchored his reputation as the archetypal eighteenth-century man of politics.

Dodington succeeded in establishing a reasonable accord with the Pelhams, but the king's prejudice against him on account of his previous connection with the prince of Wales precluded any possibility of office. On Pelham's death in March 1754 Dodington made his court to Pelham's brother the duke of Newcastle, now head of the administration, but he was unable to secure a promise of the treasurership of the navy for which he had been angling. At the ensuing general election he lost his long-held Bridgwater seat to his *bête noire*, Lord Egmont, but was elected for Weymouth, where he was able to put two other seats at the ministry's disposal.

The following year, however, Dodington forgot all thoughts of retirement as he became ineluctably drawn into the complex struggle for leadership of the House of Commons between William Pitt and Henry Fox that took place during the summer and autumn of 1755. Dodington, it must be said, had already cast himself as a Pitt supporter in March, but as spring gave way to summer he saw the benefits to be reaped from the tentative alliance forming between Pitt and the new 'reversionary interest' now centring upon the dowager princess of Wales and her young son Prince George (the future George III). In the aftermath of Prince Frederick's death, Dodington had found the princess uninterested in forming her own political party, but with Pitt's involvement the new Leicester House group had healthy prospects of success. While doing all he could throughout the late summer to encourage Pitt's aspirations, Dodington nevertheless kept up a dialogue with the duke of Newcastle. Thus in October, when the scales began to tip against Pitt in favour of Fox, Dodington was easily won over by the duke and in December, after Pitt and his friends had been finally dismissed from the administration, Dodington was given back his old office. Under repeated barracking from Pitt, however, the Fox–Newcastle ministry weakened and in November 1756 collapsed. Dodington was turned out of the navy treasurership to make way for Pitt's brother-in-law George Grenville. In February 1757 he briefly rose above his normally self-interested political stance and in delivering what Horace Walpole described as a 'humane and pathetic speech' in the Commons was one of the few to defend the unfortunate Admiral John Byng against those who desired his execution for the loss of Minorca.

Dodington returned to office for a short time from April to June 1757 during the interregnum that followed Pitt's dismissal, but again had to make way for Grenville when Pitt formed his great administration with Newcastle. By the end of the year Dodington was in contact with the prince of Wales's tutor, the earl of Bute, now resigned to await whatever rewards would follow upon the death of George II. Dodington's wait was longer than he anticipated, and when the king finally died in October 1760 old age and infirmity barred him from any post in the new administration. The young king did, however, fulfil his father's promise of a peerage, and on 6 April 1761 Dodington was duly created Baron Melcombe of Melcombe Regis. In the final year of his life Dodington gave vent to angry impatience with Pitt and the war, though soon the old confidence between himself and Bute fell away until Bute ignored him altogether. Dodington died at his Hammersmith residence on 28 July 1762 and was buried at Fulham.

Since he left no issue, the Eastbury estate went as directed in the original entail to Richard Grenville, first Earl Temple, nephew of his old antagonist Lord Cobham who had died in 1749, and his disposable property, including the manuscript diary, to another cousin, Thomas Wyndham of Hammersmith. A. A. HANHAM

Sources DNB • J. Carswell, *The old cause: three biographical studies in whiggism* (1954), 131–265 • R. R. Sedgwick, 'Bubb (afterwards Dodington), George', HoP, *Commons, 1715–54*, 1.500–03 • J. Brooke, 'Dodington (formerly Bubb), George', HoP, *Commons, 1754–90*, 2.327–8 • 'Bubb, Jeremiah', HoP, *Commons, 1690–1715* [draft] • GEC, *Peerage*, new edn, 8.640–41 • *Manuscripts of the earl of Egmont: diary of Viscount Percival, afterwards first earl of Egmont*, 3 vols., HMC, 63 (1920–23), vol. 1, p. 427 • Walpole, *Corr.*, 17.297 • *The political journal of George Bubb Dodington*, ed. J. Carswell and L. A. Dralle (1965) • H. Walpole, *Memoirs of King George II*, ed. J. Brooke, 2 (1985), 218 • Foster, *Alum. Oxon.*

Archives BL, corresp. as envoy to Spain, Egerton MSS 2170–2175 • Harvard U., papers and diary • NL Ire., corresp. • Yale U., Beinecke L., papers | BL, letters to Henry Worsley, Add. MS 15936 • Bodl. Oxf., corresp. with John Tucker and Richard Tucker • NRA, priv. coll., letters to James Oswald • NRA, priv. coll., letters to first Earl Waldegrave • Yale U., Farmington, Lewis Walpole Library, diary and poetical epistle to the earl of Bute

Likenesses G. Townshend, pencil and ink, caricature, 1751–8, NPG • line engraving, 1784, BM, NPG; repro. in *European Magazine* (1784)

Dods, Marcus (1786–1838), Church of Scotland minister and theologian, was born on 7 December 1786 near Gifford, Haddingtonshire. He was educated at the University of Edinburgh and was ordained as a minister in the Church of Scotland at Belford, Northumberland, in 1811. On 6 May 1818 he married Sarah Palliser (d. 1859); the couple had seven children of whom the most significant was Marcus *Dods (1834–1909), the Free Church minister and professor of the New Testament at New College, Edinburgh. Dods was a distinguished scholar, and used his knowledge of biblical languages, oriental literature, and patristic studies in both his preaching and his writing; the evangelical leader Thomas Chalmers described him as 'being at once rich in the scholarship of a varied and extensive erudition, and yet possessed in no ordinary degree of massive and original powers of his own' (T. Chalmers, 'Recommendary notice', in M. Dods, *On the Incarnation of the Eternal Word*, 2nd edn, 1841, v). Dods was a frequent and distinguished contributor to the *Edinburgh Christian Instructor*, the principal organ of the evangelical party in the Church of Scotland, and became its editor after the death of Andrew Thomson (1779–1831), the celebrated evangelical whose biography he was planning to write at the time of his own death. In the 1820s Dods was actively involved in the Apocrypha controversy, strongly opposing the inclusion in Bibles of the Old Testament Apocrypha. He wrote a humorous but forceful statement of his position called *Anglicanus Scotched* (1828) and in the same year produced *Remarks on the Bible*, described as 'perhaps as good a statement as the age saw of the case put forward by those who stood for an undiluted and a thoroughly inspired Canon of Scripture' (Macleod, 261).

Dods was a prominent and committed opponent of Edward Irving's views on the doctrine of the incarnation of Christ, and penned a particularly devastating review of Irving's *The Doctrine of the Incarnation Opened* in the *Edinburgh Christian Instructor* in January 1830. In that review Dods caustically remarked that Irving 'contradicts himself more frequently than any other writer probably ever did. With Mr Irving a single idea is spread over many a turgid page' (M. Dods, 'Review', *Edinburgh Christian Instructor*, Jan 1830, 2–3). A late twentieth-century biographer of Irving described Dods as 'Irving's sternest and most theologically erudite critic' (Needham, 476). Dods expanded his own views on the incarnation in his most famous work, *On the Incarnation of the Eternal Word* (1831), a powerful and closely argued statement of the doctrine of the sinlessness of Christ, which according to the writer of his obituary in the *Edinburgh Christian Instructor* 'will remain a permanent monument of his research, learning and strength of intellect … as well as of his warm, fervent and rational piety' (*Edinburgh Christian Instructor*, 544). Dods died on 29 September 1838 after more than six months of illness and was buried in Belford, where his epitaph concludes that 'he captivated his friends by his rich converse, and edified the church by his learned and eloquent pen'.

JAMES LACHLAN MACLEOD

Sources *Fasti Scot.* · *Edinburgh Christian Instructor*, 1 (1838), 543–4 · *Early letters of Marcus Dods*, ed. M. Dods (1910) · J. Macleod, *Scottish theology in relation to church history since the Reformation* (1943) · N. Needham, *Thomas Erskine of Linlathen* (1990) · d. cert.

Dods, Marcus (1834–1909), United Free Church of Scotland minister and biblical scholar, born in Belford vicarage, Northumberland, on 11 April 1834, was the youngest son of the theological writer Marcus *Dods (1786–1838) and his wife, Sarah Palliser (*d.* 1859). On the father's death in 1838 the family moved to Edinburgh, where Dods first attended a preparatory school and then Edinburgh Academy (1843–8). After spending two years in the head office of the National Bank in Edinburgh, he decided in 1850 to study for the ministry of the Free Church of Scotland. In 1854 he graduated MA at Edinburgh University and began his theological course at New College, Edinburgh; during his university career he acted as an assistant in the Signet Library. On 7 September 1858 he was licensed to preach by the presbytery of Edinburgh.

Dods had a long probationership: although he preached in twenty-three vacancies, he failed for six years to get a church. During these years of enforced leisure he edited the complete works of Augustine (1871), translated a work by Johann Peter Lange as *Life of Christ* (6 vols., 1864), and wrote his popular *The Prayer that Teaches to Pray* (1863; 5th edn, 1885) and *Epistles to the Seven Churches* (1865). Dods's characteristic humanity and humility emerge in his letters of this period: writing to his sister Marcia regarding Augustine, the 'great man' whose works he was then editing, he described Augustine's greatness and reflected on how difficult it is to be merely a 'great' and 'good little man'. As W. Robertson Nicoll remarked after Dods's death, it was above all this quality that friends, colleagues, and foes admired in Dods: his 'natural greatness of soul' coupled with his charming and utterly genuine selflessness and his complete truthfulness.

On 4 August 1864 Dods was installed as minister of the Renfield Free Church, Glasgow; from its pulpit for the next twenty-five years he exercised considerable influence. Among those who benefited from his ministry was Henry Drummond. Sermons delivered at Renfield formed the substance of his popular books: *Israel's Iron Age, or, Sketches from the Period of the Judges* (1874; 4th edn, 1880) and *The Parables of Our Lord* (1st ser., Matthew, 1883; 2nd ser., Luke, 1885). They also provided material for his editions of Genesis (Expositor's Bible, 1888), of 1 Corinthians (Expositor's Bible, 1889), and of St John's gospel (Expositor's Bible, 1897). Dods continued throughout his life to enjoy preaching, which, he wrote, 'keeps life sweet'.

Although not a theologian in the technical sense, Dods exhibited wide and exact scholarship and a gift for popularizing new critical views about the Bible. In 1877 Dods published a sermon, *Revelation and Inspiration*, which questioned verbal inspiration, the doctrine that the Bible was literally dictated to the writers of scripture by the Holy Spirit. The presbytery of Glasgow, while declining to enter on a judicial process against Dods, advised him to withdraw the sermon until it could be modified. Dods assented on conditions; the matter was brought in 1878 before the general assembly, which declined by a majority to intervene.

In 1869 Dods refused an invitation to become colleague to Robert Smith Candlish at St George's Free Church, Edinburgh, the most influential congregation in the denomination. In 1889, when he celebrated the twenty-fifth anniversary of his ordination, he was appointed to the chair of New Testament criticism and exegesis in New College, Edinburgh. The appointment implied that the Free Church of Scotland was now prepared to tolerate critical views of the Bible, for which William Robertson Smith had been removed from his chair only eight years before. At the general assembly of 1890 Dods and Alexander Balmain Bruce were charged with teaching doctrines at variance with their church. The assembly, after a protracted debate, acquitted Bruce and, while exhorting Dods to teach the faith held by his church, declined to institute a process which would formally dismiss him on the grounds of heresy. Through his gentleness and reputation for thorough, accurate scholarship Dods contributed enormously to the liberalization of the Free Church: he demonstrated an extraordinary ability to stretch conventional doctrinal boundaries in his theological tradition, while retaining the respect of those who opposed him.

Other books by Dods in his later years included *Mohammed, Buddha, and Christ* (1877), *Isaac, Jacob, and Joseph* (1880), *Erasmus and other Essays* (1891; 2nd edn, 1892), *An Introduction to the New Testament* (1891), *The Visions of a Prophet: Studies in Zechariah* (1895), *Why be a Christian?* (1896), *How to Become Like Christ and other Papers* (1897), and *The Bible: its Nature and Origin* (Bross lectures, 1905), which provides a full account of his views on inspiration. Two additional volumes of sermons, *Footsteps in the Path of Life* and *Christ and Man*, were posthumously published in 1909, while his *Early Letters … (1850–1864)* and *Later Letters … (1895–1909)* were edited by his son in 1910 and 1911 respectively.

In 1871 Dods married Catherine, daughter of James Swanston of Marshall Meadows, Berwickshire; the couple had three sons and one daughter. In 1891 he received the honorary degree of DD from Edinburgh University, and in 1901 he declined nomination for the moderatorship of the general assembly of the United Free Church of Scotland (formed in the previous year by the union of the Free and United Presbyterian churches). Appointed in May 1907, on the death of Robert Rainy, principal of New College, Edinburgh, he was prevented by ill health from taking up that office. He died at his home, 23 Great King Street, Edinburgh, on 26 April 1909, and was buried in the Dean cemetery there. W. F. GRAY, rev. MICHAEL JINKINS

Sources *Early letters of Marcus Dods*, ed. M. Dods (1910) · *Later letters of Marcus Dods*, ed. M. Dods (1911) · W. R. Nicoll, *Princes of the church* (1921) · J. S. Black and G. Chrystal, *The life of William Robertson Smith* (1912) · *British Weekly* (6 May 1909) · A. L. Drummond and J. Bulloch, *The church in late Victorian Scotland* (1978) · *CCI* (1909)
Archives U. Edin., New Coll. L., commonplace book, papers | CUL, letters to May Crum · NL Scot., corresp. with Henry Drummond
Likenesses J. Guthrie, oils, 1909, U. Edin., Rainy Hall · Maclure & Macdonald, photogravure, NPG · J. S. Rhind, bronze medallion, Scot. NPG
Wealth at death £7000 17s. 11d.: confirmation, 5 July 1909, *CCI*

Dodsley, James (1724–1797), bookseller, was born in Mansfield, Nottinghamshire, the youngest of seven children of Robert Dodsley (*bap.* 1681, *d.* 1750), a local schoolmaster, and younger brother of Robert *Dodsley (1704–1764). By 1742 James was employed in his brother's London bookshop at the sign of Tully's Head, his signature as witness appearing that year on Robert's agreement to purchase the copyright to Henry Baker's *The Microscope Made Easy*. Despite the central role Tully's Head played in the contemporary literary world, almost nothing is known of James during his first fifteen years at the shop: he is not mentioned in his brother's correspondence until 1757, and only one of his own letters survives from the period. His name was first joined with Robert's in the well-known imprint 'Printed for R. and J. Dodsley' on 2 May 1753 when the firm published Henry Jones's poem *Merit*. On 3 December 1754 he became a member of the Stationers' Company by redemption, and, in April 1759, he assumed the reins of Tully's Head at his brother's retirement.

Although James Dodsley was bequeathed only £500 at his brother's death in 1764, he inherited a small fortune in copyrights. Of these, the following, which he owned either in whole or in part, enjoyed multiple editions during James's years at Tully's Head: William Melmoth's translations of Cicero's *Letters* and Pliny's *Letters*, and his *Fitzosborne's 'Letters on Several Subjects'*; Joseph Spence's *Polymetis*; William Whitehead's *The Roman Father*; William Duncan's *Elements of Logic*; Robert's own *Preceptor* and his weekly *The World*; and Samuel Johnson's *Rasselas* and *Dictionary*. To these James added many editions of Robert Dodsley's own works, including *The King and the Miller of Mansfield* and *The Oeconomy of Human Life*, the most printed work of the century. Likewise, James continued to issue Robert's popular collections, the *Select Fables of Aesop*, *Select Collection of Old Plays*, and *Collection of Poems by Several Hands*

(the most popular poetic miscellany of the last half of the century), the latter two re-edited by Isaac Reed.

James Dodsley's own industry added many new titles to Tully's Head credits, including works by Frances Brooke, Richard Cumberland, Oliver Goldsmith, Richard Graves, Charlotte Lennox, Horace Walpole, and, notably, Laurence Sterne's *Sermons of Mr. Yorick*. Christopher Anstey's *The New Bath Guide* (1766) netted eleven editions for Dodsley in its first ten years. By far his most profitable publication, Edmund Burke's *Reflections on the Revolution in France*, passed through seven editions and 18,000 copies in 1790 alone. Other popular titles included Lord Chesterfield's *Letters to his Son* (ten editions by 1793), Soame Jenyns's *Internal Evidence of the Christian Religion* (seven editions by 1785), and Thomas Warton's *History of English Poetry*. James Dodsley's joining the London Congers in the early 1780s gave a new direction to Tully's Head's agenda, for most of his subsequent publications involved joint undertakings of large printings of multi-volume editions of established authors, such as Johnson's *Lives of the Poets*.

Some time late in 1786, after forty-four years at Tully's Head, Dodsley announced his retirement, only to resume business two weeks later. On 7 June of the next year he suffered a major loss when £2500 of uninsured stock went up in flames at his Lincoln's Inn warehouse. John Nichols, who was dining with the bookseller during the fire, reports that Dodsley bore the news 'without the least apparent emotion', and before the fire was extinguished, sold the potential waste paper to a member of the company for £100. The agreement was not fulfilled, however, and Dodsley later sold the residue for £80 (Nichols, *Lit. anecdotes*, 6.439). The following year Dodsley paid the usual fine to avoid the office of sheriff of London and Westminster. His reserved manner is reflected in his obituary printed in the *Gentleman's Magazine*: 'He kept a carriage many years, but studiously wished that his friends should not know it, nor did he ever use it on the eastern side of Temple Bar' (*GM*, 347). Some time in the 1780s Dodsley bought an estate between Chislehurst and Bromley but rarely visited it. He continued in his Pall Mall house, but, during the early 1790s, he seems to have turned over his retail business to George Nicol and to have acted merely as a wholesaler for his own productions.

Dodsley died at his home in Pall Mall on 19 February 1797. He was buried in St James's Church, Westminster, where his epitaph reads, in part: 'a man of retired and contemplative turn of mind', who was 'upright and liberal in all his dealings' and 'a friend to the afflicted in general, and to the poor of this parish in particular'. Having never married, he distributed his estate—estimated at £70,000—primarily to his nephews and nieces. His stock and copyrights were sold at the Globe tavern, Fleet Street, London, on 18 October 1797, ending the house of Dodsley.

Although he was at the helm of Tully's Head several years longer than his brother and predecessor, Robert, James Dodsley did not seem to enjoy all of Robert's energy and enterprise; nor did he possess his brother's literary talent. Besides his career as a bookseller, Robert also earned some contemporary reputation as a poet and playwright; James does not seem to have authored any works. Although James published some major works during his time, nothing approached Robert's ingenious conception and execution of such undertakings as the *Select Collection of Old Plays*, the *Collection of Poems by Several Hands*, and *Select Fables of Aesop*. Nor did James initiate any periodicals as did Robert. In short, Robert was a literary man as well as a bookseller; James was a businessman.

JAMES E. TIERNEY

Sources J. E. Tierney, 'R. Dodsley, R. and J. Dodsley, J. Dodsley', *The British literary book trade, 1700–1820*, ed. J. K. Braken and J. Silver, DLitB, 154 (1995), 106–22 · *The correspondence of Robert Dodsley, 1733–1764*, ed. J. E. Tierney (1988) · Nichols, *Lit. anecdotes*, 6.437–9 · *DNB* · H. M. Solomon, *The rise of Robert Dodsley: creating the new age of print* (1996) · R. Straus, *Robert Dodsley: poet, publisher and playwright* (1910) · M. F. Suarez, introduction, *A collection of poems by several hands*, ed. R. Dodsley and M. F. Suarez, 1 (1997), 1–119 · I. Reed, 'Memoranda from Mr. Dodsley's papers, which I received this day, 29th April 1797, from the Extors', U. Edin., New Coll. L., Chal 1 [abstracts many of Robert and James Dodsley's publishing agreements made with authors] · E. Malone, copy of Reed's extracts, Yale U., Beinecke L., Osborn collection · *GM*, 1st ser., 67 (1797), 254, 346–7

Archives BL, letters, Add. MS 28959, fol. 14 · Bodl. Oxf., corresp. · Folger, letters · NL Scot., letters, MS 582

Wealth at death est. £70,000: Nichols, *Lit. anecdotes*, vol. 6, p. 438

Robert Dodsley (1704–1764), by Sir Joshua Reynolds, 1760

Dodsley, Robert (1704–1764), bookseller and writer, was born on 13 February 1704 in Mansfield, Nottinghamshire, the eldest of seven children of Robert Dodsley (*bap.* 1681, *d.* 1750), a master of the free school in Mansfield, and his first wife. Robert's early efforts at poetry suggest that he learned something of the art from his schoolmaster father, as well as a smattering of major authors, both classical and contemporary. However, in a practical-minded move, his father apprenticed Robert, at the age of fourteen, to a local stocking weaver. It is not clear when Robert left his master or under what circumstances, but by the mid-1720s he entered into service with a series of well-connected families that eventually took him to London.

The first known verses of the aspiring young poet were composed while Dodsley was in the service of Sir Richard Howe, who kept a residence both at Langar Hall, east of Nottingham, and at Compton, in Gloucestershire. At some time before September 1729 Dodsley became a footman to Charles Dartiquenave, a well-known London epicure, friend of Swift and Pope, member of the Kitcat Club, and contributor to *The Tatler*. Dodsley's first publication, *Servitude*, a poem attempting to counter the increasing displeasure with the attitude of servants, appeared on 20 September 1729. At Dartiquenave's Dodsley became acquainted with visiting literati and probably first met Alexander Pope, who would later play a major role in his young career. Within two years Dodsley had moved to Whitehall as footman to Jane Lowther, a daughter of John, Viscount Lonsdale. On 14 February 1732, while still in Mrs Lowther's service, Dodsley married Catherine Iserloo (*d.* 1754), the beloved Kitty of his early poems. A little more than two months later, Mrs Lowther engaged a host of her

fashionable friends to subscribe to Dodsley's *A Muse in Livery, or, The Footman's Miscellany*, his most significant publication to date (the first edition had appeared in February). The more than 200 subscribers included Sir Robert Walpole, the countess of Hartford, and the duchesses of Bolton, Bedford, and Cleveland. Not until the 'second' edition, however, did Nourse, the publisher, add to the title-page: 'By R. Dodsley, now a Footman to a Person of Quality at Whitehall'.

The earliest remnant of Dodsley's acquaintance with Pope, a brief letter from the older poet on 5 February 1733, acknowledged the receipt of Dodsley's manuscript of *The Toy-Shop* and promised to recommend the one-act play to John Rich, manager of Covent Garden theatre. Pope kept his word, and Rich produced *The Toy-Shop* as an afterpiece on 3 February 1735. A moralizing satire on the town's vanities delivered by the toyshop owner himself, the play captured the fancy of audiences and enjoyed at least thirty-four performances and seven editions in its first year alone.

Shop at the sign of Tully's Head Although Pope had encouraged young Dodsley's poetic aspirations, apparently his own publishing agenda led him to convince Dodsley that his true talents would be realized in the book trade. Lacking experience in the bookselling business, Dodsley probably spent time learning the trade in the shop of Pope's current publisher, Lawton Gilliver, while Gilliver was publishing Dodsley's next three poems—*The Modern Reasoners* (1734), *An Epistle to Mr. Pope, Occasion'd by his Essay on Man* (1734), and *Beauty, or, The Art of Charming* (1735).

With proceeds from *The Toy-Shop* and other works, together with a £100 contribution from Pope, Dodsley opened his bookshop at the sign of Tully's Head in Pall Mall, London, probably in March or April 1735. Not surprisingly, his first publication found him linked in the imprint with Lawton Gilliver and James Brindley for volume 2 of the *Works of Alexander Pope*. The original site of Tully's Head is not known, but, three years later, he moved into the former quarters of Sir William Younge in Pall Mall, a large house at the end of a passageway almost directly opposite Marlborough House and running up towards King Street. Although some distance from the centre of the book trade around Stationers' Corner, Tully's Head was near the fashionable coffee houses in St James's, a short walk from parliament and government offices in Whitehall, and had no serious competition in the area, except for Brindley in New Bond Street.

During these early years Pope channelled several of his own works to Tully's Head and recommended the shop to his friends. To William Duncombe, he wrote on 6 May 1735: 'Mr. Dodsley, the Author of the Toyshop … has just set up a Bookseller, and I doubt not, as he has more Sense, so will have more Honesty, than most of [that] Profession' (*Correspondence*, ed. Sherburn, 3.454). In 1737 Dodsley issued nine publications, including a volume of Pope's letters (together with Knapton, Gilliver, and Brindley); an edition of still another of his own plays, *The King and the Miller of Mansfield*; and the year's most popular work, Richard Glover's political epic *Leonidas*. The next year saw twenty-one new works, including *London* by the not yet famous Samuel Johnson, an edition of Fénelon's *Télémaque*, a translation of Tasso's *Jerusalem*, a few more poems by Pope, and another of Dodsley's own plays, *Sir John Cockle at Court*. By 1739 Dodsley had begun to mount sufficient reserves to publish several multi-volume works on his own, including two-volume editions of Mrs Rowe's *Miscellaneous Works*, *The Philosophy of Sir Isaac Newton*, and Roger Boyle's *Dramatic Works*.

In the same year Dodsley's brief publishing career suffered a formal blow when he was prosecuted for publishing Paul Whitehead's *Manners*, a satire on various court figures and prelates. Bishop Thomas Sherlock, one of Whitehead's targets, induced the House of Lords to summon both author and publisher to Westminster Hall. Although Whitehead absconded to avoid prosecution, Dodsley was reprimanded and ordered to be detained in custody until further notice. A week later, upon the intercession of Dodsley's Pall Mall neighbour Benjamin Victor, a petition for his release was filed by one of Whitehead's victims, Lord Essex. After a formal apology upon his knees in the Lords and the payment of a £70 fine, Dodsley was released. As Alexander Chalmers later commented, 'The whole process, indeed, was supposed to be intended rather to intimidate Pope, than to punish Whitehead' (Chalmers, 16.201).

Dodsley had not been wholly innocent in the Whitehead affair. A decade of service in aristocratic gatherings had acquainted him with arrogance and incompetence in high places, and, early on, he had begun to resent the haughty imposition of a privileged social class. His struggle to reconcile his sense of his own genius with the humiliations he was forced to endure as a footman were vividly expressed in his *Miseries of Poverty* (1731). *The Toy-Shop* of 1735 had indicted the vanities and pretensions of aristocrats and clergymen. In the opening scene of his second play, *The King and the Miller of Mansfield* (1737), Henry II, lost and alone at night in Sherwood Forest, realizes that, when not surrounded by his courtiers and flatterers, he is but a 'common Man'; the king chastises Lord Lurewell for harassing the simple country folk and knights the humble, virtuous miller as Sir John Cockle, the titular character of Dodsley's next play (pp. 26, 51). Also about this time, the bookseller became acquainted with Pope's circle of patriot friends—George Lyttelton, Richard Glover, lords Chesterfield and Cobham, and the prince of Wales, major contributors to anti-ministerial literature. Dodsley also lent his shop to the cause by publishing Pope's satires on court and political figures: *The First Epistle of the First Book of Horace Imitated* (1737), *The Second Epistle of the Second Book of Horace Imitated* (1737), *One Thousand Seven Hundred and Thirty Eight*, the last published just seven months before Whitehead's *Manners*.

The 1740s Except for 1740, Dodsley's list of publications and authors, both new and established, grew at full tilt during the 1740s. He brought out the first poems of Mark Akenside, John Brown, John Gilbert Cooper, Thomas Gray, William Mason, William Shenstone, Joseph and Thomas Warton, and William Whitehead, all of whom, except the contentious Brown, continued a long-term publishing relationship with Tully's Head. Also appearing under Dodsley's imprint for the first time were poems by William Collins, Stephen Duck, William Thompson, and Edward Young, specifically *Night Thoughts*. Also during the decade, he issued Johnson's *Vanity of Human Wishes*, the last works of Jonathan Swift, including *Directions to Servants*, and the tenth volume of *Miscellanies*, as well as various editions of Pope's *Works*.

Notable also was the broadening of the subjects and types of works Dodsley was publishing during the 1740s: translations of ancient and foreign authors, works on architecture, religion, philosophy, travel, and science. These included Christopher Pitt's edition of Virgil's *Aeneid* (1740), William Melmoth's *The Letters of Pliny* (1746), and translations of Callimachus (1744), Sallust (1744), the *Decameron* (1741), and *Don Quixote* (1742); Joseph Spence's *Polymetis* (1747), John Wood's *The Origin of Building* (1741), George Lyttelton's *Observations on the Conversion and Apostleship of St. Paul* (1747), John Barr's *Summary of Natural Religion* (1749), Voltaire's *The Metaphysics of Sir Isaac Newton* (1747), William Duncan's *Elements of Logic* (1748), James Spilman's *Journey through Russia into Persia* (1742), Richard Pococke's *Description of the East* (1743), William Cheselden's *Anatomy of the Human Body* (1741), and Henry Baker's *The Microscope Made Easy* (1742) and *Natural History of the Polype* (1743).

The year 1741 saw the first of four periodicals Dodsley would publish during his career, the *Publick Register, or, The Weekly Magazine*. This threepenny sixteen-page weekly, containing foreign and domestic news, literary essays, and poetry, was aimed at capturing some of the market dominated by Edward Cave's monthly *Gentleman's Magazine*. Cave met the challenge by exerting his influence in the trade, and Dodsley was forced to discontinue the periodical with the twenty-fourth number which carried the complaint: 'the ungenerous Usage I have met with from one of the Proprietors of a certain Monthly Pamphlet, who has prevail'd with most of the common News-Papers not to advertise it, compel me for the present to discontinue it' (*Publick Register*, 332).

Engaging Mark Akenside as editor, Dodsley made his second bid for the periodical market by issuing the fortnightly *The Museum, or, Literary and Historical Register* on 29 March 1746. Running regularly forty pages, the fortnightly contained literary essays, poems, book reviews, and historical essays, and attracted original contributions from a host of notables, including William Collins, Stephen Duck, David Garrick, Soame Jenyns, Samuel Johnson, Robert Lowth, George Lyttelton, Christopher Smart, Joseph Spence, Horace Walpole, William Warburton, the Warton brothers, and the future poet laureate William Whitehead. When *The Museum* was discontinued with its thirty-ninth number on 12 September 1747, once more Cave, in the preface to the collected edition of his *Gentleman's Magazine* for 1747, smugly celebrated the demise of the supposed 'super-excellent Magazine' (*GM*, 1747). Fifteen months later, Dodsley bought a quarter-share in the *London Magazine*, the *Gentleman's* chief competitor. In the same year he purchased a share in the influential thrice-weekly *London Evening-Post*.

Dodsley's genius for envisioning new literary projects also brought to the market in the 1740s the two major works by which he is chiefly known to posterity. His love of the theatre—largely bred of his own success (three of his plays running on London stages within a single month in 1738)—inspired him to produce the twelve-volume *Select Collection of Old Plays* (1744-5). A compilation of sixty-one plays, ranging back beyond Shakespeare, the *Collection* drew upon the Harleian collection (then in his possession) and the collection of Sir Clement Dormer, to whom the work is dedicated. As announced in his preface, Dodsley's intention 'to snatch some of the best Pieces of our old Dramatic Writers from total Neglect and Oblivion' produced an unprecedented repository of texts in the English theatre tradition to which all subsequent editors would be indebted (*Select Collection*, 1.xxxv).

The advertisement to Dodsley's second major contribution to English literary history, *A Collection of Poems by Several Hands*, showed similar intent and foresight: 'to preserve to the public those poetical performances, which seemed to merit a longer remembrance than what would probably be secured to them by the Manner wherein they were originally published' (*Collection of Poems*, 1748, vol. 1.iii–iv). Given the extensive circle of poets Dodsley had cultivated by 1747, he had no trouble filling the first three volumes of the *Collection*, which appeared on 15 January 1748. Four editions were called for by March 1755 when Dodsley added a fourth volume, and, three years later, he completed the set with volumes 5 and 6. Although the earlier volumes showed many changes by their 1758 edition, the *Collection* set the canon for mid-eighteenth-century poetry, passing through several editions and supplements by other editors through the rest of the century. Although the earlier volumes show a disproportionate number of contributions by Dodsley's friends Shenstone and Akenside, except in the case of perhaps a half-dozen figures (including Swift and Young), its pages reflect the work of most major and minor practising poets of Dodsley's era.

In the late 1740s Dodsley solidified his publishing relationship with Samuel Johnson. Johnson provided the introduction and 'The vision of Theodore the hermit' to Dodsley's two-volume *Preceptor* (1748), a compilation of essays for the education of youth on such topics as mathematics, architecture, geography, rhetoric, drawing logic, ethics, trade and commerce, and law and government. The work passed through many editions, even becoming a textbook in colonial American colleges. Also, in 1749, Dodsley published Johnson's *Vanity of Human Wishes* and his tragedy *Irene*. Within a week of the last night of *Irene*'s performance at Drury Lane, Dodsley's own masque, *The Triumph of Peace*, was acted on the same stage.

The 1750s During the 1750s Dodsley reached the zenith of his career: his book production reached new highs, he became *the* London publisher of *belles-lettres*, he introduced many significant works and new talent, and his own pen enjoyed a few triumphs. He opened the decade with his own popular compilation of moral aphorisms, *The Oeconomy of Human Life* by an 'Ancient Bramin' (1750), a work that was soon translated into five languages and became the most frequently printed work of the entire eighteenth century. The next three years brought Gray's *Elegy Written in a Country Church Yard*, Richard Owen Cambridge's *Scribleriad*, the first English edition of Voltaire's *Age of Louis XIV*, Christopher Pitt and Joseph Warton's edition of Virgil's *Works*, William Duncan's translation of Caesar's *Commentaries*, William Melmoth's translation of Cicero's *Letters*, William Popple's translation of Horace's *Ars poetica*, Edward Young's *Poetical Works*, and, the least successful, Dodsley's own *Public Virtue*.

On 4 January 1753 Dodsley re-entered the periodical market with *The World*, a lively weekly on contemporary fashionable life. Immediately successful, the weekly was soon printing 2500 copies per week, ran for a full three years, and earned its conductor, Edward Moore, the amazing sum of £858. Among its many contributors were lords Bath, Chesterfield, and Hailes, the earl of Cork, Sir Charles Hanbury Williams, Richard O. Cambridge, Soame Jenyns, Joseph Warton, William Whitehead, and Horace Walpole. Two days after the close of *The World*, Dodsley ventured into the newspaper trade with William Strahan, publishing the first issue of their *London Chronicle* on 1 January 1757. Samuel Johnson provided the introduction for this thrice weekly, which ran through to the end of the century and included many contributions from James Boswell. Dodsley's last entry in the periodical market, the *Annual Register*, was begun in 1758 (published in 1759) with Edmund Burke at the helm. This annual 400-page volume chronicled the previous year's major events, and printed literary, historical, and topographical essays, as well as poetry and reviews. Burke discontinued his services in the 1760s, but James Dodsley continued the publication until 1791, when it was taken over by the Rivingtons.

Dodsley's eminent stature in the trade during the last half of the 1750s is evident in both the number and importance of his publications. Collaborating with five other booksellers, Dodsley published one of the most notable works of the century, Johnson's *Dictionary of the English Language* (1755). Johnson later acknowledged that Dodsley had given him the idea for the dictionary and, since Dodsley had published all of his significant works to date, Johnson referred to the bookseller as 'Doddy … my patron' (Boswell, *Life*, 1.326).

Other notable first editions of these years included Edward Young's *Centaur not Fabulous* (1755), James Hampton's *History of Polybius* (1756), Thomas Blacklock's *Poems* (1756), John Dyer's *The Fleece* (1757), Soame Jenyns's *Free Enquiry into the Origin and Nature of Evil* (1757), Edmund Burke's *Philosophical Enquiry into the Origin of our Ideas of the Sublime and Beautiful* (1757), Thomas Gray's *Odes* (1757), volumes 4–6 of Dodsley's *Collection of Poems* (1758), David Hume's *Remarks on the Natural History of Religion* (1758), Oliver Goldsmith's *Enquiry into the Present State of Polite Learning in Europe* (1759), and (with William Strahan and William Johnston) Johnson's *Rasselas* (1759). In 1758 Dodsley's own poetic exploration into the realm of terror and pity, *Melpomene*, appeared under Mary Cooper's imprint, and, in one week, he sold 2000 copies of his tragedy *Cleone*, as it was being acted at Covent Garden Theatre in early December. Although Dodsley baulked at the purchase of the copyright to Laurence Sterne's *Tristram Shandy* in late 1759, the first London edition would appear from the Dodsley's shop, his brother James having paid Sterne £630 for volumes 1–4 early the next year.

By the mid-1750s, Tully's Head became a fashionable gathering place of London's literati. As Joseph Warton recalled Johnson saying, 'The Noctes Atticae are revived at honest Dodsley's house' (*Correspondence*, ed. Tierney, 19), and Dodsley's correspondence frequently notes the visits and gatherings at Tully's Head. As his correspondence also reveals, Dodsley's regular literary advisers were Spence, Mark Akenside, George Lyttelton, and Horace Walpole. Outside London Dodsley relied heavily upon his Birmingham friend Shenstone and frequently on Shenstone's friend at Bath, Richard Graves. Besides his substantial contributions to Dodsley's *Collection of Poems* and *Fables of Aesop*, Shenstone entertained Dodsley on several summer visits in the 1750s where the two would revise Dodsley's works. Graves did much the same for Dodsley's writings, although most of his advice came by letter.

In 1755, as one of the earliest members of the newly founded Society of Arts (then calling itself the Society for the Encouragement of Arts, Manufactures, and Commerce), Dodsley was elected the society's first 'stationer' and was thereby responsible for providing all of its printing and publishing. He also served, along with William Hogarth, Samuel Richardson, and Jacob and Richard Tonson, on several society committees delegated to offer rewards to the public for the execution of prescribed drawings and the invention of new processes related to paper making, as well as to judge the resulting submissions.

During his later years Dodsley's own pen and genius for literary projects remained active. After protracted revisions and continuing refusals by David Garrick, Dodsley's tragedy *Cleone* was finally produced by John Rich at Covent Garden on 2 December 1758, with George Anne Bellamy in the title role. The occasion found the whole town taking sides, and a bitter exchange arising between the author and his friend Garrick. In late February 1761 appeared Dodsley's *Select Fables of Aesop and other Fabulists*, printed by John Baskerville and including ancient, modern, and 'newly invented' fables in three volumes, respectively. By his death, Dodsley, with the help of Graves, had managed to edit and publish the first few volumes of an edition of Shenstone's *Works* (1764–9), as they were simultaneously serving as the poet's executors.

In his time, Dodsley was variously described as a man of modesty, simplicity, benevolence, humanity, and true politeness. His relations with his authors seem regularly to have been conducted with cordiality and integrity, but always moderated by practical business sense. Extant evidence of copyright purchases shows that he offered the age's standard rates for authors' manuscripts, meaning that he was consistently fair, though not overly generous. Although early contributors to Tully's Head, only William Warburton and John Brown quit Dodsley in pique. Warburton associated several attacks on his works with Dodsley authors, and, as Pope's literary executor, he thought Dodsley 'not very regardfull' of the memory of his patron when the bookseller published such works as Thomas Warton's *Observations on the Faerie Queene* (1754), which accused Pope of prejudice and ignorance for enthroning Lewis Theobald as the 'prince of dullness' (*Correspondence*, ed. Tierney, 212; Warton, 11.265). The Revd Mr Brown, fearing allusions to his penchant for cursing and swearing in Sir Charles Hanbury's forthcoming response to his *Estimate*, attempted to intimidate its publisher, but then resorted to dismissing Dodsley's mediation with 'Footman's language I never return' (*Correspondence*, 357).

Dodsley and the trade Besides his brother James, Dodsley trained at least two other apprentices at Tully's Head, John Hinxman and John Walter. Both men advertised themselves as former Dodsley apprentices when they opened their own shops, Hinxman taking over John Hildyard's business in York in 1757 and Walter setting up at Homer's Head in Charing Cross, London, in 1759. James Dodsley left Walter £1000 in his will, suggesting an ongoing relationship through the last half of the century. Hinxman returned to London in 1761 to marry Mary Cooper's sister and to take over the business of Dodsley's long-time publishing associate.

During his twenty-four-year career at Tully's Head, Dodsley co-published with at least fifty-three other booksellers, including the most notable members of the London trade: Charles Bathurst, Charles Hitch, Andrew

Millar, the Knaptons, Rivingtons, Tonsons, and Longmans. Likewise, he collaborated with or served as the agent for a number of provincial booksellers including Joseph Bentham, Richard Clements, and James Fletcher. In the 1750s he also shipped some of his works to Dublin's George Faulkner for the issuing of Irish editions. By far, the names appearing most frequently in his imprint were those of Thomas (and later) Mary Cooper, Dodsley's City agents, who also occasionally published works with which Dodsley did not initially want his name connected.

Although at least thirteen printers had a hand in producing Dodsley's volumes, John Hughs seems to have been his primary printer, and the latter sometimes farmed out work to William Bowyer junior and William Strahan. John Baskerville printed Dodsley's *Fables of Aesop*, and the bookseller acted as the Birmingham printer's London agent for the sale of his Horace and Virgil, as well as for Baskerville's new typeface and wove paper. For the illustration of his publications, Dodsley enlisted the designing and engraving services of at least twenty-three hands, some among the best-known names in the trade: Francis Hayman, William Hogarth, William Kent, Samuel Wale, Charles Grignion, and Simon Ravenet.

By the time of his retirement, Dodsley's name had appeared in imprints, either as sole or joint publisher, for 468 first editions alone. He was listed as 'seller' in the imprints to another 135 publications. Beginning in 1753, James Dodsley's initial had become linked with Robert's in Tully's Head imprints, and, although Robert officially retired in March or April 1759, the familiar imprint R. and J. Dodsley continued to appear on Tully's Head publications until his death.

Death and last will and testament On 23 September 1764, in his sixty-first year, Dodsley died of complications arising from his old nemesis, gout, while visiting Durham with his close friend Joseph Spence. Spence, who held a prebend in that city, saw to Dodsley's burial in the Durham Cathedral churchyard and provided the inscription on the large brown stone that marks his grave.

Dodsley's executors were Francis Dyer, husband of his sister Alice, and his younger brother Alvory, who had served in the house of Sir George Savile (and might have been running a London pamphlet shop at the time). Over the years, Dodsley must have reinvested his profits in the business because he had comparatively little savings at the time of his death. Although he bequeathed a total of £1500 to his siblings John, Isaac, Alice, and Alvory and to his nieces Kitty (daughter of Isaac), Sarah (daughter of John), and Kitty (daughter of Alice), all of these legacies were to be paid from James's £2000 bond to his brother (perhaps the purchase price of Tully's Head at Robert's retirement in 1759). James was left the remaining £500 due, as well as the remainder of Robert's estate. Most lucrative, however, was James's inheritance of at least fifty copyrights that, by reason of continuing editions through the rest of the century, would help make the small fortune James himself left at his death (£8000 apiece to two nephews alone).   JAMES E. TIERNEY

Sources *The correspondence of Robert Dodsley, 1733–1764*, ed. J. E. Tierney (1988) · H. M. Solomon, *The rise of Robert Dodsley: creating the new age of print* (1996) · R. Straus, *Robert Dodsley: poet, publisher and playwright* (1910) · *DNB* · M. F. Suarez, introduction, *A collection of poems by several hands*, ed. R. Dodsley and M. F. Suarez, 1 (1997), 1–119 · I. Reed, 'Memoranda from Mr. Dodsley's papers, which I received this day, 29th April 1797, from the Extors', U. Edin., New Coll. L., Chal 1 [abstracts many of Robert and James Dodsley's publishing agreements made with authors] · *British Museum general catalogue of printed books … to 1955*, BM, 263 vols. (1959–66) · *The correspondence of Alexander Pope*, ed. G. Sherburn, 5 vols. (1956) · D. D. Eddy, 'Dodsley's *Oeconomy of human life*, 1750–51', *Modern Philology*, 85 (1987–8), 460–79, esp. 460, 471 · Boswell, *Life* · *London Chronicle* (8–10 Sept 1757) · *London Chronicle* (23–5 Oct 1759) · A. Chalmers, 'The life of Paul Whitehead', *The works of English poets from Chaucer to Cowper*, ed. A. Chalmers, 16 (1810), 199–205 · preface, *GM*, 1st ser., 17 (1747) · *The works of Alexander Pope*, ed. J. Warton, 9 vols. (1797) · gravestone, Durham Cathedral, churchyard · T. Warton, *Observations on the Fairy queen of Spenser* (1762); repr. (1970)
Archives Birm. CA, letter-book · Birm. CL · Bodl. Oxf., corresp. · Harvard U. · Som. ARS · U. Edin., New Coll. L., memoranda, abstracting publishing agreements with authors [copy made by Edmund Malone, in Yale U., Beinecke L.] · U. Texas | BL, letters to W. Shenstone, Add. MS 28959
Likenesses attrib. W. Alcock, oil on tin, 1760, NPG · J. Reynolds, oils, 1760, Dulwich Picture Gallery, London [*see illus.*]
Wealth at death at least £2000, plus goods; also at least fifty lucrative copyrights

Dodson, James (*c*.1705–1757), mathematician and actuary, was the son of John Dodson (*b*. 1675), citizen and freeman of the Merchant Taylors' Company, and his wife, Elizabeth, who died shortly after his birth. His grandfather, also John Dodson, was a tailor of Edmonton, Middlesex. It is not known if Dodson, who became free of the Merchant Taylors' Company by patrimony in 1733, was ever employed as a tailor, but he was at one time a student under Abraham De Moivre, and as a young man he devoted himself to the unremunerative task of calculating antilogarithms. He married on 28 October 1735 at St Clement Danes, Westminster, Elizabeth Goodwin, the ward of Sir John Chesshyre, from whom he received a loan of £300. He may thereafter have earned his living as a writing-master, for some years later he was living in Warwick Lane, near St Paul's Cathedral, under the sign of the Hand and Pen, which was widely used by such teachers. Handwriting, in the new style known as copperplate, developed during the late seventeenth and early eighteenth centuries, was a principal subject of a commercial education, along with accounting and arithmetic. In 1744 William Mountaine and Dodson produced an updated version of Edmond Halley's isogonic magnetic chart, which they published in 1746; a later updated edition was presented to the Royal Society thirteen days before Dodson's death.

At some time before 1747 Dodson removed to Bell-Dock, Wapping, where in that year he was describing himself as an accountant and teacher of mathematics. In the preface to *The Calculator* (a book of tables), Dodson claimed that he would examine accounts, advise businessmen of the form of accounting best suited to their business, and oversee their clerks until they were familiar with its working. In time Dodson built up a reputation as a consultant on the values of annuities, and his first letter to the Royal Society was a plea for more information to be given in the bills of mortality which could assist in such valuations. When the Revd William Brakenridge sent the society a life table calculated from the London bills of mortality from 1744 to 1753, Dodson wrote to the society that he felt it was his duty to compute the values of annuities according to Brakenridge's table. Dodson's major work, *The Mathematical Repository*, was published in three volumes in 1748, 1753, and 1755. The first volume was dedicated to De Moivre; the second was dedicated to David Papillon and contained a contribution by De Moivre. A classic of actuarial science, the *Repository* displayed Dodson's mastery of algebra and his knowledge of the subject of annuities, and it earned him election to the Royal Society in January 1755.

In May or early June 1755, Dodson took over the mathematics classes at Christ's Hospital in place of John Robertson who had moved to the Royal Naval Academy at Portsmouth, and on 22 July he was formally appointed master of the Royal Mathematical School, and Stone's School, institutions within Christ's Hospital. It was a brief tenure, but following his death in November 1757, his salary was paid up to April 1758 to benefit his children.

In his closing years Dodson's interest turned to life assurance. It was said that he was denied admission to the Amicable Life Assurance Society, being over forty-five years old, and that this led him to advertise asking for those interested in a project for a new form of life assurance to meet him at the Queen's Head, Paternoster Row, on 2 March 1756. He set out the operating system for mutual life assurance, showing how premiums should be calculated, and worked some examples to show how the fund would be maintained. His (unpublished) 'First lecture on insurances' was written about this time, and from a series of such meetings the Society for Equitable Assurances on Lives and Survivorships developed, though Dodson did not live to see its formation. He died on 23 November 1757, leaving a widow and three children, James (*b.* 1742), who later became actuary for the Equitable Society, as it was by then known, Thomas (*b.* 1744), and Elizabeth (*b.* 1749). In his will, Dodson made arrangements for his share of the profits (5*s.* for every £100 paid in) which would accrue once the Equitable received its royal charter, and for repayment of his debt to Sir John Chesshyre's estate. Dodson's granddaughter Elizabeth later married Colonel James De Morgan; their son was Augustus De Morgan (1806–1871), logician and professor of mathematics at University College, London.

G. J. GRAY, *rev.* ANITA MCCONNELL

Sources M. E. Ogborne, *Equitable assurances* (1962) · GL, MS 12,806 vol. 11 (Christ's Hospital), 242, 247–8 · *GM*, 1st ser., 27 (1757), 531 · M. Maty, *Mémoire sur la vie et sur les écrits de Mr Abraham de Moivre* (1755), 37 · will, PRO, PROB 11/834 sig. 353 · C. Hutton, *A philosophical and mathematical dictionary*, new edn, 1 (1815), 433 · Nichols, *Lit. anecdotes*, 5.400

Dodson, Sir John (1780–1858), judge, was born at Hurstpierpoint, Sussex, on 19 January 1780, the eldest son of the Revd Dr John Dodson (*d.* 1807), rector of Hurstpierpoint, and his wife, Frances, daughter of the Revd Mr Dawson.

He went to Merchant Taylors' School in 1790, and then to Oriel College, Oxford, where he graduated BA in 1801, MA in 1804, and DCL in 1808. He was admitted an advocate of the College of Doctors of Law on 3 November 1808, and acted as commissary to the dean and chapter of Westminster. Early cases which brought him notice included *Dalrymple* v. *Dalrymple* (husband and wife), a report of which he published in 1811. On 24 December 1822 he married Frances Priscilla, eldest daughter of George Pearson, a London doctor. They had one child, John George *Dodson, barrister and politician, created Baron Monk Bretton in 1884.

From July 1819 to March 1823 Dodson was conservative MP for Rye. On 11 March 1829 he was appointed by the duke of Wellington advocate to the Admiralty court. He was subsequently named advocate-general (15 October 1834) and knighted (29 October 1834). He was called to the bar at the Middle Temple only on 8 November 1834, and in the following year was elected a bencher. He became master of the faculties in November 1841, and vicar-general to the lord primate in 1849. From February 1852 he was judge of the prerogative court of Canterbury until the abolition of this jurisdiction on 9 December 1857, and was dean of the arches court until his death. He was sworn a privy councillor on 5 April 1852, and died at his home, 6 Seymour Place, Mayfair, London, on 27 April 1858.

Dodson's judgments on cases in the Admiralty courts were published in *Reports of Cases Argued and Determined in the High Court of Admiralty* (1811–22) and in *A Digested Index of the Cases Determined in the High Court of Admiralty* by Joshua Greene (1818). A case concerning ritualist practices in the Church of England (*Liddell* v. *Westerton*, 1857) was much discussed, and Dodson's judgment upheld on appeal.

G. C. BOASE, *rev.* HUGH MOONEY

Sources *Law Times* (26 Dec 1857), 198 · *Law Times* (1 May 1858), 87 · *The Times* (10 Dec 1857), 11 · *The Times* (19 Dec 1857), 9 · *The Times* (29 April 1858), 9 · *GM*, 3rd ser., 4 (1858), 670 · *CGPLA Eng. & Wales* (1858)
Archives Bodl. Oxf., letter-books, case notebooks, and papers · E. Sussex RO, corresp. and papers
Likenesses W. Walker, mezzotint, pubd 1835, BM, NPG · W. Walker, mezzotint, pubd 1849, BM, NPG
Wealth at death under £45,000: probate, 1 June 1858, *CGPLA Eng. & Wales*

Dodson, John George, first Baron Monk Bretton (1825–1897), politician, born at 12 Hertford Street, Mayfair, Westminster, on 18 October 1825, was the only son of Sir John *Dodson (1780–1858) and his wife, Frances Priscilla *née* Pearson. He was educated at Eton College from 1838 where he won in 1841 and 1842 the prince consort's prizes for modern languages. He matriculated from Christ Church, Oxford, on 9 June 1843, and graduated BA in 1847, when he obtained a first class in classics, and MA in 1851. In 1853 he was called to the bar at Lincoln's Inn.

On leaving Oxford in 1847 Dodson spent two years in travel in the East, going as far as Baghdad, and on his return journey visiting Albania and Montenegro. He stayed for three months in 1848–9 in Cyprus, and his account of that island, which was then little known, was reproduced in successive editions of Murray's *Handbook*

John George Dodson, first Baron Monk Bretton (1825–1897), by Spy (Sir Leslie Ward), pubd 1894

down to 1872. His eastern tour was soon followed by travel in other parts of the world—the United States in 1853 and the Crimea during the Crimean War. He possessed great facility as a linguist, which he retained throughout his life. An ardent mountaineer, he was a member of the Alpine Club. He published his narrative of an ascent of 'the passages of the Glacier du Tour and of the Col de Miage in September 1859' in *Peaks, Passes, and Glaciers* (2nd ser., 1.189–207).

Dodson unsuccessfully contested the division of East Sussex in July 1852 and March 1857 as a Liberal, but in April 1857 he was returned at the head of the poll and held the seat until February 1874. At the general election of 1874 he was elected for the City of Chester, and was again returned in April 1880, being shortly afterwards re-elected on receiving an office under the crown. But subsequently the earlier election was declared void on petition, and, although the second election remained unimpugned, he could neither sit nor vote. He consequently found a new seat at Scarborough, and represented that constituency from July 1880 until 1884, when he became a peer.

For three years (1858–61) Dodson was prominent in urging in the House of Commons the repeal of the hop duties, which Gladstone removed in 1861. In 1863 he carried through the House of Commons the act enabling university electors to vote by post (which led to Gladstone's defeat as MP for the university). He unsuccessfully introduced in 1864 a bill for the abolition of tests at the universities. From February 1865 to April 1872 Dodson was chairman of committees and deputy speaker of the House of Commons, and on 10 May 1872 he was sworn of the privy council. He was an authority on parliamentary procedure, and his speech on private bill legislation on 18 February 1868 was printed. He was financial secretary to the Treasury from August 1873 to February 1874, and for three years (1874–6) he was chairman of the committee of public accounts.

In April 1880, on the formation of Gladstone's second ministry, Dodson was made president of the Local Government Board with a seat in the cabinet. During his first year of cabinet office he carried the government's Employers' Liability Act through the Commons but failed to produce a local government bill satisfactory to the cabinet. On 20 December 1882 he was transferred to the post of chancellor of the duchy of Lancaster, an office he retained until October 1884, when he retired from the government. He was created Baron Monk Bretton of Conyboro and Hurstpierpoint on 4 November 1884 (on this curious combination in a title see GEC, 5.330). He filled political office competently and was reckoned a sound man of business, but his abilities 'did not appear on the surface, and many people were puzzled at the success he attained' (West, 1.55). In the making of policy he was fussy and pedantic. Like H. C. E. Childers, he made less impact on Victorian Liberalism than a more determined person in his position could have done.

In 1886 Lord Monk Bretton declined to accept Gladstone's home-rule policy, and thenceforth took no prominent part in politics. During the parliamentary recess he always lived a retired life in his country home at Conyboro, Sussex, and played a great role in county business. He was the first chairman of the East Sussex county council (1889–92). He wrote seven articles for the *Edinburgh Review* and contributed to the collections of the Sussex Archaeological Society an article on Sussex roads (15.138–47); he chaired the society's meetings in 1870, 1872, and 1875.

On 3 January 1856 Dodson married Florence, second daughter of William John Campion of Danny, Sussex. They had one son and three daughters. Lady Monk Bretton died on 17 February 1912, aged eighty-one. Monk Bretton died at 6 Seamore Place, London, on 25 May 1897 and was buried in the churchyard of Barcombe, Sussex, the parish of his estate of Conyboro.

W. P. COURTNEY, *rev.* H. C. G. MATTHEW

Sources GEC, *Peerage* · Gladstone, *Diaries* · *Sussex Daily News* (26 May 1897) · Boase, *Mod. Eng. biog.* · *Wellesley index* · A. West, *Recollections, 1832–1886*, 2 vols. (1899)

Archives Bodl. Oxf., corresp., diaries, and papers · E. Sussex RO, family and official corresp. and papers | BL, corresp. with W. E. Gladstone, Add. MS 44252

Likenesses F. Grant, portrait, 1874 · F. Topham, oils, 1896, repro. in *VF* (16 Dec 1871); replica, East Sussex county council chamber, Lewes · Spy [L. Ward], caricature, chromolithograph, NPG; repro. in *VF* (25 Jan 1894) [*see illus.*] · J. & C. Watkins, carte-de-visite, NPG · caricature, chromolithograph, NPG; repro. in *VF* (16 Dec 1871)

Wealth at death £135,995 3s. 9d.: probate, 12 July 1897, *CGPLA Eng. & Wales*

Dodson, Michael (1732–1799), barrister and biblical scholar, the only son of Joseph Dodson, dissenting minister at Marlborough, Wiltshire, and Elizabeth Foster, was born there on 20 or 21 September 1732. He was educated at Marlborough grammar school and then, in accordance with the advice of his maternal uncle, Sir Michael *Foster (1689–1763), justice of the king's bench, was entered at the Middle Temple on 31 August 1754. He practised for many years as a special pleader but was finally called to the bar on 4 July 1783. In 1770 he was appointed one of the commissioners of bankruptcy, a post he held until his death. On 31 December 1778 he married Elizabeth Hawkes of Marlborough.

Dodson was held in high regard as a legal expert, and among his legal writings was an edition with notes and references of Sir Michael Foster's *Report of some proceedings on the commission for the trial of rebels in the year 1746 in the county of Surrey and of other crown cases*, first published in 1762, with a third edition in 1792. In 1795 he wrote a *Life of Sir Michael Foster*. This, originally intended for the new edition of the *Biographia Britannica*, was published in 1811 with a preface by John Disney.

Dodson, who was a Unitarian in religion, was probably held in even higher regard for his critical judgement on biblical literature. His most famous publication, *A New Translation of Isaiah* (1790), which was an answer to Bishop Robert Lowth's earlier translation, brought about a long-running, but generally good-humoured, disputation with Lowth's nephew, Dr John Sturges. He wrote many other theological works, including several papers for the Society for Promoting the Knowledge of the Scriptures, and his works were much admired by his friend John Disney.

Dodson enjoyed good health until the last year of his life, when he began to suffer from a chest infection, probably tuberculosis. By October 1799 he was confined to bed, and he died at home in Boswell Court, Carey Street, London, on 13 November of the same year. He was buried in Bunhill Fields on 21 November.

FRANCIS WATT, *rev.* M. J. MERCER

Sources J. Aikin and others, *General biography, or, Lives, critical and historical of the most eminent persons*, 10 vols. (1799–1815), vol. 3, p. 416 · R. Spears, *Record of Unitarian worthies* (1877) · Watt, *Bibl. Brit.* · A. Chalmers, ed., *The general biographical dictionary*, new edn, 32 vols. (1812–17) · will, PRO, PROB 11/1335, fols. 158r–159v

Archives BL, opinions as a general pleader, Add. MS 6709, fols. 113, 131

Wealth at death several deposits of hundreds of pounds to nonconformist ministers: will, PRO, PROB 11/1335, fols. 158r–159v

Dodsworth, Roger (*bap.* 1585, *d.* 1654), antiquary, was born at Newton Grange, Oswaldkirk, near Helmsley in Yorkshire, the son of Matthew Dodsworth, the registrar of York Minster, and Elizabeth Sandwith, daughter of Ralph Sandwith of Newton Grange, and baptized on 24 April 1585 according to Oswaldkirk parish register, although Dodsworth himself gave the date as 24 July in his memoir of his life. In 1599 he entered Archbishop Hutton's School at Warton in Lancashire, founded three years earlier, where his schoolmaster was Miles Dawson, who afterwards became the vicar of Bolton. There is no record of his attending university. Few details of his youth are known, but his memoir records that in 1605 he witnessed the execution at York of Walter Calverley, whose murders formed the subject matter of the anonymous play *The Yorkshire Tragedy*. In September 1611 he married Holcroft Rawsthorne (*d. c.*1620), the widow of Lawrence Rawsthorne of Hutton Grange, near Preston, Lancashire, and daughter of Robert and Mary Hesketh of Rufford Old Hall. Mary Hesketh was the daughter of Sir George Stanley, and so by marriage Dodsworth acquired kinship with the Stanleys, earls of Derby. His wife's house at Hutton Grange became his home, which he left only on antiquarian expeditions.

Dodsworth began making antiquarian collections when he was about twenty years old. Initially he began extracting records from York Minster archives and making pedigrees of local families, these exercises being facilitated by his father's position at the minster. He soon enlarged the scope of his activities and began to travel around the churches of Yorkshire, making notes of monumental inscriptions and of coats of arms in stone and glass, and transcribing parish records. He made his first visit to the Tower of London, the principal repository of the exchequer and chancery records, in 1623. Quite early in his career he formed a friendship with Charles Fairfax of Menston, the seventh son of the first Lord Fairfax and uncle of Sir Thomas Fairfax the soldier. He transcribed many of the Fairfax family papers at Denton and Menston; by this means he came to the attention of Sir Thomas Fairfax, who eventually became the patron of his researches into monastic foundations, providing him with a pension of £50 a year.

In the mid-1630s Dodsworth determined to make collections of material relating to the history of the monasteries in England, a subject that had been first opened by three recusant scholars, all monks of the revived English Benedictine congregation, Augustine Baker, Leander Jones, and Clement Reyner, who collected many of the records of their order which were published as *Apostolatus Benedictinorum in Anglia* at Douai in 1626. Dodsworth was particularly concerned to collect monastic charters, and by 1638 he had transcribed enough of these to fill a manuscript volume that he entitled 'Monasticon Anglicanum'. In that same year William Dugdale made contact with Dodsworth through the good offices of Sir Henry Spelman (like John Selden, Augustine Vincent, and Simonds D'Ewes, a member of Dodsworth's circle of friends) and volunteered to help with the project. Dodsworth was willing to journey around England in search of monastic records, though in practice most of his research was done in London, at the Cotton Library and in the Tower, and in York. According to Francis Drake, the author of *Eboracum* (1736), St Mary's tower in York contained 'all the records taken out of the religious houses, at their dissolutions, on the north side Trent', and when the tower was blown up in the siege of the city in 1644, most of the manuscripts were destroyed, but 'our painful countryman Mr Dodsworth had but just finished his transcripts of these valuable remains' (Drake, 575).

By 1644 Dodsworth had come to believe that his undertaking was too ambitious and planned to concentrate on documenting the monasteries of the north of England, and accordingly began to assemble his collections into a 'Monasticon boreale', as he called it. Spelman, who was encouraging Dodsworth's scheme, seems to have persuaded him that a comprehensive account of English monasteries was possible. By 1650 Dodsworth believed he could proceed to publication, but needed Dugdale's help to put his papers into better order; Dugdale, however, was detained in Warwickshire, and when he did get to London found that a great deal of work had to be done to make the manuscript ready for the press. By July 1651 a hundred sheets had been printed, but then problems of finance arose, as the booksellers were not prepared to undertake the publication of a large work on a politically hazardous subject. The two men decided to borrow money to finance the publication themselves. Enough material had been gathered to produce two folio volumes, and Dugdale laboured long and hard to put Dodsworth's collections into presentable shape, for Dodsworth, though an accurate transcriber, had little ability to methodize his material, nor did he have any fluency in writing the narrative prose required for the introductory sections. Without Dugdale's help, Dodsworth's work would never have gone into print.

In the midst of the final preparations, Dodsworth died, in August 1654, at his home in Lancashire. He was buried in the church at Rufford. In his will, dated 30 June 1650, he had indicated that he wished the Monasticon Anglicanum to be dedicated to Thomas Fairfax and Dugdale to write the dedication; he hoped that John Rushworth, who had been Fairfax's secretary, would oversee the publication. At this stage, Dugdale could still refer in a letter to 'Mr Dodsworth's work of Monastery foundations' (Denholm-Young and Craster, 8). When the first volume finally appeared in 1655, it had the names of both Roger Dodsworth and William Dugdale on the title-page. There was no dedication, and it is possible that Fairfax did not want a book on monasteries dedicated to him at the height of Cromwell's republic. Dugdale claimed in a letter that it was Rushworth who suggested he add his name to the work. It is impossible at this stage to estimate how much of the material collected in the Monasticon was supplied by Dugdale, but most contemporaries regarded Dodsworth as the true compiler of the work, with Dugdale the assistant who did indeed contribute a certain amount of documentation but who was primarily the editorial figure who gave it shape and ensured its publication. Both names appeared on the second volume in 1661, but the third volume (1673), composed mainly of documents that had come to light after 1661, carried Dugdale's name alone. The English abridgement of the Monasticon by James Wright in 1693 attributed the work solely to Dugdale, as

did the much lengthier English abridgement of 1718 by John Stephens. Roger Dodsworth had been forgotten.

The perception that Dodsworth was robbed of his rightful role as the principal author and mover of the Monasticon by an unscrupulous Dugdale is of long standing, going back at least to John Anstis, the herald and genealogist who described Dugdale as 'that Grand Plagiary' in a letter to Arthur Charlett in 1713 (D. C. Douglas, English Scholars, 1660–1730, 2nd edn, 1951, chap. 2). There is some truth in this charge. As is evident, the published Monasticon was essentially the result of a collaboration, but over the years Dugdale was willing to allow the monumental labours of his deceased colleague to be ignored. For many years Dodsworth had also collected material towards a history of the baronage, an immense project, which, like those of so many contemporary antiquaries, never came to fruition. It is significant, however, that Dugdale also developed a project along similar lines in the 1640s. In 1666 he borrowed sixteen volumes of Dodsworth's notes from Lord Fairfax (into whose possession they had come) to help him with his research, which eventually came into print in 1675 as The Baronage of England. This time he acknowledged his debt to 'the elaborate collections from the Pipe Rolls made by Mr Roger Dodsworth, my late deceased friend' (Preface). Fairfax in turn bequeathed Dodsworth's manuscripts to the Bodleian Library, and Anthony Wood described how in June 1673 eighty-five volumes of manuscripts arrived from York in a rain-soaked condition, and how he spent the best part of a month drying them out on the leads of the library roof.

GRAHAM PARRY

Sources N. Denholm-Young and H. H. E. Craster, 'Roger Dodsworth and his circle', *Yorkshire Archaeological Journal*, 32 (1936) · F. Drake, *Eboracum: the history and antiquities of the city of York* (1736) · *The life, diary, and correspondence of Sir William Dugdale*, ed. W. Hamper (1827) · J. Hunter, *Three catalogues* (1838) [includes Hunter's memoir of Dodsworth's life, based on autobiographical notes, and list of surviving MSS and their location] · C. R. Markham, *A life of the great Lord Fairfax* (1870) · G. Parry, *The trophies of time* (1995) · Wood, *Ath. Oxon.: Fasti*, 1st edn · *DNB* · parish register, 1585, Oswaldkirk, Yorkshire [baptism]
Archives BL, collections relating to Northumberland and Yorkshire, Lansbourne MS 326 · BL, Harley MSS 793–804 · BL, pedigrees, SI MS 1429 · Bodl. Oxf., collections, genealogical and antiquarian notes and papers, transcripts, abstracts and extracts · Bodl. Oxf., collections, notes and pedigrees · Queen's College, Oxford · U. Hull, Brynmor Jones L., notes of epitaphs from York Minster · U. Nott. L., genealogical notes · W. Yorks. AS, Leeds, Yorkshire Archaeological Society, extracts, pedigrees and antiquarian notes and papers, MSS 282–3

Dodsworth, William (1798–1861), Tractarian clergyman and Roman Catholic writer, was born on 19 March 1798 at Kirk Ella, Yorkshire, the third son of wealthy Hull timber merchant, John Dodsworth (1765–1818), and his wife, Harriet Haydon (d. 1837). He was educated at Richmond School, Yorkshire, and at Trinity College, Cambridge, where he graduated BA in 1820 and MA in 1823. He was ordained in the Church of England, being made deacon in 1821 and priest in 1822. He served curacies at Saxby, Lincolnshire (1821), Stisted, Essex (1823), and Chiddingfold, Surrey (1826). At first he held evangelical doctrines, and

William Dodsworth (1798–1861), by unknown engraver

was for a time associated with Edward Irving and his pre-millennialism, preaching at the Albury conferences. Through this connection he became in 1829 minister of Margaret Street Chapel, London, where he was a popular and gifted preacher. Despite breaking with Irving about 1830, he was strongly influenced by his former associate's incarnational theology, which influenced his innovative sacramental practice. By 1835 his works on the eucharist and on confirmation identified him with the Tractarian movement, and he took a leading role in the diffusion of its principles in London. He married Elizabeth (1799–1856), youngest daughter of Sir Francis Yarde Buller, second bt, and sister of the first Baron Churston, on 28 October 1830. They had seven children; the youngest, Cyril Dodsworth (1844–1907), became a Redemptorist priest in America.

In 1837 Dodsworth was appointed perpetual curate of Christ Church, Albany Street, London, where, under the direction of E. B. Pusey, he put into practice the ideals of the Tractarian movement, and helped set up the first Anglican religious sisterhood at Park Village West. Although cautious in ritual matters, his services at Christ Church became important preaching venues for the Tractarian leaders. He was active in Bishop Blomfield's Metropolitan Church Building Fund, preached widely, and travelled on the continent with his friend and correspondent H. E. Manning. His faith in the Church of England was so shaken by the judgment in the Gorham case that he resigned his cure and joined the Roman Catholic church on 1 January 1851. Being married he could not take orders in that church, and after his conversion led a quiet life as a layman, publishing a small number of Roman Catholic apologetic works. After a long illness due to a stroke, he died at 7 York Terrace, Regent's Park, on 10 December 1861, and was buried in Kensal Green Roman Catholic cemetery, London.

Among his forty-seven known works the earliest reflect his evangelical and adventist period. The majority are Tractarian sermons or treatises. *Discourses on the Lord's Supper* (1835) justified his restoration of the holy communion as the central Sunday service at the Margaret Street Chapel. *The Church of England, a Protester Against Romanism and Dissent* (1836) was also influential. His Roman Catholic works included *Popular Objections to Catholic Faith and Practice Considered* (1858).

S. E. YOUNG

Sources *The Tablet* (21 Dec 1861) · Public Diocesan and Parochial Archives [Yorkshire, Lincolnshire, Winchester, Essex, London] · Venn, *Alum. Cant.* · H. W. Burrows, *The half century of Christ Church, St Pancras* (1887) · F. Oakeley, *Historical notes on the Tractarian movement* (1865) · *The letters and diaries of John Henry Newman*, ed. C. S. Dessain and others, [31 vols.] (1961–) · R. W. Franklin, *Nineteenth-century churches: the history of a new Catholicism in Württemberg, England and France* (1987) · T. J. Williams, *The Park Village sisterhood* (1965) · M. Oliphant, *The life of Edward Irving*, 2 vols. (1862) · E. S. Purcell, *Life of Cardinal Manning*, 2 vols. (1895) · St Mary, Clapham, London, Redemptorist Provincial Archives · Gladstone, *Diaries* · parish register (baptisms), Kirk Ella, Yorkshire, 15 April 1798 · register of burials, St Mary's cemetery, Kensal Green, London

Archives Birmingham Oratory, Newman archives · BL, letters to W. E. Gladstone and others · Bodl. Oxf., corresp. with H. E. Manning · LPL, Blomfield MSS · Pusey Oxf., corresp. with E. B. Pusey

Likenesses W. Walker, stipple, pubd 1835 (after E. Walker), BM, NPG · C. Baugniet, lithograph, 1845, BM, NPG · W. Walker, engraving (after E. Walker, 1834), Trinity Cam. · engraving, NPG [*see illus.*]

Wealth at death £4000: probate, 27 Feb 1862, *CGPLA Eng. & Wales*

Dodwell, Edward (1776/7–1832), traveller and archaeologist, was the son of Edward Dodwell (1747–1828), of West Molesey, Surrey, and his wife, Frances (*née* Jennings). Dodwell's sister, Frances (1771/2–1857), was a watercolour painter who married the physician Sir Alexander *Crichton (1763–1856); a younger brother, Harry, died in infancy about 1778. Dodwell was the grandson of Henry Dodwell, a London businessman, and his wife, Dulcabella. He was also the great-grandson of the prolific writer and theologian Henry Dodwell (1641–1711), fellow of Trinity College, Dublin, who from 1688 to 1691 occupied the post of Camden professor of history at Oxford.

Dodwell was educated first at Parson's Green School, Middlesex, under Mr Waring, and second at Trinity College, Cambridge, where he matriculated in 1798, and graduated BA in 1800. When young, he travelled in Scotland, Ireland, and England with his father and developed a taste for drawing buildings. Having private means he adopted no profession, though in 1823 he was described as 'a learned English architect' (*GM*, 1823). He is known to have resided for some time in Paris.

In 1801 Dodwell made a tour of Holland, Germany,

Austria, and Italy. In April 1801 he arrived at Trieste to embark on his first tour of Greece; his 'intention was to visit Greece, to explore its antiquities, to compare its past with its present state, and to leave nothing unnoticed, which, to the classical reader, can be an object of interest, or a source of delight' (Dodwell, 1.1). On this journey, he was accompanied by his friend Sir William Gell (1777–1836), who also travelled with Dodwell through Greece in 1805 and 1806. From Trieste he proceeded to Venice, and on 29 April 1801 set sail in the merchant ship *Lo Spirito Santo e la Natività della Madonna*, which was captained by Giovanni Marassi. Although this voyage was hampered by adverse weather conditions, by the end of May that year they had reached Corfu, where their passports were presented to Sir Speridion Foresti, the British consul-general. In June 1801 Dodwell travelled on to Ithaca, the island of Cephalonia, Patras, and through the provinces of Phocis and Boeotia, to Athens, and then on to the islands of the Greek archipelago, the coast of Troy, and Constantinople.

Dodwell's second tour of Greece began on 1 February 1805 when he departed from Messina with his artist, Signor Simone Pomardi, in the Greek merchant ship *Saint Speridion*. They landed at Zákinthos, and after about a week proceeded on their journey to Mesolóngion, Patras, Galaxidhion, and Ámfissa where they were met by Dr Andrea Cattani. Dodwell also visited the ruins at Delphi, Mount Parnassos, Levádhia, Thebes, and by about 26 March 1805 he had proceeded to Athens.

At Athens Dodwell was required to make a payment to the disdar, or Turkish governor, for the privilege of making drawings and observations of the Acropolis. Dodwell offered only part payment of the fee, with the promise of full payment on completion of his drawings. The disdar, however, demanded the whole sum, which Dodwell refused: in turn, he was banned from entering the Acropolis. However, on reaching the Acropolis, Dodwell procured his entrance by bribing the guards 'by throwing a few paras amongst them'. Repeatedly visiting the Acropolis by this means, he 'acquired the name of the Frank of many Paras, and for a small expense purchased the civility of the soldiers' (Dodwell, 1.293). On a later occasion, while at the Parthenon, Dodwell attempted to explain his camera obscura to the disdar, who became perturbed and called Dodwell 'pig, devil, and Buonaparte', to which Dodwell replied that if he did not leave him unmolested, he would put him into his box (camera obscura). Apparently, the disdar did not trouble him again.

From Athens, Dodwell journeyed out to the Attic Mountains, visiting Aegina, Piraeus, Thessalía, Chaeroneia and Orchomenos, Eleusis, and (about 30 November 1805) Corinth. Near Corinth, at the village of Mertese, he persuaded local villagers to open sepulchres a quarter of a mile from their village. A number of bones, vases, and an urn containing burnt remains, were extracted from these tombs; in addition he was informed by the villagers 'that a Jew of Corinth, who had lately been digging in this spot, had found several vases' (Dodwell, 2.197). On visiting this person, Dodwell found and procured an inscribed vase, the lid of which depicted a wild-boar chase, with the names of the actors written beside each painted human figure. This vase, referred to now as the 'Dodwell vase' or 'Dodwell pyxis', was one of a group of vases of Middle Corinthian oriental style now attributed to the 'Dodwell painter', who specialized in decorating vases with friezes of animals.

After leaving Corinth, Dodwell also visited Argos, the Peloponnese (including Mycenae, the ruins of Tiryns, and Epídhavros), and the ruins of Messene, Megalopolis, and Sparta. On 2 April 1806 he left Patras for Mesolóngion, and a week later set out for Ithaca. Dodwell made a prolonged stay at Corfu until 16 May 1806 when he set sail for Messina in a Russian armed brig, *Letun*. At Messina he met his acquaintance Mr Mackenzie, and on 12 August 1806 sailed in the merchant vessel *Il Redivivo* to Civita Vecchia (which had been taken by the French some weeks before). Dodwell's ship next sailed for Leghorn where the passengers had to undergo a quarantine of twenty-one days. As a former prisoner of Bonaparte's government, Dodwell felt obliged (according to the terms of his parole) to surrender himself to the French; and his two years' leave of absence to quit France (to make his tour of Greece) had expired. Therefore, following quarantine, he disembarked and visited the French general at Civita Vecchia. He was indebted to the artists Granet and Paulin du Quelar, Count Annoni of Milan, the sculptor Dupaty, and the author Lechevalier, whose exertions secured permission for him, first, to travel in Greece and, second, to surrender himself at Rome, rather than Verdun. On 18 September 1806 Dodwell arrived at Rome. In this latter city and in Naples, he reportedly resided almost continuously for the remainder of his life.

Dodwell spent two years examining Cyclopean buildings, making drawings of the walls of the cities of Argos, Tyrinthia, and Lycosurae and compared them with similar monuments in Italy. The most important of these drawings was considered to be that of Lycosurae, the ancient city of Arcadia, which was apparently discovered by Dodwell in 1805. In Greece, Dodwell also made some four hundred drawings, while his artist, Pomardi, made about six hundred. Dodwell also collected numerous coins in Greece, and during his lifetime formed an impressive collection of classical antiquities (see Braun, *Notice sur le Musée Dodwell*, 1837), including 115 bronzes and 143 vases. He sold the remarkable bronze reliefs from Perugia and an archaic head of a warrior to the crown prince of Bavaria. The location of a marble head from the west pediment of the Parthenon, once in his possession, is now unknown.

Dodwell's publications included: *Alcuni bassi rilievi della Grecia descritti e pubblicati in viii tavole* (1812); *A Classical and Topographical Tour through Greece; during the Years 1801, 1805 and 1806* (2 vols., 1819), with a German translation by F. K. L. Sickler (1821–2); *Views in Greece, from Drawings by E. Dodwell*, with descriptions in English and French (1821); and *Views and descriptions of Cyclopian or Pelasgic remains in Greece and Italy … from drawings by E. D.* (1834), which was also printed with French text and title in the same year.

In 1816 Dodwell was elected an honorary member of the

Royal Academy in Berlin, along with his friend Gell. Dodwell married late in life Theresa, the daughter of Count Giraud; she was at least twenty years his junior. There were no children from this marriage. His wife was described by Lady Blessington as 'one of the most faultless models of loveliness ever beheld' (Madden, 427); and when Moore saw Theresa Dodwell in society at Rome (October 1819), he remarked 'that beautiful creature, Mrs. Dodwell … her husband used to be a great favourite with the pope, who always called him "Caro Doodle"' (DNB). Dodwell died at Rome on 13 May 1832 from the effects of an illness contracted in 1830 when exploring the Sabine Mountains near Rome.

Dodwell was survived by his wife who married, second, in 1833, Count de Spaur, the Bavarian minister at Rome. She was responsible for organizing the pope's escape from the Vatican to Gaeta during the revolution of 1848. Gell, who acted as a trustee of Dodwell's estate, considered his friend's will most unjust towards Theresa, his widow. He left her just 12,500 scudi and, while the leased house and furniture also went to her, at the time it was doubtful whether she would inherit his museum and books. However, family records suggest that she did indeed acquire his collections of Greek, Roman, and other artefacts, including the Dodwell vase, which were later sold. The Dodwell vase, for example, now resides in the Staatliche Antikensammlungen und Glyptothek, Munich. Dodwell's sister, Lady Frances Crichton, who also survived him, inherited his Irish land. YOLANDA FOOTE

Sources DNB · GM, 1st ser., 98/2 (1828), 573 · GM, 1st ser., 102/1 (1832), 649 · E. Dodwell, A classical and topographical tour through Greece (1819) · personal information (2004) [A. Crichton] · Memoirs, journal and correspondence of Thomas Moore, ed. J. Russel, 3 (1853), 52, 64 · M. Blomberg, Observations on the Dodwell painter (1983) · Venn, Alum. Cant. · GM, 1st ser., 93/1 (1823), 110–11 · Mallalieu, Watercolour artists, vol. 1 · R. R. Madden, The literary life and correspondence of the countess of Blessington, 3 vols. (1855) · Sir William Gell in Italy: letters to the Society of Dilettanti, 1831–1835, ed. E. Clay and M. Frederiksen (1976) · A. Michaelis, Ancient marbles in Great Britain, trans. C. A. M. Fennell (1882), 72, 87

Archives BL, drawings of Egyptian, Etruscan, and Roman antiquities, Add. MSS 33958–33961

Likenesses Count D'Orsay, pencil drawing, 1828, Gov. Art Coll.

Dodwell, George Benjamin (1851–1925), merchant, was born on 3 December 1851 at Redleston Road, St Ackmund, Derby, the youngest son of the seven children of Ephraim Syms Dodwell, commercial clerk, and his wife, Sarah, daughter of Benjamin Hudson, a London builder, and his wife, Ann.

The family apparently moved to Oxford. In 1870 Dodwell left home and obtained a position as an office boy, but within two years he had joined the agency house of Adamson, Bell & Co. Sent out to China, he served briefly in Foochow (Fuzhou) before moving to Shanghai, where he was soon promoted to be the managing clerk in charge of the trading company's shipping agency. In January 1879 Dodwell married Julia Simms (d. 1906), and they had two sons and four daughters.

Adamson retired in 1887, withdrawing his investment; his partner failed to obtain new capital and, by continuing to trade at the former level and by speculation, endangered the solvency of the firm. Anticipating the completion of the Trans-Canadian Railway, Dodwell had developed the shipping side of the firm and was consequently in an influential position. Accordingly, he approached Bell, together with the firm's tea expert, A. J. H. Carlill. Bell accepted both the judgement and the dramatic solution: that sealed information should be sent out to all major clients, especially shipping and insurance companies, stating that a new partnership had been formed, and requesting that all business be transferred to Dodwell, Carlill & Co. Those receiving the letter were informed that it should not be opened until instructions, in code, had reached them. Bell became insolvent in 1891, the coded message went out, and within a few days the new partnership of Dodwell, Carlill & Co., with a London head office, had secured the business of the predecessor firm.

When the Canadian Pacific Railway reached the Pacific coast at Vancouver, Dodwell confirmed his reputation as a shipping agent by securing 'retired' Cunard steamers and inaugurating a co-ordinated trans-Pacific service, the first north of San Francisco. The Canadian Pacific, determined to organize their own shipping subsidiary, offered Dodwell the position of manager. Preferring to run his own firm, he refused, establishing instead a rival service for the Northern Pacific railroad from Tacoma, Washington, which thus reputedly became the largest steamship firm on the Pacific coast of North America. During the gold rush Dodwell successfully constructed an aerial tramway to assist the carriage of goods into the Yukon.

Meanwhile Dodwell had transferred to Hong Kong, his success leading to his being invited to serve on the board of directors of the Hongkong and Shanghai Banking Corporation (1895–8). In 1899 Dodwell, Carlill, and their colleagues incorporated as Dodwell & Co. Ltd, a private company registered in London with a capital of £500,000. The firm had several departments—for tea, silk, and shipping, for example—and it operated in a number of distinct areas, such as Japan, Ceylon, and North America, each with an expert manager. Dodwell himself diversified his business activities and was chairman of the Malacca Rubber Plantation Company. Dodwell & Co. reached a peak of success in 1919; in the inter-war period it paid dividends on three occasions only.

On his arrival in England, Dodwell established himself in Watford. In Hong Kong he had sung in the choir of St John's Cathedral and he maintained his interest in the church, becoming the senior warden of St Andrew's, Watford's parish church. Dodwell was noted for the range of his local philanthropy. On the national scene he gave testimony to the royal commission on shipping rings; he was an active member of the China Association and a member of the Overseas League. He died unexpectedly of angina, on 9 October 1925, at his house Coniston, Langley Road, Abbots Langley, Watford, Hertfordshire, and was buried at St Andrew's Church, Watford, on the 14th. On his death he was accurately described as a man of dogged determination, undaunted by temporary reverses; he had a scrupulous sense of honour, an attractive personality, and an insatiable appetite for work.　　　　　FRANK H. H. KING

Sources E. Warde [E. A. Waldron], ed., *The house of Dodwell: a century of achievement, 1858–1958* [1958] · S. Jones, *Two centuries of overseas trading: the origins and growth of the Inchcape Group* (1986) · P. Griffiths, *A history of the Inchcape Group* (privately printed, London, 1977) · *West Herts and Watford Observer* (12 Oct 1925) · *Syren and Shipping* (14 Oct 1925), 88 · *China Express and Telegraph* (15 Oct 1925), 739 · A. Wright, ed., *Twentieth-century impressions of Hongkong, Shanghai and other treaty ports of China* (1908) · 'Royal commission on shipping rings', *Parl. papers* (1909), 48.240, Cd 4685 · b. cert. · GL, Dodwell MSS, 27525, 27523 · d. cert.

Archives GL

Likenesses photograph, repro. in Jones, *Two centuries of overseas trading*, 170 · photograph, repro. in Warde, ed., *The house of Dodwell*, facing p. viii · photograph, repro. in *Syren and Shipping*, frontispiece

Wealth at death £77,860 14s. 10d.: probate, 18 Dec 1925, CGPLA Eng. & Wales

Dodwell, Henry (1641–1711), scholar and theologian, was born in late October 1641 in the parish of St Warburgh, Dublin, the only surviving son of William Dodwell (d. 1650), army officer, and his wife, Elizabeth (d. c.1651), daughter of Sir Francis Slingsby of Yorkshire. Dodwell was born a few days after the Irish rising of 1641 broke out. He spent his early years with his mother in Dublin while his father's estate in Connaught was possessed by the rebels. In 1648 the family left for London and thence to York where their relatives lived. Dodwell spent five years at the 'Free School in the Horsefair' (St Peter's School), where Christopher Wallis was his teacher. In 1650 his father died of the plague at Waterford on his way back to his estate. His mother died of consumption soon after, and Dodwell was left an orphan. He spent about a year in his uncle Henry Dodwell's house in Suffolk before continuing his education in Ireland. In 1656 he was admitted a pensioner to Trinity College, Dublin, where the eminent physician and scholar John Stearne was his tutor. Dodwell obtained a fellowship in 1662, when a bachelor of arts, and proceeded MA in 1663. He resigned the fellowship in 1666 because he did not wish to take orders when this was required by the statutes of the college. Though he always revered the priesthood, he felt personally insecure about ordination and more confident about serving the church as a lay scholar.

Early scholarship From his days of study under Stearne, whom he admired as a philosophical thinker and a theologian, Dodwell developed a strong interest in philology, classical, biblical, and patristic history, and especially chronology. In his view these were the disciplines with which to acquire knowledge useful to the church of his own day. After Stearne's death in 1669 Dodwell as his literary executor published *De obstinatione* (1672), together with a preface of his own. That same year saw the publication of *Two Letters of Advice*, a work which among other things emphasized the importance of historical and philological studies for students of divinity. The following year, he published anonymously *Introduction to a Devout Life*, an edition of St Francis of Sales's work adapted for

Henry Dodwell (1641–1711), by Michael Vandergucht, pubd 1715

protestant use. Dodwell had paid brief visits to England to study in the libraries but finally moved to London in 1674 in pursuit of learning and of contacts with English scholars. In 1675 he went to live and work with William Lloyd, then dean of Bangor, and from 1680 bishop of St Asaph. Lloyd had a reputation as a chronologist and asked Dodwell to join him in his studies. Dodwell accompanied Lloyd on his journeys in these years, and began publishing his own controversial works against Catholicism and nonconformity, for example his *A reply to Mr [Richard] Baxter's pretended confutation of … Separation of churches from episcopal government … proved schismatical* (1681). Tensions developed between the men because of the 1688 revolution, Lloyd being a latitudinarian whig and Dodwell a high-church tory. Nevertheless, their literary and personal friendship survived these differences.

In the early 1680s Dodwell's ambition to defend the Restoration church and episcopacy also led to a number of scholarly publications. At Oxford, which he visited regularly during this period, Dodwell found a congenial conservative climate and important patristic scholars who enlisted his help, such as John Fell, dean of Christ Church and bishop of Oxford, John Pearson, bishop of Chester, and Edward Bernard. Dodwell wrote *Dissertationes Cyprianicae* (1682) at Fell's request. The work was also bound with copies of Fell's famous edition of St Cyprian that came out the same year. The several works of this patristic revival argued the close relationship between the church of primitive Christianity and the Anglican episcopal church. After Pearson's death (1686), Dodwell published his friend's posthumous works together with several essays of his own in 1688.

All this time Dodwell held no university position, but his reputation for learning was growing. He was known to frequent the coffee houses in London and Oxford where he engaged in lively and learned debates on the religious and political issues of his time. With the support of William Lloyd, the biblical scholar John Mill and others at Oxford, Dodwell was elected to the Camden chair of history on 2 April 1688. He was incorporated MA at Hart Hall on 21 May and on 25 May gave a successful inaugural lecture on ancient chronology. This was followed by six lectures on the *Historia Augusta*, and a further series of sixteen on Hadrian, until 6 November 1691. Altogether nineteen lectures were published in 1692 as *Praelectiones academicae in schola rhetorices Camdeniana*, with which Dodwell impressed his contemporaries as a sophisticated humanist scholar.

Nonjuror Dodwell's public career, however, was not to last much beyond the revolution of 1688. He published anonymously his *Concerning the Case of Taking the New Oath of Fealty and Allegiance* in 1689, himself intending to refuse to take the oath to William and Mary. It was argued at the time that refusing the oath might not endanger his praelectorship, but as Dodwell wrote to Arthur Charlett on 11 March 1690, 'If I may not keep my place without Sin or Scandal, I desire not to keep it at all' (Bodl. Oxf., MS Ballard 34, fols. 2–10). When his lectures had been stopped, Dodwell felt he was being forced to resign by the institution of the new oath. Therefore, he made sure to receive a certificate from the vice-chancellor of the university stating that his dismissal was on the grounds of nonjuring. This certificate, dated 19 November 1691, confirmed to Dodwell and his nonjuring friends that he had not resigned voluntarily.

Dodwell developed his theology to justify the separation, becoming one of the first leaders of the nonjuring movement. *A Cautionary Discourse of Schism* (1691) after the suspension of the bishops was soon followed by *A vindication of the deprived bishops, asserting their spiritual rights against a lay-deprivation* (1692). This work answered Humphrey Hody's *Anglicani novi schismatis*, published in English as *The Unreasonableness of a Separation from the New Bishops* (1691). Both Hody and Dodwell argued their cases by examining historical precedents. Hody presented an ancient Greek manuscript in the Bodleian (Bodl. Oxf., MS Baroccian 142), but Dodwell proved Hody's scholarship flawed. In order to defend the deprivation of the nonjuring bishops, Hody had repressed part of the manuscript which contained canons requiring a synod to validate a deprivation. Dodwell's point that the new bishops were

schismatical was based on the writings of St Cyprian. In Dodwell's patristic theology the secular ruler could not replace bishops who had been canonically appointed. The church was envisioned as a divine society with independent jurisdiction in spiritual matters, separate from the state and its temporal affairs. Dodwell's fight against Erastianism in these and following publications considerably influenced the high-church Anglicanism of his time.

Domestic and scholarly circle After his deprivation in 1691 Dodwell wished to live in retirement and moved to Cookham, a village in Berkshire. He came to know Francis Cherry, a Jacobite squire from nearby Shottesbrooke, and the two met regularly in a Maidenhead coffee house, discussing religion and politics. Becoming close friends, Cherry desired Dodwell to move closer to a manor house he owned in White Waltham. On 29 June 1694 Dodwell married Anne Elliot (d. 1750), the daughter of his landlord from Cookham. Upon their marriage Dodwell and his wife moved to Shottesbrooke where Cherry fitted them up with a house. They had ten children, of whom two sons, Henry *Dodwell (1706–1784) and William *Dodwell (1709–1785), and four daughters survived him.

Shottesbrooke developed into an important centre for nonjurors and scholars, with regular visitors such as Thomas Ken, Charles Leslie, Robert Nelson, George Hickes, Edmund Gibson, and White Kennett. Francis Brokesby functioned as nonjuror family chaplain and was to become Dodwell's biographer. Cherry had taken the promising student Thomas Hearne into his house and Dodwell introduced the boy to the discipline of classical philology. While pursuing his own career as Oxford antiquary a decade later, a grateful and admiring Hearne filled his diaries with detailed biographical information about Dodwell. Shottesbrooke was also visited by scholars from abroad. Dodwell came to know a group of German scholars, among them Gottlieb Schelwig, C. M. Pfaff, and J. C. Wolf, who visited Oxford to work in the Bodleian Library and afterwards kept up a correspondence with Dodwell and Hearne.

Return to the Church of England Dodwell continued to defend the Church of England and episcopacy in scholarly and theological writings, but he could not be happy with the schism as a permanent situation in the church. As early as 1700, and unknown to the nonjuror bishops, he tried unsuccessfully to come to an understanding with Archbishop Tenison. Dodwell foresaw another opportunity to heal the breach when, eventually, all deprived nonjuror bishops would have either died or relinquished their sees. In his view, the schism could not be maintained once the situation of two bishops to one see or 'altar against altar' no longer existed, even though the deprivations had been invalid. Dodwell explained his position in *A case in view considered … proving that (in case our present invalidly deprived fathers shall leave all their sees vacant, either by death or resignation) we shall not then be obliged to keep up our separation from those bishops, who are as yet involved in the guilt of the present unhappy schism* (1705). The Anglican doctrines of non-resistance and passive obedience were to be heeded, despite remaining irreconcilable differences concerning liturgy and prayers. In January 1710, when Bishop Lloyd of Norwich died and Thomas Ken, the last surviving deprived bishop, ceded his claim to the bishopric of Bath and Wells, Dodwell and the Shottesbrooke group returned to the Church of England. *The Case in View now in Fact* (1711) confirmed the end of the schism. Other nonjurors followed, though it is not known how many.

Dodwell's leadership of the nonjurors, however, was no longer undisputed by this time. His tendency to present himself as the champion of Anglican religion provoked bad feelings and jealousies. Increasingly, friends had come to criticize his scholarship and theological speculations. Some, like fellow nonjuror Henry Gandy in *A Conference between Gerontius and Junius* (1711), argued that Dodwell's ideas about ending the schism were inconsistent with his earlier writings. Gandy and others were especially baffled by his ideas about the mortality of the soul in *An epistolary discourse, proving, from the scriptures and the first fathers, that the soul is a principle naturally mortal* (1706). Immortality, Dodwell maintained, was a gift of God through baptism by episcopally ordained clergy only. Though published in times of heated party debates about the constitution of the church, some of Dodwell's friends considered that his theological speculations were damaging their cause. During the next three years, attacks in sermon and pamphlet, including Edmund Chishull's charge of heresy, left Dodwell a bitter man.

Nonjurors such as George Hickes, Thomas Wagstaffe, Henry Gandy, Thomas Smith, and even Thomas Hearne among others, though supporting Dodwell's arguments against nonconformity, did not follow him in his return to the church. In fact the first two nonjuror bishops (Hickes and Wagstaffe) had been newly consecrated in secret in 1694 in order to maintain the schism. The remaining group of nonjurors led by Hickes saw no reason to end the separation on the basis of Dodwell's Cyprianic principles. With Hickes the nonjurors developed into a sect outside the Church of England, though still claiming to represent the remnant of the only true Catholic church.

Later scholarship Dodwell wished his scholarship to serve the causes of the established church. Nevertheless, his vast output of philological and historical studies remains valuable regardless of their possible application to the religious or political issues of his day. His great passion was the study of chronology and historiography of the ancient world. He produced numerous series of treatises on classical authors such as Lactantius, Irenaeus, Cicero, Thucydides, Xenophon, Velleius Paterculus, Quintilian, and Dionysius of Halicarnassus. Some were published in the classical editions of other scholars. For Bodley's librarian John Hudson, for example, Dodwell wrote introductions to the Greek geographers (published in four volumes 1698–1712) and he advised Hearne on his editions of Livy and Eutropius. Dodwell's first truly antiquarian publication was *A Discourse Concerning Sanchoniathon's Phoenician History* (1681), which showed his independent critical spirit and approach in proving the then much cited work a

forgery. Dodwell was involved in the scholarly debates of the eighteenth-century 'Battle of the books' between the ancients and the moderns. He contributed 'An invitation to gentlemen to acquaint themselves with ancient history' to a new edition of Degory Wheare's *Method and Order of Reading … Histories* (1694), and corresponded with Richard Bentley and William Lloyd about the epistles of Phalaris, trying to defend them as authentic historical documents. However, in his rather delayed publication of *Exercitationes duae* (1704), the two dissertations on the age of Phalaris and Pythagoras, Dodwell had to content himself with the discussion of minor chronological problems, tacitly granting Bentley's main point on the forgery.

Dodwell's great chronological study and life's work was *De veteribus Graecorum Romanorumque cyclis* (1701), an impressive and well-received study of all the chronological systems of the classical world. An abridged version was published by Edmond Halley and reprinted in Brokesby's *Life of Dodwell*. Other antiquarian studies, especially those on recently unearthed ancient objects, were undertaken by Dodwell when such antiquary friends as William Musgrave, Thomas Hearne, and John Woodward aroused his enthusiasm for the chronological problems involved. Thus Dodwell worked on the dating of a Latin inscription for a study of Roman Britain, *Julii Vitalis epitaphium* (1711), and on the interpretation of a relief representing the sacking of Rome on a supposedly genuine Roman shield in Woodward's possession. Woodward's shield caused a stir in the international scholarly world. Dodwell's learned and minutely detailed contribution was left unfinished at his death but published by Hearne as *Henrici Dodwelli de parma equestri Woodwardiana dissertatio* (1713).

As a scholar Dodwell was renowned for his erudition, piety, and integrity, both at home and abroad. Dodwell corresponded with important foreign scholars such as J. G. Graevius, Antonio Magliabecchi, Cardinal Noris, and Jacob Perizonius, and his works were given respectful attention in English and continental journals. He was also criticized for his obscure and digressive style, something he felt insecure about himself. Brokesby ascribed Dodwell's obscurity to his not being among people enough to know how to communicate his learning. The less charitable opinions of contemporaries such as the bishops Burnet, Kennett, and Nicolson were often coloured by political and religious prejudice. Later in the century, Edward Gibbon appreciated Dodwell's erudition but was also critical: the 'worst of this author is his method and style, the one perplexed beyond imagination, the other negligent to a degree of barbarism' (*Gibbon's Journal*, 82). Dodwell indeed presents the modern reader with intricate and at times unintelligible arguments, and scholars today agree that his conclusions were not always right (and often could not be, considering the complexity of the problems). Yet his work contains a variety and an abundance of historical detail and original observations about events in classical history. Most important was his effort, through elaborate chronological studies, to recover and reconstruct the ancient past and its historical sources. According to Joseph Levine,

Dodwell's criticism, like that of the best of his contemporaries, had advanced beyond the possibilities of Renaissance philology. Scholars of 1700 were no longer content to discover and to expose legend and forgery; they had begun the task of reconstruction as well. (Levine, *Woodward's Shield*, 210)

Dodwell struggled with deteriorating eyesight in the last years of his life. He died of a consumption on 7 June 1711 after a brief period of illness. He was buried on 9 June in the chancel of his parish church at Shottesbrooke in Berkshire. THEODOR HARMSEN

Sources Bodl. Oxf., MSS Cherry; MSS Ballard; MSS Rawlinson K (Hearne-Smith); MSS Smith; MSS St Edmund Hall [see also MSS in other collections] · *Remarks and collections of Thomas Hearne*, ed. C. E. Doble and others, 11 vols., OHS, 2, 7, 13, 34, 42–3, 48, 50, 65, 67, 72 (1885–1921) · F. Brokesby, *The life of Mr Dodwell; with an account of his works* (1715) · J. C. Findon, 'The nonjurors and the Church of England, 1689–1716', DPhil diss., U. Oxf., 1978 · J. M. Levine, *Dr Woodward's shield: history, science, and satire in Augustan England* (1977), chaps. 11–12 · M. Goldie, 'The nonjurors, episcopacy, and the origins of the convocation controversy', *Ideology and conspiracy: aspects of Jacobitism, 1689–1759*, ed. E. Cruickshanks (1982), 15–35 · J. H. Overton, *The nonjurors: their lives, principles, and writings* (1902) · N. Marshall, *Defence of our constitution in church and state* (1717) · Wood, *Ath. Oxon.: Fasti* (1820), 404–6 · *The life and times of Anthony Wood*, ed. A. Clark, 3–4, OHS, 26, 30 (1894–5) · A. T. Hart, *William Lloyd, 1627–1717: bishop, politician, author, and prophet* (1952), 79, 153–6 · T. H. B. M. Harmsen, *Antiquarianism in the Augustan age: Thomas Hearne, 1678–1735* (2000) · J. M. Levine, *The battle of the books: history and literature in the Augustan age* (1991), esp. chap. 3 · M. Feingold, 'The humanities', *Hist. U. Oxf.* 4: *17th-cent. Oxf.*, 211–358, esp. 349–57 · T. Lathbury, *A history of the nonjurors* (1845) · T. Hearne, *Henrici Dodwelli de parma equestri Woodwardiana dissertatio* (1713) · T. Hearne, 'A letter containing an account of some antiquities between Windsor and Oxford', *The itinerary of John Leland the antiquary*, 5 (1711), 103–43; 9 (1712), 188–93 · H. S. Jones, 'The foundation and history of the Camden chair', *Oxoniensia*, 8–9 (1943–4), 169–92 · A. Kippis and others, eds., *Biographia Britannica, or, The lives of the most eminent persons who have flourished in Great Britain and Ireland*, 2nd edn, 5 vols. (1778–93) · H. J. Erasmus, *The origins of Rome in historiography from Petrarch to Perizonius* (1962), 91–2, 109–10 · Dodwell's will, PRO, PROB 11/521, fols.227v–228v · M. L. Clarke, 'Classical studies', *Hist. U. Oxf.* 5: *18th-cent. Oxf.*, 513–34, esp. 514–15 · I. G. Philip, 'Libraries and the University Press', *Hist. U. Oxf.* 5: *18th-cent. Oxf.*, 725–54, esp. 734 · H. Carter, *A history of the Oxford University Press*, 1: *To the year 1780* (1975) · R. B. McDowell and D. A. Webb, *Trinity College, Dublin, 1592–1952: an academic history* (1982), 25–6 · H. Gandy, *Conference between Gerontius and Junius* (1711) · Burtchaell & Sadleir, *Alum. Dubl.* · *Gibbon's Journal to January 28th 1763*, ed. D. M. Low (1929) · E. Calamy, *An historical account of my own life, with some reflections on the times I have lived in, 1671–1731*, ed. J. T. Rutt, 1 (1829), 281–2 · [J. Walker and P. Bliss], eds., *Letters written by eminent persons in the seventeenth and eighteenth centuries*, 2 vols. (1813)

Archives Balliol Oxf., MS 401 · Bodl. Oxf., corresp. and papers, MS Eng. hist. e 183; MS Eng. lett. c 28.9 · Bodl. Oxf., letters · Bodl. Oxf., corresp. and papers, St Edmund Hall MSS 9–36 · CUL, letters, Add. MS 45, Mm. I. 51 · Worcs. RO, corresp. with William Lloyd, Hardwick Court MSS, Worcester, Box 74 | BL, letters, Add. MSS; Harley MSS; Stowe MSS · Bodl. Oxf., Ballard MSS, corresp. and papers · Bodl. Oxf., Cherry MSS, corresp. and papers · Bodl. Oxf., Hearne MSS, diaries · Bodl. Oxf., letters to Nicholas Bernard · Bodl. Oxf., letters to Thomas Hearne · Bodl. Oxf., letters to Thomas Smith · LPL, letters to Archbishop Tenison, MS 930 · TCD, corresp. with William King, MSS 1995–2008

Likenesses portrait, c.1697 (copy after an original), Bodl. Oxf. · M. Vandergucht, line engraving, NPG; repro. in Brokesby, *The life of Mr Dodwell* [see illus.]

Wealth at death see will, PRO, PROB 11/521, fols. 227v–228v

Dodwell, Henry (1706–1784), religious controversialist and barrister, was born on 25 November 1706 at Shottesbrooke, Berkshire, the fourth child and eldest son of Henry *Dodwell (1641–1711), classical scholar and theologian, and Anne Elliot (d. 1750). Educated at Magdalen Hall, Oxford, whence he matriculated on 17 April 1723, he proceeded BA on 9 February 1726 and went on to study law. He entered the Middle Temple on 15 January 1731, from where he was called to the bar on 10 February 1738. He later became a bencher (1767) of the Middle Temple and served as reader from Lent 1775 and as treasurer from 1778.

Dodwell was an early participant in the Society for the Encouragement of Arts, Manufactures, and Commerce. However, he is remembered largely because of his satirical assault on the fideism of William Law and other orthodox apologists in a book entitled *Christianity not Founded on Argument* (1741). Though it was published anonymously Dodwell was widely known to be the book's author. The supposed thesis of the work is that reason cannot be the foundation of vital Christian faith; Dodwell argued that the notion 'that your Assent to Revealed Truths should be founded upon the Conviction of your Understanding' was 'false and unwarranted' (*Christianity not Founded on Argument*, 7). Rather, belief in Christ must be maintained in opposition to the dictates of fallen reason. Moreover he questioned:

> whether that Person does not enjoy his Belief with much greater Tranquility and Confidence of Spirit, who never asked himself but one Single Question about it, than he, who by the most elaborate Discussions, and busiest Search, has attained to the utmost Degree of Moral Assurance in the Matter. (ibid., 29)

This reasoning parodies the argument contained in William Law's lucid *The Case of Reason* (1731), in which the talented and pious Law argues against the general aggrandizement of reason in all areas of human existence.

Though written by a deist and in opposition to Christian apologists *Christianity not Founded on Argument* was read by many as a serious and even important defence of the faith. The long battle with deism had taken its toll on public confidence in argument, and less discerning readers found in Dodwell a sensible retreat to a faith not dependent on an individual's capacity as a logician. Methodists in particular were drawn to Dodwell's argument and some recommended it to John Wesley himself. Dodwell's thesis complemented the Wesleyan doctrines of new birth and instantaneous conversion. Dodwell had written:

> the Holy Ghost irradiates the souls of believers at once with an irresistible light from heaven that flashes conviction in a moment, so that this faith is completed in an instant, and the most perfect and finished creed produced at once without any tedious progress in deductions of our own.

Wesley, however, was not taken in by Dodwell's satire:

> On a careful perusal of that piece, notwithstanding my prejudice in its favour, I could not but perceive that the great design uniformly pursued throughout the work was to render the whole of the Christian institution both odious and contemptible. His point throughout is to prove that Christianity is contrary to reason, or that no man acting according to the principles of reason can possibly be a

Christian. (J. Wesley, *Earnest Appeal to Men of Reason and Religion*, 1743, 14)

Wesley adds the cautionary note that Dodwell's book 'is a wonderful proof of the power that smooth words may have even on serious minds that so many have mistook such a writer as this for a friend of Christianity' (ibid.).

Dodwell's most ardent respondent, Philip Doddridge, published three letters in reply to *Christianity not Founded on Argument* in 1742–3. Doddridge asked indignantly, in response to Dodwell's charge that faith made no reference to reason:

> Can anyone indeed seriously think, that the noblest of our powers was intended only to the lowest and meanest purposes; to serve the little offices of moral life, and not to be consulted in the greatest concerns; those of immortality? Strange! (P. Doddridge, *The Perspicuity and Solidity of the Evidences for Christianity*, 1742, 10)

The most authoritative of the anti-deistic writers, John Leland, wrote an entire work on Dodwell's subject, entitled *Remarks on a Late Pamphlet, Entitled, 'Christianity not Founded on Argument'* (1744), and devoted a chapter to it in his *View of the Principal Deistical Writers* (1757). Dodwell was also answered by George Benson in *The Reasonableness of the Christian Religion as Delivered in the Scriptures* (1743) and by Thomas Randolph in *The Christian Faith a Rational Assent* (1744). Dodwell's own brother William *Dodwell preached two sermons against the book before the University of Oxford. These repudiations notwithstanding, even William Law, apparently one of the objects of Dodwell's satire, maintained the possibility that *Christianity not Founded on Argument* had been written by an earnest Christian. Dodwell died in 1784.　　JAMES A. HERRICK

Sources DNB · J. A. Herrick, *The radical rhetoric of the English deists* (1997) · J. Leland, *Remarks on a late pamphlet, entitled, 'Christianity not founded on argument'* (1744) · Foster, *Alum. Oxon.* · H. A. C. Sturgess, ed., *Register of admissions to the Honourable Society of the Middle Temple, from the fifteenth century to the year 1944*, 1 (1949), 310 · parish register, Shottesbrooke, Berkshire, 1 Jan 1706 [baptism]

Dodwell, William (1709–1785), Church of England clergyman and theologian, was born at Shottesbrooke, Berkshire, on 17 June 1709, the second son and fifth child of Henry *Dodwell (1641–1711), Jacobite and nonjuror, and his wife, Anne Elliot (d. 1750). His elder brother was Henry *Dodwell (1706–1784), religious controversialist. He matriculated from Trinity College, Oxford, on 23 March 1726 and proceeded BA in 1729 and MA in 1732. On 27 November 1740, at Bray church, he married Elizabeth Brown (b. 1712), who was probably the daughter of the Revd Thomas Brown, vicar of Bray, and Elizabeth, his wife. Dodwell took holy orders and, thanks to the patronage of the resident squire, Arthur Vansittart, became rector of Shottesbrooke, vicar of White Waltham in 1742, and vicar of Bucklesbury in 1749. Other preferment followed, due in the first instance to Dodwell's polemical skills rather than the pastoral gifts that he also possessed, perhaps in smaller measure. Thomas Sherlock, while bishop of Salisbury, awarded him the prebendal stall of Grantham Australis in Salisbury Cathedral in 1748 (collated 5 October) and he was subsequently given a residentiary canonry

there (collated 2 November 1754). In 1763 (collated 25 October) Sherlock's successor, John Thomas, made Dodwell archdeacon of Berkshire—an inspired choice, since he took seriously the need for the clergy to pursue lives of practical holiness, a concern reflected in his *Practical Discourses on Moral Subjects* (2 vols., 1748–9).

Dodwell was one of the staunchest defenders of orthodoxy produced by the Church of England in the eighteenth century. Unsurprisingly, given his background, his position was high-church in essentials but moderate withal; he took care to distance himself from both the Jacobitism and the deism that had characterized his father and brother Henry respectively. Dodwell had no doubt that faith was the highest good and comfort available to mankind. His own position was well articulated in *Two sermons on 1 Peter iii. 15 on the nature, procedure, and effects of a rational faith, preached before the University of Oxford, 11 March and 24 June 1744* (1745); in reply to his brother's *Christianity not Founded on Argument* he emphasized that 'The Fundamentals of Christianity are on all sides acknowledged to be few, plain and easy' (p. 69). But this was by no means a non-dogmatic version of Anglicanism. *The Practical Influence of the Doctrine of the Holy Trinity Represented* (1745), preached at St Mary's, Oxford, before the university, criticized those believers who had 'given up all the distinguishing Articles of Revealed [religion], in compliance with the professed advocates of natural religion' (p. 28). This could not be justified when trinitarianism was 'the very essence of the Christian Religion, the foundation of the whole Revelation, and connected with every part of it' (p. 19). Dodwell expounded his position in *Three Charges on the Athanasian Creed*, originally delivered to the Berkshire clergy but not published until 1802.

Dodwell was punctilious in defending the apostolic deposit of faith against all those who would modify, abridge, or deny it. In *The desirableness of the Christian faith illustrated and applied: a sermon preached at the triennial visitation of the Rt Rev Father in God Thomas, lord bishop of Sarum, held at Reading, 30 August 1744* (1744) he deplored the growth in number of 'speculative infidels' (p. 2) and insisted that 'an infidel in calamity is the most miserable creature, that imagination can paint' (p. 18). Bolingbroke was a particular target in *The Doctrine of a Particular Providence Stated, Confirmed, Defended and Applied in Two Sermons* (1760), a topic of central importance for contemporary defenders of Christianity. Dodwell directed most of his polemical energies against those whom he saw as distorting the faith, among them Conyers Middleton, William Romaine, and William Whiston. In *A free answer to Dr Middleton's free inquiry into the miraculous powers of the primitive church* (1749), he defended the church fathers and contested each of Middleton's four main criticisms of the primitive church and its use of miracles; there were occasions, he insisted, when they could be convincingly vindicated 'to the satisfaction of men of sense' (p. 21). He queried Romaine's grasp of the Old Testament in *Dissertation on Jephthah's Vow, Occasioned by Rev. William Romaine's Sermon on the Subject* (1745), and in *The eternity of future punishment asserted and vindicated: two sermons preached before the University of Oxford on Sunday, 21 Mar 1741*

(1743) he attacked what he believed was Whiston's blatantly heretical theology, suggesting that:

> these Attempts to distinguish away the Sense of the most vital parts of our religion, by Those, who in profession are friends to the authority of it, are rather more prejudicial than the open attacks of those, who more consistently reject the whole.　(preface)

If Dodwell was never the most feared spokesman for theological correctness, neither was his reputation tainted by a tendency to acerbity or an insistence on having the last word on any matter. His linguistic skills and his familiarity with the primary documents of the Church of England (including patristic authorities and the Caroline divines) made him also something of a liturgist. His *The sick man's companion, or, The clergyman's assistant in visiting the sick, with a dissertation on prayer* (1767) is a remarkable series of prayers, inspired by the Book of Common Prayer, for all sorts of afflicted men and women, such as 'for one that is recovered/under a relapse', 'one that wants sleep', 'prisoners before or after trial'. This work, like the rest of Dodwell's output, reflected his satisfaction with his confession's primitive character. In *A charge delivered to the clergy of the archdeaconry of Berks. at the late visitation, in May 1764* (1764) he returned to his favourite theme of the early church, insisting that the protestant religion was as old as the New Testament: 'All the primitive Churches in the world were of our religion' (p. 27). It was wholly appropriate that the degree of DD, by diploma, was conferred on him by the University of Oxford, on 23 February 1750.

Dodwell wrote copiously and published a large number of sermons in addition to those already discussed. He also published *Letter to the Author of Considerations on the Act to Prevent Clandestine Marriages*, with a postscript prompted by Stebbing's *Enquiry into the Annulling Clauses in London* (1755). He died on 23 October 1785, leaving a large family, and was buried in Shottesbrooke church. There is a monumental inscription in Salisbury Cathedral composed by his old friend Bishop Charles Moss.　　NIGEL ASTON

Sources *DNB* · *GM*, 1st ser., 55 (1785), 837, 878 · *GM*, 1st ser., 56 (1786), 32–3, 133 · *GM*, 1st ser., 73 (1803), 1138–40 · Foster, *Alum. Oxon.*, 1715–1886, 1.376 · archdeaconry of Berkshire mandates, Berks. RO, D/A2/d4, fol. 312 · Bray parish registers, Berks. RO, D/P23/1/2, D/P23/1/1 · *VCH Berkshire*, 3.170 · *Fasti Angl.*, 1541–1857, [Salisbury], 15, 45, 102
Archives Bodl. Oxf., corresp. and papers, MS St Edmund Hall 37

Doget [Doket], **John** (*d.* 1501), humanist scholar and college head, was the nephew of Cardinal Thomas Bourchier, archbishop of Canterbury (*d.* 1486), to whom Doget must have owed much of the considerable church patronage later bestowed on him. He was born in Sherborne, Dorset, and was probably educated in Bourchier's household before being admitted to Eton College as a king's scholar about 1447. From Eton he passed to King's College, Cambridge, in 1451, and became a fellow there in 1454. His humanist interests were no doubt encouraged at King's by the presence of a number of books from the library of Humphrey, duke of Gloucester (*d.* 1447), which gave King's the largest and most up-to-date collection of books in any of the Cambridge colleges. These books included

the *Phaedo* of Plato, and the *Republic* in the Latin translation of Pier Candido Decembrio (now BL, Harley MS 1705).

In 1460 Doget took orders as a priest, and was granted leave to incept in theology in 1464. But in the same year he left Cambridge for Padua, the first of a number of King's fellows to follow this route. However, he was swindled out of more than £50, intended to support him in Padua, by a London shearman named James Fynde, and had to leave, subsequently migrating to Bologna, where he studied canon law and earned his doctorate in 1469. He returned to Cambridge and continued his collection of benefices, which had begun with his appointment as archdeacon of Chichester in 1463. Papal dispensation enabled him to become a prebendary at Lincoln, Salisbury, and Southwell; to which were added by papal provision in 1479 canonries at Cambrai, St Omer, and St Mary's, Antwerp. He was also rector of Havant and Odiham, Hampshire, Eastbourne, Sussex, and Winterbourne Zelstone, Dorset, and became chancellor of Salisbury (1486) and Lichfield (1489) and master of Trinity College, Arundel (1499).

Doget was prolocutor of the clergy in the convocation of Canterbury in 1473, and was entrusted with important diplomatic duties in 1479–80. He was sent to Rome to help arrange a peace between Pope Sixtus IV (*r.* 1471–84) and Florence in 1479, dealing also with the princes of Sicily and Hungary. He was then appointed to an embassy to the king of Denmark. The standing he had attained at court was not affected either by the death of Edward IV, or by that of Richard III, whose domestic chaplain Doget had become in 1483. It was Henry VII who presented him to the provostship of his old college in 1499. At his death he bequeathed all his books on canon law and theology to King's, while also making bequests to the poor in the many parishes with which he was connected. His prosperity had taken a sad blow in 1491, when the fire that had destroyed his rectory house and outbuildings at Eastbourne cost him £600, so he claimed. John Doget's will is dated 4 March 1501. He died the following month, and was buried in Salisbury Cathedral.

Doget's principal claim to fame lies in his authorship of *Examinatorium in Phaedonem Platonis*, the first philosophical work by an English humanist. Dedicated to Cardinal Bourchier, to whom it must have been presented between 1473, when the latter became a cardinal, and his death in 1486, it survives in the British Library as Add. MS 10344. The script is italic and is probably that of Doget himself. But the parchment and illuminated vine-stem initials are English. The text of the *Phaedo* on which Doget comments is the translation of Leonardo Bruni. As Roberto Weiss has pointed out in the commentary, 'his aim appears to have been an interpretation of some of Plato's passages as Christian maxims. Because of this he deals principally with an explanation of obscure passages in the *Phaedo*, which are presented so as to emphasize their common points with Christian doctrine' (Weiss, 166). The Neoplatonic texts cited by Doget, which include Marsilio Ficino's Latin version of the *Pimander*, or *Poemander*, of Hermes Trismegistus, are seen through the prism of Christian apologetics, and the *Phaedo* was no doubt chosen in the first place as a vehicle for his commentary because it could be presented as a mythologized version of Christian doctrine. Doget's manuscript was later purchased by another humanist, Robert Sherborn, bishop of Chichester (*d.* 1536).   PETER MURRAY JONES

Sources Emden, *Cam.* · R. Weiss, *Humanism in England during the fifteenth century*, 3rd edn (1967), 57, 164–7 · R. J. Mitchell, 'English students at Padua, 1460–75', *TRHS*, 4th ser., 19 (1936), 101–18, esp. 112–14 · A. Allen, 'Skeleton Collegii Regalis Cantab.', King's Cam., vol. 1, pp. 83–4 · [A. C. de la Mare and R. W. Hunt], eds., *Duke Humfrey and English humanism in the fifteenth century* (1970), 54–7 [exhibition catalogue, Bodl. Oxf.] · N. D. Hurnard, 'Studies in intellectual life in England from the middle of the fifteenth century till the time of Colet', DPhil diss., U. Oxf., 1935 · J. Hankins, *Plato in the Italian Renaissance*, 2 vols. (1991), 2.497–501, 692

Archives BL, Add. MS 10344 · King's Cam., muniments, mundum and commons books, ledger book

Dogfael [St Dogfael, Dogwel, Dygfael, Dogmael] (*fl.* **6th cent.**), holy man, is the patron saint and presumed founder of the church of St Dogmael, known in Welsh as Llandudoch, situated on the south side of the Teifi, opposite Cardigan. In 1120 a Tironian priory was established on the site under the patronage of Robert fitz Martin, lord of Cemais, but the name remained. Robert's charter distinguishes the church of St Dogmael from the adjacent land of Llandudoch. Yet, in spite of this and of phonological objections which have been raised, it is likely that Tudoch was simply a pet form of the name Dogfael. His usual feast day was 31 October. There is no life of Dogfael, but the genealogies of the saints make his father Ithel a son of Ceredig ap Cunedda, the eponymous ancestor of the ruling kindred of Ceredigion. The centre of Dogfael's cult, however, was to the south of the Teifi in the cantrefs of Cemais and Pebidiog in Dyfed (in the north of the later Pembrokeshire), as shown by his churches: apart from St Dogmael's, they were the nearby Capel Degwel, St Dogwell's near Fishguard, Mynachlog-ddu, and Meline. The only clear trace of his cult outside north Pembrokeshire is Llanddogwel (Llanddygfael) in Anglesey (now attached to Llanfechell). The affiliation to a son of Ceredig ap Cunedda may have been in defence of the expansionist aims of the descendants of Rhodri Mawr (*d.* 878), king of Gwynedd. The saintly Dogfael is not to be confused with his supposed great-uncle, another son of Cunedda, who was the eponymous ancestor of the ruling kindred of Dogfeiling, later a commote of Dyffryn Clwyd.

                    T. M. CHARLES-EDWARDS

Sources P. C. Bartrum, ed., *Early Welsh genealogical tracts* (1966) · P. C. Bartrum, *A Welsh classical dictionary: people in history and legend up to about AD 1000* (1993) · S. Baring-Gould and J. Fisher, *The lives of the British saints*, 4 vols., Honourable Society of Cymmrodorion, Cymmrodorion Record Series (1907–13) · A. W. Wade-Evans, 'Pembrokeshire notes', *Archaeologia Cambrensis*, 90 (1935), 123–34 · F. G. Cowley, *The monastic order in south Wales, 1066–1349* (1977) · *DWB*

Dogget, John. *See* Doget, John (*d.* 1501).

Doggett, Thomas (*c.*1670–1721), actor and theatre manager, was born in Castle Street, Dublin, though nothing is known of his family or upbringing. Apparently by his early teens he was already engaged as a thespian, being

Thomas Doggett (*c.*1670–1721), by Thomas Murray, *c.*1691 [probably in the role of Nincompoop in *Love for Money* by Thomas D'Urfey]

listed in a 1684–5 manuscript cast for an intended production of John Fletcher's *The Night Walker* at Smock Alley, and various authorities have suggested that for the next several years he performed as a stroller. He eventually made his way to London, where in January 1691 his appearance at Drury Lane as Deputy Nincompoop in Thomas D'Urfey's *Love for Money* marked the beginning of a long and successful career. It was his creation of the role of Solon in D'Urfey's *The Marriage-Hater Matched* at Drury Lane a year later that marked his first triumph: the *London Mercury* remarked that the author ought 'to present Mr Dogget … with half the Profit of his Third Day' as the play's success 'was half owing to that admirable Actor' (26 Feb 1692). During the next twenty years Doggett went on to establish himself as one of the most talented and versatile comedians on the London stage, being termed by John Downes (*c.*1708) as 'the only Comick Original now Extant' (Downes, 108).

In the early years of his career Doggett performed numerous comic roles, and became a personal favourite of William Congreve. The playwright tailored characters for Doggett's talents, from Fondlewife in *The Old Bachelor* to Ben in *Love for Love*. To these successes can be added Sancho Panza in D'Urfey's *Don Quixote* (pt 1), Mass Johnny in

Colley Cibber's *The School-Boy*, Savil in Fletcher's *The Scornful Lady*, Marplot in Susannah Centlivre's *The Busy Body*, Sir Oliver in George Etherege's *She Would if she Could*, and Sir Tristram Cash in Charles Johnson's *The Wife's Relief*, to name only a few of literally dozens of parts. On occasion he could also perform roles of a quite different nature, such as Shylock in George Granville's *The Jew of Venice*, and his singing in D'Urfey's *The Richmond Heiress* earned him the praise of John Dryden.

Early in his career Doggett recognized his own acting gifts, and like his fellow performer Colley Cibber with *Love's Last Shift*, created a play featuring himself in the best role. *The Country Wake* received its première in April 1696, with Doggett in the role of Hob. This play achieved some initial success, but became wildly popular in its later revised form as *Hob, or, The Country Wake* (first performed 6 October 1711; published 1715), an afterpiece which achieved notable success for decades. There is controversy over the authorship of *The Country Wake*, with Cibber frequently being mentioned as the adapter, but no convincing evidence has surfaced to prove Cibber's hand, and Doggett was certainly competent enough to revise his own play. The enduringly successful *Hob* inspired at least three later adaptations or sequels: *Hob's Wedding* (1720, by John Leigh), *Flora, an Opera* (1729, by James Hippisley), and *A Sequel to Flora* (1732, also by Hippisley).

Always a shrewd negotiator, Doggett exhibited a keen sense for advancing his career. During 1695–6, for example, he moved back and forth several times between Christopher Rich's Drury Lane troupe and Thomas Betterton's newly formed company at Lincoln's Inn Fields, playing one offer against the other. He also realized early on that he had management potential. In 1697, uncomfortable with Rich's unjust and irregular business practices, but in apparent default of his London contract, he obtained permission under the patronage of Henry Howard, seventh duke of Norfolk, to perform in Norwich, an opportunity which he renewed several times, interspersed with intermittent and limited London appearances, through 1700. The running of the Norwich company allowed him to develop expertise that would later prove invaluable, and he evinced considerable ambition, as exemplified in his production of Betterton's *Dioclesian* in 1700, thought to be the first performance of an opera in England outside London. Nevertheless, Rich served Doggett with a warrant in Norwich in 1697, recalling him to London for a hearing. Doggett, Cibber tells us, 'was not, in the least intimidated, by this formidable Summons'. He 'was not only discharg'd, but the Process of his Confinement (according to common Fame) had a Censure pass'd upon it in Court', for the plaintiffs 'had mistaken their Man' in regard to both legal knowledge and tenacity (Cibber, 193). The vindicated Doggett returned to Norwich, but in autumn 1702 he rejoined Betterton's company, where he remained for several seasons. The 1706–7 season found him once again heading the duke of Norfolk's provincial troupe.

A turning point in Doggett's affairs took place in March 1709, when he joined with Robert Wilks and Cibber to form a partnership with Owen Swiny to perform later that year at Vanbrugh's Haymarket Theatre. After experiencing several tempestuous seasons, on 6 December 1712 he signed yet another agreement with Wilks, Cibber, and William Collier to operate at the Drury Lane Theatre, a partnership arrangement which very quickly established itself, both artistically and economically. The need to add a fourth partner, Barton Booth, in November 1713 precipitated a crisis which by summer 1714 resulted in Doggett's exit from performance and management at Drury Lane, though he still retained ownership of his share of the business. Doggett remained intransigent in demanding that his one-third share not be diluted by the addition of new partners. His position, as reported by Cibber, was simply that 'nothing but the Law, should make him part with [i.e., share] his Property' (Cibber, 259). From mid-1714 onwards Doggett was no longer actively concerned in the Drury Lane management, and the protracted legal dispute was not resolved until 6 March 1716, when Doggett received £600 and back interest on his share, terms far less favourable than he had hoped to achieve. Relations with Wilks and Cibber improved after the settlement, and he eventually returned to the company to act from time to time. However, 1 April 1717 is thought to be his last-known performance on the stage, appropriately as Hob in *The Country Wake*.

Doggett's retirement years saw large changes in his personal affairs. The *Original Weekly Journal* of 23–30 August 1718 announced that he was 'lately married to a gentlewoman of 20,000 l. fortune'. This sizeable sum, when added to his own considerable earnings from the stage, allowed him, on 1 August 1716 (being the second anniversary of the accession of George I), to establish an endowment for an annual race on the Thames and award for the Watermen's Guild, as an expression of his staunch whiggism. The race, with its award of 'Doggett's Coat and Badge' remained as a tradition enduring at least to the end of the twentieth century. The new Mrs Doggett was dead by 1721, and her husband followed her on 20 September 1721; he was buried in Eltham, Kent, on 25 September. No verifiable likenesses of Doggett are known, though a portrait reported to be his image hangs in the Garrick Club and another by Thomas Murray is at Sherborne Castle, Dorset.

WILLIAM J. BURLING

Sources C. Cibber, *An apology for the life of Colley Cibber*, new edn, ed. B. R. S. Fone (1968) · J. Milhous and R. D. Hume, 'The silencing of Drury Lane in 1709', *Theatre Journal*, 32 (1980), 427–47 · Highfill, Burnim & Langhans, *BDA* · J. Milhous and R. D. Hume, eds., *Vice Chamberlain Coke's theatrical papers, 1706–1715* (1982) · J. Downes, *Roscius Anglicanus*, ed. J. Milhous and R. D. Hume, new edn (1987) · T. Viator and W. J. Burling, *The plays of Colley Cibber*, 1 (2000) · J. Milhous and R. D. Hume, eds., *A register of English theatrical documents, 1660–1737*, 2 vols. (1991) · W. S. Clark, *The early Irish stage: the beginnings to 1720* (1955) · *Weekly Journal or Saturday's Post* (23 Sept 1721)

Likenesses T. Murray, oils, *c*.1691, Sherborne Castle, Dorset [*see illus.*] · oils, Garr. Club

Wealth at death over £20,000: *Original Weekly Journal* (23–30 Aug 1718)

Dogherty, Thomas (*d.* 1805), legal writer, was born in Ireland, the son of Patrick Dogherty of Edenderry, King's county. Educated at a country school, he later moved to England, and became clerk to Mr Foster Bower, an eminent pleader or legal writer. He spent more than sixteen years in this capacity, studying law industriously, and making from his master's manuscripts, and those of Sir Joseph Yates and Sir Thomas Davenport, vast collections of precedents and notes. However, about 1785, on Bower's advice, he became a special pleader, concerned with drawing up the written proceedings of lawsuits. Dogherty was admitted a member of Gray's Inn on 4 October 1804. For some years he held the office of clerk of indictments on the Chester circuit.

In 1787 Dogherty wrote *The Crown Circuit Assistant*, in 1790 and 1799 he edited the sixth and seventh editions of *The Crown Circuit Companion*, and in 1800 he brought out an edition of Sir Matthew Hale's *The History of the Pleas of the Crown*. Dogherty wore himself out with hard work and died at his chambers in Clifford's Inn on 29 September 1805, leaving a large family ill-provided for. Describing Dogherty as a self-taught genius, an obituary praised 'his modest and unassuming manners, his independent mind, his strict honour and probity' (*GM*, 1074).

J. A. HAMILTON, *rev.* ROBERT BROWN

Sources A. Chalmers, ed., *The general biographical dictionary*, new edn, 32 vols. (1812–17) · R. Ryan, *Biographica Hibernica: a biographical dictionary of the worthies of Ireland* (1819–21) · *GM*, 1st ser., 75 (1805), 1074 · J. Foster, *The register of admissions to Gray's Inn, 1521–1889, together with the register of marriages in Gray's Inn chapel, 1695–1754* (privately printed, London, 1889)

Dogmael. *See* Dogfael (*fl.* 6th cent.).

Doharty [Dougharty], **John** (1709–1773), land surveyor, was born on 17 January 1709 at Bewdley, Worcestershire, the son of John *Dougharty (1677–1755), a land surveyor and teacher of mathematics, and his wife, Priscilla Fereder (*d.* 1741). Nine years earlier the couple had had another son John, who died within a few days of his birth. The surviving son John was educated at the King's School, Worcester (1716–23), and the technical skill that he displayed in his first surveying commissions suggest that he had been sent thereafter to London for professional training. His brother **Joseph Dougharty** (1699–1737), also a surveyor, was born on 5 May 1699 in Kidderminster. He was educated at the King's School, Worcester (1712–14), and later in London with a view to pursuing a career in mathematics. He returned to Worcestershire to help his father as both teacher and surveyor.

The family had a flourishing land-surveying business which produced estate maps for the local gentry and aristocracy, with whom contacts were forged through pupils at the father's school and the adjacent King's School. Between 1727 and 1732 Joseph produced fine estate maps of lands in Shropshire and Herefordshire as well as Worcestershire, and between 1731 and 1733 Joseph and more especially John undertook the arduous fieldwork for their father's famous survey of Hanbury Hall, Worcestershire.

John Dougharty's last dated map was completed in 1736, and in 1737 Joseph died, leaving John Doharty junior, as he then styled himself, to continue the surveying work alone. The first map he had produced by himself was made in 1732, and some eighty of his maps and plans have now been discovered. These include surveys of the earl of Coventry's lands in Worcestershire and Gloucestershire (1738–40), apparently intended to form an estate atlas to match his father's of Hanbury Hall. Although most are of estates in the west midlands, Doharty also worked for clients, notably King's College, Cambridge (1747–51), as far afield as Middlesex and Somerset. His maps exemplify the range of a land surveyor's work, having been drawn for such purposes as boundary disputes, promoting enclosure, and assisting estate management, but they show greater technical skill and finer aesthetic judgement than many such maps. Doharty also undertook land valuation work, laid out pleasure grounds in Worcester, invested in property, and was one of the original partners in the first porcelain works in the city. His last map is dated 1755.

The death in that year of Doharty's father, whom, as he remained unmarried he had continued to live with and support, marked the start of his decline. His melancholy writings of the period indicate his insecurity and megalomania with a hint of trouble with a woman, ill health, and fire. In 1755 he left Worcester to live with his nephew John Powell on the western outskirts of London, but he was admitted a pensioner of Sutton's Hospital (the Charterhouse) on 31 March 1760. Absent for a time because of infirmity and insanity, he died there on 6 April 1773 and was buried there on 9 April.

The surviving maps and plans drawn by both brothers and their father (listed as appendix 1 to Smith, 'The Doharty family') bear witness to the skill and industry of these important west midland land surveyors.

ELIZABETH BAIGENT and BRIAN S. SMITH

Sources B. S. Smith, 'The Doharty family: eighteenth-century mapmakers', *Transactions of the Lincolnshire Archaeological Society*, 3rd ser., 15 (1996), 245–82 · B. S. Smith, 'The Dougharty family of Worcester, estate surveyors and mapmakers, 1700–60', *Worcester Historical Society, miscellany 2* (1967) · Sutton's Hospital, admissions and burials registers, governors' assembly orders, LMA, ACC/1876/PS/01/03, PS/01/07, PS/01/08, G/02/06, pp. 102–3

Doherty, John (1783–1850), judge, was born in Dublin, the son of John Doherty of Dublin. He was educated at Chester School in England and later at Trinity College, Dublin, where he obtained his BA in 1806 and his LLD in 1814. He was called to the Irish bar in 1808 and joined the Leinster circuit; he took silk in 1823. His progress at the bar was slow, but he was known for his wit and powers of oratory.

From 1824 to 1826 Doherty was the elected MP for New Ross, co. Wexford. In 1826 connections with the Bushe family and with George Canning, then premier, aided his return for Kilkenny as a liberal tory. He became solicitor-general on 18 June 1827, during Canning's administration, and was re-elected for Kilkenny. In 1828 he was elected a bencher of the King's Inns, Dublin; from July to December 1830 he was MP for Newport, Cornwall; and on 23 December 1830 he was appointed lord chief justice of the common pleas, with a seat in the privy council, on the promotion of Lord Plunket to the lord chancellorship of Ireland.

Although a committed protestant, Doherty supported Catholic emancipation and is better remembered for his political activity than for his career as a judge. He was one of Peel's chief advisers on Irish policy and impressed the house with his fluency on both Irish matters and policy in general. As solicitor-general he had led the prosecution in a case of conspiracy to murder, 'the Doneraile conspiracy', debated in the house on 15 May 1830. Daniel O'Connell represented the Catholic defendants and later in the house raised charges of impropriety against Doherty in relation to the conduct of the case. In refuting O'Connell's charges, Doherty won fame for his oratory as well as winning the case.

In 1834 Sir Robert Peel asked Doherty to retire from the judicial bench, with the view of resuming his position in parliament. However, Doherty refused, stating that he had left politics behind upon his ascension to the bench. He was a commissioner for education and lost a large fortune through railway speculation. He retired to Beaumaris, north Wales, and died from heart disease on 8 September 1850. He left a widow, Elizabeth Lucy Doherty, formerly Wall, and several children. He was buried at St Kevin's churchyard, Dublin. A portrait of Doherty by Martin Cregan was acquired by the National Gallery of Ireland and an anonymous print was obtained by the National Portrait Gallery, London.

B. H. BLACKER, rev. SINÉAD AGNEW

Sources J. F. Waller, ed., *The imperial dictionary of universal biography*, 3 vols. (1857–63) · F. E. Ball, *The judges in Ireland, 1221–1921*, 2 vols. (1926) · A. J. Webb, *A compendium of Irish biography* (1878) · [T. T. Shore], ed., *Cassell's biographical dictionary* (1867–9) · L. J. McCaffrey, *Daniel O'Connell and the repeal year* [1966] · D. Gwynn, *Daniel O'Connell* (1947) · O. McDonagh, *The emancipist O'Connell, 1830–47* (1989) · C. J. Smyth, *Chronicle of the law officers of Ireland* (1839) · [J. H. Todd], ed., *A catalogue of graduates who have proceeded to degrees in the University of Dublin, from the earliest recorded commencements to … December 16, 1868* (1869) · *GM*, 2nd ser., 34 (1850) · *Annual Register* (1850), 92 · D. J. O'Donoghue, *The poets of Ireland: a biographical and bibliographical dictionary* (1912)
Likenesses M. Cregan, oils, 1826, NG Ire. · F. C. Lewis, stipple, pubd 1830 (after a drawing by J. Hayter), NG Ire. · H. Griffiths, stipple and etching, NG Ire.; repro. in *Dublin University Magazine*, 29 (June 1847) · stipple, NPG

Doherty, John (1797/8–1854), trade unionist and political radical, was born in Ireland but his exact date of birth is not certain. He came from a labouring family and he himself began work in the local cotton industry at the age of ten. In 1816 he joined the increasing flow of Irish migrants to Britain, and worked as a cotton spinner in Manchester. From the early days he seems to have become involved in trade union activities, and for his part in the Manchester strike of 1818 he was sent to prison for two years in 1819.

At this time Doherty was still a rank-and-file militant, but quickly, as the 1820s moved along, he came to be recognized as the outstanding trade union leader in Lancashire in the textile industry. He always remained a Catholic, with a remarkable capacity for organization, straightforward, provocative oratory, and a markedly shrewd political instinct. His mentor in the early years was William Cobbett, and although in his political radicalism Doherty went beyond Cobbett, the attack upon 'Old Corruption' always remained an essential part of his attack upon contemporary society. As with many of his contemporaries in the 1820s, Doherty came to accept a version of 'the right of the labourer to the whole produce of his labour'—an analysis of bourgeois society that developed out of the writings of William Thompson (1775–1833) and his contemporaries.

By 1829 Doherty had succeeded in bringing together most of the country's cotton spinners into the Grand General Union of Operative Cotton Spinners, and, although it had disappeared by 1831, it was an important stage in the heightening of class-consciousness among certain groups of working people. In the early months of 1830 he broadened his vision with the establishment of the National Association of United Trades for the Protection of Labour and during the next four years he was at the centre of the many radical and union initiatives that were such a notable feature of the period. He was especially important in the Society for National Regeneration, and he was a major influence in the coming together of Owenism and trade unionism which culminated in the Grand National Consolidated Trades Union of February 1834.

Throughout his radical and union career Doherty produced a considerable number of journals and periodicals. They included *The Conciliator*, the *Voice of the People*, the *United Trades' Cooperative Journal*, the *Poor Man's Advocate*, and the *Herald of the Rights of Industry*. This last, which was published weekly from early February 1834 until the end of May, has become the best-known of Doherty's publications and is the least personal of all of them. Much of the *Herald* was a sustained defence of the campaign for factory reform led by John Fielden, as well as of Fielden's general ideas. None of Doherty's publications lasted very long, but they were an important part of the general ferment of radical ideas in the years leading up to the Chartist movement.

Doherty married an English girl, Laura, a milliner, in 1821, and according to the 1841 census there were four children of the marriage, two sons and two daughters. Doherty had a quick temper, and in 1835 was involved in an incident that became quite well known and was used against him. On the night of 8 July he returned home just before midnight to find that his wife had locked him out. There was a physical confrontation and Doherty was charged at the New Bailey with assault. His wife was induced not to give evidence (she too had been guilty of assault) and Doherty was discharged. The incident continued to surface, much exaggerated, during the next few years.

As a means of livelihood compatible with his politics, Doherty set up as a publisher, bookseller, and printer in

Manchester from 1832, and he seems to have remained in this business until his death. His great days were over by the middle of the 1830s, although he was still active, on a much reduced scale, until at least the middle of the next decade. In 1838 he made an important statement of evidence before the select committee on workmen's combinations. He died aged fifty-six, almost forgotten, in New Bridge Street, Cheetham, Manchester, on 15 April 1854.

JOHN SAVILLE, *rev.*

Sources E. P. Thompson, *The making of the English working class* (1963) · R. G. Kirby and A. E. Musson, *The voice of the people: John Doherty, 1798–1854, trade unionist, radical and factory reformer* (1975) · S. A. Weaver, *John Fielden and the politics of popular radicalism, 1832–1847* (1987) · d. cert.

Doherty, (Hugh) Lawrence [Laurie] (1875–1919), tennis player, was born on 8 October 1875 at Beulah Villa, Hartfield Road, Wimbledon, Surrey, the son of William Doherty, a printer, later of Clapham Park, London, and his wife, Catherine Ann Davis. His elder brother **Reginald Frank** [Reggie] **Doherty** (1872–1910), also a tennis player, was born at the same address on 14 October 1872. Both brothers were educated at Westminster School (Reggie 1883–90; Laurie 1890–94) and then at Trinity Hall, Cambridge (Reggie 1894–6; Laurie 1896–8). There they made their names as tennis players, following the example of their eldest brother William Vernon Doherty (1871–1936) of Westminster and Christ Church, Oxford, who represented Oxford University at lawn tennis in 1892 and 1893. Reggie gained lawn tennis blues for Cambridge University in 1895 and 1896, and Laurie, who at the age of fifteen won the most important junior tennis event of that time, the Renshaw cup at Scarborough, gained blues in 1896, 1897, and 1898.

Reggie Doherty won four consecutive All England singles championships at Wimbledon, his 'local' club, in 1897–1900, and with Charlotte Cooper he won the gold medal for mixed doubles at the Paris Olympics of 1900. With a perfect smash and volley game, Laurie Doherty won the Olympic men's singles in 1900. He was All England singles champion from 1902 to 1906, during which years he never lost a match in the Davis cup, despite meeting the best American players; indeed in 1903 he actually won the American championship, the only overseas player to do so between 1881 and 1925.

The Doherty brothers became a formidable doubles partnership, with Reggie's polished groundstrokes, particularly the backhand, complementing Laurie's more aggressive style. Nicknamed Big Do and Little Do, they were also a contrast in size, Reggie tall and very thin and Laurie not even medium height. Reggie relied much on anticipation, covering the court with apparent ease, whereas Laurie thought out the game more thoroughly. They were as expert on covered courts—as at Queen's Club, Kensington, where some of their best games were played—as on grass. Their doubles record was impressive: they were All England champions eight times between 1897 and 1905; Olympic gold-medal winners in 1900; American title holders twice, in 1902 and 1903; and

unbeaten in the five Davis cup matches in which they played together.

After an arduous losing doubles final in 1906 neither brother played again at Wimbledon, reputedly as a promise to their mother, who feared for their health if they again overtaxed their strength. Reggie continued to play tennis, but only in selected major events, including the 1908 London Olympic games, where he again won the men's doubles, this time with George Hillyard. In 1909 he won two titles in South Africa but his health was failing. A few hours after returning from a Swiss nursing home, he died on 29 December 1910 of heart failure and neurasthenia at his home in the Albert Hall Mansions, Knightsbridge, which he shared with his brother.

Laurie Doherty abandoned competitive tennis and took up golf, where he achieved a handicap of plus two and in 1908 reached the last sixteen of the British amateur championship at his home course of Royal St George's. In 1914 he joined the Royal Naval Volunteer Reserve but the rigours of wartime service in an anti-aircraft unit took its toll on his frail constitution. After two years suffering from tubercular nephritis and cystitis he died on 21 August 1919 of toxaemia at Leon Cottage, North Foreland, Kent. His father, with whom he lived at the Albert Hall Mansions, was with him when he died; neither of the brothers was married. The tennis feats of the brothers are commemorated by the Doherty gates at the south-western entrance to the All England club, Wimbledon.

WRAY VAMPLEW

Sources I. Buchanan, *British Olympians: a hundred years of gold medallists* (1991) · N. G. Cleather, *The Wimbledon story* (1947) · J. Arlott, ed., *The Oxford companion to sports and games* (1975) · E. Potter, *Kings of the court* (1963) · b. cert. · d. cert. · b. cert. [R. F. Doherty] · d. cert. [R. F. Doherty] · Venn, *Alum. Cant.* · *Old Westminsters*, vol. 3

Likenesses Elliott & Fry, photogravure (Reginald Frank Doherty), NPG · Spy [L. Ward], caricature, lithograph, NPG; repro. in *VF* (1 Sept 1904) · photograph (Laurence Doherty and Reginald Frank Doherty), repro. in Buchanan, *British Olympians*, p. 47

Wealth at death £950 19s. 11d.: administration, 11 June 1920, *CGPLA Eng. & Wales* · £605 18s. 6d.—Reginald Frank Doherty: administration, 10 Feb 1911, *CGPLA Eng. & Wales*

Doherty, Reginald Frank (1872–1910). *See under* Doherty, (Hugh) Lawrence (1875–1919).

Doig, David (1718/19–1800), writer on history and philosophy, was born at Monifieth, Forfarshire, where he was baptized on 17 February 1719. His father, also David Doig, who was a small farmer, died while his son was an infant, and his mother remarried. Because of poor eyesight Doig did not learn to read until he was twelve; but after only three years at the parochial school he was successful in a Latin competition for a bursary at the University of St Andrews. Having completed the classical and philosophical course with distinction, Doig graduated BA. He began the study of divinity, but scruples regarding the Westminster confession of faith prevented him from entering the ministry. From 1749 he taught in the parochial schools of Monifieth and of Kennoway and Falkland in Fife. A few years later his growing reputation gained him the rectorship of the grammar school of Stirling, an office which he held for more than forty years. In addition to Greek and

Latin, Doig mastered Hebrew and Arabic, and was generally well read in the history and literature of the Middle East and India. The University of Glasgow conferred on him the honorary degree of LLD, and on the same day he received from St Andrews his MA. He was elected a fellow of the Royal Society of Edinburgh and of the Society of Antiquaries of Scotland.

Doig published three separate works. The first was some twenty pages of annotation on the *Gaberlunzie-Man* included in *Two Ancient Scottish Poems* (1782), edited by his friend and neighbour John Callander of Craigforth. The purpose of the annotations was to illustrate etymological principles set out in Callander's preface by tracing European languages to Asian roots. In 1792 he published his most significant work, *Two Letters on the Savage State, Addressed to the Late Lord Kaims*. Dated 1774–6 and written in immediate response to Kames's *Sketches of the History of Man* (1774), the letters attack the view, prominent among the moderate literati and their friends, that human nature is perfectible and that history is progressive. Doig, whose thought was shaped by the Episcopalian traditions of St Andrews as well as by his close friendship with the Episcopal clergyman George Gleig, argued that human nature is corrupt and that history demonstrates degeneration rather than progress. Whenever progress does occur, it is the result of the direct interposition of Providence. Doig's eventual decision to publish the letters in the midst of the French Revolution, with a dedication to George Horne, bishop of Norwich and outspoken critic of David Hume and Adam Smith, suggests that he had come to see himself as part of a Scottish reaction against perfectibility, infidelity, and revolution. His third publication was a topographical poem reflecting his historical and antiquarian interests. Entitled *Extracts from a Poem on the Prospect from Stirling Castle* (1796), the poem consists of five distinct parts.

Besides his separate works, Doig contributed a dissertation, 'On the ancient Hellenes', to the Royal Society of Edinburgh's *Transactions* (1794). A continuation which he forwarded to the society was lost and never appeared. He also wrote for the third edition of the *Encyclopaedia Britannica*, edited by George Gleig, the articles 'Mythology', 'Mysteries', and 'Philology'. They attracted great attention and brought Doig into contact with such eminent scholars as William Vincent, dean of Westminster, and Jacob Bryant. In addition to Latin and English poems, he left many treatises in manuscript on a wide range of philological, religious, and historical subjects.

Doig, who married and had children, died at Stirling on 16 March 1800, aged eighty-one. A mural tablet, with an inscription in commemoration of his virtues and learning, was raised by his friend John Ramsay of Ochtertyre. The town of Stirling also erected a marble monument to his memory, which contains his own Latin epitaph.

GORDON GOODWIN, *rev.* JEFFREY R. SMITTEN

Sources D. Doig, *Two letters on the savage state* (1792); repr. with introduction by P. B. Wood (1995) · A. F. Tytler, *Memoirs of the life and writings of the Honourable Henry Home of Kames*, 2 vols. (1807) · D. Irving, 'David Doig', *Encyclopaedia Britannica*, 8th edn, 8 (1855), 90–92 · Chambers, *Scots.* (1870), 1.449–50 · D. Doig, letter to earl of Buchan, 30 June 1781, U. Edin. L., MS La. II. 588 · N. Aston, 'Horne and heterodoxy: the defence of Anglican beliefs in the late Enlightenment', *EngHR*, 108 (1993), 895–919 · H. Home, Lord Kames, *Sketches of the history of man*, new edn, 3 vols. (1813) · *GM*, 1st ser., 70 (1800), 391 · *IGI*

Archives U. Edin., letter to earl of Buchan, La. II. 588

D'Oilly, Robert (*d. c.*1092), landowner and administrator, took his name from Ouilly-le-Vicomte near Lisieux in Normandy. With his brothers Nigel and Gilbert he came to England at the conquest. He first occurs (as *minister*) in a royal writ of 1067, and his role as royal constable, which was to become hereditary in his family, suggests that he had risen in the immediate entourage of William I when he was duke of Normandy. In 1071 D'Oilly built a large castle for the king in the west suburb of Oxford, where he remained castellan for the rest of his life. He was probably sheriff of Warwickshire and possibly of Oxfordshire and Berkshire; he is addressed in three extant royal writs, appears twice in Domesday Book determining land-pleas, and evidently had custody of some of the lands of the disgraced Odo of Bayeux. He often witnesses William's *acta*, and was with him in Normandy in 1084 at the siege of Ste Suzanne.

None the less, Robert D'Oilly quickly set down roots in England. Within a year or two of the conquest he had married Ealdgyth, daughter of the wealthy collaborator Wigot of Wallingford. He inherited many manors from Wigot, whom Domesday Book calls his *antecessor* in Hertfordshire, and his Warwickshire property was mostly held from Thorkill of Warwick, another major English survivor. Robert and his Norman contemporary Roger d'Ivry were said to be 'sworn brothers allied by faith and oath' (Salter, 4.1); their estates were closely linked, and in 1074 Robert and Roger jointly founded the collegiate church of St George in Oxford Castle. Domesday Book lists Robert's landholdings in eleven counties, four-fifths of his revenues coming from Oxfordshire, Berkshire, and Buckinghamshire; his demesnes yielded some £260 yearly, manors worth a further £160 being enfeoffed to tenants.

In 1084 the future Henry I, Bishop Osmund of Salisbury, and Miles Crispin were entertained at Abingdon Abbey by Robert D'Oilly, who bestowed there 'an abundance not only of royal goods but also those of the monastery' (Hudson, 18–19). The monks remembered him as rich and rapacious, 'a plunderer of churches and the poor' who used his official status to despoil Abingdon of its lands. A nightmare in which he was condemned by the Virgin Mary, taken to one of the stolen properties and tortured by 'filthy youths' caused a change of heart, making him 'a repairer of churches and a restorer of the poor and an accomplisher of many good works', and earning him a benefactor's honourable tomb in the abbey chapter house (ibid., 326–31). Robert died in September, *c.*1092, probably at Oxford; his brother Nigel succeeded to his lands and official functions in the early 1090s, though Miles Crispin, who married Robert's daughter Maud, inherited some of Wigot's former manors and reunited them with the honour of Wallingford.

Robert D'Oilly's career was made in the service of the Conqueror, who clearly trusted him, yet it illustrates the continuities of the time as much as the changes. A Norman of relatively modest background, he allied himself with English gentry families while William was still trying to rule as an English king, and before traumatic tenurial change had become inevitable. These links would have formed attitudes capable of lasting into the different world of the 1070s and 1080s, and his interests and investments remained firmly on the English side of the channel. It is significant that he was a notable builder. His motte and massive stone keep (the west tower of St George's collegiate church, where his crypt also survives) remain among Oxford's principal landmarks, and in the 1080s he gave the princely sum of £100 towards the new monastic buildings at Abingdon (Hudson, 32–3). Most remarkable is his stupendous causeway across the Thames, which is still the southern approach to Oxford: the causeway, 700 metres long, with seventeen flood-arches, was probably the first major post-Roman stone bridge in western Europe. If Robert's castle caused short-term urban dereliction, his bridge over the ancient 'oxen-ford' helped to make Oxford one of the great towns of twelfth- and thirteenth-century England.   JOHN BLAIR

Sources J. Hudson, ed. and trans., *Historia ecclesiae Abbendonensis / The history of the church of Abingdon*, OMT, 2 (2002) · J. Morris, ed., *Domesday Book: a survey of the counties of England*, 38 vols. (1983–92) [extensive evidence for Robert's lands in Bedfordshire, Berkshire, Buckinghamshire, Gloucestershire, Hertfordshire, Northamptonshire, Nottinghamshire, Oxfordshire, Staffordshire, Warwickshire, and Worcestershire; references to his official and judicial functions in Bedfordshire (fol. 212), Berkshire (fol. 62), Essex (Little DB, fol. 61), Oxfordshire (fols. 154v, 156v, 158v), and Surrey (fol. 35)] · D. Bates, ed., *Regesta regum Anglo-Normannorum: the Acta of William I, 1066–1087* (1998) · *Ann. mon.*, 4.9–10 · H. E. Salter, ed., *Cartulary of Oseney Abbey*, 4, OHS, 97 (1934), 1 · H. C. M. Lyte and others, eds., *Liber feodorum: the book of fees*, 3 vols. (1920–31), 1.116 · K. S. B. Keats-Rohan, 'The devolution of the honour of Wallingford, 1066–1148', *Oxoniensia*, 54 (1989), 311–18 · J. Blair, *Anglo-Saxon Oxfordshire* (1994), 173–7 · A. Williams, *The English and the Norman conquest* (1995), 101–4, 200
Wealth at death demesne manors produced a yearly income of about £260; manors worth a further £160 p.a. were subinfeudated: Domesday Book (1086)

Dokett [Doket], **Andrew** (*c.*1410–1484), college head, was of uncertain origins, but there are indications from a pedigree of 1595, said in 1869 to be in the College of Arms, London, that he came of the Dukets of Grayrigg Hall, near Kendal, Westmorland, and was the second son of Sir Richard Duket of Grayrigg and Mabel Bellingham. Two of the quarterings of the Dokett arms in a late sixteenth- or early seventeenth-century light in the north-west window of the hall at Queens' College, Cambridge are arms of Bellingham and Burnishead, families in the same area. No academic record survives for Dokett, beyond the fact that in documents from at least 1439 onwards he is referred to as 'master'. There is no evidence for Fuller's assertion that he was a Franciscan, the only basis for this being that he

was admitted into confraternity with the Franciscan order in 1479.

Dokett's first recorded preferment was as vicar of St Botolph's Church, Cambridge, to which he was presented by Corpus Christi College in 1435 or 1436. In 1439 Dokett began a judicial process by which Barnwell Priory, the rector of St Botolph's by appropriation, was summoned by the bishop of Ely for neglect in maintaining the church, and subsequently renounced its rights as rector. Dokett was officially confirmed in that title on 21 October 1444, subject to the right of presentation remaining with Corpus Christi. He held the prebend of Ryton in Lichfield Cathedral from 1467 to 1470, when he exchanged it for the chancellorship of Lichfield, which he held until 1476. On 2 July 1470 he had resigned the rectory of St Botolph's.

While he was rector Dokett made those improvements to the church neglected by Barnwell, and used his wealth for the benefit of other local causes. He gave to the king a house in Milne Street (the present Queens' Lane), which was among property granted to Henry VI's new King's College in 1449; but his own great achievement in Cambridge was the establishment of Queens' College, which began its existence as the College of St Bernard in 1446. Property for its site was acquired partly through the benefactions of wealthy parishioners of St Botolph's. In August, September, and October 1446 one of these, Richard Andrew, conveyed two properties on the first site of the new college, between Milne Street and the present Trumpington Street (then High Street), to a fellow burgess, and to two clerks who were among the first four fellows of the college.

Andrew Dokett's endowment was mentioned in the first royal charter founding the college (3 December 1446), and he left it further benefactions of money and property in his will in 1461. In 1447 the original site was replaced by the present one, on the west side of Queens' Lane. Another burgess and parishioner, John Morris, donated his large messuage and garden to form the core of the new site, and another royal charter was issued on 21 August 1447. A third important parishioner was Reginald Ely, for whose soul Dokett left property by his will to establish a chantry in Queens' College. Ely was a master mason who was employed on the building of King's College, and was very likely responsible for the design of the Old Court at Queens'. After the granting of the charter Queen Margaret petitioned her husband that she might be founder of the new college, and letters patent refounding it in honour of St Margaret and St Bernard were granted on 30 March 1448. These named Andrew Dokett as president and the same four fellows mentioned in the first charter of December 1446. The queen granted her own charter of foundation, adding a dedication to the Trinity and the Virgin Mary, on 15 April.

The dedication of the college to St Bernard in all three foundations pointed clearly to the personal importance of Dokett, who besides being rector of St Botolph's governed St Bernard's Hostel, which occupied the site of the present New Court of Corpus Christi College. In 1458 a benefactor to Queens', Richard Withemarsh, received a life pension from the hostel in consideration of his donation; the upkeep of a lamp in Queens' College chapel given by another benefactor, Thomas Duffield, was to be met from the hostel rents. By Dokett's will 40s. annually from 'my hostel [hospicium] of St Bernard' was allocated for bread, wine, wax, and lamp oil to use in Queens' College chapel. He also specified that, should a benefaction of rents made to Queens' by William Lasshby not fully materialize, any shortfall was to be made good from the hostel. Finally, after his death and that of his executors, the hostel and its rents were to pass to the college, and Queens' was duly to commemorate Dokett and other benefactors.

If Dokett's local interests were vital to the foundation of Queens', his court and other connections ensured its steady growth. Both Edward IV's queen, Elizabeth Woodville, its second royal founder, and Lady Margery Roos, a benefactor of the college, had been ladies of the bedchamber to Margaret, the first royal founder. Margery granted lands and manors in Essex, Cambridgeshire, and Huntingdonshire to the college in and after 1469, and by her will in 1477 left plate to it. She also left £10 and a covered vessel engraved with her husband's arms as a personal legacy to Dokett. When Queen Elizabeth officially assumed the title of founder of Queens' in 1475, Dokett was mentioned by name in the preface to the code of statutes then issued. It was stated to be at his request that Elizabeth, as 'true foundress', had drawn up statutes and ordinances for the foundation and establishment of the college.

Dokett's activity can be seen at a humbler level in negotiations for benefactions from citizens of London. Typically, as in the case of the chantry established in 1474 for Edmund Carvell, grocer, a sum of money would be handed to the college, in return for the commemoration of the benefactor at masses and prayers said by its priestfellows. In the same year Dokett himself received at London the last instalment of a payment of £320 given by Dame Alice Wyche, widow successively of an alderman and a mercer of London, to buy lands in Lincolnshire. On 13 February 1478 a document was made at Westminster, witnessing that Dokett had received from Dame Elizabeth Yorke, widow of William Yorke of London, £40 to endow masses for the souls of the Yorkes, their children, and friends.

Dokett left another memorial of his local wealth and his efforts on behalf of charity in Cambridge. He owned a house which backed onto the first site of Queens', and he converted this to provide almshouses for three poor women, who by his will were to pray for his soul and those of the benefactors of the college; like St Bernard's Hostel, the almshouses were to be managed after his death by his executors and after their deaths by Queens'. Dokett made his will on 2 November 1484 and died on 4 November; he was buried in Queens' College chapel. In his will Dokett instructed the fellows—in so far as he was able—to elect Thomas Wilkinson as his successor as president, another sign of his proprietorial interest. Jesus College, Cambridge, has a twelfth-century manuscript, including sermons of St Ambrose, owned by Dokett while he was rector of St Botolph's. He is also commemorated by his catalogue of the books in Queens' College Library, and by a half-length representation carved on a boss over the gateway into his college's Old Court.

Malcolm G. Underwood

Sources W. G. Searle, *The history of the Queens' College of St Margaret and St Bernard in the University of Cambridge*, 2 vols., Cambridge Antiquarian RS, 9, 13 (1867–71) · J. Twigg, *A history of Queens' College, Cambridge, 1448–1986* (1987) · Emden, *Cam.* · 'Magnum journale', 1484–1518, CUL, Queens' College archives, MS BK 1 · Queens' College, Cambridge, MS BK 79 · Miscellany 'A', Queens' College, Cambridge, MS BK 77 · Miscellany 'B', Queens' College, Cambridge, MS BK 77 · Queens' College, Cambridge, boxes 29–30 · Queens' College, Cambridge, box 34 · F. R. G. [F. R. Goodman] and A. W. G. [A. W. Goodman], *St Botolph, Cambridge: guide to the church, historical notes, the patron saint* (1937) · *Register of William Gray* (1905–6) [Ely Diocesan Remembrancer] · A. Oswald, 'Andrew Dokett and his architect', *Proceedings of the Cambridge Antiquarian Society*, 42 (1949), 8–26 · M. R. James, *A descriptive catalogue of the manuscripts in the library of Jesus College, Cambridge* (1895) · G. F. Duckett, *Duchetiana, or, Historical and genealogical memoirs of the family of Duket* (1869)

Archives Queens' College, Cambridge, MS BK 79 · Queens' College, Cambridge, Miscellany 'A', MS BK 77; Miscellany 'B', MS BK 77; boxes 29–30, 34

Likenesses attrib. R. Ely, carving, Queens' College, Cambridge

Dolben, David (1581–1633), bishop of Bangor, was born at Segrwyd, Llanrhaeadr-yng-Nghinmeirch, Denbighshire, a younger son of Robert Wyn Dolben of Segrwyd, and his wife, Jane, daughter of Owen ap Reinallt of Glyn Llugwy, in Llanrwst. His family, settled at Segrwyd since 1497, when it had been given to his great-great-grandfather Robert Dolben for his support for Henry VII against the Cornish rebels at Blackheath, had supplied a recorder and several common councillors to the nearby town of Denbigh during the sixteenth century. Dolben was admitted to St John's College, Cambridge, in 1602, and proceeded MA in 1609. He was ordained in 1607 and appointed vicar of Hackney in Middlesex in January 1619. He held the living of Hackney until May 1633, but in 1621 acquired in addition the living of Llangernyw, Denbighshire, in the gift of the bishop of St Asaph. In 1626 he was promoted to the prebendary of St Asaph. This in turn led to recognition in the town of Denbigh, which made him capital burgess in 1627, in which year he was also made doctor of divinity. However, other than some undergraduate verses, Dolben published nothing, and played no significant part in the controversies in church affairs which marked the 1620s and 1630s.

The death of Lewis Bayly in 1631 provided Dolben, as a leading north Wales cleric, with an opening, and he succeeded Bayly as bishop of Bangor. He was elected on 18 November 1631, and was consecrated at Lambeth by Archbishop George Abbot on 4 March 1632. He may have owed some of his preferment to Sir Julius Caesar, master of the rolls, whose family held property in Hackney and in Beaumaris, and to whom Dolben acknowledged his gratitude for past favours. By June 1632 Dolben declared himself to be ill and a year later he was noted as 'crazy and very sickly' (*CSP dom.*, 1633–4, 110), the object of manoeuvrings for his bishopric.

Dolben died, unmarried, on 27 November 1633 at

Bangor House, Shoe Lane, in the parish of St Andrew, Holborn. Despite a wish expressed in his will to be buried in Bangor, he was buried in Hackney parish church, where he had been vicar for fourteen years. A half-length effigy of him, in ruff and lawn sleeves, complemented by an inscription and commendatory verses, was erected, and re-erected when the church was rebuilt. In his will he left £30 for lands to be bought to relieve poor families in Hackney, and for improvements to the local roads. He bestowed money also on the poor of Bangor, Llanrhaeadryng-Nghinmeirch, and Denbigh. St John's College, Cambridge, was left £20 for its library, and Jesus College, Oxford, received 20 marks for the same purpose. As he wished, his successor as bishop of Bangor was Edward Griffith, the dean.   STEPHEN K. ROBERTS

Sources T. Baker, *History of the college of St John the Evangelist, Cambridge*, ed. J. E. B. Mayor, 2 vols. (1869), 264, 339, 677 · BL, Lansdowne MSS, Bishop Kennett's collections, MS 984, fol. 132 · letter, Dolben to Sir Julius Caesar, BL, Add. MS 34324, fol. 304 · *VCH Middlesex*, 10.117, 121, 169 · *DWB* · *Fasti Angl., 1541–1857*, [St Paul's, London], 106 · will, PRO, PROB 11/165, fols. 204–5 · J. Williams, *The medieval history of Denbighshire*, 1: *The records of Denbigh and its lordship* (1860), 130 · B. Willis, *A survey of the cathedral church of Bangor* (1721), 113 · D. R. Thomas, *Esgobaeth Llanelwy: the history of the diocese of St Asaph* (1870), 246, 390 · W. Robinson, *The history and antiquities of the parish of Hackney, in the county of Middlesex*, 2 (1843), 22
Archives BL, (1 letter, holograph), Add. MS 34324, fol. 304
Likenesses effigy on wall monument, Hackney parish church, London
Wealth at death up to £100 in bequests: will, PRO, PROB 11/165, fols. 204–5

Dolben, Digby Augustus Stewart Mackworth (1848–1867), poet, was born on 8 February 1848 in Guernsey, the youngest in the family of one daughter and three sons of William Harcourt Isham Mackworth Dolben and his wife, Frances Dolben. Born William Mackworth, his father added his wife's surname to his own: they were distant cousins and she was joint heir of the manor of Finedon, Northamptonshire. Together they assumed their place in the foothills of county aristocracy. The literary interest of the family is indicated by their relationship to the poets Robert Bridges, Arthur Hugh Clough, and Winthrop Mackworth Praed.

Both of Digby Dolben's parents were deeply religious and almost violently anti-Catholic. He was first sent to a strictly protestant preparatory school in Cheam, then entered Eton College in January 1862, where his house was chosen for the 'staunch Protestant bias' of the cleric in charge. He became fag to his cousin Robert Bridges, whom he had not previously met. Dolben early developed his twin interests in extreme high-church religion and poetry, both of which were marked with strong eroticism. He was sent down from Eton in 1863 for a few months for having made a forbidden visit to a Jesuit house. Early in 1864, before he was sixteen, he became a lay member of an irregular order of English Benedictines under the leadership of 'Father Ignatius' (Joseph Leycester Lyne), and loved to wear a monk's habit and cowl with bare feet. At the end of that year he left Eton finally, to study with private tutors before taking entrance examinations for Balliol College, Oxford.

In February 1865 Dolben made a brief visit to Oxford, where he was introduced to Gerard Manley Hopkins, their only meeting in person. Hopkins was completely taken with Dolben, who was nearly four years his junior, and his private journal for confession the following year proves how absorbed he was in imperfectly suppressed erotic thoughts of him. Although Dolben was probably not emotionally interested in Hopkins, he admired him and his poetry, and the two young men deeply influenced each other in both their verse and their intentions of becoming Roman Catholic converts, an ambition Dolben had not fulfilled at his death.

Dolben was an unusually charming and humorous young man, who loved to shock both contemporaries and elders by emotional and religious excess; his poetry reflects his flamboyant interests. He demonstrated enormous fluency and ease, often in high-church devotional poems in which the physical urgency of a boy in his teens spills over into sexual imagery in describing his love of Christ. Bridges, who edited his poetry in 1911, said drily that reading it 'makes one see why schoolmasters wish their boys to play games'. Bridges regarded his work as equal to 'anything that was ever written by any English poet at his age', and it was much admired by Henry James. As it stands, it is among the best of the poetry of the Oxford Movement, and probably a longer life would have produced the mastery foreseen by Bridges and James.

After two years of preparing with tutors, Dolben fainted during his matriculation examinations for entrance into Balliol College on 2 May 1867, and failed. On 28 June 1867 he was drowned in the River Welland near Luffenham, probably having suffered a stroke, trying to save the life of his tutor's young son. He was nineteen years old, and it was the end of a life of exceptional poetic promise.

ROBERT BERNARD MARTIN, *rev.*

Sources R. Bridges, 'Memoir', *The poems of Digby Mackworth Dolben* (1911) · *The poems and letters of Digby Mackworth Dolben, 1848–1867*, ed. M. Cohen (1981) · Northants. RO, Dolben (Finedon) collection · S. J. Kunitz and H. Haycraft, eds., *British authors of the nineteenth century* (1936)
Archives Northants. RO, notebook and poems

Dolben, Sir Gilbert, first baronet (1658/9–1722), politician and judge, was the eldest son of John *Dolben (1625–1686), Church of England clergyman (and later archbishop of York), and his wife, Catherine (1626–1706), daughter of Ralph Sheldon of Stanton in Derbyshire; Gilbert Sheldon, future archbishop of Canterbury, was his great-uncle. He was educated first at Westminster School (1671–4) and then at Christ Church, Oxford, from where he matriculated aged fifteen on 18 July 1674. In the same year he was admitted to the Inner Temple, and seven years later was called to the bar.

In 1676 Dolben attended the treaty negotiations at Nijmegen, but soon abandoned diplomacy to follow his uncle Sir William Dolben into the law, at first not very successfully. By 1683 he had married well, however. His wife, Anne (d. 1744), was coheir to her father, Tanfield Mulso, of Finedon in Northamptonshire. Dolben's brother John *Dolben (*bap.* 1662, *d.* 1710) married Anne's sister, but gambled away her fortune, and eventually Gilbert was able to acquire both shares in the Finedon estate.

Dolben was returned to parliament in 1685 for the borough of Ripon, on the archiepiscopal interest. Unlike his brother John, who became a whig, Gilbert was a high-churchman of a priggishly conservative cast of mind, described even at the age of twenty-seven as 'the fustiest old gentleman you ever saw' (*Downshire MSS*, 1.389). He was also a man of scholarly interests, and is said to have assisted Dryden to publish his translation of Virgil. The fact that loyalty to the church was paramount for him was evident when he was removed from the commission of the peace in 1688 for refusing to countenance repeal of the Test Act. In the Convention, in which he represented Peterborough, probably on the cathedral interest, he was the first to give an opinion that the throne was vacant. He also declared that to have a Catholic king was 'inconsistent with the law of England' (Grey, *Debates*, 9.28). He sat in parliament almost continuously for the next two reigns, retaining his seat for Peterborough until 1698, recovering it in 1701, and transferring in 1710 to the pocket borough of Yarmouth, Isle of Wight. He was always a tory, but, as a protégé of the politically pliable secretary of state Sir William Trumbull, he supported the administration throughout the 1690 parliament, even after the king had shifted towards the whigs, and in 1693 was spoken of for the solicitor-generalship. Eventually, however, he followed his party into opposition.

Reward came in May 1701, when under the predominantly tory administration Dolben was named a justice of common pleas in Ireland. While not a permanent absentee, he refused to let judicial duties interfere with parliamentary business, and during sessions was excused attendance on circuit. For a time he was associated with Lord Nottingham, in campaigns against occasional conformity in England, and in imposing the sacramental test in Ireland in 1704, by means of a clause added by the English privy council to an Irish popery bill. In April 1704 he was created a baronet. After Nottingham left office Dolben developed a reputation as a moderate, and kept his place on the bench under the whig ministry of 1705–10. It was only on questions of religion that his prejudices were visible: resisting repeal of the Irish test, for example, or in the debates on the Anglo-Scottish union, in which he not only denounced Scottish Presbyterianism but also pressed for some mention in the union treaty of the English Test Act, recalling how, 'when the church was attacked by a papist that sat on the throne, his first and great endeavour was to get that act repealed' (Bodl. Oxf., MS Eng. lett. e. 6, fols. 9–11). He found the junto Lord Wharton hard to stomach as lord lieutenant of Ireland, but managed to avoid open insubordination.

Ultimately Dolben's success as a political survivor counted against him, when the tories returned to power in 1710: though in no danger of removal, he found promotion blocked by the 'resentments' of Lord Chancellor Harcourt. In a final political accommodation he withstood the purge of tories from office after the Hanoverian succession. A particular interest of his later years was the charity

school movement, of which he was an active supporter both in Ireland and at home, setting up a school on his own estate. He was finally obliged to retire through ill health in 1720, and died at Finedon on 22 October 1722. His will included a bequest of £500 to the Corporation of the Sons of the Clergy. His only son, Sir John *Dolben, took holy orders, and succeeded to the title.

J. M. RIGG, *rev.* D. W. HAYTON

Sources J. P. Ferris, 'Dolben, Gilbert', HoP, *Commons, 1660–90* · 'Dolben, Sir Gilbert', HoP, *Commons, 1690–1715* [draft] · 'Dolben, John', HoP, *Commons, 1690–1715* [draft] · F. E. Ball, *The judges in Ireland, 1221–1921*, 2 (New York, 1927), 27, 65–6 · Bodl. Oxf., MS Eng. lett. e. 6 · A. Grey, ed., *Debates of the House of Commons, from the year 1667 to the year 1694*, new edn, 9 (1769), 7, 28, 40, 48, 385, 529; 10 (1769), 59, 220, 305 · *Report on the manuscripts of the marquis of Downshire*, 6 vols. in 7, HMC, 75 (1924–95), vol. 1 · Gilbert Dolben to Sir William Trumbull, 31 March 1698, BL, Trumbull misc. MSS 57 · F. A. Inderwick and R. A. Roberts, eds., *A calendar of the Inner Temple records*, 3 (1901), 158, 408, 444; 4 (1933), 71 · *The manuscripts of his grace the duke of Portland*, 10 vols., HMC, 29 (1891–1931), vols. 2, 5 · *CSP dom., 1689–1704* · J. G. Simms, 'The making of a penal law (2 Anne, c. 6), 1703–4', *Irish Historical Studies*, 12 (1960–61), 105–18 · J. Simon, 'Charity schools in Northamptonshire and the S.P.C.K.', *Northamptonshire Past and Present*, 7 (1983–8), 327–38

Archives Bodl. Oxf., letter-book, MS Eng. lett. e. 6 | BL, Trumbull MSS

Likenesses G. Kneller, oils, Christ Church Oxf. · oils, Bodl. Oxf.

Dolben, John (1625–1686), archbishop of York, was born on 20 March 1625, the eldest son of Dr William *Dolben (d. 1631), prebendary of Lincoln and rector of Stanwick, Northamptonshire, and his wife, Elizabeth, *née* Williams, who had two other surviving sons and two daughters. He was baptized on 27 March. His mother was the niece of Bishop John Williams, who nominated John to be admitted as a king's scholar at Westminster School, some twelve years later, just before Richard Busby's long and influential tenure as headmaster began. In 1640 John was elected a student of Christ Church, Oxford, and in the following year he composed some Latin verses to celebrate the return of Charles I from Scotland during the deepening political crisis. When civil war came in 1642 he was among a large group of students of Christ Church who enlisted in the king's army. He fought at the battle of Marston Moor on 2 July 1644 as an ensign and was shot in the shoulder carrying the colours. He fought on at the siege of York and was wounded again, this time more seriously in the thigh, being confined to bed for a year as a result. He was promoted to the rank of major in recognition of his courage but by the time he was up and about again the civil war was all but lost.

His war service left a lasting impression on Dolben in a number of ways. His youthful royalism had resulted in serious injury. It is possible that his wounds left a certain lameness in him, which may partly explain the corpulence in later life on which contemporaries remarked. He seems to have retained throughout his life a certain military style and bearing as well as a knowledge of and interest in military affairs as is evident from his sermons.

Oxford: interregnum and Restoration Dolben returned to Oxford after the war in the hope of continuing his studies, graduating MA on 9 December 1647, without the usual

John Dolben (1625–1686), by Richard Tompson (after Jacob Huysmans, c.1670)

preliminary of a BA degree. However, he was deprived of his studentship by the parliamentary visitors of the university in 1648. Thereafter he disappears from the record until 1656, in which year he sought out episcopal ordination (from Bishop King of Chichester), as indeed did many of the clergy who conformed during the period as well as those who, like Dolben, did not. In 1657 he married Catherine Sheldon (1626–1706), daughter of Ralph Sheldon of Stanton in Derbyshire, the niece of Gilbert *Sheldon, a connection which was to have a huge impact on his subsequent career. The couple settled down in Ralph Sheldon's house in St Aldates, Oxford.

Dolben began his ministry in the context of proscribed prayer book services, held in the house of Dr Thomas Willis opposite Merton College, in collaboration with Richard Allestree and John Fell, who was Willis's brother-in-law. These services attracted wide support from Church of England loyalists at the time. Given the partly intentional laxity of interregnum regimes about local religious practice, such activity hardly now appears as daring as it seems to have done to Dolben's nineteenth-century biographers. The latter may have been misled by Dolben's own exaggerated references to the precariousness of life in the 1650s, made in a sermon of 1666 (Dolben, *A Sermon Preached before the King Aug. 14 1666*, ix). But of course, such semi-clandestine devotion did Dolben no harm when the tables were turned and the traditional Church of England was restored after 1660. It was immortalized in the famous group portrait of Allestree, Dolben, and Fell by Sir Peter Lely, painted at the time of the Restoration and now in the possession of Christ Church. All three appear in clerical garb. Fell (on the left of the picture) seems somewhat detached, while Allestree (on the right) points very emphatically at an open copy of the Book of Common Prayer, which is one of the volumes on the table before them. Dolben (in the centre) looks straight at the viewer. In this as in other portraits, he cuts a striking figure, with a full face, fine light brown hair, and a piercing eye. Altogether it conveys the strong presence to which at least one contemporary account alludes (Beddard, 420).

Dolben, along with his co-protagonists Fell and Allestree, received prompt recognition in Restoration Oxford. Dolben and Allestree petitioned for canonries of Christ Church as early as April 1660, to which they were duly appointed in July. Fell became dean. On 3 October Dolben took his DD degree alongside the other two. The three of them joined in penning Latin verses mourning the death of the duke of Gloucester, which were published in *Epicedia academiae Oxoniensis* (1660). Dolben was further rewarded with the living of Newington-cum-Britwell, Oxfordshire, on the king's presentation.

The trio had their critics, even in Restoration Oxford. Wood mocked them for trying 'to reduce the University to that condition as it stood in Laud's time'; something quite unrealistic given the intervening years (Clark, 1.348–9), though Wood may have been prejudiced by some difficulties he had had with Dolben over access to certain ecclesiastical registers while Dolben was chapter treasurer.

Meanwhile Dolben's fame as a loyalist clergyman was spreading beyond Oxford. He wrote verses mourning the death of the princess of Orange. In October 1660 he was commissioned by the king, along with Dr Barwick, to visit the condemned regicides in an abortive attempt to solicit expressions of remorse.

Preferment and politics A series of senior ecclesiastical promotions came Dolben's way soon after 1660, largely due to the influence of his wife's uncle, Gilbert Sheldon, bishop of London and soon to be archbishop of Canterbury. On 29 April 1661 he was installed as prebendary of Caddington Major in St Paul's Cathedral and on 11 October 1662 nominated archdeacon of London; and shortly after that, vicar of St Giles Cripplegate. Finally, he was raised to the deanery of Westminster, being installed on 5 December 1662. Dolben gradually reduced the number of his appointments, starting with the parochial ones and resigning the archdeaconry in 1664, the same year he became prolocutor of the lower house of convocation, in succession to John Barwick. His star continued to rise at court, culminating in his appointment as clerk of the closet, also in 1664. Dolben rapidly acquired the reputation of being a great preacher, which would be reflected some years later in a passing reference to him in Dryden's *Absalom and Achitophel* (lines 868–9). Initially Dolben tended to read the sermons which he delivered at court until a word from Charles II encouraged him to adopt a more extempore style, in which he proved highly effective. It is hard to assess Dolben on the basis of the three published sermons that survive. They certainly possess an admirable clarity and directness along with an underlying note of passion, which could have had a powerful effect on the hearers, even at the court of Charles II. A sermon which he gave before the Commons on a fast day for the fire in October 1666 (from which sadly only brief notes survive) helped to prompt MPs to appoint a committee the next day, to consider strengthening the laws against atheism and irreligious behaviour. On one occasion in Westminster Abbey, when the preacher was taken ill having only named his text and the headings of his sermon, Dolben mounted the pulpit and without any preparation 'discoursed much better on each head than the other would have don' (Beddard, 420). Even towards the end of his life, as archbishop of York, he retained a formidable reputation as a preacher. Dolben's eloquence may have contributed to his next ecclesiastical promotion, to the see of Rochester in 1666. Dolben was allowed to keep the deanery of Westminster *in commendam*, thus beginning a tradition of pluralism which would last into the early nineteenth century, on the grounds of the poverty of the see. However, he resigned as prebendary of St Paul's at this time. He was consecrated at Lambeth Palace by Sheldon on 25 November 1666, the sermon being preached by Robert South, a friend from Oxford days despite the latter's conformism under the Commonwealth.

Dolben was briefly a member of the privy council but almost immediately his standing at court began to fluctuate dramatically. After the fall of Clarendon he lost his place at court (as did Sheldon and George Morley, bishop of Winchester) and was under a cloud for several years. His well-attested contempt for flattery and his quality of plain-speaking, as Burnet noted, hardly fitted him for court life at the best of times (*Burnet's History*, 2.431). It is true that Burnet had a grudge against him for persuading Sir John Cotton to bar him from using his library while Burnet was researching his history of the Reformation, on the grounds that he was 'a great enemy of the prerogative' (ibid., 2.107). But on this, as on other aspects of Dolben's life, Burnet's judgement seems sound. Only with the rise of Danby would Dolben come fully back into favour, rising to be lord high almoner in 1675.

Just as Dolben's influence at court was waning, he was acquiring a distinctive political role elsewhere: in the Lords. He took his seat there just four days after his consecration and rapidly became a regular attender and effective operator there, with an admirable grasp of procedure. He worked closely with Sheldon and used his new found expertise to defend the church. He was linked with the parliamentary initiatives for comprehension in 1673 and 1674, though as with Morley of Winchester, this did not necessarily imply great flexibility towards dissent. When in due course under Danby defending the church became part of the court's agenda as well, it was Dolben who in 1677 introduced the far-reaching bill to safeguard the Church of England under a Roman Catholic successor.

By the late 1670s, despite Sheldon's death, Dolben was again in line for an ecclesiastical step-up. In 1678 he was offered but declined the archbishopric of Dublin, on grounds of ill health and personal inadequacy, provoking a quizzical response from Charles II (who wondered aloud if Dolben would have turned it down had he known its financial value).

Dolben was loyal to the court, but no mere 'yes-man' to any party. In parliament he supported an amendment to Danby's test bill in 1675, inspired by the country opposition, which attempted to distinguish between legal and illegal means of seeking to bring about change in the religious settlement. But in 1678 he voted against a very different test bill, apparently because of the accusation of idolatry against the Roman Catholic church which it contained. He briefly chaired the Lords committee to investigate the Popish Plot and as late as March 1679 he was said to be intimate with Sir Thomas Meres, a leading figure in the country opposition. But Meres was his half-brother and even his political stance would change over the ensuing two years. On 15 November 1680 Dolben was among the fourteen bishops in the House of Lords who helped to vote down the Exclusion Bill. Dolben's loyalty was recognized and in due course rewarded, when he was made archbishop of York in July 1683. He finally relinquished the deanery of Westminster and the almoner's place along with his southern see and moved north to the scene of his youthful military adventures.

Dolben's tenure of the see of Rochester and the deanery of Westminster had not been without its critics. Simon Patrick drew attention to the lack of progress towards weekly communion at the abbey in this period, and Burnet paid Dolben the back-handed compliment that he was later a better archbishop than he had been a bishop (*Burnet's History*, 2.431). Burnet's grudge notwithstanding, his implied criticism of the Rochester episcopate may have had some truth in it.

Dolben comes across as a vigorous dean. On the day of his installation he persuaded the chapter to enhance the financial provision for the repair and upkeep of the abbey. His commitment to its welfare and defence of its interests seem to have remained throughout his tenure. Pepys found him living 'like a great prelate' in the deanery at Westminster, 'his lodgings being very good', on 24 February 1668 (Pepys, 9.89). But it was easier to combine this with his heavy parliamentary involvement than it was to care for his diocese. He did not wholly neglect the latter though, rebuilding the episcopal residence at Bromley after civil war damage, at his own expense, and living in it, at least for a time. His securing the appointment of William Trumbull as both chancellor of the diocese and official to the archdeacon in 1671 at least prevented the clash between the two jurisdictions which occurred elsewhere in this period. The diocesan archives are too scanty to form a judgement as to how conscientiously Dolben fulfilled his episcopal duties, though Dolben Paul, one of his nineteenth-century biographers, appears to be mistaken in thinking that no episcopal register was kept between 1663 and 1683.

Archbishop of York Dolben would be active in his archdiocese for only just over two and a half years before his death but he made a vigorous start in many areas to what could have been a very significant archiepiscopate had he lived. He had Thomas Comber made precentor of York even before his own arrival there and the two would work closely together during Dolben's tenure. Dolben arrived at Bishopthorpe on 25 September 1683 amid early snow, which failed to deter a cavalcade of some five hundred local gentry and clergy from turning out to greet him. In October he initiated meetings of clergy in their own localities for mutual edification. At the same time he delicately began to explore the possibility of establishing a weekly communion in the minster, an initiative which was clearly highly controversial with the dean and chapter. This would not actually bear fruit until April 1685 but before that Dolben had managed to hold a visitation of the chapter, despite a dispute over his jurisdiction there. He also got Comber completely to reorganize the minster library and conduct a survey of the minster with a view to its repair. Dolben himself provided for a rota of vicars-choral to supervise readers and prevent thefts from the minster library. In addition, he reformed the arrangements for preaching at the minster, so that, among other things, absences were properly covered for and further sermons were provided on Wednesdays and Fridays in Lent.

Sometimes Dolben was over-ambitious in what he attempted: writing to Archbishop Sancroft on 11 August 1684, 'I know that I have undertaken too much at once to visit Chester Dioces metropolitically & mine own Dioces together'. Nottinghamshire would have to wait until the following summer (MS Tanner 32, fol. 117). But he continued to be very active in visiting the various parts of his domain and in conducting confirmations. Unfettered by rival commitments at court or (at least until 1685) in parliament, at York Dolben was able to become at once a reforming archbishop, a political broker on behalf of the government, and an invaluable interpreter of the regional political scene for Archbishop Sancroft. Dolben arrived in the north at the height of the tory reaction and this gave his role an added ideological edge. His family was caught up in the partisan divisions of the time. While he was reaching the peak of his ecclesiastical career, his brother William *Dolben suffered a reverse in his judicial one, for failing to support the *quo warranto* proceedings against London. John's elder son, Gilbert *Dolben, a lifelong tory whom his father had appointed steward of the manor of Ripon, was rapidly adopted to stand for the parliamentary seat there after the borough surrendered its charter to the archbishop personally in September 1684. His younger son, John *Dolben, would later emerge as a whig.

The archbishop's support for the regime was unflinching. Dolben featured prominently in the ceremonies to mark James II's accession in February 1685. He deliberately stayed in the north during the general election campaign which followed to support loyal candidates and was involved in promoting loyal addresses. He could be conciliatory towards those whose loyalty had been compromised but this seems to have reflected a sense of political isolation rather than any sympathy for their views. He wrote to Sancroft 'we have soe few friends that we ought to have as few enemies as we can' (MS Tanner 32, fol. 182). His conciliatoriness did not even extend to sharing a loyal address with people whose motives he suspected. Dolben backed James II's succession to the throne and put his trust in the king's assurance that the Church of England was safe in his hands. By the autumn of 1685, on his way to the second session of parliament, he was apparently beginning to have doubts, though he did not confide these to Sancroft, at least in his letters. Comber may have been wide of the mark when he wrote that Dolben's fears for the church shortened his life but there can be no doubt that by the time of his death at Bishopthorpe from smallpox on 11 April 1686 he had become a worried man. Dolben was buried on 12 April in the minster and an impressive monument was erected there in his memory. He made a number of bequests to institutions with which he had been associated, for example, leaving some 367 books to the recently reorganized minster library.

Dolben was survived by his wife for some twenty years. She was buried in due course in the church at Finedon in Northamptonshire, where Gilbert Dolben had acquired property by marriage. His other son, John, also survived him. One daughter, Catherine, had died in infancy.

From his surviving correspondence and published sermons Dolben emerges as a passionate man, sometimes hasty in his judgements of others and occasionally indiscreet but generous to those who won his favour. He was an energetic and practical-minded churchman, who really found his métier as archbishop of York towards the end of an eventful life.   ANDREW M. COLEBY

Sources Wood, *Ath. Oxon.*, new edn · *The life and times of Anthony Wood*, ed. A. Clark, 5 vols., OHS, 19, 21, 26, 30, 40 (1891–1900) · R. Beddard, 'The character of a Restoration prelate: Dr John Dolben', *N&Q*, 215 (1970), 418–20 · D. Paul, *John Dolben, dean of Westminster, bishop of Rochester and archbishop of York in the time of Charles II: his life and character* (1884) · Sancroft papers, Bodl. Oxf., MSS Tanner · *The diary of John Milward*, ed. C. Robbins (1938) · *Burnet's History of my own time*, ed. O. Airy, new edn, 2 vols. (1897–1900) · *Calendar of the manuscripts of the marquess of Ormonde*, new ser., 8 vols., HMC, 36 (1902–20), vols. 4–5 · *The autobiographies and letters of Thomas Comber, sometime precentor of York and dean of Durham*, ed. C. E. Whiting, 1, SurtS, 156 (1946) · Pepys, *Diary*, vols. 8–9 · Evelyn, *Diary*, vols. 3–4 · *Memoirs of Sir John Reresby*, ed. A. Browning, 2nd edn, ed. M. K. Geiter and W. A. Speck (1991) · J. Dolben, *A sermon preached before his majesty on Good Friday at Whitehall, March 24 1664/5* (1665) · J. Dolben, *A sermon preached before the king on Tuesday, June 20th, 1665* (1665) · J. Dolben, *A sermon preached before the king, Aug. 14, 1666* (1666) · parish records, Northants. RO, Stanwick MS 229 · DNB

Archives Northants. RO, Dolben of Finedon collection | Bodl. Oxf., corresp. with Sancroft · Northants. RO, Stanwick parish records · York Minster Library, Minster archives

Likenesses P. Lely, group portrait, oils, *c.*1660, Christ Church Oxf. · oils, before 1721, Christ Church Oxf. · oils, before 1729, Christ Church Oxf.; version, Bishopthorpe, York · attrib. J. Latham, monument, York Minster; repro. in G. E. Aylmer and R. Cant, eds., *A history of York Minster* (1977), p. 445 · R. Tompson, mezzotint (after Huyssmans, *c.*1670), BM, NPG, Westminster deanery [*see illus.*] · oils (after Lely), Westminster deanery · portrait (after Lely, *c.*1660), Christ Church Oxf.

Dolben, John (*bap.* 1662, *d.* 1710), politician, was baptized in Christ Church Cathedral, Oxford, on 1 July 1662. He was the younger son in the family of two sons and one daughter (who died in infancy) of John *Dolben (1625–1686), canon of Christ Church, Oxford, later archbishop of York, and his wife, Catherine (1626–1706), daughter of Ralph Sheldon of Stanton, Derbyshire, and niece of Gilbert Sheldon, archbishop of Canterbury from 1663 to 1677. Dolben's elder brother was Sir Gilbert Dolben, judge of the court of common pleas in Ireland. John Dolben matriculated from Christ Church, Oxford, on 23 March 1678, but his name does not appear in the printed list of graduates.

Dolben entered the Inner Temple, and was called to the bar in 1684, but having gambled away most of the money inherited from his father in 1686, he went to the West Indies, where he married Elizabeth (d. 1736), daughter of Tanfield Mulso, of Finedon, Northamptonshire. They had two sons and three daughters.

Dolben came back to England, and was returned to parliament at a by-election on 21 November 1707 as MP for the borough of Liskeard in Cornwall. In the House of Commons he worked hard as chairman of several committees until, in 1709, Godolphin put him in charge of the case against Dr Henry Sacheverell, who had preached two inflammatory sermons in Derby and in St Paul's Cathedral, directed against Godolphin and the government. On 13 December 1709 Dolben called the attention of the house to these sermons, with the result that the house decided to impeach Sacheverell in the House of Lords. The articles of impeachment against Sacheverell, drawn up by a committee of the House of Commons, were reported to the house by Dolben on 10 January 1710, and two days later he took the articles to the House of Lords. Although he was one of the managers of the impeachment, he was prevented by ill health from attending Sacheverell's trial. He died in Epsom on 29 May 1710, the day of the trial; he was buried in Finedon church.

Dolben's involvement in the case was the subject of several pamphlets, including *A Letter Written by Mr. J. Dolbin to Dr. Henry Sacheverell* (1710), composed as a letter of repentance, *An Elegy on the Lamented Death of John Dolben* (1710), and *The Life and Adventures of John Dolben* (1710). Verses were written about him, including the epitaph:

Under this marble lies the dust
Of Dolben John, the chaste and just.
Reader, read softly, I beseech ye,
For if he wakes he'll straight impeach ye.
(Wilkins, 2.84)

W. P. COURTNEY, *rev.* ANNE PIMLOTT BAKER

Sources Foster, *Alum. Oxon.* · Boase & Courtney, *Bibl. Corn.* · W. A. Speck, ed., *A critical bibliography of Dr Henry Sacheverell* (1978) · N. Luttrell, *A brief historical relation of state affairs from September 1678 to April 1714*, 6 vols. (1857) · W. W. Wilkins, ed., *Political ballads of the seventeenth and eighteenth centuries*, 2 vols. (1860) · *Remarks and collections of Thomas Hearne*, ed. C. E. Doble and others, 11 vols., OHS, 2, 7, 13, 34, 42–3, 48, 50, 65, 67, 72 (1885–1921) · J. Bridges, *The history and antiquities of Northamptonshire*, ed. P. Whalley, 2 vols. (1791)
Likenesses J. Riley, oils, 1680–89, Waddesdon Manor, Buckinghamshire

Dolben, Sir John, second baronet (1684–1756), Church of England clergyman, was born on 12 February 1684 at Bishopthorpe Palace, near York, the only son of Sir Gilbert *Dolben, first baronet (1658/9–1722), a tory MP and a judge

Sir John Dolben, second baronet (1684–1756), by John Faber junior, 1750 (after Robert Taylor)

of the common pleas in Ireland, and his wife, Anne (d. 1744), eldest daughter and coheir of Tanfield Mulso of Finedon, Northamptonshire. Dolben came from a clerical family. His great-grandfather (d. 1631) had been bishop designate of Bangor; his grandfather, John Dolben, was archbishop of York (1683–6), and his grandmother was the niece of another primate, Gilbert Sheldon of Canterbury. John Dolben was admitted on the foundation of Westminster School in 1700. He matriculated at Oxford University on 11 May 1702, having come into residence as a gentleman commoner at Christ Church on 28 April. Dolben graduated BA on 22 January 1704, proceeded MA on 8 July 1707, and accumulated the degrees in divinity on 6 July 1717.

Although Dolben entered the Inner Temple in 1707 at the request of his father (a bencher), he eventually opted for the church rather than the law, and was ordained deacon in June 1709 and priest in April 1711. He gained swift preferment, first as chaplain to Thomas Sprat, bishop of Rochester, on 11 April 1711, and then as subdean of the Chapel Royal on 20 April 1713. Although he was in charge of the thanksgiving service for the accession of George I at St Paul's Cathedral in January 1715 and was in routine control of the chapel, he was dismissed from office on 20 March 1718 together with the dean, John Robinson, bishop of London. The precise reasons for Dolben's dismissal remain obscure although, in a changed political climate, moderate tories like him were expendable.

Dolben was compensated for the loss of his Chapel Royal duties by Nathaniel, Lord Crew, bishop of Durham, who lived at Steane, near Brackley, Northamptonshire, and was thus a neighbour, as well as a tory survivor from the generation of Dolben's grandfather Tanfield Mulso. Dolben was admitted by Crewe to the sixth stall at Durham Cathedral on 2 April 1718. He exchanged it for the eleventh ('golden') stall on 17 July 1719. He kept regular residence at Durham, but lived mainly as a squire and parish clergyman at Finedon. He was presented to the vicarage of Finedon, Northamptonshire, by his father on 9 August 1714, and instituted on 30 September; he was subsequently presented to the nearby rectory of Burton Latimer on 3 February 1719, and instituted on 14 March. Dolben acted as one of the two proctors in the lower house of convocation for the clergy of the Peterborough diocese from 1714 to 1748. On 22 October 1722 he succeeded his father as second baronet. He married at Sherborne, on 28 July 1720, Elizabeth, second daughter of William Digby, fifth Baron Digby of Geashill. Lady Dolben died at Aix-en-Provence on 4 November 1730, and was buried on 12 January 1731 at Finedon. The couple had five sons and three daughters. In Aix Cathedral there is a monumental inscription to three of their sons, who, like Lady Dolben, died of smallpox. Dolben's last appointment was to the visitorship of Balliol College, Oxford, on 22 June 1728. He adjudicated in several disputes, and as the modern historian of Balliol contends, exercised his 'authority with patient and impartial wisdom' (J. Jones, Balliol College, 163). His resignation on 24 March 1755 on health grounds was widely regretted.

As the direct descendant of two primates Dolben might himself have expected a mitre, but the Hanoverian succession in 1714 dashed his hopes of crown preferment. Nevertheless, as a moderate high-churchman, Dolben did his utmost to protect the interests of the Church of England without involving himself publicly in Jacobite politics. Evidence for his direct participation in the Atterbury plot of 1720–22 is inconclusive, though in the 1740s he accepted a gift of Prince Charles Edward Stuart's portrait and was 'reckoned a staunch friend to the Pretender, or, at least, to hereditary right' (Hodgson, 200). Music was a lifelong compensation for his marginalization in the church. Dolben inherited the taste from his father, and was a minor patron in his own right. He presented Finedon church with a magnificent organ in 1717 (probably originally at Windsor) and commissioned the composer William Croft (organist of the Chapel Royal) to provide anthems for the organ's opening and music for his marriage. He was elected a member of the Academy of Vocal Music in 1726.

Dolben suffered from recurrent ill health for the last thirty years of his life; he died at Finedon on 20 November 1756, and was buried there on 11 December. He was succeeded in the baronetcy by his son William *Dolben (1727–1814). He published his sermon on brotherly love (Heb. 13: 1) preached at the sons of the clergy service at St Paul's Cathedral on 8 December 1726, and an address of 1750 welcoming the new bishop of Durham, Joseph Butler, into his see. Part of his huge theological library was placed in the monk's cell above the south porch at Finedon church as part of a 'clerical library' about 1790 by his grandson John English Dolben, later the fourth baronet.

Sir John Dolben's career symbolically linked the generation of his own grandfather (and especially Archbishop W. Sancroft and Bishop T. Sprat) to their later Georgian admirers such as George Horne, who preached his first sermon at Finedon, and William Jones (of Nayland), who was Dolben's last curate in the parish. Jones dedicated his first book to Dolben and paid tribute to 'your character and station in the Church, your firm attachment to, and experienced knowledge of the Holy Scriptures, your familiar acquaintance with Antiquities, both sacred and profane, and your unblemished life' (W. Jones, 4).

NIGEL ASTON

Sources GEC, Baronetage, 4.189–90 · J. Welch, The list of the queen's scholars of St Peter's College, Westminster, ed. [C. B. Phillimore], new edn (1852), 175, 215, 237, 238, 331 · Foster, Alum. Oxon. · F. A. Inderwick and R. A. Roberts, eds., A calendar of the Inner Temple records, 3 (1901), 400 · J. Bridges, The history and antiquities of Northamptonshire, ed. P. Whalley, 2 (1791), 224, 260 · Fasti Angl. (Hardy), 3.314, 319 · H. I. Longden, Northamptonshire and Rutland clergy from 1500, ed. P. I. King and others, 16 vols. in 6, Northamptonshire RS (1938–52), vol. 2, pp. 113–15 · J. C. Sainty and R. Bucholz, eds., Officials of the royal household, 1660–1837, 1: Department of the lord chamberlain and associated offices (1997), 56 · E. F. Rimbault, ed., The old cheque-book, or book of remembrance, of the Chapel Royal, from 1561 to 1744, CS, new ser., 3 (1872), 50 · D. Baldwin, The Chapel Royal: ancient and modern (1990) · The manuscripts of his grace the duke of Portland, 10 vols., HMC, 29 (1891–1931), vols. 5, 7 · C. E. Whiting, Nathaniel, Lord Crewe, bishop of Durham, 1674–1721, and his diocese (1940) · J. L. H. Bailey, Finedon otherwise Thingdon (1975) · J. Jones, Balliol College: a history, 1263–1939 (1988) · D. Burrows, 'Sir John Dolben, musical patron', MT, 120 (1979), 65–7 · D. Burrows, 'Sir John Dolben's music collection', MT, 120 (1979), 149–51 · D. Burrows, 'Handel and the English Chapel Royal during the reigns of Queen Anne and King George I', 2 vols., PhD diss., Open University, 1981, vol. 2, appx, section 3, 'Buildings: the Chapel Royal, St James's Palace' · H. Erskine-Hill, The social milieu of Alexander Pope: lives, example, and the poetic response (1975) · 'Diary of Thomas Gyll', ed. J. C. Hodgson, Six north country diaries, 1, SurtS, 118 (1910), 200 · J. L. M. Bolton, The vicar's gift: the organ attributed to Christopher Shrider in the parish church of St Mary the Virgin, Finedon, Northamptonshire (1986) · P. Thicknesse, Memoirs and anecdotes of Philip Thicknesse, 3 vols. (privately printed, London, 1788–91), vol. 1, pp. 13, 209–11 · W. Jones, A full answer to the 'Essay on spirit' (1753) · 'Dolben, Sir Gilbert', HoP, Commons [draft] · A. Alsop, Odarum libri duo, ed. Sir Francis Bernard (1752) · J. Jones, The portraits of Balliol College: a catalogue (1990) · will (copy), 22 May 1751, Northants. RO, Dolben (Finedon) collection, D(F) 128 · Northants. RO, Dolben (Finedon) collection, D(F) 101, 126 · parish registers, Finedon, Northants. RO · D. K. Money, The English Horace: Anthony Alsop and the tradition of British Latin verse (1998), 183–93 · [J. F. M. Carter], Undercurrents of church life in the eighteenth century, ed. T. T. Carter (1899), 193–4

Likenesses portrait, 1730; Finedon Hall, Mackworth Dolben sale, 1912 · portrait, 1756; Finedon Hall, Mackworth Dolben sale, 1912 · Claude Arnulphi?, portrait (as a young man), Balliol Oxf. · J. Faber junior, mezzotint (after R. Taylor, 1750), BM, NPG [see illus.] · attrib. R. Taylor, oils, Balliol Oxf. · attrib. R. Taylor, oils, Christ Church Oxf. · portrait (as a young man); Finedon Hall, Mackworth Dolben sale, 1912

Wealth at death Finedon estate to eldest son; proclaimed self unable to afford gifts to servants on scale he would wish: will, 22 May 1751, Northants. RO, Dolben (Finedon) collection D(F) 128

Dolben, William (1588?–1631), Church of England clergyman, was the only son of John Dolben, from Segrwyd, Denbighshire, who had become a merchant at Haverfordwest and founded the Pembrokeshire branch of the family, and Alice, daughter of Richard Myddleton of Denbigh and sister of Sir Hugh Myddleton. He was educated at Westminster School and then Christ Church, Oxford, from where he matriculated on 10 February 1604 aged sixteen, and graduated BA on 6 June 1607. He proceeded MA as from All Souls on 18 June 1610 and was incorporated in that degree at Cambridge in 1614. He was admitted BD on 13 December 1617 and was awarded his doctorate on 15 June 1619.

Dolben acquired two Pembrokeshire benefices, Stackpool Elidyr (1616) and Lawrenny (1620), and in 1623 was instituted to the rectory of Llanynys in Denbighshire. In the same year, from 11 July until November, he held the rectory of Bartholomew by the Exchange in London, but on 8 November 1623 he was instituted to the rectories of Stanwick and of Benefield, Northamptonshire. Also in 1623, he married Elizabeth Williams, daughter of Captain Hugh Williams of Cochwillan, Caernarvonshire, and Elizabeth, sister of John *Williams, bishop of Lincoln and later archbishop of York. It was undoubtedly through the agency of Bishop Williams that in 1629 Dolben was installed in the Lincoln prebend of Caistor. Dolben was reported in 1741 by his great-grandson to have been nominated for a Welsh bishopric, but this assertion is likely to rest on confusion with a relative, David Dolben, who in the year of the prebend's death became bishop of Bangor in succession to Lewis Bayly.

Dolben maintained links with his native Pembrokeshire. At his death he was still in possession of the rectory of Stackpool, leaving some of its profits to one of its parishioners, his 'most honoured and faithful friend' Henry Lort. He bequeathed £20, in addition to the provision made by his cousin William Myddleton, merchant, of London, towards the stipendiary lectureship at Haverfordwest inaugurated about 1620. He died in 1631 and was buried on 19 September at Stanwick, aged forty-two. He was survived by his sons John *Dolben (1625–1686), later archbishop of York, and William *Dolben (*bap.* 1627, *d.* 1694), later justice of king's bench. STEPHEN WRIGHT

Sources DWB · *Old Westminsters* · Foster, *Alum. Oxon.* · H. I. Longden, *Northamptonshire and Rutland clergy from 1500*, ed. P. I. King and others, 16 vols. in 6, Northamptonshire RS (1938–52), vol. 2 · will, PRO, PROB 11/160, fols. 283r–283v · *VCH Northamptonshire*, vols. 3–4

Wealth at death probably substantial: PRO, PROB 11/160, fols. 283r–283v

Dolben, Sir William (*bap.* 1627, *d.* 1694), judge, was baptized on 27 September 1627 at Stanwick, Northamptonshire, the second son of the Revd William *Dolben (1588?–1631), rector of Stanwick, and Elizabeth, daughter of Hugh Williams of Cochwillan, Caernarvonshire, and niece of Archbishop Williams. John *Dolben (1625–1686), archbishop of York, was his brother. William Dolben was admitted to the Inner Temple in 1647–8 and was called to the bar in 1655. He received the degree of MA at Oxford in 1665 on the occasion of the incorporation *ad eundem* of the earl of Manchester, for whom he acted as secretary. In 1672 he was made a bencher of his inn. He was made

recorder of London in 1676 and was knighted on 3 February 1677. Later in that year Dolben was made a king's counsel (2 May) and a king's serjeant (24 October), and a serjeant-at-law. Archbishop Sheldon made him steward of the see of Canterbury. North wrote of him that he was 'bred under a clerk of assize, and executed the office of the crown side, which gave him the habit of a loud voice, though he was but of a small person' (North, 3.110). No doubt this quality helped him when appointed a judge of king's bench on 23 October 1678. North thought him 'an arrant old snarler' (ibid.) on the bench. On 4 April 1678 he had opened the case for the crown on the trial of the earl of Pembroke for the murder of Nathaniel Cony. As a judge Dolben tried many of those implicated in the Popish Plot, including Edward Coleman (November 1678), those accused of the murder of Edmund Berry Godfrey (February 1679), the queen's physician Sir George Wakeman (July 1679), Sir Thomas Gascoigne and Oliver Plunket, as well as one of their accusers, Edward Fitzharris (April 1681).

However, Dolben did not favour the surrender of corporate charters, an integral part of Charles II's strategy for taming the whigs, North reporting that he declined to give any opinion. So at the beginning of 1683 it was reported that 'Judge Dolben sits very slippery' (*Kenyon MSS*, 156), and on 18 April he received his *quietus*. According to Luttrell 'many think the occasion of his removal is because he is taken to be a person not well affected to the *quo warranto* against the city of London' (Luttrell, 1.225). Back in practice Dolben was one of the prosecutors of Algernon Sidney in November 1683. In December 1688 Dolben was suggested by the earl of Macclesfield as a possible source of legal advice for the peers meeting to solve the problem of calling a free parliament, but he was not summoned to attend. Dolben was reinstated as a judge in king's bench on 18 March 1689. In April he gave the charge to the Middlesex grand juries, inveighing 'mightily against the corruption of juries the last seven years, and gave in charge the laws against papists' (ibid., 1.527). In June he appeared before the Lords to provide reasons why he had been dismissed, and was soon called on to deliver his opinion on the surrender of the charters, whereon he stated that there were not enough precedents to support surrender. In June 1691 he gave another characteristic charge to the grand juries of Middlesex, directing them to inquire into malcontents who disturbed the peace of the kingdom through spreading seditious news.

Dolben died 'suddenly of an apopletic [sic] fit' (Luttrell, 3.259) on 25 January 1694, and was buried four days later in the Temple Church, his funeral being attended by the lord keeper and the judges. He was unmarried. His will memorably left nothing to his nephew John Dolben because he feared that what he had gained in industry, 'for I had small beginnings' (PRO, PROB 11/418/6), would be dissipated in gambling. Instead most of the estate went to Archbishop Dolben's other son, Gilbert. STUART HANDLEY

Sources Sainty, *Judges*, 34–5 · Baker, *Serjeants*, 446, 509 · will, PRO, PROB 11/418, sig. 6 · IGI · N. Luttrell, *A brief historical relation of state affairs from September 1678 to April 1714*, 1 (1857), 82, 225, 236,

255, 527; 2 (1857), 253, 259, 262; 3 (1857), 259 • G. W. Keeton, *Lord Chancellor Jeffreys and the Stuart cause* (1965), 66, 125–33, 193–5, 208, 272 • R. North, *The lives of … Francis North … Dudley North … and … John North*, ed. A. Jessopp, 3 (1890), 110 • J. Levin, *The charter controversy in the City of London, 1660–1688, and its consequences* (1969), 27, 98 • J. E. Martin, ed., *Masters of the bench of the Hon. Society of the Inner Temple, 1450–1883, and masters of the Temple, 1540–1883* (1883), 44–5 • Sainty, *King's counsel*, 21, 87 • R. Beddard, ed., *A kingdom without a king: the journal of the provisional government in the revolution of 1688* (1988), 153 • G. Burnet, *History of his own time*, new edn, 2 (1883), 345 • Foss, *Judges*, 7.312–14 • *The manuscripts of Lord Kenyon*, HMC, 35 (1894)

Likenesses oils, Lincoln College, Oxford

Dolben, Sir William, third baronet (1727–1814), politician and slavery abolitionist, was born and baptized on 12 January 1727 at Finedon, Northamptonshire, the second and only surviving son of Sir John *Dolben, second baronet (1684–1756), rector of Burton Latimer and vicar of Finedon, and his wife, Elizabeth Digby (d. 1730). He was educated at Westminster School and matriculated from Christ Church, Oxford, on 28 May 1744, aged seventeen; he was elected a student of the house in 1744 and awarded the degree of DCL on 7 July 1763. Soon after coming down from Oxford he married, at Westminster Abbey on 17 May 1748, Judith (1730–1771), the only daughter of Somerset English of Eastergate, Sussex, housekeeper of Hampton Court Palace, and his wife, Judith, the daughter and eventual heir of Hugh Pearson of Hampnett, Sussex. She brought with her a fortune of £30,000. Dolben succeeded his father in the baronetcy on 20 November 1756 and served as high sheriff of Northamptonshire in 1760–61. He was appointed a verderer of Rockingham Forest in 1766.

Dolben's family background, his personal reputation for probity, and his attachment to a moderate toryism made him a stop-gap candidate to represent the University of Oxford in the Commons at the by-election of 3 February 1768. He had already been nominated as one of the county MPs for Northamptonshire, so when he lost his seat following the dissolution later in 1768 he was returned to the Commons for Northamptonshire. A supporter of the duke of Grafton and Lord North, he stood down in 1774 and was readopted by the university on the retirement of Sir Roger Newdigate at the general election of 1780. Dolben told his predecessor that he meant to act his 'humble part, on so great a Theatre … free from all attachments' apart from those of the university and the country (Dolben to Newdigate, 24 Sept 1780, Warks. CRO, Newdigate Papers, CR136/B1636), and his record bears scrutiny. He sat in the Commons as an independent for the next twenty-six years, supporting the governments of North, Pitt, and Addington, though none of them uncritically, and was a terse, unacerbic speaker respected throughout the house. He voted for parliamentary reform in 1783, 1785, and 1797. Seeing himself as a lay watchdog of the Church of England in the Commons, he criticized J. P. Bastard's 1787 bill to regulate the church courts, which forbade prosecutions for immorality after the lapse of six months. Dolben was also ready to defend clergy rights to resist unacceptable forms of tithe commutation in private bills. Moral issues always attracted him, and he was a

strong supporter of the royal proclamation against vice and immorality issued in 1787; in 1795 he initially backed a bill for the more effectual working of the Lord's Day Observance Act that would have made a breach of the sabbath a breach of the peace. No cause was dearer to him than the abolition of slavery, or at least the improvement of conditions for black slaves being shipped to the West Indies on the middle passage. Despite opposition from the merchants of Bristol and Liverpool, with Pitt's support he successfully piloted a bill through the Commons in 1788 designed to limit the number of slaves allowed on a vessel in proportion to its tonnage (initially, for a trial period of a year). Dolben developed a close alliance in parliament with William Wilberforce on the slave trade. He supported in principle the series of abolition bills Wilberforce brought forward in the 1790s (often acting as chairman at the committee stage), while his own annual bill to extend Dolben's Act of 1788 gave him the chance to expatiate regularly on the trade's iniquities. Influenced by Wilberforce, Dolben supported his motion for peace with France on 27 May 1795.

Dolben had a happy and relaxed family life. Following the death of his first wife, aged forty, on 6 January 1771, he married a second cousin, Charlotte Scotchmer, née Affleck (c.1739–1820), on 14 October 1789. She was the widow of John Scotchmer (d. 1786), a banker, of Pakenham, Suffolk, and the sixth daughter of Gilbert Affleck, of Dalham Hall, Suffolk, and his wife, Ann, the daughter of John Dolben, brother of the first baronet. Dolben was delighted with his new wife. He thus described her prior to their wedding:

> Her mien is erect and Generous; Her stature rather full, her shape in fine proportion slender, and her limbs grow from it with such happy elegance as gives peculiar grace to all her motions … she is a woman of real and intrinsic fashion. (Dolben to James Bland Burges, 18 Sept 1789, Bodl. Oxf., DD Bland Burges)

They had no children. Though troubled by increasing deafness, Dolben enjoyed a vigorous old age, and never wore a greatcoat or had a fire in his bedroom. As his son reported in July 1803: 'My venerable Father, tho' 76 met the Parishioners at Church Porch and vowed he would go Volunteer in the Army at reserve against French invasion, if they would not, praising God he was able' (pocket diary of Sir John English Dolben, Northants. RO, Dolben (Finedon) collection, D(F) 65). He made his last public appearance at the Northamptonshire county meeting in 1807 to thank the king for his stand against Catholic emancipation. Dolben died at Bury St Edmunds on 20 March 1814, aged eighty-seven, and was buried on 27 March at Finedon church. He was succeeded in the title and estates by (John) English Dolben (1750–1837), his only surviving son from his first marriage. His widow died on 12 March 1820.

Dolben was a country gentleman whose dedication to the Church of England, Oxford University, and the county of Northamptonshire came naturally to him. He consistently gave generously of his time and money to encourage worthy causes, such as the Sunday school movement. He was also a member of the Society for the Encouragement of Arts, Manufactures, and Commerce and of the

Marine Society, and he was a Radcliffe trustee at Oxford. It was typical of Dolben that one of his first actions after inheriting was (in 1757) to make over the great tithes of Finedon to the vicar, appreciably increasing the latter's income. But it is his single-minded dedication to the abolitionist cause for which he merits recognition. The African author of *Thoughts and Sentiments on the Evil and Wicked Traffic of the Slavery* (1787), Ottobah Cugoano, predicted that in time 'your noble name shall be revered from shore to shore' (Northants. RO, Dolben (Finedon) collection, D(F) 39, n.d., probably 1788), and though posterity has been more forgetful, Dolben's life as an enlightened lay Anglican impressed all his contemporaries. He closely resembled Richardson's fictional hero Sir Charles Grandison and remained free of any trace of priggishness to the last, 'the model of a man, a gentleman, and a Christian' (*GM*, 1st ser., 84/1, 1814, 526). As some of his sorrowing constituents put it: 'No man bore human sorrows with greater firmness nor felt a more lively compassion for those of other men … In him courtesy was but the ornament of sincerity, never its substitute' (draft letter, 16 April 1814, Northants. RO, Dolben (Finedon) collection, D(F) 52).

NIGEL ASTON

Sources GEC, *Baronetage*, 4.190 · *GM*, 1st ser., 59 (1789), 955 · *GM*, 1st ser., 84/1 (1814), 417, 526 · *GM*, 1st ser., 90/1 (1820), 286 · J. Welch, *The list of the queen's scholars of St Peter's College, Westminster*, ed. [C. B. Phillimore], new edn (1852), 330 · Foster, *Alum. Oxon.*, 1715–1886, 1.376 · J. Debrett, ed., *The parliamentary register, or, History of the proceedings and debates of the House of Commons*, 112 vols. (1775–1813), vol. 22, pp. 127–30 (20 April 1787) · Cobbett, *Parl. hist.*, 27.573 ff. · M. M. Drummond, 'Dolben, Sir William', HoP, *Commons*, 1754–90 · R. G. Thorne, 'Dolben, Sir William', HoP, *Commons*, 1790–1820 · E. G. Forrester, *Northamptonshire county elections and electioneering*, 1695–1832 (1941) · W. R. Ward, *Georgian Oxford: university politics in the eighteenth century* (1958) · J. Ehrman, *The younger Pitt*, 1: *The years of acclaim* (1969) · *Selections from the letters and correspondence of Sir James Bland Burges*, ed. J. Hutton (1885) · *Northampton Mercury* (8 Nov 1814) · J. L. H. Bailey, *Finedon otherwise Thingdon* (1975) · *DNB* · G. Isham, 'A Northamptonshire worthy: Sir John English Dolben, 4th bart. of Finedon', *Northamptonshire Past and Present*, 4 (1966–72), 277–80

Archives BL, letters relating to his election at Oxford, Add. MS 38457, fols. 1–114 · Northants. RO, corresp. mainly relating to Oxford elections · Warks. CRO, letters, CR136/B/1567–1772 | Bodl. Oxf., letters to J. B. Burges, MS 18, fols. 31, 47b, 49, 53, 63–4, 69, 74–6, 84–5, 91–2, 95, 135, 136–7, 157; MS 19, fol. 141; MS 20, fols. 15, 87, 118; MS 23, fols. 142–3; MS 24, fols. 87–8 · Yale U., letters to William Smith

Likenesses J. Tassie, Wedgwood medallion, 1779, Wedgwood Museum, Stoke-on-Trent · M. Brown, oils, exh. RA 1802, Christ Church Oxf. · group portrait (as children), repro. in Mackworth, Dolben sale catalogue for Finedon Hall, 1912 · oils (after J. Opie, c.1800), Examination Schools, Oxford · portrait, repro. in Mackworth, Dolben sale catalogue for Finedon Hall, 1912

Dolby, Charlotte Helen Sainton- (1821–1885), singer and composer, was born in London on 17 May 1821, the daughter of Samuel Dolby, a merchant. A precocious child, she first took piano lessons with a Mrs Montague. After the death of her father she entered the Royal Academy of Music, studying piano from 1832 with John Bennett and singing with Gaetano Crivelli, who advised her not to make this her main study. She won the King's scholarship in 1837 and was made an honorary RAM. She made her first public appearance at the Philharmonic Society in a

Charlotte Helen Sainton-Dolby (1821–1885), by W. & D. Downey, 1874?

quartet on 14 June 1841 and sang again for the society as a soloist on 14 April 1842. She greatly impressed Mendelssohn, who engaged her for the Leipzig Gewandhaus concerts, where she first appeared on 25 October 1845. Mendelssohn also dedicated to Dolby the English edition of his *Six Songs*, op. 57, and wrote the contralto part in *Elijah* for her. She related that during the work's composition she was dining with Mendelssohn and Robert and Clara Schumann, and on asking after the progress of the part received the reply, 'Never fear, it will suit you very well, for it is a true woman's part—half an angel, half a devil' (quoted in Edwards; the role in fact divides between the Angel and Jezebel). She also recorded that, after her singing of 'O rest in the Lord' in the revised version in London on 16 April 1847, he turned to her with tears in his eyes and said, 'Thank you from my heart, Miss Dolby.' On 27 June in the same year he accompanied her in a performance of Schubert's 'Erlkönig'. Later she toured France and the Netherlands.

On 4 February 1860 Dolby married Prosper *Sainton (1813–1890), and until her retirement ten years later, performing as Charlotte Sainton-Dolby, she was one of the most successful contraltos of her time. She was praised for 'the admirable skill with which she controlled a powerful contralto voice, the exquisite intonation, perfect enunci-ation, and noble declamation which distinguished her singing' (Edwards). What seems to have been the first use of the term 'ballad concert' (a concert sponsored by a pub-lisher and consisting of a programme of works from his catalogue) was applied to her presentation on 3 January 1866 of works issued by Messrs Chappell. In 1872 she opened a Vocal Academy, whose students included Fanny Moody. Her last public appearance was at her husband's farewell concert in June 1883. Her compositions include *The Legend of St Dorothea* (1876), *The Story of a Faithful Soul* (1879), and *Florimel* (1885), as well as many songs and bal-lads. She also published *Madame Sainton-Dolby's Tutor for the English Singer*. She died at 71 Gloucester Place, Hyde Park, London, on 18 February 1885 and was buried at Highgate. The Royal Academy founded a scholarship in her memory.   JOHN WARRACK

Sources DNB · Grove, *Dict. mus.* · F. G. Edwards, *The history of Mendelssohn's oratorio 'Elijah'* (1896) · m. cert. · *CGPLA Eng. & Wales* (1885)
Likenesses C. Baugniet, lithograph, pubd 1844, BM · W. & D. Downey, photograph, 1874?, NPG [*see illus.*] · S. Gazenave, lithograph (after a photograph by Mayall), NPG · prints, Harvard TC · two cartes-de-visite, NPG
Wealth at death £1591 13s. 4d.: probate, 23 March 1885, *CGPLA Eng. & Wales*

Dolby, Richard (*fl.* 1826–1833), writer on cookery, of whose early life little is known, was cook at the Thatched House tavern, St James's Street, London (*c.*1826–*c.*1832). He was registered by the Vintners' Company as a freeman by servitude on 5 April 1826. His residence was the Thatched House tavern, which was renowned for its clubbable atmosphere and which enjoyed the patronage of the duke of Clarence, later William IV. Dolby's *The Cook's Dictionary and Housekeeper's Directory* was published in 1830, receiving outstanding press reviews. 'It appears to contain all that the veriest gourmand in Christendom could sigh for, in a life like Methusalem's, with a throat a yard long and pal-ate all the way' (Allibone, *Dict.*). Two further revised edi-tions were published in 1832 and 1833, by which time Dolby was advertised as 'Late Cook at the Thatched House Tavern'. Dolby acknowledged his dictionary owed much to others in the profession. French influences can be traced back to Antonin Carème's works as well as Louis Eustache Ude's *The French Cook*. Dolby also made use of John Farley's *The London Art of Cookery*, Duncan Mac-donald's *The New London Family Cook*, and Mrs Rundell's *Domestic Cookery*. His 5000 recipes were necessarily very much abbreviated.   FIONA LUCRAFT

Sources R. Dolby, *The cook's dictionary and housekeeper's directory*, 2nd edn (1832) · Vintners' Company, register of freedom admis-sions, 1768–1888, GL, manuscripts section, vol. 2 · K. Bitting, *Gas-tronomic bibliography* (1939) · J. Farley, *The London art of cookery*, 11th edn (1807) · D. Macdonald, *The new London family cook* (*c.*1808) · W. Hall, *French cookery* (1836) · L. E. Ude, *The French cook*, 7th edn (1822) · M. E. K. Rundell, *A new system of domestic cookery* · D. Foster, 'Inns, alehouses, taverns, coffee houses etc. in and around Lon-don', *c.*1900, City Westm. AC, vol. 65 · Allibone, *Dict.*

Dolfin (*fl.* 1092). *See under* Gospatric, first earl of Lothian (*d.* 1138).

Dolin, Sir Anton [*real name* Sydney Francis Patrick Chippindall Healey Kay] (1904–1983), ballet dancer, was born in Slinfold, Sussex, on 27 July 1904, the second of three sons (there were no daughters) of Henry George Kay, amateur cricketer, and later master and owner of the South Coast Harriers and Staghounds, and his wife, Helen Maude Chippindall Healey, from Dublin. Patrick Kay (as he was known) took his first dancing lessons at the age of ten, in Hove, after much pleading with his reluctant father. He went to a Miss Clarice James, then to the two Cone sisters, Lily and Grace. His parents moved to London to further his stage training and he auditioned success-fully for the Black Cat in *Bluebell in Fairyland* at Christmas 1915. This role was followed by that of John in *Peter Pan*. Dolin then trained as an actor and dancer at the Italia Conti School, which arranged engagements and tours for him.

In August 1917 Dolin began serious ballet training with Serafina Astafyeva. He studied with her for five years dur-ing which he was engaged, under the name Patrikéeff, by Diaghilev to appear in his 1921 production of *The Sleeping Princess*. More commercial engagements followed and on 26 June 1923 he appeared for the first time as Anton Dolin at the Royal Albert Hall in the 'Anglo-Russian Ballet'. He was by now also studying with Nicolas Legat, who had recently escaped from Russia. In November 1923 he joined Diaghilev's Ballets Russes.

Dolin immediately established himself as an outstand-ing dancer and was particularly successful as Beau Gosse in *Le train bleu* for his Paris début in the summer season of 1924. He made his London début that autumn in the same role.

After less than two years he left Diaghilev, whose favour-ite had become Serge Lifar, during the Paris summer season of 1925. He undertook many engagements in revues and musicals in England. In 1927 he danced with Tamara Karsavina at the Coliseum, and with Ninette de Valois in *Whitebirds* at His Majesty's. He also undertook a continental tour with Vera Nemchinova, with whom in 1927–8 he founded the first English Ballet Company, which included Frederick Ashton, Harold Turner, Mary Skeaping, and Margaret Craske. Dolin created several bal-lets for his company, the best being *The Nightingale and the Rose*, Chopin's *Revolutionary étude*, and George Gershwin's *Rhapsody in Blue*. By the end of 1928 he had rejoined Diaghi-lev in Monte Carlo and danced with more great baller-inas—Olga Spesivtseva in *Lac*, Karsavina in *Petrushka*, and Aleksandra Danilova in *Le bal*. It was while filming in *Dark Red Roses* with Lydia Lopokova in August 1929 that news of Diaghilev's death reached him and he was forced to become freelance again. That autumn he performed at the London Coliseum with Anna Ludmilla, to whom he became engaged. Later she terminated the engagement.

During the 1930s Dolin appeared in various revues and as a soloist in the new Vic–Wells Ballet from 1931 to 1935. He helped to launch the Camargo Society in 1930, for which he created Satan in *Job* (1931). In 1935 he and Alicia Markova founded their own ballet company with Broni-slava Nijinska as the ballet mistress and Dolin as a director

Sir Anton Dolin (1904–1983), by Gordon Anthony, 1935 [in *David* by the Markova–Dolin Ballet]

and first soloist. The company, financed by Laura Henderson, who ran the Windmill Theatre, lasted until December 1937. During the next two years Dolin danced in Paris, Blackpool, Australia, New Zealand, Honolulu, and London.

Dolin spent the war years in America and Australia. He helped build up the American Ballet Theater, for whom he restaged several of the classical ballets and danced the lead in Michel Fokine's *Bluebeard* in Mexico City in 1941. He returned to London in 1948 as a guest star with the Sadler's Wells Ballet. In August 1950 Julian Braunsweg founded the London Festival Ballet, of which Dolin was artistic director and first soloist until 1961. The company travelled extensively, with the young John Gilpin (1930–1983) as one of its dancers. Dolin and Gilpin formed a lasting friendship, Dolin outliving Gilpin by less than three months.

After leaving the Festival Ballet, Dolin directed the ballet at the Rome Opera for two seasons and then became a freelance producer all over the world. He was hospitalized in New York in 1966 for a hernia, but later in 1967 performed as the Devil in Stravinsky's *The Soldier's Tale*. He taught at summer schools, adjudicated at festivals, and acted in his own one-man show *Conversations with Diaghilev*. In 1979 he played the part of the ballet teacher Enrico Cecchetti in Herbert Ross's film *Nijinsky*. He remounted *Giselle* in Iceland in 1982 and taught in Hong Kong and China in 1983. His last engagement was in Houston before he returned to London and Paris, where he had a medical check-up in a hospital which pronounced him in good

health, but he collapsed and died immediately afterwards in Paris on 25 November 1983.

Knighted in 1981, Dolin received the Royal Academy of Dancing's Queen Elizabeth II award in 1954 and the order of the Sun from Peru in 1959. He wrote several books, including autobiographies. He spotted and sponsored many talented young dancers, to whom his generosity was remarkable. He partnered many great ballerinas, who knew him as a most courteous partner. He was one of the best *danseurs nobles* in classical ballet and was the first British male dancer to be acclaimed internationally. He was also anxious to take his art to the widest possible public and managed to combine strict classicism with the instinct of a showman. He was unmarried.

BERYL GREY, *rev.*

Sources A. Dolin, *Autobiography* (1960) · A. Wheatcroft, ed., *Dolin: friends and memories* (1982) · *The Times* (27 Feb 1980) · personal knowledge (1990) · D. Craine and J. Mackrell, eds., *The Oxford dictionary of dance* (2000) · *CGPLA Eng. & Wales* (1984) · H. Koegler, *The concise Oxford dictionary of ballet*, 2nd edn (1982)
Archives Theatre Museum, London, photograph and cuttings album
Likenesses G. Anthony, photograph, 1935, Theatre Museum, London [*see illus.*]
Wealth at death £9049—in England and Wales: administration with will, 9 Feb 1984, *CGPLA Eng. & Wales*

Doll [*née* Rickett], **Josephine** [Jo; *performing name* Jo Douglas] (**1926–1988**), actress and television producer, was born at 146 The Green, Earlsheaton, near Huddersfield, on 6 October 1926, the eldest of the three children of Bernard Rickett (1899–1985), a manager for Fyffes banana company, and his wife, Jessie Elizabeth (1902–1986), daughter of Edward Churchill Hampson, an engineer. She attended Longley Hall secondary school until, aged fourteen, she became a shorthand typist and started a local unit of the Women's Junior Air Corps. To help raise funds for it, she wrote and produced a performance of *Hansel and Gretel*. At fifteen she won a drama prize and then joined the Huddersfield Thespians, with whom she made her stage début in December 1943, playing Hazel in J. B. Priestley's play *Time and the Conways*.

Jo Rickett joined the Women's Auxiliary Air Force (WAAF) as a wireless mechanic in 1944, but also staged and appeared in camp shows so that, in 1947, she won a wartime grant to attend the Royal Academy of Dramatic Art (RADA), taking the stage name Jo Douglas when she left in 1949. Alfred Hitchcock saw her rehearsing at the academy and gave her a role in the film *Stage Fright* (1950). Her West End stage début took place at the Vaudeville Theatre on 6 December 1949, as Nurse Brent in *Bonaventure*. Meanwhile, on 16 July 1949 she had married (Victor) Douglas Ponton (*b.* 1917), an electrician who owned a shop in Sloane Square, Chelsea; her first son, Peter, was born on 5 September 1950.

In 1951 Jo Douglas both produced and acted in an amateur performance of *The Vigil* in St Martin-in-the-Fields Church, Trafalgar Square, where Ponton was in charge of lighting the play; she had to rush from this to appear in a revue called *See You Again* at the Watergate Theatre. During

1952 she acted in three films, first donning her WAAF uniform once more to appear alongside Jack Hawkins in *Angels One Five*, then doubling for Clark Gable's leading lady, Gene Tierney, in *Never Let Me Go*—during the filming of which she met her future husband, (John) Christopher Shaboe Doll (*b*. 1919), then a camera operator with Metro-Goldwyn-Mayer—and finally appearing in *Lady in the Fog* (released as *Scotland Yard Inspector* in the USA). In 1953 she joined the actors George Cole and Sidney James in the film *Will Any Gentleman*; presented the Saturday evening television show *In Town Tonight*, in which actors were interviewed about their work; and adapted Alan Paton's novel *Cry the Beloved Country* into a play with music, which she produced with Edric Connor in the lead. She divorced Douglas Ponton in January 1954, retaining custody of her son, and married Christopher Doll on 8 May 1954.

In August 1954 Jo Douglas played herself in a television play by a fellow RADA student, Lynne Reid Banks, called *It Never Rains*. In that year she also became a regular star on the television panel game *Find the Link*, for two years (which led to her appearances in *The Name's the Same*), and acted as announcer at the national radio show at Earls Court. During 1955 she appeared as a star on *Tall Story Club*, and in April the BBC gave her a trial as a producer–artiste for six months, and she became that programme's producer. In October 1955 she was awarded a two-year contract. She thus became the only woman producer of light entertainment in Europe. As Joy Leman remarked, since 'few women were involved in the making of television programmes, either as writers or producers in the 1950s' (Leman, 108), this was a mould-breaking appointment. In July 1955 Douglas produced the popular *Saturday Night Date*, followed by *Tin Pan Alley*, with Billy Cotton, in 1956. That year also saw her visiting military bases overseas to record material for the *Forces Requests* programme. Meanwhile, in the six months prior to the birth of her second son, Christian, on 10 September 1956, she had appeared monthly on a women's programme, describing how her pregnancy was progressing.

Until 1957 the hour between 6 and 7 p.m.—known as 'the toddlers' truce'—was designed to allow parents to put their children to bed free from the distractions of television. But Independent Television, launched in September 1955, was facing financial losses and persuaded the government to remove this ban. It ended on Saturday 16 February, a few minutes after the six o'clock news, with the BBC's *Six-Five Special*, which Jo Douglas both co-produced with Jack Good and co-presented with Pete Murray. Just how revolutionary the *Six-Five Special* presentation appeared at the time is encapsulated in a comment in the *Birmingham Mail* (18 February 1957) that it was 'just the kind of thing you might have expected from ITV'. With some pride, the BBC *Handbook* of 1959 declared that 'while primarily designed for a teen-aged audience [it had become] a national institution equally enjoyed by the parents'. To *Punch* magazine it was the teenage audience who were 'the real stars of the show' (3 April 1957). After the end of her contract in October 1957, Jo Douglas stayed on for a short time, but Jack Good had been forced out and

Pete Murray soon followed. Jim Dale took over from Murray, but it was never the same. Indeed 'No-one else could do what Jack Good and Jo Douglas had done. It had been their baby, and once they were gone the party was over' (Murray, 124).

Jo Douglas briefly then returned to acting, joining Alastair Sim, Ian Carmichael, and Hatti Jacques in the television play *Left, Right and Centre*, with Sidney Gilliat directing, before going over to ITV, the 'opposition' as the BBC saw it, where she worked first for Granada Television, producing the news programme *People and Places* three nights every week, and then joined Associated Television (ATV), where she was, for a while, the sole female producer. She then switched to drama, administering a much needed transfusion to the long-running *Emergency Ward 10* (devised by Tessa Diamond), bringing in actors like James Bolam. As she remarked, 'I want more exciting bods in beds' (*The Times*, 13 July 1988), and the twice-weekly soap opera attracted audiences of over 20 million within a year. The *Arthur Haynes Show* (1957–68) was another Douglas production for ATV, as was the *Arthur Askey Show* in the spring of 1961. During 1961 she returned to presenting, on the fortnightly *Home Shopping*. Then, with the series *Love Story* (1963–7, 1969, 1972–4), she directed twenty plays by writers as diverse as Doris Lessing, Roman Polanski, and Edna O'Brien. She was also responsible for *Fire Crackers*, a 1964 sitcom about work-shy firemen, and, in 1968, *Virgin of the Secret Service*, thirteen hour-long episodes devised and written by Ted Willis as tongue-in-cheek spoofs on James Bond.

In the early 1970s Jo Douglas produced a number of films, including Danny La Rue's first film, *Our Miss Fred* (also known as *Beyond the Call of Duty*; 1972), and *Dracula AD 1972*. In 1975, with her husband Christopher directing, she produced *Pilots Royal*, a portrait of Prince Charles shown on BBC 2, which reflected her own fascination with flying. (She had gained her pilot's licence in 1967.) In that year she joined Willis Worldwide Productions as an executive producer. Beginning in 1978 she produced thirteen programmes featuring David Kossoff reading Bible stories on Majorca, where she and her husband maintained a holiday home. She worked on various projects from 1980 to 1983, but in 1984 she had an operation and, on the advice of her brother-in-law, the cancer specialist Sir Richard Doll, underwent radiotherapy and chemotherapy. She retired in 1985 and twice visited her sister Julie in Australia before succumbing to cancer on 12 July 1988 at her home, White Briars, Slinfold, Sussex. She was survived by her husband and two sons.   FRED HUNTER

Sources P. Murray, *One day I'll forget my trousers* (1976) · *The Times* (13 July 1988) · J. Corner, ed., *Popular television in Britain: studies in cultural history* (1991) · J. Hill, 'Television and pop: the case of the 1950s', *Popular television in Britain: studies in cultural history*, ed. J. Corner (1991), 90–107 · L. Reid Banks, *It never rains* (1954) · T. Valminayi, ed., *British television: an illustrated guide* (1996) · *Huddersfield Daily Examiner* (2 Dec 1949) · *Huddersfield Daily Examiner* (28 March 1952) · *Huddersfield Daily Examiner* (19 Jan 1953) · *Huddersfield Daily Examiner* (20 March 1954) · *Huddersfield Daily Examiner* (22 March 1954) · *Huddersfield Daily Examiner* (15 April 1954) · *Huddersfield Daily Examiner*

(17 Aug 1954) · *Huddersfield Daily Examiner* (24 Aug 1954) · *Huddersfield Daily Examiner* (28 Aug 1954) · *Huddersfield Daily Examiner* (23 Sept 1954) · *Huddersfield Daily Examiner* (20 June 1955) · *Huddersfield Daily Examiner* (5 Sept 1957) · *Huddersfield Daily Examiner* (21 Nov 1958) · *Huddersfield Daily Examiner* (25 Nov 1958) · *Huddersfield Daily Examiner* (14 Nov 1959) · *Huddersfield Daily Examiner* (2 March 1973) · *Huddersfield Daily Examiner* (14 July 1988) · *Evening Standard* (28 May 1955) · *Evening Standard* (16 June 1955) · J. P. Wearing, ed., *London stage, 1940–1949: a calendar of plays and players* (1991) · *The Independent* (16 July 1988) · www.whirligig-tv-co.uk/adults/rocknroll/sixfive special.htm · www.graveyard.ndirect.co.uk/Filmography/113dad 1972.htm · www.uk.imdb.com · J. Leman, 'Wise scientists and female androids: class and gender in science fiction', *Popular television in Britain: studies in cultural history*, ed. J. Corner (1991), 108–24 · b. cert. · m. cert. [Victor Douglas Ponton and Josephine Rickett] · m. cert. [John Christopher Shaboe Doll and Josephine Doll] · m. cert. [Bernard Rickett and Jessie Elizabeth Hampson, parents] · d. cert. · private information (2004)

Archives BBC WAC, T12/360/3, 4, 6, 9
Likenesses photographs, priv. coll.

Dollan [*née* Moir], **Agnes Johnston**, Lady Dollan (1887–1966), suffragette and socialist, was born on 16 August 1887 at Springburn Road, Glasgow, one of eleven children of Henry Moir, a blacksmith, and his wife, Annie Wilkinson. Forced by family poverty to leave her local elementary school at the age of eleven, she worked briefly in a factory before becoming a telephone operator. The discrimination suffered by her fellow employees inspired her to campaign for feminist and trade union rights. As a teenager she became involved with the Women's Labour League, which sought to improve female working conditions and wages, and she fought alongside Mary Reid Macarthur, a prominent trade unionist, to organize female post-office employees into a single trade union.

During the 1900s Agnes Moir's political and ideological commitments grew. She joined the Women's Social and Political Union, formed in 1903 to secure the vote for women over the age of twenty-one, and strongly favoured the Pankhursts' controversial militant campaigning tactics. Her work with the Glasgow Socialist Sunday School demonstrated both a belief in socialism and a rejection of her staunch protestant upbringing as exemplified in her father's membership of the Orange lodge. Consequently she came into contact with members of the Independent Labour Party (ILP), which she joined about 1905.

On 20 September 1912 Agnes married Patrick Joseph *Dollan (1885–1963), whom she had met a year earlier through meetings of the Clarion Scouts. Son of James Dollan, an Irish miner, Dollan was at that time working as a journalist and ILP propagandist on Tom Johnston's socialist weekly paper, *Forward*. Their relationship was to serve for years as a model partnership founded on a mutual commitment to socialism and to the Scottish labour movement. Their only child, James, born in 1913, was the first pupil in his school to be exempted from religious instruction and by the age of twelve regularly attended socialist Sunday school meetings. He was to become a successful journalist.

During the First World War the Dollans channelled their beliefs into intense, and confrontational, political activity. Strident pacifists, they formed part of a small group of anti-war protesters in Glasgow. Agnes Dollan campaigned in particular to galvanize women's natural hostility to a conflict in which, as she later put it, 'their sons are consumed as common fodder' (Corr and Knox, 90). In tandem with her suffragette friend Helen *Crawfurd, she organized anti-war demonstrations at Glasgow Green in 1914 and established a Glasgow branch of the Women's International League in 1915. Both women travelled widely throughout Scotland to disseminate the league's principles, capitalizing on their highly tuned oratorical skills. In mid-1916 they helped to form the Women's Peace Crusade, which by the following year had grown into a national movement. Dollan also played a significant role in the Glasgow rent strikes during 1915. As treasurer of the Glasgow Women's Housing Association she headed the campaign, backed largely by housewives, against the council's rent increases; its stubborn resistance prompted the government's intervention and the Rent Restriction Act in late 1915. Despite this Dollan continued to protest against high rents and was jailed briefly in 1917, at the same time that her husband was ensconced in Wormwood Scrubs in London as a conscientious objector.

With the arrival of peace Agnes Dollan plunged more deeply into municipal and provincial politics. From 1918 until the 1930s she served on a variety of bodies, furthering both Patrick Dollan's and her own political careers. Between 1918 and 1921 she was a leading advocate of improved child care, and of medical and health facilities on behalf of Glasgow education authority. In 1921 she was elected to Glasgow town council where, alongside her husband, she fought for a Labour majority and for municipal control of housing, transport, and health. In 1922 she began a six-year stint as a member of the Labour Party's executive committee, and in the 1924 general election she stood (unsuccessfully) as the first female candidate for Dumfriesshire. Following a short period in the political wilderness in the early 1930s, owing mainly to ill health, she resumed her seat on the Labour Party national executive and opposed—but could do little to prevent—the ILP's disaffiliation in July 1932. This led to her being appointed in 1933 as first president of the women's council of the Scottish Socialist Party, which Patrick Dollan had founded as an alternative to the ILP and which remained in existence until it merged with the Labour Party in 1940.

Agnes Dollan's reaction to the growing international tensions of the 1930s mirrored that of many pacifists. At a Labour Party women's conference in 1933 she appealed for united female opposition to warfare. In early 1938 she went further and professed that fascist militarism was the creation of British toryism and capitalistic aggression. A year later, however, like her husband she had transformed her views and become a supporter of rearmament and the war effort. 'It was all very well to theorise under normal conditions but we were not living under such conditions today', she told a Scottish women's Labour Party conference in February 1939. 'We were facing a crisis which might mean general mobilisation' (Corr and Knox,

91). During the war her proven talents as an organizer and propagandist were much in demand—not least by Patrick Dollan, whose position as lord provost of Glasgow included responsibility for civil defence. She also played an integral part in the women's volunteer service. For these services to the community she was appointed MBE in 1946; her husband received a knighthood.

As a mark of her new-found respectability and her knowledge of Scottish issues, Lady Dollan was appointed to the royal commission on Scottish affairs in 1953–4. Her support for a limited amount of administrative devolution echoed the Labour Party's line of policy. Through the Scottish committee she also helped to organize Scotland's contribution to the 1951 Festival of Britain, and she sat as a governor of Hutchison's grammar school between 1948 and 1955.

In her later years Lady Dollan's views on religion and war underwent radical change. Possibly affected by the atrocities committed during the Second World War, she became involved with the Moral Re-Armament movement, which preached anti-communism and religious puritanism. This corresponded with her conversion from 'free thinking' to Catholicism, which was largely influenced by her husband's taking the same route after a long period as a lapsed Catholic and an agnostic. Patrick Dollan died in 1963 after a long illness, nursed by Agnes, who was by that time retired.

Some contemporaries have argued that for all her strong attachment to feminism throughout her life, Agnes Dollan saw her role principally as that of a supporter of her husband's career and that this seriously undermined her own political development. Unlike the more pragmatic Patrick, Agnes was an idealistic socialist whose frustration with the failure to create pure socialism perhaps made her more reactionary in old age. Despite her links with Moral Re-Armament, however, she remained an outstanding advocate of socialism and feminism. Her involvement with the Labour Party from its earliest days made her a national figure and an acknowledged expert on housing, welfare, and education; and she displayed a rare ability as an organizer and public speaker, talents which added considerably to her widespread popularity within the Scottish labour movement.

Agnes Dollan died aged seventy-eight from cardiac failure on 16 July 1966 at Victoria Infirmary, Glasgow. Among those who attended her funeral were the lord provost of Glasgow and several prominent Labour MPs.

HELEN CORR

Sources H. Corr and W. Knox, 'Dollan, Patrick Joseph', *Scottish labour leaders, 1918–39: a biographical dictionary*, ed. W. Knox (1984) • b. cert. • d. cert. • H. McShane and J. Smith, *Harry McShane: no mean fighter* (1978)

Wealth at death £8148 18s. 4d.: confirmation, 25 Aug 1966, NA Scot., SC 36/48/1042/258

Dollan, Sir Patrick Joseph (1885–1963), journalist and local politician, was born in Baillieston, Lanarkshire, on 3 April 1885. He was one of thirteen children of James Dollan, a miner, and his wife, Jane Rooney (*c*.1861–*c*.1946), who were both of Irish descent. Baillieston was a mining

Sir Patrick Joseph Dollan (1885–1963), by Archibald McGlashan [*The Red Jacket*]

village, incorporated into Glasgow in 1975. Dollan's memories were of 'an independent and tough community', and he stressed his parents' indomitability, despite considerable hardship. His mother at one time ran a grocery store. In later years he made much of his childhood, to demonstrate how far working-class Roman Catholics from an Irish immigrant background could succeed in public life.

The family's fortunes improved when Dollan's father was promoted to a supervisory position at the Clydeside colliery. Nevertheless, Dollan was obliged to leave St Bridget's elementary school at the age of ten, and started part-time work in a rope-making factory. His first full-time employment was as an assistant in a Baillieston grocery store, an experience that he claimed taught him much about financial management. At the age of fifteen he joined his father as a miner in the Clydeside colliery, although with characteristic energy he also enrolled for three sessions of evening classes at Wellshot Academy, Shettleston. Here he developed a talent for writing, winning literature prizes, and finding publishers for his essays. Adopting the pseudonym of Myner Collier he made his first forays into professional journalism for the Glasgow *Evening Times*, writing on mining topics.

Dollan became active in the labour movement during the early 1900s, serving as secretary to the newly inaugurated Baillieston branch of the Lanarkshire Miners' Union. Robert Smillie, a union official and Independent Labour Party (ILP) member, was an early and enduring influence. So too was John Wheatley, another prominent ILP figure, who like Dollan came from a Catholic Irish background. In 1910 Wheatley and Dollan set up a local ILP branch and, despite the strictures of the Catholic clergy against socialism, began to win recruits. Wheatley was impressed by Dollan's skills as a propagandist and was determined that his protégé should become a full-time journalist for *Forward*, a left-wing weekly Glasgow newspaper with a lively and trenchant style. Following a brief apprenticeship with Wheatley's own publishing firm, Dollan joined *Forward* in 1911 and became assistant editor. Although he long retained the *Forward* connection, he was later appointed the Scottish editor of the *Daily Herald*.

On 20 September 1912 Dollan married Agnes Johnston Moir [*see* Dollan, Agnes Johnston (1887–1966)], a fellow ILP member and activist in the women's suffrage movement. She was not a Catholic, and the relationship was indicative of Dollan's drift from religious orthodoxy, although significantly both were later to become devout church members. In 1913 Dollan entered municipal politics, and remained a Glasgow corporation councillor until he retired in 1946. He represented the Govan Central ward, and claimed that he was initially the last-minute replacement for a candidate who had withdrawn, and that he had to be persuaded to stand by his friend John S. Taylor, Glasgow ILP organizer. Yet his writing for *Forward* revealed an enthusiastic interest in civic affairs. Effective government, he believed, originated at the community level, as citizens could relate more readily to their own home base. Dollan devoted himself to this ideal, and (apart from unsuccessfully contesting the Ayr burghs by-election in 1925) refused entreaties to embark on a parliamentary career.

From 1913 Dollan's commitment to community politics was demonstrated by his high profile on the housing issue, especially the Glasgow ILP campaign against excessive rent charges by private landlords. The demand for accommodation in the booming munitions districts after the outbreak of war intensified local protests, which took the form of rent strikes. These were notable for the pugnacious contribution of women and the role played by both Dollans in directing strategy. The events in Glasgow were decisive for the introduction of national legislation during 1915 to peg rent increases. However, Dollan did not confine his militancy to housing. He was an outspoken critic of the war, appearing on peace platforms and agitating against military conscription. In 1917 he served a prison sentence of 112 days' hard labour in London's Wormwood Scrubs for failing to comply with a directive to leave Glasgow and seek 'work of national importance'. His resistance was given widespread press coverage, and added to the wartime rebel image of 'Red Clydeside'.

The franchise reforms of 1918 opened out opportunities for the Labour Party in Glasgow and in the 1922 general election its candidates sensationally won ten out of the city's fifteen parliamentary seats. At the municipal level, despite a more restricted franchise, the Labour group also made substantial inroads, winning overall control of the corporation in 1933. Dollan was inextricably associated with these successes, his gift for organization making him a pivotal figure in the construction of Labour's expanding power base. The legend of Glasgow's electoral 'machine'

emerged at this time, a Labour juggernaut supposedly created by him, as he welded his extensive network of community connections together. Yet whatever the reality of Dollan and machine politics, Labour's forces were far from united in Glasgow, and the disaffiliation of the ILP from the party in 1932 created a crisis of allegiance. He was already disenchanted with the flamboyant individualism of ILP colleagues like James Maxton, and chose to remain within the Labour mainstream. However, a vacuum had emerged in organization because of the previous strength of ILP support in Scotland. He sought to redress the balance by forming the Scottish Socialist Party (SSP) as a campaigning alternative to the ILP. The SSP could not establish a sufficiently distinctive identity and its status as a Labour affiliate ended in 1940, when it merged fully with the national party.

Dollan held a number of key municipal positions during the inter-war period, including the city treasurership, and deflected criticism of expenditure policies by ardently espousing the common good of Glasgow during the difficult depression years. His ability to cultivate the press was evident in the blaze of publicity surrounding his election as lord provost in 1938. Not only was he the first incumbent from a Catholic Irish background but he declared that he would be a working ambassador for the city, sparing no efforts to raise its international status. For all that he was aged fifty-three, with a shock of silver-grey hair, he consciously projected a youthful, energetic image and ensured that his wife also had a prominent public profile. At the outbreak of war in 1939 he directly appealed to the community spirit of Glaswegians, in a conflict that he claimed was for the defence of 'civic and national freedom'. He went on to play a crucial co-ordinating role during the early phase of the war, when food and fuel shortages and the evacuation of children caused considerable social upheaval. For his war services he was knighted in 1941, towards the end of his three-year term as lord provost.

After his departure from civic politics, Dollan did not abandon public life, serving as chairman of East Kilbride New Town Development Corporation between 1947 and 1958. Other positions followed, including a directorship of British European Airways at a time when air transport was being nationalized. For some critics, his career path seemed to negate his early socialist commitment, and they found difficulty in coming to terms with his acceptance of a knighthood. However, as wartime lord provost Dollan was dedicated to destroying fascism and boosting Glaswegian morale, while the knighthood was perhaps the inevitable refinement to the image of the Dollans as a successful, stylish, and cultured couple. That both became associated with the right-wing Moral Re-Armament movement during the 1950s did nevertheless tarnish their reputation for progressivism. Dollan died in the Victoria Infirmary, Glasgow, on 30 January 1963 and was buried in Dalbeth cemetery on 1 February, acknowledged to be one of Glasgow's most astute and influential municipal politicians. IRENE MAVER

Sources *Glasgow Herald* (31 Jan 1963) · *Glasgow Herald* (2 Feb 1963) · *Glasgow Herald* (4 Feb 1963) · *The Times* (31 Jan 1963) · P. J. Dollan, 'Autobiography', Mitchell L., Glas. · P. J. Dollan, personal scrapbooks, 1911–42, Mitchell L., Glas. [at least 9 vols.] · P. J. Woods, ed., 'Sir Patrick Dollan, 1885–1963: a miscellany', 1982, Mitchell L., Glas. · H. Corr and W. Knox, 'Dollan, Patrick Joseph', *Scottish labour leaders, 1918–39: a biographical dictionary*, ed. W. Knox (1984) · H. Corr, 'Dollan, Agnes', *Scottish labour leaders, 1918–39: a biographical dictionary*, ed. W. Knox (1984) · 'P. J. Dollan: a future lord provost of Glasgow', *The Bailie* (2 March 1935) · *Scottish biographies* (1938) · *WWW, 1961–70* · T. Gallagher, 'Red Clydeside's double anniversary', *Journal of the Scottish Labour History Society*, 20 (1985), 4–13 · T. Gallagher, *Glasgow, the uneasy peace: religious tension in modern Scotland* (1987) · A. McKinlay and R. J. Morris, eds., *The ILP on Clydeside, 1893–1932* (1991) · NA Scot., SC 36/48/978/81
Archives Mitchell L., Glas., personal scrapbooks · U. Glas. L., papers | FILM BFI NFTVA, documentary footage · IWM FVA, news footage
Likenesses A. McGlashan, portrait (*The red jacket*), Art Gallery and Museum, Glasgow [*see illus.*] · drawing, repro. in *The Bailie* · photograph (in youth), repro. in *The Bulletin* [Glasgow] (31 July 1916) · photograph, repro. in *Evening News* (6 March 1939) · photograph, repro. in *The Post* (5 March 1939) · photograph, repro. in *The Bulletin* (6 March 1939) · photographs, Mitchell L., Glas., personal scrapbooks
Wealth at death £5025 5*s*. 8*d*.: confirmation, 9 April 1963, NA Scot., SC 36/48/978/81

Dolle, Walter (*fl.* 1662–1674), engraver, was a minor figure of the Restoration period who seems to have worked entirely for booksellers rather than print publishers. He always signed his plates 'W. Dolle', and he has often been called William Dolle (as in the *Dictionary of National Biography*). James Granger, however, called him Walter, and said that he was a pupil of Faithorne the elder; his correctness is proved by the discovery that Walter Dolle was apprenticed to William Faithorne in 1662.

Dolle appears in the diary of Robert Hooke for 3 April 1674: 'Wat Dole showed me a plate of his doing in mezzotinto I thought it had been Sir Ch. Wrens way, but it proved to be done by squeezing a file on it with a presse' (*The Diary of Robert Hooke*, ed. H. W. Robinson and W. Adams, 1935, 95). This is the only reference to Dolle's being associated with the new art of mezzotint, or with the circle of experimenters of the Royal Society, and his known work is entirely in engraving. Granger noted that 'he was a workman of a much lower class' (Granger, 4.134) than William Faithorne the elder. Dolle's work consists entirely of portraits used as frontispieces and of other book illustrations, but no complete catalogue of it has ever been compiled; many of his portraits are copied from earlier prints.   ANTONY GRIFFITHS

Sources Goldsmiths' Company records, Goldsmiths' Company, London · R. Godfrey, 'Sir Christopher Wren and the *Head of a Moor*', *Print Quarterly*, 8 (1991), 281–5 · J. Granger, *A biographical history of England, from Egbert the Great to the revolution*, 2nd edn, 4 (1775), 134 · *DNB*

Dolling, Robert William Radclyffe (1851–1902), Church of England clergyman and social reformer, was born on 10 February 1851 in the old rectory, Magheralin, co. Down, the sixth of nine children and the elder son of Robert Holbeach Dolling (*d.* 1878), a landlord in co. Down, and one

time high sheriff of Londonderry, and his wife, Eliza (*d.* 1870), third daughter of Josias Du Pré Alexander MP, a nephew of James Alexander, first earl of Caledon. Dolling's childhood was spent at Kilrea, in co. Londonderry. After education at a private school, The Grange, Stevenage, Hertfordshire (1861–4), and at Harrow School (1864–8), he matriculated in 1868 from Trinity College, Cambridge. Bad health and ophthalmia compelled his withdrawal in spring 1869, and he spent the next twelve months in foreign travel, mostly in Italy, including Florence. After his mother's death in 1870 he returned to Ireland, where he assisted his father in land agency work. His spare time in Kilrea was devoted to Bible classes and night schools for young men, and clubs for working men, and he continued this work in Dublin, where his family soon moved. After his father's death on 28 September 1878 he went to England and made London his permanent home: there he became intimate friends with Arthur Henry Stanton (1839–1913) and Alexander Heriot Mackonochie (1825–1887), two Anglo-Catholic clergymen whom he had met earlier at Cambridge. These two clerics were at that time engaged in stubbornly defending the ritualistic services which they were conducting at St Alban the Martyr, Holborn. Under their influence Dolling became warden of the south London branch of the St Martin's Postman's League in 1879. But Brother Bob, as he was called by the postmen, found more satisfying work among the poorest classes in Southwark, where he exercised a magnetic influence.

Early in 1882 Dolling entered Salisbury Theological College, where his anti-intellectual temperament and belief in practical Christianity came into conflict with student life and theological education. Ordained as a deacon on 20 May 1883 in Salisbury Cathedral by Bishop Robert Campbell Moberly, Dolling became curate of Corscombe, Dorset, and then missionary deacon of St Martin's Mission at Holy Trinity, Stepney. He was ordained as a priest by the bishop of London, Frederick Temple, on Trinity Sunday 1885 at St Paul's Cathedral. Failing health and difficulties on questions of ritual with Bishop Temple led to Dolling's retirement from Stepney on 1 July 1885. After a short stay at St Leonards, in the same year Dolling became vicar of the Winchester College Mission of St Agatha's, Landport, Portsmouth, where for ten years he did much to mitigate the social problems of slum life, especially prostitution, poverty, and drunkenness. He also supported the campaign for shorter working hours and better wages, and believed that it was 'not far distant when employers will find that the men's Unions are really a great gain in the solution of the whole Labour Question' (Dolling, 130). He was also involved in frequent controversy over liturgical practices.

Dolling believed that the colour and spectacle of ritualism drew people to religion, a belief possibly not unconnected to his own enthusiasm for the theatre, which he attended frequently. Certainly, in conjunction with his strong personality and energetic evangelistic zeal, it attracted a large congregation to his church and contributed to his strong local influence, which was greatest over women and young people. His endorsement of confession, incense, extra-liturgical practices, and a small booklet, St Agatha's, Landport, Sunday Scholars' Book (1890s?), which critics thought deviated from Anglican teaching on the eucharist, brought him into conflict with his bishops. Fresh disagreements with the newly appointed bishop of Winchester, Randall Davidson, caused Dolling's resignation of his living on 8 December 1895. St Agatha's Church had been rebuilt, and Davidson refused to grant a licence for it, as it contained an altar which would be used exclusively for requiem masses. Dolling, who had already decided to leave St Agatha's, would not compromise, and this affair provided him with a dramatic excuse. After he left Landport he wrote Ten Years in a Portsmouth Slum (1896), which gave a full account of his work and experiences at St Agatha's and his problems with Davidson.

During 1896–7 Dolling stayed in London with his sister Josephine at Earls Court, giving occasional addresses in various parts of England. In May 1897 he went to America, where he preached in numerous cities. At Chicago in March 1898 he was offered the deanery of the cathedral by Bishop William Edward McLaren, but he had already accepted the living of St Saviour's, Poplar, and returned to England in July 1898. At Poplar he again sought to solve the social and municipal problems of the district; the east London water famine of 1898, the evils of overcrowding, and the smallpox epidemic of 1901 roused all his energies, and he fiercely denounced those responsible for these scandals. In March 1901 Dolling's health failed, and after travelling abroad in hope of relief he died, unmarried, on 15 May 1902, at his sister's house in South Kensington. Solemn requiem masses were said at St Cuthbert's, Philbeach Gardens, and at St Saviour's, and he was buried next to A. H. Mackonochie at Woking on 21 May. In June 1902 a government annuity was purchased in his memory for his two sisters Elise and Geraldine, who had helped him in his work; the Dolling memorial home of rest for the working girls of Poplar and Landport was opened at Worthing under their management in 1903.

The missionary enthusiasm of Father Dolling, as he was widely known, combined an almost evangelical fervour with a strong commitment to ritualist practices and pragmatic philanthropy. Impatient of ecclesiastical authority, he was an unconventional and essentially emotional preacher who appealed potently to marginal social groups. His commitment to the disadvantaged and dispossessed was evident in his radical politics: he strongly advocated Irish home rule, church disestablishment, and the labour movement. A stout man with a generous personality, he earned an unexpected tribute at his death from the nonconformist paper British Weekly (22 May 1902), which commented aptly that he had 'lived and died in slum parishes, with outcasts sleeping under his roof, with vagabonds dining at his table'.

W. B. OWEN, rev. RENE KOLLAR

Sources R. W. R. Dolling, Ten years in a Portsmouth slum (1896) • J. Clayton, Father Dolling: a memoir (1902) • C. Osborne, The life of Father Dolling (1903) • B. Palmer, Reverend rebels: five Victorian clerics and their fight against authority (1993) • N. Yates, The Anglican revival in Victorian Portsmouth (1983) • The Times (16 May 1902) • British Weekly (22 May 1902) • R. Thomsen, Robert Dolling: et blad af den engelske statskirkes historie i det 19. aarhundrede (1908) • A. Hascombe, Robert Dolling, mission priest: a biographical sketch (1907) • G. K. A. Bell, Randall Davidson, archbishop of Canterbury, 2nd edn (1938)

Archives LPL, Randall Thomas Davidson MSS

Likenesses W. A. Attree, photographs, 1885–95, repro. in Dolling, Ten years in a Portsmouth slum • Elliott & Fry, photograph, 1885–95, repro. in Clayton, Father Dolling • Elliott & Fry, photograph, 1885–95, repro. in Osborne, The life of Father Dolling • Elliott & Fry, photograph, 1885–95, repro. in Palmer, Reverend rebels • photograph, 1885–95, repro. in Yates, The Anglican revival • W. V. Amey, cabinet photograph, NPG • cabinet photograph, NPG • portrait (after a photograph); formerly at the Dolling Memorial Home, Worthing

Wealth at death £763 12s. 0d.: administration, 16 July 1902, CGPLA Eng. & Wales

Dollond family (per. 1750–1871), makers of optical and scientific instruments, were established in London by **John Dollond** (1707–1761), originally a silk weaver. He was born in Spitalfields, London, the third child and eldest son of Jean Dollond, a Huguenot weaver, and his wife, Susanne Marie, who had both fled from France after the revocation of the edict of Nantes. His first biographer, the Revd Dr John Kelly, husband of his granddaughter Louisa, erred in giving his date of birth as 10 June 1706 (Kelly, 6), for his year of birth is entered in a family Bible as 1707. He was baptized at the French church in Threadneedle Street, in the City of London, on 24 June 1707.

Very little is known of John Dollond's early life and education, except that he was brought up as a silk weaver, like his father. He had to work to help support the family from an early age, but even as a teenager he pursued his interest in mathematics in his spare time, and he became a member of the Spitalfields Mathematical Society. On 25 February 1727 he married Elizabeth Sommelier (1708–1782); of their nine children, only two sons and three daughters survived to adulthood. John continued to pursue his studies, developing a particular interest in astronomy and optics. This enthusiasm was passed on to his eldest son, **Peter Dollond** (1731–1820), his second child, born on 13 February 1731. It was through his son that John Dollond gave up weaving and became an optician.

Peter Dollond was trained as a silk weaver and assisted in the family business, but he did not take to the work and in 1750 set up as an optician, under his father's guidance. His first shop was probably in Vine Court, Spitalfields, where the Dollond family lived. By 1752 the optician's business was sufficiently successful for John Dollond to abandon weaving and go into partnership with his son. During 1753 they moved house to Denmark Court, Westminster, and by 1759 had opened a shop 'at the Golden Spectacles and Sea quadrant, Near Exeter Exchange in the Strand'. Here they traded as J. Dollond & Son, witness the signatures on an early achromatic telescope at the Royal Museum of Scotland, Edinburgh, and a compound microscope at the Whipple Museum, Cambridge.

John Dollond's improvement of telescopes John Dollond immediately began to improve refracting telescopes, having the reports of his work communicated to the Royal

Society by his friend the optician James Short, who was a fellow. There was little competition between the two because Short made only reflecting telescopes. John Dollond's first letter, read to the society on 1 March 1753, 'concerning an Improvement of refracting Telescopes', described a method of correcting eyeglasses. This was followed by his first public contribution to the theory of optics, 'A mistake in Euler's theorem for correcting aberration in object-glasses for refracting telescopes' (PTRS, 1753, 287). This was inspired by a paper by the Swiss mathematician Leonhard Euler, which had been published by the Berlin Academy in 1749 and summarized in a letter from Euler which Short communicated to the Royal Society in November 1752. A description of a further practical improvement devised by Dollond followed in May 1753, an adaptation of the micrometer invented by Servington Savery. Instead of Savery's two separate glasses, Dollond used a single glass cut in half, with the two parts sliding against each other. He developed three versions of this device, which became known as the divided object-glass micrometer, the first of which found some use for measuring the apparent diameter of heavenly bodies, although it halved the brightness of the image. The second and third versions were less successful.

John Dollond was at the same time working on the improvement of objective lenses for refracting telescopes. His criticism of Euler in 1753 had been based on Sir Isaac Newton's laws of optics. Euler addressed the problem of chromatic aberration which resulted in coloured fringes of light distorting the images seen through refracting telescopes. He suggested that it could be removed by having two lenses with water between them, taking the human eye as his inspiration. Dollond criticized this proposal because Newton's laws, which had been verified by experiment, showed that chromatic aberration in glass lenses could not be corrected.

However, Dollond was soon led to question his previous confidence in Newton's experiments by the work of Samuel Klingenstierna, professor of mathematics and later physics at Uppsala University in Sweden. After seeing Euler's article Klingenstierna began to investigate Newton's experiments mathematically, discovering inconsistencies which led him to conclude that the experiments could not all be correct and that the general laws deduced from them were not valid. When he heard of Dollond's criticism of Euler, Klingenstierna translated his own paper into Latin and asked a pupil who was in London to show it to Dollond. It led Dollond to doubt his previous confidence in Newton's theories and to begin repeating some of the latter's experiments with prisms. Eventually he was able to produce a compound lens for refracting telescopes which was free of both chromatic and spherical aberration. In April 1758, prompted by his son, Dollond obtained a patent for his new lenses and in June he communicated the results of his experiments to the Royal Society as 'An account of some experiments concerning the different refrangibility of light' (PTRS, 1757–8, 733–43), although he did not mention what had inspired him to undertake the work. The lenses were described as achromatic, a term said to have been coined by Dr John Bevis.

The achromatic lens Ever since Dollond's own time it has been debated whether he was entitled to claim the invention of the achromatic telescope lens, or whether he merely took up ideas previously developed by Chester Moor Hall (bap. 1703, d. 1771) and the European mathematicians. Chester Moor Hall was a barrister and landed gentleman with an interest in optics. It was claimed by another eminent optician, Jesse *Ramsden, who was married to John Dollond's daughter Sarah (1743–1796), in a paper read to the Royal Society (letters and papers, decade IX, no. 146), that as far back as the 1730s Hall had developed an achromatic object-glass made from a combination of two lenses of different types of glass with different refractive powers. The optician employed to grind these lenses later mentioned the fact to Dollond, information which, combined with the ideas of Klingenstierna and his own experiments, enabled Dollond to develop his achromatic compound lens. Like Hall's, it made use of the different refractive powers of crown and flint, or lead, glass. Although the idea of using two types of glass with different refracting properties came first from Hall, neither he nor the opticians who worked with him were able to develop a method of producing achromatic lenses in commercial quantities. Dollond's contribution was first to devise a much quicker and simpler method of correcting the spherical aberration of the lenses. Second, he realized that batches of glass varied in their refractive and dispersive powers, and developed a method of measuring these values so that batches could be matched and achromatic doublet lenses reliably produced. It was the difficulty of correcting spherical aberration and of producing good-quality achromatic lenses in quantity which had inhibited the other opticians who knew of Hall's experiments from effectively exploiting their knowledge. Dollond was able to solve these problems and bring the achromatic lens successfully to the market.

In 1758 John Dollond was awarded the Copley medal of the Royal Society for his work on achromatic lenses, and on 28 May 1761 he was elected a fellow. In addition to these honours, in December 1760 he was appointed as optician to the king, George III. However, there was some resentment among the European mathematicians, who felt that their contributions to the advances in the understanding of optics and the improvement of lenses had not been properly acknowledged by Dollond and the Royal Society.

Late in the evening of 29 November 1761 John Dollond suffered what contemporaries described as an attack of apoplexy, probably a stroke, and died soon afterwards; contemporary notices record the date of his death as 29 November; Kelly (Kelly, 13) gives it as 30 November. It was said that he had been sitting by the fire at his house in the Strand studying Clairaut's treatise on the motions of the moon when he was taken ill. He was buried on 6 December at the parish church of St Martin-in-the-Fields, a short distance from his shop. Kelly provides the only character sketch of John Dollond:

In his appearance he was grave, and the strong lines of his face were marked with deep thought and reflection; but in his intercourse with his family and friends he was cheerful and affectionate; and his language and sentiments are distinctly remembered as always making a strong impression on the minds of those with whom he conversed. His memory was extraordinarily retentive, and amidst the variety of his reading he could recollect and quote the most important passages of every book which he had at any time perused. (Kelly, 14)

Dollond regularly attended services at the French protestant church in Threadneedle Street.

Patent disputes John Dollond had financed the cost of applying for the achromatic lens patent by means of a partnership agreement with fellow optician, Francis Watkins (*bap.* 1723, *d.* 1792), dated 29 May 1758. Watkins paid the expenses of the application in return for an equal share in the profits arising from the exploitation of the patent. The cost of making the tube and glass were to be deducted, then a quarter of the profit was to be retained by the seller, the remaining three-quarters divided equally. Peter Dollond inherited his father's share of the profits from the patent, and acquired the whole rights in 1763 for £200, terminating the previous arrangement on the grounds that Watkins had on occasion retained the entire profit, contrary to the articles of partnership.

On 16 August 1761, a few months before his father's death, Peter Dollond married Ann Phillips at St Martin-in-the-Fields. Between 1760 and 1767 they had two daughters, Louisa and Ann, followed by a son, John, who probably died young. After his first wife's death Peter married a Mrs Randall in 1795. Peter Dollond took an active part in London guild affairs, becoming a freeman of the Spectaclemakers' Company in March 1755 and master in 1774–82, 1797–9, and 1801–3. However, he did not become a freeman of the City until 1765, shortly before taking his first apprentice, John Berge, in December of that year. He took three more apprentices between 1769 and 1778, including his nephew John Huggins, son of his sister Susan, who had married William Huggins. He also apparently received some assistance in the business from his sister Sarah, who became estranged from her husband, Jesse Ramsden, and with their son John occupied a house in Haymarket owned by the Dollonds.

Peter Dollond was a far more ruthless businessman than his father, and set about exploiting the achromatic lens patent to the full. Towards the end of 1763 he took proceedings in the court of king's bench against Watkins for infringing the patent. In June 1764 he extracted from Martha Ayscough, widow of the optician James Ayscough, a bond of £500 that she would not make achromatic refracting telescopes. These actions brought Peter Dollond into conflict with many of the other London opticians. Thirty-five of them signed a petition to the privy council calling for John Dollond's patent of 1758 to be revoked, on the grounds that the achromatic lens had been invented by Chester Moor Hall and was already on sale in London before 1758. Their action was supported by the court of the Spectaclemakers' Company, whose master at that time was Watkins, the Dollonds' former partner. The company contributed £20 towards the expenses of presenting the petition, but to no avail as the privy council refused to hear it. It was left to those who were prosecuted by Peter Dollond for infringing his father's patent to defend themselves in the courts. In a series of cases between 1764 and 1768 Peter Dollond established his right to enjoy the privileges of the patent, and in so doing created a precedent in the case law on patents which was referred to in later judgments. Hearing Dollond's case against the optician James Champneys in the court of common pleas, Lord Mansfield gave his decision in favour of the patentee on the grounds that it was 'not the person who locked up his invention in his scrutoire that ought to profit by such an invention, but he who brought it forth for the benefit of the public' (PRO, court of common pleas, judgments, H.6 Geo III, 626 Middx, Feb 1766).

Partnership and commercial success In 1766 Peter Dollond went into partnership with his younger brother, John (1746–1804), and also moved to a new shop, acquiring for £200 the lease on premises in St Paul's Churchyard, later no. 59, from Mary Sterrop, widow of the optician Thomas Sterrop. The firm traded as P. and J. Dollond, supplying a wide range of mathematical, philosophical, and optical instruments, including several items for Captain James Cook's second voyage of exploration to the Pacific. Peter continued to improve the achromatic telescope objective, perfecting the combination of three lenses with which his father had begun to experiment. This further development of his father's work was communicated to the Royal Society on 7 February 1765. The new arrangement reduced the spherical error of the lens, and was generally accepted as a significant improvement. The Dollonds were the first to use mahogany telescope tubes, which were much more robust than the traditional vellum, and in 1783 they began to supply instruments with plated brass draw tubes, made by a process patented in 1782 by Joshua L. Martin. Peter Dollond was also working to improve other instruments. In 1772 he sent the Royal Society a description of adjustments to the glasses of Hadley's quadrant, which helped to prevent distortion, and he also patented the arrangement. In 1779 his 'Account of an apparatus applied to the equatorial instrument for correcting the errors arising from refraction in altitude' was presented to the Royal Society by the astronomer royal, Nevil Maskelyne. However, neither of the younger Dollonds was elected to the fellowship of the Royal Society. Indeed, the French astronomer, Jean Bernoulli, who visited the Dollonds during his stay in England, professed astonishment at Peter Dollond's lack of mathematical understanding, although he admitted later that he might have drawn too sweeping a conclusion from a limited conversation, and certainly Peter had sufficient knowledge to develop the use of devices for measuring the properties of lenses.

The telescopes supplied by Peter Dollond were much in demand. For the Royal Observatory at Greenwich he made an achromatic telescope of 10 ft focus with a double object-glass of 5 ins. diameter, the largest and only one of that size he made. In fact, in the closing years of the eighteenth century his workshop supplied all the new refracting lenses and eyepieces for the observatory. Dollond's refractors were also sought by customers overseas, who included J. J. Lalande, head of the Paris observatory, and Charles Messier, another Frenchman, who was responsible for the first major catalogue of nebulae. However, there were frequent complaints about the time taken to complete orders, and the high cost of Dollond telescopes. In part the delays were beyond the Dollonds' control, because of the difficulty of obtaining sufficient good-quality optical glass, especially for the larger lenses. Peter justified the cost by the care and time needed to produce high-quality achromatic refractors. Certainly Dollond instruments enjoyed a high reputation in the British Isles, to the extent that 'a Dollond' became a synonym for a telescope, but it was widely believed by contemporaries that refractors made in the latter part of Peter Dollond's lifetime by the Swiss optician Pierre Louis Guinand were superior, because Guinand developed his own process of producing improved optical glass with far fewer imperfections than the traditional methods.

Further family involvement In November 1805, the year after his brother John's death, Peter Dollond took into partnership his nephew George Huggins, who changed his name by licence to Dollond, the alteration being recorded by the College of Arms. However, the trading name remained P. and J. Dollond. **George Dollond** (1774–1852) was born on 25 January 1774, the sixth son and seventh and youngest child of Susan (or Susanne; 1728–1798), daughter of John Dollond, and William Huggins. He was educated at George Lloyd's seminary in Kennington, Surrey. His father died while he was still a child and his uncle, Peter Dollond, arranged his training. In March 1788 he was apprenticed in the London Grocers' Company to Charles Fairbone, mathematical instrument maker, but he did not take his freedom until June 1804. In 1807 he also took his freedom by purchase in his uncle's guild, the Spectaclemakers' Company; he served as its master between 1811 and 1813.

The family tradition of inventiveness continued with George Dollond, who patented a new lighting arrangement for compass binnacles in 1812. He developed an improved micrometer with a rock crystal eyepiece, which he explained to the Royal Society in 1821. He had extensive business with a variety of public institutions, supplying equipment for the observatories at Cambridge, Madras, and Trivandrum. He provided the board of longitude with some of the instruments used on the Arctic expedition of 1821, and a Dollond theodolite was used by Captain Lort Stokes in his surveys of Australia, New Zealand, and the Timor Sea. However, not everyone was satisfied with the goods supplied by Dollond. Lord Palmerston, for example, sent back a telescope, complaining of the indistinctness of the image.

Peter Dollond apparently retired from business in 1819 and George carried on the family firm alone, though in 1820 Peter and George were jointly made opticians to George IV. Peter Dollond moved his home to Richmond in

1817, but three years later moved back to Kennington, where after only a few days he died, on 2 July 1820; he was buried at the parish church of St Mary, Lambeth.

George Dollond was elected a fellow of the Royal Society in 1819. Like his grandfather and uncle, he had papers published in the *Philosophical Transactions*. He played an active role in seeking a charter for the creation of the Astronomical Society and became one of the founding fellows in 1820. He was also a founder member of the Royal Geographical Society in 1830. On the accession of Queen Victoria in 1837 he was appointed optician to her majesty. He contributed a number of papers to the *Memoirs of the Royal Astronomical Society*, notably 'A short account of a new instrument for measuring vertical and horizontal angles' (vol. 2, 1826, 125), describing improvements to enhance the accuracy of such devices. He wrote a number of short treatises on some of the instruments he sold, such as *Description of the Camera Lucida* (c.1830), a drawing aid patented in 1806 by William Hyde Wollaston and manufactured by the Dollonds. At the Great Exhibition of 1851 he was awarded the council medal for his invention, a type of weather station in which instruments which measured variations in air pressure, temperature, humidity, rainfall, and force and direction of the wind were caused to record on a roll of paper.

George Dollond died unmarried at his home at Camberwell Terrace North on 13 May 1852, and was buried on 20 May at Norwood cemetery. His property was bequeathed to his nephews and their children. He was highly respected by his contemporaries, and acquired a reputation for absolute honesty which led the Spectaclemakers' Company to entrust their investments to his care.

George Dollond had trained at least five apprentices through the Spectaclemakers' and Grocers' companies, including his nephew George Huggins (1797–1866), son of his brother John, who was bound through the Grocers in 1812 and took his freedom in 1827. The younger George succeeded to the family business on his uncle's death and, following the family tradition, adopted the surname Dollond. When the second George Dollond died in 1866 the firm was taken over by his son, William (1834–1893). In 1871 William Dollond became too ill to continue working, and he sold the firm to J. R. Chant, a former employee, who, though no Dollond family interest remained, nevertheless kept the trading name of Dollond. In 1928 the firm was acquired by James Aitchison, to become Dollond and Aitchison, and it thereafter concentrated increasingly on prescription spectacles. GLORIA CLIFTON

Sources J. Kelly, *The life of John Dollond, F. R. S.: inventor of the achromatic telescope*, 3rd edn (1808) · Dollond family tree, Society of Genealogists, London, Wagner Huguenot Pedigrees Collection · *The registers of the French church, Threadneedle Street, London*, 3, ed. T. C. Colyer-Fergusson, Huguenot Society of London, 16 (1906); 4, Huguenot Society of London, 23 (1916) · H. Barty-King, *Eyes right: the story of Dollond & Aitchison Opticians, 1750–1985* (1986) · articles of co-partnership between Mr Francis Watkins and Mr John Dollond, 29 May 1758, GL, Dollond family MSS, 14805/1 · petition for the revocation of John Dollond's patent, 1764, PRO, PC 1/7 no. 94 · court of common pleas, judgments, PRO, H.6 Geo III, 626 Middx · P. Dollond, 'Some account of the discovery, which led to the grand improvement of refracting telescopes, made by the late Mr John Dollond F. R. S., in order to correct some misrepresentations in foreign publications, of that discovery', RS, letters and papers, decade IX, no. 131 • election certificate, RS • H. C. King, *The history of the telescope* (1955) • R. Willach, 'New light on the invention of the achromatic telescope objective', *Notes and Records of the Royal Society*, 50 (1996), 195–210 • J. Short, 'Of a letter by Euler concerning the making of objective glasses for refracting telescopes', RS, letters and papers, decade II, no. 323 • Spectaclemakers' Company, court minutes, vols. 3–6, GL, MS 5213/3–5213/6 • royal appointments, Lord Chancellor's Dept, PRO, LC/3/67, p. 31, 1760; LC/3/69, p. 8, 1820; LC/5/243, p. 90, 1837 • parish registers, St Martin-in-the-Fields, City Westm. AC [marriage, 1757–62; burial, 1761] • St Martin-in-the-Fields, parish poor rate ledgers and cleansing rate ledgers, 1752–67, City Westm. AC, F531–541, F5870, F5878, F5886, F5798 • Tower Hamlets Commission of Sewers, rate books for the parish of Christ Church, Spitalfields, 1750 and 1759, LMA, THCS/174, 129; THCS/195, 209–10 • N. V. E. Nordenmark and J. Nordström, 'Om uppfinningen av den akromatiska och aplanatiska linsen. Med särskild hänsyn till Samuel Klingenstiernas insats', *Lychnos* (1938), 1–52; (1939), 313–84 [including summary in English] • W. Kitchener, *Practical observations on telescopes* (1815) • freedom certificate, CLRO, MS CF1/926 [Peter Dollond] • *Journal of the Royal Geographical Society*, 23 (1853), lxxiii–lxxiv [George Dollond] • burial register, West Norwood cemetery, London, 20 May 1852 [George Dollond] • register of births and baptisms, London, St Faith under St Paul, 1720–68 • parish register, Stepney, St Dunstan and All Saints, 25 Feb 1727 [marriage, John Dollond] • *Daily Advertiser* [London] (1 Dec 1761) [John Dollond] • *GM*, 1st ser., 90/2 (1820), 90 [Peter Dollond] • memorial, St Mary-at-Lambeth [Peter Dollond] • parish register, St Clement Danes, 14 Feb 1774 [baptism, George Dollond] • death duty registers, PRO, IR 26/818, fol. 738 [Peter Dollond] • death duty registers, PRO, IR 26/1926, fol. 383 [George Dollond]

Archives GL, family papers, MSS 14805–14807 • NMM, instruments • RS, letters and papers • Sci. Mus., trade card, corresp., treatises • Sci. Mus., instruments • Yardley, Birmingham, Dollond and Aitchison collection | Birm. CL, Boulton and Watt collections • BM, Heal collection • CUL, Royal Greenwich Observatory archives • MHS Oxf., Blundell MSS

Likenesses A. Buck, coloured drawing, 1804 (George Dollond), Dollond and Aitchison collection, Yardley, Birmingham; repro. in Barty-King, *Eyes right* • W. Witherington, oils, presented 1842 (John Dollond; after B. Wilson), RS • R. Garland, bust, presented 1843 (John Dollond), RS • lithograph, 1851 (George Dollond), Dollond and Aitchison collection, Yardley, Birmingham; repro. in Barty-King, *Eyes right* • J. Posselwhite, engraving (John Dollond), NMM • J. Thompson, engraving (Peter Dollond), NPG • B. Wilson, oils (John Dollond), Royal Observatory, Greenwich, London • oils (Peter Dollond), Dollond and Aitchison collection, Yardley, Birmingham

Wealth at death £6975 15s. 10d.—Peter Dollond: PRO, death duty registers, IR 26/818, fol. 738 • under £40,000—George Dollond: PRO, death duty registers, IR 26/1926, fol. 383

Dollond, George (1774–1852). *See under* Dollond family (*per.* 1750–1871).

Dollond, John (1707–1761). *See under* Dollond family (*per.* 1750–1871).

Dollond, Peter (1731–1820). *See under* Dollond family (*per.* 1750–1871).

Dolman, Charles (1807–1863), Roman Catholic publisher, was born at Monmouth on 20 September 1807. He was the only son of Charles Dolman, a surgeon, and his wife, Mary Frances, daughter of Thomas Booker, a Roman Catholic publisher in London. Dolman's father died in the year of

his birth, leaving his son and his two daughters to be brought up by their mother, who remarried in 1818. Dolman was educated at Downside School, near Bath, from 1817 to 1821. Subsequently he studied architecture at Preston in Lancashire, under Joseph Aloysius Hansom, the Catholic architect and inventor of the Hansom cab. Probably in the mid-1830s his mother's family, the Bookers, invited him to join their publishing establishment at 61 Bond Street, London. After the death of his uncle Joseph Booker in 1837, Dolman carried on the business with his aunt, Miss Mary Booker, and his cousin Thomas. On Mary Booker's death in 1840, Dolman and Thomas Booker went into partnership; soon after, the business became entirely Dolman's. On 12 January 1841 he married Frances, the daughter of James and Apollonia Coverdale of Ingatestone Hall in Essex; they had one son, Charles Vincent Dolman, later canon of Newport.

Dolman's early publishing career was dominated by his interest in the publication of Roman Catholic periodicals. From 1838 to 1844 he was the publisher of the *Dublin Review*, a quarterly journal founded by Nicholas Wiseman, M. J. Quinn, and Daniel O'Connell. The commencement of this publication was marked by financial problems and editorial disputes. Wiseman felt that Dolman wanted too much say in the management of the *Review*; Dolman was also criticized as inefficient, and accused of failing to advertise the *Review* properly. But Roman Catholic publishers generally had less capital and fewer trade openings than their protestant counterparts, difficulties Dolman's critics failed to appreciate. It soon became necessary to guarantee Dolman against losses of up to £400, and in 1844 arguments over the management of the journal led to Dolman's departure.

From April 1838 Dolman had been the publisher of the *Catholic Magazine*, a periodical of a more apologetic nature than the *Review*. The *Magazine* aimed to promote fellow feeling between Catholic and protestant, and to make the Roman Catholic faith attractive to a wider audience. After the *Magazine* folded in 1844, Dolman continued this tradition with his own *Dolman's Magazine and Monthly Miscellany of Criticism*. Established in July 1845, it aimed to be 'all things to all men' (*Dolman's Magazine*, April 1846, 318). Like its predecessor it avoided dealing with the controversial issues of Irish politics. It quarrelled with both the *Dublin Review* and *The Tablet* over Frederick Faber's first volume in the series Lives of the Modern Saints, his admiring account of the masochistic excesses of Rosa of Lima. In August 1849 *Dolman's Magazine* was united with Thomas Booker's *Catholic Weekly* to form the *Weekly Register*. After 1850 Dolman ceased to have any connection with it.

From the late 1840s Dolman turned his attention away from journals, though he later engaged in one further publication of this kind: from January 1856 to December 1862, he published *The Lamp*, a Roman Catholic journal intended for the edification of the lower classes. He concentrated instead on the publication of de luxe editions of Catholic classics, such as Kenelm Digby's *Broadstone of Honour*. The most significant of these productions was the fifth edition of John Lingard's *The History of England*, published in 1850 with the author's corrections. The historian's opinion of his publisher shows that Dolman's disputes with the *Dublin Review* personnel should not be permitted to obscure the strength of his commitment to the defence and propagation of his religion: Lingard, with his lingering cisalpine sympathies, found Dolman 'too fond of puffing' (Lingard to E. Price, Feb 1848) and refused to write a combative preface to the edition, indicating the errors of Macaulay's *History*. The cost of Dolman's special editions exhausted his capital; in 1858 he tried to form his business into a limited liability company called the Catholic Bookselling and Publishing Company. However, the company failed, and, probably in 1862, he went to live in Paris, where he established a small business at 64 rue du Faubourg St Honoré. He died there on 31 December 1863; his wife survived him, dying on 2 March 1885 at Erith.

ROSEMARY MITCHELL

Sources Gillow, *Lit. biog. hist.* · S. Acheson, 'Catholic journalism in Victorian Catholic society, 1830–70, with special reference to *The Tablet*', MLitt diss., U. Oxf., 1981 · R. A. Mitchell, 'Approaches to history in text and image in England, *c*.1830–1870', DPhil diss., U. Oxf., 1993 · *DNB*
Archives Ushaw College, Durham, corresp. with John Lingard; letters to Nicholas Wiseman · Westm. DA, Bagshawe MSS

Dolmetsch, (Eugène) Arnold (1858–1940), maker of musical instruments, was born at Le Mans, France, on 24 February 1858. He came from a family of musicians. His grandfather, of Bohemian origin, settled in Zürich in 1808. There his father, Rudolf Arnold Dolmetsch, was born and became a piano maker; he was also known for his performances of Bach on the clavichord. His mother was Marie Zélie Guillouard, daughter of Armand Guillouard, a piano and organ maker who taught Arnold instrument making and how to play. Arnold was the eldest son. After his father's death he went to the Brussels Conservatoire for a general musical education and took violin lessons with Henri Vieuxtemps. In 1883 he entered the newly founded Royal College of Music in London, where he studied with Henry Holmes and Frederick Bridge, and was encouraged by its director, Sir George Grove, not only in his professional career as music master at Dulwich College but also in his investigations into the early English instrumental music which he found in the British Museum in 1889.

Thereafter Dolmetsch's life work became the study of the performance of early music and the instruments on which to play it. Confronted with a lack of appropriate instruments he began to construct copies of lutes, virginals, clavichords, harpsichords, recorders, and ultimately viols and violins, and taught himself and others to play them. Dolmetsch made his first lute in 1893, his first recorder in 1919, his first clavichord in 1894; his first harpsichord, produced at the suggestion of William Morris, was shown in 1896. He also worked as an instrument builder in the USA (1905–11) and Paris (1911–14).

Dolmetsch's main contributions to the English musical renaissance, which until then had concentrated mostly

(Eugène) Arnold Dolmetsch (1858–1940), by Herbert Lambert, *c*.1925

on the repertory for voices because of the lack of authentic instruments and players who could use them, were the rediscovery of a school of English composers for consorts of viols (of whom the chief were John Jenkins and William Lawes) and the re-establishment of the recorder as an instrument of popular music. By providing the environment for its performance and instruments, he initiated a movement which has burgeoned into prolific scholarship and technical mastery. In 1915 he published a landmark performance text, *The Interpretation of the Music of the Seventeenth and Eighteenth Centuries*, the first work of its kind. He settled soon after at Haslemere, Surrey, establishing instrument workshops there and starting, in 1925, an annual festival dedicated to performing early music. Here music that Dolmetsch had unearthed was often played for the first time since its composition on the instruments for which it was intended and in what was hoped to be the original style. The performers were Dolmetsch's family and distinguished circle of friends and pupils, which eventually included the young lutenist Diana Poulton, who was a close family friend in spite of finding Arnold an impatient, bad-tempered, and otherwise poor teacher. Regardless of his shortcomings as a teacher, Dolmetsch introduced many musicians to this repertory, providing them with instruments and the impetus to teach themselves to play. Sir Henry Hadow correctly commented that he 'opened the door to a forgotten treasure-house of beauty'. The festival concerts lacked the polish that later performers were to achieve, but Dolmetsch remained unabashed. He insisted: 'This music is of absolute and not antiquarian importance; it must be played as the composer intended and on the instruments for which it was written with their correct technique; and through it personal music-making can be restored to the home, from which two centuries of professionalism have divorced it' (*DNB*). This passionate and almost obsessive belief led him to turn his children— Hélène, Cécile, Nathalie, Rudolph, and Carl—into versatile performers on many instruments. With his third wife,

Mabel, the family formed a domestic consort every evening, frequently augmented by friends, in which all the participants were expected to perform on several different instruments.

Dolmetsch's improved harpsichords encouraged the use of that instrument for the basso continuo of eighteenth-century operas and oratorios, now a standard practice. His work for viols and lute—exemplified by his three articles in *The Connoisseur* (1904)—was of the greatest antiquarian, although of less musical, interest. His restoration of the recorder reopened early music to the amateur world, and, although his work making early instruments was quickly eclipsed by other specialist builders, the family name is still synonymous with finely crafted recorders.

In 1928, in honour of Dolmetsch's seventieth birthday, the Dolmetsch Foundation was incorporated for the 'encouragement of the revival of early instrumental music'. In 1937 he was granted a civil-list pension; in 1938 he was created a chevalier of the Légion d'honneur; and in 1939 he received the honorary degree of doctor of music from Durham University.

Dolmetsch's private life was complex, especially in the decade before 1903. He was thrice married: first, on 28 May 1878 (just after the birth of their daughter, Hélène), to Marie Morel, of Namur, from whom he separated in 1894 (they were divorced in 1898); secondly, on 11 September 1899, in Zürich, to Elodie Désirée, divorced wife of Dolmetsch's brother Edgard (this marriage also ended in divorce, in September 1903); thirdly, on 23 September 1903, to Mabel (1874–1963), one of his pupils and thirteenth of the fourteen children of John Brookes Johnston, an insurance broker, of Denmark Hill. Dolmetsch's eldest daughter, Hélène, was a fine viola da gamba player, but was estranged from her father from 1901 almost until her death. With his third wife—a musicologist and viol player—he had two daughters and two sons: Rudolph, generally believed to have been the most talented of all the children, died during the Second World War, while Carl *Dolmetsch (1911–1997) perpetuated the style and approach of his father's work. Although the early music revival in Europe was largely due to Dolmetsch's work, his research did not move on as more information became available, and, despite the careful perpetuation of his tradition after his death—at his home, Jesses, Grayswood Road, Haslemere, on 28 February 1940—its influence soon waned as other views about the performance of early music came to predominate.

H. C. G. Matthew and Julia Craig-McFeely

Sources M. Dolmetsch, *Personal recollections of Arnold Dolmetsch* (1957) [with bibliography of Dolmetsch's writings] · M. Campbell, *Dolmetsch: the man and his work* (1975) · R. Donington, *The work and ideas of Arnold Dolmetsch* (1932) · *The Times* (1 March 1940) · W. McNaught, 'Arnold Dolmetsch and his work', *MT*, 81 (1940), 153–5 · *DNB* · *New Grove* · D. Poulton, 'The lute and I', *The Lute*, 33 (1993), 23–30

Archives BL, letters to Henry Newman, Add. MS 69437

Likenesses E. Kapp, drawing, 1921, Barber Institute of Fine Arts, Birmingham · H. Lambert, bromide print, c.1925, NPG [see illus.] · K. Browne, pencil drawing, 1932, NPG · M. Beerbohm, portrait, Haslemere, Surrey · E. Kapp, drawing, Bedales Junior School, Hampshire · N. Lytton, portrait, Haslemere, Surrey · W. Rothenstein, chalk drawings, NPG · W. Rothenstein, portrait, Haslemere, Surrey

Wealth at death £611 4s. 7d.: probate, 21 June 1940, CGPLA Eng. & Wales

Dolmetsch, Carl Frederick (1911–1997), musician, was born on 23 August 1911 at 3 rue de l'Audience, Fontenay-sous-Bois, near Paris, the younger son and youngest child in the family of two sons and two daughters of (Eugène) Arnold *Dolmetsch (1858–1940), musician and musical instrument maker, and his third wife, Mabel Johnston (1874–1963), bass viol player and thirteenth of the fourteen children of John Brookes Johnston, a Scottish insurance broker, of Denmark Hill, London. He had an elder half-sister, Hélène, from his father's first marriage, but saw little of her. From the age of four he was taught the viol and recorder by his father, and as a member of the family viol consort took part, with his sisters Cécile and Nathalie and brother Rudolph, in his first concert tour at the age of eight. For a time he took violin lessons with Carl Flesch and Antonio Brosa. It was he who left the bag containing his father's early eighteenth-century Bressan treble recorder on the platform at Waterloo Station in London in 1919, leading Arnold Dolmetsch, who had taken measurements of the instrument, to experiment until he was able to make his own recorder, marking the beginning of recorder making in England in the twentieth century. Although the family moved to Hampstead in 1914 they spoke French at home, and Dolmetsch never lost his Swiss accent. He was naturalized in 1931. When the Zeppelin raids began in 1917 the family moved to Jesses, Haslemere, Surrey, which remained Dolmetsch's home for the rest of his life. He was educated at St George's Wood, a girls' school in Haslemere, before leaving to work alongside his father in the Dolmetsch workshops. He took part in the first of the Haslemere festivals of early music, started by his father in 1925. On 24 February 1937 he married Mary Douglas Ferguson (1915/16–1995), daughter of James Alexander Ferguson, of Dumfries; they had twin daughters and two sons, one of whom committed suicide in 1966 at the age of twenty-one.

In 1926 Dolmetsch was put in charge of the development and production of recorders in the Haslemere workshops. From the start he experimented with ways of 'improving' the design of the recorder, and he invented a number of mechanical devices, including the tone projector, the bell key for high F♯, and the echo key: this was operated by the chin, opening a hole in the head joint, thus sharpening the pitch and making it possible to blow softly but remain in tune. He fitted these gadgets to his own instruments for his recitals. Dolmetsch made these improvements in the belief that the recorder needed to evolve if it was to survive in the modern world. In 1939 he restored the Chester recorders, four Bressan instruments discovered in 1886, to playing condition.

Dolmetsch gave his first Wigmore Hall recital on 1 February 1939 with a programme including his own *Theme and Variations* for descant recorder and piano, the first solo work written for the recorder in the twentieth century. After this concert the music critic Manuel Jacobs, a pupil of Edgar Hunt, asked ten young British composers to write solo works for the recorder, with the promise of publication by Schotts. A few months later, at the London Contemporary Music Centre, Dolmetsch, with other members of his family and Edgar Hunt, performed a whole concert of modern music for the recorder, including four of these works, most notably Lennox Berkeley's sonatina.

During the Second World War the Dolmetsch workshops were turned over to the mass production of plastic aircraft components. With the death of Arnold Dolmetsch in 1940 and the loss of his brother Rudolph at sea in 1942, Dolmetsch took on full responsibility for the Haslemere workshops. After the war he was able to use his wartime experience to begin mass production of plastic recorders, to meet the growing demand from schools, while continuing to make hand-crafted wooden recorders for the increasing number of amateur players. He became chairman and managing director of Arnold Dolmetsch Ltd in 1963. When a boardroom dispute led to his ejection in 1978, the Dolmetsch family established a rival firm, J. and M. Dolmetsch Ltd, in Haslemere, making wooden recorders and early bows, until the liquidation of Arnold Dolmetsch Ltd in 1982, when they bought back the recorder, early keyboard, and string businesses and the Dolmetsch trade marks, to form Dolmetsch Musical Instruments. Dolmetsch remained chairman until his death.

After the war Dolmetsch, encouraged by Manuel Jacobs, renewed his efforts to get leading British composers interested in writing for the recorder. Each year from 1947 to 1989 (except 1948), accompanied by Joseph Saxby (1910–1997), he gave a recital in the Wigmore Hall which included (except in 1951) at least one specially commissioned work by a British composer. Those who wrote for Dolmetsch included Edmund Rubbra, Arnold Cooke, Robert Simpson, Gordon Jacob, Alan Ridout, Alan Hoddinott, Nicholas Maw, and Michael Berkeley; forty-nine new works were composed in all. From 1955 many were for recorder and strings, or other instruments, performed by members of the Dolmetsch family and others. In response to Dolmetsch's suggestion of a work using the recorder as an obbligato instrument, Rubbra wrote *Cantata pastorale* (1957). In 1982 Donald Swann wrote *Rhapsody from Within* to celebrate the fifty years' partnership of Dolmetsch and Saxby. Although not all these pieces worked, because some composers did not understand the instrument, they were enormously important in building up a modern recorder repertory. Dolmetsch recorded many of the works, most of which were published. Although at first he was open-minded about the avant-garde music written on the continent from the 1960s for a new generation of players such as Frans Brüggen, he later came to hate it, and told his composers he did not want any avant-garde gimmicks. He also lost touch with developments on the continent in the 1960s in the performance of early music, and the style of Dolmetsch and his followers came to seem very old-fashioned to adherents of the Dutch school of recorder playing.

Dolmetsch was the first virtuoso recorder player in England in the twentieth century, and through his recitals, broadcasts, and lecture tours in England and abroad, especially in North America, which he first visited in 1935 and where he toured annually between 1961 and 1981, he did more than anyone else to establish the recorder as a serious musical instrument. In addition to making and performing on recorders, he contributed articles to journals, wrote the widely used *School Recorder Book*, and with Layton Ring edited the series Il Flauto Dolce for Universal Edition. He played in every one of the seventy-two Haslemere festivals, where he had a devoted following, from 1925 until a few weeks before his death, and was director from 1940 to 1996, for many years leading the orchestra from the violin. He also started the Dolmetsch summer school in 1948. He was one of the founders of the Society of Recorder Players in 1937, and its joint musical director.

Dolmetsch was appointed CBE in 1954. After 1960, when he was given an honorary DLitt by the University of Exeter, he was always referred to as Dr Carl. He was divorced from his first wife, Mary, in 1961. On 15 May 1997 he married Greta Florence Matthews (*b.* 1918/19), daughter of William Matthews, soldier. She had been his secretary for nearly sixty years. He died of non-Hodgkin's lymphoma at Haslemere Hospital on 11 July 1997, and was buried at St Bartholomew's Church, Haslemere, on 17 July. He was survived by his second wife, Greta.

Cécile Dolmetsch (1904–1997), musician, the eldest child of Arnold and Mabel Dolmetsch, was born on 22 March 1904 at 5 Lincoln Road, Dorking, Surrey, just before the family moved abroad to spend seven years in the United States followed by three years in France. She began viol and recorder lessons with her father at an early age, played in the family consort as a child, and performed at the Haslemere festival every year until 1990. She married Charles Leslie Clifford Ward (1901/2–1989?), a craftsman employed in the Dolmetsch workshops, on 7 September 1925; they had two sons and two adopted daughters. She became an expert on the *pardessus de viole*, a descant viol, and was for many years the only person to perform on it in public. Through her research in French libraries she found music by composers such as Thomas Marc and Jean Barrière and was able to build up a repertory for the instrument. With her sister Nathalie she founded the Viola da Gamba Society in 1948, and she became president after her sister's death in 1989. She remained active until her death from heart failure on 9 August 1997 at the Royal Surrey County Hospital, Guildford, and was buried at St Bartholomew's Church, Haslemere, on 20 August.

ANNE PIMLOTT BAKER

Sources E. O'Kelly, *The recorder today* (1990) · M. Campbell, *Dolmetsch: the man and his work* (1975) · J. M. Thomson, *Recorder profiles* (1972), 30–35 · N. O'Loughlin, 'The recorder in 20th century music', *Early Music*, 10 (1982), 36–7 · C. Dolmetsch, 'An introduction to the recorder in modern British music', *The Consort*, 17 (July 1960), 47–56 · *Recorder News* (1937–63) · *Recorder and Music Magazine* (1963–89) · *Recorder Magazine* (1990–97) · *New Grove* · *The Times* (15 July 1997) · *Recorder Magazine* (Dec 1997) · *WWW* · private information

(2004) • b. cert. [Cécile Dolmetsch] • m. cert. • m. cert. [Charles Leslie Clifford Ward and Cécile Dolmetsch] • d. cert. • d. cert. [Cécile Dolmetsch] • *CGPLA Eng. & Wales* (1997–8) • *The Independent* (14 July 1997) • *The Independent* (19 Sept 1997) • *Daily Telegraph* (15 July 1997) • *The Guardian* (14 July 1997) • *The Guardian* (15 Sept 1997)

Archives Haslemere, papers

Likenesses group portrait, photograph, 1923 (Dolmetsch family), repro. in *The Independent* (14 July 1997) • S. Hudson, photograph, repro. in *Recorder Magazine* (June 1991) • group portrait, photograph (with daughters and grand-daughter), repro. in *The Times* • photograph, repro. in *Recorder Magazine* (Dec 1997) • photograph, repro. in *Daily Telegraph* • photograph (as a young man), repro. in *The Guardian* (14 July 1997) • photograph (Cécile Dolmetsch), repro. in *The Guardian* (15 Sept 1997) • photograph (Cécile Dolmetsch), repro. in *The Independent* (19 Sept 1997) • photographs, Hult. Arch.

Wealth at death £525,434: probate, 1998, *CGPLA Eng. & Wales* • £180,000—Cécile Dolmetsch: probate, 1997, *CGPLA Eng. & Wales*

Dolmetsch, Cécile (1904–1997). *See under* Dolmetsch, Carl Frederick (1911–1997).

Domangart (*d.* 673). *See under* Dál Riata, kings of (*act. c.*500–*c.*850).

Domett, Alfred (1811–1887), writer and premier of New Zealand, was born on 20 May 1811 at Camberwell Grove, Camberwell, Surrey, the sixth of the nine children of Nathaniel Domett, a shipowner, and his wife, Elizabeth Curling. He was educated at Stockwell Park House and then St John's College, Cambridge (1829–32), but left university without completing a degree. From 1833 to 1835 he travelled in North America and the West Indies, then returned to read law at the Middle Temple in 1835; he was called to the bar in 1841. He also pursued his literary interests, publishing volumes of poetry in 1833 and 1839. Robert Browning was a family friend.

In April 1842 Domett followed the example of his cousin William Curling, and emigrated to New Zealand on the *Sir Charles Forbes*. He attained early prominence in the colony through his involvement with the *Nelson Examiner* (1843–5), while his petition of November 1845 for the recall of Governor Robert FitzRoy won settler acclaim for its cogent criticism of the humanitarian emphasis in contemporary imperial policies towards the Maori.

Domett's thirty-year career in New Zealand encompassed both political and administrative office. He was appointed by Governor George Grey to the legislative council in 1846, and later served as a provincial councillor for Nelson (1857–63) and as the elected member of the house of representatives for Nelson (November 1855–November 1860) and Nelson City (December 1860–January 1866). He led a short-lived ministry from August 1862 until October 1863, which was notable only for his advocacy of a vigorous policy of military conquest and confiscation during the New Zealand wars. In June 1866 he became a legislative councillor, a political appointment which he held, despite concurrent employment in the public service, until his retirement in 1871.

Domett's administrative contribution in these foundation years was outstanding. An energetic and efficient colonial secretary for New Munster (1848–53), he produced two significant compilations, *Statistics of the Province of New Munster, New Zealand, from 1841 to 1848* (1849); and *The*

Alfred Domett (1811–1887), by unknown photographer, after 1870

Ordinances of New Zealand Passed in the First Ten Sessions of the General Legislative Council, AD 1841 to AD 1849 (1850). In November 1851 he was also gazetted civil secretary to the general government. With the dissolution of crown colony administration, in February 1854 he took up the position of commissioner of crown lands and resident magistrate in the Ahuriri district of Hawke's Bay, and named the streets of Napier to commemorate those countrymen whose military, literary, or scientific achievements he admired. In 1856 he combined political representation with the responsibilities of commissioner of crown lands in Nelson.

A continuing interest in land administration led Domett to retain the portfolio of crown lands during his brief premiership. Political successors acknowledged his expertise by changing the position of secretary of crown lands from a political to a civil service post, with Domett taking up the appointment in January 1864. Over the ensuing eight years the brown-eyed intellectual, whose irritable public manner belied underlying qualities of gentleness and vision, transformed the crown lands office into an efficient regulatory agency for overseeing the implementation of general government land policies. Legislation passed in 1870 to prevent paid politicians from holding civil service positions specifically excluded Domett.

Upon his retirement in 1871, Domett returned to England with his wife, Mary George, a widowed Wellington schoolteacher whom he had married on 3 November 1856. He pursued his literary interests more actively, the epic verse *Ranolf and Amohia: a South-Sea Day-Dream*, long derided by critics, being published in London in 1872. His poetic accomplishments were relatively minor and his reputation derives more from his personal associations, particularly his friendship with Browning, than his own verse. A pivotal role in the establishment of the New Zealand parliament's general assembly library was his most enduring literary endeavour.

Domett was created CMG in 1880. He died at his home, 32 St Charles Square, Kensington, London, on 2 November 1887, survived by his wife. JEANINE GRAHAM

Sources B. R. Patterson, 'Reading between the lines', PhD diss., Victoria University of Wellington, 1984 · J. Graham, 'Domett, Alfred', *DNZB*, vol. 1 · A. H. McLintock, ed., *An encyclopaedia of New Zealand*, 3 vols. (1966) · W. Gisborne, *New Zealand rulers and statesmen from 1840 to 1897*, rev. edn (1897) · *CGPLA Eng. & Wales* (1887)
Archives BL, corresp. and diary, Add. MSS 45558–45561, 45876 · BL, notes on Robert Browning's *Sordello*, Ashley 247 · NL NZ, Turnbull L., annotated copy of *Flotsam and jetsam* | Auckland Public Library, letters to Sir George Grey
Likenesses photograph, after 1870, NL NZ, Turnbull L. [*see illus.*]
Wealth at death £4340 10s. 2d.: probate, 23 Nov 1887, *CGPLA Eng. & Wales*

Domett, Sir William (1752–1828), naval officer, was possibly born in Hawkchurch parish in Dorset; details of his parents and upbringing are unknown. He entered the navy in 1769 under the patronage of Captain Alexander Hood, who introduced him to Captain Reynolds, under whom he served, first as able seaman and then as midshipman, in the *Quebec* (36 guns) for three years in the West Indies. He then joined the sloop *Scorpion* (Captain Elphinstone) in the Mediterranean and was in her for two-and-a-half years before returning to England and serving in the *Marlborough* (74 guns) for a month; from her he transferred as master's mate to the *Surprise* (28 guns, Captain Linzee), in which he served for two years on the Newfoundland station. He was still in the *Surprise* when, with the outbreak of the American War of Independence, she was the advance ship of the squadron that raised the rebel siege of Quebec in May 1775. Thereafter the *Surprise* went to Newfoundland, where Linzee recommended Domett to Admiral John Montagu, who made him acting lieutenant in the *Romney* (50 guns). Domett proved a 'persevering and deserving officer' (Ralfe, 2.419) who studied his profession but he was in the *Romney* for only four months, returning to England with Montagu at the end of the year. A midshipman from 5 February 1777, he was appointed to Alexander Hood's ship, the *Robust* (74 guns), and was present at the battle of Ushant on 27 July 1778. After being appointed lieutenant on 27 December 1778 Domett remained in her under Captain Cosby until she had led Arbuthnot's line in the action off Cape Henry on 16 March 1781. He then moved to the *Invincible* (74 guns, Captain Sir Charles Saxton), and was present at the action off Chesapeake on 5 September 1781; after this he was taken, as his signal officer, to the West Indies by Sir Samuel Hood, in the *Barfleur* (90 guns). He served in that demanding capacity in the operations against St Kitts in January 1782 and in the battle of the Saints (12 April 1782). When the first lieutenant of the *Barfleur* was promoted Domett was appointed to his place. Hood, detached from Rodney's fleet, captured four enemy ships in the Mona passage on 19 April. Rodney promoted Domett to the command of one, the sloop *Ceres*, on 21 August 1782 and sent him to England with dispatches. He was advanced to post rank on 9 September 1782 and, at the particular request of Alexander Hood (now Rear-Admiral Sir Alexander Hood), was appointed his flag captain in the *Queen* (98 guns), one of Lord Howe's fleet which relieved Gibraltar and repelled the enemy attack off Cape Spartel on 20 October. The Hood 'interest' with William Pitt, and Domett's growing service reputation, served him well: though unemployed at the end of the war, on 23 June 1786 he was appointed senior officer at Leith in the *Champion* (24 guns).

On 13 May 1788 Domett was appointed to the *Pomone* (28 guns), which was bound first for the African coast and then the West Indies, and returned to England in 1789. Here, at Admiral Milbanke's request, Domett transferred, on 9 May, to the flagship *Salisbury* (50 guns), and went to Newfoundland, where Milbanke was appointed governor and commander-in-chief. On 10 May 1790 Domett was appointed to the *London*, fitting for Sir Alexander Hood's flag, in the Spanish armament, the mobilization for the Nootka Sound crisis, and joined Howe's fleet at Torbay. But being paid off he moved on 6 December 1790 to the *Pegasus* (28 guns), and once more to Newfoundland, where he stayed until returning to England at the end of 1791. Admiral Goodall, appointed commander-in-chief in the Mediterranean, then asked for Domett as his flag captain and Domett was appointed to the *Romney* (22 March 1792), but the outbreak of the French war in the following year led to his recall and appointment (14 June) as flag captain to Sir Alexander Hood in the *Royal George* (100 guns). In her he was present at the battle of 1 June 1794 and the battle off Lorient (23 June 1795) where Alexander Hood (now Lord Bridport) was commander-in-chief. After Lorient, Bridport especially commended Domett's conduct and assistance and his 'active and attentive mind' (Ralfe, 2.421) and entrusted him with dispatches of the victory. Domett remained captain of the *Royal George* for a record seven-and-a-half years, during which she was considered 'one of the best disciplined and most expert ships' (ibid.).

Domett's personal and professional loyalties lay with the Hood family, and he corresponded with Bridport after the admiral's retirement, keeping him informed of matters of naval interest. When St Vincent took command of the Channel Fleet in May 1800 Domett was critical of his abilities and wary of St Vincent's early favours to Bridport's appointees. Hearing of vacancies among the marine regiments, in May 1800 he gloomily supposed 'upwards of *thirty* years constant and faithful service' would give him no chance (Domett to Bridport, 19 May 1800, BL, Add. MS 35201, fols. 100–01), so he must have been pleased at his appointment as colonel of the Portsmouth division of marines in January 1801. His appointment as captain of the fleet in August 1800 may have been equally surprising to him, since he told Bridport that Sir

Thomas Troubridge had long been appointed to this post and was longing to take it up, but that the matter was settled between Lord Spencer and St Vincent. Domett retained his position until 29 October, taking the *Royal George* to Portsmouth to hoist Sir Hyde Parker's flag, and relieving St Vincent, whose health had broken down. Domett himself moved to the *Belleisle* (74 guns) but on 17 February 1801 he was appointed, in the *London*, captain of the fleet to Parker, commander of the fleet sent to the Baltic to break the combination of states formed there against Britain.

It was thanks to Domett's advice that the fleet entered the Baltic directly through the sound rather than through the great belt. Parker, on consulting Vansittart and Nelson, had first begun to enter by the belt; Copenhagen was then to be attacked over the grounds by the 64-gun ships and smaller vessels. Domett disagreed with this plan, arguing that the ships sent would not constitute a sufficient force, that the wind which carried the ships into the attack would prevent them returning, and that if they were crippled or repulsed, shoaling water would make it impossible to help them and the fleet would be divided, all of which the Danes knew well. Domett also reminded Parker that going into the sound they would pass closer to a fortified point of land than to Kronenborg Castle, which they sought to avoid by going through the belt. These considerations induced Parker to change his plan and enter the sound. However, he mentioned none of this in his public letter after the victory at Copenhagen, though he had told Domett that he was obliged to him 'for the *whole* and shall acknowledge it to the last day of *my Life*' (Domett to Bridport, 4 May 1801, BL, Add. MS 35201, fols. 136–9).

On arrival at Copenhagen, Parker consulted Nelson, Graves, and Domett about an attack, which Domett supported, but his name once more was not mentioned in the public dispatch. Parker apologized for this omission and said he would try to put it right, but Domett rightly felt aggrieved. 'I am left quite in the background from his neglect, or rather forgetfulness and the public know of no such man in the Fleet' (Domett to Bridport, 4 May 1801, BL, Add. MS 35201, fols. 136–9). On Parker's return to England Nelson took command and expressly asked Domett to remain captain of the fleet, which he did, in the *St George* (98 guns) from 14 May 1801, before returning to England with Nelson. On 6 July 1801 he resumed command of the *Belleisle*, but on 28 September he was appointed to the *Ville de Paris* (110 guns) as captain of the fleet to Admiral Cornwallis, commander-in-chief of the Channel Fleet, who had asked for him. He held this post until the peace of Amiens.

During that brief period of peace Domett served on the Irish station as senior officer with a broad pennant, but the renewal of war in 1803 again saw him as Cornwallis's captain of the fleet, from 6 June to 23 April 1804, when he was promoted rear-admiral of the blue. He was ordered to hoist his flag on the North Sea station (26 April), but declined on health grounds and in December was appointed one of the commissioners for revising the civil affairs of the navy, whose chairman was Sir Charles Middleton.

On 9 November 1805 Domett was promoted rear-admiral of the white and on 28 April 1808 rear-admiral of the red, while on 9 May he joined the Board of Admiralty, a position in which he served until 23 October 1813. Further promotion, to vice-admiral of the white, followed on 25 October 1809; four days after leaving the Admiralty, on 27 October 1813, he succeeded Sir Robert Calder as commander-in-chief at Plymouth, and on 4 December he became vice-admiral of the red. He served at Plymouth for fifteen months, resigning because a foot injury made him increasingly lame. He was promoted admiral of the blue (12 August 1819) and admiral of the white (27 May 1825). On 2 January 1815 he was nominated KCB, and on 16 May 1820 GCB.

Although, as he feared, he was not well known to the public, Domett was held in general esteem by his colleagues for his professional abilities. He was almost constantly employed because of these and took part in many battles. No one had more experience as captain of the fleet, under many admirals, 'an eulogium', as his monument in Hawkchurch parish church says, 'on his character and talents more eloquent than words and more durable than marble'. His ships were always in good order and discipline and ready for service, seldom suffering in bad weather and causing less expense in repairs than those of any other commander, according to Ralfe. So it is not surprising that Domett, the model of a professional seaman, backed by powerful interest earlier in his life, achieved a highly successful career. Domett never married. The family were long settled on the borders of Dorset and Devon at Hawkchurch, not far from Bridport's estate at Cricket St Thomas. Domett bought a considerable part of the manor of Phillyholm in the parish when he was one of the Admiralty commissioners, perhaps at the same time Lord Bridport bought Wild Court Manor in the same parish in 1806. Domett made his home at Westhay House, Hawkchurch, in retirement and died there, suddenly, on 19 May 1828 aged seventy-six. He was buried in a family vault in the churchyard. A monument in the parish church records his achievements.

Domett's nephew Lieutenant William Domett was lost in the schooner *Vigilant* on 9 February 1804: 'a promising young officer', wrote Commodore Samuel Hood in reporting it, 'who was succeeding fast to the skill of his gallant uncle, the captain of the Channel fleet' (*Naval Chronicle*, 11, 1804, 494). P. K. CRIMMIN

Sources J. Ralfe, *The naval biography of Great Britain*, 2 (1828), 419–25 · J. Hutchins, *The history and antiquities of the county of Dorset*, 3rd edn, ed. W. Shipp and J. W. Hodson, 4 (1874), 46–50 · D. Syrett and R. L. DiNardo, *The commissioned sea officers of the Royal Navy, 1660–1815*, rev. edn, Occasional Publications of the Navy RS, 1 (1994) · D. Lyon, *The sailing navy list: all the ships of the Royal Navy, built, purchased and captured, 1688–1860* (1993) · *Naval Chronicle*, 15 (1806), 1–13 · BL, Bridport MSS, Add. MS 35201, vol. 11, general correspondence, vol. 9 (1800–6 · lieutenants' passing certificates, PRO, ADM 6/22, 23, 24, 27, 28; ADM 107/6 · 17 letters from Domett, 1811–13, NMM, Foley MSS · J. Marshall, *Royal naval biography*, 1/1 (1823), 243–9 · *GM*, 1st ser., 98/1 (1828), 561 · PRO, PROB 11/1745–501

Archives BL, letters to Lord Bridport and others · NA Scot., corresp. with Lord Melville · NMM, letters to Sir Thomas Foley

Likenesses Bartolozzi, Landseer, Ryder, and Stow, group portrait, line engraving, pubd 1803 (*Commemoration of the victory of June 1st 1794*; after R. Smirke), BM, NPG · Ridley and Holl, stipple, pubd 1806 (after Bowyer), NPG · Ridley and Holl, lithograph (after Bowyer), repro. in W. L. Clowes, *The Royal Navy: a history from the earliest times to the present* (1897–1903), vol. 4, p. 265 · engraving (after Bowyer), repro. in *Naval Chronicle*, facing p. 1

Wealth at death £600 in annuities to family members; plus £1500 in trust to great-nephews and nieces; plus estate at Westhay and farm in Hawkchurch parish: will, PRO, PROB 11/1745–501

Dominis, Marco Antonio de (1560–1624), archbishop of Spalato and ecumenist, was born on the island of Rab off the eastern Adriatic coast. He was from a prominent family that may have been South Slavic in origin but which had used an Italian name since the fourteenth century. He received his early education at a Jesuit school in Loreto in Italy and entered the Society of Jesus in 1579. Following further education in Verona and Padua he became a professor of mathematics at the University of Padua and of rhetoric and philosophy at the University of Brescia. He made significant contributions to the science of optics during his academic career. His *De radiis visus et lucis*, published in Venice in 1611, analysed the refractions of light in droplets of water. In 1597 he resigned from the Society of Jesus in order to accept appointment as bishop of Segna, in Habsburg-controlled Croatia. He made strenuous efforts to pacify the Uskok pirates, refugees from the Ottoman empire who preyed on both Turkish and Venetian shipping, but met with little success. In 1602 he became archbishop of Spalato (Split) and primate of Dalmatia and Croatia. Spalato was in territory controlled by Venice, but much of the archdiocese was in Ottoman hands.

De Dominis took the side of Venice in the crisis over Venetian–papal relations in 1606–7 and wrote, anonymously, two manuscript treatises dealing with the jurisdictional issues in dispute. He argued that papal jurisdiction did not extend to temporal affairs and that the pope had no right to interfere in the affairs of civil governments when there was no issue of religious faith involved. He had reason to resent papal actions in the administration of his archdiocese. He was required to pay a pension to another ecclesiastic, Marzio Andreucci, who became bishop of Traù in 1604, precluding, in de Dominis's opinion, any need for a pension. During his years as archbishop he developed a theory of how the universal church ought to be governed, on the model of the early church; this was the basis of his *De republica ecclesiastica*, eventually published in three volumes. King James VI and I's ambassadors in Venice, Sir Henry Wotton, Sir Dudley Carleton, and then Wotton again, along with Wotton's chaplain, William Bedell, cultivated de Dominis's friendship, seeing in him a critic of the papacy whose activities might open the way for protestantism in the Venetian territories or who might take the protestant side in the religious and political controversies that revolved about the oath of allegiance. By 1616, de Dominis had been promised a place of dignity and modest reward by George Abbot, archbishop of Canterbury, and he made plans to migrate to England. By agreement with the papal authorities, who

were not aware of these plans, he renounced his episcopal see in favour of his nephew, Sforza Ponzone.

De Dominis set out for England in September 1616 disguised as a Ragusan merchant in the company of two British subjects. Travelling by way of northern Italy, Switzerland, the Rhineland, and the Netherlands, he arrived in England in December 1616. His *Manifestation*, explaining his departure from Italy, was published in Latin and Italian in Heidelberg (*Consilium profectionis*) in autumn 1616 and in an English translation in London after his arrival there. French and Dutch translations were also published on the continent in 1616. His migration was a sensation in the religiously divided Europe of his day. The reasons he gave included his hope of finding greater intellectual freedom in Britain and being able to encourage a reunion of the church as a community of churches sharing a common faith. It seems clear that he also wanted to find an opportunity, lacking even in Venice, of publishing his *De republica ecclesiastica*. The English Jesuits John Floyd and John Sweet wrote rejoinders accusing de Dominis of seeking material gains. They poured scorn on his intended efforts to bring unity to the warring religious sects. In England, de Dominis became a guest of Archbishop Abbot at Lambeth Palace and was given a warm welcome at court by King James. Soon afterwards he received significant appointments: dean of the Chapel Royal at Windsor and master of the Savoy, the hospital with chapel attached, in London. On occasion he preached at the Italian church, the chapel of the Mercers' Company set aside for Italian residents and visitors. In summer 1617 he visited both Cambridge and Oxford and received doctor's degrees at both universities. De Dominis assisted Archbishop Abbot in the consecration of Nicholas Felton and George Montaigne as bishops in December 1617.

De Dominis's stay in England was marked by publications widely circulated in Britain and on the continent. His sermon on 30 November 1617 at the Italian church accused the Church of Rome of having discarded the map and compass, namely the scriptures and the first four general councils, but nevertheless asserted that the churches of Christendom shared a common legacy of faith. The sermon was published in London in Italian and English in 1617 and on the continent in Latin and German in 1618 and in French in 1619. His Latin *Papatus romanus* (1617) was a collection of passages about the papacy from the church fathers, the general councils, and canon law, showing that, in earlier times, ecclesiastical power had been shared among Rome and the other major sees. His *The Rockes of Christian Shipwracke*—published in English, Italian, French, and German in 1618—argued that papal claims to supremacy were obstacles or rocks in the way of the church's successful voyage. His most important statement on how to reunite the church and to secure peace and concord in Europe was his massive Latin work, *De republica ecclesiastica*, which dealt with most of the current theological and ecclesiological controversies. The first volume, published in London in 1617, contained the first four of a projected series of ten books. The second, published in London in 1620, contained the fifth and sixth books. The third volume, containing books seven and nine (eight and ten never appeared), was published in Hanau in 1622. He sought to provide a basis on which the 'Bishops of the Holy Catholic Church', to whom the preface to the first volume was addressed, could unite to oppose papal intrusions and to overcome the dissensions that afflicted the church. In refuting the prominent Roman Catholic theologian Francisco Suarez on the exercise of the royal supremacy in England, he argued that the Church of England was an exemplary case of a reformed church in which the ancient orders of ministry had been preserved, the eucharistic recalling of Christ's sacrifice was celebrated with great solemnity, and parish churches were dedicated to the saints and martyrs and to the Blessed Virgin Mary. The universal church could best be reunited, he contended, by an ecumenical council attended by bishops from the east as well as the west and supported by the temporal rulers. Protestants whose churches lacked bishops would certainly need to be represented at the council. There, theological agreement would be sought on the basis of the scriptures and the decrees of the general councils. If perfect union could not be achieved, differences among the churches might be tolerated where they did not compromise the fundamentals of the faith.

De Dominis assisted in the publication in London of Paolo Sarpi's celebrated *Historia del Concilio Tridentino* in 1619, published in an English translation as *The Historie of the Councel of Trent* in the following year. Sarpi sought to show that the opportunity of reconciling Roman Catholics and protestants by means of a council had been lost at Trent, partly through the tactics employed by the popes and their agents. De Dominis's dedication of the work to King James implied that he had brought the manuscript to England from Venice to be published. In fact, it was sent in weekly packets from Venice by the English lawyer and scholar Nathaniel Brent to Archbishop Abbot. It was Brent who translated the work into English. But de Dominis knew Sarpi and may have brought a sample of the work to England. In 1617 de Dominis offered advice to the states general of the United Provinces on how to resolve theological disputes in the Netherlands in a moderate way, and in 1619 he wrote to Cyril Lukaris, patriarch of Alexandria, to propose that the Church of England and the Greek Orthodox church formalize the closer relations that had developed between them during James's reign.

In spring 1622, in a remarkable reversal of his earlier migration, de Dominis returned to the continent and to the communion of the Roman Catholic church. He explained his reasons in *Second Manifesto*, published in 1623 in Rome as *Sui reditus ex Anglia consilium exponit*, and in an English translation in Liège in the same year. He had found, he wrote, that the Church of England was deeply infected with heresy and he acknowledged errors in his own work since his migration to England. In a long letter to Joseph Hall, dean of Worcester, dated 1 March 1622—not published until 1660 as *De pace religionis*—he said that he had found the leaders of the English church less willing than their king to recognize the common ground shared by the Church of England and the Roman Catholic church. A further explanation is found in his written answers to interrogations by English ecclesiastical officials in early 1622, before he was given permission to leave the country. He pointed out that the recent accession of Pope Gregory XV, a friend from earlier years in Italy, had given him a potential ally in the cause of religious reconciliation. He received absolution in Brussels from the papal nuncio in May 1622 and journeyed to Rome where he was given housing, provisions, and a stipend. But Gregory XV died in summer 1623, with the result that de Dominis's position became less certain. In April 1624 he was put in prison by the Inquisition while his teachings were examined, and there he died of a fever on 9 September 1624. The Congregation of the Holy Office concluded its case by decreeing, on 21 December 1624, that he had died as a relapsed heretic. As a result his body and his books were burnt at campo dei Fiori, Rome. Among the items considered by the Inquisition was a plan, presumably written after his return, for a reunion involving the Church of Rome, the Church of England, and the reformed churches (Bibliothèque de l'Arsenal, MS 4111, 77–83). It seems to have persuaded the inquisitors that he had returned to his previous errors.

Archbishop Abbot, in a letter to Sir Thomas Roe, the British ambassador in Constantinople, described de Dominis in November 1622 as a *bestaccio* (little beast) who had never thanked his British hosts for their generosity and hospitality. Thomas Middleton's play of 1624, *A Game of Chess*, represented de Dominis as a fat bishop, worldly, proud, and gullible, who fell victim to the machinations of the black knight (the Spanish ambassador Gondomar) to return him to the kingdom of darkness. Bishop Richard Neile, who published a collection of official documents concerning de Dominis's departure, called him, in the subtitle of the book, 'a man for many masters'. Though attacked by Roman Catholic writers during his sojourn in England and by protestant writers after his return to the Roman obedience, he was a pioneer in the cause of reconciliation among Christians, a cause to which most of his contemporaries were unresponsive. His personal flaws—including, according to many observers, avarice, overweening ambition, and arrogance—also impeded the ecumenical project to which he was passionately committed. His major work, the *De republica ecclesiastica*, is a considerable achievement in the breadth of its subject matter and scholarship and in its provocative theological and historical arguments. W. B. PATTERSON

Sources N. Malcolm, *De Dominis (1560–1624): Venetian, Anglican, ecumenist, and relapsed heretic* (1984) • W. B. Patterson, *King James VI and I and the reunion of Christendom* (1997), 220–59 • D. Nedeljhović, *Marko Dominis u nauci i utopiji na delu* (1975) • A. Russo, *Marc'Antonio De Dominis, arcivescovo di Spalato e apostata (1560–1624)* (1965) • *CSP dom.*, 1611–25 • R. Neile, *M. Ant. de D[omi]nis, archbishop of Spalato, his shiftings in religion: a man for many masters* (1624) • M. A. De Dominis, *Scritti giurisdizionalistici inediti*, ed. A. Russo (1965) • *A relation sent from Rome of the processe, sentence, and execution done upon the body, picture, and bookes of Marcus Antonius de Dominis, archbishop of Spalato, after his death* (1624) • De Dominis MSS, Bibliothèque de l'Arsenal,

Paris, MS 4111, 5–84 • state papers, Venetian, PRO, SP 99/16, fols. 2r–2v; 99/17, fols. 72–75v, 190–91 • F. Yates, *Renaissance and reform: the Italian contribution: collected essays*, 3 vols. (1983), 189–217 • *The negotiations of Sir Thomas Roe, in his embassy to the Ottoman Porte, from ... 1621 to 1628*, ed. S. Richardson (1740), 102–3 • C. Hartsoeker, ed., *Praestantium ac eruditorum virorum epistolae ecclesiasticae et theologicae*, 3rd edn (1704), 482–5, 488–90 • J. H. Hessels, ed., *Ecclesiae Londino-Batavae archivum*, 2: *Epistulae et tractatus cum Reformationis* (1889), 946–54 • P. Limborch, *Historia Inquisitionis* (1692) **Archives** Bibliothèque de l'Arsenal, Paris, MSS • PRO, state papers, Venetian, SP 99/16, 99/17 | Bodl. Oxf., Tanner MSS, incl. parts of *De republica ecclesiastica* **Likenesses** J. Bill, line engraving, 1617, NPG • R. Elstrack, line engraving, 1617 (after M. Mierevelot), NPG • W. J. Delkf, line engraving (after M. Mierevelot), BM, NPG • oils, Chatsworth House, Derbyshire

Domnall Brecc (d. 642/3), king of Dál Riata, was overking of the Dalriada in Scotland and Ireland [*see also* Dál Riata, kings of]. The epithet Brecc, usually translated 'the Freckled', taken together with the name of his father, *Eochaid Buide, 'the Yellow' [*see under* Dál Riata, kings of], suggests a fair family complexion. In 622 Domnall is said to have fought at Cend Delgthen (probably in Meath) in an internal conflict between southern Uí Néill. His motives are unknown, but this is the only recorded battle in which he was on the winning side.

Eochaid Buide died about 629. His successor, Connad Cerr, was, according to one group of texts, a brother of Domnall, but there is more convincing evidence that Connad belonged to the Comgall (Cowal) branch of the Dalriada in Britain. He died in the same year, in Ireland. His successor is said to have been his son Ferchar, but there is evidence that Ferchar's reign came later, and that Connad's immediate successor was Domnall Brecc.

A badly displaced annal, which may belong to c.635, records a defeat of Domnall Brecc 'in Calathros' (A. O. Anderson, 1.158), apparently a district near Loch Awe. In 637 Congal Cáech, the overking of the Ulaid in north-east Ireland, was attacked by the head of the northern Uí Néill, Domnall, son of Áed. In the battle of Moira, in Down, Congal was killed. Domnall Brecc had been his ally, and, though apparently not personally present at Moira, was said to have wasted the province of Domnall son of Áed. His abandonment of his family's traditional loyalty to the family of Áed was thought to have brought about the fulfilment of a prophecy made by Columba to Domnall's grandfather *Aedán (or Áedan) mac Gabrán (though not, apparently, in Domnall Brecc's lifetime).

After 637 there is no word of Domnall Brecc in Ireland. In 638 there was a 'battle of Glenn Mureson in which Domnall Brecc's people fled' (A. O. Anderson, 1.163); the place is unidentified, but is assumed to be in Scotland. His last battle was fought in December of 642 or 643 in Strathcarron, east of the Kilsyth hills, against Owen, king of the Dumbarton Britons. A fragment of Welsh panegyric verse (the *Gododdin*) says that Domnall was killed after he had 'fired' a British 'town', and adds, with a note of exultation, that 'the head of Domnall Brecc, ravens gnawed it' (Jackson, 47). The cause of the affair is unknown, but it should

perhaps be placed within the context of a struggle for supremacy between Dál Riata and Dumbarton.

From 637 Domnall Brecc seems to have had to share the overkingship of the Dalriada with Ferchar, Connad Cerr's son. After Domnall's death, Ferchar reigned alone until he died, probably about 651. Domnall left at least two sons: Cathusach, who died in 650, and Domangart, who reigned from 660 to 673 and was the ancestor of the later Scottish kings.   MARJORIE O. ANDERSON

Sources *Ann. Ulster* • A. O. Anderson, ed. and trans., *Early sources of Scottish history, AD 500 to 1286*, 2 vols. (1922); repr. with corrections (1990) • M. O. Anderson, *Kings and kingship in early Scotland*, rev. edn (1980), 253, 270, 281, 286 • *Adomnán's Life of Columba*, ed. and trans. A. O. Anderson and M. O. Anderson, rev. edn, rev. M. O. Anderson, OMT (1991), 188–91 • J. Bannerman, *Studies in the history of Dalriada* (1974) • K. H. Jackson, *The 'Gododdin': the oldest Scottish poem* (1969), 47, 98

Domnall mac Áeda (d. 642), high-king of Ireland, was, in the eyes of the monks of Iona, the Irish counterpart to Oswald, king of the Northumbrians (d. 642): both were chosen to be the subjects of Columba's prophetic blessing. Adomnán tells a story of Domnall being presented to Columba on the Ridge of Cet by his foster-parents, probably on the occasion of a royal meeting between his father, Áed mac Ainmirech, Áedán mac Gabráin, king of Dál Riata, and probably others—a meeting which the annals of Ulster date to 575. Columba delivered a blessing in the manner of an Old Testament patriarch and prophet: 'This boy will in the end outlive all his brothers, and will be a very famous king' (*Life of Columba*, 1.10). He would even achieve that feat, as desirable as it was rare among Irish kings, of dying in peace on his own bed and in his own house. The chronicle of Ireland, at this stage derived from annals written on Iona, gave him the title 'king of Ireland' at his death in 642, an unusual and probably intentionally complimentary variant on 'king of Tara' (high-king of Ireland). Yet Domnall achieved this distinction only late in his career and by means of some very hard fighting.

According to the *Ban-Shenchus*, Domnall was married to Dúinsech and he probably became king of Cenél Conaill after the death in 615 of his brother, Máel Cobo, at the hands of Suibne Menn of Cenél nÉogain. Suibne Menn thereby became his principal enemy among the Uí Néill, a double misfortune in that Cenél Conaill and Cenél nÉogain had usually prospered only when in alliance, and, moreover, Suibne Menn was an energetic ruler who himself briefly gained the position of high-king. As late as 628 Domnall was defeated by Suibne Menn; but in the same year Domnall's position was again strengthened by someone else's action, when Suibne Menn was killed by the king of the Cruithni and of the province of Ulster, Congal Cáech (d. 637). Domnall, by ravaging Leinster, then demonstrated his intention to take the high-kingship. In the next year, 629, he defeated Congal Cáech at a battle not far to the west of Coleraine, close to Congal's borders. Adomnán's life of Columba refers to this battle as a victory of the Uí Néill over the Cruithni, thereby suggesting that Domnall was now accepted as the ruler of the Uí

Néill. In the next few years, however, the unity of the Uí Néill collapsed: a feud within Cenél nEógain was renewed in 630 and another among the southern Uí Néill in 634. This almost certainly allowed Congal Cáech to take the kingship of Tara until, in 635, the resolution of the feud among the southern Uí Néill allowed the rulers of Brega to combine with Domnall so as first to eject Congal Cáech from the high-kingship, and then, in 637, to defeat and kill him and his allies in two decisive battles (Mag Roth and Sailtír). Congal Cáech was the last ruler from outside the Uí Néill to take the high-kingship of Ireland until the late tenth century. Domnall mac Áeda's success was thus not just a personal triumph but a decisive victory for the leading royal dynasty in Ireland.

T. M. CHARLES-EDWARDS

Sources Adomnán's Life of Columba, ed. and trans. A. O. Anderson and M. O. Anderson, rev. edn, rev. M. O. Anderson, OMT (1991) · W. Stokes, ed., 'The annals of Tigernach [8 pts]', Revue Celtique, 16 (1895), 374–419; 17 (1896), 6–33, 119–263, 337–420; 18 (1897), 9–59, 150–97, 267–303, 374–91; pubd sep. (1993) · Ann. Ulster · G. Murphy, 'On the dates of two sources used in Thurneysen's Heldensage: 1. Baile Chuind and the date of Cin Dromma Snechtai', Ériu, 16 (1952), 145–56, esp. 145–51 · M. C. Dobbs, ed. and trans., 'The Banshenchus [3 pts]', Revue Celtique, 47 (1930), 283–339; 48 (1931), 163–234; 49 (1932), 437–89 · W. M. Hennessy, ed. and trans., Chronicum Scotorum: a chronicle of Irish affairs, Rolls Series, 46 (1866) · M. A. O'Brien, ed., Corpus genealogiarum Hiberniae (Dublin, 1962) · K. Meyer, ed., 'The Laud genealogies and tribal histories', Zeitschrift für Celtische Philologie, 8 (1910–12), 291–338 · F. J. Byrne, Irish kings and high-kings (1973)

Domnall mac Causantín. See Donald II (d. 900) under Constantine II (d. 952).

Domnall mac Murchada (d. 763), high-king of Ireland, was the first king of Tara from Clann Cholmáin, the branch of the Uí Néill that ruled Mide (approximately modern Westmeath and the northern part of Offaly). Before his time the most powerful among the southern Uí Néill had been the Síl nÁeda Sláine ('seed of Áed Sláine'), rulers of Brega, further east in the richer lands around the River Boyne. When his father, Murchad mac Diarmata, died in 715, he was given the title 'king of the Uí Néill' by the annalists. The person in question was apparently the lieutenant among the southern Uí Néill on behalf of a high-king of Ireland from among the northern Uí Néill; similarly, northern lieutenants for southern high-kings were called 'kings of the North'. Domnall, however, may have been too young in 715 to enjoy any great influence for several years; he is not noticed in the annals until 730, two years after the death of Cináed mac Írgalaig of Síl nÁeda Sláine. By this date there was again a high-king from among the northern Uí Néill, Flaithbertach mac Loingsig (d. 765) from Cenél Conaill. Domnall was married to Ailbíne, daughter of Ailill of Ard Ciannachtae. Their son, mac Domnaill *Donnchad became high-king of Ireland. Domnall had succeeded to his father's position by 730 for the annals of Ulster record 'the disturbance of an encampment against Domnall mac Murchada in the Cúla'. The Cúla were the north-west parts of Brega up the Blackwater

valley, towards Kells, ruled by a branch of Síl nÁeda Sláine, Síl nDlúthaig. Their kingdom included Tailtiu and Ráith Airthir, the former the site of the annual fair of the kings of Tara and the latter formerly the chief fortress of the kings of Brega. Among the four offences which, according to a contemporary poem, the king of the Uí Néill was entitled to judge on his own authority was 'the disturbance of an encampment' (O'Daly, stanzas 31–2). Domnall's authority, apparently as overlord of the southern Uí Néill, was thus being challenged within one of the kingdoms of the rival Síl nÁeda Sláine.

In 734 Flaithbertach mac Loingsig was replaced as high-king of Ireland by Áed Allán mac Fergaile, who went on to establish an outpost of Cenél nEógain power in the kingdom of Conailli Muirthemne (in Louth), and in 738 to win a great victory over the Leinstermen. These events may be behind Domnall's first retirement, in 740, into clerical life. In 742, however, Áed Allán personally strangled one of his principal client kings, Conaing mac Amalgada of northern Brega. This act of flagrant violence may have encouraged Domnall to return to political life; in 743 he defeated and killed Áed Allán in Tethbae. Yet, although 743 was reckoned as the beginning of Domnall's reign as high-king of Ireland, the next year saw him again retiring into clerical life. He was not mentioned again in the annals until 753 when he proclaimed the law of Columba, initiating a long collaboration between Clann Cholmáin and Iona which was to lead to the building of Kells early in the ninth century. Domnall's authority and his awareness of the threat posed by Cenél nEógain are both revealed by an entry in the annal for 756, according to which he required the Leinstermen to march up the east coast to attack Mag Muirthemne, Cenél nEógain's foothold on the Irish Sea coast. When Domnall died on 20 November 763, he had established the power of Clann Cholmáin in the midlands.   T. M. CHARLES-EDWARDS

Sources W. Stokes, ed., 'The annals of Tigernach [8 pts]', Revue Celtique, 16 (1895), 374–419; 17 (1896), 6–33, 119–263, 337–420; 18 (1897), 9–59, 150–97, 267–303, 374–91; pubd sep. (1993) · Ann. Ulster · G. Murphy, 'On the dates of two sources used in Thurneysen's Heldensage: 1. Baile Chuind and the date of Cin Dromma Snechtai', Ériu, 16 (1952), 145–56, esp. 145–51 · M. C. Dobbs, ed. and trans., 'The Ban-shenchus [3 pts]', Revue Celtique, 47 (1930), 283–339; 48 (1931), 163–234; 49 (1932), 437–89 · W. M. Hennessy, ed. and trans., Chronicum Scotorum: a chronicle of Irish affairs, Rolls Series, 46 (1866) · M. A. O'Brien, ed., Corpus genealogiarum Hiberniae (Dublin, 1962) · K. Meyer, ed., 'The Laud genealogies and tribal histories', Zeitschrift für Celtische Philologie, 8 (1910–12), 291–338 · M. O'Daly, ed. and trans., 'A poem on the Airgialla', Ériu, 16 (1952), 179–88, stanzas 31–2 · F. J. Byrne, Irish kings and high-kings (1973)

Domnall ua Néill [Domnall of Armagh] (d. 980), high-king of Ireland, was the son of *Muirchertach mac Néill (d. 943), better known as Muirchertach of the Leather Cloaks, king of Ailech, and Gormflaith, daughter of Cuilennán mac Máele Brigte. He was a dynast of Cenél nEógain and among the early Irish lords was unusual in his use of naval power to accomplish military objectives. As part of his campaigns he moved his ships overland, from one navigable water to another, in order to make rapid attacks.

Domnall became king of Ailech on the death of his father in 943 and first appears in the chronicles in 945, when he and his brother Flaithbertach attacked a viking camp at Lough Neagh and destroyed their fleet. When Flaithbertach was slain in 949 the death was a blow to Domnall and for some years he is not mentioned in the chronicles. In 954, he led an army into Brega in a challenge to the high-king Congalach mac Máele Mithig. The next year, 955, Domnall conducted the first of his interesting naval manoeuvres when he removed his ships from Lough Neagh, and had them transported first across Airgialla to Lough Erne, and then to Connacht, to Lough Oughter, in order to devastate Bréifne and take hostages. This display of military prowess was happily timed, and when Congalach was slain the following year, Domnall ascended to the high-kingship. In 960 he raided the eastern kingdom of Dál nAraidi to secure their recognition of his lordship. A demonstration of power was made by Domnall in 963 when he transported his fleet from the northern Blackwater across Sliab Fuait, in the Fews, to Lough Ennell. Two years later, during the great famine of 965, he invaded Connacht again and took the hostages of the provincial king Fergal mac Airt.

By 968 Domnall was ready to move south, and in that year he led a campaign of two months' duration against the vikings and the men of Leinster, raiding from the River Barrow to the sea. This began the hostilities between Domnall and the famous lord of Dublin named Olaf Cuarán (Sihtricson) that would continue for a decade. In 970 Domnall was defeated by Olaf and his ally, the lord of Brega, Domnall mac Congalaich, at the battle of Kilmona (Westmeath), one of the noteworthy battles of Domnall's reign. In revenge, he attacked Domnall mac Congalaich's territory and raided the monasteries of Monasterboice and Dunleer (Louth). His discomfiture at Kilmona emboldened his rivals and in the following year his troops were expelled from Meath by its ruling dynasty, Clann Cholmáin. Shaken but not discouraged, Domnall responded by leading a large army south. First, he destroyed the fortresses and churches of Clann Cholmáin, then he moved into Leinster and raided the territories of the Uí Failgi and Fothairt. Domnall's show of power seems to have had the desired effect and never again was he challenged. In 977 he raided the neighbouring Cenél Conaill and killed Gilla Coluim ua Canannáin. That same year, however, his sons Muirchertach and Congalach were slain by his old enemy, Olaf of Dublin.

By now Domnall's mind was turning from earthly to spiritual matters and there is no indication that he attempted to avenge the death of his sons. He retired into religious life at Armagh (the source of his alternative name, Domnall of Armagh) and died in 980 after a lengthy penance; he was buried there. Domnall's wife was Echrad, the daughter of Matadán mac Áeda, king of Ulster. Their son was Muirchertach (d. 977), but the most renowned of his children was Áed, king of Ailech (r. 989–1004), the identity of whose mother is not known. His other known

children were Congalach (d. 977), Muiredach, and a second son named Áed, the practice of giving the same name to two children being not uncommon among the Irish aristocracy.   BENJAMIN T. HUDSON

Sources *Ann. Ulster* · M. C. Dobbs, ed. and trans., 'The Banshenchus [3 pts]', *Revue Celtique*, 47 (1930), 283–339; 48 (1931), 163–234; 49 (1932), 437–89 · K. Meyer, 'Das Ende von Baile in Scáil', *Zeitschrift für Celtische Philologie*, 12 (1918), 232–8 · J. H. Todd, ed. and trans., *Cogadh Gaedhel re Gallaibh / The war of the Gaedhil with the Gaill*, Rolls Series, 48 (1867) · M. A. O'Brien, ed., *Corpus genealogiarum Hiberniae* (Dublin, 1962) · E. Hogan, *Onomasticon Goedelicum* (1910) · W. M. Hennessy, ed. and trans., *Chronicum Scotorum: a chronicle of Irish affairs*, Rolls Series, 46 (1866) · *AFM* · D. Ó Corráin, *Ireland before the Normans* (1972)

Domville, Silas. *See* Taylor, Silas (1624–1678).

Don, David (1799–1841), botanist, was born at Doo Hillock, Forfarshire, Scotland, on 21 December 1799, the second son among the fifteen children of George Don (1764–1814), nurseryman and field botanist. David and his brother George *Don (1798–1856) became distinguished botanists; their three brothers remained gardeners. Like his older brother, David Don was employed as a gardener in the well-stocked nursery of Messrs Dickson at Broughton, near Edinburgh, and then in the Chelsea Physic Garden. However, he was soon appointed keeper of the rich library and herbarium of Aylmer Bourke Lambert (1761–1842). His first publications were 'Descriptions of new or rare plants in Scotland' and 'Descriptions of several new plants from Nepaul', both of which appeared in *Memoirs of the Wernerian Society* (3, 1820). These were followed by 'A monograph of the genus Saxifraga' in *Transactions of the Linnean Society* (13, 1821, 341–452).

In 1821 Don accompanied his father's friend Dr Patrick Neill (1776–1851), secretary both of the Caledonian Horticultural Society and the Wernerian Society, to Paris, where he met Humboldt and Cuvier. In 1822 he became librarian of the Linnean Society, where a fellow Scot, Alexander McLeay, considered his pride and self-conceit to be intolerable. Don's important *Prodromus florae Nepalensis* (1825), based on Nepalese specimens from Hamilton and Wallich in Lambert's herbarium, contained Latin so ungrammatical that John Lindley scathingly described it as 'written in so strange a language, that we can scarcely guess its name' (*Botanical Register*, 11, 1825, 1). Yet, a friend stated in his obituary in *The Phytologist* that:

> It has never been our lot to meet with a botanist equally able and willing to afford information to the student … nothing could exceed the kindness and zeal with which he assisted every student, however complicated or however trite the subject laid before him.

Don was professor of botany at King's College, London, from 1836 to 1841. Extremely industrious, he published during his short life fifty-two papers listed in the Royal Society's *Catalogue of Scientific Papers*, acted as an editor of *Annals and Magazine of Natural History*, and produced volumes five to seven of Robert Sweet's *British Flower Garden* (1831–7). He died on 8 December 1841, after twelve months of suffering from cancer, in the Linnean Society's house at Soho Square, London, and was buried at Kensal Green on 15 December.   WILLIAM T. STEARN

Sources *Annals and Magazine of Natural History*, 8 (1842), 397–9 · *The Phytologist*, 1 (1842), 133–4 · *Proceedings of the Linnean Society of London*, 1 (1838–48), 145–9 · *Catalogue of scientific papers*, Royal Society, 2 (1868), 312–14 · W. T. Stearn, 'David Don's *Prodromus florae Nepalensis*', *Journal of Arnold Arboretum*, 26 (1945), 168 · A. T. Gage and W. T. Stearn, *A bicentenary history of the Linnean Society of London* (1988), 29–30, 45 · *Florist's Journal*, 3 (1842), 15–19
Archives Linn. Soc., catalogue and drawings · RBG Kew, *monographica crocorum* · Royal Horticultural Society, London, corresp., diary, and papers

Don, Sir George (1754–1832), army officer and colonial governor, was born in Edinburgh, the second of the three sons of John Don, a wine merchant. He entered the army as an ensign of the 51st regiment on 26 December 1770 and was promoted lieutenant in June 1774, after he had joined his regiment at Minorca. His qualities attracted the notice of General Johnstone, the lieutenant-governor and commander-in-chief, who took him on his staff as aide-de-camp, and he served General James Murray, Johnstone's successor, in the same post. General Murray also made him his military secretary. At this time he met General Murray's niece Maria Margaretta Murray (*c*.1760–1854), an illegitimate daughter of Philip Murray, fifth Baron Elibank, whom he married on his return to Britain in 1782.

Don was chief of the staff during the gallant but unavailing defence of Fort St Philip (1781–2) and was sent to London with his report on the siege by Murray, who commended him highly. In November 1783 he received a brevet majority and in April 1784 a substantive majority in the 59th regiment, which he joined in Gibraltar; he purchased the lieutenant-colonelcy in April 1789. He left Gibraltar in 1791 to take up a staff appointment in England. In 1792–3 he was with his regiment in Jersey. He was deputy adjutant-general to Sir James Murray (later Murray-Pulteney) in the duke of York's army in the Netherlands in 1793, and for his services was made aide-de-camp to the king and promoted colonel in February 1795.

Don remained on the continent after the departure of the army, as military commissioner with the Prussian army. He was promoted major-general on 1 January 1798 and appointed to command the troops in the Isle of Wight. In 1799 he joined the duke of York's unsuccessful expedition to The Helder, commanding the 3rd division under Sir David Dundas. He was captured and imprisoned by the French while carrying messages to General Brune, who accused him of carrying documents intended to subvert the Batavians, and was not released until June 1800. While in captivity he succeeded Sir John Moore as colonel of the 9th West India regiment. According to the *Dictionary of National Biography*, on his return he rejoined the staff of the Horse Guards as assistant adjutant-general. In 1802 he was in Scotland, where he was in command of the southeast, organizing a large force of militiamen against a possible invasion. He was promoted lieutenant-general in 1803. When the war with France resumed, Don returned to London to organize and command the newly formed King's German Legion, which consisted mainly of Hanoverians. With this corps and other troops, amounting in

Sir George Don (1754–1832), by Samuel William Reynolds senior, pubd 1808 (after C. G. Dillon)

all to 14,000 men, he sailed for Germany in 1805 on a diplomatic and military mission, in which he was later superseded by Lord Cathcart.

On 20 October 1805 Don became colonel of the 96th regiment and in 1806 he was appointed lieutenant-governor of Jersey, where he commanded until 1814; however, he was absent in 1809–10, when he was sent to Walcheren in order to command and supervise the withdrawal of the forces engaged in that disastrous expedition. He kept Jersey in a good state of defence, improving fortifications, building roads, and reorganizing the militia, and won the trust of the inhabitants. He was promoted general in June 1814 and appointed lieutenant-governor of Gibraltar, where he arrived in October 1814 during an epidemic of yellow fever. Recollecting the terrible toll taken by disease in the enclosed communities of Fort St Philip and Walcheren, Don improved sanitation and the water supply, built a hospital for the civilian inhabitants, and created a public park, the Alameda. The sanitary police which he established evolved in 1830 into the first British police force outside the United Kingdom. He also built Gibraltar's court house, and the charter which established Gibraltar as a crown colony was published during his term of office (1830). He repaired and completed defences which had been in disrepair since the great siege (1779–83) and built roads in Gibraltar and neighbouring parts of Spain. He was made GCH in 1816 and GCB in 1820, and received the grand cross of military merit of France in 1817 for services to the French royal family. He was appointed colonel of the 36th regiment in 1818 and transferred to the 3rd regiment (the Buffs) in 1829. In 1831 he retired as lieutenant-governor of Gibraltar and was made governor of Scarborough Castle. He died in Gibraltar of influenza on 1 January 1832 and was buried on 4 January with full military honours in the new garrison church in Gibraltar (later the cathedral of the Holy Trinity), which he had built.   S. G. BENADY

Sources correspondence of Sir George Don, 1814–31, Gibraltar Government Archives · J. Sullivan, 'General Don: an episode on the history of Jersey (1806–1814)', MS annotations to the copy of J. Sullivan, *General Don* (1884), 1884, Scottish United Services Museum, Edinburgh Castle · *Army List* · *GM*, 1st ser., 102/1 (1832), 272–3 · R. H. Mahon, *Life of Gen. the Hon. James Murray* (1921) · G. J. W. Beijnen, *De twee zendingen van den generaal Don uit het Engelsche hoofdkwortier in Noord-Holland in 1799 naar 's-Gravenhage* (Leiden, 1900?) · *DNB* · will, PRO, PROB 11/1798 · marriage settlement, 1782, NA Scot., GD2/250 · G. R. Balleine, *A history of the island of Jersey* (1950) · J. Hennen, *Sketches of the medical topography of the Mediterranean* (1830) · private information (2004) [J. Gilhooley] · H. J. M. Rey, *Essai sur le topographie medicale de Gibraltar* (1833) · *Gibraltar Chronicle* (5 Jan 1832)
Archives BL, corresp. and papers, Add. MSS 46702–46711, 46883–46884 · Gibraltar Government Archives, MSS · NAM, order book, Walcheren expedition | BL, corresp. with second earl of Liverpool, Add. MSS 38243, 38463, *passim* · Harrowby Manuscript Trust, Stafford, corresp. with Lord Harrowby · Morgan L., letters to Sir James Murray-Pulteney · PRO NIre., corresp. with Lord Castlereagh
Likenesses portrait, c.1806, Elizabeth Castle, Jersey · S. W. Reynolds senior, mezzotint, pubd 1808 (after C. G. Dillon), BM, NPG [*see illus.*] · portrait, c.1816, Gibraltar Museum · bust, c.1840, House of Assembly, Gibraltar · statue, c.1886, Royal Parade, St Helier, Jersey · portrait, repro. in W. Davies, *Fort Regent* (1971)
Wealth at death see will, PRO, PROB 11/1798

Don, George (1798–1856), botanist and plant collector, was born at Doo Hillock, Forfarshire, Scotland, on 17 May 1798, the eldest of the five sons of George Don (1764–1814), clockmaker turned nurseryman, who discovered many highland plants new to Scotland, and principal gardener (1802–6) at the Royal Botanic Garden, Edinburgh. David *Don (1799–1841) was a younger brother. After horticultural experience in the nursery of Messrs Dickson at Broughton, near Edinburgh, Don worked from 1816 to 1821 as foreman gardener in the Chelsea Physic Garden. In December 1821 he began a voyage with Captain Edward Sabine to Madeira, Sierra Leone, São Tomé, the West Indies, and Brazil, his task everywhere to collect seeds, plants, bulbs, and herbarium specimens for the Horticultural Society's garden. He returned in February 1823 having successfully assembled many new plants but, as he violated an agreement not to publish on what he had collected, the society dismissed him in 1825. He published, in 1827, *A Monograph of the Genus Allium*, a preprint from *Memoirs of the Wernerian Society* (6, 1832, 1–102). This and his 'Review of the genus *Combretum*' in *Transactions of the Linnean Society* (15, 1826, 412–41) made evident his botanical ability and he was commissioned to prepare *A General System of Botany and Gardening* (4 vols., 1831–8), an excellent work, but one which was financially unsuccessful and

never completed. He later provided the botanical section for the *Encyclopaedia metropolitana* (2, 1843). Don was elected an associate of the Linnean Society of London in 1822 and a fellow in 1831. He died, unmarried, in Kensington on 25 February 1856.   WILLIAM T. STEARN

Sources *Cottage Gardener*, 16 (1856), 152–3 · *Proceedings of the Linnean Society of London* (1855–6), xxxix–xli · H. R. Fletcher, *The story of the Royal Horticultural Society, 1804–1968* (1969), 95–6
Archives Linn. Soc., corresp. · Royal Botanic Garden, Edinburgh, daybook [copy] · Royal Horticultural Society, London, journal

Don, Sir William Henry, seventh baronet (1825–1862), actor, was born on 4 May 1825, the only son of Sir Alexander Don of Newtondon, Berwickshire, sixth baronet (d. 1826), MP for Roxburghshire, and his wife, Grace [*see* Wallace, Grace Jane, Lady Wallace], the eldest daughter of John Stein of Edinburgh. His father was a close friend of Sir Walter Scott, and a frequent attendant at his dinner parties. William Henry Don succeeded to the baronetcy when less than a year old. His mother married as her second husband Sir James Maxwell Wallace, of Ainderby Hall, near Northallerton. Don was educated at Eton College between 1838 and 1841. In August 1839 he took part in the Eglinton tournament as page to Lady Montgomerie. He entered the army as a cornet in the 5th dragoon guards in June 1842, was an extra aide-de-camp to the lord lieutenant of Ireland in 1844, and became lieutenant in the 5th dragoon guards in 1845; in November that year he retired from the army, deep in debt. The fine estate called Newtondon, left him by his father, had to be sold, and produced £85,000, which went to his creditors. He was then compelled to turn to account the experience which he had acquired as an amateur actor.

After a short starring engagement in the north of England, and following his marriage to Antonia, the daughter of M. Lebrun of Hamburg, on 1 June 1847, he went to America. He made his first public appearance there as John Duck in *The Jacobite* at the Broadway Theatre, New York, on 27 October 1850. Shortly afterwards he was seen in the character of Sir Charles Coldstream in Boucicault's comedy *Used Up*. He remained in America for nearly five years, playing with success in New York, Philadelphia, and other large towns, and on his return to England found that after all his affairs had been wound up he was still in debt about £7000. In an attempt to pay off this sum he continued as a comic actor. He began in Edinburgh and Glasgow, and after a provincial tour went to the Haymarket Theatre, London, where in 1857 he acted in J. M. Morton's farce *Whitebait at Greenwich*. His first marriage ended for unknown reasons, and on 17 October 1857, at Marylebone, he married Emily Eliza Saunders, the eldest daughter of John Saunders of the Adelphi Theatre, London. She had been well known as a lively actress in comedy and farce at the Adelphi, Haymarket, Surrey, and other theatres for some years.

In 1861 Don and his wife went to Australia, where he appeared at the Royal Theatre, Melbourne. At this period he had taken to playing female characters in burlesques. In February 1862 he visited Hobart Town, Tasmania, with a company of his own, where he fell ill with an inflammation of the lungs. On 15 March 1862 he played Queen Elizabeth in the burlesque *Kenilworth*, by Robert Reece and H. B. Farnie, and four days later, on 19 March 1862, he died from aneurysm of the aorta at Webb's Hotel, Hobart Town. He had a private burial in the same town. He left two daughters, Alexina Mary from his first marriage, and Harriette Grace Mary from his second; in the absence of any male heir, the title ended with him. Don possessed a fine sense of humour, a quick perception of the ludicrous side of life and character, a remarkable talent for mimicry, a strong nerve, a ready wit, and great self-possession.

Lady Don returned to England after her husband's death and resumed her professional career, but with no very profitable result, though she had been very popular in the Australian colonies and in New Zealand. In 1867 she went to the United States, where she made her appearance on 18 February at the New York Theatre in *Peggy Green* and the burlesque *Kenilworth*; on the close of the season she returned to England. She was for a short period lessee of the Theatre Royal, Nottingham, and assisted at the opening of the Gaiety Theatre, Edinburgh. Latterly she was in reduced circumstances and was obliged to appear as a vocalist in music halls. She died at Edinburgh on 20 September 1875. Don's first wife, Antonia, died in 1869.

G. C. BOASE, rev. NILANJANA BANERJI

Sources *The Era* (18 May 1862) · J. Foster, *The peerage, baronetage, and knightage of the British empire for 1882*, 2 [1882] · Burke, *Peerage* · T. A. Brown, *History of the American stage* (1870) · Adams, *Drama* **Likenesses** lithograph, Harvard TC · woodcut, Harvard TC **Wealth at death** under £600: probate, 6 July 1862, *CGPLA Eng. & Wales*

Donald [Dyfnwal son of Owen] (*d.* **975**), king of the Cumbrians, was the son of Owen, who as ruler of Strathclyde was active in the 930s as an ally of Constantine II, king in Scotland between 900 and 943, against Æthelstan of Wessex; it was probably Owen, rather than his son, whom Æthelstan defeated with Constantine at 'Brunanburh' in 937. Donald was apparently king by *c.*941. About that year Kaddroe, a clerical aristocrat of Pictish or British descent who was highly regarded at King Constantine's court, passed through Donald's lands intending to go to the continent.

> King Donald [Dovenaldus] ruled over the people there, and because he was a relative of [Kaddroe] he received him with all joy; after keeping him with him for some time, he brought him to the town of Loida, on the bounds of the Norse [of York] and the Cumbrians. (*Acta sanctorum*, March, 1.476)

The unidentified 'Loida' must be in the region of Stainmore Common, on the borders of Yorkshire and Westmorland; this was long recognized as the southern boundary of the kingdom of Cumbria and the diocese of Glasgow. A point that emerges from this story is that although Kaddroe was related to Donald, he is not described as a relative of Constantine; Donald and Constantine were therefore presumably unrelated.

A son of Donald, whose name appears in garbled form as Rhadarc or Amdarch (or slight variants of these; possibly Rhydderch), slew Culen, king in Scotland, somewhere in Lothian in 971, 'because of the rape of his daughter, whom the king had carried off for himself' (Anderson, *Early Sources*, 1.476). It is not stated that this Rhadarc, son of Donald, was king at the time; but he must have been an important personage among the Britons, since the king of Scotland was interested in his daughter, and since he appears to have been in command of a considerable British war band. He is not heard of again; by 973 his brother Malcolm was 'king of the Cumbrians' (Anderson, *Early Sources*, 1.478), and was one of the kings said to have rowed King Edgar on the Dee at Chester in that year. Another of the kings said to have been involved is named as Dufnal; he is not otherwise identified, and may be the same Donald, son of Owen, still living but now with his son associated in the kingship.

The death of 'Domnall, son of Eogan, king of the Britons, on pilgrimage' is recorded in the Irish annals s.a. 975; likewise a late Welsh source records that in 975 'Dunguallon, king of Strathclyde' went to Rome and received the tonsure (Anderson, *Early Sources*, 1.480). He must have resigned the kingship in Malcolm's favour by this time; possibly, indeed, *de facto* power had passed to his sons by 971. Donald (or perhaps more accurately Dyfnwal) may have been more independent of the kings of Scotland than some of his predecessors. From the 870s the kings of Strathclyde appear to have been clients of the kings of Scotland; in at least one instance the son of a king of Scotland was imposed as king of Strathclyde. From 954 to 971, however, the kingship of Scotland was disturbed by serious internal dynastic feuding, with the crown changing hands by violence four times. It was probably as a result of this, as well as the collapse of viking York, that the Strathclyde kings were able to reassert a measure of independence under Donald and under his sons—Malcolm, who at his death in 997 was described as 'king of the Britons of the north' (Anderson, *Early Sources*, 1.517), and **Owen the Bald** (*d.* 1018), king of the Cumbrians, who succeeded Malcolm and ruled in Cumbria until his death in 1018, after which his realm was finally absorbed into the kingdom of the Scots.

ALAN MACQUARRIE

Sources A. O. Anderson, ed. and trans., *Early sources of Scottish history, AD 500 to 1286*, 1 (1922), 424–80, 517 · A. O. Anderson, ed., *Scottish annals from English chroniclers, AD 500 to 1286* (1908), 66–77, 82 · 'De S. Corpteo, seu ... de s. Cadtoe', *Acta sanctorum: Martius*, 1 (Antwerp, 1668), 468–80 · A. P. Smyth, *Warlords and holy men: Scotland, AD 80–1000* (1984) · A. Macquarrie, 'The kings of Strathclyde, *c.* 400–1018', *Medieval Scotland: crown, lordship and community: essays presented to G. W. S. Barrow*, ed. A. Grant and K. J. Stringer (1993), 1–19 · D. P. Kirby, 'Strathclyde and Cumbria', *Transactions of the Cumberland and Westmorland Antiquarian and Archaeological Society*, new ser., 62 (1962), 77–94

Donald, sixth earl of Mar (*d.* in or after **1297**), magnate, was the son of *William, fifth earl of Mar (*d.* in or before 1281), and Elizabeth Comyn, his first wife. He was knighted by Alexander III at Scone in 1270 and succeeded as earl before 25 July 1281, when his name appears, with other Scots nobles, on the ratification of the treaty for the marriage of Margaret, the maid of Scotland, to Erik, king of Norway.

At Scone in February 1284 he was among those who undertook to acknowledge the daughter of that marriage, Margaret, the maid of Norway, as heir to the throne of Scotland in the event of Alexander's death without other issue. Along with many of the barons and prelates of Scotland, he wrote to Edward I of England in March 1290, agreeing to negotiate for the marriage of the king's son to the maid of Norway, and was a signatory to the resulting treaty, signed at Birgham, Berwickshire, in July 1290. After the death of the maid of Norway in September of that year, when different claimants appeared for the Scottish crown, Mar was one of those who was rumoured to be raising forces in Scotland, presumably to support Robert (V) de Brus's claim to the throne. His alignment with the Brus faction is also clearly demonstrated by his involvement with the document known as 'The appeal of the seven earls of Scotland', which seems to have been an attempt to prevent any hasty elevation of John Balliol to the throne. The relationship between the Mar and Brus families was close: Donald's daughter Isabel married Brus's grandson, the future king Robert I, probably in the mid-1290s; it has also been suggested that his son Gartnait married a sister of King Robert.

Mar was an important participant in the Great Cause, the lengthy legal proceedings by which Edward I decided that John Balliol should be king of Scots. He swore allegiance to Edward at Upsettlington, Berwickshire, on 13 June 1291, and acted as one of the forty auditors appointed by Brus to hear the case. He was a witness to Edward's protest at Berwick on 3 July 1292 as to his claim to be lord superior of Scotland. In June 1294 King John, with Mar and other Scottish nobles, was summoned to London to join the English army setting out for France. They did not attend, but instead sent 'impotent and brief excuses' (*Chronicle of Walter of Guisborough*, 264). As the Scots prepared to rebel against Edward I in 1295, Mar was one of the council of twelve elected to 'advise' Balliol; he was also one of the signatories to the ratification of the treaty of Paris in February 1296. Following the battle of Dunbar (1296) he came to Edward at Montrose, and afterwards swore fealty again at Berwick. He was, notwithstanding, ordered to accompany Edward to England, but was allowed to visit Scotland in June 1297, Edward at the same time exacting from him a pledge that he would serve him against France.

Mar then disappears from the records, and may have died about this time. In December 1297 'Alexander, son of the earl of Mar', was imprisoned in the Tower of London by order of Edward I. It is not clear, however, if this is Mar's own son or that of his son and successor in the earldom, Gartnait (father of Donald, eighth earl of Mar). Mar married Elena, daughter of the Welsh prince Llywelyn ap Gruffudd, and left at least four children: Gartnait, Duncan, Isabel, and Marjory, who married John, earl of Atholl. A daughter Mary, who is said to have married Kenneth *Sutherland, fourth earl of Sutherland [see under Sutherland family (*per. c.*1200–*c.*1510)], may be the same person.

HENRY PATON, *rev.* NORMAN H. REID

Sources W. Bower, *Scotichronicon*, ed. D. E. R. Watt and others, new edn, 9 vols. (1987–98), vol. 5, pp. 380–81 • *APS*, 1124–1423, 421–4, 428, 441–2, 451–3 • J. Stevenson, ed., *Documents illustrative of the history of Scotland*, 2 vols. (1870), vol. 1, pp. 162–73; vol. 2, pp. 62, 66, 108, 185 • E. L. G. Stones, ed. and trans., *Anglo-Scottish relations, 1174–1328: some select documents*, 2nd edn, OMT (1970), no. 14 • G. W. S. Barrow, *Robert Bruce and the community of the realm of Scotland*, 3rd edn (1988), 141 • Rymer, *Foedera*, new edn, 1.804 • *The chronicle of Walter of Guisborough*, ed. H. Rothwell, CS, 3rd ser., 89 (1957), 263–4 • E. L. G. Stones and G. G. Simpson, eds., *Edward I and the throne of Scotland, 1290–1296*, 2 (1978), 3, 104, 193–4 • *CDS*, vol. 2, nos. 872, 961, 964 • *Scots peerage*, 5.578 • G. W. S. Barrow and others, eds., *Regesta regum Scottorum*, 5, ed. A. A. M. Duncan (1988)

Donald, eighth earl of Mar (1293–1332), magnate, was the son of Gartnait, seventh earl of Mar, who died *c.*1302, when his heir was still a child. Although it has been asserted that Donald's mother was Christian Bruce, sister of the future King Robert, it seems more likely that she was an elder Bruce sibling whose name is unknown. When Robert Bruce, still earl of Carrick, submitted to King Edward in 1302, the conditions of his submission included the granting to him of the wardship and marriage of a boy who was his nephew twice over, as son of his sister and of his wife's brother (Bruce had been married to Isabel, Gartnait's sister). It can be presumed, therefore, that the young Donald, who succeeded as eighth earl of Mar in 1305, had little choice but to attend his uncle's coronation in April 1306. The lad was captured by the English a few months later, most likely in Kildrummy Castle, the centre of his earldom, which fell to Edward I in early September of that year. It was ordered that he should be sent to Bristol Castle, where he was to be spared warding in irons because of his tender years, but in the end he remained in the royal household, serving as a page of the chamber to Edward II. He became closely attached to the English king.

In 1314, as a result of the English defeat at Bannockburn, Earl Donald, together with a number of other important Scottish prisoners, was set free. Having reached Newcastle, however, he changed his mind and elected to stay in the country of his upbringing, rather than return to that of his birth. This had potentially important implications for the long overdue settlement of the Scottish succession. The Bruces claimed the throne of Scotland by virtue of being nearest in degree to David, earl of Huntingdon (*d.* 1219), through their descent from his second daughter, Isobel. If Earl Donald was indeed descended from an elder sister of King Robert, then he had an interest in the succession which, though it would probably not have taken precedence over the claims of Robert's daughter Marjorie or his brother Edward, was nevertheless of some consequence. As it was, in the absence of his nephew, King Robert (who as yet had no male child) in 1315 settled the succession on Edward and his descendants, followed by the future children of Marjorie, who was soon to be married to Walter Stewart (*d.* 1326).

Having decided to stay in England, Earl Donald was exonerated from all suspicion of rebel sympathies and was clearly high in royal favour: he received a number of grants from Edward II and in 1320 went abroad with the king. In 1321 he declared his intention of going on pilgrimage to Santiago de Compostela. As a firm supporter of the English king Donald naturally fought on the royalist side at Boroughbridge in 1322, and was also present later that year when the Scots defeated an English force near Byland. His loyalty was rewarded with the constableship of Bristol Castle in 1326, but, with the deposition of Edward II later in the year, he finally went back to Scotland, primarily in order to lobby for an attempted restoration of the errant English king. King Robert took his nephew's return at face value, restoring his lands to him and even giving him command of one of the Scottish battalions which invaded England in 1327, after the murder of Edward II and the coronation of the young Edward III. Earl Donald was still in Scotland when King Robert died in 1329; his closeness to the throne of Scotland is further underlined by the fact that on 2 August 1332 he was chosen to succeed Thomas Randolph, earl of Moray, as guardian of Scotland on behalf of his cousin David II. Nevertheless there were suspicions that Mar had retained sympathies with England and with Edward Balliol, the son of King John, whom Edward II had invited to the English court from France in 1324, and who led an English-backed invasion of Scotland in the summer of 1332. These suspicions surfaced to disastrous effect when the Scottish forces faced the invaders on Dupplin Moor on 11 August. Robert Bruce of Liddesdale, King Robert's illegitimate son, chose this moment to accuse Mar of being in league with the enemy, whereupon Mar, by way of demonstrating his patriotism, announced that he would himself be the first to engage with the enemy. The result was a thoroughly disorganized attack, which ended in a total Scottish defeat; Mar himself was killed.

Earl Donald had married Isabel Stewart, supposedly the daughter of Sir Alexander Stewart of Bonkill. They had a son, **Thomas**, ninth earl of Mar (c.1330–1377), who reached his majority in the 1350s, indicating that his parents married about 1328, after Donald's return to Scotland. On 15 January 1348 Edward III (presumably on the strength of his control of much of southern Scotland) assigned Thomas to the care of William Carsewell, Isabel's third husband, who had outlived her. But on 15 May 1350, having by now succeeded to the earldom, he witnessed a charter of David II at Dundee, and in June 1351 made an active entry into the Scottish political scene, being appointed as a commissioner for a peace treaty with England. In 1357 he became a hostage for the payment of David II's ransom, but he was back in Scotland, where he held the office of chamberlain, between 1358 and 1359. Even so he maintained close links with England and on 24 February 1360 entered Edward III's service, saving his allegiance to the king of Scots. This brought him an annual pension of 600 marks, with the additional proviso that he would receive £600 if he lost any lands in Scotland. King David regarded this relationship as unacceptable and in 1361 besieged and took Kildrummy Castle, granting it to Sir Walter Moigne. It has also been suggested that Thomas was a tyrannical overlord and practised extortion on his people; either that, or he had fallen out with Sir William

Keith, one of the king's favourites. As an incentive to mend his ways Mar was fined £1000, payable in five years under pain of losing his castle altogether. Kildrummy was still in Moigne's hands as late as 1364, although Thomas was allowed to draw on the issues of his earldom. The castle was finally restored to him at some point before August 1368. In the same year he was granted a safe conduct to go on pilgrimage to St Jean d'Amiens. He continued to travel up and down to England until his death in early 1377, from which date his brother-in-law, William *Douglas, earl of Douglas (d. 1384), styled himself earl of Mar.

Thomas married twice. His first wife was Margaret, daughter of John Graham, earl of Menteith, whom he later divorced 'at the instigation of the devil' (Scots peerage, 5.585). He subsequently married Margaret Stewart, eldest daughter and coheir of Thomas Stewart, earl of Angus; she outlived him. He had no surviving children of either marriage, and his heir was his sister Margaret, who married William, earl of Douglas.   FIONA WATSON

Sources Scots peerage, 5.581–3 · C. Moor, ed., Knights of Edward I, 3, Harleian Society, 82 (1930), 108 · G. W. S. Barrow, Robert Bruce and the community of the realm of Scotland, 3rd edn (1988) · CDS, vol. 5 · F. Palgrave, ed., Documents and records illustrating the history of Scotland (1837) · G. W. S. Barrow and others, eds., Regesta regum Scottorum, 5, ed. A. A. M. Duncan (1988) · R. Nicholson, 'The last campaign of Robert Bruce', EngHR, 77 (1962), 233–46, esp. 234 · RotS, vol. 1 · J. Robertson, ed., Illustrations of the topography and antiquities of the shires of Aberdeen and Banff, 4, Spalding Club (1862) · GEC, Peerage, 8.404 · R. Nicholson, Edward III and the Scots: the formative years of a military career, 1327–1335 (1965) · S. I. Boardman, The early Stewart kings: Robert II and Robert III, 1371–1406 (1996)

Donald I (d. 862). See under Kenneth I (d. 858).

Donald II (d. 900). See under Constantine II (d. 952).

Donald III [Domnall Bán, Donalbane] (b. in or before **1040**, d. **1099**?), king of Scots, was born before, probably not long before, August 1040, when his father, *Duncan I, king of Scots, was killed in battle 'at an immature age' (Anderson, Early Sources, 1.581). His mother was a Suthen, of unknown origin, and he had an elder brother, *Malcolm III. Another reputed brother, Mael Muire, is attested only by Orkneyinga Saga, and the relationship should be viewed with scepticism. Some physical characteristic presumably gave rise to the Gaelic name Domnall Bán, meaning Donald the Fair, by which he was commonly known. On his father's death and the succession of Macbeth (d. 1057), Donald presumably fled, and nothing is known of him during the reigns of Macbeth and Malcolm III.

On Malcolm's death, and that of Edward, the eldest son of his marriage to *Margaret, daughter of Edward Ætheling (d. 1057), at Alnwick on 13 November 1093, the Scots chose Donald to be their king. *Duncan II, Malcolm's eldest son of his first marriage, had lived in Normandy and England for twenty years, and was associated with Anglo-Norman culture; there was almost certainly a reaction also against Margaret (who died within a week), her sons (whom Donald exiled), and English immigrants.

Hence when Duncan II, with the help of William II, expelled Donald after six months in 1094, Duncan was unable to retain the throne, being forced to send his French knights packing, and then being killed when Donald returned, aided, it seems, by Edmund, second son of Malcolm III and Margaret. Edmund seems to have been given a share of the kingdom, and, if Donald had no son, may have been his intended successor.

Although Donald made no known attack on northern England (the usual means by which a new king of Scots rewarded his followers), William II set about destabilizing his rule, first recognizing *Edgar (d. 1107), the oldest surviving son of Malcolm III, as king in exile, then sending north Edgar Ætheling to put Edgar on the throne (1097). According to William of Malmesbury, Donald was killed by David, later *David I (r. 1124–53). To be preferred is the Scottish king-list, which claims that Donald was captured and blinded by King Edgar, dying in Rescobie, in Angus; the annals of Tigernach confirm this by noting that he was blinded in 1099, probably the date of his death. The king-list also claims that he was first buried in Dunkeld but that 'Iona holds his bones' (Anderson, *Early Sources*, 2.100); if so, he was the last Scottish king buried there. But the reported burial of Scottish kings on Iona may reflect only unfounded pretensions by the monastery on the island. The claim that he strangled a son of David I in revenge for being blinded is late and improbable. His part in Shakespeare's *Macbeth* derives from the fanciful tales in *Scotorum historiae* (1527) by Hector Boece or Boethius (d. 1536).

The name of Donald's wife (if he married) is unknown, but he had a daughter, Bethóc, from whom John Comyn of Badenoch (d. 1302) derived his claim to the throne in 1291.

A. A. M. DUNCAN, rev.

Sources A. H. Dunbar, *Scottish kings*, 2nd edn (1906) · A. O. Anderson, ed. and trans., *Early sources of Scottish history, AD 500 to 1286*, 2 vols. (1922) · A. O. Anderson, ed., *Scottish annals from English chroniclers, AD 500 to 1286* (1908) · H. Boece, *Scotorum historiae a prima gentis origine* (Paris, 1527) · R. L. G. Ritchie, *The Normans in Scotland* (1954) · W. Stokes, ed., 'The annals of Tigernach [8 pts]', *Revue Celtique*, 16 (1895), 374–419; 17 (1896), 6–33, 119–263, 337–420; 18 (1897), 9–59, 150–97, 267–303, 374–91; pubd sep. (1993)

Donald IV Breac. *See* Domnall Brecc (d. 642/3).

Domnall mac Alpin. *See* Donald I (d. 862) *under* Kenneth I (d. 858).

Donald, Adam [*called* the Prophet of Bethelnie] (1703–1780), spiritualist, was born into a poor family of peasant farmers at the hamlet of Bethelnie, 20 miles north of Aberdeen. Despite an extraordinarily large stature and build, which caused him to be regarded as a changeling, Donald was unable to use his hands for work. Required to find an alternative source of income, Donald 'affected an uncommon reservedness of manner, pretended to be extremely studious, spoke little, and what he said was uttered in half sentences, with awkward gesticulations and an uncouth tone of voice, to excite consternation and elude detection' (*Life and Character*). Though scarcely able to read, he was said to have studied books in all languages, and to have been particularly knowledgeable of John Gerard's *The Herball, or, Generall Historie of Plants* (1597). He made, too, a practice of haunting the ruined church of Bethelnie, where he was thought to converse with and learn from the dead.

Donald's supposed necromancy meant that he was frequently questioned about inexplicable occurrences in his community and his talent for generalized advice meant that his comments often appeared prophetic. He also acted as a quack physician and dealt principally with lingering disorders supposed to owe their origin to witchcraft. His prescriptions invariably required the application of certain unguents of his own making to various parts of the body. This was to be accompanied by particular ceremonies, described in minute detail and intended to confirm his mystical persona. Donald's assumed character provided both popularity and financial security. His house was frequently crowded with visitors seeking cures or details of their futures, for which he charged a maximum of 1s. Such was his fame that he was asked to sit for a full-length portrait, which was later engraved. To relieve the boredom of sitting he composed the prophetic lines:

> Time doth all things devour,
> And time doth all things waste.
> And we waste time,
> And so are we at last.

In later life Donald persuaded a local woman, details of whom are unknown, to marry him on account of his powers, the limitations of which proved difficult to hide in an intimate relationship. His artifice, while kept secret by his wife, was exposed by his daughter who openly mocked him. Donald died in 1780.

GORDON GOODWIN, rev. PHILIP CARTER

Sources *The life and character of Dr Adam Donald, Prophet of Bethelnie* (1815?)
Likenesses J. Harris, watercolour, BM · engraving (after portrait) · line engraving (aged sixty-nine; after J. W.), BM, NPG · portrait · woodcut, repro. in *The life and character of Dr Adam Donald*

Donald, Ian (1910–1987), obstetrician and developer of ultrasound, was born on 27 December 1910 in Liskeard, Cornwall, the eldest in the family of two sons and two daughters of John Donald, medical practitioner, and his wife, Helen Barrow Wilson, concert pianist. His education was at Warriston School, Moffat, Dumfriesshire, and Fettes College, Edinburgh, and then in South Africa at the Diocesan College, Rondebosch, Cape Town, and Cape Town University (where he obtained a BA in French, Greek, English, and music). On his return to England he entered St Thomas's Hospital medical school, London, from which he graduated MB BS in 1937. In 1937 he married Alix Mathilde, daughter of Walter Wellesley de Chazal Richards, a farmer in the Orange Free State, South Africa. Happily married for fifty years, he was the loving father of four daughters and was devoted to his women patients, as they were to him.

Donald served in the Royal Air Force medical branch from 1942 to 1946 and was mentioned in dispatches and appointed MBE (military, 1946) for acts of gallantry. He returned to St Thomas's Hospital and qualified MD and MRCOG in 1947 (FRCOG, 1955). In 1952 he became reader at Hammersmith Hospital, London, where he devised a respirator for the resuscitation of the new-born. In 1954 he was appointed to the regius chair of midwifery at the University of Glasgow. The first edition of his eminently readable textbook, *Practical Obstetric Problems*, was published in 1955. It reflected his motto, 'the art of teaching is the art of sharing enthusiasm', his sparkling wit, and his deep knowledge of English literature and the Bible.

Familiar with radar and sonar from his Royal Air Force days, Donald's mind turned to the idea that sonar could be used for medical diagnosis. With T. G. Brown of the electronics company Kelvin Hughes he produced the first successful diagnostic ultrasound machine, and with Dr John MacVicar the findings were reported in *The Lancet* of 7 June 1958 under the title 'Investigation of abdominal masses by pulsed ultrasound'. The idea of applying the principles of metal flaw detection to human diagnosis was received at first with scepticism and some hilarity, but Donald's vision of ultrasound as a new diagnostic science never faded and work with various colleagues followed, exploring the whole subject of foetal development. The impact of ultrasound on obstetric practice has been enormous and in later life Donald wrote: 'the innumerable difficulties, set-backs and disappointments have been more than compensated for by those who have turned the subject from a laughable eccentricity into a science of increasing exactitude.'

In 1964 the department moved from the Glasgow Royal Maternity Hospital to a new hospital (the Queen Mother's Hospital), for which Donald had campaigned and which he helped to design. There he directed everything with verve and panache, like a great actor–manager of the old school. He was an impressive figure as he strode its corridors, 6 feet 2 inches tall with red hair and blue eyes, and having a strong personal magnetism. He was impulsive, witty, and quick-tempered, but his sudden anger evaporated almost instantly. He had a great sense of fun and at the most solemn occasions could dissolve into helpless laughter. His hobbies were sailing (in which he persisted despite a cardiac condition), piano playing (Chopin was his favourite composer), and landscape painting in watercolour—all of which were pursued with characteristic enthusiasm.

Donald was appointed CBE in 1973 and received the order of the Yugoslav Flag with gold star in 1982. He received honorary DSc degrees from London (1981) and Glasgow (1983), the Eardley Holland gold medal (1970), Blair Bell gold medal (1970), Victor Bonney prize (1970–72), and MacKenzie Davidson medal (1975). Other distinctions included FCOG (South Africa) (1967), honorary FACOG (1976), honorary FRCOG (1982), and honorary FRCP (Glasgow) (1984). From 1961 he was hampered by ill health, but he continued to be active despite having three major heart operations. He showed enormous courage throughout and was greatly sustained by his profound Christian faith. His opposition to the Abortion Act of 1967 and its consequences stemmed from a deep respect for human life. He was opposed to experiments on embryos. His last research effort, pursued in retirement, was an attempt to achieve a perfect method of natural family planning

using a device to warn the woman of the approach of ovulation. He died at his home in Paglesham, Essex, on 19 June 1987 and was buried in St Peter's churchyard there. He was survived by his wife and four daughters.

JAMES WILLOCKS, *rev.*

Sources *The Times* (20 June 1987) · *BMJ* (11 July 1987), 126 · *The Lancet* (18 July 1987) · J. Willocks, 'Ian Donald and the birth of obstetric ultrasound', *Obstetric ultrasound*, ed. J. P. Neilson and S. E. Chambers, 1 (1993), 1–18 · J. Willocks, 'Medical ultrasound: a Glasgow development which swept the world', *Avenue*, 19 (1996), 5–7 · *College Courant*, 28/57 (1976) · J. Willocks, Ian Donald memorial lecture, British Medical Ultrasound Society (BMUS) conference, Glasgow, 1988, BMUS collection [audiotape; no script available] · J. Willocks, address, Ian Donald memorial service, 28 Oct 1987 · E. M. Tansey and others, eds., *Looking at the unborn: historical aspects of obstetric ultrasound* (2000), vol. 5 of Wellcome Witnesses to Twentieth-Century Medicine · *WWW* · personal knowledge (1996) · private information (1996) [Alix Donald, wife]

Archives BMUS collection | American Institute for Ultrasound in Medicine, 14750 Sweitzer Lane, Laurel, Maryland, MD 20707-5906 | FILM BMUS collection | SOUND BMUS collection

Likenesses 3 photographs, 1955, repro. in J. P. Neilson and S. E. Chambers, eds., *Obstetric ultrasound*, 1 (1993), 2, 12, 15 · photograph, 1980 (scanning daughter and unborn grandchild), repro. in *Avenue* (Jan 1996), 5 · BMUS collection · priv. coll.

Donald, (Mary) Jane. *See* Longstaff, (Mary) Jane (1855–1935).

Donald, Sir John Stewart (1861–1948), administrator in India, was born at Ferozepore, Punjab, on 8 September 1861, the son of Alexander John Stewart Donald (*b.* 1824), an Anglo-Indian in the Punjab provincial service, and his wife, Susan Britten (*b. c.*1830), daughter of William Edward Hilliard. He was educated at Bishop Cotton School, Simla, and in April 1882 entered the Punjab provincial service.

Initially posted to Ambala and Ludhiana, Donald was soon transferred to Dera Ghazi Khan on the north-west frontier. By 1885 his work there had attracted the attention of Robert Sandeman, who recruited him to implement his aggressive forward policy in Baluchistan. In 1890 Donald was put in charge of the newly opened Gomal pass in southern Waziristan and in the autumn of that year was attached to the Kidderzai column of the Shirani field force to pacify the Largha–Shirani territory, for which service he was admitted to the imperial civil service. This was a rare privilege for an Anglo-Indian, and in praising him in later years Donald's superiors would never quite be able to hide their surprise that one so humbly born had done so well.

In August 1893 Donald accompanied Mortimer Durand's mission to Kabul to negotiate the Indo-Afghan frontier and in the following year was charged with demarcating the southern, Waziristan, and Kurram section of the frontier. Good-humoured patience aided his success and he was created CIE and awarded, from the Afghan side, the Izzat-i-Afghani.

After eighteen months' furlough in 1896–7, Donald was appointed to Hoshiarpur, Miran Shah, and, from 1900, Bannu, a district bordering Waziristan in which the Mahsuds and Wazirs had proved less tractable than the more southern tribes of Baluchistan. In 1903 he served as

British commissioner on the Anglo-Afghan boundary commission on the Kurram and Waziristan borders, following which he took his second furlough to Britain, where on 4 January 1905, in London, he married Henrietta Mary (d. 1955), daughter of Colonel Edward Lacon Ommanney of the Indian political service. He returned to India in late 1905, and was appointed deputy commissioner of Hazara.

In 1908, at the recommendation of Sir George Roos-Keppel, Donald became the first resident of Waziristan. In 1910 he again served on the Afghan boundary commission, for which he was made CIE. From August 1913 to January 1915 he officiated for Roos-Keppel as chief commissioner of the North-West Frontier Province. He was sceptical about the efficacy of the residency system and frequently urged the full occupation of the Mahsuds' territory in Waziristan, arguing that from a distance the British could not protect the individuals who were inclined to assist them. In spite of his criticism, however, he faithfully adhered to the government's haphazard 'carrot and stick' system of tribal allowances and punitive fines, generally adopting a wait-and-see approach to tribal incursions, and counselling against over-hasty punishment.

In 1915 Roos-Keppel succeeded in getting a KCIE for Donald, even though the political department thought that he had already been amply decorated. He was due to retire in September 1916 but under wartime conditions stayed on as resident of Waziristan and additional member of the central legislative council. In 1917 he was appointed chief political officer with the Waziristan field force operating against the Mahsuds.

Not one of the big names on the frontier, Donald nevertheless commanded the respect of his colleagues and also apparently that of the Mahsuds and Wazirs, who knew him simply as Dollan. Calm, measured, and fluent in Waziri Pushtu, he was able to gauge the tone and intent of a *jirga* or tribal gathering before committing himself to action. He had a reputation for modesty but the fate of his elder son gives a clue to the pride he took in the service and instilled in his children. In June 1946 Major John Ommanney Stewart (Joss) Donald (b. 1905) was working as political agent in south Waziristan when he was kidnapped by Mahsud tribesmen. Released two weeks later, he begged to be sent back to his old post to avoid loss of face, particularly with his father, but he was perilously close to breakdown and two months later, on 25 September, shot himself dead.

Donald retired in 1920 and, having never lived for any length of time in Britain, settled first in Jersey and then in Cyprus, where he died in Amiandos Hospital on 30 July 1948. He was survived by his wife, who died in 1955, and a younger son and two daughters. KATHERINE PRIOR

Sources CUL, Hardinge MSS, vol. 89 · *History of services of officers serving under the government of the Punjab and under the chief commissioner of the North West Frontier Province*, [30th edn] (1919) · ecclesiastical records, BL OIOC · E. Howell, *Mizh: a monograph on government's relations with the Mahsud tribe* (Simla, 1931) · *The Times* (10 Aug 1948) · *DNB* · *WWW, 1941–50* · O. Caroe, 'Plain tales of the raj', interview, 1974, BL OIOC

Archives CUL, corresp. with Lord Hardinge
Wealth at death £35,189 10s. 6d.—in England: probate, 9 Dec 1948, *CGPLA Eng. & Wales*

Donald, Sir Robert (1860–1933), journalist, was born in Dufftown, Banffshire, on 29 August 1860, the son of Robert Donald, mason, and his wife, Jane McConochie. He was educated at the local parish school. Later he taught himself shorthand and French and sought to improve himself by a programme of reading. His first job was as a clerk, but already he had determined on journalism as a career. From unsolicited, unpaid contributions to the local journal, he became a reporter for the Edinburgh *Evening News*, *The Courant*, and the *Northampton Echo*. He freelanced in London, Paris, and New York before finally securing an appointment as a correspondent on the new evening daily, *The Star*. Responsible for investigating London's government, he made a detailed study of the subject. Hoping to exploit his hard-won expertise, in February 1893, funded by the Progressives, he started a campaigning journal, *London*. The enterprise quickly foundered. Undeterred, immediately he launched the *Municipal Journal*, and in 1897 the *Municipal Year Book*, editing both until 1902. These enterprises first brought him to the notice of the newspaper proprietor Frank Lloyd. Donald married in 1890 Marie-Jeanne, daughter of a French scientist, Professor Garassut. They had two daughters, one of whom predeceased him.

In March 1895 Donald became news editor of the *Daily Chronicle*. In 1899, for what then was the princely salary of £1000 a year, he became publicity manager for the Gordon Hotel group. He contemplated a parliamentary career and was adopted as Liberal and Progressive candidate for West Ham (North). But in January 1904 he accepted Frank Lloyd's invitation to edit the *Daily Chronicle*. The new editor invigorated the newspaper; its circulation rose and its influence increased. From 1906 he also edited *Lloyd's Sunday News*. In 1911 he was appointed managing director of United Newspapers. Made a fellow of the Institute of Journalists in 1909, his distinction and status in his profession were acknowledged in 1913 by his unanimous election as president.

Though broadly sympathetic to Liberalism, Donald was never a party zealot. He believed the editor of a national newspaper should maintain close contacts with Westminster. For their part, Liberal Party leaders were happy to confide in 'so well-informed and sagacious an adviser' (Taylor, 50). His proprietor required him to follow broadly Liberal policies, but the editor alone interpreted that intention and carefully preserved his independence. It was supposed he was a close ally of Lloyd George. In 1916 the two men became estranged when the *Daily Chronicle* urged that whoever replaced Kitchener as war minister should 'shine in his own orbit without infringing the orbit of the Chief of Staff' (*Daily Chronicle*, 17 June 1916). Lloyd George resented this 'most harmful … most prejudicial' (Riddell, entry for 18 June 1916) advice that seemed to imply that Donald supported the generals. The former amity between Lloyd George and Donald was not restored until 1917. Their shared aversion to a negotiated peace brought them together, but Donald continued, as he saw fit, to question the prime minister's decisions. Lesser incursions became gravely compounded by the appointment of Major-General Sir Frederick Maurice as the *Chronicle*'s military correspondent. Interpreting this as a calculated provocation, Lloyd George determined to curb Donald's independence.

In September 1918, after a series of earlier efforts had failed, Frank Lloyd was bought out for £1.6 million. Donald resigned, refusing to accept the editorship under the political control of a board chaired by Sir Henry Dalziel, who was Lloyd George's creature. Journalists generally agreed the whole transaction had been 'an especially unsavoury incident in the history of the modern political press' (Koss, 314). Donald was never to regain his former editorial prominence. In a speech that attracted much attention, he warned that editorial independence and freedom of thought were compromised when the press was controlled by ministers and run by businessmen.

Donald secured a substantial holding in the *Yorkshire Observer* and *Bradford Daily Telegraph*. From 1919 to 1921 he owned *The Globe*, London's oldest evening journal, but had to sell out. It would have been wiser to acknowledge his earlier experience with the *Echo and London Evening Chronicle* that he persuaded Lloyd to launch in February 1915; it folded within six weeks with losses of £100,000. Donald possessed neither the peculiar gifts nor the financial resources to be a successful proprietor.

Between 1922 and 1924 Donald edited two Sunday papers, *The People* and *The Referee*. His resentment at Lloyd George's treatment of him was reflected in the uncharacteristically vituperative advice he offered Andrew Bonar Law on how to deal with Lloyd George in the forthcoming general election. 'Tell him he's a liar' (Donald to A. Bonar Law, 30 Oct 1922, HLRO, Bonar Law MSS). He had long been a friend of Ramsay MacDonald, who, in 1931, made him chairman of the newly founded National Labour Party's publicity committee. Donald ran their fortnightly *News-Letter*. In the summer of 1932 he acquired the weekly *Everyman* as a vehicle for party propaganda. Donald was its chairman, managing director, editor, inspiration, and major contributor until his death.

In the last decade and a half of his life Donald was increasingly occupied with public affairs. He sat on royal commissions and committees that examined aspects of local government, wireless telegraphy, transport, and the empire. He helped to organize a series of imperial press conferences and was chairman of the Empire Press Union (1915–26). In 1920 he was made an honorary doctor of laws of the University of Toronto, an honour he valued as much as the knighthood (GBE) conferred upon him in 1924. He expressed his concern about the problems of reconstruction in post-war Europe in three books: *A Danger Spot in Europe* (1925), *The Tragedy of Trianon* (1928), and *The Polish Corridor and the Consequences* (1930).

Donald's early entries in *Who's Who* claimed he had 'no time to practise any recreations' (*WW*, 1904). Later he took up golf, for twenty-seven years was a member of the Walton Heath club, and captained the London Press Golfing

Society (1914–20). Genial and urbane, he was a shrewd observer and critic of public affairs. In controversy he was not disposed to hedge or trim and could be tenacious and combative. He never sought the limelight as an editor. He ran the *Daily Chronicle*, by his own admission, upon rather old-fashioned lines: 'No modern journalism but good solid stuff'. He was impervious to Northcliffe's ironic response, 'My dear fellow, why not print it in Gothic type?' (*Journals and Letters of Reginald, Viscount Esher*, ed. M. V. Brett, 1934, 2.275). Just and considerate, the hallmark of Donald's journalism was his honesty and independence. Donald died in London on 17 February 1933 at his home, 12 Thorney Court, Kensington. A. J. A. MORRIS

Sources H. A. Taylor, *Robert Donald* [n.d.] · *The Times* (18 Feb 1933) · *DNB* · S. E. Koss, *The rise and fall of the political press in Britain*, 2 (1984) · G. A. Riddell, *Lord Riddell's war diary, 1914–1918* (1933) · A. T. C. Pratt, ed., *People of the period: being a collection of the biographies of upwards of six thousand living celebrities*, 2 vols. (1897) · b. cert. · *WWW* · *CGPLA Eng. & Wales* (1933)

Archives HLRO, corresp. and papers | BL, corresp. with Lord Gladstone, Add. MS 46080 · CAC Cam., letters to Lord Fisher · HLRO, letters to David Lloyd George · U. Birm. L., special collections department, Dawson MSS, corresp. with W. H. Dawson

Likenesses W. Stoneman, photograph, 1924, NPG · photographs, repro. in Taylor, *Robert Donald*

Wealth at death £13,859 14s. 10d.: probate, 7 April 1933, *CGPLA Eng. & Wales*

Donaldson, Alexander (*bap.* 1727, *d.* 1794), bookseller and printer, was baptized in Edinburgh on 24 November 1727, the second son of James Donaldson (1694–1754), a wealthy linen manufacturer who served as the town's treasurer in 1726–7, and Elizabeth Weir (*d.* 1768). His grandfather Captain James *Donaldson (*d.* 1719) had published the *Edinburgh Gazette* from 1699 to 1707. Alexander later stated that he 'embarked in the trade and business of a bookseller in the year 1750 at Edinburgh' (Skinner, 4), although he is identified as the publisher of a three-volume Edinburgh reprint of Joseph Hall's *Contemplations*, dated 1749. He became a burgess and guild brother of the city by right of his father on 29 August 1750. On 10 January 1751 he married Anna Marshall or Merchall (*bap.* 1726, *d.* 1792), a merchant's daughter, with whom he had three sons, but only the eldest, James *Donaldson (1751–1830), printer and founder of Donaldson's Hospital, survived childhood. On 4 December 1751 Donaldson became a one-third seat-holder at the prestigious New Kirk in St Giles Church, and on 23 June 1752 he joined masonic lodge Canongate Kilwinning no. 2.

The period from the early 1750s to the mid-1760s was marked by a series of bookselling and printing partnerships in Edinburgh. From 1751 until May 1758 Donaldson was the junior partner of one of Edinburgh's most prominent booksellers, Alexander Kincaid (1710–1777). On their own and in collaboration with Andrew Millar of London, Kincaid and Donaldson published several new books of philosophy and medicine by Scottish authors, including Francis Home, Henry Home (later Lord Kames), James Lind, and David Hume, and from 1753 until 1784 Donaldson's name was included in the imprint of every edition of

Hume's most important collection of philosophical writings, *Essays and Treatises on Several Subjects*. They also began reprinting English literature, such as the two-volume duodecimo edition of John Milton's *Poetical Works* that appeared in 1755. Donaldson subsequently became the fourth partner in the firm which printed that work, and from 1756 to 1760 items 'printed by Sands, Donaldson, Murray, and Cochran' were common. In August 1760 he entered into a printing partnership with John Reid that was dissolved on 11 November 1765, after which Donaldson retained the large printing house he had acquired on the south side of Castlehill and sued Reid for embezzling his books.

After leaving Kincaid, Donaldson expanded his literary reprinting business, taking Alexander Pope's head as the sign of his bookshop. By the early 1760s it was the meeting place for young Scots with literary ambitions, such as James Boswell and Andrew Erskine, who lionized 'that seat of learning and genius, Mr Alexander Donaldson's shop' (*Boswell's General Correspondence*, 3 Dec 1761), and its owner, 'the great Donaldson' (ibid., 8 Dec 1761), in correspondence published in 1763 as *Letters between the Hon. Andrew Erskine and James Boswell, esq.* Boswell describes Donaldson in his harvest jaunt journal as 'a man of uncommon activity and enterprise in Business, who has a smattering of humour and a tollerable Address' and 'entertains like a Prince' (*Boswell's London Journal*, 27 Oct 1762), which he could well afford to do as a result of a £10,000 inheritance from his father. The entertaining was done in Donaldson's spacious house in the West Bow. The second volume of Donaldson's *Collection of Original Poems* by 'Scotch Gentlemen' (1760–62) provided Boswell and Erskine with a much appreciated outlet for their juvenile poetry, and accounts for Boswell's dubbing him 'the imperial sovereign of Pope's Head, Caledonian Dodsley, Scottish Baskerville, and captain-general of collective bards' (*Boswell's General Correspondence*, 2 Dec 1761). Although Donaldson published other new books in various fields, he had little to do with publishing new works by Scottish Enlightenment authors after the dissolution of his partnership with Kincaid.

Donaldson moved to London by early April 1763. He initially joined with his brother John (*b.* 1729) at 195 Strand, at the corner of Arundel Street (sometimes identified as 'near Norfolk-street'), but imprints continued to advertise both London and Edinburgh branches of the business. Although John claimed in an advertisement of 1774 to have been selling books at the same address since 1 October 1756, it was the arrival of Alexander, armed with his cheap Edinburgh reprints, that transformed 195 Strand into the notorious 'shop for cheap books' (*Boswell's London Journal*, 13 May 1763). On 24 June 1773 the partnership was dissolved 'by mutual consent' (*Edinburgh Evening Courant*, 9 Aug 1773), with John staying at 195 Strand and Alexander moving to larger quarters at 48 St Paul's Churchyard, where he remained until the late 1780s. The reasons for the dissolution of the brothers' partnership remain a mystery, but from the mid-1770s onwards imprints stating 'printed for John Donaldson' became increasingly common, at times outpacing Alexander's own. Both men issued catalogues to promote their books. In Edinburgh, with Kincaid and on his own, Alexander had used catalogues in a conventional manner to announce the sale or auction of a special collection of books, usually for a limited time, but in London he adopted a more brazen approach, as in his 1774 circular *Books Sold Cheap*, which announces prices 'thirty to fifty *per cent* cheaper than the usual London prices' on his basic stock, and editorializes about his philosophy of bookselling.

Donaldson's invasion of the London market brought to a head an ongoing struggle between the leading London booksellers, who claimed their copyrights in perpetuity, and the majority of the Scottish book trade, who believed that copyrights were limited to the maximum term of twenty-eight years set down in the statute of Queen Anne, dating from 1710. After April 1763 the copyright debate often centred on the motives and character of Donaldson himself. In a confrontation on 20 July 1763 with the Scottish MP George Dempster, who asserted that Donaldson's aim was to make books affordable to the poor, Samuel Johnson was 'loud and violent against Mr Donaldson' and said he was, at best, 'no better than Robin Hood' (Boswell, *Life*, 1.438–9). Donaldson was criticized in the press for sacrificing quality for the sake of price, as in the attack on his edition of Pope's Homer for its 'incorrectness and mutilations' (*London Chronicle*, 8–10 March 1774). He was also taken to court: eleven suits in chancery court and one in the Scottish court of session since 1763, according to a petition that Donaldson submitted to both houses of parliament in spring 1774. There, as well as in the anonymous pamphlet that he published, and allegedly wrote, in 1764 under the title *Some Thoughts on the State of Literary Property*, he consistently presented himself as the enemy of monopoly and its harmful effects on 'the advancement of learning' (p. 7), who had been obliged 'to struggle with the united force of almost all the eminent booksellers of London and Westminster', to incur 'heavy expense', and to suffer 'much trouble and anxiety' in the name of 'the general right to supply the community at large with books at a moderate price' (Donaldson, 'Petition').

At first the legal skirmishing went badly, especially when the Donaldson brothers were slapped with a perpetual injunction in *Becket* v. *Donaldson* in November 1772 for printing a cheap edition of James Thomson's *The Seasons* in Edinburgh ('printed by A. Donaldson'). But then Alexander and two others won an important challenge before the Scottish court of session in July 1773, and that case paved the way for the Donaldsons' decisive victory in *Donaldson* v. *Becket* on 22 February 1774, when the House of Lords overturned the injunction against *The Seasons* on appeal, putting an end to the legal fiction of perpetual copyright and confirming the modern concept of limited, statutory copyright. When word of this decision reached Edinburgh there was public rejoicing, and the book trade drank a toast to the Donaldson brothers 'for having the courage to stand forth in the cause of liberty, against a most powerful combination' (*Caledonian Mercury*, 2 March

1774). Alexander's petition was submitted to the House of Commons on 3 May in an unsuccessful effort to turn that body against the so-called Booksellers' Bill, which sought to provide relief to the owners of literary property by adding another fourteen years to the term of existing copyrights. The petition was also read a month later in the House of Lords, where it may have helped to quash the bill.

Despite his emigration to London, Donaldson remained closely connected to the Edinburgh book trade. In January 1764 he founded a bi-weekly newspaper, the *Edinburgh Advertiser*, which was taken over by his son James ten years later and survived until 1859. A series of Edinburgh lawsuits during the 1760s demonstrates Donaldson's continuing business interests there, and an incident in May 1769, when he had a chest containing 'eight or ten thousand guineas' (Somerville, 162) transported from London to the Bank of Scotland in Edinburgh, shows the scale of his London profits as well as where the money was going. From 1773 onwards he seems to have surrendered most of his printing work to James, and from the middle of the next decade the number of imprints stating 'printed for' or 'sold by' A. Donaldson diminished to a trickle. The last one appeared in 1789, the year in which he retired to Broughton Hall on the outskirts of Edinburgh, which he had purchased in June 1786. Donaldson died there on 11 March 1794 and was buried three days later in Greyfriars churchyard, Edinburgh, having bequeathed to his son an estate worth about £100,000.

J. J. CAUDLE and RICHARD B. SHER

Sources *Boswell's London journal, 1762–63*, ed. F. A. Pottle (1950), vol. 1 of *The Yale editions of the private papers of James Boswell*, trade edn (1950–89) · *Boswell's London journal, 1762–63*, ed. F. A. Pottle (1951), vol. 1 of *The Yale editions of the private papers of James Boswell*, trade edn (1950–89) · Boswell, *Life* · *Boswell's general correspondence, 1757–1763*, ed. D. Hankins (2002) · R. Chambers, *Traditions of Edinburgh* (1912) · [A. Donaldson?], *Some thoughts on the state of literary property, humbly submitted to the consideration of the public* (1764) · A. Donaldson, 'Petition', *Petitions and papers relating to the bill of the booksellers now before the House of Commons* (1774); in S. Parks, ed., *The literary property debate: eight tracts, 1774–1775* (1975) · J. Donaldson, book advertisement, in J. Beattie, *An essay on the nature and immutability of truth*, 5th edn (1774) [advert appended to bk] · *GM*, 1st ser., 64 (1794), 285 · W. F. Gray, 'Alexander Donaldson and his fight for cheap books', *Juridical Review*, 38 (1926), 180–203 · M. Rose, *Authors and owners: the invention of copyright* (1993) · J. Morris, 'Scottish book trade index', www.nls.uk/catalogues/resources/sbti/ · T. Somerville, *My own life and times, 1741–1814* (1861); reprint edn (1996) · R. T. Skinner, *A notable family of Scots printers* (1927) · bap. reg. Scot.

Archives Bank of Scotland, Edinburgh | Yale U., Boswell MSS

Likenesses R. Harvie, oils, repro. in Skinner, *A notable family*, facing p. 6; known to be in the Donaldson Hospital, Edinburgh, in 1927

Wealth at death about £100,000 was bequeathed to son

Donaldson, Anna Maria. *See* Falkner, Anna Maria (*d.* 1796/7).

Donaldson, Arthur William (1901–1993), politician, was born on 13 December 1901 at 27 Rosefield Street, Dundee, the third and youngest son of George Donaldson (1859–1909), yarn dresser, and his wife, Mary Ann, *née* Kerr (*b.* 1860). He was educated at Harris Academy, Dundee, where

Arthur William Donaldson (1901–1993), by Napier Studios, early 1970s

he gained five higher leaving certificate passes in 1917. His first job was as assistant registrar of births, marriages, and deaths in Dundee, but in 1919 he began a career in journalism as a reporter with the Dundee *Courier*. In 1923 he pursued new career opportunities in the USA. Employed at first in the motor industry in Detroit, he rose to become assistant secretary in the Chrysler Corporation's public procurement division, responsible for dealing with the department of defense in Washington. On 24 September 1932, in Gates' Mill, Ohio, he married Violet Glenday Bruce (*b.* 1907), from Forfar, who, like him, had come to work in America. They had one son and one daughter. In 1928, though resident in the United States, he joined the newly formed National Party of Scotland, which sought full Scottish independence to be achieved through the contesting of parliamentary elections by this party which was to be wholly free of any other political affiliations. Although these commitments were on occasion challenged, as in 1934 and 1942, Donaldson was always loyal to the original principles.

In 1937 Donaldson returned to Scotland, where he became a poultry farmer in Lugton, Ayrshire. At the same time he began to write articles presenting the nationalist view on such topics as finance, resources, land use, and economic issues in general. He revealed as himself an informed authority upon whom his colleagues relied for guidance. As war threatened he argued, first, for Scottish neutrality, and then against the imposition of conscription, in both cases because Scots had no government democratically empowered to take such decisions affecting them. These activities no doubt caused his detention under section 18B of the defence regulations in May 1941, until petitions to the secretary of state for Scotland secured his release. Donaldson's stance on the war and on conscription was shared by Douglas Young, elected in 1942 chairman of the Scottish National Party (SNP), as the National Party of Scotland had become, following its merger with the Scottish Party in 1934, and when Young contested a by-election in Kirkcaldy in 1944, Donaldson acted as his agent. In 1945 he himself was SNP candidate in Dundee. In 1948 he moved to Forfar, where he soon became editor of the *Forfar Dispatch*. He became active in municipal affairs and for some years served as a councillor and as burgh treasurer. These commitments meant that he was not active in the elections of 1950, 1951, and 1955, but in 1959 he fought the Kinross and West Perthshire constituency and he contested the same seat in a by-election in 1963.

In 1960 Donaldson became chairman of the SNP, bringing to the job exactly the qualities then required. An inspirational speaker, he enthused supporters and impressed the uncommitted. He toured branches and constituencies, and the party's growth in membership, branches, and votes throughout the decade was phenomenal. He led from the front, being a candidate in the general elections of 1964, 1966, and 1970, contesting West Perth, Moray and Nairnshire, and finally Galloway. Significantly all these areas were subsequently won by his party. He was replaced as chairman in 1969, not because he was the target of any dislike or criticism, but rather because a new generation was ready to take office. He remained active at branch, constituency, and national level well into his eighties.

A wiry and agile man, even in his later years, Donaldson's body language told of his indomitable dedication. He entered any company briskly and with a spring in his step, and his bright eyes and strong features marked him for the good-humoured but determined warrior which he was. He died of bronchopneumonia on 18 January 1993 in Forfar, and was cremated on 23 January in Dundee. He was survived by his wife and by his son, Arthur, his daughter, Beth, having predeceased him.

JAMES HALLIDAY and GORDON WILSON

Sources personal knowledge (2004) · private information (2004) [Violet Donaldson, widow] · NL Scot., Muirhead MS Acc. 3721 · NL Scot., Gibson MS Acc. 6058 · NL Scot., Donaldson MS Acc. 6038 · NL Scot., McIntyre MSS [recent accession] · *Forfar Dispatch* (21 Jan 1993) · *The Scotsman* (20 Jan 1993) · *The Guardian* (23 Jan 1993) · *Scots Independent* (Feb 1993) · R. J. Finlay, *Independent and free* (1994) · b. cert. · marriage record, USA · d. cert.
Archives NL Scot., papers · NL Scot., further personal and political corresp. and papers | NL Scot., Gibson MS Acc. 6058 · NL Scot., McIntyre MSS · NL Scot., Muirhead MS Acc. 3721
Likenesses photograph, 1963, repro. in *The Guardian* · Napier Studios, photograph, 1970–74, Scottish National Party, Edinburgh [*see illus.*]

Donaldson [*née* Lonsdale], **Frances Annesley**, Lady **Donaldson of Kingsbridge** (1907–1994), farmer and writer, was born on 13 January 1907 at Harrow, the second

of three daughters of (Lionel) Frederick *Lonsdale (1881–1954), playwright, and his wife, Leslie Brooke Hoggan.

Frances was sent to a number of schools where she received no education to speak of and her itinerant adolescence was largely spent in the company of her spendthrift father, whose favourite daughter she was and whom she regarded as mad. They moved house roughly every six months, and it was while they were living at Birchington that Daphne du Maurier, as Donaldson recalled in *Child of the Twenties* (1959), 'used to make us play Roundheads and Cavaliers in the shrubbery' (Donaldson, 27). It was the only imaginative game she could ever remember playing, and she did not enjoy it. Golf, at which she became proficient, was more to her taste, and she played tennis with the actor Ronald Squire. The youthful companionship of P. G. Wodehouse's stepdaughter later bore fruit in a biography of the enigmatic novelist. An appeal to the friendship of Ivor Novello with a view to going on the stage was impelled by romantic fantasy. She played a small 'and entirely dreary part' with 'very few speaking lines' in a touring company's production of her father's play *The Last of Mrs Cheyney* (ibid., 103). Yet she had no illusions about her abilities as an actress, and before a second tour, she 'retired from the stage' (ibid., 105). It was her future readers' good fortune that she retained not only a warm heart but the non-judgemental instincts of the true artist despite being put through a potentially very damaging youthful experience, a first dismal marriage doomed to failure from the start. On 27 September 1927 she married Ronald McKenzie Cardwell. All she would ever reveal of this disaster was to write: 'My mother forced me, by the maximum of pressure, but also through the most extraordinary duplicity in the strangest set of circumstances, to marry a man twenty years older than myself, whom I did not want to marry' (ibid., 107). He was, apparently, rich, and in the euphemistic expression employed by a close friend, Lord Healey, 'did not like women'.

Having escaped from four years of misery, on 20 February 1935 Frances married John George Stuart Donaldson (1907–1998), always known as Jack; he was a left-wing intellectual, social worker, and dilettante Gloucestershire farmer. They had three children. It was Victor Gollancz who converted Frances to socialism; her second husband, through his work with the Pioneer Health Centre at Peckham, introduced her to the realities of poverty. The farm began to prosper when the Second World War intervened and Jack Donaldson was called up, his wife so taking to agricultural life that in 1941 she achieved her real ambition to be a writer by producing her first book, *Approach to Farming*. It went into six editions in as many years. *Four Years Harvest* and *Milk Without Tears*, hardly titles to tempt the literati, followed before Donaldson tackled her first biography, a life of her father, *Freddy* (1957). *Child of the Twenties* was a continuation of her desire to make sense of a turbulent childhood (her parents eventually separated) and was also a candid and self-deprecating attempt to unravel the intricacies of the English class structure, with which she was fascinated.

With considerable courage Donaldson then broadened

the scope of her writing with an exploration of the Marconi scandal of 1912. Few political scandals had given rise to such violent passions in modern times, and Donaldson's dispassionate handling of the material earned her well-deserved praise.

In the often acerbic Evelyn Waugh, Donaldson, compassionate farmer's wife and liberal humanist, could scarcely have found herself with a west country neighbour less similar, brilliant satirist, ardent Roman Catholic, and arch-reactionary as he was. But in *Evelyn Waugh: Portrait of a Country Neighbour* (1967) Frances Donaldson produced a critical yet immensely sympathetic reassessment of a man seemingly imbued with hidden charm. For many people Donaldson redressed with tact and truthfulness Waugh's popular image, that of a thoroughly unpleasant drunken bore, an image assiduously polished by Waugh himself. He was, she wrote, the only person she had ever known 'who seemed sincerely to long for death; he was terrifying to a stranger, merciless to a friend; but it is true that his house and life revolved round jokes; very, very funny jokes' (F. Donaldson, *Evelyn Waugh: Portrait of a Country Neighbour*, 1967, xiii).

Donaldson's greatest triumph, however, was yet to come. By the 1960s, her husband having served as a cabinet minister and a director of the Royal Opera House, there were few people of influence or interest whom Frances Donaldson did not or could not know. As luck would have it, among her friends were Major Edward Metcalfe, equerry and best man to the duke of Windsor, and his wife, Lady Alexandra Metcalfe, a daughter of Lord Curzon. Few people had known the Windsors so well in the pre-war days of their exile, and they had letters and diaries never seen before. With these at her disposal Frances Donaldson embarked on what the seasoned biographer Elizabeth Longford described as a biography 'that probably had more effect on the future of the monarchy than any other single book' (*The Independent*).

Published in 1974, *Edward VIII* won the Wolfson history award. Meticulously researched, revealing of the king's dishonesty, and wonderfully well written, *Edward VIII* became required reading for anyone who wished to stand back as objectively as the author herself to relive the drama of the abdication as it was experienced not just by the king and Mrs Simpson but also by those members of his family who felt personally betrayed. The television series *Edward and Mrs Simpson*, adapted by Simon Raven and for which Donaldson was adviser, was first shown in 1978. It swept the success of her book into living rooms throughout the world; with its authentic sets, costumes, and character acting it set a benchmark for all future historical television dramas.

Donaldson's *P. G. Wodehouse* (1982) was followed up in 1990 by her edition of his letters, *Yours Plum*, which 'provided glimpses into his psyche that her earlier biography, perhaps, could not' (*The Times*). She drew on the experiences of her husband as arts minister and supported their shared interests in her books of the 1980s: *The British Council: the First Fifty Years* (1984) and *The Royal Opera House in the Twentieth Century* (1988). Her second memoir, *A Twentieth Century Life*, was published in 1992.

Donaldson was said to combine a warm heart with a cold eye, an ideal combination of characteristics for any biographer. Her straightforward approach to life was reflected in her clear prose style and unpatronizing manner: 'She loved conversation and you had to be on your mettle in her company' (*The Independent*, 9 April 1994). Jack Donaldson received a life peerage in 1967 as Lord Donaldson of Kingsbridge. Frances Donaldson died from cancer on 27 March 1994 at her home, 17 Edna Street, London.   MICHAEL DE-LA-NOY

Sources *The Times* (29 March 1994) · *The Independent* (30 March 1994) · F. Donaldson, *Child of the twenties* (1959) · m. cert. [R. M. Cardwell]
Archives King's AC Cam., letters and postcards to G. H. W. Rylands

Donaldson, Frederick Lewis (1860–1953), Church of England clergyman and Christian socialist, was born on 10 September 1860 at 49 Newhall Hill, Ladywood, Birmingham, the second son of Frederick William Donaldson, a master wire drawer, and his wife, Elizabeth Lewis. Educated as a choirboy at Christ Church Cathedral school, Oxford, he then studied at Merton College, Oxford (BA, 1884). He was influenced at school by the Christian socialist Henry Cary Shuttleworth, then chaplain of Christ Church Cathedral. It was Shuttleworth who officiated at his marriage on 31 December 1885 to Sarah Louisa (1860/61–1950), daughter of Alderman Eagleston, a JP of Oxford. They had two sons and four daughters.

Taking holy orders, Donaldson was assistant curate to Shuttleworth at St Nicholas, Cole Abbey (1884–6). An admirer of Stewart Headlam, he also joined the Guild of St Matthew (1889), founding an Oxford branch. He was one of the first members of the Christian Social Union (1889) and became chairman of the Leicester branch (1896–1906). However, considering its leaders insufficiently socialist, Donaldson joined the militant Church Socialist League in 1906 giving it the slogan 'Christianity is the religion of which socialism is the practice' (Jones, 188). He chaired the league (1913) with George Lansbury as president.

Donaldson had meanwhile worked in three poor curacies in London (1886–95): St Phillip's, Regent Street, St Peter the Great, Windmill Street (1886–9), and St John the Evangelist, Hammersmith (1889–95). He also served as rector of Nailstone, Leicester (1895–6), before achieving fame as the Red Vicar of St Mark's, Leicester (1896–1918), where he became 'chaplain of the unemployed' in a march of the latter to London and back in June 1905. This began with a service, including a prayer and sermon by Donaldson, to be followed by similar services en route. At Bedford the march was joined by Ramsay MacDonald, Labour MP for Leicester (1906–18), and his wife. Together with a by now hoarse Donaldson they headed the march to Trafalgar Square where the two men addressed a huge rally. Donaldson had written to both Edward VII and to Randall Davidson, archbishop of Canterbury, asking them to receive a delegation of the unemployed; he even knocked

Frederick Lewis Donaldson (1860–1953), by Bassano, 1936

at the door of Lambeth Palace, but both refused to receive him. However, special services for the marchers were held at Westminster Abbey and St Paul's Cathedral.

Donaldson later wrote how the march had revealed that the marchers were not 'the shiftless simpletons' as described in *The Times* but 'splendid material running to waste to the great loss of the nation', and that unemployment was not just a local but a national, parliamentary question (Binyon, 171). His reply to the archbishop had been somewhat acerbic. This fierceness was well expressed in an undated pamphlet in which he compared those he deemed responsible for the deaths of five hundred out of every thousand infants in the worst slums to King Herod massacring the innocents at Bethlehem (Jones, 261). In 1913, among other activities, Donaldson led a deputation of Church of England clergy to the prime minister, H. H. Asquith, demanding women's suffrage (*The Times*, 8 Oct 1953).

A visual expression of Donaldson's viewpoint can be found on some panels in St Mark's, Leicester, painted by J. Edie Read under the vicar's direction. Mammon is shown with his moneybags, waited on by Luxury. Workers are depicted in various states of misery but led by Christian socialists they move from the sordid world of competition to the glorious one of common ownership and co-operation. Christ appears in a centre panel as the apotheosis of labour.

A controversial pacifist in the First World War, Donaldson in 1918 moved to the rural parish of Paston, then served as a full canon of Peterborough Cathedral

(1921–4). As Labour prime minister, Ramsay MacDonald appointed him a canon of Westminster (1924–51). Among other positions Donaldson was a council member of the Industrial Christian Fellowship (1920–44) and in 1918 was appointed to the archbishop's committee on public worship. His chief interest now was world peace, being president of the London Council for the Prevention of War (1927) and chairman of the League of Clergy for Peace (1931–40). He had maintained contact with Ramsay MacDonald who, when MP for Leicester, had often stayed in his house. He wrote in September 1931 telling MacDonald, when he formed the National Government, 'that of all possible decisions you chose the better part' though he was unhappy about the National Government's prolongation (Marquand, 650). Yet he wrote congratulating MacDonald (14 February 1936) on his son, Malcolm's, victory at the Ross and Cromarty by-election, but deploring the defeat of the Labour Party. MacDonald replied that his party was the true Labour Party. 'I venture to flatter myself', he concluded, 'it was not merely as a personal friend of mine, but as an old Socialist who sticks to his faith you congratulated me on Malcolm's success' (ibid., 782). Unhappy about Labour as well as National Labour, Donaldson now devoted much of his energies to the administration and history of the abbey, being steward (1925–36), treasurer (1931–46), archdeacon (1936–46), receiver-general from 1937, and subdean from 1946. Groups of visitors whom, as a very old man, he piloted round the abbey had no idea that he was the firebrand of yester-year. Donaldson died on 7 October 1953 at 21 Dean's Yard, Westminster; his ashes were interred next to those of his wife in the Islip chantry in Westminster Abbey.

N. C. MASTERMAN

Sources *WWW*, 1951–60 · P. D'A. Jones, *The Christian socialist revival, 1877–1914* (1968) · *Church Times* (9 Oct 1953) · C. Binyon, *The Christian socialist movement in England* (1931) · D. Marquand, *Ramsay MacDonald* (1977) · G. W. E. Russell, ed., *Henry Cary Shuttleworth: a memoir* (1903) · J. Rostron, *Leicester's unemployed march to London, 1905*, ed. J. Hinton (1985) · private information (2004) [keeper of muniments, Westminster Abbey; Leicester historian, Society of Victorian History] · D. Nash, *Secularism, art and freedom* (1992), 173 · *The Times* (8 Oct 1953) · b. cert. · m. cert. · d. cert. · *CGPLA Eng. & Wales* (1953)
Archives People's History Museum, Manchester, corresp. | PRO, Ramsay MacDonald papers
Likenesses Bassano, photograph, 1936, NPG [*see illus.*] · group photograph, repro. in Rostron, *Leicester's unemployed*
Wealth at death £6314 7s. 4d.: probate, 22 Dec 1953, *CGPLA Eng. & Wales*

Donaldson, Sir George Hunter (1845–1925), art collector and dealer, was born in Edinburgh on 25 May 1845, the youngest child of Charles Alexander Donaldson (c.1800–1868), importer and exporter of furniture, and his wife, Mathilda Hunter. Although little is known about his early life and education, it is clear that Donaldson travelled extensively in Europe, settling in Paris in the late 1860s. He developed there what became a lifelong interest in historic furniture. After moving to London about 1871, he set up in business as a dealer in works of art in New Bond Street, where his shop remained until his retirement in the 1890s. In 1872 he married Alice Jessie Stronach (1851–1907), with whom he had seven children.

Perhaps in recognition of his knowledge and contacts, Donaldson was made a juror in the furniture section of the Universal Exhibition in Paris in 1867. His professional and private interests were principally in English and European furniture of the sixteenth to eighteenth centuries and early musical instruments. He built up outstanding personal collections of both and could list among his clients the collectors George Salting and John Jones, and the South Kensington (later the Victoria and Albert) Museum. The latter made its first purchase from him in 1885 and continued to receive furniture, carpets, and ceramics from him, as purchases or gifts, until his death. The Royal College of Music was the recipient of his unparalleled collection of historic musical instruments in 1894. Timed to coincide with the opening of the new college building in Prince Consort Road, Donaldson was given free rein to decorate the room of his choice in an appropriate style, which included a coffered ceiling and a Sienese minstrels' gallery. The Donaldson Room, as it became known, is now used as a library.

Donaldson's interest in international exhibitions continued with his creation of the historic music rooms for the Inventions Exhibition in London in 1885. He was a juror again at the Paris Universal Exhibition of 1889 and was made vice-president of the jury in Paris in 1900. Recognizing the 'superior ingenuity and taste' shown by the European 'new art' exhibits, he spent £500 granted by the Board of Education and several thousand pounds of his own on a collection of furniture and ceramics that he presented to the Victoria and Albert Museum for circulation among the government schools of design (new art furniture nominal file, V&A). The collection included two cabinets by Louis Majorelle, a table by Émile Gallé, and part of a music room by Charles Spindler (all V&A). It was, and remains, one of the finest collections of art nouveau—acquired contemporaneously—outside France and Belgium. However, its initial reception in England was decidedly mixed, eliciting letters of complaint to *The Times* and the *Architectural Review*.

The success of Donaldson's business can be measured by the string of homes he bought or rented in Britain and Europe from the mid-1880s. He eventually settled at 1 Grand Avenue, Hove, Sussex, where he opened his own museum. He was made a knight, first class, by the grand duke of Saxe-Coburg and Gotha in 1885, and a chevalier of the Légion d'honneur 'for artistic services to France' in 1892 (Mott, 85). In 1904 he received a knighthood. Having suffered from bronchial conditions all his life, he died at home in Hove on 19 March 1925 after a long illness and was buried on 23 March in Brighton.

SORREL HERSHBERG

Sources E. A. Mott, 'Portrait of a man: Sir George Donaldson, 1845–1925', 1983, Royal College of Music Museum, London [unpublished memoir] · *The Times* (20 March 1925) · 'Sir George Donaldson', V&A, archive and registry, nominal file · 'New art furniture', V&A, archive and registry, nominal file · G. Donaldson, 'The Victoria and Albert Museum, gift of new art furniture for circulation', *Magazine of Art*, 25 (1900–01), 466–71 · P. Macquoid, 'English furniture in Sir George Donaldson's collection', *Country Life*, 43 (1918), 115–17, 137–40 · E. Aslin, 'Sir George Donaldson and art nouveau at South Kensington', *Journal of the Decorative Art Society*, 7 (1983), 9–14 · J. A. Neiswander, '"Fantastic malady" or competitive edge?', *Apollo*, 32 (1989), 310–13
Archives Royal College of Music, London | V&A
Likenesses F. A. Sandys, watercolour, 1878, priv. coll.
Wealth at death £122,363 17s. 5d.: probate, 19 May 1925, CGPLA Eng. & Wales

Donaldson, Gordon (1913–1993), historian, was born at 140 McDonald Road, Edinburgh, on 13 April 1913, the third child and only surviving son of Magnus Donaldson (1877–1966), sorting clerk and telegraphist, and his wife, Rachel Hetherington Swan (1882–1973), daughter of William Swan, inspector with the Caledonian Railway Company, and his wife, Alice Whitehead. Educated at the Royal High School, Edinburgh, which he left in 1931 as dux, Donaldson was expected by his teachers to read classics at Edinburgh University, but, always the individualist, he chose to study history instead. Professor Robert Kerr Hannay's lectures inspired in him a lifelong fascination with documentary sources, and Donaldson took all the history class medals but one before gaining an outstanding first-class degree in 1935. Afterwards he again avoided the predictable and, instead of moving to Oxford or Cambridge, wrote his PhD thesis, 'Relations between English and Scottish presbyterian and episcopalian movements to 1604', at the Institute of Historical Research in London, under the supervision of the Tudor historian J. E. Neale. On graduating in 1938 he secured a post in the Register House, Edinburgh (now the National Archives of Scotland), where he developed his archive skills, indexing part of the register of presentations to benefices and the books of assumption as well as surveying a number of privately owned collections of muniments.

As a student Donaldson had abandoned his parents' presbyterian background to join the Scottish Episcopal church, and his deeply held faith seems to have prompted him to become a conscientious objector at the start of the Second World War (Kirk, 31–2). When several tons of the older Scottish records were evacuated to Morenish House, near Killin, in Perthshire, in 1940, he was one of the staff sent with them. He did not appreciate this exile, but it gave him further opportunities for study, and afterwards he liked to joke that he was the only person ever to have read the original manuscript of the register of the privy seal in bed. With the end of the war, the records and staff returned to Edinburgh and in 1947 William Croft Dickinson, at that time Sir William Fraser professor of Scottish historical studies and palaeography at Edinburgh University, recruited Donaldson to his staff. The Scottish history department was small and had always been somewhat overlooked, but Dickinson, a leading medievalist, was determined to develop it and he knew that Donaldson had already been contemplating a move to academic life. They collaborated on their classic three-volume *Source Book of Scottish History* (1952–4), and soon the department was famous for both teaching and research. Donaldson remained there for thirty-two years, becoming reader in 1955, and then professor when Dickinson died suddenly in 1963.

As head of his department Donaldson was an effective administrator, affable, and surprisingly democratic in style, given his reputation as an autocrat. He instituted the new degree of honours in Scottish historical studies and also attracted an impressive number of postgraduates from all over the world. A tall, thin figure with receding dark hair, horn-rimmed glasses, and neat features, Donaldson might at first sight have seemed intimidating—an austere and rigorous historian with a sharp eye for detail and an equally sharp tongue, his pencil hovering over a script, ready to swoop on any errant comma or careless generalization. His irritation with inaccuracies and his sensitivity to criticism could lead him into acrimonious public controversy but he was endlessly patient with his students, delighting them with his quick wit and always willing to find practical solutions to their problems. When they graduated he deployed them in universities, archives, and museums throughout Scotland and beyond, encouraged their careers, criticized their publications, privately boasted of their achievements, and entertained them in his house with personally cooked meals and home-made jam.

Although he was plagued for years by a duodenal ulcer, Donaldson's energy, drive, and enthusiasm led him to undertake a wide range of activities. He was president of the Scottish Ecclesiological Society (1963–5), the Scottish Church History Society (1964–7), the Scottish History Society (1968–72), the Scottish Record Society (1981–93), the Scottish Genealogy Society (1986–92), and the Stair Society (1987–93), as well as editing the *Scottish Historical Review* (1972–7) and serving on the Royal Commission on the Ancient and Historical Monuments of Scotland (1964–82) and the Scottish Records Advisory Council (1964–87). Already a fellow of the Royal Historical Society, he was elected a fellow of the British Academy in 1976 and a fellow of the Royal Society of Edinburgh two years after that.

Donaldson's publishing output was prodigious, and from the time of his university appointment he was not only editing texts such as the *Accounts of the Collectors of the Thirds of Benefices* (1949) but writing books and a stream of scholarly articles, notes, and reviews. The Scottish Reformation remained the principal focus of his attention, and in 1957 he was invited to deliver the Birkbeck lectures in ecclesiastical history at the University of Cambridge. Basing his arguments on a meticulous study of the documentary sources of ecclesiastical administration, he clearly demonstrated that the national church set up by John Knox and his colleagues in 1560 was not presbyterian, as had previously been believed. The lectures were published in 1960 as *The Scottish Reformation*, and if some of his readers were reluctant to accept this revolutionary interpretation, the book was soon recognized as a seminal work. Donaldson's writings were by no means confined to the narrowly ecclesiastical. He devised the four-volume *Edinburgh History of Scotland*, with his own contribution, *Scotland: James V to James VII* (1965), as the first part to

appear. In all, the bibliography of his works runs to twenty pages, ranging from *The First Trial of Mary, Queen of Scots* (1974) to *Northwards by Sea* (1965), an account of the ships that sailed to Shetland, his father's homeland, to which he himself was deeply attached.

Dedicated as he was to disseminating the results of recent research, Donaldson lectured widely and took part in radio broadcasts and later in television programmes. His international reputation as a scholar brought him an avalanche of enquiries. He always responded, courteously guiding a delighted German housewife and her son round the site of Kirk o'Field (thereby forming a rewarding friendship that lasted for the rest of his life), or sending a kindly response to a thirteen-year-old Canadian schoolgirl who had written: 'Since I am planning to become a History Professor, I am wondering if you could give me a few tips' (personal knowledge; Kirk, 129). Away from the academic world, he was equally active. A lay preacher in the Scottish Episcopal church, he played an important role in the Boys' Club movement, and was a governor of Coates Hall, the episcopal theological college in Edinburgh, as well as participating for more than thirty years in the ultimately unsuccessful ecumenical discussions aimed at uniting the Church of Scotland with the episcopal church. Throughout his life he was a generous and private benefactor to charitable causes.

Although he liked the company of women and had various romantic attachments in his youth, Donaldson did not marry. He was intrinsically shy, and in any case a wife would have interfered with his cherished activities. Instead, he lived with his parents until they died when he was in his fifties. He derived great satisfaction from his friendships, from sailing in small boats, digging peat at his holiday house in Benderloch, near Oban, and most of all from visiting Shetland. When he retired in 1979 he briefly considered moving there, but he realized that it was too isolated. Soon afterwards he was made HM historiographer in Scotland, an honour of which he was intensely proud. 'I am asked for historical advice', he would say, explaining his new role, and he would add with a twinkle in his eye, 'Well, I give it anyway, whether I am asked or not' (personal knowledge).

Donaldson's final years were spent in the house to which he retired in Dysart, Fife. There he could look directly out from his sitting-room windows at the waters of the Firth of Forth and go sailing in his small dinghy. As busy as ever with his historical activities, he was in 1988 invested with the insignia of a commander of the British empire at the Palace of Holyroodhouse and, to his great satisfaction, he received on 6 January 1993 the Norwegian St Olav medal for his work in promoting professional and cultural links between Scotland and Norway. By then he was terminally ill with cancer. He died peacefully in the Cameron Hospital, Windygates, Fife, on 16 March 1993, and a very large congregation filled the episcopal cathedral of St Mary, Edinburgh, on 22 March for his funeral; this was followed by a private cremation at Warriston crematorium, Edinburgh. He left the bulk of his estate to the Dalrymple Archaeological Trust for the preservation of historic buildings, with his beloved 'old kirks' particularly in mind.

Donaldson had devoted his life to writing, lecturing, and research, determined to give the Scots a meticulously accurate record of their own past. Because of his demandingly high standards, some critics have seen him as an élitist, a reactionary figure, the enemy of popularization. That was not so. He could be difficult, it is true, and he could cling tenaciously to idiosyncratic theories, but he worked tirelessly to make Scottish history the widely read and academically respected subject that it is today. Moreover, formidable though his achievements were, he remained throughout his long and distinguished career the simple, kind-hearted, unpretentious man that he had always been. Asked on a radio programme a few months before his death what epitaph he would choose for himself, he replied with characteristic modesty: 'Someone recently made, I think, the nicest remark … He said that I combined the enthusiasm of youth with the wisdom of age. Now what better a judgment could you wish for than that?' (Kirk, flyleaf). ROSALIND K. MARSHALL

Sources J. Kirk, *Her majesty's historiographer: Gordon Donaldson, 1913–1993* (1996) [incl. complete list of pubns] · T. Lothian, 'Gordon Donaldson: an appreciation', and J. Imrie, 'Gordon Donaldson and the records of Scotland', *The Renaissance and Reformation in Scotland*, ed. I. B. Cowan and D. Shaw (1983), 1–21 · W. Ferguson, 'Gordon Donaldson, 1913–93', *PBA*, 84 (1994), 265–79 · M. Merriman, 'Gordon Donaldson, 1913–93: an appreciation', *SHR*, 72 (1993), 240–43 · *The Times* (23 March 1993) · D. Shaw, 'Prof. Gordon Donaldson: leading historian', *The Scotsman* (18 March 1993) · T. Dalyell, 'Professor Gordon Donaldson', *The Independent* (18 March 1993) · *The Herald* [Glasgow] (19 March 1993) · personal knowledge (2004) · private information (2004) · b. cert. · d. cert.
Archives NRA, priv. coll., papers used for teaching · Shetland Archives, Lerwick, corresp. and papers relating to history of Shetland · U. Edin.
Likenesses photograph, 1970–79 · R. Dobson, portrait (in DLitt robes), U. Edin.; replica, Shetland Museum? · photograph, repro. in *The Isles of Home*, 2nd edn, jacket · photograph, News International Syndication, London
Wealth at death £445,382.82: confirmation, 31 May 1993, *CCI*

Donaldson, James (d. 1719), publisher and writer, is a figure whose origins are unknown, apart from his own account of them. He claimed that his father had been a landowner, and that he himself raised a company in the earl of Angus's regiment for William III in the revolution of 1688. He saw action, being wounded at Killiecrankie and imprisoned in Blair Castle, but received no reward. The company was disbanded at Candlemas 1690 and shortage of funds forced him abroad for a few years.

Donaldson took to writing with no great success. His *Husbandry anatomized, or, An enquiry into the present manner of tilling and manuring the ground in Scotland* (1697–8) was unduly neglected. It contained a programme for improved farming in advance of current thought, his most innovative proposal being for the use of potatoes as a field crop. This pamphlet was dedicated to the earl of Marchmont, then lord chancellor, and in an introduction he supplied what little is known of his family background.

Donaldson's next publication, a piece of bad verse entitled *A Picklock for Swearers, or, A Looking-Glass for Atheists and Profane Persons* (1698), was more successful for the Edinburgh council gave him an award of 10 Rex dollars 'for his paines in compyling of some poems against profanity which are dedicat to the good town' (Armet, *Extracts, 1689–1701*, 231). He wrote various other tracts, mainly on economic issues. *The Undoubted Art of Thriving* (1700) proposed the expansion of trade and laid emphasis on the Indian and African Company (the Darien scheme). In 1701 he produced *Certain and infallible measures whereby the whole begging poor of the kingdom may be alimented at much less charge*, which proposed very little more than rigorous enforcement of the existing poor law, other than calling on every parish to have a group of young men to visit each household and take the 'vicious or idle' to compulsory work. Parishes were to force those in workhouses to work more productively, so as to earn more than they ate. He seems ignorant of the lack of workhouses and assumes that profitable work is always available. He also wrote a series of verse panegyrics to various craft skills: malting and brewing (1712), weaving (1712), and wright craft (1713).

Donaldson married Jean Wedderburn (d. 1697) on 28 August 1691. Their son James (1694–1754) was a weaver, but their grandson, Alexander *Donaldson, and a further generation returned to publishing. He claimed to have a numerous family, but other members have not been traced. There is an undated verse flysheet of no literary merit entitled *An epithelanium on the jovial nuptials of Captain James Donaldson with the meritorious Mrs Jean Reid, alias Mrs Scott, composed by a lady of honour*. This may have been part of a jest or protest at his press.

Donaldson's significance lies in the fact that for fifteen years, from his printing house on the south side of Edinburgh's High Street, he was editor of the first newspaper in Scotland to have had any long-term continuity. This was the *Edinburgh Gazette*, a weekly licensed by the privy council on 10 March 1699. The paper's text was supposed to be checked before printing by Lord Cassillis for the council, but at first this was not enforced and in June 1699 a piece appeared which annoyed the council: Donaldson was imprisoned for five days, securing release by an abject statement of submission. Control in advance of printing then became a reality.

The *Gazette* consisted mainly of news from London, and British and foreign politics, passed on by the council. This was what the Scottish business community wanted for most of the eighteenth century. Donaldson also ran a business in 'buriall letters', adaptable printed formulas allowing for the insertion of specific funerals. He tried to set up a factory for producing firearms, but ran into opposition from the Edinburgh Hammermen as well as the council.

In 1705 the promise of a monopoly to Donaldson was broken by the council and one Adam Boig was allowed a similar newspaper, the *Edinburgh Courant*. Boig was also later allowed to print the names of the Scottish members of the British parliament. He got his news by post from London, for which he had to pay postage. Donaldson obtained the privilege of correspondence with France.

Both editors carried on a vigorous correspondence with the council complaining of the privileges of the other, and in Donaldson's view there was no adequate market for two papers. He received a grant of £30 from the convention of royal burghs but still felt inadequately supported. When Boig printed an advertisement which the council disliked, both editors were put in gaol. The *Courant* ceased publication soon after the quarrel with Donaldson. In 1708 the privy council was abolished but the town council of Edinburgh attempted to assert similar control. Donaldson had become a burgess and guild brother of the burgh in 1703. He died on 17 September 1719 and was buried two days later in Greyfriars churchyard, Edinburgh. He left a legacy for afflicted children.

ROSALIND MITCHISON

Sources R. T. Skinner, *A notable family of Scots printers* (1928) • W. J. Couper, *The Edinburgh periodical press*, 2 vols. (1908) • *Scottish Notes and Queries*, 3rd ser., 8 (1930), 190–93 • *Miscellany of the Maitland Club, consisting of original papers and other documents illustrative of the history and literature of Scotland*, 2 (1840) • H. Armet, ed., *Extracts from the records of the burgh of Edinburgh, 1689–1701*, [13] (1962) • H. Armet, ed., *Extracts from the records of the burgh of Edinburgh, 1701–1718*, [14] (1967) • J. Donaldson, *Husbandry anatomized* (1697) • DNB

Wealth at death legacy for afflicted children

Donaldson, James (1751–1830), newspaper editor and philanthropist, was born on 3 December 1751 at 7 West Bow, Edinburgh, and baptized the same day. He was the eldest son of Alexander *Donaldson (*bap.* 1727, *d.* 1794), an Edinburgh bookseller, and his wife, Ann, *née* Marshall. In 1763 his father opened a bookshop in London that took advantage of copyright differences between Scotland and England, thereby establishing the family fortune (about £100,000).

In 1774 Donaldson took over the editorship of the bi-weekly *Edinburgh Advertiser*, which his father had founded about ten years earlier. The paper grew into a flourishing business, particularly during the years of the American War of Independence and the French Revolution. In 1792 he married Jean Gillespie. They lived first in George Street and then in both a town residence at 85 Princes Street and a country seat at Broughton Hall. They had five children, none of whom survived childhood.

Donaldson more than doubled his inheritance through judicious investments, and although rumours of eccentricity and even miserliness seem to have circulated about him, he was extremely regular in his work habits, a fair employer, and generous in response to appeals for charity. He became a burgess and guild brother of the city of Edinburgh, and a director of the Bank of Scotland; he sat on the jury which convicted the infamous burglar Deacon Brodie in 1788. He retired in 1820.

On the death of his wife in 1828 Donaldson made a will leaving his fortune (£215,377) for the founding of a hospital for destitute children, with preference to be given to those named Donaldson and Marshall. He died at Broughton Hall on 16 December 1830, and was buried in the graveyard of St John's Church, Princes Street. Donaldson's Hospital was built at West Coates, Edinburgh, to a design by William Henry Playfair, and inaugurated in 1851; as Donaldson's College it is now a leading institution in the education of deaf people.

DOUGLAS BROWN

Sources documents supplied by Donaldson's College, Edinburgh • private information (1888) [Donaldson's nephews: James Gillespie and William Wood] • *Documents relating to Donaldson's Hospital* (1851) • bap. reg. Scot.

Likenesses A. Edouart, cut-paper silhouette, Scot. NPG

Wealth at death £215,377: Donaldson's College, Edinburgh

Donaldson, James (*fl.* 1794–1796), writer on agriculture, practised as a land surveyor in Dundee. He was also agent for the earl of Panmure. His chief work was *Modern Agriculture, or, The Present State of Husbandry in Great Britain* (4 vols., 1795–6). Donaldson was one of those employed by the board of agriculture to make surveys of the agriculture of each county, and he was responsible for *A General View of the Agriculture of the County of Banff* (1794) and similar reports on the agriculture of the Carse of Gowrie, and the counties of Elgin and Nairn, all published in 1794, and Kincardine (1795). His *General View of the Agriculture of the County of Northampton* (1794) includes an appendix comparing the systems of agriculture in Northampton and Perth.

GORDON GOODWIN, *rev.* ANNE PIMLOTT BAKER

Sources J. Donaldson, *Agricultural biography* (1854), 69

Donaldson, Sir James (1831–1915), educationist and classical and patristic scholar, was born in the Aberdeen area on 26 April 1831, son of James Donaldson (of whom nothing certain is known) and Christina McKay (subsequently married in 1849 to William Hannan, a widower). He was educated from 1842 at Aberdeen grammar school and from 1846 at Marischal College, Aberdeen, where he became a protégé of John Stuart Blackie, professor of Latin. After graduation he commenced training at New College, London, intending to become a Congregational minister. However, he already had other interests both in classical scholarship and the theory of education; moreover he studied also in Berlin, where he encountered the educational ideas of J. F. Herbart.

In 1852 Donaldson abandoned New College to become assistant to Blackie, now professor of Greek at Edinburgh. At this time, many ideas long to dominate Donaldson's thinking were shaped. He owed much to Blackie: his interest in post-classical Greek (shown by an early publication, *Modern Greek Grammar* (1853) intended for classics students, and a contribution to *Encyclopaedia Britannica* on Byzantine and neo-Hellenic literature); his admiration for the German educational tradition and for German views on the psychology of education; and perhaps also the ideological foundations for his Scottish nationalism, which was to emerge in his support for home rule for Scotland, and for his liberal politics, source of powerful support later in his career. On 4 January 1855 he married Margaret Kennedy (*d.* 1887), with whom he had two sons, born in 1857 and 1859.

After two years (1854–6) as rector of Stirling high school, Donaldson moved to Edinburgh high school where he was a classics master for ten years and rector from 1866 to 1882. In these years he made his main contributions to scholarship. His *Critical History of Christian Literature and Doctrine from the Death of the Apostles to the Nicene Council* appeared in three volumes between 1864 and 1866, the first, *The Apostolic Fathers*, in 1864 (2nd edn, 1874), and the remaining two, *The Apologists*, in 1866. With Alexander Roberts he edited and contributed to the twenty-four volumes of *The Ante-Nicene Christian Library* (1867–72). He also published *Lectures on the History of Education in Prussia and England* (1874). Donaldson's educational activity extended beyond practice to history and theory, and beyond schools to universities. He was ambitious and highly political. He expressed strong objections to the Education (Scotland) Act of 1872, in particular to the importation of 'English' ideas and the loss of the parish tradition. In 1882 he became professor of humanity in the University of Aberdeen where he continued to pursue his wide interests in education and assiduously cultivated his aristocratic contacts. At this time he opposed the foundation of teachers' training colleges, believing that the training of teachers should be done within universities.

Donaldson's appointment to the Aberdeen chair was widely viewed as having been engineered by his friend and powerful patron, Lord Rosebery; and his appointment four years later as principal of United College at the University of St Andrews (when the previous dual principalship, of St Mary's and of United College, came to an end) was attended by highly controversial political manoeuvrings. Donaldson's continued active involvement in Liberal politics was recognized in 1910 when he was one of the Liberals whom Asquith intended to create peers, to secure the passing of the Parliament Act.

After an inauspicious and unpopular start Donaldson proved an effective and forceful principal at a time of great expansion and change; his astute and pragmatic administrative style emerges in his public addresses, published in 1911. The implementation of the provisions of the Universities (Scotland) Act of 1889 engaged his energies in the early years. He presided over the difficult and protracted negotiations on the rival merits of incorporation or affiliation of University College, Dundee; these ended in 1897 with union (which he had favoured). Thereafter came a time of expansion, when Donaldson successfully raised money for extensive building projects. Notable benefactors were the marquess of Bute and Andrew Carnegie, successive rectors in this era. During Donaldson's term of office, in 1892, women were first admitted to degrees. It may have been the 'woman question' which prompted his revision and publication of earlier papers in the form of *Woman: her Position and Influence in Ancient Greece and Rome, and among the Early Christians* (1907), his last classical work.

After the death of his first wife Donaldson married again in 1890. His second wife, Mary Christie (*née* Webster, first married name Laing), had twice been widowed and predeceased him in 1908. Donaldson was knighted in 1907, and continued his work as principal until a few weeks before his death, at his home in Scores Park, St Andrews, on 10 March 1915.   E. M. CRAIK

Sources A. S. Lowson, 'Principal Sir James Donaldson: education and political patronage in Victorian Scotland', PhD diss., U. St Andr., 1988 · U. St Andr. L., special collections department, Donaldson MSS
Archives U. St Andr., papers | NL Scot., corresp. with Lord Rosebery
Likenesses G. Reid, oils, U. St Andr.
Wealth at death £8254 12s. 7d.: Scottish confirmation sealed in London, 4 June 1915, CGPLA Eng. & Wales

Donaldson, John (*b.* in or after 1737, *d.* 1801), miniature painter, was born in Edinburgh. His father was a glover 'in narrow circumstances ... [but] of so peculiar a cast of mind that he was inclined to discuss metaphysical subjects while he cut out the gloves' (*GM*, 1st ser., 71, 1801, 1056). Donaldson is first recorded in 1756, when he won a prize from the Society for the Encouragement of Arts, Sciences, Manufactures, and Agriculture in Edinburgh for a drawing from a bust of Horace. He also won a prize offered by the society in 1757 for the best drawing 'from any statue for boys under 20' (*Scots Magazine*, 19, 1757, 161). At this date he was a protégé of the engraver Richard Cooper, and several drawings are identified as by Donaldson, including a youthful self-portrait in profile in a scrapbook made by Cooper (priv. coll.). Donaldson also exhibited a portrait of Cooper in London in 1762, and a miniature portrait of Cooper by him is preserved in the Yale Center for British Art, New Haven, Connecticut.

The fullest account of Donaldson's career is the 'Memoir of the life of John Donaldson esq., miniature painter', written before 1804 in part by David Steuart Erskine, eleventh earl of Buchan, 'portions being in his own handwriting' (University of Edinburgh Library, La. IV.26), and expanding on the obituary of the artist in the *Gentleman's Magazine* (1801). Buchan records that he first met Donaldson as a young man and that he himself owned a number of his early 'imitations' of Albrecht Dürer and Wenceslaus Hollar. Such imitations are paralleled in the early work of John Runciman, also in Cooper's circle.

About 1760 Donaldson moved to London, where his first address (from *c.*1760 to 1763) was 'at Mr Coopers in Princes Street, Leicester Fields'. He seems to have remained in London. In his notes on the artist, David Laing, however, gives an account of an Edinburgh career, including membership of the Incorporation of St Mary's (the incorporation of the Edinburgh trades) in 1768, his marriage in the same year, and his election as a burgess of the city in 1781. This account seems to confuse Donaldson with a decorative painter of the same name, and has misled some later authors. It would not have been impossible for Donaldson to pursue his career in both capitals, but there is no other evidence that he did so, nor is there any other reference to his marriage. He did not entirely give up his Edinburgh connection, however, as in 1786 he applied unsuccessfully to succeed Alexander Runciman as master of the Trustees' Academy. From 1761 Donaldson exhibited regularly in London. In 1764 he won the first premium of the Society of Arts, a prize of 20 guineas, for *The Tent of Darius*, and in 1768 he won a further prize of 30 guineas from the same society for *Hero and Leander*. The latter, and *The Death of Dido* exhibited in the same year, were paintings in enamel. The earl of Buchan purchased *Hero and Leander* and presented it, incorporated into a gold box, to Marischal College, Aberdeen, where it remains. An inscription on the lid records Buchan's gift. The fact that Donaldson did exhibit enamels of this kind and the appearance of the initials 'J. D.' on a piece of Worcester porcelain have led to the hypothesis that he worked for various porcelain factories. This is unlikely. The one certain work of this kind, Buchan's gold box, bears no relationship in style to the porcelain works attributed to Donaldson. Furthermore, Buchan says of the *Hero and Leander* that 'Though he (Donaldson) was pressed by his friends to prosecute that line in the art, he never could be persuaded to paint another' (Buchan and others).

In 1763 Donaldson exhibited at the Society of Artists three miniatures, and miniatures seem to have been his principal line of work thereafter. In 1770, for instance, he exhibited a miniature of General Paoli, also at the Society of Artists. He continued to paint subject pictures, however, and in 1775 exhibited *Orlando and Olivia* at the Royal Academy. He exhibited again at the academy in 1791, *A Portrait of a Gentleman*. In 1764 he became a member of the Society of Artists and in 1789 a member of its council. The few certain works by Donaldson, including *Lady with Powdered Hair* (signed and dated 1787; NG Scot.), demonstrate that he was indeed a master of miniature painting. His miniatures were not only on ivory in the conventional manner, but were also in graphite on vellum. The drawing of Richard Cooper in the Yale Center for British Art is in this manner. In 1768 a portrait drawing by Donaldson of David Hume, presumably also in graphite, was used as the frontispiece of Hume's *Essays and Treatises*; it was used again in 1770 in an edition of Hume's *History of England*. Hume wrote to Andrew Millar, the publisher: 'The picture that Donaldson has done for me is a drawing and in everybody's opinion as well as my own is the likest that has been done of me' (Brydall, 166).

Donaldson inherited his father's speculative cast of mind and was eccentric—or radical—in his views. On 4 March 1763 James Boswell recorded in his journal: 'Donaldson the painter drank tea with me … [He] is a kind of speculative being and must forsooth contradict established systems. He defended adultery and he opposed revealed religion' (*Boswell's London Journal*, 210–11). W. D. McKay describes his views as 'socialistic' (McKay, 27), and according to his obituary not only did Donaldson never moderate these views, he actually pursued speculative thought at the expense of his art and his livelihood. Certainly such opinions would not recommend a miniature painter to a fashionable clientele, and it is not surprising that his business fell off. Perhaps in an attempt to redeem his fortunes, on 2 February 1793 he patented a system for preserving 'animal and vegetable substances on long voyages', though it brought him no profit (*GM*, 1st ser., 71, 1801, 1057). He published two books, *Elements of Beauty: also Reflections on the Harmony of Sensibility and Reason* in 1780, with a second edition in 1786, 'much improved, to which is annexed a short analysis of the human mind', and *Poems*

(1784; 2nd edn, 1786, with 'the additional poem: Danae, from the Greek of Simonides'). At his death he also left a mass of unpublished manuscripts. In 1795 he moved from Westminster, where he had been living, to Islington, where he died in poverty on 11 October 1801, 'cared for by his friends, many of whom he had lost by his sarcastic temper, during his last illness' (Buchan and others). He was buried at St Mary's Church, Islington, on 16 October.

DUNCAN MACMILLAN

Sources *Scots Magazine*, 18 (1756) · *Scots Magazine*, 19 (1757), 161 · *GM*, 1st ser., 71 (1801), 1056–8 · Earl of Buchan [D. S. Erskine] and others, 'Memoir of the life of John Donaldson esq., miniature painter, portions being in his own handwriting', U. Edin. L., MS La. IV.26 · D. Laing, 'Notes on artists', U. Edin. L., MS La. IV.26 · R. Brydall, *History of art in Scotland* (1889) · W. D. McKay, *The Scottish school of painting* (1906) · *The letters of David Hume*, ed. J. Y. T. Greig, 2 vols. (1932) · R. L. Hobson, *Worcester porcelain* (1910), 108 · W. H. Tapp, 'John Donaldson: enameller, miniaturist and ceramic artist', *Apollo*, 36 (1942), 39–42; 151–3 · D. Foskett, *A dictionary of British miniature painters*, 2 vols. (1972) · Chambers, *Scots.* (1855) · W. Tapp, notebooks, V&A NAL, M97.0003 [microfilm], vols. 2–4 · *Boswell's London journal, 1762–63*, ed. F. A. Pottle (1951), vol. 1 of *The Yale editions of the private papers of James Boswell*, trade edn (1950–89), 210–11
Likenesses J. Donaldson, self-portrait, drawing, priv. coll.
Wealth at death 'died in poverty'

Donaldson, John (1789/90–1865), composer and musicologist, was the son of a Mr Donaldson and his wife, M. S. Gregg, and appears to have started his professional career as a music teacher in Glasgow from 1811 to about 1814. In 1826 he became an advocate in Edinburgh. In 1841 he applied for the Reid chair of music at the University of Edinburgh, and was elected in 1845 as its fourth occupant. He succeeded two English holders of the chair who had regarded it as a sinecure. Such had been their indolence that the funds for the chair (endowed by General Reid) had been allowed to be appropriated by the university authorities for other purposes and, to a man of principle (which Donaldson's *Statement* on the professorship, published in 1848, clearly shows him to have been), the appointment was little short of a poisoned chalice.

Donaldson, using his legal knowledge, was the first Reid professor to establish the chair on a proper footing. He instigated proceedings in the court of session in 1850 and, after five years of litigation, gained a decision in his favour. The university was ordered by the courts to build a music room and provide adequate moneys for it to function. The university senate did not finally carry out its obligations until 1861, the battle having by then broken Donaldson's health. He was granted a civil-list pension of £75 in April 1861. The professorship being in 'the theory of music', he specialized in theory, acoustics, and even the engraving of music, as well as assembling for his department an outstanding collection of instruments, including a fine organ.

Donaldson's piano sonata in G minor, published about 1823 (reproduced in N. Temperley, *The London Pianoforte School*, 1985, 7.xviii, 275), is his only surviving composition. A powerful and ambitious work, hinting at cyclic structure, the piece is stylistically advanced in the context of

British music of the period: given its quality, it is regrettable that Donaldson appears to have abandoned composing. He died at his home, Marchfield, Cramond, near Edinburgh, on 12 August 1865. His wife, Dorothea Finlay, predeceased him. W. B. SQUIRE, *rev.* JOHN PURSER

Sources Boase, *Mod. Eng. biog.* · A. Grant, *The story of the University of Edinburgh during its first three hundred years*, 2 vols. (1884) · H. G. Farmer, *A history of music in Scotland* (1947) · d. cert. · *CGPLA Eng. & Wales* (1865)

Likenesses W. S. Watson, oils, exh. 1849, U. Edin.

Wealth at death £6790 13s.: confirmation, 19 Sept 1865, NA Scot., SC 70/1/127, 259

Donaldson, John (1799–1876), writer on agriculture, was born in Northumberland and was probably related to another agricultural writer, James *Donaldson (*fl.* 1794–1796). In all, John Donaldson wrote, contributed to, and edited more than a dozen works on agricultural topics, covering such subjects as clay lands and loamy soils, farm buildings, manures, and the management of crops, describing himself on their title pages as a professor of botany. In addition to these, he also published *Agricultural Biography* (1854) and wrote, for William Owen the bookseller, a periodical detailing country fairs to be held during the year. Donaldson was presented to the Charterhouse in Holborn, London, by the prince consort in August 1855, and died a poor brother there on 22 March 1876, leaving a will in favour of Elizabeth Paine, a widow.

THOMAS SECCOMBE, *rev.* GILES HUDSON

Sources *N&Q*, 7th ser., 8 (1889), 76 · *CGPLA Eng. & Wales* (1876) · d. cert.

Wealth at death under £100: probate, 13 May 1876, *CGPLA Eng. & Wales*

Donaldson, John William (1811–1861), philologist, born in London on 7 June 1811, was the second son of Stuart Donaldson, Australia merchant, and brother of Sir Stuart *Donaldson. His grandfather, Hay Donaldson, was town clerk of Haddington, near Edinburgh, and his mother was Betty, daughter of John Cundale of Snab Green, Arkholme, Lancashire. He was educated privately, and at fourteen was articled to his uncle, a solicitor. In 1830, while in his uncle's office, he went up for an examination at University College, London, and gained the first prize in Greek. His ability attracted the attention of the examiner, George Long, by whose advice he was sent to Trinity College, Cambridge, where he matriculated in 1831. He gained a scholarship in 1833, and in 1834 was second in the classical tripos (Dr Kennedy being first) and senior optime. He proceeded MA in 1837, BD in 1844, and DD in 1849. He was elected fellow and tutor of Trinity in 1835, and up to his marriage in 1840 devoted himself to lecturing, teaching, and making himself master of the results of German philology. He was president of the union in 1839, and in the same year he was ordained deacon and published his *New Cratylus, or, Contributions towards a More Accurate Knowledge of the Greek Language*, said to be 'the only complete treatise on inflected language then in existence either in England or on the continent'. Donaldson was right to stress the importance of the study of comparative philology, but his tone was polemical and his conclusions

were doubtful. In 1844 Donaldson published *Varronianus*, which he defined in the preface to the third edition as 'an attempt to discuss the comparative philology of the Latin language on the broad basis of general ethnography'. Although the work was unsystematic and of no lasting value, it involved him in a violent controversy with Professor T. H. Key, who accused him of plagiarism.

Donaldson lost his fellowship in 1840 on his marriage to Laetitia, daughter of Sir John Mortlock, banker at Cambridge, with whom he had two sons and two daughters. His first wife predeceased him, and he went on to marry Louisa, daughter of John Rawlins; they had three daughters. After taking pupils for a time at Winfrith in Dorset, in 1841 Donaldson was appointed headmaster of King Edward's School, Bury St Edmunds, an appointment unfortunate for the institution and for himself. He was deficient in judgement and administrative power, and the school declined under him, notwithstanding his efforts to obtain reputation by the publication of Latin and Greek grammars, which met with little acceptance beyond the sphere of his personal influence and involved him in controversy. They were probably too scientific for school use, and his conviction of the defects of standard grammars had been expressed with indiscreet candour. He was active in the cultural life of Bury St Edmunds, where he greatly improved the Athenaeum.

Donaldson resigned the headmastership in 1855 partly on account of the outcry caused by the publication of *Jashar; fragmenta archetypa carminum Hebraicorum; collegit, ordinavit, restituit J. G. Donaldson*, which appeared at the end of 1854. In this extraordinary work he endeavoured to show that fragments of a book of Jashar are to be found throughout the Old Testament scriptures up to the time of Solomon, that the book was compiled in the reign of that monarch, and that its remains constitute 'the religious marrow of the scriptures'. The work was heavily criticized and Donaldson's religious orthodoxy was questioned. Although he defended his position in a vigorous pamphlet, he failed to convince his critics.

After resigning his headmastership Donaldson took up his residence at Cambridge, where he obtained a high reputation as a tutor, and he was elected one of the classical examiners of the University of London. In 1856 he produced a lengthy essay entitled 'Classical scholarship and classical learning', which despite its characteristically intemperate style contains interesting suggestions about the improvement of university classical teaching. He prepared new and improved editions of his *New Cratylus, Varronianus, Jashar,* and *Greek Grammar*; he also wrote a disquisition on English ethnography in the *Cambridge Essays,* and the article 'Philology' in the eighth edition of the *Encyclopaedia Britannica,* and in 1858 completed K. O. Müller's unfinished *History of Greek Literature*. He began a Greek dictionary, which was to have been the great work of his life. Unfortunately he worked far too hard, both as author and teacher. When advised to take six months' rest he replied that this would cost him £1500. The neglect of the advice proved fatal. On coming to London in January 1861 he found himself unable to conduct the university examination, and on 10 February he died there at his mother's house, 21 Craven Hill, killed by overwork.

Donaldson had a brilliant mind, but he lacked the scholarly virtues of moderation and restraint. Judgement too often forsook him in his speculations, and taste in his controversies. He theorized far too boldly from insufficient data, and put forward as certainties views which should only have been advanced as suggestions. In biblical criticism more especially he can only be regarded as a brilliant amateur. He was greatly beloved by his friends, who included N. C. Thirlwall and W. H. Thompson. The diarist Henry Crabb Robinson spoke enthusiastically of the charm of his conversation. Donaldson produced a large number of other books, pamphlets, and reviews, especially in *Fraser's Magazine*, and was part author with P. W. Buckham of *The Theatre of the Greeks*, which achieved considerable popularity in its time.

RICHARD GARNETT, *rev.* RICHARD SMAIL

Sources Venn, *Alum. Cant.* · *The Athenaeum* (16 Feb 1861), 230 · *GM*, 3rd ser., 10 (1861) · *Bury and Norwich Post* (19 Feb 1861) · T. L. Peacock, 'Müller and Donaldson's *History of Greek literature*', *Fraser's Magazine*, 59 (1859), 357–77 · J. W. Burrow, 'The uses of philology in Victorian England', *Ideas and institutions of Victorian Britain*, ed. R. Robson (1967), 180–204 · T. G. Hake, *Memoirs of eighty years* (1892)
Wealth at death £18,000: probate, 3 April 1861, *CGPLA Eng. & Wales*

Donaldson, Joseph (1794–1830), soldier and surgeon, was born in Glasgow, where his father was employed by a mercantile house. With some school companions he ran away to sea and made a voyage to the West Indies, which disenchanted him of a sea life, and he returned home and was sent back to school by his father. Early in 1809 he again ran away, and without communicating with his friends enlisted in the old 94th (Scotch, or Scots, brigade). He accompanied the regiment to Jersey, then to Spain, where it took part in the desperate defence of Fort Matagorda during the siege of Cadiz, and afterwards was with Picton's division in the principal battles and sieges in the Peninsula from 1811 to 1814. After the peace in 1814 the Scots brigade was stationed in Ireland, where it was disbanded in 1818, except for the 94th, which survived. In the meantime Donaldson married a young Irish girl, alluded to in some of his writings under the name of Mary Mac-Carthy; they had ten children.

Early in 1815 Donaldson was discharged as sergeant, at the age of twenty-one, at the expiration of his limited-service engagement. Returning to Glasgow with his wife, he made a little money by the publication of his *Scenes and Sketches in Ireland*. His hopes of obtaining employment in civil life having utterly failed, Donaldson went to London with his family, enlisted in the East India Company's service, and was employed as a recruiting-sergeant, at first in London and afterwards in Glasgow. Disliking this, he got himself transferred to the district staff, and was employed as head clerk in the Glasgow district staff office for some years, during which time he published his *Recollections of an Eventful Life, Chiefly Passed in the Army* and *The War in the Peninsula*.

While in London, Donaldson had found time to study

anatomy and surgery, studies which he continued at Glasgow University. Having qualified as a surgeon, he took his discharge in 1827, and set up in medical practice at Oban in Argyllshire, where he remained until 1829, though with little success. He left his wife and children in Glasgow, and, hoping to improve his medical prospects, went to London and afterwards to Paris, where he died of pulmonary disease in October 1830, at the age of thirty-six. He was reported to have been a frequent anonymous contributor to the press. His three books, which give a vivid picture of soldier life in the Peninsula and in Ireland, were republished in 1855 as *Recollections of the Eventful Life of a Soldier* for the benefit of his widow and a surviving daughter, then in distressed circumstances in Glasgow.

H. M. CHICHESTER, *rev.* JAMES LUNT

Sources J. Donaldson, *Recollections of an eventful life, chiefly passed in the army* (1825) · C. W. C. Oman, *Wellington's army, 1809–1814* (1912); repr. (1968) · W. F. P. Napier, *History of the war in the Peninsula and in the south of France*, 3 vols. (1878) · J. Donaldson, *The war in the Peninsula: a continuation of the recollections of the eventful life of a soldier* (1825) · J. Weller, *Wellington in the Peninsula, 1808–1814*, new edn (1992)
Wealth at death left wife in distressed circumstances

Donaldson, Malcolm (1884–1973), obstetric physician and gynaecologist, was born at Tower House, Chiswick Lane, Chiswick, Middlesex, on 27 April 1884, the son of John Donaldson, a civil engineer, and his wife, Frances Sarah Thornycroft. He was educated at Charterhouse School and matriculated at Trinity College, Cambridge, in 1902. While at Cambridge he established a reputation as a great oarsman, winning the university sculls and rowing for the University of Cambridge against Oxford and Harvard in 1906. He subsequently entered St Bartholomew's Hospital, London, as a medical student and in 1909 he took the conjoint diploma of the Royal College of Physicians and the Royal College of Surgeons. He graduated MB BChir in 1912 and became FRCS in 1914.

During the First World War, Donaldson served in the Royal Army Medical Corps as a surgical specialist, and in 1921 he was elected to the staff of St Bartholomew's, where the title of physician accoucheur was still used. He later became consulting physician accoucheur to St Bartholomew's and director of its cancer department. He was also appointed gynaecologist to Mount Vernon Hospital, Northwood, and to cottage hospitals in Brentford and Potters Bar.

In 1929 Donaldson was elected a fellow of the Royal College of Obstetricians and Gynaecologists and subsequently made many distinguished contributions to the college. A member of its council for many years, he also served on the examination committee, from 1932 to 1952, the hospital recognition committee, and the scientific advisory committee; he was chairman of the first two for eight and four years respectively. He was examiner for the membership of the college, for the universities of Cambridge, Oxford, and London, and for the Central Midwives' Board. During the Second World War he volunteered as a member of a surgical team which was sent to

Southampton to attend to the casualties ferried over from the Normandy landings.

Early in his career Donaldson became deeply involved in the problems of cancer. He was one of the pioneers of the treatment of cancer of the cervix by irradiation, and he was always on very good terms with his colleagues in the department of radiotherapy, beginning with Dr N. S. Finzi, who was himself a pioneer in the field. Donaldson was a vice-chairman of the National Radium Commission and a member of the radiology committee for the Medical Research Council. His *Radiotherapy in the Diseases of Women* was published in 1933, and three years later he published *The Early Diagnosis of Malignant Disease*, a manual for the use of general practitioners. Donaldson took a tremendous interest in the education of the public about cancer. He believed that fear of cancer was the greatest factor preventing patients from seeking advice early, and he began to advocate an educational campaign aimed at promoting the early detection of cancer and dispelling the inaccurate information that clouded the issue. During the Second World War he drove many miles in the blackout to distant villages to address Women's Institutes and other associations. On his retirement from St Bartholomew's Hospital, Donaldson moved to Oxford where he founded the Cancer Information Association, and devoted his time, energy, and money to the practical application of his beliefs. He travelled widely at home and abroad to lecture on the subject, and it was not long before the requests for lectures and demonstrations were more than could be met with the resources available. During the last months of his life he was greatly encouraged to see that, with the development of the Central Cancer Council, his ideas were receiving support at the highest level.

Affectionately known as Dottie to his friends, Donaldson was a tall, elegant, and athletic man; he was widely respected and admired for his integrity, self-discipline, and devotion to work. Donaldson was twice married, first in 1919 to Evelyn Helen Marguerite Gilroy, with whom he had two sons. In 1940 he married Mia (d. 1970), widow of Gregory J. M. Whyley. He died at his home, 337 Woodstock Road, Oxford, on 16 March 1973 of coronary thrombosis.   ORNELLA MOSCUCCI

Sources *BMJ* (31 March 1973), 808 · *The Lancet* (7 April 1973), 786 · b. cert. · d. cert. · *The book of matriculations and degrees … in the University of Cambridge from 1901–1912* (1915) · WWW
Likenesses photograph, repro. in *BMJ*
Wealth at death £113,153: probate, 11 May 1973, *CGPLA Eng. & Wales*

Donaldson, St Clair George Alfred (1863–1935), bishop of Salisbury, was born at 22 Rutland Gate, Westminster, London, on 11 February 1863, the third of four sons of Sir Stuart Alexander *Donaldson (1812–1867) of Pangbourne, Berkshire, first premier of New South Wales, and his wife, Amelia, daughter of Frederick Cowper of Carleton Hall, Cumberland. He was nephew to the philologist J. W. Donaldson and younger brother of Sir Stuart Donaldson, master of Magdalene College, Cambridge, and vice-chancellor, whom he much admired. Educated at Eton College (1877–81), Trinity College, Cambridge, where he

took double firsts in classics (1885) and theology (1887), and Wells Theological College, St Clair Donaldson was made deacon in May 1888 by the bishop of London and immediately joined the diocesan mission at St Andrew's, Bethnal Green. He served simultaneously as a resident chaplain to Archbishop E. W. Benson of Canterbury, who in December 1889 priested him. In October 1891 he joined the Eton College Mission, first at St Augustine's, Hackney Wick, and then as vicar of St Mary, Hackney Wick (1894–1900) and head of the mission. In May 1901 he was mentioned as organizing secretary of the Society for the Propagation of the Gospel but in January 1902 he became rector of Hornsey, Middlesex, and rural dean nine months later. In 1903 he was elected president of the London Junior Clergy Missionary Association.

After an abortive election in 1903, the synod of the diocese of Brisbane delegated the choice of its fourth bishop to the archbishop of Canterbury alone. Randall Davidson had been resident chaplain with Donaldson at Lambeth Palace. Donaldson's Australian connections, his London experience in the East End and at Lambeth, his moderate high-churchmanship, and independent means all commended his nomination. He was consecrated in St Paul's Cathedral, London, by Davidson on 28 October 1904, and enthroned in St Luke's Pro-Cathedral, Brisbane, on 21 December. Created archbishop in 1905, he was metropolitan of Queensland, the most coherent province in Australia, and he very nearly became primate in 1909.

Upon an uneven Australian bench, Donaldson stood out for his statesmanship, spiritual leadership, common sense, and unfailing good humour. His devotion and piety in private were matched by his vision and oratory in public. As diocesan of Brisbane, he built upon the financial and administrative structures set by his predecessor, W. T. T. Webber; here he was ably assisted by two men who accompanied him in 1904, Henry Le Fanu, his archdeacon (and after 1915, his coadjutor), and Francis de Witt Batty, his chaplain. Conscious of the complaint that the diocese was a 'practising shop' for English clergy on five-year contracts, in his seventeen years in Brisbane Donaldson doubled the number of his clergy, of whom in 1921 half were Australian born and trained. In 1905 he established at Charleville the least monastic of the three Queensland bush brotherhoods. At Nundah, a Brisbane suburb, he revived as a provincial institution a former diocesan theological college, dedicated in 1907 to St Francis: as metropolitan, he controlled the placement of all its students, often favouring the weaker dioceses of the province. In 1911, within a year of the opening of the University of Queensland and largely through his private benefaction, St John's Residential College for Men was founded: it failed, however, to provide a stream of ordinands. Donaldson encouraged the diocese to eschew primary education, already provided by the state and numerous Roman Catholic convents, and to concentrate upon secondary day and boarding-schools, for boys and girls. These included the Glennie School for Girls, Toowoomba (1908), St Hilda's Southport (acquired by the church in 1911), the Southport School (1901), acquired in 1913, and the renamed Brisbane Church of England Boys' Grammar, acquired in 1914. The choir, transepts, and first bay of St John's Cathedral, Brisbane, a French Gothic revival masterpiece designed by J. L. Pearson, were consecrated on 28 October 1910, the first public occasion upon which all the bishops of the province vested in copes and mitres. St Martin's Hospital, adjacent to the cathedral, was opened in 1921 as a war memorial. Long concerned with such social and moral issues as gambling, temperance, and birth control, Donaldson finally held a general mission to the province in 1917; it was a qualified success.

Donaldson's greatest influence in Australia was felt beyond his diocese. On his election he welcomed the opportunity to work in a disestablished church; he quickly discovered the constraints imposed by the 'legal nexus' between the Australian church and the Church of England in the United Kingdom. He determined first to define that nexus, then to break it. He envisaged an autonomous Australian church, able to play an independent and prominent part in national affairs. In 1912 he helped prepare the questions upon which learned opinion was sought in England and which long remained the basis of the movement for autonomy. His farewell public speech in Australia was his peroration to the debate on this question at the 1921 general synod. The Brisbane church congress of 1913 owed much to his planning and leadership. With Bishop Gilbert White, he tried to reorganize general synod and its subsidiary, the Australian board of missions. Before the war Donaldson joined the Brisbane branch of the Round Table, which often met at Bishopsbourne; during the war, he actively encouraged recruitment. His Lenten series of addresses in the cathedral was published as *Christian Patriotism* (1915). As a senior chaplain to the armed forces he was annoyed by what he considered the indecisiveness of the primate and the chaplain-general. His speeches and correspondence with Archbishop Davidson reveal his support for imperial responsibilities but his distaste for jingoism and for national and state politicians and their sectarian outbursts, which he despised.

While Donaldson was in England in 1913–14, largely through the influence of his only sister, May, wife of the Hon. the Revd Algernon Lawley, his translation to an English see was mooted. The war intervened; but in October 1921, Donaldson was translated to Salisbury, so that he could inaugurate a post-war mission to the church overseas. His initial attempts to abandon the palace at Salisbury as his residence failed; he used it instead to entertain youth (the 'bishop's lipstick parties') and educated laity with minimal church affiliations. To lighten his administrative responsibilities, in 1925 he revived the suffragan see of Sherborne and attempted to have Le Fanu appointed. He became consultant on all matters Australian to successive archbishops of Canterbury. From 1921 to 1933 he was foundation chairman of the Church of England missionary council and inaugurated the Jerusalem Chamber Fellowship of Prayer; here he showed skill, patience, and practical wisdom, born of his Australian experience.

In 1926 he was appointed to the Church of England council of overseas settlement. He supported the 'deposited' prayer book of 1928. In 1931 he was appointed to chair the joint committee of the convocation of Canterbury on 'The church and marriage', which reported in 1935.

Donaldson received many awards, including honorary doctorates of Cambridge (1904), Durham (in civil laws, 1908), and Oxford (1920); in 1923 he became an honorary fellow of Magdalene College, Cambridge, and in 1933, knight commander and prelate of the Order of St Michael and St George. He published in his lifetime only the customary discourses of diocesan bishops; however, *A Meditation on the Acts of the Apostles* (London, 1937) reveals his intense personal piety. He died unmarried at the palace, Salisbury, on 7 December 1935 and was buried in Salisbury Cathedral on 11 December.   RUTH FRAPPELL

Sources *CGPLA Eng. & Wales* (1936) • b. cert. • LPL, Archbishop Randall Davidson MSS, vols. 90, 108, 126, 139, 141, 176, 186, 190, 192, 196, 200, 236 • LPL, Archbishop Cosmo Lang MSS, vols. 59, 97, 107, 111, 145, 157 • A. P. Kidd, 'The Brisbane episcopate of St Clair Donaldson, 1904–1921', PhD diss., University of Queensland, 1996 • K. Rayner, 'The history of the Church of England in Queensland', PhD diss., University of Queensland, 1962 • C. T. Dimont and F. de W. Batty, *St Clair Donaldson* (1939) • *Church Standard* [Sydney] (13 Dec 1935) • *The Times* (9 Dec 1935) • *DNB* • K. J. Cable, index of Australian Anglican clergy, University of Sydney • *AusDB*
Archives Anglican Diocesan Archives, Brisbane, corresp. | Trinity Cam., letters to Sir Henry Babington Smith
Likenesses O. Birley, oils, 1932, Bishop's Palace, Salisbury • W. Stoneman, photograph, 1933, NPG • photograph, repro. in Dimont and de W. Batty, *St Clair Donaldson* • photograph, NPG
Wealth at death £50,794 14s. 4d.: English probate, resworn in Australia, 3 April 1937, *CGPLA Eng. & Wales* (1936)

Donaldson, Sir Stuart Alexander (1812–1867), businessman and politician in Australia, was born on 16 December 1812, the third son of Stuart Donaldson (d. 1849), a London merchant born in Haddington, Scotland, and his wife, Betsy, the daughter of John Crundall of Snab Green, Lancashire. John William *Donaldson (1811–1861) was his brother. Family memory held that Stuart was educated privately. At the age of fifteen he entered his father's firm, which was one of the major traders with Australia. He spent part of 1830 in Hamburg and Berlin, and travelled in the silver-mining regions of Mexico between 1831 and 1834; in 1866 he published his letters on his experiences there under the title *Mexico Thirty Years Ago*.

In 1835 Donaldson migrated from England to Australia to work with his father's correspondent Richard Jones, who was the leading merchant in Sydney. Donaldson became Jones's partner in 1837 and bought his business from the beginning of 1838. This made him immediately a substantial broker, buyer, and exporter of wool and whale oil, as well as an importer and wholesaler on a grand scale. He acquired 250,000 valuable acres of sheep-runs in New England. Building on the capital and credit of the family firm, he became promoter and director of banking, insurance, steamshipping, railway, and copper-mining companies. His profits increased markedly once gold was discovered in 1851.

Donaldson had been appointed a magistrate as early as

1838, in which year he organized the Australian Club, the first club for gentlemen in the colony; in 1856 he was a founder member of the Union Club, its main rival. The capital, youthful energy, affability, bachelorhood, and self-regard that involved him in managing the social life of his peers drew him also into electoral politics, with the franchise limited to men of property. In the legislative council of New South Wales he held the rural seat of Durham, in the Hunter valley, at four polls between 1848 and 1853, when he returned to England on business. While there he married, on 21 February 1854, Amelia, the daughter of Frederick Cowper of Carleton Hall, Penrith, Cumberland. Following his return to Australia, Donaldson won the suburban seat of Sydney Hamlets in 1855 and retained it in 1856 at the first election under a new constitution (with a broader franchise) which conferred responsible government on the colony.

After two weightier conservatives failed to form a ministry, the governor turned to the clubman Donaldson as a safe alternative. Donaldson assembled his team in April 1856 and was sworn in as colonial secretary and first premier of New South Wales on 6 June. He and his backers hoped that he might gain support from some of the liberal parliamentarians, but the factional and administrative complexity of moving to responsible government brought his ministry down on 25 August 1856. Its liberal successor lasted for five weeks only. In the ensuing conservative ministry led by Henry Parker (October 1856–September 1857) Donaldson was colonial treasurer and, briefly, commissioner for railways. He was also a member of the senate of the University of Sydney from 1851 to 1861.

Having reached the limit of honour in Australia, Donaldson consolidated his wealth, placed his sheep stations in the hands of two brothers-in-law, and in 1859 retired to England. He was knighted on 23 August 1860. In that year he assumed the chair of the General Association for the Australian Colonies, an investors' lobby in London, and he joined company boards. From his arrival in England he looked for a seat in the House of Commons: *The Times* described him in April 1860 as 'a returned Australian gentleman who has been hovering about several English constituencies in the last few months'. He was the official but unsuccessful Liberal candidate at by-elections for Dartmouth in August 1859, Harwich in April 1860, and Bath in February 1861. A moderate conservative in the fast-changing Australian colonies, he presented himself as a moderate liberal in the United Kingdom, an admirer of Lord Palmerston who opposed church rates and supported a £6 franchise and the secret ballot. Donaldson visited his investments in Australia in 1861 and 1864. But his health declined drastically, and he was diagnosed with heart problems; he became gaunt where he had once been portly, and he lost his voluble joviality (which some people called bumptiousness). He died at his father-in-law's seat, Carleton Hall, on 11 January 1867, survived by his wife, their four young sons, who included St Clair George Alfred *Donaldson (1863–1935), and one infant daughter. In 1841 Donaldson had arranged a cabin passage from Sydney to London for Mrs Maria Leicester and her four-month-old son, whose paternity he acknowledged.

BARRIE DYSTER

Sources S. Draper, 'Donaldson, Sir Stuart Alexander', *AusDB*, vol. 4 · B. Dyster, 'Prosperity, prostration, prudence: business and investment in Sydney, 1838–1851', *Wealth and progress: studies in Australian business history*, ed. A. Birch and D. S. Macmillan (1967), 51–76 · *Votes and proceedings*, New South Wales Legislative Council (1848–56) · *Votes and proceedings*, New South Wales Legislative Assembly (1856–9) · *Ford's Australian Almanac* (1844) [Sydney] · *Ford's Australian Almanac* (1847) [Sydney] · *Ford's Australian Almanac* (1851–) [Sydney] · P. Loveday and A. W. Martin, *Parliament, factions and parties: the first thirty years of responsible government in New South Wales, 1856–1889* (1966) · *The Times* (15 Jan 1867) · *Sydney Morning Herald* (23 March 1867) · C. T. Dimont and F. de W. Batty, *St Clair Donaldson: archbishop of Brisbane and bishop of Salisbury* (1939) · *Sydney Morning Herald* (1835–59) · *The Times* (5 Aug 1859) · *The Times* (10 Aug 1859) · *The Times* (30 March 1860) · *The Times* (3 April 1860) · *The Times* (16 April 1860) · *The Times* (21 April 1860) · *The Times* (23–5 April 1860) · *The Times* (13 Feb 1861) · *The Times* (23 Feb 1861) · *DNB*
Archives Mitchell L., NSW · State Library of New South Wales, Sydney, Dixson Library, letters from and family corresp. | Mitchell L., NSW, Macarthur MSS · Mitchell L., NSW, Riley MSS · University of Melbourne, James Graham letter-books
Likenesses photograph, 1856, Mitchell L., NSW · C. Silvy, carte-de-visite, 1860, NPG · photograph, repro. in Dimont and Batty, *St Clair Donaldson*
Wealth at death under £40,000: probate, 19 March 1867, *CGPLA Eng. & Wales*

Donaldson, Thomas Leverton (1795–1885), architect, was born on 19 October 1795 at 8 Bloomsbury Square, London, the third son in the family of four sons and two daughters (the eldest son died in infancy) of James Donaldson (*c*.1756–1843), architect and district surveyor, and his wife, Jane, daughter of Andrew Leverton. Thomas *Leverton, the architect, was his great-uncle. He was educated at King Edward VI's Grammar School, St Albans.

In 1809 Donaldson went to the Cape of Good Hope to work for Robert Stuart, a merchant, but soon after his arrival he volunteered for the 87th regiment, for an expedition to capture Mauritius. The French surrendered, and as there was no permanent vacancy for him in the regiment, he returned to Britain at the age of sixteen, and became a pupil under his father. In 1815 he was admitted to the Royal Academy Schools, where he studied under John Soane, and was awarded the silver medal in 1817.

In 1819 Donaldson set off for the continent, and travelled for five years in Italy, Greece, and Asia Minor, measuring and sketching the most important buildings, and developing a great enthusiasm for the antique. Canova, president of the Accademia di San Luca at Rome, liked his design for a temple of victory, and Donaldson was elected a member of that academy in 1822.

On his return to Britain in 1823, Donaldson began to practise as an architect. He married Matilda Georgiana Lingham (*d*. 1876) in 1825, and they had three sons. Though unsuccessful in the competition for the completion of King's College, Cambridge, in 1825, he won the competition for Holy Trinity Church, South Kensington, with a Gothic design (1826–9). Many buildings were erected from his designs, including the library at University College, London (1848–9), in the classical style, and University Hall (now Dr Williams's Library), Gordon Square (1848–9), his best-known work, in the Tudor Gothic style, and the German Hospital, Hackney (1865). His design for the rebuilding of the Royal Exchange, which burnt down in 1838, was given first place as a design in 1840, but did not win; he also competed unsuccessfully to build the Nelson monument in Trafalgar Square and in 1860 for the memorial to Prince Albert. In addition to his practice as an architect, Donaldson was district surveyor for South Kensington for many years.

Not a major architect, Donaldson was nevertheless a prominent figure in the world of Victorian architecture and is best remembered as the founding father of the Institute of British Architects (later the Royal Institute of British Architects) in 1834. He continued to act as honorary secretary of this professional body until 1839, and then as its foreign secretary for a further twenty years. He devised the motto 'Usui civium, decori urbium', and designed the Mycenean lions medal of the institute. He was awarded the royal gold medal in 1851 and was president of the institute from 1863 to 1864. Donaldson served on the building committee for the Great Exhibition of 1851, and it is thought by some that the official design produced by the committee, which was rejected in favour of Joseph Paxton's Crystal Palace design, was almost entirely his. He also served as treasurer of the Architectural Publication Society from 1848 to 1860.

In addition to his work towards establishing the professional status of architects through the foundation of the Institute of British Architects, Donaldson is also remembered as the first professor of architecture to be elected to the newly founded chair at University College, London, in 1842. Second only to that established at the Royal Academy in 1768, this chair was established at University College in 1841 at the suggestion of William Inwood, architect. A pioneer in the academic study of architecture, Donaldson had to plan a system of work and to devise his own methods: he divided his subject into architecture as a fine art, which he treated from a historical point of view, and architecture as a science. His lectures were well illustrated with drawings and diagrams, his collection of which passed into the possession of the school. He was described as always dressed in professional black (Bellot, 265 and n.). On his retirement in 1864 the Donaldson medal was struck to commemorate his services in promoting the study of architecture; two silver impressions of the medal are given annually as prizes at the college. He was a member of the Institut de France and of various other foreign academies of the fine arts.

Donaldson also published extensively, including *Pompeii* (1827), *A Collection of the Most Approved Examples of Doorways from Ancient Buildings in Greece and Italy* (1833), and *Architectura numismatica, or, Architectural Medals of Classic Antiquity … Explained* (1859).

Donaldson died at his home, 21 Upper Bedford Place, Bloomsbury, London, on 1 August 1885, and was buried five days later at Brompton cemetery. In 1879 the prince of Wales had called him 'the father of the institute and of the profession' (Blutman, 542).

L. A. FAGAN, *rev.* ANNE PIMLOTT BAKER

Sources N. Pevsner, 'The earliest magazines and Professor Donaldson', in N. Pevsner, *Some architectural writers of the nineteenth century* (1972) [chap. 10] · E. A. Gruning, 'Memoir of the late Professor Donaldson', *Transactions of the Royal Institute of British Architects*, new ser., 2 (1885–6), 89–95 · W. Papworth, 'The late Professor Donaldson: his connection with the institute', *Transactions of the Royal Institute of British Architects*, new ser., 2 (1885–6), 96–108 · S. Blutman, 'The father of the profession', *RIBA Journal*, 74 (1967), 542–4 · H. R. Hitchcock, *Early Victorian architecture in Britain*, 2 vols. (1954) · Colvin, *Archs.* · *Dir. Brit. archs.* · *The Builder*, 49 (1885), 179–80 · H. H. Bellot, *University College, London, 1826–1926* (1929) · *The architect's, engineer's, and building-trades' directory* (1868)

Archives RIBA, corresp. and papers; drawings and sketchbooks · UCL, lecture notes | RIBA, nomination papers, F V 1 p. 4

Likenesses F. B. Barwell, lithograph, 1869, NPG · C. Martin, oils, 1872, RIBA; repro. in J. A. Gotch, *The growth and work of the Royal Institute of British Architects* (1934) · M. Jackson, woodcut, BM · photographs, RIBA BAL · portrait, repro. in *The Builder* (24 July 1869), 586

Wealth at death £7371 1s. 9d.: probate, 25 Aug 1885, *CGPLA Eng. & Wales*

Donaldson, Walter (*bap.* 1574), philosopher, was baptized at St Nicholas, Aberdeen, on 11 November 1574, the son of Alexander Donaldson, burgess of Aberdeen, and his wife, Elizabeth Lamb. He perhaps took his degree in arts at King's College, Aberdeen, and it is known that in 1598 he accompanied David Cunningham, bishop of Aberdeen, on an embassy to Denmark and to the German protestant princes. Donaldson enrolled at Heidelberg on 11 September 1599 to study the laws. By 1603 he was appointed to the protestant academy of Sedan, where he remained for sixteen years. His son recorded that Donaldson remained in France for about forty years, first as professor of natural and moral philosophy, thereafter as academy principal; in Sedan he was pastor of the protestant church. From there he was appointed principal of the new protestant academy proposed at Charenton outside Paris, a foundation opposed by Paris University. Thus his stay at Charenton was brief, though he soon became principal at the academy of La Rochelle, where John Leech wrote some verses to him and described him as poet laureate; Leech had graduated in arts at King's College in 1614. An attempt was made by Patrick Copland to have Donaldson appointed to Marischal College. Donaldson would have preferred an Aberdeen appointment to a continental one; he visited the city in 1606 to become a burgess in succession to his father and again in 1621 to renew his burgess claim.

At Heidelberg, Donaldson gave a course on moral philosophy to private pupils, one of whom printed his notes, which were published as *Synopsis moralis philosophiae* at Frankfurt am Main in 1604. Donaldson himself republished the work at Darmstadt in 1606 and further editions subsequently appeared. The publication of 1606 was dedicated to the duc de Bouillon, founder of Sedan, with verses by Zacharias Palthenus. Book 1 is concerned with definitions of ethics and its relevance to the man of politics. Its study is concerned with the pursuit of happiness; he makes the point that there are grades of happiness. Book 2 concerns virtue in general, focusing on moral virtue, though intellectual virtues are mentioned. As principal of Sedan, Donaldson published his panegyric on the death of Frederick Stuart of the Palatinate in 1613.

Donaldson also presided over several printed theses not recorded in Aberdeen bibliographies. According to *L'exégèse de l'ethique: histoire littéraire*, a Paris publication, he moderated at least the following printed theses: *De virtutibus intellectivis* (1603), *De principibus actionum humanorum* (1604), *De justitia* (1605); *De habitibus moralibus imperfectis* (1605); *De amicitia* (1605); *Disputatio publica quae est de familia primo republicae fundamento* (1606). He also seems to have lectured on Greek and on political theory. In 1628 John Leech sent some Donaldsonian verses on the marquis d'Avere to John Scot of Scotstarvit, but these do not appear in the *Delitiae poetarum Scotorum* (1637). Donaldson entices the literary student with references to classical writers, Latin and Greek, notices a few medieval writers like Thomas Aquinas and 'our Scotus', but notes more modern writers like Toledo, Lipsius, and Muret. The 1620 Paris edition of *Synopsis oeconomica* is dedicated to the future Charles I, and mentions his courtiers James Foulerton and Thomas Murray. Donaldson's ethical course is largely based on Aristotle's *Nicomachean Ethics*, and the economics course is founded on Xenophon updated. For Donaldson, society is a natural growth whose roots are in nature. His *Synopsis oeconomica* makes the family its first consideration. He writes that he was professor at Sedan of civil and natural philosophy, of Greek also, and was its principal. His book starts with the father; no word occurs oftener in sacred letters and he cites Buchanan's psalms in support. Woman is man's helper, her main job the bearing of children; the father is the ship's captain. Servants are acquired by the father to be educated, exercised, and corrected. Servants' pay must be paid faithfully, but tipping is disallowed. The virtues of servants are obedience, diligence, trustworthiness, and silence.

Donaldson was determined to popularize Dionysius Laertius, publishing a selection of his material in *Electa Laërtiana* (Frankfurt, 1625). Donaldson's theological views occasionally intrude with references mainly to Paul and he was close to the Arminian Daniel Tilenus, an important figure at Sedan. Donaldson's first wife was Catherine Dervilliers and his second Elizabeth Goffin, mother of his eldest son, Alexander, a doctor of medicine. The date of Donaldson's death is unknown.   JOHN DURKAN

Sources W. K. Leask, ed., *Musa Latina Aberdonensis*, 3: *Poetae minores*, New Spalding Club, 37 (1910) · J. M. Thomson and others, eds., *Registrum magni sigilli regum Scotorum / The register of the great seal of Scotland*, 11 vols. (1882–1914), vol. 9 · G. Toepke, ed., *Die Matrikel der Universität Heidelberg*, 1 (Heidelberg, 1884), 198 · P. J. Anderson and J. F. K. Johnstone, eds., *Fasti academiae Mariscallanae Aberdonensis: selections from the records of the Marischal College and University, MDXCIII–MDCCCLX*, 3 vols., New Spalding Club, 4, 18–19 (1889–98) · P. Mellon, *L'académie de Sedan* (Paris, 1913) · 'Le temple de Charenton, 1606–1625', *Bulletin de la Société de l'Histoire du Protestantisme Français*, 4 (1856), 40 · *Reg. PCS*, 1st ser. · *IGI* · *Antiquities of the shires of Aberdeen and Banff*, Spalding Club (1862), vol. 4, pp. 370, 380

Donally, James (*fl.* 1779–1784), blackmailer, is obscure in both his origins and ultimate fate. He warrants attention primarily because his trial and conviction established a striking legal precedent that was indicative of gender anxieties in late eighteenth-century Britain. On 18 January 1779 Donally accosted Charles Fielding, second son of the earl of Denbigh, while the latter was passing through Soho Square in London. Donally declared that he would charge Fielding with having committed sodomy upon him unless Fielding paid for his silence. Fielding gave Donally a half guinea, though he would later claim that Donally was a stranger to him. Two days later, Donally again confronted Fielding with a similar threat, and Fielding gave him a guinea, using a nearby shopkeeper as an intermediary. There the matter might have ended had Donally not further pressed his luck. On 15 February he demanded money from a man whom he took to be Fielding but who proved, in fact, to be the latter's older brother. The elder Fielding was made of sterner stuff than his sibling and attempted to seize Donally. When Donally repeated his mistake three days later, the elder Fielding grabbed hold of him and enlisted the aid of three others in taking him to the magistrates' court at Bow Street. The complaint was heard before Sir John Fielding (a distant relation), and Donally was committed to trial at the Old Bailey.

The mode of extortion which Donally had attempted was not uncommon in the eighteenth and early nineteenth centuries. A capital offence, sodomy was condemned on two counts: it was explicitly condemned in the Bible and it was also viewed as a wilful defiance of nature's ordained procreative order. Worse still, where a charge of male sodomy was involved, the defamed party had a difficult time defending himself because the 'party-witness' rule precluded him from testifying on his own behalf on the grounds that his clear and urgent interest in the outcome made his testimony worthless. An accusation of sodomy could therefore be a powerful means to blackmail and so lucrative that it sometimes formed the basis of gang activity. To add insult to injury, in most instances extortion was only a misdemeanour, so that even the most malicious and unfounded of accusations would be subject to a comparatively light punishment.

Donally's case was noteworthy because it definitively established an unusual legal principle with which to combat such blackmail attempts. At his trial, the prosecution maintained that Donally's threats to malign Fielding's character in this particular way constituted a form of highway robbery—that is, the extortion of money by threat of violence, one of the most alarming criminal offences of the era and subject to the death penalty. The presiding judge concurred: 'accusing a man with an attempt to commit sodomy ... puts him in such a state that he cannot act with his own will ... and is violence enough to constitute the crime of robbery' (*Whole Proceedings*, 197). The jury agreed and delivered a conviction, but the judge was scrupulous enough to delay Donally's sentence until the matter could be referred for the opinion of the twelve judges of the high courts. The judges heard the case on 29

April and unanimously upheld the unusual definition of highway robbery which it involved, a decision that was greeted with approbation by the *Morning Chronicle*: 'God only knows what numberless robberies of this kind would have been perpetrated by these detestable wretches, on timorous minds, if their Lordships had been of a different opinion' (1 May 1779, 3). Donally was accordingly sentenced to death on 21 May. As was the established practice with all capital convicts at the Old Bailey, his case was reviewed before a meeting of the king and an extended body of the cabinet variously referred to as the 'grand' or 'hanging' cabinet. Of the five convicts whose cases were heard on 14 July, only he and one other man were deemed worthy objects of the criminal law's ultimate sanction.

But the executioner was to be disappointed still further. One man only was hanged at Tyburn on 28 July, Donally having been respited three days beforehand (PRO, SP 44/94, p. 305). The reasons for his ultimate deliverance are uncertain, no application for his pardon having survived. An account published some thirty-four years later claimed that it had been solicited by Lord Denbigh himself after discovering that, in fact, his younger son had indeed procured Donally's sexual favours prior to the incidents in question, and the *Morning Chronicle's* assertion that 'The respite of Patrick Donally [*sic*] was entirely without the application or knowledge of Lord Denbigh' (11 Aug 1779, 2) may imply that such a rumour was current at the time. Whatever its basis, Donally's pardon aroused indignation in some circles. One newspaper correspondent wrote,

> [I]t must be sufficiently obvious to every one … [that his crime] strikes at the first grand cement of society; that it militates for ever against that peace of mind, as well as the character of the suffering individual, and is, without exception, the most dangerous hydra of a vice that ever was let loose upon mankind.   (*Morning Chronicle*, 29 July 1779, 2a)

But there was little cause for worry. Before the end of the year, another London man, John Staples, was hanged on the grounds established in Donally's case. Donally himself remained in Newgate for more than a year (during which time he briefly escaped with many other prisoners when the gaol was torched during the Gordon riots) before formally being pardoned on condition of servitude on board the prison hulks in the Thames. Six months later the condition was changed to three years' imprisonment in Newgate, from which he was finally released—into obscurity—on 2 June 1784.   SIMON DEVEREAUX

Sources *The whole proceedings on the king's commission of the peace* (1779), 191–200 [Old Bailey sessions papers, 17 Feb 1779], 325–7 [19 May 1779] · *R. v. Donnally* (1779), 1 Leach 193, 168 ER 199 · *Morning Chronicle* (1 May 1779) · *Morning Chronicle* (11 Aug 1779) · *Morning Chronicle* (29 July 1779) · A. E. Simpson, 'Blackmail as a crime of sexual indiscretion: its origins and development in the courts of eighteenth-century England', *Criminal Justice History* [forthcoming] · J. C. Oldham, 'Truth-telling in the eighteenth-century English courtroom', *Law and History Review*, 12 (1994), 95–120 · R. Trumbach, 'London's sodomites: homosexual behaviour and western culture in the eighteenth century', *Journal of Social History*, 11 (1977), 1–33 · R. Norton, *Mother Clap's molly house: the gay subculture in England, 1700–1830* (1992) · M. C. Battestin and R. R. Battestin, *Henry Fielding: a life* (1989) · A. Knapp and W. Baldwin, *The Newgate calendar, comprising interesting memoirs of the most notorious characters,* 4 vols. (1824–6) · PRO, SP 44/94, pp. 298, 305; SP 44/95, pp. 35–6, 111; PC 1/3097; HO 77/1, p. 192

Archives PRO, Secretary of State Papers, pardon, 22 July 1779, SP 44/94, p. 298 · PRO, pardon, 25 July 1779, SP 44/94, p. 305 · PRO, pardon, 23 Oct 1780, SP 44/95, pp. 35–6 · PRO, pardon, 30 April 1781, SP 44/95, p. 111 · PRO, discharge from Newgate gaol, 2 June 1784, HO 77/1, p. 192

Donat, (Frederick) Robert (1905–1958), actor, the fourth and youngest son of Ernst Emil Donat, civil engineer of Polish origin, and his wife, Rose Alice Green, was born at 42 Albert Road, Withington, Manchester, on 18 March 1905. He went to the Central School, Manchester, and later studied for the stage under James Bernard of the same city. In 1924 he joined Sir Frank Benson, whose company was not then so constantly on tour as it had been; thus Donat could alternate continuing membership with seasons in provincial repertory. This was well-varied and helpful schooling: the Shakespearian apprenticeship was valuable, for among Donat's enduring distinctions were the purity of his diction and the beauty of his voice. He worked for a while with Alfred Wareing, whose repertory seasons at the Theatre Royal, Huddersfield, had unusual ambition and quality. In 1928 he began a year at the Playhouse in Liverpool and this was followed by important work at Terence Gray's Festival Theatre in Cambridge where plays by Euripides, Pirandello, Sheridan, and Shakespeare gave him opportunities to experiment in a range of widely different and challenging leading roles. In 1929 he married Ella Annesley Voysey, having two sons and a daughter before the marriage ended in divorce.

Donat made his mark decisively in London in 1931 when he created the part of Gideon Sarn in a dramatization of *Precious Bane* by Mary Webb. His handsome features and beautiful delivery, together with the equipment of technique acquired in his repertory years, promised promotion to the front rank and there was confirmation of his powers in the Malvern festival of 1931. Again at Malvern, in 1933, he played the two Camerons in *A Sleeping Clergyman* by James Bridie; the piece was transferred to London and had a long run at the Piccadilly Theatre. Donat's performance of the two roles, the dying consumptive and his son the brilliant doctor, was memorable and was repeated in a revival of 1947. To the simulation of a man with lung trouble he brought his own knowledge of pain, for he was himself a sufferer from asthma and his later career was much impeded by illness.

Donat's success carried him to important film work, as Richard Hannay in Alfred Hitchcock's *The Thirty-Nine Steps* (1939)—one of his best performances—and with Alexander Korda, who was then recruiting remarkable casts from the leading theatre actors. His notable appearances were in *The Private Life of Henry VIII* (1933), in which Charles Laughton played the king; *The Ghost Goes West* (1935); and, as another Scottish doctor, Andrew Manson, in a screen version of A. J. Cronin's *The Citadel* (1938), for which he was nominated for an Oscar. Perhaps his most widely appreciated film role was that of Mr Chips, the ageing schoolmaster in *Goodbye Mr Chips* (1939), from the novel by James Hilton, and for which he won an Oscar.

(Frederick) **Robert Donat** (1905–1958), by Fred Daniels, 1943

Donat continued to mingle screen work with important returns to the stage, taking on the management at the Queen's Theatre in 1936 when he presented J. L. Hodson's *Red Night*. During the war he gave vigour and volume to the eloquence of Captain Shotover in a revival of Shaw's *Heartbreak House* (1943). At the Westminster Theatre in 1945 he was much liked in a plebeian comedy part in *The Cure for Love* by Walter Greenwood. His last venture as a manager was at the Aldwych Theatre in 1945 when he staged *Much Ado about Nothing* with himself as Benedick. His spirited rendering of the wordy warfare with Beatrice was exemplary at a time when Shakespearian speaking on the British stage was much criticized. He gave another lesson in delivery when he joined the Old Vic company in 1953 to play Becket in a production of T. S. Eliot's *Murder in the Cathedral*. Directed by Robert Helpmann, this was one of the most effective renderings of a play frequently revived. Donat was far from being a player attached to one type of character. He was, however, seen at his best in parts that asked for splendour of voice and dignity of bearing, and his Becket was held by those who knew the scope of his work to have a singular beauty. Asceticism was a quality that came naturally to his delicacy of feature, but he had learned in his repertory years to be richly versatile. In naming his favourite roles he included the two gusty, outspoken Camerons of *A Sleeping Clergyman*, which, with *Murder in the Cathedral*, were perhaps the summits of his achievement on the stage.

In 1953 Donat married the actress (Dorothy) Renée

Asherson (*b.* 1915). During the last five years of his life he was a constant invalid. He did not mind the seclusion since he was of a shy and retiring disposition and had never sought the bright lights of publicity. But the frustration was galling for an actor who was only just entering his fifties and should have been at the height of his powers. He died in the West End Hospital, Westminster, London, on 9 June 1958.

IVOR BROWN, *rev.* K. D. REYNOLDS

Sources J. C. Trewin, *Robert Donat* (1968) · *The Times* (10 June 1958) · J. Walker, ed., *Halliwell's film and video guide*, 12th edn (1997) · 'Renée Asherson', *Who's who in the theatre*, ed. I. Herbert, C. Baxter, and R. E. Finley, 16th edn (1977) · personal knowledge (1971) · private information (1971) · D. Quinlan, *Quinlan's film stars*, 4th edn (1996) · *CGPLA Eng. & Wales* (1958) · b. cert.
Archives JRL, corresp. and papers | CUL, corresp. with W. A. Gerhardie
Likenesses photographs, 1933–51, Hult. Arch. · F. Daniels, photograph, 1943, NPG [*see illus.*]
Wealth at death £25,236 11s. 5d.: probate, 24 Nov 1958, *CGPLA Eng. & Wales*

Donatus [St Donatus] (*d.* 876), bishop of Fiesole, was an Irishman of noble birth; nothing more is known of his ancestry. According to the *Vita sancti Donati episcopi*, preserved in two Florentine manuscripts, he decided to go abroad as a pilgrim to visit the basilica of the apostles and other sacred sites. At that time the church of Faesulae, now Fiesole, near Florence, had been plundered by the vikings and was without a bishop. The people were praying in their church when Donatus entered. As he did so, the bells pealed and the lamps burst into light miraculously. The people, realizing that their prayers had been answered, insisted that he should be their bishop. Events may not have been as fortuitous as they appear, however; he may have been tutored by Dúngal at Pavia in the years preceding his election to the episcopate of Fiesole.

The timescale of Donatus's episcopate can be established from a range of references to his presence at various church councils. In 826, at a Roman council under Pope Eugenius II, the bishop of Fiesole is named as Grusolphus; hence election of Donatus must be subsequent to that but before 844 when he is recorded as being present at the consecration of Louis, son of Lothar, as king of the Lombards. The charters at Bobbio indicate that in 850 he commissioned a church at Piacenza which he dedicated to St Brigit and granted to the monastery of Bobbio. Likewise, he was present at the Council of Ravenna in 861 or 862 and applied for redress to the emperor for the destruction wreaked by the vikings in Fiesole, an application confirmed by Charles the Bald in 875 or 876 at Piacenza. But by 877, at the Council of Florence, Zenobius was present as bishop of Fiesole. We may assume therefore that Donatus died in 876. In his epitaph, supposedly his own composition, he states that his episcopate lasted forty-seven years ('octonis lustris septenis insuper annis'). If so, it presumably began in 829.

In addition to his own epitaph, Donatus has been credited with the *Vita metrica sanctae Brigidae*, a poem of at least 2004 lines on the life of the Irish saint. It is preserved in five Italian manuscripts ranging in date from the eleventh to the seventeenth century none of which contains a full text, and, to judge from the prose version derived from it, what survives may represent only about two-thirds of it. The attribution to Donatus is based on a number of points, some more circumstantial than others. Two of the twelfth-century copies contain a twenty-eight line prologue beginning 'ego Donatus virtutes sanguine Scottus | Bricte descripsi …' (as a result of this Lapidge and Sharpe name him Donatus Scottus, but Scottus seems to be an epithet rather than part of his name). Moreover, there are close verbal parallels between the *Vita metrica* and Donatus's epitaph (*Vita sancti Donati*, chap. 27). His interest in Brigit is also evidenced by his commission of a church dedicated to her. Furthermore, according to the *De S. Brigida virgine Faesulis in Etruria*, St Brigit of Fiesole was the sister of Andreas, pupil and archdeacon to Donatus. There is, then, enough evidence to associate Donatus with Brigit, but it is not clear how much of the metrical life beyond the prologue can be attributed to him, since the closest verbal parallels to his life are with the prologue and the author of that may not be the author of all of the rest. The Brigidine sources of the poem seem to have included the *Vita prima*, the (largely) Old Irish *Bethu Brigte*, and Cogitosus. A prose life based on the poem is extant in three manuscripts and it too has been attributed to Donatus but there are sufficient misunderstandings and confusions to make it unlikely that the same person composed both. Mario Esposito (*Poems*, 129) has also attributed the poem '… Praesulis Donato abbati' to Donatus, though this has been rejected by Kissane.   PAUL RUSSELL

Sources D. N. Kissane, 'Vita metrica sanctae Brigidae: a critical edition with introduction, commentary and indexes', *Proceedings of the Royal Irish Academy*, 77C (1977), 57–192 · M. Esposito, 'The poems of Colmanus "Nepos Cracavist" and Dungalus "Praecipuus Scottorum"', *Journal of Theological Studies*, 33 (1931–2), 113–31 · M. Esposito, 'Notes on Latin learning and literature in medieval Ireland, IV: On the early lives of St Brigid of Kildare', *Hermathena*, 49 (1935), 120–65 · 'Vita sancti Donati episcopi', *Acta sanctorum: October*, 9 (Brussels, 1858), 648–62 · Anastasius, *De vitis Romanorum pontificum*, 4 vols. (1718), vol. 1, p. 352 · C. Cipolla, ed., *Codice diplomatici di S. Colombano di Bobbio*, 1 (1918), no. 44, 165–9 · M. Lapidge and R. Sharpe, *A bibliography of Celtic-Latin literature, 400–1200* (1985), 182–3 · 'De S. Brigida virgine Faesulis in Etruria', *Acta sanctorum: Februarius*, 1 (Antwerp, 1658), 243–7 · S. Young, 'Donatus, bishop of Fiesole, 829–76, and the cult of St Brigit in Italy', *Cambrian Medieval Celtic Studies*, 35 (1998), 13–26

Don Carlos. *See* O'Connor, Cathal (1540–1596), *under* O'Connor, Brian (*d*. after 1559).

Donegal [Donegall]. For this title name *see* Chichester, Arthur, first earl of Donegal (1606–1675).

Donellan, John (1737/8–1781), poisoner, was the son of Lieutenant-Colonel Donellan, army officer; further details of his background and upbringing are unknown. Donellan was educated at the Royal Military Academy, Woolwich, becoming a cadet in the Royal Artillery in 1753. By 1757 he was serving at Madras in the 39th regiment, but then transferred to the East India Company. Having been cashiered for financial irregularities he returned to England and began a mendacious campaign to re-establish his reputation. He eventually obtained a certificate of having

behaved 'as a gallant officer' but by that time he had abandoned all hope of re-establishing his military career. Instead he became part owner and master of ceremonies at the Pantheon, Oxford Street, the newly opened and very fashionable London assembly rooms. This was a situation well suited to his talents:

> He soon acquired all the frivolous accomplishments which are expected on such insignificant employments: he learned the table of precedence with great accuracy, and could tell with the most minute exactness the pretensions of every individual to rank above his neighbour: he danced with a tolerable degree of grace and was not deficient in the small-talk which is an essential requisite to the office.   (*Life of John Donnellan*, 14)

His habit of wearing a flashy diamond ring (which some suspected to be part of his illicit Indian booty) earned him the nickname Ring Donellan. In 1777 he met the wealthy, fatherless Theodosia Boughton (1757–1830), twenty years his junior, and persuaded her to elope. Not surprisingly her family objected to the union, but his charm soon won them over and in 1778 the couple went to live at Lawford Hall, the Boughton home near Rugby, where Donellan effectively became master of the house.

Donellan's wife would become still more wealthy if her brother, Sir Theodosius, died under age. On the morning of 29 August 1780 Sir Theodosius (then aged twenty) died in convulsions after drinking medicine; this, his mother later testified, smelled strongly of bitter almonds. Rumours that he had been poisoned swept the neighbourhood, although initially it was suspected that this resulted from an error in the doctor's prescription rather than murder. Sir William Wheeler, Boughton's guardian, requested a post-mortem to allay the rumours. Donellan prevented this but managed to convey the impression to Wheeler that it had been carried out. Public disquiet eventually forced an inquest and a post-mortem even though the body was by then in an advanced state of putrefaction. Again Donellan was deliberately obstructive. Suspicion was now firmly fixed upon him and the inquest jury named him as Boughton's murderer.

Donellan's case attracted widespread attention: it was unusual for persons at this level of society to be accused of murder, and poisoning was perceived as peculiarly un-English. He was tried at Warwick assizes in March 1781. During the trial, Donellan was depicted as a coldly calculating individual who had prepared several people for the death of an apparently fit young man by exaggerating Boughton's health problems; who possessed the equipment necessary to distil cyanide from laurel leaves; who had access to the medicine; who had ensured an alibi for the time of the death; and who had obstructed all attempts to investigate. Medical witnesses declared that the convulsions described by Lady Boughton indicated poisoning by laurel water, that this was confirmed by the appearance of the internal organs of the body, and went on to describe experiments with animals upon whom laurel water always had 'instantaneous and mortal effects'. A far more eminent medical witness appeared for Donellan: John Hunter impugned the adequacy of the post-mortem and of the animal experiments, and pointed out that the symptoms were as consistent with apoplexy as they were with poisoning. His testimony was treated with scorn by the presiding judge, Sir Francis Buller, and was disregarded by the jury. Donellan's credibility was not improved by his attempts to cast suspicion on his mother-in-law and by his unfounded accusations of bias against the inquest jury. It also became clear that his wife and mother-in-law believed him to be guilty. Although he claimed that his marriage settlement prevented him from profiting by his wife's inheritance, he did not produce the settlement in evidence and, given the circumstances of his runaway marriage, it seems unlikely that such a settlement existed. He was hanged at Warwick on 2 April 1781. His wife and two small children subsequently changed their names to Beauchamp (the surname of Mrs Donellan's maternal grandmother).

Donellan's death was profoundly unsettling for many people. His refusal to confess his crime undermined the central exemplary purpose of the gallows pageant. His willingness to face death without seeking divine mercy created doubts about his guilt and the conduct of his trial. Attention focused on three main issues: the prosecution's reliance on circumstantial evidence, the prejudice created by pre-trial publicity, and the rejection of Hunter's testimony in favour of that given by men whose expertise was far inferior. The indictment against Donellan was also flawed since it accused him of administering arsenic rather than cyanide. However, it was common practice to ignore flaws in indictments and, given the state of medical knowledge in 1781, the jury had little choice other than to use the balance of probabilities to decide whether Boughton had or had not been murdered. Having once decided that the death of a healthy young man in convulsions was more likely to have been caused by poisoning than by apoplexy, then the case against Donellan became overwhelming.   RUTH PALEY

Sources 'Minutes of the trial of John Donnellan', *GM*, 1st ser., 51 (1781), 209–11 • *The life of Capt. John Donnellan* (1781) • J. Donellan, *The genuine case of Capt. John Donnellan … as written by himself* (1781) • *The case of Capt. J. D.* (1772) • *The proceedings at large on the trial of John Donnellan* (1781) • Burke, *Peerage* • J. F. Stephen, *A history of the criminal law of England*, 3 vols. (1883) • G. F. C. W. Boughton-Leigh, *A Warwickshire family* (1906)
Likenesses portrait, repro. in *Life of Capt. John Donnellan*, frontispiece

Donellan [Daniel], **Nehemiah** (*b. c.*1565, *d.* in or after 1609), Church of Ireland archbishop of Tuam, was born in co. Galway and is said to have been the son of Melaghlin Donellan and his wife, Cecily, daughter of William Kelly of Calla, co. Mayo. The O'Donellans were a bardic family who originated in the south-eastern part of co. Galway. The Irish version of his name was Fearganainm Ó Domhnalláin, where Fearganainm literally means 'man without a name'.

Nehemiah was sent to Cambridge and became a sizar of King's College in January 1580. He transferred to St Catharine's College and graduated BA in 1581–2. He returned to Ireland and spent some time in Kilkenny in the diocese of Ossory. He was still in Kilkenny in 1591. In that year an

observer, probably Sir Turlough O'Brien, wrote that there were only three protestant clerics in the province capable of preaching in Irish apart from 'Nehemias o Donnellane a man of Connaught now resident in the diocese of Kilcaney'.

Thereafter Donellan became coadjutor to William Laly (Uilliam Ó Maolala), Church of Ireland archbishop of Tuam. When Laly died in 1595 Thomas Butler, earl of Ormond, recommended Donellan to the see and he was appointed in August of that year. Donellan was described at the time as 'a very honest man and recommended by many'. As was customary Donellan held other benefices along with his see, namely the rectory of Kilmore and the vicarage of Castledoagh, both in Ossory, and the vicarage of Donard in the diocese of Dublin.

In the writ of privy seal directing his appointment Donellan is praised as being 'very fit to communicate with the people in their mother tongue, and a very meet instrument to retain and instruct them in duty and religion'. It was also said that he had 'taken great pains in translating and putting to the press the Communion-Book and New Testament in the Irish language, which her Majesty greatly approved of'. There is no evidence that any part of the Church of Ireland liturgy had been translated by Donellan, but William *Daniel mentions Donellan as one of those who assisted in the translation into Irish of the New Testament. Indeed, when Donellan was elevated to the see of Tuam, part of the New Testament was actually being typeset. The whole book was published in the years 1602–3 and the dedication and preface are said to have been the work of Donellan.

Donellan married Elizabeth, daughter of Nicolas Daniel and sister of William, whom he met in all probability when he was resident in Kilkenny. They had five sons: John, James, Edmund of Killucan in Westmeath, Murtagh, and Teigue of Ballyheague in co. Kildare. James was subsequently knighted and became lord chief justice of the common pleas. Murtagh was ordained priest in the Roman Catholic church.

Nehemiah Donellan voluntarily resigned his see in 1609 and died shortly afterwards in Tuam. He was buried in the cathedral. He was succeeded as archbishop by his brother-in-law William Daniel.   N. J. A. WILLIAMS

Sources N. J. A. Williams, *I bprionta i leabhar* (1987) • *The whole works of Sir James Ware concerning Ireland*, ed. and trans. W. Harris, 1 (1739) • *DNB*

Dongan, John (*d.* in or after 1413), bishop of Down, was appointed archdeacon of Down in 1368 by Pope Urban V, and worked as papal nuncio and collector in Ireland. On 31 May or 1 June 1374, he was elected bishop of the diocese of Sodor and Man by the clergy of Man in St German's Cathedral, Peel. He received papal provision to the diocese from Pope Gregory XI, and was consecrated at Avignon by Simon Langham, cardinal-bishop of Palestrina, on 25 or 26 November 1374.

Dongan was imprisoned at Boulogne on his return from Avignon and only released on payment of a ransom of 500 marks. This delayed his installation at St German's Cathedral, Peel, until 25 January 1377, when he is said to have held his first pontifical mass and received many great offerings. He held a general chapter in February of the same year, when he inquired into the right of Whithorn Priory to hold land and churches in Man. In 1374 Dongan was also appointed papal nuncio and collector in his city and diocese and he may, therefore, have conducted an inquiry into the pattern of landholding in his diocese at this general chapter in 1377.

In 1380 Urban VI commissioned an inquiry into the allegation that John Dongan and William, bishop of Emly, apostolic nuncios and collectors in Ireland, had not handed over large sums which they had collected, thereby defrauding the apostolic chamber.

Nevertheless, Dongan must have regained Urban's trust; in the bull of 15 July 1387, the antipope, Clement VII, gives Dongan's adherence to Urban VI as the reason Dongan was removed from the diocese. In his place, Clement VII appointed Michael, formerly archbishop of Cashel, as bishop of Sodor. This appointment appears to mark the final rift between the Hebrides and the Isle of Man within the diocese of Sodor and Man, the Hebrides following a Scottish antipapal course, and the Isle of Man, a Manx papal one.

After 1387 Dongan continued to be recognized as bishop of the Manx part of the diocese of Sodor and Man while Michael was recognized in the Scottish part. Dongan appears to have worked for the bishop of Salisbury in 1390, and to have ordained in London in 1391 and 1392. He also appears to have been provided to the bishopric of Derry on 11 July 1391 and, from Derry, translated to the bishopric of Down on 16 September 1394, doing homage to the pope and receiving his temporalities on 26 July 1395.

In his later years, Dongan was active in negotiations between England and the lords of the Isles. In June 1405 he was appointed keeper of the liberty of Ulster, and authorized to deal with Gaelic Irish and Scottish enemies. In September 1407 Dongan and Janico Dartas, admiral of Ireland, were appointed to negotiate a final peace with Donald, lord of the Isles. Negotiations were still continuing in May 1408, but the grant of a royal licence in 1410 for the marriages between the son and daughter of Janico Dartas and the daughter and son of John of the Isles suggests that Dartas and Dongan may have been successful in creating a certain degree of peace.

John Dongan is said to have resigned from the bishopric of Down on 28 July 1413, and is presumed to have died soon afterwards.   EMMA CHRISTIAN

Sources E. B. Fryde and others, eds., *Handbook of British chronology*, 3rd edn, Royal Historical Society Guides and Handbooks, 2 (1986) · T. W. Moody and others, eds., *A new history of Ireland*, 2: *Medieval Ireland, 1169–1534* (1987) · T. W. Moody, F. X. Martin, and F. J. Byrne, eds., *Maps, genealogies, lists: a companion to Irish history, part 2* (1984) · J. Dowden, *The bishops of Scotland … prior to the Reformation*, ed. J. M. Thomson (1912) · W. Stubbs, *Registrum sacrum Anglicanum*, 2nd edn (1897) · C. R. Cheney, 'Manx synodal statutes', *Cambridge Medieval Celtic Studies*, 7 (1984), 63–89; 8 (1984), 51–63 · G. Broderick, ed. and trans., *Cronica regum Mannie et Insularum / Chronicles of the kings of Man and the Isles* (1979) · P. A. Munch and A. Goss, eds., *Chronicon regum Manniae et Insularum / The chronicle of Man and the Sudreys*, 2 vols., Manx Society, 22–3 (1859–1907)
Archives BL, Cotton MS Julius A.vii, fols. 50v–52r

Dongan, Thomas, second earl of Limerick (1634–1715), colonial governor, was the seventh son of Sir John Dongan of Castletown, co. Kildare, and his wife, Mary Talbot, sister of Richard Talbot, duke of Tyrconnell. He and his brothers joined the king's forces 'as soon as they were old enough to bear arms' (*CSP Ire.*, 1660–62, 50). He served on the continent, and in 1671 was appointed the lieutenant-colonel of George Hamilton's Irish regiment in French pay, which 'assuredly performed wonders' (Atkinson, 33) under his command at the battle of Enzheim (1674). He took over as colonel after Hamilton's death in 1676 until he was recalled in 1678, promoted to brigadier and sergeant-major of foot, and given the command of a new regiment to be levied in Ireland under Roman Catholic officers. On 8 November 1678 this plan became known to parliament, then in the middle of the Popish Plot crisis. The secretary of state Sir Joseph Williamson was sent to the Tower for countersigning the commissions, the regiment was never raised, and Dongan was posted to Tangier, where he served as lieutenant-governor until 1680.

In 1683 Dongan was appointed governor of New York. His five-year governorship is described as being enlightened. One of his first acts was to call an election for a general assembly of the (predominantly Dutch) freeholders, which met on 17 October 1683 and passed the charter of liberties, which provided for freedom of religion and taxation only by consent. Fearful of the growth of French influence in Canada, he established a protectorate over the Iroquois by having the duke of York's arms erected in their villages, effectively extending the area of English rule to Lake Ontario. The colony became a royal province after James II came to the throne, and the assembly was disallowed in 1686, in the same year that Dongan granted New York its charter.

When the French invaded Iroquois territory in July 1687, Dongan mortgaged his own property to raise a force to protect the colony. He armed the Iroquois and sent them on raids into Canada forcing the French to abandon Fort Niagara and sue for peace. He boasted that if he had been allowed to pursue the war for another year he would have driven the French out of Canada. When James II replaced him as governor in August 1688, Dongan remained in America, declining an offer from Tyrconnell to return to Ireland as a major-general. Following the revolution in England, warrants were issued for his arrest for his supposed Jacobite sympathies and he was obliged to flee New York and seek refuge in Massachusetts.

Dongan returned to England in 1691, where he spent his retirement seeking compensation for his service and for the family property forfeited in Ireland. He reconciled himself to King William and assumed the earldom of Limerick in succession to his brother William, who died in 1698. His right to succeed had been included in the 1686 grant of the peerage and, despite the first earl's attainder in 1691, he seems to have been generally accorded the title. He lived in London for the last years of his life, died on 14 December 1715 in the parish of St Pancras, Middlesex, and was buried in St Pancras churchyard. His wife, Mary Dongan, died in 1720. The protectorate he established over the Iroquois was recognized by the treaty of Utrecht in 1713.   PIERS WAUCHOPE

Sources The case of Thomas earl of Limerick lately call'd Colonel Thomas Dongan (1700) · M. Benjamin, 'Thomas Dungan and the granting of the New-York charter, 1682–1688', The memorial history of the city of New York, ed. J. G. Wilson, 4 vols. (1892–3), 1.399–446 · J. H. Kennedy, Thomas Dongan, governor of New York (1930) · C. Dalton, ed., Irish army lists, 1661–1685 (privately printed, London, 1907) · CSP col., vols. 11–12 · CSP Ire., 1660–62 · The manuscripts of the earl of Dartmouth, 3 vols., HMC, 20 (1887–96), vol. 1 · C. T. Atkinson, 'Feversham's account of the battle of Enzheim, 1674', Journal of the Society for Army Historical Research, 1 (1922) · GEC, Peerage, new edn, vol. 7
Likenesses portrait, repro. in Wilson, ed., Memorial history, vol. 1

Donisthorpe, Wordsworth (1847–1914), political activist, was born on 24 March 1847 at Springfield Mount, Leeds, the only son of George Edmund Donisthorpe (d. 1875), a wool merchant, and his wife, Elizabeth Wordsworth. He was educated at Leeds grammar school and Trinity College, Cambridge, where in 1869 he took a first in the moral sciences tripos. A year later he was admitted to the Inner Temple, but he was not called to the bar until 1879. In the interim he had been arrested in Strasbourg for taking part in a republican demonstration, and married (on 17 December 1873) Ann Maria, daughter of Henry Anderson, a York solicitor. In 1876 he published The Principles of Plutology, a work that endeavoured to develop a science of wealth on the same principles as Herbert Spencer's science of society.

Donisthorpe was a leading figure in a variety of organizations on the margins of late Victorian politics that had as their common purpose opposition to the growing role of the state. He was an early member of the Personal Rights Association, founded in 1871 to fight the Contagious Diseases Acts, which had empowered the police to compel women suspected of prostitution to undergo a medical examination. In 1873 he joined with William Carr Crofts to found the Political Evolution Society, the aim of which was to warn of 'the dangerous principle underlying measures of a repressive or paternal character', and which had as its instrument the abortive journal Let Be. In 1880 the society was renamed the State Resistance Union in response to Lord Elcho's advocacy, in a letter to the St James's Gazette, of a cross-party grouping to uphold personal liberty and freedom of contract. Two years later, after the publication in the Pall Mall Gazette of a further appeal by Elcho (soon to be the earl of Wemyss), and on the advice of Herbert Spencer, Donisthorpe took part in a meeting at Elcho's London home which led to the State Resistance Union being transformed into the Liberty and Property Defence League.

The league remained the chief campaigning group for the principles of laissez-faire liberalism for the rest of the nineteenth century. Its membership comprised a loose coalition of landed and commercial interests, while figures such as Auberon Herbert, Thomas Mackay, Frederick Millar, as well as Donisthorpe himself provided the league with polemical and theoretical support. In 1884 Donisthorpe published the pamphlet Liberty or Law?, effectively the league's manifesto, which argued for a realignment of the political parties to bring together all those individualists who were opposed to 'socialism' (meaning any extension of the state's role beyond the nightwatchman minimum). Donisthorpe served on the league's council until 1888, and in 1887–8 edited a journal, Jus, subsidized by the league. His final break with Wemyss occurred as a result of the latter's failure to campaign for church disestablishment.

The most sophisticated statement of Donisthorpe's political creed is his Individualism: a System of Politics (1889). His theory owed a great deal to that of Herbert Spencer, and borrowed in particular the idea that society was an organism which develops according to scientific laws of evolution. These laws, discovered by a science Donisthorpe termed 'nomology', reveal that only an ever-decreasing amount of state interference is consistent with social welfare, and that the ultimate goal of the evolutionary process is an anarchistic utopia (Donisthorpe occasionally referred to himself as a 'philosophic anarchist'). While incorporating some aspects of Spencer's thought, however, Donisthorpe repudiated his 'metaphysical' doctrine of natural rights, and drew on the positivistic conception of law associated with Hobbes and John Austin. A vigorous controversialist, his energies were as often expended in argument with fellow individualists, especially Auberon Herbert, as they were in combating what he saw as the iniquities of socialism.

Of Donisthorpe's other publications, the chapter he contributed to A Plea for Liberty (ed. T. Mackay, 1891) contains the most succinct statement of his political views. His Law in a Free State (1895) collects some of his articles and occasional pieces. In Labour Capitalisation (1887) Donisthorpe advanced the case for a form of profit-sharing and in Uropa (1913) he projected a 'philosophically-constructed' international language based on Latin. Donisthorpe died of heart failure on 30 January 1914, at Shottermill, near Farnham, Surrey.

M. W. TAYLOR

Sources Venn, Alum. Cant. · J. Foster, Men-at-the-bar: a biographical hand-list of the members of the various inns of court, 2nd edn (1885) · Wellesley index · E. Bristow, 'The Liberty and Property Defence League and individualism', HJ, 18 (1975), 761–89 · N. C. Soldon, 'Individualist periodicals: the crisis of late Victorian liberalism', Victorian Periodicals Newsletter, 6/3 (1973), 17–26 · N. C. Soldon, 'Laissez-faire as dogma: the Liberty and Property Defence League, 1882–1914', Essays in anti-labour history, ed. K. D. Brown (1974), 207–33 · M. W. Taylor, Men versus the state (1992) · b. cert. · d. cert. · CGPLA Eng. & Wales (1914)
Archives St Deiniol's Library, Hawarden, Gladstone MSS
Wealth at death £7373 19s. 4d.: administration, 25 July 1914, CGPLA Eng. & Wales

Donkin, Bryan (1768–1855), inventor and engineer, was born at Fountain Hall, near Sandoe in Northumberland, on 22 March 1768. He was the third son of a family of eight and his father, John Donkin, an acquaintance of John Smeaton, was a land agent and surveyor for a number of estates, including those of the duke of Northumberland and the Errington family. The young Donkin's aptitude for engineering was apparent in childhood; there are accounts of him, as a boy, spending almost all his spare time in the smiths' and carpenters' shops of the estates managed by his father. It was intended that he should follow his father's profession, and in 1788 he moved to Sevenoaks in Kent, where for two years he acted as agent for the duke of Dorset at Knowle Park. When he became dissatisfied with his position, he consulted Smeaton, who advised him to serve an apprenticeship with a Dartford millwright, John Hall. In 1798 Donkin married Mary Brame (d. 1858), the daughter of a Flemish refugee; they had three sons, John [see below], Bryan, and Thomas, all of whom entered the family firm.

Donkin's career path can be described as following three overlapping activities: inventor, developer of other people's inventions, and engineering consultant. His first major venture was the development of the Fourdrinier paper making machine. In 1799 a French mechanic, Louis Robert, invented a crude machine for making paper; this was taken to England by John Gamble, who assigned his patent of 1801 to Henry and Sealy Fourdrinier, who ran a successful London stationery firm. John Hall, who had business contacts with the Fourdriniers, was invited to develop the invention and he passed the project to Donkin. In 1802 Donkin began the development work, initially at Hall's plant and then at a new works at Spa Lane, Bermondsey, financed by the Fourdriniers, which was completed in April 1803. In 1807 Donkin leased the Bermondsey works and began to produce the machines on a royalty basis. By 1812 nineteen machines had been sold, a number that had increased to 191 by 1850. Although the original idea was not Donkin's the development work on the machine was due to him, and the merit of his work was recognized by the award of a gold medal at the Great Exhibition of 1851. Throughout the development phase of the paper making machine Donkin was actively engaged in other enterprises. His two most notable inventions of this period were a steel nib pen, patented in 1808, and a tachometer which he submitted to the Society of Arts in 1810 and which was awarded its gold medal. He was also involved in three other major projects, concerned with printing, canning, and scientific instrument making. In 1813, with Richard Mackenzie Bacon, a Norwich journalist and musician, he secured a patent for an improved printing machine. The machine was adopted by the Cambridge University Press but was not successful. Donkin's subsequent activities in printing were more significant; in 1820, with Sir William Congreve and John Wilks, his then partner, he contrived a method of printing stamps in two colours, and further work was commissioned from the excise and stamp office and by the East India Company at Calcutta.

Donkin has been described as the father of modern canning. In 1795 a Parisian confectioner, François Appert, had invented a method of preserving food in glass jars. An English patent was taken out in 1810 by Peter Durrant, a merchant, and this was acquired by Donkin, Hall, and Gamble for £1000. The three men formed a company with

Donkin in charge of the development work at Bermondsey, where he established the first British cannery. His innovation was to use tinned containers in conjunction with a new preservation process. In order to achieve complete sterilization, which Appert's process had failed to do, Donkin heated meat in tin cans very gradually in a bath of chloride of lime. By 1813 he felt sufficiently confident to submit samples to the prince regent for tasting; given the novel nature of the product the latter rather surprisingly agreed, and his approval was a major marketing factor in the innovation's success. A quantity of meat was supplied to the Royal Navy, and an office was opened in Cornhill and depots established in the seaport towns. Donkin's tinned meat was taken by Sir James Ross in 1829, and by Sir John Franklin in 1845, on their Arctic expeditions. Donkin himself appears to have lost interest in the project once the development problems had been tackled, but there is no doubting his vital contribution to modern canning.

Throughout his life Donkin was interested in astronomy, and in 1808–9 he collaborated with the scientific instrument maker Edward Troughton on the construction of the first mural circle for the Royal Greenwich Observatory. Donkin undertook the precision casting and machining of the large sections of this, and other astronomical apparatus and standards of length, for Troughton and subsequently for his successors, Troughton and Simms. He was a member of the Royal Astronomical Society, and he passed his enthusiasm on to his sons. He was an expert in the use of micrometers and was best known to astronomers for his dividing engine and spring level. On 6 April 1831, in the absence of Sir James South, he chaired the meeting at which the Astronomical Society was granted its royal charter.

An important spin-off from Donkin's work was his development of metal working tools, such as lathes, drills, and gear cutting engines. He stands alongside pioneer engineers, such as Maudslay and Bramah, who helped establish London as a major engineering centre. His growing reputation led him to be involved increasingly as a consultant on civil engineering projects, to be invited to give evidence before parliamentary select committees, and to act as an arbitrator when government money was used to finance innovatory projects. Thus Donkin was involved with Thomas Telford in the latter's Caledonian Canal project, supplying the engine and machinery for a dredger; he was in frequent consultation with Marc Isambard Brunel over the design of shields and pumping machinery for the Thames Tunnel Company; was called as an expert witness before the select committee on artisans and machinery in 1824; and was commissioned to make an estimate of the development costs of Charles Babbage's calculating machine. Donkin was among those instrumental in founding the Institution of Civil Engineers; he served as a member of its council for the first time in 1822, and was vice-president from 1826 to 1832, and again from 1835 to 1845. In 1828 when the institution sought its first royal charter, the cost of which was 300 guineas, Telford and Donkin advanced it 200 and 100 guineas respectively. Donkin's son Bryan became president in 1872, and his great-grandson in 1949. As early as 1803 Donkin was elected a member of the Society of Arts, and in 1807 was appointed as chair of the committee of mechanics and vice-president of the society. On 18 January 1836 Donkin was elected a fellow of the Royal Society and served repeatedly on its council. He finally retired from business in 1846, but continued to play a role in his local community, acting as a magistrate in Surrey until shortly before his death. He died at his home, 6 The Paragon, New Kent Road, London, on 27 February 1855.

His son **John Donkin** (1802–1854), engineer, was born at Dartford, Kent, on 20 May 1802. He was a partner with his father and John Wilks, and took part in many of their inventions. He became a member of the Institution of Civil Engineers in 1824 and was also a fellow of the Geological Society. He married Caroline, daughter of Benjamin Hawes; they had seven children. He died at Roseacre, near Maidstone, on 20 April 1854.

ROGER LLOYD-JONES

Sources R. H. Clapperton, *The paper-making machine: its invention, evolution and development* (1967) · S. B. Donkin, 'Bryan Donkin FRS, MICE, 1768–1855', *Transactions* [Newcomen Society], 27 (1949–51), 85–95 · A. McConnell, *Instrument makers to the world: a history of Cooke, Troughton & Simms* (1992) · *Early engineering reminiscences (1815–1840) of George Escol Sellers*, ed. E. S. Ferguson (Washington, DC, 1965) · D. M. Henshaw, 'Donkin's pentagraph engineering machine with rose engine', *Transactions* [Newcomen Society], 15 (1934–5), 77–83 · W. Walker, *Distinguished men of science* (1862), 75–7 · 'Select committee on the state of law', *Parl. papers* (1824), vol. 5, no. 51 [on artisans and machinery] · *PRS*, 7 (1854–5), 586–9 · J. Munsell, *Chronology of the origin and progress of paper and paper-making*, 5th edn (1876) · d. cert. · DNB

Archives Derbys. RO, corresp. and letter-books; journals, note-books, copy books, corresp. and papers · RAS, corresp. and papers | BL, corresp. with Charles Babbage, Add. MSS 37184–37191

Likenesses J. F. Skill, J. Gilbert, W. and E. Walker, group portrait, pencil and wash (*Men of science living in 1807–08*), NPG · portrait, repro. in Walker, *Distinguished men of science*

Donkin, Bryan (1835–1902), mechanical engineer, was born on 29 August 1835 at 88 Blackfriars Road, London, the eldest son in the family of seven children of John *Donkin (1802–1854) [*see under* Donkin, Bryan (1768–1855)], engineer, and Caroline, daughter of Benjamin Hawes. His was the third generation of the distinguished engineering dynasty founded by his grandfather, Bryan *Donkin FRS, and he was known as Bryan Donkin junior. He was educated at private schools and University College, London, before spending two years on an engineering course at the École Centrale des Arts et Métiers in Paris. At the age of twenty-one he commenced his pupillage in the family engineering works of Bryan Donkin & Co., then managed by his uncles.

In 1859 Donkin was sent to St Petersburg by the firm to superintend the construction of what was, at that time, the largest paper mill in Europe. The Donkins had obtained this contract in 1858 from the Russian government, for a mill to produce paper for banknotes and government stationery. In January 1862 he returned to London, and for the next six years worked for the family firm,

designing and superintending the installation of machinery in Britain and on the continent. His European work brought him into contact with foreign engineers and engineering practice, which was to prove important in his later career. In 1868 Donkin became a partner in the firm, and when it was converted into a limited liability company in 1889 he became chairman. Although remaining as chairman after the amalgamation with Clench & Co. of Chesterfield in 1900, he stopped having an active part in the management at that time. Donkin married his first wife, Georgina Mary (*b.* 1847/8), daughter of Frank Dillon, on 15 July 1869. They had a daughter and a son before Georgina died. On 14 February 1888 he married a widow, Edith Dunn, *née* Marshman (*b.* 1849/50); they had a daughter. Edith, who survived him, was to help him with his writing later in his career.

In the early 1870s the paper-making industry ceased to provide as much work for the firm as previously, and Donkin began to devote increasing amounts of his time to the scientific side of engine design. The earliest tests were concerned with the Farey engine, designed by Barnard William Farey, one of the partners in the firm. An example installed at a paper mill in Devon was tested with a view to measuring its efficiency and the result was published in *Engineering* (3 November 1871), giving the consumption of water and coal per horsepower hour. At that time such efficiency tests were unknown. Donkin's steam consumption test relied upon measuring the condensed water flowing over a tumbling bay or weir. He described the method in a joint paper with Salter and Martin that was presented to the Institution of Civil Engineers (*Minutes of Proceedings*, 66, 1880–81, 278–94). Supported by *Engineering*, the tests rapidly gained acceptance in the engineering community.

This work was followed by research into the behaviour of steam in cylinders, and the advantages of jacketing and superheating. The research brought him into direct contact with Professor Dwelshauvers-Devy, and led Donkin to develop his 'revealer', a glass apparatus which, attached to a steam engine cylinder, enabled him to observe the extent of condensation under varying conditions. The insight which this gave into the state of the internal work of cylinders led to a long series of trials by Donkin himself, in collaboration with other leading engineers, such as Professor Hudson Bewe, Lieutenant-Colonel English, and Alexander Kennedy (1847–1928). Kennedy and Donkin's tests on different types of boilers, initially published in *Engineering*, appeared as a book, *Experiments on Steam Boilers* (1897). A further work on steam boiler design, *The Heat Efficiency of Steam Boilers*, appeared in 1898.

In the 1890s Donkin became interested in internal combustion engines. He produced one of the earliest and most popular textbooks on the subject, *A Textbook on Gas, Oil and Air Engines* (1894), which was still in print, in its fifth edition, in 1911. He was also responsible for an early translation of Diesel's work *Theorie und Konstruktion eines rationellen Wärmemotors*. He was an early member of the Automobile Club.

Donkin was an active member of many engineering

societies, in the UK and overseas, presenting papers to the Institution of Civil Engineers, Institution of Mechanical Engineers, Incorporated Institute (later Institution) of Gas Engineers, Manchester Association of Engineers, and North of England Institution of Mining and Mechanical Engineers. He became a vice-president of the Institution of Mechanical Engineers in 1901, and was a member of its research committees on the steam jacket, marine engines, gas engines, and steam engines. For the Institution of Civil Engineers, which he joined in 1884, he served on committees on the thermal efficiency of steam engines, and on steam engine and boiler trials. At the end of his career Donkin was investigating the practicability of working gas engines using gases produced in blast furnaces, and this was the subject of his final paper in 1901.

Donkin's obituarist in *The Times* (8 March 1902, 9e) declared that no other Englishman was in such close touch with progress on the continent. The subjects of his research were reflected in developments within his firm, which had begun building internal combustion engines in the 1890s, and developing boilers using the Perret system of forced draught which he advocated. Donkin died suddenly of heart failure at the Grand Hotel, Brussels, on 4 March 1902, and was buried at Bromley, Kent.

MIKE CHRIMES

Sources PICE, 150 (1901–2), 428–33 · *Institution of Mechanical Engineers: Proceedings* (1902), 378–81 · *Engineering* (7 March 1902), 320–22 · *The Engineer* (14 March 1902), 258 · *The Engineer* (28 March 1902), 312 · *The Engineer* (11 April 1902), 366 · *A brief account of Bryan Donkin F.R.S. and of the company he founded 150 years ago*, ed. [E. R. Cross] (1953) · *The Times* (8 March 1902), 9e · *The Times* (11 March 1902), 10e · m. cert., 15 July 1869 · m. cert., 14 Feb 1888 · *CGPLA Eng. & Wales* (1902)
Archives Derbys. RO, corresp. · Inst. CE, membership records · Institution of Mechanical Engineers, London, membership records
Likenesses Maull & Fox, carte-de-visite, Inst. CE · Swain, lithograph?, repro. in *The Engineer* (14 March 1902), 258 · lithograph, repro. in *Engineering*, 321
Wealth at death £12,943 0s. 4d.: probate, 25 March 1902, *CGPLA Eng. & Wales*

Donkin, John (1802–1854). *See under* Donkin, Bryan (1768–1855).

Donkin, Sir Rufane Shaw (1773–1841), army officer, belonged to a respectable Northumbrian family, said to be of Scottish descent, and originally named Duncan. His father, General Robert Donkin (1726/7–1821), served in Flanders, the West Indies, Ireland, and America, was reputedly a personal friend of the historian David Hume, and published two books about his military experiences. In 1772 he married Mary, daughter of the Revd Emanuel Collins. Rufane Shaw was the eldest of their three children, and the only son.

On 21 March 1778 Rufane was appointed to an ensigncy in the 44th foot, in which his father then held the rank of major, advancing to lieutenant on 9 September 1779 through purely paper transactions. He was educated at Westminster School in London until the age of fourteen and appears afterwards to have been a diligent student. At one time when on leave from his regiment—probably

Sir Rufane Shaw Donkin (1773–1841), by William Holl, pubd 1831 (after Henry Mayer, 1831)

after its return from Canada in 1786—he studied classics and mathematics in France for a year, and when on detachment in the Isle of Man, read Greek for a year and a half with a Cambridge graduate. He obtained his company on 31 May 1793, and in September he sailed for the West Indies with the flank companies of the 44th foot to be involved in the capture of Martinique, Guadeloupe, and St Lucia, and the subsequent loss of Guadeloupe in 1794. After his return to England he was brigade major, and for several months aide-de-camp, to Major-General Thomas Musgrave, commanding at Newcastle upon Tyne, and advanced to major on 1 September 1795. He went back with the regiment to the West Indies in Lieutenant-General Sir Ralph Abercromby's expedition, which in April and May 1796 recaptured St Lucia (which had been again occupied by the French in 1795); here the 44th lost 20 officers and over 800 men, chiefly from fever. Donkin was removed to Martinique unconscious and afterwards invalided home dangerously ill.

Having recovered, in May 1798 Donkin was detached from the regiment to command a provisional light battalion, composed of the light companies 11th foot, 23rd Royal Welch Fusiliers, and 49th foot, with Major-General Eyre Coote's expedition to Ostend, which sought to destroy the basin, gates, and sluices of the Bruges Canal, thus hampering the concentration of French troops for an invasion of England. On 20 May Donkin distinguished himself in an action near Ostend, in which he was wounded and taken prisoner but earned Coote's special praise for his conduct. He transferred to the 11th foot as lieutenant-colonel on 24 May and joined it in temporary captivity near Douai. In 1799 the 11th sailed for the West Indies, but a regimental historian, quoting an official War Office record that he was 'in London on regimental duty' during December 1799, has noted that 'no evidence' exists for his having served in the West Indies in 1799–1800, as claimed in the *Dictionary of National Biography* (Robinson, 284). There is no doubt, however, that he did command the regiment there in 1801, when the 11th took part in the capture of numerous islands, which were returned to France after the peace of Amiens. On 29 April 1802 Donkin proposed that convicts who had opted to serve in the West Indies should not be kept there for life but be allowed to serve a normal term of engagement with a regiment, once they had proved their good conduct; this change was authorized by the War Office on 18 April 1803. His regiment remained in the West Indies but in May 1804 was declared 'unfit for service' (ibid., 292), having suffered severe loss through disease, and Donkin himself left on sick leave later that year.

On 16 May 1805 Donkin was appointed to the permanent staff of the quartermaster-general's department, serving as an assistant quartermaster-general in Kent, and then with the Copenhagen expedition of 1807. In 1808 he issued a reprint of the French text of Comte L'Espinasse's *Essai sur l'artillerie* (1800), which was translated into English forty years later. Meanwhile, he had been promoted colonel, on 25 April 1808, and in 1809 was appointed assistant quartermaster-general with the army in Portugal. As a colonel on the staff he commanded a brigade in the operations on the River Douro and at the battle of Talavera (for which he received a gold medal), but he soon returned home and was subsequently appointed quartermaster-general in Sicily. He served in that capacity in Sicily, and also in the operations in 1810–13 on the east coast of Spain where he was initially blamed for Lieutenant-General Sir John Murray's disaster at Tarragona in 1813. However, evidence at Murray's court martial showed that the general had disregarded Donkin's views, and he was vindicated. After a short period on half pay, Donkin, who had become major-general on 4 June 1811, was next appointed to a command in the Essex district, and in July 1815 to one at Madras, from which he was afterwards transferred to the Bengal presidency. Before leaving England he had married, on 1 May 1815, Elizabeth Markham (1789/90–1818), the eldest daughter of Dr Markham, dean of York, and granddaughter of Archbishop Markham.

In India Donkin commanded the 2nd field division of the grand army under the marquess of Hastings in the operations against the Marathas in 1817–18, and by skilful movements cut off the line of retreat of the enemy towards the north. He was appointed KCB on 14 October 1818, though, unfortunately, his wife died at Meerut, aged twenty-eight, on 21 August 1818, leaving him with an infant son. Much shattered in health, body, and mind, he was invalided to the Cape. While there, he was requested to assume the government of the colony during the absence of Lord Charles Somerset, and did so in 1820–21, his name being meanwhile retained on the Bengal establishment. This was the period of the settlement of the colony's eastern frontier, and Donkin named a town on the shore of Algoa Bay Port Elizabeth, after his late wife. He seems to have been popular at the Cape. However, in a communication to Earl Bathurst, the colonial secretary who appointed him, which was published in London as *A letter on the Cape of Good Hope, and Certain Events which Occurred there under Lord Charles Somerset* (1827), Donkin gave an account of his measures in Cape Colony particularly for establishing settlers there, and those pursued by Somerset 'for the total subversion of all I had done under your lordship's instructions'. Donkin had become a lieutenant-general on 19 July 1821 and was made GCH in 1824 in recognition of his services in connection with the King's German Legion (*DNB*). On 20 April 1825 he was made colonel of the 80th foot.

The rest of Donkin's life was principally devoted to literary and parliamentary pursuits. He was made a fellow of the Royal Society, was one of the original fellows of the Royal Geographical Society, and was a fellow of other learned societies. He contributed to various periodicals, including the *Literary Gazette*. He published *A Dissertation on the Course and Probable Termination of the Niger* (1829), dedicated to the duke of Wellington, in which he argued, chiefly from ancient writers, that the Niger was a river or 'Nile' bearing northwards and probably losing itself in quicksands on the Mediterranean shore (in the Gulf of Sidra, according to the subsequent *Letter to the Publisher*). This view was refuted in 1829 in the *Quarterly Review* by Sir John Barrow, who nevertheless testified, from personal knowledge, that Donkin was 'an excellent scholar, of a clear, logical, and comprehensive mind, vigorous in argument, and forcible in language' (*QR*, 81, 1829, 226). Donkin, dissatisfied and apparently not knowing who had written the review, replied with *A Letter to the Publisher* (1829). Some of his writings appear never to have been published, including 'A parallel between Wellington and Marlborough', said to have been his last work. He was described by contemporaries as a most agreeable companion, and always had many interesting anecdotes to relate. On 5 May 1832 he married his second wife, Lady Anna Maria Elliot, daughter of the first earl of Minto. They had no children, and she survived him, dying in 1855. He was returned to parliament for Berwick in 1832 and 1835, in the whig interest, each time after a sharp contest. In 1835 he was made surveyor-general of the ordnance, and he foreshadowed developments in 1855 by suggesting that the civil business of the Board of Ordnance be transferred to the War Office, and command of the Royal Artillery to the commander-in-chief of the army at the Horse Guards. At the general election of 1837 he was defeated at Berwick upon Tweed, but in 1839 returned for Sandwich in Kent. On 15 March 1837 he became colonel of his old regiment, the 11th foot, and was promoted general on 28 June 1838.

Donkin, whose health had for some time caused concern, committed suicide by hanging, at Southampton on 1 May 1841. He was buried in a vault in St Pancras old churchyard, London, together with an urn containing the heart of his first wife.

H. M. CHICHESTER, *rev.* JOHN SWEETMAN

Sources *Army List* • T. Carter, ed., *Historical record of the forty-fourth, or the east Essex regiment of foot* (1864) • R. E. R. Robinson, *The bloody eleventh: history of the Devonshire regiment*, 1: *1685–1815* (1988) • Fortescue, *Brit. army*, vol. 9 • J. Sweetman, *War and administration* (1984) • *The dispatches of … the duke of Wellington … from 1799 to 1818*, ed. J. Gurwood, 9: *Peninsula, 1790–1813* (1837)
Archives Port Elizabeth City Library, letter-book • Rhodes University, Grahamstown, South Africa, Cory Library for Historical Research, corresp. | BL, corresp. with Lord Hastings and Nicol, Add. MS 23759 • BL, corresp. with Sir Hudson Lowe, Add. MSS 20131–20150, 20226 • Mount Stuart, Isle of Bute, letters to Lord Hastings • NAM, letters to Carlo Joseph Doyle during third Maratha War • NAM, corresp. with Sir Benjamin D'Urban • NAM, corresp. with Frederick Maitland • NL Scot., letters to Sir George Murray • NMM, corresp. with Sir Benjamin Hallowell • U. Nott. L., corresp. with Lord William Bentinck, etc.
Likenesses G. Hayter, group portrait, oils (*The House of Commons, 1833*), NPG • W. Holl, stipple (after H. Mayer, 1831), BM, NPG; repro. in W. Jerdan, *National portrait gallery of illustrious and eminent personages* (1831) [*see illus.*] • H. Mayer, oils, City Hall, Port Elizabeth, South Africa

Donkin, William Fishburn (1814–1869), astronomer and mathematician, the first son of Thomas Donkin, was born at Bishop Burton, Yorkshire, on 15 February 1814. He early showed a marked talent for languages, mathematics, and music. He was educated at St Peter's School, York, and in 1832 entered St Edmund Hall, Oxford. In 1834 he won a classical scholarship at University College, Oxford, where in 1836 he obtained a double first class in classics and mathematics, and a year later he carried off the mathematical and Johnson mathematical scholarships. He proceeded BA on 25 May 1836, and MA in 1839. He was elected as a fellow of University College, and he continued for about six years at St Edmund Hall as mathematical lecturer. During this period he wrote an able 'Essay on the theory of the combination of observations' for the Ashmolean Society, which was also published in French; and he also contributed some excellent papers on Greek music to Dr Smith's *Dictionary of Antiquities*.

In 1842 Donkin was elected Savilian professor of astronomy at Oxford, a post which he held for the remainder of his life. That year he was elected a fellow of the Royal Society, and also of the Royal Astronomical Society. In 1844 he married Harriet, the third daughter of the Revd John Hawtrey of Guernsey.

Between 1850 and 1860 Donkin contributed several important papers to the *Philosophical Transactions*, including 'On a class of differential equations, including those which occur in dynamical problems' (*PTRS*, 144, 1854) and 'The equation of Laplace's functions' (*PTRS*, 147, 1857). In these and other papers he drew upon W. R. Hamilton's theory of quaternions. He also deployed the symbolic methods of solving differential equations widely used by English mathematicians at the time; a major figure was George Boole, who published some of Donkin's results in his *Treatise on Differential Equations* (1859). They included new ways of solving Laplace's equation, and also an important equation due to Laplace concerning potentials of a nearly spherical spheroid (such as the earth). He and Boole also exchanged ideas on methods of computation in probability theory. In 1861 he read an important paper to the Royal Astronomical Society entitled 'The secular acceleration of the moon's mean motion' (printed in the society's *Monthly Notices* for 1861). He was also a contributor to the *Philosophical Magazine*, his last paper in which, 'Note on certain statements in elementary works concerning the specific heat of gases', appeared in 1864.

Donkin's acquaintance with practical and theoretical music was very thorough. His work on acoustics, intended to be his *opus magnum*, was commenced in 1867, and the fragment of it which he completed was published, after his death, in 1870. Basing his mathematical treatment on Fourier series, he covered transverse and lateral vibrations of strings and rods, and free and forced oscillations. He also examined the composition of the musical scale, and had intended to present musical theory and practice in a third part. The second part would have treated elastic membranes, plates and solids, and the mathematical theory of sound. Although incomplete, his book was the principal work in English on this topic until Lord Rayleigh's *Theory of Sound* appeared in two volumes in 1877 and 1878. Among other interests, Donkin also corresponded on geometrical problems with William Spottiswoode.

Donkin's constitution was always delicate, and failing health compelled him to live much abroad during the latter part of his life. He died at his home in Broad Street, Oxford, on 15 November 1869. He was survived by his wife. W. J. Harrison, *rev.* I. Grattan-Guinness

Sources *Monthly Notices of the Royal Astronomical Society*, 30 (1870–71), 84 ff. • G. Boole, *Treatise on differential equations* (1859) • M. Panteki, 'Relationships between algebra differential equations and logic in England, 1800–1860', CNAA PhD, Middlesex Polytechnic, 1992 • d. cert. • Foster, *Alum. Oxon.*
Archives MHS Oxf., corresp. with Sir B. C. Brodie • RS, Boole MSS
Wealth at death under £5000: probate, 10 Jan 1870, *CGPLA Eng. & Wales*

Donlevy, Andrew (1680–1746), Roman Catholic priest, was born near Balymote, in co. Sligo, into a comfortably off family. He was educated locally and it is likely that he was trained as a priest and ordained in Ireland before travelling to France about 1710. There he registered in the Paris law faculty in 1718, and took his BA in 1719 and his licence in law in 1720. In Paris he sided with a reforming party (*zelanti*), which believed that the Irish church should conform to European practices, especially with regard to the education of priests. This was contentious as the Irish seminary community, housed in the Collège des Lombards, was divided into two groups: already ordained priests who had travelled to Paris for theological training, and younger clerics who were following the Tridentine discipline. Longstanding financial tensions between the two groups were exacerbated by Donlevy's proposal, as prefect of the clerics since 1722, to remove ordained priests from the seminary. He was supported by Abbé Vaubrun and Cardinal de Fleury, but excited the ire of Irish bishops who feared that exclusively Paris-formed clerics would be unlikely to return to the mission. Donlevy, exercising influence with Fleury, succeeded in having a new code of discipline drawn up for the college. Pending royal ratification, the community of priests complained to Ireland and to Rome. In the college elections of 1734 the Donlevy party was ousted. Rome intervened to allow priests to remain but removed from the students their right to elect college officers; future appointments were made the responsibility of the archbishop of Paris. Donlevy continued as superior of the clerics until his death.

Donlevy lamented the decline of the Irish language and worked to preserve its monuments. He recognized the language's importance in religious education and was anxious to modernize the increasingly scarce Franciscan catechisms in Irish of the early seventeenth century. He was helped by Philippe Joseph Perrotin, who funded a school of Irish in the college to print catechisms and works of piety for the mission. As part of this scheme Donlevy published, in 1742, the bilingual *An teagasg Críosduidhe*, to which was appended a verse abridgement of Christian doctrine, compiled by Bonaventure O'Heoghusa, and Donlevy's treatise, 'The elements of the Irish language'. Donlevy's catechism, conceived as a resource book for more advanced religious education, was written in Irish; the English version was a literal translation. It is the most complete formal text in Irish for this period and draws on the author's spoken Irish, but it was influenced too by the technical vocabulary of the early seventeenth-century Irish Louvain Franciscans.

Donlevy died at the Irish College, Paris, on 7 December 1746 and was buried in the Irish College chapel.

THOMAS O'CONNOR

Sources L. Swords, *A hidden church: the diocese of Achonry, 1689–1818* (1997) · L. W. B. Brockliss and P. Ferté, 'Irish clerics in the 17th and 18th centuries: a statistical survey' (typescript), Royal Irish Acad., 1016 · M. Tynan, *Catholic instruction in Ireland, 1720–1950* (1985) · W. Hayden, *An introduction to the study of the Irish language based upon the preface to Donlevy's catechism* (1891) · L. Swords, 'History of the Irish College, Paris, 1578–1800', *Archivium Hibernicum*, 35 (1980), 3–233 · *DNB*
Archives Irish College, Paris, archives
Wealth at death poor: Swords, *Hidden church*, 214

Donn [Donne], **Benjamin** (1729–1798), mathematician and cartographer, was born in Bideford, Devon, and baptized there on 22 June 1729, the last of six children of George Donn (*b.* in or before 1680, *d.* in or after 1750) and his wife, Elizabeth, *née* Ching. George Donn was from an old Bideford family and from about 1721 kept a well-regarded mathematical school there, in which his sons Abraham (1719–1743) and later Benjamin taught. In 1749 Benjamin began to contribute to the *Mathematical Repository*, *Gentleman's Diary*, and *Gentleman's Magazine* on astronomical and mathematical subjects. On 8 October 1759 he married Mary Anne, daughter of Henry Wilcocks.

Like other mathematicians Donn was also a surveyor, but his maps were of a quality far above the average. While still in Bideford he began his map of Devon at a scale of one inch to a mile, for which he received a premium of £100 from the Society of Arts on publication in 1765. Donn was one of the first to respond to the society's offer in 1759 of a premium for accurate, newly surveyed county maps at a scale of one inch to a mile, and he was one of the few to succeed in his application. He had apparently planned the survey independently of the society's encouragement, and, as was normal, he issued a prospectus and ultimately enlisted 528 subscribers for the map. Even with the help of assistants the fieldwork took longer than anticipated and there were further delays while Thomas Jefferys engraved the results on twelve plates. Stung by criticism from the society, Donn retorted that his map was 'not an Engraver's Job [that is an updating of a more or less out of date map], but an accurate Survey at the expense of nearly £2000 … the largest work ever done of the kind at private expense' (Harley, 120). The map is an important early county map because it was newly surveyed and because Donn was an able mathematician and judge of instruments, which increased his standards of accuracy.

In 1764 Donn moved to Bristol, where he leased rooms in the house of the city library in King Street, and from 1766 he ran an academy there to which the corporation and Society of Merchant Venturers had the right to nominate pupils. From the academy he sold his maps and instruments including his navigation scale (a Gunter's scale). In 1767 he announced his intention of publishing a map from a survey of the country 11 miles round Bristol. The city council awarded him 20 guineas on publication in 1769. The map is a valuable source of information on the then rapidly growing city. In 1768 he was elected librarian, but also continued as a mathematics teacher.

Donn was one of a number of educational reformers in Bristol at the time who wanted to stop the rote learning of words and substitute the study of things with the aid of toys or experiments, introducing children to the principles behind each subject so that they could accept rationally what they were taught, not merely believe it slavishly. He taught a practical and vocational curriculum, presenting Newtonian experimental science as an integral part of polite learning for both adults and children. His ideas were expounded in his classes and lectures, in letters to the local press, and in his publications such as *Mathematical Essays* (1764), *The Accountant and Geometrician* (1765), *The Young Shopkeeper's, Steward's and Factor's Companion* (1768), and later *An Essay on Mathematical Geometry* (1796).

Between 1765 and 1798 Donn gave at least seventy public lectures, many in Bristol but others over a wide area, in part as a means of establishing a scientific reputation and allowing him to teach a broader curriculum, and in part simply to make money, although since the supply of lecturers exceeded demand, he was not always successful. His audiences were mainly young men, with a few young women and 'mechanics'. The lectures were advertised as cultural activities and were illustrated by experiments in which he used instruments of his own making.

Donn attracted an enthusiastic following, gaining civic and public support for his projects, which were thought to be a valuable addition to Bristol's commerce and culture: however, despite his supporters, an impressive range of publications, and active self-promotion through advertisements, he was unable to sustain a local career beyond that of an ordinary mathematics teacher. Such teachers were poorly paid and there was a rapid turnover of them in the city. By 1773 Donn had lost the patronage of the corporation and the Merchant Venturers and, when a new librarian was appointed on 27 March 1773, he had to move his school out of the library house. He set up an academy at The Park, near St Michael's Church, and, when this failed, left Bristol for Kingston, near Taunton, where he ran an academy. From about 1773 he added a final 'e' to his surname, apparently reverting to the practice of his grandfather, Christopher Donne. After only two years continued financial troubles took him back to Bristol where he issued a pocket map of the city about 1775. While in Bristol he was helped by another Benjamin Donne (1764–1843), often described as his son but in fact his nephew, who was also a teacher of mathematics, surveyor, and cartographer, and who issued further maps after his uncle's death. From 1796 to his death Benjamin Donne the elder was master of mechanics to George III and the list of subscribers to his *Essay on Mathematical Geometry* (1796), which includes such figures as Erasmus Darwin, Samuel Taylor Coleridge, and Josiah Wedgwood, shows the regard in which he was held by contemporaries. He is thought to have had a son, Henry, a Church of England clergyman and minor cartographer. Donne died on 27 May 1798. ELIZABETH BAIGENT

Sources J. Barry, 'The cultural life of Bristol, 1640–1775', DPhil diss., U. Oxf., 1985 · E. Robinson, 'Benjamin Donn', *Annals of Science*, 19 (1963), 27–36 · J. B. Harley, 'The Society of Arts and the survey of English counties, 1759–1809 [pts 1–4]', *Journal of the Royal Society of Arts*, 112 (1963–4), 43–6, 119–25, 269–75, 538–43 · F. W. Steer and others, *Dictionary of land surveyors and local map-makers of Great Britain and Ireland, 1530–1850*, ed. P. Eden, 2nd edn, ed. S. Bendall, 2 vols. (1997) · R. V. Wallis and P. J. Wallis, *Index of British mathematicians*, pt 3 (1993) · E. G. R. Taylor, *The mathematical practitioners of Hanoverian England, 1714–1840* (1966) · B. Donne, *A map of the county of Devon* (1765); facs. edn with introduction by W. L. D. Ravenhill, ed. (1965) · J. E. Pritchard, 'Old plans and view of Bristol', *Transactions of the Bristol and Gloucestershire Archaeological Society*, 48 (1926), 325–53 · *GM*, 1st ser., 68 (1798), 632 · *GM*, 1st ser., 74 (1804), 999–1000
Wealth at death probably very little: Barry, 'Cultural life of Bristol'

Donn, James (1758–1813), botanist and gardener, was born in Perthshire. He began his horticultural training under William Aiton at Kew, and was appointed curator of the university botanic garden in Cambridge in 1794, in which post he remained until his death in 1813. His name is associated with a remarkable publication, *Hortus Cantabrigiensis*, the first edition of which Donn published in 1796. In the preface he explains that his book 'is not simply a catalogue of the plants actually grown in the small Walkerian garden, but contains also [plants] that are yet required to render the collection more worthy of [the botany student's] notice'. This book ran to thirteen editions, the last one dated 1845, and became, long after the original author's death, a standard reference work for both botanists and gardeners, giving compact information on the world's flora, native or exotic, as represented in British gardens. The preface to the tenth edition by John Lindley explains that Donn himself greatly enlarged the scope of his book from the fifth edition, so that it ceased to be in any way limited to what he grew in the Cambridge garden.

Donn owed his appointment at Cambridge to Sir Joseph Banks. He greatly extended the plant collections in Cambridge, especially with gifts from Kew. There are several testaments to Donn's skill in cultivating plants. Thus the entomologist William Kirby recorded in his journal his impressions of a visit to the garden in July 1797: 'Mr Newton of Jesus accompanied us to the Botanical Garden, which, by the abilities and industry of Mr Don [*sic*], the Curator, is now in excellent order; the collection of plants is greatly augmented, and the labels are in general accurate' (Freeman, 106). Donn became a fellow of the Linnean Society in 1812. He died in Cambridge on 14 June 1813.

S. MAX WALTERS

Sources B. Henrey, *British botanical and horticultural literature before 1800*, 2 (1975), 237–9 · S. M. Walters, *The shaping of Cambridge botany* (1981) · *Cambridge Chronicle and Journal* (18 June 1813) · J. Freeman, *Life of the Rev. William Kirby, M.A.* (1852)
Archives U. Cam., department of plant sciences, herbarium specimens

Donnán [St Donnán] (*d.* 617), martyr, is earliest reliably attested in the annals of Tigernach and the annals of Ulster. In their annal for the year 617, these record: 'the burning of Donnán of Eigg on 17 April with 150 martyrs' (*Annals of Tigernach*, s.a. 616; *Ann. Ulster*, s.a. 617; Adomnán, trans. Sharpe, 369). Although its date of composition is uncertain, probably the earliest fuller account of Donnán's death appears in Latin in the twelfth-century Book of Leinster. This relates how a rich woman who lived on Eigg had ill feeling towards Donnán and the monastic community that he had established on the island, and persuaded bandits to kill him. Arriving on the eve of Easter, the bandits found the community chanting psalms in the oratory, 'and they could not kill them there'. Donnán, however, instructed his monks to move to the refectory, 'since as long as we remain where we have done our all to please God, we cannot die, but where we have served the body, we may pay the price of the body' (Sharpe, 370). According to this version, fifty-four companions were killed along with Donnán. The ninth-century martyrology of Tallaght puts the number at fifty-two. The account in the Book of Leinster also appears in the scholia of the earliest glossed copies of the ninth-century *Félire Óengusso*. The scholia in two late medieval copies of that work tell in Irish that Donnán wanted Columba (*d.* 597) to be his soul-friend (*anmchara*), but Columba refused. He is supposed to have shown a preference for the white martyrdom of ascetic self-denial, rather than the red martyrdom of death, saying: 'I will be soul-friend only to people of white martyrdom; that is, I will not be your soul-friend because you and all your community with you will suffer red martyrdom' (Sharpe, 370).

Donnán's foundation on Eigg was probably located at or near the existing ruin of the church of Kildonnan in the south-east corner of the island. The name Kildonnan (or Kildonan) was also given to a church in Sutherland, indicating some small dissemination of his cult in Scotland.

MARIOS COSTAMBEYS

Sources Adomnán of Iona, *Life of St Columba*, ed. and trans. R. Sharpe (1995) [incl. full commentary on St Donnán] · R. Sharpe, 'Notes', in Adomnán of Iona, *Life of St Columba*, ed. and trans. R. Sharpe (1995) · W. Stokes, ed., 'The annals of Tigernach [8 pts]', *Revue Celtique*, 16 (1895), 374–419; 17 (1896), 6–33, 119–263, 337–420; 18 (1897), 9–59, 150–97, 267–303, 374–91; pubd sep. (1993) · *Ann. Ulster* · R. I. Best and others, eds., *The Book of Leinster, formerly Lebar na Núachongbála*, 6 vols. (1954–83), vol. 6 · *Félire Óengusso Céli Dé / The martyrology of Oengus the Culdee*, ed. and trans. W. Stokes, HBS, 29 (1905) · A. Macdonald, 'Two major early monasteries: Lismore and Eigg', *Scottish Archaeological Forum*, 5 (1973), 57–64 · W. Reeves, *The life of St Columba* (1857) [extensive, but now rather archaic]

Donnan, Frederick George (1870–1956), physical chemist, was born in Colombo, Ceylon, on 6 September 1870, the second of the six children of William Donnan, a merchant of Belfast, and his wife, Jane Rose Turnley Liggate, who was also from Northern Ireland. All Donnan's early life was spent in Ulster, where he returned at the age of three. In 1879 an accident caused the loss of his left eye, but he continued to play sport to a high standard. He attended the Belfast Royal Academy (1880–89), where his chief interest was mathematics and physical science; there being no laboratories in the academy he did some practical work externally. From there he went to the Queen's College, Belfast, where he was remarkably successful in his studies, obtaining his BA from the Royal University of Ireland in 1894.

In 1893 Donnan obtained an 1851 Exhibition scholarship. In that year, before graduating from Ireland, he went to the University of Leipzig. He did a year's chemistry under Johannes Wislicenus (1835–1902) and then joined W. Ostwald (1853–1932) to devote himself to the emerging discipline of physical chemistry. He obtained his PhD *summa cum laude* in 1896. He finished his European tour with a year in the laboratory of J. H. van't Hoff in Berlin, where he studied the hydrates of calcium sulphate and the vapour pressures of a number of saturated aqueous solutions of single and double salts occurring in van't Hoff's investigations on oceanic salt deposits.

Returning to Ireland in 1897, Donnan sat the MA examination of the Royal University of Ireland. Awarded a four-year junior fellowship, he spent a year at home, 'to read more deeply in the literature of physical chemistry', before proceeding (in 1898) to University College, London, as a senior research student in the laboratory of William Ramsay. In 1901 he became assistant lecturer in Ramsay's laboratory; in 1902–3 he was assistant professor in University College; and in 1903–4 lecturer in organic chemistry in the Royal College of Science, Dublin. In 1904, however, he accepted the new chair of physical chemistry, founded at the University of Liverpool by Sir John Brunner. He supervised the building of the Muspratt Laboratory of Physical Chemistry and was its director from 1906 to 1913. He then succeeded Ramsay at University College, London, where he remained until his retirement in 1937.

During the First World War, Donnan was a member of a number of committees including those on chemical warfare and nitrogen products. As a consultant to the Ministry of Munitions he played an important part in the early stages of the research work at University College on synthetic ammonia and nitric acid, and assisted K. B. Quinan in the designs of plant for the fixation of nitrogen and for the production of mustard gas. He was appointed CBE in 1920 in recognition of his wartime services. His connections with the chemical industry continued after the war: he was research consultant to Brunner, Mond & Co. from 1920 to 1926 and a member of the research council of Imperial Chemical Industries from 1926 to 1939. He was particularly successful in raising money from industry and other sources for scientific research.

Although pre-eminently a teacher, Donnan was internationally known as a colloid chemist and in particular for his theory of membrane equilibrium, published in the *Zeitschrift für Elektrochemie* (1911). The theory had important applications in the technologies of leather and gelatin, but particularly to the understanding of living cells, and how ions and molecules are transported within them and between the cell and its environment.

Donnan was elected FRS in 1911 and awarded the Davy medal in 1928. He received the Longstaff medal (1924) of the Chemical Society, over which he presided in 1937–9, had no fewer than eleven honorary degrees, and was an honorary member of numerous academies and learned societies. His range of interests was extraordinarily wide; his early appreciation of the necessity of a united Europe led him to the study of artificial languages, while in his old age he was much preoccupied with cosmic problems. He was tall, good looking, well built, and of great physical strength and endurance. His face in repose was often stern and rather sad, but when he began to talk he radiated charm and sympathy. A tremendous worker, he kept late hours. He was devoted to his friends but had his dislikes. To accompany him abroad was to take part in a royal progress.

After his retirement Donnan remained in his home in Woburn Square until 1940, when he left only twelve hours before it was destroyed by a bomb. He went to live at Hartlip, near Sittingbourne, Kent, and died in hospital at Canterbury on 16 December 1956. He never married and owed much to two sisters who played an unobtrusive but important part in his life and both of whom died in the same year. F. A. FREETH, *rev.* K. D. WATSON

Sources F. A. Freeth, *Memoirs FRS*, 3 (1957), 23–39 · W. E. Garner, 'Frederick George Donnan, 1870–1956', *Proceedings of the Chemical Society* (1957), 362–6 · *DSB* · C. F. Goodeve, 'Prof. Frederick G. Donnan', *Nature*, 179 (1957), 235–6 · *CGPLA Eng. & Wales* (1957)
Archives UCL, corresp. and papers | CAC Cam., corresp. with A. V. Hill · priv. coll. · RS · U. Lpool
Likenesses photograph, *c.*1900, repro. in Freeth, *Memoirs FRS* · W. Stoneman, photograph, 1922, NPG · F. A. Swaine Ltd, black and white photograph, RS · black and white photograph (negative), RS
Wealth at death £14,138 8s. 10d.: probate, 13 March 1957, *CGPLA Eng. & Wales*

Donnchad Donn mac Flainn (*d.* 944), high-king of Ireland, was the son of *Flann Sinna, high-king of Ireland (*d.* 916), and of Gormlaith, daughter of Flann mac Conaing (*d.* 868), king of all Brega (Knowth dynasty); the epithet Donn may be translated as 'the Brown-Haired'. A member of the Clann Cholmáin, the main branch of the southern Uí Néill based on the crannog of Cró-inis in the south-west corner of Lough Ennell in Westmeath, he became king of Mide in 916 and succeeded to the high-kingship in 919 on the death of the northern Uí Néill high-king, Niall mac Áeda (Niall Glúndub).

According to the Irish annals Donnchad had three wives. Cainnech, who died in 929, was a daughter of Canannán of Tír Conaill (modern Donegal). Órlaith was killed by Donnchad in 941, after what may have been a sexual relationship with his son Óengus; she was a daughter of Cennétig mac Lorcáin of the Dál gCais of Munster. Dublemna died in 943; she was a daughter of Tigernán mac Sellacháin, king of Bréifne (approximately modern counties Leitrim and Cavan). His sons were Conn (d. 944), Óengus (d. 945), and Domnall Donn (d. 952); and his daughters were Flann (d. 940) and Óebfhinn (d. 952).

Donnchad first appears in the historical record in 904 when his father, Flann, opposed him in the town of Kells, beheading many of his associates in the vicinity of the church. With his brother Conchobor he again rebelled against his ageing father in 915. They were brought to heel by Niall Glúndub, then king of Ailech, who was protecting his own future interests, especially since his attempt to oppose Flann in the previous year had failed. On succeeding his father, Donnchad ruthlessly removed opponents, blinding his brother Áed in 919, and killing his brother Domnall in 921 ('which was fitting', according to the annalist) at Bruiden Dá-Choca (Breenmore, Westmeath, on the east side of the River Shannon). This was almost certainly because of Domnall's close relationship with the Connachta, as is confirmed by Donnchad's unsuccessful raid across the Shannon in the following year. He killed his nephew, Conchobor's son Máel Ruanaid, in 928.

Donnchad campaigned with his kinsmen against the men of Bréifne in 910; and in 913 alongside Máel Mithig mac Flannacáin (his sister Lígach's husband) of the Knowth dynasty (also his mother's people) against Lorcán, son of Dúnchad (a dissident of the Knowth dynasty), who was in league with the southern Brega dynasty at Lagore and the Leinstermen. Indeed his campaigns in Brega in 939 and 940 were probably against Lorcán's two sons who were finally dispatched by Congalach, Máel Mithig's son, in 942.

After assuming the high-kingship Donnchad inflicted a massive defeat on the vikings in Louth in 920. His ally Muirchertach mac Tigernáin of Bréifne (brother of his wife Dublemna) died from his wounds. Donnchad was opposed by the northern Uí Néill king, Muirchertach mac Néill, in 927, 929, and 938, but on each occasion conflict was avoided, probably because his daughter, Flann, was married to Muirchertach. They raided Leinster and Munster jointly in 938 and 940; and in an independent campaign in 941 (following the death of Flann in 940) Muirchertach plundered Mide, Uí Failge, Osraige, and Déisi and delivered Cellachán of Cashel to Donnchad as hostage—thus demonstrating that Donnchad's power was always limited.

Through his marriages Donnchad was connected with future powerful families—that to Cainnech of the Cenél Conaill foresaw the rise of Ruaidrí Ua Canannáin, as that to Órlaith recognized the rise of the ancestors of the Uí Briain. Similarly, the marriage to Dublemna acknowledged the rise of the ancestors of the Uí Ruairc. In 939 Donnchad had a shrine made for the Book of Armagh. He died in 944.

CHARLES DOHERTY

Sources Ann. Ulster • W. M. Hennessy, ed. and trans., Chronicum Scotorum: a chronicle of Irish affairs, Rolls Series, 46 (1866) • AFM • S. Mac Airt, ed. and trans., The annals of Inisfallen (1951) • D. Murphy, ed., The annals of Clonmacnoise, trans. C. Mageoghagan (1896); facs. edn (1993) • M. C. Dobbs, ed. and trans., 'The Ban-shenchus [3 pts]', Revue Celtique, 47 (1930), 283–339; 48 (1931), 163–234; 49 (1932), 437–89 • P. Walsh, 'The Ua Maelechlainn kings of Meath', Irish Ecclesiastical Record, 5th ser., 57 (1941), 165–83

Donnchad mac Domnaill (733–797), high-king of Ireland, was a member of the Clann Cholmáin branch of the southern Uí Néill. His father, *Domnall mac Murchada (d. 763), was the first high-king of his dynasty. His mother, Ailbine, was the daughter of Ailill (d. 702) of the Fir Ardda Ciannachta (modern co. Louth). Frewin, after which he is sometimes named, lies on the west shore of Lough Owel, Westmeath. There is evidence of only two wives of Donnchad. Bé Fáil (d. 801), daughter of Cathal, of the Ulaid, eponym of Leth Cathail (barony of Lecale, Down), was the mother of his sons Óengus (d. 830) and Máel Ruanaid (king of Mide; d. 843). Less certain is a reference to his other wife, Fuirseach, daughter of a Congal of the Dál nAraidi and mother of his son Conchobar (d. 833), later high-king. His other sons were Conn, who was killed in 795, Domnall, treacherously killed by his brothers in 799, Ailill, killed by his brother in 803, Follamain, killed by the Munstermen in 830, and Ruaidrí (d. 838), prior of Clonmacnoise, Clonard, and other churches. Donnchad's daughter Gormlaith (d. 861) was the wife of the northern Uí Néill high-king *Niall mac Áeda (Niall Caille) and the mother of the high-king *Áed mac Néill (Áed Findliath). His other daughter, Euginis ('queen of the king of Tara'; Ann. Ulster, s.a. 802), died in 802. His sister Eithne was wife of Bran Ardchenn, king of Leinster; both were killed by Fínsnechta Cetharderc in Cell Chúle Dumai at Abbeyleix, in what is now Laois, on Wednesday 6 May 795.

The first phase of Donnchad's recorded career follows his father's death in 763, during succession struggles within Clann Cholmáin. He first appears in 764 in a battle against the Fir Thulach Midi (barony of Fartullagh, Westmeath, on the east shore of Lough Ennell), an isolated branch of the Leinster Uí Fhelmeda. In the same year his brother Diarmait Dub died leading the forces of Durrow unsuccessfully against the forces of Clonmacnoise, led by his brother Murchad's son Bressal. In the following year Donnchad killed Murchad in battle at Carn Fiachach (Carn, on the eastern border of the barony of Rathconrath, Westmeath). Donnchad had the support of Follaman, king of Mide. Murchad's ally Ailgal, king of Tethbae, escaped. From 769 Donnchad began to attack his neighbours. He expelled Cairpre (d. 771) from Lagore in 769 and in 770 ravaged Leinster. During the next two years he attacked the north. In 774 and again in 777 he disrupted the fair of Tailtiu.

In 775 Donnchad brought the Leinster monastery of Clonard under his control. He first campaigned against Munster in 775, and then again in 776, with the help of the forces of Durrow. In 777 he opened a new campaign against Brega by attacking the Ciannacht at the fair of Tailtiu. This war lasted into the following year culminating in the battle of 'Forcalad' (unidentified), in which Congalach, son of Conaing (of Knowth), was killed and his allies the Mugdorna, Ciannacht, and Gailenga were defeated. On the death of Niall Frossach in 778 Donnchad became high-king and hosted into the north to take hostages. In 780 he repulsed a raid on his territory by the Leinstermen, pursuing them and ravaging their territories. A royal conference under ecclesiastical leadership followed to agree a *modus vivendi*. A similar meeting between Donnchad and the Ulster king Fiachnae resulted in a stand-off when they refused to come face to face.

Following the killing of Fáeburdaith, *airchinnech* ('head') of the church of Tuilén (Dulane, just north of Kells in Meath), Donnchad defeated the Fir Chúl mBreg and their Síl nÁeda Sláine allies in battle at Lia Finn (Leafin, parish of Nobber, Meath) in 786. A supporter of the Columban community, in 789 he dishonoured the staff of Jesus and relics of Patrick at Ráith Airthir (Oristown, near Tailtiu). In 791 he drove the northern Uí Néill king Áed Oirdnide from Tailtiu along the valley of the Blackwater and the Boyne to the Cairn of Mac Caírthinn, just south of Slane. His last recorded campaign was in 794 when he helped the Leinstermen against the Munstermen. His continuous military activity allowed his dynasty to consolidate their control of the midlands during his reign. Donnchad died on Monday 6 February 797. CHARLES DOHERTY

Sources *Ann. Ulster* · W. M. Hennessy, ed. and trans., *Chronicum Scotorum: a chronicle of Irish affairs*, Rolls Series, 46 (1866) · *AFM* · S. Mac Airt, ed. and trans., *The annals of Inisfallen* (1951) · D. Murphy, ed., *The annals of Clonmacnoise*, trans. C. Mageoghagan (1896); facs. edn (1993) · R. I. Best and others, eds., *The Book of Leinster, formerly Lebar na Núachongbála*, 6 vols. (1954–83), vol. 1 · F. J. Byrne, *Irish kings and high-kings* (1973) · P. Byrne, 'The community of Clonard from the sixth to the twelfth centuries', *Peritia*, 4 (1985), 157–73 · M. C. Dobbs, ed. and trans., 'The Ban-shenchus [3 pts]', *Revue Celtique*, 47 (1930), 283–339; 48 (1931), 163–234; 49 (1932), 437–89 · M. A. O'Brien, ed., *Corpus genealogiarum Hiberniae* (Dublin, 1962)

Donne, Sir Daniel. *See* Dun, Sir Daniel (1544/5–1617).

Donne, Gabriel. *See* Dunne, Gabriel (*c*.1490–1558).

Donne [Dwn], **Sir John** (*d.* 1503), soldier and administrator, was descended from the Donne family of Kidwelly. His forebears were active soldiers, and John is said to have been born in Picardy, where his father, Gruffudd Donne (*d.* in or before 1448), served in the retinue of Richard, duke of York, perhaps about 1430. John was himself later said to have served Duke Richard in England, France, and Ireland, while after 1461 he became an esquire of the body to the duke's son, Edward IV, and was granted the office of master of the armoury in the Tower of London. But his most important services to the Yorkist cause were in Wales. Having played an important part in the campaigns

Sir John Donne (*d.* 1503), by Hans Memling, 1478? [kneeling, left; detail]

of 1460 and 1461, in the latter year he was appointed steward of Kidwelly, constable of Aberystwyth and Carmarthen, and sheriff of Carmarthenshire and Cardiganshire. On 4 March 1464, with Roger Vaughan of Tretower, he defeated a Lancastrian rebellion at Dryslwyn, near Carmarthen. His rewards included Laugharne, forfeited by the earl of Wiltshire. In 1470, following the death of the earl of Pembroke, Donne became the effective governor of west Wales under the duke of Gloucester. Consistently loyal to Edward IV, he was knighted on the battlefield at Tewkesbury, on 4 May 1471.

Donne married Elizabeth (*c*.1450–1507), daughter of Sir Leonard Hastings, some time between 24 February 1462 and 11 March 1465. During the reign of Edward IV and later he had connections with Calais, perhaps as a result of the appointment of his brother-in-law, William, Baron Hastings, as lieutenant of Calais in 1471. Donne held office at Calais in 1472. He was present in 1475 at the meeting of Edward IV with Charles the Bold, duke of Burgundy, and his wife, Margaret, King Edward's sister. In 1477 Edward sent him on missions to Louis XI of France and Maximilian, king of the Romans. He was also in command of troops at Calais in 1483. This link with Calais, which is not far from Bruges, and which was valued partly because of its connection with English wool exports to the latter city, is no doubt the explanation of the Donne altarpiece, formerly at Chatsworth House and now in the National Gallery, London. A triptych by the Bruges painter Hans Memling, it was probably made about 1479–80. Along with the coats of arms of Donne and Hastings, its central panel includes excellent portraits of Sir John, his wife, and a daughter, probably Anne. These are among the earliest sophisticated representations of British faces.

Following the usurpation of Richard III, Donne was suspected of having joined the rebellion of October and November 1483 against the new regime. The confiscation of his lands was ordered, and in February 1484 he lost his office at Calais, that of lieutenant of Ruysbank, and never recovered it. But he was able to prove his loyalty, and was even pricked as sheriff of Bedfordshire and Buckinghamshire in the autumn of 1484. Perhaps his difficulties under Richard III made it easier for him to survive the accession of Henry VII without loss of status. He may also have been seen as essentially an efficient administrator rather than a politician. His mastership of the Tower armoury was confirmed, and in 1487 he was once more appointed steward of Kidwelly. He also became keeper of Carmarthen Castle. During the 1490s, moreover, he became lieutenant of Calais, being replaced some time before 15 February 1497. His widow retained a house in that town. But he figures most prominently in the records as sheriff of Bedfordshire and Buckinghamshire, holding the lordship of Horsenden and acting as parker of the royal park at Princes Risborough in the latter county, where he was frequently a JP. He died shortly before 27 January 1503, and was buried in St George's Chapel, Windsor. He was survived by his wife, who lived until 1507, and by two sons, Edward and Gruffudd. GEORGE HOLMES

Sources K. B. McFarlane, *Hans Memling* (1971), 1–15, pl. 1–8 · *Chancery records* · *VCH Buckinghamshire* · H. T. Evans, *Wales and the Wars of the Roses* (1915) · C. Ross, *Edward IV* (1974) · R. Horrox, *Richard III, a study of service*, Cambridge Studies in Medieval Life and Thought, 4th ser., 11 (1989) · G. Williams, *Recovery, reorientation and reformation: Wales, c.1415–1642*, History of Wales, 3 (1987); repr. as *Renewal and reformation: Wales, c.1415–1642* (1993) · R. Somerville, *History of the duchy of Lancaster, 1265–1603* (1953)

Likenesses H. Memling, altarpiece, 1478?, National Gallery, London [*see illus.*]

Wealth at death see McFarlane, *Hans Memling*

Donne, John (1572–1631), poet and Church of England clergyman, was born between 24 January and 19 June 1572 at his father's house in Bread Street, London, the third of six known children of John Donne (c.1535–1576), warden of the Ironmongers' Company, and Elizabeth Heywood (c.1543–1631), youngest daughter of John *Heywood the epigrammatist and playwright. Donne claimed kinship through his father with the Dwn family of Kidwelly in Carmarthenshire, using its arms on his earliest portrait, painted in 1591, as well as on one of his seals and on his monument (the arms are azure, a wolf salient, with a crest of snakes bound in a sheaf), but there is no evidence extant concerning his father's family to support this claim. Donne's ancestors on his mother's side included John Rastell (his maternal great-grandfather), who was married to Elizabeth, daughter of Sir John More and sister of Sir Thomas More. Through his connection with the More and the Heywood families Donne was thus associated with many men and women who had remained true to the Roman Catholic faith and had suffered as a result— a fact that he was at pains to emphasize in his early work *Pseudo-Martyr* (1610). Two of his uncles, Ellis and Jasper Heywood (the translator of Seneca), ended their days as Jesuits (Jasper was the head of the Jesuit mission in England from 1581 to 1583), and Donne and his siblings were brought up as Roman Catholics. In 1576, when Donne was four, his father died; by July his mother had married John

John Donne (1572–1631), by Isaac Oliver, 1616

Syminges, a prominent physician who had trained at Oxford and Bologna and had several times been president of the Royal College of Physicians. Some time after the marriage Donne's family moved to Syminges's house in Trinity Lane, moving again in 1583 to a house in the parish of St Bartholomew-the-Less.

Oxford and the inns of court Donne was educated privately, although there is no evidence to support the popular claim that he was taught by Jesuits. On 23 October 1584, at the age of twelve, he matriculated with his brother Henry, who was a year younger than him, from Hart Hall, Oxford. It seems that the boys entered the university relatively young (and gave their ages as a year younger than they actually were) in order to avoid subscribing to the queen's religious supremacy and to the Thirty-Nine Articles—a subscription demanded of all students over sixteen. Little is known of Donne's time at Oxford, though Izaak Walton claims that he was a distinguished student, and that it was there that his long friendship with Sir Henry Wotton began (Walton, 23, 106). After Donne left Oxford without taking a degree, Walton claims that he spent some time at Cambridge; there is no evidence for this in the university records, but as R. C. Bald points out, these are imperfect for this period (Walton, 24; Bald, 46). It has recently been argued that Donne left Oxford in October 1584 for a period of exile and education among fellow Catholics on the continent (Flynn, 131–46); even if Donne did attend Cambridge after Oxford, it would have to have been for less than three years, and uncertainty remains over his movements between 1589 and 1591. It seems most likely that he travelled abroad during this period, and it is quite possible that Walton's description of his travels in the late 1590s should be redated to the earlier period (Walton, 26). If Donne was travelling on the continent at this time, he probably followed the typical itinerary for a contemporary tour, visiting France, the Low Countries, and Germany *en route* for Italy (see Bald, 52, on Donne's likely visit to Germany). During this time, Donne's stepfather John Syminges died in 1588 (he was buried in the church of St Bartholomew-the-Less on 15 July), and his mother married Richard Rainsford, probably in 1590 and certainly before 7 February 1591. In 1591 the earliest known portrait of Donne was produced: it was a miniature, possibly by Nicholas Hilliard, but now the image survives only in William Marshall's engraving of it for the frontispiece of the 1633 *Poems*. It shows him in a dark doublet, with head bared, wearing an earring in the shape of a cross and with his hand on the hilt of a sword, and bears the motto *Antes muerto que mudado* ('Sooner dead than changed') as well as the Dwn crest described above.

The next clear sight of Donne from the official records is on his admission to Lincoln's Inn on 6 May 1592, after at least a year's preliminary study at Thavies Inn. Edward Loftus and Christopher Brooke, who was to remain a close friend of Donne's, stood surety for him on his admission. It was at Lincoln's Inn that Donne also met Christopher Brooke's younger brother Samuel, their cousin John, and Rowland Woodward. Although Donne was never called to the bar, nor practised the law professionally, its language and modes of thought remained crucial to him throughout his life, and lend much of his writing its distinctive character. His *Satires* and the poems later collected as *Songs and Sonets* are not just immersed in the social world of the inns, but use the words and the distinctions of the law to conduct their business of social comment and love. Later writings, including the *Holy Sonnets*, are equally dependent upon Donne's thorough knowledge of common and canon law, and it should not be forgotten that Donne certainly used his legal knowledge in his professional life. It was in demand while he was secretary to the lord keeper, Sir Thomas Egerton; in 1603–4 he prepared a legal opinion for Sir Robert Cotton on Valdesius's *De dignitate regum regnorumque Hispaniae*; his first major published work, *Pseudo-Martyr*, is a highly professional legal exposition and defence of the oath of allegiance, and he engages in tangled questions of civil and canon law in several other works, notably *Ignatius his Conclave* and the *Essays in Divinity*. It may have been during his time at Lincoln's Inn that, as Walton claims, Donne began 'seriously to survey, and consider the Body of Divinity, as it was then controverted betwixt the *Reformed* and the *Roman Church*' (Walton, 25–6), and to undertake a systematic reading and annotation of Cardinal Bellarmine's *Disputationes*; certainly his later work shows that he was well acquainted with the Roman Catholic controversialist's works.

When Donne moved from Thavies Inn to Lincoln's Inn he probably left behind him his younger brother Henry. In May 1593 a priest, William Harrington, was found in Henry Donne's chambers by the pursuivant Richard Young. Both were arrested and committed to the Clink, then moved to Newgate, where Henry died of the plague.

Harrington was hanged, drawn, and quartered in February 1594. In the same year as Henry's death, Donne attained his majority, and in June 1593 he had received his inheritance from the chamber of the city of London.

It is difficult to date Donne's poems, most of which remained in manuscript until after his death, but it seems clear that while at Lincoln's Inn he composed verse letters to friends—such as Christopher and Samuel Brooke, Rowland and Thomas Woodward (the Westmoreland MS, one of the principal manuscripts of Donne's poems, is in Rowland's hand), Everard Guilpin, Beaupré Bell, and an unidentified Mr. I. (or J.) L.—the first two *Satires*, nearly all of the *Elegies*, the *Epithalamion Made at Lincoln's Inn*, and some of the *Songs and Sonets*. The verse letters especially show Donne experimenting with tone and form as he exchanges compliments in the world of humanist friendship, but the *Elegies* and *Satires* are remarkably assured. The speakers of the *Elegies* are rakish young men-about-town, addressing mistresses in tones of amorous and adulterous complicity (and revealing the widespread influence of Marlowe's translations of Ovid's *Amores*). They assume a tone of almost arrogant disregard for social mores and conventions, and yet here, as in much of his writing, Donne's voice, and his speakers, are as vulnerable as they are powerful. *Elegy* 2 is a persuasion to his mistress to undress that deploys the languages of religion as well as exploration and conquest in its travels over her clothing and body, but its conclusion shows that it is the poet who is naked, waiting.

The *Satires*, like the *Elegies*, are the product of, and shot through with, the social life of late sixteenth-century London; their attitudes, though, are rather different. Their speakers are urbane observers, outsiders, watching with anxious disapproval the hunt for place and promotion at court and in the courts, drawn in despite themselves (like the personae of Horace's satires, to which they are heavily indebted) to the corrupting conversation of the bore or malcontent, and finding themselves tainted by it. In the first two *Satires* there is also found a scepticism towards both learning and public life, the contemplative and the active paths, that is characteristic of the period and that informs much of Donne's work in both verse and prose. In these early poems the immediacy of voice that is so typical of Donne's writing is fully present. *Satires* 1 and 2 begin with a brusque imperative ('Away thou fondling motley humourist') and a weary epistolary salutation ('Sir; (though I thank God for it) I do hate / Perfectly all this town …') respectively; and this creation of a vital, speaking voice is one of the most striking features of Donne's poetic oeuvre, sustained by lengthy qualifying parentheses, interruption, colloquialism, and the careful disruption of metrical order. This last quality earned Donne the disapproval of the more formally orthodox Ben Jonson, who declared in his conversations with William Drummond that 'Donne, for not keeping of accent, deserved hanging' (I. Donaldson, ed., *Ben Jonson*, 1985, 596).

Soldier, secretary, and husband: 1596–1609 The last mention of Donne in the Lincoln's Inn records occurs at the end of

1594. He would certainly have ended his association with the inn by early 1596, when he was among the mass of young gentlemen who offered their services to the earl of Essex for his and Lord Howard of Effingham's expedition against Spain. The fleet set sail for Cadiz on 3 June, launching its successful attack on the harbour on the 21st; returning in triumph, the leaders of the expedition soon planned another assault, and Donne also joined this expedition, which set out in July 1597. Within a week, however, the fleet had returned in disarray after the events recorded in Donne's poem 'The Storm'; embarking again a little later, the fleets were once more separated by bad weather, and Essex's squadron set off for the Azores, where they waited for Ralegh's (in which Donne was probably sailing)—Donne describes the postponement of the rendezvous by a period of calm weather in 'The Calm'. The voyage was dogged by disorganization and ultimately achieved little: the Spanish fleet got safely into port at Angra, and only a few late ships were taken; finally, the English returned home in yet another bout of bad weather, reaching port by the end of October.

On his return to England, Donne sought civil employment, and with help from Thomas and John Egerton, whom he may have known at Lincoln's Inn and who sailed with him on the islands expedition of 1597, he was appointed secretary to Sir Thomas Egerton, lord keeper of the great seal since 1596. On his appointment Donne would have joined Egerton's substantial household at York House in the Strand and assisted his employer in the wide range of business that occupied him, from the courts of chancery, high commission, and Star Chamber to the privy council. Egerton was determined to reform legal procedures from a state of confusion and over-complexity; Donne's *Satire* 5 describes this morass and praises Egerton's attempts 'to know and weed out this enormous sin'. Donne would have spent time at court as well as in the courts during this time, where political discussion was dominated by the debates over the campaign in Ireland. When the earl of Essex was sent there in April 1599, two of Donne's friends accompanied him: Sir Henry Wotton, who was Essex's secretary, and Sir Thomas Egerton the younger. To the former Donne sent a verse letter asking why he had heard nothing from him ('H.W. in Hiber. belligeranti'); the latter was wounded in a skirmish and died on 23 August aged twenty-five. At the solemn funeral held in Chester Cathedral, Donne had the honour of bearing the dead man's sword before his coffin.

As a student at Oxford and the inns, Donne was a Roman Catholic. By 1597, however, he had sailed on an expedition against Catholic Spain and was employed by Egerton, a major public figure, if one with a recusant past. By 1601 he was a member of parliament. All of these would have been extremely difficult had he still been attached to the Roman Catholic church (although Flynn suggests that he retained important links with recusant families for a considerable time). The date of Donne's 'conversion' to the Church of England has been the subject of much scholarly debate, but is impossible precisely to determine (Bald, 69,

argues that he may have received some form of instruction from Anthony Rudd, dean of Gloucester, after Henry Donne's death). Indeed, it is probably unhelpful to conceive of it as an event, rather than as a long process. The best that can be said is that by 1600 or so Donne considered it possible that he could successfully seek advancement in areas that would be closed to a known Catholic, and that in 1601 he was married in a Church of England ceremony (if an unorthodox one). Seven years later he was writing anti-Catholic polemic, and using his own upbringing in the Roman Catholic church to lend greater force to his criticisms of that church.

In the aftermath of the Essex rebellion in February 1601 Donne may have helped the lord keeper in the long business of examining witnesses and preparing for the trial; in the autumn of the same year he was returned as one of the members of parliament for Brackley, Northamptonshire, a seat in Egerton's gift. Parliament sat from 27 October to 19 December, and there is no evidence that Donne sat on any committees or took part in any debates. During the period of his employment by Egerton, Donne's friendship with Henry Wotton was sustained by correspondence in verse and prose (the verse epistle 'Sir, more then kisses, letters mingle souls' can be tentatively dated to 1597 or 1598), and among his other friends were Sir Henry Goodyer, Robert Cotton, and the essayist Sir William Cornwallis. In 1601 Donne began his Menippean epic, 'The Progress of the Soul', or 'Metempsychosis' (the preface is dated 16 August 1601). This ambitious poem aimed to trace the migration of the soul of the apple eaten by Eve 'to this time when she is he, whose life you shall find in the end of this book', but only a portion of the first canto was completed. Jonson claimed that the soul was intended to end up 'in the body of Calvin' (I. Donaldson, ed., *Ben Jonson*, 1985, 598), but Donne indicates in stanzas six and seven that the soul is now 'amongst us' in England,

> and moves that hand, and tongue, and brow,
> Which, as the Moone the sea, moves us.

Faced with this problem, critics have suggested Queen Elizabeth and Robert Cecil as final homes for the soul. At about this time Donne was also writing his prose *Paradoxes*.

During his time as Egerton's secretary, Donne met Ann More (1584–1617), the niece of Lady Egerton and the daughter of Sir George More of Loseley Park, near Guildford in Surrey. She was brought up for some time at York House (Sir George More had for his part undertaken the education of Lady Egerton's son, Francis Wolley), and while she was there she and Donne were secretly engaged. In December 1601, when Ann was about seventeen and Donne twenty-nine, they were married in a clandestine service: Donne's friends Christopher and Samuel Brooke were in attendance, Christopher giving the bride away and Samuel, now ordained, performing the ceremony. Soon Ann returned to Loseley, and it was almost two months before Donne broke the news of their marriage to her father, using Henry Percy, ninth earl of Northumberland, as the messenger for his letter of 2 February. Sir George was horrified, and immediately demanded

Donne's dismissal from Egerton's service and arrest: along with the Brooke brothers he was committed to prison, and the lord keeper gave in to More's request. But soon Donne was released from the Fleet, and it was clear that the marriage would be proved valid (indeed, Donne himself initiated a suit in the court of audience of Canterbury to test its validity): Sir George released his daughter to Donne, but refused to support her financially, while Egerton refused to give his secretary his job back, even when the injured and reluctant father-in-law joined in the request. Without employment or a home (during the latter part of his employment by Egerton he had lived in lodgings in the Savoy), Donne and his wife had to depend on help from friends and sympathetic relatives. Ann's cousin Francis Wolley offered the most substantial help, giving the Donnes room in his house at Pyrford, near her former home at Loseley. It was there that their first children, Constance and John, were born, at the beginning of 1603 and in the spring of 1604 respectively. In August 1603 the new king, James I, and his court spent the first night of their progress at Pyrford.

Early in 1605 Donne set off to travel on the continent with Sir Walter Chute, their licence being granted on 16 February. They visited Paris, and possibly Venice, where Wotton was now ambassador, before returning to England in April 1606. While Donne was abroad, his wife, who had been staying with her sister Lady Grymes at Peckham, gave birth to their third child, George; on his return the family probably spent a short time back at the Wolley house in Pyrford until they moved, before the end of the year, to a cottage in Mitcham, Surrey. While living at Pyrford, Donne had continued his studies and his writing: it was during this time that he sent his learned opinion on Valdesius to Robert Cotton, and internal evidence suggests that he wrote at least two of the *Songs and Sonets* ('The Sunne Rising' and 'The Canonization') at about the same time.

Donne lived with his wife in Mitcham for five years, and while they were there four more children were born: Francis in 1607, Lucy in 1608 (her godmother was Lucy Harington, countess of Bedford), Bridget in 1609, and Mary in 1611. From 1607 to 1611 Donne also kept lodgings in London, in the Strand, and he spent a large amount of his time in the city, devoting his energies to making the best of his connections and seeking out some kind of public employment for himself. These attempts to resurrect what had been a promising career failed without exception: in June 1607 he sought to fill a place that had fallen vacant in the queen's household; in November 1608 he applied for a secretaryship in Ireland, through the mediation of the king's favourite, Lord Hay; in February 1609 John Chamberlain wrote to Carleton that Donne 'seekes to be preferred to be secretarie of Virginia' (*Letters of John Chamberlain*, 1.284)— and these were, most likely, only a fraction of the positions he applied for.

Among the friendships that Donne established or consolidated about this time was that with Ben Jonson (for whose *Volpone* he wrote Latin commendatory verses in 1607). From 1607 he also began his correspondence with

Lady Bedford, and at about the same time he made or renewed his friendship with Mrs Magdalene Herbert (George Herbert's mother, to whom, in July 1611, he sent what was probably the sonnet sequence 'La corona'). During winter 1608–9 he was ill with chronic neuritis, and wrote 'A Litanie', which, in a letter to Sir Henry Goodyer, he referred to as 'a meditation in verse' (Donne, *Letters*, 32). Most of the *Holy Sonnets* were probably also written at about this time. There has been much debate over how far these last form any kind of sequence, and if so in what order they should be arranged; certainly, though, the group of twelve as they appear in the Group I and II manuscripts in the 1633 edition of the *Poems* seem to have some internal coherence, and are far from being individual utterances. The *Holy Sonnets* are exhortatory, despairing, and demanding by turns, and they make use of virtually the full range of Donne's intellectual pursuits, the twelfth in particular ('Father, part of this double interest') skilfully pleading the legal case for inheritance of the kingdom of heaven to God figured as a divine judge.

Professional authorship, travels with the Drurys, and entry into the church: 1609–1615 The period during which Donne was at Mitcham was one of the most productive for his writing and research, and Bald rightly states that at this time he was 'nearer to being a professional author than at any other time during his life' (Bald, 200). Donne had been engaged for some time, it is clear, in a course of reading in canon and civil law, and in casuistry: the works that he composed from 1607 to 1610 are steeped in this learning, determined at once to display their mastery of a vast number of authorities and to cast a sceptical eye on the very use of authoritative textual testimony. The first substantial work that Donne wrote at this time, *Biathanatos* (composed in 1607–8, though work on it may have started at Pyrford), is a perfect example of his ambiguous relationship with humanism. It is a cousin to the more frivolous *Paradoxes* and *Problems* (the latter probably composed at roughly the same time) in its defence of a seeming paradox—its subtitle is 'A declaration of that paradoxe or thesis, that self-homicide is not so naturally sinne, that it may never be otherwise'—yet it is formidably researched, and its fashionably sceptical attitude can be more properly traced to a frame of mind inculcated by the study of cases of conscience that occupied Donne throughout his life. According to Walton, in Donne's study after his death were found 'divers ... cases of Conscience that had concerned his friends, with his observations and solutions of them' (Walton, 68), and Donne refers to his book of cases of conscience in two of his surviving letters. *Biathanatos* was—by contrast with Donne's other prose writings from this period—intended to be a fairly private work: it was printed in 1647, sixteen years after Donne's death, and only two manuscripts survive from Donne's lifetime. Statements made by Donne to those entrusted with a copy of the work reinforce the sense that he intended it for a restricted circle of readers: in a presentation letter to Sir Edward Herbert he suggests that the best (though he never says only) place for it is Herbert's library, and when sending a copy to Sir Robert Ker in 1619 he declared 'I forbid it only the Presse, and the Fire: publish it not, but yet burn it not; and between those, do what you will with it' (Donne, *Letters*, 22). The book was, he noted to Ker, 'upon a misinterpretable subject' (ibid., 21).

Shortly after Donne completed *Biathanatos*, he published what was to be his most substantial prose work, *Pseudo-Martyr* (1610; the book runs to 430 pages). *Pseudo-Martyr* is not merely a work more public than *Biathanatos*: it is in its own right an extremely public and deliberate intervention into a current controversy, and it announces unambiguously Donne's allegiance to the religious policies of James I, to whom it is dedicated. After the Gunpowder Plot in 1605 James had approved an act of parliament that instituted a new oath of allegiance; this oath forced Roman Catholics to deny the deposing power claimed by the pope over monarchs who opposed Catholicism, or to face imprisonment and the seizure of their property. A war of words flared up over whether English Catholics were obliged to swear the oath, the king entering the fray with his *Triplici nodo triplex cuneus, or, An Apologie for the Oath of Allegiance* (1607). The Jesuit Robert Persons soon responded to James's book in satiric vein, and William Barlow was commissioned to answer Persons. Barlow's *Answer to a Catholike English-Man* (1609) proved to be a rather feeble contribution, and Donne spoke harshly of it in a letter to Goodyer. He had been following the controversy from its beginning, and may even have been acting as an assistant to the practised controversialist Thomas Morton, chaplain to the earl of Rutland and, from 1607, dean of Gloucester—certainly Donne had read portions of the manuscript of Morton's *A Catholike Appeale for Protestants* (1609) eighteen months before its publication. *Pseudo-Martyr* is as learned a work as *Biathanatos*, and in writing it Donne turned the scepticism evinced towards human authorities in the earlier work to local ends: he was aware of the importance to the controversy of judicious and accurate quotation (Barlow's prime failing, in Donne's opinion), and went to some trouble to assert his own reliability and to expose the distortions of Catholic writers.

Pseudo-Martyr is divided into two sections, which treat in turn two arguments: first, that Catholics may take the oath of allegiance with clear consciences, and second, that therefore those who do not and who suffer as a result are not entitled to be called martyrs. In the preface Donne draws attention to the fact that he is especially well placed to pronounce on martyrdom true and false, asserting that:

> as I am a Christian, I have been ever kept awake in a meditation of Martyrdome, by being derived from such a stocke and race, as, I beleeve, no family, (which is not of farre larger extent, and greater branches,) hath endured and suffered more in their persons and fortunes, for obeying the Teachers of Romane Doctrine, then it hath done. (Donne, *Pseudo-Martyr*, 1610, sig. ¶)

In pursuing his thesis Donne argues that the temporal jurisdiction claimed by the pope is false, while the ecclesiastical jurisdiction claimed by various monarchs is legitimate. Arguing that those who suffer for obeying this false

papal authority are not true martyrs, he distinguishes between essential points of faith and things indifferent, or adiaphora: he strikes a pose of toleration and moderation, yet in claiming the authority to make this distinction he confronts and provokes his Catholic opponents. *Pseudo-Martyr* is a work that marshals profound learning in the service of the king's religious policy, yet it appears to have received little notice from other participants in the heated and drawn-out controversy over the oath of allegiance (J. P. Sommerville, 'Jacobean political thought and the controversy over the oath of allegiance', PhD diss., University of Cambridge, 1981). It may, however, have advertised Donne's skills as a controversial theologian to the king as well as to contemporaries in the church. Walton states that James at this point first suggested that Donne should enter the church, but this suggestion was clearly not received with great enthusiasm: Donne continued to pursue his civil ambitions.

In April 1610 Donne was made an honorary MA of Oxford. It was probably later that year that he wrote his next controversial work, *Conclave Ignati*, or *Ignatius his Conclave*. While *Pseudo-Martyr* tends to conceal its confrontational position behind eirenic language, *Ignatius* is a brief and biting satire against Roman Catholics in general, Jesuits in particular, and all kinds of innovators, couched in the form of a dream-vision, a Menippean journey to hell where Ignatius holds court. The book was published anonymously, first in Latin and then in Donne's own English translation. It makes much play with this anonymity, a preface 'from the Printer to the Reader' describing the author's supposed reluctance to publish while very deliberately setting the book as a companion-piece to *Pseudo-Martyr*. Once again Donne displays a studied ambivalence to learning, exposing the distortions of Roman Catholic reading practices while displaying his own erudition. He mocks the procedures of controversy (side-notes support tiny points in Donne's argument by reference to enormous volumes) while at the same time demonstrating his competence in them.

It is unclear when Donne first made the acquaintance of Sir Robert Drury and his family, but in the year following the death of their younger daughter Elizabeth in 1610, he wrote two elegies for her, 'A Funerall Elegie' and 'An Anatomy of the World', and was invited by Sir Robert to join the family on a journey to the continent. Both poems were printed, anonymously, in 1611. The party left England about November 1611, and Donne's wife and children went to stay with her younger sister Frances and her husband, John Oglander, on the Isle of Wight. Donne and the Drurys went first to Amiens, where they stayed from December until roughly the beginning of March, and where Donne wrote the next of his elegies for Elizabeth Drury, 'The Progres of the Soule'; this was published in 1612 with 'An Anatomy of the World' as the 'First' and 'Second' *Anniversaries*. Early in 1612 the Drurys moved to Paris, where Donne fell ill. He none the less witnessed the double marriage of Louis XIII and his sister, and attempted to make contact with the Sorbonnist Edmond Richer, a critic of the pope's temporal claims; he also saw the exiled

Toby Matthew. The next stage of the journey, after Easter, was to Heidelberg and Frankfurt (where the party witnessed the imperial election); from there they went on to Spa, and returned to England via the Low Countries, visiting Maastricht, Louvain, and Brussels (and possibly Antwerp).

On his return to England, Donne moved, with his family, into a house belonging to Sir Robert Drury and near to the Drurys' own substantial house on Drury Lane. He stayed here until 1621. A number of public and personal events provided the occasions for poems during the period after his travels abroad. Donne contributed an elegy for the third edition of Joshua Sylvester's *Lachrymae lachrymarum*, a memorial volume to Prince Henry, who had died in November 1612; he also wrote an epithalamion for the marriage of Princess Elizabeth to Frederick, the elector palatine ('Hail Bishop Valentine, whose day this is')—the latter a piece that deftly unites attention to the significance of the day upon which the marriage fell (St Valentine's day) with decorous celebration of the couple's equality and mutuality in love. A visit to his friend Sir Henry Goodyer in the spring of 1613 was commemorated in Donne's 'Goodfriday, 1613: Riding Westward'; Donne was probably on his way from Goodyer's house at Polesworth to Sir Edward Herbert at Montgomery Castle.

Donne was still in search of an office, and sought the patronage of those who seemed most likely to be able to help; it was during 1613 that he offered his services to Robert Carr, Viscount Rochester (later earl of Somerset). Carr was engaged in the attempt to make Frances Howard (then married to the earl of Essex) his wife, and it was at this time that Donne was presented to him by another of James's Scottish favourites, James Hay. Donne later offered to write a defence of the nullity pronounced on Howard's previous marriage, and he produced an epithalamion for her wedding to Carr, which took place in December 1613. The epithalamion is a notoriously complicated response to a marriage that was regarded with some misgivings even before the bride and groom were accused of complicity in the murder of Carr's former secretary, Sir Thomas Overbury. Donne frames his poem with an eclogue, explaining that the epithalamion was written in his absence from the court and is being delivered late, and offering to burn it. Seemingly, he removes from himself responsibility for the poem or its reception while still delivering it—an extreme example of the modesty topos, which might point to the anxieties surrounding the event being celebrated.

Also in 1613-14 the young Lord Harington, brother of Lucy, countess of Bedford, died of smallpox, occasioning Donne's long 'Obsequies to the Lord Harrington', at the end of which he announces that his muse has 'spoke her last'. Donne himself had been ill during the winter of 1613-14, as had all of his family, and in May 1614 his daughter Mary died. As well as writing to and for his powerful friends and patrons, Donne was involved once more in the daily business of politics and public life, being returned as MP for Taunton in the short-lived Addled Parliament of

April–June 1614. He served on several committees, but there is no evidence of his speaking during the session's debates. It was the search for employment that must have greatly occupied Donne during this period, as it had for some years. Before parliament assembled, he wrote to Carr (now earl of Somerset) asking him to put him forward to the ambassadorship to Venice (recently vacated by Sir Dudley Carleton), and later in the year he made more than one attempt to gain a place directly from the king. These were, however, all unsuccessful, and Donne once again was advised to enter the church, as he had been on the publication of *Pseudo-Martyr* four years earlier. He had certainly not neglected his studies: according to Walton, at this time Donne was studying Greek and Hebrew (Walton, 46); Donne himself mentions in a letter that he was employed 'in the search of the eastern tongues' (Gosse, 2.16), and he may well have made use of the visits of the scholars Isaac Casaubon and Hugo Grotius in 1613-14. As it became increasingly clear that his path to advancement lay in divine and not secular employment, Donne chose to gather his poems for publication, finding that he needed to call in manuscripts that he had sent to friends: 'by this occasion', he wrote, 'I am made a Rhapsoder of mine own rags, and that cost me more diligence, to seek them, then it did to make them' (Donne, *Letters*, 197). However, this edition appears never to have been printed.

It is impossible to tell exactly when Donne wrote his *Essays in Divinity*. When the book was published posthumously in 1651, his son John Donne the younger wrote that it was 'writ when the Author was obliged in Civill business, and had no ingagement with that of the Church', and that the essays were 'the voluntary sacrifices of severall hours, when he had many debates betwixt God and himself, whether he were worthy, and competently learned to enter Holy Orders' (*Essays in Divinity*, 3, 4), but this suggestion that the work should be dated to the years immediately preceding Donne's ordination has no other support, internal or external. Certainly at times the *Essays* read like self-conscious apprentice-work—Donne is performing a very careful kind of exegetical meditation on the beginning of Genesis and on Exodus—and their tone stands at a curious mid-point between the private and the public; at one point Donne refers to them as 'sermons' with 'no Auditory' (*Essays in Divinity*, 41). While it is likely that they were finished by 1615, however (there are no references to books published after this date), they may have been begun much earlier and added to over a long period. It may be significant that Donne uses the Geneva Bible throughout, rather than (as might be expected were he writing after 1611) the King James Version—but he can also be found using the Geneva and a range of other versions after his ordination in his sermons. The *Essays*, when they have received critical attention, have been praised for the prayers with which they conclude; but there is much more of interest to them than these short devotional pieces. The *Essays* show Donne's sceptical attitude to human authorities and testimonies engaging with

Reformation arguments about the relative status of tradition and authority in doctrine.

Priest and preacher Donne was ordained deacon and priest on 23 January 1615, in St Paul's, with John King, the bishop of London, officiating. He wrote a series of letters to friends and patrons announcing his ordination, and adopted a new seal, exchanging the sheaf of snakes for an image of Christ crucified on an anchor. Appointed soon after his ordination to a royal chaplaincy, Donne attended the king on James's visit to Cambridge in March, where he was, despite apparent reluctance on the part of the vice-chancellor, awarded an honorary doctorate of divinity. His first sermon was, according to Walton, preached at Paddington (Walton, 48); but the first to survive bears the heading 'Preached at Greenwich, April 30. 1615'. Recent research supports Jessop's contention (challenged by Bald) that the sermon was preached to the court at Greenwich, not in the parish church there. For the rest of his career Donne would combine preaching in parish churches with addressing more elevated auditories, at court, at Lincoln's Inn, and at St Paul's Cathedral, among other places.

Donne received his first benefices in the year following his ordination, being granted Keyston in Huntingdon in January 1616 and Sevenoaks in Kent in July 1616. In October 1616 he was appointed as reader in divinity at his old inn of court, Lincoln's Inn. This, along with his duties at court as chaplain-in-ordinary (he seems to have mainly preached there during Lent), was his main occupation as a preacher in the first years of his ministry. In 1617 he preached his first sermon at the outdoor pulpit at Paul's Cross, on 24 March—the anniversary of the death of Queen Elizabeth and the accession of King James—just after James had set off on a journey to Scotland. In July of the same year he preached at his living in Sevenoaks, with Lady Anne Clifford in the congregation. Another sermon from this year was on a more private and melancholy occasion: on 10 August Ann Donne gave birth to a stillborn child, and five days later she died. Donne preached the funeral sermon at St Clement Danes (the incumbent had himself died recently, and it was Donne's parish church) and he commissioned a monument from Nicholas Stone to commemorate his wife. Walton gives an affecting account of the sermon, and of Donne's ability to move his auditory:

> And indeed his very looks and words testified him to be truly such a man [one who had 'seen affliction']; and they, with the addition of his sighs and tears, exprest in his Sermon, did so work upon the affections of his hearers, as melted and moulded them into a companionable sadness. (Walton, 52)

Donne and diplomacy: travel in Germany, 1619–1620 Having sought some form of diplomatic employment during the years before his ordination, Donne was finally sent in 1619 on an embassy in the capacity of chaplain to Viscount Doncaster. James, always determined to live up to his motto *Beati pacifici* ('Blessed are the peacemakers'), believed that he could mediate between the holy Roman emperor and the Bohemian protestants and put a halt to

the conflict that would become the Thirty Years' War. Doncaster was appointed ambassador in February, but the party did not set out until May. Donne must have been chosen at least in part because of his understanding of the continental situation—indeed, about 1615 he had been entrusted with a cipher, and was sent another by Wotton in 1623. He was, through his controversial works and his wide reading, well placed to undertake such a mission. Donne appears to have been concerned for his safety on his journey, and before he departed he made preparations in case he should not return, sending his manuscript of *Biathanatos* to Sir Robert Ker. He preached a farewell sermon at Lincoln's Inn, and about this time he composed the 'Hymne to Christ, at the Authors Last Going into Germany'.

The embassy travelled from Calais to Antwerp, Brussels, and then Mariemont, where they met the archduke. After this they went on to Heidelberg to meet Frederick, the elector palatine, and Princess Elizabeth (James I's son-in-law and daughter), before whom Donne preached a sermon. Doncaster then proceeded to meetings with allies of the emperor, travelling to Ulm, Augsburg, and Munich, where he met the duke of Bavaria. In Salzburg he met Ferdinand himself, and attempted to put the case for treating with the Bohemians, but to little avail. The imperial elections took place at Frankfurt, and Doncaster and many of his party were present, though when he saw that his diplomacy was having no effect he moved on to the Spa, with Donne in attendance. Meanwhile, Frederick was chosen as king of Bohemia and Ferdinand as emperor. In the final stages of his mission, Doncaster pursued the new emperor to Graz, where he was granted an audience, and then set off on his return journey, again having failed to sway Ferdinand towards peace. The embassy travelled to The Hague, where Donne preached, and was given a medal commemorating the Synod of Dort: this gift could be seen as acknowledging his status as a moderate and sympathetic member of the European protestant movement. Finally, the party reached London on 1 January 1620: James's ambitions as peacebroker had been disappointed, and Donne and his companions had experienced the frustration of seeing their embassy exploited as a delaying tactic by the emperor while the protestant forces suffered and remained unassisted by the English.

Donne's ecclesiastical career, 1620–1631 On his return from the continent Donne resumed his duties at Lincoln's Inn; he also celebrated the wedding of Sir Francis Nethersole to Lucy Goodyer, daughter of his friend Sir Henry. He was actively seeking promotion, however, and it is known that twice in 1620–21 his hopes were frustrated. Late in August 1621, though, the bishop of Exeter died, and was succeeded by Valentine Cary, dean of St Paul's: it was decided that Donne would take Cary's place, and he was formally elected and installed on 22 November. Donne resigned from his living at Keyston in October 1621, and also from his readership at Lincoln's Inn (though it is first recorded only in early 1622). As a parting gift to the inn he donated the six-volume edition of the Vulgate with Nicholas de Lyre's commentary. Information on Donne's deanship is scarce; the act-books of the chapter for his incumbency do not survive and recent researches have failed to uncover more material. On being appointed Donne moved his residence to the deanery of St Paul's and, according to Walton, 'immediately after he came to his Deanry, he employed work-men to repair and beautify the Chapel' (Walton, 55).

As dean, Donne's preaching duties were not onerous: he was obliged only to preach on Christmas day, Easter day, and Whit Sunday. But he certainly did more than this bare minimum, and a number of sermons on other occasions survive. Nor did he preach only in the cathedral. In February 1622 Donne was appointed to the living of Blunham in Bedfordshire, in the gift of the earl of Kent, and it seems that he spent time there each summer, as had been his custom with his other livings. Moreover, he continued to preach at court, and elsewhere. In August 1622 he preached before Doncaster, the earl of Northumberland (Doncaster's father-in-law), and the duke of Buckingham at Hanworth, and later that year he was chosen to deliver a sermon on a highly sensitive political occasion. During 1622 the protestant forces had been suffering defeats in Germany, and at the same time the negotiations for a Spanish marriage for Prince Charles were progressing; there was a degree of popular unrest, and James's policies were being criticized from the pulpits. On 4 August the king issued directions to preachers, severely restricting the subjects, political and doctrinal, that could be treated by ordinary clergy, and ordered Donne to justify the directions in a sermon at Paul's Cross on 15 September. The sermon is a consummate example of orderly preaching which also has the ability to offer implicit counsel, but it received mixed reactions when it was delivered: Chamberlain suspected that Donne was not committed to his task (*Letters of John Chamberlain*, 2.451), but James was impressed, and ordered the sermon to be printed. It was quickly published with a dedication to Buckingham, the first of Donne's sermons to appear in print. This was the first of several important public sermons Donne delivered in autumn 1622. He preached the annual Gunpowder Plot sermon at St Paul's on 5 November, and James demanded to see it—though this time it was not printed. Just over a week later, on 13 November, he preached to the Virginia Company (of which he had been made an honorary member on 22 May and an honorary member of the council on 3 July), at St Michael Cornhill. This sermon was printed, and was dedicated to the company.

The next of Donne's sermons to be printed was preached and published in 1623, on the occasion of the consecration of the new chapel at Lincoln's Inn. Delivered on Ascension day, it was printed with the title *Encaenia*. As in his defence of the directions to preachers, in this sermon Donne characteristically engages with discretion in a highly controversial subject. Not only the issue of outward displays of worship (addressed by Donne in his dedicatory epistle to the masters of the bench), but also the more specific question of what the function of consecration was in a reformed church, are discussed with a polemical force that derives precisely from Donne's

choice of a moderate and moderating voice. In October 1623 Donne preached at the law serjeants' feast, although this sermon does not survive. However, the occasion is a reminder that during his time as dean Donne also had occasion to use his legal training. He served as a justice of the peace in Kent and Bedford, and he was appointed thirteen times to hear appeals from lower ecclesiastical courts and sit in the court of delegates.

During 1623 Donne was engaged in negotiations for the marriage of his daughter Constance to the former actor and founder of Dulwich College, Edward Alleyn; the wedding took place on 3 December. During this winter, however, Donne was seriously ill with what seems to have been a combination of 'relapsing fever' with the less grave 'rewme' (Donne, *Devotions*, xiii–xvii). This illness he used as the foundation of the *Devotions upon Emergent Occasions*, printed in early 1624 (it was entered in the Stationers' register on 9 January) and dedicated to Prince Charles. The book, organized into a series of twenty-three meditations, expostulations, and prayers, follows the progress of the illness through Donne's body as he observes himself and considers himself as a type of mankind. It is striking in its dogged pursuit of the possible meanings, spiritual and physical, of the symptoms Donne observes as he works away at the questions of the relation between internal and external, the corporeal and the intellectual, the human and the divine. In March 1624 Donne was appointed to the living of St Dunstan-in-the-West, whose incumbent had recently died and which was in the gift of the earl of Dorset. The parish was in the centre of the legal district as well as being surrounded by stationers' shops, and Donne's congregation there must have contained many lawyers, judges, and printers as well as other citizens. As with his personal chapel at the deanery of St Paul's, Donne initiated renovations at St Dunstan's soon after his appointment.

In 1625 Donne composed the only poem that can be dated with certainty from this period of his life—and it may well have been his last. 'An Hymne to the Saints, and to Marquesse Hamylton' was written at the request of Sir Robert Ker (Hamilton died on 2 March). The same year saw the death of James I (on 27 March) and the accession of Charles I: Donne preached the first sermon before the new king, on 3 April, and a sermon before the body of James on 26 April. He was ill once more, and was forced to leave London because of the plague that swept the city from the summer; staying in Chelsea with Sir John and Lady Danvers until December, he made use of his temporary exile by writing out many of his sermons—he refers to having completed eighty in a letter to Sir Thomas Roe of 25 November (Bald, 479). There was some familial disturbance in Donne's life, however, as he and his son-in-law Edward Alleyn quarrelled over £500 that Alleyn claimed Donne had promised to lend him and then refused to deliver.

After the plague was over, Charles was crowned in 1626 and called his first parliament. Convocation also met, and Donne was chosen prolocutor. He preached the annual Lent sermon at court, and at Charles's suggestion it was printed, with a dedication to the king. Donne clearly retained the royal favour he had enjoyed under James. 1626 was a busy year for him in the pulpit, and he was also appointed a governor of the Charterhouse. The following year his royal favour slipped briefly, as the king—via William Laud—demanded to see a copy of the sermon Donne had preached at court on 1 April. It appears that they suspected him of joining with Archbishop Abbot's criticism of James Montagu and Robert Sibthorpe, who had recently preached sermons in support of Laud's ceremonial innovations. Donne would thus, by extension, be criticizing Laud himself. The sermon was scrutinized, and Donne was cleared.

In 1627 Donne's daughter Lucy died, as well as several of his old friends: Goodyer died on 18 March; Lady Bedford on 31 May; and Lady Danvers in early June. He preached the latter's funeral sermon, and it was subsequently printed. On 19 November he preached at the wedding of Lady Mary Egerton, daughter of the earl of Bridgewater, to the son and heir of Edward, Lord Herbert of Cherbury. Little detailed information is available about Donne's activities during the final years of his life, aside from his attendance at various meetings (for instance, the vestry meetings at St Dunstan's and the meetings of the governors of the Charterhouse), his presence as judge or signatory in legal cases, and his preaching of several datable sermons at Paul's Cross, St Paul's, and the court. It is known that he continued to suffer from ill health: from August 1629 he was unwell with a quinsy, and he seems to have been frequently ill with fever during 1630—possibly a symptom of the stomach cancer that eventually killed him. Had he lived, Donne would almost certainly have been appointed to a bishopric: by summer 1630 he was listed as a candidate for a see whenever a vacancy should open. However, his health was failing, and when his daughter Constance remarried in June 1630 (Alleyn had died in 1626), he went to stay with her at Aldborough Hatch in Essex and remained there until early 1631. His mother, who had been living with him at the deanery, and who had accompanied him to Aldborough Hatch, died in January 1631. Donne had already made his will, on 13 December 1630, and he would only live for another three months.

Donne returned to London, scotching rumours of his death, and on 25 February he preached his final sermon, at Whitehall. This is an extended meditation on mortality and resurrection, later printed as *Deaths Duell* (it was entered in the Stationers' register on 30 September 1631); according to Walton many of his auditors at the time said 'that Dr. Donne *had preach't his own Funeral Sermon*' (Walton, 75). Donne spent the time remaining to him preparing for death, practically and spiritually. He dealt with the final remaining cathedral business, he posed in his shroud for a monument (the sculpture by Nicholas Stone, funded by Donne's doctor Simeon Fox, remains in St Paul's today, and the sketch for this was also the model for the engraving by Martin Droeshout on the frontispiece of *Deaths Duell*), and he bade farewell to his friends. He died at the deanery on 31 March, and Walton gives an affecting portrayal of his end (Walton, 81–2). He was buried, on 3 April, in St Paul's, and the Latin epitaph on his monument may well have been written by Donne himself. Among those who survived him was his son John *Donne the younger, author and literary executor.

Donne left his sermons to Henry King, and they later, by a rather murky process, went via Walton to John Donne the younger, who published those in his possession in three folio volumes (*LXXX Sermons* appeared in 1640, *Fifty Sermons* in 1649, and *XXVI Sermons* in 1661). One hundred and sixty of Donne's sermons survive, and they demand reading and study not just as the major productions of his maturity but also as intricate and beautiful pieces of prose. Donne's religious stance has been much debated from his lifetime on, and the sermons demonstrate that while he continued the controversial interests of his early polemical works, his concern during his ministry was most often to seek edification—of his auditors and of the English church—and, while criticizing those whom he regarded as sectarians, both puritan and Roman Catholic, to find some form of accommodation with elements of both. As Donne preaches to congregations ranging from the inhabitants of Blunham to the members of the courts of James I and Charles I, he can be seen to be mapping out a middle way that offers at the same time a strong vision of a church still seeking identity and a voice with which its ministers can speak both with and to authority.

Donne's afterlife Immediately after his death Donne's greatness was celebrated by a host of poets, especially in the collection of 'Elegies upon the Author' contained in the two first editions of the posthumously published *Poems* (1633; 1635). Writers such as John Marston, Jonson, Henry King, Richard Corbet, Thomas Carew, Lucius Carey, Jasper Mayne, Sidney Godolphin, and, of course, Izaak Walton joined in praising Donne's skill as poet, divine, and versatile intellectual. Although Carew's elegy (probably now the most famous) singled out for praise Donne's poetic inventiveness, many of the others are notable for their concentration on Donne as a preacher—perhaps surprising in a volume of his poetry. In fact, Donne's verse was not widely known during his life. The poems were initially circulated among a small coterie of readers and, although they soon moved beyond that circle to be copied and recopied in manuscript collections, the paucity of early manuscript witnesses suggests that they travelled somewhat slowly. By the 1620s Donne's secular poetry was appearing regularly in manuscript miscellanies, but by this time he had been ordained for five years and the time of many of the poems' composition was long past.

It was in the decades immediately following Donne's death that his fame as a poet reached its height. The publication of the *Poems* in 1633 made them available to a wide readership, and the printer's address to the reader emphasized that already it was taken for granted by 'the best judgements' that Donne's poetry was 'the best in this kinde, that ever this Kingdome hath yet seene'. If this was a puff, it worked: there were six editions in the twenty-three years after Donne's death. Through the middle decades of the seventeenth century he was read, admired, and imitated, with further works being printed. Although several of the elegy writers of the 1633 volume had recourse to the paradoxical topos that after Donne's death it is impossible to write, his successors in fact seized the challenge enthusiastically, finding in Donne a model of a new literary style.

However, Donne's fortunes underwent a sudden reversal in the late 1660s. In place of imitation and celebration, there is a firm rejection of his styles of thought and writing. The challenge that Carew found in Donne's prosodic inventiveness, his 'masculine expression', was considered by critics of the late seventeenth and early eighteenth centuries to be one not worth taking up. The 'roughness' of his metre condemned him as old-fashioned, and while his conceits and his wit were praised, they were alleged to overpower the poems and the reader. Dryden criticized Donne for putting wit above feeling in his love poems, and his most critical comments were taken up with enthusiasm in the eighteenth century. This line of attack was pursued most violently by Samuel Johnson in his *Life of Cowley* (1781), during the course of a general assault on the 'metaphysical poets'. Putting ingenuity above poetry, wrote Johnson, 'their thoughts were often new, but seldom natural; they are not obvious, but neither are they just; and the reader, far from wondering that he missed them, wonders more frequently by what perverseness of industry they were ever found' (Smith, 1.218). Donne was deemed indecorous, decadent, and an incompetent versifier (Pope had produced 'versions' of *Satires* 2 and 4 in an attempt to regularize them); old editions of his writings became hard to find and new ones were few and very badly produced, riddled with errors. Dissenting voices were rarely heard and the force of their arguments was necessarily reduced by the difficulty of appealing to widely known texts: the feeling against Donne was often based on, at best, a half-knowledge of the works being dismissed.

Writers of the early nineteenth century, by contrast, saw Donne as offering a mirror of some of their own most pressing concerns. Coleridge in particular stands out not only for the range and acuity of his readings of Donne but also in his treatment of the poems as arguments rather than (as Johnson did) a series of discrete and disjointed conceits. As the late eighteenth and early nineteenth centuries witnessed a surge of interest in the complex relationship between language, thought, and feeling, innovative writers like Coleridge and Godwin celebrated Donne for the individuality of his poetic voice, the force of his unusual images, and his exploration of the boundaries of genre. Coleridge made copious marginal notes in Charles Lamb's copy of the poems—notes that, among other things, show just how carefully Coleridge understood Donne's metrical inventiveness; he states that 'in poems where the writer *thinks*, and expects the reader to do so, the sense must be understood in order to ascertain the metre' (Smith, 1.266). But beyond the group of writers and intellectuals who were developing an interest in Donne in the nineteenth century (a group that included Charles Lamb, Thomas De Quincey, James Henry Leigh Hunt, Elizabeth Barrett, Robert Browning, Ralph Waldo Emerson, and Henry David Thoreau), his works were reaching a wider readership once more. The need for new editions was repeatedly asserted and, to some extent, met by Henry Alford's *Works of John Donne* (1839). The first modern edition of the poems, on bibliographical principles, was produced by Grosart in 1872 for the Fuller's Worthies Library—a milestone in the study and reception of Donne, despite its thoroughly unreliable text. Donne still remained something of an acquired taste, however, and it was the work of scholars and critics at the very end of the nineteenth and beginning of the twentieth centuries that saw a wholesale rehabilitation.

Edmund Gosse's magisterial *Life and Letters of John Donne* (1899) established a context for the understanding of his works, and the editorial labours of J. R. Lowell and C. E. Norton (1895) and E. K. Chambers (1896) went some way to providing a widely available text for the poems. It was with H. J. C. Grierson's two-volume edition of the *Poems* (1912) that modern bibliographical techniques were properly applied to Donne. Grierson's edition, along with his anthology *Metaphysical Poetry: Donne to Butler* (1921) also initiated a new interpretive framework for Donne. T. S. Eliot's review of that anthology (1921) celebrated Donne as a precursor of the modernist poet. From the early years of the twentieth century, and with the emergence and consolidation of English literature as a university subject, Donne's place in the canon was assured. Scholars using diverse critical approaches have found Donne an engaging and rewarding subject for commentary. One of the most important aspects of many of these responses to Donne has been their increasing tendency to follow Coleridge in taking Donne's argumentation seriously—a path followed especially brilliantly by the various essays of William Empson. An equally significant aspect of Donne's reputation in the twentieth century has been his popularity as a poet of love. Several of the *Songs and Sonets* in particular have been celebrated as masterpieces of the genre, and as a result feature frequently in popular and scholarly anthologies. Audio recordings of the poems (most notably an intense performance by the actor Richard Burton) also focus on the erotic affect of Donne's individuality of voice.

Both romantics and critics alike have tended to concentrate on a fairly narrow selection of Donne's works. None the less, with the appearance of the critical editions (most recently the multi-volume variorum edition of the poems), the increasing interest in manuscript studies, and the developing links between literary criticism and history, readers have the tools at hand to produce richer and more firmly grounded contributions to the ongoing debate about the meanings of Donne's life and writings. At present, his reputation is secure as one of the most significant writers of the English Renaissance.

DAVID COLCLOUGH

Sources R. C. Bald, *John Donne: a life*, ed. W. Milgate (1970) • I. Walton, *The lives of John Donne, Sir Henry Wotton, Richard Hooker, George Herbert and Robert Sanderson*, ed. G. E. B. Sainsbury (1927) •

G. Keynes, *A bibliography of John Donne, dean of Saint Paul's*, 4th edn (1973) · J. Donne, *Letters to severall persons of honour* (1651) · I. A. Shapiro, 'Donne's birthdate', *N&Q*, 197 (1952), 310–13 · W. Milgate, 'The date of Donne's birth', *N&Q*, 191 (1946), 206–8 · E. Gosse, *The life and letters of John Donne, dean of St Paul's*, 2 vols. (1899) · *The sermons of John Donne*, ed. G. R. Potter and E. M. Simpson, 10 vols. (*c*.1953–1962) · *Essays in divinity*, ed. E. M. Simpson (1952) · J. Donne, *Devotions upon emergent occasions*, ed. A. Raspa (1987) · *The letters of John Chamberlain*, ed. N. E. McClure, 2 vols. (1939) · D. Flynn, *John Donne and the ancient Catholic nobility* (1995) · J. Maule, 'Donne and the words of the law', *John Donne's professional lives*, ed. D. Colclough [forthcoming] · P. Beal, '"It shall not therefore kill itself; that is, not bury itself": Donne's *Biathanatos* and its text', *In praise of scribes* (1998), 31–57 · M. L. Brown, *Donne and the politics of conscience in early modern England* (1995) · P. Sellin, *So doth, so is religion: John Donne and diplomatic contexts in the reformed Netherlands, 1619–1620* (1988) · A. J. Smith, ed., *John Donne: the critical heritage*, 2 vols. (1975); (1996) · J. R. Roberts, ed., *John Donne: an annotated bibliography of modern criticism, 1912–1967* (1973) · J. R. Roberts, ed., *John Donne: an annotated bibliography of modern criticism, 1968–1978* (1982) · W. Empson, *Essays on Renaissance literature*, vol. 1: *Donne and the new philosophy* (1993)

Archives Folger, letters and papers · Middle Temple, London, MSS

Likenesses oils, *c*.1595, Newbattle Abbey · I. Oliver, miniature, 1616, Royal Collection [*see illus.*] · oils, 1620, St Paul's Cathedral, London, deanery; version, V&A · N. Stone, marble effigy, 1631, St Paul's Cathedral, London · W. Marshall, line engraving, pubd 1649, BM, NPG · M. Droeshout, line engraving (after N. Stone), BM; repro. in J. Donne, *Deaths duell* (1632), frontispiece · W. Hollar, etching (after N. Stone), BM; repro. in Dugdale, *St Paul's* (1658) · probably C. Janssen, oils (after portrait), St Paul's Cathedral · P. Lombart, engraving (after portrait), St Paul's Cathedral; repro. in Donne, *Letters to severall persons of honour* (1651) · P. Lombart, engraving (after portrait, 1620), BM, NPG; repro. in J. Donne, *Letters to severall persons of honour* (1654) · W. Marshall, engraving (after painting, *c*.1591), repro. in J. Donne, *Poems by J. D. With elegies on the author's death* (1633), frontispiece · W. Marshall, engraving (after N. Stone), repro. in J. Donne, *Devotions*, 4th edn (1634) · W. Marshall, portrait (after N. Stone), repro. in J. Donne, *Devotions*, 5th edn (1638) · M. Merian junior, line engraving, BM, NPG; repro. in J. Donne, *Sermons* (1640) · oils (after I. Oliver), NPG

Wealth at death £3000–£4000: will, repr. in Bald, *John Donne*

Donne, John, the younger (1604–1662/3), author and literary executor, was born about May 1604, the son of John *Donne (1572–1631), poet and dean of St Paul's, and his wife, Ann More. He was educated at Westminster School, and proceeded to Christ Church, Oxford, in 1622, where he took the degrees of BA and MA. It is usually assumed that he was the John Donne who married Mary Staples at Camberwell on 27 March 1627.

Apart from being the son and literary executor of John Donne, Donne is remembered principally for an incident that took place on 31 October 1633 at St Aldates, Oxford, when he struck with his riding whip an eight-year-old boy who had startled his horse. The boy died on 22 November and Donne was put on trial for manslaughter under Laud, who was vice-chancellor at the time, but was acquitted, as two surgeons and a physician attested that they could not find any appearance of injury on the boy. Donne left for Padua after this and took the degree of doctor of laws there, and on his return was incorporated at Oxford with the same degree in 1638. He was ordained priest about this time and was presented to the living of High Roding, Essex, that year, and also concurrently to Ufford in Northamptonshire and Fulbeck in Lincolnshire in May and June

respectively the following year. He resided at none of them. He was chaplain to Basil, earl of Denbigh, and during the rising of 1644 was under suspicion by the parliamentary party. In 1662, only months before his death, he published a small volume entitled *Donnes Satyr*, which revealed his fondness for witticisms and for playing the fool.

As early as 1637 Donne had petitioned for control of his father's estate and complained to the archbishop of Canterbury about Marriot's editions of Donne's works. He finally acquired Donne's letters, which had been left to Henry King in his will, from Izaak Walton, who was consulting them in the process of writing Donne's biography. That Walton had not consented to the acquisition is suggested by a letter of King to Walton (dated 'Novem. 17 1664' and printed as a preface to the 1670 and 1675 editions of Walton's *Life of John Donne*), in which he comments:

> How these were got out of my hands, you, who were the Messenger for them, and how lost both to me and your self, is not now seasonable to complain: but, since they did miscarry, I am glad that the general Demonstration of his Worth was so fairly preserved, and represented to the World by your Pen in the History of his Life.

Donne the younger, it seems, had acquired his father's letters despite King's desire to hold on to them. Recent scholarship has traced the course of this dispute and has suggested that, despite the acrimony, Donne and Izaak Walton worked together to some extent to assemble the volumes *Letters to Severall Persons of Honour: Written by John Donne Sometime Deane of St Pauls London* (1651) and *A Collection of Letters, Made by Sr Tobie Mathews Kt.* (1660). However, Donne's editorial methods in the first of these volumes are far from transparent or honest. As Bennett and Shapiro showed, apart from printing the letters out of chronological order and without their dates, Donne also gave many false addresses and substituted for the names or initials of his father's ordinary friends, including Sir Henry Goodyer, others suggestive of grander associations.

In 1644 Donne the younger was also involved in the publication of his father's treatise on suicide, *Biathanatos*. Caught between his father's injunction that the manuscript should be spared 'both the Presse and the Fire', Donne the younger eventually opted for publication, rather than the deliberate annihilation of the fire or the accidental damage of time and chance, remarking that the work was in equal danger of being 'utterly lost' and 'utterly found'.

Although Anthony Wood's comment that he was an 'atheistical buffoon, a banterer, and a person of over-free thoughts' has often been used to characterize the younger Donne, it seems fairer, given the pressures of his father's fame and the complicated situations of his literary executorship, to remember him by Wood's more balanced observation, that 'there is no doubt but that he was a man of sense, and parts; which, had they been applied to a good use, he might have proved beneficial in his generation' (Wood, *Ath. Oxon.: Fasti*, 1.503). In his will (dated 21 July 1657) Donne went some way towards setting his life in order: he returned to Izaak Walton's son some of his father's books and papers; he ordered that he wished to be buried plainly—'I have not lived by juggling … therefore I desire to dye and be buried without any'; and, somewhat ironically, considering his own actions, warned his executor against interpreting his Spartan wishes too freely. Donne the younger died in the winter of 1662–3 at his London house in Covent Garden and was buried on 3 February 1663 at the west end of St Paul's Church there.

JOANNE WOOLWAY GRENFELL

Sources Wood, *Ath. Oxon.: Fasti* (1815) • *The works of the most reverend father in God, William Laud*, ed. J. Bliss and W. Scott, 7 vols. (1847–60) • *DNB* • R. E. Bennett, 'Donne's *Letters to severall persons of honour'*, *Publications of the Modern Language Association of America*, 56 (1941), 120–40 • I. Shapiro, 'The text of Donne's *Letters to severall persons'*, *Review of English Studies*, 7 (1931), 289–301 • R. Krueger, 'The publication of John Donne's sermons', *Review of English Studies*, new ser., 15 (1964), 151–60 • J. Bevan, 'Izaak Walton and his publisher', *The Library*, 5th ser., 32 (1977), 344–59 • I. Walton, *The lives of Dr John Donne, Sir Henry Wotton, Mr Richard Hooker, and Mr George Herbert*, [new edn] (1675) • E. Gosse, *The life and letters of John Donne, dean of St Paul's*, 2 vols. (1899) • I. Hamilton, *Keepers of the flame: literary estates and the rise of biography* (1992) • I. Walton and C. Cotton, *The complete angler … with original notes and memoirs by Sir H. Nicolas* (1836)

Donne, William Bodham (1807–1882), essayist and examiner of plays, was born on 29 July 1807 at Mattishall, near East Dereham, Norfolk, the only child of Edward Charles Donne (1777–1819), physician, and his cousin Anne Vertue Donne (1781–1859). His grandfather William Donne was an eminent Norwich surgeon. The poet John Donne may have been his direct ancestor, and the poet William Cowper's mother was great-aunt to both of his parents. Donne was educated at the grammar school, Hingham, before going in 1819 to Edward VI Grammar School at Bury St Edmunds, where he became friends with schoolmates Edward FitzGerald (later translator of *The Rubáiyát of Omar Khayyam*) and John Mitchell Kemble, who became an Old English scholar. His lifelong friendship with the Kemble family stimulated his interest in the drama. After receiving tuition from the Revd Williams of Thornham, near Bury, in 1826 Donne entered Gonville and Caius College, Cambridge, but his objections to the Thirty-Nine Articles prevented him from taking his degree. While at Cambridge, Donne became a member of the exclusive Apostles club, which also included Kemble, Alfred Tennyson, and Arthur Hallam.

After leaving Cambridge, Donne retired to Mattishall, where, on 15 November 1830, he married his cousin Catharine (1798–1843), daughter of Charles Hewitt (1771–1847), and also a niece of Cowper's cousin and friend John Johnson. The couple had five children before Catharine's death: Charles Edward, who married J. M. Kemble's daughter Mildred; William Mowbry; Frederick Clench; Katherine Blanche; and Valentia. In 1846 Donne moved to Bury St Edmunds to educate his sons and there became friends with headmaster William Donaldson. Other friends included H. Crabb Robinson, Bernard Barton, Lamb's friend Manning, and George Borrow. A Liberal, Donne supported the repeal of the corn laws, but his scholarly nature prevented him from becoming a party

man. In 1852 he declined the editorship of the *Edinburgh Review* because he believed that 'his habits of life were too retired to keep him in the current of public opinion' (Johnson, 189). He did, however, accept the librarianship of the London Library that same year.

In 1857 Donne resigned that post to become the examiner of plays in the lord chamberlain's office. From 1849 to 1856 he had served as acting examiner for J. M. Kemble, who was consistently abroad. As both unofficial and official examiner, Donne exercised considerable influence over Victorian drama, as reflected in periodic caricatures in the illustrated papers, in which the artists emphasized his prominent nose, bushy eyebrows, and distinctive dundrearies. Best-known for his refusal to license *Camille* in 1853 and his efforts to continue the suppression of *Jack Sheppard* and *Oliver Twist* in 1859, Donne censored content that he regarded as 'indecent or profane, or politically objectionable' ('Select committee … theatres'). Genuinely interested in the state of British drama and sometimes more liberal than the general public in matters of taste, Donne nevertheless bowed to middle-class views of appropriate dramatic content and thus effectively limited the ways in which playwrights could explore serious topics. He served as examiner until 1874, when he was succeeded by E. F. S. Pigott.

Donne contributed many essays to the *British and Foreign*, *Edinburgh*, *Quarterly*, *Saturday*, and *Westminster* reviews, as well as to *Fraser's Magazine*, among others. He was complimented by contemporaries on his taste and delicate humour. Donne published *Old Roads and New Roads*, which drew on his knowledge of classical literature and modern history, in 1852, when he also edited *Magic and Witchcraft*. *Essays upon the Drama*, selected from Donne's periodical writings, was published in 1858 and reissued in 1863. In 1867 Donne edited *The Correspondence of King George the Third with Lord North* at Queen Victoria's request. Among his classical writings were the *Euripides* (1872) and *Tacitus* (1873) volumes of W. Lucas Collins's Ancient Classics for English Readers.

Donne died at his home in London at 25 Weymouth Street, Portland Place, on 20 June 1882 and was buried in Shooters Hill cemetery, Blackheath.

RUTH BURRIDGE LINDEMANN

Sources C. B. Johnson, ed., *William Bodham Donne and his friends* (1905) • *Saturday Review*, 54 (1882), 12–14 • *The Times* (22 June 1882), 9 • J. F. Stottlar, 'A Victorian stage censor: the theory and practice of William Bodham Donne', *Victorian Studies*, 13 (1969–70), 253–82 • W. E. Colburn, 'William Bodham Donne: examiner of plays, 1849–1874', MA thesis, University of Illinois, 1949 • 'Select committee to inquire into … theatres', *Parl. papers* (1866), 16.75–94, no. 373 • J. R. Stephens, *The censorship of English drama, 1824–1901* (1980) • N. C. Hannay, ed., *A Fitzgerald friendship: being hitherto unpublished letters from Edward Fitzgerald to William Bodham Donne* (1932)

Archives BL • priv. coll. • PRO • University of Illinois | Harrowby Manuscript Trust, Sandon Hall, Staffordshire, letters to earl of Harrowby and R. H. E. H. Somerset • Trinity Cam., letters to J. W. Blakesley • UCL, letters to Society for the Diffusion of Useful Knowledge

Likenesses Maull & Polyblank, photograph, *c.*1860, repro. in Johnson, ed., *William Bodham Donne* • T. Greenish, photograph, repro. in Hannay, ed., *Fitzgerald friendship* • caricature, repro. in

Johnson, ed., *William Bodham Donne* • photograph, repro. in Johnson, ed., *William Bodham Donne*
Wealth at death £16,390 8s. 11d.: resworn probate, June 1883, *CGPLA Eng. & Wales* (1882)

Donnegan, James (*fl. c.*1820–1841), lexicographer, was a doctor of medicine of a foreign university, who practised in London from about 1820 to 1835. His *New Greek and English lexicon, principally on the plan of the Greek and German lexicon of Schneider* (1826) was commended by Bishop Edward Maltby as 'an important acquisition' (Maltby, 1). Subsequent editions (1831, 1837, 1842) contain many improvements and additions; an American edition, 'revised and enlarged by R. B. Patton', was published at Boston (1836), and another at Philadelphia (1843). In his preface to the fourth edition (1842), written in 1841, Donnegan revealed that since 1837 he had been in poor health, and expressed his thanks to Sir Robert Holt Leigh, a classical scholar, of Hindley Hall, near Wigan, Lancashire, with whom he was staying.   GORDON GOODWIN, *rev.* JOHN D. HAIGH

Sources J. Donnegan, preface, *A new Greek and English lexicon*, 2nd edn (1831); 3rd edn (1837); 4th edn (1842) • E. Maltby, preface, *A new and complete Greek gradus* (1830), 1

Donnelly, Desmond Louis (1920–1974), politician and writer, was born on 16 October 1920 at Gohaingaon, Sibsagar, Assam, India, the second child of Louis James Donnelly, a tea planter of Irish extraction, and (Florence) Aimée Tucker (d. 1968), of an English Indian Civil Service family. Taken to England by his mother in 1928, he lost contact with his father, and was educated at Brightlands School, Newnham-on-Severn, Gloucestershire, and Bembridge School, Isle of Wight. In his teens, influenced by the ideas of William Morris, he joined the Labour League of Youth.

After leaving school in 1938 Donnelly worked as a London office boy. A keen sportsman, he was secretary of the London Grasshoppers rugby club, and in 1940 founded the British empire cricket eleven, raising money for the duke of Gloucester's Red Cross and the St John Fund. He joined the Royal Air Force in 1939, serving with the rank of flying officer (Bomber Command), and, in Italy, as acting flight lieutenant (desert air force). From 1945 to 1946 he lectured at the Royal Air Force Staff College, before becoming assistant editor (later editor) of *Town and Country Planning*. Between 1948 and 1950 Donnelly was director of the Town and Country Planning Association. In 1947 he married Rosemary Taggart, daughter of (William) John Taggart MD of Belfast; they had a daughter and a twin son and daughter.

In the 1945 general election Donnelly unsuccessfully contested Evesham as a commonwealth candidate. In September 1945 he joined the Labour Party, and was Labour candidate in the 1946 County Down by-election, coming second to the Ulster Unionist. In 1950 he defeated the Liberal Gwilym Lloyd-George in Pembrokeshire by 129 votes, appealing to radical sentiment and capitalizing on Liberal disquiet with Lloyd-George's close association with the

Desmond Louis Donnelly (1920–1974), by Walter Bird, 1959

Conservative Party. Subsequently he built a comfortable majority, utilizing his great vigour, organizational skills, and a publicity-seeking style. He coupled his duties as an MP with acting as adviser to the engineering firm David Brown, to Philips Industries, and to Hill Samuel.

In parliament Donnelly became a Bevanite after the resignations of April 1951, although also a friend and confidant of Hugh Dalton. Following visits to eastern Europe, however, he supported German rearmament at the 1954 Labour Party conference in a speech which marked his rejection of the left. He devoted increasing attention to international issues, striking up friendships with Dean Acheson, Barry Goldwater, Willy Brandt, Lee Kuan Yew, and Ian Smith. His anti-communism deepened following further travels in eastern Europe and China. In 1959 he wrote *The March Wind: Explorations behind the Iron Curtain*, and in 1965 *Struggle for the World: the Cold War from its Origins in 1917*. From 1959 to 1963 he was political columnist for the *Daily Herald* and from 1967 to 1970 chief political correspondent for the *News of the World*. He had a racy, gripping, if predictable, style, and his content was a mixture of shrewd observation and superficial appraisal.

A Gaitskellite from the mid-1950s, Donnelly had a deep dislike of Harold Wilson, whose election as Labour leader in 1963 left him with little chance of political advancement. Increasingly he acted as a back-bench maverick, joining Woodrow Wyatt in challenging plans to nationalize the steel industry in 1965. Deeply disillusioned with what he felt was Labour's abandonment of its commitments east of Suez after the defence review of 1967, he resigned the parliamentary whip on 18 January 1968 and on 27 March 1968 was expelled from the Labour Party. His 1968 polemic *Gadarene '68: the Crimes, Follies and Misfortunes of the Wilson Government* and his novel *The Nearing Storm* of the same year were hymns of hate against Wilson personally.

In June 1969 Donnelly founded 'Our Party', quickly retitled the United Democratic Party, which advocated the abolition of the welfare state, and the reintroduction of national service, capital punishment, and flogging. At the 1970 general election Donnelly (in Pembrokeshire) and four other United Democratic Party candidates were defeated. In 1971 he joined the Conservative Party, but failed to gain the nomination either for the Hove by-election in 1973 or for Melton, Leicestershire, for the general election in February 1974, the first in which he had failed to contest a constituency since he came of age. On 4 April 1974, clinically depressed at his political isolation and personal financial problems, he committed suicide in a hotel at Heathrow airport. He was cremated on 9 April.

Donnelly had a colourful, garrulous personality. He enjoyed walking, poetry, and an eventful private life, and he had an encyclopaedic knowledge of cricket. In party-political terms he was a rogue elephant, with great, if temporary, enthusiasms, and a passionate strain in oratory. Donnelly's enjoyment of good living, coupled with his extensive travels, meant that he was never completely free of financial worries, and his abilities, although impressive, never quite matched his political and personal ambitions.   CHRIS WILLIAMS

Sources NL Wales, Desmond Donnelly papers · *The Times* (5 April 1974) · *The Times* (13 April 1974) · *The Times* (20 April 1974) · *The Times* (28 June 1974) · *Western Mail* [Cardiff] (5 April 1974) · *Western Mail* [Cardiff] (20 April 1974) · W. Wyatt, *Confessions of an optimist* (1985) · *The political diary of Hugh Dalton, 1918–1940, 1945–1960*, ed. B. Pimlott (1986) · *The diary of Hugh Gaitskell, 1945–1956*, ed. P. M. Williams (1983) · *Sunday Telegraph* (8 June 1969) · DNB · CGPLA Eng. & Wales (1975)
Archives NL Wales, political corresp. and papers | Bodl. RH, corresp. with Sir R. R. Welensky · HLRO, corresp. with Lord Beaverbrook, BBKC/119 · U. Birm. L., corresp. with Lord Avon, ref. AP23/26 · Welwyn Garden City Central Library, corresp. with Sir Frederick Osborn, B50 | FILM BFI NFTVA, party political footage
Likenesses photograph, 1956, Hult. Arch. · W. Bird, photograph, 1959, NPG [see illus.] · cartoon, repro. in *Daily Mirror* (28 March 1968) · cartoon, repro. in *Daily Express* (29 March 1968) · cartoon, repro. in *Daily Telegraph* (9 April 1969) · cartoon, repro. in *Daily Mirror* (10 April 1969) · photographic negatives, NL Wales, Desmond Donnelly MSS, file C15 · portrait, repro. in *Penthouse*, 3/7 (28 June 1968) · portrait, repro. in *Life* (1 Nov 1954)
Wealth at death £1633: administration with will, 9 July 1975, CGPLA Eng. & Wales

Donnelly, Sir John Fretcheville Dykes (1834–1902), army officer and promoter of scientific education, born in the Bay of Bombay on 2 July 1834, was the only child of Lieutenant-Colonel Thomas Donnelly (1802–1881), deputy adjutant-general of the Bombay army, and from 1851 staff captain and afterwards staff officer at the East India Company's military college at Addiscombe until it closed in 1861. His mother was Jane Christiana, second daughter of Joseph Ballantine Dykes of Dovenby Hall, Cumberland. Educated at Highgate School (1843–8), he had a year's private tuition before entering the Royal Military Academy at Woolwich at the head of the list in August 1849. He passed out first, and was commissioned second lieutenant in the Royal Engineers on 23 June 1853, and promoted first lieutenant on 17 February 1854.

Donnelly went out to the Crimea in June, joining his corps on its march to Balaklava on 23 September, and the next month was detailed for duty with the left attack on Sevastopol. He was present at the battle of Inkerman on 5 November, and subsequently worked energetically in the trenches before Sevastopol. Through the severe winter of 1854–5 he was much in the trenches. On the day after the abortive assault on the Redan (18 June), when he was with the second column, he obtained a substantial lodgement in the Russian rifle pits at the Little Mamelon. He was mentioned in dispatches soon after the fall of Sevastopol in September 1855. In November 1855 he was appointed aide-de-camp to Colonel E. T. Lloyd, the commanding royal engineer in the Crimea, and returned home in June 1856. He received the Légion d'honneur (fifth class); he had been recommended for the Victoria Cross, but without result.

Donnelly joined the London military district in 1856, and commanded a detachment preparing for building purposes the ground purchased at South Kensington out of the surplus funds of the Great Exhibition of 1851. It was intended to erect there a permanent museum and centre of science and art. Sir Henry Cole, the director of the scheme, secured on 1 April 1858 Donnelly's services in reorganizing at South Kensington the Department of Science and Art, which was controlled by the privy council's committee of education. On 1 October 1859 he was appointed inspector for science under the department. He had been promoted second captain on 1 April 1859, but did not return to regimental duty; the rest of his career was identified with South Kensington, and in 1872 he was placed on the reserve list. His promotion continued, as he was still liable for emergency service, and he became lieutenant-colonel on 1 October 1877 and brevet colonel on 1 October 1881, retiring with the honorary rank of major-general on 31 December 1887.

The success of the scheme for national instruction in science and art was largely due to Donnelly, although some of his methods were controversial. He arranged (by minute of 1859) that grants should be made to certificated teachers on the results of the examinations of their pupils. He obtained recognition for drawing and manual training as class subjects, and having induced the Society of Arts, which he joined in 1860, to form a class in wood-carving, he procured from City companies and other sources funds to carry it on as the School of Art Wood-Carving.

In 1874 Donnelly's title at South Kensington became director of science, and his duties included the supervision not only of the science schools and classes throughout the country but of such scientific institutions as the Government School of Mines, the Museum of Practical Geology, the Royal College of Chemistry, the Edinburgh Museum of Science and Art, and the Museum of Irish Industry, which developed into the Royal College of Science for Ireland. In 1868, as a member of a commission appointed to consider the question, he had drafted a report adverse to the establishment of a separate Department of Science and Art for Ireland. In 1881 he was appointed in addition assistant secretary of the Department of Science and Art, and in 1884 secretary and permanent head of the department.

Joining the council of the Society of Arts in 1870, Donnelly was mainly responsible in 1871 for the society's scheme of technical examinations, out of which by his advice the City Guilds Institute for technical education was developed. As chairman of the council of the Society of Arts in 1894 and 1895, he led the society to organize the International Congress on Technical Education in 1897.

For many years the museums of science and art at Kensington had been in unsatisfactory temporary accommodation, and Donnelly was untiring in his efforts to secure parliamentary grants for permanent buildings. In 1896 the House of Commons appointed a select committee, on whose report in 1899 a sum of £800,000 was voted to complete the museums. Donnelly's administration was criticized by the committee in its *Report and Evidence ... on the Museums of the Science and Art Department* (1899). Whatever the quality of the educational policy, the number of science students had grown immensely under Donnelly's direction. Responding to the committee's report, he retired on 2 July 1899. A minute of the privy council dated the following day stated its full confidence in Colonel Donnelly and his staff, and Sir John Gorst, vice-president of the committee of council on education, publicly defended Donnelly.

Donnelly was made CB in 1886 and KCB (civil) in 1893. A competent artist, from 1888 to 1901 he exhibited at the Royal Academy and the New Gallery.

Donnelly was twice married. His first marriage, at Bridekirk, Cumberland, on 5 January 1871, was to his first cousin Adeliza (d. 1873), second daughter of Fretcheville Lawson Ballantine Dykes of Dovenby Hall, Cumberland; they had two daughters. On 17 December 1881 he married at Neuchâtel, Switzerland (the marriage would have been illegal in England), his deceased wife's elder sister, Mary Frances Dykes. They had two sons, Thomas and Gordon Harvey (both became Royal Garrison Artillery officers), and a daughter. Donnelly died on 5 April 1902 at his residence, 59 Onslow Gardens, London, survived by his wife. He was buried at Brompton cemetery.

R. H. Vetch, rev. James Falkner

Sources *The Times* (7 April 1902) · *The Times* (11 April 1902) · *Army List* · *Hart's Army List* · Royal Engineers Institution, Chatham, Royal Engineers Records · T. W. J. Connolly, *The history of the corps of royal sappers and miners*, 2 vols. (1855) · *LondG* (18 Dec 1855) · *The Standard* (12 April 1902) · 'Select committee on the museums of the science and art department', *Parl. papers* (1897), vol. 12, nos. 223, 341; (1898),
11.1, no. 175; 11.9, no. 327 · W. Porter, *History of the corps of royal engineers*, 2 vols. (1889)

Archives Oxf. U. Mus. NH, Hope Library · Oxf. U. Mus. NH, entomological papers | CUL, corresp. with Sir George Stokes · ICL, letters to Thomas Huxley

Likenesses H. T. Wells, oils, exh. RA 1901; formerly in possession of Lady Donnelly, 1912 · E. J. Poynter, charcoal, c.1902; formerly in possession of Lady Donnelly, 1912

Wealth at death £6870 2s. 11d.: administration with will, 29 May 1902, CGPLA Eng. & Wales

Donnelly, Sir Ross (c.1761–1840), naval officer, was the son of Dr Donnelly. After serving under Vice-Admiral Marriot Arbuthnot on the coast of North America, and at the capture of Charlestown, South Carolina, in May 1780, he was promoted on the Newfoundland station as lieutenant of the sloop *Morning Star* on 27 September 1781. After the peace (treaty of Versailles, September 1783) he served as mate in the East India Company's service, but returned to the navy in 1793, and was appointed first lieutenant of the *Montagu* (74 guns); he commanded the ship in Lord Howe's battle of 1 June 1794 in the north Atlantic after the death of her captain, James Montagu. As Howe expressed approval of his conduct and Sir Alexander Hood (Lord Bridport) wrote him a complimentary letter, Donnelly and his friends expected some more marked acknowledgement of his service than the promotion to commander's rank, which, together with the other first lieutenants of the ships engaged, he received on 6 July 1794. He had hoped (and applied) for the gold medal given to some of the flag officers and captains, but was told that it was given only to those who were post captains at the date of the battle. This rule was afterwards modified, and, after both the Nile and Trafalgar, first lieutenants who succeeded to the command by the death of their captains received the gold medal. Donnelly was, however, promoted captain on 24 June 1795, and appointed to the frigate *Pegasus* (28 guns), in the North Sea with Admiral Duncan. From her he was moved to the *Maidstone* off the French coast, in which, in 1801, he brought home a valuable convoy of 120 merchant ships from Oporto—a service for which the merchants of Oporto presented him with a handsome piece of plate. Towards the end of the year he was moved to the *Narcissus* (32 guns), which for the next three years he commanded in the Mediterranean, attached to the fleet under Nelson. Nelson had a high opinion of him, placing his own relative, W. B. Suckling, and several other young men in whom he was interested under Donnelly's immediate care. He wrote to one father, 'Your son cannot be anywhere so well placed as with Donnelly' (*GM*). In 1805, still in the *Narcissus*, he accompanied Sir Home Riggs Popham to the Cape of Good Hope, and afterwards to Buenos Aires, whence he returned to England with dispatches, in which his individual services were highly commended both by Popham and the general in command of the troops. He was then appointed to the *Ardent* (64 guns), and went back to the River Plate in command of a convoy of transports. At the capture of Montevideo he commanded the naval brigade, and rendered important service both in transporting the heavy guns and in erecting batteries. In 1808 Donnelly was appointed to the *Invincible* (74 guns), in which he joined the squadron off Cadiz, and, later on, the main fleet off Toulon under Lord Collingwood.

In 1810 cataracts in his eyes forced Donnelly to resign his command. Two years later he had so far recovered as to apply for employment again, and he was appointed to the new *Devonshire* (74 guns), which he fitted out. The conclusion of peace, however, prevented her going to sea, and Donnelly had no further service, though he was promoted rear-admiral on 4 June 1814, vice-admiral on 27 May 1825, and admiral on 28 June 1838; he was made a KCB on 28 February 1837. He died on 30 September 1840. He was married and had children; his eldest daughter, Anne Jane (*d.* 1855), married, on 18 April 1816, George John, twentieth Baron Audley. J. K. LAUGHTON, *rev.* ANDREW LAMBERT

Sources J. D. Grainger, ed., *The Royal Navy in the River Plate, 1806–1807*, Navy RS, 135 (1996) · H. Popham, *A damned cunning fellow: the eventful life of Rear-Admiral Sir Home Popham* (1991) · *GM*, 2nd ser., 15 (1841), 95 · *Navy List*
Archives BL, corresp. and papers, Add. MSS 45364–45365 · NMM, letter-book | BL, letters to Lord Nelson and logbook, Add. MSS 34919–34925, 34982

Donnet, Sir James John Louis (1816–1905), inspector-general of hospitals and fleets, born at Gibraltar, was the son of Henry Donnet, a Royal Navy surgeon. After studying at the University of Paris, where he graduated B ès L, and at Anderson College, Glasgow, he became LSA of London in 1838, LRCS of Edinburgh in 1840, and MD at St Andrews in 1857. He entered the navy as assistant surgeon in the *Benbow* in 1840. He was at once appointed to the *Vesuvius* and sent to the Mediterranean, where, on the coast of Syria, he had his first experience of war; and after the capture of Acre he was placed in charge of the wounded in a temporary hospital established on shore. In 1844 he was medical officer and secretary of an embassy to the emperor of Morocco under Sir John Drummond-Hay, who was appointed consul-general in 1845.

Donnet was promoted surgeon, and in 1849 was in the *Calypso* in the West Indies during a virulent outbreak of yellow fever. Clements Markham, who met him at this time, described him as 'handsome, with a slender aquiline nose and clear cut features, being slightly built. ... His manner was gentle and quiet, he was well-read with considerable conversational powers and the best of messmates' (Markham, 'Story of my service'). In 1850–51 he was surgeon of the *Assistance* in the Arctic with Captain Sir Erasmus Ommanney, and helped to break the tedium of the long winter by editing 'an excellent periodical, entitled the *Aurora Borealis*, to which the men as well as the officers contributed' (Markham, *Life*, 113). He married in 1852 Eliza (*d.* 1903), daughter of James Meyer; they had no children. In 1854 he was surgeon of the *President*, flagship in the Pacific, and in her was present at the disastrous attacks on Petropavlovsky in Kamchatka, Siberia, on 29 August and 7 September (Clowes, 6.429–32).

As staff surgeon at the Port Royal Hospital in Jamaica in 1866–7 Donnet prepared a detailed study of yellow fever at a time when an epidemic of the disease was raging. The study was published in the *Health Report* of 1867. Donnet thus laid the foundation of modern medical practice in dealing with this disease. Later he published *Notes on Yellow Fever*. In May 1867 he was promoted deputy inspector-general.

In 1870 he was appointed honorary surgeon to the queen, and in 1873–4 he was placed in charge of the medical wards of Haslar naval hospital, Gosport, which was crowded with cases of smallpox, enteric fever, and dysentery after the Anglo-Asante War. On 14 April 1875 he was promoted inspector-general. After this he was employed on various committees and commissions, including one in 1876 to select a site for a college for naval cadets and one in 1877 to inquire into the causes of the outbreak of scurvy in Sir George Nares's Arctic expedition (1875–6). He was awarded a good-service pension in 1878, and was made KCB at Queen Victoria's 1897 jubilee. During his last years he resided at Bognor, and he died at his home, 3 Sidlaw Terrace, Clarence Road, Bognor, on 11 January 1905.

J. K. LAUGHTON, *rev.* ANDREW LAMBERT

Sources J. J. Keevil, J. L. S. Coulter, and C. Lloyd, *Medicine and the navy, 1200–1900*, 4: *1815–1900* (1963) · *Navy List* · *The Times* (12 Jan 1905) · W. L. Clowes, *The Royal Navy: a history from the earliest times to the present*, 7 vols. (1897–1903), vol. 7 · *WWW* · C. Markham, *Life of Admiral Sir Leopold McClintock* (1909) · *CGPLA Eng. & Wales* (1905) · C. Markham, 'Story of my service [in the Royal Navy] from the point of view of a midshipman', RGS, CRM/40
Wealth at death £968 14s. 3d.: probate, 11 March 1905, *CGPLA Eng. & Wales*

Donoghue, Stephen (1884–1945), jockey and racehorse trainer, was born on 8 November 1884 at Aikin Street, Warrington, Lancashire, the eldest son in the family of three sons and two daughters of Patrick Donoghue (1862–1936), an iron puddler at the steel-wire works of Pearson and Knowles, and his wife, Mary Mitchell (*d.* 1936). He attended St Mary's Roman Catholic School, Buttermarket Street, Warrington, from the age of six until he was twelve, when he started work half-time in his father's works. In 1899, aged fourteen, he walked from Warrington to Chester races to secure employment in the Kingsclere stables of the famous trainer John Porter. Within four months, however, homesickness took him back to a job in a Warrington wireworks. Then, fearing he had killed a bully in a fight, Donoghue fled with his younger brother to the Middleham stables of Dobson Peacock, a leading northern trainer. However, the two had given assumed names and left in 1901 with the arrival of census officials, this time travelling to Newmarket, where Steve (as he was always called) joined the stables of Alfred Sadler junior.

In 1903 Donoghue went to France where he gained experience of race riding and won for the first time, on Hanoi at Hyères in April 1905. Two years later he went to ride for Philip Behan's stable in Ireland, and became the leading Irish jockey. He married Bridget Behan, the daughter of his employer, in 1908. In 1910 he was retained by H. S. 'Atty' Persse at Stockbridge, Hampshire, to replace the American Danny Maher, who was suffering from tuberculosis; by 1914 Donoghue had won the first of ten consecutive champion jockey titles. Rejected as unfit for military service, he rode two wartime Derby winners (at

Stephen Donoghue (1884–1945), by Bassano, 1920

Newmarket), in 1915 and 1917. He spent a season in South Africa, after his return from where, in November 1917, his marriage was dissolved following his wife's adultery while he was there; there were two sons of the marriage, Stevie and Patrick (who had a brief riding career), and a daughter, Kathleen. During his visit to South Africa, Donoghue himself began a long affair with Lady Torrington, the actress Eleanor Souray (c.1882–1931). Together they trained her horses and enjoyed a high social life. She divorced her husband, the ninth Viscount Torrington, in 1921.

Donoghue developed a reputation for having other riders 'jocked off' mounts in major races and was no respecter of his own contracts if he fancied the chances of another owner's horses. Although this enabled him to win four out of five Derbys between 1921 and 1925 (he won six Derbys in all), ultimately it cost him the chance of retainers later in his career as no owner or trainer would trust him to honour his obligations. After 1925 he rode no more classic winners until he piloted Exhibitionist to victory in the 1937 Oaks and One Thousand Guineas. At the end of that season he retired to become a trainer at Blewbury, though only with modest success. He also did some broadcasting and appeared in several films. Donoghue was a fearless jockey with great tactical skill, soft hands, and perfect balance, though never as strong in a finish after an accident in the 1925 grand prix de Paris in which he dislocated and fractured his left shoulder. Two horses are indelibly associated with him: at the start of his career he rode 'the spotted wonder', the unbeaten Tetrarch, and

later he piloted Brown Jack to six consecutive wins in the Queen Alexandra stakes (1929–34).

During the 1928 racing season Donoghue rode 108 consecutive losers. Worse was to follow. By then his relationship with Lady Torrington had become unhappy, not least because of financial problems due to their improvident living. In September a bankruptcy petition showed that he had debts estimated at £15,000 and assets of less than £600. His generosity to friends accounted for some of the problem but primarily it was due to illegal (for a jockey) and unsuccessful betting. Eventually he was rescued by a retainer from Sir Victor Sassoon and a decision by his creditors, early in 1929, to accept 5s. in the pound. At the start of the 1929 season, on 17 March, Donoghue secretly married Ethel Finn (b. c.1896), an American dancer. On 9 December 1931, following bankruptcy proceedings, Lady Torrington took her own life by gassing herself; a suicide verdict was returned. Donoghue's family disapproved of his 1929 marriage, which ended in separation in 1934. In April 1940 Ethel sued for arrears of maintenance payments but Donoghue showed that he had helped her on numerous occasions and her demand for £946 was reduced to £312. She died in February 1942 from an overdose of sleeping tablets; a verdict of misadventure was recorded.

Donoghue himself died suddenly of a heart attack at 24 Porchester Gate, Paddington, on 23 March 1945, during a visit to the capital. He died intestate which meant that the mementoes of his career had to be sold. His son Pat bought the Manchester cup won by Steve in 1922 and the portrait of his father in the royal colours by Sir James Lavery. Donoghue was buried on 29 March 1945 in Warrington cemetery, where a memorial stone was erected. In 1957 a pair of gates dedicated to his memory was placed at the entrance to the Epsom grandstand.

WRAY VAMPLEW

Sources M. Seth-Smith, *Steve: the life and times of Steve Donoghue* (1974) · S. Donoghue, *Just my story* (1923) · S. Donoghue, *Donoghue up! The autobiography of Steve Donoghue* (1938) · Q. Gilbey, *Champions all* (1971) · R. Mortimer, R. Onslow, and P. Willett, *Biographical encyclopedia of British flat racing* (1978) · DNB · CGPLA Eng. & Wales (1946)
Archives FILM BFI NFTVA, documentary footage · BFI NFTVA, news footage · BFI NFTVA, performance footage · BFI NFTVA, propaganda film footage (Red Cross) · BFI NFTVA, sports footage
Likenesses photographs, 1900–40, Hult. Arch. · Bassano, photograph, 1920, NPG [*see illus.*] · A. Munnings, oils, 1921, Stewards of the Jockey Club, Newmarket, Suffolk · J. Lavery, oils, 1923, Royal Scot. Acad. · L. Palmer, oils, Cottesbrooke Hall, Northamptonshire; copy, Jockey Club Rooms, Newmarket, Suffolk · A. Ritchie, cigarette card, NPG · photographs, repro. in Seth-Smith, *Steve*
Wealth at death £19,514 14s.: administration, 5 March 1946, CGPLA Eng. & Wales

Donoughmore. For this title name *see* Hutchinson, Richard Hely-, first earl of Donoughmore (1756–1825); Hutchinson, John Hely-, second earl of Donoughmore (1757–1832); Hutchinson, John Hely-, third earl of Donoughmore (1787–1851); Hutchinson, Richard Walter John Hely-, sixth earl of Donoughmore (1875–1948).

Donovan, Edward (1768-1837), natural historian and artist, is of obscure origin and little is known of his early life and education. His interest in natural history started with the collecting of shells and preservation of insects, probably before 1788. He was a prolific author and skilled artist who etched and engraved the plates for all his works. He became a fellow of the Linnean Society.

Donovan's main interest was entomology and his published works included sixteen volumes of *British Insects* (1792–1813) and three volumes on *The Insects of China, India and New Holland*, the last being dedicated to Sir Joseph Banks, and acknowledging use of his collections and library. Donovan's approach was to show species that had not been illustrated before, and many previously undescribed. Publications on other animals and plants were well received, including ten volumes of *British Birds* (1799). Donovan's other major works included *British Fishes* (1802–8), and the *Botanical Review, or, The Beauties of Flora* (1789–96). His books were not of even quality and it is generally considered that he was at his best illustrating insects. In 1805 he published two volumes, *Descriptive Excursions through South Wales*, describing his travels through Monmouthshire. Donovan's plates were all engraved, hand coloured, and accompanied by a description and synonyms for each species depicted. All were published in parts; his proposal was to issue one number every two months at 7s. 6d. for each part. His early botanical plates are signed E. O. Donovan; this led to his being quoted as O'Donovan. After about 1790 he no longer used E. O. and the confusion ceased. Some contemporaries regarded the colouring of Donovan's plates as gaudy but later nineteenth- and twentieth-century opinion was, in general, much more favourable.

Donovan was clearly endowed with a considerable fortune, spending freely to acquire specimens, including many insects from Dru Drury's collection. He bought many collections and paid high prices for some specimens (it is known he paid 7s. 6d. for a black-toed gull and 10 guineas for a great auk at the sale of the Leveren Museum). His whole natural history collection cost him several thousands of pounds and with it he established the London Museum and Institute of Natural History in Catherine Street, the Strand. The museum was opened to the public in 1807, with the general consensus that it was 'a much more valuable assortment of particular specimens than the richest Cabinets of Europe'. An entrance fee of 1s. was charged, and 6d. for the catalogue. By 1817, however, Donovan's finances began to decline. His labours of some thirty years at a cost of some £15,000 had to come to an end. A prospectus for sale of his collection was issued with the hope that funds would be raised to keep it intact, probably in the British Museum; this hope was not fulfilled and it was broken up and auctioned.

By 1833 Donovan found himself in serious financial straits. He insisted that his publishers owed him large sums of money, but in reality he had not been a good businessman. He wanted to take his case to the court of chancery, but had not the wherewithal to do so. In that year he issued a plea 'To the patrons of science, literature and fine

arts' asking for help to submit his case to the court. He described how from his first production he had verbally agreed with his publishers that they should have half the proceeds of that work and the same amount on any later publications. This would have given him a good income, since a full set of his works sold for £100; however, by withholding accounts for six years, under the existing statutes of limitation the booksellers avoided payment and Donovan was financially ruined. He was owed between £60,000 and £70,000. He had truthfully stated that there was no documentary evidence for his case, and this assured that costly legal action would not succeed.

Once a man of great substance, when Donovan died on 1 February 1837 at his home, John Street, Kennington Road, London, he left a large family in destitution.

PAMELA GILBERT

Sources *Magazine of Zoology and Botany*, 2 (1838), 292 · W. H. Mullens and H. K. Swann, *A bibliography of British ornithology from the earliest times to the end of 1912* (1917) · C. E. Jackson, *Bird etchings: the illustrators and their books, 1655–1855* (1985) · W. H. Mullens, 'Some museums of old London', *Museums Journal*, 15 (1915), 123–9, 162–72 · W. Swainson, *Taxidermy: bibliography and biography* (1840) · G. D. R. Bridson, V. C. Phillips, and A. P. Harvey, *Natural history manuscript resources in the British Isles* (1980) · E. Donovan, *To the patrons of science, literature, and fine arts: E. Donovan … solicits permission to submit … a memorial of his case with certain booksellers* (1833) · J. Parkinson, 'Letter to Mr Tilloch', *Philosophical Magazine*, 28 (1807), 346–7

Archives Oxf. U. Mus. NH, entomological corresp., drawings, notes, and papers

Donovan, Terence Daniel (1936–1996), photographer, was born at 24 Antill Road, Mile End, London, on 14 September 1936, the only child of Daniel Donovan, lorry driver, and his wife, (Lilian) Constance Violet, *née* Wright, cook. He had a fractured education—'I spent most of the war', he once said, 'in the cab of a large lorry travelling round England with my father' (Vines). Nevertheless he found time to learn the craft of photography (which throughout his life it remained, never an art). He enrolled to study lithography, as an eleven-year-old apprentice, at the London School of Photo-Engraving in Fleet Street (later relocated and renamed the London College of Printing), while also attending Fairfield Road secondary modern school. He left at fifteen to become a photographer's assistant at Gee and Watson, a blockmakers for the printing industry, and from there moved to work first with the photographer Hugh White and then with Michael Williams, a photographer for *Fleet Illustrated*. His stay there—of at least three to four years—was broken by two years of national service in the Royal Army Ordnance Corps (1955–7), where he supplemented his pay by producing picture postcards. In 1957 he joined the studio of the leading fashion photographer John French, as assistant to the photographers Adrian Flowers and John Adrian (also known as Adriaan). After a year he left with Janet Campbell Cohen (b. 1933), a stylist for French, to open a studio in Yeoman's Row, Knightsbridge. It was a success from the start, his first commission pedestrian but well paid: a photograph of a Viota sponge cake, for 27 guineas (taken on 27 January 1959). He and Janet Cohen married on 2 June 1960, and had one son, Daniel.

Unlike many young photographers Donovan was not forced to specialize in a particular discipline, thanks to a versatility that attracted a range of clients, including the leading advertising agencies and fashion and lifestyle magazines of the time. Prominent among the latter were *Vogue*, *Harper's Bazaar*, and *Man About Town* (later renamed *About Town* and then just *Town*). Donovan's expertise was sought for fashion, still life, and portraiture, both in a studio setting and on location. Shooting mostly with black and white film in the early years, his singular, *verité* style set him apart from his contemporaries and was best illustrated by a series of men's fashion pictures taken on the streets of London for *Man About Town*, published in 1961, and, for the same magazine a year later, a series of portraits of the young actress Julie Christie in her London flat. Both sets were taken with an informality untypical of the time.

Donovan brought the life of his times into the studio, too, getting his models to walk and to pose like the girls he knew from the East End. In the process he helped to give magazines a new visual language of gesture and stance—a 'working-class chic'. Again for *Man About Town* he contributed two remarkable photo-essays, the first on an artists' collective in Holland Park and the second on one day in the life of a West End stripper. He chose not to pursue straight documentary work: 'I tend to reduce my reportage to graphics', he explained later; 'I don't really want to report on life ... I'm quite happy to see a girl scratching her nose in a coffee bar and translate that via a model' (Vines). In 1963 he took his first photograph for *Vogue*—a portrait of the conductor George Solti in Covent Garden—and began an association with the magazine that ended only with his death. His last published photograph was for *Vogue* and appeared posthumously in February 1997, a grainy portrait of the London-based design team Clements Ribeiro, which in style and execution was similar to the up-to-the-minute portraits of the London fashion scene that he had created decades earlier.

Donovan's first marriage came to an end in July 1967, and on 30 April 1970 he married Diana St Felix Dare (*b.* 1942), film publicist and, later, corporate affairs consultant; they had a son, Terence, and a daughter, Daisy. In the 1970s, while continuing to shoot fashion for *Vogue*, Donovan explored the more lucrative field of advertising photography, began a series of experimental 'impressionistic' fashion photographs for *Nova* magazine, and also turned his hand to the moving image. He financed and directed a feature film, *Yellow Dog* (1973), influenced by Japanese cinema and martial arts. The film was not a popular success but he was asked subsequently to direct commercials for television and, later still, to direct for the American CBS Network films of the National Theatre stage plays *Early Days*, *On the Razzle*, and *The Importance of Being Earnest*.

By the 1980s much of Donovan's time was spent on television commercials and advertising photography, although he frequently shot fashion for *Vogue*, *Elle*, and *Marie Claire*, and the fashion collections (often twice a year) for the Italian edition of *Harper's Bazaar*. His voracious instinct for the highly colourful, for an exaggerated glamour, and for baroque fantasies in French châteaux made him a favourite with fashion editors of the 1980s and early 1990s. 'You see, fashion photography is an act of theatre', he maintained, 'and you really have to love it' ('Yellow dog'). He brought the sensibility of the glossy magazine to the fashion pages of British newspapers, much as his early employer John French had done years before at the *Daily Express*. He was also a pioneer of the pop promotional video, most notably that for Robert Palmer's song *Addicted to Love* (1986). For this he was nominated one of *Vanity Fair* magazine's 'People of the decade' in 1989.

Donovan's interests were wide-ranging, compensating perhaps for the years of disrupted schooling. He was a devotee of Zen Buddhism and a practitioner of judo. At one point he owned a chain of dress shops, a firm of building contractors, and an ironmonger's shop in Chelsea, and part-owned a restaurant with the actor Terence Stamp. He also held a successful show of his paintings at the Albemarle Gallery, London, in 1992. Like his great friend David Bailey he was a by-word for English commercial photography: 'The Falstaff of Fashion Photography', according to Francis Wyndham, 'without malice, trusted by his rivals' (Wyndham, notes). He was a photographer to the royal family, too, taking the official engagement photographs of the duke and duchess of York and photographing the princess of Wales on three occasions (8 October 1986, 24 June 1987, and 26 February 1990). Prints from these three sittings were deposited in the collection of the National Portrait Gallery, London. In 1996 he was appointed visiting professor of Central St Martin's College of Art and Design.

Donovan hanged himself on 22 November 1996 at a studio he was building in Hanwell, London, following a severe reaction to medication; he was buried at Gunnersbury cemetery on 29 November. He was survived by his wife, Diana, and his three children. He had just completed a twenty-one page portfolio for *GQ* magazine on rock'n'roll heroes in celebration of 'swinging' London's second incarnation—the 'cool Britannia' of the mid- to late 1990s. This marked a return to editorial photography that was keenly anticipated and which, published in the month of his death, became his valediction. He published three books of his photographs, *Women Through the Eyes of Smudger TD* (*c.*1964), *Glances* (1983), and *Fighting Judo* (with Katsuhiko Kashiwazaki, 1985). A retrospective exhibition of his London photographs was held at the Museum of London in 1999, and a large-format anthology of his photographs, *Terence Donovan*, was published in 2000.

ROBIN MUIR

Sources A. Vines, *British Journal of Photography* (28 Jan 1966) · L. Armstrong, *Vogue* (March 1997) · *The Independent* (25 Nov 1996) · *The Guardian* (25 Nov 1996) · *Daily Telegraph* (25 Nov 1996) · *The Times* (25 Nov 1996) · F. Wyndham, 'The modelmakers', *Sunday Times Magazine* (10 May 1964) · T. Donovan, unpublished article for *The Tatler*, *c.*July 1994, priv. coll. · A. Carter, 'Donovan's dog', *Nova* (Oct 1973) · J. Collins, *British photography, 1955–1965: master craftsmen in print* (1983) [catalogue] · 'Yellow dog', *Image*, 3/3 (1973) · J. Thrift, 'Terence Donovan', *European Creative Portfolio* (1992) · V. Williams,

Look at me: fashion and photography in Britain, 1960–present (1998) [catalogue] • M. Harrison, *Appearances* (1991) • F. Wyndham, notes, in *David Bailey's box of pin-ups* (1965) • D. Donovan, *Terence Donovan* (2000) • R. Muir, *Terence Donovan: London photographs* (1999) [catalogue] • private information (2004) [Janet Goodwin; Daniel Donovan; Diana Donovan] • personal knowledge (2004) • b. cert. • d. cert.

Archives Christies | *Vogue* office, London | SOUND Museum of London

Likenesses D. Bailey, photograph, 1961, repro. in *Vogue* (Sept 1961) • D. Bailey, photograph, c.1968, repro. in D. Bailey and P. Evans, *Goodbye baby and amen* (1969) • A. Newman, photograph, 1980–89, repro. in *The Great British* (1979) • T. D. Donovan, self-portrait, 1996, repro. in *Daily Telegraph* • A. Newman, group portrait, photograph, repro. in *The Guardian* • T. O'Leary, photograph, repro. in *The Independent* (25 Nov 1996) • photograph, repro. in Donovan, *Terence Donovan*

Wealth at death £1,658,704: probate, 3 Jan 1997, *CGPLA Eng. & Wales*

Donovan, Terence Norbert, Baron Donovan (1898–1971), judge, was born on 13 June 1898 in Walthamstow, Essex, the second son in the family of five children of Timothy Cornelius Donovan (1853–1906), Liberal political agent and private tutor, and his wife, Laura (d. 1913), daughter of James McSheedy, of Cardiff. After Brockley grammar school, he enlisted at the age of eighteen, being commissioned in the Bedfordshire regiment. He was at the front in France and Belgium in 1917 and 1918, and was later a rear gunner in the Royal Air Force, as a lieutenant. On demobilization, he won first place in an open examination for higher posts in the civil service and entered the revenue department in 1920. In his spare time he studied for the bar and was called by the Middle Temple in 1924. On 13 April 1925 he married Marjorie Florence, daughter of Leah and Charles Murray, a chemist of Winchester; they had two sons and a daughter. Lacking the financial resources and connections to support the early years of practice at the bar, he waited until 1932 before resigning his civil service appointment to begin, in chambers at 3 Temple Gardens, what soon developed into a substantial practice in revenue cases. He took silk in 1945.

It was the First World War and the unemployment which followed it that sparked Donovan's active involvement in the Labour Party, the Fabian Society, and the League of Nations Union. In the 1945 general election he was the successful Labour Party candidate for the East Leicester constituency, and in February 1950 he was returned for North East Leicester. He was a good constituency MP, particularly concerned with slum clearance in Leicester, but apart from his work as chairman of the Parliamentary Labour Party's legal and judicial group, he made relatively little impression as a back-bencher.

Donovan's real ambitions were in the legal world. His reticence about expressing those ambitions led to some surprise when he resigned his seat in July 1950 to accept appointment as a judge in the King's Bench Division. The foundation had been laid in his work, from 1946, as a JP for Hampshire, chairman of the Winchester county bench, and deputy chairman of the appeals committee of Hampshire quarter sessions. He was knighted on his appointment to the High Court where he remained until 1960

when he was promoted to the Court of Appeal and admitted to the privy council. In 1963 he was appointed a lord of appeal-in-ordinary. Surprisingly for one whose practice had been almost exclusively at the revenue bar, he was a conscientious and effective trial judge, being selected by the lord chief justice, Lord Parker of Waddington, to sit on the highly publicized and arduous trial in 1958 of several members of the Brighton police force, including the chief constable, on charges of conspiracy to obstruct the course of justice. As an appeal judge he made no significant contribution to the development of the law, but his judicial colleagues valued his expertise in tax cases, his prodigious memory, and his ability, manifest in his judgments, to express himself accurately and tersely. He was a supporter of a new activist tendency in judicial law making, led by Lord Reid. In Donovan's words, 'the common law is moulded by the judges, and it is still their province to adapt it from time to time, so as to make it serve the interests of those it binds' (*Myers* v. *Director of Public Prosecutions* [1964] 2 All England Reports, 902B). He usually had a good feeling for the policy of legislation. This was evident in his judgment in the Court of Appeal in the seminal trade union case of *Rookes* v. *Barnard* (1962) when he took the view that if a threat to strike in breach of contract constituted unlawful means for the purposes of the tort of conspiracy, a point that no one had thought of before that case, the immunities conferred on strikes by the Trade Disputes Act of 1906 would be 'largely illusory' and this would encourage lightning strikes without warning. Although the House of Lords subsequently disagreed with his view, it was restored by the amending Trade Disputes Act of 1965.

Despite his lack of experience in industrial relations, the sympathy displayed in that case towards the traditional values of collective bargaining, as well as his political background, made Donovan an acceptable choice as chairman of the important royal commission on trade unions and employers' associations (1965–8). He had previously shown his abilities as a law reformer on the Denning committee on divorce procedure (1946), on the Lewis committee on court martial procedure (1946–8), and as chairman of the criminal appeals committee (1964). He drove the royal commission on a very light rein, leaving organization and the programme of research to others. He presided graciously and wittily when evidence was heard, but did not question witnesses closely. At the internal meetings he was still less forceful, allowing his colleagues to debate and develop the themes of the report. He drafted the introduction and chapter 14 ('Changes in the law'), but left the rest to a drafting committee without the slightest intervention. When the work was done he appended his own addendum and other supplementary notes and reservations. This was a style different in most respects from those of other contemporary judicial chairmen of industrial relations inquiries such as Lord Devlin and Lord Pearson.

Donovan's views were, however, decisive on one central issue. Six commissioners proposed that collective agreements should be made legally enforceable, while the remaining six argued that this would be inconsistent with the main argument of the report. Donovan knew that there was strong support for enforcement in the Labour cabinet. Yet after careful thought, for the reasons set out in his addendum, he came to the view that there was no case for legislative enforcement of collective agreements, contrary to the will of the parties. He continued to voice these views in the subsequent debates on the Labour government's *In Place of Strife* (1969), and the Conservative government's Industrial Relations Bill (1971). He joined with a majority of the commissioners in proposing that immunity from actions in tort for inducing breaches of contract should be confined to registered trade unions and this was reflected in the Industrial Relations Act of 1971. He saw the differences between Labour and Conservatives as ones of means not ends, but was critical of the 1971 bill for not doing enough to win worker co-operation. He opposed the permanent intrusion of the High Court in this field. He regarded the essential difference between the report and the bill as being the priority the report gave to causes not symptoms, in particular the reform of procedures and the formalization of plant bargaining, but he recognized that the bill reflected some of the commission's thinking, such as the creation of the commission for industrial relations and the extension of the jurisdiction of industrial tribunals, the right for employees not to be unfairly dismissed, and the procedures to deal with disputes over trade union recognition.

Donovan was created a life peer in 1964. In 1970 he became treasurer of the Middle Temple, a strenuous task for a man who had for some years been in ill health. He died of heart failure in London on 12 December 1971.

BOB HEPPLE

Sources *The Times* (13 Dec 1971) · private information (1986) · *WWW* · b. cert. · m. cert. · d. cert. · Burke, *Peerage* (1967)
Likenesses portrait, Middle Temple, London
Wealth at death £42,685: probate, 17 Jan 1972, *CGPLA Eng. & Wales*

Doo, George Thomas (1800–1886), engraver, was born near Christ Church, Southwark, London, on 6 January 1800. Nothing is known of his parents or early life. He went in 1825 to visit the engraving schools of Paris and on his return to London set up a life and antique academy in newly built premises on the site of the Savoy Palace, the Strand. A pupil of Charles Heath, his early book engravings, mostly on steel, appeared in *Description of the Collection of Ancient Marbles in the British Museum* (1812–61), and *The Combat*, after William Etty, was published in Finden's *Royal Gallery of British Art* (1838–49). He then worked for the print publisher F. G. Moon, having taken Thomas Leeming Grundy (1808–1841) as a pupil. For Moon, Doo engraved several plates after G. S. Newton and J. Partridge, as well as *Chelsea Pensioners Reading the Account of the Battle of Waterloo* (1838) and *John Knox Preaching to the Lords of Congregation in 1559* (1838), after David Wilkie. In January 1836 he was appointed historical engraver-in-ordinary to William IV, and he occasionally submitted works to the sovereign for inspection and presentation if approved; Queen Victoria renewed the appointment in 1842. On 11 February 1836, at

George Thomas Doo (1800–1886), by Rolfe's Portrait Studio

St Pancras Old Church, he married Caroline Mary Hamilton (1812–1882), the daughter of Samuel and Caroline Mary Hamilton of Weybridge, Surrey, and the granddaughter of the engraver James Heath. Their only son, Hubert Sydney George Barrow Doo, was born in March 1847 and baptized on 1 April at Great Stanmore, Middlesex, the family home for many years.

In 1844 Doo began to engrave *The Convalescent from Waterloo*, after William Mulready, for the Art Union of London, but by January 1845 illness had supervened and it was not published until 1848, when it met with a mixed reception. He was elected a fellow of the Royal Society for distinguished services to line engraving on 5 June 1851, having been proposed by twelve gentlemen, including Robert Peel, John Burnet, and Charles Lock Eastlake. About 1853 he turned to portrait painting in oils, and was at some time a pupil of the Parisian portrait painter Charles Alexander Suisse (*fl.* 1833–1847). His first published portrait engraving was of the *Duke of York*, after Sir Thomas Lawrence (1824), and he issued one of the naturalist Baron Georges Cuvier, after H. W. Pickersgill, in 1841. In the 1850s he painted a number of portraits of naturalists and doctors (which he also engraved), many of which were exhibited at the Royal Academy. From 1826 Doo associated with those who protested against the Royal Academy's treatment of engravers, but in 1856 he was elected associate engraver; the following year he was elected Royal Academician by the chairman's casting vote, but he retired in 1866. He became president of the Artists' Annuity Fund, which he joined in 1825, and for the 1862 Paris Universal Exhibition he was chairman of Class 40, etching and engraving. For eight years he had worked on his plate of *The Raising of Lazarus*, after S. del Piombo, published by Colnaghi in 1865, and contemporaries regarded it as his finest engraving. In 1867 his engraving of *St Augustin and St Monica*, after A. Scheffer, so pleased the queen that she gave him a small gold coronation medal. The engraving was exhibited at the Paris Universal Exhibition of 1867. In July the following year Doo was granted a civil-list pension of £100 per annum. Probably his last engraving, accepted by the queen in February 1884, was of Sir Joshua Reynolds's self-portrait in doctoral robes.

Doo lectured on painting at South Kensington and elsewhere, and was an honorary or corresponding member of fine art institutions in Amsterdam, Parma, Pennsylvania, and St Petersburg. A contemporary who had known him in his younger days saw him at the age of sixty-eight as a 'very handsome old gentleman' with white hair and a courteous manner (J. Sartain, *The Reminiscences of a Very Old Man*, 1899, 241), and he was said to have 'gained a host of appreciative friends' as an artist and a gentleman (*Art Journal*, 29, 1867, 61). He died on 13 November 1886 at his home, Hill House, Sutton, Surrey.   B. HUNNISETT

Sources W. Sandby, *The history of the Royal Academy of Arts*, 2 (1862), 324–5 · *ILN* (27 Nov 1886), 573, 579 · *Art Journal*, 27 (1865), 244 · *Art Journal*, 29 (1867), 61 · *Art Journal*, new ser., 7 (1887), 63 · *Art Union*, 3 (1841), 26 · *Art Union*, 7 (1845), 11 · *Art Union*, 10 (1848), 132 · general assembly minutes, 3 Nov 1856; 1857, RA · council minutes, 27 Nov 1866, 1 Dec 1866, RA · Royal Society, election committee minutes, June 1851 · private information (2004) [Royal Arch.] · J. Pye, *Patronage of British art: an historical sketch* (1845), 192–5 · H. Guise, *Great Victorian engravings: a collector's guide* (1980), 2–3, 132, 145, 167–8 · Graves, *Artists* · IGI · d. cert. · CGPLA Eng. & Wales (1886) · B. Weinreb and C. Hibbert, eds., *The London encyclopaedia* (1983), 796
Likenesses Rolfe's Portrait Studio, photograph, NPG [*see illus.*] · wood-engraving, repro. in *ILN*, 579
Wealth at death £346 13s. 6d.: administration, 8 Dec 1886, CGPLA Eng. & Wales

Doodson, Arthur Thomas (1890–1968), mathematician and oceanographer, was born at Boothstown, near Worsley, in Lancashire, on 31 March 1890, the second son of Thomas Doodson, the manager of a cotton mill in Boothstown, who later moved to Rochdale and then to Shaw, near Oldham, and his wife, Eleanor Pendlebury, of Radcliffe, Lancashire. Doodson went to the village school and evening classes and studied as a pupil teacher before attending Rochdale secondary school and, in 1908, the University of Liverpool. He gave up the idea of teaching when he became seriously deaf and this may have led him to give up chemistry, though he was also encouraged to specialize in mathematics by Professor F. S. Carey. He gained a first-class BSc in chemistry and mathematics in

1911 and a first-class honours degree in mathematics in 1912, winning a prize for geometry.

Deafness made it difficult for Doodson to get a job and he accepted a post as meter tester for Messrs Ferranti, but two years later obtained a more congenial post at the testing and standardizing department of the corporation of Manchester. In 1916 he was appointed to a post at University College, London, under Karl Pearson to do statistics but this was soon changed to ballistics for the War Office. In 1914 Doodson had been received into one of the churches of the community known as the Churches of God in the Fellowship of the Son of God, a breakaway sect from the Plymouth Brethren, and from then on his life was dominated by religion, to the exclusion of much social intercourse. It was therefore sad and paradoxical that he was obliged to work for some years on duties to which he had a conscientious objection. Nevertheless he did some impressive computations, producing tables of Riccati–Bessel functions and of sines and cosines of radians. He was awarded the MSc degree of Liverpool University in 1914 and their DSc in 1919.

By then Doodson had acquired an aptitude and a liking for computational problems and he started what was to be the most important collaboration of his life, with Professor J. Proudman, who had persuaded shipowners to endow a Tidal Institute at Liverpool. Proudman was its honorary director and arranged for Doodson to be its secretary.

In 1919 Doodson married Margaret, daughter of J. W. Galloway, a tramways engineer, of Halifax, Yorkshire. They had a daughter, who died in 1936, and a son; Margaret died shortly after the son's birth in 1931. In 1933 Doodson married Elsie May, daughter of W. A. Carey. Doodson built up the Tidal Institute until it was recognized worldwide as an authoritative source of tidal theory, observation, and analysis. He was associate director of the institute from 1929 to 1945. Doodson's own work was mainly on the computational aspects, where his skill complemented Proudman's expertise in tidal dynamics. His engineering ability also allowed him to design and install complicated tide predicting machines in many countries. He was active in studying meteorological effects on tides and, after the Thames floods of 1928, made intensive studies of coastal flooding, adopting the word 'surge', and inventing many of the techniques which were used for many years in forecasting dangerously high high waters.

Doodson also had administrative charge of a growing institute and was skilled at the financial aspects. He was gifted, skilled, and kind, and had a quiet sense of humour. As soon as hearing aids became available he made full use of them. His probity and accounting skills were put to good purpose by the International Union of Geodesy and Geophysics when in 1954 Doodson was made president of the finance committee. He was also the first director of the permanent service for mean sea level of the International Association of Physical Oceanography.

For many years Doodson was an honorary lecturer of the University of Liverpool. In 1930 he was awarded the Thomas Gray memorial prize by the Royal Society of Arts for the benefit to navigation of his prediction of tidal currents. In 1933 he was elected fellow of the Royal Society and in 1953 an honorary fellow of the Royal Society of Edinburgh. He was appointed CBE in 1956. Doodson died at the General Hospital, Birkenhead, Cheshire, on 10 January 1968. He was survived by his second wife.

H. CHARNOCK, *rev.*

Sources J. Proudman, *Memoirs FRS*, 14 (1968), 189–205 · personal knowledge (1981) · *The Times* (11 Jan 1968), 10d · *CGPLA Eng. & Wales* (1969) · d. cert. · D. E. Cartwright, *Tides, a scientific history* (1999) **Likenesses** W. Stoneman, photograph, 1946, RS · J. Bacon & Sons, photograph, 1960, RS **Wealth at death** £18,367: probate, 7 Jan 1969, *CGPLA Eng. & Wales*

Doody, Samuel (1656–1706), botanist, was born in Staffordshire on 28 May 1656, the eldest child of the second marriage of John Doody, a local apothecary who afterwards moved to London. He assisted his father at his shop in the Strand and succeeded him in business about 1696. His interest in botany is shown in an account of an excursion he made to Gravesend in 1686, when many rare plants were found, and in his commonplace book which notes the dates of the apothecaries' herborizing expeditions for 1687 and 1688, and contains many lists of plants. Doody seems to have been a modest man, and, according to Adam Buddle (MS Sloane 2972), very slow of speech and unable to express himself adequately, but full of good argument and sound reasoning when able to exert himself. His particular interest lay in the study of mosses, fungi, and other non-flowering plants, in which little-studied field he was the acknowledged expert of his time. A possible draft for his intended publication on mosses is in the Sloane manuscripts (BL, MS Sloane 2315). His dilatoriness in passing on his observations may account for his failure to publish, although dried plant specimens sent to colleagues are found in many volumes in the Sloane herbarium. Doody was elected fellow of the Royal Society in 1695. His only publication, a letter on a case of dropsy in the breast, was published in the society's *Philosophical Transactions* (19, 1697, 390).

Among Doody's close botanical acquaintances were Ray, Plukenet, Petiver—with whom he was particularly friendly—and Sloane, and he was a member of the Temple Coffee House Botanical Club. Ray acknowledged Doody's help in 1688 in the second volume of *Historia plantarum*, and the appendix to the second edition of his *Synopsis* (1696) contains a long list of plant records due to Doody. Plukenet and other authors of the period also acknowledged his assistance. The new plants he saw on his herborizing expeditions around London, often in the company of Buddle and Petiver, are noted in his own copy of the 1696 edition of *Synopsis*, now in the British Library; some of these notes were later used by Dillenius in preparing the third edition. In 1692, having reported to the Society of Apothecaries the unsatisfactory management of their physic garden at Chelsea, Doody offered to maintain the garden for a year, free of charge, a decision applauded by Ray as likely to 'much promote botanics' (*Further Correspondence*, 175). The following year Doody was appointed to

take control for three years at a salary of £100 per annum. He continued to be involved in the running of the garden until his death.

Doody suffered much from gout, and was notorious for an unspecified failing, apparently intemperance. He never married, and died, after some weeks' illness, at the end of November 1706. He was buried at Hampstead, Middlesex, on 3 December, his funeral sermon being preached by his old friend, Adam Buddle. He is commemorated in the genus of ferns *Doodia*.

B. D. JACKSON, *rev.* RUTH STUNGO

Sources Desmond, *Botanists*, rev. edn, 212 · H. Trimen and W. T. Thiselton Dyer, *Flora of Middlesex* (1869), 376–8 · H. Field, *Memoirs of the botanic garden at Chelsea belonging to the Society of Apothecaries of London*, rev. R. H. Semple (1878), 17–22 · J. Britten and J. E. Dandy, eds., *The Sloane herbarium* (1958), 126–7 · R. Pulteney, *Historical and biographical sketches of the progress of botany in England*, 2 (1790), 108–9 · A. Buddle, BL, MS Sloane 2972 · C. Wall, *A history of the Worshipful Society of Apothecaries of London*, ed. H. C. Cameron and E. A. Underwood (1963), 167 · P. I. Edwards, 'The Botanical Society (of London), 1721–1726', *Proceedings of the Botanical Society of the British Isles*, 5 (1963), 117 · C. E. Raven, *John Ray, naturalist: his life and works*, 2nd edn (1950), 232, 245, 249, 433 · C. E. Salmon, *Flora of Surrey*, ed. W. H. Pearsall (1931), 5 · E. J. L. Scott, *Index to the Sloane manuscripts in the British Museum* (1904), 147 · *The correspondence of John Ray*, ed. E. Lankester, Ray Society, 14 (1848), 187 · *Further correspondence of John Ray*, ed. R. W. T. Gunther, Ray Society, 114 (1928), 175, 247, 250, 261 **Archives** BL, Sloane MSS, letters, notebooks, and papers · NHM, department of botany, Sloane herbarium · RS, Sherard MSS

Doolin, William (1887–1962), surgeon and author, was born on 19 June 1887 at 20 Ely Place, Dublin, the eldest child of Walter Doolin (d. 1902), an architect, and his wife, Marion, *née* Creedon. His brothers Daniel and Walter were to have careers in dentistry and architecture respectively.

Doolin was educated at the Catholic University School, Leeson Street, Dublin, at St Mary's College, Dundalk, where in 1901 he won a £20 exhibition, and at Clongowes Wood College; here he had his first experience of surgery when a surgeon named McArdle set his leg after it had been broken in a rugby game. An excellent swimmer and athlete, Doolin was later a scratch golfer and a devoted tennis player, much in demand as an umpire in his maturity.

Having matriculated at the Royal University of Ireland in 1904 Doolin entered the Catholic University medical school in Cecilia Street, Dublin. Attending his first clinic in a ward at St Vincent's Hospital the future surgeon was shown wounds sustained by a pathetic urchin who had impaled himself on an iron railing, and he promptly fainted. By the time he had completed his final examinations (taking first-class honours) in 1910, the Royal University of Ireland had been replaced by the National University of Ireland, of which he was a graduate.

Having registered on 22 June 1910, Doolin worked as a house surgeon at St Vincent's. His year on the road then took him to Edinburgh, London, Paris, and Berlin. He spent his holidays perfecting his French and German, and visiting shrines of medical history in Padua, Bologna, Montpellier, and Salerno. He became FRCSI in 1912 and in the following year embarked on practice at 9 Upper Fitzwilliam Street, Dublin; he eked out the lean period by demonstrating anatomy at Cecilia Street and administering dental anaesthetics for his brother.

Doolin was then offered a post as resident medical officer to the Anglo-German Hospital in Rosario, Argentina, and had agreed to take up duties by 31 May 1914 when, for one reason or other—possibly a dawning romance—he changed his mind. He married Clare Kennedy (d. 1937), whose parents had a grocery store in Inchicore near Dublin, in 1916. They had five children (two sons and three daughters), who, as they grew into their noisy phase, were urged to behave decorously in the afternoons, the time set aside for consultations. They knew when to be quiet. 'Hush!' they warned one another. 'There's a rat in the trap [a patient in their father's consulting room]' (private information).

In due course there had been advantageous developments in Doolin's career: he became junior consultant surgeon to St Vincent's Hospital in 1917, visiting surgeon in 1928, and visiting surgeon to the Children's Hospital, Temple Street, in 1932. He joined the council of the Royal College of Surgeons in Ireland and was its president from 1938 to 1940. Following the custom of the times he practised as a general surgeon, and took a special interest in the treatment of harelip and cleft palate.

Meanwhile T. P. C. Kirkpatrick, secretary of the Royal Academy of Medicine in Ireland, had chosen Doolin to succeed Arnold K. Henry, in 1925, as editor of the *Irish Journal of Medical Science*, to which, in 1952, would be added the editorship of the *Journal of the Irish Medical Association*. Doolin's literary flair, combined with his willingness to devote endless care to the contributions of others, gave him a special place in the affections of his colleagues. He had minimal secretarial assistance at a time when referees were not available to lighten editors' burdens and shoulder the blame for rejections.

Doolin contributed numerous articles to his own and to other journals. His books included *Wayfarers in Medicine* (1947), *Dublin's Medical Schools* (1953), and *Dublin's Surgeon-Anatomists* (1951). His book reviews were characterized by an urbanity which delighted the authors; Harvey Cushing, John Fulton, Lord Cohen of Birkenhead, and others wrote to thank him for praising their work. He did not hesitate to challenge George Bernard Shaw for his criticism of Douglas Guthrie's *A History of Medicine* (1945), concluding, 'The lowly medical reviewer cannot resist the temptation to paraphrase Chesterton: "Chuck it, P'shaw!"' (Lyons, 'Letters to an editor', 328). Doolin's wife, Clare, died in 1937, leaving him desolate. His marriage in 1942, to Maureen Clinton, theatre sister at Temple Street Hospital, with whom he had two sons, brought fresh happiness.

Doolin spoke for the profession in the editorial columns of the Irish Medical Association's journal. 'Salus populi suprema lex', he reminded an obdurate minister for health in January 1953:

Even now at the eleventh hour, we put forward the plea: let him again call into being … a Council or Commission composed of men of good will and of all shades of informed opinion, who, lifting all questions of public health above party level, will dispassionately examine all plans, taking what is best from each, thus ensuring the greatest good of the greatest number. (*Journal of the Irish Medical Association*, 1953, 32, 27)

He aimed to avoid personal animus but when the minister referred to the association's executives as 'bucket-shop share-pushers', deserving gaol sentences, he protested against this 'irresponsible and impudent levity' (Lyons, 'Letters to an editor', 325).

A handsome man, Doolin's great mane of hair, silvered with age, compounded his air of distinction. An excellent speaker after dinner, and better still on formal occasions, he delivered the Vicary lecture in London and the Lichfield lecture in Oxford. His awards included an honorary FRCS, membership of the French Académie de Chirurgie, and DLitt *honoris causa* from Dublin University and the National University of Ireland. In his seventies he suffered from coronary heart disease. His death, on 14 April 1962 at St Vincent's private nursing home, Leeson Street, Dublin, came after several weeks of congestive cardiac failure. He was buried in Glasnevin cemetery. The Doolin lecture, inaugurated by the Irish Medical Association in 1964, is given annually in the Royal College of Surgeons in Ireland.   J. B. LYONS

Sources *Irish Journal of Medical Science*, 436 (1962), 145–6 · T. C. J. O'Connell, 'A tribute to William Doolin', *Journal of the Irish Medical Association*, 54 (1964), 70–72 · J. B. Lyons, *Brief lives of Irish doctors* (1978) · J. B. Lyons, 'Letters to an editor', *Journal of the Irish Medical Association*, 73 (1980), 323–30 · J. B. Lyons, 'The portrait of an editor: William Doolin', *Irish Journal of Medical Science*, 156 (1987), 343–6 · J. B. Lyons, *A check-list of William Doolin's publications* (Dublin, [n.d., 1980?]) · private information (2004) [E. Nolan]
Archives Royal College of Surgeons in Ireland, Dublin, Mercer Library
Likenesses S. Keating, drawing, pastel on paper, St Vincent's Hospital, Dublin
Wealth at death £7461: probate, 7 April 1964, NA Ire.

Doolittle [married name Aldington], **Hilda** [H. D.] (1886–1961), poet and novelist, was born on 10 September 1886 at 110 Church Street, Bethlehem, Pennsylvania, USA, the second of the four children of the astronomer Charles Leander Doolittle (1843–1918) and his second wife, Helen Wolle (1853–1927), daughter of the botanist and Moravian minister Francis Wolle and his wife, Elizabeth. H. D. (as she was generally known) was raised in the Moravian tradition of her mother's family and began her education at the Moravian girls' seminary in Bethlehem in 1892. When her father was appointed professor of astronomy at the Flower Observatory in 1896, the family moved to Upper Darby, a suburb of Philadelphia, where she attended first Miss Gordon's school (1896–1902) and then Friends' Central School (1902–5). She went on to complete one year of university, at Bryn Mawr College (1905–6).

H. D.'s childhood was shaped by her mystical religious background, by her father's high academic expectations, and by her situation in the family as the only girl among boys, who included her older half-brother, the son of her father and his first wife, Martha, who had died in childbirth in 1876. H. D.'s interest in literature rather than in science and her struggle to define an independent and female identity came to a crisis during her year at Bryn Mawr; she experienced an emotional breakdown in 1906 and left university. Having met the young writer Ezra Pound (1885–1972) in 1901, she formed an influential friendship which would last throughout her life. The two became romantically involved in 1905 and were periodically and informally engaged over the next five years. She also developed during this time a lesbian friendship with Frances Gregg, an art student with whom she would travel abroad in 1911. Her bisexuality, which she initially confronted in these years before her departure from the United States, would become clearer to her during her sessions with Sigmund Freud in Vienna in the early 1930s, a psychoanalysis she recounted in detail in *Tribute to Freud* (1956). As a young woman, however, she experienced her sexuality with the conflict and confusion she would later depict in her autobiographical novels, particularly those written in the 1920s and only published posthumously, *Her* (1981), *Asphodel* (1992), and *Paint it Today* (1992). Except for brief holidays and a few months in New York city, where H. D. struggled to define herself as a writer, she remained at home until her trip in 1911 with Gregg and her mother to France and England, where Pound introduced her to his burgeoning literary circle. When the Greggs returned to the United States in the autumn, she remained in London.

In early 1912 H. D. met the poet Richard Aldington (1892–1962) [*see* Aldington, Edward Godfree], who fostered her interest in the classical past. At twenty-five, she was tall and slender; her delicate hands and intense eyes combined with her strong jaw to make her a dramatic presence. At nineteen, Aldington had just left University College, London, for financial reasons, and the two writers began to work together on translations from the Greek Anthology, which would influence their first published work. Having returned to London after a summer together in Paris, they showed their efforts to Pound in a tea-shop near the British Museum. He was impressed and, boldly crossing out 'Hilda Doolittle', he ascribed her poems to 'H. D.', the name by which she would thereafter be known in print. Enthusiastically sending the work of H. D. and Aldington off to *Poetry* magazine in Chicago, Pound would claim the poems as examples of 'imagism', the innovative and spare free verse which heralded literary modernism.

H. D. and Aldington married in London on 18 October 1913. Her first book of poems, *Sea Garden*, appeared in 1916, just before Aldington left for the western front. The First World War would affect both her marriage and her work. Their stillborn child in 1915 further contributed to their distress, and when Aldington began an extramarital affair in 1917, H. D. also took a lover, the aspiring composer and musicologist Cecil Gray (1895–1951). The relationship was brief, however, and Gray took no interest in their daughter, Frances Perdita, born on 31 March 1919. H. D. recounts impressionistically the difficult final months of her marriage in her autobiographical novel *Bid Me to Live* (1960). This narrative also details her intimate friendship with D. H. Lawrence and anticipates her lifelong relationship with the writer Bryher [*see* Ellerman, (Annie) Winifred (1894–1983)], the wealthy daughter of the shipping magnate Sir John Ellerman, whom she met in 1918.

H. D. and Aldington did not again live together after his demobilization in 1919, though they did not divorce until 1938, when Aldington married Netta Patmore, then pregnant with their child. Despite lack of contact in the 1920s, H. D. continued to feel deeply about Aldington; he as well as Pound and Lawrence would figure significantly in her poetry and prose as she explored issues of gender, sexuality, and artistic identity. Motherhood and femaleness would also become important matters in her work as she experimented with innovative forms and structures, breaking the boundaries of imagism as she moved towards longer poems (culminating in her epic *Helen in Egypt* in 1961) and prose which examined interiority and consciousness. Her friendship with Bryher assured her of a financial security none of the men in her life could offer, as Bryher committed herself to caring not only for H. D. but also for her daughter. Bryher could be manipulative, however, and H. D. maintained a protective distance, often living near by but in a separate household. Together they travelled to Greece, the United States, and Egypt in the 1920s and established homes in both London and Switzerland.

H. D. published most of her verse during her lifetime. Her collections include *Hymen* (1920), *Heliodora and Other Poems* (1924), *Red Roses for Bronze* (1931), and her moving war trilogy, written in part while in London during the blitz: *The Walls do not Fall* (1944), *Tribute to the Angels* (1945), and *The Flowering of the Rod* (1946). Her prose works—her modernist and fragmented autobiographical fictions—were more problematic, containing highly personal and sexually transgressive material. She often reserved these writings, returning to rework them repeatedly, even over decades. In addition to her unpublished novels, this body of prose included extensive journals (among her papers at the Beinecke Rare Book and Manuscript Library at Yale University) as well as her memoir of Ezra Pound, *End to Torment* (1979).

Hilda Doolittle, always introspective and sensitive, had seen the Second World War as a recapitulation of the first, and its conclusion left her feeling disoriented and dislocated. She experienced a serious mental breakdown in 1946 and returned to Switzerland, to a sanitorium in Zürich, where she remained until her recovery late in the year. For the rest of her life she lived in Switzerland, in elegant hotels and, as her physical health grew frail, in clinics. She rekindled her close friendship with Aldington, who visited her twice in her last years, but now her relationship with him, as with most of her other friends except for Bryher, was primarily epistolary. She travelled to the United States several times in the 1950s to visit her daughter and her grandchildren, and in 1960 she was recognized by the American Academy of Arts and Letters with the Award of Merit medal for poetry. After a cerebral haemorrhage, she died on 27 September 1961 in Zürich at the Klinik Hirslanden. She was cremated on 2 October and her ashes returned to the United States for burial in the family plot on Nisky Hill in Bethlehem, Pennsylvania.

CAROLINE ZILBOORG

Sources B. Guest, *Herself defined: the poet H. D. and her world* (1984) · *Richard Aldington and H. D.: the early years in letters*, ed. C. Zilboorg (1992) · *Richard Aldington and H. D.: the later years in letters*, ed. C. Zilboorg (1995) · C. Doyle, *Richard Aldington* (1989) · S. S. Friedman, *Psyche reborn* (1981) · S. S. Friedman, *Penelope's web* (1990) · S. S. Friedman and R. B. DuPlessis, eds., *Signets* (1990) · R. B. DuPlessis, *H. D.: the career of that struggle* (1986) · D. Hollenberg, *H. D.: the poetics of childbirth and creativity* (1991) · D. Chisholm, *H. D.'s Freudian poetics* (1992) · C. Laity, *H. D. and the Victorian 'fin de siècle'* (1996) · *Richard Aldington: an autobiography in letters*, ed. N. T. Gates (1992)
Archives Harvard U., Houghton L. · Indiana University, Bloomington, Lilly Library · Princeton University Library, Firestone Library · Ransom HRC · Southern Illinois University, Carbondale, Morris Library · Yale U., Beinecke L. | U. Leeds, Brotherton L., letters to Clement Shorter | SOUND BL NSA, H. D.'s readings of excerpts from *Helen in Egypt* and other poems
Likenesses photographs, 1910–60, repro. in Guest, *Herself defined* · photographs, 1917–19, repro. in Zilboorg, ed., *Richard Aldington and H. D.: the early years* · photographs, 1930–59, repro. in *Richard Aldington and H. D.: the later years*, ed. Zilboorg

Doolittle, Thomas (1630/1633?–1707), clergyman and ejected minister, was born in Kidderminster, Worcestershire. The evidence as to his date of birth and parentage is confusing, and he could be one of two Thomas Doolittles baptized in Kidderminster: he may be the son of William and Jane Doolittle, baptized on 20 October 1630 (a date which would be consistent with Daniel Williams's statement that Doolittle was seventy-seven when he died), but he could also be the son of Humphrey Doolittle and his wife, Anne, baptized on 12 September 1633. If he was baptized outside the parish, the suggestion of A. P. Gordon in the *Dictionary of National Biography*, that he was the third son of Anthony Doolittle, a Kidderminster glover, is also possible. Nathaniel Brokesby oversaw Doolittle's early education at the Kidderminster grammar school, which met in a converted chapel of St Mary's Church. As a teenager Doolittle heard Richard Baxter, who had returned to Kidderminster in 1647 from his civil war chaplaincy, preach the sermon series later published as *The Saints Everlasting Rest* (1650). Doolittle was converted through the influence of these sermons and thereafter considered Baxter his 'father in Christ' (Doolittle, sig. C3).

An opportunity for Doolittle to live with and assist a county lawyer ended abruptly when it became obvious that he was expected to work on Sundays. Baxter's intervention at this stage in Doolittle's life proved crucial. Seeing his academic potential, Baxter encouraged Doolittle to attend university and contributed a substantial amount of money enabling him to do so. Arrangements were made for him to attend Pembroke College in Cambridge, whose master was Baxter's friend Richard Vines. Admitted on 7 June 1649 as a sizar, Doolittle graduated BA in 1653, and MA in 1656. Surviving correspondence between Baxter and Doolittle while the latter was in Cambridge indicates Baxter's continuing close involvement in the younger man's affairs, not only with respect to financial support, but also as a mentor.

Thomas Doolittle (1630/1633?–1707), by Robert White

Upon completion of his BA degree Doolittle began the search for a pastoral position and was given the opportunity to preach in London. On 14 August 1653 the St Alfege parish account book records that Doolittle was paid £1 6s. 8d. 'for preachinge fouer tymes' before the congregation of St Alfege, London Wall, a parish within London's sixth classis which was then without a minister (London Guildhall, MS 1432/4). On 13 September the St Alfege vestry chose him 'by a generall consent' to become their minister (London Guildhall, MS 1431/2, fol. 230). In the meantime, Richard Baxter had used his own connections in Worcestershire to secure for Doolittle a living as a chaplain in the house of a squire 'with an ample salary' (Doolittle, sig. C3v). Baxter's letter informing him of the opportunity, however, arrived after he had already committed himself to St Alfege parish. Doolittle received presbyterian ordination and began his ministry later that autumn, his signature 'Thomas Doelittle Minister' first appearing in the vestry minutes on 1 November 1653 (London Guildhall, MS 1431/2, fol. 231).

During his years in London, Doolittle continued to look

to Baxter for counsel and to interact with him on theological questions, particularly with respect to universal redemption. His early pastoral efforts met with surprising success, and on 9 May 1657 he wrote to Baxter, 'God hath given me abundant encouragement in my work, by giving mee favor in the hearts and affections of the people ... & others in the city' (DWL, MS 59, i:125). Baxter himself had a high regard for Doolittle's ability as a pastor, recommending to several recently converted London correspondents that they seek him out for his preaching and counsel.

Doolittle married Mary Gill on 13 July 1655. Her influence appears to have been felt immediately, as vestry minutes record on 5 September that 'It is this day mewtually agreed upon that new river water shalbe laid into Mr. Doelittle's house our present minester by a leaden pipe & Coxke of Brase' (Hall, 37). Thomas and Mary Doolittle had at least six children, five of whose names are known—a son Samuel, and four daughters, Mary Sheafe, Tabitha Hearne, Martha Taylor, and Susannah Roades—and a fifth daughter who married Anthony Dawson.

Doolittle had a pregnant wife and three small children when he decided against accepting the terms for conforming to the Church of England set by the Restoration parliament and was ejected from his living as rector of St Alfege on 24 August 1662. He moved to nearby Moorfields, where he opened a boarding-school in his house. To accommodate a growing number of students he secured a larger house in Bunhill Fields and took on Thomas Vincent, the ejected minister of St Mary Magdalen, Milk Street, as his assistant. In the summer of 1665, at the outbreak of the plague in London, he moved his family and school to Woodford Bridge, Essex, while Vincent stayed behind to minister to plague victims. After the plague abated Doolittle, however, was presented before Romford (Essex) sessions court on 26 April 1666 as one who had lately come from St Giles Cripplegate, with the intention of settling in Essex with his wife and six children; apparently fearing that the family would become dependent upon parish charity, the court ordered them to leave.

In the chaotic aftermath of the London fire in September 1666 Doolittle and his family moved back to Bunhill Fields where in defiance of the law he opened a meeting-house and continued in public the preaching ministry he had previously undertaken privately. This site quickly proved too small and to accommodate his growing congregation he had a new meeting-house built in Monkwell Street near Cripplegate. Having thus come to the attention of the authorities he was summoned privately by the lord mayor who attempted to persuade him to desist from preaching. Doolittle refused, and the following Saturday night soldiers were sent to his home to arrest him. Doolittle escaped as they were breaking down the door. The authorities subsequently harassed the congregation and confiscated the meeting-house for use as a chapel for the lord mayor. Later, Doolittle quietly returned to his home and school, and by 1669 was reported to be preaching again at his house in Monkwell Street.

Upon Charles II's declaration of indulgence in March 1672 Doolittle received a licence (dated 2 April 1672) to hold presbyterian services in 'a room adjoining his dwelling' in Monkwell Street (*Calamy rev.*, 167), and at this time he also set up an academy at a house in Islington, Middlesex. When the king's indulgence was revoked on 3 March 1673 he was forced to move to Wimbledon, Surrey. Several of his students went as well, taking lodging in neighbours' houses and going to Doolittle's home for studies. Doolittle was able to return to Islington before 1680 but on 16 November 1682 he was convicted for having preached at Monkwell Street the previous 15 September and was fined £40. In April 1683, he was convicted of having repeated the same offence three times and fined £100, but by this time he had moved again, to Battersea, Surrey. The authorities in Battersea, however, seized and sold his possessions. Doolittle was thereby forced 'to disperse his pupils into private Families at Clapham' (Tong, 29). In 1687 Doolittle was compelled to move yet again, to St John's Court, Clerkenwell, Middlesex.

After the Toleration Act of 1689 Doolittle returned to Monkwell Street and re-established both his ministry and his academy. Despite frequent disruptions his academy was reputedly the 'leading Presbyterian academy in London', accommodating as many as twenty-eight students (McLachlan, 10). Among those who received instruction under Doolittle were the later nonconformist leaders Edmund Calamy and Matthew Henry, the Unitarian Thomas Emlyn, and nonconformist tutors John Ker and Thomas Rowe.

Doolittle's wife, Mary, died on 16 December 1692. Afterwards he seems to have stopped taking students, but within a few years he married a woman, also named Mary, who assisted him in his ministry. The second Mary Doolittle, 'my dear and loveing wife', survived her husband by only five months, dying in November 1707 (PRO, PROB 11/495, sig. 138; PROB 6/83, sig. 180v/213v).

As a pastor, Doolittle preached twice each Sunday, lectured on the Westminster assembly catechism on Wednesdays, and pursued a vigorous catechetical ministry. Already a popular author (his *A Treatise Concerning the Lord's Supper*, 1667, reached twenty-seven English editions, twenty-two Scottish editions, and twenty-six New England editions, as well as translations into Welsh and German), he was eventually the author of twenty-three treatises, tracts, and sermons, although he was valued most by his peers for his five works on catechizing.

Doolittle's surviving correspondence with Baxter demonstrates that he followed closely the theological debates between Anglicans and nonconformists and among nonconformists themselves. In most of his own published writings, however, he consistently chose to address pastoral and evangelistic concerns. His later reputation as one 'not eminent for compass of knowledge or depth of thought' is undeserved, as it is based on condescending comments by his student Thomas Emlyn, whose rejection of 'the narrow schemes of systematical divinity' and later drift into unitarianism did not predispose him to think favourably of his erstwhile tutor (*Works of Thomas Emlyn*, vi–vii). Though Doolittle suffered chronically from stone and other ailments, his final illness was brief. The Sunday before his death 'he preach'd, and Catechized with great vigour' (Williams, 32). Late the following week he became ill. He signed his will on Friday, and died the following day, Saturday 24 May 1707, in Monkwell Street, London, the last surviving London clergyman who had been ejected for nonconformity in 1662. He was buried in Bunhill Fields cemetery on 1 June.   J. WILLIAM BLACK

Sources parish register, Kidderminster, Worcs. RO · J. Smith, 'Some memoirs of the author's life and character', in T. Doolittle, *Complete body of practical divinity* (1723) · D. Williams, *Christian sincerity: described in a funeral sermon … June the first, 1707, occasion'd by the death of … Mr Thomas Doolittle* (1707) · T. Doolittle, *The Lord's last-sufferings* (1681) · St Alfege, London Wall, vestry minutes, GL, MS 1431/2 · St Alfege, London Wall, churchwardens' accounts, GL, MS 1432/4 · will, 23 May 1707, PRO, PROB 11/495, sig. 138 · DWL, Baxter letters, MS 59, i:125, vi:128 · BL, Add. MS 4275, fol. 193 · *Calendar of the correspondence of Richard Baxter*, ed. N. H. Keeble and G. F. Nuttall, 2 vols. (1991) · J. Shower, *Death a deliverance, or, A funeral discourse, preach'd (in part) on the decease of Mrs. M. Doolittle … who departed this life the 16th of Decemb. 1692* (1693) · *Calamy rev.* · administration, PRO, PROB 6/83, sig. 180v/213v [Mary Doolittle] · W. Wilson, *The history and antiquities of the dissenting churches and meeting houses in London, Westminster and Southwark*, 4 vols. (1808–14), vol. 3 · Venn, *Alum. Cant.* · *An account of the life and death of the late Reverend Mr. Matthew Henry*, ed. W. Tong (1716) · *The works of Mr Thomas Emlyn*, 4th edn, 1 (1746) · J. B. Williams, *The lives of Philip and Matthew Henry* (1974) · G. B. Hall, ed., *Records of St Alphage, London Wall* (1925) · H. McLachlan, *English education under the Test Acts: being the history of the nonconformist academies, 1662–1820* (1931) · C. D. Gilbert, *A history of King Charles I Grammar School, Kidderminster* (1980) · C. D. Gilbert, 'Richard Baxter and Nathaniel Brokesby', *Baxter Notes and Studies*, 5/2 (1997) · Tai Liu, *Puritan London: a study of religion and society in the City parishes* (1986) · *DNB* · J. Toulmin, *An historical view of the state of the protestant dissenters in England* (1814) · *The nonconformist's memorial … originally written by … Edmund Calamy*, ed. S. Palmer, 2nd edn, 1 (1777)

Archives BL, corresp., Add. MS 4275, fol. 193 · DWL, commonplace book, MS 28.5 | DWL, corresp., Baxter letters, MS 59 · GL, MS sermon preached at the funeral of his grandson, MS 2459

Likenesses J. Sturt, line engraving (aged fifty-one), BM, NPG · R. White, line engraving, AM Oxf., BM, NPG [*see illus.*] · engraving, repro. in S. Palmer, ed., *The nonconformist's memorial: … originally written by … Edmund Calamy* (1777), vol. 1, p. 80 · line engraving (in youth), BM, NPG

Wealth at death £490 cash bequests: will, 23 May 1707, PRO, PROB 11/495, sig. 138

Doort, Abraham van der (1575x85–1640), artist and curator, is thought to have been the son of Peter van der Doort, an engraver from the Netherlands who was active in Hamburg around 1590–1600, and the brother of the painters Isaak and Jacob van (der) Doort. His first known employment was at the court of Emperor Rudolf II in Prague, but about 1610 he arrived in England and joined the service of Henry, prince of Wales, who offered him the keepership of his new cabinet room, with an annual salary of £50. The prince was apparently motivated by his determination to acquire a life-sized female bust in coloured wax, which van der Doort had made to a commission from Rudolf but not yet delivered. When Henry died unexpectedly in December 1612, van der Doort made the wax hands and face of the prince's funeral effigy; he then seems to have returned to the continent, though he reappeared early in 1616 with a letter of recommendation to James I from Maurice, landgrave of Hesse-Kassel. He

was reinstated as keeper of the cabinet room of the new prince of Wales, later Charles I, and carried out other commissions for the court; these included making portrait boxes of King James and Queen Anne and drawing the king's portrait 'at length'.

After Charles I's accession in 1625, van der Doort was confirmed as keeper of the cabinet room and provider of patterns of coins; he was also appointed overseer or surveyor of pictures and master embosser and maker of medals. He encountered persistent bureaucratic difficulties in extracting payment from the exchequer of the salaries attached to these four posts, together with his daily living allowance as groom of the chamber. It may have been with the aim of providing for him more economically and reliably that the court, in the person of the secretary of state, Lord Conway, exerted its influence in 1628 to secure him a wife, one Louise Cole, the widow of an immigrant merchant from Antwerp, James Cole (d. 1628), and the daughter of the eminent botanist Mathias de l'Obel (1538–1616). They married at St Martin-in-the-Fields on 15 August 1629.

Van der Doort's achievements as an artist cannot now be judged. His works are either lost or unidentified, although his image of Charles I survives on a group of high-denomination coins and was influential on the rest of Charles's coinage. The principal achievement for which he is remembered is a detailed, but incomplete and sometimes incomprehensible, inventory of the Royal Collection at Whitehall compiled in 1637–9. Its significance was recognized a century later by George Vertue, who made a very inaccurate transcript, published in 1757. An authoritative edition, compiled from four surviving manuscripts, was published in 1960. The inventory not only describes the contents of Charles I's almost legendary collection, but also documents van der Doort's work as keeper, his friendly relationship with the king, and gifts which he made personally to the Royal Collection.

Van der Doort seems to have been oppressed by rivalries at court which hindered his work, and some time before 23 June 1640 he hanged himself, in despair at having mislaid a miniature entrusted to him by the king. The miniature was later discovered by his executors.

CHRISTOPHER MARSDEN

Sources 'Abraham van der Doort's catalogue of the collections of Charles I', ed. O. Millar, *Walpole Society*, 37 (1958–60) · T. Wilks, 'Doort, Abraham van der', *The dictionary of art*, ed. J. Turner (1996) · D. F. Allen, 'Abraham Vanderdort and the coinage of Charles I', *Numismatic Chronicle*, 6th ser., 1 (1941), 54–75 · M. Edmond, 'Limners and picturemakers', *Walpole Society*, 47 (1978–80), 60–242 · H. Walpole, *Anecdotes of painting in England: with some account of the principal artists*, ed. R. N. Wornum, new edn, 3 vols. (1849), vol. 1, pp. 265–9, 495–8 · G. Meissner, ed., *Allgemeines Künstlerlexikon: die bildenden Künstler aller Zeiten und Völker*, [new edn, 34 vols.] (Leipzig and Munich, 1983–) · J. V. Kitto, ed., 'The register of St Martin-in-the-Fields, London, 1619–1636', *Harleian Society*, 66 (1936)

Archives BL, Add. MS 10112 | Bodl. Oxf., MSS Ashmole 1513, 1514 · Royal Arch., catalogue of the contents of the cabinet room at Whitehall

Likenesses V. Green, mezzotint, 1776 (after portrait attrib. W. Dobson), repro. in *Burlington Magazine*, 19 (1911), 162 · T. Chambers, engraving, 1778 (after portrait attrib. W. Dobson), repro. in

Burlington Magazine, 19 (1911), 162 • attrib. W. Dobson, oils, The Hermitage, St Petersburg; repro. in Millar, ed., 'Abraham van der Doort's catalogue' • oils (after portrait attrib. W. Dobson), NPG; repro. in *Burlington Magazine*, 19 (1911), 162

Dopping, Anthony

Dopping, Anthony (1643–1697), Church of Ireland bishop of Meath, was born on 28 March 1643, the son of Anthony Dopping, originally from Frampton in Gloucestershire, who had bought an estate in co. Meath in 1636. His place of birth is given as Dublin by Harris (*Whole Works of Sir James Ware*, 1.394) but as Gloucester in the registers of Trinity College, Dublin (Burtchaell & Sadlier, *Alum. Dubl.*, 238), which he entered on 28 September 1655, having previously attended St Patrick's Cathedral school. He graduated BA in 1660 and MA in 1662, and was elected a fellow in 1662. In November 1669 he became vicar of St Andrew's parish, Dublin. He was appointed to the bishopric of Kildare on 16 January 1679 and consecrated in Christ Church Cathedral on 2 February. On 11 February 1682 he was translated to the bishopric of Meath, and as was normal with this senior bishopric was admitted to the privy council (5 April 1682). In the same year he was also appointed vice-chancellor of Trinity College. In these appointments he had the support both of the duke of Ormond, whose chaplain he had been while at St Andrew's, and of Archbishop Michael Boyle of Armagh.

Dopping's sermons during 1682–8 strongly upheld the traditional doctrines of divine right and passive resistance, although reports of a sermon on 31 January 1686 denouncing Catholic doctrine reached James II, who had the lord lieutenant, the earl of Clarendon, reprimand him. On 27 March 1689 Dopping led a delegation of clergy to meet James on his arrival in Dublin and assure him of their loyalty. Over the next sixteen months he acted as the principal spokesman for Irish protestants living under the Jacobite regime, repeatedly petitioning for the protection of churches, persons, and property, as well as joining William King in administering the diocese of Dublin in the absence of Archbishop Marsh. He took his seat in the House of Lords of the Jacobite parliament of May–June 1689, where he opposed legislation on tithes, liberty of conscience, the repeal of the Restoration land settlement, and other measures. On 7 July 1690, after the battle of the Boyne and the Jacobite withdrawal from Dublin, he led a deputation of clergy to William's camp at Finglas to declare their allegiance. Thereafter his declared position, both in sermons and in private correspondence, was that James had forfeited his crown by consenting to the destruction of his protestant subjects and by abandoning his kingdom.

Although Dopping's rapid changes of allegiance exposed him to some criticism, the new Williamite administration initially gave him a prominent role in both civil and ecclesiastical affairs. On 26 November 1691, however, preaching at a service of thanksgiving for the completion of the war, he forcefully denounced the treaty of Limerick, arguing that the long series of rebellions that had taken place since 1172 demonstrated the futility of any compromise settlement negotiated with the Irish. For this direct attack on government policy he was suspended from the privy council on 5 January 1692 and restored only in August 1695. His indiscretion, along with continuing doubts regarding his collaboration with the Jacobite regime, probably contributed to his failure to be appointed to either of the two archbishoprics, Cashel and Dublin, that became vacant in 1693–4.

In the early 1690s Dopping was one of the group of bishops, also including William King and Nathaniel Foy, who lobbied government for the reform of the Irish church. In March 1694 he and King, executing a royal commission to inquire into the mismanagement of the diocese of Down and Connor, deprived the bishop, Thomas Hackett, and several of his senior clergy. Dopping's own visitation records and instructions to his clergy reveal a strong commitment to high pastoral standards. In 1696 he published a treatise on episcopal visitation, *Tractatus de visitationibus episcopalibus*. William King, many years later, responded angrily to an unfavourable comparison between his own brusque treatment of his clergy and Dopping's 'mildness and gentle persuasion', insisting that he had accomplished more in five or six years in Derry than Dopping had in fifteen years in co. Meath (King, 213).

Dopping was an intermittent supporter of proposals to evangelize the Catholic Irish through the Irish language. He solicited subscriptions for the edition of Bedell's Irish translation of the Old Testament printed in 1685, and also wrote a preface, although this was mislaid and never printed. However, Narcissus Marsh complained in 1686 that Dopping subsequently 'flew off from prosecuting what he designed and promised, and has ever since been wholly unconcerned and sat neuter' (Maddison, 86). He returned to the idea of sponsoring preaching through Irish in 1693, but by 1697 had again rejected the idea. His change of heart seems to have been due in each case to fears that such efforts would retard the spread of English language and culture. Where dissenters were concerned, his anonymous pamphlet *The Case of the Dissenters of Ireland* (1695) conceded their right to religious freedom while defending their exclusion from civic office.

About 1669 Dopping married Jane Molyneux. He assisted his brother-in-law, William Molyneux, by obtaining a detailed description of co. Westmeath for a projected atlas in 1682, and at his request contributed to the financial support of the Gaelic antiquary Roderick O'Flaherty. He also shared Molyneux's interest in constitutional issues, and in 1692 published *Modus tenendi parliamenta & consilia in Hibernia*, from a manuscript left to him by Molyneux's father-in-law, William Domville. Dopping died in Dublin on 25 April 1697 and was buried in St Andrew's Church. His son Samuel was elected MP for Armagh in 1695, 1703, and 1714, and for Trinity College in 1715. Another son, Anthony, was bishop of Ossory from 1740 until his death in 1743.   S. J. Connolly

Sources M. Gilmore, 'Anthony Dopping and the Church of Ireland', MA diss., Queen's University, Belfast, 1988 • J. I. Peacocke, 'Anthony Dopping, bishop of Meath', *Irish Church Quarterly*, 2 (1909), 120–33 • J. Brady, ed., 'Remedies proposed for the Church of Ireland (1697)', *Archivium Hibernicum*, 22 (1959), 163–73 • C. C. Ellison,

'Bishop Dopping's visitation book, 1682–5', *Ríocht na Midhe*, 5/1 (1971), 28–39; 5/2 (1972), 3–13; 5/3 (1973), 3–11; 5/4 (1974), 98–103; 6/1 (1975), 3–13 • P. Loupes, 'Bishop Dopping's visitation of the diocese of Meath', *Studia Hibernica*, 24 (1984–8), 127–51 • C. S. King, *A great archbishop of Dublin, William King D.D., 1650–1729* (1906) • *Calendar of the manuscripts of the marquess of Ormonde*, new ser., 8 vols., HMC, 36 (1902–20), vols. 4, 6 • J. G. Simms, *William Molyneux of Dublin, 1656–1698*, ed. P. H. Kelly (1982) • R. E. W. Maddison, 'Robert Boyle and the Irish Bible', *Bulletin of the John Rylands University Library*, 41 (1958–9), 81–101 • *The whole works of Sir James Ware concerning Ireland*, ed. and trans. W. Harris, rev. edn, 2 vols. in 3 (1764) • Burtchaell & Sadleir, *Alum. Dubl.*, 2nd edn

Archives Armagh Public Library, corresp. and diary, MS G. II. 22–24, MS G. v. 6 • CUL, notebook • TCD, sermons, MS 1688
Likenesses portrait, TCD

Dora, Sister. *See* Pattison, Dorothy Wyndlow (1832–1878).

Doran, John (1807–1878), writer and literary editor, was born on 11 March 1807 in London, of Irish parentage. His father, John Doran, of Drogheda, co. Louth, left Ireland after the suppression of the rising in 1798, and settled in London, where he became a business contractor. In the course of his work he was captured by the French and detained in France for three years. He perfected his knowledge of the language, which he later passed on to his son, a precocious pupil who attended Matheson's academy in Margaret Street, off Cavendish Square, London. In 1819, aged twelve, the younger John Doran came first in French, geography, and elocution, winning a silver medal which was presented to him by the duke of Kent.

Before Doran was seventeen both his parents had died, forcing the youth to find employment. His excellent French immediately secured him an appointment as tutor to the first Lord Glenlyon's eldest son, George Murray, afterwards duke of Atholl. He also began to write: on 8 April 1824 his melodrama, *Justice, or, The Venetian Jew*, was produced at the Surrey Theatre, and he contributed to the London *Literary Chronicle*. Some of his Parisian sketches and Paris letters, written during his travels to Paris and other parts of the continent with his pupil, George Murray, appeared in *The Athenaeum* (into which the *Literary Chronicle* had been absorbed) in 1828, under the title 'Sketches and Reminiscences'. From 1828 to 1837 Doran was tutor to Lord Rivers, and to the sons of Lord Harewood and of Lord Portman. After 1830 he contributed lyrical translations from French, German, Latin, and Italian to the *Bath Journal*. On 3 July 1834 he married Emma Mary Harrington, the daughter of Captain Richard Gilbert RN, at Reading, a town whose history he had been researching. His book, *The History and Antiquities of the Town and Borough of Reading, in Berkshire*, was published in both Reading and London in 1835. The Dorans lived briefly at Hay-a-Park Cottage, Knaresborough, until Doran gave up his last tutorship. He then travelled on the continent for two or three years with his 'young and pretty wife' (Frith, 2.265) and took his doctor's degree in the faculty of philosophy at the University of Marburg in Prussia, using his historical research on Reading.

After returning to England Doran adopted literature as his profession and settled in St Peter's Square, Hammersmith. In 1841 he became literary editor of the *Church and State Gazette*, receiving £100 a year, and first came to public notice in 1852 for completing *Filia dolorosa*, a life of Marie Thérèse Charlotte, duchesse d'Angoulême, left unfinished by the death of its chief author, Mrs Romer. In the same year he edited a new edition of Charles Anthon's text of the *Anabasis* of Xenophon. In 1853 Doran prefixed a life of the poet the Revd Edward Young to a reissue of his *Night Thoughts*, and in 1854 rewrote his life for a new edition of Young's complete works. Reflecting on Young's line in 'Last Day': 'Man's is laborious happiness at best', Doran agreed. 'No doubt of it. Happiness comes by labour' (E. Young, *Night Thoughts*, 4th edn, 1864, lxiv).

Doran was now launched as a regular contributor to *The Athenaeum*. He became a friend of Hepworth Dixon, the editor, and during Dixon's absences acted as his substitute. Doran's first hugely successful book, *The Court of Fools* (1858), was dedicated to Dixon, 'In Friendly Homage from the Author'. In 1854 Doran had published *Table Traits and Something on Them*, and *Habits and Men*, the latter being a history of dress and costume of men and women from the Peloponnesian War to Samuel Pepys, the son of a tailor. It must have been a labour of love, since Doran wrote: 'Under trial, next to trust in God, I do not know of any better anodyne, more potent balm, than literary occupation' (p. 290). He relished writing about royalty and high society, three books having preceded *The Court of Fools*: *The Queens of the House of Hanover* (1855), *Knights and their Days* (1856), and *Monarchs Retired from Business* (1857). *New Pictures and Old Panels*, published in 1859, lacked the style and verve of *The Court of Fools*, but boasted a portrait of the author engraved by Joseph Brown from a photograph. Doran is smartly dressed, with a jewelled tie-pin in his cravat and a friendly smile on his face; his signature ends with a flourish. Also in 1859 he became a member of the Society of Antiquaries of London, and in 1876 a member of its council. In 1860 he published his most elaborate work, *Their Majesties' Servants*, a historical account of the English stage from Thomas Betterton to Edmund Kean, of which a new edition was issued in 1887. Doran never lost his critical faculty; quoting Dr Johnson's famous judgement on David Garrick, 'His death eclipsed the gaiety of nations', Doran curtly dismissed it as 'nonsense' (p. 265).

After the retirement of William John Thoms, Doran succeeded him as editor of *Notes and Queries*. In 1873 he published *A Lady of the Last Century*, which concerned Mrs Elizabeth Montagu, whom he admired for her intelligence and wit. His next book, *Mann and Manners at the Court of Florence, 1740–86* (1876), based upon the letters of Sir Horace Mann to Horace Walpole, was mainly editorial, but in 1877 he published the well-researched and engrossing *London in the Jacobite Times* (2 vols.). His conclusion was that after being a serious fact, Jacobitism became a sentiment which gradually died out (2.411). Pressed to make a book out of his articles in *The Athenaeum* on towns which the British Association for the Advancement of Science had used for its meetings, he produced *Memories of our Great Towns*. It was typical Doran. Describing the marital adventures of Henry Cecil, first marquess, he observed: 'Reality, after all, is as wonderful as romance' (Doran, 165).

On 2 January 1878 Doran, apparently his customary, jovial self, took the corrected proofs of that book to the printer, but within two weeks he contracted pneumonia, and died at his home, 33 Lansdowne Road, Notting Hill, London, on 25 January 1878. He was buried on 29 January at Kensal Green cemetery. His wife survived him, as did a son, Alban Doran FRCS, and a daughter, Florence, who married Andreas Holtz. *Notes and Queries* described Doran as an 'accomplished gentleman and warm-hearted scholar' and in April 1878 the president of the Society of Antiquaries referred to the 'kind and genial Dr. Doran, whose wonderful powers of memory made his conversations as sparkling as his writings' (*PRSA*, 1879, 384).

BRENDA COLLOMS

Sources DNB · W. P. Frith, *My autobiography and reminiscences*, 3 vols. (1887–8) · W. J. Thoms, *N&Q*, 5th ser., 9 (1878), 81 · J. F. Waller, ed., *The imperial dictionary of universal biography*, 3 vols. (1857–63) · S. Gwynn and G. M. Tuckwell, *The life of the Rt. Hon. Sir Charles W. Dilke*, 2 vols. (1917) · 'Preface', J. Doran, *Memories of our great towns—with anecdotal leanings* (1882) · *The Times* (28 Jan 1878) · *ILN* (9 Feb 1878) · *Temple Bar*, 52 (1878), 460–94 · d. cert. · *CGPLA Eng. & Wales* (1878)

Likenesses J. Brown, stipple (after photograph by H. Watkins), NPG; repro. in J. Doran, *New pictures and old panels* (1859), frontispiece · Elliott & Fry, carte-de-visite, NPG · Spy [L. Ward], watercolour caricature, NPG; repro. in *VF* (6 Dec 1873) · J. A. Vinter, lithograph (after photograph by Diamond), BM · engraving (after photograph), repro. in J. Doran, *Their majesties' servants, or, Annals of the English stage*, new edn (1897) · portrait, repro. in *ILN*, 133

Wealth at death under £3000: probate, 9 March 1878, *CGPLA Eng. & Wales*

Dorbéne mac Altaíni (d. 713). *See under* Iona, abbots of (*act.* 563–927).

Dorchester. For this title name *see* Carleton, Dudley, Viscount Dorchester (1574–1632); Pierrepont, Henry, marquess of Dorchester (1607–1680); Sedley, Catharine, *suo jure* countess of Dorchester, and countess of Portmore (1657–1717); Carleton, Guy, first Baron Dorchester (1724–1808).

Doré, (Louis Auguste) Gustave (1832–1883), illustrator, was born on 6 January 1832 in the rue Bleue, Strasbourg, France, the second of the three children of Pierre Louis Christophe Doré (d. 1849), an engineer, and his wife, Alexandrine Marie Anne Pluchart (d. 1881). His parents were both French.

A child prodigy, Doré received little formal artistic training, but his talents as a draughtsman were already apparent during his school years (at Bourg-en-Bresse, 1843–7, then at the Lycée Charlemagne in Paris, 1848–50). His first lithographic album was published by Aubert in Paris in 1847. After three years working under contract as a caricaturist for the editor Charles Philipon (1800–1862), he added book illustration to his repertory. He had achieved acclaim as an illustrator by 1854 with the publication of his first edition of the *Œuvres de Rabelais* and the *Histoire pittoresque, dramatique et caricaturale de la Sainte Russie*. He exhibited paintings in the Salon from 1850 and sculpture from 1870 but, to his great distress, was unable to match his precocious success as a graphic artist in the 'high arts'. As a young man Doré would perform acrobatic feats to astound his friends; he used his extraordinary artistic talents to astound a wider public, but often in a similarly facile manner. The speed with which he drew was legendary and his output was as noteworthy for its quantity as for its quality. He painted epic canvasses of gigantic proportions (*Le Christ sortant du prétoire*, 1867–72, priv. coll., Vienna, measures 6 metres by 9 metres). His sculpture was equally enormous, and even his etchings and watercolours were outsized (in the Salon of 1877 he exhibited a life-size watercolour portrait of his mother). Doré aspired to be the Michelangelo of the nineteenth century, and was deeply embittered by the lukewarm critical reception that his paintings and sculpture received. Time has done little to invalidate the judgement of contemporary critics, however, and it is as an illustrator that Doré is remembered today.

Doré's production as an illustrator remains unmatched for scope or ambition. Among his major works are editions of Rabelais (2nd expanded edn, 1873), Balzac (*Contes drolatiques*, 1855), Dante (*Divine Comedy*, 1861, 1868), Charles Perrault (*Fables*, 1862), Cervantes (*Don Quixote*, 1863), Milton (*Paradise Lost*, 1866), La Fontaine (*Fables*, 1867), Tennyson (*Idylls of the King*, 1867), Coleridge (*The Rime of the Ancient Mariner*, 1876), and Ariosto (*Orlando Furioso*, 1879). Doré also illustrated a host of minor works in a variety of genres. Of mixed quality, his illustrations achieved real power when he chose texts that suited his extravagant imagination and taste for excess. His editions of Dante, Rabelais, and Cervantes probably include his finest work. Too often, however, his output is marred by an overreliance on his facility and visual memory. Many of his figures lack individual character. *London: a Pilgrimage*, with a text by Blanchard Jerrold (1872), offers examples of the strengths and weaknesses of Doré's manner. The dark visions of East End poverty are magnificently evocative, but, as Jerrold himself complained, over and above the sundry inaccuracies of detail there is little that is specifically English about many of the figures that Doré drew from memory in his Parisian studio. Jerrold's criticism notwithstanding, Doré's vision of London, with its sharp contrasts between the sumptuous world of the affluent and the apocalyptic misery of the underclass, perfectly captured the public mood of horrified fascination with the burgeoning metropolis. Of the series of social investigations undertaken by journalists and graphic artists in the Victorian era, *London: a Pilgrimage* had the greatest immediate impact and has had the most enduring appeal for both the public and for later artists. Van Gogh's admiration for the London illustrations led him to paint a version of Doré's haunting image of dehumanized convicts circling a bleak exercise yard.

Doré's achievements in the field of illustration earned him polite critical applause, official honours, including the chevalier de la Légion d'honneur (1861) and officier de la Légion d'honneur (1878), and enormous public acclaim. His work was particularly popular with the British public. From 1856 until his death he worked as much for London as for Paris publishers. From 1868 the Doré Gallery in New Bond Street displayed examples of his work in every genre, and he contributed regularly to the *Illustrated London News*. Doré often visited London between 1868 and 1879, but never settled in the city or learned any English. Although he travelled widely in Europe, except for a brief exile in Versailles during the Franco-Prussian War and the Paris Commune (1870–71), he always lived in Paris after 1847. He never married. Youthful affairs with actresses (including, it seems, Sarah Bernhardt) notwithstanding, his one close emotional relationship was with his mother. As an adult, he continued to sleep in a small chamber off her bedroom in the family home in the rue St Dominique. He died there on 23 January 1883 and was buried in the Père Lachaise cemetery two days later.   DAVID KERR

Sources B. Jerrold, *Life of Gustave Doré* (1891) • A. Renonciat, *La vie et l'œuvre de Gustave Doré* (1983) • S. Nicolosi, *Gustave Doré: biografia, saggi, giudizi critici* (1989) • P. Kaenel, *Le métier d'illustrateur 1830–1880: Rodolphe Töpffer, J.J. Grandville, Gustave Doré* (1996) • B. Roosevelt, *Life and reminiscences of Gustave Doré* (1885)
Archives AM Oxf., sketchbook | Somerville College, Oxford, letters to Amelia Edwards
Likenesses G. Dorée, self-portrait, watercolour drawing, 1872, Musée des Beaux-Arts, Strasbourg, France • Nadar, photograph, Bibliothèque Nationale, Paris, France

Doreck, Beata (1833–1875), educationist, was born on 5 February 1833 in Mannheim, in the grand duchy of Baden, Germany, daughter of Herr Doreck, a jeweller. Her father provided her with a good education but he was opposed to her wish to train as a teacher, having the financial resources to enable her to remain at home without the need for employment. Her determination in pursuing her chosen career is evidence of her early sense of vocation. Beata spent three years at the normal school of Riboville, Alsace, and then went to nearby Colmar where she was examined for her diploma in teaching. Although she was only nineteen, her performance in the examination was so impressive that she was declared competent to take charge of a school without a period of probation, but she had already decided to go to England to take up a post as governess in a private family.

Beata Doreck arrived in England in 1857 and remained in this post for three years although it was not a happy period:

> It was her lot in this family to fall into the hands of employers who had neither the intelligence to appreciate nor the generosity to reward the remarkable talents which she devoted to her work. She often spoke, in after years, of the unworthy treatment she received while carrying out this engagement. (Payne, 157)

She spent the next few years as a daily governess before opening her own school in 1866 at 1 Kildare Terrace, Bayswater, London, moving to 63 Kensington Gardens Square, Bayswater, in 1869.

During the 1850s England was a place of refuge for liberal Germans fleeing the repression of democratic activity following the failed uprising of 1848–9. Froebel's ideas had been adopted by this group and the first kindergartens, opened in London and Manchester, were German speaking. However as Froebel's ideas became more widely known so a demand grew for kindergartens for English children. A major problem was the lack of English teachers who understood Froebel's ideas. At this time none of Froebel's works had been translated and very few English commentaries existed. It was recognized that the kindergarten movement needed the involvement of English teachers if it was to develop fully, although Maria Grey, in her address to the Froebel Society, 5 December 1876, acknowledged that 'Miss Doreck had lived long enough in England to understand the national peculiarities of thought and feeling' (p. 1).

The difficulties in finding suitable staff for the kindergarten she added to her existing school for girls and preparatory school for boys, led Beata Doreck to use her influence with her English and German colleagues to bring about the formation of the Froebel Society. The first meeting, chaired by her, was held at 63 Kensington Gardens Square on 4 November 1874, and she was subsequently elected president of the committee whose members included two of her close friends and colleagues, Frances Mary Buss and Joseph Payne. *The Report of the Froebel Society for the Promotion of the Kindergarten System*, June 1875, listed the methods by which the society hoped to achieve its aims, including lectures, public meetings, publications, specimen illustrations of kindergarten work, a register of kindergarten teachers, the establishment of a model kindergarten, and the formation of training classes. In addition, the members were to present papers at the monthly meetings and contact was maintained with Froebelian colleagues overseas.

Beata Doreck had been elected to the council of the College of Preceptors in June 1871 at the suggestion of Frances Mary Buss, who once said, 'We shall not have thorough education till we have the Kindergarten' (Ridley, 275). Perhaps the most important collaboration between the two women, who shared a great interest in teacher training, was the proposal presented to the College of Preceptors in October 1872 to establish a 'training class of lectures and lessons for teachers'. The college subsequently established the professorship of the science and arts of education, to which Joseph Payne was appointed in January 1873. Payne commented that Beata Doreck was largely responsible for the details of the scheme. In September 1873 she and Frances Mary Buss were elected fellows of the college, the first two women to receive the honour. In April 1874 they both formed part of a deputation to the duke of Richmond, the minister responsible for education in Disraeli's administration, urging him to establish a training college for teachers, on a par with the College of Surgeons and the law institutions, under the auspices of the College of Preceptors.

Beata Doreck was also an early supporter of the Girls' Public Day School Company, founded in 1872, and bought shares in it, although the company's plan to open a school at Notting Hill near to her own was a potential threat to her livelihood. She was also involved in the work of the Schoolmistresses' Association and served as president for a year (1873–4). She supported her own young teachers, mainly from the poorer middle class, by paying their college fees and before her death planned to take aspiring teachers into her home and to train them herself for a nominal fee. No written exposition of her ideas seems to have survived but a detailed account of her paper, *The Kindergarten in Relation to the School*, presented to the Froebel Society on 13 April 1875, is given in the society's minutes. The title refers to the Froebelian concept of harmony of development and the paper criticizes the abrupt break between kindergarten and school under the existing system. A preparatory transition class, incorporating the teaching of reading and writing, was desirable, and she argued that Froebel's principles were applicable to the teaching of *all* school subjects.

In the summer of 1875 Beata Doreck made a recuperative trip to Switzerland accompanied by her sister Anna Roth, Mme Dickerdorf, and Harriet Mann, a member of her staff. She fell ill with a fever at Interlaken and died at the Hotel Interlaken on 12 September 1875. '"Overwork" was the emphatic comment on her case pronounced by the physician who attended her dying bed' (Payne, 157).

JANE READ

Sources J. Payne, 'Miss Doreck', *Educational Times* (1 Oct 1875), 156–7 · A. E. Ridley, *Frances Mary Buss and her work for education* (1895) · Mrs W. Grey [Maria Grey], *Address delivered … at the annual meeting of the Froebel Society* (1876) · E. M. Lawrence, ed., *Friedrich Froebel and English education* (1952) · J. Liebschner, *Foundations of progressive education* (1991) · Froebel Society, minutes, 1, 1874–6 · D. Salmon and W. Hindshaw, *Infant schools: their history and theory* (1904) · *CGPLA Eng. & Wales* (1875)
Archives Girton Cam., London Association of Schoolmistresses MSS, minute books, LSM1, LSM2 · U. Lond., Institute of Education, college of preceptors · University of Surrey, Roehampton, London, Froebel Institute, minutes of Froebel Society
Wealth at death under £3000: administration, 16 Oct 1875, *CGPLA Eng. & Wales*

Dorigny, Sir Nicholas (*bap.* 1658, *d.* 1746), painter and engraver, was baptized in Paris on 2 June 1658, the second son of Michel Dorigny (1617–1665), a painter and engraver, and his wife, who was the daughter of the painter Simon Vouet. He may have had some training in art from his father, but was said by George Vertue to have been brought up to be a lawyer. In 1687, however, he joined his brother Louis Dorigny (1654–1742) in Rome, where the latter was established as a painter. There Nicholas Dorigny took up etching, imitating the new style of Gérard Audran. At first he worked for the dominant publisher Giovanni Giacomo de Rossi, producing prints after Gianlorenzo Bernini and Carlo Maratta. Dorigny's etchings of the cupola of the church of Santa Agnese in piazza Navona, after Ciro Ferri, were published by de Rossi in 1690. His next project, *The Marriage of Cupid and Psyche*, in the entrance loggia of the Farnesina (1693), was the foundation of his reputation as an interpreter of Raphael.

About this time Dorigny learned to engrave because 'he found for want of haveing learnt the handling & use of the Graver, he cou'd not arrive to the Perfection or harmony he aimed at' (Vertue, *Note Books*, 1.51). With the *Planetarium* (1695), which reproduced the ceiling of the Chigi chapel in Santa Maria del Popolo, Dorigny also began to publish his own plates. He published paintings in San Pietro, Rome, after Cigoli, Domenichino, Guercino, and Lanfranco

(1697–1700), and Domenichino's evangelists in Sant' Andrea (1707). He continued to work for de Rossi, engraving thirty-one statues for his *Raccolta di statue antiche e moderne* (1704). His large engraving of Raphael's *Transfiguration* (1705) 'got him justly the reputation of the first graver in Europe' (Vertue, *Note books*, 6.187). To this he published a companion, *The Descent from the Cross*, after Daniele da Volterra, in 1710.

In June 1711 Dorigny's pre-eminent reputation as an interpreter of Raphael secured him an invitation from Robert Harley and other virtuosi to travel to England to engrave the most important paintings in the country, Raphael's tapestry cartoons of *The Acts of the Apostles* at Hampton Court. This was the most significant commission for engravings ever yet placed in England: for this reason Vertue left detailed notes on its progress, remarking that Dorigny was enticed both by the challenge and by the prospect of making further sales of his prints in London, having already sold many to Englishmen in Rome. His arrival in England coincided with the establishment of an academy in Great Queen Street, of which, on 18 October 1711, he was elected a director.

Originally it had been intended that the cartoons would be engraved at the queen's expense in order to provide suitable presents for the nobility and for foreign ministers. However, Dorigny's demand for £4000 to £5000 'put a full stop to that affair' (Vertue, *Note books*, 6.187), and instead the novel English method of raising a subscription was attempted. After the queen had agreed to allow Dorigny an apartment at Hampton Court 'during the time he should be doing them and fireing & a bottle of Wine daily' (ibid.), this was launched on 25 October 1711 with advertisements in *The Spectator* and (repeatedly) in the *Daily Courant*. A month later Richard Steele devoted an issue of *The Spectator* to the moral value of history painting in general and of the cartoons in particular, in which he commended to his readers this initiative to engrave what the subscription described as 'the most valuable Set of portable Pictures in the World'. Tactful efforts were made to disguise the Frenchness of an artist announced as 'Signior Nicola Dorigny (lately come from Rome)'. The set was offered to subscribers for the 'modest' price of 4 guineas. This was easily the highest price ever asked in England for a set of prints.

Dorigny began work on the cartoons at Easter 1712. The first year was employed in making accurate scaled-down drawings, and in 1713 he brought over from Paris Charles Dupuis and Claude Du Bosc to help with the engraving. In January 1714 he advertised that proofs of two of the prints might be inspected by potential subscribers. Eventually, in March 1719, the subscription was closed; the plates were printed and in April the prints were delivered to subscribers. On 1 April 1719 Dorigny presented the king with two sets of the prints and gave one set to the prince of Wales and another to the princess. In recognition of these gifts Dorigny was presented with a large gold medal from the prince and with 100 guineas from the king. He was knighted by the king in June 1720 at the instance of the duke of Devonshire. A collection of ninety heads from

Dorigny's drawings of the tapestries dedicated to the princess of Wales was published in 1722.

According to Vertue, Dorigny was 'thick of hearing inclining to deafness' (Vertue, *Note books*, *Note Books*, 1.51) and did not understand English. His drawings, which Vertue admired, were sold by auction on 21 February 1723. Selling at from 6 to 12 guineas each, with 52 guineas for the cartoons, the total price realized was £320. Dorigny gave up engraving around that time owing to the impairment of his eyesight. On 9 April 1724 he retired to Paris with the means to live without working, thanks to his savings, legacies from relations, and the income he continued to derive from his engraved plates. There he was elected an *academicien* on 28 September 1725. In retirement he took up painting again and exhibited at the salons of 1739 and 1743. He died in Paris on 1 December 1746. According to Vertue, 'The Number of Plates gravd by Mr Dorigny big & small [came to] 153' (ibid., 1.56). His prints and drawings may be found in the Clarke collection at Worcester College, the Ashmolean Museum, and the Bodleian Library in Oxford, and also in the British Museum, London, the Bibliothèque Nationale, Paris, and the Nationalmuseum, Stockholm.

TIMOTHY CLAYTON

Sources T. Clayton, *The English print, 1688–1802* (1997) • A. Meyer, *Apostles in England: Sir James Thornhill and the legacy of Raphael's tapestry cartoons in England* (1996) • M. Roux and others, eds., *Inventaire du fonds français: graveurs du dix-huitième siècle*, 3 (1934), 490–507 • Vertue, *Note books* • *The Spectator* (19 Nov 1711)

Likenesses line engraving, pubd 1792, NPG • Barrett, line engraving, NPG; repro. in H. Walpole, *Catalogue of engravers* (1794)

Dorin, Joseph Alexander (1802–1872), East India Company servant, born at Edmonton, Middlesex, on 15 September 1802, was the son of Joseph Dorin, merchant, and his wife, Charlotte. He was educated at Henley School, and obtained a nomination to the Bengal branch of the East India Company's service, of which his elder brother William was already a member. At East India College, Haileybury, he was first prizeman of his year, and on his arrival in India in 1821 was made assistant to the accountant-general. During the whole of his career he was attached to the financial branch. On 12 April 1823 he married Anna Patton (1806–1863) in St John's Cathedral, Calcutta; they had two sons, Henry and James.

On his return from furlough in 1842 Dorin was entrusted by Lord Ellenborough, the governor-general, with the reorganization of Indian finance. He became the first financial secretary under the new arrangements in 1843. Praised by the authorities for his handling of the finances during the Anglo-Sikh wars, in 1851 he became one of the four members of Lord Dalhousie's council, in effect the executive of the government of India. He is credited with effecting a reduction in the rate of interest on the Indian debt, but in 1855 miscalculations of revenue and expenditures made it necessary to contract a new loan at the old rate. This occasioned a severe fall in Indian securities, and the government was harshly criticized.

While Dorin was a member of the executive council, two momentous events took place, the annexation of the kingdom of Oudh and the great uprising in north India known as the Indian mutiny. As senior member, Dorin attracted both praise and blame for decisions taken by the government in the two events. The widely circulated 'Red pamphlet' on the uprising of 1857, by G. B. Malleson, described him as utterly deficient in knowledge of India, and claimed that nowhere but in British India would he have had anything other than the most subordinate position. He was defended by another writer who argued that, while it was true that in his thirty years in India he had never been more than 16 miles from Calcutta, he was in constant touch with other officials who did know India. In regard to Oudh, its king had signed a treaty in 1837 giving the government of India the right to intervene if it considered his rule oppressive. The treaty had never been ratified by London, but Dorin argued that the king of Oudh need not be told this, for the government had the right to do what it felt was good for the country, which in this case was annexation and ending the kingdom's existence. There is some indication that Dalhousie did not wholly accept this reasoning, but it was Dorin's views that were finally accepted by the East India Company directors. In regard to the uprising, as a member of the supreme council, Dorin, like Dalhousie, at first did not believe the reports of widespread unrest in the army and among elements in the general population. In the end, however, even before the news of the decisive army mutiny on 12 May at Meerut reached Calcutta, he proposed such harsh punishment for mutinous soldiers that all the other members of the council dissented. During this time Dorin supported the governor-general in two very unpopular measures: one was the severe press censorship known as the Gagging Acts, and the other a bill prohibiting Indians from owning arms.

Dorin remained a member of the supreme council until 1858. On his return to England he was proposed for membership of the Council of India, the advisory group to the secretary of state for India, but he was not appointed. He spent the rest of his life in retirement, but under somewhat peculiar circumstances. When he returned to India in 1842 he had left his wife in Chepstow because of her ill health, but during much of the rest of his service in Calcutta, he had a companion, a widow, Margaret Christiana Twentyman, *née* Kelly (b. 1831), who returned with him to England when he retired. She lived with him in London as Mrs Dorington, with their two sons, Charles and William Dorington. After the death in 1863 of his first wife—whom he had apparently continued to visit—he married Margaret Christiana in 1864. He died at Place Street, St Lawrence Dene, Isle of Wight, on 22 December 1872, and was buried in the churchyard at St Rhadagund's, St Lawrence. His attempts to provide for his illegitimate sons in his will were overturned after a series of bitter lawsuits brought by the only surviving child of Dorin's elder legitimate son. The case of *Dorin* v. *Dorin* and others was a leading case in civil law until the Legitimacy Act of 1925.

The judgement made of Dorin by the historian Sir John Kaye, that he held high office under successive governors-general because he agreed with them, 'which saved trouble and gained favour', is perhaps not too far from the mark, but while he was not one of the famed 'Rulers of India', he was representative of those who, possessing only average abilities and no great knowledge of India, held the fabric of the British empire in India together.

RICHARD GARNETT, rev. AINSLIE T. EMBREE

Sources Bengal, Madras and Bombay Service Lists, 1753–1859 · B. M. Cook, 'The lonely lady of the Mount', Journal of the Gwent Local History Council, 81 (autumn 1996), 20–50 · East-India Register and Directory (1803–58) · India Proceedings and Consultations · J. W. Kaye and G. B. Malleson, Kaye's and Malleson's History of the Indian mutiny of 1857–8, new edn, 6 vols. (1909) · C. Allen, A few words anent the Red Pamphlet (1858) · W. Lee-Warner, The life of the Marquis of Dalhousie, 2 vols. (1904) · G. B. Malleson, The mutiny of the Bengal army (1857) [the 'Red Pamphlet'] · CGPLA Eng. & Wales (1873)
Wealth at death under £12,000 (in England): probate, 16 Jan 1873, CGPLA Eng. & Wales

Dorion, Sir Antoine-Aimé (1818–1891), lawyer and politician in Canada, was born on 17 January 1818 at St Anne-de-la-Pérade, Lower Canada, the second of the ten children of Pierre-Antoine Dorion, a merchant descended from Pierre Dorion, who had emigrated from the Basses-Pyrénées of France in 1684, and his wife, Geneviève Bureau. Antoine-Aimé was brought up in a liberal and nationalist home. His father sat in the assembly as a supporter of *patriote* causes: Louis-Joseph Papineau was a visitor to his home. Although his father later lost his fortune, Dorion, like his male peers in the Lower-Canadian bourgeoisie, received a classical education. After attending the Séminaire de Nicolet (1830–37) he studied law under Côme-Séraphin Cherrier (1838–42), and was called to the bar in 1842. On 12 August 1848 in Montreal he married Iphigénie, the daughter of Dr Jean-Baptiste Trestler, with whom he had one son and three daughters.

While politics were Dorion's first love he did practise law in Montreal with Cherrier and headed the Montreal bar in 1861–2 and 1873–5. Active in politics by the late 1840s, he was identified as a moderate Liberal among the opponents of the dominant conservatism of Louis-Hyppolyte LaFontaine and George-Étienne Cartier. By the early 1850s he had succeeded Louis-Joseph Papineau and was leader of the *rouge* party. Dorion was always perceived as a moderate and played a prominent role in founding the *rouge* newspaper Le Pays. He favoured universal suffrage, free, universal education, and an end to the corruption endemic in Canadian politics. A strong defender of private property and trade reciprocity with the United States, he supported economic development through the construction of canals and railways. Much of Dorion's energies were devoted to the issue of anti-clericalism in his party and the role of the Roman Catholic church in politics. A practising Catholic and a moderate on the issue of church-held seigneurial lands, he eventually distanced himself from the increasingly anti-clerical Institut Canadien, of which his brother Jean-Baptiste-Éric was a founder and president (1850–51). In 1854 he was elected for Montreal in the legislative assembly, a victory he owed in large measure to English-speaking voters. His signing of the annexation manifesto (1849) calling for annexation to the United States had brought him contact with liberal

members of the anglophone community. Indeed, his ties with English-speaking liberals led to nationalist charges that he was not strong enough in his defence of the French language.

In August 1858 Dorion joined George Brown in a short-lived administration. After being defeated by George-Étienne Cartier in the elections of 1861 he came back into the assembly in 1862 and became provincial secretary in the administration of John Sandfield Macdonald and Louis-Victor Sicotte. He remained in the cabinet less than a year, resigning over hostility to expansion of the Grand Trunk Railway. Although he was back in the government two months later, the government lasted less than a year, being defeated in March 1864. Dorion was not then a part of the 'Great Coalition' which shepherded the union of British North America.

Although he had earlier supported the idea of a federation of Upper and Lower Canada, Dorion opposed the Quebec Resolutions, which he described as 'the most illiberal constitution ever heard of in any country where constitutional government prevails' (cited in Young, 81). He was particularly concerned with provincial autonomy and the future of the French-Canadian minority in the proposed confederation of British North America.

Dorion's brother Jean-Baptiste-Éric Dorion (1826–1866), the *enfant terrible* of Lower Canadian politics and editor of L'Avenir, was an even more outspoken opponent of confederation, fearing that, in the long term, it would destroy French Canada, and was much stronger in his nationalism and his opposition to seigneurial tenure. Although another brother, Abbé Hercule Dorion, was a missionary, Jean-Baptiste-Éric was known for his passionate anti-clericalism.

In the post-confederation years, Antoine-Aimé Dorion played an important role in the transformation of the Liberal Party in Quebec into a moderate party acceptable to Catholic authorities. He also served as minister of justice of Canada for a short period (November 1873–May 1874) in the government of Alexander Mackenzie and was appointed a knight bachelor in 1877. Happy to leave politics, he accepted nomination in 1874 as chief justice of the court of queen's bench for Quebec, a position he held until, following a stroke, he died, on 31 May 1891, at his home on Sherbrooke Street, Montreal.

BRIAN YOUNG

Sources J. C. Soulard, 'Dorion, Sir Antoine-Aimé', DCB, vol. 12 · P. Sylvain, 'Dorion, Jean-Baptiste-Éric', DCB, vol. 9 · J.-P. Bernard, Les rouges (1971) · P. B. Waite, The life and times of confederation, 1864–1867 (1962) · J. M. S. Careless, The union of the Canadas: the growth of Canadian institutions, 1841–1857 (1967) · J. C. Soulard, 'Esquisse biographique et pensée politique d'un adversaire de la confédération: Antoine-Aimé Dorion, chef du parti rouge (1818–1891)', MA diss., Laval University, 1976 · B. Young, George-Étienne Cartier (1981)

Dorislaus, Isaac (1595–1649), scholar and diplomat, was born at Alkmaar in Holland, the son of Lieven Dorislaer (1555–1652), burgher and later Calvinist minister of Hensbrock (1627), then Enkhuizen (1628). The second of three sons (tellingly named Abraham, Isaac, and Jacob), he was educated from 1610 at Leiden, where he took the degree of LLD in 1627. He taught as conrector of the Latin school while studying law. By 1622 he was married to Elisabeth Pope of Maldon, Essex; the couple lived in his father's Leiden household, together with three English students.

In 1627 Fulke Greville, Lord Brooke, appointed Dorislaus the first incumbent of his newly founded history lectureship at Cambridge, though only after failing to secure the eminent Leiden scholar Gerhardus Vossius for the post. Dorislaus moved to England in October; lacking accommodation in Cambridge, his family settled with his father-in-law in Maldon while he himself became the houseguest of Samuel Ward, master of Sidney Sussex College.

An admirer of Francis Bacon's *Of the Proficience and Advancement of Learning*, which he owned and annotated (CUL, MS LE 7.45), Dorislaus must have found the ordinances establishing the lectureship much to his liking. Brooke's avowed aim was that 'humane learning, the use and application thereof to the practice of life, [be] the main end and scope of this foundation' (CUL, MS Mm.1.47, fol. 146). But it was just that possibility of practical application that brought the history lecture to an early demise. Dorislaus gave just two lectures on Tacitus's *Annals* before the master of Peterhouse, Matthew Wren, led a successful movement to silence him as a danger to monarchical government.

Dorislaus's first lecture, on the origins of regal authority in ancient Rome, delineated two types of monarchy, both founded on the voluntary transferral of natural sovereignty from the people to the ruler. In one form, the body of people transfers its power to a monarch without retaining sovereignty to itself; in the other, which Dorislaus clearly preferred, the people reserve particular rights for themselves, bestowing strictly limited powers upon a king. A king who by force usurps the people's rights is a tyrant and liable to deposition; his case in point was Junius Brutus's expulsion of Tarquin. His second lecture recounted at greater length the ancient tyrant's abuses of law, his deposition, and the replacement of monarchy with consular government—an act that won Brutus 'the applause of gods and men' (PRO, SP 16/86/no. 87.I, fol. 177). The lecturer identified popular consent with liberty, royal disregard of law with slavery; Matthew Wren identified the lecturer with republicanism and regicide, complaining that 'he seemed to acknowledge no right of kingdoms, but whereof the people's voluntary submission had been the constituting principle' (ibid., fol. 175). Wren found the lectures 'stored with such dangerous passages, … and so appliable to the exasperations of these villanous times', that he brought formal complaint to the vice-chancellor, Thomas Bainbridge. He was disappointed to find that the majority of the vice-chancellor's court had taken no offence at the lectures, but found that Dorislaus had spoken, as Samuel Ward reported, 'with great moderation' in 'defence of the liberties of the people' and 'with an exception of such monarchies as ours' (*Whole Works of … James Ussher*, 1843, 15.403). As it happens, Dorislaus's defenders on the university court were without exception his Calvinist co-religionists, while his opponents were, like Wren, defenders of Arminian theology and the ceremonial worship associated with William Laud. The lines

of division suggest that differences in political theory paralleled and may have been exacerbated by religious differences.

When the Cambridge heads declined to condemn Dorislaus, Wren pursued his complaint through bishops Laud and Richard Neile to the king, meanwhile delaying until 1631 Dorislaus's incorporation as a doctor of Cambridge University. Ward led the defence, marshalling the majority of the vice-chancellor's court to send letters to Brooke, the duke of Buckingham, and Laud indicating their approval of the lecturer. Wren's letters seem to have carried more weight, however, and the king prohibited Dorislaus from lecturing again. Lord Brooke declined to challenge the opposition. He offered his lecturer lodging in London, then on his own estate near Doncaster, where Dorislaus continued to collect his stipend while living, he complained, 'sunk in provincial solitude' (Bodl. Oxf., MS Tanner 72.132, fol. 284).

After Brooke's murder in September 1628, a codicil to his will was found to make Dorislaus's tenure of the lectureship lifelong and to guarantee his annuity. He took advantage of the terms of his settlement to travel extensively during the following decade, and in 1630 was resident in the Sorbonne. His scholarly interests turned for a time to military history: in 1632 he secured through Sir Kenelm Digby and the secretary of state, Coke, access to state papers to do the research for his single publication, an account of the 1600 battle of Nieuwpoort, and especially the role of Sir Francis Vere, published in 1640 as the *Praelium Nuportanum*. His family life during this period was troubled by illness: his eldest son, John, died in 1632 aged four, and by 1634 his wife was on her deathbed.

Dorislaus's principal occupation during the final decade of his life was legal advocacy. He had been admitted a commoner of the College of Advocates in 1629 and in 1640 served as judge advocate in the bishops' wars. In 1642 he threw in his lot with parliament, serving as advocate of the army. He attempted to prosecute under martial law two of Waller's accomplices in the 1643 plot to recover London for the king, but failed due to the Commons' concern about violation of parliamentary privilege. In 1644 his investigation of another royalist plot threatened to expose a link between the plot's sponsor, John Lovelace, Lord Lovelace, and Sir Henry Vane, commissioner of parliament to the army. Vane retaliated by charging Dorislaus with price-fixing in the sale of prize goods taken at Weymouth; Dorislaus, who had overseen the sale, cleared himself of the charge by a deposition before the Commons, who clearly held him in high regard: an ordinance of April 1648 made him one of the judges of the court of admiralty. This position led to his first diplomatic mission, with Walter Strickland, to the states general of the United Provinces concerning privileges being accorded 'revolted ships' by Dutch provinces sympathetic with the royalists. Cromwell's regard for the intelligence reports that the envoy brought back to England in December led to his intervention with the master of Trinity Hall to secure for Dorislaus and his remaining children chambers in Doctors' Commons in London, the residence of civil lawyers attached to the high court of admiralty.

In January 1649 the commissioners for the trial of Charles I appointed Dorislaus one of the counsel for the prosecution. He helped to draw up the charge of high treason, the preamble of which echoes the language of his Cambridge lectures, arguing for lawful deposition of tyrants who deprive subjects of their freedom and privileges. Dorislaus did not speak during the trial, but he explained to a correspondent that he would have, had the king acknowledged the court and answered the charge.

In the spring following the execution Dorislaus sought from the council of state the position of keeper of the library of St James, but agreed first to perform one last diplomatic mission as resident of parliament at The Hague. The mission proved fatal for the envoy. On 2 May 1649 a group of royalists led by Walter Whitford, son of Bishop Walter Whitford of Brechin, entered Dorislaus's inn at De Swaen and stabbed the envoy to death. The assassins were never brought to justice. Parliament had Dorislaus's body brought to Worcester House and laid in state, and issued a *Declaration on their Just Resentment of the Horrid Murther … of Isaac Dorislaus*, identifying the perpetrators as 'that party from whom all the troubles of this nation have formerly sprung' (*Acts of Parliament* (1648–50), 1.92). On 14 June, after an elaborate funeral provided by parliament at a cost of £250, Dorislaus was buried in Westminster Abbey; after the Restoration he was reinterred in St Margaret's churchyard. An act of parliament awarded £500 to each of his surviving two daughters, Elizabeth and Margaret, and an annuity of £200 to his son, Isaac [*see below*] (*JHC*, 6.209). English complaint about Dutch failure to apprehend his murderers was one of the issues brought by an English delegation to the states general in 1651; among the plaintiffs was Dorislaus's son.

The younger **Isaac Dorislaus** (d. 1688) was educated at the Merchant Taylors' School from 1639. In 1649 he became a registrar for the probate of wills in Ely and Cambridgeshire. His linguistic skills led to employment by Thurloe as a translator and intelligence agent in the 1650s. In 1653 he was appointed solicitor to the court of admiralty; in 1660 he became one of the managers of the Post Office, a position he retained after the Restoration. He was elected a fellow of the Royal Society in 1681. He died in 1688, survived by three children, Isaac, James, and Anne, and was buried in St Bartholomew by the Exchange, Bartholomew Lane.   MARGO TODD

Sources M. Todd, 'Anti-Calvinists and the republican threat in early Stuart Cambridge', *Puritanism and its discontents*, ed. L. Knoppers (2002) • P. A. Maccioni and M. Mostert, 'Isaac Dorislaus (1595–1649): the career of a Dutch scholar in England', *Transactions of the Cambridge Bibliographical Society*, 8 (1981–5), 419–70 • Wren on Dorislaus's lectures, PRO, SP 16/86/no. 87, 16/86/no. 87.I • Dorislaus to Sir Francis Nethersole, 1626, PRO, SP 16/527/no. 28 • Dorislaus's correspondence, Bodl. Oxf., MSS Tanner 71, 72, 114, 144 • ordinances of the history lecture, CUL, MS Mm.1.47, 143–52 • *Gerardi Joannis Vossii et clarorum virorum ad eum epistolae* (1690) • *Briefwisseling van Hugo Grotius*, ed. B. L. Meulenbroek and P. P. Witkam, 4 vols. (The Hague, 1981) • 'The informacion of … servants to Dr. Dorislaus deceased, who were present at his death', CUL, Mm.1.46 [read to Commons, 14 May 1649] • *CSP dom.*, 1631–3; 1644–5; 1649–52 • *The manuscripts of the Earl Cowper*, 3 vols., HMC, 23 (1888–9), vol. 1 • *Report of the Laing manuscripts*, 1, HMC, 72 (1914) • Wood, *Ath. Oxon.*, new edn, 3.666–8, 1018 • Dorislaus to Vossius, 1627, Bodl. Oxf., MS Rawl. B. 84, fols. 63–4, 157

Archives BL, Add. MSS 29960, 29974 (2), 5873 • Hunt. L., MS HM 371 | Bodl. Oxf., MS Rawl. B. 84 • Bodl. Oxf., MSS Tanner 71, 72, 114, 144

Likenesses engraving, pubd 1649, repro. in S. van Stolk, *Woedende wraeck van Isack Dorislaen* [1649] • engraving, pubd 1652 (Isaac Dorislaus?), repro. in *Dr Dorislaw's ghost* (1652) • W. Richardson, engraving, pubd 1792 (after anonymous drawing, 17th cent.), BM, NPG • I. Buys, line engraving, NPG

Wealth at death will, PRO, PROB 11/334, sig. 142, 14 Nov 1645 • Isaac Dorislaus (d. 1688): will, PRO, PROB 11/393, sig. 134; probate act book, PRO, PROB 8/81, fol. 151

Dorislaus, Isaac (d. 1688). *See under* Dorislaus, Isaac (1595–1649).

Dorman, Sir Arthur John, first baronet (1848–1931), steel manufacturer, was born at Ashford, Kent, on 8 August 1848, the son of Charles Dorman, a currier who later became a coal and timber merchant, and his wife, Emma Cage. He was educated at Christ's Hospital and spent a short period in Paris before beginning, at the age of eighteen, an apprenticeship to an iron manufacturer in Stockton-on-Tees, co. Durham. By 1873 he had become a metal broker, and in that year he married Clara, daughter of George Lockwood, a local merchant and shipbuilder. They had four sons and three daughters.

Having started with some £1500 of capital, in 1876 Dorman launched a partnership with Albert de Lande Long by taking over an existing plant, the West Marsh ironworks, Middlesbrough. With its puddling furnaces and rolling mill, the company initially manufactured iron bars and angles for shipbuilding. In the 1880s, however, the firm switched to the more productive and profitable new steel-making technologies by installing open-hearth furnaces and exploiting the breakthroughs of Percy Carlisle Gilchrist and his cousin, Sidney Gilchrist Thomas. By 1901 the company was a major manufacturer in the north-east, with a labour force of about 3000 and an output of about 180,000 tons of finished material a year. It competed for a place both at home and abroad with the principal creators of the iron and steel industry in the north-east, Henry Bolckow and Sir Isaac Lowthian Bell. Another surge of expansion occurred between 1900 and 1914, when the trend in the steel industry was towards vertical integration and merger. In 1902 Dorman Long absorbed Bell Bros. (with its distinguished but ageing head, Sir Isaac Lowthian Bell, still at the helm) and then acquired another substantial local firm, the North Eastern Steel Company. By 1914 Dorman Long, with a workforce of about 20,000, was a dominant firm on Teesside and a major British steel producer.

As both chairman and managing director, Dorman was the key decision maker in the company. Tall and imposing, he had many of the characteristics of the other great Victorian ironmasters: optimism, daring, a great capacity for hard work, and a keen interest in technical improvements. He enjoyed the trappings of wealth (though not for their own sake) and had a paternalistic attitude to his own firm and the local community. He also demonstrated some of the faults of the industry, in which many of the leading merged firms were imperfectly integrated and directed by elderly managers, who were reluctant to delegate authority and even more reluctant to retire.

These faults were exacerbated by an even more profitable and hectic phase of growth during the First World War, which saw Dorman Long become a major supplier of shells. It started to construct a £4.5 million plant at Redcar, Yorkshire, and also acquired several other large companies, such as Samuelsons and Carlton Iron. Dorman, made a KBE in 1918 and a baronet in 1923, emerged from the war more dominant and apparently more powerful than ever. But his company did not fare well in the black decade of the 1920s, and found itself crippled by inefficient plant and poor management. Although in his seventies, Dorman retained the chairmanship, working alongside the even more geriatric Sir (Thomas) Hugh Bell. Dorman's sons, Charles and Arthur, were brought into the business, though neither was able entirely to replace their father, who continued to make the key decisions through the 1920s. Most of these proved inappropriate in a period of slump, and at the end of the decade Dorman Long reflected the feebleness of its chairman. Over-capitalized and burdened with debts, Dorman sought refuge in another merger in 1929 with an equally ailing neighbour, Bolckow Vaughan. In the depression this move failed to turn the company's fortune, and not until after Dorman had departed (literally, for he never retired) were overdue managerial reforms effected.

A typical Victorian owner–founder, Dorman was better at conquering new fields than properly organizing what he had acquired. However, it has been argued persuasively that Dorman's later period of 'gerontocracy, dynastic weakness and inefficiency, superimposed on economic stress, should not be allowed to obscure his great qualities of intrepidity, resourcefulness and flair' (*DBB*). He died on 12 February 1931 at his home, Grey Towers, Nunthorpe, near Middlesbrough, Yorkshire.

GEOFFREY TWEEDALE

Sources J. S. Boswell, 'Dorman, Sir Arthur John', *DBB* · *The Times* (13 Feb 1931) · J. S. Boswell, *Business policies in the making: three steel companies compared* (1983) · S. Tolliday, *Business, banking and politics: the case of British steel, 1918–1939* (1987) · D. L. Burn, *The economic history of steelmaking, 1867–1939* (1940) · J. C. Carr and W. Taplin, *History of the British steel industry* (1962) · *CGPLA Eng. & Wales* (1931) · b. cert. · d. cert.
Archives British Steel Records Centre, Irthlingborough, Northamptonshire, east midlands region, Dorman Long records · Cleveland Archives, Dorman Long records | Durham RO, Mainsforth colliery records
Wealth at death £132,173 17s.: probate, 8 April 1931, *CGPLA Eng. & Wales*

Dorman, Sir Maurice Henry (1912–1993), colonial governor, was born on 7 August 1912, the elder son of John Ehrenfried Dorman, of Eastgate, Stafford, an engineer with W. H. Dorman & Co., and Madeleine Louise, née Bostock, dentist. Her family owned Lotus Shoes. From Sedbergh School Dorman went up to Magdalene College, Cambridge, where he took a lower second class in history.

Sir Maurice Henry Dorman (1912–1993), by Anthony Buckley, 1967

On graduation he applied for the colonial service and in 1935 was posted to Tanganyika as an administrative cadet. After only ten years' service, during which he had caught his superiors' eyes by his work as clerk of councils in Tanganyika from 1940 to 1945, he was singled out as assistant to the lieutenant-governor of Malta, the civilian deputy to the traditionally armed forces holder of the governorship of that 'fortress' colony. Already on the fast track, Dorman was promoted in 1947 as principal assistant secretary in Jerusalem, where the Palestine mandate was in its final stormy years. In 1948 he was seconded to the Colonial Office to take charge of the rapidly expanding social services department. With a successful tenure behind him, Dorman was posted to the Gold Coast in 1950, as director of social welfare and community development. By now his reputation was such that in 1952 he was chosen as colonial secretary of Trinidad and Tobago, conventionally a Colonial Office proving ground for potential governors. In 1956 the plum colonial service promotion to a governorship came with his appointment to Sierra Leone.

West Africa was already embarked on its decade of decolonization, but unlike its near neighbours Gold Coast and Nigeria, the relatively sleepier Sierra Leone (despite its conspicuous Creole élite in the capital, Freetown) was not yet prey to the exuberance of colonial nationalism. Dorman's principal political challenge was to encourage the up-country protectorate into a closer relationship with the sophisticated colony area, while at the same time ensuring that the stimulated advance towards self-government was not accompanied by any breakdown in law and order. His outstanding tact, empathy, and emphasis on good relations with the emergent political leadership were evidenced in 1961 by the request of the newly independent government of Sir Milton Margai that Dorman should stay on as the country's first governor-general. Nor was this a mere token of courtesy, for despite the constitutional fact that the post was a figurehead devoid of any executive power, Dorman's advice was in the event frequently sought, discreetly given, and often quietly taken. Coincidentally, Dorman's younger brother Richard was to become Britain's deputy high commissioner in Freetown in 1964.

By then Dorman had left. Dramatic political changes in Malta brought him back to the island in 1962. The years of political stalemate had been broken by the success of Dr Borg Olivier at the polls, a political outcome reinforced by the economic threat of the likely reduction of Britain's historic naval presence in Malta. Perceiving that what was needed was firm guidance from a civilian at the helm rather than the conventional military appointment, the Colonial Office turned to Dorman, with his proven diplomatic skills and personal experience of the art of the transfer of power. Once again his natural humanity and enlightened attitude secured local confidence, to such an extent that despite several trials and tribulations he found himself genuinely identifying with the Maltese. Once more, as in Freetown in 1961, Dorman was invited, at Malta's independence in 1964, to become the island's first governor-general. Remarkably, he remained in office for seven years, not leaving until 1971 when the new prime minister, Dom Mintoff, requested a local appointment. During his tenure Dorman turned the conventional role of the queen's representative upside-down, by speaking out against the defence cuts threatened by Britain and, to the dismay of Whitehall, declaring that he stood 'four square' with the government and people of Malta in their dispute with London.

Dorman's long service overseas was not yet finished. He was deputy chairman of the abortive Pearce commission in 1971–2 assessing African opinion on the Rhodesian government's constitutional proposals. He was to return to Rhodesia in 1980 as chairman of the British observer group monitoring the election which led to the independence of Zimbabwe.

After thirty-six years in the colonial service Dorman was ready to settle in England. With his wife, Florence Monica Churchward Smith (d. 1993), daughter of Montagu Smith of Devon, whom he had married on 4 December 1937 and with whom he had one son, John, and three daughters, he settled in Wiltshire. He turned his administrative talents to health administration, spending the next decade as chairman of the Swindon hospital management committee and then of the Wiltshire (and later the Swindon) Health Authority. He was a trustee of the Imperial War Museum and chairman of the West of England Building

Society, and also life governor of Monkton Combe School and president of the Old Sedberghians' Club. From 1972 to 1975 he was deputy lieutenant for Wiltshire.

Dorman's colonial service was recognized by his appointment as CMG in 1955; he was advanced to KCMG in 1957 and to GCMG as well as being made GCVO in 1961. A committed Christian, Dorman and his wife were both active in the order of St John, whose fortress home had long been in Malta. He was successively chief almoner and chief commander of the St John Ambulance Brigade, becoming lord prior in 1980. He was also made knight grand cross of the Maltese order of merit. Academic honours included honorary degrees from Durham University and the Royal University of Malta. His hobbies he recorded as 'once sailing, squash, and sometimes golf' (*WWW*). He and his wife were deeply appreciated in Malta as patrons of the arts, and regularly made the Palace of San Anton available to the local dramatic society. On retirement they built a private house at Fawwara in the hope of spending part of each year in Malta.

Although Dorman's career spanned the transition from the high noon of empire, when he was a district officer in Tanganyika, through the transfer of power, in which he was the last colonial governor of Sierra Leone, to the emergence of the Commonwealth, where he was the first (and last) British governor-general of an independent Malta, his part was never that of the typical pro-consul of empire. Throughout he combined the professionalism of a colonial administrator with the enlightenment and empathy of a constitutional monarch. He accepted and accomplished the challenge, as his colonial service peer Lord Grey put it, 'to look and play the part and achieve by personality what had hitherto been won by laying down the law' (*The Independent*, 10 Nov 1993). He was not only one of the last distinguished overseas career civil servants, he was also one of that handful of adaptable final colonial governors whose emollient yet fundamentally firm and fair role and capacity for personal friendship with the nationalist leadership were instrumental in effecting a smooth and mutually respecting transfer of power.

Dorman died of cancer at his home, the Old Manor, Overton, Wiltshire, on 26 October 1993. His widow, appointed dame of the order of St John of Jerusalem in her own right in 1968, died six weeks later.

A. H. M. KIRK-GREENE

Sources *The Times* (29 Oct 1993) · *The Independent* (10 Nov 1993) · *Malta Independent* (Nov 1993) · *Magdalene College Magazine and Record* (1994) · A. Abelse, *Governors of Malta* (1991) · personal knowledge (2004) · *WWW* · Burke, *Peerage* · private information [M. C. Curran] · *CGPLA Eng. & Wales* (1993)

Archives Bodl. RH, papers relating to his career | FILM BFI NFTVA, documentary footage

Likenesses A. Buckley, photograph, 1967, NPG [*see illus.*] · photograph, repro. in *The Independent* · photograph, repro. in *The Times*

Wealth at death £305,262: probate, 30 Dec 1993, *CGPLA Eng. & Wales*

Dorman, Thomas (*c.*1534–*c.*1577), religious controversialist, was born at Berkhamsted, Hertfordshire, and is of unknown parentage. His uncle, Thomas Dorman of Agmondesham in Buckinghamshire, funded his primary education under the protestant Richard Reeve. In 1547, under the auspices of Thomas Harding, he entered Winchester College. About 1550 he was made a probationer fellow of New College, Oxford, and in 1554 he was elected a full fellow of All Souls College, where he studied law, graduating BCL in July 1558. It seems probable that Dorman originally was inclined toward protestantism and only later, under the influence of Harding, embraced Catholicism. He left Oxford about 1561 and made his way to Louvain, where he pursued theological studies and received his BTh in June 1565. It was while in Louvain that he took up his pen on behalf of Harding against Bishop John Jewel.

Dorman's historical significance lies in his role as a member of the Louvain coterie of Catholic controversialists who mounted a massive response to Jewel's famous 'challenge sermon' delivered at Paul's Cross in London on 16 November 1559. In this sermon Jewel boldly challenged his adversaries: if they could produce one authentic sentence from the fathers of the first six centuries demonstrating such practices as private masses, withdrawal of the cup from the laity, the universal authority of the bishop of Rome and transubstantiation, then he would personally subscribe to these teachings of the Catholic church. During the height of the controversy, from 1564 to 1568, the Louvain Catholics published forty-five separate volumes principally against Jewel. The vitriolic nature of the controversy derives in part from the personal animosity existing between former friends and colleagues at Oxford University who subsequently chose different sides in the Reformation debate.

All three of Dorman's books derive from this controversy. The first and most important book, *A Proufe of Certayne Articles in Religion, Denied by M. Juell* (1564), and dedicated to Thomas Harding, explicitly dealt with Jewel's 'challenge sermon'. Dorman defended the Catholic cause on the whole range of issues raised by Jewel, but especially on papal authority. Jewel, in his *Defence of the Apology of the Church of England* (1562), three times mockingly cites Dorman's assertion that 'the Pope is the head and kings and princes are the feet' (Dorman, fol. 15.2). Jewel never responded directly to Dorman, but Jewel's close friend Alexander Nowell, dean of St Paul's, did. In an exchange of five books over three years Nowell took it upon himself to answer Dorman's first work as well as his second, *A Disproufe of M. Nowelle's Reproufe* (1565). Dorman turned again to Jewel with his last book, *A request to Mr. Jewel that he keep his promise made by solemn protestation in his late sermon at Paul's Cross* (1567).

In 1569 Dorman joined William Allen at the English College in Douai. He continued to be identified as a threat as late as 1576, when Archbishop Edmund Grindal instructed the English clergy to be on watch for the writings of Thomas Dorman and the Louvain Catholics, whom he charged with denying, not only the protestant faith, but also Elizabeth's supremacy over the Church of England. In Dorman's later years he took a pastoral charge in the city of Tournai, where he died about 1577.

FRANK A. JAMES III

Sources J. E. Booty, *John Jewel as apologist of the Church of England* (1963) · *The works of John Jewel*, ed. J. Ayre, 4 vols., Parker Society, 24 (1845–50) · T. Dorman, *A proufe of certayne articles in religion, denied by M. Juell* (1564) · G. E. Corrie, ed., *Nowell's catechism*, Parker Society (1853) · W. Nicholson, ed., *The remains of Edmund Grindal*, Parker Society, 9 (1843) · Wood, *Ath. Oxon.*, new edn · Wood, *Ath. Oxon.: Fasti* (1815) · A. Wood, *The history and antiquities of the colleges and halls in the University of Oxford*, ed. J. Gutch (1786) · *Hist. U. Oxf.* 3: *Colleg. univ.* · C. Haigh, *English reformations: religion, politics, and society under the Tudors* (1993) · J. Jewel, *Sermon pronounced by the byshop of Salisburie at Paul's Crosse* (1560) · *DNB*

Dormer [*née* Cottrell], **Anne** (1648?–1695), letter-writer, was the second of five children of Sir Charles *Cotterell or Cottrell (1615–1701), translator and master of ceremonies under Charles I, Charles II, and James II, and his wife, Frances West (1620–*c*.1656), of Marsworth, Buckinghamshire. Strong royalists, Anne's family, who in January 1649 were living at York House, the duke of Buckingham's London residence, left in March for the Netherlands but Anne remained 'at nurse' in England (Thomas, 2.174). Her mother returned to England in 1655 and died before Sir Charles returned in 1660. Anne spent part of her youth with her aunt and uncle, Bridget and Thomas Clayton, in Oxford. It appears that she was a favourite in her family, receiving a larger share than her siblings from her grandmother Cottrell's will and regular presents from Roger Pratt, the architect and half-brother of her mother. After attending a school in Clerkenwell, Middlesex, she lived in her father's house in Spring Gardens, St James's Park.

Anne may have enjoyed the friendship of Edward Browne, the elder son of Sir Thomas Browne, but on 10 December 1668, at St Andrew's, Holborn, she married a widower, Robert Dormer (1628?–1689), of Dorton, Buckinghamshire, and Rousham, Oxfordshire. Besides a stepson, Robert, who was ten when Anne married his father, Anne had eleven children with Dormer, eight of whom survived to adulthood. Three sons had military careers; Philip died at the battle of Blenheim and Charles at Almanza; James *Dormer (1679–1741) retired as a notable general and inherited the family estate (subsequently known as Rousham Park), which he bequeathed to his cousin Clement Cottrell.

From 1685 to 1691 Anne wrote a series of intimate and informative letters describing her life, her marriage, and her neighbours, to her younger sister Elizabeth (or Katherine; 1652?–1704) while the latter was in France and Constantinople. Elizabeth had married envoy and ambassador Sir William Trumbull. In nearly 60,000 words (BL, Add. MS 72516) the letters offer one early modern woman's representation of daily life over a six-year period and a detailed anatomy of a strife-filled marriage. They document the local and domestic repercussions of the political turmoil both before and after the revolution of 1688. They also contain a wealth of details about material culture, child rearing, daily activities, and illnesses such as the death by cancer of Anne's sister-in-law Elizabeth Cotterell. Despite Anne's claim that she had a 'soft nature' (Dormer, fol. 176r), inclined to a 'naturall bashfulness' (ibid., fol. 205r), and that she struggled with melancholy all her life she shows—in her argumentative voices and her occasional bawdy wit—that she had a strong character and a sense of righteousness, one that was strengthened by her letter-writing and even created through it. In her will, drawn up on 5 July 1695, she left money to all her children, to her father, and to charities but the bulk of her £4000 was bequeathed to her only surviving daughter, Frances (who later married Sir Samuel Daniel). Anne died shortly after making her will and was buried on 19 July at St Mary's, Long Crendon, Buckinghamshire.

MARY E. O'CONNOR

Sources A. Dormer, letters, 1685–91, BL, Add. MS 72516, fols. 156–241 · parish register, Long Crendon, St Mary, Bucks. RLSS, 5 July 1695 [burial] · R. T. Gunther, ed., *The architecture of Sir Roger Pratt* (1928), 3 · S. H. Keith-Roach, '"[T]o mingle my teares with yours": letters from Anne Dormer, c.1685–1691', MPhil diss., U. Cam., 1995 · GL, MS 6668/1 · will, PRO, PROB 11/429, fol. 232 · G. C. R. Morris, 'Sir Thomas Browne's daughters, "Cosen Barker", and the Cottrells', *N&Q*, 231 (1986), 472–9 · M. O'Connor, 'Representations of intimacy in the life-writing of Anne Clifford and Anne Dormer', *Representations of the self from the Renaissance to romanticism*, ed. P. Coleman, J. Lewis, and J. Kowalik (2000), 79–96 · M. Paige-Hagg, *The monumental brasses of Buckinghamshire*, Monumental Brass Society (1994), 52 · P. Thomas, 'Sir Charles Cotterell and Katherine Philips', in *The collected works of Katherine Philips the matchless Orinda*, ed. P. Thomas, 2 (1992), appx 4, 157–95 · HoP, *Commons, 1660–90* · *VCH Oxfordshire*, vols. 8–9 · *The life and times of Anthony Wood*, ed. A. Clark, 5 vols., OHS, 19, 21, 26, 30, 40 (1891–1900)

Archives BL, Add. MS 72516, fols. 156–241 · Rousham House, Oxfordshire, Cottrell-Dormer MSS

Likenesses G. Kneller, oils, c.1685, priv. coll. · P. Lely, oils, priv. coll.

Wealth at death £4000: will, PRO, PROB 11/429, fol. 232

Dormer, Sir Clement Cottrell-. *See* Cottrell, Sir Clement (1686–1758).

Dormer, James (1679–1741), army officer, was born on 16 March 1679, the son of Robert Dormer (1628?–1689) of Dorton, Buckinghamshire, and his second wife, Anne [*see* Dormer, Anne], daughter of the diplomat Sir Charles *Cotterell. He was appointed lieutenant and captain 1st regiment of foot guards in May 1702, in which rank he was wounded at Blenheim, and later served at Ramillies. Appointed colonel of Lord Mohun's regiment of foot in May 1708, he went to Spain, and distinguished himself at Saragossa in 1709, and was taken prisoner with General James Stanhope at Brihuega in Castile in December 1710. He was awarded £200 for his losses by pillage at Brihuega and at Bilbao on his way home on parole (*Calendar of Treasury Papers*, 137.8). He was made brigadier-general in February 1711; his regiment was disbanded in 1713. In 1715 he was commissioned as colonel to raise a regiment of dragoons in the south of England, which became the 14th hussars. He commanded a brigade during the Jacobite rising in Lancashire, and was engaged with the rebels at Preston. Transferred to the colonelcy of the 6th foot in 1720, in June 1725 he was sent as envoy-extraordinary to Lisbon, where he had a dispute with Thomas Burnett, the British consul; he was appointed a major-general in 1727 and lieutenant-general in 1735, colonel 1st troop of Horse Grenadier Guards in 1737, and governor of Hull in 1740.

Dormer was a member of the Kit-Cat Club, and, according to Nichols, the collector of a fine library. He died at Crendon, Buckinghamshire, on 24 December 1741 where he was buried on 2 January 1742. He was unmarried, and bequeathed the estates of Chearsley in Buckinghamshire and Rousham in Oxfordshire to his cousin Sir Clement *Cottrell (afterwards Cottrell-Dormer), master of the ceremonies to George II.

H. M. CHICHESTER, *rev.* JONATHAN SPAIN

Sources C. Dalton, ed., *English army lists and commission registers, 1661–1714*, 5 (1902), pt 2, pp. 1–133 [Blenheim Roll] · G. Lipscomb, *The history and antiquities of the county of Buckingham*, 4 vols. (1831–47), vol. 1, p. 119 · J. Granger, *A biographical history of England, from Egbert the Great to the revolution*, 4th edn, 4 vols. (1804), vol. 3, p. 423 · *GM*, 1st ser., 11 (1741), 166 · Burke, *Gen. GB* (1972) [Cotterell-Dormer] · J. Redington, ed., *Calendar of Treasury papers*, 4, PRO (1879), 308 · Nichols, *Lit. anecdotes*

Archives BL, dispatches, Add. MS 32753 · BL, dispatches, Egerton Ch 8224 · BL, dispatches, Egerton MS 921 · priv. coll., family MSS

Likenesses J. B. van Loo, oils, Rousham House, Oxfordshire

Dormer, Jane. *See* Suárez de Figueroa, Jane, duchess of Feria in the Spanish nobility (1538–1612).

Dormer, John. *See* Huddleston, John (1636–1700).

Dormer, John (1730–1796), army officer in the Austrian service, was born on 18 February 1730 at Grove Park, Warwickshire, the second son of John, seventh Baron Dormer (1691–1785), of Grove Park, and Mary (d. 1739), daughter of Sir Cecil Bishopp of Parkham, Sussex. The Dormers were an Anglo-Catholic family with large estates in Warwickshire and Buckinghamshire, but the career prospects in England for a younger son of the Catholic aristocracy before emancipation were poor. Consequently John Dormer left England on 24 July 1752, and studied at the military academy in Vienna between September 1752 and August 1753. According to family papers (Warks. CRO, CR895/107) he joined General Count Luquesy's regiment of cuirassiers as a cornet in May 1754 and saw action against the Prussians in the Seven Years' War. After the battle of Prague (6 May 1757) he was promoted to captain and was present at Breslau (22 November 1757) and Leuthen (5 December 1757). After the battle of Stochkerch (18 September 1757) he was given command of the 4th squadron of carabiniers. At Maxen (18 November 1759) Dormer's squadron, together with General O'Donnell's carabiniers, relieved and saved a battalion of Croats, which had been surrounded by seven squadrons of Prussian dragoons. Dormer's squadron played an equally prominent role at Torgau (2 November 1760), taking five pairs of colours. In 1762 he became 2nd captain of the regiment, now the Kleinhold cuirassier regiment, and 1st captain in 1763. When his regiment was disbanded in 1768 he was transferred to Count Serbelloni's cuirassier regiment. On 29 January 1767 he was appointed chamberlain to Empress Maria Theresa.

On 22 May 1775 Dormer married Elizabeth (1753–1824), second daughter of General Count Gabriel Buttler of Erdo-Teleck, near Eslau in Hungary. In 1777 he established his family at Gran in Hungary, where he resided until his death. Following his retirement from the service, in January 1782 he was granted the brevet rank of major.

A small group of letters from Dormer to his family in

England during the 1790s has survived; these letters record his opinions on events in revolutionary France and the legal and civil condition of Catholics in England. On 4 December 1792 he wrote to his brother Charles, eighth Baron Dormer,

> I hope our countrymen will not suffer themselves to be outdone by the French in the generous strife to extend freedom and promote the happiness of mankind. Why should Protestants view us poor Roman Catholics with scornful and suspicious eyes … if they had seen us in private life, upright, quiet and faithful in our engagements and just in our dealings, why have we been deprived so long of the Rights of Man and why are so many younger brothers … obliged to exile themselves and search precarious fortunes in foreign climates, to avoid a dependent life.

He added that 'every spirited Briton would return to his native soil if the advantages of constitutional rights were granted him' (Warks. CRO, CR895/68).

Dormer did not return to England but lived out his life in frustrated exile. He died on 19 November 1796 aged sixty-six, and was buried on 21 November in the church of St Peter and Paul, Gran. His wife, Countess Elizabeth, died on 6 April 1824. He was survived by two children (three died young): Antonia Dormer (1782–1805), who married Baron O'Brien, a general in the Austrian service; and Joseph Thaddeus Dormer (1790–1871), who, in 1826, succeeded his cousin as eleventh Baron Dormer and also inherited the family's Warwickshire estates.   JONATHAN SPAIN

Sources GEC, *Peerage* · Boase, *Mod. Eng. biog.*, vol. 5 · Burke, *Peerage* · J. Dormer, correspondence and papers, Warks. CRO, dep. 895 · Colvin, *Archs.*

Archives Warks. CRO, corresp. and papers

Dormer, Robert, first earl of Carnarvon (1610?–1643), royalist army officer, was the only son of Sir William Dormer, baronet (*d.* 1616), and Alice, daughter of Sir Richard Molyneux of Sefton, Lancashire. The Dormer family had risen to power and influence under the Tudors, gained court connections (Jane *Suárez de Figueroa, *née* Dormer, was a close friend of Mary Tudor), and were allied by marriage to such prominent midland and northern Catholic families as Catesby, Dacre, and Huddlestone. Robert Dormer's mother was a recusant and his sister married the later earl of Glamorgan. They acquired large holdings in Buckinghamshire and Oxfordshire. His grandfather, Sir Robert Dormer, prospered as a flockmaster, supplying wool and meat for the London market. He owned twenty-four manors in Buckinghamshire alone, and had an income of about £6000 p.a. (L. Stone, *The Crisis of the Aristocracy, 1558–1641*, 1965, 761). He acquired the title of Baron Dormer of Wing, Buckinghamshire, on 30 June 1615. It was said that he paid £10,000 for it in the first of the substantial sales of peerages at the Jacobean court. He was also appointed to the hereditary post of chief avenor or keeper of the king's hawks. Sir William Dormer predeceased his father, who died on 8 November 1616, leaving his grandson, a minor, heir to a great fortune. The king sold this lucrative wardship to one of his favourites, Philip Herbert, earl of Montgomery (later also earl of Pembroke) for £4000.

Dormer was educated at Eton College between 1621 and 1624, and in April of the latter year matriculated at Exeter College, Oxford. He proceeded MA on 25 May 1627. Pembroke consolidated an expensive purchase by marrying the ward to his eldest daughter, Anne Sophia Herbert (*c.*1610–1643), on 27 February 1625, when Dormer was probably fifteen. Before the wedding Dr Prideaux, vice-chancellor of Oxford, instructed the couple in religion, presumably to counteract the Catholic influence of the Dormer family. He may have had success with the bride, who refused later to take part in a court masque on a Sunday, but not with her husband. As office-holders the Dormers no doubt conformed, while retaining their old beliefs.

Shortly after the wedding Dormer set out on the grand tour. Unusually, after visiting Spain, France, and Italy, he journeyed to Turkey and the Middle East: he was a more observant traveller than most, according to Clarendon, whose eulogy on his death, in the *History of the Rebellion*, is the best source. Now a wealthy man in his own right, and well connected to the court (Pembroke was lord chamberlain of Charles I's household), he was further advanced in the peerage as Viscount Ascott and earl of Carnarvon in 1628. He was the very picture of a sumptuously attired Caroline courtier in the well-known Van Dyck portrait of the Herbert family at Wilton, painted about 1635. He too held an office in the household, and was the owner of a great house, Ascott, near Wing. He had Inigo Jones prepare plans for its enlargement, which the onset of war halted. The house fell into ruin later and is now lost. He also had a house in London, where a son, Charles (who was to succeed to the earldom), was born in 1632.

Appropriately to his position at court, Carnarvon was a keen follower of country sports. Later royalist apologists felt bound to admit that he was 'extreamly wild in his youth' (Lloyd, 372), and devoted to the 'looser exercises of pleasure, hunting, hawking, and the like' (Clarendon, *Hist. rebellion*, 3.178), if only to point the contrast with his later seriousness as a soldier. He loved gaming, and spent heavily. 'His Recreations were rather expensive than bruitish' (Lloyd, 369). He briefly served at sea, for in 1637 he was reported aboard the man-of-war *Triumph* in the Downs, presumably as a gentleman volunteer, enjoying shipboard life. After an excellent supper on a fine night, and with a good bed ready, he swore that 'by God's blood he would have three whores' (Conway to Gerrard, 10 July 1637, *Portland MSS*, 3.44).

When the bishops' wars loomed Carnarvon was appointed second in command to Pembroke of the regiment of horse raised by the royal household, and took part in the first campaign of 1639. In the second bishops' war he commanded a regiment of cavalry in 1640. A leading figure in Buckinghamshire, and acceptable to parliament, he was appointed lord lieutenant of the county in June 1641.

But early in 1642 Carnarvon detached himself from the Pembroke connection, and local opinion, by declaring for the king. He sided with his wife's brothers in deploring their father's support for the popular party, and was furious that Pembroke had used his proxy vote in the Lords against the king. In response to his father-in-law's bullying he is supposed to have said, 'leave me to my Honor and Allegiance' (Lloyd, 371). He was active in promoting the royal commission of array in Oxfordshire and Buckinghamshire, unpromising territory for the king. He joined the royal court in the north, was knighted at York in April 1642, and was one of the peers who pledged financial support for the cause in June. By August he had raised one of the first regiments of 500 horse, a complex and expensive operation, speedily accomplished. All this activity earned him an early place in the list of those to be excepted from pardon by parliament. His regiment fought with distinction in Wilmot's left wing at Edgehill in October 1642. For his good service at the battle he was awarded, with 400 others, an honorary degree at Oxford in November. His house was plundered, and a convoy of plate and jewels, destined for the king at Oxford, seized.

Carnarvon took part in Rupert's successful assault on Cirencester in February 1643, and was commended for his mercy in capturing rather than killing the many runaways. In June he was lieutenant-general, under the marquess of Hertford, of the Oxford cavalry force sent to join Hopton's Cornish army advancing from the west. In several actions against Waller's army he showed himself a resourceful and daring cavalryman, who, 'with incomparable gallantry … always charged home' (Clarendon, Hist. rebellion, 3.86). He was wounded in the leg at the battle of Lansdown on 3 July 1643, however, and was temporarily replaced. With the foot under Hopton bottled up in Devizes by Waller's superior forces, Carnarvon and Hertford with the horse made their way with difficulty back to Oxford. He returned to take part as a volunteer in the battle of Roundway down, on 13 July. According to Clarendon it was his good knowledge of Waller's tactics and prompt advice to Lord Wilmot which helped to clinch the victory (ibid., 3.85–7, 98–9).

After the fall of Bristol Carnarvon was sufficiently recovered to continue as general of the western army and lead an expedition (of about 2000 horse and dragoons) into Dorset, intended to follow up these successes in a 'malignant' area. The cavaliers' reputation for invincibility was inflated by the stories told by former soldiers of Waller's army and defenders of Bristol returning to their homes. Carnarvon's horse must have been reassuringly well disciplined as well as victorious, and himself seen as someone who could be trusted to keep his word, for Dorchester and Weymouth, both famous for godliness, quickly surrendered to him, on generous terms, without a fight, on 2 and 5 August 1643. But when the rest of the army, mainly infantry, under Prince Maurice, arrived shortly after, they plundered the inhabitants anyway. Carnarvon, 'who was full of honour and justice upon all contracts', was so disgusted that he immediately resigned his command and rejoined the main army with the king at the siege of Gloucester (Clarendon, Hist. rebellion, 3.158).

It is not certain which unit Carnarvon rode with to the first battle of Newbury, but he was one of several notables who perished that day, 20 September 1643. He had been fully engaged, charging Essex's lifeguard, as usual with success. But while he was rejoicing his men a stray trooper, recognizing him, ran him through. His body was carried to Oxford and buried in Jesus College chapel. It was removed to Wing church in 1653. His wife had died in Oxford, of smallpox, in June 1643, and her body had been buried at Wing immediately after. The church contains many monuments to the family.

Carnarvon was a prominent landlord and courtier, whose family had strong Catholic leanings. He abandoned a life of pleasure in peacetime to devote himself, against the wishes of several powerful interests, including that of his father-in-law, to the royalist cause. He showed unexpected qualities of courage and organization in building and commanding part of the king's mounted arm, and was a successful colonel and (briefly) general in the field, before losing his life in battle. As a playboy turned gallant soldier, and exemplary man of honour, he was the subject of later cavalier eulogies.   IAN ROY

Sources Clarendon, *Hist. rebellion* · D. Lloyd, *Memoires of the lives … of those … personages that suffered … for the protestant religion* (1668), 369–72 · G. Lipscomb, *The history and antiquities of the county of Buckingham*, 3 (1847) · *Collins peerage of England: genealogical, biographical and historical*, ed. E. Brydges, 9 vols. (1812), vol. 7 · GEC, *Peerage*, and addenda vol. (xiv) · W. H. Rylands, ed., *The visitation of the county of Buckingham made in 1634*, Harleian Society, 58 (1909) · P. R. Newman, *Royalist officers in England and Wales, 1642–1660: a biographical dictionary* (1981) · R. Atkyns and J. Gwyn, *Military memoirs. The civil war*, ed. P. Young and N. Tucker (1967) · P. Young, *Edgehill 1642: the campaign and the battle* (1967) · CSP dom., *1638–43* · DNB · Foster, *Alum. Oxon.* · M. A. E. Green, ed., *Calendar of the proceedings of the committee for compounding … 1643–1660*, 5 vols., PRO (1889–92) · *The life, diary, and correspondence of Sir William Dugdale*, ed. W. Hamper (1827) · R. Palmer, *The Catholique apology* (1674)

Likenesses A. Van Dyck, group portrait, oils, 1634–5, Wilton House, Wiltshire · B. Baron, line engraving, pubd 1770 (after A. Van Dyck), BM, NPG · A. Van Dyck, chalk drawing, BM · double portrait, oils (with his wife; after A. Van Dyck), Longleat, Wiltshire

Wealth at death estate valued at approx. £6000 p.a. in 1616, but big losses in Civil War probable

Dormer, Robert (*bap.* 1650, *d.* 1726), judge and politician, was baptized on 30 May 1650, the second son of John Dormer (*bap.* 1612, *d.* 1679), of Lee Grange, Quainton, Buckinghamshire, barrister and MP, and his wife, Katharine (*bap.* 1622, *d.* 1691), daughter of Thomas Woodward of Saxons Lode, Ripple, Worcestershire. Dormer matriculated on 30 April 1667 at Christ Church, Oxford, and then on 20 May 1669 entered Lincoln's Inn. He was called to the bar on 27 January 1676 and soon afterwards became attorney-general to Bishop Crew of Durham. As early as 1680 Dormer acted as junior counsel for the crown in the prosecution of Sir Thomas Gascoigne for treason and Elizabeth Cellier for libel. By 1690 he was appearing as counsel before the House of Lords. At some point before 1693 Dormer married Mary (*d.* 1729), daughter and coheir of Sir Richard Blake of London. They had two sons and five daughters, but only three daughters survived them. In March 1693 Dormer petitioned (as heir) the crown for a grant of the estate of his nephew, Sir William Dormer, second baronet (the son of his elder brother, John), who had inherited the family estates in 1675, in order to pay off the encumbrances on the estate, with William, a lunatic, being left in the care of Sir Fleetwood Dormer of Arle Court, Gloucestershire. In November 1693 Dormer was appointed chancellor of the diocese of Durham, a post which he held until 1696.

In September 1696 Dormer succeeded to his uncle's estate at Arle Court, and, if he had not already done so, gained control of his nephew's estates. In February 1698 Dormer acted as counsel for the parliamentary bill of pains and penalties against Charles Duncombe. Dormer stood for Aylesbury at the 1698 general election, but was defeated. When the election was declared void he won the subsequent by-election in February 1699. During this parliament Dormer appears to have switched sides from tory to whig and come under the influence of the leading Buckinghamshire whig Thomas, fourth Baron Wharton. He certainly proved able to defend several whig ministers, including the duke of Shrewsbury and Lord Chancellor Somers, who were under attack in December 1699 over the patent issued to Captain Kidd, who had by then turned pirate, arguing 'very strongly for the legality of the grant' (James, 2.380). By December 1700 he was being described as 'wholly Lord Wharton's' (Verney MS 636/51, Lord Cheyne to Sir John Verney, 14 Dec 1700). He stood for the county of Buckinghamshire at the January 1701 election, but lost, winning the seat at the general election held the following December. A man of 'soaring temper' (Verney, *Letters*, 1.159–60), his ambition may well have been to become lord keeper, but the king's death prevented his advancement and he then lost his seat in 1702, taking refuge at Northallerton at a by-election held in November. No doubt his local knowledge assisted the whig side in the celebrated *Ashby* v. *White* case concerning the election at Aylesbury when he argued on 21 January 1704 that voters deprived of the franchise should have recourse to the law courts and thus against the exclusive jurisdiction of the House of Commons over elections. He was returned for Buckinghamshire in 1705, vacating his seat upon becoming a judge on 11 February 1706.

Lady Gardiner had noted that Dormer's 'generous humour has made him many friends' (Verney MS 636/52, 30 July 1702) and in celebration of his elevation to the court of common pleas 'most of the Lord (Spiritual and Temporal) were invited to dine with the new judge, Mr Justice Dormer, whose Serjeant's motto, given by the Bishop of Sarum, is *Imperium Oceano, Faman Astris*' (*London Diaries of William Nicolson*, 375). Dormer's admittance to the order of serjeants-at-law was sponsored by the two leading ministers, the duke of Marlborough and Lord Treasurer Godolphin.

Dormer was reappointed to common pleas following the accession of George I and continued to grace the bench until his death. In March 1726 Dormer had succeeded his nephew to the family properties at Lee and also Purston, Northamptonshire. Dormer made his will on 15 July 1726, three days after the burial of his only surviving son, Fleetwood. Dormer died at his house in Lincoln's Inn Fields on 18 September 1726 and was buried at Quainton, where a full-sized effigy of him was set up.

STUART HANDLEY

Sources HoP, *Commons, 1690–1715* [draft] · M. W. Helms, L. Naylor, and G. Jagger, 'Dormer, John', HoP, *Commons, 1660–90*, 2.221–2 · F. G. Lee, *The history, description and antiquities of the prebendal church of the Blessed Virgin Mary of Thame* (1883), 507–8 · BL, Verney MSS, 636/51–52 [microfilms of Claydon House] · Sainty, *Judges* · Baker, *Serjeants* · Foss, *Judges* · *The London diaries of William Nicolson, bishop of Carlisle, 1702–1718*, ed. C. Jones and G. Holmes (1985), 375 · G. Lipscomb, *The history and antiquities of the county of Buckingham*, 4 vols. (1831–47), vol. 1, p. 415 · Foster, *Alum. Oxon.* · M. M. Verney, ed., *Verney letters of the eighteenth century*, 2 vols. (1930), vol. 1, pp. 159–60 · *Letters illustrative of the reign of William III from 1696 to 1708 addressed to the duke of Shrewsbury by James Vernon*, ed. G. P. R. James, 3 vols. (1841), vol. 2, p. 380

Likenesses effigy on monument, St Mary and Holy Cross Church, Buckinghamshire

Dorn, Marion V. (1896–1964), designer, was born on 25 December 1896, probably at Menlo Park, near San Francisco, California, one of five children of Diodemus Socrates Dorn (1860–1913), lawyer, and Camille Johnson (1870–1932). Educated at Stanford University from 1912 to 1916 (bachelor of arts in graphic arts, Phi Beta Kappa), thereafter she shared a studio in Russian Hill, San Francisco, with her former tutor, the artist Henry Varnum Poor (1887–1970), her husband from July 1919 to 20 October 1923. Early in 1919 they moved to New City, New York, and Dorn gained notice as a designer of batiks. In Paris in 1923 she met the poster designer Edward McKnight Kauffer (1890–1954), and subsequently resided with him at 17 John Street, The Adelphi, London, from late 1923 to 1931, at Swan Court, Chelsea, from 1931 to 1 July 1940, and in New York until his death in 1954; they lived at 40 Central Park South from about 1942, and married in 1950. Dorn's New York studio was at 54th Street and Madison Avenue.

Dorn's career was launched in Britain in the mid to late 1920s, when she maintained her graphic work and hand production of batik scarves, curtains, and decorative panels, while extending her practice to include interiors and rugs, the latter initiated about 1926. In the 1930s she ceased making batiks, instead having woven and printed fabrics made by Jean Orage, Edinburgh Weavers, and Warner & Sons Ltd. The latter two, especially Warners, also purchased her designs for their own production. Equally reciprocal was her association with the Wilton Royal Carpet Factory from 1928, resulting in the 1930s in over a hundred designs for hand-knotted carpets, some for Dorn's own clients—among them the Savoy hotel group (including Claridges Hotel, the Berkeley Hotel, and the Savoy, 1931–9) and the Cunard, Orient, and Shaw Saville ocean liner companies (1934–9). Her rugs were conceived and marketed as limited-edition fine art productions, and for these she became best known, being dubbed 'the architect of floors' in 1932. In 1933 she joined a Wilton Royal Carpet Factory sub-committee to select modern designs for the firm's production, having turned down an invitation to become a director. In 1934 she formed a design consultancy, Marion Dorn Ltd, through which she completed interior design schemes, organized the production of fabrics, wallpapers, and furniture, and undertook book illustrations and graphic and textile designs. In addition, for her own clients machine-made carpets were

Marion V. Dorn (1896–1964), by Frank Dobson, *c*.1930–31

also commissioned to supplement those hand-knotted for her by several firms other than Wiltons.

From 1927 to 1939 Dorn's work was exhibited in many influential European exhibitions including those at Dorland Hall, London (1933 and 1934), Burlington House, London (1935), and the Universal Exhibition, Paris (1937). Exports to and exhibitions in the United States from 1929 to 1939, including at the Metropolitan Museum of Art, New York (1937), and the Golden Gate International Exposition, San Francisco (1939), maintained exposure there for her work in her absence. After returning to New York she worked with at least thirteen firms, including wallpaper manufacturer Basset and Vollum and textile manufacturers A. H. Lee, Goodall Fabrics, Jofa Inc., Mitchell-David, F. Schumacher & Co., and Silkar Studios; longer and more fruitful associations were with Greeff Fabrics Inc. (1956–64), who exported her fabrics to Britain through Warners; the wallpaper manufacturer Katenbach and Warren (*c*.1947–59); and the hand gun-tufted rug and carpet manufacturer Edward Fields Inc., producing over a hundred designs (1949–62).

Known for her good looks and humour, Dorn was an astute self-publicist able to attract a fashionable clientele and collaborators—from Noël Coward to Graham Sutherland, who exhibited ceramics in Dorn's showroom in 1939—and to grasp the technical requirements of rug and fabric production. In 1957 she received an honorary fellowship of the British Society of Industrial Artists for her outstanding contribution to textile design; the society's journal recorded that 'her masterly drawing and her unerring sense of pattern, colour and texture contributed to a result that had an immense and lasting influence on textiles in this country as well as abroad' (Hunter). She made a significant contribution to British modern interiors independently and in collaboration with architects such as Oliver Hill, Robert Lutyens, Serge Chermayeff, Eric Mendelsohn, Wells Coates, and Brian O'Rorke, and interior decorators such as Syrie Maugham, designing the cream rug in the widely illustrated 'all white' drawing room in Maugham's London flat (1933). Designs for moquette seating fabric for the London Passenger Transport Board (*c*.1937) were still being rewoven in 1954 and remained in London Underground carriages for another decade or so. Her printed textile designs with casually placed areas of colour over outlined motifs, well-suiting the then new commercial technique of hand-screen printing, shaped stylistic trends from *c*.1935 to 1960. For Fields she made continued developments, promoting textured and boldly patterned floor coverings and the concept of 'area rugs'; with them she completed her last major commission (1960), the carpet for the diplomatic reception room at the White House, Washington, DC. She retired to Tangier, Morocco, in 1962, where she died on 28 January 1964 and was buried. Examples of her printed textiles are in the Gallery of Costume, Manchester, and the Victoria and Albert Museum. MARY SCHOESER

Sources C. Boydell, *The architect of floors: modernism, art and Marion Dorn designs* (1996) · P. T. Conmy, *History of the Dorn family: California pioneer settlers of Green Valley* (1965) · A. Hunter, 'Three honorary fellows', *Journal of the Society of Industrial Artists*, 55 (April–June 1957) · D. Todd, 'Marion Dorn: architect of floors', *ArchR*, 72 (1932), 107 · M. V. Dorn, 'Textiles to live with', *Craft Horizons*, 7/5 (Sept–Oct 1952), 26–9
Archives Edward Fields Inc., New York, press cuttings, designs, and photos
Likenesses F. Dobson, sculpture, *c*.1930–1931, NPG [*see illus.*] · Eric, charcoal and watercolour drawing, 1940–44, priv. coll.

Dornford, Joseph (1794–1868), Church of England clergyman, was born on 9 January 1794 in Deptford, Kent, the son of Josiah Dornford and the half-brother of Josiah *Dornford, miscellaneous writer. He was brought up in an atmosphere of evangelical piety. His mother, Esther, formerly Mrs Thomason, was by her first marriage the mother of Thomas Truebody Thomason (1774–1829), curate to Charles Simeon, the evangelical leader at Cambridge. She was described (Mozley, chap. 78) as Simeon's chief lady friend, and as pouring out the tea for his weekly gatherings.

Dornford entered young at Trinity College, Cambridge, matriculating in 1811, but he suddenly left to serve as a volunteer in the Peninsular War. Mozley explained: 'He would rather fly to the ends of the earth and seek the company of cannibals or wild beasts than be bound to a life of tea and twaddle' (Mozley, 2.56). He saw some service, and on his return home entered Wadham College, Oxford, where he gained a first in the classical school and a second in the mathematical, proceeding BA in 1816. In 1817 he was elected to a Michel fellowship at Queen's, and in 1819 to a fellowship at Oriel, where he graduated MA in 1820. In August of that year he joined Dr Joseph von Hamel on the well-known ascent of Mont Blanc in which three guides were killed, of which he subsequently wrote an account in the *New Monthly Magazine*. Ordained in 1821, he was appointed a tutor of Oriel in 1823 in succession to John Keble, a disappointment to Keble's pupils, though he proved a good lecturer. His martial exploits earned him the sobriquet the 'University Corporal' when he served as a proctor in 1830.

In 1832 Dornford was presented by his college to the rectory of Plymtree, Devon, and in 1847 he was collated by Bishop Phillpotts prebendary of Exeter Cathedral. He published nothing save a few sermons. One of these, 'The Christian sacraments', is contained in a volume edited by the Revd Alexander Watson, *Sermons for Sundays, festivals, and fasts, and other liturgical occasions, contributed by bishops and other clergy of the church* (1845). In his bearing Dornford was more of a soldier than a priest, and his talk ran much on war. He was a man of strong will, generous impulses, and pugnacious temper. Sympathetic to the Tractarians, his high-church innovations aroused opposition in his parish; further strife was caused by Dornford's gallantry towards the female members of his flock. Remaining a bachelor until late in life, despite a string of courtships, he eventually made what Mozley described as a 'quiet, domestic marriage', marrying on 31 May 1855 Emma Louisa, daughter of Lieutenant Josiah Dornford RN, a distant relative. Dornford died at Plymtree on 18 January 1868, survived by his wife and at least one son, Arthur Clifford Dornford (*b*. 1862), later a medical practitioner.

J. M. SCOTT, rev. M. C. CURTHOYS

Sources Boase, *Mod. Eng. biog.* · T. Mozley, *Reminiscences, chiefly of Oriel College and the Oxford Movement*, 2 vols. (1882) · Venn, *Alum. Cant.* · Foster, *Alum. Oxon.* · *GM*, 2nd ser., 43 (1855), 191
Wealth at death under £7000: resworn probate, Sept 1868, *CGPLA Eng. & Wales*

Dornford, Josiah (1762/3–1797), translator and writer, was the son of Josiah Dornford of Deptford, Kent, a member of the court of common council of the City of London, and the author of several pamphlets on the corporation's affairs and the reform of debtors' prisons. His half-brother was Joseph *Dornford, Church of England clergyman. He matriculated at Trinity College, Oxford, on 23 May 1781, aged eighteen, and graduated BA in 1785 and MA in 1792. He later moved to the University of Göttingen, where he took the degree of LLD. He was called to the bar at Lincoln's Inn. In 1790 he published in three volumes *An Historical Development of the Present Political Constitution of the Germanic Empire*, translated from the German of J. S. Pütter; the work was probably undertaken at Göttingen, where Pütter was professor of laws. Dornford also published in Latin a small volume of academic exercises by another Göttingen professor, the philologist Christian Gottlob Heyne, who, in a preface to this publication, speaks of Dornford as a 'learned youth' who had 'gained the highest honours in jurisprudence in our academy'. Dornford's only other known work is *The Motives and Consequences of the Present War Impartially Considered* (1793), a pamphlet

written in defence of William Pitt's administration. In 1795 he was named inspector-general of the army accounts in the Leeward Islands, and the record of this appointment shows that he had served as one of the commissaries to Lord Moira's army. He died at Martinique on 1 July 1797. J. M. SCOTT, rev. PHILIP CARTER

Sources *GM*, 1st ser., 65 (1795), 973 · *GM*, 1st ser., 67 (1797), 800 · Foster, *Alum. Oxon.*

Dorrian, Patrick (1814–1885), Roman Catholic bishop of Down and Connor, was born on 29 March 1814 at Downpatrick, co. Down, one of four sons of Patrick Dorrian, a shopkeeper, and his wife, Rose, *née* Murphy. He was educated at the classical (secondary) school in the town, which was conducted by Dr James Neilson, a Presbyterian minister. He entered St Patrick's College, Maynooth, in 1833 and was ordained priest on 19 September 1837.

From 1837 to 1847 Dorrian served as a curate in the rapidly expanding parish of Belfast. In 1841 the population was 70,500, of which, probably, one-third was Catholic. Bishop Denvir and two other priests had pastoral care of this congregation, many of whom were poor migrants from the countryside. The social conditions and the paucity of church accommodation—there were only two Catholic churches—created serious difficulties for the clergy.

Protestant–Catholic relations had been deteriorating since the granting of Catholic emancipation and the attempt in 1834 of Henry Cooke, the influential Presbyterian divine, to align his church (from which he had driven its more prominent liberal members) with the more conservative established church. The visit of Daniel O'Connell to Belfast in 1841 and the strong support afforded the movement for the repeal of the Union by the great majority of Catholics (among whom Dorrian and Bishop Denvir played prominent roles) further exacerbated these inter-denominational tensions.

Dorrian's last years as curate in Belfast were clouded by the suffering of the great famine. By 1847 the fevers associated with it were causing many deaths and taxing the medical resources of the town to the utmost. His elder brother, Bernard, who was parish priest of Lisburn, died of typhus in March 1847. In July, Patrick was transferred to the pastoral charge of Loughinisland, a rural parish situated about 7 miles from Downpatrick. There he spent thirteen years until he returned to Belfast after his appointment on 10 June 1860 as coadjutor-bishop of Down and Connor.

This appointment had been deemed necessary by the authorities in Rome, on the basis of information received from the archbishops of Armagh and Dublin, because Bishop Denvir was unable to deal with the pastoral and, to a lesser extent, social and political problems of his growing congregation. By 1860 Catholics in the town numbered about 40,000 but were served by only three churches, and were all members of one parish, over which Bishop Denvir presided. The archbishops of Armagh and Dublin wanted an active and energetic assistant for

Bishop Denvir, who would quickly address the pastoral and educational needs of his people.

Dorrian had given evidence of possessing these qualities but, until Denvir resigned, he did not have sufficient scope for applying them. When he succeeded to the see on 4 May 1865, he pushed ahead with the construction of a fourth church, which had been begun in 1860, with new buildings for the diocesan college, which would also provide a meeting-place for the diocesan clergy, and with the provision of a residence for the Christian Brothers, a teaching order, which he persuaded to come to Belfast in 1866.

In the following year Dorrian brought the Good Shepherd Sisters to Belfast and gave them charge of a female penitentiary; later they extended their work to cover a wide range of social needs. In 1872 the Bon Secours Sisters, an order devoted to nursing and welfare work, and in 1876 the Sisters of Nazareth, who looked after the poor, orphans, and the elderly, established convents and homes in the city. He also invited the Passionist Order to enter the diocese and gave them charge of a parish.

An ardent advocate of Catholic education, Dorrian encouraged his clergy to make use of the system of national education (which by 1860 was *de facto* denominational), to provide schools in every parish. He campaigned for the removal of the restrictions on national schools which prevented them from being overtly Catholic. He brought the Dominican Sisters and the Sisters of the Sacred Heart to establish schools for Catholic girls in Belfast and Lisburn, respectively, in 1870.

Politically, Dorrian was a constitutional nationalist. In the 1860s he firmly repudiated Fenianism, and with equal firmness he condemned sectarian rioting and disturbances in Belfast, pleading earnestly with Catholics to desist from giving any provocation to protestant extremists or reacting violently to their taunts or marches. He was one of the first bishops in Ireland to give his approval to Charles Stewart Parnell, then aiming for leadership of the home-rule movement, whom he described in 1879 as 'cool, confident and constitutional', and who, he believed, rightly exposed the injustices to which the poor were subjected in the late 1870s and early 1880s, as severe destitution again hit parts of Ireland. He was also one of the first bishops to throw his support behind the Land League, which campaigned for a system of just rents and fair land tenure for tenant farmers.

When the Royal University of Ireland, which was essentially an examining body, was established in 1879 to replace the Queen's University, and provision was made for students from any college to sit its examinations, Dorrian was disappointed that none of its fellowships were awarded to St Malachy's College, which he had greatly enlarged. That institution, however, like all Catholic secondary schools, had benefited from the Intermediate Education Act of 1878.

Dorrian died of a stroke at his home in Chichester Park, Belfast, on 3 November 1885 while still in office, and was interred three days later under the sanctuary of St Patrick's Church, Belfast.   AMBROSE MACAULAY

Sources A. Macaulay, *Patrick Dorrian, bishop of Down and Connor, 1865–85* (1987) · E. Larkin, *The Roman Catholic church and the creation of the modern Irish state, 1878–1886* (1975) · E. Larkin, *The Roman Catholic church and the home rule movement in Ireland, 1870–1874* (1990) **Archives** Down and Connor Diocesan Archives, Belfast | Archives of Sacred Congregation for the Evangelization of Peoples, Rome, Irish MSS · Armagh Diocesan Archives, Dixon MSS · Christian Brothers Generalate, Rome, Irish Foundations MSS · Dublin Diocesan Archives, Cullen MSS · Dublin Diocesan Archives, McCabe MSS · Irish College, Rome, Kirby MSS **Likenesses** portrait, bishop's house, Belfast **Wealth at death** £9735 1s. 1d.: probate, 18 Jan 1886, *CGPLA Ire.*

Dorrien, Sir Horace Lockwood Smith- (1858–1930), army officer, was born on 26 May 1858 at the family home of Haresfoot in Berkhamsted, Hertfordshire, the sixth and last son, and eleventh of fifteen children, of Colonel (retired) Robert Algernon Smith-Dorrien and his wife, Mary Anne, daughter of Thomas Driver MD. He was educated at Egypt House preparatory school, Isle of Wight, from 1865, then at Harrow School until 1875, where the Hon. John Fortescue became a lifelong friend.

Early career, 1871–1898 Smith-Dorrien's family was well connected in society, and he readily agreed to his father's suggestion of an army career. On 26 February 1876 he was commissioned second lieutenant in the 95th (Derbyshire) foot and attended the Royal Military College, Sandhurst, where he did well enough to earn a year's seniority, joining his regiment in Cork on 4 January 1877 as a lieutenant, and becoming adjutant a year later. His main character traits were already well established: the mischief and aggression understandable in a boy from such a large family became both courage and extravagance in the officer, and a violent and ugly temper (which his son ascribed to persistent teeth trouble) in the general. He could work hard when necessary, but throughout his life shooting, hunting, sports, and socializing were his chief interests. His diary, kept regularly from 1895 until his death, was principally a list of social engagements, supplemented by more serious meetings as his career developed, which later enabled him to be precise about events.

Smith-Dorrien's first active service came as a supernumerary transport officer in the Anglo-Zulu War of 1879, where he displayed unexpected organizational skills and attracted the attention of Evelyn Wood of the 'Wolseley ring'. Inclined throughout his career to use staff or supernumerary positions to get near the fighting, Smith-Dorrien was one of only five officers (together with fifty other Europeans and 300 Africans) to survive the catastrophic defeat by the Zulu at Isandlwana. By his own account, he helped distribute ammunition until the rout became general, and then escaped first a short distance on horse and then on foot, helping others and fighting off parties of Zulu as he went. An accomplished cross-country runner, he also noticed that like all the officers who survived Isandlwana he had worn a blue patrol jacket rather than the red coat which identified British soldiers to the Zulu. After a spell of illness he served on until the end of the campaign, being present at the battle of Ulundi on 4 July, and receiving his first mention in dispatches. He

Sir Horace Lockwood Smith-Dorrien (1858–1930), by F. A. Swaine, *c.*1918

returned to regimental duty in Britain and Gibraltar, during which his regiment was renamed 2nd battalion, the Sherwood Foresters (Derbyshire regiment). In August 1882 he was promoted captain, just as his battalion arrived in Egypt as part of the reserve under Wood for the campaign against Colonel Ahmad Arabi Pasha. Wood employed Smith-Dorrien to organize patrols of mounted infantry against Arab raids near Alexandria.

Smith-Dorrien accompanied his battalion to India in February 1883, but two months later was invalided to Britain with a recurring ailment described as a knee injury sustained when hunting (he also suffered from intermittent headaches and fevers). He was in Egypt in January 1884 on his way back to India when Wood, now sirdar of the Egyptian army, offered him an appointment. His service in Egypt brought him into contact with many later famous figures, notably Kitchener, but his knee trouble prevented him from taking part in the Gordon relief expedition. He saw active service as adjutant of the mounted infantry battalion of the Suakin field force during its brief existence (March–July 1885), and as a staff officer with the Egyptian cavalry of the Sudan frontier field force at the battle of Giniss (30 December 1885), for which he won the DSO and the Mejidiye and Osmanieh medals (both fourth class).

Spending 1886 alternating between Britain and Egypt, where he raised and commanded the 13th Sudanese battalion, Smith-Dorrien passed for the Staff College, Camberley, arriving in February 1887. He was a poor student (one story claims that after three months he had not located the library) but an enthusiastic sportsman, becoming master of the draghounds. He managed to pass the final examinations and obtained his certificate. He rejoined his battalion in India in January 1889 for almost a decade of the pleasures typical of a rich British officer in India. Regimental and staff posts alternated with long leaves, and Smith-Dorrien became involved particularly in polo and horse-racing, for which he kept a stud numbering thirty-two horses at one time, his favourite jockey being his close friend Hubert Gough. Promoted major in 1892, his only active service was with his battalion during the Tirah expedition between October 1897 and January 1898, for which he was made brevet lieutenant-colonel.

The Sudan and South Africa, 1898–1901 Smith-Dorrien's career revived in 1898 when he offered himself to Kitchener (then sirdar) for the Sudan campaign, being given the 13th Sudanese battalion once more and commanding it at the battle of Omdurman (2 September), after which Kitchener placed him in charge of his escort for the 'Fashoda incident'. He received a brevet colonelcy, and after a year in Malta commanding 1st battalion, the Sherwood Foresters, he took them to South Africa in December 1899 for the Second South African War. In February 1900 he assumed command of the 19th infantry brigade, part of the main force under Lord Roberts (with Kitchener as his chief staff officer) which included the cavalry division under John French. Smith-Dorrien's brigade saw action at Paardeberg Drift on 18–27 February, and then formed part of Ian Hamilton's column for the advance to Pretoria, taking part in the battle of Zand River on 10 May. He then commanded his own divisional-sized column in the guerrilla phase of the war under Kitchener. Already, recriminations about the war between Roberts, Kitchener, and Hamilton on one side, and French supported by his chief staff officer, Douglas Haig, on the other, marked the start of an antagonism which would affect the rest of Smith-Dorrien's career. Smith-Dorrien subsequently lent copies of his diary to Roberts, and to other favoured contacts such as Conan Doyle.

India and England, 1901–1914 In April 1901 Lord Roberts, as commander-in-chief, promoted Smith-Dorrien to adjutant-general of the Indian army with the rank of major-general. This involved him directly in the confrontation between the viceroy and the acting commander-in-chief, General Sir Arthur Power Palmer—a situation which grew worse with Kitchener's arrival to replace Palmer in November 1902, and the subsequent 'Kitchener–Curzon' affair. Smith-Dorrien was temperamentally unsuited to such positions (one of his strongest words of disgust was 'courtier'), and he requested a transfer, being given 4th (Quetta) division in April 1903. As a divisional commander he was said to know the names not only of all his officers but of their polo ponies as well.

Smith-Dorrien was married on 3 September 1902 at St Peter's, Eaton Square, London, to Olive Crofton, daughter of Colonel (retired) John Schneider of Oak Lee, Furness Abbey. In keeping with the family connections, his wife was god-daughter to Sir Donald Stewart, and her mother was stepsister to General Palmer. Their first son, Grenville, was born in 1904, followed by Peter in 1907 and David in 1911. The couple also effectively adopted the two daughters of General Palmer who were left homeless after his death in 1912.

On promotion to lieutenant-general (with a knighthood) in December 1907, Smith-Dorrien left Quetta to take over Aldershot command in succession to Sir John French, who became inspector general of the forces. This was Smith-Dorrien's first service in Britain since the Staff College. He arrived, heavily associated with Roberts and Kitchener, in the middle of the complex debate on army reform still coloured by different views of the war in South Africa. In particular, he supported Roberts in favouring compulsory military training, and sided against French on the future role of cavalry. Even so, no satisfactory explanation has ever been offered for French's mercurial attitude towards Smith-Dorrien, which from this period alternated between the highest praise and the lowest condemnation, French seeming unable to decide whether Smith-Dorrien was an enemy, a subordinate, or a rival. Some historians have identified Henry Wilson, who held various staff positions under French from 1907, as the malevolent influence between the two men. These controversies have obscured both some real achievements and reforms undertaken by Smith-Dorrien at Aldershot, and also the continuity of training between French, Smith-Dorrien, and Haig as his successor which produced the very high standards of the British expeditionary force (BEF), and made its rapid mobilization in 1914 possible. In February 1912 Smith-Dorrien was given the lesser appointment of southern command, being promoted to full general in August.

The First World War and after On the outbreak of the First World War an almost accidental sequence of events placed Smith-Dorrien in a critical position. The BEF under French consisted of 1st corps under Haig and 2nd corps under General Sir James Grierson. On 17 August Grierson died unexpectedly of a heart attack, and Kitchener, newly appointed secretary of state for war, decided to replace him with Smith-Dorrien, despite knowing that French preferred another officer and of his intermittent feud with Smith-Dorrien, who in turn stepped voluntarily into the confrontation, maintaining a private correspondence with both Kitchener and George V throughout his period of command. Smith-Dorrien took over 2nd corps on 20 August, and three days later the BEF was heavily engaged in the battle of Mons, followed by a retreat closely pursued by considerably superior German forces.

In the early hours of 26 August Smith-Dorrien was advised by Allenby, commanding the cavalry division, that for once his cavalry were too dispersed to cover the 2nd corps retreat. Fearing that the Germans would overwhelm his troops on the road, Smith-Dorrien accepted that his only choice was to stand and fight, delivering a 'stopping blow' to the enemy. Strictly, this was against French's orders to continue the retreat, but it was a situation well understood in military regulations. Smith-

Dorrien's decision was supported by others on the spot who agreed to serve under him, including Allenby, and permission to fight was received from French shortly before dawn. However, French, whose conduct of the campaign was becoming increasingly erratic, let 1st corps continue its retreat rather than moving to support 2nd corps.

The resulting battle of Le Cateau was a demonstration of one of the most difficult of all military manoeuvres, a delaying operation and retreat from contact. Smith-Dorrien's troops, with both their flanks in the air, fought a German attack of about twice their own strength to a standstill, and then marched away in broad daylight. Casualties for the battle were heavy at 7812 men (German casualties are not known), but it enabled 2nd corps to break contact, and the Germans did not locate the BEF again until 1 September. The destruction of half the BEF had Smith-Dorrien mishandled 2nd corps at Le Cateau would have had incalculable results, and his military reputation has come to rest heavily on this small but important battle.

Smith-Dorrien commanded 2nd corps through the battles of the Marne (5–10 September), the Aisne (12 September to 2 October), and the first battle of Ypres (19 October to 17 November). On 26 December his expanded command was renamed Second Army. However, his relations with French continued to deteriorate, with matters coming to a head during the second battle of Ypres (22 April to 25 May 1915). After advising a limited withdrawal on 27 April, Smith-Dorrien was ordered by French to surrender command of his troops to Lieutenant-General Sir Herbert Plumer commanding 5th corps (French's original choice to succeed Grierson). On 6 May, bowing to the inevitable, Smith-Dorrien requested to be relieved of command.

A famous anecdote has Smith-Dorrien being advised of his impending dismissal some days before this by William Robertson, chief of staff of the BEF at the time, with the words ''Orace, you're for 'ome'. Although Robertson (who liked to drop his aspirates for effect) did visit Smith-Dorrien on 29 April, the story may be apocryphal, and at least one other version: 'Well, 'Orace, I'm afraid you'll 'ave to 'op it', was in circulation (see *Lloyd George, a Diary by Frances Stevenson*, ed. A. J. P. Taylor, 1971, 114).

On Smith-Dorrien's return to Britain, Kitchener attempted to make him inspector-general of training. But this was blocked by the prime minister, Asquith, ironically because the post was being held in reserve for French as a method of dismissing him from command of the BEF, which finally took place in December. One month before this, Smith-Dorrien was offered command of the campaign in German East Africa. He left Britain in December, but was almost immediately struck down by severe pneumonia which led to his being invalided back from Cape Town, effectively ending his military career. In January 1917 he was made lieutenant of the Tower of London, and in September 1918 he was appointed governor of Gibraltar, serving for five years until his retirement from active service in November 1923.

French's dismissal of Smith-Dorrien was a by-product of

his struggle with Kitchener, and in a sense unremarkable, resembling many other cases which have established the British military convention whereby a sufficiently senior officer might remove a subordinate on grounds of mutual dislike or lost confidence, virtually regardless of the facts. What was unusual was French's own subsequent behaviour in making the dismissal both a controversy and a scandal. In April 1919 the *Daily Telegraph* began to serialize extracts from French's memoirs of the 1914 campaign. Published two months later as the book *1914*, this contained an account of Le Cateau and Smith-Dorrien's conduct so inaccurate as to verge on the defamatory, as well as contradicting the version in French's own official dispatches. Although now Viscount Ypres and lord lieutenant of Ireland, French was, like Smith-Dorrien, still on the active list, and the publication itself was of doubtful legality. Smith-Dorrien requested either a royal commission or the public right of reply, both of which were refused by Wilson, now chief of the Imperial General Staff (CIGS). But Smith-Dorrien was granted permission to record his views for posterity.

By 1919 French had few friends or supporters left, and sufficient records existed to discredit his version of events. Fortescue, now royal librarian, helped Smith-Dorrien to spread his own account, and to lodge with the British Museum in 1923 one of twenty-eight copies of his privately printed rebuttal of French, the remainder of which were discreetly circulated from December 1919 onwards to more than sixty selected members of the army, the court, and society. Smith-Dorrien's final triumph came when the first volume of the official history of the First World War, *France and Belgium, 1914*, appeared in 1922, citing official documents supporting his position. Although largely forced upon him, Smith-Dorrien's dignified public silence won him much sympathy and credence for his own memoirs, *Memories of Forty-Eight Years' Service*, which appeared in 1925 after French's death (Smith-Dorrien was one of the pallbearers at his funeral).

His supporters have seen Smith-Dorrien as a thwarted military genius. He was a fairly typical general of his era, and the events of 1914 show him to have been a good field commander, but he lacked the political sophistication to go higher. In addition to his DSO (and an unsuccessful VC recommendation after Isandlwana), Smith-Dorrien was appointed KCB in 1907, and was awarded the GCB in 1913, and the GCMG in 1915. But thereafter his involvement in the Kitchener–French feud made any further award or promotion politically impossible, and deprived him of many of the perquisites granted to his fellows.

After retirement in 1923 he settled with his family briefly in France, first in Biarritz, which proved too expensive, and then in Dinard, buying a house called Les Bocages. Photographs and paintings of Smith-Dorrien show a lantern-jawed individual with a sharp moustache and eyes that give more than a hint of his notorious temper. He was of medium height and build, but prided himself on his physical fitness (despite his illnesses), and on the smartness of his appearance. There are few photographs of Smith-Dorrien during the First World War, and little or

no film, but most unusually he chose to play himself in a brief appearance in the 1924 feature film *Mons* (British Instructional Films), which relied heavily on historical authenticity.

On 11 August 1930 Smith-Dorrien was fatally injured in a car crash on the Bath Road while visiting friends near Chippenham, Wiltshire, and died in Chippenham Cottage Hospital next day without recovering consciousness. His funeral took place at St Peter's, Eaton Square, on 16 August, and he was buried at Berkhamsted. His wife and three sons survived him. STEPHEN BADSEY

Sources H. Smith-Dorrien, *Memories of forty-eight years' service* (1925) • I. F. W. Beckett, ed., *The judgement of history: Sir Horace Smith-Dorrien, Lord French and 1914* (1993) • A. J. Smithers, *The man who disobeyed* (1970) • C. Ballard, *Smith-Dorrien* (1931) • R. R. Stein, 'Forging a rapier among scythes: Lieutenant-General Sir Horace Smith-Dorrien and the Aldershot command, 1907–1912', MA diss., Rice University, Houston, Texas, 1980 • S. D. Badsey, 'Fire and the sword: the British army and the Arme Blanche controversy, 1871–1921', PhD diss., U. Cam., 1982 • J. E. Edmonds, ed., *Military operations, France and Belgium, 1914*, 1, History of the Great War (1922) • D. R. Morris, *The washing of the spears*, new edn (1973) • Viscount French of Ypres [J. D. P. French], *1914* (1919) • B. Bond, *The Victorian army and the Staff College, 1854–1914* (1972) • *The Times* (13 Aug 1930) • *WWW* • R. Holmes, *The little field-marshal: Sir John French* (1981) • J. Fortescue, *Following the drum* (1931)
Archives BL, papers relating to First World War, Add. MSS 52767–52777 • IWM, corresp. with official historian relating to battle of Le Cateau, 1914; diary and papers • NRA, eyewitness account of battle of Isandlwana • PRO | IWM, French MSS • King's Lond., Liddell Hart C., letters to Sir J. E. Edmonds • NL Scot., Haig MSS • NRA, priv. coll., letters to Sir John Ewart • PRO, Kitchener MSS • Wilts. & Swindon RO, corresp. with Viscount Long | FILM BFI NFTVA, performance footage [playing himself in an instructional film, *Mons*, 1924]
Likenesses F. Dodd, charcoal and watercolour, 1918, IWM • F. A. Swaine, photograph, c.1918, NPG [*see illus.*] • O. Birley, oils, 1935, Harrow School, Middlesex • Bassano, photograph, The Convent, Gibraltar • J. Russell & Sons, photograph, NPG • Spy [L. Ward], caricature, chromolithograph, NPG; repro. in *VF* (5 Dec 1901) • photographs, repro. in Smith-Dorrien, *Memories* • photographs, repro. in Smithers, *The man who disobeyed* • photographs, repro. in Ballard, *Smith-Dorrien*
Wealth at death £6519 3s.: probate, 30 Dec 1930, CGPLA Eng. & Wales

Dorrington, Theophilus (1654–1715), Church of England clergyman, was born in Bow, London, on 11 November 1654 and was baptized at St Mary-le-Bow on 23 November. His father was the London clothier Theophilus Dorrington. The son of a nonconformist father, Dorrington seems to have been taught first by two ejected ministers: Mr Beard at Berden, Essex (possibly Thomas Beard), and Mr Horrax at Newington (probably Thomas Horrockes at Newington Butts, Surrey). Dorrington attended Merchant Taylors' School, London, from 1667. He was admitted on 19 December 1670 to Sidney Sussex College, Cambridge, which he left without graduating, to preach among the presbyterians.

In 1678, with Thomas Goodwin, John Shower, and James Lambert, Dorrington conducted an evening lecture at a coffee house in Exchange Alley, London, which many wealthy merchants attended. Apparently unsettled about continuing in presbyterian ministry, he enrolled on 13

June 1680 at the University of Leiden to study medicine. Dorrington spent two years in Antwerp, but when is uncertain. Encouraged by John Williams, later bishop of Chichester, he took Anglican orders as early as 1682. Probably after serving as chaplain to the mother of Elizabeth Howland, future duchess of Bedford, he entered Magdalen College, Oxford, on 16 June 1686, then became rector of Castle Hopton, Shropshire, the following year. In the summer of 1698 he toured northern Europe, collecting data for a book on Roman Catholicism. In November Archbishop Tillotson presented him with the valuable rectory of Wittersham, Kent, where he ministered for the remainder of his life. Dorrington projected an image of cultured refinement and piety—a cosmopolitan, learned divine polished in Latin and French, who cultivated patronage in high society and wrote tirelessly on establishmentarian values. Finally, on 9 March 1711, the Oxford convocation rewarded his efforts with an MA degree.

Remembered for his acerbic polemics against dissent, Dorrington was concerned ultimately to remedy the three broader but related problems of immorality, schism, and sedition. He linked immorality to declining manners and piety. Ever conscious of rank and status, he urged ladies to emulate Du Bosc's *The Excellent Woman* (1682), which he had translated from the French. In *The Right Use of an Estate* (1683) he exhorted gentlemen to exemplify discipline, duty, and religious devotion. For common folk, he published a collection of meditations resembling a Catholic breviary: his popular *Reform'd Devotions* (1696) made nine editions by 1727. He then focused on the home: *Family Devotions* was a series of discourses (1693–5) for domestic teaching on Sunday afternoons.

In *A Familiar Guide* (1695), Dorrington addressed the problem of schism by describing communion as renewal of a covenant with God that could not be observed properly outside the established church. The assassination attempt against William III (1696) prompted his *The Honor due to the Civil Magistrate*, a polemic which vindicated high-church passive obedience and linked sedition to immorality and religious schism. Hinting that dissenters were responsible for most of this, momentarily he turned his attention to an easier target. After touring the continent, he wrote *Observations Concerning … the Romish Church* (1698) to warn against harbouring its superstitious practices, to guard against divisive Jesuit influences, and to encourage protestants abroad. Next he turned to Baptists, who had 'miserably overrun' the county of Kent with error. *A Vindication of the Christian Church* (1701) was more than an apologetic for infant baptism. He claimed that the Toleration Act (1689), by removing measures of accountability, had promoted schism and the rise of heresy. Baptists were only one stage in the slide from presbyterianism to Quakerism. Disintegration of the established church had to be stopped with 'wise and moderate laws' that would protect it from such 'sects'. In the midst of this polemical barrage he published *The Divine Feudal Law* (1703), his translation (from Latin) of a work by Pufendorf, hoping, like its author, to unite protestants. Whatever goodwill created by this was quickly lost.

That year, Dorrington's *The Dissenting Ministry in Religion Censur'd* attacked the 'greatest Evil' and cause of all religious corruption: the usurping of ministry by those not qualified for that office. In a postscript to *A Defence of Moderate Nonconformity* (part 1, 1703) Edmund Calamy described Dorrington's argument as 'weak, as it is bitter and virulent' and full of 'Furious Invective' (Calamy, *Defence*, 239–40): he had misrepresented dissenters and had abandoned them because he misunderstood their principles and sought preferment in the established church.

Dorrington's shallow arguments and sharp tone had marginalized him. He returned to publishing devotional guides, but usually with commentary on the key role of lawful ministers and how nonconformity was a chief cause of impiety. *The Plain Man's Gift of Prayer* (1703) opposed the extemporaneous praying of 'sects'. *A Discourse of Singing* (1704) criticized some dissenters' plain style of worship, and *Devotions for Several Occasions* (1707) complained of others' 'instrumental verse'. *Family Instruction* (1705) labelled dissenting academies 'nurseries of errour and schism'; *The Worship of God* (1712) reinforced this attack and rebuked dissenters for abandoning sacramental worship.

In 1710 Dorrington renewed his frontal assault. In *The Dissenters Represented and Condemn'd* he opposed occasional conformity and used the presbyterian Daniel Williams's censure of a member's unlawful separation as a basis to argue against sectarian schism. To the end he maintained that true morality, unity, and loyalty could be maintained only within the established church. After the Hanoverian accession, in *The True Foundation of Obedience and Submission* (1714) he railed against dissenters as 'Republicans' whose call for personal liberty and opposition to passive obedience were just as inimical to the interests of hereditary protestant succession as were the Jacobites.

Dorrington died at Wittersham on 30 April 1715, and was buried in the church there. He was survived by his wife, Elizabeth (the daughter of Joseph Waldo of Hoxton), who lived until 1739; a daughter, Sarah; and a son, Theophilus, who became treasurer of the East India Company and died on 5 November 1768. JIM SPIVEY

Sources E. Calamy, *An historical account of my own life, with some reflections on the times I have lived in, 1671–1731*, ed. J. T. Rutt, 2 vols. (1829), vol. 2 · Venn, *Alum. Cant.* · Foster, *Alum. Oxon.* · W. Wilson, *The history and antiquities of the dissenting churches and meeting houses in London, Westminster and Southwark*, 4 vols. (1808–14), vol. 3 · DNB · T. Dorrington, dedicatory epistle, *Observations concerning the present state of religion in the Romish church* (1699) · E. Calamy, *Defence of moderate nonconformity*, pt 1 (1703), postscript, 239–61 · T. Dorrington, dedicatory epistle, *A vindication of the Christian church in the baptizing of infants* (1701) · T. Dorrington, dedicatory epistle, *Family instruction for the Church of England* (1705)
Likenesses G. Bouttats, line engraving (after C. Franck), repro. in T. Dorrington, *Family devotions*, 3rd edn, 4 vols. (1703)

Dors [*married names* Hamilton, Dawson, Lake], **Diana** [*real name* Diana Mary Fluck] **(1931–1984)**, actress, was born on 23 October 1931 in Swindon, Wiltshire, the only child of

Diana Dors (1931–1984), by Frank Buckingham?, 1955

Albert Edward Sidney Fluck (1893–1963) of Swindon, a railway clerk and former army captain, and his wife, Winifred Maud Mary Payne (1889–1955). She was educated at a local private school and when she was nine she wrote in a school essay, 'I am going to be a film star, with a swimming pool and a cream telephone.' At thirteen, pretending to be seventeen, she entered a beauty contest and came third, and during the Second World War she entertained troops at camp concerts.

At fifteen Diana Fluck enrolled at the London Academy of Music and Dramatic Art, where she was spotted in a production and put into films, making her début in a thriller, *The Shop at Sly Corner*, in 1946. After other parts she was offered a ten-year contract by the Rank Organization and she joined the Rank Charm School, which had been set up to discover and groom British stars. She changed her surname to Dors, after her maternal grandmother. Her performances in such films as *Good Time Girl* (1948), *Dance Hall* (1950), and the popular Huggett series, where she showed a flair for comedy, introduced an earthier strain into a genteel middle-class cinema. But her screen career failed to develop and the Rank contract lapsed in 1950. The publicity machine, however, was already starting to take over. With her long, platinum blonde hair, full lips, sensational figure, and colourful private life, she was projected as the British answer to Marilyn Monroe; and for the rest of her life her professional achievements came a very poor second to her status as a celebrity.

The early publicity stunts were masterminded by Dors's first husband, Dennis Hamilton (1924–1959), whom she married in 1951. Born Dennis Hamlington Gittings, he was the son of Stanley Gittings, manager of a public house in Luton. A Svengali figure, ruthless and domineering, he fed the gossip columns with a stream of Dors stories, many of them fabricated. The couple took off for Hollywood. Diana Dors continued to appear in films, most of them forgettable. An exception was *Yield to the Night* (1956), loosely based on the Ruth Ellis case, in which Dors eschewed her usual glamour roles to play a condemned murderess. It showed her potential as a serious actress, though the public found the switch from blonde bombshell difficult to take. Her marriage foundered, and ended, in the now customary blaze of publicity, in 1957. Dennis Hamilton died in 1959 and in the same year she married in New York an American comedian, Dickie Dawson. They had two sons, Mark and Gary. In 1960 she was paid £35,000 for her memoirs by the *News of the World*. Lurid by the standards of the time, the series ran for twelve weeks. The archbishop of Canterbury, Dr Geoffrey Fisher, denounced her as a wayward hussy.

By now the film parts were getting smaller. Dors put on weight and the erstwhile sex symbol gave way to a middle-aged mother figure. She had to return to England in 1966 to support her family, for she was sole breadwinner. She played Prince Charming in pantomime and did a cabaret act in the northern clubs. Her private life continued to make the headlines. Her marriage to Dawson ended after eight years and she lost custody of her two sons. On 23 November 1968 she married an actor, Alan Lake (1940–1984), son of Cyril Foster Lake, glaze maker. They had a son, Jason. In 1967 she was declared bankrupt, owing the Inland Revenue £48,413 in tax. She admitted to being hopeless with money. In October 1970 Lake was sent to prison for eighteen months for his part in a public house brawl.

Dors's acting career enjoyed a brief revival when she played a brassy widow in *Three Months Gone* at the Royal Court Theatre in London (1970) and there was a strong part in Jerzy Skolimowski's film, *Deep End* (1970). But a television comedy series written for her by the distinguished team of Keith Waterhouse and Willis Hall, *Queenie's Castle* (1970), proved disappointing. Her Jocasta in Sophocles' *Oedipus* at the Chichester Festival in 1974 was a brave, but isolated, stab at the classics.

In 1974 Diana Dors came close to death from meningitis and she underwent operations for cancer in 1982 and 1983. Resilient and cheerful in the face of such adversity, she produced further instalments of her memoirs as well as an autobiography, ran an agony column in a Sunday newspaper, and, by now over 15 stone, did a slimming series for breakfast television. A celebrity to the end, she died of cancer in hospital at Windsor, Berkshire, on 4 May 1984 and was buried on 11 May in Sunningdale. Her death was widely and genuinely mourned. Vulgar she may have been but there was admiration for her courage and tenacity. Alan Lake never got over his grief and he killed himself on 10 October 1984, the sixteenth anniversary of their first meeting.

Diana Dors was a potent early example of a media-created celebrity, who became famous more for what she was than for what she did. She was able to exploit a growing openness about sexuality, not least in the press, and she embodied, albeit in an extreme form, the ordinary person's aspiration for a better life as the nation moved from post-war austerity to 1950s affluence. Although she flaunted the trappings of her wealth, the mink coats, the Rolls-Royces, and the luxury homes, she never lost the common touch and, despite condemnation from the puritan establishment, the public stayed with her.

PETER WAYMARK

Sources J. Flory and D. Walne, *Diana Dors: only a whisper away* (1987) · contemporary newspaper reports and reviews of films and stage appearances · C. Geraghty, 'Diana Dors', *All our yesterdays: 90 years of British cinema*, ed. C. Barr (1986) · b. cert. · m. cert. · *The Times* (7 May 1984) · personal knowledge (2004)
Archives FILM BFI NFTVA, 'Dors ... the other Diana', Channel 4, 27 May 1990 · BFI NFTVA, *Arena*, BBC 2, 26 Dec 1999 · BFI NFTVA, 'The unforgettable Diana Dors', ITV, 24 March 2000 · BFI NFTVA, *Icons*, Channel 4, 23 Feb 2001 · BFI NFTVA, performance recordings | SOUND BL NSA, documentary recordings · BL NSA, performance recordings
Likenesses F. Buckingham?, photograph, 1955, Kobal Collection, London [*see illus.*] · photographs, Hult. Arch.
Wealth at death £250,167: probate, 28 May 1985, *CGPLA Eng. & Wales*

D'Orsay, Gédéon Gaspard Alfred de Grimaud [Alfred Guillaume Gabriel], styled **Count D'Orsay** (1801–1852), artist and dandy, was born in Paris on 4 September 1801, second son of Albert, Count D'Orsay, a general in Napoleon's *grand armée*, and Eleanore de Franquemont, an illegitimate daughter of the duke of Würtemburg and an Italian adventuress, Anne Franchi. His elder brother died in infancy. As befitted the son of a general, but against his staunchly imperial sympathies, Alfred D'Orsay joined the army of the restored Bourbon monarchy in 1821 with a commission in the *garde du corps*, shortly before embarking for England to attend the coronation of George IV. In England, he quickly gained a reputation as a dandy, as his biographer W. Teignmouth Shore observed: 'It was ... no small feather in D'Orsay's cap that he came to London an unknown man, was seen, and by his very rivals at once acknowledged as a conqueror. His youth, his handsome face, his debonairness, his wit, were irresistible' (Shore, 36).

D'Orsay returned to France the following year and was quartered with his regiment at Valence on the Rhône, where, on 15 November 1822, he first became acquainted with Marguerite *Gardiner, countess of Blessington, and her husband, the first earl. He accepted their invitation to travel with them and resigned his commission. On 31 March 1823 they arrived at Genoa where they met Byron, who sat to D'Orsay for his last portrait. Byron found him 'clever, original, unpretending ... he affected to be nothing that he was not' (Shore, 51). Also at Genoa, on 31 August 1823, Lord Blessington made his will, leaving all his Irish property to the daughter of his first marriage, provided she married D'Orsay. The fifteen-year-old Lady Harriet Anne Jane Frances Gardiner (1812–1869) was married to D'Orsay at Naples on 1 December 1827. The couple put up no false front of happiness: they were cold, distant,

Gédéon Gaspard Alfred de Grimaud D'Orsay, styled Count D'Orsay (1801–1852), by Sir George Hayter, 1839

and barely civil to each other. D'Orsay's interest in his new wife was merely financial; his romantic interest was in Lady Blessington. Their affair had begun some time before the marriage, and, although the earl could hardly have remained in ignorance of it, he took no action. Indeed, the possible relationships between the members of this *ménage à trois* have produced speculations that it was Blessington who was D'Orsay's admirer, and that D'Orsay himself was impotent (Sadleir, 44–8).

From Italy, the entourage moved on to Paris, where Lord Blessington died on 23 May 1829. The following year the family returned to London. Although Lady Harriet left D'Orsay and returned to her relatives in Ireland in 1831, her husband seems to have been undisturbed by either their estrangement or the scandal it caused. He busied himself by acting as host of Lady Blessington's fashionable, though bohemian, salon, first at Seamore Place, Mayfair, and then at Gore House, Piccadilly. Together they wielded a kind of influence over the artistic world of London, and gathered around them many of the social and literary celebrities of their time. Despite their precautions (D'Orsay officially lived not at Gore House, but next door) their affair was common knowledge, and had the effect of keeping away from the salon anybody with pretensions to moral respectability.

In London, D'Orsay was both a sculptor and a painter, specializing in portraiture. In 1845 he painted the portrait of Wellington, who is said to have exclaimed, 'At last I have been painted like a gentleman!', adding immediately, 'I'll never sit to any one else!' (Shore, 232). His statuettes of Napoleon and Wellington were very popular, as were engravings of many of his portraits, including those of Queen Victoria, Dwarkanath Tagore, and Lord Lyndhurst. More than 125 profile sketches of his contemporaries were published by Mitchell of Bond Street, including among them nearly all the artistic, literary, and fashionable celebrities of the time. Some sixty-one of his pencil and chalk portraits are in the National Portrait Gallery, as are the 1845 portrait of Wellington and a self-portrait in marble.

D'Orsay was chronically irresponsible about money: 'he never denied himself that which he could obtain for love or by owing money' (Shore, 131–2). Handsome, perhaps beautiful, he early developed a taste for elegant living, but had no family money to support his tastes; highly vain and profoundly selfish, he assumed he had an entitlement to live as he wished. Sadleir comments that D'Orsay decided to 'capitalise his only assets, sell his looks and fascination to the best possible advantage' (Sadleir, 47). The number of his creditors suggests he did this to some effect. He used some of the money he borrowed for philanthropic purposes, and was one of the founders of the London Société de Bienfaisance, but far more went on the gaming tables, the racetrack, his clothes, horses, and carriages. In 1838, in exchange for a legal separation and his relinquishing of all claims to the Blessington estate, Lady Harriet paid over £100,000 to his creditors—and yet still unpaid debts remained.

More important in D'Orsay's estimation than paying the debts he had incurred, was the frequenting of Gore House by the exiled Louis Napoleon (later Napoleon III). An intimate friendship grew up between the two Frenchmen, or so D'Orsay, the loyal Bonapartist, thought. Other regulars at Gore House by 1840 included Disraeli, Bulwer, Ainsworth, Dickens, Thackeray, and Marryat, drawn in part at least by D'Orsay's charm. Considered the 'prince of dandies', and widely regarded as the handsomest man in England (although French), his dandyism served no ulterior motive; unlike his admirer Disraeli, whose 'amateur' dandyism was always a means to a political end. Indeed, Disraeli included a favourable portrait of D'Orsay (as Count Mirabel) in his 1837 novel, *Henrietta Temple*. Even Tennyson was charmed: 'Count D'Orsay is a friend of mine, co-godfather to Dickens's child with me' (Shore, 266); the child rejoiced in the name Alfred D'Orsay Tennyson Dickens.

And still the debts mounted. By 1849, D'Orsay could no longer avoid his creditors, and, like the previous 'prince of dandies', Beau Brummell, he fled to France. Lady Blessington admitted defeat, sold almost all of her possessions, and joined him in Paris, where she died shortly after her arrival. Her death was a blow from which D'Orsay never fully recovered. Louis Napoleon had also returned to France from exile, and had been elected president of the new republic in 1848. D'Orsay hoped for an appointment from him, as the reward of loyalty and friendship, but Louis Napoleon was reluctant to entrust to him any affairs of state. The president finally offered him the position of director of the Beaux-Arts. Within a few months of the appointment, however, D'Orsay contracted a spinal infection, which was to prove fatal. He died on 4 August 1852 in the house of his sister Ida, duchesse de Gramont. His erstwhile friend, now Napoleon III, was conspicuous among the mourners at his funeral. D'Orsay was buried next to Lady Blessington in the grey stone pyramid which he had designed and built for her at Chambourcy, near St Germain-en-Laye.   KATHRYN M. BURTON

Sources W. Teignmouth Shore, *D'Orsay, or, The complete dandy* (1911) · M. Sadleir, *Blessington–D'Orsay: a masquerade* (1933) · R. R. Madden, *The literary life and correspondence of the countess of Blessington*, 3 vols. (1855) · *The Times* (6 Aug 1852) · *The Times* (7 Aug 1852) · *The Times* (10 Aug 1852) · *Annual Register* (1852) · *DNB*
Archives Bodl. Oxf., corresp. with B. Disraeli and his wife · Bodl. Oxf., letters to Lord Lichfield · Durham RO, letters to Lord Londonderry · Herts. ALS, letters to Lord Lytton
Likenesses E. Landseer, pen-and-wash drawing, 1832–5, NPG · R. J. Lane, lithograph, pubd 1833, NPG · Maclise, silhouette, *c*.1834, repro. in *Fraser's Magazine*, 10 (1834) · D. Maclise, group portrait, lithograph, pubd 1835, BM · F. Grant, pencil drawing, 1836, BM · G. Hayter, oils, 1839, NPG [*see illus.*] · E. Landseer, lithograph, 1840, Royal Collection · R. J. Lane, chalk drawing, 1841, NPG · W. Behnes, bust, 1843–7, Royal Collection · D. Maclise, lithograph, pubd 1873, BM, NPG · Count D'Orsay, self-portrait, marble bust, NPG · J. Doyle, drawings, BM · E. Landseer, chalk drawing, BM · E. Landseer, pen-and-ink drawings, NG Scot. · F. C. Lewis, mezzotint (after F. Grant), BM · J. Wood, oils, Hughenden Manor, Buckinghamshire · engraving (after F. Grant), repro. in S. Sidney, *Book of the horse (thorough-bred, half-bred, cart-bred), saddle and harness, British and foreign* (1875) · lithograph, BM · lithographs, NPG

Dorset. For this title name *see* Beaufort, John, marquess of Dorset and marquess of Somerset (*c*.1371–1410); Grey, Thomas, first marquess of Dorset (*c*.1455–1501); Grey, Thomas, second marquess of Dorset (1477–1530); Sackville, Thomas, first Baron Buckhurst and first earl of Dorset (*c*.1536–1608); Sackville, Robert, second earl of Dorset (1560/61–1609); Sackville, Edward, fourth earl of Dorset (1590–1652); Clifford, Anne, countess of Pembroke, Dorset, and Montgomery (1590–1676); Sackville, Richard, fifth earl of Dorset (1622–1677) [*see under* Sackville, Edward, fourth earl of Dorset (1590–1652)]; Sackville, Charles, sixth earl of Dorset and first earl of Middlesex (1643–1706); Sackville, Lionel Cranfield, first duke of Dorset (1688–1765); Sackville, Charles, second duke of Dorset (1711–1769); Sackville, John Frederick, third duke of Dorset (1745–1799).

Dorset [*née* Turner], **Catherine Ann** (*b*. in or before **1752**, *d*. in or after **1816**), children's writer, was the younger daughter of Nicholas Turner of Stoke, near Guildford, Surrey, and Bignor Park, Sussex, and his wife, Anna (*d*. 1752), daughter of William Towers. Catherine was baptized at Stoke on 15 January 1753; her mother died while she was an infant and Catherine's care consequently fell to an aunt. In 1764 her father remarried; his new wife was a Miss Meriton. Little is known of Catherine's childhood with her sister, Charlotte [*see* Smith, Charlotte (1749–1806)]. On 2 June 1779, in St Martin-in-the-Fields, Catherine married Michael Dorset (*d*. *c*.1805), a captain in the army and probably the son of Michael Dorset MA, incumbent successively of Rustington and Walberton, in Sussex.

They had two children, Lucy Smith Dorset (*bap.* 1780) and Charles Ferguson Dorset (*bap.* 1782).

In 1804 some poems by Catherine Ann Dorset appeared anonymously in her sister's *Conversations Introducing Poetry*, a temporarily popular compilation for children. Charlotte Smith, better known for her adult fiction, produced various works for children in the 1790s and early 1800s and this may have encouraged her sister to write. About 1805 Catherine Ann Dorset was widowed and in 1806 she sold the interest in Bignor Park bequeathed to her by her father. In 1807 her poem for children *The Peacock 'at Home'* was published as 'by a lady' for the second number of John Harris's Cabinet series, illustrated by William Mulready. The initial two publications in the series were to cause something of a stir; the first had been *The Butterfly's Ball* by William Roscoe, and the *Gentleman's Magazine* printed some correspondence debating the relative merits of these two numbers. Some readers asserted the superiority of Dorset's 'exquisite little Poem', and suggested that it might be a 'satire upon the manners of the times', while others attributed the poem's success merely to the gender of its author and complained also that its ornithological detail would deter young readers. Nevertheless, *The Peacock 'at Home'* was a great success, selling 40,000 copies within a year, and reaching a twenty-eighth edition by 1819. On the back of this success, Harris published eleven further numbers in this series of tiny (5 inch x 4 inch) volumes for children. These included another work by Catherine Ann Dorset, *Think before you Speak, or, The Three Wishes* (1809), a translation of a French folk story as related by Mme de Beaumont. It is also possible that another title in the series, *The Lion's Masquerade* (1807), was one of Catherine Ann Dorset's publications. Revised and unillustrated versions of *The Peacock 'at Home' and other Poems* appeared in 1809 under Dorset's married name. *The Peacock* was reprinted in 1849, illuminated by her grand-niece W. Warde, and a careful facsimile of the original edition appeared in 1883.

Catherine Ann Dorset also wrote an important memoir of Charlotte Smith, published in Walter Scott's *Miscellaneous Prose Works* (6 vols., 1827), with Scott's critical remarks appended. Little information on Catherine Ann Dorset herself emerges from the memoir, save her disapproval of the French Revolution. Catherine Ann Dorset was still alive in 1816, but nothing is known of her after this time. Her son went on to become an officer in the army and he also wrote some poetry and military works.

JENNETT HUMPHREYS, *rev.* KATHERINE TURNER

Sources D. G. C. Elwes and C. J. Robinson, *A history of the castles, mansions, and manors of western Sussex* (1876) · J. Dallaway, *The parochial topography of the rape of Arundel*, new edn, ed. E. Cartwright (1832), vol. 2/1 of *A history of the western division of the county of Sussex* · C. A. Dorset, 'Charlotte Smith', in *The miscellaneous prose works of Sir Walter Scott*, 4 (1827), 3–47 · *GM*, 1st ser., 77 (1807), 846–7, 998, 1222 · *GM*, 1st ser., 78 (1808), 206–7 · C. Welsh, introduction, 'The peacock "at home"': a sequel to 'The butterfly's ball', written by a lady, ed. [C. A. T. Dorset] (1883), iii–x, esp. vii–viii · C. Welsh, introduction, in *A lady* [C. A. Dorset], *The lion's masquerade* (1807); repr. (1883) · C. Welsh, introduction, in C. A. T. Dorset, *Think before you speak*, ed. C. Welsh (1809); repr. (1883) · M. Moon, ed., *John Harris's books for youth, 1801–1843*, rev. edn (1992) · F. J. Harvey Darton, *Children's books in England: five centuries of social life*, rev. B. Alderson, 3rd edn (1982) · *IGI*
Archives W. Sussex RO, letters to John Hawkins

Doubleday, Edward (1810–1849), entomologist, was born on 9 October 1810 at 62 High Street, Epping, Essex, the second son of Benjamin Doubleday (1771–1848), grocer and provision merchant, and his wife, Mary (1779–1846). He and his brother Henry *Doubleday (1808–1875), also a celebrated entomologist, were birthright Quakers who attended the local Friends' school, Isaac Payne's, and shared an enthusiasm for natural history. Doubleday received a good classical education, and possessing a romantic temperament dreamed of studying nature in the New World.

Doubleday contributed many articles and notes to scientific journals, notably the *Entomological Magazine*, some under the pseudonym Δ (Delta). His plans to travel widely in North America were fulfilled in 1837 when, in the company of fellow Quaker and entomologist Robert Foster, he arrived in New York. During his trip he amassed a large collection of insects, mainly Lepidoptera and Coleoptera, but also some birds and animals, which he shipped back at intervals for the Entomological Club cabinet, the British Museum, and other institutions. He met many American naturalists and his letters to Edward Newman, nearly twenty of which were printed in the *Entomological Magazine*, gave fascinating accounts of his extensive travels. On his return the following year he was dissuaded from joining the ill-fated Niger expedition.

A genial companion and a brilliant scientific lepidopterist with a worldwide correspondence, Doubleday was appointed in 1841 assistant in the zoological department of the British Museum, where he built up a magnificent lepidopteran collection. He published about thirty scientific papers of entomological importance after his return from America (among the most notable being 'Remarks on Lepidoptera of North America', *Magazine of Natural History*, 1840, and 'Description of new or imperfectly described diurnal Lepidoptera', *Annals of Natural History*, 1845–8). He enjoyed membership of many British and foreign scientific societies, including the Linnean (1843–9), and the Entomological, of which he was a founder member (1833) and secretary for the last two years of his life. He was a vice-president of the Botanical Society. Appointed curator of the collections of the Entomological Club in 1843, he was noted for his extreme liberality to fellow entomologists, to the detriment, Newman commented ruefully, of the cabinets.

Doubleday's early death at the age of thirty-nine terminated the publication of his *List of Lepidopterous Insects in the British Museum* of which three parts only, covering the butterflies, were issued (1844, 1847, and appendix 1848). Also left uncompleted was his most ambitious work, the superb two-volume serial publication *The Genera of Diurnal Lepidoptera*, illustrated with coloured plates by W. C. Hewitson. Started in 1846 but interrupted by his ill health in 1848 and later by Hewitson's illness, the *Genera* was only half completed at the time of his death. Doubleday, who never married, died of spinal disease at his home in Harrington Square, Westminster, London, on 14 December 1849, a great loss to entomological science. He was buried in the Quaker burial-ground at Epping on 19 December. The *Genera* was finally completed by J. O. Westwood in 1852, and reissued in parts in 1857–61.　ROBERT MAYS

Sources Gardeners' Chronicle (2 Feb 1850), 71 · Proceedings of the Linnean Society of London, 2 (1848–55) · Proceedings of the Entomological Society of London (7 Jan 1850) · S. H. Scudder, ed., 'Correspondence between Thaddeus William Harris and Edward Doubleday', Occasional Papers of the Boston Society of Natural History, 1 (1869), 122–73 · H. A. Hagen, Bibliotheca entomologica, 1 (1862), 179–81 · F. Hemming, 'The dates of publication of the several portions of Doubleday (E) Genera of diurnal lepidoptera and of the continuation thereof by Westwood (J. O.)', Journal of the Society of the Bibliography of Natural History, 1 (1936–43), 335–464 · E. Doubleday, 'Communications on the natural history of North America', Entomological Magazine, 4/5 (1837–8) · S. A. Neave, The centenary history of the Entomological Society of London, 1833–1933 (1933) · J. M. Chalmers-Hunt, Natural History auctions, 1700–1972 (1976) · R. South, 'The Entomological Club', The Entomologist, 32 (1899) · RS Friends, Lond.
Archives NHM · Saffron Walden Museum | Oxf. U. Mus. NH, notes relating to butterflies and MS lists of Libellulidae and Tortricidae in British Museum
Likenesses attrib. H. C., etching, 1837, RS Friends, Lond. · G. H. Ford, lithograph, 1844 (after medallion by B. Smith), NPG · B. Smith, plaster medallion, 1844, NHM · T. H. Maguire, lithograph, 1850, BM, Linn. Soc., NPG · W. Farren, carte-de-visite, Royal Entomological Society of London
Wealth at death £1000: administration, PRO, PROB 6/226

Doubleday, Henry (1808–1875), naturalist, was born on 1 July 1808 at 62 High Street, Epping, Essex, the elder of the two children of Benjamin Doubleday (1771–1848), grocer and provision merchant, and his wife, Mary (1779–1846). His brother, Edward *Doubleday (1810–1849), became a distinguished entomologist. A Quaker by birth, Doubleday attended the local Friends' school conducted by Isaac Payne. With congenial schoolfellows he studied the wildlife in the adjacent Epping Forest and the surrounding countryside, thereby laying the foundations of his life's work.

After leaving school Doubleday assisted in the family shop, and following his father's death its management devolved solely on him. This new responsibility restricted his hitherto frequent collecting trips; however, his correspondence with English and foreign naturalists continued throughout his life to be extensive, and he also contributed observations on birds, plants, and insects to scientific journals, notably *The Entomologist* and *The Zoologist*, both edited by his close friend Edward Newman. Doubleday was an original and lifelong member of the Entomological Society of London. In local affairs he succeeded his father as treasurer of the Epping and Ongar Highway Trust and Epping Poor-Law Union. An excellent shot and taxidermist, he assisted many authors of standard natural history works, including William Yarrell, for whom he provided specimens and notes for his *History of British Birds* (1837–43), and Newman, who acknowledged his invaluable help in checking and correcting every column and sheet of his *Natural History of British Moths* (1869).

Shy and retiring, Doubleday was reluctant to appear in print and published little himself. Probably his earliest

Henry Doubleday (1808–1875), by Maull & Polyblank, c.1857

scientific note was on the hawfinch in 1837, which was written after several years' study and published study in *Jardine's Magazine of Zoology*. His study of birds, particularly in his earlier years, encouraged him to publish *Nomenclature of British Birds* (1836), a catalogue which passed through four editions. However, his arrangement of species attracted criticism. Among his other contributions to natural history were his recognition of the oxlip as a species distinct from the two other members of the same family, the primrose and the cowslip; this was later confirmed by Darwin. The attraction of sallow blossom in springtime for many moth species was noted by his first published entomological observation, and he also introduced a method of attracting moths by painting tree trunks with a treacle mixture. This method, known as 'sugaring', was based on an idea suggested by P. J. Selby of Twizzell, Northumberland, but had never before been practised. In 1843 Doubleday made a two-week visit to Paris in order to compare nomenclature with European lepidopterists. As a result on his return he devoted several years to the preparation of his *Synonymic List of British Lepidoptera* (1850). A second edition, adding the Tineidae, appeared in 1859, and later supplements identified over 2000 species; for a time it became a standard authority in Britain. Of his numerous foreign correspondents it was undoubtedly Achille Guénée, the eminent French lepidopterist of Châteaudun, with whom Doubleday most closely co-operated.

Doubleday's neglect of business, for which he was unsuited, and a heavy financial loss from a bank failure in 1866, led eventually to the prospect of financial ruin and a breakdown in his health from which he never completely recovered. In December 1870 he was admitted to the Retreat, the Quaker mental institution at York, 'with his body and mind shattered', as the medical superintendent reported. After four months he returned home, where his distant cousin, Ann Main, continued to look after him. In his absence friends had contributed to a trust to provide for his maintenance and for his research, and he was thus enabled to pursue his studies at home. Doubleday died of a heart condition at his home, 62 High Street, Epping, on 29 June 1875. He was buried on 4 July in the Quaker burial-ground at Epping. Always commanding great respect for his opinions, he accumulated much practical knowledge of which little written evidence remained. He left behind a remarkably comprehensive but unlabelled British and European Lepidoptera collection for which a catalogue was published in 1877.   ROBERT MAYS

Sources J. W. Dunning, *The Entomologist*, 10 (1877), 53–61 · *The Entomologist*, 8 (1875), 240 · *Entomologist's Monthly Magazine*, 12 (1875–6), 69–71 · M. Christy, *Birds of Essex* (1890), 13–19 · R. S. Wilkinson, 'P. J. Selby, the Doubledays and the modern method of "sugaring"', *Entomologist's Record*, 88 (1976), 23–5 · RS Friends, Lond., Port. D77–81 · MSS, priv. coll. · E. Newman, *An illustrated natural history of British moths* (1869), vii · M. Christy, 'On the species of the genus Primula in Essex', *Transactions and Proceedings, iii, Essex Field Club* (1883–4) · A. Guénée, 'Avertissement', *Uranides et Phalénites*, ed. A. Guénée, 2 vols. (1857), vols. 9–10 of *Histoire naturelle des insectes: species général des lépidoptères* (1836–58), vol. 1, viii
Archives NHM, specimens · Passmore Edwards Museum, Stratford, London | NHM, Entomology Library, De Grey and Stainton collection · Oxf. U. Mus. NH, letters to J. C. Dale · RS Friends, Lond. · Saffron Walden Museum, collections
Likenesses Maull & Polyblank, photograph, *c.*1857, Royal Entomological Society of London · Maull & Polyblank, photograph, *c.*1857, RS Friends, Lond. [*see illus.*] · oils, *c.*1857 (after photograph by Maull & Polyblank), NHM, department of entomology
Wealth at death under £450: resworn probate, Feb 1876, *CGPLA Eng. & Wales*

Doubleday, Henry (1810–1902), starch manufacturer and horticulturist, was born on 24 October 1810 at Coggeshall, Essex, the fourth of eight children of William Doubleday (1777–1854) and his wife, Hannah Corder (1779–1819). His parents, staunch Quakers, were shopkeepers. A number of their ancestors had sailed with William Penn to found Pennsylvania, the Quaker colony, and one of their distant relatives had established Doubleday, the American publishers. Henry's first cousin, namesake, and contemporary, Henry Doubleday (1808–1875) of Epping, was a well-known entomologist and ornithologist who was responsible for compiling the first catalogue of British Lepidoptera.

Little is known of Henry's early life with the exception that his mother died when he was nine, and that he attended Ackworth School (1822–4). He was an enthusiastic member of the local Quaker community, involved with several activities to assist his fellow Friends. In 1851 he was awarded a bronze medal at the Great Exhibition for his lace designs, produced by cottage industries at

Coggeshall. His main career, however, was as a manufacturer producing gelatine and starch, which was used by the retail trade as a gum. At this time the newly introduced penny black stamps had to be snipped off sheets individually and then gummed on to envelopes. Doubleday utilized a new type of imported gum that would stay on the back of the stamp until wetted, securing a contract with De La Rue, who printed many of the pre-colonial stamps. (The search for alternative glues had largely been prompted by the increased demand for labour following the construction of the Suez Canal, which had in turn led to a significant decline in the workforce gathering gum arabic in north Africa.)

The publication of an article in 1871, 'Composition and nutritive value of prickly comfrey *S. asperrimum*', by Augustus Voelcker in volume 7 of the *Journal of the Royal Agricultural Society*, drew Doubleday's attention to the possibility of producing a new gum which could be grown locally at Coggeshall. The article referred to comfrey producing mucilaginous or flesh forming matter, a term frequently used at this time to denote gummy proteins which were little understood. Doubleday, who was a member of the society, assumed that prickly comfrey might produce a gum suitable for his needs. He acquired seedlings from the English head gardener at the palace, St Petersburg, Russia, where the plants were extensively cultivated. Natural hybridization had occurred between the yellow or herbalists' comfrey, *Symphytum officinale*, native throughout Europe, and another species, blue prickly comfrey, *S. asperrimum*, planted next to it. From this parent stock, Doubleday bred an F_1 hybrid strain, which was later denoted as Doubleday's solid stemmed comfrey, or Russian comfrey to distinguish it from earlier introductions. The gum it produced, however, proved unsuitable as a stamp adhesive, which contributed to his losing the De La Rue contract and led ultimately to the sale of his factory. The last thirty years of his life were devoted to researching the new hybrid comfrey in the belief that it would help feed a starving world. He estimated that it was possible to produce crop yields of 100–120 tons per acre from six to eight cuts per annum. In 1875 Doubleday was awarded a fellowship of the Royal Society but had insufficient funds to register. He made a modest living from his small-holding and occasional sales of comfrey plants. His attempts to publicize his research were confined to a letter published in the *Gardeners' Chronicle and Agricultural Gazette* on 24 October 1885.

Throughout the latter part of his life Henry Doubleday was regarded by members of his family as a poor relative, an eccentric figure who lacked the necessary business acumen to capitalize on his research. Following his death in Coggeshall on 13 December 1902, aged ninety-two, his relatives amassed his personal papers and burnt them, making it impossible to establish precisely the long-term importance of his work. He was buried in Coggeshall.

Doubleday left the marketing of comfrey to his associate **Thomas Christy** (1831–1905), a botanist of Sydenham, London. He was the son of Thomas Christy (*b.* 1801) and his wife, Jane Sandwith, and was born on 9 December 1831 at

Bedford Road, Lambeth, London. His father, grandfather (also called Thomas), and uncle, William Miller Christy (1778–1858), were prosperous hat manufacturers. In 1826 they had taken over T. and J. Worsley's factory in Stockport, which had previously made hats on commission for the London market and established the foundations of England's leading hat-making firm. The income generated from their business enabled several members of the family, including Christy's uncle, to pursue careers as botanists. Little is known about Thomas's early life or education. He belonged to a long established Quaker family but in 1853, prior to going to live in China, he relinquished his membership of the Society of Friends. This was followed later by the resignation of his father, three sisters, and brother.

During his three-year stay in China Christy was associated with Sir Thomas Hanbury. On his return he became an importer and merchant of drugs, famed for his introduction of *Strophanthus* and menthol, being closely linked with Daniel Hanbury and other leading pharmacologists. In 1876 he became a fellow of the Linnean Society, and served on its council from 1883 to 1886. In addition to several scientific papers Christy was the author of *Forage Plants and … the New System of Ensilage* (1877), *New Commercial Plants* (1878–97, in 12 vols.), and, in conjunction with C. H. Leonard, *Dictionary of materia medica* (1892). He died at his home, the Manor House, Wallington, Surrey, on 7 September 1905, three years after Doubleday. He was buried at Wallington on 11 September. Although Christy was a successful businessman and pharmacologist his achievements in popularizing Doubleday's comfrey were limited.

In the early 1950s Lawrence Donegan Hills, a well-known organic gardener and gardening correspondent for *Punch* and *The Observer*, rediscovered the merits of Russian comfrey. He found that this perennial deep-rooted plant was able to produce several cuts of foliage each year which were rich in essential plant nutrients and formed an ideal instant compost for subsequent organic crops. Hills's fifth book, *Russian Comfrey* (1953), received international acclaim. In recognition of Henry Doubleday's contribution the research association which Hills and his wife Cherry established was named after him. They were tireless environmental campaigners at a time when such activities were unfashionable. The Henry Doubleday Research Association, initially based in Essex, was relocated to a larger 22 acre site near Ryton-on-Dunsmore, Coventry, where it was formally opened on 5 July 1986. By the 1990s the association constituted Europe's largest single organic gardening organization with a prestigious reputation for researching, demonstrating, and disseminating information on environmentally friendly, sustainable growing techniques for horticulturists worldwide. The association was a fitting tribute to Doubleday, a great yet humble man, one of the first pioneers of organic methods of food production. JOHN MARTIN

Sources digest registers (births to 1837), RS Friends, Lond. [London and Middlesex quarterly meeting] · *Proceedings of the Linnean Society of London*, 118th session (1905–6), 36 · 'Dictionary of Quaker biography', RS Friends, Lond. [card index] · L. D. Hills, *Fighting like the flowers* (1989) · *Annual Report* [Henry Doubleday Research Association] (1990) · R. S. Mortimer, 'Quaker printers, 1750–1850', *Journal of the Friends' Historical Society*, 50 (1962–4), 100–33 · *Annual Monitor* (1904) · T. Christy, *Ensilage: a system for the preservation in pits of forage plants and grasses, independent of weather* (1883) · T. Christy, *Forage plants and their economic conservation by the new system of ensilage* (1877) · T. Christy, *New commercial plants and drugs: with directions how to grow them to the best advantage*, 11 vols. (1878–89) · T. Christy, *New and rare drugs; being a concise reference to the uses, doses, and preparations of over 250 of the latest introductions* (1888) · T. Christy and C. H. Leonard, *Dictionary of materia medica and therapeutics* (1892) · CGPLA Eng. & Wales (1905) [Thomas Christy]

Likenesses daguerreotype, 1851, repro. in Hills, *Fighting like the flowers*

Wealth at death died in poverty: Hills, *Fighting like the flowers* · £3028 18s. 10d.—Thomas Christy: probate, 6 Nov 1905, CGPLA Eng. & Wales

Doubleday, Herbert Arthur (1867–1941), publisher and genealogist, was born at Hamburg, Germany, on 23 November 1867, the second son of the five children of William Bennett Doubleday, a woollen factor of London, and his first wife, Agnes Hannah Newman Fenn, of Beccles. Doubleday was educated at Dulwich College and London University, and served with various booksellers and publishers in London. In 1891 he founded the firm of Archibald Constable & Co. with his stepmother's brother of that name, a grandson of Scott's publisher. Among other books they published works by Meredith and Conan Doyle, but their most important single project was the Victoria History of the Counties of England, conceived, designed, and launched mainly by Doubleday himself. On 30 September 1896 he married Katherine Alice Lucile (Kate; b. 1871, d. after 1941), the daughter of Thomas Lawrence, of Ratby, Leicestershire. They had two daughters. From 1901 to 1903 he was chief editor of the Victoria History of the Counties of England, and was then succeeded by William Page. Ten volumes of the history appeared under his sole editorship or in collaboration with Page. Doubleday possessed a keen appreciation of the qualities of good paper and type; both the History and later *The Complete Peerage* owed much to his skill and taste.

In 1903 Doubleday left Constable & Co. and for a time lived in Bruges, where he published books in English and French. With Cuthbert Wilkinson he founded in 1908 the St Catherine Press (named after the Porte Sainte Catherine in Bruges), a combination of two earlier enterprises, one in Bruges and one in London. The latter firm, Arthur Doubleday & Co., had already produced some notable fine books including a reprint of Evelyn's *Sylva*. It was to the St Catherine Press that Vicary Gibbs entrusted his new edition of *The Complete Peerage*, and Doubleday designed the layout and chose the Caslon type for it. Almost from the first Doubleday's share was more than that of an ordinary publisher, and in volumes 3 and 4 his assistance was recognized by Gibbs on the title-page. In 1916 he formally became assistant editor and in 1920 editor. After Gibbs gave up control, Doubleday became solely responsible for producing *The Complete Peerage*. Under his direction, and with various colleagues, volumes 5 to 10 and volume 13 were issued. The fact that the whole enterprise did not collapse was due entirely to his unflagging energy in simultaneously organizing the work of writing the volumes and raising the funds to produce them. He himself contributed an important appendix, 'Earldoms and baronies', to volume 4, and in 1920 replied in print to a hostile review of this by J. H. Round. Doubleday continued to work on *The Complete Peerage* to within a few weeks of his death. His wide view of the scope of the work and his scholarly desire for authoritative reference to original sources make the later volumes (especially in their medieval matter) even more valuable to scholars than the first four volumes, which he always hoped one day to re-edit.

Doubleday was a stocky man of medium height and a games player all his life. Latterly, playing golf once a week was his sole relaxation from editorial work. He had a keen sense of humour and was a kindly and understanding man. He died of cancer at his home, 27 The Terrace, Barnes, Surrey, on 27 March 1941; he was survived by his wife.   MICHAEL MACLAGAN, *rev.* P. W. HAMMOND

Sources *Herbert Arthur Doubleday* (1942) · P. Hammond, 'A brief history of *The complete peerage*', GEC, *Peerage*, new edn, 14.vi-xv · *CGPLA Eng. & Wales* (1941) · T. L. Ormiston, *Dulwich College register, 1619 to 1926* (1926) · m. cert. · d. cert.
Archives HLRO, Complete Peerage Trust MSS · NL Wales, letters to Edward Owen · W. Sussex RO, corresp. with Oswald Barron · W. Yorks. AS, Bradford, letters to W. P. Baildon
Likenesses photograph, 1930–39, repro. in *Herbert Arthur Doubleday*, frontispiece
Wealth at death £895 15s. 5d.: probate, 25 July 1941, *CGPLA Eng. & Wales*

Doubleday, Thomas (1790–1870), politician and author, born in Newcastle upon Tyne in February 1790, was the son of George Doubleday, a manufacturer of soap, tallow, and sulphuric acid, and his wife, Mary, *née* Fawcett. His political activities during the 1830s are his greatest claim to fame: although a poor orator, he was a competent organizer of political agitation, with a considerable gift for propaganda.

Under the early influence of William Cobbett, Doubleday became a leading figure in the Northern Political Union throughout the struggle for parliamentary reform in the early 1830s. After the enactment of parliamentary reform in 1832, he believed that the whigs betrayed the people. He thought the 1834 Poor Law Amendment Act to be 'a scheme, the most atrocious, probably, ever entertained by any legislators calling themselves civilised' (*A Financial, Monetary and Statistical History of England from the Revolution of 1688 to the Present Time*, 1847, 313). After the Municipal Reform Act of 1835 he entered the reformed Newcastle council, but opposed the creation of an 'Austrian-like' borough police (Newcastle watch committee minutes, 5 May 1836) in a town 'remarkable for its good behaviour' (ibid., 4 March 1837). (Newcastle police had recorded 1327 cases of 'disorderly conduct' in 1835.)

Doubleday was an enthusiastic Chartist in the early Victorian years, taking a leading part in the *Northern Liberator* during that sprightly Chartist newspaper's short life. As an elected councillor from 1835 to 1840, he defended Chartists from criticism in the reformed Newcastle town

council. Although by 1856 he claimed to have lost 'the feelings of a partisan of any line of policy' (T. Doubleday, *The Political Life of Sir Robert Peel*, 1.iii), his hostility to the whigs persisted. In 1864 he appealed to fellow radicals to vote Conservative, noting that 'If ruled by Tories, we should at all events be ruled by gentlemen' (*Crimes of the Whigs, or, A Radical's Reasons for Supporting the Tory Party at the Next General Election*). He supported the Northern Reform Union and the Reform League, but like Cobbett, his liberalism had its limits; in 1847 he denounced 'the Jew or moneyed interest' (*A Financial, Monetary and Statistical History of England*, 305), and when *The Times* supported whig foreign policy in 1861 he castigated it in a pamphlet as 'that Jew-organ' (*The French Alliance: its Origins and Authors*).

Doubleday's political activities were complemented by varied intellectual interests. His first published work (1818) comprised sixty-five sonnets, and was followed by the undistinguished verse dramas *The Italian Wife* (1823), *Babington* (1825), *Diocletian* (1829), and *Caius Marius* (1836). Such lines as 'How poor a stay has she who leans upon thy bosom for support' (from *The Italian Wife*) might well fail to achieve the desired effect on contemporary audiences. Like the sculptor John Graham Lough, Doubleday's creative talents aroused an enthusiasm in his own region that was not shared by a wider public, although his novel *The Eve of St Mark: a Romance of Venice* (1857) shows some merit. A keen angler, he co-operated with his friend Robert Roxby in writing, collecting, and publishing fishing songs (for example, *The Coquetdale Fishing Songs*, 1852). He wrote widely on political economy and similar subjects, and published a philosophical treatise *On Mundane and Moral Government* (1852). He was also much concerned with the nature and proper administration of the money supply, notably in *A Financial, Monetary and Statistical History of England from the Revolution of 1688 to the Present Time* (1847). His *Political Life of Sir Robert Peel* (2 vols., 1856) is a substantial work in which W. L. Burn rightly discerned in 1956 'considerable judgment and discernment' (Burn, 7n.). He wrote extensively on diverse topics for both local and national newspapers and reviews.

The collapse of the family business in the early 1840s was largely caused by Doubleday's absorption in political and literary activities. Other factors included a disastrous fire in 1841, speculation in lead-mining shares, and extravagant expenditure by his business partner Anthony Easterby. Doubleday's personal popularity was never in doubt, and after this catastrophe even political enemies helped to ensure that he retained enough income to live in modest comfort. He was given the post of registrar of births, marriages, and deaths for St Andrew's parish, Newcastle, and subsequently served as salaried secretary of the Tyneside coalowners' organization. In late 1870 his health failed, and he died at his home, Gosforth Villas, Bulman village, Gosforth, on 18 December. Although the evidence is incomplete, it appears probable that Doubleday had married twice; his second wife, Mary, survived him for only a few months, dying on 4 March 1871. He had three sons, all probably from his first marriage, and probably three daughters by his second marriage. He

was buried at Gosforth parish churchyard. His funeral attracted much public attention and there were laudatory
obituaries.   NORMAN MCCORD

Sources W. L. Burn, 'Newcastle upon Tyne in the early nineteenth century', *Archaeologia Aeliana*, 4th ser., 34 (1956), 1–13 · *Lawson's Tyneside celebrities* (1873), 279 · *Newcastle Daily Chronicle* (19 Dec
1870) · *Newcastle Daily Journal* (19 Dec 1870) · T. Nossiter, *Influence,
opinion and political idioms in reformed England: case studies from the
north east, 1832–1874* (1975) · R. S. Watson, *The history of the Literary
and Philosophical Society of Newcastle-upon-Tyne, 1793–1896* (1897) ·
R. Welford, *Men of mark 'twixt Tyne and Tweed*, 2 (1895), 109–19 ·
DNB · *IGI* · W. H. Maehl, 'Doubleday, Thomas', *BDMBR*, vol. 2 · private information (2004) [Roger Hawkins] · directories · *CGPLA Eng.
& Wales* (1870)

Archives Newcastle Central Library · NL Scot., letters to Black-
woods

Likenesses drawing, repro. in Welford, *Men of mark*, 1.110 · portrait, Literary and Philosophical Society, Newcastle upon Tyne

Wealth at death under £450: probate, 17 July 1871, *CGPLA Eng. &
Wales*

Douce, Francis (1757–1834), antiquary and collector, was
born on 13 July 1757 in London, the fourth and last child of
Francis Douce (*d.* 1799), attorney, of the six clerks' office,
and his wife, Ellen Tapley (*d.* 1799). His relationship with
his father was not affectionate: 'my grandfather was a
domestic despot, and tyrannized over my father, who
thought proper to retaliate upon me' (*GM*, 212); that with
his mother was very sympathetic. From his earliest years
she fostered his curiosity about books and antiquities and
his love of music, interests which were to predominate in
his adult life.

Douce was first sent to a school at Richmond but he was
suddenly removed (apparently lest he should outshine his
elder brother Thomas) to

> a French academy, kept by a pompous and ignorant Life-
> guardsman, with a view to his learning merchants' accounts,
> which were his aversion, and he made no other acquirement
> there than a little French; the second master, a Scotchman,
> knowing less Latin than himself, and no Greek. (*GM*, 213)

He wanted to go to university but was prevented, he
believed, by the machinations of the same brother. He
worked for a while under his father and on 13 January 1779
entered Gray's Inn and was admitted an attorney of the
king's bench. In that same year he was elected a fellow of
the Society of Antiquaries and in 1781 became a reader at
the British Museum.

On 2 November 1791 Douce married Isabella Maria Price,
née Corry (1754/5–1830), widow of the Revd Henry Price of
Bellevue, Ireland; they moved to 13 Upper Gower Street.
His marriage, which was childless,

> did not increase his happiness, though on his part it was a
> match of affection; some peculiarities of disposition in the
> partner of his choice occasionally embittered his life, and
> there were circumstances connected with his union which
> had a baneful influence upon his peace even to the close of
> his life. (*GM*, 213)

Isabella died at the end of July 1830, aged seventy-five; at
her burial in St Pancras churchyard no one supplied the
clerk with her Christian name.

In 1799 Douce's parents died. The disparity between his
brother Thomas's legacy from their father's estate and his
own he ascribed to 'the misrepresentations of my brother,

Francis Douce (1757–1834), by James Barry, 1803

who used to say that it was of no use to leave me money,
for I should waste it in books' (*GM*, 213). In fact, Douce's
inheritance was sufficient to enable him to amass extraordinary collections of books and manuscripts, coins,
medals, prints and drawings, and miscellaneous antiquities. His second attempt at a professional life began in
1807, when he joined the department of manuscripts at
the British Museum; he succeeded Robert Nares as keeper
later that same year, and moved into a museum residence.
He worked on the catalogues of the Lansdowne and Harleian collections, using his extensive knowledge to good
effect, and learning much in turn. However, he was too old
and independent to cope with the institutional regime,
and submitted his resignation in April 1811 on the grounds
of ill health. His own notes on the business record fourteen reasons for his decision, ranging from his damp
apartments to the 'fiddle faddle requisition of incessant
reports' by the officers of the museum (Munby, 39). Great
efforts were made to change his mind, but he was adamant, and returned to the life of a private collector and
scholar, pursuing his antiquarian researches amid a wide
circle of friends and correspondents, both at home and on
the continent.

The motive behind Douce's various collections was to
illustrate the manners, customs, and beliefs (especially
those of the common people) of all ages. It is this illustrative imperative, the desire to assemble material which
pictured the activities of humanity down the centuries,
preferably as contemporaneously as possible, which
informs his collections and provides the matter for his
two major publications. *Illustrations of Shakespeare, and of
Ancient Manners* was published in two volumes in 1807; in it

Douce endeavours to see the dramatist in his social, cultural, and historical setting, and by so doing to throw new light on the plays in particular and on Elizabethan and Jacobean customs and literature in general. Its critical reception was mostly favourable, but a vituperative review by Jeffrey in the *Edinburgh Review* (prompted by a feud against the book's publisher, Longman) hurt Douce deeply and put him off publishing for many years. It was not until 1833 that his other major work, *The dance of death exhibited in elegant engravings on wood, with a dissertation on the several representations of that subject*, appeared. He had first published on the dance of death in 1794, anonymously; during the four intervening decades he had amassed materials on, and devoted much research to, the subject, all of which was distilled in this illustrated study. In addition to several contributions to *Archaeologia* and an anonymous pamphlet attacking government economic policy, Douce collaborated with George Spencer on *Nymphaea lotus* (1804), helped Walter Scott with his edition of *Sir Tristrem* (1804), anonymously edited and augmented Joseph Ritson's *Gammer Gurton's Garland* (1810), wrote the introduction to John Thomas Smith's *Vagabondiana* (1817), and provided much material for Richard Price's edition of Thomas Warton's *The History of English Poetry* (1824).

Douce was a difficult man but, once won over, extremely generous with his knowledge, books, and affection. He was 'a perfect gentleman of the old school; a little reserved on first acquaintance; but when this was passed, easy, affable, and kind', observed the obituarist in the *Gentleman's Magazine* (*GM*, 215), adding 'his temperament was constitutionally irritable' (ibid., 216). One of Barry's portraits of 1803 shows a striking, rather severe-looking man. The obituarist in *The Athenaeum* describes him in old age 'wearing a little flaxen wig, an old-fashioned, square-cut coat … he was short and stout, somewhat near-sighted' (*The Athenaeum*, 257), much as in the pencil portrait of him aged seventy-three, by S. C. Smith.

After leaving the British Museum Douce moved to 36 Charlotte Street; in 1820 he moved to 20 Berners Street, and the following year to 34 Kensington Square. A dramatic change in his fortunes took place in 1823, when his friend Joseph Nollekens, the sculptor, died. His will became the subject of much legal wrangling and it was not until 1827 that Douce, a residuary legatee, received about £50,000, enabling him thenceforth to augment his collections on a lavish scale. His last move had been in 1825, when he returned to Upper Gower Street, to no. 15.

In July 1830 Douce and his old friend Isaac D'Israeli visited Oxford. Frederic Madden of the British Museum had given them a letter of introduction to Bodley's librarian, Bulkeley Bandinel, who enthusiastically took them round and had them to dine with him. Douce was much taken by the library's tradition of preserving the identity of its named collections. 'At this moment', records D'Israeli, 'Douce must have decided on the locality where his precious collection was to find a perpetual abode' (D'Israeli, 3.264). Douce died 'after an illness of but two or three weeks' (*The Athenaeum*, 257) on 30 March 1834 at his home, 15 Upper Gower Street, and was buried in St Pancras churchyard on 7 April. The Bodleian received his books (18,000), manuscripts (420), prints (27,000 fine, 17,000 other), drawings (1500), coins, and medals. The drawings and most of the prints were transferred to the Ashmolean in 1863, the non-fine prints being returned in 1915; the coins and medals were transferred to the same museum in 1920. Douce bequeathed his antiquities to Sir Samuel Meyrick, whose collection was dispersed in the 1870s, and his private papers to the British Museum, not to be looked at until 1900 (they were given to the Bodleian in 1930). His residuary legatees, S. W. Singer and the Revd Edward Goddard, shared an estimated £50,000.

C. HURST

Sources [S. G. Gillam], ed., *The Douce legacy: an exhibition to commemorate the 150th anniversary of the bequest of Francis Douce, 1757–1834* (1984) [exhibition catalogue] · *GM*, 2nd ser., 2 (1834), 212–17, 338 · *The Athenaeum* (5 April 1834), 256–7 · A. N. L. Munby, 'Francis Douce', *Connoisseurs and medieval miniatures, 1750–1850* (1972), 35–56 · I. D'Israeli, *Amenities of literature, consisting of sketches and characters of English literature*, 3 vols. (1841) · T. F. Dibdin, *Reminiscences of a literary life*, 2 vols. (1836) · J. G. Mann and others, 'Francis Douce centenary', *Bodleian Quarterly Record*, 7 (1932–4), 359–82 · *DNB*
Archives BL, papers relating to BM, Add. MS 42574 · BL, annotated copy of John Whitaker's *History of Manchester* · Bodl. Oxf., corresp. and papers · Bodl. Oxf., corresp., MS collection, and papers | BL, letters to George Cumberland, Add. MSS 36502–36515 · BL, corresp. with Sir Frederick Madden, Egerton MSS 2837–2840 · BL, letters to T. Sharp, etc., Add. MS 43645 · Bodl. Oxf., letters to Isaac D'Israeli · Bodl. Oxf., letters to Sir Henry Ellis · Bodl. Oxf., letters to T. Lloyd · CCC Cam., letters to Thomas Kerrich · Trinity Cam., letters to Dawson Turner · U. Edin. L., letters to David Laing
Likenesses silhouette, c.1775, Bodl. Oxf.; repro. in *The Douce legacy* · J. Barry, pen-and-ink drawing, 1803, Bodl. Oxf. [*see illus.*] · J. Barry, pen-and-ink drawing, 1803, priv. coll. · S. C. Smith, pencil drawing (aged seventy-three), Bodl. Oxf.; repro. in Hann and others, 'Francis Douce' · S. C. Smith, pencil drawing, BM · E. Turner, pencil drawing (after C. Prosperi), V&A · M. Turner, etching (after sculpted medallion by C. Prosperi, 1812), Bodl. Oxf.; repro. in *The Douce legacy*
Wealth at death under £80,000: *GM* 2/1 · 'cannot be much less than £150,000': *Athenaeum*, 336 · £9400 in monetary bequests: *GM*, 338 · residuary legatees shared about £50,000

Doudney, David Alfred (1811–1893), Church of England clergyman and educationist, was born on 8 March 1811 at 386 Mile End Terrace, Portsea, son of John Doudney (d. 1834), tallow chandler, and his wife, Sarah (d. 1838). Details of his education are unknown, but it was probably minimal. At the age of thirteen he was apprenticed to a printer at Southampton, and subsequently joined the staff of the *Hampshire Advertiser*. In 1832 he moved to London and was engaged by Messrs Jowett and Mills, printers, of Bolt Court, Fleet Street. He set up a printing business of his own in 1835, first at Holloway, and then in Long Lane, Aldersgate Street.

In 1840 Doudney purchased and became editor of the sternly Calvinist *Gospel Magazine*, which he edited for many years. He married, first, in 1834, a Miss Draper. They had three children, of whom only the eldest son, D. A. Doudney, survived. In 1842 he married Eliza (d. c.1873), daughter of William Durkin, at St Mary's, Portsea. Of their eight children, five died young. In 1846 he retired from the printing trade, and in November of that year he went to Ireland to distribute funds raised by his readers for the relief of the Irish famine. At this time he felt called to full-time Christian ministry, and underwent some training in Ireland. He was ordained in 1847 by the bishop of Cashel as a licentiate clergyman. From 1847 to 1854 Doudney was curate of Monksland, co. Waterford. Moved by the poverty and lack of facilities he found Doudney established industrial and agricultural schools at nearby Bunmahon. Here he set up a printing press, which produced his new periodical, *Old Jonathan*. An abridgement of John Gill's exposition of the Old and New testaments, which appeared in six volumes between 1852 and 1854, was also printed. The latter venture gained Doudney recognition. The lord lieutenant, the earl of Carlisle, presented him to the sinecure living of Kilcash, near Clonmel, in 1854, enabling Doudney to continue his active and highly individual work.

Doudney left Ireland in 1859 to become perpetual curate of St Luke's, Bedminster, Bristol, where again he established industrial schools. He continued to edit the *Gospel Magazine* and *Old Jonathan*, and published a large number of tracts and other devotional works. Doudney also took an active part in many charitable institutions, particularly the Printers' Corporation. He retired from St Luke's in 1890, moving to Southville, Granada Road, Southsea, where he died on 21 April 1893. He was buried at Highland Road cemetery, East Southsea, on 25 April. He married a third time in old age and had two children, who predeceased him. He left four sons and two daughters.

A. F. POLLARD, *rev.* I. T. FOSTER

Sources *Gospel Magazine* (May–June 1893) · *Record* (28 April 1893) · private information (2004) · *Hampshire Telegraph* (29 April 1893) · Allibone, *Dict.* · Boase, *Mod. Eng. biog.* · D. A. Doudney and Mrs E. Adams, eds., *Memoir of the Rev. D. A. Doudney, vicar of St Luke's, Bedminster*, 2nd edn (1894) · D. A. Doudney, *Victory through the blood of the lamb! or, Notes of the life and death-bed experiences of Edward Phillips Doudney by his brother* (1877)
Likenesses portrait, repro. in *Gospel Magazine* (May 1893)
Wealth at death £1856 11s. 4d.: probate, 13 June 1893, *CGPLA Eng. & Wales*

Doudney, Sarah (1841–1926), children's writer and hymn writer, was born at Portsea, Hampshire, on 15 January 1841, youngest of the (at least) four children of George Ebenezer Doudney (*c*.1804–1893), tallow chandler, and his wife, Lucy Clay (*c*.1806–1891). Her father ran a candle- and soap-manufacturing business, with factories at Mile End (Landport), Portsmouth, and in Plymouth, in partnership with Edward Phillips Doudney (1804–1875). Both were brothers of the evangelical clergyman David Alfred Doudney (1811–1894), editor of the *Gospel Magazine* and *Old Jonathan*. Part of a letter of Edward Phillips Doudney's about his business practice suggests the religious atmosphere of Sarah's childhood: 'After I took the order, as my custom is, if I have the opportunity, I spoke a word or two as to the unsatisfactory nature of earthly things and the importance of soul matters' (Doudney, 52).

Much of Sarah Doudney's childhood was spent in the hamlet of Love Dean, near Catherington, Hampshire, about 10 miles north of Portsmouth, and she lived there with her parents until she was past thirty. She was educated at Madame Dowell's College in Southsea, Hampshire, a school for French girls, and was also taught by a Mrs Kendall. She began writing verse and prose as a child, and when she was fifteen wrote 'The Lesson of the Water-Mill', a song which became well known in Britain and the United States. (There are four different musical settings of it in the British Library music catalogue, which also lists more than thirty other songs and hymns by Doudney.) It was published in the *Churchman's Family Magazine* in 1864, as were several other early verse works; she also published two poems in Charles Dickens's *All the Year Round*. Some of this verse was collected in *Psalms of Life* (1871). Other early works appeared in the *Churchman's Shilling Magazine* or were published by the Religious Tract Society or the Sunday School Union.

From 1871 Sarah Doudney published a long series of novels, innocuous in content and pious in tone, one of which was *Godiva Durleigh: a Novel for Girls* (1891); she also continued to publish verse. Some of her hymns are still occasionally sung, such as 'Sleep on, beloved, sleep and take thy rest' and 'Saviour, now the day is ending'. Although she was best-known for writing for young girls, she also wrote fiction for adults: in 1904, for example, she published *Silent Strings*, a love story about the five children of a doctor, and the more interesting *One of the Few*, about a middle-aged woman writer who was right not to marry. She left Hampshire to live in London, but by the turn of the century had returned to Portsmouth. She subsequently moved to Oxford, where she died of cardiac failure at her home, 69 Woodstock Road, on 8 December 1926.

CHARLOTTE MITCHELL

Sources D. M. Sale, *The hymn writers of Hampshire* (1975) · *The Post Office directory of Hampshire* (1867) · J. Julian, ed., *A dictionary of hymnology*, rev. edn (1907); repr. in 2 vols. (1915) · Allibone, *Dict.* · *Men and women of the time* (1899) · D. W. Perry, *Hymns and tunes indexed* (1980) · will index, Principal Registry of the Family Division, London · deaths index, St Catherine's House, London · L. Baillie and R. Balchin, eds., *The catalogue of printed music in the British Library to 1980*, 62 vols. (1981–7) · D. A. Doudney, *Victory through the blood of the lamb!, or, Notes of the life and death-bed experiences of Edward Phillips Doudney, by his brother* (1877) · census returns for Catherington, Hampshire, 1871 · IGI · b. cert. · d. cert.
Wealth at death £295 18s.: administration with will, 22 April 1927, *CGPLA Eng. & Wales*

Dougall, John (1760–1822), writer, was born in Kirkcaldy, where his father was master of the grammar school. He studied at Edinburgh University with a view to entering the Church of Scotland, but later abandoned this intention. For some time he was private secretary to General Robert Melville, but he ultimately settled in London and devoted himself to literary work. His writings on education were *The Modern Preceptor* (1810) and *The Cabinet of Arts* (1821). He also wrote *Military Adventures* (n.d.), and translated *España maritima, or, Spanish Coasting Pilot* (1813).

Dougall had been preparing a translation of Caesar's *Commentaries* under the patronage of the duke of York when he became seriously ill, and was unable to complete it. He had long been in financial straits, and died on 14 September 1822, at Robert Street, Little James Street, Bedford Row, London, leaving his widow destitute.

[ANON.], rev. DOUGLAS BROWN

Sources Anderson, *Scot. nat.* · *GM*, 1st ser., 92/2 (1822), 570 · Chambers, *Scots.* (1835)

Wealth at death widow left destitute

Dougall, Lily (1858–1923), novelist and religious author, younger daughter of John Dougall and his wife, Elizabeth Redpath, was born in Montreal, Canada, on 16 April 1858 and privately educated there. Her elder brother, John Redpath Dougall, became owner and editor of the *Montreal Witness*. The family was of Scottish descent and in 1878 she moved to live with an aunt in Edinburgh, where she took English, Latin, Greek, moral philosophy, logic, and metaphysics, by correspondence course at St George's Hall, to become an LLA (lady literate in arts) of the University of St Andrews in 1887. In 1891 she published *Beggars All*, the first of her ten novels, all written within the space of ten years. Their vague religiosity promoted mutual sympathy and the morally redemptive power of the love of a good woman. Many of these novels employed a Canadian setting, but enjoyed a wide audience because they addressed such contemporary topics as the ethical dilemmas faced by the 'new woman' (*The Madonna of a Day*, 1896). Preparation for *The Mormon Prophet* (1898) involved her in visiting the Mormon headquarters at Salt Lake City, Utah.

In 1900 Dougall's anonymous publication, *Pro Christo et ecclesia*, marked a decision to adopt non-fiction as her chosen mode for communicating her liberal brand of Christianity. In 1911 she moved, with her Cambridge-educated companion, Mary Sophia Earp, to Cutts End, Cumnor, near Oxford. Using this house as a conference centre, she hosted the meetings of the 'Cumnor group', a band of clerics, academics, and other writers interested in disseminating their interdenominational discussions on the moral, religious, and social issues of the day. Other prominent names in this group were Arthur Clutton Brock, art critic for *The Times*; Burnett Hillman Streeter (1874–1937), of Queen's College, Oxford; Arthur Charlewood Turner, fellow of Trinity College, Cambridge, and founder of the Anglican Fellowship; and her two co-authors, Cyril William Emmet, fellow of University College, Oxford, with whom she published essays, and Gilbert Sheldon, with whom she published a collection of light verse entitled *Arcades ambo* (1919). Theologically her position was one of liberal orthodoxy and she became a member of the Modern Churchman's Union. A photograph of a handsomely dressed woman, with a slightly quizzical smile, accords well with the assured tone of her 'modernist' diagnoses of the tendency of traditional theology to confine God within man-made images. Though increasingly frail, Dougall continued to write until her death on 9 October 1923 at Cutts End. She was buried in Cumnor churchyard on 13 October.   ELISABETH JAY

Sources B. H. Streeter, 'Introduction and biographical note', in L. Dougall, *God's way with man: an exploration of the method of divine working suggested by the facts of history and science* (1924) · *The Times* (13 Oct 1923) · *WWW* · *Oxford Chronicle and Berks and Bucks Gazette* (19 Oct 1923) · private information (2004) · Blain, Clements & Grundy, *Feminist comp.*

Archives Bodl. Oxf., corresp. and literary papers

Likenesses Elliott & Fry Ltd, photograph, repro. in L. Dougall, *God's way with man: an exploration of the method of divine working suggested by the facts of history and science* (1924), frontispiece

Dougall, Neil (1776–1862), poet and hymn writer, was born on 9 December 1776 at Greenock, the son of Neil Dougald and his wife, Jean Moir. His father was a joiner and sailor, who was pressed into the naval service and died in Ceylon when his son was four years old. His mother remarried, and Neil remained at school until he was fifteen, when he was apprenticed as a sailor in the mercantile marine service. On 14 June 1794, during celebrations of a naval victory against the French, he lost his eyesight and right arm as a result of the accidental discharge of a gun.

On recovering from his injuries, Dougall began to develop a musical talent, and became a popular teacher of singing. He married Margaret Donaldson on 28 July 1806, and through teaching, together with a business as keeper of a tavern and later of a boarding-house in Greenock, he managed to raise a family of four sons and six daughters. His daughter Lilly achieved some success as a contralto singer.

Dougall composed about a hundred psalm and hymn tunes, of which 'Kilmarnock' gained immediate popularity and became a standard melody in the Presbyterian church service. In 1854 he published a small volume, *Poems and Songs*, which contained twelve 'miscellaneous pieces', eleven songs, and thirteen 'sacred pieces', several of which he set to music. Among the miscellaneous poems are various imitations of conventional eighteenth-century pastorals and a tribute to Burns, written a few days after the poet's death. The most notable of the songs is 'My Braw John Highlandman'. Dougall died at 7 Manse Lane, Greenock, on 1 October 1862, survived by his wife.

T. W. BAYNE, rev. DOUGLAS BROWN

Sources Boase, *Mod. Eng. biog.* · Brown & Stratton, *Brit. mus.* · D. Baptie, ed., *Musical Scotland, past and present: being a dictionary of Scottish musicians from about 1400 till the present time* (1894) · N. Dougall, *Poems and songs* (1854) [with biographical notice, author uncertain] · bap. reg. Scot. · m. reg. Scot. · d. cert.

Dougharty [Doharty], **John** (1677–1755), mathematician, was born in Dublin, the son of John O'Dougherty and a descendant of the O'Doughertys of Inishowen, co. Donegal. By 1698 he was in England, marrying Priscilla Fereder (d. 1741) at Chaddesley Corbett, Worcestershire, on 5 November. They settled in Kidderminster, where their eldest child, Joseph *Dougharty (1699–1737) [see under Doharty, John], was born, then moved to Bewdley, where further children followed from 1702. There Dougharty kept a school, teaching writing, arithmetic, bookkeeping, gauging, navigation, and astronomy, and he probably surveyed land also. In 1707 he published *The General Gauger*, dedicated to the named commissioners of excise. Its sixth and last edition was in 1750. By 1711 he had moved to teach in Worcester, first in High Street, and from 1720 in Edgar Tower. The school was patronized by local gentry, some of whose estates he surveyed in partnership with his sons

Joseph and John (Doharty) the younger. Their masterpiece was the estate atlas of Hanbury Hall (1731–3), drawn by the father from the sons' surveys. In 1716 he had been appointed lay clerk and inspector of works to Worcester Cathedral, and became choirmaster. The two daughters who had survived to maturity, Elizabeth and Joyce, married and left home, and his wife, Priscilla, was buried on 8 August 1741, leaving only Dougharty and son John in the Tower. His only other book, *Mathematical Digests* [1749], encapsulating his teaching, was issued in parts from the end of 1748, the complete work having 450 pages. It was dedicated to George, Lord Viscount Deerhurst.

Dougharty died on 11 January 1755 and was buried in the cathedral cloister at Worcester. An encomium, probably by son John *Doharty, describes him as dignified, sincere, generous, cheerful, and 'ever communicative'. The combination of his amiability with talent and hard work undoubtedly led to his successful career as a mathematician, teacher, and land surveyor.   RUTH WALLIS

Sources B. S. Smith, 'The Dougharty family, eighteenth-century mapmakers', *Transactions of the Worcestershire Archaeological Society*, 3rd ser., 15 (1996), 245–82 · V. Green, *The history and antiquities of the city and suburbs of Worcester*, 2 (1796) · R. V. Wallis and P. J. Wallis, eds., *Biobibliography of British mathematics and its applications*, 2 (1986), 30

Archives Quex Park, Kent, Powell archives

Likenesses miniature, c.1740, Quex Park, Kent; repro. in B. S. Smith, 'The Dougharty family', *Transactions of the Worcestershire Archaeological Society*, 3rd ser., 15 (1996), 250

Dougharty, Joseph (1699–1737). *See under* Doharty, John (1709–1773).

Doughtie, John (1598?–1672), Church of England clergyman and religious writer, was born at Martley, near Worcester, perhaps in 1598 as asserted by Anthony Wood and indicated by his supposed age at death, but his ordination suggests an earlier date. Educated at Worcester grammar school, on 30 April 1613 he matriculated from Brasenose College, Oxford. He graduated BA on 4 November 1616, having been ordained the previous February and acquired the living of Wood Norton, Norfolk, in April. Elected to a fellowship at Merton College in 1619 he proceeded MA in 1623.

Doughtie's early writings reveal criticism of harder line Calvinism but fear of disruption of the church by Arminian innovation. In two sermons of 1628 he generally sided with Calvinists concerning doctrine and popery but, fearing schism, called for silence from dissenters. Opposed to innovation in doctrine or rite he blamed Arminius for the current doctrinal challenge, which he thought might mask popery, still the real danger. However, he may have given comfort to English anti-Calvinists by situating England's orthodox religion 'betwixt papistry and semi-Pelagianism' (*Hist. U. Oxf.* 4: *17th-cent. Oxf.*, 584), by doubting the possibility of certainty in religion (specifically concerning reprobation) and by arguing (like James I had done) that it was better to avoid public discussion of central points of faith if it meant disturbance in the church. He also emphasized reform of the individual's will and life rather than minute examination of the first

decree as a better guide to assurance. His *A Discourse Concerning the Abstruseness of Divine Mysteries* (1629), dedicated to Sir Nathaniel Brent, warden of Merton, was the last work containing Calvinist statements to be published in Oxford until the 1640s.

In 1631 Doughtie served as proctor, but in August he was made to resign by royal order after hearing an appeal from the decision of the vice-chancellor. From that year he may have been rector of Rushock, Worcestershire; Wood suggests that he was chaplain to the earl of Northumberland about this time. He was presented to the Warwickshire livings of Lapworth and Beaudesert in 1634 and 1636 respectively. In 1640 some Lapworth parishioners petitioned the House of Lords against Doughtie's alleged neglect and his supposed favouring of popery and approval of the new canons. By 1646 he had been sequestrated from both livings. That September the committee for plundered ministers ordered the payment of fifths for Lapworth to his wife, Katherine, of whom nothing else is known. John Walker claimed that Doughtie went to Oxford, then to Salisbury, where he became lecturer at St Edmund's through the patronage of Brian Duppa, and finally to London, to the home of Sir Nathaniel Brent.

Doughtie's later publications, such as *The King's Cause Rationally, Briefly and Plainly Debated* (1644), illustrate his increasing dedication to divine right or absolutist monarchy and to an ecclesiology defined by an Erastian episcopacy. A monarch, having received authority directly from God, could acknowledge no superior force on earth. Representative assemblies received their authority from subjects and were therefore inherently of inferior status. Employing Ptolemaic imagery Doughtie set the king above the three estates of the realm. Disobedience to a lawful prince led to civil wars as providential punishment. While Charles had 'somewhat swerved from the known Dictates of the Law', he had not attempted either tyranny or idolatry. Doughtie insisted that Charles had protected both religion and property. His earlier anti-popery changed here to a denunciation of the 'Popish Legend' and of the sedition it occasioned. Here and in later works, *Velitationes polemicae* (1651) and *Analecta sacra* (1658), Doughtie condemned both presbyterianism and Independency and defended the structures and practices of the Church of England and of an absolutist political authority. Monarchs properly possessed the right of coercive discipline in matters of public belief and church organization. Thus prelacy, while not scripturally mandated, had to be accepted because established by law. Monarchs should obey the law but were not accountable to it. Even illegitimate authority in a state commanded a 'submissive manner of conversation' save on matters of conscience.

In 1660 Doughtie's petition to secure the profits of his Warwickshire livings was not granted. Installed as prebendary in Westminster Abbey in July he proceeded DD on 19 October. In 1662 he was instituted to Cheam. Wood ascribes mental unsoundness to his later years. He died on 25 December 1672, said to be aged seventy-five, and was buried in Westminster Abbey.   JOHN MORGAN

Sources Merton College register, 1567–1731, Merton Oxf. • M. L. Walker, ed., *Brasenose College register, 1509–1909* (1909) • Walker's notes for annotations of Brasenose register, Brasenose College, Oxford, folder A5 • presentation deeds, Worcs. RO, 732.4/2337/22/446 and 477 • bishops' register 22, Norfolk RO • institution book, 1604–1628/9, Norfolk RO, DN/REG 16, fol. 56v • archdeacon's transcripts, parish of Wood Norton, 1627–33, Norfolk RO, esp. 1627, 1629–31, 1633 • consignation book, 1620, Norfolk RO, DN/VIS 5/2 • visitation book, 1627, Norfolk RO, DN/VIS 5/3/2 • Foster, *Alum. Oxon.* • Walker rev., 363 • W. Cooper, *The records of Beaudesert Henley-in-Arden, co. Warwick* (1931) • *Fasti Angl., 1541–1857*, [St Paul's, London] • G. C. Brodrick, *Memorials of Merton College*, OHS, 4 (1885) • Wood, *Ath. Oxon.*, new edn • *Hist. U. Oxf. 4: 17th-cent. Oxf.* • A. Hughes, *Politics, society and civil war in Warwickshire, 1620–1660* (1987)

Doughty [*née* Shackell], **Dame Adelaide Baillieu** (1908–1986), politician, was born at Vailima, Glenferrie Road, Malvern, Victoria, Australia, on 2 December 1908, the middle of the three daughters of Edward Herbert Shackell (1869–1932), public accountant, and his wife, Amy Baillieu (1870–1966). Initially she and her sisters were educated at home by governesses. Later Adelaide went to study at St Catherine's School in Melbourne from 1920 to 1925. After completing her study there she was accepted into Melbourne University. These plans soon changed during a family visit from her cousin Clive Latham Baillieu, first Baron Baillieu, the financier, and his wife, Ruby. They suggested that Adelaide return to Britain under their care. This she did, and in 1928 entered St Hilda's College, Oxford, where she gained a second in philosophy, politics, and economics in 1931.

Adelaide soon met Charles John Joseph Addison Doughty (1902–1973), the eldest son of Sir Charles Doughty, recorder of Brighton. Both were waiting in Victoria Station to catch a boat-train to Switzerland for a skiing holiday. He was then a solicitor, who had been called to the bar in 1926. They were engaged within the year and, once Adelaide finished her degree at St Hilda's, were married on 29 July 1931. They had a son and a daughter.

Adelaide Doughty's public work began in 1947, when she joined the English-Speaking Union (ESU) in what was formerly known as the Common Interests' Committee; her cousin Lord Baillieu was heavily involved in the union and later became its chairman. She worked hard for the ESU, following through with this particular side of work until the Hospitality Council was set up in 1971. She was elected as ESU club director in 1950 and devoted much of her time and interests to the affairs of the club; she was elected chairman of the board of club directors in 1969. She also served as a governor of the ESU from 1958 to 1972. Her activities with the ESU included a service on the US exchange teachers' committee and a further period as a member of the speakers' committee. She was elected to the ESU policy committee in 1970 and became joint deputy chairman of the ESU in June 1971. She resigned in September 1972 in protest against the board's 'discourtesy' in signing a lease of part of its Mayfair premises to the Grand Metropolitan Hotel Group before informing its membership.

Adelaide Doughty undertook notable work for the Conservative Party; from 1951 to 1956 she was a member of the party's south-eastern area women's advisory committee. Her husband, meanwhile, who took silk in 1954 and succeeded his father as recorder of Brighton, was elected Conservative MP for Surrey (East) in 1951 and held the seat until 1970. From 1963 to 1966 she was an outstandingly successful chairman of the Conservative Party's women's national advisory committee, doing much to shift the tory women's role towards political issues rather than administrative details. During her term in office the Conservatives elected a new leader for the first time, and she spoke in favour of Edward Heath's nomination. In 1964 she became vice-chairman of the National Union of Conservative and Unionist Associations and succeeded to the chairmanship in March 1967 following the death of Sir Robert Davies. She served as president of the party in 1978. She was appointed CBE in 1964 and DBE in 1971.

During this time, Adelaide Doughty was also a governor of the Skinners' Company's School for Girls in 1951, the director of the National Institute for Housecraft from 1966, and a member of the grand council of the cancer research campaign from 1974. She died at home at Flat 4, 89 Onslow Square, Kensington, London, on 12 August 1986.   JILL M. DAVIDSON SPELLMAN

Sources WWW, 1981–90 • WWW, 1971–80 • V. Brown and M. E. Rayner, eds., *St Hilda's College register* (1993) • matriculation records, Oxf. UA • private information (2004) [Mrs S. Clarke, Mrs A. Wallace] • m. cert. • d. cert. • 'Dame Adelaide Doughty', *Concord: English-Speaking Union Magazine* (June 1973), 10 • *Daily Telegraph* (14 Aug 1986) • general election addresses for Charles Doughty, 1951; Aston Division, Birmingham; 1959, 1964, 1966, 1970: East Surrey

Likenesses photograph, conservative party archive, election addresses of Charles Doughty, 1951–71

Wealth at death £221,426: probate, 26 Sept 1986, *CGPLA Eng. & Wales*

Doughty, Charles Montagu (1843–1926), explorer, travel writer, and poet, was born on 19 August 1843 at Theberton Hall, Leiston, Suffolk, the younger of two sons of the Revd Charles Montagu Doughty (1798–1850), landowner, and his wife, Frederica (*d.* 1843), daughter of the Hon. Frederick Hotham, prebendary of Rochester and rector of Dennington, Suffolk, and granddaughter of Beaumont, second Baron Hotham. Charles Hotham Montagu Doughty-Wylie, killed while leading a heroic charge at Gallipoli, was the son of his elder brother. Although he was a minor poet, Doughty was the most important British explorer of Arabia and one of Britain's greatest travel writers.

Early life and education The future Arabian explorer was so weak-looking at birth that his father had him baptized immediately, but in manhood Doughty was 'tall and strongly, though not heavily built, with aquiline features and a thick beard which was reddish in early and middle life', according to W. D. Hogarth (*DNB*). Within a few months of his birth his mother passed away, and when he was six his father also died, leaving Charles and his brother, Henry, in the care of an uncle, Frederick Goodwin Doughty, of Martlesham Hall, Suffolk. In school at Laleham and at Elstree, he had the reputation of being shy but too good a fighter to be bullied by the other boys. He was prepared at the Beach House School, Portsmouth, for

Charles Montagu Doughty (1843–1926), by Eric Kennington, 1921

a career in the Royal Navy, but in 1856 he was rejected owing to a slight speech impediment. His later interest in the oral poetic traditions of England and Arabia may owe something to this fact. He then left the school and spent some time with a private tutor in France. His report to the British Association's meeting in Cambridge in 1862 on the flint implements that he had excavated at Hoxne attests to his growing interest in geology and archaeology.

Doughty matriculated as a pensioner at Gonville and Caius College, Cambridge, in 1861, but he transferred in 1863 to Downing College, which was more sympathetic to his geological interests and more liberal regarding attendance at lectures and chapel. He demonstrated a rugged independence during 1863–4 when he spent nine months lodging with farmers and gamekeepers while conducting the first investigation of two remote Norwegian glaciers. He reported the results to the British Association in 1864 (and published a pamphlet, *On the Jöstedal-brae Glaciers in Norway, with some General Remarks, and a Plate*, in 1866). In 1865 he placed second in the second class of the natural sciences tripos, failing to achieve a higher result because of an inability (or refusal) to structure the wealth of details at his command. His masterpiece, *Travels in Arabia deserta* (1888), would display a similarly unstructured approach to the vast amount of material that it contains. In 1866 he returned to Caius to take his degree. A fellow student at Downing recalled him as 'rather shy and quiet but very polite' (Hogarth, 6), outward qualities that masked a fierce determination to accomplish whatever goals he set himself.

After graduation in 1865, Doughty began studying older

English literature—especially the works of Chaucer and Spenser, as well as Teutonic languages, as a means of readying himself for the writing of an epic of early Britain, intended as a patriotic substitute for his lost naval career. He hoped to reinvigorate what he regarded as a decayed Victorian English language by means of a poetic revival of earlier linguistic forms. The depreciation of his family's investments during this time left him with little money, and when he decided to travel to enhance the experience he felt necessary for writing his poem, it was as a poor student.

In 1870–71 Doughty studied Dutch in Leiden and spent some time in Louvain, and then moved southward to Provence and Italy. A manuscript diary now in the Gonville and Caius College Library records his presence at the eruption of Mount Vesuvius in 1872, an event described retrospectively with great power in *Arabia deserta*. He went on to north Africa and Spain, back to Italy, and then, in 1874, to Greece. There he decided to extend his journey eastward, and visited the holy sites of Nazareth, Jerusalem, Bethlehem, and Hebron, as well as the city of Damascus. In the autumn of 1874 he left the Holy Land via al-ʿArish and spent some time in Egypt. He then took a three-month camel journey through the Sinai peninsula beginning about February 1875, a trip described in a brief report to the Royal Geographical Society of Austria, in *Arabia deserta* retrospectively, and, nearly half a century later, in the poem *Mansoul* (1920), where he stresses its hardships. Leaving Sinai in the north-east, he arrived at Maʿan and Nabataean Petra, in what is now Jordan, in May 1875. Here he heard of the Nabataean inscriptions at Medain Salih and nearby Hejr, and resolved to return to make impressions of them, as he tells us in the opening section of *Arabia deserta*.

Travels in Arabia deserta In Damascus Doughty found that neither the British Association nor the Royal Geographical Society was willing to fund his proposed trip to Medain Salih, but he decided to make the journey anyway after studying Arabic for a year. Despite a refusal of passport documents from the British and Turkish authorities in Damascus, Doughty, now using the name Khalil, 'clothed as a Syrian of simple fortune' (Doughty, 1.4) and equipped with a few medicines to sell, embarked on the trip southward with the pilgrim caravan on 10 November 1876. He planned only a relatively brief stay in Medain Salih and the surrounding area, but he would end up wandering in Arabia for almost two years.

Travels in Arabia deserta records in more than one thousand pages of painstaking detail—much of which has been verified by later travellers—the course of Doughty's travels. The danger inherent in these wanderings was exacerbated by his lack of travel documents, by the Russo-Turkish War (which was perceived in Arabia as a Christian–Muslim conflict), and by his open admission of his Christianity and straightforward criticism of elements of Islamic culture that he did not like, such as polygamy and slavery. It did not help that he uttered these criticisms while remaining dependent upon the Arabs for hospitality and even food, but Doughty was convinced that truth may walk through the world unharmed, and he may have proved that point. The Arabs responded at some times with wry acceptance of his differences with them, and at others with passionate defences of their point of view or with overt hostility. Doughty's honest record of these debates (which he did not always win, and in which he often appears tactless) remains of great anthropological value. His various adventures, in the order in which he gives them in *Arabia deserta*, include the initial journey with the pilgrim caravan to the way station at Medain Salih, described in almost Chaucerian terms; a stay of several months with the Bedouin nearby, during which time an illness prevented him from joining a caravan to the Red Sea port al-Wajh and thereby leaving Arabia; a visit to Mohammed ibn Rashid, ruler of northern Arabia, who is described like a figure in a Shakespearian tragedy; an enforced stay at Khaybar, where a corrupt Turkish commandant, who almost appears to be a villain in a Gothic novel, made Doughty a prisoner for several months; a near escape from a riot at Buraydah; relief and good company at ʿUnayzah until he was expelled; a physically dangerous episode close to Mecca, during the climax of which Doughty handed his pistol, butt first, to one of his assailants, as if challenging him to shoot him; relief and well-being at Taʿif as a guest of the sherif of Mecca; and a final miraculous emergence on the beach at Jiddah on the Red Sea on 2 August 1878. Doughty appears almost a religious martyr toward the end of his adventure, when

> The tunic was rent on my back, my mantle was old and torn; the hair was grown down under my kerchief to the shoulders, and the beard fallen and unkempt; I had bloodshot eyes, half blinded, and the scorched skin was cracked to the quick upon my face.   (Doughty, 2.506)

Yet in spite of his suffering and his criticism of the Arabs, Doughty states at least three times in his book that the Bedouin way of life is the best in the world, and that after living with the Bedouin one 'will have all his life after a feeling of the desert' (ibid., 2.450). And Doughty's trials (many of which he caused himself) during this journey resulted in increased self-awareness, as he wrote in 1886: 'I am by nature self-willed, headstrong, and fierce with opponents, but my better reason and suffering in the world have bridled these faults and in part extinguished them' (Hogarth, 113).

Doughty left Jiddah on a ship bound for India, where he rested in a hospital, recovering from the exhaustion, ophthalmia, and bilharzia he had contracted in Arabia. While in Bombay, he read to the Royal Asiatic Society branch a paper on his journey, which was published in its journal for 1878. He made his way to England, and published his geographical results in the German periodical *Globus* in 1880–81. He addressed the Royal Geographical Society in 1883, and his paper was printed in its *Proceedings* for July 1884, but only after a struggle over his unique English style, which Doughty refused to have edited. He wrote to the society's assistant secretary, H. W. Bates, that 'as an English Scholar I will never submit to have my language of the best times turned into the misery of today—that were unworthy of me' (Hogarth, 108–9).

Doughty's records of the Nabataean documents from Medain Salih and al-ʿAla were edited by Ernest Renan and published in 1884 by the French Académie des Inscriptions as *Documents épigraphiques recueillis dans le nord de l'Arabie*. Scholars of the Nabataeans then as now have praised Doughty's contributions in the warmest terms. Indeed, *Travels in Arabia deserta*, on which Doughty laboured from 1879 to 1884 and which he continued correcting until its publication in 1888, is an unrivalled encyclopaedia of knowledge about all aspects of nineteenth-century and earlier Arabia. In a notable contemporary review in *Academy*, Sir Richard Francis Burton praised the book's scientific knowledge and its style ('pleasant for its reminiscences of the days when English was not vulgarised and Americanised'), although he felt that Doughty's forbearing attitude toward the Arabs reflected poorly on English honour. So reliable was the book's anthropology of the Bedouin peoples and its topography, that British intelligence mined it for information during the First and Second World wars. Doughty's contributions to all areas of Arabian knowledge continue to be praised by scholars. His principal geographical achievement was to confirm 'that the Wady er-Rummah system drains a large area, and definitely to the east', but his main contribution may well be the description of the land use, economy, and other features of the forty-odd settlements that he visited, according to geographer J. M. Wagstaff (Tabachnick, *Explorations*, 135, 145). His book is one of many sources that describe nineteenth-century Arabian history, but 'no single work paints an overall picture of nineteenth-century Arabian society that tells us more', according to historian Bayly Winder (ibid., 198). Geologists Reginald Shagam and Carol Faul state that, unlike some other contemporary geologists, Doughty 'failed to use the concept of faulting and he did not perceive the mass balance problem posed by the Dead Sea area', but on the other hand they find that 'his observation and mapping of the areas he travelled are correct' with few exceptions (ibid., 183, 172).

Not the least of Doughty's achievements is the style of *Arabia deserta*, one of the few truly bilingual British literary works. Walt Taylor has shown the degree to which Arabic and older English permeate Doughty's text, and Annette McCormick has demonstrated how Doughty's syntax was influenced by English translations of the Hebrew Bible. Because of the book's style, which ideally demands knowledge of older English and a Semitic language on the part of the reader, four commercial presses turned it down before Cambridge University Press agreed to publish it. Even that press recommended that Doughty's language be revised, but fortunately Doughty resisted all such attempts. As Professor Robert Fernea writes, 'With a knowledge of Arabic the connotative meanings of the dialogues become almost unsettling because unlike other contemporary ethnographic attempts one really seems to hear Arabs speaking' (Tabachnick, *Explorations*, 217).

In its authenticity, originality, and power, Doughty's English–Arabic style rivals the work of other Victorian prose masters such as Carlyle, Ruskin, and Pater. Poet Robert Bridges quickly recognized *Arabia deserta*'s uniqueness, and it was one of William Morris's favourite books toward the end of his life. W. B. Yeats, who read the work three times, may have based his desert poetry, including 'The second coming', on it. T. S. Eliot disliked Doughty's poetry, but found *Arabia deserta* a 'great work' (Eliot, 58). D. H. Lawrence, Leonard Woolf, Aldous Huxley, Herbert Read, Wyndham Lewis, Edwin Muir, Henry Green, Rex Warner, V. S. Pritchett, and the American writer Walker Percy were among the other literary admirers of Doughty's masterpiece. An abridgement was issued in 1908 under the title *Wanderings in Arabia*, and the selections *Passages from 'Arabia deserta'* appeared in 1931. Philip O'Brien's descriptive bibliography includes French, German, Hebrew, and Swedish translations (Tabachnick, *Explorations*, 223–53). Unfortunately Doughty burned the manuscript of his great work in his garden, feeling that it was a digression from his poetry and of little value; but the notebooks are held in the Fitzwilliam Museum, Cambridge, while the 'word notes'—slips of paper on which he wrote synonyms for and associations with words that interested him—are in the Caius College Library.

Later life and poetic career Doughty's life after Arabia was devoted to his family and to poetry that has not lasted. He married Caroline Amelia (*b.* 1861/2), daughter of General Sir William Montagu Scott McMurdo, on 7 October 1886. In 1892 a daughter, (Susan) Dorothy, was born, and in 1894 a second, Frederica Gertrude (Freda), followed. In 1900 his slim, clichéd volume of patriotic verse, *Under Arms*, intended to reinforce patriotic zeal for the Second South African War, was privately printed. In 1906–7 *The Dawn in Britain*, his long-meditated epic of early Britain, was published by Duckworth. This 30,000-line poem in six volumes had a mixed reception, and has since lapsed from memory outside pockets of isolated enthusiasts. This is because Doughty was unable to create convincing characters from imagination; he succeeded in *Arabia deserta* because he was describing genuine people. *Adam Cast Forth*, a 'sacred drama' based on a Muslim legend about Adam and Eve, is perhaps his sole imaginative work to achieve aesthetic success, but only because it convincingly recreates his desert sufferings. Doughty's science fiction dramas, *The Cliffs* (1909) and *The Clouds* (1912), predicted the First World War and the use of the submarine, airship, mine, torpedo, and other technical developments. But the poetic quality of these works never rises above stilted archaic dialogue and coincidental and vague plot structure, and they show that Doughty could react to an imagined attack on Great Britain with no less fanaticism than he often attributes to the Arabs in *Arabia deserta*. *The Titans* (1916), dealing with a time before Adam and Eve when giants and men battled for control of the earth, fails to come to life, and *Mansoul* (1920; rev. edn, 1923), which was Doughty's own favourite work, is a neo-medieval dream vision in which the poet as Minimus describes an underworld journey marred by simplistic philosophical speculation and overt and incongruous attacks on the Kaiser.

Visitors to the household speak of the calm outer life enjoyed by Doughty, but his wife never liked the bloody battle scenes from *The Dawn in Britain* and his other poems, which he would declaim aloud to her. There is indeed a contradiction in the poetry between Doughty's proclaimed love of humanity and his bloodthirsty attraction to patriotic gore. Moreover, in the poetry there is no counter-voice to modify Doughty's sometimes extreme opinions, while in *Arabia deserta* the Arab characters vigorously challenge them. A brief memoir by Edmund Gosse, dated 23 June 1914, records, tellingly, that toward the end of his life Doughty seemed at once very shy and very fierce.

Doughty eventually achieved recognition in the form of the gold medal of the Royal Geographical Society (1912), honorary degrees from both Oxford (1908) and Cambridge (1920), membership of the British Academy (1922), and warm admiration from the youthful (but not the older) T. E. Lawrence. Lawrence was instrumental in reviving *Arabia deserta* in 1921, and he described Doughty's masterpiece best when he called it 'a book not like other books, but something particular, a bible of its kind' (Lawrence, 17). Doughty received an inheritance in 1923 around the same time that his shareholdings fortuitously appreciated, but until then he and his family were often in difficult financial circumstances. He died on 20 January 1926 at Sissinghurst, Kent, after having moved there from Eastbourne in 1923, and was cremated at Golders Green. Charles Montagu Doughty is gone, but the staunch, stubbornly honest, and all-too-human hero Khalil will live for ever in the pages of *Travels in Arabia deserta*.

STEPHEN E. TABACHNICK

Sources D. G. Hogarth, *The life of Charles M. Doughty* (1928) · C. M. Doughty, *Travels in Arabia deserta* (1888) · T. E. Lawrence, 'Introduction', in C. M. Doughty, *Travels in Arabia deserta*, new edn (1933) · *DNB* · Gon. & Caius Cam., Doughty MSS · private information (2004) · S. E. Tabachnick, ed., *Explorations in Doughty's 'Arabia deserta'* (1987) · S. E. Tabachnick, *Charles Doughty* (1981) · W. Taylor, *Doughty's English* (1939) · R. F. Burton, 'Mr. Doughty's travels in Arabia', *The Academy* (28 July 1888), 47–8 · R. M. Robbins, 'The word notes of C. M. Doughty', *Agenda*, 18/2 (1980), 78–98 · A. McCormick, 'Hebrew parallelism in Doughty's *Travels in Arabia deserta*', *Studies in Comparative Literature* [ed. W. McNeir], Humanities ser., 11 (1962), 29–46 · T. S. Eliot, 'Contemporary English prose', *Vanity Fair* [New York], 20/5 (1923), 51–98 · S. B. Bushrui, 'Yeats's Arabic interests', *In excited reverie: a centenary tribute to William Butler Yeats, 1865–1939*, ed. A. N. Jeffares and K. G. W. Cross (1965), 280–314 · M. Morris, introduction, in *The collected works of William Morris*, ed. M. Morris, 8 (New York, 1966) · P. F. Mattheisen, 'Gosse's candid "snapshots"', *Victorian Studies*, 8 (1964–5), 329–54 · H. Scott, K. Mason, and M. Marshall, *Western Arabia and the Red sea* (1946) · Burke, *Gen. GB* (1937) · m. cert. · d. cert. [Frederica Doughty]

Archives FM Cam., notebooks relating to Arabian travels, corresp., and papers · Gon. & Caius Cam., papers · Ransom HRC, letters · RGS, Arabian travel journal | Hunt. L., letters to Sir Richard F. Burton · RGS, corresp. with Royal Geographical Society

Likenesses E. Kennington, pastel drawing, 1921, NPG [*see illus.*] · T. Spicer-Simson, bronze medallion, 1923, Golders Green crematorium; repro. in Hogarth, *Life* · F. Dodd, drypoint, NPG · oils, Downing College, Cambridge; by one of Doughty's daughters · photograph, repro. in C. M. Doughty, *Travels in Arabia deserta*, new

edn (1936) · photographs, Downing College, Cambridge · photographs, repro. in Hogarth, *Life*
Wealth at death £4691 8s. 3d.: administration with will, 11 May 1926, *CGPLA Eng. & Wales*

Doughty, William (1757–1781/2), portrait painter and engraver, born in York on 1 August 1757, was baptized on 14 August 1757 at St Michael le Belfrey, the son of John Doughty, the keeper of a fishing-tackle shop, and his wife, Anne, *née* Kirby. At the age of fourteen he produced two etchings which have survived: portraits of Thomas Beckwith after T. Barow and of Bacon Morritt after Vaslet; an earlier etched portrait of the Revd Mr Elgin has not survived. Doughty was recommended to Sir Joshua Reynolds by the Revd William Mason and, on being accepted, lived in Reynolds's house in Leicester Fields, Westminster, having enrolled as his pupil on 8 April 1775. He exhibited a portrait at the Royal Academy's exhibition in 1776. During his three years' residence with Reynolds, Doughty etched a portrait after a drawing by Mason of the poet Thomas Gray (1716–1771). On 9 August 1777, at St Martin-in-the-Fields, he married Margaret Joy, probably also from York and one of Reynolds's servants.

On leaving Reynolds in 1778 Doughty visited York and then went to Ireland, intending to reside there for a few months. In a letter to Hely-Hutchinson, Reynolds expressed a high opinion of Doughty's abilities and prospects, and Ellis Waterhouse considered him to have been 'potentially the ablest of Reynolds's students' (Waterhouse, 112). Doughty returned from Ireland at the end of 1778 and settled in Little Titchfield Street. He then produced a series of excellent mezzotints after Reynolds, who was particularly impressed with Doughty's interpretation of his portrait of Samuel Johnson. Reynolds advised Doughty to make a career as a mezzotint engraver, but Doughty was ambitious for recognition as a painter, and as his wife had friends in Bengal they decided to seek their fortune there. They embarked in 1780, but their ship was captured and Doughty was taken to Lisbon, where he died within a short time. His wife eventually reached India, but died of cholera in Calcutta, where she was buried on 10 December 1782.

TIMOTHY CLAYTON and ANITA MCCONNELL

Sources D. Mannings, 'Doughty, William', *The dictionary of art*, ed. J. Turner (1996) · J. T. Gilbert, *History of Dublin*, 3 vols. (1854–9), 3.347, 366; repr. (1972) · J. Ingamells, 'William Doughty, a little-known York painter', *Apollo*, 80 (1964), 33–7 · W. G. Strickland, *A dictionary of Irish artists*, 1 (1913); repr. with introduction by T. J. Snoddy (1989), 292–3 · J. Northcote, *The life of Sir Joshua Reynolds*, 2nd edn, 2 (1819), 33–4 · parish register, Calcutta, BL OIOC, N/1/2/460 [burial] · T. Dodd, 'History of English engravers', BL, Add. MS 33399, fol. 154 · Waterhouse, *18c painters*
Likenesses W. Doughty, self-portrait, oils, c.1776, NPG · W. Doughty, self-portrait, mezzotint, c.1780, BM

Tichborne, Roger Charles Doughty- (1829–1854?). *See under* Tichborne claimant (d. 1898).

Douglas family (*per. c.*1170–*c.*1300), barons, was of Flemish origin, possibly part of the marked Flemish settlement in upper Clydesdale, found in the reign of Malcolm IV (1153–1165). But William Douglas, the earliest known member of the Douglas family, is attested only in the last

quarter of the twelfth century. None the less, he was brother (less probably brother-in-law) of a Freskin of Kerdale, a Moray landowner, and both must have been related to the Freskin who was given land in Moray by David I, confirmed to his son William by Malcolm IV. The recurrence of these names and also of Hugh and Archibald in both families attests to their common ancestry, so that when a branch of the Moray family inherited the lordship of Bothwell in Lanarkshire in the 1240s, their near neighbours, the lords of Douglas, were distant kin. The senior line in Moray presumably procured the nomination of **Brice Douglas** (d. 1222), a son of William Douglas and prior of Lesmahagow in Lanarkshire, as bishop of Moray in 1203; the Brice (not a common name) who was a parson and dean of Christianity in Moray between 1188 and 1203 would be a Moray cousin. Bishop Brice brought his brother Freskin, parson of Douglas, to be dean, and three other brothers to be canons, of the cathedral chapter which he established in 1206–8 at Spynie, with the customs of Lincoln; hitherto the see had been peripatetic.

In November 1215 Brice was one of the Scottish bishops at the Fourth Lateran Council, and he had to visit the curia again in 1218 to seek absolution for ignoring the recent interdict on Scotland. In the same year his archdeacon and cathedral chancellor accused him at the curia of extortion of an eighth, or even a third, from his flock, of taking procurations without visitation, and of demanding money from ordinands and to grant divorces, money which he spent on women of ill fame. The truth of these allegations is unknown. Brice died in 1222.

Brice's brother, Archibald Douglas, had two sons: William and Andrew. From the latter descended the Douglases 'of Lothian', or 'of Dalkeith', later earls of Morton. The former, William, lord of Douglas, died c.1270–74, when the lordship of Douglas, with the manor of Fawdon in Northumberland which he had bought, passed to his son (possibly second son) **William Douglas** (d. 1298). This William was still under age in 1256, but had begun to earn his sobriquet of *le Hardi*, 'the Tough', by 1267, when he was severely wounded defending his father's house. Before 1288, when he was a widower, he had married Elizabeth, daughter of Alexander Stewart and sister of James *Stewart, both stewards of Scotland [*see under* Stewart family]. In that year, at Tranent in Haddingtonshire, he seized Eleanor de Lorain, the widow of William de Ferrars, who was in Scotland to take sasine of her third of Ferrars's sixth of the lordship of Galloway. Imprisoned in Leeds Castle (Kent) in 1290, Douglas fined for £100 on 18 February 1291 for the marriage of the lady. He was not named in the Great Cause of 1291–2, except that he swore fealty to Edward I as overlord, near Dunbar on 5 July 1291.

During these two years, when three men of John de Balliol came to Douglas Castle, William threw them into the dungeon, beheaded one, allowed another to die, and (most unwisely) let the third escape to John, now king. Douglas was fined for absence from John's first parliament in February 1293, but attended the August 1293 parliament to answer for his misdeeds. About 1292 he had refused to deliver her terce (or widow's portion) to his mother, and when she successfully took legal action against him, he seized the justiciar's officials who had come from Lanark to Douglas Castle to levy damages of 140 merks and to deliver sasine to the lady, detained them overnight, promised to release them, but still delayed doing so; his excuse was that he needed time to raise the money.

Whatever fine was imposed on this trouble-maker did not prevent his being placed in command of Berwick Castle in 1295 by the council set over King John to resist Edward I. When the town fell quickly to Edward I's invading army on 30 March 1296, the castle garrison of 200 surrendered for life, limb, lands, and goods, but Douglas was to be attached to Edward's household until the campaign ended. On 10 June 1296 he swore fealty to Edward, the fourth rebelling magnate to do so, and on 28 August his lands were restored. On 24 May 1297, along with other barons, he was told to hear and obey the king's agents in Scotland—doubtless to join Edward in service in France. The threat of that service may have been the factor which pushed Douglas, before the end of May, into joining the rising of William Wallace by attacking the king's justiciar at Scone. Robert Bruce, earl of Carrick (the future Robert I), to prove his loyalty to the king, ravaged Douglasdale and seized William's wife and children, but soon launched his own rebellion with James Stewart; William Douglas, possibly to save his family, joined them, both in rebelling and in their submission at Irvine on 7 July 1297.

Surrendered to the English by his allies, Douglas was taken to Berwick, and, 'very wild and very abusive', was imprisoned in Berwick Castle in irons. His gaoler begged the king 'let him not be freed, not for any profit or influence' (Stevenson, 1.205–6), and he was indeed transferred south for safe keeping after the English defeat at the battle of Stirling Bridge in September. From 13 October 1297 he was a prisoner in the Tower of London, attended by one valet, until he died there on 9 November 1298. The story in Barbour's *Bruce* that Edward I had him poisoned (after spending 4*d*. per day keeping him alive) is to be dismissed; but Edward certainly gave his estate of Douglas to Sir Robert Clifford, perhaps while he was still alive. It was a suitably dismal end of the road for a career of political expediency and physical violence.

William Douglas's first wife, Elizabeth, was a Stewart, with whom he had a son, James *Douglas, later known as the Black Douglas, who showed his father's ruthlessness and determination, but tempered by outstanding military ability; from this James's illegitimate son Archibald came the 'black' Douglases, earls of Douglas until their forfeiture in 1455. From William's son from his second marriage, also Archibald, came the 'red' Douglas line, earls of Angus, dukes of Hamilton.   A. A. M. DUNCAN

Sources *Scots peerage*, 3.132–42 · D. E. R. Watt, ed., *Fasti ecclesiae Scoticanae medii aevi ad annum 1638*, [2nd edn], Scottish RS, new ser., 1 (1969), 214, 218, 226 · G. W. S. Barrow, *Robert Bruce and the community of the realm of Scotland*, 3rd edn (1988), 83–5 · G. W. S. Barrow, *The kingdom of the Scots* (1973), 329 · Exchequer, accounts various, PRO, E101/4/10, E101/6/6 · J. Barbour, *The Bruce*, ed. A. A. M. Duncan (1997), 9 · A. O. Anderson and M. O. Anderson, eds., *The chronicle of Melrose* (1936) · J. Stevenson, ed., *Documents illustrative of the history of Scotland*, 2 vols. (1870)

Douglas, Sir Adye (1815–1906), politician in Australia, the son of Captain Henry Osborne Douglas, an army officer, and his wife, Eleanor Crabtree, was born at Thorpe, near Norwich, on 31 May 1815, and was intended for the navy. He was sent to school in Hampshire, and then to Caen, Normandy, for two years. On his return to England he was articled to a firm of solicitors in Southampton, and in 1838 was admitted to practice. He emigrated to Van Diemen's Land in 1839, and in the same year was admitted to the bar at Hobart. From 1840 to 1842, however, he and his brother were sheep farmers at Port Phillip (later Victoria). When he returned to Van Diemen's Land in 1842 he founded a legal firm in Launceston, and became one of the leading lawyers in the colony.

In 1853, on the introduction of a regular municipal administration for Launceston, Douglas became an alderman of the town, of which he was later mayor (1865–6, 1880–82). He remained alderman until 1884. About this time he won notice by his vigorous opposition to the system of transportation, which he regarded as a major obstacle to progress on the island. He was defeated at his first attempt to enter the legislative council, but in July 1855 was elected as member for Launceston, and moved to the house of assembly in 1856 under the new constitution. He actively promoted public works, particularly public water supplies and railways, and was successful despite stiff opposition, his most notable achievement being the building of the Launceston–Deloraine railway.

From 1862 to 1870 Douglas represented Westbury in the house of assembly; in 1871–2 he was member for Norfolk plains and from 1872 to 1884 for Fingal. On 15 August 1884 he became premier and chief secretary of Tasmania, and represented the island at the federal council of Australasia, a body which he had helped establish, and to which he expounded his vision of an Australasia independent of Britain. After a somewhat uneventful period of office he resigned on 8 March 1886 to go to England as first agent-general for the colony, an office he had established the previous year. In October 1887 he resigned his agency and returned to Tasmania.

From 1890 to 1904 Douglas was member for Launceston in the legislative council, and he represented Tasmania at the federal convention at Sydney in 1891. He served in the Dobson ministry as chief secretary from 17 August 1892 to 14 April 1894, when he became president of the legislative council; this position he held for ten years, and was knighted at the coronation of Edward VII in 1902. In May 1904 he was defeated at the elections for Launceston, and retired from public life.

Of striking personality, Douglas gave the impression of being brusque and unsympathetic, until he was better known. He was a good fighting leader, acute and tenacious in debate; an obituary in the Hobart *Mercury* referred to him as 'the central figure in the progressive movement' (11 April 1906). He was married four times. Of his first wife nothing is known, save that the couple had four children by the 1840s and that she had died by 10 July 1858, when

Douglas married, in London, a widow, Martha Matilda Collins, *née* Rolls. He married in Launceston on 18 January 1873 Charlotte Richards (1853/4–1876), with whom he had a daughter. His fourth wife, Charlotte's sister Ida, he married in Adelaide on 6 October 1877. They had four sons and four daughters. Douglas died on 10 April 1906 at Ryehope, Davey Street, Hobart, which had been his home for ten years; after a service in St David's Anglican Cathedral, Hobart, he was buried at the city's Cornelian Bay cemetery. C. A. Harris, *rev.* Elizabeth Baigent

Sources P. T. McKay and F. C. Green, 'Douglas, Sir Adye (1815–1906)', *AusDB*, 4.87–8 · F. C. Green, ed., *A century of responsible government, 1856–1956* (1956) · *Mercury* [Hobart] (11 April 1906) · *The Examiner* [Launceston] (11 April 1906)
Archives Tasmanian Archives, Hobart, Van Diemen's Land Company MSS

Douglas, Sir Alexander, seventh baronet (1738–1812), physician, was born in 1738, the only son of Sir Robert *Douglas of Glenbervie (1694–1770), genealogist and author of *The Peerage of Scotland*, and Margaret, eldest daughter of Sir James Macdonald of Macdonald. Douglas studied medicine at Leiden University in 1759, and was admitted MD of St Andrews on 11 July 1760. In April 1770 he succeeded his father, becoming seventh baronet, of Glenbervie. In May 1796 he became a fellow of the Edinburgh College of Physicians, and in September 1796, a licentiate of the Royal College of Physicians, London.

In June 1798 Douglas served as physician to the forces in the north of Britain, going on half pay in June 1802. It is not known whether he practised medicine subsequently, although he is described in Anderson's *Scottish Nation* as 'a physician of eminence' (Anderson, 2.59).

In 1775 Douglas married Barbara (*d.* 1815), daughter of James Carnegie of Finavon. Their only son, Robert, died in 1780 and with the death of Douglas in Dundee on 28 November 1812 the baronetcy became dormant. His wife survived him. G. T. Bettany, *rev.* Claire E. J. Herrick

Sources Munk, *Roll* · Anderson, *Scot. nat.*, 2.59 · A. Peterkin and W. Johnston, *Commissioned officers in the medical services of the British army, 1660–1960*, 1 (1968), 117 · Burke, *Peerage* · A. Jervise, *Memorials of Angus and Mearns* (1861), 97

Douglas, Alexander Hamilton. *See* Hamilton, Alexander Douglas-, tenth duke of Hamilton and seventh duke of Brandon (1767–1852).

Douglas, Lord Alfred Bruce (1870–1945), poet and biographer, was born on 22 October 1870 at Ham Hill near Worcester, the third son of John Sholto *Douglas, ninth marquess of Queensberry (1844–1900), and his wife, Sybil (1845–1935), daughter of Alfred Montgomery, a commissioner of Inland Revenue. The favourite of his mother, who dubbed him Bosie (a version of Boysie that stuck to him for the rest of his life), he was educated at private schools, then sent to Winchester College (1884–8); there he was an average student but a good runner, winning the school steeplechase in 1887. He also started a magazine, the *Winchester College Pentagram*; though it was hardly the

Lord Alfred Bruce Douglas (1870–1945), by George Charles Beresford, 1902

success hoped for—it ran for only ten issues—his contributions gave promise of his developing into a capable poet and incisive writer of prose. In 1889 he entered Magdalen College, Oxford, where he continued running and winning races. Athletic and handsome, popular with his classmates, he applied himself more to writing verse than his studies (he did not take a degree), but while at Oxford he contributed to the *Oxford Magazine* and edited the *Spirit Lamp*.

Lionel Johnson, a friend from Winchester, introduced Douglas to Oscar *Wilde in June 1891. Flattered by Wilde's fawning attention and impressed by his literary prominence, Douglas entered into a relationship that proved mutually disastrous. In March 1895 Wilde, strongly encouraged by Douglas, sued Queensberry for libel (Queensberry having provoked him by leaving a card for Wilde at his club: 'To Oscar Wilde—posing as Somdomite [*sic*]'). By his own account, Wilde abandoned the case rather than call Douglas as a witness (Ellmann, 428). Wilde was then prosecuted and, at the second of two trials in 1895, sentenced to two years' hard labour, served at Pentonville and Reading gaols. Douglas was not called to give evidence at either trial, but his letters to Wilde were entered into evidence, as was his poem, 'Two Loves'. Called on to explain its memorable concluding line—'I am the love that dares not speak its name'—Wilde answered in a great paean for the 'affection of an elder for a younger man' (Ellman, 435). Greatly distressed, Douglas wrote letters to the newspapers and unsuccessfully petitioned the queen for clemency for Wilde. Upon Wilde's release from prison in 1897, he took up with Douglas once again. They travelled through Italy together and met frequently in Paris.

After Wilde's death in 1900, Douglas established a close friendship with **Olive Eleanor Custance** (1874–1944), daughter of Colonel Frederick Hambleton Custance (1844–1925), a retired guards officer, of Weston Hall, Norwich, and his wife, Eleanor (d. 1908), daughter of Captain Hylton Jolliffe. They eloped, and married on 4 March 1902, and although their life together had a radiant beginning, after ten years of marriage they separated. Douglas lost custody of their only child, a son, Raymond (1902–1964). The Douglases did their utmost to remain respectful of each other over the remaining years of their lives. When Olive died in her seventy-first year on 12 February 1944, she was eulogized as a gifted poet. She had published her early poems under the pseudonym Opals, later works under her family name. Among her most significant publications are *Opals* (1897), *Rainbows* (1902), *The Blue Bird* (1905), and *The Inn of Dreams* (1911).

Douglas himself completed more than twenty volumes of poetry and prose. *Poems* (1896), *The City of Soul* (1899), *Sonnets* (1899), and *Lyrics* (1935) rank among his best collections of verse; his *Autobiography* (1929), *Oscar Wilde and myself* (1914), and *Oscar Wilde: a Summing Up* (1940) present vivid accounts of his creative but troubled life and his association with one of the most colourful personalities of the nineties.

Douglas was egocentric, quarrelled often, and made many enemies. In 1907, after being appointed editor of *The Academy*, he became involved in a series of violent disagreements with the publisher and an assistant editor. His disputatious behaviour cost him the editorship. In 1913 he was charged with libelling his father-in-law. In 1915 his attacks on Robert *Ross led to a prosecution for criminal libel, in which the jury disagreed. During the trial, Douglas fiercely criticized H. H. Asquith, the prime minister, for his association with Ross, and Asquith, with others, responded with a testimonial to Ross. Douglas published the most vitriolic of the many public attacks on Asquith at this time (Jenkins, 380). His vindictive nature occasioned several additional legal battles, including one with Winston Churchill in 1923, an action that resulted in Douglas's being sentenced to a six-month term in Wormwood Scrubs prison. One of the few consolations that sustained him at the time was his Roman Catholicism, to which he had converted in 1911. On 20 March 1945, while staying with friends in Lancing, he suffered a fatal heart attack. Three days later a requiem mass was said for the repose of his soul; and, as he had requested, he was interred beside his mother in the Franciscan friary cemetery in Crawley, Sussex.

Estimates of Douglas's personality and poetry vary from commentator to commentator. He has been labelled everything from 'the most complete cad in history' (Read, 1009) to 'thoroughly goodhearted and by no means the

moody, irascible revengeful person that many fancy' (Sherrard, 141). Considered opinion allows the inference that he neither ruined Wilde nor deserted him, as Douglas's enemies often alleged. The history of Wilde and his Bosie remains one of the most notorious scandals of the period. To accept Wilde's account as found in his *De Profundis* at Douglas's expense is to be less than objective. Douglas's loyalty to the imprisoned Wilde, his financial generosity, and continued concern, must be viewed in the context of a turbulent relationship involving two highly self-centred and opinionated individuals. As a poet, Douglas excelled as a sonneteer, and that his carefully crafted verse failed to win critical acclaim distressed him deeply. The attention accorded T. S. Eliot, Ezra Pound, the Sitwells, and other so-called moderns, he was certain, was misdirected. He believed that the spotlight should have fallen on *The Complete Poems of Lord Alfred Douglas* (1928), but Douglas was essentially a nineties' poet whose gifts did not survive into the twentieth century.

G. A. CEVASCO

Sources H. M. Hyde, *Lord Alfred Douglas: a biography* (1984) · R. Croft-Cooke, *Bosie: Lord Alfred Douglas, his friends and enemies* (1963) · B. Roberts, *The mad bad line: the family of Lord Alfred Douglas* (1981) · W. Freeman, *The life of Lord Alfred Douglas* (1948) · R. Ellmann, *Oscar Wilde* (1988) · G. H. Paterson, 'Lord Alfred Douglas: an annotated bibliography', *English Literature in Transition, 1880–1920*, 23 (1980), 168–200 · G. A. Cevasco, 'Lord Alfred Douglas and the *Winchester College Pentagram*', *Columbia Library Columns*, 39 (1989), 3–8 · B. Sewell, 'Olive Custance', *Like black swans* (1982), 76–96 · H. Read, 'Your affectionate friend', *The Listener* (8 Dec 1949) [review of Vyvyan Holland's edition of *De profundis*] · R. Sherrard, *Bernard Shaw, Frank Harris and Oscar Wilde* (1937) · R. Jenkins, *Asquith* (1964)

Archives Grolier Club, New York · NYPL, diaries and letters · Ransom HRC, letters and papers · Rosenbach Museum and Library, Philadelphia, papers · U. Cal., Los Angeles, department of special collections, papers · U. Cal., Los Angeles, William Andrews Clark Memorial Library, letters and memorabilia | BL, corresp. with Marie Stopes, Add. MSS 58494–58495 · Bodl. Oxf., letters to Symons, Hugh Walpole, and others; papers relating to prosecution of Herbert Asquith · NL Scot., letters to W. Sorley Brown · NYPL, Berg collection, diaries of Olive Custance · Ransom HRC, corresp. with John Lane

Likenesses double portrait, photograph, c.1893 (with Oscar Wilde), L. Cong., Kaufmann Collection · O. Wilde, photograph, 1897, U. Cal., Los Angeles, W. A. Clark Library · G. C. Beresford, photographs, 1902, NPG [*see illus.*] · H. Gaudier-Brzeska, pen-and-ink drawing, 1913, NPG · H. Coster, photographs, 1930–39, NPG · H. Leslie, silhouette, NPG · photographs, repro. in Ellmann, *Oscar Wilde* · photographs, U. Cal., Los Angeles, W. A. Clark Library · portrait (as undergraduate), repro. in A. Douglas, *Autobiography* (1929) · portrait (in his sixties), repro. in A. Douglas, *Autobiography* (1929) · portrait (aged forty-eight), repro. in A. Douglas, *Collected poems* (1919) · portrait (Olive Custance), repro. in Sewell, 'Olive Custance', 76–96

Douglas, Andrew (d. 1725), naval officer, was born in Glasgow but became domiciled in Ulster, probably in Coleraine. In 1689 he was master of the merchant ship *Phoenix*, which was laden with provisions and stores for the relief of Londonderry, besieged by the forces of James II.

For some weeks a squadron of English ships had lain in Lough Foyle, unable or unwilling to attempt to force the boom with which the river was blocked. Positive orders to make the attempt were sent to Colonel Percy Kirke, who commanded the relieving force; and two masters of merchant ships, Browning in the *Mountjoy* of Londonderry and Douglas in the *Phoenix*, volunteered for the service. With them also went Captain John Leake in the frigate *Dartmouth*. As the three ships approached the boom the wind died away; they were becalmed under the enemy's batteries, and were swept up by the tide alone. Their position was thus one of great danger; but while the *Dartmouth* engaged and silenced the batteries, the *Mountjoy* first, and after her the *Phoenix*, crashed through the boom. The *Mountjoy* ran aground and for the moment seemed to be lost. She was exposed to a heavy fire, which killed Browning; but the concussion of her own guns shook her off the bank, and on a rising tide she floated up to the city. With better fortune the *Phoenix* had passed up without further hindrance, and brought relief to Londonderry's starving inhabitants, by whom Douglas was hailed as a saviour. A certificate signed by the town's governor, George Walker, and others recommended him to the king, and in February 1690 he was accordingly appointed to the command of the sloop *Lark*.

On 30 August 1691 Douglas was promoted captain of the frigate *Sweepstakes* in which, and afterwards in the *Dover*, *Lion*, and *Harwich*, he served continuously during the Nine Years' War, employed, it would appear, on the Irish and Scottish coasts, but without any opportunity for distinction. The *Harwich* was paid off in November 1697, and for the next three years Douglas was unemployed, during which time, with no alternative profession, he wrote repeated letters to the Admiralty, asking for his case to be taken into consideration. At last, in February 1701, he was appointed to the *Norwich* (60 guns) which he commanded for eighteen months in the channel, and in July 1702 he sailed for the West Indies with a considerable convoy. He arrived at Port Royal, Jamaica, in September, where for the next eighteen months he remained senior officer; and in July 1704 he sailed for England with a large convoy. He arrived in the Thames at the end of September, and while preparing to pay off wrote on 4 October of his desire to be moved with his crew to the soon-to-be-launched *Plymouth*. Douglas's request is curious, for at the time of his writing many of his officers and men were combining to try him by court martial on charges of sutling, trading, hiring out the men to merchant ships for his private advantage, and punishing them 'exorbitantly'. He was tried on these charges at Deptford on 16 November 1704, and the court, holding them to be fully proved, 'in consideration of the meanness of his proceedings', sentenced him to be cashiered.

Douglas was reinstated in his rank on 24 September 1709 (with effect from 25 January 1710) by the earl of Pembroke, then lord high admiral, on the consideration of fresh evidence. In March 1711 he was appointed to command the *Arundel*, in which he was employed in the North Sea, and as far as Göteborg with convoy. While in her, on 15 December 1712, he was again tried by court martial, on this occasion for using indecent language to his officers and confining some of them to their cabins undeservedly, and for these offences he was fined three months' pay. He seems indeed to have been guilty, but under great provocation, especially from the lieutenant, who was at the same time fined six months' pay. In the following March the *Arundel* was paid off, and in February 1715 Douglas was appointed to the *Flamborough*, also on the home station. She was employed, mostly in the channel, in the operations concerned with the Jacobite rising of that year. The ship was paid off in October, and he had no further service. After several years on half pay as a captain he died on 26 June 1725.   J. K. LAUGHTON, *rev.* A. W. H. PEARSALL

Sources E. B. Powley, *The naval side of King William's war* (1972), 241–55 · S. Martin-Leake, *The life of Sir John Leake*, ed. G. Callender, 2 vols., Navy RS, 52, 53 (1920) · *The Byng papers: selected from the letters and papers of Admiral Sir George Byng, first Viscount Torrington, and of his son, Admiral the Hon. John Byng*, ed. B. Tunstall, 3, Navy RS, 70 (1932), 114–16, 122–3, 138 · J. Grant, ed., *The old Scots navy from 1689 to 1710*, Navy RS, 44 (1914), 7–24 · PRO, Admiralty MSS, ADM 6/424, ADM1 1692, 1693, 5265, 5269

Douglas, Andrew (1735/6–1806), physician and man-midwife, was born in Teviotdale, Roxburghshire, and educated at the University of Edinburgh. He began work as a surgeon in the navy in 1756, and later practised at Deal before returning to Edinburgh in 1775 where he graduated MD. He settled in London with the intention of practising midwifery, and was for several years physician to the Charity for Delivering Poor Married Women at their Own Houses. Douglas was admitted a licentiate of the Royal College of Physicians on 30 September 1776. He published *De variolae insitione* (his MD thesis) in 1775; *Observations on an Extraordinary Case of Ruptured Uterus* in 1785; and *Observations on the Rupture of the Gravid Uterus* in 1789. Douglas grew rich by marriage, gave up practice, and travelled abroad. From 1792 to 1796 he was detained as a prisoner in France. In 1800 he left London for Scotland and settled at Ednam House, near Kelso. He died at Buxton, Derbyshire, on 10 June 1806, aged seventy.

NORMAN MOORE, *rev.* MICHAEL BEVAN

Sources Munk, *Roll* · private information (1888) · P. J. Wallis and R. V. Wallis, *Eighteenth century medics*, 2nd edn (1988)

Douglas, Sir Archibald, lord of Liddesdale (1294?–1333), magnate, was the youngest son of Sir William *Douglas (d. 1298), lord of Douglas [*see under* Douglas family], and his second wife, Eleanor de Ferrers (d. after 1305). He was possibly born in 1294, as a two-year-old son of William Douglas, either Archibald or his elder brother Hugh, is recorded at William's manor of Stebbing, Essex, in 1296. By the time Archibald reached adulthood, his half-brother, Sir James *Douglas, had emerged as a key adherent of Robert I and Archibald benefited from the connection. During the 1320s he received estates at Morebattle in Roxburghshire and Kirkandrews in Dumfriesshire, and was granted Crimond and Rattray in Aberdeenshire; in 1327 he participated in the invasion of England.

Archibald Douglas's importance grew in the aftermath of the death of Sir James Douglas in 1330, when he became tutor to the latter's son. He himself married Beatrice (d. after 1337), daughter of Alexander Lindsay of Crawford, and their infant daughter Eleanor married Alexander Bruce, earl of Carrick, extending Archibald's connections.

The losses among the Bruce party at Dupplin Moor on 11 August 1332 increased Archibald's significance and he engineered Edward Balliol's defeat at Annan at the end of the year. This military role and the Douglas reputation made him a natural choice for guardian of Scotland after the capture of Sir Andrew Murray in April 1333. He used his authority to personal advantage, illegally occupying Liddesdale and other southern lands. When Edward III laid siege to Berwick in May, Archibald raised an army and devastated northern England. This tactic failed to force Edward's withdrawal and Douglas marched to relieve Berwick. On 19 July at Halidon Hill he was defeated and killed in the attempt. His sons, John and William *Douglas, fled into exile, and Archibald was remembered as the Tyneman or loser for this defeat, but his career shows he recognized the link between war and lordship which would allow William to become first earl of Douglas.

M. H. BROWN

Sources W. Fraser, ed., The Douglas book, 4 vols. (1885) · R. Nicholson, Edward III and the Scots: the formative years of a military career, 1327–1335 (1965) · G. W. S. Barrow, Robert Bruce and the community of the realm of Scotland, 3rd edn (1988) · W. Bower, Scotichronicon, ed. D. E. R. Watt and others, new edn, 9 vols. (1987–98), vol. 7 · M. Brown, The Black Douglases: war and lordship in late medieval Scotland, 1300–1455 (1998) · J. M. Thomson and others, eds., Registrum magni sigilli regum Scotorum / The register of the great seal of Scotland, 2nd edn, 1, ed. T. Thomson (1912)

Douglas, Archibald [*called* Archibald the Grim, Archibald the Terrible], **lord of Galloway and third earl of Douglas** (*c*.1320–1400), magnate, was the illegitimate son of Sir James *Douglas, lord of Douglas (*d*. 1330). He took his third nickname from his and his father's dark complexions. As lord of Galloway and earl of Douglas Archibald was the effective founder of the Black Douglas dynasty which dominated southern Scotland between 1388 and 1455: he had two legitimate sons, Archibald *Douglas, fourth earl of Douglas, and James *Douglas, seventh earl of Douglas and first earl of Avondale, and one illegitimate son, William *Douglas, lord of Nithsdale.

Early advancement Despite his later success, information on Archibald's origins and early life is extremely limited. He was probably born about 1320 and, to escape capture by the English, he may have been sent to France along with his cousin William Douglas, future first earl of Douglas, and David II. Although after the death of his half-brother, William Douglas, in 1333, Archibald was the only surviving son of the famous James Douglas, as a bastard he was initially excluded from any rights to the extensive lands of his father. This changed in 1342, when Archibald appears for the first time in contemporary records, being named as a possible heir to the Douglas estates. His inclusion was almost certainly the work of his distant cousin Sir William Douglas of Lothian, in whose interests the entail of 1342 was drawn up. While the document did not achieve its intended purpose in 1342, namely the diversion of the family lands to Sir William, forty-six years later Archibald used it to claim the principal Douglas estates.

In the decade from 1342 Archibald Douglas followed Sir William, witnessing one of his charters (in which he is named as a kinsman) and visiting England as his agent and servant. The death of his master at the hands of William, first earl of Douglas, in 1353 led Archibald to enter the latter's following. It was with the earl that Archibald fought for the French at Poitiers in 1356, when he escaped capture only through the efforts of a fellow knight, William Ramsay. However, the next year Archibald was taken prisoner, again as an accidental consequence of the actions of Earl William. The earl seized Hermitage Castle in Liddesdale while Archibald was visiting England, and in revenge he was detained by the English. His release was probably connected to the liberation of David II from captivity in late 1357. If so, it formed the basis of a lasting alliance between the king and Archibald. Although he continued to appear in Earl William's entourage during the late 1350s, from 1360 Archibald was moving into royal service, acting as the king's sheriff of Edinburgh and keeper of Edinburgh Castle. Adherence to the king earned Archibald his first significant estates. David II's influence was behind Archibald's marriage to Joanna Murray (*d*. after 1401) in 1362, which then brought Douglas not just Joanna's own estates, but also the lands of her first husband and cousin, Thomas Murray. By 1371 these included the baronies of Duffus, Petty, Balvenie, and Aberdour in north-east Scotland and the lordships of Bothwell and Drumsargard and a number of other baronies in Lower Clydesdale, providing Archibald with the status and resources of a major magnate. Bothwell became Archibald's favourite residence.

Royal patronage also made rivals for Archibald, among them Robert Stewart and William, earl of Douglas. When these two led a rebellion against David II in 1363, Archibald's interests lay firmly with the king, whom he accompanied throughout the crisis. His reward took the form of new opportunities. From 1364 Archibald was warden of the west march with England, and his responsibilities there included the final subjection of the province of Galloway, where strong regional identity combined with vestigial loyalty to the Balliol family to cause repeated problems for the Bruce dynasty and its allies. By 1369 Archibald had completed his task, forcing the chief local kindreds to recognize his authority. In return the king granted him the lordship of Galloway between the rivers Nith and Cree, and Douglas built a massive tower house at Threave to act as his chief stronghold. Associated with this venture was Archibald's chief ally, James Douglas of Dalkeith, the nephew of Sir William Douglas, and during the 1360s David II patronized both men as potential rivals to William, earl of Douglas.

War leader The death of David II in early 1371 seemed to pose a major threat to Archibald Douglas's prospects. The new king, Robert II, had no compelling reason to favour Archibald and quickly reached an understanding with William, earl of Douglas, who had at first opposed his accession. Although he was sent on an embassy to France in 1371, during the 1370s Archibald's position in the south-west was still at risk from the earl of Douglas and his allies, but the new lord of Galloway possessed the local backing to forestall any major challenge to his influence in the region. Indeed Archibald was able to extend that influence. In 1372 he bought the earldom of Wigtown, which neighboured his lordship of Galloway, from its lord, Thomas Fleming. Unlike Archibald, Fleming lacked the ability to control the leading kindreds of the area and, though Robert II may have had his own plans for the earldom, he accepted the purchase, recognizing the difficulties involved in supplanting Archibald.

These difficulties were increased by the gradual escalation of war with England, which had begun in the late 1360s with raids by Archibald and another protégé of David II, George Dunbar, earl of March, on English-held lands in the west and middle marches. By the early 1370s the earl of Douglas too was leading attacks against England. While the Stewart royal house was slow to participate, the conflict secured Archibald's place in the marches and the kingdom. This was in part because, despite his prosecution of the war, Archibald was also active in the border negotiations which attempted, without success, to maintain the truce which was being breached by both Scots and English. These negotiations show that Archibald retained his influence in the borders, since from the 1360s to the 1380s he was consistently named as the sole warden and commissioner for the Scots in the west march. His role in war and diplomacy was the basis for his integration into the new Stewart-dominated polity in Scotland. By the early 1380s the source of royal lordship in the south was John Stewart, earl of Carrick, the king's eldest son and lieutenant in the marches. Between 1381 and 1388 Archibald was drawn into Carrick's following, which also included the earls of Douglas and March, by a number of significant acts of patronage. Thus Archibald's bastard son, William, was made lord of Nithsdale, assigned a pension, and given the king's daughter, Egidia, as his wife. And a second marriage alliance linked Archibald and Carrick when, about 1387, Douglas's elder son from his marriage to Joanna Murray, Archibald, the future fourth earl of Douglas, married Carrick's daughter Margaret.

These marks of favour were indications of Archibald's importance as a military leader in the marches, as war with England grew in scale and intensity with the end of the truce in February 1384. To coincide with this Archibald, with Douglas and March, at once besieged and captured Lochmaben in Annandale in revenge for attacks by the garrison on his men in Galloway. His success deprived the English of their last stronghold in south-west Scotland. Archibald's value in war was recognized beyond Scotland. In 1385 the French distributed a war subsidy to the Scots king and nobility. Archibald's share of this was 5500 livres tournois, a sum equal to that of Carrick and second only to the new earl of Douglas, James Douglas. When the French sent an expedition to Scotland in 1385, Archibald showed his worth, meeting the French force in the west march and leading it in a raid on Carlisle. Much of the devastation suffered by the west march in the 1370s and 1380s was inflicted by Archibald. It was during a large-scale invasion of the English west march, by a substantial Scottish army led by Archibald and the earl of Fife, that Archibald received the news of the death of James, second

earl of Douglas, at Otterburn in August 1388, leaving the Douglas estates without an undisputed heir.

The earldom of Douglas During late 1388 and early 1389 Archibald the Grim or the Terrible as he was nicknamed, secured a share of this Douglas inheritance, which included the earldom and principal border lordships of the family. He did so despite the initial opposition of a number of leading figures, mostly relatives and followers of Earl James, who supported the claims of Malcolm Drummond, husband of Isabella, the previous earl's sister and, by normal legal standards, heir. Archibald's case rested on the 46-year-old entail of Douglas lands which limited succession to the male line and named him as ultimate heir. While Drummond sought recognition of his rights at the royal court, Archibald pressed his claim in the borders. In alliance once again with James Douglas of Dalkeith, who had his own claims to certain Douglas estates, and also with the backing of the king's second son, Robert Stewart, earl of Fife, Archibald extended his influence into Eskdale, Liddesdale, and Ettrick Forest during the autumn and winter. This success in winning over local men arguably depended less on the entail than on Archibald's pedigree as a war leader and his possession of the Douglas name, major considerations to communities in the front line of Anglo-Scottish warfare. As Archibald triumphed, Drummond's support at court crumbled. The latter's brother-in-law, Carrick, was succeeded as lieutenant by the earl of Fife, who had been on good terms with Archibald and whose interests centred on the north. Fife quickly identified Archibald as the man in possession and in April 1389 recognized him as earl of Douglas and lord of Eskdale, Lauderdale, Ettrick Forest, and the other entailed estates of the family.

Archibald Douglas spent the rest of his life defending these gains against a number of rivals. In 1389 Malcolm Drummond had in vain sought English help against Douglas, but on his return to Scotland he won support from the men round Carrick, who became king as Robert III in 1390. The focus of this faction was the king's son and heir, David Stewart, the new earl of Carrick. With this backing Drummond obtained rights to the unentailed portion of the Douglas estate, while David Stewart and his guardians began to interfere with Archibald's position in the marches. In the early 1390s Stewart himself claimed Nithsdale, following the death on crusade of Archibald's son William, who had held it by royal grant; he also took a leading role in border negotiations, squeezing out Archibald as march warden, and attracted a number of borderers to his own paid retinue. In addition to this pressure, Archibald found his position challenged by a new rival, George Douglas, earl of Angus, bastard son of William, first earl of Douglas, and his mistress Margaret Stewart, countess of Angus. From 1397 George put forward claims to the lands held by his father, and was assisted by Robert III, whose daughter Mary he married. Such claims threatened both Archibald and James Douglas of Dalkeith and were backed by force. In response Archibald seems to have transferred possession of his border lordships to his elder son, Archibald, master of Douglas, thereby ending any uncertainty over his advancing age and handing power to an active and aggressive lord who immediately renewed war with England. Royal politics confirmed Archibald's security. In late 1398 David Stewart, now duke of Rothesay, sought Archibald's support in his efforts to become lieutenant of the realm. The alliance was confirmed by Rothesay's marriage to Douglas's daughter Mary, and Archibald was left to settle the dispute between Douglas of Dalkeith and Angus, using the opportunity to build closer links with the latter. Archibald died at Bothwell Castle on Christmas eve 1400 and was buried at Bothwell collegiate church. He had secured his family's hold on the earldom of Douglas, while his son had already begun the search for still greater land and lordship.

Achievement Archibald Douglas's fame extended beyond Scotland. Like many of the Douglas family, he maintained close contact with France. He fought at Poitiers in 1356 and in 1369 and 1371 was sent as an ambassador to Charles V of France by successive Scottish kings. The scale of their payment to Archibald in 1385 suggests the French were impressed. Archibald was seen as an exceptional figure by other contemporaries. Jean Froissart wrote of him as a giant warrior, while the Scottish chronicler Walter Bower claimed that Archibald 'surpassed almost all other Scots … in worldly wisdom, resolution and daring [and] in the additions to his inheritance and wealth' (Bower, 8.35). Bower added praise for Archibald's judgements, the size of his retinue, and his generosity to the church, recording Douglas's foundation of collegiate churches at Bothwell and at Lincluden, near Dumfries. The expulsion of the existing community of nuns from Lincluden brought a characteristic element of force into his act of piety. The great rectangular tower house which he built at Threave helped to set a fashion for such residences among the Scottish landowning class, at every level, which would last into the sixteenth century. In view of his longevity and his mastery of the skills of war and politics in fourteenth-century Scotland Archibald Douglas ranks with Robert II and Robert Stewart, duke of Albany, for his impact on Scottish political society. M. H. BROWN

Sources W. Fraser, ed., *The Douglas book*, 4 vols. (1885) · W. Bower, *Scotichronicon*, ed. D. E. R. Watt and others, new edn, 9 vols. (1987–98), vols. 7–8 · J. M. Thomson and others, eds., *Registrum magni sigilli regum Scotorum / The register of the great seal of Scotland*, 11 vols. (1882–1914) · J. Froissart, *Chronicles of England, France, Spain, and the adjoining countries*, trans. T. Johnes, 2 vols. (1868) · S. I. Boardman, *The early Stewart kings: Robert II and Robert III, 1371–1406* (1996) · A. Macdonald, 'Crossing the border: a study of the Scottish military offensives against England, c.1369–c.1403', PhD diss., U. Aberdeen, 1995 · F. Michel, *Les écossais en France, les français en Écosse*, 2 vols. (1862) · *Scots peerage*, vol. 3

Douglas, Archibald, fourth earl of Douglas, and first duke of Touraine in the French nobility (c.1369–1424), magnate and soldier, was the elder son and heir of Archibald *Douglas, the Grim, third earl of Douglas and lord of Galloway (d. 1400), and Joanna Murray (d. after 1408), heir of Bothwell and Drumsagart (now Cambuslang) in Lanarkshire. The second Archibald has occasionally been called the Tyneman, or loser, on account of the defeats he suffered on the battlefields of Homildon Hill, Shrewsbury,

and Verneuil. However, it is likely that in the later middle ages this nickname belonged rather to Archibald's great-uncle and namesake who was killed at Halidon Hill in 1333. Its application to the fourth earl of Douglas is an unfair epitaph for the greatest magnate of the Douglas dynasty.

Border politics and warfare Although his father had a son, William [see Douglas, Sir William, lord of Nithsdale], from an earlier relationship, who was married to a daughter of Robert II, it was the younger Archibald Douglas who was identified as heir to both his father's lordship of Galloway and his mother's extensive inheritance in Clydesdale and in the north. The latter's status was underlined by his marriage to Princess Margaret (d. 1450/51) [see Douglas, Margaret, countess of Douglas, and duchess of Touraine in the French nobility], the eldest daughter of John Stewart, earl of Carrick, heir to the throne and lieutenant of the kingdom, about 1387. The match was designed to bind Archibald the Grim to Carrick, but instead linked the politics of the royal family to the Black Douglas dynasty in a way disastrous for Carrick's own line. This was first demonstrated in the following year when, after the death of James, second earl of Douglas, in battle in 1388, Archibald the Grim secured the earldom of Douglas and aided in Carrick's fall from power by allying with the lieutenant's younger brother Robert Stewart, earl of Fife (later duke of Albany). The events of 1388–9 made the younger Archibald heir to massive estates in southern Scotland, but his father faced problems holding the Douglas following together in the face of pressure from his Red Douglas rivals and Carrick, now King Robert III. It was as master of Douglas that Archibald the son made his first appearance in active politics in this struggle. It was perhaps in 1398 that the lands of the earldom of Douglas, including the lordships of Ettrick and Lauderdale, were assigned to the younger Archibald by his father, in an effort to ensure the former's succession to these disputed estates. The same year the master entered into war with England, breaking the truce by attacking English-held Roxburgh.

During the rest of his career Douglas combined warfare with wide political ambitions in Scotland and beyond. In 1399 he continued to lead his father's followers in attacks on England, attacks which were partly responsible for provoking the new English king, Henry IV, into launching an invasion of southern Scotland in the following year. Douglas's actions had political implications within Scotland. His father had forged an alliance with David, duke of Rothesay, elder son of Robert III and newly appointed lieutenant for his father. As part of this, Rothesay married the old earl's daughter Mary, an act which alienated the Douglases' chief southern rival, George Dunbar, earl of March. March turned to the English king to put pressure on Rothesay, but in his absence the master of Douglas seized his main stronghold at Dunbar and secured the support of many of March's chief tenants. The master clearly saw war with England and the Dunbars as the means to recover his family's influence in Lothian. By the time Henry IV led his army north in the summer of 1400, Douglas had been appointed keeper of Edinburgh Castle for life, a base for his local influence for over two decades. When his elderly father died at Christmas 1400, Douglas had already secured his place as the leader of the war in south-east Scotland. In early 1401 he routed a force led by March and Henry Percy (Hotspur), in eastern Lothian, and later in the year he established control of March's lordship of Annandale.

In these circumstances Douglas hardly wanted a cessation of Anglo-Scottish hostilities. By March 1401 the Stewart dukes, Rothesay and Albany, were anxious to secure a general truce but, when they sought to negotiate with the English, Douglas prevented them from entering his lands and continued the war. As in previous years, Stewart rivalries worked to the advantage of the Douglas earl. Amid growing political tension between them, in October 1401 Albany arrested his nephew, Rothesay. Albany's next act was to meet with Douglas at Culross in Perthshire. He needed to secure the support of Rothesay's main ally and was prepared to make considerable concessions to Douglas. The latter agreed to the death of Rothesay and in return Albany accepted an escalated war with England. Douglas, calling himself the lord of Dunbar, immediately rode to break up border negotiations and during early 1402 a series of Scottish attacks were launched across the border. In September Douglas himself took the field at the head of a massive force which included a force from Albany's retinue and a number of other magnates. However, after raiding to the Tyne the Scots were crushingly defeated on the 14th by an English army led by Hotspur and March at Homildon Hill near Wooler in Northumberland. Douglas was blinded in one eye by an arrow and taken prisoner.

English captivity Initially Douglas's defeat seemed to have exposed southern Scotland to renewed English occupation. The Percys were granted many of the earl's estates by Henry IV and in early 1403 began the campaign to make good their title. In these circumstances, Douglas was saved by conflict between his enemies. In summer 1403 the Percys rebelled against Henry IV. One of their grievances was the king's demand that they surrender those captured at Homildon Hill. Douglas in turn hoped to secure his release by providing support for Hotspur when the latter led his army south. When the Percys clashed with the royal army at Shrewsbury on 21 July 1403, Douglas, a huge and impressive fighting man, led a Scots contingent and the rebel vanguard. He wreaked considerable slaughter among Henry IV's own household, but when Hotspur was killed the rebel army fled. Douglas, who this time lost a testicle in the fight, was captured once more. Now a royal prisoner, Douglas spent much of the next six years in London. His imprisonment was not too confined: by the time of his final return to Scotland, Douglas had his own establishment in London; he shared his captivity with many other Scots, fellow prisoners like the son of Albany, Murdoch (or Murdac) Stewart, and the young king of Scots, James I, and his own household servants; and after 1405 received at least three lengthy periods of parole in Scotland.

These paroles reflected Henry IV's desire to use his prisoner to his own advantage but they also allowed Douglas to maintain his lands and lordship during his captivity. Douglas's first return in 1405 was to seek his own release in exchange for Henry Percy, first earl of Northumberland, an exile in Scotland. The failure of this scheme condemned Douglas to further captivity. His second parole in 1407 was connected to the negotiations between Albany, now governor of Scotland, and Douglas's enemies, the Dunbars, who were still in exile. In return for his release, Douglas sealed an indenture with Henry IV, becoming the king's man. Douglas's renewed presence in Scotland caused problems for Albany and the evidence suggests that friction between the two magnates and their followings ensued. When Albany allowed the Dunbars to return to Scotland in early 1408, Douglas left captivity for a third and final time, effectively absconding from his parole, even though he had left hostages for his return. A settlement between Albany and Douglas was only reached in an indenture between the two magnates in June 1409. They promised mutual friendship and agreed to settle disputes arising between them and their followers, but no mention was made of Albany's authority as governor. In return for relinquishing Dunbar to its previous lords, Douglas obtained the lordship of Annandale. The relationship between Douglas and Albany was sealed by the marriage of Douglas's daughter, Elizabeth, to Albany's second son, John *Stewart, earl of Buchan, in 1410.

Power and patronage The maintenance of Douglas's fortunes from captivity depended on the loyalty of his family and following in Scotland. The earl recognized the need to reward support. His brother James had defended family interests on the governor's council and in battle, and Douglas granted him a share of their mother's inheritance. Douglas similarly rewarded the service of other key supporters like William Crawford, his deputy in Edinburgh Castle, and James Douglas of Dalkeith, a longstanding ally of the Black Douglases. Crucially, between 1400 and 1409 Douglas was able to win the adherence of the most important local lords in the south. His influence in the old Dunbar lands was guaranteed by Douglas's good relations with Alexander and David Hume of Berwickshire, while his hold on Annandale was secured with the help of Robert Maxwell of Caerlaverock. A second Annandale man, Michael Ramsay, was also associated with Douglas. Ramsay's service rested on the dubious privilege of being husband of the earl's mistress, Christian, possibly the mother of the earl's bastard son John. Douglas gave these lords lands, money, and positions as his local deputies. Within the Douglas kindred, the support which the earl gave to William and Archibald, the bastard sons of the second earl of Douglas, weakened the power of the rival Red Douglas branch of the family.

The power of the fourth earl of Douglas rested on his leadership of a massive connection drawn from across the south. It also rested on his unparalleled accumulation of offices in the region. By 1410 Douglas was justiciar south of Forth and warden of all three marches towards England, this latter role elevated into 'Great Guardian' in the earl's own documents. As elsewhere in Scotland, the powers of government rested with the greatest private magnate of the region. The earl seems to have regarded the royal revenues of the south as a perquisite of his post. The profits of his justiciary courts and at least £500 a year from the customs of Edinburgh were siphoned into Douglas's coffers. Albany may have attempted to limit these depredations, but he had little success, and Douglas was regarded with some justice by one English writer as the real ruler of southern Scotland.

The influence of Douglas extended to the Scottish church. He was recognized by the abbeys of Dryburgh, Sweetheart, Holyrood, and Melrose, and by Coldingham Priory, as a valuable patron and protector. The earl's standing with the church, in Scotland and beyond, was raised to new levels by the ending of the great schism. By 1418 Scotland was virtually alone in continuing to support Pope Benedict XIII at Avignon when the other major kingdoms of the west were adhering to his Roman rival, Martin V. Albany remained firmly attached to Benedict, but Douglas was identified as a source of secular support for Martin, and as early as 1414 he had received letters from the king of France and elsewhere asking for his help in reuniting the church; by 1418 he had worked successfully with St Andrews University to secure Scottish recognition for Martin. The earl benefited in terms of prestige and influence from his involvement in the schism. The papacy addressed Douglas in respectful terms and churchmen and religious houses sought his sponsorship at the curia.

War and diplomacy in France Douglas's role in ecclesiastical politics also added to his reputation outside Scotland. Respected by European rulers long before 1418, Douglas was keen to play a part in international politics. He placed most weight on his family's well-established French connection. The Douglas name was already famous in France and when the earl invaded England in 1402 he had a company of French knights in his army. After Homildon Hill the French sought to ransom not just their own knights but Douglas too as a friend of their kingdom, and in 1404 there was talk of a marriage alliance between the French royal house and Douglas. The earl was eager to exploit this fame. In 1412 he travelled to France and negotiated an agreement with John, duke of Burgundy, effective regent for Charles VI. Facing a civil war and English invasion, Burgundy sought military aid and Douglas promised to lead 4000 men to the continent to fight for pay. Burgundy promised reciprocal support to Douglas, and though the plan came to nothing, it clearly established Scotland, and Douglas in particular, as a source of soldiers for wars in France. In 1419 the Dauphin Charles, facing Henry V of England's attempts to conquer France, also looked to Scotland for military assistance. He made a direct appeal to the governor and estates, having prepared the way by writing directly to Albany, Douglas, and other Scottish magnates. The expedition which the Scots sent was dominated by the retinues of Albany and Douglas. Its leaders were Douglas's elder son, Archibald *Douglas, earl of Wigtown, and his son-in-law John Stewart, earl of Buchan. Among the 6000 men the earls took to France were many who had

served the earl of Douglas in war and politics. Although Douglas himself avoided going to France at this point, he clearly committed extensive resources to the continental war and placed considerable hopes on its success.

The importance of the expeditions to France may be related to difficulties in Douglas's position in Scotland which began to show after 1410. Despite his political successes there were limits to the earl's ability to dominate the south. Most spectacularly, in 1416 Douglas was forced to besiege a hostile force in his own castle of Edinburgh, perhaps indicating a dispute with his deputy governor. This reflected wider problems, especially in Lothian. A number of feuds between baronial families in the early 1420s suggest difficulties perhaps connected to the re-emergence of the Red Douglases and Dunbars as rivals for predominance in south-east Scotland. During the same period the war leadership which was the basis of Douglas's influence across the south declined in importance. The restoration of the Dunbars in 1408 ended major Anglo-Scottish conflict. From 1415 English attention focused on France and, though Douglas led raids into northern England in that year, 1419, and 1420, and besieged Roxburgh Castle in 1417, these attacks achieved little except to provoke English retaliation.

Opportunities for greater importance and rewards lay on the continent. At Easter 1421 the Scottish army under Buchan and Wigtown defeated an English force at Baugé. The victory immediately heightened the importance of the Scots in Anglo-French conflict. While the Scots in France were showered with rewards by the dauphin, Douglas exploited the victory to seek a deal with Henry V. As he had done with other rulers, Douglas offered military service in return for significant rewards. In May 1421 he agreed to become Henry's man for life, serving him with 400 soldiers and receiving an annuity of £200 sterling. The arrangement was supported by James I who was to be temporarily released in exchange for hostages. Although James never went to Scotland and Douglas never served Henry V against his own family, and an English pension was far less than the rewards being offered by the French, the indenture had diplomatic value for Douglas. It forged links with the English and put pressure on the dauphin to bid for further Scottish help. It also allowed Douglas to move closer to his brother-in-law, James I. The two men had worked together in efforts to bring Scotland into papal allegiance between 1415 and 1418. After 1421 Douglas remained in regular contact with James and by 1423, after Henry V's death, the earl was working for the return of the king to Scotland. By the end of the year James's release was agreed.

Verneuil Douglas may have believed that James I would follow his return to Scotland with an attack on Duke Murdoch of Albany, who had succeeded his father as governor. In such Stewart rivalry the Black Douglases would hold the balance of power as they had done in 1402, and neither the king nor Albany would interfere with Douglas interests. The earl sought security in Scotland which would allow him to go to France in person. In October 1423 Douglas had promised to support the dauphin (now Charles VII) with a full-scale army and handed over his Scottish lands to the safe keeping of his wife and elder son. In February 1424 he and Buchan left for France with an army. On 7 March Douglas landed at La Rochelle and on 24 April the Scottish army of 6500 men was reviewed by Charles VII at Bourges. Douglas was well paid for his support. He was granted the duchy of Touraine and was named lieutenant-general of the king for the war against England. A non-royal foreigner, Douglas had been given rank and powers without precedent in medieval France. He moved quickly to take possession of his new lands. On 7 May the citizens of Tours reluctantly welcomed their new duke, who was made a canon of the cathedral and also took custody of the castles at Loches and Tours.

During the next three months Douglas and his army lived off the land in Touraine, running up debts and arousing local hostility. Then in August he led an army of Scots, French, and Italians northwards to enter the war against the English in Normandy. Although his attempt to relieve the town of Ivry (Eure) failed, on 16 August Douglas captured Verneuil-sur-Avre (Eure). This provoked the advance of the English under John, duke of Bedford. Against the advice of many French nobles, Douglas offered battle next day outside Verneuil. The fight was the fiercest of the war. The Scots threatened to break the English opposite them but, led by the Italians, the rest of the army fled. Douglas, who was in the thick of the fight, was killed along with his younger son James, Buchan, and almost the entire Scottish contingent. He was buried with his son and son-in-law in St Gatien's Cathedral at Tours. The fourth earl of Douglas had used the resources built up by magnates of his family to carve out a role for himself in Scotland and in European politics. His ambitions were enormous and rested on his military following. Douglas may have hoped to found a Franco-Scottish princely house but his death and the destruction of his army left the way clear for the revival of royal power in Scotland.   M. H. BROWN

Sources W. Fraser, ed., *The Douglas book*, 4 vols. (1885) · M. Brown, *The Black Douglases: war and lordship in late medieval Scotland, 1300–1455* (1998) · S. I. Boardman, *The early Stewart kings: Robert II and Robert III, 1371–1406* (1996) · W. Bower, *Scotichronicon*, ed. D. E. R. Watt and others, new edn, 9 vols. (1987–98), vol. 8 · G. Burnett and others, eds., *The exchequer rolls of Scotland*, 2–4 (1878–80)

Douglas, Archibald, fifth earl of Douglas, and second duke of Touraine in the French nobility (*c.*1391–1439), magnate and soldier, was the elder son of Archibald *Douglas, fourth earl of Douglas and first duke of Touraine (*c.*1369–1424), and Margaret *Douglas, *née* Stewart (*b.* before 1373?, *d.* 1450/51), daughter of *Robert III. His early career was dictated by the ambitions of his father in Scotland, England, and France. During the fourth earl's English captivity his heir acted as a hostage for his good behaviour on temporary release from custody and, while in London, the younger Archibald witnessed two of his father's charters. Similarly, in Scotland Archibald and his younger brother, James, were associated with an indenture designed to regulate possibly uneasy relations between their father and the governor, Robert Stewart, duke of Albany, in 1409. The assumption by Archibald of

the title earl of Wigtown (the lands of which earldom had been held by the Black Douglases since 1372) may have been part of his father's attempt to raise the status of his house in Scotland and beyond. More particularly, occurring as it did between 1417 and September 1419, Archibald's elevation was probably connected with his co-leadership of an army in France.

In the autumn of 1419 Archibald, earl of Wigtown, was one of the principal commanders of a Scottish force of up to 6000 men sent to France. He and the other main leader, John Stewart, earl of Buchan, second son of the duke of Albany and husband of Archibald's sister, Elizabeth, had been sent to support the dauphin, Charles (the future Charles VII), in his war against Henry V. Although he returned to Scotland on recruiting missions in early 1420 and late 1422, between 1419 and 1423 Wigtown's career was as a French commander. The high point of his efforts was the victory won by the Scots and their French allies at Baugé in Anjou on Good Friday 1421 in which Henry V's brother Thomas, duke of Clarence, was killed. Wigtown was rewarded for this success with the lands of Dun-le-roi in Berri and the title of count of Longueville (then in English hands). His role at Baugé and his prizes indicate that in the leadership of Scots troops on the continent he played a junior part to Buchan, who was made constable of France after the battle. Wigtown probably represented his father both at the French court and in the Scottish army—the latter contained considerable numbers of kinsmen, tenants, and adherents of the Black Douglases.

The return of Wigtown to Scotland in 1423 was once more in response to the ambitions of his father. The fourth earl was preparing for his own entry into the French war, encouraged by the offer of the duchy of Touraine from Charles VII, the imminent return of James I from English captivity, and the death of Henry V, whom the earl had promised to serve in France. Wigtown was again to stand in for his father, this time in Scotland. Since 1419 Wigtown had been confirming grants made by Archibald the elder. Such confirmations by an heir of alienations by his father are commonplace, but these may also reflect the fourth earl's long-standing intention to serve in France. Between late 1423 and the departure of the fourth earl to France in March 1424 Wigtown was given power to run the Douglas lands in his place, with the exception of Galloway, where his mother, Margaret, was left in authority. Although he had helped secure the king's release, the fourth earl was apparently not prepared to experience James's rule. Wigtown's marriage, around 1423, to Euphemia Graham (*d.* 1468), sister of Malise Graham, earl of Strathearn, and great-niece of Walter Stewart, earl of Atholl (*d.* 1437), forged connections with other magnates which could be valuable in the uncertain circumstances of the king's return.

In the event Wigtown found his uncle James I anxious to maintain Black Douglas support. Though he relinquished part of his father's dominance in the marches, Wigtown successfully forged a working relationship with the king; James knighted him in May 1424, which seemed to secure his family's power. This position was weakened in August by the death of the fourth earl and the destruction of the Scottish army at Verneuil. The French lands received by both Douglases were quickly repossessed by Charles VII and given to new owners, despite continued complaints from the family. More damagingly, the removal of the earl and so many of his adherents meant that his son had to concede influence in Lothian and Berwickshire to the king. Archibald, now fifth earl of Douglas, backed the king's attack on Murdoch Stewart, duke of Albany, in March 1425 not because he was the mainstay of royal power envisaged by the fourth earl, but in hope of reward. The support of the Black Douglas connection was none the less crucial to the assize which condemned Albany, and Douglas had his title to the lordship of Bothwell confirmed in return. Further recompense was not forthcoming. Instead in 1426 the king confirmed his sister, Douglas's mother, in her hold on Galloway and displayed his ability to intervene in the family's border power base.

The fifth earl was clearly dissatisfied with the limitations on the regional powers established by his father. He continued to concern himself in Galloway after 1426, and in 1429 sought to exert influence in Carrick in a dispute between members of the Kennedy kindred. James I distrusted such activities and, although Douglas was given the rank and role of a trusted councillor at court and served on James's 1429 highland campaign, the king blocked his local ambitions. Tension increased with the king's move towards a war in the highlands and with England, which Douglas saw as potentially disastrous. The earl was removed as a march warden and in 1431 was arrested, once again perhaps in connection with the feuding Kennedys. He was quickly restored to lands and offices, but his local role remained curtailed. While he did not go to France, as David Hume of Godscroft later claimed, his activities were confined to the heartlands of the family, Bothwell, Annandale, and Selkirk Forest, and his support drawn largely from those regions.

Throughout James's reign Douglas benefited from the rise of family servants. Men such as his uncle James Douglas of Balvenie, John Cameron, and William Crichton maintained contact between king and earl and prevented wider conflict. They were also vital in the earl's promotion following the assassination of James in February 1437. Douglas had no part in a plot which sought power for his rival, Walter, earl of Atholl. To many, though, he was the most acceptable lieutenant for the young James II, no doubt in part because of his descent from Robert III. In June he received the office from a general council, forcing Queen Joan to relinquish power. All the same, it is arguable that his rise owed less to legitimacy than to the support of Balvenie and Crichton. Both profited from his brief period of power, in which Douglas showed himself aware of the need to forge agreements with the other major Scottish magnates, the earl of Crawford and the lord of the Isles, and widened his own basis of support in Ayrshire and Lothian. However, the earl's own death on 26 June 1439 at Restalrig, Edinburghshire, was to prove the dangers of reliance on such powerful servants as Balvenie and Crichton, who orchestrated the murder of Douglas's sons,

David and William *Douglas, the following year. The earl was buried in an impressive tomb in the church of Douglas, St Bride's, on which were recorded his full titles—earl of Douglas and Wigtown and lord of Galloway, Bothwell, Selkirk and Ettrick Forest, Eskdale, Lauderdale, and Annandale in Scotland, and duke of Touraine, count of Longueville, and lord of Dun-le-roi in France.

M. H. BROWN

Sources W. Fraser, ed., *The Douglas book*, 4 vols. (1885), vols. 1, 3 · M. Brown, *James I* (1994) · C. McGladdery, *James II* (1990) · W. S. Reid, 'The Douglases at the court of James I', *Juridical Review*, 56 (1944), 77–88 · A. I. Dunlop, *The life and times of James Kennedy, bishop of St Andrews*, St Andrews University Publications, 46 (1950) · G. Burnett and others, eds., *The exchequer rolls of Scotland*, 4–5 (1880–82) · B. G. H. Ditcham, 'The employment of foreign mercenary troops in the French royal armies, 1414–1470', PhD diss., U. Edin., 1978 · A. I. Dunlop, ed., *Calendar of Scottish supplications to Rome*, 3: *1428–1432*, ed. I. B. Cowan, Scottish History Society, 4th ser., 7 (1970)
Likenesses effigy on funeral monument, *c.*1440, St Bride's Church, Douglas, Lanarkshire

Douglas, Archibald [nicknamed Bell-the-Cat], **fifth earl of Angus** (*c.*1449–1513), magnate and rebel, was the elder of the two sons of George *Douglas, fourth earl of Angus (*c.*1417–1463), and his wife, Isabel, daughter of Sir John Sibbald of Balgonie in Fife. The steady advance of this comital family to a position of great power, especially on the borders, was based on unswerving loyalty to the crown over two generations. Earl Archibald's career displays no such consistency; indeed, he may be regarded as the great political maverick of the reigns of James III and James IV, an earl who rose to be chancellor, yet whose last years were spent trying to preserve his family's inheritance from the encroachments of a predatory crown.

Early manoeuvrings On 4 March 1468 Earl Archibald, who had succeeded his father in 1463 at the age of about fourteen, married Elizabeth (*d.* 1498), eldest daughter of Robert, Lord Boyd (*d.* 1482), the chamberlain, whose power rested on his seizure of the adolescent James III in July 1466. Boyd earned the king's undying hatred by marrying his son Thomas to James's elder sister Mary in 1467; so the Angus–Boyd alliance of 1468, although doubtless made with a view to advancing the fortunes of both families, soon misfired badly. In November 1469 the king took control of government, and the Boyds, forfeited, finished up in exile or on the block. The young Earl Archibald, having backed the wrong side, hastened to make amends to the king by sitting on the parliamentary assize of November 1469 which condemned his Boyd kinsmen.

Thereafter, during most of the 1470s, Angus was rarely at court, and was only occasionally in parliament. His territorial interests lay mainly, though not exclusively, in the south and west, where he had inherited lordships stretching from Haddingtonshire to Kirkcudbright; and by the early 1480s, if not before, he was justiciar south of Forth. Together with his near neighbour Alexander Stewart, earl of March and duke of Albany, the king's brother, Angus appears to have disliked James III's obsessive concern for peace and alliance with England. Albany's opposition to the king's Anglophile stance led to a royal attack on his castle of Dunbar in the spring of 1479. The duke fled to

France (moving to England in the late spring of 1482), and James III's unconvincing indictment of Albany failed to secure a parliamentary sentence of forfeiture in October 1479. In the following spring the king's foreign policy collapsed, and Angus was first off his mark in the war with England which ensued, raiding Northumberland and burning Bamburgh Castle.

Treason and plots Angus played an important, if rather obscure, role in the Lauder crisis of July 1482, when James III, mustering the host to resist the invasion of a huge English army commanded by Richard, duke of Gloucester, and the exiled Albany, was seized by his own magnates and incarcerated in Edinburgh Castle. Angus was certainly present at Lauder—he had probably no further to come than from Tantallon Castle in Haddingtonshire and, according to the chronicler Robert Lindsay of Pitscottie, writing in the 1570s, he played a major part in arresting and hanging Cochrane and other offensive royal familiars—but his motives are difficult to ascertain. He can hardly have been the prime mover in the Lauder *coup*, for he played no obvious part in the governmental regime which followed it; control of the king fell to James III's half-uncles, the earls of Atholl and Buchan, and Andrew Stewart, bishop-elect of Moray. Angus may, indeed, have been a committed Albany man throughout, looking to the duke as 'Alexander IV', a suitable replacement for James III; he may have taken part in an embassy to the exiled duke in France in the spring of 1482, and therefore been in collusion with Albany before the Lauder crisis; and later, when Albany had acquired a new backer in Edward IV of England, Angus may have been one of those twenty-six Scottish magnates who gave a written commitment to the English king to support the duke in his efforts to displace James III. What is clear beyond doubt is that, early in 1483, Angus was acting as one of Albany's commissioners to Edward IV, travelling south to Westminster to negotiate a treasonable treaty with the English king. According to this agreement (11 February 1483), Albany and his supporters, including Angus, would become liegemen of the English king, and Edward IV promised to assist Albany in his efforts to acquire the Scottish crown.

Thus Angus's role in the crisis of 1482–3 was overtly treasonable, a far cry from the later portrayal of the patriotic earl acting out of concern for his king, misled as he was by evil counsellors who had to be removed for the good of the kingdom. This latter view of the earl has persisted, however, thanks to the efforts of sixteenth- and seventeenth-century chroniclers to portray Angus in a flattering light. Among these, David Hume of Godscroft, in his *History of the Houses of Douglas and Angus* (1644), was the first writer to apply the epithet Bell-the-Cat to the fifth earl. According to Godscroft, when the nobles were holding their conference in Lauder kirk to decide what could be done to remove the royal favourites, Lord Gray told the old story of the mice who resolved to hang a bell about the cat's neck, to give warning of its approach, but lacked the courage to do so, whereupon Earl Archibald volunteered to bell the cat. In spite of the fact that no earlier chronicler—not even Pitscottie, the *locus classicus* for this event—mentions

the story, the tag has stuck as an inappropriate nickname for the fifth earl.

Tacking between James III and James IV The recovery of power by James III and the death of Edward IV in April 1483 doomed Albany's schemes, and left Angus and the rest to make what terms they could. Given his recent treasons, the fifth earl was treated remarkably leniently, losing his justiciarship and keepership of Threave, but acquiring, astonishingly, the wardenship of the middle marches. However, uncertainty as to his standing with James III made Angus a rebel in the crisis of 1488 when Prince James (the future James IV) took arms against his father at the head of a huge and diverse body of disaffected magnates.

As in 1482, Angus's initial role in this crisis is obscure. James III may have tried to buy his support, for the earl remained at court until early March 1488, more than a month after the start of the rebellion, and he was at best a lukewarm rebel. When the end came for James III at Sauchieburn (11 June), no contemporary record, no later chronicler even, mentions Angus's prowess at the battle, and he may not have been there at all. Perhaps significantly, many of the earl's relatives and tenants—Lindsay of Auchtermonzie, lords Forbes and Glamis, David Scott of Buccleuch, and William Douglas of Cavers—did not join him in rebellion.

The advent of the fifteen-year-old James IV produced a temporary improvement in the fifth earl's fortunes; he was the king's friend, who gave James presents and who on occasions played cards and dice with him. More to the point, Angus acquired the wardenships of all three marches at the start of the reign. But there was no room for him in the new government, dominated as it was by Patrick Hepburn, recently created earl of Bothwell, and his Hume allies. Fearing Angus's power on the borders and facing a serious rebellion against their authority in 1489, the leaders of the new regime gradually stripped the earl of his lands and offices: all his march wardenships, the sheriffdom of Lanark, the Berwickshire lands of Earlston, and the lands and castle of Broughty in Angus. The earl also disappeared from the royal council and from parliament for three years (1489–92).

Under severe threat in the borders, Angus renewed his treasonable links with England, this time with Henry VII, promising by an agreement of November 1491 to hand over Hermitage Castle in Liddesdale to the English king in return for lands of equal value in England, if he could not move the Scottish government towards peace with England. About this time he also sought to have himself recognized as heir-at-law to the last earls of Douglas, a chilling prospect for his Hepburn and Hume rivals in southern Scotland. In October 1491 the king laid siege to Angus's castle of Tantallon; the outcome is unknown, but in spite of a reconciliation between King James and Angus at Christmas, the Bothwell-dominated royal council was taking no chances with Angus's future loyalty. On 29 December 1491 the earl was forced to exchange his border lordship of Liddesdale and castle of Hermitage (which went to

Bothwell in regality) for the lordship of Kilmarnock in Ayrshire.

Gains and losses Angus–Bothwell rivalry continued for much of the rest of the reign, with Earl Archibald generally on the losing side. In January 1493 he made a spectacular political comeback by acquiring the chancellorship, an office which fell to him partly through the growing importance of his Ayrshire relatives, for his niece, Marion Boyd, was James IV's first mistress. But advancement acquired in this way was difficult to sustain. Within a few years the king was an adult, Marion Boyd was discarded, and the Anglo-Scottish war of 1496–7 made Angus, with his earlier English affiliations, a highly unsuitable chancellor. He was dismissed to make way for the earl of Huntly in the autumn of 1497 and thereafter Angus's career was visibly in decline. In 1498 he made the tactical mistake of granting the baronies of Braidwood and Crawford-Lindsay in Lanarkshire to his mistress Janet Kennedy, only to see Janet transfer her affections to the king, who was quite happy to confirm the earl's Lanarkshire grants to the woman who was to become the most durable of his mistresses.

Angus suffered some losses in the royal revocation of 1498; and Hepburn rivalry may account for Earl Archibald's being warded in Dumbarton Castle in 1501 and, much more seriously, on the island of Bute for the remarkable period of seven years (1502–9). Perhaps significantly, he was not freed until after the death of Patrick Hepburn, earl of Bothwell, in 1508, and then only to be savagely pursued by the crown on the legal technicality of non-entry—forty-five years of it—to his lands of Kirriemuir in Angus and his border lordship of Eskdale, and presented with an appalling bill of £45,000 Scots for Kirriemuir alone. Angus, endeavouring to preserve some of his inheritance in the face of relentless and cynical royal demands, settled for a composition of 5,000 merks, not all of which had been paid when he died.

In his last years, though a chastened old man, Angus re-emerged at court. According to Buchanan, he opposed the Anglo-Scottish war of 1513; yet his two eldest sons, George, master of Angus, and Sir William Douglas of Glenbervie, were both killed in James IV's army at Flodden (9 September 1513). Angus's survival left him one of Scotland's senior earls, but towards the end of October 1513 he died at Whithorn, Wigtownshire, aged about sixty-four. He was succeeded by his grandson Archibald Douglas (d. 1557), another political high-flyer who came to grief even more spectacularly than his grandfather.

The fifth earl of Angus was twice married. He and his first wife, Elizabeth Boyd, had four sons and three daughters: George, master of Angus, and Sir William Douglas (both killed at Flodden), Gavin *Douglas, the poet and bishop of Dunkeld, Archibald *Douglas of Kilspindie (d. before 1540), Marion, Elizabeth, and Janet. Angus's second marriage, to Katherine Stirling, daughter of Sir William Stirling of Keir, in the summer of 1500, produced no children and had ended in divorce or separation by 1512.

NORMAN MACDOUGALL

Sources J. M. Thomson and others, eds., *Registrum magni sigilli regum Scotorum / The register of the great seal of Scotland*, 11 vols. (1882–1914), vol. 2, index • T. Dickson and J. B. Paul, eds., *Compota thesaurariorum regum Scotorum / Accounts of the lord high treasurer of Scotland*, 1–4 (1877–1902) • *APS, 1424–1567*, index • W. Fraser, ed., *The Douglas book*, 4 vols. (1885), vol. 3 • *Scots peerage*, vol. 1 • *LP Henry VIII*, vols. 1/1–2 • [G. Buchanan], *The history of Scotland translated from the Latin of George Buchanan*, ed. and trans. J. Aikman, 6 vols. (1827–9), 253–5 • D. Hume of Godscroft, *The history of the houses of Douglas and Angus* (1644), 226–7 • M. G. Kelley, 'The Douglas earls of Angus: a study in the social and political bases of power in a Scottish family from 1389 to 1557', PhD diss., U. Edin., 1973 • N. Macdougall, *James III: a political study* (1982), index • N. Macdougall, *James IV* (1989), index • *The historie and cronicles of Scotland … by Robert Lindesay of Pitscottie*, ed. A. J. G. Mackay, 1, STS, 42 (1899), 173–6
Archives NA Scot., APS • NA Scot., RMS • NA Scot., TA

Douglas, Archibald, sixth earl of Angus (c.1489–1557), magnate and lord chancellor of Scotland, was the eldest son of George Douglas, master of Angus (c.1469–1513), and his wife, Elizabeth, widow of Sir David Fleming of Monycabo and daughter of John Drummond, first Lord Drummond.

Inheritance and first bids for power Douglas's first involvement in dynastic politics may have been his marriage in 1509 (contract 26 June) to Margaret, daughter of Patrick Hepburn, first earl of Bothwell, a rival of his grandfather Archibald *Douglas, fifth earl of Angus, nicknamed 'Bell-the-Cat'. She died childless in 1514. His father was killed at Flodden on 9 September 1513, and in November Douglas succeeded to the earldom of Angus on the death of his grandfather. His inheritance was scattered over a wide area: Crawford Douglas in Lanarkshire, Tantallon in Haddingtonshire, the regalities of Jedburgh Forest and Selkirk, and the advowson of Abernethy collegiate church in Perthshire, to mention only a few. He maintained a persistent claim to Coldingham Priory, Berwickshire, important both for its potential wealth and for its position near the border, though here he faced competition from the Humes. He was also well connected: the Cunningham earls of Glencairn, the Graham earls of Montrose, the Hays of Yester, and the Lyonses of Glamis were all close relatives. His considerable power and worth to the monarchy lay in his extensive kin and in the large number of armed retainers he could call upon for support.

In 1514 Angus began to attend the council regularly. In August 1514 (probably, though not certainly, on the 6th) he made a secret marriage at Kinnoul in Perthshire to James IV's widow, Margaret Tudor [see Margaret (1489–1541)]. The priest who performed the ceremony was Angus's kinsman John Drummond, and it is likely that the groom's maternal grandfather helped to arrange the match. This was barely eleven months after the king had been killed at Flodden and only four months after the birth of James's last child, Alexander. At that time Margaret was not only queen dowager, the mother and protector of the royal children, but also regent of the kingdom of Scotland. She also was a major landowner, holding not only her dower of Stirling Castle, but estates as widely scattered as Dunbar, Methven, and Crawford. In one bound, the youthful Angus leapt close to real power.

Angus's ambition was so blatant that Margaret was

removed from the regency in September. The lords of the council then invited John Stewart, second duke of Albany, eldest son of James III's brother and the heir to the throne should the infant sons of James IV both die, to come from France and assume the governorship. Albany arrived in May 1515, a development which displeased Margaret's brother Henry VIII, who had counted on her to create and maintain good Anglo-Scottish relations and to keep him informed of Scottish affairs. Albany, by contrast, was seen as essentially an agent of France. So unpopular was her new union that Margaret fled to England, where in October she gave birth at Harbottle, Northumberland, to a daughter, Margaret *Douglas. Angus and his wife had no more children; Angus lost interest in Margaret during her absence and took a mistress, Lady Jane Stewart of Traquair (to whom he had earlier been briefly betrothed). The queen responded by beginning divorce proceedings shortly afterwards, a goal which she attained only early in 1527. Yet despite their acrimony she begged James V to be 'good and gracious' to her former husband as she died at Methven, Perthshire, the home of her third husband, Henry Stewart, Lord Methven, in October 1541.

Angus's influence in Scotland was restricted while Albany was in Scotland, but soon after the duke returned to France in June 1517 his arrangements for the government of Scotland began to break down. There was fierce competition for power between Angus and James Hamilton, earl of Arran, with control of Edinburgh in particular a bone of contention. Their rivalry culminated in the skirmish known as Cleanse the Causeway at the end of April 1520, in which the Hamiltons were driven from the town. But Albany returned late in 1521 and used his authority to restore order; thereupon Angus retired to France, where he stayed until 1524. It was Albany's leaving Scotland for France at the end of May in that year which enabled Angus to make the same crossing but in the opposite direction. He did not go directly, however, but made the journey via England—he arrived in London on 28 June. He had been maintained by an English pension of 1000 marks since 1521, and in 1525 this was raised to £1000. This reflected his importance in Scottish government by that date. In July 1524 Queen Margaret and her supporters had declared James V of age in order to ensure against Albany's return; as James was still only twelve they intended to govern in his name. Margaret was very anxious to prevent her estranged husband's return, but by October Angus had secured English agreement to his going home. He was perceived as popular in Scotland, and as a valuable counterbalance to the influence there of France. About the beginning of November he crossed the border.

The exercise of power For several months Angus and Margaret competed for power. Margaret's coup of the previous July had led to the dismissal of Chancellor James Beaton, who now made common cause with the earl. Hence the proclamation issued in the king's name in January 1525 against consorting with Beaton, who had 'kept up private councils and trysts' with Angus 'and other broken men' (*LP Henry VIII*, 4/1, no. 1030). But Angus soon held the initiative, and by mid-February had enough noble support

to be able to force the queen to surrender control of the realm to a council, in which he rapidly became predominant. As the queen dowager's husband, Angus held a 'special position' within the realm. He was never formally designated regent to James V, whose person was instead entrusted on 17 July 1525 to a rota of four groups of lords, each of which was to be attendant on the boy as administrators of his realm for three months at a time. Angus was a member of the first group to have custody of James, but when the time came for the king to be passed to the second, at the beginning of November, he refused to surrender his charge.

Between 1525 and 1528 Angus had almost complete control over the person of the king, reinforcing his own position when he took the post of chancellor in August 1527. He also advanced the interests of his relations. His uncle Gavin *Douglas was nominated to the see of Dunkeld; another uncle, Sir Archibald *Douglas of Kilspindie, became treasurer; his brother George *Douglas of Pittendreich was master of the royal household; yet another brother, William, was given the revenues of Holyrood Abbey and Coldingham. His kinsman James Douglas of Drumlanrig had watch over the royal wine cellar. Some historians have seen Angus's administration as marking the low point of sixteenth-century Scottish political morality, but such a condemnation is anachronistic as well as exaggerated; it was expected that a nobleman would use power to further the interest of his kin. Moreover, Angus performed his duties in government, both those attached to his various offices and the broader responsibilities involved in trying to punish wrongdoing and disorder. These often overlapped with his efforts to keep peace with England. Between 1525 and 1528 he made no fewer than six judicial raids into the borders, more than any of his predecessors had done, and though their effects were usually transient, some observers (for instance the English ambassador Thomas Magnus) still felt able to declare that the region had never been better ruled. Angus's work here provided a model for later policy: thus James V's hounding of the Armstrongs in the early 1530s was a direct continuation of Angus's attempts to tame them in 1527–8, when he was warden of the east and middle marches. Both in September 1525 and in January 1526 Angus was also a commissioner in negotiations for a lasting peace with England, and his efforts here, too, enjoyed at least a temporary success, with a treaty being concluded at Berwick on 15 January 1526.

Despite his achievements Angus faced growing opposition. The queen was unreconciled to her loss of power, and Angus also had to face the continuing hostility of the Hamiltons and of the Humes (over whom Angus exercised a technical overlordship), who resented his activities in border areas they regarded as their own preserve. In January 1526 Margaret and Arran led an attempted coup, but this was quickly suppressed. Then in August 1527, while Angus was engaged in a judicial raid into the borders with the king, Sir Walter Scott of Buccleuch attempted to ambush them at Melrose in order to take control of the monarch; this attempt also failed. Appreciating the developing threat to his position, Angus manoeuvred to maintain a coalition of supporters, but John Stewart, twelfth earl of Lennox, a key figure in any grouping, had become irremediably alienated, partly by Angus's refusal to share the custody of the king and partly by the extent to which government patronage was now monopolized by the Douglases, and on 4 September 1526 he made his own bid to secure the person of James V. The 'Lennox affair' which took place at Manuel near Linlithgow perhaps deserves to be called only a skirmish, but it resulted in Lennox's being killed, leaving Angus still very much in control of Scottish government.

Defeat and exile From 1526 the problem of Angus's relations with his fellow Scottish nobles was increasingly overshadowed by those with his young king. His hold on power depended entirely on his hold on James, who was therefore effectively kept a prisoner, with his every move being closely watched, and as far as possible distracted from thoughts of power by being encouraged into debauchery. These dubious pleasures notwithstanding, James came to loathe the Douglases in general, and Angus in particular, with a fine and near hysterical fervour. Finally, at the end of May 1528, he escaped from Edinburgh and fled to Stirling, where in the following month he raised the country against Angus, who was replaced as chancellor by Gavin Dunbar, archbishop of Glasgow, while Lord Hume became warden of the east march. On 23 June James announced that a convention would be held in Edinburgh on 10 July, with the purpose of investigating charges of maladministration against Angus. He wrote to Henry VIII giving details of his former chancellor's deficiencies, and on 13 July had Angus summoned on a charge of treason. The summons was served on the earl at Dalkeith five days later, and he was finally forfeited on 5 September. Angus and his brother George withdrew to the great Douglas castle of Tantallon, where they were able to resist the Royal Artillery, mocking the ineffectiveness of both the king and his guns. But efforts to secure English support came to nothing, and when Magnus tried to intercede for Angus with King James he was rebuffed. Fighting continued throughout the winter, but the pressure which the king was able to exert on the Douglases began to tell, and on 23 March 1529 Angus agreed to surrender Tantallon and his other castles and retreat to England. The only concession he was able to extract was that his earldom would retain its integrity. Thus began a thirteen-year exile, during which James conducted a relentless hounding of members of the Douglas family, justified by his conviction that Angus and his brother wanted to return to Scotland and see the king dead.

Although he travelled intermittently to the English court, Angus resided mostly at Berwick upon Tweed, which served as a base for numerous raids into Scotland and where he gathered information for forwarding to Henry VIII. He was now totally dependent upon the English king's goodwill and on 25 August 1532 signed a contract (deemed a treaty in English records) recognizing Henry as supreme lord of Scotland, to whom he rendered homage. His knowledge of the borders exceeded that of many English march wardens, and his attacks upon Scotland were often bloodily effective. When James went to France in 1536 it was suggested that the French king be asked to try to reconcile him to Angus, but nothing came of this, and James's campaign of violence against the Douglases continued, culminating in the burning at the stake of Angus's sister Janet *Douglas, Lady Glamis, in 1537. She had been charged with treason, for having both conspired to poison the king and communicated with her exiled brothers. Even this failed to satisfy the king's hostility and vindictiveness, for in December 1540 the Scottish parliament declared all Angus's estates forfeited and he was again branded a traitor. The earl's lands were now comprehensively redistributed by James.

During his thirteen years of exile Angus became a skilled and experienced soldier, as he showed again when war between England and Scotland erupted once more in the summer of 1542, leading a number of highly destructive raids over the border; John Dudley, Lord Lisle, praised his diligence. He was a member of the English army which the Scots roundly defeated at Haddon Rig on 24 August and was almost captured. It was rumoured after the Scottish defeat at the battle of Solway Moss on 24 November 1542 that James V was considering calling Angus home so that he could bring order to the Scottish armies and lead them effectively. The earl was one of the first to hear of James's death on 14 December, so efficient was his information-gathering network (as Lord Lisle observed).

Return to Scotland After the death of James V, James Hamilton, second earl of Arran, emerged as governor and immediately set about reversing almost all James's policies. The central plank of his programme was to return the Scottish aristocracy to the centre of politics, and he invited Angus to return home, which he did with his brother early in 1543. Before leaving England he signed a set of articles in which he promised to secure the person of the infant Queen Mary for Henry VIII, not to mention a string of powerful castles. On 16 January 1543 Arran issued a proclamation restoring Angus's estates, and in the March parliament his forfeiture was voided.

Angus was so attached to Henry that he became the effective head of an English party in Scotland, advocating protestantism and the marriage of Queen Mary to Prince Edward. It was to Angus that the English ambassador, Sir Ralph Sadler, repeatedly turned for information and advice, and when Sadler was hounded out of Edinburgh in September 1543, it was to Coldingham and Tantallon that he retired. During Arran's short-lived protestant phase (January to August 1543) Angus wielded considerable influence. On 9 April 1543 he married his third wife, Margaret (d. 1594), daughter of Robert Maxwell, fifth Lord Maxwell. It might have been a useful political alliance had not Maxwell spent the years between January 1544 and his death in 1546 almost entirely in gaol, in Blackness Tower in Scotland and in the Tower of London. None of the children of Angus's marriage to Margaret survived to maturity.

When Arran returned to the Catholic faith in September and rejected the English marriage, Angus opposed him, increasingly by armed force. At this time Angus remained loyal to Henry as did others of his party, men like William Cunningham, third earl of Glencairn. In January 1544 Angus and his allies formed a small army and issued defiance to the governor at Leith, but Arran was too quick and too strong for him, and at Greenside Chapel Angus was forced to submit and give pledges: Maxwell was gaoled, as was George Douglas. Angus escaped to his estates and lay low, but in April 1544 was warded in Blackness. He was freed in May when Edward Seymour, earl of Hertford, sacked Edinburgh.

Gradually Angus transferred his allegiance from Henry VIII to Arran's regime, and late in 1544 showed himself a true Scotsman. Arran had mustered a small army, strengthened by artillery from Edinburgh Castle, proposing to retake Coldingham Priory, which the English had fortified. But when he heard that an English army intended to attack him, he fled and his army almost disintegrated. Angus, however, kept his nerve. Though an adroit practitioner of mounted warfare characteristic of the border regions, he also appreciated the potentially decisive role that artillery could now play on the battlefield. At this juncture he made sure that the Scottish guns were not abandoned, storing them at Dunbar. This was the act of a man who knew (as Arran then did not) how to fight wars and who had a firm grip on military imperatives. Others appreciated his qualities, to the extent that in December 1544 he was appointed lieutenant-general of the south, given money to hire soldiers, and encouraged to attack England's Scottish allies—his own former associates—in Teviotdale and the Merse.

Ancrum Moor Angus's martial qualities were still more strikingly displayed at his famous triumph at Ancrum Moor, fought on 27 February 1545. A massive English raiding party, over 5000 strong, under the command of Sir Ralph Evers and Brian Layton, had invaded the borders, setting fire to numerous tower houses and desecrating Melrose Abbey, where many Douglas tombs lay. At the time it was widely reported that Angus turned on his erstwhile allies in revenge for this sacrilege, but he had already abandoned his English alliance. Using his own and Arran's troops, Angus lured the English into a trap. Just before the battle at Ancrum Moor commenced, a heron flew over him, prompting him to remark: 'Would that I had my goose hawk [goshawk] with me now: I could thus have two good meals in one day.'

The massive defeat which Angus inflicted on the English was in no small measure due to the revolt of the contingent of 'assured Scots' in English service, something Angus may have engineered in advance. Over 1000 English were made prisoners and both their commanders were killed. Moved to tears, Arran embraced Angus, and trumpeted how the earl was now 'ane true Scottisman' again. In the words of a seventeenth-century poet, 'the honour of the victory was wholly given to him' (Hume, ed. Reid, 2.121). François I of France was overjoyed at the victory, and a printed report (*La deffaicte des anglois par les ecossois faicte le jour de jeudi sainct dernier*) was published in Rouen and widely circulated. François then sent an expeditionary army to help the Scots during the summer of 1545. Its commander brought with him Angus's admission to the order of St Michel, an honour Angus deeply cherished. This was rehabilitation indeed, and yet more rewards followed, in particular the revenues of Arbroath Abbey, one of Scotland's richest monasteries. When a massive English army attacked Scotland in 1547, Angus again showed his military skills. At the battle of Pinkie, fought on 10 September, he commanded the Scottish right wing, and when the main battle under Arran and the left wing under George Gordon, fourth earl of Huntly, began to disintegrate under the impact of sophisticated English firepower, Angus kept his head and suffered the fewest casualties. He also extricated himself (by hiding in a ditch), as Huntly did not.

Drumlanrig Angus's skills as a soldier did not lie only in steadfastness; he also had a grasp of strategy which he displayed tellingly in the aftermath of Pinkie, which seemed to lay Scotland at the feet of the invader. In February 1548 a force under Thomas Wharton, first Baron Wharton, and Matthew Stewart, thirteenth earl of Lennox, invaded the west marches. Their intention was to attack James Douglas of Drumlanrig, one of the few Scots in the west not to have assured. Again, Angus laid a trap. One of the key elements in Wharton's force was some 1000 assured Scots under the command of John Maxwell, master of Maxwell, who had submitted to the English with great reluctance at the end of 1547. Maxwell clearly kept Arran informed of this attack and promised that he would 'revolt' if the governor would only allow him to marry the crown's richest ward, Agnes Herries, Lady Herries, of Terregles. Arran agreed, whereupon Angus assembled a small army and despite the wintry conditions took it over the Lammermuir Hills and fell upon Wharton's force, defeating it piecemeal. Angus's triumph on this occasion was even more timely than his victory at Ancrum Moor, for England's 'pale' in the south-west utterly collapsed. Utterly routed, Wharton withdrew via Dumfries to Carlisle, while his report to the English commander at Haddington (carried by his son, in a state of near hysteria) so alarmed the latter that he abandoned the town and removed the English garrisons at Yester and Hailes to Berwick. Angus's reputation soared.

With these victories under his belt Angus became unabashedly hostile to Edward Seymour, formerly earl of Hertford (and as such Angus's rescuer in 1544) but now duke of Somerset and lord protector, and to all his works. This loathing was fully reciprocated: the English made at least two determined attempts to capture Angus. The earl, increasingly assiduous in attending council and parliament meetings, now worked vigorously with Arran to have Queen Mary sent to France, for marriage to the dauphin. He played a conspicuous part in the parliament held at Haddington Abbey in July 1548, when he presented the Scottish regalia to the French commander, and commanded half of the Scottish force besieging the town nearby. In September he was rewarded with another order of

St Michel and a pension to enable him to finance a company of cavalry, while in November he helped to raise a force to push the English out of Dundee; December found him attacking their garrison at Broughty. The English garrisons stood increasingly on the defensive, and were unable to attack the Scots as Somerset had intended. The cost to the English exchequer became insupportable, and in September 1549 Haddington had to be abandoned; by the end of March 1550 Scotland was utterly lost to England. All this had stemmed largely from Angus's victory at Drumlanrig.

Retirement and death   Once the wars were over Angus set about trying to restore his estates and regalities. He had been regranted most of his forfeited lands by the lords of council in July 1546 and July 1547. Then at the parliament of February 1552 both he and his brother George were declared exempt from any claims brought against them as a result of their devastations in the borders around Berwick between 1529 and 1542. The rest of his life was spent not on the battlefield but in the law courts, as he set about recovering his former properties which James V had given away. As a result he largely left the central stage of high politics, attending only a few meetings of the privy council in June and August 1553, signing a bond in favour of Arran in February 1554, and standing caution the next year for Huntly. By the end of his life he had virtually reconstituted the inheritance he received in 1514. A further factor in his withdrawal from politics was the mutual dislike between him and Mary of Guise, who became regent of Scotland in April 1554. Attempts were made to tame him, to make him behave in a respectful and obedient manner. They all failed. Mary of Guise once rebuked him for turning up to a meeting in armour. Angus rejoined: 'It is only my old dad Lord Drummond's coat, a very kindly coat to me. I cannot part with it.'

To the end of his life Angus retained a strong sense of family loyalty. When walking across the courtyard at Douglas one day in 1550, he encountered a messenger sent from his daughter Margaret, countess of Lennox, then in England. He paused to ask after the family's health and general well-being. And he gossiped that the French were coming to take over the kingdom, 'and frenche lawes and thei be sharpe'. How was it with his grandson, Lord Darnley ('that young boy there'), whose residence so far away in England 'brekes my hart?' Patience was a virtue he had clearly cultivated in his many years of exile. 'The worlde ys very strange and I have sene mony changes' (BL, MS Cotton Calig., fol. 423). The tales many recorded about him may well be apocryphal in their details, but they often accord with firsthand accounts of his deeds and sayings, as well as with his contemporary reputation.

Angus died at Tantallon shortly before 22 January 1557. As he lay dying, a retainer commented that it was ironic that such a formidable warrior should expire in his bedclothes and not have been killed in battle, underneath his heart standard. 'Lo,' Angus barked, grasping a crucifix, 'Here is the standard under which I shall die' (Merriman, 353). He was buried in the collegiate church of Abernethy, Perthshire, of which he was patron.

Despite many frustrations, especially in the years of his exile, Angus showed some accomplishment in the exercise of power, both in the mid-1520s and later. Moreover he was a soldier of notable skill in an age which knew many such. But he failed in a dynast's most important duty, leaving no male heir to succeed to his inheritance. His daughter Margaret, countess of Lennox, had put pressure on him to deed the honour and lands of Angus to her and her heirs, but instead he created an entail which laid down that all should go only to heirs male. The earldom thus passed to Angus's nephew, David Douglas, who lived only until June 1557, after which his great-nephew Archibald *Douglas (c.1555–1588) succeeded as eighth earl of Angus.   MARCUS MERRIMAN

Sources   *Scots peerage*, 1.190–92 · J. Cameron, *James V: the personal rule, 1528–1542*, ed. N. Macdougall (1998) · W. Fraser, ed., *The Douglas book*, 4 vols. (1885) · M. Merriman, *The rough wooings: Mary queen of Scots, 1542–1551* (2000) · G. Phillips, *The Anglo-Scots wars, 1513–1550: a military history* (1999) · J. Kerr, *Margaret Tudor, queen of Scots* (1989) · G. Donaldson, *Scotland, James V–James VII* (1965) · A. J. Slavin, *Sir Ralph Sadler* (1966) · B. Bradshaw and J. Morrill, *The British problem, c.1534–1707* (1996) · *LP Henry VIII*, vols. 1–21 · BL, MS Cotton Calig. · P. Buchanan, *Margaret Tudor, queen of Scots* (1985) · T. I. Rae, *The administration of the Scottish frontier, 1513–1603* (1966) · *David Hume of Godscroft's The history of the house of Douglas*, ed. D. Reid, 2 vols., STS, 4th ser., 25–6 (1996)
Archives   BL, Cotton MSS, letters and papers

Douglas, Sir Archibald, of Kilspindie (*b. c.*1490, *d.* before 1540), administrator, was the fourth son of Archibald *Douglas, fifth earl of Angus (*c.*1449–1513), and his first wife, Elizabeth Boyd (*d.* 1498). Old enough to witness charters in 1509, he was probably born about 1490. His principal seat was Kilspindie Castle and estate in Perthshire, but he was not a major landowner, and his advancement resulted mainly from political influence and from his having property in Edinburgh, some of which he acquired through his marriage to Isobel Janet Hoppringle, widow of John Murray, which had taken place before 27 May 1519. Kilspindie owed his political career to his nephew Archibald *Douglas, sixth earl of Angus, who in the confusion of James V's minority won control of Edinburgh in 1519. Angus failed to secure the castle, where the young king was in the keeping of Lord Ruthven, but his grip on the town was strengthened by the election of his uncle Douglas of Kilspindie to the office of provost. However, this proved unacceptable to Angus's rival, James Hamilton, first earl of Arran, who demanded that Kilspindie relinquish the office. In 1520 the regent, John Stewart, duke of Albany, attempted to solve the tension by barring either a Douglas or a Hamilton from holding the provostship, and Kilspindie duly ceded office to a neutral burgess, Robert Logan of Coitfield. The arrival of Albany in Scotland in 1521 led to several years in the political wilderness for the Angus faction, including Kilspindie.

The trust placed in Kilspindie by his nephew is demonstrated by the positions of influence afforded to him on the restoration in 1525 of Angus, following Albany's departure for France the previous year. Douglas dominance was based on control, principally within that family, of offices of state and patronage, and Kilspindie was at the heart of this strategy. On 21 June 1526 he was one of the lords appointed to be a member of the royal council and he had acquired the office of treasurer by 15 October. By November he had regained the provostship of Edinburgh and held the important office of keeper of the privy seal. He appears to have formed a close relationship with the young king, in the light of the legend (first related by Hume of Godscroft in 1644) that James V called him Greysteil. The nickname derives from an epic poem, known to have been popular at court no later than 1498, whose hero, Sir Greysteil, is a powerful, almost invincible, swordsman, and points to James's youthful admiration for the man who was at the centre of court administration. Kilspindie sat continuously upon the session of lords of council; that the government was under severe financial strain is suggested by the substantial debt of £3654 8s. 1d. which appeared in the account which he submitted as treasurer for the period October 1526 to August 1527.

Political ascendancy could be personally lucrative, however; Kilspindie received 1000 merks from Archbishop Beaton and shared in the profits from the forfeiture of Patrick, Lord Lindsay of the Byres. But dissatisfaction with the Douglases—with Angus's former wife, Queen Margaret, prominent among the malcontents—was never far beneath the surface of political life, and the escape of James V from Angus-controlled Edinburgh to Stirling in early June 1528 caught the Douglases off guard. According to John Law's contemporary account, the king's flight occurred while Angus was absent from court and Kilspindie was visiting his mistress in Dundee. The Observantine friar Adam Abell adds the opinion that the overbearing pride of Kilspindie's wife, Isobel, referred to scathingly as 'my lady thesaurer' (NL Scot., Add. MS 1746, fol. 116v), had also alienated support from the Douglases.

With the effective commencement of James V's personal rule in 1528 Kilspindie lost the keepership of the privy seal to George Crichton, bishop of Dunkeld, and as Kilspindie's accounts for the Edinburgh customs were being audited in July, Lyon king, unable to find Kilspindie in person, proclaimed a summons against him from Haddington market cross. On 19 July Robert Cairncross, provost of the collegiate church of Corstorphine, was appointed treasurer in place of Kilspindie, who had ignored instructions to enter into ward at Edinburgh Castle, and in August Robert, fifth Lord Maxwell, was appointed provost of Edinburgh. Roger Lascelles, the English captain of Norham Castle, describes Maxwell arriving in Edinburgh and proceeding to surround the provost's house where Kilspindie was hosting dinner for his nephews George and William, suggesting that the king's control of Edinburgh was still not secure. The Douglases retreated to Tantallon (according to Lascelles, accommodation at Norham had been offered to the Douglases, including Kilspindie and his wife). On 5 September 1528 sentence of forfeiture of life, lands, and goods was passed against Kilspindie, his possessions being divided between Hugh Montgomery, first earl of Eglinton, and Robert Cairncross. His stepson, Andrew Murray of Blackbarony, Peeblesshire, bailie of Ballencrieff, had to seek remission for association with his

stepfather after the latter's forfeiture, although he was sufficiently in favour to have secured the office of sheriff of Edinburgh by 1536.

A period of exile in England followed. In February 1529 Kilspindie was involved in tentative negotiations with Sir James Hamilton of Finnart at Cockburnspath, possibly aimed at seeking political rehabilitation. Nothing came of these discussions, and in 1540 charges were brought against Hamilton which included the accusation that in 1529 he had plotted with Kilspindie and others to kill the king at Holyrood. Kilspindie joined Northumberland's raid on Haddingtonshire and the Merse on 11 December 1532, but he appears to have approached Thomas Erskine, secretary to James V, while Erskine was on business at the English court, with a view to sounding him out on the possibility of returning to Scotland. An undated letter to Erskine from the king warns him against association with the Douglases, probably in response to these encounters, yet Kilspindie, encouraged by the peace treaty between Scotland and England, risked returning to seek clemency in August 1534. While he had a cold reception from the king, he did not suffer imprisonment. Instead James V commanded that he should be conveyed overseas, probably to France, which amounted to effective banishment, as Kilspindie seems to have died abroad before 1540. His son, also Archibald, succeeded to Kilspindie in 1543, upon the lifting of the sentence of forfeiture.

C. A. McGLADDERY

Sources W. K. Emond, 'The minority of James V, 1513–1528', PhD diss., U. St Andr., 1988 • J. Cameron, *James V: the personal rule, 1528–1542*, ed. N. Macdougall (1998) • W. Fraser, ed., *The Douglas book*, 4 vols. (1885) • J. M. Thomson and others, eds., *Registrum magni sigilli regum Scotorum / The register of the great seal of Scotland*, 11 vols. (1882–1914), vol. 3 • NL Scot., Additional MS 1746 (Adam Abell), fol. 116v • J. Purser, 'Greysteil', *Stewart style, 1513–1542*, ed. J. H. Williams (1996), 142–52 • *Scots peerage*, vol. 1 • N. Macdougall, *James III: a political study* (1982)

Douglas, Archibald (c.1540–c.1602), conspirator and Church of Scotland minister, was the second son of William Douglas of Whittingham and Janet Matheson; he had an elder brother, also William (d. c.1572). Educated for the priesthood in France, Archibald graduated MA and by June 1562, probably in his early twenties, was parson of Douglas. An early convert to protestantism, in February 1566 he was appointed subdean of Orkney in recognition of his work as a royal clerk. Three months earlier, probably through his knowledge of canon law, he had been appointed an extraordinary lord of session in place of Adam Bothwell, bishop of Orkney. Douglas held his new positions only for a short time. In March 1566, with his brother William and his kinsman James Douglas, fourth earl of Morton, he was involved in the conspiracy to murder David Rizzio, secretary to Mary, queen of Scots. Charged for his part in the crime, Douglas fled to France, where he found favour with Charles IX. After his return to Scotland he successfully negotiated the pardons of the other conspirators and attached himself to the company of James Hepburn, fourth earl of Bothwell. In February 1567, with Bothwell, Douglas was implicated in the plot to murder Henry Stuart, Lord Darnley, the queen's husband. Despite widespread belief in his guilt, however, no immediate proceedings were taken against him.

Following Queen Mary's deposition in June 1567, Douglas helped secure the casket letters for Regent Moray (it has been suggested that he was responsible for forging them). On 2 June 1568 Douglas was appointed an ordinary lord of session in place of John Leslie, bishop of Ross, and in 1570 he was presented to the parsonage of Glasgow through Morton's intercession. However he was refused letters testimonial by the commissioner and this decision was confirmed by the general assembly in March 1570. At length he was allowed possession, on 23 January 1572, but an account of his examination for the benefice stated: 'when he had gottin the psalme buike, after luking, and casting ower the leives thereof a space, he desyrit sum minister to mak prayer for him; "for", said he, "I am not used to pray"' (Pitcairn, *Memoriales*, 312). Indeed Douglas was more of a politician than a cleric: in September 1570 he acted as ambassador to the earl of Sussex, and in April 1572, having been detected sending money and supplies to the queen's party besieged within Edinburgh Castle, he was imprisoned in Stirling Castle (when it was alleged he plotted to kill his kinsman Morton, now regent). The rift did not last long, and for the remainder of the 1570s Douglas remained prominent, mainly owing to his close alliance with the regent. He was restored to his place on the bench in November 1578.

A year earlier Douglas had married Janet Hepburn (*d. c.*1586), Bothwell's only sister and widow successively of John Stewart, Lord Darnley (an illegitimate son of James V) and of John Sinclair, master of Caithness. They appear to have had at least one son, John. The marriage was not successful, however, and by 1581 Janet Hepburn was seeking a divorce. Meanwhile, on 31 December 1580 Douglas had been accused (along with Morton) by Captain James Stewart (afterwards earl of Arran) of 'heigh treason and foreknawlege of the king's murthour' (Thomson, *James the Sext*, 180–81). Hearing of Morton's imprisonment—and aware of orders issued for his own arrest—Douglas fled from Morham Castle to England and then France. His wife did not accompany him. He was degraded from the bench in April 1581, and a decree of forfeiture was pronounced against him on 28 November 1581.

In France and England, Douglas remained heavily involved in Scottish affairs and was primarily responsible for the forged letters which implicated Esmé Stewart, duke of Lennox, in popish plots. Although Elizabeth refused James VI's requests to return Douglas for trial in Scotland, she did temporarily imprison him in the Tower of London. After six months Douglas gained his release by disclosing his private transactions with the imprisoned Queen Mary; he then remained at the English court as an unofficial agent to various Scots who sought his aid (including the king). From mid-1583 he was also a paid agent for the English secretary, Sir Francis Walsingham, acting as a spy in the household of Michel de Castelnau, the French ambassador to England. In spring 1586 he was permitted to return to Scotland, and on 1 May an act of rehabilitation was passed under the Scottish great seal restoring him, but at the same time providing that if he should be found guilty of King Henry's murder then the act should have no effect. On 21 May Douglas received a pardon for all his crimes except the murder, and five days later he was put on trial for it. The indictment declared that Douglas had been present at the blowing up of Henry's lodgings in Kirk o' Field, and claimed that while perpetrating the crime Douglas 'tint his mulis [lost his dancing slippers]', which, being found upon the spot the next day, were acknowledged to be his (Pitcairn, *Criminal Trials*, 1.146). The rigged jury unanimously acquitted him.

The continuing association between Douglas and the Scottish administration fluctuated depending on who was in favour at court. He had a close relationship with his stepson Francis *Stewart, first earl of Bothwell, but was greatly disliked by the more powerful Chancellor Maitland. Although known to be an agent of Elizabeth, Douglas returned to England as the official Scottish ambassador. Highly sensitive to political realities, he was well aware of the ambiguities of King James's position with regard to his mother, Mary, queen of Scots—her execution would damage the Scottish king's honour while at the same time greatly strengthening his claim to be Elizabeth's heir. Faced with the task of securing the promise of the English succession for his king while also attempting to preserve Mary's life, Douglas treacherously revealed royal letters to Walsingham and Elizabeth, and informed the earl of Leicester that, even if Mary was executed, it was unlikely that James would break amity with England. In spite of such acts of disloyalty, Douglas remained a well-used conduit for official and secretive cross-border communication. Following Mary's death James employed him to try to secure his English heritage, and he continued to use his services until at least 1596.

Douglas was also active on his own behalf. He attempted to co-ordinate English support for his stepson Bothwell after the murder of the second earl of Moray in February 1592; he was approached by the rebel Roman Catholic earls in an attempt to secure English support in 1594; and he involved himself in the various continental (largely Spanish) plots to invade England and Ireland. He was deposed from his parsonage for non-residence and neglect of duty on 13 March 1593, though it was not until July 1597 that he ceased to use his ecclesiastical style. The date of his death is unknown, but it appears that he was alive until at least the summer of 1602 (resident in Lime Street, London) when he was 'unfit for ony service', of 'poor estate', and desiring to return to Scotland (*Salisbury MSS*, 12.252).

ROB MACPHERSON

Sources G. Brunton and D. Haig, *An historical account of the senators of the college of justice, from its institution in MDXXXII* (1832) • *CSP Scot.*, *1547–1603* • W. Fraser, ed., *The Douglas book*, 4 vols. (1885) • H. Maxwell, *The history of the house of Douglas*, 2 vols. (1902) • M. Livingstone, D. Hay Fleming, and others, eds., *Registrum secreti sigilli regum Scotorum / The register of the privy seal of Scotland*, 5–8 (1957–82), vols. 5–8 • G. H. Johnston, *The heraldry of the Douglases* (1907) • D. Calderwood, *The history of the Kirk of Scotland*, ed. T. Thomson and D. Laing, 8 vols., Wodrow Society, 7 (1842–9) • R. Pitcairn,

ed., *Ancient criminal trials in Scotland*, 7 pts in 3, Bannatyne Club, 42 (1833) • R. Bannatyne, *Memoriales of transactions in Scotland, 1569–1573*, ed. [R. Pitcairn], Bannatyne Club, 51 (1836) • *Reg. PCS*, 1st ser., vols. 1–6 • D. Moysie, *Memoirs of the affairs of Scotland, 1577–1603*, ed. J. Dennistoun, Bannatyne Club, 39 (1830) • [T. Thomson], ed., *The historie and life of King James the Sext*, Bannatyne Club, 13 (1825) • *Fasti Scot.* • R. G. Macpherson, 'Francis Stewart, fifth Earl Bothwell, 1562–1612: lordship and politics in Jacobean Scotland', PhD diss., U. Edin., 1998 • J. Spottiswood, *The history of the Church of Scotland*, ed. M. Napier and M. Russell, 3 vols., Bannatyne Club, 93 (1850) • *APS, 1424–1625* • J. M. Thomson and others, eds., *Registrum magni sigilli regum Scotorum / The register of the great seal of Scotland*, 11 vols. (1882–1914), vols. 4–6 • T. Thomson, ed., *A diurnal of remarkable occurrents that have passed within the country of Scotland*, Bannatyne Club, 43 (1833) • T. Thomson, ed., *Acts and proceedings of the general assemblies of the Kirk of Scotland*, 3 pts, Bannatyne Club, 81 (1839–45) • J. Kirk, ed., *The books of assumption of the thirds of benefices: Scottish ecclesiastical rentals at the Reformation* (1995) • G. Donaldson, ed., *Accounts of the collectors of thirds of benefices, 1561–1572*, Scottish History Society, 3rd ser., 42 (1949) • J. Bain, ed., *The border papers: calendar of letters and papers relating to the affairs of the borders of England and Scotland*, 2 vols. (1894–6) • *Calendar of the manuscripts of the most hon. the marquis of Salisbury*, 24 vols., HMC, 9 (1883–1976), vols. 1–14 • R. S. Rait and A. I. Cameron, *King James's secret* (1927) • H. G. Stafford, *James VI of Scotland and the throne of England* (1940) • J. Bossy, *Under the molehill: an Elizabethan spy story* (2001)
Wealth at death died in poverty

Douglas, Archibald, eighth earl of Angus and fifth earl of Morton (*c*.1555–1588), magnate, was the only son of David Douglas, seventh earl of Angus (*c*.1515–1557), and Margaret Hamilton, daughter of John Hamilton of Samuelston, a natural son of James Hamilton, first earl of Arran. He was only about two years old when his father died, and in his early years his uncle James *Douglas, fourth earl of Morton, supervised Angus's affairs. Since he was an infant this would in any circumstance have been necessary, but the support of a powerful figure like Morton was doubly important because of the bitter legal wrangle which developed over his inheritance with Margaret, countess of Lennox, the daughter of his great-uncle Archibald Douglas, sixth earl of Angus. This prolonged dispute was resolved only in May 1565 when the countess, eager to obtain Morton's support for the wedding of her son Lord Darnley to Mary, queen of Scots, renounced all her claims. A mutual contract between the two parties confirmed Angus in his possession of Tantallon Castle, one of the most formidable strongholds in the lowlands, the regality of Bothwell, in Lanarkshire, and 'the Landis, lordschipps and baroneys of Abernethy, Jedburgh Forest, Bonkle, Preston, Dryburgh and Selkirk' (Fraser, 2.261). He had established himself as a territorial magnate in central and south-east Scotland.

Morton's influence is also evident in Angus's education, which took place at St Andrews University under the tutelage of the provost of New College, John Douglas, a kinsman and protégé of his uncle, who subsequently became the first protestant archbishop of St Andrews. While the future primate was no radical, it is quite possible that Angus was influenced by Douglas's tutoring, since he undoubtedly became a devout Calvinist, indeed, he was unusual among the Scottish nobility of this period in the earnestness of his religious observance. As head of one of

the principal families in Scotland, Angus played a leading role in a number of ceremonial occasions; in spite of his youth he carried the crown at the state opening of parliament in 1567 and again in 1571. But his career took off when Morton became regent in November 1572. One of Angus's main responsibilities during Morton's regency was to assist his uncle with the administration of the borders, an area of Scotland with a long tradition of disorder and unrest, where between 1573 and 1580 Angus held a number of appointments. In 1573, for instance, he was appointed sheriff of Berwickshire, one of the key administrative posts in the crown's possession while from July 1575 to February 1576 he was warden of Liddesdale, subsequently holding a similar position on the west march between May 1577 and March 1578. But his most important office, one placing him in overall control of the whole region, was as lieutenant from July 1574 to March 1578. In that capacity he took part in several judicial and military operations, notably Morton's expedition to Lauder and Jedburgh in November 1576; on that occasion Angus was personally in charge of the campaign against local lawbreakers. Morton's deposition as regent in March 1578 spurred Angus, who had been recently rewarded with the hereditary stewardship of Fife and the captaincy of Falkland Palace, into considerable activity on his uncle's behalf. Throughout the crisis he acted as the latter's spokesman and also kept him in touch with developments at Stirling, where James VI's parliament was bringing the regency to an end.

In summer 1578, with Morton effecting a political comeback, his nephew also returned to play a significant role in the new administration. In August 1578 Angus was put in command of the forces which Morton had assembled against the league raised against him by the disaffected earls of Argyll and Atholl. The rival armies faced each other near Falkirk but Angus's military capabilities were not on this occasion put to the test, since the parties accepted a truce and signed a joint agreement ending hostilities. Angus was also prominently involved in the vendetta pursued by Morton's government against the Hamilton family in 1579, being one of the commissioners appointed to enforce the measures prescribed against the outlawed family.

Although Angus reputedly had some kind of disagreement with Morton during 1580, he made strenuous efforts in support of his uncle following the ex-regent's arrest on 31 December 1580, an event at which Angus was present. Having abandoned plans to rescue Morton on his way to incarceration in Dumbarton Castle prior to his trial, Angus concentrated his energies into rallying noblemen sympathetic to his cause and making appeals for assistance to Thomas Randolph, the English ambassador, and Lord Hunsdon, the governor of Berwick. In the end nothing significant came of these endeavours, but his activities did result in March 1581 in the new administration of Lennox and Arran ordering him into exile beyond the River Spey. Initially he ignored this decree, but when it became obvious that his support was dwindling—a large number of border lairds withdrew their allegiance by renouncing their bonds of manrent in March—Angus reconsidered his position. Consequently, on 8 July 1581, six days after his uncle's execution, Angus and his followers arrived at Carlisle, to be taken under the protection of Henry, Lord Scrope, governor of that city and warden of the English west march, and as such an official with whom he had been on amicable terms since his own years as a border administrator.

Morton's downfall signalled the start of a bewildering series of fluctuations in Angus's fortunes, the outcome of the complex religious struggle within Scotland in these years. The immediate consequence was a period of exile in England. By summer 1581 Angus had moved to London, where he relayed his version of events to Elizabeth and her ministers. He also, apparently, became sufficiently friendly with Sir Philip Sidney for the latter to show him a manuscript copy of his *Arcadia*. Then in August 1582 the ultra-protestant faction to which Angus was aligned, headed by William Ruthven, earl of Gowrie, seized James VI and ousted the Lennox–Arran administration. Although the Ruthven raiders survived in power for less than a year, during their short ascendancy Angus received a royal pardon and was reconciled with the young king. He also persuaded James to order the removal of Morton's head from the Edinburgh tolbooth so that it be 'layed in a fyne cloath, convayed honorabilie and layed in the kist where his bodie was buried' (Calderwood, 3.692).

By summer 1583, following James VI's escape from the control of the Ruthven faction and a comeback by Arran and his supporters, Angus found himself in an awkward position. Once again ordered to take himself beyond the Spey he spent the winter of 1583–4 in Elgin. However, his involvement in an unsuccessful coup by the Ruthven party in April 1584 forced him to leave the country altogether and return to England. There followed a year of frantic intrigue by Angus and other Scottish exiles against Arran's regime. They were aided and abetted in their plotting by Elizabeth's minister Sir Francis Walsingham and by her Scottish ambassador, Sir Edward Wotton, both of whom had doubts of Arran's political reliability in England's conflict with Spain. The eventual upshot was that in October 1585 Elizabeth agreed to allow Angus and his associates to return to Scotland to assist in the overthrow of Arran. Their capture early in November of the town and castle of Stirling signified that Arran had been ousted, just as the return of their estates shortly afterwards to Angus, Mar, and the Hamiltons confirmed that Arran's opponents were back in royal favour.

These events heralded another upturn in Angus's career, and for the rest of his life (apart from an interval early in 1587 when Arran made a brief recovery) he once again played a significant role in the government of Scotland. Thus he was prominent at traditional ceremonial events such as the opening of parliament in July 1587 when he carried the royal sceptre. He was also restored to his old position in the borders, being appointed lieutenant and justiciar for the whole region on 2 November 1586. Moreover, he became warden of the west march from around March 1587.

While he was lieutenant, Angus took part in four judicial raids on the borders, during which he held courts and dispensed justice over the length and breadth of the region. In January 1587, for example, he held a court of justice at Jedburgh at which he had sixteen offenders hanged and took pledges for good behaviour from a number of others. In his last expedition, which took place in May–June 1588 and was directed against the rebellious Maxwell family, he accompanied James VI and the chancellor, John Maitland, into south-west Scotland. Lord Maxwell himself was arrested and several of his strongholds were captured.

Angus died on 4 August 1588 at Smeaton, near Dalkeith. The latter had been one of the principal residences of his uncle, whose lands and title Angus had inherited in July 1587, following ratification in parliament. His body was buried at Abernethy (Perthshire), a Douglas burgh of barony since 1459, although his heart was apparently interred separately at Douglas (Lanarkshire), another family possession. In all likelihood he died of tuberculosis, although Angus's biographer and younger contemporary, David Hume of Godscroft, made some curious references to sorcery and to the activities of a certain Agnes Sampson, who would feature in the witchcraft trials conducted by James VI in 1591. Angus married three times. His first wife was Mary Erskine, daughter of the seventeenth earl of Mar, whom he married at Stirling on 13 June 1573. She died less than two years later, on 3 May 1575, and Angus married, on 25 December following, Margaret Leslie, daughter of the fourth earl of Rothes; he was divorced from her in 1587 because of her liaison with John Graham, third earl of Montrose. Neither of these marriages produced children. Immediately afterwards, on 29 July 1587, Angus took as his third wife Jean (d. 1608x10), widow of Robert Douglas and daughter of John Lyon, eighth Lord Glamis. Their daughter, Margaret, who died aged fifteen, was born after her father's death. For want of a male heir Angus's title was inherited by the nearest claimant, Sir William Douglas of Glenbervie, great-grandson of the fifth earl.

Angus was held in high regard by contemporary churchmen, especially those who shared his ultra-protestant inclinations. Thus the presbyterian historian David Calderwood was to declare that Angus was 'more religious nor anie of his predecessors, yea, nor anie of all the erlis in the countrie much beloved of the godlie' (Calderwood, 3.498). Archbishop John Spottiswoode, who obviously did not share Calderwood's views on church polity, nevertheless described Angus in glowing terms as

> a nobleman in place and rank, so in worth and virtue, above other subjects; of a comly personage, affable, and full of grace a lover of justice, peaceable sober and given to all goodness and which crowned all his virtues, truly pious. (*History of the Church*, 2.371)

The diarist James Melville, too, was greatly impressed by Angus when he met him in England in 1584.

> This nobleman was felon weill myndit, godlie, devot, wyse and grave, and by and besyde their comoun was given to reiding and privat prayer and meditation and ordinarlie efter dinner and super haid an houres and sum tyme mair nor twa

houres, conference with me about all maters; namely concerning our Kirk and comoun-weill, what war the abusses thairof and whow they might be amendit.
(*Autobiography and Diary*, 185)

But all these eulogies notwithstanding, Angus's impact on the affairs of the kirk was marginal, and it is as a border administrator that he principally deserves recognition. In a letter written in August 1577 Lord Scrope, the English warden and Angus's border colleague, wrote, 'I am well assured of your lordschippis honourable meaning and intention to reformacion of such disorders' (Fraser, 4.232). His words underline the high regard in which Angus was held, and show that his contribution to the difficult task of taming the borders was a substantial one.

G. R. HEWITT

Sources D. Hume of Godscroft, *The history of the house and race of Douglas and Angus*, 2 (1743) · *Scots peerage*, 1.193–7 · W. Fraser, ed., *The Douglas book*, 4 vols. (1885), vols. 2, 4 · *Reg. PCS*, 1st ser., vols. 2–3 · *CSP Scot., 1571–81* · D. Calderwood, *The history of the Kirk of Scotland*, ed. T. Thomson and D. Laing, 8 vols., Wodrow Society, 7 (1842–9), vol. 3 · J. Spottiswood, *The history of the Church of Scotland*, ed. M. Napier and M. Russell, 2, Bannatyne Club, 93 (1850) · T. I. Rae, *The administration of the Scottish frontier, 1513–1603* (1966) · G. R. Hewitt, *Scotland under Morton, 1572–80* (1982) · *The autobiography and diary of Mr James Melvill*, ed. R. Pitcairn, Wodrow Society (1842)
Archives NRA, priv. coll., papers | BL, Cotton MSS, corresp. and papers · NRA, priv. coll., corresp. with Sir George Bowes

Douglas, Archibald (*d.* 1667), army officer, whose origins are obscure although he was probably Scottish by birth, was commissioned captain on 5 July 1666 in Colonel Lord George Douglas's regiment of foot (the Royal Scots). In 1667 the regiment was brought back from four years' garrison duty in France to confront the Dutch threat during the Second Anglo-Dutch War. As the Dutch fleet under De Ruyter advanced on the Medway estuary, Colonel Douglas's regiment was reinforced and assigned to the defence of Chatham. Captain Douglas was sent with a detachment of soldiers to defend HMS *Royal Oak*.

On 12 June the Dutch got their fireships over the chain across the mouth of the Medway and entered the river. They missed the *Royal Oak* on the first attempt but on the following day John Clapham reported to Pepys that he saw the *Royal Oak* and other vessels 'fired and aflame' (*CSP dom.*, 1667, 185). Douglas defended the vessel with great courage and when advised to retire, refused, allegedly saying, 'it shall never be told that a Douglas quitted his post without orders' (Lediard, 589). Douglas perished in the flames on 13 June; it is not known whether his body was recovered for burial but on 18 October of the same year his widow, whose name is not stated, was given the sum of £100 by royal warrant.

ANITA MCCONNELL

Sources J. Charnock, ed., *Biographia navalis*, 1 (1794), 291–2 · *GM*, 2nd ser., 33 (1850), 394 · *CSP dom., 1667*, 185, 189 · A. M. Brander, *The royal Scots* (1976) · T. Lediard, *The naval history of England*, 2 vols. (1735), 588–9

Douglas, Archibald, styled earl of Angus and Ormond (*c.*1609–1655), nobleman, was the eldest son of William *Douglas, eleventh earl of Angus and first marquess of Douglas (1589–1660), and his first wife, Margaret (1584/5–1623), daughter of Claude Hamilton, first Lord Paisley. In

his early years he was known by the titles Lord Douglas and master of Angus, but after his father was promoted to the rank of marquess in 1633 he became known as earl of Angus. By contracts dated November 1629 and May 1630 he married Lady Anne (*d.* 1646), daughter of Esmé *Stuart, third duke of Lennox. In 1630 he received permission to travel abroad for two years, and on 4 May 1636 he was admitted as a member of the Scottish privy council.

When conflict broke out between Charles I and his Scottish subjects Angus acted indecisively, his inclination to support the king's opponents being countered by his father being a royalist and a Roman Catholic. He was present in the privy council in December 1636 when it approved the new Scottish prayer book, the introduction of which provoked the emergence of open opposition to the king, but he was one of those whom Robert Baillie hoped in September 1637 would 'speik plaine Scottish' (*Letters and Journals of Robert Baillie*, 1.14) to the king's cousin, the fourth duke of Lennox, when he visited Scotland, indicating that Angus was considered to have sympathy for the opposition. In February 1638 he was one of the councillors who signed a royal proclamation demanding the submission of the Scots, but he then declared repentance for his rashness in doing so. In September 1638 he signed the king's covenant, the abortive rival of the national covenant, and in February 1639 the king appointed him one of the noble extraordinary lords of the court of session, no doubt hoping this would strengthen his loyalty. But in April 1639 he made clear his wish to avoid involvement in the approaching first bishops' war by seeking permission to leave Scotland.

In May 1639 the bishop of Bath and Wells investigated reports of two mysterious strangers whose speech was incomprehensible who had appeared in Wells. One of them—'a tall man, black haired, having a little beard, with a visible blemish in one of his eyes' (*CSP dom.*, 1639, 200)—proved to be Angus. He explained with embarrassment that he had visited the royal court at York, gone to London, and was now sightseeing incognito. The inconclusive result of the bishops' war of 1639, leaving the king's covenanter enemies in control of Scotland, persuaded Angus that he now had to commit himself. It was clear that his father's support for the king would provoke the covenanters into occupying the family estates. After seeing the king again, Angus returned to Scotland and swore the national covenant. He presented what he had done as a necessity, writing to his father on 28 February, 'I have now done that which I told you I should be necessitated to do' (*CSP dom.*, 1639–40, 495) and 'I have done nothing else than what before my parting from Court I told his Majesty I would be necessitated to do.' 'What is done cannot be undone' (*CSP dom.*, 1640–41, 376). Taking over his father's lands, he raised men and led them in defence of the border against the threat of invasion by the king's army. His father bitterly denounced 'the unnatural courses of my eldest son to denude me of my whole estate and people' (*CSP dom.*, 1640, 199), but received assurance from Charles that 'I will not lay the follies of your son to your charge' (Fotheringham, 2.602).

When the king reached a settlement with the covenanters in November 1641 Angus was reappointed a member of the privy council of Scotland. As intervention by the covenanters in the English civil war to assist parliament against the king approached he again gave his support. In August he sat as an elder in the general assembly which agreed the solemn league and covenant as the basis for alliance with the English parliament, and from 1643 to 1651 he was annually appointed a member of the commission of the general assembly. This, and the fact that he did not support the engagement whereby moderate covenanters and royalists allied to try to help Charles I in 1647–8, indicates real commitment to the covenanting cause, though he was not prominent in state affairs, perhaps being distrusted because of his father's continuing royalism. Relations between father and son remained bitter, as is indicated by a report by a French agent in August 1647: Douglas 'named to me while in tears the Earl of Angus as the principal author of the hardships that he has been made to endure' (Fotheringham, 2.226).

In 1647, on the death of his brother James, Angus was appointed colonel of the Scottish regiment the former had commanded in the French service, but although he retained the post until 1653 his only contributions to it were efforts in 1646–7 and 1650 to send recruits to France, some of them royalist prisoners of war. He supported the bringing of Charles II to Scotland in 1650, and at the coronation at Scone on 1 January 1651 he acted as 'chamberlane appoynted by the King for that day' (Nicoll, 42). On 3 April the king ordered that Angus be created earl of Ormond, so he would be an earl in substance as well as style during his father's lifetime but, with the administration collapsing in the face of the Cromwellian conquest, the grant never passed the great seal and was therefore never regarded as valid. Angus sat in the general assembly of July 1651, but the English advance forced the assembly to flee from St Andrews to Dundee, and thereafter he accepted English rule. His first wife having died in 1646, he had married on 2 January 1649 Lady Jean (d. 1715), daughter of David *Wemyss, second earl of Wemyss [see under Wemyss, David], who was to outlive him for sixty years; their eldest son was Archibald *Douglas, first earl of Forfar. He was probably ill in his final years: in February 1651 he referred to himself as 'a creple man' (Fraser, 4.258). Under the Cromwellian Act of Grace and Pardon of 1654 he was fined £1000 sterling, and his efforts to have this cancelled, by persuading the English authorities that he was a staunch protestant who had lived quietly in the Canongate for years, were thwarted by his death, which occurred in Edinburgh on 16 January 1655. He was buried at Douglas, Lanarkshire. In 1654 Robert Baillie, mourning the decline of the Scottish nobility, had remarked that 'Dowglas and his sonne Angus are quyet men, of no respect' (Letters and Journals of Robert Baillie, 3.249).   DAVID STEVENSON

Sources DNB · GEC, Peerage · Scots peerage · CSP dom., 1639–41 · The letters and journals of Robert Baillie, ed. D. Laing, 3 vols. (1841–2) · The memoirs of Henry Guthry, late bishop, ed. G. Crawford, 2nd edn (1748) · J. G. Fotheringham, ed., The diplomatic correspondence of Jean de Montereul and the brothers de Bellièvre: French ambassadors in England and Scotland, 1645–1648, 2 vols., Scottish History Society, 29–30 (1898–9) · W. Fraser, ed., The Douglas book, 4 vols. (1885) · J. Nicoll, A diary of public transactions and other occurrences, chiefly in Scotland, from January 1650 to June 1667, ed. D. Laing, Bannatyne Club, 52 (1836)

Douglas, Archibald, first earl of Forfar (1653–1712), nobleman, was born in Lanarkshire on 3 May 1653, the eldest son of the second marriage of Archibald *Douglas, earl of Angus (c.1609–1655), to Lady Jean Wemyss (d. 1715), eldest daughter of David Wemyss, second earl of Wemyss. On his father's death, in January 1655, Douglas ought to have succeeded to the title of second earl of Ormond, which his father obtained from Charles II in April 1651 for himself and the heirs-male of his second marriage. However, owing to Charles's defeat at Worcester and the establishment of the Commonwealth, the patent never passed the great seal, and the title of earl of Ormond was never borne by either father or son. Nevertheless, after the Restoration, by patent dated 2 October 1661, the king created Douglas earl of Forfar, Lord Wandell and Hartside, with precedency dating from the original grant of 1651.

Forfar sat in parliament in 1670, but there appears to be little record of the earl's public life until the revolution of 1688. This is probably due to his apparent dissatisfaction with aspects of the Scottish policy of both Charles II and James VII and II. Like his father, he seems to have held covenanting sympathies. In 1685 a complaint was brought before the privy council that Forfar, along with various others, had since August 1679 'attended house and field conventicles in the shires of Lanerk … or elsewhere, and heard divers rebels and vagrant preachers, "these trumpets of sedition and rebellion"', and had 'proposed to levy money for rebels, prisoners or banished persons' (Reg. PCS, 10.121).

After the revolution Forfar was sworn of the privy council, and regularly attended parliament and council. He was appointed one of the commissioners for executing the office of keeper of the privy seal, and in March 1689 subscribed both the act declaring the convention to be a lawful meeting of the estates, and the letter of congratulation to King William. Throughout the period from 1689 to 1702 he was actively employed on a number of committees dealing with a variety of subjects, receiving the praise of the duke of Hamilton for having carried himself very well in parliament.

Following the accession of Queen Anne, Forfar remained active in public affairs. He was a member of the privy council, and one of the lords of the Treasury—an office he held until the dissolution of that court, in consequence of the treaty of Union. Queen Anne promised him an equivalent post, and until it was obtained gave him in compensation a yearly pension of £300, although, ultimately, no similar position was forthcoming. During the debates concerning parliamentary Union, Forfar appears to have steadily voted with the government.

Forfar married Robina (1661/2–1749), daughter of Sir William Lockhart of Lee and a close friend of Queen Mary. He possessed the baronies of Bothwell and Wandell in Lanarkshire, but resided chiefly at Bothwell Castle. He died at Bothwell on 23 December 1712 and was buried in

Bothwell church, where his countess erected a monument to his memory. He was succeeded as earl by their only son, Archibald *Douglas (1692–1715).

HENRY PATON, rev. DEREK JOHN PATRICK

Sources Scots peerage · APS, 1689–1701 · Reg. PCS, 3rd ser., vol. 10 · B. Burke, A genealogical history of the dormant, abeyant, forfeited and extinct peerages of the British empire, new edn (1883) · W. H. L. Melville, ed., Leven and Melville papers: letters and state papers chiefly addressed to George, earl of Melville ... 1689–1691, Bannatyne Club, 77 (1843) · GEC, Peerage

Douglas, Archibald, second earl of Forfar (1692–1715), army officer, son of Archibald *Douglas, first earl of Forfar (1653–1712), soldier and politician, and his second wife, Robina Lockhart (d. 1741), was born on 25 May 1692. In his early years he bore the courtesy title of Lord Wandell, and Queen Anne about 1704 granted him a yearly pension of £200 to assist his education. In 1712, on the death of his father, he succeeded as second earl. In the following year, though only twenty years of age, he was appointed colonel of the 3rd, or Buff, regiment of infantry. In 1714 he petitioned Anne for payment of arrears, both of his father's pension and his own, amounting together to £1400; he pointed out at the same time that in her majesty's service he had incurred a debt of about £3000. He was appointed envoy-extraordinary to Prussia in 1715 (credentials dated 14 July) but never took up his post.

In 1715 Forfar served as a brigadier-general in the army raised by the duke of Argyll for quelling the Jacobite rising in Scotland, and was present on 13 November at the indecisive combat at Sheriffmuir, where he fought bravely, but sustained wounds that were to prove fatal. He was taken prisoner to Stirling, and died there on 8 December. He was buried in Bothwell church, where a monument was erected to his memory. As he died unmarried the title of earl of Forfar became extinct, and his estates passed to Archibald, first duke of Douglas.

HENRY PATON, rev. MAIRIANNA BIRKELAND

Sources GEC, Peerage · P. W. J. Riley, The English ministers and Scotland, 1707–1727 (1964) · Scots peerage

Douglas, Archibald, duke of Douglas (bap. 1694, d. 1761), landowner, the son of James *Douglas, second marquess of Douglas (c.1646–1700), and his second wife, Mary Kerr (Ker; bap. 1674, d. 1736), daughter of Robert *Kerr, first marquess of Lothian, was baptized on 13 October 1694. He succeeded his father as marquess of Douglas in February 1700. He was created duke of Douglas by Queen Anne in 1703 at the behest of his kinsman James Douglas, second duke of Queensberry, ostensibly in recognition of the loyalty and deeds of his forebears, but more immediately to balance the elevation of the rival marquess of Atholl to a dukedom.

As he was head of the senior line of one of Scotland's most illustrious families and heir to a great fortune, much was expected of Douglas as a young man. Such hopes, however, went unfulfilled. His public career was brief and spotty. In 1712 he joined nineteen other Scottish peers in a remonstrance to the queen against the decision of the House of Lords that those who had held Scottish peerages at the time of the Union could not subsequently sit in the house by virtue of British peerages. During the Jacobite rising of 1715 he was commissioned lord lieutenant of Forfarshire, and raised 500 men for the government; he also fought as a volunteer at the battle of Sheriffmuir.

It became apparent, however, that Douglas was not cut out for political or social leadership. He was, for one thing, barely literate. Late in life he confessed to the earl of Shelburne (who characterized him as 'the last of the feudal lords') that 'he could neither read nor write without great difficulty' (Fitzmaurice, 1.6–7). Proud, irascible, and reclusive by nature, his eccentric conduct raised doubts about his mental stability. Such concerns were intensified in 1725 when, at Douglas Castle, his chief seat, he killed John Kerr, the illegitimate son of his brother-in-law, Lord Mark Kerr, and a suitor for the hand of his sister, Lady Jane *Douglas. Douglas fled to the Netherlands for a time, but eventually returned to Scotland and was never prosecuted. The affair, Horace Walpole suggested, 'had been winked at on supposition of his insanity' (Walpole, 3.201n.). No certificate of lunacy was ever issued, but the duke 'retired from the world', in the words of the duke of Queensberry, and 'lived like a prisoner' (Laing MSS, 2.455), surrounded by retainers sympathetic to the duke of Hamilton, next heir after his sister. Douglas never participated in peers' elections, and he allowed the family's parliamentary interests in Lanarkshire, Forfarshire, and elsewhere to languish. Events occasionally intruded on his isolation. During the Jacobite rising of 1745 he denied Lord George Murray admittance to Douglas Castle on the Jacobite army's return from England. However, he was later obliged to open his door to the Young Pretender himself (Charles Edward Stuart), whose troops did much damage. In 1758 Douglas Castle burnt down, forcing the duke to divide his time between Holyrood Palace, where he had apartments, and Bothwell Castle. He began the reconstruction of Douglas Castle (unfinished in his lifetime) to plans from John Adam, with the intention, it was said, of building a house 10 feet wider and 10 feet higher than the duke of Argyll's new seat at Inveraray.

The last decades of Douglas's life were dominated by speculation over the eventual disposition of his considerable estate, which included property in eight Scottish counties and was said to be worth more than £12,000 a year. His relationship with his only sibling, Lady Jane Douglas, was strained after Kerr's death. In 1746 she married—without his knowledge—Colonel John Stewart of Grandtully (from 1759, third baronet), a former Jacobite sympathizer, mercenary, and sometime bankrupt, and fled to the continent. In 1748 she reported her marriage from Paris and then informed the duke of the birth (in her fifty-first year) of twins. Douglas cut off Lady Jane's support and refused either to see her before her death in 1753 or to accept her offspring as genuine. He instead entailed his estates on the Hamiltons.

Douglas, who had often stated that he would never marry, surprised many when on 1 March 1758 he wed Margaret (d. 1774) [see Douglas, Margaret], the daughter of James Douglas of Mains. (When Alexander Carlyle first met her in 1745, he noted that she had even then 'Sworn to be Dutchess of Douglas, or never mount a Marriage Bed' (Carlyle, 56). An eccentric in her own right, she took a sympathetic view of the claim of Lady Jane's only surviving son, Archibald [see Douglas, Archibald James Edward, first Baron Douglas], and eventually persuaded the duke to reconsider the case and recognize him as heir. This set the stage for the famous Douglas cause that would, nearly eight years after the duke's death, confirm young Archibald, now called Douglas, in possession of the Douglas estates.

The duke died on 21 July 1761 at Queensberry House, Edinburgh, and was buried on 4 August with his ancestors in the parish church at Douglas, Lanarkshire, contrary to his wish to be buried in the bowling green. The marquessate and other titles he had inherited passed to the seventh duke of Hamilton; the dukedom and other titles conferred on him in 1703 became extinct. Once the object of high hopes, Douglas led an eccentric and reclusive life, posthumously overshadowed by the titanic legal battle to become his heir.   WILLIAM C. LOWE

Sources DNB · L. de la Torre, *The heir of Douglas* (1953) · W. Fraser, ed., *The Douglas book*, 4 vols. (1885) · GEC, *Peerage*, new edn, vol. 4 · Marchioness of Tullibardine [K. M. Stewart-Murray, duchess of Atholl], ed., *A military history of Perthshire, 1660–1902*, 2 vols. (1908) · *Life of William, earl of Shelburne … with extracts from his papers and correspondence*, ed. E. G. P. Fitzmaurice, 2nd edn, 2 vols. (1912) · J. S. Shaw, *The management of Scottish society, 1707–1763* (1983) · A. Carlyle, *Anecdotes and characters of the times*, ed. J. Kinsley (1973) · H. Walpole, *Memoirs of the reign of King George the Third*, ed. G. F. R. Barker, 4 vols. (1894) · P. W. J. Riley, *The Union of England and Scotland* (1978) · *Report on the Laing manuscripts*, 2 vols., HMC, 72 (1914–25) · David, Lord Elcho, *A short account of the affairs of Scotland in the years 1744, 1745, 1746*, ed. E. Charteris (1907) · C. Sinclair-Stevenson, *Inglorious rebellion: the Jacobite risings of 1708, 1715 and 1719* (1971)
Archives NRA, priv. coll., corresp. and papers
Wealth at death over £12,000: de la Torre, *Heir of Douglas*, 156, 187 · received over £5000 for regalities when hereditable jurisdictions abolished in Scotland, 1747: GEC, *Peerage*, 439n.

Douglas [*formerly* Stewart], **Archibald James Edward**, **first Baron Douglas** (1748–1827), litigant and politician, the son of Sir John Stewart of Grandtully, third baronet (1687–1764), and his wife, Lady Jane *Douglas (1698–1753), was born on 10 July 1748 at faubourg St Germain, Paris. His early life was dominated by the efforts of his parents and supporters to establish his identity as nephew and heir of Archibald *Douglas, duke of Douglas (*bap.* 1694, *d.* 1761). His mother, the duke's only sister, had in 1746 married without her brother's knowledge Colonel John Stewart, a former Jacobite sympathizer and veteran of the Swedish army, and fled to the continent. Two years later she informed the duke of the marriage and notified him that she was (at the age of fifty) pregnant. Subsequently she reported the birth on 10 July 1748 of twin boys, named Archibald and Sholto. The irascible and eccentric duke disapproved of the marriage, cut off his sister's allowance, and—encouraged by the duke of Hamilton's family, who stood next in line to the sister as heir—refused to recognize the twins as hers. In 1751 the family returned to

Archibald James Edward Douglas, first Baron Douglas (1748–1827), by George Willison, 1769

Britain, where they lived a hand-to-mouth existence as Colonel Stewart was soon imprisoned for debt. Sholto and Lady Jane both died in 1753. Archibald's upbringing was taken over by Lady Schaw of Greenock, and, after her death in 1757, by the duke and duchess of Queensberry, who saw to his education, first at Rugby School (1759–61) and then at Westminster School (1761–5). The reclusive duke of Douglas surprisingly married in March 1758, and the new duchess, Margaret Douglas of Mains, became an aggressive advocate of Archibald's claim to the Douglas estates, which were said to be worth in excess of £12,000 a year. Before the duke died, she convinced him to reinvestigate the case and to name Archibald as his heir. Following the duke's death in July 1761, Archibald Stewart was duly served heir and took the surname Douglas.

This set the stage for one of the eighteenth century's most famous legal battles, the Douglas cause. Archibald's inheritance was challenged by the Hamiltons, who argued that he and his brother were supposititious. The Hamilton lawyers put together a plausible circumstantial argument that Archibald was actually Jacques Louis Mignon, the son of a Parisian glassworker, who had disappeared in July 1748. The case was litigated at great length and expense (the two sides spent £54,000 between them). It attracted tremendous interest, especially in Scotland. Not only was a large estate at stake, but many felt that requiring Archibald Douglas to in effect prove his identity raised a question that could endanger the security of inheritance in general. In Scotland the Douglas side enjoyed broad popular support, with James Boswell an especially eager partisan, though many of the literati favoured the Hamilton side. In 1767 the court of session decided by the casting vote of the lord president against Douglas. Douglas appealed to the House of Lords which, following the opinions of law lords Mansfield and Camden, reversed the decision without a division.

Douglas settled easily into the life of a landed magnate. He was an improving landlord who continued the rebuilding of Douglas Castle begun by his uncle, though investment in the Ayr bank of Douglas, Heron & Co., which failed in 1772, complicated his finances during the 1770s. He also achieved a degree of political prominence as he worked to resurrect the Douglas interest in Lanarkshire, Berwickshire, Forfarshire, and elsewhere. He was elected member for Forfarshire in 1782, and was made lord lieutenant of the county in 1794. During the following year he raised a regiment of fencibles. In parliament he was a loyal, if silent, follower of Henry Dundas and William Pitt, a status that facilitated his successful pursuit of a peerage. Although he would have preferred an earldom, he was created Baron Douglas of Douglas in 1790.

Douglas married twice into ducal families: first, on 13 June 1771, Lady Lucie Graham (1751–1780), daughter of the second duke of Montrose, and second, on 13 May 1783, Lady Frances Scott (1750–1817) [see Douglas, Frances, Lady Douglas], sister of the third duke of Buccleuch; among the children born of this second marriage was Caroline Lucy *Scott, novelist. Horace Walpole commented that 'it is proof of *his* sense, that he can forgive her person in favour of her merit' (to Lady Ossory, 17 April 1783, Walpole, *Corr.*, 33.399). Douglas died on 26 December 1827 at Bothwell Castle, Lanarkshire. He was buried in Douglas parish church in the same county. Forever identified with the Douglas cause, as an adult he proved a rather unexceptional aristocrat.   WILLIAM C. LOWE

Sources DNB · L. de la Torre, *The heir of Douglas* (1953) · A. F. Steuart, *The Douglas cause* (1909) · *Boswell in search of a wife, 1766–1769*, ed. F. Brady and F. A. Pottle (1957), vol. 6 of *The Yale editions of the private papers of James Boswell*, trade edn (1950–89) · W. Fraser, ed., *The Douglas book*, 4 vols. (1885) · E. Haden-Guest, 'Douglas, Archibald', HoP, *Commons, 1754–90*, 2.330–31 · GEC, *Peerage*, new edn, vol. 4 · R. M. Sunter, *Patronage and politics in Scotland, 1707–1832* (1984) · *Collins peerage of England: genealogical, biographical and historical*, ed. E. Brydges, 9 vols. (1812), vol. 8 · Walpole, *Corr.*, vol. 33 · H. Hamilton, 'The failure of the Ayr Bank, 1772', *Economic History Review*, 2nd ser., 8 (1955–6), 405–17 · J. Dwyer, R. A. Mason, and A. Murdoch, eds., *New perspectives on the politics and culture of early modern Scotland* (1982) · *The letters and journals of Lady Mary Coke*, 4 vols. (1970)
Archives priv. coll., deeds, family and estate papers | NL Scot., letters to Lord Lynedoch · NRA Scotland, priv. coll., letters to Robert Graham of Fintry · NRA Scotland, priv. coll., letters to David Scott
Likenesses G. Willison, oils, 1769, Lennoxlove House, East Lothian [*see illus.*] · T. Lawrence, oils, *c.*1790, Buccleuch estates, Selkirk
Wealth at death in 1761 estates allegedly worth at least £12,000 p.a.: de la Torre, *Heir of Douglas*, 156, 187 · later inherited Amesbury, a property in Wiltshire, from third duke of Queensberry; lands in eight Scottish counties valued for land tax at £29,910 9s. 7d. Scots, however assessments based on values set in 1650s: L. R. Timperly, ed., *A directory of landownership in Scotland, c.1770* (1976)

Douglas, Archibald Ramsey (1807–1886). *See under* Douglas, William (1780–1832).

Douglas, Aretas Akers-, first Viscount Chilston (1851–1926), politician, was born on 21 October 1851 at St Leonards. He was born Aretas Akers, son of the Revd Aretas Akers (1824–1856), of Malling Abbey, Kent, and Frances Maria (*d.* 1900), daughter of Francis Holles Brandram of Underriver, Kent. He had two younger sisters. His father was a 'squarson', but the Akers family had only recently settled in Kent; on his father's side, he was descended from six generations of West Indies sugar planters and slave owners. He was educated at Eton College and at University College, Oxford, and was called to the bar by the Inner Temple in 1875.

In the same year Akers inherited the estates of his kinsman James Douglas of Baads, Midlothian, consisting of 6629 acres in Dumfries, 3106 in Midlothian, and 2190 in Lanark, as well as Chilston Park and 3753 acres in Kent. He assumed the additional surname of Douglas, and soon afterwards (10 June 1875) married Adeline Mary (*d.* 1929), daughter of Horatio Austen-Smith of Hayes, Kent. They settled at Chilston Park (Malling Abbey, the family home, belonged to his grandmother for life), and had seven children—two boys and five girls—but the marriage was not a happy one. Adeline was gifted but deeply eccentric, making impossible the social life normal for that time and class.

As a young Kentish landowner and an excellent shot, Akers-Douglas came under the eye of Lord Abergavenny of Eridge Castle, Disraeli's unofficial adviser and chief of the 'Kentish gang' of Conservative Party managers. Encouraged by Abergavenny, he stood and was elected as a Conservative for East Kent in 1880. The constituency was reshaped as the St Augustine's division in 1885, and Akers-Douglas represented it until his retirement in 1911. In parliament he spoke rarely, but his sympathies were with the tory democratic wing of the party: he may have met Disraeli at Eridge, and he was friendly with Lord Randolph Churchill and the Fourth Party. Any signs of independence were checked, however, by his appointment as an opposition whip in 1883. In 1884 he was promoted second whip, and in June 1885, at the age of thirty-three, he became chief whip and patronage secretary to the Treasury in Salisbury's minority government (June 1885 – January 1886). He returned to the Treasury in July 1886, continuing as government chief whip in Salisbury's second ministry until 1892.

Effective whipping was at a premium in the parliament of 1886–92. Not only was the government paralysed by obstruction from the Irish party in the house, making necessary the use of the closure and guillotine to force through government business, but the government's seventy-five Liberal Unionist allies, led by Hartington and Chamberlain, required diplomatic handling in the house and brought friction with Conservatives in the constituencies. As chief whip Akers-Douglas was responsible for a dramatic tightening in party discipline. Voting against

Aretas Akers-Douglas, first Viscount Chilston (1851–1926), by Elliott & Fry

party lines virtually disappeared after 1886, and conformity became in practice total. He managed the parliamentary party in tandem with central office and the constituencies, working through Richard Middleton (the 'Skipper'), whom he had recommended as chief party agent in 1885, and who remained at central office until 1903. In the house, Akers-Douglas formed a close partnership with W. H. Smith, leader of the house in 1887–91, with whom he dined nightly; the intelligence he collected from the party he regularly transmitted to Salisbury. He was sworn of the privy council in 1891.

Smith was succeeded as leader of the house by A. J. Balfour in 1891, and in opposition to the Liberal government of 1892–5 Akers-Douglas continued as Conservative chief whip. He was the perfect foil to Balfour, playing tortoise to Balfour's hare; where Balfour was dexterous, agile in debate but languid and aloof, Akers-Douglas was assiduous, a natural conciliator and manager of men. 'No one knew better the changing mood of the lobby, the exact value of the *frondeur*, or the extent of an intrigue', wrote J. S. Sandars (*DNB*). For Akers-Douglas the whips' room provided the utterly absorbing escape from an unhappy marriage. 'The Room', with its clubbishness, its talk of 'old boy' and 'pal', played a crucial part in cementing party loyalty—a function of key importance after 1886 as the Conservative Party lost its socially homogeneous character and the ranks of country gentlemen were swollen by recruits from newly won seats in the big towns.

In July 1895, when Salisbury formed his third government, Akers-Douglas was appointed first commissioner of works with a seat in the cabinet. Adjusting from the whip's role, at the centre of the party's nervous system, to a junior department was not easy. He had no direct experience of government administration, but his running of his own estates helped him at the office of works, where his responsibilities included building new government offices, as well as acting as a kind of estates' bursar to the royal family. Ably assisted by his permanent secretary, Lord Esher, he presided over the preparations for the coronation of King Edward VII. But he owed his influence in cabinet not to his departmental work but to the sagacity of his advice, to his knowledge of men, and to his intuitive understanding of the party and the country. At Salisbury's request, he acted as adviser to Sir William Walrond, his successor as chief whip, and he continued to control party funds. He predicted the result of the 1900 election with remarkable accuracy. In 1900 he was used by Balfour to persuade the ageing Salisbury to give up the Foreign Office when he resumed office as prime minister; it was, wrote Akers-Douglas, 'a difficult and unpleasant mission'. In 1901–2 he chaired the committee on military education and officers' training, which published a report condemning officers' education at Woolwich and Sandhurst. When Balfour succeeded as prime minister in 1902, he rewarded the faithful Akers-Douglas by promoting him to home secretary (1902–5).

As home secretary Akers-Douglas was responsible for the Aliens Bill, tightening the restrictions on immigration. The bill as originally introduced in 1904 was dropped, and a milder bill passed in 1905. After 1902 Akers-Douglas remained close to Balfour and his party managers; he was deeply involved with the government reshuffle of 1903 which followed the resignations of Joseph Chamberlain and the Unionist free-traders. In the house, he acted as deputy to Balfour, who combined the office of leader of the house with the premiership. To Akers-Douglas fell the duty of writing the nightly parliamentary letter to the king, and when Balfour was away Akers-Douglas took his place. In February 1904, he wound up a crucial debate on the fiscal question with an inept appeal for party unity—an episode which appeared to epitomize his shortcomings as a politician. 'He is a most skilful wirepuller, and his methods of organization are wonderful', wrote Balcarres, then a junior whip: 'but as a speaker and debater his abilities are nil.' However, as the seasoned parliamentary journalist Henry Lucy perceived, Akers-Douglas's low-calibre performance was in fact a deliberate ploy:

> With fine art, the greater because it is concealed, the Home Secretary, questioned by unreasonable members opposite, absolutely looks as if he knew nothing on the particular subject submitted, or indeed on any other ... Mr Akers-Douglas, surveying the inquisitive members opposite as if they were a field of buttercups and daisies, with childlike blandness says he doesn't know. And there the matter ends.

Akers-Douglas was returned for St Augustine's with an increased majority in the 1906 election, but he let it be known that he was no longer a contender for cabinet. Nevertheless, he continued to sit on the Unionist front bench, and behind the scenes he acted as adviser to the party leadership. In 1911 Balfour appointed him chairman of the Unionist Organization Committee, which was appointed to inquire into the party machine in the light of the double election defeat of 1910. When the committee called for the heads of both the chief whip, Acland-Hood, and the principal agent, Percival Hughes, Akers-Douglas refused to sign the report. None the less, he agreed to convey the committee's criticisms privately to Balfour; and Acland-Hood resigned shortly afterwards. It was an exercise in damage limitation characteristic of Akers-Douglas, for whom loyalty to the party came before all else. In the coronation honours of 1911 he received a peerage, becoming Baron Douglas, of Baads, and Viscount Chilston, of Boughton Malherbe, Kent.

After 1911 Akers-Douglas retired completely from public life. His last years were spent at Chilston Park, surrounded by his collections of butterflies and birds' eggs. He wrote no memoirs, and he destroyed many of his papers, including fifty-three letters from Queen Victoria and over sixty from Lord Salisbury. The wealth of papers remaining provided the material for the illuminating biography, *Chief Whip*, published by his grandson in 1961.

Akers-Douglas was a tall man, who developed an abundant Edwardian figure in middle age. Though a poor speaker, his smiling manner masked a quick mind; the soul of discretion, he could be secretive but was never duplicitous. He disliked women, especially fashionable women who meddled in politics. His world was the man's world of the lobby and the house: his loyalty to the party was absolute. He died at 34 Lower Belgrave Street, London, on 15 January 1926.　　　　　　　　　　　　JANE RIDLEY

Sources E. A. Akers-Douglas, third Viscount Chilston, *Chief whip: the political life and times of Aretas Akers-Douglas, 1st Viscount Chilston* (1961) · *DNB* · [J. S. Sandars], *Studies of yesterday by a privy councillor* (1928) · H. W. Lucy, *The Balfourian parliament, 1900–1905* (1906) · P. Marsh, *The discipline of popular government: Lord Salisbury's domestic statecraft, 1881–1902* (1978) · *The Crawford papers: the journals of David Lindsay, twenty-seventh earl of Crawford … 1892–1940*, ed. J. Vincent (1984) · *CGPLA Eng. & Wales* (1926) · Burke, *Peerage*
Archives CKS, corresp., diaries, and papers | BL, corresp. with Arthur James Balfour, Add. MS 49772 · Bodl. Oxf., corresp. with Sir William Harcourt · Bodl. Oxf., corresp. with J. S. Sandars · CAC Cam., corresp. with Lord Randolph Churchill · Hatfield House, Hertfordshire, Salisbury MSS · W. H. Smith, London, Hambledon MSS
Likenesses Spy [L. Ward], cartoon, 1885, repro. in *VF* · Russell & Sons, photograph, c.1894, NPG · A. S. Cope, portrait, 1910, Chilston Park · Elliott & Fry, photograph, NPG [*see illus.*] · P. May, watercolour, caricature, NPG · Mayall & Co, photograph, NPG · B. Stone, photograph, NPG
Wealth at death £21,841 17s. 6d. save and except settled land: probate, 18 Feb 1926, *CGPLA Eng. & Wales* · £111,162 6s. 1d. limited to settled land: further grant, 8 March 1926, *CGPLA Eng. & Wales*

Douglas, Aretas Akers-, second Viscount Chilston

(**1876–1947**), diplomatist, was born in London on 17 February 1876, the elder son in the family of two sons and five daughters of Aretas Akers-*Douglas, first Viscount Chilston (1851–1926), politician, and his wife, Adeline Mary (d. 1929), daughter of Horatio Austen-Smith, of Hayes, Kent. His father was Conservative MP for East Kent (1880–85)

and St Augustine's, Kent (1885–1911), and was home secretary from 1902 to 1905; he assumed the surname Akers-Douglas by royal licence in 1875, under the terms of the will of his cousin, Alexander Douglas of Baads, and was created first Viscount Chilston and Baron Douglas of Baads in 1911.

Akers-Douglas was educated at Eton College from 1889 to 1895, and served briefly in the Royal Scots before entering the diplomatic service in October 1898. (From 1899 to 1907 he served as a captain in the 3rd battalion of the Royal Scots militia.) He was fortunate to be posted to Cairo in October 1899, where he served under Lord Cromer, whom he impressed, and where he showed evidence of a flair for languages which later assisted his diplomatic career. He was promoted third secretary in December 1900, and was employed at Madrid from September to December 1901. In January 1903 he was transferred to Constantinople, returning to London in June 1903. On 6 August that year he married Amy Constance (d. 1962), daughter of John Robert Jennings-Bramly, officer in the Royal Horse Artillery. They had two sons, Aretas (1905–1940) and Eric Alexander (1910–1982).

In September 1904 Akers-Douglas was appointed to Athens, where he was promoted second secretary in April 1905. He was acting agent and consul-general at Sofia from February to April 1907. Already identified as a high-flyer, he then served as head of Chancery in Rome and then in Vienna from May 1909. He was promoted first secretary in April 1912. On three occasions between 1911 and 1914 he was posted to rugged Montenegro, and from March to July 1912 he served as chargé d'affaires at Bucharest; all this at the time of the Balkan wars when the area was highly unstable and communication with London was difficult. He was transferred to Bucharest in April 1914, returning in February 1915 to the Foreign Office, where he remained for the rest of the First World War. He was appointed CMG in 1918.

After the First World War, Akers-Douglas was sent to Paris as a member of the British delegation to the Versailles peace conference. When he returned to London in August 1919 he was appointed diplomatic secretary to the secretary of state, Lord Curzon. He was promoted counsellor the following month. Robert Vansittart, then Curzon's private secretary, wrote later that Curzon 'underrated my assistants Allen Leeper and Akers-Douglas, later our Ambassador to Moscow and one of those mute Britons whose immobile faces effortlessly belie their shrewdness' (Vansittart, 274). But Akers-Douglas's merit was recognized by the diplomatic service when he was sent as minister to Vienna in November 1921, thus renewing his pre-war acquaintance with that city.

Akers-Douglas remained in Vienna for almost seven years at a time when the rump Austrian state, all that was left of the old Habsburg empire, was surviving a difficult birth under its clerical chancellor Seipel. While in Vienna, Akers-Douglas became the second Viscount Chilston following his father's death on 15 January 1926. He was promoted KCMG in 1927. From Vienna he was transferred in June 1928 to Budapest, the other half of the old imperial tandem, where he dealt skilfully with Hungarian revisionist claims to Transylvania, and other territories lost under the treaty of Trianon.

In October 1933 Chilston was appointed ambassador to Moscow, capital of what was then a pariah state in Europe. He took the trouble to learn Russian but found the post exacting. 'It is not what an ambassador can do', he later remarked, 'but what he can stand' (Craig and Gilbert, 657). It was very difficult to get access to the Kremlin, and Neville Chamberlain wrote of him in 1937: 'He gets no information and the condition of the country is a mystery to him' (Andrew, 407). His term as ambassador coincided with the infamous Stalinist purges, a process which puzzled many foreign diplomats and journalists. On first meeting Stalin, Chilston remarked to his staff: 'I think the chap's a gentleman' (de Jonge, 243), but he soon had cause to revise his opinion. He reported to the Foreign Office in 1937 that the indictment of Old Bolsheviks such as Radek and Piatokov was 'utterly unworthy of belief', and he was convinced (rightly) that their false confessions had been extracted by means of 'unavowable methods'. Nevertheless he was pleased that the trials helped to discredit Stalin's tyranny abroad (*Documents on British Foreign Policy*, ser. 2A, documents 14, 23, and 31).

It was perhaps surprising, given the dearth of accurate intelligence available to the embassy, that Chilston opposed the appointment of a passport control officer in Moscow, the normal role of such officers being to gather intelligence. However, he did campaign for a new cohort of consular officials who would get an intensive training in Russian before being posted to the Soviet Union. This would have followed the US practice of appointing 'experts' to Moscow, but the diplomatic service rejected the proposal and continued to employ 'generalists', partly because the Treasury flatly refused to provide the necessary funds. Chilston, whose character has been described as 'shrewd and sardonic' (Cameron Watt, 118), left Moscow in December 1938, before the abortive talks with Britain and France for a security pact. He then retired from the service. He was sworn of the privy council on retirement, having been promoted GCMG in 1935.

Chilston lived out his remaining years at the family estate of Chilston Park, Maidstone, Kent. During the war he served as a Home Guard officer. He died at his home on 25 July 1947. He was survived by his wife and his younger son, who succeeded him as third viscount, his elder son having died in a motor accident in 1940.

PETER NEVILLE

Sources DNB · A. de Jonge, *Stalin and the shaping of the Soviet Union* (1986) · M. Hughes, *Inside the enigma: British officials in Russia, 1900–39* (1997) · M. Hughes, 'British and American diplomatic reporting on Russia', *Diplomacy and Statecraft*, 11/2 (July 2000) · *Documents on British foreign policy*, 2nd and 3rd ser. (1949) · Lord Vansittart, *The mist procession* (1958) · C. Andrew, *Secret service* (1985) · D. Cameron Watt, *How war came* (1989) · G. A. Craig and F. Gilbert, *The diplomats*, 2 (Princeton, 1953) · S. Aster, *The making of the Second World War* (1973) · earl of Avon [A. Eden], *Facing the dictators* (1962) · J. Haslam, *The Soviet Union and the struggle for collective security in Europe* (1984) · *FO List* (1939) · *WWW*, 1941–50 · Burke, *Peerage* · register, Eton

Archives CKS, corresp. · PRO, FO 800 series · PRO, FO 800/309–328 | Borth. Inst., Lord Halifax papers
Likenesses W. Stoneman, photograph, 1933, NPG · Lady Chilston, portrait, Chilston Park, Maidstone, Kent
Wealth at death £120,694 7s. 1d.: probate, 29 April 1948, CGPLA Eng. & Wales

Douglas, Basil William, Lord Daer (1763–1794). *See under* London Corresponding Society (*act.* 1792–1799).

Douglas, Brice (d. 1222). *See under* Douglas family (*per.* c.1170–c.1300).

Douglas, Catherine [Kitty], **duchess of Queensberry and Dover** (1701–1777), literary patron, was the second daughter of Henry Hyde, second earl of Rochester, later fourth earl of Clarendon (1672–1754), son of Laurence *Hyde, first earl, and his wife, Jane *Hyde (d. 1725), daughter of Sir William Leveson-Gower, though Lady Mary Wortley Montagu always said that Kitty's real father was Henry *Boyle, first Baron Carleton. Henry *Hyde, Baron Hyde, was her brother. Her mother was a great beauty and Catherine, usually known as Kitty, was brought up in a household frequented by literary celebrities such as Alexander Pope and Matthew Prior. They made much of her, and when she was about sixteen Prior composed his well-known poem 'The Female Phaeton: upon Lady Kitty Hyde's First Appearing in Publick'.

On 10 March 1720 Kitty married her second cousin Charles *Douglas, third duke of Queensberry and second duke of Dover (1698–1778), at a magnificent ceremony in her father's house in Whitehall, London. Both were tall and slim, Kitty with large brown eyes, fair hair, and a famously graceful figure. They were a devoted couple. The duke, who had inherited great wealth when he was only twelve, was a quiet, patient man, a good listener, and a natural diplomat. This was fortunate, for Kitty had strong opinions and no hesitation in voicing them. Perhaps as a reaction to the flattery heaped upon her in her mother's house, she hated artifice. She could dress magnificently when she chose, but she rarely wore jewellery, as her portraits show, and she often startled her friends by appearing at court in the simplest of garments. She avoided alcohol, loved walking, and was an enthusiastic planter of trees on her husband's estates. Convinced that she knew best, she was all too ready to tell other people how they should live their lives, but in spite of her blunt manner she had a kind heart and her friends valued her common-sense advice. She and the duke had two sons, Henry, Lord Drumlanrig, born in 1723, and Charles, born in 1726. A daughter, Catherine, died in infancy.

The duke was lord of the bedchamber to George II, and at their London residence, Queensberry House, their regular guests included Handel, Pope, Prior, William Kent the architect, Charles Jervas the painter, and John Gay the playwright. When, in 1729, Gay was refused a licence for *Polly*, a sequel to his immensely successful *Beggar's Opera*, Kitty took up his cause, quarrelled with the lord chamberlain, offended the king, and was ordered to withdraw from court. London society was horrified at her temerity, but the duke stood by her and resigned his appointment as vice-admiral of Scotland, despite the king's kindly urgings that he should stay on. When Gay fell ill, Kitty took him in and nursed him tenderly. The duke and duchess, he told Swift, could not have treated him more kindly had he been their nearest relative. On his death in 1732 they arranged his magnificent funeral in Westminster Abbey and put up a monument by Rysbrack, describing him as 'the warmest friend, the gentlest companion, the most benevolent man'.

For the next fifteen years the duke and duchess divided their time between Amesbury, their Wiltshire and Oxfordshire estates, and Drumlanrig Castle, the duke's ancestral home in Dumfriesshire. Kitty was finally received back at court in 1747. By then her sons were grown up, but her happy family life was shattered when the recently married Lord Drumlanrig apparently committed suicide in 1754 while suffering from depression, and his younger brother died of tuberculosis the following year. After that, Kitty and the duke preferred to live quietly at Amesbury. Even in her seventies she was as tall, upright, and energetic as ever. She died at Queensberry House in London on 17 July 1777, after a brief illness caused, according to Horace Walpole, by a surfeit of cherries. Her servants said that she had been suffering from a chest complaint. She was buried in the duke's family vault at Durisdeer, near Drumlanrig, Dumfriesshire.

ROSALIND K. MARSHALL

Sources V. Biddulph, *Kitty, duchess of Queensberry* (1935) · *Letters written by Jonathan Swift D.D., dean of St Patrick's, Dublin*, ed. J. Hawkesworth (1767) · W. Fraser, ed., *The Douglas book*, 4 vols. (1885) · *A catalogue of the royal and noble authors of England, Scotland and Ireland … by the late Horatio Walpole*, ed. T. Park, 5 vols. (1806) · W. Fraser, *The Scotts of Buccleuch*, 2 vols. (1878) · *Boswell's London journal, 1762–63*, ed. F. A. Pottle (1950), vol. 1 of *The Yale editions of the private papers of James Boswell*, trade edn (1950–89) · H. Bleackley, *The story of a beautiful duchess: an account of the life and times of Elizabeth Gunning, Duchess of Hamilton* (1908) · *Scots peerage*, 7.143–4 · GEC, *Peerage*
Archives NA Scot., corresp. between duchess and female friends, GD24/5/98, GD24/5/106, GD24/5/111 | NRA Scotland, priv. coll., letters to Lady Lucy Graham · priv. coll., letters to Lord Cathcart
Likenesses attrib. A. Forbes, oils, priv. coll. · H. D. Hamilton, pastel, priv. coll. · attrib. T. Hudson, oils, priv. coll. · attrib. C. Jervas, oils, NPG; version, Petworth House West Sussex; version, Penicuik House, Midlothian, Scotland · attrib. studio of van Loo, group portrait (with her husband and children), priv. coll. · attrib. C. Read, pastel, priv. coll. · C. Zincke, miniature, priv. coll.

Douglas, Cathleen Sabine. *See* Mann, Cathleen Sabine (1896–1959).

Douglas, Charles, third duke of Queensberry and second duke of Dover (1698–1778), courtier and politician, the son of James *Douglas, second duke of Queensberry and first duke of Dover (1662–1711), and his wife, Mary Boyle (1670/71–1709), daughter of Charles, Lord Clifford, was born at Edinburgh on 24 November 1698. Having been created earl of Solway in the Scottish peerage in 1706 in recognition of the services of his father and grandfather, in 1711 he succeeded his father as third duke of Queensberry (in the Scottish peerage) and second duke of Dover (British).

After returning from the grand tour, in 1719 Queensberry unsuccessfully sought his seat in the House of Lords

Charles Douglas, third duke of Queensberry and second duke of Dover (1698–1778), attrib. Thomas Hudson

as duke of Dover, the house applying its 1712 decision that no peer of Scotland at the time of the Union could sit by virtue of a British peerage. On 10 March 1720 he married his second cousin Lady Catherine Hyde (1701–1777), the second daughter of Henry, second earl of Rochester and later fourth earl of Clarendon, and Jane, daughter of Sir William Leveson-Gower [*see* Douglas, Catherine, duchess of Queensberry and Dover]. Catherine was a major figure in her own right as a literary patron and socialite. Queensberry was a successful courtier under George I: lord of the bedchamber (1721), vice-admiral of Scotland (1722), and privy councillor (1726). In 1729 his wife's outrage at the lord chamberlain's refusal to license the performance of John Gay's *Polly* (which satirized Sir Robert Walpole) led George II to bar her from court and Queensberry to resign his offices. Thereafter they joined the opposition, the duke serving as a gentleman of the bedchamber to Frederick, prince of Wales, from 1733. In 1734 Queensberry took an active part in an unsuccessful attempt to elect a slate of opposition Scottish representative peers, standing as a candidate and voting in a peers' election for the only time in his life. After the accession of George III, Queensberry regained his place on the privy council and became keeper of the great seal of Scotland (1761–3) and lord justice-general (1763–78). Often solicited by Scots seeking patronage, the duke was not always able to oblige, as James Boswell found.

The Queensberrys lived mostly in England, where they were prominent in the social life of the capital. The duke periodically returned to Scotland and remained involved in affairs there, exercising over his long life the predominant parliamentary interest in Dumfriesshire and Dumfries burghs. An improving landlord, he sought to promote Scottish economic development. He was the chairman of the Firth and Clyde Canal Company and a major backer of the Ayr Bank (whose failure in 1772 put a dent in the duke's considerable fortune).

Queensberry's political influence was probably less than his contemporaries thought, and was likely limited by his exclusion from parliament. He was regarded as an amiable and benevolent aristocrat, Boswell characterizing him as 'a man of the greatest humanity and gentleness of manners' and 'good plain sense' (*Boswell's London Journal*, 63). Many sympathized with the duke and duchess for their fortitude in the face of sorrow when their adult sons, Henry, Lord Drumlanrig, and Charles, died within two years of each other in the mid-1750s. Queensberry died on 22 October 1778 from 'mortification of the leg after an accident alighting from a carriage' (GEC, *Peerage*, 10.699), and was buried at Durisdeer, Dumfriesshire. He was succeeded in his title and estates (said to be worth £18,000 p.a.) by the earl of March and Ruglen, the son of his first cousin.   WILLIAM C. LOWE

Sources DNB · *The letters and journals of Lady Mary Coke*, ed. J. A. Home, 4 vols. (1889–96) · A. Murdoch, *'The people above': politics and administration in mid-eighteenth-century Scotland* (1980) · *Autobiography of the Rev. Dr. Alexander Carlyle … containing memorials of the men and events of his time*, ed. J. H. Burton (1860); repr. as *Anecdotes and characters of the times*, ed. J. Kinsley (1973) · *Report on the manuscripts of Lord Polwarth*, 5, HMC, 67 (1961) · W. Robertson, *Proceedings relating to the peerage of Scotland, from January 16, 1707 to April 29, 1788* (1790) · *Scots peerage*, vol. 7 · GEC, *Peerage* · *Boswell's London journal, 1762–63*, ed. F. A. Pottle (1950), vol. 1 of *The Yale editions of the private papers of James Boswell*, trade edn (1950–89) · John, Lord Hervey, *Some materials towards memoirs of the reign of King George II*, ed. R. Sedgwick, new edn, 3 vols. (1952) · J. S. Shaw, *The management of Scottish society, 1707–1764: power, nobles, lawyers, Edinburgh agents and English influences* (1983) · HoP, *Commons, 1715–54* · H. Hamilton, 'The failure of the Ayr Bank, 1772', *Economic History Review*, 2nd ser., 8 (1955–6), 405–17
Archives NRA, priv. coll., family corresp. · Wilts. & Swindon RO, letters | Mount Stuart, Isle of Bute, corresp. with the earl of Bute · NRA, priv. coll., letters to Archibald Douglas · PRO, letters to first earl of Chatham, PRO 30/8
Likenesses J. Wootton, group portrait, oils, 1740 (*The shooting party*), Royal Collection · A. Forbes, oils, 1772, Penicuik House, Midlothian · V. Green, mezzotint, 1773 (after G. Willison), BM, NPG · N. Dance, oils, Buccleuch estates, Selkirk · attrib. T. Hudson, group portrait, oils (with duchess and two sons), Buccleuch estates, Selkirk · attrib. T. Hudson, oils, Buccleuch estates, Selkirk [*see illus.*] · attrib. T. Hudson, oils, Scot. NPG
Wealth at death wealthy; left estate of £18,000 p.a.: *Scots Magazine* (Oct 1778)

Douglas, Sir Charles, of Carr, first baronet (d. 1789), naval officer, was descended from a younger son of William Douglas of Lochleven, sixth earl of Morton. The record only begins with his passing his examination for lieutenant in the British navy in February 1747, having attracted the attention of Admiral Francis Holburne who in 1757 described him as a 'good clever sensible man' (PRO, ADM 1/481, fol. 467). From 1749 to 1752 he served as a lieutenant

in the Dutch navy (admiralty of Amsterdam). He was promoted to that rank in the Royal Navy on 4 December 1753 and on 24 February 1759 he was made commander. He served through that summer in command of the armed ship *Boscawen* attached to the fleet under Sir Charles Saunders during the capture of Quebec.

In 1761 Douglas had command of the *Unicorn* (28 guns) attached to the squadron employed in blockading Brest, and in 1762 he was in charge of the *Syren* (20 guns) on the coast of Newfoundland, where he commanded the naval force which covered Lieutenant-Colonel William Amherst's landing at Torbay on 13 September. He was still in the *Syren* at the peace, and when transferred to the *Tweed* (32 guns) was able to ensure that James Cook could complete his survey of St Pierre and Miquelon before those islands passed to the French. In 1764 and 1765 he served as a flag officer in the Russian navy. From 1767 to 1770 he commanded the *Emerald* (32 guns), and from 1770 to 1773 the *St Albans* (64 guns), both on the home station. In 1775 he was appointed to the *Isis* (50 guns), and was sent with reinforcements and stores for Quebec, then threatened by American rebel forces commanded by Benedict Arnold. He did not reach the coast of America until too late in the season; the St Lawrence was closed by ice, and he was obliged to return without having effected the object of his voyage. He was again sent out early in the next year, and, pushing through the ice with great difficulty, arrived off Quebec on 6 May. The town, which had been closely blockaded during the winter, was relieved, and the governor, assuming the offensive, drove the enemy from their entrenchments in headlong flight. Douglas then proceeded to construct a squadron of small vessels on Lake Champlain, with which he defeated Arnold's flotilla in the battle of Valcour Island (11–13 October 1776). On his return to England, Douglas was rewarded with a baronetcy on 23 January 1777. A few months later he was appointed to the *Stirling Castle* (64 guns); in her he took part in the action off Ushant on 27 July 1778. In the subsequent courts martial his testimony was distinctly to the advantage of Admiral Augustus Keppel.

Douglas was afterwards appointed to the *Duke* (98 guns), and commanded her in the Channel Fleet for the next three years; during this time he experimented with moving standards from the gun decks, in order to open greater arcs of fire, thereby enabling several ships to engage a single target at a quarter mile range, or a single ship to engage several. He also introduced improvements in gun tackles and equipment which significantly increased rates of fire.

Douglas was selected by Sir George Rodney towards the end of 1781 as his first captain or captain of the fleet, accompanied him to the West Indies on board the *Formidable*, and was with him in the battle of the Saints on 12 April 1782. The claim, recounted years later by Admiral Sir Charles Dashwood, who had been a midshipman on the *Formidable*, that Douglas persuaded Rodney to make the decisive tactical movement to cut the enemy battle line, is doubtful, and Brian Tunstall largely accepts Samuel Hood's criticism of Douglas's failure as Rodney's staff officer to ensure that the older man's weakness of memory was overcome. In particular Hood criticized Douglas's failure to support Hood's efforts to persuade Rodney, who was exhausted after four sleepless nights, to order 'general chase' in the pursuit of De Grasse following the battle (Tunstall, 113–20). Captain Thomas White, who dismissed the claim for Douglas, also reported that when the *Formidable* was passing the *Glorieux*, and pouring in her a tremendous broadside at very close range, Douglas exclaimed: 'Behold, Sir George, the Greeks and Trojans contending for the body of Patroclus'; to which Rodney replied, 'Damn the Greeks, and damn the Trojans; I have other things to think of'. Later, the story goes, he returned to Douglas and said, smiling, 'Now, my dear friend, I am at the service of the Greeks and Trojans, and the whole of Homer's "Iliad"; for the enemy is in confusion and our victory is secure'. White said that the remark attributed to Douglas was 'in perfect accordance with his usual style of expression', and 'the answer to it is agreeable to that of Sir George Rodney' (*Naval Researches*, 112). To set against the tittle-tattle is Douglas's real and very important contribution to the victory provided by his gunnery innovations, which had been approved by the Admiralty in the early months of 1781, and at Rodney's instructions had been introduced into some at least of the ships under his command.

When Rodney was recalled Douglas remained with Admiral Hugh Pigot as captain of the fleet, before returning to England at the peace in 1783. In October he was appointed commodore and commander-in-chief on the Halifax station, but in 1786 he asked for his recall when the Admiralty would not support him in a dispute with the dockyard commissioner, Henry Duncan. On 24 September 1787 he was promoted rear-admiral, and in January 1789 he was again appointed to the command in North America.

Douglas was married three times. His first wife was Lydia Schimmelpinck; the couple produced two sons and a daughter, the eldest son, William Henry, inheriting as second baronet. His second marriage was to Sarah (*d.* 1779), daughter of James Wood, who gave birth to a daughter and a son, Howard *Douglas, who subsequently inherited the title as third baronet, and became inspector of artillery. Major-General Sir Howard Douglas was the chief advocate for his father's claims at the battle of the Saints, and served a term as governor of New Brunswick. His third marriage was to Jane Baillie. Douglas died suddenly of apoplexy in early February 1789 as he was about to take up his command in North America.

NICHOLAS TRACY

Sources DNB · W. A. B. Douglas, 'Douglas, Sir Charles', *DCB*, vol. 4 · B. Tunstall, *Naval warfare in the age of sail: the evolution of fighting tactics, 1650–1815*, ed. N. Tracy (1990) · B. Tunstall, *Flights of naval genius* (1930) · D. Spinrieg, *Rodney* (1969) · D. Syrett and R. L. DiNardo, *The commissioned sea officers of the Royal Navy, 1660–1815*, rev. edn, Occasional Publications of the Navy RS, 1 (1994) · PRO, ADM 1/481, fol. 467
Archives NA Canada, corresp. and papers, MG 24A3; 18L4 pkt20 · NMM, corresp. and papers · PRO, ADM 1/481, fol. 467; 1/482, fols. 413, 429–435, 441; 1/487; 1/491; 1/1704; 1/1706; 1/1709 | NMM, letters to Sir Charles Middleton · NMM, letters to Lord Sandwich

Douglas, Sir Charles Whittingham Horsley (1850–1914), army officer, was born on 17 July 1850 at the Cape of Good Hope, the second son of William Douglas of Lansdown House, near Bath, and his second wife, Caroline, daughter of Captain Joseph Hare. Educated privately, he was commissioned (by purchase) into the 92nd highlanders in December 1869; he was made lieutenant (by purchase) in October 1871. He was adjutant of the 2nd Gordon Highlanders from 1881 to 1884, and first saw active service in the Second Anglo-Afghan War (1878–80), where he took part in Sir Frederick Sleigh (later Earl) Roberts's famous march from Kabul to Kandahar. After the action at Kandahar (1 September 1880), in which he had a horse shot from under him, Douglas was mentioned in dispatches. Promoted captain in July 1880 and brevet major in March 1881, he served with the Gordon Highlanders in the First South African War (1880–81). Although he did not take part in the battle of Majuba Hill (27 February 1881) he wrote a detailed account of it from survivors' recollections, criticizing Major-General Sir George Pomeroy Colley and his staff, praising the Boers' marksmanship and skirmishing, and admitting that some of the British 'should have behaved better' (Douglas to Lieutenant-Colonel George White, 5 April 1881, BL OIOC, Sir George White MSS). In 1884 he was given a staff appointment (deputy assistant adjutant and quartermaster-general) for the Suakin expedition, where he was again mentioned in dispatches. In May 1885 he was promoted major, and in 1893 was appointed brigade major to the 1st infantry brigade. In 1895 he became lieutenant-colonel on appointment as deputy assistant adjutant-general, Aldershot. In 1898 he was promoted assistant adjutant-general, Aldershot, with the brevet rank of colonel, and later that year was appointed aide-de-camp to Queen Victoria and made full colonel. In the Second South African War (1899–1902) he served initially as an assistant adjutant-general on the headquarters staff of Sir Redvers Buller's field force, before serving as chief staff officer to Lord Methuen and later commanding the 9th brigade and, finally, in 1900, a column of all arms in the South Africa field force. He was mentioned in dispatches twice, and was promoted major-general for distinguished service in the field.

In 1901 Douglas was given command of the 1st infantry brigade at Aldershot, and, in 1902, of the 2nd division of the First Army corps. From 1904 to 1909 he was adjutant-general at the War Office and second military member on the first Army Council under the reforms introduced by Lord Esher's committee after the Second South African War. He advocated, without success, the restoration of corporal punishment in the army, and took part in protracted arguments with H. O. Arnold-Forster, the secretary of state for war, over the latter's opposition to the adoption of an 18½-pounder field gun and his wish to introduce simultaneous recruiting for long and short service enlistments. As adjutant-general, Douglas strongly opposed the creation of a separate list of officers for the general staff, coupled with accelerated promotion opportunities for the newly proposed general staff, and also participated in the planning to reduce the volunteers. However, he subsequently tried to dissociate himself from a highly contentious circular (issued 20 June 1905, requesting reports from general officers commanding on volunteer units that might be disbanded or amalgamated for inefficiency or lack of numbers) that he had approved which was sent to volunteer commanding officers; on account of the 'considerable opposition' provoked by the circular, he argued that the policy of reduction had to be abandoned (Douglas to Arnold-Forster, 26 Sept 1905, BL, Arnold-Forster MSS). After the Liberals' triumph in the 1906 general election, Douglas found the incoming secretary of state for war, R. B. Haldane, much more congenial and he loyally assisted him with his reforms, particularly in the conversion of the militia infantry into a special reserve for the regular army.

In 1909 Douglas was made general officer commanding-in-chief, southern command. Having been promoted lieutenant-general in 1905, he was made a full general in 1910. Created KCB in 1907, he was promoted GCB in 1911, and appointed colonel of the Gordon Highlanders in June 1912. Also in 1912 he was appointed inspector-general, home forces, and proved so conscientious that his staff tours were regarded as models of their kind. He had married Ida de Courcy, daughter of George Tomline Gordon JP, of Cuckney, Nottinghamshire, on 9 August 1887; they had no children, and she survived her husband.

Naturally shy and reserved, Douglas gave the impression of being 'a hard man' (Macready, 135) who could be abrupt and overbearing to subordinates. Yet he had a 'unique knowledge of the details of all army matters' (Robertson, 195), and so his appointment as chief of the Imperial General Staff after Sir John French's resignation in 1914 was widely acclaimed. When Lord Kitchener was appointed secretary of state for war on the outbreak of the First World War he concentrated authority in his own hands, and the Army Council and general staff were allowed to drift into abeyance. Douglas rendered him considerable assistance as Kitchener knew little about the administration of the home army. Douglas found Kitchener difficult to serve, but worked indefatigably under him; indeed, the combination of stress and long hours on duty may have contributed, after a few days' illness, to his death (certified as from renal colic, bronchitis, and pulmonary congestion) at his home, 68 Eaton Square, Belgravia, London, on 25 October 1914. EDWARD M. SPIERS

Sources BL, H. O. Arnold-Forster MSS · Army Council minutes and memoranda, PRO · I. Beckett and J. Gooch, eds., *Politicians and defence: studies in the formulation of British defence policy, 1845–1970* (1981) · J. Gooch, *The plans of war: the general staff and British military strategy, c.1900–1916* (1974) · E. M. Spiers, *Haldane: an army reformer* (1980) · W. Robertson, *From private to field-marshal* (1921) · I. F. W. Beckett, ed., *The army and the Curragh incident, 1914* (1986) · *Journals and letters of Reginald, Viscount Esher*, ed. Oliver, Viscount Esher, 3 (1938) · N. Macready, *Annals of an active life*, 2 vols. [1924] · *Aldershot News* (10 Aug 1901) · *The Times* (26 Oct 1914) · *Debrett's Peerage* (1912) · *WWW* · *Hart's Army List* (1891) · Burke, *Peerage* (1914) · *DNB* · BL OIOC, Sir George White MSS

Archives PRO, army council minutes and memoranda, WO 163/9; 163/11 | BL, H. O. Arnold-Forster MSS, Add. MSS 50312, 50342, 50349, 50351, 50350, 50352 · BL, A. J. Balfour MSS, Add. MSS 49723 · BL OIOC, Sir George White MSS, Eur. F 108/91
Likenesses photograph, repro. in *Aldershot News*
Wealth at death £12,828 9s. 0d.: probate, 27 Nov 1914, *CGPLA Eng. & Wales*

Douglas, Claude Gordon (1882–1963), physiologist, was born in Leicester on 26 February 1882, the second son of Claude Douglas, honorary surgeon to Leicester Royal Infirmary, and his wife, Louisa Bolitho Peregrine, of London. His elder brother, J. S. C. Douglas, was professor of pathology at Sheffield University, and his cousin, J. A. Douglas, was professor of geology at Oxford. He was a scholar at Wellington College, but moved to Wyggeston grammar school, Leicester, to study science. In 1900 he went up to Oxford, where he was a demy of Magdalen College. In 1904 he obtained first-class honours in natural science (animal physiology), after which he stayed on in the physiological laboratory, working for the research degree of BSc under the supervision of J. S. Haldane. In 1905 Douglas took up a London University scholarship at Guy's Hospital and completed his medical degree of BM, BCh (Oxon.) in December 1907. Six months earlier he had been elected to a fellowship and lectureship in natural science at St John's College, Oxford, a position he held for forty-two years. He became DM in 1913.

Douglas's scientific career falls into three parts: the first, his collaborative work up to 1914 with J. S. Haldane on human breathing; the second, his work during the First World War on physiological aspects of gas warfare; and the third, back in Oxford, after Haldane's departure from the physiological laboratory, on general human metabolism, successively as university demonstrator (1927), reader (1937), and titular professor (1942), and, after he had passed the retiring age, as departmental demonstrator up to 1953.

It was Douglas's good fortune to join the physiological laboratory when work on the regulation of body oxygen and carbon dioxide concentrations, and exchange of these gases through the lungs, was still developing. He quickly became the best-known and the most permanent of the younger colleagues of Haldane, whose work since the turn of the twentieth century had transformed the subject of respiration. Douglas's name appears on some ten of the most important papers over this period, which show an insight into the principles of control physiology three or four decades ahead of their time. Douglas and Haldane provided a quantitative description of the transport of carbon dioxide by the blood between cells and lungs, and the facilitatory effect on it of oxygen transport in the opposite direction. This work complemented the earlier work of Christian Bohr, K. A. Hasselbalch, and S. A. S. Krogh, of Copenhagen, who had shown the facilitatory effects of carbon dioxide on oxygen transport. Work of this kind allowed Douglas and Haldane to develop a practical and bloodless method for measuring the rate of pumping of blood by the human heart under various conditions.

Detailed and meticulous measurement allowed Douglas and J. S. Haldane (with some mathematical assistance from J. B. S. Haldane) to elucidate the equilibria between the oxygen-carrying substance haemoglobin and the concentrations of oxygen and carbon monoxide. They went on to show that certain conditions, notably residence at high altitude, altered the equilibria. Ingenious reasoning led them to conclude from this observation that oxygen could be transported against the concentration gradient across the lung capillary membranes (oxygen secretion). The question was open at the time, and the resulting controversy between them and their friends Krogh and Joseph Barcroft, of Cambridge, was one of the entertainments of early twentieth-century physiology. Subsequent developments decided the controversy against Oxford, but the basic observation remained unexplained.

During this period Douglas began to measure the rate of uptake of oxygen and of the output of carbon dioxide by collecting expired air in a large canvas gasbag. The Douglas bag became well known for its convenience for measuring energy expenditure in people in various occupations.

Douglas served in the Royal Army Medical Corps in the First World War, reaching the rank of lieutenant-colonel. When gas warfare started in 1915, he was the serving officer in France with the detailed knowledge and deep understanding of respiratory physiology that allowed interpretation of the effects of the alarming new weapon. He held several appointments in the British expeditionary force related to gas warfare before being appointed physiological adviser in 1917 to the Directorate of Gas Services, where he worked with Harold Hartley. He was awarded the MC in 1916, was four times mentioned in dispatches, and was appointed CMG in 1919. He contributed extensively to the official history of the war, and Hartley felt that his chapter dealing with the development of gas warfare was by far the best summary of the use of the new weapon.

After the war Douglas returned to Oxford, where he collaborated with J. G. Priestley in setting up and running a novel and thorough practical course in human physiology. The course was taken by all Oxford medical undergraduates over a period of some thirty years.

After J. S. Haldane left the physiological laboratory, Douglas's interests moved towards the assessment of metabolic processes in humans in the light of the new insights provided by the rapid expansion of biochemistry. With a succession of research students, including F. C. Courtice, he applied the new knowledge to the interpretation of quantitative measurements. His conclusions put him in the vanguard of those who questioned the fashionable, though erroneous, view that carbohydrate was the sole source of energy for muscular contraction. Between the wars the departure of Haldane and the scanty material support received by his branch of physiology rendered difficult any achievement in his field of interest; the Oxford laboratory was more concerned with the exciting advances in neurophysiology of the school of C. S. Sherrington.

During the Second World War Douglas remained in Oxford, teaching and helping with administration in college and the laboratory. After the war and before his final retirement in 1953 he supervised the work of three more research students, including Roger Bannister.

From 1920 onwards Douglas was increasingly involved in government committee work, some of which he took over from J. S. Haldane, on such topics as chemical warfare, muscular activity in industry, health and safety in mines, conditions in hot and deep mines, research on pneumoconiosis, breathing apparatus for the National Fire Service, the Gas Research Council, heating and ventilation of buildings, and diet and energy requirements. As a chairman or member, Douglas prepared his papers meticulously, listened carefully, but spoke comparatively seldom.

Douglas was a devoted senior member of St John's College, which was his home for twenty-eight years. He was a formidable walker, and a keen and very knowledgeable gardener and photographer. He was an excellent host in college and at home. Douglas was unmarried and lived with his younger sister, Margaret Douglas, for twenty-four years.

In 1911 Douglas won the Radcliffe prize; in 1922 he was elected FRS and was on the council of the Royal Society (1928–30). He was an *ad hominem* professor at a time when Oxford had few such. In 1945 he was awarded the Osler memorial medal, and in 1950 he was elected to an honorary fellowship of St John's.

Douglas's early and best-known joint work in academic physiology probably stemmed in large part from Haldane's genius. However, his extraordinarily high standards of accuracy, his energy, his rare common sense and general competence must have contributed greatly to the joint achievement. His capacity as an independent scientist was obvious to his younger colleagues and to readers of his writings on chemical warfare.

Douglas died in the Radcliffe Infirmary on 23 March 1963 after a street accident in Oxford.

D. J. C. CUNNINGHAM, *rev.*

Sources D. J. C. Cunningham, *Memoirs FRS*, 10 (1964), 51–74 · personal knowledge (1981) · *CGPLA Eng. & Wales* (1963)
Archives U. Oxf., History of Neuroscience Library, corresp. and papers | CAC Cam., corresp. with A. V. Hill
Likenesses A. Pán, oils, 1950–51, St John's College, Oxford
Wealth at death £77,147 12s. 0d.: probate, 6 June 1963, *CGPLA Eng. & Wales*

Douglas, Clifford Hugh (1879–1952), economic theorist, was born in Stockport, Cheshire, on 20 January 1879, the youngest son of Hugh Douglas, draper, and his wife, Louisa Arderne Hordern. Douglas was a complex and intensely secretive character, and little is known of his life. What biographical information he did release tended to magnify his importance, creating a public image that in some respects differed significantly from the reality. Having been educated at Stockport grammar school, he entered on an engineering and mechanical career, and was a member of the Institution of Electrical Engineers (1904–20) and of the Institute of Mechanical Engineers

(1918–36). It is possible that his employment took him for a time to India, where he claimed to have been chief engineer and manager of the British Westinghouse Company, although the company has no record of his having worked for the firm. In 1910, at the late age of thirty-one, he went up to Pembroke College, Cambridge. In later life he was keen to give the impression of having been educated there in the fullest sense, when in fact he spent four terms only and left without taking a degree. During the First World War he was taken on at the Royal Aircraft Establishment in Farnborough, where he reorganized production and cost accounting. He was promoted to temporary captain in the Royal Flying Corps on 1 January 1916, and soon afterwards to temporary major on 1 June 1916.

Douglas had already been reflecting on society's failure to exploit the full possibilities of modern technology; his work at Farnborough suggested an explanation of this, which in turn led to the theory of social credit. In every productive establishment the amount of money issued in a given period as wages, salaries, and dividends—which he took to be the amount available to purchase the goods produced in that period—was less than the collective price of those products. To remedy the supposed chronic deficiency of purchasing power he advocated issuing additional money to consumers, or subsidies to producers to enable them to set prices below costs. By these devices, which came to be known as social credit, production was to be liberated from the price system, inaugurating an era of plenty, freedom, leisure, and human dignity, without altering the system of private ownership, profit, and enterprise.

Convinced that his analysis was the sole key to understanding and remedying the world's ills, Douglas devoted himself to developing its implications and pressing its claims. His critique of the economic system first appeared in articles in *The Organiser* in 1917, and later in the *English Review* (December 1918 – October 1919). In the meantime he was introduced to the journalist A. R. Orage, editor of the intellectual weekly *New Age*, which offered another platform for his views. In time the journal became completely devoted to advancing social credit theory. Orage's own critique of society had anticipated Douglas's, and he became an enthusiastic convert to Douglas's economic theory, publishing Douglas's first book, *Economic Democracy* (1920), serially in the *New Age* (June–August 1919) and collaborating in his second, *Credit-Power and Democracy* (1920). Douglas's utopian vision of society rejected conventional politics, whether of the right or the left, as a means of change: 'There is no hope whatever in the hustings; but a modified credit-system could transform the world in five years' (Douglas, *Credit-Power*, 86). In 1921 and 1922 these ideas attracted considerable public attention but were opposed by socialist writers and the Labour Party, which formally rejected social credit doctrine in 1922. In 1923 Douglas was brought to Ottawa by some Canadian admirers to expound his views to the Canadian House of Commons committee on banking and commerce.

Public discussion of social credit declined in Britain after 1922, but with the depression of the thirties it revived in greater volume, supported now by the *New Age*, the *New English Weekly*, Douglas's own weekly *Social Credit*, and various pamphlets and books, some of which went through several editions. 'What gave the Douglas movement its persistent strength, even after the complete fallacy of the social credit monetary theory had been repeatedly demonstrated, was its cutting denunciation of existing society and its epochal vision of a new society' (Macpherson, 96). Douglas testified to the Macmillan committee on finance and industry (1930) and lectured as far afield as New Zealand and Canada in 1934.

By the late thirties the British social credit movement under Douglas's rather autocratic leadership had dwindled into an esoteric sect. But it had struck roots in western Canada, where Douglas had had a following from the early twenties. When he visited Alberta in 1934 he won such wide support that the ageing United Farmers government, in spite of being sceptical about social credit, appointed him (early in 1935) principal reconstruction adviser to the government of Alberta, with a two-year contract. However, the government was swept out of office by the more zealous Social Credit League in the elections of August 1935. Relations between Douglas and the new government soon became strained. He resigned as adviser in 1936, and published his account of the matter in *The Alberta Experiment* (1937). In this lengthy work of self-justification Douglas did not conceal his contempt for the Alberta legislators: it was they who had failed the theory of social credit, and not the reverse. At the same time his writing showed deep compassion for the poor and a refusal to accept that in a land 'fertile, rich, and reasonably developed', such as Alberta, there should ever exist 'desperate poverty at the lower end of the social scale, and economic and political insecurity amongst all classes not in actual want' (Douglas, *Alberta*, 90). A back-benchers' revolt in the province in 1937 compelled the government to ask Douglas's further help. He sent two of his staff, who prepared legislation which, when enacted, was invalidated by federal authorities. The provincial government remained social credit in name but virtually abandoned Douglas's principles.

Douglas's earlier writings were remarkable for their reasoned protest against the frustration of individuality by business civilization. But his economic theory never surmounted his initial fallacy of reasoning from one firm to the whole economy. And his social and political theory was vitiated by his engineering concepts. He saw social credit 'as an engineering solution to an engineering problem', and naïvely believed that he had only to identify the solution for the necessary change to be effected (Macpherson, 121). The failure of the political and financial establishments to take up his ideas in Britain forced him to seek public support, but when this too failed to realize his vision he was forced into increasing isolation. Ultimately he could explain this failure only in terms of a 'world plot' that aimed to undermine Christian civilization. He was driven to attribute the thwarting of technology, and hence of human freedom, to a conspiracy of world Jewry, freemasonry, international finance, Bolshevism, and Nazism, and finally to denigrate democracy and denounce the secret ballot. 'He died a lonely and embittered man, cut off even from the main body of his own supporters' (Finlay, 88).

Douglas was married twice: first to Constance Mary, daughter of Edward Phillips, of Royston House, Hertfordshire. His second wife was Edith Mary, daughter of George Desborough Dale, of the Indian Civil Service; they had one daughter. He was a fisherman and yachtsman, and for a time ran a yacht-building shipyard at Swanwick, Southampton. He died in Dundee on 29 September 1952; his second wife survived him.

C. B. MACPHERSON, rev. MARK POTTLE

Sources C. B. Macpherson, *Democracy in Alberta* (1953) · C. H. Douglas, *The Alberta experiment: an interim survey* (1937) · C. H. Douglas, *Credit-power and democracy, with a draft scheme for the mining industry* (1920) · J. L. Finlay, *Social credit: the English origins* (1972) · W. van Trier, 'Every one a king: an investigation into the meaning and significance of the debate on basic incomes with special reference to three episodes from the British inter-war experience', PhD diss., University of Louvain, 1995 · *The Times* (1 Oct 1952) · J. Eatwell, M. Milgate, and P. Newman, eds., *The new Palgrave: a dictionary of economics*, new edn, 4 vols. (1998) · *CGPLA Eng. & Wales* (1953) · A. Clooney, *Clifford Hugh Douglas* (1997) · F. Hutchinson and B. Burkitt, *The political economy of social credit and guild socialism* (1997)
Archives CAC Cam., corresp. with R. G. Hawtrey
Likenesses A. John, oils, exh. RA 1934
Wealth at death £12,996 11s.: probate, 13 April 1953, *CGPLA Eng. & Wales*

Douglas, David (1799–1834), plant collector and traveller, was born on 25 June 1799 at Scone, Perthshire, one of six children of John Douglas, a stonemason, and his wife, Jean, *née* Drummond. Quick to learn but often truant from school owing to his passion for natural history, he was apprenticed at the age of ten in the gardens of the earl of Mansfield at Scone. In 1818 he became under-gardener to Sir Robert Preston at Valleyfield, near Culross in Perthshire, whence, about 1820, he moved to the botanical garden at Glasgow. There he attended the botanical lectures of W. J. Hooker, whom he accompanied on several excursions to the highlands. According to Hooker, Douglas's 'great activity, undaunted courage, singular abstemiousness, and energetic zeal, at once pointed him out as an individual eminently calculated to do himself credit as a scientific traveller' (Hooker, 87). These qualities led Hooker to recommend Douglas as a plant collector to Joseph Sabine, secretary to the Horticultural Society of London.

In 1823 the society sent Douglas to America, where he spent four months collecting in the eastern parts of the United States and Canada. Soon after his return to London Douglas was commissioned again by the society, this time for a more ambitious journey to the Columbia River in America's Pacific north-west. After arriving at Fort Vancouver in April 1825 he spent two years combing the mountainous regions of the north-west in pursuit of new species of plants, birds, and mammals. He endured continual hardship from exposure, fatigue, lack of food, and native hostility. In March 1827 he left for England by an overland route, bearing a profusion of live plants

unknown in the gardens of Europe. The botanical world was astonished by the wealth of Douglas's collection, and received him with great enthusiasm. This pleased him at first, but at length the lionization caused revulsion and irritability, 'so that his best friends could not but wish, as he himself did, that he were again occupied in the honourable task of exploring North-west America' (Hooker, 142). John Murray offered to publish his travel journals, but they did not finally appear in print until 1914.

In 1829 Douglas embarked once again for north-west America, this time travelling via Cape Horn and the Sandwich Islands. He reached the mouth of the Columbia River in June 1830, and spent the summer and autumn making journeys into the interior. In December he took ship for Monterey in California where he stayed nineteen months collecting along the Spanish mission trail before returning to the Columbia. In October 1833 he sailed to the Sandwich Islands where, in Laupahoehoe Forest near Mauna Kea on the island of Hawaii on 12 July 1834, he met his death when he fell into a pit trap and was gored by a wild bull. He was buried at Kawaiahao church cemetery, Honolulu, on 4 August.

Douglas's introductions to the horticultural world number over 200, including the famous Douglas fir (*Pseudotsuga taxifolia*) and the sugar pine (*Pinus lambertiana*). The Royal Society's catalogue credits him with fourteen papers. He was described by his fellow traveller, F. McDonald, as 'a sturdy little Scot, handsome rather, with a head and face of a fine Grecian mould; of winning address, and withal the most pious of men' (Coats, 310). His death at the age of only thirty-five cut short what was certain to have been a great career in plant collecting.

CHERYL PIGGOTT

Sources W. J. Hooker, 'Brief memoir of the life of Mr David Douglas, with extracts from his letters', *Companion to the Botanical Magazine*, 2 (1836), 79–182 · A. G. Harvey, *Douglas of the fir* (1947) · Desmond, *Botanists*, rev. edn · *Journal kept by David Douglas during his travels in North America, 1823–1827* (1914) · W. F. Wilson, *David Douglas, botanist at Hawaii* (1919) · A. M. Coats, *Quest for plants* (1969), 304–14 · S. D. McKelvey, *Botanical exploration of the trans-Mississippi west, 1790–1850* (1955, [1956]) · F. A. Stafleu and R. S. Cowan, *Taxonomic literature: a selective guide*, 2nd edn, 1, Regnum Vegetabile, 94 (1976), 674–5 · D. Douglas, letters, RBG Kew, directors' correspondence · *Catalogue of scientific papers*, Royal Society, 2 (1867), 327
Archives Lindley Herbarium, Cambridge · Linn. Soc. · NHM · RBG Kew · Royal Horticultural Society, London, journals, letters, and papers
Likenesses D. Macnee, crayon, 1828, RBG Kew · Atkinson, pencil, 1829, Royal British Columbia Museum, Vancouver · charcoal, Linn. Soc. · engraving (after Macnee), repro. in *Companion to the Botanical Magazine* (1836–7), frontispiece · lithograph (after Atkinson), repro. in *Gardeners' Chronicle* (1885/1915) · lithograph, BM

Douglas, Evelyn. See Barlas, John Evelyn (1860–1914).

Douglas, Frances, Lady Douglas (1750–1817), friend of Sir Walter Scott and Lady Louisa Stuart, was born on 26 July 1750, the sixth and posthumous child of Francis Scott, earl of Dalkeith (1721–1750), eldest son of the duke of Buccleuch, and Lady Caroline Campbell (1717–1794) [see Townshend, Caroline, *suo jure* Baroness Greenwich], eldest daughter of John Campbell, duke of Argyll. She was brought up in the family's residence at Grosvenor Square,

Frances Douglas,
Lady Douglas
(1750–1817), by
unknown artist

London, where she experienced a difficult childhood: her mother showed her little affection and was, according to her aunt, the redoubtable Lady Mary Coke, 'insensible to her merits' (*Letters and Journals*, vol. 1). The saving grace of her early years was her mother's second marriage in 1755 to the mercurial politician Charles Townshend (1725–1767). Recognizing her many qualities, he was the most important influence on her early education and development. Alexander Carlyle, minister at Inveresk, later a great friend and correspondent, met her at Dalkeith in 1767 and noted her good taste, knowledge of *belles-lettres*, and ready wit. He also saw how the stepfather, her 'enlightened instructor', protected her from the tyranny of her mother (*Autobiography*, ed. Burton, 515). The growing intimacy between Townshend and the highly strung adolescent could have developed into something more dangerous had not Lady Frances used the occasion of her brother's marriage in 1767 to escape to Scotland. Townshend's death some months later removed her protector, but Lady Frances blossomed in the literary society at Dalkeith Palace. In 1779 the death of her aunt Lady Jane Scott afforded her financial independence as well as a house at Petersham, Surrey.

In 1782 Lady Frances visited Dublin with her brother as the guests of Lady Carlow, sister of Lady Louisa Stuart, but also to sort out the finances of her stepsister Anne Townshend, who had married disastrously. For someone who in her youth had claimed to prefer the armchair to society, her stay in Ireland was the making of her. In a series of lively letters to her sister-in-law, the duchess of Buccleuch, she describes herself as 'recherchée and fetée', a success Lady Carlow ascribed to her having been so much 'mortified and neglected at home' (Stuart, *Gleanings*, 1.185). She stayed on to introduce her friend Lady Portland, the wife of the new lord lieutenant, into society, returning to England via Wales, where she visited the ladies of Llangollen, later petitioning successfully for royal pensions for Sarah Ponsonby. Her Irish letters, subsequently annotated by Lady Louisa, her literary executor, were, following the conventions of her circle, never published. Like the verse journals of her tour in Scotland in

1780, and of another to the Lake District in 1781 (written at the request of Queen Charlotte), they were copied or circulated among friends and family, and greatly admired.

On 13 May 1783 Lady Frances married Archibald James Edward *Douglas, first Baron Douglas of Douglas (1748–1827), at her brother's London residence in Grosvenor Square. The marriage to a 'safe … and comfortable man' seems to have been, if not a love match, one of convenience and mutual affection. Douglas's first marriage to her friend Lady Lucy Graham, who died in 1780, had produced four children. Lady Lucy's attachment to her friend and Lady Frances's affection for her children played no small part in the union, which was itself to produce a further eight offspring. She parodied her role as 'wicked stepmother' in a prose and verse version of Cinderella written in 1801. At Bothwell Castle with its ruined medieval castle and 'romantick solitudes' she created an 'air of ease, comfort and gaiety' (Stuart, *Memoire*, 96), where the Douglases welcomed authors and poets, including Mary Berry and M. G. Lewis, and the French émigré aristocracy. It was there, in 1799, that she introduced Sir Walter Scott to her great friend and confidante Lady Louisa Stuart, who became one of his most valued critics and one of the few to share the secret of the authorship of his novels. Through their auspices Scott also met the classical scholar J. B. S. Morritt of Rokeby. She and Lady Louisa had formed a close bond through their family connections, and a shared passion for poetry and literature. Lady Douglas's early life is related in Lady Louisa's frank *Memoire of Frances, Lady Douglas*, written some years after her death for her daughter the novelist Lady Caroline *Scott. There she encapsulated the character of this charming woman whom Jane, duchess of Gordon, described as 'a most uncommon sort of young lady' (NA Scot., GD1/479/15/2). Lady Louisa asked Sir Walter Scott to memorialize Frances Douglas in one of his novels, and believed he had done so in the character of Jeanie Deans in *The Heart of Midlothian* (1818).

Lady Douglas was small and undistinguished in appearance—even the favourably inclined Carlyle described her as 'far from handsome'—but surviving portraits of her scarcely seem to justify Sir Walter Scott's description of her as 'quite the ugly old woman of a fairy tale', though, he adds, 'still [with] the *air d'une grande dame*'. Although she characterized herself as a 'weak, unsteady creature', her strength and generosity of mind, modesty, loyalty, and wit nevertheless made her greatly admired; her only fault, mentioned by all, was her laziness. Lady Douglas was prone to nervous exhaustion; her many pregnancies took their toll on her health, and in middle age she lost the sight of one eye. But her sudden death in May 1817 at Bothwell Castle, Lanarkshire, came as a shock to her friends and family. She was buried in the Douglas aisle in Douglas parish church, Lanarkshire.   ALISON ROSIE

Sources Lady Stuart [L. Stuart], *Memoire of Frances, Lady Douglas*, ed. J. Rubenstein (1985) · Lady Stuart [L. Stuart], *Gleanings from an old portfolio*, ed. G. Clark, 3 vols. (1895–8) · *The letters of Lady Louisa Stuart*, ed. R. B. Johnson (1926) · *Letters of Lady Louisa Stuart to Miss Louisa Clinton*, ed. J. Home, 2 vols. (1901–3) · *Selections from the manuscripts of*

Lady Louisa Stuart, ed. J. A. Home (1899) • NRA, priv. coll., earl of Home MSS • *The autobiography of Dr Alexander Carlyle of Inveresk, 1722–1805*, ed. J. H. Burton (1910); facs. edn with introduction by R. B. Sher (1990) • *The letters and journals of Lady Mary Coke*, ed. J. A. Home, 4 vols. (1889–96) • *The letters of Sir Walter Scott*, ed. H. J. C. Grierson and others, centenary edn, 12 vols. (1932–79) • NA Scot., Abercairney muniments, GD 24/5/105–6, 111–12 • NA Scot., Drummond Forbes MSS, GD1/479 • F. MacCunn, *Sir Walter Scott's friends* (1909)

Archives NA Scot., Abercrombie muniment • earl of Home MSS **Likenesses** J. Reynolds, oils, *c*.1760 (of Frances Douglas?), NG Scot. • F. Ferrière, miniature, oils, *c*.1794, repro. in Stuart, *Memoire of Frances, Lady Douglas* • F. Coates, portrait, priv. coll. • J. Reynolds, group portrait, oils (with her brothers Henry and Campbell), priv. coll. • miniature, priv. coll. [*see illus.*]

Douglas, Francis (*bap.* **1719**, *d. c.***1790**), writer, was baptized on 6 February 1719 in the parish of Logie Coldstone, near Aberdeen, the third son of Robert Douglas of Blackmiln. He was apprenticed to a baker in Aberdeen and after the completion of his training in the late 1730s he went to London to practise his trade. During this time he wrote *Rural Love, a Tale in the Scotish Dialect* that he printed in Aberdeen in 1759. From 1743 he was back in Aberdeen and became a baker in the Netherkirkgate. From 1744 to 1747 he was a juror for the fixing of the fiars' prices. He married Elizabeth Ochterloney of Pitforthey on 22 April 1745 in the church of St Nicholas in Aberdeen. They had seven children: Robert (*b*. 1746), Mary (*b*. 1747), Elizabeth (*b*. 1748), Mary (*b*. 1750), Ann (*b*. 1754), Bathia (*b*. 1756), and Margaret (*b*. 1759). The family became Episcopalian in the late 1740s and joined St Paul's in Aberdeen.

In 1748 Douglas started book selling and advertised that 'catalogues … may be had at his house in the Nether Kirkgate' (*Aberdeen Journal*, 31 May 1748). Two years later he had now 'taken himself entirely to the trade' (ibid., 8 May 1750). He was importing new and second-hand books from London as well as selling maps, prints, and stationery. With William Murray, a druggist, he set up a printing house and published books and a weekly Jacobite newspaper called the *Aberdeen Intelligencer*, in opposition to the *Aberdeen Journal*. The *Intelligencer* existed from 1752 to 1757. In 1755 Douglas published the first of his own works, *The History of the Rebellion in 1745 and 1746*, extracted from the *Scots Magazine*. Murray would appear to have withdrawn from an unprofitable partnership in 1757. Douglas continued until at least 1768, and published more of his own works, *A Pastoral Elegy to the Memory of Miss Mary Urquhart* (1758) and *Life of James Crichton of Clunie, Commonly Called the Admirable Crichton* (1760).

In the early 1760s Douglas moved to a farm near Drumoak belonging to Mr Irvine of Drum. Here he was moderately successful and in 1763 won a £10 prize for planting the most trees (*Aberdeen Journal*, 1 Aug 1763), although Chalmers writes that his mutton was of such poor quality and so badly butchered that it never sold (*N&Q*, 1861, 222–3). When the Douglas peerage case came before the House of Lords, he advocated in the *Scots Magazine* the claim of the successful litigant, Archibald, son of Lady Jane Douglas. A pamphlet by him entitled *Observations on the Douglas Cause* (1768) was printed by James Chalmers and published

by Dilly, neither of whom was aware that they had committed a breach of privilege. The House of Lords ordered them to be carried to London, but Dilly induced Lord Lyttelton and some other peers to interfere, and the printer and publisher were excused on account of ignorance. When Archibald Douglas succeeded to the estate of his uncle the duke, Francis Douglas was gifted with the liferent of Abbotsinch, a farm near Paisley, for his services. He continued to write and publish such works as *Reflections on Celibacy and Marriage* (1771), *Familiar letters, on a variety of important and interesting subjects, from Lady Harriet Morley and others* (1773), *The Birthday; with a Few Strictures on the Times; a Poem in Three Cantos* (1782), and his most reprinted book, *A General Description of the East Coast of Scotland from Edinburgh to Cullen* (1782).

Douglas died at Abbotsinch about 1790 and was buried in the churchyard of Paisley Abbey. He was survived by two married daughters living in the Paisley area.

THOMPSON COOPER, *rev.* H. LESLEY DIACK

Sources G. M. Fraser, 'Francis Douglas, a notable Aberdeen printer …', *Aberdeen Book-Lover*, 2/1 (May 1916), 2–9 • W. R. McDonald, 'The *Aberdeen Journal* and the *Aberdeen Intelligencer*, 1752–7', *The Bibliotheck*, 5 (1967–70), 204–6 • *Aberdeen Journal* (1747–70) • W. R. McDonald, 'Some aspects of printing and the book trade in Aberdeen', *The hero as printer*, ed. C. A. McLaren (1976) • D. W. Nichol, 'Aberdeen imprints and the ESTC …', *Aberdeen and the Enlightenment*, ed. J. J. Carter and J. H. Pittock (1987), 309–15 • I. Beavan, 'Bibliography of the Enlightenment: … notes on the Aberdeen booktrade', *Aberdeen and the Enlightenment*, ed. J. J. Carter and J. H. Pittock (1987), 316–22 • I. Beavan, 'The nineteenth-century book trade in Aberdeen', PhD diss., Robert Gordon University, 1992 • *N&Q*, 2nd ser., 12 (1861), 222–3 [letter from James Chalmers to his brother dated 11 April 1805] • parish register, Logie Coldstone, 6 Feb 1719 [baptism] • parish register, St Nicholas, Aberdeen, 22 April 1745 [marriage]

Douglas, Francis Wemyss-Charteris-, eighth earl of Wemyss and sixth earl of March (1818–1914), politician, the eldest son of Francis Wemyss-Charteris-Douglas, seventh earl of Wemyss and fifth earl of March (1795–1883), and his wife, Lady Louisa Bingham (1798–1882), third daughter of Richard, second earl of Lucan (of Balaklava fame), was born in Edinburgh on 4 August 1818. He was educated at Edinburgh Academy, at Eton College, and at Christ Church, Oxford, where John Ruskin was his contemporary; he graduated BA in 1841. The eighth earl was tall and lean with a hawk-like visage and Dundreary whiskers. Although 56,739 acres of the Wemyss estates were in East Lothian, over 4000 acres were in Gloucestershire and as a result in 1841 he entered parliament to represent East Gloucestershire as a tory protectionist. His conversion to the repeal of the corn laws forced his resignation in January 1846. The next year he was elected as MP for East Lothian, a seat he held until he was called to the House of Lords on the death of his father in 1883. In 1843 he married Lady Anne Frederica Anson (*d*. 1896), second daughter of Thomas William Anson, first earl of Lichfield (1795–1854), and his wife, Louisa Catherine (*d*. 1879); they had six sons and three daughters.

Wemyss enjoyed early political success. He was made a lord of the Treasury with the formation of the earl of Aberdeen's ministry late in 1852. From his grandfather's death in 1853 he was styled Lord Elcho. He retired with the Peelites in 1855 when Lord Palmerston became prime minister and he did not subsequently hold office. From that time Elcho acted independently, styling himself a Liberal-Conservative. In 1859, though he supported the earl of Derby's Reform Bill, he later opposed the reform proposals of Lord John Russell. On the introduction of the Franchise Bill of 1866 he joined Edward Horseman, Robert Lowe (afterwards first Viscount Sherbrooke), and others in forming the 'cave of Adullam', to oppose giving the vote to the 'ignorant masses' of men. The meetings of the 'cave' took place at Elcho's St James's home; Reform League supporters stoned the windows. Elcho so opposed the opportunism of Gladstone, Bright, and Russell that he later voted for Disraeli's Household Suffrage Bill.

Elcho was a member of the royal commission on trades unions in 1867. He developed a close friendship with Alexander *Macdonald (1821–1881), the moderate president of the National Miners' Association and one of the first two trade unionist MPs (1874–81). By using his political position to pass the Master and Servant Amendment Act of 1867, which made it a civil rather than a criminal offence for an employee to breach a contract, he is viewed as an 'old Liberal, New Model Employer, Whig Aristocrat' who tried up to a point to cope with economic and political change through paternalism. Co-operation between Macdonald and Elcho lasted until the depression of 1873 caused Macdonald to advocate restrictive measures to lower the supply of coal and to raise miners' wages.

Elcho took an active part in the proceedings of the House of Commons. He introduced a Medical Practitioners Bill in 1854 and, in great measure, it was due to his exertions that the act of 1858, which created the General Medical Council, became law. In 1869 he called for government inspection and regulation of fertilizer and animal food and in 1872 he supported increased inspection of mines. At the behest of the Metropolitan Reform Association in 1874, Elcho unsuccessfully introduced a bill to extend the City corporation of London and have the association assume the duties of the City, the Metropolitan Board of Works, and the vestries. It was the reforms of Gladstone's first ministry, 1868–73, and especially the Irish Land Act of 1881 that enraged Elcho, as well as British landlords, publicans, and business interests. These events led him with others on 5 July 1882 to found the Liberty and Property Defence League to fight socialism, trade unionism, and 'promising' politicians; Elcho was the founder, chairman, and a major source of financial support of this organization until he died in 1914. It attracted whigs, ultra-tories, landlords, employers, individualist philosophers, and members of the Personal Rights Association, the last a society that attempted to combat harmful legislation affecting the poor and women's right to work. While the league attempted to win the votes of the blue-collar worker, it had to settle for influencing the middle classes and the rate-payers. The Liberty and Property Defence League included 208 trade or defence associations; it launched a four-pronged counter-attack through the Free Labour Protection Association (FLPA) founded in

July 1897 aimed at defeating the growth of the militant new unionism; the Employers' Parliamentary Council aimed at defeating legislation harmful to business; the co-partnership movement attempted to narrow the gulf between employers and employees by profit sharing plans; and a journal, the Liberty Review, was published monthly from 1888 to 1907. The FLPA was a key weapon in defeating the engineering strike of 1897. Unfortunately for the league and its allies, the FLPA's success in this instance led to the formation of the Labour Representation Committee in 1900 which eventually spawned the Labour Party.

The cause of the 1897 strike, a scenario played out a number of times during the twentieth century, was the debate over the open shop and the definition of intimidation and interpretation of the Conspiracy and Protection of Property Act of 1875. At its core the strike was an attempt by the skilled engineers of the now socialist-led Amalgamated Society of Engineers to frustrate efforts by the Employers' Federation of Engineering Associations to stay competitive by increasing productivity through the introduction of labour-saving devices and methods. The FLPA tactics were based on those used by William Collison's National Free Labour Association established in 1893 to oppose the tyranny of socialistic trade-union leaders by using the courts, the police, the open shop, and free labour. Sir George Livesey of the London Metropolitan Gasworks and Frederick Millar, editor of the league's journal, the Liberty Review, were intermediaries between Collison's National Free Labour Association and the FLPA, which was led by Colonel Dyer, chairman of the Armstrong Works at Elswick, and Alexander Siemens, of the famous engineering firm, who was a charter member of the league. After Dyer's death in 1898 leadership of the Engineering Employers' Federation passed to Benjamin Browne, chairman of Hawthorn Leslie. On 15 November 1898, under the auspices of the league and the FLPA, a meeting attended by a veritable who's who of British industry, and representing over £1000 million of property, formed the Employers' Parliamentary Council. Regional, personal, inter-, and intra-industrial differences proved difficult to overcome and the league also encountered even greater problems given its diverse constituencies. The efforts of Wemyss to build pressure groups and other structures to combat the growth of the state and its attack on liberty and property through 'socialist' legislation were his greatest legacy.

Elevation to the House of Lords in 1883 as Lord Wemyss did not diminish his interest in public affairs. His persistent opposition to the steady growth of state interference brought him into conflict with each administration in its turn. His libertarian beliefs made it difficult for him to support any political party but by 1899—as licensed victuallers, Irish landlords, and employers rapidly lost faith in the Salisbury government—he and other league officials called for the formation of a free bona fide conservative party. His hope that Lord Rosebery would take up the banner of an independent-individualist party came to naught.

Lord Wemyss had many interests outside politics. He was an accomplished sculptor and painter in watercolours. Throughout his career he rendered valuable service to successive administrations with his wise counsel in matters of art and architecture, and his watchfulness over the public buildings of London. In 1856 he was largely instrumental in preventing the removal of the National Gallery to Kensington Gore.

While Wemyss played a significant role in the economic history of the period between Chartism and the First World War, he also played a role in matters of military reform and national service from the Crimean War to the outbreak of the First World War. As a member of the Aberdeen ministry, 1852–5, Elcho became aware of the deficiencies of the army. When the government authorized the formation of a corps of rifle volunteers in May 1859, he threw himself enthusiastically into the movement and was a founder of a London Scottish regiment (originally the 15th Middlesex corps). As lieutenant-colonel of this regiment he was present at the first review in Hyde Park on 23 June 1860 when 19,000 volunteers paraded before Queen Victoria. Elcho relinquished command of the regiment in 1879 and became an aide-de-camp to the queen in 1881. Elcho was also ensign-general of the Royal Society of Archers and he served on the royal commission of 1862, which produced the Volunteer Act of 1863.

In a related area Elcho presided over the meeting that inaugurated the National Rifle Association in 1859; he was first chairman of the association in 1859–67 and again in 1869–70. He presented the association with the Elcho challenge shield for yearly competition by teams representative of England and Scotland, later including Ireland and Wales, and he regularly attended the Wimbledon meetings of the association.

Lord Elcho was a persistent advocate of the militia ballot. He was frankly critical of Edward (afterwards Viscount) Cardwell's military reforms, and in 1871 he printed a series of letters published as *Letters on Military Organization*. In 1907, when he reached his ninetieth year, he vigorously protested in the House of Lords against the reforms of R. B. Haldane. Six years later in a letter to *The Times* (3 June 1913) he referred to the military system of the country as having been 'fatuously destroyed several years ago'.

In 1900 Wemyss married, as his second wife, Grace (d. 1946), daughter of Major John Blackburn, army officer, and his wife, Maria. Wemyss died after a short illness on 30 June 1914 at his London residence, 23 St James's Place, and was buried on 4 July at Aberlady, the village next to his vast estate and house, Gosford, on the southern shores of the Firth of Forth. He was succeeded by his fourth—the eldest surviving—son, Hugh Richard (1857–1937), whose wife was Mary Constance *Charteris, a prominent member of the Souls and a close friend of A. J. Balfour.

NORBERT C. SOLDON

Sources C. J. Kauffman, 'Lord Elcho, trade unionism and democracy', *Essays in anti-labour history*, ed. K. D. Brown (1974), 183–207 · N. C. Soldon, 'Laissez-faire as dogma: the Liberty and Property Defence League, 1882–1914', *Essays in anti-labour history*, ed. K. D. Brown (1974), 207–33 · Lord Freemantle, *History of the National Rifle Association, 1859–1909* (1914) · E. J. Bristow, *Individualism vs. socialism in Britain, 1880–1914* (1987) · M. Cowling, *1867: Disraeli, Gladstone and revolution* (1967) · McCready, 'British labour and the royal commission on trade unions, 1867–1869', *University of Toronto Quarterly*, 25 (1954–5), 390–409 · R. Harrison, *Before the socialists: studies in labour and politics, 1861–1881* (1965) · B. L. Farr, 'The development and impact of right-wing politics in Great Britain, 1903–1932', PhD diss., University of Illinois, 1979 · K. D. Brown, 'The anti-socialist union, 1908–49', *Essays in anti-labour history*, ed. K. D. Brown (1974) · DNB · GEC, *Peerage* · Earl of Wemyss and March [F. W. C. Douglas], *Memories, 1818–1912*, 2 vols. (1912) · *CGPLA Eng. & Wales* (1915) · *The Times* (1 July 1914)

Archives NA Scot., MSS · NRA Scotland, priv. coll., corresp. and MSS | BL, letters to Sir Austen Layard, Add. MSS 38985–39048 · BL OIOC, letters to Lord Tweeddale, MSS Eur. F 96 · Bodl. Oxf., corresp. with Benjamin Disraeli · Co-operative Union, Holyoake House, Manchester, corresp. with George Holyoake · CUL, corresp. with Sir Edwin Chadwick · NAM, letters to Lord Roberts · U. Durham L., archives and special collections, letters to third Earl Grey

Likenesses D. O. Hill and R. Adamson, photograph, 1843–8, NPG · P. A. de Laszlo, oils, 1908, Scot. NPG · Ape [C. Pellegrini], chromolithograph caricature, NPG; repro. in *VF* (23 July 1870) · L. Caldesi, carte-de-visite, NPG · A. Edouart, cut-paper silhouette, Scot. NPG · J. Leslie, pen-and-pencil sketch, Shugborough, Staffordshire · J. Phillip, group portrait, oils (*The House of Commons, 1860*), Palace of Westminster, London · J. S. Sargent, portrait, NPG · J. Watkins and C. Watkins, carte-de-visite, NPG · pastel drawing, Scot. NPG · photographs, repro. in Earl of Wemyss and March, *Memories* · photographs, Scot. NPG · prints (after photographs), BM

Douglas, Frederick Sylvester North (1791–1819). *See under* Douglas, Sylvester, Baron Glenbervie (1743–1823).

Douglas, Gavin (c.1476–1522), poet and bishop of Dunkeld, was the third son of Archibald *Douglas (Bell-the-Cat), fifth earl of Angus (c.1449–1513), and Elizabeth (d. 1498), daughter of Robert *Boyd, Lord Boyd [see under Boyd family]. The earliest surviving reference to Douglas, in a supplication to the papal curia dated 13 February 1489, stated that he was in his thirteenth year, and he himself, in July 1515, claimed to be a 'man of forty yeris or tharby [thereabouts]' (Bawcutt, 'New light', 95–6). It is likely that Douglas was born in Tantallon Castle, Haddingtonshire, one of the chief seats of the fifteenth-century earls of Angus.

Early years and education Douglas was educated at the University of St Andrews: having matriculated in 1490 he became a licentiate, or master of arts, in 1494. There is no firm evidence that he later studied at the University of Paris—though John Mair (Major) stated in 1516 that he had enjoyed Douglas's friendship both at home and in Paris—or that he had higher degrees in theology or law. None the less Douglas was a learned man and well read, both in vernacular poetry and in classical and humanistic authors. His writings reveal an intensely bookish man, who was acquainted with recently printed editions of Ovid and Virgil, and who read Mair's *Historia majoris Britanniae* ('History of greater Britain', 1521) almost as soon as it was published. In later life he travelled to England, France, and Italy.

Douglas was designed, from an early age, for the church.

During the late middle ages the church in Scotland, as elsewhere in Europe, was characterized by nepotism, pluralism, and frequent struggles for wealthy benefices. Douglas was highly ambitious, and was aided in the search for ecclesiastical preferment by his intelligence, noble birth, and the favour of James IV. In the competitive and litigious climate of the age, however, he did not retain permanently all the benefices with which his name was associated in the 1490s. According to an entry in the chancery register of Pope Alexander VI, Douglas was granted the deanery of Dunkeld in 1496, but his right to that office was vigorously contested by George Hepburn; though Douglas had royal support, Hepburn's persistence in litigation seems to have been ultimately successful. On 6 May 1498 Douglas was 'presented' with the parsonage of Glenholm, when it should become vacant, but there is some doubt as to whether it ever came into his possession, since the presentation was provisional. There is more certainty as to the parsonage of Linton, a small village in Haddingtonshire, not far from Tantallon, which had been appropriated to the collegiate church of Dunbar in the fourteenth century. Douglas probably became parson of Linton and canon of Dunbar about 1504, though the precise date is not known.

Douglas's first important benefice was the provostry of St Giles, Edinburgh, a rich and well-endowed collegiate church, whose patron was the king. Douglas was in possession by 11 March 1503. During his time as provost St Giles was substantially enlarged, and several side chapels were added. There are only a few sparse testimonies to Douglas's activities at St Giles: on 30 July 1510, for instance, he supplicated the pope that he should be granted a special faculty to dispense those within the fourth degree of consanguinity who wished to marry, 'for the making of peace and avoidance of bloodshed', and on 27 February 1511 he and the other prebendaries bound themselves to celebrate the mass of the holy blood regularly throughout the year. There is no reason to doubt Douglas's genuine piety, which is evident in his poetry. Between 1503 and 1513, however, there is far more evidence for Douglas's involvement in secular affairs. He was present at meetings of the lords of council in February and March 1505, and again in 1509. He was one of those appointed to counsel the rector of St Andrews University in 1512 and 1513 ('Acta rectorum', vol. 1, fols. 59 and 61). He frequently witnessed charters for his father and other members of the Douglas family. He also served as their legal representative: on 11 October 1503 he acted as procurator for his brother George in a dispute concerning lands in Jedworth Forest, and on 26 November 1512, in another dispute concerning property, he was one of the procurators for his sister-in-law, Elizabeth Auchinleck.

Douglas's friendship with John Mair played some part in the offer to Mair, in December 1509, of the treasurership of the Chapel Royal, Stirling. Mair draws an interesting portrait of Douglas, clearly based on life, in the 'Dialogus inter duos famatos viros magistrum Gawinum Douglaiseum et magistrum Davidem Crenstonem', which

is prefixed to his commentary on Peter Lombard's *Sentences* (29 April 1510). In the 'Dialogus' Douglas aligns himself with the opponents of scholastic theology, and advocates a return to the biblical and patristic sources of Christianity.

Poetical works All Douglas's surviving poetry belongs to the early years of his life, during the reign of James IV. In the brief 'Mensioun of hys pryncipall warkis' (*Virgil's Aeneid*, 4.139), Douglas refers to a mysterious juvenile translation 'Of Lundeys lufe the remeid'; this is no longer extant, but was possibly a translation of Ovid's *Remedium amoris*. His second work, completed c.1501 and dedicated to the king, was *The Palice of Honour*. This long and complex poem employs an ancient but still very popular form, the allegorical dream, to explore the nature of honour. The varied processions, led by Minerva, Diana, Venus, and the Muses, that pass before the dreamer represent some of the different paths by which men and women have sought to attain honour, such as learning, asceticism, love, or poetry. From the fourteenth to the sixteenth century this was a topic that fascinated poets, who frequently placed a deified Honour in temples and palaces. Douglas's dreamer is taught, at the end, that true honour must be distinguished from worldly glory, and that pre-eminence should be given to heroic honour won by martial virtue. Yet the central section of *The Palice of Honour* is dominated by the Muses, and voices Douglas's tribute to the power of imaginative literature. This is the poet–dreamer's preferred route to honour. The poem shows evidence of Douglas's wide reading: it abounds in allusions to Ovid's *Metamorphoses*, and the humorous self-mocking characterization of the dreamer owes much to Chaucer. Yet, despite the highly literary framework, there are interesting links with Douglas's own career. One is the trial scene, which makes comic use of the terms and procedures of the Scottish law courts. There must have been much piquancy for contemporary readers in finding the poet who had recently litigated with George Hepburn now bandying legal precedents with Venus. Two other poems are attributed to Douglas in the Maitland folio, a literary miscellany compiled in the 1580s. The longer of these, usually known as 'King Hart', is an impressive homiletic allegory; Douglas's authorship of this poem, however, has been vigorously contested on stylistic and linguistic grounds. The attribution to him of 'Conscience', a witty, punning poem on corruption in the church, is more convincing.

Douglas's greatest claim to fame rests upon the *Eneados*, a translation of Virgil's *Aeneid*. In the early 1500s no major classical work had been translated into English, and Douglas's *Eneados* was a pioneering work; what is more, it was not a free paraphrase nor a mere sample of one or two books, but a careful translation of the whole of Virgil's great poem. Douglas was aware of the novelty of his undertaking. He proudly asserted his own fidelity to Virgil's text, and voiced pungent criticisms of William Caxton's recent version of the *Aeneid*, which was no more like Virgil 'than the devill and Sanct Austyne' (prologue 1, 143). It might well seem inconsistent that Douglas also translated the so-called thirteenth book, written by the

Italian humanist Maffeo Vegio, but it should be recalled that most editions of Virgil included this supplement to the *Aeneid* until the seventeenth century. The *Eneados* was affectionately dedicated to Henry, Lord Sinclair, whom Douglas characterized as a keen bibliophile and 'fader of bukis' (prologue 1, 85). He did not design his translation, however, solely for aristocratic readers, but envisaged a wider audience, including 'masteris of grammar sculys', teaching on their 'benkis and stulys' (*Virgil's Aeneid*, 4.189). Douglas shared the values of the humanists: an antipathy to scholasticism, respect for classical authors, and a zeal for education. He wished to communicate to his countrymen a knowledge of the *Aeneid*, and also to enrich his native 'Scottis' tongue with something of the 'fouth', or copiousness, of Latin.

Douglas attempted to acquaint his readers with the Virgilian scholarship of his age. Much in his translation that might seem extraneous is closely related to the contents and apparatus of contemporary editions of Virgil. He is thought to have used an edition published in Paris by Jodocus Badius Ascensius (1501), and often incorporates into his translation the explanatory glosses of Badius and Servius. He is occasionally diffuse and over-explicit, but this springs from a desire to convey the full implications of Virgil's 'sentence', or inner meaning. Douglas, like many translators, is better at rendering some aspects of the *Aeneid* than others. He seems to have found particularly intractable those passages which are densely packed with historical or mythological allusion. He is more successful with narrative, portraiture, and battle scenes, where a debt to the vernacular tradition of alliterative poetry is evident. Douglas excels at rendering the more timeless parts of the *Aeneid*—the similes, and descriptions of nature or of the underworld. At his best he is a responsive and sensitive translator: 'he makes the world of the *Aeneid* seem almost contemporary; Virgil's characters might be just around the corner' (R. G. Austin, *Some English Translations of Virgil*, 1956, 16–17).

Knowledge of Douglas's critical ideas on a wealth of topics, including Virgil and Chaucer, and the problems of translation, derives largely from the prologues which he furnished for each book of the *Eneados*, and the series of epilogues, in which he took a leisurely farewell of Virgil, his patron, his readers, and even his critics. The prologues vary greatly in tone, length, and metrical form—this includes rhyme royal, the decasyllabic couplet (used also for the translation), and the archaic 13-line alliterative stanza of prologue 8. Critics have debated the relevance of some of them to the *Aeneid*, and whether they might better be regarded as independent poems. There is no doubt, however, that they contain much of Douglas's finest and most original writing. Several offer glimpses of the poet in the process of composition; prologue 7 contains a brilliant vignette, in which the poet rises from bed on a wintry morning and shudders at the cold, before he turns to resume work at his lectern. Douglas's tone is often highly colloquial: sometimes he chats familiarly with his readers, sometimes he exhorts them to read poetry attentively—'Considir it warly, reid oftar than anys [once]'

(prologue 1, 107). Prologues 7, 12, and 13, commonly entitled the 'nature prologues', are outstanding for their perceptive description of the natural world in winter and summer, moving from tiny and vivid details to grand panoramic vistas.

After Flodden Douglas completed the *Eneados* on 22 July 1513; on 9 September 1513 occurred the disastrous battle of Flodden, at which James IV died, to be succeeded by James V, a child of eighteen months. Flodden marked a watershed in Douglas's life. Poetry seems to have been abandoned, and his attention diverted to the power struggles within Scotland, and the advancement of himself and his family. On 30 September 1513 Douglas was made a free burgess of Edinburgh: this, though possibly a tribute to his poetry, is more likely to be a sign of the high status of the Douglases in the city. In August 1514 his nephew Archibald *Douglas, now the sixth earl of Angus, married James IV's widow, Margaret Tudor. Henceforward Douglas's fortunes were closely linked with those of his nephew. The queen was held to have forfeited the regency by her marriage to a powerful nobleman, and the duke of Albany, who had lived in France for most of his life, was summoned to be the governor. The queen's supporters, led by Angus and Gavin Douglas, were opposed by many of the lords of council, including James Beaton, the chancellor. Beaton was temporarily deprived of the great seal, and its keys were handed over to Douglas, who himself for a short time had pretensions to the high office of chancellor.

Many important churchmen died at Flodden, and at a time when several rich benefices were vacant Douglas's family connection with the queen was at first advantageous to him. During 1514 Margaret wrote several letters, in the name of the infant James V, to Pope Leo X, urging Douglas's appointment to the abbey of Arbroath. She also supported his claim to the archbishopric of St Andrews, and on 23 November 1514 persuaded Henry VIII to write on his behalf to Rome. Henry praised Douglas lavishly—though hardly from firsthand acquaintance—for his extraordinary learning, probity, and great zeal for the public good. Douglas was so confident that he occupied St Andrews Castle with his servants, but was forced to surrender it. There were more powerful contestants for both benefices: Leo X granted Arbroath *in commendam* to James Stewart, earl of Moray, and Andrew Forman, bishop of Moray, was appointed archbishop of St Andrews.

Douglas was thus doubly disappointed. In January 1515, however, another benefice fell vacant, on the death of George Brown, bishop of Dunkeld. A letter written by Douglas on 18 January to Adam Williamson, one of his agents, leaves no doubt concerning his resentment towards Forman: 'yon evyll myndyt Byschop of Murray trublys all our promociones, and has sped Sanct Andris to himself'. No less evident is his ambitious desire for Dunkeld, 'a rycht gud Byschopry of rent and the thryd Seyt of the realm' (*Poetical Works*, 1.xxxvi). The queen, with the consent of some lords of council, presented him to the bishopric on 20 January 1515. Leo X consented to the appointment, but in May 1515 the governor, Albany, gave his support to another contestant, Andrew Stewart, brother of the powerful earl of Atholl. In July Albany and those lords of council hostile to Douglas charged him with breaking the laws concerning the purchase of benefices at Rome. He was imprisoned for nearly a year, but was released some time before 30 July 1516, and was officially appointed to the see of Dunkeld on 16 September 1516. Even when Douglas arrived in Dunkeld, after his consecration, he still met with armed resistance from Andrew Stewart. One of the canons, Alexander Myln, who was probably an eyewitness, gives a vivid account of the incident, describing how 'shooting began from the steeple and the episcopal palace, and the nobles who were with the bishop disposed themselves for his defence' (Myln, 333).

According to Myln, Douglas now devoted himself to good works, one of which was to complete the building of a bridge over the River Tay, begun by his predecessor. But his life as bishop was by no means calm and uneventful. Dunkeld, which is in the highlands, was notorious as the haunt of criminals and outlaws: Queen Margaret, in urging Douglas's preferment, had written that it required 'a strong man to curb an unruly people' (Letters of James V, 17). Douglas's hostility to Andrew Forman continued: as late as 1518 he refused to render obedience to Forman as archbishop of St Andrews, and when Forman sent messengers to Dunkeld, Douglas's servants repelled them forcibly, threatening to throw them in the Tay. Douglas seems to have yielded at last, possibly because of papal pressure. He was often absent from Dunkeld, travelling to Edinburgh for consultations with Albany, or attending meetings of the lords of council. In the spring of 1517 Douglas was sent on a diplomatic mission to France, together with Patrick Panter, the royal secretary, and Robert Cockburn, bishop of Ross. The chief object of the embassy was to renew the alliance between France and Scotland, and to arrange for a marriage between James V and a daughter of Francis I. Douglas returned to Scotland in the autumn, shortly after the treaty of Rouen was confirmed on 26 August 1517.

After Albany's departure to France in June 1517, Scotland grew more anarchic and faction-ridden. There was a long-running dispute between the Hamiltons and the Douglases, which had as its focus the office of provost of Edinburgh. When this dispute turned to pitched battle on the streets of Edinburgh (30 April 1520), Gavin Douglas took no part in the fighting, but acted as a mediator between the two sides. Lindsay of Pitscottie, a vivid but unreliable historian, describes a picturesque conversation between Douglas and James Beaton, bishop of Glasgow, on this occasion, and states that Douglas later intervened to save Beaton's life.

After 1517 the marriage of Margaret Tudor and the earl of Angus grew increasingly troubled. Margaret accused her husband of wrongfully appropriating to his own use the revenues of her properties. In this quarrel Douglas supported Angus, and acted as his advocate when the legal dispute was heard before the lords of council on 28 February 1519. It is not surprising that he lost the friendship of

Margaret, who considered him partly responsible for Angus's harshness towards her. When Albany returned to Scotland in November 1521, Douglas again supported his nephew, who had fled to the borders and was openly rebellious. In December of that year Douglas travelled to London, and attempted to secure English support for Angus. His last surviving letters, written to Cardinal Wolsey between December 1521 and January 1522, vividly illustrate Douglas's hatred of Albany, whom he called a 'dedelie inimye to me and all my hous' (Poetical Works, 1.xcix), and exasperation with his nephew, that 'young wytless fuyll' (ibid., 1.civ).

Douglas's spirit was by no means crushed. About this time he formed a new friendship, with the Italian historian Polydore Vergil, resident in London since 1502. Vergil reports that they discussed Scottish history, and that Douglas, ever a controversialist, 'vehementlie' criticized John Mair for his scepticism concerning Gathelus and Scota, the mythical founders of Scotland. Despite his absence from Scotland, Douglas sought to obtain the archbishopric of St Andrews, vacant upon the death of Andrew Forman. He seems to have enlisted the support of Wolsey, who wrote on his behalf to the pope. On 21 February 1522, however, James V ratified a decreet issued by Albany, proclaiming Douglas guilty of treason and stating that letters were to be sent to the pope to prevent his promotion. (The Scottish parliament later declared this charge of treason unfounded.) On 8 April James Beaton, Albany's nominee to St Andrews, sought the aid of the king of Denmark to 'impede the ambitious schemes of a proscribed exile' (Letters of James V, 90).

Death and reputation Whatever Douglas's schemes, they were frustrated by his death, in London, apparently from the plague, in September 1522. In his will, dated 10 September 1522 and made while he was staying in the house of his friend Lord Dacre, he requested that his body should be buried in the hospital church of the Savoy. A brass tablet, reading 'Gavanus Dowglas, natione Scotus, Dunkellensis praesul, patria sua exul', formerly marked his grave.

Douglas attained high office in the Scottish church, and he briefly played an important political role in the turbulent years of James V's minority. He cannot be regarded as a great bishop or statesman, comparable in stature to James Kennedy, bishop of St Andrews, or William Elphinstone, bishop of Aberdeen. But his career is more richly documented than those of other early Scottish churchmen and poets, and vividly illuminates many aspects of contemporary Scotland, such as the strong attachment to kin and 'house', and the intense rivalries and power struggles within the church. More positively, Douglas throws valuable light on the education and literary culture of Scotland in the early sixteenth century, through his friendships (and occasional quarrels) with scholars such as John Mair and Polydore Vergil, through the impressive width of his reading, and, above all, through his own writings. Douglas's lasting importance lies in his poetry, which was highly esteemed, in England as well as Scotland, throughout the sixteenth century. The *Eneados* circulated in several manuscript copies (five of which survive) and in an edition printed at London (1553). No manuscript survives of *The Palice of Honour*, but it was printed at least three times, in Edinburgh (c.1540 and 1579) and in London (c.1553). It was the *Eneados*, however, that was most famous and influential: it was imitated by Tudor poets, notably Henry Howard, earl of Surrey. In later centuries Douglas's reputation remained high, assisted in part by the association of his name with that of Virgil, and also by the interest of his language to antiquarians and scholars, such as Francis Junius. More recently critics have debated whether Douglas should be regarded as a medieval or Renaissance figure, and to what extent he had a political purpose in translating the *Aeneid*. The *Eneados*, however, has an importance that is more than merely historical. In Ezra Pound's opinion 'Douglas gets more poetry out of Virgil than any other translator' (*Literary Essays*, 1954, 245). In all Douglas's writings, including his letters, a distinctive voice may be heard, trenchant, acerbic, and often witty.

PRISCILLA J. BAWCUTT

Sources P. Bawcutt, *Gavin Douglas: a critical study* (1976) · *The poetical works of Gavin Douglas*, ed. J. Small, 4 vols. (1874) [incl. introduction by J. Small; also letters] · P. Bawcutt, 'New light on Gavin Douglas', *The Renaissance in Scotland: studies in literature, religion, history, and culture offered to John Durkan*, ed. A. A. MacDonald and others (1994), 95–106 · P. Bawcutt, 'The correspondence of Gavin Douglas', *Stewart style, 1513–1542: essays on the court of James V*, ed. J. Hadley Williams (1996), 52–61 · *Virgil's Aeneid translated into Scottish verse*, ed. D. F. C. Coldwell, trans. G. Douglas, 4 vols., STS, 3rd ser., 25, 27–8, 30 (1957–64) · *The shorter poems of Gavin Douglas*, ed. P. Bawcutt, STS, 4th ser., 3 (1967) · W. Fraser, ed., *The Douglas book*, 4 vols. (1885) · A. Mylne, 'Lives of the bishops of Dunkeld', *Rentale Dunkeldense*, ed. and trans. R. K. Hannay, Scottish History Society, 2nd ser., 10 (1915) · *The letters of James V*, ed. R. K. Hannay and D. Hay (1954) · *A history of greater Britain … by John Major*, ed. and trans. A. Constable, Scottish History Society, 10 (1892) [incl. *Dialogus inter duos famatos viros*] · A. I. Dunlop, ed., *Acta facultatis artium universitatis Sanctiandree, 1413–1588*, 2 vols., Scottish History Society, 3rd ser., 54–5 (1964) · P. Vergil, *Polydore Vergil's 'English history'*, ed. H. Ellis, CS, 36 (1846) · acta rectorum, U. St Andr., vol. 1, fols. 59 and 61 · J. Lauder, G. Donaldson, and C. Macrae, eds., *St Andrews formulare, 1514–1546*, 1, Stair Society, 7 (1942) · *The historie and cronicles of Scotland … by Robert Lindesay of Pitscottie*, ed. A. J. G. Mackay, 1, STS, 42 (1899) · *Scots peerage*, 1.178ff. · F. Ridley, 'Douglas', *A manual of the writings in Middle English, 1050–1500*, ed. A. E. Hartung, 4 (1973), 1180–204

Archives BL, Cotton MSS, MSS · LPL, MS of *Eneados* · NA Scot., will, GD, 254/331 · PRO, corresp., SP 49/1/127, 128, 130 · Trinity Cam., MS of *Eneados* · U. Edin., MSS of *Eneados*

Wealth at death see will, *Poetical works*, ed. Small, vol. 1, pp. cxix–cxxv

Douglas, George, first earl of Angus (1378x80?–1403?), magnate, was the illegitimate son of William *Douglas, first earl of Douglas (c.1330–1384), and Earl William's sister-in-law, Margaret Stewart (b. 1353x62, d. in or before 1418), eldest daughter and heir of Thomas Stewart, earl of Angus, and wife of Thomas, earl of Mar, whose sister, also Margaret, was Douglas's wife. The liaison between George's parents presumably began after the death of Thomas, earl of Mar, early in 1377. Thomas died childless, and his estates and titles passed to his sister's husband,

George's father, who was made earl of Mar in July 1377. Margaret Stewart became Earl William's mistress and by January 1379 was residing in Douglas's fortress of Tantallon in Haddingtonshire. The relationship produced a son, George. Despite George's illegitimacy, Margaret Stewart was determined to arrange his succession to the estates and title of his maternal grandfather, the earl of Angus. In 1388–9 she was able to exploit a political struggle for control of the kingdom between two of Robert II's sons, John, earl of Carrick, and Robert, earl of Fife, to obtain royal ratification of George's right to inherit his grandfather's earldom and lordships. On 10 April 1389 Robert II confirmed Countess Margaret's resignation of the earldom of Angus and the lordships of Abernethy and Bunkle in favour of her son, who became first earl of Angus of a new creation in 1397.

Between 24 May and 9 November 1397 Angus married Mary Stewart, a daughter of Robert III. As part of the marriage settlement the earl's lands in Forfar and his lordships of Abernethy and Bunkle were elevated to the status of a regality. Under the terms of the marriage contract Robert III was obliged to confirm all resignations of land made in George's favour by his half-sister Isabella Douglas, countess of Mar, and his cousin Sir James Sandilands of Calder. This arrangement gave Angus claims to many of the lordships which had been the property of his father. After the latter's death his estates and title had passed to his legitimate son, James, who, however, was killed at the battle of Otterburn in August 1388. The title of earl of Douglas and possession of many of Earl William's estates had passed, by means of an entail drawn up in 1342, to Earl James's illegitimate kinsman Archibald Douglas, lord of Galloway, who became third earl of Douglas in April 1389. Robert III seems to have encouraged George Douglas's claims to the wider Douglas inheritance in 1397 in order to undermine Earl Archibald and his allies, who were associated with the king's brother and political rival, Robert, earl of Fife. The arrangement made in 1397 essentially gave Angus rights to all the lordships not covered by the 1342 entail, including Liddesdale, Cavers, and Jedworth; his attempts to recover control of Liddesdale led to a serious feud with an alternative Douglas claimant, Sir James Douglas of Dalkeith.

Angus was briefly active in Anglo-Scottish diplomacy, but on 14 September 1402 he was among the Scottish noblemen captured by English forces at the battle of Hamildon Hill. He is said to have died in England shortly after his capture during an outbreak of plague. When his son, William *Douglas, was served as heir to his father in Liddesdale on 27 March 1409, it was noted that the lordship had been in the crown's hands for six years, suggesting that George died early in 1403. His widow, Mary, had certainly married Sir James Kennedy of Dunure before 25 January 1406. Angus and his wife had two children, William, who succeeded as earl of Angus and was the first of the so-called Red Douglases, and Elizabeth, who married Sir Alexander Forbes before 4 November 1423 and, surviving him, Sir David Hay of Yester. Mary Stewart was to remarry three times in all. After Kennedy's death in 1408 she became the spouse of Sir William Graham of Montrose, who died in 1424. Finally, widowed yet again, she married Sir William Edmonstone of Duntreath in 1425. She seems to have died some time after 1458, and is said to have been buried in the parish church of Strathblane. All her marriages produced children. S. I. BOARDMAN

Sources W. Fraser, ed., *The Douglas book*, 4 vols. (1885), vol. 3 · W. Bower, *Scotichronicon*, ed. D. E. R. Watt and others, new edn, 9 vols. (1987–98), vols. 7–8 · NA Scot., Register House charters, RH6/nos. 167/168/169/173 · *The manuscripts of the marquess of Abergavenny, Lord Braye*, G. F. Luttrell, HMC, 15 (1887), 77–8 · NA Scot., Ailsa muniments, GD25 · J. Anderson, ed., *Calendar of the Laing charters, AD 854–1837, belonging to the University of Edinburgh* (1899) · *CEPR letters*, vol. 3 · G. Burnett and others, eds., *The exchequer rolls of Scotland*, 2 (1878) · NA Scot., Crown Office writs, AD1/23

Douglas, George, fourth earl of Angus (*c*.1417–1463), courtier and soldier, was the second son of William *Douglas, second earl of Angus (*c*.1398–1437), and his wife, Margaret (*fl*. 1410–1484), daughter of Sir William Hay of Yester. He succeeded to the earldom on the death of his childless elder brother, James *Douglas, in 1446. William Douglas, who had been a prominent crown servant in the reign of James I, died shortly after the king, and his eldest son failed to make his mark at court. Earl George, however, seems to have established himself quickly there after his succession, but managed to avoid entanglement with the notorious Livingston faction, whose fall in late 1449 had widespread ramifications. Furthermore, although he continued to witness crown charters thereafter, he was not caught up in the collapse of the Black Douglases either, and indeed it was the final defeat of the earls of Douglas in May 1455 which brought him further prestige.

Angus was by this time seldom at court, yet James II granted him the lordship of Douglas, Lanarkshire, which had been forfeited by James, ninth earl of Douglas. Earl George already possessed major estates (most of them held in regality) in Forfarshire (Angus), Fife, Perthshire, Haddingtonshire, Dumfriesshire, Selkirkshire, Berwickshire, and Roxburghshire. His becoming lord of Douglas represented a significant accretion of honour, marking that he was now the senior member of the house of Douglas. He had succeeded his brother as warden of the east marches (against England), and after the defeat of the Black Douglases he obtained the wardenship of the middle marches as well. He shared the military preoccupations of his father. He and others invaded England to counter raids from the south and burnt Alnwick, probably in 1448. He may have had a role in the rout of the Douglases in 1455; and some accounts suggest that he was standing beside James II at the siege of Roxburgh in August 1460 when the king received the fatal blow from a Scottish gun which shattered when fired, and was himself injured.

Although the family historian, David Hume of Godscroft (*d*. *c*.1630), relates that at the coronation of the eight-year-old James III on 10 August 1460 Angus seized the crown and put it on the head of the new king, challenging anyone else to remove it, he seems to have played little part in political life during the opening years of the minority administration. It is certain, however, that the earl sought to profit from the civil war in England. When Henry VI fled with his family to Scotland, in 1461, he contracted with Angus to enlist his support against the Yorkists, in return for which Angus would be created an English duke and would obtain a castle and territory to the value of 2000 marks, on the north side of the rivers Trent and Humber. Angus supplied material help in January 1463 by relieving Edward IV's forces' siege of Alnwick, where French troops raised by Henry VI's spouse, Margaret of Anjou, had taken refuge. But before Angus could capitalize on this he died, on 12 March 1463; he was apparently buried beside his ancestors in the collegiate church of St Bride, Abernethy, Perthshire.

Hume of Godscroft regards Angus as the earl who securely founded the family's fortunes, and gives him the sobriquet 'the Great Earl'. After the fall of the Black Douglases, Earl George was careful to build up his following, particularly when he had assumed the lordship of Douglas. Most notably, he persuaded some greater and lesser barons to effect bonds of manrent to him. Recent scholarship has suggested that these bonds, which first appear in the 1440s, indicate efforts by a new nobility within Scotland to establish their status. Forfeitures in the reigns of James I and James II fell hard on many old noble families. The new nobility sought to assure themselves of support among the lairds by securing written, personal promises of loyalty, often for life, in return for maintenance of the subscribers' interests. Angus received bonds from barons whose estates lay in Roxburghshire, Lanarkshire, and Forfarshire, including two lords of parliament: James Hamilton, first Lord Hamilton of Cadzow (*d*. 1479), and John Somerville, second Lord Somerville (*d*. 1491). Hamilton, formerly a leading adherent of the Black Douglases, had changed sides in 1455 and been given forfeited Douglas estates. His giving a bond to Angus represents a striking demonstration of regional supremacy on the latter's part. Earl George is also said to have taken a wider perspective of his family estates, moving their centre from Perthshire and Forfarshire to his border strongholds, notably Jedburgh and Hermitage in Liddesdale; but he is often found in Edinburgh, presumably with the king's court, and in 1455 he received the king's permission to construct and fortify a castle at Broughty, Forfarshire.

Earl George married, apparently before his elder brother's death, Isabel, daughter of Sir John Sibbald of Balgonie, master of the king's household in the 1440s. They had two sons, one of whom was Archibald *Douglas, fifth earl of Angus, and six daughters. Shortly before Earl George died Archibald was contracted to marry a daughter of Alexander Seton, first earl of Huntly, but the marriage is not known to have occurred. After her husband's death Isabel married John Carmichael of Balmedie (by 1477) and then Sir Robert Douglas of Lochleven (by 1489). She had died by February 1503. ALAN R. BORTHWICK

Sources The Hirsel, Berwickshire, Home Muniments · W. Fraser, ed., *The Douglas book*, 4 vols. (1885), vols. 2–3 · D. Hume, 'History of the house and race of Douglas and Angus', MS, Lennoxlove, East Lothian, Hamilton Muniments · J. M. Thomson and others, eds., *Registrum magni sigilli regum Scotorum / The register of the great seal of Scotland*, 11 vols. (1882–1914), vol. 2 · G. Burnett and others, eds., *The exchequer rolls of Scotland*, 5–7 (1882–4) · various collections of manuscript estate and other papers in archive offices and in private hands in Scotland and England · *RotS*, vol. 2 · M. Brown, *The Black Douglases: war and lordship in late medieval Scotland, 1300–1455* (1998)

Archives priv. coll. | The Hirsel, Berwickshire, Home muniments

Douglas, Sir George, of Pittendriech (1490?–1552), nobleman, was the second son of George Douglas, master of Angus (*c*.1469–1513), who was killed at Flodden, and his wife, Elizabeth Drummond. Archibald *Douglas, sixth earl of Angus, was his elder brother. George's early years are obscure, but he emerged as a force to be reckoned with in the confusion which followed the killing in 1517 of Antoine de la Bastie, the principal agent of the duke of Albany. Although Douglas's involvement in the crime could not be proven, he was bustled off to France after incarcerations in Blackness and Inchgarvy. Throughout his life he collaborated with his elder brother, in a partnership in which Angus (while clearly not stupid) provided the brawn, George the brains. And there is no doubting the latter's intelligence and wide-ranging adventurousness. Behind his inveterate evasiveness a lively mind can always be seen at work. Few of his ingenious schemes saw fruition, but they all required considered replies from the English privy council, the council of the north, and even the king.

George Douglas aimed to secure independence in life and eventually achieved a fair measure of success. He had become a laird by about 1516 through his marriage to Elizabeth, heir to David Douglas of Pittendriech, whose lands lay near Elgin; they had two sons, David, who became seventh earl of Angus, and James *Douglas, later earl of Morton and regent of Scotland in the 1570s. Pittendriech also had an illegitimate son, George of Parkhead, and four illegitimate daughters. Marriage to an heiress brought wealth, and he transformed Dalkeith Castle into something of a palace (in March 1543 Cardinal David Beaton was imprisoned there). Because Angus had no male children, George Douglas was styled master of Angus as his brother's heir presumptive. He was indeed very much Angus's man, acting for him on numerous occasions; rarely did their ambitions clash, and much of Pittendriech's story is the biography of Angus as well. He had been knighted by 3 October 1524, when he was described as 'a man of more knowledge and experience than the Earl' (*LP Henry VIII*, vol. 4, pt 1, no. 701). Master of the royal household from 1526, he shared power with Angus during the latter's ascendancy (1525–8), and when James V took control went into exile with the earl in England, where he remained from 1529 to 1543. Having been forfeited in 1528, Sir George was several times involved in efforts to recover his family's lost position. In 1532 and again in 1542 he took part in English raids into Scotland, and he seems to have maintained spies in Scotland throughout his years in exile.

Following the death of James V on 14 December 1542—for which his dispatch is a vivid if uncertainly reliable source—Douglas returned to Scotland with Angus early in 1543; not everyone was pleased to see them, but eventually the two men recovered their estates and positions. Douglas was quick to profit from his return, by marrying his son James to the youngest daughter of the third earl of Morton in 1543, with a settlement securing the earldom of Morton for them. The exiled Douglases came back with English encouragement and ostensibly at least they were committed to the furtherance of Henry VIII's plans for Anglo-Scottish union. Sir George also seems to have become a committed protestant. Thereafter he was seldom out of the records and featured in the English ones almost as frequently as his apparently much more powerful brother.

Pittendriech owed his prominence to qualities peculiarly suited to the confused political position prevailing in Scotland in the early 1540s—abounding energy, a wide-ranging intelligence, and an almost pathological deviousness. He had an uncanny memory for faces and for gossip; he knew everyone that mattered and most of their secrets. He was also unusually sensitive to geographical factors; thus his outlined schemes for invasion routes for English armies were infinitely detailed and quite accurate. Moreover he had great personal charm and was a negotiator of high skill. This took a number of forms, not least his manipulation of the rather guileless English ambassador Sir Ralph Sadler and a mastery of the art of telling people what they wanted to hear. In spring 1543 Scottish ambassadors were dispatched to London to conclude what became the treaties of Greenwich: the betrothal of Queen Mary and Prince Edward. When the envoys needed stiffening, it was Pittendriech (along with the earl of Glencairn) who was sent early in May, in part because he had become familiar with Henry VIII, in part because he was avowedly in favour of the marriage, but also because of his reputation as a canny and forceful diplomat. In this he was largely successful: the resulting treaty secured much of what the Scots wanted.

At this time Pittendriech and his brother appeared to be staunch 'Englishmen'. Early in January 1544 they were captured by the governor, the second earl of Arran, and Cardinal Beaton, and were reported to be in danger of execution. When he was released from Blackness in May by the earl of Hertford, then leading an army of invasion, Douglas told him that 'bothe his brother and he shuld have loste their heddes, and the daye prefixed for the same' (Bain, 2.372). But although he maintained an overtly Anglophile stance, at least to the extent of being free with his advice, doubts soon arose as to his trustworthiness. By December 1544 Henry VIII's agents were complaining how 'thErle of Anguishe and George Douglas have nowe opened their untrew, false and disloyall hartes' (ibid., 2.525–6), and soon after Henry himself ordered that the two men be captured and offered 1000 marks to whoever should bring Douglas in. So complete was his rapprochement with Beaton that on 18 March 1545 it was reported that 'the Cardinall and George Dowglas rulith the realme of Scotland this tyme as they thynk good' (ibid., 2.583). Pittendriech and Angus had recently both fought in the victorious Scottish army at Ancrum Moor on 27 February, while by the beginning of 1546 each was receiving a French pension. Sir George's position survived the murder of Beaton on 29 May 1546 and he continued to be the target for English detestation and distrust, only just escaping when Dalkeith Castle was captured on 3 June 1548. A member of the Scottish council at that time, he took part in Mary of Guise's visit to France in October 1550. In 1552 he accompanied Arran (now duke of Châtel-herault) to the north of Scotland and during this expedition he died at Elgin, some time before 10 May, worth £3582 Scots. His widow lived until at least 1560.

Douglas is one of the more fascinating figures of his time, not least because so much of his correspondence survives and because so much was written about him by contemporaries. Bishop John Lesley spoke for many when he described him as 'sa well knawin' in Scotland, England, and France for his 'inventionis' and for his 'politique and wechtie effertis' (Lesley, 244). His 'falsehood' enraged Englishmen, then and later, and has led to his coming to be perceived as treacherous and unpatriotic, ready to sell out his country for gain. However, the circumstances of sixteenth-century Scottish political life were such as to make a certain slipperiness essential for survival, and in any case there were limits to Pittendriech's unreliability. The one man he never played false was his brother, and he was ever loyal to his kinsfolk; when Dalkeith was taken in 1548, the house was full of them. Like Angus, he lived and died in the faith of the Douglases.

MARCUS MERRIMAN

Sources LP Henry VIII, vols. 3–21 · J. Bain, ed., The Hamilton papers, 2 vols. (1890–92) · J. Lesley, The history of Scotland, ed. T. Thomson, Bannatyne Club, 38 (1830) · Scots peerage, 1.186–8 · M. Merriman, The rough wooings: Mary queen of Scots, 1542–1551 (2000) · R. K. Marshall, Mary of Guise (1977) · M. H. B. Sanderson, Cardinal of Scotland: David Beaton, c.1494–1546 (1986) · J. Cameron, James V: the personal rule, 1528–1542, ed. N. Macdougall (1998) · G. Hewitt, Scotland under Morton, 1572–80 (1982)

Wealth at death £3582 Scots

Douglas, George, earl of Dumbarton (c.1636–1692), army officer, was the second son of the second marriage of William *Douglas, first marquess of Douglas (1589–1660), to Lady Mary Gordon (1610/11–1674), daughter of George Gordon, first marquess of Huntly. In 1647 he received permission from Charles I to go to France for five years. He took military service under Louis XIV, receiving by 1656 the colonelcy of the regiment formerly commanded by his elder half-brothers, Lord James *Douglas and Archibald *Douglas, styled earl of Angus and Ormond. The regiment was recalled in 1666 during the Second Anglo-Dutch War, upon which its arrears, and his pension, were withheld. Charles II returned part of the regiment 'as a present' in 1667, whence it was used as a diplomatic tool by Louis XIV in order to endanger British trade with the Ottoman Porte by making it part of the invasion force of Candia (Crete) in 1668/9. Though a great favourite of Louis XIV, he was said to be very much 'in their black book' (PRO, SP 78/122/122)

after deserting the service in 1669, and Arlington had to forward him 242 livres so that he could afford to leave France. He soon returned to French service and was a maré-chal de camp at the time when his regiment fought alongside the duke of Monmouth's régiment royal anglais in the French army during the Third Anglo-Dutch War. On 9 March 1675 Charles II granted him the titles of earl of Dumbarton and Lord Ettrick, though he owned no land anywhere in Scotland. He was appointed a lieutenant-general in the French army in 1676/7 after considerable manoeuvring at the French court. His brother the duke of Hamilton was told that the appointment would gain him nothing save a further debt of the 20,000 livres he was forced to spend on his equipage for the French encampment at Cambray. In the same year the regiment of his younger brother Lord James was collapsed into his own. His regiment was formally disbanded from the French army in June 1678, but was re-formed on the English establishment as the 1st Royal regiment of foot, or the Royal Scots. He again recruited Scots for French service in 1679. From 1680 onwards his regiment served in Ireland, with 200 of his men also being sent to Tangier.

Dumbarton was a great royal favourite; in 1684 Charles II granted him £1500 to cover fines imposed on him for ecclesiastical irregularities resulting from his Catholicism. Following James VII and II's accession to the throne he assisted in the suppression of Argyll's rebellion and was appointed commander-in-chief of the army in Scotland. He was an integral member of James's Catholic court party, supporting the policies in Scotland of his brother-in-law James Drummond, earl of Perth, chancellor of Scotland, and Perth's brother John, earl of Melfort, secretary of state for Scotland. In 1687 he became one of the founding knights of the 'restored' Order of the Thistle, and was appointed a gentleman of James's bedchamber. He received the estate of the attainted Andrew Fletcher of Saltoun in the same year, upon which he wrote to his brother-in-law the duke of Queensberry, saying of his sister that 'now I am a Scots Laird I may hop[e] to see herr' (NL Scot., Salt. MS 17498, fol. 57). The king also helped pay off his many debts. He was one of the courtiers who advised James to flee in 1688. He followed James to Rochester, being one of the three courtiers, including his nephew the earl of Arran, who accompanied him there. He died at St Germain-en-Laye on 20 March 1692 and was buried, possibly the same day, at St Germain-des-Prés. He married, in or about 1686, Anne, daughter of Robert Wheatley, of Bracknell, Berkshire. She was supposedly a sister of the duchess of Northumberland, but Dumbarton's brother the duke of Hamilton would never consent to meet her. She died at St Germain-en-Laye on 25 April 1691. He and Anne had a son, George, second earl of Dumbarton, born in April 1687. He wanted to be a monk, but was dissuaded by Mary of Modena in 1704. He returned to Britain, having been pardoned of high treason as a Jacobite in 1710, and attained high rank in the British army and the diplomatic service, being appointed ambassador to Russia in 1716. He died without issue and the title became extinct.

M. R. GLOZIER

Sources *Scots peerage* · NA Scot., GD 406/1/5997–5998, 6014; GD 100/317A, 406/1/7650, 7652 · PRO, SP 78/122/96–97, 122 · *Reg. PCS*, 3rd ser. · *The autobiography of Sir John Bramston*, ed. [Lord Bray-brooke], CS, 32 (1845), 280–81 · NL Scot., Saltoun MS 17498, fol. 57 · *Calendar of the Stuart papers belonging to his majesty the king, preserved at Windsor Castle*, 7 vols., HMC, 56 (1902–23), vol. 1, p. 97 · NL Scot., MS 5370, fol. 28 · Douglas charter chest, NL Scot. · *CSP dom., 1660–85* · Bibliothèque Nationale, Paris, Collection Châtre de Congé, 32/189 · NA Scot., RH 9/18/30 · Marquise Campana de Cavelli, ed., *Les derniers Stuarts à Saint-Germain en Laye*, 2 vols. (Paris, 1871) · J. Childs, *The army of Charles II* (1976)
Archives BL, Add. MSS · NRA, priv. coll., papers about raising men for the French Scots regiment | Bibliothèque Nationale, Paris, Châtre de Congé MSS · BL, letters to Duke of Lauderdale, Add. MSS 23124–23138 · NA Scot., Hamilton MSS · Service Historique de l'Armée de Terre, Vincennes, France
Likenesses H. Gascars, oils, c.1680–1681, priv. coll.; repro. in S. Stevenson, 'Armour in seventeenth-century portraits', *Scottish weapons and fortifications, 1100–1800*, ed. D. Caldwell (1981), 366 · J. Scougal, oils, c.1681–1682, priv. coll.; repro. in S. Stevenson, 'Armour in seventeenth-century portraits', *Scottish weapons and fortifications, 1100–1800*, ed. D. Caldwell (1981), 366

Douglas, George, fourth Lord Mordington (d. 1741), political writer, was the only son of James Douglas, third Lord Mordington (1651–1706?), and his wife, Jean Seton (b. 1651), eldest daughter of Alexander Seton, first Viscount Kingston. On 16 November 1704 he married Mary Dillon (d. in or after 1745). He was imprisoned for debt at Newgate on 22 April 1706, and abandoned his wife soon after. On 1 April 1715, while his wife still lived, he went through a form of marriage with Catherine (d. 1741), daughter of Robert Lauder, rector of Shenty, Hertfordshire. She styled herself Lady Mordington; they had one son, Charles, and two daughters, Mary and Campbellina.

Mordington's principal political study was *The Great Blessing of a Monarchical Government* (1724), a rambling work of patriotic and anti-Catholic sentiment which he dedicated to George I. In the preface he wrote of his not being 'insensible that what I sent into the world at two different times about three years since, occasioned by a weekly paper called "the Independent Whig", created me some enemies', referring to two tracts: *Aminadab, or, The Quaker vision: a satirical tract in defence of Dr Sacheverell's sermon before the lord mayor*, which was answered anonymously in *The Tory Quaker*; and *A Letter from Lord Mordington to the Lord Archbishop of York* (1721).

Mordington died in Covent Garden, London, on 13 May 1741 and was buried at Paddington, Middlesex. He was survived by both Catherine Lauder, who died on 3 June of the same year, and his estranged wife. His son, Charles, did not assume the title in 1741, having no landed property. He was imprisoned in December 1745, first at Preston and later at Carlisle, for his supposed Jacobite sympathies. He then pleaded his peerage, and the trial was postponed. However, he was still in Carlisle gaol in 1750 and may have remained there until his death in 1755. His sister Mary, who was married to William Weaver, an officer of the Horse Guards, then assumed the title of Mordington; but she died childless, and it finally lapsed in July 1791.

ALSAGER VIAN, rev. PHILIP CARTER

Sources Lord Mordington [G. Douglas], 'Preface', *The great blessing of a monarchical government* (1724) · GEC, *Peerage*

Douglas, George Cunninghame Monteath (1826–1904), Hebrew scholar, was born on 2 March 1826, in Kilbarchan, west Renfrewshire, one of six children of Robert Douglas, minister of the parish, and his wife, Janet, daughter of John Monteath, minister of Houston. His brother, Carstairs Douglas (1830–1877), became a missionary, and was a Chinese scholar of repute. George was educated at home by his father with such success that he entered the University of Glasgow in 1837 at the early age of eleven, and took a distinguished place in the classes of languages and philosophy. He graduated BA in 1843, the year of the Disruption, and was awarded a DD in 1867. Deciding to become a minister in the Free Church, he took the prescribed four years' training in theology at New College in Edinburgh, which the Free Church had established with Dr Thomas Chalmers at its head. He was duly 'licensed to preach' by his presbytery, and, after some years spent in 'assistantships', was ordained in 1852 minister of Bridge of Weir, near Paisley, Renfrewshire. In 1856 the Free Church built a third theological college, at Glasgow, and Douglas was appointed tutor of Hebrew there. On 26 May 1857, aged thirty-one, he became professor, and he held this position until his retirement on 23 May 1892. On the death of Dr Patrick Fairbairn, Douglas succeeded him as principal (22 May 1875), and held office until 26 May 1902. His entire life was spent in Glasgow and his activities closely connected with university and educational matters. He took a keen interest in the establishment of a Scottish system of national education, was chairman of the Free Church committee on the matter, and was sent to London in 1869 to see the Education Bill through parliament. He was member of the first two Glasgow school boards, and for several years an active member of Hutcheson's educational trust. He was also chairman of the university council's committee on university reform. Douglas was an early member of the Old Testament Revision Company established for the revision of the Authorized Version of the Bible (the Revised Version, afterwards replaced by the Revised Standard Version) and worked on the project until its completion in 1884. His knowledge of the Hebrew text made him a useful contributor. He died at Woodcliffe, Bridge of Allan, Stirlingshire, on 24 May 1904, and was buried in the necropolis, Glasgow.

Douglas was a biblical scholar of the old school whose learning was considerable but whose approach became dated during his own lifetime. He had an exact and minute acquaintance with the Massoretic text of the Old Testament and with extra-canonic Hebrew literature. He read widely and kept up with Hebrew scholarship in German, French, and English. But he was profoundly mistrustful of what he called 'the hasty generalisations' of the higher criticism, which changed the face of biblical scholarship and left Douglas of no intellectual interest to academics in his field. *Why I Still Believe that Moses Wrote Deuteronomy* (1878) is a typical example of his conservatism. He wrote on a wide range of Old Testament topics, but by the end of his own lifetime his writings were thought to have failed to do justice to his talents.

T. M. LINDSAY, rev. GERALD LAW

Sources WWW • W. Ewing, ed., *Annals of the Free Church of Scotland, 1843–1900*, 2 vols. (1914) • private information (1912)
Likenesses G. S. Calvert, portrait; Free Church College, Glasgow, 1912

Douglas, George William (1859–1947), woollen and worsted dyer, was born on 14 August 1859 at 26 Spring Gardens, Bradford, in the West Riding of Yorkshire, the son of David Maitland Douglas and his wife, Margaret, *née* McConnell. He was educated at Bradford grammar school and at the Yorkshire College, Leeds. His father was a manager and later a partner in the important merchanting establishment in Bradford of A. and S. Henry. Between school and college George worked in his father's firm and while there gained experience in technical and commercial matters, particularly textile materials and their distribution throughout the markets of the world. He accompanied his father on several visits to the United States. On leaving the Yorkshire College in 1878, George Douglas found employment with Edward Ripley & Son, dyers, of Bowling, near Bradford. The firm enjoyed a high reputation in the worsted trade. From very small roots it had progressed to being capable of handling almost every kind of piece-goods manufactured in the Bradford area, and some Lancashire cotton goods. Douglas rose rapidly in the firm, graduating to the position of general manager and junior partner.

The Yorkshire dyeing industry in the last third of the nineteenth century was facing immense competition from the continent, particularly Germany, and was struggling to achieve the standards the wool textile industry needed for its products to be competitive. In particular the invention and innovation of artificial dyestuffs was putting traditional dyers under much pressure. Douglas led the reorganization of the Ripley business and the redevelopment of the dyeworks, enabling the firm to cope with a wider variety of trade and to encompass broader technological innovation. He joined the campaign to reform the organization of the piece-dyeing industry in Bradford and district, where competition was severe and prices unremunerative. Short-time working was commonplace and standards were suffering. Douglas took the lead in the establishment of the Bradford Dyers' Association, formed to rationalize the local dyeing industry. In 1898 the association was founded, combining twenty-two of the firms engaged in the dyeing and finishing of textile piece-goods in the Bradford district, some ninety per cent of the total business. Edward Ripley & Sons was by far the largest in the amalgamation. The association was floated with a capital of £3 million. Douglas was appointed managing director, and he led attempts to restore remunerative prices for dyeing and to improve the quality of the output of the industry in order to allow it to face foreign competition. Economies were accomplished through the sharing of technical expertise and the centralization of organization and administration. Uneconomic works were closed and work was allocated according to the capabilities of various plants. A monopoly price situation enabled a very high return on assets in the early years of the association.

In the early twentieth century the association expanded rapidly, incorporating many other dyeing businesses in Yorkshire and Lancashire. By 1906 it employed about 7500 people, having in the previous year ranked as the seventeenth largest industrial company in Britain, in terms of capital employed. Douglas led the association through the First World War and into the textile depression of the interwar years. He became sole managing director in 1909, and held that position until his retirement in 1946. From 1924 he was also chairman of the association. He was a founder member of the Society of Dyers and Colourists in 1884, serving as its vice-president from 1894 to 1912, and as president from 1912 to 1914. He was appointed an honorary member of the society in 1934. Although, in principle, he favoured free trade, he recognized the need for subsidies to help the dyeing industry in the 1930s, and campaigned for them. He also advocated industrial reorganization in the textile industry at that period to eliminate surplus capacity, maintain prices, and promote exports.

George Douglas was recognized as having a clear vision about the needs of the industry, and an alert, analytical mind in confronting its problems. He was described as an accomplished organizer and a thoughtful but determined businessman. He shunned personal publicity. He was reported to have been a substantial benefactor, but few details of his bequests were ever published.

Douglas was married, but the date of the marriage and the name of his wife, who died in France in 1923, are unknown. They had one son and one daughter. From 1908 he lived at Farfield Hall, Addingham, Skipton, West Riding of Yorkshire, spending his leisure hours fishing and shooting on this estate. He died of a cerebral thrombosis at Farfield Hall on 26 November 1947, and was buried at Bolton Abbey church on 29 November.   D. T. JENKINS

Sources D. T. Jenkins, 'Douglas, George', *DBB* • *Journal of the Society of Dyers and Colourists*, 64 (1948), 133–5 • The Bradford Dyers Association Ltd., typescript history, 1950, Bradford Local History Library • A. F. Ewing, *Planning and policies in the textile finishing industry* (1972) • *Dyer, Textile Printer, Bleacher and Finisher* (Dec 1947), 149–50 • *Yorkshire Post* (27 Nov 1947) • *To mark a notable occasion in the history of the Bradford Dyers' Association Ltd* (1946) • b. cert. • d. cert.
Likenesses photograph, repro. in *To mark a notable occasion* • photograph, repro. in *Bradford Dyers' Association Staff Guild Journal*, 1
Wealth at death £391,248 5s. 3d.: probate, 25 Feb 1948, *CGPLA Eng. & Wales*

Douglas, Sir Howard, third baronet (1776–1861), army officer and colonial official, the third son of Vice-Admiral Sir Charles *Douglas, first baronet (*d.* 1789), and his second wife, Sarah (*d.* 16 Aug 1779), the daughter of James Wood, was born at Gosport, Hampshire, on 23 January 1776. His mother died when he was three and, his father being away at sea, he was brought up by his aunt Helena, the wife of James Baillie of Olive Bank, Musselburgh, near Edinburgh.

Education and early military career He was educated by a governess, then by a tutor, and finally at Musselburgh grammar school, but his early boyhood was spent largely with fishermen, from whom he gained knowledge of boats and the sea. He was intended for the navy, but his

Sir Howard Douglas, third baronet (1776–1861), by William Holl junior, pubd 1863 (after Thomas Richard? Williams, c.1860)

father died suddenly in early 1789 and his guardians—without consulting him and to his bitter disappointment—obtained for him a nomination to the Royal Military Academy, Woolwich. Douglas initially failed the simple entrance examination in reading, writing, and arithmetic, but passed a few weeks later and entered as a cadet on 29 June 1790. He soon showed mathematical ability and became a favourite with Dr Charles Hutton. He appears to have been a daring boy: he spent his spare time on the river, and improved his seamanship by working his passage to and from the north on Leith and Berwick smacks.

Douglas passed out as second lieutenant, Royal Artillery, on 1 January 1794, and was promoted first lieutenant on 30 May 1794. Reportedly he served under the duke of York on the continent, but this appears doubtful. He commanded the artillery of the northern district during the spring 1795 invasion alarms, and in August of that year he embarked for Quebec as senior officer of a detachment of troops on board the transport *Phillis*, which was wrecked off Little Bay Head, Cape Ray, Newfoundland. Douglas suppressed an attempted mutiny among the soldiers, and the survivors were rescued by a trader and taken to Great Jervais, a fishing port on Fortune Bay, Newfoundland, where they passed the winter. They were then taken to Halifax, Nova Scotia, where Douglas served three months, and then to Quebec, where he remained for a year. In summer 1796 he commanded a schooner scouting for the French fleet said to be making for Quebec, and in 1797 and 1798 he served at Kingston, Upper Canada, where he hunted and fished among the native people and was sent on a Canadian government mission to the Cherokees. He once skated from Montreal to Quebec to attend a ball, a feat

which cost the life of a brother officer who accompanied him. He also had an affair with a young Quebec woman, and they had a daughter. Douglas returned home in 1798, and his seamanship saved the timber-laden brig in which he travelled.

In July 1799 Douglas married Anne (c.1781–1854), the eldest daughter of Captain James Dundas of Edinburgh, who was in the East India Company's marine service; they had six sons and three daughters.

Douglas became a captain lieutenant in the Royal Artillery on 2 October 1799 and served at Plymouth, with one of the new horse artillery troops at Canterbury and Woolwich, and for ten months with Congreve's mortar brigade (1803–4). This last, organized by General Congreve (father of the rocket pioneer Sir William Congreve), comprised twenty 8 inch mortars and a battery of field guns. The intention, if the enemy landed, was to bombard them at night with continuous shell fire, preparatory to a dawn attack. Douglas became captain in 1804, but as he was required at the Royal Military College he was placed on half pay, retired from the artillery, and appointed major in the 1st battalion of the army of reserve on 12 October 1804 and the following day placed on half pay of the York rangers. He continued on the retired list of that corps until promoted major-general.

At Sandhurst, and the Napoleonic wars The Royal Military College (later at Sandhurst) was formally established in 1801 with its senior department, to train staff officers, at High Wycombe, Buckinghamshire. From 1804 to 1808 Douglas was superintendent of the senior department, and also held until 1820 the post of inspector-general of instructions. He improved and extended the training and improved discipline. Among his students were Philip Bainbrigge, Henry Hardinge, and other well-known officers of the Peninsular period. However, opinions on him differed. Lieutenant-Colonel Charles Napier, who graduated from the senior department in 1817, alleged: 'Sir Howard Douglas is perfectly ignorant of military affairs and anything but "able" and could not *teach* what he did not *know* … Sir Howard is *quite ignorant* of fortification' (Bond, 53–4). He became brevet lieutenant-colonel on 31 December 1806.

In 1808 Douglas was appointed assistant quartermaster-general in Spain. He joined Sir John Moore's retreating army in December at Benevente, and was present at the battle of Corunna on 18 January 1809. In July 1809 he accompanied the disastrous Walcheren expedition as assistant quartermaster-general and took part in the artillery attack on Flushing; he wrote the journal of the expedition appended to the report of the parliamentary commissioners. Douglas succeeded to the baronetcy on the death of his unmarried elder half-brother, Vice-Admiral Sir William Henry Douglas, second baronet, on 23 May 1809. He then resumed his college duties. Concerned with naval warfare, he studied navigation and developed his 'improved reflecting circle and semicircle for land and marine surveying' (patented in July 1811), for which he was elected FRS in January 1816. In 1811 Lord Liverpool sent him to the north of Spain to report on the state of the Spanish armies in Galicia and Asturias and on Spanish military resources, including the guerrillas, and how they could be assisted. After conferring with Wellington he went on his mission, and was present at the operations on the Orbigo and Esta, in the combined naval and military operations of the Spaniards and Sir Hope Popham's naval squadron on the north coast in the early part of 1812, in the capture of Lequertio, in the siege of Astorga, in operations on the Douro, in the siege of Zamorra, and at the attack on the Douro ports. At the end of August 1812 he joined the army on the advance to Burgos. The British government, expressing satisfaction with his work, then recalled him to the Royal Military College. He became brevet colonel on 4 June 1814, major-general on 19 July 1821, and lieutenant-general on 10 January 1837.

At the end of the Napoleonic wars Douglas had been appalled to witness the low standard of gunnery and gun drill aboard some British warships. Inspired by the brilliant training regime of Captain Philip B. V. Broke and the capture of the USS *Chesapeake* in 1813, he realized that naval officers required a basic knowledge of gunnery as part of their basic training, and that seaman gunners should be encouraged to remain in the service. In 1818 he presented his findings to the Admiralty, without success. He then began to correspond with Broke. Among the naval lords between 1815 and 1830 only Henry Hotham, who had served on the North American station and seen HMS *Shannon*, favoured modern gunnery methods. His interest may well have been reflected in the initial impetus for the gunnery training ship HMS *Excellent*, set up in 1830. Douglas's *Treatise on Naval Gunnery*, which went through five editions between 1820 and 1861, remained the basis of study until the late 1840s, when Douglas fell out with the captain of the ship, Henry Chads RN, over the significance of the new shell-firing guns. Unlike members of the 'liberal' school, Douglas considered shells unreliable and inaccurate. War experience would prove him largely correct. Douglas's book was more than a mere artillery training manual; it encompassed key elements of national strategy, notably the development of new weapons and tactics for the bombardment of foreign naval bases—initially Cherbourg in France. He considered that mortars, and later Armstrong breech-loading cannon, enabled naval forces to lay off at long range and destroy naval bases. In the Crimean War his ideas were applied at Sveaborg in August 1855 with devastating results.

In 1816 Douglas published his *Essay on the Principle and Construction of Military Bridges*, initially compiled in 1808 as a manuscript textbook for the Royal Military College, which reportedly gave Telford the idea of the suspension principle in bridge construction. In 1808 he had also submitted to the authorities a plan for a corps of pontooners. In 1819 he published *Observations on the Motives, Errors, and Tendency of M. Carnot's System of Defence*. His criticism of Carnot drew a reply from a French engineer, M. Augoyat. Copies of the latter work were forwarded by Douglas, then residing in Paris, to Wellington, who was officially interested

in the Prussian Rhine frontier fortresses then under construction, and led to artillery experiments at Woolwich, in accordance with Douglas's suggestions, in 1822.

Douglas in North America From 1823 to 1831 Douglas was lieutenant-governor of New Brunswick, where he arrived in August 1824. He was dynamic, effective, and popular. He identified with the province and encouraged its development, reorganizing local government and the militia. In 1825 fires destroyed Government House, forests, and much of the capital, Fredericton; Douglas directed the fire-fighting, relief, and reconstruction. He favoured British immigration but opposed the British government's pauper emigration, and he wanted adequate reserves for native North Americans. He improved communications and promoted rural schools, agricultural societies, and fairs. He saw the North American colonies as a source of strength to Britain and urged the British government to continue financial support to New Brunswick, opposing Treasury policy on the payment of customs officials. He was a founder and first chancellor of King's College, Fredericton (later the University of New Brunswick), which received its royal charter in 1829 and where he endowed an annual prize. He resisted American encroachments. The boundary dispute with the United States was referred to arbitration by the king of the Netherlands, and in March 1829 Douglas was ordered to England to advise the British delegation. While there he was awarded an honorary DCL degree by Oxford University (1 July 1829) for his work in New Brunswick, especially with King's College, and was enthusiastically cheered by the undergraduates. His presence at The Hague when the Belgians rebelled in 1830 led to his being sent on a secret observation mission on the Dutch frontier. In February 1831 he resigned as lieutenant-governor in order to campaign publicly for continued British protective tariffs for British North American timber, against the ascendant free-traders. He published a pamphlet, *Considerations on the Value and Importance of the British North American Provinces* (1831). When the House of Commons rejected a whig government bill to reduce duties on Baltic timber, Douglas was acclaimed for saving the North American timber trade, and in New Brunswick a public subscription was raised to send him a service of silver plate. However, he was not favoured by the whig government, who disliked his firmness on the boundary question and also his opposition to the Reform Bill and to emancipation.

In 1832 Douglas published *Naval Evolutions on the Battle of the Saints*, defending his father's claim as originator of the manoeuvre of 'breaking the line'. This work was suggested by a conversation with his old friend and school companion Sir Walter Scott. Douglas unsuccessfully contested Liverpool as a Conservative in 1832 and again in 1835. From March 1835 to December 1840 he was lord high commissioner of the Ionian Islands. The post was a difficult one, but despite criticism at home he governed firmly, if sometimes high-handedly. He foiled conspiracy, domestic and foreign, and countered Russian intrigue, promoted education and public works, and improved the revenue. He introduced a new code of laws based on the

Greek model, known as the Douglas code, and founded a prize medal (the Douglas medal) at the Ionian College. At his departure the Ionian states erected a column at Corfu commemorating the achievements of his government. In 1837 he became lieutenant-general and in 1841 colonel of the 99th foot, and in 1851 was transferred to the 15th foot. In November 1851 he was promoted general. Douglas was elected a Conservative MP for Liverpool in 1842. A frequent and moderate speaker on service questions, he warned against the French naval threat, advocated a naval reserve, and attempted to gain better treatment of army surgeons. In 1846 he voted against the repeal of the corn laws, and at the 1847 dissolution withdrew from parliamentary life.

Later life For the rest of his life Douglas took an active interest in professional subjects. He was consulted by politicians on service matters, as by Sir Robert Peel in 1848 on the introduction of iron ships into the navy, which Douglas opposed; by Lord Aberdeen in 1854 on the descent on the Crimea, which Douglas opposed on the grounds that the season was too far advanced and the army insufficiently provided; by Lord Panmure in 1855 on army education—Douglas having called attention to the decline of military education; and by Sir John Pakington on ship armour, which Douglas strongly and controversially opposed, maintaining that ordnance would in the end always prove superior to any armour that could be carried. He told the 1855 select committee on the Royal Military College of the potential value of a revived staff school. He also developed an improved screw propellor. In 1859 he was invited to be chairman of the royal commission on the defences of the United Kingdom, but declined because of his age. He was 'a steady assertor of the doctrine that ships could not stand against forts' (*GM*, 3rd ser., 14, 1863, 91), and he recommended that the government substantially implement the recommendations of the commission's 1860 report, which resulted in the 'Palmerston's follies' fortifications. Though in some respects a reformer, in others Douglas was conservative: for example, in the early 1850s he opposed replacement of muskets by rifles.

Douglas's later output included the significant study *Naval Warfare under Steam* (1857) and *Modern Systems of Fortification* (1859). Lord Palmerston, prime minister from 1855 to 1858, and again from 1859 to 1865, held Douglas in the highest regard as an adviser on defence. Douglas's work on steam tactics was overly geometric, but it inspired more practical work, at Palmerston's direction, in Admiral Sir William Fanshawe Martin's Mediterranean Fleet (1860–63). His publications showed the wide scope of his scientific and technical attainments, and it has been claimed that the value of his labours lay in his peculiar capacity for grafting new discoveries on old experience and hitting the wants of the generation which had sprung up since his own youth.

Douglas's last service to his country was to raise doubts about the value of ironclad warships in a heated debate with John Scott Russell and the Institution of Naval Architects. Although he was wrong, Douglas had forced the exponents of the new system to think through their ideas and express their arguments with greater clarity than had hitherto been the case.

Although a theoretical, and conservative, contributor to the development of naval gunnery, Douglas provided a critical professional element to supplement the work of Broke and other reformers.

Douglas was one of the first fellows of the Royal Geographical Society and was elected an associate of the Institution of Naval Architects (1861). He was made CB in February 1817, GCMG in March 1835, KCB in July 1840, and GCB, civil division, in August 1841. Shortly before his death Palmerston offered him the military GCB, but he declined, saying he was 'too old for such vanities' (Fullom, 423). He had the grand cordon of Charles III of Spain and the Peninsular medal with clasp for Corunna. He was a commissioner of the Royal Military College, a patron of the Royal United Service Institution and of Wellington College, in which he took a lively interest, president of the Royal Cambridge Asylum, and supported other charities. He was colonel of the 99th regiment from 1841 to 1851 and of the 15th from 1851 until his death. For many years he was a gentleman of the bedchamber to the duke of Gloucester.

On 22 September 1859 Douglas's unmarried daughter, Christina Helena Emma, his companion since his wife's death, died, and the shock apparently contributed to the deterioration of his health. He died at Tunbridge Wells, Kent, on 9 November 1861, and was buried beside his wife at Boldre, near Lymington, Hampshire. His three elder sons had died in the service of their country, and he was succeeded in the baronetcy by his fourth son, Robert Percy (1805–1891), army officer and lieutenant-governor of the Cape of Good Hope (1863–8).

H. M. CHICHESTER, rev. ROGER T. STEARN

Sources S. W. Fullom, *The life of General Sir Howard Douglas, Bart., G.C.B., G.C.M.G., F.R.S., D.C.L.* (1863) · *GM*, 3rd ser., 14 (1863), 89–91 · *DCB*, vol. 9 · GEC, *Peerage* · Boase, *Mod. Eng. biog.* · Burke, *Peerage* (1924) · private information (2004) [A. D. Lambert] · *Dod's Peerage* (1858) · *Hart's Army List* (1854) · J. G. Lockhart, *The life of Sir Walter Scott*, [new edn], 10 vols. (1902) · A. D. Lambert, *The last sailing battlefleet: maintaining naval mastery, 1815–1850* (1991) · B. Bond, *The Victorian army and the Staff College, 1854–1914* (1972) · J. G. Wells, *Whaley: the story of HMS Excellent, 1830 to 1980* (1980) · J. Smyth, *Sandhurst: the history of the Royal Military Academy, Woolwich, the Royal Military College, Sandhurst, and the Royal Military Academy, Sandhurst, 1741–1961* (1961) · M. S. Partridge, *Military planning for the defense of the United Kingdom, 1814–1870* (1989) · H. Strachan, *From Waterloo to Balaclava: tactics, technology and the British army, 1815–1854* (1985) · J. Philippart, ed., *The royal military calendar*, 3rd edn, 5 vols. (1820) · F. Duncan, ed., *History of the royal regiment of artillery*, 1 (1872)

Archives NA Canada, corresp., letter-books, and papers, MG 24 A3 · University of New Brunswick, Harriet Irving Library, letter-book, E3B 5H5 · University of New Brunswick, letter-books | All Souls Oxf., corresp. with Charles Richard Vaughan · BL, corresp. with Lord Aberdeen, Add. MSS 43123–43250, *passim* · BL, corresp. with Sir Robert Peel, Add. MSS 40310–40608, *passim* · Bodl. Oxf., letters to Sir William Napier, MS Eng. lett. c 245 · Lpool RO, letters to fourteenth earl of Derby, 920 Der 14, box 137 · Metropolitan Toronto Reference Library, letters and papers relating to New Brunswick's defences · NA Scot., letters to Lord Dalhousie, GD4S · NA Scot., letters to G. W. Hope · NL Scot., letters to Lord Melville,

MS15 • NMM, Broke MSS • U. Durham L., letters to Viscount Ponsonby • W. Sussex RO, letters to Admiral Lord Lyons
Likenesses W. Holl junior, stipple and line engraving, pubd 1863 (after T. R.? Williams, c.1860), NPG; repro. in Fullom, *Life of General Sir Howard Douglas*, frontispiece [*see illus.*] • F. Chantrey, pencil drawing, NPG
Wealth at death £16,000: probate, 16 Jan 1862, *CGPLA Eng. & Wales*

Douglas, Hugh Osborne (1911–1986), Church of Scotland minister, was born in Glasgow on 11 September 1911, the son of the Revd Robert Baillie Douglas (1870–1943) and his wife, Mary Isabella Osborne (1870–1955). His parents served as missionaries in India. His early years were spent in India, first in Jalna and then in Bombay. He returned to Glasgow for his schooling at Glasgow Academy (1919–28), and stayed with his maternal aunts. Through his school days he was to see his parents only when they were home on furlough. He was joint dux of the academy, and in 1928 went on to study classics at Glasgow University. His experience as a child had not given him any enthusiasm for the organized church, and his aim was to be a lawyer. But the Scottish Schoolboys' Club had encouraged a healthy, liberal religious commitment which the Student Christian Movement was to mature, and he came to find a vocation to the ministry.

In 1932 Douglas graduated with a first in classics, though it is questionable whether that gave him greater pleasure than his blue for rugby. During his theological study at Trinity College he became assistant to the Revd Dr George MacLeod at Govan, and continued to work there for five years, as probationer and then as ordained assistant. These years in an industrial parish in a time of depression shaped his entire ministry. MacLeod's vision gave him hope that the church could be relevant to the whole of life, to the slum and the street as well as to the sanctuary. In 1938, when MacLeod left to found the Iona community, Hugh Douglas continued in Govan until the appointment of MacLeod's successor. In March 1939 he was inducted to St John's, Leven. He took a bit of Govan with him, however, for on 29 April he married the girls' club leader, Isabella Crammond Rutherford (1910–1995), who was to be his lifelong companion and helpmeet. During their time in Leven their three children, Molly, and then twins, Colin and Ruth, were born. At the outbreak of war he wished to volunteer as a chaplain, but his congregation persuaded him to stay.

In November 1942 Douglas was called to the parish of North Leith. Here he developed more fully his style of ministry, using many of the insights of Govan. A congregation used to an individual gospel soon warmed to the demands made on it, in a mission of friendship to the parish and in many other ways. Yet although the influence of Govan was always there, Douglas was never an imitator of MacLeod. His style was his own. He did not aspire to be the visionary orator. He was a pastor who cared intensely for his people and who preached quietly, persuasively, and comfortingly to their needs in a world at war.

The church building had suffered bomb damage in 1941, and not until war restrictions ended was it possible to think of full restoration. Then structural damage and rot were found and costs escalated. But by 1950 Ian Lindsay's scheme of restoration of the Georgian building was complete and paid for, and George MacLeod preached at the rededication. In 1951 came a call to Dundee: St Mary's, the original parish church of Dundee. The congregation was spread citywide, and the minister was called on for many civic duties. These Douglas could take in his stride. His main concern was to develop the life and witness of his congregation, and here he had the help of a succession of young assistants and deaconesses. Those he trained in this way kept their affection for him until his death.

In 1945 Douglas had written a pamphlet, *What is Christian Marriage*, and he became the founder chairman of the Dundee Marriage Guidance Council. He was a natural broadcaster with his persuasive, almost confidential style, and became known to a wide public through a series of talks, later published as *Coping with Life* (1964). Life in Dundee was not all work. A month each summer was spent with the family, usually on Iona, and Monday mornings were frequently spent on the golf course.

The wider church began to use Douglas's gifts in committee work. He convened the committee which organized the celebration of the fourth centenary of the Scottish Reformation in 1960, when the queen attended a special session of the general assembly. But he had overstretched himself with unremitting pastoral work, meticulous pulpit preparation, and demanding committee work. A coronary thrombosis sounded a warning. He learned to pace himself better, and in 1970 was able to undertake the onerous duties of moderator of the general assembly.

In 1958 Douglas received a DD from St Andrews University, and in 1971 an LLD from the University of Dundee. In 1959 he became one of the queen's chaplains in Scotland, and in 1974 dean of the Chapel Royal, a post from which he retired on his seventieth birthday in 1981. In 1961 he was appointed CBE, and in 1981 was made a knight commander in the Royal Victorian Order. In 1977 he retired from St Mary's and settled in St Andrews. He had given many talks to ministers on how to cope with retirement, and now he put his own advice into practice. He served as locum tenens in Hope Park church, and later accepted the invitation of the new minister to become his part-time associate. It was a happy association in which the younger man had the responsibility and the older man now did as he was asked. Douglas loved it, and the people loved him. Sadly it ended when a further series of heart attacks took his life on 4 January 1986 at Broomlea, Windmill Road, St Andrews, Fife. He was buried at the western cemetery, St Andrews, on 9 January.

Douglas was a shy man, whose reserve could be misinterpreted as aloofness. Yet he attained distinction both in church and in state, carried both without any pretension, and earned the affection of all who worked and worshipped with him.   JAMES A. WHYTE

Sources *WW* (1985) • *Fasti Scot.*, new edn, vols. 9–10 • H. Douglas, *One man's ministry* (1993) • personal knowledge (2004) • private information (2004) • *CCI* (1986)
Archives priv. coll.

Likenesses photograph, General Assembly of the Church of Scotland, Edinburgh · photographs, priv. coll.
Wealth at death £43,912.77: confirmation, 21 April 1986, *CCI*

Douglas, Sir James [*called* the Black Douglas] (*d.* **1330**), soldier, was the son of Sir William *Douglas [*see under* Douglas family] and of Elizabeth, daughter of Alexander, the steward of Scotland; she had died by 1289. William Douglas's arrest (1297) and imprisonment and death (1298) allowed Edward I to grant his lands of Douglas to Sir Robert Clifford, leaving James to find his own way in the world.

First battles About 1301–4 Douglas went to Paris (where he sowed his wild oats), possibly as valet to William Lamberton, bishop of St Andrews, because after the latter's return to Scotland Douglas served him as his carver. Lamberton interceded with Edward I, asking that Douglas have his lands restored to him, but merely angered the king. When Robert I made his bid for the throne in 1306, Douglas soon joined him. He is said to have been present at the battle of Methven on 19 June 1306 and to have shared Robert's subsequent hardships in the highlands, though it is unlikely that he went to Kintyre, Rathlin, and the Isles with the king between September and December 1306.

In 1307 Douglas began his long campaign to recover his heritage. He took Douglas Castle about 1 May 1307, but ingratiatingly sent the garrison back to Clifford (who repaired the castle); he was at Loudoun on 10 May, seeking to negotiate terms with the advancing force of Aymer de Valence, before joining King Robert in halting them. In the following months he harassed the English and, while he was hounded near Paisley in September 1307, defeated the pursuers at 'Edirford' near Fenwick, Ayrshire. He remained in Ettrick Forest when Robert went north in September 1307 and on Palm Sunday (7 April) 1308 caught the garrison of Douglas Castle in Douglas kirk, took the undefended castle, and beheaded the prisoners in a cellar, mingling their blood and limbs with emptied sacks of provisions and tuns of wine from the castle stores; the well was polluted with salt and dead horse. The name Douglas Lardner needs no further explanation. Later in the year he joined the king to defeat the men of John of Argyll, whom they sandwiched between their forces on the slopes of Ben Cruachan, and after his return to Ettrick captured a small body of Anglo-Scots including the king's nephew, Thomas Randolph.

Between Douglas's appearance as a baron, though not a knight, at the St Andrews parliament of March 1309 and Bannockburn in 1314, little is heard of him, partly because the war was relatively quiet in 1309–11, and partly because King Robert himself led the incursions into enemy territory thereafter. Douglas is not named at the attacks on Dundee, Berwick, or Perth in 1312–13, but early in 1314, when Randolph, now earl of Moray, was besieging Edinburgh, he again had a signal success from his Ettrick base by taking Roxburgh Castle at night on 27 February 1314, his men creeping close to the walls under cloaks and securing a rope ladder to the wall-head. Later in the year he and his young cousin Walter Stewart were knighted on

the eve of Bannockburn—he must have been at least twenty-six years old—and, according to Barbour's *Bruce*, he was in command of one of four Scottish divisions there. But all other sources are agreed on three divisions, and it is likely that he served under Edward Bruce. When the English broke and Edward II fled, King Robert allowed Douglas to pursue him, but the Scots dared not send a large enough cavalry force lest the English rally (or so Barbour claims); despite being followed by Douglas all the way, Edward and his men rode by Winchburgh to Dunbar and safety.

Campaigns in northern England The victory of Bannockburn, though not complete, established Robert I's rule firmly, and led to an intensification of attacks on northern England, attacks in which the king rarely participated, the leaders being Moray, when not in Ireland, and Douglas. In the summer of 1315 when the Scots invaded co. Durham, the king sent Douglas to Hartlepool, formerly a Bruce possession; Douglas despoiled the town, took men and women prisoner, and rejoined the king to return home. Later in the year, in Cumberland, Douglas ravaged in Copeland, robbing the priory of St Bees of its vestments, before joining the king at the siege of Carlisle. In the final assault, on 30 July, his men seem to have reached the wall-head, but were driven off, and Douglas himself is said to have been wounded; the army withdrew. On 13 January 1316, in an unsuccessful surprise attack on Berwick, Douglas barely escaped with his life in a small boat; according to one source, he was jointly responsible for the taking of the town in April 1318, having bribed a defender to allow Scots to climb the wall:

> At dawn, with the gates opened, they had James Douglas, who was waiting outside, come in. This James entered the town with such lightness and joy in his heart that he claimed he had come into the city more cheerfully and happily than even paradise. For they despoiled all that they found and killed those who resisted them, throwing the rest into prison. (Stevenson, 5)

Barbour gives the credit elsewhere.

Meanwhile, in the first half of 1317 the king and Moray diverted their energies to Ireland and Douglas was left in Scotland, according to Barbour, as 'Warden' and 'Warden of the March'. The former, which implies a regency, is unlikely; the latter is independently attested. Seeking advantage from the king's absence, the English warden, the earl of Arundel, invaded Roxburghshire with a large force in March 1317, and aimed:

> at Lintalee, where James Douglas was staying in a certain fortified place with 200 men. Hearing of their coming, Douglas took to flight, leaving the place empty, which a noble freebooter called Elias the clerk, with 30 companions entered, eating up the many victuals he found there. But James, having ascertained the sloth of the English, who made little effort to approach the place, recovered his boldness, entered the place, cut off the head of Elias and stuck its face inhumanely in the anus, killing the rest by the sword. Then he violently attacked the army of the English, which conducted itself very carelessly, and killed Sir Thomas Richmond. (Stevenson, 3–4)

Barbour has another version, omitting Douglas's initial flight and the fate of Elias's face, but describing how

Douglas knocked Richmond to the ground, dismounted, turned him over, and dispatched him with a dagger—no time for taking prisoners in the heat of combat.

When the succession was regulated in 1315, it was laid down that in the event of a child succeeding Robert I, Moray was to be guardian; three years later, in revised provisions after the death of Edward Bruce, Moray was again to serve or, if he had died, Douglas. Although he was not an earl nor any kin of the king and the extent of his comradeship with Robert may well have been overdrawn by Barbour, Douglas's military capacities had nevertheless won him recognition as the outstanding man in the kingdom, and a series of brushes with the enemy in these years confirmed his abilities as a brilliant tactician and ruthless field commander, to whom winning was all. The women of the English borders silenced their children with the threat that mewling would bring the Black Douglas upon them. The name is not derived from his coat of arms, so presumably refers to the colour of his hair.

Douglas with Moray led the force which penetrated to near York in 1319, defeated a local force mustered by the archbishop at the 'Chapter of Myton' (because so many clerics were killed), and pulled Edward II away from the siege of Berwick. There was a truce in 1320–21, and in 1322 Douglas was deep in the negotiations between an invalid King Robert and the traitor Thomas, earl of Lancaster. Later in that year, as Edward II withdrew from his vain march to Edinburgh, Douglas caught and destroyed a scouting party at Melrose, then joined his king and Moray in a swift and secret invasion of England which sent the queen fleeing for refuge from York, defeated Edward's force in a brilliant uphill assault near Byland, and almost caught him as he fled from Rievaulx Abbey, abandoning his plate and equipment to the Scots; again Barbour presents Douglas as commander, but it is likely that he served under Moray and the king.

Victory and its rewards After the truce of 1323–7 Douglas was a leader either with or, more probably, under Moray of the 1327 campaign in Northumberland which drew Edward III in pursuit. It is brilliantly described by Jean le Bel (who was with Edward) and by Barbour, and if the latter prettifies the planning of the Scots, there can be no doubt that the English stumbled about in a strategic and tactical fog. Barbour ascribes two brilliant moves to Douglas: in Weardale he led a night force round the English and attacked their camp on the far side, cutting tent-ropes to confuse and immobilize them and almost reaching King Edward's tent; and on 6–7 August 1327, silently by night, the Scots evacuated Stanhope Park with no loss other than of horses and equipment—in large amounts, says le Bel. The former enterprise was certainly his.

The English made peace in 1328, and Douglas and Moray were at Berwick for the rumbustious marriage of the young David, earl of Carrick, to Joan of the Tower; the kirkyard wall was knocked down by the revellers. Douglas had been well rewarded by his king with grants of the lands, castle, and forest of Jedworth, of Ettrick Forest, Lauderdale, and Bedrule in the east and the baronies of Staplegordon and Westerkirk in Eskdale in the west, as well

as a more generous definition of his lordship of Douglas in Lanarkshire. After the peace the family's English lands (at Fawdon in Northumberland) were restored to him, despite the king's wish not to revive such double loyalties. At Byland he had taken three French knights prisoner; in return for 4400 merks he was persuaded to release these men to his king, who wished to send them home to win over Charles IV of France. As payment of this sum the king, by putting an emerald ring on Douglas's finger, gave him the revenues of criminal justice from all his lands and baronies and freed them from any services due; it was a unique mark of favour, and at the same time a taste of the gravy which dripped from the roast of chivalric warfare.

Death in Spain In 1329, as Robert I lay dying, Douglas undertook for his lord, troubled by the murder of Comyn in a church in 1306, the responsibility of carrying the king's heart to the Holy Land 'to the help of Christians against Saracens' (*CDS*, vol. 3, nos. 990, 991) and returning it for burial at Melrose Abbey. On 1 February 1330, the day of Douglas's patron, St Brigit, he made a gift to Newbattle Abbey, then set out for the Mediterranean by sea with an English safe conduct. In Spain he joined Alfonso XI of Castile in his war against the Moors of Granada, and was involved in a battle at Turon near the siege of Teba, Malaga province. He seems to have been rash, as he became isolated and was cut down and killed on 25 August 1330. His body was boiled, the flesh buried in Spain and the bones brought back for burial at Douglas, where decades later his illegitimate son, Archibald, provided the tombstone in that kirk. The political consequences of sending Douglas away were catastrophic, for Moray died as guardian a week before the war was renewed in 1332, leaving the Scots without the one leader who might have discouraged Edward III.

Barbour's *Bruce* describes Douglas memorably:

> his face was somewhat grey and he had black hair, as I heard say; but his limbs were well made, with big bones and broad shoulders. His body was well-made and lean, as those who saw him said to me. When he was cheerful he was attractive, meek and sweet in company, but if you saw him in battle, he had another face altogether. He lisped in his speech a little, but that suited him very well.   (Barbour, 64)

When he was in Spain, an English knight was astonished that so fierce and famous a veteran had no scars on his face. He has left only one known charter as grantor, and most of our knowledge of him comes from *The Bruce*, behind which surely lies a life, perhaps by Douglas herald, written not long after his death; such a source is suggested by Barbour's knightly league-table entry: 'he was beaten thirteen times, and won victory fifty-seven' (Barbour, 312).

The name of Douglas's wife is unknown, but they had a son, William, who was killed, childless, at Halidon Hill on 19 July 1333. James also had an illegitimate son, Archibald *Douglas, who, through an entail of 1342, succeeded to the lands and (by then) earldom of Douglas in 1388, and from whom the earls down to 1455 were descended.

A. A. M. DUNCAN

Sources J. Barbour, *The Bruce*, ed. A. A. M. Duncan (1997) • J. Stevenson, ed., *Chronicon de Lanercost, 1201–1346*, Bannatyne Club, 65 (1839) • *Scalacronica, by Sir Thomas Gray of Heton, knight: a chronical of England and Scotland from AD MLXVI to AD MCCCLXII*, ed. J. Stevenson, Maitland Club, 40 (1836) • J. Stevenson, ed., *Illustrations of Scottish history, from the twelfth to the sixteenth century*, Maitland Club, 28 (1834) • G. W. S. Barrow, *Robert Bruce and the community of the realm of Scotland*, 3rd edn (1988) • W. Fraser, ed., *The Douglas book*, 4 vols. (1885) • *Scots peerage*, 3.142–6 • W. Bower, *Scotichronicon*, ed. D. E. R. Watt and others, new edn, 9 vols. (1987–98), vol. 7
Likenesses marble effigy on monument, *c.*1380, Douglas kirk • lithograph, repro. in Fraser, ed., *Douglas book* • photograph (of effigy), National Monuments Record, Edinburgh

Douglas, James, second earl of Douglas and earl of Mar (*c.*1358–1388), magnate and soldier, was the son of William *Douglas, first earl of Douglas, and his wife, Margaret of Mar. He was probably born in the late 1350s and was old enough to make a favourable impression on the chronicler Jean Froissart when he visited Scotland during the 1360s. In 1371 the newly crowned Robert II, in an attempt to win over James's father, knighted the Douglas heir and agreed a marriage alliance between James and his second daughter, Isabella (*d. c.*1410). In connection with this match James received annuities worth £266 from the king. This generosity may have been in part intended to compensate Douglas for the exclusion of his new wife from the succession under the male entail that was subsequently created, as well as representing the exercise of crown patronage on behalf of a great noble.

During the later 1370s James Douglas assumed an active role in his family's affairs and was assigned the lordship of Liddesdale by his father. As Earl William's title to this estate was dubious, his grant forestalled future difficulties of James's inheritance. James's emergence as an active political figure was also marked by a royal grant of customs revenue to him in return for his service as a retainer of the king and his son John Stewart, earl of Carrick. Probably intended to finance Douglas's own military following, the grant symbolized a growing alliance between Carrick and the Douglases, one centred on the war with England. James clearly supported his father's prosecution of warfare in the marches and in 1381 was associated with Carrick in border diplomacy. The two men also received gifts from John of Gaunt for their hospitality when the latter took refuge briefly in Scotland in 1381.

In spring 1384 full-scale war erupted with England. Shortly after leading an attack on Teviotdale in early April, Earl William died. James Douglas succeeded to the extensive southern estates of the Douglas earldom and to his mother's earldom of Mar in Aberdeenshire. The new earl immediately made his mark in war and politics. While Robert II and many Scots wished to suspend warfare and join the recent Anglo-French truce, Douglas was determined to continue the conflict and to respond to an English raid on Lothian in April. A significant group of magnates, led by Carrick, seems to have backed Douglas, perhaps after secret talks in Edinburgh, and there was a series of Scottish raids into northern England during the summer of 1384. Although a short truce was agreed, it is unlikely that Douglas observed its terms. Moreover, in

November Robert II was sidelined politically and Carrick was appointed as lieutenant of the realm. Douglas gave Carrick vital support in this coup. In return he expected the lieutenant to give full support to the war with England. In a manner which would be repeated, Douglas military ambitions in the south had been a determining factor in the rivalries of the Stewart dynasty.

In spring 1385 the war was resumed with active French help. A war subsidy was sent by the French to various Scottish magnates and Douglas received 7500 livres tournois, the largest sum given to any Scottish lord. In May an expeditionary force arrived from France at Leith to be met by Douglas and John Dunbar, earl of Moray. Douglas, whose father had had strong ties to France, may have been the sponsor of the whole venture. He went to the west to escort Robert II to Edinburgh to meet the French, and was one of the few Scots to make a favourable impression on these allies. However, even Douglas urged the French to be cautious in their attacks on the English and probably hoped to use the army for the capture of Roxburgh Castle, whose English garrison was based amid the earl's border lands. But after brief local campaigning the army withdrew in the face of a major English counter-attack and the French returned home.

Douglas's role in war and politics depended in his extensive network of adherents in southern Scotland. He inherited much of this following from his father. The earl's closest allies were his cousin James Lindsay of Crawford and Sir Malcolm *Drummond [*see under* Drummond family], the husband of his sister Isabella. These men also formed a bridge to Carrick. Other kinsmen, like his uncle Patrick Hepburn, and his cousin James Sandilands, were men who had built connections with the old earl. However, in his short spell at the head of the Douglas lordships, James sought to extend his connection. That his father's rivals in the Douglas kindred, James Douglas, lord of Dalkeith, and Archibald Douglas, lord of Galloway, appeared on the new earl's council suggests improved relations, perhaps fostered by Carrick. James also sought to strengthen his kindred, as well as to provide for his own children, when he granted his bastard son William the lordship of Drumlanrig in Dumfriesshire in return for one knight in the earl's army. The marriage of his widowed mother to Sir John Swinton may have been encouraged by Earl James for military reasons. Swinton was an experienced soldier, and his good relations with his stepson are suggested by the earl's reference to him as 'our dearest father'. When Robert Colville, a Teviotdale lord who returned to Scottish allegiance only in 1384, married the daughter of James Lindsay, it was an alliance designed to bring a new recruit into the Douglas affinity. The needs of warfare were never far from Earl James's lordship.

Given the importance of the earl of Douglas in Carrick's regime and his overriding interest in war with England, it is not surprising that the Scots renewed the conflict on a major scale in 1388 and that Douglas played a leading role in the campaign which was fought that summer. In late July 1388 Douglas assembled an army which was dominated by his own adherents. In the army were Drummond, the Lindsays, Swinton, Sandilands, and Hepburn, as well as the Dunbars, George, earl of March, and John, earl of Moray. The other leaders of the host were Lothian knights whose connections with James's father stretched back to the 1350s and marchers who traditionally followed the Douglas banner. Although some retainers of Carrick were also present, the bonds of Douglas lordship and kinship held the army together. Rather than as part of a national host, this force was raised and deployed as the earl's army. Douglas led his army into north-east England raiding as far south as Newcastle. In a skirmish outside the walls, Douglas's men captured the pennon of Henry Percy, Hotspur. This loss is supposed to have provoked Hotspur to pursue the Scots as they withdrew. On about 5 August 1388 the English army caught up with the Scots at Otterburn in Redesdale, attacking them in the evening. Led by Earl James, the Scots recovered from the surprise to defeat the English, but in the confused night-fighting Douglas was killed. His body was recovered by his men and carried back for burial alongside his father in Melrose Abbey.

Although James Douglas had two bastard sons, William and Archibald, and one daughter, Eleanor, he had no children from his marriage to Isabella Stewart. James's death created a succession dispute over his estates during late 1388 and early 1389, which ended in the inheritance of the earldom of Douglas by Archibald the Grim, rather than by James's ally and brother-in-law Malcolm Drummond. This competition in turn precipitated the downfall of Carrick as lieutenant and his replacement by Robert Stewart, earl of Fife. The death of Douglas thus caused a major readjustment of political power in Scotland. His friends lost power to men who were, at best, ambivalent in their attitude to James. This upheaval had a major effect on the earl's posthumous reputation and has obscured the events of Douglas's last campaign. The contemporary Scottish account, used in the chronicles of Andrew Wyntoun and Walter Bower, is critical of the earl. It portrays him as rash and unwise, first in refusing to join the Scottish army assembled in the west march, then in rushing into battle without armour or bodyguard. By contrast, Fife and Archibald Douglas, the western leaders, are said to have showed wisdom in bringing their army home. The new regime wished to highlight the failings of the dead earl for political purposes. This account was not the only view of the 1388 campaign, however. Jean Froissart wrote an account of Otterburn based on the views of knights in Douglas's force which claims that Douglas's separate invasion was the result of a previously agreed plan. Froissart also presents the Scottish leaders as coolly planning to meet the English attack. Although Douglas was killed in the fight, Froissart portrays him as heroic rather than stupid, winning the fight but dying at the moment of triumph. Significantly, a similarly heroic tone was used in a poetic account of Otterburn written in the 1390s. Its author, Thomas Barry, was a clerical servant of Archibald Douglas and its approach may reflect the desire of the new Douglas earl to glorify his predecessor and smooth over past divisions. The earl's last fight similarly entered popular imagination. On both sides of the border,

ballads were composed about the Otterburn campaign. While these vary in perspective and in their views of the outcome of the battle, they both present James as 'the dowghtye Douglas', a chivalrous enemy or a valiant leader. While Earl James's death may have divided historians, all agreed on his warlike character and readiness to fight the English.   M. H. BROWN

Sources S. I. Boardman, *The early Stewart kings: Robert II and Robert III, 1371–1406* (1996) · A. Grant, 'The Otterburn war from the Scottish point of view', *War and border societies in the middle ages*, ed. A. Goodman and A. Tuck (1992), 30–65 · J. Reed, 'The ballad and the source: some literary reflections on *The battle of Otterburn*', in A. Goodman and A. Tuck, *War and border societies in the middle ages* (1992), 94–123 · M. Brown, *The Black Douglases: war and lordship in late medieval Scotland, 1300–1455* (1998) · W. Fraser, ed., *The Douglas book*, 4 vols. (1885) · W. Bower, *Scotichronicon*, ed. D. E. R. Watt and others, new edn, 9 vols. (1987–98), vol. 7

Douglas, Sir James, of Dalkeith (*d.* 1420), magnate, was the eldest son of Sir John Douglas and his wife, Agnes. His father came from a minor branch of the Douglas kindred, whose importance was raised in the 1330s and 1340s through the activities of James's uncle, William Douglas of Lothian. John Douglas was killed in 1349, and by 1351 James was named as William's heir-male for his lands of Aberdour in Fife and Dalkeith. In return James served as a hostage for his uncle's release from English captivity and returned to Scotland only after William was killed in 1353. His killer, William, first earl of Douglas, proceeded to occupy many of his victim's estates, including Liddesdale and Dalkeith.

Through the 1350s James Douglas was powerless to recover his uncle's lands. His principal connections during this period were with his five brothers and his more distant kinsman, Archibald Douglas, known as the Grim, another associate of William Douglas. It was probably through Archibald that James obtained access to David II's favour. In the early 1360s the king confirmed James's right to Aberdour and other lands of William and granted him holdings in Annandale—minor patronage, but a sign of growing royal support. In 1367 James claimed the lands of Mary, daughter of William Douglas, who had died in childbirth along with her child. Her husband, Robert Erskine, claimed the estates in right of the dead infant, James, as Mary's heir. A judicial duel between the claimants was planned over the lands, and, before this, James was knighted by Archibald Douglas. The king ultimately decided the dispute in James's favour. In late 1369 and early 1370 David II granted James lands near Kinghorn, Fife, and confirmed his rights to Dalkeith and to lands at Buittle in Galloway. These latter rewards reflected David's animosity towards Earl William, who lost these estates, but they were also royal compensation. James had been betrothed to Agnes Dunbar, David's mistress and intended third wife.

Sir James Douglas of Dalkeith was linked to the king's southern allies, Archibald Douglas and George Dunbar, earl of March. On David's death in 1371, James strengthened these bonds. He married Agnes Dunbar and received the lands of Morton in Dumfriesshire, Mordington in Berwickshire, and Whittingham in Haddingtonshire from her sister March. In 1372 he accompanied Archibald on an embassy to France. Tensions with Earl William were eased by James's agreement to become the earl's retainer in 1372, while following the death of Agnes, James's marriage to Egidia (d. before 1406), the widowed sister of Robert II, secured his acceptance in 1378 by the new king, who gave his brother-in-law a series of rights and privileges, including the erection of Dalkeith and other lands into a regality. However, when the earl of Douglas was killed in 1388, James Douglas exploited the crisis. It was his horse that kicked the lieutenant, John, earl of Carrick, precipitating a change of regime; but more directly, James renewed his claims to Liddesdale, and to lands in Eskdale, as heir to William Douglas of Lothian. James occupied these lands and gained limited acceptance of his rights. The next decade saw James seeking to defend these gains both on the royal council and locally, against pressure which may have encouraged James to produce detailed wills in 1390 and 1392. In 1397 a series of attacks led by George Douglas, son of Earl William, devastated James's Lothian estates in an attempt to force him to surrender Liddesdale. In a negotiated settlement, James relinquished Liddesdale but retained his Eskdale lands.

After 1400 Sir James Douglas continued his association with the Black Douglases. When the new earl was captured at Homildon Hill in 1402, Douglas of Dalkeith sent his son and grandson to act as hostages for him and was associated with the earl's servants in border negotiations. He was rewarded by the erection of his lands at Buittle in Galloway into a regality. By the early fifteenth century he was recognized as a major Scottish magnate and was one of a small group who received a letter from James I in 1415. When he died in 1420, in his eighties, of a disease called 'le Quhew', James Douglas had assembled a major collection of southern Scottish estates later valued at 1500 merks, a figure which placed the Douglases of Dalkeith among the richest Scottish barons.

This picture of Dalkeith's wealth is supported by the exceptional survival of Sir James Douglas's records, especially his wills and a rental of his lands. These give a unique picture of the activities, concerns, and tastes of a late fourteenth century Scottish nobleman. The wills of 1390 and 1392, in particular, demonstrate that, far from being backward and uneducated, a Scottish magnate could possess objects of value and learning. For example, Douglas possessed a small library. He owned books of grammar, dialectic, statutes of the realm, and romances. His 'best book' was red and embroidered and clasped with fetterlocks. An entry thoughtfully instructing his executors to return those volumes which James had borrowed to their owners, suggests he was a reader and not simply an owner of books. Armour for jousting and war, golden circlets, collars, rings and belts, jewels and fur robes, at least one of which came from Flanders, and relics of the true cross and St Mary Magdalene indicate that James possessed many objects of opulence and luxury. Among the beneficiaries of the will were his immediate family and magnate friends like the earls of Douglas and March. Remembered too were a number of his servants, who received money and gifts. James instructed that all his household servants should be paid their fees up to the day of his death. Religious institutions were also prominent among the beneficiaries. Newbattle Abbey in Edinburghshire, where James wished to be buried alongside his first wife, received money for the repair of the buildings, while the chapel of St Nicholas in Dalkeith was bequeathed a missal, vestments, and money by Douglas. James's patronage of the chapel culminated in 1406 with its erection into a collegiate church. By founding the college James was following a growing trend among Scottish lords.

The rental, drawn up in 1376–7, is one of only two such documents from this period. It does not include all of James Douglas's estates, only those in Peeblesshire, Dumfriesshire, and Fife, while an extent detailing the lands of Liddesdale, Westerkirk, and Staplegordon in Dumfriesshire was added in the decade after 1388, when these estates were in James's possession. The rental provides unique evidence of local landholding. It records eighty-eight holdings each held by one or more tenants, the vast majority of whom held their lands under twelve-month leases. Such short leases seem to have been a standard feature of Scottish landholding. The value of the lands included in the rental was £483.

Sir James Douglas was succeeded in his estates by his namesake, another **Sir James Douglas of Dalkeith** (d. 1441), the eldest son of his father's marriage to Agnes Dunbar. In 1378 James was betrothed to Elizabeth Stewart, daughter of John, earl of Carrick (later Robert III), and the marriage took place before 1387. Knighted between 1390 and 1392, in 1402 he was captured with the fourth earl of Douglas at the battle of Homildon Hill, and after his own release acted as a hostage for the earl's temporary parole. His second marriage, to Janet, daughter of William Borthwick, some time before 1439, linked James to an Edinburghshire neighbour who was a councillor of the Douglas earl before 1424. However, after his succession to his father's lands, James's links to the Black Douglases diminished. His eldest son, William, died as a hostage for James I's ransom, and his second son, James, was later declared unfit to hold the family's lands. Towards the end of his life James himself may have been under the influence of his ambitious neighbours, the Crichtons. In 1440 he granted William Crichton lands in Dumfriesshire, while within weeks of James's death in early 1441 Janet Borthwick married George Crichton, later earl of Caithness, who laid claim to her lands. She died some time after 1460. Subsequent years would see conflict over the Dalkeith estates between the Crichtons and James's third son, Henry.

M. H. BROWN

Sources M. Brown, *The Black Douglases: war and lordship in late medieval Scotland, 1300–1455* (1998) · A. Grant, 'The higher nobility in Scotland and their estates, c.1371–1424', DPhil diss., U. Oxf., 1975 · S. I. Boardman, *The early Stewart kings: Robert II and Robert III, 1371–1406* (1996) · W. Bower, *Scotichronicon*, ed. D. E. R. Watt and others, new edn, 9 vols. (1987–98), vols. 7–8 · *Scots peerage*, vols. 2, 6 · C. McGladdery, *James II* (1990) · T. Thomson, A. Macdonald, and

C. Innes, eds., *Registrum honoris de Morton*, 2 vols., Bannatyne Club, 94 (1853)
Wealth at death approx. 1500 marks: Thomson, Macdonald, and Innes, eds., *Registrum honoris*, vol. 1

Douglas, Sir James, of Dalkeith (d. 1441). *See under* Douglas, Sir James, of Dalkeith (d. 1420).

Douglas, James, of Balvenie [*called* James the Gross], **seventh earl of Douglas and first earl of Avondale** (d. 1443), magnate, was the younger son of Archibald *Douglas, third earl of Douglas (c.1320–1400), and Joanna Murray, lady of Bothwell and Drumsargard (d. after 1401). His exceptional rise to dominance in his family and in the kingdom began with the disastrous defeat of his elder brother, Archibald *Douglas, fourth earl of Douglas, at Hamildon Hill in 1402. After the capture of the earl and his leading followers James was left to maintain Black Douglas influence in southern Scotland. He deputized for the earl as warden of the Scottish marches and keeper of Edinburgh Castle, but when he tried to maintain his family's position found himself increasingly challenged by a rival faction in the south led by Robert III's councillors, Sir David Fleming and Henry Sinclair, second earl of Orkney. Most worryingly for James, Fleming's and Orkney's support of the rebel Henry Percy, first earl of Northumberland, created tensions with England which led to attacks on Douglas lands and jeopardized negotiations for the earl's release. In early 1406 these tensions resulted in open conflict. James Douglas led a force from Edinburgh which caught Fleming, Orkney, and the young heir to the throne, the future James I, in Haddingtonshire. Orkney and Prince James escaped by sea, but Fleming was killed by Douglas's men in a running fight.

James Douglas's success preserved Black Douglas dominance in the south. Between 1406 and the release of his brother in 1409 he managed the family's interests in the kingdom. He supervised the demolition of Jedburgh Castle in 1409, and the governor of Scotland, Robert Stewart, duke of Albany, recognized his significance by calling him 'our lieutenant' in 1407. Despite this importance James was never more than his brother's deputy and, when the earl returned to Scotland, James assumed the role of councillor to his senior kinsmen which would continue until 1440. His service to the earl brought rewards, albeit in a form which suggests a certain wariness on the latter's part. The grant of estates in 1408 included Balvenie in Banffshire, Avoch in Inverness, Aberdour in Buchan, Petty and Duffus in Moray, and Strathaven and Stonehouse in Lanarkshire, and without much doubt represents an attempt to direct James's interests and energies to the north. This appanage was created from the inheritance of James's mother, Joanna Murray, but in terms of James's future interests the earl's most notable grant to his brother was Abercorn Castle in Linlithgowshire. For the rest of his life Abercorn was James's principal residence. Between 1408 and 1424 it served as a base for his plundering of the Edinburgh and Linlithgow customs and

as the basis for connections with the neighbouring Crichtons and Livingstons, which would later be of vital importance.

During this period James Douglas remained a councillor of his brother and in the early 1420s he acted as the link between the earl and Murdoch Stewart, duke of Albany, the new governor. Although there may have been plans for him to marry into the Albany Stewarts, James Douglas's links with the duke did not prevent his appearing as a councillor of James I when the king returned in 1424, and he was on the assize which condemned Albany and his sons in 1425. In these roles Douglas acted in his family's interests, but his marriage (before March 1426) to Beatrix Sinclair (d. in or before 1463), daughter of his former enemy the earl of Orkney, cemented his own connection with the royal council, and the king quickly appreciated the importance of Douglas's support for his relationship with Archibald *Douglas, now fifth earl of Douglas, who was the nephew of both men. In 1426 James received royal confirmation of his lands at a time when the king was putting pressure on the earl, and in 1430–31, while his nephew was briefly imprisoned by the king, James replaced him as warden of the west march and remained a royal councillor. This backing from the earl's senior kinsman was vital to the king to prevent a clash with the Douglas affinity, and in the 1430s James received continued royal favour. His eldest son, William *Douglas, was knighted by the king in 1430 and by 1435 he himself was sheriff of Lanark, confirming his place among the king's principal followers.

Despite the often difficult relationship between the king and the earl of Douglas, James Douglas successfully maintained his place in family councils and, when, in 1437, the king was assassinated, he transferred his support to the earl. Along with two other Douglas adherents in royal service, Sir William Crichton and John Cameron, bishop of Glasgow, James backed the earl's appointment as lieutenant-general for the young James II, contrary to the expectations of James I, who had planned that in the event of his death his wife, Joan, should act as regent. Return to family loyalty paid James Douglas well. Within months he was made earl of Avondale and justiciar, and, with his grateful nephew in power, he was guaranteed an influential role on the lieutenant's council. Along with Crichton, he probably engineered the downfall of Bishop Cameron in April 1439, further securing their place in government.

This security was shaken by the death of the fifth earl of Douglas in June 1439. Though James acted for his great-nephew William *Douglas, sixth earl of Douglas, the future was now threatening. James's influence in the minority government and in the Douglas family were both at risk, the first from Queen Joan, the second from the new Douglas earl. Characteristically, both problems were resolved in James's favour by force applied by his allies with no certain guilt being attached to Douglas himself. In August 1439 the queen was arrested by Sir Alexander Livingston in Stirling Castle and released only when she surrendered her son, the king. Douglas was present throughout and had well-established links with Livingston. The settlement, which gave custody of the king to his ally, safeguarded Douglas's interests, and he produced his great-nephew to seal the agreement. Over the next year it was this great-nephew who caused James anxiety. Earl William was a potential rival who would have the lands and men to back any claim to his father's lieutenancy. James was no more prepared than Livingston and Crichton to risk this dominance and on 24 November 1440 Earl William and his brother, David, were arrested and executed at a feast in Edinburgh Castle. The deed was carried out on the direct order of Crichton, but to the chief advantage of James, who at the same time took the opportunity to remove Sir Malcolm Fleming, a close associate of the sixth earl who was also a local rival. This 'Black Dinner' left James as heir by male entail to the Douglas earldom and, together with the coup of 1439, made him the most powerful figure in the kingdom.

In spite of his career as a royal councillor it is significant that, as seventh earl of Douglas and lord of Lauderdale, James concentrated on family aggrandizement, leaving custody of the king to Crichton and Livingston. The new Douglas earl sought to create a network of lands and alliances which was not limited to the southern interests of his predecessors. He directed his younger sons towards north-east Scotland. His third son, Archibald, was married to Elizabeth Dunbar, coheir of the earldom of Moray, and in 1442 was created earl of Moray. Archibald's twin brother, James *Douglas, the future ninth earl of Douglas, was chosen as bishop of Aberdeen in 1441, a mark of his father's influence with the conciliar party, though the appointment proved ineffective; after the elder James's death his two youngest sons, Hugh and John, were provided for from his own northern estates. Earl James clearly intended to implant the Douglas family into the disturbed political society of the north. In the south he followed a similar course. In Berwickshire he intervened in a complex feud within the Hume family. His principal aim was to re-establish the influence exercised by his brother in the east march before 1424. James did not ignore the traditional territorial interests of the Black Douglases. Before his death he probably arranged the marriage of his eldest son, William, future eighth earl of Douglas, to Margaret, sister of William, the sixth earl. To achieve this he had to obtain a papal dispensation. Through this match Galloway, which James did not inherit, would be reunited with the earldom. By inclination and experience, Douglas was not a border magnate like his predecessors. His main residences at Abercorn and Lanark confirm him as a magnate whose lands and personal connections centred on Clydesdale and Lothian. The marriages of his daughters to landowners in these two sheriffdoms support this impression. It was thus appropriate that it was at Abercorn Castle that Douglas died on 10 March 1443. His grossly fat body, which earned him his nickname and which at his death reportedly contained 4 stone of tallow, was buried in a magnificent tomb in St Bride's Church in Douglas.

Douglas's career as earl was one of superficial success. Family aggrandizement created enemies, including Crichton, Bishop James Kennedy, and the earls of Angus, without any secure increase in Douglas power. Relative neglect of the family's place in the marches loosened loyalties already shaken by the 'Black Dinner'. Finally, by centring his interests on Lothian, a heartland of royal interests, Earl James risked future conflict with James II. Douglas's career had parallels with that of his father. Both combined roles as royal servants, family councillors, and ambitious and forceful magnates, and both their long careers culminated in the acquisition of the Douglas earldom. But the 1440s were not the 1390s. Changes in Scottish political society and attitudes meant that the achievements of James Douglas would leave his sons a difficult legacy.

M. H. Brown

Sources M. Brown, *James I* (1994) · C. McGladdery, *James II* (1990) · A. I. Dunlop, *The life and times of James Kennedy, bishop of St Andrews* (1950) · W. Fraser, ed., *The Douglas book*, 4 vols. (1885) · J. M. Thomson and others, eds., *Registrum magni sigilli regum Scotorum / The register of the great seal of Scotland*, 11 vols. (1882–1914), vols. 1–2 · S. I. Boardman, *The early Stewart kings: Robert II and Robert III, 1371–1406* (1996) · A. Fraser, ed., *The Frasers of Philorth* (1879)

Likenesses tomb effigy, c.1443, St Bride's Church, Douglas, Lanarkshire

Douglas, James, third earl of Angus (c.1415–1446), magnate, was the eldest son of William *Douglas, second earl of Angus (c.1398–1437), and his wife, Margaret (fl. 1410–1484), daughter of Sir William Hay of Yester. Earl William had performed distinguished service to the crown in the reign of James I and would probably have been a significant figure in the minority administration of James II had he not died in late 1437. James seems to have lacked the experience to assume his father's mantle, although he did hold the wardenship of the east march against England, a well-nigh hereditary office. He is little heard of during the political intrigues of the minority, when such men as William Crichton, the chancellor, the Livingstons, and the earls of Douglas were jockeying for power. Angus's most public role was to mediate in the early 1440s in the dispute involving David Hume of Wedderburn, his nephew Alexander Hume of that ilk, and Coldingham Priory, a cell of Durham Priory, principally over the office of bailie on Coldingham's extensive lands.

Nevertheless, Angus was singled out for an important distinction, namely marriage to Princess Joanna, third daughter of James I. A contract was drawn up in October 1440, when the intended bride would have been about twelve years old, but it is thought that the marriage did not take place, and in 1445 the princess was sent to France. The earl was by then in serious trouble. The king's exchequer rolls show that the annual pensions he lifted from the burghs of Haddington and North Berwick were being seized from, rather than willingly released by, the burghs. Angus appears to have allied himself with the group surrounding the queen mother, Joan Beaufort (probably explaining in part the proposed marriage alliance), but this group was increasingly removed from authority. The earl was charged with treason in parliament in June 1445, although the cause is unknown, and was consequently forfeited. It seems that the forfeiture was lifted before his death, which had occurred by September 1446. As he had no children, he was succeeded by his brother, George *Douglas (c.1417–1463), who was able to enter into his landed patrimony without dispute. Earl James held estates in Fife, Perthshire, Haddingtonshire, Angus, Berwickshire, Selkirkshire, and Roxburghshire, and was apparently buried in the ancestral graveyard at the collegiate church of St Bride, Abernethy, Perthshire.

ALAN R. BORTHWICK

Sources The Hirsel, Berwickshire, Home Muniments · W. Fraser, ed., *The Douglas book*, 4 vols. (1885), vols. 2–3 · G. Burnett and others, eds., *The exchequer rolls of Scotland*, 5 (1882) · D. Hume, 'History of the house and race of Douglas and Angus', MS, Lennoxlove, East Lothian, Hamilton Muniments · J. Raine, ed., *The correspondence, inventories, account rolls and law proceedings of Coldingham Priory*, SurtS, 12 (1841) · various collections of manuscript estate and other papers in archive offices and in private hands in Scotland and England · M. Brown, *The Black Douglases: war and lordship in late medieval Scotland, 1300–1455* (1998)
Archives priv. coll. | The Hirsel, Berwickshire, Home Muniments

Douglas, James, ninth earl of Douglas and third earl of Avondale

(c.1425–1491), magnate and rebel, was the second son of James *Douglas, seventh earl of Douglas and first earl of Avondale (d. 1443), and Beatrix Sinclair (d. in or before 1463), daughter of Henry Sinclair, second earl of Orkney.

Entry into national life In his earliest years Douglas seemed destined for an ecclesiastical career. His father favoured the Council of Basel against the pope, representing a minority view within Scotland, and sought preferment from the anti-pope Felix V for James to the bishopric of Aberdeen in 1441 (despite his youth). As Scotland remained loyal to Eugenius IV, however, James's hopes were dashed. Although he seems to have matriculated at the University of Cologne in mid-1443, no more is heard of his ecclesiastical ambitions. That is probably no accident. He had a twin brother, Archibald, earl of Moray, and in 1447, after evidence was taken from his mother and other women, a decision was made that James was the elder and might therefore succeed to the title and estates if their brother, William *Douglas, eighth earl of Douglas, remained childless.

A more martial turn to James Douglas's career had already been demonstrated in late 1446, when he was briefly keeper of Hailes Castle. It was underlined by his fighting in the lists at Stirling in February 1449 in the presence of James II, with two other Scots against three Burgundians, all of whom were knighted by the king at the time. His own opponent, Jacques de Lalain, had apparently become aware of Douglas's prowess and issued a challenge to him, and was successful in their encounter.

The occasion of Douglas's succession to the earldom could scarcely have been less propitious. He was among the notable entourage who accompanied his brother Earl William when he visited Rome in the jubilee year of 1450. On their return James spent part of 1451 in England, perhaps seeking English support, as the absence of the

Douglases had brought to the surface discontent at court about the earl's posturing. The king harboured doubts about the earl's ambitions and about his confederacies with other nobles, and summoned him under a safe conduct to Stirling in February 1452, ostensibly to discuss his bonds with the earls of Crawford and Ross. When on 22 February Earl William refused to break them, the king suddenly stabbed him, setting in train a chain of blows from other courtiers standing near by from which he died instantly.

Conflict, accommodation, and revolt A month passed before Earl James displayed his anger at the circumstances of his brother's death, when he and his allies wreaked havoc in Stirling, after denouncing the king and his courtiers to the blast of twenty-four horns and dragging the safe conduct through the town tied to a horse. It must have been a remarkable sight. The king was absent, and made no immediate effort to confront Douglas. In (probably) May 1452 the earl conferred with John MacDonald, lord of the Isles, in Knapdale, rewarding MacDonald's entourage with wine and clothes, perhaps as an inducement to foment trouble. When parliament met in Edinburgh in June and exonerated the king from blame for the slaying of Earl William, Earl James and others, including James, Lord Hamilton, fixed a letter on the parliament house door renouncing their allegiance to the king and saying that they would not hold their lands of him. This has been considered an example of *diffidatio*, the breaking by a vassal of his fealty to his lord. Meanwhile, Douglas was also holding negotiations with Henry VI of England. King James had to react, and he conducted a destructive raid upon the border areas where Douglas might have found followers.

This military action seems to have persuaded Douglas to draw up a bond in August 1452 under which, among other matters, he and his party agreed to forgive those who had taken part in the killing of his brother and to make no bonds which threatened the king. Such notable concessions by Douglas imply that he considered that an accommodation with the king would serve him better in the long run. It was a useful boost for the king; he showed his uneasiness by sealing at the same time in parliament a pardon for the surviving members of the Livingston family who had been disgraced and forfeited in 1449–50.

Perhaps to underline his concern to negotiate with Douglas, James II made a further accord with him in January 1453, whereby the earl promised to give manrent and service to the king in return for restoration of certain lands. About the same time the king granted Douglas permission to marry his brother's widow and cousin, Margaret, the fair maid of Galloway (c.1432–c.1476?), daughter of Archibald Douglas, fifth earl of Douglas, if the necessary dispensation could be obtained from the pope. This was a significant act of patronage, for Margaret was the sister and heir of the sixth earl of Douglas (d. 1440), and therefore possessed the lordship of Galloway and other estates. Earl William's marriage to her had been engineered by his father to ensure that the Douglas patrimony was not sundered; but that marriage lacked offspring and the patrimony would have been divided had the king not been prepared to allow James to marry his sister-in-law. The marriage was duly celebrated, and Douglas was then accepted back into court circles, to the extent that he, as ambassador, sealed a new truce with England in May 1453. Even so, he remained a fringe figure. The only formal offices he held in Scotland were those of sheriff of Lanark, a post hereditary in his family, to which he succeeded on his brother's death, and warden of the west and middle marches (against England).

Notwithstanding his concord with the king, Douglas seems to have continued to intrigue with potential supporters. Douglas castles in Moray, Kirkcudbrightshire, Lanarkshire, and Linlithgowshire were fortified, and the queen's dower lands and a grange of the king's justiciar were burnt. Early in 1455, however, the king, intending to pre-empt (and perhaps also to provoke) further manoeuvres by Douglas, besieged and threw down Douglas's castle of Inveravon near Linlithgow, and then began to sweep west and south to ravage Douglas lands. By April he was besieging Abercorn, Linlithgowshire, which Douglas attempted to defend with all his forces; but his lack of strength was all too clearly shown when Lord Hamilton, sensing that Douglas was wavering, switched sides, causing Douglas to flee to England. Without him his men were no match for a force of borderers loyal to the king when they met at Arkinholm on 1 May 1455.

The consequences of defeat included the forfeiture in parliament in June of the earl, his mother, and brothers after a charge of treason, and also the execution of his younger brother Hugh, earl of Ormond. The sentence on Douglas was carried out in his absence since he was in England, where he remained for almost all the rest of his life. His extensive estates were split up, some being annexed in perpetuity by the crown and others forming significant prizes for its supporters. One of the Douglas kindred, George Douglas, fourth earl of Angus, the head of the so-called Red Douglases, was rewarded with the lordship of Douglas, and quickly sought to establish authority over former Douglas vassals in Lanarkshire. The Douglas estates formed a substantial bloc, and are estimated to have brought the king gross cash rents of about £2000 Scots, approximately one-third of the total for all crown lands. They comprised land in Dumfriesshire, Kirkcudbrightshire, Wigtownshire, Lanarkshire, Linlithgowshire, Edinburgh, Haddingtonshire, Berwickshire, Peeblesshire, Roxburghshire, Selkirkshire, Aberdeenshire, Ayrshire, and Renfrewshire: the largest accumulation of property held by one individual in Scotland apart from the king. The lands in the western and mid-borders lay at the traditional heart of the Douglas domains, but Earl James drew most of his support from his father's patrimony in Lanarkshire and Linlithgowshire.

Pensioner of England Douglas had now to rely on charity from the king of England. His first gift from Henry VI was received as early as 4 August 1455, a pension of £500 until his estates were restored by James II. Douglas, however,

had already surrendered Threave Castle, his principal stronghold, to Henry in return for succour and provisions (an ineffectual move, as the castle was annexed by James II). The comparative peace between Scotland and England in the next few years provided no opportunities for Douglas, apart from a possible raid on Kirkcudbright in 1457 in the company of the Stanleys, English lords of the Isle of Man (a retaliation for an earlier Scottish attack on the island).

The circumstances surrounding the accession of Edward IV in England in 1461, and the death of James II on 3 August 1460, renewed Douglas hopes of political influence in Scotland. The Lancastrians had made a successful bid for Scottish support in December 1460, and in response Edward sent Douglas, together with his brother John Douglas, Lord Balvenie, to communicate with John MacDonald, who as earl of Ross as well as lord of the Isles had continued to be a thorn in the flesh of successive Scottish kings. The result was the document known as the treaty of Westminster–Ardtornish, made in February 1462, by which Ross and his associates bound themselves to become vassals of Edward and to co-operate with his forces in the conquest of Scotland. Should this occur, the reward for Douglas would include the restoration of his estates and the division of the remainder of Scotland with the earl of Ross, all these lands to be held of the king of England. As Ross swiftly rebelled against James III, this approach brought some short-term benefit. The following spring Douglas, again with Edward's connivance, was in the field in the borders, culminating in early March in an encounter in which the earl of Crawford, among others, was temporarily imprisoned; Douglas also appears to have been in Galloway in the early summer.

The Scots themselves had been pursuing an aggressive policy towards England, but this could not be sustained once a truce between England and France was agreed in October 1463, and they sealed their own truce with England in December. At that time Douglas, apparently at his own request, was appointed governor of Carrickfergus in Ireland by Edward. For his services Edward made Douglas a knight of the Garter, the first Scot to receive the distinction.

Revanche and retirement The more stable relations between England and Scotland thereafter gave Douglas little leeway. He continued to collect his annuity from Edward, and served with the English army during Edward's major expedition to France in 1475, while in 1480 he was paid for services on the Anglo-Scottish border. Soon afterwards Douglas became involved with Alexander Stewart, duke of Albany (James III's brother but a fellow exile). In 1482 Albany had engaged, with English assistance, in a campaign to re-establish himself in Scotland. The attempt failed, but in February 1483 Edward made a treaty with the duke, whereby Albany renounced his Scottish allegiance in return for English help in capturing the Scottish throne; for his part Albany undertook to assist Douglas in recovering his Scottish estates. The childless Douglas apparently also made an agreement with Archibald Douglas, fifth earl of Angus, who was also a rebel against James III, perhaps about the destination of Douglas's estates after his death. All these manoeuvres came to nothing. In July 1484 Douglas accompanied Albany and about 500 men when, without English support, they raided Lochmaben, in a lordship formerly held by his family where Douglas clearly expected to receive support. Instead they were attacked by local forces and easily defeated on 22 July, and Douglas was made captive. The king evidently now feared Douglas little, as he permitted him to reside thenceforth in the abbey of Lindores in Fife, where he died in mid-1491 and where he was most probably buried. By then he had become a pensioner of James IV. The later historian of the Douglas family, David Hume of Godscroft, claims that James III, aware of the pressure he had to face in 1488—he was eventually defeated in battle by forces including his son and heir, and was killed during his flight from the fray—personally sought assistance from Douglas, offering restoration of his titles and possessions in return. The offer was curtly rebuffed. Hume was anxious to paint Douglas in a favourable light. He makes little reference to the earl's career as a liegeman of successive English kings; and he told this tale to emphasize Douglas's resolution against a suppliant king whose father had brought about the violent death of the earl's brother and had later forfeited the earl himself.

Douglas's first marriage, to Margaret Douglas, probably occurred in early 1453. She fled to England with him, but (after apparently obtaining a divorce) returned to Scotland c.1459, and then married the king's half-brother John Stewart, earl of Atholl; she may have died c.1476, when Stewart remarried. Douglas's second marriage was to Anne (c.1430–1486), daughter of John Holland, duke of Exeter (d. 1447), and his first wife, Anne Stafford (d. 1432). Relict successively of John Neville (d. 1450) and of the latter's uncle John, Lord Neville (d. 1461), she married Douglas some time after 1461. She predeceased him, dying on 26 December 1486. From neither marriage did Douglas have children.   ALAN R. BORTHWICK

Sources J. M. Thomson and others, eds., *Registrum magni sigilli regum Scotorum / The register of the great seal of Scotland*, 11 vols. (1882–1914), vol. 2 · *APS*, 1424–1567 · *CDS*, vol. 4 · *RotS*, vol. 2 · *The Asloan manuscript*, ed. W. A. Craigie, 2 vols., STS, new ser., 14, 16 (1923–5) · various collections of manuscript estate and other papers in archive offices and private hands in Scotland and England · David Hume of Godscroft's MS history of the house of Douglas and Angus, Hamilton Muniments, Lennoxlove, East Lothian · F. Devon, ed. and trans., *Issues of the exchequer: being payments made out of his majesty's revenue, from King Henry III to King Henry VI inclusive*, RC (1837) · A. I. Dunlop, *The life and times of James Kennedy, bishop of St Andrews*, St Andrews University Publications, 46 (1950) · G. Burnett and others, eds., *The exchequer rolls of Scotland*, 23 vols. (1878–1908) · N. Macdougall, *James III: a political study* (1982) · *CEPR letters*, 10.130–31 · M. Brown, *The Black Douglases: war and lordship in late medieval Scotland, 1300–1455* (1998)
Archives priv. coll. | Hamilton Muniments, Lennoxlove, East Lothian
Likenesses portrait, repro. in *David Hume of Godscroft's The history of the house of Douglas*, ed. D. Reid, 2 STS, 4th ser., 26 (1996)

Douglas, James, first earl of Morton (d. 1493), magnate, was the only child of James Douglas (d. before 11 Oct 1457), lord of Dalkeith, and Elizabeth, daughter of James Gifford

of Sheriffhall. Formal ownership of the extensive Dalkeith regality was transferred to him in July 1456, and the full inheritance came by 11 October 1457, when he was still legally a minor, following his father's death. Shortly afterwards, on 14 March 1458, James II created him earl of Morton. This reflected partly his estates and partly his opposition to the last two earls of Douglas, which had been provoked by their support for his uncle Henry Douglas of Borg in the take-over of the Dalkeith lands from his simple-minded father during the 1440s. Royal favour may further have resulted from the earl's agreement to marry Joanna (b. c.1428, d. after 16 Oct 1486), the king's deaf and mute sister and the third daughter of *James I. They were married by 15 May 1459 and had a son, John.

There was a problem over the title of Morton, however. The barony of Morton, Nithsdale, had previously been alienated, as part of her jointure, to Janet Borthwick, second wife of the earl's grandfather, and she protested in parliament about the title on behalf of her son William Douglas. The chancellor replied that the earldom was called after Morton in Calderclere, in the sheriffdom of Edinburgh, not Morton in Nithsdale. But Earl James clearly wanted the barony back, and on 30 June 1466 he made an indenture with Patrick Graham (d. 1478), bishop of St Andrews and a close associate of the ruling Kennedy faction, that his heir should marry the bishop's niece, essentially in return for Graham's aid in recovering Morton and his other alienated lands. Morton's flirtation with the politically influential lasted just nine days, until 9 July, when the Kennedys were replaced by the Boyds in a *coup d'état* and as a result the marriage did not take place. The earl eventually forced William Douglas to resign Morton to him in 1474, and the same year saw him make his cousin Henry, the son of Henry Douglas of Borg, renounce any claim to the Dalkeith estates. Apart from the 1466 indenture and witnessing the parliamentary forfeiture of the Boyd family in November 1469, Morton remained remote from political affairs, and he may well have seen the recovery of these estates as his main achievement. In so doing he was acting very much in a family tradition.

Although his son was involved in the treasonable actions of the duke of Albany in 1482–3, Morton stayed loyal to James III in the 1480s. In May 1488 he made one of his rare appearances at court, indicating continued support of the king in the developing crisis. It is not known if he followed his sovereign to the battle of Sauchieburn on 11 June. In the reign of James IV he attended parliament frequently, but otherwise still took no part in affairs of state. He died between 22 June and 22 October 1493 and was probably buried in Dalkeith church. He was succeeded by his son, John.   ROLAND J. TANNER

Sources C. A. Kelham, 'Bases of magnatial power in later fifteenth-century Scotland', PhD diss., U. Edin., 1986, 135–211 · T. Thomson, A. Macdonald, and C. Innes, eds., *Registrum honoris de Morton*, 2 vols., Bannatyne Club, 94 (1853) · N. Macdougall, *James III: a political study* (1982) · *APS*, 1424–1567 · J. M. Thomson and others, eds., *Registrum magni sigilli regum Scotorum / The register of the great seal of Scotland*, 11 vols. (1882–1914), vol. 2 · NA Scot., Morton MSS, GD 150 · A. Grant, 'The higher nobility in Scotland and their estates, c.1371–1424', DPhil diss., U. Oxf., 1975 · [T. Thomson], ed.,

The acts of the lords auditors of causes and complaints, AD 1466–AD 1494, RC, 40 (1839), 182 • [T. Thomson], ed., *The acts of the lords of council in civil causes, 1478–1495*, 1, RC, 41 (1839), 308 • *Scots peerage*
Archives NA Scot., Morton MSS, GD 150 • NL Scot., MSS 72–4

Douglas, James, **fourth earl of Morton** (*c*.1516–1581), regent and chancellor of Scotland, was the second son of Sir George *Douglas, master of Angus (1490?–1552), of Pittendreich, near Elgin, Moray, and his wife, Elizabeth (*d*. *c*.1560), only daughter of David Douglas, also of Pittendreich.

Early career Details of Douglas's early life are sketchy. The quarrel of his paternal uncle, Archibald *Douglas, sixth earl of Angus, with James V in 1528 forced some of the family, including his father, into exile in England. Whether James Douglas accompanied them is uncertain, and he is described by David Hume of Godscroft, the family biographer, as having spent the rest of James V's reign sheltering from the crown on the estates of his cousin Douglas of Glenbervie. On the other hand, the existence of a charter from 1536 which names James Douglas as heir to his mother suggests that he spent this period comparatively undisturbed on the Douglas lands at Pittendreich. It was claimed, however, that his education suffered from neglect. Between 18 March and 22 April 1543 Douglas married Lady Elizabeth Douglas (*d*. in or after 1581), youngest daughter of James Douglas, third earl of Morton (*d*. 1548), and Catherine Stewart (*d*. in or after 1554), illegitimate daughter of James IV. As part of the marriage settlement Douglas became heir to the earldom of Morton; until his father-in-law's death he was known as master of Morton. He and his wife were childless, but according to Hume he had four natural sons. Only two of them, Archibald and James, played any part in his career.

In the 1540s Morton's actions were largely dictated by his father and his uncle. As a result of the former's allegiance to Henry VIII as a diplomat and border official while in England, Morton and his elder brother, David, were drawn into collaboration with the earl of Hertford when in 1544 he invaded Scotland on behalf of Henry, frustrated at the pro-French policies of the Arran administration. However, in 1548 pensions to the Douglases from Henri II persuaded the family to support France. The outcome was Morton's defence of Dalkeith against the forces of Lord Gray, in the process of which he was not only 'sore hurt in the thigh' (*CSP Scot.*, 1.118) but also taken as a prisoner to the Tower of London. Following his father-in-law's death, which probably occurred in December 1548, he succeeded as fourth earl of Morton; he was certainly using the title by mid-1550, on his release from captivity and return to Scotland.

On 14 October 1552 Morton became a privy councillor in Arran's government. His rise to prominence was assisted when, following the death of his brother David in 1557, he became the tutor or guardian of his nephew Archibald *Douglas, eighth earl of Angus (*c*.1555–1588). During Archibald's minority Morton administered on his behalf the regality of Bothwell, Tantallon Castle, Jedburgh Forest, and various other Douglas possessions in the borders. This role brought Morton considerable financial benefits.

James Douglas, fourth earl of Morton (*c*.1516–1581), attrib. Arnold Bronckorst, *c*.1580

With the onset of the Reformation, Morton pursued what can only be described as an equivocal policy. Certainly in 1557 he was one of those who signed the 'first band', a declaration protesting allegiance to the reformed faith, but thereafter his behaviour vacillated so much that John Knox was led to comment that he 'promised to be ours but never did plainly join' (*John Knox's History of the Reformation in Scotland*, ed. W. C. Dickinson, 2 vols., 1949, 1.261–2). However, once English support for the lords of the congregation was guaranteed through the treaty of Berwick, which Morton helped to ratify in May 1560, he backed the reformers wholeheartedly and was a signatory of the first Book of Discipline in January 1561.

Politician and courtier, 1561–1572 The start of Mary's personal rule marked the emergence of Morton as a leading figure on the Scottish political scene, and later in 1561 he actively assisted the earl of Moray in his restoration of law and order in the borders. In the following year he played a prominent role in the campaign against the rebellious earl of Huntly. His reward in 1563 was to become chancellor, the key post in the administrative system. In 1565 he gave his approval to the proposed marriage between Mary and Henry Stewart, Lord Darnley, though his decision to do so was probably greatly influenced by the eventual agreement of the bridegroom's mother, Margaret Stewart, countess of Lennox, to renounce any claims to the inheritance of Morton's nephew, the earl of Angus.

However, the queen's marriage was undoubtedly a turning point in Morton's relations with her. Although in

August 1565 Morton helped Mary to suppress the chaseabout raid, the earl of Moray's ill-advised attempt at rebellion, a few months later he became deeply implicated in the conspiracy against David Riccio, the queen's unpopular Italian secretary. His motive for an involvement which extended to being actually present at Riccio's murder in March 1566 may have been based on a suspicion that he was about to lose his post as chancellor; but it is much more likely that Morton saw an opportunity to win the favour of Darnley, who hated Riccio, and in association with Morton create a situation where the queen's husband became a mere figurehead in a government dominated by the two powerful noblemen. Whatever his motivation, the upshot for Morton was the loss of his chancellorship and another period of exile in England. This lasted until December 1566 when, being granted a remission for his complicity in the Riccio affair, he arrived back in Edinburgh shortly before the next violent episode in Mary's reign, the Darnley murder. Morton's part in the mysterious events at Kirk o' Field remains uncertain, though he later insisted that while he had known about the plot he had not personally participated in the events.

Thereafter, Morton initially supported Bothwell, being a signatory of the Ainslie bond in which several noblemen agreed to the proposition that Bothwell should marry the queen. However, like most of the nobility Morton quickly changed his attitude once the wedding took place, and he became a prominent member of the party in revolt against Mary and her new husband. He was consequently at Carberry, where the queen surrendered, though not before Bothwell had challenged him to a duel to settle outstanding issues between the two of them. Perhaps fortunately, considering Morton's age, Mary intervened and refused to countenance such a contest.

Mary's abdication marked another significant stage in the fourth earl's career. On 29 July 1567 Morton took the coronation oath on behalf of the infant James VI; at the same time he became a member of the council in charge of the country until the earl of Moray returned from France; in December he was reappointed chancellor. During Moray's regency he remained a key figure, commanding the vanguard at the battle of Langside in May 1568 and later acting as a commissioner for the king's party at the inquiry into Mary's conduct organized at York by Elizabeth I. Moreover, it was Morton who possessed what he claimed was incriminating evidence against Mary, namely, the casket letters. These 'lettrez, missives, contractis sonnettis and utheris writles' (*CSP Scot.*, 2.730) had, he said, been discovered by his agents eighteen months before, inside a box in a house in Edinburgh.

In some ways Moray's assassination in January 1570 might seem to have been an appropriate occasion for Morton to seize control of the country. Yet he supported the claims of the earl of Lennox for the regency, acting in this fashion because, presumably, he judged the time inappropriate and the queen's party still in a strong position. In fact it was another year before Mary's most significant supporters, including Argyll, Eglinton, and Cassillis, forsook her. Again, in September 1571, when Lennox was killed at Stirling, Morton hesitated to contest the succession as regent of the earl of Mar, and it was not until the latter's sudden death in October 1572 that he felt absolutely convinced that his moment had arrived. Finally on 24 November 1572 at a convention of the Scottish estates in Edinburgh Morton was elected regent 'be pluralitie of votes of the saidis estaittis' (Calderwood, 3.242–3).

Relations with the nobility Although on 12 January 1573 Morton placated one of his most powerful antagonists, Archibald Campbell, fifth earl of Argyll, by appointing him chancellor, he still faced internal opposition. First, certain members of the nobility were against him—the Gordons, Hamiltons, and Setons, linked with the earl of Atholl; second, under Kirkcaldy of Grange's command within the strategically important Edinburgh Castle, there were such diehard Marians as Lord Home and Maitland of Lethington. To some extent the hostility of the former proved to be the lesser problem. With the considerable assistance of the English ambassador, Henry Killigrew, in February 1573 the agreement known as the pacification of Perth was reached with the Gordons and Hamiltons. In return for ending their allegiance to Mary, promising religious conformity, and recognizing the regent's authority, the two families were given an amnesty for their previous actions and much of their forfeited property was restored. When the earl of Atholl submitted separately in April, Morton's outstanding difficulties with the nobility were over.

The struggle against the so-called Castilians lasted a bit longer, largely because Grange and the others, convinced that the fortress was impregnable, rejected Morton's attempts at mediation. Morton did not possess the military strength to capture the castle. Consequently it was not until May, when the English government provided the requisite artillery firepower, that Grange and his associates were eventually forced to agree to an unconditional surrender.

For nearly five years thereafter, with an administration largely dominated by his relatives and trusted supporters, Morton ruled Scotland on James VI's behalf. For much of the time he experienced little serious opposition from the nobility. Unquestionably there were the occasional problems: George Gordon, fifth earl of Huntly (*d.* 1576), and his exiled brother, Adam Gordon of Auchindoun, the Perth settlement notwithstanding, were still restless and disaffected. Morton countered this threat by placing the earl under house arrest in the south of Scotland and undertaking a punitive expedition to Gordon territory in the northeast in August 1574. Again, a dispute with Colin Campbell, sixth earl of Argyll, who had succeeded his brother the chancellor on the latter's sudden death in September 1573, was resolved in the regent's favour. At issue here were certain royal jewels retained by Argyll's wife, the earl of Moray's widow, which Morton insisted must be restored to the crown. However, in his handling of the feud which developed in 1576 between Argyll and John Stewart, twenty-third earl of Atholl, Morton was much less successful. In this instance disagreements between the earls over rights of jurisdiction with their respective territories escalated into a bitter wrangle which created widespread disorder between their followers. The regent attempted to tackle the situation by summoning both noblemen before the privy council, denouncing their actions, and demanding an end to the disturbances. But all he achieved was a hardening of Argyll's resolve and the disillusionment of Atholl, who became convinced that Morton had not done enough on his behalf.

Whether Morton might have dealt with this affair more effectively and thus forestalled the coup against him in 1578 is a moot point. Certainly the outcome was unfortunate for him since it resulted in Atholl's retaliating by aligning himself with his recent enemy, Argyll. Furthermore, the two earls were a formidable coalition since they also had a crucial ally in Sir Alexander Erskine, the king's guardian, who was only too willing to give the regent's opponents access to James VI. The upshot was that they persuaded the twelve-year-old monarch to summon a convention at Stirling in March 1578 for the express purpose of ending Morton's regency. Sensing a *fait accompli*, the latter meekly offered his resignation, and after handing over Edinburgh Castle to the new regime he retired from the scene to contemplate events; a letter written at this time gave his age as sixty-one.

In temporary retirement Morton must have reflected on how he had been outmanoeuvred by Argyll and Atholl, not to mention all those other noblemen who joined their faction. Included among these were the earl of Montrose, at odds with the regent over a disputed charter; the earl of Eglinton, aggrieved at being imprisoned for offences against the Hamiltons; Lord Maxwell, displeased at his dismissal as warden of the west march; Lord Herries, Maxwell's uncle, who sympathized with his nephew; and Lord Ogilvie, an incorrigible Marian who had also been imprisoned by Morton. The latter must also have realized how his opponents exploited his failure to devote sufficient attention to James VI who, at such an impressionable age, could easily be manipulated by older men. The former regent in his turn used this lever to recover his former position. Within three months he had himself restored to his previous status in all but title, by deploying the influence of the youthful earl of Mar over the king (at the end of April 1578 Mar had displaced his uncle, Sir Alexander Erskine, as the royal guardian). Although Morton subsequently denied any involvement in this change of personnel it certainly suited his purposes. In no time he was conducting negotiations with his former enemies and at a convention held at Stirling on 12 June 1578 persuaded a majority of those present that he should not only be restored to the privy council but should also have 'first rowme and place' on that body (*CSP Scot.*, 5.296).

However Morton's troubles were not quite over. That summer the Argyll–Atholl faction rallied to challenge him, and by August matters had come to such a head that civil war seemed imminent as the supporters of the rival parties faced each other at Falkirk. But wiser counsels prevailed, and largely through the intervention of the English ambassador, Robert Bowes, a settlement was reached which satisfied both sides. Further conciliatory meetings

over the next few months tended to confirm that at least for the present Morton's position was reasonably secure. Morton, who had survived his most recent crisis by granting some of his rivals greater access to the king and admitting others to the privy council, was undoubtedly aware that he must tread warily in the future. Consequently he was attracted to a diversion which would prevent, as Hume of Godscroft put it, his opponents having 'leisure to think of him and his late greatness' (*History of the House of Douglas*, 2.262). The stratagem of launching an attack on the Hamiltons early in 1579 was not only diversionary but also a popular move against a family with considerable financial assets. On the grounds that the terms of the pacification of Perth were no longer in force, on 1 May the Hamiltons were proscribed. Lords John and Claud escaped to France but their deranged brother, the earl of Arran, and his mother, the duchess of Châtelherault, were seized and forced to hand over the Hamilton possessions to the crown. The morality of Morton's actions against the Hamiltons is obviously questionable, and certainly Queen Elizabeth was critical of his tactics. None the less it did win favour with James VI, who was reported as saying that 'no nobleman's service to Scotland was to be compared to Morton's' (*CSP Scot.*, 5.337).

Relations with the kirk While Morton's relations with the nobility were highly significant and the breakdown in them led ultimately to his downfall, his dealings with the kirk formed another important aspect of his administration. Here, the two main issues were the finances and the organization of the church. Morton inherited a financial system adopted in Mary's reign whereby the former members of the unreformed church retained two-thirds of their income while the remaining third was shared between the state and the new kirk. In 1567 a further change had given the latter first claim to the thirds and the right to appoint its own collectors. However, John Knox and his colleagues had neither the organizational ability nor the clout to make these concessions effective, and when Morton took over in 1572, having coincidentally become regent on the day of Knox's death, he found the collectory in a chaotic condition.

One of Morton's first tasks was to have the outstanding accounts audited while at the same time encouraging the clergy to collect the current thirds or duties from the members of their own parishes. To make this possible he had a new register of members compiled; one minister was responsible for three or four parishes on average. Additionally Morton revived the office of collector-general, and the state once again became responsible for the collection of the thirds. These innovations, which were introduced in 1573–4, were mostly received quite favourably by members of the kirk. However, there was one outspoken critic, John Davidson, regent of St Leonard's College, St Andrews, who, before fleeing into exile, protested that 'Four parish kirks are over a great charge for one minister', and that 'the order that would appoint so many was evil and consequentlie devilish' (Calderwood, 3.314). Some of the clergy were also unhappy about lay collection of the thirds, but there is little doubt that under Morton they were far more efficiently collected and administered than hitherto.

The regent was less successful in the recovery of thirds which had been lost as a result of remissions and the granting of pensions, and there is little evidence that he was either very innovative or energetic enough to recover the kirk's wealth. Conversely, he certainly looked after his own family: always alert to the interests of his sons Archibald and James, he appointed the latter commendator of Pluscarden Abbey and awarded him a pension from Balmerino Abbey. Other kinsmen who benefited from his generosity with ecclesiastical revenues included Archibald Douglas, senator of the college of justice; William Douglas, commendator of Melrose Abbey; and George Douglas, bishop of Moray. However, it was the polity or constitution of the reformed church that gradually became the key issue dominating Morton's relations with its members, particularly in the later stages of his career. In 1571, before he became regent, Morton had his first taste of clerical opposition over the question of the appointment of bishops to the church and, in particular, that of his elderly kinsman John Douglas as archbishop of St Andrews. A conference at Leith in January 1572 seemed to resolve this at least for the time being, since the kirk's leaders agreed to a settlement whereby the government would continue to appoint bishops, but the latter would require the approval of the chapter concerned and also be subject to the discipline of the general assembly. It was not until 1574 with the return from Switzerland of the more radically inclined Andrew Melville and his appointment as principal of Glasgow University that the kirk acquired a leader prepared to challenge the regent and that Morton found himself under increasing pressure from the church. As it happened, it took Melville and his colleagues until 1578 to reach a position to seek approval from Morton's government of their revised blueprint for the reformed church, the second Book of Discipline. While it reiterated many of the proposals of the first book, there were undoubtedly a number of controversial aspects within it. The reformed kirk now sought to obtain all the revenues of the old one, to abolish bishops altogether, and to seek acceptance of the so-called doctrine of the 'two kingdoms', whereby the church had sole control of ecclesiastical matters.

To Morton, who was strongly convinced that the church should be subordinate to the state, the proposed reforms were totally unacceptable. However, faced with the political instability which existed between 1578 and 1580, he had to proceed cautiously and avoid antagonizing the Melvillian party too much, since the latter, as he discovered, were quite prepared to make difficulties for him by fraternizing with his adversaries. Therefore Morton's strategy was to procrastinate; conferences were held and committees were duly appointed. When the second Book of Discipline was presented in June 1578 Morton told the kirk's commissioners that 'the said buik bein red and considerit … and mony headis thairof being found of so

great wecht and consequence … na resolution nor determination can be presentlie gevin thairin' (*APS*, 3.105). The final result was little different.

The borders and other domestic matters The governmental system which Morton took over in 1572 was one in which the central authorities depended largely on the local wardens to impose law and order on their respective territories. These comprised three areas known as the east, west, and middle marches, with in addition Liddesdale—technically part of the middle march but often assigned a separate keeper. While the virtually hereditary nature of the positions gave Morton little choice in selecting the wardens, his appointments nevertheless performed competently. On the east march between 1573 and 1578 Hume of Coldenknowes carried out his duties effectively as did his replacement, Hume of Wedderburn, between 1578 and 1580. Similarly, Morton had little to complain of in the efforts of Ker of Cessford and John Carmichael of that ilk on the middle march and Liddesdale respectively. But the situation was somewhat different on the west march, where Lord Maxwell's quirky personality (a characteristic also of the other wardens) proved too much for the regent, who in 1577 had him replaced by his nephew the earl of Angus. After the upheaval of 1578 the west march became more unstable; first Maxwell and then his uncle Lord Herries were in charge, until, perhaps unwisely, Morton appointed their great family rival, John Johnstone of that ilk.

In the administration of the borders there were occasions when Morton reinforced the power of the wardens by attending in person. For instance, eight judicial and military raids on various parts of the frontier were planned between 1573 and 1578, of which six were implemented. Morton was present on all of these. Again, in 1574–5 he gave instructions for a detachment of 100 infantrymen and forty light horsemen to carry out operations in Liddesdale and the middle march, a tactic repeated at the suggestion of Lord Herries in 1579. Finally, the system of taking pledges was tightened up. The prevalent practice, which had been subject to various forms of abuse, was that prominent borderers, as a guarantee for the good behaviour of their family or dependants, were placed in a form of mild detention remote from their homes. Morton now insisted that any keeper who allowed a pledge to escape would be subject to a statutory fine of £2000.

Lawlessness and disorder in other parts of Scotland also received Morton's attention. An expedition to the northeast in 1574 was aimed both at the suppression of the troublesome Gordon family and at 'the establishment of justice and punishment of disordouris and enormittis attemptit aganis our Soverane lordis authoritie and commonweill of the realme' (*Reg. PCS*, 2.388). Undoubtedly there were still numerous turbulent outbreaks in various parts of the country, notably the Black Isle, where the Mackenzies of Kintail were the offenders. None the less, there seems good ground for believing the verdict of the Edinburgh burgess, Robert Birrell, that, overall, Morton 'kept the country in great justice and peace' (Dalyell, 21).

The other main aspect of Morton's domestic administration was his supervision of the country's finances. Commendable efforts were made to obtain the outstanding revenues from the crown lands and customs. In addition Campveere in the Netherlands was at last established as the staple port for Scottish merchants. To some extent Morton's actions eased the financial position of the comptroller, William Murray of Tullibardine, yet escalating commodity prices ensured there was still a huge deficit in his department. In the context of rampant inflation the treasurer, Lord Ruthven, was faced with the expenses of the civil war (including the rebuilding of Edinburgh Castle with its famous half-moon battery) and of dealing with the unrest of 1578 and the Hamilton vendetta the following year. In response to constant financial difficulties Morton drew on his personal wealth and made regular loans to the treasury. He then recovered the debt from the profits which he made by manipulating the currency, an amount described by one modern commentator as 'unquantifiable' (Lynch, 227).

However, while debasement was a fairly common measure in the sixteenth century it was inflationary and in the long term did little to improve the situation or enhance the regent's popularity with his subjects. Other expedients adopted by Morton included the placing of an embargo on the export of silver, a request to the convention of royal burghs for a subsidy, and, in an attempt to tackle the shortage of bullion, encouragement of attempts at gold and silver mining. Notwithstanding Morton's efforts, both financial departments registered continuing and substantial deficits.

Anglo-Scottish relations France still exercised some influence in Scottish affairs, especially at the beginning of Morton's regency, and there was a certain amount of diplomatic activity with Sweden and the Netherlands over the recruitment of Scottish mercenaries. Relations with England unquestionably dominated Morton's foreign policy, however, and Elizabeth and her government welcomed his appointment, correctly anticipating that the regent would continue to display those Anglophile tendencies which had been a feature of his earlier career. Morton's immediate task was to convince the English government of the necessity of providing support for his efforts at overcoming the resistance of the Castilians, backed as they were by France and actively seeking the latter's intervention on their behalf. Military and financial aid was crucial if the regent was ever to capture Edinburgh Castle, but fortunately for Morton both Lord Burghley and Sir Francis Walsingham appreciated his problems and supported his appeals to Queen Elizabeth for assistance. In April 1573, following the breakdown of further attempts at persuading the garrison to surrender, an alliance was signed between Morton's government and England. The unconditional surrender of the castle in May brought an end to the first chapter of Morton's relations with England. The last serious threat to the regent's authority had been removed, while the collapse of the Marian faction was popular in England and advantageous to Elizabeth.

Thereafter, until his deposition in March 1578, the main feature of Morton's policy towards England was his attempt to persuade Elizabeth and her ministers to conclude a defensive pact with their neighbour. What the regent envisaged was an alliance in which both sides would give guarantees to defend the protestant cause, while at the same time promising mutual assistance in the event of a foreign attack. However, Morton's efforts were doomed to failure. In the 1570s Elizabeth experienced few serious threats from either France or Spain, and since there was little likelihood of Scotland being used as a base for attacking England she was not interested in Morton's proposition. Quite clearly she regarded Scotland as a minor power and treated its regent accordingly. In 1575 Morton required all his diplomatic skill to defuse the Redeswyre crisis, which arose when an English warden was killed in a border incident and Elizabeth furiously overreacted.

None the less, when he recovered his position later in 1578, Elizabeth was not prepared to forsake Morton in his subsequent struggles with his opponents. During the threat from the Argyll–Atholl faction that summer he could take some reassurance from the knowledge that English forces were poised at Berwick to swoop, if necessary, on his border adversaries. Again in August 1578 it was largely through the diplomacy of Robert Bowes, the English ambassador, that a possible civil war was averted and Morton's position secured. The final occasion when there was a flurry of activity in Anglo-Scottish relations occurred late in 1579, when Esmé Stewart, a kinsman of James VI, arrived from France. His influence with the impressionable young king (who created him earl of Lennox in April 1580), combined with his political connections, supposedly with both France and Spain, caused concern not only to Morton but also to Elizabeth. But embroiled as she was in negotiations for a possible marriage to the duc d'Alençon, the queen vacillated between sending modest subsidies to the Scottish government and ignoring Morton altogether. As Lennox tightened his grip on the country and gathered increasing support, Morton was left to reflect on the ineffectual nature of his partnership with England. Once Elizabeth perceived that the threat posed by Lennox was much less serious than originally imagined, she was prepared more or less to abandon her ally. Her reluctance to commit herself to Morton's cause was to have even more damaging consequences for him when he was finally overthrown by his enemies.

Downfall In the course of a year Lennox had become the focus for all those who for one reason or another wished to end Morton's regime. Many of them were members of that group of Morton's opponents of the summer of 1578 referred to by Robert Bowes, the English ambassador, as the 'Fellowship of Falkirk' (*CSP Scot.*, 5.378). The earl of Atholl had died in controversial circumstances in April 1579 amid allegations that he had been poisoned on Morton's instructions, but there were others who by this juncture had aligned themselves to the Lennox bandwagon, notably William Ruthven, Lord Ruthven, the treasurer, and Robert Pitcairn, commendator of Dunfermline and royal secretary, as well as a new star on the political horizon, Captain James Stewart. After his return from military service abroad Stewart, who was the second son of Lord Ochiltree, enjoyed a meteoric rise in the favour of both Lennox and James VI, who eventually elevated him to the earldom of Arran. It was Stewart who, at a meeting of the privy council on 31 December 1580 attended by the king, suddenly accused Morton of being an accessory to the murder of Lord Darnley. Following Morton's furious denial of the charge, the royal advocate, David Borthwick of Lochhill, recommended that the regent should be placed in custody pending his trial. Morton's political career ended; he was briefly imprisoned in Holyrood Palace and then in Edinburgh Castle before being transferred to Dumbarton, a fortress which was deep in Lennox territory, and chosen, according to the English ambassador, because the privy council was worried about 'what practices his friends would use either to give him intelligence or to carry him away' (ibid., 5.580).

These fears were not groundless, since during the early part of 1581 Morton's followers attempted to rally support for him. Morton's principal agent was his nephew the earl of Angus, who at one point in February even contemplated attacking Dumbarton Castle. But in the end Angus found himself outmanoeuvred. The backing for the Lennox administration was too widespread, and it outflanked him by arresting his relatives Archibald Douglas, senator of the college of justice, William Douglas of Whittinghame, George Auchinleck of Balmanno, and William Hume of Spot, and by exiling his sons Archibald and James and his kinsmen John Carmichael of that ilk, Malcolm Douglas of Mains, and William Douglas of Lochleven. While the sympathies of Elizabeth and her ministers tended to lie with the former regent, they pursued a realistic foreign policy. Elizabeth instructed Lord Hunsdon, governor of Berwick, to raise troops for possible action on the borders, and her ambassador Thomas Randolph condemned the Lennox administration in front of the Scottish estates. Ultimately, however, the English government placed its own interests first. Consequently, when Elizabeth reflected upon the growing threat from Spain, the actual cost of intervention in Scottish affairs, and the poor condition of her border levies, it made sounder political sense to abandon Morton and concentrate on the maintenance of friendly relations with France.

By April 1581 support for Morton within Scotland had dwindled even further: on 8 April his cousin, Douglas of Lochleven, was instructed to go into exile 'beyond the wattir of Cromartie' (*Registrum honoris de Morton*, 1.127); and on 22 April John Johnstone of that ilk, one of his main allies in the borders, lost his wardenship of the west march to Lord Maxwell, one of Lennox's adherents. The same month, as a result of pressure from his uncle Alexander Erskine, the earl of Mar abandoned Angus and handed over the strategically important Stirling Castle to the government. Shortly afterwards Angus, recognizing the inevitable, prepared with the remnant of his followers to seek refuge in England.

At this stage, confident that the opposition had been nullified, Lennox began to set in motion the arrangements for Morton's trial. On 23 May Morton was taken from Dumbarton to Edinburgh. Initially he faced a lengthy list of charges ranging from supporting Bothwell at the time of his marriage to Mary, committing various currency offences, plotting the removal of the master of Mar as royal guardian, conspiring to seize James VI in April 1580, and accepting English pensions, to the crucial charge of being implicated in the murder of Darnley. Significantly, there was no mention of the poisoning of the earl of Atholl; this suggests that his opponents, despite their efforts, had still insufficient evidence to offer against him. None the less, there was considerable substance to many of these accusations. For example, like numerous others Morton had briefly supported Bothwell; quite likely he was guilty of certain malpractices relating to the treasury; he may well have plotted the overthrow of Lennox and the seizure of the king; undoubtedly he pursued an Anglophile foreign policy and received some financial aid from England.

Finally, however, the Lennox administration decided that it would merely accuse Morton of complicity in the murder of Darnley and that it would ignore all the other charges. This was a wise move considering the delay which might well have ensued in hearing nearly twenty charges, not to mention the embarrassment for some prominent figures which would have ensued from the raking up of the past. It remained only for Lennox to guarantee the verdict he wanted; hence the selection of a jury almost totally antagonistic to Morton. Obvious candidates were old foes such as the earls of Argyll, Glencairn, and Montrose, and lords Maxwell and Seton. Others with grievances against the former regent were the earl of Sutherland, a kinsman of Adam Gordon of Auchindoun, Lord Ogilvie (whom Morton had imprisoned between 1576 and 1578), Sir Patrick Learmonth of Dairsie, and Hepburn of Waughton. The last two were closely connected to Kirkcaldy of Grange, whose execution had been ordered by Morton after the fall of Edinburgh Castle in 1573. Lord Innermeath, the master of Livingston, and Sir William Livingston too were linked one way or another to the Lennox faction. Only the earls of Eglinton and Rothes with Lord Somerville could be regarded as in any way impartial. With such a jury the odds were stacked against Morton.

After a brief hearing, the outcome of which was a foregone conclusion, on 1 June 1581 the earl of Montrose, on behalf of the jury, pronounced the accused guilty of 'airt, pairt, foir knowledge and conceling of the tresonable and unnatural murthow foirsaid' (Pitcairn, 1.114). The next morning, Friday 2 June, Morton had a lengthy discussion with some of the leading members of the kirk. Two of the churchmen present, Walter Balconquhall and John Durie, subsequently recorded the conversations which have become known as Morton's 'confession'. In fact it hardly merited this description since it was mainly a refutation of all the previous allegations, including a denial of any knowledge of the poisoning of Atholl. Morton conceded that he might have been 'a filthie abusare of my body in the pleasures of the flesh' (Calderwood, 3.574); yet, he insisted, he had always put the interests of the kirk at the forefront of his considerations. This questionable statement was followed by a final warning to the clergy: the king was surrounded by those 'knowin to he papistis' and 'the estait of the religion in this country appeired never to be in sic danger' (ibid., 575). About 2 o'clock that afternoon Morton had his last meal. Two hours later he was executed at the cross, Edinburgh, by the 'maiden', an instrument similar to the guillotine which he himself had allegedly introduced into Scotland from England. That evening his body was buried in Greyfriars churchyard.

It seems clear that the Lennox administration eliminated Morton because it feared a possible repetition of his performance of 1578 and recovery of his position for a third time. Equally, there was the attraction of the various spoils attendant on the downfall of the Douglases. Not surprisingly Lennox and Arran did particularly well; the former acquired, among other rewards, the lordship, regality, and barony of Dalkeith and the baronies of Aberdour, Mordington, and Whittinghame; the latter obtained a substantial pension from Balmerino Abbey, formerly in the hands of Morton's natural son James, and a lease of the lead mines previously belonging to Morton's cousin George Douglas of Parkhead. Other members of the Stewart family were also handsomely rewarded, as were their close allies, especially John Maxwell, Lord Maxwell, who was created earl of Morton only three days after the execution. This particular victory was short-lived, however. Morton's attainder was reversed on 29 January 1586, and the earldom reverted to his heir of entail, his nephew the earl of Angus. Morton's wife survived him, but on 12 July 1581 a jury pronounced that she had been insane for twenty-two years.

Morton's political performance must be regarded as uneven. He handled the turbulent nobility quite skilfully for much of the time, yet he failed to prevent the Argyll–Atholl partnership from undermining his position in 1578 and, even more crucially, to take decisive action against the partnership of Lennox and Captain James Stewart in 1580. The attack on the Hamiltons the previous year was a questionable stratagem. However, Morton was comparatively old when he took office in 1572 and by 1579 he was complaining of both his 'grit aige' and his 'disesis and infirmiteis' (Livingstone and others, 7.2093), so it is quite possible that his enthusiasm for day-to-day government waned while his judgments became less perceptive. The vexed question of the institution of the kirk was still very much unresolved at his downfall. Since, like the king, he had little time for the policies of Andrew Melville and the radical wing of the kirk, it seems unlikely that the favourable opinion held of him by certain presbyterian authors at the time of his death would have endured had he remained in power. In domestic affairs his administration of the borders displayed all the signs of an efficient regime, at least until the crisis of 1578. Elsewhere, despite his efforts, he was ultimately unable to prevent rising deficits occurring within the exchequer office. Moreover, his

manipulation of the currency and certain other questionable practices gave rise to probably justifiable allegations that he 'was inclined to covetousness' (Spottiswoode, 2.197).

Undoubtedly Morton was not a paragon of virtue in either public or private life. Nevertheless he did have one outstanding characteristic, a powerful personality. Consequently, he was the best individual available to administer Scotland during James VI's minority and for eight years gave the country a relatively strong and effective government. In the circumstances prevailing, this was a commendable achievement and one for which Morton should be principally remembered.   G. R. HEWITT

Sources CSP Scot., 1547–1603 · Reg. PCS, 1st ser., vol. 2 · D. Calderwood, The history of the Kirk of Scotland, ed. T. Thomson and D. Laing, 8 vols., Wodrow Society, 7 (1842–9), vol. 3 · M. Livingstone, D. Hay Fleming, and others, eds., Registrum secreti sigilli regum Scotorum / The register of the privy seal of Scotland, 6–7 (1963–6), vols. 6 and 7 · T. Dickson, J. B. Paul, and C. T. McInnes, eds., Compota thesaurariorum regum Scotorum / Accounts of the lord high treasurer of Scotland, 13 vols. (1877–1978), vols. 11, 13 · J. M. Thomson and others, eds., Registrum magni sigilli regum Scotorum / The register of the great seal of Scotland, 11 vols. (1882–1914), vols. 3–5 · CSP for., 1569–80 · APS, 1567–92 · Registrum honoris de Morton (1853), vol. 1 · J. Spottiswoode, History of the Church of Scotland, ed. M. Napier and M. Russell, 2, Spottiswoode Society, 6 (1851) · Scots peerage, vol. 6 · GEC, Peerage · T. Thomson, ed., Acts and proceedings of the general assemblies of the Kirk of Scotland, 3 pts, Bannatyne Club, 81 (1839–45) · G. Hewitt, Scotland under Morton (1982) · W. Fraser, ed., The Douglas book, 4 vols. (1885), vol. 2 · T. I. Rae, The administration of the Scottish frontier, 1513–1603 (1966) · J. G. Dalyell, ed., Fragments of Scottish history (1798) · M. Lynch, Scotland: a new history (1991) · R. Pitcairn, ed., Ancient criminal trials in Scotland, 7 pts in 3, Bannatyne Club, 42 (1833) · David Hume of Godscroft's The history of the house of Douglas, ed. D. Reid, 2 vols., STS, 4th ser., 25–6 (1996)
Archives NA Scot., papers · NA Scot., letters and documents | BL, Cotton MSS, corresp. and papers · NA Scot., letters to Sir John Ogilvy and others · NL Scot., letters to David Borthwick
Likenesses oils, 1577, Scot. NPG · attrib. A. Bronckorst, oils, c.1580, Scot. NPG [see illus.] · D. Allan, pencil, grey ink, and wash drawing

Douglas, James, second earl of Queensberry (d. 1671), nobleman, was the eldest son of William *Douglas, first earl of Queensberry (d. 1640), and Isobel (d. 1628), daughter of Mark Ker, first earl of Lothian, and his wife, Margaret Maxwell. In 1622 he was conjoined with his father in the charter by which the barony of Torthorwald was added to the family estates. By a contract dated 4 June 1630 he married Lady Mary Hamilton (d. 1633), third daughter of James *Hamilton, second marquess of Hamilton; the marriage produced no children. By a contract dated 26 March 1635 he married Lady Margaret Stewart (d. 1673), eldest daughter of John *Stewart, first earl of Traquair, with whom he had four sons, including William *Douglas, later first duke of Queensberry, and five daughters. As heir to the earldom of Queensberry from 1633 he was styled Viscount Drumlanrig until he succeeded his father in 1640 as second earl of Queensberry, second viscount of Drumlanrig, and second Lord Douglas of Hawick and Tibberis.

Initially Queensberry was a supporter of the Scottish national covenant. He was appointed a commissioner for the apprehension of papists in 1642, to the committee of war for Dumfriesshire in 1643, and the following year to the committee for the south. However, in 1645 he changed his allegiance to the king. He set out to join Montrose after his victory at Kilsyth, but on the way was captured and taken prisoner to Carlisle. William, first marquess of Douglas, who had accompanied him on his ill-fated journey, but had evaded capture, and others tried to bribe the governor of Carlisle to win his release, but they failed and were fined. Queensberry was fined 120,000 marks Scots by parliament for his delinquency, but in 1647, after half the amount had been paid, the remainder was discharged. Nevertheless, he remained out of favour during the rule of the kirk party. On 2 March 1649 parliament ruled against Queensberry in a case brought by the heritors of Glencairn, who wanted to remove the gift of the barony of Glencairn from the earl. In July 1649 he supplicated the general assembly to be received to the covenant, and his situation eased as Scottish divisions diminished in the face of invasion from England. In December 1650 his complaint to parliament about his treatment at the hands of the army of the western association was referred to the committee of estates, while in March 1651 he regained a command in the army. In 1654 he was fined £4000 by the protectorate's Act of Pardon and Grace, but this was reduced by three-quarters the following year. In 1656 he took advantage of the government's order for the relief of debtors in Scotland, registering debts of £290,000 Scots.

After the Restoration Queensberry exploited the more favourable political climate to relieve his straitened financial position. In June 1661 a report estimated his losses to have been £234,879 Scots. Significantly, in addition to other grants, parliament ordered £2000 to be paid to him by those attached to the forces of the western association in 1650, when goods and cattle had been seized and the gates of Drumlanrig Castle burnt. He was appointed a commissioner of excise in 1661 and a JP in 1663. He added to his estates with the acquisition, among others, of the lands of Kininmont, Locharwood, and Cummertrees. He died in 1671 and was survived by his wife.

DAVID MENARRY

Sources Scots peerage · APS · Reg. PCS, 1st ser. · D. Stevenson, ed., The government of Scotland under the covenanters, 1637–51 (1982), 8, 16, 22–3, 30, 32 · D. Stevenson, Revolution and counter-revolution in Scotland, 1644–1651, Royal Historical Society Studies in History, 4 (1977), 36 · J. R. Young, The Scottish parliament, 1639–1661: a political and constitutional analysis (1996), 130, 177 · The diary of Mr John Lamont of Newton, 1649–1671, ed. G. R. Kinloch, Maitland Club, 7 (1830), 9 · DNB · Book of debts, 18 June 1656–6 Jan 1657, NA Scot., CS 4/24, pp. 168–70 · The manuscripts of his grace the duke of Buccleuch and Queensberry … preserved at Drumlanrig Castle, 2 vols., HMC, 44 (1897–1903), vol. 1, p. 6 · W. Fraser, ed., The Douglas book, 4 vols. (1885), vol. 3, pp. 331–2 · H. Maxwell, A history of the house of Douglas, 2 vols. (1852), vol. 2, pp. 263–5 · P. Donald, An uncounselled king: Charles I and the Scottish troubles, 1637–1641 (1990), 123 · GEC, Peerage

Douglas, Lord James (c.1617–1645), army officer in the French service, was the third son of William *Douglas, first marquess of Douglas and eleventh earl of Angus (1589–1660), and his first wife, Margaret Hamilton (1584/5–1623), daughter of Claud *Hamilton, first Lord Paisley. He

was born during a three-year period when his father was travelling in Europe after his Catholicism had exposed him to criticism by presbyterian clergy in Scotland. One of his two older brothers, William, died in childhood and there is some suggestion that James may have assumed the Christian name William in consequence. His eldest brother, Archibald, predeceased his father in 1655 and the Angus earldom and Douglas marquessate were inherited by Archibald's son in 1660.

Lord James Douglas took the opportunity offered by the recruitment of Sir John Hepburn's regiment for service in France in 1633 to begin a military career, and by the time of Hepburn's death in 1636 had become first captain of the regiment. He was narrowly passed over for command in favour of Sir James Hepburn, who was himself killed in Lorraine in October 1637. Douglas had previously been favoured by Cardinal Richelieu for the regimental command on grounds of his Catholicism, and since James Hepburn died without a relative or designated successor in the regiment, Douglas's candidacy could be revived with success, the regiment subsequently being retitled Douglas. The appointment seems to have excited some tension among the established officers, however. In April 1638 a list of absentee captains from the regiment was publicized by the secretary of state for war, and concern was expressed that significant numbers of soldiers had deserted to other Scottish units. The shortfalls in officers and men led to disputes over appropriate levels of pay during the winter of 1638–9, and the unit limped through the campaign of 1639 with little distinction. The regiment would probably have been formally disbanded had it not, by a royal ordonnance of 28 November 1636, acquired entretenu (maintained) status, a royal undertaking to keep the unit on a permanent footing.

In January 1640 Douglas was sent back to Scotland with 30,000 livres to levy 2000 men—effectively a commission to raise the regiment again from scratch. This mission proved a failure and in July 1640 he was ordered to return the money that he had received for recruitment. The deepening crisis in Anglo-Scottish relations and Douglas's own Catholicism may well have contributed to this failure. The regiment remained in service in 1641 as a handful of compagnies réformées with the army of Marshal Châtillon, and once again Douglas was ordered to return to Scotland with some of his officers to carry out levies. Strongly supported by the French ambassador, Douglas had more success and in January 1642 disembarked at Dieppe with 2000 recruits. Confusion with his brother, George Douglas, has led to the erroneous assumption that James was appointed to the highest rank of lieutenant-général in the French armies. In fact he served ably as colonel of his regiment in the campaigns from 1642 to 1645, but was not promoted above this rank, which George Douglas himself did not receive until 1677. On 21 October 1645 James Douglas was leading his regiment on the Flanders frontier and was killed in a small-scale combat between Douai and Arras. His corpse was taken to Paris and buried in the abbey of St Germain des Prés near the remains of his grandfather,

William, tenth earl of Angus. His brother George ultimately succeeded him in command of the regiment, which was to suffer extremely heavy casualties at the battle of Lens in 1648.   DAVID PARROTT

Sources Service Historique de l'Armée de Terre, Vincennes, Archives de la guerre, A 1 45, fol. 188; A 1 50, fol. 110; A 1 50ii, fols. 146, 211; A 1 52, fols. 43, 293, 328; A 1 57, fol. 322; A 1 58, fols. 228, 395; A 1 59, fol. 720; A 1 65, fols. 170, 173, 345, 362; A 1 66, fol. 142 • Archives des Affaires Etrangères, Paris, AAE, mémoires et documents, vol. 842, fol. 228v • *Scots peerage* • *Lettres, instructions diplomatiques et papiers d'état du cardinal de Richelieu*, ed. D. L. M. Avenel, 8 vols. (Paris, 1853–77) • Pinard, *Chronologie historique-militaire*, 8 vols. (Paris, 1760–78), vol. 4, pp. 302–3 • A. Aubery, *Mémoires pour l'histoire du cardinal duc de Richelieu*, 1 (Paris, 1660), 653–4, 660, 681, 694 • GEC, *Peerage* • R. Douglas, *The peerage of Scotland*, 2nd edn, ed. J. P. Wood, 1 (1813) • F. Michel, *Les écossais en France, les français en Écosse*, 2 vols. (1862), vol. 2, pp. 291–318

Douglas, James, second marquess of Douglas (*c.*1646–1700), nobleman, was the only son of Archibald Douglas, earl of Angus (*c.*1609–1655), and his first wife, Lady Anna (*bap.* 1614, *d.* 1646), daughter of Esmé *Stuart, third duke of Lennox (1579?–1624), and his wife, Katherine Clifton. Following the death of his father in 1655 he bore the courtesy title of earl of Angus, and he was still under age in 1660 when he succeeded his grandfather, William *Douglas, first marquess of Douglas, as second marquess. On his father's request he had been placed in the care of his paternal aunt, Margaret, Lady Alexander, but she died at about the same time as her father. The family estates at Douglas's entry were in such an embarrassed condition, mainly because of accumulated debts, that it was estimated that his clear disposable income amounted to just £1000 Scots yearly. On 8 September 1668, after the attainment of his majority, he was served heir to his father in the earldom of Angus. In 1670, by a contract dated 7 September, he married Lady Barbara Erskine, eldest daughter of John Erskine, earl of Mar. Douglas Castle, which had fallen into disrepair, was renovated for their use. The marriage was not a happy one: the marchioness complained that her husband treated her with contempt, while he accused her of not affording him the respect he was due. A contract of separation, agreed in 1681, was made the subject of a popular ballad entitled 'Lord James Douglas' or 'The Marchioness of Douglas', beginning 'O Waly, waly up the bank' (C. Mackay, *The Legendary and Romantic Ballads of Scotland*, 1861, 189–94). The marchioness, with whom he had one son, died about August 1690.

William *Lawrie, tutor of Blackwood, the marquess's trusted factor and chamberlain, who was blamed by many for the estrangement, had since his appointment in 1670 exacerbated rather than improved Douglas's financial state. A royal commission of investigation into the marquess's affairs, initiated in 1684 by Charles II, came to nothing. When, following the battle of Bothwell Bridge, Blackwood was condemned to be beheaded, Douglas begged successfully for his life, asserting that Blackwood was the only man who knew his affairs. In 1692 the marquess married, by contract dated 13 December, his second wife, Lady Mary Kerr (*bap.* 1674, *d.* 1736), daughter of Robert *Kerr, first marquess of Lothian. They had two sons

and one daughter, Lady Jane *Douglas. Mary refused to allow Blackwood's interference in domestic affairs and after acquainting herself with the financial condition of the estate accused him of gross mismanagement. With the help of her father she managed to secure the appointment of a commission to take charge of the estate in 1698. It found debts in excess of £240,000 Scots. The commissioners dismissed Blackwood, but it was to be a few months before the marquess's view of him was changed.

Douglas was frequently present in parliament, and after his admission to the privy council in 1671 he regularly attended its meetings, but he was not at the forefront of politics during the reigns of Charles II and James VII. In the spring of 1689, however, he was a member of the committee of estates that ushered in the revolution, and in May was named as one of William III's council. About 1690 the new king granted him the forfeited estates of John Graham of Claverhouse, Viscount Dundee, and he was also appointed to the heritable office of constable of the castle and town of Dundee. He died at Douglas on 25 February 1700 and was buried in the old chapel of St Bride on 1 March.   DAVID MENARRY

Sources W. Fraser, ed., *The Douglas book*, 4 vols. (1885) • *Scots peerage* • APS • *Reg. PCS*, 1st ser. • *DNB* • GEC, *Peerage*

Archives NL Scot., papers • NRA, priv. coll., materials relating to estates and finances | BL, letters to duke of Lauderdale and Charles II, Add. MSS 23126–23137, 23244–23247

Douglas, James. *See* Hamilton, James, fourth duke of Hamilton and first duke of Brandon (1658–1712).

Douglas, James, second duke of Queensberry and first duke of Dover (1662–1711), politician, was born at Sanquhar Castle, Dumfriesshire, on 18 December 1662, the eldest son of William *Douglas, third earl and first duke of Queensberry (1637–1695), and Lady Isabel Douglas (*d.* 1691), sixth daughter of William *Douglas, first marquess of Douglas. He entered his studies at Glasgow University in 1676 and thereafter travelled in continental Europe, returning in 1684. On 1 December 1685, aged nearly twenty-three, he married Lady Mary Boyle (1670/71–1709), second daughter of Charles Boyle, styled Viscount Dungarvan, and Jane Seymour, daughter of William, duke of Somerset; the marriage produced four sons and five daughters. His title was lord and then earl of Drumlanrig, before he succeeded his father in March 1695.

Early political career Drumlanrig appears to have first entered the political scene in February 1684, when he was named by the privy council as one of the commissioners for the borders, and on 15 July 1684 he was sworn of the new privy council. On the same day he was appointed to the privy council's committee for public affairs, and he was also made a lieutenant-colonel of the regiment of John Graham of Claverhouse. On 1 August Drumlanrig's troop of horse was ordered to lie at Dumfries as part of the privy council's policy of suppressing conventicles. He was issued with a licence from the privy council on 12 August for importing English cloth to clothe his troop. Following a petition by the partners of Newmilns cloth manufactory against the imports, on 19 August the privy council set up

James Douglas, second duke of Queensberry and first duke of Dover (1662–1711), attrib. Sir Godfrey Kneller

a committee on which Drumlanrig sat to consider the claim that these partners were capable of providing Scottish cloth. The privy council received a letter from Charles II on 6 September ordering members of the council to 'proceed to the disaffected shires with the object of securing obedience to the laws' (*Reg. PCS*, 8.155–6). In line with the king's instructions, Drumlanrig and John Graham of Claverhouse (later first Viscount Dundee) were to be sent to Dumfriesshire and Wigtownshire. On 13 September Drumlanrig's troop of horse and Captain Strachan's dragoons were ordered by the council to proceed to Dumfries to attend the district commissioners appointed as part of the policy of the suppression of religious disorders in the western shires. On 15 November five rebels and fugitives subscribed the Test Act in the presence of Drumlanrig at Sanquhar Castle, and on 5 December he was appointed to a privy council committee to consider the cases of gentlemen and their wives in Teviotdale who were fined for their 'irregularities' (ibid., 10.47). The activities of Drumlanrig and Graham of Claverhouse in the south-western shires were applauded by the privy council on 12 December, and they were given 'hearty thanks for ther so good and acceptable service done to the King on this occasione' (ibid., 10.58). In 1685 Drumlanrig was appointed as a member of the new privy council on 9 April. His father was summoned to court in 1685, and on 7 August the privy council allowed Drumlanrig to accompany him. On 12 August a precept for £500 sterling was issued to cover Drumlanrig's expenses at court. He was appointed to the privy council in 1686 and 1687, though he

attended only once, on 30 March 1686. With the escalating tension in the reign of James VII and II, a commission to Drumlanrig as a lieutenant-colonel of horse was issued from Whitehall on 19 September 1688. Nine days later, on 27 September, orders were sent from Whitehall to the Scottish privy council ordering troops to march into England and magazines to be removed from Edinburgh Castle to Stirling Castle. Acting on the king's orders, John Drummond, first earl of Melfort, was to instruct Drumlanrig to go to his command in Scotland.

Servant of King William Drumlanrig was present at the privy council meeting of 1 October 1688, but he was shortly to change his allegiance to William of Orange, following his landing in England. Along with Prince George and the duke of Ormond, Drumlanrig joined Prince William at Sherborne, Dorset, on 30 November 1688. Drumlanrig's shift in allegiance away from James to William was scathingly commented on later by the Jacobite George Lockhart of Carnwath. According to Lockhart, Drumlanrig was 'the first Scotsman that deserted over to the Prince of Orange, and from thence acquired the epithet (among honest men) of Proto-rebel, and has ever since been so faithful to the revolution party, and averse to the king and all his advisers, that he laid hold on all occasions to oppress the royal party and interest' (*'Scotland's Ruine'*, 11). Drumlanrig did not attend the convention of estates (1689), nor was he present in the parliamentary sessions of 1689–90 which enacted the revolution settlement in Scotland. A commission for William's privy council was issued from Hampton Court on 27 May 1689. Drumlanrig was included on the king's council, and he attended the diets of 6 and 17 July 1689. That he had found favour with William was further reflected in his appointment as one of the gentlemen of the bedchamber and his appointment as colonel of the sixth or Scottish troop of Horse Guards.

In April 1690 Drumlanrig wrote to William Carstares seeking the position of extraordinary lord of session, an office which had been held by his father before the revolution. However, he failed to secure this position, which was later bestowed on his father on 23 November 1692. Drumlanrig served William's military cause against his former associate, now Viscount Dundee, in the first Jacobite rising. Drumlanrig was also a member of the 1690 privy council and, from 16 April, of a specialized committee dealing with artillery. Later, in September 1690, he was sent to Stirling with government forces for the potential defence of the town, and was instructed by the privy council to be ready to attack enemy forces should they proceed towards Dumbarton to the west or Perthshire to the east. Drumlanrig was present at the extraordinary meeting of the privy council on 4 November 1691 which issued a proclamation celebrating William's safe return from Ireland following his military success there. Having been appointed as a Treasury commissioner on 3 March 1692, he made his first formal appearance in the Scottish parliament in the fourth session of the parliament of William and Mary, which sat from 18 April to 15 June. George, first earl of Melville, the parliament's high commissioner, produced a letter from William authorizing Drumlanrig to sit and vote as lord high treasurer. Drumlanrig took his place in the 1693 parliamentary session as an officer of state. In accordance with current parliamentary legislation, he took the oath of allegiance, the parliamentary oath, and he signed the assurance.

On 28 March 1695 Drumlanrig succeeded to the dukedom following the death of his father, and thereafter attended that year's parliamentary session (9 May to 17 July). On 25 May 1696 he was appointed as lord privy seal, and on 26 June he took his seat as an extraordinary lord of session. In the next parliamentary session (7 September to 12 October 1696) Queensberry was present in the capacity of an officer of state as lord privy seal, and on 10 September he signed the association directed against Jacobite conspiracy towards King William, which also acknowledged the king as the rightful and lawful monarch. On 25 September he was named as one of the commissioners of supply for Dumfriesshire. Queensberry also attended the parliamentary session of 19 July to 1 September 1698 as lord privy seal. He was reappointed as a commissioner of supply for Dumfriesshire on 30 July, and on 31 August parliament passed legislation which ratified his earldom and regality of Drumlanrig. His general political and specific parliamentary profile was raised by the Darien disaster in 1699. Owing to public outcry William was reluctantly forced to summon a parliament in Scotland, and Queensberry was appointed as high commissioner to the parliamentary session which met from 21 to 30 May. He also served as high commissioner in the remaining sessions of the Williamite parliament (29 October 1700 to 1 February 1701 and 9 to 30 June 1702, the latter sitting under Queen Anne's authority after William's death). Queensberry's political credit was significantly enhanced by his successful political handling and containment of the Darien crisis in Scotland on William's behalf. As a reward for these services, Queensberry was made a knight of the Garter on 18 June 1701. He maintained his important political profile with the accession of Queen Anne, not only being retained as high commissioner to parliament, but also being appointed as one of the secretaries of state for Scotland, along with George Mackenzie, first earl of Cromarty. The 1702 session fulfilled the last wish of William III and met with the first request of Queen Anne by empowering the crown to appoint commissioners to treat for a union of the kingdoms. However, Queensberry had to bring the session to a sudden end on 30 June.

Moves to union, and personal crisis Queensberry played an important role in the abortive negotiations of 27 October 1702 to 3 February 1703 for a treaty of union with England. As the spokesman for the Scottish commissioners, on 10 November he made a speech in which he spoke of the union as 'highly advantageous for the peace and wealth of both Kingdoms and a great security for the Protestant Religion everywhere'; he also stressed the 'sincere intentions' of the Scottish commissioners to 'advance this great design' (APS, 1670–1707, 11, appendix, 148). Queensberry was appointed as high commissioner to the 1703 parliamentary session, which met from 6 May to 16 September and was the first session of a newly elected parliament which met over four sessions between 1703 and 1707. On 1 July the earl of Seafield wrote to Sidney, first earl of Godolphin, informing him that he and Queensberry had worked together in parliament concerning the disputed elections of the commissioners of the shires for Orkney. Seafield and Queensberry had therefore used their influence to secure 'the electione by a great majority' of those 'very well inclined' for the queen's service (*Letters Relating to Scotland*, 2). Nevertheless, in the face of aggressive constitutional nationalism in the 1703 session and the possibility that Scotland and England might have different monarchs in the future, Queensberry prorogued the session on 16 September.

Soon after, the duke's political fortunes suffered a severe setback with the exposure of the 'Scotch' or 'Queensberry plot'. Queensberry was discredited by his involvement with Simon Fraser, later Lord Lovat, a political charlatan closely associated with the exiled Jacobite court, who had returned to Scotland in summer 1703 (as a result of a government indemnity allowing Jacobite exiles to return to Scotland) ostensibly to co-ordinate a Jacobite rising. Fraser was driven by personal ambition to secure the restitution of his estates, following their earlier confiscation and his being declared an outlaw for the rape of, and forced marriage to, the daughter of the marquess of Atholl (she was the widow of the previous chieftain of the Frasers) in his drive to secure the Lovat title and chieftainship of the Frasers. The unreliable Fraser turned Jacobite informer and sought Queensberry's protection in an attempt to secure these personal objectives. Fraser implicated some of Queensberry's main Scottish political rivals in the Jacobite plot, especially John Murray, second marquess and first duke of Atholl. Without exploring the details of the plot in full, Queensberry secretly passed on the information to the queen, and provided Fraser with a feigned name and pass to go to France and report on Jacobite activity. However, the conspiracy was exposed when Fraser unwittingly passed on the details to one Robert Ferguson, who then warned Atholl and others of their implication in the supposed plot. Lockhart of Carnwath later argued that Queensberry and his associates deliberately 'resolved one way or other to frame such a plot, as, when lodged upon those they designed it against, should, in all humane probability, be their utter ruin and destruction' ('Scotland's Ruine', 49). Queensberry's subsequent fall from favour was accelerated by two key events. Firstly, following a memorial presented to the queen by Atholl, exposing the conspiracy against him, the House of Lords resolved that there had been a dangerous conspiracy in Scotland in favour of the Pretender (James Stuart). Secondly, a deputation from Scotland, consisting of politicians from the country party who were shortly to become part of what was known as the 'new party', arrived in London to protest at Queensberry's behaviour. Queensberry was replaced as high commissioner to the 1704 parliamentary session by John Hay, second marquess of Tweeddale, and the 'new party' was installed in power.

Revival of fortunes and the Union Yet Queensberry's power base in Scotland was too strong to be ignored, and the demands of the escalating crisis in Anglo-Scottish relations resulted in his rehabilitation in 1705 when he was reappointed as lord privy seal and made a lord of the Treasury. John Campbell, second duke of Argyll, was appointed as high commissioner to the parliamentary session which met from 28 June to 18 September 1705. Queensberry attended in the capacity of lord privy seal, but Lockhart of Carnwath argued that Argyll operated in liaison with Queensberry. Indeed, Lockhart claimed that Queensberry 'used him as the monkey did the cat in pulling out the hot roasted chestnuts' ('*Scotland's Ruine*', 85). It is clear, however, that lobbying took place for the rehabilitation of Queensberry, within the court interest in general and in the run-up to the 1705 parliamentary session in particular. Accordingly, David Boyle, first earl of Glasgow, wrote to the earl of Godolphin on 12 May, informing him that 'It is my opinion that the only means and way to setle the succesion is that the Duke of Queensberrie come down to Scotland as soon as possible and cordially assist my Lord Duke of Argyll, her Majesties Commissioner' (*Letters relating to Scotland*, 179). In response to the outrage among Scottish politicians caused by the English Alien Act, Queensberry introduced a motion in the 1705 session that a separate address should be made to Queen Anne informing her of the indignation of the nation at the interference of the House of Lords in Scottish affairs. Queensberry's motion was successfully carried, and his personal anger at the Lords may have been related to its stance over and interference in the recent 'Scotch plot'. Of greater importance is the fact that Argyll and Queensberry collaborated to ensure that James Douglas, fourth duke of Hamilton, was not nominated to the 1705 council of trade. Chancellor Seafield informed Godolphin of this in a letter from Edinburgh on 18 August 1705. Hamilton was not to be nominated, despite his own intense personal lobbying, because of his leading role in ensuring that the council of trade was to be elected by the parliament and not nominated by the queen. Accordingly, Argyll and Queensberry were 'positive not to have him named, nor any that voted against the Queens nominatione' (ibid., 71).

Queensberry was one of the Scottish commissioners who negotiated the treaty of union with their English counterparts in the summer of 1706, but, unlike the 1702–3 negotiations, Chancellor Seafield, and not Queensberry, was their spokesman. As high commissioner, Queensberry played a crucial role in the last session of the Scottish parliament, sitting from 3 October 1706 to 25 March 1707, which ratified the treaty of union. Instructions issued to Queensberry from Anne at Windsor on 31 July stressed that 'an entire Union' was the only acceptable political option for 'the Peace and happiness of our Subjects of this Island' (*Letters relating to Scotland*, 190–91). Thus Queensberry was instructed to endeavour to obtain

the ratification of the articles of the treaty in the forthcoming session of the Scottish parliament. Moreover, he was clearly informed that if 'a Federal Union or any other measure in opposition to an entire Union will carry in Parliament' then he was 'in that case to adjourn the Parliament' (ibid., 191).

Queensberry was also empowered to give the royal assent to any parliamentary legislation for the security of the presbyterian Church of Scotland for the post-Union future, as well as being instructed that the Scottish parliament was to decide on the manner of choosing the sixteen elective peers for the House of Lords and the forty-five MPs as the Scottish representation for the new British parliament. He was in correspondence with Godolphin prior to the opening of the parliamentary session on 3 October, and during the actual progress of the session. In a letter of 22 September John Erskine, twenty-second earl of Mar, secretary of state, wrote to Godolphin from Edinburgh and informed him that Queensberry and the court interest were currently considering 'what are the most advisable methods and measurs for manadging and cairying on business when the Parl. Meets' (*Letters Relating to Scotland*, 176). Popular disquiet at the Union meant that Queensberry was subjected to verbal abuse by the Edinburgh mob, suffered an attack on his coach, and saw his guards and servants wounded on a regular basis. Despite these external pressures, Queensberry played a crucial part in steering the treaty through the house, and he had a key role in the covert distribution of the £20,000 sterling sent north to pay the debts and arrears due to government servants. He worked closely with Chancellor Seafield and the Scottish treasurer, David Boyle, first earl of Glasgow, along these lines. On 4 October Glasgow wrote to Godolphin informing him that he had been ordered by Queensberry to acquaint Godolphin that:

> you would be pleased to remitt the s[d] money to Scotland so soon as possible, in regard that many of our nobility who are come to Parliament, that want their bygone pensiones, are calling for some money, and it is for her Maties service that they have a part at this juncture. (ibid., 182–3)

Ironically, Queensberry received the bulk of this money with a payment of £12,325, though he actually had recorded arrears of £26,756 9s. ½d.

British politician As a reward for his services to the queen and securing the treaty in Scotland, Queensberry was rewarded with a British peerage. On 26 May 1708 he was created duke of Dover, marquess of Beverley, and earl of Ripon, with remainder to his third son, Charles *Douglas, earl of Solway, who was later to succeed him as third duke of Queensberry. Queensberry's post-1707 political career was consolidated by his appointment as joint keeper of the privy seal, and on 9 February 1709 he was appointed as third secretary of state. This latter appointment gave Queensberry a continued significant influence in the management of Scottish affairs. Yet his position as a British peer aroused controversy during the general election of 1708, in the context of the election of the sixteen

Scottish peers to be represented in the new British parliament. His vote was protested against at the general election of the Scottish peers on 17 June 1708. This resulted in a more general resolution issued by the House of Lords on 17 January 1709. Accordingly, the Lords resolved that a peer in Scotland, who chose to sit in the House of Lords by virtue of a patent under the great seal of Britain, was to have no voting rights in the election of the Scottish representative peers. Nevertheless, it would appear that the Queensberry interest secured a strong profile in the 1708 election. One Alexander Rigby, writing from Edinburgh on 19 June 1708, stated that prior to the election nine of the sixteen elected peers were 'supposed to be for D. Queensberrys party', and that 'the D. of Dover and his friends have the greatest stroak in the Kn^ts of the Shires and in the burroughs' (*Letters Relating to Scotland*, 185–6). As secretary of state, in January 1711 Queensberry was in correspondence with the Board of Trade and Plantations concerning the reopening of trade to ports in Livonia and Ingria.

Queensberry died in London on 6 July 1711, just under two years after his wife's death in October 1709. He was buried at Durisdeer, near Drumlanrig, Dumfriesshire. He is remembered as one of the Scottish statesmen and politicians who were responsible for securing the safe passage of the treaty of union through the Scottish parliament. In an essay written in 1703 on the 'character of families', Lord Cromarty stated that Queensberry was 'in estate as great as any mentioned, and considerable in his following; but the more by his being now the most considerable family of Douglass, who ever were the most eminent family and most active in Scotland, or perhaps elsewhere' (*Letters Relating to Scotland*, 130).   JOHN R. YOUNG

Sources DNB · *Scots peerage* · *Reg. PCS*, 3rd ser., vols. 8–16 · *APS*, 1670–1707 · *Letters relating to Scotland in the reign of Queen Anne by James Ogilvy, first earl of Seafield and others*, ed. P. Hume Brown, Scottish History Society, 2nd ser., 11 (1915) · *The letters and diplomatic instructions of Queen Anne*, ed. B. C. Brown (1935) · S. M. Dixon, ed., *Britain and Russia in the age of Peter the Great: historical documents* (1998) · P. W. J. Riley, *King William and the Scottish politicians* (1979) · P. W. J. Riley, *The Union of England and Scotland* (1978) · W. Ferguson, *Scotland's relations with England: a survey to 1707* (1977) · P. H. Scott, *Andrew Fletcher and the treaty of union* (1992) · *'Scotland's ruine': Lockhart of Carnwath's memoirs of the union*, ed. D. Szechi, Association of Scottish Literary Studies, 25 (1995)
Archives Drumlanrig Castle, Dunfriesshire, muniments of duke of Buccleuch · Dumfries and Galloway Archives, estate papers · NRA, priv. coll., corresp. | Hunt. L., letters to earl of London · NA Scot., corresp. with Lord Leven · U. Nott. L., letters to Lord Portland
Likenesses G. Kneller, oils, *c*.1692, Buccleuch estates, Selkirk · studio of G. Kneller, oils, *c*.1703, Plymouth City Museum and Art Gallery · J. van Nost, marble effigy, 1711, Durisdeen church, Dumfries · attrib. J. Baptiste de Medina, oils, Scot. NPG; repro. in Scott, *Andrew Fletcher*, 198 · L. du Guerrier, line engraving (after G. Kneller), BM · attrib. G. Kneller, oils, Buccleuch estates, Selkirk · attrib. G. Kneller, portrait, Chatsworth House, Derbyshire [*see illus.*] · oils (with garter sash), Scot. NPG

Douglas, James (*bap.* **1675**, *d.* **1742**), anatomist and man-midwife, was the third child of a family of eight sons, four of whom became fellows of the Royal Society, and five

daughters of William Douglas (*d.* 1705), of Baads, West Calder, 5 miles west of Edinburgh, and his wife, Joan Mason. The date of his birth is not known but he was baptized on 21 March 1675. Nothing is known of his early education, although a James Douglas graduated MA at Edinburgh University in 1694. In 1698 Douglas was a medical student at Utrecht and may have spent time in Paris before graduating MD at Rheims in 1699. In London by 1700 he became associated with Paul Chamberlen in the practice of midwifery, and on one occasion, in 1702, used (unsuccessfully) *modo nostro* (forceps), the Chamberlens' secret instrument. A large collection of Douglas's case histories, both midwifery and clinical, survive for the period 1700–11 and illustrate contemporary medical practice. The accuracy with which symptoms are recorded often makes modern diagnosis possible. After 1711 only records of patients' prescriptions survive, an indication that Douglas had a considerable practice among the upper class.

In 1706 Douglas began teaching anatomy, for which he published a syllabus. Cadavers not being available, students dissected dogs. Douglas intended publishing a series of handbooks comparing the anatomy of dogs and humans but got no further than *Myographiae comparatae specimen, or, A comparative description of all the muscles in a man and in a quadruped* (1707), long used as a dissecting guide, and republished in 1760 and 1775 with a Latin translation (1729). In 1705 he reviewed Valsava's *De aure humana tractatus* for the Royal Society (*PTRS*, 25.2214) and on 4 December 1706 he was elected a fellow of the society. Eleven of his papers on medical, botanical, and zoological subjects were published in *Philosophical Transactions* and he read at least fifty-seven unpublished papers. In 1740 he was excused further annual subscriptions. The Barber-Surgeons' Company elected him Gale osteology lecturer for 1712, and to the Arris lectureship on the muscles in 1716, for which a syllabus survives. He resigned this lectureship over disagreement with the masters of surgery.

Interested in all aspects of medicine Douglas published *Bibliographiae anatomicae specimen, sive, Catalogus omnium pene auctorum, qui ab Hippocrate ad Harveum rem anatomicum … scriptus illustravat* (1715) with another edition in 1734. All his medical and other writings started with a historical review. A number of assistants helped Douglas with his work over the years. His brother George worked with him for many years and he had other able assistants in Robert Nesbitt, Joseph Hurlock, William Douglas (no relation), James Parsons, and, finally, William Hunter. Douglas's published work was often illustrated by talented artists and engravers. Many of his papers are in the handwriting of amanuenses. Hunter acquired all Douglas's papers, some of his medical books, and preparations from the latter's famous anatomy museum.

Douglas's interest in comparative anatomy covered not only mammals, birds, reptiles, amphibia, and fish but also extended to invertebrates. From about 1719 he took an interest in botany, possibly as a result of acquiring a garden. At first he lived in Fetter Lane, London, an area of dense housing. In 1721, when he was made an honorary fellow of the Royal College of Physicians, he was living in

Bow Lane, where most houses had gardens. Moving to the Grand Piazza, Covent Garden, he grew in his garden many medicinal plants for observation and experiment. He gave to the Royal Society a series of papers on medicinal plants including wild valerian that he had found plant hunting near Ilford. Plants were part of his interest in materia medica and in 1724 he published *Index materia medicae, or, A catalogue of simple medicines that are fit to be used in the practice of physic and surgery*. In 1733, together with Thomas Wilkins, a chemist, he considered setting up a laboratory for the preparation of 'curious medicines'. His most important botanical work, although it contains nothing of medical interest, is *Lilium sarniense, or, A description of the Guernsay-Lilly; to which is added, the botanical description of the coffee berry*. On the title page Douglas is described as physician-extraordinary to the queen. In 1726 he sent the gardener Thomas Knowlton to Guernsey to learn what he could of the history and cultivation of the Guernsey lily there and in 1729 published a second edition incorporating Knowlton's findings; it was reprinted in 1737. In 1727 Douglas published *The Description and History of the Coffee Tree* and *A Supplement to the Description of the Coffee Tree*. His work on chocolate and tea was not published.

An advertisement in *Lilium sarniense* told readers that George I had given Douglas £500 'to communicate the observations and discoveries he has made in anatomy' and 'a treatise on diseases incident to women'. Douglas had been working on an osteology since at least 1713; the plan was monumental: the book was to comprise plates of all the bones, together with their weights, chemical composition, connections, cartilages, glandulae, and sacculi mucosi (first described by Douglas), and associated muscles and ligaments. It was also to include sections on diseases of bones and a history of osteology and osteological figures. It was virtually complete at his death, but his assistant William Hunter's wish to publish it remained unfulfilled. All that remains extant is a large collection of drawings of dissections of normal and abnormal reproductive systems, gravid uteri and foetuses for the treatise on diseases of women. In order to assist his brother, the surgeon John *Douglas, James undertook an investigation of the relevant anatomy to enable John to reintroduce safely suprapubic lithotomy. Indeed, Douglas intended a complete history of lithotomy but got no further than *The History of the Lateral Operation* (1726), reprinted 1731 with an *Appendix Containing Mr Cheselden's Present Method* with French (1726) and Latin (1733) translations. Much unpublished material survives.

Douglas was also involved in the case of Mary Toft, of Godalming, who claimed in 1726 to have given birth to a number of rabbits. Toft was brought to London and examined by Sir Richard Manningham and Douglas. She eventually admitted her deception and it was Douglas who took down her confession. When Manningham published his diary of the case Douglas became concerned that Manningham had implied that he (Douglas) had been duped by Toft. He therefore defended himself in *An Advertisement Occasioned by some Passages in Sir R. Manningham's Diary Lately Published* (1727). A satire on Douglas's account of the Toft affair and his earlier actions in it was *'Flamingo', a shorter and truer advertisement by way of supplement, to what was published the 7th instant, or, Dr D-g-l-s in an extasy, at Lacy's Bagie, December 4th 1726* (1727).

Douglas's most important medical work, *A Description of the Peritoneum*, was published in 1730. In it Douglas described the fold in the peritoneum between the rectum and the bladder, later called the pouch of Douglas. In an early draft of this work he acknowledged Winslow's priority in describing this fold but this was left out in the published version. Douglas described the fold as being:

> where the pertionaeum leaves the foreside of the rectum, it makes an angle and changes its course upwards and forwards over the bladder; and a little above this angle there is a remarkable transverse stricture or semi-oval fold of the peritonaeum which I have constantly observed for many years past, especially in women.   (J. Douglas, *A Description of the Peritoneum*, 1730, 37)

In 1734 Douglas attended Princess Anne, daughter of George II and wife of the prince of Orange. Setting out for a return to the Netherlands in November 1734 after a visit to England the princess became ill. She was believed to be pregnant and Douglas and a midwife were sent to attend her. Douglas thought it was inadvisable for her to make a sea crossing but George II insisted on her return to the Netherlands. Whether or not Douglas accompanied her on this trip, he was in the Netherlands in 1735 when she was found not to be pregnant. Queen Caroline awarded Douglas an annuity of £500 for his attendance on the princess. However, the princess had taken a dislike to him and he did not attend her pregnancy in 1736, but did so in 1739 when her daughter lived only half an hour.

About 1735 Douglas began working on a treatise on aneurysms. The work remained unpublished although much of the material still remains. He also produced the papers on English, Latin, and Greek languages which may have been written for his children. Assessments of these papers have been made by Holmbert (1956) and Michael (1970). Alexander Pope (1743) described Douglas as 'above all curious in what related to Horace' (Pope, 4.187). In the *Dunciad* Pope refers to Douglas in the couplet:

> There all the learn'd shall at the labour stand,
> And Douglas lend his soft obstetric hand.

Douglas collected editions of Horace and published *Catalogus editionum Quinti Horatii Flacci ab 1476 ad an 1739 quae in bibliotheca Jacob Douglas … adservantur* (1739). He also made a translation of Horace's first ode.

Douglas married twice. The identity of his first wife is unknown, but there was a daughter of this marriage. His second wife was Martha Wilkes (*d.* 1752), aunt of John Wilkes the radical politician. They had two sons, Israel James, an apothecary, and William George, who studied medicine, and a daughter, Martha Jane, who was said to have been engaged to William Hunter but who died in 1744. Nothing is known of Douglas's private life. His friends tended to be colleagues and others who shared his interests. Latterly Douglas lived in Red Lion Square, London, where he died on 2 April 1742; he was buried on 9 April in St Andrew's Church, Holborn. His wife applied to administer his will, but the will has not survived. William Hunter helped William George Douglas to assemble, from his father's notes, the substance of what would have been James Douglas's second Croonian lecture on the bladder, which George read to the Royal Society on 27 May 1742. In 1748 he published *Nine Anatomical Figures Representing the External Parts, Muscles and Bones of the Human Body*, being the proposed first plates in Douglas's osteology.

HELEN BROCK

Sources U. Glas., James Douglas papers · C. H. Brock, *Dr James Douglas papers and drawings ... a handlist* (1993) · K. B. Thomas, *James Douglas of the pouch and his pupil William Hunter* (1964) · C. H. Brock, 'James Douglas (1675–1742), botanist', *Journal of the Society of the Bibliography of Natural History*, 9 (1978–80), 137–45 · B. Holmbert, *James Douglas on English pronounciation c1740* (1956) · I. Michael, *English grammatical categories and the tradition to 1800* (1970) · A. Pope, *The Dunciad in four books*, rev. edn (1743), bk 4 · A. Wilson, *The making of man-midwifery: childbirth in England, 1660–1770* (1995) · DNB

Archives Hunterian Museum and Art Gallery, Glasgow, pathology department, Royal Infirmary, pathological preparations · Royal Society, The Hague, Netherlands, Dutch Royal Archives, journal book and classified papers · U. Glas. L., special collections department, medical and scientific papers | BL, Sloane MSS · Bodl. Oxf., Rawl. MSS · NHM, Bankesian MSS

Douglas, James, fourteenth earl of Morton (1702–1768), natural philosopher, was born in Edinburgh, the eldest of three sons of George Douglas, thirteenth earl of Morton (1662–1738), politician, and his second wife, Frances, daughter of William Adderley of Halstow, Kent. He graduated MA from King's College, Cambridge, in 1722; he may also have attended the University of Edinburgh. Upon leaving Cambridge he embarked on the grand tour, and established connections with French scientists. After returning to Scotland he entered scientific circles in Edinburgh, and became close friends with the mathematician Colin Maclaurin. Lord Aberdour, as he was known at this time, was elected a fellow of the Royal Society of London on 19 April 1733. With Maclaurin and several others, Aberdour observed a solar eclipse in February 1737. He was one of the six men (Maclaurin, Lord Hope, Andrew Plummer, Alexander Lind of Gorgie, and Alexander Monro *primus* were the others) who in May 1737 proposed the formation of the Philosophical Society of Edinburgh, which expanded the Medical Society founded in 1731 by Monro into a broader society devoted to natural philosophy and related subjects. Aberdour was named the society's president. Early recipients of his patronage via the society include the applied mathematician and Church of Scotland minister Alexander Bryce.

In 1738 Aberdour succeeded to the title of fourteenth earl of Morton, and was invested with the Order of the Thistle. The following year, after the death of the earl of Selkirk, he was appointed a lord of the bedchamber, and succeeded Selkirk as a representative peer for Scotland. He regularly spoke in the House of Lords. Before 1731 he had married Agatha (*d.* 1748), daughter and heir of James Halyburton of Pitcur, Forfarshire; they had five sons and two daughters.

Morton was involved in many scientific activities. He was a patron of the instrument maker James Short (whom he hired to tutor his children) and owned several of Short's telescopes. With Maclaurin and the earl of Hopetoun he was successful in establishing an observatory at the University of Edinburgh, and gave £100 toward the

James Douglas, fourteenth earl of Morton (1702–1768), by Jeremiah Davison, 1740 [with members of his family]

fund in 1740. A member of the Honourable Society for Improvement in the Knowledge of Agriculture in Scotland, he was also interested in mining and chemistry, and was keen to exploit resources of lead and coal on his estates. One of the two articles he published in the *Philosophical Transactions* of the Royal Society, concerning the validity of a supposed cure for hydrophobia, further demonstrates Morton's involvement in the study of medicine. The paper well displays his critical and empirical turn of mind: after reading a newspaper story that an Italian cured the illness by administering draughts of vinegar, he wrote to a friend in Venice to ascertain the truth of the story, which turned out to be false.

In 1739 Morton travelled to Orkney to survey his estates there and also to measure a degree of latitude. These lands were held under form of mortgage to the crown, and Morton obtained an act of parliament in 1742 which made the grant of Orkney and Shetland absolute to himself. During the 1739 visit he was assaulted by Sir James Murray, bt, during a dispute over property. Murray was fined and imprisoned, but his action showed the troublesome nature of the management of these lands, and Morton sold them in 1766 to Sir Laurence Dundas for £63,000.

Morton's politics are unclear, though he was associated with the duke of Newcastle in parliament. In September 1746, during a visit to Paris, he was imprisoned in the Bastille (along with his wife, child, and sister-in-law) for three months for failure to produce documentation to validate his residence. Horace Walpole commented on Morton's 'imprudence' and the *Daily Advertiser* claimed a private cipher was found in his papers with Jacobite connections. (Walpole, *Corr.*, 19.301). Having been released in late 1746, the family did not return to Britain until May 1747, but Morton must have gone back to France a year later, for he reported in the *Philosophical Transactions* (vol. 45) on an eclipse of the sun he observed in Paris in July 1748. He had hoped to make his observations in Scotland, but the meridian line set by Maclaurin had been destroyed during the rising of 1745–6. Morton's first wife died on 12 December 1748, and on 31 July 1755 he married Bridget (1722/3–1805), eldest daughter of Sir John Heathcote, bt, of Normanton, Rutland; they had one son, John (1756–1818), and a daughter, Bridget (1758–1842).

In the 1750s Morton acted as an intermediary between Robert Wallace and the French *philosophe* Montesquieu, in regard to Wallace's debate over ancient population with David Hume. In 1760, after the death of the Hon. Alexander Hume Campbell, Morton was named lord clerk register of Scotland, and developed plans to preserve the archives. A trustee of the British Museum and member of the longitude commission, he was also one of the commissioners of annexed estates between 1755 and 1760, but never attended a meeting. Having been elected to the council of the Royal Society on 30 November 1763, he was elected president following the death of the earl of Macclesfield six months later. He also filled Macclesfield's place as a foreign member of the Académie Royale des Sciences in Paris. During Morton's presidency of the Royal Society the Greenwich observatory was placed under the

society's management, Mason and Dixon were charged to measure a degree of latitude during the course of their famous survey, and preparations were made for the observation of the 1769 transit of Venus for which Morton, in his capacity as a commissioner of longitude, had obtained government funding. Unfortunately, he did not live to see Cook embark, but died at Chiswick on 12 October 1768. Morton was anatomized by Sir John Pringle of Edinburgh, where he was probably buried. He was survived by his wife, who died on 2 March 1805. Of the surviving children of his first marriage, his second son, Sholto Charles (1732–1774), succeeded his father as fifteenth earl, and the younger daughter, Mary (1740?–1816), married Charles, fourth earl of Aboyne, in 1774.   ANITA GUERRINI

Sources DNB · C. R. Weld, *A history of the Royal Society*, 2 vols. (1848) · R. L. Emerson, 'The Philosophical Society of Edinburgh, 1737–1747', *British Journal for the History of Science*, 12 (1979), 154–91 · *Scots peerage*, vol. 6 · GEC, *Peerage* · A. Murdoch, 'The people above': *politics and administration in mid-eighteenth-century Scotland* (1980) · H. A. Bruck, *The story of astronomy in Edinburgh* (1983) · E. C. Mossner, *The life of David Hume* (1954); repr. (1970)
Archives RS · U. Aberdeen · U. Edin. | BL, corresp. with Lord Hardwicke, Add. MSS 35446–35910 · BL, corresp. with Sir Andrew Mitchell, Add. MS 58286 · BL, corresp. with duke of Newcastle, etc., Add. MSS 32699–33056 · NA Scot., letters to John Drummond · U. Nott. L., letters to Henry Pelham
Likenesses J. Davison, group portrait, oils, 1740 (with members of his family), Scot. NPG [*see illus.*]

Douglas, Sir James, first baronet (1703–1787), naval officer, was the son of George Douglas of Friarshaw, Roxburghshire, and Elizabeth, daughter of Sir Patrick Scott, baronet, of Ancrum, in the same county. Douglas, despite entering the navy in 1715, had to wait until 1732 to be commissioned. However, he was—and remained—politically well-connected. In 1741, when he was serving at Cartagena in the *Tilbury*, his patron was William Pulteney. On 14 March 1744 Douglas was posted to the *Mermaid* (40 guns) and he commanded her at the capture of Louisbourg in 1745. On that station in 1746 he commanded the *Vigilant* (64 guns). From 1754 to 1768 he was MP for the seat of Orkney and Shetland, a constituency which provided a number of men for the navy. Often absent from parliament, he followed his patron, the earl of Morton, in his support of the duke of Newcastle.

In 1756 Douglas commanded the *Bedford* in the Home Fleet and in December and January he sat on Admiral John Byng's court martial. In the following year he commanded the *Alcide* (64 guns) on the fruitless Rochefort expedition. In 1759, while in the same ship, he served at the capture of Quebec. Admiral Charles Saunders valued his knowledge of 'the French language, and particularly their sea-terms' and found him 'very useful' in dealing with 'the French pilots' (PRO, ADM 1/482, part 1, fol. 50). In September Saunders sent Douglas home with the tidings of victory and the king duly rewarded him with a knighthood and a gift of £500. In 1760 Douglas was appointed to the *Dublin* as commodore and commander-in-chief at the Leeward Islands. Here he displayed administrative and diplomatic skills, and dealt effectively with troublesome enemy privateers. In 1761 he moved swiftly and successfully, in conjunction with Lord Rollo and his troops, to take the island of Dominica.

In 1762 Douglas was understandably surprised to be superseded by Rear-Admiral George Rodney, and he served as Rodney's second-in-command at the capture of Martinique. Later that year Douglas was appointed to the chief command at Jamaica where he handled the local planters with characteristic tact. He gave indispensable support to the Havana expedition but, to his chagrin, did not share in the lavish subsequent rewards. On 21 October he was promoted rear-admiral of the white. During the peace he went out again to the West Indies as commander-in-chief. Douglas was twice married: first in 1753 to Helen (d. 1766), daughter of Thomas Brisbane of Brisbane in Ayrshire; the couple had four sons and three daughters. His second wife was Lady Helen Boyle, daughter of John, second earl of Glasgow and Helenor, née Morison.

In October 1770 Douglas advanced to vice-admiral, and from 1773 to 1777 he was commander-in-chief at Portsmouth. In January 1778 he became an admiral of the blue and, in April 1782, an admiral of the white. Having been created a baronet on 27 June 1786, he died on 2 November 1787 and was survived by children from his first marriage.　　RUDDOCK MACKAY

Sources DNB · N. A. M. Rogers, 'The Douglas papers', *The naval miscellany*, 5, Navy RS, 125 (1984), 244–83 · D. Syrett, ed., *The siege and capture of Havana, 1762*, Navy RS, 114 (1970) · N. A. M. Rodger, *The wooden world: an anatomy of the Georgian navy* (1986) · R. Pares, *War and trade in the West Indies, 1739–1763* (1936) [repr. 1963] · E. Haden-Guest, 'Douglas, James', HoP, *Commons, 1754–90* · Vice-Admiral Charles Saunders's dispatches from North America, 1759, PRO, ADM 1/482, pt 1 · *The Vernon papers*, ed. B. McL. Ranft, Navy RS, 99 (1958) · D. Spinney, *Rodney* (1969) · D. Syrett and R. L. DiNardo, *The commissioned sea officers of the Royal Navy, 1660–1815*, rev. edn, Occasional Publications of the Navy RS, 1 (1994)

Archives NMM, corresp. and papers · U. Mich., Clements L., letter-books, logbooks, accounts, and memoranda | NMM, letters to Sir Charles Middleton · NMM, letters to Lord Sandwich · PRO, Admiralty records

Wealth at death gathered much less prize money than he might have reasonably expected: Rodger, ed., 'Douglas papers'; Syrett, ed. *Siege and capture of Havana*

Douglas, James (1753–1819), antiquary and geologist, third and youngest son of John Douglas (d. 1762), innkeeper of the Hercules Pillars in Hyde Park Road, and Mary Gardiner (d. 1766), was born in London on 7 January 1753. Of nine siblings only the three boys survived. After the deaths of his parents he was brought up by his elder brother William (1745–1810) in Manchester, where James belatedly attended Manchester grammar school.

The chronology of Douglas's next few years remains obscure, but he was employed by his brother William, a cloth merchant, and was eventually sent overseas as his agent in Italy—only to be dismissed and cut off when he misappropriated some of the funds with which he had been entrusted. Desperate to support himself, he entered the Austrian army as a cadet and was soon in Vienna. After some time in that service he was sent on a mission to England and decided to remain there. He certainly toured the Low Countries in 1773 and he may have briefly attended a military college in Flanders. In 1777 and 1778, however, he

was a student at Peterhouse, Cambridge, though he did not graduate. In 1779 he accepted a commission as a lieutenant in the Leicester militia, served on the staff of Colonel Hugh Debbieg, and was put to work as an engineer fortifying Chatham Lines (1758–1807), on the Medway, adjacent to Rochester in Kent.

On 6 January 1780 Douglas married Margaret (1760–1820), daughter of John Oldershaw of Rochester, a surgeon. In 1781 Douglas published a two-volume translation from the French of J. A. H. Guibert entitled *A General Essay on Military Tactics* 'by an Officer'. The next year he likewise issued and illustrated an anonymous *Travelling Anecdotes, through Various Parts of Europe* (1782), which was successful enough to require London editions in 1785 and 1786, with a Dublin one following in 1787—by which time the author's name had been added. Written primarily at Cambridge during his student years, and in an unconventional manner reminiscent of *Tristram Shandy*, the *Anecdotes* (some of them military) recalled the author's earlier experiences at Vienna and in the Low Countries, where, at Tongres especially, his antiquarian interests had been aroused.

At one point in his youth Douglas had been associated with the noted collector and antiquary Sir Ashton Lever, even assisting him in stuffing some of the birds later displayed in Lever's Leicester Square museum (1774–88). In 1783, sponsored by Lever and others, Douglas was elected a fellow of the Society of Antiquaries, a learned society that meant more to him than any other. He was ordained the same year. Though Douglas would later exemplify his clerical devotion with *Twelve Discourses on the Influence of the Christian Religion on Civil Society* (1792), he identified himself on the title-page first as a fellow of the Society of Antiquaries and only second as chaplain in ordinary to the prince of Wales.

Between 1785 and 1793 Douglas wrote the two works for which he is most often remembered. The first of these, *A Dissertation on the Antiquity of the Earth* (1785), had been presented originally on 12 May as a paper before the Royal Society. Without having been refereed, the paper was then withdrawn (and retitled) for publication as an independent work. In its final form Douglas's *Dissertation*, illustrated with aquatints by himself, consisted of three inductive 'cases' and a lengthy appendix commenting on previous geological theories. The first case comprised a group of relics from a barrow on Chatham Hill that Douglas had had opened in 1779; the second, another group from a barrow at Kingston opened by Bryan Fawsett in 1771; and the third, fossils from the Isle of Sheppey collected by himself and Sir Joseph Banks. Though Douglas, like most men of his time, believed in the reality of the Noachian flood, the Sheppey fossils and others demonstrated independently of Genesis—for him, at least—that there had been an inhabited antediluvian world full of animals (and probably human beings) subsequently destroyed by just such a global catastrophe as the Flood.

At the time Douglas was writing, the vast duration of geological time was entirely unrecognized. His final remarks nevertheless emphasized four important points:

the fossilized animals and plants, though tropical, had lived where they were found; the climate then was much warmer than in his day; a forty-day flood (as in Genesis) would not have sufficed to transport animal remains from afar (as other theorists had contended); and the earth had some unknown power within it to fossilize organic remains. These conclusions, though not unique to himself, were of far-reaching intellectual significance.

Douglas's second major work, and no less important than the *Dissertation*, was *Nenia Britannica, or, A sepulchural history of Great Britain from the earliest period to its general conversion to Christianity*, which was published in twelve parts from May 1786 to 1793 and as a book in 1793, again with his own illustrations. Consisting primarily of archaeological reports, the book (*nenia* meaning 'dirge') aspired to be a general history of the funerary customs of ancient Britons, whether Celtic, Anglo-Saxon, Roman, or Danish. Douglas therefore described excavations by himself of barrows at Chatham Lines (1779–93) and of graves at Ashford, Kent (1771 and 1783), and in Leicestershire (undated). Other portions of the book discuss some early barrow diggings on Chartham Downs, Kent, near Ashford, by Cromwell Mortimer (an early founder of the Society of Antiquaries) in 1730; miscellaneous antiquities; the opening of ditched barrows in Greenwich Park; and the contents of numerous 'small barrows' recognized for the first time as being Anglo-Saxon. Douglas also describes Roman graves in Britain and at Tongres in Flanders. Finally, there is a lengthy analysis of Stonehenge. His interest in funerary monuments may have been caused by his many bereavements, having lost both parents, his six sisters and two brothers. Douglas's personal copy of *Nenia Britannica* in the British Library includes his original drawings, twenty-six extra illustrations, and some manuscript additions. Many of the relics he described are now in the Ashmolean Museum at Oxford. He also published several other papers on antiquarian subjects, of which 'Two dissertations on the brass [in fact, bronze] instruments called Celts' (1785) is the most important.

Finally, Douglas tried his hand at novels, of which there were three, though none were of permanent literary value: *Fashionable Infidelity* (3 vols., 1790; no surviving copy); *The Maid of Kent* (3 vols., 1790); and *The History of Julia d'Haumont* (2 vols., 1797). In addition to the illustrations for his own works, he painted some excellent portraits of his friends, both in oils and miniature, and engraved a full-length portrait of his fellow antiquary Francis Grose. He also contributed an engraving of Coston church to John Nichols's *History and Antiquities of the County of Leicester*.

Douglas's wandering ministry brought him livings successively in Chiddingfold, Surrey, in 1785; Litchborough, Northamptonshire, in 1787; Middleton, Sussex, in 1799; and Kenton, Suffolk, in 1803. After 1809 he lived in several further locations in Sussex, and he died of a chill at Vicarage House, Preston, near Brighton, Sussex, on 11 November 1819. He was buried in the local churchyard three days later. He was survived by his wife, who died the next year, and by three sons and one daughter.

DENNIS R. DEAN

Sources R. Jessup, *Man of many talents: an informal biography of James Douglas, 1753–1819* (1975) · *DNB* · D. R. Dean, *Gideon Mantell and the discovery of dinosaurs* (1999) · *GM*, 1st ser., 89/2 (1819), 564–5 · Venn, *Alum. Cant.*
Archives AM Oxf. · BL · Bodl. Oxf. · NL NZ, Turnbull L. | Cornwall RO, corresp. with John Hawkins · Devizes Museum, Wiltshire Archaeological and Natural History Society, letters to William Cunnington · NRA, priv. coll., letters to Lord Egremont, accounts, etc. · S. Antiquaries, Lond., letters to H. G. Faussett · Wilts. & Swindon RO, letters to William Cunnington and Sir R. C. Hoare
Likenesses attrib. T. Phillips, oils, AM Oxf.

Douglas, James, fourth Baron Douglas (1787–1857), Church of England clergyman and aristocrat, fifth son of Archibald Stewart Douglas, first Baron Douglas (1748–1827), and his second wife, Lady Frances Scott (1750–1817), youngest daughter of Francis Scott, earl of Dalkeith, was born on 9 July 1787. Having been educated for the church at Christ Church, Oxford, he was appointed in 1819 rector of Marsh Gibbon, Buckinghamshire, and in 1825 rector of Broughton in Northamptonshire. At the time of these appointments, which he held concurrently until 1848, there was little prospect of his succeeding to the title and estates, as he was then the third surviving son. But both his elder brothers died unmarried—Archibald, second Baron Douglas, in 1844, and Charles, third Baron Douglas, in 1848, when the estates and title fell to him. On 18 May 1813 James Douglas married Wilhelmina (1791–1857), daughter of General James *Murray, fifth son of the fourth Lord Elibank. They had no children and, on his death at Bothwell Castle on 6 April 1857, the title of Lord Douglas became extinct, and the estates passed to his sister, Lady Montagu. He was buried at Douglas.

HENRY PATON, *rev.* K. D. REYNOLDS

Sources GEC, *Peerage* · *GM*, 2nd ser., 35 (1851), 616

Douglas, Sir James (1803–1877), governor in Canada, was born on either 5 June or 15 August 1803 in Demerara, British Guiana, the second of three children and the younger son of John Douglas, a merchant, of Glasgow, and an unknown, probably coloured, woman whom he never married, whose surname may have been Ritchie. After a childhood in Lanark, Scotland, where he attended preparatory school, Douglas went to Canada in 1819, employed by a firm soon absorbed by the Hudson's Bay Company. A hot-tempered individual, he early on fought a duel and beat to death a Native American accused of murder. In 1828 he married, 'according to the custom of the country', Amelia, the half Native American daughter of William Connolly, chief factor at Stuart Lake, a marriage which was religiously regularized in 1836. They had thirteen children, of whom one boy and five girls lived to maturity.

After being transferred to Fort Vancouver as an accountant, Douglas rapidly improved its management and was given more responsibilities, including negotiating with the Russians to the north and the Mexicans in California. Having founded Fort Victoria in 1843, he was sent there as chief factor in 1849. Two years later he was appointed governor of Vancouver Island. Despite opposition to the duality of his role and criticism of his creating a judgeship for his brother-in-law, Douglas presided over the steady growth of both company and colony. During the gold rush of 1858 he moved boldly to close Fraser River to non-company trade, organized the policing of claims, assumed authority over the mainland, and sternly maintained law and order in the face of social upheaval. His effectiveness was admired as his arrogance and conflict of interest were deplored, and he was made governor of the new colony, formed when Vancouver Island was incorporated with British Columbia, on condition he leave the company. In 1859 he went to the brink of war with American troops over San Juan Island, despite his council's urging restraint. He seemed disappointed when the dispute was settled at higher levels. The project of a road connecting the Cariboo goldfields to the coast occupied him from 1862. He was appointed KCB when his governorship of Vancouver Island ended in 1863, and he retired from his British Columbia post in the following year, citing the state of his health as the cause.

A physically vigorous, tall, and muscular man of dark complexion, moderate in personal habits, industrious but volatile, Douglas spoke fluent French and several Native American dialects. Stiff and cold in personal relations, he was pompous and excessively attached to the trappings of power. He died in Victoria, British Columbia, on 2 August 1877. J. M. McCarthy, *rev.*

Sources M. A. Ormsby, 'Douglas, Sir James', *DCB*, vol. 10 · D. B. Smith, *James Douglas in California, 1841: being the journal of a voyage from the Columbia to California* (1965) · D. Pethick, *James Douglas, servant of two empires* (1969) · B. A. McKelvie, 'Sir James Douglas, a new portrait', *British Columbia Historical Quarterly*, 7 (1943) · W. N. Sage, *Sir James Douglas and British Columbia* (1930) · R. H. Coats and R. E. Gosnell, *Sir James Douglas* (1908) · *The Times* (6 Aug 1877) · *The Times* (12 Aug 1877)

Archives British Columbia Archives and Records Service, Victoria, corresp. and papers

Wealth at death under £35,000 (in England): probate, 13 Nov 1877, *CGPLA Eng. & Wales*

Douglas, Sir James Dawes (1785–1862), army officer, was born on 14 January 1785, the elder son of Major James Sholto Douglas of Grange in Jamaica (first cousin of the fifth and sixth marquesses of Queensberry) and Sarah, daughter of James Dawes. He was commissioned ensign in the 42nd regiment (Black Watch) and was at once taken on the staff of Major-General Sir James Duff, commanding at Limerick, where he became a close friend of his fellow aide-de-camp, William Napier, the military historian. In 1801 he was promoted lieutenant and joined the Royal Military College at Great Marlow. He was promoted captain in 1804, and, being pronounced fit for staff duty, was appointed deputy assistant quartermaster-general with the force sent to South America in 1806. He was praised in dispatches, and in 1807 was nominated in the same capacity to the corps proceeding to Portugal under Sir Arthur Wellesley, and was present at the battles of Roliça and Vimeiro. He advanced into Spain with Sir John Moore, and served with the 2nd division through the disastrous retreat from Salamanca and at the battle of Corunna.

When Beresford was sent to Portugal in 1809 to organize the Portuguese army, Douglas accompanied him; he was in February 1809 promoted major in the English army and appointed lieutenant-colonel of the 8th Portuguese regiment. He soon got his regiment fit for service, and was present at the brilliant passage of the Douro in May 1809; at the end of the year his regiment was attached to Picton's, the 3rd division, and brigaded with the 88th and 45th regiments. At the battle of Busaco this brigade had to bear the brunt of the French attack, and Douglas's Portuguese were praised for their conduct, which was specially mentioned in Lord Wellington's dispatch.

Douglas commanded this regiment all through the campaign of 1811, and in 1812, when the Portuguese were considered sufficiently disciplined to be brigaded alone, it formed part of Pack's Portuguese brigade. This was the brigade which distinguished itself at the battle of Salamanca by its gallant though vain attempt to carry the hill of the Arapiles, and Douglas was again mentioned in dispatches. At the beginning of 1813 Major-General Pack was removed to the command of a British brigade, and Douglas, who had been promoted lieutenant-colonel in May 1811, succeeded him in the 7th Portuguese brigade, part of Sir John Hamilton's Portuguese division. At the head of this brigade he distinguished himself at the battles of the Pyrenees, where he was wounded, of the Nivelle, the Nive, Orthez and Toulouse, where he was twice severely wounded and lost a leg (for which he received a pension of £350 per annum). At the conclusion of the war he received a gold cross and three clasps for the battles in which he had been engaged with a regiment or brigade, and was made knight of the Tower and Sword (Portugal) and KCB (January 1815). In 1815 Douglas married Marianne, daughter of William Bullock of Jamaica, and they had eleven children; she predeceased him.

Douglas was deputy quartermaster-general in Scotland (1815–22) and in Ireland (1825–30). He was promoted colonel in 1819 and major-general in 1830, when he received the command of the south-western district of Ireland. From 1837 to 1842 he was lieutenant-governor of Guernsey. He was promoted lieutenant-general in 1838, and was made a GCB in May 1860. He had been made colonel of the 93rd foot in 1840 and of the 42nd highlanders in 1850, and was promoted general in 1854. After leaving Guernsey he retired to Clifton, Bristol, where he died at his residence, 25 Royal York Crescent, on 6 March 1862.

H. M. Stephens, *rev.* James Lunt

Sources J. Philippart, ed., *The royal military calendar*, 3 vols. (1815–16) · *GM*, 3rd ser., 12 (1862) · Boase, *Mod. Eng. biog.* · *Dod's Peerage* (1858)

Wealth at death under £300: administration, 19 April 1862, *CGPLA Eng. & Wales*

Douglas, Lady Jane (1698–1753), noblewoman, was the second child and only daughter of James *Douglas, second marquess of Douglas (*c.*1646–1700), and his wife, Lady Mary (*bap.* 1674, *d.* 1736), daughter of Robert *Kerr, first marquess of Lothian, and his wife, Lady Jean Campbell. Jane was born on 17 March 1698; her father died when she was two, but her mother made sure that she was carefully educated. Slim, beautiful, intelligent, and devout, she was highly eligible and when she was twenty-two she almost

Lady Jane Douglas (1698–1753), by Allan Ramsay, *c*.1735

married Francis, earl of Dalkeith, later second duke of Buccleuch. However, the duchess of Queensberry broke the match so that the earl could marry her own sister-in-law, another Jane Douglas. Jane fled to the continent where, the story goes, she planned to enter a nunnery, but was retrieved by her mother and brother. This seems unlikely for, by her own account, Jane had been brought up as a Presbyterian, but she certainly declined all subsequent suitors, though they included the dukes of Hamilton and Atholl, and the earls of Hopetoun, Aberdeen, and Panmure.

Living with her mother at Merchiston Castle, Edinburgh, Lady Jane Douglas initially enjoyed a good relationship with her difficult, eccentric brother, Archibald *Douglas, third marquess and first duke of Douglas. He granted her an allowance and made her his sole executor. Having decided to remain a bachelor (though he was later to marry), he now began to urge his sister to find a husband and carry on the family line. When she met the handsome, dashing, but penniless Jacobite widower, Colonel John Steuart of Grandtully (1687–1764), Jane encouraged him. The colonel courted her for two years until the day when she unaccountably refused to see him, returned all his love tokens and sent back his letters unopened. Steuart left the country to resume his continental military career and did not return for another ten years. By then, living on her own at Drumsheugh House since the death of her mother in 1736, Jane sent him a note, explaining

that she had broken off their friendship because she had believed false rumours about him. He promptly called on her, they resumed their relationship, and they were married in August 1746 at Drumsheugh by the well-known episcopal minister Robert Keith. Jane's faithful serving-woman, Helen Hewat, was the only witness.

The marriage was kept secret because of the duke of Douglas's disapproval. A Hanoverian, he had turned against Colonel Steuart and had also quarrelled with Jane, perhaps after hearing how she had sheltered the Jacobite James, Chevalier de Johnstone, at Drumsheugh for two months after the battle of Culloden. The newly married couple left Scotland separately, Jane using the name Mrs Gray. Reunited at Huntingdon, they sailed from Harwich to the Low Countries and settled first at The Hague, later moving to Utrecht and then Aix-la-Chapelle. Not until the summer of 1748 did the very pregnant Jane reveal that she was Steuart's wife. The couple had by now run up such large debts that their friends advised them to escape their creditors by moving to Paris. This they did, Jane allegedly having to be lifted into the stagecoach by two men because she was so heavy.

After taking up residence at the Hôtel Châlons in the rue St Martin, Lady Jane gave birth to non-identical twin sons on 10 July 1748, or so she claimed. Many people were incredulous, for she was fifty years old. Such late births were not unknown, but her enemies soon began to circulate the rumour that became the centre of a *cause célèbre* fifteen years later. Jane had never been pregnant, people said. She and Steuart had obtained two French babies which they passed off as their own, in the hope of securing the duke of Douglas's inheritance. The voluminous papers in the complex court case known as the Douglas cause record these accusations and the very different evidence provided by Helen Hewat and Jane's other servants and friends. According to them, Sholto Thomas, the younger child, was very delicate, and had been baptized immediately after birth by Pierre la Marr, the man-midwife who delivered him. When Jane and the colonel decided to return to Rheims they took the older twin, Archibald James Edward *Douglas (formerly Steuart), with them but left Sholto with a wet-nurse, fearing that he would not survive the journey.

Four weeks after Archibald's public baptism in Rheims, Lady Jane found that she was pregnant again, but she miscarried at three months. Meanwhile Sholto was thriving in the care of his wet-nurse, and in November 1749 his parents travelled to Paris to collect him. They had resolved to return to Britain in the hope of improving their financial situation, more desperate than ever since the duke had cut off Jane's allowance on hearing the rumours about the twins. When Jane appealed to George II for financial assistance, writing pathetically, 'Presumptive heiress of a great estate and family, with two children, I want bread' (Fraser, *Douglas Book*, 2.498), he granted her an annual pension of £300, the equivalent of her brother's allowance. Meanwhile Steuart had been incarcerated in the king's bench prison at the instigation of his creditors.

Sending affectionate messages to her husband almost

every day, Lady Jane decided to take her sons to Scotland to see the duke. He, however, declined to answer her letters and, when she and the twins arrived at Douglas Castle in April 1753, they were turned away. 'The children, poor babies, have never yet done any fault', Jane protested. 'May I not then plead for their being admitted and allowed to see you and to kiss your hands?' (*Letters*, 125). The duke ignored her pleas. Anxious about her husband, Jane set off for London a few days later, leaving the twins with her law agent. Two days after she left, Sholto fell ill, and on 5 May he died. Jane was inconsolable. She wrote to her brother to give him the news. Still he did not reply.

Now seriously ill herself, with violent pains in her stomach, Lady Jane travelled back to Edinburgh that August and tried once more to see the duke. It was no use. Weak and emaciated, she died in her Edinburgh lodgings at noon on 21 November 1753 and was buried five days later in her mother's grave in the Chapel Royal at Holyrood. With her brother's death in 1761, the scandal surrounding the birth of the twins was revived, as Archibald's claim to the Douglas estates was contested on behalf of the duke's kinsman James-George, seventh duke of Hamilton. Years of legal debate followed, with both sides sending investigators to Paris to try to discover what had really happened there in the summer of 1748. Finally, the House of Lords decided in favour of Archibald, and Lady Jane Douglas was publicly vindicated.   ROSALIND K. MARSHALL

Sources *Service of Archibald Stewart, now Douglas of Douglas esq., as heir of provision to Archibald, duke of Douglas his uncle (1761)* • *The petition of George-James, duke of Hamilton, 19 December 1763 (1764)* • *Replies for George-James, duke of Hamilton, 20 June 1764 (1764)* • *Proof for Archibald Douglas of Douglas Esq., defender* [n.d.] • *Proof for Archibald Douglas of Douglas Esq., defender, 28 January 1766 (1766)* • *Proof in the conjoined processes, George-James, duke of Hamilton ... against the person pretending to be Archibald Stewart (1766)* • *Memorial for George-James, duke of Hamilton ... against the person pretending to be Archibald Stewart, January 1767 (1767)* • *Letters of the Right Hon. Lady Jane Douglas (1767)* • *A survey of the speeches, arguments and determinations (1767)* • *The speeches and judgement ... upon the important cause (1768)* • W. Fraser, ed., *The Douglas book*, 4 vols. (1885), vol. 2 • W. Fraser, ed., *The Red Book of Grandtully*, 2 (1868), 306 • *DNB* • *Scots peerage*, 1.207–10; 5.475–7 • GEC, *Peerage*, 4.438–9
Archives The Hirsel, the earl of Home's archives, letters | Lennoxlove, Hamilton archives, MSS relating to Douglas cause and depositions of witnesses relating to her marriage and birth of twins
Likenesses J. Vanderbank, oils, 1721, priv. coll. • A. Ramsay, portrait, c.1735; Christies, 20 Nov 1964, lot 187 [*see illus.*] • W. Aikman, oils, priv. coll.; negative, Scot. NPG • engraving, Scot. NPG

Douglas, Janet, Lady Glamis (c.1504–1537), noblewoman, was the daughter of George Douglas, master of Douglas, who was killed at Flodden in 1513 and so predeceased his father, Archibald *Douglas, fifth earl of Angus, by a few weeks, and of his wife Elizabeth Drummond. Archibald *Douglas, sixth earl of Angus, and Sir George *Douglas of Pittendriech were her brothers; she also had at least one other brother and four sisters. In 1520, when she was probably aged about sixteen, she married John Lyon, sixth Lord Glamis. He died on 17 September 1528, leaving a minor as his heir, and three other children. In the same year James

V succeeded in escaping from the control of his step-father, the sixth earl of Angus, who had married James IV's widow Margaret Tudor and established his own authority. James had come to loathe his guardian, a development evident in the proclamation made at Stirling on 29 June that year, that Angus should not come within 7 miles of the king, ostensibly because of his misrule and failure to maintain justice. Within a year Angus was in exile in England.

The king's antagonism extended to other members of the Douglas family, and particularly to Janet, who in December 1528 and again in January 1529 was summoned to appear before parliament to answer the charge of art and part assistance to her brothers given at Edinburgh the previous June. Her husband had made his final appearance on the council early in July 1528, so it is certainly possible that his wife could have been in Edinburgh at that time. Patrick Charteris of Cuthilgurdy, Hugh Kennedy of Girvanmains, and John Hume of Blackadder were summoned for the same offence, but Kennedy and Hume received a remission, whereas (perhaps as an alternative to remission) Janet and Charteris were granted licence to go overseas on pilgrimage on 20 September 1529, being given respite from actions against them until their return. However, Janet does not appear to have left the country, as she was pursuing a legal action against John Lyon of Knockany through the winter of 1529–30.

Janet Douglas had come under suspicion again by June 1531, when she was described as 'fugitive fra the law and at the horne ... for intercommonying with our soverane lordis rebellis' (Livingstone, no. 951). By 31 January 1532 she was being prosecuted for the alleged poisoning of her late husband, whose early death was obviously now being viewed as suspicious. However, the assizes which followed in January and February were drawn from the localities of Forfar, Perth, Aberdeen, and Fife, areas where the Lyon family held estates, and the reluctance of local lairds to serve on them is reflected in the numerous fines which were levied for default. The prosecution against Janet was dropped, and James V's suspicions against her seem to have been allayed, since by July 1532 she had contracted a second marriage, to Archibald Campbell of Skipness (d. 1537), the younger son of Archibald Campbell, second earl of Argyll, and uncle of the fourth earl. They had no children.

In the years which followed Janet brought several legal actions concerning rents and payments, mostly with success, but events were to turn against her in 1537. On 15 June her son John *Lyon, the young seventh Lord Glamis, was ordered to remain in ward in Edinburgh Castle, and on 17 July Janet Douglas herself was convicted on two points of treason: conspiring and imagining the death of the king by poison, and assisting and communicating with her brothers. This assize was mixed in composition, with no overwhelming local bias; the sentence which followed, that Janet should be burned on Edinburgh's castle hill, was carried out at once. Her husband, who had been imprisoned in Edinburgh Castle, broke his neck while trying to escape on the following day. Her son was convicted, also on 18 July, of concealing his mother's conspiracy to poison the king, though the sentence of hanging and drawing was commuted to imprisonment. On 22 August John Lyon of Knockany was convicted of concealing Janet's conspiracy, and of plotting to use the same poison to kill the earl of Rothes. One Alexander Mackie was convicted of supplying the poison, and was sentenced to be banished to Aberdeenshire, while Lyon was hanged and beheaded. After the death of James V, Lord Lyon claimed that he had been tortured into confessing to a poison plot, and in any case, given the king's obvious suspicion of Janet, it is difficult to see how she could have been in a position to poison him, as she does not appear to have attended court. It is possible that the antipathy felt by the earl of Rothes to the Glamis family played some part in the poison allegations, as he certainly stood to benefit from their downfall, though in the event he profited less than he would have liked: the king's annexation of the Glamis estates, of Janet's terce in Aberdeenshire, and of the estate of John Lyon of Knockany raised £5770 for the exchequer between 1538 and the end of James's reign.

The real motive behind the king's pursuit of the case against Janet Douglas is far more likely to have been implicit in the second part of the charge, the assistance she had allegedly given to her brothers. The popular sympathy said to have been felt for her as a beautiful young woman, taken together with the fact that she was the highest-ranking person to be executed during the personal rule of James V, may obscure the fact that the king genuinely detested the Angus faction and had just returned from a nine-month absence in France during which various potentially treasonable plots had been reported. Unlike her sisters Janet had always been suspected by the king of close links with her brothers, and he was anxious to underline his supremacy on his return and to emphasize the end of Angus influence, not least by his commitment to a French alliance, rejecting the foreign policy once pursued by his stepfather. Notwithstanding its brutality the public execution of Janet Douglas was not without a rationale, in that it sent an unmistakable message not only to the Douglases but also to any other potential rebels.

C. A. McGLADDERY

Sources J. Cameron, *James V: the personal rule, 1528–1542*, ed. N. Macdougall (1998) · R. Pitcairn, ed., *Ancient criminal trials in Scotland*, 1, Bannatyne Club, 42 (1833), pt 1 · M. Livingstone, D. Hay Fleming, and others, eds., *Registrum secreti sigilli regum Scotorum / The register of the privy seal of Scotland*, 2 (1921) · *Scots peerage*, 1.189–90; 8.278–81

Douglas, Jo. *See* Doll, Josephine (1926–1988).

Douglas, John (*c*.1500–1574), archbishop of St Andrews and educational reformer, was born in Longnewton, Roxburghshire, the son of Robert Douglas. His cousin Hugh Douglas was the son of William Douglas of Bon-Jedburgh, but nothing else is known of John Douglas before he matriculated in St Leonard's College, St Andrews, in 1515, with other future reformers, John Winram and Alexander Alesius (Allane or Alan). Douglas graduated MA in 1517, when he would have been in his mid- to late teens.

Tracing his subsequent university career depends partly on identifying one and the same John Douglas in dispersed records, and, since false identifications vitiated earlier accounts, caution is suggested. Douglas probably moved to Glasgow in 1518, his incorporation coinciding with that of John Mair (Major) on his return from Paris. He would then have followed Mair to St Andrews in 1523, where Douglas matriculated in the pedagogy on 25 June. He may even have followed Mair back to Paris in 1525, where for more than ten years, from 1526 until at least 1537, a John Douglas of the diocese of Dunkeld, already bachelor and master of arts, is recorded in several roles in the university. He was preceptor in the colleges of Presles (1528, 1531) and Montaigu (1533), elected procurator of the German nation in 1531 and dean in 1532, and paid fees to become bachelor of medicine from 1532 to 1536. Douglas later owned medical books published in Paris between 1528 and 1531. George Buchanan was in Paris during this period, and Douglas's interests were advanced by Robert Wauchope, later archbishop of Armagh. In 1537 Archbishop James Beaton of St Andrews granted Douglas financial support. Another of Douglas's presumed Paris associates was Archibald Hay, proponent of a trilingual college in St Andrews. In Hay's *Oratio pro collegii erectione*, published in Paris in 1538, the author commended Douglas to Beaton as eminently qualified to implement this plan. The outcome was the new college (St Mary's) established by Beaton in 1539. Hay was provost in 1546–7 and succeeded by Douglas, who was presented by the crown on 27 September 1547 and collated on 1 October; Douglas retained the office until his death. From 28 February 1551 he was also rector of the university, re-elected twenty-three times by the end of his life.

Douglas's humanist formation matched the vision of John Hamilton, archbishop of St Andrews from 1547 to 1571, and he carried through Hamilton's 'new foundation' of St Mary's in 1555. During the 1550s Douglas's provostship espoused a humanist's reforming Catholicism. Particular stress was placed on the study of the Bible, and to advance the college's work scholars were recruited from far and wide, including at least one exiled professor from England. Among Douglas's deputies in St Mary's was Richard Marshall, the main author of 'Hamilton's catechism'. According to Lindsay of Pitscottie (but no other source), Douglas was among those, including Winram, who condemned Walter Milne to death for heresy in 1558—the last protestant martyr in Scotland. In mid-1559, however, Douglas probably supported the formation of a reformed congregation in St Andrews parish church, and by 1560 he was sufficiently identified with the Reformation to be appointed to the six-man (and six-John) commission that compiled the Scots confession and the First Book of Discipline in that year. Along with Winram, Douglas is generally credited with the book's precise recommendations on the universities. He seems to have proceeded to the degree of doctor under St Andrews' post-Reformation statutes, and with others from St Mary's he was approved by the general assembly in December 1560 as qualified for the ministry. (Winram and twenty others from St Andrews had been approved at the March assembly.) That same year Douglas and Winram received recantations from former priests. On 1 October 1561 Douglas was elected an elder on St Andrews kirk session, and he was re-elected every year thereafter, even after becoming archbishop.

Douglas presided over St Mary's and the university during a quarter-century of upheaval and reconstruction. He taught many of the new leaders of the Scottish kirk—for instance, James Lawson, Knox's successor in St Giles's, Edinburgh; and the young orphan Andrew Melville, who was treated with almost paternal solicitude by Provost Douglas. Yet no writing by him has survived or is attested apart from a Latin letter which, as first signatory among forty Reformation luminaries, he sent on 4 September 1566 to Beza in Geneva in response to a request for Scottish subscription to the second Helvetic confession. The letter reported thorough scrutiny by the superintendents and others in St Andrews and their enthusiastic approval, except for the chapter on the festivals of the church calendar. The general assembly ratified this position on 27 December 1566.

Douglas was frequently at the assembly after 1560. In 1564 he concurred with Winram that, if the queen opposed the new religion, she could justly be resisted. He regarded her private mass as idolatry, but was unsure whether it should be forcibly suppressed. His reformism, like Winram's, retained a conservative streak. When, after Archbishop John Hamilton's execution on 6 April 1571, Douglas was nominated the first protestant archbishop of St Andrews, on 6 August following, by his kinsman and namesake Regent Morton, the assembly protested and Winram as superintendent of Fife inhibited him from assuming office. Only the concordat reached at the convention of Leith on 16 January 1572 enabled the appointment to proceed, with both election by ministers (on 6 February) and royal presentation (on 9 February). Douglas's inauguration on the 10th by Winram, using the service for superintendents, may have been condoned by Knox at a distance; but his retention of his university offices and his physical incapacity provoked complaints of dereliction from the assemblies of 1573–4.

Douglas died in St Andrews on 31 July 1574, according to an early tradition while in the pulpit for once, and left goods and chattels valued at nearly £4000 Scots. He was buried in the public cemetery, without a monument. He was not immediately replaced in the discredited role of 'tulchan' (titular) bishop. It had earned him in his last years aspersions of ambition and accommodation which his earlier career, intelligent and purposeful if not distinguished, did not warrant.   D. F. WRIGHT

Sources K. Hewat, *Makers of the Scottish church at the Reformation* (1920) · D. H. Fleming, ed., *Register of the minister, elders and deacons of the Christian congregation of St Andrews*, 1, Scottish History Society, 4 (1889) · W. A. McNeill, 'Scottish entries in the *Acta rectoria universitatis Parisiensis*, 1519 to c.1633', SHR, 43 (1964), 66–86 · T. Thomson, ed., *Acts and proceedings of the general assemblies of the Kirk of Scotland*, 3 pts, Bannatyne Club, 81 (1839–45) · J. K. Cameron, 'A trilingual college for Scotland: the founding of St Mary's College', *In divers manners*, ed. D. W. D. Shaw (1990), 29–42 · J. K. Cameron, 'St Mary's College, 1547–1574: the second foundation', *In divers manners*, ed. D. W. D. Shaw (1990), 43–57 · A. I. Dunlop, ed., *Acta facultatis artium universitatis Sanctiandree, 1413–1588*, 2 vols., Scottish History Society, 3rd ser., 54–5 (1964) · J. Durkan and A. Ross, *Early Scottish libraries* (1961) · H. Meylan and others, eds., *Correspondance de Théodore de Bèze*, 3 (1973), 346–9 · J. Kirk, *Patterns of reform: continuity and change in the Reformation kirk* (1989) · M.-L. Concasty, *Commentaires de la faculté de médecine de l'Université de Paris (1516–60)* (1964) · C. Egasse du Boulay, *Historia Universitatis Parisiensis*, vol. 6: *1500–1600* (1673) · R. Wodrow, 'Collections on the life of Mr. John Douglas, rector of St Andrews', U. Glas. L., GEN. 1211, item 8 [16 pp.] · E. Cameron, 'Archibald Hay's "Elegantiae": writings of a Scots humanist at the Collège de Montaigu in the time of Budé and Beda', *Acta conventus neo-Latini Turonensis*, ed. J.-C. Margolin (1980), 1.277–301 · M. Livingstone and others, eds., *Registrum secreti sigilli regum Scotorum / The register of the privy seal of Scotland*, 3–4 (1936–52), 6 (1963) · *The historie and cronicles of Scotland … by Robert Lindesay of Pitscottie*, ed. A. J. G. Mackay, 2, STS, 43 (1899) · J. Lee, *Lectures on the history of the Church of Scotland* (1860), vol. 1 · D. E. R. Watt, ed., *Fasti ecclesiae Scoticanae medii aevi ad annum 1638*, [2nd edn], Scottish RS, new ser., 1 (1969) · A. Petrie, *A compendious history of the Catholick church, from the year 600 untill the year 1600*, 2 vols. (1662), vol. 2 · R. Bannatyne, *Memoriales of transactions in Scotland, 1569–1573*, ed. [R. Pitcairn], Bannatyne Club, 51 (1836) · J. Scott, *History of the lives of the protestant reformers in Scotland* (1817) · T. Thomson, ed., *A diurnal of remarkable occurrents that have passed within the country of Scotland*, Bannatyne Club, 43 (1833) · *The autobiography and diary of Mr James Melvill*, ed. R. Pitcairn, Wodrow Society (1842) · J. Durkan, 'The French connection in the sixteenth and early seventeenth centuries', *Scotland and Europe, 1200–1850*, ed. T. C. Smout (1986), 19–44 · C. J. Lyon, *History of St Andrews* (1843), vol. 1 · R. K. Hannay, *The statutes of the faculty of arts and the faculty of theology at the period of the Reformation*, St Andrews University Publications, 7 (1910) · MSS, U. St Andr. L. · private information (2004) [Dr John Durkan] · J. K. Cameron, 'Humanism and religious life', *Humanism in Renaissance Scotland*, ed. J. MacQueen (1990), 161–77

Wealth at death £3925 18s. 4d.: NA Scot., CC 8/8/3, register of Edinburgh testaments, 14 Feb 1575, fols. 213r–215v; Kirk, *Patterns of reform*, 179

Douglas, John (d. 1743), surgeon, was one of the seven sons of William Douglas (d. 1705) and his wife, Joan, daughter of James Mason of Park, Blantyre. James *Douglas (bap. 1675, d. 1742) was his brother. In 1712 he became chirurgeon-general of the Leeward Islands, where his brother Walter was governor from 1711 to 1714; by June 1714 he was in Antigua. He was admitted a foreign brother to the Company of Barber-Surgeons in 1717. In 1719 Douglas was giving anatomical lectures at his house in Fetter Lane, London; he was living in Lad Lane, near Guildhall, in 1735, and Downing Street from 1739. Douglas's first publication was *A syllabus of what is to be performed in a course of anatomy, chirurgical operations, and bandages* (1719).

Douglas came to prominence in 1719 when he introduced the supra-pubic operation for the stone, details of which he published in his *Lithotomia Douglassiana, or, An account of a new method of making the high operation, in order to extract the stone out of the bladder, invented and successfully performed by J. D.* (1720). An enlarged second edition was published in 1723 and translations appeared in France (1724) and Germany (1729). Douglas's invention won him in 1723 the freedom of both the City of London and of the Company of Barber-Surgeons. It also brought him letters of congratulation from Boerhaave, Winslow, and Heister. Douglas's operation was, however, superseded in 1726 by

William Cheselden's lateral operation, a development which caused Douglas much bitterness.

Douglas, who believed that he had never received due credit for his work on lithotomy, became embroiled in a number of medical controversies, one of them causing him to publish *Animadversions on a late pompous book intituled 'Osteographia, or, The anatomy of the bones' by William Cheselden, esq* (1735). Douglas, who had been appointed surgeon to the Westminster Hospital in 1721, then published *A Short Account of the State of Midwifery in London and Westminster* (1736), in which he attacked Edmund Chapman, William Giffard, and Hugh Chamberlen the elder, who had all criticized midwives and claimed that men-midwives such as themselves should be responsible for all difficult deliveries. Douglas considered that midwives, if trained correctly, could be responsible for most births, and put forward a five-point plan for their instruction (see Wilson, 111–12). Adrian Wilson argued that Douglas's defence of the midwives arose from a fear that the incursion into midwifery of practitioners skilled in the use of forceps would upset the traditional division of labour established between the midwife, who delivered live babies, and the surgeon, who delivered dead infants. Forceps practitioners would be able to monopolize most of the work carried out by both surgeons, such as Douglas, and midwives.

Douglas was married and had one daughter, who married the surgeon Robert Owen. Owen managed his father-in-law's practice during his illness and carried it on after Douglas's death on 25 June 1743. Douglas, who was survived by his wife, left Owen his silver, his prints, and his 'fine coat-of-arms in the fore-parlour' (Peachey, 258).

MICHAEL BEVAN

Sources A. Wilson, *The making of man-midwifery: childbirth in England, 1660–1770* (1995) · *DNB* · G. C. Peachey, *A memoir of William and John Hunter* (1924) · J. Langdon-Davies, *Westminster Hospital* (1952) · S. C. Lawrence, *Charitable knowledge: hospital pupils and practitioners in eighteenth-century London* (1996) · D. P. Henige, *Colonial governors from the fifteenth century to the present* (1970) · *GM*, 1st ser., 13 (1743), 333 · will, PRO, PROB 11/727, sig. 228
Wealth at death see will, PRO, PROB 11/727, sig. 228

Douglas, John (1721–1807), bishop of Salisbury and writer, was born on 14 July 1721 in Pittenweem, Fife, the second son of Archibald Douglas, a merchant, and his wife, who was the daughter of Melvill of Carsender in Fife. His paternal grandfather was a distinguished minister in the Scottish Episcopal church, who, in 1669, had succeeded the historian Gilbert Burnet in the living of Saltoun, Haddingtonshire. Douglas attended the grammar school at Dunbar, where he received a good classical education, and was then sent for a short time to two private schools in London. In 1736 he was entered as a commoner at St Mary Hall, Oxford, and two years later he was elected to a Warner exhibition at Balliol College, where Adam Smith, a distant relative, was his contemporary. He graduated BA (1740) and MA (1743). He was sent abroad by his father, from 1740 to 1742, to learn French, and on taking deacon's orders in 1743 he embarked on a highly successful career as a clergyman. In July 1744 he became chaplain to the 3rd

John Douglas (1721–1807), by Sir William Beechey, exh. RA 1789

foot (Scots) guards, serving as an aide-de-camp at the battle of Fontenoy (29 April 1745). He resigned his commission on the army's return home the next year to fight the Jacobites, and was elected Snell exhibitioner at Balliol (1745–7).

Ordained priest in 1747, Douglas became curate of Tilehurst, near Reading, and also of Duns Tew, Oxfordshire. At about this time friends of his mother introduced him to William Pulteney, first earl of Bath, whose wealth and political and literary connections made him a highly desirable patron. An early assignment was to take Bath's 'difficult' heir, Lord Pulteney, on a grand tour of Holland, Germany, and France between July 1748 and October 1749. In Paris Douglas met Montesquieu but his journal of his tour devoted more pages to the Jansenist controversy and to the exposure of the miracles at deacon Pâris's tomb, which later figured in his pamphlet on supernatural phenomena, *The Criterion*. On his return to England he was presented by Lord Bath to the free chapel of Eaton Constantine and to the donative of Uppington in Shropshire, exchanging the latter, in 1750, for the vicarage of High Ercall, also in Shropshire. He seldom visited his livings but spent the winter in London, in a house next to that of his patron, whom he accompanied in the summer to Bath, Tunbridge Wells, and to nobles' houses, acting as Bath's chaplain and secretary. Douglas's first marriage, to Dorothy Pershore (*d.* 1752), sister of Richard Pershore of Reynolds Hall, Staffordshire, in September 1752, ended with her death in December of the same year. In April 1765 he married Elizabeth Rooke, daughter of Henry Brudenell Rooke. They had two children: William, who became chancellor of the diocese of Salisbury, and Elizabeth.

Douglas began to earn a reputation as a critic and controversialist, first by exposing the forgeries of William Lauder, who had accused Milton of plagiarism. His pamphlet on this subject, *Milton No Plagiary*, went into two editions (1750–51 and 1754), and caused Samuel Johnson, who had written a preface to Lauder's book, to dictate to Lauder a letter to Douglas, confessing to the imposture. Douglas then sought to elude David Hume's arguments against miracles in *The Criterion* (1752, 1754, and 1757), which made much of differences between alleged modern contraventions of the laws of nature and those presented in the Christian gospels. Later Douglas dined in a friendly spirit with Hume, who in 1773 considered him a 'better hand' than either Sir John Dalrymple or James Macpherson (Ossian) for continuing his *History of England* beyond 1689 (*Letters*, 2.269). After trouncing the Hutchesonian sect in an *Apology for the Clergy* (1755), Douglas then turned on the Scottish Jesuit mole Archibald Bower in several pamphlets published between 1756 and 1758, pillorying him for dishonesty and plagiarism.

Oxford University granted Douglas a DD in 1758, and Lord Bath presented him to the perpetual curacy of Kenley, Shropshire, also securing him a canonry at Windsor in 1762. The previous year Douglas had exchanged his Shropshire livings for the rectory of St Augustine with St Faith, Watling Street, London. He worked for Bath and his heir in Shropshire politics and wrote several political pamphlets, mainly under his patron's direction. He assisted Samuel Johnson in 1762 in the detection of the Cock Lane ghost. In the following year he edited the *Diary and Letters* of the second earl of Clarendon and accompanied his patron to Spa, where he made the acquaintance of the duke of Brunswick. Bath died on 1 July 1764, leaving his library to Douglas, who sold it for £1000 to Bath's brother and heir, General Henry Pulteney; on inheriting it a second time, on the latter's death, Douglas sold it again, on the same terms, to Sir William Pulteney so that it would remain at Bath House. He is believed to have been prevented from writing a biography of Lord Bath by General Pulteney's destruction of his brother's papers.

Douglas wrote more political articles, in 1766, 1767, and 1768, which were published by the *Public Advertiser*; he also contributed all the letters signed by Tacitus and by Manlius which appeared in that periodical in 1770 and 1771. In 1775–6, at the request of Lord Sandwich, he helped Captain James Cook to edit his journals (*Voyage towards the South Pole*, 1777); he also edited and wrote an influential introduction to Cook's last journals (*Voyage to the Pacific Ocean*, 1784). The second earl of Hardwicke enlisted him to edit his *Miscellaneous Papers*, for publication in 1778, and the same year he was elected FRS and FSA. In March 1787 he was appointed a trustee of the British Museum, which had opened on 15 January 1759.

Throughout these years Douglas advanced steadily in his clerical career. In 1776 he exchanged his Windsor canonry for one at St Paul's; on 18 October 1787 he became bishop of Carlisle, on 21 March 1788 dean of Windsor, and on 28 July 1791 bishop of Salisbury. James Boswell obtained anecdotes and information from Douglas for his *Life of Johnson* and proposed him for membership of the Johnson Club on 14 December 1790; he was elected on 22 December 1792. Acknowledging his 'advanced years and infirmities' Douglas made a will, on 21 April 1806, which reflected his wealth, his fairness but not excessive charity to dependants, and his complete trust in his son William as executor. He died of a gradual decay on 18 May 1807, his wife having predeceased him. He was buried a week later, on 25 May, in St George's Chapel, Windsor.

Average for his time in the performance of clerical duties, Douglas was regarded as a likeable, sociable, and respectable figure in the Church of England. As a man of letters he was notably industrious, and his family rarely saw him without a pen or a book in his hand when company was absent. He was well read in history and literature as well as in the church fathers and English divines, and made a telling case in controversies within his knowledge. Of his writings his introduction to Cook's last explorations had perhaps the greatest impact, drawing wide European and American attention to the resources of the Pacific north-west.   IAN SIMPSON ROSS

Sources Anderson, *Scot. nat.* · J. K. Barnett, 'Alaska and the north Pacific: a crossroads of empires', *Enlightenment and exploration in the north Pacific, 1741–1805*, ed. S. Haycox, J. Barnett, and C. Liburd (1997), 3–21 · J. C. Beaglehole, *The life of Captain James Cook*, Hakluyt Society, 37 (1974) · *The correspondence of James Boswell with certain members of the Club*, ed. C. N. Fifer (1976), vol. 3 of *The Yale editions of the private papers of James Boswell*, research edn (1966–) · Boswell, *Life* · J. Cook, *A voyage towards the south pole and round the world*, 2nd edn, 2 vols. (1777) · J. Cook and J. King, *A voyage to the Pacific Ocean*, ed. J. Douglas, 3 vols. (1784) · W. Macdonald, biographical memoir, in J. Douglas, *Select works with a biographical memoir by William Macdonald* (1820) · *The letters of David Hume*, ed. J. Y. T. Greig, 2 vols. (1932) · *Fasti Angl.* (Hardy) · E. C. Mossner, *The life of David Hume*, 2nd edn (1980) · L. B. Namier, *The structure of politics at the accession of George III* (1960) · L. B. Namier, 'Pulteney, William', HoP, *Commons, 1754–90* · A. Smith, *Wealth of nations*, ed. R. H. Campbell, A. S. Skinner, and W. B. Todd, 2 vols. (1976) · *DNB*

Archives BL, autobiography, corresp., and papers, Egerton MSS 2177–2186 · Wilts. & Swindon RO, papers | BL, letters to earl of Hardwicke, Add. MS 35403 · Bodl. Oxf., letters to Henry Bowdler · Bodl. Oxf., corresp. with Richard Scrope · Glos. RO, letters to Brudenell and Hayman Rooke · U. Edin. L., letters to Alexander Carlyle

Likenesses W. Beechey, oils, exh. RA 1789, LPL [*see illus.*] · R. Muller, oils, exh. 1797, Balliol Oxf. · G. Bartolozzi, stipple (after R. Muller), BM; repro. in *Contemporary portraits* (1810)

Wealth at death £23,000 in 3 per cent annuities of the Bank of England; 'consolidated stock'; £1000 in East India stock; £2000 in bank stock; £500 and more in ready money or money due to Douglas as part of his emoluments as bishop of Salisbury; 'accumulation of private property during a long life', and of furniture, plate, books, pictures, and prints: will

Douglas, John (1830–1911), architect, was born at Park Cottage, Sandiway, Cheshire, on 11 April 1830 and baptized on 16 May that year at St Mary's Church, Weaverham, the only son of John Douglas (*c*.1798–1862), builder, and his wife, Mary Swindley (1792–1863), daughter of John Swindley of Aldford, Cheshire. He was articled to E. G. Paley (1823–1895), architect, of Lancaster, and after completing his articles became Paley's chief assistant. He established himself in practice in Chester in either 1855 or 1860. In the latter year he moved into 6 Abbey Square, which served as

John Douglas (1830–1911), by G. Watmough Webster

his office for the rest of his life, and married Elizabeth (1827/8–1878), daughter of Mr Edmunds, farmer, of Bangor Is-coed, Flintshire; they had four sons and one daughter, of whom one son and the daughter died in infancy. Another son died at the age of twelve, and the eldest son, Colin Edmunds Douglas (b. 1864), who trained as an architect, died in 1887. The only surviving child was Sholto Theodore Douglas (1867–1943).

From Paley Douglas learned to build in a Decorated Gothic style in accordance with the precepts of A. W. N. Pugin and the Cambridge Camden Society. His decision to set up practice in his own county town is not surprising, and he must have been attracted by its many ancient buildings, and especially those in half-timber, the revival of which had begun in the 1850s. His earliest patronage came from Lord Delamere, whose seat, Vale Royal, he greatly enlarged in 1860–61, and for whom he built St John's Church, Over (1860–63). In 1865 he carried out his first works for the Grosvenor family, being commissioned by the second marquess of Westminster to design the architectural works for the Grosvenor Park, Chester (1865–7), and a new church at Aldford (1865–6). Another important early patron was R. E. Egerton-Warburton, of Arley Hall, who also employed William Eden Nesfield (1835–1888) for some of his many architectural projects: Douglas was clearly much influenced by Nesfield and the 'Old English' domestic revival.

Douglas showed, in some of his works of the 1860s, a remarkably bold high Victorian style. These include the polychrome brick Congregational (now United Reformed) chapel at Over (1865), a substantial stone country house,

Oakmere Hall, Sandiway (1867), and the strikingly radical brick St Anne's Church, Warrington, Cheshire (1868–9; now adapted for another use), with its broad aisleless nave. Douglas's chief patron was the first duke of Westminster (1825–1899), son of the second marquess; he carried out an astonishing number and variety of works, including lodges, farms, cottages, schools, and churches on the duke's estates in Cheshire and north Wales, and in Chester itself. These included large houses at Eccleston, Cheshire, for the duke's agent and secretary: one of these, The Paddocks (1882–3), shows the romantic side of Douglas's genius, with its Germanic conical turrets. The duke was particularly keen on the use of half-timbering, although Douglas's own tastes moved towards a preference for stone and brick. This is clearly shown by the intriguingly complex terrace he built at his own expense at 6–11 Grosvenor Park Road, Chester (1879–80), whereas for the east side of St Werburgh Street, Chester, which he also built as a private speculation (c.1895–7), the duke persuaded him to substitute half-timber for the Flemish-style brick and stone scheme which he first designed. This is one of a number of Douglas's contributions to the streets of Chester which have become well loved. The best-known is perhaps the Eastgate clock (1899).

Douglas was particularly gifted as a church architect. He showed an outstanding talent for adapting earlier churches, such as: St Mary's, Whitegate, Cheshire (1728; remodelled 1874–5); St Paul's, Boughton, Chester (1830; rebuilt 1876; enlarged 1902); and Maentwrog, Merioneth (1814; remodelled 1896). He sometimes used half-timber, uniquely for a whole church at St Michael's, Altcar, Lancashire (1879). At Halkyn, Flintshire (1877–8), he used stone for a sophisticated church with a fine tower. His churches are characterized by broad naves and narrow aisles, with comparatively short, well-raised chancels. He had a particular fondness for crossing towers. Good examples include St Paul's, Colwyn Bay, Denbighshire (1887–8), St John's, Barmouth, Merioneth (1889–95), and Christ Church, Bryn-y-Maen, Denbighshire (1897–9).

Douglas was responsible for several country houses, the largest being the Elizabethan-style Abbeystead, Over Wyresdale, Lancashire (1885–7), for the earl of Sefton. Outstanding among his public buildings is St Deiniol's Library, Hawarden, Flintshire (1899–1906), built in memory of W. E. Gladstone. Towards the end of his life, in 1896, Douglas built for himself a very large sandstone house, dramatically sited above the River Dee, and called Walmoor Hill. It seems to have been intended to instil into his only surviving son, Sholto Theodore Douglas, a sense of family pride.

Douglas was especially knowledgeable about timberwork, having received instruction in joinery in his father's workshop, and he put this knowledge to excellent use in the fitting-up of his buildings. His maternal grandfather was a blacksmith, and he also showed great skill in the design of ironwork. His buildings were characterized by 'sure proportions, imaginative massing and grouping (with tendencies to verticality and attenuated forms), immaculate detailing and a superb sense of craftsmanship and feeling for materials' (Hubbard, 210). In 1884 Douglas took into partnership Daniel Porter Fordham (*c*.1846–1899), and, on Fordham's retirement in 1897, Charles Howard Minshull (1858–1934).

Douglas is one of a number of nineteenth-century architects who, although preferring to practise in the provinces, was fully the equal of his London contemporaries. This was recognized both by British critics and by foreign writers on architecture. Maurice B. Adams said that he 'well deserved the Royal Gold Medal [of the RIBA] which he did not get' (*Journal of the Royal Institute of British Architects*, 3rd ser., 19, 1911–12, 644); both Paul Sédille and Hermann Muthesius illustrated and praised his work. At the Paris Universal Exhibition of 1889 Douglas and Fordham were awarded a gold medal for their drawing of Abbeystead.

Douglas died on 23 May 1911, at his home, Walmoor Hill, Dee Banks, Chester, and was buried on 25 May in Overleigh old cemetery, Chester.   PETER HOWELL

Sources E. Hubbard, *The work of John Douglas* (1991) · *British Architect*, 75 (1911), 362–3 · *The Builder*, 100 (1911), 697 · *Building News*, 100 (1911), 731 · *Cheshire Observer* (27 May 1911) · *Chester Chronicle* (27 May 1911) · *Chester Courant* (24 May 1911) · G. A. Humphreys, 'The late John Douglas', *RIBA Journal*, 18 (1910–11), 589–90 · *British Architect*, 49 (1898), 360–61 · P. Sédille, *L'architecture moderne en Angleterre* (1890), 86–9 · H. Muthesius, *Die englische Baukunst der Gegenwart* (1900) · H. Muthesius, *Das englische Haus*, 3 vols. (Berlin, 1904–5) · *CGPLA Eng. & Wales* (1911)

Archives Eaton estate office, Eccleston, Cheshire, Eaton estate MSS · Arley, Cheshire, Arley Hall MSS | Croxteth Hall, Lancashire, Molyneux muniments

Likenesses G. W. Webster, photograph, RIBA BAL [*see illus.*] · T. A. Williams, pen-and-wash caricature sketch, Design Group Partnership, Chester · photograph, repro. in *Building News*, 58 (1890), 686

Wealth at death £32,088 17s. 7d.: probate, 6 Oct 1911, *CGPLA Eng. & Wales*

Douglas, John Sholto, ninth marquess of Queensberry (1844–1900), sportsman and controversialist, was born in Florence on 20 July 1844, the first son of Archibald William Douglas, eighth marquess (1818–1858), and Caroline Margaret (1821–1904), daughter of Lieutenant-General Sir William Clayton of Harleyford, Buckinghamshire. He was the brother of the author and traveller Florence *Dixie (1857–1905). Such formal education as he received was gained at the naval training school, Portsmouth, before his transfer to the naval training ship *Britannia*. Douglas became Viscount Drumlanrig in 1856, the year in which he first went to sea as a twelve-year-old midshipman. He remained a sailor after inheriting the marquessate in 1858, following his father's apparent suicide, and became a lieutenant in the navy in 1859. He returned to dry land only in 1864 to matriculate at Magdalene College, Cambridge. While an undergraduate he became engaged to Sybil Montgomery (1845–1935), daughter of Alfred Montgomery, commissioner of the Inland Revenue, and Fanny Charlotte Wyndham, daughter of George, first Baron Leconfield. The couple married at St George, Hanover Square, on 26 February 1866.

John Sholto Douglas, ninth marquess of Queensberry (1844–1900), by Richard William Thomas, pubd 1896

Sport and the Queensberry rules At Cambridge Queensberry distinguished himself at hunting, steeplechasing, running, and cricket: he left after two years without graduating, and would maintain throughout his life that he had 'never known a degree to be worth twopence to anybody' (Roberts, 27). His sporting education would indeed prove more useful to him than any academic work he might have undertaken. In 1866 he embarked on a tour of the United States in the company of the duke of Manchester and the lightweight boxing champion J. G. Chambers to promote the sport of boxing, then somewhat in disrepute, across the Atlantic. The chief outcome of the trip was the formulation of the Queensberry rules, devised to replace the permissive London prize ring rules of 1839. The rules established the fundamental provisions which have governed the sport ever since, concerning, for instance, the conduct of fighters, the length of rounds, and the duration of the count following a knock-out. Though Queensberry was said to have been responsible for the definition of boxing weights, most of the Queensberry rules were drawn up by Chambers, the aristocratic title being adopted in the hope of enhancing the sport's respectability. Queensberry's own pugilism was not, in fact, always respectable—as a sailor he had briefly been imprisoned following a fracas in Madeira, and in 1872 he would be fined 20s. by Bow Street magistrates for assaulting a man who had attempted to prevent him assaulting a hotel porter—but he was said to be the finest amateur boxer of his time and was at one point amateur lightweight champion. He was also said, though, to care more for steeplechasing than for boxing. He gained his first success in the Dumfriesshire Hunt Club chase in 1865, but 'his ambition as a rider was greater than his abilities', according to one authority: in the course of his career he would break both arms and legs, twice fracture his collar bone and frequently sustain concussion (Roberts, 71). He rode his last winner at Sandown Park in 1883. Though a member of the Grand National Hunt committee, he never realized his ambition of winning the National. A last-minute substitution deprived him of a ride on the victorious Old Joe in 1886—a cause of lasting distress to him.

Queensberry was also a keen huntsman, becoming master of the Worcester foxhounds in 1870. His move south reflected his alienation from his wife. Four sons were born in the first six years of the marriage—Francis Archibald (1867-1894), Percy Sholto Douglas (1868-1920), Alfred Bruce *Douglas (1870-1945), and George Sholto (1872-1932)—but marital friction was evident almost from the start. Queensberry returned to the family home of Kinmount in Dumfriesshire in 1872, when he was elected a representative Scottish peer, but from that year he and his wife 'met only to quarrel' (Roberts, 70). His children grew up under the wing of a doting mother, and would side with her in the developing family dispute. 'The truth is that we hardly ever saw him', Lord Alfred Douglas said of his father, 'while his own public conduct was hardly such as … to command the sort of slavish obedience to his orders which he seemed to expect from his children' (A. Douglas, *Without Apology*, 236). Queensberry's private conduct was hardly more edifying: he underlined his estrangement from his wife by establishing a London home in James Street, Marylebone, where he entertained a succession of mistresses.

Politics, the peerage, and private hedonism Queensberry's peerage did not confer the right to sit in the House of Lords, which he attained only by virtue of election by the body of Scottish peers. He had hoped for elevation to the British peerage by Derby's government in 1867—his father had been a Conservative and he would generally vote with the tories as a representative peer—but the Conservatives' defeat in 1868 ended any immediate prospect of a British title. The position of a Scottish elective peer was generally secure enough, and Queensberry was re-elected in 1874, but he was unseated by his peers in 1880, in explicit reaction to his unorthodox views on religion, which he expressed with increasing emphasis during the 1870s. Queensberry had been brought up a high-churchman, though his mother and one of his brothers converted to Catholicism in the early 1860s. The sequence of family tragedies which befell Queensberry—the premature deaths of his father, two brothers, and his eldest son, three of them probably by suicide—would have tested anybody's faith. It is not clear whether Queensberry's move towards agnosticism was prompted by the death of his brother Francis in a mountaineering accident on the Matterhorn in July 1865, but it is the case that the

most extended statement of Queensberry's creed took the form of a poem, *The Spirit of the Matterhorn*, written in Zermatt in 1873. He published the poem in 1881, dedicating it to the peers of Scotland who had denied him re-election. It represents an unconventional attempt to come to terms with the concept of death without recourse to consoling doctrines of the afterlife. Queensberry denied that the soul was an entity separate from the body and refused to categorize as 'God' a power which he believed 'undefinable by man' (preface, 5-6). He argued that in death souls slept, surrendering their individuality 'in the great essence of an Eternal Power' before gaining fresh identities in new human frames: 'for death is life and life eternity' (ibid., 17, 21). This process tended towards the perfection of man (indeed, the sinful were held to 'possess no right to be progenitors'), a perfection defined as 'man's complete adaptation, socially, morally and physically, to his surroundings' (ibid., 24; preface, 15). The poem is an idiosyncratic confection of theism, humanism, and social Darwinism (Herbert Spencer was the only authority cited in Queensberry's 1881 preface, and Alfred Douglas believed Spencer and Huxley to be the only non-fiction writers to have captured Queensberry's attention). It defined Queensberry, in his own mind, as an agnostic rather than an atheist, but the distinction carried little weight in the eyes of polite society when, influenced by the freethinkers G. J. Holyoake and Moncure Conway, he fell into the company of the London secularist community. Queensberry became president of the British Secularist Union on its formation in 1877. This body was a secession from Charles Bradlaugh's National Secular Society, and Queensberry played little part in the debates over Bradlaugh's refusal to take the parliamentary oath in the early 1880s, but he did attain notoriety in November 1882 with a public protest to interrupt a performance of Tennyson's only stage play, *The Promise of May*, with its unflattering portrayal of a freethinker. In 1884, though, the disbandment of the British Secularist Union robbed Queensberry of his public platform, and he returned to a life of private hedonism. This life was led largely in London. At the Pelican Club in Gerrard Street he entertained his fellow sporting aristocrats with songs delivered in what Alfred Douglas remembered as a pleasant baritone voice. He continued to entertain women at James Street and various hotels, conduct which provided the grounds for his eventual divorce from Sybil in November 1887, when two servants testified to his adultery with Mabel Gilroy of Camden Town (*The Times*, 24 Jan 1887; Ellmann, 366).

Second marriage Queensberry's second marriage, at Eastbourne register office on 7 November 1893, remains mysterious. The new marchioness, whom Queensberry was said to have met on the Eastbourne promenade, was Ethel, daughter of Edward Charles Weeden of Eastbourne. The union was unsuccessful. After only four months of marriage, spent entirely in hotels in London and the Isle of Wight, Ethel petitioned for annulment, alleging at an *in camera* hearing in October 1894 that Queensberry had been 'wholly unable to consummate [the marriage] by reason of the frigidity and impotence of his parts of generation, ... incurable by art or skill'. Queensberry claimed in response to be 'apt for coition as will appear on inspection', but the annulment was eventually granted on the grounds not only of frigidity and impotence, but also of 'malformation of the parts of generation of the said Respondent'. What effect this private humiliation had on Queensberry's attitude during the legal contest with Oscar Wilde, over the next few months, remains unknowable, but he is unlikely to have felt entirely temperate about sexual issues (PRO, J77/532/16267).

Oscar Wilde The context for the battle with Wilde was another family tragedy, the death of Queensberry's eldest son, Francis, Viscount Drumlanrig, in October 1894. Drumlanrig had become a protégé of the prime minister Lord Rosebery during Rosebery's tenure of the Foreign Office in 1892–4. Rumours that he had been drawn into a homosexual relationship with the statesman led to Queensberry's quixotic trip to Bad Homburg in the hope—unrealized—of horse-whipping Rosebery. Queensberry, like many others, believed his son's death during a shooting party to have been suicide. His sensitivity to any hint of homosexuality in the family had already been evident in his claims that his father-in-law was a homosexual (Hyde, *Douglas*, 8) and in his insistence that Alfred Douglas should not follow his closest prep school friend to Eton College (Roberts, 150). The ill-concealed sexual basis of Alfred's friendship with Oscar Wilde provided a constant public provocation to Queensberry. He attempted first to humiliate Wilde with an exercise in audience participation similar to his Tennyson protest, arriving for the first performance of *The Importance of being Earnest* with a bunch of carrots which he hoped to throw at Wilde. Denied entry to the theatre, he sought other means of goading Wilde, and succeeded spectacularly with a card left at Wilde's club, said to depict him 'posing as a somdomite [sic]'. Wilde's response, an ill-advised libel action, brought not only Queensberry's acquittal, to public acclaim, but also the clear advertisement of Wilde's homosexuality—a criminal offence under the 1885 Criminal Law Amendment Act. Wilde was prosecuted, convicted, and imprisoned and Queensberry lionized, 'taking the place of the great Duke of Wellington in the hearts of the British people', in Alfred Douglas's sardonic words (Roberts, 255).

Decline, disintegration, and death This unfamiliar adulation did not last long, and Queensberry lapsed rapidly during the remainder of the decade into obscurity, decline, and death. It seems likely—though this is a conjecture and an induction—that he fell victim to syphilis, a common—and commonly concealed—cause of aristocratic death in the late Victorian period. It is clear that neither the impotence nor the 'malformation' attested in the 1894 annulment were the lifelong afflictions of a man who had fathered four children and been divorced for adultery. Syphilis would be consistent both with Alfred Douglas's claim that his father's mental powers deteriorated rapidly after the age of forty (A. Douglas, *Without Apology*, 247) and

with his temperamental volatility in his relationships with those around him. He disowned his second son, Percy, 'that so-called skunk of a son of mine' (Douglas and Colson, 63), for marrying a clergyman's daughter in 1893, affected an emotional reconciliation with him on his return from Australia, assaulted him in the street during the Wilde trial (both parties were bound over for £500), and finally acknowledged a deathbed visit by spitting at his son and heir. Syphilitic dementia would be consistent with the delusions of Queensberry's last years, when he believed that he was being persecuted by the 'Oscar Wilders' (Hyde, *Trials of Oscar Wilde*, 10), and syphilitic paresis could explain his early death on 31 January 1900, attributed publicly to 'a serious illness of a paralytic nature' after a stroke two months earlier had confined him to a bed in his club in Welbeck Street (*Dumfries and Galloway Standard*, 3 Feb 1900; Roberts, 270). One who had once invoked as man's destiny the 'perfection of the body and the mind' (J. S. Douglas, 21) endured the erosion of both in his final months. Queensberry was cremated at Woking crematorium on 2 February 1900, his ashes being buried at the family burial-ground at Kinmount the following day. The burial-ground was part of only 2000 remaining acres of the 30,000 acres of Scottish estate that Queensberry had inherited. The rest had been sold, as had paintings by Kneller, Lely, Stubbs, and Reynolds in 1897, to fund his London lifestyle, his allowances to his first wife and sons, and the costs—estimated at £2000—of pursuing Wilde.

The Victorians could be most tolerant of the shortcomings of their aristocracy, but Queensberry's combination of profligacy and violence, of adultery, promiscuity, and family neglect, went beyond the limits of society's tolerance. *The Times*, in a critical obituary (1 February 1900), considered him representative of 'a type of aristocracy which is less common in our time than it was a century ago—the type which is associated in the public mind with a life of idleness and indulgence'. An eighteenth-century Queensberry had in fact been the model for the dissolute Lord March in Thackeray's *The Virginians*, and *The Scotsman* (2 February 1900) observed that 'it cannot be said that the eighth [ninth] Marquis ... did anything to bring the title into better repute'. Newspaper obituaries were notably sparse for one who had been a celebrity only five years earlier, and those that did appear made little effort to extend the usual courtesies to the dead. The *Dumfries and Galloway Standard* (3 February 1900) noted soberly that 'a want of certain commonplace but useful and admirable qualities' had prevented him from playing an appropriate role in public life. *The Field* (3 February 1900) even questioned his competence as a boxing referee.

Queensberry left a relieved family which, Wilde claimed, had 'often discussed the possibility of getting him put into a lunatic asylum so as to keep him out of the way' (Hyde, *Trials of Oscar Wilde*, 29). Within three weeks of the funeral Wilde recorded receiving Percy and Alfred Douglas in Paris, 'in deep mourning and the highest spirits. The English are like that' (Hyde, *Douglas*, 126). Driven by this sense of euphoric release, Percy, who succeeded to his father's title, dissipated what remained of the family fortune in less than eighteen months, being sued for bankruptcy in December 1901.   JOHN DAVIS

Sources B. Roberts, *The mad, bad line: the family of Lord Alfred Douglas* (1981) • A. Douglas, *The autobiography of Lord Alfred Douglas* (1929) • A. Douglas, *Without apology* (1938) • J. S. Douglas, *The spirit of the Matterhorn* (1881) • R. Ellmann, *Oscar Wilde* (1988) • H. M. Hyde, *Lord Alfred Douglas: a biography* (1984) • H. M. Hyde, *The trials of Oscar Wilde* (1948) • F. A. F. Douglas, tenth marquess of Queensberry and P. Colson, *Oscar Wilde and the Black Douglas* (1949) • F. A. F. Douglas, *The sporting Queensberrys* (1942) • *The Times* (1 Feb 1900) • *The Scotsman* (2 Feb 1900) • *Dumfries and Galloway Standard and Advertiser* (3 Feb 1900) • private information (2004) [S. Prawer] • m. cert. • d. cert.
Likenesses engraving, 1866, repro. in Roberts, *Mad, bad line*, following p. 148 • Spy [L. Ward], caricature, chromolithograph, pubd 1877, NPG; repro. in Hyde, *Trials of Oscar Wilde*, facing p. 32 • P. May, silhouette, 1889, NPG • R. W. Thomas, photograph, pubd 1896, Horsham Museum, Sussex [*see illus.*] • P. May, sketch, repro. in Roberts, *Mad, bad line*, 149 • photograph (in later life), repro. in Roberts, *Mad, bad line*, following p. 148

Douglas, Keith Castellain (1920–1944), poet, was born on 24 January 1920 at the Garden Road Nursing Home, Tunbridge Wells, Kent, the only child of Captain Keith Sholto Douglas MC, soldier and chicken farmer, and his wife, (Marie) Josephine (*b.* 1887), daughter of Charles Castellain, a man of private means. His childhood was spent in Cranleigh, Surrey, and he was educated at Edgeborough School, Guildford, where he revealed precocious talents as artist, poet, and sportsman, and at Christ's Hospital, London. In 1927 his father left home and, in due course, remarried. Like Lord Byron, who suffered a similar deprivation and whom he would grow to resemble in other ways, Douglas hero-worshipped the absent captain, at twelve beginning an autobiographical essay: 'As a child he was a militarist, and like many of his warlike elders, built up heroic opinions upon little information—some scrappy war stories of his father.'

In 1938 Douglas won a scholarship to Merton College, Oxford, where his influential tutor was Edmund Blunden, soldier–poet of an earlier war than that for which Douglas enlisted in 1940. A year later, now a second lieutenant, he sailed to Palestine to join the Nottinghamshire Sherwood Rangers yeomanry, a cavalry regiment that had recently exchanged its horses for tanks. Moving with them to north Africa, he was initially held in enforced inactivity behind the lines, a problem which he solved in characteristic style:

> The Battle of Alamein began on the 23rd of October, 1942. Six days afterwards I set out in direct disobedience of orders to rejoin my regiment. My batman was delighted with this manoeuvre. 'I like you, sir,' he said, 'You're shit or bust, you are.' This praise gratified me a lot.

So ends the introduction to Douglas's prose memoir of that battle and its aftermath, *Alamein to Zem Zem*. Published posthumously in 1946, with his own illustrations and an appendix of poems, this rendered the war in the western desert as graphically as Blunden's *Undertones of War* (1928) had depicted life and death on the western front.

Douglas had an artist's eye for the horrors—and also the absurdities—of battle. Technically, his war poems show

Keith Castellain Douglas (1920–1944), by unknown photographer, *c.*1942

the influence of those of Wilfred Owen, but their language is simpler, more direct, and they have nothing of his indignation. There was less cause for indignation in the desert than in the trenches, and Douglas never lost his insatiable appetite for experience. Where Owen's preface to his poems had declared 'This book is not about heroes', Douglas in both his poetry and prose celebrates the last stand of the chivalric hero, men such as his colonel, Piccadilly Jim. In his poem 'Aristocrats' he asks:

> How can I live among this gentle
> obsolescent breed of heroes, and not weep?

His language, finely responsive to his theme, fuses ancient and modern: his fellow officers are 'gentle', like the 'verray parfit gentil knight' of Geoffrey Chaucer, and at the same time 'obsolescent'.

Douglas was wounded by a mine in January 1943, but survived the desert campaign. Back in England for Christmas, he wrote some of his best poems, collected and copied others, and by the end of March had completed manuscripts of *Alamein to Zem Zem* and a volume of poems.

Douglas commanded a tank troop in the main assault on the Normandy beaches, and his death outside the village of St Pierre, on 9 June 1944, robbed English literature—as had Owen's death in 1918—of the most individual and accomplished poet of his generation. He was unmarried, and was buried in the war cemetery at Tilly-sur-Seulles, France.   JON STALLWORTHY

Sources K. Douglas, *Alamein to Zem Zem*, ed. D. Graham (1979) • *The complete poems of Keith Douglas*, ed. D. Graham (1978) • *Keith Douglas: a prose miscellany*, ed. D. Graham (1985) • D. Graham, *Keith Douglas, 1920–1944: a biography* (1974)

Archives BL, corresp., literary MSS, and papers, Add. MSS 53773–53776, 56355–56360, 57977, 59833–59835 · U. Leeds, Brotherton L., corresp., literary MSS, and papers | BL, letters to Brenda Jones · BL, letters to Margaret Stanley-Wrench, Add. MS 57977
Likenesses photograph, c.1942, U. Leeds, Brotherton L. [*see illus.*] · K. C. Douglas, self-portrait, BL · photograph, NPG · photographs, U. Leeds, Brotherton L.
Wealth at death negligible: Graham, *Keith Douglas*

Douglas, Sir Kenneth. *See* Mackenzie, Kenneth, first baronet (1754–1833).

Douglas, Margaret, countess of Douglas, and duchess of Touraine in the French nobility (*b.* before 1373?, *d.* 1450/51), landowner, was the eldest child of *Robert III (*d.* 1406) and his wife, *Annabella, *née* Drummond (*d.* 1401), and thus the sister of *James I. She married Archibald *Douglas, fourth earl of Douglas and first duke of Touraine (*c.*1369–1424), probably in the late 1380s. Archibald died in 1424 fighting for the French, having apparently entrusted the administration of Galloway to Margaret in his absence abroad and the rest of his estates to his eldest son. In 1426 James I gave Margaret a life grant of the lordship of Galloway, and she ruled for twenty-three years as widowed countess of Douglas and duchess of Touraine from her *caput*, Threave Castle. Galloway's snail-pace recovery from the disasters of the fourteenth century complicated her task.

Margaret had to live through the brutal conflict between successive kings of Scots and the Black Douglases. Stewart by birth and Douglas by marriage, she seems to have attempted to do her conventional duty by both. If as a ruler her horizon was confined to the promotion of family interests, this helped to bring some order into the countryside and economy. The few surviving charters written in her chancery at Threave or quoted in royal confirmations record her conduct of business. In eastern Galloway she enlarged the estates of the Stewarts and other relatives, while in the west she raised the lands of William Douglas of Leswalt to a barony. She endorsed and added to her husband's endowment of a chapel in Whithorn Cathedral and made her secretary and chancellor provost of the collegiate church of Lincluden, Kirkcudbrightshire, where she endowed a chaplaincy for the souls of her husband and their respective kin. She granted the Franciscans the tolls of Dumfries Bridge. This patronage, meagre by comparison with the prodigality of the Balliols in better times, bears witness to her limited means.

Margaret Stewart had three known children and probably a fourth, but she lost her younger son, her husband, and her son-in-law at the battle of Verneuil in 1424. Her elder son, Archibald *Douglas, fifth earl of Douglas and second duke of Touraine, predeceased her, dying of plague in 1439. Her brother James I was murdered in 1437, and two grandsons, William *Douglas, sixth earl of Douglas and third duke of Touraine, and his younger brother, were judicially murdered in 1440. This left Margaret in old age without any close male relative to protect her. William *Douglas, eighth earl of Douglas, put pressure on her to resign Galloway. Dreading impoverishment, she petitioned the French king for a widow's portion from the

duchy of Touraine. It was refused. In 1448 the English burnt Dumfries, threatening her border, and the next year she relinquished Galloway to the eighth earl. She is said to have died at Threave, apparently before April 1451, although the exact date is unknown. No chronicler romanticized Margaret. An elegant tomb with her recumbent effigy was erected at Lincluden collegiate church.

DAPHNE BROOKE

Sources APS, 1424–1567, 64 · J. M. Thomson and others, eds., *Registrum magni sigilli regum Scotorum / The register of the great seal of Scotland*, 11 vols. (1882–1914), vol. 1, appx 2, no. 1817; vol. 2, nos. 12, 86–7, 133, 183, 255 · G. Burnett and others, eds., *The exchequer rolls of Scotland*, 4, 6–7 (1880–84) · J. Stevenson, ed., *Letters and papers illustrative of the wars of the English in France during the reign of Henry VI, king of England*, 1, Rolls Series, 22 (1861), 20–21; 2 (1864), 569 · A. I. Dunlop, ed., *Calendar of Scottish supplications to Rome*, 2: 1423–1428, Scottish History Society, 3rd ser., 48 (1956) · *Transactions of the Dumfriesshire and Galloway Natural History and Antiquarian Society*, new ser., 21 (1909) · F. McGurk, ed., *Calendar of papal letters to Scotland of Benedict XIII of Avignon, 1394–1419*, Scottish History Society, 4th ser., 13 (1976) · M. Brown, *James I* (1994), 31, 78 · R. C. Reid, ed., *Wigtownshire charters*, Scottish History Society, 3rd ser., 51 (1960), 161–2 · S. I. Boardman, *The early Stewart kings: Robert II and Robert III, 1371–1406* (1996)
Archives NA Scot., GD 23 VIII.1.143; GD 10; GD 154.11; RH6 i.296
Likenesses tomb effigy; formerly at Lincluden collegiate church [now destroyed]

Douglas, Lady Margaret, countess of Lennox (1515–1578), noblewoman, only child of Archibald *Douglas, sixth earl of Angus (*c.*1489–1557), and his second wife, Margaret Tudor [*see* Margaret (1489–1541)], daughter of *Henry VII of England and *Elizabeth of York, was born on 8 October 1515 at Harbottle Castle in Northumberland.

Early years Margaret's mother's first husband had been James IV, king of Scots, and her childhood was complicated by her parents' matrimonial adventures and the bitter power struggles in which they engaged during the minority of her half-brother, *James V. Having lost the regency of Scotland by her hasty second marriage, Queen Margaret had been fleeing south to the court of her brother, *Henry VIII, when she was seized with labour pains and forced to seek shelter in the castle of Thomas, second Lord Dacre, at Harbottle. A hastily arranged baptism was held the day after her daughter's birth, 'with such provisions as couthe or mought be had in this baron and wyld country' (Ellis, 265–7), so Lord Dacre told Henry VIII. The queen dowager was ill for a long time after the birth, but the following spring she took Margaret to the English court, and the baby stayed in the royal nurseries at Greenwich Palace until in June 1517 Henry VIII sent mother and daughter back to Scotland.

Margaret's parents were reunited, but their domestic harmony was brief. When she was three, her mother discovered that Angus was keeping a mistress; a violent quarrel erupted and the earl, conscious of his daughter's dynastic significance, snatched her from her mother's arms and took her first to his fortress of Tantallon in Haddingtonshire, probably to France, then to England, and finally back to Scotland again. Ignoring his wife's attempts to marry her to James IV's illegitimate son, James Stewart,

Lady Margaret Douglas, countess of Lennox (1515–1578), by unknown artist

fourteenth earl of Moray, Angus kept custody of the child and when he was driven out of Scotland in 1528, found shelter for her at Norham Castle and then at Berwick, with Thomas Strangeways, comptroller of the household of Cardinal Wolsey, who was her godfather. After Wolsey's death in November 1530, Margaret's aunt Princess Mary came to the rescue and invited her to London. Henry VIII then decreed that she should live at Beaulieu, in Mary's household. With only four months between them in age, the two girls became lifelong friends, despite the fact that in 1536 Henry removed both his daughters from the succession on the grounds of their alleged illegitimacy, and for a time treated his niece as heiress presumptive.

Margaret was a great favourite at court. The French ambassador, Louis de Perreau, noted in 1534 that she was both 'beautiful and highly esteemed' (LP Henry VIII, 7, appx 13). Apart from a Holbein miniature in the Royal Collection speculatively reidentified as Lady Margaret, the surviving portraits show her in later life. In these her hair is covered and so its colour is not shown, but she had heavy-lidded, deep-set eyes, a long nose, broad jaw, and fairly thin lips. Lively and attractive, she was somehow able to charm reformers and Catholics alike. Sent to be lady-in-waiting to Anne Boleyn, she got on surprisingly well with the new queen, and fell in love with Anne's uncle, Thomas

*Howard. The two became secretly engaged but Henry VIII was furious when he found out, declaring that Howard was aiming at the throne by trying to capture a royal bride. Henry sent him to the Tower and imprisoned Margaret there too, until she fell ill with a recurring fever. He then allowed her to live at the abbey of Sion, near Isleworth, under the supervision of the abbess, who was soon complaining about the large number of servants she kept and her constant stream of visitors. She was finally released on 29 October 1537. Howard died in the Tower two days later.

When Henry VIII's son, Edward, was born, the king convinced himself that Margaret, like his daughters, was illegitimate. Thus rendered harmless, she was restored to favour, becoming successively first lady of honour to Anne of Cleves and Katherine Howard. However, when she fell in love with Katherine's brother Charles, Henry sent her back to Sion and then to Kenninghall, in Norfolk, where Thomas Cranmer reproved her for 'over much lightness', warning her to 'beware the third time' (Fraser, Lennox, 1.427). She remained at Sion until Henry VIII decided to use her father again to promote his own interests in Scotland and allowed her to return to court. On 10 July 1543 she was a bridesmaid at his wedding to Katherine Parr and the following year Henry arranged her own marriage.

Countess of Lennox On 6 July 1544, in St James's Palace, London, Margaret married Matthew *Stewart, thirteenth earl of Lennox (1516–1571), one of Scotland's leading noblemen. A descendant of James I of Scotland, he had been brought up in France by an uncle, and was well educated and handsome, 'a strong man, of personage well shaped … fair and pleasant faced, with a good and manly countenance' (Historie and Cronicles, 2.16–18). He had been lured back to Scotland with promises that Mary of Guise might marry him, but he soon realized that she simply wanted to use him as a counterpoise to his hereditary enemy, James Hamilton, second earl of Arran. Disillusioned, he entered into negotiations with the pro-English earl of Angus, asking for Margaret as his bride in return for his future support of Henry VIII. On his wedding day he became a naturalized Englishman, receiving from the king grants of property in London and Yorkshire.

Margaret and her husband were deeply in love with each other, but Lennox had to leave London almost at once to attempt to advance Henry's policies in Scotland and was forfeited by the Scottish parliament on 1 October 1545 as a result. His wife remained in the south, first in the household of Queen Katherine and then in her own residence of Stepney Palace, where she gave birth to a son, Henry, Lord Darnley, named after the king. Leaving the baby at Stepney, she moved to Temple Newsam, one of Lennox's properties in Yorkshire, to be closer to Scotland. Her first child died on 28 November 1545 and was buried in St Dunstan's Church, Stepney, but just over a week later she gave birth to another son, a second Henry *Stewart, Lord Darnley.

Shortly before Henry VIII's death in 1547 Margaret quarrelled bitterly with him over her attachment to the

Roman Catholic church, and when he made his will he cut her out of the succession. Her parents were by now divorced and she began a lengthy dispute with her father when he too bypassed her and entailed his property on his heirs male. After Queen Margaret's death he remarried and had two sons, but although neither survived infancy, he still insisted that his titles would eventually go to his brother, not to his daughter, and they were on bad terms for several years.

When Edward VI succeeded his father, Margaret hastened to court with little Lord Darnley to show him off to the young king, but for much of protestant Edward's reign she found it prudent to stay at Temple Newsam, her household becoming the centre for Roman Catholics in England. In 1553 Edward VI died, Mary I became queen, and Margaret suddenly found herself at the centre of court life once more. Mary granted her apartments in Westminster Palace, sent her luxurious furniture and tapestries, authorized the provision of food and drink for her household free of charge, and showered her with gifts: new gowns, a girdle of gold set with diamonds and rubies, diamond rings, and revenues of nearly 3000 marks a year from taxes on the wool trade. Moreover, as Mary's relations with her half-sister, Elizabeth, deteriorated, she began to give Margaret precedence over the latter, treating her as though she were heir presumptive once more. When Mary married Philip of Spain, Margaret was in attendance as first lady and soon afterwards she named her next child Philip.

Margaret and her father were reconciled shortly before his death in 1557. For a time she styled herself 'countess of Lennox and Angus', but the fact that her husband had forfeited his Scottish lands complicated her claim and in the end her father's earldom passed to a male cousin. Mary was by now seriously ill; she died the following year. As always the earl and countess of Lennox were among the first to congratulate the new monarch, and Elizabeth I received them graciously. In private Margaret made no secret of the fact that she thought she had the better claim to the throne, for she considered Elizabeth to be illegitimate. Once more Roman Catholics in England looked to the countess of Lennox for leadership and she moved from Temple Newsam to Settrington House, near Burlington Bay, where she could have more direct contact with France, and with her niece Mary, queen of Scots. Soon her house was full of secret agents, plotting both for and against Elizabeth I.

Lord Darnley Margaret had always envisaged a splendid future for her son Lord Darnley. Tall and fair, with a ready smile, handsome, athletic, well-educated, and apparently intelligent, he was the focus of her life and she had long cherished hopes that he would one day marry her niece Mary, queen of Scots. Mary was the wife of the French dauphin, of course, but François was delicate and immature. Perhaps he would not survive. Determined to draw Mary's attention to the boy, Margaret sent him across with congratulations when François succeeded his father, and again with condolences when he died. Now all her hopes

could be realized. Lennox, who according to a contemporary was 'wholly governed by his wife' (Strickland, 2.366), was happy to go along with her plans.

When Mary, queen of Scots, arrived safely back in Scotland in August 1561, Margaret was so delighted that she forgot to be discreet, telling people openly that her son would marry Mary, they would rule Scotland together, claim the English throne and dispose of protestant Elizabeth. Needless to say, the various spies in the Lennox household were quick to report this to the English queen, who immediately summoned Margaret and her family to London, imprisoned Lennox in the Tower, and sent Margaret and two of her younger children to the custody of Sir Richard and Lady Sackville at Sheen. When Lennox fell ill Margaret pleaded for his release, reminding Elizabeth that he suffered from an illness that made him unable to tolerate being alone, but it was not until November 1562 that he was allowed to join his wife and the following February before they were released.

Undeterred by their recent reverses Margaret set about winning Elizabeth's confidence once more by means of flattering letters. By July 1564 she was back at court, acting with the queen as godmother to William Cecil's new daughter, while Lord Darnley carried the sword before Elizabeth on official occasions, as the prince nearest to the throne. Gratifying though that might be, Margaret had not abandoned her ambitious plans for him, and although her husband and son later denied it, she may well have had a hand in Elizabeth's puzzling decision to allow Darnley to travel to Scotland, where his father had recently gone to reclaim his estates. Lennox's restoration and his wife's final abandonment of her claims to the earldom of Angus in November 1565 were the key events that ushered in the reshaping of the Scottish court as a prelude to Queen Mary's marriage to Darnley. Moreover Lady Lennox plied Mary with letters urging her son's virtues, and sent gifts of jewellery to the Scottish nobility to encourage them to favour the union.

It had suited Elizabeth to divert Queen Mary with thoughts of Darnley as a possible husband, but when Mary took her at her word and announced her betrothal to him, the English queen was appalled. Realizing that she had made a dreadful mistake, she immediately summoned Darnley and Lennox back to London. They refused to go and so Margaret was sent to the Tower once more, arriving by water at Traitors' Gate on 20 June 1565. At the same time the privy council seized all the Lennox properties. An inventory of the contents of Temple Newsam, made for the court, records sumptuous furnishings, portraits of Margaret and her husband, her mother, and Henry VIII, and some touching personal items such as the ermine-trimmed crimson velvet and crimson satin bearing cloths used at the baptisms of the all too often short-lived Lennox children.

Margaret was still in the Tower on the afternoon of 19 February 1567 when William Cecil's wife and Lady William Howard arrived with terrible news. Lord Darnley had been murdered, and they mistakenly told her that Lennox had been killed too. This was later contradicted, but Margaret was in such a state of shock that her visitors had to summon Dr Huick, one of the royal physicians, and the dean of Westminster to come to her assistance. She was later allowed to go back to Sheen, while Lennox remained in Scotland, trying to prosecute James Hepburn, fourth earl of Bothwell, for his son's murder.

Bothwell was acquitted, and Lennox left Scotland in disgust. He joined his wife at Sheen and Elizabeth gave them the dilapidated royal palace of Coldharbour in London as their residence. They were desperately short of money, but although the queen at last permitted them to have the revenues from their estates she refused to allow them to administer their properties themselves. In spite of these difficulties, in January 1568 they commissioned a large picture showing the body of Darnley in gilded armour, with the earl, countess, their younger son, Charles, and their grandson James VI grouped around, calling for vengeance. According to one of the many inscriptions, the countess commissioned the painting so that if she and her husband did not live long enough to see their grandson and tell him to seek revenge, the picture would convey the message for them.

When they heard that autumn that Mary, queen of Scots, had arrived in England, the earl and countess hurried to court, clad in deepest mourning, and threw themselves on their knees before Elizabeth, begging for justice. Margaret's face 'was all swelled and stained with tears' (Strickland, 2.423) but her passionate cries for vengeance lasted so long that Elizabeth's initial sympathy turned to impatience and she told her not to prejudge the issue. In 1570, however, when the Scottish regent, the earl of Moray, was assassinated, Elizabeth agreed to consider a plan for bringing James VI to England. At her urging Lennox became the next regent, and set off for Scotland, intending to bring his grandson south. Margaret stayed with the queen to guarantee his good faith.

Widowhood It seems to have been Elizabeth I herself who broke the news to Margaret when Lennox was shot in the back in a fracas outside Stirling Castle on 4 September 1571 and died at four o'clock that same afternoon, asking his friends to 'remember my love to my wife Meg, whom I beseech God to comfort' (Fraser, *Lennox*, 1.416). He was buried in the castle chapel, and Margaret put up an elaborate monument. According to some accounts she commissioned the famous Lennox jewel, now in the Royal Collection, at this time. A locket made in the shape of a heart, it is richly enamelled, set with a large sapphire and decorated with allegorical figures, her husband's initials and enigmatic inscriptions which seem to refer to her future hopes for James VI.

Margaret's son Charles was now the only one of her eight children still alive. In 1574 she obtained the queen's permission to visit Scotland with him, but from the very beginning Elizabeth was suspicious, believing that she might be plotting with Mary, queen of Scots. Margaret's passionate grief and rage at Mary had long since passed and soon after the death of Lennox the two women had been reconciled, united by their shared concern for their

'peerless jewel', James VI (Fraser, *Lennox*, 2.449). Knowing this, Elizabeth was convinced that Margaret would try to see Mary, but although Margaret does not seem to have done so, she found herself in trouble for another reason. Staying at Rufford on the way north, Charles fell in love with Lady Shrewsbury's daughter, Elizabeth Cavendish (better known as Bess of Hardwick), and the two mothers arranged their marriage. Her suspicions redoubled, the queen summoned them to London and sent both Margaret and Lady Shrewsbury to the Tower. During this imprisonment Margaret corresponded regularly with Mary, queen of Scots, sending her the gift of a small piece of lace made partly from her own white hairs.

Released in the autumn of 1574, Margaret lived at Stepney with her son, his wife, and their baby daughter, Arabella Stuart. By now she was deeply in debt and Charles, earl of Lennox, was seriously ill with tuberculosis. When he died in 1576, his mother fell into 'a languishing decay' (Strickland, 2.448) but she roused herself to try to claim the earldom of Lennox for Arabella. Her efforts were unsuccessful, and on 7 March 1578 she was taken violently ill after entertaining Robert Dudley, earl of Leicester, to supper. She died peacefully two days later, on the evening of 9 March. There was talk of poisoning, but such rumours often accompanied a sudden death in court circles at the time. In fact, Margaret had long been suffering from a colic, presumably a digestive disorder. She was buried in Henry VII's chapel in Westminster Abbey on 3 April, at the expense of the queen, and a quarter of a century later her grandson James VI and I erected a fine monument in her memory.

Margaret Douglas's position as granddaughter of Henry VII of England, aunt of Mary, queen of Scots, and countess of Lennox drew her into many of the complex political events of her time. She never hesitated to employ her consummate charm as well as her taste for devious scheming in her efforts to advance the interests of both her family and the Roman Catholic religion. It was her tragedy that her ambitions brought nothing but disaster to herself, her husband, and her adored son Lord Darnley.

ROSALIND K. MARSHALL

Sources A. Strickland and [E. Strickland], *Lives of the queens of Scotland*, 2 (1851), 271–452 · W. Fraser, *The Lennox*, 2 vols. (1874), vol. 1, pp. 364–418, 426–69; vol. 2, pp. 432, 448–9 · W. Fraser, ed., *The Douglas book*, 4 vols. (1885), vol. 2, pp. 255–9, 263, 281, 289–92, 323–5 · P. Buchanan, *Margaret Tudor, queen of Scots* (1985) · 'Observations on a picture representing the cenotaph of the Lord Darnley', D. Jacques, *A visit to Goodwood* (1822), 103–27 · G. Donaldson and R. S. Morpeth, *Who's who in Scottish history* (1973) · C. Bingham, *Darnley: a life of Henry Stuart, Lord Darnley* (1995) · *LP Henry VIII*, vols. 4–21 · *CSP dom.*, 1547–80 · *State papers published under … Henry VIII*, 11 vols. (1830–52), 4–5 · J. Phillip, *A commemoration of the right noble and vertuous Lady Margrit Douglasis, countis of Lennox* (1578) · S. Adams, 'The release of Lord Darnley and the failure of amity', *Innes Review*, 38 (1987), 123–53 · R. Marshall and G. Dalgleish, eds., *The art of jewellery in Scotland* (1991) · E. W. Crossley, 'A Temple Newsam inventory, 1565', *Yorkshire Archaeological Journal*, 25 (1918–20), 91–100 · S. James, 'Lady Margaret Douglas and Sir Thomas Seymour by Holbein: two miniatures re-identified', *Apollo*, 147 (May 1998), 15–20 · H. Ellis, ed., *Original letters illustrative of English history*, 2nd edn, 1st ser., 1

(1825), 265–7 · *The historie and cronicles of Scotland … by Robert Lindesay of Pitscottie*, ed. A. J. G. Mackay, 2, STS, 43 (1899), 16–18 · DNB
Likenesses L. de Vogelaare, group portrait, oils, 1567–8 (*The memorial of Lord Darnley*), Royal Collection; version, Goodwood House, West Sussex · N. Hilliard, miniature, 1575, Mauritshuis, The Hague · H. Holbein, miniature, oils, Royal Collection · marble tomb effigy (not contemporary), Westminster Abbey; electrotype, NPG · miniature, oils, priv. coll. · oils, Royal Collection [*see illus.*]

Douglas, Margaret, duchess of Douglas (1714–1774),

noblewoman, was the eldest daughter of James Douglas (formerly Campbell) of Mains, Dunbartonshire, a member of a cadet branch of the family of the earls of Morton, and his wife, Isabel, daughter of Hugh Corbet of Hardgray. She probably had very little formal education, and in later years was renowned for her lack of sophistication. Homely in appearance but shrewd and with an outspoken wit, Douglas (usually known as Peggy) remained unmarried for many years. About 1746, when a friend teased her about being an old maid, she retorted in typically jocular manner that she would never marry unless she could be duchess of Douglas. According to tradition, twelve years later she visited Douglas Castle in Lanarkshire to persuade the duke to grant her nephew an army commission. She was by then forty-three. Archibald *Douglas, duke of Douglas (*bap.* 1694, *d.* 1761), was sixty-three, still a bachelor, and, according to C. K. Sharpe, 'a person of the most wretched intellects—proud, ignorant and silly, passionate, spiteful and unforgiving'. However, 'he possessed a handsome form' (Wilson), and Peggy told him briskly that he needed a wife. Not long afterwards, on 28 February 1758, she drove up to the castle in a hired chaise for their wedding.

Within months there was trouble between them. A fire started in a small room next to the duchess's bedchamber, all her jewels were destroyed in the blaze, and the duke refused to replace them. They then became embroiled in a violent argument over the parentage of his sister's supposed twins. Lady Jane Steuart [*see* Douglas, Lady Jane] claimed that, at the age of nearly fifty, she had produced two baby boys. One had died, but she asserted that the other, Archibald Steuart [*see* Douglas, Archibald James Edward, first Baron Douglas], was her brother's heir. Peggy was inclined to believe the story but the duke did not, and they quarrelled so fiercely about it that they separated, he promising her £250 sterling a year on condition that she make no effort to see or speak to him. A few months later, however, they were reconciled and he replaced her jewels at a cost of more than £3000 sterling.

Peggy subsequently managed to convince the duke that Archibald was indeed his nephew. She and her husband had not agreed a marriage contract before their wedding, but they now signed a post-nuptial contract stating that, if there were no children of their own marriage, the Douglas estates should go to Archibald instead of the duke's kinsman, James George Hamilton, seventh duke of Hamilton, as he had previously intended. When he died in 1761, Peggy renewed her efforts on the young man's behalf, even visiting France in an attempt to prove that he really had been born there to Lady Jane. The prolonged legal struggle became famous as the 'Douglas cause', and when

in 1767 the court of session in Edinburgh delivered a verdict in favour of the duke of Hamilton, Duchess Peggy and her lawyers immediately appealed to the House of Lords. After a dramatic debate, the Lords reversed the previous decision and found that Archibald was the true heir to the Douglas estates.

Duchess Peggy enjoyed her triumph for another seven years. In 1773, during the last months of her life, Boswell and Dr Johnson met her at a tea party in Edinburgh. As usual, she was ostentatiously clad, 'with all her diamonds' (Wilson), a fellow guest noticed, and although Johnson described her as 'an old lady who talks broad Scotch with a paralytic voice and is scarce understood by her own countrymen' (ibid.), he could not resist the attentions of a duchess and allowed himself to be monopolized by her all evening, Boswell struggling to translate 'the unintelligible gaucherie of her ladyship into palatable commonplaces for his guest's ear' (ibid.). She was remembered as 'the last of the nobility to be attended by halberdiers when going about the country. When she visited she left her dress behind her as a present' (GEC, *Peerage*, 4.440n.). Duchess Peggy died at Bothwell Castle, Lanarkshire, on 24 October 1774 and was buried beside her husband in a vault beneath the new church at Douglas. Her deliberately cultivated eccentricities had shocked and amused polite society, but Archibald Steuart's triumph in the courts owed much to her energy and determination.

Rosalind K. Marshall

Sources W. Fraser, ed., *The Douglas book*, 4 vols. (1885), vol. 2, pp. 469, 524–6 · *Scots peerage*, 1.211 · D. Wilson, *Memorials of Edinburgh in olden times*, 2nd edn, 2 vols. (1891), vol. 1, p. 208 · GEC, *Peerage*, new edn, 4.439–40 · H. Bleackley, *The story of a beautiful duchess* (1908) · P. FitzGerald, *Lady Jean: the romance of the great Douglas cause* (1904) · R. K. Marshall, *Women in Scotland, 1660–1780* (1979)
Archives NA Scot., letter, GD61/119
Likenesses oils, *c.*1760, priv. coll. · G. Willison, oils, *c.*1769, priv. coll. · J. Reynolds, oils, priv. coll. · J. Reynolds, oils; Sothebys, 9 March 1997, lot 39 · photograph, Scot. NPG

Douglas, Mary Alice (1860–1941),

headmistress, was born at Salwarpe rectory, Worcestershire, on 29 November 1860, eighth child and fifth daughter of the nine daughters and seven sons of William Willoughby Douglas (1824–1898), rector of Salwarpe, and his wife, Frances Jane, daughter of W. Wybergh How. She was educated at home by a governess in this tight-knit, deeply religious family. As they grew older the daughters took part in parish work, teaching in the Sunday school and visiting the sick and infirm. Aged twenty-two, she persuaded her father to allow her to work as Alice Ottley's assistant at the newly opened Worcester Girls' High School. She quickly became a supernumerary, teaching the first eleven pupils there. Anxious to improve her education, she attended Lincoln Diocesan Training College and then Westfield College, London, for a year. There she became friendly with the only other woman student in the constitutional history class, Sara Burstall, later headmistress of Manchester Girls' High School. She returned to work under Alice Ottley in Worcester, becoming second mistress and head of the sixth form.

In 1890 Mary Alice Douglas was appointed headmistress

of Godolphin School in Salisbury, taking up her post in January 1891, when there were twenty-two girls at the school. Inspired by Alice Ottley, her single most important friend and influence, she developed a large, thriving school dedicated to a Christian vocation to selfless service, combining a thorough academic curriculum with a healthy, well-ordered community. In 1892 the school moved into new purpose-built premises for eighty girls. She subsequently opened four houses, which she had bought and later gave to the school on her retirement, eventually expanding the school to more than 200 girls.

Miss Douglas made a systematic education in an academic curriculum for public examinations in preparation for public service the hallmark of the school. A sixth form preparing girls for the higher school certificate was started, and the school regularly sent pupils to the women's colleges at Oxford and Cambridge. Her aims were 'to teach the girls to think for themselves, to desire what is good and true and to overcome difficulties by perseverence' (*Godolphin School Magazine*, spring 1900, 27). She was always concerned that academic work did not become too dominant. Games became more varied and important. Lacrosse, cricket, and swimming were introduced, though her beliefs about femininity made her initially fearful that cricket was unsuitable for girls (ibid., spring 1896, 2). She was active in the Association of Headmistresses and was chair from 1911 to 1913, at a time when the association supported the enfranchisement of women as both just and expedient while deploring the militant methods used by Mrs Pankhurst and her followers.

Miss Douglas was chair of the headmistresses' curriculum subcommittee during the first decade of the twentieth century, when there was a vigorous debate about the claims of academic and domestic subjects in the curriculum of girls' schools. Miss Douglas believed firmly in the value of a liberal academic education with the purpose of 'helping girls to understand the great social problems of the day and to give them the hope of some day helping to solve them' (school diary, 1916). In her contribution to *Public Schools for Girls: a Series of Papers on their History, Aims and Schemes of Study* (1911), which she edited with Sara Burstall, she argued that the curriculum was already overcrowded and examinations were the cause of too much anxiety. More choice was needed, less teaching, and more time for reflection. Her solution was to provide a broad academic curriculum until the age of sixteen, after which girls specialized in the subject they would study at college for ten hours a week with four hours of domestic science as part of their accompanying general education. She regretted the division this would require between the education of those preparing for a profession and those who would return home. The school's distinguished alumnae reflect this emphasis, and include the Cambridge mathematician Dame Mary Cartwright and the writer Dorothy L. Sayers.

Miss Douglas always gave a series of Lenten addresses and sent an annual Easter letter to old girls, in which the message was entirely spiritual. Like Alice Ottley and other headmistresses of the period a belief in service was at the centre of her religious and educational creed. The highest value at Godolphin School was to be useful through service in the home, the community, and wider society. She gave illustrated talks on her foreign travels and the current political situation, and invited missionaries and travellers to lecture at the school. The Godolphin School was one of the founder members of the United Girls' School Mission Settlement in Southwark. During the First World War teams of senior girls accompanied by a mistress were sent to work in the local hay fields, and later in the war girls received instruction in milking, sitting a test and being certified as efficient by the instructor. In May 1917 five teams of twenty girls planted potatoes on land lent to local widows and poor wives.

Mary Alice Douglas was a pioneer in her views on school discipline. The newly established girls' schools had to gain acceptance among the middle classes as a more suitable method of education for their daughters than home instruction by family and governesses. In consequence great emphasis was placed upon femininity imposed by a plethora of school rules covering every aspect of girls' behaviour. At Godolphin more freedom was allowed; unlike most other schools, talking was allowed in passages, form rooms, and dormitories. Girls went to and from their houses unaccompanied by mistresses. Older girls particularly appreciated being allowed to go for walks in fours without a mistress as chaperone. Known affectionately as MAD, Miss Douglas was a small, slight figure with shining blue eyes, who conveyed serenity and kindness. Her outstanding characteristics were her sincerity, generosity of spirit, and Christian faith.

Miss Douglas retired as headmistress of Godolphin School in 1919, though true to her philosophy of public service she remained prominent in the civic life of Salisbury, serving on the education committee for many years. She died on 7 November 1941 at Framland, Wantage, Berkshire, where she had lived with one of her brothers, a retired preparatory school master, and a sister since 1930.

CHRISTINE HEWARD

Sources E. Douglas, *Memoir of Mary Alice Douglas* (privately printed, c.1942) · school diary, 1890–1920, Godolphin School · *The Godolphin School Magazine* (1895–1921) · M. A. Douglas and C. R. Ash, eds., *The Godolphin School, 1726–1926* (1928) · M. A. Douglas, *Lucy Jane Douglas* (privately published and circulated) · *The Times* (17 Nov 1941) · *The Wiltshire Chronicle* (15 Nov 1941) · b. cert.
Wealth at death £5960 6s. 1d.: probate, 6 Dec 1941, CGPLA Eng. & Wales

Douglas, (Constance) Mona (1898–1987), folklorist, was born on 18 September 1898 at 49 Allerton Road, Much Woolton, Liverpool (although she claimed to have been born on the *Ellan Vannin*, on passage between the Isle of Man and Liverpool). She was the daughter of Frank Beardmore Douglas (c.1864–1943), shop manager, and his wife, Frances Mona Holmes (c.1873–1953). She was an only child who, because of ill health, was educated at home. Her childhood holidays were usually spent with her grandparents in the Isle of Man, where she roamed the countryside, striking up conversations with men and women who worked on the land and at sea. Her interest in folklore was kindled by Sophia Morrison, who encouraged her to write down the stories and songs that she heard, a task that she took very seriously. Morrison also developed Mona's interest in all things Celtic, an interest that was to preoccupy her for the rest of her life. By 1921 she was the secretary of the Manx branch of the Celtic Congress and had already had published two books of poetry (*Manx Song and Maiden Song*, 1915, *Mychurachan*, 1917) and three plays. In 1917 she was admitted to the third order of the Gorsedd of Bards at the 'Black' eisteddfod in Birkenhead. She came into contact with many influential writers, scholars, and politicians, including W. B. Yeats, George Russell (AE), and Maud Gonne. In 1925 she moved to Harlech where she worked as a secretary to the poet A. P. Graves while he was writing his autobiography *To Return to All That*. Graves encouraged her to go to London to widen her horizons. There, she strengthened her links with the English Folk Dance Society, corresponding with A. G. Gilchrist and apparently contributing to A. G. Gilchrist's three issues (1924–6) of the society's journal devoted to Manx traditional music. She also collaborated with Arnold Foster on the first of three sets of arrangements of Manx songs (Stainer and Bell, 1928, 1929, and 1957).

In the 1930s Douglas returned to live in the Isle of Man and work in the Rural Library. Her boundless energy enabled her to work tirelessly up until the end of her long life, teaching young people Manx songs, dances, stories, and the island's history, continuing to write poetry and articles for learned journals, and writing and producing Manx Gaelic and Manx dialect plays. After her 'retirement' she fulfilled another ambition, working as a journalist for a further twenty-five years. She also published two novels (*Song of Mannin*, 1976, and *Rallying Song*, 1981) that embody her cultural, political, and religious beliefs. In 1976 she revived Yn Chruinnaght, a festival of Manx dance, music, and literature that, in spite of gloom-mongerers' predictions, went from strength to strength. This was to be one of her greatest memorials, inspiring generations of young people to participate in and enjoy the music and dance that was so close to her heart.

Mona Douglas never married but had a long and close relationship with the colourful Nikolai Giovannelli from before the Second World War until his death in the early 1980s. For six years they ran a brave but unsuccessful experiment in upland farming at the Clarum, which had to be sold in 1949 to meet increasing debts. She seemed to be equally comfortable worshipping in a Methodist chapel or a Roman Catholic church but felt particularly close to the mystical Christian spirituality of the early Celtic church. The spirit of the sea-god Manannan and 'the shining fellowship' was central to her visionary poetry and prose. Her character was a remarkable mixture of practicality and mysticism. She was utterly single-minded and determined, with an extraordinary stamina. From her friends and colleagues she expected a commitment to all things Manx that was equal to her own. Animals, particularly cats, were important to her and her car driving was

famous for its excitement and eccentricity. Her hospitality was generous. She was a talented singer and actress, who was able to produce memorable performances, particularly in comic roles. Her dream of a Manx theatre to rival the Abbey in Dublin did not come to fruition.

After a lifetime of dedication, Douglas's work was finally recognized with an MBE in 1982, awarded for outstanding services to Manx culture; she also received the Mannanan trophy (1972), was patron of the Manx Heritage Foundation (1986), was awarded membership of the principal order of the Gorsedd of Bards in 1987, and the Reih Bleeaney Vanannan was awarded posthumously in 1988. Just before Christmas 1986 Douglas fell and broke her leg but, in spite of her friends' urgings, refused to move from her remote cottage in the hills. However, within months she had to return to Noble's Hospital, where she died peacefully on 8 October 1987 in her ninetieth year. She was cremated in Douglas a few days later. In the following months her achievements were celebrated in a series of memorial services and concerts.

FENELLA CROWE BAZIN

Sources Mona Douglas bequest, Manx National Heritage Library, Douglas, Isle of Man · M. Douglas, *This is Ellan Vannin* (1965) [see also *This is Ellan Vannin again* (1966); *They lived in Ellan Vannin* (1968); *We call it Ellan Vannin* (1970)] · F. Bazin, ed., *Mona Douglas: a tribute* (1998) · b. cert.
Archives Manx Museum, Douglas, Isle of Man, Manx National Heritage Library, bequest · Vaughan Williams Memorial Library, London
Likenesses V. Cottle, photographs, priv. coll.

Douglas, Sir Neil (1779/80–1853), army officer, born in Glasgow, was the fifth son of John Douglas, a Glasgow merchant, and descendant of the Douglases, earls of Angus, through the Douglases of Cruxton and Stobbs. He entered the army as second lieutenant in the 95th regiment (later the Rifle brigade) on 28 January 1801. He was promoted lieutenant on 16 July 1802, and captain into the 79th (Cameron Highlanders) on 19 April 1804. This was the regiment with which he served most of the rest of his military career.

Douglas first saw active service in the siege of Copenhagen in 1807, and then he and his regiment accompanied Sir John Moore to Sweden and Portugal. He served throughout Moore's retreat and in the battle of Corunna, in the expedition to the Walcheren and at the siege of Flushing in 1809, and in the Peninsula from December 1809; he served in Portugal until he was promoted major on 31 January 1811. The only great Peninsular battle at which he was present in this period was Busaco, during which he was shot through the left arm and shoulder; on promotion he left the Peninsula to join the 2nd battalion of his regiment.

Douglas was promoted lieutenant-colonel on 3 December 1812, and in the following April rejoined the 1st battalion in the Peninsula. He commanded this force, which was attached to the 2nd brigade of Cole's division, in the battles of the Pyrenees—the Nivelle, the Nive, and Toulouse—and at the end of the war he was rewarded with a gold cross for these victories. In the following year the regiment was reduced to one battalion, which Douglas commanded both at Quatre Bras, where he was wounded in the right knee, and at Waterloo. After this campaign he was made a CB (June 1815) and also received a wound pension of £300 a year. In 1816 Douglas married the daughter of George Robertson, a banker, of Greenock. They had one son.

Douglas continued to command his regiment for twenty-two years until he became a major-general, and during that period many distinctions were conferred upon him. In 1825 he was promoted colonel, and from 1825 to 1837 he was an aide-de-camp to the king; in 1831 he was knighted (September), made a KCH, and permitted to wear the orders of Maria Theresa and St Vladimir, conferred for his services at Waterloo. In July 1838 he was made a KCB. He was promoted major-general in June 1838, and lieutenant-general on 9 November 1846. In 1845 he was made colonel of the 81st regiment, from which he was transferred to the 72nd in 1847, and to the 78th, in 1851. From April 1842 to January 1847 he was governor of Edinburgh Castle.

Douglas died in Brussels on 1 September 1853 and was buried that month. His son was General Sir John Douglas GCB (1817–1887), a distinguished commander in India during the suppression of the mutiny.

H. M. STEPHENS, rev. ROGER T. STEARN

Sources GM, 2nd ser., 40 (1853) · Hart's Army List · Boase, Mod. Eng. biog. · J. Haydn, The book of dignities: containing rolls of the official personages of the British empire (1851) · A. J. Guy, ed., The road to Waterloo: the British army and the struggle against revolutionary and Napoleonic France, 1793–1815 (1990) · R. Muir, Britain and the defeat of Napoleon, 1807–1815 (1996)
Likenesses B. W. Crombie, caricature, coloured etching, 1845, NPG; repro. in B. W. Crombie and W. S. Douglas, Modern Athenians: a series of original portraits of memorable citizens of Edinburgh (1882) · J. Watson-Gordon, oils, 1866, Scot. NPG

Douglas, Niel [pseud. Britannicus] (1750–1823), poet and minister of the Relief church, was educated at the University of Glasgow, and married Mary Anne Isabella Millar on 26 August 1787. As minister of the Relief church at Cupar, Fife, he published Sermons on Important Subjects, with some Essays in Poetry in 1789. Among the poems are two extremely loyal odes on the king's illness and recovery, to which their author referred nearly thirty years later when charged with disaffection to the royal family. Under the pseudonym of Britannicus, Douglas next published A Monitory Address to Great Britain in 1792, lamenting the degeneracy of the times and calling upon the king to abolish the anti-Christian practices of the slave trade, duelling, and church patronage. That same year he published The African Slave Trade, and the year after, Thoughts on Modern Politics, also concerned with the slave trade.

By 1793 Douglas had moved to Dundee, where he officiated as a minister of relief charge at Dudhope Crescent. The following year he brought out The Lady's Scull, a sermon in verse upon the text 'A place called the place of a skull'. Another collection of sermons, Britain's Guilt, Danger, and Duty, appeared in 1795, and Dialogues on the Lord's Supper and The Duty of Pastors in 1796.

In the summer of 1797 Douglas, who was fluent in Gaelic, went on a mission to remote regions of Argyll, after first collecting some funds by preaching at Dundee and Glasgow Messiah's Glorious Rest in the Latter Days, published that year. On his return he described his experiences in a series of letters published as A Journal of a Mission to Part of the Highlands of Scotland in 1799. At this time he issued proposals for publishing the Psalms and New Testament in Gaelic, but abandoned the project through lack of encouragement. After resigning his charge at Dundee, Douglas moved in 1798 to Edinburgh, where he published Lavinia, based on the book of Ruth. He moved afterwards to Greenock, where he published Leonidas and Sign of the Times in 1805. That year Douglas settled in Stockwell Street, Glasgow, and in 1807 he published The Messiah's Proper Deity. About 1809 he seceded from the Relief church to set up on his own account as a 'preacher of restoration', or 'universalist preacher'. As such he published The Royal Penitent in 1811, on the repentance of King David, then King David's Psalms in 1815. His sermons advocated peaceful political reform, and he was a delegate to the Convention of the Friends of the People in Edinburgh.

In 1817, while promulgating his restoration views in Glasgow, Douglas was indicted for sedition in drawing a parallel between George III and Nebuchadnezzar, the prince regent and Belshazzar, and representing the House of Commons as a den of thieves. He appeared before the high court of justiciary, Edinburgh, on 26 May, aged sixty-seven and, in his own words, 'loaded with infirmities'. Cockburn, one of his four advocates, after referring to him as 'a poor, old, deaf, obstinate, doited body', says:

> The crown witnesses all gave their evidence in a way that showed they had smelt sedition because they were sent by their superiors to find it. The trial had scarcely begun before it became ridiculous, from the imputations thrown on the regent—and the difficulty with which people refrained from laughing at the prosecutors, who were visibly ashamed of the scandal they had brought on their own master. (manuscript note on flyleaf of J. Dow, ed., The Trial of the Rev. Niel Douglas, BL)

A unanimous verdict of acquittal was returned, and Douglas left the court loyally declaring, 'I have a high regard for his Majesty and for the Royal Family, and I pray that every Briton may have the same' (Dow, 50). He had prepared for the worst, as he published soon after the trial An Address to the Judges and Jury in a Case of Alleged Sedition, which was intended to be delivered before sentence was passed.

Douglas was not perceived as belonging to the Scottish establishment, and was described as a 'wavering nonconformist' (N&Q, 3rd ser., 1, 1862, 92). A Catechism with Proofs, published in 1822, gives a statement of the religious views of Douglas and his church. 'The analogy', attributed to him, is found in A Collection of Hymns for universalists (1824). He also wrote numerous tracts, such as 'Causes of our public calamity', 'The Baptist', 'A word in season', and others.

Douglas died at Glasgow on 9 January 1823, aged seventy-three. His wife had died before him, and his only surviving son, Neil Douglas, was a constant source of trouble to him and narrowly escaped hanging (see his trial for 'falsehood, fraud, and wilful imposition', 12 July 1816, in the *Scots Magazine*, 78.552–3).

GORDON GOODWIN, *rev.* SARAH COUPER

Sources Irving, *Scots.*, 100 · G. Struthers, *The history of the rise, progress, and principles of the Relief church* (1843) · *N&Q*, 2nd ser., 12 (1861), 472 · *N&Q*, 3rd ser., 1 (1862), 18–19, 92–4, 139 · J. Dow, ed., *The trial of the Rev. Niel Douglas* (1817) · N. Douglas, *An address to the judges and jury, in a case of alleged sedition, on 26th May, 1817* (1817) · 'Account of the trial of Neil Douglas, universalist preacher, for sedition', *Scots Magazine and Edinburgh Literary Miscellany*, 79 (1817), 417–22 · P. B. Ellis and S. Mac A'Ghobhainn, *The Scottish insurrection of 1820* (1970) · *IGI* · m. reg. Scot.

Likenesses B. W. [J. G. Lockhart?], etching, 1817, NPG; repro. in Dow, ed., *Trial of the Rev. Niel Douglas* · J. Brooks, drawing, repro. in N. Douglas, *King David's Psalms* (1815), prefixed

Douglas, (George) Norman (1868–1952), travel writer, was born on 8 December 1868, at Thüringen, Vorarlberg, Austria, the third son of John Sholto Douglass (1838–1874), mountaineer and archaeologist, and his wife, Vanda (1840–1902), daughter of Baron Ernst von Poellnitz and granddaughter of James Ochoncar, seventeenth Lord Forbes. When Douglas was five, his father was killed in a mountaineering accident, and in 1876 he was sent to be educated at Yarlet Hall, Lancashire, following his mother's second marriage. In 1881 he began two unhappy years at Edward Thring's Uppingham School, and later in life he recalled an ultimatum to his mother: either she remove him, or he would arrange to be expelled for 'sexual malpractice' (Holloway, 43). The threat worked, and he continued his education at the Karlsruhe *Gymnasium*, where he specialized in natural history, contributing scholarly articles to *The Zoologist*.

At twenty-one Douglas entered the Foreign Office, and was posted to St Petersburg, where after two years he was promoted to third secretary. While in Russia Douglas continued to contribute to *The Zoologist* and other natural history periodicals, and published two monographs, *The Herpetology of the Grand Duchy of Baden* and *On the Darwinian Hypothesis of Sexual Selection*. In 1896 he resigned his post with the Foreign Office; he wished to leave the country, having impregnated Helen Demidoft, the daughter of an élite Russian family. He bought a villa at Posilipo in the Bay of Naples, intending to dedicate himself to botanical studies and travel.

On 25 June 1898 Douglas married his cousin Elizabeth Louisa Theobaldina (Elsa; 1876–1916), daughter of Augustus FitzGibbon, at Fulham register office, London. The couple married secretly and in haste: Douglas thought himself syphilitic, while Elsa was two months pregnant. They lived at Posilipo, where their first child, Archie, was born, and a second son, Robin, the following year. While travelling in India and Tunisia in 1900, the couple collaborated on *Unprofessional Tales*, published under the joint pseudonym Normyx and dedicated to the popular novelist Ouida. Although the collection was not successful, Douglas later revised and republished one short story from it, 'Nerinda'. Towards the end of 1902 Douglas's mother died, and by 1903 his prolonged visits to Capri contributed to the breakdown of his marriage. He obtained a divorce in

(George) Norman Douglas (1868–1952), by Sir Cecil Beaton

1904 on the grounds of Elsa's adultery, gaining custody of their two sons.

Douglas moved to Capri, sending his sons to boarding-school in England, and over the next few years privately published eight monographs about the island. Late in 1904 Joseph Conrad moved to the island for several months, and the two became friends. When by 1907 Douglas found himself short of money, he sold his Capri property, and in January 1908 moved to London, successfully contesting his wife's attempt to regain custody of her children on the grounds of her husband's 'rather faunesque pursuit of young boys' (Holloway, 161). His wife's lawsuit gave an early indication of the paedophilia which dominated Douglas's later years.

By mid-1909 Douglas was establishing himself in London literary circles, writing for the *Cornhill Magazine* and the *English Review*. His eyewitness account of devastating earthquakes in Capri was serialized in the *Cornhill Magazine*, and later articles were incorporated into three books, *Siren Land* (1911) about the Sorrento peninsula, *Fountains in the Sand* (1912) on Tunisia, and *Old Calabria* (1915). These were not financially successful, but *Old Calabria* especially made him known. He was appointed assistant editor of the *English Review* in 1912. Regular work at the *English Review* brought him not only a necessary income, but also weekly contact with contributors—including Edward Thomas, Rupert Brooke, James Elroy Flecker, Compton Mackenzie, and D. H. Lawrence.

While working at the *English Review* Douglas was drafting his best-known book, *South Wind*. Meanwhile, he published *London Street Games* (1916), in his terms a social document, intended to 'demonstrate the inventiveness of children' (Holloway, 225). Much of the material came from his friendship with Eric, an East End street urchin whom Douglas had adopted in 1911 and had taken touring with him around Europe. The book became a major source for James Joyce's *Finnegans Wake*, and was still acclaimed by child psychologists in the 1960s. Later in 1916 a darker aspect of Douglas's interest in young boys became evident when he was arrested and charged with sexually assaulting a sixteen-year-old boy. In January 1917 he was charged with further offences against two brothers aged ten and twelve. On the advice of Compton Mackenzie, Joseph Conrad, and other friends, he broke his bail conditions and returned to Capri.

At Capri Douglas completed the proofs of *South Wind*, which enjoyed an immediate success. Its ironic questioning of conventional morality appealed to a war-weary public, and its humane values were praised by Virginia Woolf in the *Times Literary Supplement*. It sold particularly well in America, but as Douglas was not protected by copyright there, his financial situation was not ameliorated. In 1917 he moved to Paris and later to St Malo, where poverty extending to near-starvation made it impossible to complete his next book. He finished it at Menton, and after protracted negotiations with various publishers, it appeared as *They Went* in 1920. It was received with respectful acclaim, but without the enthusiasm which greeted *South Wind*.

From 1920 until 1937 Douglas was settled in Florence, where his financial troubles steadily abated. As his fame grew, he became much visited by inter-war writers, and forged close friendships with D. H. Lawrence and Bryher. During these years he lived with the publisher Giuseppe (Pino) Orioli, who helped him publish several limited editions, most of which were later commercially published in London. *Alone* (1921) was the mellowest, most relaxed of his travel writings, the author's favourite and the last about Italy. It was followed by *Together* (1923), a recollection of his Vorarlberg childhood which brought glowing tributes in the press, and admiring letters from Lytton Strachey and E. M. Forster.

In 1925 Douglas published *D. H. Lawrence and Maurice Magnus: a Plea for Better Manners*, a biting polemic against Lawrence's 'ungentlemanly' biographical preface to the memoirs of their mutual friend Magnus, who had committed suicide two years earlier. The pamphlet was surprisingly successful: 500 copies were sold in the first fortnight, and the literary controversy was debated in the *Times Literary Supplement*. The quarrel was continued in *Experiments* (1925), causing Lawrence to retaliate in the *New Statesman* where, he explained, he was 'weary of being slandered'. The two were reconciled in 1927, but a continuing rivalry with Lawrence was behind the private publication of *Some Limericks* (1928), in Douglas's words 'one of the filthiest books in the English language, written for the Dirty Minded Elect', and in obvious dialogue with *Lady Chatterley's Lover* (Holloway, 367).

Douglas published *Looking Back* in 1933, a discursive, leisurely autobiography drawing upon material accumulated over several decades, and brought out as a two-volume limited edition of 535 copies under the guidance of Charles Prentice, his friend and patron at Chatto and Windus. The entire edition was sold prior to publication, and Douglas left off writing for several years, turning down even light reviewing work. He spent the next few years travelling through India, revisiting Calabria, and assisting Orioli with his novel *Moving Along*.

In 1937 Douglas was forced to flee Florence after the police made enquiries concerning his friendship with a ten-year-old local girl. By his own account Douglas escaped the wrath of the girl's family 'with only an hour to spare', eventually settling in Lisbon with Orioli, though he spent much of 1940 in France. After Orioli's death in January 1942, he moved to London, where he eked out a living as a language teacher and publisher's reader. Later that year the second British edition of *South Wind* was published, and *The Bookseller* used the novel, which it characterized as 'one of the most famous books of the present century', to illustrate its campaign for the copyright protection of British books in the USA (*The Bookseller*, Feb 1943).

Douglas returned to Capri in 1946, publishing *Late Harvest*, in part an annotated anthology of extracts from earlier books, which contributed further chapters to his interrupted autobiography. During 1949 the Italian Lux Films company began to produce a film of *South Wind*, but by November that year the project had collapsed. Douglas died on Capri on 7 February 1952 after several months of illness, and was buried there. *Footnote on Capri*, a 10,000-word essay outlining the history of the island and accompanying Islay Lyons's photographs, was published posthumously.   KATHERINE MULLIN

Sources M. Holloway, *Norman Douglas: a biography* (1976) · N. Douglas, *Looking back* (1933) · D. C. Browning, *Everyman's dictionary of literary biography* (1962) · H. M. Tomlinson, *Norman Douglas* (1952) · C. Fitzgibbon, *Norman Douglas* (1953) · *CGPLA Eng. & Wales* (1952)

Archives Boston PL, papers · Dartmouth College, Hanover, New Hampshire, corresp., literary MSS, and papers · NL Scot., corresp. and papers · Ransom HRC, papers · Temple University, Philadelphia, papers · U. Cal., Berkeley, Bancroft Library, letters and papers · U. Cal., Los Angeles, corresp., literary MSS, and papers · Yale U., Beinecke L., corresp., notebooks, diaries, and literary MSS | Harvard U., Houghton L., letters to Martin Secker · King's AC Cam., letters to E. J. Dent · NL Scot., letters to R. M. Dawkins · University of Bristol Library, editorial corresp.

Likenesses D. Harmsworth, oils, 1933, U. Texas · B. Brandt, photograph, 1946, NPG · M. Ayrton, ink and wash drawing, 1948, NPG · M. Ayrton, oils, 1948, Sheffield City Art Gallery · photograph, 1949 (with bust of himself when a boy), NPG · C. Beaton, bromide print, NPG [see illus.] · H. Coster, photographs, NPG · G. Harard Thomas, bust, RA · photographs, repro. in Holloway, *Norman Douglas*

Wealth at death £3098 11s. 11d.—in England: administration with will, 28 June 1952, *CGPLA Eng. & Wales*

Douglas, O. *See* Buchan, Anna Masterton (1877–1948).

Douglas, Sir (Henry) Percy (1876–1939), hydrographer, was born at Dacre Hill, Higher Bebington, Cheshire, on 1 November 1876, the second son of Admiral Sholto Douglas (1833–1913) and his first wife, Maria Louisa, the only daughter of William Bickford, of Stonehouse, Devon. He entered the training ship *Britannia* as a naval cadet in 1890 and in 1892 was appointed to the *Cleopatra* on the North America and West Indies station as midshipman. At the end of 1895 he was transferred to the *Majestic*, the flagship of Lord Walter Kerr in the channel squadron, and in 1896 he was promoted sub-lieutenant. Then followed the usual courses at Greenwich and Portsmouth. Having decided to enter the surveying branch, he served in the *Stork*, a surveying ship, in the Pacific for nearly three years; he was promoted lieutenant in 1898. In that year he married Katherine Chute, the second daughter of Captain John Mackenzie, Lincolnshire militia, of Belmont, near Kirkcudbright. They had one daughter.

Until the end of 1906 Douglas was continuously employed on surveying work in the Red Sea, the Mediterranean, China, the west coast of Africa, and home waters. He then had a short spell ashore as naval assistant to the hydrographer, and in June 1907 joined the *Egeria* at Esquimalt for survey work in the north Pacific. A year later he was selected for command of the *Waterwitch* for the survey of the Malacca Strait and other Far Eastern waters. In March 1910 he was brought to Whitehall to be superintendent of charts in the hydrographic department, a post he held for nearly five years, and at the end of the year was promoted commander. By this time Douglas was recognized as one of the ablest of the younger surveying officers, and when Admiral John de Robeck, at the beginning of the Dardanelles campaign, asked the Admiralty for the addition to his staff of a good surveying officer, Douglas was sent out in February 1915 and joined the flagship *Inflexible*. Later he transferred to the *Queen Elizabeth* and *Lord Nelson*. De Robeck's dispatches contain several mentions of his 'work of inestimable value to the fleet'. His expertise was in fact indispensable for successful landing operations: he compiled and printed new local charts and dealt with problems of minefields, ranges, and indirect bombardment. His zeal and ability were recognized by promotion to acting captain in October 1915, confirmed two months later.

In June 1916, after the evacuation of the Gallipoli peninsula, Douglas returned to the hydrographic department and held the new office of director of the naval meteorological service from April 1917 until January 1918. Then Admiral Roger (afterwards Lord) Keyes, who had been chief of staff to de Robeck, asked for Douglas's assistance on his staff at Dover in preparation for the Zeebrugge and Ostend exploits. He was accordingly appointed to the *Arrogant* (Keyes's flagship) for indirect firing duties. Keyes reported that his services were invaluable and his dispatches of May 1918 stated that the preparation of the routes from the starting point of attack by the removal of obstructions and the placing of navigational marks and marks for the long-range bombardments were carried out by Douglas and his assistant. For this service he was appointed CMG and received the Belgian order of Leopold and the Italian silver medal for valour.

From February 1919 until July 1921 Douglas was assistant hydrographer, after which he resumed duty at sea in command of the *Mutine*, and later the *Ormonde*, for surveys in British Guiana and the West Indies. He received the official commendation of the governors of Honduras, Jamaica, and Bermuda for surveying work in their waters.

Douglas returned to the Admiralty as hydrographer of the navy in October 1924 and, on completing the normal five years in that office, was offered and accepted an extension for three more years on condition of retiring from the active list. He was appointed CB in 1929 and KCB in 1933. He reached flag rank in February 1927 and was promoted vice-admiral on the retired list in 1931.

Douglas was much interested in the technical side of his professional work and had a probing, inventive mind for the discovery of new aids to navigation. When in command of the *Waterwitch* he developed the Douglas–Schafer sounding gear, which did much to facilitate the accurate determination of the depth of water in from 20 to 100 fathoms. He received the thanks of the Board of Admiralty 'for devising and perfecting a sounding traveller for rapid sounding for ships under weigh' and was given a money prize for this service. He was an enthusiastic advocate of echo-sounding, and it is mainly owing to his enterprise that this valuable invention was adopted for general use. Various improvements in surveying apparatus are due to him, especially the development of the 45° prismatic astrolabe.

In hydrography, Douglas's interest was chiefly in improvements of instruments and the geodetic and astronomical control of marine surveys, and he did much to improve both; he maintained his study of meteorology, begun officially in 1917. He was from 1928 to 1932 Admiralty representative on the *Discovery* executive committee, appointed by the Colonial Office for the promotion of research in the southern and Antarctic seas, and took a leading part in the design, equipment, and manning of the new ship built for that purpose. He gave close and invaluable personal attention to all her proceedings until she was finally laid up shortly before the outbreak of war in 1939. This work led to his being associated with other polar exploration schemes, in which his expert help was readily and unobtrusively given. He had many intimate friends, particularly in the scientific world, and seldom made enemies. He was a younger brother of Trinity House.

After retirement from the service Douglas was appointed acting conservator of the Mersey and chairman of the Dover Harbour Board. On the outbreak of war in September 1939 he was employed as commodore superintendent of Dover, where he died on 4 November following; he was buried at sea on 7 November at his own wish in the Strait of Dover.   V. W. BADDELEY, *rev.*

Sources private information (1949) · *GJ*, 95 (1940), 326–7 · M. E. Day, ed., *The engineers' who's who* (1939) · *Ostend and Zeebrugge, April 23 – May 10, 1918: the dispatches of Vice-Admiral Sir Roger Keyes … and other narratives of the operations*, ed. C. S. Terry (1919) · *WWW* · *CGPLA Eng. & Wales* (1940)
Likenesses W. Stoneman, two photographs, 1919–33, NPG
Wealth at death £2993 7s. 3d.: resworn probate, 7 Feb 1940, *CGPLA Eng. & Wales*

Douglas, Philip (1758–1822), college head, was born at Witham, Essex, on 27 September 1758, one of the family of six sons and five daughters of Archibald Douglas (1707–1778) and Elizabeth, daughter of Edmund Burchard of

Witham. His father was colonel of the 13th dragoons and sat as MP for Dumfries Boroughs (1754–61) and for Dumfriesshire (1761–74). Philip was educated at Harrow School, where he was a scholar in 1777, and matriculated from Corpus Christi College, Cambridge, at Michaelmas 1778. He graduated BA in 1781, when he was third in the second class of the mathematical tripos, and won the members' prize in 1782; he proceeded MA (1784), BD (1792), and DD (1795). He was elected fellow of his college in 1782 and joint tutor in 1787, and proctor of the university in 1788.

Ordained deacon on 26 May 1782 and priest on 10 November 1783, Douglas was made curate of Whittlesford, Cambridgeshire, in 1785. From 1 January 1795 he was master of his college, an office that he held until his death; he twice served as vice-chancellor of the university, in 1795–6 and 1810–11. In 1796 he was presented by the crown, on the recommendation of William Pitt, then MP for the university, to the vicarage of Gedney, Lincolnshire. On 15 June 1797 he married Mary (d. 1809), daughter of Anthony Mainwaring, of Shirrall Hall, Staffordshire, and niece of Dr Mainwaring, Lady Margaret professor of divinity. In the same year he was defeated by Thomas Kerrich in the election for principal librarian of the university.

By that time Douglas lived almost entirely in his lodgings, confined by poor health and the loss of sight in one eye. Despite his infirmities he presided over the installation of the duke of Gloucester as chancellor of the university in 1811, and in his address drew attention to the fact that the duke was the first of the Hanoverian dynasty to have been educated at the university. He also warmly praised the duke's support for the movement to abolish the slave trade. Douglas died in college, after a short illness, on 2 January 1822, aged sixty-three, and was buried in the chapel. He was survived by two of his children, Philip William and Mary.   J. W. CLARK, rev. S. J. SKEDD

Sources Venn, *Alum. Cant.* · *Masters' History of the college of Corpus Christi and the Blessed Virgin Mary in the University of Cambridge*, ed. J. Lamb (1831), 258 · Nichols, *Illustrations*, 6.715 · E. Haden-Guest, 'Douglas, Archibald', HoP, *Commons, 1754–90* · will, PRO, PROB 11/1652, fols. 90r–91r

Likenesses Kirkby, oils, CCC Cam.

Douglas, Robert, Viscount Belhaven (1573/4–1639), politician, was the third son of Malcolm Douglas (d. 1585) of Mains, Dunbartonshire, and his wife, Janet, daughter of John Cunninghame of Drumquassle. His father was executed at Edinburgh Cross on 9 February 1585 for his alleged complicity in the plot of the banished lords to assassinate James VI. Having been page of honour to Prince Henry, he later became his master of horse. He was knighted by the king on 7 February 1609. On 12 January 1611 he married at St Mary Woolnoth, London, Nicola, the eldest daughter of Robert Moray of Abercairny. She died in November 1612 giving birth to their only child, who did not survive.

Following the death of Prince Henry the same month, Sir Robert was appointed one of the king's gentlemen of the bedchamber, and his wealth and standing increased. He had charters of an annual rent out of the lordship of

Torthorwald (3 June 1613 and 11 September 1617) and Carlyle (3 June 1613), as well as the lands of Spott and the office of chamberlain (1622) and baillie of the lordship of Dunbar, which were united into the free barony of Spott (24 April 1624). In 1631 he also acquired a charter of annual rent of lands in the Dunbar lordship. Douglas continued as a gentleman of the bedchamber under Charles I and was appointed master of the household. However, Sir Archibald Primrose related to Gilbert Burnet a story which, if true, indicated that Douglas might be ruthless in opposing royal policy. When in the third year of Charles's reign Robert Maxwell, earl of Nithsdale, arrived in Scotland with a commission for the resumption of church lands and tithes, the interested parties agreed in Edinburgh, 'if no other argument did prevail to make the earl of Nithisdale desist, they would fall upon him and all his party in the old Scotish manner, and knock them on the head'. Douglas, who was blind, asked to be placed next to one of the commissioners to 'make sure of' him. Sitting with the earl of Dumfries, 'he was all the while holding him fast', an action he put down, when challenged, to his blindness, but 'he had all the while a poinard in his other hand, with which he had certainly stabbed Dumfrize, if any disorder had happened' (*Bishop Burnet's History*, 1.36–7). Nithsdale and his party were duly intimidated, and temporarily abandoned their mission.

In the long term Douglas's career was not adversely affected. On 5 July 1631 he was admitted to the Scottish privy council. He was one of the many aspirants who were raised to the Scottish peerage during the period of the king's coronation visit to Scotland, being on 24 June 1633 created Viscount Belhaven in the county of Haddington. That he was a favourite of Charles I is apparent from the report of Sir Robert Pye in 1637, in which it is stated that Belhaven had:

> received out of the exchequer since his majesty's accession, besides his pension of 666l. 13s. 14d. per annum and his fee for keeping his majesty's house and park at Richmond, 7000l. by virtue of two privy seals, one, dated 5 Aug 1625, being for 2000l. for acceptable services done to his majesty, and the other, dated 25 June 1630, for 5000l. in consideration of long and acceptable services.   (*CSP dom.*, 1637, 130)

On 22 September 1638 Belhaven signed the 'king's covenant', a royally approved alternative to the national covenant, in the presence of the Scottish privy council, and was appointed to superintend its subscription in the sheriffdom of Renfrew. Belhaven died at Edinburgh on 12 January 1639 and was buried in the abbey church of Holyrood, where a monument to him was erected by his nephews, Sir Archibald and Sir Robert Douglas. Since Belhaven was childless, the viscountcy became extinct.

G. F. R. BARKER, rev. JOHN J. SCALLY

Sources APS · *Reg. PCS*, 1st ser. · *Reg. PCS*, 2nd ser. · *Reg. PCS*, 3rd ser. · *The historical works of Sir James Balfour*, ed. J. Haig, 4 vols. (1824–5) · *Scots peerage* · GEC, *Peerage* · R. Douglas, *The peerage of Scotland*, 2nd edn, ed. J. P. Wood, 2 vols. (1813) · *The historical works of Sir James Balfour*, ed. J. Haig, 4 vols. (1824–5)

Likenesses I. Herbert, effigy, Savoy chapel, London · J. Schurman, effigy on wall monument, Abbey Church, Holyroodhouse,

Edinburgh · engraving (after effigy, Savoy chapel), repro. in J. Pinkerton, *Iconographia Scotica, or, Portraits of illustrious persons of Scotland* (1797)

Douglas, Robert (1594–1674), Church of Scotland minister, was the son of George Douglas, in turn the illegitimate son of Sir George Douglas of Lochleven and, according to commonly held contemporary opinion, of Mary, queen of Scots. However, while Robert never denied the rumour of his royal heritage, there is no historical evidence to substantiate it. Little is known of his early life other than that he was educated at the University of St Andrews and that he graduated MA in 1614. Licensed to preach the gospel about 1617, he was ordained to the second charge of Kirkcaldy in 1628 and, soon after, became chaplain to one of the brigades of Scottish auxiliaries sent to aid Gustavus Adolphus in the Thirty Years' War. By all reports Douglas was a man of majestic appearance, great wit, and strength of character which, combined with the rumours of his parentage, caused many of his contemporaries to stand in awe of him. According to the historian Robert Wodrow, Gustavus was so impressed with him that upon Douglas's departure he declared, 'There is a man who, for wisdom and prudence, might be a counsellour to any king in Europe' (Wodrow, *Analecta*, 3.82).

In 1638 Douglas subscribed the national covenant and was a member of the famous Glasgow general assembly that abjured episcopacy. The following year he was translated to the second charge of St Giles, Edinburgh, and on 24 December 1641 he was removed to the city's north-west quarter, or Tolbooth parish. He was elected moderator of the 1642 general assembly and at its close was chosen moderator of the assembly's revived standing committee, the powerful commission for the public affairs of the kirk. The next year he was named as one of the Scottish commissioners to the assembly of divines at Westminster, but did not serve because of other responsibilities. From January to November 1644 he served as moderator of the presbytery of the Scottish army and as chaplain to the earl of Leven during the army's expedition into England. By the summer of 1646 Douglas's first wife, Margaret Kirkaldy, whom he had married at an unknown date, had died, and on 20 August 1646 he married Margaret Boyd (*d.* 1692).

During the remainder of the decade Douglas emerged as the kirk's leading minister. He was elected moderator of the general assembly three more times, in 1645, 1647, and 1649, and served as moderator of its commission from 1646 to 1650. During the period known as the theocracy, or kirk regime, following the duke of Hamilton's failed engagement, his sphere of power was greatly expanded as the assembly and its commission exercised an unprecedented influence on the affairs of state. Accordingly, in early 1649 he was translated again to Edinburgh's High Kirk, this time to the prestigious first charge, where he remained until the Restoration.

In February 1650 Douglas joined with the marquess of Argyll and other leading moderates in kirk and state in calling for renewed negotiations with the exiled Charles II. During the ensuing controversy between the regime's radical and moderate wings he led the moderates in a staunch defence of the king's royal prerogatives. Following the Cromwellian invasion of Scotland in the summer of 1650 he resisted the radicals' desire to purge all royalist malignants and former engagers from the covenanting army, and instead advocated the raising of all fencible men in the nation's defence. From December 1650 to May 1651 he led the commission in passing a number of public resolutions which resulted in parliament's full repeal of the 1646 and 1649 acts of classes and the readmittance of royalists and engagers to the military and public office. On 1 January 1651 he officiated at the coronation of Charles II at Scone, and preached a sermon in which he reminded the king of his covenanted responsibility to establish presbyterianism in all three of his kingdoms. In July he was elected moderator of the infamous 'pretended' general assembly at St Andrews and Dundee, which ratified the commission's public resolutions, and saw the kirk irreparably divided between resolutioners and protesters.

On 28 August 1651 Douglas and other leading members of the commission and committee of estates were captured at Alyth, near Dundee, by a large troop of English horse. He was transported to England and imprisoned in the Tower of London. During his confinement Douglas continued to have a large influence on the affairs of the national kirk, even going so far as to send his resolutioner colleagues detailed instructions on how to conduct the business of the 1652 general assembly.

In early April 1653 Douglas was released from the Tower and returned to Edinburgh amid much public jubilation. Immediately upon his arrival in the city he began to preach against sectarianism and religious toleration and persuaded the synod of Lothian to emit a protestation 'against the usurpation of the English' (*Letters and Journals of Robert Baillie*, vol. 3, appendix 1, 446). He also encouraged the resolutioner ministers to give covert support to the royalist rebellion in the highlands known as Glencairn's rising. For his suspected complicity in this matter he was identified by the commander of the English army in Scotland, Colonel Robert Lilburne, as 'the principall man in their plott' (Firth, 160). With the failure of the rising he changed tack and, together with his colleagues 'the Ministers of Edinburgh', led the national party in pursuing an accommodation with the English authorities. In September 1655 he and his ministerial colleagues reached an accord with the Lord Broghill and the Scottish council wherein the resolutioners agreed to suspend their public prayers for the king. The following year he was instrumental in the party's decision to grant tacit recognition to the English regime's authority in ecclesiastical matters. During the years 1657 and 1659 he directed the activities of the resolutioners' agent, James Sharp, during his struggles with the protesters in London.

In late 1659 and early 1660 Douglas assisted General Monck, soliciting support for his intervention in England, and using his influence to ensure that Scotland remained calm after the general's march into England. During the remainder of 1660 he also continued to direct Sharp in his ill-fated attempts to secure a presbyterian settlement for the Scottish church. Due to his efforts in effecting the Restoration, in the autumn of 1661 Douglas was offered, via Sharp, a bishopric. Douglas flatly refused, but perceiving Sharp's intention to take the archbishopric of St Andrews, told him, 'take it, and the curse of God with it' (Kilpatrick, 44). Douglas was removed from his charge at St Giles in June 1662 to make way for the new bishop of Edinburgh, and translated to Greyfriars, Edinburgh. On 1 October that year he was deprived from his new charge for refusing to conform to episcopacy. Virtually nothing is known of his activities during the remainder of the 1660s, but in the spring of 1669 Douglas supported the government's plan to settle deposed presbyterian ministers in vacant parishes. He accepted the resultant indulgence and, on 2 September 1669, at the age of seventy-five, was admitted to the parish of Pencaitland in Haddingtonshire, where he continued quietly until his death there in February 1674. He was buried on 6 February at Edinburgh. He was survived by his second wife, Margaret, who died in July 1692.

K. D. HOLFELDER

Sources *Fasti Scot.*, new edn, 1.59, 64, 385–6 · R. Wodrow, *Analecta, or, Materials for a history of remarkable providences, mostly relating to Scotch ministers and Christians*, ed. [M. Leishman], 4 vols., Maitland Club, 60 (1842–3), vol. 1, p. 166; vol. 2, pp. 136–8, 324–5; vol. 3, pp. 82–3, 87 · *The letters and journals of Robert Baillie*, ed. D. Laing, 3 vols. (1841–2) · A. Peterkin, ed., *Records of the Kirk of Scotland* (1838) · A. F. Mitchell and J. Christie, eds., *The records of the commissions of the general assemblies of the Church of Scotland*, 3 vols., Scottish History Society, 11, 25, 58 (1892–1909) · W. Stephen, ed., *Register of the consultations of the ministers of Edinburgh*, 2 vols., Scottish History Society, 3rd ser., 1, 16 (1921–30) · R. Wodrow, *The history of the sufferings of the Church of Scotland from the Restoration to the revolution*, ed. R. Burns, 1 (1828); 2 (1829) · J. Kilpatrick, 'The Rev. Robert Douglas, A.M., 1594–1674', *Records of the Scottish Church History Society*, 12 (1954–6), 29–46 · C. H. Firth, ed., *Scotland and the Commonwealth: letters and papers relating to the military government of Scotland, from August 1651 to December 1653*, Scottish History Society, 18 (1895), 160, 163
Archives NL Scot., Wodrow collection, papers and letters

Douglas, Robert, Count Douglas in the Swedish nobility

(1611–1662), army officer in the Swedish service, was born at Standingstone Farm, near Haddington, on 17 March 1611, the youngest of at least three sons of Patrick Douglas of Whittingehame and his wife, Christina Leslie. The document proving Douglas's ancestry, obtained from the Scottish parliament in the name of Charles I in 1648, listed his father as *comarchus* of Standingstone, which later became translated as marquess in Sweden, although Patrick Douglas was only a laird.

Not much is known of Douglas's early years, but by 1628 he had taken a path common to many young Scotsmen and entered Swedish service in Colonel James Ramsay's regiment, along with his two brothers, William and Richard, who both died shortly thereafter. Douglas was taken into service as a page for the elector palatine Johann Casimir, the brother-in-law of the Swedish king, Gustavus Adolphus, and as a result Douglas came to know the future king Karl X rather well. Douglas soon became an ensign in the service of Gustavus Adolphus, and saw action during the joint Swedish–Danish defence of Stralsund from 1629 to 1630, where he served under the command of the governor, Colonel Alexander Leslie (the

future earl of Leven). Although his autobiographical notes maintain he was still a personal page to the Swedish king, the Swedish army muster rolls reveal that Douglas entered the Green regiment in 1631. Douglas also served as captain-lieutenant of some of the British troops recruited by the marquess of Hamilton for Swedish service. He then became a major with a dragoon corps from 1632, was promoted lieutenant-colonel two years later, and finally rose to a colonelcy in 1636.

Douglas decided to travel home that year to sort out domestic issues in Scotland, and the Riksråd (Swedish state council) arranged accreditation for him to Charles I. The intercessory letter they provided concerned his inheritance troubles, while Chancellor Oxenstierna also employed him for personal affairs in London. Douglas therefore had both official and private sponsorship from the highest echelons of the Swedish government for his journey, and by November 1636 he had arrived in London. He avoided involvement in the covenanting wars of Scotland and returned in the late summer of 1637 to Sweden to continue his military career. Although Douglas remained on the margins of British political developments throughout his life, Charles II personally requested his support in providing Scottish recruits for his use in 1655. He was not able to comply, but he had already sent him 5200 riksdaler two years previously. Douglas also sought Swedish intercession in 1658 on behalf of John Maitland, marquess and duke of Lauderdale, who was imprisoned by Cromwell. Although this did not lead to Lauderdale's immediate release, his prison conditions improved.

By 1643 Douglas had been promoted general of the Swedish cavalry. He further consolidated his social standing in 1645 by marrying Hedvig Mörner (c.1624–c.1671), the sister-in-law of Baron Erik Stenbock. His wife and family followed him on his foreign appointments, as shown by the birth of his sixth child in Poland in 1655. His position as governor of Schwaben caused him problems owing to the drastic shortage of funds, frequently complained about in the Riksråd. His military promotions continued and he became major-general in 1647. He spent a month in Stockholm that year participating in the meetings of the Riksråd, often in the presence of Queen Kristina, where he provided information on the army's situation in Germany, and advised the queen against entering into land exchanges with the French.

In 1649 Douglas was promoted lieutenant-general and, having become firmly established in Sweden, planned to build a house at Qvarnholmen in Stockholm. Douglas was ennobled in 1651 with the title of Baron Douglas of Skälby, which gave him land at Kalmar. He was also appointed a member of the military council, despite his open Calvinism. His integration into Swedish noble and court society was confirmed by service as the royal stablemaster in 1652. Two years later he gained another title, being made Count (Greve) Douglas of Skenninge, and was introduced to the Swedish house of nobility. He also continued to participate in meetings of the Riksråd.

Sweden's war with Poland, beginning in 1655, saw

Douglas active as general and successfully taking a fortress barely 6 miles from Crakow. He became a lieutenant-field marshal of the infantry and cavalry in the same year. Douglas personally accompanied Karl X on his march towards Riga in 1656, and became a full field marshal in the following year. On account of war with Denmark–Norway, Douglas was recalled from Riga, with his family, to help defend Sweden. He not only participated in the Riksråd again that year, but also served as a military adviser to the Swedish government on defence tactics. He commanded 3000 men at the battle of Laholm, defeating the Danish forces. His military expertise led the Riksråd to send him to the Dal and Norrland regions with 2000 soldiers and 300 cavalry in order to take Trondheim from the Norwegians. In 1658 he received a pass to travel in Sweden, and he again served on the military council which was organizing the garrisons in the territories newly won through conquest from Denmark–Norway.

When the Polish campaigns resumed towards the end of 1658 Douglas replaced governor Magnus de la Gardie as military commander in the Baltic states of Estonia and Livonia. His military assignment in the Baltic was to regain territories occupied by the Russians, who had joined in the Polish war against Sweden. Indeed Douglas's most notorious duty involved kidnapping the duke of Courland and his family. Once peace had been established at Kardis in 1661 Douglas became responsible for demobilizing his Swedish troops. Karl X, with whom Douglas had a personal relationship (he had twice entertained the Swedish royal couple at his Göteborg home in 1658) died and Douglas and his family returned to Sweden in September 1661. Douglas continued to participate in meetings of the Riksråd and military council until his death in Blasieholmen, Stockholm, on 28 May 1662. He was buried in Riddarholms church, Stockholm.

Militarily, Robert Douglas was probably the most successful British immigrant to Sweden during the Thirty Years' War. Although Alexander Leslie also attained the rank of field marshal, his love for Scotland was so strong that he left Sweden in 1638, never to serve its crown again. Douglas, on the other hand, only briefly considered moving to Scotland with his family when he temporarily fell out of favour with the new Swedish king, Karl XI, in 1660. In his adopted country he has been regarded as 'a great Swedish man' and his biographer has concluded that, through high military rank, baronial privileges, wealth, and marriage, 'despite all the retained Scottish idiosyncrasies', he had become a Swede (Douglas, 16).

A. N. L. GROSJEAN

Sources G. Elgenstierna, *Den introducerade svenska adelns ättartavlor med tillägg och rättelser*, 9 vols. (1925–36), vol. 2 • A. Douglas, *Robert Douglas en krigaregestalt från vår storhetstid* (1957) • 'Svenska sändebuds till utländska hof och deras sändebud till Sverige', 1841, Riksarkivet, Stockholm • 'Katalog öfver sköldebref', Riddarhusarkivet, Stockholm, Sweden • military muster rolls, Krigsarkivet, Stockholm, 1659/13; 1660/4, 11, 17 • N. A. Kullberg, S. Bergh, and P. Sondén, eds., *Svenska riksrådets protokoll*, 18 vols. (Stockholm, 1878–1959), *passim* • S. Bergh and B. Taube, eds., *Sveriges riddarskaps och adels riksdags-protokoll*, 17 vols. (1871) • A. Kugelberg, W. A. Douglas, and B. Hilderbrabd, 'Robert Douglas', *Svenskt biografiskt lexikon*, ed. B. Boëthius, 11 (1945), 372–8 • M. Roberts, ed., *Swedish diplomats at Cromwell's court, 1655–1656: the missions of Peter Julius Coyet and Christer Bonde* (1988) • J. Kleberg, *Krigskollegii historia biografiska anteckningar, 1630–1865* (1930) • C. H. Firth, ed., *Scotland and the Commonwealth: letters and papers relating to the military government of Scotland, from August 1651 to December 1653*, Scottish History Society, 18 (1895) • *The diary of Bulstrode Whitelocke, 1605–1675*, ed. R. Spalding, British Academy, Records of Social and Economic History, new ser., 13 (1990) • T. A. Fischer [E. L. Fischer], *The Scots in Sweden* (1907)

Archives Lund University, Sweden, De la Gardieska Samlingen, biographica minora | Lund University, Sweden, De la Gardieska Samlingen, Släktarkiven, Douglas • Lund University, Sweden, De la Gardieska Samlingen, Kurzer Verlauff seiner hoch-gräfflichen Excellence Herren General Douglas geführten Lebens so viel man sich besinnen kan • Riksarkivet, Riksarkivarien Ingvar Anderssons Arkiv, Stockholm, Kartong 13, F.12 • Royal Library, Stockholm, Sweden, Rålambskasamlingen, Douglas

Douglas, Sir Robert, of Glenbervie, sixth baronet (1694–1770), genealogist, was the son of Sir Robert Douglas of Glenbervie (*c.*1662–1748), fourth baronet, and his second wife, Janet Paterson (1655–1750). His father, who inherited the baronetcy from a cousin in 1692, changed the name of his lands at Ardit, Fife, to Glenbervie, the name of the family's original barony in Kincardineshire. Details of Douglas's early life are few. The Glenbervie line was descended from a younger son of the fifth earl of Angus who died at Flodden in 1513. Born a younger son, Robert developed an abiding interest in the genealogy of Scotland's landed families that became his life's work.

Douglas is best known as the author of the most influential eighteenth-century account of the Scottish peerage. The field was pioneered by George Crawford's peerage of 1716. In 1759 Nathaniel Salmon's *Short View of the Families of the Scottish Nobility* appeared, noting that 'there has been no good account of the Scottish Peerage for several years past' (Salmon, iv). The 'indefatigable and judicious Douglas' (Almon, ii) spent many years gathering material. He gained access to numerous collections of family papers and public records, and also drew on the work of the antiquary Walter MacFarlane (*d.* 1767). Douglas gave peers a chance to correct or add to the entries on their families, if they could provide 'sufficient Documents in Support of any Alteration made' (Douglas, *Peerage of Scotland*, 1764, v). *The Peerage of Scotland* was published in Edinburgh in one folio volume in 1764, and was much acclaimed. Dedicated to James Douglas, fourteenth earl of Morton, the work was strongly supported by the Scottish aristocracy. The subscription list numbered 396, including some 56 peers (approximately sixty per cent of the Scottish peerage). Sections on individual families were excerpted and privately printed; that on the Wemyss family, for example, appeared in French in 1765. Having inherited his half-brother's baronetcy in 1764, Douglas reissued the peerage in 1768 with a new title-page denoting the author as 'Sir Robert Douglas of Glenbervie, Bart.'

Douglas's peerage was generally accepted as authoritative in its day and served as the base for later efforts, particularly John Philp Wood's *Peerage of Scotland*, published in two volumes in 1813. Wood's Douglas, as the revision became known, remained the dominant reference work for the rest of the nineteenth century. In the early twentieth century Sir James Balfour Paul edited the massively expanded and revised *Scots Peerage, Founded on Wood's Edition of Sir Robert Douglas's Peerage of Scotland* (9 vols., 1904–14). As his subtitle indicated, Paul saw himself in direct succession to Douglas and Wood, and retained some of their wording.

During his lifetime Douglas also gathered much material for a companion work on the Scottish gentry, some of it with the help of James Cummyng (*d.* 1793), herald-painter and Lyon clerk depute. Though announced as forthcoming in 1767, the work was left in manuscript at Douglas's death. The first—and only—volume of *The baronage of Scotland, containing an historical and genealogical account of the gentry of that kingdom* appeared posthumously in 1796, with Douglas's name on the title-page and a notation that it had been completed by 'other hands'. Douglas used the term 'baronage' in the Scottish sense of those who held land in free barony as tenants-in-chief of the crown. The work was well known long before publication, and at least parts of it circulated in manuscript during Sir Robert's lifetime. Indeed, his death notice in the *Scots Magazine* (1770, 24) described Douglas as 'author of the Peerage and Baronage of Scotland'.

Douglas married three times. His first wife was Dorothea, daughter of Anthony Chester, attorney-general of Barbados. At some time before 1738 he married Margaret, daughter of Sir James MacDonald of Slate, sixth baronet. Finally, he wed Anne (*d.* 1770), daughter of Alexander Hay of Huntingdon. He died at Edinburgh on 24 April 1770, and was survived by Anne (who died on 17 September) and his only surviving son (from his second marriage) and heir, Alexander *Douglas (1738–1812), a prominent physician.

WILLIAM C. LOWE

Sources DNB · *Scots Magazine*, 29 (1767) · *Scots Magazine*, 32 (1770) · GEC, *Baronetage*, vol. 2 · J. Almon and others, *The peerage of Scotland* (1767) · N. Salmon, *A short view of the families of the Scottish nobility* (1759) · *Scots peerage* · *The general correspondence of James Boswell, 1766–1769*, ed. R. C. Cole and others, 1 (1993), vol. 5 of *The Yale editions of the private papers of James Boswell*, research edn · Walpole, *Corr.*, vol. 42 · W. Fraser, ed., *The Douglas book*, 4 vols. (1885) · R. Douglas, *Généalogie de la maison de Wemyss* (1765) · J. H. Stevenson, 'The Scottish peerage', *SHR*, 2 (1904–5), 1–13
Archives NL Scot., genealogical papers, Adv MSS 19.1.21, 20.1.6–20.1.11 | NA Scot., letters to Sir A. Grant, GD 345/1170 · U. Edin. L., letters to James Cumming, La ii 82

Douglas, Robert (1747–1820), Church of Scotland minister, was born in Kenmore, Perthshire, on 19 July 1747, the eldest son of the Revd John Douglas (*d.* 1768) and Beatrix Ainslie (1710–1794?). His father was also a parish minister, of 'uncommon prudence and agreeable manners' (Somerville, 173), a description which could be applied equally to the son. Robert was educated at Marischal College and King's College, Aberdeen, and ordained minister of Galashiels, Selkirkshire, in the Scottish borders, on 17 July 1770. In the borders he moved in a cultivated and enlightened society. Many letters to him from the poet Alison Cockburn survive, a good deal more elegant and amusing than one might expect in Scottish Presbyterian circles. He

Robert Douglas (1747–1820), by Sir Henry Raeburn, 1813

was, in fact, a representative figure of the Church of Scotland's moderate party, a parish minister who refused to confine his kindness to members of his own church, but regarded every inhabitant of Galashiels as worthy of interest and assistance. It is characteristic of him that he published a sensible and temperate essay on the danger of needlessly multiplying oaths (1783). His memoir of the Leith minister and poet John Logan, prefixed to editions of his poems in 1805 and subsequently, showed him to be equally averse to austere and unnatural restraints on the one hand, and to reckless infidelity on the other. He was the author both of a brief account of Galashiels in Sir John Sinclair's *Statistical Account* and a substantial *General View of the Agriculture in the Counties of Roxburgh and Selkirk* (1798). The *General View* was prepared for the board of agriculture at the request of Sinclair, who used his influence to persuade King's College, Aberdeen, to award Douglas the degree of DD 'as a worthy respectable clergyman' (NL Scot., MS 3117, fol. 13). The book itself is a striking illustration of the attitudes of 'improving' farmers, and shows little patience, for example, with the 'mighty clamour' raised about the enclosure of commons.

Douglas's younger brother Walter was a military officer in the East India Company's service, work that was dangerous but financially rewarding. In February 1780 he wrote to Robert that he intended to settle his fortune on him, and since Walter was killed in battle near Cuddalore in south India on 17 June 1783, Robert became unusually wealthy for a parish minister and felt in a position to marry, on 4 June 1784, Robina Lothian (1755–1837), daughter of an Edinburgh jeweller. He evidently invested much of his capital in buying land and developing a farm. He put his resources to good use during the trade depression that followed the Napoleonic wars, guaranteeing the credit of Galashiels manufacturers until better times returned. They were so grateful for this generous intervention on their behalf that on their trades' holiday, 12 October 1819, they went in procession to the manse, Walter Scott's piper John of Skye at their head, to present Douglas with an engraved silver cup. By this time he was in very poor health, and his frail appearance when he accepted the gift reduced many of those present to tears.

Douglas was a good friend of Walter Scott, who greatly enjoyed his conversation, describing him once as 'our principal resource in bad weather' (*Letters of Sir Walter Scott*, 7.454). Scott addressed to him a letter in his *Paul's Letters to his Kinsfolk* (1816) concerning the state of religion in France. Scott's confidence that French Catholicism was entering on a gradual and slow reformation probably reflects the tolerant benevolence of his correspondent. It was from Douglas that Scott bought the land on which he built Abbotsford. Friend or not, Douglas had a strong business sense, and when Scott tried to reduce the price from 4000 guineas to £4000, he insisted on the guineas. Douglas died on 15 November 1820 at Galashiels and was buried there on 26 November.   GEOFFREY CARNALL

Sources correspondence, NL Scot., Douglas MSS 3116–3121 · A. R. Cockburn, *Letters and memoir of her own life*, ed. T. Craig-Brown (1900) · *Fasti Scot.*, new edn, vol. 2 · J. G. Lockhart, *Memoirs of the life of Sir Walter Scott*, 7 vols. (1837–8) · T. Craig-Brown, *The history of Selkirkshire* (1886) · T. Somerville, *My own life and times, 1741–1814*, ed. W. Lee (1861) · *The letters of Sir Walter Scott*, ed. H. J. C. Grierson and others, centenary edn, 12 vols. (1932–79), vol. 7, p. 454
Archives NL Scot.
Likenesses H. Raeburn, oils, 1813, priv. coll. [*see illus.*]

Douglas, (William) Sholto, Baron Douglas of Kirtleside

(1893–1969), air force officer, was born in Oxford on 23 December 1893, the second of the three sons of the Revd Robert Langton Douglas (1864–1952), secretary of the Church of England Temperance Society, and his first wife, Margaret Jane (*d.* 1958), the daughter of Percival Cannon, a printer. His father left the priesthood in 1898 after his marriage to Margaret Douglas was dissolved (his first divorce), and later became an authority on the history of Italian art, director of the Irish National Gallery, a citizen of the United States, and a Roman Catholic; he was married twice more and—according to Douglas's reckoning—fathered a total of ten legitimate and eight illegitimate children. Brought up in straitened circumstances by his mother, Douglas overcame the handicap of unsettled early years to flourish at St Clement's School, Headington, Oxford; Emmanuel School, Wandsworth; and Tonbridge preparatory school and Tonbridge School in Kent (1908–13), where he won a classical scholarship to Lincoln College, Oxford, in October 1913. He sang in the Bach Choir, attended Fabian Society meetings, and joined the artillery section of the Oxford OTC.

First World War: the western front Douglas was commissioned as a second lieutenant in the Royal Field Artillery on 15 August 1914 and served in France, but transferred to

(William) Sholto Douglas, Baron Douglas of Kirtleside (1893–1969), by Howard Coster, 1942

the Royal Flying Corps as an observer with 2 squadron at Merville in northern France (flying BE 2a and b reconnaissance biplanes) from December 1914 to April 1915. He returned to England for pilot instruction in May and qualified in July. In August he was posted to 8 squadron on the western front, where he was promoted captain and flight commander in December and awarded a Military Cross in January 1916. On promotion to major in May he was sent to Montrose on the Scottish east coast where he formed and trained 43 squadron (equipped with the oddly named Sopwith One and a Half Strutter, a versatile machine, used for bombing and reconnaissance), which he took to France in January 1917. He was appointed to command 84 squadron, equipped with the SE 5a, an excellent single-seat fighter, in August. By the end of the war he was a lieutenant-colonel (promoted on 9 November 1918), a proven administrator, and an experienced pilot (awarded a Distinguished Flying Cross in February 1919), but he met with surprisingly little success in aerial combat: he achieved certainly fewer than the five victories which identify an ace, and perhaps none at all. In later years, however, he rated his performance during the First World War very highly: 'I was a well-known fighter pilot and an expert on air fighting when in its infancy', he told the literary agent A. D. Peters, on 29 March 1961. 'I commanded two crack fighter squadrons [the Sopwith was not a fighter] on the Western Front for a total period of nearly two years and was awarded three decorations for gallantry, ending up as the youngest lieutenant-colonel in the RAF at 23 [actually almost 25]' (Douglas papers).

RAF appointments between the wars Douglas left the RAF in 1919, but did not return to Oxford to complete a degree. Instead, he joined the Handley Page Company as an air transport pilot, obtaining a commercial pilot's licence and flying from London to Manchester and Brussels. In October 1919 he married May Howard. A chance meeting with Sir Hugh Trenchard, chief of the air staff (CAS), encouraged him to return to the service in March 1920 with a permanent commission as a squadron leader. Trenchard decided to present a 'tournament' at Hendon, a display of flying skill, and Douglas suggested a fly-past by three four-engined Handley Page V/1500 bombers. He and Keith Park flew two of the machines on 3 July 1920 in what the editor of *The Aeroplane* regarded as the highlight of the show. 'It was truly a terrifying sensation', he wrote, 'as the twelve Rolls-Royce Eagles roared towards the railings' (7 July 1920, 5), clearing them by no more than 15 feet. Trenchard delivered a stinging rebuke to all concerned. Nevertheless, both Douglas and Park were selected to attend the world's first air force staff college, at Andover in Hampshire, from April 1922 to January 1923—long enough to offer practical instruction in efficient management of paperwork and to sow the seeds of a 'school of thought'. Among the twenty officers selected were seven who occupied vital positions during the Second World War, but even in that august company three stood out: Charles Portal, Douglas, and Park—and among their instructors was Wilfrid Freeman, one of the RAF's greatest officers.

Douglas's education was further broadened in 1927 by a year at the Imperial Defence College (IDC) in London. He won the prestigious and well-rewarded (£30 plus books) R. M. Groves memorial prize in 1928 for an essay on how aircraft could best help to develop imperial communications. He served in the Middle East, mainly in Egypt and the Sudan, from August 1929 until March 1932, when he returned to the IDC as an instructor. His first marriage was dissolved in 1932, and in September 1933 he married Joan Leslie, the daughter of Colonel Hubert Cuthbert Denny.

In January 1936 Douglas began an exceptionally long stint in the Air Ministry: first as director of staff duties (responsible for framing and amending the tasks assigned to senior operational and staff officers) until February 1938; next as assistant CAS until April 1940 (where his daily concerns were weapons and equipment, including the possibility of airborne radar, for the new fighters and bombers coming into service); and finally as deputy CAS (involved in operational policy at the highest level) until 25 November 1940. He then succeeded Sir Hugh Dowding as head of Fighter Command at Bentley Priory in Stanmore, north-west London. Appropriate promotions accompanied his rise towards the top: wing commander (January 1925), group captain (January 1932), air commodore (July 1935), air vice-marshal (January 1938), and air marshal (on arrival at Bentley Priory). He was appointed CB in July 1940 and knighted (KCB) a year later.

Head of Fighter Command By October 1940 moves to replace Dowding at Fighter Command were gathering momentum. He had failed to settle a bitter—and increasingly public—quarrel between his two principal group commanders (Keith Park and Trafford Leigh-Mallory) over the most effective tactics to employ against German daylight raids during the battle of Britain. The Germans had switched to an increasingly destructive night offensive in September, and Dowding seemed at a loss, energetic only in brusquely rejecting Air Ministry suggestions made (or at least supported) by Douglas. Several powerful men, among them Trenchard, Sir John Salmond (also a former CAS, currently conducting an investigation into the problems of night defence), Sir Archibald Sinclair (secretary of state for air), and Harold Balfour (his under-secretary), wanted Dowding's head—and that of the CAS, Sir Cyril Newall, long regarded as a lame duck. The situation was ideal for new commanders to step forward: young, confident, articulate, aggressive and (not least) untainted by what Trenchard and others regarded as mistakes in strategy and tactics since the outbreak of war.

Douglas supported Leigh-Mallory's opposition to the emphasis on defence by Dowding and Park throughout the day battle. As far back as 11 August 1938 he had declared that it was 'immaterial in the long view whether the enemy bomber is shot down before or after he has dropped his bombs on his objective' (Orange, 121). Douglas agreed with Leigh-Mallory that targets should be defended primarily by anti-aircraft guns, balloons, and searchlights, while a concentrated attack was prepared by massed fighters on enemy bombers—if necessary, after they had bombed. It was a risky policy, especially given Fighter Command's lack of combat-hardened pilots by October 1940. Douglas, however, never accepted a distinction between flying ability and fighting experience. On 31 October, for example, he wrote that the pilot position had undergone a 'kaleidoscopic change' recently: 'in the case of Fighter Command we are actually faced with a surplus'. Two days later, Douglas Evill (Dowding's chief staff officer) reported realistically that the command was 'at about the lowest ebb in operational pilots', as opposed to young men who could more or less control high-performance aircraft, at which it could function (Orange, 107).

Some years later, in February 1956, Douglas was given an opportunity to comment on a draft of Basil Collier's official history of this period, *The Defence of the United Kingdom* (1957). Douglas argued that causing heavy casualties and therefore using large forces was one way to diminish and end an assault. Interception before the enemy reached his target obliged the use of small forces and the risk of defeat in detail. In the short run the effect of bombing was minimized by interception, but in the long run the best answer might be to withhold attack until large fighter forces were massed. 'Of course, I realise that Dowding and Park were under pressure from the government to try and break up the attacks before they reached their objective at any cost, and that they could not afford to disregard this pressure' (Orange, 134–5). This political reason (not mentioned by Douglas in 1940) weighed less with Dowding and Park than the military reason. Douglas and his supporters thought constantly in terms of a single raid on a single target. Had that been the normal pattern of the attack, it would certainly have made sense to assemble a massive counter-attack, but the Luftwaffe rarely made it so easy for the defence.

Meanwhile, on 17 October 1940, Douglas had presided (in the absence of the 'indisposed' Newall) over an Air Ministry meeting with Dowding and his group commanders that has become famous. The subsequent minutes, about which Park protested in vain, made many critical points concerning the conduct of operations and left no doubt in the minds of Dowding's many opponents that he and Park (who was deemed to be exhausted) should be replaced by Douglas and Leigh-Mallory; Portal should also succeed the ineffectual Newall.

During his Air Ministry days Douglas had clearly recognized that aerial combat in daylight and darkness required completely different machines. He therefore strongly advocated the development of a twin-engined, two-seat machine—the Bristol Beaufighter—for work at night. Its long endurance, heavy armament, and airborne radar helped Britain's defences to take an increasing toll of German bombers before the blitz was suspended in May 1941. And yet as head of Fighter Command Douglas also encouraged the use at night of a single-engined, single-seat day fighter, the Hawker Hurricane. Its long nose, exhaust glare, and short range made it entirely unsuitable for such operations, which served only to illustrate Douglas's commitment to aggression at all costs. From December 1940 onwards, Spitfires and Hurricanes carried out large-scale 'sweeps' across the channel, but short-range fighters, denied help from radar chains and the observer corps, proved as vulnerable over occupied Europe as did German fighters over England. As early as 12 February 1941 Douglas was unhappy. 'Our idea', he complained to Leigh-Mallory, 'was to go over the other side and leap on the enemy from a great height in superior numbers; instead of which it looks as though we ourselves are being leapt on' (Orange, 138). Evill vainly urged Douglas to insist on intensive training during this lull in the daylight offensive, rather than on offensive sweeps of little military value over territory where the Luftwaffe had every advantage.

Tragically, Douglas followed Trenchard in his belief that continuous offensive enhanced morale. This belief was bolstered after the German assault on the Soviet Union in June 1941 by the hope—unrealized, in fact—that fighter sweeps might oblige the Luftwaffe to retain strong forces in the west or even withdraw units from the eastern front. Fighter Command lost more pilots and inflicted far fewer casualties in 1941 than during the battle of Britain and achieved no comparable strategic advantage.

The main event of 1942, so far as Fighter Command was concerned, was its participation in the raid on Dieppe in August. An ill-planned and poorly executed venture, it cost more than 4000 casualties, mainly Canadians; Fighter Command lost 106 aircraft, the Luftwaffe only forty-eight.

Although Douglas was not among those primarily responsible for the disaster, neither he nor Leigh-Mallory voiced reservations about employing short-range fighters far beyond their bases. Nothing had been learned by either man from their mishandling of the command in 1941. Douglas was promoted air chief marshal in July 1942.

RAF Middle East and Coastal Command In December 1942 Douglas succeeded Sir Arthur Tedder in Cairo as head of RAF Middle East. During 1943 the centre of operations moved westwards, to Tunisia, Sicily, and Italy, and planning for operation Overlord (the allied attempt to liberate western Europe) became serious. But the British prime minister, Winston Churchill, hoped to generate a new campaign in the Balkans and the Dodecanese Islands that might add Turkey to the allied coalition. Although Douglas eagerly supported Churchill's plans, General Dwight D. Eisenhower (supreme allied commander) and his principal army, navy, and air subordinates, General Harold Alexander, Admiral Andrew Cunningham, and Tedder, did not. Such a campaign, they argued, diverted attention from Italy, the short-term target, and Overlord, the long-term target. Tedder's unwavering support for American resistance to operation Accolade helped to ensure him a high place in Overlord. Denis Richards, an official British historian, castigated Accolade: 'this rash experiment … ill-judged from the beginning, had been the result of overconfidence, an unconscious flouting of a cardinal principle of modern warfare' (Richards and Saunders, 2.345). Douglas and his army and navy colleagues in Cairo did what they could with their own resources and received some assistance from Eisenhower's subordinates, but it was never sufficient. Douglas shared Churchill's intense excitement over these adventures in the eastern Mediterranean, but he—of all men—quite overlooked the fact that the Luftwaffe enjoyed local air superiority, and neither Douglas nor Churchill had a convincing answer to the question asked by President Franklin D. Roosevelt in October 1943: where do the allies go from the Aegean? Accolade collapsed in November, at a cost of some 5000 British casualties, and Turkey remained neutral. The collapse deeply angered Douglas, who even contemplated resignation; he went to his grave convinced that a great opportunity had been wasted by the timidity of others.

While he was still pressing on with his 'rash experiment', Douglas learned that the Americans had vetoed his appointment as allied commander in south-east Asia, an appointment prematurely offered to him by Sinclair with Churchill's approval. The Americans were unimpressed by his conduct of operations at Fighter Command, still less by his support for Accolade, and some of them regarded him as a difficult colleague, overbearing and self-satisfied. Their reservations about Douglas's personality were soon confirmed. During December 1943 it was decided that Lieutenant-General Ira C. Eaker be made first commander-in-chief of the newly formed Mediterranean allied air forces, with Douglas as his deputy. Douglas was upset, although he liked Eaker, 'and respected his ability. But it was a strange state of affairs in which an officer of my seniority in high command could be appointed as deputy to an American officer so much junior in rank and experience' (Douglas papers). Even granting these objections, which are arguable, Douglas overlooked the fact that in a coalition the partner providing most of the equipment and manpower must sometimes be allowed overall command. 'Tedder was sympathetic', Douglas continued, 'but the way he expressed it angered me. "The great chess players do not, I think," he wrote, "have much regard for pawns like you and me." I have never been able to regard myself as a pawn' (ibid.).

Douglas accepted the position, with a bad grace, but at the last moment Portal offered to bring him back to England in January 1944 as head of Coastal Command—an appointment which delighted him, even though he knew nothing about its highly specialized war against submarines, surface warships, and coastal shipping. Sir John Slessor, an officer of greater ability and wider experience who understood the realities of coalition warfare, took over as Eaker's deputy. Coastal Command had become, under Slessor, a large and successful organization, stretching from Iceland to Gibraltar, and working closely with the Royal Navy. Under Douglas's direction, it kept open for Overlord the vital cross-channel links before and after D-day, 6 June 1944.

Occupation of Germany and retirement from the RAF In August 1945 Douglas was appointed head of British air forces of occupation (BAFO) in Germany under Field Marshal Montgomery. He was responsible for overseeing the disarmament of the Luftwaffe in a devastated land, securing access to the western sectors of Berlin, dealing with Soviet suspicion and reluctance to co-operate in restoring something approaching 'normal' life in Germany, and returning Polish and Czech airmen, who had served with the RAF, to their homes—if they still had any. It was an appointment he hated, not only for the long hours and hard travelling, but for the constant sense of wrestling with problems which had no satisfactory solutions in any foreseeable future. Consolation came in January 1946, when he was knighted again (GCB) and promoted to the rank of marshal: only he and Sir Arthur Harris, head of Bomber Command, reached five-star status in RAF history without serving as chiefs of the air staff. In May he succeeded Montgomery as head of all British forces in Germany, military governor of the British zone, and British member of the four-power Allied Control Commission. Although he doubted the propriety of the Nuremberg war trials, he found himself obliged to confirm the sentences passed. He retired in November 1947, ending what he described as the unhappiest period of his life.

Douglas's military career, though distinguished, left him unsatisfied. He arrived in Fighter Command *after* the battle of Britain, in Egypt *after* Rommel's last departure, in Coastal Command *after* victory over the U-boats, and in Germany *after* the defeat of Hitler. Historians express reservations about his conduct of Fighter Command and his Aegean campaign; he was denied a great allied command in the Far East and, although Churchill often spoke warmly of his merits, both Tedder and Slessor stood ahead of him as candidates for the succession to Portal as CAS.

Peer and chairman of BEA Douglas was created a peer in February 1948 and sat on the Labour benches. At the suggestion of Lord Pakenham he was appointed a director of the British Overseas Airways Corporation (BOAC) in 1948, but resigned in March 1949 when he was appointed chairman of British European Airways (BEA), which had been created as a result of the Attlee government's nationalization of civil aviation. His appointment was regularly renewed until 1964. During his time, BEA grew rapidly—from about 750,000 passengers in 1949 to 5.6 million in 1964—and was turned around from making serious losses to a net profit. Under his chairmanship BEA expanded both business and leisure travel into Europe, encouraging demand by introducing reduced tourist fares in 1953, and achieved economies by using larger aircraft. Jet airliners were introduced and commercial agreements were made with companies outside the EEC. The longest-serving, and one of the most successful among chairmen of nationalized industries, he 'handled the board and the politicians with a direct firmness which brooked no interference' (Masefield).

After his second marriage was dissolved in 1954 Douglas married, in 1955, Hazel, the daughter of George Eric Maas Walker and the widow of Captain W. E. R. Walker. They had a daughter, Katherine, Douglas's only child. He produced two volumes of memoirs, *Years of Combat* and *Years of Command*, in 1963 and 1966, with essential assistance from his former personal assistant, Wing Commander Robert Wright. Although valuable, both volumes suffer from the fact that most official records were then withheld from public scrutiny. Douglas was a burly man, well aware that his face usually wore a forbidding frown, which he protested was beyond his power to control. He could certainly be charming, to men as well as women, for he had a powerful personality. He was often ill in his last years and died in hospital in Northampton on 29 October 1969. He was buried privately at St Clement Danes in the Strand, London, on 4 November. VINCENT ORANGE

Sources W. S. Douglas and R. Wright, *Years of combat* (1963) · W. S. Douglas and R. Wright, *Years of command* (1966) · Douglas papers, IWM · J. P. Ray, *The Battle of Britain: new perspectives* (1994) · H. Probert and S. Cox, eds., *The battle re-thought: a symposium on the battle of Britain* (1991) · V. Orange, *Sir Keith Park* (2001) · D. Richards and H. St G. Saunders, *Royal Air Force, 1939–1945*, 3 vols. (1953–4); rev. edn (1974–5) · B. Collier, *The defence of the United Kingdom* (1957) · J. J. Sbrega, 'Anglo-American relations and the selection of Mountbatten as supreme allied commander, South East Asia', *Military Affairs*, 46 (Oct 1982), 139–45 · I. C. B. Dear and M. R. D. Foot, eds., *The Oxford companion to the Second World War* (1995) · *Daily Telegraph* (31 Oct 1969) · *The Times* (31 Oct 1969) · P. Masefield, 'Douglas, William Sholto', *DBB* · CGPLA Eng. & Wales (1970)

Archives IWM, corresp. and papers · RAF Bentley Priory, Stanmore, Middlesex, Air Historical Branch, papers | IWM, corresp. with Tizard and memoranda | FILM BFI NFTVA, documentary footage · BFI NFTVA, news footage · IWM FVA, actuality footage · IWM FVA, news footage

Likenesses W. Stoneman, photographs, 1938–45, NPG · H. Coster, photographs, c.1940–1949, NPG [*see illus.*] · E. Kennington, pastel drawing, 1941, IWM · W. Bird, photograph, 1961, NPG · H. A.

Freeth, drawing, priv. coll. • J. Gunn, oils, IWM • portrait, Air Historical Branch, Bentley Priory, Stanmore, London

Wealth at death £34,138: probate, 10 Feb 1970, *CGPLA Eng. & Wales*

Douglas, Sylvester, Baron Glenbervie (1743–1823), politician and diarist, was born in Fechil, Aberdeenshire, on 24 May 1743, the elder and only surviving son of John Douglas (1713/14–1762), landowner, of Whiteriggs, Kincardineshire, and his first wife, Margaret Gordon (*d.* 1747), daughter and coheir of James Gordon of Fechil. His father was descended from a brother of Sir William Douglas of Glenbervie, later earl of Angus, and resided at Fechil after having bought out his wife's two sisters, who were second cousins of George Keith, the Jacobite Earl Marischal. Douglas's pride in his genealogy is displayed in the account of his family which he published in the third edition of *Lyric Poems* (1806) by his brother-in-law, the poet James Mercer (1734–1804), who had married his only sister, Katherine Douglas.

Douglas was educated at Foveran School, Aberdeen, where bullying by a young kinsman, so he later alleged, damaged his development. From 1754 his father engaged tutors (Alan Gordon, John Calder, and Alexander Gall) to teach him at home, until in 1757 he entered King's College, Aberdeen, of which he later became rector from 1805 to 1814. He lived at home, his father having moved to Aberdeen, and left college without a degree in 1760. After his father's death he spent some time in Edinburgh, proceeded to London in 1765, and took a medical degree at Leiden in 1766, with a dissertation 'De stimulis'. He travelled to Paris, then toured Italy and progressed to Vienna, from where he visited Hungary; his first publication was to be an account of Tokay wines in the *Philosophical Transactions* (1773). He returned to London in 1769, switched from medicine to the law, and entered Lincoln's Inn in 1771. When called to the bar in 1776 he had already embarked on reporting the disputed parliamentary elections to the 1774 House of Commons, which were published in four volumes in 1775 and 1777. From 1778 he reported Lord Mansfield's judicial decisions in king's bench, published in 1783. He was elected FSA in 1781 and FRS 1795.

By 1784 Douglas's election reports were said to earn him £3000 a year. He had also, since his call, practised on the Oxford circuit, and for a decade to 1794 he was king's attorney. Tall and high-nosed with beetling black brows, he was more remarkable for his assimilative capacity and ambition than for any originality. One of the prosecuting counsel for Warren Hastings's impeachment, he moved in whig circles, joining Brooks's Club and the Whig Club in 1789, when he made a momentous marriage on 25 September that year. His bride, Catherine Anne North (1760–1817), to whom he had been introduced by Lord Sheffield, was the eldest daughter of Frederick *North, second earl of Guilford (1732–1792), the former premier, and his wife, Anne Speke, and was her father's match for wit and ugliness. They had a son, Frederick Sylvester North Douglas [*see below*], but both of their daughters were stillborn. Douglas's whig friends had encouraged him to look to high legal office during the Regency crisis, but even the

Sylvester Douglas, Baron Glenbervie (1743–1823), by Sir Thomas Lawrence, *c.*1792–3

solicitor-generalship would have left him much poorer than his professional income, and he was in no hurry to enter parliament, which served him better with its crop of election and canal disputes.

The death of his father-in-law in 1792 freed Douglas from whig shackles. He joined the phalanx of Portland whigs who went over to Pitt the younger's administration. He took silk on 7 February 1793, and became a bencher of his inn (of which he was to be treasurer in 1799). After complaining loudly of not having been made solicitor-general to the prince of Wales, he was offered a commissionership at Toulon, captured from the French, in September 1793. As this appointment was worth £1500 a year and not pensionable, Douglas declined, preferring an under-secretaryship at the Foreign Office. In January 1794, however, he agreed to become chief secretary to the lord lieutenant of Ireland, and was sworn of the Irish privy council on 20 January and of the British privy council on 4 May. Report had it that having failed to 'bustle himself into the Chancellorship of Ireland', he 'bullied himself into the Secretaryship' (Walpole, 12.124). He sat for St Canice in the Irish parliament. Recalled from Dublin with Viceroy Westmorland in January 1795, he was unable to obtain the sinecure Irish secretaryship of state, being told this was reserved for Irishmen, but he was offered compensations: the first vacant lordship of the Treasury at home, a seat at the Board of Control for India, a pension of £800, half of which was to descend to his son, and a seat in parliament. The latter was for Fowey, where he was by-elected on 14 February 1795 with ministerial backing, having failed in his negotiations elsewhere. His pension, awarded on 21 March 1795, was actually set at £600 for life and the same in survivorship for himself or his son unless he accepted office of £1000 a year (a condition which reflected his stated aspiration to succeed John Robinson as surveyor of woods and forests). He gave his maiden speech on disputed elections on 14 April 1795, but was shouted down when he defended Westmorland's Irish administration on 19 May. In June he took his seat at the Board of Control, but chafed for further employment. Lord Camden would not have him as his chief secretary at Dublin, although the king had suggested it, and he tried to make himself useful to ministers in debate, coming to the defence of Henry Dundas and of Pitt, whose Poor Relief Bill he helped to prepare. In March 1796 he obtained a seat at the Board of Trade.

Douglas sat for Midhurst on Lord Carrington's interest in the 1796 parliament. In September he was invited to accompany Lord Macartney to the Cape with the promise of succeeding him as governor in eighteen months' time, and of receiving a £2000 pension two years later. He agreed, on condition that he would be raised to the Irish peerage, but his wife disapproved, and her influence on his decisions was paramount. He jobbed with Dundas to place him at the Treasury board instead. In the Commons he served as committee chairman and teller, and was a notable promoter of the Irish union: his speech of 22 April 1799 answering objections to it was published in 1800. When in January 1800 he was again offered the governorship of the Cape, his wife took the blame for his refusal. After talk of a continental mission, he settled for the Cape in October 1800, and was duly created Baron Glenbervie on 30 November. Pitt's resignation spared him the Cape, and from Addington he requested the Home Office. Instead he was appointed joint paymaster-general, in March 1801, to which he would have preferred a return to Dublin or promotion on the Board of Control, and finding himself second fiddle at the pay office, he angled to replace Dundas in charge of Scottish affairs. As his Irish peerage enabled him to sit at Westminster, he was by-elected for Plympton Erle as a government nominee on 6 July 1801; he made himself useful in debate, and was offered the presidency of the Board of Control. This still did not satisfy his ambitions as he would have preferred the vice-presidency of the Board of Trade, presiding in Lord Liverpool's absence, or better still, the speakership. He scorned, as Lord North's son-in-law, Addington's proposal of a diplomatic mission to the United States in December 1801, even though he introduced a bill easing commercial relations with America, and on 24 May 1802 reminded Addington that he had no objection to negotiating a commercial treaty with France.

In January 1803 Glenbervie, who sat for Hastings as a Treasury nominee in that parliament, succeeded Robinson as surveyor of woods and forests, thereby enabling Addington's brother to replace him at the pay office, although he would have preferred to have held both. He obtained £3000 a year, but not for life, and promotion in the peerage might have compensated him. Ostensibly for health reasons he took little part in debate, and in February 1804 gave up the Board of Trade. On Pitt's return to power that year he was a doubtful supporter, and offered to relinquish office only if compensated. By September he was listed as a reliable government supporter, and in 1805 defended Lord Melville against charges of naval maladministration. He was mortified to lose his surveyorship when the Grenville administration took over in February 1806. He complained that the pension he negotiated was only a fifth of what he had been earning in 1793, and tried to obtain compensatory employment hearing appeals to the privy council. He did not seek re-election to parliament that year. The Portland ministry restored him to the surveyorship of the woods and forests in April 1807, reducing his salary but not sufficiently to allow him to retain his pension: this saved the public £1600 a year. In July 1810, when his office was reformed, he became first of three commissioners. Then, and in 1812, he was criticized as a jobber in the Commons, and Lord Liverpool was reluctant to let him serve in 1814 in view of his pension claims. He travelled on the continent, and his later years were devoted to a vain attempt to guide his son's career. His wife died on 6 February 1817 and his son in 1819. Cared for by his daughter-in-law, he turned to literary pursuits. Nothing came of a projected biography of Lord North, but he managed a translation of part of the Italian poet Fortiguerri's *Ricciardetto*, published in 1822. From 1812 he was a trustee of the British Museum. He died at Cheltenham on 2 May 1823, whereupon his title became extinct. His journals and diaries, published piecemeal in 1910 and 1928, are a record of his aspirations and disappointments, interlaced with scandalous anecdotes, political gossip, and travel notes, which account for their attraction as a period piece.

His son, **Frederick Sylvester North Douglas** (1791–1819), politician and classical scholar, was born in Bedford Square, London, on 8 February 1791 and christened at home by the rector of St Giles-in-the-Fields, Bloomsbury. Delicate and precocious, he was educated at Sunbury School, proceeding to Westminster School in 1801 and Christ Church, Oxford, in 1806. Admitted to Lincoln's Inn in 1807, he was not called to the bar. Taking a first in classics and a top second in maths at Oxford in 1809 (MA, 1813), he went to Edinburgh to pursue his studies, but was taken ill. Physically he resembled his mother's family. In 1810 he embarked on a two-year tour of Greece and the Near East, under the aegis of his philhellenic uncle Frederick *North, fifth earl of Guilford (1766–1827), colonial governor in Ceylon. His *Essay on Certain Points of Resemblance between the Ancient and the Modern Greeks* went into a second edition in June 1813, in which year he acted as Germaine de Staël's guide to Oxford and deputy secretary of the politically ambivalent Grillion's Club. He had entered parliament in 1812 for Banbury, the North family borough, of which his father was recorder. His political independence soon alarmed his father. His maiden speech was lukewarm in support of the Christianization of India and he consistently voted for Catholic relief and abolition of the slave trade. More conventionally he was shy of parliamentary reform, apart from sponsorship of a bill (lost on 16 May 1814) to stop payment of non-resident electors' expenses. He opposed the peacetime reduction of the militia in 1815; he had been a major in the Surrey militia since 1813, and was a captain in the Oxfordshire yeomanry in 1817. During the recess in 1814 he interviewed Bonaparte, who liked him best of his English visitors on Elba. From February 1816, when he consulted the speaker about his debating style, which was disliked by reporters, he acted increasingly under the whig opposition, joining Brooks's Club on 7 May. He voted against the address and tried to exempt Scotland from measures against sedition in the 1817 session, to the chagrin of his father, whom he joined on a continental tour in the autumn. In spite of defending his father and uncle in debate in 1818, he also delivered a speech on 15 May against the Aliens Bill which went unanswered by the administration. In 1819 he conceded the need for piecemeal parliamentary reform, and in his last speeches in June, he spoke in favour of South American independence and educational reform. On 19 July 1819 he married a whig bride, Harriet Wrightson (d. 1864), eldest daughter of William Wrightson of Cusworth, Yorkshire. He died on 21 October 1819, after a bout of jaundice, in Brook Street, Westminster. According to one obituary, he had 'enlivened every society by his presence' (GM, 1st ser., 89/2 1819, 468). His widow married in 1825 Colonel Henry Hely Hutchinson and died on 16 July 1864.

ROLAND THORNE

Sources HoP, Commons, 1790–1820 · The diaries of Sylvester Douglas (Lord Glenbervie), ed. F. Bickley, 2 (1928), 340–82 [incl. autobiographical memoir] · Baron Glenbervie [S. Douglas], The Glenbervie journals, ed. W. Sichel (1910) · GM, 1st ser., 93/1 (1823), 467–8 · S. Douglas, Baron Glenbervie, 'An account of the life of James Mercer, Esquire', in Lyric poems by the late James Mercer, with an account of the life of the author, by Sylvester Lord Glenbovie, 3rd edn (1806), xi–lxiv · MS extracts from the diaries, History of Parliament Trust · DNB · Walpole, Corr. · GM, 1st ser., 89/2 (1819), 468–9 [Frederick Sylvester North Douglas] · GEC, Peerage · P. J. Anderson, ed., Officers and graduates of University and King's College, Aberdeen, MVD–MDCCCLX, New Spalding Club, 11 (1893), 17, 245 · R. W. Innes Smith, English-speaking students of medicine at the University of Leyden (1932) · W. P. Baildon, ed., The records of the Honorable Society of Lincoln's Inn: admissions, 1 (1896) · Scots Magazine, 24 (1762), 227
Archives BL, memorandum on French society, Add. MS 62319 · Bodl. Oxf., letters to his wife · CKS, corresp. and papers · E. Sussex RO, letters to first earl of Sheffield · NL Scot., corresp., literary MSS, papers incl. family papers; corresp. and diaries; papers relating to European tour | Birm. CA, letters to Boulton family · BL, letters to Lord Auckland, Add. MSS 34456–34461, passim · BL, corresp. with F. S. N. Douglas, Add. MSS 61876, 61981–61983, 61986 · BL, corresp. with first and second earls of Liverpool, Add. MSS 38235–38236, 38308–38311, 38428, 38473, 38570, passim · BL, corresp. and papers relating to Lord North, Add. MS 61876 · NA Scot., corresp. with Lord Melville · NA Scot., letters to Alexander Ross · NL Scot., letters to Archibald Constable · NL Scot., letters to Sir William Forbes · NL Scot., letters to Lord Melville · NL Scot., letters to first earl and countess of Minto · PRO, letters to William Pitt, PRO 30/8 · PRO NIre., corresp. with Lord Castlereagh
Likenesses T. Lawrence, portrait, c.1792–1793, priv. coll. [see illus.] · E. Harding, stipple, pubd 1794 (after T. Lawrence), BM, NPG · J. Gillray, caricature, 1801, repro. in U. D. George, Catalogue of political and personal satires, 8, no. 9722 · J. Henning, chalk drawing, 1805, Scot. NPG · J. Henning, porcelain medallion, 1808, Scot.

NPG · J. D. Ingres, lithograph, 1815 (Frederick Sylvester North Douglas), BM, NPG · J. D. Ingres, portrait, 1815, BM, NPG · C. S. Taylor, stipple, 1823 (after A. Buck), BM, NPG; repro. in New European Magazine (1823) · F. C. Lewis, engraving (after J. D. Ingres, 1815), NPG · F. C. Lewis, engraving (Frederick Sylvester North Douglas; after J. Slater), BM, NPG

Douglas, Thomas (d. c.1684), ejected minister and physician, is of unknown parentage and background. He graduated MA of the University of Edinburgh on 23 May 1655 and by at least 1661 was the rector of St Olave, Silver Street, London. Douglas wrote several tracts including Theanthrōpos, or, The Great Mysterie of Godlines (1661) in which he described ceremonial in worship as 'derogatory … to the ripe and mature age of the church' (p. 56). By March 1662 he had been ejected from his parish as a result of the Restoration religious settlement and during 1664 he was reported to have preached on three occasions at conventicles in London. He then became involved in a scandal of which the details are unknown and left the country, travelling abroad for some time, and then settling at Padua, where he was admitted to the university on 15 September 1665 and eventually received the degree of MD. Douglas afterwards returned to London where he practised medicine and where, as a widower, he married Elizabeth Juxon, aged twenty-eight, of co. Meath, Ireland, by licence dated 28 October 1678. Records suggest that they lived at St Dunstan-in-the-West, but they later moved to Ireland. Little is known of Douglas's later life except that he died in debt in Ireland in or about 1684 and was survived by his widow.

CAROLINE L. LEACHMAN

Sources Calamy rev., 168 · The nonconformist's memorial … originally written by … Edmund Calamy, ed. S. Palmer, 1 (1775), 137 · D. Laing, ed., A catalogue of the graduates … of the University of Edinburgh, Bannatyne Club, 106 (1858), 76 · DNB
Archives DWL, Turner MS 3A
Wealth at death £34 2s.: will, PRO, PROB 6/59, fol. 101; Calamy rev., 168

Douglas, Thomas, fifth earl of Selkirk (1771–1820), colonist and proponent of colonization in North America, was born at St Mary's Isle, Kirkcudbrightshire, Scotland, on 20 June 1771, the youngest of the seven sons of Dunbar Douglas, fourth earl of Selkirk (1722–1799), and his wife, Helen Hamilton (1737/8–1802), the daughter of the Hon. John Hamilton and his wife, Margaret, née Home. His father was an obscure Scottish nobleman of 'true whig' political proclivities who had been educated under Francis Hutcheson at the University of Glasgow and spent most of his life improving his estates. Only around the time of Thomas's birth did he begin to become involved in a prolonged political struggle for the independence of the Scots peerage from English ministerial authority. During the war against America he was an outspoken critic of government conduct.

Early life Like several of his elder brothers, Thomas was educated at Palgrave, a Unitarian dissenting academy located about 30 miles north of Cambridge and run by the Revd Rochemont Barbauld and his wife, Anna Laetitia. Mrs Barbauld was a minor poet who believed in the unity of moral and intellectual development. Besides English

Thomas Douglas, fifth earl of Selkirk (1771–1820), by unknown artist, c.1800

accents, the Douglas boys probably acquired at Palgrave the consumptive tendencies that bedevilled them throughout their adult lives. While Thomas was attending Palgrave, his father and his eldest brother, Basil William *Douglas (Lord Daer) [see under London Corresponding Society], increased the intensity of the family campaign not only for the reform of the political privileges enjoyed by the Scottish peerage but for wide-ranging parliamentary reform, which made the family politically and socially unacceptable to most of its contemporaries.

In 1785 Douglas matriculated at the University of Edinburgh, where he was taught by Dugald Stewart and joined 'the Club', an informal association of students that included Walter Scott, William Clerk, Adam Ferguson, and George Abercromby. He entered the undergraduate Speculative Society of Edinburgh in 1789 and was active at its meetings until he left Edinburgh in early April 1791 for revolutionary Paris with his brother-in-law Sir James Hall. Douglas never returned to student life or obtained a degree. If Edinburgh had provided an undergraduate education, Paris provided graduate-level training. Sir James Hall was a well-known scientist with a wide acquaintance among the French *philosophes*, and Lord Daer was a notorious radical who personally transported Thomas Paine and *The Rights of Man* to Britain in 1791. Young Douglas was able to mingle—and even argue informally—with the likes of Condorcet, Brissot de Warville, and du Chastellet. Paris provided him with several exemplary lessons, including the dangers of totally ignoring reform and the possibility of intellectuals also becoming men of action. Throughout

the early 1790s he continued to travel, mainly abroad, although he made an eye-opening tour of the highlands of Scotland in 1792. His brother Lord Daer became increasingly involved in radical political agitation and Scottish nationalism, and died in 1794 in Devon, just before repressive action was taken by the government.

With the death of Daer, followed over the next few years by the deaths of his other brothers, Douglas moved inexorably closer to the family title: he became Lord Daer himself in 1797 and the fifth earl of Selkirk in May 1799. That same year saw the publication of his first writing in political economy, an anonymous and untitled pamphlet describing the poor relief system of Galloway as lately reformed under his direction. Little is known of his movements between late 1799 and 1801. In Kirkcudbrightshire he worked to settle the sale of the family estate at Baldoon agreed between his father and Lord Galloway in 1793, which brought a substantial sum to the family coffers. Late in 1801, however, the Roman Catholic vicar-general of the highland district, John Chisholm, informed his superiors in Edinburgh that the earl of Selkirk wanted to discuss matters of importance with him, and in February 1802 Selkirk prepared the draft of a memorial to the British government proposing that he take charge of a plan for Irish Catholics to set up a colony in Louisiana. Selkirk's lifelong involvement with North American colonization had begun.

North American colonization The British government found the Louisiana proposal—and a revision proposing to relocate the scheme at the confluence of the waters which fell into Lake Winnipeg and the rivers which drained into Hudson Bay—unacceptable. Selkirk was prepared to change locations, and subsequently offered Upper Canada or Prince Edward Island as well, but was initially more stubborn about the source of his colonists. Lord Hobart, secretary of state for the colonies, suggested that Selkirk shift from Irish to Scottish families, and the earl eventually took up this idea with enthusiasm. Thus was he manoeuvred into the midst of the highland emigration crisis, which was becoming a major public issue in Scotland. Characteristically, he plunged into emigration mania with little thought for the implications of his actions. He was soon in the highlands, especially the Hebrides, actively recruiting settlers. When in late 1802 a number of books and pamphlets began to appear criticizing the highland operations of unscrupulous promoters of North America, Selkirk was a principal target. Matters became more complicated when his negotiations over land concessions with the British government broke down late in 1802, forcing him to buy land in Prince Edward Island on the open market. The passage of parliamentary legislation regulating the emigrant trade in the spring of 1803 was a godsend for Selkirk, for he was the only promoter whose project seemed likely to survive the stringent new laws. He acquired many new recruits as a result. Ultimately Selkirk sent more than 800 highlanders to Prince Edward Island aboard three ships in the spring of 1803, and, as promised, accompanied the party to the island. It proved his only successful colonization venture.

Selkirk spent a month on Prince Edward Island organizing his settlement, and then made a tour of the United States and Upper Canada. Here he still had plans of creating a personal estate, at Baldoon on the Chenail Écarte, near Windsor, which would, he envisaged, breed the finest possible sheep for North America. He left Baldoon in July 1804, just before the arrival of 102 settlers for the estate. They later experienced a malaria epidemic, and the settlement eventually succumbed to the disruptions of the Anglo-American War. After his return to Britain Selkirk began writing the manuscript that would become *Observations on the Present State of the Highlands of Scotland* (1805), his major contribution to political economy and the debate over emigration. In this work he emphasized the illogical self-interest of the various objections against highland emigration to North America, arguing that highlanders were entitled to move to preserve their language, culture, and manners. The hearty applause he received from the reviewers helped him in December 1806 to gain election to the House of Lords as a representative Scottish peer, loosely associated with the reform whigs. Once elected, he continued the family tradition of arguing for reform of the Scottish peerage, with a pamphlet, *A Letter to the Peers of Scotland*. He made a sufficient impact upon his contemporaries that the newly installed tory government offered to support him at the general election of 1807. Once re-elected, he shifted his energy to advocating reform of the militia, calling for the establishment of a citizen army under a system of universal military training. On 29 November 1807 he married Jean Wedderburn, the daughter of James Wedderburn (later Wedderburn-Colvile) of Inveresk, a distinguished Scottish lawyer.

In 1808 Selkirk became involved with the noted explorer Sir Alexander Mackenzie in purchasing stock in the Hudson's Bay Company, a process that continued through 1809, the year he published *A Letter Addressed to John Cartwright*, disavowing parliamentary reform for its encouragement of popular demagogues and the abuses of the American political system. He was now poised on the verge of the great project and adventure of his life: the establishment of a colony at Red River, the first European settlement in what is now western Canada. As with his previous scheme, Selkirk started by establishing a goal that many thought chimerical, surrounded that goal with well-conceived theoretical justifications, and then proceeded to improvise his way towards its realization. He assumed that his title, status, and connections would make it possible to work within the system and gain its support. This turned out not to be the case.

The Hudson's Bay Company was in serious difficulty by 1809, its shares of stock declining in value on the London market in the face of aggressive competition from its Montreal-based rivals. Selkirk and his merchant brother-in-law Andrew Wedderburn proposed drastic reforms in early 1810, calling initially for profit-sharing with the employees and an orderly inland expansion based upon newly recruited highlanders. A year later Selkirk unveiled his great scheme, by which he would accept a grant of land within the bounds of the company's territories in return for supplying the necessary recruits for expansion. Agents of the North West Company desperately, but unsuccessfully, opposed the grant at the stockholders' meeting and then turned to opposing the recruitment of highlanders in Scotland itself. Nevertheless, the first party, headed by Miles Macdonell, departed in July 1811.

Because of his place in the House of Lords (he was re-elected as a representative peer in 1812) and his position as lord lieutenant of Kirkcudbright (from 1807), Selkirk found it impossible during wartime to cross the Atlantic to lead his people personally, as he had planned. Instead, he sought to take advantage of the worsening military situation in North America for the benefit of both Red River and the British empire, and he proposed to the secretary of war that he should raise and lead a corps modelled on the Canadian fencible regiment. A stipulation added that the men should settle in Red River at the close of service, and their families should be transported there beforehand at government expense. The regiment received cabinet approval, but was eventually rejected by the commander-in-chief, the duke of York. During the months when its acceptance seemed likely, Selkirk had discussed the possibility of recruiting his regiment from among the tenants of the marquess of Stafford in Sutherland, whose lands were being cleared for sheep. Instead, he was forced to transport to Red River families recruited without his consent, on his own account.

The Sutherland settlers, sent to North America beginning in the summer of 1813, put additional pressures upon the limited food supply at the settlement. The potential for conflict between the settlers and the Montreal-based traders of the North West Company who dominated the western fur trade was always high, and was exacerbated by the decision of Selkirk's local governor, Miles Macdonell, to issue on 8 January 1814 a proclamation forbidding the export of provisions from the territory without licence. Open warfare resulted from the subsequent decision of the Hudson's Bay Company to establish a large trading presence in the rich Athabasca territory to compete directly with the Montreal traders. Selkirk was helpless to provide much assistance to his beleaguered settlement, and spent his spare time doing research on the fur trade of North America. This work resulted in the publication in 1816 of *A Sketch of the British Fur Trade in North America*, a systematic exposure of the abuse of the aboriginal peoples of the west by the North West Company, based chiefly on Hudson's Bay Company documents. Selkirk's health remained precarious, with increasing signs of consumption.

After the end of the wars in Europe and America, Selkirk and his family planned to visit America, and departed in September 1815. In the meantime, earlier in the year and unbeknown to Selkirk, the Nor'Westers (agents of the North West Company), with a mixture of threats and promises, convinced many of Selkirk's settlers to move to Upper Canada with the canoe brigades. In the wake of this disaster Miles Macdonell was replaced as governor by Robert Semple. In Montreal, Selkirk was unable to gain any military protection from the government for the Red

River settlement, and he decided to recruit a small mobile force of well-armed and well-disciplined men from among the disbanded De Meuron regiment of Swiss mercenaries. With a large party of these mercenaries, Selkirk started west for Fort William (the North West Company's headquarters on the western shore of Lake Superior) in July 1816. *En route*, he learned that Governor Semple and twenty-one settlers had been killed by a party of mixed-race men at Seven Oaks on 19 June 1816. The Selkirk party hastened to Fort William and captured it easily. Selkirk arrested the leading partners, who happened to be present for the annual company meeting, and shipped them east for trial. But he then proceeded to make one of the great blunders of his life: he purchased all the furs held in Fort William from one of the more vulnerable North West Company partners for a pittance, and thus exposed himself to charges of personal profiteering.

Despite the successful seizure of Fort William, the forces arrayed against Selkirk grew in confidence, particularly when the governments in Canada and in London agreed that none of the various parties to the fur trade war in the west was entitled to claim any moral advantage in the controversy. A considerable pamphlet war, in which Selkirk was worsted, erupted in Montreal, Toronto, and London in late 1816 and 1817. Selkirk's forces recaptured Red River early in 1817, while he wintered at Fort William. He finally arrived at his settlement in the spring of 1817. Meanwhile, the colonial secretary, Lord Bathurst, angrily ordered the governor of Lower Canada, Sir John Sherbrooke, to arrest Selkirk. Sherbrooke had already appointed an investigating commission headed by W. B. Coltman, which arrived at Red River on 1 July 1817. Coltman's approach was to regard all parties involved as equally culpable, a position that Selkirk abhorred, since he regarded his settlers as innocent victims of North West Company aggression. If Selkirk did not succeed in gaining the support of Coltman, whose published report did indeed blame everyone, he did manage to put his settlement back on its feet before heading south on horseback in September 1817. His decision to return east via the United States was prudent, given the hostility to him in many parts of Canada: he arrived back in York, Upper Canada, in January 1818.

Selkirk spent the next few months embroiled in legal complications in the Canadian courts, his health continually deteriorating through the ensuing period of turmoil. He had remained in remarkably good health during his time in the western outdoors, but this condition did not long survive his return to the east. He was unable to vindicate his position in the courts, and was not re-elected to the House of Lords in 1818 despite government support, ostensibly because of his prolonged absence in America. He returned to Britain late in 1818, and, despite increasing illness, spent long hours at his desk preparing a series of statements outlining his interpretation of events in North America and defending his conduct. Because of his death most of these explanations were not published at the time, and have appeared in print only a century and a half later. Some contemporary breakthrough did occur in his

favour when his brother-in-law Sir James Montgomery called successfully in the House of Commons in June 1819 for the tabling of the relevant Colonial Office documents of the Red River settlement. The papers were printed within weeks and made clear that the North West Company had indeed criminally conspired against Selkirk's settlement, as he had always claimed. On doctor's orders he headed for southern Europe in September 1819, and had reached as far as the town of Pau in the foothills of the Pyrenees when the languor of ill health forced him to stop. He died there on 8 April 1820, and was buried in the protestant cemetery at Orthez. Although his efforts to vindicate his name were largely unsuccessful in his lifetime, Selkirk has since become a mythical figure in the development of the Canadian west and a prophet of western agricultural settlement.   J. M. BUMSTED

Sources NA Canada, Selkirk collection · J. M. Bumsted, ed., *The Selkirk papers*, 2 vols. (1984–8) · *Papers relating to the Red River settlement* (1819) · J. M. Gray, *Lord Selkirk of Red River* (1963) · US Naval Academy, Annapolis, Maryland, USA, Selkirk MSS · J. Hall of Dunglass, journal, NL Scot. · J. M. Bumsted, *The people's clearance: highland emigration to British North America, 1770–1815* (1982) · Speculative Society minutes, U. Edin. L. · *Lord Selkirk's diary, 1803–04*, ed. P. C. T. White (1965) · C. Martin, *Lord Selkirk's work in Canada* (1916) · R. J. Adam, ed., *Papers on Sutherland estate management, 1802–1816*, 2 vols., Scottish History Society, 4th ser., 8–9 (1972) · *Scots peerage* · *Edinburgh Advertiser* (28 Nov 1807) · gravestone, Orthez protestant cemetery, France

Archives McCord Museum of Canadian History, Montreal, corresp. and papers · Minnesota Historical Society, St Paul, papers · NA Canada, corresp. and papers · NA Scot., MSS · NL Scot., MSS · US Naval Academy, Annapolis, Maryland | Hornel Library, Broughton House, Kirkcudbright, Daer MSS · McGill University, Montreal, McLennan Library, letters to Miles Macdonnell · NL Scot., letters to Alexander Marcet · Scottish Catholic Archives, Edinburgh, Blair letters · Scottish Catholic Archives, Edinburgh, Sir James Hall MSS · U. Edin. L., special collections division, corresp. with Alexander MacDonald

Likenesses portrait, c.1800, Glenbow Archives, Calgary, Alberta [*see illus.*] · Chantrey, bust, repro. in G. Bryce, *History of Manitoba* (1880)

Wealth at death many assets in the form of colony of Red River, which had no value at death but for which the Hudson's Bay Company paid £35,000 in 1835: correspondence in Selkirk MSS

Douglas, Sir Thomas Monteath (1788–1868), army officer in the East India Company, was born on 25 November 1788 at Hanover, Jamaica, the son of Thomas Monteath. He took the surname Douglas on 18 December 1850, on inheriting the estate of Douglas Support, which had been entailed to the descendants of his paternal grandmother by her sister Margaret, duchess of Douglas.

Monteath entered the East India Company's service as a cadet in 1805. He was appointed an ensign in the Bengal army on 4 December 1806, and was at once attached to the 35th Bengal infantry, with which he served throughout his long career. He was promoted lieutenant on 9 September 1808. He first saw service under Sir Gabriel Martindall in the campaigns in Bundelkhand in 1809 and 1810, during which Monteath was twice wounded. He next served throughout the Gurkha and Nepalese campaigns in 1814 and 1815 under generals Sir Jasper Nicolls and Sir David Ochterlony. He was present at the battles of the Timli Pass and of Kalanga, and at the assaults of Jountgarh and Srinagar, where he was again wounded. In the marquess of Hastings' campaign against the Pindaris in 1818, the 35th Bengal native infantry was attached to the brigade which was sent to Bikaner in the extreme east of Rajputana, in order to drive the Pindaris back into central India, where Lord Hastings was waiting for them. Douglas was next engaged in the Merwara campaign of 1820, and was promoted captain on 24 May 1821. In 1826 he was present at Viscount Combermere's successful siege of Bharatpur and took part in the assault. On 20 July 1826 Monteath married Mrs Lucinda Florence Whish, at Meerut. He and his wife had at least one daughter, before his wife died at Lucknow in 1837, at the age of thirty-nine.

Monteath was promoted major on 17 January 1829 and lieutenant-colonel on 2 April 1834, and commanded his regiment throughout the First Anglo-Afghan War of 1838–42. His regiment was one of those which, under Sir Claude Wade, forced the Khyber Pass and co-operated with Sir John Keane's army from Bombay in the storming of Ghazni and the capture of Kabul in 1838. For his services Monteath was made a CB on 20 December 1839 and selected by Shah Shuja as one of the officers to receive his newly formed Durani order. Monteath's regiment was one of those left to garrison Kabul, and remained there until October 1841, when it was ordered with the 13th light infantry to return to India under the command of Sir Robert Sale. Hardly had this brigade started when the Afghans resumed hostilities and Sale had to fight his way to Jalalabad, where he was besieged. In the defence of that city Monteath, who from his rank was second in command, greatly distinguished himself. On 16 April 1842 the garrison was relieved by General Sir George Pollock, and in the campaign which followed Monteath commanded a brigade. For his gallant conduct he was appointed an aide-de-camp to the queen on 4 October 1842. On 7 September 1845 he was appointed colonel of his old regiment, and on 10 March 1846 he was given command of the district of Ambala, with the rank of brigadier. Soon after he left India.

Douglas was promoted major-general on 20 June 1854, lieutenant-general on 18 March 1856, and general on 9 April 1865. On 28 March 1865 he was made a KCB for his long services during the early years of the century. He died at Stonebyres in Lanarkshire on 18 October 1868.

H. M. STEPHENS, rev. ALEX MAY

Sources Army List · Indian Army List · V. C. P. Hodson, List of officers of the Bengal army, 1758–1834, 2 (1928) · The Times (24 Oct 1868) · G. R. Gleig, Sale's brigade in Afghanistan: with an account of the seisure and defence of Jellalabad, 2nd edn (1861) · G. N. Molesworth, 'The defence of Jallalabad, 1841–43', Journal of the Society for Army Historical Research, 46 (1968), 146–53 · J. A. Norris, The First Afghan War, 1838–1842 (1967) · J. Pemble, The invasion of Nepal: John Company at war (1971) · M. Edwardes, Glorious sahibs: the romantic as empire-builder (1968) · J. G. Elliott, The frontier, 1839–1947 (1968) · T. A. Heathcote, The Afghan wars, 1839–1919 (1980) · H. T. Prinsip, History of the political and military transactions in India during the administration of the marquess of Hastings, 2 vols. (1825) · C. R. Low, The life and correspondence of Field-Marshal Sir George Pollock (1873) · P. Macrory, Signal catastrophe: the story of a disastrous retreat from Kabul, 1842 (1966)

Wealth at death £46,487 19s. 8d.: confirmation, 11 Dec 1868, NA Scot., SC36/48/60/676

Douglas, William (d. 1298). See under Douglas family (per. c.1170–c.1300).

Douglas, Sir William, lord of Liddesdale (c.1310–1353), soldier and magnate, was the eldest son of Sir James Douglas of Lothian, who was a young valet in 1306, and his wife, Joan. He had possession of his heritage in April 1323, when his father was dead, but seems not yet to have been of age; he was knighted between 1323 and 1330. In 1330 he was a warden of the marches, probably in succession to Sir James Douglas, his distant cousin, and this probably kept him in the south of Scotland when the 'disinherited' attacked in 1332. On 25 March 1333, in response to a Scottish incursion into Cumberland (though the two realms were nominally still at peace), Sir Anthony Lucy raided across the Solway, and on his return was attacked by the garrison of Lochmaben, including Douglas of Lothian, as he was known. The Scots were beaten and Douglas was carried off to two years' captivity in Carlisle Castle. When back in Scotland he engaged with Edward Balliol's supporters in Galloway, attended the guardian's parliament at Dairsie in April 1335, and later in the same year served with the guardian (John Randolph, earl of Moray) in fighting the count of Namur, come to help Edward III, driving him into Edinburgh and securing his promise to depart the Scottish war. As Namur's escort made its way to the border it was set upon; the guardian was taken and Douglas was lucky to escape.

Douglas joined the new guardian, Sir Andrew Murray, in refusing the submission which others made to Edward III, and together they cornered and killed David Strathbogie, titular earl of Atholl, a leading supporter of Edward Balliol, at Culblean in Aberdeenshire on 30 November 1335. For his actions in leading the van, the Lanercost chronicle claims that Douglas was given the earldom of Atholl; but it is more likely that he was only promised the earldom. While Edward III was at Perth, and his brother John was ravaging in the south-west in 1336, the latter was harassed by Douglas, who in 1337 was active with Murray in Fife and elsewhere. In 1338, during a truce granted by Edward III, Douglas visited the court of David II at Château Gaillard, whence he came with a hired pirate and five galleys to the Tay in 1339. Perth was blockaded, and Douglas bribed the constable of Cupar Castle to surrender it and join in the assault on Perth, which surrendered on 17 August 1339. In 1341 he took part in the ruse which led to the taking of Edinburgh Castle (bogus supplies were lodged in the entrance, so that the gates could not be closed), and by the return of David II in that year he was outstanding among the military commanders on the patriotic side. He had charters of lands in various parts from Robert the Steward and others, possibly as part of the arrangements to finance his war.

The king saw Douglas's value and heaped rewards upon him: the earldom of Atholl, lands in Peeblesshire, Eskdale, and Ewesdale, and a charter of the barony of Dalkeith. He is not known to have used the title of Atholl. In

February 1342 the Steward claimed Liddesdale, which Douglas opposed as guardian of William, the heir of Archibald Douglas (d. 1333). Archibald Douglas had in effect seized Liddesdale during wartime disturbance, and the council found for the Steward, to whom William Douglas promptly surrendered Atholl in return for Liddesdale. The whole transaction was clearly fixed to transfer Liddesdale to William's possession, and he is thereafter known as William Douglas of Liddesdale. But his ambitions now took him into more dangerous territory. Jealous of Sir Alexander Ramsay, who had won a high reputation in both war and tournament and was sheriff of Roxburgh, an office Douglas coveted, Douglas seized Ramsay while holding a sheriff court on 20 June 1342, and took him to Hermitage Castle in Liddesdale, where Ramsay died, in effect murdered. Douglas obtained a royal pardon, but the feud won him few friends.

In 1345 the truces with England came to an end, and when, in 1346, David II invaded England in support of the hard-pressed French king after Crécy, he and Douglas were taken prisoner at Nevilles Cross on 17 October 1346, fortunate not to be among the many dead. Douglas now languished in the Tower of London, but about 1348 became involved in the efforts of David II to secure liberty. By 1350 Edward III had once more conceded the title of king to David, and in November negotiations for the latter's release were under way at York. By the end of the year Douglas was in Scotland, evidently with a proposition that David II be ransomed for £40,000, that he be succeeded, if he died childless, by a younger son of Edward III, and also that the 'disinherited' be restored. Douglas was back in England with some kind of response by March 1351; negotiations were pushed ahead and Douglas was again allowed to go home. Eventually proposals were agreed at Newcastle, and David II returned to Scotland in November 1351 with Douglas to secure their acceptance. This they failed to do in a parliament held at Scone in February–March 1352, though in February 1352 Edward III had given leave to all the Scots in his allegiance to join Douglas in putting down any Scots who rebelled against David over acceptance of the Newcastle terms.

Once more in prison, Douglas clearly despaired of a general political settlement and of his own freedom; it is not known why his ransom was not negotiated, when that of, for example, the earl of Fife seemed to give little trouble. Instead he entered into an agreement on 17 July 1352, whereby he promised allegiance to Edward, service in war except against Scots, free passage through his lands at all times to invade Scotland, and hostages, and he received in return the assurance of his English-occupied lands as well as release. In August 1353 he was back in Scotland, his treason still unknown, when his cousin William, later first earl of Douglas, the boy who in effect had lost Liddesdale in 1342, killed him in Williamhope, Ettrick Forest. He was buried at Melrose Abbey, Roxburghshire.

According to Bower, Douglas was killed in revenge for the death of Ramsay; but Fordun's annals, Bower's source for the death, do not make that claim. Nor does Fordun have the verdict passed by Bower, that Douglas was 'an

energetic man when fighting, who endured much for the freedom of the kingdom, expert in war, faithful to his promises, a scourge of the English and a wall to the Scots' (Bower, 7.275). His career was also marred by cupidity for baronies and rents. He did not fear the risks of war, and showed considerable tactical skill in siege and battle, but the defeat of Nevilles Cross and consequent imprisonment seem to have altered his priorities and consigned him to the category of shameful Scot.

Douglas married an Elizabeth of unknown family before 1346. Their daughter, Mary, who was surrendered as a hostage in 1352, eventually returned to Scotland and married, but died without issue. In 1351 William had entailed his lands on the son of his deceased brother John, from whom the lords of Dalkeith and earls of Morton descended.   A. A. M. DUNCAN

Sources R. Nicholson, *Scotland: the later middle ages* (1974), vol. 2 of *The Edinburgh history of Scotland*, ed. G. Donaldson (1965–75) • A. A. M. Duncan, 'Honi soit qui mal y pense: David II and Edward III, 1346–52', *SHR*, 67 (1988), 113–41 • The 'Original chronicle' of Andrew of Wyntoun, ed. F. J. Amours, 6, STS, 1st ser., 57 (1908) • W. Bower, *Scotichronicon*, ed. D. E. R. Watt and others, new edn, 9 vols. (1987–98), vol. 7 • Johannis de Fordun Chronica gentis Scotorum / John of Fordun's Chronicle of the Scottish nation, ed. W. F. Skene, trans. F. J. H. Skene, 1 (1871) • Scots peerage, 6.339–42 • RotS, vol. 1

Douglas, William, first earl of Douglas and earl of Mar

(c.1330–1384), magnate, was the younger son of Archibald *Douglas (1294?–1333), guardian of Scotland in 1332–3, and Beatrice, daughter of Alexander Lindsay, lord of Crawford.

Securing an inheritance The deaths in the battle of Halidon Hill both of William's father and of his cousin, William, lord of Douglas, son of Sir James Douglas, made William and his elder brother, John, heirs to the Douglas estates. Their uncle Hugh succeeded to lands which had largely passed into English or Balliol allegiance but, a former ecclesiastic, he does not seem to have married, and may have designated his nephews as his heirs. The significance of William and John explains their dispatch to France for safety, probably in 1334, when David II also went into exile. For the next thirteen years William remained in France. In 1340 his brother John was in David II's household at Château Gaillard in Normandy and it is likely that William also reached adulthood in this Franco-Scottish environment. The death of John in France between 1340 and 1342 made William heir to the Douglas estates. Probably because of his youth, though, he stayed in France in 1341, when King David returned to Scotland.

While he was in France, William Douglas's rights were eroded by the impact of war on southern Scotland. Active leadership in the Douglas family's border lordships was provided not by Hugh, nicknamed the Dull, but by a distant, junior kinsman, Sir William *Douglas of Lothian. Douglas of Lothian recovered the local communities of the forest of Selkirk, Liddesdale, and upper Annandale from English allegiance and in the early 1340s was looking to secure his local leadership by obtaining formal rights in the lands of the senior Douglas line. He sought to achieve this through championing the rights of the young and exiled heir to the Douglas lands, who was also his godson. In 1337 the interests of the young Douglas heirs were represented by their mother, but by 1342 Douglas of Lothian was claiming to act as William's guardian. His aims in this role were predatory. In February 1342 his ward's claim to Liddesdale was rejected, and he subsequently secured the lordship for himself. On 26 May Douglas of Lothian engineered a charter of entail to the Douglas estates. In this Hugh the Dull resigned his rights to Douglasdale, Selkirk Forest, Lauderdale, and other estates, which were granted to his nephew William. The succession of the younger William to these lands was overshadowed by the insertion of Douglas of Lothian as his heir, an act followed by the grant of a number of estates by Hugh to this ambitious kinsman. Although he had become lord of Douglas, William remained in France. The threat to his survival now came not from England, but from his own guardian and heir. The rights of the absentee lord were usurped by his well-backed and aggressive relation.

The lessons of this situation were not wasted on William, lord of Douglas. He recognized the Scottish defeat at Nevilles Cross in 1346, in which Sir William Douglas, now lord of Liddesdale, was captured, as his own opportunity. In 1347 he returned to Scotland with the aim of recovering his southern lands from English allegiance. He regained his ancestral lordship of Douglas and was received into Edinburgh Castle by his uncle David Lindsay of Crawford. With the support of the Edinburgh burgesses he then moved south. He was welcomed by the men of Selkirk Forest and defeated a force of English garrison troops and men from Teviotdale, forcing some of the latter to return to Scottish allegiance. For the next decade Douglas's activities centred on local warfare against the English and their allies in the marches, leading campaigns in the Merse, Tweeddale, and Galloway. Such war leadership had a political purpose. The submission of the local landowners of these regions combined a return to Scottish allegiance with the acceptance of Douglas's own lordship. When, for example, Dungal MacDowell and the men of Galloway 'surrendered' to him at Cumnock in 1353, this may have marked the extension of Douglas's influence into the province where he held the lands of Buittle, the traditional seat of the lords of Galloway.

William's achievements in local warfare were complicated by the continued ambitions of his godfather, Sir William Douglas of Liddesdale. Although an English prisoner, Douglas of Liddesdale was allowed increasing liberty to return to Scotland, where he acted as David II's agent in discussions with the Scottish estates for the king's release on English terms. His appearances on William's council, attested by three charters, suggest he was also seeking to maintain influence in the marches. The tension this must have created between William, lord of Douglas, and Douglas of Liddesdale burst into open conflict in 1352. Initially with David II's backing, Douglas of Liddesdale worked against his kinsman with English help, using Liddesdale, Eskdale, and English-held Teviotdale as bases for his efforts. Despite this opposition, William retained his hold

on Scottish border communities and a charter of 1353 suggests that Douglas of Liddesdale may have been brought to recognize the former's lordship. In any event, William took advantage of any improvement in relations that resulted to have his rival ambushed and killed in Ettrick Forest in August 1353, ensuring there was no renewal of the conflict.

War and lordship William Douglas's success in border warfare and in dealing with Douglas of Liddesdale stemmed from the wide network of allies and adherents he had built up since 1347. With considerable long-term significance for Scotland, he provided a focus of lordship for men in the middle marches. While his hold on Teviotdale families, such as the Kerrs, Rutherfords, and Colvilles, remained insecure into the 1380s, he probably brought families based in the upland areas of the borders, such as the Glendinnings, Gledstones, and Pringles, firmly into Scottish allegiance; by 1355 he was also warden of the east march. Douglas acted as a principal leader for important Lothian families which had been active in resisting the English since 1334, winning support and a commitment to further warfare by grants of land in Lauderdale. The maintenance of this community's backing was crucial to his regional dominance. He arranged three successive marriages between his frequently widowed sister, Eleanor, and influential Lothian knights, and, as a base for his influence, constructed Tantallon Castle in his barony of North Berwick. His position in Lothian was aided by close relations with Patrick Dunbar, earl of March. The two magnates generally co-operated in war and politics and in a truce of 1356 Douglas specifically included Dunbar's lands in his protection. By 1356, though, Douglas was the senior partner. His status in the marches was confirmed by his leadership of Scottish resistance to Edward III's invasion of that year. In the aftermath of the attack Douglas rounded off this period of military success by capturing Hermitage Castle in Liddesdale.

David II had already recognized Douglas's importance. In 1354 he had confirmed Douglas in all the lands of his uncle Sir James and his father, including many granted previously to Douglas of Liddesdale. David also gave William powers to lead the men of upper Clydesdale, Roxburghshire, Selkirkshire, and Peeblesshire, acknowledging Douglas's military role. When the king was released by the English in 1357, his apparent benevolence went further: in early 1358 William was created earl of Douglas. Although the terms of this creation are unknown, it secured William's status. David also either confirmed or appointed Douglas as justiciar south of Forth, and may have consented to his marriage about 1357 to Margaret, sister and heir of Thomas, earl of Mar. However, this political honeymoon was short-lived. By 1363 David was successfully promoting royal authority, especially in Lothian, winning such men as William Ramsay and Douglas's own cousin Archibald Douglas, known as Archibald the Grim, to his service. At the same time the king displayed hostility towards the earl's allies. Douglas's associate Thomas Stewart, earl of Angus, died in royal custody in 1361 and in early 1363 David seized Mar's castle of Kildrummy. Douglas feared that the settlement between Mar and the king would end his hopes to succeed his brother-in-law, and this may have been one of the reasons for his joining Robert Stewart and Patrick, earl of March, in open rebellion in 1363, claiming to be acting to obtain 'wiser government'. While Stewart quickly came to terms, Douglas stayed in arms for several weeks before being defeated at Lanark.

Relations with the crown, 1363–1371 David's principal aim after the revolt was to detach Douglas from Stewart. He exacted no major retribution from Douglas, but appears to have associated him with attempts to deny Stewart's rights of succession to the throne. At the same time, though, David also supported rivals for Douglas's lands and influence in the south. These included two of William's kinsmen, Archibald the Grim and James Douglas of Dalkeith, the nephew and under form of law the coheir of Douglas of Liddesdale. William was made to relinquish several estates, among them Dalkeith and Buittle, to James and to accept Archibald as lord of Galloway and leading magnate in the west march. The succession of another royal protégé, George Dunbar, as earl of March in 1368 further isolated Douglas in the south. If the period of Anglo-Scottish truce since 1356 removed one threat to his lordship, the king seemed increasingly to represent another.

On the sudden death of David II in 1371 Earl William displayed his determination to prevent renewed royal pressure. In an assembly at Linlithgow Douglas challenged Robert Stewart's right to the throne. Later accounts suggest Douglas sought to become king himself, but his aims were clearly more limited. Though he may have threatened Robert with the revival of proposals made in the 1350s and 1360s to offer the throne to John of Gaunt, son of Edward III, his likeliest motive was a wish simply to demonstrate his own power, one which may have been directed as much against the Erskines, favourites of the late king, as against David II's successor. In the event, Douglas allowed himself to be bought off by Robert. He was restored to the justiciarship south of Forth, his son James *Douglas was married to the new king's daughter, and both Douglases received large sums in cash and annuities. Moreover, while they had ultimately backed away from open defiance of Robert II, in 1371 William had received support from many former adherents of King David, who now needed a new protector. Old allies, such as Douglas's cousins the Lindsays, and new ones, such as the earl of March, worked closely with him in the 1370s. Even the marriage of his daughter, Isabella, to David II's favourite Sir Malcolm *Drummond [see under Drummond family], which had probably occurred against Douglas's will during the 1360s, worked in his favour after 1371.

Further gains Drummond, the Lindsays, and his son's marriage made Douglas, who was a constant witness of royal charters, a member of the extended royal family and formed the basis for his alliance with John Stewart, earl of Carrick, the heir to the throne, and the only son of Robert II with interests in the south. Douglas's favoured position

helped him to achieve his ambitions, implicit in his marriage, with regard to the earldom of Mar. In July 1377, following the death of Earl Thomas, Douglas travelled north with the king and was made earl of Mar, issuing his first charter from Kildrummy Castle on 27 July. He had obtained Kildrummy from the widowed countess, Margaret Stewart (b. 1353x62, d. in or before 1418), who received in return a 200 merk annuity for her terce and the right to reside in Tantallon. This arrangement had a personal side. Margaret became William's mistress and probably about 1380 gave birth to his son George *Douglas, the future earl of Angus. This relationship also brought William the support of Margaret's own connection. She was the daughter and heir of Douglas's former associate Thomas, earl of Angus, and would prove to be a determined defender of her inheritance and an influential figure in Haddingtonshire.

Despite his new northern earldom, Earl William's interests continued to focus on the marches. In the 1370s he participated in escalating warfare in the region led by him, his fellow wardens, and lesser men, many of whom were his adherents. In 1380 he was leader of a raid which destroyed Penrith, and before this the renewal of warfare with the English march warden, Henry Percy, earl of Northumberland, over Jedforest resulted in efforts by their respective governments to control their conflict. However, in spite of the active role in border diplomacy played by John Stewart, earl of Carrick, as 'lieutenant on the marches', by the early 1380s Douglas was taking a more aggressive line. This attitude was probably forced by the desire of his southern associates for warfare. Earl William, in particular, was looking beyond Scotland for allies in any conflict and, when the period of formal truce ended in early 1384, he immediately led an attack on Teviotdale which secured the lasting adherence to the Scottish crown of many local landowners. Appropriately, this proved to be the earl's last public act. Before 24 April he had died at Douglas Castle, Lanarkshire, of a fever contracted during the campaign.

A national and international figure Douglas was not simply a Scottish magnate. The effect of his formative years in France was to give him European interests. In 1356, once he was established in Scotland, he took a retinue of forty knights through England to France, with the aim of travelling as pilgrims, perhaps to Spain. Instead he joined the French army, which met defeat at the battle of Poitiers. Douglas was knighted by Jean II of France before the fight and consulted for his military experience, but escaped the field only through the efforts of his household. He also held lands in France, at St Saëns in Normandy, and retained his continental connections throughout his life. He had co-operated with French troops in Scotland in 1355, and in 1378 one of his servants, Andrew Mercer, led a combined Scottish, French, and Castilian fleet in attacks on English shipping, his efforts possibly reflecting an alliance entered by his master (at a time when effective royal leadership was lacking) with kingdoms involved in war with England. As the actions of Douglas's successors would show, such a continental perspective was not beyond the capacity of the Douglas family, and may have prepared the way for the Franco-Scottish campaign of 1385. Earl William certainly impressed foreign contemporaries. The chronicler Jean Froissart clearly retained a good impression of the Douglas castle of Dalkeith, which he visited in 1365, and spoke favourably of both William and his son James.

Earl William was also aware of his image within Scotland. To enhance his own status during the 1340s and 1350s he consciously appealed to the heroic reputation of his uncle Sir James Douglas. He adopted the red heart in his coat of arms as a reminder of James's expedition to Spain in 1330, carrying Robert I's heart against the Moors. He himself may have intended to repeat his uncle's journey when he crossed to France in 1356 and, despite periods of friction, established close relations with Melrose Abbey, where King Robert's heart was buried on its return to Scotland. These attempts to glory in his predecessor's achievements owed much to William's own difficulties, in particular with Sir William Douglas of Liddesdale. In his leadership and in this image building William sought first to supplant his rival and then to heal the rifts within the Douglas family caused by Douglas of Liddesdale's murder. In 1360 he went so far as to endow masses for his guardian at Melrose Abbey. On his own death in 1384 Melrose was chosen as the site of his tomb. The site symbolized his successful creation of his family's dominance in the central borders and of a dynastic image which his successors exploited to great effect in extending their lordship.   M. H. BROWN

Sources W. Fraser, ed., *The Douglas book*, 4 vols. (1885) · W. Bower, *Scotichronicon*, ed. D. E. R. Watt and others, new edn, 9 vols. (1987–98), vol. 7 · *The 'Original chronicle' of Andrew of Wyntoun*, ed. F. J. Amours, 2, STS, 1st ser., 50 (1903) · J. M. Thomson and others, eds., *Registrum magni sigilli regum Scotorum / The register of the great seal of Scotland*, 11 vols. (1882–1914) · J. Froissart, *Chronicles of England, France, Spain, and the adjoining countries*, trans. T. Johnes, 2 vols. (1868) · S. I. Boardman, *The early Stewart kings: Robert II and Robert III, 1371–1406* (1996) · A. Goodman, 'A letter from an earl of Douglas to a king of Castile', *SHR*, 64 (1985), 66–78 · F. Michel, *Les écossais en France, les français en Écosse*, 2 vols. (1862) · A. Macdonald, 'Crossing the border: a study of the Scottish military offensives against England, *c*.1369–*c*.1403', PhD diss., U. Aberdeen, 1995 · M. H. Brown, 'The development of Scottish border lordship, 1332–58', *Historical Research*, 70 (1997), 1–22 · *Scots peerage*, vol. 3

Douglas, Sir William, lord of Nithsdale (*c*.1360–1391), soldier, was the illegitimate son of Archibald *Douglas, third earl of Douglas (called Archibald the Grim; *c*.1320–1400), and an unknown mother. He was presumably prominent as a warrior by September 1384, when, already a knight, he was awarded a royal annuity of a type used to maintain participants in border conflict with England. Scottish chronicle accounts relate some of his early military exploits. They are not possible to date accurately, but probably refer to the Anglo-Scottish warfare of 1384 and 1385, and suggest that Douglas was particularly active in the fighting on the western marches. The details of his triumphs as recorded in the chronicles cannot, however, be relied upon: he is depicted as a conventional chivalric hero with all the requisite attendant qualities. Among these is a comely and statuesque physical appearance, a detail which gives no accurate guidance as to how Sir William looked. The accumulation of enthusiastic chronicle tales regarding his military activities do, none the less, point to his being an effective border warrior. At a time when attacking England was an important plank of royal policy, such prowess had its rewards. His chivalric reputation helped him to secure marriage to Egidia, a daughter of *Robert II and allegedly an internationally renowned beauty, by 26 December 1387. On that date Douglas and his new wife were granted the substantial annuity of £300 from the royal customs. By then, too, he had been granted the royal lordship of Nithsdale, which probably brought him little in the way of land, but conferred substantial jurisdictional authority—rights as warden, sheriff, justiciar, and chamberlain—within the area between Galloway and Annandale. This area was also, of course, a handy base from which to launch attacks on Cumbria or oppose English incursions into south-west Scotland.

When Anglo-Scottish war recommenced in 1388, Douglas was again heavily embroiled in the fighting. In June of that year he led a seaborne expedition to Ulster which defeated the local defensive forces, sacked the town of Carlingford, and then raided the Isle of Man before returning to Galloway. The exercise was hugely successful for Douglas and his colleagues. On one level the plundering provided the opportunity for personal profit: the chronicler Walter Bower claims the raiders were greatly enriched by their journey across the Irish Sea. On another level the naval venture was part of a carefully organized and fruitful national offensive in 1388 which involved simultaneous invasions of the western and eastern marches of England, culminating in victory for the Scottish eastern force at the battle of Otterburn. One repercussion of this battle was to propel Douglas into an even more prominent position among the aristocracy of Scotland. The second earl of Douglas died at Otterburn, and Archibald the Grim inherited the title and lands of the earldom. Douglas of Nithsdale was now the son of indisputably the most powerful magnate in southern Scotland.

Scotland's war effort, as fighting with England continued into 1389, was led by the third earl of Douglas and his political ally Robert Stewart, earl of Fife and Menteith and guardian of Scotland in the name of Robert II. In these circumstances it seems likely that Douglas of Nithsdale continued to fight on the marches, yet no details of his participation are known. We know, however, that a personal animosity rose at about this time between Douglas and Thomas, Lord Clifford. This may well have been connected to grants made by Edward I in 1298 and Edward Balliol in 1333, giving lands belonging to the Douglases to members of the Clifford family. Whether fundamentally territorial or not, the dispute was serious enough for Douglas to seek and receive English safe conducts in June 1390 for a judicial combat to be fought with Clifford. It is thought that the proposed duel was never fought, but Douglas went to France to buy armour for it and while he was there exchanged insults with Clifford, who accused him of cowardice.

The hostility between the two men was ultimately to have fatal consequences for Douglas when he was on crusade in the Baltic in 1391. He was in Bruges in December 1390, accompanied by other Scottish knights who had been his companions in the recent Anglo-Scottish conflict, and they were intending to be in Danzig by Easter 1391. Douglas probably took part in the summer *Reise* of the Teutonic knights, although Scottish chronicle accounts of his prominence in the fighting and of his status among the assembled chivalry cannot be relied upon. In any case it is entirely fitting that a figure whose career was founded on martial activity should have taken the well-worn path to the northern crusades when opportunities for fighting had dried up at home. Indeed, a fifteenth-century chronicler suggests that Douglas was a frequent crusader in the Baltic. The crusade of 1391 was to be his last. Some time between June and August of that year, according to the most reliable account, the Westminster chronicle, he and his party attempted to attend mass in Königsberg, but were turned away on the grounds of their adherence to Clement VII, the Avignon pope. Douglas blamed a group of English crusading knights for this rebuff. While the group was certainly associated with Clifford, he himself may not have been present. The Scots allegedly ambushed their English adversaries outside the church, and in the ensuing struggle Douglas was killed. The communal aristocratic ethos of the crusade had clearly been unable on this occasion to overcome personal and national animosities. Nor were the Scots and English alone in this, for other crusaders are recorded as involving themselves in the dispute. All were apparently supportive of the English cause, save only the French contingent.

ALASTAIR J. MACDONALD

Sources W. Bower, *Scotichronicon*, ed. D. E. R. Watt and others, new edn, 9 vols. (1987–98), vol. 8 · J. M. Thomson and others, eds., *Registrum magni sigilli regum Scotorum / The register of the great seal of Scotland*, 11 vols. (1882–1914); facs. repr. (1984), vol. 1 · D. Ditchburn, 'Merchants, pedlars and pirates: a history of Scotland's relations with northern Germany and the Baltic in the later middle ages', PhD diss., U. Edin., 1988 · S. I. Boardman, *The early Stewart kings: Robert II and Robert III, 1371–1406* (1996) · L. C. Hector and B. F. Harvey, eds. and trans., *The Westminster chronicle, 1381–1394*, OMT (1982), 475–7 · G. Burnett and others, eds., *The exchequer rolls of Scotland*, 3 (1880) · *RotS*, vol. 2 · F. J. H. Skene, *Liber pluscardensis*, 2 vols. (1877–80) · Crown Office writs, NA Scot., AD1 · F. R. H. Du Boulay, 'Henry of Derby's expeditions to Prussia, 1390–1 and 1392', *The reign of Richard II: essays in honour of May McKisack*, ed. F. R. H. Du Boulay and C. M. Barron (1971), 153–72 · *Scots peerage*, 3.164

Douglas, William, second earl of Angus (c.1398–1437), magnate, was the only son of George *Douglas, first earl of Angus, lord of Liddesdale and Jedburgh (1378x80?–1403?), and of Mary Stewart (d. in or after 1458), daughter of Robert III. He succeeded his father between 1402 and 1404. His interests were safeguarded by his grandmother, Margaret Stewart, countess of Angus, and her half-brother, Sir William Sinclair of Herdmanston. Although they secured Angus's rights to the earldom and to the lordships of Abernethy and Bunkle, his claims to the share of the Douglas estates held by his father were opposed. Liddesdale and Jedburgh were eventually obtained, but other lesser estates to which he had a claim were granted to rival kinsmen by Archibald, fourth earl of Douglas (d. 1424). The dominance of the Black Douglas earl limited Angus's influence in southern Scotland. His marriage about 1415 to Margaret, daughter of William Hay of Yester, represented an attempt to strengthen his following in the south-east, and may also, since Hay was a very prominent retainer of the earl of Douglas, have been intended to promote a reconciliation between the two earls. But the potential rapprochement came to nothing, and from 1420 Angus was a rival to his Douglas cousins.

The turning point of Angus's career occurred in 1424 with the return of his uncle, James I, who included him in the group of nobles whom he knighted at his coronation in May that year. Angus was to be one of the king's closest allies among the nobility and the marriage of his sister Elizabeth to Alexander Forbes (d. 1448), a trusted royal councillor, reinforced his links with the royal circle. He backed the king's attacks on the house of Albany in 1425 and the lord of the Isles in 1429, and his castle of Tantallon, Haddingtonshire, was used as a gaol for two royal captives, the duchess of Albany and Alexander MacDonald of the Isles. The rewards of this service came in the south. Angus's efforts to replace the fourth earl of Douglas as the principal magnate in the region after the latter's death in 1424 were aided by the king, who secured Angus's appointment as protector of Coldingham Priory in 1428 and made him warden of the east and middle marches. This promotion brought him into conflict with George Dunbar, earl of March (d. 1456). Friction between Angus and March, combined with Anglo-Scottish tension, persuaded James I to intervene. In 1434 Angus seized March's castle at Dunbar and became the king's lieutenant on the border; he defeated an English attempt to aid the Dunbars at Piperdean, near Cockburnspath, in 1435. The bond between Angus and James I was evident in the crisis which followed the king's murder on 21 February 1437. Angus's capture of the earl of Atholl was the crucial victory of the king's adherents. The death of Angus himself, in October 1437, deprived the queen mother of the earl's support when she and his sons, James *Douglas (who became third earl of Angus) and George, were eclipsed by the Black Douglases.

M. H. BROWN

Sources M. Brown, *James I* (1994) · M. G. Kelley, 'The Douglas earls of Angus: a study in the social and political bases of power in a Scottish family from 1389 to 1557', PhD diss., U. Edin., 1973 · W. Fraser, ed., *The Douglas book*, 4 vols. (1885), vols. 2–3 · C. McGladdery, *James II* (1990) · C. C. H. Harvey and L. MacLeod, eds., *Calendar of writs preserved at Yester House, 1166–1625*, Scottish RS, 55 (1930), 42–3

Douglas, William, sixth earl of Douglas, and third duke of Touraine in the French nobility (1422/3–1440), magnate, was the elder son of Archibald *Douglas, fifth earl of Douglas (c.1391–1439), and Euphemia Graham (d. 1468/9), sister of Malise Graham, earl of Menteith (d. 1490). Although he survived only into his eighteenth year, his career marked a crisis in the history of the Black Douglas family. His earliest appearance was in 1430 when he was knighted, along with other nobles 'of tender years', by James I at the baptism of the king's twin sons. Despite his youth, he may have assumed a political role during the lieutenancy of his father for the young James II between 1437 and 1439. His younger brother, David, acted as an auditor in this period, and William's marriage to Jean Lindsay (d. 1482x4), daughter of David Lindsay, third earl of Crawford (d. 1446), about 1437 forged an alliance with another major magnate house.

When Douglas succeeded his father in June 1439 he was still a minor. His tenure of the earldom of Douglas would last just seventeen months and was overshadowed by its violent end. Contemporary accounts are uninformative, but later accounts provide circumstantial details of the so-called Black Dinner, the feast in Edinburgh Castle on 24 November 1440 to which the young earl and his even younger brother were lured. The placing of a bull's head on the table by Sir William Crichton was the signal for their being seized, given the barest formality of a trial, and beheaded. The background to this act is uncertain. The near contemporary Auchinleck chronicle restricts itself to the bald facts, while later chroniclers indulge in sermons on the pride of youth. It is clear, though, that Douglas fell victim to the instability of minority politics. The men held responsible for his death were the chancellor, Sir William Crichton, and Sir Alexander Livingston, the custodian of the king. The power of these men was based on the accumulation of royal offices, and Douglas may have appeared to threaten this by reclaiming the lieutenancy of his father on the basis of his descent from Robert III. He was certainly beginning to exercise his rights as the greatest magnate in the kingdom, but this threatened the power of his great-uncle James *Douglas of Balvenie, earl of Douglas and of Avondale, rather than that of Livingston and Crichton.

Avondale was the senior kinsman of the sixth earl and had been a major figure in royal and Black Douglas circles for decades. Following the fifth earl's death it would have been Avondale who stepped in to act as tutor, or guardian, for William. In September 1439, when William's signet was appended to the agreement between the queen mother and Livingston, Avondale represented the family on the council. The prospect of relinquishing his power to William would not have been welcome, especially as there may have been tension between the two. This is suggested by the appearance of Malcolm Fleming of Biggar (who was arrested with William and executed a day later) as William's 'speciall counsellor' in November 1440. Avondale had killed Fleming's father in 1406 and was a local rival of the family in Lanarkshire. William's association with Fleming may have been a further reason why Avondale encouraged or accepted the attack on the earl, to which, as justiciar south of Forth, Avondale could have given an appearance of legality.

The involvement of Avondale and Crichton in the Black Dinner indicates flaws in the Black Douglas support by 1440. Both men had strong and well-established ties to the family, but both were prepared to see the young earl executed in pursuit of their interests. These interests were not just those of minor baronial families. Service to James I and the Douglases had allowed Crichton and Avondale to exercise power on a large scale, and in 1440 they were not prepared to withdraw into the following of a magnate lieutenant. William Douglas's death was part of the changing structure of the Scottish nobility. Avondale was certainly the main beneficiary of his kinsman's death, inheriting the earldom and the bulk of the Douglas lands. William's grandmother Margaret Stewart and sister, Margaret, retained the rights to Galloway and Bothwell, and Annandale, where Crichton had his own interests, was annexed to the crown. While the new earls of Douglas—Avondale and his sons—dominated Scottish politics after 1440, the Black Dinner left a powerful legacy of mistrust which affected their affairs and support.

M. H. BROWN

Sources W. Fraser, ed., *The Douglas book*, 4 vols. (1885), vols. 1, 3 · C. McGladdery, *James II* (1990) · A. I. Dunlop, *The life and times of James Kennedy, bishop of St Andrews*, St Andrews University Publications, 46 (1950) · W. Bower, *Scotichronicon*, ed. D. E. R. Watt and others, new edn, 9 vols. (1987–98) · *Scots peerage*, 3.172

Douglas, William, eighth earl of Douglas and second earl of Avondale (1424/5–1452), magnate, was the eldest son of James *Douglas, seventh earl of Douglas and first earl of Avondale, known as the Gross, and Beatrix Sinclair, daughter of Henry, earl of Orkney. An adult when he succeeded his father in 1443, William must have been born within a year of his parents' marriage in early 1424. He is first recorded at the baptismal celebrations for the twin sons of King James I on 16 October 1430 at Holyrood Abbey. As a mark of favour to William's father, a trusted royal councillor, the young William was knighted by the king alongside the two princes and a number of other noble children, including his cousin and namesake, the future sixth earl of Douglas.

Inheritance and marriage It was the violent death of this other William Douglas at the so-called 'Black Dinner' on 24 November 1440 which led to the succession of James Douglas to the earldom of Douglas and to the bulk of the family lands which passed by entail to the heirs male. William was heir to the greatest magnate inheritance in Scotland but his father sought to add to his fortune by arranging the marriage of his son and Margaret Douglas, the Fair Maid of Galloway (c.1426–c.1476). Margaret was the sister of the sixth earl and heir to the lordship of Galloway. The match between these cousins was intended to reunite the Black Douglas estates, but Earl James's attempts to achieve it antagonized many other councillors of the young King James II. The earl's leading enemies were the chancellor, William, Lord Crichton, and his family, but there were many other Scottish magnates who were reluctant to see the power of the Black Douglases reconstituted and, when Earl James died in March 1443, his son was still unmarried.

William Douglas succeeded his father in extensive lands, titles, and offices, and also in his readiness to dispense with legalities. Along with the earldom of Douglas, William also inherited his father's lands in Clydesdale and Lothian which had been united to form the earldom of Avondale in 1437. The lord of castles like Abercorn, Bothwell, Douglas, and Newark in Ettrick Forest, Earl William was the greatest magnate in southern Scotland and assumed his father's offices of justiciar, sheriff of Lanark, and warden in the west and middle marches towards England. The new earl may well have spent the spring and summer of 1443 securing this southern inheritance and building new alliances with those on the royal council and especially the Livingston family, which had custody of the young king. With the backing of these allies Douglas sought to defeat those who remained opposed to his marriage and the other interests of his house.

On 22 August 1443 Douglas led a large army against the lands of the Crichtons where they bordered his own in Linlithgowshire. The earl presented his attack as more than a private feud. The young king was in his force and Douglas flew the royal banner, demanding that his opponents surrender to the crown. Control of the king was further exploited in the aftermath of military victory. In November the Crichtons were summoned to parliament to answer for their resistance and, on their failure to appear, were stripped of their offices. Although he had not finally defeated the Crichtons, during late 1443 Douglas had successfully allied physical force and legal justification to achieve private goals. It was an approach to politics which would characterize the rest of his career. Earl William's ascendancy was evident in 1444. He abandoned his father's support of the conciliar movement in the church, and thereby removed the last obstacle to his marriage, receiving a papal dispensation (dated 24 July) for a match which reunited Galloway with the rest of the Douglas lands. Elsewhere, too, Earl William secured his family's interests where his father had failed, imposing his will in local disputes in Lothian and Berwickshire.

Extensions of power These actions demonstrated Douglas's predominance in southern Scotland but by the end of the year the earl was looking to extend his family's influence in the north of the kingdom. In alliance with a group which included David Lindsay, earl of Crawford, and the Livingstons, Douglas participated in a series of attacks on their enemies, a group headed by Queen Joan, Bishop Kennedy of St Andrews, and Crichton. This sporadic conflict lasted from late 1444 until the following summer and ended with the eclipse of Crichton and the death of Queen Joan while under siege in Dunbar Castle. Even before victory had been secured Douglas and his allies held a parliament to secure their gains. Two of Douglas's brothers, Archibald and Hugh, were created earls of Moray and Ormond. These new Douglas earldoms lay in the north, and to ensure his brothers' ability to enjoy their estates, Douglas sought friends in the north. Initially these included Alexander Gordon, earl of Huntly. However, Huntly soon clashed with Douglas's other northern ally, the earl of Crawford, and it may have been in March 1446 that Douglas entered into a band, or private alliance, with Crawford and Alexander, earl of Ross and lord of the Isles. Designed to secure Douglas lands in the north, this agreement would ultimately prove fatal to Earl William.

However, in the later 1440s the position of Douglas and his brothers seemed secure. Control of king and council was largely left to the Livingstons, while Douglas sought

to increase his status further. During 1447 Earl William secured direct control of the lordship of Galloway. His wife's grandmother, Margaret Stewart, the widow of the fourth earl of Douglas, had been given custody of Galloway for life but Douglas forced her to spend her last years in the priory of Lincluden near Dumfries, and took possession (illegally) of her principal castle of Threave. In the late 1440s Douglas also followed the example of his forebears in attitudes to European politics. The ascendancy of Douglas over the king's council from late 1444 coincided with the adoption of a closer relationship with Charles VII of France. Three sisters of James II (and of the dauphin's wife, Margaret) were sent to the continent to become pawns in French diplomatic ventures, and in 1448 the alliance with France was formally renewed. During the negotiations with France, Douglas put forward a claim to a share of the duchy of Touraine on behalf of the recently dispossessed Margaret Stewart. His claim was politely denied, but Douglas still sought fame abroad. In the border war with England which broke out in 1448 Douglas and his brothers took a leading role, defending the Scottish marches and raiding into northern England.

Such echoing of traditional Douglas roles had a serious domestic purpose. For all Earl William's political successes since 1443, his lordship rested on shallower roots than that of his predecessors. The Black Dinner had brought his family to power but had weakened the cohesion of the traditional Douglas following. The murder of James Auchinleck by Richard Colville in 1449, which Earl William punished, was the killing of one Douglas adherent by another. When, during 1448, the earl reissued a code of march law established by his predecessors, he was not just reorganizing border defence. He was also emphasizing the link between his lordship in the marches and that of earlier Douglas magnates. Earl William had other problems. In 1447 his brother James *Douglas was designated as his heir and was consistently referred to as master of Douglas. An exceptional instance of such a title being held by a magnate's brother, this may in part have reflected problems in the earl's marriage, which had produced no offspring in nearly a decade. Without children from this match the earl's hold on Galloway remained uncertain, which in turn emphasized his difficulties with local men who resented his treatment of Margaret Stewart.

Conflict with the crown By 1449 Earl William had established his branch of the Douglas family at the head of Scottish political society. However, flaws remained in this strength and, with hindsight, the emergence of James II as an active force with his destruction of his Livingston keepers in September 1449 heralded a new political atmosphere. There was no obvious sign of impending conflict between crown and Douglases, nor of personal animus between the two young men at the head of Scottish politics. Earl William had aided and benefited from the fall of the Livingstons. In January 1450 he received royal charters confirming his hold on Galloway and Ettrick Forest, and he joined a number of major magnates in giving loans to the king. Like others, Douglas was seeking to secure his position with the king while maintaining his family's gains since 1437. The only indication of the earl's anxiety was his decision to leave Scotland on a pilgrimage to Rome in October 1450. Yet his journey had other purposes. Douglas travelled with an impressive entourage via the courts of Burgundy, France, and England. As well as winning papal blessings, William may have been offering his services at a moment of crisis in the Anglo-French conflict.

However, in his absence the king launched an assault on the estates of the pilgrim. In December 1450 James II travelled to Melrose, in the middle of Douglas's border lordships, and called together the earl's local enemies. Early the next year the king went south-west to Annandale and Galloway, this time using force to obtain the submission of the earl's tenants. His aim was not the destruction of Douglas power but the establishment of control over lands to which Douglas's rights were dubious. James II was able to win over a significant number of the earl's allies and may have expected Douglas to accept his losses. When Earl William returned to Scotland in April 1451, though, it was to resist not submit. He secured English support and may have been acclaimed lieutenant by his followers to justify his opposition to the king. During May and early June Douglas clearly forced the king to recognize his failure. In a parliament in late June Douglas resigned his lands to receive a fresh grant and a remission for his actions. Only the lands of Wigtown and of Stewarton in Ayrshire were withheld by James. In October these too were restored to the earl.

Violent death Douglas's ability to withstand royal attack was testament to his power. It was also a product of the king's wider problems. During late 1451 royal actions had driven two of the major northern magnates, the earls of Crawford and Ross, to take up arms. In this crisis, the king turned to Douglas and his brothers, Moray, Ormond, and John, lord of Balvenie, to provide support in the north. At a series of meetings during the winter of 1451–2, the king sought Douglas's aid in an increasingly tense atmosphere. By late February Douglas would only attend the king's council at Stirling with a written safe conduct. When the two men met in Stirling Castle on 22 February 1452 Douglas once again refused to take action which would break his band with Ross and Crawford. In response the king replied that if Douglas would not break the band he would, and stabbed William in the neck. The wounded earl was then killed by others at the council, among them his own former adherents.

Earl William's killing precipitated a conflict which the king was fortunate to survive. Ultimately he failed for a second time to defeat the Douglases and was forced to recognize William's brother James Douglas as heir to all the dead earl's lands and as the husband of his widow. Subsequently the death of Douglas became recognized as a defining moment in crown–magnate relations in fifteenth-century Scotland. To sixteenth-century historians like Hector Boece and Robert Lindsay of Pitscottie, Douglas epitomized the overmighty subject, arrogant, lawless, and heedless of royal justice. Stories of the earl's tyrannous treatment of his own vassals justified the

king's killing of a protected guest, but may also derive from Douglas's own difficulties in maintaining the support of his own followers after the disruption of his family's lordship between 1424 and 1449. In his short career, Douglas represented the power, ambition, and independence of the greatest Scottish magnate dynasty at its fullest extent.   M. H. BROWN

Sources W. Fraser, ed., *The Douglas book*, 4 vols. (1885) · M. Brown, *The Black Douglases: war and lordship in late medieval Scotland, 1300–1455* (1998) · C. McGladdery, *James II* (1990) · A. I. Dunlop, *The life and times of James Kennedy, bishop of St Andrews*, St Andrews University Publications, 46 (1950) · A. I. Dunlop, ed., *Calendar of Scottish supplications to Rome*, 4: *1433–1447*, ed. D. MacLauchlan (1983) · J. M. Thomson and others, eds., *Registrum magni sigilli regum Scotorum / The register of the great seal of Scotland*, 11 vols. (1882–1914), vols. 1–2 · M. G. Kelley, 'The Douglas earls of Angus: a study in the social and political bases of power in a Scottish family from 1389 to 1557', PhD diss., U. Edin., 1973

Douglas, William, ninth earl of Angus (1532/3–1591), magnate, was the son of Archibald Douglas of Glenbervie and Agnes Keith, daughter of William, second Earl Marischal. In 1552 he married Egidia, daughter of Robert Graham of Morphie; they had thirteen children—nine sons and four daughters. His paternal grandfather having been a son of Archibald, fifth earl of Angus, William Douglas succeeded to the earldom under an entail on 25 December 1588 following the death of Archibald, the eighth earl, on 4 August, after his right had been contested in the court of session by James VI. The king claimed the title through his grandmother Margaret, countess of Lennox, a daughter of Archibald, the sixth earl, whereas Douglas of Glenbervie based his claim on Archibald's will, drafted in 1547, and on Countess Margaret's renunciation of her claims in 1565. Although Douglas was awarded the title, under pressure from the king he had to pay James 35,000 merks and also relinquish his lands at Braidwood to the crown. James immediately conferred Braidwood on his chancellor, John Maitland of Thirlestane, who (perhaps significantly) was a prominent member of the court which had decided in the new earl's favour.

Shortly before he succeeded to the earldom, Douglas had begun to be actively involved in national affairs. In 1585, in association with Maitland, he presented a petition to the king seeking to revive the system whereby lairds attended parliament and took part in its business. In 1589 he took part in the suppression of the rising by the sixth earl of Huntly and his fellow 'northern earls', serving as chairman of the jury at the trial of the earl of Bothwell, a leading insurgent. Shortly afterwards he was a member of the body responsible for the government of Scotland while the king was in Scandinavia for his marriage to Anne of Denmark, and on 7 May 1590 he carried the sword at the new queen's coronation. But overall his career was uneventful, and he has been justly described as 'one of the most pacific of all the earls' (Lee, 222). Angus died on 1 July 1591, in his fifty-ninth year, at Glenbervie, where he was also buried. His widow was still living in 1606. His eldest son, William *Douglas, succeeded as tenth earl.

G. R. HEWITT

Sources W. Fraser, ed., *The Douglas book*, 4 vols. (1885), vol. 2 • D. Hume of Godscroft, *The history of the house and race of Douglas and Angus*, 2 (1743) • *Scots peerage*, 1.197–9 • *Reg. PCS*, 1st ser., vols. 2–3 • *CSP Scot.*, 1571–81 • D. Calderwood, *The history of the Kirk of Scotland*, ed. T. Thomson and D. Laing, 8 vols., Wodrow Society, 7 (1842–9), vol. 3 • M. Lee, *John Maitland of Thirlestane* (1959) • GEC, *Peerage*, 1, 157–9

Douglas, William, sixth earl of Morton (*c*.1540–1606), magnate, was the son of Sir Robert Douglas of Lochleven (killed at the battle of Pinkie in 1547) and Lady Margaret *Erskine [*see under* James V, mistresses and children of], daughter of John, fifth Lord Erskine. His parents, who were married in 1527, had two other sons, Robert (earl of Buchan in right of his wife, Christian Stewart) and George, and three daughters, Euphemia, Janet, and Katherine. In 1531 Margaret Erskine bore a son to James V, Lord James *Stewart (1531/2–1570), later earl of Moray and regent of Scotland, a half-brother whom William Douglas thus shared with Mary, queen of Scots. William spent some time in France during his minority after his father's death, when his mother managed his affairs. His 'Memoir', an extended testament-cum-memoir written by him in 1568 during an illness, throws light on his participation in and attitude to the events of the 1550s and 1560s (Morton muniments, GD 150/2234). In the 1550s he identified with the movement for religious reform and developed an admiration for some of its leaders, including both his half-brother James and John Knox, whose preaching impressed him during the reformer's visit to Scotland in 1555–6. His marriage to Lady Agnes *Leslie, eldest daughter of George, fourth earl of Rothes (contract 19 August 1545, revised 1554), strengthened his association with the protestant party; the Leslies were ringleaders in the assassination of Cardinal David Beaton in 1546.

In 1559–60 Douglas joined the army of the protestant lords of the congregation in their military confrontation with the French-backed forces of the regent, Mary of Guise, which resulted in the withdrawal of the French from Scotland and the treaty of Edinburgh between France and Scotland's new ally, England. Only the prospect of victory for protestantism, he admitted, enabled him to accept Scotland's political alignment with England, the former enemy:

> quhilk wes a begynning of the reconciliatioun amang us, and that the hairtis of thaim quhilkis wer in malice aganis thaim [the English] throw want of thair predecessouris in battaill wes begun to be slokinit [quenched] as I knaw be experience in my selff for the want of my fader at the feild of Pinky, quhilk wes the first occasioun that I did remit the sam with my hairt. (Douglas, fol. 14*r*)

He was present at the parliament of August 1560 which confirmed the reformation settlement.

In Mary's personal reign (1561–7) Douglas was a staunch supporter of the protestant establishment. During the brief uprising of 1565 against the queen's marriage to Henry, Lord Darnley, known as the chaseabout raid, Douglas was commanded to hand over Lochleven Castle, with the munitions stored there by Moray, one of the leaders, but he was allowed to retain it on a plea of illness and on promising to surrender it on twenty-four hours' notice if

required. He shared the resentment of others towards the queen's Italian secretary, David Riccio, whose growing influence, they claimed, prevented their direct access to the queen. Douglas himself says that he approached Riccio with an offer of £1000 if the secretary would 'stay the earl of Moray's forfaltour' for his part in the chaseabout raid, 'bot his answer wes twenty thowsand' (Douglas, fol. 20*v*). He was denounced as one of those implicated in the murder of Riccio on 9 March 1566, although he maintained that he never intended that the secretary should be dealt with other than by process of law. After the event he retired to Argyll 'ane whill in quiet maner' (ibid.). He rejoiced at the birth of Prince James on 19 June 1566 and thereafter kept a watchful eye on the prince's interests in the light of his parents' estrangement and the queen's growing attachment to the earl of Bothwell, whom Douglas believed had 'crually put doun his [the prince's] fader in ane maist abominabill maner in Edinburt' (ibid., fol. 21*r*) in February 1567. He was gratified when the prince was placed in the guardianship of his own uncle and his wife, the earl and countess of Mar, in Stirling Castle. He was periodically associated with Mar in his keepership of that castle.

After Mary's marriage to Bothwell in May 1567 Douglas joined the confederate lords who pledged themselves to protect the prince and avenge his father's murder. He was far from happy, however, when after the queen's surrender to the lords at Carberry in June 1567 they chose to detain her in his own castle of Lochleven, where on 24 July she was compelled to demit the crown. Four days later Douglas formally protested that her demission had taken place in his absence, 'in respect thereof [he] protestit that her majestie suld not be comptit heirefter as captive or in prisoun with hym. Quhilk her majestie allowit and admittit' (Thomson, Macdonald, and Innes, 1.26–7). 'I desirit', he recorded, 'that [the] nobilitie wald haiff relevit me off my burden, quhilk I culd nott get' (Douglas, fol. 22*r*). During her ten-month stay at Lochleven Mary maintained friendly relations with Douglas and members of his family, including his wife and his mother, and with his brother George and a young orphaned relative, who between them contrived her escape on 2 May 1568. He himself was never charged with failure of his trust as custodian. At the battle of Langside, near Glasgow, on 13 May 1568 Douglas led the rearguard of the king's forces and he later accompanied Moray to York for the investigation into the so-called Casket Letters, which allegedly incriminated Mary in Darnley's murder. On the collapse of the northern rising in 1569 the earl of Northumberland took refuge in Scotland, only to be imprisoned at Lochleven. His extradition to England to stand trial on a charge of treason was delayed while Douglas haggled with the English government for substantial remuneration; they eventually guaranteed him £2000.

On the assassination of Moray in January 1570 Douglas and his brother Robert, as the regent's nearest of kin, called for the summary execution of the killer, James Hamilton of Bothwelhaugh, and in 1575, when Lord John

Hamilton was reported to be intending to bring the murderer home, Douglas raised 1200 men to confront them. As a result of his attack on Lord John Hamilton while he was travelling through Fife both Douglas and Hamilton were called before the privy council to give assurances for their good behaviour. Douglas also quarrelled with Lord Ruthven over the earldom of Buchan, of which he had received a crown gift of ward on his brother Robert's death in 1580, a gift contested by Ruthven. William was closely associated with his cousin James Douglas, fourth earl of Morton, who became regent in 1572, although Morton reprimanded him for his vendetta against the Hamiltons, which threatened to wreck the regent's attempts at reconciliation with potential opponents. When Morton lost the regency in 1578, he went to his cousin's castle of Lochleven, where Douglas kept him informed of political movements that might help Morton to recover power; in 1580 Douglas co-operated with his kinsman the earl of Mar in a final attempt to build up support for Morton. Douglas served as a commissioner for musters in 1574, commissioner for the laws in 1578, when he also took part in musters for the pacification of the borders, and was sheriff principal of Banff in 1584. He was knighted before 1581.

After Morton's arrest in 1580 on a charge of complicity in Darnley's murder Douglas with others of the regent's party was summoned before the privy council to answer questions, and was ordered to ward himself in the north on penalty of £10,000. His son participated in the attempt of the so-called Ruthven raiders on 22 August 1582 to remove King James from the influence of Esmé Stewart, first duke of Lennox. Douglas, released from detention on security of £20,000, but still suspected of alliance with the ultra-protestant Ruthven raiders, went into exile in France. From there he co-operated with those in Scotland who plotted the downfall of the earl of Arran in October 1585, and he returned to Scotland in 1586. In 1587 he was made a commissioner for executing acts against the Jesuits. In 1588, on the death of Archibald Douglas, eighth earl of Angus, who had acquired the earldom of Morton in 1585 following the revocation of a grant of the title made to Lord Maxwell in 1581, William Douglas succeeded as earl under the will of the former regent Morton. Strictly speaking this made him sixth earl of Morton, but the continued claim of Lord Maxwell caused personal animosity between the two men. In 1592 Maxwell's title was revived, with the ambiguous proviso that this should in no way prejudice Douglas's rights; the claimants came to blows over precedence in 1593. Eventually in 1620 the tenth Lord Maxwell was made earl of Nithsdale.

Douglas's 'Memoir' and surviving letters give the impression of a serious, almost introspective personality. For much of his life he suffered from recurrent bouts of illness, which required a constant supply of medicines, the services of a nurse, and the use of a litter when travelling around his estates, which after he became earl of Morton in 1588 were scattered over ten sheriffdoms, from Angus (Forfarshire) in the north-east to Roxburghshire in the borders. His wife, Agnes, with whom he enjoyed a

married life of over fifty years, survived him. She played an active part in the running of these estates, going regularly to Auchterhouse in Angus for that purpose, from where she wrote to her husband about her activities. They had four sons, all of whom predeceased their father, and seven daughters. The earl died on 27 September 1606 and was succeeded in the earldom and estates by his grandson William *Douglas (1582–1648).

MARGARET H. B. SANDERSON

Sources M. H. B. Sanderson, 'Sir William Douglas, laird of Lochleven, earl of Morton', *Mary Stewart's people: life in Mary Stewart's Scotland* (1987), 55–74 • W. Douglas, 'Memoir', NA Scot., Morton muniments, GD 150/2234 • *Scots peerage*, 6.369–74 • T. Thomson, A. Macdonald, and C. Innes, eds., *Registrum honoris de Morton*, 2 vols., Bannatyne Club, 94 (1853), vol. 1 • M. Livingstone, D. Hay Fleming, and others, eds., *Registrum secreti sigilli regum Scotorum / The register of the privy seal of Scotland*, 8 (1982) • D. Calderwood, *The history of the Kirk of Scotland*, ed. T. Thomson and D. Laing, 8 vols., Wodrow Society, 7 (1842–9), vol. 2, p. 526 • NA Scot., Mar and Kellie muniments, GD 124
Archives NA Scot., Morton muniments

Douglas, William, tenth earl of Angus (c.1554–1611), magnate, was the eldest son of William *Douglas, ninth earl of Angus (d. 1591), and his wife, Egidia or Giles Graham (d. in or after 1606), daughter of Robert Graham of Morphie. He studied at St Andrews University and then served his great-uncle James Douglas, earl of Morton, before going to France in 1577. While there he was converted to Roman Catholicism, to the annoyance of his protestant family. In 1585 (contract dated 12 April) he married Elizabeth Oliphant, eldest daughter of Laurence, Lord Oliphant, a supporter of Queen Mary in the Scottish civil war and a Catholic sympathizer. Douglas was ordered to leave the country on account of his religion in September 1589. He took legal instruments the following month affirming that he had gone to Aberdeen in obedience to this instruction, but found the sailing season over and was therefore obliged to remain at home. In May 1591 he was again ordered into exile, but the death of his father on 1 July that year prevented him from complying.

Having succeeded to the earldom, Angus took a notable part in public life, opposing James VI's wish to promote his favourite the duke of Lennox to prominence in the parliament of 1592. In the same year he was employed as king's lieutenant in the north, where he was successful in healing the feud between the earls of Atholl and Huntly which had arisen following the latter's murder of the earl of Moray. At the end of that year he was accused of involvement in the 'Spanish blanks' affair, a putative conspiracy among Huntly and his Catholic associates, who were alleged to be encouraging Spanish intervention in Scotland in furtherance of the Catholic cause. On 3 January 1593 Angus was imprisoned in Edinburgh Castle, but on 13 February he escaped with the help of his wife. She was said to have smuggled a rope into his cell with which he got out. It was also claimed that the authorities were aware of the possibility of his escape and that one of his warders connived at it. He made his way north and entered into a bond of mutual defence with the earls of Huntly and Erroll.

Later in February 1593 King James and an army marched to Aberdeen against the Catholic earls, who proved reluctant to oppose the king personally and fled to Caithness. A parliament met in July, but James ensured that proceedings against the earls were impeded and that they were not forfeited. He was perhaps concerned at the threat from ultra-protestant elements in the kirk and wished, by protecting the earls, to ensure the survival of a Catholic counter-weight to strict Calvinist influence. An act of oblivion was offered to the earls should they submit to the reformed kirk; if they refused to accept this, they were to go into exile, but be allowed to retain their estates. The earls rejected the accommodation and in June 1594 were tried at the parliament in Edinburgh. Angus's possessions were forfeited and given to the duke of Lennox, while all three earls were excommunicated by the general assembly of the church.

During this time the earls remained at large in the north-east, where they mounted a punitive raid on the burgh of Aberdeen to release some unnamed foreign emissaries who had been imprisoned in the town on their way to meet Huntly. In the autumn the king sent the young earl of Argyll, a rival of Huntly, north to settle matters. He was defeated at Glenlivet on 3 October 1594. James then came in person, the earls once more declined to meet him in the field, and Huntly's castle and lands were ravaged. Although Angus was not present at Glenlivet, he had associated with the earl of Bothwell in stirring up unsuccessful diversionary activities in the south of Scotland. Erroll and Huntly now agreed to go abroad, but Angus remained in hiding in the north. In 1595 he reached a partial settlement with the king, in negotiations which were still in progress when Huntly and Erroll returned from exile in June 1596. In March 1597 the countess of Angus petitioned the general assembly, then sitting at Perth, to depute some ministers to confer with her husband on religious matters, and in June the three earls were publicly reconciled with the kirk.

Soon afterwards, on 29 June 1598, Angus was appointed lieutenant of the borders, where he discharged his duties so effectively, financing his administration from his own resources, that his post was renewed after a year. Doubts persisted about the sincerity of his protestant convictions, however, and in 1602 the church authorities appointed James Law, later bishop of Orkney, to act as his chaplain—in effect he was a spy in the earl's house, charged with the daily catechizing of the family, removing suspected Catholics from the earl's service, and ensuring the appointment of reliable protestant pastors in the earl's territory. During this time Angus was reported to be wearing a cross openly and refusing to communicate in the kirk, and in 1608 the church once more began proceedings against him. He was briefly imprisoned in Glasgow before retiring to France. In 1609 he passed through England on his way to exile; he requested an interview with King James and also that he might take his second son with him to France, but permission for both was refused. Later that year, in October, he asked the king if he might

return to Scotland to settle his affairs and to put his house in order, but this was once more denied.

A few of Angus's letters survive from this period in which he describes himself as old and sick, although he was no more than fifty-five years old. He lived near the abbey of St Germain-des-Prés in Paris, where he was recognized as a regular attender at mass and the monastic offices. He died in Paris on 3 March 1611, and was buried in St Christopher's aisle in the abbey church. His son William *Douglas, first marquess of Douglas, erected a monument to his memory in the shape of a sarcophagus of black marble, on which lies a white marble effigy of the earl clad in armour, with an inscription recording his life and achievements. The earl's wife survived him and subsequently married James Hamilton. She and Angus had three sons and three daughters: William, who succeeded his father as eleventh earl; James, who was raised to the peerage by Charles I in 1641 as Lord Mordington and who married Anne, only child of Laurence, fifth Lord Oliphant; Sir Francis Douglas of Sandilands; Catherine; Mary, who became the second wife of Alexander Livingstone, second earl of Linlithgow; and Elizabeth, who married John Campbell, fiar of Cawdor. ALLAN WHITE

Sources Scots peerage, 1.198–202 · GEC, Peerage, new edn, 1.159–60; 2.380–411 · W. Fraser, ed., The Douglas book, 4 vols. (1885), vol. 2, pp. 405, 407, 409–10; vol. 3, pp. 322, 323; vol. 4, pp. 40, 195 · R. Gordon and G. Gordon, A genealogical history of the earldom of Sutherland ... with a continuation to the year 1651 (1813) · D. Calderwood, The history of the Kirk of Scotland, ed. T. Thomson and D. Laing, 8 vols., Wodrow Society, 7 (1842–9) · R. Pitcairn, ed., Ancient criminal trials in Scotland, 7 pts in 3, Bannatyne Club, 42 (1833) · J. Bouillart, Histoire de l'abbaye royale de Saint Germain des Prez (1724) · T. I. Rae, The administration of the Scottish frontier, 1513–1603 (1966)
Archives NL Scot., letters and papers · NRA, priv. coll., papers

Douglas, William, **first earl of Queensberry** (d. 1640), landowner, was the eldest son of Sir James Douglas of Drumlanrig (d. 1615) and his wife, Mary, eldest daughter of John Fleming, fifth Lord Fleming, and his wife, Elizabeth; his parents married in 1581. By a contract dated 20 July 1603 he married Isobel (d. 1628), later Lady Isobel, daughter of Mark *Ker, Lord Newbattle (b. in or before 1559, d. 1609), who was created earl of Lothian in 1606, and his wife, Margaret Maxwell. They had four sons and two daughters.

Having been knighted before 14 July 1612, Douglas entered into possession of the regality of Drumlanrig on the death of his father. He was active in his family's often violent disputes with their neighbours, being rebuked by the privy council in 1606 and fined in 1614. Nevertheless, in 1617 he entertained James VI at Drumlanrig, and he played a leading role in the government's attempts to tackle the lawlessness of the middle shires. In the early 1620s he was involved in the discussions on the wool trade and manufacturing, and, a decade later, on Charles I's plans for fishing. He was created viscount of Drumlanrig, Lord Douglas of Hawick and Tibberis in 1628, and earl of Queensberry in 1633. He added the barony of Torthorwald to his estates in 1622, the town of Hawick in 1623, and the baronies of Sanquhar and Cumnock in 1637. He died on 8 March 1640, and was succeeded by his eldest son, James *Douglas (d. 1671).

ALSAGER VIAN, rev. DAVID MENARRY

Sources *Scots peerage* · M. D. Young, ed., *The parliaments of Scotland: burgh and shire commissioners*, 2 vols. (1992–3) · *Reg. PCS*, 1st ser. · *Reg. PCS*, 2nd ser. · *APS* · *The manuscripts of his grace the duke of Buccleuch and Queensberry ... preserved at Drumlanrig Castle*, 2 vols., HMC, 44 (1897–1903), vol. 1, pp. 84–5 · *Diary of the public correspondence of Sir Thomas Hope*, ed. [T. Thomson], Bannatyne Club, 76 (1843), 29 · *DNB* · H. Maxwell, *A history of the house of Douglas*, 2 vols. (1852), vol. 2, pp. 262–3 · GEC, *Peerage*

Douglas, William, seventh earl of Morton (1582–1648),

politician and nobleman, was the son of Robert Douglas of Lochleven (d. 1585) and Jean Lyon (d. 1608x10), daughter of John *Lyon, eighth Lord Glamis (c.1544–1578). Following his father's death in March 1585 his mother married Archibald *Douglas, eighth earl of Angus (c.1555–1588), and then, before 31 May 1590, Alexander *Lindsay, first Lord Spynie (c.1563–1607); Alexander *Lindsay, second Lord Spynie (c.1597–1646), was thus his half-brother. Little is known of Douglas's early life, although he seems to have had a good education. On 5 March 1604 he was contracted to marry Lady Anne Keith (d. 1649), daughter of George *Keith, fourth Earl Marischal (1549/50–1623), and in June 1605 was served heir to his father.

Douglas and his grandfather, William *Douglas, sixth earl of Morton (c.1540–1606), waged a jurisdictional feud against the Maxwells, who had held the earldom of Morton after 1581. Both sides were discharged from holding justiciary courts in Eskdale on the western border, and on 3 September 1606 were forbidden any armed convocations in the middle shires, Edinburgh, or Fife. On 4 November, still in his early twenties, Douglas succeeded his grandfather, becoming seventh (sometimes rendered eighth) earl, and began his political career by attempting to mitigate this longstanding civil conflict. On 14 July 1607 the privy council accused John Maxwell, ninth Lord Maxwell, of holding courts in Eskdale, a charge that he ably deflected on a legal technicality; at this stage his feud with Morton had reached such a pitch that both parties were forbidden from sitting in parliament that month, sent home, and made to find caution of £10,000 each. Ignoring this order, on 3 August Maxwell dispatched a cartel with messages to intimidate Morton, whose own political loyalty was assured through the oath of allegiance, and his subsequent sitting at the convention of estates on 20 May 1608. In November 1610 Morton was appointed to the new Scottish peace commission for Peeblesshire, Edinburgh, Fife, and Kinross, an indication of his status and general reliability, which resulted in further appointments as a JP between 1613 and 1615. A landowner with extensive property Morton also partook of taxations worth over £800 derived from Melrose Abbey and, having resigned the barony of Dunfedling to the king in March 1613, he received a charter of Segy barony on 9 October 1616.

On 16 January 1617 Morton received a special licence to

William Douglas, seventh earl of Morton (1582–1648), by unknown artist

travel in France, Germany, or Italy for up to three years 'without skaith to his person, lands, and goods, provided he behave as a loyal subject' (*Reg. PCS*, 1st ser., 9.10; NL Scot., MS 73, no. 83). He did not leave immediately, probably because he had to attend King James VI; he appeared at the convention of estates in March 1617 and from 11 to 14 June entertained the king at Dalkeith Palace. His continental tour began shortly afterwards, and in July he joined his cousin, William Douglas, eleventh earl of Angus, and Henry Erskine at Bourges. By spring 1618 they were in Paris, where Morton feared that he had contracted a fatal disease. He had returned to Scotland by 1621, if not before: on 13 September 1620 he was appointed a JP for Edinburgh. Morton attended parliament at Edinburgh on 25 July 1621, and by November had been officially admitted as a Scottish privy councillor and a member of a select conciliar cabinet to undertake the king's 'most weyghtie affairis' (*Reg. PCS*, 1st ser., 12.604). The following year he cemented an alliance with the new lord chancellor, Sir George Hay, by marrying his eldest daughter, Ann, on 7 September to Hay's heir, George Hay (d. 1644), later second earl of Kinnoull. In 1623 he attended an exhausting number of conciliar committees, discussing the exclusive export of undraped wool into England, serving on the commission of grievances, and presiding over the commission of manufactures. His political focus changed dramatically in January 1624, when he was appointed to the prince's council—the first step in his career as a court-based statesman. Thereafter he spent much of his time at Whitehall and was present during the changeover of administration following the death of James, whose funeral Morton attended as standard-bearer with the second earl of Mar.

By November 1625 Morton had returned to Scotland to attend the convention of estates, and on 6 December he received a charter of the baronies of Aberdalgy, Dupplin, and Gask. After being reappointed to the Scottish privy council in March 1626 he was soon assigned to the commission of the exchequer and later, in February 1627, to the controversial commission of surrenders and teinds. It was during this period that Morton made two more strategic marriages, between his teenage daughter Margaret and Archibald Campbell, Lord Lorne, in August 1626, and between his eldest son, Robert, and Buckingham's niece Anne Villiers in April 1627. The latter secured Morton's place in the British court and formed the backdrop to his command of between 2000 and 3000 Scottish troops in the expedition to La Rochelle that August. By 12 April 1630 he had replaced the ageing Mar as lord high treasurer of Scotland, inheriting 'an empty cupboard' and facing the prospect of a new taxation (Lee, 31, 87). His record as treasurer was unexceptional but did coincide with the king's first return visit to Scotland in June 1633, for which Morton had been appointed to a seven member preparatory committee in the previous January. By June 1634 the earl's accounts as treasurer were audited by John Maitland, first earl of Lauderdale, and David Carnegie, first earl of Southesk, the first indication that Morton was about to be shuffled out of office. However, this shift permitted him to concentrate on his active court life: on 21 April he was promoted to the Order of the Garter and in 1635 he was appointed captain of the yeomen of the guard. He willingly stepped down as treasurer on 24 June 1636, but only on the king's personal assurance of protection against his creditors and the repayment of his substantial debts; Charles had earlier written to the Edinburgh financier William Dick, asking him to forgive Morton's loan of £5000.

Morton was at court during the signing of the national covenant in 1638, and he was awarded a charter incorporating all of his lands into the earldom of Morton and Aberdour. He was sent home to make preparations for James Hamilton, marquess of Hamilton, who had insisted that a royal faction be established at Edinburgh before he himself set out as lord high commissioner. Morton witnessed the king's proclamation at the Scottish camp in Duns Law on 22 June 1639, but as the conflict between the king and the covenanting movement intensified Morton found himself losing control of the properties he had used as pledges during the 1620s and 1630s. In September 1640 he attended the assembly of peers with the earls of Traquair and Lanark, later helping to draw up the treaty of Ripon in the following month. Morton personally accompanied the king to Edinburgh in 1641, and on 18 August was himself obliged to sign the covenant before sitting in parliament. In September he tactfully declined the king's offer of the chancellorship in light of the loud protestations as to his unsuitability by his son-in-law Argyll.

In March 1642 Morton attended the king at York as a member of the council of peers, returning temporarily to his palace of Dalkeith, which he was obliged to sell on 14 July to mitigate his debts. He accepted a charter of the regalities of Orkney and Shetland from the king, who had the option of redeeming them for £30,000, but immediately afterwards the Scottish commissioners passed an act to apprehend Morton and other 'incendiaries between the two kingdoms' (GEC, *Peerage*). He eluded capture and apart from his sporadic participation in the civil wars (including attendance on Charles at Newcastle in 1646), Morton used Kirkwall as his base and served as commissioner of justiciary for Shetland and Orkney. His last major act was to sign an obligation to pay Michael Shaw of Kirkwall £2000 Scots on 1 May 1648. As the political conflict in England reopened that year Morton sheltered his son-in-law Kinnoull, who had recently evaded the parliamentarian sea blockade in a vain attempt to spur support for a royalist land campaign. The earl himself died on 7 August 1648 at Kirkwall Castle, where he was also buried; his remarkable wife, Anne, who had long attempted to manage his estates during his prolonged absences, died a few months later on 30 May 1649. Their eldest son, Robert, succeeded to the earldom of Morton, but himself died at Kirkwall on 12 November 1649, leaving as his heir his son William (d. 1681).   J. R. M. SIZER

Sources R. Douglas, *The peerage of Scotland*, 2nd edn, ed. J. P. Wood, 2 (1813) · *Scots peerage* · *Reg. PCS*, 1st ser., vols. 7–14 · *Reg. PCS*, 2nd ser., vols. 1–5 · GEC, *Peerage*, new edn, vol. 9 · M. Lee, *Road to revolution: Scotland under Charles I, 1625–37* (1985) · K. Brown, *Noble society in Scotland: wealth, family and culture, from Reformation to revolution* (2000) · K. Brown, 'Courtiers and cavaliers: service, Anglicisation and loyalty among the royalist nobility', *The Scottish national covenant in its British context*, ed. J. Morrill (1990), 155–94 · *APS, 1593–1625* · H. Paton, ed., *Supplementary report on the manuscripts of the earl of Mar and Kellie*, HMC, 60 (1930) · J. Spalding, *The history of the troubles and memorable transactions in Scotland and England, from 1624 to 1645*, ed. J. Skene, 2 vols., Bannatyne Club, 25 (1828–9) · NL Scot., MS 78 · *Ninth report*, 3 vols., HMC, 8 (1883–4)
Archives NA Scot., papers · NL Scot., NLS MS 7384
Likenesses oils, Scot. NPG [see illus.]
Wealth at death 'one of the richest men of his day in Scotland'; said to have drawn annual income of £100,000 from Dalkeith property alone; this, like many of mainland possessions, was sold to subsidize royalist war effort during civil wars: *Scots peerage*, 6.377; GEC, *Peerage*, 9.295; NL Scot., MS 78

Douglas, William, first marquess of Douglas (1589–1660), magnate and scholar, was the eldest son of William *Douglas, tenth earl of Angus (c.1554–1611), and his wife, Elizabeth (d. in or after 1611), daughter of Laurence *Oliphant, fourth Lord Oliphant. From early childhood, the master of Angus was affected by the repercussions of his father's involvement in Catholic conspiracies. Taken into custody as a royal hostage, in 1596 he received by special arrangement the Douglas estates, which had been granted temporarily to the duke of Lennox, and in the following year he was released after suffering an accident. However, the conditions of his father's reinstatement stipulated that the Angus heir be handed over to his kinsman William Douglas, sixth earl of Morton (d. 1606), for education as a protestant. At the exceptionally young age of twelve he was contracted on 11 July 1601 to marry Margaret (1584/5–1623), daughter of Claud *Hamilton, Lord

Paisley (1546?–1621), and sister of James Hamilton, later first earl of Abercorn (1575–1618). Although Lord Claud was a Catholic, his son, who had inherited the estates following the former's insanity, was a prominent protestant privy councillor. Meanwhile, the tenth earl of Angus had been reconciled to the kirk, but his allegiance became increasingly suspect and in 1608 he left Scotland, dying in exile in Paris on 3 March 1611.

In May 1612 William Douglas, now eleventh earl of Angus, appeared before the privy council as a result of altercations with the Kerrs of Ferniehirst over their respective rights to hold bailie courts in Jedburgh Forest. Angus's case was upheld by conciliar decision on the understanding that he could not hold a court with a gathering of more than sixty retainers. However, his more hotheaded brother Lord James Douglas was imprisoned at Blackness Castle for his part in antagonizing the Kerr family. On 8 August 1616 Angus obtained a royal licence to travel on the continent—officially to relieve 'his disease and seikness' (Fraser, 2.416)—a journey in which he was joined by William Douglas, seventh earl of Morton (1582–1648), grandson of his former guardian. In August 1617 the earl of Mar's European agent, Schau, reported from Bourges that this Douglas party had 'concludit to begin thair travelling upon the 4 of September' (*Supplementary Mar and Kellie MSS*, 78), in a journey that was to encompass Lyons, Geneva, Marseilles, Bordeaux, La Rochelle, and Orléans. On his return to Scotland in 1619 Angus assumed a greater interest in the political affairs of the nation, attending the special conference of the council and nobility in November 1620, when he served on the committee to recommend fund-raising possibilities for the war effort in the Palatinate. Controversially, he insisted (unsuccessfully) on claiming, as traditional crown-bearer to the Scottish king, precedence over the marquess of Huntly in the procession which opened the ensuing parliament in January 1621. Angus very early demonstrated his loyalty to the Anglicizing policies of James VI and I, openly supporting the parliamentary ratification of the controversial five articles of Perth.

However, Angus's political activities soon gave way to his lifelong fascination with travel and genealogical research, both of which led him on 26 May 1623 back to the continent, leaving his wife, who died on 11 September, and the earl of Morton to assume responsibility for his financial affairs and the administration of his estates. He travelled throughout France and Italy, probably drawn to the latter mainly through his correspondence with the Italian nobleman Marc Antonio Scoto d'Agazano, who claimed kinship with the Douglases, albeit 'on somewhat mythical grounds' (*Scots peerage*, 1.203), but divided his time mainly between Paris (where he is known to have been based in November 1623) and Rome, where he paid a controversial visit to St Peter's in early 1625. The apparent lure of continental Catholicism alarmed his home presbytery of Lanark, whose elders interrogated him upon his return to Scotland that September, exhorting him to reassure his parishioners by attending services at his local parish kirk. Their concern over his religious integrity and

annoyance at his sporadic church attendance continued to be expressed until his death.

Angus appears to have been favoured by Charles I, possibly owing to his careful political inactivity as a suspected Catholic and consistent covert loyalty to the king's manifestly episcopalian policies. On 10 March 1631 the king officially regranted him the earldom of Angus, restoring in addition his heritable rights to carry the crown during parliamentary processions and to cast the first vote. On 15 September 1632 at the Gordon stronghold of 'the Bog' he married Lady Mary Gordon (1610/11–1674), third daughter of the ageing marquess of Huntly. After spending a fortnight in Aberdeenshire, during which they visited the earl of Moray, Angus and Mary returned to a comparatively quiet life divided between Douglas Castle in Lanarkshire and Tantallon on the Lothian coast. In the following year Angus resumed his political career at Edinburgh in preparation for the king's state visit, having been personally selected by the king as commissioner of articles for parliament alongside the Catholic noble Winton. After bearing the crown in the coronation ceremony on 17 June 1633, Angus was made marquess of Douglas, earl of Angus, and lord of Abernethy and Jedburgh Forest. Yet he never exploited royal favour to gain national prominence, choosing this time to retreat from the increasingly complex political problems and ecclesiastical issues developing between Whitehall and Edinburgh and concentrate on his studies and expanding family, which eventually numbered six sons and ten daughters. He also began to strengthen his administrative control over his territories in Lanarkshire and Roxburghshire, an authority enhanced by his commission of justiciary for Walston parish, Lanark (1 August 1634), and appointment as justice of the peace for Lanark (18 September). Following the apparent increase in frontier lawlessness throughout the western border, Douglas was also enlisted in 1635 to appear on the new conjunct commission, an Anglo-Scottish collective originally instituted by King James thirty years earlier. In the following year the presbytery of Lanarkshire again registered its annoyance with the truant marquess, alleging that he had refused to permit his daughter to attend local church services.

After the renewal of his place on the border commission in September 1636 little was heard of Douglas until the signing of the national covenant in February 1638 and the subsequent outbreak of war. Douglas himself escaped to England before the troops of John Fleming, Lord Fleming began besieging Douglas Castle. Expecting a harsh reception and resistance, Fleming was surprised at how easily he was able to take the stronghold, which was occupied by the marchioness; she was permitted to remain in the castle due to her 'delicate health' (Baillie, 1.420). After the imposition of an uneasy peace in Scotland, on 27 March 1640 Charles forewarned both Douglas and his border kinsman Robert Maxwell, earl of Nithsdale, to re-garrison their castles in the light of his impending breach with the covenanters. In the context of further destabilization, the marquess shied away from active involvement in politics, and conspicuously absented himself from parliament on

17 November 1641, when his place as crown-bearer was assumed by the earl of Argyll.

By the time civil war broke out in England in 1642 Douglas was firmly established as a border magnate and scholar who only rarely participated in national events. His half-hearted commitment to the covenant can be observed in his refusal to assist Lanark presbytery in disciplining the 'braincracked' young James Baillie of Todholes for regularly assaulting the minister of Dunsyre throughout 1642 (Fraser, 2.421 n. 4), and it was only under some pressure that he eventually signed the covenant in his parish kirk in Lanark in July 1644. His true interests lay in his genealogical work and in the preparation for publication of David Home of Godscroft's *History of the House of Douglas*, which was ultimately published by Evan Tyler in 1644. Encouraged by the marquess of Montrose's military success at Kilsyth in August 1645 Douglas was inspired to side with the royalist movement, which was then gaining new momentum in Scotland. After being awarded the lieutenancy of Clydesdale by Montrose, Douglas led a march on Hawick but found himself obliged to escape the defeat suffered by Montrose's forces at Philiphaugh on 13 September. This humiliation was followed by the death on 21 October of Douglas's third son, Colonel James Douglas, while serving in the French army at Douai. In April 1646 Douglas was himself imprisoned in Edinburgh Castle by the committee of estates, but later freed after admitting his breach of the terms outlined in the covenant and upon the payment of a fine.

In 1647 and 1648 Douglas maintained contact with the French diplomatic agent Montereul, with whom he discussed the plight of Catholic Scots and the breakdown of his relationship with his eldest son, Archibald Douglas (c.1609–1655), styled since 1633 earl of Angus, who was initially a covenanter sympathizer and considered by his father as 'the principal author of the hardships that he has been made to endure' (Fotheringham, 225). However, both Douglas and his son Angus attended the coronation of Charles II on 1 January 1651, and the marquess took part in the Scottish parliaments at Perth and Stirling in 1651, when he served on the committees for the army and estates. His allegiance to the royalist effort earned him the distrust of Cromwell, who had him (and his son) charged with a fine of £1000 under the 1654 Act of Grace, though this was later reduced to £333 6s. 8d. on 6 April 1655 in recognition of his good faith and disempowerment. Despite this reduction, Cromwell's fiscal penalty symbolized the nullification of his powers as head of the house of Douglas and led him to reduce permanently his political activity, including any outward support for the exiled Stuart court. On 19 July 1654 the presbyterian Robert Baillie—an erstwhile polemicist for the covenanters—lamented that 'Dowglass and his sonne Angus are quyet men, of no respect' (Baillie, 3.249), a glaring indication of the deleterious social upheavals endured by the Scottish nobility over the previous decade. By 30 October eighteen Lanarkshire landholders certified the conformity and continuing good behaviour of the marquess, a sign that the presbytery of Lanark had won its long struggle with its patron, or that

Douglas himself had given up the fight in favour of the quiet scholastic life. Angus died in Edinburgh on 16 April 1655, and Douglas's virtual disappearance from the political and ecclesiastical affairs of Scotland after this date made his own death at Douglas Castle on 19 February 1660 and subsequent burial in Douglas church something of a non-event, and one considerably overshadowed by the ensuing Restoration. He was succeeded as second marquess of Douglas by his grandson James *Douglas (c.1646–1700). J. R. M. SIZER

Sources W. Fraser, ed., *The Douglas book*, 4 vols. (1885), vols. 2, 4 · *Scots peerage* · GEC, *Peerage* · *The letters and journals of Robert Baillie*, ed. D. Laing, 3 vols. (1841–2) · J. G. Fotheringham, ed., *The diplomatic correspondence of Jean de Montereul and the brothers de Bellièvre: French ambassadors in England and Scotland, 1645–1648*, 2 vols., Scottish History Society, 29–30 (1898–9) · J. Spalding, *History of the troubles*, 1 (1822) · M. Lee, *Road to revolution: Scotland under Charles I, 1625–37* (1985) · P. Donald, *An uncounselled king: Charles I and the Scottish troubles, 1637–41* (1990) · R. Douglas, *The peerage of Scotland*, 2nd edn, ed. J. P. Wood, 1 (1813) · *Reg. PCS*, 2nd ser., vol. 7 · *Ninth report*, 3 vols., HMC, 8 (1883–4) · *Report on manuscripts in various collections*, 8 vols., HMC, 55 (1901–14), vol. 5 · *David Hume of Godscroft's The history of the house of Douglas*, ed. D. Reid, 2 vols., STS, 4th ser., 25–6 (1996) · H. Paton, ed., *Supplementary report on the manuscripts of the earl of Mar and Kellie*, HMC, 60 (1930)
Archives NL Scot., letters and papers · NRA, priv. coll., corresp.
Wealth at death very little: Fraser, *Douglas book*, vol. 3, pp. 343–4; Baillie, *Letters*, vol. 1, p. 196; *Diplomatic correspondence*, 427

Douglas, William, first duke of Queensberry (1637–1695), politician, was the eldest son of James *Douglas, second earl of Queensberry (d. 1671), and Lady Margaret Stewart (d. 1673), daughter of the first earl of Traquair. Born on the eve of the revolutionary upheavals of the 1640s and 1650s, he did not receive the usual education of a young nobleman, 'but being a Man of very good natural Parts, and of a clear Judgment, when he came to engage in publict Business, he made a good Figure, and managed Affairs with great Dexterity and Address' (Crawfurd, 419). He served a political apprenticeship locally in the 1660s, obtaining appointments as a commissioner of excise in 1661, as a justice of the peace in 1663, and as sheriff and coroner of Dumfriesshire in 1664 and 1667. In 1667 he also made his entry into national politics when he was appointed a privy councillor. It was during these years that he started a family. He married Lady Isabel Douglas (bap. 1642, d. 1691), daughter of the first marquess of Douglas, in 1657, and together they had four children. Their son James *Douglas (1662–1711) succeeded in due course as the second duke of Queensberry; William became the first earl of March; George, who died unmarried in 1693, left a valuable library which his father donated to the Faculty of Advocates; and their daughter, Anne, married the third earl of Wemyss in 1697.

Queensberry was well placed to benefit from the collapse of the Lauderdale regime at the end of the 1670s. He was appointed justice-general of Scotland on 1 June 1680, an extraordinary lord of session on 1 November 1681, and constable and governor of Edinburgh Castle on 21 September 1682. But it was as high treasurer of Scotland that he was to make his mark. After his father's death in 1671 he had demonstrated a gift for financial management in restoring his family's wealth, greatly depleted by the war and by the imposition of a severe financial penalty by Cromwell. On 12 May 1682 he was appointed high treasurer with instructions to raise £40,000 per annum for the king and with permission to retain any surplus for himself. According to Sir John Lauder, 'he, like a new byssom, fell on sundry methods to inrich the Tresurie' (*Historical Notices*, 359). According to Gilbert Burnet, he 'was for every thing that would bring money into the treasury' (*Bishop Burnet's History*, 378). Husbands were to be fined when their wives failed to attend church, dissidents were to be prevented from travelling to the colonies until every fine possible had been extracted from them, new powers were to be exercised in reviewing the financial administration of burghs and other bodies, and generally no opportunity was to be missed in recovering the payments due to the crown. Not surprisingly, both the king and the duke of York held Douglas in high esteem. He was created marquess of Queensberry on 11 February 1682 and duke of Queensberry on 3 February 1684. In 1685 he was appointed commissioner to the first session of the parliament of James VII and II, and the shires through which he passed on his journey from London to Edinburgh as the king's representative were ordered to wait upon him. He had reached the zenith of his political career.

Burnet noted that Queensberry was reckoned by his colleagues to be 'haughty' and 'imperious', and his own view was that he had difficulty in maintaining an alliance with anyone because he 'loved to be absolute, and to direct every thing' (*Bishop Burnet's History*, 418, 613). When he first came to office as treasurer he worked closely with the chancellor, the earl of Aberdeen, but a deep antipathy developed between them which manifested itself in a series of public confrontations. In December 1683 the power of the chancellor was curbed and in July 1684 he was ousted from office and replaced by the earl of Perth, who had contrived with Queensberry to bring about his downfall. For a few months Queensberry worked in harmony with the new chancellor, but within a year he was leading one faction in the privy council and the chancellor another. Although the chancellor failed in his attempt to gather evidence of malpractice in the Treasury and could only present the king with a series of complaints that were deemed to be lacking in substance, he did manage to undermine the king's confidence in Queensberry. He was not appointed royal commissioner to the second session of the 1685 parliament and in March 1686 he was deprived of overall control of the Treasury. Technically he became one of a commission of five treasurers, another of whom was the chancellor, and at the same time he was made president of the privy council, but as Lauder observed, this was 'first to break his head, and then to put on his kowll' (*Historical Notices*, 712). Little over a week later he was replaced as constable and governor of Edinburgh Castle by the duke of Gordon, and the cloak of continuing favour finally slipped away in June 1686 when he was deprived of his places in the Treasury, privy council, and session, under orders to remain in Edinburgh until the accounts of the Treasury could be audited.

During his brief period in high office Queensberry had concentrated his attention on financial administration and had gained and retained power partly by gathering in the king's revenues with exceptional efficiency, partly by paying the king's creditors with uncommon promptness, and partly by using government funds to buy influence. Ultimately, however, his survival had not been dependent on his financial dealings. If Queensberry's differences with the earl of Aberdeen over the treatment of conventiclers had been motivated by a desire to draw in as much revenue from the imposition of fines as he could, what had pleased Charles II was the firm line he appeared to be taking against religious dissent. Similarly, what had turned James VII and II against him had not been any malpractice in the management of the Treasury but his refusal to offer assistance in the promotion of Catholicism. When James first came to the throne Queensberry warned the king that he would be party to no assault on the established religion, and it was on the basis of an assurance from the king that no such assault was intended that he saw a series of acts through the parliament of 1685 to secure the revenues of the crown, to authorize the privy council to impose a religious test on all levels of society, and to clamp down further on religious dissent. In the following year the earl of Perth was able to suggest that the programme of legislation devised by the king could have been carried through the parliament without all the promises Queensberry made on behalf of the king that there would be no change in religious policy. Unlike the earl of Perth, Queensberry refused the attempts made to convert him, including, he claimed, an offer of some £20,000, and he was praised for his public demonstration of commitment to the reformed faith.

Despite prolonged efforts to find fault with the Treasury accounts and a search for informants to testify to maladministration, Queensberry was able to retire quietly from public life until the arrival of William and Mary. He then equivocated, hoping on the one hand that if James survived he would turn again to his successful ministers, and on the other hand that if James was deposed the new monarchs would look favourably on the experienced father of the first notable Scot to join their ranks after the landing at Torbay. In fact, it was not until after the duke's death on 28 March 1695, at the age of fifty-eight, that his eldest son was able to obtain one of the major offices of state again for the family. Although Queensberry had been appointed an extraordinary lord of session once more in 1693, he had spent most of the early 1690s in retirement from political life, devoting his time to the construction of Drumlanrig Castle. He was laid to rest in the parish church of Durisdeer, Dumfriesshire.

J. D. FORD

Sources *The manuscripts of his grace the duke of Buccleuch and Queensberry … preserved at Drumlanrig Castle*, 2 vols., HMC, 44 (1897–1903), vol. 1 • G. Crawfurd, *The lives and characters, of the officers of the crown, and of the state in Scotland* (1726), 419–23 • *Bishop Burnet's History* • *Historical notices of Scotish affairs, selected from the manuscripts of Sir John Lauder of Fountainhall*, ed. D. Laing, 2 vols., Bannatyne Club, 87 (1848) • P. W. J. Riley, *King William and the Scottish politicians* (1979) • *Scots peerage*, 7.137–40 • GEC, *Peerage*

Archives NRA Scotland, priv. coll., corresp. and papers | BL, letters to duke of Lauderdale and Charles II, Add. MSS 23117–23129, 23244–23247, *passim* · Dumfries and Galloway Libraries, letters to Sir Robert Grierson
Likenesses G. Kneller, oils, Buccleuch estates, Selkirk

Douglas, William (*b.* 1710/11), physician and satirist, was born in Forfarshire, but his parentage has not been traced. By 1729 he was in London, apprenticed to James Douglas (1675–1742), the obstetrician and anatomist. He matriculated at the University of Leiden on 18 May 1733, aged twenty-two, and studied there under Boerhaave, but his degree of MD, awarded on 27 January 1738, was from the University of Rheims. By 1739 he was back in London, practising as a physician and man-midwife, and living in Covent Garden—in Southampton Street to 1745, thereafter in Henrietta Street. By 1746 he had become a physician-in-ordinary to Frederick, prince of Wales, recommended by his opposition whig politics.

When the politician Thomas Winnington died on 23 April 1746 under the treatment of Thomas Thompson, another of the prince's physicians, and controversy arose over Thompson's methods, Douglas published a vituperative *Letter to Dr. Thomson* (June 1746), and was, in his turn, attacked in *Thomsonus redivivus* (October 1746), a satirical pamphlet attributed to Smollett. The next work published over Douglas's name, *The Resurrection* (April 1747), was an impudent plagiarism. This devotional poem was written years earlier by Hugh Blair (1718–1800) and his cousin George Bannantyne; Douglas came by a manuscript and printed the work as his own in a pompous folio with a dedication to his patroness the princess of Wales. It was ridiculed as Douglas's in *The Town* (March 1748), a verse satire by William Kenrick (1725–1776), who was a libeller as coarse as Douglas himself.

In 1748 Douglas returned to clinical controversy with two published letters attacking the obstetric methods of William Smellie (1697–1763) and a scurrilous satire on Richard Mead (1673–1754) entitled *The Cornutor of Seventy-Five … the Life, Adventures, and Amours, of Don Ricardo Honeywater*. There was an undated second edition of this last work with enlarged introduction and footnotes. Though Douglas published all his earlier attacks on fellow practitioners under his own name, this clumsy fiction is absurdly attributed to Cervantes. A withering reply, *Don Ricardo Honeywater Vindicated* (1748), perhaps by Smollett, included a calumnious biography of Douglas, in which events before 1746 are almost certainly fanciful. In 1749 Douglas was appointed man-midwife and in 1750 physician to the Middlesex Hospital; he resigned both posts in 1752. By 1758 he had returned to Scotland and, according to Smellie, had gone mad (Johnstone, 119). It is not known when he died.   JAMES SAMBROOK

Sources R. W. Innes Smith, *English-speaking students of medicine at the University of Leyden* (1932) · W. Douglas, 'The cornutor of seventy-five' (1748) and 'Don Ricardo Honeywater vindicated' (1748), ed. R. A. Day (1987) · R. A. Day, 'When doctors disagree', *Études anglaises*, 32 (1979), 312–34 · R. W. Johnstone, *William Smellie, the master of British midwifery* (1952), 119 · J. Glaister, *Dr William Smellie and his contemporaries* (1894), 68–97 · *The parish of St Paul, Covent Garden*, Survey of London, 36 (1970), 209 · W. Douglas, *A letter to Dr. Thomson* (1746) · D. F. Foxon, ed., *English verse, 1701–1750: a catalogue of separately printed poems with notes on contemporary collected editions*, 2 vols. (1975), D414 · Boswell, *Life*, 1.360

Douglas, William, fourth duke of Queensberry (1725–1810), sybarite and politician, only son of William Douglas, second earl of March (*c.*1696–1731), and his wife, Anne Hamilton, *suo jure* countess of Ruglen (1698–1748), was born on 16 December 1725 at Queensberry Lodging, Peebles. He succeeded his father as earl of March in 1731 and was known by that title until succeeding his father's first cousin as duke of Queensberry in 1778. The latter also acted as March's guardian after the second earl's death on 7 March 1731, and was instrumental in the decision to educate him at Winchester College, which he attended from 1735 to 1740. He succeeded to the earldom of Ruglen on his mother's death on 21 April 1748.

After reaching his majority, March settled in London and dedicated himself to the pursuit of pleasure in a variety of forms. By the time he became heir to the third duke of Queensberry in 1756, he had established himself as a leading man about town. Lady Louisa Stuart noted that by then he was:

> the most fashionable, most dissipated young man in London, the leading character at Newmarket, the support of the gaming table, the supreme dictator of the Opera-house, the pattern whose dress and equipage were to be copied by all who aimed at distinction and … the person most universally admired by the ladies.   (*Letters and Journals*, 1.lxxiii)

No crude sensualist, March was a man of discerning taste and common sense who single-mindedly devoted himself to whatever interested him.

Admitted to the young club at White's in 1747, March soon became known as an active and successful gambler. His reputation soared after the 'chaise match' in 1750 in which he and the earl of Eglinton bet Theodore Taafe and Andrew Sproule 1000 guineas that a carriage could carry a passenger 19 miles in one hour. March arranged for the construction of a skeletal vehicle of lightweight materials that barely fitted the definition of a carriage and trained horses specially to pull it. The trial was held at Newmarket, and March's vehicle completed the 19 miles in under fifty-four minutes. As in much of his gaming, March shrewdly assessed the variables before committing to the wager and stretched the terms of the bet to his advantage. He seldom risked more than he was prepared to lose and manifested a degree of self-control that often eluded his fellow gamblers.

Success in the match was facilitated by March's expert knowledge of horses. He had run his first horses at Newmarket in 1748—winning three out of three races. Five years later he bought a house overlooking the racecourse. Though not a charter member of the Jockey Club, he was an early recruit and influential member. He was a careful breeder of horses and occasionally rode himself in the crimson colours that marked his stable. One of the turf's most successful and visible patrons, he continued to run horses until his eighty-first year.

Another passion was music. A founder member of the

Catch Club in 1762, March became better known as a patron of the opera. He continued to attend the latter, according to Nathaniel Wraxall, even after losing much of his hearing in order to gratify 'his wish of being still seen upon the great arena of the world' (*Historical and Posthumous Memoirs*, 4.359). To contemporaries, March's musical interests seemed keyed more to opera singers and ballet dancers, and some of his better-known mistresses, such as Teresina Tondino and Anna Zamparini, were divas.

Indeed it was as a pursuer and seducer of the opposite sex that March would be most remembered. He had a long string of mistresses, whom he neither flaunted nor concealed. Despite his lecherous reputation, he was regarded as one of the most eligible bachelors in the kingdom, especially after he became heir to the Queensberry title and estates. Though often rumoured to be on the verge of marriage, he successfully eluded all attempts to get him to the altar and died unmarried. He was probably the father of at least one daughter (with the Marchesa Fagnani). The child, Maria Emily Fagnani, familiarly known as Mie-Mie (later Maria Emily Seymour-*Conway, marchioness of Hertford) [*see under* Conway, Francis Ingram-Seymour-, second marquess of Hertford], was raised largely by his best friend, George Selwyn, and in 1798 married the heir of the marquess of Hertford.

Though his career as a pleasure-seeker tended to predominate in the public mind, March was also a figure of at least middling importance in politics. His paternal inheritance gave him the dominant parliamentary influence in Peeblesshire and as heir to the dukedom of Queensberry he gained a similar influence in Dumfriesshire and a less commanding interest in Dumfries burghs. He generally followed the lead of the third duke of Queensberry during the 1750s, becoming associated with the Leicester House group clustered around the prince of Wales. On the latter's accession, as George III, March was named a lord of the bedchamber and elected a representative peer in 1761. Honours and sinecures followed: knight of the Thistle (1763), vice-admiral of Scotland (1766–76), and first lord of police (1776–82). In 1763 he played a role in the prosecution of John Wilkes when his chaplain, the Revd John Kidgell, helped the government obtain a copy of Wilkes's privately printed poem 'Essay on Woman'.

As a representative peer March was more regular than most in attending the House of Lords but sought no reputation as a speaker. He usually supported the ministry of the day, though in 1766 he opposed the first Rockingham administration on the repeal of the Stamp Act, and in December 1783 opposed by proxy the Fox–North coalition's India Bill. He was in many ways a nominal Scot. Usually voting in peers' elections by sealed list, he attended in person only in 1747, 1761, and 1784, and generally spent little time in Scotland. In 1786 he was created a British peer as Baron Douglas of Amesbury. In 1789 he made the major political miscalculation of his career when he backed the prince of Wales and voted against William Pitt on the regency question, the only lord of the bedchamber to do so. He approached the issue as he would a prospective wager and had obtained from the king's doctor an opinion

that a recovery was unlikely. When the king's health did improve, Queensberry was dismissed and subjected to much criticism. He tried unsuccessfully to make amends with the king and thereafter ceased to be a prominent figure at court. In the 1790s he frequently offered hospitality to aristocratic refugees from the French Revolution. In 1794 he became lord lieutenant of Dumfriesshire when that office was revived for Scottish counties.

Already comfortably off, on the inheritance of the Queensberry estates in 1778 (said to be worth £18,000 a year) the duke became one of the richest men in the kingdom. As he grew older, his actions brought increasing notoriety and criticism. To some, perhaps, he was emblematic of aristocratic licence, to others merely a dirty old man. He was often referred to as Old Q, his continued pursuit of young women grist to the mill of caricaturists and salacious biographers. His decision to cut down large stands of timber on his Scottish estates provoked the ire of major poets. Thus Burns concluded his 'Verses on the Destruction of the Woods Near Drumlanrig':

> The worm that gnaw'd my bonnie trees,
> That reptile wears a ducal crown.

Wordsworth reacted: 'Degenerate Douglas! Oh, the unworthy lord!' (Blyth, 184–5). None of this bothered Queensberry, who remained contemptuous of public opinion. He did enjoy seeing and being seen, however, and fitted a balcony to his Piccadilly house so that he might watch the traffic below. Among other things he interested himself in underwriting the defence of Sir Thomas Picton, accused of brutality as governor of Trinidad. Prior to his death, the prospective disposition of his estate occasioned much speculation. He continued to add codicils to his will (twenty-five in all) until his death on 23 December 1810 at 138 Piccadilly, London. According to Wraxall he was then worth £900,000. He made numerous bequests and was notably generous to his male servants, though the largest share of his estate went to his natural daughter. He was buried on 31 December at St James's, Piccadilly, under the communion table.

Perhaps the most remarkable feature of Queensberry's career is that despite slender contributions to public life, he has remained a subject of popular interest. Refuting the obituary prediction of the *Scots Magazine* that because he had 'fulfilled none of the present duties of society, self-preservation only excepted', his name would be forgotten by all but his legatees and racing aficionados (Melville, 15), he has remained in the popular mind one of the best-known of eighteenth-century peers. He has been the subject of three serious biographies since the late nineteenth century, a statement that cannot be made about many of his noble contemporaries.   WILLIAM C. LOWE

Sources *DNB* · H. Blyth, *Old Q, the rake of Piccadilly* (1967) · L. Melville, *The star of Piccadilly: a memoir of William Douglas* (1927) · J. H. Jesse, *George Selwyn and his contemporaries, with memoirs and notes*, new edn, 4 vols. (1882) · E. S. Roscoe and H. Clergue, eds., *George Selwyn, his letters and his life* (1900) · *The letters and journals of Lady Mary Coke*, ed. J. A. Home, 4 vols. (1889–96); facs. repr. (1970), esp. vol. 1 · *The historical and the posthumous memoirs of Sir Nathaniel William Wraxall, 1772–1784*, ed. H. B. Wheatley, 5 vols. (1884), vols. 4–5 · J. R.

Robinson, *'Old Q': a memoir of William Douglas, fourth duke of Queensberry* (1895) • *Scots peerage*, vol. 7 • GEC, *Peerage*, new edn, vols. 8, 10, 11 • W. Robertson, *Proceedings relating to the peerage of Scotland, from January 16, 1707 to April 29, 1788* (1790) • A. Hamilton, *The infamous essay on woman or John Wilkes seated between vice and virtue* (1972) • *The later correspondence of George III*, ed. A. Aspinall, 5 vols. (1962–70)

Likenesses A. Ramsay, oils, 1742, Buccleuch estates, Selkirk • J. Reynolds, oils, 1759, Wallace collection, London • J. Sayers, caricature, etching, pubd 1789, NPG • stipple and line engraving, pubd 1795, NPG • R. Dighton, etching, pubd 1796, NPG • stipple, pubd 1803, NPG • caricature, line engraving, pubd 1807, BM, NPG • J. Gillray, caricature, coloured stipple, pubd 1811, NPG • attrib. J. Opie, oils, NPG • caricatures, BM

Wealth at death £900,000–£1,200,000: Melville, *Star*, 317; *Historical and posthumous memoirs*

Douglas, William [W. D.] (**1780–1832**), miniature and portrait painter, a descendant of the family of Douglas of Glenbervie, was born in Fife on 14 April 1780. He received a liberal education and showed an interest in painting at an early age. This led to his being placed as an apprentice to the engraver Robert Scott in Edinburgh, the engraver John Burnet being one of his fellow apprentices. However, he decided to specialize in miniature painting, generally producing miniatures in watercolour on ivory, but also full-length pencil drawings with the head often finished in watercolour, and oil paintings. His favoured subjects on a large scale were combined portraits of sitters and their animals, and his expertise at landscape painting meant that he often included extensive landscape backgrounds in both his drawings and oil paintings. Latterly he also painted miniatures of animal subjects alone. His work was usually signed, either with his initials W. D. and the date, or, in the case of his miniatures, in full on the reverse (for example, 'W. Douglas Edinburgh Pinxt 1816'). He achieved considerable success in Scotland and England, exhibiting at the Royal Scottish Academy in 1808–9 and the Society of Associated Artists between 1808 and 1816. His patrons in Scotland included numerous members of the Edinburgh middle classes and members of the Scottish aristocracy such as the ninth earl of Dalhousie and the fourth duke of Buccleuch, who commissioned him to paint portraits of their families and retainers, such as his oil painting of Thomas Hudson, keeper at Bowhill, of about 1810 (Bowhill, Selkirk).

On 9 July 1817 Douglas was appointed miniature painter in Scotland to Prince Leopold of Saxe-Coburg-Saalfeld and was commissioned to paint a miniature of his wife, Princess Charlotte of Wales, the only daughter of George IV. He then visited London, undertaking several commissions for William Balliol Best of Chilston Park, Kent. Although he subsequently returned to Edinburgh, he continued to exhibit at the Royal Academy in London from 1818 to 1826. In 1822 he painted a miniature of Sir Walter Scott's son, Walter. He died in Edinburgh on 30 January 1832. A pencil and watercolour drawing and a miniature by Douglas are in the Scottish National Portrait Gallery, Edinburgh.

Douglas and his wife, whose name is unknown, had one son and two daughters, the eldest of whom was Miss **Archibald Ramsey Douglas** (1807–1886), miniature painter, born on 23 April 1807 in Edinburgh. She learned the art of miniature painting from her father. She exhibited four works at the Royal Academy between 1834 and 1841 and nine works at the Royal Scottish Academy between 1835 and 1847, practising from 13 Hart Street, Edinburgh. She died in Edinburgh on 25 December 1886.

V. REMINGTON

Sources P. J. M. McEwan, *Dictionary of Scottish art and architecture* (1994), 177 • C. B. de Laperriere, ed., *The Royal Scottish Academy exhibitors, 1826–1990*, 4 vols. (1991) • D. Irwin and F. Irwin, *Scottish painters at home and abroad, 1700–1900* (1975), 80, 216 • *DNB* • private information (1888) [J. M. Gray] • D. Foskett, *Miniatures: dictionary and guide* (1987), 218, 530 • B. S. Long, *British miniaturists* (1929), 130 • L. R. Schidlof, *The miniature in Europe in the 16th, 17th, 18th, and 19th centuries*, 1 (1964), 211 • *CCI* (1887)

Wealth at death £278 0s. 2d.—Archibald Ramsey Douglas: confirmation, 3 Feb 1887, *CCI*

Douglas, William (**1783/4–1821**), lawyer and politician, was the eldest son of James Douglas of Orchardton, Kirkcudbrightshire, and his wife, Elizabeth, daughter of William Douglas of Worcester. His exact date of birth is unknown but after education at Edinburgh high school he was admitted as a fellow-commoner at Trinity College, Cambridge, on 12 October 1804, aged twenty. He became a member of the Faculty of Advocates in Scotland in 1806 and was admitted at Lincoln's Inn, London, on 20 June of the same year. At the general election of 1807 he initially intended to stand on the interest of the fifth earl of Selkirk at Kirkcudbright but withdrew before the poll. In 1810 he referred to himself in a letter to Henry Dundas, first Viscount Melville, as being 'from my heart a sturdy adherent to the principles of Mr. Pitt' (NA Scot., GD 51/5/470). In the general election of 1812 he went to the poll at Kirkcudbright but, having lost the confidence of his erstwhile patron Selkirk, he was defeated by General James Dunlop of Dunlop. None the less Douglas, said by James Shaw to possess 'a mind of considerable delicacy' (NA Scot., GD 51/1/179), was soon returned to the Commons on the pro-government interest of the Treby family at Plympton Erle, Devon (26 December 1812). He had an undistinguished parliamentary career. He voted mostly, but not often, with the government and in 1813 supported Catholic relief. He is not known to have spoken in the House of Commons. In June 1816 he vacated his seat, possibly because of the tour of Europe he undertook, probably with the artist Hugh W. Williams, in 1816–17. He died, unmarried, in London on 9 July 1821.

STEPHEN M. LEE

Sources Venn, *Alum. Cant.* • D. R. Fisher, 'Douglas, William', HoP, *Commons, 1790–1820* • NA Scot., Melville Castle muniments • *GM*, 1st ser., 91/2 (1821), 93

Archives U. Edin. L., special collections division, letters describing European tour | NA Scot., Melville Castle muniments

Douglas, William Alexander Anthony Archibald. *See* Hamilton, William Alexander Anthony Archibald Douglas-, eleventh duke of Hamilton and eighth duke of Brandon (1811–1863).

Douglas, Sir William Fettes (**1822–1891**), painter, antiquary, and curator, was born in the parish of St Cuthbert, Edinburgh, on 29 March 1822, eldest son of Douglas James

Douglas, accountant with the Commercial Bank of Scotland, and Martha Brook, great-niece of Sir William Fettes, bt, the founder of Fettes College. He was educated at the Southern Academy and the Royal High School in Edinburgh. In 1836 he took up a post as a clerk in the Commercial Bank where he remained for about ten years. During this period he resolved to become an artist and devoted his spare time to drawing and painting. However, his formal art training was limited: he enrolled at the Trustees' Academy for a few months in 1848 and attended the Royal Scottish Academy Life School for the 1851–2 session. More informally, in 1848 he joined the Smashers' Club. This was a group of Edinburgh-based artists whose meetings combined sketching sessions and criticisms of each other's work with general drinking and socializing. As the members migrated south, the group re-formed in London in the 1860s and Fettes Douglas was an occasional visitor there. He also attended botany and anatomy classes at Edinburgh University. In addition he travelled with the painter Alexander Fraser to Warwickshire and the Lake District in 1851.

Fettes Douglas first exhibited at the Royal Scottish Academy in 1845 and thereafter became a regular exhibitor. Although he showed portraits, figure studies, and a few landscapes to begin with, he very quickly immersed himself in historical, literary, and occult subjects. He frequently used the works of Shakespeare and Walter Scott as source material but picture titles show his wider interests, for example *Benvenuto Cellini Showing a Chased Salver* (1856; Hospitalfield House, Arbroath), *The Summons to the Secret Tribunal: an Incident in the Life of Vesalius the Great Anatomist* (1860; Perth Museum and Art Gallery), and *The Spell* (1864; National Gallery of Scotland, Edinburgh). His paintings were meticulously researched, particularly in the details of furnishings, costumes, and *objets d'art*. It is likely that he was influenced by Pre-Raphaelitism through Millais's painting *Mariana* (1851), which was exhibited at the Royal Scottish Academy in 1852. Unlike many of his Scottish contemporaries whose brushwork is characterized by a looseness and freedom of handling, Fettes Douglas relied on thin layers of oil carefully applied with linear precision. His paintings were signed with his monogram in the Douglas heart, usually painted in red.

In 1857 Fettes Douglas first visited Italy. This trip fostered his antiquarian interests and he began to collect coins and medals. His collection expanded to include costume, furniture, ceramics, glass, and silver and he used it in his paintings. He also acquired an important library which reflected his serious interest in history, particularly that of Scotland. After his death his collection of antiquities and fine art was sold at auction over four consecutive days and his library over five.

During the 1860s Fettes Douglas travelled widely in Europe and in 1866–7 he made a lengthy journey through France, Italy, and Sicily. Not only did his travels feed his antiquarian imagination but he also began to paint his immediate surroundings. For example *On a Housetop, Rome* (1871; Royal Bank of Scotland) is one of a series of paintings of contemporary Italian subjects. Later in his career he turned increasingly to landscape, for example *The Village of the Water of Leith from a Window in Rothesay Terrace* (1879; Edinburgh City Museums and Art Galleries), painted on a strong vertical format. In the late 1870s, due to ill health, he began painting in watercolours, particularly landscapes, for example *On the Shores of the Lake of Menteith* (1887; Dundee Museums and Art Galleries).

Fettes Douglas was elected an associate of the Royal Scottish Academy in 1851, and an academician in 1854. He was involved with the raising of the Artists' company of the City of Edinburgh artillery volunteers in 1859. During the late 1860s he served as a visitor to the Royal Scottish Academy Life School and from 1869 to 1870 was the academy's secretary. In 1877 he was appointed curator of the National Gallery of Scotland but he resigned in 1882 in order to become president of the Royal Scottish Academy, a position he retained until his death. In 1880 he married Marion Barclay Grahame (c.1836–1916), the second daughter of Baron Grahame of Morphie; they had no children. He was knighted on 17 May 1882 at Windsor Castle. Fettes Douglas died at Monkswell, Abdie, near Newburgh, Fife, on 20 July 1891. After a funeral in Edinburgh his body was taken by train to St Cyrus, Kincardineshire, for burial in the Barclay family plot on 28 July.   JOANNA SODEN

Sources J. M. Gray, *Sir William Fettes Douglas PRSA* (1885) · *Annual Report of the Council of the Royal Scottish Academy of Painting, Sculpture, and Architecture*, 64 (1891), 11–13 · W. D. McKay, *The Scottish school of painting* (1906), 334–40 · J. L. Caw, *Scottish painting past and present, 1620–1908* (1908), 172–4 · D. Irwin and F. Irwin, *Scottish painters at home and abroad, 1700–1900* (1975), 305–7 · C. B. de Laperriere, ed., *The Royal Scottish Academy exhibitors, 1826–1990*, 4 vols. (1991), vol. 1, pp. 439–43 · W. Armstrong, *Scottish painters* (1888), 82 · P. J. M. McEwan, *Dictionary of Scottish art and architecture* (1994), 177–8 · Wood, *Vic. painters*, 2nd edn · Graves, *RA exhibitors*, 2 (1905), 358 · b. cert. · d. cert. · archives, Royal Scot. Acad.
Archives Royal Scot. Acad. | U. Edin. L., letters to David Laing
Likenesses G. Reid, oils, 1883, Royal Scot. Acad. · J. Faed, watercolour and pencil drawing, Scot. NPG · W. Graham Boss, pencil drawing, Scot. NPG · photograph, Royal Scot. Acad.
Wealth at death £2078 3s. 9d.: confirmation, 10 Oct 1891, CCI · £2052 12s. 2d.—additional estate: 4 June 1892, CCI

Douglas, William Gerald [Bill] (1934–1991), film-maker, was born on 17 April 1934 at 14 Third Avenue, Newcraighall, Edinburgh, the only son of John James Douglas (1913–1988), coal miner, and Rose McEwen Beveridge (1912–1996), hosiery worker. He was brought up initially by his maternal grandmother, also Rose Beveridge, and then, following her death, by his father and his paternal grandmother. After a period of national service in Egypt, during which he met his lifelong friend and companion, Peter Jewell, he moved to London and embarked on a career of acting and writing. After spending some time with Joan Littlewood's Theatre Workshop company in Stratford East he was cast in the Granada television series *The Younger Generation* in 1961, and had a musical, *Solo*, produced in 1962 at Cheltenham. In 1968 he enrolled at the London International Film School, where he wrote the screenplay for a short autobiographical film, *Jamie*. Encouraged by the distinguished British film-maker Lindsay Anderson he secured a commission from the British Film Institute for the project, now entitled *My Childhood*.

Released in 1972 the film's considerable success on the international festival circuit helped to pave the way for the second and third instalments of what became a trilogy of Douglas's formative years, *My Ain Folk* (1973) and *My Way Home* (1978).

The Bill Douglas trilogy recounts the harrowing experiences of a young boy, Jamie, growing up in crippling poverty. *My Childhood* depicts his life with his cousin Tommy and their maternal grandmother towards the end of the war, the harsh material and emotional impoverishment alleviated only by his friendship with a German prisoner of war. After the grandmother's death Tommy is sent away to a children's home and Jamie is taken in by his father's family. The harrowing privations that he endures at the hands of his cold and vindictive paternal grandmother become the primary focus of *My Ain Folk*, culminating in Jamie's being incarcerated in a similar manner to that of his cousin. *My Way Home* picks up the story a few years later, with Jamie now old enough to leave the home. After ill-fated attempts to live first with his father and then with a foster mother he spends a period in a hostel for down-and-outs before being called up for national service. It is during his posting in Egypt that he finds redemption through his friendship with Robert, a young middle-class Englishman who introduces him to books and the possibility of a more optimistic and fulfilling future.

The austere black and white images of Douglas's films embodied a stillness and intensity reminiscent of silent cinema, far removed from the kind of film-making associated with the 1970s. The use of non-professional actors in several key roles recalled the work of similar film poets like Robert Bresson and Satyajit Ray, and served to enhance Douglas's interrogation of the experience of poverty and deprivation, the pain palpably etched on the face of young Stephen Archibald, as Jamie, and conveying infinitely more about the human condition than the most skilful acting could ever hope to do. Douglas's visual style was augmented by the equally spare and precise use of sound. Just as the stillness of the image forced the audience to look, so the relative silence encouraged greater attention to specific sounds—boots scraping on asphalt, the chirping of birds, and the timbre of voices—granting an emotional power lost in the aural bombardment characterizing much contemporary cinema.

Despite a wealth of critical plaudits Douglas struggled to fund his next project and was forced to find other ways of earning a living. In 1978 he was invited by former head of BFI Production, Mamoun Hassan, to teach at the National Film and Television School, where he proved an inspiring presence. As director of the National Film Finance Corporation, Hassan also helped to realize *Comrades*, Douglas's film about the Tolpuddle martyrs, six Dorset farm labourers who were arrested in 1834 and tried for forming a trade union, and subsequently transported to Australia. But it had been a long and frustrating struggle to raise the £3 million budget for a film that finally appeared in 1987, seven years after the screenplay had been completed. Dubbed a 'poor man's epic', *Comrades* continued Douglas's interest in the perseverance of the human spirit in the face of material adversity. It also alluded to his fascination with the world of optics and image-making by way of several references to various forms of pre-cinematic optical toys and media, such as the magic lantern, the zoetrope, the peep-show, and the camera obscura. The story itself is ostensibly mediated by the character of an itinerant magic lanternist, who reappears in a number of roles.

Comrades was Douglas's last film. He died of cancer at his home, Ashpool, Park Lane, Barnstaple, Devon, on 18 June 1991 and was buried at the church of St John the Baptist, at nearby Bishop's Tawton, on 24 June. He left two unmade screenplays, *Justified Sinner*, an adaptation of James Hogg's celebrated novel, and *Flying Horse*, based on the life of the pre-cinema pioneer Eadweard Muybridge. Another posthumous script, *Ring of Truth*, written during a fellowship at Strathclyde University in 1990, was produced by BBC Scotland in 1995. But Douglas's legacy was not confined to his films. With Peter Jewell he was a voracious collector of books, memorabilia, and artefacts relating to the history and prehistory of cinema. In 1995 Peter Jewell donated their collection of some 50,000 items to the University of Exeter; two years later a museum and study centre, the Bill Douglas Centre for the History of Cinema and Popular Culture, was officially opened to the public.

DUNCAN PETRIE

Sources E. Dick, A. Noble, and D. Petrie, eds., *Bill Douglas: a lanternist's account* (1993) • A. Noble, 'Bill Douglas's trilogy', *From limelight to satellite: a Scottish film book*, ed. E. Dick (1990) • M. Hassan, 'His ain man', *Sight and Sound*, new ser., 1/7 (1991), 22–6 • D. Petrie, *Screening Scotland* (2000), 148–71 • *The Independent* (20 June 1991) • *The Times* (2 July 1991) • b. cert. • d. cert.
Archives University of Exeter, Bill Douglas Centre for the History of Cinema and Popular Culture, Bill Douglas and Peter Jewell collection
Likenesses photograph, repro. in *The Independent* • photograph, repro. in *The Times*
Wealth at death under £125,000: probate, 27 Nov 1991, CGPLA Eng. & Wales

Douglas, William Scott (1815–1883), editor, was born in Hawick on 10 January 1815, the son of Alexander Douglas and his wife, Isabella Scott. He was educated at Heriot's Hospital, Edinburgh. On 5 June 1862 he married Isabella Forbes, with whom he had at least five children: William (*b*. 1863), Daniel (*b*. 1865), David Gordon (*b*. 1868), Isabella Scott (*b*. 1873), and Jessie Irving (*b*. 1874).

Douglas worked as a mercantile accountant, like his father before him, but in his leisure time he put much effort into studying the life and works of Burns, acquiring perhaps a more thorough mastery of them than any previous editor of Burns's works. In 1850 he read a paper on the 'Highland Mary' incident of Burns's life before the Society of Antiquaries of Scotland. His principal publications were a reissue of the Kilmarnock, 'popular edition' of *The Complete Poetical Works of Robert Burns with Memoir, &c* (1871; rev. edn, 1876); *Descriptive Picture of the County of Ayr* (1874); and a splendid, six-volume library edition of *The Works of Robert Burns* (1877–9). The poems in this edition are arranged chronologically, and while it was the most sumptuous yet published it was also the most complete and correct regarding both text and notes. He also supplied letterpress for an edition of B. W. Coombie's *Modern Athenians*, published in 1882. In 1877 he succeeded James Ballantine as secretary of the Edinburgh Burns Club. He was found, drowned, off the East Pier at Leith on 23 June 1883.　　　　　　　T. F. HENDERSON, *rev.* JAMES HOW

Sources Allibone, *Dict.*, suppl. • Irving, *Scots.* • IGI • bap. reg. Scot. • d. cert.

Archives NL Scot., corresp.

Douglas, Sir William Scott (1890–1953), civil servant, was born in Edinburgh on 20 August 1890, the elder child and only son of Daniel Douglas, solicitor, and his wife, Margaret Dougal. William Scott *Douglas (1815–1883) was his grandfather. Douglas went to George Heriot's School and Edinburgh University, where he won the Lanfine bursary in economics (1911) and graduated with second-class honours in history (1912). In 1914 he passed into the first division of the civil service, in which his career was astonishingly varied. He had a natural talent for administration and could turn his hand to any administrative task without becoming deeply involved with the subject. What fascinated him was negotiation and management of both people and things; at these he was superbly good.

Douglas started in the customs and excise department, but in 1920 he was appointed financial adviser to the Allenstein plebiscite commission which dealt with adjustments to the frontiers between East Prussia and Poland. There he attracted the notice of Sir John Bradbury, principal British delegate to the reparation commission in Paris, whose private secretary Douglas became on first joining the delegation. He greatly enjoyed his period in Paris, becoming a fluent French speaker. Customs and excise, to which he returned in 1926, was never his spiritual home, but in those days civil servants were seldom consulted about their wishes. However, in 1929 he transferred to the Ministry of Labour to face the tremendous problem of unemployment, as divisional controller for the midlands (1931–3), for Scotland (1933–5), and as an assistant secretary (1935–7). In 1937 he became secretary of the Department of Health for Scotland, where he was a popular chief and did a great deal to bring the department into the administrative structure of the service and to lay the foundations of its future.

In 1939 Douglas moved to the Treasury as third secretary in charge of the establishment division, succeeding the greatly loved Sir James (Jimmy) Rae who had done so much to make the service one service and so enable it to take the strain of war. Douglas was probably not at his happiest without his own machine to manage; the endless struggle to keep the fast expanding departments amenable to some kind of financial discipline in pay and complements hardly suited his style. The story goes that he settled one battle with his old Scottish department by playing for it at golf; probably the Treasury came off best since he was a scratch performer. His major contribution in the Treasury lay in the planning and manning of the new departments needed for war, and in starting the 'exchange and mart' by which the Treasury sought to place experienced men where they were most needed.

In 1942 Sir Andrew Duncan returned to the Ministry of Supply and picked Douglas to replace the permanent secretary, who was ill. The two made an excellent team. Douglas was both adviser and friend to the minister, and under the two of them the department worked both hard and effectively. It was a difficult ministry to manage, because of the nature of some of the individuals with whom he had to deal, and his personal skills were both necessary and effective.

In 1945 came Douglas's last and longest job, with his transfer to the Ministry of Health, where Aneurin Bevan was setting up the National Health Service. There his gift for negotiation proved invaluable. It was not the detail, even the purpose, of the health service which absorbed him, but getting it across. It was an immense help that he got on extremely well with the, to him, new world of the medical profession and all its auxiliaries. Less personally involved than either the minister or the departmental officers who were closest to the operation, he could often smooth over difficulties or suggest a solution to an impasse. Surprisingly, given their different backgrounds and views, he and Bevan had a comfortable and productive working relationship. Douglas considered Bevan the best minister he had ever worked for; Bevan returned the compliment by specifically mentioning Douglas in his speech to the House of Commons on the tenth anniversary of the National Health Service. On the housing side he took a great interest in the building of non-traditional houses.

When in 1951 the housing and local government side of the ministry joined with the Ministry of Town and Country Planning, and the health side became a separate ministry, Douglas stayed with the health work but retired later in the same year. He acquired several directorships and particularly enjoyed one at Slazengers, for golf was always a ruling passion. He was chairman of the civil service preparatory commission which investigated the form the public service should take under the proposed federation of central Africa, whose draft report was published in 1952. He was appointed CB in 1938, KBE in 1941, KCB in 1943, and GCB in 1950. He was also awarded the American medal of freedom (with gold palm) in 1947.

In 1919 Douglas married Vera Paterson, daughter of George Macpherson Duffes, chief assistant keeper of the Sasines in Edinburgh, whom he had met while she was still at school. They had two daughters and took care that both should be born in Scotland. His retirement promised to be as varied and active as his civil service career, but was cut short by his death on 17 February 1953, at the hospital, Rye Street, Bishop's Stortford, Hertfordshire. He was survived by his wife.　　　　　SHARP, *rev.* JOHN STEWART

Sources private information (1971) • personal knowledge (1971) • M. Foot, *Aneurin Bevan: a biography*, 2 (1973) • C. Webster, ed., *Aneurin Bevan on the national health service* (1991) • CGPLA Eng. & Wales (1953)

Archives Nuffield Oxf., corresp. with Lord Cherwell

Likenesses W. Stoneman, photograph, 1942, NPG

Wealth at death £11,422 0s. 1d.: administration with will, 20 Aug 1953, CGPLA Eng. & Wales

Douglass, David (*d.* 1789). *See under* Hallam, Lewis (1714?–1756?).

Douglass, Dorothea Katharine. *See* Chambers, Dorothea Katharine Lambert (1878–1960).

Douglass, Sir James Nicholas (1826–1898), civil engineer, eldest son of Nicholas Douglass of Northumberland, and his wife, Alice, daughter of James Douglass of Winlaton, co. Durham, was born on 16 October 1826 at Bow, London, where his father was employed by the engineering firm of Hunter and English. He was educated at Blaydon, co. Durham, on the Tyne, and at Bridgend under the Revd E. Jones, and was then apprenticed to Hunter and English at Bow. His father, meanwhile, having ventured his own capital on an engineering and shipbuilding business on the Thames which failed, joined the engineering staff of Trinity House in 1839 and rose to be superintending engineer.

In 1847 Douglass became assistant to his father in the erection of the Bishop's Rock lighthouse in the Isles of Scilly. He then became manager at R. J. and R. Laycock's railway carriage works on the Tyne. He returned briefly to Scilly in 1854 to marry Mary, second daughter of Captain James Tregarthen, shipowner of St Mary's. They had two sons and a daughter. In 1855 he was appointed resident engineer of the Gun Fleet Pile lighthouse, and afterwards of the Smalls Rock lighthouse near Milford Haven. This latter work was one of extraordinary difficulty and danger. Douglass always accompanied the working party, and was the first to land and the last to leave. He had many narrow escapes; during the terrible gale of October 1859, when the passenger steamer *Royal Charter* was wrecked, it was thought that the whole of the working party had been drowned, but the small sailing tender in which the party embarked from the rock succeeded at length in making Swansea harbour.

In 1861 Douglass became resident engineer on the Wolf Rock lighthouse, situated in deep water between Land's End and the Isles of Scilly. The structure was not completed until 1870, and the dangerous nature of the work was made plain in Douglass's account to the Institution of Civil Engineers. In October 1862 he was appointed chief engineer to the corporation of Trinity House in succession to James Walker. Foremost among the many important lighthouses which he designed was his replacement of John Smeaton's famous Eddystone lighthouse, necessitated by the disintegration of the rock upon which it stood. Douglass found a new site, and took down most of the old lighthouse, which was re-erected on Plymouth Hoe, itself a difficult task. Work was begun on 17 July 1878, and the new lighthouse was opened on 18 May 1882, the cost (below the original estimate) being £59,250. On the completion of this work he was knighted in June 1882.

Douglass carried out, in conjunction with John Tyndall and Michael Faraday, many exhaustive experiments with fog signals and on lighthouse illumination by Argand oil lamps and by electric arc lamps. In 1884 he was a member of the committee appointed by Trinity House to assess the effectiveness of different kinds of light for lighthouse work. The committee made its experiments at the North Foreland, reporting that oil was the most economical and suitable illuminant for ordinary lighthouses, but that electric lighting was preferable for the more important structures on lofty headlands.

Douglass became a member of the Institution of Civil Engineers on 5 February 1861, and was elected to the council in 1881. He was elected a fellow of the Royal Society in 1887, and in 1886, at the Birmingham meeting of the British Association, he served as president of the mechanical section. He attended the Montreal meeting of the association in 1884, preceding it by travelling with his wife and daughter across Canada to the Rocky Mountains and back by train, a tour which, with the meeting, lasted some three months. He was a governor of Dulwich College and of University College, London, and retained his position with Trinity House until an attack of paralysis in 1892 obliged him to resign. He spent his last years at Stella, Bonchurch, on the Isle of Wight, where he died on 19 June 1898. He was buried at Bonchurch.

T. H. Beare, *rev.* Anita McConnell

Sources *Nature*, 58 (1898), 177 · T. Williams, *Life of Sir James Nicholas Douglass* (1900) · *PICE*, 134 (1897–8), 403–5 · *CGPLA Eng. & Wales* (1898)
Likenesses photograph, repro. in Williams, *Life*, frontispiece
Wealth at death £9464 7s. 0d.: probate, 9 Dec 1898, *CGPLA Eng. & Wales*

Douglass, John (1743?–1812), vicar apostolic of the London district, was born at Yarm, Yorkshire, probably in December 1743, the son of John Douglass, originally from Scotland, whose occupation is unknown, and his wife, Bridget Semson. His sister Ann became a Carmelite nun. He was educated by the secular priest Simon Bordley at Salwick Hall, Lancashire, and from October 1757 at the English College, Douai. After ordination and after graduating DD, he set out on 20 May 1768 with eight students from Douai to the English College, Valladolid, from which the Jesuits had recently been expelled. Here he taught humanities and philosophy, a contemporary noting:

> He is young and has a great narrowness of mind and thinking, as yet; such persons stick close to their own few ideas, and to try and persuade them directly not to cleave to their own preconceived and narrow notions, is the way to throw them entirely off their hinges and to get their ill will for one's pains. (Williams, 76)

Owing to ill health he left Valladolid on 30 July 1773 and became a mission priest at Linton upon Ouse, Newton upon Ouse, and York by 24 March 1776.

In 1790 he was chosen to succeed James Talbot as vicar apostolic of the London district against the wishes of the Catholic committee, composed of liberal lay Catholics, who insisted that he was being 'imposed by a foreign power' (Nelson, 146). The success of the conservative vicars apostolic in having Douglass appointed against the wishes of the leading laity suggests a decline in the gentry's influence on English Catholicism. He was consecrated on 19 December 1790 as bishop of Centuria *in partibus infidelium*—in the chapel at Lulworth Castle, Dorset—by Dr William Gibson, the northern vicar apostolic, the Jesuit Charles Plowden giving a discourse on episcopal authority. The Catholic committee—which demanded that bishops be elected, and campaigned for Catholic emancipation, a reduction of papal influence in England, and more accommodation with the British government—identified him, not altogether correctly, as siding with the conservative vicars apostolic. Douglass certainly provided his fellow bishops with essential information, and was in communication with politicians like William Pitt the younger and Edmund Burke, whom he called 'our sincere friend' (diary, 72). In the interests of unity he supported the substitution of the Irish oath of allegiance, adopted from the 1779 Irish Catholic Relief Act, and this was included in the Catholic Relief Bill which became law on 24 June 1791.

Douglass exploited the new opportunities brought about by the act, helping religious orders to establish themselves, and he began publishing an annual 'new year's gift' and Lenten pastoral letter. About 1790 he had moved to his official residence at 4 Castle Street, Holborn, where, in his wainscoted study, surrounded by portraits of English Catholic clergy and martyrs yellow with smoke, Douglass, a tall thin man in a 'suit of black, not very fresh, with a little close white wig' (Ward, *Catholic London*, 64), would openly wear his pectoral cross and amethyst ring. Despite some protestant opposition, he began to pontificate with mitre and crosier at high mass in the new London chapels, and in 1805 ordered a Te Deum and prayers for the royal family after Trafalgar. After 1791 he acted as mediator in further disputes between the orthodox party and the Catholic committee, now called the Cisalpine Club, and remained a close friend of the leading Cisalpine, Charles Butler. From 1792 until 1801 he struggled with another Cisalpine, Sir John Throckmorton, by refusing to give priestly faculties to his outspoken and liberal chaplain, Joseph Berington. It was hard for one so mild as he to resort to harsh measures; in the parable of the tares, he saw 'encouragement to leave doubtful doctrine uncondemned till the Last Day' (Duffy, 'Doctor Douglass', 262), and therefore more aggressive bishops, like John Milner, insinuated that he had 'deserted the faith of his fathers' (Duffy, 'Ecclesiastical democracy', part III, 125). Still, his enhancement of episcopal authority can be said to have paved the way for the grand Catholic prelates of the following century. He remained from 1808 a determined opponent of the veto by which the crown would exercise some control over episcopal appointments. In the apocalyptic gloom of the 1790s he had to face the problem of hundreds of émigré clergy without direction or means of livelihood swarming into London during the French Revolution, and insisted that they, as well as the Irish in the capital, be subject to his immediate jurisdiction. In 1808 he suspended the Blanchardist schismatics who opposed Pius VII's concordat of 1801 with Napoleon.

To ensure a continuity of Catholic education after the closure of English institutions in France during the Revolution, Douglass used his influence and financial resources to begin in November 1793 the foundation of a college at his property at Old Hall Green, Hertfordshire, as the successor of Douai College in France, which ultimately became the seminary of St Edmund, Ware. He appointed its president and was a frequent visitor. After a long illness Douglass died at his residence, 4 Castle Street, Holborn, London, on 8 May 1812, leaving money in his will to his brother James, at Ealing, and to his two nephews. He was buried at St Pancras churchyard on 15 May 1812, and in 1906 his remains were translated to St Edmund's, Ware. He was 'a man of unusual kindness of disposition, with a calmness of judgment and action in keeping with his Scotch descent, while by no means wanting in firmness when occasion demanded' (Ward, *Catholic London*, 64).

GEOFFREY SCOTT

Sources B. Ward, *The dawn of the Catholic revival in England, 1781–1803*, 2 vols. (1909) · B. Ward, *The eve of Catholic emancipation, 1803–1829*, 3 vols. (1911) · B. Ward, *Catholic London a century ago* (1905) · E. Duffy, 'Doctor Douglass and Mister Berington: an eighteenth-century retraction', *Downside Review*, 292 (1970), 246–70 · J. Douglass, diary, 2 vols., 1792–1811, Westm. DA · Gillow, *Lit. biog. hist.*, vol. 2 · F. Blom and others, *English Catholic books, 1701–1800: a bibliography* (1996) · L. Gooch, ed., *The revival of English Catholicism* (1995) · G. Anstruther, *The seminary priests*, 4 (1977) · G. L. Nelson, 'Charles Walmesley and the episcopal opposition to English Catholic Cisalpinism, 1782–1797', PhD diss., Tulane University, 1977 · M. E. Williams, *St Alban's College, Valladolid* (1986) · E. Duffy, 'Ecclesiastical democracy detected, pt II (1787–1796)', *Recusant History*, 10/6 (1970), 309–31 · E. Duffy, 'Ecclesiastical democracy detected, pt III (1796–1803)', *Recusant History*, 13/2 (1975), 123–48
Archives Birmingham archdiocesan archives · Clifton Roman Catholic diocese, Bristol, diocesan archives · Hexham and Newcastle diocesan archives · Leeds diocesan archives · St Edmund's College, Ware, archives · Ushaw College, Durham · Westm. DA, corresp., diary, notes, papers, and sermons
Likenesses stipple, pubd 1812, NPG · portrait, 1893, St Edmund's College, Ware · Meisenbach, oils, St Edmund's College, Ware · P. Turnerelli, bust, St Edmund's College, Ware · engravings (after Turnerelli), repro. in *Laity's Directory* (1813)
Wealth at death see will, proved, 23 June 1812, Anstruther, *Seminary priests*

Doulton, Sir Henry (1820–1897), pottery manufacturer, was born on 25 July 1820 at Vauxhall Walk, London, the second of the eight children of John Doulton (1793–1873), pottery manufacturer, and his wife, Jane Duneau, a widow from Bridgnorth in Shropshire. His father had become a partner in the Vauxhall Walk pottery in 1815, establishing the Doulton name in the industry with functional brown stoneware products. Henry spent two years at University College School in Gower Street, London, where his love of literature was fostered. John Doulton fully expected the most bookish of his sons to take to the cloth or the bar when he left school in 1835 but instead Henry expressed his desire to follow his elder brother, John junior, into the pottery business. Four of Henry's brothers also joined the company, but Frederick Doulton (1824–1872) became MP for Lambeth in 1862 and remained so for six years.

After a brief apprenticeship, Henry Doulton had learned enough by 1846 to leave home and initiate and control his own branch of the business, making ceramic pipes for the sanitary market. It was the first factory to provide such products, meeting the rising demand for effective sanitation. In 1849 Doulton married Sarah,

Sir Henry Doulton (1820–1897), by Vandyk

daughter of John L. Kennaby. They settled at 7 Stockwell Villas, Lambeth, where they had three children: Sarah Lilian, Henry Lewis, and Katherine.

At the Paris Exhibition of 1867 Doulton presented the first examples of art pottery to be made by the company. Ten years previously John Sparkes, principal of the Lambeth School of Art, had approached Doulton with the idea of producing such ware but while the business of functional pottery was proving so successful there had seemed no need to add any new products. But Sparkes had not been dissuaded and, with the help of Edward Cresy, an engineer and lifelong friend of Henry Doulton, he eventually convinced him to experiment with purely artistic designs. The production of art ware had been fraught with technical problems and it was not until 1870 that they began to be resolved. John Sparkes had already introduced one student of the art school to Doulton, namely the sculptor George Tinworth, who was immediately employed for his modelling skills. Other artists like Hannah Barlow followed, and by 1872 a great variety of work was being produced. These early examples prompted Doulton to enlist a batch of Sparkes's students to decorate his products, providing them with studio facilities and blank pots of soft clay to work on. The resulting richly coloured salt-glazed stoneware with a range of decorative motifs was so distinctive of the company that it became known as Doulton Ware.

In 1877 Doulton was approached by Shadford Pinder, a potter from Burslem, Stoke-on-Trent, with a proposition to become a partner in the firm of Pinder, Bourne & Co. for an outlay of £12,000. This he agreed to, but the money was unwisely spent and differences of opinion caused such a rift between the two concerns that only arbitration resolved the matter. Indeed Pinder retired from the business and in 1882 the name changed to Doulton & Co., Burslem. It was John Slater, art director at Pinder Bourne, who, after travelling among the European potteries, convinced Doulton to produce china as well as earthenware. Again the marriage of art and industry facilitated some of the finest hand-painted china of the time with artists Percy Curnock and David Dewsberry among others. Such was the success of Doulton's efforts to create a vast array of art wares as well as functional designs at Lambeth and Burslem that in 1885 the Society of Arts, of which he had been a member since 1851 and later served as vice-president (1890–94), awarded him the Albert medal, which was presented by the prince of Wales (later King Edward VII). In 1887 Doulton was knighted by Queen Victoria at Osborne House. A year after his knighthood, in October 1888, Doulton's wife died and after a succession of highly renowned exhibitions Doulton spent most of his remaining years at Woolpit Farm, his home in Ewhurst, Surrey. He died at his London residence, 10 Queen's Gate Gardens, on 17 November 1897 and was buried on 22 November at Norwood cemetery.   ALEXANDER JAMES CLEMENT

Sources E. Gosse, *Sir Henry Doulton: the man of business as a man of imagination*, ed. D. Eyles (1970) · D. Eyles, *The Doulton Lambeth wares* (1975) · D. Eyles, *The Doulton Burslem wares* (1980) · D. Eyles, *Royal Doulton, 1815–1965* (1965) · d. cert.
Archives Lambeth Archives, London · Royal Doulton, Burslem, Stoke-on-Trent, Sir Henry Doulton Gallery
Likenesses F. Sandys, drawing, mixed media, 1861, Royal Doulton, Burslem, Stoke-on-Trent, Sir Henry Doulton Gallery · G. Tinworth, terracotta bust, 1888, Royal Doulton, Burslem, Stoke-on-Trent, Sir Henry Doulton Gallery · W. & D. Downey, cabinet photograph, c.1890, NPG · E. Roberts, oils, 1898, Potteries Museum and Art Gallery, Stoke-on-Trent · C. Melbourne, bronze statue, 1986, Burslem, Stoke-on-Trent · Vandyk, photograph, priv. coll. [see illus.]
Wealth at death £310,544 13s. 9d.: resworn probate, Aug 1898, CGPLA Eng. & Wales

D'Ouvilly, George Gerbier (*fl.* 1638–1661), playwright and translator, was the eldest son of Sir Balthazar *Gerbier (1592–1663/1667), art agent, miniature painter, and architect, and his wife, Deborah Kip (*b.* 1601). Balthazar Gerbier later styled himself Baron d'Ouvilly. Descended from a Huguenot family which had sought refuge in establishing the French church in Middelburg, Zeeland, after the St Bartholomew's day massacre, George showed early educational promise and, while still a youth, 'had all the exercises fitt for a gentleman', possessing the ability to speak 'eight several languages prompt' (*Manifestation*, 3–4; Sainsbury, 318). By 1638, however, D'Ouvilly had enlisted as a captain in the regiment of William, Lord Craven, who was financing attempts to restore the Palatinate, held by Ferdinand II, to the former king and queen of Bohemia. In 1637–8 campaigns were fought in the Low Countries, and it is possible that D'Ouvilly was taken prisoner there with Craven and Elizabeth of Bohemia's son, Prince Rupert.

D'Ouvilly's military links may have been instrumental in securing a commission from 1662 for his father to design and supervise the rebuilding of Craven's house at Hampstead Marshall, Berkshire.

D'Ouvilly appears to have been resident in England throughout the period of the protectorate and on 18 March 1651 was ordered by the Committee for Examinations to offer securities that he would not 'do anything to the prejudice of the commonwealth, and to appear before the Council on summons' (*CSP dom.*, 1651, 94).

D'Ouvilly's literary works differed in genre, reputation, and success. In 1657 his tragi-comedy *The False Favourite Disgrac'd. And the Reward of Virtue* was printed in London, but remained unacted. Set in Florence, the plot revolves around a series of misunderstandings which are ultimately resolved in the closing scene when concord, hierarchy, and true vision are re-established within the court. D'Ouvilly's linguistic talents, however, proved to be more apparent in his translation of a selection of French biographies by André Thevet, cosmographer to Henri III. Introduced under the title, 'Prospographia, or, Some select Portraitures and Lives of Antient and Modern Illustrious Personages ... newly translated into English by some Learned and Eminent Persons; and generally by Geo: Gerbier, alias D'Ouvilly', the passages form the third part of the stationer William Lee's edition of North's *Plutarch* (1657).

D'Ouvilly's final work, *Il trionfo d'Inghilterra overo racconto et relatione delle solennità fatte & osservate nella ... incoronatione ... di Carlo Secondo ... nel terzo giorno di Maggio, 1661, insieme con la descrittione degl' archi trionfali ... e altre ... dimostrationi d'allegrezze ... nella ... Città di Londra ... anco la superba cavalcata fatto ... il giorno innanzi ... Il tutto transportato nella lingua italiana, per il Capitan Giorgio Gerbieri D'Ouvilly*, was printed in Venice in 1661.   ELIZABETH HARESNAPE

Sources BL cat. • Wing, STC • A manifestation by S' Balthazar Gerbier (1651), 3–4 • DNB • H. R. Williamson, 'Sir Balthazar Gerbier', Four Stuart portraits (1949), 26–60 • W. N. Sainsbury, ed., Original unpublished papers illustrative of the life of Sir Peter Paul Rubens, as an artist and diplomatist (1859), appx F • D. E. Baker, Biographia dramatica, or, A companion to the playhouse, rev. I. Reed, new edn, 2 vols. (1782), 1.345, 2.116 • CSP dom., 1651, 94

Likenesses A. Van Dyck, group portrait, 1629–30, Royal Collection

Dovaston, John Freeman Milward (1782–1854), naturalist and poet, the younger child and only son of John Dovaston (1740–1808) and his wife, Ann, *née* Price, was born on 30 December 1782 in the villa known as The Nursery which his father had personally built on a small ancestral estate developed into a prosperous tree nursery near the village of West Felton, between Oswestry and Shrewsbury, Shropshire. To his remarkable father, the self-educated son of a feckless wheelwright, Dovaston was to owe a life of propertied leisure, manual skills, a fondness for natural history, and a love of the classics and of Welsh music and literature. His father had been an intimate of Shenstone and a taste for poetry and its composition in particular extended also to an uncle and a cousin. But it was music that was latterly to claim him pre-

eminently, reflected in his ownership of two organs, a grand piano, a set of harmonica glasses, and a cello.

After successively attending Oswestry grammar school and, more briefly, Shrewsbury School, Dovaston went up in 1800 to Christ Church, Oxford, on a Careswell exhibition. After graduating in 1804 he read for the bar, augmenting his then slender means by acting as drama critic for a newspaper. Called in June 1807, he practised, however, only for a year or two before the death of his father enabled him to abandon a profession he found uncongenial and spend the rest of his life in rural retirement.

At least since undergraduate days Dovaston had been composing poems and in 1812 a volume of these was published locally under the title *Fitz-Gwarine, a ballad of the Welsh border, with other rhymes, legendary, incidental and humorous*. The main piece was an evident imitation of Scott's *Marmion* of four years earlier. This made him sufficient of a celebrity locally for the freedom of the borough of Oswestry to be conferred on him in 1814. It also won him a national publisher for an enlarged edition (in 1816), followed in 1817 by a collection of songs, *British Melodies*, set to music by Clementi, further poems in 1822, and finally a volume of his collected work in 1825. Though he himself doubtless set much store by this *oeuvre*, its overall impact seems to have been slight.

It is rather for his pioneer experiments in ornithology and his friendship with Thomas Bewick that Dovaston is principally notable. So trifling by comparison with his literary work did he regard the former, however, that details of them were divulged almost apologetically and published so obscurely that their impressively innovatory character lay overlooked for a century and a half. Though the most important of his discoveries saw print in Loudon's widely read *Magazine of Natural History*, it was communicated in the guise of a mock Socratic dialogue, his authorship semi-concealed behind an anagram of his name. The choice of Von Osdat was accidentally appropriate, though, for while several others had long anticipated him in noting that robins have individual territories, the only one to have appreciated the biological significance of this was an Austrian counterpart, Baron Von Pernau. Until the 1920s, however, no one but Dovaston seems to have pursued matters to the point of trapping and marking birds and, albeit unsystematically, discriminating territories. This work was a by-product of his no less pioneer use of a feeding device for wild birds, punningly termed by him an 'ornithotrophe'. Similarly advanced were his regular resort to a spyglass for watching birds, when almost everyone else relied still on a gun, and his creation on his estate of artificial nesting holes and boxes. He even did some rudimentary ringing of migrants, utilizing his cello wire for the purpose, and made abortive attempts to translate bird songs into musical notation. Nor were birds the only focus of his thoughtful curiosity: he also succeeded in growing mistletoe on over a score of different tree species.

Regrettably, Dovaston was content to be a dilettante and through diffidence or inertia was disinclined to trawl for converts or penetrate further in his experiments. His most substantial publication in natural history was a mere list of local birds contributed to W. A. Leighton's *Guide to Shrewsbury* in 1850, following many plant records supplied to the same author's *Flora of Shropshire* of 1841. But a mass of notes dating from boyhood onwards which he sent to Bewick for the sixth edition of his *History of British Birds* was little drawn on, to his chagrin. A great admirer of Bewick's work, Dovaston had called on him in Newcastle while on a walking tour in 1823 and the two remained in touch until Bewick's death five years later. Dovaston procured orders for Bewick's works among his friends, passed on specimens and notes from his naturalist neighbours, and drafted the preface for the last edition of the *History*. The account of Bewick he subsequently published in the *Magazine of Natural History* has ever since been the main source for the artist's biographers.

As well as an unpublished account of a tour through Scotland as far as the Hebrides that he made with his friend J. E. Bowman in 1825, which characteristically includes valuable observations on the bagpipe and its music, much of Dovaston's correspondence has survived. Forthright and decided in his views, he reveals in this a coolness towards the church and a whig stance politically which none the less failed to alienate the many devoted friends won by his liveliness, warmth, and humour.

After several serious illnesses from digestive disorders Dovaston's health finally failed in 1847, leaving him permanently bedridden. He died at home on 8 August 1854 and was buried in the churchyard at West Felton. A lifelong bachelor, he left his estate to a nephew, but his library of over 3000 volumes was dispersed by auction in 1910. He is commemorated in the Dovaston Yew, *Taxus baccata* var. *dovastonii*, a pendulous variety derived from a bush found by his father in a local hedge.

D. E. ALLEN

Sources D. E. Allen, 'J. F. M. Dovaston, an overlooked pioneer of field ornithology', *Journal of the Society of the Bibliography of Natural History*, 4 (1962–8), 277–83 · D. E. Allen, 'An overlooked pioneer', *Birds*, 2 (1969), 296–7 · *GM*, 2nd ser., 42 (1854), 395–6 · H. E. Forrest, 'Two old Shropshire naturalists', *Transactions of the Caradoc and Severn Valley Field Club* [for 1910], 5 (1911), 125–35 · C. Hulbert, *The history and description of the county of Salop* (1837), 222 · A. T. McKenzie, 'Thomas Bewick and John F. M. Dovaston: a record of their friendship', *The Library Chronicle*, 24 (1968), 67–77 · A. Roberts, 'Oswestry grammar school', *Transactions of the Shropshire Archaeological and Natural History Society*, 5 (1882), 1–88, esp. 51 [biographical notice] · 'An old local celebrity', *Oswestry Commercial Circular* (5 March 1910) · O. Clare, 'Dovaston and Bewick — letters which tell of their friendship', *Shropshire Magazine*, 6 (1955), 13 · S. Bagshaw, *History, gazetteer and directory of Shropshire* (1851) · *Bewick to Dovaston: letters 1824–1828*, ed. G. Williams (1968) · d. cert.
Archives Bodl. Oxf., corresp. · Duke U., Perkins L., corresp. · NL Wales, notes and poems · Shrops. RRC, corresp. and papers · U. Birm. L., lecture notes | BL, corresp. with Thomas Bewick, Egerton MS 3147 · Bodl. Oxf., letters to Harriett Pigott · Liverpool Museum, botanical specimens · Lpool RO, corresp. with William Roscoe · NL Wales, letters to Charles M. D. Humphreys · Shrops. RRC, letters to Thomas Archer · Yale U., Beinecke L., autograph manuscripts of poems
Likenesses T. Bewick, woodcut silhouette, 1823, repro. in *Bewick to Dovaston*, ed. Williams · J. W. Giles, sketches

Dove, Evelyn Mary (1902–1987), singer and actress, was born on 11 January 1902 at the Lying-in Hospital, Endell Street, London, the daughter of Francis Dove (d. 1949), a barrister born in Sierra Leone, and his English wife, Augusta, *née* Winchester. Francis Dove was the son of William Dove, who had made a fortune from trading out of Freetown, Sierra Leone. Evelyn's older brother Frank, born in London in 1897, studied law at Oxford and enlisted in the British army, joining the élite Royal Tank Corps in 1915. He fought at the battle of Cambrai in 1917, the first breach of the German lines in over three years, and was awarded the Military Medal.

From 1917 Evelyn Dove studied singing, piano, and elocution at the Royal Academy of Music and, when she graduated in 1919, she was awarded a silver medal. As a contralto she hoped for a career on the concert platform but the world of jazz and cabaret was more welcoming. In the early 1920s the all-black jazz revues that were popular in America were being recreated in Europe. In 1925 the cast of *Chocolate Kiddies* was assembled in New York and sent to Europe to give overseas audiences an opportunity to see some of America's top black entertainers. A young Duke Ellington contributed to the score and, after the tour commenced, Dove was invited to join them from England to replace Lottie Gee who had to return to America. *Chocolate Kiddies* toured western Europe for a year, then headed for Russia, playing in Leningrad and Moscow, where the audience included Stalin.

In the 1920s and 1930s Dove's career went from strength to strength. After replacing Josephine Baker as the star attraction in a revue at the Casino de Paris, she travelled to New York in 1936 to appear in cabaret at the famous nightclub Connie's Inn. This rivalled the Cotton Club as a showcase for top black talent. In 1937 her travels took her to Bombay, India, where she performed with great success for white colonials at the Harbour Bar. This review of her opening night appeared in the *Evening News of India* on 7 October 1937:

> She is an artist of international reputation, one of the leading personalities of Europe's entertainment world. She is described as the closest rival of the great Josephine Baker herself. Evelyn didn't get just the big hand. She got an ovation, a roaring welcome.

Dove's greatest professional success was her work with the BBC. From 1939 to 1949 she broadcast in many popular music and variety programmes, including *Rhapsody in Black*, *Calling the West Indies*, *Variety Bandbox*, and *Caribbean Carnival*. She also made over fifty broadcasts with the Trinidadian folk-singer Edric Connor in *Serenade in Sepia* (1945–7). This series was so popular with listeners that the BBC transported Dove and Connor to their studios at Alexandra Palace where they appeared in a television version. At the height of her radio popularity, one of the BBC's top producers, Eric Fawcett, gave the following recommendation to one of his colleagues in a memorandum dated 6 June 1948:

> She is a contralto with a perfect microphone quality and although I have used her mostly in music of negro origin this has ranged from spirituals to Samuel Coleridge-Taylor. She

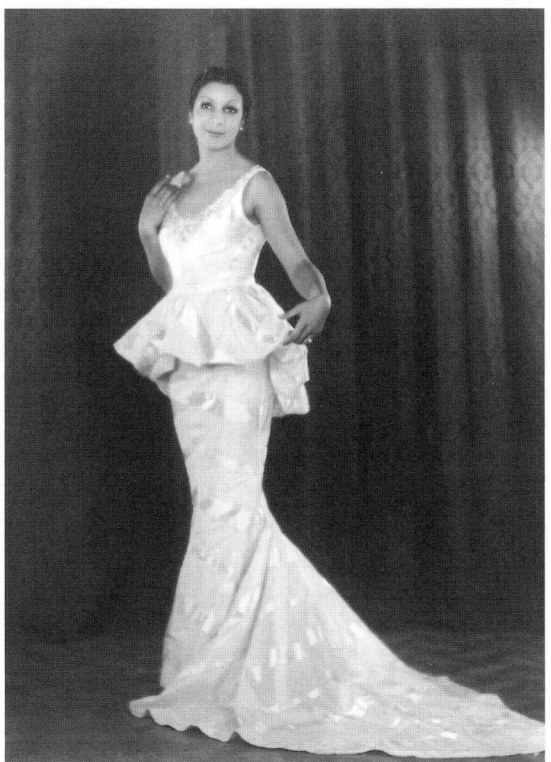

Evelyn Mary Dove (1902–1987), by Macari

is, of course, a highly trained singer. She is an extremely charming person with a very attractive personality. I would rate her the best coloured contralto in this country. (Bourne, 'Spirit of a Dove')

In 1949 Dove left the BBC to work in cabaret in India, Paris, and Spain, but on her return to Britain at the end of 1950 she found it difficult to find employment. Work became scarce, though she did appear in the cast of *London Melody* with ice-skater Belita and comedian Norman Wisdom at London's Empress Hall in 1951. Despite her experience and talent, she found herself understudying Muriel Smith in the role of Bloody Mary in the Rodgers and Hammerstein musical *South Pacific* at Drury Lane. Then, in 1955, broke and desperate for work, she applied for a job as a Post Office telephonist, asking the BBC for a reference. In 1956 things began to look up when the BBC cast her as Eartha Kitt's mother in a television drama called *Mrs Patterson*. More television work followed and she returned to the West End musical stage, not as an understudy, but as one of the stars of Langston Hughes's *Simply Heavenly*, directed by Laurence Harvey. Also in the cast of *Simply Heavenly* was the singer and actress Isabelle Lucas, who later recalled: 'We became friends, but Evelyn's life took a bad turn. Her reputation as a singer faded, and she became very ill. She lost contact with her family. Her spirit was broken' (Bourne, 'Spirit of a Dove'). In 1972 Dove was admitted to a nursing home, Horton Hospital, in Epsom, Surrey, where she died of pneumonia on 7 March 1987.

STEPHEN BOURNE

Sources S. Bourne, 'Spirit of a Dove', *Pride* (July 1999), 112–13 · S. Bourne, *Black in the British frame: black people in British film and television, 1896–1996* (1998) · b. cert. · d. cert.
Likenesses photograph, 1945, repro. in Bourne, *Black in the British frame*, following p. 116 · Macari, photograph, priv. coll. [*see illus.*]

Dove, Dame (Jane) Frances (1847–1942), founder of Wycombe Abbey School, was born at Bordeaux, France, on 27 June 1847, the eldest of the ten children of the Revd John Thomas Dove (1821–1906), vicar of Cowbit, Lincolnshire, for more than forty years, and chairman of the Spalding board of poor-law guardians and of the South Holland magistrates' bench, and his wife, Jane Ding, daughter of Thomas Lawrence of Dunsby, Lincolnshire. Her education began at home in London, where she was taught by her father, with her two brothers. Subsequently she attended Queen's College, Harley Street, for nearly three years. At this time her father was curate to the Revd Llewelyn Davies, rector of Christ Church Marylebone. This association with the Davies family and their acquaintances brought an early exposure to the debate on women's education. At the age of fifteen her formal education was interrupted when her father was appointed to Cowbit, which in 1862 was an isolated fen village. There was little diversion for the Dove children beyond 'watering cabbages'. At her own request, Frances Dove was sent to a boarding-school, which she later described as being 'everything a school should not be' (Bowerman, 15). After a year away she returned home to a much busier life, educating the younger children, making their clothes, and undertaking parish visiting.

In 1871, at the age of twenty-four, Frances Dove was prompted to enter Girton College by news of the new college for women brought from London by her father. She prepared for the entrance examination virtually unaided and, although the aggregate of her marks placed her sixth of the eleven candidates, her performance in the arithmetic paper was outstanding. She was one of the nine students who, with Emily Davies (Llewelyn Davies's sister) as mistress, migrated from Hitchin to Girton in 1873. Her story of Davies's meeting her, the first student to enter the new building, surrounded by builders' debris, passed into college history. She and another member of her year were the first women to sit the natural sciences tripos, and as such were the first to be admitted to university lectures in anatomy, physiology, and chemistry. In 1874 she attained the standard of the ordinary degree; this she was able to convert to an MA in 1905 when Trinity College, Dublin, offered suitably qualified women *quasi ad eundem* degrees.

While she was still at Girton, Dove was engaged by Miss Beale to teach mathematics and physiology at Cheltenham Ladies' College. Constance Maynard, a contemporary at Girton, called it a 'capital beginning'. Maynard and another Girtonian, Louisa Lumsden, were to follow Frances Dove to Cheltenham, and when in 1877 Lumsden was invited to become the first headmistress of St Andrews School for Girls, Dove and Maynard joined her on the staff. However, their incompatible temperaments made them uneasy colleagues. In 1882, when Louisa Lumsden

Dame (Jane) Frances Dove (1847–1942), by Lafayette, 1928

resigned, Frances Dove was appointed headmistress in her place. It was under her supervision that the school was rehoused in new buildings and changed its name to St Leonards. Her most important task was to establish a tradition of excellence which would outlast the pioneer enthusiasm which had carried the school in its early years. By the time she announced her resignation in 1895 the school had more than doubled in size.

Dove's decision to leave St Andrews to found a sister school in England was, as she later admitted, 'a great venture of faith'. The prospectus of the Girls' Education Company, which she founded in 1896 to raise the necessary finance for the enterprise, stated that, 'The proposed system of education aims at doing for girls, with suitable modifications, what the existing great Public Schools do for boys' (Bowerman, 79). Lord Carrington's house near High Wycombe, Buckinghamshire, was purchased, and Wycombe Abbey School opened in September 1896. Although she never spoke of the school in proprietary terms, it was nevertheless the realization of Frances Dove's educational ideals, brought about largely by her own energy and organizational ability. Starting with forty girls, she built up the numbers to 230, with fifty mistresses, by the time of her retirement in 1910. Her success inspired the foundation of Benenden School in 1923, and made her an important figure in disseminating the model for girls' boarding-schools pioneered at St Leonards.

The underlying principle of Dove's educational thinking was education for citizenship. She set out her philosophy in her essay 'Cultivation of the body' in the volume which she edited with Dorothea Beale and Lucy Soulsby, *Work and Play in Girls' Schools* (1898). She argued that women should be taught corporate virtues, and that to be good citizens it was essential to have wide interests, a sense of discipline, and *esprit de corps*. She applied these principles at Wycombe, believing that the best place to instil ideals of citizenship was the school. Like headmasters of boys' public schools, she regarded team games as the best medium for developing character, and introduced cricket, hockey, and lacrosse as compulsory activities. A regime of daily cold baths and unheated dormitories was intended to develop hardiness in the girls; she was comparatively uninterested in their clothes or appearance, though she favoured 'rational dress'. The curriculum at Wycombe included gardening, carpentry, and Swedish gymnastics as well as more conventional academic subjects, though she was suspicious of music, fearing that the emotional nature of girls might be 'overstimulated by excessive time spent on music, especially if the music is of a certain kind' ('Cultivation of the body', 55). A devout high-church Anglican, she ensured that the religious life of the school was centred on the parish church at High Wycombe.

Dove regarded the school as a preparation for a life of service. Pupils were expected to become involved in community work through the United Girls' School Mission at Camberwell, and in missionary work abroad by contributing to the Melanesian mission. On her own retirement she devoted her time to public work in High Wycombe. In 1906 she had inaugurated the Central Aid Society in the town, involving welfare work with invalid children and workhouse girls, and infant health. She was a governor of schools and raised funds for church schools. She was a committed suffragist, believing that women could exercise a wholesome influence upon public life. At the first elections open to women candidates for borough and county councils, held in November 1907, she stood for High Wycombe town council, one of the women candidates co-ordinated by the Women's Local Government Society. Staff at Wycombe Abbey School assisted in her campaign, after which she was returned at the top of the poll. Her nomination to the mayoralty in October 1908 appeared to be a formality, but unexpected opposition, stirred up by a reaction against the suffragettes, defeated the motion for her appointment, preventing her from becoming the first woman mayor in England. She lost her council seat in 1913. Thereafter she continued to undertake voluntary work for the diocese and the county education committee, and was made a JP for Buckinghamshire in 1921, learning to drive at an advanced age in order to fulfil her many commitments in the county. She was a member of Girton College council from 1902 to 1924, becoming thereafter a life governor. In January 1928 she was created DBE.

A photograph taken in the year of Wycombe Abbey's foundation shows a youthful-looking Frances Dove with clear dark eyes and upswept white hair in a high-necked, smocked dress. It is a great deal less intimidating a portrait than that painted by Sir William Richmond and presented to her in 1904. There is no doubt that both pupils and peers sometimes found her forbidding. However, just as her spartan lifestyle was tempered by a love of fine art, so those who recalled her indomitable will and autocratic manner remembered an affectionate and generous nature. Frances Dove died, unmarried, at her home, 24 Priory Avenue, High Wycombe, on 21 June 1942.

KATE PERRY

Sources I. E. Bowerman, *Stands there a school* (1966) · J. F. Dove, 'Remembrances', Girton Cam., Stephen MS · K. T. Butler and H. I. McMorran, eds., *Girton College register, 1869–1946* (1948) · *Girton Review*, Michaelmas term (1942) · *The Times* (23 June 1942) · *Daily Telegraph* (24 June 1942) · *Yorkshire Post* (24 June 1942) · J. Grant and others, *St Leonards School, 1877–1927* (1927) · Register of terms and examinations; entrance and scholarship examination, June 1871, Girton Cam. · C. L. Maynard, diaries and unfinished autobiography, Queen Mary College, London, Queen Mary and Westfield College Archives · L. I. Lumsden, *Yellow leaves: memories of a long life* (1933) · P. Hollis, *Ladies elect: women in English local government, 1865–1914* (1987) · *DNB* · d. cert.
Archives Girton Cam. · Wycombe Abbey School, High Wycombe, speeches, articles, and addresses
Likenesses photograph, 1896, repro. in Bowerman, *Stands there a school* · W. Richmond, oils, 1904, Wycombe Abbey School, High Wycombe · Lafayette, photograph, 1928, NPG [*see illus.*] · W. Stoneman, photograph, 1930, NPG · Lafayette, photograph, Girton Cam. · E. Sweetland, photograph, Girton Cam.
Wealth at death £11,403 8s. 7d.: probate, 1 Dec 1942, CGPLA Eng. & Wales

Dove, Henry (*bap.* 1641, *d.* 1695), Church of England clergyman, was baptized at Ilsington, Devon, on 2 November 1641, the son of Robert Dove (*d.* 1645) and his wife, Elizabeth. His father, rector of Ilsington and of Elm and Emneth in the fens, was sequestered from his East Anglian parishes for deserting his cure for the royal army, and proceedings were in train to deprive him from Ilsington when he died there in September 1645. Educated at Westminster School, where he was a boarder from 1656, Henry Dove was elected to Trinity College, Cambridge, in 1658. He graduated BA in 1661 and MA in 1665, was incorporated MA at Oxford on 6 May 1669, and proceeded DD in 1677. Ordained deacon at Ely in March 1665, he became vicar of St Bride's, Fleet Street, London, on 12 January 1673 and on 3 December 1678 was collated to the archdeaconry of Richmond. He was chaplain to his uncle John Pearson, bishop of Chester, who recommended him to the king for the mastership of Trinity College, Cambridge, in 1683. He was also chaplain successively to Charles II, James II, and William and Mary.

Although Dove was married twice no record can be found of his first marriage, which produced a daughter, Susan. In 1680 he married his second wife, Rebecca Holworthy (*bap.* 1657), who was described in the marriage licence of 2 July as 'of St. Margaret, Westminster, spinster, aged 23' (Chester, 414).

Described as 'an able preacher' (*Old Westminster*, 1.279), Dove published several sermons. In 1680 he published *A Sermon Preached before the Honourable House of Commons … Nov. 5, 1680* which commented on the furious political debate surrounding Titus Oates's Popish Plot revelations in 1678 and the subsequent parliamentary attempts to exclude Charles II's brother, James, from succeeding the throne. Thanking God for his 'deliverance of the King and Kingdom from the bloody designs of Popish Traytors', Dove nevertheless railed against 'all Sedition … Heresie and Schism' and encouraged a 'hearty Loyalty and Fidelity to our King', thus declaring his support for Charles and all those who opposed the whig attempts to pass bills of exclusion.

Narcissus Luttrell refers to Dove preaching a sermon 'exhorting to unity and loyalty', which was later published as *A Sermon Preached before the Right Honourable Lord Mayor … on the Feast of St. Michael, 1682* (Luttrell, 1.225), while John Evelyn mentions Dove's *A Sermon Preached before the King at Whitehall, January 25, 1685*. Dove also published *A Sermon Preached before the Queen at Whitehall, February the Fifteenth, 1691* and *Albania: a Poem Humbly Offered*, in memory of Queen Mary in 1695. His relationship to the queen, rightful heir in the absence of James and the model of Anglican piety, suggests how Dove's loyalist churchmanship could accommodate itself to the revolution of 1688. A further pointer to his continuing religious sensibilities is provided by his presence among those who witnessed the will of Francis Atterbury.

Dove died on 11 March 1695, leaving his second wife and his daughter, Susan. His will detailed a gift of £5 for the poor of his parish, 40 shillings for each of his servants and £400 for his daughter, to be received on her twenty-first birthday or her marriage, if earlier. Susan also received copyhold lands in Sutton, Lincolnshire, left him by his first wife. His second wife, Rebecca, inherited the remainder of his goods and estate. He was buried in St Bride's Church.

SARAH CARR

Sources *Old Westminsters* · Foster, *Alum. Oxon.* · J. Welch, *The list of the queen's scholars of St Peter's College, Westminster*, ed. [C. B. Phillimore], new edn (1852) · Wood, *Ath. Oxon.*: *Fasti*, new edn · R. Newcourt, *Repertorium ecclesiasticum parochiale Londinense*, 2 vols. (1708–10) · *Fasti Angl., 1541–1857*, [York] · Evelyn, *Diary* · N. Luttrell, *A brief historical relation of state affairs from September 1678 to April 1714*, 6 vols. (1857) · J. L. Chester and J. Foster, eds., *London marriage licences, 1521–1869* (1887) · will, PRO, PROB 11/425, sig. 46 · *IGI* · *Walker rev.*
Wealth at death left £400 and copyhold lands to daughter, £5 for the poor, and 40s. each for servants; remainder to second wife: will, PRO, PROB 11/425, sig. 46

Dove, John (1561–1618), Church of England clergyman, a Surrey man, was a scholar of St Peter's College, Westminster, from which he was elected to Christ Church, Oxford, in 1580. He graduated BA on 5 February 1584 and proceeded MA on 16 March 1587, BD on 22 November 1593, and DD on 1 July 1596. He was presented to the rectory of Tidworth, Wiltshire, in 1596 by Lord Chancellor Thomas Egerton and collated by Archbishop Whitgift on 5 November of that year to the rectory of St Mary Aldermary, London, which he held for the rest of his life. In 1597, however, he received a licence from the privy council to travel abroad for three years.

Aside from his pastoral duties Dove was an author of some repute, publishing seven tracts between 1594 and 1613 in which he revealed himself to be a capable and a loyal defender of the Church of England as established by law. In a 1594 tract containing a sermon originally preached at Paul's Cross he identified the Roman Antichrist as that Antichrist spoken of in scripture, and, following on from the theological controversies at Cambridge University in 1595–6, he published another sermon (again previously preached at Paul's Cross) in which he advocated the Calvinist interpretation of the doctrine of divine predestination. In 1601 he published a sermon upon the legality of divorce, arguing that the word of God did not allow a man to divorce his wife and marry another, even if his wife had previously committed adultery. In *A Perswasion to the English Recusants, to Reconcile themselves to the Church of England* (1603), dedicated to James I, he appealed to the recusant population to frequent holy communion as celebrated by the Church of England; he played down the differences between the two churches, although he was careful to add a section addressed 'to the protestant reader' which laid out his impeccable protestant credentials. A tract confuting atheism in the realm (1605) was followed in 1606 by *A Defence of Church Government*, in which he defended against puritan criticism both the use of episcopacy by the church and the employment of the sign of the cross in the baptismal rubric of the Book of Common Prayer. Dove died in April 1618. WILL ALLEN

Sources DNB · Foster, *Alum. Oxon.* · *CSP dom.*, 1595–7, 398 · Register Whitgift, LPL, 2, fol. 339r · J. Dove, *A sermon preached at Paul's Cross the 3 of November 1594* (1594) · J. Dove, *A sermon preached at Paul's Cross the 6 of February 1596* (1597) · J. Dove, *Of divorcement: a sermon preached at Paul's Cross the 10 of May 1601* (1601) · J. Dove, *A perswasion to the English recusants, to reconcile themselves to the Church of England* (1603) · J. Dove, *A confutation of atheisme* (1605) · J. Dove, *A defence of church government* (1607) · J. Dove, *The conversion of Solomon: a direction to holiness of life* (1613)

Dove, John (*d.* **1664/5**), politician, was the son of Henry Dove (*d.* 1616), mayor of Salisbury at the time of his death. John Dove was married with four children, but little else is known of his family. Perhaps a brewer by trade, he was an alderman of Salisbury and served as mayor in 1635. A zealous parliamentarian, he was elected MP for Salisbury in 1645 in place of the town recorder, Robert Hyde, an ejected royalist who was also a personal enemy. With his brother Francis (mayor in 1645 and 1650), Dove served on the Wiltshire county committee and most subsequent militia and assessment commissions. As an MP he was nominated to several parliamentary committees but took no part in the king's trial beyond attending when the sentence was agreed, on 26 January 1649. He also amassed considerable wealth, purchasing the manors of Fountell in Hampshire, Blewbury, Berkshire, and Winterbourne Earls, Wiltshire, from the sales of bishops' lands, plus other lands in Wiltshire. He was named colonel of foot in the Wiltshire militia on 10 August 1650. On 25 August 1651 the council of state commended him for his zeal in raising the militia against Charles II.

Dove was chosen high sheriff of the county in 1655, the year of the abortive royalist rising. On 14 March, Sir Joseph Wagstaffe, Colonel John Penruddock, and some 150 men entered Salisbury early in the morning, and seized Dove, Chief Justice Rolle, and Lord Nicholas, who were there for the county assizes. After the royal proclamation had been read Wagstaffe proposed hanging both judges and the sheriff on the spot. This violent proposal was overruled by the local gentry but Dove, for refusing to read the proclamation, was reserved for future punishment. He was carried to Yeovil, but after two days was allowed to return on parole to Salisbury, where he found that Major Boteler had freed the city. Dove's actions immediately afterwards graphically illustrated his vindictive and grasping nature. On 29 March he asked Thurloe that only those of the 'honest and well-affected party' be allowed to serve on juries to try the rebels (Thurloe, *State papers*, 3.319). Later, sixty-three citizens of Salisbury petitioned for clemency for a condemned rebel, John Lucas, who had intervened to save Dove's life. Lambert, Disbrowe, and Rous were sent to discuss this with Dove, but Lucas was duly hanged. When another rebel, Hugh Grove, was beheaded at Exeter on 14 May, he called from the scaffold for God to forgive, among others, 'Mr Dove and the rest for so falsely and maliciously swearing against me' (Hoare, 17–18); perhaps significantly, Dove had been granted Grove's sequestered estate at Chisenbury Priors in 1650.

In September 1656 both Doves were listed among the aldermen and assistants to be removed from the corporation when the new charter reduced the numbers, their presbyterian faction having been outflanked by radicals. He took his seat in the restored Rump in 1659, while the recent borough charter was replaced by the old one in August of that year. At the Restoration Dove made an abject submission and was allowed to depart unpunished. He and his brother were still aldermen in 1662, when the Act for the Well Governing and Regulating of Corporations removed them. He retired to his estate at Ivy Church, Alderbury, Wiltshire, where he died between October 1664, when his will was made, and March 1665 when it was proved.

GORDON GOODWIN, *rev.* ANDREW WARMINGTON

Sources R. Benson and H. Hatcher, *Old and New Sarum or Salisbury*, 2 vols. (1843) · R. C. Hoare, *The history of modern Wiltshire*, 2/1: *Hundreds of Everley, Ambresbury, and Underditch* (1826) · *CSP dom.*, 1650–51; 1655 · D. Brunton and D. H. Pennington, *Members of the Long Parliament* (1954) · C. H. Firth and R. S. Rait, eds., *Acts and ordinances of the interregnum, 1642–1660*, 3 vols. (1911) · J. Easton, *A chronology of remarkable events relative to the city of New Sarum*, 5th edn (1824) · Thurloe, *State papers* · will, PRO, PROB 11/316, sig. 24 · VCH Wiltshire, vol. 5

Wealth at death £70 in cash legacies; plus house and estate in Ivy Church and houses and lands in and near London: will, PRO, PROB 11/316, sig. 24

Dove, John (**1872–1934**), colonial official and journalist, was born on 6 November 1872 in Birkenhead, Cheshire, the second son of John Matthew Dove, of Birkenhead and Boreatton Hall, Shropshire, managing director of the Liverpool, London and Globe Insurance Company, and his wife, Amy Gordon, *née* Wood. He was educated at Rugby School and New College, Oxford, where he was an exact contemporary of Lionel Curtis and two years senior to Lionel Hichens and Richard Feetham, all of whom became close friends. He took a third in classical moderations in 1893 and a fourth in *literae humaniores* in 1895. He then read in chambers with J. A. Hamilton (later Lord Sumner), and was called to the bar by the Inner Temple in 1898.

A lifelong propensity to ill health was made worse by the effects of an early hunting accident, and it was partly in the hope that the warm, dry climate of the veldt would improve his health that in 1903 Dove applied successfully (with the help of a recommendation from Sir William Anson) for the post of assistant town clerk of Johannesburg. There he worked directly under Feetham (in whose house he lived) and joined Curtis and Hichens in the activities of Lord Milner's 'kindergarten'. He succeeded Feetham as town clerk in 1905, but resigned following the victory of Het Volk in the Transvaal elections of February 1907. He then worked directly for Lord Selborne (Milner's successor as governor of the Transvaal and high commissioner of South Africa) as chairman of the Transvaal land settlement board, set up to protect the interests of British settlers in the colony. He was closely involved in the kindergarten's activities in support of the unification of the South African colonies, spending autumn 1908 in England attempting to drum up support, and then helping Curtis in the organization of Closer Union societies.

Dove returned to England in spring 1910, exhausted. Nevertheless he was pressed into service as Curtis's assistant in forming Round Table groups around the empire, to discuss and (their founders hoped) agitate for imperial federation, prompting Lady Selborne to comment that 'it was clear that his duty was now to die for the Empire, though on the whole not to die in the Transvaal' (Lavin, 101). He undertook a successful tour of Australia, but shortly after his return to England in March 1911 suffered a physical collapse, necessitating a major operation and a long period of convalescence. He recovered sufficiently to serve in France in the intelligence department of the War Office from late 1917. At the end of 1918 he became a director of the Commonwealth Trust, set up to administer the properties of German and German-Swiss missionary bodies which had been sequestrated during the First World War. On behalf of the trust he undertook journeys to India in 1919 and Mesopotamia in 1919–20.

Late in 1920 Dove was persuaded to become editor of the *Round Table* in succession to Geoffrey Dawson. He wrote little for the journal (most editorials still being written by Philip Kerr), and when he did he tended, as he admitted, 'to make bricks without straw or rather you may say to steal some of other peoples' straw' (May, 254). Nevertheless he was an assiduous editor, and one whose style suited the collegiate nature of the journal's editorial board. He remained a firm believer in imperial federation, though under his editorship the journal moved with the times in accepting co-operation as the theme of Anglo-dominion relations. He travelled frequently to Germany and Switzerland to seek cures, and some of his observations on central European politics were published in the journal. He was assisted as editor by H. V. (Harry) Hodson from 1931.

After Dove's death Robert Brand recalled his 'inexhaustible courage, battling to the very last of his days with ill-health, with physical difficulties and with still more baffling difficulties of the mind and spirit too' (Brand, *Letters*, vi). Profoundly religious, he was nevertheless prone to doubts and uncertainties, and was not at all dogmatic. Dougal Malcolm thought that he 'came as near to real saintliness as is given to our frail humanity' (May, 59). A keen chess player, in his youth he enjoyed hunting, fishing, shooting, and golf, but had progressively to give up these pursuits. He retained an interest in art, and at the end of his life hoped to enrol as a student at the Slade School of Fine Art. He made light of his physical difficulties, and had an impish sense of humour. He was fortunate in having a private income which allowed him to live in comfort, though he was not extravagant and had a streak of austerity. He was unmarried. He died at his home, the Lower House, North Aston, Oxfordshire, on 18 April 1934. After his death a volume of his letters (mainly from travels in India, Mesopotamia, and Europe) was published, edited by Robert Brand. ALEX MAY

Sources DNB · *The Times* (19 April 1934) · [R. H. Brand], 'John Dove', *Round Table*, 95 (June 1934) · *The letters of John Dove*, ed. R. H. Brand (1938) · W. Nimocks, *Milner's young men: the kindergarten in Edwardian imperial affairs* (1966) · J. E. Kendle, *The Round Table movement and imperial union* (1975) · D. Lavin, *From empire to international commonwealth: a biography of Lionel Curtis* (1995) · A. C. May, 'The Round Table, 1910–1966', DPhil diss., U. Oxf., 1995
Archives Bodl. Oxf., R. H. (Baron) Brand MSS · Bodl. Oxf., corresp. with L. G. Curtis and Round Table corresp. · Bodl. Oxf., Geoffrey Dawson MSS · Bodl. Oxf., Lionel Hichens MSS · Bodl. Oxf., Alfred (Viscount) Milner MSS · Bodl. Oxf., second Earl Selborne MSS · Bodl. Oxf., Maud, Countess Selborne MSS · Bodl. RH, Richard Feetham MSS · NA Scot., corresp. with Lord Lothian and others · Queen's University, Kingston, Ontario, Edward Grigg (Baron Altrincham) MSS · University of Cape Town, Patrick Duncan MSS
Likenesses photographs, Bodl. Oxf., Lionel Curtis papers
Wealth at death £80,833 11s. 2d.: resworn probate, 11 June 1934, CGPLA Eng. & Wales

Dove, Nathaniel (1711–1754), writing master, trained in London under Philip Pickering, a writing master in Paternoster Row. Almost nothing is known of his life, except that he described himself as 'Master of the Academy at Hoxton' (Heal, 46) and was one of the schoolmasters recommended in T. Dilworth's *A New Guide to the English Tongue*. He is chiefly known for his book *The Progress of Time* (1740), where verses on the seasons and months are composed in a mixture of calligraphic styles, including 'German' text and 'Gothic' hands. Dove's designs for these plates were engraved by Thomas Gardener and the work was dedicated to Prince George, the eldest son of the prince of Wales. Between 1738 and 1740 Dove also contributed twenty designs to George Bickham's luxury engraved copybook *The Universal Penman* (1733–41), and a survey of these shows his facility in a variety of hands, including the businesslike round hand and the more ornamental square and German texts. Although he was evidently fond of decorating his texts with flourishes, the greater part of his work in *The Universal Penman* was of a more practical orientation, providing exemplary formats for tradesmen's bills and accounts. According to William Massey's conclusion, in his *The Origins & Progress of Letters* (1763), these performances must have recommended Dove to his final lucrative position as a clerk in the 'Victualling-office, on Tower-hill' (Massey, 2.76). It was while in this employment that he died in 1754. LUCY PELTZ

Sources W. Massey, *The origin and progress of letters: an essay in two parts* (1763) · A. Heal, *The English writing-masters and their copy-books, 1570–1800* (1931)

Dove, Patrick Edward (1815–1873), political theorist, son of Henry Dove, naval officer, and his wife, Christiana Paterson, was born at Lasswade, near Edinburgh, on 31 July 1815. Thomas Dove, bishop of Peterborough, was an ancestor. His family, originally from Surrey, had been connected for many generations with the navy. They lived in Devon after 1716, when Francis Dove RN was appointed 'commissioner of the navy' at Plymouth. Henry Dove had retired from active service in 1815 at the end of the Napoleonic wars, and held an appointment at Deal connected with the Cinque Ports.

Dove had a desultory education in England and France, until he had to leave school for heading a rebellion against the headmaster. His father would not allow him to follow his own strong desire for naval service. He was sent in 1830 to learn farming in Scotland. He afterwards spent some time in Paris, in Spain, and finally in London, where he became a close friend of Seymour Haden, who was impressed by his 'enormous energy, physical and moral'. In 1841 he took the estate of the Craig, near Ballantrae, Ayrshire, where he lived as a quiet country gentleman. A man of great physical power, he was a first-rate rider, a splendid shot with gun and rifle, an expert fly-fisher, a skilful sailor, and an excellent mechanic. Dove wrote the article on gunmaking for the eighth edition of the *Encyclopaedia Britannica*. He was the agricultural adviser of the neighbouring farmers, and, objecting on principle to the game laws, refused to employ a gamekeeper. In the potato famine of the 1840s he did a great deal to provide work for his starving neighbours.

In 1848 Dove lost most of his fortune by an unlucky investment. In 1849 he married Anne, daughter of George Forrester, an Edinburgh solicitor. He spent the next year at Darmstadt, Germany, pursuing the philosophical studies to which he had long been devoted. The first result was a book published while he was still in Germany, *The Theory of Human Progression, and Natural Probability of a Reign of Justice* (1850), the first part of a projected treatise on the 'science of politics'. It was praised by Sir William Hamilton and Thomas Carlyle; Charles Sumner had it stereotyped in America, and at Sumner's request Dove wrote an article on slavery called 'The elder and younger brother', which appeared in the *Boston Commonwealth* (21 September 1853). The main principle of the book is that liberty and equality could be reconciled only if rent income were socialized, either as a surrogate for the nationalization of land or as a complement to it. That principle, arrived at independently by Dove, is familiarly associated with more illustrious writers on the 'land question', especially with Herbert Spencer, at least in the first edition of his *Social Statics* (1851), and with Henry George, notably in his *Progress and Poverty* (1880). Dove was praised by George at a public meeting in Glasgow (*Daily Mail*, 19 Dec 1884). However, Dove's theories are closer to Spencer than to George, who saw the socialization of rent as a surrogate for the nationalization of land, not as a complement.

After leaving Germany Dove settled in Edinburgh. He lectured at the philosophical institution in 1853 on 'Heroes of the Commonwealth', in 1854 on 'The wild sports of Scotland', and in 1855 on 'The crusades'. He took a special interest in volunteer militias. In April 1853 he was captain of the Midlothian rifle club. For six months in 1854 he edited *The Witness* during the illness of his friend Hugh Miller, and in the same year he published the second part of his work on politics, called *Elements of Political Science*. It included 'An account of Andrew Yarranton, the founder of English political economy' (also published separately). In the *Elements*, Dove developed his arguments on the ownership of land and on its taxation. This was a continuation of his theoretical ambition of devising a property system that would secure for individuals entitlements not only to the produce of their labour, but also to those natural resources which were distinctively not the product of (human) labour. The third and concluding part was written, but never published, and the manuscript was lost. In 1855 he published *Romanism, Rationalism, and Protestantism*, a defence of orthodox protestantism. In 1856 Dove stood unsuccessfully for the chair of logic and metaphysics at Edinburgh University vacated by the death of Sir William Hamilton, but he impressed his successful rival, Alexander Campbell Fraser, as a man who powerfully combined determined practicality with speculative insight. J. S. Blackie, who knew Dove well, spoke of him in similar terms. In the same year Dove published *The Logic of the Christian Faith*. In 1858 he published a small book on *The Revolver*, with hints on rifle clubs and on the defence of the country, lamenting the depopulation of the highlands. In 1858 Dove moved to Glasgow, where he edited *The Commonwealth* newspaper, and was general editor of the *Imperial Dictionary of Biography* for its first twenty issues. He also edited with Professor Macquorn Rankine the *Imperial Journal of the Arts and Sciences*, and wrote the article 'Government' for the 1860 edition of the *Encyclopaedia Britannica*. He had now developed a rifled cannon with 'ratchet grooves'. It was tested by the eminent shipbuilder J. R. Napier, and shown to have great range and accuracy. The ordnance committee before whom it was brought refused to test it further unless the inventor would pay the expenses, which he could not at the time afford.

In 1859 Dove accepted the command of the newly formed 91st Lanarkshire rifle volunteers, and in 1860 he took part in the first meeting of the National Rifle Association at Wimbledon, and won several prizes. He soon afterwards suffered what appears to have been a stroke, which left him partially paralysed. He went to Natal in May 1862 for a change of climate, but returned in April 1863. He died in Edinburgh on 28 April 1873, leaving a widow, two daughters, and a son.

[ANON.], *rev.* JOHN CUNLIFFE

Sources private information (1888) · *The Scotsman* (1 May 1873) · *Glasgow Herald* (29 April 1873) · *People's Journal* (1 March 1884) · *People's Journal* (3 May 1884) · J. Morrison Davidson, *Concerning four precursors of Henry George and the single tax* (1904) · J. Cunliffe, 'The neglected background of radical liberalism: P. E. Dove's theory of property', *History of Political Thought*, 11/3 (1990), 467–89 · Boase, *Mod. Eng. biog.*

Dove, Thomas (1555–1630), bishop of Peterborough, was born in London, the son of William Dove. He was a scholar at Merchant Taylors' School between 1564 and 1571, whence he proceeded to Pembroke College, Cambridge, as a Watts scholar, graduating BA in 1575 and MA in 1578. In 1575 he was nominated one of the first scholars at Jesus College, Oxford, but preferred to remain at Pembroke as *tanquam socius* (equivalent to a fellow), having come second in the competition for the sole vacant fellowship to his illustrious contemporary at Merchant Taylors' and Pembroke Lancelot Andrewes. Dove was ordained deacon and priest by Bishop Cox of Ely on 21 December 1578, and became vicar of Saffron Walden, Essex, in 1580 on the presentation of the crown; he was rector of the college living of Framlingham from 1584 until his death, and briefly vicar of Heydon in Essex (1586–8). About this time he married Margaret, daughter of Oliver Warner of Eversden, Cambridgeshire; they had three daughters and two sons, the older being William, later knighted, and the younger Thomas, baptized in 1587, who later became archdeacon of Northampton and predeceased his father.

Dove's further preferment owed much to his preaching, which so impressed Elizabeth I that she remarked after first hearing him that 'she thought the Holy Ghost was discended againe in this Dove' (Harington, 147–8). He became a royal chaplain, preaching three times before the queen in Lent 1586, and occupying the Good Friday slot from 1590 to 1601. In 1589 he became dean of Norwich, being installed on 16 June. Here he worked with local gentry against patentees for concealed lands, which resulted in 1593 in the statutory confirmation of the possessions of the dean and chapter; his appointment as a JP in 1591 was one mark of his local standing, and another followed in 1602, when seven local gentlemen wrote to Sir Robert Cecil requesting that Dove fill the vacant bishopric of Norwich. By this time Dove had left East Anglia, however, having been consecrated bishop of Peterborough on 26 April 1601. He was to remain at Peterborough for the rest of his life, despite lobbying the earls of Suffolk and Northampton for promotion to Lincoln in 1608. Also in 1601, he received the local living of Polebrooke to augment his slender income.

The accession of James I was probably the major reason why Dove rose no higher. He was one of nine bishops to attend the Hampton Court conference in January 1604, but his only recorded contribution, on lay baptism, provoked the king's scorn. When Dove cited a patristic source that in case of necessity sand might be used instead of water, James retorted with 'a turd for the argument, he might as well have pissed on them' (Usher, 2.342). In the winter of 1604–5, as James enforced conformity on puritan clergy, Dove misread the signals and deprived sixteen

Thomas Dove (1555–1630), by unknown artist

ministers, more than any other diocesan, and had to defend his conduct to the privy council, pleading that his diocese was 'the nest and nursery of factious ministers' and that those he had ejected were of 'such invincible obstinacy, as never any bishop met with' (*Salisbury MSS*, 17.46–7, 58–9). He then faced the embarrassment of a petition from forty-five Northamptonshire gentry to the king against the deprivations. Dove's vigour against nonconformists also betrayed his anti-puritanism, and in his early years at Peterborough he assembled a team of proto-Arminian officials, among them Richard Butler, John Buckeridge, and John Lambe, his chancellor in 1615–16 and later Archbishop William Laud's dean of the arches.

Dove had learned caution from the events of 1604–5, however, and in any case he had to co-operate with the puritan gentry in the workings of local government. In 1611 and 1614 he was rebuked by Archbishop George Abbot, acting on royal orders, for his indulgence to intransigent nonconformists; earlier, in 1611, Dove also had to assure the privy council that he had not been negligent in tendering the oath of allegiance to Roman Catholics. This impression of a somewhat slack administration in the years after 1605 is no doubt heightened by the chance survival of such letters in Lambe's archive among the state papers, but independent evidence, such as Dove's rather casual practices at ordination (a significant number of his ordinands were later ejected for nonconformity), points in the same direction. Nevertheless Dove was active in diocesan affairs, regularly leading his triennial visitations and preaching to his clergy, and until about 1616 hearing disciplinary cases in his consistory or audience court. No fewer than nine different sets of his visitation articles are extant, and are remarkable for the regular revisions that he or his chancellor made to them.

Dove resided at Peterborough Palace, making occasional forays to the Jacobean court in order to preach, again with some applause—a sermon delivered in August 1605 won praise from many, including Queen Anne. He played some part in secular affairs too, attending the commission of sewers, especially in 1618–21, a time of controversial projects to drain the fens. But as the 1620s progressed he took less part in local affairs, delegated his visitations of 1626 and 1629, and missed the parliaments of 1624, 1625, 1626, and 1628–9. Dove composed his will in August 1626, leaving bequests to his large family, including £500 for the education of five grandchildren, and appointing his son Sir William Dove of Upton, Northamptonshire, as his executor. His wife had predeceased him. He died on 30 August 1630 and was buried in Peterborough Cathedral, where a monument, demolished in 1643, was erected to his memory. KENNETH FINCHAM

Sources prerogative court of Canterbury, wills, PRO, PROB 11/158/95 · CSP dom., 1598–1631 · BL, Cotton MS Julius C III, fol. 156 · W. J. Sheils, The puritans in the diocese of Peterborough, 1558–1610, Northamptonshire RS, 30 (1979) · K. Fincham, Prelate as pastor: the episcopate of James I (1990) · P. E. McCullough, Sermons at court: politics and religion in Elizabethan and Jacobean preaching (1998) [incl. CD-ROM] · Calendar of the manuscripts of the most hon. the marquess of Salisbury, 17, HMC, 9 (1938) · Report on the manuscripts of Lord De L'Isle and Dudley, 3, HMC, 77 (1936) · Venn, Alum. Cant., 1/2.59 · I. Atherton and others, eds., Norwich Cathedral: church, city and diocese, 1096–1996 (1996) · J. Harington, A supplie or addicion to the catalogue of bishops to the yeare 1608, ed. R. H. Miller (1979) · R. G. Usher, The reconstruction of the English church, 2 vols. (1910) · Fasti Angl., 1541–1857, [Bristol], 115 · J. Ingamells, The English episcopal portrait, 1559–1835: a catalogue (privately printed, London, 1981)

Archives PRO, state papers, domestic | Northants. RO, Peterborough diocesan records

Likenesses oils, bishop's palace, Peterborough [see illus.]

Wealth at death reasonably wealthy; cash bequests: PRO, PROB 11/158/95

Dover. For this title name see Jermyn, Henry, third Baron Jermyn and Jacobite earl of Dover (bap. 1636, d. 1708); Douglas, James, second duke of Queensberry and first duke of Dover (1662–1711); Douglas, Charles, third duke of Queensberry and second duke of Dover (1698–1778); Douglas, Catherine, duchess of Queensberry and Dover (1701–1777) Yorke, Joseph, Baron Dover (1724–1792); Ellis, George James Welbore Agar-, first Baron Dover (1797–1833).

Dover, John (1644–1725), lawyer and playwright, was born in October 1644 at Shirley Farm, Barton on the Heath, Warwickshire, and baptized on 28 October, the second son of Captain John Dover (bap. 1614, d. 1696) and his wife, Elizabeth Vade (d. 1700). In 1661 he was admitted as a foundation scholar of Magdalen College, Oxford, matriculating on 12 July, and left the university in 1665 without taking a degree. He entered Gray's Inn on 19 May 1664 and was called to the bar on 21 June 1672.

In 1667 Dover's play, The Roman Generalls, or, The Distressed Ladies, an unacted tragedy in heroic verse, was published. In his dedication to his patron, Robert, Lord Brook, he declared that he had written the play to lessen the severity of his legal studies, 'for after I had read a sect or two in Littleton, I then to divert my self took Caesar's Commentaries, or read the Lives of my Roman Generalls out of Plutarch' (dedication). Dover practised law at Banbury, Oxfordshire. Wood stated that he wrote 'one or two more plays' (Wood, Ath. Oxon., 4.597), one of which may have been the comedy The Mall, or, The Modish Lovers (1674). In 1680 The White Rose, or, A Word for the House of York, Vindicating the Right of Succession: in a Letter from Scotland, 9 March 1679 was published. On 30 August 1682, at the herald's visitation of Warwickshire, Dover made an unsuccessful attempt to claim that his grandfather Robert *Dover (1581/2–1652) had been granted supporters and augmentations to a Dover coat of arms by James I because of his Cotswold Olimpick Games. He provided Wood with information about Robert Dover for his Athenae Oxonienses (1691) (Wood, Ath. Oxon., 4.222).

About 1684 Dover took holy orders and from 1688 was rector of Drayton near Banbury, where, to quote Wood, he was 'resorted to by fanatical people' (Wood, Ath. Oxon., 4.597), probably Anabaptists. He died unmarried at his Drayton rectory on 3 November 1725, aged eighty-one, and was buried on 6 November in the chancel of the church where there is an inscription to him.

GORDON GOODWIN, rev. F. D. A. BURNS

Sources parish register, Drayton, 6 Nov 1725, Oxon. RO [burial], 6 Nov 1725 · parish register, Barton on the Heath, 28 Oct 1644, Warks. CRO [baptism] · parish register, Barton on the Heath, 20 Oct 1700, Warks. CRO [burial] · J. R. Bloxam, A register of the presidents, fellows … of Saint Mary Magdalen College, 8 vols. (1853–85), vol. 5, pp. 239–40 · D. E. Baker, Biographia dramatica, or, A companion to the playhouse, rev. I. Reed, new edn, 1 (1782), 195; 2 (1782), 219 · Wood, Ath. Oxon., new edn, 4.222, 597 · Bodl. Oxf., MS Rawl. B. 400 F, fol. 62 · J. Foster, The register of admissions to Gray's Inn, 1521–1889, together with the register of marriages in Gray's Inn chapel, 1695–1754 (privately printed, London, 1889), 297 · W. H. Rylands, ed., The visitation of the county of Warwick … 1682 … 1683, Harleian Society, 62 (1911), 95–6 · R. M. Ingersley, 'John Dover', Warwickshire poets, ed. C. H. Poole (1914), 113–14 · K. Dewhurst, The quicksilver doctor (1957), 6–7, 34

Dover, Robert (1581/2–1652), organizer of the Cotswold Olimpick games, was born in Great Ellingham, Norfolk, the second son of John Dover, gentleman. He went to Queens' College, Cambridge, as a sizar, matriculating on 15 June 1595, but left without taking a degree. In 1599, at the age of seventeen, he was examined at Wisbech Castle as a gentleman's son, sent by his father to serve one of the priests held captive there. On 27 February 1605 he was admitted to Gray's Inn and was called to the bar probably six years later. On 23 May 1623 he was further called to be of the Grand Company of Ancients of Gray's Inn. By 1611 he had followed his sister Anne and his brother Richard to the Vale of Evesham, Worcestershire, settling initially at Saintbury, Gloucestershire. Some time before he had married Sibilla Sanford (d. 1653), daughter of William Cole, dean of Lincoln and at one time president of Corpus Christi College, Oxford, and widow of John Sanford, a Bristol merchant. They had four children, Abigail (b. 1611), Sibella (b. 1612), John (1614–1696), and Robert (b. 1616), who died soon after his birth.

Dover lived and undertook legal work in the Cotswolds

or the Vale of Evesham for almost the rest of his life, residing at Saintbury and Chipping Campden, Gloucestershire, and from 1628 at Childswickham, Worcestershire. In 1612 he became involved in organizing the games held on the hillside above Chipping Campden which subsequently became known as Robert Dover's Cotswold Olimpick games. Although many of his contemporaries considered that Dover had founded the games, it seems more likely that he became involved with a traditional Cotswold Whit festivity and revitalized it with his own distinctive form of entertainment. Dover's games were held on the Thursday and Friday of Whitsun week near the site of the stone that marked Kiftsgate hundred. Shakespeare may have attended them.

The most detailed contemporary accounts of the games are to be found in *Annalia Dubrensia: upon the yeerely celebration of Mr. Robert Dover's Olimpick games upon the Cotswold Hills*, published in London on 11 January 1636. This work included thirty-three poems by such recognized poets as Michael Drayton, Ben Jonson, Thomas Randolph, Shackerley Marmion, Owen Feltham, William Basse, Sir John Mennes, and Thomas Heywood, with a response from Robert Dover. Many of the contributors had clearly attended the games, and all were enthusiastic about Dover's character, referring to him as jovial, generous, mirth-making, heroic, and noble-minded. He had a reputation for being fair in legal dealings, trying to settle differences out of court. The frontispiece depicted the games in progress, with Robert Dover as master of ceremonies. He is portrayed as an impressive figure, dressed ceremonially in clothes, including hat, feather, and ruff, which originally belonged to James I, from whom he had authority to organize the event. The games offered activities for all levels of society—horse-racing, coursing, backswords, wrestling, jumping, tumbling, spurning the bar, throwing the sledge-hammer, and pike exercises—with dancing for ladies as well as feasting in tents on the hillside. A castle was erected from which guns were fired to introduce events. Competitors and spectators came from more than 60 miles around, and prizes included Dover's yellow favours which as many as 500 gained in any year.

Dover was probably supported initially by Sir Baptist Hicks, the city merchant who was building the almshouses and the market hall in Chipping Campden, and he later certainly had the support of Endymion Porter, groom of the bedchamber to Charles I, who acquired the royal clothes and whose home was nearby at Aston-sub-Edge. Prince Rupert attended the games in 1636. For many the games conveyed the ideals of the original Greek Olympic games; Michael Drayton's poem in particular, written by 1630, made detailed comparisons. In addition Dover, in referring to his sports as honest and harmless, criticized puritan views of games and showed his support for the Book of Sports, first published by James I in 1618 and reissued by Charles I in 1633.

The games overseen by Dover continued until 1644. He remained at Childswickham until 1650, serving as steward for the court of Wickhamford, and then went to live with his son, John, at Barton on the Heath, Warwickshire.

He died there, at Shirley Farm, and was buried at Barton on 24 July 1652; his wife died fifteen months later. Dover's games were revived after the Restoration and continued annually, their location becoming known as Dover's Hill. They were described by William Somervile (Somerville) in his poem *Hobbinol*, first drafted as 'The Wicker Chair' in 1708. They were the setting for a humorous scene in Richard Graves's *The Spiritual Quixote* (1775), first drafted by 1758. Posters for the 1812 and 1849 games, where they continue to be described as 'Olimpick', advertise horse-racing, wrestling, backsword fighting, jingling, dancing, leaping, and running in sacks. They continued until 1852 when they were brought to an end, largely owing to the pressure exerted by Canon G. D. Bourne, JP and rector of Weston, and his supporters, who were concerned about the rowdyism the games brought to the area. The parish of Weston-sub-Edge was enclosed, and Dover's Hill became private property, to be bought by the National Trust in 1928. The Olimpick games were revived for the Festival of Britain in 1951, and have been an annual event on Dover's Hill since 1966 on the Friday after the spring bank holiday.

F. D. A. BURNS

Sources parish register, Childswickham, Glos. RO · parish register, Saintbury, Glos. RO · Venn, *Alum. Cant.* · *CSP dom.*, 1598–1601 · J. Foster, *The register of admissions to Gray's Inn, 1521–1889, together with the register of marriages in Gray's Inn chapel, 1695–1754* (privately printed, London, 1889), 110 · Wood, *Ath. Oxon.*, new edn, 4.222 · M. Walbancke, ed., *Annalia Dubrensia: upon the yeerely celebration of Mr Robert Dovers Olimpick Games upon Cotswold-hills* (1636) · W. Somervile, *Hobbinol, or, The rural games* (1740) · R. Graves, *The spiritual Quixote*, ed. C. Tracy (1967) · F. Burns, *Heigh for Cotswold! A history of Robert Dover's Olimpick games* (1981) · C. Whitfield, *Robert Dover and the Cotswold games* (1962) · E. A. B. Barnard, 'Old days in and around Evesham', *Evesham Journal Notes and Queries*, 12.687–695 · parish register, Barton on the Heath, Warks. CRO, 24 July 1652 [burial] · F. Burns, 'Robert Dover's Cotswold Olimpick games: the use of the term "Olimpick"', *Olympic Review* (1985), 210, 230–36 · C. J. Bearman, 'The ending of the Cotswold games', *Transactions of the Bristol and Gloucestershire Archaeological Society*, 114 (1996), 131–41 · parish register, Barton on the Heath, Warks. CRO, 5 Nov 1653 [burial of Sibilla Dover]

Likenesses line engraving (after woodcut for *Annalia Dubrensia*, 1636), BM, NPG; repro. in J. Caulfield, *Portraits, memoirs, and characters of remarkable persons from the reign of Edward the Third, to the revolution*, 1 (1794)

Dover, Thomas (*bap.* 1662, *d.* 1742), physician and privateer, was baptized on 6 May 1662 at Barton on the Heath, Warwickshire, the third son of John Dover (*bap.* 1614, *d.* 1696), gentleman, and his wife, Elizabeth, daughter of Thomas Vade. Thomas was grandson of Robert Dover (1581/2–1652), lawyer and reviver of the Cotswold games, with whom he has occasionally been confused, and the brother of the dramatist John *Dover. Thomas followed John to Oxford, matriculating on 1 December 1680 at Magdalen Hall. He took his BA on 1 July 1684 and moved to Gonville and Caius College, Cambridge, as a pensioner in November 1686, graduating MB the following year. Dover subsequently went to live and study in Westminster at the house of Thomas Sydenham. While there, Dover contracted smallpox and was treated by his mentor. After being bled and purged:

I went abroad, by his Direction, till I was blind, and then took to my Bed. I had no Fire allowed in my Room; my Windows were constantly open, my Bed-Clothes were order'd to be laid no higher than my Waist. He made me take twelve Bottles of Small-Beer, acidulated with Spirits of Vitriol, every Twenty-four Hours. (Dover, 119–20)

Dover was cured and retained a lifelong affection for Sydenham, urging the public to '[r]ead the Man whose Reason was much superior to mine, the honest and good Dr. *Sydenham*' (Dover, 103). Some time during this period Dover married Joanna (d. 1727); they had twin daughters, Magdalen and Elizabeth, baptized on 27 April 1688, who died within weeks. A third daughter, Sibilla, born in 1693, later married John Hunt, and a fourth, Elizabeth, married John Opie.

By 1695 Dover had moved to Bristol, where he set up practice. He later reports that at this time spotted fever 'raged much … so that I visited from twenty-five to thirty Patients, a Day … besides their poor Children taken into their Workhouse, where I engaged … to find them Physick, and give them Advice at my own Expence and Trouble, for the two first Years' (Dover, 107–8). That such a practice was unusual at the time is suggested by the reaction of one of Dover's detractors, H. Bradley, who labels it '[t]he first laudable action I have yet met with from this practitioner' (Strong, 161). On 9 December 1697 Dover 'offered himself to be Phisitian to the New Workhouse gratis' (ibid., 71). Before 1708 Dover had travelled to the West Indies, perhaps aboard a Bristol slaver; he subsequently states that he cured the surgeon Jonathan Keate of diabetes in Port Royal 'more than forty Years since' (Dover, 28). Dover was subsequently described as someone 'who hath been a sea captain for many years, and who pretends to have learnt the method of cure in the West Indies where no one is known to die of the small-pox' (Dewhurst, 54). Whether owing to an inheritance, success in his practice or in the slave trade, or a combination of these, Dover was in a position to invest heavily in the Bristol syndicate backing Woodes Rogers's 1708 privateering venture to the south seas. This was not unique for the time: the physician John Radcliffe himself speculated in a vessel bound for the West Indies, which was captured by the French.

Rogers's expedition was, however, responsible for much of Dover's fame and not a little of his notoriety, causing Sir William Osler subsequently to stigmatize him as 'Dover, the Buccaneer' (Osler, 19). Owing to his stake Dover was appointed second captain of the *Duke* under Rogers, captain of the marines and president of the council, having two votes. His reason for personally participating in the venture is unknown, but may be reflected in his subsequent revision of advice offered by Dr Radcliffe to would-be practitioners:

Perhaps he had done better, if he had obliged those Gentlemen to practice Physick at least ten Years, before their setting out for foreign Parts: They would then have been much more capable of making such Observations, as might be of singular Use to them; and 'tis further my Opinion, that if he had ordered them to visit the most intemperate Climates, where all acute Diseases are the most violent, they would have returned Masters of greater Knowledge and Experience. (Dover, 7)

Dover modestly added that '[i]f Traveling be necessary to make an accomplished Physician, I am very sure that I have travelled more than all the Physicians in *Great Britain* put together' (Dover, 7–8). Prior voyages may well have provided the contacts or inclinations leading to Dover's involvement with Woodes Rogers.

The privateering expedition sailed on 1 August 1708. Before sighting Tenerife, Dover helped quell a mutiny on the *Duke* when Rogers had gone aboard a Swedish vessel to examine her cargo, and he also commanded the first expedition boat to land at Juan Fernandez on February 1709, where Alexander Selkirk, Defoe's Robinson Crusoe, was rescued. The ships revictualled here, and Woodes Rogers recalls the island's

green piemento trees, which cast a refreshing smell. Our house being made by putting a sail round four of 'em, and covering it a top with another; so that Capt. Dover and I both thought it a very agreable seat, the weather being neither too hot nor too cold. (*Life Aboard a British Privateer*, 66–7)

Unfortunately, this appears to be the last time Rogers and the doctor agreed on anything during the cruise; Rogers's *Cruising Voyage* is generally silent about Dover, although, probably significantly, it omits him from its dedication 'To the worthy Gentlemen my surviving owners' (*Life Aboard a British Privateer*, 4). The breach presumably stemmed from disputes over precedence and tactics, particularly the successful April attack on Guayaquil which Dover insisted on leading, although once ashore he was prominent in urging caution. Dover later transmutes this: 'I took by Storm the two cities of *Guciaquil*' (Dover, 100)—although, again significantly, this statement in his *Ancient Physician* appeared the year of Rogers's death. Against doctors' traditional adversary, disease, Dover was more in his element. Sleeping in Guayaquil's churches, where 'We were very much annoy'd with the Smell of dead Bodies' (Dover, 100), some one hundred and eighty privateers came down with the plague. Dover administered physic to all, and lost only seven or eight owing 'to the strong Liquers which their Mess-Mates procured for them' (Dover, 102). Rogers mentions the illness without ascribing its cure to Dover. Dover does not note that one of the deceased was his brother-in-law, Samuel Hopkins. By October, Dover had transferred from the *Duke* to the *Dutchess*, and his claim to captain the captured Manila ship *Nostra Signora de la Incarnacia del Singana* was met with the protest that he was 'utterly incapable of the office' (Powell, 128). (In a compromise, he was made the equivalent of a 'social captain'.) The expedition successfully returned to England via the East Indies, where Dover appears to have made at least some medical enquiries. His return of £6689 more than doubled his initial outlay and temporarily made the doctor a wealthy man before he lost much of this through investments in the South Sea Company.

By 1717 Dover had settled in London, being admitted a licentiate of the Royal College of Physicians on 30 September 1721. Despite some early success Dover fell foul of his fellows, and was admonished by the committee of censors in 1722 on a complaint by Dr Wagstaffe over interference with his treatment of a case. Plagued by South Sea debts,

Dover sold his property at Barton on the Heath in July 1727 after the death of his wife. He spent three years in Gloucestershire, where he cured several individuals during the epidemic of 1728–9 and tried unsuccessfully to set up a practice in Bristol. Dover then returned to the capital, seeing patients daily at the Jerusalem Coffee House.

It seems clear from his writings that Dover held some beliefs which might be termed holistic: '[n]ature will neither be forced nor driven, and is often very hard to be led; but will do wonders when properly assisted' (Strong, 145). He was unprejudiced in many aspects of his practice: after a surgeon refused to bleed Miss Corbett in one case about 1720, Dover noted that '[c]olours were all the same to the blind' and summoned 'a *black man* who blooded very well' (Dewhurst, 131). At the same time Dover's attitude toward professionals appears to have been acerbic and confrontational; he had little good to say about apothecaries, whom he believed overcharged, or the College of Physicians, whom he termed a 'clan of prejudiced gentlemen' (Dover, 150), and in criticizing treatments, he was prepared to name names. In 1732 Dover published *The Ancient Physician's Legacy to his Country*, chiefly noted for his touting of mercury as a remedy for many diseases, which inevitably led to his nickname, the Quicksilver Doctor.

There followed much published criticism based on Dover's suggested remedies, his attitude toward fellow physicians, and, one suspects, inspired not a little by the doctor's invitation to patients to self-diagnose. H. Bradley referred to Dover's 'ungentlemanlike way of treating mankind, together with his blind zealous boasting of himself', adding, 'I fear our worthy author … has an itch, which all the cold baths in Europe cannot heal, I mean that itch of the tongue which not being well cured in his youth became so inveterate as not to be rooted out' (Strong, 159–60). Daniel Turner noted that 'his conversation, you know, has been much with tars, and he thinks that the most tender constitutions of our citizens will bear the same rough handling' (ibid., 163), while the author of a *Treatise on Mercury* affirmed 'that some nurses, and even the grave-diggers' were obliged to Dover for his publication (ibid., 161). One of Dover's supporters opined that in writing his opus, 'You must have been under the strong Influence of some very Inauspicious Planet, not your Friend Mercury', adding that while the doctor's opposers 'swim in Shoals with the Current, … You … labour against the Stream, friendless and unaccompanied, and whoever meets you in his Way, helps to sink you'. Dover's treatise did, however, go through numerous editions (largely unrevised, although he did occasionally 'improve' his testimonials). He was the originator of the formerly well-known 'Dover's powder', whose composition has changed since the publication of *The Ancient Physician's Legacy*.

In the 1740s Dover spent time at Stanway House, in Gloucestershire, belonging to his friend Robert Tracy, to whom the *Ancient Physician* was dedicated. Dover died there in April 1742 and was buried on 20 April in the Tracy family vault in Stanway church.

SAMUEL PYEATT MENEFEE

Sources T. Dover, *The ancient physician's legacy to his country, being what he has collected himself, in fifty-eight years practice, or, An account of the several diseases incident to mankind; described in so plain a manner, that any person may know the nature of his own disease. Together with the several remedies for each distemper, faithfully set down*, 7th edn (1762) • K. Dewhurst, *The quicksilver doctor: the life and times of Thomas Dover, physician and adventurer* (1957) • L. A. G. Strong, *Dr. Quicksilver, 1660–1742: the life and times of Thomas Dover, M.D.* (1955) • J. A. Nixon, 'Thomas Dover: physician and merchant adventurer', *The Bristol Medico-Chirurgical Journal*, 27 (1909), 31 • J. W. D. Powell, 'Thomas Dover', *Bristol privateers and ships of war* (1930), 127–30 • *Life aboard a British privateer in the time of Queen Anne: being the journal of Captain Woodes Rogers, master mariner*, ed. R. C. Leslie (1894) • J. A. Nixon, 'Further notes on Thomas Dover', *Proceedings of the Royal Society of Medicine*, 6 (1913), 233–7 [section of the history of medicine] • D. N. Phear, 'Thomas Dover, 1662–1742: physician, privateering captain, and inventor of Dover's powder', *Journal of the History of Medicine and Allied Sciences*, 9 (1954), 139–56 • M. P. Russell, 'Thomas Dover: 1660–1742', *Edinburgh Medical Journal*, 3rd ser., 49 (1942), 259–65 • W. Osler, 'Thomas Dover: physician and buccaneer', *An Alabama student and other biographical essays* (1908), 19–36 • 'Archaeologica medica XXVII: "Dover's ancient physicians' legacy"', *BMJ* (13 March 1897), 671–2 • 'Nova et Vetera: Thomas Dover, physician and circumnavigator', *BMJ* (22 March 1913), 619–20

Archives BL, Sloane MSS

Likenesses double portrait (with Alexander Selkirk), repro. in Strong, *Dr. Quicksilver*, frontispiece

Doveton, Sir John (1768–1847), army officer in the East India Company, was born in London, the son of Frederick Doveton, merchant, of Upper Wimpole Street, London, and his wife, Mary, *née* Slade, of Deptford. His brother was Sir William Doveton, for many years governor of St Helena.

Doveton entered the 1st Madras light cavalry as a cornet on 5 December 1785. He served all through the three campaigns of Lord Cornwallis against Tipu Sultan, and was promoted lieutenant on 12 June 1792. He also served in the campaign of Lieutenant-General George Harris against Tipu Sultan during the Fourth Anglo-Mysore War of 1799. He specially distinguished himself at the head of part of his regiment in the rapid pursuit of the notorious warlord Dhundia Wagh, under the direction of Colonel Arthur Wellesley.

Doveton was promoted captain on 8 May 1800, major on 2 September 1801, and lieutenant-colonel on 15 October 1804. In 1808 he was appointed to command the expedition against Bhangarh Khan, whose camp at Amritnair he stormed on 28 December. On 14 June 1813 he was promoted colonel, and in the following year appointed with the rank of brigadier-general to command the Hyderabad contingent, which was officered by Englishmen and kept under the control of the East India Company's government, while paid by the nizam. This force, which comprised nearly 10,000 men, was cantoned round Aurangabad, and was soon brought to a high pitch of efficiency by Doveton. In the Pindari war, conducted by the marquess of Hastings, the Hyderabad contingent played an important part.

Doveton's most important services were rendered during the Third Anglo-Maratha War of 1817–18. The Bhonsla ruler of Nagpur, Apa Sahib, who had succeeded his cousin after having him strangled, lent a ready support to the peshwa's scheme of assisting the Pindaris to overthrow British power in India. He therefore directed his troops, who were chiefly Arab mercenaries, to attack the British resident, Richard Jenkins. Though the resident's escort, commanded by Colonel Scott, beat off the assailants from the fortified hill of Sitabaldi in November 1817, its position soon became critical. Doveton, on hearing of this, advanced by forced marches on Nagpur, which he reached on 12 December. On the following day Apa Sahib surrendered himself, but his troops refused to surrender likewise. After a fierce battle, in which Doveton lost 141 men killed and wounded, the Arabs were defeated with a loss of 75 guns and 40 elephants. But they still held the city and palace of Nagpur, which Doveton attempted to storm on 24 December. The attack was repulsed, and Doveton lost over three hundred men in the assault. Yet the obstinacy of his attack terrified the Arab soldiers, who soon after agreed to evacuate the city. For his share in these operations, Doveton was made a CB on 14 October 1818 and a KCB on 26 November 1819.

In April 1819 Doveton commanded the forces which besieged and captured Asirgarh. On 12 August the same year he was promoted major-general. The following year he resigned his command and retired to Madras. He was promoted lieutenant-general and made a GCB on 10 January 1837. He died at his house in Madras on 7 November 1847, aged seventy-nine.

H. M. STEPHENS, rev. ALEX MAY

Sources Army List · East-India Register · W. J. Wilson, ed., History of the Madras army, 3, 4 (1883–8) · M. Edwardes, Glorious sahibs: the romantic as empire-builder (1968) · D. Forrest, Tiger of Mysore: the life and death of Tipu Sultan (1970) · R. G. Burton, The Mahratta and Pindari wars (1910) · R. G. Burton, Wellington's campaigns in India (1908) · H. T. Prinsep, History of the political and military transactions in India during the administration of the marquess of Hastings, 2 vols. (1825)
Archives BL OIOC, corresp. relating to India, Home misc. series · NAM, letter-books | NL Scot., corresp. with Lord Minto and papers

Dow, Alexander (1735/6–1779), army officer in the East India Company and author, was born in Perthshire, Scotland. Alexander Dow's father was 'of the customs at Dunbar' and Alexander himself was said to be apprenticed at Eyemouth to be educated for a mercantile career. In 1757, however, he joined the King of Prussia, a private ship of war, as a midshipman. One explanation given for this sudden career change was that he was forced to leave Scotland because of a fatal duel. In the course of the following three years he somehow made his way to Bengal, some say via Bencoolen, in Sumatra, where he entered the East India Company's military service as a cadet in 1760. Later that same year he was raised to the rank of ensign. In 1763 he became lieutenant and a year later he raised the 19th battalion of sepoys at Murshidabad. Appointed captain in April 1764, he took part in the assault on the Chunar Fort on 2 December that same year, during which he sustained a skull fracture. In 1766 he participated in the officers' association to protest against Clive's measure to abolish the double field allowance. Probably in consequence of his involvement in this affair, Dow found himself in Britain in 1768.

In that year Dow published Tales Translated from the Persian of Inatulla of Delhi and the first two volumes of the History of Hindostan. The latter work is a translation of the Persian text by Muhammad Kasim Ferishta, to which Dow added a dissertation on the religion and philosophy of the Brahmans and an appendix containing the last forty years of the history of the Mughal empire. His dissertation on Hindu religion and philosophy did not add much to existing knowledge of Hinduism but reached a wide audience and was extensively reviewed and discussed in Britain. It was therefore of some influence in shaping British views on India and on the religion and philosophy of its people until real advances in knowledge were made by William Jones and his fellow orientalists during the last two decades of the eighteenth century. Dow's treatise also influenced the views of Voltaire, and a French translation of his work appeared in 1769. In London Dow shared his lodgings with James Macpherson, another Scot with literary tastes, who would make a name for himself as the perpetrator of the Ossian hoax. In 1769 Dow published Zingis, a tragedy in five acts, which played with some success at Drury Lane. His qualities as a Persian scholar were called into question by John Shore, who supposed that he had had his Persian interpreter read and explain the stories of Inatulla to him, after which he had freely rewritten the substance of them in English. Shore considered Dow's translation of Ferishta's work, however, to be more correct, and in some places even exact in its translation. In his memoirs John Macdonald, in those days Dow's personal servant, wrote that his master spent so much money on women that he was tired of waiting on them. But Macdonald also recognized that Dow was a generous employer and when the latter set out for Bombay in April 1769, the footman agreed to accompany him.

During the voyage Dow worked on the third volume of his History of Hindostan. From Macdonald we learn that Dow spoke to inland princes in their own language and felt much at ease in their company as he 'knew their ways'. From this we may conclude that Dow's acquaintance with the Persian language went beyond his having a capable interpreter. Once arrived in India, his servant said that as his 'master made his fortune in Bengal and was a single man, he did not mind money' and 'kept the best house in Bombay' (John Macdonald: Memoirs, 117). But Bombay did not agree with Dow, and when, early in 1771, Eyre Coote passed through the settlement on his way overland to Britain, Dow asked Lieutenant-Governor Hodges for leave to accompany him. During the voyage they met with various 'fatiguing, dangerous and disagreeable accidents of detention' (Dow to Philip Francis, 8 Nov 1777, BL OIOC, MS Eur. F/5, fols. 329–31) which seem to have called forth Coote's notoriously quick temper.

Back in Britain in 1772 Dow considerably added to the public clamour raised against the East India Company in that year by publishing the third volume of his History of Hindostan, to which he prefixed two essays: 'A dissertation on the origin and nature of despotism in Hindostan', and 'An enquiry into the state of Bengal, with a plan for restoring that Kingdom to its former prosperity and splendour'.

The essays, like the writings published earlier that year by William Bolts, were openly critical of Clive, but Dow, unlike Bolts, expressed himself more charitably about Clive's successor, Harry Verelst, whom he qualified as a man of 'probity and honour'. But even his friendship for Verelst did not prevent Dow from criticizing him for failing to implement many obviously necessary regulations. Dow's ideas on improvement centred around the introduction of paper money to relieve Bengal commerce from the stranglehold caused by a lack of specie, the introduction of property rights in Bengal, the establishment of a board of revenue, and the introduction of a proper judicial system under a supreme court with jurisdiction over all of the Bengal territory. Dow's plan for property rights in Bengal was an early expression of the ideal of the permanent settlement. He expected that the enhanced security such a measure would provide would induce the new owners to improve the cultivation of their lands while at the same time strengthening their loyalty to the British. However, he saw the introduction of property rights not as an aim in itself but as a measure that would revive commerce by an increased agricultural output. His ideas were essentially mercantilist. In 1774, while Dow himself was in India, his new verse tragedy was published in London under the title *Sethona*. It was staged by Garrick at Drury Lane but was acted only for nine nights.

In March 1772 the directors, having already cleaned the slates of many other officers involved in the officers' association of 1766, decided to restore Dow to the rank he would have held in Bengal had he never participated in that transaction. Dow now ranked as a lieutenant-colonel but was to receive the pay of a captain until a lieutenant-colonelcy became available in Bengal. A year later he took his passage on the *Stormont* via Madras. In 1775 he was appointed commissary-general, an administrative post taking care of the military stores of all the factories and stations of the company's Bengal establishment. While executing his function diligently and to his employers' satisfaction, he grew impatient about being kept occupied 'in the detail of Brigade duty on the scanty pittance of 240 Rupees per month', obliging him 'to expend the greater part of a small independent fortune' he possessed (Dow to Francis, 11 Oct 1777, BL OIOC, MS Eur. F/5). Finally, he was rewarded for his services by an appointment as commander of the fort at Chunar for the limited duration of two years. But after one year he received notice that Lieutenant-Colonel Upton was appointed to succeed him. By such setbacks Dow was driven into the camp of Philip Francis, the opponent of Warren Hastings, hoping to receive more favourable treatment should Francis succeed Hastings as governor-general. Dow was now stationed at Barrackpore and, after notice of the war with France was received in Bengal, Hastings, despite Dow's allegiance to his great opponent, entrusted him with the task of investing the French settlement at Chandernagore. Dow executed this order at daybreak on 10 July 1778.

Towards the end of that year Dow felt his constitution deteriorating. He left Calcutta to try to retrieve his health.

On 18 July 1779 he wrote to Francis from Murshidabad: 'From some remaining obstruction in my liver I have been necessitated to recommence, or rather to prolong my course of mercury, which prevents so sudden a restoration of strength as I had once reason to expect' (BL OIOC, MS Eur. E/17). Thirteen days later, on 31 July 1779, Dow died at Bhagalpur, aged forty-three. Two years later an inventory was made up of his possessions in Bengal. From his papers it appeared that they amounted to Re146,720 (about £18,000), but his administrators had by that time only been able to recover half of that sum.

WILLEM G. J. KUITERS

Sources *John Macdonald: memoirs of an eighteenth-century footman*, ed. E. Denison-Ross and E. Power (1927) · V. C. P. Hodson, *List of officers of the Bengal army, 1758–1834*, 4 vols. (1927–47) · PRO, PROB 11/1091, no. 277 · inventory of the estate of Alexander Dow in India, BL OIOC, L/AG/34/27/2, no. 18 · DNB · *Memoir of the life and correspondence of John, Lord Teignmouth*, ed. C. J. Shore, second Baron Teignmouth, 1 (1843) · D. E. Baker, *Biographia dramatica, or, A companion to the playhouse*, rev. edn, rev. I. Reed, new edn, rev. S. Jones, 3 vols. in 4 (1812) · BL OIOC, MSS Eur. · K. K. Datta and others, eds., *Fort William–India House correspondence*, 6–7 (1960–71) · R. Guha, *A rule of property for Bengal: an essay on the idea of permanent settlement* (Paris, 1963) · P. J. Marshall, *The British discovery of Hinduism in the eighteenth century* (1970)
Archives BL OIOC, MSS Eur.
Likenesses J. Reynolds, oils, 1771–2, Petworth House, West Sussex
Wealth at death Rs146,720 [£18,000]: inventory, 28 May 1781, BL OIOC, L/AG/34/27/2, no. 18

Dow, (John) Christopher Roderick (1916–1998), economist, was born on 25 February 1916 at 6 Wordsworth Crescent, Harrogate, West Riding of Yorkshire, the son of Warrender Beganie Dow, company secretary, and his wife, Amy Langdon Grimwade. He was educated at Bootham School, York, at Brighton, Hove, and Sussex grammar school, and at University College, London. He served in the Royal Air Force in the Second World War. He joined the Treasury as an economic adviser in 1945 and worked in the economic section until 1954, by which time he was a senior economic adviser; then, with the support of the head of the section, Sir Robert Hall, he moved to the National Institute of Economic and Social Research (NIESR) as deputy director. In his eight years there he set up its quarterly review (first published in January 1959) and arranged for civil-service economists to be seconded for a period to undertake research.

A turning point came in Dow's private life in 1960 with his conversion to Roman Catholicism and his marriage on 31 December to Clare Mary Keegan (*b*. 1935), a librarian. Theirs was a particularly close and happy union. There were four children, three daughters and a son, James, who too became an economist, although of a very different type from his father—deploying rigorous North American micro-economics and finance theory at the London Business School.

During this period Dow's own research (much of it then, as later, carried out jointly with L. A. Dicks-Mireaux) was focused on wage inflation, then embryonic, with articles in *Oxford Economic Papers* in 1956 and 1958 and one in the *Journal of the Royal Statistical Society* in 1959. But the main fruit of his labours was his magisterial work *The Management of the British Economy, 1945–60* (1964). This work reflected fully his detachment from, and scepticism about, policies with which he was quite clearly involved—as later with monetarism. At this time he favoured Keynesian 'fine tuning', as it later became known—the attempt to stabilize the economy by managing demand—and thought it had prevented 'the heavy unemployment that accompanied the pre-war trade cycle' (p. 364). This was an era of extensive economic and financial controls—a fixed exchange rate (devalued in 1946) and tight controls on international capital movements—and it was only after the mid-1950s that monetary policy involved much reliance on interest rates rather than hire-purchase controls. These and budgetary instruments were used primarily to maintain the exchange rate. As a result, Dow wrote:

> The Major Fluctuations in the Rate of Growth and Output in the years after 1952 were thus chiefly due to government policy. This was not the intended effect; in each phase, it must be supposed, policy went further than intended, as in turn did the correction of those effects. As far as internal conditions are concerned then, budgetary and monetary policy failed to be stabilizing, and must on the contrary be regarded as having been positively destabilizing.   (p. 384)

He also expressed support for indicative planning of the type practised in France and subsequently by the National Economic Development Office of 1962 and in George Brown's national plan of 1965.

By the time the book appeared, Dow had spent another year (1962–3) in the Treasury before moving, as assistant secretary-general and chief economist, to the Organization for Economic Co-operation and Development in Paris. Having been founded to co-ordinate European responses to the Marshall plan of 1947, the organization continued to address questions of policy and its co-ordination in the industrial world—and of economic development more widely. Under his guidance it employed more macro-economists and used them to work along lines he had developed at the NIESR, publishing in the *Economic Outlook* (from 1967) analyses designed to facilitate co-ordinated demand management. The context of economic policy changed with the collapse of the Bretton Woods system of fixed (but adjustable) exchange rates in 1970, the diminishing role for controls, and the development of international financial markets.

In 1973, while considering the offer of the Oxford chair of applied economics, Dow accepted an invitation from the governor, Leslie O'Brien, to become executive director (economics) at the Bank of England on the eve of the first oil-price shocks (and of O'Brien's departure). He formed a very close relationship with O'Brien's successor, Gordon Richardson. As at the NIESR and the Organization for Economic Co-operation and Development, Dow strengthened the economics department; he also upgraded the content of the *Quarterly Bulletin* which the bank had published (on the recommendations of the Radcliffe commission) since 1960. He was elected FBA in 1982 (but declined the official honours he was offered).

Though remaining at the Bank of England until 1984 (as adviser to the governor after retiring from his directorship in 1981) while the tide of monetarism rose, Dow was consistently sceptical. Despite sharing some of Milton Friedman's reservations on fiscal fine-tuning, he did not share his faith in either the desirability or the feasibility of achieving the steady growth of any particular monetary aggregate. The depth of his dissent became public only with the appearance in 1988 of his *Critique of Monetary Policy*. By then Dow had returned to the NIESR as a visiting fellow. Iain Saville was seconded from the bank to help him on this project, and became a joint author. The book was not a great success, tending to suggest not merely that money was difficult to measure or control and endogenous but also that it was essentially irrelevant: in this Dow went further than most pragmatists.

Already over seventy, Dow embarked on his last major work, which was in press when he died: *Major Recessions* (1998) reverted to the success with which he had credited demand management in his first book. He adopted a novel (and questionable) methodology, but struck several chords with his timing, and with the blame that he attached to expansionary excesses (such as were then becoming evident in the USA) for subsequent slumps. He was cautious in his prescriptions but revealed some hankering for the instruments of control available in earlier decades.

The seminar to launch this book was already announced when, as was his wont, Christopher Dow attended mass at the Brompton Oratory on Sunday 29 November 1998 and collapsed during the course of the service. He died with his family at his bedside in the Chelsea and Westminster Hospital, Chelsea, London, two days later, on 1 December; his wife, Clare, survived him. A well-attended requiem mass was held at the oratory on Friday 11 December.

Christopher Dow contributed to the development of economic policy analysis over four decades. His careful, thoughtful, and independent work always stood apart from any of the excesses that tended to discredit forecasting. Shy and withdrawn, he surprisingly added membership of the Garrick late in life to his lengthy membership of the Reform Club. A cultured person, in both literature and art, especially of France, he painted seriously and worked in wood to a high standard of craftsmanship. Similar dedication and fastidiousness were evident in all he did, said, and wrote. His style—described by one colleague as 'invisible'—became well known in all the organizations for which he worked: he himself was heard to extol the merits of 'nuanced tautology' when writing (defensively) for official publication.

JOHN S. FLEMMING

Sources *The Times* (4 Dec 1998) · C. W. McMahon, *The Independent* (4 Dec 1998) · W. Keegan, *The Guardian* (4 Dec 1998) · A. J. C. Britton, *British Academy Memoirs* (1999–2000), 397–413 · K. Jones, 'Fifty years of economic research: a brief history of the NIESR, 1939–1988', *National Institute Economic Review* (May 1988) · b. cert. · m. cert. · d. cert. · personal knowledge (2004)
Likenesses photograph, repro. in *The Times* · photograph, repro. in *The Independent* · photograph, repro. in *The Guardian*

Dow, Robert (1553–1588), music copyist, was the eldest of
five sons born to Lettice Bull and Robert Dow (1523–1612),
citizen and merchant taylor of London. His father was collector of tonnage and poundage for the port of London. He
may have attended Merchant Taylors' School before going
up to Corpus Christi College, Oxford, where he was admitted BA on 14 January 1574, having supplicated for the
degree on 12 October 1573. Although his name does not
appear in the Corpus registers, Dow wrote Lord Burghley
three Latin letters in 1573, 'Oxoniae in Collegio Corporis
Christi'. This correspondence sought to secure royal support for Dow's efforts to gain admittance to All Souls College as a student of civil law, but while this was not immediately forthcoming, he was eventually elected to a probationary fellowship there on 28 November 1575. At this
time he was giving lessons in penmanship, and could
count Robert Sidney among his pupils.

On 14 January 1577 Dow was admitted to All Souls as BA
and student in laws. He supplicated for the degree of BCL
on 29 March 1582 and was admitted on 26 April following.
From 1585 to 1587 he was bursar of laws at All Souls, and in
the latter year he contributed to *Exequiae Illustrissimi equitis*,
a collection of verse in memory of Sir Philip Sidney; his
elegy reveals that Dow had travelled to Poland and met
King Stephen Báthory. Dow died intestate on 10 November 1588, presumably at All Souls. The inventory of his
goods included a library of over 300 volumes, among
them a set of music partbooks in his own fine italic hand
which survives today as Oxford, Christ Church, MSS 984–
988. It contains instrumental pieces, songs, anthems, and
motets, some of which bear annotations in Latin about
their composers. Dated 1581, it is one of the most important sources of Elizabethan music, even if in the vocal
pieces the scribe occasionally modernizes the composer's
setting by altering notes and text underlay. Dow's music
manuscripts are the major source of the compositions of
Robert White. The content of his library may suggest recusant sympathies.   DAVID MATEER

Sources Christ Church Oxf., MSS 984–988 · Bodl. Oxf., Univ.
Oxon. Arch. Hyp. B12, inventories D–F · D. Mateer, 'Oxford, Christ
Church music MSS 984–8: an index and commentary', *Royal Musical
Association Research Chronicle*, 20 (1986–7), 1–18 · D. Mateer, 'John
Baldwin and changing concepts of text underlay', *English choral
practice, c.1400–c.1650*, ed. J. G. Morehen (1995), 143–60 · R. Cooke,
Visitation of London, 1568, ed. H. Stanford London and S. W. Rawlins,
[new edn], 2 vols. in one, Harleian Society, 109–10 (1963) · M. H.
Curtis, *Oxford and Cambridge in transition, 1558–1642* (1971) ·
W. Gager, ed., *Exequiae Illustrissimi equitis D. Philippi Sidnaei,
gratissimae memoriae ac nomini impensae* (1587) · N. R. Ker, *Records of
All Souls College Library, 1437–1600* (1971) · H. B. Wilson, *The history of
Merchant-Taylors' School*, 2 vols. (1814) · C. T. Martin, *The archives in the
muniment rooms of All Souls College* (1877) · *Oxford University register of
congregation and convocation, 1564–82*
Archives BL, Add. MS 22583 · Christ Church Oxf., the 'Dow' partbooks, MSS 984–988 | BL, Lansdowne MS xvii, nos. 77, 80, 84
Wealth at death £68 7s. 2½d.: inventory, Oxf. UA Hyp. B12, inventories D–F

Dowdall, George (1487–1558), archbishop of Armagh,
according to the Dowdall pedigrees, was the son of
Edward Dowdall and grandson of Henry and Jeneta
Dowdall of Newtown Termonfeckin, co. Louth. His family

were probably landowners. Sir Thomas *Cusack, later
lord chancellor of Ireland, was his cousin. On 8 July 1518
Dowdall, described as a cleric, was not yet a fully professed
member of the community of crutched friars at Ardee, co.
Louth. He was employed as a proctor in a number of suits
in Armagh's consistory court, suggesting a training in
canon law. By 1522 he was being styled 'magister', a title
normally reserved for university graduates, although no
record of his graduation has been preserved. By June 1524
Dowdall had become the prior of the hospital of the
crutched friars at Ardee.

It is not known whether Dowdall joined Archbishop
George Cromer in the Kildare revolt of 1534–5, though Sir
Thomas Cusack described him as 'such a papistical fellow,
being able to corrupt a whole country' (Bradshaw, 126). His
hospital was dissolved in 1539 and he became Armagh's
official principal. Despite his commitment to Catholic
doctrines Dowdall acquiesced in Henry VIII's royal
supremacy. By 1540 Cromer was terminally ill and
Dowdall was increasingly responsible for the administration of the archdiocese. He visited the English royal court
in 1542 in the company of the lord deputy, St Leger, and
was promised that he would be the next archbishop of
Armagh.

Dowdall was appointed as archbishop of Armagh and
primate of all Ireland by Henry VIII on 29 April 1543. His
career as archbishop may be traced by means of Dowdall's
register, the last in the series of volumes of medieval
records which survive for Armagh. His administration
may be characterized as conservatively reformist (that is,
accepting of the royal supremacy) rather than pro-
reformation. None of his actions had a distinctly protestant character. Indeed, Dowdall resisted the extension of
protestantism into his diocese during Edward VI's reign.
By the summer of 1551, however, faced with imminent
imprisonment, he left Ireland precipitately, declaring
that he would 'never be bishop where the holy Mass was
abolished' (Shirley, 54–60). He was subsequently removed
from office. He spent some time with the abbot of Centre,
in the Netherlands, and is supposed to have translated a
History of Ireland from a manuscript belonging to Conn
Bacach O'Neill at Armagh in 1551 (Lambeth MS 623). He
was reconciled with the Roman Catholic church and
received a papal provision on 1 March 1553. Mary restored
him as the crown acknowledged archbishop of Armagh in
October 1553, and he was also a member of her council of
Ireland. The title of 'primate of all Ireland', granted to the
archbishop of Dublin, George Browne, in 1551, was
restored to Dowdall on 12 March 1554.

Following his return, Dowdall convened a major synod
to restore and revitalize the Catholic religion throughout
the ecclesiastical province of Armagh. Several of its
decrees reimposed long-standing obligations. Other
decrees on the exaction of burial fees from widows and
orphans, and on fees for the administration of sacraments, show that Archbishop Dowdall tried to defuse
sources of tension between the laity and its priests. The
synod also authorized the appointment of inquisitors to

identify and prosecute persons expressing heretical opinions. Heretical books were ordered to be burnt. Within the archdiocese of Armagh the work of restoration was quickly carried out. The decrees issued in the annual diocesan synods in Mary's reign were wholly traditional. Protestantism, clerical negligence, or immorality in Armagh *inter Anglicos* presented no problem in the primate's eyes. His provincial synod of 1556 did no more than confirm a number of feast days as holy days of obligation, though agricultural labourers were not forbidden to work on those days.

Dowdall was a member of a royal commission established in April 1554 to remove all married clergymen in Ireland from office, the counterpart of similar commissions established in England and Wales. Several Henrician and Edwardian bishops were deprived of office as a result, together with some lesser clergymen, though it seems that there were very few married priests in Ireland. Dowdall was appointed to another commission in December 1557 to inquire into the location of all chalices and ornaments, bells, houses, and lands belonging to parish churches and chapels in co. Louth, with the aim of restoring to the use of the church any such items which had been confiscated. There seems, however, to have been no need in Ireland for the herculean efforts required in England to reconstruct the ritual and sacramental framework of traditional religion following Edward's reign.

With the married bishops deprived, the way was clear for Cardinal Pole to promote two local men, William Walsh, one of his chaplains, and Thomas Leverous, whom he met in Rome, to Meath and Kildare respectively, two important dioceses which encompassed significant portions of the pale. Pole relied on Walsh and Leverous, as well as Dowdall, to spearhead the Marian restoration in Ireland. Following the revocation of the Henrician and Edwardian ecclesiastical legislation by the English parliament in January 1555 the Marian restoration gathered pace. St Patrick's Cathedral, Dublin, was restored on 25 March 1555, a powerful centre of Catholic piety and preaching at the heart of the English lordship in Ireland. Dowdall was appointed as a prebendary of the cathedral, giving him a residence in the capital whenever he had to attend the council of Ireland.

Mary's Irish parliament of 1557 repealed all statutes and proclamations made against the papacy in Ireland since 1534. Statutes for the suppression of heresy were revived but no persecution of protestants ensued. The crown renounced its claim to the first fruits and twentieths, tithes, glebes, and advowsons which, as in England, Cardinal Pole hoped to use for a concerted assault on clerical poverty. Pole also hoped to establish diocesan seminaries to enhance the training of priests. George Dowdall doubtless approved of Pole's strategy. Yet it seems significant that he intended to found a chantry near his archiepiscopal residence at Termonfeckin, rather than a school or seminary, shortly before he died in London on 15 August 1558. In the event his intention, like Pole's plans, came to naught on Mary's death. One study has concluded that Dowdall 'was one of the finest figures of the late medieval Irish Church' and that, while he did not anticipate the Counter-Reformation in Ireland, he had 'laid foundations which helped to ensure that the counter-reformation would find receptive congregations during Elizabeth's reign' (Jefferies, *Priests*, 170).   HENRY A. JEFFERIES

Sources G. Dowdall, register, PRO NIre., MS D10 4/2/13 · H. A. Jefferies, 'Primate George Dowdall and the Marian restoration', *Seanchas Ardmhacha*, 17 (1998–9), 1–18 · H. A. Jefferies, *Priests and prelates of Armagh in the age of reformations, 1518–1558* (1997) · *The whole works of Sir James Ware concerning Ireland*, ed. and trans. W. Harris, rev. edn, 2 vols. in 3 (1764) · E. P. Shirley, ed., *Original letters and papers in illustration of the history of the church in Ireland during the reigns of Edward VI, Mary and Elizabeth* (1851) · J. Morrin, ed., *Calendar of the patent and close rolls of chancery in Ireland, of the reigns of Henry VIII, Edward VI, Mary, and Elizabeth*, 1 (1861) · A. Gwynn, *The medieval province of Armagh, 1470–1545* (1946) · B. Bradshaw, *The dissolution of the religious orders in Ireland under Henry VIII* (1974) · Dowdall pedigrees, TCD, MS F4.18

Archives PRO NIre., MS D10 4/2/13 · TCD, pedigrees, MS F4.18

Dowden, Edward (1843–1913), literary scholar and poet, was born on 3 May 1843 at Cork, the second son of John Wheeler Dowden (1799–1891), linen merchant and landowner, and his wife, Alicia Bennett (d. 1869). His elder brother, John *Dowden (1840–1910), became bishop of Edinburgh in 1886. There were two sisters, Margaret and Anna. Edward was educated at home and at Queen's College, Cork, from 1858, before being admitted in 1859 to Trinity College, Dublin, where he graduated in 1863. On 23 October 1866 he married Mary (d. 1892), daughter of David Clerke; they had four children, a son and two daughters, and a fourth child who died before 1914. Also in 1866 he became professor of English at Alexandra College, Dublin, a post he resigned in July 1867. The same year he was appointed to the newly founded chair of English literature in Trinity College.

At Trinity College, Dublin, in 1873 Dowden prepared a number of lectures entitled 'The mind and art of Shakespere', lectures that were, eventually, the materials for what was to be his most influential work, *Shakespere: a Critical Study of his Mind and Art* (1876). The book went through a number of editions and was translated into a number of languages. Dowden's view of Shakespeare's philosophy was coloured by his study of the positivism of Auguste Comte. There followed a spate of books, biographies, editions, and articles, prominent among which were a *Shakespere Primer* (1877), *Studies in Literature* (1878), and *New Studies in Literature* (1895). Short biographies of Southey, Browning, and Montaigne were crowned by his most extensive work, the biography of Shelley (2 vols.) on which he laboured from 1883 to its publication in 1886. In the biography of Shelley Dowden was faced with the problem of the poet's marriage to Harriet Westbrook and its unsavoury aftermath. Harriet, estranged from Shelley, drowned herself in the Serpentine on 13 December 1816. Dowden wrote of her:

> There is no doubt that she wandered from the ways of upright living; how far she wandered we need not inquire. If she sinned, she also sorrowed; we would think of her, not as a desperate fugitive from life, but as the fair, bright, innocent, kind-hearted Harriet of her early wedded days. That no act of Shelley's during the two years which

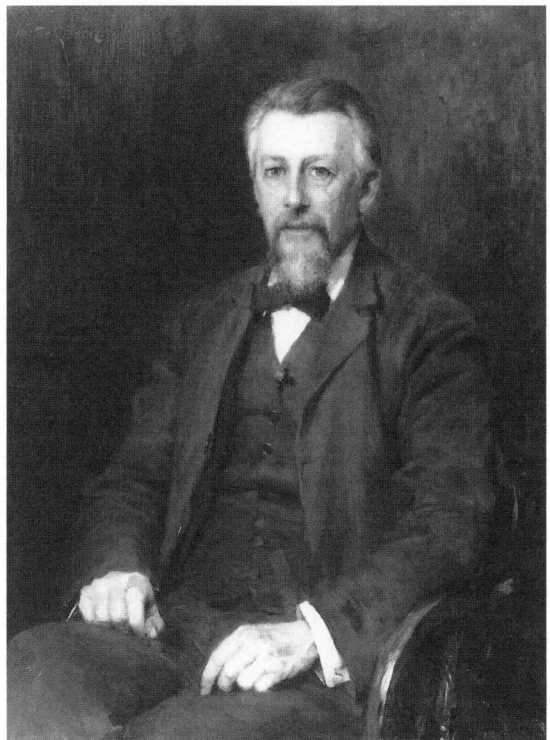

Edward Dowden (1843–1913), by Walter Frederick Osborne, 1891

immediately preceded her death tended to cause the rash act which brought her life to its close, seems certain.

(E. Dowden, *The Life of Percy Bysshe Shelley*, 1950, 332–3)

The biography was both damned and praised. Dowden was an early admirer of Whitman's poetry and devoted one chapter of his *Studies in Literature* to 'The poetry of democracy' in which he discussed Whitman's poetry extensively.

On 12 December 1895 Dowden married Elizabeth Dickinson West, daughter of John West, dean of St Patrick's Cathedral, Dublin. She was a minor poet and translator, a student of his at Alexandra College, with whom he corresponded throughout his first, unsatisfactory, marriage. For her he wrote a little volume of poems, *A Woman's Reliquary*, published posthumously in 1913. There were no children of this marriage.

Dowden was an opponent of a national Anglo-Irish literature as well as an outspoken opponent of home rule. In the introduction to his *New Studies in Literature* (1895) Dowden disclaimed any desire to be thought of as an Irish writer, stating 'I confess that I am not ambitious of intensifying my intellectual or spiritual brogue' (p. 19), with more in the same vein. He was not, understandably, popular with, among others, W. B. Yeats. Dowden had praised the young Yeats, son of his friend, J. B. Yeats, on the publication of the younger Yeats's 'The Wandering of Oisin', when such praise was very welcome. Indeed, the younger Yeats later admitted to having virtually worshipped Dowden. But Dowden's lack of sympathy for Anglo-Irish literature alienated Yeats, and in an article, 'The poetry of

Samuel Ferguson', in the *Dublin University Review* for November 1886, he wrote:

> It is a question whether the most distinguished of our critics, Professor Dowden, would not only have more consulted the interests of his country, but more also, in the long run, his own dignity and reputation which are dear to all Irishmen, if he had devoted some of those elaborate pages which he has spent on the much bewritten George Eliot, to a man like the subject of this article.   (Yeats, *Prose*, 89)

In his *Autobiographies: Reveries over Childhood* (1915), Yeats devoted sections 24 and 25 to his recollections of Dowden, in which he records his final damning estimation of him. In his essay 'At Stratford-on-Avon', of May 1901, Yeats wrote that he had read Dowden's *Shakespere … his Mind and Art* diligently and went on to disagree radically with his characterization of Richard II in Shakespeare's play. But the two did not become enemies, and Dowden writes in a letter of 14 April 1907 of a visit by Yeats, of whom he says that he 'comes and goes and is always intelligent and interesting—but after all, wisdom is better than folly, and he ought to be attending to his higher sense' (*Letters*, 351). Dowden died on 4 April 1913 at Rochdale, Orwell Road, Rathgar, Dublin. With the exception of visits to the United States and Canada, he had spent his entire life in that city.   E. J. GWYNN, *rev.* ARTHUR SHERBO

Sources K. R. Ludwigson, *Edward Dowden* (1963) · W. B. Yeats, *Uncollected prose*, ed. J. P. Frayne, 2 vols. (1970–75) · W. B. Yeats, *Autobiographies*, new edn (1927) · *Letters of Edward Dowden and his correspondents*, ed. E. D. Dowden and H. M. Dowden (1914)
Archives TCD, corresp. and literary papers · TCD, diaries | Birm. CA, letters to Wilson King and Rachel King · BL, letters to W. H. Griffin, Add. MS 45564 · BL, corresp. with Hodgsons, MS 54717 · BL, corresp. with Macmillans, Add. MS 55029 · Bodl. Oxf., letters to Bertram Dobell · Hunt. L., letters to Robert Perceval Graves and poems · NL Ire., letters to Robert Perceval Graves · NL Ire., letters to A. E. Thiselton · NL Scot., corresp. with John Dowden · TCD, letters to W. Macneile Dixon · TCD, letters to John Todhunter · TCD, letters to Herbert Martin Oliver White · U. Edin. L., corresp. with James Halliwell-Phillipps · U. Leeds, Brotherton L., letters to Sir Edmund Gosse · University of British Columbia Library, letters to W. K. Magee
Likenesses W. Osborne, oils, 1891, NG Ire. [*see illus.*] · J. B. Yeats, oils, Hugh Lane Municipal Gallery of Modern Art, Dublin · two portraits, repro. in *Letters*, ed. Dowden and Dowden
Wealth at death £1558 15s.—in England: probate, 13 June 1913, CGPLA Eng. & Wales

Dowden, John (1840–1910), Scottish Episcopal bishop of Edinburgh and scholar, was born on 29 June 1840 at Cork, the fifth of the five surviving children of John Wheeler Dowden (1799–1891), linen draper, and his wife, Alicia Bennett (d. 1869), daughter of John Barter Bennett, surgeon and chemist. His father, a leading merchant in the town, had interests in literature and contemporary thought which were not restricted by his devout Presbyterianism. His mother was an equally devout member of the Church of Ireland. Throughout his life Dowden was close to his father, and to his younger brother Edward *Dowden, later professor of English literature at Dublin University.

In Cork Dowden attended both the Scots Church and the local parish church. Educated at the diocesan school, by private tutors, and at Dr Douglas's school, at the age of sixteen he matriculated at Queen's College, Cork, gaining scholarships in his first and second years. But throughout his education uncertain health prevented him from realizing his full intellectual potential. Previously set on a medical career, he began to consider becoming a clergyman in the Church of Ireland, and accordingly his father sent him in October 1858 to Trinity College, Dublin, while he made up his mind.

Dowden attended Trinity College from 1858 to 1864, exhibiting a lifelong love of literature and music. He graduated BA in 1861 with first-class honours in logic and ethics, and then joined the divinity class, becoming known for his attachment to the theology of the Oxford Movement. Although reverencing John Henry Newman, he was never attracted to ritualist extremes. He was ordained deacon by Bishop Verschoyle of Kilmore on 17 July 1864 to the curacy of St John's, Sligo. On 15 September 1864 he married Louisa Jones, daughter of Francis Jones, a civil engineer, and they had six children. Ordained priest in 1865, with his delicate health and scholarly bent he found the ministry in a small county town difficult, being generally regarded by the parishioners as high-church. In 1867 he was appointed perpetual curate of Calry, a suburb of Cork. Not a natural, but a conscientious pastor, Dowden also began to develop his liturgical scholarship in articles in the new *Contemporary Review*. In 1870 he was appointed one of the chaplains to Lord Spenser, the lord lieutenant. A more congenial appointment came in 1872 when the rector of the fashionable Dublin church, St Stephen's, invited him to be one of the curates.

In September 1874 Dowden accepted the appointment as Pantonian professor of theology at the Scottish Episcopal church's Trinity College, Glenalmond, the warden being an acquaintance from his parish days in Cork. Before leaving for Scotland he graduated BD at Trinity College, Dublin. Glenalmond was founded in 1846 to be both a public school and a divinity institution, but the latter was struggling when he arrived in 1874, owing to the school's remoteness and the age differences between divinity students and schoolboys. A fire in the school the next year saw the theological institution move to Edinburgh, which gave Dowden the combination he wanted of a liberal theological environment with a devotional grounding, and student numbers began to increase. An exacting though sympathetic teacher, Dowden was devoted to the advancement of Scots in the higher offices of the church as against the contemporary Episcopalian preference for educated Englishmen. In 1876 he was awarded a DD from Trinity College. His scholarship bore lasting fruit in 1884 in his still authoritative annotated edition of the Scottish communion office, the eucharistic liturgy of the eighteenth-century nonjuring Episcopalians which continued to be used by various congregations of the Scottish Episcopal church. The work contributed to a renewed sympathy for the Scottish office among Scottish Episcopalians. Widening recognition of his scholarship saw the University of Dublin appoint him Donnellan lecturer in 1885–6, and in 1886–7 he was select preacher there and in 1888 at the University of Cambridge.

In 1886 Dowden was elected bishop of Edinburgh (after the refusal of the position by Canon Henry Liddon); he was consecrated on 21 September, the most scholarly Episcopal bishop of his day. This scholarship could have unfortunate consequences: he adopted the archaic Latin title of John Edenburgen which, by its apparent territorial implications, offended presbyterian sensibilities, as did also his hard line against Episcopalians preaching in Presbyterian churches in his diocese. But Dowden continued to be best known as a theologian. In 1896 he was invited to the United States as the Paddock lecturer at the General Seminary, New York. Back in Scotland he became involved in possible prayer book and canonical revision from 1894, and his work was to make an important posthumous contribution to eventual revision in 1912. In the latter part of his episcopate his scholarship brought recognition in Scotland, where he had been one of the founders of the Scottish History Society in 1886. The University of Edinburgh awarded him in 1904 an honorary LLD. An acknowledged authority in liturgical history, his *Scottish Communion Office, 1764* (1922) is still authoritative. He contributed to the *Scottish Historical Review* and wrote works on the medieval church history of Scotland, including *The Medieval Church in Scotland* (1910). Developing a later interest in Christian reunion, he was a regular attender at the meetings of the Christian Unity Association. Dowden died at his home, 13 Learmonth Terrace, Edinburgh, on 30 January 1910. His funeral was held in St Mary's Cathedral, Edinburgh, from where he was buried in the Dean cemetery.

ROWAN STRONG

Sources A. Mitchell, 'John Dowden bishop of Edinburgh', *Biographical studies in Scottish church history* (Milwaukee, WI, 1914), 258–88 · *Scottish standard bearer*, 21 (1910) · NL Scot., Dowden MS Dep. 171 · A. Dowden, 'A biographical sketch of Bishop Dowden', in J. Dowden, *The medieval church in Scotland* (1910) · *Scottish Guardian* (1910)
Archives NL Scot., corresp. and papers; papers mainly relating to Scottish church history | NA Scot., Scottish Episcopal Church MSS · NL Ire., letters to Alice Stopford Green
Likenesses R. Lorimer, bronze tablet, 1911, Edinburgh Cathedral · photograph, NPG · photographs, NL Scot., Dowden MSS, Dep. 171 · photographs, repro. in Mitchell, 'John Dowden', 258
Wealth at death £4534 18*s*. 1*d*.: confirmation, 28 March 1910, *CCI* · £433 8*s*. 4*d*. in Ireland: probate, 12 May 1910, *CGPLA Ire.*

Dowdeswell, William (1721–1775), politician, was born on 12 March 1721, the first surviving son of William Dowdeswell (1682–1728), landowner and politician, and his second wife, Amy Hammond (*d.* in or after 1728), daughter of Anthony Hammond of Somersham, Huntingdonshire. The Dowdeswell family had been settled at Bushley, near Tewkesbury, on the Gloucestershire and Worcestershire border, since Elizabethan times and purchased Pull Court in 1628. They amassed considerable property locally, giving them an important electoral interest in Tewkesbury, for which no fewer than nine Dowdeswells had sat since 1660, including William's father and grandfather. William inherited while a minor, following his father's early death on 5 September 1728.

Education and entry into politics In 1730 Dowdeswell was sent to Westminster School, for which he developed a lasting affection that culminated in his position as a Busby trustee (1769–75). He proceeded in 1737 to Christ Church, Oxford, where he contributed a set of Latin verses to the university collection of poems on the death of Queen Caroline in the following year. He does not appear to have taken an Oxford degree but in 1745 he went to the University of Leiden, where he associated, among others, with Charles Townshend, John Wilkes, Anthony Askew, and Alexander Carlyle. From the Netherlands he toured Italy, travelling through Sicily and Greece and returning to England by 1747. On 6 November 1747 he married Bridget (d. 1818), fifth and youngest daughter of Sir William Codrington, first baronet (d. 1738), of Dodington, Gloucestershire, and Elizabeth Bethell (d. 1761), and sister of Sir William Codrington, second baronet (1719–1792). The couple had six sons, including William *Dowdeswell, army officer and art collector, and seven daughters, several of whom died young.

In 1747 Dowdeswell was returned as MP for Tewkesbury but he declined to stand for re-election in 1754, when certain constituents made their support conditional on a contribution of £1500 towards the local roads. He resumed his parliamentary career in 1761 as MP for Worcestershire, which he represented until his death, and enjoyed great popularity as MP. In his early career he was often mistaken for a tory because he supported continued commemoration of Charles I's execution, but his politics were more complex. As a typical country gentleman he opposed government expenditure levels but he upset the tories with his comments during the proceedings on the Westminster election in 1751 and with his dislike of the militia. In December 1762 he voted against the peace preliminaries.

Opposition to the cider excise Dowdeswell was catapulted to prominence by the cider tax controversy of 1763. Considerable resentment was provoked in the western counties when Sir Francis Dashwood's budget extended the excise duties to domestic cider in March 1763. James Harris, the parliamentary diarist, noted between 9 and 14 March that Dowdeswell 'was the chief opponent and had taken great pains', making 'by far the best figure on that side' (Harris) and unsuccessfully pressing a series of amendments. In the summer of 1763 Dowdeswell sought further support by composing *An Address to such of the Electors of Great Britain as are not Makers of Cyder and Perry*, in which he contended that this widening of an 'arbitrary' excise system foreshadowed the eventual subjection of all freeborn Englishmen in a sinister Machiavellian 'plan for *power* not for revenue' (p. 8). He also supported the extra-parliamentary campaign to petition the legislature, instruct local MPs, and collect examples of excise grievances; he attended the Worcestershire county meeting on 29 August and guided discussions in the Tewkesbury common council on 13 September. On 18 November George Grenville, the new first lord of the Treasury, sought a compromise solution in discussions with Dowdeswell and other interested MPs but his apparent prevarication led Dowdeswell to conclude that the western members should seek a full repeal through their own efforts. On 24 January 1764, Harris records, Dowdeswell moved for a

committee in a 'decent, temperate, and reasonable' speech. On 31 January he:

> entered into a detail of the grievances of the excise laws upon ignorant countrymen, the enormity of the penalties, the trials without juries, the partiality of what he called revenue injustices, the dreaded consequences that were these laws extended commissioners of excise might nominate Members for the cider counties. (Harris)

On 10 February he seconded an unsuccessful repeal motion, following which Grenville pushed through conciliatory modifications. Dowdeswell also voted against Grenville on Wilkes and general warrants but he supported the Regency Bill. He criticized Grenville's spending plans in the budget debate on 27 March and was almost alone that day in warning prophetically against provoking the American colonies by new taxation.

Chancellor of the exchequer When Rockingham took office in July 1765 both Sir William Baker and Henry Seymour Conway declined the chancellorship of the exchequer. Rockingham therefore turned to Dowdeswell, who was sworn of the privy council on 10 July and accepted the exchequer three days later. The appointment surprised many contemporaries, since Dowdeswell had never sided unequivocally with the opposition, or belonged to the opposition Wildman's Club. However, his Commons performances had highlighted his self-made expertise on financial matters, his honest integrity, and his ability to deliver solid argument based on a clear command of the issues. Rockingham's desire to court popularity 'out of doors' neatly complemented Dowdeswell's hostility towards the cider excise. Dowdeswell himself was under few illusions: 'I am called to the office I hold', he observed on 24 July:

> only because I am supposed to have some talents in the execution of it. In the business of that office I shall set myself down. If either inability, or the disposition of the times shall put me out of power to do good, I know what I then have to do. (Buccleuch MSS)

On 17 September he still adhered to the outdated 'country' belief that 'every man in office or out of it may vote with his opinion' (Dowdeswell MSS). By 12 October George Onslow was enthusiastically forecasting that 'he will be our great stay' on the Treasury bench (West MSS), and he was soon playing a major and respected role in all government business, particularly commercial affairs.

Though not formally a member of cabinet Dowdeswell was in regular attendance and Rockingham, who soon recognized the value of consulting him, invited him to many of the dinners at which public affairs were discussed. Dowdeswell assisted Conway in conducting the business of the house and, when the latter was taken gravely ill during March and April 1766, he led the government in the Commons. He was present at the crucial meetings on 19 and 21 January 1766 to discuss the Stamp Act repeal. His silence in the great debate of 21–22 February gave Harris the impression that 'he was in his private sentiments rather for a modification than a repeal' (Harris) but on 24 February he spoke in favour of repeal. On 4 March he stressed the need for a declaratory act to prevent any impression that parliament had surrendered the right of taxation. Repeal of the 1763 cider duty was the predictable centrepiece of Dowdeswell's budget on 7 March, the removal of 103,000 private households from the excise administration being trumpeted as a restoration of liberty. The 'Apple Chancellor' (*St James's Chronicle*, 8–10 April 1766) now raised the existing retail cider duties by 6*s.* per hogshead and tightened legislation against fraud but provoked controversy with a new window tax. Such a record belies Horace Walpole's acid depiction of Dowdeswell as 'a duller version of Mr. Grenville, though without his malignity'. He was allegedly:

> so suited to the drudgery of the office, as far as it depends on arithmetic, that he was fit for nothing else. Heavy, slow, methodical without clearness, a butt for ridicule, unversed in every graceful art, and a stranger to men and courts, he was only esteemed by the few to whom he was personally known. (Walpole, *Memoirs … George III*, 2.219, 139)

Equally cheap was Bishop Warburton's sarcastic observation of a visit from Lord Lyttelton to Dowdeswell: 'there … goes a man who cannot tell that two times two is four going to dine with a man who knows nothing else' (H. Thrale, *Thraliana*, ed. K. C. Balderston, 2 vols., 1942, 1.2).

Rockingham opposition leader in the Commons When Chatham's administration was being formed in July 1766 Grafton, the new first lord of the Treasury, felt inclined to retain Dowdeswell at the exchequer 'for the general good, and very likely for my own private ease of mind' (*Correspondence of William Pitt*, 2.460). These prospects were ruined when Chatham learned from George III 'that Lord Rockingham's being quiet would much depend' on such an arrangement and insisted on Dowdeswell's immediate dismissal (*Correspondence of George III*, 1.380). Compensatory offers of a place as joint paymaster-general or first lord of trade followed but Dowdeswell refused them, to the surprise of many political commentators who were aware of his straitened financial circumstances. Burke later portrayed Dowdeswell's stance in terms of highly principled loyalty, in contrast to those careerists who abandoned Rockingham in order to remain in office, but the truth was more prosaic. In his last audience with the king, on 29 July 1766, Dowdeswell stressed his belief that he had discharged his office both to the royal satisfaction and 'with no small degree of public approbation', adding: 'It might be a misfortune sometimes to have been raised too high. Men could not after being much exalted stoop to certain offices, which they might have at first accepted' (Dowdeswell MSS). On 16 September 1766 Lord Harcourt recorded that Dowdeswell had returned to Worcestershire 'very much out of humour and indeed with reason after the treatment he has met with' (*Jenkinson Papers*, 430). Thereafter Dowdeswell distrusted Chatham and was drawn irrevocably towards Rockingham in a way that might not otherwise have occurred, becoming his close friend, faithful adviser, and trusted strategist. As the leader of the Rockingham group in the Commons his political life was thereafter essentially 'the history of the Rockingham party' (Brooke, 'Dowdeswell', 335). He was a conspicuous and respected figure in the house, preparing many of the key opposition motions and making some 500 speeches on all manner of subjects. Although these were generally dry, legalistic, and narrow his more flamboyant junior colleague Edmund Burke none the less wrote to Rockingham on 7 January 1773 that he was sure 'we cannot find a leader whom a man of honour and judgment would so soon choose to follow' (Rockingham MSS).

In February 1767 Dowdeswell sought to rally a confused and demoralized opposition by proposing a reduction in the land tax from 4*s.* to 3*s.* in the pound, arguing that £1 million of debt could still be repaid. Critics noted that Dowdeswell had not acted in his own budget, but this opportunistic measure had a natural appeal for the independent country gentlemen and ensured successful *ad hoc* co-operation with the Bedfords and Grenvilles. Dowdeswell triumphantly carried the motion by 206 votes to 188 but Chatham's normal majority was not affected and in subsequent months Dowdeswell failed to exploit the ministry's divisions regarding the affairs of the East India Company. Renewed thoughts of a possible permanent opposition alliance none the less highlighted Dowdeswell's growing importance. On 8 July 1767 Rockingham urgently requested his presence 'because it is a very great ease and satisfaction to my own mind to have the assistance of your calm judgement within reach' (Rockingham MSS). Dowdeswell attended both of Rockingham's discussions with Bedford, on 20 and 21 July, about the outlines of a possible new administration but these reached deadlock over Rockingham's insistence on Conway as leader of the Commons. Bedford suggested Dowdeswell instead but the latter declined 'for many reasons which he then gave, and for many more which he kept in his own breast' (ibid.). Conway now invited the Rockinghams to join Chatham's administration, suggesting Dowdeswell as chancellor of the exchequer. The latter's memorandum of 23 and 24 July advised Rockingham to decline unless 'the King should send for him to give him powers from his own mouth without any of his ministers' (ibid.).

Dowdeswell's paper is a crucial summary of the principles that were subsequently to guide Rockingham. He attributed the current political instability to the court's malign use of secret influence, and insisted that only a broad and comprehensive ministry, dominated by a single party, could withstand this. Rockingham 'must consider himself as the former of an Administration and answerable for its success, and would therefore preserve in all offices of business a manifest superiority for his own friends' (Rockingham MSS). Gloomily Dowdeswell saw 'no fair prospect' of forming such a grand coalition, in which case the wisest course of action was for the Rockinghams to 'finish with honour', 'to stand still and enjoy the reputation we have, not risk it for something new'; maintaining their 'honour as individuals' took precedence over any weakening as a party (ibid.). This was a principled approach but Dowdeswell's implicit notion that Rockingham should himself make ministerial appointments would have severely curtailed the royal prerogative. The failure of the July 1767 negotiations condemned the Rockinghams to remain in opposition for the next fifteen years, although Dowdeswell's name was periodically mentioned in any speculations about ministerial changes.

America and Wilkes On America, Dowdeswell displayed a pragmatic awareness of the colonies' great importance for British trade and manufactures, and in October 1766 he advised his successor, Charles Townshend, to help the East India Company to sell tea there and thereby reduce smuggling. On 17 May 1767 Dowdeswell none the less criticized the inadequacy of Townshend's proposals for coercive action against a recalcitrant New York and urged the quartering of soldiers in private houses. Despite this he became involved in a full-scale altercation with Grenville in late November 1767, when the latter attacked the apparent weakness of the Rockinghamite approach. On 14 August 1768 Dowdeswell sent Rockingham a lengthy appraisal of the American situation, apportioning blame for the Townshend duties crisis to Chatham's irresponsible 'folly' in encouraging the colonists, their provocation by the 'obstinacy' and 'threatening language' of the Grenvilles, and Townshend's weak imposition of a 'foolish tax' simply so that 'it might be collected in America' (Dowdeswell MSS). American opposition was now essentially to 'the general principle of raising *any* revenue in America', which constituted a clear challenge to parliamentary sovereignty: 'It must either be admitted, which is timidity, weakness, irresolution, and inconsistency; or it must be resisted, and the arms of this country must be exerted against her colonies' (ibid.). Only two courses of action were available:

> either, to fight to the last, in which case this country will be undone, or to treat with the contending party, depart from your own dignity, weaken your authority, and by giving up in time a part of your rights preserve the rest. (ibid.)

Once British control was restored the offending duties should be repealed on grounds of economic distress to 'add good humour to submission' (ibid.). Parliament's right to taxation was not thereby denied but left in reserve for some future contingency when it might appear to both sides 'equitable as well as necessary to exert' (ibid.). 'Upon the whole', Dowdeswell argued, 'moderate measures are less dangerous, and if we come off at last with a loss those must answer for it who have wantonly and unnecessarily revived the question' (ibid.). His subsequent placatory approach was consistent with this honest and perceptive analysis; he argued on 8 November 1768 that the ministry should have come to the house before threatening to dissolve the colonial assemblies, and supported a call on 7 December for a general inquiry into the ministry's American decisions.

In 1769 Dowdeswell played a prominent role in debates on the Middlesex election controversy, pressing unsuccessfully on 5 February for a statement of the reasons for Wilkes's expulsion, questioning on 17 March whether it was prudent to have a Middlesex election every month, and seeking on 8 May to define the question as to whether Lutterell was duly elected. In early May he was involved in discussions with leaders in the City of London and attended a dinner at the Thatched House tavern to consider the petitioning movement. Dowdeswell's influence in Worcestershire, Herefordshire, and Gloucestershire was potentially important but he was sensitive to the need to proceed cautiously in a region where the gentry were suspicious of radicalism and repelled by Wilkes's dubious character. Although Dowdeswell subscribed to the eventual Gloucestershire petition and also signed in Wiltshire, his signature does not appear on the Herefordshire or Worcestershire documents and he did not even speak at a great meeting at Worcester Guildhall on 9 August. He composed a pamphlet entitled *Sentiments of an English Freeholder*, in which he argued for effective checks and balances to ensure ministerial accountability and to protect the freeholder's electoral property. He cautiously delayed publication until November 1769, pending scrutiny of the text by the lawyer Alexander Wedderburn.

The petitions were designed to bolster a renewed attack upon the ministry in January 1770. On 9 January Dowdeswell lamented what he perceived as a ubiquitous discontent, arguing that the petitions 'call loudly for the exertion of public virtue, to strike at the roots of that corruption, by which the State is reduced to the most deplorable conditions both at home and abroad' (Cobbett, *Parl. hist.*, 16, 1765–71, 680). His subsequent motions were carefully crafted to cause embattled ministers the maximum difficulty. On 25 January his proposition that in election cases the house was bound to judge according to the law of the land was defeated by only 44 votes, by the device of a destructive amendment, and Grafton resigned the next day. On 31 January Dowdeswell's simple premise 'that, by the law of the land and usage of Parliament, no person, eligible by common right, can be incapacitated by vote or resolution of the House, but by Act of Parliament only' (ibid., 800) placed North in danger of immediate defeat but he circumvented it by resorting to a procedural motion to leave the chair.

Frustrated opposition and illness As North subsequently proceeded to strengthen his position Dowdeswell experienced endless and increasingly disheartening frustration. On 12 February 1770 his renewed proposal to disenfranchise the lower revenue officers, first attempted two years earlier, was defeated by 263 votes to 188. He also foreshadowed later economical reform by challenging ministers over the civil-list debt. During the following year he supported an abortive motion to repeal the American tea duty, criticized the government's handling of the Falkland Islands crisis, and defended the responsible reporting of parliamentary debates in the printers' case. When the lord mayor, Brass Crosby, and Alderman Richard Oliver were subsequently committed to the Tower Dowdeswell was among the leading whigs who visited them there. On 7 March 1771 his draft bill defining the role of juries in press libel cases was rejected. The vehement condemnation from Chatham, adamant on his own leadership on this issue, shattered any residual opposition unity, making Dowdeswell's task drearier still. On 2 April 1771, now deeply suspicious of any financial innovation, he castigated North's innocent Lottery Bill as 'an iniquitous project' by which the crown might attack the independence of parliament (Cobbett, *Parl. hist.*, 17, 1771–4, 166). In March 1772 he led the opposition to the Royal Marriage Bill but declined to support moves to modify subscription to the Thirty-Nine Articles. Faced with the futile prospect of a permanent, paralysed opposition Dowdeswell now supported Burke's idea of a partial secession from the Commons. However, during 1773 and 1774 he opposed government proposals concerning the East India Company, criticized both the Boston Port Bill and the Massachusetts Bay Regulation Bill, and again urged repeal of the tea duty. In what was to be his last major parliamentary utterance, on 19 April 1774, he accused ministers of 'struggling to obtain a most ridiculous superiority' over the colonists (ibid., 1198).

Dowdeswell's health now began to deteriorate, apparently from tuberculosis, and he wrote wearily to Rockingham on 8 June 1774: 'Impossibility of doing good in opposition and despair of being able to do it if we were again called into Administration, has long left me hopeless in politics' (Rockingham MSS). Seeking a cure he went to Bath and, later in the summer, he visited Bristol, but he burst a blood vessel. When the physicians recommended a change of climate he went to Nice, in November 1774, but he grew weaker and he died there on 6 February 1775. His body was brought back to England and buried in a vault in Bushley church on 9 April 1775. Shortly afterwards Bridget Dowdeswell asked Burke to compose the monumental inscription to her husband's memory that was erected at Bushley in 1777. Burke replied on 13 June 1775 with glowing affection, noting that in nine years of close political participation:

> we have scarcely ever had a difference in opinion … we never had a momentary coldness of affection; no disgust; no peevishness; no political or personal quarrels; no reconciliations. There never was a soul so remote as his from fraud, duplicity, or fear; so perfectly free from any of those little passions or from any of that capricious unevenness of temper which embitters friendships and perplexes business. (Dowdeswell MSS)

Unsurprisingly Burke's lengthy epitaph was highly eulogistic, praising Dowdeswell's virtuous citizenship, financial knowledge, mastery of parliamentary procedure, and inflexible honesty in refusing all emoluments 'contrary to his engagements with his party' (Nash, 1.183). Dowdeswell's library was sold in 1775. Bridget Dowdeswell died at Sunbury, Middlesex, on 27 March 1818 and was placed in the same vault as her husband. Their sixth son, John Edmund Dowdeswell (1772–1851), MP for Tewkesbury (1812–32), who had a distinguished career as a master in chancery, wrote a manuscript memoir of his father's life, which was printed in John Wright's edition of Sir Henry Cavendish's debates.   PATRICK WOODLAND

Sources U. Mich., Clements L., Dowdeswell MSS · Rockingham MSS, Sheff. Arch., Wentworth Woodhouse muniments · J. E. Dowdeswell, 'Memoir of the Right Hon. William Dowdeswell', in *Sir Henry Cavendish's Debates of the House of Commons during the thirteenth parliament of Great Britain*, ed. J. Wright, 1 (1841), 575–90 · Cobbett, *Parl. hist.*, vols. 16–17 · J. Harris, diary, Hants. RO, Malmesbury MSS [transcript, History of Parliament Trust, London] · H. Walpole, *Memoirs of the reign of King George the Third*, ed. G. F. R. Barker, 4 vols. (1894) · R. C. Simmons and P. D. G. Thomas, eds., *Proceedings and debates of the British parliaments respecting North America, 1754–1783*, 1–4 (1982–5) · G. Thomas, earl of Albemarle [G. T. Keppel], *Memoirs of the marquis of Rockingham and his contemporaries*, 2 vols. (1852) · [E. Burke], *The correspondence of Edmund Burke*, 2, ed. L. S. Sutherland (1960) · *Correspondence of William Pitt, earl of Chatham*, ed. W. S. Taylor and J. H. Pringle, 4 vols. (1838–40) · *The correspondence of King George the Third from 1760 to December 1783*, ed. J. Fortescue, 6 vols. (1927–8) · H. Walpole, *Memoirs of the reign of King George the Second*, ed. Lord Holland [H. R. Fox], 2 vols. (1846) · *The letters of Horace Walpole, earl of Orford*, ed. P. Cunningham, 9 vols. (1857–9) · *The last journals of Horace Walpole*, ed. Dr Doran, rev. A. F. Steuart, 1 (1910), 13, 49, 55, 63, 468 · *The Grenville papers: being the correspondence of Richard Grenville … and … George Grenville*, ed. W. J. Smith, 3–4 (1853) · *The Jenkinson papers, 1760–1766*, ed. N. S. Jucker (1949) · Buccleuch MSS [transcript at History of Parliament Trust, London] · BL, West MSS, Add. MS 34728 · J. Brooke, 'Dowdeswell, William', HoP, *Commons* · P. D. G. Thomas, *British politics and the Stamp Act crisis: the first phase of the American revolution, 1763–1767* (1975) · P. D. G. Thomas, *The Townshend duties crisis* (1987) · P. D. G. Thomas, *John Wilkes: a friend to liberty* (1996) · F. O'Gorman, *The rise of party in England: the Rockingham whigs, 1760–1782* (1975) · P. Langford, *The first Rockingham administration, 1765–1766* (1973) · J. Brooke, *The Chatham administration, 1766–1768* (1956) · G. Rudé, *Wilkes and liberty: a social study of 1763 to 1774* (1962) · P. Woodland, 'Extra-parliamentary political organization in the making: Benjamin Heath and the opposition to the 1763 cider excise', *Parliamentary History*, 4 (1985), 115–36 · P. Woodland, 'Political atomization and regional interests in the 1761 parliament: the impact of the cider debates, 1763–1766', *Parliamentary History*, 8 (1989), 63–89 · J. Brewer, *Party ideology and popular politics at the accession of George III* (1976) · *VCH Worcestershire*, 4.47–8 · T. Nash, *Collections for the history of Worcestershire*, 1 (1781), 183 · *Autobiography of the Rev. Dr. Alexander Carlyle … containing memorials of the men and events of his time*, ed. J. H. Burton (1860) · Nichols, *Lit. anecdotes*, 3.620 · *DNB*

Archives U. Mich., corresp. | BL, corresp. with duke of Newcastle, Add. MSS 32975–32991 · Sheff. Arch., Wentworth Woodhouse muniments, corresp. with marquess of Rockingham, Rockingham MSS

Dowdeswell, William (1760–1828), army officer and art collector, was born on 27 February 1760, the third son of the Right Hon. William *Dowdeswell (1721–1775) of Pull Court, near Upton-on-Severn, Worcestershire, and his wife, Bridget (*d.* 1818), youngest daughter of Sir William Codrington, first baronet, of Dodington, Gloucestershire, and aunt of Sir Edward Codrington, the admiral. Educated partly at Westminster School (1770), Dowdeswell entered the army as ensign in the 1st or Grenadier Guards on 6 May 1780 and acted as aide-de-camp to the third duke of Portland, lord lieutenant of Ireland, who had befriended him. In 1782 he was promoted lieutenant and on 4 May 1785 captain.

Dowdeswell was elected MP for Tewkesbury, about 4 miles from Pull Court, where the Dowdeswells had long possessed much property and parliamentary influence, on 19 March 1792. In 1793 at the close of the session he joined the brigade of guards, under Gerard Lake, at Tournai, and served throughout the 1793 campaign, being present at the affair of Lincelles, the siege of Valenciennes, and the battles before Dunkirk. He returned to England in the winter, and was promoted captain and lieutenant-colonel on 8 February 1794, but he did not again go to the Netherlands. Portland procured

Dowdeswell's appointment as governor of the Bahamas, so he vacated his parliamentary seat in November 1797, and was succeeded as MP by his cousin, Christopher Bethell Codrington. Dowdeswell was governor of the Bahamas from 1797 to 1801. He was promoted colonel on 25 June 1797, and after acting for a short time as commander of a battalion of the 60th regiment, he went to India in 1802 as private secretary to Portland's son, Lord William Henry Cavendish-Bentinck, governor of Madras.

On 25 September 1803 Dowdeswell was promoted major-general, and in 1804 he was requested to take command of a division of Lord Lake's army, then engaged in a trying campaign with the Maratha chieftain, Jeswant Ráo Holkar. He joined the army on 31 December 1804, and commanded a division during Lake's unsuccessful operations against Bharatpur, and in the field until the start of the hot weather. In October 1805, on the opening of the new campaign, Dowdeswell was detached with a division of 8000 men to protect the Doab; he remained there until Lord Cornwallis made peace with Holkar, and then took command of the Cawnpore division, a position which he held until February 1807, when he temporarily succeeded Lake as commander-in-chief in India. Soon afterwards he was compelled to leave India on account of his health. He received the thanks of the government and of the directors of the East India Company, and was promoted lieutenant-general on 25 July 1810.

In 1811 Dowdeswell retired from the army (with full rank, but no pay), on inheriting the family estates after the death of his elder brother, Thomas. He then devoted himself to collecting prints, especially by old English engravers, and his collection was sold by auction in 1820, 1821, and 1828; some items were later acquired by the British Museum. He was one of the first collectors to make a speciality of 'grangerizing', and the most important item in the 1820 sale was his copy of Gough's *British Topography*, enlarged by him from two to fourteen volumes by the insertion of more than 4000 views and portraits. In 1821 his unequalled collection of Hollars was sold, realizing £505 16s. 6d. He was promoted general in 1821.

Dowdeswell died at his residence, Pull Court, on 1 December 1828, and was interred in the family vault at Bushley, Worcestershire, on 8 December. As he never married his Worcestershire estates devolved on his brother, John Edward Dowdeswell (1772–1851), MP and master in chancery, and his Lincolnshire estates on the Revd Dr Edward Christopher Dowdeswell (c.1765–1849), canon of Christ Church, Oxford.

H. M. STEPHENS, *rev.* ROGER T. STEARN

Sources GM, 1st ser., 99/1 (1829) · HoP, *Commons* · J. Philippart, ed., *The royal military calendar*, 3 vols. (1815–16) · J. Bennett, *History of Tewkesbury* (1830) · P. Moon, *The British conquest and dominion of India* (1989) · T. C. W. Blanning, *The French revolutionary wars, 1787–1802* (1996) · A. Griffiths, ed., *Landmarks in print collecting: connoisseurs and donors at the British Museum since 1753* (British Museum Press, 1996) [exhibition catalogue, Museum of Fine Arts, Houston, TX, 1996, and elsewhere]

Archives BL, corresp. with Shaw, Add. MS 13636

Likenesses R. Graves, line engraving, pubd 1826, BM, NPG

Dowding, Hugh Caswall Tremenheere, first Baron Dowding (1882–1970), air force officer, was born in Moffat, Dumfriesshire, on 24 April 1882, eldest of the four children of Arthur John Caswall Dowding (1855?–1932), founder and headmaster of St Ninian's preparatory school in Moffat, and his wife, Maud Caroline (1855?–1934), daughter of Lieutenant-General Charles William Tremenheere, chief engineer in the public works department, Bombay presidency. Dowding's two brothers also made their mark: Arthur Ninian Dowding (1886–1966) was superintendent of the Devonport naval dockyard from 1938 to 1945, and Kenneth Tremenheere Dowding (b. 1889) joined the Royal Flying Corps in 1914, qualified as a pilot, ended the war as a major and squadron commander, and was awarded the DFC in January 1919. Their sister, Hilda Dowding, never married.

The happiest days: India, 1904–1910, and Staff College Dowding was educated at St Ninian's and, like his father, at Winchester College (1895–9), but ancient Greek proved beyond him. Unable therefore to follow his father to New College, Oxford, he entered the Royal Military Academy, Woolwich, in September 1899 and was commissioned in the Royal Garrison Artillery on 18 August 1900. After service in Gibraltar, Ceylon, and Hong Kong, he transferred in 1904 to the mountain artillery based in Rawalpindi, India. The next six years, he assured both his biographers, were the happiest of his entire career: plenty of shooting, fishing, polo, and interesting military exercises in a grand country. During one such exercise, he and his men 'annihilated' two companies of Gurkhas commanded by Cyril Newall, an officer who would later be preferred to him as head of the RAF.

Lieutenant Dowding was accepted by the Staff College, Camberley, in January 1912, having returned to England in 1911 with a year's leave on reduced pay in order to prepare for an exacting entrance examination. Promoted to captain on 18 August 1913, he learnt to fly (at his own expense, in his own time) at Brooklands, and was awarded a pilot's certificate—after a mere 100 minutes in the air, few of them in sole charge—by the Royal Aero Club on 20 December 1913, the day he passed out from Camberley. It was during these staff college years that he earned his lifelong nickname Stuffy, visited Switzerland, and began his lifelong addiction to skiing, a hobby which became an off-duty obsession.

Highly promoted, undervalued, 1914–1918 Dowding spent the first three months of 1914 at the Central Flying School, Upavon, where he became known to two officers who reached the highest air rank: John Salmond (his flying instructor) and Hugh Trenchard (assistant commandant). Neither Trenchard nor Salmond ever warmed to him—few men did—although they learnt to respect his uncompromising character, devotion to duty (as he saw it), and sheer professional knowledge. At the end of 1940, however, both men actively sought his removal from Fighter Command.

Dowding resumed his gunner career at Sandown, Isle of Wight, in April 1914, but transferred to the Royal Flying

Hugh Caswall Tremenheere Dowding, first Baron Dowding (1882–1970), by Vandyk, *c.*1931

Corps on the outbreak of war in August. He was sent to Dover to organize the departure of four squadrons joining the British expeditionary force, and then to Farnborough, to help form 7 squadron. Persistent pestering finally provoked Trenchard into sending him abroad in October with 6 squadron—but as an observer, not as a pilot. Although he soon regained pilot status, he never made a name in aerial combat, even though he was reputedly a fine shot. Perhaps he was too old (in his thirty-third year) to learn new tricks. Or perhaps, given his long experience of military procedures, he was considered too valuable an asset on the ground for such a new service to risk losing him in the air, where younger men were more at home.

He therefore found himself employed as a staff officer in France, but in January 1915 he managed a return to Brooklands to command (as a major, from March) a 'wireless experimental establishment'. This appointment introduced him to the exciting challenges of rapid communication, a field in which his practical direction of the work of scientists and technicians would lie at the root of Britain's successful air defence system in 1940. His unit was charged to find a means of using Marconi's discovery (not yet twenty years old) that messages could be sent between two places without connecting cables. The military advantages for all armed services were obvious. Dowding claimed to be 'the first person, certainly in England if not in the world, to listen to a wireless telephone

message from the air' (Collier, 103). Unfortunately, he was sent back to France in July 1915 and took no further part in this important work.

For six unhappy months he took command of 16 squadron, near Merville, some 18 miles west of Lille. In 1933 Duncan Grinnell-Milne, a squadron pilot, recorded his impressions of the major:

> He was efficient, strict and calm; he had a sense of duty. But he was too reserved and aloof from his juniors; he cared too much for his own job, too little for theirs … he was not a good pilot, seldom flew, and had none of that fire which I then believed and later knew to be essential in the leader of a good squadron.   (Grinnell-Milne, 42–3)

Recalled to England in January 1916, Dowding was promoted to lieutenant-colonel and in June took command of 9 wing (responsible for four squadrons, under the eye of Trenchard himself) at Fienvillers (west of Albert on the Somme front) for six happier months, absorbed in problems of supply and replacement of men and equipment, and devising an efficient organization. He returned to England, was promoted to colonel in January 1917 and to brigadier-general in June, but never served in another operational theatre. Instead, he commanded southern training brigade in Salisbury until April 1918, and was then sent to York as chief staff officer to the RAF's senior administrative officer in that area.

Dowding married on 16 February 1918 Clarice Maud Vancourt, daughter of Captain John Williams of the Indian army and widow of an army officer named Vancourt who was killed before 1914. They had one child, a son. Clarice died suddenly on 28 June 1920.

The armistice in November 1918 seemed likely to mark the end of Dowding's aviation career, even though he was made a CMG in January 1919. He had quarrelled with Trenchard, soon to be confirmed as head of a very small post-war air force and influential in the choice of senior officers to be offered permanent commissions. Dowding believed that Trenchard's insistence on offensive action cost too many casualties for too little military advantage. He also believed that Trenchard failed to emphasize the need for sufficient realistic training before sending men into combat. For his part, Trenchard believed that Dowding's limitations as a field commander were not outweighed by any value he might have in post-war administrative, training, or technical appointments.

Earning Trenchard's respect, 1919–1929 Trenchard, however, was persuaded to change his mind for once, perhaps because the demand for field commanders was likely to be small in the foreseeable future, and Dowding accepted a permanent commission on 1 August 1919 in the rank of group captain (equivalent to colonel in the army). As head of no. 1 group at Kenley from February 1920 he was responsible for two of Hendon's enormously popular annual air pageants: and nothing, he recalled, including presumably the darkest days of 1940, 'has ever induced in me a comparable state of prostration' (Wright, 46). Promoted to air commodore—brigadier-general—in January 1922, he served as chief staff officer at Inland Area headquarters,

Uxbridge, from February 1923 and then at the headquarters of Iraq command, Baghdad, from September 1924.

Dowding's first influential post came in May 1926 when he was appointed director of training in the Air Ministry. Working closely with Trenchard in a demanding task which enthused him, he gradually earned that formidable man's respect, was made a CB in January 1928, and promoted to air vice-marshal a year later. Trenchard sent him to Palestine and Transjordan in September to study security problems in the light of Arab–Jewish unrest. His long reports—considered sensible and constructive by Trenchard—paved the way for further elevation.

Member of the Air Council, 1930–1936 The new decade began with a tragedy for which Dowding was partly responsible. He joined the Air Council in September 1930 as air member for supply and research, and one of his first acts was to sanction the issue of an airworthiness certificate to a new airship (the R101), which crashed on 5 October, killing forty-eight of those on board. He was aware of severe pressure to permit the flight—intended to carry Lord Thomson, secretary of state for air, to India—and accepted without question optimistic technical reports. 'I think I was wrong not to insist on much more extensive trials and tests', he later admitted (Wright, 53).

In his new position Dowding soon became aware that dramatic improvements to the design, construction, and production of airframes and aero-engines were pending. These improvements coincided, from 1933 onwards, with a steadily growing fear that another major war was also pending. Although without scientific or technical training, he now confirmed (as his wireless experiments of 1915 suggested) that he had a rare capacity—among senior RAF officers—for grasping scientific and technical principles, and gave vital practical support to the work of experts, service or civilian.

Dowding was promoted to air marshal in January 1933 and made a KCB in June. In January 1935 his title was changed to air member for research and development, to reflect his actual responsibilities at a time of rapid expansion, when the RAF was receiving (and devising) new equipment on the ground as well as in the air. Matters of supply and organization were assigned to Newall.

Two single-engined monoplane fighters—the Hurricane and the Spitfire—were under development in 1934. They eventually had the unprecedented armament of eight wing-mounted machine-guns (no previous British fighter had more than two). Work also began on four-engined long-range bombers. Radios were improved and research into what became known as radar—a method of detecting hostile aircraft at a distance—was encouraged.

Organizing an air defence system, 1936–1940 Dowding was appointed first head of the newly created Fighter Command in July 1936, with his headquarters at Bentley Priory in Stanmore, north-west London, and received his last promotion—to air chief marshal—in January 1937. There he prepared the world's first effective air defence system, based on two excellent fighter aircraft (some of which were assigned to photo-reconnaissance duties), two chains of coastal radar stations (one to detect high-flying intruders, the other to spot those approaching at low levels), and operations rooms, equipped to receive information not only from radar stations but also from members of a revived and ever-expanding observer corps. The human eye (assisted by binoculars) remained a necessary supplement to a fallible radar system, which in any case looked only seaward. Information came also from anti-aircraft gunners, and those working searchlights, barrage balloons, and wireless interception stations. Air-raid warning was controlled from Bentley Priory.

On Dowding's initiative, or with his active encouragement, fighters gradually received vital equipment: improved radios, bulletproof windscreens, armoured seats, self-sealing fuel tanks, and an electronic device to distinguish them from enemy fighters. Hard runways began to be constructed. If he had died *before* the battle of Britain was fought, 'his work in the field of technical development would place him high among his country's saviours' (*The Times*, 16 Feb 1970).

To go or not to go, that is the question: 1937–1940 Dowding learnt in February 1937 that he had been passed over for the RAF's highest office—chief of the air staff (CAS)—in favour of Cyril Newall, who succeeded Sir Edward Ellington in September. He was somewhat consoled in July by a most unusual elevation for an airman, the GCVO. His personal grief turned out to be a national blessing, however, as he himself later recognized. He had all the qualities needed at Fighter Command, few of those needed in Whitehall, and during the next three critical years he and Newall proved to be round pegs in round holes.

Even so, it was Newall who advised Dowding in July 1938 that he must leave his command in June 1939. He would by then have held it for three years (longer than many appointments) and Newall was justified in wishing to promote a younger officer to replace one past his fifty-seventh birthday. The ever-escalating crisis with Germany (and hindsight) may make that decision seem unwise, but it is the subsequent dithering in the Air Ministry—resulting in brief extensions of his tenure, tardily notified—that merits criticism. He was to have been replaced by Christopher Courtney, an officer without air defence experience.

In June 1939, shortly before he was injured in an aircraft accident, Courtney learnt that he would not now take over Fighter Command until 1 April 1940. He was in fact appointed air member for supply and organization in January 1940, and remained in that position for the rest of the war. On 31 March 1940, the day before Dowding expected to leave Bentley Priory, he was invited by Newall to stay on for a further fifteen weeks, until 14 July. Newall wrote again, on 5 July, to ask him to remain in office until the end of October. In view of Britain's desperate situation, Fighter Command's key role in remedying it (and his own conviction that he was still the best man available for the job), Dowding asked to remain in office until 24 April 1942, his sixtieth birthday, unless the war ended before then, or he wished to leave. Both Newall and Sir Archibald Sinclair (secretary of state for air) apologized for past discourtesy, and on 13 August 1940 Newall informed him that he was to remain in office indefinitely (Wright, 138–43, 158).

The battle of Britain 'Since I was a child', Dowding later recalled, 'I have never accepted ideas purely because they were orthodox, and consequently I have frequently found myself in opposition to generally-accepted views', adding, somewhat smugly, 'Perhaps, in retrospect, this has not been altogether a bad thing' (Collier, title-page). His opinions, he believed, were soundly based; once they were formed and expressed, he proved most reluctant to change them. He argued forcefully and constantly that the needs of his command should prevail over those of any other—and, indeed, over any other branch of the armed services, except those of the Royal Navy. Britain's security, resting on command of the air and sea approaches, must have absolute priority over offensive action.

He therefore resisted using fighters, especially Spitfires, to support operations in France. Their presence could not affect the issue there, whereas their absence from the home base would leave Britain vulnerable to invasion. On 16 May 1940, when a German invasion—then in its seventh day—was sweeping virtually unchecked through western Europe, he wrote out his case against sending more fighters to France in what has become a famous letter to the Air Ministry, often quoted. The framed original now hangs in the RAF College at Cranwell. It is less well known that Newall attached this letter to a clear statement on air defence weakness which he circulated to his fellow chiefs of staff that same day. Fighter Command, he argued, could give no further assistance to France:

> if we are to have any chance of protecting the United Kingdom, the Fleet, our sea-borne trade, our aircraft industry, and all the vital centres throughout the country on which we must depend for our ability to continue the war. (Wright, 116)

Dowding appeared before the cabinet on 3 June to reinforce that statement. The Dunkirk evacuation was then drawing to a close and no more fighters were sent to France.

Dowding delegated the actual conduct of the battle to his group commanders, especially to Keith Park, his second in command at Bentley Priory from July 1938 until April 1940, when he went to Uxbridge, west London, as head of no. 11 group, the most important of the command's four subdivisions, covering London and southeast England. Trafford Leigh-Mallory, head of no. 12 group in central England, advocated the use of large formations—three or more squadrons working together in a single wing—but most historians agree that these were ill-suited to defensive fighting because they took so long to assemble and move into action; they were also difficult to control, either from the ground or in the air. Park disagreed strongly with Leigh-Mallory's tactics and Dowding failed to decide between them.

The system, nevertheless, withstood the German challenge admirably. That said, German errors made a major contribution to Fighter Command's avoidance of defeat. The German assault, hastily mounted, suffered from inept leadership, faulty tactics, and poor target selection, as a result of inadequate intelligence information about either Fighter Command's organization or the key centres of British industry. German bombers were incapable of carrying a devastating load and German fighters lacked the range to afford them continuous escort or to engage British fighters in prolonged combat.

The daytime assault had been rebuffed by mid-September, and the Germans then mounted a much more destructive night offensive. But Fighter Command was neither equipped nor trained for night fighting. In Park's words, tactics at night were 'those of a cat stalking a mouse rather than a greyhound chasing a hare' (Orange, 116). Different aircraft, aircrews, ground organization, methods of control, and, above all, a radar set small enough to be carried in an aircraft, were needed, but not yet available. A night air defence committee was formed in September 1940, chaired by Salmond. Both Salmond and most members—among them Wilfrid Freeman, Arthur Tedder, and Sholto Douglas—wanted a new commander in Bentley Priory.

Dowding was undermined by his antipathy to those who worked in the Air Ministry; his blunt resistance to suggestions made by Salmond's committee; his failure to control his group commanders; his vocal enthusiasm for Lord Beaverbrook, minister of aircraft production (hated, as he well knew, by most senior officers); the active opposition of Trenchard and Salmond behind the scenes; the alarming success of German night bombers; and a strong feeling that it was time for new blood.

Removed, retired, rewarded: 1940–1943 Dowding was informed by Sinclair on 13 November 1940 that he must go, but Sir Charles Portal (who had succeeded Newall as CAS in October) asked him to stay on until 25 November, when Douglas—deputy CAS—took over. Leigh-Mallory succeeded Park at no. 11 group in December. At that time Britain was suffering severe nightly attack, aerial defences were evidently impotent, and winter had hardly begun. Come the spring, a heavier and better managed daytime attack was likely. Consequently, the mood in governing circles, air force or civilian, was more fearful of future destruction than grateful for past deliverance. It was a time for new faces and new methods. Few who knew Dowding regretted his impending departure—sweetened, incidentally, in October with yet another honour, the GCB.

In June 1943 Dowding became the first RAF officer since Trenchard in 1919 to be offered a barony. Accepting, he most appropriately added the territorial designation Bentley Priory to his title. He might also have been promoted to the highest rank—marshal of the RAF—at that time, when the significance of the battle of Britain as a turning point in the war was already obvious. Quite apart from the recognition, the promotion would almost have doubled his income. But he was overlooked, as he was again in January 1946, when Arthur Harris and Sholto Douglas were elevated despite an alleged prohibition against officers who had not served as CAS. He was, however, offered and refused a highly desirable appointment as governor of Southern Rhodesia (Zimbabwe), and he expressed disdain—'guinea pigging', he called it—when directorships in the City of London were mentioned. In 1957 he declared in a preface to the first biography of him that he had 'no sense of grievance' (Collier, 12) over his removal from Fighter Command. But a decade later, while co-operating with Robert Wright in the writing of another biography, he was encouraged—or decided—to tell a very different story.

Dowding was persuaded by Churchill and Beaverbrook to go to the United States in 1940 on an ill-defined mission to look into the purchase or production for Britain of American aircraft or engines. A delicate task, it required diplomatic and commercial skills that he conspicuously lacked. As early as 25 March 1941 Lord Halifax (British ambassador to the United States) asked Churchill to send him home because he was expressing personal views in contradiction of official policy. By June he was back in England and took up the more congenial task of composing a detailed account of the battle. Completed in October, it was published in 1946. Churchill then found him another delicate task—inquiring into the RAF's economic management—which he thankfully abandoned in July 1942, when he actually retired.

A contented spiritualist, vegetarian, and icon Churchill barred publication until 1946 of Dowding's essay, *Twelve Legions of Angels*, the last work he wrote based on his military experience. From 1942 onwards he gradually became as single-mindedly devoted to spiritualism as he had once been to the organization and equipment of Fighter Command. He was also attracted by theosophy, a movement seeking some universal truth supposed to be common to all religions. He published four books on these themes: *Many Mansions* (1943), *Lychgate* (1945), *God's Magic* (1946), *The Dark Star* (1951), and became a regular lecturer on occult subjects. His 'very unfashionable' retirement interests, as he described them, 'may appear to the orthodox as being strange, heretical and, still worse, "non-U"' (Collier, 12); they included belief in fairies, flying saucers, and the possibility of intelligent communication between the living and the dead.

Dowding married again, at Caxton Hall on 25 September 1951; his second wife was Muriel (1908–1993), [*see* Dowding, Muriel] daughter of John Albino and widow of Jack Maxwell Whiting (a flight engineer in Bomber Command, killed in 1944). Muriel shared her new husband's spiritual beliefs, and converted him to her own hatred of cruelty to animals. He gave up shooting, became a vegetarian, and they lived contentedly at her home, 1 Calverley Park, Tunbridge Wells.

Dowding was elected president of the Battle of Britain Fighter Association and regularly attended its reunions, at which he was regarded as a revered icon. During the summer of 1968, he visited Hawkinge, an airfield near Folkestone, where scenes for a film about the battle were being shot. Dowding was portrayed by Laurence Olivier, Park by Trevor Howard. Dowding told Howard: 'If it hadn't been for Keith Park's conduct in the battle, and his loyalty to me as his Commander-in-Chief, we should not be here today'

(Wright, 281). His last public appearance was at the London première of that film in September 1969. Sadly crippled by arthritis and confined to a wheelchair, he was given a standing ovation by some 350 of his former pilots: 'Dowding's chicks', as Churchill called them. He died at his home on 15 February 1970 and his ashes reside below the battle of Britain memorial window in the RAF chapel, Westminster Abbey. His son, Derek Hugh Tremenheere Dowding (1919–1992), who served as a fighter pilot during the battle of Britain and retired as a wing commander in 1956, succeeded him as second Baron Dowding.

For good or ill, Dowding was not a man to compromise, thereby provoking anger, exasperation, respect, and devotion—sometimes all of these in a single day—but he was also a man who cared deeply about casualties and always did his best to keep these down. Although well read, with a dry wit, he was too abstemious and intensely serious to be easy company, even off duty. He had no ready flow of words and did not impress in debate across a table, preferring instead to state his case or to give instruction in writing: always cogently, often bluntly, and sometimes offensively. His appearance matched his personality: upright, lean, correct, unsmiling. He mellowed in his last years, cherished by Muriel, but the 'loving-kindness' he then radiated was 'redeemed from mawkishness by a sense of fun and an undimmed eye for human foibles' (*The Times*, 16 Feb 1970). The queen mother unveiled a statue of him outside St Clement Danes (a church specially dedicated to the RAF) in the Strand, London, on 30 October 1988. His expression blends 'surprise, severity and faint disapproval' of this ultimate elevation (Ray, 7).

VINCENT ORANGE

Sources J. P. Ray, *The Battle of Britain: new perspectives* (1994) · R. A. Hough and D. Richards, *The battle of Britain* (1989) · S. Bungay, *The most dangerous enemy: a history of the battle of Britain* (2000) · H. Probert, *High commanders of the Royal Air Force* (1991) · B. Collier, *Leader of the few: the authorised biography of Air Chief Marshall, the Lord Dowding of Bentley Priory* (1957) · R. Wright, *Dowding and the battle of Britain* (1969) · E. B. Haslam, 'How Lord Dowding came to leave fighter command', *Journal of Strategic Studies*, 4/2 (June 1981), 175–86 · G. Lyall, 'Air Chief Marshal Lord Dowding', *The war lords*, ed. M. Carver (1976), 202–12 · P. Flint, *Dowding and headquarters fighter command* (1996) · Salmond–Trenchard correspondence, RAF Museum, Hendon, Salmond papers, B/2638 · A. Rose, 'Radar and air defence in the 1930s', *Twentieth Century British History*, 9/2 (1998), 219–45 · D. Grinnell-Milne, *Wind in the wires* (1933) · *The Times* (16 Feb 1970) · *DNB* · *CGPLA Eng. & Wales* (1970) · V. Orange, *Park: the biography of Air Chief Marshal Sir Keith Park* (2000)

Archives Royal Air Force Museum, Hendon, department of research and information services, corresp. and papers | HLRO, corresp. with Lord Beaverbrook · IWM, corresp. with Sir Henry Tizard and related papers · King's Lond., Liddell Hart C., corresp. with Sir B. H. Liddell Hart

Likenesses Vandyk, photograph, *c*.1931, NPG · Vandyk, photograph, *c*.1931, NPG [*see illus.*] · W. Rothenstein, sanguine drawing, 1939, IWM · A. Bates, oils, *c*.1969, Royal Air Force Museum, Hendon · F. Kenworthy-Browne, portrait, repro. in Collier, *Leader of the few*, frontispiece · W. Russell, oils, IWM · W. Russell, portrait, RAF Bentley Priory, Stanmore, Middlesex, Air Historical Branch · statue, St Clement Danes Church, London

Wealth at death £22,038: probate, 1 May 1970, *CGPLA Eng. & Wales*

Dowding [*née* Albino; *other married name* Whiting], **Muriel, Lady Dowding** (1908–1993), animal rights campaigner, was born on 22 March 1908 at 74 Castellain Mansions, Paddington, the elder of the two daughters of John Angelo (Jack) Albino, goldsmith, and his wife, Hilda Gertrude, *née* Barnes. After attending St Thomas's School for the sons of gentlemen, in Porchester Terrace—she was the only girl on the roll—she attended Walthamstow Hall, in Sevenoaks, and then the Convent of the Holy Child in Sussex. Although her father had been a Catholic she was influenced by her mother's spiritualist and theosophical views from her teenage years. Interested in astrology and spiritualism, she became a member of the theosophist lodge in Tunbridge Wells—and subsequently its lecture secretary for many years—and, later, a member of the White Eagle lodge run by the spiritualist Grace Cooke. She married her first husband, Jack Maxwell (Max) Whiting, businessman, on 24 August 1935 and their only child, David Maxwell, was born in September 1938. During the Second World War her husband served as a bomber pilot in the RAF, and went missing in action over Norway in May 1944. She contacted Air Chief Marshal Hugh Caswall Tremenheere *Dowding, later first Baron Dowding (1882–1970), for information about the circumstances of her husband's mission. Her meeting with Dowding, also a keen spiritualist, led both to their marriage at Caxton Hall on 25 September 1951 and to joint public campaigns on behalf of animals.

Both Dowdings were active anti-vivisectionists. Hugh used his position in the House of Lords to speak against animal experimentation and against the cruel ways in which animals were poisoned in the wild; indeed most of his speeches in the Lords were on animal welfare. Although Muriel was at first reluctant to speak in public she soon became a member of the committee of the Animal Defence and Anti-Vivisection Society, founded by Louise Lind af Hageby, and a council member. She then for many years chaired the National Anti-Vivisection Society (NAVS), and in that role, and later as president of the NAVS, she led demonstrations, presented petitions to parliament, represented the organization at international conferences, and helped to increase the public profile of the anti-vivisectionist cause. Her writing for the NAVS drew attention to the part played by women such as Anna Kingsford and Frances Power Cobbe in earlier campaigns. In 1967 she attempted unsuccessfully to re-unite the NAVS and the British Union for the Abolition of Vivisection (BUAV), the two leading anti-vivisectionist bodies in Britain. The BUAV had broken away in 1898 over disagreements about the best tactics for ending animal experimentation.

In the late 1950s Muriel Dowding, with like-minded friends, founded Beauty without Cruelty, originally to campaign against existing cruel practices in the fashion and cosmetics industry. She helped to publicize the ingredients of cosmetics, in particular the use of whale oil in lipsticks and civet in scent, and the testing of cosmetics and shampoos on animals; she also compiled lists of brands free from cruelty. Beauty without Cruelty held its first official meeting in autumn 1959. Imitating the practice of animal rights campaigners such as Louise Lind af Hageby, Muriel Dowding organized alternative fashion shows in London, New York, and Amsterdam, demonstrating synthetic and cruelty-free alternatives to furs. The Beauty without Cruelty fashion and cosmetic business followed, and boutique premises were obtained in the 1960s. The organization attracted much publicity, helped by the participation of 1960s fashion model and pro-animal activist Celia Hammond.

Hugh Dowding acted as president of Beauty without Cruelty and as patron of the International Association against Painful Experiments. Three years after his death, in February 1970, the Lord Dowding Fund for Humane Research, to promote practical alternatives to animal experiments, was established by the NAVS, as was the annual world day for laboratory animals, on his birthday, 24 April.

Muriel Dowding continued her campaigning work after her husband's death, promoting the fund and speaking at a number of public events. As a participant in a televised debate in November 1970 she declared: 'If we can put a man on the moon, surely we are clever enough if we put our minds to it to evolve the alternatives to using animals' (*Animals' Defender*, Jan–Feb 1971, 68–73). In the early 1970s she was described as an indefatigable person who devoted 'abounding time and energy to the pursuit of compassion for all living things' (ibid., editorial). Having for many years taken stray animals into her own home, in 1977 she established the Lychgate Animal Sanctuary in Coldwaltham, Sussex. In November 1979 she received the Richard Martin award of the RSPCA, the society's highest recognition for outstanding service to animal welfare for those not associated with the organization. She continued her high-profile work for the NAVS until incapacitated by a stroke in the 1980s. She died, of heart failure and a brain haemorrhage, at her home, The Pines, Furze Hill, Hove, Sussex, on 20 November 1993. She was survived by the son of her first marriage.

While much of the work of promoting Beauty without Cruelty was undertaken after Hugh Dowding's death the activity of both husband and wife was commemorated on Muriel's death. As a NAVS obituary stated somewhat optimistically, 'Both Lord and Lady Dowding were vegetarians and pioneers of a humane movement that we now take for granted' (*The Campaigner*).   HILDA KEAN

Sources M. Dowding, *Beauty—not the beast* (1980) · *Animals' Defender* (1959–71) · *Animals' Defender* (1981) · *The Campaigner* (Oct–Dec 1993), 59 · B. Collier, *Leader of the few: the Dowding story* (1957) · S. Cranstoun, *HPB: the extraordinary life and influence of Helena Blavatsky* (1993) · C. Amory, *Man kind? Our incredible war on wildlife* (1974) · *The Times* (24 Nov 1993) · b. cert. · d. cert.
Likenesses portrait, repro. in Dowding, *Beauty*, frontispiece · portrait, repro. in *The Campaigner*, 59 · portrait, repro. in *Animals' Defender* (Sept 1960), 95 · portrait, repro. in *Animals' Defender* (Oct 1965) · portrait, repro. in *Animals' Defender* (July–Aug 1966), 90–91 · portrait, repro. in *Animals' Defender* (May–June 1967)

Dowell, Stephen (1833–1898), legal and historical writer, born at Shorwell in the Isle of Wight on 1 May 1833, was the eldest son of Stephen Wilkinson Dowell (1802–1870), rector of Mottiston and Shorwell, and from 1848 until his death vicar of Gosfield, Essex; his mother was Julia, daughter of Thomas Beasley of Seafield, co. Dublin.

Dowell was among the first intake to Cheltenham College in 1841 and was afterwards educated at Sherborne and Highgate schools. Proceeding to Corpus Christi College, Oxford, he matriculated on 7 June 1851, graduating BA in 1855 and MA in 1872. In 1855 he was articled to R. Bray, a solicitor of 99 Great Russell Street, London, and on 1 May 1863 he was admitted student of Lincoln's Inn. In the same year Palmerston appointed him assistant solicitor to the Board of Inland Revenue, a post he held until he retired through ill health in August 1896. Dowell died of pneumonia at his home, 46 Clarges Street, London, on 28 March 1898; he was unmarried.

Besides writing various legal tracts, one of which, entitled *The Income Tax Laws* (1874), went through nine editions, Dowell made a valuable contribution to historical knowledge with his four-volume *History of Taxation and Taxes in England from the Earliest Times to the Present Day* which reached a second edition in 1888 and was reprinted in 1965. Though its coverage of remoter periods is sketchy and outdated, its compendious account of more recent centuries meant that it remained a valuable source of reference in the late twentieth century.

A. F. POLLARD, *rev.* PATRICK POLDEN

Sources *Law Journal* (18 June 1898), 328 · *Solicitors' Journal*, 42 (1897–8), 575 · *The Times* (16 June 1898) · Boase, *Mod. Eng. biog.* · Foster, *Alum. Oxon.* · Allibone, *Dict.* · A. A. Hunter, ed., *Cheltenham College register, 1841–1910* (1911), 71 · [W. J. Bensly], ed., *The Sherborne register, 1550–1937*, 3rd edn (1937), 55 · *Highgate School: a roll* (1913), 66 · W. P. Baildon, ed., *The records of the Honorable Society of Lincoln's Inn: admissions*, 2 (1896), 307 · A. T. C. Pratt, ed., *People of the period: being a collection of the biographies of upwards of six thousand living celebrities*, 2 vols. (1897) · *VCH Hampshire and the Isle of Wight*, 5.252 · private information (1901) · *CGPLA Eng. & Wales* (1898)

Wealth at death £10,314 11s. 5d.: probate, 2 May 1898, *CGPLA Eng. & Wales*

Dower, Kenneth Cecil Gandar- (1908–1944), sportsman and explorer, was born on 31 August 1908 at his parents' home at 17 Sussex Place, Regent's Park, London, the fourth and youngest son of Joseph Wilson Gandar-Dower (1848–1919), of independent means, and his wife, Amelia Frances Germaine (*d.* 1932). Two of his elder brothers, Eric Leslie Gandar Dower (1894–1987) and Alan Vincent Gandar Dower (1898–1980), sat as Conservative members of parliament. At Harrow School, which he attended from 1922 to 1927, he played soccer, Eton fives, rackets, and cricket, and wrote for *The Harrovian* alongside Terence Rattigan. He was admitted to Trinity College, Cambridge, in 1927 and left in 1931 with an upper second in history. At Cambridge he won seven athletic blues. The sports included cricket and billiards together with variants of tennis, rackets, and fives. He was also prominent in intellectual life, editing *Granta* and chairing the Trinity debating society.

Gandar-Dower competed at Wimbledon in the 1930s with limited success. At the London championship of 1932

Kenneth Cecil Gandar-Dower (1908–1944), by unknown photographer, 1937

he defeated the great Australian Harry Hopman. As a tennis player, he is remembered for fine tactical awareness together with excellent footwork and anticipation. He represented England against Scotland at lawn tennis and squash in 1932 and 1939 respectively. In June 1932 Gandar-Dower entered a Puss Moth for the king's cup air race and he soon became one of the most colourful aviators of his era. Some months later, despite rudimentary navigational techniques, he made the first flight from England to India. The trip is described in his *Amateur Adventure* (1934). In the autumn of 1934 Gandar-Dower explored Mount Kenya and the Aberdares in pursuit of a half-mythical spotted lion of which he found no trace. He spent 1935 and 1936 in the Belgian Congo and Kenya, where he scaled several active volcanoes and produced a definitive map of the Sattima Mountain. In 1937 he returned to England with a team of cheetahs, which he raced against whippets at greyhound stadiums. He caused uproar at the Queen's club when he brought a two-year-old male into the bar on a lead. Despite co-operation from the White City stadium, the cheetah-racing failed. The animals do not hunt in packs and could not negotiate tight bends. In 1938 Gandar-Dower wrote two volumes of satire with James Riddell. *Inside Britain* and *Outside Britain* have much gentle irony and are occasionally clairvoyant in their political speculation.

At the outbreak of war Gandar-Dower was photographing gorillas in the Belgian Congo. He spent 1940 working on the mass-observation project with Tom Harrisson before serving as a press representative in Nairobi. Later he covered campaigns in Abyssinia and Madagascar, travelling vast distances by bicycle and canoe. At Tamatave in eastern Madagascar he landed with the east Lancashires under heavy fire. He is said to have leapt from an amphibious vessel carrying a bowler hat, a typewriter, and an umbrella. In February 1944 Gandar-Dower boarded the SS *Khedive Ishmael*, a troopship bound for Colombo out of Mombasa. While approaching Addu Atoll in the Maldives, on 12 February 1944, the vessel was attacked by a Japanese submarine. Gandar-Dower was among a death toll of 1297. JEREMY MALIES

Sources private information (2004) · J. W. Moir, ed., *The Harrow School register, 1885–1949*, 5th edn (1951) · Burke, *Gen. GB* (1937) · b. cert. · *Sunday Telegraph* (13 Dec 1994)
Likenesses photograph, 1937, Hult. Arch. [*see illus.*]
Wealth at death £75,855 14s. 8d.: probate, 5 Jan 1945, *CGPLA Eng. & Wales*

Dowie, John Alexander (1847–1907), faith healer and leader of a religious group, was born in Leith Street Terrace, Edinburgh, on 25 May 1847, the son of John Dowie, a breeches maker, and his wife, Ann Macfarlan. At a school in Arthur Street, Edinburgh, he gained a silver medal at the age of fourteen (1861). His parents emigrated to Adelaide, South Australia, in 1860 and Dowie soon followed them. In 1868 Dowie, who had been working for a grocery wholesaler, returned to Scotland, and, with a view to entering the Congregational ministry, attended Edinburgh University for two sessions, 1869–71. His first place of ministry was the Congregational church at Alma, near Adelaide, from where he soon moved to the charge of Manly church, Sydney, and later to a church at Newton, a suburb of Sydney. On 26 May 1876 he married his cousin Jane Dowie in Adelaide. At this period he was well known as a social reformer, a temperance advocate, and a pleader for free, compulsory, and undenominational education. In 1878 he declared himself against a paid ministry and resigned his charge. Two lectures, which he delivered in the Victoria Theatre, Sydney, in 1879, entitled 'The drama, the press, and the pulpit', attracted attention and were published. By 1880 he was regarded as eccentric, and was subjected to ridicule in the press. He began to be involved in injudicious financial loans and schemes. After a period at the Sackville Street Tabernacle, Collingwood, in 1882—which led to a rupture with the congregation described in *Sin in the Camp* (1882)—Dowie built a new tabernacle in Johnston Street, Fitzroy. Disputes about its ownership led to his imprisonment. At these tabernacles, Dowie developed a ministry of faith healing. He claimed that over a period of ten years he laid hands on 18,000 sick people and healed most of them. He made expeditions to New Zealand, San Francisco (1888), and Nebraska (1890), and in July 1890 made Chicago his headquarters, though extending his travels to Canada. In May 1893 he opened Zion's Tabernacle, at Chicago, as a centre for the Divine Healing Association.

Dowie's move for the independent organization of a new religious community in November 1895 led to trouble in the law courts. About 100 charges were brought against him, but none succeeded. On 22 January 1896 he established the Christian Catholic Church in Zion, with a hierarchy of overseers, evangelists, deacons, and deaconesses. On 22 February Dowie was made general overseer; his wife, Jane, was the only woman overseer. The wives of overseers were usually made elders; no unmarried man could be more than deacon. Zion City, on Lake Michigan, 42 miles north of Chicago, was chosen as the site for the

community on 22 February 1899; on 1 January 1900, 6500 acres of land were secured, the title deeds being held by Dowie as proprietor and general overseer. If Dowie is to be believed, his following had by 29 April 1900 increased from 500 to 50,000; his critics say that he never had more than half that number. The site of Zion Temple was consecrated on 14 July 1900. Dowie now announced himself as 'Elijah the restorer', otherwise 'the prophet Elijah' and 'the third Elijah'.

The gates of Zion City were opened on 15 July 1901; by 2 August the first residence was ready. The religious organization of the community, completed on 7 April 1902, was supplemented on 21 September by the formation of a body of picked men, known as the 'Zion restoration host'. The city was ostentatiously planned with winter and summer residences for its inhabitants. Dowie distinguished himself by a showy costume of oriental appearance. On 18 September 1904 he consecrated himself First Apostle, with authority to elect eleven others; the title of the body was enlarged to Christian, Catholic, Apostolic Church in Zion, and its purpose, frankly avowed by Dowie, was 'to smash every other church in existence'. Its members were bound to minute particulars of personal and ceremonial observance, alcohol and tobacco being prohibited. The leading motive was evidently the establishment of a sheer autocracy, wielded by Dowie. The publications of this body, including their journal, *Leaves of Healing*, were translated into German and French, some of them into Danish, Norwegian, and Dutch, and some even into Chinese and Japanese. Dowie twice visited England, where a congregation of disciples had been formed in London. In 1903 he was not well received in London and Manchester; in 1904 some disrespectful allusions to Edward VII, uttered in Australia, caused an uproar at the Zionist tabernacle in Euston Road, London.

In April 1906, while Dowie was in Mexico for his health, there was a revolt in Zion led by his chief follower, Wilbur G. Voliva. Dowie was charged with having advocated polygamy in private, and was deposed by the officers of his church, who, with the agreement of his wife and son, put Deacon Granger in possession not only of the church property but even of Dowie's private belongings. Dowie began a suit in the United States district court for reinstatement, estimating the value of the property at £2 million. The court decided that, as the property had been made by contributions to Dowie in his representative capacity, it passed to his successor in the office of general overseer. In the course of the suit it was stated that Dowie's account in Zion City Bank was overdrawn more than $480,000, that he had been drawing for his personal use at the rate of $84,000 a year, and had lost $1.2 million on Wall Street in the slump of 1903–4. Dowie was now a broken man. He was afflicted with partial paralysis, and with strange illusions as to the importance of his intervention in international politics. He died on 9 March 1907 at Shiloh House, Zion City, Illinois.

Dowie was an attractive personality, a man of fine build, though obese and bow-legged, with brilliant, sparkling eyes and a flowing white beard; a turban covered his baldness, and his ostentatious dress was tasteful and picturesque. He did not shine as a speaker, being long-winded and dull. After his death a rival fanatic, Mirza Ghulam Ahmad, 'the promised Messiah', published a pamphlet (n.d., but written in April 1907), in which the fate of Dowie was interpreted as a 'divine judgment' on his opposition to Islam.

ALEXANDER GORDON, rev. H. C. G. MATTHEW

Sources The Times (11 March 1807) · AusDB · E. S. Kiek, An apostle in Australia (1927) · R. Harlan, J. A. Dowie and the Christian Catholic Apostolic Church in Zion (1906) · A. Newcomb, Dowie, anointed of the Lord (1930)
Likenesses portrait, repro. in Newcomb, Dowie · portraits, repro. in Harlan, J. A. Dowie

Dowie [married names Norman, FitzGerald], **Ménie Muriel** (1867–1945), writer and traveller, was born at 7 Dingle Hill, Toxteth Park, Liverpool, on 15 July 1867, the second of the three children of James Muir Dowie, corn merchant, and his wife, Annie, daughter of Robert *Chambers (1802–1871), author of Vestiges of Creation and founder of Chambers's Dictionary. Baptized Mary Muriel Dowie, after her maternal grandmother, she acquired the familiar name Ménie even before birth and used it all her life. About 1869 the Dowie family moved to Whetstones, West Kirkby, Deeside. Dowie was educated first at home, then—from eight to eleven—at a private school in Liverpool, after which she was sent abroad to complete her education first at Queen Olga's School in Stuttgart, then at the protestant seminary in Bordeaux. On her return to England the family took a house (The Golland) near Loch Leven, before moving for three years to a remote 'shooting' in Kinross-shire where, under her father's instruction, Dowie became a proficient fisher and huntswoman. She continued her studies for a time through private tuition and St George's correspondence classes in Edinburgh, but her formal education ended at fourteen. An early ambition to be a surgeon had to be relinquished (the profession was still closed to women) and at eighteen she left home to train as an actress and dramatic reciter in London, where she made the acquaintance of Mrs Kendall. She enjoyed modest success on the stage in Scarborough in the late 1880s.

While still in her teens Dowie began publishing regular articles, short stories and occasional poetry in newspapers and magazines. Most were unsigned, some appeared under her initials or under pseudonyms—among them, Princess Top-Storey, Judith Vermont, and M. Nugent. In spring 1890 she travelled to Austrian Poland to begin a six-month tour of the Carpathian mountains, journeying on horseback with only a peasant guide and eschewing petticoats in favour of a detachable skirt worn over knickerbockers and leggings. She ate the vegetarian diet of the peasant families with whom she stayed, smoked cigarettes, bathed in the streams, and spent her twenty-third birthday sharpening her revolver skills in case she encountered a wild bear. On her return to England she acquired immediate celebrity as a 'woman adventurer' and the book of her adventures, A Girl in the Karpathians,

appeared on 7 May 1891. It went through five British and four American editions within the year and for the rest of her writing career she was known to the popular press as the 'Girl in the Karpathians'.

In mid-1891 Dowie was appointed London correspondent to a syndicate of newspapers in the north of England. She began to involve herself in labour politics, speaking in support of the shop assistants' Weekly Half-Holiday Bill and advocating rational dress and exercise for women. On 28 August she married the journalist and travel writer Henry *Norman (1858–1939). Over the next eight years they travelled extensively around Europe, Asia, and north Africa. On their return from Egypt and Sudan in 1892 Dowie toured the north of England, lecturing on their travels. A serious bout of malaria put paid to her new political involvements, but she remained a favourite with the society columnists, who were fascinated by her extravagantly stylish dress sense—most memorably, a leopard- (some reports said tiger-) skin dress in which she appeared at the first-night performance of Hypathia. Dowie edited a collection of essays entitled Women Adventurers (1893), reviewed regularly until 1898 for Norman's paper, the Daily Chronicle, and wrote its weekly column 'A woman's view' during most of 1896.

Gallia, Dowie's first novel, appeared in 1895. The 'sheer audacity' (in one early reviewer's phrase) of its treatment of sex caused a sensation, making her one of the most prominent of the New Woman novelists. She contributed short stories to the Yellow Book and Chambers's Journal in the mid-1890s, collected with other work in Some Whims of Fate (1896), and made the acquaintance of many of the leading figures in the English 'decadence' movement. Dowie published two further novels, The Crook of the Bough (1898) and Love and his Mask (1901).

In November 1896 the Normans purchased Kitcombe Farm, near Winchester. Her only child, Henry Nigel St Valery Norman, was born on 21 May 1897. Early in 1901, however, Norman discovered that his wife had been having an affair with his close friend, the mountain-climber and millionaire Edward Arthur *FitzGerald (1871–1931). In February 1902 Norman filed for divorce on the grounds of her adultery. A decree nisi was awarded at the start of 1903, with custody of their child awarded to him, and full details of the case were published in The Times on 30 January. Dowie was forbidden access to her son and did not see him again until he was fifteen. Her literary career appears to have ended abruptly at this point. She married FitzGerald on 13 August 1903 and spent most of the next decade abroad with him.

About 1918 the FitzGeralds purchased Marsden Manor, near Cirencester. There Dowie established herself as a highly successful breeder of cattle, polo ponies, and sheep. In 1929 she separated from FitzGerald. A sizeable part his fortune was lost in the Wall Street crash, and at his death in January 1931 much of the remainder was found to have been squandered or, allegedly, embezzled by a secretary. The Marsden estate was sold, and from 1931 to 1941 Dowie lived principally at Shepherd's Crown, near Winchester, though she continued to travel extensively. In

1941 she emigrated to America, partly on health grounds (she suffered badly from asthma) and partly because she believed Britain was going to lose the war. She died at Tucson, Arizona, on 25 March 1945. Her ashes were returned to England and scattered in Clifferdine Wood, near Marsden Manor.

Besides being one of the sources for Mrs Jardine in Rosamond Lehmann's *The Ballad and the Source*, Dowie is the model for Lil in Ethel Heddle's novel *Three Girls in a Flat* (1896) and is thought by some scholars to have influenced Hardy's portrayal of Sue Bridehead in *Jude the Obscure* (1895). Her reputation now seems secure as a leading New Woman writer of the 1890s, but her views on sexual politics were in many respects less radical than they appeared to her contemporaries. 'The dangerous experiment' of writing in 'an ironic sense', she said in an interview in 1901, had caused her novels to be misinterpreted as advocating sexual revolution, when they were 'studies, as faithful as I could make them, of women who made rather a grotesque mess of trying to rearrange life'.

HELEN SMALL

Sources private information (2004) [family] · *The Times* (2 April 1945) · *The Times* (5 Jan 1931) · *New York Times* (27 March 1945) · *The author's and writer's who's who and reference guide* (1935), 288 · *WW* (1903–22) · *WWW*, 1929–40, 1007–8 · *WWW*, 1941–50 · Burke, *Peerage* (1952) · *Men and women of the time* (1891–5) · A. T. C. Pratt, ed., *People of the period: being a collection of the biographies of upwards of six thousand living celebrities*, 2 vols. (1897), vol. 1, p. 336, vol. 2, p. 217 · P. French, *The life of Henry Norman* (1995) · M. M. Norman [M. M. Dowie], 'Recollections of my schooldays', *Lady's Magazine* (8 Aug 1901), 163–5 · E. F. Heddle, 'The Chamberses: a family portrait', unpublished typescript. Xerox passed on by Patrick French. · E. F. Heddle, *Three girls in a flat* (1896) · E. F. Heddle, 'Celebrated lady travellers. 1. -Ménie Muriel Dowie (Mrs Henry Norman)', *Good Words* (Jan 1901), 15–20 · *Young Woman* (Feb 1997), 208 · *The Queen* [numerous short articles during the 1890s] · *Woman's Herald* (21 Feb 1891), 274: 'Miss Dowie at Liverpool' · *Woman's Herald* (12 Sept 1891), 742 · *Daily Chronicle* (6 Jan 1893), 3 · 'A journey through the Balkans: a chat with Mr and Mrs Henry Norman', *The Sketch* (22 Jan 1896), 672–4 · *The Times* (30 Jan 1903), 9 · *The life of Liza Lehmann, by herself* (1919) · R. Lehmann, *The swan in the evening: fragments of an inner life*, rev. edn (1982), 67 · J. Adlard, 'A Girl in the Karpathians', *Journal of the Eighteen Nineties Society*, 12 (1981), and 13 (1982), 12–17 · *The diaries of Charlotte Perkins Gilman*, ed. D. D. Knight, 2 vols. (1994) · *The living of Charlotte Perkins Gilman* (1935) · *The collected letters of George Gissing*, ed. P. F. Mattheison, A. C. Young, and P. Coustillas (1990–97) · *London and the life of literature in late Victorian England: the diary of George Gissing*, ed. P. Coustillas (1978) · *Army List* (1900–20) · R. Evans, *The story of the fifth royal Iniskilling dragoon guards* (1951) · *Post Office directory of Cheshire* (1878) · M. S. Wade, *Mackenzie of Canada* (1927) · *Journal of the Red Poll Breed* (1926–31)

Likenesses engraving, repro. in *Queen* (3 June 1893)

Wealth at death £27,357: *The Times* (29 Aug 1945), 71

Dowland, John (1563?–1626), lutenist and composer, was, according to Thomas Fuller (*Worthies*, 244), born in Westminster; however, nothing certain is known about Dowland's parentage or place of birth. The dedication of the song 'From Silent Night' in *A Pilgrimes Solace* (1612), 'To my loving Country-man Mr. John Forster the younger, Merchant of Dublin in Ireland', has been taken to mean that he was Irish (W. H. Grattan Flood, *GM*, 301, 1906, 287–91); but in *Lamentatio Henrici Noel* (1597) Dowland signs himself as 'infœlice Inglese', and elsewhere he describes himself as an Englishman.

Early years Nothing is known about the first seventeen or so years of Dowland's life, but he probably received his musical education as an apprentice in the service of one or more of the noblemen and gentlemen to whom he paid tribute in later life, such as Sir Henry Cobham, George Carey, and Henry Noel. In 1580 he went to Paris in the service of Cobham when the latter was appointed ambassador to the French court. In this capacity Dowland must have witnessed many of the masques and other court entertainments that Cobham describes in his letters home, and the airs and dances that were so prominent a feature of them would have been an important part of his own early musical experience.

The date of Dowland's return to England is not known, but he seems to have been in France for about four years. Although virtually nothing is known about his musical activities in these early years, by 1588 his reputation had spread beyond the immediate environment in which he worked. Anthony Munday specified one of his tunes, identified only as 'Dowlands Galliard', for one of the poems in his *A Banquet of Daintie Conceits* (1588, but registered in 1584), and John Case, in his *Apologia musices* (1588), listed Dowland among the most famous musicians of the day. In that year, too, he was admitted to the degree of bachelor of music at Oxford.

It was probably Dowland's setting of the poem 'My [later 'His'] golden locks time hath to silver turnd' that was performed in November 1590 at the tiltyard in Westminster when Sir Henry Lee resigned as the queen's champion. In 1592 Dowland had a speaking part in the entertainments for the queen at Sudeley Castle, when another song by him, 'My heart and tongue were twinnes', was performed. One of the lines given to 'Do.' in this little scene—'I have plaide so long with my fingers, that I have beaten out of play al my good fortune'—already evokes the air of luckless melancholy that was to become a hallmark of both the man and his music. In the same year he contributed six harmonizations to Thomas East's *Whole Booke of Psalmes*, some of which (such as his setting of the 'Old Hundredth') are still in use in English hymnbooks.

By this time Dowland was married: his son Robert *Dowland was born *c.*1591, and there were other children, but the date of the marriage is unknown, and nothing whatever is known about his wife. She is mentioned in a few letters in the 1590s, but after 1601 is heard of no more.

Travels in Germany and Italy In 1594 Dowland applied for a post as one of queen's lutenists, on the death of John Johnson. The application was rejected, and echoes of this disappointment reverberated through his life for years to come. He decided to seek his fortune abroad, and set out on a journey that took him to the courts of two music-loving princes—'miracles of this age for vertue and magnificence', as he later described them—Heinrich Julius, duke of Brunswick, at Wolfenbüttel, and Moritz, land-grave of Hesse, at Kassel. Thence Dowland proceeded to Italy, visiting Venice (where he met Giovanni Croce), Padua, Genoa, Ferrara, and Florence, where he played before the grand duke of Tuscany, Ferdinando I. In 1595, while in Florence, he became caught up in the intrigues of some English Catholics living abroad and, taking fright, decided to curtail his Italian trip (including a planned visit to Luca Marenzio at Rome) and to return to Kassel. Sensing that he had become compromised, from Nuremberg he wrote a long and emotional letter to Sir Robert Cecil, which not only provides much biographical information, but also sheds light on his troubled mental state. Before going into details about his encounter with English Catholics in Florence, he explains that he was first won over to Catholicism while in France fifteen years earlier. He attributes his failure to secure an appointment at the English court to his reputation as an 'obstinate papist', but says that he has now forsaken this religion and vows his loyalty to the queen, pledging his 'bounden duty and desire of God's preservation of my most dear sovereign Queen and Country: whom I beseech God ever to bless & to confound all their enemies what & whom soever' (letter to Sir Robert Cecil, 10 Nov 1595, Hatfield House, marquess of Salisbury's papers, vol. 172, no. 91).

It seems that Dowland's Catholicism was in the nature of a youthful enthusiasm, and in the distressed mental state so apparent in the letter he may have exaggerated its impact on his subsequent career. He must have kept quiet about it to obtain his Oxford degree (and by 1597, one from Cambridge as well), and if his loyalty was at all suspect he would hardly have obtained a licence—signed by Cecil and the earl of Essex—to travel abroad in 1594, since restrictions were placed on Catholics for that very reason. Nor did his Romish reputation prevent him from enjoying hospitality at the staunchly protestant courts of Brunswick and Hesse.

In 1596 Dowland was back at Kassel, where he received a letter from his friend and former master, the popular courtier Henry Noel, assuring him that 'her Matie hath wished divers tymes your return'. But any hopes that Noel might help him to obtain a position in the queen's service were dashed when the courtier died on 26 February 1597. Dowland wrote seven pieces as a memorial to him, under the title *Lamentatio Henrici Noel*.

In 1596 seven lute solos by Dowland were included in William Barley's *A New Booke of Tabliture*. But the publication which set the seal upon Dowland's fame was *The First Booke of Songes or Ayres*, published in 1597 and dedicated to Sir George Carey. Many of the twenty-one ayres were already well known as lute pieces, but in decking them out so that they could be sung either as solos to the lute (or similar plucked instrument) or as partsongs for four voices, Dowland ensured that they would appeal to various types of music-lover. *The First Booke* was the most successful of all Elizabethan music publications, going through four more editions between 1600 and 1613. It also encouraged other composers, like Thomas Campion and Robert Jones, to publish works of similar type, and it

established the 'table book' format that was characteristic of the spate of lute songs published between 1597 and 1622. The following year Richard Barnfield invoked Dowland's name to epitomize the art of music in the famous sonnet:

If music and sweet poetry agree,
As they must needs (the sister and the brother),
Then must the love be great 'twixt thee and me,
Because thou lov'st the one, and I the other.
Dowland to thee is dear, whose heavenly touch
Upon the lute doth ravish human sense;
Spenser to me, whose deep conceit is such
As, passing all conceit, needs no defence.
Thou lov'st to hear the sweet melodious sound
That Phœbus' lute (the queen of music) makes;
And I in deep delight am chiefly drowned
Whenas himself in singing he betakes:
One god is god of both (as poets feign),
One knight loves both, and both in thee remain.

Denmark In 1598 Dowland was appointed lutenist at the court of Christian IV of Denmark, with a generous salary of 500 daler a year. He retained this appointment until 1606, but he was frequently back in London, sometimes for prolonged periods, and had a house in Fetter Lane. In 1603–4 he was in England for about year, though he explains that 'I have been twice under sayle for Denmarke … but by contrary windes and frost, I was forst backe again, and of necessitie compeld to winter here'. The Danish court records give some intimation of his employer's chagrin at this extended absence, but show that Dowland was paid in full, and often in advance.

This period saw the consolidation of Dowland's fame with the publication of two more books of ayres (1600 and 1603) and *Lachrimæ, or, Seaven Teares Figured in Seaven Passionate Pavans* (registered 1604). *The Second Booke of Songs or Ayres*, dedicated to Lucy, countess of Bedford, was the cause of a series of lawsuits between the publisher, George Eastland, and the printer, Thomas East, the records of which provide interesting insights into the economics and practices of Elizabethan music publishing—as well as the last known reference to Dowland's wife. *Lachrimæ, or, Seaven Teares* was dedicated to the new queen, Anne (the sister of his Danish employer), to whom he had 'had accesse' at Winchester in September or October 1603.

On at least one occasion while in Denmark, Dowland was asked to pass on information that might be of use to the English government. In 1602, following the breakdown of negotiations between England and Denmark over fishing rights, the English diplomat Stephen Lesieur wrote to him:

I shalbe very glad from tyme to tyme to heere from yow of as much as may concerne her ma.stie or her subjects, yt shall come to yr knoledge … spare not any reasonable charge to do it for I will see yow repaid. (Copenhagen, Kongelige Bibliotek, MS NKS 1305 in-fol.)

This has led to the suggestion that he may have been acting as a secret agent for the English, or even have been a double agent. At that time it was not unknown for court musicians to be employed in this capacity, but beyond this one request for information, there is no reason to believe that Dowland was employed in such activities.

Later years Little is known about Dowland's life immediately following his departure from the Danish court early in 1606. In 1609 he published a translation of the *Micrologus* of Andreas Ornithoparcus. In the following year he contributed three songs to an anthology by his son Robert, *A Musicall Banquet*, as well as some observations on lute playing to Robert's *Varietie of Lute-Lessons*, which appear to be all that was ever completed of a promised treatise on the subject. In 1612 he published his final book of ayres, *A Pilgrimes Solace*, dedicated to Theophilus, Lord Walden, in whose service he was at the time. By now a younger generation of composers was coming to the fore—men like Alfonso Ferrabosco the younger, Robert Johnson, and Nicholas Lanier—providing songs and instrumental music for the sumptuous masques presented at the Jacobean court. Dowland might have been excused for feeling that his time had passed, and in the preface to *A Pilgrimes Solace*, after reminding his readers of his fame on the continent, he goes on to say that he has found 'strange entertainment' since his return from Denmark, singling out the 'ignorant' singers and the young 'professors of the lute', who say that 'what I doe is after the old manner'. In the same year his friend Henry Peacham painted this poignant picture of him in *Minerva Britannica*:

Here Philomel in silence sits alone,
In depth of winter, on the bared brier,
Whereas the rose had once her beauty shown,
Which lords and ladies did so much desire;
But fruitless now, in winter's frost and snow,
It doth despis'd and unregarded grow.

So since (old friend) thy years have made thee white,
And thou for others hast consumed thy spring,
How few regard thee, whom thou didst delight,
And far and near, came once to hear thee sing;
Ingrateful times, and worthless age of ours,
That lets us pine, when it hath cropped our flow'rs.

In October 1612, at the age of forty-nine or fifty, Dowland was at last appointed one of the king's lutenists, the position that he had so long coveted. It seems that the post was specially created for him, and did not come about as the result of a vacancy. But he was only one of several musicians with this title, and his name appears only occasionally in the records of royal occasions. The last of these was the funeral of James I in 1625. Already, in 1610, Robert Dowland had described his father as 'being now gray, and like the Swan, but singing towards his end', and the only music that came from his pen after 1612 was two pieces for William Leighton's *Teares or Lamentacions of a Sorrowful Soulle* (1614) and a psalm setting for Thomas Ravenscroft's *Whole Booke of Psalmes* in 1621. By 1620 he had been awarded a doctorate, presumably from Oxford, since Thomas Lodge's *Learned Summary* (1621) refers to 'Doctor Dowland, an ornament of Oxford'. Dowland's last payment from the court was on 20 January 1626, and he was buried at St Ann's, Blackfriars, London, on 20 February 1626.

Musical style and reputation John Dowland was the most famous English musician of his age, and in the preface to *A Pilgrimes Solace* he could justly claim that his music had been published 'in eight most famous Cities beyond the Seas'. He was first and foremost a lutenist, and the essential characteristics of his art are to be found in the pieces that he wrote for his instrument—fantasies, pavans, galliards, almains, jigs, and settings of ballad tunes. Many variant readings are to be found in the sources (most of them manuscript) in which they were circulated, and it is not easy to establish an authoritative text for many of the pieces. No doubt there was an element of improvisation in Dowland's own performances. Nevertheless, there is no hiding his exceptional gift for melody, combined with a warm, vibrant harmonic style, and there is evidence of his imaginative exploration of the technique of the instrument.

Dowland's outstanding contribution to the repertory of instrumental consort music is the *Lachrimæ* collection of 1604. It is a cycle of meditations on his famous 'Lachrimæ' tune, together with other dances, for a five-part consort of viols (or, alternatively, instruments of the violin family) and lute. Although many of the pieces exist also as lute solos, and are considered to have been originally composed as such, there is ample evidence of the care and thought that the composer put into this 'long and troublesome worke' (as he described it in the preface). The titles of the seven pavans suggest some sort of spiritual journey, while the linking of them all by the use of common thematic material is ground-breaking in the evolution of instrumental music.

In his songs Dowland began by building on the success of his lute music, adding words to pieces such as *The Earl of Essex Galliard* ('Can she excuse my wrongs'), *The Frog Galliard* ('Now O now I needs must part'), and the *Lachrimæ pavan* ('Flow my teares'). As is the case with most of the other lute ayres of the time, the authorship of most of the lyrics of Dowland's ayres is unknown, but there is reason to believe that some of them at least were by the composer himself, who elsewhere showed himself capable of writing quite respectable commendatory verse. Certainly, the words as well as the music of 'Flow my teares' and 'Sorrow stay' epitomize the brooding melancholy of the composer who styled himself 'Semper Dowland semper Dolens' ('Ever Dowland, ever doleful'). In his later ayres he shows himself aware of the new declamatory style emanating from Italy, and in the powerful 'In darknesse let mee dwell' he achieves a rare fusion between this and the more traditional English polyphonic idiom within which he normally worked. In his final collection, *A Pilgrimes Solace*, he turns from the familiar concerns of the courtly lover to themes of a penitential nature.

Although a few of his ayres remained in the popular repertory after Dowland's death, interest in him during the eighteenth and nineteenth centuries was largely antiquarian, stimulated in many cases by his contemporaneity with Shakespeare. In the early twentieth century the development of historical musicology in England revived interest in his music, thanks in large measure to the pioneering work of E. H. Fellowes and Peter Warlock, later consolidated by Diana Poulton. In the latter half of the century this interest was further stimulated by developments in the performance of early music and the associated attention that this received from the recording industry. Benjamin Britten pays tribute to two of Dowland's pieces in *Lachrymae: Reflections on a Song of John Dowland* for viola and piano (op. 48, 1950) and *Nocturnal: Reflections on 'Come, Heavy Sleep'* for guitar (op. 70, 1963). Hans Werner Henze also draws on music by Dowland in his *Kammermusik 1958*. The composer's alleged Irish origins receive fanciful treatment in a short story by Cathal O'Byrne, 'Will Shakespeare's Friend' in *Ashes on the Hearth* (1948).

DAVID GREER

Sources D. Poulton and B. Lam, eds., *The collected lute music of John Dowland* (1974), 3rd edn (1981) • E. H. Fellowes, *The English lute-songs*, rev. T. Dart, 1st ser., 1–2, 5–6, 10–11, 12–14 (1965–70) • D. Greer, ed., *John Dowland: ayres for four voices*, Musica Britannica, 6 (2000) • D. Poulton, *John Dowland* (1972), 2nd edn (1982) • J. M. Ward, 'A Dowland miscellany', *Journal of the Lute Society of America*, 10 (1977), 5–153 • *New Grove*, 2nd edn, vol. 7, pp. 531–8 • A. Ashbee, ed., *Records of English court music*, 9 vols. (1986–96), vols. 3–5 • A. Ashbee and D. Lasocki, eds., *A biographical dictionary of English court musicians, 1485–1714*, 1 (1998), 354–7 • J. Craig-McFeely, 'English lute manuscripts and scribes', DPhil diss., U. Oxf., 1994 • I. Spink, *English song: Dowland to Purcell* (1974), repr. with corrections (1986) • E. Doughtie, *Lyrics from English ayres, 1596–1622* (1970) • E. Doughtie, *English Renaissance song* (1986) • E. B. Jorgens, *The well-tun'd word: musical interpretations of English poetry, 1597–1651* (1982) • R. Toft, *Tune thy musicke to thy hart: the art of eloquent singing in England, 1597–1622* (1993) • P. Holman, ed., *Lachrimae (1604)* (1999) • M. Dowling, 'The printing of John Dowland's *Second booke of songs or ayres*', *The Library*, 4th ser., 12 (1931–2), 365–80 • P. Warlock, *The English ayre* (1926) • D. Greer, 'The part-songs of the English lutenists', *Proceedings of the Royal Musical Association*, 94 (1967–8), 97–110 • J. M. Ward, 'The so-called "Dowland lute book" in the Folger Shakespeare Library', *Journal of the Lute Society of America*, 9 (1976), 4–29 • M. Spring, *The lute in Britain: a history of the instrument and its music* (2001) • parish register, St Ann Blackfriars, London, 20 Feb 1626 [burial] • Dowland to Sir Robert Cecil, 159X • J. Dowland, preface, *A pilgrimes solace* (1612) • P. Hauge, 'Dowland in Denmark, 1598–1606: a rediscovered document', *The Lute*, 41 (2001), 1–27

Dowland, Robert (*c*.1591–1641), musician, was the son of John *Dowland (1563?–1626), lutenist and composer. The likely year of his birth is indicated by his marriage documents, dated 11 October 1626, which state that he was 'aged about xxxv yeares'. His godfather was Sir Robert Sidney. During his father's absence abroad he received part of his education in the household of Sir Thomas Monson. Between May 1612 and January 1616 he was employed by William Cavendish, earl of Devonshire, and in February 1613 he was one of the lutenists who played in George Chapman's *Masque of the Inner Temple and Lincoln's Inn* which formed part of the wedding festivities of Princess Elizabeth and Frederick, elector palatine. During the early 1620s Dowland travelled abroad with English actors: his name appears among those who sought permission, on 30 August 1623, to return home from the duke of Wolgast in Pomerania.

In 1626 Dowland succeeded his father as one of the royal lutenists, and in the same year he married Jane Smalley (*b.*

c.1601). The registers of St Anne's, Blackfriars, record the burial of a son, John, in December 1627, and the baptism of a daughter, Mary, in April 1629.

There are few surviving lute compositions by Robert Dowland, and he is chiefly remembered for two anthologies published in 1610. *A Varietie of Lute-Lessons*, dedicated to Sir Thomas Monson, contains forty-two lute solos, including nine by his father. *A Musicall Banquet*, dedicated to his godfather and namesake Sir Robert Sidney, contains one lute solo by John Dowland and twenty ayres for voice, lute, and bass viol, by English, French, Italian, and Spanish composers. Among the English ayres are three by his father, including the powerful 'In darkness let me dwell', but the collection is also interesting for containing songs by other important English lutenists—Daniel Batchelar, Robert Hales, Anthony Holborne, and Richard Martin—who are not generally known as composers of vocal music. Among the foreign pieces is the famous 'Amarilli mia bella' by Giulio Caccini.

The records of St Andrew's, Holborn, state that 'Robert Doling a man sometyme servant to the king died in his house in the New Buildings in Chancery Lane the 28th buried the 29th November 1641'.

DAVID GREER

Sources D. Poulton and R. Spencer, 'Dowland, Robert', *New Grove*, 2nd edn • A. Ashbee and D. Lasocki, eds., *A biographical dictionary of English court musicians, 1485–1714*, 1 (1998), 357 • A. Ashbee, ed., *Records of English court music*, 9 vols. (1986–96) • D. Poulton, *John Dowland*, 2nd edn (1982) • E. Doughtie, *Lyrics from English ayres, 1596–1622* (1970) • *Robert Dowland: a musicall banquet* (1610), ed. P. Stroud, The English Lute-Songs, 2nd ser., 20 (1968) • J. Craig-McFeely, 'English lute manuscripts and scribes', DPhil diss., U. Oxf., 1994 • *DNB* • marriage documents, GL, MS 1009/11, fol. 34 • parish register, Holborn, St Andrew's

Dowley, Philip (1789–1864), Roman Catholic priest and Vincentian father, was born at Ballyknock, Mothel, co. Waterford, on 3 December 1789, the son of Maurice Dowley, a farmer, and his wife, Honora, *née* Corbett. He was educated at St John's College, Waterford, and at St Patrick's College, Maynooth, which he entered in 1812.

After ordination to the priesthood in 1816 Dowley remained on the staff at Maynooth, becoming senior dean in 1820. One of his duties was to conduct retreats for ordinands, and he was much esteemed as a spiritual director. When in 1832 four senior students at Maynooth resolved to establish a religious community modelled on the Congregation of the Mission, originally founded in France by St Vincent de Paul, they invited Dowley, some twenty years their senior, to join them as their superior. He was appointed vice-president of Maynooth on 25 June 1834, but resigned the following day in order to commit himself to the new venture. Under the patronage of Archbishop Daniel Murray of Dublin, they had already opened a school at 24 Ushers Quay, Dublin, on 28 August 1833. The original aim of the community was to concentrate on the conduct of parish missions, but Murray invited them to take charge of a new diocesan seminary, which was established at Castleknock, co. Dublin, on 28 August 1835. The first pupil was John Lynch, later the first Roman Catholic archbishop of Toronto. In 1839 Dowley served a novitiate of six months at the mother house of the Congregation of the Mission in Paris, where he took his religious vows. An Irish province of the congregation was established in 1848, with Dowley as its visitor.

From its beginning the community was divided between the competing claims of the seminary and its mission work. After the appointment of Paul Cullen as archbishop of Armagh in 1849, Dowley soon became one of his most trusted associates. This caused some cooling off in his relations with Murray, who in 1850 withdrew his students from Castleknock and founded his own seminary. Thenceforward Castleknock increasingly functioned as a secondary school. Following the appointment of Cullen as archbishop of Dublin in 1852 the Vincentian fathers played an important role in promoting his policy of establishing tighter clerical discipline and turning the Irish church in an ultramontane direction. When J. H. Newman arrived in Dublin in 1854 to take charge of the Catholic university, Cullen recommended Dowley to him as an adviser on practical matters.

Dowley's last years were overshadowed by ill health and by disagreement within his community over the direction of policy. Moderate by temperament, he was averse to confrontation. He died at Castleknock College on 31 January 1864, and was buried there. His successor, Thomas Macnamara, reorientated the congregation towards its original work of parish missions, but this attempt was short-lived. By the time of Dowley's death, the congregation numbered some twenty-four religious, in seven Irish houses. Castleknock became the leading college for the education of the rising Irish Catholic middle class.

G. MARTIN MURPHY

Sources E. J. Cullen, *The origin and development of the Irish Vincentian foundations, 1833–1933* (1934) · J. H. Murphy, ed., *Nos Autem: Castleknock College and its contribution* (1996) · private information (2004)
Archives Castleknock College, co. Dublin, archives · Congregation of the Mission, 4 Cabra Road, Dublin, archives
Likenesses photograph, repro. in Murphy, ed., *Nos Autem*

Dowley, Richard (*bap.* 1622, *d.* 1702), Presbyterian minister, was baptized on 5 February 1622 at Burghfield, Berkshire, the son of John Dowley (*d.* in or after 1662), vicar of Alveston in Warwickshire. He matriculated from All Souls College, Oxford, on 10 October 1639, but in 1640 was admitted demy at Magdalen College, which he remained until 1648, graduating BA on 13 May 1643. At an unknown date he married; he is known to have had a family, but the names of his wife and children are unknown.

With the advent of civil war Dowley's father sent him to Coventry, where he continued his preparation for the pastoral ministry under the tutelage of John Bryan. While in Coventry he probably became acquainted with Richard Baxter, who had moved to the city in September 1642 after hostilities forced him to flee Kidderminster. Baxter was the designated preacher for the town's parliamentary garrison until he decided to join Edmund Whalley's regiment as a chaplain following the battle of Naseby in June 1645. After spending several years in Coventry Dowley accepted a position as chaplain to Sir Thomas Rous's family at Rous Lench in Worcestershire. On 26 April 1650 he became vicar of Bishampton in the same county. By 1655 he was

the minister at Stoke Prior near Bromsgrove in Worcestershire. Baxter writes that 'Mr Dowley of Stoke' was a member of the Worcestershire association and one of those 'meeting weekly at our Lecture, and monthly at our Disputation' (*Reliquiae Baxterianae*, pt 1, p. 90).

Although both his father and his uncle Robert Dowley conformed at the Restoration, Dowley refused and was subsequently ejected from Stoke Prior on 24 August 1662. With the reinstatement of the sequestered minister John Toy, under the terms of the Act of Uniformity, he moved to Elford in Staffordshire where he is said to have assisted his uncle, who was minister there. He 'liv'd for some Time privately, went to Church, and apply'd himself to Country Business for a Subsistance' (*Calamy rev.*, 169). His uncle's will of 3 May 1664 mentions that his 'cosen' Richard was in possession of the 'messuage' at Comberford, Staffordshire (ibid.).

By the late 1660s Dowley maintained an active preaching ministry in Warwickshire villages such as Newton Regis, Austrey, and Shuttington despite government legislation against nonconformists. After the declaration of indulgence in 1672 he took out a licence as a presbyterian to preach at his house in Orton on the Hill in Leicestershire. About 1680 he moved to London, 'where he taught a school, and preached occasionally, attending on John Howe's ministry when not engaged himself'. On one occasion in 1683 when Howe was holding a service the meeting was raided and Dowley was one of seven members of the congregation who were arrested and imprisoned in Newgate. They were examined by the lord mayor, after which they were indicted for inciting a riot and bound over until the next sessions. Dowley was subsequently fined £10 for attending a conventicle and was forced to give up teaching. He was later arrested a second time. When he was once again brought before the lord mayor he took the Oxford oath rather than suffer imprisonment.

Following the Toleration Act of 24 May 1689, Dowley lived in London at Bird-in-Hand Alley, Cheapside. He took a position as minister at Godalming, Surrey, for which he received a grant from the Common Fund on 6 June 1692. He returned to London and lived with his children until his death in 1702.

GORDON GOODWIN, *rev.* J. WILLIAM BLACK

Sources *Calamy rev.* · *IGI* · Foster, *Alum. Oxon.* · *Reliquiae Baxterianae, or, Mr Richard Baxter's narrative of the most memorable passages of his life and times*, ed. M. Sylvester, 1 vol. in 3 pts (1696) · *Walker rev.* · *Calendar of the correspondence of Richard Baxter*, ed. N. H. Keeble and G. F. Nuttall, 2 (1991), 257

Dowling, Alfred Septimus (1805–1868), law reporter, brother of Vincent George *Dowling and Sir James *Dowling, and fourth son of Vincent Dowling (1756–1825) of Queen's county, Ireland, was probably born in London. Admitted to Gray's Inn in February 1823, he was called to the bar on 18 June 1828, became a special pleader in the common-law courts, and went on the home circuit.

Already the compiler of two collections of recent statutes (1830–33), Dowling turned to law reporting and his *Reports of Cases in the King's Bench, Common Pleas, and Exchequer* (9 vols.; 1833–8) were continued in association first with his brother Vincent and then with John James Lowndes until 1851. The series, essentially a continuation of Chitty's reports, is usually known as 'Bail court cases'.

Dowling was admitted a member of Serjeants' Inn on 12 November 1842, and made a judge of county courts for Yorkshire by Lord Chancellor Cottenham on 9 November 1849. He made a good impression at first, was immediately chosen for the county court rule committee, and on 20 August 1853 he became one of the Romilly commission for inquiring into the state and practice of the county courts. Later, however, there were complaints of persistent lateness for his courts and rough and hasty justice. He died of cancer at his residence, 34 Acacia Road, St John's Wood, London, on 3 March 1868. He was survived by his wife, Bertha Eliza, who died on 25 March 1880, aged sixty-seven.

G. C. BOASE, rev. PATRICK POLDEN

Sources Boase, *Mod. Eng. biog.* • *Solicitors' Journal*, 12 (1867–8), 410 • *Law Journal* (13 March 1868), 202 • *GM*, 4th ser., 5 (1868), 547 • J. W. Wallace, *The reporters*, 4th edn (1882) • J. Foster, *The register of admissions to Gray's Inn, 1521–1889, together with the register of marriages in Gray's Inn chapel, 1695–1754* (privately printed, London, 1889) • J. Whishaw, *Synopsis of the members of the English bar* (1835) • *Law Times* (1849–68) • Baker, *Serjeants* • *London street directories* (1881–1927) • *CGPLA Eng. & Wales* (1868) • Allibone, *Dict.* • *Debrett's Illustrated House of Commons and the Judicial Bench* (1868), 435

Wealth at death under £5000: probate, 14 March 1868, *CGPLA Eng. & Wales*

Dowling, Frank Lewis (1823–1867), newspaper editor, son of the journalist Vincent George *Dowling (1785–1852), was born, most probably in London, on 18 October 1823, and called to the bar at the Middle Temple on 24 November 1848. He became editor of *Bell's Life* the leading sporting newspaper of its time, on the illness of his father in 1851. He married, on 29 October 1853, Frances Harriet, fourth daughter of Benjamin Humphrey *Smart, of 55 Connaught Terrace, Hyde Park, London.

Dowling was remarkable for his urbanity, and for the fair manner in which he discharged the duties of arbiter and umpire in numerous cases of disputes connected with the prize-ring. He had the control of the arrangements of the international fight between Tom Sayers and the American John Camel Heenan held at Farnborough, Hampshire, on 17 April 1860, and it was by his advice that the combatants agreed to consider it a drawn battle, and to receive a belt each. He was also widely trusted by competitive pedestrians and *Bell's Life* was holding £15,000 annually in stake money at the end of his career. He died from consumption at 4 Norfolk Street, the Strand, London, on 10 October 1867. He was survived by a widow, Isabel Dowling, presumably after a second marriage. Dowling also edited and brought out the annual issues of *Fistiana, or, The Oracle of the Ring* from 1852 to 1864, besides preparing a further edition which did not appear until the year after his death.

G. C. BOASE, rev. DENNIS BRAILSFORD

Sources *GM*, 4th ser., 4 (1867), 690 • *Bell's Life in London* (1852–64) • *Illustrated Sporting and Theatrical News* (19 Oct 1867), 657

Likenesses portrait, repro. in *Illustrated Sporting and Theatrical News*

Wealth at death under £3000: probate, 31 Oct 1867, *CGPLA Eng. & Wales*

Dowling, Sir James (1787–1844), judge in Australia, was born in London on 25 November 1787, the second son of Vincent Dowling (1756–1825), at various times a journalist, bookseller, and vendor of patent medicines, of Queen's county, Ireland, and London. Alfred Septimus *Dowling and Vincent George *Dowling were his brothers.

Dowling was educated at St Paul's School, London, before becoming a parliamentary and general reporter. In 1815 he was called to the bar at the Middle Temple through the system, as his son described it, of being able to 'deposit what is known as "caution money" with the Society … to pay his "call dues"' (Dowling, 43). He produced, with Archer Ryland QC, the king's bench reports from 1822 to 1831, as well as other well-received legal works. On 3 September 1814 he married Maria (d. 1834), the daughter of J. L. Sheen of Kentish Town, London; they had ten children, four of whom died in infancy. Following her death, on 1 September 1835 he married Harriott Mary Ritchie (d. 1881), the widowed daughter of the Hon. John Blaxland of Newington, New South Wales.

Dowling had become a 'protégé' (Ward, 85) of Lord Brougham and other influential individuals, and in 1827 he obtained the position of a judge on the supreme court in New South Wales. He arrived in the colony in February the following year. When Chief Justice Forbes retired in 1837, Dowling's claim to succeed to the post, as senior puisne judge, created controversy. He had previously offended, during a case, the influential local politician James Macarthur, who offered the opinion that Dowling's appointment to the position would be 'a public calamity … a man of no ideas' (ibid., 84–5). The retiring chief justice, however, came to the point in his recommendation that 'Dowling's is the stronger claim and … is … backed by Lord Brougham' (ibid., 85). Dowling became chief justice, and was knighted the following year.

Despite the controversy, in his new position Dowling gained the respect of his colleagues, as they later said of him, for his 'indefatigable industry' in applying himself to his duties, as well as his good humour and 'kindly nature' (Dowling, 49–50). However, as Sir Alfred Stephen expressed it, Dowling's 'painstaking and anxious' approach to his job (Currey, 320) led him to illness through overwork. In May 1841 he applied for extended leave to recover his strength, but this was delayed. In June 1844 he collapsed while sitting on the bench; he was preparing to return to England when he died at his home, Brougham Lodge (named after his benefactor), in Darlinghurst, Sydney, on 27 September 1844. He was buried in the Devonshire Street cemetery, Sydney.

MARC BRODIE

Sources J. S. Dowling, *Reminiscences of a colonial judge*, ed. A. Dowling (1996) • C. H. Currey, 'Dowling, Sir James', *AusDB*, vol. 1 • J. M. Ward, *James Macarthur: colonial conservative, 1798–1867* (1981) • *Gipps–La Trobe correspondence, 1839–1846*, ed. A. G. L. Shaw • IGI • DNB

Archives Mitchell L., NSW, letters and notebooks | Mitchell L., NSW, Gipps dispatches

Likenesses J. Backler, oils, *c.*1840, Sydney, Supreme Court of New South Wales collection · T. Dennis, oils, 1840, repro. in Dowling, *Reminiscences,* following p. 76 · J. Dennis, oils, State Library of New South Wales, Sydney; repro. in J. M. Bennett, *Portraits of chief justices* · J. B. East, pencil and watercolour drawing, State Library of New South Wales, Sydney · H. S. Sadd, engraving, State Library of New South Wales, Sydney, Dixson collection · W. Sargent, photograph, Mitchell L., NSW

Dowling, John Goulter (1805–1841), Church of England clergyman and schoolmaster, the eldest son of John Dowling, innkeeper of the King's Head, Westgate Street, Gloucester, alderman, and sometime mayor of Gloucester, and his wife, Elizabeth Goulter of Hawkesbury, was born on 18 April 1805 in Gloucester. He was educated at the Crypt Grammar School, Gloucester, and at Wadham College, Oxford (1823–6). In 1827, soon after taking his BA degree, he became headmaster of the Crypt Grammar School, appointed by the governors, the corporation of Gloucester. He was ordained deacon in 1828 and priest in 1829 by Bishop Christopher Bethell, then of Gloucester. In 1834 Lord Chancellor Brougham presented him to the rectory of St Mary-de-Crypt with St Owen, Gloucester. He remained as headmaster of the school, and held both positions until his death. In addition to several sermons, Dowling published *An Introduction to the Critical Study of Ecclesiastical History* (1838), and *Notitia scriptorum ss. patrum aliorumque veteris ecclesiae monumentorum* (1839), which was described in the *Gentleman's Magazine* as 'a valuable assistance to all engaged in theological researches'. He died on 9 January 1841 in Gloucester. Held in high esteem, he was commemorated by the stained glass in the east window of his church, placed there by his pupils and the people of Gloucester.   J. R. WASHBOURN, *rev.* PAULINE NASH

Sources *VCH Gloucestershire,* 4.213–14 · parish register, Hawkesbury, Glos. RO, ref. P120 IN 1/7 [marriage] · *GM,* 2nd ser., 15 (1841), 327 · Foster, *Alum. Oxon.*

Dowling, Thady (1543/4–1628), ecclesiastical administrator and antiquary, was probably a native of Laois, where the O'Dowlins or Dowlings were a landholding sept. Most of what is known of his life is derived from the brief autobiographical memoir (dated 12 March 1602) which was enclosed with his account of the Irish sees. His family, who were 'true husbandmen', sent him to be fostered in Old Leighlin, co. Carlow, the cathedral town of the diocese of Leighlin. After some local education he went on to Dublin, where he studied civil and canon law for four years, attending Patrick Cusack's school, frequenting the consistory and admiralty courts, and learning from the local practitioners, including John Ball, archdeacon of Glendalough and official-principal to the archbishop of Dublin. He became a proficient civil and canon lawyer, although he never attended a university or received a degree.

Being invited back to Leighlin (as he tells us) by the Church of Ireland bishop and chapter, Dowling was appointed to the treasurership of the cathedral, with the right of reversion to the better endowed chancellorship when it fell vacant. This did not occur until 1591, when he resigned the treasurership. During this period he acted as vicar-general of the diocese, at first jointly with another and then alone, when he combined the post with that of official-general. He also twice acted as keeper of the spiritualities during vacancies of the see (presumably in 1587 and 1597). During the wars of the 1590s, when the archives of the cathedral were destroyed, he was forced to flee and lost all his movable goods. After the war he returned his office and remained chancellor until his death in 1628 at the age of eighty-four. It is not known whether he ever married or had children.

In his memoir Dowling described himself as having completed two works, one an 'Abstract of histories' and the other a collection of Irish statutes concerning ecclesiastical jurisdiction, with a commentary and citation of cases. The former is presumably the collection of annals which was printed in 1849 from a copy in MS 834 of Trinity College, Dublin. At least three other seventeenth-century copies exist (BL, Add. MSS 4788, 4791; Armagh Public Library, MS Kh II, 1), but the autograph appears to be lost. The annals extend from the fabulous period to 1600, and are largely derived from English printed sources. They show no knowledge of the native annalistic material. At the time of the memoir (1602) Dowling was working on a handbook which would contain an introduction to the Irish language, with a calendar and almanac, and other material in Irish. This, like his legal treatise, appears to be lost, but other historical material by Dowling survives, including succession lists of governors of Ireland and fragments of genealogy and local history. He was also apparently the author of a set of annals from 1534 to 1590 (quite distinct from those mentioned above) which were entered in the now lost register of Duisk Abbey as a continuation of the annals which it contained. As a scholar Dowling seems to have been an industrious collector of local traditions, but lacking in a critical sense, even by the standards of his age. His knowledge of Irish would appear to have been purely colloquial, and he was quite ignorant of the Gaelic learned tradition. The lists of bishops which are included in his account of the Irish sees, often based on records which he tells us were subsequently destroyed, are however of value, and seem to have been largely drawn on by James Ware.   K. W. NICHOLLS

Sources PRO, SP 61 · autobiographical memoir, PRO, SP 63/210, no. 62 · PRO, SP 63/210, nos. 74–6 · *CSP Ire., 1601–3,* 330–34, 353–4 · H. Cotton, *Fasti ecclesiae Hibernicae,* 2 (1848) · K. W. Nicholls, 'The annals of Duisk', *Peritia,* 2 (1983), 93–4 · BL, Add. MS 4788 · BL, Lansdowne MS 418 · *The annals of Ireland by Friar John Clyn and Thady Dowling: together with the annals of Ross,* ed. R. Butler, Irish Archaeological Society (1849) · 'Two books of the writers of Ireland', *The antiquities and history of Ireland, by … Sir James Ware* (1704), 26

Archives BL, autograph, Add. MS 4788, fols. 147–154v · PRO, autograph, SP 63/10, no. 24 · PRO, autograph, SP 63/210, no. 78 · PRO, autograph, SP 63/210, nos. 62, 74, 75, 76 · TCD, MS 578, fols. 18, 37–42 [copies] | BL, Lansdowne MS 418, fol. 64–64v

Dowling, Vincent George (1785–1852), journalist, was probably born in London. His father was Vincent Dowling (1756–1825) of Queen's county, Ireland, a journalist, bookseller, and patent medicine vendor. Vincent George's brothers included Alfred Septimus *Dowling and Sir

James *Dowling. He received his early education in Ireland. He returned to London with his father early in the new century and occasionally helped him with his work on *The Times*, which Dowling senior had just joined. The younger Dowling then worked for the *Star*, contributed pieces to *The Observer* from 1804, and went to the *Day* in 1809. He was clearly building a reputation as an energetic and reliable reporter, a reputation enhanced by his eyewitness account of the assassination of Spencer Perceval in the lobby of the House of Commons on 11 May 1812, and later by his being first to arrive in London with the news that Queen Caroline was to return there from France after the accession of George IV in June 1820. His twelve-hour crossing of the channel in an open boat on a stormy night was evidence of a determined and romantic spirit. But, during the same period, Dowling also worked as a government informer. On 6 December 1816 he reported to government officials on the tone of political conversation in London public houses. He had already been employed by the government to give details of the meeting of radicals at Spa Fields on 2 December 1816, and the following year he gave evidence from that report at the trial of James Watson for treason.

In August 1824 Dowling was appointed editor of *Bell's Life in London*, by its new proprietor, William Clement, who also owned *The Observer*. *Bell's Life* was one of Britain's earliest and most successful sporting newspapers. It first appeared in January 1822, the property of Robert Bell, a London printer and newsvendor. It set out to depict life in London 'as it really was', and police intelligence was more prominent than sport in its early issues. Dowling was to remain editor for twenty-eight years, during which time *Bell's Life* became Britain's leading sporting newspaper, without which no gentleman's Sunday was quite complete. The verdict on *Bell's* of T. C. Sanders in 1856 would probably have satisfied Dowling. The paper had little vulgarity in it, 'it judges with a kind of solemn honesty; and it imposes laws really fair and just on a great many who very much need such laws to control them' (Sanders, 275–6).

In 1824 the circulation of *Bell's Life* was probably less than 10,000. By the time of Dowling's death in 1852 it had been making profits estimated at £10,000 a year for some time. Dowling made the paper a reliable and respectable commentator on contemporary sport. *Bell's* could be trusted so much so that it was often the stakeholder for bets and prize fights. It was estimated that between £8000 and £10,000 a year passed through the paper's hands in this way by the 1850s. At a time when the organizational infrastructure of most sports was embryonic, *Bell's* played an important role in the early development of modern sport. Dowling told the select committee of the House of Lords on gaming in 1844 that the popularity of all sports had increased, and that whereas he had 200 letters a week 'in former times, I have now 1500 or 1600' ('Select committee', q. 236). He was convinced that *Bell's Life* had been instrumental in this growth of sports, even attributing the expansion of interest in cricket 'to the Paper of which I am the Editor … the Moment the Cricketers found themselves the Object of Attention almost every village had its Cricket Green. The Record of their Prowess in print created a desire still more to extend their Exertions and their Fame' (ibid., question 234).

Dowling was particularly identified with prize-fighting, which had been proscribed by law since 1750. For him it was the most manly of English sports and a means to maintain 'a love of fairness in single combat, and an abhorrence of the cowardly and murderous use of the knife' (*Bell's Life*). He recognized the need to restrain its excesses, supporting the Pugilistic Club in its attempts at control between 1814 and 1828, and near the end of his life helping to promote the short-lived Pugilistic Benevolent Association. He was much in demand as a referee, although his reputation for fair play did not prevent his being knocked about by 'roughs' after Bendigo's fight with Tom Paddock in 1850. In 1840 Dowling wrote *Fistiana, or, The Oracle of the Ring*, which became a classic work on the noble art, including informative sections on fitness training and sparring. It was a book which was regularly updated and went through fourteen editions before his death. It was continued by his son Frank Lewis *Dowling (1823–1867), who also succeeded to the editorship of *Bell's* on his father's death, which took place at Stanmore Lodge, Kilburn, Middlesex, on 25 October 1852. Dowling had been suffering from a heart condition for two years and it was this, accompanied by paralysis and dropsy, which finally caused death. He was survived by his wife and children.

TONY MASON

Sources *Bell's Life in London* (31 Oct 1852) • *ILN* (13 Nov 1852) • *DNB* • 'Select committee of the House of Lords on … gaming: minutes of evidence', *Parl. papers* (1844), 6.85–91, no. 604 • D. Brailsford, *Bareknuckles: a social history of prize fighting* (1988) • T. Mason, 'Sporting news, 1860–1914', *The press in English society from the seventeenth to nineteenth centuries*, ed. M. Harris and A. Lee (1986) • J. C. Reid, *Bucks and bruisers: Pierce Egan and Regency England* (1971) • Boase, *Mod. Eng. biog.* • [T. C. Sanders], 'The sporting press', *Saturday Review*, 1 (1855–6), 275–6 • D. Griffiths, ed., *The encyclopedia of the British press, 1422–1992* (1992)

Likenesses engraving (after bust by T. Butler), repro. in *ILN* (13 Nov 1852)

Down, John Langdon Haydon Langdon- (1828–1896), physician and expert in mental science, was born in Torpoint, Cornwall, on 18 November 1828, the youngest of seven children (three daughters and four sons) of Joseph Almond Down (d. 1853), apothecary, and his wife, Hanna Haydon; his eldest sister's descendants included Walter Langdon Brown, J. Maynard (later Baron) Keynes, and Geoffrey Keynes. Down was educated at local schools, including the Devonport Classical and Mathematical School, from 1839 to 1842, and became an apprentice to his father. He also attended a local literary and scientific institution. In 1846 he went to London to work in the laboratory of the Pharmaceutical Society, where he helped Michael Faraday with his work on gases. A breakdown in his health forced him home. During this period he lectured at mechanics' institutes and wrote a prize-winning essay: 'The wisdom and beneficence of the creator as displayed in the compensation between the animal and vegetable kingdoms'.

After the death of his father in 1853 Down decided to

move from chemistry to the more lucrative field of medicine, and became a student at the London Hospital (MRCS and LSA, 1856), where he won many prizes. In 1858 he took the London MB and was appointed medical superintendent at the Earlswood Asylum for Idiots in Redhill, Surrey, maintaining a lectureship in comparative anatomy at the London Hospital. In 1859 he took the MD and the MRCP and was appointed assistant physician to the London Hospital; he became FRCP in 1869. In 1868 Down retired from Earlswood to establish a private home for mentally handicapped people at Normansfield, Hampton Wick, which he ran with the assistance of his wife, Mary (d. 1900), daughter of Philip Crellin, outfitter, of London, whom he had married in 1860. They had three sons and a daughter. Down remained at Normansfield for the rest of his career, while maintaining a consultant position at the London Hospital and a private Harley Street practice, and established himself as the leading British expert on idiocy. Normansfield proved a great success: it pioneered education training and grew to hold 200 residents by the time of Down's death, attracting foreign visitors, and hosting medical meetings in its beautiful grounds. As a model it showed the need for specialized institutional care for idiocy.

Down was vice-president and a Lettsomian lecturer of the Royal Medical and Chirurgical Society, a member of the Anthropological Institute, the Medico-Psychological Association, and the Neurological, Clinical, and Pathological societies, and a founder member of the Thames valley branch of the British Medical Association. In politics he was a Liberal and a supporter of women's education. In 1884 he was made a JP for London, Westminster, and Middlesex, and in 1889 he became an alderman of Middlesex county council. His handsome appearance, high principles, and genial manner won him a powerful influence over his patients and the real affection of his colleagues.

Down's appointment as medical superintendent at Earlswood, so soon after qualification, was based on his outstanding promise as a student. With his qualities of zeal, right-mindedness, and an eminently practical turn of mind, he promised to cast new light on the causes of idiocy. His background in comparative anatomy and outpatient care of women influenced his research at Earlswood. He published papers on maternal health, tuberculosis, obstetrics, and birth order as causes of idiocy, and on the anatomy of the mouth, teeth, and skull. He is best-known for recognizing the 'Mongol' as a distinct type of idiot in his 1866 paper, 'Observations on an ethnic classification of idiots' (*London Hospital Reports*, 3, 1866, 259–62). His theory was that these idiots (and others—the 'Malay' and 'Negroid' types, for instance) were products of racial degeneration. This supported the idea that all races were simply variations within a unified mankind, and was intended to counter the polygenist theories which had supported slavery in the American Civil War. The theory of Mongolian origins was dismissed in the early twentieth century, but the idea of a distinct type persisted and was generally given the name Down's syndrome. Many of Down's most important findings were published in his

only major publication, *On some of the Mental Affections of Childhood and Youth* (1887).

Langdon-Down (he had changed his name by deed poll) died suddenly on 7 October 1896 at Normansfield. He was survived by his wife, and by his sons Reginald and Percival, who carried on his work there, as did his grandson. He was cremated at Woking on 10 October and a memorial service was held for him at St Thomas's, Portman Square, London.   JAMES OGDEN, *rev.* MATHEW THOMSON

Sources *The Lancet* (17 Oct 1896) · *BMJ* (17 Oct 1896) · Munk, *Roll* · W. R. Brain, 'Chairman's opening remarks: historical introduction', *Mongolism*, ed. G. E. W. Wolstenholme and R. Porter (1967), 1–5 · private information (1993) · C. A. Birch, 'Down's syndrome: John Langdon Haydon Langdon-Down', *The Practitioner*, 210 (1973), 171–2 · *Surrey Comet* (10 Oct 1896) · L. S. Zihni, 'The history of the relationship between the concept and treatment of people with Down's syndrome in Britain and America from 1866 to 1967', PhD diss., U. Lond., 1989
Archives LMA, corresp. and papers
Likenesses oils, Royal Society of Medicine, London, Marcus Beck collection · photograph, LMA, Normansfield MSS, H29/NF/PH/OG/1
Wealth at death £19,947 12s. 1d.: probate, 18 Jan 1897, *CGPLA Eng. & Wales*

Downe. For this title name *see* Pope, Thomas, third earl of Downe (1598–1668) [*see under* Pope, Thomas, second earl of Downe (*bap.* 1622, *d.* 1660)]; Pope, Thomas, second earl of Downe (*bap.* 1622, *d.* 1660).

Downe, John (1570?–1631), Church of England clergyman, was born at Holdsworthy, Devon, the son of John Downe and his wife, Joan, daughter of John Jewel; his uncle, who exerted a strong influence on Downe, was John *Jewel, bishop of Salisbury. Downe was admitted as a pensioner to Emmanuel College, Cambridge, on 1 July 1586. He proceeded BA in 1590, MA in 1593, and BD in 1600, and was elected a fellow in 1594. In July 1600 he was incorporated at Oxford. He took orders, and was presented by his college to the vicarage of Winsford, Somerset, which he held from 1602 to 1604. In 1604 he was preferred to the living of Instow, in his native county.

Although Downe was a productive and wide-ranging author on issues of Anglican belief and liturgy, it seems that he published nothing during his lifetime and his writings emerged posthumously, under the auspices of his friend George Hakewill, archdeacon of Surrey. Prefixed to *Certain Treatises of the Late Reverend and Learned John Downe* (1633) is Hakewill's funeral sermon for Downe, which contains much information about his life. As well as heaping acclamation on his social virtues, in particular his wise and affectionate raising of his family and inexhaustible hospitality, Hakewill dwells long on Downe's erudition, describing him as knowing well the 'Hebrew, Greek, Latin, French, Spanish, and I think Italian' languages (*Certain Treatises*, 45). In addition, Downe was so deeply versed in theology and patristics that 'many, and those not unlearned Divines were content, nay glad to draw water from his well, and to light their candles at his torch' (ibid., 46). Such, in fact, was his learning in all fields that he was thought extremely unlucky not to have been granted a doctorate, an honour that Hakewill hints he ought to have received.

The ten sermons contained within *Certain Treatises* demonstrate Downe to have been an admirable stylist of English. Lucid and elegant, they also show that, despite being renowned for his piety, he was capable of liberal views. Justifying those who gamble 'moderately, seasonably, and peacefully', he concludes 'A defence of the lawfulness of lots in gaming' by asking 'why should the distemper and irregularity of others prejudice them in the free use of their liberty?' (*Certain Treatises*, 51). His 'Prayer to saints and angels neither necessary nor commanded' is a reasoned attack on Catholicism in which he declares 'it is now high time to beat down Popery by all meanes' (ibid., 85).

The diversity of Downe's accomplishments is best illustrated in a second volume, *A Treatise of the True Nature and Definition of Justifying Faith* (1635), which contains, as well as several more sermons, some original sacred poems and hymns, translations of the Psalms, and a verse rendering of Marcus Antonius Muretus's 'Institution for children'. A letter from Joseph Hall, bishop of Exeter and Norwich, included in *Certain Treatises* (pp. 55–6) praises his ability in Latin verse, 'in which faculty, I dare boldly say, few if any of our age exceed him'. None of this work, unfortunately, appears to have survived.

Downe died, still incumbent of the rectory of Instow, in May 1631. He was buried in the chancel of Instow church, where are also the tombstone of his first wife, Rebecca, who was buried on 6 October 1614, and a monument to John, a son born during his second marriage, to Agnes. Bishop Hall's letter sums up the affection in which Downe was held by his contemporaries: 'How much ingenuity, how much learning and worth, how much sweetness of conversation, how much elegance of expression, how much integrity and holiness have we lost in that man?'

ROSS KENNEDY

Sources Venn, *Alum. Cant.*, 1/2.60 • Wood, *Ath. Oxon.: Fasti* (1815), 286 • J. Prince, *Danmonii orientales illustres, or, The worthies of Devon* (1697), 262 ff. • Foster, *Alum. Oxon.* • F. W. Weaver, ed., *Somerset incumbents* (privately printed, Bristol, 1889), 467 • will, PRO, PROB 11/161, sig. 51

Downer, Anne. *See* Whitehead, Anne (c.1624–1686).

Downes. For this title name *see* individual entries under Downes; *see also* Burgh, Ulysses Bagenal de, second Baron Downes (1788–1863).

Downes, Andrew (c.1549–1628), Greek scholar, was born in Shropshire of unknown parentage. He was educated at Shrewsbury School under the first headmaster, Thomas Ashton, who was subsequently tutor to Robert Devereux, second earl of Essex. He became acquainted with Essex at Cambridge. He was admitted to a Lady Margaret Beaufort scholarship at St John's College, Cambridge, on 7 November 1567, proceeded BA in 1570–71, and was elected a fellow of his college on 6 April 1571. He proceeded MA in 1574, was ordained deacon at Peterborough, Lincolnshire, on 25 June 1575, was admitted a senior fellow of St John's on 30 January 1580, and graduated BD in 1582.

With his pupil John Bois, Downes was active in the revival of the study of Greek at St John's and in 1585 he was elected regius professor of Greek at Cambridge. In 1586 he was among the signatories of a letter to William Cecil, first Baron Burghley, pressing the case for William Whitaker as master of St John's. He was appointed one of the translators of the Authorized Version of the Bible in 1605 and assigned to the company, along with Bois, charged with the Apocrypha. Both also served as members of the company for the review of the whole work. These men earned 30s. a week, working in London, 'where, meeting (though Mr Downes would not go 'till he was either fetcht or threatened with a Pursuivant) their four Fellow-Labourers, they went dayly to Stationers' Hall, and in three Quarters of a year finished their Task' (Peck, vol. 2, bk 8, p. 48). Shortly after the completion of their work Downes and Bois were both engaged on Sir Henry Savile's edition of the works of John Chrysostom, Bois meeting with slightly more approbation than Downes, who resented it.

On 1 October 1608 Downes married, at Great St Mary's, Cambridge, Anna Delves and, no doubt on this account, wrote in that year to Robert Cecil, first earl of Salisbury, requesting part of the £160 per annum assigned for the better maintenance of the Lady Margaret professorship, then vacant. In the following year a warrant was issued for payment to him of £50 of James I's free gift. In 1610 he wrote to Dr Samuel Ward wishing to succeed to some of the preferments of Richard Clayton, dean of Peterborough. On 27 October 1613 he was collated to the Bath and Wells prebend of Dinder in Somerset and was duly installed on 18 April 1614. He had, though, resigned it by 17 February 1617.

The most vivid account of Downes is to be found in the diary of Simonds D'Ewes, who declined to attend his private lectures on account of their expense. However, he changed his mind and attended several in March 1619 on Demosthenes' Greek orations, *De corona*. He understood that Downes was regarded as 'the ablest Grecian of Christendom, being no native of Greece'. He went on to write:

> When I came to his house near the public Schools, he sent for me up into a chamber, where I found him sitting in a chair with his legs upon a table that stood by him. He neither stirred his hat nor body, but only took me by the hand, and instantly fell into discourse (after a word or two of course had passed between us) touching matters of learning and criticism. He was of personage big and tall, long-faced and ruddy-coloured, and his eyes very lively, although I took him to be at that time at least seventy years old. (*Autobiography*, 139)

Apart from his contribution to the Authorized Version, Downes's major publications were directly related to his Cambridge lectures: *Eratosthenes, hoc est brevis et luculenta defensio Lysiae pro caede Eratosthenis* (1593), of which a copy in Cambridge University Library is annotated, perhaps by one of his auditors; and *Praelectiones in Philippicam de pace Demosthenis* (1621). He also contributed verses to Sir Francis Nethersole's memorial volume for Henry, prince of Wales, in 1612. His fluency in Greek is witnessed by his

Greek letters to Isaac Casaubon, Metrophanes Krito-poulos, and others.

Downes died at Coton, near Cambridge, whither he had retired having reluctantly resigned his chair in 1625 after almost forty years' tenure, on 2 February 1628, and was buried there on 5 February. He left a book each to Trinity and St John's colleges, £5 to a kinsman, and the residue of his estate to his wife. His monument in the church is illustrated by William Cole. His arms were: azure, a buck lodged, armed or, with a crescent for difference.

ELISABETH LEEDHAM-GREEN and N. G. WILSON

Sources DNB · J. E. Sandys, A history of classical scholarship, 3 vols. (1906–21), vol. 2, pp. 336–7 · BL, Add. MSS 5805, 5867 · CUL, MS Ff.1.7 · Bodl. Oxf., MS Tanner 74 · F. Peck, ed., Desiderata curiosa, 1 (1732) · W. Allen, Translating for King James (1970) · The autobiography and correspondence of Sir Simonds D'Ewes, ed. J. O. Halliwell, 2 vols. (1845) · T. Baker, History of the college of St John the Evangelist, Cambridge, ed. J. E. B. Mayor, 2 vols. (1869) · Fasti Angl., 1541–1857, [Bath and Wells] · I. Casaubon, Epistolae, ed. T. Janson ab Almeloveen (1709) · C. Davey, 'Letters of Metrophanes Kritopoulos, c. 1618–24', Theologia [Athens] (1970) · CSP dom., 1603–10 · J. Strype, Annals of the Reformation and establishment of religion … during Queen Elizabeth's happy reign, new edn, 3/1 (1824)
Archives BL, letters to Isaac Casaubon, Burney 363 · CUL, Ff.1.7

Downes, (Robert) Douglas (1878–1957), Church of England clergyman and Franciscan friar, was born at 5 Abbey Road, Brighton, on 8 April 1878, the youngest of the children of Robert Percival Downes (1842/3–1924), a Wesleyan Methodist minister, and his wife, Clara Elizabeth Trouncer (1844/5–1921). Douglas followed his mother's Anglicanism and was confirmed in the Church of England as a schoolboy at Dulwich College. In 1896 he went up to Corpus Christi College, Oxford, reading classics and then history; after a year at Wycliffe Hall in 1900–01 he was ordained, serving curacies in Walthamstow and then Lambeth. From 1908 to 1914 he was vice-principal of the Society for the Propagation of the Gospel in Foreign Parts college at Trichinopoly in India, before serving as a chaplain during the First World War and then spending the immediate post-war years in student chaplaincy work in Oxford. Throughout these years Douglas revealed a deep commitment to the poor and disadvantaged, living with great simplicity and avoiding the privileges which might have automatically followed from his background and position.

In Oxford Douglas arranged for wayfarers and students to meet, and supported projects to provide facilities for the destitute and unemployed. One project initiated from Oxford was the founding of a settlement for wayfarers at Hilfield in Dorset. Douglas had encouraged this idea, even though his evangelical sympathies made him uncomfortable about the new venture being run by a newly formed religious community known as the Brotherhood of St Francis of Assisi. When Brother Giles, the founder, withdrew from the work after less than a year, Douglas was persuaded to take over as warden in late 1922, despite his reluctance to become a habited friar himself. But when his attempts to pass the work on to someone else were unsuccessful, he began to realize the value of the customs

of religious life, and took vows as a friar on 14 February 1931.

The work at the friary was a model of a more humane treatment of wayfarers and contrasted with the degrading conditions found in the workhouses and casual wards run by local authorities. With two others, Brother Douglas, as he was known, formed the Vagrancy Reform Society in 1928, which, with other pressure groups, succeeded in 1930 in improving these conditions. During the 1920s and early 1930s, Douglas was also tireless in mission work for the church, preaching in parishes, schools, and even before George V. His mixture of genuine humility and deep faith made him inspiring and moving as a speaker.

Brother Douglas proved less effective at administering the brotherhood. So he encouraged the movement to unite different Anglican Franciscan communities for men into one order, and with the formation of the Society of St Francis in 1936–7, he was able to hand over community leadership to Father Algy Robertson. Although he continued as father minister of the society until his death, he was a somewhat detached figurehead for the brothers. Most of his later work was away from the friaries: chaplain to the forces in the early years of the Second World War; mission work in western Canada; ministering to—and campaigning for—refugees in Germany after 1945; running a services hostel in Portsmouth. Finally, he settled in Goodworth Clatford, near Andover, to run a home—mainly for men recovering from mental illness. His practical help and public advocacy of all those he saw as outcast by society was his most powerful witness, which proved of lasting influence on his community and on the church. Brother Douglas developed cancer in his final years and died on 7 September 1957 under the care of the Sisters of St Margaret at the Hostel of God, Clapham. His ashes were interred at Hilfield friary on 8 October.

PETÀ DUNSTAN

Sources P. Dunstan, This poor sort: a history of the European province of the Society of St Francis (1997) · Fr Francis, Brother Douglas (1959) · Hilfield Friary archives, Dorset · G. Seaver and C. Jennings, eds., Tales of Brother Douglas (1960) · b. cert. · d. cert. [Robert Percival Downes, father; Clara Elizabeth Downes, mother]
Archives Hilfield Friary, Hilfield, Dorchester, Dorset, archives, MSS
Likenesses photographs, Hilfield Friary archives, Dorset

Downes, Hubert Downes Cherry- (1876–1964), maltster, was born on 23 September 1876 at Hemington vicarage, near Oundle, Northamptonshire, the third of the four surviving children of Benjamin Newman Cherry (1840–1905), vicar of Hemington, and his wife, Rosa Georgina, daughter of Edward Barratt-Lennard of Belhus Park, Essex. In 1909 he inherited from his godfather, Samuel Downes, the family's Cheshire estate, on condition that he assume by royal licence the name and arms of Downes. Hubert was educated at Winchester College. Afterwards he trained for two years with the old-established millers and maltsters Thorpe & Sons of Newark-on-Trent, Nottinghamshire, spending a final year in London studying the technical aspects of malting. In 1897 he was offered a partnership in the Burton upon Trent malting firm of L. and G. Meakin but, with two other Burton maltsters, founded Richards, Cherry and Yeoman. Three years later, the business was registered as a limited liability company (renamed Yeomans, Cherry and Curtis), but soon after, Hubert returned to Thorpes to manage the grain side of the business.

In 1901, Cherry-Downes married Adeline Rachel Barclay (*b.* 1872), daughter of Colonel Hanbury Barclay, chairman of the London brewers, Barclay Perkins. There were two sons, both of whom followed their father into his malting business, and one daughter. The elder son, Hubert Arthur Downes Cherry-Downes, also took over the Cheshire estate. Although later sold to counter heavy taxation, land on the Nottinghamshire–Lincolnshire border, including North Clifton Manor, was purchased and farmed.

Following his inheritance in 1909, Cherry-Downes decided to leave Newark, but after the death of Thomas Earp MP was asked to become managing partner of the prestigious maltsters Gilstrap, Earp & Sons. He accepted, and assumed effective control, and, when in 1921 the firm was incorporated with a capital of £100,000, became its first managing director. The following year, at the depth of the post-war slump, Cherry-Downes proposed a scheme to rationalize the malting industry by the closure of redundant maltings. His ideas were too radical and found little support, but six years later he merged Gilstrap, Earp & Sons with four other substantial malting firms; the company was renamed Associated British Maltsters (ABM) in 1929. Cherry-Downes served as joint managing director, 1928–54, and non-executive director until his retirement, aged eighty-two, in 1958. An expert barley buyer (so influential he was said to control local markets), he was also a driving force behind the rapid expansion which took ABM to the forefront of European malting.

Cherry-Downes worked tirelessly to promote the interests of the malting industry. In 1917, with trade halted by war controls and threatened by the possible nationalization of brewing, he was instrumental in reviving the Maltsters Association of Great Britain, which had lapsed since the repeal of the malt tax in 1880. As its chairman (1920–24 and 1935–45), he served the executive committee for thirty years. During both wars he was appointed to the joint advisory committee of brewers and maltsters which worked in conjunction with the Ministry of Food, and in 1923 served the departmental committee advising the Treasury on barley import duties.

Cherry-Downes' great love was the countryside. Always to be seen in his favoured dress of plus fours, he was a lifelong member of the Newark and Nottinghamshire Agricultural Society, its president in 1924, and vice-president thereafter. A great authority on horses, he rode to hounds and was for many years a steward at Southwell racecourse. In 1925 he became a racehorse owner, his greatest success coming three years later when his horse Hank won the Foxhunters' Chase at Liverpool. A talented sportsman, he was also a keen shot and golfer. He was a JP for Newark and, although not deeply involved in local politics, a member of Newark Conservative Association. Cherry-Downes

died of heart failure at his home, Southfield House, Millgate, Newark, on 1 October 1964 and was cremated at Wilford Hill, Nottingham, two days later. He was survived by his wife, and left an estate valued at more than £100,000.

CHRISTINE CLARK

Sources Pauls Malt Limited, Ipswich, Associated British Maltsters archives · Newark on Trent, Maltsters Association of Great Britain archives · private information (2004) · *Brewers' Journal* (19 Nov 1947), 519 · *Newark Advertiser* (7 Oct 1964) · *Newark Advertiser* (14 Oct 1964)
Likenesses A. E. Cooper, oils, 1947, priv. coll. · A. E. Cooper, photograph, repro. in *Brewers' Journal*, 519
Wealth at death £102,832: probate, 30 Sept 1965, *CGPLA Eng. & Wales*

Downes, John (*bap.* 1609, *d.* in or after 1666), regicide, was baptized on 16 July 1609 at Manby, Lincolnshire, the eldest surviving son of Richard Downes (*d.* 1618/19) of Manby and his wife, Elizabeth. Although characterized as having come from a 'mean family' (Noble, 191), the family's fortunes were probably rising. Downes was admitted to the Inner Temple in November 1631 and called to the bar on 1 May 1642. By that stage he had married twice; his first marriage was to Joanna, daughter of Richard Mosely of Tunstall in Staffordshire, and his second, by a licence of 11 April 1634, was to Catherine (*d.* before 1653), daughter of Francis Townley of Littleton in Middlesex.

In October 1633 Downes became one of the two auditors of the duchy of Cornwall, and the contacts made in connection with his employment probably included the patron who secured his return to parliament for Arundel, in a county to which he had no prior connection, in a by-election in December 1641. Downes was returned amid controversy and opposition from the secretary to Thomas Howard, fourteenth earl of Arundel, a Catholic, but was able to take his seat with support from prominent godly MPs. He made little impact in the house before Pride's Purge, and was reported as having said that 'I do not often trouble you with speeches' (Fry, 18). Nevertheless, he became one of the most zealous parliamentarians in Sussex during the civil war, and helped ensure that parliament, rather than the king, secured the income from duchy lands. By 1647 he was aligned with the independents at Westminster, and became more active after the purge. He was involved in suppressing pamphlets by the secluded members, joined the powerful army committee, and was appointed to the high court of justice to try Charles I. He later claimed that his name was inserted in the act late in the day, and that he was pressurized into taking part in the trial, and succumbed 'through weakness and fear' (Downes), although he attended ten of the meetings in the painted chamber. It was in one of these that Downes clashed with another MP, John Fry, whom he accused of blasphemy for his unitarian views. Downes subsequently attacked Fry in the Commons, and was instrumental in securing his suspension from the house. Furthermore, Downes developed reservations about the proceedings against the king, and on 27 January, having attended all four days of the trial, expressed his objections to fellow commissioners. As the sentence was about to be read Downes rose to declare his dissent and demanded an adjournment, in which he said that the king ought to be allowed to speak. Cromwell, who called Downes a 'peevish man', said that 'he would fain save his old master' (*State trials*, 5.1213). Downes refused to return to the high court, and although he signed the death warrant he later claimed to have done so only under duress. He also claimed to have hoped that the trial would force a settlement rather than result in Charles's execution.

Although Downes faced hostility for his actions, including a pamphlet attack by John Fry entitled *The Accuser Sham'd*, he continued to fulfil his duties on committees and in relation to the duchy of Cornwall. He re-emerged in the Commons in July and was awarded £3000 when he resigned his post as auditor, and thereafter government finances and the affairs of the army came to dominate his career. Although he later claimed that he was 'never of any junto or cabal' (Downes), Downes worked closely with the civilian republicans, with whom he shared a religious and social conservatism. A member of the committee for plundered ministers from July 1650, Downes was a religious independent but zealous against sectarians, although he later claimed to have protected a group of presbyterian divines who faced the death penalty for their part in the 'Love plot' during the early 1650s.

In recognition of his hard work as an administrator Downes was elected to the council of state in November 1651, although his activity was slight, and his career continued to be dominated by his work as chairman of the army committee and in matters regarding the treasury, which eventually resulted in his nomination to the powerful revenue committee in October 1652. He was obviously an important figure during the Anglo-Dutch War, although this perhaps resulted in his removal from the council of state in November 1652. Although he played little part in the political machinations in the dying days of the Rump, he appears to have acquiesced to its dissolution, and continued to fulfil his responsibilities in the weeks which followed. However, during both Barebone's Parliament and the protectorate Downes withdrew from political and administrative affairs, and apparently retired to his estate at Hampstead. Some time before 1653 he married for the third time, although the background of his wife, Hannah, is unknown.

Downes re-emerged during 1659, and resumed his position of influence in the Commons when the Rump was recalled in May as an ally of the civilian republicans and in relation to financial affairs. He was also named to the council of state, although he withdrew from the house shortly before its sittings were interrupted by the army in October, returning to Westminster in December and to membership of the army committee. He appears to have withdrawn from the Commons in early February 1660, shortly after the arrival of General Monck and shortly before the readmission of the secluded members. Downes faced arrest as a regicide in May 1660, which prompted his publication of a vindication of his career and actions. This

failed to prevent his arrest in June or his trial in the following October, at which he 'pleaded ignorance, and acknowledged the guilt, but denied the malice' (Ludlow, 267). He denied being instrumental in the proceedings, and pleaded that he had signed the death warrant only after death threats. He was found guilty, but was reprieved from execution and sent to the Tower. Although considered for release in February 1662, he remained in prison and in poverty. In April 1663 he appealed to John Robinson, the lord mayor, begging to be 'thrust into some hole where he might silently be slain' (PRO, SP 29/71, fol. 20). The date of Downes's death is unknown, although it was after November 1666, when he was still listed among the prisoners in the Tower.

J. T. PEACEY and IVAN ROOTS

Sources J. T. Peacey, 'Downes, John', HoP, *Commons, 1640–60* [draft] · *JHC*, 2–8 (1640–67) · C. H. Firth and R. S. Rait, eds., *Acts and ordinances of the interregnum, 1642–1660*, 3 vols. (1911) · *CSP dom.*, 1649–67 · M. Noble, *The lives of the English regicides* (1798) · *State trials*, vol. 5 · D. Underdown, *Pride's Purge: politics in the puritan revolution* (1971) · B. Worden, *The Rump Parliament, 1648–1653* (1974) · E. Ludlow, *A voyce from the watch tower*, ed. A. B. Worden, CS, 4th ser., 21 (1978) · A. Fletcher, *A county community in peace and war* (1975) · J. Fry, *The accuser sham'd* (1648) · J. Downes, *A true and humble representation* (1660) · IGI

Downes, John (*d.* 1712?), theatre prompter and historian, is first heard of in June 1661 when he took the part of Haly in the première performance of part 1 of Sir William Davenant's *The Siege of Rhodes* at the opening of the Lincoln's Inn Fields Theatre in the presence of royalty, and, as he himself reports, was 'spoil'd … for an Actor' by stage-fright (Downes, 1987, 73). According to the lord chamberlain's records, Downes was sworn as a comedian in the Duke of York's Company on 27 June 1664, and as a comedian in the King's Company successively on 12 January 1688, 22 February 1695, and about 20 April 1697. Some time in the 1660s he became prompter to the Duke's Company. Following the merger of the Duke's and the King's companies in 1682 he worked for the United Company until the split of 1694; thereafter he was a member of Betterton's Company at Lincoln's Inn Fields and, from 1705, at the Haymarket, until his retirement in October 1706.

'[B]eing long Conversant with … Plays and Actors' (Downes, 1987, 2), Downes produced the first substantial work of theatre history in English: *Roscius Anglicanus, or, An Historical Review of the English Stage* (1708). Usually written by outsiders, earlier publications on the subject had been either scrappy and amateurish in their treatment of Restoration theatre (for example James Wright's *Historia histrionica*, 1699) or chiefly concerned with printed drama (such as Gerard Langbaine's *Momus triumphans*, 1688, and *An Account of the English Dramatick Poets*, 1691). However quirky its chronology, chaotic its narrative, and spotty its coverage of the King's Company, *Roscius Anglicanus* is the most comprehensive account of repertory, acting personnel, and casting in the Restoration theatre. Much maligned by earlier critics, Downes's accuracy has been vindicated by modern scholars. When approached with a suitable degree of caution—for instance, the cast lists it provides for stock plays should not be taken to reflect the casting of the earliest performance—*Roscius Anglicanus* is a surprisingly reliable source of information about casting, especially of new plays, about actors, their parts and particular strengths and weaknesses, about the commercial success of individual plays, the length of their original runs, and their place in the repertory, and, to a lesser extent, about their authorship. Downes treats plays as scripts for performance, not literary artefacts, and thus is less interested in the artistic quality of the drama. What matters to him is whether the play was profitable to the company (and the playwright) and whether it became a stock offering. He routinely records any major outlay on costumes, scenery, and special effects. For instance, he attributes the success of 'The Tragedy of *Macbeth*, alter'd by Sir *William Davenant*' to its 'being drest in all it's Finery, as new Cloath's, new Scenes, Machines, as flyings for the Witches; with all the Singing and Dancing in it'; and he notes the loss incurred by the Duke's Company when the first run of John Dryden's opera *Albion and Albanius* was interrupted by Monmouth's rebellion, the play 'not Answering half the Charge they were at' (Downes, 1987, 71, 84).

We know nothing about Downes's marital situation, but he seems to have had a son who aspired to be a musician. A letter of 27 January 1707 addressed to the lord chamberlain by Owen Swiney, the manager of the Haymarket Company, explains that 'young Downes' had been denied employment because of lack of qualifications (LC 7/3, fols. 94–5, quoted in Downes, 1987, xi). However, the letter expresses readiness to grant a pension to Downes *père* according to the lord chamberlain's suggestions. Downes may have died in 1712, for according to *The Registers of St Paul's Church, Covent Garden, London* a John Downes was buried there on 4 June 1712.   PAULINA KEWES

Sources J. Downes, *Roscius Anglicanus*, ed. J. Milhous and R. D. Hume, new edn (1987) • B. Podewell, 'New light on John Downes', *N&Q*, 223 (1978), 24 • J. Downes, *Roscius Anglicanus*, ed. F. G. Waldron, another edn (1789) [with additions by T. Davies]

Downes, Mary Patricia [Mollie] **Panter-** (1906–1997), writer, was born on 25 August 1906, possibly in Ireland, the daughter of Edward Martin Panter-Downes (1873–1914) and his wife, Marie Kathleen Cowley (1868–1950), who was of Irish origin. From 1911 to 1914 her father, a major in the 2nd battalion Royal Irish regiment (and distinguished for winning the Royal Humane Society bronze medal), was seconded as acting colonel to the Gold Coast regiment. He took his wife with him, leaving Mollie with friends in Brighton; just after their return, in August 1914, he was killed at Mons. His widow and daughter went on living in different places in Sussex including Brighton (in a flat at 3 Vernon Terrace), and Rudgewick, a village on the Sussex–Surrey border; they subsisted on a small widow's pension and occasional help from relations. Mollie learned early on how to be the breadwinner by writing her first, extremely accomplished novel, *The Shoreless Sea*, when she was sixteen. A story of doomed love (Deidre and Guy fall innocently in love but when they at last find each

other again she has married someone else), its maturity of style astonished the critics. Instalments were published in the *Daily Mirror* in autumn 1923: contemporaries (such as the writer Elizabeth Jenkins) remembered large advertisements on the side of London buses; subsequently the novel went into eight editions in a year and a half. *The Chase* (about Charles Standish's life and loves) appeared in 1925.

On 12 July 1927 Mollie Panter-Downes married Aubrey Clare Robinson (1903–1997), a businessman; they lived in Walton Street, London, for two years before her husband's employer, British Celanese, sent him round the world to explore export markets. Mollie wrote short stories and two more romantic novels in 1929 and 1931; later, however, and particularly after her involvement with the *New Yorker* began, she disowned her early work entirely. Two daughters were born, in 1932 and 1935. In 1931 she and her husband bought a house in rural Surrey, between Chiddingfold and Haslemere—Roppeleghs, originally a fifteenth-century tile-hung house, surrounded by gardens and fields. Here she had a small writing hut in the woods to which she would retire each day with her lunch in a basket; her writing took precedence even over her daughters.

It was Panter-Downes's idea that she should write for the *New Yorker*, something which her agent, Nancy Pearn, or 'Pearnie', at Curtis Brown, scornfully rejected, but Mollie persisted and in 1938 published the first of thirty-six short stories for them (most have been republished, in *Good Evening, Mrs Craven*, covering 1939–44, and *Minnie's Room*, covering 1947–65). Then, in September 1939, she began her column, 'Letter from London', and continued it until 1984, by which time she had written no fewer than 852 pieces for the *New Yorker*. A volume of the letters, *Letters from England*, appeared in 1940. During the war she travelled up to London to glean material for her 153 wartime letters. These are some of the most memorable pieces ever written about civilian life in Britain at this period. In 1947 she published *One Fine Day*, which is set on a July day in 1946 and evokes the life of Laura and Stephen as they struggle to adapt to post-war life: 'wretched victims of their class, they still had dinner' (p. 21). Its style is poignant, poetic, observant, and funny, and it is one of the great British novels of the twentieth century. *One Fine Day* was serialized in *Atlantic Monthly* and published as a book in Britain, but not reprinted again until 1985.

Mollie Panter-Downes was deeply modest, almost diffident, about her professional achievements but this belied a strong sense of self-worth and an intense pride in her fifty-year connection with the *New Yorker*. Her self-contained, mysterious air, derived perhaps from her girlhood, and from years of being Mollie Robinson among neighbours who never read what she wrote—her work is unusual in being very English without being read by the English. Her obituary in the *New Yorker* described her as 'A strikingly good-looking woman, with a tremendously patrician nose and startling blue eyes'. Mollie Panter-Downes also published two excellent non-fiction works,

Ooty Preserved: a Victorian Hill Station in India (1967), an evocation of Anglo-Indian life that explores the same territory as Paul Scott's novel *Staying On*, and *At The Pines: Swinburne and Watts-Dunton in Putney* (1971), which describes the poet's thirty years with his devoted friend in their house at 11 Putney Hill; both books were first serialized in the *New Yorker*. The wartime *New Yorker* letters were further collected in *London War Notes* (1972). Mollie Panter-Downes never left Roppeleghs, although in her last months she was looked after at Eastbury Manor, Compton, Surrey, where she died on 22 January 1997. She was cremated, and her ashes were scattered round her writing hut in the woods at Roppeleghs. NICOLA BEAUMAN

Sources *New Yorker* (10 Feb 1997) · P. Parker and F. Kermode, eds., *The reader's companion to the twentieth century novel* (1994) · N. Beauman, introduction, in M. Panter-Downes, *One fine day* (1985) · personal knowledge (2004) · private information (2004) [Lady Baer and Mrs Virginia Chapman]
Archives priv. coll.
Likenesses portrait, priv. coll.
Wealth at death £429,902: probate, 26 June 1997, *CGPLA Eng. & Wales*

Downes, Ralph William (1904–1993), organist, was born on 16 August 1904 at 61 Arthur Street, Derby, the only child of James William Downes (1873–1954) and his wife, Constance Edith, *née* Platt (1876–1922). He was educated at Derby municipal secondary school, which he left at 'exactly 16' (Downes, 19). Compulsively drawn to the organ from about the age of nine, he became thoroughly soaked in the sounds of the Derby instruments over his remaining years at school. He was for a time deputy organist of All Saints' Church (later the cathedral), and made his first acquaintance with the Mustel harmonium in a local cinema. Faced with the necessity of finding a job he played the organ, first in cinemas in Nottingham, and then, back in Derby, as 'star performer' on the Mustel in 1922. From the autumn of that year he studied at the Royal College of Music, London, taught by Walter Alcock, Henry Ley, and Edgar Cook; he was Cook's assistant at Southwark Cathedral from 1923 to 1925, at which point he went to Oxford as organ scholar of Keble College. He was active in the University Musical Club, becoming president in 1927, and directed the orchestral ensemble for several Keble summer plays, some of the music being composed or transcribed by him. Jack Westrup, his contemporary and later professor of music in the university, played trombone in the orchestra; he once described Downes as appearing 'almost dashing' at this time (personal knowledge).

On leaving Oxford in 1928 Downes departed in August for Princeton University where he became the first organist and director of music of the new Gothic chapel; this appointment came about after an interview in England. In 1929 he married Agnes Mary Rix (1889–1980), daughter of John Joseph Helsdon Rix, an English schoolteacher settled in the Netherlands, where she herself was private secretary to the US envoy. They had one son, the art historian Professor Kerry Downes (*b.* 1930). Downes remained at Princeton until 1935, becoming also a lecturer in the

music department, which was started in 1934. His experience of Princeton was not all he hoped, as the organ, which had an excellent specification, was badly balanced, the imposing-looking chapel contained large amounts of acoustic tiling disguised as stonework, and the academic level of undergraduate students in music was not up to the standard that he expected. As he later recounted, he tried to improve the organ at various times and learned much from American organ builders, principally Donald Harrison of the Aeolian-Skinner company.

Downes converted to Roman Catholicism in 1930 and, at the beginning of 1936, became organist of Brompton Oratory, London, retaining this post until 1978 when he became organist emeritus. He did not have responsibility for the choir, but provided accompaniments on the organ to all the church music. In 1937 he was able to obtain a Mustel harmonium for the oratory, and in the same year visited Paris, where particularly the great Cavaillé-Coll organs made a revelatory impression on him. It was in his first years at Brompton Oratory, and those immediately after the Second World War, that Downes was probably at his finest as an organist. He performed the major works of Reger, Hindemith's organ sonatas, and Schoenberg's *Variations on a Recitative*, as well as countless other modern works largely neglected by the general run of organists; many of these were played in recitals for the Organ Music Society, and he was a frequent broadcasting recitalist for the BBC. Although he played Messiaen's organ compositions he seemed to be not over-enthusiastic about them—'bad music' was one description. One particular association was with the Aldeburgh Festival, in which he took part (almost without a break) from its beginning in 1948 until 1985.

Downes is most widely perceived as having been the guiding light in transforming people's attitudes to the organ in mid-twentieth-century Britain. He did this most decisively in the design for the organ in the Royal Festival Hall, London, on which he worked from 1948. As newly appointed organist of the London Philharmonic Orchestra, intended to be the resident orchestra of the as yet unbuilt hall, Downes was the natural choice to be designer of the organ; and while this may have seemed to the London county council (LCC) harmless enough, in a very short time the project became extremely contentious, with damaging interventions from the LCC's musical advisers and other influential persons. In the end Downes's quiet persistence persuaded a distinctly uneasy LCC, in May 1950, that the planned scheme should go ahead.

For Downes life was something of a balancing act, with home life, church (there were many demands at the oratory in addition to Sunday services), performing both as soloist and in concerted music, organ building and maintenance, teaching, examining, and adjudicating. As an interpreter, he had metamorphosed from the youth who had 'got the bug' into a discriminating musician by his early twenties; he gave entertaining accounts of some of his adventures in *Baroque Tricks* (1983). My own experience comes to mind when, as a brash former national service-man, I said to him at a lesson that taking a rarefied view was all very well, but what would Bach do if he had our conditions. 'Ah', he replied, quietly and tellingly as always, 'you are taking a subjective view, while I am trying to be objective'. When, on a much later occasion, we were having a conversation about teaching, he remarked that he had never felt himself particularly suited to it because many of the practical elements of organ playing had come to him naturally, and he could not readily explain them to a student who found things difficult.

Downes was, in his son's description, a romantic, one who was forever seeking the ideal means of expression, in one instrument, of styles which could be strange bedfellows. He repeatedly claimed, before it was built, that the Royal Festival Hall organ was to be an all-purpose instrument, yet the reeds were given twentieth-century French voicing (by Louis-Eugène Rocheson) which made their use perilous, particularly in such a location. He was strongly influenced by the American reform movement of the 1930s, which was wedded to electric actions for many years to come, and indeed the principal instruments with whose construction he was associated (at the Royal Festival Hall, Buckfast Abbey, Brompton Oratory, Paisley Abbey, and St Albans and Gloucester cathedrals) had electric rather than mechanical action to their keyboards. The great leap, for him, to mechanical action came with the design for the organ in St David's Hall, Cardiff, which was completed in 1982.

Downes was appointed CBE in 1969 and a knight of the order of St Gregory the Great (an honour conferred by the pope) in 1970. He died of pneumonia in London on 24 December 1993 and was buried in Kensington borough cemetery, London, on 7 or 8 January 1994. He was survived by his son. A solemn mass for him was celebrated at Brompton Oratory on 10 May 1994.　　　JAMES DALTON

Sources R. Downes, *Baroque tricks* (1983) · London county council committee reports and council minutes, 1948–54, LMA · *WWW*, 1991–5 · *New Grove* · private information (2004) [K. Downes] · personal knowledge (2004) · *The Times* (3 Jan 1994) · *The Independent* (1 Jan 1994) · council minutes, Keble College, Oxford · SBC (Royal Festival Hall) Archive
Archives British Institute of Organ Studies, papers connected with instruments and organ building | SOUND BL NSA, performance recordings
Likenesses photograph, repro. in *The Times* · photograph, repro. in *The Independent*
Wealth at death £166,633: probate, 4 March 1994, CGPLA Eng. & Wales

Downes, Theophilus (1657/8–1726), nonjuror and author, was born at Purslow, Shropshire, between March 1657 and March 1658, the son of John and Knightley Downes. He became a commoner of Balliol College, Oxford, in March 1673, graduating BA on 17 October 1676 and MA on 10 July 1679. He was elected a fellow of Balliol College, but was ejected in 1690 following his refusal to take the oath of allegiance to William III. In support of this view he published several pamphlets, most notably *An examination of the arguments drawn from scripture and reason, in Dr. Sherlock's case of allegiance, and his vindication of it* (1691), and wrote the introduction to the nonjuring Jacobite volume *The Hereditary Right of the Crown of England Asserted* by George Harbin (1713). After his ejection he acted at least until 1711 as a travelling tutor on the grand tour in France and Italy, occasionally visiting the exiled Stuart court in France. Among his students were James Scudamore and Thomas Thynne, whose family members continued to support Downes. He also received financial support via a network of well-off nonjurors when staying in London. Having acquired first-hand knowledge of Roman antiquities during his numerous travels, he participated in the famous debate about the antiquity of the iron shield in the possession of John Woodward, rejecting Henry Dodwell's view of its ancient origin. It was only after his death, on 26 July 1726 in the parish of St George the Martyr, London, that his contribution to the dispute was published. He remained a bachelor throughout his life.　　　CHRISTOPH V. EHRENSTEIN

Sources Foster, *Alum. Oxon.* · letter of administration, PRO, PROB 6/102, fol. 93 · *Remarks and collections of Thomas Hearne*, ed. C. E. Doble and others, 11 vols., OHS, 2, 7, 13, 34, 42–3, 48, 50, 65, 67, 72 (1885–1921) · J. M. Levine, *Dr Woodward's shield: history, science, and satire in Augustan England* (1977) · J. Ingamells, ed., *A dictionary of British and Irish travellers in Italy, 1701–1800* (1997) · PRO, PROB 3/25/132 [inventory] · T. Downes, letters to Hilkiah Bedford, 1700–04, Bodl. Oxf., MSS Rawl., letters 42, fols. 36–8 · J. C. Findon, 'The nonjurors and the Church of England, 1689–1716', DPhil diss., U. Oxf., 1978 · J. H. Overton, *The nonjurors: their lives, principles, and writings* (1902) · Wood, *Ath. Oxon.*, new edn · H. Dodwell, letter to Th. Downes, 12 May 1711, Bodl. Oxf., MS St Edmund Hall 14, fol. 60 · W. G. C. Maxwell, ed., 'The register of Clunberry', *Diocese of Hereford*, ed. W. P. W. Phillimore, 2, Shropshire Parish Registers, (privately printed, London, [1901])
Archives Bodl. Oxf., MS Eng. th. e. 20 | Bodl. Oxf., MSS Rawl., letters 42 · Bodl. Oxf., MS St Edmund Hall 14
Wealth at death £652; incl. more than £600 from bonds and mortgages: inventory, PRO, PROB 3/25/135

Downes, William, first Baron Downes (1751–1826), judge, was born at Donnybrook, co. Dublin, the third and youngest son of the six children of Robert (Robin) Downes (1708–1754) of Donnybrook (MP for Kildare, 1735–54), and of Elizabeth (Lily), daughter of Thomas Twigg, also of Donnybrook; he was grandson of Dive Downes, bishop of Cork (d. 1709). He was aged only two or three when his father was found dying in the parlour of their home in Dawson Street, Dublin, with a sword run through his body; the circumstances were never explained.

In 1768 Downes entered Trinity College, Dublin, from which he graduated BA in 1773, the same year that he was admitted to the Middle Temple. He was called to the Irish bar in 1776, and soon acquired a reputation for industry and competence. In 1788 he successfully defended the future Major-General Gillespie, who had been charged with the murder of Sir Jonah Barrington's brother. The Irish government thought sufficiently highly of Downes to arrange in 1790 for his election as an MP for Donegal borough, a seat that lay within its gift. Two years later he was made a puisne judge in the Irish king's bench. Although criminal business constituted but a portion of Downes's judicial work it was here that his performance was most jealously scrutinized. Conservative critics were not always impressed, the presumed pro-defence stance

William Downes, first Baron Downes (1751–1826), by John Comerford, c.1822

of the judge in a high-profile 1796 trial causing one complainant to label Downes 'a phlegmatic, cowardly heap' (McDowell, 547).

The rising of the United Irishmen in 1798 and the manner of that rising's suppression had a profound effect on Downes, both as judge and man. He was distressed by the execution after court-martial in June of that year of an old friend, Sir Edward Crosbie. 'The melancholy situation of the country', Downes confided in July, 'has so much heated the minds of most people … that a ready ear is lent to reports which tend to criminate' (*An Accurate and Impartial Narrative of the Appeal, Trial and Execution of Sir E. W. Crosbie, Bart.*, 94). In October he remonstrated with Castlereagh, the Irish chief secretary, over an incident that had occurred on the opening day of the assizes at Waterford. As presiding judge Downes had been shocked to learn that that morning six 'rebels' scheduled to be tried before him had been transferred into military custody:

> The law cannot appear to the public to be weak without losing that respect which it ought to have with the people especially if they shall feel only its terrors, and shall believe it is not strong enough to extend benefits to them. (*Correspondence of … Cornwallis*, 3.14)

Downes was promoted to the chief justiceship of king's bench in 1803 to fill the vacancy caused by the murder of Viscount Kilwarden. 'As a judge, lawyer and citizen, Downes … then the senior puisne was by universal admission the fit man' (Ball, *The Judges in Ireland*, 2.244). Three years later he was given an honorary LLD on becoming vice-chancellor of the University of Dublin, a position he held until his death.

Downes was to fill the office of chief justice for nearly nineteen years. Few specimens of his written judgments survive, but both these and contemporary accolades indicate that he contributed a good deal to such dignity as the immediate post-union Irish bench was able to muster. This praise counted for little in the turbulent years that preceded Catholic emancipation, however, and in 1812, in a deteriorating political atmosphere and in what was a remarkable twist to events, Downes himself was to be sued over the arrest of a prominent Catholic, an arrest that he had personally sanctioned under the terms of the Irish Convention Act of 1793: *Taaffe v. Downes*. Taaffe's suit failed. Downes's conduct of the trial of John Magee the following year, on a charge of criminal libel, in turn incensed the government. Daniel O'Connell, Magee's defence counsel, had mounted a savage attack on Dublin Castle rule. Peel, as chief secretary, was horrified at Downes's indulgence of O'Connell, and expressed the hope to a correspondent that the chief justice would not 'allow the court to be again insulted and made the vehicle of treason' (Parker, 1.117). O'Connell, for his part, did not reciprocate the indulgence, variously describing Downes as a 'scoundrel' and a 'plausible tool of bigotry' (*Correspondence of Daniel O'Connell*, 2.152, 384).

Downes resigned the office of chief justice in February 1822, on a pension of £3800 a year. On 10 December he was created Baron Downes of Aghanville in King's county, with a special remainder in favour of his cousin Sir Ulysses Burgh. About 1805 Downes had bought Merville, near Stillorgan in co. Dublin, a property then reputed to possess the best garden in Ireland. Downes died at Merville on 3 March 1826 and, like his two elder brothers, died unmarried. At his special request he was buried in the same tomb in the vault of St Ann's Church in Dawson Street, Dublin, as a colleague and fellow king's bench judge, William Tankerville Chamberlain (1751–1802), who had been laid to rest some twenty years earlier. An inscription in the church records: 'Their friendship and union was complete. They had studied together, lived together, sat together on the same bench of justice, and now by the desire of the survivor they lie together in the same tomb.'

W. N. OSBOROUGH

Sources F. E. Ball, *The judges in Ireland, 1221–1921*, 2 (1926) · Burtchaell & Sadleir, *Alum. Dubl.*, 2nd edn, 242 · E. Keane, P. Beryl Phair, and T. U. Sadleir, eds., *King's Inns admission papers, 1607–1867*, IMC (1982), 141 · E. M. Johnston, 'The state of the Irish House of Commons in 1791', *Proceedings of the Royal Irish Academy*, 59C (1957–9), 1–56 · GEC, *Peerage*, new edn, 4.455–6 · F. E. Ball, *A history of the county Dublin*, 6 vols. (1902–20), vol. 2, p. 79 · *An accurate and impartial narrative of the appeal, trial and execution of Sir E. W. Crosbie, bart.* (1801), 94 · J. Hatchell, *A report of the arguments and judgment upon demurrer in the case of H. E. Taffe, esq. agst Rt Hon Wm. Downes* (1815) · *Correspondence of Charles, first Marquis Cornwallis*, ed. C. Ross, 2nd edn, 3 vols. (1859), vol. 3, p. 14 · *The correspondence of Daniel O'Connell*, ed. M. R. O'Connell, 2–3, IMC (1972–3) · *Report on the manuscripts of Mrs Stopford-Sackville*, 1, HMC, 49 (1904), 214–15 · *Journal of the Association for the Preservation of the Memorials of the Dead, Ireland*, 2 (1892–4), 88–9 · C. S. Parker, ed., *Sir Robert Peel: from his private papers*, 1 (1891),

117 · R. B. McDowell, *Ireland in the age of imperialism and revolution, 1760–1801* (1979), 547
Archives BL, corresp. with Robert Peel, Add. MS 40206 · PRO NIre., letters to first earl of Sheffield
Likenesses G. F. Joseph, oils, 1820, TCD · J. Comerford, oils, c.1822; Sothebys, 19 Dec 1977 [*see illus.*] · M. Cregan, oils, c.1827, King's Inns, Dublin · S. W. Reynolds, mezzotint, pubd 1827 (after M. Cregan), BM · W. Brocas, engraving (after H. Hamilton) · H. Hamilton, oils · T. Lupton, engraving (after J. Comerford) · oils, priv. coll.

Richard Joseph Downey (1881–1953), by Lafayette, 1928

Downey, Richard Joseph (1881–1953), Roman Catholic archbishop of Liverpool, was born on 5 May 1881 in Kilkenny, the eldest of three children and only son of Thomas Downey, chemist, and his wife, Mary (Minnie) Casey. The family moved to Liverpool and he attended St Edward's College junior seminary in 1894. In 1901 he moved to the senior seminary, St Joseph's College, at Upholland, near Wigan, where he was ordained priest in 1907. Sent to Rome to pursue higher studies at Beda College and the Gregorian University, Downey gained a doctorate of divinity with distinction in 1911. In that year he was appointed a member of the Catholic Missionary Society, dedicated to the conversion of non-Catholics to the Roman Catholic faith. This involved him in preaching and lecturing throughout the British Isles. In 1918 he became co-founder and first editor of the *Catholic Gazette* (a successor to the *Missionary Gazette*) which began to cater for a more educated Catholic readership. During these years he also had part-time posts teaching philosophy and theology. In 1926 he returned to teach at Upholland, and became vice-rector there the following year.

In 1928 Downey was appointed archbishop of Liverpool, and was consecrated in the pro-cathedral on 21 September, a meteoric rise to ecclesiastical power. At forty-seven he was the youngest Roman Catholic archbishop in the world. With a Catholic population of 374,000 it was by far the most populous diocese in England and Wales. Downey was decisive in manner, unashamedly triumphalist, and would not compromise over Catholic principles. A good conversationalist with a ready wit, he was able to relax in an easy manner with his senior clergy (who referred to him as Dickie). Almost immediately he began to grapple with the thorny question of Catholic education. In his Advent pastoral letter of 1928 he argued that the funding of Catholic schools was not merely a political matter but was a question of justice for Catholics and that the church had to be vigorously involved in the debate. In October 1928 Downey coined the slogan 'The cathedral in our time'. He subsequently engaged the prominent architect Sir Edwin Lutyens to design a cathedral that would be worthy of the city and diocese, and which would be second in size only to St Peter's in Rome. In order to finance this Downey established a Catholic Emancipation Fund, and put a lot of his energy into fund-raising.

With his Liverpool background Downey was familiar with the bitter sectarian divisions which bedevilled politics in the city—and with which a Catholic archbishop had to contend. The powerful Working Men's Conservative Association was strongly Orange in composition. The local Labour Party had reached its inter-war peak with fifty-seven councillors facing seventy-nine Conservatives. However, one third of the Labour councillors were Roman Catholic and the party had strong support from the Roman Catholic working-class population. Even so, Downey had misgivings about the socialist tendencies of the Labour Party. He banned his clergy from electioneering and forbade the Catholic Representation Association (founded by his predecessor) from using the word 'Catholic' in its title. (It subsequently became the Centre Party.) Downey forged a close personal friendship with Sir James Reynolds, a prominent Catholic businessman, high sheriff of Lancashire (1927–8), and Conservative MP for Liverpool Exchange (1929–32).

In 1930 the 9 acre site of Brownlow Hill workhouse came on the market as the city corporation of Liverpool took over responsibility for poor relief. Downey put in a bid of £100,000 for it as a site for his projected cathedral. There was bitter Orange opposition: Councillor Longbottom said that he would prefer 'a poison germ factory' there rather than a Catholic cathedral. Eventually the Catholic bid, the only one standing, was accepted by an overwhelming vote in the city council. The foundation stone was laid at Whitsuntide 1933 in the presence of a papal legate. Because of the war building had to cease in 1941, when only the massive crypt had been partially completed. After the war escalating costs made it impracticable to continue building on Lutyens's scale or design.

The Hadow report of 1926 (the consultative committee on the education of the adolescent) had recommended replacing the system of parallel secondary and all age elementary schools with a diversified education after the age of eleven according to age, ability, and aptitude of the child. It also recommended raising the school-leaving age to fifteen. The Catholic bishops welcomed these suggestions, but could not sustain the costs which this would entail. Archbishop Downey, both in articles and by addressing mass rallies in Liverpool and in many centres throughout the country, pressed the Catholic claim that they should be given financial support for this reorganization parallel to that given to local education authorities. In the run-up to the general election of 1930 Downey questioned fifty-nine parliamentary candidates in the Liverpool area as to whether they were willing to support the Catholic cause; thirty-eight agreed to do so. An Education Bill drawn up by the Labour government proved unacceptable to the Catholic bishops because it allowed local education authorities (LEAs) to appoint teachers in denominational schools except for a few reserved places. After five years of campaigning the Catholic bishops under Cardinal Hinsley agreed to accept the terms of the 1936 Education Act which allowed LEAs to give grants of up to 75 per cent of the cost of reorganizing denominational schools (although by now Church of England and free church authorities had agreed to use LEA schools with an agreed syllabus for religious education). The first school built under this act was a Catholic one in Southport, in the Liverpool archdiocese. Because of the sectarian opposition to 'Rome on the rates' Liverpool city council refused to pay any grants to Catholic schools and Downey called upon Catholics to make it an issue at the forthcoming local election. The Catholics lost this fight, but in 1938 the Board of Education stepped in and withheld £180,000 of Liverpool's grants. Eventually, by means of a private act, a solution was reached whereby the diocese rented schools from the LEA.

Archbishop Downey was not on friendly terms with the Church of England diocesan bishop of Liverpool, Dr Albert David (1923–44). Their differences became public when David criticized Downey for refusing to join protestants even to sing hymns at the Cenotaph, and attacked the Roman Catholic clergy, and also the Catholic Evidence Guild for bringing relentless pressure to bear upon non-Catholic partners in mixed marriages. Downey rejected David's invitation to an ecumenical service: 'an Archbishop of the Catholic Church can hardly be expected to accept the spiritual leadership of an Anglican Bishop', he wrote (*The Times*, 3 Dec 1930). At a later stage he was to lead the opposition among the Catholic bishops to Cardinal Hinsley's ecumenical prayers with Bishop George Bell at meetings of the 'Sword of the Spirit' in May 1941. None the less his popularity as an after dinner speaker and his power as an orator at public functions built many bridges at the secular level.

Downey suffered from obesity and in 1932, although he was only 5 feet 4 inches, he weighed 18 stone. This did not restrict his activity but it alarmed his doctor. By rigid dieting he had reduced his weight by half by 1939. He was a capable administrator, increasing the number of deans from fourteen to twenty. Through them he kept in touch with every part of the diocese, whose population grew from 374,000 to 437,000. At the same time the number of clergy, both secular and regular, grew steadily from 445 in 1928 to 683 in 1953. Downey met the need for more clergy partly by recruiting newly ordained priests from Ireland. Some of these priests gained a reputation for fund-raising and the building of new churches and schools. Under the nickname of the Kerry gang they were believed to have considerable unofficial influence with the archbishop.

Meanwhile, the number of churches had increased from 152 to 195.

After a brief illness Downey died in Gateacre Grange, a convent nursing home in Woolton, Liverpool, on 16 June 1953. His requiem mass took place at the pro-cathedral of St Nicholas and he was buried on 23 June in a tomb designed by Lutyens in the unfinished crypt of the cathedral of which he had dreamed. MICHAEL GAINE

Sources *DNB* · G. A. Beck, ed., *The English Catholics, 1850–1950* (1950) · P. J. Waller, *Democracy and sectarianism: a political and social history of Liverpool, 1868–1939* (1981) · press cuttings, Upholland Northern Institute, Lancashire, Roman Catholic Diocesan Archives · *The Tablet* (20 June 1953) · A. Hastings, *A history of English Christianity, 1920–1990*, 3rd edn (1991) · private information (2004) · *The Times* (3 Dec 1930) · *The Times* (17 June 1953) · *Liverpool Daily Post* (16 Oct 1953) · WWW

Archives Upholland Northern Institute, Lancashire, Roman Catholic diocesan archives, official corresp., press cuttings, printed pastoral letters | Bodl. Oxf., corresp. with Sir James Marchant · TCD, corresp. with Thomas Bodkin

Likenesses Lafayette, photograph, 1928, NPG [*see illus.*] · S. Reed, oils, *c*.1949–1950, Upholland Northern Institute, near Wigan, Lancashire · S. Reed, oils, *c*.1949–1950, NPG · H. Coster, photographs, NPG

Wealth at death £55,996 10s. 3d.: probate, 14 Sept 1953, CGPLA Eng. & Wales

Downham. For this title name *see* Fisher, William Hayes, Baron Downham (1853–1920).

Downham, George (*d.* 1634), bishop of Derry, was the elder son of William *Downham (1510/11–1577), bishop of Chester; John *Downham (1571–1652) was his younger brother. He matriculated pensioner from Christ's College, Cambridge, in 1581, graduated BA in 1584, was made a fellow in 1587, and proceeded MA in 1588. In the earlier part of his career at Cambridge, Downham joined in the controversy (and signed the petition) over the dispute concerning the later separatist Francis Johnson, whom he supported. He was also one of the complainants who drew up a summary against Peter Baro's sermon on universal redemption, which demonstrated his strict adherence to the Calvinist doctrines of predestination. He was a renowned logician, and because of his proficiency and learning in the logic of Ramus he was appointed professor of logic at the university in 1590. He was canon of Gloucester in 1593 and prebendary of Chester in 1594, and was awarded his BD in 1595. On 13 December 1598 he was appointed prebendary of Caddington Minor in St Paul's and he was rector of St Margaret, Lothbury, London, from September 1596 to August 1601, when his brother John succeeded him. It is likely that some time during this period he married his first wife, Ann (*d.* 1615), daughter of William Harrison, with whom he had seven children. On 10 September 1601 he was installed as rector of Great Munden, Hertfordshire.

In addition to publishing devotional and moral works such as *The Christians Sanctuarie* (1604) and *Lectures on the XV Psalme* (1604), Downham became involved in some of the great controversies in this period. His *A Treatise Concerning Antichrist* (1603) upheld the doctrine that the pope was the

Antichrist as foretold in a number of passages of scripture. This particular tract is a good example of his vehement anti-Catholicism, arguing that Roman religion consists 'not only in respect of the worship, of manifold superstition and most gross idolatry, but also in respect of the doctrine, of many hundred Antichristian errors and doctrines of devils' (sig. A3v). The doctrine that the pope was the Antichrist was at the heart of his condemnation of the Church of Rome and argued that it was 'the cheefe of all controversies betwixt us and the papists, and of the greatest consequence'.

On 17 April 1608 Downham gave the consecration sermon for James Montagu, bishop of Bath and Wells. In an enlarged version, published as *Two Sermons* (1608), he defended *jure divino* episcopacy, the lawfulness and excellence of bishops, and argued that episcopacy was an apostolic and divine institution. Significantly, he tried to do so without driving a wedge between advocates of the existing Church of England settlement and those who commended a presbyterian form of church government. For him '*jure divino* episcopacy should be construed as exclusive and immutable only by those who chose to promote the Presbyterian church polity in a similarly exclusive manner' (Milton, 480). This sermon caused much controversy and provoked a wealth of tracts and treatises that were still appearing a decade later, especially from the pen of Paul Baynes. Downham's views on episcopacy were, however, greeted favourably by the king, who on account of this sermon appointed him as one of his chaplains. It is suggested that Archbishop Richard Bancroft stood at Downham's shoulder when he composed this sermon. Downham's dedicatory epistles to the archbishop in his earlier sermons provide further evidence of links between them, as does Bancroft's use of Downham in his attempt to prevent Francis Walsingham (*bap.* 1577, *d.* 1647) from converting to Catholicism. Downham was one of the first candidates to be mentioned by James I as a possible successor to Edward Barwell as master of Christ's College, after the void election of September 1609. He was, however, rejected, possibly at the instigation of Bancroft, because of the perceived need for a stricter man at the helm.

Having become prebendary of Yatton in the diocese of Bath and Wells, Downham resigned this when in September 1616 he was appointed bishop of Derry. He was consecrated on 16 October. His first wife had died in 1615, and on 22 April 1617 he married at St Margaret, Lothbury, Jaell (or Jaél) (*née* de Pergne), widow of Sir Henry *Killigrew. Downham had probably known her for quite some time as he preached the funeral sermon for Sir Henry at Easter 1603. A Frenchwoman, naturalized in 1601, she had a daughter and two sons from her first marriage.

On his appointment to the Irish see, Downham continued in earnest his crusade against Catholicism, but experienced difficulties in spreading the Reformation. It appears that he was utterly dissatisfied with the support he received from the secular and civil authorities and their role in enforcing conformity. Indeed, Downham thought it was the duty of the state to use its power to coerce the conversion of Catholic recusants. Moreover, because of the influential Hamilton family, many of the Catholic priests enjoyed immunity from persecution and were able to continue their ministry as normal. Downham's frustration in the face of this situation is reflected in a short memoir he wrote in 1624 where he said that:

> for the removing of popish priests our laws are weak and powerless, neither can I get the assistance of the military men I desire, and that which discourageth me most is that when I have gotten any of them apprehended, convicted and committed they have been by corruption set at liberty to follow their former courses. (Burke, 1–2)

He also became embroiled in long-standing disputes with the Irish Society of London concerning the uncertainty of ownership between secular and church property and the question about fishing rights in the Foyle. It is likely, therefore, that anonymous accusations made against him in a letter of May 1617, accusing him of appropriation of moneys for his own advantage and neglect of his diocese, were made in the context of these disputes. Downham, however, promptly defended himself in a letter to the lord deputy, but it seems that the issue remained unresolved.

Despite Downham's hostility to the Irish he still fought for improvements to be made to the physical condition of his diocese. For example, in November 1630 he, Sir John Vaughan, and George Carey sent identical petitions to the Goldsmiths', Grocers', and Skinners' companies, requesting them to build a bridge over the Faughan, at a total cost of £90, which they thought would be of great advantage to the inhabitants. In his visitation report he also noted that Derry was deprived of an educational endowment. The most famous story told of Downham is of when he read the protestation against the 'graces' in a sermon preached before the lord deputy on 23 April 1627 in Christchurch, Dublin. Downham, along with many others, opposed the granting by Charles I of toleration to Catholics in return for money. It is reported that after the reading of the protestation Downham asked that everybody should say Amen, 'and suddenly the whole church almost shaked with the great sound their Amens made' (*CSP Ire.*, 239–40). Later, in May 1628, Downham took part in an inquiry into the sequestration of the Londonderry rents ordered by the king that was soon after revoked by the House of Lords in England.

Downham had continued to publish. *An Abstract of the Duties Commanded, and Sinnes Forbidden in the Law of God* (1620) and *The Christian Duke of Thriving* (1620), were followed more controversially, in the more Arminian climate then prevailing, by *A Treatise of Justification* (1633) and *The Christians Freedome* (1635). His Paul's Cross sermon of two decades earlier, which had first appeared as *A Treatise upon John 8.36 Concerning Christian Libertie*, was published in Dublin in 1631 as *The Covenant of Grace*. Charles I ordered the suppression of this work because it contained an appendix defending the thirty-eighth Irish article on perseverance. Downham died in Londonderry on 17 April

1634 and was buried in the cathedral church on 21 April. He had married a third wife, Margery (*d.* 1656), daughter of Sir Nicholas Bagnall and widow of Sir Francis Roe (*d. c.*1620), a landholder in co. Tyrone.

KENNETH GIBSON

Sources A. Ford, *The protestant Reformation in Ireland, 1590–1641* (1985) · J. Peile, *Biographical register of Christ's College, 1505–1905, and of the earlier foundation, God's House, 1448–1505*, ed. [J. A. Venn], 1 (1910) · *Fasti Angl., 1541–1857*, [Bath and Wells] · J. E. Cussons, *History of Hertfordshire*, 3 vols. (1870–81); facs. repr. (1972) · E. Freshfield, ed., *The vestry minute book of the parish of St Margaret, Lothbury, in the City of London, 1571–1677* (privately printed, London, 1887) · H. C. Porter, *Reformation and reaction in Tudor Cambridge* (1958) · T. W. Moody, *The Londonderry plantation, 1609–1641: the City of London and the plantation in Ulster* (1939) · T. W. Moody and J. G. Simms, eds., *The bishopric of Derry and the Irish Society of London, 1602–1705*, 2 vols., IMC (1968–83) · F. G. James, *Lords of the ascendancy: the Irish House of Lords and its members, 1600–1800* (1995) · *CSP Ire., 1625–32* · W. A. Reynell, ed., 'The estate of the diocese of Derry compiled by Dr. George Downham', *Ulster Journal of Archaeology*, new ser., 1 (1894–5), 165–77, 243–53 · W. P. Burke, 'The diocese of Derry in 1631', *Archivium Hibernicum*, 5 (1916), 1–6 · *IGI* · A. Milton, *Catholic and Reformed: the Roman and protestant churches in English protestant thought, 1600–1640* (1995), 452, 459, 460, 480–81 · J. B. Leslie, *Derry clergy and parishes* (1937), 7 · private information (2004)
Archives Derry Diocesan Library, student notebook · TCD, 'The Ulster visitation book', 1622

Downham, John (1571–1652), Church of England clergyman and author, was born in Chester, the younger son of William *Downham (1510/11–1577), bishop of Chester. He matriculated pensioner from Christ's College, Cambridge, in 1589, graduated BA in 1693, and proceeded MA in 1596 and BD in 1603. Ordained deacon and priest in London in 1598 at the age of twenty-seven, Downham was vicar of St Olave Jewry, London, from 1599 to 1602, when he was presented to the consistory court for 'that he ministreth to men as he finds them, some sitting and some kneeling' (LMA, consistory court correction book, 1601–3, DL/C/303, fol. 56r, 20 Jan 1602). From 1602 to 1618 he was, in succession to his brother George *Downham, rector of St Margaret, Lothbury, where he was presented in 1607 for preaching without a licence. Subsequently he seems to have avoided the attentions of the diocesan authorities: whether he actually conformed or whether his nonconformity was simply not reported cannot be determined, but eminent patrons and extensive publications may provide some explanation for his immunity.

In the course of his long life Downham published nineteen treatises, biblical concordances, and collections of sermons, the most famous of which was *The Christian Warfare*, published in four parts between 1604 and 1618, which aimed to arm the Christian against the temptations of 'our spiritual enemies'. Although many of his works, such as *A Guide to Godlyness* (1622), were 'discourses of practical divinity, tending to stir up devotion', and aimed to stir up those who 'waxing weary of the truth … desire to return to the fleshpots of Egypt' (Sir Robert Harley owned a copy of *A Guide*), he also published a popular exposition of reformed theology, *The Summe of Sacred Divinitie* (1620?), which went through three editions. The second edition of

The Christian Warfare (1608) was dedicated to George Abbot, archbishop of Canterbury, and *The Second Part of the Christian Warfare* (1611) to Thomas Egerton, Lord Ellesmere, chancellor of England, 'from whom I have had … all the means of my maintenance'.

About 1614 Downham joined with Richard Stock and William Gouge in supporting George Walker in his controversy with Anthony Wootton, another puritan preacher, who was charged with antinomian opinions. On 1 February 1615 the Haberdashers' Company appointed Downham the first William Jones lecturer at St Bartholomew Exchange. His inaugural lecture, published as *The Plea of the Poore* (1616), praised Jones's munificent bequest, which included almshouses and schools as well as endowed lectureships, and which was held up as a model of intelligent charity. Downham continued to preach what came to be known as the 'Golden' lecture until the infirmities of old age led to his retirement on 8 May 1650. Within two years of his initial appointment Downham had become an adviser of the Haberdashers' Company, regularly consulted on the exercise of its ecclesiastical patronage. The company paid him a pension of £80 for the first year of his retirement and £70 yearly thereafter.

In, or shortly after, 1623 Downham, already apparently a widower with at least one son, George, probably born in 1608, married Katherine, *née* Little, widow of his friend Thomas Sutton; Sutton had been lecturer at St Saviour's, Southwark, from 1615 to 1623, and his *Lectures upon … Romanes* Downham subsequently edited and published in 1632. Downham became rector of All Hallows-the-Great in Thames Street on 3 November 1630, a living he held until his death. From 1633 he was a member of a steering committee of London ministers set up to oversee the English contribution to John Dury's project for the preparation of a manual of practical divinity. In 1640 he reportedly joined other London puritans in petitioning the privy council against Archbishop Laud's new canons and the 'etcetera' oath (PRO, SP 16/263/53). In 1643 he was appointed one of the licensers of the press. However, Downham was not appointed to the Westminster assembly, although he was appointed by the assembly on 18 September 1644 to a committee for the ordination of ministers, and he appears not to have been involved in the debate between the presbyterians and Independents, being simply known, as Thomas Fuller put it (and Fuller was no puritan) as 'a grave divine' and 'a painful and profitable preacher' (Fuller, 82).

By the time Downham came to draw up his will on 26 February 1652 he had two surviving sons, Francis and William, and three daughters, Sarah Ward, Joan Harrison, and Elizabeth Kempe, all of whom were remembered in his will; his wife also survived him. Another son, George, who had been curate of St Stephen Walbrook, London, between about 1637 and 1639 was dead, but his four children were also remembered. Downham also left his stepson, Thomas Sutton, a Greek Testament and a Latin and Greek Bible. He died 'a venerable and celebrated divine' (Brook, 2.497) in his eighty-first year, in 1652 (before 13

September when his will was proved), at his house in Bunhill in St Giles Cripplegate. His will asked that he should be buried by his pew door in All Hallows-the-Great.

P. S. SEAVER

Sources B. Brook, *The lives of the puritans*, 3 vols. (1813) · T. Fuller, *The worthies of England*, ed. J. Freeman, abridged edn (1952) · Wood, *Ath. Oxon.*, new edn · P. S. Seaver, *The puritan lectureships: the politics of religious dissent, 1560–1662* (1970) · W. M. Hetherington, *History of the Westminster Assembly of Divines* (1843) · Venn, *Alum. Cant.* · J. T. Cliffe, *The puritan gentry: the great puritan families of early Stuart England* (1984) · consistory court (London), correction books, LMA, DL/C.303, DL/C/306 · Haberdashers' Company, court of assistants minutes, 1583–1652, GL, MS.15,842/1 · St Bartholomew Exchange, vestry minutes, 1567–1642, GL, MS.4384/1 · will, PRO, PROB 11/223/187 · T. Webster, *Godly clergy in early Stuart England: the Caroline puritan movement, c.1620–1643* (1997), 257 · PRO, SP 16/263/53
Wealth at death see will, PRO, PROB 11/223/187

Downham, William (1510/11–1577), bishop of Chester, was born in Norfolk and became a brother of the Bonshommes' priory of Ashridge, Hertfordshire; he received a pension of £6 13s. 4d. on the dissolution of that house in 1539. In the same year he entered Exeter College, Oxford, and in 1541 was a chaplain of All Souls. He became probationer fellow of Magdalen College on 26 July 1542 and fellow exactly a year later, vacating by 1545. He had meanwhile graduated BA (4 February 1541) and incepted MA (11 July 1543); he would receive his DTh by special resolution on 30 October 1566. On 14 September 1548 he was instituted to the rectory of Datchworth, Hertfordshire, which he retained until 1554, by when he was married. On 27 October 1554 he became vicar of Edlesborough, Buckinghamshire, vacating in 1555 when he became rector of Ayot St Peter, Hertfordshire. By 12 July 1555 he was rector of Holywell with Needingworth, Huntingdonshire.

Downham's steady career was probably assisted by Princess Elizabeth, who occupied the house at Ashridge which had once been his. On 8 July 1559 Elizabeth, now queen, presented Downham, her chaplain, to the rectory of Brington with Old Weston, Huntingdonshire. The queen further advanced him to the archdeaconry of Brecon (20 January 1560) and to a canonry at Westminster on the refoundation of the collegiate church (21 May 1560, vacated by March 1564). By December 1560 he had been designated bishop of Chester, and thereafter he resigned all his preferments except (for the time being) his stall at Westminster. The queen gave her assent to his election on 1 May 1561, and he was consecrated three days later. On the following day he was appointed an ecclesiastical commissioner for the northern province.

Chester was among the poorest sees in England, and in November 1561, by royal warrant, Downham was excused the first of six instalments due for his first fruits and allowed to pay the residue over three years. In the same month he was given an annuity accidentally omitted from the original endowment of Henry VIII, with arrears of over £500, and personally allowed to hold two livings *in commendam* for seven years. Although he conducted a primary visitation of his cathedral in 1561, he was slow to fill posts in his administration, and allegedly compounded with the archbishop of York in lieu of a general visitation,

not wanting to 'trouble the country nor put them to charge' (Bruce and Perowne, 222, misdated). On 25 July 1562 Downham's authority was ostensibly strengthened by the creation of a twenty-one-man special commission, headed by the earl of Derby, to assist his enforcement of uniformity. In 1563 the bishop visited some parts of his diocese and compiled a survey of its 19,000 households; but he tolerated widespread evasion of subscription to the royal supremacy and the 1559 settlement among his mostly conservative clergy. In the following year he instructed rural deans and churchwardens to remove altars and effect other reforms, again facing much disobedience.

To his enemies Downham was an obvious papist, but he had an almost impossible task in remote country, where a third of the population was not integrated into the parochial structure. Because the see was financed almost wholly from spiritual revenues the bishop had no manor houses to serve as local headquarters; when he travelled he was obliged to lodge with the very gentry who impeded reform. Downham also knew that to deprive Catholic clergy would leave churches and chapels unserved. Instead he ordained large numbers to the priesthood, but with little regard to quality: in his seventeen years he ordained over 300 men, but only four were graduates. When he did send out a graduate chaplain to preach, the man was pelted with rotten eggs. Downham was also forbearing in his treatment of moral lapse: a fornicating rector was quietly dealt with 'lest it should redound to the reproach of the ministry' (Haigh, *Lancashire*, 242).

By 1568 Downham's laxity was of serious concern to the government, and on 3 February the Chester commission was ordered to proceed against the leading recusant gentry. This was followed on 21 February by a personal letter to Downham from the queen, in her severest manner: 'we find great lack in yow, being sorry to have our former expectation in this sort deceaved' (PRO, SP 12/46, no. 33). On 31 July the commission examined eight prominent recusants, but they were merely bound over to conform. During the summer Downham at last toured the full extent of his diocese. Back at Chester on 1 November he sent Cecil a sanguine report on his progress, claiming that the people were 'verie tractable', nowhere more so than in the far north. He took the opportunity to explain that his income of 500 marks a year ('bare rent, and much of it evill payd': that is, no profitable manorial casualties) was only enough to support the household of forty he needed. For the present he was solvent, but asked to have his two *commendams* renewed for life (SP 12/48, no. 36).

Downham's 1568 measures were ineffective, and by 1570 the York high commission was obliged to intervene over the bishop's head. In November 1570 Downham was summoned to London, where the privy council on 14 January appointed Parker to investigate his conduct; by 19 February the archbishop had been joined by a committee of other bishops. As a result, from April 1571 to summer 1572 Downham was inhibited from jurisdiction, and in his place Bishop Barnes of Carlisle conducted a visitation which revealed much further disorder. Twice in 1574 and again in 1577 Downham was urged to act more vigorously against recusants, but the returns he compiled were perfunctory. He died, by now much in debt, in Chester late in 1577 and was buried in the choir of his cathedral. A memorial (no longer extant) gave his age as sixty-six and 3 December as the date of either his death or his burial.

His wife, much stronger-willed than her husband, bore two sons, George *Downham and John *Downham, a bishop and a puritan: Downham sat so long on the fence that his seed fell either side of it.   C. S. KNIGHTON

Sources Emden, *Oxf.*, 4.174 · G. A. J. Hodgett, ed., *The state of the ex-religious and former chantry priests in the diocese of Lincoln, 1547–1574*, Lincoln RS, 53 (1959), 96 · F. O. White, *Lives of the Elizabethan bishops of the Anglican church* (1898), 167–71 · R. V. H. Burne, *Chester Cathedral: from its founding by Henry VIII to the accession of Queen Victoria* (1958), 39, 46–9, 54 · C. Haigh, 'Finance and administration in a new diocese: Chester, 1541–1641', *Continuity and change: personnel and administration of the Church of England, 1500–1642*, ed. R. O'Day and F. Heal (1976), 145–66, esp. 145, 150, 155–7 · C. A. Haigh, *Reformation and resistance in Tudor Lancashire* (1975), 22, 210–13, 220, 223–4, 225–6, 239, 242, 250–52, 262–3 · *Correspondence of Matthew Parker*, ed. J. Bruce and T. T. Perowne, Parker Society, 42 (1853), 222 · state papers domestic, Elizabeth I, PRO, SP 12/46, no. 33; 12/48, no. 36; 12/118, no. 49 · *CSP dom.*, 1547–80, 203, 305, 307, 321–2, 568; 1595–7, 404; *addenda, 1566–79*, 340–41 · *CSP for.*, 1560–61, 462 · APC, 1558–70, 399; 1571–5, 5, 258, 317 · CPR, 1558–60, 89, 255, 397; 1560–63, 170–71, 227; 1563–6, 85 · P. Collinson, *The Elizabethan puritan movement* (1967), 206–7 · P. Hughes, *The Reformation in England*, 3 (1954), 46, 422 · F. Heal, *Of prelates and princes: a study of the economic and social position of the Tudor episcopate* (1980) · exchequer, first fruits office, PRO, E337/4, no.21 · Ches. & Chester ALSS, EDA 2/1 [incl. episcopal register]
Archives BL, 1563 survey of diocese, Harley MS 594, fols. 101–8
Wealth at death heavily indebted: Haigh, 'Finance and administration', 156

Downie, Allan Watt (1901–1988), medical microbiologist, was born on 5 September 1901 in Rosehearty, Aberdeenshire, the fifth child in the family of seven sons and one daughter of William Downie, a deep-sea fisherman, and his wife, Margaret Watt, daughter of a fisherman from Fife. The younger of identical twins, he and his twin, Ricky Downie (1901–1978), grew up close to Rosehearty harbour and became familiar with the sea. They were educated at Rosehearty School, where their unusual ability was spotted, and at Fraserburgh Academy. In 1918 they entered Aberdeen University medical school, from which in 1923 they graduated MB ChB with first-class honours and the distinction of collecting between them every subject prize in every year of the course. In 1923 Allan Downie was in general medical practice in Sheffield and from 1924 to 1926 was a lecturer in bacteriology at Aberdeen University. He obtained his MD in 1929 and DSc in 1938. In 1927 he moved to the department of pathology in Manchester University, where he turned to the new science of virology. With a veterinary pathologist he for the first time demonstrated, in tissue culture, the cellular changes which characterized in its natural animal host, the disease mousepox, a model for human smallpox. This little-noted paper opened a new chapter in methods for studying viruses and virus diseases.

In 1935 Downie married Annie (Nancy), schoolteacher, daughter of William Alan McHardy, wood engineer; they had two daughters and a son. That year he also won the senior Freedom research fellowship at the London Hospital medical school. First, however, he had to spend a nine-month academic year at the Rockefeller Institute in New York City under O. T. Avery and alongside the future leaders of American microbiology. At the London Hospital, Downie initiated work on pox viruses and defined for the first time the distinction between vaccinia and cowpox viruses. This later led him on to smallpox and to its ultimate eradication. The outbreak of the Second World War stalled his work on pox viruses, when he was directed to head the Emergency Public Health Laboratory Service in Cambridge, one of the regional laboratories providing expertise in public health for disease control, water-supply monitoring, and possibly bacterial warfare. (The east coast was a probable front line should invasion happen.) Downie was at Cambridge until 1943, when he was appointed professor of bacteriology in Liverpool.

Returning troops and the resumption of foreign trade after the war brought numerous imports of smallpox into Britain. Downie's laboratory in Liverpool became the world centre for the study of smallpox: of how the virus entered its victims, spread inside them, and then passed to others; of precisely when the patient became infectious and for how long. These studies progressed for twenty-two years, and then the World Health Organization recognized that an effective smallpox eradication plan was possible. With Downie's guidance the intensified and successful programme was launched in 1966, the year of his retirement. Since 1978 there has been no smallpox case; there are no human carriers and no animal cases or carriers. The disease which in the 1960s was killing ten million people per year has ceased to exist. Many thousands of public health workers took part in the programme and the credit, as Downie would have wished, has been spread worldwide. None can doubt that in the laboratory in Liverpool, in the field in India, and after his retirement at the World Health Organization at Geneva and in training courses in Denver, Colorado, Downie's contribution was paramount. It was the greatest medical triumph of the century. Downie helped to train more than 3000 doctors and published 110 outstanding papers. A founder fellow of the Royal College of Pathologists, he was made an honorary LLD at Aberdeen University (1957). He became a fellow of the Royal Society in 1955 and an FRCP in 1982.

Short and wiry, Downie had a great affection for sport. In Manchester he played left-half for Whalley Range Football Club in the Lancashire amateur league. He spent every summer holiday in Rosehearty, with Ricky and his family, sailing in the heavy old family sailboat, with grandchildren or friends, and happy to be on the water and under sail. He loved to fish and to identify sea birds, but it was at golf on the Royal Birkdale course, near Southport, that he excelled and was never satisfied, striving always to reduce his (most enviable) handicap. When he retired from his Liverpool chair in 1966, the *Southport Visiter* heralded the news with the headline 'Noted Local

Golfer Retires'. He was a smoker, as was his twin, Ricky; both died of lung cancer. Allan Downie died on 26 January 1988 in Southport, Lancashire, and was cremated there.

K. McCARTHY, rev.

Sources *The Independent* (1 Feb 1988) · *Journal of Medical Microbiology*, 28 (1989), 291–5 · D. A. J. Tyrrell and K. McCarthy, *Memoirs FRS*, 35 (1990), 97–112 · *University of Liverpool Recorder* (1966), 20–22 · personal knowledge (1996) · *Journal of Hygiene*, 89 (1982), 353–4 · *Society for General Microbiology Quarterly* (Aug 1988) · *ALMS Newsletter* [Association of Liverpool Medical School], 6 (Sept 1988) · *Aberdeen University News* (c.1957), 179 · *Aberdeen Post Grad. Med. Bulletin*, 22/2 (May 1988), 38–9 · J. Howie, *Portraits from memory* (1988), 131–4 · *The Times* (28 Jan 1988) · *The Lancet* (6 Feb 1988) · K. McCarthy, *Bulletin of the Royal College of Pathologists*, 62 (April 1988), 13–14 · Munk, *Roll* · *Liverpool Echo* (Jan 1988) · *Daily Telegraph* (6 Feb 1988) · *Liverpool Medical Institution Transactions and Report* (1988), 52–3 · *ALMS Newsletter* [Association of Liverpool Medical School], 7 (March 1989), 4
Archives U. Lpool L., papers
Likenesses double portrait, photograph (with Ricky, aged five), repro. in *Journal of Medical Microbiology*, 293 · photograph (on his retirement), U. Lpool, Special Collections and Archives, S71
Wealth at death £46,418: probate, 14 April 1988, *CGPLA Eng. & Wales*

Downing, Arthur Matthew Weld (1850–1917), mathematician and astronomer, was born on 13 April 1850 at Carlow, Ireland, the younger son of Arthur Matthew Downing (b. 1809/10), and his wife, Mary Weld. He was educated at Nutgrove, then a well-known school near Rathfarnham, co. Dublin, and at Trinity College, Dublin, which he entered in November 1866. He specialized in mathematics and graduated in 1871, in which year he won a scholarship in science. In the following year he was successful in an open competition for appointment as an assistant at the Royal Observatory, Greenwich, and he commenced his duties in January 1873.

Downing remained at the observatory for nineteen years, during which time he was concerned primarily with the accurate determination of the positions and motions of stars from very precise measurements made with a variety of astrometric telescopes. He observed regularly for most of this time, but his main concern was with the onerous computations that were required to derive the data published in the catalogues from, for example, the observed times and angular altitudes of the stars as they crossed the spider thread of the telescope. It was necessary to analyse the data to determine the errors of the measurements and to improve the mathematical models that related the telescope on the earth, as it rotated on its axis and revolved around the sun, to the reference frame of the star catalogue.

The principal products of this work were the published star catalogues and the improved accuracy of the determinations of Greenwich time, but Downing also wrote more than fifty scientific papers. The value of his work was recognized by the granting in 1893 of an honorary degree of DSc by Trinity College, Dublin, and by his election in 1896 as a fellow of the Royal Society.

On 1 January 1892 Downing took up the post of superintendent of the *Nautical Almanac* following the resignation of Dr J. Russell Hind. At that time the *Nautical Almanac* office was separate from the Greenwich observatory. Hind had been largely content to leave the almanac unchanged from year to year, but Downing introduced improvements, such as those suggested by the Royal Astronomical Society in 1891, as opportunities arose. He continued to make other investigations; he predicted, correctly, but too late for publication, that the Leonid meteor shower in 1899 would be very disappointing.

In the first edition of the *Nautical Almanac and Astronomical Ephemeris* for which he was responsible, that for 1896, Downing announced that its first part, which contained the data that were needed by navigators at sea for the determination of their positions, would be published separately so that seamen would not need to pay for, or carry, the high-precision data provided for the use of astronomers. In the preface to the edition for 1907 he announced that the tabulations of 'lunar distances', which had been the principal innovation in the first edition for 1767, had been omitted; the widespread use of accurate chronometers had made them unnecessary.

Downing was a major participant in the International Conference on Fundamental Stars that was held at the Paris observatory in 1896. The conference adopted several resolutions concerning the computation and publication of star positions and also led to the adoption for the British and American almanacs of new theories for the computation of the ephemerides of the planets. Downing was strongly criticized by some astronomers for introducing these changes in the edition for 1901 without formally consulting the Royal Astronomical Society, but his decisions were upheld. He retired from the post of superintendent on reaching the age of sixty.

In common with other astronomers at the Greenwich observatory, Downing took an active interest in the affairs of the Royal Astronomical Society and was one of its secretaries (1889–92); he subsequently served as a vice-president. He was one of the founder members of the British Astronomical Association, which was primarily for amateur astronomers, and he served as its president in 1893–5. He organized its first eclipse expedition to the Scandinavian Arctic in 1896 and contributed many articles and unsigned items to its *Journal* and other publications. Some of these would almost certainly have been prompted by the many enquiries that he dealt with in the *Nautical Almanac* office.

Downing was methodical and careful in all his work, and he was fair, courteous, and considerate in his relations with his staff. After his retirement he suffered increasingly from heart disease, and he died at 30 New Oxford Street, Bloomsbury, on 8 December 1917, leaving a widow, Ellen Jane Downing, and their only child, a married daughter. He was cremated on 13 December at Golders Green crematorium.

GEORGE A. WILKINS

Sources W. F. D. [W. F. Dyson] and E. W. M. [E. W. Maunder], *Monthly Notices of the Royal Astronomical Society*, 78 (1917–18), 241–4 · A. S. D. Maunder, *Journal of the British Astronomical Association*, 28 (1917–18), 67–9, 72–3 · A. C. D. Crommelin, *Nature*, 100 (1917–18), 308–9 · *History of the Royal Astronomical Society*, [1]: *1820–1920*, ed. J. L. E. Dreyer and H. H. Turner (1923), 217–18 · d. cert. · Boase, *Mod. Eng. biog.* · Boylan

Archives CUL, archives of the Royal Greenwich Observatory ·
RAS, letters to Royal Astronomical Society
Wealth at death £1584 4s. 6d.: probate, 1 Feb 1918, *CGPLA Eng. &
Wales*

Downing, Calybute (1606–1644), Church of England clergyman and author, was born in Shenington, Gloucestershire, the son of Calybute Downing (d. 1644), lord of the
manor of Sugarswell in Tysoe, Warwickshire, and his
wife, Ann Hoogan (d. 1630), daughter of Edmund Hoogan
of Hackney. He matriculated in 1623 at Emmanuel College, Cambridge, but in the same year migrated to Oriel
College, Oxford, from where he graduated BA in 1626. He
then seems to have been curate at Quainton, Buckinghamshire, where on 2 December 1627 he married Margaret Brett, daughter of the rector, Richard *Brett (1567/8–
1637) [see under Authorized Version of the Bible, translators of the (act. 1604–1611)]. Three daughters and a son of
the couple were baptized at Quainton between 1628 and
1636. Having entered Peterhouse, Cambridge, Downing
proceeded MA in 1630 and LLD in 1637.

By 1632 Downing was chaplain to the earl of Salisbury.
That year he became rector of Ickford, Buckinghamshire,
but resigned in 1636, and in 1637 became both rector of
West Ilsley, Berkshire, and through the influence of Mary,
Lady Vere, vicar of Hackney; he retained the latter
through the support of Archbishop Laud despite the
objections of the previous incumbent.

Other hopes for advancement were disappointed. An
unsuccessful competitor against Gilbert Sheldon for the
wardenship of All Souls College, Oxford, Downing was,
according to Anthony Wood, 'a great suitor to be chaplain
to … [the earl] of Strafford … thinking that employment
the readiest way to be a bishop. And whilst he had hopes of
that preferment, he writ stoutly in justification of that
calling' (Wood, *Ath. Oxon.*, 3.106). His *A Discourse of the State
Ecclesiasticall of this Kingdome, in Relation to the Civill* (1632),
dedicated to the earl of Salisbury, argued that 'aristocratic' or episcopal church government was best suited to
the English state, which he conceived as 'a free
Monarchie, erected and protected by free concent' (*Discourse of the State Ecclesiasticall*, 3). He condemned both
'monarchical' (papist) and democratic church government, and deplored the authority granted by the latter to
lay elders: Calvin, he said, did not intend the rule of lay
elders 'as an universall perpetuall government' (ibid., 19).
The contrast with Downing's later position is striking, but
the seeds of its evolution were already present. Although
his perspective was aggressively protestant, his argument
was political and legal as much as religious; it revealed his
background in civil law, which gave his opinions a markedly secular and international dimension. The form of
church government was not immutable but should be
that 'which is most agreeing with the Civill State' (ibid., 2)
and its safety, and under its 'dominion and protection'
(ibid., 43). Here Downing praised the 'happie hartie unitie'
(ibid., 19) of English church government, but his views of
the church's and the country's happiness were to change
radically.

By 1640 Downing was associated with the leading puritan clergy in London, although he was probably not, as
has been said, Cornelius Burgess's partner in the circulation of the ministers' petition against the Laudian canons.
On 1 September 1640, in *A Sermon Preached to the Renowned
Company of the Artillery*, he blamed the Jesuits for breeding
bad blood between 'the best of Princes' and his people,
and for 'breaking … the happy Union of the Kingdomes' (*A
Sermon*, 27, 31). The king nevertheless remained ultimately
responsible: 'when a party in power breaks the Laws of
the Land' subjects may be forced 'to make a stand'. The
'Laws of Nations' allowed that the principle of *salus populi*
could override even good laws that had been so abused
that the subject's security was endangered (ibid., 27–8, 36–
7). In conclusion Downing quoted 'Rationall Grotius' (discreetly in Latin) to confirm that in such cases the law of
non-resistance to the prince did not hold, and declared
that the representative body of a kingdom 'may goe very
far, before they can be counted rebels' (ibid., 37–8). This
influential sermon, which rejected the major arguments
for undeviating obedience to the state and was published
in 1641 by order of the House of Commons, marked a
decisive stage in the legitimization of resistance to the
king. *A Letter from Mercurius Civicus to Mercurius Rusticus*
(1643) declared that Downing was the willing tool of the
puritan leaders who wished 'to feele the pulse of the Citty'
in response to the doctrine 'that for defence of Religion
and Reformation, it was lawfull to take up armes against
the King' (p. 8).

After preaching the sermon Downing had taken refuge
at Leez, the earl of Warwick's house in Essex, 'the common Randevous of all Schysmaticall Preachers' (*Letter from
Mercurius Civicus*, 8). Two of the products of his retirement,
A Discoverie of the False Grounds (1641) and *A Discourse upon the
Interest of England* (1641), urging intervention in support of
the Palatinate, primarily reflected Downing's interest in
civil and international law and geopolitics, in particular
the threat of the extension of Austrian power. *Considerations toward a Peaceable Reformation* (1641) argued for moderation in religious reformation as the way to compose
differences, while *A Discoursive Conjecture upon … the Present
Troubles of Great Britaine* (1641) was more vindictive, but
none the less held out the hope that punishment of evil
advisers offered the king the opportunity to prevent civil
war and open the way to 'new endearing obligations' (*A
Discoursive Conjecture*, 42).

Downing's position was hardening, however. In late
1641 or early 1642 he published anonymously *An Appeale to
Everye Impartiall, Judicious and Godly Reader*, which
unequivocally put the case for a presbyterian form of
church organization. It was republished in 1644 as *The
Cleere Antithesis or Diametricall Opposition betweene Presbytery
and Prelacy* (when George Thomason identified Downing
as the author), and again in 1645. On 31 August 1642 Downing preached what Simonds D'Ewes called a 'dangerous
seditious' fast sermon to the House of Commons (Greaves
& Zaller, *BDBR*, 1.234), possibly that in which he declared, 'I
have studied obedience as much as in me lyeth … I find
obedience due to the king as king in parliament, but not as

head of factious villains, and the very scum of the kingdom' (Ellesmere MS 6874).

By mid-1642 Downing was lecturer at Stepney, but in August he was appointed chaplain to Lord Robartes's regiment in the earl of Essex's army, and served until May 1643. He preached at Reading after Essex's capture of the town in April 1643. On 20 June he was appointed by parliament one of the licensers of books of divinity. According to Wood in 1643 he took the covenant and was a member of the Westminster assembly, but left them and sided with the Independents, preaching so assiduously in their support and against rapprochement with the king that he was known as Young Peters or Hugh Peters the Second. That year he also resigned his livings at Hackney and West Ilsley.

Early in 1644, in Hackney, Downing suddenly died, 'to the great grief of his aged father' (Wood, *Ath. Oxon.*, 3.108). In the course of his relatively short career he had progressed from upholder of the status quo in church and state to advocate of resistance and radical change. This progression was shared by many of his countrymen; Downing's was one of the public voices that gave it impetus and legitimacy.   BARBARA DONAGAN

Sources Wood, *Ath. Oxon.*, new edn, 3.105–8 · A. Laurence, *Parliamentary army chaplains, 1642–1651*, Royal Historical Society Studies in History, 59 (1990), 122 · *A letter from Mercurius Civicus to Mercurius Rusticus* (1643), 8–9 · Foster, *Alum. Oxon.* · Venn, *Alum. Cant.* · Greaves & Zaller, *BDBR*, 233–4 · *JHL*, 4 (1628–42), 117 · *JHC*, 2 (1640–42), 694, 746–7; 3 (1642–4), 138 · *The works of the most reverend father in God, William Laud*, 4, ed. J. Bliss (1854), 298 · Hunt. L., Ellesmere MS 6874 · *Fourth report*, HMC, 3 (1874), 2–114, esp. 33, 35 [House of Lords] · V. Pearl, *London and the outbreak of the puritan revolution: city government and national politics, 1625–1643* (1961), 41–2 · P. S. Seaver, *The puritan lectureships: the politics of religious dissent, 1560–1662* (1970), 367–8
Wealth at death see will, PRO, PROB 11/192, sig. 15

Downing, Sir George, first baronet (1623–1684), diplomat and financial reformer, was born in Dublin in August 1623, the son of Emmanuel Downing (1585–1659), attorney and clerk, of the Inner Temple and Lucy (1601–1679), sister of John Winthrop, first governor of the colony of Massachusetts Bay. Emmanuel Downing, the son of an Ipswich schoolmaster, attended Trinity Hall, Cambridge, in 1602. His first marriage was to Anne Ware, and following her death he married Lucy Winthrop in 1622. In 1626 he returned from Dublin to London to become an attorney of the court of wards. In 1638, at Winthrop's invitation, the godly Downings emigrated to Salem, Massachusetts, where their minister was Emmanuel's 'cosen', the future regicide Hugh Peter. George Downing later stated that his father had been 'banished to New England'. Emmanuel and Lucy remained in the colony until 1655, when George secured his father's appointment as clerk to the Scottish council. Thereafter they lived happily in Cromwellian Edinburgh until Emmanuel's death in 1659.

Early life In 1640 George Downing attended Harvard College and in 1642 became the second ranking member of its first graduating class. On 27 December 1643 he was appointed, on a stipend of £4 per annum, 'to read to the Junior pupills as the Prsident shall see fit' (De Kay, 56B–C). His mother having 'perceive [d that] he is strongly inclined to travill', Downing left Salem in 1645, as ship's chaplain, for Barbados and elsewhere in the Caribbean (*Winthrop Papers*, 5.42–5). From there he made his way to England, where, in 1646, he became chaplain in the dragoon regiment of Colonel John Okey in the New Model Army. Thomas Edwards describes a sermon delivered at Hackney in August of the same year by 'one Master Downing a preacher of the Army, and a young Peters, as he was called' (T. Edwards, *Gangraena*, 1646, pt 3, 81–2). On 8 March 1648 Downing informed Winthrop that 'Sir Arthur Hezilrige (with whom I live) is appointed Governour of New Castle upon Tyne ... and I am suddainely to go with him thither' (*Winthrop Papers*, 5.207–8). Downing became chaplain to Hesilrige's regiment at Newcastle. In 1657 John Thurloe was still keeping Downing informed of the 'horrible ... blusterings' of 'your old great friend, of the North' and in January 1660 Pepys reported: 'Mr Downing this day feasted Sir Arth Haselrig and a great many more of the Parliament' (BL, Add. MS 22919, fol. 11; Pepys, 1.23). As Okey had once been a major in Hesilrige's regiment, so Hesilrige's military superior was now Cromwell. Cromwell signed Downing's appointment as scoutmaster-general of the English army in Scotland on 1 November 1649 at a salary of £365 per annum. By October 1654 he was reporting from London on the health of 'his hyghnesse' to the commander-in-chief of forces in Scotland, Monck (BL, Egerton MS 2618, fol. 46). His principal duty as scoutmaster was the gathering of intelligence: such a person 'generally kept spies in his employment' (C. H. Firth, *Cromwell's Army*, 1962, 65). These skills were to play a major part in Downing's subsequent interpretation of his role as a diplomat.

Republic and protectorate In Scotland, Downing fought in 'the great victory' of Dunbar (3 September 1650) where he 'received 3 great wounds on his arme besides others' (*Winthrop Papers*, 6.184). He participated in the 'crowning mercy' of the defeat of Charles II at Worcester one year later, of which he furnished one of the most important written descriptions (H. Cary, *Memorials of the Great Civil War*, 2 vols., 1842, 2.357–9). He worked closely with the council of state in London, both by letter and in person. Some of his letters and accounts of Scottish affairs were published in the contemporary newsbook *Mercurius Politicus*; others appear in later compilations. By October 1652 Hugh Peter was remarking upon Downing's wealth. In 1654 he married Lady Frances Howard (d. 1683), sister of the future earl of Carlisle. 'Under ... Countenance ... [of] particular credit' with Cromwell, reported Clarendon, 'he married a very beautiful Lady of a very Noble Extraction ... which was the fate of many bold men in that presumptuous time' (Clarendon, 2.50). In 1656 he became a teller of the receipt in the exchequer on a salary of £500 a year.

Downing was a member of all three protectoral parliaments, first for Edinburgh (1654) and then Carlisle (1656,

1659). In this context he distinguished himself by his economic warnings against the Dutch—'they are far too politic for us in point of trade, and do eat us out in our manufactures' (*Diary of Thomas Burton*, 1.181)—and by his pragmatic speech on 19 January 1657 in favour of return to the old constitution: 'The people must not be fitted to the government but the government to the people' (Beresford, 73). His first diplomatic mission had followed the massacre of protestants in Piedmont in April 1655. His instructions were to proceed via Paris and Geneva to Turin to protest on Cromwell's behalf. By the time he reached Geneva in early September, French pressure had already ended the conflict and he was recalled. In Paris, however, he had enjoyed a two-hour conversation of notable cordiality with Mazarin (conducted in Latin) which registered the new reality of English power on the European stage. 'Of all things in the world' he reported, Mazarin 'desired a right understanding with his hyghnesse; that he would do anything in his power to evidence it' (Thurloe, *State papers*, 3.734).

Downing's next assignment, as envoy to The Hague from November 1657, was crucial to protectoral foreign policy as also to the remainder of his own career. His general mission was to cement an Anglo-Dutch amity of 'very deep concernment to all protestants and Reformed Princes and States' against the Counter-Reformation enemy (Downing, letter book, pp. 3–6). More particularly he sought to deter Dutch support for Spain against Portugal, and for Denmark against Sweden. In addition he applied himself vigorously to altering the conditions which had 'made this place a meere nursery of cavaleerisme' (Thurloe, *State papers*, 246). This involved lobbying the Dutch republican government for action against those 'phanatiques … Charles Steward and other rebels of England' (ibid., 7.379, 444–5). It involved establishing a network of spies reporting through Downing to Thurloe. So successful was he in this, he reported, that a group of royalist assassins, including the 'one that killed Dr Dorislaus … [had] come with designe and order to kill me' (ibid., 7.334).

Finally it was during this period that Downing began to apply himself to the study of Dutch fiscal and economic policies. One feature of Dutch state revenue was its reliance upon the excise, combined with a low revenue yield from customs duties, which were regarded as inhibiting trade. Downing accordingly accompanied his 'playne truth' to Monck in 1659 that 'if you will be able to pay taxes you must lower your customes very greatly, and raise it by way of excise' with detailed proposals to this effect (Firth, 3.178). More generally Dutch success hinged upon the interdependence of fiscal and military power. On the one hand a precondition for Dutch success in trade was the state's willingness to protect it militarily. 'In this very thinge', Downing wrote [the fact that merchant fleets were convoyed] 'is the mystery of this state' (Scott, 34). This in turn made the Dutch prepared to pay enormous taxes. Downing first noticed this observing the great 'sea equipage' being prepared to assist Denmark in 1659. It is

strange to see with what readyness this people doe consent to extraordinary taxes, although their ordinary taxes be yett as great as they were dureinge the warr with Spaine … men doe not heere beleeve that you will be able to possess any English parliament … to contribute in a farr lesser degree. (Firth, 3.174–5)

It was not simply that 'Downing's lasting contribution to England's economic destiny was that he brought to bear his observation of Dutch economic practice on English economic theory and policy' (Wilson, 95). It was crucial to Downing's subsequent contribution to English statebuilding that his situation outside the country exposed him to a European perspective upon the process.

[I]t's not enough to say what moneyes were sufficient for England in former times, for then England's revenue though small, yet held proportion with the revenues of neighbouring Princes and States about them, and that must be the rule now, or England is undone. (Firth, 3.178)

Restoration politics It was with understandable anxiety that, in March 1660, Downing wrote to Thurloe: 'I shold be infinitely obliged to you, that you would a little let me know what things are like to come to' (Thurloe, *State papers*, 7.837–8). The following month he made his approach to Charles (still in exile) through one of his agents, Thomas Howard. Howard assured the marquess of Ormond that Downing

wished the promoting of your Majesty's service, which he confessed he had endeavoured to obstruct … alledging to be engaged in a contrary party by his father who was banished to New England, where he … had sucked in principles that since his reason had made him see were erroneous … and to assure me that he was real in [this desire] … he shewed me a letter he received that morning (all in cypher …) from Thurloe, which gave him an account of the intention of the army. (T. Carte, *A Collection of Original Letters and Papers*, 2 vols., 1739, 5 April 1660)

His overture accepted, he was knighted, on 12 May 1660, calling his secretary, Pepys, to him the following day 'to tell me that I must write him *Sir G. Downing*' (Pepys, 1.153). Thereafter, reassigned to The Hague, Downing sought to demonstrate his usefulness by putting the skills learned during the 1650s to service in the royal cause. As he later boasted to Pepys: he

had so good spies, that he hath had the keys taken out of De Witts pocket when he was a-bed, and his closet opened and the papers brought to him and left in his hands for an [hour], and carried back and laid in the place again and the keys put in his pocket again. (ibid., 9.402)

His efforts culminated in 1662 in the triumph of scoutmastering from which his personal reputation would never recover: the apprehension and return for execution in England of the three regicides John Okey, Miles Corbet, and John Barkstead. It was not simply that the men had effectively been kidnapped on the territory of a foreign sovereign state. On the scaffold it fell to Okey to forgive his own 'Chaplaine who pursued my life to the Death' (*Speeches*).

This achievement brought Downing a baronetcy (1662) and the personal attention of the king. Lucrative offices followed, culminating in a commissionership of customs from 1671 at a salary of £2000 a year, until Evelyn could report that 'From a pedagogue and fanatic preacher not worth a groat he has become excessive rich' and parliamentary gossip that 'He keeps 6 whores in pay and yett has got £40,000' (BL, Lansdowne MS 805, p. 86). As the tone of these remarks suggests, however, the action which secured his fortune also established him as the new standard in unscrupulous self-interest. Pepys recorded: 'all the world takes notice of him for a most ungrateful villaine for his pains … though the action is good and of service to the King, yet he cannot with any good conscience do it' (Pepys, 3.44, 47–8). In 'New-England … it became a proverbial expression, to say of a false man who betrayed his trust, that he was an arrant George Downing' (De Kay, 56B; Hutchinson, 97).

Yet it would be misleading to mistake Downing's royalist overcompensation for royalism proper. His deeper allegiance was to his own experience in studying the source of national fiscal and military power, first under the English, and then the Dutch republics. Accordingly he found the restoration not only of monarchy, but monarchical military ineffectuality, deeply exasperating. 'This is that', he reported to the earl of Clarendon in 1661, 'with which continually heer they shune the king and trifle wt can he do he hath no money' (Bodl. Oxf., MS Clarendon 105, fol. 152). In July Clarendon was forced to warn Downing to restrain his bellicosity—'I pray remember the streights … we are in for money, the emptiness of all our stores and magazines, etc,'—and to reprimand him for claiming a diplomatic status to which he was not entitled—'I was sure there must be some mistake, and that you knew too well the formes to be observed, to demand anything that was not your dew' (Bodl. Oxf., MS Clarendon 104, fols. 3, 8). The following year Pepys was informed

> of a speech [Downing] made to the Lords States of Holland, telling them to their faces that he observed that he was not received with the respect and observance now, that he was when he came from that Traitor and Rebell Cromwell. (Pepys, 3.45)

When rumours circulated in 1662 of the sale of the Cromwellian acquisition of Dunkirk Downing could not contain himself.

> I … give no credit thereunto … I confesse that I am such a doting foole in this point that I had rather … let his Majesty have … the litle I have in the world … then that he should want where withall to maintaine this place: England was never considerable … since it wanted a footing on this side the water … should [France] thus go about to take it away … they would find there is now alive, that old brave English blood and spirit that hath shewed itself on this side the water in former ages. (BL, Egerton MS 2538, fol. 35)

From 1661 to 1665 Downing's insistence upon resolute English action against Dutch pretensions was sufficiently aggressive to be accounted a cause of the ensuing war. Following failure in that war Pepys recorded:

> He … alway[s] had their most private debates … but between two or three of them, brought to him in an hour after, and an hour after that … sent word thereof to the King—but nobody here regarded them. (Pepys, 9.402)

Downing's disregard for the judgement of his superiors culminated in six weeks in the Tower in 1672 for disobeying his instructions during a disastrous final mission to the United Provinces. This had featured a remarkable letter from the king:

> because I find you … divided in your opinion betwixt what seemes good to you for my affaires … and what my instructions direct you … I have thought fitt to send you my last minde … in my owne hand … that you may know … it is your part to obey punctually my orders, instead of putting yourselfe to the trouble of finding reasons why you do not do so. (BL, Add. MS 35858, fol. 262)

Restoration finance It is against the same background, however, that Downing's extraordinary contribution to Restoration fiscal reconstruction and state building, the basis of his real historical importance, must be understood. In 1661 he wrote to Clarendon:

> I would to God … something [were] done … for the augmentation of his Majesties Revenue … his Majesty cannot keepe … neither honour nor interest with his neighbours, and … the Trade of England cannot have its necessary protection and incouragement unlesse his Majesty have a much greater Revenue. (Bodl. Oxf., MS Clarendon 104, fol. 37)

There followed eleven proposals to this end, including a variety of new taxes, especially excise taxes, a range of new charges and licences, and proposals for 'Additional Acts for the better collecting of both Customes and Excises' (Bodl. Oxf., MS Clarendon 104, fols. 252–254). In fact, as a member of the Convention, Downing had already had a major influence on the initial Restoration fiscal settlement. He had been instrumental in its retention of the Commonwealth's excise and had overseen its revision and re-enactment of the 1651 Navigation Acts. More broadly, 'Downing's name appears, after 1656, in connexion with every important Act affecting navigation and colonial trade for more than a century' (Wilson, 94–103). Between 1656 and 1681 he

> was nominated to over four hundred [parliamentary] committees, in several cases as the leading member. In the Restoration Parliaments alone he participated actively in framing nearly seventy public statutes as well as some fifty private bills … Of economic legislation his hand was on two thirds … Over one hundred recorded speeches confirm and amplify the record. On this showing Downing emerges as one of the most remarkable legislative entrepreneurs of his times. (Roseveare, 'Prejudice', 138)

His most spectacular achievement came in 1665. The reform embodied by the Act for the Additional Aid was 'the most important financial experiment of the period'. By its 'technique of raising credit upon Orders, registered and repayable in course … an entirely new credit structure was erected' (Chandaman, 216–17). That this was Downing's brainchild is confirmed both by Clarendon and Pepys. Although it began as an emergency wartime measure the principle of appropriation was regularized and applied to the ordinary revenue from 1667.

Most important, Downing's 'new Method' applied to English state finances for the first time the two features that were to be fundamental to its longer term success between 1689 and 1714. The first of these was 'the acquisition by the Commons of the power of appropriating its supplies, the first significant limitation of the financial freedom of the action of the executive' (Chandaman, 278). The second was the importation into English fiscal practice of those features of Dutch public credit which would stand at the heart of the subsequent 'financial revolution' of the 1690s. It did these things despite the fact that in 1665 the United Provinces was a republic and England a monarchy. Its effect was to strengthen the English state by reducing monarchical power. It is for just these reasons that Downing's scheme was opposed by Clarendon with a passion which helped to end Clarendon's political career.

> Downing ... told them ... by making the Payment with Interest so certain and fixed, that ... it should be out of any Man's Power to cause any Money that should be lent To-morrow to be paid before that which was lent Yesterday ... he would make [the] Exchequer ... the best and the greatest Bank in Europe ... and all Nations would sooner send their Money into [it] ... than into *Amsterdam* or *Genoa* or *Venice*. And it cannot be enough wondered at, that this Intoxication prevailed so far that no Argument would be heard against it ... without weighing that the Security for Monies so deposited in Banks is the Republick itself, which must expire before that Security can fail; which can never be depended on in a Monarchy, where the Monarch's sole word can cancel all those formal Provisions.   (Clarendon, 2.195–6)

Thereafter his majesty having announced that he wished to 'new-model' the Treasury itself in the hands of 'rough and illnatured men, not to be moved with Civilities or Importunities in the Payment of Money', it was no surprise when Downing became secretary to the new commissioners (ibid., 2.215). In the subsequent fundamental reform of Treasury management, administration, and record keeping he played the most important role.

Downing's achievement built not only upon his experience and ability, but upon his ruthlessness, ambition, and energy. To the latter, hundreds of diplomatic letters remain as testimony. As he put it to Thurloe in 1658: 'I have so much to doe, that I have halfe kild them that are about me, wanting help' (Thurloe, *State papers*, 6.851–3). He was, said Pepys, 'a man of the old ways, for taking pains' (Roseveare, 'Prejudice', 136). Thus if he ended his days on his estate at Gamlingay, East Hatley, the richest landowner in Cambridgeshire, and yet still notorious for his meanness, he had contributed far more still to the fiscal development of a kingdom soon to become a great power. Downing died in Gamlingay in July 1684, a year after his wife, and was buried beside her on 24 July in the chancel of Croydon church, Cambridgeshire.

JONATHAN SCOTT

Sources J. Beresford, *The godfather of Downing Street: Sir George Downing, 1623–1684* (1925) · G. Downing, letters to the earl of Clarendon, Bodl. Oxf., MSS Clarendon 104–108 · Pepys, *Diary* · Thurloe, *State papers* · *The Winthrop papers*, ed. W. C. Ford and others, 4–6 (1944–92) · G. Downing, letters to Edward Nicholas, BL, Egerton MS 2538 · H. Colenbrander, ed., *Bescheiden uit vreemde Archieven omtrent de groote Nederlandsche Zeeoorlogen, 1652–1676*, 2 vols. (1919), vol. 1 · *The life of Edward, earl of Clarendon ... written by himself*, 2 vols. (1760) · J. Scott, 'The pragmatic republicanism of Sir George Downing, 1623–1684', *Essays on the history of Downing College*, ed. P. Millett (2000) · H. Roseveare, 'Prejudice and policy: Sir George Downing as parliamentary entrepreneur', *Enterprise and history: essays in honour of Charles Wilson*, ed. D. C. Coleman and P. Mathias (1984), 135–50 · G. Downing, *A reply of Sir George Downing knight and baronet ... to the remarks of the deputies of the estates-general, upon his memorial of December 20 1664* (1665) · G. Downing, letter-book, 1658, Downing College, Cambridge · G. Downing, *A discourse written by Sir George Downing vindicating his royal master* (1664) · *Mercurius Politicus* (1650–51) · C. D. Chandaman, *The English public revenue, 1660–1688* (1975) · *The Clarke papers*, ed. C. H. Firth, 3, CS, new ser., 61 (1899) · O. De Kay, 'George Downing: "As Arrant a Rascal as Lives Amongst Men"', *Discovery* [special supplement of *Harvard Magazine*] (March–April 1981) · C. Wilson, *Profit and power: a study of England and the Dutch wars* (1957) · H. Roseveare, *The treasury, 1660–1870: the foundations of control* (1973) · T. Hutchinson, *The history of the colony and province of Massachusetts-Bay*, ed. L. S. Mayo, 1 (1936) · *Diary of Thomas Burton*, ed. J. T. Rutt, 4 vols. (1828) · *The speeches, discourses and prayers of ... Barkstead, ... Okey, and ... Corbet* (1662)

Archives BL, corresp. and papers, Add. MSS 22919–22920 · Downing College, Cambridge | All Souls Oxf., letters to Sir William Temple · BL, Egerton MSS 2618, 2538 · BL, letters to Sir Edward Nicholas, Egerton MSS 2537–2538 · Bodl. Oxf., Clarendon MSS · Bodl. Oxf., Rawlinson MSS A · Bodl. Oxf., Thurloe state MSS · PRO, state papers, foreign, Holland

Likenesses oils, priv. coll.; repro. in Beresford, *Godfather of Downing Street*, frontispiece · oils, Harvard U.

Wealth at death extensive estates in Cambridgeshire and valuable property, with buildings in progress, in London (site of future Downing Street): Beresford, *Godfather of Downing Street*, ch. 7 and appx C

Downing, Sir George, third baronet (1685–1749), benefactor of Downing College, Cambridge, was born at East Hatley, Cambridgeshire, the only son of Sir George Downing, second baronet (d. 1711), and Catherine (d. 1688), eldest daughter of James, third earl of Salisbury. His grandfather was Sir George *Downing, first baronet. After his mother's death on 13 August 1688 he was brought up chiefly by his uncle Sir William Forester of Dothill, near Wellington, Shropshire, and his wife, Mary, third daughter of Lord Salisbury. In February 1700 Sir William took the opportunity of secretly marrying Downing, then aged fifteen, to his thirteen-year-old daughter, Mary. Soon afterwards Downing went abroad, and on returning home, after about three years' absence, refused either to live with or acknowledge his wife. In 1715 he supported her unsuccessful petition for divorce and two years later secured legal sanction for the couple to live separately. Downing had one daughter with a Mary Townsend, for whom he provided a dowry of £20,000.

Downing succeeded his father as third baronet in June 1711. He was elected for the pocket borough of Dunwich, Suffolk, in the parliaments of 1710 and 1713, but lost the election of 1715. In 1722, however, he regained his seat which, with the aid of a 99-year lease from the crown for the borough, he secured and occupied until his death. He was a dutiful if uninspiring supporter of the Walpole and Pelham ministries, for which he was created a knight of the Bath on 30 June 1732. Downing died at his seat, Gamlingay Park, Cambridgeshire, on 10 June 1749 having, according to the Cambridge antiquary William Cole, 'for the latter part of his life led a most miserable, covetous, and sordid existence' (Sedgwick, 1.620). In a codicil to his will, dated 23 December 1727, he left £500 p.a. to his daughter and £200 p.a. to Mary Townsend. By the original document, drawn up in 1717, he had bequeathed estates in

Sir George Downing, third baronet (1685–1749), by unknown artist

Cambridgeshire, Bedfordshire, and Suffolk in trust for his cousin Jacob Garrard Downing (c.1717–1764) and his male heirs, with remainder to other relatives in like manner. Should the male line fail the trustees were directed to purchase

> some piece of ground lying and being in the town of Cambridge, proper and convenient for the erecting and building a college, which college shall be called by the name of Downing's College; and my will is, that a charter royal be sued for and obtained for the founding such college, and incorporating a body collegiate by that name.

Upon Downing's will being proved (13 June 1749) it was found that the trustees had predeceased him. His cousin, who married Margaret Price in 1750, died without children on 6 February 1764. In addition all the parties entitled in remainder were now deceased without heirs.

In the year of Jacob Garrard Downing's death an information was filed in the court of chancery at the relation of the chancellor, masters, and scholars of Cambridge University against the heirs-at-law. The lord chancellor gave judgment on 3 July 1769,

> declaring the will of the testator well proved, and that the same ought to be established, and the trusts thereof performed and carried into execution, in case the king should be pleased to grant a royal charter to incorporate the college. (Willis and Clark, 2.756)

The estates, however, remained in possession of the Downing family, and afterwards of its devisees, without any real title. Their opposition, coupled with additional litigation, delayed the charter, which passed the great seal on 22 September 1800. Debate over the location and design of the college further delayed building work, which eventually began on 18 May 1807.

GORDON GOODWIN, rev. PHILIP CARTER

Sources R. R. Sedgwick, 'Downing, George', HoP, Commons, 1715–54 · R. Willis, *The architectural history of the University of Cambridge, and of the colleges of Cambridge and Eton*, ed. J. W. Clark, 4 vols. (1886); repr. (1988) · P. Searby, *A history of the University of Cambridge*, 3: 1750–1870, ed. C. N. L. Brooke and others (1997) · GM, 1st ser., 19 (1749), 284 · GM, 1st ser., 34 (1764), 97

Likenesses oils, Downing College, Cambridge [see illus.]

Wealth at death £500 for daughter; £200 p.a. for partner; estates bequeathed to trustees for establishment of Downing College, Cambridge, in event of end of male line through cousin: will, 13 June 1749

Downing, Joseph (1676–1734), printer and bookseller, was born into a family of London printers, the second of four sons of William and Ann Downing. He learned his trade in the family printing shop in Bartholomew Close, near West Smithfield, and took over responsibility for the business on his father's death. Shortly afterwards Downing became free of the Stationers' Company by patrimony, and by 1705 he was binding apprentices in his own right. He took the company's livery in 1706 and held minor office in 1713–14, but never became a member of the court. From 1703 Downing was closely associated with the Society for Promoting Christian Knowledge (SPCK), later also with the Society for Propagating the Gospel. The former, founded in 1698, had as one of its major aims the dissemination of devotional literature among sections of the population that were losing a formal connection with the church. The association with the SPCK enabled Downing to build up a substantial business, specializing in printing and distributing large quantities of cheap, improving tracts intended to be read by a wide and increasingly literate public.

Downing was not the society's servant. His imprint (unlike those of his successors) does not refer to the SPCK directly, nor do his catalogues make explicit reference to the connection between the titles listed and the society. Although the society distributed only those it selected, publication was probably regarded by Downing almost as having its imprimatur. This explains incidents such as that in December 1703, when Downing was reprimanded by the society's committee for printing a translation from the French that contained 'many dangerous points' (Jefcoate, 321). After this the minutes of the twice-monthly SPCK committee meetings record relatively few signs of dissatisfaction with their printer, though they occasionally sought to advise him on matters such as appropriate binders or advertising. He rarely appeared before the committee in person, often sending a representative if requested to do so. As membership changed with time, the committee sought to establish the society's precise relationship with Downing. On occasion, he was obliged to renounce his right in the society's titles printed by him. Nevertheless, the connection continued, apparently to mutual benefit, for the remainder of his life.

Downing's achievement was to develop a profitable business in a specialist area of the book trade at a time when the spread of literacy was creating a market for such material. This was based on the printing of large quantities of a relatively small number of tracts on social topics of particular concern to SPCK members—for example swearing, drunkenness, uncleanness, lying, and breaches of the Lord's day. Some were intended for specific groups, such as prisoners, soldiers, or even London boatmen. Downing's interest in spreading literacy took practical expression with his own published *Proposal for Teaching Poor Children to Read*, in which he calculates that a child could be taught to read for an investment of only 10s. He was a trustee of London charity schools, and left £50 to the charity school of his own parish.

A catalogue issued in 1707 (wholly revised in 1708) was addressed to 'all pious and charitable persons (especially as live in the country) who are religiously disposed to give any number of [books] to their friends, dependents, or others' (Jefcoate, 322). Prices are supplied for books singly or 'by the hundred &c.' Items could be selected to make up parcels of improving tracts on a range of subjects. Nevertheless, Downing's publishing activities were not restricted entirely to mass markets for cheap print, as his long connection with the German pastor Anton Wilhelm Böhm (1673–1722) demonstrates. This enabled the distribution in the English-speaking world of translations and adaptations of many of the key texts of Lutheran pietism. In addition Downing printed Böhm's sermons and other works for London's own Lutheran parishes, some of the first examples of printing in London in the German vernacular. Downing died in 1734, after which the business (and SPCK connection) was continued by his widow, Martha, of whom further details are unknown.

GRAHAM JEFCOATE

Sources G. Jefcoate, 'Joseph Downing and the publication of pietist literature in England, 1705–1734', *The German book, 1450–1750*, ed. J. L. Flood and W. A. Kelly (1995), 319–32

Downman, Hugh (1740–1809), physician and poet, son of Hugh Downman (*d*. 1789), of Newton St Cyres, Exeter, and his wife, Anne, was born on 7 February 1740 at Alphington, near Exeter. He was educated at Exeter Free Grammar School and entered Balliol College, Oxford, in 1758. After graduating BA in 1763 he was ordained by Bishop Keppel on 3 July that year. In the meantime he had formed an attachment to Frances (1748–1822), second daughter of Dr Andrew, an eminent physician in Exeter and a near relative of Lord Courtenay. Seeing that his prospects as a priest offered scant reward, Downman decided on a career in medicine and moved to Edinburgh where he spent three years, boarding at the house of the blind poet and orator Thomas Blacklock. Here he met and befriended, as fellow lodgers, three west country medical students, Penny, Warren, and Birdwood.

In 1769 Downman moved to London where he attended hospital practice during one winter, proceeding MA at Jesus College, Cambridge, in 1770, and receiving a licence to practise. On 18 July 1771, on the death of Dr Andrew, Downman was appointed one of the physicians to the Devon and Exeter Hospital, at the same time receiving the degree of MD of Aberdeen. His marriage to Frances

Andrew took place on 20 December that year; they lived in St Paul's Street, Exeter, and despite his chronic ill health they lived in uninterrupted harmony for nearly forty years, often interspersed with distressing scenes of pain and sickness.

Downman had already published in 1768 *The Land of the Muses*, a poem in the manner of Spenser, and wrote a number of lightweight poems in adoration of his future wife and under the influence of the merry Blacklock, himself an average if prolific poet. Now Downman embarked on his best known poem, a long didactic work in three books, *Infancy, or, The Management of Children*, published in 1774–6. It was well received and eventually published as a single volume; Downman just lived to see the ninth edition in 1809. The poem is written in Miltonic blank verse in a style that combines flowery classicism somewhat incongruously with medical phraseology. It is full of good sense, and crusades against superstition and meddlesome practices, often personified in the baleful figure of the 'vaunting midwife', presuming upon her nostrums. Cameron points out a telling deviation from the main theme in which the author refers to his own fractured health, a thumbnail sketch of a sufferer from consumption:

Can I then hope, whom sickness long hath drench'd
In her Lethean dews, with feeble limbs
And wan complection …
(Cameron, 106)

Three cardinal symptoms—fever, weakness, and pallor—appear in this short passage. Downman was an early advocate of breastfeeding, with notes on choosing a wet nurse, hygiene, and nutrition. He also advocated smallpox inoculation and lauded Lady Mary Wortley Montagu. His *Poems to Thespia* appeared first in 1781, also in 1791 and 1792, 'the accumulated annual offering at the shrine of conjugal affection'. Thespia was his wife, Frances, but there were many sonnets dedicated to medical and literary colleagues. Less known, published in 1775, were *The Drama, an Elegy Written under a Gallows*, and *The Soliloquy*. He wrote a number of plays, with indifferent success, which were subsequently published in one volume as *Tragedies* (1792). The best of these, *Lucius Junius Brutus* (1779), was never performed. *The Death Song of Ragnar Lodbrach* (1781) he translated from the Latin of Olaus Wormius, and also in 1781 he was one of the translators of an edition of Voltaire's works into English. He also contributed in large measure to his friend Richard Polwhele's *Collections of the Poetry of Devon and Cornwall* (1792).

After seven years Downman was obliged to resign from the hospital on 20 August 1778 on grounds of ill health, described as 'a chronic complaint'. He made some recovery, however, and was reinstated on 28 December 1781. Among his literary activities was the foundation of a literary group, the Society of Gentlemen at Exeter, which published a volume of essays in 1796; Downman wrote the introduction and three additional pieces. The society originally had nine members, subsequently increased to twelve, all of some distinction; they included Richard Polwhele and Isaac d'Israeli, father of Benjamin Disraeli, who became a friend and patient of Downman in 1795. While at Exeter d'Israeli wrote some verses in Downman's praise which were published in an anonymous pamphlet in 1807. The society survived for nearly twelve years but enthusiasm waned with the health of its founder and meetings were discontinued. Downman's portrait (painted in oils by his cousin John Downman in 1796) shows a strong, wide-eyed, well-proportioned face, youthful considering his fifty-six years. He resigned from the hospital for the second time on 31 October 1802 and finally gave up his practice in 1805. With his frequent periods of ill health, it seems unlikely that he died a wealthy man; during one bout of illness he spoke of 'living on the verge of want'. In his will a substantial property known as Ford, situated in the parish of Newton St Cyres, was left to trustees, the income to provide a small annuity for his kinsman John Downman and his wife, and for his own wife. A codicil mentions a manganese mine, in the same location. It seems likely that the conjugal home in St Paul's Street was disposed of in 1806, since an auction sale of the contents was advertised in June of that year. Downman died at Alphington on 23 September 1809 and was buried near the altar rail of St David's Church, Exeter. All commentators paid tribute to his charm, his high moral standards, and his beneficence. His widow passed the rest of her life in Bedford Crescent, Exeter, until her death on 20 July 1822.

ALICK CAMERON

Sources GM, 1st ser., 80 (1810), 81–4 · DNB · Devon and Cornwall Notes and Queries, 13 (1924–5), 244 · G. Oliver, 'Biographies of eminent Exonians', Stone's scrapbooks, Devon and Exeter Institution, 1.226 · W. Munk, 'The medical worthies of Devon', Western Times (10 Nov 1855) · J. M. S. Tomkins, 'The didactic lyre', The polite marriage (1938), 41–57 · Critical opinions and complimentary verses on the poems of H. Downman M.D. (1807) · A. Cameron, Thomas Glass, MD: physician of Georgian Exeter (1996), 104–7 · J. D. Harris, The Royal Devon and Exeter Hospital (1922), 76–7 · Trewman's Exeter Flying Post (26 June 1806)
Likenesses J. Downman, chalk drawing, 1778, FM Cam. · J. Downman, oils, 1796 · J. Downman, pencil and watercolour drawing, 1796, BM · J. Fittler, engraving (after J. Downman, 1796), repro. in H. Downman, Infancy, or, The management of children, 7th edn (1809)
Wealth at death household goods and furniture auctioned: Exeter Flying Post, 26 June 1806

Downman, John (1750–1824), portrait and subject painter, was born in Ruabon, Wales, the son of Francis Downman, attorney, and Charlotte Goodsend, eldest daughter of George I's private secretary. Downman studied briefly in Liverpool, then, from 1769, under Benjamin West, president of the Royal Academy, whom he referred to as his 'most beloved teacher' (Munro, 8, 19). In 1773 he travelled to Italy with Joseph Wright of Derby, remaining there until 1775. Before 1773 he married his first wife, Elizabeth, who seems to have died or disappeared by 1804. They had three children: one daughter, Isabella Chloë, who was baptized at St Anne, Soho, London, on 2 July 1787, and two sons.

From 1776 to 1777 Downman worked in Cambridge, where he established himself as a portrait painter. In 1778 he was in London and the west country, to which he

returned periodically over the next thirty years. Within a few years of his return to London in 1779, he gained a reputation as one of the most fashionable portraitists of the day, and was patronized by the royal family, as well as such fashion icons as the duchess of Devonshire, the duchess of Richmond, and Mrs Siddons. His popularity was largely dependent on his ability to work quickly and in quantity. In order to do so he gave up portraits in oil and devised a technique of working in chalks on a lightweight wove paper that allowed him to reproduce up to ten or twelve versions of the same portrait (for example, his portraits of the countess of Tyrconnel, 1792, and Mrs Thornhill, 1786: Munro, 13). Downman exhibited 148 works at the Royal Academy between 1770 and 1819. A small number of these were history paintings (for example, *Edward IVth on a Visit to the Duchess of Bedford*, exh. RA, 1797, and *A Late Princess Personifying Peace Crowning the Glory of England Reflected on Europe*, 1815, exh. RA, 1819; National Museum and Gallery of Wales, Cardiff); however, his treatment of the subject is often muddled and on the whole these were badly received. In some cases, such as *The Return of Orestes* (1782; Hinton Ampner, Hampshire), these so-called 'historical' paintings were in fact a form of group portrait of amateur thespians among the gentry and nobility, including Charles James Fox, depicted in theatrical performance. His closest involvement with amateur theatricals came in 1787, when he was engaged by the duke of Richmond to paint the portraits of those who acted in the highly fashionable performances at Richmond House, including Richard, second earl of Mount Edgcumbe, the Hon. Mrs Bruce, and Major Arabin (Fitzwilliam Museum, Cambridge). Downman became an associate of the Royal Academy in 1795, but never gained full membership. His reputation as snobbish, undemocratic, and slow-witted may have lost him the essential support of his peers. In the 1790s his critical popularity began to flag, and towards the end of that decade he developed a style of chalk portraiture which was larger in scale, bolder in execution, and more penetrating in the description of personality. The majority of these later portraits are in the British Museum. After 1800 his career was itinerant. From about 1804 to 1806 he lived at West Malling in Kent and from 1806 to 1807 lived in Exeter during the year of his brief second marriage. His second wife, whom he married in St Peter's Cathedral, Exeter, on 20 October 1806, was Mary Jackson (d. 1807), daughter of William Jackson, composer. Thereafter he was based in London, but made trips to Northumberland and Yorkshire (1811 and 1812) and to Oxford (1814, 1818). He exhibited publicly for the last time in 1819 and retired to Chester in the same year. He then moved to Wrexham, north Wales, where he died in 1824.

During his retirement Downman systematically assembled into albums a number of preliminary studies for portraits of 'Distinguished Persons' which he bequeathed to his only daughter, Isabella Chloë Benjamin. These were arranged in four series, roughly chronological in sequence, each series containing between four and eight volumes, with twenty-five to thirty-five drawings in each.

The first series was dispersed after it was sold by Mrs Benjamin in 1825; three of the eight albums, some individually mounted, are now in the Fitzwilliam Museum, Cambridge. The remaining three series were acquired from Downman's daughter by the Hon. George Neville, later dean of Windsor. These became known as the Butleigh Court sketchbooks, after Neville's seat near Glastonbury. They are now divided between the Fitzwilliam Museum and the British Museum. Other examples of his work are in the National Museum and Gallery of Wales, Cardiff, and the Grosvenor Museum, Chester. JANE MUNRO

Sources J. Munro, *John Downman, 1750–1824* (1996) · G. C. Williamson, *John Downman A.R.A.: his life and works* (1907) · Farington, *Diary* · J. Ingamells, ed., *A dictionary of British and Irish travellers in Italy, 1701–1800* (1997) · IGI
Archives BM, William T. Whitley MSS
Likenesses group portrait, line engraving, pubd 1798 (*Sketches taken at print sales*; after P. Sandby), BM · J. Downman, self-portrait, 1813, BM; repro. in Munro, *John Downman*, 6

Downman, Sir Thomas (1776–1852), army officer, was born at St Neots, Huntingdonshire, the elder son of Lieutenant-Colonel Francis Downman and his wife, a daughter of Thomas Day of Pontefract; he was a nephew of John Downman (1750–1824) the artist. After attending the Royal Military Academy, Woolwich, he was commissioned second lieutenant, Royal Artillery, on 24 April 1793. He joined the army in the Netherlands, and served with the guards in the campaigns of 1793 and 1794; he was at the battles of Cateau, Lannoy, Roubaix, and Mouveaux, and was taken prisoner by the French hussars on 18 May 1794, during the retreat after Mouveaux. Exchanged in July 1795, he was appointed to the B troop, Royal Horse Artillery (RHA), and promoted captain-lieutenant in November 1797.

In 1798 Downman was sent to the West Indies with the 3rd brigade, Royal Artillery, serving in San Domingo until November 1800, when he was invalided and returned to England. In 1801 he was again attached to the RHA, in 1802 promoted captain, and in 1804 made captain of the A troop, RHA. In 1809 his troop was ordered to Spain with Sir David Baird's reinforcements for Sir John Moore's army, and on its arrival it was attached to the cavalry division under Major-General Lord Paget. Downman was engaged in all the brilliant actions fought by the cavalry while covering the retreat of Sir John Moore, and he was especially mentioned for his gallantry in the affairs of Sahagun and Benevente.

In January 1810 Downman was promoted brevet major, and in September commanded the reinforcement of artillery sent to join the British army in the lines of Torres Vedras. In December 1810 he returned to England, but in May 1811 he again joined the army in the Peninsula at Fuentes de Oñore, and was attached to the headquarters as field officer commanding all the horse artillery with the army. In this capacity he remained with the army for two years, and satisfied Wellington, which was more than his rapidly changing commanders of the field artillery could do. With the headquarters' staff and in the field with the cavalry headquarters Downman was present at the affair

of Aldea da Ponte and other engagements in 1811, at the siege of Ciudad Rodrigo (though not actively engaged here), at the various cavalry actions of 1812—notably Llerena and Castrejon—at the battle of Salamanca and the advance on Madrid, and then in the advance on Burgos. During the siege of Burgos, Downman commanded the artillery upon the right of the British position; and in the retreat he commanded the whole of the artillery, both horse and field, of the rearguard, and was frequently engaged. He was specially mentioned in Wellington's dispatch for his bravery at the action of Celada. For his services at Salamanca he received a gold medal, and he was promoted brevet lieutenant-colonel on 17 December 1812.

Downman returned to England invalided in 1813, and handed over the command of the RHA with the army to Major Augustus Frazer. He was appointed to the command of the Royal Artillery in the eastern district and then in Sussex, and was promoted lieutenant-colonel in the RHA on 20 December 1814; in 1815 he was made a CB on the extension of the Order of the Bath. He was promoted colonel in 1825, knighted (September) and made KCH in 1831, promoted major-general in January 1837 and lieutenant-general in November 1846, and made KCB on 6 April 1852. He became a colonel-commandant of the RHA in 1843, was director-general of artillery in 1843–4, and was appointed to the command of the Woolwich district and garrison in 1848. He married first in 1804 the second daughter of William Holmes of Kent, and second the only daughter of John Marsh of Brighton. Downman died at the Royal Arsenal, Woolwich, Kent, while still holding his command there, on 11 August 1852.

H. M. STEPHENS, *rev.* ROGER T. STEARN

Sources J. Philippart, ed., *The royal military calendar*, 3rd edn, 4 (1820) · F. Duncan, ed., *History of the royal regiment of artillery*, 2 vols. (1873) · J. Kane, *List of officers of the royal regiment of artillery from the year 1716 to the year 1899*, rev. W. H. Askwith, 4th edn (1900) · *GM*, 2nd ser., 38 (1852) · Boase, *Mod. Eng. biog.* · A. J. Guy, ed., *The road to Waterloo: the British army and the struggle against revolutionary and Napoleonic France, 1793–1815* (1990) · R. Muir, *Britain and the defeat of Napoleon, 1807–1815* (1996) · T. C. W. Blanning, *The French revolutionary wars, 1787–1802* (1996) · J. Haydn, *The book of dignities: containing rolls of the official personages of the British empire* (1851)
Archives NAM, corresp. and papers · Royal Artillery Institution, Woolwich, London, papers

Downshire. For this title name *see* Hill, Wills, first marquess of Downshire (1718–1793); Hill, Mary, marchioness of Downshire and *suo jure* Baroness Sandys of Ombersley (1764–1836).

Downton, Nicholas (*bap.* 1561, *d.* 1615), sea captain, was baptized on 10 February 1561, son of John Downton (*d.* 1593) and his wife, Katherine (*d.* 1593), at Bushley, Worcestershire. He is known to have had two brothers, Roger and Edward, and one sister, Elizabeth. His will suggests that he had at some point lived in Gosport, Hampshire, because he owned land there, and in the parish of St Mary Woolnoth, London, since he left money to the poor of that parish. He may also have lived at some point in the parish of St Botolph, Aldgate, where his son was baptized. The first that is firmly known of him as an adult is that in 1594 he sailed to the Azores in the expedition of the earl of Cumberland which resulted in the destruction of the Portuguese carrack *Las Cino Chagas*. Downton was in command of the *Samson* and was severely wounded in the expedition. In 1605 Downton made a trading voyage to Cumana and other ports in the Caribbean as commander of a small merchantman the *Pilgrim*. Downton and the earl of Cumberland were principal shareholders of the voyage which shipped tobacco home and thus probably sailed to England via Virginia.

Early in 1610 Downton was appointed to command the East India Company's ship *Peppercorn* in the company's sixth voyage, led by Sir Henry *Middleton in the *Trade's Increase*. With a third ship, *Darling*, they sailed on 1 April 1610 with instructions to try to establish trade at Surat in western India. They arrived at Aden on 7 November 1610 where *Peppercorn* remained while Middleton went on to Mocha. Middleton was imprisoned there, but subsequently escaped, and for the following eighteen months he and Downton sailed the Red Sea, visiting ports and trying to establish trading relations, though with little success. Frustrated by lack of progress on a voyage hampered by the Turks, the Dutch, and the Portuguese, and by rivalry with the commander of the company's eighth voyage, John Saris, Middleton ordered Downton to take the *Peppercorn* to England and he set sail on 4 February 1613. It proved a difficult journey. Many men died, most contracted scurvy, Downton himself became very ill, and the ship was delayed by unfavourable winds, reaching England only in October 1613. Her arrival brought some reassurance to the subscribers (the company did not yet operate as a joint-stock company) though financial results were very modest and the sixth voyage failed in its more general aim of opening up the Surat trade.

Downton himself however had proved a reliable and skilful servant of the company and was pressed to command its next voyage and to be general of the company's ships in the East Indies. Downton's fleet of four ships, *New Year's Gift* (650 tons), *Hector* (500 tons), *Hope*, and *Solomon* (200 tons), put to sea on 7 March 1614 with the aim of consolidating the progress in the Surat trade which had been made since his own unsuccessful visit with Middleton. The fleet arrived at Surat on 15 October 1614. However, they found the Portuguese determined to resist their efforts to expand trade there. The viceroy of Goa had also quarrelled with the nawab of Surat, Mukarrab Khan. Hoping simultaneously to deter the English and force the nawab to submit to more favourable terms of trade, the Portuguese had collected at Surat all their available shipping, comprising 6 large galleons, several smaller vessels, and 60 rowing boats, carrying in all 134 guns and manned by 2600 Europeans and 6000 local sailors. Downton had only his fleet of 4 ships and 3 or 4 country vessels, known as galivats, and fewer than 600 men. The disparity of the English and Portuguese fleets however was less than the figures suggest since Downton's guns were better than the Portuguese, and the Indian volunteer swordsmen in the Portuguese service were notoriously ill-disciplined

and unreliable. None the less, Downton was at a clear disadvantage. On 18 January 1615 the fleet arrived at Surat. Mukarrab Khan sued for peace but the viceroy of Goa, Don Hieronymo de Azebedo, refused, and on 20 January the battle began. The English were lying in the Swally, later known as Sutherland Channel, inside a sheltering shoal, which kept the Portuguese ships at a distance. This was a canny, if not heroic, plan but Downton clearly set prudent management of company affairs as his highest goal and engaging the Portuguese on hazardous terms he judged unjustifiable. The smaller Portuguese vessels crossed the shoal and swarmed round the *Hope*, the smallest of Downton's four ships. The Portuguese boarded *Hope* setting fire to her mainsail and mainmast. The English guns set fire to the boarding vessels and many Portuguese sailors drowned because, having been beaten off the *Hope*, they could not re-board their own vessels. *Hope*'s fire was put out and the burning ships cast off. In the next three weeks the Portuguese repeatedly sent fireships towards the English ships but without success and on 13 February the Portuguese withdrew, allegedly with the loss of nearly 500 men compared with only 5 on the English side.

The victory enormously increased the English influence although Downton's position at Surat remained difficult. On 3 March 1615 Downton, with his four ships, left Surat intending to go to Bantam on the island of Java. They were immediately joined by the Portuguese fleet and for three days the ships sailed within sight of each other before the Portuguese withdrew. The *Hope* then sailed direct for England where she unloaded a valuable cargo. *Hector* sailed to Sumatra in search of pepper and *New Year's Gift* and *Solomon* sailed for Bantam which they reached in June 1615. Downton, whose health had been severely tried in his East Indies voyages, died there on 6 August 1615 from causes unknown. His place of burial is not known but was probably on the island of Panjang in the Bay of Bantam, where East India Company servants who died in the region were generally buried.

Downton's only son, George (*bap.* 16 Dec 1593), who accompanied him on both his East India voyages, died at Surat on 3 February 1615, while the English were expecting the renewal of the Portuguese attack and when Downton noted in his journal for 3 February 'I had least leasure to mourne' (Foster, 25). George was buried on shore at Surat. It is unlikely that Downton's wife survived him as she is not mentioned in his will. He also had a daughter, Sarah, wife of Francis Wright (*d.* 1621), a sailor. Downton willed £200 of the money owed to him by the East India Company to her son, who had died by February 1626.

Of the rest of Downton's fleet *Hector* sank in 1616, an unsurprising fate for an old vessel; *New Year's Gift* arrived in England with a cargo worth more than £140,000; and *Solomon* was kept in the East Indies to serve the company there. Though his two voyages did not result in any spectacular commercial advances for the company, Downton proved a skilful and prudent servant.

ELIZABETH BAIGENT

Sources W. Foster, ed., *The voyage of Nicholas Downton to the East Indies, 1614–15*, Hakluyt Society, 2nd ser., 82 (1939) · will and sentences, PRO, PROB 11/128, fols. 62r–v; PROB 11/129, fols. 348r–v · K. N. Chaudhuri, *The English East India Company: the study of an early English joint-stock company* (1965) · IGI

Dowriche [*née* Edgcumbe], **Anne** (*d.* in or after 1613), poet and historian, was the daughter of Sir Richard Edgcumbe (*d.* 1562) and Elizabeth Tregian. Her actual birth date is unknown, but her father's will of 1560 provided for the education of both her and her sister, suggesting she was still very young. Her father was reputedly a learned man and poet. His explicit provision for Anne's education and the nature of her published work suggests that she received a humanist and protestant education. She married Hugh Dowriche [*see below*], rector of Lapford, in 1580 at Exeter, and they had at least six children: Elkana, Walter, Mary (1587), Elizabeth, Anne (1589), and Hugh (1594). Her father-in-law's will of 1590 omits Anne, who may have died in childhood.

In 1589 Dowriche published *The French historie: that is, a lamentable discourse of three bloodie broiles in France for the gospell of Jesus Christ*, a polemical verse history of the French religious wars in alternating iambic heptameters and hexameters, based upon Jean de Serres's work, translated by Thomas Tymme and published as *The three parts of commentaries containing the whole and perfect discourse of the civil wars of France* (1574). She used additional source material, including an unpublished version of Simon Paterick's translation of the *Contre-Machievel* (not published in English until 1602), and possible manuscript versions of political speeches, weaving a dramatized story of three key 'moments' in the protestant struggle against Catholicism in France: an attack on a reformist prayer meeting in 1557; the trial and execution of the protestant senator Annas Burgeus; and the murder of the Huguenot leader Gaspard de Coligny, whose death preceded the St Bartholomew's day massacre in 1576.

Dowriche outlines sophisticated religious and political aims and a lucid historical and poetic method in her prefatory 'Epistle to the Reader'. Her religious fervour is explicit and directed: 'my onelie purpose in collecting and framing this worke was to edifie and comfort, and stir up the godly minds unto care, watchfulness, zeal and ferventness in the cause of God's truth … by the chusing and ordering of these singular examples' (sig. A4). She justifies dramatic expansion of events and the creation of imagined speeches: 'many of these orations that are here fully and amply expressed were in the *French Commentaries*, but only in substance lightly touched, and the sum set down without amplifying the circumstance' (sig. A4). The function of the devil as an allegorical morality character is defended: 'wheresoever … the Divel [is] brought in Poeticallie to make any oration … understand, that under those speeches are expressed all the subtilties, villanies, cruelties, and policies … put in practice against the godly, more lively to set them down in their colours' (sig. A4).

Dowriche's historical method intersperses the factual with anecdotes of 'the great plagues and just judgements of God against the persecutors in every several history'

(sig. A4), complemented by marginal biblical glosses. The self-conscious structural, poetic, and dramatic devices act as a moral and providential commentary on recent French history, and implicitly on English political and religious turmoil. It is also a sophisticated engagement in English protestant poetic theory.

Dowriche was conscious of her marginal status as a woman writer, and attempted to defuse criticism in a prefatory epistle to her brother, Pearce Edgcumbe, an MP in six Elizabethan parliaments, by claiming that the 'manner' may be 'base and scarce worth the seeing', but the 'matter' contained 'comfortable tast of the inward substance' (sig. A3), an orthodox defence of women's religious writing in the period.

There were no further editions of her work. Dowriche contributed commendatory verses to her husband's work, *The Jaylor's Conversion*, which explicitly draw attention to the sermon's Calvinist message. Her historical and poetic method, combined with her evangelical protestantism, provides a picture of a highly educated, alert, intellectual, and creative woman. Although the date of her death is not known, she was still alive in 1613.

Hugh Dowriche (*b.* 1552/3), Church of England clergyman and author, the son of Sir Richard Dowriche, was educated at Hart Hall, Oxford, and was licensed to preach in 1583. He was rector of Lapford until 1587, and then of Honiton from 1587 to 1598. He is the author of *The Jaylor's Conversion* (1596), an extended sermon which comments explicitly on the perceived lack of progress in the purification of the reformed English church. This, combined with the work's dedication to Valentine Knightley ('my approved good friend'), a prominent puritan, illustrates that both Dowriches were engaged in puritan activism, albeit of a literary nature. KATE AUGHTERSON

Sources E. V. Beilin, 'Anne Dowriche', *Sixteenth-century British nondramatic writers: fourth series*, ed. D. A. Richardson, DLitB, 172 (1996), 79–84 · G. E. Trease, 'Dowrich and the Dowrich family of Sandford', *Devon and Cornwall Notes and Queries*, 33 (1974–7), 208–11 · W. H. Edgcumbe, *Records of the Edgcumbe family* (1888) · E. V. Beilin, *Redeeming Eve: women writers of the English Renaissance* (1987), 101–7 · E. V. Beilin, '"Some freely spake their minds": resistance in Anne Dowriche's *French historie*', *Women, writing, and the reproduction of culture in Tudor and Stuart Britain*, ed. M. Burke and others (2000), 119–40 · R. Martin, 'Anne Dowriche's *The French history*, Christopher Marlowe and Machiavellian agency', *Studies in English Literature* (1999), 69–87 · Foster, *Alum. Oxon.*

Dowriche, Hugh (*b.* 1552/3). *See under* Dowriche, Anne (*d.* in or after 1613).

Dowse, Richard (1824–1890), politician and judge, son of William Henry Dowse of Dungannon and Maria, daughter of Hugh Donaldson of the same town, was born in Dungannon on 8 June 1824, and received his early education in the royal school there. In 1845 he entered Trinity College, Dublin, obtaining a sizarship; he gained a classical scholarship in 1848 and graduated with honours in 1850. In 1852 Dowse was called to the Irish bar. In the same year he married, on 29 December, Catherine (*d.* 1874), daughter of George Moore of Clones, co. Monaghan. Having joined the north-west circuit, he early displayed marked forensic ability, and in 1863 became a QC. In 1869 he was appointed one of the queen's serjeants-at-law, and in the same year was elected a bencher of the King's Inns.

A Liberal in politics, Dowse was elected MP for Londonderry City on 18 November 1868, with strong Presbyterian support. He was a supporter of Gladstone's Irish Church Act, and was appointed in February 1870 solicitor-general for Ireland, being re-elected for Londonderry on 15 February. In the House of Commons, where the prominence of Irish questions gave him exceptional opportunities, Dowse quickly obtained a high reputation for both ability and wit, his speeches being marked by a racy humour and a keen incisiveness. In January 1872 he became attorney-general for Ireland in succession to Charles Robert Barry, was raised to the bench, and was sworn of the Irish privy council; but in November of the same year his parliamentary career ended with his acceptance of the office of a baron of the Irish court of exchequer, a title which Dowse was the last among Irish judges to accept.

Dowse remained a member of the Irish bench until his death, which occurred suddenly, from a heart attack, in the court house at Tralee, where he was sitting as judge of assize, on 14 March 1890. Dowse's career as a judge was not one of special distinction, nor did he ever attain the reputation of a lawyer of the first rank; but his judgments were marked by sound common sense and breadth of view, and pointed by his always ready wit.

Dowse was a visitor of the Queen's College, Galway, and was twice appointed a lord justice for the government of Ireland in the absence of the viceroy. As a member of the Bessborough commission into Irish land (1880–81), he favoured legislation enacting the '3Fs' to protect the interests of tenancy. He was critical of coercion, and quashed convictions in the Court of Appeal of people charged under the 1887 Coercion Act.

C. L. FALKINER, rev. PETER GRAY

Sources WWBMP · D. Thornley, *Isaac Butt and home rule* (1964) · P. Bew, *Land and the national question in Ireland, 1858–82* (1978) · J. L. Hammond, *Gladstone and the Irish nation* (1938) · *Annual Register* (1890) · *The Times* (15 March 1890) · *Freeman's Journal* [Dublin] (15 March 1890) · F. E. Ball, *The judges in Ireland, 1221–1921*, 2 vols. (New York, 1927) · Boase, *Mod. Eng. biog.*
Archives BL, memoranda and letters to W. E. Gladstone, Add. MSS 44307–44616
Likenesses Ape [C. Pellegrini], caricature, chromolithograph, repro. in *VF* (25 March 1871) · line engraving (engraved), repro. in *Our judges, by Rhadamanthus* (1890), 61–5 · line engraving, repro. in *ILN* (8 Jan 1881), 42 · wood-engraving (after a photograph by Chancellor & Son of Dublin), NPG; repro. in *ILN* (22 March 1890), 358
Wealth at death £14,282 17s. 11d.: administration, 15 April 1890, *CGPLA Ire.*

Dowsing, William (*bap.* 1596, *d.* 1668), iconoclast, was baptized in Laxfield church, Suffolk, on 2 May 1596. He was the younger son of a prosperous and godly yeoman farmer, Wolfran Dowsing (*d.* 1607), and his wife, Joan Cooke (*d.* 1632), heir of another Laxfield farmer. As a younger son Dowsing inherited the lesser part of the family's property, none of it within the home parish of Laxfield. He appears to have been educated in a grammar school, for he had both Latin and Greek, but there is no

evidence that he attended university. By his early twenties, he was laying the foundation of a substantial library of religious books, and his earliest known purchases were of illegal separatist works printed in the Netherlands and smuggled into England. In the early 1620s he married Thamar Lea, daughter of a minor (but godly) gentleman, and he moved to farm a small estate from a substantial six-room longitudinal farmhouse just outside her home village of Coddenham. She died in 1640 or early 1641 (after bearing him ten children), and shortly afterwards he sublet his land at Coddenham and moved to a copyhold tenancy at Stratford St Mary in the Stour valley. It is possible that he wished to move away from his in-laws for reasons unknown, but it is more likely that his strong puritan views tempted him to settle close to an area where the godly still held sway. This was not in Stratford itself, with a Catholic lord of the manor and a Laudian vicar, but in the contiguous parish of Dedham, with its great puritan legacy. Dowsing's name can be found amid those of the godly of Dedham from 1642 right down to his death in 1668, for it was they who witnessed his will and benefited under it. In 1646 he was married again, this time to Mary (*d.* 1678), daughter of Henry Cooper, physician, and widow of John Mayhew, with whom he had three more children. But at the time of his iconoclastic activities (1643–4) he was a widower bringing up five young children.

For all his adult life William Dowsing was a working farmer. By the end of his life he had freehold and copyhold land in four scattered parishes, all but the land in Stratford being let or sub-let to tenants. His income appears to have been in the range £50–£80 a year, consistent with possession of a five-hearth house listed in the hearth tax returns for 1674. He was a working farmer who possessed a substantial library of religious books. Since he put his name in his books and heavily annotated them, often including cross-references to other books he owned, it is possible to reconstitute part of the library (which his son sold off piecemeal through a London bookbinder in 1704). He had a number of biblical commentaries, an eclectic collection of works of religious controversy from the sixteenth and seventeenth centuries (including works by Tyndale, Bullinger, Bale, and the exiled John Robinson and Thomas Dighton), no less than three separate editions of Foxe's *Acts and Monuments*, and an almost complete set of the fast sermons preached to the Long Parliament between 1640 and 1646 (but significantly, perhaps, not thereafter). He also possessed a collection of works by Roman historians (Plutarch, Livy, Josephus) and modern historians (Bacon, Hayward, and Ralegh). The last books he is known to have bought—almost twenty years before his death—related to the debate on the regicide, together with an edition of Polybius purchased in 1651. This was a serious collection, and he was a serious man, purposefully acquiring a guide for masters and servants a fortnight after the death of his first wife (presumably because he now had to take on more responsibility for the servants), and making provision in his will for his wife to inherit a commentary on the book of Job to help her get over his death. This was a grave, earnest, godly man who appears to have held no public office or sought any public notice over his seventy-two years of life, except for an explosive period of fifteen months at the height of the civil wars.

In August 1643 Dowsing was appointed provost marshal of the armies of the eastern association by its incoming commander, Edward Montagu, second earl of Manchester. Zeal and not experience must explain this appointment. Back in March 1643, Dowsing had drafted a personal letter to Matthew Newcomen, preacher at Dedham since 1636 and a close friend of close friends of Manchester, in which he called for action to be taken against all the 'blasphemous crucifixes, all superstitious pictures and reliques of popery' in the town and university of Cambridge (Morrill, 'Bureaucratic puritan', 188). He had thus drawn attention to himself as someone anxious to see the puritan cause prosper. As provost marshal, Dowsing helped to supply the army during the siege of King's Lynn and an expedition into Essex, and he made arrangements for the care of prisoners of war. In the course of December 1643, however, he surrendered this office for an appointment as commissioner for removing the monuments of idolatry and superstition from all the churches of the eastern association. In thus appointing him, Manchester was acting *ultra vires*. But appoint him he did, and in the months that followed, Dowsing personally supervised the 'cleansing' of most of the churches of Cambridgeshire, and, in conjunction with at least eight deputies appointed by himself, he 'cleansed' most of the churches of Suffolk. There are traces of him, and more particularly of his deputies, in north Essex and south Norfolk, but it seems that with the lapse of Manchester's commission at the end of 1644 Dowsing laid down his commission. What might have been a much wider iconoclasm was abandoned. Dowsing has no parallel elsewhere in the country. Under parliamentary ordinances of August 1643 and May 1644, the work of removing monuments of idolatry and superstition was entrusted to (and imposed under sanction upon) churchwardens. It was also quite commonplace for troops on the march to undertake acts of impromptu iconoclasm. But Dowsing's work was the most systematic and the best recorded. For he kept rough notes of what he had done and what he had ordered to be done and he subsequently wrote up all these notes into a single journal in chronological sequence, thus mingling entries for his work in churches and chapels in Cambridge and Cambridgeshire with his notes on his visits to churches in Suffolk. The manuscript has been long lost, but not before the entries for each county were published separately from one another by local antiquaries.

Dowsing visited the chapels of all sixteen Cambridge colleges between 20 December 1643 and 2 January 1644 (during which time he also visited fourteen parish churches within the city). Between 6 and 20 February 1644 he swept through the northern deaneries of Cambridgeshire (this part of his journal has not survived), and between 6 and 26 March he swept through the southern deaneries, recording visits to eighty-two parishes. He visited churches in Suffolk on his journeys to and from home during both his February and March visits to Cambridgeshire. He also made a succession of 'sweeps' (each centred on one of the places where he owned property) in late January, late February, mid-April, late August, and late September. In all, he recorded visits to 147 Suffolk parishes, around 30 per cent of the total. It is possible that he carried out unrecorded visits elsewhere, but more likely that over the summer months he was preoccupied with his farm, and that Manchester's waning star brought activity to a halt in the autumn. Certainly his eight deputies, several of whom lived close by him or were related to him by marriage, and each allocated one or more deaneries, seem to have covered most of the area he did not cover himself. We know that he intended to appoint deputies in other counties of East Anglia, but it seems probable that he did not proceed to do so.

Dowsing stuck closely to the terms of the ordinances. In the early months he concentrated on levelling chancels, removing any altar rails that had survived the parliamentary instruction for their destruction in 1641, removing any inscriptions on tombs or in glass which invited the living to pray for the souls of the dead, and the breaking of all representations in glass, wood, or stone of the persons of the Trinity or of the heavenly host. Later—after a new ordinance required it—he started to take an interest in holy water stoups and organs. Initially he was comprehensive in his inventory of monuments of idolatry and superstition and, together with the troopers who escorted him, he undertook much of the work himself. As the magnitude of his task became clearer to him, he scaled back in two ways: he concentrated on those images and monuments which were a visual distraction to the worshipper and those which represented a discredited doctrine of the communion of saints (the efficacy of prayer to and for the dead) and he left alone those things which were out of sight or 'mere' representations of the divine (such as bench ends and misericords); and he did not wait to undertake the destruction himself, but identified a reliable person—sometimes a churchwarden, sometimes a constable, occasionally a local gentleman—who undertook to carry out the work. Good illustrations of the records he took include the entry for Hadleigh (Suffolk):

> Feb 2. We brake down 30 superstitious pictures, and gave order for the taking down of the rest, which were about 70; and took up an inscription, *quorum animabus propitietur deus*; and gave order for the taking down of the cross on the steeple; gave 14 days (*Journal*)

and the entry for Madingley (Cambridgeshire):

> March 6. John Ivett and Theodore Witcham, churchwardens, Edward Dantry, cunstable. There was 31 pictures superstitious, and Christ on the cross and two thieves by him, and Christ and the Virgin Mary in another window, a Christ in the steeple window. Ordered the steps to be levelled and 14 cherubim in wood to be taken down, which promised. (ibid.)

Generally he met with acquiescence, sometimes sullen, but at Pembroke College, Cambridge, he had a heated verbal exchange with several fellows, who denied the authority of the parliamentary ordinance, of Manchester's warrant, and of the scriptural texts he cited as underwriting his work. In a display of biblical pyrotechnics, he and the fellows exchanged citations until (in his own version at least) the fellows were silenced.

Dowsing's marginalia to his library show a deep providentialism and faith in an immanent God. He told Newcomen that God had given the protestant armies of Edward VI victory over the Scots at Musselburgh in 1549 because that very day the Charing cross was pulled down in London. Thus he believed that his work made possible the victories of the parliamentarian armies.

But those same marginalia show Dowsing's surging confidence in the justice of the puritan–parliamentarian cause peak in the middle of 1644 and then increasingly turn to doubt and anxiety as divisions among the godly and the abuses of Christian liberty among the sectaries undermined the moral authority of the cause. By 1646 he was a truly alarmed and distressed man. He retreated into himself and appears to have played no further part in public affairs. He was—at least at the end of his life—obviously also troubled by disputes between the children of his first and second marriages. After his death in 1668 one of the executors of his will refused to leave money to the poor because he had paid enough to them through fines levied under the Conventicle Act. Like him, perhaps, Dowsing's life ebbed away in disillusion at a cause betrayed and lost.   JOHN MORRILL

Sources J. S. Morrill, 'William Dowsing, the bureaucratic puritan', *Public duty and private conscience in seventeenth-century England: essays presented to G. E. Aylmer*, ed. J. S. Morrill, P. Slack, and D. Woolf (1993), 173–204 · J. S. Morrill, 'William Dowsing and civil war iconoclasm', *The journal of William Dowsing*, ed. T. Cooper, Ecclesiological Society (1999), 1–28 · *The journal of William Dowsing*, ed. T. Cooper, Ecclesiological Society (1999) · M. Aston, *England's iconoclasts* (1988) · A. Kingston, *East Anglia and the great civil war* (1897) · J. Blatchly, *The town library of Ipswich provided for the use of the town preachers in 1599: a history and catalogue* (1989) · J. Phillips, *The Reformation of images: destruction of art in England, 1535–1660* (1973) · J. G. Cheshire, 'William Dowsing's destructions', *Transactions of the Cambridgeshire and Huntingdonshire Archaeological Society*, 3 (1914), 77–91 · C. H. Evelyn White, *The journal of William Dowsing of Stratford*, new edn (1885) · will, Suffolk RO, Ipswich, Archdeaconry of Suffolk wills, IC/AA1/98/14G · Bodl. Oxf., MS Tanner 257, fol. 186 [genealogy of William Dowsing] · BL, Add. MS 19127, fols. 126–7 [genealogy of William Dowsing] · BL, Harleian MS 6071, fols. 353–8 [genealogy of William Dowsing]
Archives S. Antiquaries, Lond., diary
Likenesses portrait, Ipswich Museum

Dowson, Ernest Christopher (1867–1900), poet, was born on 2 August 1867 at 11 The Grove, Lee, Kent, the elder son (there were no daughters) of Alfred Christopher Dowson (d. 1894), nephew of the colonial politician and poet Alfred Domett and friend of Robert Browning and Robert Louis Stevenson, and his wife, Annie Chalmers Swan (d. 1895), of Scottish descent. Both parents committed suicide, Dowson's mother by hanging. After irregular schooling he went up to Queen's College, Oxford, in 1886. He left in March 1888 after five terms, without completing the papers for honour moderations.

After leaving Oxford, Dowson worked supervising the dry dock which his father had owned, Bridge Dock, on the Thames at Limehouse, which later featured as 'Rainham's

Dock' in *A Comedy of Masks*. His work there was not characterized by any great commitment; he preferred instead to be in the London literary society of Lionel Pigot Johnson, Richard Le Gallienne, Oscar Wilde, and Aubrey Beardsley. He contributed to the principal aesthetic magazines: the *Century Guild Hobby Horse*, the *Yellow Book*, and *The Savoy*. He was a member of the Rhymers' Club and contributed poems to the two collections of their work (1892 and 1894). The club met at a pub in Fleet Street, as Yeats, its most famous member, remembers in 'The Grey Rock':

> Poets with whom I learned my trade,
> Companions of the Cheshire Cheese.
> (W. B. Yeats, *Responsibilities*, 1914)

In the same poem he particularly singles out Dowson and Johnson:

> Dowson and Johnson most I praise—
> To troop with those the world's forgot.
> (ibid.)

In 'The tragic generation' (book 4 of *The Trembling of the Veil*, 1922) Yeats recalled the personalities of the 1890s, including Dowson, and helped to create the myth of the decadent *poètes maudits*. The myth has been revised and modified slightly since Yeats, but the general picture of Dowson as a decadent, prizing artistic production above all else and living a life opposed to Victorian views of propriety and probity, remains. Dowson collaborated with Arthur Moore on the novel *A Comedy of Masks* (1893). His principal published works were *Dilemmas* (1895), *Verses* (1896), *The Pierrot of the Minute: a Dramatic Phantasy in one Act* (1897), *Adrian Rome* (1899; with Moore), and *Decorations* (1899). He was assistant editor on the short-lived magazine *The Critic* in 1890, for which he wrote 'Between the acts', 'The cult of the child', and articles on music-halls.

The principal love affair of Dowson's life was with Adelaide Foltinowicz (Missie), who was twelve when he first met her serving in a restaurant, The Poland, in Sherwood Street in London. She was his Beatrice and the dedicatee of *Verses*. She married the tailor August Noelte, causing Dowson great mental anguish. He regarded his unsatisfied love for her as something like Keats's for Fanny Brawne. Through the letters and poetry there runs a strong current of paedophilia, which has an erotic strain; but it is tempered by a humane and romantic appreciation of the freshness and generosity of children not yet tainted by the manners of society. In his letters this positive appreciation runs alongside outbreaks of striking misanthropy. 'Youth' is an important poem on the loss of childhood. Dowson's poetry is lyrical, mannered, literary, mellifluous, and in a diction operating on a narrow register. The principal modern influence is A. C. Swinburne, but one can also trace the influence of the French symbolists, especially Verlaine, as well as that of the classical Latin poets. T. S. Eliot felt Dowson to be the most gifted and technically perfect poet of his age. His most famous poem is 'Non sum qualis eram bonae sub regno cynarae', modelled on the first ode in book 4 of Horace and containing the well-known refrain 'I have been faithful to thee, Cynara! in my fashion'. 'Vitae summa brevis spem nos vetat incohare longam', with its reference to 'the days of wine and roses', is a quintessentially 1890s piece.

About 1891–2 Dowson was received into the Roman Catholic church, and he produced certain religio-aesthetic poems, such as 'Nuns of Perpetual Adoration' and 'Carthusians'. The dry dock was relinquished to the foreman in 1894 and Dowson lived in Brittany, principally in Pont-Aven. Leonard Smithers paid him a salary for producing translations. His best work in this field included Emile Zola's *La terre* (1894), Louis Couperus's *Majesté* (1894), Honoré de Balzac's *La fille aux yeux d'or* (1896), Pierre Choderlos de Laclos's *Les liaisons dangereuses* (1898), Guillaume Dubois's *Mémoires du Cardinal Dubois* (1899), Voltaire's *La pucelle d'Orléans* (1899), and Edmond and Jules de Goncourt's *Les maîtresses de Louis XV* (as *The Confidantes of a King: the Mistresses of Louis XV*, 1907). Smithers was also editor of *The Savoy* and encouraged Dowson to submit work. But Smithers's dissolute lifestyle had an adverse influence on Dowson. The combination of self-indulgence, drink, opiates, depression caused by the failure of the dry dock, his parents' suicides, the betrayal (as he saw it) of Missie, and the tuberculosis he contracted in 1894 weakened his resistance, and he spent the last six months of his life being looked after by R. H. Sherard and his wife. He died, unmarried, on 23 February 1900 at the Sherards' house, 26 Sandhurst Gardens, Catford, London, and was buried on 27 February in Ladywell cemetery, Lewisham, London.

BERNARD RICHARDS

Sources V. Plarr, *Ernest Dowson, 1888–1897: reminiscences, unpublished letters and marginalia* (1914) · W. B. Yeats, *The trembling of the veil* (1922) · B. I. Evans, *English poetry in the later nineteenth century*, 2nd edn (1966), 402–8 · E. Jepson, *Memories of a Victorian*, 1 (1933) · J. Gawsworth [T. I. F. Armstrong], 'The Dowson legend', *Essays by Divers Hands, being the Transactions of the Royal Society of Literature of the United Kingdom*, new ser., 17 (1938), 93–124 · M. Longaker, *Ernest Dowson*, 3rd edn (1967) · T. B. Swann, *Ernest Dowson* (1964) · *The letters of Ernest Dowson*, ed. D. Flower and H. Maas (1967) · L. Dakin, *Ernest Dowson* (1972) · D. Stanford, ed., *Three poets of the Rhymers' Club: Ernest Dowson, Lionel Johnson and John Davidson* (1974) · J. Gardner, *Yeats and the Rhymers' Club: a nineties perspective* (1989) · G. A. Cevasco, *Three decadent poets: Ernest Dowson, John Gray and Lionel Johnson, an annotated bibliography* (1990) · N. Alford, *The Rhymers' Club: poets of the tragic generation* (1994) · B. Gardiner, *The Rhymers' Club: a social and intellectual history* (1988) · b. cert. · d. cert.

Archives University of British Columbia, Vancouver, papers | Morgan L., letters to A. C. Moore

Likenesses C. Conder, pencil drawing, NPG · photograph (as an undergraduate), Philadelphia, Lessing Rosenwald collection · photograph, L. Cong., Lessing F. Rosenwald collection

Wealth at death £1119 18s. 7d.: administration, 15 May 1901, CGPLA Eng. & Wales

Dowson, Sir Ernest MacLeod (1876–1950), colonial administrator and expert on land registration, was born on 19 November 1876 in India, the only son of Ernest Dowson, superintendent of the Indian government telegraph department. He was educated at the Isle of Wight College and the Central Technical College, London.

In 1898 Dowson joined the Egyptian Delta Light Railways as assistant engineer. After two years he moved to the Egyptian survey, where he became the director of topographical survey in 1905 and succeeded Sir Henry Lyons as director-general in 1909. He married Hilda Fanny

(*b.* 1881/2), the youngest daughter of the Revd Samuel Pascoe of Newquay, on 19 July 1910; they had one son. As director-general of the Egyptian survey Dowson accepted on its behalf a number of additional responsibilities, and the outbreak of the First World War severely taxed his resources. The survey undertook in 1914 to compile and supply all maps required by the Egyptian expeditionary force in the advances against Ottoman forces that culminated in the capture of Damascus in October 1918. Dowson was three times mentioned in dispatches for his mapping work. A more curious demand on his time during the war was made by the design, in collaboration with T. E. Lawrence, of a set of postage stamps for the emir of Mecca, Sharif Hussein ibn Ali, who expected to be recognized by the British as the king of an independent Arab state once the war ended.

From 1917 to 1921 Dowson chaired a mixed commission appointed to recommend measures for the settlement of title to land in Egypt. With its cosmopolitan make-up, the commission sought to consider systems of registering rights to land that were in force in various parts of the world, but found it impossible to benefit from other experiences except through slow and costly *ad hoc* studies. From this frustrating experience emerged Dowson's deep interest in the comparative study of land registration, a subject which increasingly absorbed his time and energy. In 1919 he was appointed financial under-secretary in the Egyptian government, and in the following year he became financial adviser, a post he held until his retirement from the Egyptian service in 1923.

Having concluded his work in Egypt, Dowson was called upon to advise on land questions in the newly created mandated territories of Palestine, Transjordan, and Iraq and, later, on agricultural indebtedness in Zanzibar. His numerous reports to the Colonial Office consistently argued that a national settlement of rights to land would benefit these countries, particularly by encouraging development and as the basis for the extension of agricultural credit and the equitable levying of taxation. In Palestine and Transjordan Dowson's investigations led to the promulgation of new laws and regulations (from 1926 to 1927 he was named commissioner of lands for Palestine in order to oversee the implementation of his recommendations), but his report for Iraq failed to receive the full support of powerful landed interests. Dowson's recommendation that direct links be developed between government and individual cultivators threatened the position of large landholders and, with Iraq set to join the League of Nations, British officials there lacked the power and interest to push through such reforms. On Dowson's pioneering advice, cadastral maps in Zanzibar were compiled from aerially surveyed mosaics. He consistently but unsuccessfully advocated compulsory registration of land ownership on cadastral maps in England and Wales, but he could not overcome opposition from self-interested conveyancing lawyers or government fears that a cadastral survey would prove unjustifiably expensive.

Dowson's enthusiasm for the comparative study of land registration in various jurisdictions led directly to the establishment in the 1930s of the cadastral survey and land records office. What began as an exhibit at the 1931 Empire Survey Conference of cadastral maps, plans, and supporting records was later developed into an international reference centre. Often working from home, and in close collaboration with his lifelong friend and colleague Vivian Sheppard, Dowson continuously enlarged the collection of cadastral material, kept it up to date, and made it as accessible as possible. The two men already had numerous personal connections from around the world, and they received logistical support from the Colonial Office. Accommodation was provided first by the Royal Geographic Society and then by the Ordnance Survey.

Work was suspended upon the outbreak of the Second World War, but in 1946 Lord Hailey, chairman of the colonial land tenure advisory panel, asked Dowson for an analysis of prominent systems of land registration around the world. Co-written with Sheppard, this memorandum achieved a wide circulation and was immediately used for instruction by the Royal Institution of Chartered Surveyors. A revised version, together with some articles that Dowson and Sheppard wrote for the *Empire Survey Review*, was published in 1952 by HMSO with the title *Land Registration*. The book provided a wealth of information in an uncharted field and rapidly became a standard source: student demand for the monograph remained high until its place was taken by S. R. Simpson's *Land Law and Registration* (1976), which drew significantly on Dowson's and Sheppard's renowned collection of cadastral records and related material (later integrated into Cambridge University libraries).

Ever impressed by Dowson's breadth of knowledge and his commitment to his work, the Colonial Office relied on him for expert advice. Although some thought him incapable of relaxing even for short periods, Dowson was none the less a man of great personal charm and generosity, always finding time to devote to hospital work in particular: while in Cairo, he chaired for some years the board of the Anglo-American hospital, and on retiring from the Egyptian service to Wrotham, Kent, he supported the care of a local hospital there.

In 1907 Dowson received the Ottoman order of the Osmania (fourth class), and in 1912 the Ottoman order of the Mejidiye (third class). He was created CBE in 1918, invested with the insignia of the grand cordon of the order of the Nile in 1923, and promoted KBE in 1924. In 1937 he received the Brilliant Star of Zanzibar (second class). He died at his home, Downlands, Wrotham, Kent, on 26 June 1950, survived by his wife.

MARTIN BUNTON

Sources V. L. O. Sheppard, *Empire Survey Review*, 10/78 (1950), 383–4 · S. R. Simpson, *Land law and registration* (1976) · R. Porter, 'The Dowson and Sheppard Collection of cadastral survey and land registration records: a note on the origin, history, and current whereabouts of the collection', 1993, Ordnance Survey, Southampton [typescript] · E. Dowson and V. L. O. Sheppard, 'Work of the cadastral survey and land records office, 1932–1945', *Empire Survey Review*, 8/56 (1945), 42–52 · WWW, 1941–50 · m. cert. · d. cert. · *CGPLA Eng. & Wales* (1950) · R. J. P. Kain and E. Baigent, *The cadastral map in the service of the state* (1992)

Archives CUL, Dowson and Sheppard collection, collection of cadastral survey and land registration material
Wealth at death £1890 4s. 5d.: probate, 21 Sept 1950, *CGPLA Eng. & Wales*

Dowson, John (1820–1881), orientalist, was born at Uxbridge, Middlesex. His uncle, Edwin *Norris, then assistant secretary to the Royal Asiatic Society, encouraged him from the age of sixteen to specialize in Eastern languages and he appears eventually to have mastered Arabic, Persian, Sanskrit, Telugu, and Hindustani. For a time tutor at the East India College, Haileybury, in 1855 he was appointed professor of Hindustani and Telugu at University College, London, and subsequently, about 1859, professor of Hindustani at the newly reorganized staff college at Camberley, a post he held until 1877. As oriental languages ranked poorly in the staff college's educational priorities, Dowson had ample time for research. In 1862 he produced a popular *Grammar of the Urdu or Hindustani Language*, followed in 1869 by a translation of a Hindustani reader commonly used in language examinations, *Ikhwanu-s safa, or, Brothers of purity*.

In the early 1860s Edward Thomas, adviser to the widow of Sir Henry Miers Elliot, approached Dowson to edit Elliot's massive bibliographical index to the manuscript histories of medieval India. Under Dowson the final eight volumes of extracts from Persian and Arabic chronicles (*The History of India, as Told by its Own Historians: the Muhammadan Period*, 8 vols., 1867–77) acquired more of a historical emphasis than Elliot had planned. It was a huge job. Dowson translated about half of the extracts himself and, although the volumes were well received and established Dowson's academic reputation, in the small, precious world of oriental scholarship there were inevitably attacks on his competence and methods. Ironically, in the longer term, the apparent comprehensiveness of his work seriously retarded scholarly re-examination of the manuscripts on which it was based. In 1879 Dowson published *A Classical Dictionary of Hindu Mythology and Religion*, compiled from numerous European authorities, but he returned to Elliot's papers to work on a volume on medieval Gujarat. Unfinished at his death, it was afterwards completely recast by a new editor, E. C. Bayley. Dowson's final work, reflecting his skills in palaeography, was an article on Indian inscriptions for the ninth edition of the *Encyclopaedia Britannica*.

Little is known of Dowson's personal life. An 1864 photograph of the staff college professors shows a large, stout man, plainly dressed and in appearance more like a respectable merchant than an orientalist. The image accords with his reputation in the Royal Asiatic Society as a self-taught man—a helpful and thorough scholar who resisted claiming too much for his achievements. He died at his home, Sandhurst Lodge, Worthing, Sussex, on 24 August 1881. He was survived by his wife, Henrietta Cowley Dowson, and at least one child, a son.

KATHERINE PRIOR

Sources *Journal of the Royal Asiatic Society of Great Britain and Ireland*, new ser., 14 (1882), xiv–xv · H. M. Elliot, *The history of India, as told by its own historians: the Muhammadan period*, ed. J. Dowson, 8 vols.

(1867–77) • *The Times* (6 Sept 1881), 4 • A. R. Godwin-Austen, *The staff and the Staff College* (1927) • *DNB* • *CGPLA Eng. & Wales* (1881) • d. cert. **Likenesses** group portrait, photograph, 1864, repro. in Godwin-Austen, *Staff and the Staff College*
Wealth at death £2900 4s. 9d.: administration with will, 19 Oct 1881, *CGPLA Eng. & Wales*

Dowton, Henry (b. 1798). *See under* Dowton, William (1764–1851).

Dowton, William (1764–1851), actor, the son of an innkeeper and grocer at Exeter, was born in that city on 25 April 1764. At an early age he worked with a marble cutter, but in 1780 he was articled to an architect. During his apprenticeship he occasionally performed at a private theatre in Exeter. His success on stage prompted him to run away from home and join a company of strolling players at Ashburton, where, in 1781, he made his appearance in a barn as Carlos in *The Revenge*. After enduring many hardships he was engaged by Hughes, the manager of the Weymouth theatre, and eventually returned to Exeter, where he played Macbeth and Romeo. In September 1791 he joined Sarah Baker's company in Kent. Here he changed his line of acting, and took the characters of La Gloire, Jemmy Jumps, Billy Bristle, Sir David Dunder, and Peeping Tom, in all of which he was well received by a Canterbury audience. In 1794 he married the daughter of Sarah *Baker, also Sarah (or Sally) Baker (1768–1817). Their eldest son, **William Dowton** (1794x7–1883) was theatre manager on the Kent circuit from 1815 to 1835. He appeared in London at Drury Lane in December 1832 as Tangent and was afterwards a brother of the Charterhouse for thirty-seven years. He died there on 19 September 1883 and was buried at Bow on 24 September 1883. Another son, **Henry Dowton** (b. 1798) was also an actor. He was known for his performances of the parts most closely associated with the comic actor John Liston. He married a Miss Whitaker, an actress, who after his death became the wife of John Sloman, an actor. She died at Charleston, South Carolina, on 7 February 1858.

Dowton made his first appearance in London at Drury Lane under Wroughton's management, as Sheva in Richard Cumberland's comedy *The Jew*, in October 1796, and was received with much applause. He was extremely versatile at this period of his career. His version of Sir Hugh Evans in *The Merry Wives of Windsor* was excellent, and he was considered the best representative of Malvolio on the English stage. He played with great success Mr Hardcastle in Goldsmith's *She Stoops to Conquer*, Sir Francis Wronghead in Vanbrugh's *The Provoked Husband*, Cacafogo in Beaumont and Fletcher's *Rule a Wife and have a Wife*, Sir Fretful Plagiary in Sheridan's *The Critic*, and a number of minor Shakespearian characters, such as the First Gravedigger in *Hamlet* and Feste in *Twelfth Night*. After his successful London season he spent the summer of 1797 performing at Margate, Richmond, and Canterbury, and became very popular as Frank Oatland in Thomas Morton's *A Cure for the Heartache* at Tunbridge Wells. He was back in Drury Lane again in 1798, taking on the new roles of Sir Anthony Absolute in *The Rivals*, Clod in *The*

Young Quaker, Peachum in *The Beggar's Opera*, and Orzembo in *Pizarro*.

Dowton continued at Drury Lane for the next two decades, playing at the Haymarket in the summer months. In August 1805 members of the guild of tailors rioted in protest against his production at the Haymarket of *The Tailors*, a burlesque. The disturbance was quelled by a detachment of Horse Guards. Other engagements away from Drury Lane included a brief visit to Manchester in 1806, to the New Theatre, Worthing, in 1812, and to Canterbury again in 1814. In October 1815 he played Shylock at Drury Lane at the desire, as it was stated, of Lord Byron. Although his conception of the character was said to be excellent, it was not well received by the public, who preferred him in comic parts. In 1815–16, Dowton assumed managerial duties at the Haymarket. He was afterwards manager of theatres at Canterbury and Maidstone, but he finally transferred these to his son, and confined himself to acting. He gave evidence before the committee on dramatic literature in August 1832.

In June 1836 Dowton went to America, and made his first appearance in New York at the Park Theatre in his favourite character of Falstaff. During this engagement he played only elderly characters. He also performed at the Chesnut Street Theatre, Philadelphia, in September 1836, as Sir Robert Bramble. His quiet and natural style of acting was not at first understood by his audiences, and just as they were beginning to warm to him he decided to return home, and took his farewell benefit in November 1836.

In his old age, not having invested in the Theatrical Fund, Dowton became destitute, and would have been in absolute poverty but for a benefit at Her Majesty's Theatre in June 1840, when Colman's *The Poor Gentleman* was played with an excellent cast, in which Dowton took the part of Sir Robert Bramble. With the proceeds of this benefit an annuity was purchased, which amply provided for his final years. He enjoyed good health to the last, and died at his home, 27 Brixton Terrace, Brixton, Surrey, on 19 April 1851. His wife had predeceased him, at Rochester on 16 October 1817.

G. C. BOASE, rev. NILANJANA BANERJI

Sources Highfill, Burnim & Langhans, *BDA* • Adams, *Drama* • *Oxberry's Dramatic Biography*, 4/63 (1826) • P. Hartnoll, ed., *The Oxford companion to the theatre* (1951); 2nd edn (1957); 3rd edn (1967) • P. Hartnoll, ed., *The concise Oxford companion to the theatre* (1972) • J. N. Ireland, *Records of the New York stage, from 1750 to 1860*, 2 vols. (1866–7) • *The thespian dictionary, or, Dramatic biography of the present age*, 2nd edn (1805) • *The biography of the British stage, being correct narratives of the lives of all the principal actors and actresses* (1824) • *Illustrated Sporting and Dramatic News* (30 Oct 1880) • T. Gilliland, *The dramatic mirror, containing the history of the stage from the earliest period, to the present time*, 2 vols. (1808) • T. A. Brown, *History of the American stage* (1870) • Hall, *Dramatic ports.* • d. cert.
Likenesses S. De Wilde, group portrait, exh. RA 1805, Garr. Club • S. De Wilde, group portrait, exh. RA 1810, Garr. Club • S. De Wilde, chalk and watercolour, 1812, BM • S. De Wilde, watercolour, 1812, Garr. Club • R. W. Buss, two sketches, Garr. Club • J. W. Gear, pencil and ink, NPG • portrait, repro. in Gilliland, *The dramatic mirror* • portrait, repro. in J. Cawthorne, ed., *Cawthorne's Minor British theatre*, 6 vols. (1806) • portrait, repro. in *Monthly Mirror* (1804) • portrait, repro. in *European Magazine* (1813) • portrait, repro. in

Oxberry, *New English drama* (1818) [and 1820] • portrait, repro. in *Oxberry's Dramatic Biography* • prints, BM, NPG

Dowton, William (1794x7–1883). *See under* Dowton, William (1764–1851).

Dowty, Sir George Herbert (1901–1975), aeronautical engineer and industrialist, was born on 27 April 1901 at Pershore, Worcestershire, the son of William Dowty, a druggist and chemist in Pershore, and his wife, Laura Masters. He was the elder of twin boys by half an hour and the seventh son in the family. The twins were educated in a small private school in Pershore until 1913, when they both entered the Worcester Royal Grammar School, which they were obliged to leave at the age of fourteen because their older brothers had been conscripted into the army and they had to help in running the various family businesses. At the age of twelve George Dowty lost his right eye during some experiments with photographic materials, when a bottle of magnesium powder exploded.

Dowty spent a year in the family business, but his early interest in engineering and applicational science led him to join Heenan and Froude as a workshop boy entrant. His first job, pressure testing, using a hydraulic hand-pump, of the cast-iron cylinder for aero-engines, introduced him to hydraulics, which was later to be so important to him. Realizing his need for a special engineering education he began what became a lifetime of study and joined evening classes at the local Victoria Institute, paying his own fees. At the same time he took postal courses on the internal combustion engine. This interest in engineering was soon noticed by a benevolent foreman who encouraged Dowty to move through a variety of departments in order to widen his experience and knowledge. He finally joined the drawing office, the centre of decision making for engineering products and an excellent training ground for a future engineering designer.

In July 1918 Dowty answered an advertisement in *Flight* and obtained a new job as a draughtsman with the British Aerial Transport Company in London. The company's chief designer was Bobby Noorduyn, a Dutchman and a pioneer of aircraft design in Britain and later in Canada. Dowty, eager to learn, worked on undercarriages and, in Noorduyn's creative environment, accelerated his career rapidly and perhaps impatiently.

After a brief post-war flirtation with several non-aircraft companies (for example, he designed moulds for golf balls at Dunlop in 1920) he joined the design office of the A. V. Roe Company at Hamble, Southampton. There he specialized in undercarriages, for which his further hydraulics reading was useful; he knew the formulae for determining the resistance of oil through an orifice (vital for calculating the energy absorption of an aircraft undercarriage). By the age of twenty-one he had designed landing gear for the first Cierva Autogyro and for the Avro Aldershot.

In 1924 Dowty left A. V. Roe to join the Gloucestershire Aircraft Company (later the Gloster Aircraft Company). By this time he had read a number of papers on undercarriage design to the Institution of Aeronautical Engineers,

Sir George Herbert Dowty (1901–1975), by unknown photographer

and was already working at home on several ideas that he was later to patent. He also wrote articles for the technical press to supplement his income, and examined the application of his hydraulics theory to other fields—for example, in his 'Balanced and servo control surfaces' (National Advisory Committee for Aeronautics, Tech. Memo. No. 563, 1926). This was a principle so advanced that it was not to be developed for nearly thirty years. In 1927 he took out a patent for a wheel incorporating oil shock absorbers, steel springs, and brakes operating on the wheel rims. In 1931 he set up his own one-man company while still employed at Gloster Aircraft—the Aircraft Components Company, which was designed to answer a need to provide main aircraft design companies with specialist accessories and equipment. It advertised many of Dowty's designs and patents, at first to no avail, but June 1931 saw a change of fortune when he received his first order, worth £1500, from Kawasaki in Japan, to fit Dowty internally sprung undercarriage wheels to its Type 92 aircraft. Dowty left Gloster Aircraft the same month, borrowed against a life assurance, and established single-handed the first foundations of a vast international engineering enterprise. With one order and no factory, using subcontract manufacture and the help in the evenings of two friends, Dowty designed, ordered, and assembled two of his wheels and within nine weeks shipped them to Japan, being paid on shipment.

Dowty recruited his first two employees in November 1931. A major breakthrough occurred in 1934 when he offered to H. P. Folland a pair of oleostruts of new design for the Gloster Gauntlet aircraft. This gave him his first large production order and was followed by a similar order for the Gladiator. Dowty leased a factory and bought Arle Court, Cheltenham. Company growth was now possible and the pioneer work on aircraft hydraulics and seals also paid off. The firm went public in 1936 with Dowty holding only a small percentage of the equity. Thanks to the concurrent technical revolution in aircraft design to include retractable undercarriages, brakes, and flaps, his work and knowledge expanded rapidly. During the Second World War Dowty's inventive and creative engineer's mind was fully unleashed. Twenty-eight different aircraft were fitted with Dowty equipment, which included 12,900 sets for the Hurricane, over 90,000 other undercarriage units, and more than a million hydraulic units. Plants were set up throughout Britain and in Canada and the USA.

After the Second World War Dowty applied his new approaches to hydraulics to wider fields—motorcycle forks, hydraulic pit props and a prime support system, industrial pumps, and hydraulic control systems. In 1954 a group holding company was formed with the Canadian operation generating 50 per cent of the total turnover. Rotol Propellor Ltd was acquired in 1954, Boulton and Paul in 1959, and Meco of Worcester in 1964.

From 1935 Arle Court in Cheltenham was both the company's headquarters and Dowty's home. He walked along the corridor to his office until three years before he died, when he took up semi-retirement on the Isle of Man. Like many of his contemporaries he was a hands-on inventor, engineer, and manager, whose life was his company. In 1948 he married Marguerite Anne Gowans, daughter of M. J. H. Lockie, of Newmarket, Ontario, Canada; they had a son and a daughter.

Dowty was active in the Royal Aeronautical Society, being elected its president for 1952–3. The society made him an honorary fellow and awarded him the gold medal in 1955. He was also president of the Society of British Aircraft Constructors in 1960–61 and its treasurer in 1961–8. He was knighted in 1956 and received honorary doctorates from Bath University (1966) and Cranfield Institute of Technology (1972). In 1971 he was master of the Worshipful Company of Coach Makers and Coach Harness Makers. He was an honorary freeman of Cheltenham (1955) and Tewkesbury (1964) and chairman of the Industrial Development Board, Malta.

Keenly interested in cricket, Dowty put the Worcestershire County Cricket Club on to a sound financial basis during his term as its president (1962–6). He played tennis and golf well and captained England against Scotland at curling. Chess and snooker were other interests, also bloodstock breeding. He was very much involved in the community and social activities in the area around Tewkesbury and Pershore. Dowty died on 7 December 1975 at his home in the Isle of Man.

M. G. FARLEY, rev. ROBIN HIGHAM

Sources DBB · *The Aeroplane Yearbook* (1961) · *WW* · *DNB* · B. Gunston, *By Jupiter: the life of Sir Roy Fedden* (1978) · G. Dowty, 'Aviation – the pacemaker', *Journal of the Royal Aeronautical Society* (1966), 227–9

[centenary issue] · B. Stait, *Rotol: the history of an airscrew company, 1937–1960* (1990)
Likenesses photograph, Royal Aeronautical Society Library [*see illus.*] · portrait, Dowty Group, Arle Court, Cheltenham

Doxat, Lewis (1778–1871), journalist, was born at Calcutta, India. He came to London when a boy, and at an early age obtained work in the office of the *Morning Chronicle*, where he remained for twenty-five years. He afterwards joined the staff of *The Observer*. His connection with *The Observer* had started as far back as 1804 and was continued until 1857, a period of fifty-three years. During most of this time he was manager of the paper and contributed greatly to its success. But notwithstanding his possession of literary ability and of extensive and varied information, it is said of him that he never wrote a single article or paragraph for the journal.

When, in 1821, after the death of James Perry, the *Morning Chronicle* was bought by William Clements, the proprietor of *The Observer*, Doxat returned to his old office and became manager of the *Morning Chronicle*, suffering great trials of patience from the dilatory ways of its editor, John Black. In 1834 the two papers ceased to belong to the same proprietor, and the official connection between them ended. Doxat confined his attention again to *The Observer*, which stood higher in reputation than any contemporary for its early and exclusive information on political affairs. According to the 1851 census, Doxat was widowed by this date; in 1857 he gave up his position and moved from 30 Henrietta Street, Covent Garden, to 17 Haverstock Hill, and then to 13 Queen's Crescent, where he died peacefully on 4 March 1871.

ROBERT HARRISON, rev. NILANJANA BANERJI

Sources *The Observer* (12 March 1871) · J. Grant, *The newspaper press: its origin, progress, and present position*, 3: *The metropolitan weekly and provincial press* (1872) · D. Griffiths, ed., *The encyclopedia of the British press, 1422–1992* (1992) · *Newspaper Press*, 5 (1871), 94 · *CGPLA Eng. & Wales* (1871–5) · *The Times* (10 March 1871), 12d · census returns, 1851
Wealth at death under £9000: resworn probate, May 1875, *CGPLA Eng. & Wales*

Doxford, Sir William Theodore (1841–1916), shipbuilder, was born at Bridge Street, Bishopwearmouth, Sunderland, co. Durham, on 1 February 1841, the first of four sons in a family of ten children of the merchant shipwright William Doxford (1812–1882) and his wife, Hannah (1814–1895), daughter of Robert Pile, a glassworker. His father made several abortive attempts to set up in business as a wooden shipbuilder before finally succeeding during the 1850s; in 1858 he opened a shipyard at Pallion on the south bank of the River Wear, near Sunderland. Doxford began work there after being educated at Bramham College, and in 1863 he married Margaret (d. 1916), daughter of Richard Wilkinson, a Sunderland shipbuilder. They had one son and five daughters.

Only after the decision was taken in 1864 to build iron ships did the Doxford shipyard make significant progress. The output of 3000 tons of shipping in 1864 had trebled to 9500 tons by 1872. In order to build their own marine engines the Doxfords erected engine and boiler shops in

1878, with a younger brother, Robert Doxford, in charge. When their father died in 1882, all four sons were involved in the management of the business. By this time Doxfords had probably the leading shipyard on the River Wear.

The Doxfords had an eye for technical innovation. In 1875 they built their first naval vessels, and twelve years later the firm installed oil-burning boilers in a torpedo boat. However, the Admiralty proved uninterested in this novel idea at that time. Doxford dominated the family management, and in 1891 the firm became a limited liability company with a capital of £200,000, all owned by the Doxford family. In the following year the firm introduced its 'turret ship', a design which brought Doxfords both fame and fortune.

The turret ship was based on the American whaleback steamer then active on the Great Lakes. The hull bent inwards from a little way above the waterline to give a curved deck—a whaleback—across the top of the vessel. Steering platforms and other openings projected from the whaleback in vertical structures or 'turrets'. One of these American vessels visited Liverpool in the early 1890s and attracted great interest. Doxfords was commissioned to build a similar vessel under licence. While it did so, A. H. Havers, the firm's chief draughtsman, prepared his own design for a turret ship, and it was patented in the name of Charles Doxford. The principal innovation was that there was now one long turret running the length of the ship.

The first Doxford turret ship appeared in 1892 and after some initial reluctance from shipowners the type soon became very popular, the Clan Line alone taking no fewer than thirty such ships. In all, between 1892 and 1911, Doxfords built 176 turret ships at Sunderland, while six others were built under licence in other British shipyards and one in Spain. In 1903 Havers sued the company, demanding recognition as the inventor of the turret ship. Doxfords showed that Havers had been handsomely rewarded by the firm, but the jury still awarded him damages of £1250. Nevertheless, this was still only a small slice from the £150,000 profit which Doxfords was said to have made by that time out of the turret ship.

Besides its inherent strength, helped by a cellular double bottom, the turret ship was also popular with shipowners in the bulk trades because its net tonnage (often used to calculate harbour charges) was low in relation to its deadweight tonnage (the actual weight of cargo carried). Also, the Suez Canal dues were based on the breadth of the upper deck, which on a turret ship was usually half the actual width of the vessel; however, the success of the turret ship led to the canal rules being altered. Between 1907 and 1909 a number of losses and accidents involving turret ships caused alarm, but these were found to be largely due to incorrect loading rather than to faults in the design of the ship. Nevertheless, the popularity of the turret ship waned and the last one was built in 1911.

The turret ship brought great prosperity to the Doxford shipyard. It launched over 100,000 tons of shipping in 1906 and while the totals for 1905 and 1907 were only about 90,000 tons, this was sufficient to make Doxfords the most productive shipyard in the world in those years.

Such productivity was possible because in 1904 the shipyard had been rebuilt. The original five building berths were scrapped to make way for three berths of greater length, each capable of building a 12,000 ton ship. By 1914 the capital of William Doxford & Sons Ltd was £450,000 and it made a profit of £160,000.

Doxfords also took the bold step of beginning the development of a marine diesel engine. At that time diesel technology was dominated by continental European firms, but, under the engineer K. O. Keller, Doxfords began research and design work in 1906. The first experimental engine was ready by 1912 and the first opposed-piston engine was built in 1913. The Doxford engine did not become a commercial success until after the First World War, but the basis had been laid before 1914 for the firm to achieve the distinction of being the only British company to produce a successful marine diesel engine.

As well as the technical side of shipbuilding, Doxford took a close interest in labour relations, being aware from his own family history of the hardships that could be caused by the fluctuations in the shipbuilding trade. He helped to make a success of the conciliation board established in Sunderland in 1885 and he was a witness to the royal commission on labour in 1892. He often represented Wearside on the National Federation of Shipbuilding Employers and was chairman of the Wear Shipbuilders' Association from 1908 to 1912.

Doxford was the first Conservative to be elected for Sunderland for forty years when he became a Unionist MP in 1895. Knighted in 1900, he retired from parliament in 1906. He was actively involved in local affairs, serving on the Sunderland town council and as a River Wear commissioner, in addition to being a magistrate in both the town of Sunderland and co. Durham. He was also a deputy lieutenant of the county. He was a foundation member and second president of the North-East Coast Institution of Engineers and Shipbuilders. He joined the Institution of Naval Architects in 1878, and was elected a council member in 1896 and vice-president in 1908.

Still head of the family firm, Doxford died on 1 October 1916, at his home, Grindon Hall, Silksworth, Sunderland, co. Durham, a few months after the death of his wife. An obituary in the *Transactions of the Institution of Naval Architects*, surveying Doxford's career, noted that he had been 'associated with all the principal developments in shipbuilding and marine engineering from the days of wooden ships' (49, 1917, 233).   ALAN G. JAMIESON

Sources *William Doxford and Company* (1921) · J. W. Smith and T. S. Holden, *Where ships are born: Sunderland, 1346–1946*, rev. edn (1953) · D. Dougan, *The history of north east shipbuilding* (1968) · J. F. Clarke, *A century of service to engineering and shipbuilding: a centenary history of the North East Coast Institution of Engineers and Shipbuilders, 1884–1984* (1984) · J. F. Clarke, 'Doxford, Sir William Theodore', *DBB* · *Transactions of the Institution of Naval Architects*, 49 (1917), 233 · *CGPLA Eng. & Wales* (1916) · b. cert. · d. cert.

Archives Tyne and Wear Archives Service, Newcastle upon Tyne, Sunderland Shipbuilders Ltd, Doxford archives

Likenesses photograph, repro. in Clarke, 'Doxford, Sir William Theodore'

Wealth at death £151,110 5s. 11d.: probate, 27 Dec 1916, *CGPLA Eng. & Wales*

Doyle, Andrew (1809–1888), newspaper editor and civil servant, was born on 22 November 1809 in Dublin, the third son of another Andrew Doyle, a merchant. He was enrolled at Trinity College, Dublin, in 1829 and proceeded to Lincoln's Inn in 1834. He was called to the bar in 1842. On 22 August 1843 he married Louisa (1813–1896), the youngest child of John Easthope. Easthope was the proprietor of the *Morning Chronicle*, a newspaper which then rivalled *The Times* in influence. The *Morning Chronicle* maintained close relations with a number of leading liberal politicians, but especially with Lord Palmerston, who was supposed sometimes to draft the leading articles himself. Doyle became its editor in 1843, but after Easthope sold the paper in 1847 he sought a new career.

In 1848 Doyle became a poor-law inspector. He remained a senior civil servant until his retirement in 1876, becoming a local government inspector in 1871 when the Local Government Board took over the functions of the poor-law board. His district included most of Wales and some of the border counties. The work continually expanded in these years and Doyle was responsible for a number of important reports, including those on vagrancy in 1849 and 1865, and on pauper education in 1860 and 1862. He pioneered work on statistics, and his reports were supported by pages of tabulated figures. The collection of statistics from the agricultural population was not popular, and when Doyle tried to obtain them from Denbighshire and Shropshire in 1854, many of the forms were burnt. One farmer cut his in pieces and returned it endorsed, 'The idea of such questions. What next!' (Hawkins, 4).

Doyle has sometimes been portrayed as a rigid bureaucrat (Parr, 51), but he seems to have been a humane man who believed that lax administration benefited the exploiters at the expense of the vulnerable. He disliked the casual ward in the workhouses, believing that

> so far from being the temporary refuge of the deserving poor [including those moving to seek work], [it] is a place of rendezvous for thieves and prostitutes and other vagabonds … gangs of whom 'work' allotted districts, and make their circuits with as much regularity as the Judges. ('Reports on vagrancy', 35.677)

He provided numerous examples of abuse from his own district. If such wards could not be closed, he believed that they should be strictly controlled. For similar reasons he disliked outdoor relief, by which paupers were helped in their own homes rather than in the workhouse. In 1872 he contrasted the situation in Brecknockshire, where 93 per cent of the relief was outdoor, with Shropshire, where only 77 per cent was. As a result the Welsh poor rate was 1*s*. 2¼*d*. in the pound; in Shropshire less than 5*d*. (Mackay, 526; 'Local government board: second annual report', 29.118–30). He opposed the boarding out of workhouse children, which was becoming fashionable, believing that the children were better supervised and received a better education in workhouse schools.

The most famous controversy of Doyle's later years centred on the sending of pauper children to Canada. Two philanthropists, Maria Rye and Annie Macpherson, pioneered this in the late 1860s. In 1870 Rye's schemes to send out workhouse children received the blessing of the poor-law board. Rumours, however, began to circulate that all was not well. Perhaps the investigative journalist was not quite dead in Doyle: in 1874, although nearing retirement, he went on an official mission of inquiry. He discovered a number of cases of ill treatment and exploitation and suggested that the whole scheme should be suspended at least until a proper system of supervision, similar to that which he had advocated for 'boarded out' children in Britain, could be put in place. Maria Rye had powerful supporters, including Lord Shaftesbury and the archbishop of Canterbury, and a battle royal ensued. The Canadians, too, were angry, claiming that in most cases they had behaved more than fairly to children whose prospects at home could hardly have been worse. The scheme was ultimately suspended until 1883, when it resumed under tighter control.

Doyle was an acknowledged expert on what would later be called social security questions, and in the 1870s he was sent on fact-finding missions to Germany and France. He concluded that the poor-law system in Elberfeld, which was much admired, was unsuited to the very different conditions in Britain, and his report to that effect was published in 1870. In 1879, after his retirement, he was appointed an assistant commissioner on the royal commission on the depressed condition of agricultural interests, chaired by the sixth duke of Richmond. Doyle was responsible for investigating conditions in Staffordshire, Oxfordshire, Warwickshire, Gloucestershire, Worcestershire, Shropshire, Herefordshire, and most of Wales, including Monmouthshire. He set to work with vigour, reactivating his poor-law contacts, summoning meetings, and promising confidentiality to correspondents. He submitted his report on the English counties in 1879 and on Wales in 1882. He added lengthy memoranda on local taxation and, to his 1882 report, on railway rates. The reports contained a wealth of statistical information, as well as comparisons with conditions in France. He gave detailed oral evidence before the royal commission in March 1881 and again in February 1882.

Although Irish by birth, Doyle came to associate himself with Wales. He settled first at Llanddulas in Denbighshire and lived there from about 1852 to 1879, but in 1868 he began to acquire property in Llangenni, near Crickhowell, in Brecknockshire. John Easthope, his father-in-law, had died in 1865 and left the bulk of his property to his grandson, John Andrew Doyle, the son of Andrew and Louisa, born on 14 May 1844, naming Andrew as executor. Father and son together developed a country estate. The house, Pendarren, with views over the Vale of Grwyne, was completed in 1876. Lavish provision was made for stables, reflecting the family interest in horse breeding. He was remembered in the parish for his philanthropy, including the improvement of the water supply and the donation to the village school of swings and seesaws, as well as a room in which the children could eat their dinners.

Doyle died at Pendarren on 13 December 1888 and was

buried in the family grave at Llangenni on 18 December. His wife, Louisa, died on 20 December 1896 and was buried beside him.   MURIEL E. CHAMBERLAIN

Sources A. R. Hawkins, *The Doyles of Pendarren* (Brecon Museum, [n.d.]) · *The Times* (25 Dec 1888) · 'Reports on vagrancy to … the poor law board', *Parl. papers* (1866), 35.677, no. 3698 · 'Local government board: second annual report', *Parl. papers* (1873), 29.56–68, C. 748 [outdoor relief] · 'Report … on the emigration of pauper children to Canada', *Parl. papers* (1875), 63.255, no. 9; (1877), vol. 71, no. 263 · 'Royal commission on the depressed condition of agricultural interests', *Parl. papers* (1881), 16.258–360, C. 2778-II; 17.92–123, C. 3096; (1882), 14.357–74, C. 3309-I; 15.363–455, C. 3375-II · A. Doyle, *The poor law system of Elberfeld* (1870) · S. E. Koss, *The rise and fall of the political press in Britain*, 1 (1981) · T. Mackay, *A history of the English poor law*, 3: *From 1834 to the present time* (1899) · M. E. Chamberlain, 'Child emigration from Merthyr Tydfil workhouse', *Merthyr Historian*, 10 (1999), 71–9 · W. B. Turner, 'Miss Rye's children and the Ontario press, 1875', *Ontario History*, 68 (1976), 169–203 · J. Parr, *Labouring children: British immigrant apprentices to Canada, 1869–1914* (1980)

Archives PRO, poor law and local government records | U. Southampton L., corresp. with Palmerston

Wealth at death £5310 9s. 5d.: administration, 15 Feb 1889, *CGPLA Eng. & Wales*

Doyle, Sir Arthur Ignatius Conan

Doyle, **Sir Arthur Ignatius Conan** (1859–1930), writer, was born at 11 Picardy Place, Edinburgh, on 22 May 1859, the eldest son and third of the nine children of Charles Altamont Doyle (1832–1893), an artist and draughtsman in the Edinburgh office of works, and his wife Mary, *née* Foley (1838–1921), daughter of Catherine Foley, *née* Pack. Mary and her mother were immigrants from Ireland and were descended from landed Irish Catholic and protestant stock. They supplemented their meagre income by taking in lodgers, one of whom was Charles Doyle. In 1864 Charles's growing alcoholism led to a temporary breakup during which Arthur was domiciled at Liberton Bank with sisters of the historiographer-royal for Scotland, John Hill Burton, who influenced the young Doyle's development as historian and bibliophile.

Early life and education In 1867 the Doyle family reunited and inhabited the overcrowded tenement flats at 3 Sciennes Place, Edinburgh, the poorer half of a Newington cul-de-sac. Arthur headed a local street gang of boys, from whom he later evolved Sherlock Holmes's youthful allies, the Baker Street Irregulars. Funded by wealthy uncles, he attended Hodder preparatory school from 1868 to 1870 and then its senior school, Stonyhurst College, from 1870 to 1875. He was happy at Hodder, less happy at Stonyhurst, but developed talents as a story-teller and sportsman. Homesickness increased his love of Sir Walter Scott, possibly the greatest single literary influence on his work in general. The school grounds in the Ribble valley later reappeared in his fiction, notably the building, yew walk, observatory, and mists which transferred to the Dartmoor terrain of *The Hound of the Baskervilles*. Loneliness was offset by a close friendship with a fellow Scot, James Ryan of Glasgow, presumably the initial basis for the Holmes–Watson companionship. He spent a final year of schooling at Feldkirch, Austria, in 1875–6, which added to his remarkable ability to view the past from non-British perspectives. Yet he lost his belief in Catholic doctrine while at Stonyhurst, although he later regained some of its

Sir Arthur Ignatius Conan Doyle (1859–1930), by Emil Otto Hoppé, 1912

attendant cults (guardian angels, the communion of saints) when fashioning his spiritualist faith.

Conan Doyle, as he became known, entered Edinburgh University medical school in 1876 and witnessed a variety of medical characters, chief among them his mentor, Joseph Bell. Bell was a master of deduction from minutiae of evidence, such as gravel on a shoe conveying a patient's route to work, the better to impress the patient and his own attendant students. Otherwise, Bell was austere and scientific with students and patients, in contrast to Sir Patrick Heron Watson, of whom it was said that 'nobody in Scotland was ready to die until they had first seen Watson'. The contrast between Bell's and P. H. Watson's manners survives in Holmes's cold-bloodedness contrasted with John Watson's humanity.

First writings and medical practice During his student days Conan Doyle sent his earliest surviving fictional work, 'The Haunted Grange of Goresthorpe' (unrelated to a similar title published in 1883), to *Blackwood's Edinburgh Magazine*, but it was not used. His first published story was a mock-authentic South African yarn, 'The Mystery of Sasassa Valley', which appeared in *Chambers's Edinburgh Journal* on 6 September 1879. Later that month, on 20 September, he published his first non-fictional article, 'Gelseminum as a poison' in the *British Medical Journal*. Neither was noteworthy in itself, but each presaged fine work to come. His university studies were interrupted by work as a doctor's assistant in Birmingham where he passed an examination in pharmacology extramurally and by service as a ship's doctor on the Greenland whaler *Hope* of Peterhead from February to September 1880. Conan Doyle graduated MB CM in 1881. From October 1881 to January 1882 he was surgeon on the steamer *Mayumba* to west Africa, where he met and treated the dying African-American anti-slavery leader Henry Highland Garnet, who inspired his hostility to the Ku Klux Klan and sympathy for racial intermarriage as expressed, unfashionably at the time, in the Holmes stories of 1891 and 1893, 'The Five Orange Pips' and 'The Yellow Face'. To his other degrees, he added his MD, also from Edinburgh, in 1885 (on aspects of syphilis, using literary as well as medical evidence).

After an ill-fated partnership in Plymouth general practice with George Turnavine Budd, Conan Doyle settled in Southsea, Portsmouth, and built a successful practice. One of his patients, Major-General Alfred Wilks Drayson, fellow of the Royal Astronomical Society, exposed him to theosophy. While Conan Doyle became suspicious of the Blavatsky cult, it nevertheless gave him the plot of his first novel, *The Mystery of Cloomber* (not published until 1888). He also built up a fine portfolio of short stories, particularly two derived from his seafaring. 'The Captain of the *Pole-Star*' takes place on a whaler haunted by the ghost of the captain's dead love while his ship is temporarily cut off from further voyage by icebergs. 'J. Habakuk Jephson's Statement' offered a solution to the sea mystery of the *Mary Celeste*. The latter was so successful that posterity has always employed its orthography, '*Marie Celeste*'. Its explanation of an ex-slave's vengeance derived from Garnet's passionate account of his people's suffering under slavery. The homicidal Septimius Goring supplies Conan Doyle's most memorable narrator up to that time—a black voice. It won a place in Thackeray's old magazine, *The Cornhill*, in January 1884.

On 6 August 1885, Conan Doyle married Louisa (Louise) Hawkins (1856/7–1906), sister of one of his patients, John Hawkins, who died while in residence at Conan Doyle's Southsea surgery. Charles Doyle had by now succumbed to alcoholism and epilepsy. Confined in a number of Scottish mental institutions, he nevertheless was given some commissions for illustrations for his son's books. Mary Doyle continued to live in a cottage on the estate of their former lodger, Bryan Charles Waller, at Masongill, on the Yorkshire border.

Conan Doyle's fiction made astonishing progress in the early 1880s. He learned the economics of the short story from the work of Guy de Maupassant and from the Edinburgh medical journals with their logical progress from case-statement to collection of symptoms, rival diagnoses, and finally to ultimate conclusion and explanation. His first translation of these techniques into fiction ended in what is now called *A Study in Scarlet*. The story brought together Sherlock Holmes and Dr Watson for the first time and a lifelong series was launched. Both *A Study in Scarlet* and *Micah Clarke*, Conan Doyle's historical novel set during the Monmouth rebellion, struggled to find publishers. *A Study in Scarlet* found a badly paid home with Ward Lock, who gave Conan Doyle £25 for all his rights on 20 November 1886. The story was published a year later in *Beeton's Christmas Annual* and was singled out for enthusiastic review in *The Scotsman* and the *Glasgow Herald*. A sequel, *The Sign of the Four*, was commissioned and published by *Lippincott's Magazine* in co-operation with Ward Lock (February 1890) but Conan Doyle's anger against Ward Lock for exploiting the innocence of a struggling author left book publication to Spencer Blackett. Meanwhile Ward and Downey had published *The Mystery of Cloomber* in December 1888, after serialization in the *Pall Mall Gazette*. The *Cornhill* serialized and Smith Elder published his medieval romance, *The White Company*, a remarkable piece of research on fourteenth-century English mercenary warfare in France and Spain. *Micah Clarke* was taken on by Longmans in 1889 after a recommendation from Andrew Lang. *The Captain of the 'Pole-Star' and other Tales* appeared in 1890, as did his partly autobiographical long thriller *The Firm of Girdlestone*.

Success with Holmes and the Strand Magazine It was still medical ambition that took Conan Doyle and his family (now including his daughter Mary, born in 1889) from his successful Southsea practice to residence in London, first at Montague Place and then at South Norwood in 1891. His attempt at eye specialization foundered, partly because of his success in transferring Watson and Holmes to the short story in the newly founded *Strand Magazine* edited by H. Greenhough Smith. Introduced into the July 1891 number towards the back, it rapidly won its way to the front and the magazine's circulation nearly doubled. Conan Doyle had now perfected the formula of a series of stories featuring the same characters but without continuous plot, so that the occasional number might be lost without injury to the suspense. The new arrangement, positing a Watson married since the love interest of *The Sign of the Four*, increased audience identification. They were radical stories in the ways in which they singled out social wrongs, a king's betrayal of an opera singer, a stepfather's deception of his ward as a fictitious lover, an aristocratic crook's exploitation of a failing pawnbroker, a beggar's extensive estate in Kent. The early stories in particular are sharply critical of official incompetence and aristocratic privilege, and at least two in the first dozen short stories ('A Scandal in Bohemia' and 'The Beryl Coronet') are thinly disguised versions of the amorous and financial chicanery of Edward, prince of Wales. Against that, the stories praised a new professionalism: the struggles of the well-qualified aspirant in an unjust world reflected the anxieties of both author and readers.

But now Conan Doyle faced the danger of too much success. The *Strand Magazine* demanded another six stories after the first series and then a further twelve. Conan Doyle twice raised his rates, without demur. Holmes became so famous that the author feared that he would be known only as the detective's creator. He therefore confronted Holmes with the evil genius of Professor Moriarty, a confrontation which resulted in their apparent mutual destruction in 'The Final Problem' (*Strand Magazine*, Dec 1893). The author left himself a slight loophole, but the death story itself was a miniature epic of such dramatic force that it consolidated Holmes's hold over the public.

It was essentially to realize his capabilities in historical fiction, particularly with a view to mastering the era of Napoleon, that Conan Doyle ditched Holmes. His first attempt here had been founded on medical experience: 'A Straggler of '15', the last days of a Waterloo veteran, was published in *Black and White* (21 March 1891). It became a roaring success on the stage as *Waterloo*, starring Henry Irving (1895). A novel, *The Great Shadow* (1892) gave a Scottish boy's impression of the crisis leading to Waterloo, with a cameo appearance of Walter Scott as literary homage. Conan Doyle published collected medical stories in 1894 as *Round the Red Lamp*, which ranged from elegant defence of elderly unscientific medical wisdom in 'Behind the Times' and of woman doctors ('The Doctors of Hoyland') to horrific manoeuvre, where a surgeon unwittingly mutilates his adulterous mistress ('The Case of Lady Sannox'). The Brigadier Gerard stories, which looked at Napoleon's Europe through the eyes of a besotted, somewhat absurd, but profoundly heroic and unquestionably lovable French devotee, replaced Holmes in the *Strand Magazine*. All save one were composed between 1894 and 1903. The Gerard stories are distinguished achievements in intellectual no less than military and social history. They were later collected in *The Exploits of Brigadier Gerard* (1896) and *Adventures of Gerard* (1903), with the late story 'The Marriage of the Brigadier' included in *The Last Galley* (1911). Even without Holmes, Conan Doyle successfully invaded historical fiction using deductive methods and mistakes for Gerard and others.

For all of Holmes's identification with London, Conan Doyle's time there was short. His son Alleyne Kingsley Conan Doyle was born in 1892, but Louise, his wife, contracted tuberculosis and, after visits to Switzerland, the family moved from 12 Tennison Road, South Norwood, to the therapeutic neighbourhood of Hindhead, Haslemere, Surrey. He accepted a lecturing tour in the United States for much of 1894 in company with his younger brother Innes. He took his wife on a recuperative journey down the Nile, which stimulated *The Tragedy of Korosko* (1898), about the adventures of a band of travellers during a Muslim rising. In 1898–9 he produced 'Round the Fire Stories' for the *Strand Magazine*, a mystery series worthy of recognition alongside the best of the Holmes cycle. They were not given book publication until 1908 on an absurd plea of inadequacy: it is more likely that they were withheld because of content. Charles Doyle died in 1893, and passages echo details of his certification ('The Beetle Hunter'), alcoholism ('The Japanned Box'), and incarceration ('The Sealed Room'). Furthermore, 'The man with the Watches' deals with homosexuality and cross-dressing and culminates in a man's saving the gambler who has debauched and accidentally killed his brother.

War, social issues, and personal grief Conan Doyle enthusiastically supported the British effort in the Second South African War and served as a doctor in the volunteer-staffed Longman Hospital in 1900, after which he defended British policy if not always British practice in *The Great Boer War* (1900) and in *The War in South Africa: its Cause and Conduct* (1902). The latter, translated into many foreign languages and braille, became the major international advocate of the British case in the controversial war, and bowing to his mother's insistence a somewhat reluctant Conan Doyle accepted a knighthood for it in 1902. Hitherto his finest work on warfare in modern fiction had been 'The Green flag' and 'The Lord of Chateau Noir', short stories portraying Irish mutiny in British imperial ranks in the 1880s and French guerrilla resistance after German conquest in 1870. *The Hound of the Baskervilles*, supposedly an overlooked adventure of Holmes from before his death, was published in 1902. In response to an offer of $45,000 from *McClure's Magazine* in the United States, Conan Doyle revealed that his famous creation had not died when Moriarty was killed at the Reichenbach Falls. *The Return of Sherlock Holmes*, a collection of thirteen new stories, appeared in 1905 after *Strand* serialization (1903–04).

Conan Doyle celebrated martial virtues, notably in *Sir Nigel* (1906), a violently anti-clerical account of the youth of his medieval hero in the thick of the Hundred Years' War. But he was no bellicose warmonger in the years before the First World War, being converted to the belief in a German threat only two years before its outbreak: he had cherished the memories of his schooldays among German speakers and drew on Goethe and Heine. Yet his stories published in the last years of peace reflect a disintegrating world. He confronted this in his crusade against the Belgians' continuation of Leopold's slave state in Congo, in his support for the legalization of divorce, and in his part in the exposure of grave miscarriages of British justice, namely those of George Edalji, convicted of a series of horse and cattle mutilations, and Oscar Slater, imprisoned for the murder of an elderly Edinburgh spinster, Marion Gilchrist. Conan Doyle also championed Irish home rule after two Unionist candidacies in Scotland in 1900 and 1906. His sense of the glory and nonsense of scientific advance found happy resolution in *The Lost World* (1912), where academic vendetta at its most ludicrous continually punctuates a thrilling quest to establish the survival of dinosaurs.

Louise Conan Doyle succumbed to tuberculosis on 4 July 1906. On 18 September 1907 Conan Doyle married Jean Blyth Leckie (1872/3–1940), daughter of James Blyth Leckie of Glebe House, Blackheath, whom he had known for over ten years. Each year he marked their anniversary by presenting Jean with a single snowdrop. They had three children: Denis (b. 1909), Adrian (b. 1910), and Jean Lena Annette (b. 1912), later Air Commandant Dame Jean Conan *Doyle, head of the Women's Royal Air Force.

Conan Doyle's most valuable piece of reminiscence is *Through the Magic Door* (1907), his appreciation of some of the major literary influences, including Scott, Macaulay, Carlyle, Boswell, Stevenson, Melville, and Froissart. In it he evangelizes for great literature; he believed his works stood in a great tradition but also that they were accessible rather than élitist. He read, as he wrote, for everybody. The last Holmes story, *The Valley of Fear*, was serialized in 1914–15. Conan Doyle also served as military correspondent and pro-ally historian in the First World War, with several volumes culminating in the *British Campaign in France and Flanders* (1920), the original six volumes recording each year of war as soon as possible thereafter, with two volumes for 1918.

Champion of spiritualism and last years Death had been an unobtrusive but lifelong companion for Conan Doyle. His memoirs, *Memories and Adventures* (1924–30), describe his grandmother's corpse as his first memory. His Jesuit schooling reinforced his hope for a life after death, which his loss of faith undermined; his medical training exposed him to scientific scepticism, but left him critical of what seemed to be professional callousness. His first marriage evidently originated in his sorrow—and possibly his guilt—at the death of John Hawkins, and much of it was overladen by the battle to save his wife from tuberculosis. His fiction became death-obsessed, beyond the detective story norm. Death in his writing is not the occasion of a puzzle but the inevitability of an adventure. His son Kingsley died in 1918 from influenza aggravated by war wounds in the British army, where he had won the rank of captain. His brother Innes Doyle, a general, died of pneumonia in the wake of the war. Like other war propagandists, he had to measure the magnitude of the slaughter against the reality of its justification. Spiritualism—denial of death—gave him some degree of peace. The 1920s were dominated for him by a world crusade to evangelize for spiritualism, resulting in most of his last books, including *The Wanderings of a Spiritualist* (1921), *The History of Spiritualism* (1926), and *Pheneas Speaks: Direct Spirit Communications in the Family Circle* (1927). *The Case-Book of Sherlock Holmes* (1927) made no attempt to interfere with Holmes's scepticism, but sexual themes were handled much more vigorously than hitherto, and Holmes denounced human cravings for artificial prolongation of life as well as rejecting suicide.

Conan Doyle's *The Coming of the Fairies* (1922) showed an endearing credulity for fairy phenomena which now appear to have been faked by two little girls at Cottingley, Yorkshire, Elsie Wright and Frances Griffiths. His gallantry and enthusiasm may have prevented their confession at the time. Belatedly but firmly the verdict that his novels have 'no claim to literary distinction' (*DNB*) has been overturned. While he was no remarkable poet, his three volumes of verse, collected as *Poems* (1927), include judicious economic instruction ('Advice to a Young Author') as well as self-analysis ('The Inner Room'), as he lists the many contrasting personalities within himself.

Sir Arthur Conan Doyle died at his home, Windlesham, Crowborough, Sussex, on 7 July 1930, and was buried on 11 July 1930 in the rose garden of Windlesham. He was reinterred with his wife in Minstead churchyard in the New Forest, Hampshire.

Posthumous reputation Edmund Wilson, in 'Mr Holmes, they were the Footprints of a Gigantic Hound' (*Classics and Commercials*, 1950), observed that 'Sherlock Holmes *is* literature on a humble but not ignoble level … by virtue of imagination and style'. While Conan Doyle most wanted to be remembered as a champion of spiritualism and as a

historical novelist, it is Sherlock Holmes who has continued to capture the imagination of the public. The stories have inspired numerous imitators and have lent themselves to stage and screen adaptation. The first Holmes film was made in 1908, and a number of actors have become forever associated with 'the Great Detective'. The American William Gillette played Holmes on the stage from 1899 to 1932. Basil Rathbone starred as Holmes alongside Nigel Bruce as Dr Watson in fourteen films between 1939 and 1946, while Jeremy Brett recreated the role in the Granada television series between 1984 and 1993. The Holmes character has equally inspired parodies, musicals, and even a Disney film. Countless Holmes societies exist all over the world, from the Societé Sherlock Holmes de France to the Baker Street Irregulars, an exclusive, invitation-only club founded in London in 1934. In the United States regional groups pay homage to the detective, from the Diogenes Club of Dallas to the Noble and Most Singular Order of the Blue Carbuncle in Portland, Oregon.

Recent biographies and critical studies have gone some way to presenting a more rounded view of Conan Doyle, his work, and his beliefs. The Arthur Conan Doyle Society was founded in 1989.   OWEN DUDLEY EDWARDS

Sources O. Dudley Edwards, *The quest for Sherlock Holmes* • O. Dudley Edwards, ed., *The Oxford Sherlock Holmes*, 9 vols. • R. Lancelyn Green and J. M. Gibson, *A bibliography of A. Conan Doyle* • *ACD: Journal of the Arthur Conan Doyle Society* (1988) • H. Pearson, *Conan Doyle: his life and art* • J. Dickson Carr, *The life of Sir Arthur Conan Doyle* • P. [Weil-]Nordon, *Sir Arthur Conan Doyle: l'homme et l'oeuvre* • C. Higham, *The adventures of Conan Doyle* • J. Symons, *Portrait of an artist: Conan Doyle* • private information (2004) [Dame Jean Conan Doyle, daughter; John Doyle] • Archives of the British Province of the Society of Jesus, Stonyhurst College, Lancashire, archive of the Society of Jesus • P. G. Wodehouse, *Performing flea*
Archives Free Library of Philadelphia, MS collection • NL Scot., letters • Ransom HRC, corresp. and MSS • Toronto Public Library • U. Edin., MSS | BL, corresp. and papers relating to his petition for the reprieve of Roger Casement, Add. MS 63596 • BL, corresp. with T. A. Guthrie (pseudonym of F. Anstey), Add. MS 54267 • BL, corresp. with Society of Authors, Add. MSS 56694, 63223, 63224 A, B • BLPES, corresp. with E. D. Morel • Bodl. Oxf., corresp. with H. A. Gwynne • CUL, Society for Psychical Research archives, corresp. with Sir O. Lodge • Indiana University, Bloomington, Lilly Library, MS collection, incl. original MS of *The adventure of the Bloomsbury lodger* • Lpool RO, corresp. with Sir Hugh Jeudwine relating to his *History of the battle of the Somme* • LUL, letters to Harry Price • NL Ire., letters to Roger Casement, MS 13073 • NL Scot., letters to E. Bruce Low relating to his political ambitions • Portsmouth Museums and Records Service, letters to patients and colleagues while in Southsea • Richmond Local Studies Library, London, corresp. with Douglas Sladen | FILM BFI NFTVA, *Crime writers*, BBC1, 5 Nov 1978 | SOUND BL NSA, recorded talks
Likenesses London Stereoscopic Co., photograph, 1900, U. Texas, Gernsheim collection • E. O. Hoppé, photograph, 1912, Curatorial Assistance, Inc., Los Angeles, E. O. Hoppé Trust [see illus.] • H. L. Gates, oils, 1927, NPG • B. Partridge, pencil, ink, and wash caricature, NPG; repro. in *Punch* (12 May 1926) • J. Russell & Sons, photograph, NPG • studio Cigarini, photograph, NPG
Wealth at death £63,491 3s. 1d.: probate, 13 May 1931, CGPLA Eng. & Wales

Doyle, Sir Charles Hastings (1804–1883), army officer and colonial administrator in Canada, the eldest son of

Sir Charles Hastings Doyle (1804–1883), by Margaret Sarah Carpenter

Lieutenant-General Sir Charles William *Doyle, CB GCH (1770–1842), and his wife, Sophia Cramer, the daughter of Sir John Coghill, was born on 10 April 1804 in London. He was educated at Sandhurst, and entered the army as an ensign in the 87th, the regiment of his great-uncle, Sir John Doyle, on 23 December 1819. He was promoted lieutenant (27 September 1822), captain (16 June 1825), major (28 June 1838), and finally lieutenant-colonel (14 April 1846). After having served with his regiment in the East and West Indies and in Canada, he went on the staff in 1847 as assistant adjutant-general at Limerick. He was promoted colonel on 20 June 1854, and was appointed assistant adjutant-general to the 3rd division of the army. Ill health prevented him from serving in the Crimea. He next acted as inspector-general of the militia in Ireland until promoted major-general on 15 September 1860, and in the following year he was appointed to command the troops in Nova Scotia. His command was complicated by the American Civil War, but he showed great tact in handling several crises in Anglo-American relations. He dealt adroitly with the *Trent* affair in 1861–2, and in 1863 with the *Chesapeake* affair, when he successfully demanded the release of three Nova Scotians wrongfully detained by the northern steamer, but then pursued the Nova Scotians through the courts for piracy. After having successfully pre-empted a Fenian invasion of New Brunswick in April 1866, he was made the province's administrator in October that year and on 1 July 1867 became its first lieutenant-governor. In October 1867 he became lieutenant-governor of Nova Scotia, where those in favour of repealing the British North America Act had won an overwhelming

majority in the provincial election. Showing considerable political acumen, Doyle wooed the moderates among the repealers and acted as a middleman in the negotiations which led to Joseph Howe's entry into the federal cabinet and the collapse of the repeal movement. In May 1868 he became colonel of the 70th regiment, in 1869 KCMG, and in 1870 lieutenant-general and colonel of his old regiment, the 87th. In May 1873 he resigned his governorship and left Nova Scotia. He acted as general commanding the southern district at Portsmouth from April 1874 to May 1877, and in 1877 was promoted general and placed on the retired list. He died suddenly of heart disease at 18 Bolton Street, Piccadilly, London, on 19 March 1883. He never married. Doyle's time in Canada was marked by a succession of controversies, all of which he managed, by skilful negotiation and, where necessary, resolute action, to resolve peacefully.

H. M. STEPHENS, *rev.* ELIZABETH BAIGENT

Sources *The Times* (20 March 1883) · *Hart's Army List* · *DCB*, vol. 11 · *CGPLA Eng. & Wales* (1883) · *CGPLA Eng. & Wales* (1884)
Archives Bodl. Oxf., corresp. and papers · NA Canada · Public Archives of Nova Scotia, Halifax | New Brunswick Museum, Saint John, corresp. with Sir William Fenwick Williams · U. Nott., Pelham MSS, letters to duke of Newcastle
Likenesses M. S. Carpenter, portrait, priv. coll. [*see illus.*] · Spy [L. Ward], caricature, watercolour study, NPG; repro. in *VF* (23 March 1878)
Wealth at death £56,249 7s. 10d.: resworn probate, March 1884, *CGPLA Eng. & Wales* (1883)

Doyle, Sir Francis Hastings Charles, second baronet (1810–1888), poet and civil servant, the only son of Major-General Sir Francis Hastings Doyle, first baronet (1783–1839), and Diana Elizabeth (d. 1828), eldest daughter of Sir William Milner, was born at the house of his grandfather Sir William Mordaunt Milner, at Nunappleton, near Tadcaster in Yorkshire, on 21 August 1810. Doyle was first sent to a well-known private school at Chelsea, kept by a Frenchman named Clément, where Walter Kerr Hamilton and Henry John Codrington were among his contemporaries. At the beginning of 1823 he entered Eton College as the pupil of Richard Okes, and under the headmastership of John Keate. There, through the debating society held at Miss Hatton's, 'a cook and confectioner', he formed friendships with W. E. Gladstone, A. H. Hallam, James Bruce (afterwards eighth earl of Elgin), and Charles John Canning (afterwards Earl Canning). He heard Gladstone's maiden speech delivered to this society, and assisted him in editing the *Eton Miscellany*.

At Christmas 1827 Doyle left Eton to study with a private tutor, Henry De Foe Baker, rector of Greetham in Rutland. He attended Christ Church, Oxford, from 1828 to 1832, when he obtained a first-class degree in classics. He graduated BCL in 1843 and MA in 1867. He was elected a fellow of All Souls in 1835, retaining his fellowship until his marriage. Among his Oxford friends were Thomas Dyke Acland, Sidney Herbert (afterwards Baron Herbert), and Robert Joseph Phillimore. He was a close friend of Gladstone during their student days and in the 1830s, acting as

Sir Francis
Hastings Charles
Doyle, second
baronet (1810–
1888), by unknown
engraver, pubd
1888

best man at Gladstone's marriage in 1839, but the friendship slowly dissolved thereafter, Doyle professing in his *Reminiscences* 'a continually increasing dislike to Mr. Gladstone as a statesman, and a continually deepening distrust of his character as a man' (Doyle, 404).

After completing his university studies Doyle turned his attention to the law. On 11 October 1832 he entered the Inner Temple as a student, and in 1834 and 1835 was taken on the northern circuit as marshal by Sir James Parke (afterwards Baron Wensleydale), an old family friend who was at that time baron of the court of exchequer. On 17 November 1837 Doyle was called to the bar and joined the northern circuit, where he was shortly appointed a revising barrister. He succeeded to the baronetcy on his father's death on 6 November 1839. On 12 December 1844 at St George's, Hanover Square, he married Sydney (d. 1867), youngest daughter of Charles Watkin Williams *Wynn; they had two sons and a daughter. After his marriage Doyle sought more remunerative employment than the law, and in 1845 Sir Robert Peel offered him the assistant solicitorship of the excise, with the promise that after a year he should be appointed receiver-general of customs. These offers he accepted, and abandoning his early ambition for legal or parliamentary distinction, he continued to hold the receiver-generalship until 1869.

Doyle's earliest verses appeared in the *Eton Miscellany*. In 1834 he published his first volume of poetry entitled *Miscellaneous Verses*, which he reissued in 1840 with a number of additional poems. These early verses were considered somewhat immature, several of the best poems, including 'The Eagle's Nest', 'Mehrab Khan', 'The Crusader's Return', and 'The Catholic', appearing for the first time in the second edition. In 1844 he issued *The Two Destinies*, a poem dealing with social questions; in 1849 *Oedipus, King of Thebes*, a translation from the *Oedipus tyrannus* of Sophocles; and in 1852 *The Duke's Funeral*, in memory of the duke of Wellington. For the next fourteen years he published nothing; but in 1866, finding Matthew Arnold's tenure of the professorship of poetry at Oxford coming to an end, and desiring to be appointed his successor, he published *The Return of the Guards and other Poems*, with the stated aim

of bringing his work to the attention of the younger members of the university. This volume is thought to contain almost all his best poems, including one or two which had appeared in his former collection.

Doyle was elected professor of poetry in 1867 (the year of his wife's death), and was re-elected in 1872 for a further period of five years, holding a fellowship at All Souls with his university appointment. On resigning the professorship he received the honorary degree of DCL on 11 December 1877. His *Lectures* were published in 1869, a second series appearing in 1877. Although full of interest, they were held to be discursive and without much unity of plan, and they inevitably suffered by comparison with those of his predecessor, Matthew Arnold. The first series contains an appreciation of the Dorset poet William Barnes. The second series is more elaborate, consisting of studies of Wordsworth, Scott, and Shakespeare, and a lecture on Newman's *Dream of Gerontius*, which was translated into French in 1869.

In 1869 Doyle exchanged his post of receiver-general of customs for that of commissioner of customs, an appointment which he retained until 1883. He died in London on 8 June 1888 at 46 Davies Street, Berkeley Square. His eldest son, Francis Grenville Doyle, a captain in the 2nd dragoon guards, died in the Egyptian campaign on 2 December 1882. His second son, Everard Hastings, succeeded as third baronet.

Doyle's poetic work is chiefly notable for his use of the ballad form. Traditionally archaic in both subject and expression, the ballad was employed by Doyle for the treatment of contemporary events. He believed that modern deeds of national bravery were 'as susceptible as any in the far past of free ballad treatment, with all the old freshness, directness, and simplicity' (Japp, 249). Among his better-known ballads are 'The Red Thread of Honour', which was translated into Pushtoo and became a favourite among the villagers on the north-western frontier of India, 'The Private of the Buffs', 'The Fusilier's Dog', 'The Loss of the Birkenhead', and 'Mehrab Khan'. The poetic reputation of Doyle in the late nineteenth century rested chiefly on these works. Although he attempted a variety of other verse forms, the majority of his poetry was considered commonplace and pedestrian, lacking in both feeling and technique.

E. I. CARLYLE, rev. CHARLES BRAYNE

Sources F. H. C. Doyle, *Reminiscences and opinions* (1886) · A. H. Japp, 'Memoir', *The poets and poetry of the century*, ed. A. H. Miles, 4 (1892), 103–8 · *Macmillan's Magazine*, 58 (1888), 286–91 · *Saturday Review*, 65 (1888), 712–13 · *National Review*, 12 (1888–9) · *Oxford Magazine* (13 June 1888) · W. E. Gladstone, 'Personal recollections of A. H. Hallam', *Daily Telegraph* (5 Jan 1898) · *Memoirs of James Robert Hope-Scott, with selections from his correspondence*, ed. R. Ormsby, 2 vols. (1884), vol. 1, pp. 72–4 · Gladstone, *Diaries* · H. C. G. Matthew, *Gladstone*, 2 vols. (1986–95); repr. in 1 vol. as *Gladstone, 1809–1898* (1997) · J. Foster, *Men-at-the-bar: a biographical hand-list of the members of the various inns of court*, 2nd edn (1885) · Foster, *Alum. Oxon.*
Archives BL, corresp. with W. E. Gladstone, Add. MS 44150 · Bodl. Oxf., corresp. with Sir Henry Taylor · Bodl. Oxf., letters to Henry Halford Vaughan · Herts. ALS, corresp. with Lord and Lady Lytton · NL Scot., letters to J. R. Hope-Scott · NL Wales, letters to George Stovin Venables · Trinity Cam., letters to Lord Houghton

Likenesses Spy [L. Ward], caricature, watercolour study, NPG; repro. in *VF* (24 Nov 1877) • wood-engraving, NPG; repro. in *ILN* (23 June 1888) [*see illus.*]

Wealth at death £5323 0s. 1d.: probate, 4 July 1888, *CGPLA Eng. & Wales*

Doyle, Henry Edward (1827–1892), painter and museum director, was born in Dublin, the third of seven children of John *Doyle (1797–1868) and his wife, Marianna Conan (d. 1832). John Doyle, also born in Dublin, had trained initially as a miniature painter with John Comerford before settling in the 1820s in London, where he achieved fame as a political cartoonist, under the pseudonym H. B. All four of his sons became artists and illustrators, the best-known being Richard *Doyle (pseudonym Dick Kitcat; 1824–1883), illustrator and painter of fairy themes. The children were privately educated at their home in London and Henry went on to receive some art training in Dublin. He worked briefly for *Punch* in 1844 and later from 1867 to 1869 drew cartoons for *Fun*, signing himself Hen or Fusbos. A devout Catholic, he used his family's religious reputation to gain patronage, and his best-known oil portrait is that of Cardinal Wiseman (exh. RA, 1858). Other portraits of note include an oil portrait of his brother Richard (NG Ire.), and a pencil portrait of John Ruskin (NG Ire.). Through the influence of the cardinal, Doyle was appointed commissioner for the Papal States to the London International Exhibition of 1862 and was created a knight of the order of Pope Pius IX. His religious paintings include some frescoes for the chapel of the Dominican convent at Cabra, near Dublin. He also illustrated Mary Frances Cusack's *An Illustrated History of Ireland: from the Earliest Period* (1868).

In 1869 Doyle was appointed the second director of the National Gallery of Ireland, after George Mulvany (1809–1869). Doyle's period of directorship, cut short by his untimely death in 1892, was marked by flair and innovation. With a limited amount of money from the Treasury, he purchased a number of pictures of international importance, including Rembrandt's *Rest on the Flight into Egypt* (1647), *The Attempted Martyrdom of Saints Cosmos and Damian with their Brothers* (1438–40) by Fra Angelico, and *Lamentation over the Body of Christ* (c.1657/1660) by Poussin. He instigated the rehanging of the entire collection by national schools rather than displaying works in the order of their acquisition. Doyle, above all, was responsible for bringing a strong Irish dimension to the collection. He initiated a policy of buying pictures by native artists in order to promote an Irish school of art and set aside a special room for their display. In his twenty-three years as director, over 170 oil paintings were purchased by the gallery. Of these, forty-six were of Irish origin. This is in marked contrast to the acquisition policy at the time of the opening of the gallery in 1864. At that time the policy was to display a selection of European old master paintings with a view to providing stimulus for young aspiring Irish artists while at the same time raising public appreciation of art. On his appointment Doyle extended that policy to include the work of eighteenth- and nineteenth-century Irish artists such as George Barrett, Daniel Maclise, and

William Mulready, in the belief that they had much to contribute to the legacy of European art.

Doyle was also responsible for the establishment of the National Portrait Collection. This was not without opposition. The Treasury refused to increase funding for such a project on the grounds that eminent Irish personages were already acknowledged in the portrait gallery in London. It argued that a separate collection in Dublin would materially lessen the importance and interest in the existing portrait collection. In spite of lack of financial backing, Doyle went ahead and a room termed the National, Historical and Portrait Gallery was officially opened in 1884. On display were 148 portraits of different media, and the collection has been substantially added to since that time. One of the finest of the portraits, purchased by Doyle for this collection in 1875, is Joshua Reynolds's *Charles Coote, First Earl of Bellamont* (1773). Henry Doyle was made companion of the Bath in 1880, and JP for Wicklow in 1884. He married, in 1866, Jane Isabella, daughter of Nicholas Ball. They had no children. He died suddenly of heart disease on 17 February 1892 at his home, 55 South Street, Mayfair, London. Greatly loved for the simplicity of his nature and for his charming manners, Doyle was mourned in both Dublin and London.

SÍGHLE BHREATHNACH-LYNCH

Sources W. G. Strickland, *A dictionary of Irish artists*, 2 vols. (1913); facs. edn with introduction by T. J. Snoddy (1969) • letter books, NG Ire. • minute books, NG Ire. • correspondence, NG Ire. • annual reports, NG Ire. • R. Engen, *The artist and his critic, Richard Doyle*, 2 (1983) • *Pall Mall Gazette* (20 Feb 1892) • *The Times* (20 Feb 1892) • *CGPLA Eng. & Wales* (1892)

Archives NG Ire., annual reports; corresp.; letter copy books; minute books; newspaper cuttings | BL, letters to Sir Austen Layard, Add. MSS 38997–39046, *passim*

Likenesses H. J. Brooks, group portrait, oils (*Private view of the Old Masters Exhibition, Royal Academy, 1888*), NPG

Wealth at death £238 6s.: probate, 30 May 1892, *CGPLA Ire.*

Doyle, James Warren (1786–1834), Roman Catholic bishop of Kildare and Leighlin, political controversialist, and educationist, was born in September 1786 in New Ross, co. Wexford, the last of four children of James Doyle, a farmer, and his second wife, Anne Warren.

Doyle was educated by the Augustinians in New Ross and entered the Augustinian noviciate in 1805. In 1806 he went to Coimbra in Portugal and matriculated at the University of Coimbra in 1807 but his studies were interrupted by the French invasion. As a British subject Doyle was arrested by the French; on his release he aided the Portuguese resistance. He was recalled to Ireland in 1808 and was ordained priest in Enniscorthy, co. Wexford in the following year. From 1809 until 1813 he taught seminarians in the Augustinian friary in New Ross. In 1813 he was appointed to the chair of rhetoric in Carlow College, and in 1814 to the chair of theology. In 1819 he was appointed bishop of Kildare and Leighlin at the age of thirty-three.

As bishop Doyle entered on a systematic programme of religious renewal and reform. Doyle was a disciplinarian and clerics who did not conform were removed from the mission. He reformed a relatively easy-going culture of church and enforced Tridentine standards. Frequent pastorals urged greater religious exertion and also established Doyle's reputation as a firm opponent of political and agrarian terrorism. Confraternities, Sunday school catechesis, and chapel libraries were significant elements of his programme aimed at improving the faith and morals of the laity. A modernizing voice in pre-famine Ireland, he advocated the reform of popular mores. In 1829 he anticipated Father Mathew by promoting temperance. Doyle held exhaustive biennial visitations. His reputation as a preacher was unequalled. His building of Carlow Cathedral (1828–33) exemplified a great surge of church building throughout the diocese. In his 1829 *relatio status* Doyle reported to Rome that there was hardly any aspect of the religious life of the clergy or the laity which was not very satisfactory.

Politically, Doyle's first major public intervention was his *Vindication of the Religious and Civil Liberties of the Irish Catholics*, published in 1823 under the contentious rebus J. K. L. (James, Kildare and Leighlin). This monogram made a territorial claim forbidden in law to Catholic bishops. The *Vindication* was an aggressive rebuttal of attacks made on Catholicism and burnt with grievance and a sense of historical oppression. It signalled the arrival of a self-confident episcopal spokesman for Irish Catholics who had jettisoned the traditional low profile of the hierarchy. Doyle became the Catholic Association's bishop *par excellence* though his important relationship with Daniel O'Connell was often strained. His book *Letters on the State of Ireland*, published in 1825, is an outstanding work of great passion, brimming with savage indignation—one of the finest examples of modern Irish polemic. Doyle's evidence before the parliamentary inquiry on the state of Ireland in 1825 was a *tour de force*. His name dominated *Hansard* debates on Ireland and the Catholic question throughout his era. In 1826 Doyle addressed *An Essay on the Catholic Claims* to the prime minister, Lord Liverpool, which sought to prove that the allegiance of Catholics was not divided. In 1828 he publicly supported O'Connell's decision to stand in the County Clare election.

When emancipation was conceded in 1829 Doyle envisaged that it would signal a new era in Anglo-Irish relations, but this proved to be a vain hope. When O'Connell announced that he would agitate the repeal of the union, Doyle supported repeal in principle but did not see how it could be achieved in practice without recourse to violence. He believed that O'Connell should seek legislative reform for Ireland on issues such as poverty rather than pursue the unpromising cause of repeal. Doyle gave extensive evidence before the parliamentary inquiry on the state of the Irish poor in 1830 and became the leading theoretician of an Irish poor law. In March 1831 O'Connell, having read Doyle's *Letter to Thomas Spring Rice*, declared himself for the first time fully convinced of the validity of Doyle's stance on the issue; but when, in December of the same year, O'Connell declared that repeal was his poor law for Ireland, they engaged in a public dispute on this issue.

Throughout his episcopacy Doyle was at the centre of fierce religious controversy. In 1822 he denounced a visitation charge of Archbishop Magee of Dublin which attacked the Catholic church. Magee's charge is often seen as the starting point of the Irish evangelical crusade to convert Catholics to protestantism known as the New Reformation. In 1824, in an effort to turn the New Reformation on its head, Doyle published a *Letter on the Re-Union of the Churches* which advocated an ecumenical solution to the political ills of Ireland. A passage in the letter stating that 'if a rebellion were raging from Carrickfergus to Cape Clear no sentence of excommunication would ever be fulminated by a Catholic prelate' attracted much hostile attention, but the ecumenical dimension was largely ignored. In 1825 Doyle forbade his clerics from engaging in public controversy with evangelical clergy, stating that it was contrary to the public peace. In 1827, the year a conversion crusade in Carlow failed, Doyle entered the lists of controversy against Archbishop Magee and the evangelical nobleman Lord Farnham. In 1828 he had a pamphlet dispute with Bishop Elrington of Leighlin and Ferns. In his public works Doyle was always very critical of the wealth of the established church.

In a period when education was a source of great interdenominational tension, Doyle favoured the education of Catholic and protestant children together but he objected to protestant schools, particularly those of the Kildare Place Society, which insisted that Catholic pupils should read the Bible without note or comment. Throughout the 1820s Doyle led a strong Catholic attack on this state-funded society, arguing that it did not offer a proper national use of public finances since its religious principles excluded Catholics. In 1831 he enjoyed success when the state withdrew its support from the Kildare Place Society and inaugurated the national system of education. Doyle thought the new system the best which Catholics could expect to achieve at that time and he urged his clergy to seek aid from the national board for their parish schools.

The damage done to interdenominational relations in the 1820s was confirmed in the 1830s by the outbreak of the tithe war which saw many violent episodes. The tithe war began in this final phase in December 1830 in Graiguenamanagh, co. Kilkenny, within Doyle's diocese. The refusal of the parish priest, Martin Doyle, a cousin of the bishop, to pay tithes to the protestant minister sparked the campaign in which Doyle's clergy took a prominent part and in which he himself provided intellectual leadership. Although he abhorred violence, Doyle wrote that citizens could not be disbarred from their lawful right to protest against an iniquitous law even though violence might occur. His phrase 'may your hatred of tithes be as lasting as your love of justice' became a slogan of the tithe war. In February 1832 Doyle defended his stance before parliamentary committees of both houses on the Irish tithe question with contemptuous éclat.

Doyle was often ill. His health failed entirely from 1832 onwards and he died on 15 June 1834, probably of tuberculosis, at the age of forty-eight. He was buried before the altar of Carlow Cathedral. Doyle was pastorally, politically, and educationally the outstanding Irish Catholic bishop of his time, playing a leading role in public affairs during the era of Catholic emancipation and achieving renown as a brilliant advocate of the rights of Catholics and of Ireland.   THOMAS MCGRATH

Sources T. McGrath, *Religious renewal and reform in the pastoral ministry of Bishop James Doyle of Kildare and Leighlin, 1786–1834* (1999) · T. McGrath, *Politics, interdenominational relations and education in the public ministry of Bishop James Doyle of Kildare and Leighlin, 1786–1834* (1999) · W. J. Fitzpatrick, *The life, times, and correspondence of the Right Rev. Dr Doyle, bishop of Kildare and Leighlin*, 2 vols. (1861)
Archives Kildare and Leighlin Diocesan Archives, Bishop's House, Carlow, MSS · St Patrick's College, Maynooth, account book | Dublin Diocesan Archives, Clonliffe, Dublin, Murray MSS · NL Ire., letters to Thomas Wyse
Likenesses Irish school, plaster bust, 19th cent., NG Ire. · R. Cooper, stipple, pubd 1824 (after drawing by J. C. Smith), NPG, NG Ire. · W. Holl, stipple, pubd 1834 (after P. Turnerelli; after bust), BM; NPG · J. Hogan, statue, 1840, Carlow Cathedral · J. P. Haverty, lithograph, Carlow College · J. P. Haverty, lithograph, NPG · J. P. Haverty, lithograph (after his oil portrait), NG Ire. · J. P. Haverty, oils, Carlow College · T. Kelly, line and stipple (after portrait, Irish school, *c*.1820), NG Ire. · death mask, NG Ire.

Doyle, James William Edmund (1822–1892), illustrator and antiquary, was born in London on 22 October 1822, the eldest of the four sons of the caricaturist John *Doyle (1797–1868), who used the pseudonym HB, and his wife, Marianna Conan (d. 1832). He was the brother of the artist and illustrator Richard *Doyle and of Henry Edward *Doyle, the director of the Irish National Gallery; he was also the uncle of Sir Arthur Conan *Doyle, the creator of Sherlock Holmes.

The Doyles were a close-knit, happy, and very devout Catholic family, who collaborated on various juvenilia. All the brothers were taught to draw by their father and did not attend school; they were instructed instead in French, history, and dancing by a tutor who came to their home at 17 Cambridge Terrace, off the Edgware Road. James early became fascinated by history: his scholarly instincts earned him the family nickname of the Priest, an epithet which later matched well with his tall and austere appearance and prolonged bachelorhood (apparently Jones of Brown, Jones, and Robinson, Richard Doyle's three famous clerks, was partially modelled on James).

James Doyle's first career was as an oil painter: *A Literary Party at Sir Joshua Reynolds'* was his first success. His painting of *Dr Johnson Reading the Manuscript of 'The Vicar of Wakefield'* was engraved as a large print in 1848, and proved very popular: it sold out in two years and went into a second edition in 1851. Doyle also painted scenes from Walter Scott's novels as frescoes in the summer house at Buckingham Palace. However, he soon turned from painting to pursue historical and genealogical research. His only existing oil painting is *The Black Prince on the Eve of the Battle of Poitiers* (exh. RA, 1849). In 1852 he did a little pencil sketch of John Henry Newman at the Oratory in King William Street: lithographed as a private plate, it is believed to be the only portrait from that period of the future cardinal.

Doyle was the main illustrator of a new edition of *The History of England* by the Catholic historian John Lingard, published in 1854–5 by the Catholic publisher Charles Dolman. His illustrations suggest an attraction to the 'German manner' of line drawing which was increasingly popular in mid-nineteenth-century England, and also reflect the influence of the Nazarene school of history painters, who shared Doyle's romantic commitment to promoting the Catholic faith. His illustrations in Lingard's *History*—elegantly composed, with statuesque figures, but essentially lifeless—bear a remarkable resemblance to those of *A Chronicle of England, B.C. 55–A.D. 1485* (1864), which Doyle published in 1864. Probably originally intending it to be a Christmas present for his father, he had started work on it in the 1840s. Here his images were engraved and printed in colour by Edmund Evans, and the book is one of the earliest (and finest) examples of Victorian colour printing.

In the same year in which the *Chronicle* was published, the Doyle family moved to 54 Clifton Gardens, Maida Hill. James continued to live there after his brothers left home and married only late in life: no details are known of his wife. He moved in aristocratic Catholic circles, and spent his honeymoon, by invitation, at the duke of Norfolk's seat, Arundel Castle. His grave appearance contrasted with a dry wit: his obituarist in *The Athenaeum* recalled that 'the drollest of his stories was always told without the movement of a muscle in his face' (*The Athenaeum*, 921). He managed the estate of his brother Richard after his death, and published in 1886 Richard's *Scenes from English History*, cartoons originally drawn about 1840, for which he wrote the letterpress.

In 1886 Doyle published his *Historical Baronage of England … from 1066 to 1885*, which covered all ranks except barons and gave exhaustive lists of the offices held by peers. It also included illustrations based on portraits, coats of arms, and facsimile signatures. It was not a financial success, despite the 'extraordinary pains and research [Doyle] bestowed upon the book' (*The Athenaeum*, 921), and ceased publication after three volumes. However, the *Baronage* remains a standard work of reference for the College of Arms, and was the basis of a close friendship between James and his sister-in-law Mary Doyle, the mother of Arthur Conan Doyle and a fellow enthusiast for heraldry. James Doyle died on 3 December 1892 at his home, 38 Dorset Square, Marylebone, London, and was buried in Kensal Green cemetery on 9 December.

     ROSEMARY MITCHELL

Sources *The Athenaeum* (31 Dec 1892), 921–2 · *The Times* (16 Dec 1892) · R. Engen, *Richard Doyle* (1983) · L. Lambourne, R. Engen, and M. Heseltine, *Richard Doyle and his family* (1983) [exhibition catalogue, V&A, 30 Nov 1983 – 26 Feb 1984] · R. K. Engen, *Dictionary of Victorian wood engravers* (1985), 76 · R. Mitchell, *Picturing the past: English history in text and image, 1830–1870* (2000), 184–8 · R. McLean, *Victorian book design and colour printing*, rev. edn (1972) · d. cert.

Doyle, Dame Jean Lena Annette Conan [*married name* Dame Jean Lena Annette Bromet] (**1912–1997**), director of the Women's Royal Air Force, was born Lina Jean at Windlesham, Crowborough, Sussex, on 21 December 1912, the only daughter and second of three children of Sir

Arthur Ignatius Conan *Doyle (1859–1930), writer, and his second wife, Jean Blyth, *née* Leckie (1872/3–1940). The most bookish of the children, Jean was the only one allowed in her father's study when he was working. He regarded his young daughter as something of an enigma: 'You know the boys, you never feel you quite know the girl. Something very strong and forceful seems to be at the back of that wee body. Her will is tremendous' (Conan Doyle, 6). Given the nickname Billie in order to distinguish her from her mother, Jean was a tomboy who played cricket with her brothers and was no less accomplished than they at boxing: as a nine-year-old 'she could swing a fine loose left' (Conan Doyle, 82). Educated at Granville School, Eastbourne, she also accompanied her father on his numerous lecture tours abroad. She was only seventeen and just out of school when Conan Doyle died in 1930: 'I knew that life would never be the same again', she said (Roden, 117). She spent the following years living with and looking after her widowed mother.

In 1938 Jean Conan Doyle joined no. 46 (County of Sussex) RAF company, attached to the Auxiliary Territorial Service, enlisting as aircraftwoman, second class. In March 1940 she was commissioned in the Women's Auxiliary Air Force (the predecessor of the Women's Royal Air Force) as assistant section officer. She served throughout the Second World War in various postings in England and Northern Ireland, achieving promotion at nearly every stage, before joining the British forces of occupation at Buckeburg air headquarters in 1947. She was appointed OBE in 1948 and received the air efficiency award in 1949. During the 1950s she held a variety of posts, which culminated in her appointment as director of the Women's Royal Air Force—the first to have risen through the ranks—in 1963. In that year she was made DBE. From 1963 to 1966 she was honorary aide-de-camp to the queen, a post which she held with such discretion that even her closest friends knew nothing of it until they saw it listed in her *Who's Who* entry. Described as a good listener who had time for everyone, Jean Conan Doyle saw the 'wastage' that occurred when newly married women left the WRAF. She encouraged them to stay, and through her initiative, which at first raised eyebrows, married couples became the norm. 'Tidiness' and 'order' were her catchwords.

On 11 June 1965 Jean Conan Doyle married retired Air Vice Marshal Geoffrey Rhodes Bromet (1891/2–1983), a widower. She retired in 1966, but remained active in charity work as a governor of the Royal Star and Garter Home (1968–72), a member of council of the Officers' Pension Society (1970–75; vice-president, 1981–8), and a member of committee of the Not Forgotten Association (1975–91; president from 1981 to 1991). The copyright on her father's works ran out in Britain in 1980, but European legislation revived it. Nevertheless, acrimonious litigation between members of the family and others continued for many years, to be resolved only in 1996. In America the estate held copyright for seventy years from the date of each publication. On the death of her brother Adrian, Jean Conan Doyle became literary executor and utilized this control of books and films for the American market by assiduously upholding the reputation and legacy of her father and his creations. When her husband died in 1983, she reverted to her maiden name. They had no children. She died at her home, Flat 6, 72 Cadogan Square, London, on 18 November 1997 and was buried near her parents at Minstead churchyard in the New Forest (having in 1955 overseen the transfer of their remains from the grounds of their home in Crowborough). JANE POTTER

Sources *The Independent* (22 Nov 1997) · *Daily Telegraph* (21 Nov 1997) · *The Times* (19 Nov 1997) · b. cert. · m. cert. · d. cert. · C. Roden, 'In conversation with … Air Cmdt. Dame Jean Conan Doyle', *ACD: The Journal of the Arthur Conan Doyle Society*, 1/2 (1990), 113–20 · A. Conan Doyle, *The three of them* [1923]
Likenesses photograph, 1990, repro. in Roden, 'In conversation with … Air Cmdt. Dame Jean Conan Doyle', 2.112
Wealth at death £1,888,772: probate, 18 Dec 1997, CGPLA Eng. & Wales

Doyle, Sir John, baronet (1756–1834), army officer and politician, was the fourth son of Charles Doyle (*d.* 1769) of Bramblestown, co. Kilkenny, and Claughmoney, co. Carlow, and his wife, Elizabeth, daughter of the Revd Nicholas Milley of Johnville, co. Kilkenny. He was educated by the Revd Benjamin Hobart of Carlow and at Trinity College, Dublin. Destined for a legal career, he was admitted to Lincoln's Inn in 1769, but in 1771 the example of his younger brother, Welbore Ellis [*see below*], who had already joined the army, inspired him to purchase an ensigncy in the 48th foot. Having been promoted lieutenant, he transferred to the 40th foot in 1775 and sailed with his new regiment to quell the rebellion in America. He fought throughout General Sir William Howe's New York and Philadelphia campaigns, particularly distinguishing himself at Brooklyn, where he rescued the body of his commanding officer, and Germantown, as one of the defenders of Chew House. In 1778 he was given a captaincy in Lord Rawdon's loyalist regiment, the 'Volunteers of Ireland', recruited from Irish-American deserters. With this corps he saw action at Monmouth, New Jersey, and in the southern campaigns at Charlestown, Camden, and Hobkirk's Hill. Promoted major in March 1781, he showed himself adept at partisan warfare and was in the forefront of the defeat of Francis Marion's brigade at Wambaw Bridge, South Carolina, on 24 February 1782. He also served as assistant adjutant-general to the British commander-in-chief in the south, General Paston Gould, and his two successors. At the end of the American war he returned home and went on half pay.

In 1783 Doyle was brought into the Irish parliament by Lord Granard, an opposition peer, as member for Mullingar. An eloquent speaker, he held the seat until 1799. In 1788 the lord lieutenant in Dublin hoped to win over Granard by granting Doyle his wish to resume an army career; but in spite of Prime Minister William Pitt's endorsement, George III would not allow Doyle a preferential return to the full-pay list. Doyle moved further into opposition. A founder member of the Irish Whig Club, he was an early advocate of Catholic emancipation. In 1791 Lord Rawdon

Sir John Doyle, baronet (1756–1834), by Sir Thomas Lawrence, c.1792–3

secured him the position of secretary-extraordinary to the prince of Wales, a post which he held until 1796. When war with France broke out in 1793, Doyle raised a corps—the 87th foot—styled the Prince of Wales's Irish regiment. He was appointed its lieutenant-colonel commandant and remained regimental colonel all his life. He then served in Flanders as quartermaster-general to his old chief, Lord Moira (formerly Rawdon), until wounds received at Alost on 15 July 1794 saw him invalided home. In January 1795 the appointment of the coalition whig Earl Fitzwilliam as Irish viceroy saw Doyle made his military under-secretary. However, Fitzwilliam's administration survived barely two months and the consequent abandonment of measures of Catholic relief ensured Doyle's own resignation shortly afterwards.

Promoted colonel on 3 May 1796, Doyle returned to active service the following October when, as a temporary brigadier, he was instructed to land troops in the northern Netherlands to help in the elimination of the Dutch fleet. Disembarkation having proved impossible, he returned to England and, after recovering from a bloody encounter with highwaymen, received a posting as brigadier-general to Gibraltar in 1798. Two years later, upon the arrival of Sir Ralph Abercromby's expeditionary force in the Mediterranean, he was given command of the 4th brigade for the invasion of Egypt. At the battle of Alexandria on 21 March 1801 he moved adroitly to the support of John Stuart's brigade. On 17 May, during the advance on Cairo, his enterprise at the head of 250 cavalry led to the capture of a French dromedary regiment comprising 600 troops, 200 horses, and 460 camels. And in August, hearing that the final attack was to be made on Alexandria, he rose from his Rosetta sickbed, rode 40 miles, and arrived in time to supervise his brigade's successful assault on the Green Hill. General Hutchinson's dispatch failed to mention Doyle's contribution or even his presence on this occasion, but once Doyle pointed this out, the omission was rectified and he received the particular thanks in parliament of the war minister, Lord Hobart. The Turks awarded him the order of the crescent.

Promoted major-general on 29 April 1802, Doyle was sent to Guernsey and appointed the island's lieutenant-governor on 17 May 1803. He improved the state of defence, building roads, repairing fortifications, and reinvigorating the militia. To fund the work he persuaded the Guernsey legislature to vote a tax on property which yielded £20,000 within two years. So biddable did Doyle's easy manner render the independent-minded islanders (not for nothing was his army nickname Popularity Jack) that after his departure in 1815 they erected a large column bearing the inscription 'Doyle—Gratitude'. The government rewarded his success on Guernsey with a baronetcy in October 1805.

Doyle was returned to parliament, through Lord Moira, in 1806 as member for the pocket borough of Newport, Isle of Wight, whose patron sold the seat. He spoke against the slave trade but left parliament after the dissolution of 1807. Promoted lieutenant-general in 1808, he was offered command of the Portuguese army the following January. The letter conveying the offer to Guernsey was delayed by gales, however, and the government sent William Carr Beresford instead. In February 1813, after many years of petitioning, Doyle was made a knight of the Bath. The governorship of Charlemont was bestowed upon him in 1818, followed by promotion to full general in 1819. In later years anxiety for the well-being in Portugal of his nephew John Milley Doyle undermined Doyle's health. He died aged seventy-eight on 8 August 1834 in Somerset Street, Portman Square, London. As he had remained unmarried, the baronetcy became extinct on his death.

Doyle's brother **Welbore Ellis Doyle** (1758–1798), also an army officer, served with him in America as lieutenant-colonel of the 'Volunteers of Ireland'. Placed on half pay at the peace, he apparently spent some time as a military envoy to Poland before receiving the lieutenant-colonelcy of the 14th foot in 1789. While in Flanders at the head of his regiment at the battle of Famars on 23 May 1793, he famously steadied his men by shouting: 'Come on, my lads, let's break these scoundrels to their own damned tune. Drummers, strike up *Ça ira*' (Doyle, 54); the French revolutionary tune became the regimental march thereafter. Following his promotion to major-general in 1795, Doyle was given command of the expedition to the Isle d'Yeu, off Brittany. A year later he was appointed commander-in-chief and acting governor of Ceylon, where he died on 2 January 1798. He left a widow, Frances Rainsford, afterwards Princess Joseph of Monaco, and two sons.   ALASTAIR W. MASSIE

Sources A. Doyle, *A hundred years of conflict* (1911) · B. Murphy and R. G. Thorne, 'Doyle, Sir John', HoP, *Commons, 1790–1820* · J. Philippart, ed., *The royal military calendar*, 3rd edn, 5 vols. (1820) · *GM*, 2nd ser., 2 (1834), 534–6 · Doyle family papers, Bodl. Oxf., MSS North c. 18, e. 21 · *The correspondence of George, prince of Wales, 1770–1812*, ed. A. Aspinall, 8 vols. (1963–71) · *Report on the Laing manuscripts*, 2, HMC, 72 (1925) · *The later correspondence of George III*, ed. A. Aspinall, 5 vols. (1962–70), vols. 1–2 · *The manuscripts of J. B. Fortescue*, 10 vols., HMC, 30 (1892–1927), vols. 1, 3 · *Report on American manuscripts in the Royal Institution of Great Britain*, 4 vols., HMC, 59 (1904–9), vol. 2 · W. Berry, *The history of the island of Guernsey* (1815) · P. Mackesy, *British victory in Egypt, 1801* (1995)

Archives Bodl. Oxf., corresp. and papers | Bodl. Oxf., MSS North, 'Memorandum for army officers on the treatment and discipline of soldiers written by Welbore Ellis for his brother' (121ff.), e. 21 [W. E. Doyle] · Mount Stuart Trust, Isle of Bute, letters to Lord Hastings

Likenesses T. Lawrence, portrait, *c*.1792–1793, priv. coll. [*see illus.*] · miniature (Welbore Ellis Doyle), repro. in Doyle, *Hundred years of conflict*, facing p. 49 · portraits, repro. in M. Cunliffe, *The Royal Irish Fusiliers, 1793–1950* (1952), facing pp. 4, 190

Doyle, John [*pseud.* H. B.] (**1797–1868**), cartoonist and painter, was born in Dublin. 'His father … belonged to a family which had come from the King's or Queen's county' (Strickland, 1.297). Engen noted that Doyle's 'ancestors traced back to the fourteenth century, and in the seventeenth century were granted large estates and their own coat of arms emblazoned with "Fortitudine Vincit" under a crown and stag' (Engen, 11). The family suffered for their religion and were dispossessed; Doyle's father set up in business as a silk mercer in Dublin. The elder of two sons, Doyle was sent to learn landscape painting under Gaspare Gabrielli and to the Royal Dublin Society's drawing school. There he was a pupil of the miniature painter John Comerford, and he won a gold medal in 1805. He had a good eye for detail, and his love of horses led to early commissions for equestrian portraits from the marquess of Sligo and Lord Talbot, the Irish viceroy. In 1822 he produced six prints entitled *The Life of a Racehorse*, and that year left Dublin for London with his wife, Marianna Conan (*d.* 1832), who also came from an old Irish family.

By 1832 the Doyles had seven children, five sons: James William Edmund *Doyle (1822–1892); the painter Richard *Doyle (1824–1883); Henry Edward *Doyle (1827–1892), who became director of the National Gallery of Ireland; Charles (*b.* 1832), who was the father of Arthur Conan *Doyle; and Francis (*d. c.*1840), and two daughters: Adelaide (who died young) and Annette. They moved house four times in ten years from Berners Street to Lambeth, then to Euston and Somerstown in north London. Noted to have inherited the 'austere aloof nature of his father' (Engen, 12), Doyle became further withdrawn after the death of Marianna in 1832 following the birth of their youngest son. After Marianna's death her brother, Michael Conan, and his wife, Anne, moved in to the family home to help take care of the children. During this time Doyle supported his family by painting miniature portraits. Though he continued to exhibit miniatures at the Royal Academy until 1835, it was his painting *Turning out the Stag*, exhibited there in 1825, that brought him recognition.

John Doyle [H. B.] (1797–1868), by Henry Edward Doyle

Working in the new reproductive medium of lithography, Doyle began to make portraits 'from reminiscence', and his prints of *The Duke of Wellington on his Charger*, *Princess Victoria in her Pony Phaeton*, and small portraits of noted politicians including the prime minister, George Canning, were popular and sold well. It is for his political prints, dating from 1827, however, that Doyle is now remembered. These were signed with the initials 'HB' (a conjunction of two Is, which are printed like Js, and two Ds, these two letters singly being Doyle's initials), and the artist's anonymity was preserved until his popularity began to wane. The political sketches of H. B. were issued usually once a month during parliamentary sessions, and ran for over twenty-two years. The drawings, whose 'subjects are treated with a distinctly sarcastic humour but with an absence of exaggeration' in which 'likeness is faithfully preserved' (Everitt, 238), 'were called for in a mysterious hackney coach, mysteriously deposited in a mysterious lithographic printing office, and mysteriously printed and mysteriously stored until the day of publication' (ibid., 239). Engen noted that so great was H. B.'s following that *The Times* printed a key to his drawings as did the publisher McLean in the 1840s. Thackeray observed that:

> You never hear any laughing at 'H. B.'; his pictures are a great deal too genteel for that [they are] polite points of wit, which strike one as exceedingly clever and pretty, and cause one to smile in a quiet, gentlemanlike way. (*Westminster Review*, June 1840)

By 1840 Doyle's prosperity had enabled him to move to

the fashionable address of 17 Cambridge Terrace, Hyde Park, where he became the nucleus of a circle of artistic and literary figures, including David Wilkie, Scott, Wordsworth, Coleridge, Dickens, Thackeray, Macaulay, and the poets Thomas Moore and Samuel Rogers. He remained careful, however, to preserve the secret of his identity as the cartoonist H. B.

Though Doyle's later work is sometimes criticized as slovenly, the political sketches are carefully drawn in a restrained style well suited to their reproduction in soft, indistinct lithographic prints. Their gentle humour often lies in evoking a scene from a current play where the political figures are substituted for dramatic characters. During a debate on the Reform Bill, for example, the duke of Cumberland intervened in a heated exchange between lords Grey and Kenyon. The scene was transformed by H. B. into an incident from the current farce *I'll be your Second* where Cumberland appears as the character Placid, interposes between the intending duellists, and delivers the play's punchline, 'Can't this affair be arranged?' H. B.'s subjects included Lord Brougham, Sir Francis Burdett, Sir Robert Peel, Lord Melbourne, Lord Palmerston, George IV, William IV, and Queen Victoria. In *English Caricaturists and Graphic Humourists*, Everitt's reference to the view in *Blackwood's Magazine* (August 1863) that H. B.:

> would have been a greater artist had he worked on the same material and with the same tools as Gillray and Cruikshank, but we should probably not have possessed so complete a gallery of portraits, comprising all the men of note who took part in political affairs from before the passing of the Catholic Relief Bill until after the repeal of the Corn Laws (Everitt, 274)

indicates both the range of his subject matter and his status as a satirical artist.

In 1843 Doyle wrote a seventeen-page letter to Sir Robert Peel in which he revealed his identity as H. B. and claimed that his drawings were 'governed by a steadiness of moral and political principle. Although commenced in sport' they were of 'some little influence' and avoided 'indelicacy, private scandal and party bitterness' (Engen, 36). An affectionate father, Doyle encouraged his children's artistic and musical skills, and on Sunday evenings they gave concerts and entertainments for him at home. John Doyle died at his home, 54 Clifton Gardens, Maida Hill, London, on 2 January 1868. His son Richard (Dickie) Doyle's painting *The Enchanted Tree*, exhibited at the Royal Academy five months later, was a tribute to him.

The rapid fading of Doyle's reputation was signalled by the delayed publication of his obituary in the *Art Journal*, which did not appear until three months after his death. A posthumous sale (*c.*1882) at Christies of a large number of his original sketches was cancelled, because there were no buyers. Everitt noted that 'it is surprising how completely his [political sketches] have passed into oblivion' (Everitt, 139). His view that Doyle's:

> chief merits are to be found in the facility with which he grasped an idea; the harmlessness and playfulness of his satire, which wrought a complete revolution in the style and manner of the caricaturists; and above all in the excellence of his likenesses (ibid.)

is unlikely to be challenged. As the founder of 'the modern school of graphic satirists represented by Richard Doyle, John Leech and John Tenniel' (ibid.) Doyle prepared the way for *Punch*. 'The name of "caricature" disappeared, and the modern word "cartoon" assumed its place' (ibid.). Over 900 of Doyle's drawings are in the British Museum.

KENNETH BAKER

Sources R. Engen, *Richard Doyle* (1983) · G. Everitt, *English caricaturists and graphic humourists of the nineteenth century* (1886) · W. G. Strickland, *A dictionary of Irish artists*, 1 (1913), 297–8 · *DNB* · *CGPLA Eng. & Wales* (1868) · G. M. Trevelyan, *The seven years of William IV, a reign cartooned by John Doyle* (1952) · M. D. George, introduction, *Catalogue of political and personal satires preserved ... in the British Museum*, ed. F. G. Stephens and M. D. George, 11 (1954), xiii–liv
Archives PRO NIre., letters to James Emerson Tennent
Likenesses H. E. Doyle, pencil and chalk drawing, NPG [*see illus.*] · C. Moore, plaster bust, NG Ire.
Wealth at death under £450: resworn administration, Oct 1868, *CGPLA Eng. & Wales*

Doyle, John Andrew (1844–1907), historian, was born on 14 May 1844, the only child of Andrew Doyle (d. 1888), one-time editor of the *Morning Chronicle* and later a poor-law inspector, and Louisa (d. 1896), daughter and coheir of Sir John *Easthope (1784–1865). He was educated at Eton College (1853–62) and then, after a year of private tuition, at Balliol College, Oxford, where he graduated in 1867 with first-class honours in *literae humaniores*. Doyle remained in Oxford to study history, and in 1869 won the Arnold prize for an essay entitled 'The English colonies in America before the Declaration of Independence'. Later in the same year he was elected to a fellowship at All Souls College, which he held for the rest of his life.

Of sufficient private means not to have to earn a living, Doyle pursued two largely separate careers. In Oxford he was active and conscientious as a fellow of his college, serving as librarian (1881–8) and helping to frame the revised All Souls statutes arising from the commission of 1887. His scholarly interest was in the British North American (mainland) colonies of the seventeenth and eighteenth centuries, on which he wrote a series of volumes over the course of twenty-five years. This work presumably originated in his prize essay of 1869, which may in turn have reflected an interest arising from the American Civil War. His first publication was a textbook on the history of the USA (1875). Although Doyle's writings are seldom consulted today and have only a limited historiographical interest, they constitute the fullest and fairest treatment of colonial America by any British historian; they were only superseded by the works of American scholars in the early and mid-twentieth century. Apart from state papers in the Public Record Office (which were not then fully calendared), Doyle worked from printed sources and secondary works. Although he made at least one visit to the United States, it is not clear how well he knew the country, even those parts which had been settled by 1763. None the less, for someone writing in the reigns of Victoria and Edward VII, his grasp and relatively detached judgement are commendable.

When he was not in Oxford, Doyle lived with his parents, first in north Wales and then from 1880 in Brecknockshire, where after their deaths he remained in the house which they had had built for the rest of his own life. He took an active part in local affairs, and served as a justice of the peace, county councillor, deputy lieutenant, and sheriff. He was interested in the provision of higher education for the poor as well as the rich, but even more in field sports, notably the breeding of racehorses and fox-terriers. Mountain rock-climbing too was among his pastimes.

One interest drew together the Oxford and the Welsh halves of Doyle's life: rifle-shooting and the volunteer movement. Whether or not he was stimulated in this by his knowledge of American superiority over the British as marksmen in the eighteenth century, the efforts of such as Doyle surely contributed to the quality of British rifle-shooting in the Second South African War of 1899–1902 and again in 1914. His health never seems to have been robust, and he died on 4 August 1907, after a long but unspecified illness, at his home, Pendarren, Crickhowell, Brecknockshire. His near contemporary and the author of his article in the *Dictionary of National Biography*, the warden of All Souls, Sir William Anson, would seem to have been his closest friend. A photograph reproduced in Doyle's posthumous *Essays on Various Subjects* (1911) shows a good-looking man in early middle age, with a terrier perched on his knee. G. E. AYLMER

Sources *Brecon County Times* (Aug 1907) · W. Anson, Introduction, in J. A. Doyle, *Essays on various subjects*, ed. W. P. Ker (1911) · *The Times* (7 Aug 1907) · college records, All Souls Oxf. · college records, Balliol Oxf.
Archives Bodl. RH, corresp. relating to *The English in America* | All Souls Oxf., letters to Sir William Anson
Likenesses Hill & Saunders, photograph, repro. in Doyle, *Essays on various subjects*
Wealth at death £57,891 18s. 4d.: probate, 21 Nov 1907, CGPLA Eng. & Wales

Doyle, Sir John Milley (1781–1856), army officer, was the second son of the Revd Nicholas Milley Doyle, rector of Newcastle, co. Tipperary, who was third son of Charles Doyle of Bramblestown, Kilkenny, and therefore nephew of General Sir John *Doyle and General Welbore Ellis Doyle, and cousin of Lieutenant-General Sir Charles William *Doyle. He was commissioned ensign in the 107th regiment on 31 May 1794, and was promoted lieutenant into the 108th on 21 June 1794. He first saw service in the suppression of the Irish insurrection of 1798, and in the following year accompanied his uncle, Brigadier-General John Doyle, to Gibraltar as aide-de-camp. As such he served throughout the expedition to Egypt, being present at the battles of 8, 13, and 21 March, and at the capture of Alexandria. He was recommended for promotion, but did not obtain his captaincy into the 81st regiment until 9 July 1803.

Doyle eventually exchanged into the 87th, Sir John Doyle's regiment, in December 1804, and in the following year joined him in Guernsey, where he acted as his uncle's aide-de-camp and as inspector-general of the Guernsey militia until 1809. In that year he was one of the officers selected to assist Beresford in reorganizing the Portuguese army, and was promoted major in the British army in February and lieutenant-colonel in the Portuguese service in March 1809. He was placed in command of the 16th Portuguese regiment of infantry, which was sufficiently well disciplined to take part in Sir Arthur Wellesley's advance on the Douro, and the pursuit after Soult's army. When the Portuguese brigades were formed in 1810, his regiment was made one of Pack's brigade, which was attached to Picton's (3rd) division, with which he served until January 1812, being present at the battle of Fuentes de Oñoro and the storming of Ciudad Rodrigo.

On 26 September 1811 Doyle was promoted lieutenant-colonel in the British army, and on 1 January 1812 he was made colonel in the Portuguese service, and was transferred to the 19th regiment of Portuguese infantry, which formed part of Le Cor's Portuguese brigade, attached to Lord Dalhousie's (7th) division. He commanded this regiment in the battles of Vitoria and the Pyrenees, and was made a knight of the Tower and Sword (Portugal) in October 1812. In the winter of 1813, when Lord Dalhousie went to England on leave, General Le Cor took command of the 7th division, and Doyle succeeded him in the 6th Portuguese brigade, which he commanded in the battles of the Nivelle and of Orthez, and afterwards in the march on Bordeaux. On the conclusion of the war Doyle left the Portuguese service. He was knighted by the prince regent at Carlton House on 28 July 1814, and made KCB on 2 January 1815. He was subsequently appointed once more inspecting officer of militia in Guernsey.

Doyle still continued to take a keen interest in the affairs of Portugal, and in June 1823 he chartered a steamer at his own expense in which he took dispatches for Dom Pedro to Cadiz. This and other similar acts caused his arrest by Dom Miguel, and he was imprisoned for several months in a cell in Lisbon, and not released until the strongest representations had been made by the English minister, Sir F. Lamb, later Lord Beauvale. Doyle was MP for county Carlow in 1831–2. He still continued to assist Dom Pedro, with both his purse and his services, and acted as major-general and aide-de-camp to Dom Pedro in the defence of Oporto (1832).

At the end of the war in 1834 Doyle was disgracefully treated. He was made to resign his commission on the promise of being paid in full for his expenditure and his services, but he was then put off with excuses and left unpaid. It was Doyle who, by pamphlets and petitions, got the mixed commission appointed to liquidate the claims of the English officers, and this commission paid every English officer except himself. He was apparently made a scapegoat for having initiated the appointment of the commission. For many years he was engaged in lawsuits to obtain this money, but he never got it and only sank deeper into difficulties. At last he gave up, and in July 1853 he was appointed a military knight of Windsor and a sergeant-at-arms to the queen. He died in the lower ward, Windsor Castle, on 9 August 1856, and was buried with military honours on the green, at the south side of St George's Chapel. H. M. STEPHENS, *rev.* JAMES LUNT

Sources J. Philippart, ed., *The royal military calendar*, 3rd edn, 4 (1820), 2 · *GM*, 3rd ser., 1 (1856) · C. W. C. Oman, *Wellington's army, 1809–1814* (1912); repr. (1968) · A. Brett-James, *Life in Wellington's army* (1972) · J. Weller, *Wellington in the Peninsula, 1808–1814*, new edn (1992) · Boase, *Mod. Eng. biog.*

Doyle, Martin. *See* Hickey, William (1787–1875).

Doyle, Richard [*pseud.* Dick Kitcat] (**1824–1883**), illustrator and watercolour painter, was born in September 1824 in London, the second of the seven children of John *Doyle (pseudonym H. B.) (1797–1868), caricaturist and painter, and his wife, Marianna Conan. His parents were both Irish, having come to England in 1817 to further his father's career as a painter. Marianna died in 1832 shortly after giving birth to Charles, her seventh child, and from then on the family was brought up and educated at home under the careful supervision of John Doyle. Richard Doyle showed remarkable talent for imaginative and humorous drawings at a very early age. At the age of twelve he produced a series of fifteen designs titled *Homer for the Holidays* (eighteen watercolours; Ross County Historical Society, Chillicothe, Ohio) parodying Flaxman; he also produced hundreds of highly finished drawings in letters to his father; a journal for 1840 (British Museum); several 'books of nonsense' (three in V&A); illustrated manuscripts of 'Beauty and the Beast' with text by his sister Adelaide (Pierpont Morgan Library, New York); 'Jack the Giant Killer' and 'Comic Histories' with text by his brother James; other unfinished tales; and three published works. The first of these was a delightful pictorial record of the ill-fated Eglinton tournament, based on his father's account of the proceedings in 1840, followed by a series of pictorial envelopes by Doyle and his brother James commissioned later that year. *A grand historical allegorical classical and comical procession of remarkable personages ancient modern and unknown* (1842) was an adaptation of the watercolour of the christening procession of the princess royal made for his father in 1840, the first work published under his pseudonym Dick Kitcat. Both the tournament and procession are recorded at some length in the journal of that year.

At the age of eighteen Doyle provided five very successful etched plates to join those of John Leech in *The Fortunes of Hector O'Halloran* by W. H. Maxwell (1842), his first and only attempt to work in this medium. The following year he was introduced by his uncle Michael Conan to Mark Lemon, editor of *Punch*, and became a regular contributor, supplying pictorial borders, whimsical historiated initials, and full-page political cartoons, the first being *The Modern Sisyphus* in March 1844. Doyle's contributions raised the pictorial content of the magazine immediately, causing other artists such as Hine and Leech to look to their laurels. He also designed the famous cover, in use with only minor changes for over one hundred years, and innovative page layouts where lines of type were divided by a large illustration such as the Z-shaped new year greeting, 1844. Doyle was soon a household name, with his series of *Manners and Customs of ye Englishe* impressing the young Pre-Raphaelites and W. M. Thackeray as well as the general public. His career with *Punch* finished abruptly in

Richard Doyle [Dick Kitcat] (**1824–1883**), by John & Charles Watkins

1850 when he resigned from the magazine, having taken exception to the religious stance of the editorial board during the anti-papal controversy. He was by then a well-established illustrator, popular with his contemporary artists, writers, and society hostesses, but sadly he was never again to achieve the same financial security for himself and other members of the family.

During his seven years at *Punch*, Doyle provided illustrations for eighteen books and three almanacs as well as over one thousand drawings for the magazine. His fascination with fairy tales and legends, already apparent in so much of his early work, anticipated growing public interest in the subject. Fairy paintings by artists such as Daniel Maclise, Noël Paton, and Richard Dadd were shown at the Royal Academy, and writers were producing new fairy tales. Doyle was invited by Charles Dickens to join Maclise, Leech, Clarkson Stanfield, and Edwin Landseer as illustrators of *The Chimes*, *The Cricket on the Hearth*, and *The Battle of Life*, published annually from 1844 to 1846. Other new tales illustrated by Doyle were *The Enchanted Doll* by Mark Lemon (1850), and John Ruskin's *The King of the Golden River* (1851). Doyle was also commissioned to provide the designs for *The Fairy Ring*, a collection of the Grimm brothers' tales (1846); *Fairy Tales from All Nations*, by Anthony Whitehill (pseudonym Anthony R. Montalba; 1849); and *The Story of Jack and the Giants* (1851). Doyle's first major fairy picture to be published appeared in his anonymous *Selections from the Rejected Cartoons* (1848). The fifteen plates parody designs for historical frescoes by Maclise, A. W. N. Pugin, and others submitted to the Westminster Hall cartoon competition. All are accompanied by his own descriptive text written in the style of a disgruntled artist. Four other important books of this period that Doyle illustrated are Leigh Hunt's *A Jar of Honey from Mount Hybla* (1848); *The Lover's Stratagem* by Heinrich Zschokke (1849), the only occasion when Richard and his brothers James and Henry worked together on the same book; *Manners and Customs of ye Englishe* (1849), a reprinting of the illustrations and Percival Leigh's text serialized in *Punch*; and Thackeray's historical romance *Rebecca and Rowena* (1851).

Following his resignation from *Punch*, Doyle's career suffered from a lack of routine and self-discipline, coupled with bouts of ill health, depression, and indecisiveness: a constant concern for authors and publishers commissioning work from him. He was far happier socializing with other artists and writers, at his club or at the homes of Arthur Lewis or Mrs Prinsep. Many of these, such as William Holman Hunt, became lifelong friends. Invitations to some of the country's finest homes including Chatsworth, Longleat, Isel Hall, and Cortachy Castle were another welcome distraction. Thus his drawings for the fine panoramic *Overland Journey to the Great Exhibition* (1851) finally reached the block-makers just as the exhibition was closing. The Dalziels had also commissioned *The Story of Jack and the Giants* (1851) as the first of a series of fairy tales, but drawings for the second title were so late that the project was abandoned. The illustrations were finally published in 1865 in *An Old Fairy Tale Told Anew*, a version of 'Sleeping Beauty' by J. R. Planché. The model for the heroine was Blanche Stanley, whom Doyle had met and fallen in love with in 1850. Despite her marriage to Lord Airlie soon afterwards he remained devoted to her. She appears repeatedly in his drawings, and he never married.

In 1853 Thackeray invited Doyle to illustrate *The Newcomes*. What should have been an ideal partnership developed into a disaster. As work proceeded the artist recognized both himself as J. J. Ridley and Blanche Stanley as Ethel Newcome. This and the usual lateness created a rift between the two friends. Fortunately Doyle's most successful title to date appeared while the novel was in progress. *The Foreign Tour of Brown, Jones and Robinson* was published in 1854, following a brief appearance of the characters in *Punch*, based on Doyle's travels in Europe with his friends Tom Taylor and Watts Phillips in 1850. Further problems occurred with *The Scouring of the White Horse* by Thomas Hughes (1859) and *A Selection from the Works of Frederick Locker* (1865), but Doyle was at least able to draw on his social activities for *A Bird's Eye View of Society*, first published in the *Cornhill Magazine* (1861–2) and in book form in 1864, and echoed in the illustrations to Laurence Oliphant's *Piccadilly* (1870).

Doyle's greatest book appeared in 1869. Carefully prepared designs varying from vignettes to full-page plates for an album of fairy pictures were produced without the usual pressures from publisher or author. The verses by William Allingham were added only after the drawings had been completed. *In Fairyland*, printed in colour by Edmund Evans, is generally considered to be one of the greatest books of the nineteenth century both for its illustrations and production. It was sufficiently popular for a second edition in 1875, and a reworking in 1884 with a story entitled 'The Princess Nobody' written around the illustrations by Andrew Lang.

In the mid-1870s Doyle gave up illustration to concentrate on his watercolours. These were very different to such early works as *The Fairy Tree*, painted in 1845 and exhibited at the Royal Academy in 1868. The whimsical humour still evident in the *In Fairyland* illustrations had disappeared from *The Haunted Park*, exhibited at the Royal Academy in 1871. A number of landscapes and views of stately homes were painted while Doyle stayed with friends, but his more successful pictures were those of witches, dragons, and fairy or romantic figures seen among the Scottish hills or the Lake District, a ruined tower sometimes adding to the sense of desolation. A total of thirty-seven works were shown at the Grosvenor Gallery between 1878 and the artist's death on 11 December 1883 at his home, 7 Finborough Road, West Brompton, following an apoplectic seizure. He was buried at Kensal Green cemetery on 17 December. In 1885 a large exhibition was organized at the same gallery by his brother James, who also arranged publication of his brother's journal and other early pieces in an attempt to maintain Doyle's reputation. The exhibition was not a success, and much reappeared the following year in the estate sale held at Christies. Fashions had changed and for years he was virtually forgotten. Contemporary critics and later historians could compare him to other artists but never place him in any particular group. The revival of interest in this unique illustrator culminated with the exhibition at the Victoria and Albert Museum to commemorate the centenary of his death. Some of his large watercolours, purchased by Henry Doyle from the estate sale, are in the National Gallery of Ireland, Dublin. Others are in the Victoria and Albert Museum, London.

MICHAEL HESELTINE

Sources R. Engen, *Richard Doyle* (1983) · L. Lambourne, R. Engen, and M. Heseltine, *Richard Doyle and his family* (1983) [exhibition catalogue, V&A, 30 Nov 1983 – 26 Feb 1984] · *A journal by Dick Doyle, 1841*, ed. J. H. Pollen (1885) · [G. Dalziel and E. Dalziel], *The brothers Dalziel: a record of fifty years' work ... 1840–1890* (1901) · M. H. Spielmann, *The history of 'Punch'* (1895) · D. Hambourg, *Richard Doyle* (1948) · L. Lusk, 'The best of Richard Doyle', *Art Journal*, new ser., 22 (1902), 248–52 · P. Leigh, *God's Englishmen* (1948) [introduction by M. Sadleir] · *Mr Punch's pageant, 1841–1908: a souvenir catalogue* (1909) [exhibition catalogue, Leicester Galleries, London, Jan–Feb 1909] · F. G. Green, 'Memoir', *The Doyle fairy book*, trans. A. R. Montalba [A. Whitehill], 3rd edn (1890) · Richard Doyle sale catalogue (1886) [Christies] · *CGPLA Eng. & Wales* (1884)

Archives Hunt. L., letters · Morgan L., corresp. and papers · NL Scot., logbook | Hunt. L., letters to Frederick Locker-Lampson · Morgan L., letters to John Doyle

Likenesses woodcut, 1885, repro. in Pollen, ed., *Journal by Dick Doyle*, frontispiece · H. Doyle, oils, NG Ire. · J. & C. Watkins, carte-de-visite, NPG [*see illus.*] · wood-engraving (after photograph by Watkins), repro. in Green, 'Memoir' · woodcut, BM

Wealth at death £1569 5*s.* 0*d.*: administration, 3 April 1884, *CGPLA Eng. & Wales*

Doyle, Thomas (1793–1879), Roman Catholic priest, was born in London, of Irish parents, on 21 December 1793. He was sent to St Edmund's College, Ware, where he served as organist. Before he had finished the theological curriculum, a lack of clergy led Bishop Poynter to ordain him priest. In 1820 he was sent to St George's, London Road, Southwark, then to the Royal Belgian Chapel, Southwark; in February 1829 he became first chaplain there. In the 1820s the chapel had a large and steadily growing congregation, composed mainly of Irish immigrants. Doyle proved himself a devoted parish priest, serving unstintingly during the cholera epidemic of 1832. He was an energetic promoter of Catholic services and devotions: in 1840 he established the Guild of Our Blessed Lady and St George to further devotions for the dead and provide funerals. He is credited, too, with the inauguration of Sunday evening services for the London poor. He was claimed by some to have been the first priest since the Reformation to preach publicly on the Virgin Mary.

The growth of his congregation led Doyle to plan the building of a new, larger, church. He began to raise money for the scheme, which sceptics called 'Father Doyle's folly', through collections at his own chapel and appeals to other Roman Catholics. In 1838, when sufficient money had been collected, a local architect drew up plans, but these were set aside when the earl of Shrewsbury intervened to suggest A. W. N. Pugin as architect. After some initial problems, Pugin's second set of designs was accepted in late 1839, and land was purchased. Work began on 8 September 1840 and the church was substantially complete by 1848. In the intervening years, Doyle had continued and extended his appeals, travelling throughout the British Isles and Europe. Nor did he neglect other causes: he collected £207 for the Irish people during the great famine of 1845–9. A fellow cleric aptly described Doyle as 'the very prince of beggars' (Bogan, 82). The new church, St George's, was officially consecrated on 4 July 1848 in a lavish service attended by Wiseman, the earls of Shrewsbury and Arundel, and a number of Irish, Scottish, English, and continental bishops, as well as over 250 clergy, regular and secular. The Protestant Association distributed a pamphlet entitled *The Opening of the New Popish Mass House in St George's Fields*, and there was considerable comment in the London press. Although St George's was originally intended to be a parish church, it became the cathedral of the newly created diocese of Southwark in July 1852, with Doyle as its provost. It was here that Wiseman preached his famous sermons on the restoration of the hierarchy in 1850.

In 1851 Doyle was accused of persuading his ward, Augusta Talbot, niece of the earl of Shrewsbury, to enter a religious order while under age, so that, at her majority, her large fortune would accrue to the church. The matter went to court, but the finding was in Doyle's favour; he continued as Miss Talbot's guardian, although she was removed from the convent at Taunton where she had been living.

Doyle remained active after the completion of St George's. From the early 1840s, he had contributed, writing as Father Thomas, a weekly letter to *The Tablet*, which discussed the affairs, ceremonies, and needs of St George's, and gave a vivid picture of the life of a hard-working Roman Catholic priest in mid-Victorian London. His *Times* obituary described these letters as 'full of a quaint humour peculiar to himself, and generally ... very true to the mark' (9 June 1879). His last contribution to *The Tablet* was published in November 1876. From September 1873 Doyle was in poor health; in 1875 he had a paralytic stroke. He died on 6 June 1879, and was buried in St George's.   ROSEMARY MITCHELL

Sources *The Tablet* (14 June 1879), 756–7 · *The Times* (9 June 1879) · B. Bogan, *The great link: a history of St George's Cathedral, Southwark, 1786–1958*, 2nd edn (1958) · Gillow, *Lit. biog. hist.*
Archives St George's Roman Catholic Cathedral, Southwark Roman Catholic diocesan archives, corresp. and papers
Likenesses Eryall?, portrait, *c.*1869, repro. in Bogan, *The great link*, facing p. 205 · alabaster memorial, 1882, St George's Cathedral, Southwark · oils (in youth), St George's Cathedral, Southwark, London
Wealth at death under £450: probate, 16 June 1879, *CGPLA Eng. & Wales*

Doyle, Welbore Ellis (1758–1798). *See under* Doyle, Sir John, baronet (1756–1834).

Doyle, Sir (Charles) William (1770–1842), army officer, was born at Bramblestown, co. Kilkenny, the eldest son of William Doyle (*d.* 1792) of Bramblestown, KC and master in chancery in Ireland, and his second wife, Cecilia, daughter of General Salvini of the Austrian service. William Doyle was the eldest son of Charles Doyle of Bramblestown and elder brother of General Sir John *Doyle, baronet, and General Welbore Ellis Doyle. He had children only from his second marriage; his second son, Cavendish Bentinck Doyle, a captain in the navy, died on 21 May 1843.

Charles William Doyle entered the army on 28 April 1783 as an ensign in the 14th regiment commanded by his uncle, Welbore Doyle. He was promoted lieutenant on 12 February 1793, in which year he accompanied his regiment to the Netherlands. The 14th was one of the 'ragged' regiments which Sir Harry Calvert, in his *Journals and Correspondence*, compares to Falstaff's soldiers in Shakespeare, but Major-General Ralph Abercromby soon got them into better condition, in which task he was helped by Doyle, whom he appointed his brigade major. Abercromby's brigade was conspicuous for its efficiency throughout the ensuing campaigns. With it Doyle was present at the battle of Famars, where Welbore Doyle led the attack at the head of the 14th regiment. Charles William Doyle was publicly thanked by Abercromby for carrying a redoubt on the heights above Valenciennes, and he then acted as orderly officer to the Austrian generals during the siege of that town, at which time he was wounded in the head. His next service was at the battle of Lannoy, where he acted as aide-de-camp to Abercromby, and was wounded in the hand, being selected to take the dispatch announcing the battle to the duke of York. At the close of the campaign he was transferred to the adjutancy of the 91st regiment, and in June 1794 he purchased the captain-lieutenancy and adjutancy of the 105th, from which he soon exchanged into the 87th commanded by his uncle, John Doyle. He accompanied this regiment to the West Indies in 1796 and acted first as brigade major and then as aide-de-camp to Abercromby, whose public thanks he received in 1797 for covering the embarkation of the troops from Puerto Rico. He also received the thanks of the governor of Barbados in 1798 for having driven off a dangerous French privateer and retaking two of her prizes—all of which was accomplished in an open boat with only thirty soldiers. He was recommended for a majority, but this came to nothing, and in the following year, after acting as brigade major at Gibraltar, he was again recommended for a majority; however, the governor's recommendation arrived just two days too late. He threw up his staff appointment to serve in the expedition to The Helder, in the Netherlands, in 1799, but was again too late, and he was immediately afterwards appointed a brigade major to the army, sailing to the Mediterranean under Abercromby. He was attached to Lord Cavan's brigade and was present with it at Cadiz and Malta, and finally in Egypt, where he served in the battles of 8, 13, and 21 March, in the last of which he was severely wounded. While lying injured at Rosetta he learned from some French prisoners that the garrison of Cairo was weak, and by giving timely information to General Lord Hutchinson, he ensured the fall of that city. He was heartily thanked by Hutchinson and again recommended, for the fifth time, for a majority, which, however, he did not receive until 9 July 1803, after the conclusion of the peace of Amiens. In the same year he was appointed brigade major to Sir J. H. Craig, commanding the eastern district.

Doyle married, on 21 May 1802, Sophia Cramer, daughter of Sir John Coghill, first baronet. They had a daughter, and three sons: Lieutenant-General Sir Charles Hastings *Doyle (1804–1883); Colonel John Sidney North (1804–1894) MP, privy councillor, who took the name of North in 1838 after marrying Baroness North of Kirtlington; and Percy William Doyle (d. February 1887) CB, British minister in Mexico. In 1804 Doyle first commanded the volunteers and directed the defences of Scotland, for which he was thanked by General Sir Hew Dalrymple; he then commanded the light infantry on Barham downs and published his Military Catechism, and was at the end of the year appointed assistant quartermaster-general in Guernsey. On 22 August 1805 he was promoted lieutenant-colonel into his uncle's regiment, the 87th, and commanded it for three years during Sir John Doyle's lieutenant-governorship of that island.

On the outbreak of the Peninsular War in 1808, the British government determined to send aid to the Portuguese and Spanish insurgents, Doyle being one of a number of officers dispatched to the Iberian peninsula with orders to make contact with the rebels and send back information on their political and military situation; he was also given the particular responsibility for conducting several hundred Spanish prisoners to Galicia, where they

were formed into a regiment known as the Blendengues de Buenos Aires. The activities of these liaison officers gave rise to much criticism, in that they were accused of becoming more and more embroiled in the politics of the insurrection. In the case of Doyle in particular, whom Wellington later accused of 'attending to anything and everything but his own business' (Wellington to H. Wellesley, 23 May 1813), this complaint was certainly justified, the fault being compounded by the fact that he chose to give his support to some of the least worthy figures in the patriot camp. After first attempting to promote the efforts of the singularly vacuous duque del Infantado to become commander-in-chief—for which Doyle earned a severe reprimand from the secretary for war, Viscount Castlereagh—he travelled to Saragossa and became a fierce partisan of the faction headed by its ambitious and bombastic dictator, José Palafox; for good measure, he also played a leading role in the formation of the disastrous plan of operations that led to the French reconquest of Madrid in December 1808. He travelled on to the Levant and spent the first months of 1809 struggling both to obtain help for Saragossa, which was now besieged, and to strengthen the defences of Valencia. Unable to save Saragossa, he then became attached to the British embassy in Seville, where he also secretly assisted the Palafoxists in their efforts to seize power. Sent to Catalonia late in 1809 as British liaison officer, he distinguished himself in the allied victory at La Bisbal on 14 September 1810 and served at various other minor actions, as well as at the sieges of Tortosa and Tarragona; in the process, he was not only wounded twice but also had two horses killed under him. He was ordered home in late 1811, and while passing through Cadiz he was asked by the British ambassador, Henry Wellesley, to accept command of a depot being established there to train fresh conscripts. He carried out the task with some success, but his efforts to obtain either an active command or a post on the staff were rebuffed by Wellington, who regarded him with great distrust; on 4 June 1813, however, he was at least promoted colonel and appointed as an aide-de-camp to the prince regent. After the war he was knighted and made a CB; in addition, the Spanish had awarded him several decorations, including the order of Charles III, made him a lieutenant-general, and paid him various other honours. (In 1808 Palafox had named an infantry regiment after him, and he was also invited to add the arms of Tortosa to his own.)

In 1819 Doyle was promoted major-general, made colonel of the 10th (Royal Veteran) battalion, and created a KCH. From 1825 to 1830 he commanded the south-western district of Ireland, and in 1837 he was promoted lieutenant-general. On 21 April 1838 he married his second wife, Sophia, widow of William Steir. In 1839 he was made a GCH. He died in Paris on 25 October 1842.

H. M. STEPHENS, rev. CHARLES ESDAILE

Sources PRO, War Office MSS · PRO, Foreign Office MSS · U. Southampton L., Wellington MSS · C. W. C. Oman, *A history of the Peninsular War*, 7 vols. (1902–30) · Burke, *Peerage* (1959)
Archives BL, corresp., Add. MS 15675 · Bodl. Oxf., papers · University of Kansas, Lawrence, Kenneth Spencer Research Library,

journal kept during English expedition against Puerto Rico and in West Indies | Bucks. RLSS, letters to Lord Hobart • PRO, War Office MSS • Scottish United Services Museum, Edinburgh, Dalrymple MSS • U. Southampton L., Wellington MSS

Likenesses J. Godby, stipple, pubd 1813 (after Walton), NPG • M. Carpenter, oils, Boston Museum of Fine Arts • stipple, BM; repro. in F. L. Clarke, *The Life of Wellington*, new edn, 3 vols. (1814?)

Doyley, Edward (1617–1675), colonial governor, was born at Albourne, Wiltshire, the second son of John Doyley and his wife, Lucy, daughter of Robert Nicholas of Chiselhampton, Oxfordshire. Following study at the inns of court, he committed himself to the parliamentarian cause, serving in the New Model Army in Wiltshire and in Ireland, where he received a land grant in recompense for his services. In December 1654 Doyley, now a lieutenant-colonel in General Robert Venables's regiment, sailed for the West Indies. Cromwell had dispatched Venables and his men in order to advance the western design, by which he hoped to gain control of the lucrative and strategically important islands of the Caribbean by defeating the Spanish forces there, and simultaneously stamping out the pro-royalist sentiment which flourished among many English settlers. Having arrived in Barbados in March 1655, Venables raised a local regiment, of which he appointed Doyley colonel. From then on Doyley rose slowly but steadily within the ranks; after Major-General Richard Fortescue's death in November 1655 the parliamentary commissioners in Jamaica selected him as commander-in-chief of the island's forces, which were embroiled in a struggle to defeat the Spanish and gain control of the island for England. Although Doyley was temporarily superseded by the Cromwellian protégés Robert Sedgwick and William Brayne, neither man survived for long, and after September 1657 the Jamaican command devolved permanently upon Doyley.

Doyley soon proved himself worthy of his responsibilities, leading his men successfully against Spanish forces sent from Cuba with the intention of reconquering Jamaica. In 1657 he defeated General Ysassi's troops at Ocho Rios, and did the same the following year at Rio Nuevo, in the largest single engagement ever fought on Jamaican soil. Having inflicted a decisive defeat upon the Spaniards and established himself as Jamaica's first English governor, he described his endeavours in a pamphlet entitled *A narrative of the great success God hath been pleased to give his highness's forces in Jamaica against the king of Spain's forces*, which was printed in London in 1658.

Although Doyley was a staunch parliamentarian, he was sufficiently competent as a governor that, upon the Restoration, Charles II confirmed him in his post and requested that he establish a council to assist in the task of governing the island. In one historian's evaluation Doyley was 'too much a soldier to feel much enthusiasm for the institution of civil government and, beyond swearing in the councillors as Justices of the Peace and establishing courts of law at Morant Bay, Port Royal, and Spanish Town, he did little to alter the shape of things' (Spurdle, 25). It was in his role as commander-in-chief that Doyley made

his mark; he succeeded in defending Jamaica against all Spanish attempts to reconquer it. He was willing to take unorthodox measures in order to defeat the Spanish, as is shown by his inviting the English buccaneers of nearby Tortuga to transfer their headquarters to Jamaica in order that he might use them as a deterrent to Spanish attack. By the early 1660s approximately 1500 buccaneers had settled in the environs of Port Royal, which became notorious as a pirates' haven until its destruction by earthquake in 1692.

In 1662 Doyley was superseded as governor by Thomas, Lord Windsor, later first earl of Plymouth, a protégé of Charles II. Upon Windsor's arrival in Jamaica, Doyley returned to England, where he established himself in the London parish of St Martin-in-the-Fields. He is not known to have married and died in London in March 1675.

NATALIE ZACEK

Sources DNB • F. G. Spurdle, *Early West Indian government* (privately printed, New Zealand, [n.d.]) • R. S. Dunn, *Sugar and slaves* (1972) • 'Mitchell's West Indian bibliography', www.books.ai, 2 Sept 2002 • S. A. G. Taylor, *The western design* (1969)

Archives BL, order book, journal kept whilst chief commander of Jamaica, and other papers, Add. MSS 12410, 12411, 12423 | Hunt. L., letters to William Blathwayt

D'Oylie [Doyley, D'Oyly], **Thomas** (c.1548–1603), physician and lexicographer, was the third son of John D'Oyly of Greenland House, Hambleden, Buckinghamshire, and his wife, Frances, daughter of Andrew Edmonds of Cressing Temple, Essex. Having been elected fellow probationer of Magdalen College, Oxford, in 1563, he graduated BA on 24 July 1564 and proceeded MA on 21 October 1569. His name appears in the account of a visitation to Magdalen in September 1566 by Bishop Hore's commissary, Dr George Ashworth: another fellow, Thomas Turner, was on that occasion charged with quarrelsome behaviour for attempting to get D'Oylie expelled for wearing a surplice (Turner appears to have been of puritan leanings). In 1567 D'Oylie was one of a group of bachelor fellows who were admonished to be more diligent in attending divine service. D'Oylie supplicated for the BM degree and was licensed to practise medicine in Michaelmas term 1571, but resigned his fellowship the same year after marrying Anne, daughter of Simon Perrott MA of North Leigh, Oxfordshire, who was also a fellow of Magdalen. They had six children: Norris, Michael (who became an army captain who settled in Ireland), Francis, Frances, Margery (who was the mother of Hugh Paulinus *Cressy, the Benedictine monk and ecclesiastical historian), and Katharine.

After his marriage D'Oylie travelled abroad in the company of Anthony Bacon, with whom he was connected by marriage. (His eldest brother, Sir Robert D'Oylie, married Elizabeth Bacon, who was half-sister to Anthony and Francis; a copy of a letter dated 11 July 1580 from Francis Bacon to Thomas D'Oylie survives in the British Library.) Before 1582 D'Oylie proceeded MD at Basel; he must have become doctor by 1582 because he is described thus in an endorsement by the earl of Leicester on one of D'Oylie's letters to the earl from Antwerp dated 28 May 1582. Two further letters from November 1585 to Leicester survive, and suggest that D'Oylie was employed on Leicester's business in the Low Countries during the early 1580s. The first, from Calais, dated 12 November, tells how the ship on which D'Oylie was sailing was captured by two men-of-war off Dunkirk on 14 October; the passengers were 'rifled of all our goods and apparrel unto our dubletts and hose'. D'Oylie and others were imprisoned in Dunkirk and questioned by the governor about English affairs in Flanders; D'Oylie was later ransomed by two merchants (Messrs Hudson and Beal) for 500 guilders. D'Oylie writes to the earl that he had escaped lightly, nothing but 'phisick and astronomie books' being found in his chest, and he reassures Leicester that all letters and notes relating to the earl's business had been disposed of through a porthole when the ship was boarded. D'Oylie's connection with Dunkirk continued later in his life: a letter from Robert Whyte to Sir Robert Sidney in 1597 records that the governor was 'at Dr Doileys House', where he was said to be resolved to die rather than pay his ransom of 20,000 crowns (Collins, 78). D'Oylie accompanied Sir Robert Cecil to France in that same year.

In the meantime D'Oylie continued his medical career. He was admitted a licentiate of the College of Physicians on 21 May 1585, and became a candidate on 28 September 1586 and a fellow on the last day of February 1588. He was censor in 1593, 1596, and 1598. According to Anthony Wood, D'Oylie was 'much frequented for his successful practice in his faculty' (Wood, *Ath. Oxon.*, 1.737), and on 18 July 1592 D'Oylie was incorporated MD at Oxford. He was also physician to St Bartholomew's Hospital, London.

D'Oylie was a lexicographer as well as a physician. On 19 October 1590 a book was entered in the Stationers' register by the bookseller and printer John Wolfe, described as

A Spanish Grammer conformed to our Englishe Accydence. With a large Dictionarye conteyninge Spanish, Latyn, and Englishe wordes, with a multitude of Spanishe wordes more then are conteyned in the Calapine of x: languages or Neobrecensis Dictionare. Set forth by Thomas D'Oyley, Doctor in phisick, with the co[n]firence of Natyve Spaniardes. (Arber, *Regs. Stationers*, 2.565)

D'Oylie's grammar and dictionary were never published, but his work was incorporated into Richard Percyvall's *Bibliotheca Hispanica. Containing a grammar, with a dictionarie in Spanish, English, and Latine, gathered out of divers good authors: very profitable for the studious of the Spanish toong. The dictionarie being inlarged with the Latine, by the advise and conference of Master Thomas Doyley doctor in physicke* (1591). Percyvall informs the reader that 'seeing mee to bee more foreward to the presse then himselfe, [D'Oylie] very friendly gave his consent to the publishing of mine; wishing me to adde the Latine to it as hee had begunne in his; which I performed' (sig. A2r). This dictionary was expanded and reissued by John Minsheu in 1599 and 1623.

D'Oylie died at some point between 7 March 1603, when he drew up his will, and 11 March, when he was buried, at his request, in the hospital church, St Bartholomew-the-

Less. His lengthy and detailed will, which included the bequest of 'my border of Spanish worke', was proved on 25 June 1603 (PRO, PROB 11/101, fol. 368r).

HELEN MOORE

Sources W. D'Oyly Bayley, *A biographical, historical, genealogical and heraldic account of the house of D'Oyly* (1845), 148–51 • will, PRO, PROB 11/101, sig. 46 • *Reg. Oxf.*, 1.253, 2.374 • *CSP dom.*, 1601–3, 190 • J. L. Chester and J. Foster, eds., *London marriage licences, 1521–1869* (1887), col. 417 • J. Peller Malcolm, *Londinium redivivum: an antient history and modern description of London*, 1 (1802), 308 • J. Strype, *Annals of the Reformation and establishment of religion … during Queen Elizabeth's happy reign*, new edn, 2/2 (1824), 210 • T. Wright, *Queen Elizabeth and her times*, 2 (1838), 266–9, 270–71 • J. R. Bloxam, *A register of the presidents, fellows … of Saint Mary Magdalen College*, 8 vols. (1853–85), vol. 2, pp. lxxiv–lxxvi; vol. 4, p. 233 • W. D. Macray, *A register of the members of St Mary Magdalen College, Oxford*, 2 (1897), 36, 165–6; 3 (1901), 199 • Foster, *Alum. Oxon.*, 1500–1714, 1.421 • Wood, *Ath. Oxon.*, new edn, 1.737 • Munk, *Roll* • G. Stein, *The English dictionary before Cawdrey* (1985) • R. J. Steiner, *Two centuries of Spanish and English bilingual lexicography* (1970) • H. Sydney and others, *Letters and memorials of state*, ed. A. Collins, 2 vols. (1746), 78 • Arber, *Regs. Stationers*
Archives BL, letter, Add. MS 4109, fol. 122 | BL, letter, Cotton MS Galba C.vii. f.233

D'Oyly, Sir Charles, seventh baronet (1781–1845), administrator in India and artist, born at Murshidabad, India, in September 1781 and baptized on 16 September 1781, was the elder son of Sir John Hadley D'Oyly, sixth baronet (1754–1818), the East India Company's resident at the court of the nawab of Bengal at Murshidabad, and of his wife, Diana Cotes, *née* Rochfort, of Clontarf, co. Dublin. There were three other children: a younger son, and two daughters. The family, originally of Shottisham Hall, Norfolk, had had to sell its lands early in the eighteenth century. Sir John D'Oyly used the Murshidabad post—'the most lucrative office in the Company's service' (*Memoirs of William Hickey*, 3.236)—to restore his fortunes. He returned to England in 1785, where he was MP for Ipswich from 1790 to 1796, and acquired an estate, Newlands, near Lymington in Hampshire. Sir John was intimate with Warren Hastings, while Charles was godson to Marian Hastings, and the two families visited each other continually.

Young Charles was educated at home, and in 1797, while not yet sixteen, sailed for India, with introductions from Warren Hastings. These advanced him quickly to membership of the 'family' of young men around the governor-general, Lord Wellesley: by 1803 he was head of the private office with a salary of 1000 rupees per month. He felt assured enough in this position to take a wife, and was married at Tamluk in 1805 to his childhood sweetheart and cousin Marian Greer (*b. c.*1775). His father, who had returned a widower to India with his daughters, leaving his other son in Hastings's care, was opposed to marriages between cousins, but quickly became reconciled. The entire family lived together for a while at Alipore. Marian D'Oyly died on 9 January 1814. There were no children of this marriage, nor of D'Oyly's subsequent marriage to Elizabeth Jane, *née* Ross (cousin to the wife of the governor-general, the marquess of Hastings), whom he married in Cawnpore on 8 April 1815. D'Oyly inherited the baronetcy in 1818.

Sir Charles D'Oyly, seventh baronet (1781–1845), by George Chinnery

After a brief period out of employment on Wellesley's departure in 1805 (time he used to practise his drawing), D'Oyly's official career followed a conventional path through the ranks of the Bengal civil service. His first major appointment was as collector at Dacca (1808–12). This was followed by a period in Calcutta, as deputy collector and then collector, where he was at the centre of Calcutta society and of its artistic and musical life. In 1820 he moved to Patna as opium agent, becoming commercial resident there in 1831. His house was a centre of hospitality for local society (both British and Indian) and for visitors on their way to and from upper India. His duties did not keep him too busy and 'his pencil like his hookah-snake was always in his hand' (William Prinsep, manuscript memoir, BL OIOC). After a long leave spent at the Cape of Good Hope (1832–3) he returned to Calcutta as senior member of the board of customs, salt and opium, and of the marine board.

D'Oyly is of significance only as an artist. He drew as a child, and was sending drawings home from India soon after arrival. Like many amateurs in India, his work came under the influence of George Chinnery; the two men were constantly in each other's company between 1807 and 1820. D'Oyly's views in pencil of Dacca, with some input from Chinnery, were engraved by John Landseer between 1814 and 1827. With his removal to Patna, D'Oyly freed himself sufficiently to be able to develop his own style. A fine draughtsman, his topographic drawings in pen or pencil can be of great skill and sensitivity, whether of India or the Cape, but he failed to develop any really interesting artistic individuality in watercolour painting.

D'Oyly is at his best depicting the villages and monuments of Bengal set against subtropical greenery and lush waters, or the harsher, more mountainous regions of south Bihar. His lack of training in perspective drawing becomes apparent in his more ambitious architectural views of the great Indian cities. Calcutta's Palladian architecture fortunately did not greatly interest him, for his surviving drawings of it are among his weakest. His views of Calcutta, worked up anonymously for publication by George Francis White, were published as lithographs by Dickinson & Co. posthumously in 1848. He experimented with lithography, a process newly introduced into Calcutta in 1822. By 1825 he had his own press in Patna, which he ran (with assistance from Indian artists) under the name The Behar Amateur Lithographic Press; with it he published, from 1828 to 1831, many hundreds of drawings done by himself and his artistic circle, both in various scrapbooks, and in volumes devoted to ornithology and the hunt. Many of these he drew on stone himself, as he did his most serious lithographic work, a series of views published in 1830 as *Sketches of the New Road in a Journey from Calcutta to Gyah*. In Patna he and his friends founded a society of dilettanti, the Behar School of Athens, 'for the promotion of the arts and sciences and for the circulation of fun and merriment of all descriptions', and his other published works reveal this more frivolous side: amusing drawings illustrating life in India, with texts by Thomas Williamson (*The Costume and Customs of Modern India*, and *The Europeans in India*, both published by Edward Orme in 1813), and his doggerel epic poem *Tom Raw, the Griffin: a Burlesque Poem* (published anonymously in 1828), on the adventures of a new arrival in Calcutta, illustrated with his own drawings. D'Oyly also worked in oils from at least 1811; these are rarely signed, and his work has only in recent years been distinguished from that of other artists of the Indian scene. These paintings are, none the less, often of considerable distinction. The more painstaking effort required for oils forced him finally to express his feelings for India in a mature style of his own, at its best combining Chinnery's picturesqueness with Wilson's landscape style, and an almost impressionist approach to colour.

D'Oyly's promising start to his Indian career owed more to the influence of Warren Hastings and to his own personality than to any conspicuous administrative talents. He frankly acknowledged his character to be 'an indolent one' in a letter to Hastings in 1803. As a boy he was good-natured, lovable, and handsome, and he remained so throughout his life; he charmingly mocks his indolence by always drawing himself as rather portly. His love of society and his well-known position within it can only have contributed to his artistic fame, for he was judged by his contemporaries the most talented of all the amateur artists in India: 'the best gentleman artist I ever met with' (Heber, 1.314). There were other contemporary talented and interesting amateurs in India, for example the three Prinsep brothers, William, James, and Thomas, and George Francis White, but D'Oyly's fame above theirs is perhaps owing to his having devoted himself so conspicuously to art, in his own words to Warren Hastings, 'beyond perhaps what an amateur ought'.

D'Oyly retired in 1838 'obliged by severe ill-health' (D'Oyly Bayley, 134), although he took only one full leave and no apparent sick leave in forty years. He spent the remainder of his life in Italy, where he lived in a large villa outside Florence, still drawing prolifically. He died on 21 September 1845 at Leghorn, where he was buried.

J. P. LOSTY

Sources W. D'Oyly Bayley, A biographical, historical, genealogical and heraldic account of the house of D'Oyly (1845) · J. P. Losty, 'Sir Charles D'Oyly's lithographic press and his Indian assistants', India: a pageant of prints, ed. P. Rohatgi and P. Godrej (1989), 135–60 · J. P. Losty, 'Sir Charles D'Oyly: a career in art', Under the Indian sun: British landscape artists, ed. P. Rohatgi and P. Godrej (1995), 81–106 · BL, Warren Hastings MSS · E. Dodwell and J. S. Miles, Bengal civil servants, 1780–1838 (1839) · BL OIOC · HoP, Commons · Memoirs of William Hickey, ed. A. Spencer, 4 vols. (1913–25) · R. Heber, Narrative of a journey through the upper provinces of India, 2 vols. (1828) · DNB
Archives BL OIOC · Yale U. CBA, Paul Mellon collection | BL, corresp. with Warren Hastings, Add. MSS 29174–29192 passim
Likenesses G. Chinnery, portrait (with his second wife), Hong Kong and Shanghai Bank [see illus.]

D'Oyly, Christopher (bap. 1717, d. 1795), politician, was baptized on 23 December 1717 in Banbury, Oxfordshire, the eldest son of Christopher D'Oyly (1682?–1752) of Banbury, an attorney in the court of common pleas, and his wife, Susanna (d. 1758). There is no record of his early education, but he was admitted to the Inner Temple in 1741 and called to the bar on 5 June 1744. He sold his chambers in 1764, but it is said that he ceased to practise in 1754 on succeeding to an estate at Walton-on-Thames, Surrey (Bayly, 64). On 2 December 1765 he married Sarah Stanley (1725–1821), the younger daughter of George Stanley (d. 1734) of Paultons, Hampshire, and his wife, Sarah (d. 1764), and the granddaughter of Sir Hans Sloane. There were no children of the marriage.

Having been appointed first clerk in the war office in December 1761, D'Oyly was promoted to deputy secretary on 1 January 1763. His replacement as first clerk was Philip Francis, with whom he forged political links and a candid friendship. Both continued in post when Lord Barrington succeeded Welbore Ellis, D'Oyly's future brother-in-law, as secretary at war in 1765. On 21 December 1771 D'Oyly informed Francis that he had resigned, but offered no reason why. His departure was followed three months later by that of Francis, who quit the war office in circumstances that remain unclear. On appointment to the Bengal supreme council in 1773, Francis negotiated for D'Oyly to stand in for him at the next general election at Wareham, for which seat D'Oyly was returned in October 1774. D'Oyly maintained a regular correspondence with Francis in India about politics and family affairs. If the replies that he received were sometimes intemperate and occasionally graceless, he retained goodwill and equanimity towards his correspondent.

In May 1776 D'Oyly was appointed under-secretary in the colonial department and commissary-general of the musters, which drew him into planning the conduct of the war in America. A friend of the naval and military commanders Admiral Lord Howe and General Sir William Howe, he was dissatisfied by what he took to be the tepid support accorded them by his superior, Lord George Germain. He resigned abruptly on 6 February 1778, only days after the dispatch of a notice recalling Sir William Howe. In a letter to Francis he wrote: 'My reasons for giving up are many, but must not be trusted in a letter' (Memoirs of Sir Philip Francis, 2.133).

D'Oyly declared his intention to retire from parliament in 1780. Following the dissolution in September, Lord North offered him a deal by which he would become comptroller of army accounts in exchange for the commissary-general, which North required for a sitting member of parliament. D'Oyly declined the offer but then changed his mind about leaving parliament, and was returned for Seaford on 4 December 1780. He finally retired from parliament and public life in 1784.

For much of his official life D'Oyly's London home was in Mayfair, first in Charles Street and from around 1779 in Curzon Street. He enjoyed Twickenham as a retreat, and there he became a friend of Horace Walpole. D'Oyly was frequently in demand as a family lawyer. Besides acting as an attorney for Francis during his absence in India he fulfilled the same function for Henry Strachey. He was an executor to Clive's will, adviser to his widow, Margaret Clive, and cleared up Charles Townshend's financial affairs after his death in 1767. More administrator than politician, D'Oyly made no impact in the house; indeed, he is not recorded as having spoken.

D'Oyly died at Twickenham on 19 January 1795 and was buried on 27 January at St Mary's Church, Walton-on-Thames. Sarah D'Oyly long outlived him, and died on 28 November 1821, aged ninety-five. A marble monument in St Mary's Church by Sir Francis Chantrey commemorates both D'Oyly and his wife, who, as a widow, was among the sculptor's first patrons. D'Oyly is well characterized in the inscription, which eulogizes 'his professional abilities ... ever exercised in acts of humanity, in allaying animosities, in composing differences'.

T. H. BOWYER

Sources J. Parkes and H. Merivale, Memoirs of Sir Philip Francis, 2 vols. (1867) · W. D'O. Bayly, 'D'Oyly of Adderbury ... Hampton and Twickenham ... 1580–1840', A biographical, historical, genealogical and heraldic account of the house of D'Oyly (1845), 60–66 · L. B. Namier, 'D'Oyley, Christopher', HoP, Commons · E. W. Brayley, 'Walton-upon-Thames', in E. W. Brayley, J. Britton, and E. W. Brayley, jun., A topographical history of Surrey, 2nd edn, 4 vols. (1878–81), vol. 2, pp. 84–107 · M. M. Spector, The American department of the British government, 1768–1782 (1940) · GM, 1st ser., 99/1 (1829), 506–7 · F. A. Inderwick and R. A. Roberts, eds., A calendar of the Inner Temple records, 4–5 (1933–6) · A. Valentine, Lord George Germain (1962) · Walpole, Corr. · J. Holland, Memorials of Sir Francis Chantrey [1851] · G. S. Brown, The American secretary: the colonial policy of Lord George Germain, 1775–1778 (1963) · parish register (baptism), 10 April 1682, Adderbury · parish register (baptism), 23 Dec 1717, Banbury · parish register (marriage), 2 Dec 1765, Rotherwick, Hampshire · parish register (death), 1795, Walton-on-Thames, St Mary's · monumental inscription, Walton-on-Thames, St Mary's Church
Archives BL OIOC, corresp. with Philip Francis, Eur MSS C 8, D 18, E 12–22, F 5–6
Likenesses F. Chantry, marble effigy, 1821, St Mary's Church, Walton-on-Thames

Wealth at death left land and property in Oxfordshire, Buckinghamshire, and Surrey; much to wife for life; remainder to nephews: will, PRO, PROB 11/1255, sig. 76; Brayley, 'Walton-upon-Thames'

D'Oyly, Sir Francis (d. 1815). *See under* D'Oyly, Sir John, baronet (1774–1824).

D'Oyly, George (1778–1846), Church of England clergyman and theologian, fourth son of the Ven. Matthias D'Oyly (1743–1815), archdeacon of Lewes and rector of Buxted, Sussex, and his wife, Mary, *née* Poughfer, was born on 31 October 1778. He belonged to a branch of the D'Oyly family which settled at Bishopstone, in Stone parish, Buckinghamshire, in the reign of Elizabeth, and his brothers included Sir John *D'Oyly and Sir Francis *D'Oyly [see under D'Oyly, Sir John]. He went to schools at Dorking, Putney, and Kensington, and in 1796 he entered Corpus Christi College, Cambridge. In 1800 he graduated BA as second wrangler and second Smith's prizeman, and in 1801 won the member's prize for the Latin essay. In the same year he was elected a fellow of his college. Ordained deacon in 1802 by the bishop of Chichester, and priest in 1803 by the bishop of Gloucester, he was curate to his father for a few months in 1803, and in 1804 became curate of Wrotham in Kent. He was moderator in the University of Cambridge from 1806 to 1809, select preacher in 1809, 1810, and 1811, and proctor in 1808. In November 1811 he was appointed Hulsean lecturer at Cambridge, and in that capacity attacked Sir William *Drummond's theistic work *Oedipus Judaicus* in *Letters to Sir William Drummond* and *Remarks on Sir William Drummond's 'Oedipus Judaicus'* (1813), accusing him, in an acrimonious series of exchanges, of blasphemy and plagiarism. In 1813 he was appointed domestic chaplain to the archbishop of Canterbury, and married Maria Frances, daughter of William Bruere, formerly one of the principal secretaries to the government of India. In 1815 he was presented to the vicarage of Hernhill in Kent, but before he came into residence he was appointed, on the death of his father, rector of Buxted, Sussex. In 1820 he accepted the rectories of Lambeth, London, and of Sundridge, Kent, and held those preferments during the remainder of his life.

D'Oyly was well known in his day as a theologian. He was also an admirable parish priest, and while he was rector of Lambeth thirteen places of worship were added to the church establishment of the parish. He was treasurer to the Society for Promoting Christian Knowledge, a member of the London committee of the Society for the Propagation of the Gospel, and one of the principal promoters of the establishment of King's College, London. Indeed, in a resolution passed by the council on 13 February 1846 it was said that 'by giving the first impulse and direction to public opinion he was virtually the founder of the college', a reference to his pamphlet (signed Christianus) opposing the secularism of University College, London.

Besides his controversy with Sir William Drummond, D'Oyly published *Two discourses preached before the University of Cambridge on the doctrine of a particular providence and modern unitarianism* (1812) and a volume of *Sermons* (1827). He assisted Richard Mant in the preparation of the annotated Bible published by the SPCK and known as 'D'Oyly and Mant's Bible' (1814 and later edns). He also wrote a life of William Sancroft (2 vols., 1821). D'Oyly died on 8 January 1846 and was buried in Lambeth church, where a monument was erected to his memory. His son, Charles John D'Oyly, edited his sermons in two volumes (1847), with a memoir.   L. C. SANDERS, *rev.* H. C. G. MATTHEW

Sources G. D'Oyly, *Sermons …: with a memoir by his son*, ed. C. J. D'Oyly, 2 vols. (1847) · W. D'Oyly Bayley, *A biographical … account of the house of D'Oyly* (1845) · J. D'Oyly, *Letters to Ceylon, 1814–1824*, ed. P. E. Pieris (1938) · Venn, *Alum. Cant.*

D'Oyly, Sir John, baronet (1774–1824), administrator in Ceylon, was the second son of Matthias D'Oyly (1743–1815), archdeacon of Lewes and rector of Buxted, a descendant of the D'Oylys of Stone in Buckinghamshire, and his wife, Mary, daughter of George Poughfer of Leicester. He was born on 11 June 1774 and was educated at Westminster School, where he was a favoured pupil of William Vincent, and at Corpus Christi College, Cambridge. A distinguished Latin scholar, he was elected a fellow of Corpus Christi in 1798 and proceeded MA in 1799.

In 1801, having obtained a writership through the patronage of Lord Liverpool, D'Oyly went to Ceylon and set himself to mastering Sinhalese. He rose rapidly in the service through a series of judicial and revenue posts in the districts of Matara and Colombo, and in 1805 was appointed chief translator to the government. In February 1815 his linguistic and intelligence skills were indispensable to General Brownrigg, the governor of Ceylon, in his campaign against the kingdom of Kandy, in the interior of the island. Resenting the encroachments of the encircling English, the king of Kandy had resorted to increasingly desperate assaults on them and their Sinhalese allies, eventually incurring the might of the army's retribution. The king was captured, and on 2 March 1815 his kingdom was annexed by proclamation. On 1 October 1816 D'Oyly was appointed resident and first commissioner of government in the Kandyan Provinces, offices which he held until his death. For years the only Sinhalese scholar in the Ceylon civil service, he produced a work on the Kandyan constitution and laws, which was published by the Royal Asiatic Society in 1832, and translated many poems from the Sinhalese, few of which have survived. On 29 August 1821 he was created a baronet for his services. He died of fever at Kandy on 25 May 1824 and was buried there in the old garrison cemetery. D'Oyly never married and he had not been back to England since his departure in 1801. His colleagues considered him something of a recluse, half-Sinhalese in his habits, and much preferring his Sinhala poems to the company of his fellow officers. The baronetcy ceased with his death.

Sir Francis D'Oyly (d. 1815), third son of Matthias, went up to Corpus Christi College, Cambridge, in 1794. He enjoyed a distinguished military career with the guards and acted as assistant adjutant-general to the 1st division throughout the Peninsular War. He received a gold cross and three clasps for the battles of Busaco, Fuentes de Onoro, Salamanca, Vitoria, the Nivelle, the Nive, and

Orthes. He was made a KCB on the extension of the Order of the Bath, and acted as assistant adjutant-general in the campaign of 1815 to Picton's division. He was killed by a cannon-ball on 18 June 1815, early in the battle of Waterloo. There is a graveyard inscription in his memory in Walton-on-Thames.

H. M. STEPHENS, rev. KATHERINE PRIOR

Sources J. P. Lewis, *List of inscriptions on tombstones and monuments in Ceylon of historical or local interest, with an obituary of persons uncommemorated* (1913), 11, 298–300 · Venn, *Alum. Cant.*, 2/2.332 · *Memoirs of the life of the Right Honourable Sir James Mackintosh*, ed. R. J. Mackintosh, 2 vols. (1835) · *Diary of Mr John D'Oyly*, ed. H. W. Codrington (1917) · J. Burke and J. B. Burke, *A genealogical and heraldic history of the extinct and dormant baronetcies of England, Ireland and Scotland*, 2nd edn (1841); repr. (1844) · P. E. Pieris, *Letters to Ceylon, 1814–1824. Being correspondence addressed to Sir John D'Oyly* (1938) · G. Powell, *The Kandyan wars: the British army in Ceylon, 1803–1818* (1973)
Archives CCC Cam., diary as undergraduate and fellow | PRO, letters to William Pitt, PRO 30/8
Likenesses watercolour drawing, c.1800, V&A

D'Oyly, Samuel (*bap.* 1681, *d.* 1748), translator, was baptized on 24 November 1681 at St Margaret's, Westminster, the son of Charles D'Oyly (*d.* in or before 1692) and his wife, Martha, whose background is unknown but who married Nehemiah Arnold in 1699. His father was the fourth and youngest son of Sir William D'Oyly, first baronet, of Shottisham, Norfolk. He was admitted to Westminster School, as a scholar, in 1697. He entered Trinity College, Cambridge, as a pensioner, on 5 June 1700, was elected scholar on 2 May 1701, and took his BA in 1703/4. He was appointed minor fellow of his college on 2 October 1706 and promoted major fellow on 25 April 1707, the year in which he proceeded MA. He did not immediately take orders.

Much of D'Oyly's time at Cambridge was taken up with a property dispute. His father had been left the manor of Cosford Hall, in the parish of Hadleigh, Suffolk, by Sir William D'Oyly. The hall was part of the jointure of Bridget, Lady Astley, widow of Edmund D'Oyly, Sir William's cousin, who had died in 1638. D'Oyly's father predeceased Lady Astley and therefore did not inherit the property, but before his death he had mortgaged it to Thomas Manning. When Lady Astley died, in 1700, Manning took over Cosford Hall and began felling trees to raise money to retrieve his loan. D'Oyly began chancery proceedings against Manning in 1705, but Manning questioned whether D'Oyly was Charles D'Oyly's natural son; the matter was settled amicably in 1707, when D'Oyly sold his interest in the estate to Manning. Manning's allegations were thought by William Bayley in his history of the D'Oyly family to explain why, in his contribution on the family to Thomas Wotton's *English Baronetage* in 1729, D'Oyly failed to mention himself or his mother. However, he still had enough confidence in his identity to prove the will of Philippa Wetenhall, *née* D'Oyly, as her nephew, in 1717.

D'Oyly took orders no later than November 1710, when he was presented by Thomas Sprat, bishop of Rochester and former dean of Westminster, to the vicarage of St Nicholas, Rochester, which he held until his death. The position proved amenable to his career as a translator. In 1718 he published *Christian Eloquence in Theory and Practice*, translated from the French of Blaise Gisbert. His greatest project was the translation of Augustin Calmet's *Dictionnaire historique, critique, chronologique, geographique et litteral de la Bible*, in which he collaborated with his neighbour John Colson. The work was begun before the publication of the second French edition, in 1730, but was revised to take account of Calmet's changes and published in 1732, in three folio volumes, as *An historical, critical, geographical, chronological and etymological dictionary of the Holy Bible*.

By this time D'Oyly had married Frances (*d.* 1780), of whose family nothing is known; they had no children. He also befriended Thomas Herring, the future archbishop of Canterbury: in 1735 Herring wrote to William Duncombe (whose brother John married D'Oyly's half-sister Elizabeth Arnold) that D'Oyly was 'much your humble servant, and a very genteel and agreeable companion' (*Letters*, 32). According to John Nichols, D'Oyly was appointed a chaplain to the army but in 1741 was unable to perform the task as he had become so corpulent that no horse would carry him. He died in Rochester at the beginning of May 1748, and was buried on 9 May near the west door of the cathedral, without an inscription. Herring expressed interest in buying his books but they were acquired by John Whiston, a bookseller in Fleet Street, London. His wife survived him, and lived in Rochester until her death in 1780.

GORDON GOODWIN, rev. MATTHEW KILBURN

Sources W. D. Bayley, *A biographical, historical, genealogical, and heraldic account of the house of D'Oyly* (1845) · *Old Westminsters* · Venn, *Alum. Cant.* · J. Welch, *The list of the queen's scholars of St Peter's College, Westminster*, ed. [C. B. Phillimore], new edn (1852), 141–2 · letters to Thomas Wotton, 1729, BL, Add. MS 24120, fols. 264–9 · *Letters from the late most reverend Dr. Thomas Herring, lord archbishop of Canterbury, to William Duncombe, Esq; deceased, from the year 1728 to 1757* (1777), 32, 113–14 · J. L. Chester, ed., *The marriage, baptismal, and burial registers of the collegiate church or abbey of St Peter, Westminster*, Harleian Society, 10 (1876) · E. Hasted, *The history and topographical survey of the county of Kent*, 4 vols. (1778–99), 2.51 · *The miscellaneous works of Bishop Atterbury*, ed. J. Nichols, 5 vols. (1789–98), vol. 2 · T. Wotton, *The English baronetage*, 4 vols. (1741) · IGI · GEC, *Baronetage* · W. A. Copinger, *The manors of Suffolk*, 7 vols. (1905–11)
Archives BL, letter to Thomas Wotton, Add. MS 24120, fols. 264–9
Wealth at death see will, PRO, PROB 11/762, sig. 145

D'Oyly [Doyle], **Thomas** (*b. c.*1530, *d.* after 1598), antiquary, was the second son of Sir Henry Doyle (*c.*1500–1563) of Pond Hall, Hadleigh, Suffolk, and his second wife, Jane, daughter of William Elwyn of Wiggenhall St Germans, Norfolk. Henry, a Suffolk JP from 1538 to 1561, was knighted by Henry VIII at Boulogne in 1547, and on 16 July 1553 he took his sons Henry and Thomas with him in the retinue of Thomas, Lord Wentworth, to be among the first to give their loyalty to the new Queen Mary at Framlingham Castle. When Thomas was scarcely seventeen he married Elizabeth, daughter and heir of Ralph Bendish of Toppesfield Hall, Hadleigh; she also brought him Overbury Hall at nearby Layham and bore him two sons and four daughters between 1548 and 1553, but died that 2 August after giving birth to the fourth. Two years later

Thomas was admitted to Gray's Inn, where his studies fitted him to become steward to Archbishop Matthew Parker at Croydon Palace. The letter his father wrote thanking Parker for seeing Thomas is dated March 1560; it was probably from Parker (who was chancellor of Cambridge University) that he received the degree of DCL. Sir Henry, as sheriff of Norfolk and Suffolk, had presided at the burnings of protestant heretics on the Cornhill at Ipswich, the last occasion only thirteen days before the death of Mary; he died in 1563. On 11 February 1565 Thomas married his second wife, Anne Crosse of Hadleigh, and they had three more sons. The eldest, Thomas, died, but the next, also Thomas, married Parker's niece Joane Baker. The children of both marriages were baptized at Layham, but the registers there are seriously defective; the burials of Thomas and his wives are not recorded.

Parker's interest in antiquities and his support for those who studied them is well known, but there is no evidence that he initiated gatherings of antiquaries (to include Thomas D'Oyly) in the early 1570s as has been alleged. What is certain is that 'Mr Doyley, Dr of the lawe' was among those who met as 'the Assembly of the Antiquaries' headed by 'Mr Garter Dethicke, Mr Clarenceaux Cambden', and Sir Henry Spelman, but this cannot be earlier than 1597, the year in which Camden became Clarenceux. Two short contributions to debate by 'Doctor Doylye' were printed by Hearne in his *Curious Discourses* (1771, 1.174–5, 183–4): 'Of the antiquity of arms' was discussed on 2 November 1598, and 'Of the etymology, dignity and antiquity of dukes in England' on the 28th following. Concerning the first, D'Oyly begins by stating that 'it is likely that warrs and weapons are almost coetanea', and goes on to suggest that 'Warrs at the first were but rapine … but when civility produced discipline, arms were martialled by discipline. Then virtue was rewarded with honour and cowardness with shame'. On dukes, he wrote in French, beginning with the titles of 'Comptes' given to the sons of early French kings. Dukes were commanders on the battlefield, at first leading four, and then twelve, counts. On both occasions Arthur Agard and another, anonymous, contributor spoke, or wrote, at great length.

J. M. BLATCHLY

Sources D. MacCulloch, 'The *Vita Mariae Angliae Reginae* of Robert Wingfield of Brantham', *Camden miscellany, XXVIII*, CS, 4th ser., 29 (1984), 181–301 · H. D'Oyley, letter to Matthew Parker, CCC Cam., Parker MS, 114/246 · Assembly of Antiquaries, list of members, BL, Harl. MS 5177, fol. 141 · T. Hearne, ed., *Curious discourses* (1771), 1.174–5, 183–4

Drabble, George Wilkinson (1823?–1899), merchant and banker, was born at Sheffield, the fourth son of James Drabble (1781/2–1841), merchant, and his wife, Marianne, *née* Brownell (1794/5–1876). He had six brothers and three sisters. Drabble was educated at Sheffield grammar school. His father, who became wealthy, died in 1841, aged fifty-nine, having made provision for his sons' business training among family and associates in Sheffield and London. His mother lived to be eighty-one; she died at Worthing in 1876.

In the early 1850s, Drabble and his brother Charles Thompson Drabble set up as Drabble Brothers, commission merchants in Manchester, specializing in the export of textiles. To develop South American business, Drabble went to the River Plate, calling at Uruguay in 1847 and Argentina in 1848. Drabble became a leading figure in Buenos Aires, extending his interests to the acquisition of *estancias* (ranches) for sheep farming and winning the confidence of Argentine politicians at a time when British investment was shaping the local infrastructure. About 1856, Drabble married Isabel White (*c*.1834–1899), who was born in Buenos Aires. They had four sons and a daughter.

In 1862 Drabble played a key role in establishing the Buenos Ayres Great Southern Railway Company. He became the first chairman of the Buenos Ayres Western Railway and in 1884 he reorganized the Campaña railway and extended it to Rosario and Tucumán. In Uruguay, too, Drabble revolutionized communications, becoming chairman of three railway companies. In 1870 he was responsible for the City of Buenos Ayres Tramways Company, which made dramatic growth despite the initial restriction that every tram had to follow a mounted trumpeter. He also pressed for the installation of a clean water supply for the city, which was badly affected by cholera, and assisted in raising money for dock schemes.

Drabble's recruitment to the London and River Plate Bank (founded in 1862 as the London, Buenos Ayres and River Plate Bank) was effected by his friend John Fair, already a director, when both men were in London in 1868. Fair reported to colleagues that Drabble 'evinced an inclination to join this Board' (minute book No. 1, 412). He was elected immediately (July 1868), and became chairman from 1870 until his death nearly thirty years later. He visited Argentina only twice more.

Drabble was never comfortable being categorized as a banker. He was still describing himself (in census records) as a South American merchant in 1871 and 1881, and as a company director in 1891. His bank colleagues were clearly tolerant of the overlap as, when Drabble returned to Argentina in 1872 at the urgent request of the Buenos Ayres Great Southern Railway, 'to endeavour to arrange some matters for that company', he went at the bank's expense. His rather short obituary notice in *Bankers' Magazine*, inaccurate as to the date of death, and giving equal weight to his achievements in banking and in the public utilities, seemed to underline the ambivalence of his position. Drabble was, nevertheless, recognized as a fair and prudent banker who kept his company strong through difficult years. He told shareholders 'we do all in our power to eliminate from our books risk of every character' (AGM report, 1882). He has been criticized for poor managerial appointments, but his own integrity and authority were never in question. In the last years of his chairmanship, the bank's success, judged by return on shareholders' equity, placed it in the first flight of British international banking.

Drabble's stature is illustrated by the 'Rosario incident'. In 1875 the provincial government of Santa Fé deprived the London bank's local branch of its right of note issue, and then ordered it into liquidation. When its gold was seized and the manager arrested, an international incident was in the making. Drabble travelled rapidly to Argentina in June 1876, to the relief of the British minister in Buenos Aires who saw him 'as the harbinger of better times' (PRO, FO 6/345, St John to Derby, 14 July 1876). The dispatch of a British warship to Rosario reinforced Drabble's credibility: the manager was freed, the order for liquidation was rescinded, and the branch regained its gold. But it was Drabble's excellent relations with the Argentine foreign minister which were at the heart of the resolution of the crisis. The same credentials made Drabble a member of the committee of bankers under Lord Rothschild to negotiate a financial settlement with the Argentine government after the Baring crisis of 1890.

In 1882 Drabble set up in London the River Plate Fresh Meat Company, the first *frigorífico* (freezing plant) to export mutton, and later beef, to Europe; thus began one of the staples of the Argentine economy. A visitor to his plant in 1883 could 'well remember the imposing and novel sight the freezing-rooms offered, with their long rows of sheep's carcases, swathed in spotlessly clean linen as in their winding sheets, and disappearing in the dim perspective of the snow-covered chamber' (Gibson, 160). Drabble died of kidney failure on 2 October 1899 at Los Altos, Sandown, Isle of Wight, having chaired board meetings at the bank until 20 June. His wife died in the same year, on 26 December. He was succeeded immediately on the bank's board by his eldest son, Charles William Drabble, who later joined his own son, Edward G. Drabble, in a stock-raising firm in Argentina, independent of Drabble Brothers. This latter firm continued in Buenos Aires under the management of the sons of Charles Thompson Drabble, turning to the management of *estancias* and the breeding of championship stock.   JOHN BOOKER

Sources *Bankers' Magazine*, 68 (1899), 630 • R. Lloyd, *Twentieth century impressions of Argentina* (1911) • J. T. Critchell and J. Raymond, *A history of the frozen meat trade*, 2nd edn (1912) • *Commercial encyclopedia*, British and Latin American Chamber of Commerce (1922) • H. S. Ferns, *Britain and Argentina in the nineteenth century* (1960) • D. Joslin, *A century of banking in Latin America* (1963) • D. C. M. Platt, ed., *Business imperialism, 1840–1930: an inquiry based on British experience in Latin America* (1977) • R. C. Conde, *Dinero, deuda y crisis: evolución fiscal y monetaria en la Argentina, 1862–1890* (1989) • minute book no. 1, UCL, London and River Plate Bank archives, 412 • AGM report of London and River Plate Bank, 1882, Lloyds TSB Group Archives • H. Gibson, *The history and present state of the sheep-breeding industry in the Argentine Republic* (1893) • census returns, 1871, 1881, 1891 • d. cert.

Archives Lloyds TSB Group, London, archives, records of London and River Plate Bank • PRO, FO 6/345 • UCL, BOLSA archive, letter books, etc., London and River Plate Bank

Likenesses photograph, repro. in Critchell and Raymond, *A history of the frozen meat trade*, facing p. 76 • photograph, repro. in Joslin, *A century of banking*, facing p. 116

Wealth at death £438,263 11s. 8d.: probate, 1 Dec 1899, CGPLA Eng. & Wales

Drage, William (*bap.* 1636, *d.* 1668), physician and apothecary, was baptized at Raunds, Northamptonshire, on 8 January 1636, the son of William and Elizabeth Drage, who were able to provide him with a good grammar-school education. He was then apprenticed to an apothecary, and in 1658 settled in Hitchin, Hertfordshire, where he opened an apothecary's shop and established himself as a physician, with a large practice that included local gentry. On 5 October 1659 he married Elizabeth Lawndy, of Baldock, who embarrassed him in 1664 by turning Quaker. Drage read very widely in English and continental medical works, compiling from them in 1658–9 several treatises on specific diseases, which he incorporated in his major work, *A Physical Nosonomy* (1664), a compendium of medical symptoms and treatments, reissued in 1665 and again with different title-pages in 1666 and 1668. In a combative introduction Drage condemned the reverence still given to ancient writers, contrasting 'the Sons of Superstition and Tradition' with 'the Sons of Experience' (*Physical Nosonomy*, 1665 edn, 8) and championing modern authors, such as Felix Platter, who relied on their own observations. The work also drew on Drage's own notes on 1400 medical case histories. Despite his pugnacious spirit he accepted traditional medical theories based on the four humours and on herbal and other therapies designed to restore a proper balance between them. His work upheld the importance of astrology in medical practice but cautioned that more weight should always be given to observed symptoms than to the astrological chart. In 1665 Drage published *Pyretologie*, a treatise on fevers, in both English and Latin editions. Another work, 'Physiology, iatrosophy and pneumatography', was then ready for the press but was never published, though Drage referred frequently to it in his *Nosonomy*.

In 1665 Drage also published *Daimonomageia*, a short work for physicians treating diseases caused by witchcraft and possession. Drage was more concerned to find cures than to punish witches, and though he considered it legitimate to frighten them with threats, he pointedly did not advocate execution. The subtitle explained that the tract was also designed to '*confute Atheistical, Sadducistical, and Sceptical Principles*', and it was heavily influenced by the writings of Henry More, as well as by Drage's own wide reading in continental demonology. Though this work now appears highly credulous, accepting accounts of possessed people able to walk upside down across ceilings, Drage's critical faculties had not altogether deserted him. He freely acknowledged that some cases of possession were fraudulent and others wrongly diagnosed, but was overwhelmed by the volume of well-authenticated case studies from different places and times, and by his own first-hand experience. The tract included a vivid account of the recent local case of Mary Hall of Little Gaddesden, Hertfordshire, the teenage daughter of pious nonconformists, who was possessed by two spirits in 1663. Drage was summoned after Baptist preachers and the specialist Dr Woodhouse of Berkhamsted had attempted in vain to cure her. Drage too was unable to help, but used his meetings in 1664 with Mary, her family, and Woodhouse to pen one of the best accounts we have of demonic possession. The 'spirits', speaking through Mary, declared they had tried to kill her father, and their blasphemous outbursts that 'God was a Bastard', and demands that she should have a new gown, hoods, scarves, and 'Ribbons, Hay! Ribbons, Ribbons, Ribbons, Ribbons' (*Daimonomageia*, 34, 38) suggest powerfully the role of possession in providing an outlet for suppressed desires in a highly repressive environment.

Drage suffered poor health throughout his life, being subject to dropsy and convulsions. He died at Hitchin on 17 November 1668, and was buried there on 23 November at St Mary's Church. By his will, drawn up in 1666 and revised on 12 November 1668, he left his house and shop to his widow, his patrimony at Raunds to his eldest son, William, and property at Morden, Cambridgeshire, to his younger sons Theodorus and Philogithus, and his daughter Lettice. BERNARD CAPP

Sources R. L. Hine, *Hitchin worthies: four centuries of English life* (1932) · C. Drage, *Family story: the Drages of Hatfield* (1969) · *DNB* · *IGI*
Archives BL, Sloane MSS, lecture notes taken by Henry Coley
Wealth at death house (assessed at five hearths in hearth tax) plus shop in Hitchin; patrimony at Raunds, Northamptonshire; land and malting at Morden, Cambridgeshire: will, PRO, PROB 11/329, sig. 31, cited by *DNB*; Drage, *Family story*

Draghi, Giovanni Battista (*c.*1640–1708), musical performer and composer, may have been a brother of Antonio Draghi (1635–1700), who was born in Rimini and became a leading court musician in Vienna. Giovanni Battista Draghi served at a continental court (now unidentified) before going to England to join an ensemble of Italian musicians established under royal patronage in 1663. He is first mentioned on 12 February 1667, when Samuel Pepys heard him perform from memory a complete act of an opera of which Draghi had written the libretto as well as the music. 'Seignor Baptista', as Pepys called him, and the English equivalent, 'Mr Baptist', became the names by which he was generally known.

Over the next two decades Draghi established an enviable reputation as a performer and composer. John Evelyn later described him as famous for 'his playing on the harpsichord, few if any in Europe exceeding him' and as 'that excellent and stupendious Artist' (Evelyn, 4.384–5, 25 July 1684; 4.404, 28 Jan 1685). Little evidence of his performing career survives: most of the few references to his playing describe him accompanying singers, and his solo harpsichord music was probably improvised or played from memory. Many of the keyboard works extant in manuscripts or eventually collected in his *Six Select Sutes of Lessons for the Harpsichord* (1707) seem to be teaching material written for a select group of privileged pupils: the antiquarian and librarian Humphrey Wanley stated that Draghi was 'Music-Master to Her Most Excellent Majesty Queen Anne' and that he 'instructed her Majesty in Music' (*Catalogue of the Harleian Manuscripts*, 1.643, 2.271). BL, MS Mus. 1, a keyboard book containing music in Purcell's hand at one end and probably in Draghi's autograph at the other, may have belonged to a family which employed both musicians at different times.

In many respects Draghi adapted his compositional style to English expectations, but a few works are uncompromisingly Italianate, notably a long solo cantata, *Qual*

spaventosa tromba (BL, Harley MS 1863). A trio sonata appears in BL, Add. MS 33236, a score which contains some of Purcell's earliest instrumental music and perhaps reflects the kind of repertory Purcell studied in the 1670s, although Draghi's composition does not provide a direct model for Purcell's own sonatas. Draghi contributed instrumental music, now unfortunately lost, to two major theatrical ventures of the 1670s: Thomas Shadwell's musical version of *The Tempest* (1674) and his *Psyche* (1675). The epilogue to *Psyche* identifies Draghi as 'Master of the *Italian* Musick to the King'. Between 1673 and 1677 he may have taken over some duties in Queen Catherine's Roman Catholic chapel at Somerset House from Matthew Locke, with whom he collaborated on *The Tempest* and *Psyche*, and he officially succeeded Locke as the queen's organist in 1677. At some time after this date he commissioned a painting from Benedetto Gennari the younger, who had been employed as an artist for the chapel since 1674: its subject, the Christ child with St John the Baptist, was probably of special personal significance.

As a Catholic and a foreigner Draghi must have felt insecure at the time of the Popish Plot, and on 18 November 1679 he and three other Italian musicians petitioned the king for payment of four years' arrears of wages, on the grounds that they were about to be forced to leave the country. Draghi's position in the queen's chapel, however, provided him with protection during the immediate political crisis, and he remained a prominent figure in London musical life. A number of songs, some written for plays, were published in the four volumes of *The Theater of Music* (1685–7) and elsewhere. An English anthem, 'This is the Day' (William Andrews Clark Library, Los Angeles, MS fC6966/M4/A627/1700), was copied by Daniel Henstridge, probably in the mid-1680s when Henstridge was organist of Rochester Cathedral. In 1684 the rival organ builders Bernard Smith and Renatus Harris both set up instruments in the Temple Church, and Draghi was chosen to demonstrate Harris's organ in competition with Smith's, which was played by Blow and Purcell.

In 1687 Draghi was invited to compose the ode for the annual London celebration of St Cecilia's day. In his setting of John Dryden's *From Harmony, from Heavenly Harmony* Draghi produced a modern Italianate work grander in conception than any ode so far written by an English composer: its impact on his contemporaries is shown by the survival of four complete manuscript copies of the full score, and its influence is clearly apparent in later music by Blow and Purcell. About Christmas 1687 Draghi was appointed organist of James II's new Catholic chapel at Whitehall: this post was destined to be short-lived, but after the revolution of 1688 he continued to serve Queen Catherine until she returned to Portugal in 1692, and also enjoyed the patronage of Princess Anne. Draghi promoted public concerts, and in late 1692 brought to England a promising Italian female singer whom he took to sing to the princess (BL, Sloane MS 1388, fols. 77r–78v). In 1695 he was named as one of the organ and harpsichord teachers at a proposed royal academy, and on 25 July 1696 he witnessed a contract whereby the dancer Joseph Sorin joined

Thomas Betterton's theatre company. On 24 February 1697 a birthday ode composed by him for Princess Anne, now lost, was performed at York Buildings.

By 1698 Draghi was seriously ill with gout and unable to earn his living. Concerts for his benefit took place on 30 March 1698 and 24 March 1701; in 1698 he was granted a pension of £100 a year by William III 'in consideration of near 30 years' service in the royal family', and this was later renewed by Queen Anne, from whom he received a separate pension of £50 (Shaw, 17, pt 2, 71). At the time of his death he lived in the parish of St Giles-in-the-Fields, at which church he was buried on 13 May 1708; probate was granted to his widow, Sybilla, in the commissary court of London on 8 September (Guildhall Library, London, MS 9168/30, fol. 212), and on 28 July 1708 Queen Anne gave her £25 to cover the costs of her husband's funeral. It is not known whether Sybilla is to be identified with a 'Mrs Baptist' mentioned in May 1669 (Ashbee, *Records*, 8.194) or whether the Draghis had any children.

ROBERT THOMPSON

Sources *New Grove*, 2nd edn · A. Ashbee and D. Lasocki, eds., *A biographical dictionary of English court musicians, 1485–1714*, 2 vols. (1998) [incl. bibliography] · *A catalogue of the Harleian manuscripts in the British Museum*, 4 vols. (1808–12) · J. Redington, ed., *Calendar of Treasury papers*, 2, PRO (1871) · W. A. Shaw, ed., *Calendar of treasury books*, 17–18, PRO (1936–47) · R. T. Dart, 'Purcell's chamber music', *Proceedings of the Royal Musical Association*, 85 (1958–9), 81–93, esp. 93 · Evelyn, *Diary* · Pepys, *Diary* · A. Ashbee, ed., *Records of English court music*, 9 vols. (1986–96), vols. 5, 8 · P. Leech, 'Musicians in the Catholic chapel of Catherine of Braganza, 1662–92', *Early Music*, 29 (2001), 570–87 · D. Baldwin, *The Chapel Royal ancient and modern* (1990) · C. Hogwood, 'A new English keyboard manuscript of the seventeenth century: autograph keyboard music by Draghi and Purcell', *British Library Journal*, 21 (1995), 161–75 · Highfill, Burnim & Langhans, *BDA* · C. L. Day and E. B. Murrie, *English song-books, 1651–1702* (1940) · M. Tilmouth, 'A calendar of references to music in newspapers published in London and the provinces (1660–1719) [2 pts]', *Royal Musical Association Research Chronicle*, 1 (1961); 2 (1962), 2–15 · P. Holman, *Four and twenty fiddlers: the violin at the English court, 1540–1690* (1993)

Dragonetti, Domenico Carlo Maria (1763–1846), double bass player and composer, was born on 7 April 1763 in the parish of San Gervasio and San Protasio, Venice. Of his parents, Pietro Dragonetti and Cattarina Calegari, little is known, although it is speculated that his father played both the double bass and the guitar and may have been a gondolier. His mother bore at least one other child, Marietta, who married Giovanni Zimolo, son of a public notary in Caorle. Dragonetti provided financial support for his seemingly ungrateful parents later in life.

From lowly beginnings as a street musician in Venice, Dragonetti rose to the very top of his profession. His story is one of progress from rags to riches, from anonymity to adulatory fame. In Venice he studied with Michele Berini, played in various opera houses, and, after a failed attempt aged twenty-one, auditioned again and joined the orchestra of St Mark's on 13 September 1787 as the last in a section of five players. By December the players had reshuffled and Dragonetti led the section. He composed and played concertos and became a familiar soloist in St Mark's, other sacred venues, and in theatres and the

Domenico Carlo Maria Dragonetti (1763–1846), by Johannes Notz

homes of the nobility. His fame soon reached foreign shores. On 13 December 1791 the procurators of St Mark's issued a gratuity of 310 ducats to him by extraordinary decree in recognition of his refusal of offers of work in London and Moscow. By 1794, however, they had given him a two-year leave of absence (later extended by another three years) and he left for the glittering opportunities of London secure in the knowledge that he could return to his former post.

In the autumn of 1794, aged thirty-one, Dragonetti arrived in London. The capital was a hotbed of musical activity. Dragonetti's Italian roots were an important factor in the success of his English career and gave his virtuosity a fashionable added dimension. His engaging facility as a raconteur and his generosity to friends and family are well documented. He was an astute entrepreneur. He based his activities in London, residing at various Westminster addresses, and combining employment at the King's Theatre, the Concerts of Antient Music, and Drury Lane with further engagements at benefit concerts, subscription series, and public and private concerts. Later he added the Philharmonic Society and the classical concerts of Nicolas Mori and Robert Lindley as well as his own subscription series to this list. His income from these sources was supplemented by teaching and financial investments; he also dealt in fine art and musical instruments. His engagements were seasonal; several months each year were spent playing at provincial festivals and in the country residences of the aristocracy. He also travelled outside Britain, famously encountering Beethoven in Vienna in 1799. He spent time in Venice and then Vienna between 1808 and 1814, and was reputedly expelled from Venice in 1809 following imprisonment. His Viennese friends included the Starhemberg family and the composer Simon Sechter (1788–1867), who wrote accompaniments for some of Dragonetti's compositions in response to a commission from the bass player in 1839. Dragonetti returned to England from Vienna via Amsterdam and Rotterdam in May 1814.

Dragonetti destroyed perceptions of the capabilities of the double bass, carving a new niche for the instrument and firmly establishing its significance as the foundation of sonority and ensemble. His performances as a soloist in the 1790s were greeted with reverence and astonishment. A typical review of his playing is found in the *Bath Chronicle* for 14 November 1799: 'Dragonetti, who, by powers almost magical, invests an instrument, which seems to wage eternal war with melody, "rough as the storm, and as the thunder loud", with all the charms of soft harmonious sounds.' Dragonetti's playing was founded on his outwardly curved bow pattern. Unadjustable and held underhand, this bow type gave Dragonetti's playing the reputation of powerful projection and rhythmic impetus. His bow pattern was introduced with limited success at the Paris Conservatoire in 1827 at Rossini's instigation.

On Dragonetti's return from Vienna in 1814 a new phase of his career began. After establishing his reputation through unprecedented solo virtuosity he moved on to make a long-term commitment to chamber and orchestral music. The Concerts of Antient Music became a regular forum for works by Corelli and Handel. At a time when conducting was in its infancy, his orchestral role was one of substantial responsibility and effect. His reputation as an orchestral anchor benefited from his engagement by the Philharmonic Society from 1816 onwards. The inclusion of his name in advertisements was enough to establish the quality of any event to the public. His reputation enabled him to bargain with the directors of the Philharmonic Society for fees which consistently outstripped those of his colleagues between 1837 and his final season in 1842.

Dragonetti composed many works for his own use—the British Library houses eighteen volumes of manuscripts, including concerto and concerto-like works, quintets, variations on, and obbligato parts for, popular operatic arias, and multi-movement pieces for double bass and piano. These compositions reflect his considerable virtuosity within popular genres. Other works exclude his instrument and these include vocal and piano pieces and caprices for violin and piano. He was a collector of music, musical instruments, paintings, dolls, and snuff-boxes. Many of the manuscripts from his music collection are housed at the British Library and his considerable correspondence reveals his interest in amassing scores of contemporary operas. There is no doubt that he had a sense of humour but this was certainly combined with an understanding of the art of self-promotion. Anecdotes such as those by Henry Phillips and Ignaz Moscheles recall his apparent eccentricity and suggest that away from the double bass he was 'a mere child'. His doll collection and faithful dog, Carlo, were sources of curiosity which only enhanced his profile as a performer. He never married,

but a letter from one Teresa Battagia, held by Northwestern University, dated 6 October 1794, suggests that he broke her heart when he left Venice that year.

The 'Dragonetti havoc affair' in 1839 was played out in the pages of the *Musical World* and saw his friend Vincent Novello rising to his defence following some unfortunate inferences in a review of the fifth Philharmonic Society concert of the season. Mention of Dragonetti's tardiness was combined with the statement, 'we regret to state that age and illness are now making sad havoc with this venerable artist' (*Musical World*, 12/164, 9 May 1839, 29), and aroused Dragonetti to such anger that he and Novello issued a circular refuting the 'calumnious insinuation' ('From Signor Dragonetti to the Musical Public', 15 May 1839, MS, Northwestern University). Through this high-profile contretemps Dragonetti managed to inject his career with considerable publicity: his public was left in no doubt as to his continued verve. Following nomination by Gaspare Spontini, Dragonetti was made a member of the Accademia di Santa Cecilia, Rome, in February 1839.

Dragonetti died of dropsy, aged eighty-three, at his apartments at 4 Leicester Square on Thursday 16 April 1846 and was buried at the Roman Catholic chapel, Moorfields, eight days later. In 1889 his remains were moved to the Roman Catholic cemetery at Wembley, Middlesex. His financial security is evidenced in his bank account with Coutts & Co., which shows a balance of £937 17s. 7d. in the month of his death. Dragonetti's will bears testimony to his gift for friendship and the impact and success of his career.

FIONA M. PALMER

Sources F. M. Palmer, *Domenico Dragonetti in England (1794–1846): the career of a double bass virtuoso* (1997) · F. Caffi, *Storia della musica sacra* (1987) · [V. Novello], 'Orchestral sketches', *Musical World* (18 March 1836), viii–xvi · T. Baumann, 'Musicians in the marketplace: the Venetian guild of instrumentalists in the later 18th century', *Early Music*, 19 (1991), 345–55 · C. Brown, 'Discovering bows for the double bass', *The Strad*, 101 (1990), 39–45 · T. B. Milligan, *The concerto and London's musical culture in the late 18th century* (1983) · H. Phillips, *Musical and personal recollections during half a century*, 2 vols. (1864) · BL, Add. MS 17838 · BL, Philharmonic Society Archive, Loan 48 · *The Harmonicon*, 1–11 (1823–33) · *Musical World* (1836–46) · *The Times* (1800–23) · *The Times* (1834–5) · *The Times* (18 April 1846), 7d · parish register, Venice, San Trovaso, 9 April 1763 [baptism]
Archives BL, Add. MS 17838 · Northwestern University, Illinois | BL, Philharmonic Society Archive, Loan 48
Likenesses J. P. Dantan, plaster sculpture, 1834, Musée Carnavelet, Paris · T. Fairland, lithograph, pubd 1846 (after C. Doane), NPG · F. Bartolozzi, engraving, NPG · M. Gauci, lithograph, BM · F. Hillemacher, etching, BM · J. Notz, engraving, NPG [see illus.]
Wealth at death £937 17s. 7d.—bank account balance: the accounts of Signor Dragonetti, Coutts & Co., 20 Oct 1840–14 May 1853

Drakard, John (1774/5–1854), newspaper proprietor and publisher, was baptized on 10 February 1775 in Boston, Lincolnshire, the son of Henry and Ann Drakard. He began as a printer and bookseller at Stamford, but on 15 September 1809 he started a weekly newspaper called the *Stamford News*. On 13 March 1811 he was tried at Lincoln before Baron Wood and a special jury on an *ex officio* information for libel, and was sentenced to eighteen months' imprisonment in Lincoln Castle, and fined £200. The subject matter of the libel was an article published in Drakard's paper for 24 August 1810, entitled 'One thousand lashes', which dealt with the question of corporal punishment in the army. Drakard was defended by Henry Brougham, but neither his eloquence, nor the fact that the Hunts, as proprietors of *The Examiner*, had been previously acquitted on the charge of libel for publishing the greater portion of the very same article, were of any avail. Drakard was also the proprietor of the *Stamford Champion*, a weekly newspaper which first appeared on 5 January 1830, under the name of the *Champion of the East*.

In politics Drakard was an advanced radical. He was a defendant in several libel suits, and is said to have been horsewhipped in his own shop by Lord Cardigan for some remarks which had appeared in the *Stamford News*. Although two books have been attributed to Drakard (*Drakard's Edition of the Public and Private Life of Colonel Wardle ... 1810?*, and *The History of Stamford*, 1822), it is likely that his only connection with them was that of publisher. In 1834 both his newspapers ceased publication and Drakard retired to Ripley, Yorkshire. He had married a woman named Ann, and they had a daughter, Sophia Ann. Drakard died in poverty at Ripon on 25 January 1854, aged seventy-nine.

G. F. R. BARKER, rev. M. CLARE LOUGHLIN-CHOW

Sources [J. Watkins and F. Shoberl], *A biographical dictionary of the living authors of Great Britain and Ireland* (1816) · *Lincoln, Rutland and Stamford Mercury* (3 Feb 1854) · G. Burton, *Chronology of Stamford* (1846) · *State trials* · Boase, *Mod. Eng. biog.* · N&Q, 7th ser., 3 (1887), 89, 176, 196, 235, 375 · will, proved London, 31 Oct 1855 · IGI

Drake [*née* Meinertzhagen], **Barbara** (1876–1963), political activist and author, was born on 3 October 1876, at 10 Rutland Gate, London, the second of the ten children of Daniel Meinertzhagen, a merchant banker, and Georgina, daughter of Richard Potter and sister of Beatrice Webb. Drake spent her childhood mostly in the country with her mother, brothers, and sisters, while her father worked and lived in London. She had very little formal education, although governesses came and went. In adolescence she went briefly to her aunt's cookery school, since her family apparently 'regarded university ... only as a place of punishment for girls' (Caine, 141). She was usually known as Bardie. On 20 December 1900, when aged twenty-four, she married her family's solicitor, Bernard Harpur Drake (*d.* 1941). For most of their married life they lived in Sheffield Terrace, London. They had no children.

It was, initially, through her family connections that Barbara Drake seems to have developed her skills and interests into a life devoted to public service of a particularly Fabian kind. She is frequently mentioned in both the diaries and letters of her aunt Beatrice, to whom she became not only favourite niece but the nearest thing to an heir: a diary entry of 3 November 1914 describes Drake as 'an intellectual and attractive woman following in my footsteps as an economic writer and a Fabian'. Drake was a leading member of the Fabian Women's Group from 1913 and shared their anxiety about the effects of wartime employment on women's employment. She wrote reports in 1913–15 for the Women's Industrial Council on women's labour in the brush-making trades and in the bar trade, and on women shop assistants and sub-postmistresses, which were published in the *Women's Industrial News*, refining her investigative and reporting skills at a time of great interest in women's labour and of vigorous trade union organization and some militancy (Branson, vii). Her first substantial piece of writing, *Women in the Engineering Trades*, published in 1917, was strikingly well researched and lucid, making it a valuable primary source as well as an interesting statement of the Fabian Women's Group attitude to the expansion of the female factory workforce. It is written in clear, impersonal Fabian prose, but presents a strong indictment of the working conditions of these workers and the limits of any lasting opportunity created by munitions work. She was also critical of the failure of male trade unionists to recognize their own interest in encouraging trade union organization among war-workers, and in this she was, as so often, correct in her predictions. This led, during the war, to the formation of a research committee by the Fabian Women's Group and the Fabian Research Bureau to monitor the impact of war-work in industry on women, which was largely supplied with information by Drake, and in the last years of war to another inquiry, published in 1920 as *Women in Trade Unions*. This too was systematic, based on primary research, and clearly argued a point of view which criticized the refusal of the skilled men to recognize the capacities of women to organize and thus protect conditions and wages, and was thus disliked by those representing skilled men. A reviewer, fellow writer-member of the Fabian Women's Group B. L. Hutchins, commented that the prose was less clear than usual as a result of speed. In retrospect all seems clearly written and well informed, if perhaps a little dull for the general reader, but exciting and persuasive for anyone closely concerned with her themes. The book enabled her to use her unpublished historical account for Mr Justice Atkin's inquiry on behalf of the war cabinet committee on the relation between men's and women's wages, on which sat Drake's aunt, Beatrice Webb, the only woman on the committee and the only person to recognize (in a minority report) the essential falsity of the final conclusion, which was that although men and women had not had equal earnings, this was because they had not been 'worth' equal rewards.

Drake not only ran the Fabian Women's Group and acted as host for many of their meetings, she was also a researcher at the Fabian Research Bureau during the war. Her three major reports of the war years reflect extensive research and a sensitivity to the differences between the unions representing skilled men and the general unions, at a time when both were associated with attempts to recruit women to trade unionism and efforts to prevent wartime employment leading to exploitation. Drake herself provided a careful, detailed refutation of the argument that women were 'naturally' incapable either of arduous manual employment or of loyalty to a trade union. Her political interests and activities changed focus in 1921 when she left the Labour Research Department (as the Fabian Research Bureau became in 1918) in the dispute over funding from the Soviet Union, which, she believed, threatened to jeopardize the bureau's independence (Branson, xi).

Drake embarked upon the second phase of her career in public life when she was co-opted onto the education committee of the London county council (LCC) by the Labour members in 1925. She had tried and failed previously to win a parliamentary seat (at West Lewisham) in October 1924 and a seat on the LCC, having fought several London wards. When Labour won control of the LCC in 1934 she became an alderman until 1946, again serving on the education committee, frequently as chair until 1949, when deafness forced her retirement, and served on the executive committee of the Fabian Society from 1921 until 1947.

Barbara Drake was trustee under Beatrice Webb's will and, with Margaret Cole, edited from her diaries the second volume of autobiography, published in 1948 as *Our Partnership*. What exactly Drake's own views were and how far they differed from her aunt's is not clear, since she left no biographical views nor personal papers, and her published writings, although filled with enthusiasm and commitment, are nearly all written as either a researcher or representative of a larger body. Her relationship with her aunt became closer in Beatrice's old age and Barbara Drake's middle years. The affection is plain from Webb's frequent diary references: on 18 April 1928, for instance, she described Drake as her 'only friend' among the descendants of the Potter sisters. Drake's Kensington house became the London base for both Sidney and Beatrice Webb when they moved to the country: they frequently went to the theatre together, and Drake regularly entertained them and invited people to dinner on their behalf. This familial and intellectual kinship perhaps reached its highest point when Drake accompanied Sidney Webb on a five-week visit to the Soviet Union in 1934. In her diary Beatrice Webb cited Drake's amused recollection of Sidney's growing enthusiasm for the way in which the Soviet Union had demonstrated the value of centralized planning, 'Sidney would whisper to me, with the relish of a scientist whose theoretical proposition has stood the test of practical experiment: "See, see, it works, it works"'. The only place in Webb's comments where Drake's voice is heard indicates that she too became an enthusiast for the Soviet Union when she reported, on 11 June 1940, 'Barbara Drake received me with her usual affectionate greetings and abuse of our ruling class'. After Bernard Drake died in December 1941 their house continued to serve as the family meeting place.

Drake's visit to the Soviet Union gave her great enthusiasm for Soviet welfare measures. She became a champion of simple material measures to improve the lives of the capital's children, on which she wrote pamphlets and made speeches. The New Fabian Research Bureau published *Technical Education* and *State Education: an Immediate Programme for a Socialist Government* in 1936 and 1937 respectively, but she achieved arguably her most lasting fame by introducing milk in all London schools, despite post-war austerity, in 1946: one of the most successful initiatives in municipal socialism. She continued to write on schooling and nutrition, having always linked the state of the nation to the health of its children, as in her 1933 Fabian tract *Starvation in the midst of Plenty*. In 1922 her analysis, *Some Problems of Education*, went beyond many contemporaries, as she was to do in her 1929 memorandum to the new president of the Board of Education, Trevelyan, on behalf of the Labour education advisory committee, entitled 'A unified system of post-primary education'. When Labour won control of the LCC she chaired the special joint subcommittee to consider education for children of secondary age, which was to recommend a unified system of education for all, a policy which eventually took shape in the London plan of 1947, recommending the comprehensive school. She was closely involved in the discussion of post-war reconstruction in the 1940s, as she had been in 1917, and wrote pamphlets and articles on community feeding and women in the post-war world. She died on 19 July 1963, at her home in Sheffield Terrace, Kensington, and was thus described by Margaret Cole in a *Times* obituary (27 July): 'Withal, she was a charming and generous personality, highly individual and loved by all who knew her'.   D. Thom

Sources N. Branson, 'Introduction', in B. Drake, *Women in trade unions* (1983), vii–xiv · B. Caine, *Destined to be wives* (1986) · *The letters of Sidney and Beatrice Webb*, ed. N. MacKenzie, 2–3 (1978) · *The diary of Beatrice Webb*, ed. N. MacKenzie and J. MacKenzie, 4 vols. (1982–5), vols. 3–4 · *Fabian News* (1910–63) · *The Times* (27 July 1963) · b. cert. · m. cert. · d. cert.

Archives Hassocks, Brighton, Fabian Society archive, Harvester microform OR 1975

Wealth at death £68,515 3s. 0d.: probate, 16 Sept 1963, CGPLA Eng. & Wales

Drake, Sir Bernard (c.1537–1586), sea captain, was the eldest son of John Drake, gentleman, of Ashe in Devon, and his wife, Amy, daughter of Sir Roger Grenville. He may have been a kinsman of Sir Francis Drake. Bernard succeeded his father in 1558, and at an unknown date married Gertrude Fortescue; they had six children, John, Hugh, a third son, Margaret, Ellen, and Mary. His life was uneventful until he became associated with Sir Humphrey Gilbert, perhaps through his relatives Richard Grenville and Walter Ralegh. In December 1582 Drake was among the adventurers in a corporation established by Gilbert to exploit his royal grant in North America, although Drake's involvement seems to have been limited to his investment. By 1585, however, Drake had joined with Ralegh and Humphrey Gilbert's brother, John, in activities connected with the Roanoke Island Colony. When, in May, the Spanish government placed an embargo on English shipping in its ports, Ralegh commissioned Drake to warn English fishermen in Newfoundland of the embargo and to seize Spanish shipping. Dropping plans for a privateering voyage to the West Indies *en route* for Roanoke, Drake left for Newfoundland in July.

The voyage was both successful and profitable, beginning with the capture of a Portuguese ship laden with Brazilian sugar. Once at Newfoundland Drake alerted the fishermen to the danger of heading directly to markets in

Spain and captured both Spanish and Portuguese fishing ships. Sending some of his ships back to England with the prizes, he joined forces with another of Ralegh's associates, George Raymond, and sailed for the Azores. There they seized Spanish ships coming from the West Indies with cargoes of sugar, wine, and ivory, and a French ship carrying some gold. In all they probably took more than twenty ships, though not all reached England safely. Estimates of the value of the prizes vary but the voyage likely returned a profit of at least 600 per cent. As their share Drake and his eldest son John were given four of the most valuable ships by Ralegh and Sir John Gilbert. Strategically the raid had the result of depriving the Spanish navy and merchant marine of 60,000 quintals of the dried fish so important to the victualling of ocean-going ships. In a precautionary move the following year the Spanish government forbade ships to sail to Newfoundland. Thereafter Spanish fishing ships tended to frequent the island's south coast, away from the English area of dominance. The Portuguese fishery seems never to have fully recovered from Drake's attack.

On 9 January 1586 Bernard Drake was knighted by Elizabeth I at Greenwich. A couple of months later the surviving Portuguese prisoners, whom Drake had had imprisoned in Exeter, were put on trial. Those who lived to come to trial were so weak and ill that Drake was reprimanded by the judge for his neglect. Shortly afterwards the judge, some of the jurors, and a number of justices of the peace who had been exposed to the prisoners died, probably of typhus. Ill himself, Drake tried to reach home but died in Crediton on 10 April 1586. Drake's son John inherited Ashe as well as the profits of the Newfoundland voyage.   GILLIAN TOWNSEND CELL

Sources D. B. Quinn, ed., *The Roanoke voyages, 1584–1590: documents to illustrate the English voyages to North America under the patent granted to Walter Raleigh in 1584*, 2 vols., Hakluyt Society, 2nd ser., 104, 105 (1955) • G. T. Cell, *English enterprise in Newfoundland, 1577–1660* (1969) • D. B. Quinn, ed., *Sir Humphrey Gilbert*, 2 vols. (1940) • *DCB*, vol. 1 • D. B. Quinn, A. M. Quinn, and S. Hillier, eds., *New American world: a documentary history of North America to 1612*, 3–4 (1979) • *CSP dom.*, *1581–90* • PRO, HCA 13/27 • PRO, HCA 13/101 • F. T. Colby, ed., *The visitation of the county of Devon in the year 1620*, Harleian Society, 6 (1872) • *DNB* • R. Holinshed and others, eds., *The chronicles of England, Scotland and Ireland*, 2nd edn, ed. J. Hooker, 3 vols. in 2 (1586–7) • administration, PRO, PROB 6/4, fol. 18r

Drake, Charles Frederick Tyrwhitt (1846–1874), naturalist and explorer in the Middle East, the youngest child of Colonel William Montague Tyrwhitt Drake (1785–1848) and Emma Halsey (1806–1897), was born at Amersham, Buckinghamshire, on 2 January 1846. He had two sisters and two brothers, a third brother having died before his birth. He was educated at Rugby School and Wellington College, where asthma interrupted his studies. Thence he proceeded to Trinity College, Cambridge, matriculating in 1864; but ill health prevented him from taking a degree. He passed the winters of 1866–7 in Morocco, shooting, hunting, collecting natural history specimens, and learning Arabic. In 1867 and 1869 he published accounts of the bird life of Morocco.

In the winter of 1868 Drake visited Egypt and the Nile,

and the following spring went to Sinai. Here he met the officers of the Ordnance Survey of the Sinai expedition, and visited all the places of interest which they had discovered, together with better known attractions. After returning to England for a few months in order to make his preparations, in the autumn of 1869 he returned to the East in company with Professor Edward Palmer. They travelled with little baggage and explored on foot, starting from Suez, the whole of the desert of the Tih for the first time, the Negev, or south country of scripture, the mountains on the west side of the Araba, and the previously unknown parts of Edom and Moab. Many new sites were discovered and useful geographical work performed. After visiting Palestine, Syria, Greece, and Turkey, Drake returned to England, but again set out to the East in the winter of 1870, in order to investigate for the Palestine Exploration Fund Society the inscribed stones at Hama, the ancient Hamath. After accomplishing this task he and Richard Burton, then consul at Damascus, explored the volcanic regions east of that city and then the highlands of Syria. They described their journeys in *Unexplored Syria* (2 vols., 1872). For the next two and a half years Drake continued as a member of the survey of western Palestine, having particular responsibility for the collection of place names and for natural history.

Drake contracted the fever common to the low-lying plains of Palestine, and he died on 23 June 1874 at Jerusalem, aged only twenty-eight. He had earned a great reputation as an explorer, naturalist, archaeologist, and linguist. He was liked by colleagues for his enthusiasm, hard work, and easy manner, and also got on well with the local peoples whose lands he visited. As well as his *Modern Jerusalem* (1875), Drake's main published work was in reports for the Palestine Exploration Fund, to which he also gave many unpublished reports, letters, and an important collection of early photographs, which, with his watercolours, are a valuable record of the lands he explored.

GRAHAM WALLAS, *rev.* ELIZABETH BAIGENT

Sources C. R. Conder, *Palestine Fund Reports* (1874), 131–4 • *The Times* (27 June 1874) • private information (1888, 2004) • *CGPLA Eng. & Wales* (1874) • W. Besant, 'Memoir', in C. F. T. Drake, *The literary remains of the late C. F. T. Drake* (1877) • Venn, *Alum. Cant.* • S. Gibson, 'C. F. Tyrwhitt-Drake: the earliest photographer in the Negev of Southern Palestine', *Palestine Exploration Quarterly* [forthcoming]
Archives Palestine Exploration Fund, London, corresp. and reports relating to Palestine
Wealth at death under £12,000: resworn administration, May 1875, *CGPLA Eng. & Wales*

Drake, Sir Francis (1540–1596), pirate, sea captain, and explorer, was born about February or March 1540 in Crowndale, near Tavistock, Devon, the eldest of five known children of Edmund Drake (d. 1566) of Tavistock. Edmund's wife is unknown, though she may have been named Anna Milwaye. Edmund Drake was a shearman (of woollen cloth) at Crowndale, where his family had occupied the same farm for generations. Edmund was almost certainly a priest as well, perhaps one of those deprived of a living during Henry VIII's sequestration of religious property. In 1548 he was involved in a fracas with other clerics and laymen and forced to flee from Devon.

Sir Francis Drake (1540–1596), by Jodocus Hondius?

Edmund soon gained a royal pardon, and found a place as curate at Upchurch in Kent. He was not an obvious partisan of either side in the religious debates, being Catholic enough to serve as curate at Upchurch in 1553 and protestant enough to be appointed vicar there when Elizabeth became queen.

Early training Francis Drake had earlier begun living in Plymouth with his kinsman William *Hawkins (*b.* before 1490, *d.* 1554/5), whose family included sons William *Hawkins (*c.*1519–1589) and John *Hawkins (1532–1595). Francis Drake's brothers John and Joseph may also have lived there, though his two other brothers, Edward and Thomas, very likely did not. This association with the Hawkins family had a lasting influence on young Francis Drake. As he grew up, he served for several years under John Hawkins and seemed to model himself on this older relative. Originally from Tavistock, the Hawkins family had moved to Plymouth about the turn of the century and established a reputation in trading and seafaring. William Hawkins made trips to the Guinea coast of Africa and even to Brazil. He was a leading figure in Plymouth politics and on occasion represented the town in parliament. His sons John and William went to sea as boys, as did Francis Drake and the other boys in the household. They met people who knew how to live well, dress well, and speak well in conversations that covered politics, religion, trade, and foreign affairs. At home the boys learned to read and write and count. At sea they learned that a profit could be made by seizing ships and cargoes from foreign merchants who were themselves shading the law. A daring sea captain

with a little luck could commit piracy and suffer nothing in consequence.

The Hawkins household was as flexible in religion as it was in morals. William Hawkins was neither a devout Catholic nor an ardent protestant, but something in between. His son John Hawkins was the same. John Hawkins not only attended mass during trading visits to Spanish Tenerife but did so with such apparent fervour that his Spanish friends thought he was a committed Catholic. Young Francis Drake adopted the moderate religious practices of the Hawkins family, travelling with them to Dutch, French, and Spanish ports, and attending either Catholic or protestant churches, just as circumstances might dictate.

Learning to be a pirate Among Devon's merchant seamen piracy was not the only part-time business. The slave trade was also common, and members of the Hawkins family made a good deal of money in this noxious enterprise. As early as 1560 Francis Drake sailed on one of the Hawkins slave ships, and in 1562 he went to sea with them again. John Hawkins commanded the four-ship fleet, which paused for a time in Tenerife, where the family had friends and business associates. From there he sailed on to Cape Verde and down the Guinea coast to Sierra Leone, where he loaded his ships with slaves bought from the Portuguese, stolen from other slavers, or captured in fierce battles at native villages. He took so many that he had to commandeer a Portuguese vessel to carry the slaves he could not cram into his own holds. Trading thus far had been so successful that Hawkins sent a small vessel home with the profits, Francis Drake apparently being one of the crew. The other ships continued to the West Indies for a round of trading at the ports of La Española.

Astonished at the profits made in the voyage of 1562–3, Hawkins hurried through the preparations for a return trip, which began in October 1564, with young Francis Drake sailing again as a seaman on one of his four ships. The fleet stopped once more in the Canaries, but met with somewhat less cordiality than before. The Englishmen captured a load of slaves in Sierra Leone, then sailed to the West Indies and the coast of South America, where the slaves and trade goods were sold at a substantial profit. This time the Spanish king had forbidden his subjects to trade with the foreigners, so Hawkins pretended to attack the colonial ports, after which the people surrendered to his demand and bought his cargo at good prices.

By the time Hawkins returned to Plymouth the Spanish and Portuguese governments had entered such strong protests that Queen Elizabeth forbade him to go again. Consequently Hawkins sent a trusted captain, John Lovell, with Francis Drake again as one of the crew. Lovell lacked the subtlety and good judgement of John Hawkins, so the trip was marred by hostile clashes and outright piracy. Even so, the slaves and trade goods were sold for a profit, and Francis Drake returned home in time to sail once more with his kinsman and mentor John Hawkins.

The fleet that left Plymouth in October 1567 consisted of the usual four ships, Francis Drake commanding for the first time in the little *Judith*. Two royal vessels also joined the fleet, and the *Jesus*, one of the queen's ships, became Hawkins's flagship. When the fleet stopped as usual in the Canaries, two of the gentlemen adventurers began arguing, and in the heat of the argument one of the men struck Hawkins with a knife. As a result Hawkins condemned the man to die, saying this was an insult to the queen, on whose ship they were. At the urging of several people, including the local priest, Hawkins forgave the condemned man, but Francis Drake remembered this example of royal discipline.

Hawkins assembled his cargo of slaves in the usual way, partly by trade and partly by raids on native villages, and supplemented his fleet by taking French and Portuguese vessels. At sea as at home Hawkins dressed in fine clothes, lived in a richly appointed cabin, dined at a table set with linen and silver, and had a band of musicians for entertainment. This impressed young Francis Drake as it no doubt impressed local Spanish officials. Even so, some of them now refused to trade with the English merchants, and the hurricane season was well advanced before all goods and slaves had been sold.

Heading home by way of the Yucatan Channel and the Florida Strait, the fleet was battered by a severe storm and forced to head for San Juan de Ulúa for repairs. Arriving in the middle of September 1568 at this island near Vera Cruz, Hawkins seized the fort and sent the inhabitants to the mainland. The following day a fleet arrived from Spain, carrying the viceroy of New Spain. Taken unawares, he agreed that Hawkins could retain control of the island while he repaired his ships and bought necessary supplies. Nevertheless, a few days later Spanish forces mounted a surprise attack on the Hawkins ships and the island fortifications. Fire ships that drifted down on the English vessels came slowly enough that Hawkins and many of his men managed to escape aboard the *Minion*, as did Drake on the *Judith*. Although Drake was ordered to come alongside and take some of the men from the overloaded *Minion*, he ignored the order and sailed away in the darkness. 'The *Judith*', said Hawkins, 'forsooke us in our great myserie' (Hakluyt, *Principall Navigations*, 556).

Stopping first along the coast of New Spain, Hawkins released a hundred or so men who said they would rather risk capture by Spaniards than attempt the trip home in a leaky and overloaded ship. Sick to the point of collapse, Hawkins and his crew suffered through a four-month voyage homeward. The *Judith* took nearly as long, though Drake arrived in such obvious good health that William Hawkins dispatched him immediately to London with a message reporting the probable loss of his brother and the rest of the fleet.

It is impossible to know whether the voyage made or lost money. Early on, when William Hawkins thought everything was lost except Drake and the *Judith*, he estimated probable losses at £2000. After John Hawkins returned home, and it suddenly appeared that the Spanish might be made to pay damages for lost ships and goods, he claimed losses amounting to £25,000. But Hawkins also sent an entire pack train of gold, silver, and trade goods to London, and the Spanish ambassador reported that profits for the voyage amounted to 28,000 pesos in gold, plus a small trunk full of pearls. Even so, Drake continued to talk about the losses suffered by his cousin and himself at San Juan de Ulúa, 'not onely in the losse of his goods of some value but also of his kinsmen & friends' (Nichols, 2). This may well be, but the Spanish historian Herrera claimed that Drake himself brought home the treasure, then tried to hide it from the authorities, and was jailed for three months for doing so.

Raids on the Spanish main Whatever happened on his return, Francis Drake had made enough on the voyage to take a wife, and on 4 July 1569 he married Mary Newman (*d.* 1583) in St Budeaux parish church near Plymouth. Details about her family are scarce, but it is customary to say her brother was a shipmate of Francis Drake, perhaps the one named Harry Newman. Romance did not keep Drake long at home. Late in November 1569 he sailed again on a Hawkins ship, commanding the 50 ton *Brave* on a voyage to the Guinea coast. From this point Hawkins returned home, while Francis Drake took the three-ship fleet to the Indies on a trading voyage about which nothing else is known.

In 1571 Drake sailed once more to the Indies, commanding a 25 ton pinnace called the *Swan*, probably part of a pirate fleet organized by William Wynter and his brother George. In February 1571 Drake and his crew joined French pirates in a raid on Spanish outposts in the Isthmus of Panama. With a captured *cimarron* (an escaped black slave) as guide, Drake and his allies took a Spanish vessel loaded with goods worth about 50,000 pesos. Over the next few months Drake and the pirates made repeated attacks on coastal and inland trading posts, taking ships and goods to the value of 250,000 pesos, or so the Spanish owners claimed. Even allowing for exaggeration, the booty was probably worth more than £100,000, a good portion of which went to Drake and his men.

While resting back in Plymouth, Drake began to plan a new raid on the Spanish Indies. With his brothers John and Joseph, Drake assembled a fleet of two light ships, plus three small pinnaces, boats that were light enough to be rowed into the shallow bays and inlets around the isthmus, but small enough to be knocked down for easy transport on the other vessels. Leaving Plymouth in May 1572 the fleet sailed through the Canary Islands, then straight across to Dominica in the West Indies. After resting for a time Drake took the ships to meet his partner, the English pirate James Raunse, in a place on the isthmus called Port Pheasant. Here Drake and his men built a log fort, while his carpenters assembled the pinnaces. By the end of July he was ready to attack Nombre de Dios, where treasure and goods were loaded for shipment to Spain. Twenty years later Philip Nichols wrote that Drake and his men found a great hoard of treasure in the town but were unable to take it because Drake himself was badly wounded and his men feared he might die. This is probably untrue. There was no treasure in the town, which was defended only by a few locals parading around behind their barricades with burning matches as though they were a huge armed force ready to launch a counter-attack.

Disgusted with the outcome of the raid, Raunse withdrew from the partnership. Drake sailed off to Cartagena, and spent the next few months in desultory attacks on small vessels and settlements between there and the isthmus. During this time his brother John Drake managed to conclude an alliance with local *cimarrones*, who befriended anyone who was an enemy of the Spanish settlers. Before anything could come of this alliance, John was 'sodenlie stroken with a gunne shott' and died (PRO, PROB 11/56, sig. 7). A little later his brother Joseph died from a disease that was ravaging the fleet. In an act of extreme callousness Drake ordered the surgeon to cut open the body, so he could learn the cause of death.

Undiscouraged by the failure of his raids or the deaths of his brothers, Drake decided to wait for the annual treasure shipment from Peru. Early in January 1573 he led his pirates and their *cimarron* allies across the isthmus and came within sight of Panama, where he sent a scout for information about the next treasure train. The man came back with the news that a pack train would cross that very night with fourteen mule-loads of gold and jewels. Although Drake tried to ambush the pack train, his plot was discovered, and the Spanish mule drivers took their treasure packs back to Panama. Returning to his base camp Drake met a French pirate named Guillaume Le Testu. Quickly joining forces Drake and Le Testu took a shore party back to the isthmus, where by luck they surprised the treasure train. This time they drove off the Spanish guards and seized the treasure. Drake and his men loaded themselves with the gold and buried the silver, but Le Testu was badly wounded, and they left him in the road where he fell. Drake returned to the coast, loaded the treasure on board the ships, then sent a search party back to the isthmus. Le Testu was dead, and the rest of the treasure was gone, but Drake and his pirates could at last return home with a good profit. The English share of the booty was at least £20,000, a princely sum for that time and enough to make Drake rich. In addition Drake was equipped to be a merchant, having acquired two small ships taken at Cartagena in the early days of the voyage.

Drake probably used some of his new wealth to buy property on Notte Street in Plymouth, where he was listed as a merchant in 1576. Rich enough to have a servant, he took his cousin John Drake as his personal page. Still he wanted more. When the earl of Essex needed assistance in his efforts to occupy Antrim in northern Ireland, he found that Francis Drake was willing to invest in the enterprise and even to use his own ships. It was a bloody affair, culminating in July 1575 with a surprise attack on Rathlin Island, where 500 men, women, and children were put to the sword. Drake's own role in the massacre is unclear, but the Antrim operation brought him into a close relationship with the earl's retainer, Thomas Doughty.

Voyage around the world Either through Doughty or through Essex, Drake was introduced to Sir Francis Walsingham, and this association led to a plan for Drake to take a fleet into the Pacific and raid Spanish settlements

there. The general outline of the scheme is contained in a draft memorandum of about May or June 1577 (BL, Cotton MS, Otho E.viii), but the exact details were kept secret, even from some of the participants. Ostensibly a trading venture to Alexandria, the fleet actually intended to continue the programme of piracy Drake had developed. Investors included Walsingham, Christopher Hatton, John Hawkins, William and George Wynter, and even Queen Elizabeth. Leadership was left unclear from the start, with Francis Drake, John Wynter, and Thomas Doughty listed as 'equall companions and frindly gentlemen' in the enterprise, though Drake was always spoken of as commander of the fleet (BL, Harley MS 540, fol. 93). Drake's ship was the 150 ton *Pelican*, double-planked, lead-sheathed, and armed with 18 guns. John Wynter contributed his own 80 ton *Elizabeth*, which carried 11 guns. Another 12 guns were distributed among the 50 ton *Marigold*, the 30 ton *Swan*, and the 15 ton *Benedict*.

The trip began inauspiciously in November 1577 with a storm that disabled the *Pelican* and the *Marigold*. The fleet was not able to leave port again until 13 December. Stopping at an island off the Moroccan coast Drake had the carpenters assemble one of the pinnaces he had brought along for raiding purposes. By the end of the month the work was completed, and six Spanish and Portuguese ships were taken in quick succession, then looted and eventually set free. The unlucky captain of a Spanish fishing smack was forced to accept the little *Benedict* in exchange for his own 40 ton vessel, which was renamed *Christopher*.

At the end of January 1578 the fleet paused to raid Maio in the Cape Verde Islands but found that other pirates had beaten them to the place. After loading wood and water the fleet sailed on to São Tiago, where they captured a Portuguese merchant vessel, *Santa Maria*, loaded with wine and other cargo. The commander was Nuño de Silva, a Portuguese pilot who knew the coast of South America. Taking Silva to serve as pilot of his own fleet Drake set the rest of the crew adrift in a pinnace, and put Thomas Doughty in charge of the ship, which was thereafter called the *Mary*. The cargo of wine proved too much of a temptation for Doughty's crew, and after one ugly incident Doughty accused Drake's brother Thomas of stealing from the cargo. Hearing this, Drake flew into a rage, and after a terrible row put Doughty in command of the *Pelican*. Francis Drake himself went on board the *Mary*, with Thomas Drake as the new captain.

During the next few weeks Thomas Drake and his friends took every opportunity to vilify Doughty, and Francis quickly convinced himself that Doughty was a threat to the entire enterprise. Finally, Drake summoned Doughty back to the *Mary*, where he took the man into custody and sent him as a virtual prisoner to the *Swan*. Thus humiliated and separated from his friends, Doughty began to grumble about Drake, who in turn became obsessed with the idea that Doughty was an enemy and wished to do him harm. Finally, on 17 May 1578 at the Rio Deseado on the lower coast of South America, Drake brought Doughty aboard the *Pelican* once more, then ordered the *Swan* to be stripped and burnt. Outraged, Doughty reminded Drake of their partnership agreement; Drake was incensed, and after a heated argument struck Doughty and had him bound to the mast. The *Swan* was burnt, as was the *Christopher*, and Doughty and his brother John were sent to the *Elizabeth* as prisoners.

Late in June 1578 the fleet arrived at Port St Julian, Magellan's old winter quarters on the southern coast of Argentina, where Drake put Thomas Doughty on trial for mutiny. As authority for his action Drake claimed to have a document from the queen, giving him supreme command of the fleet; thus, an offence against him was an offence against the queen, as John Hawkins had claimed in 1567. The nature of the offence was obscure, but as Drake explained it, Doughty was somehow involved in 'takynge away of my good name and altogether discreditinge me, and then my life' (BL, Harley MS 540, fols. 103v–104). Bullied and threatened by their commander, the seamen finally agreed that Doughty was indeed guilty. He was beheaded on 2 July 1578. Just how these two friends had come to be enemies is not clear. According to Richard Madox's diary, gossips in Plymouth said that Doughty had 'lived intimately' with Drake's wife and while drunk boasted of his exploit to Drake himself. Whatever the reason, John Wynter, the third 'equall companion', began to realize that his own friendship with the commander was in jeopardy, as did other officers and men in the fleet, motivated no doubt by Drake's constant threats against those he saw as friends of Doughty and thus his own enemies. Grown daily more suspicious of his associates, Drake finally called the captains and crew together, then announced that all the officers, who held their appointments from the owners of the ships, were relieved of command. He then reappointed them or most of them as officers responsible only to him.

Many of Doughty's friends were placed aboard Wynter's ship *Elizabeth*. When Drake finally led his fleet through the strait and into the Pacific, Wynter took advantage of a storm to absent himself from the fleet and finally took his ship back to England. The *Marigold*, commanded by Doughty's friend John Thomas, also disappeared, and the *Mary* was abandoned at Port St Julian. Thus Drake was left with only the *Pelican*, renamed the *Golden Hind*. This reduced fleet was much more to Drake's liking, as he was not comfortable with the responsibility for a large number of ships. After John Wynter returned home, the English government began to circulate the story that Wynter had gone through the Strait of Magellan but that he had come home without passing through the straits again. When Francis Drake came home, the story changed to name him as the Englishman who first sailed into the open sea south of the American continent. Whether Drake actually sailed there or not is unclear. After passing through the straits, he did go south for a time, then headed north along the coast of South America, but John Drake and others with him seem not to have been aware of a new route around the tip of South America.

Eighty or more men were lost in Drake's passage through the straits. Some died from cold, hunger, and disease. Twenty souls were lost when the *Marigold* disappeared without a trace. Another two dozen seem to have perished on the pinnaces. Wynter took fifty men home with him, and these were effectively lost to the expedition as well. Undaunted, Drake sailed up the Pacific coast with renewed enthusiasm for piracy. He reached the island of Mocha on 25 November 1578, intending to help himself to the treasure from the rich Madre de Dios mines. Instead he met fierce Indian resistance, losing two men in battle and two more who died later from their wounds. Others were also injured, including Drake himself, with an arrow wound beneath the right eye and another that just grazed his head. Further north, at Valparaiso he took a ship carrying 200,000 pesos in gold, then went ashore and raided the church and the warehouses. The most valuable booty was a *derrotero* (a set of charts and navigation instructions) for all the ports on the Pacific coast.

Moving north with both ships, Drake stopped at Bahía Salada to assemble another knocked-down pinnace and to bring out the guns he had stored beneath the ballast stones. With the *Pelican* thus turned into a floating artillery battery, he set sail again. On 5 February 1579 he arrived at Arica on the north coast of Chile and captured a merchant ship carrying thirty or forty bars of silver. A second ship loaded with wine and clothing was accidentally burnt when a drunken English sailor dropped a lamp in the hold. At Chule on the southern coast of Peru he took another ship, but it was empty, the crew having been warned ahead of time that Drake was on the way. Putting to sea, Drake took everything usable out of the three captured ships, then hoisted their sails and watched them move out to sea.

At this point battles and sickness had reduced Drake's crew to little more than seventy men. Only thirty of them were fit to fight, but that was enough, since the merchant ships Drake met were unarmed. Continuing to move north Drake sailed into the harbour of Callao de Lima. After a brief fight he took one ship, only to release it outside the harbour. There were similar encounters at other ports until 28 February 1579, when he took a ship from Guayaquil, loaded with tackle, maize, salt pork, and hams, plus 18,000 pesos' worth of gold and silver. On 1 March he met and captured the richest ship of all, *Nuestra Señora de la Concepción*, carrying much valuable cargo and 362,000 pesos in silver and gold. An English sailor later insisted the Spanish ship was called *Cacafuego*. After Drake's cannon ripped through the sails and rigging and carried away the mizzen mast, her Spanish pilot is supposed to have said, 'Our ship shalbe called no more the Cacafogo [shitfire] but the Cacaplata [shitsilver]' (BL, Harley MS 280, fols. 84–6).

Sailing again up the coast of Central America and Mexico, Drake took a few more ships and raided several more ports. A vessel taken just west of Panama carried two pilots, one of whom had charts of the Manila galleon route across the Pacific. Another captured ship carried silks and linens and crates of fine china. A rich merchant surrendered a large gold chain and 7000 pesos in silver and goods. Two other merchant ships yielded up as many black slaves, along with 'a proper negro wench' (BL, Harley MS 280, fol. 86v) who could relieve the tedium of the long journey home.

As success piled onto success Drake became expansive. He told his Spanish captives that the queen had given him a licence to rob Spanish subjects and recover the money Hawkins had lost at San Juan de Ulúa. Taking his cue from John Hawkins, he draped himself in fine clothes and set a fine table, using silver dishes that he said were a gift from the queen, decorated with his own coat of arms. His men bowed and doffed their hats when he walked by. Ignoring his chaplain, Drake began to lead religious services, showing the captives that he was a man of God. Taking choice items from his vast store of loot, Drake made gifts to some of his captives, not to the seamen, but to the officers and especially to one hidalgo. He pulled maps out of a case and boasted that he could go wherever he pleased in the Pacific. He showed the captives how he had come into the Pacific and said he intended to sail home by way of the Moluccas. Finally, realizing that he might have talked too much, Drake carefully primed his Portuguese pilot Silva with plans for a return journey by a supposed northern passage. The man, who had considered himself to be part of the pirate band, was then put ashore at Guatulco with the other Spanish prisoners, and Drake sailed out into the Pacific with the *Pelican* and a bark captured off the Nicaraguan coast.

Just where Drake went from this point is unclear. The *Pelican* was leaking badly and needed to be careened. Sixteenth-century accounts and maps can be interpreted to show that he stopped anywhere between the southern tip of Baja California and latitude 48° N. John Drake said they careened the ship on an island in latitude 44° or 46° or 48°. A Dutch commentator at the time, van Meteren, said it was 33°. A map of the period shows the island in 42°. Richard Hakluyt said 38°, and an account published in 1628 said 38°30′. These two latitudes correspond closely with the modern port of San Francisco, where a brass plate was discovered some years ago and said to be the one Drake used to mark his encampment. The plate is generally thought to be a hoax, while the anthropological and zoological data from the various accounts is similarly unreliable. The most logical guess about Drake's anchorage would place it somewhere along the coast of Baja California or in the San Benito Islands.

Drake had his ship repaired by July or August 1579, when he abandoned the captured bark and perhaps a dozen of his men and set sail across the Pacific in the *Pelican*. Very likely following the Manila galleon route, Drake made his first landfall in the Palau Islands, where he fired a cannon at some overenthusiastic islanders and killed twenty of them. South of the Davao Gulf he met another ship and fired on it as well, then sailed into the Molucca Passage. At one small island a merchant advised him to head for the island of Ternate in the Moluccas, which he did. There the king supplied Drake's crew with provisions, a cargo of spices, and entertainment. Anchoring once more in a deserted island off the Celebes, Drake careened

his ship again. There he decided to leave the two black men, along with the black woman who was pregnant. The identity of the father is unknown. One account spread the blame widely, saying she was 'gotten with child between the captaine and his men pirats' (BL, Harley MS 280, fol. 86v).

Somewhat later in the journey the ship ran aground on a reef and could not be towed free. Trying to lighten the ship, Drake ordered the recently acquired food and spices to be tossed overboard, along with several cannon, but nothing seemed to help. Chaplain Fletcher announced that the grounding was God's punishment for the execution of Doughty. Most of the men agreed and thought they were going to die, but a sudden gale blew the ship off the rocks, little the worse for the experience. Drake however was livid. He called the poor chaplain on deck, declared him excommunicated, gave him an insulting label to wear, and told him to spend the rest of the journey with the crew, saying that if he came before the mast again or took off the label he would be hanged.

During a later stop in Java Drake and his crew found the local people most cordial, particularly the women, from whom some of them managed to catch the French pox. Having loaded plenty of food they sailed through the Indian Ocean, and around the Cape of Good Hope. According to one account the provisions lasted until 20 July 1580 when they reached Sierra Leone on the Guinea coast. Beyond that nothing much is known of the return voyage. One intriguing document in Spanish archives says Drake and his men stopped for supplies at the French port of La Rochelle (Pedro de Rada to Gomez de Santillan, 29 July and 17 Aug 1580, Archivo General de Indias, Patronato 266, ramo 41), but this is probably another one of the many rumours about Drake then circulating in the chanceries of Europe. Everyone seemed to know that he had sailed unopposed through the Spanish possessions, taking everything of value that came his way. Drake and the *Pelican* arrived in Plymouth on 26 September 1580, ending an astonishing three-year voyage around the world and carrying treasure beyond imagination.

Honours and riches Once home Drake's first move was to send a message to London, notifying the queen and the other investors of his arrival. The first replies were ominous, speaking of royal embarrassment and Spanish demands for restitution, but private messages from the queen told Drake that he had nothing to worry about. He thereupon put most of his treasure under guard in a tower near Plymouth and set off for London with several horses carrying packs of gold and silver. In a private audience with the queen that lasted all day a decision was made on how these astonishing riches would be handled. Most of Drake's booty had not been registered by the owners, who were trying to evade the Spanish levy on shipments of gold and silver. Therefore, Drake advised that it might be better to make no inventory. If the Spanish government did not know how much he had stolen, there could scarcely be an intelligent request for its return. As a result Drake and the queen knew what he had brought home, but no one else did. No doubt Drake kept a large part of the treasure for himself. The Spanish ambassador reported that 20 tons of silver were placed in the Tower, together with five huge boxes of gold and a great quantity of pearls. Investors were said to have received double their money. The crew may have shared £40,000 and Drake had an extra £10,000 for himself. But the real total was vastly larger. The Spanish ambassador thought it might have reached a million and a half pesos. Others thought it was 2 million.

Though tight-fisted with his crew, Drake showered rich gifts on the queen and others. The queen was well pleased and ordered Drake's ship to be taken ashore at Deptford as a permanent memorial of his astonishing voyage. Then, with royal approval, Drake bought Buckland Abbey, a former Cistercian monastery near Plymouth that had been converted into a private estate when Henry VIII suppressed the religious houses. Typical of Cistercian foundations, most of Buckland's buildings were simple, austere structures. Only the church possessed ornate architectural features, and it became a home with the installation of two wooden floors inside the nave. The arcades were blocked with stone and a great hall was formed in the space under the crossing tower, where the south transept was removed to allow for the installation of windows. When Drake bought the place it was already remodelled and furnished, and he seems to have made few or no changes during his occupancy.

In the spring of 1581 the queen knighted Drake, making a gentleman of the one-time pirate. That same year Nicholas Hilliard painted his portrait, a miniature that can be seen at the National Portrait Gallery, and the best of several likenesses made just after his return. Even without the pictures Drake could be recognized from descriptions made by Nuño de Silva and others. He was short, stout, and extremely strong. The reddish-blond beard did not quite hide the arrow wound on his right cheek, but a bullet wound in the right leg apparently left no limp. As time passed Drake became decidedly heavy. A painting in the National Maritime Museum, usually attributed to Marcus Gheeraerts and dated 1591, shows a decidedly older Drake, thick of body and thin of hair, with a beard going grey and a somewhat sinking chin.

Worried, perhaps, that their most prominent citizen might abandon the town, the aldermen and burgesses of Plymouth named Francis Drake mayor for a term beginning in September 1581. His accomplishments in office are unclear, the sole record mentioning only a 'newe compasse made upon the Hawe' (Plymouth black book, Devon RO, W46, fol. 7), which may be a reference to a new wall built adjoining the castle on Plymouth Hoe. Some years later Drake took a municipal contract to reconstruct a shallow canal bringing water to the town. This business arrangement, in which Drake obtained the right to build and operate grist mills on the canal, has given rise to a fanciful tale that Francis Drake brought the first supply of water to the grateful citizens of Plymouth.

It was almost inevitable that a man so popular would be named to sit in parliament, which Drake did in 1581 (for an unknown constituency) and again in 1584 (for Bossiney); in the latter parliament he was appointed to a committee considering a bill for Walter Ralegh's colonization in America. In 1593 he was elected one of the members for the significant constituency of Plymouth, and took a more active role in the Commons than previously. Not a parliamentary leader, Drake none the less had the opportunity to serve on committees with such men as Philip Sidney, Christopher Hatton, and Richard Grenville, whose friendship and influence he was glad to have. These associations also gave Drake the opportunity to acquire some of the sophistication and polish lacking in his training at sea. Even so, some thought he was a bit too pushy, and they resented his attempts to buy favour with costly presents. On one occasion Lord Burghley rejected a gift of ten gold bars, saying he could not accept stolen goods. On another, when Drake was boasting about his exploits, Lord Sussex declared that it was no great accomplishment to capture an unarmed vessel with a well-armed ship. But if there were some who disliked this pushy pirate, many admired him, including the queen, who enjoyed his company. After Drake's first wife died, in January 1583, he courted and married Elizabeth Sydenham (d. 1598), only child of a rich and well-connected Somerset family, about 9 February 1585. Elizabeth was young, beautiful, intelligent, and well mannered—just the wife for a newly rich gentleman seeking social advantage.

The West Indies raid During this same period Drake planned and invested in a number of trading enterprises, with mixed success. Finally at the end of 1584 he received royal approval for a new raid on Spanish ports and shipping in the West Indies. In addition to the queen, Drake's investors included the earl of Leicester, John and William Hawkins, and Sir Walter Ralegh. The original plan was probably never written out in detail, but Drake was very likely expected to intercept the Spanish treasure fleet. If successful, he would return home immediately. Otherwise, he would continue to the Indies and raid Santo Domingo, Cartagena, and Panama. It was war without a formal declaration, and the queen reserved the right to disavow Drake if necessary. The fleet included about two dozen ships, the largest of which was Drake's flagship or admiral, the 600 ton *Elizabeth Bonaventure*, commanded by Thomas Fenner. Drake probably owned three or four of the smaller ships in the fleet, one of which his brother Thomas commanded. Christopher Carleill, commander of the military force, was also in charge of a ship, as was Martin Frobisher on the vice-admiral.

Drake intended to keep a careful account of the voyage, very likely depending on his chaplain, Philip Nichols, who later wrote about the voyage of 1572–3 and probably had a hand in the preparation of a narrative about Drake's circumnavigation. However, no such journal has survived, and the best firsthand account is the one drawn up by Captain Walter Bigges (*Summarie and True Discourse*, 1589). Never a man for attention to detail, Drake took his fleet to sea on 14 September 1585 without any sailing orders, then called his captains aboard to help in preparing a set. In this conference Drake found again that he did not like the responsibility of command, particularly the need to ask for opinions before taking action. Within a few days he had decided on an informal advisory group of Frobisher and Carleill, plus two men from his own ship, Nichols and Fenner.

Heading south, as usual, Drake captured several French vessels, one of which he renamed *Drake*, adding it to his fleet. Within a few days he was at Bayona in the mouth of the Vigo River, a Spanish port where he decided to stay and take on supplies, daring the king of Spain to send troops against him. Fearless in the extreme, Drake was none the less inclined to rash decisions of which this was an example. He remained for two weeks at Vigo and Bayona, pillaging houses, convents, and churches of loot worth perhaps 6000 ducats. The delay allowed enough time for the Spanish fleet to reach San Lucar unmolested, and deprived Drake and his raiders of the richest cargo brought from the Indies in recent years.

The English fleet reached the Canaries in late October. In the harbour at Palma they were met with a blistering fire from the fortress. One cannon ball 'strake atwixt our Generalls legges' (BL, Harley MS 2202, fol. 57v), but Drake was uninjured. Faced by such firm resistance, he ordered the fleet to sail on. By mid-November the fleet was at São Tiago in the Cape Verde Islands, where Carleill landed his troops for an attack on the town. The place was occupied without resistance, and the loot included a huge supply of provisions plus more than fifty pieces of brass ordnance. Despite this success Drake was increasingly uneasy about the responsibility of commanding such a large fleet, and began to fret about the loyalty of his captains. With no advance discussion, Drake had Nichols draw up an oath similar to the one administered to the officers and men at San Julian. Once announced, the oath provoked great controversy. Francis Knollys, rear-admiral, refused to sign and was eventually removed from command.

Drake lingered at São Tiago until the end of the month; he finally set fire to the town and sailed away. However, the stop had lasted long enough for the men in the fleet to be infected by an epidemic that had filled the local hospital with patients. Several hundred men died before the fleet reached the West Indies, and others were permanently disabled by the disease. Still, there was no question of changing plans.

On 1 January 1586 Drake landed 1000 men at Santo Domingo on the island of Española and occupied the town. When local officials asked about ransoming the place, they were told it would take a million ducats to convince the Englishmen to leave. The officials refused, so Drake ordered part of the town to be set afire. After three weeks of alternate refusal and torching, the locals paid 25,000 ducats to ransom what remained of the town. Drake promptly set fire to everything that could not be moved and took his fleet to Cartagena, which he captured on 9 February 1586 in a brief battle. Again he demanded ransom for the town, and again he destroyed a few buildings each time his demands were refused. He finally agreed to accept something more than 100,000 ducats, though some men grumbled that this amount did not include a large sum that disappeared into Drake's possession. Indeed, there was not much other wealth to be had.

Warned ahead of time, the citizens had spirited most of their goods out of the city. Lacking booty, many Englishmen decided to take a few slaves instead, most of them women. For these and other reasons discipline became a serious problem at Cartagena before Drake finally took his fleet out of the bay on 31 March.

Sailing across to Cuba, then up the Florida coast, Drake stopped to attack the Spanish fort at San Augustín, which he captured, looted, and burnt at the end of May. Continuing north he passed the Outer Banks and noticed a signal fire from Croatoan Island. It was a party from the English settlement at Roanoke, founded a year earlier by Sir Richard Grenville. After brief consultation, the demoralized settlers decided to abandon the place and return to England on Drake's ships. His fleet reached Plymouth on 28 July 1586, ending a voyage that cost more than it brought home.

Drake had proved himself once again to be brave and unrelenting in battle, but he had displayed little understanding of the command process, and his idea of capturing isolated towns to hold for ransom was a complete failure. Even so his reputation in Spain grew enormously, for he was an embarrassment to the king and an object of fear in every colonial town. More than this, Drake was beginning to be seen abroad as something more than just a pirate. Spanish officials girding for war began to see Sir Francis Drake as the greatest threat in the English arsenal.

The Spanish Armada During the period of alternate peace and hostility Dom Antonio, pretender to the throne of Portugal, had appeared in England, telling Drake, the queen, and anyone else who would listen that people in Portugal were eager for him to arrive and end the Spanish occupation. Amid all this, in March 1587 Drake signed a contract with a group of London merchants who would supply a number of ships for a new raid, with pillage to be split evenly between the crown and the investors. As usual with Drake's ventures, the objective was not well defined. Starting with a possible move to place Dom Antonio on the throne of Portugal, it changed over time to an attack on Spanish ships at sea and in port. As it turned out, Drake's fleet left Plymouth in early April 1587, just as the permission to attack Spanish ports was withdrawn, and he probably never received that order. Instead, he sailed directly for the Spanish coast. By chance capturing a small boat in the outer bay of Lisbon, Drake learned about a great merchant fleet in the harbour at Cadiz and immediately headed there.

Menaced only by a small fleet of Spanish galleys, Drake was able to enter the harbour at Cadiz and drive the galleys back with his long-range guns. Much of the resistance came from an armed Genoese merchantman and a Biscayan galleon, both of which he quickly dispatched. Many of the Spanish ships were without crews or sails and thus easy prey for a determined raider. Moving past treacherous shoals to the inner bay, Drake calmly plundered and burnt the rest of the Spanish ships, more than two dozen vessels in all. Meanwhile Drake resupplied his own fleet from the huge stores of provisions available there. Spanish authorities later estimated their losses at 172,000 ducats, including four Spanish ships that Drake added to his fleet. It was a stunning victory for Drake, not in an open battle at sea, at which he had little experience, but in a surprise attack on a lightly defended port, at which he was a master.

Not everyone shared his elation. Caught in the mêlée of battle, Drake failed to recall that he was commander of a fleet. William Borough, his second in command, was left in the outer harbour to take the fire from the heavy guns on shore, uncertain what to do because he did not know where Drake was. Angry at Drake for leaving him to the mercy of the Spanish, as he thought, Borough later reacted badly when Drake proposed to land his troops on the south coast of Portugal. Giving his opinion in writing, as was the custom, Borough called the plan rash and ill-conceived. Beyond this, he said that Drake's method of command was an affront to experienced captains.

Drake was furious. Seething for two days, Drake told his old friends Philip Nichols and Thomas Fenner to draw up a list of charges against Borough, just as they had done against Knollys. Once this was done, he summoned Borough to his flagship, accused him of insubordination, and removed him from command. Thoroughly shaken, Borough wrote a letter of apology, but Drake was unmoved. It was his main character defect. Always suspicious, always wary of a plot, Drake became ever more anxious under the isolation of command at sea. He seemed to need a scapegoat like Doughty, Fletcher, Knollys, or Borough to serve as an object of his scorn and ridicule.

Landing on the Algarve coast on 4 May 1587, Drake put 1000 soldiers ashore. The men marched overland a few miles to Lagos, but the guns of the fortress drove them back to their ships. Retracing his route a short distance, Drake next landed his troops at Sagres, where they burnt some huts and fishing boats. They bombarded the castle at Sagres and captured it, sacked a nearby monastery, then went back to their ships. For several weeks Drake kept his fleet in the waters between Lisbon and Sagres, menacing shipping, and burning what he could not carry away. By late May disease began to make its way through his fleet, and some ships, including Borough's, headed for home. Drake then took his remaining vessels to the Azores, where he had heard there was a big merchant ship, waiting to be taken. This was the king's own *San Felipe*, coming from the East Indies with a cargo of china, silks and velvet, a small quantity of jewels, and some black slaves. Despite the illness of his crew, Drake was able to capture the ship in a surprise attack. Adding the *San Felipe* to his fleet Drake then returned to Plymouth, where he arrived on 26 June 1587. As usual there was grumbling about the spoils. Some of the investors claimed that Drake kept a great part of the loot for himself. The Spanish ambassador said 300,000 ducats in cash had been taken from the *San Felipe*, but less than a third of this amount was distributed among the investors.

There was happiness in London, where Drake as usual boasted of his success. Some thirty-five years later Francis Bacon recalled Drake's description of the raid on Cadiz as 'The Cingeing of the king of Spaines Beard' (Bacon, 40).

There was also the problem of Borough, whom Drake had accused of insubordination, cowardice, and desertion. Defending himself in court, Borough described his own role in the fight at Cadiz, battling alone against the Spanish fort and the galleys, while the other ships were off looting. He then reminded the court of Drake's own chequered past, including his desertion of Hawkins at San Juan de Ulúa and the execution of Thomas Doughty. Perhaps of most importance in his acquittal was a decision by the queen to apologize to Spain for Drake's raids. Aware that the English fleet was not yet ready to take on Spain, her representative pulled the orders of late March out of the files and used them to claim that 'unwittingly, yea unwillingly, to her Majesty those actions were committed by Sir Fras. Drake, for the which her Majesty is as yet greatly offended with him' (Burghley to De Loo, 28 July 1587, *CSP for.*, 1583–8, 21, 3, 186). Of course, no one believed this, particularly the Spanish officials, who began to refer to Drake as a 'captain general' of the English navy.

During the voyage to Spain and Portugal, Drake began to concern himself with the record he would leave for posterity. Accordingly he called upon two friends to help with his reports, Thomas Fenner and Philip Nichols, the latter of whom was a university graduate and cleric. Both may have contributed parts of the wonderfully literate messages Drake sent home describing the voyage, but Nichols alone is probably responsible for the invocations of the deity, prayers for the queen and her council, and requests for prayers for the fleet. Nichols was also no doubt the author of the most famous letter from this voyage, one addressed 'To the Reverend Father in God John Fox, my very good friend' on 27 April 1587. The letter to Foxe is apparently not extant in the original, and there is nothing to indicate that he was a friend of Drake. Moreover, none of the letters from this voyage was written in Drake's hand. Even so, the correspondence has given Drake an undeserved reputation for great personal piety. In fact, none of the letters in Drake's own hand shows Drake as a particularly devout protestant. Instead, he seems to have thought that 'God would receive the good work that he might perform in either law, that of Rome or that of England', though He no doubt preferred the latter (Archivo General de la Nación, Mexico City, Ramo de Inquisicion, tomo 75, fol. 115r–v).

In the course of his raid on Cadiz and the coast of Portugal, Drake gathered sufficient information to show conclusively that the Spanish government was seriously preparing to invade England, so English preparations took on new vigour. While many favoured meeting the Spanish threat at the English coast, Drake preferred taking the battle to Spain. Not everyone agreed, nor did many think Drake himself should have the command. In May 1588 Drake was summoned to London, where he was told that Lord Howard was to be commander of the English fleet, while Drake himself could have the post of second in command. With anyone else Drake might have rebelled, but Howard was a man of great charm and courtesy, and the two struck up a good relationship from the start. Howard joined Drake at Plymouth in late May 1588 and immediately called his captains into conference. Once more Drake explained his plan to attack the Spanish fleet in Spanish waters, and Howard admitted Drake was probably right. Twice Howard attempted to take his fleet to the Spanish coast, but storms forced him back to port on each occasion. Finally, on 19 July 1588, word arrived that the Armada had been sighted off the Lizard heading towards Plymouth.

In one tale told and retold, Drake was bowling on the Hoe at Plymouth with some of the other captains when word came that the Spanish Armada had just arrived. Rather than going to his ship immediately, Drake is supposed to have remarked that there was plenty of time to finish the game and then to finish the Spaniards. Whether the story has any factual basis is unknown. It first appeared in print in 1624 in a pamphlet by Thomas Scott, an English clergyman who said only that the fleet's 'Commanders and Captaines were at bowles upon the hoe of Plimouth' (Scott, 6). Another century passed before Drake's name was connected to this fictional game of bowls, and the direct quotation of Drake is even later. Still, it is a wonderful story about Drake's legendary equanimity in battle.

The English and Spanish fleets were approximately equal in effective strength, some 130 ships in the Spanish Armada and about 120 in the combined English fleets. At first the Spanish commander, Medina Sidonia, had a great advantage, with Howard's fleet caught in Plymouth harbour. However, Medina Sidonia also had orders to head straight for the channel, where he was to rendezvous with the Spanish invasion troops from Flanders and convoy them to the English coast. Consequently he sailed past Plymouth, allowing Howard and Drake time to warp their ships out to sea against the heavy wind and currents. The work went on all night, and at dawn on 21 July 1588 the Spanish commander, with his ships arranged in an arc, found the English fleet in two squadrons bearing down on him. Drake, leading the attack on the right wing, engaged his opponent in a heavy artillery battle. When the Spanish ships tried to close for the hand-to-hand fighting at which their troops excelled, Drake declined. After two or three hours of inconclusive duelling the Spanish commander finally broke off the fight and sailed towards the Isle of Wight.

The most severe damage to the Spanish fleet came by accident. First a disgruntled German artilleryman deliberately set a match to a barrel of gunpowder on board the *San Salvador*, which began to burn uncontrollably and had to be abandoned. While this ship was still aflame, there was a second accident. The *Nuestra Señora del Rosario* of Don Pedro de Valdés lost its bowsprit and foremast in a collision with a sister ship and began to drop astern of the Armada. Rather than delay his own fleet waiting for the straggler, Medina Sidonia abandoned the *Rosario* as well. It was an opportunity that Drake recognized immediately. Though ordered by Howard to lead the pursuit of the Spanish fleet, keeping his stern lantern lit all night as a beacon for the other ships, Drake extinguished his lantern and sailed off in the darkness to capture the *Rosario*. At dawn on 22 July the Spanish captain woke to find Drake's *Revenge* two or three cables away from his disabled ship. He surrendered without firing a shot. The *Rosario* was one of the pay ships of the Armada, carrying perhaps 50,000 gold ducats, of which Drake seems to have kept about a third for himself. In addition, there were 46 great guns and large stores of powder and shot. The captured ship was sent to Torbay, but the gold was loaded onto the *Revenge*, along with the commander and other important prisoners whom Drake intended to hold for ransom.

Late that same day Drake rejoined the fleet, and the Spanish tried once again to grapple with the elusive English ships. Details are unclear, but Drake was almost certainly the English commander who attacked the Spanish armed merchantman *Gran Grifón* on 23 July. Wallowing in heavy seas, the *Grifón* straggled behind the rest of the Armada. Suddenly a daring English galleon, doubtless Drake's *Revenge*, came up on her beam and loosed a broadside at her. Then turning swiftly about, the English ship came across the stern of the *Grifón* and raked her once more with heavy fire. Fearing the loss of another vessel, Medina Sidonia quickly sent several rescue ships to drive the English vessel out of range and take the *Grifón* in tow. During the rescue, fire from the relief vessels put Drake's *Revenge* out of commission temporarily, with heavy damage to the main top.

Seeing the need for better control of the fleet, Howard reorganized his forces into four squadrons, with himself, Drake, John Hawkins, and Martin Frobisher as commanders. The Spanish also revised their formation, sailing in a sort of roundel, rather than an arc. On 25 July Howard's reorganized fleet engaged the Armada in a fierce gun battle. With his *Revenge* still under repair, Drake missed the engagement in which Hawkins and Frobisher were knighted for gallant service under fire. Meanwhile Medina Sidonia took the Armada across the channel to Calais, where he hoped to meet Parma and his invasion army. This did not happen. Instead, the pursuing English fleet sent fire ships in among his Armada, scattering the vessels, and forcing the Spanish captains to cut their cables and sail away. Medina Sidonia and four other commanders were isolated from the rest of the Armada, and on 29 July, off Gravelines, Drake brought his squadron up to attack them. Other ships from both fleets joined the battle, fighting at a range so close the men could exchange taunts and curses with their opponents.

Though his squadron remained in the fight, Drake himself withdrew after the first hour or so, probably to take his captives to safety. His withdrawal led Frobisher to declare later that Drake was either 'a cowardly knave or a traitor'. He was unsure which, but added, 'the one I will swear' (deposition of Matthew Starke, 11 Aug 1588, PRO, SP 12/214/63 and 64, fols. 139–140v, 141–2). Drake, of course, was no coward, as he was at some pains to prove. A year later, when Petruccio Ubaldino issued his account of the Armada campaign, Drake insisted that the author compose a revised edition, including more about his own role in the fighting, especially the account of cannon balls at Gravelines that pierced his own cabin and injured at least one of the occupants.

Gravelines was the last great battle of the Armada campaign. Stormy seas drove the Spanish ships northwards, and after a few days the English fleet broke off the pursuit. The great Armada battle was over.

The invasion of Portugal The English fleet returned to port, but within a few months plans were under way for Drake to go to sea again. This time he was to command a fleet in a joint commission with Sir John Norris, who would lead a land force. The objective was twofold, an attempt to put Dom Antonio on the throne of Portugal, and the capture of the Spanish treasure fleet off the Azores. As usual plans changed over the next few months. By the time the fleet sailed from Plymouth on 18 April 1589 there were more than 100 ships, organized into 5 squadrons, with perhaps as many as 19,000 officers and men. Queen Elizabeth had her own objective, giving Drake and Norris strict orders to go first to Santander and other Spanish ports in the Bay of Biscay and destroy the warships there.

Instead Drake took his fleet directly to La Coruña, where he had heard the Spanish fleet had taken shelter. Once arrived, he found the harbour almost completely deserted, but Norris landed the army anyway and began to attack the town. In heavy fighting, in which Drake took part, the English troops captured the fortress and put the defenders to the sword. However, there was nothing worth taking except a great quantity of wine, which the soldiers began drinking as usual. Many fell ill and blamed the wine for their sickness. Finally, on 8 May, the troops embarked once more. This time the fleet stopped further south at Peniche, where the Spanish garrison abandoned the town after two days of hard fighting. From that point Norris marched his army overland to Lisbon, where Drake and the fleet were to reinforce him. The march was badly organized. Many men were still sick, and the local people showed little enthusiasm for Dom Antonio. Arriving at Lisbon on 23 May, the English troops found the fortress was too strong and the army too weak. Meanwhile Drake brought the fleet up to the mouth of the Tagus River but made no attempt to reach Lisbon. Puzzled by his delay, Norris abandoned Lisbon, leaving behind many of his sick and wounded troops.

Together once more, Drake and Norris decided to head for the Azores, the second part of the grand plan. Before they could leave the harbour, a dozen or so Spanish galleons appeared, sailing downriver from Lisbon, and attacked the English ships that were scattered across the bay. Probably not understanding the need for a tactical grouping, Drake did not draw his ships into the squadrons into which they were supposedly organized. Instead he allowed the galleons to pick off English stragglers, until a wind finally came up and allowed his fleet to sail away. Driven north the partners decided to take Vigo, where they landed on 18 June. This attack was also a failure, for the inhabitants had abandoned the place and left nothing worth taking except the usual supply of wine. Realizing that the army was too weak to continue the campaign,

Drake and Norris decided that Drake would take the twenty best ships and the healthiest soldiers and sailors and continue to the Azores. Norris and the rest of the force would return to England. Once out of the harbour, however, Drake found his fleet beset by a storm, and he headed back for Plymouth, where Norris found him waiting a few days later.

The queen was furious at the failure of the campaign and the direct violation of her order to attack the ports in the Bay of Biscay. Beyond this, some men accused Drake of cowardice for his failure to come upriver at Lisbon. Both Drake and Norris were brought before the privy council to answer charges about their conduct of the campaign, but in the end no action was taken against them.

The last voyage For a time thereafter Drake concentrated on matters at home, but soon there were discussions about a new raid on the West Indies. Again organized as a profit making venture, the plan was for Francis Drake and John Hawkins to be joint commanders, attacking various ports in the West Indies, and perhaps even capturing Panama. The new fleet left Plymouth on 28 August 1595, but there was bickering between the two commanders from the very start. Drake wanted to attack the Canaries; Hawkins did not. Finally Hawkins conceded, and on 25 September 1595 Drake tried to land his troops at Las Palmas on the island of Gran Canaria. However, the surf was high, the defenders entrenched, artillery fire heavy, and Drake had to abandon the attack. Similar attacks the following day met similar results, and finally the fleet sailed away.

A month later Drake and Hawkins were in the Lesser Antilles, where the commanders differed again. Drake wanted to head immediately for Puerto Rico and attack San Juan, while Hawkins thought it would be better to wait a few days and put the fleet into some sort of order. This time Drake conceded, for Hawkins was ill. On 11 November 1595, just as the fleet reached Puerto Rico, John Hawkins died. The attack went on, but the Spanish had erected formidable fortifications, and Drake was unable to capture the town despite a fierce battle.

After raiding a few small ports on the mainland, Drake landed his troops once more on 27 December 1595 at Nombre de Dios, where he intended to begin a march on Panama. Here, too, the English troops were driven away by determined Spanish soldiers, and Drake took his fleet to sea again. By late January a deadly fever was running through the fleet, making everyone ill. Drake himself was racked with a bloody dysentery. Seeing the end was near, he signed a will, talked to his brother and friends, and on 27 January 1596, in the harbour at Porto Bello, he died. Contrary to his express wish to be buried on land, the body of Francis Drake was sealed in a lead coffin and buried at sea the next day. His officers tried for several days to reorganize the expedition, but the men were too sick and too demoralized. Following a battle with a Spanish fleet off the Isla de Pinos the ships dispersed, each vessel making its own way home, the whole voyage a disaster.

Writing about Francis Drake When Francis Drake died his reputation at home was in eclipse, but the Spanish rejoiced at the passing of a powerful foe. The Spanish cleric and dramatist Lope de Vega celebrated the event in 1598 with an epic poem, *La Dragontea*, recounting some of the stories of the English dragon that had preyed on Spanish possessions and threatened the Spanish religion. A few years later the Spanish historian Antonio de Herrera devoted a long section of his *Historia general del mundo* to the exploits of Francis Drake, while Bartolomé Leonardo de Argensola used much of the same material in his own *Conquista de las Islas Malucas*.

English chroniclers such as Edmund Howes and William Camden also wrote about Drake, but to them he was just one of many brave and resourceful seamen who helped make England a seafaring nation. Finally in 1625 Drake's nephew, also named Francis Drake, published the manuscripts of Philip Nichols in a successful attempt to revive Drake's faltering reputation. The book that Nichols completed, *Sir Francis Drake Revived*, was quickly followed by *The World Encompassed by Sir Francis Drake*, a work that was extensively revised by the younger Francis Drake. The former title caught the public imagination, and it was reissued several times during the next quarter-century. In 1681 Nathaniel Crouch added considerable material of his own and reprinted the work under the title *The English Hero, or, Sir Francis Drake Reviv'd*, and this went through many editions during the following century.

A major theme of these works was that Drake's unfortunate attraction to piracy was more than offset by his devotion to English protestantism. This was also the theme of Henry Holland, who in 1620 included Francis Drake in his *Herōologia*, a sort of illustrated pantheon of English heroes. The same theme was taken up by Thomas Fuller in his book of 1642, *The Holy State and the Profane State*, in which he showed Drake as the very model of a Christian sailor, agonizing about the circumstances that drove him to piracy, but justifying it on the grounds that he robbed England's Catholic enemies.

With remarkably few exceptions this theme has been adopted by Drake's biographers ever since. George William Anderson, in his work of 1781, *A New, Authentic, and Complete Collection of Voyages Round the World*, was one of the first historians to make effective use of the manuscript collections in the British Museum and one of the few to show that Drake's heroism was tinged with villainy. His work has been almost completely ignored by later biographers. Instead, Victorian England embellished the Drake legend, producing novels, plays, and poems by dozens of authors. A sort of culmination was reached in 1895 with the work of Sir Henry Newbolt. His poem 'Drake's Drum' has reminded English boys for more than a century that when they go to sea in warships they do so in the company of Drake and his sailors. The drum itself, preserved at Buckland Abbey, is clearly of sixteenth-century origin and retains many original features. Newbolt's poem was set to music by Sir Charles Stanford: one of his *Songs of the Sea*, it was first performed in 1904. Other Drake relics, some of dubious authenticity, have been preserved at Buckland and elsewhere. Among the best-known are eight banners, now hanging in the gallery at Buckland, that are said to have decorated the *Golden Hind* at Deptford when Drake was knighted by the queen. Pieces made from the timbers of the ship include a chair which has been at Oxford's Bodleian Library since 1662.

In 1898 a respected naval historian, Julian Corbett, used Drake family papers and other manuscript sources to produce a two-volume work (*Drake and the Tudor Navy*) showing that Francis Drake was a great seaman, a leader of men, a protestant gentleman, a fine naval strategist, and the real founder of the English navy. This interpretation was revised somewhat by James A. Williamson in 1938 to make room for John Hawkins, but it remained the standard view of English historians until 1967. In that year Kenneth R. Andrews published *Drake's Voyages*, showing that both Drake and Hawkins were important figures in Elizabethan maritime expansion, but scarcely the founders of a true naval tradition. None the less, the myth lives on, and every few years a new biography appears declaring that Francis Drake had an important role in founding the English navy and explaining his piracy as the patriotic conduct of an intensely religious man. These tales do an injustice to Sir Francis Drake, who was both more interesting and less admirable than the Drake of myth.

HARRY KELSEY

Sources R. Hakluyt, *The principall navigations, voiages and discoveries of the English nation* (1589) · A. de Herrera, *Primera parte de la historia general del mundo* (1606) · P. Nichols, *Sir Francis Drake revived* (1626) · *An Elizabethan in 1582: the diary of Richard Madox, fellow of All Souls*, ed. E. S. Donno, Hakluyt Society, 2nd ser., 147 (1976) · [W. Bigges], *A summarie and true discourse of Sir Francis Drakes West Indian voyage* (1589) · *CSP for., April–Dec 1587* · T. Scott, *The second part of 'Vox populi'* (1624) · R. B. Wernham, ed., *The expedition of Sir John Norris and Sir Francis Drake to Spain and Portugal, 1589* (1988) · B. de Argensola, *Conquista de las Islas Malucas al Rey Felipe III, nuestro señor* (1609) · F. Drake, *The world encompassed by Sir Francis Drake* (1628) · N. Crouch, *The English hero, or, Sir Francis Drake reviv'd* (1681) · H. H. [H. Holland], *Herōologia Anglica* (Arnhem, 1620) · F. Bacon, *Considerations touching a warre with Spaine* (1629) · T. Fuller, *The holy state and the profane state* (1642) · G. Anderson, *A new, authentic, and complete collection of voyages round the world, undertaken and performed by royal authority* (1781) · J. S. Corbett, *Drake and the Tudor navy*, 2 vols. (1898) · K. R. Andrews, *Drake's voyages: a re-assessment of their place in Elizabethan maritime expansion* (1967) · H. Kelsey, *Sir Francis Drake: the queen's pirate* (1998) · J. A. Williamson, *Sir John Hawkins: the time and the man* (1927) · E. Eliott-Drake, *The family and heirs of Sir Francis Drake*, 2 vols. (1911) · R. Hakluyt, *The principal navigations, voyages, traffiques and discoveries of the English nation*, 2nd edn, 3 (1600) · E. van Meteren, *Belgische ofte Nederlandische Historiae*, 1599, bk 10, fols. 174–175v · N. van Sype, *La herdike enterprinse faict par le signeur Draeck davoir circuit toute la terre* (1581?) · Z. Nuttall, *New light on Drake* (1914), 339 · 18 Dec 1548, PRO, C82/893 5079 · will, CKS, PRC 16/43-D · will, PRO, PROB 11/56, sig. 7 [John Drake] · Plymouth and West Devon Record Office, Plymouth, 277/1–12 · BL, Harley MSS 280, 2202 · BL, Add. MS 26056C, fols. 127, 208 · Archivo General de Indias, Seville, Patronato 266, ramo 10; ramo 19, fols. 1v–2; ramo 37, no. 2, fol. 1; ramo 41; ramo 49, fol. 49; ramo 54, fol. 8 · J. Stow and E. Howes, *The annales, or, Generall chronicle of England … unto the ende of the present yeere, 1614* (1615) · parish register, St Budeaux, Devon RO, 1569 [marriage] · J. Stow, *A survay of London*, rev. edn (1603); repr. with introduction by C. L. Kingsford as *A survey of London*, 2 vols. (1908); repr. with addns (1971) · *A full relation of another voyage to the West Indies made by Sir Francis Drake* (1652) · Bibliothèque Nationale, Paris, MS Anglais 51

Archives BL, abstract of voyage, Cotton MS Otto E. viii · BL, Cotton MSS, letters and papers · BL, Add. MS 26056C, fol. 208 · BL, Harley MSS, papers · Buckland Abbey, Devon, papers · CCC Cam., MS 580 · CKS, papers, P/377 · Devon RO, clipping book, T/1258 · Devon RO, black book, W46, fol. 7 · Karpeles Manuscript Library, will of 30 May 1588 · NMM, BHC 2622 · Plymouth and West Devon RO, Plymouth, Eliott-Drake collection, 346/M · Plymouth City Museum and Art Gallery, accounts, PCM 1971.5 · Westcountry Studies Library, Exeter | Archivo de Simancas, near Valladolid, Secciones de Estado and Guerra Marina · Archivo General de Indias, Seville, Patronato 266, ramo 10; ramo 19, fols. 1v–2; ramo 37, no. 2, fol. 1; ramo 41; ramo 49, fol. 49; ramo 54, fol. 8 · Archivo General de Indias, Seville, Secciones de Patronato, Santa Fe, and Santo Domingo, Panama 13, ramo 13, no. 49 · Archivo General de la Nación, Mexico City, Ramo de Inquisición, tomo 85, no. 13, fol. 92; tomo 75, fols. 115–115v · Biblioteca Apostolica Vaticana, Vatican City, Urbinates Latini 1115, fol. 138 · BL, Egerton MSS · BL, Harley MS 540, fols. 1303v–104; MS 280, fols. 84–84v · BL, Lansdowne MSS · BL, account of his final voyage by Robert Leng, Add. MS 21620 · BL, Royal MSS · BL, Sloane MS 3962, fol. 39v · BL, Stowe MSS · Canterbury Cathedral, archives, act books · Canterbury Cathedral, archives, archdeacon's transcripts · Canterbury Cathedral, archives, archdiaconal visitations · Canterbury Cathedral, archives, bishop's transcripts · Canterbury Cathedral, archives, libri cleri · Canterbury Cathedral, archives, MS 2-3-6, fol. 56v · Folger, Mary Frear Keeler Collection · L. Cong., Arthur Riggs papers · LPL, Registrum Matthei Parker · PRO, state papers, domestic, 12/49/36, fol. 75; 12/214 · PRO, state papers, Spanish · V&A NAL, letter to Lord Burghley relating to the preparations for the invasion of England **Likenesses** portrait, c.1580–1585, NPG · studio of N. Hilliard, miniature, oils, 1581, NPG · portrait, c.1590 (after W. Segar?), Plymouth City Museum and Art Gallery · M. Gheeraerts, oils, 1591, NMM; version, Plymouth City Museum and Art Gallery · M. Gheeraerts or A. Janssen, oils, 1594 · portrait, c.1594 (after M. Gheeraerts), NMM · J. Barry, group portrait, oil mural, 1777–84 (*The Thames or the triumph of navigation*), RA · J. Barry, group portrait, etching and line engraving, 1791 (*The Thames or the triumph of navigation*; after his oil mural, 1777–84), NG Ire. · bronze statue?, 1853, Offenberg, Germany; [probably destroyed during WWII] · C. Claesz, engraving on broadside, repro. in *Corte beschryvinghe van die seer heerliicke voyagie, die Capteyn Draeck inde Zuydersche Zee* (c.1596) · J. Hondius?, line engraving on map (after unknown artist, c.1583), BM, NPG [*see illus.*] · I. Oliver, miniature, oils (authenticity disputed) · C. van de Passe, line engraving, BM; repro. in C. Passaeo [C. de Passe], *Effigies regum ac principum* (Cologne, 1598) · J. Rabel, line engraving (after unknown artist), NPG · N. van Sype, engraving on map, repro. in van Sype, *La herdike enterprise* · W. M., line engraving (after unknown artist), NPG · bronze statue, Plymouth Hoe · bronze statue, Tavistock · line engraving (after unknown artist), BM, NPG · line engraving (after unknown artist), NPG **Wealth at death** estates of Buckland Monachorum, Sherford, Yarcomb, and Samford Spinney; mills on the leat near Plymouth; houses and business property in Plymouth; cash assets, jewellery, and precious metal unknown: Plymouth and West Devon RO, 277/12

Drake, Francis (*bap.* 1696, *d.* 1771),

antiquary and surgeon, was baptized in Pontefract on 22 January 1696, the son of Francis Drake (1654–1713), vicar of Pontefract and canon of York, and his second wife, Elizabeth, daughter and heir of John Dickson, town clerk of Pontefract.

Family and early career Drake came from an old Yorkshire family long seated at Horley Green, near Halifax. His grandfather Samuel *Drake (*bap.* 1622, *d.* 1679), was vicar of Pontefract from 1660 to 1678; his great-grandfather Nathan Drake of Godley, Halifax, fought in the royalist army and left a manuscript account of the sieges of Pontefract in 1644 and 1645. He had two half-brothers from his

Francis Drake (*bap.* 1696, *d.* 1771), by Philip Mercier, 1743

father's first marriage: John Drake (1678–1742), who succeeded his father in the Pontefract living, and Samuel *Drake (1687/8–1753), antiquary. By contrast with his half-brothers, who were educated at Cambridge, Francis Drake lamented that he had received 'only a moderate share of school learning' and was 'bred a surgeon' (F. Drake, *Eboracum*, preface, d1v), having been apprenticed at an early age to Christopher Birbeck (*d.* 1717) in York.

On his father's death in 1713 Drake succeeded to the manor of Warthill, near York, and a house in Pontefract; four years later Birbeck died and Drake stepped into his master's medical practice in York. He soon gained a reputation as an expert practitioner, and in May 1727 the corporation of York appointed him city surgeon, an office of little profit but considerable prestige. He was a freemason, having been admitted to the York grand lodge on 6 September in the year that it was established, 1725; on 27 December 1726, as junior grand-warden, he delivered a speech, mainly on the history of the craft, that was printed in York by Thomas Gent about 1727 and reprinted in London in 1729. In 1761, when the York grand lodge was revived after an interval, Drake was made grand master. He was also a member of Spalding Gentlemen's Society.

On 19 April 1720 Drake married Mary Woodyeare (1692/3–1728) at York Minster. His bride, who was from Crook Hill, near Doncaster, was the daughter of George Woodyeare (*d.* 1710), one-time secretary to the diplomatist Sir William Temple; after her father's death she and her mother had moved to York. The couple had five sons, of whom two died in infancy and a third did not survive childhood. After only eight years of marriage Mary herself died in May 1728, aged thirty-five, and was buried in the church of St Michael-le-Belfrey, York, where she is commemorated in a memorial tablet bearing a long Latin inscription by Drake's half-brother Samuel. Her two surviving sons were William *Drake (*bap.* 1723, *d.* 1801), antiquary and master of Felsted grammar school, and **Francis Drake** (*bap.* 1721, *d.* 1795), Church of England clergyman. He was baptized on 5 June 1721 at St Michael-le-Belfrey, York, and in 1739 entered Lincoln College, Oxford, whence he graduated BA in 1743. He proceeded MA in 1746, the year in which he was elected a fellow of Magdalen College, Oxford, BD in 1754, and DD in 1773. He held a series of livings in Yorkshire, first as lecturer of Pontefract and vicar of Womersley, then as vicar of St Mary's, Beverley (1767–75), and lastly as rector of Winestead in Holderness (1775–95). On 31 July 1764, at Womersley, he married Susanna Wilson, with whom he had at least one son, Francis (*bap.* 1766, *d.* 1847), rector of Langton-on-Swale. He died at Doncaster on 2 February 1795.

Eboracum Drake never remarried, and it seems that after his wife's death he sought consolation by devoting his off-duty hours to the study of history, and especially to the writing of a history of York. 'History and antiquity', he states in the preface to his most important work, *Eboracum*, 'were always from a child, my chiefest taste' (preface b1r). He had inherited some historical manuscripts: a copy of his ancestor Nathan Drake's journal of the first siege of Pontefract and a 'very ancient' manuscript on freemasonry found at the demolition of Pontefract Castle in 1649, which he presented to his grand lodge in 1738; in 1740 he is reported as possessing a cartulary of Fountains Abbey. In August 1729 he wrote to the botanist and antiquary Dr Richard Richardson that 'I am … incited [to publish the Antiquitys of this city] by a very valuable manuscript I have in my possession, wrote by Sir Thomas Widdrington, some time Recorder of this place'. This statement seems to have been premature, for in October 1729 Drake wrote to Thomas Hearne that he only 'had the perusal of a copy' of the Widdrington manuscript; furthermore he later wrote that the first copy that he saw was in the city records, which he was unlikely to have seen before 1731, and that he acquired his own copy about 1734–5 (*Extracts from the … Correspondence of Richard Richardson*, 299–300; Walker, vol. 2, pt 1, pp. 76–9). He asked both Richardson and Hearne to lend him books and 'a helping hand to one who, swayed by no thirst of interest or vainglory, undertakes to deliver down to posterity the transactions of this famous city' (F. Drake, *Eboracum*, preface, c2v), but met with no favourable response. He received more encouragement and assistance from the Revd Thomas Barnard, a schoolmaster in Leeds and the husband of Drake's half-sister Frances. He paid the following tribute to Barnard:

> To [him] the whole performance is, in some measure, owing. He it was that principally encouraged me to undertake it; lent me several very scarce historians out of his own collection; and, upon perusing some part of the manuscript, gave it as his judgment, that I needed not despair of success. (ibid., d1r)

Drake bought some manuscripts from the York bookseller Thomas Hammond, which Thomas Gent, his rival

historian of York, complained that he was not allowed to see. Those who lent him manuscripts and gave other assistance included Roger Gale, Brian Fairfax, Benjamin Langwith, John Anstis, Browne Willis, and George Holmes, all of whom were acknowledged in the published history. The dean and chapter of York Minster allowed him to read in their library, where he made particularly good use of the manuscripts of James Torr and, through the recommendations of Canon John Bradley (his wife's uncle by marriage) and Canon Thomas Lamplugh, in 1729 he borrowed William Dugdale's *Monasticon* and some volumes of medieval chronicles. When in April 1731 he wrote to the corporation 'that the work was so far completed that he should be able to put out his proposals in a short time, and he desired liberty to inspect the ancient registers, cartularies, &c., belonging to the city' the corporation immediately made an order giving him access to these documents 'and such things as he should think requisite for completing and illustrating his proposed history' (Davies, *Memoir*, 39). In September 1735, when Drake was anxious to add to his already numerous illustrations engravings of the two market-crosses, Ouse Bridge, a map of the Ainsty, the front elevation of the newly built mansion house, and an interior view of its state room, the corporation voted him, under certain conditions, a contribution of £50.

There survives a slim folio notebook in which Drake made some preliminary collections for his history (York Minster Library, MS XVI.I.2), which possibly dates from 1729. It suggests that Drake originally intended to publish no more than a slim volume and that it was the appearance in 1730 of Gent's modest octavo *The Antient and Modern History of the Famous City of York* that stimulated him to emphasize the difference between their rival histories. In 1731 a trial title-page was printed, and on 3 August 1732 proposals were issued from the London press of William Bowyer, comprising four pages in the format of the projected book, for printing the work by subscription. Nearly three years passed before Drake issued revised proposals announcing that his 'History was in the press, and that the many copper plates necessary to the work were under the hands of the best masters in that art' (*GM*, 1st ser., 5, 1735, 280). The book, an imposing folio of some 800 pages, was at last issued late in 1736 under the title *Eboracum, or, The History and Antiquities of the City of York, from its Original to the Present Time; together with the History of the Cathedral Church and the Lives of the Archbishops* and printed for the author by William Bowyer. Priced at 5 guineas for large paper copies and half as much for copies on small paper, the work attracted nearly 540 subscribers, many of whom were clerical, but the name of the archbishop of York, Lancelot Blackburne, is conspicuously absent. He 'not only refused', wrote Drake, 'upon my repeated applications to him, to accept of the dedication of the church account, but even to subscribe to the book' (*Eboracum*, preface, d1v), even though the archbishop of Canterbury and the bishop of London were subscribers. Drake supposed that Blackburne disapproved of a layman daring to write ecclesiastical history but alternatively it may be conjectured that

Blackburne felt that he should have been the dedicatee of the whole book, or that he disagreed with the author's tory-Jacobite politics, which are plainly displayed in the history. Drake took his revenge with a series of insulting references and omissions in his book, for example leaving out an account of Blackburne's life and an illustration of his coat of arms.

On 26 November 1736 Drake attended a full meeting of the corporation at the guildhall in York and presented to them six copies of his book, one 'richly bound in blue Turkey leather, gilded and beautifully painted and illuminated, in two large folio volumes on royal paper' (Davies, *Memoir*, 40), to be kept among the city records. He expressed his gratitude to the corporation in a speech in which he explained that he could not dedicate his history to them, as he was bound in gratitude to dedicate it to the earl of Burlington. Drake's motives were genuine. In the preface to *Eboracum* he alluded somewhat mysteriously to a sojourn in London, and this allusion is explained in a letter from the antiquary Benjamin Forster to Richard Gough, dated 12 November 1766. Happening one day, probably in spring or early summer 1736, to put up at an inn in Knaresborough, Drake found Sir Harry Slingsby, MP for the borough, negotiating with a farmer for a loan of £600, and he was persuaded to put his name to the bond. Slingsby, protected by his position as an MP, repudiated the debt and allowed Drake to be arrested and imprisoned for the money. As Forster wrote:

> He might have lain in the Fleet to this day had not Lord Burlington interposed, who assured Sir Harry he would use all his interest to prevent him his being rechosen for Knaresborough unless he paid the debt and made a compensation to Mr Drake.   (Nichols, *Illustrations*, 5.298)

In addition Burlington gave Drake £50 towards completing his history. In 1741 Drake further demonstrated his gratitude to Burlington by acting as his electoral agent in the parliamentary election at York.

Antiquarian pursuits   On his return home from prison Drake found that his long-enforced absence had seriously interfered with his practice. Although he accepted the post of honorary surgeon to the York County Hospital on its foundation in 1741, and held it until 1756, he henceforth devoted himself almost entirely to historical and antiquarian research. Having shown 'abundance of curious drawings which he has design'd for his History of the Antiquitys of York' to a meeting of the Society of Antiquaries on 15 January 1735 (Society of Antiquaries minute book, 2, 1732–7), he read before the society a paper entitled 'Introduction to the Aspilogia of John Anstis' and, until 2 December 1736, attended many of the weekly meetings. In June 1740 Drake, together with Roger Gale, showed William Stukeley the antiquities of York, and in July accompanied them on a tour of antiquities in east Yorkshire. Elected a fellow of the Royal Society in 1736, Drake published a medical paper in the *Philosophical Transactions* for 1747–8, and an appendix to John Burton's paper on the location of the Roman station Delgovitia, after their joint visit to the supposed site in the Yorkshire wolds in the spring of 1745. He also contributed a description,

apparently written by his friend John Ward from notes by Drake, of a Roman Mithraic relief sculpture that had recently been found in Micklegate. In October 1754 he and Burton visited Skipwith Common, 10 or 12 miles from York, where they opened a number of small barrows called Danes' hills. He resigned his fellowship of the Royal Society in 1769, having withdrawn from the Society of Antiquaries in November 1755 after a disagreement about his unpaid subscription. At the close of his preface to *Eboracum* he had disclaimed all desire or expectation of another edition, but changed his mind after the first edition had been sold off, though he had no intention of producing it himself. In a letter to John Ward dated 5 April 1755 he referred to 'an interleav'd book I keep of my Antiquitys of York' (BL, Add. MS 6181, fol. 27). This copy, which contains large manuscript additions by the author, was at one time in the possession of his son William, who according to John Nichols would have republished *Eboracum* if the plates could have been recovered, and even contemplated having them engraved anew. As early as 1740 Drake had complained that some of the plates had been lost or stolen from Bowyer's premises.

The Parliamentary history   Writing to Dr Zachary Grey on 1 February 1748 Drake mentioned 'a great work which I am upon' (BL, Add. MS 6396, fol. 9), and 1751 saw the publication of the first eight volumes of *The parliamentary or constitutional History of England from the earliest times to the restoration of King Charles II, collected from the records, the rolls of parliament, the journals of both houses, the public libraries, original manuscripts, scarce speeches and tracts, all compared with the several contemporary writers, and connected throughout with the history of the times, by several hands*. In 1753, 1755, and 1757 a total of twenty further volumes appeared, and in 1760 the final two, comprising an appendix and a copious index. A second edition, in twenty-four handsome octavo volumes, was issued in 1763. There is little doubt that the Cambridge antiquary William Cole was right to assert that Drake and Caesar Ward, bookseller and printer of York, were the sole authors of what he described as this 'most excellent illustration of our English history' (BL, Cole MSS, xxvi, fol. 3b). A surviving volume containing thirty pamphlets, mostly dating from 1647–8, marked up for printing in volume 17, has a manuscript note 'Ask FD', which further confirms Drake's part in the production (York Minster Library, MS XV.L.21).

Character and final years   In person Drake was 'tall and thin', and reserved before strangers in as much as he 'never did or could ask one subscription for his book' (BL, Cole MSS, xxvi, fols. 3b, 4b). A sturdy Jacobite in politics, he could not always disguise his opinions even in the generally sober pages of his history. Having persistently refused to take the oaths to government he was called upon at the height of the Jacobite rising of 1745 to enter into recognizances to keep the peace and not to travel 5 miles or more from home without a licence. He was moreover superseded in the office of city surgeon at a meeting held by York corporation on 20 December 1745. It was not until July 1746 that he obtained a discharge from his recognizances. By the late 1750s his health had begun to fail, and in November 1757 he took the waters at Bath in the company of his friend George Lane Fox. In 1767 he left York to pass the remainder of his life at Beverley, in the house of his eldest son, Francis. He died there on 16 March 1771, in his seventy-sixth year, and was buried in the church of St Mary's, where a tablet to his memory was erected by his son.

Drake's *Eboracum*, though inevitably now outdated in many respects and superseded by the works of later and more critical writers, contains much that would otherwise have been forgotten and is particularly valuable upon points of pure topography. His repeated declarations in 1754 and 1755 that he was not going to produce a new edition may have become known to the booksellers who, knowing that there was a market for one, took action themselves. First, in 1755, the York bookseller John Hildyard, in conjunction with his London counterpart William Sandby, produced a slim folio volume, without any author's or editor's name, entitled *An accurate description and history of the metropolitan and cathedral churches of Canterbury and York*, with a reprint in the following year. A decade later the book trade perceived a new market from the growing number of tourists eager for pocket descriptions and histories to collect on their travels. Accordingly in 1768 the York booksellers published in duodecimo, again anonymously, *An Accurate Description and History of the Cathedral and Metropolitan Church of St Peter, York*; this was a selection from the minster section, with many of the original plates reprinted and heavily folded. Revised editions of this text were published in 1783 and 1790, and a second volume, containing further material relating to the minster, was added in 1770 but not reprinted; each of these editions contained some additional material, such as monuments, clergy lists, and a few historical events. The larger section of *Eboracum*, relating to the city, similarly was reprinted, in three volumes with little abridgement, as *The History and Antiquities of the City of York* (1785). Thus the whole of the original was substantially available in five pocket volumes, and some sets exist uniformly bound. In 1786 the book began to be serialized as a supplement to the *Yorkshire Magazine*; though the magazine ceased at the end of that year the history continued to be published in parts until 1788, when it was reissued in two octavo volumes comprising both city and minster sections. Finally, in 1818 William Hargrove in his *History and Description of the Ancient City of York* professed to give in the compass of two moderate octavo volumes 'all the most interesting information already published in Drake's *Eboracum*, enriched with much entirely new matter from other authentic sources' (title-page). In the 1820s ambitious proposals were issued for a new, enlarged edition of Drake, but nothing was published.

C. BERNARD L. BARR

Sources R. Davies, *York Archaeological and Topographical Journal*, 3 (1875), 33–54 · Nichols, *Illustrations* · Nichols, *Lit. anecdotes* · *The family memoirs of the Rev. William Stukeley*, ed. W. C. Lukis, 3 vols., SurtS, 73, 76, 80 (1882–7) · *Dugdale's visitation of Yorkshire, with additions*, ed. J. W. Clay, 3 (1917), 30–35 · R. Davies, *A memoir of the York press*, new edn, ed. C. B. L. Barr (1988) · J. Evans, *A history of the Society of Antiquaries* (1956), 55 · W. Hargrove, *History and description of the ancient city of York*, 2 (1818), pt 2, 475–80 · Foster, *Alum. Oxon.* · *Extracts from the literary and scientific correspondence of Richard Richardson*, ed. D. Turner (1835), 299–300, 304 · J. Walker, ed., *Letters written by eminent persons in the seventeenth and eighteenth centuries—from originals in the Bodleian Library*, 2 (1813), pt 1, 76–9 · T. Gent, *The antient and modern history of the famous city of York* (1730) · E. Brunskill, *18th century reading: some notes on the people who frequented the library of York Minster in the eighteenth century, and on the books they borrowed* (1950) · T. C. Barnard and J. Clark, eds., *Lord Burlington: architecture, art and life* (1995), 214 · *York Courant* (19 March 1771) · W. J. Sheils, 'Yorkshire: the North Riding and the city of York', in C. R. J. Currie and C. P. Lewis, *English county histories: a guide* (1994), 445–60 · *GM*, 1st ser., 65 (1795), 174 · *IGI* · R. F. Gould, *The history of freemasonry*, 6 vols. (1884–7), 4.273, 284, 404–5

Archives BL, corresp., Add. MSS 4305, 6181, 6210, 6396, 28536 · BL, papers, Add. MSS 5830, 6183, 11249, Egerton MSS 2577–2578 | BL, letters to Charles Lyttelton, Add. MSS 753–754 · BL, letters to Sir Hans Sloane, Add. MSS 4052, 4054–4055, 4435 · Bodl. Oxf., corresp. and notes on Dodsworth collection · Bodl. Oxf., papers relating to Civil War · York Minster Library, Drake's notebook on the history of York, MS XVI.I.2

Likenesses P. Mercier, oils, 1743, York City Art Gallery; on loan to Mansion House, York [*see illus.*] · N. Drake, oils, 1756, York City Art Gallery · V. Green, mezzotint, 1771 (after N. Drake), BM, NPG

Drake, Francis (*bap.* **1721**, *d.* **1795**). *See under* Drake, Francis (*bap.* **1696**, *d.* **1771**).

Drake, Sir Francis Samuel, baronet (*b.* in or after **1725**, *d.* **1789**), naval officer, was the younger son of Sir Francis Henry Drake, and Anne, *née* Heathcote, of Hursley, Hampshire, and Clapton House, Hackney, Middlesex. His family was descended from that of Francis Drake of Armada fame. His older brother, Francis William, was born in June 1724 (parish register, Hursley, *IGI*) so that it is probable that Francis Samuel was born in 1725 or 1726. The date of his joining the navy is not known but he was made lieutenant on 24 August 1749. His name first appeared on the muster roll of the *Torrington* in May 1751 (PRO, ADM 36/4307) and he also served on the sloops *Otter* and *Windsor* before being given the command of the sloop *Viper* on 20 March 1756. On 15 November 1756 he was made post captain and given the *Bideford*. He succeeded his brother, Francis William, as captain of the *Falkland* (50 guns) and in her was with Vice-Admiral Knowles in November 1756. He stayed in the *Falkland* until 1762, serving in the Leeward Islands under Commodore Moore from 1757 to 1758, and returning to England in the spring of 1759 while protecting the homeward bound trade. In the autumn of 1759 he went to Quiberon Bay in the squadron of Commodore John Reynolds and in November he joined Admiral Hawke between Ushant and Belleisle in a detachment commanded by Captain Robert Duff and was present at the defeat of the French in Quiberon Bay on 20 November 1759.

Drake was with Commodore Swanton in the St Lawrence in the summer of 1760, with Admiral Colville at Halifax, and then in 1761 with Sir James Douglas in the Leeward Islands; he stayed there with Sir George Rodney, taking part in the attack on Martinique in 1762. While with Rodney he transferred to the *Rochester* (being replaced in the *Falkland* by Captain Tucker) and stayed with her until the peace of Paris in 1763. In 1766 he commanded the *Burford* and from 1772 to 1775 he was captain of the *Torbay* (74 guns), guardship at Plymouth. In June 1773 the *Torbay* was one of four ships from Plymouth to join the fleet at Spithead for review by George III.

In the spring of 1778 Drake was appointed to the *Russell* (74 guns) and sailed with Vice-Admiral Byron's squadron for North America. The crossing was disastrous. Damaged and scattered by gales soon after leaving England, the ships of the squadron completely lost touch with one another in thick fog on the banks of Newfoundland, and Byron arrived in Halifax on 27 August 1778 quite alone. Earlier Drake's *Russell* had been so damaged by the storms that he was forced back to England. In April 1779, refitted, he joined Vice-Admiral Mariot Arbuthnot at St Helens and sailed with him to North America. The squadron arrived at Sandy Hook, New York, on 29 August 1779, the '*Russell* being so sickly as not being able to proceed' (PRO, ADM 1/486).

In September 1779 Drake was sent to Jamaica as commodore with a convoy of transports carrying 5000 soldiers. In February 1780 he was again with Arbuthnot at the entrance to the Savannah and in April he was ordered to join Sir George Rodney in the West Indies. On 26 September 1780 he was promoted rear-admiral of the blue and hoisted his flag in the *Princessa* (70 guns). In January 1781 news was received in the West Indies of the rupture of relations with the Netherlands and Drake took part with Rodney in the operations against the Dutch islands and the capture of St Eustatius. On 29 April, in the leading division of Hood's detached squadron and with his flag in the *Gibraltar*, he was warmly engaged in the battle against De Grasse off Fort Royal, Martinique.

In August 1781, once more in the *Princessa*, Drake sailed with Hood to reinforce Admiral Graves in New York, and he took part in the battle of the Chesapeake on 5 September. The preliminary manoeuvring put his division into the van which, with part of the centre, was heavily engaged with De Grasse. His own ship was so badly damaged that he shifted his flag to the *Alcide*. He returned with Hood to the West Indies and in January 1782 was with him in the unsuccessful defence of St Kitts. In Sir George Rodney's great victory at the Saints on 12 April Drake again commanded the van. His conduct on this occasion deservedly won him a baronetcy, gazetted on 28 May 1782. He continued in the West Indies until the peace in 1783 after which he had no further service.

It seems certain that Drake was married first, in 1763, to Elizabeth Hayman of Kent, and secondly on 22 January 1788 to Pooley, daughter of George *Onslow, MP for Guildford. On 12 August 1789 Drake was made a lord of the Admiralty but he died, shortly after his appointment, on 19 October 1789 at Whitehall in the parish of St Martin-in-the-Fields, London. He was survived by his second wife. As he died without children Drake's baronetcy became extinct.   KENNETH BREEN

Sources letters, PRO, ADM 1, esp. 486 · lieutenants' passing certificates, PRO, ADM 107 · ships' muster books, PRO, ADM 36 · D. Syrett and R. L. DiNardo, *The commissioned sea officers of the Royal Navy, 1660–1815*, rev. edn, Occasional Publications of the Navy RS, 1 (1994) · J. Charnock, ed., *Biographia navalis*, 6 vols. (1794–8) · R. Beatson, *Naval and military memoirs of Great Britain*, 2nd edn, 6 vols. (1804) · Burke, *Peerage* · J. Burke and J. B. Burke, *A genealogical and heraldic history of the extinct and dormant baronetcies of England, Ireland and Scotland*, 2nd edn (1841); repr. (1844) · *GM*, 1st ser., 58 (1788) · will, PRO, PROB 6/164, fol. 221v

Archives NRA, dispatches | PRO, corresp. with Admiral Rodney, PRO 30/20

Drake, James (*bap.* 1666, *d.* 1707), political and medical writer, was born in Cambridge and baptized on 4 December 1666 at the town's Great St Mary's Church, the son of Robert Drake, a solicitor. 'By the Care of an indulgent Father' he enjoyed 'a very Liberal Education' (Drake, *Memorial*, iii). Educated first at Wivelingham and at Eton College he was then admitted to Gonville and Caius College, Cambridge, in March 1685. He took his BA at some time before the revolution of 1688, 'having declaimed and disputed in the Schools with very great Applause' (ibid., iv). He went on to take his MA 'with unusual Honours paid him by Men of the Brightest Parts'. In 1693 he went to London, where 'he was very much admir'd at all places frequented by Men of the *Belles Lettres*' (ibid.). 'Having a particular Genius to the Study of *Physick*' he was encouraged to pursue it by Sir Thomas Millington 'the most eminent practitioner in the College of Physicians' (ibid.). He became MB in 1690 and MD in 1694. In 1701 he was elected fellow of the Royal Society, and five years later he became fellow of the Royal College of Physicians. In the transactions of the Royal Society is a paper by Drake, entitled 'Some influence of respiration on the motion of the heart hitherto unobserved'.

Described as 'a lover of literature', in 1697 Drake contributed to a pamphlet, *Commendatory Verses upon the Author of Prince Arthur and King Arthur* (*N&Q*, 8.346). He was also keenly interested in the theatre, particularly in the nature of comedy. In the preface to his *Antient and Modern Stages Survey'd* (1705), which is a reply to the views of Jeremy Collier, 'some of Mr Collier's mistakes are rectified'. Drake also wrote plays. *The Sham Lawyer, or, The Rich Extravagant* was an adaptation of John Fletcher's *Spanish Curate*. Another of Drake's plays, *Wit without Money*, was acted at Drury Lane in 1697; it was later printed as 'it was Damnably ACTED at the Theatre Royal' (Nichols, *Lit. anecdotes*, 1.341). It is suggested that Drake became a playwright either through straitened financial circumstances or by 'mistaking his talents and neglecting physic' (ibid., 1.133). Temporarily abandoning his scientific studies Drake became propagandist for the tory party. In 1702 he published *The History of the Last Parliament*, which was 'highly resented by the House of Peers' and seen as critical of King William (ibid.). He was summoned before parliament, which ordered him to be prosecuted; he was tried and acquitted.

In 1703 Drake published *Historia Anglo Scotica*, which he held was based on a manuscript by an unknown author although he gave no indication of where he had found it. It purported to trace relations between England and Scotland from the time of William the Conqueror to that of

Queen Elizabeth. The Scots reacted with fury and held that the work contained 'many false and injurious reflections' (N&Q, 3.519). The text was burnt at Mercat Cross, Edinburgh, on 30 June 1703.

Drake was disappointed at his failure to become a commissioner of the sick and wounded, a post which had been promised him. He was also upset by the rejection of the bill to prevent occasional conformity, and the disgrace into which some of his friends, ardent supporters of the bill, had fallen. In 1704, with Henry Poley, MP for Ipswich, he published *The Memorial of the Church of England*; it was 'represented to the Queen as an Insult upon her Majesties Honour, and an Intimation that *The Church was in Danger under her Administration*' (Drake, *Memorial*, v). Parliament decided to punish the author and offered a reward for the printer, who surrendered on promise of a pardon. The pamphlet was proscribed by the House of Commons and burnt by the common hangman at the Royal Exchange. Although Drake escaped punishment some statements in the paper *Mercurius Politicus*, of which he was the author, led to his prosecution. Drake endured a long trial and, although found guilty of writing the pamphlet, again avoided punishment through a simple error in the wording of the indictment—the word 'Nor' was mistakenly substituted for the word 'not'.

But the accusations made against Drake, his abandonment by the tories, and the threat of punishment had taken its toll. His health deteriorated and he died of a fever at Westminster on 2 March 1707. It was said that he died 'raving against cruel persecutors, and patrons not much more humane' (N&Q, 8.346). Not long before his death his scientific interests appear to have revived and he published *Anthropologia Nova, or, A New System of Anatomy*. It was said to have been published by his wife, the author and medical practitioner Judith *Drake. It was a very popular treatise and ran to three editions in the next twenty years. It is a sad reminder of the great talent that Drake sacrificed to politics.   BRIDGET HILL

Sources DNB · J. Drake, *The memorial of the Church of England* (1711) · [J. Drake], *The antient and modern stages survey'd, or, Mr Collier's view of the immorality and profaneness of the English stage set in a true light* (1699) · Nichols, *Lit. anecdotes*, 1.133, 340–41 · N&Q, 3 (1851), 519 · N&Q, 8 (1853), 272, 346 · A. Boyer, *The history of Queen Anne* (1735) · *Remarks and collections of Thomas Hearne*, ed. C. E. Doble and others, 1, OHS, 2 (1885), 59, 65, 186 · Munk, *Roll* · H. Smith, 'English "feminist" writings and Judith Drake's *An essay in defence of the female sex* (1696)', *HJ*, 44 (2001), 727–47
Likenesses M. Vandergucht, line engraving (after T. Foster), BM, NPG; repro. in J. Drake, *Anthropologia nova*, 2 vols. (1707)

Drake, Sir James (1907–1989), civil engineer, was born on 27 July 1907 at 69 Prospect Terrace, Whalley Road, Altham, Burnley, the son of James Drake, a commercial clerk, and his wife, Ellen Hague. He was educated at Accrington grammar school (1918–1924) and at the Victoria University of Manchester (1924–7), where he graduated BSc in civil engineering, with first-class honours. He passed the professional exams of the Institution of Civil Engineers in April 1931, and was accepted as an associate in 1933 and as a full member in 1943. He married Kathleen Shaw (b.

1913/14), daughter of Richard Shaw Crossley, company director, on 6 July 1937; they had two daughters. He served Stockport county borough council (1927–30), then Bootle county borough council (1930–37), where he built a sports stadium and cycle track and an eighteen-hole golf course, and prepared plans for an arterial road 84 feet wide. He then moved on to work for Blackpool county borough council, first as deputy, and from 1938 as chief, engineer and surveyor, and constructed a number of municipal offices, housing estates, libraries, and schools. He designed sea defences costing £950,000, an 18 mile sewerage system with three pumping stations costing £750,000, and a 7 mile ring road and other road improvements costing £670,000. He was also responsible for the construction of Britain's first multi-storey car park, with a bus station below, which anticipated modern multi-modal policy.

In the later 1930s many new road schemes were projected. In 1936 the Institution of Highway Engineers published a plan for 2826 miles of motorways and the first Trunk Roads Act (1936) brought central government into road building for the first time. Drake had viewed Germany's autobahns in 1937 for the County Surveyors' Society, which published its own plans for 1000 miles of motorway in Britain in the following year. At this time Drake became a persistent, often acerbic, advocate of motorways for access, speed, and safety. From the mid-1950s he was also a prime administrator of contracts in the field when post-war construction of houses and schools, and relief from rearmament for the Korean War, had progressed far enough to release exchequer money for the Special Roads Act (1949). As county surveyor and bridgemaster of Lancashire (1945–72) Drake devised a road plan for the county, published in 1949, resting on measurement and projection of traffic flows, as the basis of the county's development plan. His document was seminal for the highway strategies of his county for more than thirty years and was the forerunner of national highway planning procedures. His deep Lancastrian knowledge kept the public inquiry to a single hearing, at which the sole objector did not appear. His method was to anticipate obstacles by sequential contracts for advance works: for example, for the lofty Thelwall Viaduct, 4114 feet long, which the M6 would later require.

From 1946 government plans incorporated a new north–south trunk route through Lancashire. So did Drake's plan, which he pressed on government from 1949 to 1955. Work began in 1956 on the Preston bypass with the county as the government's agent. This became the first section of Britain's motorway system, opened to traffic in 1958. His Lancaster bypass followed in 1960, along with the Stretford–Eccles bypass which became part of the M63, including the Barton high-level bridge, 2425 feet long, over the Manchester Ship Canal; and the Warrington–Preston section in 1963. Drake's planning envisaged linking Preston, Liverpool, Manchester, Blackpool, and eventually Hull by the M6, M61, and M62. He was involved in intense discussion in 1962–4 between the Ministry of Transport, the Scottish development department, the

Association of County Councils, and the County Surveyors' Society over the local and national economic benefits of motorways.

Detailed studies of the new rigid concrete road pavements built for the Grantham and Newark bypasses convinced Drake of the need to improve upon what the road research laboratory and the Cement and Concrete Association recommended. He headed a technical delegation to Switzerland comprising staff from Alfred McAlpine, Fairclough Construction, and Ribblesdale Cement to study Swiss construction and maintenance techniques and frost-resistance. In 1964–5, as president of the County Surveyors' Society, he took a team of highway engineers to North America, and sent another to Europe, to gather information on motorway specifications, methods, costs, and productivity. A resultant conference of 800 delegates exchanged their findings and led to *Motorways*, edited by Drake and others, published in 1968. Drake's research trips led to major changes in the standard Ministry of Transport specification for rigid concrete pavements on motorways and the methods of building them from 1971. Other innovations he had tested and successfully introduced were the use of 'Bunter', a red sandstone from south Lancashire and north-east Cheshire substituted for the usual sand and gravel sub-base, and crushed limestone or 'crusher run' to top it. The Lancashire motorways incorporating these features far exceeded their expected design lifetimes. In 1967–8 Drake was seconded to the Ministry of Transport as director of the first road construction unit, for the north-west of England, constructing the M6 through the Lune valley and planning the M53 and M56 in Cheshire. In 1968 he returned to his Lancashire office, adding the duties of chief engineer of the Lancashire sub-unit of his former unit to complete construction of the M61 and part of the M62 and to prepare plans for the M55, the M58, and the M66 before retiring in 1972.

The author of many technical papers, Drake was elected fellow and member of the council of the Institution of Civil Engineers and a fellow and president of the Institution of Highway Engineers. In 1973 he was knighted (having been appointed CBE in 1962) and awarded an honorary DSc degree by Salford University and an honorary fellowship of Manchester Polytechnic. On retiring, he served as a director and later a consultant for the Fairclough construction group. He enjoyed playing golf at Royal Lytham St Anne's, near his home at 11 Clifton Court. Drake died on 1 February 1989 at the Victoria Hospital, Blackpool.

PETER BALDWIN

Sources Archives of the Institution of Highways and Transportation, London · Lancs. RO, Highways and Bridges Committee papers, CC/MBA series · motorway files, PRO, MT 117, MT 121 · personal knowledge (2004) · private information (2004) · *20 years of British motorways: proceedings of the Institution of Civil Engineers conference* [London 1980] (1980) · G. Charlesworth, *A history of British motorways* (1984) · A. Smith, *A history of the County Surveyors' Society, 1885–1985* (1985) · A. Gray, *The road to success: Alfred McAlpine, 1935–1985* (1987) · b. cert. · m. cert. · d. cert. · Inst. CE
Archives Inst. CE | Lancs. RO, MSS of highways and bridges committee

Wealth at death £204,128: probate, 19 April 1989, *CGPLA Eng. & Wales*

Drake, John Poad (*bap.* 1794, *d.* 1883), inventor and artist, son of Thomas Drake and his wife, Frances Poad, was born in Stoke Damerel, Devon, where he was baptized on 20 July 1794. A shipwright in the naval dockyard at Plymouth, Thomas Drake was a man of independent character, whose career was damaged by his refusal to connive at malpractice. None the less, after leaving the service of HM dockyard he continued to receive a pension of £24 per annum until his death in Jersey on 20 May 1835. John Poad Drake married Susannah Johns Holman at Stoke Damerel on 24 March 1819.

After observing Napoleon Bonaparte on board the *Bellerophon* in Plymouth Sound, Drake produced a picture of the scene and took it to be exhibited in North America, where he practised as an artist. Joseph Bonaparte saw the picture in New York. Drake was commissioned to paint a portrait of Justice Blowers to hang in the court house of Halifax, Nova Scotia, where the Drakes' son was born on 2 March 1820. In Montreal he painted an altarpiece and continued to describe himself as an artist, although no corpus of his creative endeavours has been traced in published works or in British gallery records. He returned to England in 1827.

While continuing to paint, Drake engaged in more technical pursuits. Among them were improvements in shipbuilding, in which a diagonal arrangement of ribs and planking was substituted for the 'parallelogrammatic'. From 1829 to 1837 he occupied himself with schemes for breech-loading guns, and from 1832 to 1840 laid before Admiralty committees his proposals for iron-cased floating batteries and steam rams. In 1837 he described himself as 'Artist' of Arundel Street, the Strand, London, in an application for which he was granted letters patent no. 7406 in respect of improvements in the design of ships, including a screw trenail fastening for their timbers. It was said that any benefit from patents that might have accrued to him was dissipated when Drake fell into the hands of adventurers.

By 1851 Drake was in St Austell, Cornwall, where he was granted letters patent no. 13,736 in respect of 'Improvements in Constructing Ships and Other Vessels'. The content of the application reveals that he believed that others had benefited from his earlier designs having been passed by the Admiralty to the mercantile marine. Between 1854 and 1856 he presented before Board of Ordnance committees schemes for facilitating the working of heavy cannon and for 'impregnable revolving redoubts'.

The Standard of 26 November 1866 reported that Drake should receive some credit for, in 1835, drawing to attention of the Board of Ordnance the 'fundamental principle of the now called Snider Enfield' (a new service rifle) but no modern arms historian mentions his involvement. John Poad Drake continued to invent, pressing his claims steadily on an unappreciative government, receiving compliments, but failing to persuade the authorities to adopt his innovations. He died of senile decay at the Esplanade, Fowey, Cornwall, on 26 February 1883. His wife died at St Austell on 4 October 1865, aged sixty-eight. Drake's only son, Henry Holman Drake, was editor of a new *History of Kent*, publishing the first part, 'The hundred of Blackheath', in London in 1886.   WILLIAM REID

Sources private information (2004) [H. H. Drake] · Boase & Courtney, *Bibl. Corn.*, 3.1160 · J. Maclean, *The parochial and family history of the deanery of Trigg Minor in the county of Cornwall*, 1 (1873), 320 · 'Paddle wheels', *Civil Engineer and Architect's Journal*, 15 (1852), 113 · 'Drake's breech-loading cannon'; 'Extensive naval and military improvements'; 'Drake's improvements in cannon', *Mechanic's Magazine*, 67 (1857), 242, 251–4, 393, 422, 493–5, 538 · 'Drake's improvements in cannon'; 'Strengthened cast-iron guns'; 'Iron defences'; 'Our coast defences', *Mechanic's Magazine*, 68 (1858), 107, 181, 542, 609 · 'Drake's long-range duplex breech-loading cannon' (letter), *Mechanic's Magazine*, 69 (1858), 61 · Dockyard pensions lists, PRO, ADM 42/1046 · d. cert.

Drake, Judith (*fl.* **1696–1723**), writer and medical practitioner, was the wife of James *Drake (*bap.* 1666, *d.* 1707), physician and political writer. Although no marriage is traceable the register of St Andrew's, Holborn, records the baptism of 'Ann daughter of James Drake and Judith'. It was probably from James Drake, a fellow of the Royal Society and of the College of Physicians, that she acquired her medical knowledge. In 1723, summoned to appear before Sir Hans Sloane, president of the Royal College of Physicians, she defended herself against accusations of medical malpractice made by 'a malicious informant'. Apparently she regularly dispensed medicines to 'those not in acute distempers' among her 'own sex and little children'. She little suspected that this would make her 'obnoxious to the censure of the College'. The complainant had made no objection 'against the price (which he all along knew) nor the success of the medicines, till they came to be pay'd for'. He had accused her of administering poisons, but, as she retorted, 'the only poison … administered was to his Ears—in a demand for money'. Since he had made the accusation his mistress had three times sent for more medicines. As Drake commented, 'when a man permits that to be taken by his Friend which he calls poison, he must not wonder if we reflect upon him for want of sense or sincerity' (Sloane MS 4047, fol. 38).

Drake is best known for her probable authorship of the anonymous pamphlet *An Essay in Defence of the Female Sex* (1696), frequently ascribed to Mary Astell. It was included in a catalogue of second-hand books sold after 1741 by the publisher Edmund Curll, where it was described as written by 'Mrs. Drake, probably a sister of Dr. James Drake, who attended to the publication of the pamphlet' (F. M. Smith, appendix). The author's preface refers to 'the gentleman, who was so kind as to take care of the Publication of it, only to excuse me from appearing'. 'The same gentleman' persuaded her not to put her name to the pamphlet for fear of the malice of men who 'greedily … suck in anything to the prejudice of A Woman'. She wrote that there were 'some Men, (I hear) who will not allow this Piece to be written by a Woman'. The true author, they held, was James Drake. She saw no reason why her sex 'shou'd be robb'd of the Honour of it, since there have been Women in all Ages whose Writings might vie with those of the greatest Men' (Drake, *Essay in Defence of the*

Female Sex). James Drake in the preface wrote an elegant poem in praise of his wife's work.

Written in a lively and witty style, Drake's pamphlet defends women against the accusations of vanity, impertinence, enviousness, dissimulation, and inconstancy which men make against them. In satirical sketches of the Scholar, the Country Squire, the Beau, the Virtuoso, the Poet, and the Coffee-house Politicians she revealed the weaknesses of men. While admitting to 'a very great Veneration' for the Royal Society in general, she thought there was 'a vast difference between the particular Members'. She attacked the '*Mushrome* and *Cockel-shell* Hunters'. What 'noble Remedies, what serviceable Instruments' had they produced to equal 'so good a Med'cine as Stew'd *Prunes*, or so necessary an Instrument as a *Flye-Flap*'? She argued that women by nature were no less talented than men. 'Never design'd for Fatigue', they were 'chiefly intended for Thought and the Exercise of the Mind'. Men's physical strength made them more fitted 'for Action and Labour' (Drake, *Essay*, 18). Aware of women's potential to 'become their Superiours' men had denied them access to education (ibid., 21). She had sharp words for those men who believed time spent in women's company was 'mis'employ'd' (ibid., 6) but admitted that among the 'inferior sort', 'the Condition of the two Sexes' was 'more level' than among their social superiors (ibid., 15–16).

Drake appears to have abandoned writing after 1696, but when her husband died on 2 March 1707, having just completed his second volume of *Anthropologia Nova, or, A New System of Anatomy*, Judith published it, edited the text, and was responsible for the dedication to Henry, duke of Beaufort. In it she described herself as a 'Retir'd Disconsolate Woman, whose Great Misfortune it is that it was not offer'd to Your Grace by a better Hand'.

BRIDGET HILL

Sources [J. Drake], *An essay in defence of the female sex* (1696) · BL, Sloane MS 4047, fol. 38, 1 Sept 1723 · F. M. Smith, *Mary Astell* (1916) · Munk, *Roll* · J. Drake, *Anthropologia nova, or, A new system of anatomy*, 2 vols. (1707) · Venn, *Alum. Cant.* · H. Smith, 'English "feminist" writings and Judith Drake's *An essay in defence of the female sex* (1696)', *HJ*, 44 (2001), 727–47

Drake, Nathan (1726–1778), painter, was born on 6 December 1726 in the parish of St Peter Eastgate, Lincoln, the son of Samuel Drake (*b. c.*1698), a minor canon at Lincoln and MA of Magdalen College, Oxford, and his wife, Elizabeth. Nothing is known of his training, and his earliest work is a *View of Boston* (Lincolnshire), engraved by J. S. Muller in 1751. A view *Newport Arch, Lincoln* (Usher Art Gallery, Lincoln) may also date from this time. On 26 December 1752 he advertised in the *York Courant* as a 'Limner and landscape painter' willing to teach drawing or watercolour painting at his rooms in Colliergate. His younger brother, Thomas, had already been apprenticed as a cabinet-maker in York in 1750 and was to remain in practice until 1784. In 1756 Drake's *New Terrace Walk, York*, was engraved by C. Grignion, the original painting existing in two versions (both in York Art Gallery). His 1756 painting of the York antiquary Francis Drake (1696–1771), a remote kinsman (York Art Gallery), was engraved by Valentine Green in 1771. Drake then 'met with little encouragement and was more successful in miniature' (Davies) and a miniature signed ND (now in York Art Gallery) of an unknown man is probably by him. On 31 May 1763 he married Martha Carr at St Michael-le-Belfrey, York, and moved from Colliergate to Precentor's Court, York, where their two sons were born: Nathan *Drake (1766–1836), the physician and essayist, and Richard (b. 1767), a surgeon.

By 1767 Drake had met William Tufnell Joliffe of Nun Monkton Priory, York, for whom he painted three bucolic portraits (all priv. coll.): of the earth-stopper Arthur Wentworth of Bulmer (engraved by Valentine Green in 1767), of Joliffe himself with his huntsmen in the grounds of Nun Monkton (1769), and of the bailiff John Redman (1773). Drake's most elaborate portrait is that of the aged York printer Thomas Gent (1693–1778) (York Archaeological Society, Leeds), presumably the portrait of an old man shown by Drake at the Society of Artists in London in 1771, and engraved in 1774 by Valentine Green. Drake was elected a fellow of the Society of Artists in 1771 and went on to exhibit with the society in 1773 (A Family; in Little), 1775 (A View of a Gentleman's Seat in Yorkshire, with Two Gentlemen Going out a-Hawking, Sacarissa from James Thomson's The Seasons, and a miniature of a lady), and in 1776 (A Madona and Child), on each occasion giving his address as 'At Mr Drake's, Colourman, Long Acre', that is, Nathaniel Drake, the well-known artists' agent, who had been in practice in London since 1763 and was presumably related. In 1776 Valentine Green engraved two paintings by Drake illustrating Thomson's The Seasons, one doubtless being the picture exhibited in 1775. Drake died in York on 19 February 1778 and was buried in St Michael-le-Belfrey, where his tombstone gives his age as fifty.

Drake's talent was modest, but William Mason described him as 'an ingenious artist' (W. Mason to T. Wharton, 11 Aug 1772, BL, Egerton MS 2400) on the occasion of their collaboration on a posthumous portrait of the poet Thomas Gray (probably that now in York Minster Library). It is of particular interest that, despite their mediocrity, many of Drake's works were engraved by good hands. JOHN INGAMELLS

Sources J. Ingamells, 'Art in 18th century York', Country Life, 149 (1971), 1530–32 • Catalogue of paintings, City of York Art Gallery, 2: English school, 1500–1850 (1963), 14–15 • J. Ingamells, York Art Gallery catalogue supplement (1974), 23 • B. Barr and J. Ingamells, eds., A candidate for praise: William Mason, 1727–97, precentor of York (1973), 26 [exhibition catalogue, York Art Gallery and York Minster Library, York, 16 June – 15 July 1973] • Robert Davies, MSS notes, York Reference Library • York Courant (26 Dec 1752) • J. Harris, The artist and the country house: a history of country house and garden view painting in Britain, 1540–1870, new edn (1985), 225, 241 • Graves, Soc. Artists • IGI

Drake, Nathan (1766–1836), essayist and physician, belonging to a well-established Yorkshire family, was born on 15 January 1766 at York, where his father, Nathan *Drake (1726–1778), was an artist, and where his younger brother, Richard, was afterwards a surgeon. His mother was Martha Carr. Young Nathan received a scanty preliminary education. His father died in 1778, and in the following year Drake began his professional studies as apprentice to a general practitioner in York. He went to Edinburgh University in 1786, where he graduated MD in 1789, with an inaugural thesis, 'De somno'. He first practised as a physician at Billericay, Essex, but moved in 1790 to Sudbury, Suffolk. Here he became acquainted with Mason Good, who was established as a general practitioner. A shared interest in medical and literary matters drew them together, and resulted in an intimate friendship, which continued until Dr Good's death in 1827. Drake moved in 1792 to Hadleigh, Suffolk, where he continued with his professional and literary labours.

Drake's first publication was a volume of essays, Literary Hours (1798), which was followed by other volumes, such as Essays Illustrative of the 'Tatler', 'Spectator', and 'Guardian' (1805); Essays Illustrative of the 'Rambler', 'Adventurer', 'Idler' (1809); Winter Nights (1820), and Evenings in Autumn (1822). He was married in 1807 and became the father of three children. He continued to publish various other collections of miscellaneous essays, critical, narrative, biographical, and descriptive, but his only professional writings consisted of a few papers contributed to medical periodicals. Five of these were published in the Medical and Physical Journal (1799–1800) as 'On the use of digitalis in pulmonary consumption', on which subject he was considered an authority.

Drake's most ambitious work was Shakespeare and his Times (1817), which was the result of such hard work that it was felt to have impaired his health. It received quite a few favourable reviews, as it brought together for the first time the scattered material of the various editions, and of the work of other scholars, such as Tyrwhitt. Drake published a supplementary work, Memorials of Shakespeare, or, Sketches of his Character and Genius by Various Writers (1828). A posthumous work, The Harp of Judah, or, Songs of Sion, being a Metrical Translation of the Psalms, appeared in 1837. Drake was an honorary associate of the Royal Society of Literature and was universally esteemed as a good and religious man. He died in Hadleigh, Suffolk, in 1836 survived by his wife and children.

W. A. GREENHILL, rev. NILANJANA BANERJI

Sources Annual Register (1836) • Nichols, Lit. anecdotes, 2.87 • GM, 2nd ser., 6 (1836) • O. Gregory, Memoirs of the life, writings, and character of the late John Mason Good, M.D. (1828)
Archives CUL, letters to James Plumptre
Likenesses P. W. Tomkins, stipple (after H. Thomson), BM, NPG

Drake, Nicholas Rodney [Nick] (1948–1974), singer and songwriter, was born on 19 June 1948 in Rangoon, Burma, the only son of Rodney Drake (1908–1988), an engineer, and his wife, Molly, née Lloyd (1915–1993). An elder sister, Gabrielle (b. 1944), became well known as an actress. The Drake family returned to Britain from Burma when Nick was four, and at eight he was sent to Eagle House School, a preparatory school at Sandhurst, Berkshire. After following his father and grandfather to Marlborough College (1962–6)—where he learned to play the piano, clarinet, saxophone, and, latterly, the guitar—he went up to Cambridge to read English at Fitzwilliam College (1967–9). He left before taking his degree to pursue a career in the music business. As a musician he was influenced by the Scottish singer–songwriter Bert Jansch and the Americans Bob Dylan and Jackson C. Frank, and it is songs by these artists that feature on the earliest known recording of him singing, taped on a schoolfriend's machine in Aix-en-Provence in the south of France during the spring of 1967. It was also during this four-month period he spent studying French in Aix that Nick Drake first began to write his own songs, accompanied by his own guitar-playing.

In the following year at The Roundhouse in London, during one of his earliest professional performances, Drake was spotted by Ashley Hutchings, then bass player with the folk-rock group Fairport Convention, who recommended him to Fairport's producer and manager, Joe Boyd. Impressed by the demo tape he was sent, Boyd soon signed him to Island Records, the leading independent record label of the time. Drake's début album, *Five Leaves Left* (1969), featured esteemed musicians such as guitarist Richard Thompson and double bass player Danny Thompson and lavish string arrangements by Drake's Cambridge contemporary Robert Kirby. The album attracted favourable reviews on its release, but sold few copies.

Drake was strikingly good-looking and charismatic, with trademark shoulder-length hair. He had been happy enough to play live in public while in groups at Marlborough College but the concerts he gave to promote his début recording showed him as a reluctant solo performer. Contemporary accounts speak of a shy figure, clearly uncomfortable in front of an audience; and in that pre-video age when live shows were the only way for new artists to be seen, his continued reluctance to perform inevitably restricted his audience. No live footage of Drake's few performances survives.

For his second album, *Bryter Layter* (1970), Drake was accompanied by Fairport Convention's Dave Pegg and Dave Mattacks, and the Velvet Underground's John Cale. The record was a musical triumph which on its release drew favourable comparisons with Van Morrison's *Astral Weeks* (1968), and nearly thirty years later was hailed by *The Guardian* as the greatest cult album ever made. Drake himself was convinced that this was the record that would help him achieve the success he longed for. But he faced tough competition from the many other singer–songwriters: Leonard Cohen, Joni Mitchell, Neil Young, Cat Stevens, Elton John, Carole King, James Taylor. They were reaching their peak at the same time, and this, together with a lack of radio airplay, sparse press interest, and his growing distaste for live performance, resulted once again in low sales.

Disillusioned by the commercial failure of his first two records and the decision of his manager, Joe Boyd, to relocate to America, Drake became more silent and withdrawn and friends began to notice the first signs of the depression which eventually killed him. Despite his increasingly fragile state, he found the inner strength to make one last album, *Pink Moon* (1972). Recorded totally solo and in just two brief sessions, this stark and haunting collection has been praised posthumously as the best of Drake's three albums, but at the time it suffered the same commercial ignomy as its predecessors.

In 1972, with his depression deepening and his career effectively over, Drake left London in despair and returned to the family home in Warwickshire, where he spent the rest of his life. Shocked by their son's condition, his parents sought medical help and soon after his return home Drake spent five weeks in a local psychiatric hospital. But on his release the depression persisted and he was forced, reluctantly, to rely on the drugs prescribed by his psychiatrist.

In 1974 Drake went into the studio for one last time. He spent a day recording, hoping that this would be the start of his fourth album, but what emerged from that session were the four final tracks of his life: 'Rider on the Wheel', 'Black Eyed Dog', 'Hanging on a Star', and 'Voice from the Mountain'. That autumn his parents were delighted when he announced he was going to Paris to visit some friends and to see the chanteuse Françoise Hardy, who had earlier expressed interest in recording some of his work. However, any improvement was short-lived and within weeks of returning home he was dead. It was in his childhood bedroom at Far Leys, Bates Lane, in Tanworth in Arden, Warwickshire, that Drake's mother found the body of her only son on the morning of 25 November 1974. He had overdosed on Tryptizol, one of the powerful antidepressants he had been prescribed to help fight his illness. The coroner's verdict was suicide, although many who knew him remain convinced that the overdose was accidental. He was buried in St Mary Magdelene churchyard, Tanworth in Arden. He was unmarried.

Thereafter Drake's parents received a steady stream of visitors to Far Leys. The cult burgeoned in 1979 with the release of the box-set *Fruit Tree*, which included the final four tracks recorded in 1974, which had previously remained unreleased. A subsequent posthumous collection, *Time of No Reply* (1987), and the compilations *Heaven in a Wild Flower* (1990) and *Way to Blue* (1994) have all further enhanced Drake's musical legacy.

Nick Drake has been called the first singer–songwriter whose career began after he died; while other fatalities such as Jimi Hendrix, Jim Morrison, and John Lennon enjoyed a posthumous resurgence of interest in their work, they had all achieved a considerable degree of fame prior to their deaths, whereas during his lifetime Drake's music was known only to a select few. In later years he was cited as an influence by such major talents as REM, Blur, Radiohead, Paul Weller, and Lucinda Williams; to this day guitarists remain mesmerized by his inimitable technique and listeners are drawn in by his intimate, essentially English style of singing. In 2000 a prize-winning short documentary film, *A Skin too Few*, was made about his life and music, and his songs are increasingly heard on film soundtracks. But his biggest commercial breakthrough came during 1998, when Volkswagen used the song 'Pink Moon' in an American television commercial. In the weeks following its first airing American sales of the eponymous album outstripped those for Drake's entire output during his lifetime. A quarter of a century after his death Nick Drake had achieved the success and recognition which had eluded him during his short life.

PATRICK HUMPHRIES

Sources P. Humphries, *Nick Drake: the biography* (1997) • K. Danielsson, nickdrake.net, 212.209.231.144/nickdrake/default. asp, 19 April 2002
Archives SOUND 'Fruit tree - the Nick Drake story', first broadcast on Radio 2, 20 June 1998
Likenesses K. Morris, photograph
Wealth at death £4394: administration, 24 Jan 1975, *CGPLA Eng. & Wales*

Drake, Richard (1609–1681), Church of England clergyman, was born in the parish of St Peter Westcheap, London, on 21 April 1609, the second son of Roger Drake (d. 1650/51), a London mercer, and his wife, Margaret, daughter of John Allyn of Uttoxeter. He was educated at Eppingham from 1616 to 1624, until in June that year he was admitted to Pembroke College, Cambridge. He was elected Greek scholar in 1626, and graduated BA in 1627, MA in 1631, BD in 1639, and DD in 1661. In 1631 he was elected a fellow of his college, which had become well known for espousing anti-Calvinistic beliefs and practices. Drake was one of several younger scholars closely associated with and profoundly influenced by Lancelot Andrewes and Matthew Wren. In 1635 he contributed Latin verses to the preface of Robert Shelford's *Five Pious and Learned Discourses*, a tract whose arguments for free will and Laudian ceremonial made it notorious. In 1640 a report for the House of Commons on religious innovation at the university described Drake as an 'active and forward man to promote the new practises' and listed him among those who 'gave great offence in theire sermons' (BL, Harley MS 7019, fol. 63). In 1639 Drake had preached on Romans 2: 22 on the provocative theme that those who abhor idols commit sacrilege.

Drake was ordained in 1635, and was licensed to preach in Norwich diocese by Matthew Wren in 1636. In 1638 he became rector of the Essex parish of Radwinter, a living to which his father had purchased the right of presentation. Drake set about repairing and decorating the church in accordance with his advanced ceremonialist beliefs. This deeply offended the puritans among his parishioners and precipitated a violent conflict. Drake's manuscript account of that conflict, 'Affronts and insolencies com-[m]itted in the parish of Radwinter, against the divine service, and the ministers therof', provides one of the most detailed accounts of the troubles suffered by a royalist clergyman in the prelude to, and during, the English civil war. Trouble began in 1640 when the images erected by Drake were destroyed by a group of soldiers who, finding Drake absent from the parish, were reported to have thrown the head of a duck into the church, saying, 'they would serve the Drake so if they could Catch him' (BL, Add. MS 21935, fol. 89r). Drake's response, repeating for the benefit of his parishioners the provocative sermon he gave in 1639, betrays something of the combative character which contributed to his problems.

After a series of clashes with his parishioners Drake was forced to flee Radwinter in 1643. Following his ejection he lived in London, where he met and on 29 May 1654 married Jane Lambert (d. 1662), a widow; shortly thereafter he moved to Richmond, Surrey. His Latin autobiography, covering his life to 1658, detailed what he saw as his continuing political persecution at the hands of parliament and its committees. His elder brother, Roger *Drake, a physician and later a presbyterian minister, was able to use his good offices to offer him some protection. But in 1651 both brothers were arrested and briefly imprisoned for their supposed part in the conspiracy to help the Scots bring Charles II to the throne of England. The plot, in which their brother William Drake was a ringleader, became known as Love's plot—after the principal victim of official retribution, Christopher Love. Drake's autobiography also offers valuable evidence of the successful attempt of loyalists in the revolution to continue to live their lives by the rites of the Anglican church. In 1647 Drake had an audience with the king, and in 1648 he dedicated to the future Charles II his translation of Andrewes's Greek prayers—*A Manual of the Private Devotions and Meditations of the Right Reverend Father in God Lancelot Andrews*—Andrewes's great testament to prayer-centred piety.

After the Restoration Drake came into his own. Restored to his living of Radwinter, he became a chaplain to Charles II. In September 1662, shortly after the death of his wife, he was collated prebendary of Alton Borealis in Salisbury Cathedral. He was chancellor from 1663 until his death. Drake resigned at Radwinter in 1667, and when he died on 16 October 1681 he was also rector of Wyke Regis, Dorset. He was buried in Salisbury Cathedral.

JOHN WALTER

Sources Latin autobiography, Bodl. Oxf., MS Rawl. D. 158 • *Walker rev.* • Venn, *Alum. Cant.* • BL, Add. MS 21935, fol. 89r • will, PRO, PROB 11/368, sig. 161 • *The visitation of London, anno Domini 1633, 1634, and 1635, made by Sir Henry St George*, 1, ed. J. J. Howard and J. L. Chester, Harleian Society, 15 (1880) • BL, Harley MS 7019, fols. 52–93 • *A manual of the private devotions and meditations of the Right Reverent Father in God Lancelot Andrews*, trans. R. D. [R. Drake] (1648) • *Calamy rev.* • H. Smith, *The ecclesiastical history of Essex under the Long Parliament and Commonwealth* [1933] • *Mr Love's case …* (1651) • *Fasti Angl., 1541–1857*, [Salisbury] • PRO, PROB 11/221, sig. 55, fols. 37r–38r [will of Roger Drake]
Archives Bodl. Oxf., Latin autobiography, MS Rawl. D. 158 • Pembroke Cam., Notae MSS in *Nicetae Chonitae*, etc.
Wealth at death approx. £1500; also left property in London: PRO, PROB 11/368, sig. 161

Drake, Roger (1608–1669), physician and minister of religion, was born in London, the eldest son of Roger Drake (d. 1650/51), a wealthy mercer of Cheapside, London, and his wife, Margaret Allyn, of Uttoxeter, Staffordshire. Richard *Drake was his younger brother. He received his early education from the London schoolmaster Thomas Farnaby, and went on to matriculate at Pembroke College, Cambridge, in 1624. He became a scholar in 1626, and graduated BA in 1628, and MA in 1631. His movements between 1631 and 1638, when he entered as a medical student at Leiden, are unclear. Drake was strongly drawn to puritan theology and the presbyterian form of church government, so a career in the Anglican church was unlikely; he may have continued to read medicine at Cambridge, perhaps influenced by Francis Glisson, who became regius professor of physic there in 1636. It is not unlikely that he practised medicine in or around Cambridge, or possibly in London, or its environs. Glisson's students were already beginning to discuss William Harvey's theory of the circulation of the blood in their disputations. This trend continued at Leiden among the medical students of Professor Waleus, of whom Drake was one of the first to defend the circulation, drawing in 1640 the *Animadversiones* of an old Harveian enemy, James Primrose. Returning to London in 1640, Drake wrote a Latin vindication of his ideas, Waleus, and the circulation, all directed against Primrose's attack: *Vindiciae contra animadversiones d.d. Primirosii*. Drake had hoped for the official approval of the College of Physicians, London, but the college maintained a studied neutrality in its meeting of 19 April 1641. Drake published his vindication later that year, and it was reprinted at Leiden in 1647, along with other authors' contributions relevant to the Harveian debate, all under the title *Recentiorum disceptationes*.

In his student years at Leiden Drake published at least three sets of medical theses—the first on the circulation; the second, *De tremore*; and the last, *De convulsione*, which earned him his Leiden MD on 18 September 1640. His long list of dedicatees, prefixed to these theses, indicated the strength of his theological and presbyterian sympathies. There were at least five ministers listed as friends and relatives, the most notable being the Revd Francis Cheynell, one of the greatest presbyterian polemicists of the seventeenth century. Also notable among Drake's friends and dedicatees were Nathaniel and John Fiennes, the sons of the puritan earl of Saye and Sele. The former led the presbyterian effort to abolish episcopacy in the parliament of 1641, and may have been the unnamed nobleman Wood spoke of who rescued Drake from complicity in the royalist plot of Christopher Love in 1651.

Drake was back in London by 3 December 1640, at which time he was first examined, successfully, by the College of Physicians. Eventually, on 22 December 1643 (presumably after incorporating his Leiden degree at Cambridge), Drake was elected a candidate of the college. He attended college meetings in 1644 and 1645, but on 4 December 1646, in a letter from his house in Seething Lane, he resigned his candidacy, 'with much profession of humility and thanks' (annals, 1646, bk 3, 567). The English church became presbyterian by law in 1646: this must have appeared to Drake like a dream come true, a dream whose practical implementation he very much wanted to be a part of, as an administrator, a minister, or a theoretician.

Drake was by this time a husband and a father. Shortly after his return to London in 1640 he had married Susan Middlemore (d. 1680), younger daughter of a 'pious' London merchant, Samuel Middlemore. They had one son, Roger Drake, and four daughters, at least two of whom, Sarah and Mary, were unmarried at the time of his death. Middlemore's eldest daughter, Mary, had also married a

puritan physician, Edmund Trench, in 1639. The brothers-in-law Drake and Trench remained friends for life. Drake also had a strong influence on Trench's son, Edmund Trench, who, like many who knew Drake, admired his sincerity and humility, and followed his example in becoming a nonconformist minister. Drake's best-known published work as a minister was *Sacred Chronologie* (1648). Dedicated to his father, and to his uncle, Thomas Burnell, it is a history of the world, drawn out of scripture, from the creation to the death of Christ. Drake's decision to leave medicine for the ministry in 1646 is described in the dedication as being 'the last great turn in my life, wherein I seemed unto many a sign and a wonder, by relinquishing that honourable profession of physic, to attend upon a higher calling (though very mean in the eyes of the world)'.

Drake's duties in 1649 included that of scribe to the Presbyterian London Provincial Assembly. In 1650 he was elected by its parishioners rector of St Peter Westcheap, London, but he did not formally take office until the death of the last incumbent in 1653. In that year he also served as moderator of the London Assembly. Along with other defendants he was pardoned for life and estate for his role in Love's plot of 1651, but not before his imprisonment for nearly a month in the Tower of London.

Always respected for his intelligence, judgement, and character, Drake served on the London commission of 1654; was commissioner for the approbation of ministers in 1660; and as a commissioner was selected as a representative to the Savoy Conference in 1660, although he did not attend. He was ejected from his living at St Peter Westcheap in the same year, but continued occasionally to preach and serve Presbyterians at St Giles-in-the-Fields and at Cripplegate. He maintained a house in Burnham, Kent, and also had a newly built house in Cheapside at the time of his death in 1669. Drake was admired by the great Presbyterian leaders Richard Baxter and Samuel Annesley, the latter also giving his funeral sermon, which was filled with praise for Drake's piety and learning. He tithed regularly for the poor. Drake was also the author of two pieces of controversial literature: *A Boundary to the Holy Mount, or, A Barre Against Free Admission to the Lord's Supper* (1653); and a later rejoinder, *The Barre Against Free Admission to the Lord's Supper Fixed* (1656).

Towards the end of his life Drake retired to Stepney, Middlesex, where he seems to have also practised medicine. He died and was buried there in the summer of 1669. His will, dated 24 July 1669, in which he mentions properties in Ireland, was proved on 12 August following (PRO, PROB 11/330/93). His wife survived him.

WILLIAM BIRKEN

Sources annals, RCP Lond., 3.567 · Munk, *Roll* · Venn, *Alum. Cant.* · G. Clark and A. M. Cooke, *A history of the Royal College of Physicians of London*, 1 (1964) · R. W. Innes Smith, *English-speaking students of medicine at the University of Leyden* (1932) · Wood, *Ath. Oxon.* · R. French, 'Harvey in Holland: circulation and the Calvinists', *The medical revolution of the seventeenth century*, ed. R. French and A. Wear (1989) · *New England Historical and Genealogical Register* (1847) · C. Hill, 'William Harvey and the idea of monarchy', *Past and Present*, 27 (1964), 54–72 · *Some remarkable passages in the holy life and death* *of the late Reverend Mr Edmund Trench, most of them drawn out of his own diary*, ed. [J. Boyse] (1693) • *The obituary of Richard Smyth ... being a catalogue of all such persons as he knew in their life*, ed. H. Ellis, CS, 44 (1849) • *The visitation of London, anno Domini 1633, 1634, and 1635, made by Sir Henry St George*, 2, ed. J. J. Howard, Harleian Society, 17 (1883) • *Calamy rev.* • will, PRO, PROB 11/330, sig. 93

Drake, Samuel (*bap.* 1622, *d.* 1679), Church of England clergyman, was born in Pontefract and was baptized on 29 September 1622, the first of the three children of Nathan Drake (1587–1658) of Halifax and Elizabeth Higgins (*d.* 1672) of Hardwick, Pontefract. His was an old family of west Yorkshire yeomen, and about 1633–7 his father bought a small estate near Halifax called Godley. From there Samuel was sent to Pocklington School and was admitted a pensioner to St John's College, Cambridge, on 26 June 1637. He became a Dowman scholar in November and graduated BA in 1641. In 1643 he was admitted a fellow of St John's by royal mandate, and in 1644 received the degree of MA. Shortly afterwards he was ejected from his fellowship for refusing to take the covenant. Drake then joined the royalist 'marching army and the garrison of Pontefract and of Newark until the close of the war' (PRO, SP 29/44, fol. 25 I). His father, also at Pontefract, described the siege of 1644–5 in his diary. On 12 May 1647 Drake became the first priest to receive clandestine ordination from Thomas Fuller, bishop of Ardfert, and was soon followed by many other candidates, including his college friend John Lake, from Halifax. About the same time Drake married Jane Abbot (*d.* 1701), daughter of Robert Abbot of Whitwood, near Pontefract. They had eight children and were the grandparents of the antiquaries Samuel Drake and Francis Drake. Although Nathan Drake took the covenant and oath in 1647 in order to retain his estate, Samuel remained a disaffected royalist. He served as curate at South Kirkby, Yorkshire, 1650–59. In 1651 the parliament ordered him and several other ministers to be tried by the high court of justice on suspicion of conspiracy, but he obviously evaded punishment.

At the Restoration, partly in recognition of his father's loyalty, Drake was presented to the living of Pontefract, which the family retained for three generations. (A family connection with that parish continued through its Fothergill lectureship until 1821.) Drake and John Lake, then vicar of Leeds, travelled together to London and Cambridge, successfully petitioning the king to issue royal mandates for their degrees of DD. Their service in the king's army had interrupted the normal course of their studies, so degrees were an inexpensive way to repay the royal debt. In 1669 Drake delivered two assize sermons in York, published the following year as *Totum hominis*, a sermon on justice, mercy, and humility, drawn from Micah 6: 8, and as *Theou Diakonos, or, The Civil Deacon's Sacred Power*, a sermon on Romans 13: 6, full of royalist zeal. In the same year (1670) Drake and Lake were both collated to prebends at Southwell, from which Drake resigned in 1672 after receiving the rectory of Hansworth near Sheffield, which he held from 1671 to 1678. In 1677 Drake and Lake, meeting at York Minster, decided to correct the many spurious editions of cavalier poems written by their

Cambridge mentor, John Cleveland, and jointly published *Clievelandi vindiciae*, a vehement tribute to their college as well as to the bombastic loyalism of their tutor. Samuel Drake died two years later on 3 April 1679 at Pontefract under mysterious circumstances, including rumours of poisoning, and was buried at All Saints' Church, Pontefract. He was succeeded by his son Francis Drake MA (1654–1713), who helped John Walker compile his *Sufferings of the Clergy*.   H. H. POOLE

Sources DNB • J. Watson, *The history and antiquities of the parish of Halifax, in Yorkshire* (1775), 248–50 • J. S. Fletcher, 'Nathan Drake', *Yorkshiremen of the Restoration* (1921), 11–28 • T. Baker, *History of the college of St John the Evangelist, Cambridge*, ed. J. E. B. Mayor, 2 vols. (1869) • J. E. B. Mayor and R. F. Scott, eds., *Admissions to the College of St John the Evangelist in the University of Cambridge*, 3 vols. in 4 pts (1882–1931) • Venn, *Alum. Cant.* • W. H. D. Longstaffe, introduction to Nathan Drake's diary, *Miscellanea*, SurtS, 37 (1861), iii–xix • *Walker rev.*, 40 • J. Hunter, *Familiae minorum gentium*, ed. J. W. Clay, 4 vols., Harleian Society, 37–40 (1894–6) • B. Morris and E. Withington, 'Introduction', *The poems of John Cleveland*, ed. B. Morris and E. Withington (1967) • J. Ogen, 'Langley's Farm, Hipperholme', *Papers read before the Halifax Antiquarian Society* (1906), 88–91 • C. E. Davies, 'Robert Anderson, Restoration bishop: his administration of the diocese of Lincoln, 1660–1663', BLitt diss., U. Oxf., 1969, 179 • PRO, SP 29/44 • Southwell Minster library, Southwell, Nottinghamshire, act book 6, 138, 140 • supplications and mandates, CUL, department of manuscripts and university archives • parish register, Halifax, Wakefield RO • parish register, Pontefract, Wakefield RO • will, 2 Dec 1658, proved, 6 Feb 1659, Borth. Inst. • institution books, PRO, E331 • calendar of the committee for compounding, 3.1746 ordination, Borth. Inst., MS R/IV/C/13, fol. 31 • Bodl. Oxf., MS Top Yorks c.18, fols. 126, 130 • R. Tangye, 'J. Potkin to S. Drake. 9 Aug. 1642', *The two protectors* (1899), 56

Likenesses A. Birrell, line engraving, BM, NPG

Drake, Samuel (1687/8–1753), antiquary, was born in Pontefract and baptized on 23 April 1688, the son of Francis Drake, vicar of Pontefract, and elder brother of the historian Francis *Drake (*bap.* 1696, *d.* 1771). His grandfather was Samuel *Drake (*bap.* 1622, *d.* 1679). After being educated at Sedbergh School, Drake was admitted sizar at St John's College, Cambridge, aged sixteen, on 4 May 1704, and graduated BA in 1707; he proceeded MA in 1711, BD in 1718, and DD in 1724. He was ordained deacon on 5 March 1710, priest on 16 June 1717, and was a fellow of St John's from 1710 to 1735. He was vicar of Hutton-Buscel, Yorkshire, from 1722 to 1728, when he became rector of Treeton, Yorkshire; in 1733 he also became vicar of Holme-on-Spalding Moor. On 21 October 1734 he married Elizabeth, daughter of Darcy Dalton, at St Benet Paul's Wharf, London.

In 1720, while a fellow at St John's, Drake issued a proposal to reprint Archbishop Matthew Parker's great work on ecclesiastical antiquities. This was printed in 1729 by William Bowyer under the title of *Matthaei Parker ... de antiquitate Britannicae ecclesiae*, and the work contained twenty-three new folio copperplates. Drake also edited several Latin discourses to the clergy, defending himself in 1721 against a reply to one of these by Thomas Wagstaffe the nonjuror. He died on 5 March 1753 and was buried in Treeton church.

JOHN WESTBY-GIBSON, *rev.* J. A. MARCHAND

Sources Venn, *Alum. Cant.* · Nichols, *Lit. anecdotes*, 1.171, 193, 204, 243, 414, 420–21, 550 · B. Boothroyd, *The history of the antient borough of Pontefract* (1807), 369 · J. Hunter, *Hallamshire: the history and topography of the parish of Sheffield in the county of York*, new edn, ed. A. Gatty (1869), 495

Drake, William (*bap.* 1723, *d.* 1801), antiquary and philologist, was the second surviving son of Francis *Drake (*bap.* 1696, *d.* 1771), historian, and Mary Woodyear (1692/3–1728), third daughter of George Woodyear of Crook Hill, near Doncaster. He was born in York and baptized at St Michael-le-Belfry, York, on 10 January 1723. He matriculated at Christ Church, Oxford, on 21 March 1741, graduated BA on 19 October 1744, and took holy orders.

For a few years Drake was third master of Westminster School until 1750, when he was appointed master of Felsted grammar school, Essex. In 1764 he became rector of Layer Marney in the same county. He continued to hold both appointments until 1777, when he became vicar of Isleworth, Middlesex.

Drake was elected a fellow of the Society of Antiquaries on 29 March 1770. Between 1777 and 1789 he contributed six papers to *Archaeologia*, four of which were on the origins of the English language. The fifth paper was a description of two Roman stations in Essex and the sixth an account of some discoveries in Brotherton church, Yorkshire.

Drake died at Isleworth vicarage, Middlesex, on 13 May 1801.   Gordon Goodwin, *rev.* J. A. Marchand

Sources Nichols, *Illustrations*, 4.620 · C. R. J. Currie and C. P. Lewis, eds., *English county histories: a guide* (1994), 452 · *GM*, 1st ser., 20 (1750), 237 · *GM*, 1st ser., 71 (1801), 574 · Nichols, *Lit. anecdotes*, 2.87 · D. Lysons, *The environs of London*, 3 (1795), 108 · D. Lysons, *Supplement to the first edition of 'The environs of London'* (1811), 204 · [R. Gough?], *A list of the members of the Society of Antiquaries of London, from their revival in 1717, to 19 June 1796* (1798), 23 · Foster, *Alum. Oxon.* · R. Davies, 'Memoir of Francis Drake', *Yorkshire Archaeological and Topographical Journal*, 3 (1873–4), 33–54 · G. J. Aungier, *The history and antiquities of Syon Monastery, the parish of Isleworth, and the chapelry of Hounslow* (1840), 145, 161, 183 · P. Morant, *The history and antiquities of the county of Essex*, 1 (1768), 409; 2 (1768), 421

Likenesses W. Bromley, line engraving (after N. Drake), BM, NPG

Drakoules [*née* Lambe; *other married name* Lewis], **Alice Marie** (*c.*1850–1933), humanitarian and campaigner for animal welfare, was born near Brussels, the daughter of Henry Lambe. In 1876 she married William Burrows Lewis (*b.* 1820/21), the managing director of the Union Assurance Company. They adopted a daughter. After Lewis's death, on 9 October 1907 she married Platon Eustathios Drakoules (*b.* 1857/8), a journalist, sociologist, and former member of the Greek parliament. Like her, he lived his life according to humanitarian principles, and was a founder of the Greek Anti-Carnivore Society.

Alice Drakoules was a lifelong humanitarian, vegetarian, and campaigner for animals. As Mrs Lewis in 1887 in Weybridge in Surrey she founded the Band of Mercy, the children's group within the Royal Society for the Prevention of Cruelty to Animals (RSPCA). In 1891 her London home by Regent's Park became a meeting place for representatives of intellectual and spiritual movements. She played a key role in establishing the Humanitarian League, founded by Henry Salt, to 'prevent the perpetration of cruelty and wrong—to redress the suffering, as far as is possible, of all sentient life' (Henry Salt, *Humanitarianism*, 1893, 15). She hosted its inaugural meeting in her fashionable London home and was treasurer of the league at its inception and at its demise in 1919. Although she was known primarily neither for her writing nor for her public eloquence she co-ordinated the work of the league, and was a member of its executive committee for most of its history. When former members of the Humanitarian League regrouped in the 1920s to organize the League for the Prohibition of Cruel Sports (which still exists as the League against Cruel Sports) she was one of its earliest supporters.

Alice Drakoules was also a founder member of the executive council of the Animal Defence and Anti-Vivisection Society, initiated by Louise Lind af Hageby in 1906 to campaign against all forms of cruelty to animals, and remained a member until her death nearly thirty years later. According to her colleague Nina, duchess of Hamilton, in her twenty-seven years of service she scarcely missed a meeting. She was particularly active in the society's campaigns for humane slaughter and the establishment of municipal slaughterhouses, and for legislation to prohibit the use of performing animals.

Alice Drakoules was known for her unswerving commitment to principled, but often unpopular, causes. Her circle of friends and acquaintances included the leading animal rights' activists of her day and the spiritualists Edward Maitland and Anna Kingsford. She subsequently joined the circle of Nina, duchess of Hamilton, and Louise Lind af Hageby with whom she campaigned for many years.

Through her behind the scenes work and steady influence Alice Drakoules was seen as a 'spiritual mother' of the humanitarian movement. She died on 15 January 1933 at her London home, 14 Park Square East, Regent's Park. Four years after her death her friends erected an appropriate memorial to her in St John's Wood churchyard, near where she had lived most of her life. As the inscription on it tells, she was 'for forty years a devoted and generous worker in London for animal welfare' (memorial inscription, St John's Wood churchyard gardens). The bird-bath memorial depicts a range of animals—fox, stag, squirrel, horse, bird, cat, dog, and heron—which appropriately epitomizes her concern for the broad spectrum of animals and her opposition to all forms of hunting and experimentation on animals. Alice Drakoules is less well known than many of her Humanitarian League colleagues, but the work and influence of the organization owed much to her commitment and unflinching support.   Hilda Kean

Sources H. Kean, *Animal rights: political and social change in Britain since 1800* (1998) · *Cruel Sports*, 8/5 (May 1934), 18 · *Cruel Sports* (July 1927), 80 · *Annual Report* [Humanitarian League], 3 (1893) · *Annual Report* [Animal Defence and Anti-Vivisection Society] (1933) · *Annual Report* [Animal Defence and Anti-Vivisection Society] (1937) · *Annual Report* [Animal Defence and Anti-Vivisection Society] (1938) · *Cruel Sports*, 1/2 (Feb 1927) · memorial inscription, London, St John's Wood, St John's Wood churchyard gardens · m.

cert. · d. cert. · census returns, 1881 · census returns, 1901 · index of marriages, freebmd.rootsweb.com

Wealth at death £16,061 11s. 3d.: probate, 1 March 1933, *CGPLA Eng. & Wales*

Drane, Augusta Theodosia [*name in religion* Francis Raphael] (1823–1894), prioress of Stone and author, born at Bromley St Leonard's, Middlesex, on 28 December 1823, was the youngest daughter of Thomas Drane, managing partner in an East India mercantile house, and his wife, Cecilia, *née* Harding. Her father, who was widely travelled, had amassed a large library and collection of curiosities, and it was from these two sources that Drane developed a precocious reading ability and interest in the natural sciences. Drane's formal education was received at home from governesses and for two years at a school in Kensington conducted by a Miss James. When she was fourteen years old the family moved to Babbacombe in Devon. Brought up in the established church she soon came under the influence of Tractarian teaching at Torquay, and in June 1850 was received into the Roman Catholic church at Tiverton. In the same year she published anonymously a pamphlet entitled *The Morality of Tractarianism*, which has sometimes been attributed to Newman. Soon after her conversion Drane first made the acquaintance of the Dominican sisters at Clifton, whose convent had been founded several years earlier at Coventry by Margaret Hallahan. In the autumn of 1851 Drane went to Rome where she spent six months. On her return Mother Margaret Hallahan received her as a postulant in the Dominican convent at Clifton. She was clothed in the habit on 7 December 1852, receiving the name Sister Francis Raphael. The following year the noviciate was transferred to the new mother house of the congregation at Stone, Staffordshire. Here she professed her vows on 8 December 1853.

From the time of her entry into the community Drane's intellectual gifts were encouraged. In 1857 she produced her first major work, *The Life of St Dominic*, and before 1872 nine further works appeared, including a *History of England for Family Use* (1864), which went through six editions; her masterpiece, *Christian Schools and Scholars* (1867); and *The Life of Mother Margaret Mary Hallahan*, which appeared in 1869, only months after the founder's death. Drane was appointed novice mistress in 1860 and mistress of studies three years later. In 1872 she was elected prioress of Stone, and for the next nine years her administrative obligations limited her publications to a volume of poetry and *The History of St Catherine of Siena and her Companions*, which was published in 1880 to mark the 500th anniversary of the saint's death. In November of the following year she was elected to succeed Mother Mary Imelda Poole as mother provincial of the order, an office which she held until shortly before her death.

In addition to directing some 150 religious sisters in four convents engaged in a wide variety of works, Drane found time to write several works of fiction, a series of school readers in five volumes, and a second biography of St Dominic, and also produced editions of the autobiography and letters of Bishop Ullathorne. Her final work, *The*

Augusta Theodosia Drane (1823–1894), by Netterville Briggs

Spirit of the Dominican Order (1896), was published two years after her death. Besides her own writing, she also translated several French works, most notably Père Cocharne's biography of the French Dominican Lacordaire. This work, in common with others, was completed while supervising the evening study of the girls in the boarding-school at Stone. A number of her own works were, in turn, translated into French, German, and Italian.

As a religious superior Drane was committed to deepening the intellectual and liturgical life of the community along traditional Dominican lines. Several notebooks of instructions given to the community, circular letters to the various convents, and hundreds of letters to friends inside and outside the order testify to her remarkably wide range of interests. Nor were her intellectual development and interests limited to the sacred sphere. Her correspondence shows that she was equally at ease discussing Shelley's *Lament* or other contemporary works of literature, philosophy, or even politics. She was curious to know about George Eliot, and read the three volumes of journals and letters edited by Cross and published in 1885. Despite being unable to sympathize entirely with Eliot's aims or principles as expressed in her works, she clearly recognized her genius. Drane also possessed artistic talent: an album in the archives at Stone shows caricatures and cartoons in strikingly modern style, full of movement; many of the subjects are clearly recognizable. Her breadth of vision, spiritual insight, and intellectual rigour place Drane in the vanguard of nineteenth-century Dominican revival. Her scholarship anticipated by many years the development of a strong intellectual tradition among the friars of the English province. Mother Francis Raphael Drane died at the convent in Stone on 29 April 1894 and was interred on 1 May in the choir of the conventual church alongside Mother Margaret Hallahan.

ANSELM NYE

Sources B. Willberforce, *A memoir of Mother Francis Raphael, O.S.D.* (1895) · *The conventual third order of St Dominic and its development in England, by a Dominican of Stone* (1923), 55–7
Archives St Dominic's Convent, Stone, Staffordshire, archives of the English Dominican Sisters, corresp. and papers
Likenesses Netterville Briggs, photograph, St Dominic's Convent, Stone [*see illus.*] · photographs, St Dominic's Convent, Stone

Drant, Thomas (*c.*1540–1578), poet and Church of England clergyman, was born at Hagworthingham, Lincolnshire, the son of Thomas Drant, a farmer. He matriculated as a pensioner at St John's College, Cambridge, on 18 March 1558, probably aged about eighteen, and became a protégé of Richard Curteys, one of the fellows and later bishop of Chichester. Drant graduated early in 1561, became himself a fellow of St John's on 21 March that year on Dr Thimbleby's foundation, and proceeded MA in 1564. When Queen Elizabeth visited the university in August, he presented her with copies of verses he had composed in English, Greek, and Latin. At the commencement of 1565 he performed a public exercise on the doctrinal issue 'Corpus Christi non est ubique'; this later appeared in his *Medicinable Morall*.

Drant's first published work was *Impii cuiusdam epigrammatis quod edidit R. Shacklockus in mortem Cuthberti Scoti apomaxis, also certayne of the speciall articles of the epigramme, refuted in Englyshe* (1565), an anti-Catholic commentary on the translation of Richard Shacklock's epitaph for Cuthbert Scott, sometime bishop of Chester, composed earlier that year. There followed a translation of Horace, *A Medicinable Morall, that is, the Two Bookes of Horace his Satyres Englyshed* (1566), albeit with Horace's book 5 replaced by Drant's own anti-Catholic satire. In 1567 he published a translation of Horace's *Epistula ad Pisones*, under the title *Horace his Arte of poetrie, Pistles and Satyrs Englished, and to the earle of Ormounte by T. Drant addressed*, which incorporates the earlier translations of the satires. Here Drant was breaking new literary ground. Translations of the first five books of the *Iliad*, the Psalms, and the 'Book of Solomons proverbs, epigrams, and sentences spirituall', remained unpublished, although the last was licensed for the press in 1567. In 1568 Drant published *Epigrams and Sentences Spirituall in Vers*, a translation of Gregory of Nazianzus. Although epigrams in Latin had been published in the early sixteenth century by Sir Thomas More and others, followed about 1550 by English ones in the native tradition of Piers Plowman by John Heywood and Robert Crowley, Drant's efforts brought the classical epigram and the English language together, anticipating what later became a fashionable Elizabethan genre

employed by many better-known poets, such as Ben Jonson. Francis Meres's treatise *Poetrie* lists Drant among those who wrote epigrams in English.

Meanwhile Drant had been singled out for high ecclesiastical preferment. At some point during the 1560s he became a domestic chaplain to Edmund Grindal, bishop of London, and was appointed divinity reader in St Paul's. In May 1569 he was collated to the vicarage of St Giles Cripplegate by the dean and chapter of St Paul's. Admitted BTh at Cambridge the same year, he was collated to the prebend of Chamberlainwood in St Paul's by Grindal on 2 July. On 8 January 1570 he preached before the court at Windsor, inveighing against the vanity of secular attire. Drant's close relationship with Curteys, now dean of Chichester, further advanced his career. At the end of January 1570 he was admitted rector of Slinfold, Sussex, and prebendary of Firle in Chichester Cathedral. Then on 4 March he was installed archdeacon of Lewes, despite competition from William Overton, the cathedral treasurer and later bishop of Coventry and Lichfield. On 4 April Drant attended the chapter meeting which elected Curteys as bishop of Chichester, subsequently announcing the outcome. At Easter that year he preached at St Mary Spital in London, denouncing the worldly ways of the citizenry. On 15 July 1571, in recognition of his preaching skills, the Chichester chapter granted Drant's petition for maintenance in the city, despite the bitter feud that had developed between Curteys and Overton factions within its ranks. Thwarted over the archdeaconry, Overton had subsequently made suit for the bishopric, and then for the vacant deanery after Curteys's elevation. Drant attacked him from the pulpit for pride, ignorance, and hypocrisy.

Little more can be said of Drant's ecclesiastical career except that he became rector of East Hatley, Cambridgeshire, in 1575. Meanwhile a further translation had appeared, *In Selomonis regis et praeconis illustris ecclesiasten paraphrasis poetica* (1572). Drant also wrote a number of dedicatory verses for the works of others, including the second edition of John Foxe's *Acts and Monuments* (1570). In 1576 he published *Thomae Drantae Angli Advordingamii praesul eiusdem sylva*, dedicated to Grindal, now archbishop of Canterbury, in which he implies that he has given up his classical studies in favour of religious writing, apparently at Grindal's request. Despite his strong connections with Chichester it seems that Drant lived mainly in Cripplegate, at least towards the end of his life. Two daughters, Dorcas and Elizabeth, were baptized there, in 1576 and 1578 respectively. Dorcas was buried on 1 May 1577, and Drant himself on 16 April 1578. Administration of his goods was granted to his widow, Alice. He would appear to have been a heavily built man; Gabriel Harvey makes posthumous reference to him as 'your gorbellyed Maister' and as 'a fat-bellyed Archdeacon' (Smith, 1.97, 118).

Drant drew up a set of rules for the metrification of English poetry. They are not known to have survived, but are mentioned in the correspondence between Edmund Spenser and Gabriel Harvey published in 1580. They were also discussed by Philip Sidney, Edward Dyer, and Fulke Greville and, though finally rejected as a basis for English poetry, must have stimulated poets seeking a new direction. William Ringler has analysed a note in the manuscript of Sidney's *Arcadia* (St John's College, Cambridge, MS 208) which may be Sidney's version of them. Drant's influence is certainly suggested by Spenser's claim in a letter to Harvey (1579) that he had breached Drant's rules in his own verse. But Harvey, though professing himself 'a favorer of his deserved and just commendation', disclaimed all knowledge of such rules (Smith, 1.96–7). In 1580 Spenser mentioned to Harvey the rules that are 'mine, that M. Philip Sidney gave me, being the very same which M. Drant devised, but enlarged with M. Sidneys own judgement, and augmented with my own Observations' (ibid., 1.99). Harvey expressed a desire to see them, although questioning their value. His allusion to the 'Dranting of verses' in *Pierce's Supererogation* is often quoted out of context (ibid., 2.272), but his view of Drant is certainly not negative (*Pierce's Supererogation*, 74, 48, 190–91). Nevertheless Drant's contribution as poets began to experiment and seek new forms was significant, and awaits fuller appreciation.   R. W. MCCONCHIE

Sources DNB · *Fasti Angl., 1541–1857*, [Chichester] · *STC, 1475–1640* · G. G. Smith, *Elizabethan critical essays*, 2 vols. (1937) · N. Mukherjee, 'Thomas Drant's rewriting of Horace', *Studies in English Literature 1500–1900*, 40/1 (2000), 1–20 · Venn, *Alum. Cant.*, 1/2.65 · *Horace his arte of poetrie, pistles, and satyrs Englished* (1567) *by Thomas Drant*, ed. P. E. Medine (1972) · G. Harvey, *Pierce's supererogation* (1593) · W. Ringler, 'Master Drant's rules', *Poetry Quarterly*, 29/1 (1950), 70–74 · *Francis Meres's treatise 'Poetrie': a critical edition*, ed. D. C. Allen (Urbana, IL, 1933) · F. B. Williams, *Index of dedicatory and commendatory verses in English books before 1641* (1962) · C. Burrow, 'Horace at home and abroad: Wyatt and sixteenth century Horatianism', *Horace made new: Horatian influences on British writing from the Renaissance to the twentieth century*, ed. C. Martindale and D. Hopkins (1993), 27–49 · W. D. Peckham, ed., *The acts of the dean and chapter of the cathedral church of Chichester, 1545–1642*, Sussex RS, 53 (1959) · E. Spenser, *Three proper, and wittie, familiar letters* (1580) · administration, PRO, PROB 6/2, fol. 143*v*
Archives GL, MS 6419/1

Drapentier, Jan (*fl.* 1674–1713), engraver, was the son of D. Drapentier or Drappentier, a native of Dordrecht, Netherlands, who engraved some medals commemorative of the great events connected with the reign of William and Mary, and also a print with the arms of the governors of Dordrecht, published by Balen in his *Beschryving van Dordrecht* (1677). Apprenticed in The Hague between 1669 and 1674 and in London by 1674, Jan Drapentier was probably identical with the Johannes Drapentier who, with his wife, Dorothea Tucker, had a son, Johannes, baptized at the Dutch church in Austin Friars on 7 October 1694. At that time he was best known as an engraver of portraits and book illustrations, later judged, somewhat unfairly, to be 'very indifferent' (Strutt, 1.262). Some of his earliest work is represented by the plates and portrait of the author done for William Hopkins's *The Flying Pen-Man* (1674), and he later engraved title-pages for several other books, notably Perkins's *The Seaman's Guide* (1682). He also found topographical work, and engraved views of country seats for Sir Henry Chauncy's illustrated folio *History of Hertfordshire* (1700). Among his portraits, which are executed in a bold and distinctive manner, are *Richard Baxter*,

The Earl of Athlone, Viscount Dundee, Dr Henry Sacheverell, and a group of *The Seven Bishops*. His miscellaneous output included at least one satirical print, *Le beau service*, an allegorical broadside on the theme of the peace of Utrecht (1713), and an ephemeral etching, *A Trew Draught of the Whale as he was Seen at Blackwall-Dock* (*c*.1690). An engraving of the House of Commons (1690) is also probably by him.

Following the example of his father, Jan Drapentier also applied his engraving skills to the production of coins and medals. His earliest medal commemorated the death of Queen Mary in 1694. Later medals, for the peace of Ryswick (1697) and the peace of Utrecht (1713), were produced in response to commissions from the magistrats of Amsterdam and Friesland respectively, and Drapentier can probably be identified with the person who held the post of engraver to the mint at Dordrecht during this period. His date of death is not known.

RICHARD SHARP

Sources Thieme & Becker, *Allgemeines Lexikon* · Vertue, *Note books* · J. Strutt, *A biographical dictionary, containing an historical account of all the engravers, from the earliest period of the art of engraving to the present time*, 2 vols. (1785–6) · E. Hawkins, *Medallic illustrations of the history of Great Britain and Ireland to the death of George II*, ed. A. W. Franks and H. A. Grueber, 2 vols. (1885) · S. O'Connell, *The popular print in England* (1999) · DNB

Draper, Edward Alured (1776–1841), army officer and colonial official, a cousin of General Sir William Draper (1721–1787), was born at Werton, Oxfordshire, on 22 October 1776, and was educated at Eton College, where he showed ability. While there he was made a page of honour to George III, and seems to have acquired the lasting friendship of the king's sons. He was appointed ensign in the 3rd foot guards in 1794, and became a lieutenant and captain in 1796. He served with his regiment in the Netherlands and Egypt. As a brevet major he accompanied Lieutenant-General Grinfield to the West Indies as military secretary in 1802, and brought home the dispatches after the capture of St Lucia in 1803, receiving the customary step and gratuity of £500.

Early in 1806 Sir Thomas Picton, then a brigadier-general, was tried for acts of cruelty allegedly committed during his brief government of Trinidad. Draper, who had known Picton in the West Indies, published *Address to the British Public* (1806), in which, with much irrelevant detail, he accused Picton's two official colleagues in Trinidad, Colonel William Fullarton and the Right Hon. John Sullivan, of wilful and corrupt misrepresentation. Sullivan filed a criminal information for libel against Draper, who was convicted by the court of king's bench and underwent three months' imprisonment; this drew much sympathy from his friends, the first to visit him at Newgate being the prince of Wales, attended by Sir Herbert Taylor.

Draper served with his battalion in the Walcheren expedition, but was afterwards compelled by financial difficulties to sell his commission, despite the efforts of his friends to save it. In 1813 he was appointed chief secretary in the island of Bourbon, and virtually administered the government during the temporary suspension of the acting governor, Colonel Keating. When Bourbon reverted to

France, Draper was transferred to Mauritius and held various posts: chief commissioner of police, acting colonial secretary, acting collector of customs, civil engineer and surveyor-general, registrar of slaves, stipendiary magistrate of Port Louis, and treasurer and paymaster-general. On one occasion his independent line of action displeased the governor, General Hall, who suspended him, but when the case was referred home Draper was reinstated and Hall recalled.

Mauritius was an island of slave-worked sugar plantations, dominated by the planters and their associates. From 1823 to 1835 (when the 1833 Emancipation Act came into force in Mauritius and its dependencies), the imperial government attempted the 'amelioration' of colonial slavery by regulatory legislation. This the Mauritian planters resisted. Following pressure in Britain by members of the Anti-Slavery Society, dissatisfied with 'amelioration' in Mauritius as elsewhere, the British (whig) government in 1832 appointed John Jeremie, a well-known abolitionist, as *procureur général* (public prosecutor) and advocate-general in Mauritius. The slave-owning establishment there rallied against him with Draper, a member of the colony's council, one of the leaders, and Jeremie was forced to leave. However, the imperial government appointed a new governor, General Sir William Nicolay, who, on its instructions, in 1833 dismissed Draper from his appointments. He returned to England, and after an interview with William IV was awarded a pension of £500 a year until another appointment could be found for him in Mauritius. Soon afterwards he was appointed joint stipendiary of Port Louis, and later colonial treasurer and paymaster-general, a post which he held until his death.

Draper was reportedly a man of agreeable manners, apparently had a powerful interest in Britain, and was popular with the slave owners. In his young days he was a gentleman rider, and he inaugurated horse-racing in Mauritius. In 1822 Draper married a Creole woman, Mlle Krivelt; they had several children, two of whom—a son, afterwards in the colonial service, and a daughter, married to General Brooke, son of Sir Richard Brooke, baronet—survived him. Draper died in Mauritius on 22 April 1841.   H. M. CHICHESTER, rev. ROGER T. STEARN

Sources GM, 2nd ser., 16 (1841) · E. Draper, *Address to the British public* (1806) · M. D. E. Nwulia, *The history of slavery in Mauritius and the Seychelles, 1810–1875* (1981)

Draper, Elizabeth (1744–1778). *See under* Sterne, Laurence (1713–1768).

Draper, John William (1811–1882), chemist and historian, was born in St Helens, Lancashire, on 5 May 1811, the third child and only son of John Christopher Draper (*d.* 1828/9), a Wesleyan minister of Heptonstall, Yorkshire, and his wife, Sarah Ripley (*d. c.*1834). It is thought that his father had assumed the surname Draper after being disowned by his Roman Catholic parents following his conversion to Methodism. Draper was educated at Woodhouse Grove School (a Wesleyan Methodist academy near London) and showed early promise in science. From 1829 to 1831 he attended London University, studying chemistry with

Edward Turner. Draper then emigrated to Virginia, where his mother's relatives were already established. He arrived in 1832 accompanied by his mother, his three sisters, and the two children of Daniel Gardener (1775–1831), late physician to the emperor of Brazil. Gardener had befriended the Drapers shortly before his death, while visiting London. In 1836 Draper married Gardener's daughter Antonia Pereira (*d.* 1870); Draper's sister Sarah Ripley married Antonia's brother, Daniel Gardener (1818–1853). Antonia and Daniel's mother may have been Princess Isabella Maria, daughter of John VI of Portugal; some sources say merely that she was of aristocratic background.

Draper's sister Dorothy remained single, and her earnings as a teacher supported him at the University of Pennsylvania. In 1836 he graduated MD and became professor of chemistry and physiology at Hampden Sidney College, Virginia. By 1839, when he moved to the University of New York, Draper had published over a dozen scientific papers, on osmosis, analytical chemistry, galvanism, and photochemistry. He held the New York chair of chemistry until just before his death, often concurrently with other posts. In 1841 he helped found the New York school of medicine, and in 1850 became its president. Multiple appointments and royalties from textbooks were necessary to support the growing family. Draper and his wife had four sons and two daughters, and assumed responsibility for the six children of their brother-in-law Daniel Gardener after his death. The unmarried Draper sisters, Dorothy and Elizabeth, also remained in residence. After Antonia's health deteriorated Dorothy ran the home—at first a town house on Fourth Street, later a spacious country residence at Hastings-on-Hudson, New York state. Family reminiscences depict a happy household. However, Elizabeth quarrelled bitterly with her brother about religion, eventually converting to Catholicism.

Though an opponent of all that he regarded as superstition, Draper was not a thoroughgoing materialist. He declared 'The vital force which pervades the world is what the illiterate call God' (Draper, *History of the Conflict*, 25). An interest in the forces affecting living and non-living matter pervaded his own scientific researches. Early studies of photosynthesis led to other photochemical investigations, and from 1837 he was experimenting with photography. After learning of Daguerre's work in 1839 he attempted to produce a picture of a human subject and succeeded in December 1839 (probably a few weeks after a fellow New Yorker, Alexander Wollcott). An image of his sister Dorothy remains the earliest surviving photographic portrait. During the winter of 1839–40, Draper took the first known photographs of the moon, and remained involved with astronomical photography thereafter. (By 1850 he had also taken some of the earliest photomicrographs.) Draper strove to identify the photochemically active rays, and in 1841 demonstrated that light reflected from one daguerreotype plate had no effect on a second. His inference—that only absorbed rays were effective—became known as Draper's law. The credit was eventually shared with C. J. D. Grotthus, who had made a similar claim in 1817. Draper was interested in every type of radiant energy, and in 1847 published results indicating that all solid bodies became incandescent at the same temperature, while the region of maximum radiant energy in their spectra moved towards the shorter wavelengths with increasing temperature. By 1857 he had shown that the maxima of solar luminosity and heat occurred at the same point in the visible spectrum.

To isolate these active rays, Draper constructed powerful spectroscopes—at first with prisms, but from 1844 with diffraction gratings. By 1843 he had photographed spectral lines and developed a sensitive instrument—the tithonometer—for measuring the intensity of chemically active rays. It involved monitoring a photo-catalysed reaction between hydrogen and chlorine, but experiments convinced him that light affected the chlorine alone, converting it from a passive to an active state. He compared this transformation with the allotropy recently noted by J. J. Berzelius in elementary phosphorus, and in 1849 proposed that the enhanced activity of certain elements (particularly nitrogen) in organic combinations might derive from similar allotropic changes, catalysed by solar radiation in plants, and by other forms of energy in animal tissue. In 1857 he suggested that intense radiation might even transmute one element into another. Draper's experimental work was internationally admired, but his theories were less popular. (Wilhelm Bunsen and Henry Enfield Roscoe were particularly critical of them, although their own research owed something to Draper's innovative techniques.) Draper's reputation for speculative theorizing may explain his absence from the founding group of the American Association for the Advancement of Science (AAAS) in 1863. He was admitted in 1877, having received the Rumford medal of the American Academy of Arts and Sciences in 1875, and became president of the American Chemical Society in 1876. However, his outspoken comments on religious topics may also have provoked his initial exclusion from the AAAS.

Draper's influential *History of the Intellectual Development of Europe* (1863) was already completed when he summarized its theory of cultural evolution for the 1860 British Association meeting at Oxford. His otherwise uneventful discourse included provocative references to Charles Darwin's *Origin of Species* (1859), and the ensuing discussion culminated in the notorious confrontation between Bishop Samuel Wilberforce and Thomas Huxley. Further controversy surrounded Draper's *History of the Conflict between Religion and Science* (1874), which went through ten English editions, with translations into twenty other languages. It indicted most Christian denominations for persecution and censorship, and outraged many believers (though Draper remained a welcome speaker at Unitarian meetings). His other books included: *Human Physiology, Statical and Dynamical* (1856), *Thoughts on the Future Civil Policy of America* (1865), *History of the American Civil War* (3 vols., 1867, 1868, and 1870), and *Scientific Memoirs: being Experimental Contributions to a Knowledge of Radiant Energy* (1878). He also published over fifty scientific papers, gave many public addresses, and was a prolific correspondent.

Draper died at his home in Hastings-on-Hudson on 4 January 1882 and was buried at Greenwood cemetery, Long Island. He was survived by five children, of whom Henry became a prominent astronomer and Daniel became director of the New York Meteorological Observatory. MICHAEL A. SUTTON

Sources D. Fleming, *John William Draper and the religion of science* (1950) • D. Gardener, 'Dr John William Draper and his co-workers', 1948, University of Pennsylvania, Special Collections Library • J. W. Draper, letters, L. Cong., manuscript division • J. W. Draper, *A history of the intellectual development of Europe* (1863) • J. W. Draper, *A history of the conflict between religion and science* (1874) • J. W. Draper, *Scientific memoirs: being experimental contributions to a knowledge of radiant energy* (1878) • DAB • D. Fleming, 'Draper, John William', DSB • H. Plotkin, 'Henry Draper, Edward C. Pickering, and the birth of American astrophysics', *Symposium on the Orion nebula to honor Henry Draper, Annals of the New York Academy of Sciences*, 395 (1982), 321–30
Likenesses N. Sarony, photograph, 1878, NPG • N. Sarony, photograph, *c.*1880, Smithsonian Institution, Washington, DC

Draper, Sir William (1721–1787), army officer, was born in Bristol, the youngest of the four surviving children of Ingleby Draper (*d.* 1722), an officer of customs, and his wife, Mary (*c.*1694–1764), the daughter of Alexander Harrison. Ingleby Draper was the second of the seven sons of William Draper of Beswick in the East Riding of Yorkshire, a famous fox-hunting squire.

Ingleby's early death at the age of about twenty-five meant that his children were brought up under conditions of considerable financial hardship. Nevertheless, William attended Bristol Cathedral school and went on to Eton College as a king's scholar from 1733 to 1740. From Eton he gained a scholarship to King's College, Cambridge, where he graduated BA in 1744. By then the War of the Austrian Succession made the prospect of a military career attractive. He obtained an ensigncy in March 1744 in the 48th regiment of foot, commanded by Lord Henry Beauclerk. The 48th distinguished itself at the battle of Falkirk in January 1746 against the Young Pretender's forces and was also present at Culloden in April. Within a month of Culloden, Draper was transferred from the 48th foot to be adjutant of the 2nd battalion, 1st foot guards, whose colonel was the duke of Cumberland. Transfer to this élite regiment represented a singular mark of approval from the duke, who was also captain-general.

The 1st guards fought in the Flanders campaigns of 1747, including the battle of Laffeldt. During the winding down of the war before the treaty of Aix-la-Chapelle in 1748 Draper returned to King's, where he proceeded MA in 1749 and was elected a fellow. He chose to continue his military career in preference to an academic one, while enjoying the peacetime pleasures of a guards officer's life. He was a skilled all-rounder at sports, particularly real tennis, and in 1751 made the highest batting score in the first three-day series of cricket matches between an Etonian side and the rest of England.

During this period Draper shared a London residence with two of his brother officers in the 1st guards, the Hon. Robert Brudenell and Richard Peirson, and between them they were 'enabled to make a figure' (*The Times*, 18 Jan 1787,

2c). On 21 February 1756 Draper married Caroline Beauclerk (*c*.1730–1769), the younger daughter of Lord William Beauclerk and the niece of the duke of St Albans, 'though her relations rather opposed the connection' (ibid.). In the same month Draper was appointed aide-de-camp to the third duke of Marlborough, master-general of the ordnance, with whom he also regularly played tennis.

In 1757 Draper was commissioned as lieutenant-colonel commandant to raise a regiment of foot, a thousand strong, for service in the East Indies. The regiment took rank as the 79th foot and embarked in January 1758, split between a number of East Indiamen. The *Pitt*, on which Draper and two of the regiment's companies were travelling, reached Madras in September 1758, having lost more than fifty men through sickness during the voyage. Their arrival just preceded the siege of Madras by the French army under Count Lally-Tollendall, and tilted the balance in favour of the British forces under the command of Stringer Lawrence. Early in the siege Draper led a sally from Fort St George which, despite his conspicuous personal courage, was unable to achieve any decisive result.

The French siege collapsed after three months. In its aftermath, command of the British forces on the Coromandel coast was offered to Draper by the East India Company. He declined the offer, pleading ill health. He left Madras on the East Indiaman *Winchelsea* in April 1759 on a voyage which took in a trading visit to Canton (Guangzhou) on the China coast. The idea of the expedition to Manila three years later arose during this voyage.

In the autumn of 1761, when it appeared that Spain might be entering the Seven Years' War in support of France, Draper submitted to Lord Egremont a memorandum for a strike against the Spanish base at Manila. The plan gained the personal backing of Lord Anson, first lord of the Admiralty, who ensured that it received the approval of both the government and the East India Company. Draper was promoted to the rank of 'Brigadier-General in the East Indies only' after the outbreak of war with Spain in January 1762, and was dispatched to organize and command the expedition to be mounted from royal and company forces available in Madras. Uniquely, it was agreed that without his presence there would be no expedition.

Despite the misgivings of the company servants in Madras, the expedition was swiftly organized, and sailed on the six-week voyage under the joint command of Draper and Vice-Admiral Samuel Cornish. Speed was essential, and the British forces arrived off Manila on 25 September 1762, with the advantage of surprise before news of the outbreak of war had reached the Philippines. A landing was effected despite a tropical storm, and the combined forces maintained their momentum to such effect that the city and citadel of Manila were captured on 6 October.

In the immediate aftermath of the conquest Draper and Cornish ransomed the city against pillage for £1 million sterling. The fact that there had already been uncontrollable looting, linked with the reality that there was much less to seize in Manila than the victors had expected, resulted in the governor of the Philippines, Archbishop Rojo, agreeing to draw bills for 2 million pesos on the Spanish treasury in Madrid. But the ransom pledge was disavowed as soon as it was received in Madrid, the Spanish choosing to regard the seizure of Manila more as an act of piracy than a legitimate conquest of war. It was to remain a subject for wrangling between the British and Spanish governments over the next decade.

Draper departed for England within weeks of the conquest. By the time he arrived home in April 1763 his achievement had already been overtaken by events. Anson was dead, and Pitt was out of office. The treaty of Paris, ending the Seven Years' War, had been signed. Manila was to be restored to Spain without compensation. The distant conquest was no longer a negotiating counter or even much cause for celebration. Nevertheless Draper was allowed to enjoy some of the fruits of victory, while pressing the government to push for settlement of the ransom. He presented the Spanish colours captured at Manila to his old Cambridge college, where they were placed in the chapel. He and Admiral Cornish received the thanks of the House of Commons. The £5000 which he received from the East India Company as an initial tranche of the prize money of the victors allowed him to build a small mansion, named Manilla Hall, at Clifton, near Bristol, to which he retired with his wife, Caroline. His mother, Mary, died there in September 1764.

By then it was apparent that the Spanish had little intention of resolving the ransom issue. At the end of 1764 Draper published a pamphlet entitled *Colonel Draper's answer to the Spanish arguments claiming the galleon and refusing payment of the Manilla ransom from pillage and destruction*, a document typifying the lack of constraints then felt by serving officers wishing to present their case to the public. The British government maintained pressure for payment of the ransom over the next few years but made no progress in the face of Spanish intransigence. Draper meanwhile in 1765 received a knighthood of the Bath and retained his sinecure governorship of Great Yarmouth. In June 1765 he was made colonel of the 16th foot, in succession to his old friend Robert Brudenell, his own regiment, the 79th, having been disbanded. In March of the following year he received permission to exchange with Colonel James Gisborne to the Irish half pay of the late 121st (King's Royal volunteers). During these years both he and Caroline were painted by Thomas Gainsborough. He also commissioned memorial tributes to his old regiment and to William Pitt for the garden of Manilla Hall. These memorials still stand on Clifton Down near the site of the mansion, which was demolished early in the twentieth century.

Draper suddenly came back to public attention when he risked challenging the anonymous writer Junius. On 21 January 1769 the *Public Advertiser* published the first of the famous letters of Junius, containing a vitriolic and well-informed attack on most of the senior figures of the government, including the marquess of Granby as commander-in-chief. The letter was immediately raised in public awareness in producing a response from Draper, writing under his own name. Sir William, who was vain about his own scholarship and claimed 'very long, uninterrupted and intimate friendship with Lord Granby', defended Granby, apparently uninvited, against his anonymous assailant.

Junius, with senior ministerial figures in his sights, was thus forced to divert his attention to disposing of this unforeseen challenge. He bent to the task in an exchange of long public letters, retorting with sarcasms on Draper's tacit renunciation of the Manila ransom, and on his exchange with Colonel Gisborne, an everyday transaction in military circles at that time. 'By what accident', asked Junius:

> did it happen in the midst of all this bustle and all these claims for justice to your injured troops the name of the Manila ransom was buried in a profound, and since then an uninterrupted silence? … Was it the blushing ribbon which is now the perpetual ornament of your person? Or was it the regiment which you afterwards, (a thing unprecedented among soldiers), sold to Colonel Gisborne? Or was it the governorship, the full pay of which you are content to hold with the half-pay of an Irish colonel? (*Letters of Junius*, letter 3)

Draper as part of his reply stated that, in September 1768, only four months earlier, he had waited on Lord Shelburne in respect of the Manila claims and had been frankly told, as by previous secretaries of state, that any rights must be sacrificed to the national convenience. He went on to explain that the exchange with Colonel Gisborne was as much on grounds of poor health as for any other reasons, and was certainly not to his financial advantage. In a public reply to another correspondent at the same time Draper revealed that he had turned down a bribe of £50,000 offered to him by Archbishop Rojo in Manila to cut the ransom demand by half.

A further insinuation from Junius that Draper had made a false declaration on accepting his half pay was easily rebutted, but by then Sir William was embarrassingly on the defensive. He compounded his folly in returning to challenge Junius again later in the same year, defending the duke of Bedford against further accusations. The correspondence, which aroused immense public interest, finally closed in October 1769 with Junius's brilliant dismissal of Sir William. The furore over this public humiliation must have accelerated the early death of Caroline, Draper's wife, who died childless in the autumn of 1769.

At the end of that disastrous year Draper left England for a tour of America. He travelled to New York, where the commander of the British troops was General Thomas Gage, who had been an exact contemporary in the 48th foot. Gage probably introduced Draper to the powerful de Lancey family, and on 13 October 1770 he married Susannah de Lancey, the daughter of Oliver de Lancey, who was to become the senior loyalist commander in New York during the War of Independence.

Draper and Susannah returned to England early in 1771, and she gave birth to the first of their daughters in August. Sir William was promoted to major-general in 1772. He remained in close touch with the club and military life of London, and in February 1774 was chairman of a 'Committee of Noblemen and Gentlemen' which produced the revised laws of cricket, to shape the game thereafter. He also continued to be a devotee of the gaming tables, which were largely responsible for his chronic state of financial disarray.

Draper was promoted to lieutenant-general in 1777, but his need for active service increased when Susannah died in August 1778, leaving him with two young daughters. In 1779 his dilemma was relieved when he was appointed lieutenant-governor of Minorca, under Lieutenant-General the Hon. James Murray. Draper arrived in Minorca shortly before the invasion of the island in August 1781 by a combined force of French and Spanish which led to the siege of Fort St Philip. The small garrison was eventually forced to capitulate in February 1782, defeated by the ravages of scurvy.

The later months of the siege had been bedevilled by an unnecessary and increasingly bitter row between Murray and Draper over the limits of their operational authority. This resulted in Draper being relieved of his command shortly before the end of the siege. After returning to England, Sir William, in an effort to restore the balance of honour, made twenty-nine miscellaneous charges against Murray. A general court martial sat at the Horse Guards between November 1782 and January 1783.

The court acquitted Murray of all charges save two—some arbitrary interference with auction dues on the island and the issuing of an order in October 1781 'tending to discredit and dishonour the Lieutenant Governor'—for which he was sentenced to be reprimanded. George III also:

> expressed much concern that an officer of Sir William Draper's rank and distinguished character should have allowed his judgement to be so perverted by any sense of personal grievance as to view the general conduct of his superior officer in an unfavourable light, and in consequence to exhibit charges against him which the court after direct investigation have considered to be frivolous and ill-founded. (PRO, WO 71/100)

To avoid the possibility of a subsequent duel the court dictated an apology which was agreed by Draper and accepted reluctantly by Murray. As Draper's rejoinder to Murray's defence had not appeared in the newspapers, he published it later under the title *Observations on the Hon. Lieutenant-General Murray's Defence* (1784).

The matter effectively terminated the careers of both senior soldiers. Draper was still in pressing financial need and later wrote to various contacts urging his claims for compensation for his services. His pleas were no more effective than those of many other needy claimants. He lived the remaining three years of his life mostly in Bath, where he died on 8 January 1787, cared for by his surviving daughter, Anna Susannah. A tablet to his memory, bearing a Latin epitaph by his friend the poet Christopher Anstey, was erected in Bath Abbey. A 'Characteristic sketch' in *The Times* of 18 January 1787 concluded: 'his amiable manners, his generous nature and his cultivated understanding made him esteemed by all'.

JAMES DREAPER

Sources J. Dreaper, *Bristol's forgotten victor* (1998) · BL OIOC, Gps: B/D/E/H/L/Mar/L/P&S/MssEur/Madras Diary, etc. · PRO, WO 1/4/5/25/26/40/45/47/55/64/65/71 · PRO, ADM 1/51 · calendar of home office papers, 1755–85, PRO · PRO, SP 78, vols. 269–76; SP 94, vols. 165–84 · wills and probates, PRO · PRO, CO 77/20; CO 174/12–14 · correspondence between Draper and college, 1763, King's AC Cam. · A. Allen, 'Skeleton Collegii Regalis Cantab.', King's Cam. · BL, Newcastle MSS · *The letters of Junius*, ed. J. Cannon (1978) · Walpole, *Corr.* · *LondG* (Dec 1765) · parish register, Bristol, St Augustine-the-Less, 3/1723 [baptism]
Archives BL, letters to Charles Jenkinson, Add. MSS 38200–38217, 38305–38308, 38480 *passim*
Likenesses T. Gainsborough, oils, 1766–9, M. H. de Young Memorial Museum, Golden Gate Park, San Francisco · E. Bocquet, stipple, pubd 1782 (after drawing by T. Gainsborough), NPG · W. Ridley, engraving, 1805 (similar to stipple by E. Bocquet), BM; repro. in Cannon, ed., *Letters of Junius* · T. Gainsborough, engraving, BM
Wealth at death £6000 in debt: administration, PRO, PROB 6/164; will [Anna Susanna Gore], 1793, PRO, PROB 11/365

Drax, Sir Reginald Aylmer Ranfurly Plunkett-Ernle-Erle- (1880–1967), naval officer, was born in London on 28 August 1880, the second of the two sons of John William Plunkett, later seventeenth Baron Dunsany (1853–1899), and his wife, Ernle Elizabeth Louisa Maria Grosvenor Burton (*d.* 1916), only child of Colonel Francis Augustus Plunkett Burton, of the Coldstream Guards. In 1916, on inheriting estates from his mother, he assumed by royal licence the additional names of Ernle-Erle-Drax. Thereafter he was usually known by the surname of Drax. His elder brother was Edward John Moreton Drax *Plunkett, eighteenth Baron Dunsany.

After attending Cheam School Plunkett joined the Royal Naval College, Dartmouth, and began service at sea in 1896. He was promoted lieutenant in 1901 and went on to specialize in torpedo. His request to attend the Staff College, Camberley, was granted and there he took an intense interest in 'the subject of staff training and its application—then quite unthought of in higher naval circles—to the needs of the navy' (*The Times*, 12). In 1912 he received early promotion to commander and when in 1913 Admiral Beatty was given command of the battle-cruiser squadron, he chose Plunkett as his war staff officer. In this capacity he served in the *Lion* at the actions of Heligoland Bight, Dogger Bank, and Jutland. He was promoted captain in 1916 and ended the war in the cruiser *Blanche* which was employed in laying minefields in the Heligoland Bight close to the enemy's main ports. For his services in the *Lion* he was mentioned in dispatches and he was appointed to the DSO when commanding the *Blanche*. On 15 April 1916 he married Kathleen (*d.* 1980), only daughter of Quintin Chalmers MD and sister of the future Rear-Admiral W. S. Chalmers, the naval biographer. They had four daughters and one son.

Prior to the war Drax had been a founding member of the Naval Society which from 1913 had issued the quarterly *Naval Review* to encourage new ideas on naval matters. He was one of the group of younger officers of the Grand Fleet known as the Young Turks who increasingly criticized the defensive approach of the Admiralty. During the later years of the war Drax privately wrote at length on what he saw as the failings of the navy leadership. In 1917 he noted of the strategies adopted by the Admiralty that 'Masterly strategy, deep knowledge of the Art of War, keen and rapid brain-work—these were pitiably absent' (Marder, 5.325). Drax kept up such criticism of ineffective policy throughout and following his career, and later wrote *The Art of War* (1943) and other works which attacked aspects of defence strategy.

Intellectually Drax 'stood out among his brother officers' (*The Times*, 12), and his talents were recognized within the navy. In 1919 he became first director of the new Royal Naval Staff College at Greenwich where he served until 1922. Having proved himself a brilliant staff officer and thinker and also as a fine captain of a cruiser, he was the ideal person for this appointment as he showed it was possible to be both. He did much to make staff work respectable in a navy where thinkers were apt to be regarded with suspicion. He went next as president of the Inter-Allied Naval Control Commission in Berlin until 1924. In 1926–7 he commanded the *Marlborough* in the 3rd battle squadron.

In 1928 Drax was promoted rear-admiral and in 1929 appointed to command the 1st battle squadron in the Mediterranean. As director of manning at the Admiralty (1930–32) he was involved in the recovery of the navy's morale after the Invergordon mutiny, an episode for which he had had no responsibility. In 1932–4 he was commander-in-chief, America and West Indies, where he cruised widely in his flagship and did much to promote friendly relations with the United States navy. He was promoted vice-admiral in 1932 and admiral in 1936, having been appointed CB in 1928 and KCB in 1934. In 1935–8 he served as commander-in-chief, Plymouth. In 1939 he headed the British section of the ineffectual Anglo-French military mission to Russia to attempt to gain agreement on opposition to German aggression. But John Weitz wrote of this mission that it 'had no real power to negotiate … Drax was, politically speaking, a eunuch' (Weitz, 195). The British and French were outmanoeuvred by Ribbentrop, the German foreign minister, who negotiated a Russo-German treaty of non-aggression while Drax's group was engaged in vague staff talks in Leningrad.

In 1939–41 Drax was commander-in-chief at the Nore. He was involved in the evacuation of British troops from Dunkirk and the preparation of defensive measures for the anticipated German invasion. In 1941 Drax retired and returned to his estates in Dorset where he served as a private in the Home Guard. In the spring of 1943 he volunteered for duty as a commodore of convoy and served until 1945, with the distinction of never losing a ship.

Drax was in many ways a radical, with his belief in the study of war and promotion of new ideas, and the additional concern he exhibited for the welfare, and training, of junior officers and men. In retirement he remained busy with the management of his estates at Charborough Park, near Wareham, Dorset, and wrote articles on a range of subjects. He developed ideas for the solar-heated swimming pool. He died in Poole, Dorset, on 16 October 1967.

PETER GRETTON, *rev.* MARC BRODIE

Sources *The Times* (18 Oct 1967) · Burke, *Peerage* (1999) · A. J. Marder, *From the Dreadnought to Scapa Flow: the Royal Navy in the Fisher era, 1904–1919*, 5 vols. (1961–70) · J. T. Sumida, *In defence of naval supremacy: finance, technology and British naval policy, 1889–1914* (1989) · *WWW* · J. Weitz, *Joachim von Ribbentrop: Hitler's diplomat* (1992) · d. cert. · personal knowledge (1981) · private information (1981) · *CGPLA Eng. & Wales* (1968)

Archives CAC Cam., corresp. and papers | Plunkett Foundation, Long Hanborough, Oxfordshire, corresp. with Sir Horace Plunkett

Likenesses photograph, repro. in *The Times*, 12

Wealth at death £105,102: probate, 8 Feb 1968, *CGPLA Eng. & Wales*

Draxe, Thomas (d. 1618/19), author and Church of England clergyman, was born at Stoneleigh, near Coventry, possibly (as Thomas Fuller suggests) a member of the Draxe family of Woodhall near Wombwell, Yorkshire. He matriculated pensioner at Christ's College, Cambridge, in December 1588, graduated BA probably in 1595, and was admitted BD in 1609. It is possible that he is the Thomas Draxe of Walton in Shropshire who married Mary Ottley on 5 January 1595. He seems to have lived mainly in Warwickshire, since all his early writings are signed from Stoneleigh or Coventry, beginning with *The Churches Securitie* (1608). In all he is known to have published eleven books, including three catechisms. *The Worldes Resurrection*, dedicated from Coventry in November 1608 to Lucy, countess of Bedford, is remarkable for its millenarian interest in the Jews: the epistle dedicatory describes them as 'the faithful keepers of the Old Testament', but the magistrates are none the less to 'repress their vile and intolerable usuries' and 'compel them to hear the gospel', for their conversion is 'dayly expected', and with its advent 'we shall all in short time be fully and finally perfected and glorified'. On 2 August 1612 Draxe preached at Paul's Cross in London, and dedicated to William, fourth Baron Paget, the version published as *The Earnest of our Inheritance* (1613).

Draxe was also a Latin scholar, translating the works of William Perkins for publication in Geneva. His *Callipeia, or, A Rich Store-House of Proper, Choise, and Elegant Latine Words and Phrases* was dedicated from Coventry on 20 November 1612 to Thomas Leigh, Stoneleigh's largest landowner. On 12 January following Draxe was instituted vicar of Colwich, Staffordshire, and it was here that he dedicated a second Latin work, *Novi coeli et nova terra*, to the master of his old college of Christ's, Valentine Carew. The living of Colwich had been valued at £20 per annum in 1604 but Draxe held it for less than three years, his successor being instituted on 12 July 1615. On 9 May 1615 he was instituted vicar of Dovercourt, Essex, to which was annexed the chapelry and port of Harwich. It was from Harwich, for several years home port of the *Mayflower*, that in 1617 he signed *Ten Counter-Demands*, a pamphlet urging separatists to choose between returning to the English church and creating a plantation in America. It is not known whether his argument influenced their decision. Draxe did not live much longer. Fuller believed that it was 'the change of the aire', his exposure to the rains and fogs of the Essex coast, which led to his death (Fuller, 3.283–4). Thomas Draxe was

buried at Harwich on 29 January 1619. He may have been related to an older namesake, possibly the man ordained by the bishop of Gloucester on 8 January 1573, who was vicar of Kirmington, Lincolnshire, by 1585, and vicar of Tetney in the same county from 1591 to 1595.

STEPHEN WRIGHT

Sources Venn, *Alum. Cant.*, 1/2.66 · Fuller, *Worthies* (1662), pt 3 · C. W. Foster, ed., *The state of the church in the reigns of Elizabeth and James I*, Lincoln RS, 23 (1926) · W. N. Landor, 'Staffordshire incumbents and parochial records, 1530–1680', *Collections for a history of Staffordshire*, William Salt Archaeological Society, 3rd ser. (1915 [i.e. 1916]) · T. Draxe, *The worldes resurrection* (1608) · T. Draxe, *Ten counter-demands* (1617?) · L. T. Weaver, *The Harwich story* (1975) · *The works of William Perkins*, ed. I. Breward (1970) · J. C. Challenor-Smith, 'Some additions to Newcourt's *Repertorium*—volume 2 [pt 1]', *Transactions of the Essex Archaeological Society*, new ser., 6 (1896–8), 228–57 · 'Extracts of the registers of Pitchford', *Shropshire Archaeological and Natural History Transactions*, 2nd ser., 7 (1895), 369–74

Draycot, Anthony (d. 1571), Roman Catholic priest, was born into an old Staffordshire family taking its name from Draycott in the Moors. First recorded in 1508 as a scholar of White Hall, Oxford, he was admitted BCL on 3 February 1511, before becoming principal of White Hall on 29 November 1514; about this time he also practised as a proctor in the chancellor's court. He subsequently also took the degrees of BCnL and DCnL on 23 June and 21 July 1522 respectively. In the meantime he had taken orders, being ordained deacon on 16 February 1516 and priest on 8 March following. Ordination at once brought preferments, starting in his native Staffordshire with the rectory of Checkley in March 1516. In 1526 he was made warden of St Leonard's Hospital at Grantham, and in 1527 rector of Hitchin, in 1531 exchanging that living for the rectory of Cottingham, Nottinghamshire. Other benefices included the family living of Draycott in the Moors (1533–48), the Derbyshire rectories of Wirksworth (1535–60) and North Wingfield (1543–4), the rectory of Kettering, Northamptonshire (1540–60), and another Derbyshire living, at Grindon (1544–60).

Draycot also held a number of higher ecclesiastical offices. In February 1532 he was referred to as a royal chaplain, but his career came to centre on the diocese of Lincoln, where by 1537 he had become vicar-general to Bishop John Longland. On 11 February 1539 he was collated to the prebend of Bedford Major in Lincoln Cathedral. He was also successively archdeacon of Stow (1543) and Huntingdon (1543–60). As vicar-general Draycot played an active and very prominent part in the administration of the diocese; he is also recorded as preaching at least once, at Bedford. He later also became chancellor to Ralph Baynes, bishop of Coventry and Lichfield, and on 8 September 1556 was admitted a canon of Lichfield Cathedral, with the prebend of Longden. Theologically conservative, he supported both Longland and Baynes in their pursuit of heretics, earning condemnation by John Foxe as a result. Under Mary, according to the martyrologist, Lichfield diocese was afflicted by 'a cruel bishop there, called Rafe Bane, and a more cruel chancellor named Dr Draicot' (*Acts and Monuments*, 8.255), and he tells how Draycot preached before the burning of Joan Waste at

Derby, and then returned to his inn to sleep while the execution took place. He also admits, however, that many more were compelled to do penance than went to the stake.

Following Elizabeth's accession Draycot refused to take the oath of supremacy and was accordingly deprived of all his benefices. In 1560 he was recorded as a prisoner in the Fleet, but it would appear that he was eventually released, for a later source reports—with some confusion of dates—that 'Dr Draycott, long prisoner, at length getting a little liberty, went to Draycot, and there died', on 20 January 1571 (Morris, 35). He was buried at Draycott.

GORDON GOODWIN, rev. ANDREW A. CHIBI

Sources Emden, *Oxf.*, 4.176 • *Fasti Angl.* (Hardy) • J. Strype, *Memorials of the most reverend father in God Thomas Cranmer*, 2 vols. (1848) • *The acts and monuments of John Foxe*, ed. J. Pratt, [new edn], 8 vols. (1877) • J. Strype, *Ecclesiastical memorials*, 3 vols. (1822) • *CSP dom.*, *1547–65* • Wood, *Ath. Oxon.: Fasti* (1815), 61 • *Fasti Angl., 1300–1541*, [Lincoln] • *Fasti Angl., 1541–1857*, [Lincoln] • M. Bowker, *The Henrician Reformation* (1981) • J. Morris, ed., *The troubles of our Catholic forefathers related by themselves*, 3 (1877), 1–60
Archives BL, Lansdowne MS 980

Drayton, Harold Charles Gilbert [Harley] (1901–1966), financier, was born on 19 November 1901 at Streatham, the elder of two sons of Bob Drayton and his wife, Annie Keep. His father, who came from Lincolnshire, was employed by the London county council as a gardener. His mother died when the boys were still very young and they were subsequently brought up mainly in the house of a family called Low, who had recently arrived in Croydon from Dinnet in Aberdeenshire. Alexander Low, a sanitary inspector, had several children and in 1926 Drayton married one of the daughters, Christine Collie.

Soon after leaving school at the age of thirteen Harley Drayton, as he was always known, got a job as office boy in the St Davids group of companies in Dashwood House, Old Broad Street, London. He was hired by J. S. Austen, an able solicitor whom Lord St Davids had enlisted to help run his investment trust companies. Austen spotted the boy's talent, encouraged and befriended him, and indeed subsequently bequeathed to him his estate in Suffolk. Drayton had at that time read little except the Bible (he later always maintained that Ecclesiasticus contained all the principles of finance that any businessman needed) and he now turned his attention to reading what was lying around the office—financial newspapers, journals, and company reports. It became apparent that he had an uncanny knack of assimilating and remembering figures, and the encyclopaedic knowledge that he acquired made him indispensable. By 1928 he was manager of the securities agency and it was not long before the economic blizzard swept across the world and his powers were tested. He revealed the courage and tenacity of purpose for which he became known. Lord St Davids died in 1938 and Drayton became *de facto* head of the group, but the outbreak of war prevented him for some time from exercising his new responsibilities to the full.

The first assignment on which Drayton's reputation began to be built was the management and liquidation of the Lloyd George Political Fund. This entailed close co-operation with certain companies in which there were large shareholdings. His success led to the adoption of a new policy in the St Davids investment trusts of buying into companies in difficulty or in their infancy and helping them with money and advice. Some 20 per cent of the trusts' money was committed in this type of investment, largely unquoted on the stock exchange, and the policy was the subject of criticism by those who thought that investment trusts should not interfere in company management. In fact the technique was so successful that in 1945 a larger-scale operation was launched in the Industrial and Commercial Finance Corporation. The financial results were most gratifying; Drayton picked his companies well and, without interfering with their managements, was a source of inspiration to them.

During the war Drayton was appointed to the three-man commission sent to Argentina to prepare the ground for the sale of the then British-owned Argentine Railways. The sale was consummated a year or two after the war ended and shareholders got their money and had reason to be satisfied.

In the 1945 general election Drayton stood as Liberal candidate for Bury St Edmunds, where at least he saved his deposit. He took no further active part in politics, but was always ready to give his views in favour of freedom of action and thought. For the next twenty-one years he settled down to heading the group which in 1971, five years after his death, was renamed the Drayton group. He was chairman of the larger trusts in the group. He was elected to the board of British Electric Traction in 1933 and in 1947 he took over the chairmanship, being responsible for two big decisions during his term of office. He successfully resisted the nationalization of the provincial bus companies under the Attlee government and a good many opponents of nationalization were encouraged by his show of independence. Then he took the decision to back independent television; and it needed great courage to see this through. After two years the losses amounted to £6 million, at which point some of the largest participants wanted to withdraw, but typically Drayton bought them out; his faith was justified and the reward was rich.

Drayton had many other business interests. He was chairman of Mitchell Cotts, which led to journeys all over Africa. He was chairman of United Newspapers and was largely responsible for building up the group because of his ability to make acquisitions. He was a director of the Midland Bank and of Eagle Star Insurance. He served his term as chairman of the Association of Investment Trusts and was treasurer of the Institute of Directors on its resuscitation in 1946.

In all these offices Drayton showed his constructive independence and a personal touch. He had originality, conviction, and courage. Smoking his pipe, he would make quick decisions on which he never went back. He was forthright, obstinate, and reliable, like the countryman he always remained. He never received any official recognition of his achievements—perhaps on account of his unwillingness to compromise and conform. Had he been a better public speaker he might have been more widely known.

Drayton's chief interests outside the City were country pursuits which centred around Plumton Hall, Whepstead, near Bury St Edmunds, in Suffolk, which J. S. Austen had left to him. He became an enthusiastic farmer, pampered his pigs, loved his garden, and enjoyed entertaining his friends at shooting parties. He was high sheriff of Suffolk in 1957. He collected pictures and books, at first specializing in eighteenth-century pamphlets, then Kiplingiana, and later in fine illustrated books, which also reflected his interest in ornithology. He learned to like the best, and this applied not least to claret, which he dispensed generously.

There were no children of the marriage to Christine Collie Low, which was a very happy one, but he was exceedingly popular with the children of his friends. Indeed, Drayton gave confidence to all with whom he came into contact, and was an active ally and friend. He died on 7 April 1966 at his London house, 20 Kensington Palace Gardens; Princess Alexandra was present at his funeral at St Petronella, Whepstead, near Bury St Edmunds, on 14 April, and an enormous concourse attended his memorial service in St Paul's Cathedral.   ANTONY HORNBY, rev.

Sources R. Fulford, *The sixth decade, 1946–1956* (1956) · G. E. Mingay, *Fifteen years on: the B.E.T. group, 1956–1971* (privately printed, London, 1973) · *The Times* (9 April 1966), 10e · *The Times* (13 April 1966), 15c · *The Times* (15 April 1966), 14b · *ILN* (16 April 1966), 10 · *New York Times* (9 April 1966), 25 · *CGPLA Eng. & Wales* (1966)

Likenesses D. Jagger, portrait; British Electric Traction office, Stratton House, London, in 1981 · photograph, repro. in Fulford, *Sixth decade*, frontispiece · photograph, repro. in *ILN*

Wealth at death £2,121,321: probate, 13 May 1966, *CGPLA Eng. & Wales*

Drayton, Michael (1563–1631), poet, was born early in 1563 at Hartshill, near Atherstone, in north Warwickshire. His origins were humble. John Aubrey's *Brief Lives* says his father was a butcher. The more reliable Bernard Newdigate tentatively identifies William Drayton, a tanner, as his grandfather and another William (*d.* 1616?), probably also a tanner, as his father; his mother's name may have been Katherine. He had connections with the Goodere family, though the precise nature of these is not certain. A dedication to the earl of Bedford prefixed to one of Drayton's *Englands Heroicall Epistles* (1597, 'Isabel') says the poet had been recommended to the earl's wife by that 'accomplished Gentleman, Sir Henry Goodere (not long since deceased,) whose I was whilst he was: whose patience pleased to beare with the imperfections of my heedlesse and unstaied youth'. A dedication to Sir Henry in the same volume ('Mary the French Queene') says that the poet was beholden to 'the happy and generous family of the Gooderes' for 'the most part of my education'. This would indicate close ties to the Goodere household at Polesworth. Jean Brink has shown, however, that Drayton tended to overstate his connections with the fashionable. He seems, rather, to have entered, by 1580 and probably earlier, the service of Sir Henry's younger brother, Thomas, at Collingham, Nottinghamshire, some 70 miles from Polesworth.

Michael Drayton (1563–1631), by William Hole, 1613

On 16 August 1598 'Mychaell Drayton of London gent of the age of xxxv yeres or therab[ou]tes' was deposed in chancery court in the case of *Engelbert v. Saunders* (PRO, C 24/261/28). This was a suit over property, filed by Thomas Goodere's widow, Margaret, now also the widow of her fourth husband, Lawrence Engelbert, against Goodere's youngest brother, William, and Margaret's brother, Edmund Saunders. According to Drayton, in winter 1584–5 he had been a servant to Thomas Goodere. He denied any involvement with Thomas Goodere's estate after his death, but said that he visited his dying master in his sickroom. According to the testimony of one Nicholas Moon, he had been summoned there, a few days before Thomas died on 5 January, to witness Thomas's instructions to his wife concerning the lease of Collingham Manor. The depositions show Drayton's familiarity with the household, for he could note that Thomas 'was wont' to call his wife 'by the name of Gyrle' and, said Moon, Margaret had called for Drayton after her husband said to choose 'some more of those that be thy frendes that thou best lykest of' (ibid.). There is no evidence that after Thomas's death Drayton attached himself to Sir Henry or that he attended a university.

Early works By 1590 Drayton was settled in London, looking for laurels and patrons. His first printed work, *The Harmonie of the Church*, a versification of various biblical passages, appeared in 1591 with a preface—dated London, 10 February 1591—that thanks 'the godly and vertuous' Lady Jane Devereux for her 'bountifull hospitalitie'. This book was once confused with *The Triumphes of the Churche*, which was ordered to be destroyed by church authorities, but Drayton's is another work entirely. In 1593 came *Idea: the Shepheards Garland*, nine eclogues dedicated to young Robert Dudley and modelled on Spenser's *Shepheardes Calender*. Drayton later revised them, smoothing their diction and metre. The fourth laments the death of Sir Philip Sidney at the battle of Zutphen in 1586; it is probably this elegy to which Nathaniel Baxter refers in his *Sir Philip Sydneys Ourania* (1606):

> O noble Drayton! well didst thou rehearse
> Our damages in dryrie sable verse.

In 1593 Drayton also published the first of his historical poems in the complaint mode made famous by *The Mirror for Magistrates*: *Peirs Gaveston, Earle of Cornwall*. This was followed in 1594 by *Matilda: the Faire and Chaste Daughter of the Lord Robert Fitzwater*, and both poems, revised, were reissued in 1596 with *The Tragicall Legend of Robert, Duke of Normandy* and dedicated to the countess of Bedford.

Before leaving Warwickshire, according to a posthumous tradition, Drayton had courted a lady from Coventry living near the River Anker, long identified as Sir Henry Goodere's daughter, Anne. It was in her honour, supposedly, that in 1594 Drayton published a sequence of fifty-one sonnets under the title *Ideas Mirrour: Amours in Quatorzains*. The evidence for a lifelong and idealized love for Anne does not wholly bear scrutiny, however, and the unromantic may find 'Idea' as unsubstantial as her name. Some of Drayton's wordplay in fact seems better suited to the countess of Pembroke: compliments to 'Marygold' or 'Meridianis' (for example, sonnet 51) recall or anagrammatize 'Mari Sidnei'. In later years Drayton may have come to think that Anne made a good 'Idea'; at least he wanted to give the woman of the sonnets a local habitation, if not an actual name. A 'hymne to his ladies birthplace' in the 1606 *Poemes* identifies the town as Coventry, and the 1627 collection includes an epistle, perhaps composed in 1614, 'Of his Ladies not Coming to London' that locates that lady in the snowy north. Whatever the reality of 'Idea' outside Drayton's mind, the poet was dissatisfied with the collection of 1594, never reprinting twenty-one of its sonnets. His later revisions and additions edge his love poems away from simpler versions of Petrarchism and towards a complexity and irony that may paradoxically be more genuinely Petrarchan. Witness, for example, the exaggerations and self-mockery in his sonnet 'Since there's no help, come let us kiss and part', first printed in 1619.

In 1595 Drayton published *Endymion and Phœbe*, dedicated to the fourteen-year-old Lucy Harington, now countess of Bedford. Its 516 couplets recount a sleeping shepherd's enraptured vision of the cosmos, with perhaps a glance at Elizabeth as her nation's moon, or possibly at 'Lucy', whose name means 'light'. Drayton later revised this pretty exercise in what one might call the poetics of levitation as *The Man in the Moone* (1606). He, or more likely the printer, included the sonnet of 1595 to Lucy Harington in later editions of the poems, although by now the poet had abandoned hopes for her patronage.

The year 1596 saw *Mortimeriados* (on the civil wars during the reign of Edward II), a brief quasi-epic republished in 1603, with many alterations and informative marginalia, as *The Barrons Wars*. An address to the reader in 1603 explains that 'the cause of this my second greater labour was the insufficient and carelesse handling of the first'; the 1619 edition makes it clear that the carelessness was the printer's, not Drayton's vexed comment on the book industry. *Mortimeriados* is in rhyme royal, but for the *Barrons Wars* Drayton reworked these stanzas into *ottava rima*, a pattern the prefatory epistle calls 'of all other the most complete and best proportioned'. Many more revisions followed before *The Barrons Wars* saw its final shape. *Mortimeriados* had been dedicated to the countess of Bedford; but in 1603 the disappointed poet withdrew the dedication and cancelled various other references to her. He seems to have been genuinely angry, for the eighth eclogue in the 1606 *Poemes* inveighs against one 'Selena' who once befriended 'faithfull Rowland' but now favours 'deceitefull Cerberon'. Rowland is Drayton's pastoral name for himself; Cerberon's identity is uncertain, but Selena probably represents the countess. Later editions charitably—or prudently—cancel the invective.

Englands Heroicall Epistles (1597) was to be among the most popular of Drayton's works. Modelled on Ovid's *Heroides*, at least in terms of genre but with more focus on history than on remote legend, it comprises paired epistles between famous lovers. Later editions added more lovers. As though to stress the historical nature of these mostly English lovers, Drayton appends notes to each epistle and dedicates most to some distinguished aristocrat; that so many of his narratives involve the fall of princes doubtless increased their political interest. The letters themselves show Drayton's interest in imagining his way into other people's interests and outlooks; half of the letters, after all, voice what he takes to be a female subjectivity. Not surprisingly, then, and doubtless also in need of cash, Drayton turned to playwriting, collaborating with Anthony Munday, Henry Chettle, Thomas Dekker, and others. From late 1597 to 1604 he wrote more than twenty plays for the Lord Admiral's Men (Harbage and Chambers differ in their counts) on such topics as the French civil wars, 'Conan, Prince of Cornwall', 'The Madman's Morris', and 'Caesar's Fall'; 1598 alone saw about a dozen, although some were perhaps never completed. The *First Part of Sir John Oldcastle*, written with Robert Wilson, Richard Hathway, and Munday (printed in 1600) and later sometimes included with Shakespeare's works, is the only one of these to survive. Unlike Ben Jonson, Drayton omitted his plays from his collected works (1619), whether because he thought them poor stuff, too collaborative to suit the laurel-wreathed bard he wanted to be, or too ephemeral, simply as stage plays, to deserve the solidity of print.

Writings under James I It is possible that in 1599 Drayton visited Scotland: a resentful crane in *The Owle* who may speak for the poet mentions that it had gone in search of preferment 'unto the happie North' and 'there arriv'd, disgrace was all my gaine'. Upon Elizabeth's death Drayton evidently believed that something 'happie' might come to him from the new king, for in 1603 he published *To the Majestie of King James: a Gratulatorie Poem*; the following year saw *A paean triumphall: composed for the societie of the goldsmiths of London, congratulating his highnes magnificent entring the Citie*. All in vain, for James ignored Drayton and his flattery. Henry Chettle's *Englandes Mourning Garment* (1603) suggests that Drayton had been tasteless in so speedily courting his new monarch:

Thinke twas a fault to have thy Verses seene
Praising the King, ere they had mournd the Queen.

Perhaps, though, the king merely associated Drayton too closely with the previous reign. As time went on, moreover, he might have perceived in Drayton (if he looked at the verse, which would not be unlikely, for James was well read and a poet) a disdainful hostility towards the court and the king's attempted absolutism. Disillusion with the new regime certainly sharpened Drayton's bite, although even before James's arrival he had begun to share the relish for indignant satire popular among smart young men in the late 1590s.

Printed some time before late April in 1604 (but, says Drayton, written before his congratulatory poem on James), *The Owle* comments with dyspeptic courage on the despotism of the great, the avarice of the rich, corruption everywhere, and the misuse or neglect of learning. A dream vision of talking birds and personified vices (a sort of avian estates satire), it may allude to specific events; except for an arrogant oak who recalls the rebellious earl of Essex, however, it does so too obscurely for modern comprehension. Drayton dedicated it to Sir Walter Aston, a rich and appreciative young gentleman. At his investiture as knight of the Bath in 1603, Aston had made Drayton one of his esquires, a title that the poet afterwards often displayed proudly on the title-pages of his books, sometimes giving the word 'Esquire' a whole line. It was to Aston that the poet dedicated the 1603 version of *The Barrons Wars* and *Moyses in a Map of his Miracles* (1604). This last is a venture into the biblically based poetry made fashionable by the French Huguenot Du Bartas, a writer whom James much admired and whose *L'Uranie* he had translated.

In 1605 appeared a collected *Poems*, dedicated to Aston and ushered into print with poetic flourishes by Thomas Greene, Sir John Beaumont, Sir William Alexander, and others. Perhaps meant as a companion volume, *Poemes Lyrick and Pastorall: Odes, Eglogs, the Man in the Moone* saw print shortly after, probably in 1606. It contains some of Drayton's best poems, such as the spirited 'Ballad of Agincourt', the ode 'To the Virginian Voyage' with its ambiguous mix of colonizing fervour and anticipatory nostalgia for a new world's lost paradisical innocence, and the delicate 'To Cupid'. Other editions followed, that of 1610 with a commendatory sonnet by the antiquary and scholar John Selden. The 1619 folio drops a semi-Stoic ode to the lawyer John Savage (its allusion to 'base tyrants' may have

seemed incautious) and an ode to a rose that could conceivably be read as nostalgia for Elizabeth, so unlike Britain's new Scottish thistle.

Poly-Olbion (1612) In 1607 came *The Legend of Great Cromwel*, reprinted in 1609 and included in the 1610 *Mirror for Magistrates*, and then, in 1612, Drayton published the first eighteen songs of his longest poem, *Poly-Olbion, or, A chorographicall description of all the tracts, rivers, mountaines, forests, and other parts ... of Great Britaine*. He had been working on this well-researched *magnum opus* at least since 1598, when Francis Meres reported in his *Palladis tamia* that 'Michael Drayton is now penning, in English verse, a Poem called *Poly-Olbion*', accurately calling it 'Geographicall and Hydrographicall'. The title-page shows an enthroned 'Great Britain' with a faint smirk on her face, positioned so as to give her the same shape as her nation. Draped in a map of the lands she personifies, she is as prettily blonde as any Petrarchan mistress but with a cornucopia symbolizing fertility. She is surrounded by four lovers/conquerors: the Trojan Brute (Drayton affected to believe the legend that Britain was first settled by Trojans and hence shared in the legacy of Rome's ancient empire), the Roman Caesar, the Saxon Hengst, and the Norman William. It is she who holds a sceptre, though, for Drayton's celebration of British history, legends, cities, hills, vales, and rivers suggests a nation with an identity, realized or potential, beyond any one conqueror's scope. 'Poly-Olbion' means 'Many blessings', but also 'Multiple Albion'—a greater Britain in which, as Alexander Gardyne wrote to James hopefully in *A Garden of Grave and Godlie Flowres* (1609), various nations might 'Al[l]-be-on[e]'. Albion is the heroine of this epic, not some male equivalent of Spenser's Gloriana. The impressive volume included a portrait of Prince Henry, the poem's dedicatee, whose appreciation for Drayton, if only as a means further to distinguish himself from his father, shows in the £10 annuity listed in his privy purse accounts; unfortunately his death that November precluded further patronage. The volume has maps and copious annotations by Selden that comment with amused but friendly scepticism on the poem's legends and descriptions. Drayton wrote twelve more sections, although the airborne muse whose narrative voice he sometimes adopts never did reach Scotland. Either because the poem's manner—locally patriotic, leisurely, sometimes a little earnest—was now less in style or simply because of its length, Drayton had trouble finding a publisher. In a letter dated 14 April 1619 he wrote to 'dear, sweet [William] Drummond', with whom he maintained a lively correspondence, thanking him for his 'good opinion' of *Poly-Olbion*. The new part, he says, 'lyeth by me; for the Booksellers and I are in Terms: They are a Company of base Knaves, whom I both scorn and kick at'. Eventually, in 1622, he published all thirty sections, although without additional annotations by Selden.

In 1619 there appeared *Poems by Michael Drayton Esquyer*, containing all the poetry except *Poly-Olbion* that the author wished to preserve together with new lyrics. Dedicated to

Aston, this small but handsome folio with a title-page allegorizing various genres has seven parts, each with its own title-page. The second state has a portrait by Hole of the author, laurel-wreathed yet looking discontented; the surrounding inscription says 'Effigies Michaelis Drayton armigeri, poetæ clariss. ætat. svæ L. A. Chr. M.DC.XIII' ('Image of Michael Drayton, esquire, a most famous poet, in his fiftieth year AD 1613'). A volume of miscellaneous works, *The Battaile of Agincourt*, appeared in 1627. Drayton may have hurried the title poem into print as background marching music for the duke of Buckingham's imminent campaign in France. The collection's best-known poem is 'Nimphidia, the Courte of Fayrie', an entertaining mock-heroic; its fascination with the materials, costumes, and stuffs of its minuscule fairies has been read as satirizing the court's obsession with fancy dress and imported goods. In the same volume are 'The Shepheards Sirena', which combines nostalgia for Elizabeth with anti-court satire, an interminable complaint by Margaret, wife of Henry VI, and 'The Quest for Cynthia'. Among the 'elegies', several of which had already appeared in Henry Fitzgeffrey's *Certain Elegies* (1617), is an epistle to Henry Reynolds that comments on English poets, including Shakespeare:

> in thy naturall braine,
> As strong conception, and as Cleere a rage,
> As any one that trafiqu'd with the stage.

The volume is prefaced by liminary verses from friends and admirers, not least Ben Jonson. In 1619, on a visit to Drummond, he had said (recorded his host) that he 'esteemed not' of Drayton, that he disliked the choice of hexameter for *Poly-Olbion*, and that 'Drayton feared him'. Perhaps age and illness had taught Jonson tact, or perhaps, argues Thomas Cogswell, he perceived in Drayton's Agincourt poem a welcome if belated support for Stuart policies.

Drayton's last book was *The Muses Elizium, lately discovered, by a new way over Parnassus … Noah's floud, Moses, his birth and miracles, David and Golia* (1630). In the main body of the volume, ten exquisite 'nimphalls' describe a green world, a 'Poets Paradice', in which the muses, fairies, and poets can wander far from the corruptions of power and the greed of printers. These poems are dedicated to the earl of Dorset (a dedication to his wife precedes the biblical poems). The poignant tenth nimphall tells how an aged satyr finds himself among elegant nymphs who fear his shagginess until, hearing his just complaint, they 'make him an Elizian Saint'. Drayton and satire have found a pastoral home unlike the Stuart court and yet perhaps also representing an idealized and newly hopeful version of it.

Final years and reputation In 1627 Drayton was involved in another lawsuit, noted by Bernard Capp, which is more eyebrow-raising than the first. On 8 March 1627 Drayton appeared before the London consistory court in St Paul's, accused of 'suspicion of incontinency with Mary Peters, wife of John Peters'. Elizabeth Welsh, keeper of a lodging house in St Clement Danes, had charged that one January afternoon in 1627 a maidservant had seen Mary Peters raise her skirts

> unto her navel before Mr Michael Drayton and that she clapt her hand on her privy part and said it was a sound and a good one, and that the said Mr Drayton did then also lay his hand upon it and stroke[d] it and said that it was a good one.

Mrs Peters, hotly denying this, and launching a counter-suit, called Drayton as a witness. Possibly feeling relaxed because of his innocence and age, Drayton said he had gone to the inn to see Mr Peters, denied having seen any skirt-raising, and joked, when asked about his finances, that although worth only 20 nobles, debts paid, he was 'worth at least 2000 li. in good parts'. He also confirmed that he had been born in Hartshill, Warwickshire, and had been living in the parish of St Dunstan-in-the-West for fifteen years. Although the verdict is lost, the evidence suggests that Welsh, whose credibility several witnesses impugned, was lying.

Commending a woman's private parts, if only as a courtesy, would be out of character for Drayton. According to Meres's *Palladis tamia*, 'among schollers, souldiours, Poets, and all sorts of people' he was 'helde for a man of vertuous disposition, honest conversation, and well governed cariage', and an anonymous play, *The Returne from Parnassus* (1605), notes ironically that he lacked 'one true note of a Poet of our times, and that is this, hee cannot swagger it well in a Taverne, nor dominere in a hothouse'. Did he ever marry? In 'Pleasant notes upon Don Quixot' (1654) Edmund Gayton says he did, but there is no record of a marriage. Indeed, the luxurious sympathy with which he could describe male beauty and imagine (if not explicitly approve) homoerotic desire could indicate that, except as a writer, he found heterosexual passion uninteresting.

In appearance, Drayton was short and line 63 of 'Robert, Duke of Normandie' refers to the writer's 'Swart and Melancholy face'. There is no evidence for chronic or serious disease, but once when down with a tertian fever Drayton was cured by Dr John Hall, Shakespeare's son-in-law, who gave that 'excellent Poet' an emetic mixed with syrup of violets; this, he recorded in notes later translated by James Cooke (1657), 'wrought very well both upwards and downwards'. Drayton died in London in 1631, probably in Fleet Street below St Dunstan's Church, and probably in late December. He left an estate of £24 2s. 8d. A manuscript in the Bodleian Library, Oxford (MS Ashmole 38, fol. 77) contains a love poem with a note saying, 'By Michaell Drayton Esquier Poett Lawreatt the night before hee dyed'. He was buried in Westminster Abbey, attended by gentlemen of the inns of court and other notables. A monument erected to him by the countess of Dorset is inscribed with lines variously credited to Jonson, Thomas Randolph, and Francis Quarles.

Drayton fretted when not recognized as Britain's laureate bard, and he rightly sensed that his interests and manner were remote from the cavalier poets on the one hand, whatever the lyric lightness he could summon, and from the metaphysicals on the other, whatever the witty compression that often strengthens his lines. Even his acidity can seem a reversion to a tone more suiting late Elizabethan satire. In a common if not wholly useful or valid taxonomy, he is a late 'Spenserian' poet. Yet he had distinguished friends and drew praise from such fellow poets as Richard Barnfield, Thomas Lodge, Joshua Sylvester, Sir William Alexander, Francis Beaumont, and William Browne. He in turn wrote commendatory poems for books ranging from Thomas Morley's *First Booke of Balletts* (1595) to George Chapman's translation of Hesiod (1618). In the small theatre world he would have known Shakespeare, although no written evidence for this remains except an implausible note made around 1662 by John Ward, vicar of Stratford upon Avon, that mentions a 'merry meeting' at which Shakespeare, Drayton, and Jonson 'dranke too hard, for Shakespear died of a feaver there contracted'. Drayton's epistolary friendship with Drummond brought him great pleasure. And, even if disappointed by the countess of Bedford and James, he found a refreshing welcome at Aston's estate, Tixall, and at the Gloucestershire home of Anne Goodere and Henry Rainsford.

Much read and published in his own day, less so in the eighteenth century, Drayton appealed to the Romantic poets and his stock rose in the nineteenth century. The twentieth century saw a rapid increase in scholarship devoted to him, together with an invaluable edition begun by William Hebel and completed by Kathleen Tillotson. Its biographical chronology (with many contemporary allusions to Drayton), lists of variants, and bibliographical analyses by Bent Juel-Jensen, contain much material ignored here. Newdigate's companion volume traces Drayton's ties to friends and patrons, although its statements concerning his love for Anne Goodere and service to her father should be read against Brink's scepticism.

Writing in an array of genres, Drayton can move from Neoplatonic flights to pastoral retreats free of royal neglect and the sad need to scramble for funds; to grieved witness of Time's hungry destruction of women and walls; to ironic visions of court life; and to an image of the British landscape in which rivers with excellent historical memories, boastful hills that look down on equally voluble valleys, rivers that run on at the mouth, self-assured towns, and lively fauna leave scant room for monarchy as the Stuarts conceived it. Drayton will seldom excite the enthusiasm many feel for Spenser, Donne, or Jonson: sensing himself estranged from his own age, he may still remain too much of it. Yet he repays the reader, especially one looking less for the stolid moralism or simple patriotism with which he has been too often identified than for sardonic melancholy, political resistance, airy delicacy, and access to realms invisible to the merely well born or rich. Any poet who can, in the poem *Robert, Duke of Normandie*, have Fortune tell Memory, with a savage pun, that 'Written with Bloud, thy sad Memorials lye' deserves attention.   ANNE LAKE PRESCOTT

Sources M. Drayton, *Works*, ed. W. Hebel and K. Tillotson, 5 vols. (1961) · B. H. Newdigate, *Michael Drayton and his circle* (1961) · J. Brink, *Michael Drayton revisited* (Boston, 1990) · R. Hardin, *Michael Drayton and the passing of Elizabethan England* (Lawrence, 1973) · K. Tillotson, 'Drayton and the Gooderes', *Modern Language Review*, 35 (1940), 341–9 · B. Capp, 'The poet and the bawdy court: Michael Drayton and the lodging-house world in early Stuart London', *Seventeenth Century*, 10 (1995), 27–37 · D. Taylor, 'Drayton and the countess of Bedford', *Studies in Philology*, 49 (1952), 214–28 · W. B. Hunter, 'The date of Michael Drayton's first elegy', *N&Q*, 240 (1995), 306 · J. Robertson, 'Drayton and the countess of Pembroke', *Review of English Studies*, 16 (1965), 14 · T. Cogswell, 'The path to Elysium "lately discovered": Drayton and the early Stuart culture', *Huntington Library Quarterly*, 54 (1991), 207–33 · M. Swann, 'The politics of fairylore in early modern English literature', *Renaissance Quarterly*, 53 (2000), 449–73 · J. Hall, *Select observations on English bodies*, trans. J. Cooke (1657), 26 · J. Aubrey, *Brief lives: a modern English version*, ed. R. Barber (1982) · A. Harbage, *Annals of English drama, 975–1700*, 2nd edn, ed. S. Schoenbaum (1964) · E. K. Chambers, *The Elizabethan stage*, rev. edn, 4 vols. (1951); repr. (1961), vol. 3 · S. Giantvalley, 'Barnfield, Drayton, and Marlowe: homoeroticism and homosexuality in Elizabethan literature', *Pacific Coast Philology*, 16/2 (1981), 9–24 · A. Hadfield, 'Spenser, Drayton, and the question of Britain', *Review of English Studies*, new ser., 51 (2000), 599–616 · R. Helgerson, *Forms of nationhood: the Elizabethan writing of England* (Chicago, 1992) · A. L. Prescott, 'Marginal discourse: Drayton's muse and Selden's "Story"', *Studies in Philology*, 88 (1991), 307–28

Archives Bodl. Oxf., MS Ashmole 38, fol. 77 · GL, MS 9189/2 · PRO, C 24/261/28 | LMA, Consistory Court Act Book 1626/7, p. 174, DL/C/622

Likenesses W. Hole, line engraving, 1613, BM [*see illus.*] · oils, 1628, Dulwich Picture Gallery, London · attrib. E. Marshall, marble bust, *c.*1631, Westminster Abbey · W. Hole, engraving, facsimile, 1796, BM, NPG · attrib. P. Oliver, miniature on a locket, Welbeck Abbey, collection of the Duke of Portland

Wealth at death £24 2*s.* 8*d.*: letters of administration, 17 Jan 1632, *Works*, ed. Hebel and Tillotson, vol. 5

Drayton, Nicholas (*d.* in or before **1379**), ecclesiastic and justice, was a fellow of the royal college of the King's Hall, Cambridge, from 4 May 1360 until 26 August 1362. He was already a king's clerk when appointed warden of the King's Hall on 1 December 1363, the third holder of this position. He retained it for only one year, and vacated it in December 1364. As warden he had been given an allowance of 4*d.* a day, and also received 8 marks (£5 6*s.* 8*d.*) yearly for two sets of robes per annum. His wardenship coincided with a challenge to the authoritarian rule of the warden. The brevity of Drayton's tenure of office suggests that all was not well, but few details are supplied by the records of the college.

Among Drayton's ecclesiastical livings were the rectorship of St Martin Vintry, London, which he had acquired by 1363 and held until his death, and the canonry of Hereford and prebend of Bullinghope, which he held in 1377 and likewise retained until his death. Drayton specialized in the Roman or civil law, and had been awarded the degree of BCL by 1355 and LicCL by 1376. On 14 November 1376 he was appointed a baron of the exchequer, and was reappointed to this position on 26 June 1377. He died at the Roman curia before February 1379. Drayton is probably not to be identified with the Nicholas Drayton who was charged with heresy before the bishop of London, Simon Sudbury, in 1370.   ALAN B. COBBAN

Sources *Chancery records* · *CPR* · Rymer, *Foedera*, 3rd edn, 3/2.716, 889, 1064 · Foss, *Judges* · Emden, *Cam.* · A. B. Cobban, *The King's Hall*

within the University of Cambridge in the later middle ages, Cambridge Studies in Medieval Life and Thought, 3rd ser., 1 (1969)

Drayton, William Henry (1742–1779), planter and revolutionary leader in America, was born in September 1742 at Drayton Hall, St Andrew's parish, South Carolina, the son of John Drayton (1713?–1779), a wealthy planter and public official, and Charlotta (1719–1743), daughter of Lieutenant-Governor William Bull. Sent to England in 1753 for his education, William Henry attended Westminster School (1753–61), and Balliol College, Oxford (1761–3), but his father, angered by his presumed extravagance, cut off funds before he received a degree. William Henry returned to South Carolina and on 28 March 1764 married a rich heiress, Dorothy Golightly (1747–1780). This marriage brought him a rice plantation in St Bartholomew parish where the couple made their home; they had four children, two of whom survived to adulthood.

Elected to the South Carolina Commons house of assembly in 1765, Drayton failed to play a conspicuous part in the opposition to the Stamp Act, parliament's attempt to tax internal American transactions, and was therefore not returned in 1768. He opposed the coercive aspects of the American non-importation movement against the Townshend duties, another parliamentary attempt to tax the Americans, and in 1769 argued his position under the pen-name Freeman in the *South Carolina Gazette*. Public policy, he maintained, should not be made by men who knew only how 'to cut up a beast in the market to the best advantage … or to build a necessary house' (*Letters of Freeman*, 31). Ostracized, Drayton sailed for England in January 1770; there he republished most of the essays in the non-importation debate under the title *The Letters of Freeman, etc.* On 1 February 1771 the crown rewarded him with an appointment to the South Carolina council.

Despite his initial support of the royal governor in an ongoing dispute over the right of the Commons house to draft money bills, Drayton soon suffered several setbacks. During the winter of 1770–71 his uncle, Lieutenant-Governor William Bull II, temporarily appointed him interim deputy postmaster-general for the southern district of North America and recommended him for an associate judgeship. Royal authorities rejected him for both positions. Later, when Drayton proposed that Catawba Indian lands be granted to him in trust so that he could 'protect' the occupants, the superintendent for Indian affairs, John Stuart, suspected fraud and blocked the move. In August 1773 Drayton and his father, who was also a councillor, broke with their colleagues and published a dissent to the majority's refusal to act on a money bill passed by the Commons. With Drayton again objecting, the council then gaoled the printer for contempt. Perhaps hoping to quiet him, Bull made Drayton an associate justice to fill a temporary vacancy, and he served for most of 1774, during which he charged grand jurors to hold their civil liberties 'dearer' than their lives (*Letters of Freeman*,

xxxiv). In August Drayton also published *A Letter from Freeman of South-Carolina, to the Deputies of North-America*, addressed to the deputies assembled in the first continental congress, in which he denounced British attempts 'to exercise despotism over America' (Dabney and Dargan, 56) and advocated establishment of 'a High Court of Assembly of North America' (ibid., 58) with power to tax the colonies. On 1 March 1775, after he again protested against his colleagues' rejection of a bill sent to them by the Commons, Drayton was suspended by Bull from the council. British officials later confirmed the action, declaring him unfit to serve the king in any office.

Meanwhile Drayton, courting popularity, energized South Carolinians. In mid-March he advocated strict enforcement of the inter-colonial non-importation of British goods effort because, he claimed, the people demanded it and 'the people ever are in the right' (Drayton, *Memoirs*, 1.186). Elected to the revolutionary first provincial congress (January 1775), he became an active member of several committees—including the council of safety—that enabled him to plan local defences. To acquire arms and information he also headed parties that raided provincial armouries and the Post Office. Accurately termed one 'of the most virulent incendarys' (*Letters of Freeman*, xxxvi) by one royal observer, he and a few associates toured the Carolina backcountry from July to September 1775 in a largely futile attempt to enlist support for the American patriot cause. He achieved only a treaty of neutrality with some loyalists.

Shortly after his return to Charles Town, Drayton helped to precipitate the first local battle of the war in a bloodless naval skirmish at Charles Town. Elected president of the second provincial congress, he advocated independence from Great Britain as early as 6 February 1776. In March the provincial congress adopted a temporary constitution and transformed itself into the general assembly, which elected Drayton chief justice. As such he delivered a number of noteworthy charges to grand juries in which he declared that 'The Almighty created America to be independent of Britain' (Dabney and Dargan, 124). After the American Declaration of Independence (4 July 1776) he sought to strengthen American defences in Georgia by convincing its inhabitants to accept unification with South Carolina. Local leaders baulked and eventually offered a reward for his arrest.

During 1777 and 1778 Drayton also played an important part in two constitutional debates. The first involved a new South Carolina constitution to replace the temporary document adopted in 1776; the other concerned the articles of confederation proposed by the continental congress as a temporary national constitution. As finally approved, the South Carolina constitution of 1778 provided for popular election of the senate and partial disestablishment of the Anglican church, both of which Drayton supported. But the articles of confederation contained insufficient safeguards for the southern interest and slavery to satisfy him, and he accordingly proposed numerous amendments.

On 31 January 1778 the legislature chose Drayton as one

of its delegates to the second continental congress, and for a year and a half he was among its most active members, serving on more than eighty committees, supporting the alliance with France, quarrelling with colleagues, and collecting materials for a projected history of the American War of Independence. After his unexpected death in Philadelphia on 3 September 1779 from a 'putrid fever' (presumably typhus), the former president of congress, Henry Laurens, helped to arrange his burial next day in Christ Church cemetery, Philadelphia, as well as the destruction of his secret papers.

Drayton's obituary maintained that 'he had a head to contrive, a temper to persuade, and a hand to execute plans of the most extensive utility to his country' (Jervey, 204), but an observant visitor to Charles Town recorded in 1778 that Drayton had 'acquired a large share of popularity, but his private character is bad' (Merrens, 191). Both assessments of this leading revolutionary were probably accurate.   ROBERT M. WEIR

Sources *The letters of Freeman, etc: essays on the nonimportation movement in South Carolina collected by William Henry Drayton*, ed. R. M. Weir (1977) · J. Drayton, *Memoirs of the American Revolution as relating to South Carolina*, 2 vols. (1821); repr. (1969) · R. W. Gibbes, ed., *Documentary history of the American revolution*, 3 vols. (1853–7); repr. (1972) · P. H. Smith and others, eds., *Letters of delegates to congress, 1774–1789*, 26 vols. (1976–2000) · *The papers of Henry Laurens*, ed. P. M. Hamer and others, 15 vols. (1968–) · W. C. Ford and others, eds., *Journals of the continental congress, 1774–1789*, 34 vols. (1904–37) · K. Krawczynski, *William Henry Drayton: South Carolina revolutionary patriot* (2001) · W. H. Drayton, *A charge on the rise of the American empire, delivered by the Hon. William Henry Drayton, esq., chief justice of South Carolina, to the grand jury for the district of Charlestown* (1774) · W. H. Drayton, *A letter from Freeman of South-Carolina, to the deputies of North-America, assembled in the high court of congress at Philadelphia* (1774) · journals of the South Carolina royal council, South Carolina Archives and History Center, Columbia, · 'Journal of the Council of Safety for the province of South Carolina, 1775', *Collections of the South Carolina Historical Society*, 2 (1858), 22–64 · papers of the first and second councils of safety, 1775–6, *South Carolina Historical and Genealogical Magazine*, 1 (1900), 41–75, 119–35, 183–205, 279–310; 2 (1901), 3–26, 97–107, 167–93, 259–67; 3 (1902), 3–15, 69–85, 123–38, 193–201; 4 (1903), 3–25, 83–96, 195–214 · W. E. Hemphill and W. A. Wates, eds., *Extracts from the journals of the provincial congresses of South Carolina, 1775–1776* (1960) · W. E. Hemphill, W. A. Wates, and R. N. Olsberg, eds., *Journals of the general assembly and house of representatives, 1776–1780* (1970) · journals of the South Carolina house of representatives, South Carolina Archives and History Center, Columbia, · British Public Record Office records relating to South Carolina, South Carolina Archives and History Center, Columbia, · South Carolina loyalist claimants Thomas Knox Gordon, Thomas Irving, and Edward Savage, American loyalists, PRO, audit office papers · *South Carolina Gazette* · *South Carolina and American General Gazette* · *South Carolina Gazette and Country Journal* · H. R. R. Merrens, 'A view of coastal South Carolina in 1778: the journal of Ebenezer Hazard', *South Carolina Historical Magazine*, 73 (1972), 177–93 · K. Krawczynski, 'Drayton, William Henry', *ANB* · W. B. Edgar and N. L. Bailey, eds., *Biographical directory of the South Carolina house of representatives*, 2 (1977) · E. H. Jervey, ed., 'Death notices from the *Gazette of the State of South-Carolina*, Charleston, SC', *South Carolina Historical and Genealogical Magazine*, 50 (1949), 204 · W. M. Dabney and M. Dargan, *William Henry Drayton and the American Revolution* (1962) · E. C. Burnett, *The continental congress* (1941) · A. S. Salley, ed., 'The Bull family of South Carolina', *South Carolina Historical and Genealogical Magazine*, 1 (1900), 76–90

Archives Hist. Soc. Penn., Confederation of the US MS | South Carolina Historical Society, Charleston, H. Laurens MSS · University of South Carolina, Columbia, J. Glen MSS · Virginia Historical Society, Richmond, Lee family MSS

Likenesses B. L. Prevost, engraving, 1780, Smithsonian Institution, Washington, DC · B. B. Ellis, stipple, 1783, Smithsonian Institution, Washington, DC · B. Reading, stipple, 1783, Smithsonian Institution, Washington, DC

Drebbel, Cornelis (1572–1633), inventor and mechanical engineer, was born in Alkmaar in the Netherlands, the son of Jacob Janszoon Drebbel (d. 1591). His father, whose family name was originally Dremmel, was a well-to-do burgher of Alkmaar, a town in the province of North Holland, and in all probability a landowner or farmer. Nothing is known of Drebbel's mother. He was an Anabaptist, and attended the Latin school in his home town. About 1587 he went to Haarlem, where he was apprenticed to the well-known painter and engraver Hendrik Goltzius (1558–1617). Here Drebbel was instructed in drawing and copperplate-engraving, and became an excellent etcher. He also assisted Goltzius, an expert in alchemy, in his experiments, and from him acquired an interest in and a knowledge of the subject.

In 1595 Drebbel married Sophia Jansdochter, Goltzius's younger sister, who was a little older than Drebbel. They settled at Alkmaar, where their first-born son was buried on 6 November 1596. The couple had at least six more children: two sons, Jan and Jacob, two daughters, Anna and Catharina, and twins, who died in 1602. The marriage seems to have been very unhappy, and Sophia's prodigal way of life led to Drebbel's constant lack of money and finally to bitter poverty. Drebbel worked as an engraver, painter, and cartographer, and also as an instrument maker and an engineer. That he was a competent pupil of Goltzius is shown by a number of extant engravings in his hand.

On 21 June 1598 the states general granted to Drebbel a patent for a water-supply system and for a perpetual clockwork (a self-winding and -regulating clockwork); on 16 February 1602 he obtained a patent for a chimney with a good draught. We know that about 1600–01 he built a fountain for the city of Middelburg. His patents indicate that Drebbel was primarily an inventor. Perpetual motion machines and ingenious devices played an important part throughout his life. In particular, his perpetuum mobile appeared to be pre-eminently suitable to spread his reputation elsewhere. His inventions were mainly based on the recently known works of the Alexandrian engineers Philo of Byzantium (*fl. c.*250 BC) and Hero of Alexandria (*fl.* AD 62), and of the Roman writer Vitruvius (*d. c.*25 BC). In these years he worked on the grinding of lenses and the construction of optical instruments (the magic lantern and camera obscura), so that when he later came to England he was a skilled optical worker.

At the end of 1604 or in early 1605 Drebbel moved to London, where he came into the service of James I and soon into the special service of the ten-year-old Henry, prince of Wales. He was installed at Eltham Palace and assisted in the technical preparations of the theatrical performances and innumerable entertainments at the Stuart court.

had a glass-grinding machine. In 1620 he was experimenting to prepare glass that would be a substitute for rock crystal. It is probable that in 1622 he taught Constantijn Huygens how to grind glass, and that Huygens passed his knowledge to his son Christiaan. Robert Hooke may have learnt glass-grinding from Drebbel's son-in-law Johannes Sibertus Kuffler, with whom he was acquainted.

About 1620 Drebbel constructed an oar-driven submarine, which was based on the principle of a diving bell: the bottom was open, and a rower sitting above the water level controlled the submarine. In this boat Drebbel travelled down the Thames from Westminster to Greenwich under the surface of the water, and in a short time the story of his submarine became grossly exaggerated. Drebbel did not invent the submarine, nor did he discover oxygen, which he obviously needed to stay in the boat under water. He refreshed the air in the boat by heating saltpetre in a retort, which—as was known—gave an 'air' in which one could breathe. Drebbel's two sons-in-law promoted his discoveries and inventions so strongly that today it is hardly possible to reconstruct exactly the true facts of the matter.

These sons-in-law, Abraham Kuffler (1598–1657) and Johannes Sibertus Kuffler (1595–1677), were sons of a Dutchman who had taken up residence in Cologne. About 1620 they came to England, where they became closely associated with Drebbel as his assistants. Abraham married Drebbel's eldest daughter, Anna, in 1623 and Johannes Sibertus the second daughter, Catharina, in 1627. The dyeworks operated by Drebbel, probably since 1607, in Stratford by Bow (14 miles from London) was not flourishing. About 1622 the brothers Kuffler became Drebbel's business partners, but only after their father-in-law's death did they succeed in bringing the factory to prosperity.

During this time (1622–33) Drebbel made his most important contribution in the field of chemical technology, namely his discovery of a tin mordant for dyeing scarlet with cochineal. It is said that he also introduced into England the manufacture of sulphuric acid by burning sulphur with saltpetre, and that he discovered the mercury and silver fulminates.

From 1626 until 1629 Drebbel was in the service of the Royal Navy, concerning himself mainly with the famous expedition to La Rochelle to assist the Huguenots being besieged by French troops. He manufactured explosives and fireships, and participated in the last English expedition of 1628. This ended in failure, and Drebbel was dismissed from the service. In 1630 we find him involved in planning an extensive drainage scheme, which was carried out under the direction of the Dutch engineer Sir Charles Vermuyden (c.1590–1677), who with Dutch colonists had been trying since 1627 to reclaim the marshlands north of London and round Cambridge and Huntingdon.

Drebbel left very few writings of his own, and none of them was concerned with his inventions. His perpetuum mobile was described in Thomas Tymme's *Dialogue philosophicall, wherein natures secret closet is opened and the cause of all motion in nature shewed out of manner and forme:*

Cornelis Drebbel (1572–1633), by unknown engraver, pubd 1628

Soon Drebbel drew attention with his perpetuum mobile, automatic and hydraulic organs, optical instruments, and the like. In December 1607 he demonstrated to James I his perpetuum mobile, a kind of air thermometer, which operated on fluctuations in atmospheric temperature and pressure. It made such a deep impression that Ben Jonson refers to it in his *Silent Woman* (1609), when he makes Morose say: 'My very house turns round with the tumult! I dwell in a Windmill! The Perpetual Motion is here, and not at Eltham' (act 5, scene 3).

Drebbel's fame as an inventor soon became well known outside Britain. In 1607 Emperor Rudolf II invited him to Prague, and Drebbel and his family moved to the city in October 1610. He demonstrated to Rudolf his perpetuum mobile, constructed pumps for mining, and devoted himself to alchemy. After Rudolf's brother Matthias conquered Prague in 1611, Drebbel was imprisoned; late in 1612 he was set free. At some time after February 1613 Drebbel returned to England, where he occupied himself with the manufacture of telescopes and compound microscopes, and with the construction of thermostats (temperature regulators for ovens and furnaces) and an incubator for hatching duck and chicken eggs.

Drebbel's compound microscopes with two convex lenses were known over western and southern Europe and bought by several eminent persons, among them Constantijn Huygens. At his house near London, Drebbel *together with the wittie invention of an artificiall perpetual motion* (1612). Drebbel's most famous work was *Van de natuyre der elementen* (1604), which was reprinted and translated many times and mainly dealt with the transmutation of the four elements fire, air, water, and earth. A second edition appeared in 1607 with a new title, *Wondervondt van de eeuwighe beweging die den Alcmaarschen philosooph Cornelis Drebbel … te weghe gebracht heeft* ('The wonderful discovery of perpetual motion which the philosopher of Alkmaar had contrived …'); the book was dedicated to James I, who—as noted above—witnessed Drebbel's demonstrations. His *De quinta essentia tractatus* (1621) described the alchemical process in vague and general terms.

The last years of Drebbel's life were far from easy. From 1629 until his death he was extremely poor and earned his living by keeping an alehouse beside the Thames below London Bridge. He died in the parish of Holy Trinity, in the Minories, London, some time before 7 November 1633, on which date administration of his estate was granted to his two sons.   H. A. M. SNELDERS

Sources F. M. Jaeger, *Cornelis Drebbel en zijne tijdgenooten* (1922) · G. Tierie, *Cornelis Drebbel (1572–1633)* (Amsterdam, 1932) · L. E. Harris, *The two Netherlanders: Humphrey Bradley and Cornelis Drebbel* (1961) · H. A. M. Snelders, 'Alkmaarse natuurwetenschappers uit de 16de en 17de eeuw', *Alkmaarse Historische Reeks*, 4 (1980), 101–22 · F. W. Gibbs, 'The furnaces and thermometers of Cornelius Drebbel', *Annals of Science*, 6 (1948–50), 32–43 · R. L. Colie, 'Cornelis Drebbel and Salomon de Caus: two Jacobean models for Salomon's house', *Huntington Library Quarterly*, 18 (1954–5), 245–60 · J. R. Partington, *A history of chemistry*, 2 (1961), 321–4 · H. Michel, 'Le mouvement perpetuel de Drebbel', *Physis*, 13 (1971), 289–94 · municipal archives, Alkmaar

Likenesses engraving, pubd 1628, NPG [*see illus.*] · C. von Swichem, wood-engraving, repro. in Jaeger, *Cornelis Drebbel* · P. Velyn, copper engraving, repro. in Jaeger, *Cornelis Drebbel*

Dredge, James (1840–1906), civil engineer and journalist, was born in Bath on 29 July 1840, the younger son of James Dredge and his wife, Anne Vine. The elder James Dredge was an engineer who designed and patented a form of suspension bridge with inclined suspension rods carrying the roadway. The younger James's elder brother, William, under whom he served articles, was also an engineer. After education at Bath grammar school Dredge spent three years (1858–61) in the office of D. K. Clark; in 1862 he entered the office of John Fowler, and was engaged for several years in London on work connected with the Metropolitan District Railway. However, Dredge soon gave up practical engineering for engineering journalism. From the start in January 1866 of the weekly periodical *Engineering*, which was founded by Zerah Colburn on his retirement from the editorship of *The Engineer* in 1865, Dredge helped in illustrating and occasionally wrote for the paper. On Colburn's death in 1870 Dredge and W. H. Maw, the sub-editor, became joint editors and proprietors. Dredge helped actively in the management until May 1903, when he was disabled by paralysis. He published several books on technical subjects, which mainly derived from his writings in *Engineering*.

Dredge was keenly interested in international exhibitions. He described for his journal those at Vienna (1873), Philadelphia (1876), and Paris (1878 and 1889), publishing his reports of the first and last in book form. He was also officially connected as a British commissioner with exhibitions at Chicago (1893), Antwerp (1894), Brussels (1897), and Milan (1906). For services at Paris in 1889 he was appointed an officer of the Légion d'honneur and for his work at Brussels he was made CMG in 1898.

As a close friend of the American engineer Alexander Lyman Holley he delivered an address in Chickering Hall, New York, on 2 October 1890, at the installation of a bronze bust of Holley in Washington Square, New York. He was also elected in 1886 an honorary member of the American Society of Mechanical Engineers. He was elected a member of the Institution of Civil Engineers on 4 February 1896, and of the Institution of Mechanical Engineers in 1874, and was a member of the council of the Society of Arts (1890–93). In 1901 he founded, as a monthly supplement to *Engineering*, a journal called *Traction and Transmission*, which he edited with much care until it ceased in 1904. Dredge died at Pinner Wood Cottage, Pinner, Middlesex, on 15 August 1906. He was long a widower; an only child, Marie Louise, survived him.

W. F. SPEAR, *rev.* RALPH HARRINGTON

Sources *Engineering* (24 Aug 1906) · *PICE*, 166 (1905–6), 382–4 · *CGPLA Eng. & Wales* (1906)

Likenesses portrait, repro. in *Engineering*

Wealth at death £78,366 18s. 10d.: probate, 15 Nov 1906, *CGPLA Eng. & Wales*

Dreghorn. For this title name *see* MacLaurin, John, Lord Dreghorn (1734–1796).

Drelincourt, Peter [Pierre] (1644–1722), dean of Armagh, was born in Paris on 22 July 1644, one of sixteen children of Charles Drelincourt (1595–1669), minister of the French Reformed church at Charenton (on the outskirts of Paris) and author of religious works; his mother's family name was Bolduc. He studied theology at Geneva (1666), Oxford (1671), and later Leiden (1675), where his brother Charles held the chair of anatomy. By 1678 he had returned to Oxford as the private tutor to the thirteen-year-old Lord James Butler, grandson of the duke of Ormond, who in that same year was appointed lord lieutenant of Ireland for the third time. For three years, at an annual salary of £50, Drelincourt was responsible for part of the education (French, history, geography, and religion) and for the physical and financial well-being of his charge—a task at which he was, at least initially, less than successful. Sir Robert Southwell attributed this to a lack of authority, informing Ormond that 'our young lord … has in his rage struck him and rogued him like a lackey; and he has brooked all rather than let go his hold' (*Ormonde MSS*, 5.550). But Ormond seems to have had a higher opinion of Drelincourt, since he retained him as his 'domestick chaplain' in 1681 and sought to promote him in the Church of Ireland.

In the spring of 1681 Drelincourt graduated MA from Trinity College, Dublin, and was appointed precentor of

Christ Church; in 1683 he was made archdeacon of Leighlin (collated 31 October, installed 11 November; resigned February 1691). In the spring of 1691 he graduated LLD from Trinity College and was appointed dean of Armagh (patent, 28 February, installation, 14 March) and also rector of Armagh and Clonfeacle; while he ceded the archdeaconry of Leighlin, he remained precentor of Christ Church. These combined benefices placed Drelincourt among the wealthier clergy of his time, providing him with an annual income of some £900 and no doubt making it possible for him to marry Mary (d. 1755), daughter of Peter Maurice, dean of Derry, who brought to the marriage landed estates in the parish of Wrexham in Wales. They had one daughter, Anne (d. 1775), who married Lieutenant-Colonel Hugh, third and last Viscount Primrose, on 21 June 1739. Although Drelincourt did not reside much at Armagh, but mostly in London and Dublin, he did carry out restoration on the cathedral, which had suffered during the Williamite wars. He also contributed significantly to the cost of constructing the churches at Eglish in Clonfeacle and St Dolough in Glasnevin, Dublin, and made a generous donation to the hospital and free school of King Charles II (now the King's Hospital, Dublin) in return for a seat on the board, whose meetings he attended from 1711 to 1715.

Although from a family of scholars and writers, Drelincourt published only two pamphlets, *De l'état présent d'Irlande* (1681) and *A Speech Made to his Grace the Duke of Ormond* (1682), both inspired by the flight of Huguenot refugees from France. These slight publications and his absenteeism may have inspired Archbishop William King's harsh comment to Primate Lindsay after Drelincourt's death: 'Your grace is sensible what a clog and how useless the last Dean was to the Church' (Reeves, fol. 187). During his lifetime, however, King not only praised Drelincourt's judicious 'management of … difficult affairs' in 1701 but also appealed unreservedly to his generosity to meet various needs of the Church of Ireland. Drelincourt died in London on 7 March 1722. He was buried in Armagh Cathedral, where his wife erected a monument to his memory by the Belgian sculptor Jean-Michel Rysbrack. This praised the way he 'To sacred service … his wealth consigned', and it is for his munificence that his memory endures within the Church of Ireland. Mary Drelincourt founded the Drelincourt charity school in Armagh in 1747, and another on her estate in Wrexham, called the Berse-Drelincourt School. RUTH WHELAN

Sources D. W. Reeves, 'Memoirs of the deans of Armagh, 1550–1875', Armagh Public Library, fol. 187 · TCD, MS 750/2/2/92–3 · Burtchaell & Sadleir, *Alum. Dubl.*, 2nd edn, 244 · H. Cotton, *Fasti ecclesiae Hibernicae*, 5 vols. (1848–60), vol. 2, pp. 53, 398; vol. 3, p. 33 · S. Stelling-Michaud, *Le livre du recteur de l'Académie de Genève* (1559–1878), 6 vols. (Geneva, 1959–80), vol. 3, p. 437 · J. McKee, 'Pierre Drelincourt et sa contribution à la vie intellectuelle en Angleterre et en Irlande', *La vie intellectuelle aux Refuges protestants*, ed. J. Häseler and A. McKenna (Paris, 1999), 269–88 · P. Bayle, 'Drelincourt, Charles', *Dictionnaire historique et critique* (1697); (1702) · *The manuscripts of the marquis of Ormonde*, [old ser.], 3 vols., HMC, 36 (1895–1909), vols. 1–2 · *Calendar of the manuscripts of the marquess of Ormonde*, new ser., 8 vols., HMC, 36 (1902–20) · will, PRO, PROB 11/584, fols. 190r–190v

Likenesses portrait; formerly at King's Hospital, Dublin
Wealth at death see will, PRO, PROB 11/584, fols. 190r–190v

Drennan, James. *See* Allen, William Edward David (1901–1973).

Drennan, Martha. *See* McTier, Martha (1742–1837).

Drennan, Thomas (1696–1768). *See under* Drennan, William (1754–1820).

Drennan, William (1754–1820), physician, poet, and political reformer, was born in Belfast on 23 May 1754, the child of the Revd **Thomas Drennan** (1696–1768) and his wife, Anne, *née* Lennox (1719–1806). Of Thomas Drennan, the minister of Belfast's First Presbyterian Congregation, very little is known. He was born on 25 December 1696. Having graduated from Glasgow in 1716, he seems to have moved to Dublin shortly after 1720, where he assisted the philosopher Francis Hutcheson in running a private academy for protestant dissenters. In 1726 he was licensed to preach by the General Synod of Ulster, and he accepted a call from the congregation of Holywood (co. Down) in 1731, following Hutcheson's appointment to the chair of moral philosophy at Glasgow. In 1736 he moved to the First Congregation of Belfast, affiliated to the non-subscribing Presbytery of Antrim, where he became the ministerial colleague of the Revd Samuel Haliday. Although he published no sermon, he was regarded as an elegant preacher and an accomplished scholar; his close friends and correspondents included not only Hutcheson but the Revd John Abernethy, the Revd James Duchal, and James Arbuckle, the poet and editor of the *Dublin Weekly Journal*. In 1741 he married Anne Lennox. Of their eleven children only three survived: William, Martha (1742–1837), and Anne (1745–1825). Thomas Drennan died on 14 February 1768.

William Drennan was educated by his father and by the Revd Matthew Garnet, an Anglican clergyman who conducted a local school. At the age of fifteen he matriculated at the University of Glasgow, graduated MA in 1772, and then took a degree in medicine at Edinburgh between 1773 and 1778. Even before his return to Ireland, Drennan had already been caught up in the excitement surrounding the volunteers, the independent militia companies raised to defend Ireland during the American War of Independence; and he supported their campaigns to secure 'free trade' and 'legislative independence' for Ireland, publishing his first political pamphlet in 1780. Towards the end of 1782 he moved to Newry, co. Down, where he set up practice as an obstetrician, and where he continued to be active as a volunteer and an advocate of parliamentary reform. His influential *Letters of Orellana, an Irish Helot* (1785), published first in the *Belfast News-Letter* and then as a pamphlet, established his reputation in radical circles.

When in December 1789 Drennan moved to Dublin, he was caught up in the radical revival which followed the outbreak of the French Revolution. He joined The Monks of the Screw, a group of prominent patriot politicians, and a political club founded by Thomas Addis Emmet, Peter Burrowes, Wolfe Tone, and Whitley Stokes. In June

1791 he circulated in Dublin and Belfast a prospectus for an Irish brotherhood, a secret society to be organized along masonic lines and dedicated to radical reform; the paper was one of several initiatives which led to the formation of the Society of United Irishmen soon after. It is for his role as a founder and prominent member of the society (1791–4) that he is best-known; he served several terms of office as president of the Dublin branch, was responsible for framing the United Irish test, and was the author of many of the society's publications. One of these, the 'Address to the volunteers', dated 14 December 1792, eventually led to his trial for seditious libel on 29 June 1794. Although acquitted, he withdrew from the United Irishmen and played no part in the insurrectionary phase of the republican movement, though his ballads 'Erin' (1795) and 'The Wake of William Orr' (1797) demonstrate his continuing sympathy for the national cause.

On 3 February 1800 Drennan married Sarah Swanwick (1770?–1866x70) from Wem, Shropshire. Following the death of his cousin, Martha Young, he inherited a small property at Cottown, near Bangor, co. Down, and retired to Belfast in 1807. At local political meetings, and in the editorials of his *Belfast Monthly Magazine* (1808–13), he continued to support parliamentary reform and Catholic emancipation, though he became reconciled to the Act of Union, a measure which he had passionately opposed in 1799–1800. He helped to establish the Belfast Academical Institution (1810). His poems are now seldom read, but a number of his patriotic verses achieved popularity at the end of the eighteenth century, and he was the first to call Ireland the 'emerald isle'. His poetry was collected in *Fugitive Pieces in Prose and Verse* (1815) and his translation *The Electra of Sophocles* (1817) was published two years later. In 1931 a volume of his correspondence was edited by D. A. Chart and published as *The Drennan Letters … 1776–1819*; it is highly valued by historians as a remarkable portrait of the political, social, and cultural life of late eighteenth-century Ireland.

William Drennan died on 5 February 1820 at Cabin Hill, Belfast, and was buried in the Old Clifton Street graveyard. His funeral procession, at which the coffin was borne by six protestants and six Catholics, was a symbolic testimony to the liberalism which once distinguished a city later better known for its religious animosities.

I. R. MCBRIDE

Sources *The Drennan–McTier letters*, ed. J. Agnew, 3 vols. (1998–9) • *The Drennan letters*, ed. D. A. Chart (1931) • A. T. Q. Stewart, '"A stable unseen power": Dr William Drennan and the origins of the United Irishmen', *Essays presented to Michael Roberts*, ed. J. Bossy and P. Jupp (1976), 80–92 • A. T. Q. Stewart, *A deeper silence: the hidden roots of the United Irish movement* (1993); repr. as *A deeper silence: the hidden origins of the United Irishmen* (1998) • I. McBride, 'William Drennan and the dissenting tradition', *The United Irishmen: republicanism, radicalism and rebellion*, ed. D. Dickson and others (1993), 49–61 • C. P. Hill, 'William Drennan and the radical movement for Irish reform, 1779–94', MLitt diss., University of Dublin, 1967 • A. Rice, 'The lonely rebellion of William Drennan', *The poet's place: Ulster literature and society: essays in honour of John Hewitt*, ed. G. Dawe and J. W. Foster (1991), 77–95 • correspondence, PRO NIre., Drennan-McTier, D 591 [typescript, T 765]; Drennan-Bruce, D 553; letters to Sarah Drennan, T 2884 [with biographical notes by M. Duffin] • wills and land documents, PRO NIre., Drennan MSS, D 270 • W. I. Addison, *A roll of graduates of the University of Glasgow from 31st December 1727 to 31st December 1897* (1898) • W. I. Addison, ed., *The matriculation albums of the University of Glasgow from 1728 to 1858* (1913) • J. Mackay, *The happiness of the righteous in a future state, explained and improved. A sermon preached in the Old Meeting-House in Belfast, February 28th, 1768. On occasion of the death of the late Reverend Mr Thomas Drennan, pastor of that congregation, who departed this life, February 14, 1768* (1768) • W. Bruce, 'The progress of nonsubscription to creeds', *Christian Moderator*, 1 (1827), 429–31 [Thomas Drennan] • A. Gordon and G. K. Smith, *Historic memorials of the First Presbyterian Church of Belfast* (1887) [Thomas Drennan]

Archives PRO NIre., corresp. and papers • PRO NIre., wills and land documents relating to Drennan family, D 270 | PRO NIre., papers relating to Belfast Academical Institution, D 4137/A/8/1–6 • PRO NIre., corresp. with Bruce, D 553 • PRO NIre., letters to Sarah Drennan, biographical notes on William and Sarah by Maria Duffin, T 2884 • PRO NIre., D 591 with notes by Ruth Duffin, T 765 [typescript copy] • PRO NIre., corresp. with McTier, D 591

Likenesses attrib. R. Home, portrait, Ulster Museum, Belfast

Wealth at death £300 left to a number of relatives; £2000 left to three younger children; the townland of Cottown, parish of Bangor, Down: will, PRO NIre., D270/30

Dreschfeld, Julius (1845–1907), pathologist and physician, was born on 13 October 1845 at Niederwären, near Bamberg, Bavaria, the youngest son in a family of five sons and five daughters of Samuel Dreschfeld, a well-to-do merchant, and his wife, Giedel. His parents were well-respected Orthodox Jews; his father lived until the age of ninety-two, and his mother to ninety-seven. In 1861, after completing his early education at the Bamberg Gymnasium, he came to Britain to live with his brother Leopold Dreschfeld (1824–1897), a dentist in Manchester. Julius entered Owens College (the forerunner of Manchester University), and gained prizes in English, mathematics, and science, including the Dalton chemical prize (1863) and the Dalton junior mathematical scholarship (1864). He attended the Manchester Royal School of Medicine in Pine Street, but in 1864 he returned to Bavaria to continue his medical study at the University of Würzburg. In 1866 his studies were interrupted by the 'seven week' Austro-Prussian War, during which he acted as assistant surgeon in the Bavarian army. On his return to Würzburg he graduated MD in 1867 with a thesis 'Reflex action of the vagus nerve on blood pressure'. He acted as assistant to Albert von Bezold (1838–1868), professor of physiology, and made a special study of pathology, the area of medicine in which he was to specialize. In 1869 he returned to Britain, and after becoming licentiate of the Royal College of Physicians, London, he set up in practice in Manchester. In 1872 he was appointed honorary physician to the Hulme Dispensary, Manchester, and the following year honorary assistant physician at the Manchester Royal Infirmary; in 1883, on the resignation of Sir William Roberts, he was made a full honorary physician, and in due course senior honorary physician in 1899, and the first honorary consulting physician in 1905.

Dreschfeld's most important contributions were to the study of pathology, especially related to diseases of the nervous system. In 1875 he was asked to supervise and catalogue the pathological collection in the Owens College medical museum, and the following year he was promoted to lecturer in pathology. Under his influence the pathology department rapidly expanded and played an increasingly important role in the medical school. In 1881 he was appointed as professor of general pathology, morbid anatomy, and morbid histology, the first chairs in these subjects in England. Dreschfeld's knowledge of the French and German medical literature was encyclopaedic, and he travelled widely throughout Europe visiting medical laboratories to learn new techniques. His pathology laboratory at Owens College, one of the first of its kind in Britain, was modelled on those in the continental medical schools. He stressed the importance of pathology in medical training, and argued that a good knowledge of pathology was essential to the practice of clinical medicine. He was said to be an extremely good teacher both at the bedside and in the lecture theatre; the number of his students rose from 3 in 1873 to 110 in 1891. He urged his students to look beyond the superficial manifestations of disease, and to try to explain their patients' symptoms in terms of the underlying pathology. It was mainly due to Dreschfeld's influence that pathology became established as an essential part of the medical curriculum in Britain. His most enduring research contribution to pathology was his paper 'A new staining fluid' in the *Journal of Anatomy and Physiology* (1876), which described the use of eosin dye to stain tissue slides to reveal microscopic detail—this became a standard technique, still in present use. His work on rabies during the 1882–3 epidemic in Manchester is also well known—he attempted to develop an attenuated anti-rabies vaccine by injecting infected spinal tissue into rabbits. His technique was similar to that used by Louis Pasteur for anthrax in 1881 (Pasteur's own anti-rabies vaccine was not available until 1888). Dreschfeld's work on rabies may have succeeded, but it was never completed because of the Cruelty to Animals Act (1876). He explained in the *British Medical Journal* (14 August 1886) that the experiments had to be carried out immediately after the death of a rabies victim, and there was never sufficient time to apply for the necessary animal licence. He thought the act was too restrictive, and was holding back medical research in Britain.

In 1891 Dreschfeld gave up his chair in pathology to take over the chair of medicine from John Edward Morgan—a unique achievement, and a tribute to his breadth of medical knowledge. Dreschfeld was one of the best-known physicians in England, his opinion was greatly respected, and he was widely consulted, especially for neurological problems. Apart from his work at the Royal Infirmary he held honorary posts at the Manchester Skin Hospital, the Manchester Jewish Hospital, and the Christie Cancer Hospital. He became a member of the Royal College of Physicians in 1875 and a fellow in 1883; he delivered the Bradshawe lecture on 'diabetic coma' in 1887. He was married twice: first in 1888 to Selina (d. 1904), daughter of Felix Gaspari of Berlin, with whom he had two sons and two daughters; and again in 1905, to Ethel, daughter of Dr James Harvey Lilley of Leamington Spa, who survived him.

Dreschfeld took a prominent part in many local medical, scientific, and philanthropic societies. He helped to form the Pathological Society of Manchester (1885), and was a founder member of the Pathological Society of Great Britain (1906); he was president of the Manchester Medical Society in 1888, and president of the Manchester Therapeutics Society in 1899. He took an active part in the British Medical Association, acting as president of the pathological section in 1886, and president of the section of medicine in 1902. He was a strong supporter of the Manchester Society for Aiding Distressed Foreigners, and was medical adviser to the Manchester Royal School of Music.

A slowly progressive disease of the spinal cord from which he suffered since 1897 (said by some of his colleagues to be a form of multiple sclerosis) impaired his walking, but scarcely affected his varied industry. While preparing his forthcoming Lumleian lecture to the Royal College of Physicians, he died suddenly at his home, Stanley House, Wilmslow Road, Withington, Manchester, from heart failure on 13 June 1907. He had previously converted to Christianity, and following a Church of England service, attended by a large congregation of friends and colleagues from Manchester, he was buried in a family vault in Holy Trinity churchyard, Hoghton Street, Southport, on 18 June. He was remembered by a memorial scholarship, founded by his wife and colleagues, for new medical students.

Dreschfeld wrote over 120 papers in English, French, and German; a full bibliography can be found in the *Dreschfeld Memorial Volume* compiled by Professor E. M. Brockbank in 1908. Dreschfeld's published works covered all aspects of general medicine; he made important observations on the metabolic effects of diabetes, and the classification of Hodgkin's disease; he wrote the sections on peptic ulceration, endocarditis, and typhoid for Clifford Allbutt's textbook *System of Medicine* (1896–8). He was an authority on diseases of the nervous system and his most important contributions were in this area; he described the pathology of motor neurone disease, alcoholic paralysis, neurosyphilis, and numerous other rare neurological disorders. His work in clinical medicine and neurology is well known; he can be regarded as one of the founders of neuropathology, and many of his observations can still be traced in modern-day medical practice. However, it is arguable that his contribution to British medical education was even more important than his clinical and laboratory work; his introduction of pathology into the medical curriculum signalled a new approach to the understanding of disease, and raised the standard of medical teaching. In this respect Dreschfeld should be remembered not only as a great teacher, but also as one of the founders of modern scientific medicine.

PETER D. MOHR

Sources S. Oleesky, 'Julius Dreschfeld and late 19th century medicine in Manchester', *Manchester Medical Gazette*, 51 (1971–2), 14–17, 58–60, 96–9 · *The Times* (15 June 1907) · *Manchester Guardian*

(15 June 1907) · *Manchester City News* (15 June 1907) · *Manchester Evening News* (18 June 1907) · *BMJ* (22 June 1907), 1519–20 · *The Lancet* (29 June 1907) · *Medical Guild Quarterly* (July 1907) · *Manchester University Magazine* (Oct 1907) · *Medical Chronicle* (Nov 1907) · E. M. Brockbank, *Dreschfeld memorial volume* (1908) · G. Steell, *Manchester Medical Students Gazette*, new ser., 7 (1907), 98–101 · W. Brockbank, 'Who were they?', *Manchester Medical Gazette*, 43 (1964), 18–20 · W. Brockbank, *The honorary medical staff of the Manchester Royal Infirmary, 1830–1948* (1965) · E. M. Brockbank, 'Julius Dreschfeld', in *The book of Manchester and Salford*, British Medical Association [1929], 55–6 · W. J. Elwood and A. F. Tuxford, eds., *Some Manchester doctors: a biographical collection to mark the 150th anniversary of the Manchester Medical Society, 1834–1984* (1984) · Munk, *Roll* · 'Professor Julius Dreschfeld', *Manchester Faces and Places*, 4 (1892–3), 35–6 · 'Professor Julius Dreschfeld MD', *Owens College Union Magazine* (June 1895), 137–8 · 'Professor Julius Dreschfeld', *Manchester Faces and Places*, 16 (1905), 2–4 · S. Coates, 'Manchester German gentlemen: immigrant institutions in a provincial city, 1840–1920', *Manchester Regional History Review*, 5/2 (1991), 21–30 · B. Williams, *The making of Manchester Jewry, 1740–1875* (1976); repr. (1985), 311 · *DNB*

Archives JRL, Manchester collection
Likenesses G. Harcourt, oils (posthumous), Manchester Royal Infirmary, Professor of Pathology Office, Directorate of Pathology · photograph, repro. in *Manchester Faces and Places*, 4 (1892–3), 37
Wealth at death £71,016 15s. 10d.: probate, 25 July 1907, *CGPLA Eng. & Wales*

Dresdel, Sonia [*real name* Lois Obee] (1909–1976), actress, was born on 5 May 1909 in Hornsea, East Riding of Yorkshire, the daughter of John Henry Obee (*b.* 1868/9), a music-seller, and his wife, Florence Binks. Shortly afterwards the family moved to Grimsby and thence, in 1915, to Aberdeen, where she was educated at the girls' high school, and in 1926–7 studied briefly at the university before opting for a stage career; she entered the Royal Academy of Dramatic Art in 1930. Having completed her training and won the Kendal prize, she made her professional début in 1931 as Rosalie Quilter in Walter Ellis's farce *Almost a Honeymoon*. She subsequently worked in provincial repertory theatres, seen as the accredited apprenticeship for any aspiring performer, throughout the 1930s. She was engaged for the 1931–2 season at the New Theatre, Northampton, then spent five years with the White Rose Players at Harrogate, and finally acted in similar companies managed by H. M. Tennent in Edinburgh and Glasgow. In August 1939 she joined the Old Vic company, first appearing at the Buxton festival as Abigail in Norman Ginsbury's *Viceroy Sarah* and reappearing with them in October at the Streatham Hill Theatre, London, and later on tour, in this and other parts, including Lady Capulet in *Romeo and Juliet*, Judith Anderson in G. B. Shaw's *The Devil's Disciple*, the Duchess de la Trémouille in his *Saint Joan*, and Olivia in Oliver Goldsmith's *The Good-Natured Man*. She again toured with the Old Vic in 1940 and 1941, playing Viola in *Twelfth Night*, Portia in *The Merchant of Venice*, Lady Faulconbridge in *King John*, and the eponymous heroine in an adaptation of Du Maurier's *Trilby*.

In September of the following year this early promise came to fruition with an outstanding interpretation of Hedda Gabler at the Mercury—a sensitive, highly intelligent performance which drew rhapsodic praise from no less fastidious a critic than James Agate. Dresdel followed it in November with a shrewdly calculating Millamant in William Congreve's *The Way of the World*, also directed by Ashley Dukes at the Mercury, in 1943 with an exquisitely flirtatious Clotilde in his version of Henry Becque's *La Parisienne* at the St James's, and in January 1944 scored an even more remarkable success, particularly in box-office terms, as Olivia Russell in Joan Morgan's *The Dark Potential* at the Q. Retitled *This was a Woman* for its transfer in March to the Comedy, this melodramatic story of a homicidally paranoid and manipulative suburban housewife ran in war-damaged London for almost a year. It was a success which proved a mixed blessing in that it identified Dresdel with the persona of the villainess or heartless conniver and initiated a strain of type-casting which never quite deserted her. It also created a pattern for the next phase of her working life, characterized by leading roles in a succession of unmemorable plays for West End commercial managements—leavened by occasional revivals such as W. S. Maugham's *The Sacred Flame* at the St Martin's in November 1945, in which she played the repressed Nurse Wayland, and Leo Tolstoy's *The Power of Darkness* at the Lyric in April 1949, in which she was cast as the murderous, adulterous Anisya, and several productions at the Arts Theatre Club. Other highlights during this period were her appearances at two Edinburgh festivals—in 1950 as Juno in the première of James Bridie's *The Queen's Comedy* and in 1955, when she repeated her Hedda—a tour of Australia with James Parish's *Message for Margaret* in 1951, and in 1958 a further tour of South Africa and Kenya with *Hedda Gabler* and Ugo Betti's *The Queen and the Rebels*.

The year 1959 signalled an exploratory change of direction, which in the event led nowhere, when Dresdel was appointed director of productions for a season at the Harrogate Theatre, presenting a weekly repertory of routine farces and thrillers interlarded with rather more ambitious fare in plays by John Osborne, Ugo Betti, Terence Rattigan, Noël Coward, Aldous Huxley, and Frederick Lonsdale. Returning to the Old Vic in November 1961 as Christine Mannon in Eugene O'Neill's *Mourning Becomes Electra*, she gave an electrifying performance which the *Times* reviewer described as 'a bravura display of Christine's rattlesnake charms and quick threatening tensities' (22 Dec 1961) and which persuaded another commentator to designate her 'actress of the year'. Between October 1963 and August 1965 she appeared in five productions at the Mermaid, enabling her to demonstrate some of the versatility for which the majority of her stage work allowed little scope: as Varvara Stavrogin in Albert Camus's version of Dostoyevsky's *The Possessed*, Amalia in Luigi Pirandello's *Right You Are! (If You Think So)*, Jocasta in Sophocles' *Oedipus the King*, Queen Eleanor in John Arden's *Left-Handed Liberty*, and Georgina Tidman in Sir Arthur Wing Pinero's *Dandy Dick*. In the last decade of her life her most notable performances were as the erupting woman spectator in Robert Shaw's *The Man in the Glass Booth* at the St Martin's in July 1967 and Judith Bliss in Noël Coward's *Hay Fever* at the Bristol Old Vic in August 1970. She also appeared frequently on television and rarely without distinction, whether in single plays, series, or classic adaptations, but was poorly served by the cinema, making only twelve films; only two, *The Fallen Idol* (1948, as the evil Mrs Baines) and *The Trials of Oscar Wilde* (1960, as Lady Wilde), offered her any creative stimulus.

Sonia Dresdel's leisure time was spent gardening at her home, Ransley House, Mersham, Kent. She died in the Kent and Canterbury Hospital, Canterbury, on 18 January 1976. In reviewing her career it is difficult not to account her an unlucky actress who never fully realized her considerable potential. Despite her obvious gifts—a riveting stage presence, a dynamic yet velvet-like voice, and a sustained emotional power which some thought excessive, but was eminently theatrical—she found herself progressively under-employed and under-extended, denied the opportunity in her prime to measure herself against the great tragic roles, so that one can only speculate upon what she might have made of Lady Macbeth, Phèdre, or Medea. Nevertheless, she remained an accomplished artiste, who set an example of professionalism and left behind a worthy record of achievement.

DONALD ROY

Sources I. Herbert, ed., *Who's who in the theatre*, 16th edn (1977) · *WWW*, 1971–80 · *The Times* (19 Jan 1976) · *The Guardian* (19 Jan 1976) · D. Quinlan, *The illustrated directory of film character actors* (1985) · J. Agate, *Ego 6: once more the autobiography of James Agate* (1944) · J. Agate, *Ego 8: continuing the autobiography of James Agate* (1946) · J. Agate, *The contemporary theatre, 1944 and 1945* (1946) · S. D'Amico, ed., *Enciclopedia dello spettacolo*, 4 (Rome, 1957) · E. M. Truitt, *Who was who on screen*, 3rd edn (1983) · R. May, *A companion to the theatre* (1973) · J. Agate, *Ego 7: even more of the autobiography of James Agate* (1945) · East Riding of Yorkshire Archives Service, Beverley · J. Agate, play reviews, *Sunday Times* (1942–6) · review of *Mourning becomes Electra*, *The Times* (22 Dec 1961) · *Theatre World* (Oct 1944), 27–8

Archives FILM BFI NFTVA, performance footage | SOUND BL NSA, performance recordings

Likenesses A. Akerbladh, portrait, c.1943 (as Hedda Gabler), repro. in *Theatre World* (March 1945), 7 · photographs, 1949–65, Hult. Arch. · D. de Marney, photograph, repro. in *Plays and Players* (March 1977) · A. McBean, photograph (as Christine Mannon in *Mourning becomes Electra*), repro. in *Plays and Players* (Jan 1962) · photograph, repro. in Quinlan, *Illustrated directory* · photograph (in middle age), repro. in *The Times* · photograph (as Olivia Russell in *This was a woman*), repro. in *The Times* (16 March 1944) · photograph (as Amalia in *Right you are! (if you think so)*), repro. in *Plays and Players* (May 1965) · photograph (as Jocasta in *Oedipus the king*), repro. in *Plays and Players* (July 1965) · photograph (as Varvara Stavrogin in *The possessed*), repro. in *The Times* (24 Oct 1963) · photograph (as Laura in *Laura*), repro. in *The Times* (15 Feb 1945) · photograph, repro. in *Theatre World* (May 1948), 3 · photograph, repro. in *Theatre World* (Dec 1949), 32

Wealth at death £18,041: probate, 8 March 1976, *CGPLA Eng. & Wales*

Dresser, Christopher (1834–1904), designer and botanist, was born on 4 July 1834 in Glasgow, the second son and third of six children of Christopher Dresser, excise officer, of Yorkshire, and his wife, Mary Nettleton, of Norton, near Doncaster, Yorkshire. The family was posted to Sussex in 1847 and Dresser was educated at the Government School of Design at Somerset House in London from 1847 to 1854. He became arguably the first industrial designer,

identified by name on his work, which included ceramic, glass, metal, furniture, wallpapers, and textiles. He was influential as a theorist in Britain and America and anticipated, especially in his metalwork, the functional style of the modern movement.

The interests that provided a consistent source of inspiration throughout his career, botany and oriental art, developed while Dresser was still at the School of Design. He also came under the influence there of Henry Cole, Richard Redgrave, and Owen Jones, whose *Grammar of Ornament* of 1856 included Dresser's first published illustration.

Unlike William Morris, who was in some ways influenced by him, Dresser believed it necessary to co-operate with industry to bring well-made objects within reach of the widest possible public. He made a point of working with modern materials such as cast iron and linoleum. His design theory was based on the belief that natural forms should be abstracted and made geometric for use in ornamentation, and he likened the designer's mind to 'the vital force of the plant ever developing itself into forms of beauty'. His personal motto was 'truth, beauty, power'. His interest in natural sciences ran parallel with his design work at the beginning of his career, and his appointments included the chair of botany applied to the fine arts at the Department of Science and Art, South Kensington (1860), and the chair of ornamental art and botany at the Crystal Palace (1862). In 1854 he had married Thirza, daughter of William Perry, a lay missionary of Madeley, Shropshire. They had five sons and eight daughters, and Dresser's hectic career was driven in part by the need to support them all.

Among Dresser's first important writings were 'On the relation of science to ornamental art', a paper given to the Royal Institution in 1857, and *The Rudiments of Botany* and *Unity and Variety*, both of 1859. On the strength of the two latter he was awarded a doctorate by Jena University in 1860. He was always extremely proud of this and made a point of being known as Dr Dresser. He was disappointed in the same year when his application for the chair of botany at London University was unsuccessful.

In 1862 Dresser published *The Art of Decorative Design*. It shows the influence of A. W. N. Pugin and was important as the first popular book on design to show readers how to create designs themselves. In the battle of the styles, however, Dresser remained neutral, declaring that no style of ornament had yet arisen which had not possessed 'some beautiful feature'. In 1880 he set up the Art Furnishers' Alliance at Bond Street to sell 'artistic house furnishing material'. Gradually his scientific interests took less of Dresser's time. In 1876–7 he made his first visit to Japan and this confirmed his admiration for oriental design and inspired much of his best work, as well as a book, *Japan: its Architecture, Art, and Art Manufactures* (1882). Dresser's unusually prominent role as a named designer and the 'rediscovery' of his work in the 1930s have perhaps caused him to be overrated as an innovator. His work forms a distinguished part of Victorian design, but is not *sui generis*. Dresser died suddenly at the Hôtel Central, Mulhouse,

Alsace, Germany, of a heart attack while on a business trip, on 24 November 1904, and was buried at Mulhouse in an unmarked grave. His work was largely forgotten until 1936 when Nikolaus Pevsner acclaimed him as one of the pioneers of modern design. A sketchbook of his designs is at Ipswich Museum.   ROSEMARY HILL

Sources M. Collins, S. Durant, and P. Atterbury, *Christopher Dresser, 1834–1904* (1979) [exhibition catalogue, Camden Arts Centre, London, 3 Oct – 25 Nov 1979] · W. Halén, *Christopher Dresser* (1990) · private information (1993) [Stuart Durant] · *CGPLA Eng. & Wales* (1904) · N. Pevsner, *Pioneers of modern design* (1936) · S. Jerris, *The Penguin dictionary of design and designers* (1984) · R. Allwood, 'Christopher Dresser', *The dictionary of art*, ed. J. Turner (1996) · *Christopher Dresser, 1834–1904* (1990) [exhibition catalogue, Fine Art Society and Haslam & Whiteway Ltd, London, 17 Sept – 6 Oct 1990] · *DNB*
Archives Ipswich Museum, sketchbook
Likenesses photograph, NPG
Wealth at death £3891 1s. 3d.: probate, 19 Dec 1904, *CGPLA Eng. & Wales*

Dressler, John (*fl.* 1777–1808), musician, was probably from Germany. He first appears on 6 April 1777 when, as a single man and professional musician, his name was put forward for membership of the Royal Society of Musicians. On this occasion, however, he withdrew his name, and he did not join until March 1785. As a performer he was among the double bass players in the Handel memorial concerts at Westminster Abbey and the Pantheon, Oxford Street, in May and June 1784. He also appeared at the charity concerts of the Royal Society at St Paul's in May of the following year and on a regular basis from 1789 to 1796. On 24 February 1792 he was performing at the King's Theatre in *The Redemption* (probably Samuel Arnold's oratorio based on the works of Handel), and on 7 March in Handel's *Acis and Galatea*. While it is unclear on which instrument he was performing on these occasions, on 15 February 1793, in an oratorio concert at the King's Theatre, he made his first recorded performance on the trombone. The following year (12 March) he was playing at the opening of the new Drury Lane Theatre. His address at this time, according to Doane, was King Street, Soho. There were engagements at Covent Garden (including Handel's *Alexander's Feast* on 12 February 1796, Handel's *Messiah* on 3 March 1797 and 23 February 1798, and the Handel concerts on 8 February 1799 and 28 February 1800) and the Haymarket Theatre (*Messiah* on 15 January 1798). However, regular employment came in the band of Drury Lane. The accounts show that he played the trombone there from 27 October 1798 for nearly a decade, to January 1808, earning £3 a week during the 1803–4 season.

There is little further information on Dressler after this point. According to Sainsbury he published some concertos and quartets for wind instruments, which do not appear to have survived. The claim that he introduced the trombone to British orchestras appears to originate with Sainsbury, but has no merit. He had a daughter, who married Samuel Thomas Lyon, and Raphael (or Rafael) Dressler (1784?–1835?), a flautist and probably Dressler's son, issued numerous pieces for the flute, including studies, arrangements, and *New and Complete Instructions* op. 68

(1828). Raphael's name was put forward for membership of the Royal Society of Musicians in 1829, but on 6 December of that year his name was withdrawn by a Mr Lyon, possibly his brother-in-law.   DAVID J. GOLBY

Sources Highfill, Burnim & Langhans, *BDA* · [J. S. Sainsbury], ed., *A dictionary of musicians*, 2 vols. (1824), vol. 1, p. 219 · J. D. Brown, *Biographical dictionary of musicians: with a bibliography of English writings on music* (1886), 217 · J. Doane, ed., *A musical directory for the year 1794* [1794]

Drew, Catharine (1825/6–1910), journalist and women's rights activist, was born in Belfast, only daughter of Revd Thomas Drew, a militant Orange Church of Ireland clergyman who was for twenty-seven years incumbent of Christ Church, Belfast, and subsequently rector of Seaforde, co. Down, and precentor of Down Cathedral. Her brother was Sir Thomas *Drew (1838–1910), the distinguished ecclesiastical architect, who became president of the Royal Society of Antiquaries, Ireland. She was educated at home.

In 1862 Thomas Drew moved to work in a Dublin architectural practice and soon began to contribute articles to the *Irish Builder*, becoming, briefly, its temporary editor. Catharine went to live with her brother in Dublin for four years and helped him edit the magazine. In 1871, shortly after the death of her father, she moved to London. Aged forty-six, she now embarked on a freelance career and was able to use contacts she had made in Dublin with the *British Architect*, *London Society*, and, later, the *Literary World* to establish herself. She also wrote fiction. Her principal journalistic achievement at this time was to write a column for the *Belfast News-Letter* devoted to women's interests. This was one of the first 'Ladies' letters', a popular feature of many newspapers by the end of the century. From 1896 to 1906 Drew was on the London staff of the National Press Agency.

Catharine Drew was an active worker for various philanthropic causes connected with women. She was a pioneer in the setting up of the Institute of Journalists (IOJ) in 1885 and was the first woman to be elected an honorary vice-president and a councillor of the IOJ in 1895. She successfully advocated establishing the Institute Orphan Fund, formally ratified at the annual IOJ conference in Dublin in 1891, and worked passionately for the fund until she died. She was also on the council of the work and leisure court of the United Sisters Friendly Society and was one of the founders of the Caroline Biggs Memorial Fund, which lent women students fees for technical training. It was on account of her work for the Orphan Fund, her concern for the education of orphan children of journalists, as well as her passionate defence of the rights of women journalists that, on her retirement from the IOJ in 1908, she was presented with a gold bracelet, with the seal of the institute as a medallion. On her death in 1910 she bequeathed the bracelet to the institute with a request that it be worn by the president's wife, or lady assisting the president in his duties.

In 1894 Drew represented the IOJ at the first International Conference on the Press in Antwerp and the following year was again chosen as one of the delegates at the second international conference in Bordeaux. In 1894, speaking at the IOJ conference in Norwich, she made a powerful plea for women journalists to be paid the same rate as their male counterparts. She pointed out that the woman's wage was often far from being a living wage and rarely allowed her to make any provision for old age. 'Many women have aged and invalid relatives dependent on them and some are widows bravely doing their best for their little children. For the woman journalist the eight hours day has yet to dawn, for her work is never done' (IOJ Archives). Drew maintained that one of the dangers of failing to pay women adequately was that they might be tempted to accept small bribes, such as a hat from a milliner, in return for writing about the product. The following year she delivered another lecture on journalism in which she insisted that women journalists were not in need of patronage, but warned again that, as they were paid so little for their writing, they could rarely afford to become experts on any subject unless they had independent means.

Catharine Drew was once described as 'sharp of tongue' by her colleague Mary F. Billington, but perhaps this was no more than a family talent for public speaking, which might well have been derived from listening to her father's sermonizing in childhood, as her brother was also renowned for his fluent and witty talks. By the time of her death, at her home, 25 Holland Street, Kensington, London, on 26 August 1910, following a stroke three years previously, Catharine Drew was one of the most respected women journalists of her day. She was eighty-four and she had never married. Her funeral was at the nearby St Mary Abbot's Church in Kensington.   ANNE M. SEBBA

Sources C. Bainbridge, ed., *One hundred years of journalism: social aspects of the press* (1984) · *Journalist and Newspaper Proprietor* (14 April 1894) · Cambs. AS, Huntingdon · 'Drew, Sir Thomas', *DNB* · *Journalist and Newspaper Proprietor* (16 March 1895) · F. Hunter, 'Women in British journalism', *The encyclopedia of the British press, 1422–1992*, ed. D. Griffiths (1992), 686–90 · d. cert. · *CGPLA Eng. & Wales* (1910) · News International database
Archives Institute of Journalists, Huntingdon
Likenesses photograph, repro. in *Journalist and Newspaper Proprietor*
Wealth at death £637 5s.: probate, 19 Oct 1910, *CGPLA Eng. & Wales*

Drew, Edward (*c*.1540–1598), lawyer, was the eldest son of Thomas Drew (*b*. 1519) and his wife, Eleanora, daughter of William Huckmore of Devon. He was probably born at the family seat of Sharpham, in the parish of Ashprington, near Totnes. He is named in the records of Exeter College, Oxford, in 1557, but evidently left without taking a degree. He was admitted to the Inner Temple in November 1560, and was called to the bar in 1574. Developing his career in the west country as well as in London, he was clerk of assize for the western circuit in 1577 and a justice of the peace in Devon from about 1579. Judging from the ages of their seven children when Drew made his will in 1598, it is likely that he and his wife, Bridget, the daughter of George Fitzwilliam of Mablethorpe, Lincolnshire, married at about this time.

Drew became a master of the bench at the Inner Temple in 1581, and Lent reader there in 1584. In the same year he was elected to parliament for Lyme Regis, possibly due to a connection with the second earl of Bedford, of whose will he was an overseer. Having been retained regularly by the city of Exeter for some years previously, Drew served as its MP in 1586 and 1589. It is one measure of his reputation as a lawyer that in December 1588 he was asked to help draw up a list of statutes that were ripe for repeal, and to present ideas for further law reform. In Michaelmas 1589 he was called to the order of the coif, one of eight new serjeants-at-law who chose the phrase *Lex reipublicae vita* as the motto on their ceremonial gold rings.

Drew was appointed recorder of Exeter in May 1592, but resigned almost immediately to take up the more prestigious post of recorder of London on 17 June. He made a speech before the queen when he introduced the new mayor of London, Sir Cuthbert Buckle, to her in 1593, and he was elected member of parliament for the city in the same year. In this, as in previous parliaments, he appears to have served primarily as an active committee man, but on 21 March 1593 he made a speech on the problems caused by alien retailers in London. Noting that 'charity' to 'strangers' had to be tempered by consideration for 'our countrymen' (HoP, *Commons, 1558–1603*, 2.56) who felt themselves disadvantaged by competition from traders who had not gone through the prescribed apprenticeship and obtained the freedom of the city, he argued that it would be wrong to introduce a measure that applied retrospectively, but was in favour of one that would restrain the activities of those who set up trade in the future.

The city gave Drew a basin and ewer in silver gilt in recognition of his service when he resigned the recordership on 27 March 1594 to become a justice of assize and gaol delivery for Essex and Kent. In 1596 he was made a queen's serjeant and commissioned a justice for the northern assize circuit. Obviously enjoying favour with the government, he was regularly employed by the privy council in the examination of political prisoners and on other legal business. During the meeting of parliament in 1597 he was very active as a judicial assistant to the House of Lords. Evidently at the peak of his career, he died suddenly at Broad Clyst, Devon, on 11 May 1598, having contracted gaol fever while riding the northern circuit. According to his countryman and contemporary Tristram Risdon, Drew's 'knowledge and counsel won him a general love' (Risdon and Taylor, 43), but a brief collection of manuscript law reports is evidently all that survives from his professional archive. During his lifetime he purchased lands in Broadhembury and Awliscombe, and his will provided comfortably for his children. Probably towards the end of his life, he sold the family seat at Sharpham for £2250, and established his residence at Killerton in the parish of Broad Clyst. He is buried alongside his wife in the parish church there, where a sumptuous monument, depicting him in his robes, was erected in 1622.
                                                                        CHRISTOPHER W. BROOKS

Sources HoP, *Commons, 1558–1603*, 2.55–6 · *DNB* · will, PRO, PROB 11/91, fols. 345–6 · a contemporary obituary, CUL, MS 8080, fol. 26*v* · J. H. Baker and J. S. Ringrose, *A catalogue of English legal manuscripts in Cambridge University Library* (1996), 118 · Baker, *Serjeants* ·

T. Risdon and J. Taylor, *The chorographical description or survey of the county of Devon: printed from a genuine copy of the original manuscript, with considerable additions*, 2nd edn (1811) · J. Prince, *Danmonii orientales illustres, or, The worthies of Devon*, 2nd edn (1810), 334–7 · D. Dean, *Law-making and society in late Elizabethan England: the parliament of England, 1584–1601* (1996)
Likenesses effigy, Broadclyst, Devon
Wealth at death wealthy, but not quantifiable; incl. Sharpham, and other properties; left his three daughters £1800: will, PRO, PROB 11/91

Drew, Frederick (1836–1891), geologist, was born at Southampton on 11 August 1836, the youngest son of John *Drew (*bap.* 1809, *d.* 1857), astronomer, and his wife, Clara, daughter of Nicholas Peter Phené, solicitor, of Melksham, Wiltshire. Following an education at the school run by his father in Southampton he entered the Royal School of Mines in 1853, passed through it with distinction, and joined the geological survey as an assistant geologist in August 1855. He was employed for seven years in the south-east of England, working primarily on the stratigraphic geology of the weald, especially in mapping the subdivisions of the Hastings sands. In October 1861 he was promoted to geologist grade.

In February 1862, following representations by the British military commander of the Punjab and the mediation of Sir Roderick Murchison, Drew resigned the geological survey to enter the service of the maharaja of Jammu and Kashmir, Ranbir Singh. He was initially engaged in a mineral reconnaissance of the territories, was then charged with the management of the forest department, and finally, in 1871, was appointed vizier (governor) of the province of Ladakh. In addition, he probably acted unofficially as a British political agent, providing intelligence on a state on India's northern frontier which was considered to be of great strategic importance as a bulwark against Russian expansion. He acquired a detailed knowledge of the geology, topography, and anthropology of the country, which he employed in his major work, *The Jummoo and Kashmir Territories: a Geographical Account* (1875), which was written following his return to London in 1872. In 1877 he published an abridged, popular account under the title *The Northern Barrier of India*.

Drew was elected a fellow of the Geological Society of London in 1858—serving on its council from 1874 to 1876—and of the Royal Geographical Society in 1872. In the autumn of 1875 he was appointed an assistant master in science at Eton College, where he became a housemaster in 1887. He remained at Eton for the rest of his life, but in his last years suffered severely from sciatica. He died at Pier View, South Cliff, Bournemouth, on 28 October 1891. He was survived by his wife, Sara Constance, daughter of Alfred Waylen, one of the first settlers in West Australia, and two sons and two daughters. Nothing further is known about his marriage or family. Besides the works already cited, Drew was the author of a *Memoir of the Geological Survey* on the Romney Marsh area (1864), two further papers relating to English geology, and six papers concerning his geological and anthropological researches in

Kashmir. He edited the second edition of his father's *Practical Meteorology* (1860), and his notes were used by William Topley in his 'The geology of the weald', *Memoir of the Geological Survey* (1875). E. M. LLOYD, *rev.* ANDREW GROUT

Sources *Geological Magazine*, new ser., 3rd decade, 9 (1892), 142–4 · A. Geikie, *Quarterly Journal of the Geological Society*, 48 (1892), 49–50 · R. A. Stafford, *Scientist of empire: Sir Roderick Murchison, scientific exploration and Victorian imperialism* (1989), 120, 129 · C.-J. Charpentier, 'Preface', in F. Drew, *The Jummoo and Kashmir territories* (1976), v*–xv* · W. T. Blanford, *Proceedings* [Royal Geographical Society], new ser., 14 (1892), 52–4 · *Eton College Chronicle* (12 Nov 1891), 1 · J. F. Kirkaldy, 'William Topley and *The geology of the weald*', *Proceedings of the Geologists' Association*, 86 (1975), 373–88 · private information (1901) · private information (2004) · d. cert. · CGPLA *Eng. & Wales* (1891)
Archives BGS
Likenesses photograph, BGS, IGS 1/639
Wealth at death £3961 17s. 9d.: probate, 10 Dec 1891, CGPLA *Eng. & Wales*

Drew, George Smith (1819–1880), Church of England clergyman and biblical scholar, son of George Drew, tea dealer, of 11 Tottenham Court Road, London, was born at Louth, Lincolnshire. Admitted a sizar of St John's College, Cambridge, on 22 January 1839, he took his BA degree as 27th wrangler in 1843, and was ordained the same year. After serving a curacy at St Pancras, London, for about two years, he was presented to the incumbency of St Pancras Old Church in 1845, in which year, on 20 May, he married Mary, eldest daughter of William Peek of Loddiswell, Devon. He became incumbent of the church of St John the Evangelist, in the same parish, in 1850. He was one of the earliest promoters of evening classes for young men, and published three lectures in support of the movement in 1851 and 1852. He had taken his MA degree in 1847, and became vicar of Pulloxhill, Bedfordshire, in 1854. During the winter and spring of 1856–7 he made a tour in the East, and as the result he wrote *Scripture Lands in Connection with their History* (1860), several times reissued. Drew was vicar of St Barnabas, South Kensington, from 1858 to 1870, was select preacher to the University of Cambridge in 1869 and 1870, and rector of Avington, Hampshire, from 1870 to 1873, but returned to London in that year as vicar of Holy Trinity, Lambeth, a preferment which he retained until his death. In 1877 he was elected Hulsean lecturer at Cambridge, and the following year he published his lectures as *The Human Life of Christ Revealing the Order of the Universe … with an Appendix*. Drew was a fellow of the Royal Geographical Society and at one time an active member of the British Association for the Advancement of Science. He published a number of scriptural expositions and sermons and wrote for the *Imperial Bible Dictionary* and Cassell's *Bible Dictionary*, as well as for the *Christian Observer*, the *Contemporary Review*, and the *Sunday Magazine*. He died suddenly at Holy Trinity vicarage on 21 January 1880, his wife surviving him. Their son Julius Charles *Drewe is separately noticed. GORDON GOODWIN, *rev.* H. C. G. MATTHEW

Sources *The Guardian* (28 Jan 1880) · Crockford (1879) · Venn, *Alum. Cant.*
Wealth at death under £1500: probate, 31 March 1880, CGPLA *Eng. & Wales*

Drew, John (*bap.* **1809**, *d.* **1857**), astronomer, the son of John and Ann Drew, was baptized at Bower Chalk, Wiltshire, on 1 March 1809. His father died shortly afterwards, and Drew had little if any formal education; nevertheless, at the age of fifteen he was able to take up teaching. After two years as an assistant at Melksham, Wiltshire, he moved to Southampton, where for the next sixteen years he ran his own school. He married, probably about 1830, Clara, who survived him; four sons were born between 1831 and 1836.

Drew's first astronomical observations were made with a small refracting telescope, which was later replaced by an excellent 5 foot equatorial by Dollond, installed in a small observatory which he built in his garden. With a transit circle by Thomas Jones, and the Beaufoy clock lent by the Royal Society, he very accurately determined the time, and supplied it for many years to the ships leaving Southampton. Drew published on astronomy, its apparatus, and the need for greater co-operation, and he reviewed the astronomy section of the Great Exhibition of 1851 for the *Civil Engineer and Architect's Journal*, to which he contributed several articles on astronomy and meteorology.

Drew turned to meteorology to search for some correlation between weather conditions and the cholera outbreaks in Southampton. He procured meteorological instruments, including a barometer of special design, from John Newman, but his regular observations from 1848 to 1853 did not suggest any correlation with the disease, as he informed the British Association, to whom he presented a summary of his results. In earlier years Drew had travelled on the continent, visiting Brussels observatory and Basel, where he obtained the degree of doctor of philosophy at the university. At Basel he met C. F. Schönbein, professor of chemistry, who, having in 1839 discovered ozone, wished to establish a network of observers to measure its atmospheric distribution; he encouraged Drew to recruit volunteers in Britain. Drew helped to found the Meteorological Society in 1850, and was on its first council. His essays describing suitable instruments for meteorology, and the evaluation of the observations, were circulated informally to members, then published serially and in book form as *Practical Meteorology* (1855); the latter volume was reissued by his son Frederick *Drew in 1860. Drew was elected to the Royal Astronomical Society in 1846, and contributed several papers to its *Monthly Notices*; he was also a corresponding member of the Philosophical Institute of Basel. Shortly before his death he moved to Surbiton, Surrey. He died there on 17 December 1857.

Frederick Drew shared his father's interest in local geology. He was educated at his father's school and then at the Royal School of Mines in Kensington, where he gained all the prizes on offer. After pursuing a successful career in the British Geological Survey and in Kashmir, he returned to England in 1872 to end his days as a schoolmaster at Eton College.   A. M. CLERKE, *rev.* ANITA MCCONNELL

Sources *Monthly Notices of the Royal Astronomical Society*, 18 (1857–8), 98 · J. Drew, 'On the construction of a small observatory, a new stand for a transit instrument, and an eyepiece for the rectification of instrumental errors by reflexion', *Monthly Notices of the Royal Astronomical Society*, 10 (1849–50), 68–70 · C. L. F. André, *L'astronomie pratique et les observatoires en Europe et en Amérique*, 1: *Angleterre* (Paris, 1874), 166–9 · Boase, *Mod. Eng. biog.* · d. cert. · IGI

Archives RAS

Wealth at death under £7000: probate, 8 March 1858, *CGPLA Eng. & Wales*

Drew [*née* Gladstone], **Mary** (1847–1927), private secretary and author, was born at 13 Carlton House Terrace, London, on 23 November 1847, the third of the four daughters and fifth in the family of eight children of William Ewart *Gladstone (1809–1898), statesman, and his wife, Catherine *Gladstone, *née* Glynne (1812–1900). Her childhood and youth were spent between Hawarden Castle, Flintshire, the London homes necessary to her father as a rising politician, and the houses of her extended family of cousins the Lytteltons, of Hagley Hall, Worcestershire. Unlike the rigorous educational standards that Gladstone applied to his sons, his daughters' schooling was haphazard, and in later life Mary admitted that she always found it difficult to concentrate on a sustained piece of work. Music was her passion: when she was less than forty days old her father observed her 'great susceptibility to musical sounds' (Gladstone, *Diaries*, 1 Jan 1848); and she was a talented pianist, but even there the lack of rigorous teaching showed: she was heard to comment: 'I know Beethoven wrote it like *that*, but I like to play it like *this*' (Masterman, 13).

Mary Gladstone's father was the greatest influence on her life. In many ways the Gladstone household lived up to the Victorian archetypal family: everything revolved around the needs and demands of the man at its head, and the daughters especially were expected to subordinate themselves to their parents' lives. The commandment to honour one's father and mother was held particularly strongly by the Gladstones, and religious duty was allied to the profound belief that their father was a truly great man, with genuinely important work to do. The most obvious effect of Mary's relationship with her father was the long delay of her marriage, for few men could live up to her father in her estimation, and still fewer had the temerity to approach the daughter of the prime minister. (The absence of a significant family fortune also played a part.) She had several suitors, including Edward Bickersteth Ottley and Hallam Tennyson, the son of the poet laureate, and was at least twice in love, unrequitedly—with Lord Lorne (later ninth duke of Argyll and Queen Victoria's son-in-law) and with the family friend (and later prime minister) A. J. Balfour. Mary witnessed the marriages of her closest friends and relatives during her twenties with a growing sense of crisis about her own identity: there were no alternatives to marriage for women of her class and she clearly felt some dismay at the prospect of remaining a child in her parents' house. Fortunately one of the causes of her dilemma provided the relief from it, as she became an important member of Gladstone's (unpaid and unacknowledged) auxiliary staff.

Mary's interest in politics had a fitful start: the rightness of her father and the demerits of his opponents pretty

Mary Drew (1847–1927), by Hayman Selig Mendelssohn, c.1880

much encompassed her views well into the 1870s. But about 1876 there came a marked change, and she began recording in detail in her diary the issues of the day and the actions of the government. Mary, like her father, was galvanized by the Bulgarian atrocities, and when he came out of retirement she began to work for him as an unofficial private secretary. When he became prime minister again in 1880 she continued in her work, having special responsibility for correspondence concerning ecclesiastical patronage. Her duties included writing many routine letters to applicants for patronage, decoding cipher telegrams, and finding suitable candidates for vacant livings. She also undertook many of the duties associated with managing a political household which her mother found onerous and uninteresting: entertaining eminent visitors, colleagues, supporters, and potential allies required significant resources of time and energy which Catherine Gladstone would not spare from her husband.

The other consolation Mary Gladstone found in this period was the friendship of a number of eminent, older men, among them Lord Acton, John Ruskin, James Stuart, Edward Burne-Jones, Lord Stanmore, Canon Henry Scott Holland, the Revd John Illingworth, Sir George Grove, and Lord Rosebery. Some sought initially to use correspondence with Mary as a means of gaining the ear of the prime minister but they soon came to place a high value on his daughter. Acton, in particular, wrote extensively to Mary, using the correspondence as a place in which to work out his ideas. Although he sometimes intended her to pass on

information and opinions to Gladstone she was more than a conduit; an intelligent, informed woman, Mary Gladstone was the sympathetic reader that Acton had always needed. After 1886 Acton's daughter Mamie (Marie) served as his confidante, and it was with some reluctance that he resumed writing to Mary in 1892 as 'a way of conveying some things which I cannot say right off [to Gladstone]' (Hill, 313). Her social circle was not confined to politicians, nor indeed to men. Through her sisters Agnes and Helen and her cousin Lavinia Talbot she had strong links with the academic circles in Oxford and Cambridge, while her friend Frances Graham (later Horner) introduced her to the artists' studios. Clergymen and musicians were her natural constituency; she was less at home with the Souls, for though she counted many of them among her friends (particularly Laura and Alfred Lyttelton, Arthur Balfour, Margot Asquith, and Frances Horner) she was too much her father's daughter to accept their rejection of Victorian Christian earnestness and moral strictures.

After so many years as the indispensable daughter at home it came as something of a shock to many of Mary's friends when, on Christmas day 1885, she became engaged to the curate of Hawarden, Harry Drew (1856–1910). They were married in Westminster Abbey on 2 February 1886, at the height of a political crisis; Gladstone gave his daughter away and went straight to Windsor, where he once again accepted the prime ministership. Marriage did not separate Mary from her ageing parents, as she made her home at Hawarden, and she continued to be indispensable, but she no longer played such a prominent part in their London and political lives. In August 1886 she miscarried a son and was dangerously ill for five months. In March 1890, at the age of forty-two, she gave birth to a daughter, Dorothy. She had a further miscarriage in May 1893.

In 1897 Harry Drew accepted the living of Buckley, 3 miles from Hawarden, and for the first time Mary had her own home. The last illnesses and deaths of her parents, in 1898 and 1900, inevitably dominated these years but she established herself thoroughly in her role as a clergyman's wife; in 1904 Harry Drew became rector of Hawarden. She also began arranging to publish some of the letters that she had received from eminent men. First to appear was *Letters to M. G. and H. G.* (1903), which contained a selection of Ruskin's rather sickly letters to Mary and her sister Helen. More controversially Herbert Paul edited *Letters of Lord Acton to Mary, Daughter of the Right Hon. W. E. Gladstone* (1904). Mary had urged Acton to allow her to publish his letters but he had refused; now that he was dead the volume was hurried into print, with disastrous consequences for Acton's reputation. Although personal material had been removed from the letters enough was left to offend members of his family, and both Catholics and Anglicans found matter for concern in his freely expressed views on his own church and on the affairs of the other; a second, slightly amplified edition appeared in 1913. *Some Hawarden Letters*, edited by Lisle March-Phillipps and Bertram Christian, appeared in 1917, containing letters from Burne-Jones, Lord Stanmore, James Stuart,

Henry Sidgwick, and George Wyndham, among others; *A Forty Years' Friendship* (1919), edited by S. L. Ollard, contained Henry Scott Holland's letters to Mary. In 1919 Mary Drew produced her only full-length book, a biography of her mother, *Catherine Gladstone*, a lightweight volume heavy on anecdote and inconsequential letters from the great and good. In 1924 she published *Acton, Gladstone and Others*, a collection of essays and reviews, including accounts of Gladstone's books and the foundation of St Deiniol's Library, and of Ruskin's infatuation with Rose La Touche.

Mary Drew was both lessened and liberated by her parents' deaths. She no longer had a direct connection with the great affairs of the nation, and her perspective on politics remained resolutely Gladstonian: she gave no support to the Second South African War, was repulsed by the military character of Queen Victoria's funeral, lamented the resurgence of the Eastern question in the form of the Balkan wars of 1912–13, and reflected ironically on the passage of the Home Rule Bill in 1920. The sudden and unexpected death of Harry Drew, in 1910, was a devastating blow: 'I don't quite know how to bear *anybody* now I can't have him', she wrote (Masterman, 460). She travelled for a time and was restored somewhat by the marriage of her daughter to Francis Parish, in 1912, and the births of five grandchildren. She made her home at 2 The Boltons, Earls Court, London, developed arthritis, and became a zealous vegetarian. She continued to take a vigorous interest in politics, viewing the rise of the Labour Party with interest and more than a little sympathy. She spent Christmas 1926 at a family party at Hawarden, and died there on 1 January 1927, having been 'rather particularly lively at dinner in the evening' (ibid., 491). She was buried at Hawarden on 5 January, and a memorial service was held on the same day at St Margaret's, Westminster. An edited selection from her diary and family correspondence appeared in 1930 and remains a valuable source for Gladstone studies and for the portrait it paints of the interactions between social, political, and cultural circles in late-Victorian London.   K. D. REYNOLDS

Sources *Mary Gladstone (Mrs Drew): her diaries and letters*, ed. L. Masterman (1930) · Gladstone, *Diaries* · P. Jalland, *Women, marriage and politics, 1860–1914* (1986) · O. Chadwick, *Acton and Gladstone* (1976) · [A. Schlüter], *A lady's maid in Downing Street*, ed. M. Duncan [n.d.] · R. Hill, *Lord Acton* (2000) · L. March-Phillips and B. Christian, eds., *Some Hawarden letters* (1917) · *The Times* (3 Jan 1927) · *The Times* (6 Jan 1927)

Archives BL, corresp., diaries, and papers, Add. MSS 46219–46271 · St Deiniol's Library, Hawarden, family corresp. | BL, corresp. with Arthur James Balfour, Add. MS 49794, *passim* · BL, corresp. with Lord Gladstone, Add. MS 46044 · BL, letters to Sir Edward Walter Hamilton, Add. MS 48611 · BL, letters to Sir Arthur Hamilton-Gordon, Add. MSS 44321–44322 · BL, corresp. with Macmillans, Add. MS 55244 · CUL, corresp. with Lord Acton and others · King's AC Cam., letters to Oscar Browning · NL Scot., corresp. with Lord Rosebery · U. St Andr. L., corresp. with Wilfrid Ward

Likenesses Jamblin, Penmaenmawr, photograph, 1860, repro. in *Strand* (1898), vol. 14, p. 297 · Elliott & Fry, photograph, 1869, repro. in *Strand* (1898), vol. 14, p. 297 · E. Burne-Jones, drawing, *c*.1875, repro. in *Mary Gladstone*, ed. Masterman · H. S. Mendelssohn, photograph, *c*.1880, NPG [*see illus.*] · photograph, *c*.1880, repro. in *Mary Gladstone*, ed. Masterman · A. Hughes, photograph, repro. in *Strand* (1898), vol. 14, p. 297

Wealth at death £11,618 6*s*. 1*d*.: probate, 12 March 1927, *CGPLA Eng. & Wales*

Drew, Samuel (1765–1833), metaphysical writer, born on 6 March 1765 near St Austell in Cornwall, was the son of Joseph Drew and his second wife, Thomasin Osborne. Joseph Drew made a hard living in the parish by streaming for tin and a little small farming. He had been impressed by a sermon from George Whitefield and was one of the early Cornish Methodists. Samuel Drew was put to work in the fields when seven years old. His mother died in 1774, and his father married again; Drew, finding home disagreeable, was apprenticed to a shoemaker nearby at St Blazey when between ten and eleven. He was a wild lad and joined in smuggling expeditions, but was discouraged for a time (as he always asserted) by meeting one night a being like a bear with fiery eyes which trotted past him and went through a closed gate in a supernatural manner. Soon afterwards he ran away from his master, but was found at Liskeard and brought back to his father, now farming successfully south of St Austell at Polplea, near Par. He afterwards worked for a time at Millbrook, Plymouth, and was nearly drowned in a smuggling adventure, from which he had not been deterred by any bogy.

Returning to his home, Drew became a journeyman shoemaker in a shop at St Austell in January 1785. The death of an elder brother, who had been a studious Methodist, and the funeral sermon preached by Adam Clarke had a great effect upon his mind, and he joined the Wesleyan society in June 1785. He took a keen interest in politics, began to read all the books he could find, and was much impressed by a copy of Locke's *Essay*. He set up in business for himself in 1787. He became a class leader and a local preacher in 1788. Though some accusation of heresy led to his giving up the class leadership for many years, he continued to preach throughout his life. On 17 April 1791 he married Honour Hills. They had seven children, of whom six survived him. Drew began to write poetry, always kept a notebook by the side of his tools, and used his bellows for a writing-desk. His first publication, *Remarks upon Paine's 'Age of Reason'*, prompted by some controversy with a freethinking friend, appeared in 1799 and was favourably noticed in the *Anti-Jacobin Review* for April 1800. He made the acquaintance of the antiquary John Whitaker, the vicar of Ruan Lanihorne, and of John Britton. In July 1800 he published some 'observations' upon Richard Polwhele's *Anecdotes of Methodism*, defending his denomination against Polwhele's charges. Whitaker now encouraged him to complete a book upon which he had long meditated, published by subscription in 1802 as *Essay on the Immateriality and Immortality of the Soul*; it enjoyed considerable success. After the first publication Drew sold the copyright to a Bristol bookseller for £20. When four editions had appeared in England and two in America, he brought out a fifth with additions in 1831, which he sold for £250. His old adversary, Polwhele, generously reviewed him with high praise in the *Anti-Jacobin* for February 1803.

Drew became famous as the Cornish Metaphysician and made many friends among the Anglican clergy, though he declined to become a candidate for its orders. He formed a close friendship with Adam Clarke, through whose influence he was elected in 1804 a member of the Manchester Philological Society. Another friend was Thomas Coke, who was writing various books for the Wesleyan conference. Coke was also superintendent of the Wesleyan missions, and, being overwhelmed with work, employed Drew to write for him. The books appeared under the name of Coke, and were in fact from his notes, but it seems that Drew was the chief author, though he did not complain of the concealment of his name. Drew later wrote a *Life of Thomas Coke*, published after the subject's death in 1815. In 1806 Drew was invited through Clarke to revise metaphysical works for the *Eclectic Review*, but the connection did not last long. In 1809 he published an *Essay on the Identity and Resurrection of the Body*, which attracted little interest, though it reached a second edition in 1822. About the same time he began to write an essay for the Burnett prize, which, however, went in 1814 to J. L. Brown and J. B. Sumner. He published his essay in 1820, but it enjoyed little notice.

In 1814 Drew undertook a history of Cornwall. Part of it had been written by F. Hitchens, on whose death the composition was entrusted to Drew. Though he is described only as editor, he wrote the greater part. It marks a significant development in local history writing and compilation. In 1819 he moved to Liverpool, again through the recommendation of Clarke. He was to edit the *Imperial Magazine*, started in March 1819, and superintend the business of the Caxton Press. A fire destroyed the buildings at Liverpool, and the business was transferred to London, where Drew settled. Here he was employed in absorbing work, which seems to have tried his health. In May 1824 the degree of MA was conferred on Drew by Aberdeen University, inadvertently styling him 'Reverend'. Hopes of providing for retirement to Cornwall were disappointed by financial losses. He made short visits to Cornwall, during one of which his wife died at Helston on 19 August 1828, at the house of a son-in-law. Drew rapidly declined in strength after this blow. On returning to his work in London he declined an offer of nomination to the chair of moral philosophy at the university in 1830, being reluctant to stay in the city. He went back to Cornwall and died at Helston on 29 March 1833, while staying with his son-in-law.

Drew was among the Methodist laity what Adam Clarke was among the ministers, the foremost thinker and writer of his day, offering a sober and analytical description of religious experience and Methodist piety.

LESLIE STEPHEN, *rev.* TIM MACQUIBAN

Sources W. J. Townsend, H. B. Workman, and G. Eayrs, *A new history of Methodism*, 2 vols. (1909) • J. H. Drew, *The life, characters, and literary labours of Samuel Drew* (1834) • R. Polwhele, *Biographical sketches in Cornwall*, 1 (1831), 96–103 • Boase & Courtney, *Bibl. Corn.*
Archives Bodl. Oxf., letters to Mary Ann Clarke

Likenesses Hicks, stipple, pubd 1819 (after Griffiths), NPG • W. T. Fry, stipple, pubd 1834 (after J. Moore), NPG • R. Hicks, line engraving, 1835, BM

Drew, Sir Thomas (1838–1910), architect, born at Victoria Place, Belfast, on 18 September 1838, came from a well-known Limerick family. His father, Thomas Drew (*d.* 1870), a staunch Orangeman, was long rector of Christ Church, Belfast, before becoming rector of Seaforde, co. Down, and precentor of Down Cathedral. A sister, Catharine *Drew (1825/6–1910), was a well-known journalist in London. Thomas was educated in Belfast, and in 1854 was articled to Charles Lanyon. After serving his apprenticeship he formed a brief partnership in Belfast with another pupil of Lanyon, Thomas Turner (1820–1891), before moving to Dublin, where he was to settle for the rest of his life. In 1862 he entered the office, in Dublin, of William George Murray (*d.* 1871). Next year he began to write for the *Dublin Builder*, and subsequently acted for a time as editor, introducing articles on antiquarian subjects. In 1864 he was awarded a special silver medal by the Royal Institute of the Architects of Ireland for his set of measured drawings of the Portlester Chapel in St Audoen's Church, Dublin. In 1870 he was elected associate of the Royal Hibernian Academy and the following year he became a full member. He married in 1871 Adelaide Anne, daughter of William Murray, formerly architect of the board of works, Ireland, and a collateral descendant of the architect Francis Johnston, founder of the Royal Hibernian Academy.

In 1875 Drew began independent practice in North Frederick Street, Dublin; he subsequently moved to Upper Sackville Street (now O'Connell Street), and then to 6 St Stephen's Green, a house designed by himself, and finally to 22 Clare Street. Noted by a contemporary for 'a robust and virile Gothic' (*DNB*), Drew built up a reputation for ecclesiastical work which was the basis of his independent practice, almost all of it for the Church of Ireland denomination. As diocesan architect for Down, Connor, and Dromore, he designed a significant number of churches in the eastern part of Ulster in the 1860s and 1870s. His most important ecclesiastical work was St Anne's Cathedral in Belfast, in a Romanesque style, which was started to his designs in 1899 but completed by others following his death. He was also responsible for the restoration of Waterford Church of Ireland Cathedral and consulting architect to a number of other Church of Ireland cathedrals.

Among the other chief buildings designed by Drew were several in Dublin, including Rathmines town hall (1890–94), the Ulster Bank in College Green (1888–91), and the graduates' tercentenary memorial building at Trinity College (1899–1902). He was also the only Irish architect to be invited to submit a design for the Queen Victoria memorial in London in 1901.

In 1889 Drew was elected fellow of the Royal Institute of British Architects. In 1892 he was elected president of the Royal Institute of Architects of Ireland and in 1902 he became the first president of the Ulster Society of Architects. Known to his contemporaries as a fluent and witty speaker, he delivered from 1891 an annual lecture on St

Stephen's day, in Christ Church Cathedral, on its history and fabric. He was also instrumental in establishing in the crypt a museum of Irish antiquities. In 1895–7 he was president of the Royal Society of the Antiquaries of Ireland.

Drew was elected tenth president of the Royal Hibernian Academy on 18 October 1900, on the death of Sir Thomas Farrell, the sculptor, and was knighted the same year by the lord lieutenant of Ireland, Earl Cadogan. In 1905 Dublin University conferred on him the honorary degree of LLD, and in 1910 he was asked by the National University of Ireland to fill the newly established chair of architecture at University College, Dublin. Drew died in hospital in Lower Mount Street, Dublin, on 13 March 1910 and was buried in Dean's Grange cemetery, co. Dublin. His wife survived him. [ANON.], rev. PAUL LARMOUR

Sources Irish Builder and Engineer, 52 (1910), 168–73 · Belfast News-Letter (14 March 1910) · Irish Times (14 March 1910) · P. Larmour, 'The first president of the R.S.U.A.', Perspective, 4/5 (May/June 1996), 61–3 · P. Larmour, Belfast: an illustrated architectural guide (1987) · H. Maguire, 'Drew, Sir Thomas', The dictionary of art, ed. J. Turner (1996) · CGPLA Eng. & Wales (1910) · WW (1906)
Likenesses W. Osborne, oils, 1891, NG Ire. · W. Osborne, portrait, repro. in Irish Builder and Engineer (30 Jan 1901) · photograph, repro. in Irish Builder and Engineer (19 March 1910)
Wealth at death £868 5s. in England: Irish probate sealed in London, 25 May 1910, CGPLA Eng. & Wales · £5277 9s. 7d.: probate, 4 May 1910, CGPLA Ire.

Drewe [formerly Drew], **Julius Charles** (1856–1931), retailer and architectural patron, was born on 4 April 1856 at Pulloxhill vicarage, Pulloxhill, Ampthill, Bedfordshire, the sixth child in a family of four sons and three daughters of the Revd George Smith *Drew (d. 1880) and his wife, Mary Peek. Drew's most recent ancestors had made their living through commerce: his great-grandfather had practised as a surveyor, and his grandfather George Drew became a tea broker in Marylebone, London. Although his mother's family came from Devon, they also made their living through tea; and following schooling at Bournemouth, Drew was sent by his uncle Francis Peek, a partner in the Liverpool tea importing firm of Peek and Winch, to China as a tea buyer. Drew stayed in the Far East for some years and returned shortly after his twenty-first birthday. A staid job with the firm in Liverpool proved not to his taste, however, and in 1878 Drew opened his own 'Willow Pattern Tea Store' in that city.

In order to develop the business, in 1883 Drew went into partnership with John Musker. This was a shrewd alliance as Musker's knowledge of the retailing end of the trade was complemented by Drew's expertise as a tea buyer. The establishment of a London shop at 268 Edgware Road was the first fruit of their partnership; this was followed by the establishment of large stores at Islington, Birmingham, and Leeds, as well as a number of smaller tea stores. In 1885 Drew and Musker formed the Home and Colonial Trading Association, with Drew holding a majority of the shares.

Tea, and especially the fashionable Indian tea personally selected by Drew, remained the core of their business; but there was also a considerable trade in other groceries.

Specializing in good quality products at low prices, the firm's turnover, and also profits, were very high. The number of retail outlets also continued to expand at a phenomenal rate: the number of shops peaked at 500 in 1903, and annual profits at £220,000 in 1901.

Although founder of the grocery chain, Drew ceased from 1888 to have any active role in its management. Wishing to lead the life of a country gentleman, he was able to do so in his mid-thirties because of the increasingly powerful role played by his solicitor, William Capel Slaughter. The leading partner of the City firm of Slaughter and May, Slaughter had acted as Drew's adviser at the time of the launch of Home and Colonial, and had the entrepreneurial drive and City connections that were needed to mastermind the continued expansion of the firm. When the business was converted to a private limited company in March 1888, Slaughter undertook the chairmanship. Henceforth a very wealthy rentier, Drew nevertheless remained a director of the new firm, and he also personally retained more than half of the 150,000 ordinary £1 shares.

Two years later Drew took the first step towards the establishment of a landed dynasty: on 16 September 1890 he married Frances, daughter of Thomas Richardson of Buxton, a cotton manufacturer. The couple had two daughters and three sons, and their first home was a romantic mock castle, Culverden, near Tunbridge Wells in Kent. In 1899 Drew acquired Wadhurst Hall in Sussex from the estate of the bankrupt Adrian de Murietta, a Spanish banker and extravagant friend of the prince of Wales. This mansion, along with its tapestries and exotic Spanish furniture, remained the family home for the next two decades and should have been enough to satisfy the ambitions of any nouveau riche shopkeeper. However, family tradition maintained that the Drews came from ancient Devon landowning stock, and Julius and his elder brother William investigated this further. With the aid of a professional genealogist they produced a family tree: this showed that one of their putative ancestors was Drogo or Dru, who had accompanied William the Conqueror to England; and his descendant, Drogo de Teign, gave his name to the parish of Drewsteignton (Dru-his-town on the Teign) in Devon in the twelfth century.

Drew was already familiar with the area, as his first cousin Richard Peek was rector of Drewsteignton; and it was probably on one of his visits there that he conceived the notion of building a castle on his ancestral domain. Moreover, the perfect site was available on glebe land belonging to his cousin: on a narrow ridge overlooking the steep gorge of the River Teign to the south and Chagford Vale to the north. Purchasing the site in 1910, along with 450 acres, he also changed his name by deed poll to the more authentic Drewe.

In need of an architect, Drewe was advised by Edward Hudson, the proprietor of Country Life, that Edwin Lutyens was 'the only possible architect' (Aslet, 168). Although the latter had not yet designed any grand buildings, his domestic architecture would have been familiar to Drewe; and he had also recently remodelled Lindisfarne

Castle for Hudson in Northumberland. Lutyens accepted the commission and by 3 August 1910 he was writing to Emily, his wife, that:

> Mr Drew writes a nice and exciting letter. I go on with drawings not more than £50,000 and £10,000 for the gardens … Only I do wish he didn't want a castle—but just a delicious loveable house with plenty of good large rooms in it.
> (*Letters of Edwin Lutyens*, 199)

The site was staked out one day in early September, but Drewe's ideas were still developing. The principal modification required, Lutyens wrote, was that 'He wants to build a large keep or commemorative tower to commemorate the first Drogo … and this we planned and plotted and he was mighty pleased and proud'. They got on 'famously', and, instead of returning that day to London, Lutyens 'went on to Sidmouth to talk more castles that night'. Although his motoring expenses alone came to £5 5*s.*, Lutyens noted that he would get it all back, adding that 'Drewe travels and hotels en prince' (ibid., 205).

Despite what Lutyens had written to Emily, his preliminary sketches suggested a building of heroic proportions. Christopher Hussey noted that:

> As first conceived Drogo would have occupied the whole summit of its heather-clad promontory, approximating in extent and effect to a feudal castle such as Richmond, built of the glittering granite as massively as Durham, and growing out of its summit like a geological outcrop. (Hussey, 219)

Yet because Drewe insisted that the castle had to be built in traditional fashion, using only solid granite laid 6 feet thick, this was never realistic. In the event the original design was scaled down by two-thirds, leaving two wings joined at an angle of 120°, with the commemorative entrance tower and the great hall along the south front.

The foundation stone of Castle Drogo was laid on 4 April 1911. Lutyens was in overall control from his office in London, with Drewe's agent, John Walker, directing operations on site. There was a workforce of up to 100, many of whom hewed and dressed the stone; but, in an almost medieval fashion, every piece of granite was laid by two Devon stonemasons, Cleeve and Dewdney. Drewe's children soon discovered that Lutyens was 'a perfect tease', who would use the pepper and salt containers at table 'to illustrate a point connected with the design and he would make a lot of very quick sketches' (*Castle Drogo*, 49).

In the event Castle Drogo took more than twenty years to complete. Construction was delayed by the continued shortage of worked granite, but the major hold-up was caused by the outbreak of the First World War. More than three-quarters of the workers were called up, and progress was 'fearfully slow' (*Castle Drogo*, 50). Drewe, like so many other parents, also suffered a personal disaster in 1917, with the death of his eldest son, Adrian, who had been serving in Flanders. A room in the castle was later furnished as a memorial to him.

The last stone was laid at Castle Drogo on 22 December 1925, and two years later the family were able to start living at the house. Yet Drewe hardly lived long enough to enjoy being seigneur of Castle Drogo: he had suffered a stroke in 1924, and he died at Kilmorie, Asham Marine Drive, Torquay, on 10 November 1931, survived by his wife.

His remains were buried in the churchyard at Drewsteignton, amid the shades of his ancestors, and covered by a simple granite tombstone designed by Lutyens.

Castle Drogo itself proved to be the lasting memorial to the medieval vision to which Julius Drewe, in alliance with Sir Edwin Lutyens, attempted to give material shape. Although an anachronism, and only a fragment of what was originally conceived, its massive and rugged features are genuinely fortress-like. 'The ultimate justification of Drogo is that it does not pretend to be a castle. It *is* a castle' (Hussey, 225). Another and more modern view, however, sees it as 'a great country house masquerading as a fortress' (Greeves and Trinick, 55).

In 1974 Drewe's grandson Anthony gifted Castle Drogo to the National Trust. Although it was the first twentieth-century house to pass into the trust's possession, the first thing visitors see as they approach the great entrance tower is, fittingly, the large heraldic Drewe lion carved above the doorway. Beneath it is carved the family motto, *Droge nomen et virtus arma dedit* (Drewe is the name and valour gave it arms).   ROBERT BROWN

Sources *Castle Drogo* (1990) [The National Trust] · P. Mathias, *Retailing revolution: a history of multiple retailing in the food trades based upon the Allied Suppliers group of companies* [1967] · *The letters of Edwin Lutyens to his wife Lady Emily*, ed. C. Percy and J. Ridley (1985) · C. Aslet, *The last country houses* (1982) · C. Hussey, *The life of Sir Edwin Lutyens* (1950); repr. (1989) · D. J. Jeremy, 'Drew, Julius Charles', *DBB* · L. Greeves and M. Trinick, *The National Trust guide* (1989) · A. S. G. Butler, *The domestic architecture of Sir Edwin Lutyens* (1950); repr. (1989) · D. Gough, ed., *The work of the English architect Sir Edwin Lutyens* (1981) · J. Brown, *Lutyens and the Edwardians: an English architect and his clients* (1996) · *CGPLA Eng. & Wales* (1932) · b. cert. · d. cert. · m. cert.

Archives National Trust

Likenesses photograph, Castle Drogo, Devon

Wealth at death £207,673 3*s.* 11*d.*: resworn probate, 4 Jan 1932, *CGPLA Eng. & Wales*

Drewe [Drue], **Thomas** (*c.*1586–1627), actor and playwright, was the eldest son of George Drewe, fishmonger. On 17 February 1612 he married Margaret Hart at St James's, Clerkenwell, Middlesex, where the couple had four children baptized: Elizabeth (*bap.* 21 March 1613, *bur.* 29 March 1613); Francis (*bap.* 10 July 1614, *bur.* 19 June 1617); a second Elizabeth (*bap.* 18 May 1617); and Robert (*bap.* 20 Sept 1618).

About the time of his marriage Drewe joined Queen Anne's Men as an actor at the Red Bull, just as the company was entering a tumultuous period. Their leading actor and financial manager, Thomas Greene, died in August 1612 and they were eventually forced to pay Greene's widow, Susan, a substantial portion of each day's takings as partial payment for an old debt. The company suffered a further blow on 4 March 1617, when rioting apprentices destroyed their costumes and playbooks at the new Cockpit playhouse. Drewe, a sharer in the company by this time, later testified that they 'would have put downe the Flag, being weary of the payment', except that Susan agreed to reduced payments in late 1618 (PRO, 24/500/9).

It was too late, however. Drewe, according to his own testimony, left Queen Anne's Men at Christmas 1618, and the death of their patron in March 1619 caused the company's effective dissolution. On 11 October 1619 Drewe claimed his freedom in the Fishmongers' Company by patrimony, being described as the son of 'Georg Drewe deceased' (Guildhall Library, MS 5576/1). Soon afterwards he moved to Tower Street in the parish of All Hallows Barking, where he was living when he testified in November 1623 in the chancery case *Worth* v. *Baskerville*, recounting the history of Queen Anne's Men and describing himself as thirty-seven years old and free of the Fishmongers.

Though he appears to have given up acting after receiving his freedom Drewe stayed involved in the theatre by writing plays. On 2 January 1624 Sir Henry Herbert licensed a play for the Palsgrave's Men, called *The History of the Dutchess of Suffolk*, 'written by Mr. Drew'. This play was entered in the Stationers' register on 13 November 1629, with a fuller attribution to 'Thomas Drue', and it was printed anonymously in 1631. Herbert noted in his licence that the play 'being full of dangerous matter was much reformed' (Bentley, 3.284) and it is difficult to tell, from the reasonably innocuous extant text, what that dangerous matter might have been. It concerns the popular story (also told by Hall, Holinshed, and balladeer Thomas Deloney) of Katherine, the sixteenth-century duchess of Suffolk, her flight from religious persecution, and her return to England under Queen Elizabeth.

In September 1624 Herbert licensed a now lost play by 'Mr. Drew' about a sensational contemporary murder that was also dramatized by Dekker, Webster, Ford, and Rowley as *Keep the Widow Waking* (also lost, but known from a subsequent lawsuit). Bentley speculated that this play might be identical with *The Woman's Mistake*, entered in the Stationers' register in 1653 as a work of Drewe and Robert Davenport. Drewe may be the T. D. who wrote *The Bloodie Banquet*, printed in 1639 but possibly written much earlier, though Thomas Dekker is also a likely candidate, and Thomas Middleton almost certainly contributed as well. This play, a rather crude melodrama based on a story in William Warner's *Syrinx* about the tyrant of Cilicia, was listed on 10 August 1639 as the property of William Beeston, the son of Drewe's old acting colleague Christopher Beeston. Drewe paid quarterage dues as a member of the Fishmongers until early 1627, when the notation 'mort' in the quarterage books indicates that he had recently died.

DAVID KATHMAN

Sources G. E. Bentley, *The Jacobean and Caroline stage*, 7 vols. (1941–68), vol. 2, p. 427; vol. 3, pp. 280–86 • C. J. Sisson, 'Notes on early English stage history', *Modern Language Review*, 37 (1942), 25–36 • C. J. Sisson, 'The Red Bull company and the importunate widow', *Shakespeare Survey*, 7 (1954), 57–68 • Fishmongers' Company, register of freedom admissions, GL, MS 5576/1 • M. Eccles, 'Elizabethan actors, I: A–D', *N&Q*, 236 (1991), 38–49, esp. 46 • T. D., *The bloodie banquet, a tragedie* (1639); repr. as *The bloody banquet, 1639* (1962) • Fishmongers' quarterage book, 1610–42, GL, MS 5578A/1

Dreyer, Sir Frederic Charles (1878–1956), naval officer, was born on 8 January 1878 at Parsonstown, King's county, Ireland, the second son of the Danish-born John Louis Emil *Dreyer (1852–1926), then astronomer to the fourth

earl of Rosse, and his wife, Katherine Hannah (*d.* 1923), daughter of John Tuthill, of Kilmore, co. Limerick. From the Royal School, Armagh, Dreyer entered the Royal Naval College, Dartmouth, in 1891 and in his final examinations was placed fifth in his term. He continued to obtain class 1 certificates in nearly all his courses for sub-lieutenant and lieutenant (promoted July 1898) and for gunnery lieutenant; in 1900 he was the author of *How to Get a First Class in Seamanship*. In 1901, on the demanding advanced course for gunnery and torpedo lieutenants at Greenwich, he came first, with honours, in his class of three; he then joined the staff of the gunnery school, Sheerness. On 26 June 1901 Dreyer married Una Maria (1876–1959), daughter of John Thomas Hallett, vicar of Bishop's Tachbrook, Warwickshire; they had three sons and two daughters.

In 1903 Dreyer became the gunnery officer of *Exmouth* and, after the battleship was recommissioned in 1904 as the flagship of the Home (later Channel) Fleet, gunnery adviser to Admiral Sir Arthur Wilson. For three years to 1907 the *Exmouth* was first in the Channel Fleet in both gunlayers' test and battle practice. In 1905 Dreyer served on the calibration committee chaired by Rear-Admiral Percy Scott and, in January 1907, joined *Dreadnought* for her first cruise as experimental gunnery officer. On his return he went to the Admiralty as an assistant to the director of naval ordnance (DNO), Captain John Jellicoe, but was quickly selected by Sir John Fisher (on Wilson's recommendation) to advise the nucleus crews of the Home Fleet in their gunnery training. At the close of 1907 he was promoted commander and then assisted Wilson during the trials of Arthur *Pollen's rangefinder mounting and plotter in *Ariadne*. Afterwards Dreyer returned to the DNO's department (now under Captain Reginald Bacon) until he was appointed commander of *Vanguard* in late 1909. A year later he was invited by Jellicoe to be his flag commander, first in *Prince of Wales* and, from December 1911, in *Hercules*, appointments which established their 'long and close connection which has been so valuable to me' (Jellicoe). Jellicoe also arranged for Dreyer to take command of the new cruiser *Amphion* in 1913, and promotion to captain followed in June. *Amphion* was first in the whole navy in that year's gunlayers' test and first in its category at battle practice. In October 1913 Dreyer became flag captain to Rear-Admiral Sir Robert Arbuthnot in *Orion*, and in 1914 he received the civil CB for services to gunnery.

From 1899 onwards Dreyer had submitted a number of gunnery inventions. These were not successful until he and his elder brother, Captain John Tuthill Dreyer RA (1876–1959), who was himself a prolific inventor, put forward a device for obtaining range-rates from a plot of ranges against time. This led directly to the improvised rate plot used by Wilson shortly after the trials on *Ariadne* had finished, and from 1908 there was open rivalry between Frederic Dreyer and Pollen. However, the Royal Navy continued to experiment with manual course-plotting and it was not until Dreyer became commander of *Vanguard* that he first assembled a fire control system based on standard service instruments and a range-rate plotter patented by both Dreyer brothers in 1908. In September 1910 Frederic applied for a patent on a fire control table comprising a Dumaresq (an instrument, named after its inventor, modelling the relationship between speeds, courses, target bearing, range-rate, and deflection), range clock, and rate plotters for both range and bearing. Its novelty lay mainly in the integration of the components so that the results from the plots could be used to refine the settings of the Dumaresq. The 'original Dreyer table' was designed and built by the firm of Elliott Brothers under the direction of Keith Elphinstone and installed in *Prince of Wales* in September 1911. After successful trials an order was placed for five improved mark III tables, which incorporated manually set range and bearing clocks and a drive controlled from a gyrocompass receiver; subject to the limitations of manual working, the last feature (which was not included in Pollen's contemporary Argo clocks marks III and IV) enabled the table to continue predicting ranges and bearings during changes of course, even if the target was obscured. The Dreyer table mark IV (the first was installed in *Iron Duke* in 1914) was fully automatic, though its design was mainly the work of Elphinstone. In 1916 Dreyer was awarded £5000 for his inventions (which also included a range of tactical instruments). Although the Argo clock was superior mechanically, the automatic two-axis follower of the later Dreyer tables was equally innovative: these tables proved adaptable (in ways inconceivable for the separate and unconnected Argo clock and plotter) to new gunnery methods. The post-war Admiralty fire control tables used Argo- or Ford-type variable speed drives, but their integrated design with separate plotting of ranges and bearings derived from the earlier Dreyer tables.

In 1915 Dreyer became Jellicoe's flag captain in *Iron Duke*. After Jutland he and his ship's gunnery were praised in the commander-in-chief's dispatches and he was apppointed a military CB. He then accompanied Jellicoe to the Admiralty, initially as assistant director, anti-submarine division, but from March 1917 as DNO. Proving himself 'outstandingly able and of great energy and pertinacity' (Chatfield, 157), with the aid of a small committee, which included his elder brother (now colonel and eventually major-general and director of artillery), he drove through the development and supply of new and effective armour-piercing shell for the Grand Fleet, despite conflicts with the controller of armament production, Sir Vincent Raven. In 1918 he joined the naval staff as director of naval artillery and torpedoes. In 1919 he was appointed commodore and chief of staff for Jellicoe's empire mission and was made CBE. On his return Dreyer in 1920 resumed his staff duties as director of the gunnery division until he took command of the battle cruiser *Repulse* in 1922. He was promoted rear-admiral at the end of 1923; in the following year he became assistant chief of the naval staff and was responsible for founding the Tactical School at Portsmouth. In 1927 he hoisted his flag in *Hood* in command of the battle-cruiser squadron (which included two aircraft-carriers). He was promoted vice-admiral in 1929 and became deputy chief of the naval staff in 1930. Thus

Dreyer was a member of the board at the time of the Invergordon mutiny and had to accept that he would not, as he had hoped, be appointed commander-in-chief, Atlantic Fleet; instead, after promotion to admiral in 1932, he served as commander-in-chief, China station, from 1933 to 1936. He was promoted KCB in 1932 and GBE in 1936, and was placed on the retired list in 1939.

On the outbreak of war Dreyer immediately volunteered as a commodore, Royal Naval Reserve, of convoys. In 1940 he joined the staff of the general officer commanding-in-chief, home forces, on anti-invasion measures, and was then chairman of the Admiralty committee assessing U-boat losses. From 1941 he was a highly effective inspector of merchant navy gunnery until a temporary appointment as chief of naval air services in 1942. He briefly held the position of deputy chief of naval air equipment early in 1943 before finally returning to the retired list.

Dreyer died on 11 December 1956 at his home, Freelands, St Cross, Winchester, a year after publishing his memoirs, *The Sea Heritage: a Study in Maritime Warfare*. His body was cremated and his ashes scattered at sea. All three sons and both sons-in-law were naval officers; the second son, Sir Desmond Parry Dreyer, also commanded in the Far East and subsequently became second sea lord.

Beginning with Captain Stephen Roskill, who acknowledged an antipathy (Roskill, *Naval Policy*, 2.130), and Jon Sumida, later historians have been very critical of Dreyer himself and of the fire control tables. Yet Dreyer rate-plotting could make better use than the Argo true-course plotter of the intermittent and inaccurate target data actually available and, in battle, when conditions were comparable, German ships shot as well as or better than the British using a system of meaning ranges which was similar in principle to Dreyer's. At the end of the First World War Dreyer's ability and achievements were widely praised by senior officers; Jellicoe thought him 'one of the best captains of ships I have ever known' (F. C. Dreyer, 238). However, he was unapologetically ambitious and a disciplinarian who did not seek popularity. 'A large man without much sense of humour' (King-Hall, 247), he acquired a reputation as 'one of the most outspoken of twentieth-century admirals' (Marder, 1.35) who was also prolix on paper (Roskill, *Naval Policy*, 2.130); particularly in his defence of the board after Invergordon and as commander-in-chief, China (though also in early 1943), his lack of tact caused offence. Even so Dreyer more than Pollen established the foundations on which subsequent developments in British fire control were based, and he accomplished much, both in command afloat and at the Admiralty.

JOHN BROOKS

Sources F. C. Dreyer, *The sea heritage: a study in maritime warfare* (1955) · A. E. M. Chatfield, *The navy and defence: the autobiography of Admiral of the Fleet Lord Chatfield*, 1 (1942) · J. Jellicoe, letter to F. C. Dreyer, 20 Feb 1920, CAC Cam., DRYR 3/1–2 · S. King-Hall, *My naval life, 1906–1929* (1952) · A. J. Marder, *From the Dreadnought to Scapa Flow: the Royal Navy in the Fisher era, 1904–1919*, 5 vols. (1961–70) · S. W. Roskill, *Naval policy between the wars*, 2 vols. (1968–76) · CAC Cam., Dreyer MSS · J. Brooks, 'Fire control for British Dreadnoughts: choices of technology and supply', PhD diss., U. Lond., 2001 · J. T.

Sumida, *In defence of naval supremacy: finance, technology and British naval policy, 1889–1914* (1989) • *The Beatty papers: selections from the private and official correspondence of Admiral of the Fleet Earl Beatty*, ed. B. Ranft, 1, Navy RS, 128 (1989), 522–31 • D. Dreyer, 'Early development in naval fire control', *Naval Review* (July 1986), 238–41 • S. W. Roskill, *The war at sea, 1939–1945*, 1–2 (1954–6) • *DNB* • *The Times* (12 Dec 1956) • d. cert. • private information [Cmdr Christopher Dreyer]
Archives CAC Cam., personal and naval papers • PRO, official papers, ADM 137, 205, T. 173 | NMM, corresp. with Lord Chatfield
Likenesses photograph, 1914, CAC Cam. • photograph, 1916, IWM • W. Stoneman, photograph, 1936, NPG • photographs, 1941, IWM

Dreyer, Georges (1873–1934), pathologist, was born at Shanghai on 4 July 1873, the second son and third and youngest child of Captain Georg Hannibal Napoleon Dreyer, of the Royal Danish Navy, and his wife, Dagmar Alvilde, daughter of Judge W. T. Qvistgaard, a well-known jurist of Fredensborg. They lived in Copenhagen, but at the time of Dreyer's birth his father was in Shanghai as diplomatic adviser to the Great Northern Cable Company. Dreyer went to the Borgerdydsskolen at Christianshavn, then to the University of Copenhagen, where he graduated MD in 1900. His unusually rich education in mathematics, physics, and chemistry, and periods of postgraduate research in Denmark, Germany, and England under Carl Julius Salomonsen, Niels Ryberg Finsen, Albert Neisser, and Sir J. Burdon Sanderson, gave him a command of languages and supremely fitted him for a scientific career. He married, in 1900, Margrete Caroline, daughter of Laurits Jörgersen, of Söllestedgaard Manor, Laaland, Denmark, who survived him. There were no children.

Dreyer's first appointment as demonstrator of pathology in the University of Copenhagen combined research with arduous routine. In collaboration with Thorvald Madsen he contributed to the knowledge of diphtheria toxin and anti-toxin, and studied the effects of ultraviolet radiations on micro-organisms. From the beginning a passionate precision of technique and a loathing of slipshod thought characterized all his work, and it was in the accurate quantitative measurement of biological processes that he made many of his most notable contributions to science.

Appointed in 1907, when only thirty-four, to the chair of pathology at Oxford, which he held until his death, Dreyer revolutionized the teaching, and by his vivid personality, enthusiasm, and learning attracted a steady succession of collaborators. Among the varied fields of research pursued in his department were the principle and practice of the serological diagnosis of intestinal infections; quantitative studies of blood volume, the size of the aorta, vital capacity, and their relations to height and weight; the calculation of the dosage of toxins and drugs according to the surface area of the individual; inoculation against typhoid and paratyphoid fevers, and its effects on the Widal reaction; and methods of serological diagnosis in syphilis.

Dreyer was naturalized in 1912. During the First World War he was appointed to the pathological advisory committee where he pressed for triple inoculation in the place of typhoid inoculation only. He was commissioned in the Royal Army Medical Corps in 1915 and sent to Wimereux to organize the laboratory diagnosis of enteric fever and dysentery. In the course of this project he instituted, in 1915, the standards laboratory at Oxford which for the next thirty years provided this country and the dominions with scientifically standardized reagents for serological diagnosis. Later came investigations on the quantitative estimation of tuberculin, on variations in the virulence of the tubercle bacillus, and on the preparation and use of immunizing reagents against tuberculosis. His field test of the latter in Danish cattle did not, however, live up to its early promise.

Although in his later years he paid increasing attention to university business and to the building of the Sir William Dunn School of Pathology, which is his monument, Dreyer could not be parted from his own research, which in this period turned to the action of radiations on bacteria (a revival of an earlier interest) and the devising of quantitative methods for the estimation of bacteriophage potency.

Dreyer was elected a member of the Kongelige Danske Videnskabernes Selskab in 1909, and in 1913 received the French order of Officier de l'Instruction Publique. For his war work on the oxygen supply to aircrews and on the diagnosis of enteric fever he was appointed CBE in 1919, and he was elected FRS in 1921.

In 1912 Dreyer was elected a fellow of Lincoln College, Oxford, which profited greatly from his interest and wise counsels. He served for many years on the hebdomadal council where his unusual power of understanding the points at issue, shown in university, college, and scientific matters, caused his opinions and judgement to command respect. He died suddenly while on holiday at Söllestedgaard on 17 August 1934.

H. G. HANBURY, rev. ANITA MCCONNELL

Sources S. R. Douglas, *Obits. FRS*, 1 (1932–5), 569–76 • M. Dreyer, *Georges Dreyer: a memoir by his wife* (1937) • E. W. A. Walker, 'Georges Dreyer's scientific work at Oxford', *BMJ* (24 Nov 1934), 946 • *BMJ* (25 Aug 1934), 376 • *Journal of Pathology and Bacteriology*, 39 (1934) • private information (1949) • personal knowledge (1949) • *CGPLA Eng. & Wales* (1934)
Likenesses W. Stoneman, photograph, 1933, NPG • J. Russell and Sons, colour photograph, Wellcome L. • photomechanical print (after J. Russell and Sons), Wellcome L.
Wealth at death £437 14s. 1d.: probate, 30 Nov 1934, *CGPLA Eng. & Wales*

Dreyer, John Louis Emil (1852–1926), astronomer and historian of astronomy, was born at Copenhagen on 13 February 1852, the third son of John Christopher Dreyer, lieutenant-general in the Danish army, and his wife, Ida Nicoline Margarethe Rangrup. At the age of fourteen he read a book about Tycho Brahe which inspired him to 'be an astronomer and nothing else'; he 'admired the bold use of large instruments and the ambitious cataloguing undertaken by his countryman' (Gingerich, 'Dreyer and his NGC', 621). During monthly visits to the Copenhagen University observatory he was encouraged by Hans

John Louis Emil Dreyer (1852–1926), by unknown photographer

Schjellerup, an assistant there. He entered the university in 1869 to study logic, mathematics, and astronomy, and by 1870 he was given free access to the instruments of the observatory and encouraged to compute. In 1874 he was awarded a gold medal by the university for an essay on 'Personal errors in observations'. He graduated MA, and received a PhD in 1882 for his memoir on 'The constant of precession'.

Dreyer's wife, Katherine Hannah, whom he married in 1875, was the daughter of John Tuthill of Kilmore, co. Limerick, Ireland. This connection and Dreyer's reputation gained him an invitation the previous year to succeed as astronomer in charge of the fourth earl of Rosse's observatory at Birr Castle, Parsonstown, King's county. His task was to complete the third earl's observations of nebulae and clusters made between 1848 and 1867 and prepare the work for publication. With the great 36 inch and 72 inch reflecting telescopes he made many observations. There was no good catalogue of nebulae and clusters: Messier had catalogued 109 objects, John Herschel 5079 more. In an important supplement to Herschel's catalogue of 1864, Dreyer provided notes and corrections to Herschel's objects and added 1172 more. This completed the work at Birr, and demonstrated Dreyer's skills in assessing errors and making precision measurements and his painstaking scholarship. In 1878 he became an assistant at the Dublin University observatory at Dunsink, and took charge of the new meridian circle.

In June 1882 Dreyer became the fourth director of the Church of Ireland's observatory at Armagh. The best candidate in Ireland, he was the first incumbent not to be Irish, clerical, and a graduate of Trinity College. He completed and reduced the meridian observations made by his predecessor, T. R. Robinson, since 1859, and the accuracy of the positions after his analysis of the systematic errors of the observations, together with his identification of the proper motions of twenty-nine stars, gave the *Second Armagh Catalogue of 3300 Stars* (1886) lasting value. The observatory's meridian instruments of 1827 were obsolete. The site, noted for 'extreme unfavourableness' of climate in 1796, had been rendered 'never again [suitable] for fundamental measurement' by a railway in 1874 (Bennett, 46, 150). The 1869 disestablishment of the church had halved observatory income; in 1884 Dreyer's salary was reduced, and his assistant paid only enough for meteorology. The Treasury declined support, but made a one-off grant of £2000. Dreyer installed a new 10 inch Grubb equatorial refractor in 1885, and until the early 1900s made micrometric positional measurements of nebulae with respect to comparison stars.

In 1886 Dreyer submitted to the council of the Royal Astronomical Society (RAS) a second supplementary catalogue of nebulae, but the council invited him instead to compile a complete catalogue of all known nebulae. Dreyer completed the enormous task in only two years. It was published as *A new general catalogue of nebulae and clusters of stars, being the catalogue of Sir John Herschel, revised, corrected and enlarged* (1888) (NGC), and contained the positions and descriptions of 7840 nebulae and clusters. Two index catalogues of 1895 and 1908 added 5386 more, all listed in order of right ascension, with their north polar distances. A major contribution to astronomy, the NGC numbers remain the universally employed nomenclature.

Dreyer's historical curiosity and empathy disposed him to many years studying all sources on Tycho Brahe. In 1890 he published a biography of his hero, which was superseded only by Victor Thoren's *Lord of Uraniborg* (1991). Dreyer complemented his work with the classic *History of the Planetary Systems from Thales to Kepler* (1906). This drew on original sources, and explained man's conception of the universe from about 500 BC to Kepler's mathematical proof of the Copernican system.

Dreyer 'enriched astronomy by three monumental works of research, collection, and editing' (*DSB*). The first was the NGC of 1888–1908. In 1908 Dreyer began the second, a complete edition of the observations of Tycho Brahe, under the auspices of the Carlsberg Institute. Later, the generosity of G. A. Hagemann of Copenhagen made it possible to include all the works and correspondence of Brahe, published and unpublished. The fourteen volumes of *Tychonis Brahe opera omnia* (1913–26) in Latin include two long introductions by Dreyer, one an account of Brahe's work, the other regarding the quality of his observations, both translated into Latin. Despite its inaccessibility, it remains the foundation of contemporary work on Brahe. Dreyer's third monumental work resulted from the councils of the Royal Society and the RAS inviting him to edit a complete edition of the works of Sir William Herschel. *The Scientific Papers of Sir William Herschel* (2 vols., 1912) contain seventy-one published and some thirty unpublished papers. Dreyer checked the original observations and reductions of nebulae and double stars, and added a fine introductory biography based mainly on unpublished material.

Meanwhile, Dreyer never lost interest in practical astronomy. Recognizing that visual micrometer work had been superseded, in 1898 he purchased a micrometer microscope to enable him to measure photographic plates of nebulae supplied by Isaac Roberts. That work, 'a step on Dreyer's path from the dome to the study' (Bennett, 168), engaged him from 1899 until Roberts's death in 1904.

After a new financial crisis in 1897, Dreyer's salary slumped to £140, that appropriate to a junior assistant, and the whole situation must have been dispiriting. Dreyer promptly applied for the newly vacant Radcliffe observership at Oxford, but the appointment went to Arthur Alcock Rambaut from Dunsink. He applied on 30 July to William Christie, the astronomer royal, for a reference to support his application to return to Dunsink in place of Rambaut. After all his underpaid service to Irish astronomy he was surely bitter to receive a reply on 5 October that Christie was supporting two 'very well qualified' young Cambridge candidates from his own staff, and would support no others (Christie to Dreyer, 5 Oct 1897, CUL, RGO 7 156 Radcl.). Meanwhile Trinity College appointed Charles J. Joly (1864–1906), a mathematician and one of their own fellows since 1894, but a man who had no knowledge of practical astronomy.

In 1916 Dreyer was awarded the RAS gold medal for the NGC and historical work. Fortunately the Carlsberg Institute enabled him to retire to Oxford and devote himself to writing. He served on the council of the RAS from 1917, and was president in 1923 and 1924. In that office he collaborated with Professor H. H. Turner and supervised *A History of the Royal Astronomical Society, 1820–1920* in commemoration of the society's centenary.

Dreyer's astronomical posts were less important than his linguistic, historical, and scientific skills, and the thoroughness of his scholarship, 'such as rarely decorates our science' (Sampson, 'Dreyer's "Tycho Brahe"', 159), gave his astronomical as well as his historical work lasting importance. His gifts were matched by an unsparing devotion to astronomy. He was endeared to many friends by his gentle and amiable disposition. In late 1925 his health began to fail as a consequence of stomach cancer, and he died at his home, 14 Staverton Road, Oxford, on 14 September 1926. He had been naturalized a British citizen in March 1885, and received an honorary DSc from Queen's University, Belfast, and an honorary MA from Oxford. Dreyer's wife had died in 1923; they had a daughter and three sons, the second of whom was Sir Frederic *Dreyer (1878–1956).

F. W. DYSON, *rev.* ROGER HUTCHINS

Sources J. A. Bennett, *Church, state, and astronomy in Ireland: 200 years of Armagh observatory* (1990) · O. Gingerich, 'J. L. E. Dreyer and his NGC', *Sky and Telescope*, 76 (1988), 621–3 · E. B. K. [E. B. Knobel], *Monthly Notices of the Royal Astronomical Society*, 87 (1926–7), 251–7 · R. A. Sampson, 'Dreyer's "Tycho Brahe"', *The Observatory*, 49 (1926), 159–62 · P. Moore, *The astronomy of Birr Castle* (1971) · 'Letter of application to the Radcliffe trustees from J. L. E. Dreyer, PhD, candidate for the post of Radcliffe observer', 1897, CUL, Royal Greenwich Observatory papers, RGO 7 156 Radcl. · O. Gingerich, 'Dreyer and Tycho's world system', *The great Copernicus chase and other adventures in astronomical history* (1992), 251–6 · D. Abbott, ed., *The biographical dictionary of scientists: astronomers* (1984), 45–6 · *The Observatory*, 49 (1926), 293–4 · A. F. O'D. Alexander, 'Dreyer, Johann Louis Emil', *DSB* · R. A. Sampson, presidential address on presenting the gold medal to Dr J. L. E. Dreyer, *Monthly Notices of the Royal Astronomical Society*, 76 (1915–16), 368–75 · J. L. E. Dreyer, letter to W. H. M. Christie, 30 July 1897, CUL, Royal Greenwich Observatory papers, RGO 7 156 Radcl. · W. H. M. Christie, letter to J. L. E. Dreyer, 5 Oct 1897, CUL, Royal Greenwich Observatory papers, RGO 7 156 Radcl. · R. A. Sampson and F. E. Brasch, 'John Louis Emil Dreyer (1852–1926)', *Isis*, 21 (1934), 131–44 · *CGPLA Eng. & Wales* (1926) · d. cert. · O. Gingerich, *The great Copernicus chase and other adventures in astronomical history* (1992)

Archives Armagh Observatory, MSS · RAS, files, MS, and photographs · RAS, papers | Birr Castle, Offaly, archives, letters to earl of Rosse · CUL, letters to Sir George Stokes · RAS, letters to Royal Astronomical Society

Likenesses Elliott & Fry, photograph, repro. in *The Observatory*, 293 · photograph (in youth), repro. in Gingerich, 'Dreyer and Tycho's world system', 251 · photograph (as an old man), Armagh Observatory; repro. in Gingerich, 'J. L. E. Dreyer', 621 · photograph, University of California, Mary Lea Shane Archives of the Lick Observatory [*see illus.*]

Wealth at death £1213 12s. 10d.: probate, 25 Oct 1926, *CGPLA Eng. & Wales*

Dreyer, Rosalie (1895–1987), nurse, was born on 3 September 1895 in Bern, Switzerland, the eldest child in the family of four daughters and one son of Johann Dreyer, manager of a dairy co-operative, and his wife, Elisabeth Neuenschwander. Her father's work necessitated travel in the Lausanne area, and the two eldest daughters of this Lutheran family received their education from Roman Catholic nuns. The young Rosa was encouraged to travel by a cosmopolitan aunt. She went to England in 1914 as an au pair girl to the Saltzburgers, a Swiss family settled there; for many years afterwards she kept links with her young charges.

In May 1918 Rosalie Dreyer began to train as a nurse at Guy's Hospital, London. Despite a bout of glandular fever, she gained her state registration certificate in March 1922, excelling in practical nursing and sick-room cookery. After a year's private nursing she went back to Switzerland to work in the Rollier Clinic, a tuberculosis sanatorium in Leysin, canton Vaud.

In 1924 Rosalie Dreyer returned to the staff of Guy's. She gained her midwifery qualification in 1926 and rose through the nursing hierarchy to become assistant matron in 1931. In 1934 she secured the post of matron at the Bethnal Green Hospital, which since the 1929 Local Government Act was under the control of the London county council (LCC). The next fifteen years of her career were spent in the service of the LCC, as principal matron (1935–40), principal matron in charge (1940–48), and chief nursing officer (1948–50). The move to the LCC was to a world vastly different from Guy's and the voluntary sector. The LCC nursing service had been built up from over

120 different institutions, employing approximately 8000 female nursing staff. It offered a comprehensive training, uniformity of conditions of employment, and probably the most integrated service in existence prior to the inception of the National Health Service. In the course of her work Rosalie Dreyer frequently met Herbert Morrison, leader of the LCC from 1934 to 1940. She was well aware of her uniquely powerful position, seeing herself as a policy maker and using her opportunities to promote nursing and to professionalize the former workhouse infirmary staff. Younger women at London matrons' meetings and her own ward sisters were in awe of her. Her charm and sense of humour were also much appreciated.

During the Second World War Rosalie Dreyer's organizational abilities were fully utilized. She had to deal with the immense challenges presented by the urgent need to evacuate and disperse hospitals into the surrounding countryside. Personnel and equipment had to be relocated and both had eventually to return together. Her memos give eloquent testimony to her managerial skills as patients (many of them chronically sick), staff, student nurses, their teachers, equipment, anatomical charts, and life-sized manikins were moved about London and the home counties in what was logistically the most difficult task to face a nurse manager so far in the twentieth century. With a car and a driver at her disposal, she visited bombed and evacuated hospitals to assess the extent of the damage and morale of her staff. Her opinion was esteemed by her LCC colleagues, for she had an acute grasp of the realities of the situation. In negotiations with the Ministry of Health on the production of a nursing recruitment film to be shown in cinemas, she stressed the need for the filming to be undertaken in a hospital where the uniform was up to date and visually appealing to potential new nurses.

Rosalie Dreyer had become a British citizen in 1934, shortly before her appointment to Bethnal Green Hospital. Her wartime experience was marred by the xenophobic agitation of Ethel Bedford Fenwick, who described her appointment as matron-in-chief as unpatriotic. Rosalie Dreyer received messages of support from the Royal College of Nursing and was publicly defended by the LCC leader, Charles Latham. After the war she supervised the assimilation of the LCC nursing service into separate new National Health Service units which had their own hospital management committees. She became chief nursing officer, in charge of domiciliary nursing services, but she disliked this work, which was in no way comparable with her previous post, and in 1950 she moved to the World Health Organization (WHO) as nursing adviser, touring the war-torn countries of Europe and advising on nursing reconstruction, until her retirement in 1953. Despite her significant contribution to the health provision for Londoners, she received no civic or public honours.

Rosalie Dreyer was a life member of the Royal College of Nursing, president of one of its London branches (South East Metropolitan), and a member of the Royal College of Nursing committee on the assistant nurse, chaired by the first Baron Horder. She believed in the formal recognition of the second-level nurse, and was chosen as first president of the National Association of State Enrolled Nurses. Within the National Health Service she served on three hospital management committees (South West Middlesex from 1950 to 1958, Stepney from 1952 to 1964, and Lewisham from 1955 to 1964) and was a governor and honorary secretary to the friends of the Royal National Throat, Nose and Ear Hospital on the Whitley Council.

Rosalie Dreyer was birdlike, tall, and slim (until she worked for the WHO), with dark hair which she complained was squashed by nurses' caps. While at Guy's she was an avid theatregoer, with a wide circle of friends. She regarded her nurses as her family. Her retirement was an active one, sustained by her love of sewing, cooking, and travelling. She travelled to Australia in her sixties, partly by mail boat. She kept up her lifelong links with nursing friends such as Dame Elizabeth Cockayne. During her last illness she was nursed by one of her sisters and district nurses, some of whom knew her background. She died, unmarried, at her flat, 5 Kingsthorpe Court, Raymond Road, Wimbledon, London, on 21 May 1987 from the effects of a cerebral tumour. STEPHANIE KIRBY, *rev.*

Sources records, London, Guy's Hospital, LMA · records, London county council, LMA · membership archives, Royal College of Nursing Archives, Edinburgh · *The Times* (5 June 1987) · *The Telegraph* (5 June 1987) · private information (1996) [M. Dreyer (sister), P. Nuttall (professional colleague)] · *CGPLA Eng. & Wales* (1987)
Likenesses photographs, priv. coll.
Wealth at death £292,845: probate, 11 Sept 1987, *CGPLA Eng. & Wales*

Dreyfus, Henry [Henri] (1882–1944), industrialist, was born in January 1882 into a Jewish family in Switzerland; he was the son of Abraham Dreyfus. Trained as a chemist, he held a doctorate of the University of Basel. In 1912, in conjunction with his elder brother, Camille, and a silk dyer, Alexander Clavel, he set up in Basel a company for the manufacture of cellulose acetate and other chemicals. Cellulose acetate had been the subject of patents for various uses: as a base for cinematograph film; for paints and varnishes including 'dope' used for treating the outer skin of early aircraft; and for spinning into artificial silk. Dreyfus was among those who took out such patents, though his were hotly contested and were rejected in Germany.

At the outbreak of the First World War the sole sources of dope available to the allied powers were a firm in France and the Dreyfus plant in Switzerland, and in 1915 the British War Office accepted a tender from the latter for the supply of the chemical. In 1916 the Dreyfus brothers and Clavel went to Britain and, in association with some other businessmen, set up the British Cellulose and Chemical Manufacturing Co. Ltd. Work began on the erection, near Derby, of a factory to make cellulose acetate dope and related chemical products. With the aid of tax concessions and loans from the government, production finally started in 1917. So, too, did trouble for the company in the form of complaints about delays, about the government-sponsored monopoly which it had secured, and about some dubious share pushing and speculation.

Dreyfus's name first came into the public eye in Britain

during 1918–19, when a House of Commons select committee, followed by a special government tribunal, reported on the company in connection with what had come to be called the 'dope scandal'. The name also elicited some antisemitic comments, notably, in August 1918, from G. K. Chesterton. But the adverse publicity died down and in 1920 the enterprise was launched as a public company with the stated intention of making artificial silk by the cellulose acetate process. In the following year it began to market the yarn under the name of Celanese and in 1923 the company changed its name to British Celanese Ltd. By 1927 Henry Dreyfus had become chairman and managing director. In the course of the 1920s and 1930s he built up the business into a remarkable example of a vertically integrated chemical and textile concern, undertaking the basic chemical processes, the spinning of yarn, weaving, knitting, and dyeing, and the manufacture of garments. A vigorous selling and advertising campaign ensured that Celanese became a household name in Britain in the 1930s, especially for women's underwear.

There seems little doubt that it was Dreyfus himself, as both businessman and technical expert, who gave to British Celanese the dynamic qualities which it exhibited at that time. But the price of that contribution was high. He was autocratic and difficult to work with, and his brash optimism, disregard of costs, and extravagant pursuit of goals caused financial chaos and a disastrous profit record. The need to repay government loans, together with the high development costs in the early 1920s, saddled it with a large proportion of preference capital and a heavy burden of debt. Despite a substantial rise in sales and in trading profits, preference dividends remained in arrears and no dividends were paid on the ordinary shares until 1944.

The personal qualities which Dreyfus brought to bear upon business life also included a pugnacious determination to defend his patents at all costs. But just as the Germans had rejected his original patents, so the validity of later patents which he took out was successfully questioned elsewhere. Undeterred, in 1931 he issued writs against Courtaulds, the dominant firm in rayon manufacture, alleging infringement of patents. Judgment was given against him in 1933; it was upheld by the Court of Appeal and then by the House of Lords in 1935. Still undeterred, Dreyfus persisted in further litigation, now alleging false evidence. Again he lost and prepared to go to appeal. By this time, 1937, an incensed body of shareholders, calling themselves the British Celanese Shareholders Union, had come into being. Dreyfus finally withdrew his appeal. Attempts to secure an understanding with Courtaulds came to nothing; merger negotiations were abandoned in 1940. British Celanese was finally taken over by Courtaulds in 1957.

In 1938 Dreyfus married Elizabeth Deborah Jenkinson, daughter of John Banks *Jenkinson, and twenty-nine years his junior. He died of heart failure on 30 December 1944, at the Hyde Park Hotel, Knightsbridge, London. His estate passed to his brother, Camille.   D. C. COLEMAN

Sources D. C. Coleman, *Courtaulds: an economic and social history*, 3 vols. (1969–80) · D. C. Coleman, 'War demand and industrial supply: the "dope scandal", 1915–1919', *War and economic development: essays in memory of David Joslin*, ed. J. M. Winter (1975), 205–27 · D. C. Coleman, 'Dreyfus, Henry', *DBB* · *CGPLA Eng. & Wales* (1945) · m. cert.
Archives Courtauld Inst.
Wealth at death £2,499,492 7s. 7d.: administration with will, 27 June 1945, *CGPLA Eng. & Wales*

Driberg, Thomas Edward Neil, Baron Bradwell (1905–1976), journalist and politician, was born on 22 May 1905, at Uckfield Lodge, Crowborough, Sussex, third and last son of John James Street Driberg (1841–1919), and his wife, Amy Mary Irving Bell (1866–1939). His father had retired from the Indian Civil Service in 1896 after thirty-five years in Assam. Driberg was awarded a scholarship to Lancing College in 1918. He relished the Anglo-Catholic tendencies of the school (becoming head sacristan) but at the age of fifteen also joined the Communist Party. In September 1923 he became head of his house and deputy head of the school. Shortly afterwards he made sexual overtures to a fellow pupil, who denounced him; Driberg was isolated from the other boys for the rest of the term, and then excluded from the school. After several months' private tutoring by Colin Pearson, afterwards Lord Pearson, Driberg won the third scholarship in classics at Christ Church, Oxford, in 1924.

The undergraduate Driberg swiftly bought lurid green Oxford bags, and joined the raffish set. He first read T. S. Eliot's *The Waste Land* in company with W. H. Auden, and had pretensions as an avant-garde poet. Driberg's Sitwellian poem 'London Square' was reprinted in *Oxford Poetry 1926* by Auden, who referred to Driberg and Eliot in the titles of two poems of 1926, 'Thomas Prologizes' and 'Thomas Epilogizes'. On the outbreak of the general strike Driberg was motored to London by A. J. P. Taylor and was arrested while helping to circulate communist strike bulletins. In the same year he won seventy-five votes as the Communist candidate for the presidency of the Oxford Union. Geoffrey Grigson recalled him at this time:

> the black hair, the white face, the nervous insolence, the elegant tailoring—Stendhal might have seen him and modelled upon the sight a young priest, machiavellian and subfuscly burning with ambition; or Balzac might have transformed him from the brilliant undergraduate into a schemer sliding into power through the *salons* of Paris … this exceedingly able man was … the white embryo of a dark cardinal … or a prince of the Renaissance. (Grigson, 114–15)

He left Oxford without taking a degree.

Throughout adulthood Driberg had a consuming passion for fellating handsome, lean, intelligent working-class toughs. He sympathized with a soldier of the Black Watch who told him in bed in 1938, 'Only sissies like women. Real men prefairr male flesh' (Wheen, 189). He was acquitted of indecent assault in 1935, and released without charge after being discovered by a policeman fellating a Norwegian sailor in 1943. Throughout his life he was thrilled by foolhardy sexual risks.

Edith Sitwell's support obtained Driberg's appointment to the staff of the *Daily Express* in 1928. He became an allusive and satirical chronicler of the Chelsea and Mayfair

Thomas Edward Neil Driberg, Baron Bradwell (1905–1976), by Ronald M. Franks, 1966

sets in a social column entitled 'The talk of London'. In 1933 he was allotted his own column which he compiled under the pseudonym William Hickey. His egalitarian sympathies and political radicalism permeated his commentaries on political events, social trends, and artistic fashions. His writing was wry, compassionate, and brimmed with his open-minded intelligence. Recognizing that his powers as a columnist were stimulated by travel, he visited Spain (1937; 1939), the Middle East (1938), *Mitteleuropa* after the Munich agreement, and the USA (1937, 1939, and 1941).

Having opposed the Nazi–Soviet pact, and probably after being identified as communicating information to MI5's counter-subversion section, Driberg was expelled from the Communist Party in 1941. Reginald Paget said, 'he couldn't have been a spy because no-one would have trusted him with a secret' (Wyatt, 1.299). In a by-election of June 1942 Driberg was elected as independent MP for Maldon. He joined the Labour Party before the general election of 1945, and continued to represent that constituency until 1955. He was initially a diligent constituency member, but as MP for Barking from 1959 to 1974 he haughtily neglected his local party and constituents. Driberg was a sincere if eccentric Christian socialist who detested racism and colonialism. Within the Parliamentary Labour Party in the late 1950s he strenuously advocated nuclear disarmament.

Driberg's position as Beaverbrook's employee became impossible after he entered the Commons, and from 1943 he was an influential columnist on *Reynolds News*. He was a

courageous war correspondent both with the allied armies after the Normandy invasion (1944) and with British troops in Korea (1950). In April 1945 he was a member of the British parliamentary delegation that inspected Buchenwald concentration camp. As a result of his celebrity as a *Reynolds News* columnist, he was elected to the national executive committee of the Labour Party throughout 1949–72 and, despite the hostility of many trade unionists, was chairman of the party in 1957–8.

On 30 June 1951 Driberg married Ena Mary Binfield (1902–1977), daughter of Myer Lyttelton, former wife of Joe Berger, and common-law widow of Robert Binfield (d. 1948), whose surname she had assumed. Driberg was a misogynist and never consummated his marriage. Despite his sexual and financial incontinence, Driberg was over-fastidious about food and wine, notoriously strict as a grammarian, and punctilious about ecclesiastical ritual. Although his company was often amusing, he could be pompous, mannered, wayward, self-indulgent, ungrateful, bullying, and indiscreet.

Driberg, who was a television reviewer for the *New Statesman* (1956–61), published several books. *Colonnade* (1949) contains a lively and versatile sample of his journalism from 1937 to 1947, including some items of enduring historic interest. *The Best of both Worlds* (1953) mixes his later journalism and diary jottings with less success. Despite being gutted by libel lawyers, his biography *Beaverbrook* (1956) is subtle and fair-minded. *Guy Burgess* (1956) is a sequel to the climax of his journalistic career: his exclusive interview in Moscow with the fugitive spy. Driberg, who had been a passionate critic of Frank Buchman's Christian revivalism since 1928, published *The Mystery of Moral Rearmament* in 1964. Though his biography of Hannan Swaffer (1974) was a feeble pot-boiler, his posthumous memoir *Ruling Passions* (1977) is playful and mischievous; its erotic emphasis 'horrified, and nauseated' Sir Sacheverell Sitwell (Lees-Milne, 169).

The opportunism of the Labour government of 1964–70 estranged Driberg, although he asked Harold Wilson to appoint him as legate to the Holy See. As a substitute for political engagement, this ageing *enfant terrible* became infatuated with the youth culture of the 1960s. His antics became increasingly ludicrous as his financial position deteriorated. His sexual prowling never abated: he came to resemble 'a sort of stout Dracula' (Vidal, 199). In January 1975 a life barony was gazetted in Driberg's name. On 12 August 1976 he had a fatal heart attack while travelling in a taxi from Paddington Station to his flat in the Barbican. He was interred in Bradwell cemetery, Essex, on 19 August.   RICHARD DAVENPORT-HINES

Sources F. Wheen, *Tom Driberg* (1990) · T. Driberg, *Ruling passions* (1977) · T. Driberg, *Colonnade* (1949) · T. Driberg, *The best of both worlds* (1953) · G. Grigson, *The crest on the silver* (1950) · *The journals of Woodrow Wyatt*, ed. S. Curtis, 3 vols. (1998–2000), vol. 1 · J. Lees-Milne, *Through wood and dale* (1998) · G. Vidal, *Palimpsest* (1995) · R. Davenport-Hines, *Auden* (1995) · *DNB* · *The Times* (2 Jan 1975) · *The Post Office London directory*

Archives Bodl. RH, corresp. relating to colonial affairs · Christ Church Oxf., papers | HLRO, corresp. with Lord Beaverbrook and related papers · People's History Museum, Manchester, corresp.

with Morgan Phillips |FILM BFI NFTVA, news footage · BFI NFTVA, performance footage |SOUND BBC WAC
Likenesses photographs, 1938–69, Hult. Arch. · R. M. Franks, photograph, 1966, NPG [*see illus.*] · M. Boxer, cartoon, repro. in Wheen, *Tom Driberg* · photographs, repro. in Wheen, *Tom Driberg*
Wealth at death £37,181: probate, 7 Feb 1977, *CGPLA Eng. & Wales*

Dring [*married name* Lord], **Madeleine Winefride Isabelle** (1923–1977), composer, was born on 7 September 1923 at 66 Raleigh Road, Hornsey, London, the younger child of Cecil John Dring (1883–1949), an architect and surveyor, and his wife, Winefride Isabel (1891–1968), the daughter of John Austin Smith of Fochabers, Morayshire. A Roman Catholic, she was initially educated at La Retraite Convent, Clapham Park. Since she showed precocious musical talent, in 1934 she was awarded an exhibition to the junior department of the Royal College of Music to study the violin. Her youthful diaries (1935–43), written in school exercise books and full of amusing drawings, give a witty commentary on her life, from national events to holidays at the seaside, ghastly visits to the dentist, troubles at school in the form of a jealous music teacher, the joys of the Royal College of Music, her early compositions, and, in 1940, the news that her brother Cecil (*b.* 1918) was reported missing in action in France. She won a further scholarship to the college as a senior student, where she studied composition with Herbert Howells, Ralph Vaughan Williams, and Gordon Jacob, as well as furthering her studies of the violin, piano, singing, drama, and mime; she left in 1944.

During the 1950s Madeleine Dring was involved in various musical radio programmes in collaboration with D. F. Aitken and others. She wrote items of a gently satirical nature for Laurie Lister's 'intimate revues', sometimes providing words as well as music, notably for *Airs on a Shoe String* (1953) and *Fresh Airs* (1955), at the Royal Court Theatre, where she made many friends, including Michael Flanders and Donald Swann. She also had a happy association with the Players' Theatre, where she had the opportunity to sing and act as well as compose.

Of striking appearance, very pale, with long blond hair, Madeleine Dring was highly intelligent and prepared to work intensively at the things which interested her—mainly music and theatre. She had perfect pitch, and also synaesthesia, in which musical sounds and keys had individual colours. Some of her compositions were influenced by George Gershwin and Cole Porter, and she used a syncopated or blues style in the *Colour Suite* (1963) for piano, for example, and in her setting of John Betjeman's 'Song of a Nightclub Proprietress' (1976). She also admired Poulenc, whose influence may be traced in her chamber and instrumental pieces and in her many songs. On 12 August 1947 she married Roger Frewen Lord (*b.* 1924), an oboist, with whom she had a son, Jeremy, born in 1950. She wrote several pieces for the oboe, of which two trios, one for flute, oboe, and piano (1968), the other for oboe, bassoon, and harpsichord (published 1986), are the most important. Two pianos and four hands appealed to her, and she wrote

various dance movements for this combination. Not sympathetic to the fashionable idioms of the atonal and the serial, she continued in the mainstream tradition of English songwriting, using mainly classical texts in a lyrical way. Her use of subtle and sophisticated harmonies to grace a melody gives her songs an individual voice.

In later life Madeleine Dring became interested in parapsychology; she attended lectures and conferences of the Centre for Spiritual and Psychological Studies, and occasionally gave talks there on music. She died unexpectedly from a brain haemorrhage on 26 March 1977 at her home, 52 Becmead Avenue, Streatham, London, and was buried in Lambeth cemetery. Her wind music seems to have a secure place in the chamber repertory, and her settings of five poems by Betjeman, which were published in 1980, continue to be performed.   ROGER LORD

Sources personal knowledge (2004) · M. W. I. Dring, diaries, 1935–43, priv. coll. · b. cert. · m. cert. · d. cert. · M. G. Matthews, *RCM Magazine*, 73/2 (1977), 49 · J. A. Sadie and R. Samuel, eds., *The new Grove dictionary of women composers* (1994) · R. Hancock-Child, *Madeleine Dring: her music, her life* (2000)
Archives priv. coll., MSS |SOUND BL NSA, 'Madeleine Dring', BBC Radio 3, 31 Jan 1994 · British Music Information Centre, London
Likenesses M. Boys, photograph, 1960–69, priv. coll. · C. Dunn, oils, 1960–69, priv. coll.

Dring, Rawlins (*bap.* 1660), physician, son of Samuel Dring, was baptized at Bruton, Somerset, on 8 April 1660. He was educated at Wadham College, Oxford, of which he became first scholar and a fellow in 1682. He proceeded BA on 27 June 1679, MA on 24 May 1682. Then entering on the physic line he practised at Sherborne, Dorset. He was the author of *Dissertatio epistolica ad amplissimum virum & clarissimum pyrophilum J. N. Armigerum conscripta; in qua crystallizationem salium in unicam et propriam, uti dicunt, figuram, esse admodum incertam, aut accidentalem ex observationibus etiam suis, contra medicos & chymicos hodiernos evincitur* (1688). According to Wood, 'the reason why 'tis said in the title that it was printed at Amsterdam is because the College of Physicians refused to license it, having several things therein written against Dr. Martin Lister'. The rest of Dring's life remains obscure.
                          GORDON GOODWIN, rev. MICHAEL BEVAN

Sources Wood, *Ath. Oxon.*, new edn, 4.738 · Wood, *Ath. Oxon.: Fasti* (1815), 369, 381 · IGI

Drinkwater, Francis Harold (1886–1982), Roman Catholic priest, was born on 3 August 1886 at Wednesbury, Staffordshire, the first of the seven children of Francis James Drinkwater (1860–1951), draper, and his wife, Frances Angela Moore (1864–1943), from Wolverhampton. He was educated at St Wilfrid's College, Cotton, Staffordshire (1898–1903), before entering the diocesan seminary Oscott College, Sutton Coldfield, in 1903. After his ordination to the priesthood in 1910 Drinkwater was appointed as curate to William Barry, parish priest of St Peter's, Leamington Spa, who encouraged the interest in social questions he had picked up from his Oscott tutor, Monsignor Henry Parkinson.

A formative period for Drinkwater was his posting, in

1915, as chaplain to the forces on the western front. It was a traumatic experience: he was forced to retire from service after suffering a mustard gas attack; while recuperating he learned that his brother, Edward Oscar Drinkwater, had been killed in action.

It was during his time as chaplain that Drinkwater began to reflect on the quality and character of Catholic education. His pioneering contribution to catechetical education is the achievement for which he is most remembered. The journal he founded in 1919, *The Sower*, exposed the inadequacies of the 'penny catechism' approach to religious instruction with its heavy stress on learning by rote. Instead, Drinkwater's teaching emphasized the need to engage pupils in a practical manner— 'religion should be presented to children as something to be done, something to be lived' (Crichton, 19). *The Sower* played a pioneering role in the movement for a new approach to catechesis which emerged internationally in the early twentieth century. Drinkwater's appointment as diocesan inspector of schools in 1922 and secretary to the National Board of (Catholic) Religious Inspectors in 1924 provided the opportunity to put his ideas, as outlined in *The Sower*, into practice; and in 1929 his scheme was adopted by the Birmingham archdiocese. A key pedagogical principle, expounded in his widely read aid book, *Teaching the Catechism* (1936), was that good methods were those that enlisted the interest and activity of the child in a concrete and vivid manner, so for instance at infant level the child should be taught religion through stories, drama, and the visual arts. Drinkwater's pioneering work brought him international recognition and at the International Congress of Catechetics in Antwerp in 1956 he was hailed as the 'patriarch of the catechetical movement in Europe' (Crichton, 33).

In 1920 Drinkwater became parish priest of the Holy Family Church, Small Heath, Birmingham, where he would remain until 1941. After the church suffered extensive bomb damage he moved to a smaller parish at Lower Gornal, near Dudley. He was not reluctant to speak out on political issues, frequently conflicting with the views of the ecclesiastical authority in the process. Although he was rather shy in company his views were as robust as his physique. His friend Mgr J. D. Crichton described him as 'tall, large-boned and well-made, always with something of the air of a countryman, a quality that he no doubt inherited from his family who had been farming people in Warwickshire' (Crichton, 11).

In the 1930s Drinkwater wrote several books urging a reform of the financial system, notably *Money and Social Justice* (1934) and *Seven Addresses on Social Justice* (1937). A more controversial intervention came when Drinkwater challenged the view that the Spanish Civil War was a battle between godless communism represented by the republicans and Christianity represented by Franco. He was highly critical of the Catholic press, and to one editor expressed his unbelief at 'the moral disaster that has happened to us—a surrender to war-time mentality, untruth and hatred' (F. H. Drinkwater to Michael de la Bedoyere, 7 June 1937, F. H. Drinkwater papers, FHD/Q2, Birmingham

Archdiocesan Archives). This stance made Drinkwater appear a very isolated figure and drew a sharp response from Arthur Hinsley, cardinal archbishop of Westminster (ibid., Arthur Hinsley to F. H. Drinkwater, 16 June 1937). During the 1950s Drinkwater, by then a canon, became exercised about the nuclear threat (and wrote a book about it, *Conscience and War*, 1950) although he was always concerned to distinguish his own critique of what he saw as the indiscriminate nature of modern warfare from outright pacifism.

Drinkwater retired from his parish responsibilities in 1964 but remained a prolific correspondent and writer. On issues such as contraception he was a progressive, outlining his views in a work entitled *Birth Control and Natural Law* (1965), but on a matter like the scriptural proof for the resurrection he was more conservative, as demonstrated in his *The Fact of the Resurrection* (1978). In 1970 the pope made him prelate of honour in recognition of his path breaking catechetical work. Drinkwater spent the last years of his life at Aston Hall, Aston by Stone, where he died on 11 December 1982. He was buried at the cemetery attached to Oscott College. KESTER ASPDEN

Sources J. D. Crichton, *The secret name* (1986) · Birmingham Archdiocesan Archives, Cathedral House, St Chad's, Birmingham, F. H. Drinkwater papers · CGPLA Eng. & Wales (1983) · b. cert. [Frances Moore, mother]
Archives Birmingham Archdiocesan Archives, Cathedral House, St Chad's, Birmingham, diaries, corresp., and papers
Wealth at death £4394: probate, 22 Feb 1983, CGPLA Eng. & Wales

Drinkwater, John [later John Drinkwater Bethune] (1762–1844), army officer and military historian, was born at Latchford, near Warrington, on 9 June 1762, the eldest son of John Drinkwater, a medical practitioner at Salford (then a suburb of Manchester) and formerly a navy surgeon. In 1777, aged fifteen, Drinkwater joined as ensign a regiment of volunteers raised in Manchester, at a time of indignant excitement produced by the news of General Burgoyne's surrender at Saratoga. The Manchester regiment or, more properly, the 72nd regiment or Royal Manchester volunteers, was not, however, sent to America, but to Gibraltar. The garrison was besieged in June 1779 by a Franco–Spanish force. Throughout the siege, which lasted until February 1783, Drinkwater kept a careful record of events. Thereafter the 72nd, in which he had become a captain, was ordered home and disbanded. From his memoranda Drinkwater compiled *A history of the late siege of Gibraltar, 1779–1783, with a description and account of that garrison from the earliest period* (1785), dedicated by permission to the king. It went through four editions in four years. In 1787 Drinkwater purchased a company in the 2nd battalion of the 1st or Royal regiment, then stationed at Gibraltar, where he established a garrison library, which served as a model for others.

Drinkwater accompanied his regiment to Toulon, acting as military secretary during its occupation by the British. He became secretary for the military department and deputy judge-advocate during the subsequent occupation of Corsica and the viceroyalty of Sir Gilbert Elliot (afterwards earl of Minto). After Corsica's evacuation Drinkwater returned with Sir Gilbert in the *Minerva*, which flew the pendant of Nelson as commodore, whom he had befriended while in Corsica. Sir John Jervis's squadron off Cape St Vincent having been reached, Drinkwater witnessed the battle of St Vincent, and brought the news of it to England. Drinkwater was of the opinion that the services of Nelson, who was not mentioned in the published dispatches, had been underestimated, and he published anonymously *A Narrative of the Battle of St Vincent*, in which justice was done to Nelson. A revised edition, with Drinkwater's authorship stated, was published in 1840.

Between 1794 and 1796 Drinkwater purchased first the rank of major and then lieutenant-colonel of his regiment. After Sir Gilbert Elliot had strongly recommended him to Pitt, he was placed on half pay with the rank of colonel and embarked on a long association with the administration of the army, accepting a commission to arrange and settle the complicated accounts connected with the British occupation of Toulon and Corsica. On 6 June 1799, at St Mary's, Putney, he married Eleanor, daughter of Charles Congalton of Congalton, Edinburghshire. That year he was appointed commissary-general of the force which was being dispatched to The Helder, and which he accompanied. In 1801 he accepted an honorary appointment in the household of the duke of Kent, and became his close friend. In 1805 he was nominated a member of the parliamentary commission of military inquiry, later becoming its chairman. In 1807 he declined the under-secretaryship of state for war and the colonies offered to him by Windham. In 1811 he was appointed comptroller of army accounts, and filled the office for twenty-five years, until it was abolished in 1835. After his withdrawal from public life, and on the death of his brother-in-law, whose property, Balfour Castle in Fife, his wife inherited, he assumed the surname Bethune. His eldest son was John Elliot Drinkwater *Bethune, administrator in India and educationist.

In his last year Drinkwater was almost totally blind. Nevertheless he was preparing an enlarged edition of the history of the siege of Gibraltar when he died, aged eighty-one, on 16 January 1844, at Thorncroft, near Leatherhead, Surrey. Besides the works already mentioned Drinkwater also published *A Compendium of the Regent's Canal, Showing its Connection with the Metropolis* (1830), and in 1835 he printed for private circulation *Statements respecting the late departments of the comptrollership of the army accounts, showing the inconveniency which will probably result from its abolition.*

FRANCIS ESPINASSE, rev. DAVID GATES

Sources GM, 2nd ser., 21 (1844), 220 · J. Drinkwater, *A history of the late siege of Gibraltar* (1785) · J. Drinkwater, *A narrative of the battle of St Vincent*, 2nd edn (1840) · IGI

Archives BL OIOC, home misc. series, corresp. relating to India · NAM, corresp. and papers · NL Scot., autobiography | BL, letters to Charles Babbage, Add. MSS 37184–37200 · NL Scot., corresp. with first earl of Minto · NL Scot., letters to second earl of Minto

Drinkwater, John (1882–1937), poet and playwright, was born at Leytonstone, Essex, on 1 June 1882, son of Albert Edwin Drinkwater (1852–1923), schoolmaster and, later,

John Drinkwater (1882–1937), by Sir William Rothenstein, *c*.1918

actor, and his wife, Annie Beck, *née* Brown (*d*. 1891). He was educated at Oxford high school from 1891 to 1897, leaving before his sixteenth birthday. Like his contemporary Harley Granville Barker, in later life he frequently expressed regret and embarrassment at not having had a university education. He had some leanings towards a theatre career but his father, who himself had deserted schoolteaching to become an actor in 1896, nevertheless steered his son in the direction of commerce, securing for him an appointment in the Nottingham offices of the Northern Assurance Company. The young Drinkwater did fairly well in his new profession, though he hated it throughout the twelve years of it that he had to endure. It provided (though only just) a livelihood and gave him independence of a sort, but he was desperately poor. He wrote in his autobiography that the very first book that he was able to buy for himself was *The Ingoldsby Legends*, and he had to wait until he was twenty before he dared lash out so extravagantly. He effected his escape eventually, partly by discovering his own writing talent and partly by way of an invitation from Barry Jackson, who was setting up a new and exciting provincial theatre in Birmingham. Jackson's invitation, founded upon some modest amateur acting experience that Drinkwater had had in Nottingham, was to play Feste in an amateur production of *Twelfth Night* in the extensive garden of The Grange, the palatial mansion belonging to Barry Jackson's father. Jackson was two years senior to John Drinkwater. Both were passionate about the theatre, and liked each other. In 1907 they joined forces to found a group of amateur actors which they called the Pilgrim Players. Eschewing light, popular fare, the Pilgrim Players gradually gained a serious-minded Birmingham audience for plays of quality. Among the players was

Drinkwater's wife, Kathleen Walpole (Cathleen Orford; *b.* 1881/2), whom he had married on 11 January 1906. After five years, with Jackson's money behind them, they turned their amateur theatre company into a professional one and erected a theatre building of their own, calling it the Birmingham Repertory Theatre. It opened in 1913 with a production of *Twelfth Night*, with Drinkwater as Malvolio and Cathleen Orford as Maria. Drinkwater had also written a prologue-like celebratory verse, 'Lines for the Opening of the Birmingham Repertory Theatre', to be spoken by Barry Jackson. It is among Drinkwater's *Poems, 1908–1914* (1917). He became the new theatre's general manager—a position that included acting, directing, and play-writing as well as the more ordinary managerial duties. By 1918, when he left Birmingham in triumph to take his own play, *Abraham Lincoln*, to London and thence to New York, he had played about forty parts at the new Repertory Theatre and directed sixty productions in six years.

Also during his Birmingham years Drinkwater had established himself as a published poet whose lyric verses had begun to win a good deal of respect and to find their way into the better anthologies. In the second volume of his unfinished autobiography (*Discovery*, 1932) he tells about the moment, walking home late one night along the Moseley Road in January 1903, when he realized that poetry was his true vocation. His first small book of verse was *The Death of Leander and other Poems* (1906), and in the next twelve years he published three more, and contributed individual poems to eight or nine leading national magazines: these poems included the beautiful and much-anthologized 'Moonlit Apples', which appeared in his collection called *Tides* in 1917.

Drinkwater returned from America in 1920 a temporarily famous man, much respected for his plays and his poetry. But his writing, in the later 1920s and early 1930s—except in the case of *Bird in Hand* in 1927—failed to live up to the promise of his first, fine, careless rapture and his fame gradually declined. *Bird in Hand* was produced at the Birmingham Repertory Theatre in 1927, with Laurence Olivier and Peggy Ashcroft in the leading parts, under Drinkwater's direction. After an absence of many years he also returned to acting, though not at Birmingham. He played Prospero at the Regent's Park Open Air Theatre in 1933 and Duke Senior, also at Regent's Park, in 1934. Also in 1934 he played Malvolio at His Majesty's Theatre. All in all, it must in honesty be said that his reputation died before he did.

Drinkwater's marriage to Cathleen Orford was dissolved in 1920, and on 16 December 1924 he married, at the Kensington register office, the violinist Daisy Fowler (*b.* 1892/3); she was the daughter of Joseph Arthur Kennedy, schoolmaster, of Norwood, Adelaide, Australia, and formerly wife of Benno Moiseiwitsch, the Russian pianist. Their daughter, Penelope, was born in 1929. She is saluted in a group of six poems in *Summer Harvest: Poems, 1924–33* (1933). *Qua* poetry they are mawkishly embarrassing; but as snatches of overheard private conversation or glances

at the kind of private diaries that ought never to be published, they are interesting, informative, and moving.

There are signs in one of his books that Drinkwater, for all his passion and fervour, may have inadvertently missed his true calling. The book is *The Gentle Art of Theatre-Going*, commissioned for a Gentle Art of … series and published in 1927. The circumstances of its publication strongly suggest that it was mere bread-and-butter work, but the text itself rises above this level. Its liveliness and persuasiveness suggest that he would have made a first-class theatre critic if he had given himself to that occupation on a regular and long-term basis.

Through the 1920s and 1930s Drinkwater lived a busy and useful public life. He belonged to many societies and committees, he travelled quite widely, he wrote a new play for Barry Jackson's new festival at Malvern (not a very good play, unfortunately), he wrote two volumes of autobiography—*Inheritance* (1931) and *Discovery* (1932); and throughout he retained to a large extent a boyish enthusiasm combined with a middle-aged worthiness. And he left behind, among a fair amount of lesser material, one extremely fine play (though just short of greatness), several short plays that ought still to be played but are not, and some poetry that still glints and gleams here and there (and was never as nerveless as its more severe critics made out). He had once been condemned by Middleton Murry (*The Athenaeum*, 5 Dec 1919), as being guilty of 'a false simplicity'. The criticism is not without substance but there are among Drinkwater's various works some vivid and still-resonant exceptions. His total output amounted to seventeen plays (including an adaptation into English of a play about Napoleon by Benito Mussolini), nine volumes of verse, biographies of Pepys and Shakespeare, critical studies of Byron, Swinburne, and William Morris, and the two volumes of autobiography.

Drinkwater died at his home, North Hall, Mortimer Crescent, Maida Vale, London, of heart disease, on 25 March 1937. Several times, from quite early days onward, one finds him—in effect—writing his own epitaph, as in his poem about his family ancestors, 'who were before me' (*Seeds of Time*, 1921). The poem 'Petition' in the collection *Olton Pools* (1916) concludes:

That, when I die, this word may stand for me—
He had a heart to praise, an eye to see,
And beauty was his king.

ERIC SALMON

Sources DNB · J. C. Trewin, *The theatre since 1900* (1951) · D. Perkins, *A history of modern poetry* (1976) · J. Drinkwater, *Inheritance* (1931) · J. Drinkwater, *Discovery: being the second book of an autobiography, 1897–1913* (1932) · J. C. Trewin, *The Birmingham Repertory Theatre, 1913–1963* (1963) · T. C. Kemp, *The Birmingham Repertory Theatre*, 2nd edn (1948) · G. W. Bishop, *Barry Jackson and the London theatre* (1933) · CGPLA Eng. & Wales (1937) · b. cert. · m. certs. · d. cert.
Archives BL, corresp. mainly with second wife, Add. MSS 62564–62567 · Dickinson College, Carlisle, Pennsylvania, corresp., literary MSS and papers · Indiana University, Bloomington, letters and literary papers · Ransom HRC, corresp. and literary MSS · Rutgers University, New Jersey, corresp. · Yale U., Beinecke L., papers | BL, corresp. with Society of Authors, Add. MS 63237 · JRL, letters to Allan Monkhouse · King's Cam., memoir of Rupert Brooke · Royal

Society of Literature, letters to Royal Society of Literature · Somerville College, Oxford, letters to Percy Withers · U. Leeds, letters to Sir Edmund Gosse |FILM BFI NFTVA, home footage |SOUND BL NSA, documentary recording · BL NSA, performance recordings **Likenesses** photograph, 1907 · W. Rothenstein, pencil drawing, 1917, Minneapolis Institute of Arts · W. Rothenstein, oils, *c.*1918, priv. coll.; on loan to NPG [*see illus.*] · A. Boughton, vintage bromide print, 1920–29, NPG · photographs, 1930–33, Hult. Arch. · W. Stoneman, photograph, 1931, NPG · photograph, 1933 · H. Coster, photographs, 1934, NPG · J. W. Thompson, chalk drawing, 1935, NPG · A. B. Sava, bronze head, RS · photograph (after Sava, 1931)
Wealth at death £1577 16*s.* 6*d.*: probate, 5 May 1937, *CGPLA Eng. & Wales*

Drinkwater, Peter (1750–1801), cotton manufacturer, the son of Thomas Drinkwater of Whalley, Lancashire, was born at Whalley and baptized there on 29 June 1763. Nothing further is known of his life until 14 May 1771, when he married Margaret Bolton of Preston. They had four children. On 28 March 1785 he married Grace Bower, who may have died in 1789.

Drinkwater is an example of those eighteenth-century merchant manufacturers who invested in the mechanization of the cotton industry and were responsible for the centralization of production in the factory. He enjoyed a successful career as a fustian manufacturer (under the 'putting out' system) and as a foreign merchant in Bolton and Manchester in the 1770s and 1780s. By 1782 he had moved into factory production, buying a newly erected water-powered cotton spinning mill on the River Weaver in Northwich, Cheshire. Subsequently, he was one of those accused by William Arkwright of having infringed his water-frame patent. In 1789 Drinkwater began the construction of his second factory, a four-storeyed building near Piccadilly, Manchester, known as the Bank Top Mill. This was the tenth cotton mill to be powered by a Boulton and Watt rotary steam engine and the first in Manchester, which, during the 1790s, became the centre of the increasingly important cotton industry. Thus, he played a significant role in the mechanization of cotton production and the early history of the factory system in Lancashire. He was ahead of Arkwright in utilizing the rotary steam engine. Although Arkwright and Simpson had used an atmospheric engine at their Manchester mill of 1783, it was not until 1790 that Arkwright used the rotary engine.

Drinkwater's Manchester mill illustrates the mixture of traditional and new technologies at this early stage of factory production. Steam power was used for the preparatory processes only, spinning being undertaken using a large number of hand-powered mules. Drinkwater's venture was one of the 'giant' firms of the 1790s. He employed a series of managers to supervise production and oversee the workforce of 500. The first of these, George Lee, left him in 1792 to assume a partnership in the Salford firm later known as Philips and Lee. Lee's successor was the young Robert Owen in his first significant managerial position.

Owen worked as Drinkwater's manager from about 1792 to 1794. Owen's autobiography portrays Drinkwater as something of a 'sleeping partner' who lacked technical

knowledge. This may not be a reliable portrait: according to Chaloner (87–91) the Boulton and Watt correspondence in Birmingham Central Library reveals Drinkwater as an innovative industrialist with an exhaustive eye for detail in both the construction of his mill and the specifications of his steam engine. Moreover, he paid close attention to the sanitary conditions provided for his workforce and attempted to ensure that his factory should be well ventilated and admit plenty of daylight. This paternalism may have influenced Owen. Certainly this period was a formative one in Owen's life, and he claimed later that his intention at New Lanark was 'to introduce principles in the conduct of the people which I had successfully commenced … in Mr Drinkwater's factory' (Owen, 56–7).

Drinkwater was a prominent figure in the Manchester business community and in the broader public life of the town. His wealth and liberality were reflected in his support of relevant causes. He and Arkwright led the subscription list in support of the Committee of the Fustian Trade in the mid-1780s, set up to oppose Pitt's tax on the cotton manufacture, and Drinkwater was among the first to join the Commercial Society of Merchants Trading on the Continent of Europe in 1794. His business interests prospered. Owen reports that Drinkwater's wealth enabled him to survive unscathed the commercial crisis of 1792–3. Certainly by 1794 he was sufficiently well off to purchase a country estate in Prestwich—Irwell House—where he lived in the summer, travelling up to his town house at 42 Fountain Street, Manchester, on two or three days a week.

He found a niche in the local establishment serving as a constable in the 1780s and as a magistrate for the county of Lancaster (Salford hundred) by the mid-1790s. He was a supporter of the established religion and a churchwarden of the collegiate church of Manchester. A patron of patriotic causes in the 1790s, he was one of the biggest contributors (giving £500) to the voluntary fund of March 1798 to raise moneys to fight the war with France. He participated in the life of some of the town's leading voluntary institutions, being a member of the Manchester Literary and Philosophical Society from 1786 and a notable subscriber to the Royal Infirmary.

Drinkwater died suddenly and unexpectedly of causes unknown on his way to London on 15 November 1801. According to Burke's *Landed Gentry*, his purchase of the Irwell estate had established another branch of the ancient family of Drinkwater. His eldest son Thomas adopted the arms of the Drinkwaters of Shrewsbury.

ALAN J. KIDD

Sources R. Owen, *The life of Robert Owen written by himself*, 1 (1857) · W. H. Chaloner, 'Robert Owen, Peter Drinkwater, and the early factory system in Manchester, 1788–1800', *Bulletin of the John Rylands University Library*, 37 (1954–5), 78–102 · R. S. Fitton, *The Arkwrights: spinners of fortune* (1989) · R. L. Hills, *Power in the industrial revolution* (1970) · C. H. Drinkwater and W. G. P. Fletcher, *The family of Drinkwater* (1920) · Burke, *Gen. GB* (1848) · E. Baines, *History of the cotton manufacture in Great Britain* (1835) · A. Ure, *The cotton manufacture of Great Britain*, 1 (1836) · Birm. CL, Boulton and Watt collection · parish registers, Whalley, Lancashire, Lancs. RO, 1750 and 29 June 1763 [birth, baptism]

Archives Birm. CL, Boulton and Watt MSS

Driscoll, James [Jim] (1880–1925), boxer, was born on 5 December 1880 at 12 Ellen Street in Newtown, Cardiff's main Irish quarter, the second son of the four surviving children of Cornelius Driscoll (1856–1881), a railwayman on the docks who died in an accident at work soon after Jim's birth, and his wife, Elizabeth (*née* Burns). His first job was in the printing works of the local *Evening Express*, where there was a boxing club, and despite its rudimentary facilities—'gloves' were made from waste paper and string from the packing department—the fistic skills of club captain Driscoll soon brought him to the attention of larger and better-organized clubs in Cardiff. By seventeen he was appearing regularly in Jack Scarrott's fight booths in the south Wales valleys, and in 1901 he graduated into professional boxing. On 30 June 1907 he married Edith Gwynne (Edie) Wiltshire (*b.* 1880/81).

At 5 feet 6 inches tall and weighing 9 stone, the clean-limbed, dark-haired Driscoll was fast and skilful; upright in stance, he possessed a flashing blade of a left hand with which he would beat his opponent into submission before employing a devastating right to deliver the final blow. These trademarks were all in evidence when he beat Joe Bowker on 25 September 1906 at the National Sporting Club (NSC) for the British featherweight title. The world title at that weight was held by Abe Attell, the 'little Hebrew' of New York, who won it in 1904. Attell's most difficult fight during the six years he held the title was against Driscoll on 19 February 1909 at the National Athletic Club in New York. The Irish–Welshman's success against each of his nine opponents during his four-month tour of the US between November 1908 and February 1909 made him a worthy opponent for Attell and they met on a 'no decision' basis, which meant that to claim the fight a boxer had to knock out or otherwise stop his opponent. For the entire ten rounds Attell was given a master class in the 'sweet science' in a performance which, though it failed to achieve the knockout which would have brought Driscoll the championship, earned him the name Peerless Jim. This nickname was first bestowed on him by the gunslinging scourge of Dodge City turned sports journalist and former US marshal Bat Masterson. Attell offered Driscoll a return bout for the world title, but Jim had promised to return home to box an exhibition match at the annual charity show of the Nazareth House Roman Catholic Orphanage in Cardiff. There would never be another chance to challenge for the title.

At home Driscoll was naturally, if inaccurately, hailed as world champion. In February 1910 he beat Seaman Arthur Hayes for the British featherweight title over six rounds, and retained it by defeating Frank (Spike) Robson, twice, to become the first British boxer to become an outright holder of one of the coveted belts donated by Lord Lonsdale. In challenging his compatriot Freddie Welsh for the British welterweight title, however, he was conceding several pounds to his sturdier opponent. On a night choking with tension, 20 December 1910, at Cardiff's American Roller Rink arena, Welsh's street-fighter tactics of elbowing, gouging, and rabbit-punching drove an increasingly frustrated Driscoll into reckless retaliation in the tenth round, when he flagrantly and repeatedly butted Welsh across the ring and was immediately disqualified.

From then on Driscoll fought infrequently. The second match with Robson was his sole contest in 1911, and he fought only once in 1912, though it was to win the European featherweight title by knocking out the French champion Jean Posey in the twelfth round. He drew with the experienced Owen Moran at the NSC in January 1913, then announced his retirement. On the outbreak of war he was drafted into the army as a physical training and boxing instructor, and celebrated the peace by training the British army team to win the allied boxing tournament at the Royal Albert Hall.

At this point Driscoll, now in the early stages of tuberculosis and in financial straits, sought to revive his own boxing career. Although in March 1919 he easily beat the ageing Pedlar Palmer, who had challenged for the world bantamweight title in 1899, two months later he could only draw with the much younger and less experienced Francis Rossi of Pontypridd. Then he ill-advisedly agreed to fight Charles Ledoux, the thickset and stumpy French bantamweight champion known as the 'little assassin' who was 6 inches shorter but twelve years his junior. At the NSC on 20 October 1919 the immaculate left jab of a drawn and haggard Peerless Jim kept him well ahead for fourteen rounds, but at the end of that round he was shaken by a desperate right to the body from which he never recovered, and his seconds threw in the towel at the start of the sixteenth. Had this contest been over fifteen rounds instead of twenty, Driscoll, by common consent, would have won. The reluctant victor, Ledoux, paid him a handsome tribute: 'Jim Driscoll is the master. He is the greatest man I have ever met or ever shall meet. He played with me for fourteen and a half rounds and I could do absolutely nothing' (Hails, 16).

Jim Driscoll died at home in the Duke of Edinburgh Hotel at 18 Ellen Street, Cardiff, on 30 January 1925 and his military-style funeral took place on 3 February. After requiem mass at St Paul's Roman Catholic Church 100,000 mourners accompanied his coffin, draped in the union flag and carried behind a gun carriage, to burial at Cathays cemetery. He was survived by his wife, Edie.

GARETH WILLIAMS

Sources Jim Driscoll cuttings file, Central Library, Cardiff, Local history division · D. Smith, *Aneurin Bevan and the world of south Wales* (1993), chap. 12 · H. Mullan, *Heroes and hard men* (1989) · J. Hails, *Classic moments of boxing* (1989) · *Western Mail* [Cardiff] (31 Jan 1925) · *Western Mail* [Cardiff] (3 Feb 1925) · *Western Mail* [Cardiff] (23 March 1949) · *South Wales Echo* (3 Feb 1925) · F. Deakin, *Welsh warriors* (1990) · *CGPLA Eng. & Wales* (1926) · census returns · m. cert. · d. cert.
Archives Cardiff Central Library, file and cuttings book | FILM BFI NFTVA, documentary footage · BFI NFTVA, sports footage
Likenesses J. Gronow, photograph, 1910, repro. in J. Huntington-Whiteley, ed., *The book of British sporting heroes* (1998), 90 [exhibition catalogue, National Portrait Gallery, London, 16 Oct 1990–24 Jan 1999] · photograph, repro. in Deakin, *Welsh warriors*
Wealth at death £10: probate, 9 April 1926, *CGPLA Eng. & Wales*

Driver, Christopher Prout (1932–1997), journalist and writer on food, was born in India on 1 December 1932, the son of Arthur Herbert Driver, a Presbyterian medical missionary, and his wife, Elsie Kathleen Shepherd. When the family returned to England, Dr Driver ran Book in Hand, an antiquarian bookshop in Shaftesbury, Dorset, which his son continued to operate until selling it in 1995. Christopher Driver was educated at the Dragon School, Oxford; at Rugby School (where he was head boy); and at Christ Church, Oxford, where he read Greats, graduating in 1955. His affinity with the Latin classical writers was evident in his own writing, and indeed it was this background that was the first bond with Raymond Postgate, who had gained a first in classics moderations at Oxford and whom Driver succeeded as editor of *The Good Food Guide* in 1970.

A conscientious objector, Driver did his national service in the Friends' Ambulance Unit, where most of his work was with Hungarian refugees who had been made homeless in the uprising of 1956. He later said that this was when he first learned to cook, though 'I first ate a Good Food Guide meal in 1954, as a bumptious Oxford undergraduate' (*The Times*, 22 Oct 1994). The ambulance corps's atmosphere of intellectual and religious dissent was congenial; probably more so than that of the Liverpool *Daily Post*, which he joined in 1958 in order to become a journalist. In the same year, on 3 May, he married Margaret Elizabeth Perfect (b. 1932/3), a hospital almoner. They had three daughters. Driver was more at home when he joined the Manchester *Guardian* in 1960, an association he retained, with occasional interludes, for the rest of his life. He was features editor from 1964 to 1968, food and drink editor from 1984 to 1989, and worked on the obituaries page at the end of his career.

The Good Food Guide grew out of an article Postgate wrote in 1949 vilifying the standard of public eating in Britain, which led to the formation of the Good Food Club in the following year. By 1963, when Postgate sold the publication (which he continued to edit) to the Consumers' Association, it had become an important institution in a country that no longer had food rationing as an excuse for its terrible restaurant food. The *Guide* was an informal democracy, with members of the club acting as unpaid inspectors. Until Driver took over as editor in 1970, most of the editor's work was collating these reports; these, however varied their standards of judgement and knowledge, at least had the merit of being disinterested.

Driver's approach was different; he immediately pruned the number of restaurants listed from 1634 to 761, which should have meant that inclusion in the *Guide* was a prima facie recommendation. However, Driver's waspish wit often expressed itself in writing negative reviews: in 1978 he wrote of the restaurant at the National Gallery that it was 'a below-stairs abortion of a room, where below-standard motorway-level food is dispensed in surroundings of challenging ugliness' (*Daily Telegraph*, 19 Feb 1997).

Driver was not an obvious choice to be the country's number one restaurant critic. There was something austere about his character, and his dissenting religious beliefs and left-liberal opinions seemed to rule out high living in favour of high thinking. He was totally unfrivolous—though this did not mean that he was unable to have a good time. He once agreed that he was a puritan at heart, 'but not puritanical. And we tend to forget that the puritans used to feast and dance at their weddings' (personal knowledge). His appearance in his middle years, tall and lean, bearded and tweedy, meant that headwaiters sometimes seated him where he would not attract the attention of other diners. He simply did not look like someone who enjoyed the trappings of luxury in grand restaurants, though in fact he hugely enjoyed good food, and was much more knowledgeable about food than those who ran any of the rival guides, for whom he had an amiable contempt. He had little time for the entertainment aspect of eating out, and was a little horrified by the theatrical practices (such as the synchronized lifting of cloches by a gaggle of waiters) that accompanied the growth of the *nouvelle cuisine* in the 1980s.

Driver also showed little sympathy for the business side of restaurants, despising those whose only motive was to make a profit. So it was no surprise that more modest Chinese and Indian restaurants caught the *Guide*'s attention more easily than French establishments with pretensions and ambitions to Michelin stars. This led to a comic episode in 1978, when a conspiracy of fancy restaurateurs was hatched in a building opposite Harrods with the objective of getting Driver deposed from the *Guide*. It failed, and he remained in the post until 1982, when he handed over to Drew Smith, who he insisted in print was 'not my choice' (*The Times*, 22 Oct 1994).

Driver's greatest contribution to food, however, was scholarly. His slim 1983 volume, *The British at Table, 1940–1980*, is of incalculable importance to the historian of food and of the period, and he was certainly correct to point out that the British were better nourished under war-time rationing than ever before or since. But he was a man of many interests, and his publications covered a wide range of subjects. A fine musician (he played the violin and viola, and two of his three daughters became professional musicians), in his last year he orchestrated for strings Schubert's *Grand Rondeau* in A minor for piano; and in 1994 he published *Music for Love: an Anthology of Amateur Music-Making*. His first book had been *A Future for the Free Churches* (1962); worried by the relations between professing Christians and the poor, particularly of the third world, he was on the board of Christian Aid from 1972 until 1984. In 1964 he wrote *The Disarmers*, a pioneering study of the Campaign for Nuclear Disarmament, a book which lasted well, and in 1968 he took leave of absence from *The Guardian* to write *The Exploding University*. In 1984 he collaborated (with Michelle Berriedale-Johnson) on *Pepys at Table*, adapting seventeenth-century recipes for modern cooks. He returned to India in the early 1980s on a press trip, where he greatly amused his colleagues by collecting up the badly oxidized bottles of Goan wine they had discarded to give to a Christian community in Bombay, which, he was certain, 'can find a use for anything' (personal knowledge).

Driver suffered a stroke in 1978; it, and a brain tumour discovered in 1993, slowed his speech, but not his intellect; he published a volume of poetry, *Strokes* (1996), and only a month before his death, *John Evelyn, Cook*. He died at his home, 6 Church Road, Highgate, London, on 18 February 1997. PAUL LEVY

Sources personal knowledge (2004) · *Daily Telegraph* (19 Feb 1997) · *The Independent* (22 Feb 1997) · *The Guardian* (19 Feb 1997) · *The Guardian* (26 Feb 1997) · *The Herald* [Glasgow] (22 Feb 1997) · *The Times* (22 Feb 1997) · S. Jenkins, 'Two faces of Englishness', *The Times* (5 March 1997) · C. Driver, 'Good food, good wine and good company', *The Times* (22 Oct 1994) · C. Driver, *The British at table, 1940–1980* (1983) · m. cert. · d. cert. · WWW

Driver, Sir Godfrey Rolles (1892–1975), Hebraist and Semitist, was born in Oxford on 20 August 1892 as the eldest of three sons and two daughters of Samuel Rolles *Driver (1846–1914), regius professor of Hebrew and canon of Christ Church, and his wife, Mabel, *née* Burr (1866/7–1947). After attending a Miss Owen's school, and Summer Fields School in Oxford, he won a scholarship to Winchester College. In 1911 he went as a scholar to New College, Oxford, and was placed in the second class in classical moderations in 1913. He was awarded the Gaisford prize for Greek prose in 1913 and for verse in 1916, and (having learned Hebrew from his father) the junior Hall–Houghton Septuagint prize and the Pusey and Elerton Hebrew scholarship in 1913. War service (1915–19) took Driver to the Balkans (where he was wounded in Serbia), France, and the Near East (including Palestine). He attained the rank of major, was awarded the MC, and was mentioned in dispatches.

Driver was elected a fellow of Magdalen College, Oxford, in 1919 and served the college as a classical tutor until 1928, serving as pro-proctor in 1923, librarian in 1923–40, and vice-president in 1931–2. He was elected senior Kennicott Hebrew scholar in 1921, and was a visiting professor at the University of Chicago in 1925. Oxford University appointed him a lecturer in comparative Semitic philology in 1927 and reader in 1928, and the title of professor of Semitic philology was conferred on him in 1938; he became emeritus professor in 1962. He was also Grinfield lecturer on the Septuagint in 1935–9.

Driver married Madeleine Mary (1902–1991), the daughter of John Goulding, an accountant, on 18 December 1924. The marriage was a happy one, and they had three daughters.

Since the regius professorship of Hebrew was attached to a canonry, Driver, who remained a layman of the Church of England, was not eligible for appointment, but he served as deputy professor during a vacancy in 1934, and again in 1959. In 1938 he was offered the regius chair of Hebrew at Cambridge University, which was no longer attached to a canonry, but he declined the offer and David Winton Thomas, whom he had once taught, was elected.

During the Second World War, Driver again served in Palestine, and later in the Ministry of Information in London. Afterwards, he returned to his work in Oxford, where he played a leading part in planning the Oriental Institute and in the discussion that led to the separation of the regius chair of Hebrew from a canonry. He was a member of the Old Testament panel for the *New English Bible* and became the convener in 1957 and joint director (with C. H. Dodd) in 1965; their translation was eventually published in 1970. After a heart attack in 1967, Driver's health was poor, and he died in Oxford on 22 April 1975. He was buried in Wolvercote cemetery, Oxford.

Driver served on several Old Testament or theological bodies. He was an editor of the *Journal of Theological Studies* from 1933 to 1940, the president of the Society for Old Testament Study in 1938, and the International Organization for the Study of the Old Testament in 1953–9, and a member of the advisory committee of its journal *Vetus Testamentum* until his death. He was a member of the council of Wycliffe Hall, an Anglican theological college in Oxford.

Driver's contribution to his field was recognized with various honours. He was elected a fellow of the British Academy in 1939, gave the academy's Schweich lectures in 1944, and received the Burkitt medal for biblical studies in 1953. He was elected an honorary fellow of Magdalen College in 1962 and of New College shortly before his death, and of the School of Oriental and African Studies, London, in 1963. Honorary doctorates were conferred by the universities of Durham (1945), Aberdeen (1946), Manchester (1956), Cambridge (1964), and Oxford (1970). He was made a CBE in 1958 and a knight in 1968. He also received two Festschriften: the *Journal of Semitic Studies*, 7/2 (1962), and a volume edited by D. W. Thomas and W. D. McHardy, *Hebrew and Semitic Studies* (1963). The latter included a list of his publications that was brought up to date in *Vetus Testamentum*, 30 (1980), 185–91.

Driver's books and articles were concerned with Hebrew and other Semitic languages. *Problems of the Hebrew Verbal System* (1936) investigated the development of the verb in Semitic languages in general, and *Semitic Writing* (1948) discussed the origin of the alphabet and the various Semitic scripts. He published a grammar of colloquial Palestinian and Syrian Arabic (1925), editions of Babylonian letters (1925) and, with Sir John Miles, Assyrian (1935) and Babylonian (1952 and 1955) laws, a translation from the Syriac of *The Bazaar of Heracleides* (1925), and editions of Aramaic papyri (1957) and Ugaritic mythological texts (1956).

Driver's historical judgements on the Dead Sea scrolls were, initially (in *The Hebrew Scrolls*, 1951) that they should be dated between AD 200 and 600. Subsequently, in his *The Judaean Scrolls* (1965) he identified the Dead Sea community as Zealots, and placed the 'event' of the 'killing' of the 'teacher of righteousness' during the time of the siege of Jerusalem in AD 69.

Driver's central interest was the vocabulary of the Hebrew Bible studied in the light of other Semitic languages, and his theories influenced the *New English Bible*. Together with D. W. Thomas, he collected material for a Hebrew lexicon, but the project was never completed. Driver explained many obscure words—and some not previously regarded as obscure—by comparing cognates in other

Semitic languages, and claimed support for some explanations in Greek, Latin, Aramaic, and Syriac versions of the Bible.

Driver had an honest, forthright personality and a strong sense of humour. He was a stimulating teacher with an infectious enthusiasm for his subject, and was always ready to answer—usually on barely legible postcards—enquiries from former pupils and any serious scholar.   J. A. EMERTON

Sources J. A. Emerton, 'Godfrey Rolles Driver, 1892–1975', *PBA*, 63 (1977), 345–62 • 'Select bibliography of the writings of Godfrey Rolles Driver', *Hebrew and Semitic studies presented to Godfrey Rolles Driver*, ed. D. W. Thomas and W. D. McHardy (1963), 191–206 • J. A. Emerton, 'A list of G. R. Driver's publications since 1962', *Vetus Testamentum*, 30 (1980), 185–91 • *WW* • private information (2004) [M. Driver] • personal knowledge (2004) • *CGPLA Eng. & Wales* (1975) • m. cert.

Archives U. Oxf., Griffith Institute, collection of nineteenth-century photographs of Jerusalem, Lebanon, etc. | Bodl. Oxf., corresp. with C. D. Darlington • U. Birm. L., corresp. with W. C. T. Onions

Likenesses W. Stoneman, photograph, 1944, NPG • W. Dring, oils, 1961, Magd. Oxf. • W. Dring, portrait, Oriental Institute, Oxford

Wealth at death £90,644: probate, 28 July 1975, *CGPLA Eng. & Wales*

Driver, Robert Collier (1816–1897), surveyor and auctioneer, was born on 28 August 1816, one of the five sons of Charles Burrell Driver (1788–1852), of Cornhill, City of London, stationer, and his wife, Ann Manning. He was educated at a school in Epping, and in 1832 he was articled to James Marmont, land surveyor, in Bristol. Destined to join his three uncles in their surveying business, his father was odd man out in not being a surveyor himself.

Family tradition holds that the Drivers' surveying business was started in 1725 by Samuel (I) Driver (1692–1741), but this is doubtful since all that is known is that this Samuel was a baker in Wandsworth, and also had a market garden in the same parish. His son, Samuel (II) Driver (1720–1779), however, besides becoming a Quaker in 1754 when he married Jane Purshouse, from Tipton, Staffordshire, and continuing both the baking and market gardening businesses, definitely practised as a land valuer and property auctioneer, and the Driver family link with surveying is firmly established from his lifetime onwards. In the next generation Samuel (II)'s sons, Abraham Purshouse (1755–1821) and William (1758–1819), made the move from multi-occupation as nurserymen, market gardeners, and surveyors, working from the Old Kent Road, to specialized professional practice as surveyors and land agents. In 1816 they moved their office north of the river to New Bridge Street, Blackfriars. The brothers Abraham and William were joint authors of the *General View of the Agriculture of Hampshire* (1794), and received some commissions for surveying and valuing farms on the crown estates.

The business expanded considerably when three of Abraham's five sons—that is, Robert Collier Driver's uncles—entered the partnership from about 1810: Edward (1783–1852), Samuel (III) (1785–1857), and George Neale (1794–1855). The eldest, Edward, became the principal partner after his father's death in 1821 and in 1826 he

moved the firm's office to Richmond Terrace, Whitehall, in recognition of the growing importance of official business and of business involving parliamentary proceedings. The leading example of this trend was the large-scale survey and report on the Isles of Scilly which Edward Driver carried out for the duchy of Cornwall in 1829. This report revealed a state of neglect and mismanagement by the lessee, the duke of Leeds, and his agent, who paid the duchy a rent of £40 a year for land and buildings worth more than £4000 a year; the survey also foresaw a future for the Scillies as a holiday and health resort. Edward Driver followed this, like many prominent surveyors of the time, with extensive involvement in purchasing land for railway construction in the 1830s: he purchased the land for the first 60 miles of the Great Western Railway's route out of London, and he also bought most of the land on the Brighton line.

Robert Collier Driver joined his three uncles in the family firm in 1837, and he became the sole partner from about 1855 when they had all died or retired. Initially Driver had assisted his uncles, chiefly in the railway land purchases, but increasingly he specialized in selling property by auction and by private treaty, and the centre of his activity became Garraways and the Auction Mart in the City as much as the Whitehall office. In his prime, from about 1860 to 1875, it was reckoned that Driver's property sales amounted to about £1 million annually. These included the large estates of the Greenwich Hospital (Admiralty) in Northumberland, the Claremont estate in Surrey, Vauxhall Gardens, and properties of Lord Lytton, the king of the Belgians, and Napoleon III. Driver was engaged in the development of many London suburban building estates, and in many of the metropolitan improvements of the time, notably the construction of Holborn Viaduct, the freeing of the Thames bridges from tolls, and the acquisition of the site for the law courts. He acted for the crown, and later for the corporation of the City, over encroachments on Epping Forest and the negotiations leading to its opening to the public in 1882. He was one of the founder members of the Institution of Surveyors in 1868, and he became a vice-president in 1883 and its president in 1890. He had also been a member of the Land Surveyor's Club for many years previously. Driver was a strong advocate of making entry into the surveying profession subject to a qualifying examination, which was introduced from 1881, whereupon he offered an annual prize of £25 for the best candidate in the examination. Later this prize was reduced to 15 guineas at the suggestion of the council, for obscure reasons, for which Driver provided a permanent endowment in his will. Active in the City, he was warden of the Clothworkers' Company (1874–5) and master (1880–81), and a deputy lieutenant of the City.

Driver married Maria (d. 1888), daughter of William and Rachel Robson of Darlington, on 21 October 1852, possibly a Quaker connection, though the Drivers appear to have lapsed by the 1830s; they had three sons and one daughter. The youngest son, James (1857–1936), became a solicitor, whereas the two older sons, Charles William (b. 1853) and

Robert Manning (1856–1935), entered the family firm and became partners. Charles was drummed out and banished to South Africa in 1898 in mysterious circumstances. Driver's daughter, Maria (1854–1888), married in 1878 Henry Jonas (d. 1928), son of Samuel Jonas of Chrishall Grange, Essex, one of the largest and most efficient farmers of the period; Henry Jonas, articled to a surveyor in 1860, joined the Drivers in 1874 and was made a partner at the time of his marriage. From the end of 1894, when Robert Collier Driver retired, the firm became known as Drivers, Jonas & Co. The partners in Drivers Jonas continued into the 1990s to include direct descendants of Henry Jonas. Robert Collier Driver died on 13 April 1897 at his home, Melrose House, Cromwell Road, London, after a long illness.

F. M. L. THOMPSON

Sources Drivers, Jonas & Co. Archives, 18 Pall Mall, London · *Transactions of the Surveyors' Institution*, 30 (1897–8), 555–9 · Boase, *Mod. Eng. biog.*
Archives Drivers, Jonas & Co., 18 Pall Mall, London, archives
Likenesses oils, 1893, Drivers, Jonas & Co., London
Wealth at death £216,387 16s. 5d.: probate, 21 June 1898

Driver, Samuel Rolles (1846–1914), biblical scholar and Church of England clergyman, was born at Southampton on 2 October 1846, the only son of Rolles Driver, of that city, and his wife, Sarah, daughter of H. F. Smith, of Darlington. His parents were originally Quakers. At the age of sixteen he entered Winchester College as a commoner, and it was at school that he began the study of Hebrew. From Winchester he passed with a classical scholarship to New College, Oxford, in 1865. A distinguished undergraduate career (BA, 1870; MA, 1872) was followed by a fellowship in 1870 and a tutorship in classics in 1875 at his college. His reading had been unusually wide, and the scientific bent of his mind had declared itself early, a factor of importance later in his career.

During this period Driver wrote *A Treatise on the Use of the Tenses in Hebrew* (1874, revised in 1881 and 1892). It was the first attempt in English to expound the principles of Hebrew syntax on lines at once philosophical and scientific, and it established his reputation as a Hebraist. As a result he was appointed to the Old Testament Revision Company (1875–84). Meanwhile, on 16 September 1882, E. B. Pusey died; and on 23 October W. E. Gladstone offered Driver the vacant regius professorship of Hebrew, and canonry of Christ Church, Oxford. At the time (December 1881) Driver was only in deacon's orders; he was ordained priest in December 1882, and the letters patent were dated 5 January 1883. From June of that year until his death he lived in Christ Church.

In England, Driver faced a difficult task, that of reconciling Christian faith with biblical criticism and with the scientific outlook engendered by the work of Darwin. John William Colenso and Samuel Davidson had already questioned traditional Old Testament scholarship; subsequently, the translation of the works of the continental scholars, Heinrich Ewald and Abraham Kuenen, had introduced English scholars to new techniques of biblical criticism. Further, in *The O.T. in the Jewish Church* (1881) and *The*

Prophets of Israel (1882), W. Robertson Smith had passionately advocated biblical criticism from an evangelical perspective. Driver more than any one else came to be trusted as a guide through this period of transition. His published sermons showed how faith could be reconciled with science, and his Genesis commentary of 1904 was said to have saved the faith of a generation; it was said that he taught the faithful criticism, and the critics faith.

During the thirty-one years of his professorship Driver devoted himself to teaching and writing and to encouraging the work of younger men. His publishing record in this period was remarkable. His *Notes on Samuel* (1890; enlarged edn, 1913) and his contributions to the Oxford *Hebrew Lexicon* (1891–1905) set a standard which raised the whole level of Hebrew scholarship. He wrote distinguished if unoriginal commentaries in one form or another on nearly half of the Old Testament. But of all his books the *Introduction to the Literature of the Old Testament* (1891; 9th edn, 1913) had the widest influence in scholarly circles. Characteristically Driver did not accept the so-called Graf–Wellhausen theory of the Pentateuch, which identified and dated sources for the books of Moses, until he had worked over the field for himself. Between 1882 and 1889, however, he became convinced, and in the *Introduction* he explained and cautiously endorsed this transformation of Old Testament studies. To enthusiasts Driver's moderation seemed disappointing; in general, however, the book was welcomed as authoritative, and it was singularly well timed. It remains the best account of the documentary hypothesis in English.

Driver visited Palestine in 1888 and in 1908 he gave the first of the Schweich lectures of the British Academy, under the title *Modern Research as Illuminating the Bible*. For his pupils he insisted on a firm grounding in Hebrew grammar and vocabulary, before any engagement with 'higher criticism'. Many a preface acknowledges the time and trouble he would spend on the work of others, and though he was retiring and self-effacing by nature, he did not shrink from necessary controversy. Moreover, through the revolution in biblical studies which he helped to bring about, his own Christian faith remained unshaken.

Driver married on 7 July 1891 Mabel (b. 1866/7), elder daughter of Edmund Burr, of Burgh, Norfolk; they had three sons and two daughters. Their eldest son was Sir Godfrey Rolles *Driver (1892–1975), Hebraist and Semitist. Driver died on 26 February 1914, aged sixty-seven, at Christ Church, Oxford, and was survived by his wife.

G. A. COOKE, rev. J. W. ROGERSON

Sources S. R. Driver, *Ideals of the prophets*, ed. G. A. Cooke (1915) · F. Brown, 'Samuel Rolles Driver', *Biblical World*, 43 (1914), 291–4 · G. B. Gray, 'S. R. Driver: the character and influence of his work', *Contemporary Review*, 105 (1914), 484–90 · A. E. Cowley, 'Samuel Rolles Driver, 1846–1914', *PBA*, [7] (1915–16), 540–44 · A. S. Peake, 'Professor S. R. Driver', *The Expositor* (1914), 385–400 · W. Sanday, *The life-work of S. R. Driver* (1914) · G. A. Cooke, 'Driver and Wellhausen', *Harvard Theological Review* (1916), 249–57 · J. W. Rogerson, 'S. R. Driver', *Theologische Realenzyklopädie*, ed. G. Krause, G. Müller, and S. Schwertner, 10 (Berlin, 1982), 190–92 · J. B. Wainewright, ed.,

Winchester College, 1836–1906: a register (1907), 181 · Gladstone, *Diaries* · m. cert. · *CGPLA Eng. & Wales* (1914)

Archives Bodl. Oxf., corresp. with George Ridding

Likenesses B. Rivière, oils, exh. 1910, Christ Church Oxf.

Wealth at death £25,247 14s. 2d.: probate, 18 April 1914, *CGPLA Eng. & Wales*

Droeshout, John (*bap.* 1599, *d.* 1652). *See under* Droeshout, Martin (1565x9–*c.*1642).

Droeshout, Martin (1565x9–*c.*1642), engraver, the second son of John Droeshout (*d.* 1598/9) and his wife, Mary, was born, like his elder brother Michael, in Brussels; his family moved to London as protestant refugees about 1569. Returns of aliens (published by the Huguenot Society) are essential sources of information for the lives of the Droeshouts, as are the registers of baptisms and marriages at the Dutch church in Aldgate ward. John Droeshout is sometimes described as a 'painter', a word then used for men who worked on metal, wood, and stone as well as with pigments ('stainers' applied colours to fabrics for such things as wall hangings and banners). The Company of Painter–Stainers, incorporated in 1581, did its best, like other companies, to round up immigrants practising in the City, admitting them for a fee and making them obey the ordinances; the first reference to John Droeshout as a 'painter', a freeman of the new company, is dated 1583. His son 'Michaell Drowswoot alien'—who had rejoined the family about 1590 after travelling on the continent and learning to engrave on copper in Brussels—was rounded up by the Goldsmiths' Company in 1617, but 'paide nothing quia paup[er]' (Goldsmiths' Hall, wardens' accounts and court minutes, 1611–17, vol. P, pt 1, 321).

Martin Droeshout would have become a freeman of the Painter–Stainers' Company by patrimony; he too may have studied on the continent, but evidence is lacking. By 1587 he was living with his parents near the Dutch church, and he stayed with his mother after John Droeshout's death in 1598 or 1599. Ann Winterbeke from Brussels, whom he married on 26 October 1602, soon died, and on 30 October 1604 he married Janneken Molijns from Antwerp, with whom he had six children who survived to adulthood. The family lived in Crutched Friars, Aldgate ward, close to the church of St Olave, Hart Street. Shakespeare's editors, John Heminges and Henry Condell, chose this prominent member of the immigrant artistic community to adorn the title-page of the First Folio with the most familiar and almost only undisputed likeness of the playwright. 'Mr Drosset(t)' appears in the first surviving court minutes of the Painter–Stainers' Company, on 19 September 1634 and 28 February 1641; on 26 December 1641 Droeshout testified at the admission of his youngest son Daniel to the Dutch congregation. He probably died soon after that, and would have been buried at St Olave, Hart Street. A few surviving portraits include one of James, second marquess of Hamilton, which—like the Shakespeare image—dates to 1623.

John Droeshout (*bap.* 1599, *d.* 1652), engraver, baptized on 20 May 1599, was the first surviving son of Michael Droeshout and his first wife, Susanneken van der Ersbek.

He settled in the parish of St Bride's, Fleet Street, and married an Englishwoman, Anne Ward, by licence dated 4 June 1627. She died in 1640, and John's will was proved on 18 March 1652 by a second wife, Elizabeth. In his will he names a nephew, Martin Droeshout, and two 'sons in law' (stepsons), and leaves his apprentice two books of prints and two of his 'owne drawing' and some engraving tools. There is no evidence that his younger brother Martin, born in 1601, was an engraver.   MARY EDMOND

Sources M. Edmond, 'It was for gentle Shakespeare cut', *Shakespeare Quarterly*, 42 (1991), 339–44 · I. Scouloudi, *Returns of strangers in the metropolis, 1593, 1627, 1635, 1639: a study of an active minority*, Huguenot Society of London, 57 (1985), 1–368 · L. Cust, 'Foreign artists of the reformed religion working in London from about 1560 to 1660', *Proceedings of the Huguenot Society*, 7 (1901–4), 45–82 · parish registers, Dutch Church, baptism and marriage, 1571–1601, 1602–1874, GL, MSS 7381, 7382 · aliens' returns for Aldgate ward, 12 November 1635, PRO, SP16/305/II.ii · Painter–Stainers' Company, court minute book, 1623–49, GL, MS 5667/1, 97, 155 · A. M. Hind, *Engraving in England in the sixteenth and seventeenth centuries*, 2 (1955), 341–66 · H. A. Harben, *A dictionary of London* (1918), 189 · R. M. Glencross, ed., *A calendar of the marriage licence allegations in the registry of the bishop of London*, 1, British RS, 62 (1937), 69 · GL, MS 6538 · will, PRO, PROB 11/221/55 [John Droeshout] · wardens' accounts and court minutes, 1611–17, Goldsmiths' Hall, vol. P, pt 1, 321

Drogheda. For this title name *see* Moore, Charles, first marquess of Drogheda (1730–1822); Moore, (Charles) Garrett Ponsonby, eleventh earl of Drogheda (1910–1989).

Drogheda, William of (1200x10?–1245), civil and canon lawyer, has no known association with the Irish town of Drogheda. He made provisions—in a charter which survives in the Queen's College, Oxford, charter 287, sealed with his seal—for his parents (and himself) to be buried in the priory church at Monk Sherborne, Hampshire. His presentation to the living of Grafton Underwood, Northamptonshire, his only certain benefice, was by the Norman priory at St Fromund which, like Monk Sherborne, was dependent on the abbey of St Vigor, Cérisy, in Normandy. His connections, therefore, are likely to be with Hampshire, and Drogheda may be a local place-name in that county. He may not have been priested until he received the Northamptonshire living in 1242–3. A dispensation to hold an additional benefice was granted to him in 1245, and this may have been Petham in Kent, if a model case in his book is to be believed.

Drogheda's career was associated with Oxford. His mastership apparently postdates Trinity 1237; his regency is mentioned in 1239. There is no evidence that he ever studied at the great Bolognese law school. Drogheda's particular claim to fame is as an Oxford teacher of the late 1230s, who produced a successful law book at a time when legal studies were in a state of transition. This work, the *Summa aurea*, served as a handy manual for both student and practitioner. Only one book of the projected six which are promised in the preface (and were to include one on marriage) has survived. It has been edited by L. Wahrmund (1914) and since then only two further manuscripts have been discovered: Bruges, Stadsbibliotheek, MS 355, and Worcester Cathedral, Dean and Chapter MS 74 (incomplete). Drogheda knew and cited the works of the two civilians, Azo and Roffredus of Benevento. Azo's *Summe* of the first nine books of the *Code* and of the *Digest* was in circulation in 1211 and Roffredus's *Libelli de iure civili* after 1235. He also knew and used Gregory IX's *Decretals* of 1234 and he cites the canons of the legate Otto in the Council of London of 1237. The *Summa aurea* is likely to date from 1237, though it may have been in use in various stages of completion before that date. Included in Gregory IX's *Decretals*, and so more widely circulated by them, was the bull of Honorius III of 1219 banning the study of the civil law by the clergy. It was the particular importance, therefore, of Drogheda's treatise that following the prohibition it retained and passed on the civilian knowledge which was needed by practitioners in the English canon-law courts. It is a procedural textbook, built on examples, possibly based on actual cases and their documents, and giving advice on how to win cases. There is little doubt that it influenced two generations of Oxford students.

Drogheda himself was an accomplished advocate and proctor: Matthew Paris informs us that William of Montpellier gave up his claim to the bishopric of Coventry and Lichfield on hearing of the death of his advocate, William of Drogheda. The great Bolognese doctor of the fourteenth century, Giovanni d'Andreae, gave Drogheda's work a posthumous fame by adding it to a list of notable civilian treatises which had originally been compiled by the French canonist William Durandus (*d.* 1296). Drogheda's work, in spite of its local examples, had already found its way abroad, and the manuscript was certainly copied in the thirteenth century in France and in Italy, and perhaps also in the empire and the Low Countries. His career was brought to an untimely end when he was murdered by his servant in 1245. The house in Oxford which he gave to the prior and convent at Monk Sherborne was supposedly on the site of 33 High Street, which is still called Drawda Hall. JANE E. SAYERS

Sources F. N. Davis, ed., *Rotuli Roberti Grosseteste, episcopi Lincolniensis*, CYS, 10 (1913), 213 · F. W. Maitland, *Roman canon law in the church of England* (1898), 100–131 · *Les registres d'Innocent IV*, ed. E. Berger, 4 vols. (Paris, 1884–1921), no. 1140 · *Curia regis rolls preserved in the Public Record Office* (1922–) · *Die Summa aurea des Wilhelmus de Drokeda*, ed. L. Wahrmund (Innsbruck, 1914) · *Paris, Chron.*, 4.423 · F. de Zulueta, 'William of Drogheda', *Mélanges de droit romain dédiées à Georges Cornil*, 2 (Gand, 1926) · Charter 287, Queen's College, Oxford · assize roll, PRO, Just. Itin. I/700 m ll d [Oxford eyre midsummer 1247] · J. E. Sayers, 'William of Drogheda and the English canonists', *Seventh International Congress of Medieval Canon Law* [Cambridge 1984], ed. P. Linehan (1988), 205–22 · Emden, *Oxf.*
Archives City Library, Bruges, MS 355 · Worcester Cathedral, dean and chapter MS 74 [incomplete]

Drokensford, John. *See* Droxford, John (d. 1329).

Dromgoole, Thomas (d. 1824x9?), political activist, came from Ireland; nothing else is known of his life until he graduated MD at the University of Edinburgh in 1800 with his thesis 'De rheumatismo'. He settled as a physician in Dawson Street, Dublin, though he possessed a 'small fortune which rendered him independent of patients' (Sheil, 2.177).

Dromgoole became a prominent member of the Roman

Catholic board, which was established in the early nineteenth century to further the cause of Catholic emancipation. An anti-vetoist, he was opposed to the purchase of freedom for the Catholics at the price of giving the government a veto in the appointment of their bishops. In 1813 he made some vigorous speeches on the subject, which materially contributed to the temporary defeat of the Catholic Emancipation Bill. These speeches were published in 1814 together with an anonymous 'Vindication', said by William John Fitzpatrick to have been written by John Lanigan, the biblical scholar. Fitzpatrick also alleged that Lanigan had provided the theological arguments used by Dromgoole, though they were 'enunciated through the ponderous trombone of Dromgoole's nasal twang' (Fitzpatrick, 171–2).

Dromgoole's staunch defence of the rights of Irish Roman Catholics was regarded as intemperate and sectarian by moderate Catholics and Dublin protestants alike, drawing down a hornets' nest around his ears. Condemned by the *Freeman's Journal* and lampooned by Dr Brennan in the anti-Catholic *Milesian Magazine* as 'Dr Drumsnuffle', Dromgoole was also censured by the Catholic board at its meeting of 24 December 1812. This was later rescinded when wider Catholic opinion came out in the doctor's support. Daniel O'Connell confessed privately that he hated Dromgoole 'most cordially' (*Correspondence of Daniel O'Connell*, 1.360) for his role in exacerbating divisions among Catholics on the veto question. Yet Dromgoole's defence of the autonomy of the Irish Catholic church revealed the growing importance of that institution in the development of the idea of Irish nationhood in the first half of the nineteenth century—a point O'Connell was equally aware of.

For Dromgoole the whole affair caused a breakdown in health. From about 1815 he retired from public life and lived in exile at Rome in the shadow of the Vatican. Richard Lalor Sheil, who met Dromgoole in Paris on a visit in 1819, described him as a clever, well-educated man, in private very good and gentle. But on the veto question, 'he was scarcely master of himself' (Sheil, 2.178). Describing Dromgoole's mode of emphasizing the end of each sentence in his speeches by knocking loudly on the ground with a heavy stick, Sheil spoke of him as 'a kind of rhetorical paviour who was busily engaged in making the great road of liberty and paving the way to emancipation' (ibid., 2.177). Dromgoole died at Rome, probably between 1824 and 1829. L. C. SANDERS, *rev.* JONATHAN SPAIN

Sources T. Dromgoole, *The speeches of Dr Dromgoole, a physician, at the Catholic board in Dublin, December 8, 1813; with a commentary, by a protestant of Ireland* (1820) · T. Dromgoole, *The speeches of Dr Dromgoole, against surrendering the government of the Catholic church in Ireland to the discretion of parliament, accompanied by a vindication of his statements and principles* (1814) · R. Musgrave, *Observations on Dr Dromgoole's speech, delivered in the Catholic board, December 8, 1812*, 3rd edn (1817) · *Dublin Evening Post* (Dec 1812) · T. Wyse, *Historical sketch of the late Catholic Association of Ireland*, 2 vols. (1829) · T. Bartlett, *The fall and rise of the Irish nation: the Catholic question, 1690–1830* (1992) · R. L. Sheil, *Sketches, legal and political*, 2 vols. (1855) · *The correspondence of Daniel O'Connell*, ed. M. O'Connell, 8 vols. (1972–7), 1.373, 392, 460, 465 · *Library catalogue of the Royal College of Physicians of Edinburgh*, 1 (1898) · W. J. Fitzpatrick, *Irish wits and worthies, including Dr Lanigan,* *his life and times* (1873) • A. J. Webb, *A compendium of Irish biography* (1878) • *List of the graduates in medicine in the University of Edinburgh from MDCCV to MDCCCLXVI* (1867)

Wealth at death small fortune rendering him independent of patients: Sheil, *Sketches*

Dronfield, William (1826–1894), trade unionist, was, according to local obituary notices, born in Sheffield in April 1826, the son of Andrew Dronfield, a gardener, and apprenticed to the printing trade. Little is known about his early years before his marriage, on 30 November 1848, at St Mary's Church, Sheffield, to Harriet (1826x8–1897), the daughter of George Allen, a cutler.

A committed trade unionist by his early twenties, Dronfield was present at the foundation conference, held in Sheffield in June 1849, of the Provincial Typographical Association. He was an executive committee member of the Typographical Association for fifteen years and secretary of the Sheffield Journeymen Printers' Society, a post he held for thirty-five years. A trade dispute with the proprietor of a local newspaper in 1858 led Dronfield and others to create the Association of Organised Trades of Sheffield and the Neighbourhood (later, in 1872, reconstituted as the Sheffield Federated Trades Council). For several years, as secretary of the association, he was an important provincial figure in advancing the claims of trade unionism. He was also in contact with several prominent trade union leaders, notably in the campaign against the Master and Servant Acts; in May 1864 he attended the conference held in London to promote this cause and on 29 May 1866 he gave evidence before the select committee appointed to inquire into the law.

Dronfield spoke at the annual meeting of the National Association for the Promotion of Social Science, held in Sheffield in October 1865. However, he felt slighted when the published transactions merely noted 'Mr. Dronfield read a paper pointing out the advantages of Trades' Unions'. His paper was printed in the seventh annual report of the Association of Organised Trades and gave impetus to the view that workers should develop further their own organizations. In June 1866 he called trade union delegates to a conference in Sheffield to discuss the creation of a national body that would resist employers' lock-outs. The conference lasted five days and attracted 138 delegates representing 187,771 workers. Out of it came the United Kingdom Alliance of Organised Trades, with Dronfield in his customary role as secretary, but it did not flourish and was wound up after a few years. However, influenced by his remarks at the conference of 1866, two Manchester delegates—William Wood and Samuel Nicholson, who were also compositors—resolved to call a congress of trades councils and societies. Held in Manchester in 1868 (with Dronfield present on behalf of the Sheffield Association of Organised Trades) it can be regarded as the founding conference of the Trades Union Congress.

Dronfield advocated conciliation as a means of settling industrial disputes. In public at least he deplored what were termed 'outrages': the use of physical violence and 'rattening' (interference with tools and equipment to enforce the interests of trade societies in the local grinding trades). As the honorary secretary of the Sheffield Trades Defence Committee he was summoned to give evidence in June 1867 before the Trades Unions Commission inquiring into the 'Sheffield outrages'. Although the chairman of the commission referred to him as 'a respectable man' (*Report*, Q. 15, 332), Dronfield had to fend off several ticklish questions about his knowledge of the actions of William Broadhead, a fellow trade unionist and the chief instigator of violent practices.

In common with other mid-Victorian working-class radicals, Dronfield was involved in a range of progressive causes. He was a Reform League supporter and, along with his friend and fellow trade unionist Robert Applegarth, prominent in persuading A. J. Mundella to stand for Sheffield in the general election of 1868. Mundella defeated the incumbent, J. A. Roebuck, who had come to be regarded as hostile to working-class interests (Dronfield especially deplored Roebuck's sympathies for the Confederate states during the American Civil War). In the Social Science Association transactions for 1865, in the discussion of another paper, Dronfield's remarks on the benefits of schooling and the need for state aid were printed. In the early 1870s he was able further to press for these reforms as a committee member of the Sheffield branch of the National Education League, the pressure group formed by Joseph Chamberlain and others to connect radicalism with the call for free and secular education. However, he was not apparently a freethinker, preferring to leave religious instruction to the various denominations.

In July 1870 Dronfield was in London as a representative of his town at the Workmen's International Exhibition, held at the Agricultural Hall, Islington; he was introduced to the prince of Wales, who opened the proceedings, and guided him through the Sheffield exhibits. From the early 1870s he was a local voluntary sanitary inspector, which offered opportunities to press for improvements in public health. A directory of 1883 gave the sanitary department as an address of his, and also stated his occupation as traveller and collector. It was not until the mid-1880s, however, when his health was failing, that he resigned as secretary of the local Typographical Association branch. Towards the end of his life he furnished Sidney and Beatrice Webb with information that was incorporated into their history of trade unionism.

Dronfield died at his home, 120 William Street, Sheffield, on 24 August 1894; his death was attributed to hemiplegia—he had suffered from paralysis since 1885—and cerebral haemorrhage. Survived by his wife, son, and two daughters (another daughter died in 1871), he was buried in the general cemetery, Sheffield, on 29 August.

D. E. MARTIN

Sources V. Thornes, *William Dronfield, 1826–1894: influences on nineteenth century Sheffield* (1976) • W. H. G. Armytage, 'William Dronfield and the good name of the Sheffield workman in the 1860s', *N&Q*, 193 (1948), 145–8 • W. H. G. Armytage, *A. J. Mundella, 1825–1897: the liberal background to the labour movement* (1951) • D. Smith, *Conflict and compromise: class formation in English society, 1830–1914: a comparative study of Birmingham and Sheffield* (1982) •

Sheffield and Rotherham Independent (27 Aug 1894) • *Sheffield Daily Telegraph* (27 Aug 1894) • 'Sheffield outrages inquiry: report presented to the trades unions commissioners', *Parl. papers* (1867), 32.397, no. 3952-I; repr. with introduction by S. Pollard as *The Sheffield outrages* (1971) • A. E. Musson, 'The origins and establishment of the Trades Union Congress', *Trade union and social history* (1974), 23–63 • A. E. Musson, *The Typographical Association: origins and history up to 1949* (1954) • S. Pollard, *A history of labour in Sheffield* (1959) • J. Mendelson, W. Owen, S. Pollard, and V. Thornes, *Sheffield Trades and Labour Council, 1858 to 1958* [1958] • D. E. Fletcher, 'Aspects of liberalism in Sheffield, 1849–1886', PhD diss., University of Sheffield, 1972 • B. C. Roberts, *The Trades Union Congress, 1868–1921* (1958) • *Transactions of the National Association for the Promotion of Social Science, Sheffield meeting, 1865* (1866) • m. cert. • d. cert. • census returns for Sheffield, 1881

Likenesses photograph, repro. in Thornes, *William Dronfield*
Wealth at death £178 18s. 9d.: probate, 12 Oct 1894, *CGPLA Eng. & Wales*

Drope, Francis (1629?–1671), arboriculturist, was born at Cumnor vicarage, Berkshire, a younger son of the Revd Thomas Drope BD, vicar of Cumnor and rector of Ardley, near Bicester, Oxfordshire. He became a demy (or foundation scholar) of Magdalen College, Oxford, in 1645, and graduated as BA in 1647. In 1648 he was expelled by the parliamentary visitors, probably for having borne arms for the king, and he then became an assistant master in a private school kept by William Fuller at Twickenham. After the Restoration he received his MA (23 August 1660), and in 1662 he was made a fellow of Magdalen College. He graduated as BD (12 December 1667), and served as a prebendary of Lincoln (17 February 1669–1670).

Drope's one work, *A Short and Sure Guide in the Practice of Raising and Ordering of Fruit-Trees*, was published in 1672, and praised in *Philosophical Transactions*. It was rare at that time to have a treatise on gardening based on practical experience rather than classical theory. Drope died on 26 September 1671, and was buried in the chancel of Cumnor church.

Drope's elder brother, **John Drope** (1626–1670), became a poet and physician. He was a demy of Magdalen College, Oxford, in 1642, and was awarded a BA on 12 July 1645. He also bore arms for the king in the garrison of Oxford, and he was made a fellow of Magdalen College in 1647. Ejected by the parliamentary visitors the next year, he became a master at John Fetiplace's school at Dorchester about 1654. After the Restoration he finally received his MA (23 August 1660), and was restored to his fellowship. He subsequently studied medicine, which he practised at Borough, Lincolnshire; he died at Borough in October 1670. He was a minor poet, and published *An Hymenaean Essay* on the marriage of Charles II in 1662, and a poem on the Oxford Physic Garden in 1664.

G. S. BOULGER, *rev.* ANNE PIMLOTT BAKER

Sources Wood, *Ath. Oxon.* • S. Felton, *On the portraits of English authors on gardening* (1828) • Desmond, *Botanists*

Drope, John (1626–1670). *See under* Drope, Francis (1629?–1671).

Drout, John (*fl.* 1570), poet, was, from the evidence of the title-page of his only known work, an attorney of Thavies Inn. He also may have been the John Drowte recorded as having matriculated at Cambridge in 1567 as a sizar from Trinity College. What is known with certainty, however, is that Drout was the author of a black-letter tract of thirty leaves entitled *The pityfull historie of two loving Italians, Gaulfrido and Barnardo le vayne: which arived in the countrey of Grece in the time of the noble Emperoure Vaspasian and translated out of Italian into Englishe meeter* (1570). Drout and his poem were forgotten until the late eighteenth century when Edmond Malone, in his preliminary remarks on *Romeo and Juliet*, erroneously supposed *Gaulfrido and Barnardo* to be a prose narrative of the story from which Shakespeare's play was constructed (*Plays and Poems of William Shakespeare*, 6.4). Malone, however, knew of Drout's work only through its entry in the Stationers' register. It was not until 1844, when John Payne Collier reprinted the text from a copy (believed to be unique) lent to him by Charles Wycliffe Goodwin, fellow of St Catharine's, Cambridge, that it became apparent that the text is in fact in verse. Furthermore, the history of Romeo and Juliet comprises only a small part of it (Lowndes, 2.869; appendix, 250). Collier, in his 1844 edition, expressed doubt as to whether Drout really translated the story from Italian, and suggested that he had described his work as a translation in order to take advantage of the Elizabethan vogue for Italian novels (Drout, ii). Because Collier had earlier forged an entry in Henslowe's diary about a non-extant play called 'Galfrido and Bernardo', and was then the first to discuss Drout's work, the latter was long suspected of being a fake also.

GORDON GOODWIN, *rev.* ELIZABETH GOLDRING

Sources J. Drout, *The pityfull historie of two loving Italians, Gaulfrido and Barnardo le vayne … 1570*, ed. J. P. Collier (1844) • *The plays and poems of William Shakespeare: comprehending a life of the poet, and an enlarged history of the stage*, ed. J. Boswell and others, 21 vols. (1821) • W. T. Lowndes, *The bibliographer's manual of English literature*, ed. H. G. Bohn, [new edn], 6 vols. (1869) • Venn, *Alum. Cant.*, 1/2

Drower [*née* Stevens], **Ethel May Stefana**, Lady Drower (1879–1972), orientalist and novelist, was born on 1 December 1879 in North Road, Highgate, Middlesex, the first of the four daughters of the Revd Silas William Stevens (1856–1916), rector of Burley, Hampshire, and then St Lawrence, Southampton, and his wife, Susan Ellen (1845?–1932), formerly Dean, daughter of William Carpenter and his wife, Ann. She attended a boarding-school near Bournemouth and then worked as a freelance journalist, travel companion, and novelist. Several journeys took her to different countries in the Near East and find their reflection in her early novels: *The Veil* (1909), *The Mountain of God* (1911), and *The Earthen Drum* (1911), a collection of oriental tales. On her travel to Sudan, of which she gives an account in *My Sudan Year* (1912), she met in Khartoum Edwin Mortimer Drower (1880–1951), a lawyer whom she married in 1911. They had three children: one daughter, Margaret (*b.* 1911) and two sons, William (*b.* 1915) and Denys (*b.* 1918). Having children did not stop her from writing, and numerous novels appeared during this period, all of which were published under her maiden name. They are entertaining, but for the most part have no great literary value. However, *The Mountain of God* does have lasting value as the story centres around the belief, cult, and political persecution of the sect of the Baha'is who have their sanctuary, the tomb of Baha' 'Ullah, on Mount Carmel in Haifa.

This novel demonstrated an observational and descriptive talent that was also apparent in Drower's many travel books and articles on the cult and rites of various minor religious and ethnic groups in the Near East (Iraq, Persia, Syria), including *By Tigris and Euphrates* (1923), *Cedars, Saints and Sinners* (1926), and *Peacock Angel* (1941). In the last book Drower describes a religious sect in northern Iraq, the Yezidis, devil worshippers. Her husband was a British government official, stationed from 1919, in Basrah; and later he was (until 1947) adviser to the minister of justice in Baghdad; he was knighted in 1941. But Drower did not restrict herself to the role of an 'official' wife. Some of her time she devoted to travel and to learning Arabic. As a woman she had access to the women's quarters which were normally denied to men. A remarkable outcome is her collection from the vernacular of many folk and fairy tales from Baghdad, Mosul, and surroundings. A selection of those forms the well-known book *Folk-Tales of 'Iraq* (1931). She was the first to collect stories from this area. It was just in time before modern inventions such as the gramophone and the cinema replaced this oriental art of entertainment.

The second period of Drower's life was devoted to the only surviving gnostic group from antiquity, the Mandaeans, who are called in Arabic as-Subbis, 'baptizers', a sect of observers and owners of secret rites and knowledge who are a product of the ancient oriental and hellenistic syncretism, the gnosis. A detailed description is found in her study of this sect, *The Mandaeans of Iraq and Iran* (1937) which by the close of the twentieth century had not been superseded. She won the trust of the Mandaeans so that some members of this sect sold her copies of manuscripts which were allowed to be read and studied only by their priests. These formed the basis of *The Secret Adam* (1960). The fifty-four manuscripts are kept now in the Bodleian Library, Oxford, as the Drower collection. *Water into Wine* (1956), a comparison of baptismal rites, owes much to her study of different religious groups. Without any scholarly education Drower learned Aramaic and mastered the translation of very important Mandaic manuscripts; these publications are of great value for the study of the culture and language of the only remaining gnostic sect in the twentieth century: *Book of the Zodiac* (1949), *Diwan Abathur* (1950), *Šarḥ ḏ Qabin ḏ Šišlam Rba* (1950), *Haran Gawaita and the Baptism of Hibil-Ziwa* (1953), *The Canonical Prayerbook of the Mandaeans* (1959), *The Thousand and Twelve Questions* (1960), *The Coronation of the Great Šišlam* (1962), and *A Pair of Naṣoraean Commentaries* (1963). She also contributed many articles to scholarly journals such as *Iraq* and the *Journal of the Royal Asiatic Society*. *A Mandaic Dictionary* (1963) was drawn from her vast word collection, in collaboration with Rudolf Macuch. She was honoured for her scholarly achievements with several degrees, an honorary DLitt from Oxford University and an honorary DD from Uppsala University, as well as being made an honorary fellow of

the School of Oriental and African Studies of London University. On 1 October 1964 she was awarded the greatest honour for a scholar in semitic languages, the Lidzbarski gold medal, for her work on Mandaic, a very important and interesting branch of eastern Aramaic. She died on 27 January 1972 in London.   CHRISTA MÜLLER-KESSLER

Sources R. Macuch, 'Lady Ethel Stefana Drower', *Zeitschrift der Deutschen Morgenländischen Gesellschaft*, 124 (1974), 6–12 · R. Macuch, *Handbook of classical and modern Mandaic* (1965) · private information (2004) [Margaret Hackforth-Jones, daughter] · *CGPLA Eng. & Wales* (1972) · b. cert.
Archives Bodl. Oxf.
Wealth at death £65,227: probate, 13 April 1972, *CGPLA Eng. & Wales*

Droxford [Drokensford], **John** (d. 1329), administrator and bishop of Bath and Wells, probably came from Droxford in Hampshire, where he was baptized; he later built a tomb for his mother in the church of Droxford and undertook restoration work there. He had at least three brothers: Philip, Michael, and Richard. His family held land in Hendon and Finchley in Middlesex. Droxford is first found in royal service in Gascony in 1286. Unusually for a southerner he made his career in the wardrobe, obtaining promotion as cofferer (May 1290), controller (November 1290), and keeper (November 1295 – July 1307), on each occasion in succession to Walter Langton (d. 1321), for whom he also deputized as treasurer, and who may have been his patron. Like Langton, Droxford had no university education. However, he was richly rewarded for his royal service. In September 1298 Edward I secured him a papal dispensation to retain four churches and eight canonries and prebends, and he was appointed to the honorary post of papal chaplain. He participated in the Great Cause concerning the Scottish succession in 1291–2. In the spring of 1297, together with the elder Hugh Despenser (d. 1326) and other councillors, he took the initiative in extending the wool prise (seizure for the king's benefit) to include wealthy English merchants, an action later disavowed by the king. He was also very closely involved in the financing of the Scottish war, for which he personally provided a retinue in royal service.

Like Walter Langton, Droxford was removed from office on Edward II's accession. However, as prince of Wales, the new king had already written to the pope on his behalf in April 1306, and in March 1308 he obtained for him two further generous papal dispensations for pluralism, one of them for a benefice worth £200. In May 1308 Droxford was appointed chancellor of the exchequer, but in July he returned to his old job as keeper, which he held for a year. During that year, on 5 February 1309, he was elected to the bishopric of Bath and Wells. Archbishop Winchelsey arranged for his consecration to take place at Canterbury in August 1309 in order to draw prelates away from the king's parliament at Stamford; but Droxford, owing his appointment to the crown, attended the parliament, obtaining a letter from the king on his behalf asking the pope to relieve his burden of debt. The consecration eventually took place on 9 November. The following month Piers Gaveston (d. 1312) and two other earls obtained for him a grant that he be allowed to repay his debts at the exchequer at the rate of 100 marks p.a., an important concession given the chaotic state of his wardrobe accounts, although one that was not permitted to stand in 1319, when five auditors were appointed to hear these accounts. In 1310 he was one of only five bishops allowed to fine to be excused military service in Scotland. So far as can be discerned he supported the king during the conflict over the ordinances.

By 1313 Droxford was one of the leading men in the English government. Many writs were witnessed by him during the summer of that year, and he was one of four men commissioned on 1 July to open and conduct parliament in the king's absence. He remained high in royal favour afterwards, and attended Gaveston's funeral on 2 January 1315. At the Lincoln parliament in 1316, and again at York in October 1318 and Westminster in October 1320, he was an auditor of Gascon petitions. However, he fell from favour when the king became convinced that he had sided with the barons during the war against the Despensers in 1321–2. On 2 February 1323 Edward petitioned the pope for his removal from his see, and on 10 October 1323 he requested that William, abbot of Langdon, Kent, replace him. The pope refused to condemn Droxford unheard and later interceded with the younger Despenser on his behalf. In July 1323 Droxford was also reprimanded for procrastinating to account for 45,000 marks for his keepership of the wardrobe between 1295 and 1298. It may be that the more informal practices of Edward I's day were unacceptable by the more stringent standards of the 1320s. Most of Droxford's accounts were never enrolled, and on his death his goods and chattels were taken into the king's hands as security.

Droxford must have enjoyed considerable wealth. By March 1308 he occupied sixteen prebends and five other churches, while still only in deacon's orders. As bishop he was often non-resident, and he was a great nepotist; for instance, he briefly secured the precentorship of Wells for his nephew Richard Droxford. From 1319 to 1321 he was at odds with Dean Godley and the cathedral chapter in a dispute that the chapter claimed had been occasioned by the bishop's official and in which the bishop eventually gave way. He died at Dogmersfield in Hampshire on 9 May 1329, and was buried in St Katherine's Chapel in Wells Cathedral.

M. C. BUCK

Sources Chancery records · E. Hobhouse, ed., Calendar of the register of John de Drokensford, Bishop of Bath and Wells, Somerset RS, 1 (1887) · Rymer, Foedera · M. Prestwich, Edward I (1988) · M. Prestwich, War, politics, and finance under Edward I (1972) · Calendar of papal letters · exchequer, queen's remembrances, memoranda rolls, PRO, E.159 · chancery, charter rolls, PRO, C.53 · L. S. Colchester, ed., Wells Cathedral: a history (1982) · Fasti Angl., 1300–1541 · J. H. Denton, Robert Winchelsey and the crown, 1294–1313: a study in the defence of ecclesiastical liberty, Cambridge Studies in Medieval Life and Thought, 3rd ser., 14 (1980) · N. G. Brett-James, 'John de Drokensford, bishop of Bath and Wells', Transactions of the London and Middlesex Archaeological Society, new ser., 10 (1951), 281–301 · C. M. Church, 'The rise and growth of the chapter of Wells from 1242 to 1333', Archaeologia, 54 (1894–5), 1–40 · W. Hunt, ed., Two chartularies of the priory of St Peter at Bath, Somerset RS, 7 (1893) · The liber epistolaris of Richard de Bury, ed. N. Denholm-Young, Roxburghe Club (1950) · F. J. Baigent, ed., The registers of John de Sandale and Rigaud d'Asserio, bishops of Winchester, Hampshire RS, 8 (1897), 25
Archives Som. ARS, episcopal register

Druce, George Claridge (1850–1932), botanist, was born at Potterspury, south Northamptonshire, on 23 May 1850, the illegitimate son of Jane Druce, who came of farming stock from Woughton on the Green, Buckinghamshire. Little is known of his early life: circumstances were evidently difficult for his mother and in 1855 she took a situation in the nearby village of Yardley Gobion, where he attended the village school. Two ministers of the independent chapel at Potterspury, J. and T. B. Slye, took an interest in the boy and assisted his education. From his earliest years Druce had an eye for plants and a remarkable memory for their occurrence; as a child his chief relaxation and interest were the collection and study of local butterflies and wild flowers.

In 1866 Druce was apprenticed to P. Jeyes & Co. of Northampton, a firm of retail and manufacturing chemists. After long hours in shop and laboratory, in which he was soon given considerable responsibility, culminating in promotion to acting manager at the age of nineteen, he somehow found time for hard study and in 1872 passed all his pharmaceutical examinations with high honours. Once these were out of the way he felt free to give time to field botany. He began to form a herbarium, to write on the local flora, and helped to found and organize the activities of a local pharmaceutical association (from 1871) and of the Northamptonshire Natural History Society (from 1876). He also became one of the two honorary secretaries of the Midland Union of Natural History Societies. For six years after qualifying he remained with his employer, but in June 1879 he suddenly broke all connections with Northampton and took the risk of setting up in business in Oxford, investing his savings of about £400 in a chemist's shop at 118 High Street. The cause of this complete break with Northampton was probably the entry into the firm of his employer's son, which left Druce convinced that he would never head the firm. However, he could not start his own business in Northampton because, in common with other employees, he had given a legal undertaking not to set up in competition within a radius of 30 miles.

As soon as he was settled in Oxford, Druce began to take part in activities similar to those abandoned at Northampton. In 1880 he helped to found the Ashmolean Natural History Society of Oxfordshire and began to investigate the county flora. A Flora of Oxfordshire followed in 1886— and the degree of honorary MA from the university, in recognition of that achievement, three years later. Further recognition came from the university in 1895 with conferment on him of the title of special curator to the Fielding Herbarium. His labours to resurrect the department of botany's long-neglected early collections were to be long-lasting and devoted, though marred by overmuch haste and too little attention to detail. The first instalment of his scholarly account of these appeared in print after only two years' work. He followed that up in 1907 with a substantial monograph, edited by the then professor, S. H.

George Claridge Druce (1850–1932), by Philip A. de Laszlo, 1931

Vines, on the particularly valuable herbaria left by the latter's eighteenth-century predecessor, Dillenius. The two again collaborated on an account of the herbarium of Robert Morison, a still earlier professor, in 1914. When a fourth and final contribution was published in 1919, the university granted him an MA by decree in recognition of his efforts. Three years later he was awarded the degree of DSc, by examination. His subsequent election to fellowship of the Royal Society in 1927, a singular achievement for a largely self-educated amateur, is said to have been primarily in recognition of this scholarly work under the university's auspices. He also received the honorary degree of LLD from the University of St Andrews, and there was keen disappointment among his friends that Oxford did not similarly honour him.

It was as a field botanist, however, that Druce was best known and on his series of large floras of the four south midlands counties that his reputation most widely rested. After his early completion of one on Oxfordshire, he moved on to Berkshire (1897), then Buckinghamshire (1926), then Oxfordshire afresh (1927), and finally his native Northamptonshire (1930). The last was an enlargement of work he had embarked upon in his youth, much of it originally published in parts by the Northamptonshire Natural History Society in its journal in 1880–94. That was one publication he manifestly left until too late; another was his sadly unreliable *Comital Flora of the British Isles* (1932), intended as an updating of H. C. Watson's mammoth compendium of half a century earlier, *Topographical Botany*, but devoid of the crucial documentation

of each record that had made that influential precursor so definitive. A sizeable percentage of the records in Druce's book had been made in the course of his travels over the years in every county of Great Britain and Ireland. Those included several visits to the Shetlands and the Channel Islands, which seemed to him to offer the greatest potential for adding further species to the national list.

While the flora of the British Isles always remained Druce's foremost concern, affluence and abundant leisure in his later years stimulated him to go farther afield. He accompanied the British Association to Australia and made visits independently to many other parts of the world. Everywhere he collected avidly and assiduously, his personal herbarium extending to some 200,000 specimens by the time of his death (though many were acquired from others). Always in a hurry, he commonly took little more than scraps, just as he never studied any group of plants intensively, happy to rely on the expertise of specialists, too often quite uncritically. Many species were erroneously claimed for the flora of these islands in consequence. Indeed the soundness of Druce's taxonomic judgement may frequently be questioned, unduly eager as he was to add to the tally of entities bearing Latin names, many of them minor variants scarcely warranting such distinction or even of doubtful constancy.

The unrestrained character of Druce's collecting, a relic of an earlier era, often provoked the wrath of an increasingly conservation-minded British botanical community. It was therefore incongruous that he also played a leading role in the Society for the Promotion of Nature Reserves from its founding in 1912, drawing up at the request of his friend Charles Rothschild a pioneering register of plant sites most deserving protection.

By that time Druce's prominence in the world of floristics had brought him a much more enduring and onerous commitment. This was the honorary secretaryship of the Botanical Exchange Club, which he took on in 1903, two years before his retirement from business. It was a body with which he had long been closely connected and which at that point was in danger of petering out. Its sole purpose was the enrichment of the members' herbaria with authoritatively named specimens of difficult or otherwise interesting higher plants of the British Isles. This involved the distributor in making up numerous parcels once each year, such a backbreaking task that the club was kept deliberately tiny. Druce decided this was much too limited and took it upon himself to change its character and build it up into the major national society that field botany glaringly lacked. In this he had great success, though only by acting without reference to the other members, some of whom were so angered by his unilateral actions and so opposed to his policy that they campaigned, vainly, to unseat him. Accustomed to being his own master and unable to take criticism, Druce steadfastly refused to operate democratically, undertaking all the duties himself and largely writing the progressively fatter annual reports until they turned effectively into a journal; this he used as a mouthpiece for his unorthodox views, particularly on the international rules governing plant naming. His untiring helpfulness and rapport with the inexperienced, especially if they were young, nevertheless won him a large body of loyal supporters, a body in the end sufficiently well-cemented to survive his death and form the basis of what was later to become the Botanical Society of the British Isles.

The cares of his business and the pursuit of his hobby did not exhaust Druce's energies. He was prominent in freemasonry and took an active part as a Liberal in municipal affairs. He served on the Oxford city council from 1892 until his death, was chairman of the public health committee for thirty years, and was sheriff in 1897 and mayor in 1900. He also served on the council of the Pharmaceutical Society and was president in 1901–2 of the British Pharmaceutical Conference.

The wide respect and affection which were felt for Druce were impressively demonstrated in the celebrations of his eightieth birthday. Two years later, on 29 February 1932, he died at his home, Yardley Lodge, 9 Crick Road, Oxford, after a short illness and was buried in the city's Holywell cemetery. He was unmarried, and many years of careful saving and astute investment had left him a man of considerable wealth. After numerous bequests to friends his will provided that his house, library, and collections were to be offered to Oxford University to serve as an institute of systematic botany. The Botanical Exchange Club, which had nursed hopes of being generously endowed by its effective begetter, merely received indirectly the services of Druce's assistant. The university and the Society for the Promotion of Nature Reserves were named as the residuary legatees to what was eventually established, after protracted wrangling in the courts over various ambiguities, as about £90,000.   D. E. ALLEN

Sources D. E. Allen, *The botanists: a history of the Botanical Society of the British Isles through a hundred and fifty years*, St Paul's Bibliographies (1986), 91–118 · G. C. Druce, *Flora of Buckinghamshire* (1926), cvi · G. C. Druce, *Flora of Northamptonshire* (1930), cxxi · F. Perring, 'Druce in Northamptonshire', *Watsonia*, 20 (1995), 185–94 · D. E. Allen, 'Druce in Oxford', *Botanical Society of the British Isles News*, 67 (1994), 41–5 · A. B. Rendle, *Obits. FRS*, 1 (1932–5), 12–14 · D. E. Allen, 'The discoveries of Druce', *Scottish Naturalist*, 98 (1986), 175–89 · T. B. L. Churchill, memoir, 1977, NHM, Botanical Society of the British Isles Archives [photocopy; orig. in priv. coll.] · F. A. Bellamy, incomplete biography, Oxford, Druce MSS · H. Dunkley, 'Some personal recollections of George Claridge Druce', *Botanical Society of the British Isles News*, 67 (1994), 45–6 · *Nature*, 129 (1932), 426–7 · *The Times* (1 March 1932) · *The Times* (5 March 1932) · J. Wake, 'The early days of the Northamptonshire Natural History Society', *Northamptonshire Past and Present*, 1/5 (1952), 39–52 · will, proved (admin), London, 8 April 1933

Archives Bodl. Oxf., corresp. and MSS · MHS Oxf., scrapbook · RBG Kew, corresp. · S. Antiquaries, Lond., antiquarian MSS · U. Oxf., department of plant sciences, botanical specimens · U. Oxf., department of plant sciences, corresp. and papers relating to publication of *Flora Graeca* · U. Oxf., Forestry Institute, corresp. | NL Wales, letters to J. E. Griffith · Royal Society for Nature Conservation, Newark-on-Trent, corresp. with N. C. Rothschild

Likenesses photograph, before 1914, Ashmolean Natural History Society, Oxford; repro. in D. E. Allen, *The naturalist in Britain* (1976) · P. A. de Laszlo, oils, 1931, Bodl. Oxf., Radcliffe Science Library [*see*

illus.] · W. Stoneman, photograph, 1931, NPG · R. Chalmers, photograph, repro. in G. C. Druce, *The comital flora of the British Isles* (1932), frontispiece · F. Lascelles, bronze bust, U. Oxf., department of plant sciences · P. A. de Laszlo, oils, Oxford city hall · photograph, repro. in Allen, *Botanists*, facing p. 134

Wealth at death £92,307: resworn probate, 18 Jan 1934, *CGPLA Eng. & Wales*

Druce, (John) Gerald Frederick (1894–1950), chemist and schoolmaster, was born on 8 December 1894 at 14 St John's Road, Leamington Spa, the son of Frederick Druce, an assistant manager of a coffee house (and later a gardener), and his wife, Hannah Freeman. Following the family's move to Reading, he was educated at Kendrick School and at University College, Reading (1911–12), before studying chemistry and botany at University College, London, where he graduated BSc in 1915. Following war service he pursued independent research, obtaining an MSc from the University of London in 1920. At University College he had met the Czech chemist, Jardslav Heyrovský (1890–1967), who inspired him to visit Czechoslovakia in 1920 and to learn Czech and other Slavonic languages. He studied chemistry with Heyrovský at the Charles University in Prague and was awarded a doctorate in 1923. In the same year Druce began to teach chemistry and botany at Battersea grammar school, where he set up a temporary research laboratory in the playground at St John's Hill, Clapham. Later, he built a laboratory in his garden. In 1921 he married Elsie Olive (b. 1895/6), the daughter of Edward James Caudell, a blouse manufacturer; they had one son.

Mendeleyev had predicted the existence of two missing elements, eka- and dimanganese, in group VII of the periodic table, and the likely existence of elements of masses 43 and 75 had been confirmed from X-ray spectra by H. G. J. Moseley in 1915. Using his school facilities to concentrate solutions of pyrolusite, and in collaboration with the physicist F. H. Loring (d. 1944), in 1925 Druce announced the discovery of missing element, atomic number 75, in the form of potassium per-rhenate. While Druce's preparation of a rhenium salt was undoubtedly genuine, the international community allowed the honour of discovery of the pure element to go to the Germans W. Noddack, I. Tacke, and O. Berg, who in the same year gave the name rhenium to the element they had isolated from columbite and molybdenite. Druce's findings were corroborated by Heyrovský, who had also identified rhenium by means of polarography. Druce compiled the first textbook on the preparation and properties of this rare element in 1948.

Druce was elected a fellow of the Chemical Society in 1915 and became a licentiate (1919) and fellow (1925) of the Royal Institute of Chemistry. He travelled extensively in eastern Europe, visiting Czechoslovakia at least once a year and wrote two books (1930 and 1936) on the country, as well as a monograph on the Czech scientists B. Brauner and F. Wald. He was a personal friend of the first Czech president, Thomás Masaryk (1850–1937) and shared his conviction that 'truth prevails' ('pravda vítězí'). Druce was awarded the order of the White Lion by the Czech government for his cultural and scientific work as well as membership of several Czech learned societies. His strong interests in the history of science were reflected in a book in 1925, and a London MA thesis in 1943. He published many articles on preparative inorganic chemistry, was a regular contributor to *Chemical News*, and served in an editorial capacity during its declining years, 1924–31.

A quiet, unassuming man, Druce was an inspiring teacher who impressed his pupils with his experimental skills. He was probably the last chemist to find ways and means of doing original research in a secondary school environment. He died at the Royal Cancer Hospital, Fulham Road, London, on 22 June 1950.　　W. H. BROCK

Sources *JCS* (1950), 3358 · *Nature*, 166 (1950), 134–5 · *The Times* (24 June 1950), 6 · J. C. Poggendorff and others, eds., *Biographisch-literarisches Handwörterbuch zur Geschichte der exacten Naturwissenschaften*, 7b, pt 3 (Berlin, 1970) · J. G. F. Druce, *Wanderings in Czechoslovakia* (1930) · d. cert. · m. cert. · b. cert. · *CGPLA Eng. & Wales* (1950) · J. G. F. Druce, *Rhenium* (1948)

Wealth at death £3200 18s. 9d.: administration with will, 4 Oct 1950

Drue, Thomas. *See* Drewe, Thomas (c.1586–1627).

Drugger, Abel. *See* Hardham, John (d. 1772).

Druitt, Robert (1814–1883), general practitioner and medical writer, the son of Robert Druitt, a medical practitioner at Wimborne, Dorset, was born in December 1814. After being educated at the local grammar school he spent four years as a pupil of his uncle, Charles Mayo, surgeon to the Winchester Hospital. He entered King's College as a medical student in 1834 (where another relation, Herbert Mayo, was a professor), and also trained at the Middlesex Hospital, London. He became LSA in 1836 and MRCS in 1837, and settled in general practice in Bruton Street, Berkeley Square. In 1845 he married Isabella Hopkinson, daughter of William Hopkinson, corn merchant. They had at least three sons and four daughters.

In 1839 Druitt published the *Surgeon's Vade-Mecum*. Written in a very clear and simple style, it became a great favourite with students, and Druitt spent much time preparing further editions. The eleventh edition appeared in 1878, and in all more than 40,000 copies were sold. It was reprinted in America, and translated into several European languages. In 1845 Druitt became FRCS by examination, and in 1874 he was elected FRCP; he later received the Lambeth degree of MD. He practised successfully for many years, and also engaged in literary work, editing the *Medical Times and Gazette* between 1862 and 1872. He was an earnest advocate of improved sanitation, and from 1856 to 1867 was one of the medical officers of health for St George's, Hanover Square. From 1864 to 1872 he was president of the Metropolitan Association of Medical Officers of Health, before which he delivered numerous addresses.

In 1872 Druitt's health broke down, and he for some time lived in Madras, India, whence he wrote a series of 'Letters from Madras' to the *Medical Times and Gazette*. On his retirement 370 medical practitioners and other friends presented him with a cheque for £1215 in a silver cup. After an exhausting illness Druitt died at 8 Strathmore Gardens, Kensington, London, on 15 May 1883.

Druitt was a man of wide culture, being well versed in languages, as well as in science and theology. Church music was one of his special studies, and as early as 1845 he wrote *A Popular Tract on Church Music*. He also wrote a small work entitled 'Cheap wines, their use in diet and medicine', which appeared first in the *Medical Times and Gazette* in 1863 and 1864, and was twice reprinted in an enlarged form in 1865 and 1873. In 1872 he contributed an important article on inflammation to Samuel Cooper's *Dictionary of Practical Surgery*. A minor writing worthy of mention is his 'Construction and management of human habitations, considered in relation to the public health' (*Transactions of the Royal Institute of British Architects*, 1859–60).　　G. T. BETTANY, *rev.* RICHARD HANKINS

Sources *Medical Times and Gazette* (19 May 1883), 561–2 · *Medical Times and Gazette* (26 May 1883), 600–1 · *Medical Directory of Great Britain and Ireland* (1845) · Munk, *Roll* · b. cert. · *CGPLA Eng. & Wales* (1883) · m. cert.

Archives BL OIOC, family corresp. relating to India, MSS Eur. B 231

Likenesses R. B. Parkes, mezzotint, BM

Wealth at death £8853 19s. 8d.: probate, 27 June 1883, *CGPLA Eng. & Wales*

Drummond family (*per.* 1363–1518), nobility, was a Perthshire family of purely local importance until the mid-fourteenth century. Their rise began when *Margaret (*née* Drummond), widow of John Logie, became the second consort of King *David II in 1363. Thereafter David promoted the interests of his new wife's relatives, including her nephew **Sir Malcolm Drummond** (d. 1402?), who benefited from a series of grants of Perthshire lands. The Drummond family's growing importance at David's court undoubtedly explains the marriage of Malcolm's sister *Annabella, between 13 March 1366 and 31 May 1367, to the king's likely successor, John Stewart of Kyle, the future earl of Carrick and King *Robert III. The exact date of Drummond's own prestigious marriage to Isabella (d. 1408), daughter of William *Douglas, first earl of Douglas, is unknown, but may also have dated from the period of Queen Margaret's influence at the heart of royal government. The political ascendancy of the Drummond family was threatened first by David's decision to divorce Queen Margaret (who had failed to produce an heir in the late 1360s), and then by the king's own early death on 22 February 1371. Despite these setbacks, Drummond retained a number of powerful political allies after 1371, and in particular he enjoyed a close relationship with his two brothers-in-law, John Stewart, earl of Carrick, and James *Douglas, second earl of Douglas. In the 1380s, by now a knight, Sir Malcolm was an active participant in the border raids and Anglo-Scottish warfare promoted by Carrick and Douglas. In 1385 he received 400 livres tournais from a French war subsidy designed to encourage and reward Scottish noblemen involved in that year's joint Franco-Scottish assault on northern England. In August 1388 Drummond was a member of a raiding force led by the earl of Douglas which encountered and defeated a northern English army at Otterburn, and was said to have played a leading role in the battle.

The death of the second earl of Douglas at Otterburn had a profound effect on Sir Malcolm Drummond's career. Earl James died childless and Drummond, as the husband of James's sister, had a powerful claim to control the extensive estates, titles, and offices of the Douglas earls by right of his wife. Moreover, his claims were supported by Carrick, at that stage guardian of the kingdom on behalf of the incapacitated Robert II. Despite this powerful backing, Drummond lost out in the struggle for possession of the Douglas lordships to Archibald Douglas, lord of Galloway, who became third earl of Douglas in April 1389 on the basis of an earlier entail of the Douglas estates. Drummond stayed away from the council meeting which ruled against him, claiming to fear for his life, and may even have hoped to recover his losses with English support—a possibility ruled out by an Anglo-Scottish truce shortly afterwards. He was more successful in upholding his wife's claim to estates in the earldom of Mar, and by October 1393 at the latest he was accorded the courtesy title lord of Mar.

In the 1390s Drummond offered consistent support to the political ambitions of his nephew David *Stewart, earl of Carrick (later duke of Rothesay), the eldest son and heir of Robert III. In 1399 he and his sister Queen Annabella acquiesced in a coup which saw Rothesay established as lieutenant and guardian of the kingdom at the expense of Robert III. Late in 1401, however, having alienated many of the most powerful magnates in the kingdom, Rothesay was arrested on the orders of his uncle the duke of Albany, and imprisoned in Falkland Castle, where he died in March 1402. Drummond may well have been arrested at about the same time as his nephew, as part of a campaign to neutralize Rothesay's supporters. The chronicler Wyntoun records that Sir Malcolm was surprised and captured (by unspecified persons) and kept in close confinement under conditions which eventually caused his death. The exact date of his demise is unknown, but he was certainly dead by 8 November 1402.

There were no children of Drummond's marriage to Isabella Douglas, who in 1404 married Alexander Stewart, son of the earl of Buchan and a nephew of Robert III. Consequently the main line of the family descended through Malcolm's brother John Drummond of Cargill (d. 1424). John, his son Sir Walter (d. 1455), and his grandson Sir Malcolm (d. 1470), were once again of only local consequence. But the second Sir Malcolm's son **John Drummond**, first Lord Drummond (d. 1518), restored the family to national prominence, beginning in the 1470s. On 20 March 1474 King James III confirmed the resignation by Maurice Drummond of Concraig of his hereditary right to the offices of steward, coroner, and forester of the earldom of Strathearn in favour of his kinsman John Drummond of Cargill. The Strathearn offices had, however, been occupied since c.1437 by members of the Murray of Tullibardine family who immediately objected to the new grant. By September 1475 James III had reversed his decision and

revoked his earlier grant. Although John Drummond was occasionally to be found in royal service thereafter, most notably as one of the men appointed to negotiate a peace treaty and marriage alliance between James III and Richard III of England in 1484, his relationship with James never seems to have recovered from the events of 1474-5. On 29 January 1488, when he was facing intense political opposition, the king made John a lord of parliament with the title of first Lord Drummond. If the creation was designed to secure his loyalty to James's regime, then it was in vain. In the spring of 1488 Drummond joined the rebellion against James III which was nominally led by the latter's own son and heir, the future James IV. James III's death at the battle of Sauchieburn on 11 June paved the way for Prince James's supporters to dominate the new royal establishment, and Drummond immediately displaced Sir William Murray of Tullibardine as steward of Strathearn and organized the removal of Murray's kinsmen from royal lands in the earldom. A fierce feud ensued, culminating in 1490 in the massacre of twenty of Sir William's men in the kirk of Monzievaird by a party of Drummonds led by John's son David. Lord Drummond and Sir William Murray were briefly taken into royal custody in 1491 in an effort to contain the dispute, while David Drummond seems to have been executed by May 1492. Drummond's influence in James IV's administration may have waned briefly as a result of this dispute, but a revival of his fortunes during 1495 saw him appointed as royal justiciar in February (an office he held until 1501) and confirmed in the disputed Strathearn offices in October. His place in the young king's favour was secured by the romantic liaison between James and Drummond's daughter Margaret *Drummond who was resident in the royal castle of Stirling by June 1496, and who bore the king an illegitimate daughter in the following year.

John Drummond appears to have retained the goodwill of James IV (despite the ending of the king's liaison with Margaret in 1498) until the end of the king's reign and life at the battle of Flodden in 1513. One of the few Scottish lords of note to escape unscathed from Flodden, Drummond soon became embroiled in the faction-fighting of the minority of James V. He was identified with the pro-English faction headed by his own grandson Archibald Douglas, sixth earl of Angus, and supported Angus's marriage in 1514 to James IV's widow, Margaret. A reaction against Angus's influence saw John, duke of Albany, appointed as regent and tutor to the young James V. When Sir William Cumming, Lyon king of arms, was sent by Albany to summon Angus before the regency council, John Drummond struck him. Drummond was tried before parliament in July 1515 for, among other things, his violent conduct against the royal herald. Found guilty, he was forfeited and imprisoned in Blackness Castle. However, in 1516 he pledged his support to Albany's regime and on 22 November was pardoned and restored to some of his estates. Drummond died shortly thereafter, perhaps on or about 4 August 1518. He was reputedly buried in the kirk of Innerpeffray.

John Drummond was married before 3 February 1483 to Elizabeth Lindsay, thought to have been the daughter of Alexander *Lindsay, fourth earl of Crawford [see under Lindsay family, earls of Crawford]. They had several children. Three of their sons, Malcolm, William, and David, predeceased their father, as did William's eldest son, Walter. John was thus succeeded by his great-grandson David, who became second Lord Drummond. Of their daughters the most famous was Margaret, the mistress of James IV, who seems to have died c.1502. Another, Elizabeth, married George Douglas, master of Angus, as her second husband, and was the mother of the sixth earl of Angus.

S. I. BOARDMAN

Sources G. Burnett and others, eds., *The exchequer rolls of Scotland*, 23 vols. (1878–1908), vols. 1–14 · *APS*, 1124–1567 · J. M. Thomson and others, eds., *Registrum magni sigilli regum Scotorum / The register of the great seal of Scotland*, 11 vols. (1882–1914), vols. 1–3 · G. W. S. Barrow and others, eds., *Regesta regum Scottorum*, 6, ed. B. Webster (1982) · *CDS*, vol. 4 · J. Robertson and G. Grub, eds., *Illustrations of the topography and antiquities of the shires of Aberdeen and Banff*, 4 vols., Spalding Club, 17, 29, 32, 37 (1847–69) · Andrew of Wyntoun, *The orygynale cronykil of Scotland*, [rev. edn], ed. D. Laing, 3 vols. (1872–9) · W. Robertson, ed., *An index, drawn up about the year 1629, of many records of charters* (1798) · *CSP Scot. ser.*, 1509–89 · *LP Henry VIII*, vols. 1–2 · S. I. Boardman, *The early Stewart kings: Robert II and Robert III, 1371–1406* (1996) · N. Macdougall, *James III: a political study* (1982) · N. Macdougall, *James IV* (1989)
Archives NA Scot.

Drummond, Alexander (d. 1769), traveller, was the son of John Drummond (d. 1709) of Newton, merchant burgess of Edinburgh, and Mary Menzies. His elder brother was George *Drummond. The George Drummond of Newton said in the *Dictionary of National Biography* to be his father was in fact a kinsman for whom his father worked. Little is known of Alexander Drummond's early years. The *Travels* describe his journey via Harwich (where he embarked in May 1744) and Hellevoetsluis and across Europe to Venice. From there he sailed to various Greek islands including Delos, Cephalonia, Zante, and Crete, and on to Smyrna, where he established a lodge of freemasons (commemorated in some indifferent verse in the *Travels*). He reached Cyprus in March 1745 and used the island as a base for several years, during which he made excursions into Syria ('the desarts of Arabia') and as far as the Euphrates. His host for much of the time was the British consul, George Wakeman. The last letter in the *Travels* is dated 13 November 1750. Drummond was British consul at Aleppo between 1754 and 1756, and died at Edinburgh on 7 August 1769.

In 1753 George Drummond engaged the then impecunious Tobias Smollett to prepare his brother's manuscript letters for publication and the work appeared the following year, entitled *Travels through different cities of Germany, Italy, Greece, and several parts of Asia, as far as the banks of the Euphrates*. Smollett's editorial work undoubtedly influenced the writing of his own *Travels through France and Italy* (1766), and Drummond's careful register of the weather seems to have inspired Smollett's similar subsection in his own work. The nature and extent of Smollett's revisions

are not known, but they are likely to have been substantial since he received 100 guineas for the work. G. M. Kahrl (*Tobias Smollett: Traveler-Novelist*, 1945, 87) suggests that Smollett may have inserted some of the cross-references and allusions to Addison, Breval, Tournefort, and other travellers. The *Monthly Review* gave a long and enthusiastic notice of the impressive folio volume in 1754, praising Drummond's 'masculine' taste and 'sprightly' style; Smollett's editorship was not then known (*Monthly Review*, September 1754, 198–211). The title-page of the *Travels* advertises the authorship of 'Alexander Drummond, Esq: His Majesty's Consul at Aleppo', which would no doubt have increased the volume's attractions for the book-buying public. The *Travels* probably owe their elegant epistolary form to Smollett. Most of the letters are addressed to George Drummond ('dear brother'). Although the attractions of Italy were familiar to British travellers and readers, Greece, Syria, and Turkey were more novel territories. Drummond paints a lively picture of places and people, exhibiting particular interest in antique sculpture (especially the nude female variety) and comparative religion and culture. He displays the characteristic attitudes of many British travellers of his age: patriotic and protestant, he is critical of Catholic superstition, Turkish disrespect for antiquities, and the confinement of women in Italian nunneries or Eastern harems. His account is a quintessential travelogue of the mid-eighteenth century: it blends conventional objective description (the topics so described are depicted symbolically on the complex frontispiece) with hints of an inward subjectivity, and declares that 'every man is an original in his own remarks and observations' (Drummond, 2). The work contains some interesting plates; these are mostly architectural and archaeological, but also include charming sketches of Drummond's pet chameleon in locomotion and drawings of the Cypriot tarantula.

KATHERINE TURNER

Sources *Scots Magazine*, 31 (1769), 447 · A. Drummond, *Travels through different cities of Germany, Italy, Greece, and several parts of Asia* (1754) · *Court and City Register* (1753–8) · *The letters of Tobias Smollett*, ed. L. M. Knapp (1970), 27–8 · L. L. Martz, *The later career of Tobias Smollett* (1945), 11, 23, 72, 89 · private information (2004) [A. L. Foley] · M. Hook and others, *Lord Provost George Drummond, 1687–1766* (1987)
Archives BL, letter-books, Add. MSS 45932–45933

Drummond, Andrew (1688–1769), goldsmith and banker, was born at Machany, Perthshire, the great-great-grandson of James *Drummond, first Lord Maderty, and the son of Sir John Drummond (d. 1707) and his wife, Margaret, the daughter of Sir William Stewart of Innernytie. Little is known of his early life, though he had four elder brothers, of whom only William *Drummond, who succeeded as fourth viscount of Strathallan in 1711, survived to adulthood. A decree of forfeiture was passed against Drummond's father in 1690 for his attachment to the Stuarts, and he was imprisoned for a while in Stirling Castle; on proof that his mind was deranged, he was released on 28 July 1692.

Drummond was apprenticed to Colin McKenzie, a goldsmith of Parliament Close, Edinburgh, on 4 May 1705, but in 1712 he is recorded as practising his trade in London, at the sign of the Golden Eagle, Charing Cross. On 7 November 1716 he married Isabella (d. 13 Feb 1731), the daughter of Alexander Strahan or Strachan, a London-Scottish merchant; they had three sons and two daughters. Two of their children survived to adulthood: John (1723–1774), who married Charlotte Beauclerk; and Isabella (c.1720–1740).

In 1717 Drummond began to offer banking services in addition to his goldsmithing work, by which time he was the tenant of one of six newly constructed brick houses alongside Northumberland House. His business came to an abrupt halt on 3 October 1745, when the entries in his customer account ledger for that year were ruled off and balances calculated. A notice was placed in the press arranging to pay off his debts in two 'dividends' by March 1746. Tradition has it that the ledger was seized or inspected because Drummond was suspected of Jacobite sympathies, as his brother, Lord Strathallan, was a leading participant in the Jacobite rising of 1745. However, on 15 October 1745 a new ledger was started for those customers who wished to continue with him, although fewer than half of those named in the earlier ledger elected to do so. Drummond took his son John into partnership at that time, and his nephews Robert and Henry also began to work in the bank in 1749.

The banking business gradually recovered, and in 1760 Drummond moved into specially commissioned premises on the west side of Charing Cross (now Whitehall). He lived on the bank premises until 1729, when he purchased Stanmore House, Middlesex. In 1763 work began on the virtual reconstruction of the house to designs of John Vardy, and following Vardy's death in 1765 Sir William Chambers completed and added to the existing works. In 1755 Drummond also bought the family's former estate at Machany, which had been attaindered after the Jacobite rising.

Drummond died on 2 February 1769 at Stanmore House; a memorial to him was placed in Great Stanmore church. At the time of his death the bank was owned jointly with his son John and nephew Robert; it had more than 1500 accounts on its books and annual profits of over £10,000. The clientele included various titled and landed families, but the business was also noteworthy for the number of artists and craftsmen it served, including the painter Thomas Gainsborough, the sculptor Henry Cheere, the plasterer Joseph Rose, the architects Sir William Chambers and Henry Holland, and the landscape gardener Capability Brown. Another distinctive feature was the number of army agents who banked at Drummonds, including from the 1750s Drummond's nephew Henry *Drummond, who acted as agent to a number of regiments and obtained lucrative contracts as joint paymaster to the Royal Artillery and the British forces in North America.

A contemporary, John Ramsay of Ochtertyre, remembered Drummond's boast: 'I have done great things, and have almost everything I could desire. My son is married into a noble family, and I have planted a colony of Drummonds round Charing Cross which appears to thrive' (Allardyce, 304). PHILIP WINTERBOTTOM

Sources H. Bolitho and D. Peel, The Drummonds of Charing Cross (1967) · Royal Bank of Scotland, London, Drummonds Bank partnership papers · Scotland and Scotsmen in the eighteenth century: from the MSS of John Ramsay, esq., of Ochtertyre, ed. A. Allardyce, 2 (1888), 304
Archives Royal Bank of Scotland, London, Drummonds branch
Likenesses J. Reynolds, oils, 1762, priv. coll. · J. Zoffany, oils, 1766, Royal Bank of Scotland, London · J. Zoffany, oils, 1766, priv. coll. · J. Zoffany, group portrait, oils, after 1769 (with his family), Paul Mellon, Virginia · G. Halse, bust, 19th cent., Royal Bank of Scotland, London · J. B. Closterman, oils, Royal Bank of Scotland, London · oils (after T. Beach), Royal Bank of Scotland, London
Wealth at death wealthy; estate incl. Stanmore House, Middlesex; share of banking business

Drummond, Annabella. See Annabella (d. 1401).

Drummond, Dugald (1840–1912), railway engineer, was born on 1 January 1840 in Ardrossan, Ayrshire, the son of George Drummond, a permanent-way inspector on the Bowling to Balloch railway, and his wife, Christina Thomson. He had at least one brother, Peter *Drummond. In 1856 he commenced an engineering apprenticeship with Forrest and Barr of Glasgow. After gaining experience with his father's railway and with Peto, Brassey, and Betts at Birkenhead, he worked under Samuel Waite Johnson at the Cowlairs (Glasgow) works of the Edinburgh and Glasgow (later North British) Railway. In 1865 he became foreman erector at the Inverness workshops of the Highland Railway, under William Stroudley, and works manager in the following year. In 1870 he followed Stroudley, with whom he had developed a close friendship, when the latter moved to the London, Brighton, and South Coast Railway as locomotive and carriage superintendent, and Drummond became locomotive and carriage works manager of that railway.

In 1875 Drummond was appointed locomotive superintendent of the North British Railway, where he found the locomotive stock and workshops somewhat run down. He rapidly took steps to improve and re-equip the Cowlairs workshops and to introduce new passenger and freight locomotives of improved performance, initially closely following Stroudley's designs. He then introduced a new type of 4-4-0 express locomotive, with a leading bogie which gave a much smoother and safer ride over curved track at speed, and these ran for fifty years from their entry into service in 1876. This type of locomotive was repeated by him after he transferred to the Caledonian Railway in 1882 and was further developed by his successors on that railway for the next thirty years. Some of these locomotives took part in the railway 'race' from London to Aberdeen in 1895, when there was keen competition between the west and east coast routes for Anglo-Scottish passenger traffic, and averaged well over 60 m.p.h. from Carlisle to Aberdeen on severe gradients. Drummond also carried out extensive tests to improve the efficiency of his locomotives.

In 1890 Drummond resigned from the Caledonian Railway to establish an engineering works in Queensland,

Australia. This project was abortive and he returned to form the Glasgow railway engineering works, where industrial locomotives were built. In 1895 he was appointed to succeed William Adams as locomotive superintendent of the London and South Western Railway, where he had new and well-equipped locomotive workshops built in Eastleigh to replace the existing inadequate facilities in Nine Elms in London. He introduced new main-line and suburban passenger and freight locomotives developed from those he had designed in Scotland, which gave excellent results and had similarly elegant outlines, although his later and more powerful 4-6-0 type locomotives were less successful. He was a highly innovative engineer, introducing developments in boiler design and the use of locomotive exhaust steam for pre-heating the feed water.

Drummond was a forceful personality and could be dour and difficult, although fair in dealings with his men, who appreciated his locomotives and respected him personally. He was a member of the Institution of Civil Engineers and the Institution of Mechanical Engineers, becoming a Telford medallist of the former for his outstanding paper in 1897 on locomotive efficiency trials on the Caledonian Railway. He was married and had one son and four daughters. Drummond died at his home, Morves, South Bank, Surbiton, Surrey, on 7 November 1912, while still in office.　　　　　　　　GEORGE W. CARPENTER, rev.

Sources PICE, 195 (1913–14), 371–2 · Engineering (15 Nov 1912), 685 · C. S. Lake, 'Some C.M.E.s I have known', Railway Magazine, 89 (July–Aug 1943), 213–15 · H. Ellis, 'Famous locomotive engineers', Locomotive Carriage and Wagon Review (15 June 1938), 192–6

Archives London and South Western Railway | National Railway Museum, Drummond, 4-4-0 express locomotive

Drummond, Edward (1792–1843), civil servant, the second son of Charles Drummond, banker, of Charing Cross, and his wife, Frances Dorothy, second daughter of the Revd Edward Lockwood, was born on 30 March 1792, and in June 1814 became at an early age a clerk in the Treasury, where he was successively private secretary to the earl of Ripon, Canning, Wellington, and Peel. So highly did Wellington think of him that he spoke in the House of Lords of his satisfaction with Drummond's services. Having been seen travelling alone in Scotland in Peel's carriage and coming out of Peel's London house by Daniel Macnaghten (1815?–1865), a wood-turner of Glasgow, Drummond was shot by him in the back in mistake for Peel as he was walking towards Downing Street on 20 January 1843. Medical treatment of him may have been incompetent; he died at 9 a.m. on 25 January, at Charlton, near Woolwich, where he was buried on 31 January. Macnaghten was acquitted on the ground of insanity and the criteria for this judgement became known as the 'Macnaghten rules'.

　　　　　　　　J. A. HAMILTON, rev. H. C. G. MATTHEW

Sources GM, 2nd ser., 19 (1843), 320 [states Drummond died on 1 Jan.] · The Times (21 Jan 1843) · The Times (27 Jan 1843) · Gladstone, Diaries · C. S. Parker, ed., Sir Robert Peel: from his private papers, 3 vols. (1891–9) · [S. Dickson], Who killed Mr Drummond, the lead or the lancet? (1843)

Archives BL, Peel MSS

Drummond, (James) Eric, seventh earl of Perth (1876–1951), diplomatist, was born on 17 August 1876 at the White House, Fulford, near York, the eldest of three sons and two daughters of James David Drummond, tenth Viscount Strathallan (1839–1893), army officer, of Machany, Perthshire, and his second wife, Margaret (d. 1920), daughter of William Smythe, of Methven Castle, Perthshire. He had one half-brother and two half-sisters from his father's first marriage, to Ellen (d. 1873), daughter of Cuthbert B. Thornhill, of the Indian Civil Service. He succeeded to the earldom on 20 August 1937, on the death of his half-brother William Huntly Drummond, succeeding also to the titles Lord Drummond of Cargill and Stobhall, Lord Maderty, twelfth Viscount Strathallan, Lord Drummond of Cromlix, hereditary thegn of Lennox, hereditary steward of Menteith and Strathearn, and chief of clan Drummond.

Educated at Eton College, Drummond was captain of the Oppidans and won the prince consort's first French prize in 1895, the year he left. In April 1900 he entered the Foreign Office, where he served as private secretary to the parliamentary under-secretary, Lord Fitzmaurice, in 1906–8; précis writer to the foreign secretary, Sir Edward Grey, in 1908 and 1910–11; private secretary to the parliamentary under-secretary, Thomas McKinnon Wood, in 1908–10; private secretary to the prime minister, Herbert Asquith, in 1912–15; private secretary to the foreign secretary, Sir Edward Grey, in 1915–16; and private secretary to Grey's successor, A. J. Balfour, in 1916–18. He accompanied Balfour on a mission to the United States in 1917.

In 1919 Drummond was attached to the British delegation to the Paris peace conference, which drafted the League of Nations covenant. Because the league's secretary-general would play an important directing role, it was thought fitting that the office-holder should be an eminent statesman. None was available. Instead, on 5 May 1919, Drummond was appointed secretary-general. He was highly regarded by British and American leaders who knew him through his wartime work, and he had bolstered his reputation at the peace conference by his sincerity, grasp of detail, procedural knowledge, and detached approach to complicated and difficult questions.

Drummond had to create from scratch the multinational secretariat that serviced the league, and in so doing he chose carefully and well. He also bore in mind political considerations: appointees had to be acceptable to their home governments, and senior positions were quietly earmarked for nationals of leading states. As the administrative head of the league, Drummond was skilful and efficient. He read all important papers, often late into the evening, and returned them, with comments, within twenty-four hours. He was financially prudent and had an eye for detail. He was also open-minded and knew how to delegate, giving much latitude to heads of departments. He appeared distant and aloof to the lower echelons but was always approachable to higher officials, who valued his advice.

Contrary to myth Drummond was a politically very

(James) Eric Drummond, seventh earl of Perth (1876–1951), by Walter Stoneman, 1917

active secretary-general—but always behind the scenes. Scope for political initiative arose partly because league meetings were infrequent (each year the council held just three or four week-long meetings and the assembly met for roughly a month), and partly because permanent missions were in their infancy. He was also able to give a lead because he was in direct contact with policy makers and paid them visits; he knew their delegates to the league; he had contacts with non-governmental bodies; and senior secretariat officials acted as confidential channels of communication with members and non-members. He was thus privy to much confidential information and he never betrayed a confidence. He contributed to league discussions and readily made suggestions to governments on issues arising before the league, and foreign ministers often consulted him, not only on league matters. He was listened to because he gave sound advice and appeared more concerned with helping governments to find agreed solutions than with pushing his own specific policies. Sometimes there were complaints that he had trespassed on the prerogatives of states, but there was no serious friction: Drummond well understood that his only power was that of persuasion and that he was the servant of the member states.

Drummond also recognized that the league could be successful only to the extent that states were willing to use its machinery. Most crucially, as a collective security organization it needed the support of the great powers.

The absence of the USA meant that in this respect the league was severely weakened. After Japan invaded Manchuria in 1931, Drummond worked hard, but to no avail, at finding a diplomatic solution. Japan was intent on aggression and neither the USA nor leading league members felt able to act firmly.

Drummond's term as secretary-general had no legal time limit. In 1932 he gave notice of his intention to resign and did so on 30 June 1933. A United Nations secretary-general later described his own job as the most difficult in the world and several have stumbled at its political pitfalls. It is remarkable that Drummond departed amid universal regret and with a higher stature than in 1919. The friend and confidant of most of the leading statesmen of the day, he had firmly established the idea of an international civil service and made the secretary-generalship a vital international office.

Drummond now returned to the British Foreign Office (from which he had been seconded). He was keen to become ambassador at Washington, a post for which he had been a contender in 1919. The prime minister, Ramsay MacDonald, vetoed it (and also denied Drummond the permanent under-secretaryship of the Foreign Office and the ambassadorship at Paris). This was allegedly because MacDonald never forgave his fellow Scot's conversion to Roman Catholicism at the age of twenty-seven. Instead, Drummond became ambassador at Rome in October 1933.

When Mussolini invaded Abyssinia in 1935, Drummond was keenly aware of the dilemma confronting Britain. As a leading league member Britain was committed to upholding the covenant, but she was very worried about the German and Japanese threat and did not want to drive Mussolini into Hitler's arms. Personally, Drummond found the situation 'hateful'; the 'boasting, the posturing, the rampant nationalism, the gross misrepresentations of the British attitude, the absurd egotism and conceit … [were] enough to turn the least Anglo-Saxon stomachs' (Gelardi, 23, 114). However, he was sceptical about the usefulness of league sanctions and believed concessions by Abyssinia were a lesser evil than war with Italy. His conciliatory advice chimed with the thinking of policy makers in London, who agreed, after Abyssinia's annexation in 1936, that good Anglo-Italian relations were essential. Trying to implement that policy was a thankless and, in retrospect, futile endeavour. However, London much appreciated his services which included paving the way for, and concluding, the 1938 Anglo-Italian agreement. He had a personal friendship with Ciano and, thanks to his 'patience, even temper, good sense and transparent honesty of purpose' (The Times, 17 Dec 1951) he enjoyed good personal relations with Mussolini.

Drummond (now earl of Perth) left Rome in April 1939 and retired from the Foreign Office in May. He became director-general of the Ministry of Information on 3 September 1939 but resigned on 9 September on being appointed chief adviser on foreign publicity at the Ministry of Information, a position he held until July 1940. In

1941 he took his seat in the House of Lords and in 1946 became deputy leader of the Liberal Party in that house.

Drummond was brown-haired and of medium height and aristocratic bearing. A shy man who did not put on diplomatic airs, he disliked speech-making and his large acquaintance included few intimate friends. He enjoyed golf, bridge, and, above all, fishing. He was optimistic and had

> a pleasant sense of quiet humour, reflecting the general poise of his temperament. But he had no temptation to the dangers of the witty and memorable epigram. Nor did he have the kind of uncompromising precision of thought and language which sometimes handicaps a chairman or a negotiator who is seeking a solution through compromise. (*DNB*)

He was industrious, sensible, prudent, practical, tactful, discreet, discerning, resourceful, cautious, and circumspect. He was also 'far from being either as frank, or as simple, as he appeared' (Walters, 558). He was appointed CB in 1914, KCMG in 1916, and GCMG in 1934, was sworn of the privy council in 1933, and was awarded the Wateler peace prize in 1931. He also received honorary doctorates from Oxford and Liverpool universities.

A devout Roman Catholic, Drummond married on 20 April 1904 into a family of that faith, his wife being (Angela) Mary (1877–1965), younger daughter of Marmaduke Francis Constable-Maxwell, eleventh Baron Herries of Everingham Park, Yorkshire, and Terregles, Kirkcudbrightshire, and his wife, Angela Mary Charlotte Fitzalan-Howard, second daughter of the first Baron Howard of Glossop. There were three daughters of the marriage, Margaret Gwendolyn Mary (*b.* 1905), Angela Alice Maryel (*b.* 1912), and Gillian Mary (*b.* 1920), and one son, John David (*b.* 1907), who succeeded Drummond in his titles when he died of cancer at his home, Fyning House, Rogate, Midhurst, Sussex, on 15 December 1951.

LORNA LLOYD

Sources J. Barros, *Office without power: secretary-general Sir Eric Drummond, 1919–1933* (1979) • *DNB* • *The Times* (17 Dec 1951) • *The Guardian* (17 Dec 1951) • *FO List* (1933) • A. J. P. Gelardi, 'Sir Eric Drummond, Britain's ambassador to Italy and British foreign policy during the Italo-Abyssinian crisis of 1935–1936', MA Diss., Simon Fraser University, British Columbia, Canada, 1998 • D. N. Dilks, 'British reactions to Italian empire-building, 1936–39', *Imperialism: the British and Italian experiences compared. Proceedings of the second British-Italian historian's conference held at Catania, 2–4 October 1987*, ed. F. Serra and C. Seton-Watson (1989), 165–94 • F. P. Walters, *A history of the League of Nations*, 2nd edn (1969) • valedictory letter from Lord Halifax, 30 June 1939, PRO, R5264/1604/22 FO 371/23865 • b. cert. • d. cert. • D. T. Rotunda, 'The Rome embassy of Sir Eric Drummond, 16th earl of Perth, 1933–1939', PhD diss., U. Lond., 1972 • *WWW* • Burke, *Peerage* • *The Eton register*, 8 vols. (privately printed, Eton, 1903–32) • *CGPLA Eng. & Wales* (1952)

Archives BL, corresp. with Lord Cecil, Add. MSS 51110–51112 • Bodl. Oxf., corresp. with Gilbert Murray • Bodl. Oxf., corresp. with Sir Horace Rumbold • Bodl. RH, corresp. with Lord Lugard • CAC Cam., corresp. with Philip Noel-Baker • CAC Cam., corresp. with E. L. Spears • CUL, corresp. with Sir Samuel Hoare • HLRO, letters to David Lloyd George • NA Scot., corresp. with Lord Lothian, GD40 • PRO, corresp. of Lord Robert Cecil, FO 800/195–8 • PRO, corresp. of Sir Eric Drummond, FO 800/329, 383–5 | FILM BFI NFTVA, news footage

Likenesses W. Stoneman, two photographs, 1917–39, NPG [*see illus.*] • photograph, 1938, repro. in *New York Times* (17 Dec 1938) • G. Kelly, portrait, Palais des Nations, Geneva, Switzerland; repro. in Barros, *Office without power*, 4, 4141

Wealth at death £28,870 16s. 11d.: probate, 9 Feb 1952, *CGPLA Eng. & Wales*

Drummond [*née* Gibson; *other married name* Simpson], **Flora McKinnon** (1878–1949), suffragette, was born on 4 August 1878 at 12 Elizabeth Ann Street, Manchester, the daughter of Francis Gibson, a tailor, and his wife, Sarah (*née* Cook). In her early childhood, Flora's family returned to the Isle of Arran where she attended high school. She left at fourteen and took up a summer post as telegraphist, returning to study at a civil service school in Glasgow in winter. There she qualified as a postmistress, but was unable to follow this career owing to new regulations which raised the height standard to 5 feet 2 inches, an inch above her height. Instead, she took further classes in shorthand and typing, funded by her father's relatives. She achieved a prestigious Society of Arts certificate, but remained bitterly disappointed at the loss of her chosen career and angry at the regulation which she felt discriminated against women because of their lower height average.

As a young woman, Flora Gibson was a keen athlete and a leader among her peers. On 26 September 1898 she married Joseph Percival Drummond (*b.* 1876/7), a journeyman upholsterer from Manchester who was a local celebrity in her small community following his fall from a steamer during a holiday trip to Arran. The couple settled in Manchester, and became involved with the socialist culture surrounding the Independent Labour Party (ILP), the Fabian Society, and the *Clarion* newspaper. Flora Drummond took several short-term posts in local factories to share and understand the conditions of local women workers, but stopped when poor trade left Joseph unemployed and herself the main wage earner; she then worked as manager of the Oliver Typewriter Company.

In October 1905 Manchester socialists organized a series of indignation meetings to protest at the imprisonment of Christabel Pankhurst and Annie Kenney, ILP activists who, as members of the Women's Social and Political Union (WSPU), had been arrested following their interruption of a local Liberal rally. Flora Drummond attended one of these meetings in Stevenson Square, where she joined the WSPU. She quickly became part of its leadership, forming an especially close friendship with Annie, whom she followed to London in 1906. There, Flora Drummond put her secretarial talents at the disposal of the WSPU. From December 1906 the WSPU employed her as a salaried organizer.

Flora Drummond proved popular and innovative in this role. Her small, rotund figure and her Scottish origins gave her the nicknames Bluebell and the Precocious Piglet, and her consistently cheerful manner won a sympathetic audience as she worked to build the WSPU's London branches. Supporters and opponents consistently praised her witty speeches. Outdoor meetings in working-class

Flora McKinnon Drummond (1878–1949), by unknown photographer, after 1907

districts, to which she was used from her socialist work, were her forte. She initiated a group of suffrage bicycle scouts as a mobile propaganda corps who paraded and delivered leaflets on bicycles, a technique borrowed from the *Clarion* movement. She also demonstrated a talent for original forms of protest, bursting into 10 Downing Street, finding subterranean entrances to parliament, and dancing a highland fling outside Holloway prison. Once she hired a motor launch and moored on the River Thames opposite the terrace of the House of Commons to harangue members taking afternoon tea.

In June 1908 Flora Drummond was placed in charge of organizing processions for 'Women's Sunday', the largest franchise demonstration to date. Her flair and enthusiasm earned her the nickname General, which she proudly adopted. From this point, she was rarely given any other name, and completed her military persona by regularly sporting a peaked cap, epaulettes, and a sash embroidered 'general', all in the WSPU colours of purple, white, and green. A skilled horsewoman, she often rode at the head of WSPU processions in her regalia, or reviewed her suffragette 'troops' on horseback.

Flora Drummond's central role in the WSPU was acknowledged when she was summonsed along with Mrs Pankhurst and Christabel in October 1908 for distributing

a leaflet urging the general public to 'help the suffragettes to rush the House of Commons'. She and Mrs Pankhurst received heavy sentences of three months, but Flora was released after nine days when it became apparent to the authorities that she was pregnant, and not in good health. The child was named Keir Hardie Drummond in honour of the Labour leader and of his parents' socialist beliefs. Motherhood did nothing to curb Flora's frantic public schedule, but as militancy became more violent her role was increasingly one of organizer rather than participant. This was not unusual; it was essential to retain a core of experienced workers to direct suffragettes in campaigns which became daily more dangerous. Flora's flair for organizing working women made her more valuable in the field than in prison, and she conducted several national tours to recruit women workers. She remained close to the Pankhursts and was again summonsed on conspiracy charges as one of the WSPU leadership in June 1913. This time ill health and an urgent, unspecified operation saved her from a lengthy prison sentence. She remained willing to face arrest, however, and also undertook a hunger strike in 1914.

When war broke out in 1914, Flora Drummond's loyalty to Christabel and Emmeline Pankhurst meant that she stopped suffrage work and joined their anti-German crusade. Working women still remained her favourite targets for propaganda. She toured the country reviewing lines of female munitions workers in her 'general's' regalia, often accompanied by former adversaries including Lloyd George, whom she now enthusiastically supported. However, as the WSPU became increasingly anti-Bolshevist, she rejected the last vestiges of her socialist past which she now dismissed as 'sentimental'. When the war ended she was one of the few former suffragettes who attempted to continue the popular, jingoistic campaigning which the WSPU had followed from 1914 to 1918. With Elsie Bowerman, another former suffragette, she founded the Women's Guild of Empire, an organization aimed at furthering a sense of patriotism in working-class women and defeating such socialist manifestations as strikes and lock-outs. The guild, which continued working throughout the Second World War, claimed 40,000 members in more than 30 branches at its peak in 1925. In 1926, in an echo of her WSPU work, Flora led 20,000 of its supporters through the streets of London to a meeting at the Albert Hall against a barrage of jeers from socialist protesters. Yet despite the size of the guild, it was as a suffragette that Flora remained best-known. She presided at the unveiling of Mrs Pankhurst's statue in March 1930 where she proved her famous wit remained intact, informing the prime minister that 'half the women here are gaol birds!' (*The Guardian*, 18 Jan 1949).

Although a very public figure, Flora kept her private life concealed. In 1922 she and Joseph Drummond divorced, and later the same year she married Alan Simpson, a marine engineer, but she retained the name Drummond in public life. Simpson, about whom little is known, was killed by a bomb in 1944. Flora herself died on 17 January

1949 at Carradale, Argyll. She was determined and independent to the last: her death followed a stroke, brought on by the effort of attempting to build herself a new house, single-handed, on the shore at Carradale.

KRISTA COWMAN

Sources *The Times* (18 Jan 1949) · *New York Times* (18 Jan 1949) · *Daily Herald* (18 Jan 1949) · E. S. Pankhurst, *The suffragette movement: an intimate account of persons and ideals* (1931); another edn (1935); repr. of 1st edn (1977) · D. Mitchell, *The fighting Pankhursts* (1967) · O. Banks, *The biographical dictionary of British feminists*, 1 (1985) · A. Raeburn, *The militant suffragettes* (1973) · b. cert. · m. cert.
Archives Women's Library, London, biographical clippings | FILM BFI NFTVA, news footage
Likenesses photograph, after 1907, Museum of London, Suffragette Fellowship collection [*see illus.*] · F. Lion, oils, 1936, Scot. NPG · photographs, Museum of London, Suffragette Fellowship collection; repro. in D. Atkinson, *The suffragettes in pictures* (1996)
Wealth at death £780 11s. 6d.: confirmation, 6 Sept 1949, *CCI*

Drummond, George (1687–1766), accountant-general of excise in Scotland and local politician, was born on 27 June 1687, probably at Edinburgh, although in some accounts his place of birth is given as Newton Castle in Perthshire, where his father had business and family connections. He was one of at least three children of the factor and merchant John Drummond (d. 1709), record having survived of a sister, May *Drummond, and a younger brother, Alexander *Drummond. His mother died in 1736. He attended the Royal High School, Edinburgh, from 1699 to 1704. On leaving the school he was employed by Sir John Clerk of Penicuik, one of the Scottish commissioners negotiating the terms of the treaty for the proposed parliamentary union of Scotland with England, who commented in his *Memoirs* that Drummond was his 'amanuensis' in drawing up two reports to the Scottish parliament at the time; 'he was then about eighteen years of age, and he wrote a good hand' (*Memoirs*, 54).

Drummond's work with Clerk introduced him into government circles: when the excise tax was introduced into Scotland after the treaty of union, as part of the integration of the Scottish Treasury with that for England, he was appointed to the post of accountant-general of excise in Scotland. He remained in public employment for the rest of his life, although he did engage in trade. His father had been a burgess and guild brother of Edinburgh, which allowed him to trade, and his younger brother Alexander pursued a career as a merchant. Drummond himself was a member of a co-partnership formed in 1712 with James Nimmo, another Edinburgh merchant and civil servant, and John Campbell of Skipnish, who was a brother of the Glasgow merchant and MP Daniel Campbell of Shawfield. This firm effectively ceased trading about 1720, and for many years Drummond 'was dunned by creditors and threatened with ruin' (Shaw, 75). When he became involved with the project of founding a public medical infirmary in Edinburgh in 1725, it was by making a suggestion

> that the owners of a fishery company that Drummond had managed were about to dissolve their business but could be persuaded to sell and sign their stock certificates over to a newly established fund created for the specific purpose of opening a voluntary hospital. (Risse, 26)

George Drummond (1687–1766), by Sir George Chalmers, 1764

This led to a public appeal with the support of the magistrates of Edinburgh, the Bank of Scotland, and the Scottish College of Physicians to raise the £2000 to purchase the stock.

Drummond had become an adult at the time of the treaty of union between Scotland and England, had entered public employment as a result of that treaty, and thereafter devoted his life to its defence. At the time of both the Jacobite risings in Scotland, in 1715 and 1745, this involved risking his life in military activity at a time when few other members of the public in Edinburgh, whatever their politics, were willing to follow his example. He was at the battle of Sheriffmuir in 1715 when the Jacobite army was prevented from progressing beyond the River Forth, and in 1745 his efforts to organize an active defence of Edinburgh against the approaching Jacobite army exceeded those of any other inhabitant, although they were ultimately unsuccessful and he had to flee the city.

In the aftermath of both rebellions Drummond was thus one of the few citizens of Edinburgh undoubtedly loyal to the interests of the Hanoverian monarchy and its government, which led to his election to the town council. Like all Scots burghs at the time, outgoing members of the council elected their successors, which effectively confined local political power to a small group of merchants and craftsmen open to direct influence by the representatives of the government. Drummond first became a member of the town council in 1716. In 1717 he was made treasurer, in 1722 he became dean of guild (an office involving approval of building undertaken in the town), and in 1725 he was elected lord provost for the first time. This success in local politics was matched in public employment. As part of government attempts to improve tax collection in Scotland Drummond was made a member of an expanded board of customs in 1723, having previously served as a commissioner of excise.

It was as lord provost of Edinburgh that Drummond became closely involved with the infirmary project on the model of the Westminster Infirmary which had opened in London in 1720. This also brought him into contact with the College of Edinburgh, which operated largely under the patronage of the town council of Edinburgh. He also even at this early date had thoughts of encouraging the expansion of Edinburgh beyond its medieval boundaries, drawing on ideas which were first put forward in 1688 in a charter granted to Edinburgh by James VII but never confirmed by a Scottish parliament. Thomas Somerville recorded in his memoirs a conversation he recalled having with Drummond in which the latter declared that the expansion of the city north towards its port of Leith was an object he had kept in mind 'since the year 1725, when I was first elected Provost' (Somerville, 47–8).

Under Drummond's leadership the public subscription in aid of the infirmary was completed and a house was opened with six beds in Robertson's Close in association with the Scottish Royal College of Physicians and the professors of medicine at the College of Edinburgh. By 1738 the foundation stone of a larger purpose-built Royal Infirmary of Edinburgh was laid, in which the Edinburgh College of Surgeons co-operated with the Royal College of Physicians and the town council. Drummond also came to co-operate closely with John Monro, sometime deacon of the Incorporation of Surgeons on the town council of Edinburgh, who had studied at Leiden and had sent his son there to be trained in medicine. With Drummond's support, Monro secured the election of his son Alexander by the town council to the college's chair of anatomy, thereby founding a dynasty of father, son, and grandson that held the position into the nineteenth century. Drummond and Monro set out to create a medical faculty at Edinburgh's college on the model of Leiden and other Dutch universities and they succeeded. By the time of Drummond's death wealthy students from England and beyond travelled to Edinburgh in preference to the Netherlands or London for a medical education which was of high quality yet economic in cost compared to other centres. On this success others built to expand the reputation of the college.

Yet although Drummond had exerted considerable influence in the Scottish civil service and the Edinburgh town council, by 1727 he was no longer a member of the council, although he was made a member of the board of trustees for the encouragement of fisheries and manufactures established by the British government in Edinburgh that year to administer a modest fund intended for economic development, and at the same time he also became a founder member of the board of directors of the new Royal Bank of Scotland. What had happened was that he had fallen foul of the Scottish political establishment. His Edinburgh career after 1715 had benefited from the support of the second duke of Argyll, victor over the Jacobites

in 1715 and the leader of a powerful political interest in Scotland. English political pressure to reform the Scottish tax system had led to his promotion in 1723, but also to widespread public demonstrations in 1725 against the extension of the English malt tax to Scotland. Drummond travelled to London in 1726 as representative of the Scottish convention of royal burghs to petition parliament for Scottish exemption from this tax without consulting Scottish politicians working with the ministry of Sir Robert Walpole, such as the earl of Ilay, younger brother of the second duke of Argyll. Ilay wrote to his agent in Edinburgh, Lord Milton, that 'our Scotch members are very angry and think it impertinent in George to undertake what is their business' (Shaw, 126).

Drummond was a unionist and a Hanoverian but not enough of a follower of the Argyll interest in Scotland to earn the complete trust of Ilay, its principal operative. Drummond's manuscript diary, the only surviving personal manuscript relating to him, records in 1738 an entry for 13 June that indicates considerable misgivings about 'great men', written after attending the second duke of Argyll on a visit to Edinburgh.

> I wish to behave wisely and with becoming respect to great men—but neither their frowns nor smiles stand with me in that point of light they have done. I see future things in faiths views so strong, that I view great men with pity and concern, because I am afraid they do not mind them. (Edinburgh University Library, Laing MSS)

This indicates a degree of strong religious commitment which the great and the good clearly sometimes found hard to take. The future fourth duke of Argyll, John Campbell of Mamore, referred to him (in 1747) as 'that coxcomb', 'that vain prig' (Shaw, 89). By 1737, at a time of renewed unrest in Edinburgh, and following several failures to consult the Argyll political interest in making Scottish customs appointments as a commissioner, Ilay got Drummond sacked. The period of personal crisis recorded in Drummond's surviving diary coincides with this period of professional uncertainty and its financial implications. Eventually a 'humble epistle', as Ilay recorded it, led to a demotion to the board of excise rather than a complete lack of employment. Drummond remained a commissioner of excise in Scotland for the rest of his life.

Drummond recovered from this political humiliation eight years later when, in the aftermath of the Jacobite rebellion, he was chosen as lord provost of Edinburgh for a second time, but on this occasion by a free poll of the burgesses (taxpayers) of Edinburgh. He was almost the only creditable candidate known for his loyalty to the union and the Hanoverian monarchy at a time when preparations were already under way to put his predecessor, Archibald Stewart, on trial for treason in the light of the abject surrender of the city to the Jacobite army in 1745. Drummond was a witness for the prosecution at the trial. There was even talk of making him MP for Edinburgh, but again his lack of respect for Scottish 'great men' limited his success. His failure to gain election to parliament did not prevent him from embarking on a late and eminently successful career as a leader of the town council of Edinburgh and from making efforts to modernize the town. He was elected lord provost a further four times, from 1750 to his last election in 1762—the constitution of the burgh prohibiting continuous service as lord provost. He remained a member of the council throughout, however, serving on it from the age of sixty until he was seventy-seven. In 1755 his fourth marriage brought him enough wealth to purchase a small estate on land that is now part of the New Town of Edinburgh, which he named Drummond Lodge, and where his entertainments enabled him to encourage plans for civic development. These included the construction of a modern Royal Exchange on the High Street with the help of an act of parliament, begun in 1753, and attempts to extend the boundaries of Edinburgh that would not be successful until after his death. Under the influence of his son-in-law the Revd John Jardine, he became sympathetic to a more moderate brand of Presbyterianism which established its influence in the town's kirks and its colleges under the leadership of Jardine and his friend William Robertson. He was a keen mason, and as grand master of the Scottish freemasons laid the cornerstone of both the Royal Exchange in 1753 and, a decade later in 1763, the north bridge intended to encourage suburban development northwards.

Drummond married four times. His first marriage, in 1707, was to Mary Campbell (d. 1718), the daughter of Mungo Campbell of Burnbank, Perthshire; they had five children, three of whom died young. His second marriage, in 1721, was to Catherine Campbell (d. 1732), the daughter of Sir James Campbell of Aberuchill, his colleague on the board of customs; the couple had nine children, eight of whom survived. Six years after her death Drummond wrote in his diary of his 'dear Partner carried away from me'. In 1739 he married Hannah Parson (d. 1742), a widow of some means, after an introduction effected by a mutual female acquaintance concerned at Drummond's uncertainty over his ability to meet his financial and family commitments. His fourth and final marriage was in 1755 to Elizabeth Green, an English widow and a member of the Society of Friends, who brought a fortune of £20,000. Drummond died of an unspecified illness at his home, Drummond Lodge, on 4 December 1766. He was buried in Canongate churchyard on 8 December, and a memorial concert was held in his honour at St Cecilia's Hall in the Old Town by the Edinburgh Musical Society on 19 December.   ALEXANDER MURDOCH

Sources G. Drummond, diary, 1738, U. Edin. L., special collections division, MS Dc. 1.83, vol. 2 · M. Hook and others, *Lord Provost George Drummond, 1687–1766* (1987) · A. C. Chitnis, 'Provost Drummond and the origins of Edinburgh medicine', *The origins and nature of the Scottish Enlightenment*, ed. R. H. Campbell and A. S. Skinner (1982), 86–97 · J. S. Shaw, *The management of Scottish society, 1707–1764: power, nobles, lawyers, Edinburgh agents and English influences* (1983) · W. Baird, 'George Drummond: an eighteenth century lord provost', *Book of the Old Edinburgh Club*, 4 (1911), 1–54 · T. C. Smout, *Provost Drummond* (1978) · A. J. Youngson, *The making of classical Edinburgh, 1750–1840* (1966) · A. Murdoch, 'The importance of being Edinburgh: management and opposition in Edinburgh politics, 1746–1784', *SHR*, 62 (1983), 1–16 · T. Somerville, *My own life and times, 1741–1814*, ed. W. Lee (1861) · *Autobiography of the Rev. Dr. Alexander Carlyle … containing memorials of the men and events of his time*, ed. J. H. Burton (1860); repr. as *Anecdotes and characters of the times*, ed. J. Kinsley (1973) · *Memoirs of the life of Sir John Clerk of Penicuik*, ed. J. M. Gray, Scottish History Society, 13 (1892) · R. Scott, 'The politics and administration of Scotland, 1725–48', PhD diss., U. Edin., 1982 · G. B. Risse, *Hospital life in Enlightenment Scotland: care and teaching at the Royal Infirmary of Edinburgh* (1986) · R. B. Sher, *Church and university in the Scottish Enlightenment: the moderate literati of Edinburgh* (1985) · A. Murdoch, *'The people above': politics and administration in mid-eighteenth-century Scotland* (1980)
Archives NA Scot., corresp., papers · U. Edin. L., diaries | BL, corresp. with duke of Newcastle, Add. MSS 32729–32894 *passim* · NL Scot., corresp. with Duncan Forbes · U. Nott. L., corresp. with Henry Pelham
Likenesses J. Alexander, oils, 1752, Royal Infirmary of Edinburgh · G. Chalmers, oils, 1764, Scot. NPG [*see illus.*] · A. Bell, mezzotint (after J. Alexander, 1752), BM, NPG · Nollekens, bust, Royal Infirmary of Edinburgh

Drummond, Sir George Alexander (1829–1910), entrepreneur and politician in Canada, was born in Edinburgh on 11 October 1829, the son of George Drummond, a contractor, and his wife, Margaret Pringle. He was educated at the high school and university in Edinburgh. In 1854 he emigrated to Canada at the invitation of John Redpath, his brother-in-law, to become technical manager and later partner in John Redpath & Son of Montreal, sugar refiners. In 1857 he married Redpath's daughter Helen. They had two daughters and five sons, including Sir Huntly Redpath Drummond, who succeeded his father in the sugar business. In 1879 the firm became the Canada Sugar Refining Company with Drummond as its first president.

Drummond entered politics in 1872, when he unsuccessfully contested the seat of Montreal West as an advocate of a protectionist trade policy. The defeat of this policy brought crisis to Redpath & Son, but, when it gained favour after 1878, Drummond's advice was sought by politicians and he became a spokesman for the Montreal business community. As president of the Montreal board of trade (1886–8) he persuaded the government to assume the debt resulting from the deepening of the St Lawrence to make it navigable to ocean-going vessels. He gained further influence as director (1882), vice-president (1887), and finally president (1905) of the Bank of Montreal. His appointment to these prestigious positions showed the growing influence of manufacturers within the bank. He became involved in many other enterprises closely linked with the bank, which under his influence expanded and favoured loans to industry. From 1888 until his death he was senator in the parliament of Canada. He was created KCMG in 1904 and CVO in 1908.

Drummond took a keen interest in civic affairs: he was a benefactor to the Royal Edward Institute for the prevention of tuberculosis and endowed a home in Montreal for the dying. A successful and discriminating collector, he built up one of the most important private collections of European art in Canada. In later life he and his second wife, Grace Julia, the daughter of A. D. Parker of Montreal, whom he married in 1884 after the death of his first wife, spent much time at their country house, Huntlywood, near Montreal, with their two sons, breeding animals and playing golf. He suffered from a heart complaint from about 1908 and died in Montreal on 2 February 1910. He was buried in Mount Royal cemetery. He was one of the city's foremost entrepreneurs in a formative period of its history. ANDREW MACPHAIL, *rev.* ELIZABETH BAIGENT

Sources *DCB*, vol. 13 · private information (1912) · H. J. Morgan, ed., *The Canadian men and women of the time*, 2nd edn (1912) **Likenesses** R. Harris, priv. coll. · G. Reid, priv. coll. · Trondetski, priv. coll. · P. Troubetskoy, portrait, National Gallery of Canada, Ottawa · J. Walker, Mount Royal Club, Montreal, Canada **Wealth at death** £6718 15s.: administration with will, 29 Dec 1910, *CGPLA Eng. & Wales* · £80: confirmation, 29 July 1910, *CCI* · valuable estate in Canada

Drummond, George Henry Charles Francis Malcolm, **Viscount Forth** (1834–1861), dipsomaniac, was born on 13 May 1834, in Naples, the only surviving child of George Drummond (1807–1902), soldier, and his first wife, the Countess Rapp, *née* Baroness Albertine von Rothberg Rheinweiler Coligni, (*d.* 1842). In 1853 his father was restored as fifth earl of Perth and second earl of Melfort, but failed to recover the Drummond Castle estates from the Willoughby de Eresby family. From this date George Henry Drummond took the title Viscount Forth. He joined the 42nd highlanders in December 1853, and reached the Crimea on 14 September 1854. At the battle of the Alma (20 September) he carried the regimental colours. He served on trench and picket duty before requesting leave to sell out as soon as Sevastopol was taken. He then clashed with his commanding officer, Lieutenant-Colonel D. A. Cameron. By Forth's account, having not eaten for twenty-four hours, he refused to accompany a covering party until he had dined. Cameron, however, charged him with cowardice or insubordination. Forth resigned his commission on 17 October 1854. Detrimental versions of this incident circulated widely.

Forth married on 24 October 1855, at St Peter's Church, Pimlico, Harriet Mary (1836–1868), daughter of the Hon. Adolphus Capel. They lived with her parents at Wroughton in Wiltshire, where Forth soon manifested delirium tremens. He was violent and abusive to his wife, and threatened to contract syphilis so as to infect her and their only child, a son (*b.* 1856). She separated from him in 1858, and in 1860 petitioned for divorce on the grounds of his cruelty and adultery. After the queen's proctor intervened (1861) to prevent her suit on the grounds of her adultery with Edward Cholmeley Dering, Sir Cresswell Cresswell ruled that a wife 'guilty of adultery' could not petition for relief on account of cruelty (*The Times*, 19 April 1861, 11d). Shortly afterwards Forth (who wished to avoid his creditors in London) settled at the Spa Hotel in Gloucester under the name of Captain Drummond, together with a woman who passed as his wife. She fell ill after delivering a daughter on 19 September 1861, and was devotedly nursed by Forth in a hotel room. Following her death on 8 October of that year he raved with grief, drank three-quarters of a pint of brandy, and swallowed a half bottle of laudanum, dying at the hotel from its effects

after a few hours. A verdict of suicide was recorded. Forth was buried at Gloucester. The lives of his widow and son also ended miserably young.

RICHARD DAVENPORT-HINES

Sources *GM*, 3rd ser., 11 (1861), 576–7 · *Annual Register* (1861), 201 · *The Times* (23 April 1855) · *The Times* (29 May 1855) · *The Times* (19 April 1861) · *The Times* (11 Oct 1861) · *The Times* (12 Oct 1861) · [G. Arthur], *Some letters from a man of no importance, 1895–1914* (1928), 140–41 · GEC, *Peerage*

Drummond, Sir Gordon (1772–1854), army officer, fourth son of Colin Drummond, paymaster-general of the British forces at Quebec, and the maternal grandson of Robert Oliphant of Rossie, Scotland, was born at Quebec, Lower Canada, on 27 September 1772. He entered the army as an ensign in September 1789, joining the 1st (Royal Scots) regiment in Jamaica. He was soon transferred to the 41st regiment, becoming a lieutenant in March 1791 and a captain in January 1792. After being promoted major of the 23rd regiment in January 1794, he was made a lieutenant-colonel of the 8th (King's Liverpool) regiment on 1 March 1794. At Guadeloupe in June 1794, Drummond led the brave but ultimately futile resistance of the 43rd regiment at Fort Fleur d'Épée against an overwhelming French attack. Later in the year he led the 8th regiment in the Netherlands, taking part in the winter retreat of 1794–5, having distinguished himself at the siege of Nijmegen. In late 1795 he served in Sir Ralph Abercromby's campaign in the West Indies.

In 1799, after having been promoted colonel on 1 January 1798, Drummond accompanied Abercromby to the Mediterranean. After a brief period in Minorca, the 8th regiment formed part of Major-General Cradock's brigade in Egypt. Drummond distinguished himself throughout this campaign, particularly at the capture of Cairo, and then of Alexandria. When the campaign was over the 8th served in Malta and then Gibraltar. In 1804 he left his regiment to take command of a brigade in England. On 1 January 1805 he was promoted major-general, and in May he assumed command of a division in Jamaica; his old comrade Sir Eyre Coote was governor and commander-in-chief of that colony until August 1807.

In December 1808 Drummond was transferred to serve in Canada, where he was promoted lieutenant-general on 4 June 1811, which made him second in command to Sir George Prevost. He played an important role on the Canadian frontier during the Anglo-American War, assuming command in Upper Canada in December 1813. During that year the inadequate British fleet on the Great Lakes had suffered several setbacks. However, on 29–30 December Drummond led a column of 1500 men south down the Niagara River, burning the city of Buffalo and the Black Rock naval yard. During 1814, having been reinforced by regiments recently freed from the Peninsula, he achieved further successes on the Niagara front. On 25 July, at the battle of Lundy's Lane near Niagara Falls, his force of under 3000 men clashed with the 2600 battle-hardened troops of General Jacob Brown. The fighting lasted five hours and ended at midnight, when the Americans fell back on Fort Erie with heavy losses; but the ferocity of the battle may be judged from the British casualties, which amounted to 878 men killed, wounded, and missing.

Drummond next besieged the enemy's headquarters at Fort Erie and actually captured it on 25 August, when a massive explosion forced his troops to evacuate it. The siege resumed, and on 18 September an American sortie from the fort was repulsed by him at heavy cost to his force: 609 losses in all. Eventually, on 6 November, the position was abandoned by the Americans. Peace was made with the United States in 1815, but the efforts of the army, which had wiped out the disgrace of the defeats of 1813, were not forgotten, and Drummond was made a KCB on 2 January 1815.

Drummond returned to England in 1815, and after being made colonel of the 97th regiment in 1814, the 88th in 1819, the 71st in 1824, and the 49th in 1829, and being promoted general in 1825, he was transferred in 1846 to the colonelcy of his old regiment, the 8th, which had distinguished itself on the Niagara front in 1814. He was made a GCB in 1827. He married Margaret Russell (*d.* 1842), eldest daughter of William Russell of Brancepeth Castle, co. Durham; they had two sons and one daughter. Drummond died at his home, 25 Norfolk Street, Park Lane, London, on 10 October 1854, aged eighty-two.

H. M. STEPHENS, *rev.* S. KINROSS

Sources Fortescue, *Brit. army*, vols. 4, 9–10 · R. E. Dupuy and T. N. Dupuy, *The Collins encyclopedia of military history*, 4th edn (1993) · J. Haydn, *The book of dignities: containing rolls of the official personages of the British empire* (1851) · A. B. Rodger, *The war of the second coalition: 1798–1801, a strategic commentary* (1964) · J. Philippart, ed., *The royal military calendar*, 3 vols. (1815–16) · *GM*, 2nd ser., 42 (1854), 625 · Boase, *Mod. Eng. biog.*

Archives NA Canada, letter-book

Drummond, Henry (*c.*1730–1795), banker, was born about 1730, the son of William *Drummond, fourth viscount of Strathallan (1690–1746), and his wife, Margaret (1692–1773), the daughter of Lord William Murray, later Lord Nairne. He was one of at least thirteen children. In 1744, with his brother Robert, he was entrusted to the care of his uncle Andrew *Drummond (1688–1769). His father, who had taken part in the 1715 Jacobite rising, joined Prince Charles Edward Stuart in 1745 and commanded the Jacobite forces in Scotland during the period of the advance into England; he was killed at the battle of Culloden in April 1746.

Henry Drummond was employed in his uncle's banking business in Charing Cross, London, from 1749, and during the Seven Years' War he acted as agent to the 42nd (the Black Watch), 46th, 87th, and 89th regiments of foot. In 1763 he was financial agent for New Jersey, and from 1764 he was associated with the army agent Richard *Cox (1718–1803). He went into partnership with Cox from premises in Craig's Court, Whitehall, in 1765. The two men acted as joint paymasters to the Royal Artillery from 1766 and by 1771 had eighteen regiments on their books. From 1767 Drummond was also involved in the contract for the payment of the British forces in North America, and in 1770 replaced his cousin John (1723–1774) in the partnership with Thomas Harley (1730–1804).

Henry Drummond (*c.*1730–1795), by Thomas Gainsborough, *c.*1775–80

Drummond joined his brother Robert and cousin John as a partner in the family banking firm in 1772, from which time his partnership with Cox ceased, although they continued to have a business connection until 1774. From the early 1770s the volume and profits of the banking business increased significantly, and by the time of Drummond's death in 1795 the firm had almost 3200 accounts—double the number at Andrew Drummond's death in 1769—and average annual profits approaching £30,000.

In December 1774 Drummond purchased a seat in parliament at Wendover, Buckinghamshire, from Lord Verney. He consistently supported Lord North, but by 1777 had become disillusioned over North's policy in North America. In June 1777 Harley and Drummond were given a year's notice of termination of their contract; however, in the event they were able to secure its renewal and extension to the West Indies, and the work continued until 1783. At the 1780 general election, at North's recommendation, Drummond purchased a seat at Midhurst, Sussex. Drummond supported North until his fall, but he was not present at the divisions on Fox's East India Bill. Being a friend of Henry Dundas (whose daughter Anne married Drummond's son in 1786), he may have followed the latter's political lead, and by 1784 he was listed among Pitt's supporters. He held his seat at Midhurst until 1790.

As a young man Drummond lived at the bank and also had a property at Lawers, Perthshire. Later he acquired a house in St James's Square, London, and owned a country residence, first at Langley Park, Buckinghamshire, and from 1787 The Grange, near Alresford, Hampshire. He married Elizabeth (*d.* 1819), the daughter of Charles Compton MP (*d.* 1755) and his wife, Mary, the daughter of Sir Berkeley Lucy, on 23 March 1761; they had two children, Henry (1762–1794) and Anne.

Drummond was a member of 'the Gang', an informal circle of friends which, in addition to his brother Robert, included William Amherst, Thomas Bradshaw, Lord Frederick Campbell, Anthony Chamier, Richard Cox, Thomas Harley, Sir Robert Murray Keith, Richard Rigby, and Sir John Sebright. It started out as a bachelors' monthly dining club and soon became the forum for wild activities and jocular camaraderie. As time went on the friendships matured and extended to incorporate the members' families.

Drummond died on 24 June 1795 at The Grange.

PHILIP WINTERBOTTOM

Sources H. Bolitho and D. Peel, *The Drummonds of Charing Cross* (1967) · Royal Bank of Scotland, London, Drummonds Bank customer accounts ledgers · Royal Bank of Scotland, London, Drummonds Bank partnership papers · HoP, *Commons* · parish register (marriage), St James's, Westminster

Archives Royal Bank of Scotland, London, Drummonds branch | Alnwick Castle, Northumberland

Likenesses T. Gainsborough, oils, *c.*1775–1780, priv. coll. [*see illus.*] · portrait (style of H. Raeburn), Royal Bank of Scotland, London

Drummond, Henry (1786–1860), politician and apostle of the Catholic Apostolic church, eldest son of Henry Drummond (1762–1794), banker, of The Grange, near Alresford, Hampshire, and his wife, Anne (*d.* 1852), daughter of Henry Dundas, first Viscount Melville, was born at Alresford on 5 December 1786. His father died in 1794, and when his mother remarried and went to India in 1802 the boy was left in the care of his grandfather, Lord Melville, at whose house he often saw and became a favourite of the prime minister, William Pitt. He was educated at Harrow School from 1793 to 1802, and at Christ Church, Oxford, from 1802 to 1804, leaving without taking a degree. He was made a partner in his father's bank at Charing Cross and continued in the business, purchasing a London house in Belgrave Square. In 1807 he made a tour of Russia, and on his return married on 28 June 1807 Lady Henrietta (or Harriet) Hay-Drummond (*d.* 1854), eldest daughter of the tenth earl of Kinnoull, with whom he had two daughters, one of whom married Lord Lovaine, heir to the dukedom of Northumberland, and the other Sir Thomas Rokewood Gage, bt; they also had three sons, who all died young.

Drummond entered parliament in 1810 as member for Plympton Erle and was instrumental in the passing of the act against the embezzlement by bankers of securities entrusted to them for safe custody, but in 1812 he gave up his seat on the grounds of ill health. In June 1817, 'satiated with the empty frivolities of the fashionable world' (*DNB*), he sold The Grange and broke up his hunting establishment to travel with his wife to Palestine. They arrived in Geneva just as Robert Haldane, who was conducting a vigorous evangelical campaign there against the Socinianism of the governing bodies and encouraging ministers who upheld pure Calvinism to secede from the official church, was about to leave. Drummond took over this

Henry Drummond (1786–1860), by William Holl (after George Richmond, 1856)

campaign but, when summoned before the council of state, thought it wiser to withdraw from his house at Sêcheron within the Genevan jurisdiction to the Campagne Pictet, a villa in Montauban, France. From there he continued the movement with some success, a secession taking place in September 1817, and financed a mission to Alsace. While still in Geneva, at his own expense he sent out the traveller John Lewis Burckhardt to sell copies of the gospels in Muslim towns, and he later co-financed the great missionary traveller Joseph Wolff, a converted Jew, and in 1819 co-founded the Continental Society, formed to give protestant teaching in Roman Catholic countries.

In the same year Drummond purchased Albury Park, Surrey, becoming the chief landowner in the district and patron of the parish living, much appreciated as a conscientious and caring landlord and a pioneer of the allotment system. Later, in 1842, he was to finance the building of a new parish church, though he was no longer an Anglican. A high tory, he became known for his frequent sarcastic attacks on political economists in parliament and elsewhere, but in 1825 endowed a chair of political economy at Oxford. He became especially celebrated for his generous involvement with many good causes—a newly found friend, Edward Irving, writing: 'He is in all chairs—I fear for him' (Flegg, 36). He was active in the Jews' Society, being greatly influenced by Lewis Way.

Irving introduced Drummond to Thomas Carlyle, at that time a little-known writer in London, who, after dining at Belgrave Square, wrote: 'He was a singular mixture of all things—of the saint, the wit, the philosopher—swimming, if I mistake not, in an element of dandyism'

(J. A. Froude, *Life of Carlyle*, 1882, 2.177). Later, in his *Reminiscences*, Carlyle was to describe him as 'a sharp, elastic, haughty kind of man' with 'a disorderly force of intellect and character' and 'an enormous conceit of himself' which rendered his life 'a restless inconsistency' (ibid., 2.199). By contrast William Watson Andrews, an American Congregationalist and later in the episcopate of the Catholic Apostolic church in New York, was to describe him in 1843 as 'a very plain, unassuming man, but of great mental activity and industry'. He became a close friend of John Wilson Croker, and was described by him as possessing 'an unusually large fund of common sense' and 'an understanding peculiar to himself for all he saw, and language and manner as original as his thoughts'. Kinglake described him as 'a man often soaring into mystic, spiritual realms … gifted with a piercing cleverness, with a keen lively wit, and a nature devoid of fear' (Kinglake, 7.317).

In November 1826 Drummond summoned the first of five annual conferences at Albury, the purpose of which was to study unfulfilled biblical prophecies with particular emphasis on the Jews, the visions of Daniel and the Revelation of John, and the second advent of Christ. Participants were drawn from the various protestant churches, though with Anglicans in the majority. They included Irving, Wolff, Hugh McNeill (rector of Albury), J. Hatley Frere (commentator on the Apocalypse), Spencer Perceval (son of the former prime minister), John Tudor (secretary of the Prophetic Society), and some thirty-five others. Drummond published important premillennial conclusions in *Dialogues on Prophecy* (1827), co-edited with Irving. These included the restoration of the Jews to Palestine and imminent judgments on Christendom prior to the millennium. The fifth and final conference was called to consider reports of charismatic religious revival occurring in south-west Scotland associated with Isabella and Mary Campbell of Rosneath and the Macdonald family of Port Glasgow. These events were investigated and pronounced upon favourably by a committee from England which included J. B. Cardale, and were followed by similar manifestations in England, most notably at Irving's church, for which Irving was subsequently deposed.

Convinced that the manifestations were of the Holy Spirit, Drummond set up prayer-meetings at Albury and Guildford despite the hostility of the rector, McNeill. On 7 November 1832, during prayers at Irving's house, he ecstatically declared Cardale to be an apostle, the latter using this apostolic authority to ordain Drummond to the episcopate on 26 December as Angel (or Minister in charge) at Albury following prophetic utterances. On 24 September 1833, during a service at Albury, Drummond was called to be the second apostle, and during 1834 and 1835 toured England and Scotland with Cardale, ordaining ministers for various local congregations of the Catholic Apostolic church. In June 1836, during apostolic deliberations at Albury, he prophetically called for the division of Christendom into twelve 'tribes' and was given responsibility for Scotland and protestant Switzerland. In 1838 he travelled abroad with an apostolic colleague to deliver the apostles' *Great Testimony* (1838) to the heads of the nations and churches, handing copies to Cardinal Acton (for the pope) and Prince Metternich (for the emperor), but failing to deliver that for King Louis-Philippe because of court mourning.

In 1847 Drummond circulated a letter entitled *On Foreign Work*, in which he complained about a lack of enthusiasm, especially for evangelization at home, on the part of Catholic Apostolic congregations, with the result that the apostles introduced the sacrament of sealing. He partly financed Raphael Branden's great Central Church in Gordon Square, London, consecrated on Christmas eve 1853, having entirely financed the £16,000 Apostles' Chapel at Albury, built in 1840. He was frequently out of sympathy with the 'Catholic' trend of Cardale's Catholic Apostolic liturgy, opposing, for example, the reservation of the sacrament; in 1849 he published his own service book for Scotland, subsequently withdrawn on the insistence of the other apostles.

Also in 1847 Drummond returned to parliament as member for West Surrey, and retained the seat until his death. By this time he had shifted from giving qualified support to free trade in corn—in his pamphlet *Cheap Corn Best for Farmers* (1825)—to viewing the repeal of the corn laws as initiating 'the destruction of all those things which God has instituted in a Christian monarchy' (Hilton, 44). None the less, he did not align himself with the protectionists, and it has been suggested that he even welcomed the 'catastrophe' of repeal in 1846 as signalling the breakdown of society and the second coming. Drummond took a more prominent role during this second period in parliament, becoming well known as an active debater, adopting an independent line but invariably supporting the budget whichever party was in power. An ideological paternalist, he 'extolled monarchy, aristocracy, and property and berated all who demanded equality as of unsound mind' (Roberts, 241). He was fierce in his hostility to Roman Catholicism, virulent in his support for the Ecclesiastical Titles Act of 1851, and persistent in his demands for the regulation of convents, publishing *A Plea for the Rights and Liberties of Women Imprisoned for Life under the Power of Priests* (1851). He supported the government in its conduct of the Crimean War, and was a member of the Roebuck committee of inquiry, for which he prepared a minority report (neutralized in the final draft) placing the blame for the military shambles on the 'plea for economy during the peace by the continued pressure of the House of Commons' (Taylor, 253–4).

During the late 1850s Drummond revisited Switzerland, receiving five Roman Catholic priests and sealing some 200 members of Catholic Apostolic congregations. He died at Albury on 20 February 1860 and was buried in the thirteenth-century chapel of Albury Old Church, decorated by Pugin, with the Drummond motto 'Gang warily' carved on the screen. Drummond was a prolific author, producing some 140 works on ecclesiastical subjects. Notable among them were *Tracts for the Last Days* (1844), *Abstract Principles of Revealed Religion* (1845), *Elements of the*

Christian Religion (1845), and *Discourses on the True Definition of the Church* (1858), which put forward the Catholic Apostolic church's views on the contemporary apostasy of the churches, the second coming of Christ, the need for renewal, and its progress under the new apostles. His son-in-law, Lord Lovaine, later sixth duke of Northumberland, published two volumes of Drummond's parliamentary speeches in 1860.   COLUMBA GRAHAM FLEGG

Sources R. A. Davenport, *Albury Apostles*, rev. edn (1973) · T. Carlyle, *Reminiscences*, ed. C. E. Norton, 2 vols. (1887) · C. G. Flegg, *Gathered under Apostles* (1992) · M. Oliphant, *The life of Edward Irving*, 2 vols. (1862) · A. L. Drummond, *Edward Irving and his circle* [1937] · *The Croker papers: the correspondence and diaries of … John Wilson Croker*, ed. L. J. Jennings, 3 vols. (1884) · A. W. Kinglake, *The invasion of the Crimea*, 7 (1887) · J. Aarsbo, *Komme dit Rige*, 1 (1930) · B. Hilton, *The age of atonement: the influence of evangelicalism on social and economic thought, 1795–1865* (1988) · D. Roberts, *Paternalism in early Victorian England* (1979) · M. Taylor, *The decline of British radicalism, 1847–1860* (1995)

Archives Alnwick Castle, Northumberland, archives, corresp. and papers · Catholic Apostolic Church Library, London | BL, corresp. with W. E. Gladstone, Add. MSS 44366–44388 *passim* · BL, corresp. with Sir Robert Peel, Add. MSS 40243–40603 *passim* · BL, letters to Francis Place, Add. MSS 37949–37950 · Bodl. Oxf., corresp. with Benjamin Disraeli · Duke U., Croker MSS · NA Scot., corresp. with Lord Melville

Likenesses H. Edridge, watercolour, 1813, Clive Lodge, Albury · A. Murier-Romilly, chalk and wash drawing, 1836, Clive Lodge, Albury · J. Doyle, pencil caricature, 1848, BM · W. Walker, stipple, pubd 1849, BM · G. Richmond, chalk drawing, 1856, Clive Lodge, Albury · W. Holl, engraving (after G. Richmond, 1856), NPG [*see illus.*] · T. Lawrence, red chalk drawing, Clive Lodge, Albury · T. Phillips, portrait, Clive Lodge, Albury · portrait, repro. in Aarsbo, *Komme dit Rige* · portrait, repro. in *Neue Apostelgeschichte* (1982) · portrait, repro. in Davenport, *Albury Apostles*

Wealth at death under £16,000: administration, 13 June 1860, *CGPLA Eng. & Wales*

Drummond, Henry (1851–1897), writer on theology, born at 1 Park Place, Stirling, on 17 August 1851, was the second son of the four sons and two daughters of Henry Drummond (*d.* 1888) and his wife, Jane (*née* Blackwood), of Kilmarnock, and grandson of William Drummond, a land surveyor and nurseryman. His father, who became head of the firm of William Drummond & Sons, seedsmen, of Stirling and Dublin, was a pillar of the Free North Church in Stirling; his uncle, Peter Drummond, was the founder of the Agricultural Museum in Stirling and of the Stirling Tract Enterprise. Henry junior was educated at Stirling high school (1856–63) and at Morrison's academy, Crieff, before matriculating in 1866 at Edinburgh University, where he studied classics, philosophy, mathematics, and natural science; he left the university without a degree. In 1868 he helped to start a magazine, *The Philomathic*, where he wrote about such topics as hypnotism, which he practised enthusiastically. In 1870 he entered the divinity course of the Free Church at New College, Edinburgh, spending a summer semester at Tübingen, Germany, in 1873. In the autumn of the same year he was drawn into the Edinburgh campaign of the American evangelists Dwight L. Moody and Ira D. Sankey. From April 1874 to July 1875 he travelled with them to the cities of Ireland and

Henry Drummond (1851–1897), by T. & R. Annan & Sons

England, speaking himself, editing Moody's evangelistic addresses, and counselling prospective converts in the enquiry room.

In spite of many invitations to conduct missions Drummond returned to New College, Edinburgh, in the autumn of 1875. Most of the addresses published posthumously in *The Ideal Life* (1897) were originally delivered while he was assistant at Barclay Church, Edinburgh, during 1876–7. From 1877 he acted as lecturer in natural science at the Free Church college, Glasgow, spending the summer of 1878 as his church's chaplain in Malta. In 1879 he joined a geological expedition to the Rocky Mountains under Professor Archibald Geikie of Edinburgh. Afterwards he returned to his Glasgow lecturing and to the Possilpark mission, Glasgow, until 1882, when he again assisted Moody during his second evangelistic tour of Britain. Drummond became a fellow of the Royal Society of Edinburgh in 1880.

In 1883 Drummond published the book which contributed so largely to his contemporary fame, *Natural Law in the Spiritual World*. Based on lectures delivered to working men at Possilpark, the book contended that the same principles operated in the world of nature and in the spiritual experience of human beings. The thesis was founded on a series of brilliant figures of speech rather than on a chain of reasoning, and the fallacies in Drummond's argument were pointed out, for instance, in an anonymous work by the Free Church theologian James Denney. The book, however, proved amazingly successful; its popularity, due in the first instance to the beauty of the writing, was strengthened by a most enthusiastic review in *The Spectator*, and over the next five years some 70,000 copies were sold.

Within a few days of the publication, in June 1883, Drummond set out on a visit to the southern equatorial region of Africa. His commission was to make a scientific, and especially geological, exploration of the district between lakes Nyasa and Tanganyika for the African Lakes Corporation. Although he failed to reach Lake Tanganyika he subsequently drew from his journal to publish *Tropical Africa* (1888), in which he argued that British involvement in the region was essential to put down the slave trade. So powerful was his animus against the trade that he looked forward to the extinction of the elephant, whose ivory was the reason for the presence of the Arab slavers. Shortly after his return, in 1884, he was promoted by the Free Church to a professorship in theology, a status that entailed ordination, though he never used the title Reverend. In December he delivered his inaugural address, 'The contribution of science to Christianity', which was reprinted in the posthumous collection of papers *The New Evangelism* (1899). In the following month, after two evangelistic missions to Edinburgh students by Stanley Smith and C. T. Studd, volunteer China missionaries from Cambridge, Drummond took over responsibility for continuing Sunday evening meetings that aroused enormous enthusiasm, particularly among medical students. The series at Edinburgh continued, with intermissions, until 1894 and led to similar campaigns in Oxford (1885) and several German universities (1886). In May 1885, during the height of the London season, he gave three addresses in Grosvenor House on the subject of conversion, at the invitation of the earl and countess of Aberdeen to whom he became closely attached. He was strongly but vainly urged by Gladstone to contest the Partick division of Lanarkshire as a Liberal in 1886. In the following year he accepted Moody's invitation to speak at his annual Northfield convention, addressing students at several universities on the same American visit. A hectic programme at this period included another set of Grosvenor House lectures (1888) and a leading part in the foundation of a Glasgow University settlement (1889). He actively promoted the Boys' Brigade, a uniformed evangelistic organization, earning the title Apostle of the Boys' Brigade. He used a tour of Australian colleges in 1890, for instance, to commend the movement, but also seized the opportunity to visit the New Hebrides. On his return to Scotland he encountered a barrage of criticism for neglecting the fundamentals of Christianity in his teaching, and by 1893, when he again spoke at Northfield, he was regarded by the theologically conservative as totally unsound.

In that year Drummond delivered the Lowell lectures in Boston, Massachusetts, publishing them as *The Ascent of Man* (1894). Designed as a response to Charles Darwin's work *The Descent of Man* (1871), it attempted to harmonize Christianity and evolution. Drummond's general thesis that the struggle for life gradually became altruistic in character, or 'struggle for the life of others', was severely criticized by men of science. At the same time he was attacked by many theologians on account of too close an adherence to Darwin and Herbert Spencer. With the publication of *The Ascent of Man* Drummond's career as a public teacher virtually ended because he became the victim of a painful bone disease that particularly affected the spine. In 1895 he travelled to Dax and Biarritz in the south of France, and was then taken to Tunbridge Wells, where he died on 11 March 1897. He was buried in Holy Rude churchyard, Stirling.

Much of Drummond's profound impact on young men can be attributed to his personal bearing: he was dignified, smartly turned out, with angular features, a drooping moustache, and a penetrating eye. He was thought to be indifferent to female company, 'sexless … towards women' (J. Watson, 519), and never married. He was also entirely unclerical in manner, preaching no formal sermons after about 1882, and seemed simply a cultivated amateur man of science. His eye for detail, originally developed under the influence of reading John Ruskin and vividly expressed in *Tropical Africa*, gave him an aesthetic interest in natural phenomena that was the foundation of his scientific approach. The American transcendentalists R. W. Emerson and W. E. Channing also shaped his mind, and Herbert Spencer provided the framework of social evolution in which he cast his mature thought. Human beings, he taught, gradually grew towards a higher life when guided by Christ. His addresses, as his critics noted, lacked a strong sense of sin and therefore placed little emphasis on the atonement. He came to suppose that everything in nature was moving away from the physical towards the spiritual and so disbelieved in the resurrection of the body. His teaching, which was originally individualistic, eventually embraced a social dimension based on the principle of love, which, as his most celebrated address put it, was 'The greatest thing in the world'. The international renown of his books was a sign of the eagerness of his age to reconcile religion with science. Drummond is now usually treated as the extreme case of an English-speaking evangelical who welcomed the principle of evolution.   D. W. BEBBINGTON

Sources G. A. Smith, *The life of Henry Drummond* (1899) · C. Lennox [J. H. Napier], *Henry Drummond: a biographical sketch* (1901) [with bibliography] · J. Y. Simpson, *Henry Drummond* (1901) · J. Watson [I. Maclaren], 'Henry Drummond', *North American Review*, 164 (1897), 514–25 · H. Drummond, I. Maclaren, and W. R. Nicoll, *The ideal life and other unpublished addresses; with memorial sketches by Ian Maclaren and W. Robertson Nicoll*, 3rd edn (1899) · *The Times* (12 March 1897), 10 · D. W. Bebbington, 'Henry Drummond, evangelicalism and science', *Records of the Scottish Church History Society*, 28 (1998), 129–48 · J. R. Moore, 'Evangelicals and evolution', *Scottish Journal of Theology*, 38 (1985), 383–417 · J. Denney ['A brother of the natural man'], *On 'Natural law in the spiritual world'* (1885) · R. A. Watson, *Gospels of yesterday: Drummond, Spencer, Arnold* (1888) · R. Watts, *Prof. Drummond's 'Ascent of man' and Principal Fairbairn's 'Place of Christ in modern theology'* (1895?) · H. M. Cecil [E. Newman], *Pseudo-philosophy at the end of the nineteenth century. An irrationalist trio: Kidd, Drummond, Balfour* (1897)

Archives Haddo House, Tarves, Aberdeenshire, MSS · NL Scot., corresp. and papers · U. Edin. L. | BL, Gladstone MSS

Likenesses S. Rankin, wash drawing, 1893, repro. in Lennox, *Henry Drummond*, frontispiece · T. and R. Annan & Sons, photograph, NPG [see illus.] · T. and R. Annan & Sons, photographs, repro.

in Smith, *Life of Henry Drummond*, frontispiece · photographs, repro. in Lennox, *Henry Drummond* · wood-engraving (after photograph by Lafayette), NPG; repro. in *ILN* (20 March 1897)

Wealth at death £12,501 13s. 10d.: confirmation, 25 May 1897, *CCI* · £1 10s. 5d.—additional estate: confirmation, 19 Nov 1897, *CCI* · Scottish confirmation sealed in London, 18 June 1897, *CCI*

Drummond, Sir Jack Cecil (1891–1952), nutritional biochemist, was born at Leicester on 12 January 1891, the only child of John Drummond, a retired major of the Royal Horse Artillery, who died the following June. He was brought up by his aunt and her husband, Captain George Spinks, a Crimean veteran and keen amateur gardener, from whom Drummond probably derived his interest in wild flowers and birds. An early talent for drawing led him on to photography and thence to chemistry. After attending Roan School, Greenwich, and King's College School in the Strand, he entered East London College and graduated in 1912 with first-class honours in chemistry. In 1913 he became a research assistant in the department of physiology at King's College, London, under Otto Rosenheim, who (together with the professor, W. D. Halliburton) exerted a profound and lasting impression upon Drummond. In March 1914 he became an assistant at the Cancer Hospital Research Institute where collaboration with Casimir Funk started his interest in nutrition. In 1915 Drummond married a former fellow student, Mabel Helen, daughter of Philip Straw, schoolmaster.

In 1917 Halliburton, as a member of the food (war) committee of the Royal Society, invited Drummond to join him in experimental work on substitutes for butter and margarine. The work introduced Drummond to fat soluble vitamins, which became one of his major fields of experimental work. More important, it immediately led him to practical problems of human nutrition; he published in *The Lancet* in 1918 a paper on infant feeding. In the same year he received a DSc from the University of London and succeeded Funk as biochemist at the Cancer Hospital. In 1919 he became a research assistant in physiological chemistry at University College, London. He was subsequently appointed reader (1920) and then to the newly created professorship of biochemistry (1922).

Drummond's department was never autonomous and for many years received inadequate financial resources. A variety of lines of research was pursued, too various for errors to be avoided or major contributions made; Drummond's artistic temperament was better suited to the broad sweep of the canvas than to dull attention to detail. Nevertheless his energy and enthusiasm inspired his colleagues and students, and his department was among the most important in the country for training biochemists; at the time of his death no fewer than nine of his colleagues or pupils were holding or had held chairs. The breadth of his interests and his approachability caused him to be much in demand as a lecturer and as a consultant to industry to which he devoted much time.

In the early 1930s the need to apply the new knowledge of nutrition was becoming increasingly clear. This realization, together with Drummond's interest in gastronomy, led him to study the dietary habits of the English over the previous 500 years. This unique survey was published in 1939 as *The Englishman's Food* (jointly with his secretary, Anne Wilbraham).

When the Second World War broke out Drummond was consulted by the Ministry of Food on gas contamination of food, and on 16 October 1939 he was appointed chief adviser on food contamination to the ministry. Once there he interested himself in its various scientific aspects and in that December he urged the creation of a co-ordinating unit in the ministry with a scientific liaison officer in charge. On 1 February 1940 he was appointed scientific adviser to the Ministry of Food.

When Lord Woolton became minister of food in April 1940 policy became a blend of scientific theory and practical possibilities, for the minister believed that his scientific experts should have a hand in framing policy. Lord Woolton, Drummond, and their colleague Sir Wilson Jameson in the Ministry of Health took the opportunity to combat nutritional ignorance and to improve—rather than merely to maintain—the nutriture of the population. The result was described by the Lasker awards committee of the American Public Health Association as 'one of the greatest demonstrations in public health administration that the world has ever seen' and named Lord Woolton, Sir Jack Drummond (he was knighted in 1944), Sir Wilson Jameson, and Sir John Boyd Orr as 'the four great leaders in this historic enterprise'.

In 1944 Drummond became an adviser on nutrition to Supreme Headquarters Allied Expeditionary Force and the following year to the allied control commissions for Germany and Austria (British elements). That year, 1945, he resigned his professorship on appointment as director of research to Boots Pure Drug Company, but he was seconded to the ministry until 1946.

Drummond's first marriage had broken up in 1939 and in the following year he married his secretary and co-author, Anne (1905/6–1952), daughter of Roger Wilbraham. Drummond was elected FRS in 1944. He received the United States medal of freedom with silver palms, was made a commander of the order of orange Nassau, and received an honorary doctorate from the University of Paris.

Drummond was small, neat, sprightly, and gay, abounding with energy. He enjoyed the company of others as well as the delights of good food and wine. He also enjoyed travel and it was in France, on the night of 4–5 August 1952 that he, his wife, and their ten-year-old daughter, Elizabeth, were murdered when camping in the French Alps at La Grande Terre, Lurs, near Digne-les-Bains, Provence. The subsequent murder case became one of the most sensational of the 1950s in France. Suspicion immediately fell on the Dominicis, a family of peasant farmers on whose land the Drummonds had been camping. Gustave Dominici (1918/19–1996) claimed to have discovered the bodies, and allegedly told an acquaintance that Elizabeth had still been alive when he found her. As a result he was sent to prison for two months for 'depraved indifference' (Young). He subsequently alleged that his father, Gaston Dominici (1876/7–1965), was the real killer, an allegation retracted, remade, and retracted again before Gaston's trial. Gaston Dominici himself made (but later retracted) a confession to the effect that he had shot Sir Jack after having been caught embracing Lady Drummond. He was sentenced to death in 1954, but was reprieved in 1957 and pardoned in 1960.

It is likely that Drummond's real killer will never be known. Sir Jack's involvement with the government led to speculation that foreign agents may have been involved. In addition, at one point, a German, Wilhelm Bartwoski, allegedly confessed to British special investigation branch officers that he and three accomplices had perpetrated the crime. Following Drummond's murder over £30,000 was contributed to a memorial fund for the foundation of a research fellowship in nutrition.

H. M. SINCLAIR, *rev.* PETER OSBORNE

Sources F. G. Young, *Obits. FRS*, 9 (1954), 99–129 · *British Journal of Nutrition*, 3 (1954) · G. F. Marrian, *JCS* (1953) · private information (1971) · personal knowledge (1971) · R. Young, 'Murder riddle outlives last member of the cast', *The Times* (23 Feb 1996) · *CGPLA Eng. & Wales* (1952)
Likenesses W. Stoneman, photograph, 1944, NPG
Wealth at death £6680 14s. 3d.: probate, 23 Dec 1952, *CGPLA Eng. & Wales*

Drummond, James, first Lord Maderty (1551×61–1623), courtier, was the second son of David, second Lord Drummond (*d.* 1571), and his wife, Lilias Ruthven (*d.* 1579), a daughter of William, second Lord Ruthven. Drummond first became important through his acquisition of Inchaffray Abbey in Strathearn. The previous commendator of the abbey was Alexander Gordon, bishop of Galloway, whose mother married Sir John Drummond of Innerpeffray as her second husband; Gordon consequently became close to his mother's Drummond connections. A series of transactions led Queen Mary to appoint James Drummond commendator of the abbey of Inchaffray on 26 July 1565. These acquisitions established him, though still a child, as a substantial landowner in Perthshire. Drummond married Alexander Gordon's niece, Jean Chisholm (*d.* 1589), granddaughter of Sir John Drummond, and thereby acquired the lands of Innerpeffray.

Drummond was active in the politics of the nation. On 15 October 1580 James VI appointed him a gentleman of the chamber. His commendatorship gave him the right to sit in parliament, and between 1578 and 1617 Drummond attended ten parliaments, from 31 January 1609 as a peer with the title Lord Maderty (taken from the parish next to Inchaffray). In his own locality he was the steward depute of Strathearn and in 1613 was appointed a JP for Perthshire. When his brother Patrick, third Lord Drummond, was absent, James Drummond assumed responsibility for his affairs, both private and public.

Drummond's religion was intimately connected with his politics. In the 1580s he was associated with the protestant faction known as the Ruthven raiders. As late as September 1589 he was identified as a follower of the protestant earl of Mar, and a friend of England. However, on 23 February 1591 Sir Robert Bowes, the English ambassador,

reported a rumour that Drummond was to go to the duke of Parma as an ambassador from the Scottish Catholics. Why the change occurred is unknown, but for the rest of the 1590s and beyond Drummond was associated with the Catholics. In 1594, at the treason trial of the Catholic earls, Andrew Melville accused him of being in league with the latter, and Drummond was indeed one of five out of eighteen men who voted to acquit them. In 1598 it was rumoured that he would be sent to the pope as an ambassador. In April 1604 he was charged before the privy council with sheltering Jesuits, but there is no evidence that he was convicted, and Drummond never seems to have suffered for his Catholicism. This was probably due to his personal loyalty to King James, shown by the support he gave James on 5 August 1600 during the Gowrie conspiracy. On 2 June 1607 he took the oath of allegiance. His wife died in November 1589 and Drummond never remarried. They had two sons and five daughters: John (who became second Lord Maderty), James, Lilias, Jean (or Jane), Margaret, Catherine, and Agnes. Lord Maderty died in September 1623.   MICHAEL WASSER

Sources *Scots peerage*, vols. 7–8 · *APS*, 1567–1625 · *Reg. PCS*, 1st ser., vols. 2–10 · D. Calderwood, *The history of the Kirk of Scotland*, ed. T. Thomson and D. Laing, 8 vols., Wodrow Society, 7 (1842–9), vols. 4–5 · *CSP Scot.*, 1589–95; 1597–1603 · W. A. Lindsay, J. Dowden, and J. M. Thomson, eds., *Charters, bulls and other documents relating to the abbey of Inchaffray*, Scottish History Society, 56 (1908) · J. M. Thomson and others, eds., *Registrum magni sigilli regum Scotorum / The register of the great seal of Scotland*, 11 vols. (1882–1914), vols. 4–7 · Edinburgh commissary court, NA Scot., CC8/8/38, 26 Nov 1603 · R. Douglas, *The peerage of Scotland*, 2nd edn, ed. J. P. Wood, 2 (1813) · GEC, *Peerage*, new edn, 8.347
Wealth at death wife's debts exceeded assets by £166 13s. 4d.: will, NA Scot., CC 8/8/38

Drummond, James, fourth earl of Perth and Jacobite first duke of Perth (1648–1716), politician, born on 7 July 1648, was the elder son of James Drummond, third earl of Perth (*d.* 1675), and Lady Anne (1616?–1656), eldest daughter of George Gordon, second marquess of Huntly. Known by his courtesy title of Lord Drummond, he was educated at St Andrews University and at an academy in Angers. On 18 January 1670 he married his cousin Lady Jane Douglas (*d.* 1678), daughter of William *Douglas, first marquess of Douglas (1589–1660), with whom he had one son, James *Drummond (1674–1720), and two daughters, Mary *Drummond (1675–1729) and Anne. In 1675 he succeeded his father as fourth earl.

Perth was keen to restore his family's fortunes, which had suffered during the civil wars. He was also ambitious, and by the end of the 1670s was actively involved in Scottish politics. At first he offered his services to the duke of Lauderdale and was made a member of the Scottish privy council in 1678. But he soon joined 'the party', a group of noblemen under the leadership of his brothers-in-law William Douglas, third duke of Hamilton, and William Douglas, third earl of Queensberry, who opposed Lauderdale. During the exclusion crisis Perth and his brother, Lord John *Drummond (1649–1714), attached themselves to the interests of the duke of York, who was sent by Charles II to govern Scotland. In May 1682 Perth

James Drummond, fourth earl of Perth and Jacobite first duke of Perth (1648–1716), by Nicolas de Largillière, *c.*1714

was made justice-general and an extraordinary lord of session, and later the same month was with the duke when his yacht the *Gloucester* was shipwrecked off Yarmouth. In August of the same year he was appointed one of the commissioners for the trial of Lauderdale's brother the treasurer-depute, Charles Maitland, for irregularities in the administration of the Royal Mint. When the latter was found guilty, Perth obtained the post for his own brother. The following year Perth and his brother became members of the 'secret committee' of the Scottish privy council. The other members included Queensberry and John Murray, first marquess of Atholl and fifth earl of Tullibardine. Perth had meanwhile married his cousin Lilias Drummond (*d.* 1685), the widow of James Murray, fourth earl of Tullibardine, in 1678 or early 1679, after his first wife's death in 1678. They had two sons, John and Charles, born in 1679 and 1681 respectively.

During the last years of the reign of Charles II, Perth and his brother became steadily more powerful and supplanted rivals such as Hamilton and Queensberry. In 1684, when they engineered the fall of Lord Aberdeen, Perth replaced him as lord chancellor, and also became sheriff-principal of the county of Edinburgh and governor of the Bass. Lord John Drummond (created Lord Melfort in 1685) became secretary for Scotland, an important appointment which ensured that Perth's interests were well represented at Whitehall. Both men were continued in office by James II when he became king in 1685. Although Perth's mother had been a Catholic, he had so far confessed himself a convinced episcopalian. The details of

the deathbed conversion of Charles II, however, had a profound effect on him, particularly when supported by a private correspondence with Bishop Bossuet of Meaux. As a result Perth converted to Catholicism in June 1685 and persuaded his wife and his brother to do the same shortly after. When his wife died later the same year, he was free to remarry. His third wife, whom he married in January 1686, was his widowed first cousin Lady Mary Gordon (1653/4–1726), widow of Adam Urquhart of Meldrum, who was also a Catholic; they had two sons, William and Edward, born in 1687 and 1689 respectively, and a daughter, Theresa. Many people at the time, and subsequently, accused Perth and his brother of converting to Catholicism for purely political reasons, but their sincerity is no longer in doubt. Nevertheless, becoming Catholic did considerably increase their influence with the new king and when Queensberry, a protestant, was shortly after dismissed as lord treasurer, Perth and Melfort succeeded in gaining complete control over the government of Scotland. In 1687 they were among the original eight knights of the newly revived Order of the Thistle. In the same year Perth resigned his earldom and his heritable offices in favour of his thirteen-year-old son by his first marriage, Lord Drummond.

Until the revolution of 1688 Perth remained the chief agent in James II's administration of Scotland and made himself unpopular with many people because of his willingness to sanction the use of torture to obtain confessions. He was also responsible for extending there the king's policy of religious toleration and on one occasion there was rioting in Edinburgh against the Catholic chapel he established for the king in Holyroodhouse. When the news reached the city in December 1688 that James II had retreated from Salisbury before William of Orange, the mob, in the absence of troops whom Perth had unwisely disbanded, rioted. Perth retreated to Drummond Castle, but finding himself unsafe there fled in disguise to Burntisland where he boarded a vessel for France. He had, however, been recognized and his vessel was overtaken at the mouth of the Forth by some watermen from Kirkcaldy. He was then arrested and taken to Stirling Castle where he remained until March 1692. When the news of his arrest reached James II in Dublin in March 1690 the king issued a warrant whereby he was created duke of Perth, but this was not made public.

After an extended negotiation, during which he was allowed to live for most of the time in his country house at Stobhall, Perth was eventually released in June 1693 on condition that he went abroad permanently and persuaded his eldest son, who had been at the court of James II at St Germain-en-Laye, to return. Having written to his son, Perth left Scotland in September 1693 on a ship bound for Rotterdam. For the next year he lived mainly at Antwerp, but did not go to St Germain, where Melfort was secretary of state. For some reason Perth's letter had never reached his son and he blamed his brother for this. In July 1694 he discovered that his son's possessions in Scotland were to be seized. He then ordered him once more to return and the two men met briefly in Antwerp that September, when Lord Drummond was on his way to London. Perth's own possessions, and indeed those of his two daughters by his first marriage, the elder of whom had married the ninth Earl Marischal in 1691, had been entrusted to his sister the countess of Erroll at Slains Castle, and he now felt free to travel. He determined to visit Italy and particularly Rome, where he could also freely indulge his passion for music and painting. In March 1695 he reached Venice, where he received credentials from James II appointing him his ambassador-extraordinary to the pope. His instructions were to obtain political and financial support for the Jacobite cause, in liaison with Cardinal Caprara, who already represented James's interests at the Holy See. He remained ambassador at Rome from May 1695 to March 1696.

At St Germain the prince of Wales had celebrated his seventh birthday in June 1695 and James II needed to appoint a governor to supervise his education. It was decided to recall Perth from Rome and to give him the new post. Perth reached Paris in May 1696 and formally assumed his new duties at the end of July, when his wife was also appointed a lady of the bedchamber to the queen. The 'Rules for the family of the prince of Wales' had been drawn up the previous year, when the prince's tutors had also been appointed. Perth was not therefore responsible for the basic policy adopted in educating the prince. He was, however, in charge of the detailed management of that policy and probably exercised a determining influence on the development of the personality of the future James III. In particular he allowed the prince to be exposed to Jansenist thought to an extent which was later criticized by both Mary of Modena and Louis XIV.

Perth had considerable influence with James II and was with him when he died in September 1701. The two letters that he wrote to the abbé de La Trappe provide the best and most detailed account of the king's death. Perth then paid for an impressive monument to be erected to the memory of James II in the chapel of the Scots College in Paris where the king's brain was deposited. From this point onwards Perth, who was now finally declared a duke, began to feel neglected and unappreciated at court. This was partly because there were very few Scots at St Germain and Perth felt that the favour of Mary of Modena was reserved for the English. It was partly also because he wished to play a more important political role and found himself thwarted by the greater influence of the two secretaries of state, Lord Middleton and Lord Caryll. Two developments weakened his position. In 1703 he supported the intrigues of Lord Lovat and refused to believe that he was a traitor until he was finally exposed and imprisoned at the beginning of 1704. At the same time James III's preceptor John Betham was investigated for his suspected Jansenism and eventually ordered to resign. In the summer of 1704 Perth was reprimanded by Mary of Modena after he had engaged in a public dispute about Scottish affairs with his opponents at the court.

Perth was keen to organize an invasion of Scotland and became increasingly frustrated by what he regarded as the obstruction of Middleton and Caryll. In July 1705 he complained that he had not had any 'mark of favour' since his arrival at St Germain: 'I have not been kindly used … Had I been an English man … I had been more distinguish'd' (Joly, 414). But in June 1706, when James III reached his majority, Perth was made a knight of the Order of the Garter, and in March 1708 he accompanied James on his unsuccessful attempt to invade Scotland. Perth had already been appointed gentleman of the bedchamber in February 1703, but he relinquished the post to his son Edward when the latter married one of the daughters of Lord Middleton in November 1709. Perth was then given the honorary title of first gentleman of the bedchamber, but he was in effect unemployed, so when James III and Middleton left in 1712 for Bar-le-Duc, Perth remained with Mary of Modena at St Germain and handled some of her secret correspondence. In 1711 he developed a stone in his bladder and in 1714 his health began to deteriorate. In December 1714 Mary of Modena appointed him to be her lord chamberlain and he held that post until his death, which occurred at the Château-Vieux de St Germain-en-Laye, as a result of an operation to remove his stone on 11 May 1716. He was buried the following day in the chapel of the Scots College at the foot of his monument to the memory of James II. He lived just long enough to witness the failure of the Jacobite rising of 1715, which resulted in the exile and attainder of his eldest son, Lord Drummond. The latter, however, had followed Perth's advice and handed over his title and estates to his own son in 1713. Perth's widow remained at St Germain with their son Edward until her death in 1726, their son William having died in 1703.

Perth was noted for his loyalty but he did not have good political judgement and Mary of Modena was wise to prefer the counsels of other men. He had a tendency to condemn moderation and caution as laziness or disloyalty and then to become over-pessimistic when his advice was not accepted. Posterity has judged him harshly because his administration of Scotland was unpopular and because Bishop Burnet's contemptuous opinion of him was given wide circulation by Macaulay. The publication of his biography in 1934 revealed the nobility of his character and should have laid to rest all doubts about the sincerity of his conversion to Catholicism.

EDWARD CORP

Sources A. Joly, *Un converti de Bossuet: James Drummond, duc de Perth, 1648–1716* (1934) · D. Nairne, journal, 1655–1708, NL Scot., MS 14266 · G. Scott, 'John Betham et l'éducation du prince de Galles', *Revue de la Bibliothèque Nationale*, 46 (winter 1992), 32–9
Archives BL, corresp., Add. MS 19254 [copies] · Drummond Castle, Perthshire · U. Aberdeen, letters [transcripts] | Archives Diplomatiques, Paris, 'correspondance politique, Angleterre', corresp. · BL, Lauderdale MSS, Add. MSS · BL, corresp. with Lord Lovat and Cardinal Gualterio, Add. MSS 20296, 31253, 31256 · Bodl. Oxf., Nairne papers · NL Scot., corresp. mainly with first and second marquesses of Tweeddale · Scottish Catholic Archives, Edinburgh, Blairs MSS · W. Sussex RO, letters to marquess of Huntly
Likenesses W. Faithorne, line engraving, 1679, BM, NPG · J. Riley, oils, 1680–84, Scot. NPG · G. Kneller, oils, 1682, Scot. NPG; version, priv. coll. · R. White, line engraving, 1682 (after G. Kneller), BM, NPG · R. White, line engraving, 1686 (after J. Riley), BM, NPG · oils,

1713 (after A. S. Belle), Scot. NPG • N. de Largillière, oils, c.1714, priv. coll. [see illus.] • attrib. A.-S. Belle, oils, Scot. NPG • miniature (after J. Riley), NPG • oils (after N. de Largillière), Musée d'Art et d'Histoire, Neuchâtel

Drummond, James, styled fifth earl of Perth and Jacobite second duke of Perth (1674–1720), Jacobite army officer, was born in Perthshire, the eldest son of James *Drummond, fourth earl of Perth and Jacobite first duke of Perth (1648–1716), and his first wife, Lady Jane Douglas (d. 1678), fourth daughter of William *Douglas, first marquess of Douglas; following the fourth earl's death the family's title was forfeited on account of James's support of the Stuart cause. The younger James joined his uncle, the earl of Melfort, in France shortly after the deposition of James VII and II, having, like his father, become a Roman Catholic in 1686. He began studying at the Scots College, Paris, in 1689, but on James's going to Ireland joined the expedition, and was present at all the engagements of the campaign. He then resumed his studies in Paris, and afterwards travelled in France and Italy. In 1694 his father, released on condition of his leaving Scotland, met him at Antwerp after five years' separation, and describes him as 'tall, well-shaped, and a very worthy youth'; at both Versailles and the Jacobite court-in-exile he had made a good impression.

In 1695 Drummond was allowed to return to Scotland, where he was effectively in control of the family estates in Perthshire. After his father became duke of Perth in the Jacobite peerage in 1701, the younger James was known as the marquess of Drummond. In 1707–8, from Castle Drummond in Strathearn, he was at the very heart of the widespread Jacobite conspiracy in association with the attempted French descent on the Firth of Forth in March 1708. For his part in this, Drummond was summoned to Edinburgh, sent to London, and imprisoned briefly in the Tower. In 1713 he made over his estates to his infant son, James *Drummond, later styled sixth earl and Jacobite third duke of Perth (1713–1746), the result of his marriage on 5 October 1706 to Lady Jean Gordon (1682/3–1773), daughter of the first duke of Gordon. In the rising of 1715 he undertook with 200 of his highlanders and some Edinburgh Jacobites to surprise Edinburgh Castle, but the scheme miscarried. He commanded the cavalry at the battle of Sheriffmuir, but was not to blame for the earl of Mar's failure in overall command on that day. John, master of Sinclair, who left a full account of the 'Fifteen in his *Memoirs of the Insurrection* (published 1858), had, however, little good to say of him.

Drummond escaped from Montrose in February 1716 with the Pretender (James Stuart) and lords Melfort and Mar. He was subsequently with the Pretender at the court-in-exile at Avignon and at Rome. He succeeded his father as second Jacobite duke of Perth in May 1716. Though a devoted Jacobite and Catholic, Perth was always tolerant of his protestant neighbours. However, he skilfully resisted attempts to foist Presbyterian ministers onto his Perthshire estates in place of the incumbent pastors. Perth died in Paris on 6 April 1720 and was buried beside his father at the Scots College. He was survived by his son

James Drummond, styled fifth earl of Perth and Jacobite second duke of Perth (1674–1720), by Sir John Baptiste de Medina, c.1700

and heir, James, and his younger son, John *Drummond, Jacobite fourth duke of Perth. His wife, who entertained Charles Edward Stuart, the Young Pretender, at Drummond Castle in 1746, and was imprisoned for nine months at Edinburgh for collecting taxes for the Jacobite cause, died, aged ninety, at Stobhall on 30 January 1773.

J. G. ALGER, *rev.* JOHN SIBBALD GIBSON

Sources D. Malcolm, *A genealogical memoir of the most noble and ancient house of Drummond* (1808) • J. S. Gibson, *Playing the Scottish card: the Franco-Jacobite invasion of 1708* (1988) • W. Scott, *Tales of a grandfather* • B. P. Lenman and J. S. Gibson, *The Jacobite threat: a source-book* (1990) • G. Dickson, *Jacques III Stuart, un roi sans couronne: extraits de la 'Gazette de Hollande' (1716), du 'Journal du Medecin Brun' (1716)* (Paris, 1993) • J. L. Carr, *Le Collège des Ecossais à Paris, 1662–1962* (1963) [intro. by G. Dickson] • A. M. Smith, *Jacobite estates of the Forty-Five* (1982) • B. Lenman, *The Jacobite risings in Britain, 1689–1746* (1980) • GEC, *Peerage* • R. Douglas, *The peerage of Scotland* (1764)
Likenesses J. B. de Medina, oils, c.1700, Scot. NPG [see illus.] • portrait (after hand-coloured lithograph on paper by F. de Troy), Scot. NPG
Wealth at death exiled; attainted; estate made over to son

Drummond, James, styled sixth earl of Perth and Jacobite third duke of Perth (1713–1746), Jacobite army officer, was born on 11 May 1713 at Drummond Castle, Perthshire, the eldest son of James *Drummond, styled fifth earl and Jacobite second duke of Perth (1674–1720), and Lady Jean Gordon (1682/3–1773), daughter of George Gordon, first duke of Gordon. He was brought up by his mother at Drummond Castle from the outset of the Jacobite rising of 1715 until his father's death in exile in 1720, when his mother took him and his younger brother, John *Drummond, Jacobite fourth duke of Perth, to France

James Drummond, styled sixth earl of Perth and Jacobite third duke of Perth (1713–1746), by François de Troy

that they might receive a Catholic education. He was accordingly educated at Douai, then sent to Paris to learn 'accomplishments'. He returned to Scotland in 1732, where he set to managing his estates effectively and, despite his father's attainder, was known as the third duke of Perth. He also involved himself wholeheartedly in the Jacobite cause, and in 1741 headed the list of seven Jacobite nobility and gentlemen (the Association) who entered into a treaty with Louis XV's ministers pledging to raise 20,000 from the highland clans to bring about a Stuart restoration if supported by Louis's famous Irish brigade. In the build-up of the ensuing conspiracy Perth took a prominent role, and offered in early 1745 to mortgage his estates for £10,000 to aid the Jacobite interest.

In the summer of 1745, fearing a Jacobite rising, the lord justice clerk at Edinburgh attempted unsuccessfully by subterfuge to have Perth arrested at Drummond Castle. Perth, however, outwitted and eluded his would-be captors, escaping on a horse taken from a peasant woman. Perth declared himself immediately for Prince Charles Edward after his landing in the west highlands in July 1745. In deference to his rank, and to the prominent part he had played in the conspiracy, Perth was made a lieutenant-general of the highland army, and it was in this

capacity that he participated at the victorious battle of Prestonpans in September.

In the prince's council, formed thereafter at Holyrood, Perth sided with Charles Edward against Lord George Murray, who argued heatedly for a 'fortress Scotland' strategy that would have consolidated in Scotland and waited for the arrival of military help from France. In the march into England, Perth negotiated the surrender of Carlisle but magnanimously relinquished his post as lieutenant-general following protests over a Roman Catholic's holding a high-ranking military position. At Derby, Perth initially favoured the onward march on London, as strenuously advocated by the prince. Despite his resignation from office he continued to take a prominent role in the highland army, and was fully involved particularly in the hazardous retreat to the north.

Perth was not at the battle of Falkirk, having been detailed to take charge at the (unsuccessful) siege of Stirling Castle. Thereafter he distinguished himself in the ousting of Lord Loudoun and his Hanoverian highlanders from Sutherland in March 1746. He commanded the Jacobite rearguard facing the duke of Cumberland's army as it crossed the Spey and advanced towards Inverness. At the battle of Culloden in April 1746 Perth attempted, but failed, to induce the clan regiments on the left wing to close with the enemy. Escaping from the ensuing débâcle to the west coast of Inverness-shire he was taken aboard the large French privateer *La Bellone* which had belatedly arrived with money and supplies for the highland army. Worn out by the privations of the campaign he died at sea on 13 May of that year.

John Murray of Broughton described Perth as 'six foot high, of slender make, fair complexion and weakly constitution', with 'a good genius for improvement in which he spent much of his time, and fired with an extraordinary love for his country'. He had

> an unparalleled affection for the exiled family of Stuart. … He never attained to the perfect knowledge of the English language, and what prevented this in a great measure was his over-fondness to speak broad Scots. … He was Roman Catholic, but far from being bigoted. … In short, never was man possessed of more shining qualities, nor attended with a worse fortune. (*Memorials*, 188–9)

Perth died unmarried, the role of 'hostess' to the cause at the brief court at Holyrood in the autumn of 1745 having been taken on by his formidable mother.

John Sibbald Gibson

Sources D. Malcolm, *A genealogical memoir of the most noble and ancient house of Drummond* (1808) · *Memorials of John Murray of Broughton*, ed. R. F. Bell, Scottish History Society, 27 (1898) · W. B. Blaikie, ed., *Origins of the 'Forty-Five and the papers relating to that rising*, Scottish History Society, 2nd ser., vol. 2 (1916) · F. J. McLynn, *The Jacobite army in England, 1745: the final campaign* (1983) · R. Douglas, *The peerage of Scotland* (1764) · GEC, *Peerage*
Likenesses J. S. Stuart, ink drawing (with Lord Seaforth); copy, Scot. NPG · F. de Troy, portrait, priv. coll. [*see illus.*] · line engraving · oils (after F. de Troy), Floors Castle, Borders region · portrait, Scot. NPG

Drummond, James (*bap.* **1787**, *d.* **1863**), botanist and collector, was born in Inverarity, Scotland and baptized there on 8 January 1787. He was the elder son of Thomas Drummond, gardener; his younger brother, Thomas *Drummond, became a collector of North American plants. Little is known of Drummond's early years but in the summer of 1808 he became curator of Cork Botanical Gardens in Ireland. Shortly afterwards he married Sarah Mackintosh (1782–1864); they had six children. Drummond became an associate of the Linnean Society in 1810, and published a botanical textbook (1823) and several papers on Irish plants.

In 1829 Drummond and his family emigrated to the new Swan River Colony of Western Australia. He was superintendent of the government gardens until 1834. By 1835 he had a grant of land at Helena, but in 1836 he exchanged this for one of 2900 acres near Toodyay, which he named Hawthornden, after the ancestral seat in Scotland. His family managed the farm while he collected plants and seeds for museums. He made many of his journeys with his son Johnston (1820–1845) and the zoologist John Gilbert. Drummond's collections, comprising plants from more than 3500 species, were from a huge area of Western Australia, and were used to describe hundreds of new species. One set went to Sir William Hooker at Kew, who was a lifelong correspondent; there are Drummond specimens in at least twenty-five herbaria worldwide. Many plants were named after James Drummond, including the genus *Drummondita* Harvey, which is named for both James and Thomas Drummond—the 'i' for James, the 't' for Thomas.

Drummond also proved that severe stock losses were due to poisonous plants and his observations were published by *The Inquirer* (1842–3). In 1846 Drummond received an honorarium of £200 from the Queen's Bounty for services rendered to botanical science; he went on collecting until old age. He died at Hawthornden, Western Australia, on 26 or 27 March 1863, and was buried in the family grave plot there.   CLEMENCY THORNE FISHER

Sources R. Erickson, 'Drummond, James', *AusDB*, vol. 1 · R. Erickson, *The Drummonds of Hawthornden* (1975) · E. C. Nelson, 'James and Thomas Drummond: their Scottish origins and curatorships in Irish botanic gardens', *Archives of Natural History*, 17 (1990), 49–65 · baptism cert.
Archives Linn. Soc., letter · Melbourne Herbarium, primary collection of plants · NHM, numbers and names of plants of western Australia collected, MS 1880 · RBG Kew, collection of plants | Liverpool Central Library, letter (thirteenth earl of Derby) · RBG Kew, Australian letters to Sir William Hooker
Likenesses probably E. Mackintosh, photograph, c.1860, repro. in Erickson, *The Drummonds of Hawthornden*, frontispiece

Drummond, James (1816–1877), historical genre painter, was born in Edinburgh on 1 September 1816 at 49 High Street, John Knox's house in the Canongate, the son of James Drummond, an Edinburgh merchant noted for his historical knowledge of the Old Town, and his wife, Isabella Borthwick. He attended George Watson's Hospital, Edinburgh, before entering the employment of Captain Brown, an ornithologist, as draughtsman and colourist. He did not, however, remain long in that position, and found more congenial work in the teaching of drawing before becoming a student at the School of Design, under William Allan. He was eighteen years of age when he first exhibited in the Royal Scottish Academy; the subject was *Waiting for an Answer* (exh. Royal Scottish Academy 1835). Later pictures exhibited, like *The Love Letter* (exh. Royal Scottish Academy 1836), by title alone recall works by contemporaries like William Mulready. He became an associate of the academy in 1846, and was elected an academician in 1852. He had a prominent role teaching drawing and in 1857 was chosen as librarian of the academy. In 1858, with Noël Paton and James Archer, he prepared a report upon the best mode of conducting the life school of the academy which met with unanimous approval. He was remembered by students for his 'bright, cheery, quick, suggestive advice or his equally kindly word of warning' (*Annual Report of the Royal Scottish Academy*, 1877). On the death of W. B. Johnstone in 1868, Drummond was appointed curator of the National Gallery of Scotland.

From an early period of his life Drummond devoted himself closely to the study of historical art and collected European and Eastern antiques, jewellery, costume, arms, and armour. Many of his topographical drawings recording the vanishing buildings of Edinburgh, in crayon and pencil, are now in the Scottish National Portrait Gallery, Edinburgh. His artistic training, along with his archaeological interests, laid an emphasis on historical accuracy in costume and architectural detail in his paintings of scenes from the Scottish past, often subjects from Sir Walter Scott. These elements can be seen successfully combined in works like *George Wishart* (exh. Royal Scottish Academy 1845; Dundee Art Gallery), *James Graham, First Marquis of Montrose on his Way to Execution* (exh. Royal Scottish Academy 1859; NG Scot.) and *The Return of Mary Queen of Scots to Edinburgh* (exh. Royal Scottish Academy 1870; NG Scot.). He made his name with *The Porteous Mob* (exh. Royal Scottish Academy 1855; NG Scot.), which was purchased and engraved by the Association for the Promotion of the Fine Arts in Scotland in 1862. His two contrasting pictures of the 'good knight': *Peace* and *War* (exh. British Institution 1850; Royal Collection) were purchased by Prince Albert for Queen Victoria's birthday in 1850 and engraved in the *Art Journal* of 1860 and 1861.

Drummond was elected a fellow of the Royal Scottish Society of Antiquaries in 1848 and curator of the National Museum of the Antiquaries of Scotland between 1851 and 1854 and from 1861 to his death. He was one of their most active members, and at meetings of the society read numerous papers, which were generally illustrated, and later published as separate volumes. Many of these are now regarded as classic texts and include *Scottish Market Crosses*, *Highland Targets and other Shields*, *Ancient Scottish Weapons*, and *Sculptured Monuments in Iona and the Western Highlands*. He died, unmarried, from a malignant tumour, at his home, 8 Royal Crescent, Edinburgh, on 12 August 1877. The Royal Scottish Academy, National Library of Scotland, and Scottish National Portrait Gallery, Edinburgh, hold numerous sketches and drawings by Drummond.   L. A. FAGAN, *rev.* AILSA BOYD

Sources E. Cumming, *James Drummond RSA: Victorian antiquary and artist of Old Edinburgh* (1977) · W. Hardie, *Scottish painting, 1837 to the*

present (1990) · *Art Journal*, 39 (1877), 336 · F. Lewis, *A dictionary of British historical painters* (1979) · J. Halsby and P. Harris, *The dictionary of Scottish painters, 1600–1960* (1990) · Redgrave, *Artists*, 2nd edn · Wood, *Vic. painters*, 3rd edn · O. Millar, *The Victorian pictures in the collection of her majesty the queen*, 2 vols. (1992) · W. D. McKay and F. Rinder, *The Royal Scottish Academy, 1826–1916* (1917) · Graves, *RA exhibitors* · d. cert.

Archives Royal Scot. Acad., letters | Scot. NPG, letters to D. O. Hill · U. Edin. L., letters to David Laing

Likenesses D. O. Hill, collotype, *c.*1845, Scot. NPG · seven, photographs, *c.*1854, Royal Scot. Acad. · D. W. Stevenson, terracotta, 1875, Royal Scot. Acad. · D. O. Hill & R. Adamson, photograph, NPG

Wealth at death £2626 2*s.* 3*d.*: confirmation, 14 Sept 1877, *CCI* · £3154 10*s.* 0*d.*: additional inventory, 30 Dec 1878, *CCI*

Drummond, James (1835–1918), Unitarian minister and theologian, was born in Dublin on 14 May 1835. He was the third and youngest son of the Revd William Hamilton *Drummond (1778–1865), minister of Strand Street Chapel, Dublin. His mother (his father's second wife) was Catherine (*d.* 1879), daughter of Robert Blackley, of Dublin. He entered Trinity College, Dublin, in 1851 and graduated in 1855, gaining the first classical gold medal.

Deeply admiring, as were most Unitarians of the time, of the American theologian William Ellery Channing (1780–1842), in 1856 Drummond chose the ministry and entered Manchester New College, London, where John James Tayler was principal and James Martineau professor of philosophy. His first and only pastorate was at Cross Street Chapel, Manchester, where he became assistant to William Gaskell in 1860. On 5 March 1861 he married Frances (1834/5–1920), the youngest daughter of John Classon, from a family of Dublin corn merchants and proprietor of the Northumberland Baths and the Abbey Music Hall. They had two sons and six daughters.

In 1869 Drummond left Manchester to succeed Tayler as professor of biblical and historical theology. He succeeded Martineau as principal in 1885, and when the college was moved to Oxford in 1889 he went with it. He retired from the principalship in 1906, continuing to live in Oxford until his death at home at 18 Rawlinson Road on 13 June 1918. The funeral service was held at Manchester College on 18 June, and the interment was at Wolvercote cemetery.

As theologian and scholar Drummond showed great independence. He was a loyal and trusted member of the Unitarian denomination—R. D. Darbishire (1826?–1908), a prominent layman, once said of him, 'we have our own St. James' (*The Inquirer*, 11 May 1935)—but it was not the dogmatic negations with which Unitarianism is popularly identified that appealed to him. It was rather the principle of theological freedom and the repudiation of doctrinal tests for its ministers or members, repeatedly affirmed within the denomination and captured in the college motto, 'Truth, Liberty, Religion'. 'A pledge', Drummond said in *Old Principles and New Hopes*, his opening address at Oxford on 25 October 1889, 'which binds teacher or learner to any foregone conclusion, even if that conclusion should be true, may yet bias the intellect and strain the conscience, and so impair the faculty by which truth is apprehended' (Drummond, 13).

He had little use for a priori methods in his critical or historical enquiries. For example, he rejected as circular David Hume's argument that miracles are antecedently incredible, treating the problem as a question of fact but departing dramatically from the conclusions of Unitarians a century earlier who had answered Hume by appealing to incontrovertible testimony in the Bible. Close examination of the narratives, he told his students, showed the evidence for the gospel miracles and for the resurrection to be insufficient.

On the other hand, Drummond broke away from Tayler and Martineau and the general body of advanced New Testament critics in his acceptance of the Johannine authorship of the fourth gospel. But here again his independence came out, not simply in the way in which he rested his case on external far more than on internal evidence, but especially in his contention that, though apostolic in origin, the gospel is largely unhistorical in its record of the ministry of Jesus. He disliked over-curious theological speculation: profoundly conscious of the limitations of human faculties, he thought that speculation on high theological mysteries such as the Trinity might easily become irreverent. He regarded Jesus as Lord and Saviour, the religious and moral leader of the race, and the supreme revelation from God to man.

Drummond's longer contributions to theological literature were all of them important, and in some instances opened out new paths for British scholarship. They exhibited full knowledge of the best authorities of the day, but rested even more on close and prolonged study of the original documents. *The Jewish Messiah* (1877), *Philo-Judaeus* (1888), *Via, veritas, vita* (the Hibbert lectures for 1894), *The Character and Authorship of the Fourth Gospel* (1904), and *Studies in Christian Doctrine* (1908) were his most notable works. With his colleague C. B. Upton he published *The Life and Letters of James Martineau* (1902). He was awarded the LLD degree by Trinity College, Dublin, in 1882 and the LittD in 1892. The degree of DD was given by Tufts University in 1905.

As a preacher Drummond displayed great eloquence and passion. Vividly conscious of the divine presence, profoundly convinced of the great truths on which his whole ministry rested, he searched the conscience of his hearers, braced their moral energies, kindled their spiritual imagination, and communicated some sense of those unseen realities of which he was himself so intensely aware. His innate shyness and an impetuous temper had been disciplined by rigorous self-control. His ardent humanitarianism and sympathy with the oppressed led him to support campaigns for peace, for temperance, and the enfranchisement of women; he was a Liberal and a home-ruler in politics. His love of nature—he was an enthusiastic walker and climber—and deep religious experience combined to produce a character of great elevation and nobility, in which integrity and loyalty to principles were balanced and completed by a singular openness and graciousness of disposition.

A. S. Peake, *rev.* R. K. Webb

Sources E. D. Hicks and G. D. Hicks, 'Memorial introduction', in J. Drummond, *Pauline meditations* (1919), vii–lxii · *The Inquirer* (22 June 1918) · V. D. Davis, 'Our own Saint James', *The Inquirer* (11 May 1935) · J. Drummond, *Old principles and new hopes: an address* (1889), 13; repr. in [R. D. Darbishire], ed., *Theology and piety, alike free: from the point of view of Manchester New College, Oxford* (1890), 374–95 · *The Times* (14 June 1918) · *The Post Office Dublin directory and calendar* (1856) · m. cert. · d. cert.
Archives Harris Man. Oxf., register
Likenesses G. Reid, oils, 1906, Harris Man. Oxf. · photographs, DWL; repro. in Trustees' Album
Wealth at death £14,164 6s. 1d.: probate, 7 Sept 1918, CGPLA Eng. & Wales

Drummond, James Lawson (1783–1853), anatomist and naturalist, was born at Larne, co. Antrim, in May 1783, the second son (there was also a daughter) of William Drummond (*d. c.*1786), a Royal Navy surgeon, and his wife, Rose (*née* Hare). His elder brother was William Hamilton *Drummond (1778–1865). Of Presbyterian upbringing, Drummond attended Belfast Academy, a school run under enlightened Scottish educational principles. After preliminary surgical training, he served as an apprentice surgeon with the navy from 1807 to 1813, then in May of the latter year he went to Edinburgh University to study medicine further. He graduated in 1814 with a thesis entitled 'De oculi anatomia comparativa'. In the same year he was appointed attending physician and dispensary attendant at the Belfast Fever Hospital, but the newly opened Belfast Academical Institution, a collegiate school open to all religious denominations, held considerable interest for him. In 1818, following his offer of an unsalaried lecture course on anatomy and physiology, the institution established its first chair, of 'anatomy and medical physiology', to which Drummond was elected the following year. Apart from the required medical elements he taught 'a very wide field of natural history and a good deal of natural theology'. His position integrated the major strands which were to involve him for the rest of his life—medicine, natural history, and the younger generation.

In 1820 Drummond published *Thoughts on the Study of Natural History*, which revealed his deeply held belief that 'conceptions of the power of Deity will be infinitely enlarged by a study of nature', further expounded in his *First Steps to Botany* (1823). In June 1821 he and seven naturalist friends founded Belfast Natural History Society (from 1840 'and Philosophical' was added to the name) and Drummond served as president until 1842. The society attracted wide public interest and collected a great range of natural history specimens—displayed and explained in its impressive museum, built through public subscription, in College Square North beside the institution. Drummond's popular *Letters to a Young Naturalist* (1831) was a revealing exposition of his theological, moral, and scientific views, and on 1 November 1831 he delivered the museum's opening address.

Apart from actively promoting a botanical garden for Belfast, and a long-standing involvement with Belfast Literary Society, Drummond pursued the foundation of the Academical Institution's medical department, which eventually opened in September 1836 with Drummond as first dean and professor of anatomy and physiology; his *First Steps to Anatomy* was published in 1845. Drummond took retirement in 1849 after thirty years at the institution, when the new Queen's College took over medical teaching. He was married three times, first to a Miss Getty, then to Catharine Mitchell, and finally to Eliza O'Rorke, who alone survived him (they had no family). Following several years of declining health, he died at 8 College Square North on 17 May 1853 and was buried at Ahoghill, co. Antrim, two days later.   HELENA C. G. CHESNEY

Sources *Centenary volume, 1821–1921*, Belfast Natural History and Philosophical Society, ed. A. Deane (1924) · W. Gray, *Science and art in Belfast* (1904) · *Belfast Daily Mercury* (20 May 1853) · *Belfast News-Letter* (20 May 1853) · *Northern Whig* (20 May 1853) · W. Thompson, *The natural history of Ireland*, ed. R. Patterson, 4 vols. (1849–56), vol. 4 · R. Blaney, *Presbyterians and the Irish language* (1996), 155–9
Archives U. St Andr. L., botanical notebooks
Likenesses W. C. Day, portrait, repro. in Deane, *Centenary volume*

Drummond, Jane. *See* Ker, Jane (*b.* in or before 1585, *d.* 1643).

Drummond, John, first Lord Drummond (*d.* 1518). *See under* Drummond family (*per.* 1363–1518).

Drummond, John, styled first earl of Melfort and Jacobite first duke of Melfort (1649–1714), politician, was the younger son of James Drummond, third earl of Perth (*d.* 1675), and Lady Anne (1616?–1656), eldest daughter of George Gordon, second marquess of Huntly, and younger brother of James *Drummond, later fourth earl of Perth and second Jacobite duke of Perth (1648–1716). His early years were influenced by the civil war in Scotland, when his family home at Drummond Castle was occupied by Cromwellian soldiers and his parents had to take refuge at Stobhall nearby. Educated at St Andrews University and at an academy in Angers, he grew up with a hatred of rebellion and rebels.

Early career Known as Lord John Drummond, he joined the army and was appointed captain of the Scottish foot guards in 1673. On 30 April 1670 he married Sophia (*d.* in or before 1680), the heir of Robert Maitland and Margaret Lundin, with whom he had four sons and three daughters. His father-in-law was a brother of John Maitland, duke of Lauderdale, and this connection probably secured Drummond the post of deputy governor of Edinburgh Castle in 1679. The following year he was promoted lieutenant-general and appointed master of the ordnance. He then distanced himself from Lauderdale and supported a group of his opponents known as 'the party', a move that was helped by the death of his first wife. In 1680 he married Euphemia (1652/3–1743), the daughter of Sir Thomas Wallace of Craigie, a lord of session, and in 1682 he became treasurer-depute after the fall of Lauderdale's other brother, Charles Maitland.

During the exclusion crisis Drummond had succeeded in obtaining the favour of the duke and the duchess of York, and in 1683 he was sent to Whitehall by the 'secret committee' of the Scottish privy council to persuade them that Lord Chancellor Aberdeen should be dismissed. In

John Drummond, styled first earl of Melfort and Jacobite first duke of Melfort (1649–1714), by Sir Godfrey Kneller, 1688

the consequent reshuffle of posts, in 1684 he was appointed one of the secretaries for Scotland. His brother Perth had meanwhile been given the post of lord chancellor and the two brothers steadily established an almost complete control over the government of Scotland. After the death of Charles II in 1685 they were confirmed in office by James II, who elevated Drummond as viscount of Melfort in April 1685 and earl of Melfort in August 1686. The new peer was granted some of the confiscated Argyll estates, and exchanged them in 1686 for Riccartoun, Castlemains, and other estates which had been forfeited by Sir Hugh Campbell of Chesnock. Unusually Melfort took his new title from the name of a loch, while his subordinate title, viscount of Forth, was taken from the name of a river.

Servant of James II, 1685–1689 In the summer of 1685 Melfort was converted to Catholicism by his brother, who had been strongly influenced by the papers concerning the deathbed conversion of Charles II. Melfort was inevitably accused of converting for purely political reasons, but his entire future career testifies to his sincerity. As the children of his first marriage remained protestant and would inherit the Lundin estates, he arranged that his new titles and estates should pass to the children of his second marriage. His heir, John, styled viscount of Forth, had been

born in 1682 and was eventually followed by five more sons and six daughters. Melfort lived at Whitehall from 1684 until the end of 1688. In 1687 he was one of the eight original knights of the Order of the Thistle, which he had persuaded the king to revive, and the full-length portrait of him by Kneller shows him wearing his spectacular robes, at the height of his power, before the revolution of 1688. However, his close association with James II's policy of religious toleration made him unpopular and his position was threatened by the invasion of William of Orange in 1688. When the news of the latter's successful landing reached Whitehall in November, Melfort immediately resigned his estates to the crown and had them regranted to his wife, with reversion to their eldest son. He urged the king to stand firm, arrest the whigs, and fight the invader, but when James's nerve failed Melfort advised him to send the baby prince of Wales to France for safety. Intending to meet the prince and his attendants at Dieppe, he left London on 3 December and three days later reached Ambleteuse, where he was soon afterwards joined by his wife and children. However, Lord Dartmouth's refusal to transport the prince meant that Melfort's plan had to be abandoned, so he made his way to the French court and was already at St Germain-en-Laye when first the queen and the prince, and then, shortly afterwards, James II arrived there.

Melfort now became James II's principal secretary of state and accompanied the king to Ireland. There he quickly found himself in opposition to the duke of Tyrconnell and the French ambassador, the comte d'Avaux, both of whom believed that James II should remain in Ireland and overcome all opposition there before crossing over to Great Britain. Melfort urged the king to push on instead to Scotland and link up with the Jacobites under Dundee. He opposed making constitutional concessions and was responsible for the king's ill-judged letter to the Scottish convention in March. D'Avaux found Melfort's opposition so inconvenient that he used his influence with Louis XIV to have him sent back to France to report on the situation. James II showed his appreciation of Melfort's work by giving him an English peerage as Baron Cleworth before his departure in August 1689. The eventual outcome of the Irish campaign and the collapse of the Jacobite position in Scotland suggest that Melfort was probably right to urge the king not to remain in Ireland.

Ambassador and secretary, 1689–1694 Melfort reached St Germain at the beginning of October 1689 and continued in vain to press for an invasion of either Scotland or England. Louis XIV and Mary of Modena then decided that he should be sent as ambassador to Rome. A previous Jacobite ambassador had failed to secure the moral and financial support of the papacy, but the death that summer of Pope Innocent XI, bitter enemy of France, had made a second attempt worthwhile. Immediately after the election of Alexander VIII, Melfort left St Germain for Rome, where he arrived in December. While he was there he discovered that he had been outlawed in February 1690 and that all the estates he had surrendered to his wife had been sequestrated. The following February all his goods were seized in London and later auctioned for £1182. It is unlikely that any Jacobite ambassador could have succeeded at this time. The papacy had taken the anti-French side in the Nine Years' War and James II was now irrevocably associated with Louis XIV. Melfort's embassy at Rome was a considerable social success and he did obtain 30,000 crowns for the relief of British and Irish Catholics, but he failed to persuade the pope to support James II. His presence was badly needed at St Germain after the king's return from Ireland, but the early death of Alexander VIII in February 1691 obliged him to delay his departure by several months. The new pope, Innocent XII, was keen to end the breach with France, but no more disposed than his predecessors to provide the necessary financial support for James II until after the return of peace. Once this had become clear, in the autumn of 1691, Melfort was recalled to St Germain, where he arrived in November. He was then appointed sole secretary of state and became the dominant voice at the Jacobite court.

Melfort maintained that James II would only regain his throne through military conquest, and that political concessions and compromises would be no help and would indeed be harmful to the royal prerogative in the long run, for he was confident that a second Stuart restoration would take place sooner or later. He worked with energy and dedication and persuaded Louis XIV to prepare an invasion of England in the summer of 1692. He argued that there was enough Jacobite support in the English fleet to ensure a successful landing in the south-west and sufficient loyalty among the people to guarantee the overthrow of William III. He also persuaded James II to issue a stern declaration in April 1692 making clear to waverers that, although the privileges of the Church of England would be fully protected after a restoration, no royal pardon would be forthcoming for those who failed to show their loyalty. Before leaving with James II to join the army near Cherbourg, Melfort was made a knight of the Garter by the king in a ceremony at St Germain. A week later the king gave him a warrant creating him duke of Melfort and marquess of Forth, though these titles were to be kept secret until the restoration had been achieved.

The Anglo-Dutch naval victory off La Hogue in June 1692 meant that the invasion had to be abandoned and Melfort had the unenviable task of bearing the bad news to Louis XIV at Namur. His position at the French court was seriously undermined and he was accused of having exaggerated the extent of Jacobite support in England and of stiffening the opposition there by the tone of the king's declaration. He had already made himself unpopular at St Germain, where he favoured religious toleration for dissenters, and various factions began to intrigue against him. The English, who constituted the great majority of the court and who disliked him because he was Scottish, pointed out that he was distrusted by the Jacobites in England, who were not prepared to have any dealings with him. The 'compounders', who believed that James II would now have to make political concessions if he were ever to recover his throne, argued that Melfort's intransigence was making a restoration impossible. Melfort

enjoyed the support of the king and queen, but he rapidly lost that of the French ministers. The Abbé Renaudot, an agent used by the French to act as a liaison between Versailles and St Germain, sided with his enemies and began to make unfounded accusations against him, even that he was a secret agent of William III. His position was steadily weakened. In the spring of 1693 the French and the compounders persuaded James II to change his policy and issue a new declaration offering considerable political concessions. At the same time Lord Middleton arrived from England to become joint secretary of state. From then onwards Middleton handled the correspondence with England and Scotland, while Melfort was only allowed to deal with Catholic (mainly Italian) affairs. Eventually Renaudot's intrigues against him had their effect. In May 1694 Louis XIV formally asked James II to dismiss Melfort as joint secretary of state and he resigned on 2 June. When Louis also asked that Melfort be sent away from St Germain, James advised him that it would be better to live in the provinces than in Paris.

Eclipse and rehabilitation, 1694–1705 The summer of 1694 was a particularly bad time for Melfort. One month after these events he was outlawed by the government in London. Meanwhile his relations with his brother Perth (then at Antwerp) were particularly strained, and in July his wife had a miscarriage while travelling to their new provincial exile. His relations with James II, however, were not undermined, and before his departure the king gave him a formal pardon for all 'treasons' committed against both himself and Charles II. The Melforts took a holiday at Bourbon, then settled at Orléans, where they remained until the end of 1695. They then moved to Rouen in January 1696 and lived there for another year and a half. It was while Melfort was at Orléans that he discovered that he had been attainted in July 1695. It was specified that the children of his first marriage would not be affected by this so there was now a permanent rift in the family. Of his first seven children he seems to have remained on good terms with only one, his son Charles who joined him in France.

In October 1697, after the treaty of Ryswick, Melfort was allowed to live in Paris. He then began to visit the court of St Germain, where he was appointed gentleman of the bedchamber, and in October 1698 he accompanied James II to Fontainebleau. He owed his partial rehabilitation to the influence of his brother, who had been appointed governor of the prince of Wales in 1696, and with whom he had effected a reconciliation. Yet any chance that Melfort might recover his political influence at St Germain was destroyed in February 1701 when one of his letters to his brother was accidentally sent to London. It seems that a mistake was made by a French messenger, who assumed that the letter was addressed to the English court at Whitehall rather than to St Germain. The letter referred to the Jacobite party in Scotland and included some indiscreet speculation about the possibility of a French invasion. It was obviously intended for Perth's eyes only, but William III had it published and Melfort was wrongly accused of having sent it to London deliberately to cause problems between the French and English governments and encourage the prospects of another war. When James II heard the news on 4 March he had a stroke from which he never really recovered. Louis XIV banished Melfort to a second term of provincial exile, this time at Angers, where he had been educated.

Melfort was not allowed to return to Paris until 1705, by which time the War of the Spanish Succession had started and France was once again prepared actively to support the Jacobite cause by invading Scotland. After a secret nocturnal visit to St Germain in February, he was finally declared a duke in March and allowed to visit the court publicly. (It should be added, however, that the often repeated story that Melfort was created duc de Melfort by Louis XIV is without foundation and based on a misunderstanding.) By this time Melfort's health was no longer good and he seems to have lost all interest in resuming his political career. He did not accompany James III (James Francis Edward Stuart) when he attempted to invade Scotland in March 1708.

Private life Although Melfort had a large family, only three of the twelve children from his second marriage were married during his lifetime. In May 1707 John, viscount of Forth, married the duchess of Albemarle, the French widow of James II's illegitimate son who had estates at Lussan in Languedoc. (Their descendants managed to reclaim the earldoms of Melfort and Perth during the nineteenth century.) In April 1710 his daughter Frances was married to an extremely wealthy pro-Jacobite Spanish nobleman named Don José de Rosas y Mélendez de la Cueva, count of Castelblanco. When she died in December 1712 the count then married her elder sister Mary. Later, in 1721, Melfort's son Andrew married an heiress with large estates in Poitou. Melfort's grandchildren achieved important positions both in France and in Spain, where a great-granddaughter married the brother of Charles III.

Melfort had a strong personality and provoked deep feelings among those who knew him. He had many admirers, including both James II and Mary of Modena, and his private secretary from 1689 to 1694 wrote that 'I cannot but love him' because of his 'generous heart', his 'infatiguable labour … and the sweetest of humours' (letters of David Nairne, Scottish Catholic Archives, Blairs MSS. BL. 1/124, 181). But he was doubly on the losing side in politics, first as a Jacobite and then as a non-compounder, and his posthumous reputation reflected the opinions of those who strongly disliked him at the time and rejected the policies that he advocated. The criticisms of d'Avaux and Renaudot were echoed in the influential memoirs of Saint-Simon and he has been consistently vilified by British historians as an irresponsible 'absolutist' without political judgement.

Melfort was very keen on music and was also an accomplished dancer, but he was particularly notable as a connoisseur of painting who created two important collections. The first was assembled at Whitehall before 1688 and included nearly 150 works, including several by Van Dyck, Rubens, Bassano, and Holbein, and portraits commissioned from Kneller. He lost the entire collection when he left England in 1688, but he managed to bring with him a large amount of money. He then began to create another collection while he was in Rome, helped by having large pensions from both James II and Louis XIV, and after his return he made the Stuart court at St Germain an important centre of Italian culture. His collection mainly reflected his taste for seventeenth-century Italian works, but he also acquired portraits by Rembrandt and Van Dyck, while for family portraits he turned to Carlo Maratta and Francesco Trevisani in Rome and François de Troy in France. After his return to Paris in 1705 he opened his collection to the public in his apartment in the Hôtel de Soissons (near St Eustache) and then transferred it in December 1712 to 'la plus belle maison' in the rue des Petits Augustins (now the rue Bonaparte, off the quai Malaquais) (Corp, 'Melfort', 44). Melfort himself also started to paint and sent some of his works to his sister in Scotland.

Melfort died at his house in the rue de la Planche, Paris, on 25 January 1714, after a long illness, when the chances of a Jacobite restoration seemed particularly hopeful. He was buried at St Sulpice. The *Memoirs of John, Duke of Melfort*, published in London later that year 'from the original papers found in the closet of the said Duke, since his death', were a forgery. His widow had financial worries because his French pension was stopped and his money had all been invested in the Hôtel de Ville. After her husband's death she was appointed a lady of the bedchamber by Mary of Modena and in 1715 she sold his collection of paintings. She died in Paris at the age of ninety in March 1743.

EDWARD CORP

Sources E. Corp, 'Melfort: a Jacobite connoisseur', *History Today*, 45/10 (1995), 40–46 · D. Nairne, journal, 1655–1708, NL Scot., MS 14266 · A. Joly, *Un converti de Bossuet: James Drummond, duc de Perth, 1648–1716* (1934) · [E. T. Corp and J. Sanson], eds., *La cour des Stuarts* (Paris, 1992) [exhibition catalogue, Musée des Antiquités Nationales de Saint-Germain-en-Laye, 13 Feb – 27 April 1992] · *Scots peerage* · W. A. Shaw, ed., *Calendar of treasury books*, 9, PRO (1931), esp. pt 4; 10 (1935), esp. pt 1 · E. T. Corp, 'The exiled court of James II and James III: a centre of Italian music in France, 1689–1712', *Journal of the Royal Musical Association*, 120 (1995), 216–31 · E. Corp, ed., *Lord Burlington: the man and his politics* (1998) · *House of Lords sessional papers, 1852–3*, 26 [evidence before Lords committees for privileges and before the house, July 1846, April 1847, June 1847, August 1848] · M. Glozier, 'The earl of Melfort, the court Catholic party and the foundation of the Order of the Thistle, 1687', *Scottish Historical Review*, 79 (2000), 233–8

Archives BL, corresp., Lansdowne MSS 1163 A, B, and C · BL, letter-books, Add. MSS 37660, 37661 · priv. coll., MSS | Archives Diplomatiques, Paris, 'correspondance politique, Angleterre', corresp. · BL, letters to Cardinal Caprara, Add. MS 31246 · BL, letters to duke and duchess of Lauderdale, Add. MSS 23134–23138, 23242–23250, *passim* · Bodl. Oxf., Nairne MSS · NRA Scotland, priv. coll., letters to duke of Queensberry · Scottish Catholic Archives, Edinburgh, Blairs MSS

Likenesses G. Kneller, oils, 1683, priv. coll. · P. Vanderbank, engraving, 1683 · G. Kneller, oils, 1688, Scot. NPG [*see illus.*] · miniature, 1692–4, Belton House, Lincolnshire · I. Beckett, mezzotint (after G. Kneller), BM, NPG; repro. in R. Sharp, *The engraved record of the Jacobite movement* (1996), following p. 182 · P. Vanderbank, line engraving (after G. Kneller), BM, NPG · group portrait, oils (*La* *reception faite au roy d'Angleterre par le roy à St Germain en Laye le VIIe Janvier 1689)* • oils (after G. Kneller), priv. coll.

Drummond, John, styled seventh earl of Perth and Jacobite fourth duke of Perth (*c*.1714-1747), Jacobite army officer, was born in France, the son of James *Drummond, styled fifth earl of Perth and Jacobite second duke of Perth (1674-1720), attainted of his earldom in 1716, and his wife, Lady Jean Gordon (1682/3-1773). A lifelong Roman Catholic, from early youth Drummond, a handsome man as well as 'a most quarrelsome person' (Tayler, 115), was active in the cause of the Stuarts. In 1736, and again in 1741, he visited Scotland, on the latter occasion writing a 28-page memorial, which among other things suggested that the duke of Atholl might stay out of any conflict between the Jacobites and government. In 1739 Lord John was a member of the Society of Young Gentlemen Travellers at Rome, five of whom were painted by Domenico Duprà, whose portrayal of Drummond is our main surviving image of the duke.

In the early 1740s Drummond was prominent among the associators in Scotland who were intent on restoring the Stuarts. In 1743-4 the royal Ecossais was formed in France under his command: recruitment for this regiment was carried out in Scotland, 'notwithstanding the utmost vigilance of the Government' (Allardyce, xx). Kept in the background in 1744 to avoid raising British government suspicions, during the rising of the following year the Royal Scots formed the backbone of the French expeditionary force. Probably following news of the victory at the battle of Prestonpans, Louis XV determined to send Drummond with his Royal Scots to aid the Jacobites. Drummond was ordered to land 'between Edinburgh and Berwick' (McLynn, *France and the Jacobite Rising*, 87), to obey Charles Edward Stuart's commands on arrival (he did not), and to try and recruit a further battalion for his regiment in Scotland. In mid-November 1745 the Royal Scots sailed, together with six picquets of the Irish brigade under Brigadier Stapleton from Ostend for Montrose in *La Fine* (Drummond's frigate), *La Rénommée* (26 guns), *Espérance*, and 'five Dunkirk privateers' (Gibson, 18). *L'Espérance* was taken by the *Sheerness* off Dogger Bank, and two other ships were lost, including *Le Louis XV*, together with about 300 men. *La Fine* grounded at Montrose, while, after she had successfully disembarked her troops, the covering fire from *La Rénommée's* guns enabled the companies from the 2nd battalion of the Forfarshires on shore to capture the sloop *Hazard* from the government forces. Drummond landed on 22 November with at least 700 men, and France dispatched many more, few of whom got through.

None the less, Drummond's arrival placed indisputably French troops in the field and thus (as he pointed out to them) forced the Dutch to withdraw from giving active military help to the government, as the soldiers they had offered were bound by the terms of the surrender of Tournai not to take arms against France until 1 January 1747. News of Drummond's landing, accompanied by an exaggeration of the numbers with him, also helped to stiffen the resolve of senior Jacobite officers to retreat from Derby, at least to some extent in pursuit of the impractical

John Drummond, styled seventh earl of Perth and Jacobite fourth duke of Perth (*c*.1714-1747), by Domenico Duprà, 1739

'fortress Scotland' policy which none the less had an appeal for figures such as Cameron of Lochiel. Lord John himself remained in Scotland rather than join the main army in the south, as instructed by Charles Edward.

Drummond's troops moved south towards Perth in early to mid-December with limited supplies of artillery, including one 16-pounder, while Drummond himself was asked by the Earl Marischal on 14 December to raise Aberdeenshire and the Mearns. Heavy lowland recruitment was also carried on under Lord John's subordinates, including the earl of Cromarty (Fife), Lord Lewis Gordon (Aberdeen and Banffshires), James Moir of Stoneywood (Aberdeen), Sir Alexander Bannerman (Mearns), and Sir James Kinloch (Forfarshire). By the time the army returned from England, Drummond and William, fourth viscount of Strathallan had raised an equal force of 5000 men, which joined Charles's troops at Glasgow on 1 January 1746. Later in the month, with help from the Camerons, Lord John defended Alloa against a landing from Lieutenant-General Henry Hawley. At Falkirk (where he received a flesh wound in the arm), Drummond's troops were in the second and third lines. Subsequently, he acted as 'governor of Fort Augustus' (McLynn, *Charles Edward Stuart*, 227) and as commander on the Spey, engineering the Jacobite victory at Keith in March. After commanding the retreat from the Spey, Drummond was in favour of the abortive night march before Culloden, in which the failure of his Franco-Scottish and Irish regulars to keep up with the clansmen played a significant part. At the battle of Culloden they fought in the second line under his cousin, Lieutenant-Colonel Lord Lewis Drummond, while Lord John commanded the centre, where he attempted to draw the government fire, so that their musket-line could be charged by the Jacobite left: he 'even walked between the lines with his pike in his hand' (Tomasson and Buist, 186). As the rout began, he stayed on the field to rally the troops. The day after Culloden he arrived at the rallying point of Ruthven in Badenoch. Drummond boarded a French ship at Loch nan Uamh on 30 April with his brother, James *Drummond, Jacobite third duke of Perth, who died on 13 May on the return voyage, leaving Lord John to inherit the Jacobite title as fourth duke.

Perth was attainted in 1746, but by this time had returned to what promised to be a glittering career under Marechal Saxe in the French service. Promoted to major-general, the duke served at the siege of Bergen op Zoom in 1747, dying, unmarried, of a fever (possibly combined with wounds) on 28 September. He 'was buried in the Chapel of the English nuns at Antwerp, where there is a monument to himself and his brother' (Scots peerage, 7.56).   MURRAY G. H. PITTOCK

Sources DNB · F. McLynn, France and the Jacobite rising of 1745 (1981) · J. Allardyce, ed., Historical papers relating to the Jacobite period, 1699–1750, 2, New Spalding Club, 16 (1896) · J. Gibson, Ships of the '45 (1967) · Scots peerage · E. Cruickshanks, Political untouchables: the tories and the '45 (1979) · S. Reid, 1745: a military history of the last Jacobite rising (1996) · NL Scot., MSS 17514, 17523 · J. Stuart, ed., The miscellany of the Spalding Club, 1, Spalding Club, 3 (1841) · G. B. Bailey, Falkirk or paradise! The battle of Falkirk Muir, 17 January 1746 (1996) · A. H. Millar, ed., A selection of Scottish forfeited estates papers, Scottish History Society, 57 (1909) · M. Pittock, Jacobitism (1998) · F. J. McLynn, The Jacobite army in England, 1745: the final campaign (1983) · F. J. McLynn, Charles Edward Stuart: a tragedy in many acts (1988) · K. Tomasson and F. Buist, Battles of the '45 (1962) · F. P. Lole, A digest of the Jacobite clubs (1999) · A. Livingstone, C. W. H. Aikman, and B. S. Hart, eds., Muster roll of Prince Charles Edward Stuart's army, 1745–46 (1984) · H. Tayler, ed., Jacobite epilogue (1941) · GEC, Peerage
Likenesses D. Duprà, oils, 1739, Scot. NPG [see illus.]

Drummond, Sir Malcolm (d. 1402?). See under Drummond family (per. 1363–1518).

Drummond, Malcolm Cyril (1880–1945). See under Camden Town Group (act. 1911–1913).

Drummond, Margaret. See Margaret (d. in or after 1374).

Drummond, Margaret (d. 1502), royal mistress, was the eldest of the six daughters of John *Drummond of Cargill, first Lord Drummond (d. 1518) [see under Drummond family (per. 1363–1518)], and his wife, Elizabeth Lindsay. *James IV may have met Margaret when he visited Drummond Castle on 25 April 1496, and she appears to have succeeded Marion Boyd as James's mistress about this time. Coupled with the growing influence of Archibald Campbell, second earl of Argyll, whose sister Isabel was Drummond's daughter-in-law, Margaret's affair with the king helped in the advancement both of her father, who held the office of justiciar from February 1495 until 1501, and of his kinsman Walter Drummond, dean of Dunblane, who became clerk register in 1497. Official acknowledgement of the relationship came on 3 June 1496, when James installed Margaret in apartments in Stirling Castle;

a reference by the Spanish ambassador, Don Pedro de Ayala, to a lady being kept by the king in great state in a castle describes this arrangement.

Margaret Drummond lived at Stirling Castle under the care of its keeper, Sir John Lundy, and of his wife until 30 October 1496, when she was moved to Linlithgow, possibly to give birth to the daughter, also called Margaret, whom she bore the king. The liaison effectively ended in March 1497, when Margaret and her daughter were sent home to Drummond, but although James IV had embarked on his long-running affair with Janet Kennedy in 1498, Margaret received a crown lease for nine years of lands in the earldom of Strathearn, dated 23 January 1498, possibly at the time of her marriage—according to de Ayala she was married off after her return to Drummond, although there is no supporting evidence for this. The king certainly seems to have accepted a measure of responsibility for his erstwhile mistress, as payments to her of £21 and 41s. for her daughter's nurse were made as late as June 1502. When Margaret died, towards the end of 1502, James had their daughter Margaret brought from Drummond Castle to Stirling, where royal children were traditionally brought up, and he paid a quarterly fee until at least 1508 for two priests in Dunblane Cathedral to sing masses for Margaret Drummond.

A number of stories concerning Margaret Drummond's time as royal mistress appear in the eulogistic history of the Drummond family which William Drummond, later first viscount of Strathallan, completed in 1681. He states that the king had known Margaret since 1488 and had desired to marry her, but in 1502 some courtiers, determined to help the king to a far more advantageous marriage, and fearing that his infatuation with Margaret would prevent this, caused her and two of her sisters, with whom she happened to be dining, to be poisoned. There is no contemporary evidence for these stories, and official records attest a much briefer and less dramatic liaison than the exaggerated account presented by William Drummond.   C. A. McGLADDERY

Sources N. Macdougall, James IV (1989), 113–14 · W. Drummond, The genealogy of the most noble and ancient house of Drummond, ed. D. Laing (1831), 138–9 · Scots peerage, 7.40–45

Drummond, Dame (Edith) Margaret (1917–1987), director of the Women's Royal Naval Service, was born on 4 September 1917 at 101 Dundonald Road, Kilmarnock, Ayrshire, one of at least two daughters of Robert James Drummond, professor at the dairy school of the West of Scotland Agricultural College, and his wife, Marion Street. She was educated at Park School, Glasgow, and Aberdeen University. She joined the Women's Royal Naval Service (WRNS) as a Wren writer in April 1941 and, after her administrative skills had been made apparent, she was commissioned as an officer in September that year.

Rising swiftly through the ranks, Drummond served early in 1944 as a first officer on the staff of the commander-in-chief, Plymouth command, and was responsible for the administration and paperwork relating to the command's role in operation Neptune, the

Dame (Edith) Margaret Drummond (1917–1987), by Walter Bird, 1965

allied landings in Normandy in June 1944. She was the first woman to know about the invasion; as Dame Katharine Furse recounted, 'About two months before D-Day she received twenty copies of the naval plans for invasion; she signed for them, and almost slept with them in the strong room, one of the cellars under Mount Wise' (Furse, 232).

After D-day Drummond sailed for India where she worked as assistant secretary to the flag officer, helping with the instruction of the Wrens of the Indian navy, then became superintendent on the staff of the commander-in-chief, East Indies. Back in Britain, her tours of duty included that of officer in charge of HMS *Dauntless*—the Wrens' initial training establishment, as superintendent of the WRNS officers' training course at Greenwich, and as superintendent of training and drafting. She rose to be deputy director, became an OBE in 1960, and was appointed director in June 1964.

During her tenure Drummond oversaw the organization of the new WRNS units in Singapore and Mauritius. She was also called before a Commons select committee to explain how it had come about that the WRNS was not subject to the Naval Discipline Act, an anomaly that was rectified only in 1977. She was created DBE in 1966, and she retired in 1967.

Dame Margaret Drummond settled at Somersham Cottage, Saxlingham, on the north Norfolk coast, where she immersed herself in village life and, as a devoted Christian, to local church activities. A keen gardener, she still found time to chair a civil service interview board. She

was a popular member of the community, and was affectionately remembered for her kindness, dignity, sincerity, and honour. Drummond died at her sister's house, Manor Cottage, 15 High Street, Holt, on 21 April 1987, after several years of failing health. She never lost contact with the service she loved, and was a life member and vice-president of the Association of Wrens and of the WRNS Benevolent Trust. LESLEY THOMAS

Sources V. S. Mason, *Britannia's daughters: the story of the WRNS* (1992) · V. L. Matthews, *Blue tapestry* (1948) · *Daily Telegraph* (24 April 1987) · *The Wren* (Oct 1987) · G. Mills, 'The late Dame Margaret Drummond, D. B. E.', *St Margaret's Church, Saxlingham, Newsletter* · *North Norfolk News* (1 May 1987) · *CGPLA Eng. & Wales* (1987) · b. cert. · m. cert. · K. Furse, *Hearts and pomegranates* (1940)
Likenesses W. Bird, photograph, 1965, NPG [*see illus.*]
Wealth at death £128,576: probate, 15 July 1987, *CGPLA Eng. & Wales*

Drummond [*married name* Keith], **Mary**, **Countess Marischal** (1675–1729), Jacobite sympathizer, was the daughter of James *Drummond, fourth earl, and Jacobite first duke, of Perth (1648–1716), and his first wife, Lady Jane Douglas (*d.* 1678), the fourth daughter of William Douglas, first marquess of Douglas. According to the *Red Book of Grandtully* Mary (or Maria) was born in Scotland on 14 July 1675. About 1690 she married **William Keith**, ninth Earl Marischal (*c.*1664–1712), Jacobite politician, the son of George Keith, eighth Earl Marischal (*d.* 1694), army officer, and Lady Mary Hay (*d.* 1701), courtier and third daughter of the second earl of Kinnoull. The date of Lady Mary's marriage means that she did not accompany her father into exile for Jacobitism in 1693, though she would have witnessed the unpopularity which demanded that exile and his earlier imprisonment at Kirkcaldy between December 1688 and 1693.

William Keith succeeded to the earldom in March 1694. In politics an anti-union tory, he took the oaths to the *de facto* monarchy and his seat in the Scottish parliament in July 1698 and was sworn of the privy council in June 1701. Created a knight of the Thistle by James III (James Francis Edward Stuart) in 1705, his known Jacobite leanings led to his imprisonment in Edinburgh Castle during the rising of 1708 (when his father-in-law accompanied King James to Scotland) and to his being sent for trial in London in its aftermath. Notwithstanding, he was made one of the sixteen representative peers at Westminster in 1710 and remained so until his death in London on 27 May 1712. The earl founded, but did not endow, a chair of medicine at Marischal College, Aberdeen. John Macky described him in colourful terms which enrich his committed but sober political career:

> He is very wild, inconstant and passionate; does everything by starts; hath abundance of flashy wit, and by reason of his quality, hath good interest in the country; all Courts endeavour to have him at their side for he gives himself liberty of talking when he is not pleased with the Government. He is a thorough Libertine, yet sets up mightily for Episcopy; a hard drinker; a thin body; a middle stature; ambitious of popularity. (GEC, *Peerage*, 8.484)

The marriage of Lady Mary and Lord Keith produced an heir, George *Keith, later tenth and last Earl Marischal, a second son, James Francis Edward *Keith, and two daughters: Mary (d. 1721), who married John, sixth earl of Wigtown, and Anne (d. 1728), who married Alexander, sixth earl of Galloway. As the name of her second son suggests, Lady Mary was a committed Jacobite throughout her life. She died on 7 March 1729 at Edinburgh and was buried at Holyrood Abbey. The ascription to her of the song 'When the king comes o'er the water', sometimes called 'Lady Keith's lament', has no solid foundation, and the song itself (printed in James Hogg's *Jacobite Relics* of 1817) has been dated to later in the eighteenth century. Consequently, while in her kinship networks and their combination of Roman Catholicism and Episcopalianism she is representative of the private sphere in which Jacobite sympathies were sustained among the Scottish élite, her principal contribution to Jacobite history remains the parenthood of her soldier sons.

EIRWEN E. C. NICHOLSON

Sources *Scots peerage*, 7.53 · GEC, *Peerage*, new edn, vol. 8 · A. K. Merrill, ed., *The Keith book* (Minneapolis, 1934) · J. Hogg, *Jacobite relics* (1817) · M. G. H. Pittock, *Jacobite politics and poetry* (1994) · W. Donaldson, *Jacobite song* (1988) · W. Fraser, ed., *The Red Book of Grandtully*, 2 vols. (1868)
Archives NRA, priv. coll., corresp. with Mary, fourth countess of Traquair

Drummond, May (1709/10–1772), Quaker minister, was born in Edinburgh, the daughter of John Drummond (d. 1709), a factor and merchant, and his wife, who died in 1736. Her brother George *Drummond (1687–1766) was lord provost of Edinburgh six times and another brother, Alexander *Drummond (d. 1769), was consul in Aleppo. In 1731 May attended the Quaker yearly meeting in Edinburgh and was convinced by the travelling minister Thomas Story that she should become a Quaker. Her family, members of the Church of Scotland, were very much against her choice but she persevered and was soon recognized as a minister. She began to travel extensively in the ministry in Scotland and then, about 1735, she moved to England, where she created a stir among the general public.

May Drummond was a tall, handsome woman, who spoke very eloquently and drew large crowds, on much the same scale as John Wesley, from all social classes. She was even granted an audience by Queen Caroline, which increased her fame. She was particularly appealing to young women, for whom she held special, often very emotional meetings. A poem by 'a young lady', published in the *Gentleman's Magazine* in 1735, gives some idea of her impact:

No more O Spain! thy saint Teresa boast,
There's one outshines her on the British coast …
Too long indeed, our sex has been deny'd,
And ridiculed by men's malignant pride …
That woman had no soul was their pretence,
And woman's spelling past for woman's sense
'Til you, most generous heroine, stood forth,
And shew'd your sex's aptitude and worth.
(*GM*)

In 1736 May published, first in Reading and then in Bristol,

a book of letters, *Internal Revelation the Source of Saving Knowledge*. She travelled widely in England, and visited Ireland in 1738 and again in 1753. Some Friends, however, distrusted her eloquence and her popularity, fearing that she was in danger of acting for her own glory rather than God's.

William Cookworthy (1705–1780) of Plymouth met May in 1744 and was kinder in his estimation. Writing to a friend he said that she was:

one of a surprising genius, her apprehension being quick, lively, penetrating … a great connoisseur of the human heart in all its emotions, passions and foibles, her own open, generous, tender and humane … I had forgotten her person which seems contrived to enforce and embellish truth, not excite desire. Her face and gesture are aimed at the mind. (Miller, 60–61)

He approved the religious content of her speech but was critical of her style: 'rather too learned; her epithets rather swell too much' (ibid.). 'But', he adds, 'I really believe all this to be owing to her education and not to any affectation or want of simplicity' (ibid.). May continued to travel but gradually more doubts were raised about her ministry. Her habit of often mentioning her noble relatives and acquaintances made Friends uneasy and there was a feeling that she demanded too much attention for herself.

In the late 1750s May Drummond returned to Scotland but she was not welcomed in her own country. Edinburgh Quakers felt that she spoke in meeting too often and refused to accept their discipline. Rumours circulated that May, having fallen upon hard times financially, had stooped to pilfering food from the houses of Friends whom she visited. It was also insinuated that she had become a drunkard. Eventually, in 1764, she was officially requested not to preach and her certificate as a minister was withdrawn. She returned to England and continued to travel, becoming a shadow of her former self. Friends treated her kindly but could not acknowledge her ministry. In May 1772 she was in London but later that year she made her way back to Edinburgh, where she died, unmarried, aged sixty-two. Her family forgave her sufficiently to allow her to be buried in the family vault.

GIL SKIDMORE

Sources W. F. Miller, 'Episodes in the life of May Drummond', *Journal of the Friends' Historical Society*, 4 (1907), 55–61, 103–11 · S. Hobhouse, *William Law and eighteenth-century Quakerism* (1927) · E. E. Moore, *Travelling with Thomas Story: the life and travels of an eighteenth-century Quaker* (1947) · *The records and recollections of James Jenkins*, ed. J. W. Frost (1984) · *GM*, 1st ser., 5 (1735), 555
Archives RS Friends, Lond., letters
Likenesses J. Richardson, oils, priv. coll.; photograph, RS Friends, Lond.

Drummond, Peter (1850–1918), locomotive engineer, was born on 13 August 1850 in Polmont, Stirlingshire, the son of George Drummond, who was then a permanent-way inspector on that section of the Edinburgh and Glasgow (later North British) Railway, and his wife, Christina Thomson. When Peter was young the family moved to Maryhill, Glasgow, where he served an apprenticeship with Forrest and Barr, general engineers and millwrights, with whom his elder brother Dugald *Drummond, ten years his senior and a much more forceful character, had also been apprenticed. In 1871, after serving his time, Drummond moved to the locomotive works of the London, Brighton, and South Coast Railway in Brighton where Dugald was already working under William Stroudley. On 29 August 1876 Drummond married Mary McLay Phillips, a dressmaker, the daughter of John Phillips, a Maryhill joiner. They had at least one daughter. When Dugald returned to Glasgow in 1875 to become the locomotive superintendent of the North British Railway, Peter too came north, securing a position at that railway's Cowlairs works. In 1882 when Dugald 'crossed the tracks' to become the locomotive superintendent of the rival Caledonian Railway he took Peter with him, Peter being appointed assistant locomotive engineer—a post reputed to have been created especially for him. Whether originally appointed on merit or not, Drummond possessed good organizational skills and is credited with reorganizing St Rollox works into a far more efficient unit. In 1890 the two brothers' paths diverged: Dugald left to set up a private concern while Peter stayed at St Rollox, supervising the production of many famous Caledonian locomotive classes and being appointed works manager in 1895.

In 1897 Drummond moved to Inverness to become the locomotive, carriage, and wagon superintendent of the Highland Railway. As an astute engineer who was never afraid to copy, he built a 4-6-0 express passenger locomotive that his predecessor, David Jones, had on the drawing board when he was appointed, merely replacing the Jones style chimney and cab with designs similar to contemporary practice on the Caledonian. These engines proved so successful that fifty similar machines were purchased by the French Chemins de Fer de l'Est. He reorganized the locomotive works at Lochgorm along modern lines and designed a variety of successful snowploughs. When he turned his attentions to new locomotive designs he looked more to the Caledonian and to his elder brother's design than to any previous Highland tradition for inspiration—indeed throughout his design career he was highly influenced by Dugald, borrowing many features both good and bad and producing engines which possessed a 'family likeness'. He perhaps only became his own man in terms of design after Dugald's death in 1912. Among the bad features borrowed were firebox cross water tubes and steam reversing, both of which were disliked by crews; otherwise his locomotives were simple and robust. In 1906 his status was elevated to chief mechanical engineer.

Drummond moved to Kilmarnock in 1912 to become the locomotive, carriage, and wagon superintendent of the Glasgow and South Western Railway at a salary of £1100 per annum. Overbearing, and in open contempt of his predecessor, James Manson, he made sweeping changes to established practice, including the imposition of the 'Drummond Standard' left-hand drive, and built a series of huge engines—his first three designs were the heaviest of their wheel arrangement in the UK at the time. Unfortunately these engines, encumbered with typical Drummond gadgetry of feed pumps and steam driers, were not very successful and were disliked by the crews and maintenance staff alike. After about three years at Kilmarnock an unexplained and total change took place in him. Previously rough and overbearing, not unlike his brother, he became a quiet man, fair in dealing with his men and building engines which were sound in design and even brilliant in performance.

Drummond was elected a member of the Institution of Mechanical Engineers in 1898. He took a keen interest in the education of his men and in their improvement societies. On 30 March 1918 he became ill and died of cancer on 30 June 1918 at Belmont, Grange Terrace, Kilmarnock, aged sixty-seven. RONALD M. BIRSE, rev. JIM SMELLIE

Sources T. Middlemas, *The Scottish 4-4-0: its place in history* (1994) • D. L. Smith, *Locomotives of the Glasgow & South Western Railway* (1976) • C. Highet, *Scottish locomotive history, 1831–1923* (1970) • J. R. H. Cormack and J. L. Stevenson, *The Drummond Smith & Cummings classes* (1990), vol. 2 of *Highland railway locomotives* • B. Haresnape and P. Rowledge, *Drummond locomotives: a pictorial history* (1982) • *Institution of Mechanical Engineers: Proceedings* (1918), 449–50 • bap. reg. Scot., 13 Aug 1850, 8 Sept 1850 • m. cert. • d. cert.
Archives General Register Office for Scotland, Edinburgh, RHP collection, locomotive carriage and wagon drawings (ex BR) • National Railway Museum, York, Railprint collection

Drummond, Peter Robert (1802–1879), bookseller and agriculturist, was born at Madderty, Perthshire, the son of John Drummond, a small farmer, and his wife, Jean Gow. He was educated in Madderty, and in early life worked as a carpenter. He attained skill as a maker of picture frames, which brought him into the society of picture dealers and allowed him to gain some knowledge of art.

While working in Glasgow as assistant to his uncle, a provision merchant, Drummond developed a love of literature. Towards the end of 1832 he opened a circulating library at 15 High Street, Perth. During the same year he made the acquaintance of the poet Robert Nicoll who was then apprenticed to a nearby grocer. On Drummond's advice Nicoll gave up grocery and started a bookselling business in Dundee.

A few years later Drummond was able to move to larger premises at 32 High Street, where he largely relinquished his circulating library and entered fully into the bookselling trade. From here he introduced Perth audiences to Jenny Lind, Grisi, and other famous singers. Drummond then moved to 46 George Street from his High Street premises, and built what was to become the Exchange Hotel. He intended to use the premises as a printing office, and perhaps to start a newspaper. He resolved, however, to turn to farming, and, having completed the building as a hotel, made over his bookselling business to his cousin John. He took the holding of Balmblair, in the parish of Redgorton, Perthshire, from Lord Mansfield. Drummond wrote several pamphlets on political and agricultural subjects, including *The Tenants and the Landlords versus the Free Traders* (1850), in support of the agricultural interest. He was also something of an inventor, and was awarded a medal for a churn at the Great Exhibition of 1851, and received an honourable mention for an agricultural rake at the exhibition of 1862. He became an enthusiastic collector of paintings and engravings, and about 1859 he exhibited his collection in the Exchange Hall, Perth.

By 1873 Drummond had retired from farming, and devoted himself to writing. He died suddenly at his home, Ellengowan, Almond Bank, near Perth, on 4 September 1879, and was buried at Wellshill cemetery, Perth. Drummond had been married twice, first to Helen Bryce, and then to Ellen Gow, both of whom predeceased him. He had at least two sons. His *Perthshire in Bygone Days: one Hundred Biographical Essays* was published posthumously in 1879, and *The Life of Robert Nicoll*, which he had intended to issue with a complete edition of the poet's works, was edited by his son James, and appeared in 1884.

GORDON GOODWIN, rev. DOUGLAS BROWN

Sources Boase, *Mod. Eng. biog.* · private information (1888) [James Drummond] · *Perthshire Constitutional* (8 Sept 1879), 2–3 · *Perthshire Advertiser* (5 Sept 1879), 2 · *Perthshire Advertiser* (11 Sept 1879), 2 · *Perthshire Courier* (9 Sept 1879), 3 · bap. reg. Scot.
Archives Perth and Kinross council archive, papers
Wealth at death £532 15s. 10d.: inventory, 7 Aug 1880, CCI

Drummond, Sir Peter Roy Maxwell (1894–1945), air force officer, was born on 2 June 1894 in Perth, Western Australia, and registered as Roy Maxwell, the son of John Maxwell Drummond, a merchant, and his wife, Caroline Lockhart. Having been educated at the Scotch College in Melbourne he joined the cadet corps and passed the senior and higher public examinations then set by the University of Adelaide. On 10 September 1914 he enlisted in the all-volunteer Australian Imperial Force (AIF), giving his occupation as bank clerk. Precluded from active service by his slight build, he was posted to the 2nd stationary hospital as a medical orderly. In December 1914 he embarked for the Middle East, and by April 1915 he was assisting surgeons operating by candlelight in a hospital ship off Gallipoli. Later, suffering from dysentery and debility, he was evacuated to England and hospitalized.

With what he described as 'mixed feelings', Drummond was discharged from the AIF on 14 April 1916 and accepted the commission he had applied for with the Royal Flying Corps. After flying training as a temporary second lieutenant at Shoreham-on-Sea, Sussex, he was attached as a pilot to 1 squadron, Australian Flying Corps, based in Egypt. With this unit he won the Military Cross (16 August 1917) for an action involving six enemy aircraft; the citation noted his 'skill and courage on all occasions'.

On promotion to temporary captain in October 1917, Drummond joined 111 squadron, Royal Flying Corps, equipped with Nieuports and SE 5as. In December he and his observer encountered three German fighters over Tul Keram, Palestine, and destroyed them all. Drummond was awarded the DSO. In March 1918 his single-handed action against six enemy fighters resulted in the destruction of two and the award of a bar to his DSO. From July 1918 he commanded 145 squadron, Royal Air Force. After being promoted acting major in September he was mentioned in dispatches for the attacks he made on Turkish infantry in the following month. The war ended with Drummond

credited with seven and a half confirmed victories, including six over the formidable Albatross DV type. In August 1919 he accepted a permanent commission in the RAF.

As acting squadron leader, in 1920 Drummond commanded H unit, which accompanied a punitive expedition against the Garjak Nuers in south-eastern Sudan. After four weeks of bombing and machine-gunning this rebel faction capitulated. On his return to England in 1921 Drummond was appointed OBE. Following graduation from the RAF Staff College, Andover, in 1923, he worked directly under Air Chief Marshal Sir Hugh Trenchard at the Air Ministry. Between 1925 and 1929 Drummond was on loan to the Royal Australian Air Force (RAAF) and served as director of operations and intelligence at their headquarters in Melbourne. He acted as aide to Air Marshal Sir John Salmond, who visited Australia in 1928 to report on the RAAF. On 17 July 1929 he married Isabel Rachael Mary Drake-Brockman, a member of a prominent Western Australian family, at the fashionable St John's Anglican Church, Toorak. She was the daughter of Paris Frederick Drake-Brockman, a barrister. The couple had a son and two daughters.

After returning to England in 1930 Drummond attended the Imperial Defence College, and in the following year, on his promotion to wing commander, was given command of Tangmere, Sussex, an important fighter station in Britain's air defence system. Between 1933 and 1936 he was again at the Air Ministry. In January 1937, while commanding RAF station, Northolt, Middlesex, he was promoted group captain.

Drummond returned to the Middle East in November 1937 as senior air staff officer in the RAF Middle East command, based at Cairo. There he took part in building the infrastructure for a modern air force. This task was almost completed when Italy entered the war on 10 June 1940. By then Drummond had been promoted air commodore, and in January 1941 he attained the rank of air vice-marshal. On 1 June 1941 Air Chief Marshal Arthur Tedder took over as air commander-in-chief, Middle East, and Drummond was appointed his deputy, as acting (temporary June 1943) air marshal. Drummond and Tedder developed the concept of a mobile strike force capable of operating fully with the other two services.

In 1942 Drummond was offered but rejected the post of chief of the air staff, RAAF. In an attempt to solve the problems which had arisen in that service's higher command structure, the Australian government raised the matter of Drummond's appointment again in April 1943. On this occasion the Air Ministry refused to release Drummond, who had been selected to become air member for training, with a seat on the Air Council, the RAF's ruling body. In Tedder's opinion the Air Ministry's decision was wise: he later referred to Drummond's ability and support as important factors in winning the war in north Africa.

As air member for training, Drummond was partly responsible for managing the supply and training of aircrew made possible through the functioning of the empire air training scheme. By 1944 it had become obvious, through investigations made by Winston Churchill as prime minister and minister of defence, that there was a massive surplus of aircrew available, under training and into the foreseeable future. By May 1944 Drummond thought that only high casualty rates in the planned invasion of Europe would counteract this surplus of aircrew. He was appointed CB in 1941 and promoted KCB in 1943. At that point he formally took his nickname Peter, which he had acquired at Scotch College, as an additional forename.

Drummond was 5 feet 7 inches tall with a fair complexion, brown eyes, and brown hair, and he possessed a pleasant unaffected personality which made him a popular officer. On 27 March 1945, *en route* for Canada to mark the achievements of the empire air training scheme, the Liberator in which he was travelling, *Commando*, was lost near the Azores. No trace of the aircraft (which had been used on several occasions by Churchill) or of Drummond and its other occupants was ever found. All the passengers, who included Sir John Abraham, deputy undersecretary of state for air, Rupert Brabner, joint undersecretary for air, and H. A. Jones, director of public relations at the Air Ministry, were presumed to have died that day. JOHN MCCARTHY

Sources DNB · P. Firkins, *The golden eagles* (1980) · *The Times* (17 Aug 1917) · *The Times* (27 March 1918) · *The Times* (27 July 1918) · *The Times* (26 Aug 1918) · *The Times* (13 April 1945) · *The Aeroplane* (20 April 1945), 452–3 · PRO, AIR 2/5943 · Australian War Memorial records · *AusDB* file on Sir Peter Drummond, Australian National University, Canberra · private information (2004) [J. McCarthy] · [Lord Tedder], *With prejudice: the war memoirs of marshal of the Royal Air Force, Lord Tedder* (1966) · V. Orange, *Coningham* (1990) · b. cert.
Likenesses W. Stoneman, photograph, 1943, NPG · H. A. Freeth, pencil drawing, IWM · E. Kennington, pastel drawing, IWM · C. Orde, oils, Gov. Art Coll. · photographs, Hult. Arch.
Wealth at death £5819 16s. 5d.—in England: Australian probate sealed in England, 24 April 1946, *CGPLA Eng. & Wales*

Drummond, Robert Hay (1711–1776), archbishop of York, was born Robert Hay in London on 10 November 1711, the second son of George *Hay, eighth earl of Kinnoull (1689–1758), then known as Viscount Dupplin, and his wife, Abigail, *née* Harley (d. 1750), second daughter of Robert *Harley, first earl of Oxford and Mortimer. In 1718 he entered Westminster School, at that time noted for high-church, tory, and nonjuring principles, complementary to his family's tory and Jacobite connections. It is said that his singular presence of mind when the ostrich plumes on his costume caught fire during a school production of *Julius Caesar* first brought him to the notice of Queen Caroline, whose patronage continued until her death in 1737. After Westminster, Hay went up to Christ Church, Oxford, matriculating on 12 April 1728. He was elected canoneer student that year, and graduated BA on 25 November 1731. Having spent several years on the grand tour with his cousin Thomas Osborne, fourth duke of Leeds, he returned to Oxford to read in preparation for holy orders. After taking his MA on 13 June 1735, he was ordained deacon on 26 June 1736 and priest the following day by John Potter, bishop of Oxford and later archbishop of Canterbury, and was presented immediately by his uncle Edward Harley, second earl of Oxford, to the rectory of Bothal,

Robert Hay Drummond (1711–1776), by Andrea Soldi, 1755

Northumberland, which he retained until 1761. In the same year, 1736, through the interest of Queen Caroline, he was appointed a royal chaplain, and later rose to be a deputy clerk of the closet. In 1739 Hay assumed the name and arms of Drummond, as heir to his great-grandfather William Drummond, first viscount of Strathallan, who had entailed the estates of Cromlix and Innerpeffray, Perthshire, on the younger son of the Kinnoull family. On 29 April 1743 he was appointed to a prebendal stall at Westminster, but did not take up the duties of the post until after he had returned from attendance on George II during the German campaign in 1743. This arduous experience served well to prepare him for gruelling diocesan duty later in life. After the battle of Dettingen, Drummond preached the sermon (on Psalm 8: 5) at the thanksgiving service attended by the king at Hanau on 7 July 1743.

Drummond took his BD and DD degrees at Oxford on 9 June 1745, and was consecrated bishop of St Asaph at Kensington church on 24 April 1748, when he gave up the stall at Westminster. He made a point of residing for several months every summer in the diocese, which he 'constantly mentioned … with peculiar affection and delight' (DNB). Energy and stamina characterized his episcopate, and he conducted full visitations in 1749, 1753, and 1758, taking a close interest in the condition of church buildings, the regularity with which parish registers were kept, and the educational and pastoral standards of the clergy. He made significant use of rural deans' reports, and demonstrated a sympathetic awareness of the importance of the Welsh language. On 31 January 1749 Drummond married Henrietta (d. 1773), daughter of Peter Auriol, a London merchant. Six surviving sons (the eldest of whom, Robert, became tenth earl of Kinnoull) and three daughters attested to the success of the union, but their happiness was later marred by the death, in late childhood, of all three daughters: Henrietta, Abigail, and Charlotte, in 1765, 1766, and 1769 respectively. The children were educated at home, in great part by Drummond himself, who paid particular attention to history and religious instruction.

Drummond was a kinsman of Henry Pelham and Thomas Pelham-Holles, first duke of Newcastle, and, unsurprisingly, regularly attended the House of Lords throughout his time at St Asaph. He was much involved in routine committee work, particularly in connection with road improvements. He also became noted as a preacher, not only before the House of Lords on several state occasions, but also for the Society for the Promotion of Christian Knowledge and the Society for the Propagation of the Gospel. His reputation was further enhanced during a long debate in the House of Lords on 22 February 1754, when his earnest and eloquent contribution was largely instrumental in deflecting a charge of Jacobitism that had been levelled against Andrew Stone, sub-governor to the prince of Wales (afterwards George III), James Johnson, bishop of Gloucester, and William Murray, afterwards earl of Mansfield, all, like Drummond himself, old Westminsters and Christ Church men. Later, Drummond's connections to Westminster would be recognized by his appointment as a Busby trustee of the school (11 April 1764).

Drummond had been seen by some as a possible successor to Matthew Hutton at Canterbury in 1758, and neither his promotion to the see of Salisbury on 11 June 1761 nor his rapid translation to York on 23 October of the same year were unexpected. Horace Walpole noted that Drummond was seen as 'a man of parts, and of the world' (Walpole, 3.14) and 'a dignified and accomplished prelate' (*DNB*), and he was in favour with the court. On 22 September 1761, shortly before his formal election as archbishop of York, Drummond preached the sermon at the coronation of King George III and Queen Charlotte. Taking his text from 1 Kings 10: 9, 'Because the Lord loved Israel for ever, therefore made he thee King, to do judgement and justice', Drummond, though hesitating to assert the new king's title in terms of hereditary right, presented an explicit account of monarchy as a divinely sanctioned ordinance and concluded with a powerful (and effective) exhortation to the young king about the binding sanctity of the coronation oath. He was sworn of the privy council on 7 November 1761. His close involvement with the court, epitomized by his appointment as lord high almoner, soon caused him to lament the factiousness of many of his former whig colleagues, and led to estrangement from the duke of Newcastle. Drummond wrote to Newcastle in November 1763:

> In this infamous affair of Mr Wilkes … I neither think it for the honour of any person, nor for the good of the cause of the whigs to espouse such a man and put yourselves so totally in the wrong in the eyes of all the world. I would wish

to look up always to the support of the King's person and family, and the essentials of the Constitution. (BL, Add. MS 32952, fol. 370, cited in Sykes, 55)

In consequence of these developments, Drummond became less active in parliament, and instead he devoted his considerable energies to the affairs of the archdiocese of York, badly neglected during the primacy of his predecessor, the invalid John Gilbert. Having an estate at Brodsworth, near Doncaster, which had been acquired by his father in 1713, Drummond and his family were able to continue to reside within the diocese while extensive improvements and new building in the gothick taste were being carried out at the archepiscopal palace in Bishopthorpe between 1761 and 1769, to the designs of Thomas Atkinson. A new gatehouse and west front to the palace were constructed in a style to rank with 'the foremost displays of Gothic fantasy in mid-eighteenth century England' (Pevsner, *Yorkshire, West Riding*, 1967, 109), the chapel was refurbished, and the parish church rebuilt.

> The see of York was fortunate in … Drummond, who was … enabled by his private fortune to maintain the most magnificent traditions of episcopal entertainment and by his territorial connections with the county to establish the most cordial relations with its chief laity. (Sykes, 68)

He was an enthusiastic art collector, owning many notable works, among them Benjamin West's *Agrippina at Brundisium with the Ashes of Germanicus*, engraved in mezzotint by Richard Earlom in 1773. According to the memoir by his sixth son George, prefixed to the 1803 publication of his *Sermons*, 'Wherever he lived, hospitality presided; wherever he was present, elegance, festivity, and good humour were sure to be found. His very failings were those of a heart warm even to impetuosity' (*DNB*).

However, Drummond was more than just a magnificent prelate. His primacy occurred at a time when the large archdiocese of York, containing 650 parishes, was on the point of great change, marked by population growth, industrial invention, and religious revivalism. Drummond was not unaware of these developments. Just as at St Asaph, he made systematic attempts to assemble information about the diocese by means of diligent correspondence and extensive travelling, for visitations and to ordain and confirm, in a manner that has been fairly compared with the itinerant ministry of John Wesley. Between 1768 and 1771 alone, Drummond is estimated to have confirmed an estimated total of 41,600 people. His visitations, in 1764 and 1770, drew upon experience already gained in 1758, when Drummond had carried out a York visitation on behalf of Archbishop Gilbert. The surviving documentation for the 1764 visitation, which has been described as 'the most important of the century' (Jago, 62), gives a detailed impression of the church's activity and effectiveness, offering an interesting opportunity for comparison with Archbishop Herring's better-known returns of 1743. Drummond's returns indicate that the church was 'broadly conscientious and successful by its own standards' (Jago, 265), with particular strengths in preaching, catechizing, and charitable activity.

Drummond was also aware of his responsibilities as a

metropolitan, and worked particularly closely with Thomas Secker, archbishop of Canterbury from 1758 to 1768. They collaborated regularly with regard to ordinands and dispensations, and shared a practical sympathy for the episcopal cause in North America. In June 1764, at Secker's request, Drummond prepared a report, *Thoughts upon the Present State of the Church of England in America*, acknowledging the deficiency of jurisdiction by commissary of the bishop of London and re-stating the case (which was not new) for a colonial episcopate. The proposal to establish four suffragan bishops, with handsomely endowed incomes, at Burlington in New Jersey, William and Mary College in Virginia, Charlestown in South Carolina, and Codrington College in Bermuda, was received cordially, though ineffectually, by the marquess of Rockingham, prime minister from 1765 to 1766, and by William Petty, second earl of Shelburne, secretary of state for the south in the succeeding Chatham administration, who met with Secker and Drummond in 1767 to discuss the matter. However, the rapidly deteriorating political situation in North America ensured that practical progress was impossible. Despite this disappointment, Drummond retained his sympathetic interest in this forward-thinking cause, and in 1776 he subscribed £30 to a fund for the distressed episcopalian clergy.

Drummond's advice was also sought with regard to the ecclesiastical settlement of Canada at the end of the Seven Years' War. In a substantial and thoughtful report prepared for Shelburne as first lord at the Board of Trade in April 1764, *Thoughts upon the Ecclesiastical Establishment in Canada*, he proposed a plan which anticipated the eventual provisions of the Quebec Act in 1774. Although anxious to use the evidence of his visitation returns to limit and control recusancy in England, Drummond accepted that it would be expedient to allow limited freedom of worship to Roman Catholic French Canadians, while hoping that the advancement of the Anglican Church in Canada might then occur gradually, by means of missionary endeavour and the establishment of free schools. In his own churchmanship, he was regarded as 'pious without enthusiastic flame' (Abbey, 2.210), deeply attached to 'the decent services and rational doctrines of the Church of England' (*DNB*). His dislike for Calvinism was manifested in a freely expressed criticism of some passages in the articles and homilies, and in his refusal to accept John Newton as a candidate for holy orders in 1764. His *Letter on Theological Study*, originally intended for private circulation, showed evidence of wide reading, not only in divinity. Unlike his predecessors at York, he did not insist on rigid conformity in the matter of clerical dress, and irritated the high-churchman William Cole by walking about without his gown and cassock, 'habited in every respect like a layman' (Mather, 261, n. 34).

The death of Drummond's wife in 1773 affected him deeply. Having made his will early in 1776, he died at Bishopthorpe on 10 December and was buried beneath the altar at the parish church of St Andrew, Bishopthorpe. At his own request, no memorial was erected. A collected edition of his six previously published sermons, together with the *Letter on Theological Study* and a short *Memoir* by his son, George William Auriol Hay Drummond, prebendary of York, appeared in Edinburgh in 1803.

RICHARD SHARP

Sources J. Jago, *Aspects of the Georgian church* (1997) • P. M. Doll, *Revolution, religion and national identity: imperial Anglicanism in British North America, 1745–1795* (2000) • S. H. Cassan, *Lives of the bishops of Sherborne and Salisbury* (1824), 284–303 • *DNB* • F. C. Mather, 'Georgian churchmanship reconsidered: some variations in Anglican public worship 1714–1830', *Journal of Ecclesiastical History*, 36 (1985), 255–83 • N. Sykes, *Church and state in England in the XVIII century* (1934) • J. Ingamells, *Catalogue of portraits at Bishopthorpe Palace* (1972) • J. Ingamells, *The English episcopal portrait, 1559–1835: a catalogue* (privately printed, London, 1981) • *Engraved Brit. ports.*, vol. 2 • *Debrett's Peerage* (2000) • *Scots peerage* • GEC, *Peerage* • Burke, *Peerage* (1999) • C. J. Abbey, *The English church and its bishops, 1700–1800*, 2 vols. (1887) • *Old Westminsters* • H. Walpole, *Memoirs of King George II*, ed. J. Brooke, 3 vols. (1985)
Archives Borth. Inst., corresp. and papers, Bp C&P VII • NL Wales, corresp. and papers • W. Yorks. AS, Leeds, Yorkshire Archaeological Society, estate papers, DD 132 | BL, corresp. with duke of Newcastle, etc., Add. MSS 32700–33082, *passim* • Hunt. L., letters to Elizabeth Montagu • NRA Scotland, priv. coll., Kinnoull MSS • U. Nott. L., letters to third duke of Portland
Likenesses A. Soldi, oils, 1755, York City Art Gallery [*see illus.*] • J. Watson, mezzotint, 1764 (after J. Reynolds), BM, NPG • J. Reynolds, oils, 1764–5, City Art Museum, St Louis; version, Scot. NPG • T. Hudson, oils, *c*.1765, Bishopthorpe Palace, York; version, Christ Church Oxf.

Drummond, Samuel (1765?–1844), history and marine painter, was born, according to Redgrave, in London on 25 December 1765; however, Farington records Drummond himself telling him that he 'did not know where He was born but He believed in Scotland', and that in 1808 he was 'abt. 41 years old' (Farington, *Diary*, 9.3247, 27 March 1808). At about thirteen he was apprenticed to the sea service, working the Baltic trade for six or seven years, and reportedly serving in three naval engagements. At twenty he married a widow with five children; they had two children of their own who subsequently died. His wife also died some two and a half years after their marriage.

Having given up the sea, Drummond worked for a short time as a clerk, but was set on a career as a painter. In 1791 he entered the Royal Academy Schools and submitted his first works to the academy exhibition; otherwise he appears to have been self-taught, not unusual for a marine painter at this time. He continued to exhibit at the academy for the rest of his life, a total of 303 works. About 1794 he remarried, and was the father to five children. He supported his family by doing portraits and work for the publisher Asperne, for the *European Magazine*. He achieved some celebrity in portraiture, which his facility enabled him to produce very quickly. Farington noted that he could produce a portrait in a single sitting lasting an hour and a half, and charged 5 guineas for a head and 8 guineas for a three-quarter length. He had ambitions, however, to work in the highest rank of painting, that of history painting, and produced several works relating to the naval campaigns of the Napoleonic wars. His *Death of Nelson*, exhibited at the British Institution in 1807, received good notices and was engraved. His background and manner, however, appear to have impeded his progress in the art establishment. At his application to the academy in 1807 to become an associate, John Constable referred to him as 'the king of a Pot House, [with] such low habits & notions that he seemed unfit to be associated with men of rank' (Farington, *Diary*, 8.3142, 16 Nov 1807). Yet he was elected an associate in 1808, and thereafter achieved some success in painting naval historical subjects. His *Battle of Camperdown, 11 October 1797: Duncan Receiving the Surrender of Admiral de Winter*, commissioned by the British Institution, was exhibited in 1827 and subsequently presented to Greenwich Hospital. It is now in the collection of the National Maritime Museum, Greenwich, which houses the most substantial collection of Drummond's work. His later pictures were increasingly of biblical and poetic subjects.

Although very competent, Drummond's history paintings are generally somewhat stiff compositions, and derivative of the major history painters of the period, particularly Philippe-Jacques de Loutherbourg and Benjamin West; Waterhouse notes a growing tendency in his work towards a chalkiness of finish. He died on 6 August 1844 in London. GEOFF QUILLEY

Sources Farington, *Diary* · Redgrave, *Artists* · E. H. H. Archibald, *Dictionary of sea painters* (1980) · Graves, *Brit. Inst.* · A. Graves, *A century of loan exhibitions, 1813–1912*, 5 vols. (1913–15) · Graves, *RA exhibitors* · Waterhouse, *18c painters* · A. Wilson, *A dictionary of British marine painters* (1967) · B. Stewart and M. Cutten, *The dictionary of portrait painters in Britain up to 1920* (1997) · *Concise catalogue of oil paintings in the National Maritime Museum* (1988)
Likenesses W. Barnard, mezzotint, pubd 1805 (after S. Drummond), BM · G. H. White, ink and pencil drawing, 1842, NPG · J. T. Smith, pencil drawing, BM

Drummond, Thomas (*bap.* 1793, *d.* 1835), horticulturist and botanical collector, was baptized on 8 April 1793 at Inverarity, Forfarshire, Scotland, the second son of Thomas Drummond, gardener at Fotheringham near Inverarity. He was the younger brother of the botanical collector James *Drummond (*bap.* 1787, *d.* 1863). He trained as a gardener, becoming manager of George Don's Doo Hillock nursery, Forfar, after Don's death in 1814. He married Isobel Mungo on 18 November 1820 in Forfar; they had three children, Ann, James, and Isabella.

Being well schooled in botany and a protégé of Dr William Jackson Hooker, then professor of botany in the University of Glasgow, Drummond was chosen to join Captain John Franklin's second Arctic expedition (1825–7) as assistant naturalist to Dr John Richardson. The expedition travelled from New York westward to the Mackenzie River in Canada. On 20 August 1825 Drummond left the main party at Cumberland House, Saskatchewan, and explored westwards into the Canadian Rockies, discovering numerous new plants. He sailed from York factory on Hudson Bay in the same ship as his 'old botanical acquaintance' (Coats, 309), another of Hooker's protégés, David Douglas, early in September 1827 and reached England on 11 October 1827. He returned to Forfar, bringing with him some of his American collections.

By 7 August 1828, Drummond had moved to Belfast as the first curator of the Belfast Botanic and Horticultural

Society's new botanical garden. He was constantly to complain about the lack of qualified staff and shortage of funds, and there was considerable conflict between him and committee members. By August 1830 he was determined to resign but on 24 November 1830 he was dismissed because he refused to apologize for 'hasty words' to a member of the committee. Drummond, who, according to Mrs Katharine Templeton (11 December 1830) in a letter to Professor William Hooker, had a 'fatal propensity for strong drink', then returned to Scotland, promising her not to 'take fermented Liquors for a year' (Templeton to Hooker, 11 Dec 1830, W. J. Hooker correspondence). He was determined to return to North America as a plant collector and on 25 April 1831 landed in New York. He had a moderately successful few years gathering plants, seeds and birds especially in Louisiana and Texas, but *en route* by sea from Apalachicola for Key West, Florida, some time between 9 February and 11 March 1835, he died in unexplained circumstances in Havana, Cuba.

Drummond produced two exsiccatae of mosses; *Musci Scotici* (Forfar, 1824–5) and *Musci Americani* (Glasgow 1828). He is commemorated in the names of numerous North American plants (including *Dryas drummondii*, *Oenothera drummondii*, and *Phlox drummondii*) and an Irish horsetail (*Equisetum drummondii*, now *E. pratense*). William H. Harvey cleverly commemorated both Thomas and his elder brother, James, in *Drummondita*—'i' for 'j' for James, and 't' for Thomas—which is the botanical name for a genus of Australian shrubs belonging to the rue family.

E. CHARLES NELSON

Sources E. C. Nelson, 'James and Thomas Drummond: their Scottish origins and curatorships in Irish botanic gardens', *Archives of Natural History*, 17 (1990), 49–65 · S. D. McKelvey, *Botanical exploration of the trans-Mississippi west, 1790–1850* (1955, [1956]) · A. M. Coats, *The quest for plants* (1969) · G. Sayre, *Memoirs of the New York Botanical Garden*, 19 (1971), 193–6 [Thomas Drummond's exsiccatae] · W. J. Hooker correspondence, RBG Kew · parish register, Inverarity and Methy, Angus, Scotland, 8 April 1793 [baptism] · parish register, Forfar, Scotland, 18 Nov 1820 [marriage]
Archives RBG Kew, herbarium specimens | RBG Kew, W. J. Hooker corresp.
Likenesses D. Macnee, coloured crayon, *c.*1830, RBG Kew
Wealth at death not wealthy; left very little; some specimens and books of little value: Nelson, 'James and Thomas Drummond'

Drummond, Thomas (1797–1840), administrator in Ireland and military engineer, was born in Castle Street, Edinburgh, on 10 October 1797. His father, James Drummond (1764/5–1800), a member of the Society of Writers to the Signet, belonged to an old landed Scottish family. In 1792 James Drummond married Elizabeth (Betsy) Somers, daughter of James Somers of Edinburgh. Thomas was the third of four children of this marriage, the others being James Patrick, John, and Elizabeth. When James Drummond, an improving landlord, died in 1800, at thirty-five, he left his family encumbered with debt, much of it inherited from his father, Patrick Drummond. Though the widowed Elizabeth Drummond got some help from her brother-in-law William Macfarlane, the young

Thomas Drummond (1797–1840), by Henry William Pickersgill, c.1838

family struggled with the burden of an honourable name but no fortune.

Education and early scientific work The Drummonds lived in a small house on the banks of the River Esk, near Musselburgh. Thomas survived some unpleasant tutors at the local grammar school, and in 1810 was sent to Edinburgh, where for three years he studied mathematics, natural philosophy, and chemistry at the University of Edinburgh. Professor Leslie said of him, 'No young man has ever come under my charge with a happier disposition or more promising talents' (O'Brien, 9). At sixteen he entered as a cadet at the Royal Military Academy, Woolwich, in London. Though he disliked aspects of the military regimen and was financially hard-pressed, he won academic honours by the perseverance that would be a lifelong personality trait. In July 1815, one month after Waterloo, he joined the corps of Royal Engineers, the army's most scientific branch. Lieutenant Drummond served at Plymouth and then at Chatham, and was posted briefly (1817) to France before being sent to Edinburgh in July 1818. Disillusioned with army life, he was now considering beginning legal studies in London.

Lengthy discussions in Edinburgh, in 1819, with Colonel Thomas Frederick Colby (1784–1852) persuaded Drummond that he could combine a scientific with a military career. Colonel Colby had been conducting the military survey of the Scottish highlands; Drummond joined the survey team and was actively involved in 1820–23 with the mapping of districts in Scotland and England. In 1824 the Ordnance Survey in Ireland was commenced, in part

to apportion local taxes more equitably than had been done hitherto by the county grand jury assessments. This surveying project, headed by Colonel Colby, introduced Drummond to Ireland.

While in Edinburgh, Drummond had resumed chemistry studies at the university, and in London in the early 1820s he had attended lectures and worked in laboratories at the Royal Institution. Drummond would put his scientific and mathematical knowledge to considerable practical use in the surveying of Ireland. He constantly tinkered with improving three devices not of his own invention: the heliostat, the compensation (or measuring) bars, and the limelight. The heliostat (or heliotrope) was a recent (1822) invention by the German mathematician and scientist Carl Friedrich Gauss (1777–1855), in the course of his geodetic surveying of Hanover. The compensation bars are credited for invention to Colonel Colby, head of the Irish Ordnance Survey; the limelight, to the scientist Sir Goldsworthy Gurney (1793–1875), Drummond's contemporary in London scientific circles.

The heliostat is a device used by surveyors. It reflects the sun's rays by means of a mirror that, initially, was fixed between two telescopes. In his Irish surveying, Drummond's sustained experimentation with the heliostat enhanced its practicality by adding a theodolite (an instrument for measuring angles), dispensing with the telescopes, and reducing the size of the mirror and connecting it to a stand by a ball-and-socket joint so that overall the heliostat was made smaller, portable, and easier to set up and adjust.

The Colby–Drummond compensation bars, used in geodetic surveying for the accurate measurement of baselines, are a complex mechanism of brass and iron bars and microscopes. Drummond continuously tinkered with Colby's design, seeking ways to improve the 'self-compensating' mechanism of the bars, which from their metallic nature expand or contract in different temperatures. A friend and colleague from the Irish Ordnance Survey, Sir Thomas Larcom (1801–1879), who was named Colby's assistant in 1828, paid homage to Drummond's 'indefatigable exertions' to achieve increasingly accurate measurements. Drummond 'never claimed to be the inventor' of the bars, noted Larcom, who emphasized that it was Lieutenant Drummond who 'made the bars, [and] was the deviser and planner of the numerous and beautiful contrivances and experiments by which they were brought to perfection' (McLennan, 103).

The 'Drummond light' The limelight was the third scientific innovation associated with Drummond, so much so that through the 1830s it was called the 'Drummond light'. But the invention is correctly attributed to Sir Goldsworthy Gurney, and Drummond himself credited Gurney in a letter to Joseph Hume, chair of the House of Commons committee on lighthouses (1834). Drummond's experiments with the limelight, both in London and in Ireland, caused his name to be initially associated with the light. The limelight was a breakthrough because its light, produced by the burning of lime with magnesia and harnessed in a reflector, is many times brighter than the light generated by the conventional Argand whale-oil lamp. Drummond published articles on the limelight in the Royal Society's *Philosophical Transactions* (1826, 1830). He also arranged demonstrations in London of the limelight's intensity compared with that of other lights, such as the Argand burner and the Fresnel lamp used in French lighthouses. At one demonstration, at the end of a long darkened hall in the Tower of London, Sir John Herschel reported that the limelight was so 'overpowering, and as it were, annihilating both its predecessors, which appeared by its side, … [that] a shout of triumph and admiration burst from all present' (McLennan, 73). The intensely bright, white limelight Drummond found to be extremely useful for surveying at night and in Ireland's often dark and murky weather. Drummond was experimenting with the application of the limelight to British lighthouses when, in the early 1830s, he became sidetracked by his new political career.

All three devices—heliostat, compensation bars, and limelight—were employed in the survey of Ireland. The survey was authorized in June 1824, and Colonel Colby and Drummond first toured the country together that autumn. They selected the stations for the future triangulation of the country, and chose the most fitting place for measuring a base. The next year, the triangulation commenced on Divis Mountain, near Belfast. Districts in co. Antrim and co. Down were surveyed in 1825–6, and in 1828 a critical point was passed, under Drummond's direct supervision, when the base at Lough Foyle was accurately measured. Drummond's tendency to overwork, and his constant exposure to cold, damp weather (he would often remain during storms at his self-devised hilltop meteorological stations), caused him to have recurrent periods of ill health. For a time in 1825–6 he returned to Edinburgh, and in 1828–9 to Dublin, the survey's headquarters, in order to recoup his health.

From 1829 to 1834 Drummond resided chiefly in London, where his scientific reputation from the Drummond light caused him to gain a widening circle of friends. One demonstration led him to meet the lord chancellor, Henry Brougham, who, terrified by the light's brilliancy, not only refused to look directly at it but even fled the room. Thus had Thomas Drummond made contact with the whigs. At thirty-three, the fragile, modest, hard-working Lieutenant Drummond was about to enter politics.

Early political career Drummond's first political appointment came in 1831, when, on Brougham's recommendation, the home secretary, Melbourne, named him chairman of the Parliamentary Boundary Commission. The movement to broaden the parliamentary suffrage had raised the question of the relative disenfranchisement of borough residents. Under Drummond's personal leadership, the commission—comprising eighteen commissioners and thirty surveyors and draftsmen—measured borough jurisdictions and applied mathematical formulae incorporating statistics on the boroughs' population (houses) and wealth (assessed taxes). Using the 'Drummond list', analyses and judgements were then made on the equity of pre-Reform Bill borough representation. This novel concept of 'algebraic' or 'scientific' representation was cheered by liberals and opposed by traditionalists. The tory John Wilson Croker called Drummond's list 'a blind guide to form a new constitution' (McLennan, 151). But various professors testified on behalf of the accuracy of Drummond's calculations, which served as a general basis for the subsequent reform (1832) of some of the boroughs' representation in the House of Commons. (Drummond's principles would be more fully embodied in the Electoral Redistribution Act of 1885.) Drummond's fellow commissioners were so impressed by his labours that they commissioned and paid a noted painter, H. W. Pickersgill, to execute a portrait of Drummond; finished in 1835, it was the first of two by that artist.

The Pickersgill three-quarter-length portrait shows the 38-year-old Drummond to be a handsome man of short to medium height, with a small physique, almost frail. Most noticeable is the large head with the wide-set, active, and arresting eyes. The face captures Sir Thomas Larcom's assessment of Drummond's character as one of 'determined perseverance', with 'an aptitude to seize on information of every kind' (O'Brien, 16–17). In personality Drummond was quiet and reserved; all commented on his amiable disposition. He also had a tendency in argument to take the side of the underdog. At the time of this portrait he was still a bachelor. In his work habits he tended to push himself so hard that he regularly suffered periods of illness or physical exhaustion.

With the boundary commission behind him, Drummond briefly rejoined the Ordnance Survey in London in 1832. In November he declined the offer of a professorship in natural philosophy at the University of Edinburgh. (In 1865 Drummond's sister would endow, with £2500, a scholarship in his name in mathematics and philosophy at this university.) Drummond had now resolved on a political career. In 1833–4 he served as private secretary to Lord Althorp, then chancellor of the exchequer.

Under-secretary in Ireland In 1835 the whig government chose Drummond to be under-secretary at Dublin Castle. Drummond's appointment placed him in Ireland at a critical juncture. Catholic emancipation had raised popular expectations but not satisfied them, the tithe war had produced bloody clashes between police and peasants, and Daniel O'Connell had begun to agitate for repeal of the union. Both to return themselves to office and to pacify Ireland, the English whig party had formed an alliance with O'Connell's Catholic Irish party. In exchange for the Irish leader's agreement to suspend his demand for repeal, Melbourne's government pledged itself to a broad programme of reform in Ireland.

The new Irish administration consisted of the second earl of Mulgrave, the lord lieutenant; Viscount Morpeth, the chief secretary; and Drummond, the under-secretary. Through this office—one that was immediately below the

Irish chief secretary and responsible for all domestic correspondence to and from the English headquarters in Ireland—Drummond would be in charge of enforcing the London government's policies in the country. The under-secretaryship had long been held (1812–30) by William Gregory, a reactionary tory. His successor (1830–35), Colonel Sir William Gosset, a whig appointee, was more liberal but fractious and difficult to work with. Drummond's appointment was widely greeted with praise. The London *Sun* editorialized that the choice of Drummond furnished 'another convincing proof that Ministers are fully in earnest in their endeavours to ameliorate the condition of that distracted country' (McLennan, 184).

Drummond arrived in Ireland in July 1835. Four months later, back in England, on 19 November he married, at Weston House, Warwickshire, seat of Sir George Philips, an accomplished, attractive, and intelligent woman, Maria Kinnaird (d. 1891), the ward and adopted daughter of Richard ('Conversation') *Sharp, a man who was active in the literary world. Thomas and Maria's marriage was to be a happy if short-lived one; Maria outlived her husband by half a century. The Drummonds would have three children: Mary Elizabeth, who in 1863 married Joseph Kay QC, author of *The Social Condition and Education of the People of Europe* and *Free Trade in Land*; Emily; and Fanny Eleanor.

In December 1835 Thomas and Maria Drummond took up their residence at the under-secretary's lodge in Phoenix Park, Dublin. The new under-secretary's attention was first directed to reforming the Dublin Castle-controlled Irish rural police. Created in 1822, the 8000 man constabulary had by now taken over most of the duties of Robert Peel's much smaller riot police, the Peace Preservation Force (1814). Both forces were protestant-officered, but since the late 1820s Catholics had increasingly filled the rank and file. Drummond eagerly implemented whig policies, begun in the early 1830s, of making the constabulary a much less sectarian force. Developing a bill whose draft form dated to 1832, Drummond laboured with Morpeth to pass the Irish Constabulary Act (1836), which abolished the Peace Preservation Force and gave the constabulary a single inspector-general, where before there had been four provincial inspectors-general. Recruiting was standardized and a reserve force and depots established, more Catholic officers as well as constables were appointed, and the force generally became more professional, if also more bureaucratic. Drummond also consolidated in 1836 various irregular forces into a thousand-man armed revenue police.

Second, Drummond worked with Morpeth to reform the Dublin police. The city police had undergone major reforms in 1786 and 1808, but by the 1830s the force—consisting of a small number of day constables and about 400 night watch—was in serious decay. Using the model of the London Metropolitan Police (1829), Drummond and Morpeth drafted bills which became the Dublin Metropolitan Police Acts (1836, amended 1837), creating from January 1838 an unarmed, fully Castle-controlled, uniformed force of one thousand day and night constables.

Third, Drummond implemented judicial reforms. He was appalled by the cases of biased or inefficient justice from Ireland's local county magistrates. He continued whig policies of weeding out men from the commission lists. He scrutinized judicial proceedings and required that Dublin Castle be furnished quarterly returns of not only quarter sessions and assizes but also petty sessions. An act of 1836 gave local taxpayers more control over tax assessments (presentments) made by the often oligarchic county grand juries. A decade earlier the London government had begun to create Castle-controlled stipendiary magistrates, to whom the local magistrates had to defer. The Drummond–Morpeth administration expanded their numbers from twenty-nine to fifty-four; as to the local magistrates, 'their wings are clipped' (McLennan, 278), exulted Drummond in a letter to his mother in July 1836. As Drummond added Catholics to the constabulary, so too he injected them into the legal system. Catholics were named judges and crown law advisers and solicitors. Vacant positions were frequently filled by the appointment of qualified Catholics. Greater access to the law, Drummond believed, would produce less breaking of the law among Ireland's Catholic majority.

Drummond's place in history stems not simply from his actions but from his tone and attitude toward the Catholics of Ireland. A decade earlier, working on the Irish Ordnance Survey, he had brought his intellect and emotions to the Irish question; the scientist-surveyor was moved by what he saw of the miseries of the people. An outsider, a Scottish Presbyterian by upbringing, Drummond as under-secretary at Dublin Castle came to form a bond with the Irish Catholics. For a person in his position this attitude was unprecedented.

New attitudes and policies Ireland had long been the scene of political agitation, social disorder, religious acrimony, and protestant ascendancy. Extreme protestants, the Orangemen, alarmed at the emancipation of the Catholics, had formed a huge secret army to uphold the prerogatives of the dominant class. Orange processions and armed demonstrations terrorized Ulster and historically had overshadowed the executive in Dublin. From 1835 on Drummond eagerly carried out new English whig policies to break up the Orange Society. Its mythic founding event, the battle of the Diamond in Armagh in 1795, Drummond repudiated (in a famous official circular) as a 'lawless and most disgraceful conflict' (McLennan, 297). Orange lodges in the army and constabulary were disbanded, Orange secret signs and passwords prohibited, Orange processions banned, and Orange magnates reprimanded. The Orange order was dissolved in 1836.

New whig policies, enforced by Drummond, also aimed to promote 'civility' among the poorer Catholic population. Previous police policy had been to allow faction fighters at fairs to settle their differences among themselves. Drummond insisted on police intervention and suppression of fairs where disorder was great. By the late 1830s faction fighting had declined significantly.

Drummond's policies on the use of police in tithe and rent collection were less novel. He continued Castle policies of refusing aid in collection expeditions unless there were certified cases of 'previous forcible resistance'. Drummond gained popularity with Catholic Ireland by stating his opinion that it was wrong to force 6 million Catholics to pay tithes to the church of 800,000 protestants, especially at a time when parliament was discussing reform of the tithe system. Under Drummond, the Dublin Castle executive no longer appeared as the instrument of minority oppression of the majority of the Irish population. The whig government's Tithe Commutation Act of 1838 reformed but did not abolish the tithe, which was reduced by a quarter and converted to a rent surcharge.

It is misleading to credit Drummond's undersecretaryship with having any direct impact on crime trends in Ireland. No one person can of course control the volume of such phenomena. Drummond claimed credit for a decline in crime in the late 1830s. In fact, total criminal committals were relatively stable and conviction rates actually falling. But Drummond was correct that many agrarian offences—such as shooting at persons, attacking houses, and administering oaths—were on the decline. One crime, homicide, did resist the downward trend; the most spectacular case was the murder in January 1839 of an Irish landlord, the second earl of Norbury. Months earlier there occurred a famous exchange of letters between Tipperary landlords and Drummond. About thirty county magistrates, among them several peers, had written to Dublin Castle concerning the murder of a Mr Cooper, and had pleaded for stringent legislation for the suppression of crime. Drummond's lecturing reply (22 May 1838) included a famous sentence, 'Property has its duties as well as its rights.' He added, 'To the neglect of those duties in times past is mainly to be ascribed that diseased state of society in which such crimes take their rise' (O'Brien, 284). Though such views infuriated protestant Ireland (and led to Lord Roden's 1839 parliamentary inquiry into crime), they would gain credence with the passage of time. William Gladstone, in a speech in October 1864, cited Drummond's quotation of 'property has its duties', and stated that this notion 'has now become a domesticated idea' (on Gladstone and the controversial history of this aphorism, see McLennan, 327–39).

Drummond was a scientist and military man turned politician. A member of the Society for the Diffusion of Useful Knowledge, he viewed politics as a means to a practical end. At his suggestion a four-member Irish railway commission, over which he presided, was appointed in October 1836. Its dual aim was to modernize Ireland by developing the country's infrastructure and to provide public works-type employment for the poor. Issuing two reports (March 1837, July 1838), the commission proposed the construction of trunk lines from Dublin to Cork, with branches to Kilkenny, Limerick, and Waterford, and from Dublin north to Navan, branching to Belfast and Enniskillen. For Irish railways, Drummond believed, exchequer grants should supplement funds from private enterprise. Unfortunately, owing to tory opposition and private speculators' jealousies, Drummond's scheme was defeated in parliament. The idea was ahead of its time: massive state intervention in Irish affairs would not occur until the last quarter of the nineteenth century. Nevertheless, the railway reports remain remarkable documents. Mostly the work of Drummond himself, they offer a wealth of detail, argument, and analysis of Ireland's demographics and socio-economic condition. Text, maps, and appendices offer a mine of information on subjects far beyond proposed railways.

Overwork, death, and reputation During three years Drummond had worked night and day. His health and family life suffered. Maria Drummond wrote to her mother-in-law in June 1838:

> I often say that I might as well have no husband, for day after day often passes without more than a few words passing between us. … From last Monday until this morning—a week all but a day—he never even *saw* his baby, although in the same house with her. … [H]e is very thin and very much older in appearance than when you last saw him. (McLennan, 411)

A family trip to the continent (September–October 1838) temporarily restored his health. He was back in harness in November—'Thank God, the Railroad Report is done' (ibid., 415) he wrote his mother—but his long hours again began to take their toll. Friends and family urged him to resign the under-secretaryship. Drummond himself at this point seems to have been considering a change: he talked of running for a borough seat in the House of Commons. Though contemporaries judged him only an average speaker, they believed that Drummond's services would have been unsurpassed in the labours of committee work.

Throughout 1839 Drummond continued to overwork himself. He lobbied for acceptance of his railway report and testified at length (14–27 June) before Lord Roden's select committee on Irish crime. In the winter of 1839–40 Drummond suffered recurrent bouts of influenza. After a spell in England, in February 1840 he returned to Ireland and resumed his duties. After working nine hours at his office on Saturday 11 April, he became seriously unwell on Sunday. He died in Dublin on Wednesday 15 April 1840, aged forty-two. His death was attributed to erysipelas. Drummond's exact last words are in dispute but not their meaning. He told his physician, a Dr Johnstone, that he wished to be buried in Ireland, the land of his adoption, in whose service he had given his life.

Thomas Drummond was buried at Mount Jerome cemetery, Harold's Cross, in Dublin, on 21 April 1840. The tributes were numerous for the public servant whose life had been cut short. Sir Thomas Larcom said simply: 'He had died for Ireland'. Another friend, Harriet Martineau, accurately stated, 'He lived too fast, knowingly and willingly' (McLennan, 429, 433). Throughout the United Kingdom the public press was unstinting in its praise. Even the ultra-protestant Dublin *Evening Packet* candidly reported its dislike of many of Drummond's policies, yet called him 'the sheet-anchor of the Irish executive' and observed of his toil on the railway commission that 'it proves him to have been a great man' (O'Brien, 389).

Drummond had evolved from soldier to scientist to politician. He is most remembered for being an able, conscientious 'British' public servant: a Scot who served the English government by carrying out policies for the improvement of Ireland. The Irish dramatist and politician Richard Lalor Sheil described him as a man 'who, not born in Ireland, was more than an Irishman in his love of Ireland' (McLennan, 246).

There is general agreement among historians, past and present, that the political administration of Ireland in the late 1830s is accurately described, not as the age of Mulgrave–Morpeth, but as the age of Drummond. But scholars' views of the nature of Drummond's contributions have changed in recent years. The traditional view (McLennan, O'Brien) credited Drummond with introducing numerous reformist policies in Ireland. Recent scholars have argued that Drummond's administration had a twofold importance: first, his steady, insistent, and at times controversial enforcement of whig policies, some dating to 1830; and second, the setting of a more liberal and inclusive tone of governance that, by contrast to earlier times, would characterize the remaining decades of British government in Ireland.   STANLEY H. PALMER

Sources J. F. McLennan, *Memoir of Thomas Drummond, undersecretary to the lord-lieutenant of Ireland, 1835–1840* (1867) · R. B. O'Brien, *Thomas Drummond, under-secretary in Ireland, 1835–40: his life and letters* (1889) · M. A. G. Ó Tuathaigh, *Thomas Drummond and the government of Ireland, 1835–41* (1978) · 'Select committee of the House of Lords on the state of Ireland', *Parl. papers* (1839), 12.960–1306, no. 486 [evidence of Thomas Drummond] · A. J. Webb, *A compendium of Irish biography* (1878) · W. Yolland, *An account of the measurement of the Lough Foyle base* (1847)
Archives Irish State Paper Office, Dublin Castle, Dublin · PRO, HO 100 (Ireland) · UCL, letters to the Society for the Diffusion of Useful Knowledge | Castle Howard, Yorkshire, Howard MSS · Mulgrave Castle, Yorkshire, Phipps MSS · NL Ire., O'Connell MSS · PRO, corresp. with Lord John Russell, PRO 30/22
Likenesses H. W. Pickersgill, oils, 1835, U. Edin.; repro. in McLennan, *Memoir of Thomas Drummond* · H. W. Pickersgill, oils, *c.*1838, NG Ire. [*see illus.*] · mezzotint, pubd 20 June 1841 (after H. W. Pickersgill), NG Ire. · J. Hogan, bronze statue, 1843, Dublin City Hall · J. C., lithograph, BM

Drummond, Victoria Alexandrina (1894–1978), marine

engineer, was born on 14 October 1894 at Megginch Castle, Errol, Perthshire, the second of four children of Captain Malcolm Drummond of Megginch (1856–1924), groom-in-waiting to Queen Victoria, and his wife, Geraldine Margaret (*née* Cherry; 1865–1956), the sixth of seven daughters of William Amherst Tyssen-Amherst, first Baron Amherst of Hackney, and his wife, Margaret Mitford, of Didlington, Norfolk. She was a god-daughter of Queen Victoria, after whom she was baptized at Megginch Castle. Victoria's childhood was spent between Megginch and her grandparents' home at Didlington, Norfolk, and she was educated at home. She showed an early enthusiasm for mechanics, and the onset of the First World War allowed her to enter the engineering trade, her avowed intention being to become a marine engineer.

From 1916 to 1918 she served as apprentice at the Northern Garage in Perth, and from 1918 to 1922 as apprentice at the Caledon Ship Works in Dundee. On 29 August 1922 she sailed overnight on the SS *Anchises*, Blue Funnel Line, from Liverpool to Glasgow, and on 2 September on a round trip to Australia as tenth engineer, calling at Las Palmas, Cape Town, Adelaide, Melbourne, Sydney, and Brisbane. It was the first of four voyages to Australia on SS *Anchises*; on the fifth she sailed to China. After her father died Drummond left the Blue Funnel Line and worked for two years on her second engineer's examination, which she passed at the third attempt. In April 1927 she joined the British India Company and sailed as fifth engineer to Africa on TSS *Mulbera*, followed by four voyages to India; she left the company in December 1928. During the depression in the 1930s there was little demand for marine engineers and none at all for a woman. Victoria Drummond took the chief engineer's examination thirty-seven times. Each time she failed. Finally she was convinced this was because she was a woman. She did however have a Panamanian chief engineer's certificate.

At the beginning of the war Victoria Drummond became an air raid warden with her two sisters in Lambeth, but in March 1940 she went to sea as second engineer on a small Dutch boat, SS *HarZion*, which sailed round the Mediterranean loading rice, and also rescued the British consul and some of the British expeditionary force from Marseilles. In August 1940 she joined SS *Bonita* at Southampton and sailed to Fowey to load china clay before sailing across the Atlantic. 'The ship was attacked for 25 minutes by a bomber, when 400 miles from land', says the citation for her MBE in *The Times*,

> But by skilful handling many hits were avoided. When the alarm was sounded Miss Drummond at once went below and took charge. The first salvo flung her against the levers and nearly stunned her. When everything had been done to increase the ship's speed she ordered the engine room and stokehold staff out. After one attack the main injection pipe just above her head started a joint and scalding steam rushed out. She nursed this vital pipe through the explosion of each salvo, easing down when the noise of the aircraft told her that bombs were about to fall, and afterwards increasing steam. Her conduct was an inspiration to the ship's company, and her devotion to duty prevented more serious damage to the vessel.   (*The Times*, 10 July 1941)

She was also awarded Lloyd's war medal, for bravery at sea. When they landed at Norfolk, Virginia, she received a heroine's welcome. Money was subscribed for a Victoria Drummond canteen which stood in Lambeth North throughout the war providing sustenance to those who were bombed out.

In 1941 sailing back from Lisbon on SS *Czikos* Drummond was again under attack by enemy aircraft. The second mate was killed and two men injured. She then did a coastal voyage on SS *Auk*, and in April 1942 joined SS *Manchester Port* as fifth engineer, sailing in convoy to Quebec and back, in which many ships were lost. After two coastal voyages on SS *Elizabeth Lensen* and SS *Danae II*, she sailed round the world on TSS *Perseus* in 1943—to New York, Panama, Sydney, Cape Town, Freetown, and Gibraltar. In 1944 she joined MV *Karabagh*, in which she sailed intermittently until after the end of the war—first in a convoy to Russia, and then standing by off the Isle of Wight for the invasion, in which she took part. She then took a cargo of high explosives to Kiel, and after the war ended went to Abadan in west Africa.

After 1945 Victoria Drummond superintended some shipbuilding in Dundee, relieved on various Cunard ships, and did short coastal trips round the Mediterranean, or on tankers, and passed her second engineer's motor examination. In 1952 she supervised building SS *Master Nikos* at Burntisland, and from 1952 to 1954 sailed round the world on SS *Markab* as second engineer. In the next two years she served on the tanker MV *Lord Canning*, and on several smaller coastal or continental boats. In 1957 she sailed to Japan and back via the Panama Canal and Vancouver on MV *British Monarch*, and in 1958 was chief engineer on an antique yacht, MY *Adventuress*, which sailed into the Mediterranean. Photographs of her in uniform show a tall woman with a commanding presence and an air of quiet competence. From 1959 until she retired in March 1962 she sailed as chief engineer on various Hong Kong owned boats, which she delivered from Europe, then voyaged mostly around China.

After the death of her sisters in 1974 she moved to St George's Retreat in Sussex, where she died on Christmas day 1978 and was buried at Megginch Castle beside her sisters and parents six days later.   CHERRY DRUMMOND

Sources b. cert. · d. cert. · private information (2004) · personal knowledge (2004) · C. Drummond, *The remarkable life of Victoria Drummond* (1994)
Archives priv. coll., MSS
Likenesses watercolour, 1898, priv. coll. · P. Lamb, oils, 1960, priv. coll. · photographs, priv. coll. · photographs, Institute of Marine Engineers, London · photographs, Hult. Arch.

Drummond, William, of Hawthornden (1585–1649), poet and pamphleteer, was born at Hawthornden Castle, Lasswade, Edinburghshire, on 13 December 1585, the eldest of the seven legitimate children of Sir John Drummond (1553–1610), laird of Hawthornden, and his wife, Susanna (1562–1623), sister of the poet William Fowler, secretary to James VI's queen, Anne. The Drummond family is ancient and royally connected: from the siblings of Annabella Drummond, daughter of Sir John Drummond of Stobhall, by her marriage to Robert III of Scotland in 1367, the various branches of the family could, and did, claim kinship with the royal house of Stewart. As second son of Sir Robert Drummond of Carnock, Stirlingshire, John Drummond bought his own estate at Hawthornden, 6 miles from Edinburgh by the River Esk, and conveniently near to the Scottish court at Holyrood, where he was gentleman usher to James VI. Sir John was knighted in 1603 when James acceded to the English throne. He had two illegitimate sons previous to William's birth, John (d. c.1615) and Alexander (d. 1622); following William within his marriage came Anna, Jane, Rebecca, James, Alexander, and John, all of whom survived to adulthood.

Drummond was educated at the high school of Edinburgh, and at fifteen proceeded to the University of Edinburgh, then known as the College of Edinburgh, later the

William Drummond of Hawthornden (1585–1649), by unknown artist, 1612

College of King James, where he passed four years under the supervision of James Knox and the tuition of John Ray. His Latin was and remained fluent, his Greek moderate, and his Hebrew fairly modest, and he graduated MA in 1605. Aiming for a career in law, he went via London to Paris in September 1606, armed with letters of recommendation from his kinsman James Drummond, now earl of Perth, and attended lectures. In April 1607 he was in Bourges studying law. He returned through Paris to Scotland in November 1608, and nearly lost his life when his ship collided with another off Scarborough. He brought back with him nearly a quarter (399 volumes) of what was to be a fine private library, with a heavy emphasis upon literature, in French, Italian, Spanish, and English, rather than law. His lists of the books he read at that time confirm his interest in contemporary poetry and romance.

About 1609 Drummond's sister Anna (1592–1636) married John Scot, later Lord Scotstarvet, of Tarvet in Fife, who was Drummond's lifelong friend, and who assisted with the posthumous publication of Drummond's collected poems and prose. In 1610 Drummond visited London, where he is alleged to have met some of the famous poets of the city, but returned before his father died of a stroke on 21 August. This made him the laird of Hawthornden, by then a modest but prosperous estate. Intending, as he later said, 'vivere infra fortunam' ('to live well within his means'; Masson, 21), he abandoned law and embraced in his private life the Horatian ideal of a gentlemanly rural simplicity. He corresponded with courtiers and was willing to flatter sovereigns, but he received no honours from either James VI and I or Charles I.

Early works and literary acquaintances For some years from 1610 Drummond read at his leisure in several languages, acquiring a working knowledge of Italian and Spanish as well as French. He bought and read the works of contemporary English poets and dramatists, including Shakespeare; he himself, some few early letters excepted, even for his own private use wrote in English, not Scots. He first played a part in the Anglification of Scottish writing when, in response to the death of Prince Henry on 6 November 1612, the Edinburgh printer and bookseller Andro Hart published a collection of epitaphs by English and Scottish poets, *Mausoleum, or, The Choisest Flowres of the Epitaphs* (1613), containing one by Drummond, and also Drummond's first independent work, *Teares on the Death of Meliades* (1613), a six-leaf black-bordered poem. He became acquainted, as surviving letters show, with the leading Scottish poets at the English court, Sir Robert Kerr, Sir Robert Aytoun, Sir David Murray, and, most notably, William Alexander of Menstrie, whom he first met in 1614 on a chance visit to his house near Stirling. The two became firm friends, as Alexis and Damon, for the rest of their lives.

In 1616 appeared *Poems by William Drummond of Hawthorne-denne*: it contains sixty-eight sonnets mixed with other lyric poems in two sections, a reprint of *Teares on the Death of M[o]Eliades*, a set of spiritual poems, and a group of madrigals and epigrams. Since the sonnets are love sonnets, and the two sections relate to a mistress alive and a mistress dead, a legend has persisted that Drummond wrote the set to mourn the death of a fiancée, identified by Drummond's eighteenth-century editors in 1711 as a Miss Cunningham of Barns in Fife, from a family with whom Drummond was certainly closely acquainted. Only one piece of evidence connects her to him: a single printed leaf, unsigned and undated, the unique copy of which is now in Edinburgh University Library, containing a sonnet probably Drummond's, 'In Pious Memorie of … Euphemia Kyninghame, who … Died the 23 of Julie 1616'. The date of her death (known since 1957) and the complicated printing history of the 1616 *Poems* make it in the last degree unlikely that the mourning sonnets were indeed composed for her. The sonnet on the printed leaf is not one of these in the *Poems*, and is a rather stilted and frigid poem. When Drummond later in life in his 'Memorialls' recorded births and deaths in his family and accidents in his own life, he made no mention of her at all.

Visit from Jonson In 1617 James VI and I revisited Scotland, and Drummond responded to the event with a long poem, *Forth Feasting: a Panegyricke to the Kings most Excellent Majestie*, published by Andro Hart in the same year. No honours came to Drummond among all the largesse of the king's visit, but as a poet he now became known in London, and Michael Drayton corresponded with him affectionately. Possibly this acquaintance influenced Ben Jonson, on his visit to Scotland in 1618, to stay at Hawthornden for almost three weeks in the winter of 1618–19. Drummond recorded their conversations, first printed in full from a transcript in 1842. Jonson compiled an account of his Scottish visit, with Drummond's assistance, but it was lost in a fire in 1623, and there is no further contact between them recorded.

Late in 1620, Drummond was so seriously ill with pleurisy that he wrote to Alexander that he might well die (Masson, 121), but though he suffered intermittently from gout and from kidney stones his health seems to have been good. On 29 May 1622 he was made burgess of Haddington, 17 miles from Edinburgh. A severe famine in Scotland in 1623, in which many poor people died in the streets in Edinburgh, brought Drummond the loss of many near friends; his mother, too, died on 23 October. These griefs may have encouraged him to his next publication, *Flowres of Sion* (1623). This consisted entirely of religious and philosophical lyrics (some reprinted from the 1616 *Poems*), two long poems in couplets, and a prose essay, 'A cypresse grove', a meditation upon death. It also contained a commemorative sonnet on Jane, countess of Perth, the wife of Drummond's family head. Rather remarkably this proves to be a recycled version of the sonnet on Euphemia Kyninghame—something which, if noticed, might well have offended both families.

Drummond was still at Hawthornden, living, as one of his friends said, the sweet solitary life (*Works*, 153), when the news of the death of King James (27 March 1625) arrived, and he responded to it with a sonnet which he included in the second edition of *Flowres of Sion* (1630). Almost immediately, however, he embarked upon a relationship with an unknown woman, by whom he had three illegitimate children: Anna, born 21 December 1625, lived only 18 days; Marie, born 12 August 1627, and Lodowick, born 4 December 1628, survived and were remembered in Drummond's will. Where their encounters took place is not known, but Marie, at least, cannot have been conceived far from Edinburgh, for on 8 December 1626 Drummond was made a burgess of Edinburgh; he recorded proudly that at a banquet in the lower council house his burgess ticket was given him in gold letters. Prior to that he had overseen a most generous donation of books to the University of Edinburgh, recorded on 22 November 1626, of more than 360 volumes and manuscripts. There is no indication of his motive in thus dismembering his library, and the books themselves, Drummond's catalogue of which was published in 1627, are miscellaneous. Probably the most unaccountable event of these years is the granting of a patent to Drummond by Charles I at Hampton Court, on 29 September 1626, for the production of sixteen military machines, from a new kind of pike to a perpetual motion machine: this patent was sealed at Holyrood on 24 December 1627. Drummond had never shown any interest in or aptitude for such work, nor did his library contain any relevant books; certainly no subsequent actions suggest any technical inventiveness.

In February 1629 Drummond was in Stirling, but his mind was rather on literary matters than military: confined to his room for five weeks with a feverish colic, he thought of the long-delayed Scottish coronation of Charles I, and wrote a series of pageants for the monarch's proposed entry to the city of Edinburgh. This did not happen until 15 May 1633, when Drummond's contributions were printed as *The entertainment of the high and mighty monarch Charles, king of Great Britaine, France and Ireland* (1633).

Marriage and family The arrival of Charles in Scotland heralded trouble for Drummond, and changed the interest of the rest of his life from literature to politics and history. But before that, in 1632, his life had changed more rewardingly when, apparently rather suddenly, he married Elizabeth Logan (d. 1679), who was to bear him nine children and survive him by thirty years. It was later claimed that she was the granddaughter of Sir Robert Logan of Restalrig (d. 1606), but the evidence supports the view that she was the daughter of James Logan, minister of Eddleston near Peebles (d. 1624), of the family of the Logans of Coitfield in Edinburgh. The marriage was celebrated on 12 February 1632 by John Adamson, principal of the College of King James. The first child, and only daughter to survive infancy, Eliza, was born on 10 September 1632. No doubt because of his marriage, Drummond undertook a massive renovation of his house at Hawthornden (finished, as an inscription over the doorway records, in 1638), and from 1633 to 1637 he and his wife lived at Linlithgow, 16 miles from Edinburgh, where Drummond had inherited the lands of Kingsfield and Boghall, subsequently transferred to his wife. In February 1633 Drummond was made a burgess of Linlithgow, his third such honour: in 1631 he had been made a burgess of the Canongate, now the area of Edinburgh at the foot of the Royal Mile before Holyroodhouse. Four children were born in the Linlithgow years: John (1633–1636), Margaret (1634–1635), William, his second son and heir, who was born in 1636 and lived until 1713, and Annabella, who died in 1637, the year of her birth. Four more were born after Drummond's return to Hawthornden: Robert (1638–1687), Richard (1639–1641), James, born in 1641, who died in early childhood, and Jane (1644–1646). Eliza married Dr Henderson, a physician in Edinburgh, and had one daughter; Robert died without issue. William had three sons and six daughters.

Later works: politics and history On 15 June 1633 Charles I entered Edinburgh in triumph, greeted by the words of William Drummond and the images of George Jamesone on the various arches and pageants along the route. Chosen as the leading poet of his city and country, Drummond now enjoyed a literary esteem as the foremost Scots seventeenth-century poet, a reputation he has kept ever since. He also had a wide acquaintance with, and the respect of, the Scottish nobility, to whom his blend of conservatism, learning, and peaceableness seems to have appealed.

About this time Drummond was consulted by his kinsman John Drummond, second earl of Perth, about the Drummond family arms and motto. William Drummond bore the 'or, three bars wavy within a bordure gules' of the earls of Perth, but with a different crest (a Pegasus proper) and motto (*Hos gloria reddit honores*). Thinking it, as he said, 'a great spur to virtue to look back on the worth of our line' (*Works*, 136), he communicated to the earl a genealogy of the Stobhall line, preserved in note form in his 'Memorialls', as well as *A Short Discourse upon Impresas and Anagrams*, printed in the 1711 *Works*. At the same time (1633) Drummond embarked upon what was to be the longest of all his works, the *History of Scotland from the Year 1423 until the Year 1542*, usually known as the *History of the Five Jameses*, finished about 1644, but printed only after his death, through the good offices of Lord Scotstarvet (London, 1655).

Drummond's first overtly political pamphlet came in 1635 in what is known as the Balmerino affair: as rivalries and hostilities among the aristocracy of Scotland were sharpened by the conflicts over the policies of Charles and Archbishop Laud, John Elphinstone, Lord Balmerino, was arrested, tried, and convicted upon a capital charge of libel against the king, for merely possessing a document thought to be treasonable. Scottish support of Balmerino was strong, and Drummond's friend the earl of Traquair, who had given the casting vote against Balmerino, worked with William Alexander to obtain his pardon. Just before the trial Drummond wrote *A Letter Apologeticall, Concerning the Divulging of a Paper to his Majestie*, dated 2 March 1635 and addressed to R[obert] K[er, earl] of A[ncrum], protesting sharply against the folly of bringing the matter to trial. Drummond had all his life avoided trouble, but on this occasion he cannot have been unaware that he was writing the kind of criticism that Balmerino was being tried for merely possessing.

Throughout the controversies over the introduction of the Book of Common Prayer, culminating in the Edinburgh riots (July 1637), Drummond kept silent. The death in August 1637 of the younger son of Sir William Alexander, now earl of Stirling, occasioned his last poem in print, *To the Exequies of the Honourable Sir Antonye Alexander: a Pastorall Elegie* (1638). Although the piece is anonymous it is certainly by Drummond, and, unlike much of his ceremonious verse, is from the heart, as his correspondence shows. The signing of the national covenant in March 1638 prompted him to write and circulate a few private copies of *Irene: a Remonstrance for Concord, Amity and Love amongst his Majesty's Subjects*, which contains Drummond's political philosophy of passive obedience to the king tempered by hostility to any kind of compulsion of belief, whether from kings, bishops, or presbyteries. In a more sarcastic vein, as Scottish Presbyterianism strengthened and the country moved to war in 1639, he wrote 'The magical mirror', 'Queries of state', 'The idea', and 'The load starre' (all first printed in *Works*, 1711), and attacked the consequences of civil war in 'A speech to the noblemen'.

During the bishops' wars of 1639 and 1640, Drummond was offered protection by the marquess of Douglas and the earl of Perth, but he remained at Hawthornden, where he was appointed to the committee of the shire. After the explosion at Dunglass Castle (30 August 1640) Drummond wrote that he had been directed to 'ravage and plunder' some of his neighbours (Masson, 336), but simply did nothing. He continued quietly at Hawthornden, but the huge disagreements in Scotland caused by the English civil war and its repercussions made him write what was his last substantial tract, *Skiamachia* [*Shadow Boxing*], *or, A*

Defence of a Petition, January 1643. This referred to the marquess of Hamilton's so-called 'cross-petition', one of the documents flying about in the king's struggle to stop the Scots aiding the English parliament, and Drummond's defence of it shows his extreme anti-clericalism, as what he saw as the tyranny of Presbyterianism became absolute. Despite his authorship of this, he was not persecuted, though a draft 'Speech of the author's when he should have been questioned' among his papers shows that he anticipated interrogation, and the troubles of the times impelled him to make his will (1 September 1643).

During the marquess of Montrose's campaign for the king, Drummond's kinsmen were closely involved, and a letter from Montrose to Drummond in 1645 asks for his monarchist tracts for publication. After Philiphaugh, Montrose remembered Drummond with gratitude enough to write thanking him for his loyalty (19 August 1646).

Death and reputation Drummond died at Hawthornden Castle on 4 December 1649, at the end of the year in which his king had been executed, from complications of the pyelonephritis which had plagued him intermittently for more than twenty years. He is thought to have been buried on the following day, against the wall of Lasswade church, in a grave deep enough for his wife to be buried above him in 1679. His son and heir William placed a stone with W:D cut on it just above his father's remains.

William co-operated with Lord Scotstarvet in the printing of Drummond's *History of Scotland* with some other prose tracts and letters in 1655, and again with Scotstarvet and Milton's nephew Edward Phillips, in a reprint of Drummond's published poetry along with some manuscript verses, *Poems, by … William Drummond of Hawthornden* (1656; reissued in 1659). The macaronic dog-Latin poem 'Polemo-Medinia', persistently ascribed to Drummond from 1691 onward and frequently reprinted, appeared in Edinburgh in 1684. In 1711 Bishop John Sage and Thomas Ruddiman edited the *Works of William Drummond*, reprinting all previously published work and adding many of the political tracts and letters, accessible through Drummond's son, who died two years later. Drummond's poems, and his prose essay 'A cypress grove', were reprinted a number of times in the nineteenth century by editors who annotated his poems with varying degrees of fullness: this culminated in the scholarly edition of L. E. Kastner (2 vols., 1913), whose bibliographical accuracy and care in tracing Drummond's sources laid the foundation for all subsequent scholarship.

Appreciations of Drummond tend to reveal more about the critic in his time than the writer: it is not known what John Milton thought of Drummond, though he borrowed from him; his nephew, Edward Phillips, thought him 'a famous wit … a polite and verdant genius', and (less fulsomely) said that his *History of Scotland* was 'florid and ornate'. Sage and Ruddiman in their 1711 edition of his works said nothing about Drummond's prose writing, and contrived to give the impression that Drummond had, in best Augustan fashion, been a loyal tory member of a circle of poet–wits. When the criterion of poetic wit gave way to that of poetic sentiment, Drummond was praised in the nineteenth century for what *Chambers's Cyclopaedia* called his 'elevation of sentiment, natural feeling, play of fancy and melancholy mysticism' (1901, 1.510), and this essentially Romantic view of Drummond lasted at least as far as French Rowe Fogle's *Critical Study of William Drummond of Hawthornden* (1952). There has still been little interest in Drummond's prose writing, but late twentieth-century critical interest in rhetorical artifice and intertextuality focused attention on Drummond's borrowings. R. D. S. Jack attempted to reconcile some of these opinions in his study of Drummond's debt to Italian poetry by calling him 'first among literary chameleons, and yet … an intensely personal poet' (Jack, 123). Once Drummond's use of his sources is understood, he does indeed appear to be a Mannerist poet, and that enables him to exhibit to his readers wit, sensuous feeling, and fanciful and mystical imagery, all in the confessional mode of Petrarchist verse.

Drummond's manuscripts, printed and unprinted, came in 1782 to the Scottish Society of Antiquaries from Abernethy Drummond, husband of the poet's great-great-granddaughter Mary Barbara (*d.* 1789), and later bishop of Brechin, Edinburgh, and Glasgow. They were arranged in fifteen volumes, now in the National Library of Scotland, by David Laing, who published a valuable account of them with extracts in *Archaeologia Scotica* (4/1 and 4/2, 1831–2). Nineteenth-century editors of Drummond's works, and David Masson's *Drummond of Hawthornden: the Story of his Life and Writings* (1873), drew upon this new material. Drummond's 'Memorialls', an autograph manuscript compiled by Drummond and his son of births, marriages, deaths, and notable events in the family, was made available in 1962 on permanent loan from Brechin Diocesan Library to the University of Dundee in the manuscript collection of the university archives, and was used by R. H. MacDonald for his study *The Library of Drummond of Hawthornden* (1971). MacDonald identifies about 1300 of Drummond's books, of which about 800 are known still to exist, the majority being in the library of the University of Edinburgh. A transcript of Drummond's will and some land transfer documents of the family are in the General Register House, Edinburgh.　　MICHAEL R. G. SPILLER

Sources W. Drummond, 'Memorialls', University of Dundee Archives · will of William Drummond of Hawthornden, registered 22 July 1653, Edinburgh register of testaments, General Register Office for Scotland, Edinburgh, commissariat records, CC8/8/67/158 · W. Drummond, NL Scot., Hawthornden MSS · D. Masson, *Drummond of Hawthornden: the story of his life and writings* (1873) · D. Laing, 'Extracts from the Hawthornden manuscripts', *Archaeologia Scotica*, 4/1–2 (1831–2) · R. H. MacDonald, *The library of Drummond of Hawthornden* (1971) · W. Drummond, *The genealogy of the most noble and ancient house of Drummond*, ed. D. Laing (1831) · *The poetical works of William Drummond of Hawthornden*, ed. L. E. Kastner, 2 vols., STS, 2nd ser., 3–4 (1913) · *The poems of William Drummond of Hawthornden*, ed. T. Maitland (1832) · *The works of William Drummond, of Hawthornden*, ed. J. Sage and T. Ruddiman, [3 pts] (1711) · F. R. Fogle, *A critical study of William Drummond of Hawthornden* (1952) · R. D. S. Jack, *The Italian influence on Scottish literature* (1972) · M. Spiller, 'Poetry after the Union', *The history of Scottish literature*, ed. C. Craig, 1: *Origins to 1660*, ed. R. D. S. Jack (1987), 141–62

Archives NL Scot., literary papers; tracts · U. Edin. L. · University of Dundee, archives, diary, MSS, and 'Memorialls'
Likenesses oils, 1609, Scot. NPG · oils, 1612, Scot. NPG [*see illus.*] · R. Gaywood, etching, 1654 (after oil painting), BM, NPG; repro. in W. Drummond, *A history of Scotland* (1655) · J. Finlayson, mezzotint, pubd 1766 (after C. Johnson?), BM, NPG · engraving (after oil painting at Hawthornden Castle), repro. in W. Drummond, *Poems* (1614?) · engraving (after oil painting at Hawthornden Castle), repro. in W. Drummond, *Poems* (1616) · oils, Scot. NPG · two oil paintings, Hawthornden Castle, Lasswade, Edinburgh
Wealth at death £3936 Scots: will, CC8/8/67/158

Drummond, William, first viscount of Strathallan (*c.*1617–1688), royalist army officer, was the fifth son of John Drummond, second Lord Maderty (*d.* 1649×51), and Margaret Leslie, eldest daughter of Patrick Leslie, first Lord Lindores. Drummond attended the University of St Andrews, and served as a captain in the Scottish army in Ireland in 1642–8. He was commissioned on 5 October 1645 and 30 June 1646 to negotiate on the army's behalf with the Scottish committee of estates and the English parliament, and spent several months in London in 1646–7. He was with the contingent of the army which returned to Scotland in 1648 to support the engagement to help Charles I, and was present when it dispersed the marquess of Argyll's levies near Stirling in August.

Facing punishment in Scotland for his support for the engagement, Drummond considered taking part in a scheme Cromwell was considering whereby the Spanish would recruit Scottish troops for service in Flanders, and he was present at Cromwell's invitation in January 1649, when the latter debated with Scottish commissioners opposing the execution of Charles I. However, Drummond left London the day after the execution to join Charles II in the Netherlands. Returning to Scotland in 1650 he was appointed a colonel in the forces opposing Cromwell's invasion in December. He was captured at the battle of Worcester (3 September 1651), but on being granted bail fled to rejoin Charles II in Paris. By 1653 he was back in Scotland, serving with the royalists who had risen in the highlands against English rule. He was sent to the Netherlands to invite Charles II to come to Scotland, but the king dispatched him again to the highlands in November with just 'good words and a few kind letters' (*Bishop Burnet's History*, 1.111). Now holding the rank of major-general, Drummond had some success in delaying the collapse of the fragmented and demoralized royalist resistance, but in May 1655 he and his friend Major-General Thomas Dalyell obtained passes from the English to withdraw to the continent. High regard for him at this time is indicated by Edward Hyde's description of him in 1653 as 'a very discreet, honest, gallant person' (Firth, *Scotland and the Commonwealth*, 245n.) and by the comment in 1654 that he was 'not only a good souldier, but a sober, rationall man' (Firth, *Scotland and the Protectorate*, 123).

With the permission of the king, Drummond and Dalyell served Tsar Alexis I of Russia against the Poles and Tartars in 1655–65. Drummond became 'Lieut-General of the Strangers' (foreign troops) and governor of Smolensk after defeating the Poles near Chausy in 1662 (Dalton, pt 1, 70), and was credited on one occasion with having saved a retreating Russian army from total defeat by his rearguard action with a small body of men. The generals were recalled by Charles II in 1665, as he feared unrest in Scotland during the Second Anglo-Dutch War, and Drummond was appointed major-general of the forces in Scotland in May 1666. The king declared himself 'very sensible of the share' he had in the dispersal of presbyterian dissidents at Rullion Green in November 1666 (ibid., pt 1, 71) and he was sworn of the privy council in January 1667. But the disbanding of the army in Scotland in September left Drummond unemployed, and he is said to have pressed for harsh military repression of dissidents—Gilbert Burnet later alleged that Drummond, being 'ambitious and covetous', was disappointed at the failure to implement a proposal to treat all who refused to denounce the covenants as traitors, as that would have led to 'great dealing in bribes and confiscations' (*Bishop Burnet's History*, 1.439). Drummond came to be associated with those opposed to the earl of Lauderdale's policies (he represented Perthshire in the 1669–74 parliament), and this led to his imprisonment in Dumbarton Castle between September 1674 and February 1676; he was made an example of in this way, it was said, because he 'was of all the military men he that had the best capacity and the greatest reputation' (ibid., 2.57). In April 1678 he accompanied a delegation of Scottish politicians opposed to Lauderdale to court, and is said to have complained to the king that though he had always been a loyal subject he had been imprisoned without explanation. He had now come to seek employment 'in the ware', and if there was no employment for him he would rather the king hanged him than treated him as a slave (O. Airy, ed., *The Lauderdale Papers*, 3 vols., CS, new ser., 34, 36, 38, 1884–5, 3.151).

The expected war with France did not take place, and Drummond remained unemployed. These years of respite from military duties allowed him to turn to personal matters. He married Elizabeth Johnston (*d.* 1679), daughter of Sir Archibald Johnston of Wariston and widow of Thomas Hepburn of Humbie, at Holyrood Abbey on 28 February 1668. The marriage ceremony was held at midnight, doubtless to avoid scandal, as the couple's daughter had been born ten days before. Drummond is said to have been instrumental in having his father-in-law's head removed from the Netherbow Port, Edinburgh, where it had stood since his execution in 1663. Their only son, William, later second Lord Strathallan, was born in 1670. The general also developed his literary interests, completing *The Genealogy of the most Noble and Ancient House of Drummond* (which was not published until 1831); the work was dedicated to the head of his kin, James Drummond, fourth earl of Perth, in 1681.

The decline of Lauderdale's power eventually brought Drummond renewed employment. He was appointed master-general of the king's ordnance in Scotland (8 September 1682), and in the years that followed he played an active part in the suppressing of disorder in the west and in the highlands. On 4 June 1685 he was made lieutenant-general of all forces in Scotland, and he took part in the suppression of the earl of Argyll's uprising. On a visit to court in March 1686 he resisted pressure from James VII to convert to Roman Catholicism, being, as his brother-in-law James Johnston put it, 'a bad Christian but a good Protestant' (T. B. Macaulay, *History of England*, 6 vols., 1913–15, 2.774). Drummond's first wife, Elizabeth, died in 1679. He probably contracted a second marriage, to Grisel Drummond, in or before 1685, because their son was baptized in that year without mention of illegitimacy. Drummond was created viscount of Strathallan and Lord Drummond of Cromlix on 16 August 1686; he died on 23 March 1688, and was buried on 4 April 1688 at Innerpeffray, Perthshire, a funeral sermon being preached by Alexander Monro, the principal of Edinburgh University.

Gilbert Burnet's comment about Drummond that there was 'yet too much of the air of Russia about him, though not with Dalziel's fierceness' (*Bishop Burnet's History*, 1.439), and the rumour that he was (with Dalyell) responsible for introducing the thumbscrew as an instrument of torture to Scotland from Russia, are not backed up by specific allegations against him. Even Sir John Lauder of Fountainhall, who spread the thumbscrew rumour, admitted that in fact it was already used in Scotland under another name—'the pilliewincks' (J. Lauder, *Historical Notices*, 2 vols., 1848, 2.557). However, he undoubtedly could be brutal. In 1685 he referred to some mutinous soldiers as 'thes miserable unhappy divells' but added 'I wishe they wer all shot to death'—though he admitted that this would be inexpedient (NA Scot., RH15/12/123/70). Burnet refers to Drummond's 'great measure of knowledge and learning, and some true impressions of religion', while Ewen Cameron of Lochiel described him as 'ane honest man, a faithfull and sinscear friend and ane incorruptible patriot; besides he distinguished himsel by his learning and parts' (E. Cameron, *Memoirs*, 1842, 219).   DAVID STEVENSON

Sources DNB · GEC, *Peerage* · *Scots peerage* · C. Dalton, *The Scots army, 1661–1688*, 2 pts (1909) · A. Monro, *Sermons* (1693) · *Bishop Burnet's History*, vols. 1–2 · *CSP dom.*, 1642–89 · *Reg. PCS*, 2nd ser., vol. 8 · *Reg. PCS*, 3rd ser., vols. 1–14 · C. H. Firth, ed., *Scotland and the Commonwealth: letters and papers relating to the military government of Scotland, from August 1651 to December 1653*, Scottish History Society, 18 (1895) · C. H. Firth, ed., *Scotland and the protectorate: letters and papers relating to the military government of Scotland from January 1654 to June 1659*, Scottish History Society, 31 (1899) · M. D. Young, ed., *The parliaments of Scotland: burgh and shire commissioners*, 2 vols. (1992–3) · D. Stevenson, *Scottish covenanters and Irish confederates* (1981) · transactions of the army in Ireland, NL Scot., Adv MS 33.40.8 · D. Stevenson, *The government of Scotland under the covenanters*, Scottish History Society (1982) · S. Murdoch and A. Grosjean, 'Scotland, Scandinavia and Northern Europe, 1580–1707', www.abdn.ac.uk/ssne/
Archives BL, Lauderdale MSS, letters to earl of Lauderdale and Charles II, Add. MSS 23122–23130 · Buckminster Park, Grantham, corresp. with earl of Lauderdale
Likenesses attrib. L. Schuneman, oils, Scot. NPG

Drummond, William, fourth viscount of Strathallan (1690–1746), Jacobite army officer, was born at Machany, Perthshire, the fourth but eldest surviving son of Sir John Drummond of Machany (*d.* 1707) and Margaret, daughter of Sir William Stewart of Innernytie. In the year of Strathallan's birth his father was outlawed for adhering to the house of Stuart. On 26 May 1711 Drummond succeeded his cousin William as fourth viscount of Strathallan. In 1712, by a contract dated 1 November, he married Margaret (1692–1773), eldest daughter of William Murray, second Lord Nairne, and his wife, Margaret. They had thirteen children, including Henry *Drummond, banker; Drummond's eldest son, James Drummond, the master of Strathallan, was 'out' with his father in 1745, and was attainted in the following year. Lady Strathallan, herself from a Jacobite family, was held prisoner in Edinburgh Castle from 11 February to 22 November 1746, and proceedings for treason were considered against her.

Strathallan was one of the first to participate in the Jacobite rising of 1715, attending the earl of Mar's hunting party. In the campaign he led a battalion from Perthshire, serving under the command of Brigadier William Mackintosh of Borlum. Taken prisoner at Sheriffmuir, Strathallan was removed to Stirling, but under the terms of the Act of Grace of 1717, suffered neither prosecution nor forfeiture. In 1745 he joined the army of Charles Edward Stuart at Perth on 3 September. Strathallan commanded the Perthshire horse, with two troops under him led by Lieutenant-Colonel Lawrence Oliphant of Gask and Major John Haldane (who joined after Prestonpans); he was also named as a member of the prince's privy council. At Prestonpans Strathallan's was the only cavalry unit in the Jacobite ranks, at that time consisting of some thirty-six troopers and their servants: subsequently numbers rose to about seventy. When Prince Charles marched south, Strathallan as major-general was appointed general officer commanding in Scotland, stationed at Perth; meanwhile his cavalry squadron went south under the command of the earl of Kilmarnock. Strathallan remained in overall command in Scotland until superseded by Lord John Drummond after the latter's landing at Montrose. In January 1746 he wrote from Perth as commander to pass on Charles's orders to the marquess of Tullibardine, requesting one hundred men for the garrison and fifty to raise 'tax and excise in Perthshire and Fife' to replace the Banffshire troops, who had been relieved (Burton and Laing, 160). At Falkirk the Perthshire horse were in the rear, taking little part in the action. As the government lines closed round the Jacobites at Culloden and began to move forward against the undeployed second line and third line reserve (many of whom had, however, run away), Strathallan 'resolved to die in the field rather than by the hand of the executioner' (Tomasson and Buist, 197). He may have charged the government line in a heroic counter-attack, possibly at the head of his cavalry, officially a squadron, but now probably fewer than forty strong. Strathallan's horse was killed under him, and he himself was run through, according to tradition, by Colonel George Howard of the 3rd foot. As he lay dying on the battlefield he received the last sacrament, reportedly under the kinds of oatmeal or oatcake and whisky or water, from John Maitland of Careston, episcopalian chaplain to the Forfarshire regiment.

Strathallan played a key role in the rising of 1745 and

died a heroic death at Culloden, two well-matched roles which guarantee this brave but not particularly distinguished Scottish nobleman a place in national history.

MURRAY G. H. PITTOCK

Sources DNB · GEC, *Peerage* · *Scots peerage* · K. Tomasson and F. Buist, *Battles of the '45* (1962) · A. Tayler and H. Tayler, *Jacobites of Aberdeen and Banffshire in the Forty-five* (1928) · S. Reid, *A military history of the last Jacobite rising* (1996) · NL Scot., MSS 1498, 17523 · J. Baynes, *The Jacobite rising of 1715* (1970) · F. McDonnell, ed., *The Jacobites of 1745: northeast Scotland* (1996) · A. H. Millar, ed., *A selection of Scottish forfeited estates papers*, Scottish History Society, 57 (1909) · J. H. Burton and D. Laing, eds., *Jacobite correspondence of the Atholl family* (1840) · A. Tayler and H. Tayler, eds., *Jacobite letters to Lord Pitsligo* (1930) · M. G. H. Pittock, *Jacobitism* (1998) · F. J. McLynn, *The Jacobite army in England, 1745: the final campaign* (1983) · F. J. McLynn, *Charles Edward Stuart: a tragedy in many acts* (1988)

Archives NA Scot., forfeited papers, E782 · NL Scot., MSS 1498, 17523

Drummond, Sir William, of Logiealmond (1770?–1828), classical scholar and diplomatist, was the eldest son of John Drummond, the laird of Logiealmond, and his wife, Lady Catherine Murray, sister of John, earl of Dunmore. He succeeded his father on the latter's death in 1781. He studied philosophy briefly (*c*.1786–7) at St Andrews but matriculated at Christ Church, Oxford, in January 1788. On 12 December 1794 he married Harriet Anne, the daughter of Charles Boone MP, of Lee in Kent, who in 1819 inherited a considerable fortune (in excess of £500,000) from her father.

In 1795 Drummond was returned to parliament in the tory interest for the borough of St Mawes, and in the following parliament, which lasted from 1796 to 1802, he sat for Lostwithiel. Diplomacy, however, attracted him more than debate. He was chargé d'affaires in Denmark in 1800–01 and was then sent as minister-plenipotentiary to Sicily and Naples in 1801. In 1803 he succeeded Lord Elgin as ambassador to the Ottoman Porte. On his way to Constantinople he wrote an important dispatch to his government, in which he advised it to retain possession of Malta, even though this would probably end (as it did) the peace of Amiens, since he suspected the French were preparing to invade Greece. The sultan treated him with unusual honour and bestowed the order of the Crescent on him (*London Gazette*, 8 Sept 1803) but he remained only a few months, from May to November 1803, perhaps discouraged by the burning down of the British embassy. He was sworn of the privy council in 1804 and returned to Sicily in 1807 but was recalled in 1808. His relations with the government were strained and he did not hold another diplomatic appointment. In 1808 Drummond was an unsuccessful claimant of the Roxburghe peerage.

In the latter part of his career Drummond returned to his scholarly interests. He was an active member of the Dilettanti Society, which was by this time an important patron of classical archaeology. He had already published a *Review of the Governments of Sparta and Athens* in 1795, and the *Satires of Persius, Translated* in 1798, which had been well received, as well as the (anonymous) *Philosophical Sketches on the Principles of Society and Government* (1793). In 1805 he wrote for the *Edinburgh Review*, with the young earl

of Aberdeen, a devastating review of William Gell's book *The Topography of Troy*, in which Gell claimed to have located Troy at the village of Burnabashi. In 1810 Drummond published, with Robert Walpole, *Herculanesia, or, Archaeological and Philological Dissertations, Containing a Manuscript Found among the Ruins of Herculaneum*. In 1821 he published a *Memoir on the Antiquity of the Zodiacs of Emeh and Dendera* and between 1824 and 1829 four volumes entitled *Origines, or, Remarks on the Origins of Several Empires, States, and Cities*, which contained bold speculations on the origins of Assyria and Babylon in particular. In 1817 he had published a blank verse poem, 'Odin', in which Odin was identified with Pharnaces, the son of Mithridates.

It was Drummond's religious speculations, however, that caused a sensation. In 1805 he published his *Academical Questions*. He wrote to Aberdeen:

> I have attempted to veil its real meaning; but I am afraid that our bigots will take the alarm … I have avoided all remarks upon our peculiar religion. The constitution of the country has given us a creed … We must expect the hoi polloi to be under the guidance of some superstition or another; and I do not think ours the most mischievous I know. (Aberdeen MSS, BL, Add. MS 43229, fols. 33–4)

The book was severely handled in the periodicals and Drummond was threatened with prosecution, but his speculations grew wilder and in 1811 he printed for private circulation his *Oedipus judaicus*, in which he attempted to prove that the Old Testament was an extended astrological allegory. Again criticism was severe and George D'Oyly accused Drummond of plagiarism as well as blasphemy, alleging that he had appropriated the ideas of Charles François Dupuis. A writer using the pseudonym Vindex (probably Drummond himself) replied in 1812 in *Letters to G. D'Oyley* [*sic*]. Further exchanges followed in 1813 and 1814. Drummond also tried his hand at dramatic poetry in *Byblis, a Tragedy in Five Acts* (privately printed, 1802). He was made a fellow of the Royal Society on 4 April 1799 and a DCL (Oxford) on 3 July 1810. He lived abroad, mainly in Italy, in his latter years and died in Rome on 29 March 1828.

MURIEL E. CHAMBERLAIN

Sources D. Malcolm, *A genealogical memoir of the most noble and ancient house of Drummond* (1808) · HoP, *Commons* · *Annual Register* (1828), 228 · *GM*, 1st ser., 98/2 (1828), 90–91 · *GM*, 1st ser., 89/1 (1819), 284 · *FO List* (1828) · BL, Aberdeen MSS, Add. MS 43229 · M. E. Chamberlain, *Lord Aberdeen: a political biography* (1983) · Foster, *Alum. Oxon.*

Archives Yale U., Beinecke L., holograph travel journal | BL, letters to Lord Aberdeen and notes on coins, Add. MSS 43229, 43345 · BL, corresp. with Fox, Add. MS 37050 · BL, letters to Lord Grenville, Add. MS 59023 · BL, corresp. with Lowe, Add. MSS 20108, 20163–20171 · BL, letters to Arthur Paget, Add. MSS 48391, 48395 · BL, corresp. with Lord Wellesley, Add. MSS 13791–13792 · NRA, priv. coll., letters to Lord Grenville [drafts] · The Dingle, Witts MSS · U. Durham L., letters to Viscount Ponsonby

Likenesses stipple (after A. de Meyer), NPG

Drummond, William Abernethy (*b*. before 1720, *d*. 1809), Scottish Episcopal bishop of Edinburgh and Glasgow, was born William Abernethy; he was descended from the family of Abernethy of Saltoun in Banffshire. Nothing is known of his early years until he became governor to the sons of Colonel Hackett of Pitfirran. On 30

William Abernethy Drummond (*b.* before 1720, *d.* 1809), by David Martin, 1788

May 1744 he was made deacon by Bishop John Alexander of Dunkeld on the recommendation that 'the lad is very deserving' (A. Livingstone to J. Alexander, 20 March 1744, NA Scot., CH12/23). He was ordained priest on 19 December 1744 and between 1744 and 1746 ministered at Logiealmond, Perthshire, before becoming presbyter to the Jacobite nonjuring congregation at Carrubber's Close, Edinburgh. These were perilous times for nonjurors, especially after the Jacobite rising of 1745, and both their property and their lives were at stake. Drummond—known as Abernethy until his marriage—unsuccessfully explored the possibility of becoming a nonjuring clergyman in England before deciding to study medicine at the University of Edinburgh. He graduated doctor of medicine in 1754 with a dissertation on asthma. He remained obsessively aware of the threats to nonjurors, and chose to wear the dress of a physician. On 25 October 1760, in Edinburgh's Tron Kirk, he married Mary Barbara Macgregor (*d.* 1789), widow of Robert Macgregor and heir of William Drummond, laird of Hawthornden, near Edinburgh. The family claimed connection with the Scottish royal house and henceforth Abernethy styled himself Abernethy Drummond. By his marriage he returned to the Hawthornden estate which his family had relinquished in 1388.

Drummond was over sixty before he came to prominence in Scottish church affairs and an explanation lies both in his personality and his opinions. Bishop John Skinner called him a man 'who scolded and threatened in various underhand ways' (1 Dec 1782, NA Scot., CH 12/2) while his less than enthusiastic support for the Jacobite cause also prompted criticism. He was consecrated bishop of Brechin on 26 September 1787, having earlier been rejected as a candidate for the same see 'for his imperious and arbitrary character' (Farquhar, 31). Drummond himself turned down the bishopric of Dunkeld, writing to the dean 'because you all know how ill I stand with those who rule over us' (Drummond to Skene). He stipulated to the electors of Brechin that he must have a coadjutor and a few weeks later he resigned on being elected to the see of Edinburgh, shortly afterwards accepting responsibility for Glasgow as well.

With the death of Prince Charles Edward in 1788 Drummond was in the forefront of those who believed the time had come for nonjurors to accept the Hanoverians. His family connections—the Drummonds were related to Henry Dundas, then treasurer of the navy—and his own political sympathies made him acceptable to George III. Lord Sydney wrote to Drummond expressing the king's satisfaction 'at the resolution of your body to pray, by name, for the King and royal family' (Skinner, 83). With Bishop Skinner, his critic, and Bishop Strachan, his successor at Brechin, Drummond made the four-day journey to London in April 1789 to urge the passage of a bill through parliament repealing the penal laws against nonjurors. His kinship with Dundas was valuable in winning the support of Lord Thurlow, the lord chancellor, and his meeting with the archbishop of Canterbury paved the way for the support of those English bishops who had hesitated to accept a legal, non-Erastian episcopacy. Drummond also secured the support of leading Scottish Presbyterians in both houses of parliament and the Repeal Act duly became law in 1792. Yet the tolerance which Drummond sought he had for long publicly denied to Roman Catholics. He had published in 1776 the first of two pamphlets in the form of *Letters* to the Roman Catholic bishop George Hay, and this hostility towards Catholic relief had won him praise from leading Presbyterians. His motive was primarily to distance episcopacy from Catholicism in their eyes.

It was with Jonathan Boucher, vicar of Epsom and formerly a priest in colonial America, that Drummond corresponded at length on another matter. After the repeal of the penal laws Drummond had turned his attention to unifying the continuing divisions among Episcopalians. Those ministers who had, since the Toleration Act of 1712, taken an oath of loyalty to the crown and declared their allegiance to the established Church of England had become 'qualified' and had remained distinct from the nonjurors. Drummond was willing to relinquish the see of Edinburgh to allow Boucher to become bishop but Presbyterian alarm at this prospect led him to withdraw his name. In 1800 Drummond offered another possible English candidate £80 a year from his own resources and 'plenty of good, wholesome victuals' (21 July 1800, NA Scot., GD 230/578) to come to Edinburgh with the bishopric in view. Finally, in 1805 he relinquished the see in favour of Daniel Sandford, another Englishman already serving the 'qualified' congregation of St John's, Edinburgh. Drummond, although by now in his mid-eighties, retained responsibility for Glasgow.

Drummond could be vituperative in correspondence and 'hasty and resolute' as Bishop Jonathan Watson observed in 1781 (Farquhar, 13). He could display 'teazy and troublesome impertinence' (J. Skinner to R. Kilgour, 1 Dec 1782, NA Scot., CH 12/2), yet there was a generous and kindly streak to his nature. Bishop Alexander Jolly called him 'the good bishop' (Archibald, 93). He supplied one hundred carts of coal to an orphan hospital, paid for a child's coffin and established a fund for clergy widows, raising the first £1000 by his own efforts. In addition to his writings against Roman Catholics Drummond wrote several tracts on doctrinal matters. He was a spirited controversialist and Bishop Michael Russell, writing less than twenty years after Drummond's death, called him a good theologian and a well-meaning man 'whose intemperate manner defeated in many cases the benevolence of his intentions' (Keith, 529). It was a fair, if stern assessment.

In his old age Drummond—whose wife and only child had predeceased him—sought lodgings in Hawthornden, Mrs Allen giving him a couple of rooms, a closet, and a meal a day. There he died on 27 August 1809, at least in his ninetieth year. He left the substantial sum of £2673.

GERALD M. D. HOWAT

Sources NA Scot., Drummond of Hawthornden MSS, GD 230 [especially 230/571–78] · NA Scot., Alexander MSS, episcopal chest, CH 12/23 · NA Scot., miscellaneous MSS, episcopal chest, CH 12/2; 12/23, GD 1; 18; 417 · G. T. S. Farquhar, *Three bishops of Dunkeld* (1915) · G. Grub, *An ecclesiastical history of Scotland*, 4 vols. (1861) · J. Skinner, *Annals of Scottish episcopacy* (1818) · W. Stephen, *History of the Scottish church*, 2 vols. (1894–6) · R. Keith and J. Spottiswoode, *An historical catalogue of the Scottish bishops, down to the year 1688*, new edn, ed. M. Russel [M. Russell] (1824) · W. A. Drummond, *The lawfulness of breaking with heretics* (1778) · W. A. Drummond, *A second letter to G. H.* (1779) · T. Lathbury, *A history of the nonjurors* (1845) · J. Archibald, *History of the episcopal church at Keith* (1890) · F. J. Grant, ed., *Edinburgh marriage register, 1751–1800* (1922) · *Scots Magazine*, 51 (1789), 466 · *Scots Magazine and Edinburgh Literary Miscellany*, 71 (1809), 719 · *GM*, 1st ser., 30 (1760), 542 · *Nomina eorum, qui gradum medicinae doctoris in academia Jacobi sexti Scotorum regis, quae Edinburgi est, adepti sunt, ab anno 1705 ad annum 1845*, University of Edinburgh (1846) · Dunkeld Cathedral Library, Perth, loose MSS, W. Drummond to G. Skene, 10 Oct. 1786

Archives Dunkeld diocese, Perth, loose MSS and diocesan minute books · NA Scot., corresp. and papers · NA Scot., episcopal chest · NRA Scotland, corresp. and MSS | BL, letters to Bishop Douglas, Egerton MSS 2185–2186 · BL, Egerton MSS, Drummond / Skinner letters relating to Hanoverian succession, index, catalogue, Add. MSS 1854–1875, 448 · NA Scot., Alexander MSS · NL Scot., Fettercairn MSS, letters · University of Dundee, Brechin MSS 2/1/7, 2/1/14, 3, DC/60, DC/61, DC/64, DC/82, DC/115, DC118/18

Likenesses D. Martin, oils, 1788, Scot. NPG [*see illus.*]

Wealth at death £2673 6*s.* 7¾*d.*: NA Scot., SC 70/1/2

Drummond, William Hamilton (1778–1865), non-subscribing Presbyterian minister and poet, was born at Larne, co. Antrim, in August 1778, the eldest son of William Drummond (*d. c.*1786), surgeon, RN, and his wife, Rose Hare. James Lawson *Drummond (1783–1853), anatomist, was his brother. His father, paid off in 1783, died of fever soon after taking up practice at Ballyclare. Left without resources, his mother moved to Belfast with her three children and went into business. After studying at Belfast Academy, Drummond was placed with a manufacturing

William Hamilton Drummond (1778–1865), by Henry O'Neill (after William Henry Collier, exh. Royal Hibernian Academy 1846)

firm in England. His sister maintained that cruel treatment which his employer would not or could not control turned the sensitive boy against a commercial career and towards the ministry; he himself said that the change arose from his preference for intellectual life.

Drummond entered the University of Glasgow in November 1794, but his course was interrupted, apparently because of poverty, and he left without a degree. He had, however, acquired considerable classical learning and as a student began to publish poetry, in which the revolutionary ideas of the time are evident. *The Man of Age* (1798) pleaded the cause of Ireland through a tale of an impoverished peasant family tyrannized by a powerful neighbour. Reportedly, on a visit to Larne in 1798 he was threatened with a pistol by a loyalist cavalry officer furious over such 'infernal poetry' (Porter, 'Memoir', iv).

Drummond became tutor in a family at Ravensdale, co. Louth, while pursuing his studies under the direction of the Armagh presbytery, which he chose for the high standard of proficiency it demanded from ministerial candidates. On his return to Belfast in 1799 he was transferred to the Antrim presbytery—neither presbytery required subscription to the Westminster confession of faith—and was licensed on 9 April 1800. He received calls from the First Holywood and Second Belfast congregations, and, accepting the latter, was ordained on 26 August 1800. Shortly afterwards, he married Barbara, daughter of David Tomb of Belfast; of several children, one son and two daughters survived him.

On his marriage Drummond opened a boarding-school

at Mount Collyer. He was a founder member of the Belfast Literary Society in 1801. Of his ten contributions to the society's transactions, four were poems, including a verse translation of Lucretius' *De rerum natura* (1808), which attracted the attention of Thomas Percy, bishop of Dromore and the editor of the famous *Reliques*, who was instrumental in obtaining for Drummond the degree of DD from Marischal College, Aberdeen, on 29 January 1810. His long poem *The Giant's Causeway* (1811) is an evocation of Irish history and the stunning coastline of the north-west, and is notable for its author's acquaintance with geology and for his defence of the uniformitarian hypothesis of James Hutton (1726–1797).

In 1815 Drummond was an unsuccessful candidate for the chair of logic and *belles-lettres* in the newly founded Belfast Academical Institution, and on 15 October in that year he was called to Strand Street, Dublin, as colleague to James Armstrong, where he was installed on 25 December. Several members of his Belfast congregation who were electors for the chair cast their votes against him, apparently fearing his distraction from pastoral work; he denied that the loss of the election figured in his decision to move south, emphasizing rather the opportunity that a joint ministry would give him for a wider intellectual life. He was elected a member of the Royal Irish Academy, contributed frequently to its *Transactions*, and for many years held the office of librarian. He took a scholarly interest in Celtic literature, but some of his poetical pieces are graceful paraphrases of ancient Irish sources rather than close translations. In 1830 his prize essay for the academy established that a recent Gaelic publication of the poems of Ossian was a translation from the English and not the alleged original, thus vindicating the authorship of the poems by James Macpherson (1736–1796). He also edited for publication in 1840 the autobiography of his friend Archibald Hamilton Rowan, the United Irishman. His writings show very wide reading, facilitated by an insatiable habit of book collecting.

In Belfast, Drummond was a highly popular preacher, particularly in demand by philanthropic organizations for his gift for charity sermons. He is said to have preached only one doctrinal sermon there, and that at the request of a member of the congregation troubled on a theological point. While he continued in that vein in Dublin he emerged as a formidable controversialist in the Unitarian cause. *The Doctrine of the Trinity* (1827), which he injected into a protestant–Catholic debate to illustrate a third alternative, went through three editions in Britain and one in America. His *Life of Michael Servetus* (1848) is a continuous onslaught on what he supposed to be the unamiable tendencies of Calvinism.

Drummond's second marriage was to Catherine (d. 1879), daughter of Robert Blackley of Dublin. One daughter died young and another survived him, as did two sons, Robert Blackley Drummond (1833–1920), minister of St Mark's, Edinburgh, and James *Drummond (1835–1918), principal of Manchester College.

Drummond's tastes were simple, and his kind and singularly sweet character was enlivened by a bright vein of humour. A fine countenance dignified his short stature; in Belfast he was known as 'little God Almighty'. He was very near-sighted and, although he wrote many much-admired hymns, he had no ear for music. In his old age recurring attacks of apoplexy led to progressive loss of memory and wider mental deterioration. He died at his home in Lower Gardiner Street, Dublin, on 16 October 1865 and was buried at Mount Jerome cemetery, Dublin, on the 20th.

R. K. WEBB

Sources J. S. Porter, 'Memoir', in W. H. Drummond, *Sermons* (1867) · *The Inquirer* (28 Oct 1865) · J. S. Porter, *Unitarian Herald* (27 Oct 1865), 345 · *CGPLA Ire.* (1866) · private information (2004) **Archives** Royal Irish Acad., essays | NL Scot., letters to Dr Robert Anderson **Likenesses** W. H. Collier, oils, c.1846, Unitarian Church, 112 St Stephen's Green West, Dublin · H. O'Neill, lithograph (after W. H. Collier, exh. Royal Hibernian Academy 1846), NG Ire. [*see illus.*] **Wealth at death** under £10,000: administration, 9 June 1866, *CGPLA Ire.*

Drummond [*formerly* Drumm], **William Henry** (1854–1907), poet and physician in Canada, was born on 13 April 1854 near Mohill, near Carrick-on-Shannon, co. Leitrim, Ireland, the eldest of the four sons of George Drumm (d. 1866), an officer in the Royal Irish Constabulary, and his wife, Elizabeth Morris Soden (d. 1906). He attended school in Tawley, co. Leitrim, where his parents had moved shortly after his birth. His father was dismissed from his post after a quarrel with Lord Leitrim and the Drumms emigrated to Lower Canada, arriving in Montreal in 1864. After his father's death in 1866 the family was left in poverty. Mrs Drumm opened a small shop, and her sons all sold newspapers, but lack of money led William at the age of fourteen to leave school to become a telegrapher's apprentice. He worked at Bord-à-Plouffe on the Rivière des Prairies during the summer and at Montreal during the winter. In 1875 he changed his surname and that of his mother and brothers to Drummond, of which he believed Drumm was a corruption.

Drummond returned to school at Montreal high school (1876–7) and then studied medicine at McGill College (1877–9) and Bishop's College (1879–84). After qualifying in 1884 he practised in various areas before in 1888 returning to Montreal to work from the family home. He was a conscientious doctor who often treated poor patients for little financial reward, but he also held professorships at Bishop's College from 1893 to 1905. On 18 April 1894 he married May Isobel Harvey in Savanna la Mar, Jamaica. Of their five children, one son and one daughter survived infancy.

In the late 1870s Drummond began writing poetry. His first poem, 'The wreck of the *Julie Plante*', circulated widely and achieved huge popular success many years before its publication. From the 1890s his poems started to appear in print and he began recitations of his works. With the encouragement of the poet Louis Fréchette, who provided a preface, Drummond published *The Habitant and other French-Canadian Poems* in 1897. In the work he sketched the French-Canadian rural *habitants*, using the language which they themselves would have used to English speakers. The volume won him wide popular and scholarly fame, a string of lecturing engagements throughout North America, and demand for further collections of verse, which followed in 1898, 1901, and 1905. Honorary degrees from Toronto (1902) and Bishop's College (1905) were matched by election to the (British) Royal Society of Literature (1898) and the Royal Society of Canada (1899).

The deaths of his third son in 1904 and of his mother in 1906 moved Drummond deeply. In 1905 he closed his medical practice in Montreal and turned his attention to managing the silver mines of Cobalt, northern Ontario, in which he and his brothers had an interest. After tending patients in a smallpox epidemic in Cobalt, despite his own poor health, he died there of a cerebral haemorrhage on 6 April 1907, and was buried on 8 April in Mount Royal cemetery, Montreal.

Collections of Drummond's poems appeared posthumously in 1908 and 1912, and his continued inclusion in anthologies of Canadian poetry kept his fame alive, although by the 1970s there were suggestions that his portrayal of French Canadians as simple and unlettered, if honest, was patronizing. Yet his portraits were never caricatures, and the majority have continued to admire his unique and sympathetic portrayal of French Canadians through their own dialect.   ELIZABETH BAIGENT

Sources M. J. Edwards, 'Drummond, William Henry', *DCB*, vol. 13 · [N. Story], *The Oxford companion to Canadian history and literature*, ed. W. Toye, suppl. (1973) · J. F. Macdonald, *William Henry Drummond* [1925] · M. Drummond, 'Memoir', in W. H. Drummond, *The great fight* (1908) · G. Noonan, 'Drummond—the legend and the legacy', *Canadian Literature*, 90 (1981), 179–87 · L. J. Burpee, 'W. H. Drummond (1854–1907)', *Leading Canadian poets*, ed. W. P. Percival (1948), 71–8
Archives McGill University, Montreal · NA Canada
Likenesses photograph, repro. in Macdonald, *William Henry Drummond*

Drummore. For this title name *see* Dalrymple, Hew, of Drummore, Lord Drummore (1690–1755) [*see under* Dalrymple, Sir Hew, first baronet, Lord North Berwick (1652–1737)].

Drury family (*per.* 1485–1624), gentry, of Hawstead, traced its descent from Drieu, allegedly one of the companions of the Conqueror. A connection with St Edmund's Abbey in west Suffolk was confirmed by Abbot Baldwin before 1088 through land held in Thurston and remained unbroken until the surrender of the abbey in 1539, and it was in Rougham, conveniently close to Bury St Edmunds, that the senior branch of the family settled. A second branch which settled at Hawstead, west of Rougham and 4 miles south of Bury St Edmunds, first attained more than local importance with Sir Robert *Drury (*b.* before 1456, *d.* 1535). Speaker of the House of Commons in 1485 and probably three times MP for Suffolk, Sir Robert typified the rising gentry of Suffolk who with long-established links as clients to the old aristocracy now increasingly acted as executors of their wills and administrators of their estates. Through kinship and shared local interests the Drurys joined other gentry families to form a network of common loyalties and concerns. When Sir Robert died

on 2 March 1535 at least four years after his wife, Anne Calthorpe, the greater part of his property in land and profitable flocks of sheep was concentrated in west Suffolk, but he also owned a house in London on the site that was to become Drury House in Drury Lane.

Sir Robert's heir was his eldest son, **Sir William Drury** (*c.*1500–1558), who was already established in the royal service at the time of his father's death. William had accompanied Cardinal Wolsey to Calais in 1521 and was knighted in 1533 at Anne Boleyn's coronation, while in 1540 he was appointed a groom of the privy chamber at the arrival of Anne of Cleves. He married twice. His first wife, Joan St Maur, died in 1517 after barely a year of marriage. His second wife, Elizabeth Sotehill (*d.* 1575), whom he married on 11 February 1521, brought him a considerable marriage portion from her father, whose sole heir she was. This and the wealth he inherited from his father enabled Sir William to raise and equip 100 men for the duke of Norfolk's expedition against the Pilgrimage of Grace in 1536. In that same year he was sheriff of Suffolk and Norfolk, while in 1539 he was appointed commissioner for the defence of the Suffolk coast. Although on friendly terms with John Reeve, until 1539 abbot of Bury, he benefited from the dissolution of St Edmund's Abbey in that year to consolidate his estates on the south side of the town near his properties at Hawstead; his acquisitions included the manor and advowson of Whepstead and half the manor of Rede. Like many of the Suffolk gentry he declared for Princess Mary in 1553, although the duke of Northumberland had expected his support. He continued to be returned as knight of the shire until 1555, but took little part in parliamentary business. Following the sudden death of his eldest son, Robert, in December 1557 Sir William drew up his own will on 26 December. The administration of his Hawstead estate was left to his widow during the minority of their second grandson, William. No specific bequests were made to the church or to the poor and the preamble to his will has the briefest formula commending his soul 'to almighti god our ladye Saincte Marye and to all tholly companye of heaven' (PRO, PROB 11/40, fol. 127v). Sir William died a fortnight later, on 11 January 1558, and was buried in Hawstead church where a memorial brass commemorates him.

Sir William Drury (1550–1590) was only just seven when he inherited the family estates. His education followed family tradition, with a brief residence in Cambridge followed by admission to Lincoln's Inn. His marriage to Elizabeth Stafford (*d.* 1600), daughter of Queen Elizabeth's mistress of the robes and herself one of the ladies of the bedchamber, introduced him into court circles. Their first child, Robert, was born at Durham House, Westminster, on 30 January 1575, followed by two daughters, Frances, born at Hawstead on 13 June 1576, and Elizabeth, born on 4 January 1578, by which date Drury had been knighted. The year 1578 was a momentous one for the young couple. For some time the house at Hawstead had been undergoing considerable refurbishment. Not only had the domestic apartments been altered but the outside walls had been spectacularly transformed by the insertion of sparkling particles of glass. In short Hawstead Place was ready to receive a royal visit. The queen spent a night in August 1578 there with 'a costly and delicate dinner' (J. Nichols, *Progresses of Queen Elizabeth*, 1823, 2.117). Tradition maintains that during this visit the queen dropped a silver-handled fan into the moat.

The Drurys were a favoured couple, exchanging new year's gifts with the queen, but not all Sir William's time was taken up by his attendances at court. He was sheriff of Suffolk in 1582–3. Like his grandfather he seems to have taken little interest in theological controversy, but his position as a JP inevitably involved him in religious disputes. In 1583 he acted against puritanism by bringing Richard Bancroft to preach at Bury against the defacement by the separatist Thomas Gibson of the new royal arms set up in St Mary's Church. He was returned as MP for Suffolk in the following year. But Sir William increasingly hankered after a military career, and in 1587 he followed the earl of Leicester to the Netherlands, where he was appointed temporary governor of Bergen-op-Zoom during the absence of its governor, and then given the command of the forts outside the town. His portrait of about this date—depicting him outside a richly decorated tent, half armed and with his helmet and gauntlets at hand against a backdrop of men apparently reconnoitring a walled town—mirrors his self-image. When the Spanish siege of Bergen-op-Zoom was abandoned Sir William returned to England but was almost immediately ordered to re-embark for France as colonel of a thousand men to assist Henri IV. Passing through Bergen-op-Zoom once again he quarrelled with Sir John Borough. In the ensuing duel Sir William received a wound in his arm, which subsequently had to be amputated. He died on 18 January 1590.

On his deathbed Sir William begged Sir Francis Walsingham to entreat the queen 'to be good to his wife and children, and for his eldest sone to leave him to his wife or grandmother' (Campling, 55). His will, drawn up in 1587, contained the appropriate bequests to secure the dower of his wife and the upbringing of his children, and to provide generous marriage portions for his four daughters. He left the plate and household furnishings from Drury House to his wife, and property in Bury St Edmunds to his second son, Charles. Most of the estate, including the mansion house at Hawstead and all the silver plate 'by Inventory remayninge in the butlers charge there' (PRO, PROB 11/86, fol. 11r), was inherited by his fifteen-year-old son Robert. Such bequests give a misleading impression of opulence. Sir William owed £3000 to the exchequer and another £3000 in private debts. Despite his dying appeal to the queen the entire Drury estate was seized by the crown in 1591 as surety for the debt to the exchequer, and probate of his will was not granted until 1595. Sir William himself was not buried until 6 May 1593, more than four years after his death.

The young **Sir Robert Drury** (1575–1615) inherited a heavily burdened estate. His guardianship and that of his younger brothers and sisters was in the hands of his mother, who in 1590 married Sir John Scott of Nettlestead,

Kent. After tutoring by Richard Brabon, vicar of Whepstead, in 1588 he went to Corpus Christi College, Cambridge, but did not complete his residence there, for in 1591 he joined the army in France under the command of the earl of Essex. He was knighted by Essex during the siege of Rouen and seems to have been intent upon following a military career. Meanwhile the responsibility for unravelling the complexities of Sir William Drury's estate gradually passed into the hands of Sir Nicholas Bacon of Redgrave, whose eldest daughter, Anne, married Robert Drury on 30 January 1592. By a series of negotiations with the crown and with Sir John and Lady Scott the debts were finally settled so that marriage portions and other legacies could be paid. Sir Robert appeared content to leave to Bacon the management of his affairs and the maintenance of his wife and two daughters, both born at Bacon's house at Redgrave, while he continued to campaign out of England. During her husband's absences abroad **Anne Drury**, Lady Drury (1572–1624), oversaw the households in London and Suffolk. Puritanically inclined in religion, in 1601 she presented Joseph Hall, a fellow of Emmanuel College, Cambridge, who later became bishop of Norwich, to the living of Hawstead, and drew her household from likeminded women.

More constant than his attachment to his wife, Sir Robert's loyalty to Essex took him on the Cadiz expedition (1596) and to command a company in Ireland. Perhaps in search of a change of career he visited Paris in late 1599, offering the queen's covert support to the Huguenot cause. Restless, ambitious, and quick to take offence, earlier that year he had been set upon and seriously injured in an ambush laid by an East Anglian acquaintance, Sir William Woodhouse, while in 1600 he was involved in a lawsuit which resulted in his being taken into custody. At least this saved him from direct implication in the Essex rebellion of 1601, although Drury House had been the venue for the meetings of the conspirators. Once cleared of treason Sir Robert returned to Paris and remained abroad until after Elizabeth's death.

Thanks to the efforts of his father-in-law Drury's finances were now improving. He also established a good relationship with James I, resulting in the remission of the outstanding portion of his debt to the exchequer. In spite of continued absences in London and abroad Sir Robert began to assume some of the county responsibilities associated with his family's traditions of service. He was a member of the muster commission in 1597 for Suffolk, and was returned as a knight of the shire for the county in 1604. In the parliamentary session of 1606 he moved an amendment to the recusancy laws inhibiting the residence of Roman Catholics from in and near London, and aligned himself with the king's party in voting for an increased subsidy. Journeys to Newmarket in the royal entourage and a grant of £500 in 1608 'as of his Majesties free guift in regard of his service' (Bald, 66) indicate a place at least on the fringe of James I's inner circle. He also speculated in the development of Drury House into a complex of rentable properties arranged round the courtyard of the family's own house, with open grounds or gardens behind each of them. By 1608 the whole property had been cut up into 'twelve messuages and twenty gardens with thappurtenances' besides the 'Cappital massuage or mancion called Drury House' (Bald, 111). At the same time Hawstead Place was being remodelled, perhaps under the direction of Lady Drury, while its garden and park were enriched by rare plants: Sir Nicholas Bacon gave seeds of plane trees brought from Constantinople and medlar trees were planted against the walls of the inner courtyard.

Sir Robert now hoped for a diplomatic post, but his hopes to be appointed ambassador to Spain in 1609 were disappointed, and in mid-August 1610, with Lady Drury and their daughter Elizabeth, he began an extended journey to Spa and then to Paris. In December, after their return to London, Elizabeth Drury suddenly died. Her funeral was held in St Clement's Church and on 17 December she was buried in Hawstead church. Elizabeth's death was a devastating blow to her parents. Not only did it mean the end of the line of Drurys of Hawstead but she was recognized to be a girl of great charm who had been considered as a possible bride for Henry, prince of Wales. The Latin epitaph on her tomb at Hawstead is reputedly by John Donne; certainly his poems 'A Funerall Elegie' presented to her parents and 'The Anniversaries' commemorating Elizabeth Drury's death mark an increasingly close relationship with the Drurys. Between 1611 and 1612 he travelled with the Drurys on the continent, in the Low Countries and Germany, partly as congenial companion, partly as amanuensis, and on their return to London brought his wife to one of Sir Robert's new houses adjoining Drury House.

Sir Robert and Lady Drury returned to Suffolk, to Hardwick House on the outskirts of Bury St Edmunds. They had been fitting it up since 1609 and it became their preferred residence, perhaps because of the memories of their daughter Elizabeth at Hawstead Place. Sir Robert was occupied with estate affairs and with buying Snareshill near Thetford, a considerable property. In the following year Sir Robert embarked on a generously endowed charitable project to provide almshouses for six poor widows from his estates. A complex endowment provided an annual rent of £52 for its beneficiaries, to which Sir Robert added a further annuity of £20 in his will. The money was probably drawn from an estate at Hardwick, north of Hawstead, which had been bought for £1100 in 1609.

In 1614 Sir Robert was returned to parliament as one of the members for Eye. Soon afterwards he tried once more to obtain a diplomatic posting, this time to Venice, but was again disappointed. Restlessly unoccupied he continued with building work on the Drury House site and also started work again on improvements to Hawstead Place. But in spring 1615 he contracted a fever, and died at Hardwick House on 2 April; his funeral took place on 1 June in Hawstead church under the direction of the Richmond and Chester heralds. The monument was ordered by Lady Drury from Nicholas Stone at a cost of £140. Sir Robert's will left £100 for a bust of his father in full armour to be placed on his own monument, a son's tribute to the father whose career he had tried to emulate. John Donne contributed the epitaph which sums up such lofty hopes so sadly disappointed:

> Quem et bellicae expeditiones, et exterae peregrinationes et aulicae occupaciones, satis (ipsa invidia, qua saepe tactus, fractus nunquam, teste) instruxerant, tam ad exercitus ducendos, quam ad legationes peragendas, aut civiles pertractandos. (The envy by which he was often afflicted but never broken bears witness that he was a man whom military enterprises, foreign travels, and attendance at court had well prepared to lead armies, carry through embassies, and perform his public obligations.)

Sir Robert Drury died a rich man. The Drury House properties were bringing in rents of £300 per annum and his inventory included further rents of £650 and debts owed to Sir Robert of £3615. The Hardwick estate had been settled on Lady Drury at the time of its purchase. Other properties settled on her for life included the mansion of Drury House, all his possessions, and tithes in and around Bury St Edmunds and Snareshill. The almshouses were to receive a generous endowment out of rents from Hawstead and Hardwick leases and £5000 was to be raised to pay Sir Robert's debts 'to a noble personage'. By the time the final draft of the will was drawn on the day of his death this indebtedness had been reduced to £2500, releasing a further £2000 for Lady Drury. Smaller bequests included an annuity of £20 'to my honest Tutor Mr Brabon parson of Whepstead £20 by yeare to be levyed out of my manor of Whepstead all the tyme of his life'. In a codicil he received an additional £100 'to buy him bookes withall' (PRO, PROB 11/126, fols. 252v–253r).

There seem to have been some fears that Sir Robert's sisters and heirs Lady Burghley, Lady Wray, and Diana Drury might raise difficulties over the administration of the will, and steps were taken to obtain probate with all speed on 27 November 1615. No problems arose and Lady Drury showed all the firmness of purpose in executing her husband's will that she had learned in the years of his absences from home. A very wealthy woman, she was expected by her family to marry again. Instead, she continued to supervise the properties bequeathed to her by her husband and invested shrewdly in property. Perhaps it was the loneliness of much of her married life that kept her close to her Bacon relatives and made her a loyal friend not only to her intimates like Lady Caesar but also to her household. Richard Brabon was generously remembered among her legatees. She suffered from recurrent ill health after Sir Robert's death and gradually withdrew from London society, spending much time enlarging Hardwick House. At her death on 5 June 1624 her goods and chattels were valued at £4522 5s. 6d. True to her religious principles her will provided for the simplest of funerals 'with noe funerall pompe bestowed nor anie blackes but onlie to my servantes' (PRO, PROB 11/143, fol. 400r).   JOY ROWE

Sources A. Campling, *The history of the family of Drury in the counties of Norfolk and Suffolk* (1937) · J. Cullum, *History of Hawstead*, 2nd edn (1813) · R. C. Bald, *Donne and the Drurys* (1959) · D. MacCulloch, *Suffolk and the Tudors: politics and religion in an English county, 1500–1600* (1986) · A. Simpson, *The wealth of the gentry* (1961) · HoP, *Commons,*

1509–58 • HoP, *Commons, 1558–1603* • Venn, *Alum. Cant.*, 1/2.68–9 • C. L. S. Linnell, 'Suffolk church monuments: a preliminary survey', *Suffolk Institute of Archaeology*, 27/1 (1955), 1–24 • J. Gage, *The history and antiquities of Suffolk: Thingoe hundred* (1838) • Coll. Arms, MS 442 • will, PRO, PROB 11/127, fols. 169v–179r • *LP Henry VIII*, 15, no. 282 (116) • *CSP dom.*, 1547–1610 • will, PRO, PROB 11/25, fol. 3 [Sir Robert Drury] • parish register, Hawstead [burial; Lady Elizabeth Drury], 19 May 1575 • will, PRO, PROB 11/40, fols. 127v–128v [Sir William Drury] • PRO, PROB 11/86, fols. 10r–12v [Sir William Drury] • parish register, Hawstead [burial; Sir William Drury], 6 May 1593 • parish register, Hawstead [birth; Robert Drury], 30 Jan 1575 • parish register, Hawstead [death; Anne, Lady Drury], 5 June 1624 • parish register, Hawstead [burial; Sir Robert Drury], 1 June 1615 • will, PRO, PROB 11/126, fols. 252v–253r [Sir Robert Drury] • will, PRO, PROB 11/143, fols. 399v–400r [Anne, Lady Drury]

Archives Derbys. RO, legal notebook and precedent book [Sir Robert Drury] • Suffolk RO, Bury St Edmunds, deeds • Suffolk RO, Bury St Edmunds, Drury estate papers [microfilmed] • University of Chicago, Redgrave muniments, Drury MSS

Likenesses oils, *c.*1550–1600 (Sir Robert Drury), Courteenhall, Northamptonshire • bust on monument, 1617 (Sir Robert Drury), Hawstead church • oils (Sir William Drury), Yale U. CBA; repro. in Campling, *History of the Drury family*

Wealth at death £4522 5s. 6d.—Anne, Lady Drury: will, PRO, PROB 11/143, fols. 399v–400r

Drury, Sir Alan Nigel (1889–1980), experimental pathologist, was born in Hackney, London, on 3 November 1889, the youngest of five children, the eldest of whom was a girl, of Henry George Drury MVO (1839–1941), superintendent of the Great Eastern Railway, and his wife, Elizabeth Rose Seear (1847–1937). Alan Drury's great-great-grandfather, John, born in the early 1700s, was a surgeon to the East India Company.

Born into a comfortable middle-class family Drury attended a day school in Dalton Lane before entering Merchant Taylors' School (which was then a day school in Charterhouse Square, London) in 1902, at a time when it was developing a good scientific side; his interest in biology was stimulated also by an elder brother-in-law, William Stokes, secretary of the Quekett Microscopical Club. Drury entered Gonville and Caius College, Cambridge, as an ordinary student in 1909 and at the end of his first year was awarded a scholarship. He obtained first classes in both parts of the natural sciences tripos (1910 and 1913). In 1913 he was awarded the Schuldam Plate prize and the Shuttleworth studentship. He started research under W. B. Hardy at whose suggestion he went to work at the Marine Biological Research Station, Plymouth. In 1914 he was awarded the George Henry Lewes studentship and re-awarded the Shuttleworth studentship, both of which were held over for the duration of the First World War. Late in 1914 Drury entered St Thomas's Hospital, London, and, as he had already done some clinical work at Addenbrooke's Hospital, Cambridge, soon took his final medical examinations. He qualified MRCS, LRCP, and MB BS in January 1916. In April the same year he married Daphne Marguerite (1887–1975), elder daughter of H. A. Brownsword, a lace manufacturer, of Nottingham; they had a daughter and a son.

Drury joined the Royal Army Medical Corps in 1916 and was posted to Mount Vernon Hospital, Hampstead, for the study and treatment of 'disordered action of the heart' which caused invalidism in young soldiers. There he met Thomas Lewis. After only a few months he was drafted to India and attached to the Secunderabad Pathological Laboratory. In 1918 he was promoted major and appointed to the 9th divisional headquarters staff at Bangalore as deputy assistant director of medical services (sanitary) having the care of 50,000 troops in relation to epidemic disease and a large clinico-pathological laboratory to direct.

Drury returned briefly in 1919 (the year in which he gained his MD) to the pathology department in Cambridge and then, in 1920, supported by the Medical Research Council (MRC), joined Thomas Lewis at University College Hospital, London, in developing the basic electrocardiological procedures for the experimental and clinical study of auricular fibrillation and flutter. This fruitful and intensive collaboration ended abruptly in 1926 when Drury developed a tuberculous lung lesion. After a year's recuperation in 1927 he rejoined the Cambridge pathology department under H. R. Dean, where, with H. W. Florey, he organized the new part two of the tripos course in pathology. He continued experimental cardiological research in animals with A. Szent-Gyorgi, examining the effects of nucleic acid derivatives. In 1934 he was appointed Huddersfield lecturer in pathology and a fellow of Trinity Hall, Cambridge.

Discussions initiated by Janet Vaughan with the MRC in 1939 led to the establishment of four blood transfusion centres in the London region to facilitate the treatment of air-raid casualties. Drury went to London to administer these for the MRC and became chairman of the associated MRC blood transfusion research committee which had an outstanding impact in solving biomedical and logistical problems of blood transfusion practice. Later a draft scheme drawn up by Drury and Philip Panton led to similar centres, administered by the Emergency Medical Service and covering the whole country, being established in provincial towns. Drury was instrumental in obtaining finance and expediting the construction at Cambridge of large-scale plant for freeze-drying human plasma essential for the treatment of war casualties.

In 1943 Drury succeeded Sir J. C. G. Ledingham as director of the Lister Institute of Preventive Medicine in London, while still continuing his MRC work. Departments of the institute were widely dispersed because of war conditions and he immediately began its successful reintegration. By incorporating some MRC units he established it after the war as a national centre for research on blood transfusion problems and for the provision of blood products for clinical use. After a period of poor health Drury resigned in 1952 and went to live in Cambridge.

At that time I. de Burgh Daly, who was establishing the new Agricultural Research Council Institute of Animal Physiology at Babraham, Cambridge, invited Drury to develop its department of experimental pathology. The department's overall pattern of research was defined by the choice he made of scientists to join him. These included E. J. H. Ford, A. E. Pierce, and D. C. Hardwick.

With Elizabeth Tucker he examined various characteristics of erythrocyte behaviour in sheep and new-born lambs especially in relation to natural and immune haemolysins and the formation and persistence of foetal haemoglobin. He retired from Babraham in 1960 but continued an interest in research in the department of pathology at Cambridge. Although he contributed notably by his own research, his greatest contribution came from his profound impact on the scientific development of blood transfusion. He was a quiet man with an ironic sense of humour and had wide cultural interests.

Drury was elected FRS (1937) and was a council member (1940–41 and 1955–6) and vice-president (1955–6). He was appointed CBE (1944), knighted (1950), and admitted FRCP (1951). He was a member of the Agricultural Research Council (1947–51) and of the Medical Research Council (1944–8), and he was chairman of many MRC committees. He was secretary of the Beit memorial fellowships for medical research (1944–52) and honorary secretary of the Physiological Society (1938–43). He died in St Catherine's Nursing Home, Letchworth, Hertfordshire, on 2 August 1980. A service of thanksgiving was held in Trinity Hall Chapel, Cambridge, on 29 November 1980.

R. A. KEKWICK, *rev.*

Sources R. A. Kekwick, *Memoirs FRS*, 27 (1981), 173–98 · private information (1986) · personal knowledge (1986) · *CGPLA Eng. & Wales* (1980)

Archives Wellcome L., corresp. with Lister Institute

Likenesses S. Flett, photograph, 1951, repro. in Kekwick, *Memoirs FRS* · D. Fildes, oils, 1952, RS

Wealth at death £51,936: probate, 1 Oct 1980, *CGPLA Eng. & Wales*

Drury, (Edward) Alfred Briscoe (1856–1944), sculptor, was born in London on 11 November 1856, the son of Richard Drury, a tailor, and his wife, Emma Rachel Tombs. He grew up in Oxford, where he attended New College choir school and the Oxford School of Art. At the National Art Training School, South Kensington (*c.*1877–1881), he was taught by F. W. Moody, a protégé of Alfred Stevens, and later by Jules Dalou. Drury won three consecutive gold medals in the national art competition (1879–81) and in 1881 followed Dalou on the latter's return to Paris. He then served as Dalou's assistant, and worked with him on *The Triumph of the Third Republic* monument (1879–99; place de la Nation, Paris), a landmark of late nineteenth-century French sculpture.

On his return to London in 1885, Drury briefly worked as an assistant to Edgar Boehm. Although he regularly exhibited at the Royal Academy, several years elapsed before he received serious critical attention. Until the early 1890s his sculpture was profoundly influenced by Dalou and was criticized for this by Edmund Gosse, who called Drury 'a mannered Kensington student' ('The New Sculpture', *Art Journal*, 1894, 310). Drury's works of this period include the exuberantly neo-rococo *Triumph of Silenus* (1885; see Spielmann, *British Sculpture and Sculptors*, 109) and the sentimental *First Lesson* (1885–6; Birmingham Museum and Art Gallery). Drury made his name with the life-sized *Circe* (bronze version, 1894; Park Square, Leeds) which was

awarded the gold medal at the Paris Universal Exhibition in 1900. While its original inspiration was again French, it has a symbolist resonance all of its own. Circe is portrayed not so much as a decorative sexual object as a powerful temptress, in command of the boars beneath her. Drury followed this with *Griselda* (1896; Tate collection) and *The Age of Innocence* (1897; Laing Art Gallery, Newcastle upon Tyne and elsewhere). These pensive mood portraits responded to George Frampton's *Mysteriarch* (1892; Walker Art Gallery, Liverpool) but lack its sinister, Medusa-like qualities. In 1900 Drury married Phebe Maud Turner (*c.*1884–1928). They had two sons, one of whom was the engraver (Alfred) Paul Dalou *Drury (1903–1987).

Drury's chief claim to distinction is in his public space and architectural sculpture. M. H. Spielmann wrote of this: 'Drury's quiet, suave and contemplative art lends itself well as decorative sculpture to architectural embellishment' (Spielmann, 'Modern British sculpture', 505). For the garden of Barrow Court, near Bristol (*c.*1897–1898), he carved twelve busts representing the months of the year, each one mounted on a pier. The same character is used throughout: she evolves from the youthful *January* to the careworn *December*. Far better known are the so-called Drury Dames, eight semi-draped female torch-bearers (*c.*1898; City Square, Leeds. Cast from two moulds, four represent Evening and four Morning. They combine 'sensuality and aestheticism in a way that proved irresistible to the Edwardians' and still exert 'a peculiar magic' (Beattie, 114). Located nearby is Drury's bronze *Joseph Priestley* (1899) which reveals his proficiency in historical portrait statuary.

Drury's eight colossal stone groups for the War Office building, Whitehall (1904–5), representing War, Peace, Truth and Justice, and Victory and Fame, are masterpieces of the New Sculpture. Their neo-baroque vigour and drama are tempered by sensitivity towards their scale and context. A. L. Baldry wrote of them:

> Each of the figures and each of the groups signifies something that is nobly imagined and finely thought out; each is an independent and original conception; and yet each one takes its proper place in the story which the whole series sets forth, and takes it as rightly as the work itself agrees with the architectural design. (Baldry, 'A notable sculptor', 16)

Another major commission, Drury's four meditative, female allegories for Vauxhall Bridge, London (*c.*1905), probably influenced Jacob Epstein's British Medical Association building figures (1908; Strand, London), though this was never acknowledged. Drury's relief panels and statue of Prince Albert for the Victoria and Albert Museum (*c.*1905–1908) were executed with typical grace but their effect is somewhat bland. For the Victoria memorial (unveiled 1911; The Mall, London), Drury carved charming gatepost figures representing Canada, South Africa, and west Africa.

Drury's statues of Queen Victoria in Bradford, Hove, and Wellington, New Zealand, and of Edward VII in Birmingham, Sheffield, and Aberdeen are successful examples of the genre; Spielmann called such works 'good, reticent and full of character' (Spielmann, 'Modern British sculpture', 505). One of Drury's best-known war memorials, the bronze *St George* (1905; Clifton College, Bristol), commemorates the Second South African War. Brave yet vulnerable, it 'epitomizes everything that Clifton of those years stood for' (M. Girouard, *The Return to Camelot*, 1981, 174). Drury's London troops memorial (1920–23; Royal Exchange, London) ennobles ordinary soldiers, but was criticized for its conservatism. Another First World War commission, a struck medal issued by the department store Derry and Toms (c.1918), demonstrates Drury's effectiveness on a smaller scale.

Drury retained his skills in later life. The bronze statue of Sir Joshua Reynolds (RA), unveiled in December 1931, when Drury was seventy-five, convincingly conveys Reynolds's energetic working methods and accurately records his elegant costume. The statue earned Drury a Royal Society of British Sculptors silver medal (1932) and its success showed how, long after its supposed decline, the New Sculpture was 'by no means dead' (Read, 'Whatever happened', 24).

Besides sculpture, Drury occasionally exhibited paintings and drawings. He was made an associate of the Royal Academy in 1900 and a full member in 1913, and was also a member of the Society of Medallists. His recreations were music and rose cultivation, and he formed a major collection of Alfred Stevens drawings, most of which were acquired after his death by the British Museum, London, and the Walker Art Gallery, Liverpool. Drury died at his home, Lancaster Lodge, 40 Lancaster Road, Wimbledon, on 24 December 1944. He was described in his obituary as 'a good all-round sculptor' (*The Times*, 27 Dec 1944); Spielmann's belief that he represented 'the highest contemporary standard of English sculptors' is, however, nearer the mark (Spielmann, 'Modern British sculpture', 505).
MARK STOCKER

Sources S. Beattie, *The New Sculpture* (1983) · A. L. Baldry, 'A notable sculptor: Alfred Drury', *The Studio*, 37 (1906), 3–18 · M. H. Spielmann, *British sculpture and sculptors of to-day* (1901) · A. L. Baldry, 'Our rising artists: Alfred Drury, sculptor', *Magazine of Art*, 24 (1899–1900), 211–17 · M. Meade, 'The versatile art of Alfred Drury', *Antique Collector*, 55 (1984), 60–65 · B. Read, *Victorian sculpture* (1982) · 'Some new sculpture by Alfred Drury', *The Studio*, 46 (1909), 100–05 · A. L. Baldry, 'The art movement: decorative sculpture by Mr Alfred Drury', *Magazine of Art*, 22 (1897–8), 442–5 · J. Darke, *The monument guide to England and Wales* (1991) · 'Drury, Alfred', *The dictionary of art*, ed. J. Turner (1996) · M. H. Spielmann, 'Modern British sculpture', *Encyclopaedia Britannica*, 11th edn (1911), vol. 24, p. 505 · B. Read, 'Whatever happened to the New Sculpture?', *Reverie, myth, sensuality: sculpture in Britain, 1880–1910*, ed. J. Glaves-Smith (1992) [exhibition catalogue, Stoke-on-Trent City Museum and Art Gallery, 26 Sept 1992–29 Nov 1992, and Cartwright Hall, Bradford, 12 Dec 1992–7 March 1993] · J. Christian, ed., *The last Romantics: the Romantic tradition in British art* (1989) [exhibition catalogue, Barbican Art Gallery, London, 9 Feb – 9 April 1989]
Archives PRO, MSS, Works 12, 91/12 (1–7) | RA, Spielmann MSS
Likenesses P. Drury, crayon drawing, 1937, BM · P. Drury, pencil, 1943, NPG · P. Drury, pen and ink, 1944, NPG · photograph, NPG
Wealth at death £24,363 0s. 7d.: probate, 20 April 1945, CGPLA Eng. & Wales

Drury, Anne, Lady Drury (1572–1624). *See under* Drury family (*per*. 1485–1624).

Drury, Sir Dru (1531/2–1617), courtier, was the fifth, but third surviving, son of Sir Robert Drury (*b.* before 1503, *d.* 1577), landowner, and Elizabeth, daughter of Edmund Brudenell of Chalfont St Peter, Buckinghamshire. His father owned substantial Buckinghamshire estates, including Hedgerley. He was being educated at St Edmund's Hostel, Cambridge, in 1544 and may have completed his education at one of the inns of court or inns of chancery. A younger brother of Sir William *Drury (1527–1579), he was made a gentleman usher of the privy chamber in 1559, a position he retained until his death. Drury was elected MP for Mitchell, Cornwall, in 1559 but took little part in the proceedings. He became a good friend of Thomas Howard, duke of Norfolk, and may even have been one of his clients. He supported the duke in his conflict with Sir Robert Dudley, later earl of Leicester, over Elizabeth I's marital status and was imprisoned from December 1559 until early 1561 for his participation in a brawl over it. He was suspended from office until 1572 or 1575 as a result. Despite this, Drury was personable and able enough to recommend himself to the protestant Francis Russell, second earl of Bedford, and probably owed his election as MP for Camelford, Cornwall, in 1563 to him. He continued to act as a counsellor to Norfolk but did not participate in the duke's involvement in treason in 1569–72.

About 1565 Drury married Elizabeth Woodhouse (*d.* 1582). She was a daughter of Sir Philip Calthrop of Cockthorpe, Norfolk, and had been widowed twice, her first husband being Sir Henry Parker and her second Sir William Woodhouse. Her dowry consisted of the lordship of the manor of Riddlesworth, Norfolk. Following their marriage, the Drurys moved there and built Riddlesworth Hall. They appear to have had no children. After her death, Drury married Katherine (1555/6–1601), daughter and heir of William Finch of Lynsted, Kent, who brought with her the manor of Sewards and lands at Preston in Kent. They had four children, a son, Dru, and three daughters, Elizabeth, Anne, and Frances. Their son was later created a baronet (7 May 1627). Their daughter Elizabeth married twice: her first husband was Sir Thomas Wingfield of Leveringham, Suffolk, and her second was Harry Reynolds. Anne married John Deane of Deane, Essex, while Frances married Sir Robert Boteler of Woodhall, Hertfordshire. Drury benefited from his marriages in political and social terms too. He was appointed JP for Norfolk from about 1566 and for Middlesex from about 1596. His position in Norfolk grew over the years; he was sheriff in 1576–7 and *custos rotulorum* from 1583.

A 'sincere honest man', Drury was knighted at Wanstead, Essex, in September 1579 (Kennett, 2.501). He served with his brother in Ireland in 1579. By 1584 he had enough standing to be elected MP for Norfolk and he was much more active in this parliament, sitting on a series of committees. In November 1586, together with Sir Amias Paulet, he was charged to supervise the imprisonment of

Mary, queen of Scots. He may have been appointed because of his puritan leanings; she found him kind and gracious. Drury was made a lieutenant of the Tower in 1595-6. He was less active during his last years and died at Riddlesworth Hall on 29 April 1617, aged eighty-five. He was buried in Riddlesworth parish church, where a monument erroneously gives his age at death as ninety-nine. He gave generously to the poor of London, Kent, and Norfolk.   J. ANDREAS LÖWE

Sources F. Blomefield, *An essay towards a topographical history of the county of Norfolk* (1736-9) • E. Hasted, *The history and topographical survey of the county of Kent*, 2nd edn, 12 vols. (1797-1801) • J. Cullum, *The history and antiquities of Hawsted* (1784) • Fuller, *Worthies* (1840) • [J. Chambers], *A general history of the county of Norfolk*, 2 vols. (1829) • *CSP dom.*, 1547-1625 • HoP, *Commons, 1558-1603*, 2.56-8 • HoP, *Commons, 1509-58*, 2.58-9 • A. Campling, *The history of the family of Drury in the counties of Norfolk and Suffolk* (1937) • W. H. Kennett, *A complete history of England: with the lives of all the kings and queens thereof* (1706) **Likenesses** R. Peake, oils, Courteenhall, Northamptonshire • manuscript, Northants. RO, Delapré Abbey

Drury, Dru (1725-1804), silversmith and naturalist, was born on 4 February 1725, probably in Lad Lane, Wood Street, London, the son of Drew Drury, silversmith, and only surviving child of the eight children of his father's second marriage, to Mary Hesketh. (The unusual forename was bestowed through many generations, from Sir Dru Drury (1531/2-1617), courtier, into the twentieth century.) Drury was apprenticed in 1739 to his father in the Goldsmiths' Company, obtained his freedom in 1748, and became a liveryman in 1751. When Drury was twenty-three he succeeded to his father's business, and on 7 June 1748 he married Esther, or Easter, Pedley (d. 1787), a daughter of his father's first wife's previous marriage. Of their seventeen children, only three survived him; the rest died young. Through this marriage he became the owner of several freehold houses in London and Essex, which brought him an annual income of between £250 and £300. In 1771 he purchased a silversmith's shop and stock at 32 Strand, where he made nearly £2000 per annum for some years. In 1777 he was made bankrupt as a result of deception by two Yorkshire cutlers, but was helped by generous friends to resume business the following year. In 1789 he retired from the business, which was carried on by his son William.

Drury's private and business income enabled him to indulge to the full his interest in natural history and especially entomology. He persuaded ships' officers and other travellers to collect for him, providing them with the necessary equipment. He had printed and distributed a pamphlet of three quarto pages entitled *Directions for Collecting Insects in Foreign Countries* (1772?), offering 6*d*. per insect, 'whatever the size'. His collection soon became famous. Henry Smeathman (d. 1786), noted for his researches on termites, was one of his collectors, and the naturalist Edward Donovan (1768-1837) spoke admiringly of his magnificent collections. Fabricius, Olivier, Kirby, and other workers based descriptions of new species on his specimens.

Between 1770 and 1782 Drury published *Illustrations of* *Natural History*, a work in three parts with parallel texts in English and French. The illustrations, based on specimens in his collection, were prepared by Moses Harris, who also coloured the plates of the best copies. Through his own efforts Drury succeeded in selling a number of copies into Europe. The work was much admired in his lifetime and the plates are undoubtedly very fine, though by modern standards the descriptions leave much to be desired. Westwood (1837) and Panzer (1885-8) published enlarged French and German editions. Drury's letter-books and other surviving papers show that he kept up a lively correspondence, mainly on natural history, with Linnaeus, Pallas, Haworth, and other friends and acquaintances at home and abroad. From 1780 to 1782 he was president of the Society of Entomologists of London, the precursor of the Royal Entomological Society of London. He was also an early member of the Linnean Society.

In retirement Drury divided his time between London and his home at Broxbourne, Hertfordshire, where he continued to collect insects. He was a lover of gardening, and enjoyed angling in the River Lea and the New River. For several years he amused himself by making wines from different sorts of fruit, and conducting experiments in distillation. Always of an active mind, he persuaded many travellers to join his speculative searches for gold. In this connection he published a booklet and plate entitled *Thought on precious metals, particularly gold: its general dissemination over the face of the globe with descriptions and hints to travellers, captains of ships etc., for obtaining them, from the rough diamond down to the pebble-stone* (c.1801). His projects were generally fruitless.

About 1797 Drury moved to Turnham Green, to the west of London. A complication of ailments began to afflict him, principally stones in the bladder, from which he died at his son's house in the Strand on 15 January 1804; he was buried in the church of St Martin-in-the-Fields, Westminster, on 21 January.

Drury's remarkably fine collection of over 11,000 specimens, many unique, built up over thirty years, was dispersed by auction at a three-day sale in May 1805. It brought £614 8*s*. 6*d*., with about £300 more for the cabinets, books, and copperplates of the *Illustrations of Natural History*.   C. M. F. VON HAYEK

Sources C. H. Smith, 'Memoir of Dru Drury, with a portrait', *The Naturalists' Library*, 13 (1842), [17]-71 [Introduction to the Mammalia] • A. G. Grimwade, *London goldsmiths, 1697-1837: their marks and lives, from the original registers at Goldsmiths' Hall*, 3rd edn (1990), 494-7, 746 • T. D. A. Cockerell, 'Dru Drury, an eighteenth-century entomologist', *Scientific Monthly* (Jan 1922), 67-82 • H. B. Weiss, 'Dru Drury, silversmith and entomologist of the eighteenth century', *Entomological News*, 38 (1927), 208-14 • B. Noblett, 'Dru Drury's *Directions for collecting insects in foreign countries*', *Bulletin of the Amateur Entomologists' Society*, 44 (1985), 170-78 • C. M. F. von Hayek, 'On the type material of the species of coleoptera described from the Drury collection by D. Drury and J. C. Fabricius with notes on some coleoptera from the Milne collection preserved in the British Museum (Natural History)', *Archives of Natural History*, 12 (1985), 143-52 • W. Noblett, 'Dru Drury, his *Illustrations of Natural History* (1770-82), and the European market for printed books', *Quaerendo*, 15/2 (1985), 83-102 • W. Noblett, 'Publishing by the author: a case study of Dru Drury's *Illustrations of Natural History* (1770–82)', *Publishing History*, 23 (1988), 67–94 • F. J. Griffin, 'The first entomological societies, an early chapter in entomological history in England', *Proceedings of the Royal Entomological Society of London*, ser. A, 15 (1940), 49–68 • E. B. Poulton, 'The Society of Entomologists of London for the Study of Insects: 1780–82', *Proceedings of the Royal Entomological Society of London*, 8 (1933), 97–104 • C. D. Sherborn, 'Dru Drury', *Journal of the Society of the Bibliography of Natural History*, 1 (1936–43), 109–11 • W. Drury, signed statement, notebook no. 28, NHM, entomology library

Archives NHM, corresp. and papers • Oxf. U. Mus. NH, Hope Library, entomological notebooks • University of Sydney, MacLeay Museum

Likenesses W. H. Lizars, engraving, repro. in Smith, 'Memoir of Dru Drury'

Drury, Henry (1812–1863), Church of England clergyman, eldest son of Henry Joseph Thomas *Drury (1778–1841) and his wife, Caroline Tayler, and grandson of Joseph *Drury (1751–1834), was born at Harrow, Middlesex on 11 May 1812. After a distinguished school career at Harrow School he was admitted minor pensioner of Gonville and Caius College, Cambridge, in 1831, and held a scholarship there from 1832 to 1834. In 1833 he won the Browne medal for the Latin ode, and in 1835 that for the epigrams. An eye complaint prevented further academic successes as an undergraduate. In 1837 he took the ordinary BA degree, proceeding MA in 1840. In 1838 he became classical lecturer at Caius, but, having been ordained, he left Cambridge in 1839 to take sole charge of Alderley, Gloucestershire, a curacy which he exchanged the following year for that of Bromham, Wiltshire. Drury, together with some friends, projected and published the *Arundines Cami* (1841), a collection of translations into Latin and Greek verse by Cambridge men, which had four further editions in Drury's lifetime. A sixth edition, after Drury's death, was edited by Henry John Hodgson in 1865.

Drury became rector of Alderley in 1843, and shortly afterwards, on 13 December 1843, he married Amelia Elizabeth, eldest daughter of Revd Giles Daubeny, rector of Lydiard Tregoze, Wiltshire. In 1845 he became vicar of Bremhill with Foxham and Highway, Wiltshire, a preferment which he received from Edward Denison, bishop of Salisbury, to whom, and his successor in the see, Walter Kerr Hamilton, he was examining chaplain. In 1855 he was installed prebendary of Shipton in Salisbury Cathedral, and in 1857 was appointed chaplain to the House of Commons by the speaker, John Evelyn Denison. He became archdeacon of Wiltshire in July 1862.

Drury was a genial and affectionate friend and companion, 'possessed of lively wit and humour, full of anecdote and badinage, but tempered with excellent tact and judgment, all combined with a modesty and absence of self-assertion' (H. J. Hodgson, quoted in *DNB*). He died at Bremhill vicarage on 25 January 1863 after two days' illness.

GORDON GOODWIN, *rev.* M. C. CURTHOYS

Sources Boase, *Mod. Eng. biog.* • Venn, *Alum. Cant.* • private information (1888) • *GM*, 2nd ser., 21 (1844), 194

Wealth at death under £7000: probate, 30 May 1863, *CGPLA Eng. & Wales*

Drury, Henry Joseph Thomas (1778–1841), classical scholar, son of the Revd Joseph *Drury (1751–1834) and

Louisa (*bap.* 1753), daughter of Benjamin Heath DCL, of Exeter, was born at Harrow on 27 April 1778. He was educated at Harrow School, Eton College, and King's College, Cambridge (BA 1801, MA 1804), where he was a fellow from 1799 until 1808, when he married Caroline, daughter of Archdale Wilson Tayler of Boreham Wood, Hertfordshire. They had eleven children, of whom the eldest, Henry *Drury, became archdeacon of Wiltshire. Drury became an assistant master at Harrow in 1801, where he remained until his death, serving from 1833 to 1841 as master of the lower school. In his early years as a teacher he was stimulating and inspiring, but his energy faded and he increasingly found himself out of sympathy with a younger generation of ambitious masters. The responsibilities of his large family, however, prevented his retirement. His nephew, Charles Merivale, attributed his sloth to the fact that he had been 'put too early into an easy position beneath his abilities' (Tyerman, 188). He was ordained in 1811 and in 1820 he was presented to the rectory of Fingest. He died at Harrow on 5 March 1841.

Drury had a great reputation in his day as a classical scholar, but contented himself with editing selections from the classics for the use of Harrow School. He also formed a valuable library of the Greek and Latin classics, both printed editions and manuscripts, two parts of which were sold in 1827 for £8917 13*s.*, and the third, in 1841, for £1693. He was an original member of the Roxburghe Club, London, and contributed to their collection a reprint of *Cock Lorell's Boat* (1817) and *The Metrical Life of Saint Robert of Knaresborough* (1824), from a manuscript in his possession, which was deciphered and transcribed by Joseph Haslewood. Among Drury's numerous friends were Thomas Dibdin, the bibliographer, who mentioned him several times in *The Bibliographical Decameron*, and Lord Byron who was in his house at Harrow. Moore's *Life of Lord Byron* published several letters from the poet to his former tutor, written in affectionate terms and without much regard to the propriety later thought usual to preserve in a correspondence with a clergyman.

L. C. SANDERS, *rev.* M. C. CURTHOYS

Sources *GM*, 2nd ser., 16 (1841), 323 • W. R. Drake, *Heathiana: notes, genealogical and biographical, of the family of Heath* (privately printed, London, 1881) • *Letters and journals of Lord Byron, with notices of his life*, ed. T. Moore, 1 (1830) • Venn, *Alum. Cant.* • C. Tyerman, *A history of Harrow School, 1324–1991* (2000) • F. MacCarthy, *Byron: life and legend* (2002)

Archives BL, corresp. with Samuel Butler and others, Add. MSS 28653, 34585, 34587–34590

Likenesses T. Hodgetts, mezzotint (after M. S. Carpenter), BM, NPG

Drury, Joseph (1751–1834), headmaster, was born in London on 11 February 1751, the elder son of Thomas Drury (1717/18–1805), who came from a Norfolk gentry family, and Elizabeth, daughter of John Hilton, of the City of London. He was educated at Westminster School as a king's scholar from 1765 under John Hinchcliffe and Samuel Smith; among his closest school friends were the brothers Cyril and William Jackson, respectively future dean of Christ Church, Oxford, and bishop of Oxford. In June 1768 he was admitted a pensioner of Trinity College, Cambridge, where he was tutored by Richard Watson, but his father's financial difficulties forced him to leave after a few terms without completing his degree. He was warmly recommended by Watson to Robert Carey Sumner, headmaster of Harrow School, who was seeking a new assistant master, and in 1769 he began his thirty-five-year career at the school.

Harrow School was then flourishing under Sumner, and Drury, together with Samuel Parr, gained valuable experience teaching for him in an atmosphere of 'easy conviviality' (Tyerman, 129) among the staff. Sumner's sudden death in September 1771 sparked off a hotly fought contest to succeed him. The pupils' dismay at the choice of Benjamin Heath, an Eton College master, over Parr was shared by Drury, and he considered accepting Parr's invitation to join him in his rival school at Stanmore. Drury's decision to stay at Harrow proved a happy one both for his career and his personal life. Despite Parr's very public defection the school's academic and social reputation was maintained during Heath's fourteen years as headmaster, and Drury virtually guaranteed his own succession as head when in 1777 he married Heath's youngest sister, Louisa (bap. 1753). It was a double wedding, for on the same day Louisa's sister Rose married Drury's colleague Thomas Bromley; the sisters were daughters of the scholar and book collector Benjamin *Heath and his wife, Rose Marie Michelet, of Exeter. Of the Drurys' six children two died in infancy; their three sons—Henry Joseph Thomas *Drury, Benjamin, and Charles—all took holy orders; and their only daughter, Louisa, married John Herman *Merivale. Their marriage founded a formidable educational dynasty whose influence stretched into the mid-nineteenth century. Drury's younger brother Mark came to Harrow as assistant master in 1785 and his son William also taught at the school; Louisa's brother Dr George Heath became headmaster of Eton in 1792; and Drury's own son Henry and his grandson Benjamin Henry Drury were assistant masters at Harrow.

Having been ordained Drury was appointed rector of Aldwinkle, Northamptonshire, in 1778 and of Pilton, in the same county, in 1794, parishes that he resigned in 1806. Awarded a BD in 1784 by Cambridge University, he proceeded DD in 1789. When Heath resigned as headmaster of Harrow, in 1785, after accepting a fellowship at Eton, Drury was unanimously elected his successor at Easter, despite his being only thirty-four and the fact that he was the first headmaster of Harrow in a century not to have been educated at Eton. He decided at the outset that he would retire after twenty years in the post, on account of his wife's indifferent health, but in those twenty years he brought Harrow 'to an apogee of fame and glamour' (Tyerman, 166). Although initially the school roll fell from 150 by 20 or 30 pupils, by the end of the 1790s numbers rose to over 200, and a high of 351 was reached in 1802–3. Drury assiduously courted patronage from aristocratic and gentry families, and an exceptional number of his pupils entered public life, including five future prime ministers: Perceval, Goderich, Peel, Aberdeen, and Palmerston. The speech days established by Heath in place of the traditional archery day offered the boys a chance to show off their oratorical skills, and Drury encouraged his pupils to declaim the best of their English essays to the rest of the school. His enthusiasm for oratory and public speaking was prompted by his love of the stage rather than of the pulpit, for he was fonder of Drury Lane than of his preaching duties.

The curriculum conventionally concentrated on Latin and Greek, yet Drury sought to stimulate a comparative approach to literature:

> In reading the poets, especially the Greek tragedies, he was fond of illustrating their sentiments or descriptions, by citations from our own poets; while, at the same time, he invariably pointed out all the passages which the more servile Romans had imitated or translated from their prototypes. (Drury, 18)

He frequently set the boys English prose composition and encouraged their efforts at writing English verse. He certainly fostered the literary talents of Byron, who, though a difficult and disruptive pupil, later affectionately described Drury as 'the best and worthiest friend I ever possessed, whose warnings I have remembered but too well, though too late when I have erred,—and whose counsels I have but followed when I have done well or wisely' (George, Lord Byron, *Childe Harold's Pilgrimage*, canto 4, stanza 75n.). By design Drury inspired affection among his pupils: he took care to counsel them in private and preferred to admonish them through ridicule rather than with the cane. His innovation of exempting the upper forms from corporal punishment, however, did not rid the school of flogging, which instead was delegated to the senior boys, who acted as monitors.

Drury kept his promise and resigned the headmastership at Easter 1805; against his wishes he was succeeded by Dr George Butler and not by his brother Mark. Drury had astutely supplemented his salary and had accumulated considerable savings through the lucrative practice of taking private pupils, who boarded at his house, which was run by his wife. Tyerman has calculated that he made over £80,000 during his twenty years as headmaster from an annual income that fluctuated between £2500 and £4000. He retired to his estate at Cockwood, by the Exe estuary in Devon, where he busied himself with farming some 300 acres, acting as a county magistrate, and indulging his love of music and the theatre. After watching Edmund Kean act at Teignmouth playhouse Drury took advantage of his contacts at Drury Lane theatre to promote Kean's career. He took a keen interest in landscape gardening, studying the writings of William Gilpin and Uvedale Price and consulting Humphrey Repton for guidance on creating picturesque surroundings. He kept in close contact with many former pupils both through correspondence and visits, and toured Ireland, the Lake District, north Wales, and Shropshire. In 1812 he was instituted to the prebend of Dultincote, at Wells Cathedral, which he held until his death. In his memoir of his father Charles Drury speculated that Drury might have received further preferment in the church had his principal patron, Spencer Perceval, not been assassinated in 1812.

Drury died at Cockwood on 9 January 1834 and was buried next to Benjamin Heath's grave in a vault in St Leonard's, Exeter, on 17 January. Unusually for such a successful schoolmaster Drury published nothing; he methodically destroyed all his correspondence and papers and evaded all attempts to paint his portrait.   S. J. SKEDD

Sources C. Drury, 'Rev. Joseph Drury', *Annual Biography and Obituary*, 19 (1835) • C. Tyerman, *A history of Harrow School, 1324–1991* (2000) • P. M. Thornton, *Harrow School and its surroundings* (1885) • Venn, *Alum. Cant.* • *Fasti Angl.* (Hardy), 1.203 • W. R. Drake, *Heathiana: notes, genealogical and biographical, of the family of Heath* (1881) • *Old Westminsters* • *DNB*

Drury, (Alfred) Paul Dalou (1903–1987), artist and teacher of art, was born on 14 October 1903 at Crescent Lodge, 2 Tressillian Crescent, Brockley, in south-east London, the elder of the two sons of (Edward) Alfred Briscoe *Drury RA (1856–1944), sculptor and painter, and Phebe Maud Turner (c.1884–1928), painter, daughter of the Revd George Lyon Turner. In 1912 the family moved into Lancaster Lodge, a purpose-built house with a large studio in Lancaster Road, Wimbledon; this was Paul's home until his marriage, and there he not only assisted his father but also shared the studio for his own work. Drury displayed an early talent for drawing and by the age of ten had decided to be an artist. He attended King's College School in Wimbledon (1910–13) and then Bristol grammar school (1913–17), where in 1914 he suffered the tragic loss of an eye in a shooting accident. Undeterred he continued to draw; while at Westminster School, in London (1917–21), he honed his draughtsmanship by making architectural drawings of the abbey cloisters, and his considerable talents in both art and music received particular encouragement.

Drury's enrolment in 1921 at the University of London's Goldsmiths' College, where he remained until 1926, marked the formal beginning of his artistic career and his lifelong association with the college's school of art (where his father still taught). Among his contemporaries were Graham Sutherland, William Larkins, and Edward Bouverie Hoyton, part of the group of landscape etchers in the pastoral tradition who came to be known as the Goldsmiths' School; in Sutherland particularly he found a kindred spirit and lifelong friend, and their landscape subjects reveal many similarities in ideas, motifs, and stylistic influences.

Drury was a gifted portraitist, and even his earliest student print is a work of astonishing virtuosity and maturity: *Old Frost* (1922; needled by Drury but etched by his tutor) demonstrates not only his masterly draughtsmanship, a sharp eye, and command of mass and form but also his sensitivity and humanity. A year later, after several more portrait heads, he etched his first landscape, *Hayling Island: Barn with Cart* (1923), a straightforward rural scene. In 1924 he won the British Institute scholarship for etching but later sacrificed the prix de Rome in order to assist his father, whose health was failing; he also exhibited for

the first time at the Royal Academy, and continued to do so almost annually until 1985. In 1926 he was elected an associate of the Royal Society of Painter-Etchers and Engravers; he was also invited (with Sutherland) by F. L. M. Griggs to take his plates to Griggs's studio to watch him print from them. His technical development was further enhanced by a major exhibition of Samuel Palmer's prints and drawings at the Victoria and Albert Museum, London, which displayed working proofs in progressive states accompanied by the artist's detailed notes. Drury's admiration of Palmer's glowing landscape etchings had already led him to experiment with the expressive use of light but it was not until *September* (1928), Drury's most important work, that the mystical influences were fully assimilated and he transcended the tranquil countryside to enter a visionary world of his own.

At the same time Drury was working on a series of portrait drawings (1927–8) commissioned by New College, Oxford, and by Trinity College, Cambridge; he also produced *A Man of Fifty* (1928), a particularly sensitive portrait etching. Following an article, 'The etchings of Graham Sutherland and Paul Drury', in the authoritative journal *Print Collector's Quarterly* in January 1929 his first one-man show was held at the Twenty-One Gallery, London; he also co-founded the National Society of Painters, Sculptors, Engravers and Potters. Helping his father to complete his statue of Sir Joshua Reynolds, commissioned by the Royal Academy, left little time for his own work during 1929–31.

In the 1930s Drury was busy teaching at several art schools, including Goldsmiths' College, the Royal Academy, the Central School of Arts and Crafts, Heatherley's, the Sir John Cass, and Kingston School of Art. His work began to be acquired by both public and private collections, and he continued to exhibit in Britain and (through the British Council) abroad. In 1932 he was elected fellow of the Royal Society of Painter-Etchers and Engravers. He had been exhibiting regularly since 1926 and was to play an increasingly active role in the society, ultimately becoming its president, in 1970–75. His reforms modernized and revitalized the society, broadening the membership, widening the scope of techniques, and establishing a more democratic ethos.

In 1936 Drury fell in love with and subsequently married one of his students. Though born into a Jewish family Enid Marie Solomon (1910–1996), a talented painter, had already embraced Christianity, and they were married on 21 December 1937 in the parish church of St Marylebone, London. Having settled in London at 114 Haverstock Hill they joined the British Red Cross Society in 1938, when war was looming. Drury used his modelling experience to create plaster casts for limb prostheses at Queen Mary's Hospital, Roehampton, prompting a move to Athelenary Cottage, 8 King's Road, Richmond, Surrey. War casualties provided subject matter for his constant drawing habit, and two small works from this period are in the Imperial War Museum's collection.

A son, Jolyon Victor Paul, was born on 19 November

1946, when the Drurys were living at Greville Lodge, 9 Greville Road, Richmond. They moved once more, to 13 King's Road (1956), before leaving Richmond in 1958 for Ranger's Cottage, Nutley, near Uckfield, Sussex, where Drury was to live for the remainder of his life. He had left Goldsmiths' in the late 1930s but returned to teaching there after the war. In 1947 he was elected chairman of the exhibitions committee of the Artists' International Association and also of the National Society of Painters, Sculptors, Engravers and Potters. He joined the faculty of engraving at the British School in Rome (1948–74) and during the 1960s and 1970s also taught drawing and composition at summer schools at Urchfont Manor, near Devizes, Wiltshire, and at Attingham Park, Shropshire.

Drury was an inspirational if demanding teacher driven by his own love of the creative process to exact the highest standards through meticulous craftsmanship and attention to detail, yet he dispensed advice gently and with humour. His extended association with the school of art at Goldsmiths' College culminated in his appointment as principal (1967–9), shortly before he retired. A witty and convivial character never without a cigarette, he was popular with both students and staff, and was renowned for his prowess as raconteur and songwriter at Goldsmiths' social events. He was an erudite man of scintillating intellect who spoke Latin fluently, read musical scores with ease, adored Bach, and played the piano; one of his compositions for harpsichord was broadcast on BBC Radio 3. He also enjoyed watching cricket. He was dark-haired, with intense and sparkling grey eyes; in middle age he wore glasses or a monocle.

Drury continued to create and exhibit in his retirement, and also joined the governing body of the West Surrey School of Art (1969–74). Two exhibitions of his work were held in his last years—one, a major retrospective, in 1984 at Goldsmiths' College Gallery, and the other at Garton and Cooke, London, in 1987. He died at his home, Ranger's Cottage, Nutley, on 19 May 1987, after a succession of small strokes, and was buried in Putney cemetery on 26 May.

Drury created ninety-two prints, most unpublished and unsigned, all but a few being intaglio processes. The portrait etchings, which form the majority, are striking in their humanity; among the best are *Head of a Negro* (1925), *Old Man Reading II* (1932), *Mrs. Douglas James* (1936), and *Carel Weight* (1938–9). Published works, in editions varying up to 100, were sometimes signed in the plate with the initials 'PD' (or 'P. D.') and date, or 'Paul Drury' and date, but were just as likely to be unsigned; a catalogue raisonné of the prints was published by Robin Garton in 1992. Drury also left a large body of richly-coloured oil paintings (landscapes and portraits), most of which remain in the family but some major works were sold at the Royal Academy's summer exhibitions. With their loose and freely applied brushstrokes his paintings are the antithesis of the controlled precision of his delicately drawn etchings. A substantial archive, including sketchbooks, drawings, and prints in several states, is held by the Art Gallery of Greater Victoria, British Columbia; other works are held

in Boston Public Library, Massachusetts; the Ashmolean Museum, Oxford; the British Museum, London; the National Museum and Gallery of Wales, Cardiff; the National Gallery of Canada, Ottawa; and the Victoria and Albert Museum, London.

Drury was a leading printmaker and accomplished painter who strove after perfection and devoted himself to instilling his values in the young. A modest man, he shunned the limelight, and his works were therefore little known, even by his pupils. But his importance lies in his contribution to the continuity of traditional printmaking skills, both in his own work and through his influence on generations of art students during a lifetime of teaching. A major biography and critical appreciation was prepared by Jolyon Drury to celebrate his father's centenary in 2003.

RUTH WALTON

Sources R. Garton, *The catalogue raisonné of the prints of Paul Drury, 1903–1987* (1992) · private information (2004) [Jolyon Drury] · D. Ogg, 'The etchings of Graham Sutherland and Paul Drury', *Print Collector's Quarterly*, 16 (Jan 1929), 77–99 · *Catalogue of drawings and etchings by Paul Drury, ARE*, Twenty-One Gallery (1929) [exh. cat.] · I. Mackenzie-Kerr, ed., *Paul Drury: artist and printmaker* (1984) [exhibition catalogue, Goldsmiths' College Gallery in association with Garton and Cooke, 1984] · M. Hopkinson, *No day without a line: the history of the Royal Society of Painter-Printmakers, 1880–1999* (1999) · *Catalogue of an exhibition of drawings, etchings & woodcuts by Samuel Palmer and other disciples of William Blake … with an introduction by A. H. Palmer* (1926) [exhibition catalogue, V&A] · N. Aldred, *Graham Sutherland: the early years, 1921–40* (1986) [exhibition cataloge, Goldsmiths' College Gallery] · Goldsmiths' College, delegacy minutes, 24 Oct 1924–27 July 1925 · Goldsmiths' College Delegacy, annual reports, 20, 1924/5; 21, 1925/6 · prospectuses, 1963–4, 1966–7, 1967–8, 1968–9, Goldsmiths' College, London · b. cert. · m. cert. · d. cert. · *CGPLA Eng. & Wales* (1987) · *The exhibition of the Royal Academy* [exhibition catalogues, 1924–30; 1932–67; 1970; 1972–4; 1976; 1978; 1979; 1985] · *Catalogue* [exhibition catalogues, Royal Society of Painter-Etchers and Engravers, 1926–30; 1932; 1934–40; 1944–63; 1965; 1967; 1971]
Archives Art Gallery of Greater Victoria, British Columbia
Likenesses P. Drury, self-portrait, drypoint etching, 1923–4, repro. in Garton, *Catalogue raisonné* · P. Drury, self-portrait, etching, 1925, repro. in Garton, *Catalogue raisonné* · photograph, 1926–9, repro. in Garton, *Catalogue raisonné*
Wealth at death £28,781: probate, 27 Aug 1987, *CGPLA Eng. & Wales*

Drury, Sir Robert (*b.* before **1456**, *d.* **1535**), lawyer and speaker of the House of Commons, was born before 1456 at Hawstead, Suffolk, the first of four sons and two daughters of Roger Drury (*d.* 1496), an important landowner in that county, and his wife, Felice, daughter and heir of William Denston of Besthorpe, Norfolk, whom he married in 1455. Robert Drury's family was long established in Suffolk, but he was its first member to make connections at court after training as a lawyer. There is no evidence, as was once thought, that he was educated at Gonville Hall, Cambridge. He was admitted to Lincoln's Inn in 1473 and became a leading figure there, serving several times as governor from 1488 onwards, and as Lent reader in 1491. When his son William was admitted in 1517, Drury paid the annual salary of a chaplain in order to obtain certain privileges, and after Robert's death William provided a chaplain to sing for his father's soul.

By 1499 Drury was the chief steward of John de Vere,

thirteenth earl of Oxford, and also one of his feoffees. He may have served under Oxford at the battle of Blackheath in 1497, after which he was knighted (on 17 June). Oxford was 'relied on by the government to mediate its policies to East Anglia' (MacCulloch, 225), and he in turn depended for support on a group of leading landowners from west Suffolk of whom Drury was the most reliable. When Oxford died in 1513, Drury was appointed an executor and given an annuity of £6 13s. 4d. and the Ellesmere Chaucer, while the other executors retained him with an annuity of £2 13s. 4d. He concerned himself with de Vere family affairs until his death.

Drury was active on Henry VII's council, for example considering a case concerning the Merchant Adventurers and the Staplers in 1504. He was the beneficiary of the grant of several wardships, and also had a grant of forfeited lands in north Norfolk for life. However, he was also one of a group caught by Henry VII's fiscal devices, possibly as a security for the earl of Oxford.

Drury was a councillor and knight of the body under Henry VIII. In the early years of the reign he served on several commissions, devoting much time to resolving border disputes with Scotland. He was present at the funerals of Henry VII in 1509 and Prince Henry in 1511 and the marriage of Princess Mary in 1518, and in 1520 attended the Field of Cloth of Gold and the king's subsequent meeting with Charles V. He gave advice on legal matters and was one of the councillors who became particularly associated with Star Chamber as a court. In 1523 Drury was appointed to a commission which investigated Dr John Stokesley's record as a judge in the court of requests. There had been hostility in the legal profession to the principles on which Stokesley's decisions were given, especially in real property cases, and proceedings ended with his being dismissed from his post.

Drury first became a JP for Suffolk in 1488 and thereafter served on many local commissions until his death. He was MP for Suffolk in 1491, 1495, and perhaps in 1510. In 1495 he was elected speaker in parliament, while in 1510 he announced in the upper house the election of Thomas Englefield as speaker. In 1525 he assisted the dukes of Norfolk and Suffolk in dealing with the threat of a major popular rebellion in East Anglia over the so-called 'amicable grant'. According to Hall's *Chronicle* it was the agreement which the duke of Suffolk made with the rich clothiers which caused the trouble, for they claimed to their workers that they would have to lay off labour. Hall reports that the duke of Suffolk attempted to disarm the crowds at Stansted, 'but when that was knowen, then the rumour waxed more greater, and the people railed openly on the Duke of Suffolke, and Sir Robert Drurie, and threatened them with death, and the Cardinall alsoe' (*Hall's Chronicle*, 698–9). This problem would recur, and in 1528, another year of acute economic distress, Drury arrested some rioters who wanted to go to the king to beseech a remedy. He wrote several anxious letters to Wolsey and others asking what to do next and acted with the duke of Norfolk to ease tension. The duke subsequently 'urged Wolsey to convey appropriate thanks to Drury' (MacCulloch, 226).

Drury enlarged his property in East Anglia. In 1501 he received a papal licence for a chapel and in 1510 a royal licence to impark over 2000 acres and to crenellate Hawstead. He married twice. With his first wife, Anne, daughter of Sir William Calthorpe of Burnham Thorpe, Norfolk, whom he had married by 1494, he had two sons and four daughters. His second wife, whom he had married by 1531, was Anne, daughter of Edward Jerningham of Somerleyton, Suffolk, and successively widow of Lord Edward Grey (d. in or before 1517); one Berkeley; and Henry Barley of Albury, Hertfordshire, who died on 12 November 1529. After Drury's death, she married a fifth husband, Sir Edmund Walsingham, and died in 1558.

Drury made his will on 1 May 1531 and died on 2 March 1535, probably at Hawstead. He asked to be buried in St Mary's Church, Bury St Edmunds, where a stone monument with effigies of himself and his first wife bears the inscription 'Such as ye be, sometimes were we, such as we are, such shall ye be. Miserere nostri.' He left his household hangings, his goods and plate, and large flocks of sheep to his wife and sons. As well as Hawstead, he had a house in College Street, Bury St Edmunds, and a 'place' in St Clement Danes, London, which later gave its name to Drury Lane. PATRICIA HYDE

Sources HoP, *Commons, 1509–58*, 2.57–8 · A. Campling, *The history of the family of Drury in the counties of Norfolk and Suffolk* (1937), 42–7 · J. S. Roskell, *The Commons and their speakers in English parliaments, 1376–1523* (1965), 304 · J. C. Wedgwood and A. D. Holt, *History of parliament, 1: Biographies of the members of the Commons house, 1439–1509* (1936), 284 · CIPM, *Henry VII*, 1, no. 53 · N. H. Nicolas, ed., *Testamenta vetusta: being illustrations from wills*, 2 (1826), 526 · will, PRO, PROB 11/25, sig. 32 · will, PRO, PROB 11/42B, sig. 17 [Lady Anne Grey] · R. Somerville, *History of the duchy of Lancaster, 1265–1603* (1953), 431 · W. P. Baildon, ed., *The records of the Honorable Society of Lincoln's Inn: the black books*, 1 (1897) · LP *Henry VIII*, vols. 1/1, 4/2 · CCIR, *1500–09*, no. 412 · Emden, *Cam.*, 195 · W. A. Shaw, *The knights of England*, 2 vols. (1906) · J. A. Guy, *The cardinal's court: the impact of Thomas Wolsey in star chamber* (1977) · D. MacCulloch, *Suffolk and the Tudors: politics and religion in an English county, 1500–1600* (1986) · C. G. Bayne and W. H. Dunham, eds., *Select cases in the council of Henry VII*, SeldS, 75 (1958) · *Hall's chronicle*, ed. H. Ellis (1809)

Archives Derbys. RO, legal notebook and precedent book
Likenesses oils, *c.*1550–1600, Courteenhall, Northamptonshire · tomb, St Mary's Church, Bury St Edmunds

Drury, Robert (1567–1607), Roman Catholic priest, was the second son of Robert Drury (d. 1592) of Hedgerley, Buckinghamshire, a gentleman who was pricked as sheriff in 1577. His mother was Ann Boorman (d. after 1592), the daughter of Nicholas Boorman of Brook, Isle of Wight. He arrived at the English seminary at Rheims on 1 April 1588, and was given minor orders at Rheims on 18 August 1590. He then departed with other students for the English College recently founded at Valladolid in Spain. He was ordained priest by the bishop of León and in the autumn of 1595 he left Spain for England to become a missionary priest. He was taken under the wing of the Jesuit John Gerard and lived for two years in a house in London belonging to Gerard which was kept by Mistress Anne Line. Gerard says, 'He was well born and well educated … and he could move about in the best society without suspicion. I gave him an introduction to my friends among the gentry and he was a great assistance to them' (*Autobiography*, 86). Although he had been educated at Valladolid by Jesuits and lodged by Gerard in London, he took the appellant side in the archpriest controversy. He signed the appeal against the appointment of Blackwell, the archpriest, dated from Wisbech on 17 November 1600, and was officially suspended from his priestly functions by Blackwell as a result. Like thirteen other supporters of the appellants he signed a protestation of allegiance to the queen on 31 January 1603.

Drury continued to work as a missionary priest in the reign of James I, but was arrested, along with another priest and various lay people, on 10 February 1607 in the house of John Stansby in London. He was tried and sentenced to death under the statute which made being a seminary priest a capital offence. He was offered the oath of allegiance to the king, a new test which had been devised in the wake of the Gunpowder Plot, and was in the words of Challoner, 'worded on purpose in such a manner that the Catholics might be divided in their opinions about the lawfulness of it' (Challoner, 2.18). Drury, after some initial prevarication, took the heroic view that the oath was not lawful and refused to take it. Had he done so, he would have saved his life. It may seem odd that he swore allegiance to Elizabeth but not to her successor, but the Jacobean oath required the juror to deny papal power in temporals, and many (but not all) Catholics rejected it for that reason. He wrote an account of his own arrest and trial which circulated in manuscript, with a description of his execution, among Catholics; the government also printed its own report of these events. He was executed at Tyburn on 26 February 1607 apparently in the garb of a Benedictine, but probably did not belong to that order. A report claimed that he was admitted to the Society of Jesus two days before his martyrdom, but this was denied by the seculars.   PETER HOLMES

Sources DNB · G. Anstruther, *The seminary priests*, 1 (1969) · R. Challoner, *Memoirs of missionary priests*, another edn, 2 vols. (1878), vol. 2, pp. 16–18 · *John Gerard: the autobiography of an Elizabethan*, trans. P. Caraman, 2nd edn (1956), 86–7, 140, 252 · T. F. Knox and others, eds., *The first and second diaries of the English College, Douay* (1878), 218, 232, 234 · A. Campling, *The history of the family of Drury in the counties of Norfolk and Suffolk* (1937), 78–9, 102 · Gillow, *Lit. biog. hist.* · C. Dodd [H. Tootell], *The church history of England, from the year 1500, to the year 1688*, 2 (1739), 258–9, 292–3 · 'A true report of the arraignment … of Robert Drewrie', *The Harleian miscellany*, ed. W. Oldys and T. Park, 3 (1809), 38–47 · M. Lunn, 'English Benedictines and the oath of allegiance, 1606–1647', *Recusant History*, 10 (1969–70), 146–63 · E. Henson, ed., *The registers of the English College at Valladolid, 1589–1862*, Catholic RS, 30 (1930), 9–10

Drury, Sir Robert (1575–1615). *See under* Drury family (*per.* 1485–1624).

Drury, Robert (c.1588–1623), Jesuit, was born in Middlesex, the son of William *Drury DCL (c.1534–1589), of Brett's Hall, Tendring, Essex. William Drury was a judge of the prerogative court of Canterbury who was reconciled to the Catholic faith on his deathbed. He was married to Mary, daughter of Sir Richard Southwell of Woodrising, Norfolk, a relative of Father Robert Southwell, the poet

and martyr. Their son was educated in London, while living at Drury House, Drury Lane. At the age of fourteen he was sent to the Jesuit college at St Omer. On 9 October 1605 he entered the English College, Rome, for his higher studies. After receiving minor orders he joined the Society of Jesus on 16 October 1608, subsequently went to Louvain to finish his theological studies, and was ordained priest in 1614. In 1621 he was professor of moral theology and confessor of the college at St Omer, and afterwards was sent on the mission to his native country, where he became a distinguished preacher. He was professed of the four vows on 8 September 1622. Occasionally he went under the names of Bedford and Sanger.

Drury died on Sunday 26 October 1623 at the 'fatal vespers' in Blackfriars. On the afternoon of that day about 300 persons assembled in an upper room at the French ambassador's residence, Hunsdon House, Blackfriars, for a religious service by Drury and William Whittingham, another Jesuit. While Drury was preaching the great weight of the crowd in the old room suddenly snapped the main summer-beam of the floor, which instantly crashed in and fell into the room below. The main beams there also snapped and broke through to the ambassador's drawing-room over the gatehouse, a distance of 22 feet. Part of the floor, being less crowded, stood firm, and the people on it cut a way through a plaster wall into a neighbouring room. The two Jesuits were killed on the spot. About ninety-five persons lost their lives, while many others sustained serious injuries. The event was seized on in puritan circles as a providential judgment on the Catholics and a pamphlet was issued. Catholic views were expressed by John Floyd's *A word of comfort, or, A discourse concerning the late lamentable accident of the fall of a roome at a Catholicke sermon, in the Blackfriars* (St Omer, 1623). A number of protestant accounts of the accident were published including *The Doleful Even-Song* (1623), written by Thomas Goad, and *The Fatall Vesper* (1623), ascribed to William Crashaw, father of the poet Richard Crashaw.

THOMPSON COOPER, *rev.* G. BRADLEY

Sources T. M. McCoog, *English and Welsh Jesuits, 1555–1650*, 1, Catholic RS, 74 (1994), 115 · G. Holt, *St Omers and Bruges colleges, 1593–1773: a biographical dictionary*, Catholic RS, 69 (1979), 89 · G. Anstruther, *The seminary priests*, 2 (1975), 87–8 · P. Caraman, ed., *The years of siege: Catholic life from James I to Cromwell* (1966), 30–34 · B. Basset, *The English Jesuits, from Campion to Martindale* (1967), 168, 193 · Gillow, *Lit. biog. hist.*, 2.108 · H. Foley, ed., *Records of the English province of the Society of Jesus*, 1 (1877), 77–97; 5 (1879), 1002; 6 (1880), 235; 7 (1882–3), 21 · A. Freeman, 'William Drury, dramatist', *Recusant History*, 8 (1965–6), 293–7 · G. Oliver, *Collections towards illustrating the biography of the Scotch, English and Irish members, SJ* (1838), 83 · A. Kenny, ed., *The responsa scholarum of the English College, Rome*, 1, Catholic RS, 54 (1962), 151–2 · A. Walsham, 'The fatall vesper': providentialism and anti-popery in late Jacobean London', *Past and Present*, 144 (1994), 36–87

Drury, Robert (1687–1734?), traveller, was born on 20 July 1687, in or near Crutched Friars, London, the eldest of the three surviving children of John Drury (d. 1716), keeper of the King's Head inn, Old Jewry, and his first wife, Mary Elizabeth (d. 1703). Robert went to sea at thirteen aboard the *Degrave*, on a trading voyage to Bengal, where the ship was delayed and sustained some damage. She sailed on the return voyage in December 1702 but a leak obliged her to call at Mauritius for repairs which proved ineffectual. On the resumed voyage to the cape the ship continued to take water and had to make for the nearest land, the southern coast of Madagascar, where nearly all aboard were able to scramble or swim ashore before she broke up. They were then detained by the local king, whom they seem to have suspected of intending to kill them. They took him hostage, therefore, with his wife and a nephew, and set off east across the country to the adjoining territory of another king, but were pursued and induced to give up their hostages on false promises of a safe passage. Some who were suspicious of these promises (including the *Degrave*'s second mate, John Benbow) slipped away at night but all those who remained were massacred except for a few boys, among them Robert Drury.

From this point Drury's own account of his life on Madagascar lacks corroboration, but those with knowledge of the history of the peoples of the island have found his story credible in general and a valuable if not entirely reliable source of ethnographic information. According to his account he was kept as a slave or servant to various kings or chiefs, and functioned as bee-keeper, cattle-herder, hunter, and fighter, while periodically absconding and transferring allegiance to improve his conditions. He lived and dressed as a man of Madagascar, and had a wife whom he abandoned when escaping from his first chiefly patron, the king's grandson, to another, further north in the Angavo hills. After some time with this chief he escaped again, walking alone from the territory of the Antandroy peoples in the south to the territory of the Fiherenana in the south-west, 'singing Madagascar songs, for I had forgot to sing in English', and supporting himself on yams and wild honey and by hunting with his javelin (Drury, 291). In his last years on the island, after having been captured by the Sakalava peoples controlling the west coast, he acquired another wife, cattle, and even a slave.

An Englishman Drury encountered was able to escape from the island by ship, and word reached Drury's father, who arranged for a Captain Mackett of the *Drake* to contact him with a letter addressed 'To Robert Drury on the Island of Madagascar' (Drury, 429). Captain Mackett purchased Drury, 'naked except the Lamber' (the *lamba*, the local dress, in Drury's cockney rendering), in exchange for 'a handsome, and very good Buccaneer Gun' (ibid.). In gratitude Drury presented Mackett with his slave. Before leaving Madagascar he helped to procure more slaves for Mackett from the north-west, where he met another survivor from the *Degrave*, living with some of the pirates who frequented the island at the time. Drury sailed with the *Drake* and her slaves to Jamaica before reaching England in September 1717.

Drury had left London at thirteen, and he returned at thirty to find his mother had died in 1703 and his father in 1716. A year after his repatriation he sailed again with a Captain White in the *Mercury* for slaves from Madagascar, who were sold in Virginia, from where the *Mercury*

returned to England with tobacco and Robert Drury in September 1720. Little is known of his later life, but in 1729 appeared *Madagascar, or, Robert Drury's Journal, during Fifteen Years Captivity on that Island*, which declared that 'I am every Day to be spoken with at Old Tom's Coffee-house in Birchin-Lane'. A preface explained that, although the 'Original was wrote by Robert Drury', a 'Transcriber' had 'put it in a more agreeable Method'. The author of the preface also stated that he expected the work would be 'taken for such another Romance as *Robinson Cruso*' but, 'so far as every Body concern'd in the Publication knows, it is nothing else but a plain, honest Narrative of Matter of Fact'. It seems to have been taken as fact on publication and for many years subsequently, but the editor of an edition in 1890 suspected that the 'Transcriber' was none other than Daniel Defoe, the author of *Robinson Crusoe*, and by the middle of the twentieth century the book was indeed taken as a work of fiction by Defoe, to whom it is ascribed in many libraries. There is no evidence, however, to connect Defoe with *Robert Drury's Journal*, even as 'Transcriber', and careful research has confirmed much of the maritime background of the work, and reaffirmed Robert Drury's status as a real person, not a character in a novel by Defoe.

A writer in the *Gentleman's Magazine* in 1769 reported that Drury after his travels 'was known to many, being a porter at the East India House'. He lived 'at his house in Lincoln's Inn Fields', where he was often seen to throw a javelin with Malagasy accuracy, 'and strike a small mark at a surprizing distance' (Duncombe, 172). He is probably the Robert Drury whose burial was recorded at St Clement Danes, London, on 15 March 1734. NEIL RENNIE

Sources R. Drury, *Madagascar, or, Robert Drury's journal, during fifteen years captivity on that island* (1729) • W. Duncombe, 'An account of William Benbow, son to the admiral', *GM*, 1st ser., 39 (1769), 171–2 • H. C. V. Leibbrandt, *Précis of the archives of the Cape of Good Hope: letters despatched, 1696–1708* (Cape Town, 1896), 310–12 • A. W. Secord, 'Robert Drury's journal' and other studies (Urbana, Illinois, 1961)

Drury [married name Warter], **Susanna** (b. 1698?, d. in or after 1770), landscape painter, was, on her father's side, from a family of East Anglian origin which had been established in Ireland since Elizabethan times, a branch having settled in Dublin by 1675. Susanna was one of five children of Lieutenant Thomas Drury (who was baptized at St Peter and St Kevin, Aungier Street, Dublin, on 11 November 1683), the son of John Drury and his wife, Ann, née Leeson, who married there in 1675; Susanna's mother was Rebeckah, née Franklin (buried at St Ann's, Dawson Street, Dublin, on 27 September 1732). Susanna's date of birth is not certain, but her parents were probably the Thomas Drury and Rebecca Franklin who were married on 28 August 1695 at North Elmham, Norfolk, where their two eldest children, Thomas and Rebecca, were also baptized. Their other children were Mary Drury (baptized at St Catherine's, Dublin, on 23 September 1714); the Revd John Drury (1716–1791), vicar of Powerscourt, co. Wicklow; Franklin Drury, miniature painter, who died at Powerscourt, in 1771; and Elizabeth Drury, who married John

Dudley at St Anne's, Dublin, on 6 November 1750 and by 1770 was a widow. Neither is it certain where Susanna was trained, but it may have been London, as her only dated work is *View of London from One-Tree Hill, Greenwich Park* (1733; sold in Dublin 1905; in Frank Sabin collection, London, in 1954).

A pair of landscapes or perspectives, *The Giant's Causeway*, won the £25 premium of the Dublin Society in 1740, and Susanna Drury's identity was disclosed to the society by Gabriel Maturin, a Huguenot, then dean of Kildare and later Jonathan Swift's successor at St Patrick's, Dublin. Her views of the Giant's Causeway were engraved in London in 1743–4 by François Vivarès, another Huguenot. These engravings, the first-ever accurate views of the site, were circulated throughout Europe and provided the French geologist Nicolas Demarest with evidence to support his 'Vulcanist' theory of the origin of basalt, against the current 'Neptunist' theory held by Abraham Gottlob Werner. Mary Delany, Swift's friend, wrote to her sister on 8 October 1758: 'Mrs Drury, who took the draughts (of which you have the prints) lived three months near the place, and went almost every day. I can do nothing so exact and finished' (*Autobiography … Mrs Delany*, 3.519). Two pairs of Susanna Drury's gouache paintings on vellum of the Giant's Causeway are known, one pair in the Ulster Museum, Belfast, and the other in the collection of the knight of Glin at Glin Castle, co. Limerick. Apart from her view of London, the only identified works by Susanna Drury are the views of the Giant's Causeway, which remain landmarks both in Irish topography and in European scientific illustration. Her married name was probably Warter, as a 'Susanna Warter … she a painter of landscape' appears in her brother Franklin Drury's will of 1770.

MARTYN ANGLESEA

Sources 'Drury family trees', unpubd MS, priv. coll. • 'Pedigrees of the Drury family of Dublin and Roscommon', (7 photocopied sheets), c.1900, PRO NIre., T 590 • *The autobiography and correspondence of Mary Granville, Mrs Delany*, ed. Lady Llanover, 1st ser., 3 vols. (1861); 2nd ser., 3 vols. (1862) • W. G. Strickland, *A dictionary of Irish artists*, 2 vols. (1913) • A. Crookshank and the Knight of Glin [D. Fitzgerald], *The painters of Ireland, c.1660–1920* (1978) • M. Anglesea and J. Preston, 'A philosophical landscape: Susanna Drury and the Giant's Causeway', *Art History*, 3 (1980), 252–73 • *The Cambridge encyclopedia of earth sciences* (1982) • S. Rousham, *The story of the causeway stones* (1987) • *Irish women artists: from the eighteenth century to the present day* (1987) [exhibition catalogue, NG Ire., the Douglas Hyde Gallery, TCD, and the Hugh Lane Municipal Gallery of Modern Art, Dublin, July–Aug 1987] • M. Anglesea, 'The iconography of the Antrim coast', *The poet's place: essays in honour of John Hewitt, 1907–1987*, ed. G. Dawe and J. W. Foster (1991), 31–44 • A. Crookshank and the Knight of Glin [D. Fitzgerald], *The watercolours of Ireland: works on paper in pencil, pastel and paint, c.1600–1914* (1994) • M. Anglesea, 'Irish artists with Huguenot backgrounds', *Proceedings of the Huguenot Society*, 26 (1994–7), 59–70 • IGI

Drury, Sir William (*c.*1500–1558). *See under* Drury family (*per.* 1485–1624).

Drury, Sir William (1527–1579), soldier and lord justice of Ireland, was born on 2 October 1527 at Hawstead, Suffolk, the third of five sons of Sir Robert Drury (*b.* before 1503, *d.* 1577), landowner, of Hedgerley, Buckinghamshire, and his wife, Elizabeth, daughter of Edmund Brudenell of

Sir William Drury (1527–1579), attrib. George Gower, *c.*1570–75

Chalfont St Peter, Buckinghamshire. His brothers included the MP Robert Drury (1525–1593) and the courtier Sir Dru *Drury (1531/2–1617). At an unknown date he matriculated at Gonville Hall, Cambridge, but does not appear to have graduated.

Drury embarked on a military career in the service of John Russell, Baron Russell, who was his father's Buckinghamshire neighbour, and whose aunt Agnes Bowreman was married to William Drury's elder brother. He accompanied Russell during Henry VIII's invasion of France in 1544, taking an active part in the sieges of Boulogne and Montreuil. He was subsequently taken prisoner during a skirmish near Brussels. Having been ransomed, he is said to have pursued a short but successful maritime career. In 1549 he assisted Russell in the suppression of the western rebellion, which had broken out in defiance of the evangelical reforms of the lord protector, Edward Seymour, duke of Somerset. Like his patron, Drury was a staunch supporter of the protestant Reformation promoted in the name of Edward VI. However, he refused to countenance the attempt of John Dudley, duke of Northumberland, to divert the rightful succession to secure the nascent protestant church, and it is said that at the death of the young king on 6 July 1553 Drury was one of the first to declare for Princess Mary. It is claimed that his religion and his connection with Russell (now first earl of Bedford) strongly influenced his withdrawal from the court during the new reign, but such considerations evidently did not preclude his serving the Marian regime. Drury sat in the 1554 parliament for Chipping Wycombe, Buckinghamshire, and appears to have acted in some capacity on diplomatic missions, going to Spain shortly before Mary's marriage, for example.

Drury's public service attained far greater prominence after 1559, however, despite some initial hesitancy about his loyalty owing to doubts arising from his well-known association with the imperial ambassador in England, Lamoral Egmont, count of Egmont. Having persuaded the new regime of his inwardness and discretion Drury became an active and effective instrument of Elizabeth I's Scottish policy at a time when the privy council looked north with some anxiety, and sought to combat the burgeoning influence in Scotland of the French party under Mary of Guise. Drury was first dispatched to Edinburgh in October 1559 to investigate the state of the parties there, and to view the new French fortifications at Leith, then said to be rapidly nearing completion. On 10 October 1560, at St Alfege, London Wall, he married Margaret (d. 1587), daughter of Thomas Wentworth, first Baron Wentworth of Nettlestead, and his wife, Margaret, and widow of John Williams, first Baron Williams of Thame. The couple were to have three daughters. Resuming his public duties, Drury provided an important link between the Elizabethan regime and the Scottish lords of the congregation, while also maintaining valuable links with the most important Marians. His position was not without its dangers, and he was subjected to grave personal hazard on numerous occasions, supposedly instancing eight attempts on his life by the time he left Scotland in 1576. In April 1567 he was challenged by James Hepburn, fourth earl of Bothwell, who perceived himself the victim of foul reproaches by Drury. Nothing came of the earl's own sharp words once Drury had expressed a willingness to meet with him.

In February 1564 Drury was appointed to succeed Sir Thomas Dacre as marshal and deputy governor of Berwick. From October 1567, when Francis Russell, second earl of Bedford, was recalled as warden of the east march, until the appointment of his successor, Henry Carey, first Baron Hunsdon, in August 1568, Drury was personally responsible for the security of the region. Amid the suppression of the northern uprising of 1569–70, Drury was commissioned, with Sir Henry Gater, as a special ambassador to negotiate with the regent of Scotland, James Stewart, earl of Moray, for the surrender of the insurgents' leader, Thomas Percy, seventh earl of Northumberland, who had been betrayed into the hands of the Scots and detained at Lochleven Castle. Talks, including an audience with the regent on 19 January 1570, began barely a fortnight before the assassination of Moray by James Hamilton of Bothwellhaugh, supporter of the Marian cause, on 23 January. At the same time, Drury himself escaped assassination. He took part that spring in the punitive raids over the border aimed at laying waste the lands of those Scots who had assisted, and were still harbouring, the English rebels. Ninety castles and strongholds were razed, and 300 towns and villages torched in a three-pronged assault on the Ferniehirst and Buccleuch strongholds of Teviotdale, Liddisdale, and the Merse. On 11 May, having been knighted by Thomas Radcliffe, third earl of Sussex, lord president of the queen's council in the north, Drury marched once more into Scotland at the head of a 1500-strong army dispatched to intervene in the open civil war which had now broken out between the respective camps of the deposed queen, Mary, and her infant son, James VI.

Failing to broker a cease-fire at Edinburgh, and finding the siege of Glasgow lifted by the time he arrived there, little remained for Drury to do but waste the Hamilton territories in Clydesdale. On 20 May 1571 he was sent as special ambassador to try to broker a truce between the queen's and the king's parties. He was sent again on 31 January 1572, arriving in the middle of February. This time he was paid £2 per day and probably took Nicholas Errington as his secretary. Again, he failed and, as in 1571, narrowly escaped assassination. Before he ventured north the third time he wrote to William Cecil, Baron Burghley, beseeching him to protect his wife and children in the event of his untimely demise on the queen's service. He was special ambassador from 5 July to 1 August 1572. Coinciding with the arrival of an ambassador with instructions from Charles IX to persuade the queen's party to submit to the regent, James Douglas, fourth earl of Morton, this third attempt to secure by diplomacy the ascendancy of the king's party nevertheless came unstuck, and Drury was left expressing the fervent wish to be stood down from the hapless task, saying that 'he would sooner serve the queen in Constantinople' (DNB). However, rather than have his wish, he now found himself at the head of the army which Elizabeth dispatched to achieve by arms that which talks had failed to obtain. Coming to Morton's assistance with an army and a heavy train of artillery, Drury brought the siege of Edinburgh to a close in a week, the Marians, under the command of Sir William Kircaldy of Grange, surrendering on 28 May 1573. Drury and Morton clashed over the subsequent treatment of Kircaldy, with whom Drury had evidently enjoyed some kind of friendship after several years of acquaintance, association, and frequent communication. His solicitation on behalf of Kirkcaldy may also have reflected an unwillingness on the part of Elizabeth to upset Charles more than was necessary. Morton's order for Kirkcaldy's execution caused some serious friction between himself and Drury. Their antagonism was exacerbated by the lengths to which the regent was forced to go subsequently in order to recover from Drury the crown jewels and regalia entrusted to him by Kirkcaldy at the fall of the castle.

In 1574 Drury was appointed one of the members of the newly reconstituted council of the north. However, the privy council had considered sending him with an army to Munster in response to the increasingly tense state of affairs there. The danger passed, and with it the necessity for immediate action, but on 20 June 1576 Drury was appointed president of Munster. The lord deputy, Sir Henry Sidney, had set in train a number of reforms designed, albeit somewhat theoretically, to entrench English authority in Ireland, and measures for the pacification of Munster were well in hand by the time Drury arrived in July. The key to the problem lay in establishing a reasonable working relationship with Gerald fitz James Fitzgerald, fourteenth earl of Desmond, the greatest magnate in western Munster, who had only recently returned from imprisonment in England. Sidney continued on-going attempts to undermine the system of coign and livery which maintained the armed followings on which Irish and Old English power depended, and succeeded in persuading Desmond to abandon his own cousin and principal mercenary commander, James fitz Maurice Fitzgerald, who went into exile in March 1575. Drury was a governor from an altogether different mould. He was determined to undermine Desmond and Thomas Butler, tenth earl of Ormond, and followed up Sidney's initiative for the creation of what was, in effect, a crown affinity in the province, as a means of supplanting the traditional patterns of overlordship. This led to the execution of 400 'masterless men' in the space of a year and a half. The president's more aggressive bearing, especially in holding sessions within Desmond's palatine liberty at Tralee in July 1577, twice pushed the earl close to the point of overt hostility. However, while he remained in Ireland, Sidney's more conciliatory policy just about held and an open breach was averted. 'Desmond became not merely compliant but actively cooperative', as some of the financial benefits accruing to him from the commutation of his traditional military exactions began to take effect, while for his part Drury learned eventually to appreciate the advantages of co-operating with the earl; 'but appearances were deceptive' (Ellis, 306–7).

Sidney was recalled in 1578, and Drury was appointed lord justice in his place on 27 April, transferring himself to Dublin. By then Fitz Maurice had assembled the wherewithal to carry into Ireland the papal crusade against Elizabeth and protestant England, making landfall at Smerwick in co. Kerry on 17 July 1579 with a band of several dozen Spanish and Italian soldiers. This puny force would have achieved nothing on its own, but before long Fitz Maurice had raised sufficient support in Munster for Desmond to fear the consequences of his own disengagement from his followers more than he feared the government. Drury's response, initially as vigorous as might be in the absence of an army in Munster, was gravely weakened by the onset of a fatal illness. He delegated responsibility for the suppression of the rising to Sir Nicholas Malby, president of Connaught. Malby, who did not have the ties with Desmond which Drury had cultivated, behaved in such a way as to present the earl with no option other than to join a rebellion which proved to be a watershed in relations between the government and Irish society in the south of Ireland. As Desmond's rebellion took hold, Drury himself lay dying at Waterford, where he expired on 13 October 1579. His body was embalmed and taken to Dublin for burial. The monument bearing his effigy erected in his memory in St Patrick's Cathedral, Dublin, does not survive. Administration of his estate was granted to his widow on 14 June 1580, by which time she had married James Croft of Weston in Oxfordshire. She was dead by 20 July 1587.   SEAN KELSEY

Sources C. Brady, *The chief governors: the rise and fall of reform government in Tudor Ireland, 1536–1588* (1994) · J. S. Brewer and W. Bullen, eds., *Calendar of the Carew manuscripts*, 6 vols., PRO (1867–73) · *CSP dom.*, 1547–53 · *CSP Ire.*, 1574–85 · *CSP Scot.*, 1563–74 · G. R. Hewitt, *Scotland under Morton, 1572–1580* (1982) · S. G. Ellis, *Ireland in the age of the Tudors* (1998) · T. W. Moody and others, eds., *A new history of Ireland*, 3: *Early modern Ireland, 1534–1691* (1976) · *DNB* · D. L. W. Tough, *The last years of a frontier: a history of the borders during the reign of Elizabeth* (1928) · HoP, *Commons, 1509–58*, 2.56–60 · C. Brady, 'Faction and the origins of the Desmond rebellion of 1579', *Irish Historical Studies*, 22 (1980–81), 289–312
Archives BL, Cotton MSS, corresp. · PRO, state papers, Ireland, SP 63 · PRO, state papers, Scotland, SP 52 · University of Chicago Library, Bacon MSS
Likenesses attrib. G. Gower, portrait, version, *c.*1570–1575, priv. coll. [*see illus.*] · oils, *c.*1570–1575, Guildhall, Thetford · portrait, version, Courteenhall, Northamptonshire · portrait, version, NPG

Drury, William (*c.*1534–1589), civil lawyer, was the third son of John Drury of Rougham, Suffolk, and Elizabeth, daughter of John Goldringham of Belstead in the same county. He was educated at Trinity Hall, Cambridge, where he graduated LLB in 1553. In January 1560 he was appointed regius professor of civil law, proceeding to the degree of LLD. Appointed advocate at Doctors' Commons in May 1561, he shortly afterwards became secretary to Matthew Parker, who in 1562 made him his commissary for the faculties. By 1567 he was a member of the high commission, and in June that year was appointed visitor of the diocese of Norwich.

In 1571 Drury, along with other advocates of Doctors' Commons, was consulted on the legal implications raised by the intrigues, on behalf of Mary, queen of Scots, of John Leslie, bishop of Ross, who twice committed to prison on charges of endeavouring to raise a conspiracy, but who claimed that he had entered England under a safe conduct with the full privileges of ambassador. The lawyers were asked whether an ambassador 'procuring an insurrection or rebellion' was entitled to such diplomatic immunity. Their verdict—that he was not so entitled, and might 'jure gentium et civili Romanorum' be punished as an enemy, traitor, or conspirator—became the reference point for all subsequent discussion of the question, but it was never upheld either in England or elsewhere, the bishop of Ross himself being detained without trial until his banishment from the realm.

In 1571 Parker had to seek the approval of the council, grudgingly given, for Drury's admission as master of the prerogative court of Canterbury after an unspecified 'oversight' had led to his imprisonment in the Tower, whence he had been summoned to appear in the Star Chamber. On several subsequent occasions, proceedings in which Drury was engaged in the ecclesiastical courts were subject to prohibitions emanating from the council, who nevertheless consulted him on a number of maritime and mercantile cases. He is recorded as having been present at Parker's funeral, but won the confidence of Archbishop Grindal, being appointed in November 1577, along with Laurence Hussey, as auditor of the court of audience, vicar-general in spirituals, and official principal in place of Thomas Yale, who had until his death acted singly as vicar-general; their tenure lasted barely two months, being rescinded by joint orders of the queen and the council in favour of William Aubrey and William Clark in January 1578.

Drury was sworn master-extraordinary in chancery in October 1580, and master-in-ordinary in 1585. In 1584 Whitgift asked him how the revenues of the church might be defended against a feared confiscation by the crown under cover of a writ of *melius inquirendum*. Drury's response, which may explain why he appears to have been suspected of 'popish' views, reveals him as an uncompromising and resourceful champion of the church against those who claimed that they wanted reformation but who were really aiming at 'destruction and spoliation'. He advised that special care be taken in the forthcoming parliamentary elections. The church should be ready to counter criticism of the ecclesiastical courts with counter-accusations of abuses in the temporal courts, together with an account of every prohibition of the last seven years, 'whence may be gathered the rough violence and absurdities therein used'. Similarly, they should prepare details of all lay impropriations of church revenues: were they to be restored, he suggested, the queen would have more profit from first fruits, tenths, and subsidies than she presently received from the laity in fines and rents (Strype, appendix 1, no. 40; 3/1.230–31).

Drury married Mary (d. 1622), daughter of Sir Richard Southwell of Woodrising in Norfolk, and they had four sons, including William *Drury, Latin playwright, and two daughters. He died in 1589 possessed of several properties in Essex. The family seat of Brett's Hall, in the parish of Tendring, together with other holdings in Weeley and Little Holland, was left during her life to his wife and thence to his eldest son, John, who acquired in his own right the manor of Tendring Hall, the advowson of the parish church, and other property. Two other sons, George and Robert *Drury (c.1588–1623), and his two daughters, Bridget and Elizabeth, acquired other properties at Poplar, West Ham, and Geddyhall. Drury was buried in the church of St Mary Magdalen, Old Fish Street, London. His son John was knighted in 1604.

P. O. G. WHITE

Sources J. Strype, *Annals of the Reformation and establishment of religion … during Queen Elizabeth's happy reign*, 3rd edn, 4 vols. (1731–5) · J. Strype, *The life and acts of Matthew Parker* (1711) · APC, 1571–82, 1588–9 · J. Strype, *The history of the life and acts of … Edmund Grindal* (1710) · J. Strype, *Historical collections of the life and acts of … John Aylmer* (1701) · J. Strype, *The life and acts of … John Whitgift* (1718) · will, PRO, PROB 11/75, sig. 1 · Cooper, *Ath. Cantab.*, 2.74 · P. Morant, *The history and antiquities of the county of Essex*, 1 (1768) · *Correspondence of Matthew Parker*, ed. J. Bruce and T. T. Perowne, Parker Society, 42 (1853) · DNB · P. Collinson, *Archbishop Grindal, 1519–1583: the struggle for a reformed church* (1979) · R. Phillimore, *Commentaries upon international law* (1882), vol. 2, pp. 162–3, 205 · *CSP dom.*, 1547–80
Wealth at death several properties in Essex: will, 1589, PRO, PROB 11/75, sig. 1

Drury, Sir William (1550–1590). *See under* Drury family (*per.* 1485–1624).

Drury, William (*bap.* 1584, *d.* in or after 1643), Latin playwright, was the third of the four sons of the lawyer William *Drury (*c.*1534–1589) and his wife, Mary Southwell (d.

1622); his younger brother was the Jesuit priest Robert *Drury. William was baptized at Tendring, Essex, on 11 October 1584 and was educated in London and at St Omer from 1601 to 1605. He entered the English College at Rome on 9 October 1605 and was ordained on 10 April 1610. Imprisoned in England on account of his Catholicism, Drury was liberated and banished on 26 June 1618. He repaired to the English College at Douai where he began by teaching music and was later placed in charge of rhetoric and poetry. There he made his name as a writer of highly popular Latin plays in verse, three of which were published in *Dramatica poemata* (Douai, 1628, reprinted at Antwerp, 1641). *Alvredus* is a humorous rendering of Alfred the Great's deliverance of his people from the Danes. In *Mors*, 'an excellent Latin comedy' in Douce's opinion (Douce, 175), a dissolute son enrols Death to do away with his miserly father, unaware that the latter has pledged the son's soul to the Devil in return for greater riches. This is Drury's finest work, in which his lively, colloquial Latin, influenced by the comedies of Plautus and Terence, is well suited to the droll predicament. These plays had been published together previously at Douai in 1620, but the collected edition of 1628 also includes a new piece entitled *Reparatus*; this contains some excellent repartee and demonstrates the author's wide comic range, extending from farce to fast wit. Appended to the plays is the elegant elegiac poem 'De venerabili eucharistia ab apibus inventa', on the celebration of the eucharist by bees. Drury was released from an incarceration in the Clink in Southwark on 24 March 1635 and was apparently still alive in 1643 (Anstruther, 89).

THOMPSON COOPER, *rev.* ROSS KENNEDY

Sources F. Douce, *The dance of death* (1833), 175 · A. Freeman, 'William Drury, dramatist', *Recusant History*, 8 (1965–6), 293–7 · G. Anstruther, *The seminary priests*, 2 (1975), 87–8 · A. F. Allison and D. M. Rogers, eds., *The contemporary printed literature of the English Counter-Reformation between 1558 and 1640*, 1 (1989), 49 · H.-R. Duthilloeul, *Bibliographie douaisienne*, rev. edn, 1 (Douai, 1842), 63 · W. Kelly, ed., *Liber ruber venerabilis collegii Anglorum de urbe*, 1, Catholic RS, 37 (1940), 139 · A. Kenny, ed., *The responsa scholarum of the English College, Rome*, 1, Catholic RS, 54 (1962) · E. H. Burton and T. L. Williams, eds., *The Douay College diaries, third, fourth and fifth, 1598–1654*, 2, Catholic RS, 11 (1911), 146, 148, 172, 185, 186 · G. Holt, *St Omers and Bruges colleges, 1593–1773: a biographical dictionary*, Catholic RS, 69 (1979), 89 · A. Campling, *The history of the family of Drury in the counties of Norfolk and Suffolk* (1937), 26 · DNB

Drust (*d.* 729). *See under* Picts, kings of the (*act. c.*300–*c.*900).

Drust (*d. c.*848). *See under* Picts, kings of the (*act. c.*300–*c.*900).

Dry, Sir Richard (1815–1869), politician in Australia, was born on 15 June 1815 at Elphin Farm, near Launceston, Tasmania, the elder of the two sons and the third of the five children of Richard Dry (1771–1843), a former convict from Ireland and chief assistant in the government store, and his wife, Anne Maugham (d. 1836). He was educated at Kirklands School at Campbell Town and at the Revd Mr Thompson's academy in Hobart. When he was twenty-one he travelled to Mauritius and India, after which he returned to assist his family in running the large Western

River estate, Quamby, purchased by his father in 1828. He inherited the property in 1843. The following year he was appointed as a member of the Tasmanian legislative council.

Dry was a leading figure in the attempt by the council to force an inquiry into the expense and effects on the colony of the convict system. Coming into conflict with the lieutenant-governor, Sir John Eardley-Wilmot, he was one of the 'patriotic six' who resigned from the council on 31 October 1845 over the issue. Dry in particular gained widespread popularity as a result of this action. He became a leader of the Anti-Transportation League, which then supported his election to the newly democratized council in 1851, and was unanimously elected speaker of the council. On 27 April 1853 he married Clara (*d.* 1904), the daughter of George Meredith of Cambria, Swanport. They had no children.

In 1854 Dry was forced to step down from his positions as a result of ill health. He and his wife then travelled extensively through Europe, returning to Tasmania in 1860. He received a knighthood from the queen while in England in 1858. In December 1862 he returned to the legislative council by means of election for the seat of Tamar. On the resignation of the Whyte ministry in 1866, the popular Dry was called upon to take up the premiership. He retained this position—with some controversy resulting from perceptions of his 'self-interest and parochialism' in promoting railway development in the northwest of the state near his constituency (Baker, 100)—until his death, on 1 August 1869, at his Hobart residence, Holbrook. He was buried at St Mary's, Hagley. His death brought 'unprecedented tributes of sorrow from all classes' (Reynolds, 330). Extravagant, 'colourful', and 'equalitarian' (ibid.), Dry was widely regarded as 'perhaps the most popular statesman Tasmania ever possessed' (Baker, 108).   MARC BRODIE

Sources A. D. Baker, *The life and times of Sir Richard Dry* (1951) · J. Reynolds, 'Dry, Sir Richard', *AusDB*, vol. 1 · W. V. Teniswood, 'Dry, Richard', *AusDB* [father], vol. 1 · W. A. Townsley, *The struggle for self-government in Tasmania* (1951) · IGI · DNB
Archives Mitchell L., NSW, Caldor MSS
Likenesses L. Hecter, pencil and watercolour drawing, 1802, Mitchell L., NSW · C. Harb, oils, 1855, Parliament House, Hobart · R. Dowling, portraits, Queen Victoria Museum, Launceston, Tasmania · A. Norte, tinted crayon portrait, Mitchell L., NSW · portrait, repro. in Baker, *Life and times*, frontispiece

Dryander, Francis. *See* Enzinas, Francisco de (1518?–1552).

Dryander, Jonas Carlsson (1748–1810), botanist and librarian, was born on 5 March 1748 in Göteborg, Sweden, son of Carl Leonard Dryander (*d.* 1757), lecturer, and Brita Maria Montin. His uncle, Dr Lars Montin, a botanist and pupil of Linnaeus, advised him on his education after the early death of his father. After attending school in Göteborg, he went to Uppsala University in 1765, where he came under the influence of Linnaeus; he finally graduated from Lund University in 1776 and his thesis was published as *Dissertatio gradualis fungos regno vegetabili vindicans* (1776). He was never on good terms with Linnaeus the

Jonas Carlsson Dryander (1748–1810), by William Daniell, pubd 1811 (after George Dance, 1795)

younger and gave the young James Edward Smith advice over the purchase of Linnaeus's library and herbarium.

In 1777 Dryander moved to England and on the death of his fellow Swede, Solander, in 1782, succeeded him as librarian to Sir Joseph Banks at his home in Dean Street, Soho; his duties included visiting all important gardens and nurseries in and around London, supervising Banks's garden at Spring Grove, and making more than 160 visits to William Aiton at Kew. He also became librarian of the Royal Society and the first librarian and vice-president of the Linnean Society, founded in 1788 by his friend Sir James Edward Smith. When the society was incorporated in 1802, Dryander was the chief author of its laws. Both societies benefited from duplicate books from Banks's library. Dryander assisted Robert Brown (who succeeded him as Banks's librarian) with the taxonomic framework of his books, and both of them helped Banks to choose which plants, collected in the south seas expedition, were to be drawn in colour. Bishop Goodenough of the Linnean Society described Dryander as 'a dull plodding genius', but conceded that 'plodding was the first quality of a librarian'. He also wrote that 'his bluntness had its great effect with innovators, impertinents and popinjays' (Goodenough to Smith, Linn. Soc., Smith MSS, 9.171).

Dryander was the main author of the first edition of Aiton's *Hortus Kewensis*, published in 1789, and part of the second edition issued between 1810 and 1813, and he edited Roxburgh's *Plants of the Coromandel Coast* between 1795 and 1798; his *magnum opus* was the *Catalogus bibliothecae historico-naturalis Josephi Banks, baronetti* (5 vols., 1796–1800), which has been described as a 'lasting monument of erudition, perseverance and sound judgment' (*GM*, 1st ser., 80, 1810, 398). Dryander died from complications arising from haemorrhoids on 19 October 1810, at

Banks's house in Soho Square and was buried in St Anne's Church, Soho. Banks wrote to Home (Dryander's surgeon): 'I have lost my right hand man … my chief pleasure, that of my library, is reduced almost to a shadow …' (Banks to Home, Natural History Museum, Dawson Turner copies, 18.88a). Brown was asked 'to see the remains of my FRIEND properly laid in the ground' (Natural History Museum, Dawson Turner copies, 18.84–9). Dryander's services to botany were commemorated by his friend Thunberg in the genus *Dryandra*, a group of South African Proteaceae.   G. S. BOULGER, *rev.* MARGOT WALKER

Sources *A selection of the correspondence of Linnaeus, and other naturalists, from the original manuscripts*, ed. J. E. Smith, 2 vols. (1821) • *The Banks letters*, ed. W. R. Dawson (1958) • H. B. Carter, *Sir Joseph Banks, 1743–1820* (1988) • R. Desmond, *Kew: the history of the Royal Botanic Gardens* (1995); repr. (1998) • D. J. Mabberley, *Jupiter botanicus: Robert Brown of the British Museum* (1985) • *Swedish Linnean Society Year Book* (1939), 46, 53, 58 • *Swedish dictionary of national biography* (1859–60) • A. H. Uggla, 'Jonas Carlsson Dryander', *Svenskt biografiskt lexikon*, ed. B. Boëthius, 11 (1945), 468–72 • Nichols, *Lit. anecdotes*, 9.43
Archives NHM, corresp. and papers | FM Cam., letters to Sir Joseph Banks • Linn. Soc., Smith MSS • NHM, Banks MSS • NHM, Robert Brown MSS • NRA, corresp. with Sir Joseph Banks
Likenesses G. Dance, drawing, 1795 • W. Daniell, soft-ground etching, pubd 1811 (after G. Dance, 1795), BM, NPG [*see illus.*]

Dryburgh, Adam of [Adam Scotus, Adam Anglicus, Adam the Carthusian] (*c*.1140–1212?), abbot of Dryburgh and theologian, was born in the Anglo-Scottish borders. His parents are unknown. Nationality and political control there were very mixed, giving rise to the variety of names by which he was known. In his *De tripartito tabernaculo* Adam wrote that at Dryburgh he was 'in the land of the English and in the kingdom of the Scots' (*Patrologia Latina*, 198, col. 723). His family was of sufficient wealth to see that he obtained a good education (hence he was sometimes known as Master). After rejecting a career in the secular church he entered Dryburgh, a Premonstratensian house, probably not long after its foundation in 1150. There he became a priest at the age of twenty-five, and from *c*.1184 acted for about four years as abbot, when Abbot Gerard became incapacitated by illness. Adam refused episcopal blessing while Gerard lived, but was summoned to Prémontré by the abbot who on account of his preaching skill took him with him on a series of visits to French houses of the order. These visits included the Carthusian priory of Val St Pierre (diocese of Lyons), where the first abbot of Dryburgh had retired. The life there so impressed Adam that on returning to Britain he consulted Hugh of Lincoln (*d.* 1200) and received his encouragement to enter the only Carthusian house in England, at Witham, Somerset, of which Hugh had himself been prior. The bishop helped to get Adam formally released by the Premonstratensians, and at Witham Adam remained for twenty-four years until his death during the interdict, probably on 20 March 1212. Knowledge of his career rests largely upon a fragmentary account written at Witham by a man with whom he had shared a cell for ten years, but the dates derived from it can only be approximate. It tells how Hubert Walter, archbishop of Canterbury (*d.* 1205), heard Adam preach and then went to

his cell, confessed, and submitted to discipline at his hands. On occasion he also upbraided Bishop Hugh on his annual visits. He is said to have been of medium height, and at Dryburgh to have been known for his cheerful speech, charming manners, insight, and memory. With old age he had become rather stout, while his cheerfulness shone out from his face, under a balding head with some white hair.

Adam's own extensive writings reveal much more. There is no scholarly edition, even though some works were printed as early as 1518. Most of what is extant dates from Dryburgh; only the *Liber de quadripartito exercitio cellae* survives from Witham. Dedicated to Prior B[ovo] it must have been completed before 1200, but, until the discovery of the Witham account, was credited to Guigo, the second prior of the Grande Chartreuse. His writings are very significant since few other works by early British Premonstratensians or Carthusians survive to explain their own life and spirituality. His skill as a preacher is seen in over sixty sermons, while for the *Liber de ordine, habitu et professione canonicorum ordinis Praemonstratensis* he deliberately chose the sermon form because he thought it would be more lively. There he discusses many sides of his order's life, from use of the parlour, or complaints about food, to the election of abbots. More spiritual issues occupy the *De triplici genere contemplationis*. The single Carthusian work deals with practical matters like the obligations of priors to the general chapter, and then turns to explore the meaning of the four occupations of the cell: reading the Bible, meditation, prayer, and manual work.

Adam of Dryburgh stands out as well read in the fathers, including Dionysius the Pseudo-Areopagite, and near contemporaries like Anselm (*d.* 1109), Bernard of Clairvaux, and more unusually Andrew of St Victor (*d.* 1175), quoted in *De tripartito tabernaculo* of 1180. One part of this, describing a mental tabernacle adorned with portraits of popes and saints, emperors and rulers, leads him to give an account of the rulers of England and Scotland. At first sight this suggests that he knew King David and his family, which is not impossible since Dryburgh was a house in which they took an interest, but most of his words are derived from Ailred of Rievaulx's *Genealogia*, to which he makes no reference. Elsewhere he often took care to cite the authors whom he used with some precision. The fact that he makes much use of Hugh of St Victor, as well as of Andrew, suggests that he could have studied under the former. Adam's works deserve more examination.

CHRISTOPHER HOLDSWORTH

Sources J. Bulloch, *Adam of Dryburgh* (1958) • E. M. Thompson, 'A fragment of a Witham Chronicle and Adam of Dryburgh', *Bulletin of the John Rylands University Library*, 16 (1932), 482–506 • R. Sharpe, *A handlist of the Latin writers of Great Britain and Ireland before 1540* (1997), 10–12 • Adam of Eynsham, *Magna vita sancti Hugonis / The life of Saint Hugh of Lincoln*, ed. D. L. Douie and D. H. Farmer, 2 vols., OMT (1961–2) • B. Smalley, *The study of the Bible in the middle ages*, 3rd edn (1983) • D. Knowles, C. N. L. Brooke, and V. C. M. London, eds., *The heads of religious houses, England and Wales, 1: 940–1216* (1972) • H. M. Colvin, *The white canons in England* (1951) • D. M. Smith, ed., *Lincoln, 1186–1206*, English Episcopal Acta, 4 (1986) • F. Petit, *La spiritualité* *des Prémontrés aux XIIe et XIIIe siècles* (Paris, 1947) · Adamus Scotus, *Patrologia Latina*, 198 (1855)

Dryden, Alice (1866–1956). *See under* Dryden, Sir Henry Edward Leigh, fourth baronet and seventh baronet (1818–1899).

Dryden, Charles (1666–1704). *See under* Dryden, John (1631–1700).

Dryden, Sir Erasmus-Henry, fifth baronet (1669–1710). *See under* Dryden, John (1631–1700).

Dryden, Sir Henry Edward Leigh, fourth baronet and seventh baronet (1818–1899), archaeologist and antiquary, was born on 17 August 1818 at Adlestrop, Gloucestershire, the eldest of the three children of the Revd Sir Henry Dryden, third baronet (1787–1837), and Elizabeth (1782–1851), daughter of the Revd Julius Hutchinson, of Woodhall Park, Hertfordshire, and Owlthorpe, Nottinghamshire. He was educated at Shrewsbury School, where, according to Dr Butler, he 'didn't at all shine in academic subjects, but he was good at drawing' (Sargant, 86). He was nineteen and studying at Trinity College, Cambridge, when he inherited the baronetcy and its debts. In 1874 he enlarged the title by succeeding to that of his cousin Sir Edward Page-Turner, as seventh baronet. By then, however, he was a much-loved squire in Northamptonshire, where he was a deputy lieutenant and local magistrate and had been high sheriff in 1844 when Queen Victoria and Prince Albert visited the county.

Sir Henry, as he was universally known, owed his popularity to a genial nature formed by his old-fashioned values, sharp yet kind wit, and notable eccentricity. He was scrupulous in observing the English Sunday and had a paternalistic view of Christian duty towards the community. He regularly practised with local church choirs, among which he introduced the Hullah-Wilhem method for teaching singing. He built schools for his neighbours, together with cottages and other vernacular buildings, and was the first chairman of Canons Ashby parish council. He had his clothes made in the villages, and dressed in an out-of-date fashion. In these outfits he would befriend tramps and recommend Canons Ashby House as a place to beg a meal; getting there by a short cut, he would astonish the subsequent caller by becoming his host.

Dryden acquired the nickname 'the Antiquary' from his passion for exploring ancient churches, ruins, and other monuments, all of which he investigated with close attention to detail. His methods were truly archaeological, involving careful observation and recording by accurate drawing and measured survey. The exactness of his plans was notorious among contemporaries, who told how he had travelled 200 miles across France in order to check a half-inch discrepancy of measurement. His lifelong interest in history, archaeology, ecclesiology, and medieval architecture was characterized by thoroughness, which occasionally bordered upon the obsessive, such as setting the type for one of his publications. He deplored shoddy

work, and condemned what he called the 'decadent and bastard type' of heraldry which it was proposed to include in the Victoria History of the Counties of England series.

Because Dryden collected information about many historic structures since destroyed or subsequently altered, his drawings and notes remain of value. Over 500 portfolios of plans, elevations, and other records survive, mostly as a gift to Northampton Public Library, where he helped to establish the town's museum and was its honorary curator of antiquities, costumes, and leather work. Together with letters exchanged with the leading authorities at the time, the material illustrates the wide range of his researches. These extended from British antiquities and sites of all ages to Scandinavian prehistory and the megaliths of Brittany, which he surveyed with the Revd William Collings Lukis FSA. He also worked in the Orkney and Shetland islands, in particular making measured drawings of St Magnus Cathedral in Kirkwall, Orkney, which formed the basis of a published description (1868).

Dryden was made an honorary fellow of the Society of Antiquaries of Scotland in recognition of his archaeological work in the north. He was president of the Oxford Archaeological Society, a member of the Peterborough Diocesan Church Building Association, and a founding vice-president of the architectural society for the archdeaconries of Northampton and Oakham, in whose journal he published various papers. He was a popular contributor to the annual series of Saturday evening talks at Northampton town hall, where his inevitable banter with the audience was eagerly looked forward to, in spite of the often abstruse subject matter. According to one observer, he was a restless speaker:

> pacing rapidly from one illustration to another: now sketching an old gable on a blackboard; now calling for someone to come up and try on some ancient armour, then giving measured details of medieval houses; then thanking God that there were no Radicals in those days. (Adkins, 4–5)

Dryden died at Canons Ashby House on 24 July 1899 after succumbing to septicaemia from gangrene of his right leg, which he had scratched three months earlier while working on the estate. His brother, Sir Alfred Erasmus Dryden (1821–1912), succeeded him as baronet. Sir Henry's only child from his marriage on 24 January 1865 to Frances (1825–1899), eldest daughter of the Revd Robert Tredcroft, prebendary of Chichester and rector of Tangmere, Sussex, was **Alice Dryden** (1866–1956), historian, who was born at Canons Ashby on 3 August 1866. She left the area shortly after her father's death and married John Marcon (*d.* 1928) on 6 April 1913, eventually settling in Oxford, where she died on 4 February 1956 at 7 Hamilton Road.

Alice inherited her father's sense of service, becoming an earnest worker for the Primrose League and founding the Northamptonshire Home Arts and Industries Association, through which she sought to revive local lacemaking. She also had his bent for historical research, revising Mrs Bury Palliser's *History of Lace* (1902) and compiling a series of county studies, beginning with *Memorials of Old*

Northamptonshire in 1903. Her publication of medieval manuscripts on *The Art of Hunting* (1908) reissued some of Sir Henry's work.   BRIAN DIX

Sources *Northampton Mercury Daily Reporter* (24 July 1899) · *North-ampton Mercury* (28 July 1899) · *Northampton Herald* (29 July 1899) · D. Sargant, 'Sir Henry Dryden, Baronet (1818–1899): a centenary tribute', *Northamptonshire Past & Present*, 52 (1999), 85–7 · J. W. [J. Wake], 'Alice Dryden', *Northamptonshire Past & Present*, 2/3 (1956), 157–9 · T. J. George, *A catalogue of the collection of drawings, plans, notes on churches, houses, and various archaeological matters, made by the late Sir Henry E. L. Dryden, Bart. of Canons Ashby, Northamptonshire, and pre-sented to the corporation of Northampton by Miss Alice Dryden* (1912) · R. J. C. Atkinson, 'Lukis, Dryden and the Carnac megaliths', *To illus-trate the monuments: essays on archaeology presented to Stuart Piggott*, ed. J. V. S. Megaw (1976), 111–24 · Dryden family papers, Northants. RO · W. R. D. Adkins, *Our county: sketches in pen and ink of representa-tive men of Northamptonshire* (1893)

Archives AM Oxf., drawings and plans of megalithic monu-ments · Northampton Central Museum, collection · Northamp-ton Library, drawings, papers, and corresp. · Northants. RO, papers | BL, plans and notes of Broughs, etc., in Scotland, Add. MSS 37329–37335 · Bodl. Oxf., corresp. with Sir Thomas Phillipps and papers · Royal Commission on the Ancient and Historical Monuments of Scotland, Edinburgh, National Monuments Record of Scotland, drawings and plans of churches, mainly in Orkney and Shetland · U. Edin. L., letters to James Halliwell-Phillipps

Likenesses A. Dryden, group portrait, photograph, *c.*1890, Northants. RO; repro. in *Canons Ashby, Northamptonshire*, National Trust handbook (2001), 43 · F. N. Street, oils, 1891, Canons Ashby House, Northamptonshire; repro. in *Canons Ashby, Northampton-shire*, National Trust handbook (2001), 48 · W. B. Shoosmith, pen-and-ink sketch, repro. in Adkins, *Our county*, facing p. 4

Wealth at death £5666 8*s*.: probate, 20 Sept 1899, *CGPLA Eng. & Wales*

Dryden, John (1631–1700), poet, playwright, and critic, was born on 9 August 1631 at Aldwincle, Northampton-shire, the eldest of the fourteen children of Erasmus Dry-den (*c.*1602–1654), son of Sir Erasmus Dryden (1553–1632) of Canons Ashby, and his wife, Mary (*d.* 1676), daughter of the Revd Henry Pickering (1564–1637) of Aldwincle. The family lived in the nearby village of Titchmarsh. Both par-ents were from puritan gentry families who were not well disposed to the king, and the young Dryden was doubtless brought up in a godly environment. No record of his early education survives, but he probably attended the village school.

Education and government service, 1644–1659 It was prob-ably about 1644 that Dryden was sent to Westminster School, famous for the quality of its education under Rich-ard Busby. Here he received a thorough grounding in clas-sical culture which left its mark on his later work: his poetry and criticism show a deep knowledge of, and delight in, Greek and Roman literature. Ovid and Virgil were perhaps his principal companions, but he also prized Horace, Lucretius, and (in later life) Homer. These writers contributed both to his imagery and to his view of the world, and classical translation was the mainstay of his late career. Introducing his version of Persius's third satire in 1692, he recalls translating the poem for a Thurs-day night's exercise while a king's scholar at Westminster (*Works*, 4.293). In due course Dryden entrusted the educa-tion of his sons Charles and John to Busby. Westminster, however, had a strongly royalist and Anglican ethos

John Dryden (1631–1700), by Sir Godfrey Kneller, 1697

which was at variance with the religious temper and polit-ical allegiances of his home. Perhaps Westminster was formative in this sphere too, for there is no indication in his adult life of any puritan sympathies: indeed, *Religio laici* and *The Hind and the Panther* exhibit a strong (and well-informed) antipathy to protestant sects and to the more radical elements of Reformation theology and ecclesio-logy. But if he recoiled from ignorant zeal and violent sect-arianism, he was just as averse to clerical power and venal-ity, and a thread of anti-clerical satire runs through his writing, directed equally at Anglican and at Roman Cath-olic clergy, 'For Priests of all Religions are the same' (*Absa-lom and Achitophel*, l. 99). It was as a Westminster schoolboy in 1649 that he published his first poem, conceitful and somewhat ungainly verses in *Lachrymae musarum*, a memorial volume for Lord Hastings.

From Westminster Dryden proceeded in 1650 to Trinity College, Cambridge, as one of five Westminster scholars; his tutor was John Templer. He presumably followed the usual undergraduate curriculum in the classics, rhetoric, and mathematics, along with biblical study. The ethos of the college at this difficult period was puritan but not fan-atic; the master, Thomas Hill, was a noted preacher and pastor who was also vicar of Dryden's home village of Titchmarsh. But Dryden also had sufficient contact with the Cambridge Platonist divine John Smith to write memorial verses for him. Cambridge in general, and Trin-ity in particular, was a crucible of the new science, but such studies were not expected of undergraduates; per-haps, however, Dryden assimilated enough to stir a lay interest in scientific matters, for *Annus mirabilis* (1667) includes an encomium on the Royal Society, of which he was elected a fellow in 1662 (though it was not long before he was expelled for non-payment of dues). His time at Trinity was marred by an incident in 1652 when he was punished for some unspecified disobedience to the vice-master, but he distinguished himself academically, graduating in February 1654 at the top of the list of Trinity men. His contemporary Robert Creighton recalled that Dryden:

> was reckoned a man of good Parts & Learning while in Coll: he had to his knowledge read over & very well understood all the Greek and Latin Poets: he stayed to take his Batchelors degree; but his head was too roving and active, or what else you'll call it, to confine himself to a College Life; & so he left it & went to London into gayer company, & set up for a Poet. (Trinity College Muniments, 'The great volume of miscellany papers III', no. 42)

Though the college held his place open until April 1655, Dryden did not stay in Cambridge; the death of his father in June 1654 brought new responsibilities, and though he inherited a farm there was insufficient income to make him financially comfortable. At some point, at least by 1657, he joined the civil service of the new protectorate, probably introduced by his cousin Sir Gilbert Pickering, who was Cromwell's lord chamberlain. The record of Cromwell's funeral procession in 1658 shows Dryden walking along with Milton and Marvell as secretaries of the French and Latin tongues. This occasion prompted his first important poem, the *Heroique Stanza's* (printed 1659), which celebrates Cromwell as a strong and intelligent ruler in dignified, sober quatrains, displaying a patriotic rather than a partisan judgement. Unhappily, the poem remained in the memory of readers, and was circulated both in manuscript and in print in the late 1670s and early 1680s to embarrass the Stuart laureate.

Marriage and early literary career, 1660–1667 As the protectorate crumbled, its servants sought other employment, and some rethought their loyalties. In the late 1650s Dryden had received casual work from the bookseller Henry Herringman, probably writing occasional prefaces and advertisements for him. With the restoration of the monarchy Dryden set out to establish a literary career, and greeted the returning king in June 1660 with an accomplished poem *Astraea redux* ('Justice brought back'), which saw Charles II as a second Augustus. It was followed in April 1661 with a poem *To His Sacred Majesty, a Panegyrick on his Coronation*, and in 1662 with new year verses *To my Lord Chancellor*. In these pieces Dryden was courting favour with the new regime, and his change of allegiance would later bring accusations that he was a mere mercenary time-server. Such charges were heard with more frequency and bitterness after 1685, when his conversion to Catholicism, coinciding with the accession of the Catholic James II, made it appear to some that his principles went no deeper than his pocket. Of his shift of allegiance in 1660 Dr Johnson observed that 'if he changed, he changed with the nation' (Johnson, 1.334). *Astraea redux* actually shows strongly held beliefs which were to run through Dryden's later work—a distrust of the easily misled populace, a reverence for kingship, and a faith in the workings of divine providence. The *ex officio* respect for Charles in these early poems deepened as the reign progressed into a regard for his tolerance and an affection for his person, despite the provocation of a salary frequently in arrears, and encouragement which too rarely took tangible form. From 1660 onwards Dryden's writing shows a reverence for the divinely instituted office of kingship, but also with a wry recognition of the failings of its particular incumbents; indeed, in *Absalom and Achitophel* he cannot restrain his Chaucerian sense of the comic disparity of man and image.

It was probably in 1660 that Dryden began lodging in London with Sir Robert Howard, son of the earl of Berkshire, and in that year he contributed commendatory verses to Howard's *Poems*. Soon the bond became closer, for on 1 December 1663 Dryden married Howard's sister, Lady Elizabeth (*c*.1638–1714). The marriage lasted until his death, but there is little evidence about how they lived as a couple. There were three sons: Charles, John, and Erasmus-Henry [*see below*]. It is possible that Elizabeth was a Roman Catholic, and likely that his sons' conversion preceded Dryden's own. The only sexual scandal which attached to Dryden was the belief (probably true) that the actress Anne Reeves was his mistress in the 1670s. Satires such as Rochester's *An Allusion to Horace* and the anonymous *The Medal of John Bayes* represent Dryden making obscene boasts in an attempt to demonstrate his libertine credentials, but such behaviour would seem forced and out of character. He was no libertine, in a milieu where such behaviour was routine. Some poems (such as his late verses to his cousin John Driden of Chesterton) make barbed references to the pains of marriage, but we do not know whether they have any autobiographical resonance.

Though his literary career began with poetry, it was in the theatre that Dryden established his profession. His first play, *The Wild Gallant*, was staged at the Theatre Royal on 5 February 1663, and then at court on 23 February, probably through the influence of the king's mistress Lady Castlemaine, to whom Dryden wrote some grateful verses. But Dryden's naïvety in matters of dissipation was apparent, and Pepys commented that:

> it was ill acted and the play so poor a thing as I never saw in my life almost, and so little answering the name, that from beginning to end I could not, nor can at this time, tell certainly which was the wild gallant.   (Pepys, 23 Feb 1663)

A second play, the tragi-comedy *The Rival Ladies*, was performed in late 1663 or early 1664. *The Indian Queen*, written jointly with Howard, was the first of Dryden's ventures into heroic drama, a form in which he was to gain success, though he eventually tired of its posturing and inflated rhetoric. Its first recorded performance was on 25 January 1664, in the presence of the king. Its sequel, *The Indian Emperour*, Dryden's unaided work, was performed early in 1665 (published 1667).

When the plague struck London in 1665, and the theatres closed, Dryden retired to the country, to his father-in-law's estate at Charlton in Wiltshire. It was there that his first son was born, and there that he wrote a new play, *Secret Love*, and two major works, the essay *Of Dramatick Poesie* and the poem *Annus mirabilis*. When he returned to London late in 1666 or early in 1667, these works marked him out as a major force in the new Restoration culture.

Drama and the laureateship, 1667–1680 *Annus mirabilis: the Year of Wonders, MDCLXVI*, published in January 1667, addressed two events from 1666 which puritan oppositional voices had represented as signs of divine displeasure at Charles's government and morals: the inglorious Second Anglo-Dutch War, and the fire of London. Dryden saw these as testimony to individual heroism, the king's care for his people, and divine providence; and although a late metaphysical wit animates the poem, sometimes producing extravagant images, it does not gloss over the human suffering. Simultaneously, in his dialogic essay *Of Dramatick Poesie* (1668), Dryden explored the theory and practice of drama, using four fictional characters (based on the earl of Dorset, Sir Charles Sedley, Sir Robert Howard, and Dryden himself) who debate the relative merits of Renaissance and modern playwrights, of English and French drama, of blank verse and rhyming couplets. The essay is specially notable for its critique of Shakespeare and Jonson (particularly appreciative of the former's rare natural abilities), and for Dryden's evident desire that the Restoration stage should lead a cultural renaissance in England.

Dryden was committed now to the drama as his principal literary medium, and his main source of income. Three plays were premièred in 1667: the tragi-comedy *Secret Love* in March (published 1668) and the comedy *Sir Martin Mar-All* on 15 August (published 1668), and on 7 November the adaptation of *The Tempest* which he had written with Sir William Davenant (published 1670): here Miranda, the girl who has never seen a young man, is provided with a male counterpart, Hippolito, who has had an equally sheltered upbringing. Double recognition of Dryden's status came in spring 1668. First, he signed a contract with the King's Company to write three plays a year in return for a share of the profits; and although he never kept up the promised rate of production, his work was a mainstay of the company until it foundered in 1682. Secondly, on 13 April he was appointed poet laureate; appointment as historiographer royal followed on 18 August 1670. But events in 1668 also showed that this eminence was not without its detractors. Howard attacked Dryden's views on rhyme in his preface to *The Duke of Lerma*, while Shadwell used his preface to *The Sullen Lovers* to inveigh against Dryden's criticism of Jonson. Dryden replied in 'A Defence of an Essay of Dramatique Poesie' prefixed to the second edition of *The Indian Emperour* (September 1668), but the debate with Shadwell was destined to run on through a series of prefaces, dedications, prologues, and epilogues, in which the two writers debated with somewhat acerbic politeness the reputation of Jonson, charges of plagiarism, and the question whether comedy should primarily instruct or please. Matters came to a head in *Mac Flecknoe* (1676).

Meanwhile, Dryden was turning to the heroic drama, and particularly to scenarios which allowed him to explore personal dilemmas of passion and duty within the larger context of the clash of cultures and ideologies. Questions of fate and free will often trouble his characters, and many of their speeches have an outlook and idiom influenced by Hobbes. *Tyrannick Love* (staged June 1669, printed 1670) shows St Catharine disputing with the Roman emperor Maximin, while Moors and Spaniards meet in the two-part play *The Conquest of Granada* (staged December 1670–January 1671, printed 1672). And Dryden still kept his company supplied with comedies of wit and love, competent pieces, albeit lacking the sparkle and social penetration of Etherege or Wycherley at their best: *An Evening's Love* (staged 12 June 1668, printed 1671); *Marriage à-la-mode* (staged November 1671, printed 1673), probably his best comedy; and *The Assignation* (staged 1672, printed 1673). Often the songs from these plays enjoyed an independent life in manuscript circulation and in musical miscellanies. The jingoistic play *Amboyna* (staged and printed 1673) seemed designed to inflame anti-Dutch opinion during the Third Anglo-Dutch War. On 25 January 1672 the Theatre Royal was destroyed by fire, and the company had to move into temporary quarters. Dryden wrote a prologue for the occasion, which appropriately featured a revival of *Wit without Money* by Beaumont and Fletcher. He became a master of the occasional prologue, renowned for pieces which engaged in a witty, bantering rapport with the audience, sometimes flattering, sometimes insulting them, cajoling them into indulging a new playwright or (in the 1680s) supporting a beleaguered king. Southerne told Pope that Dryden:

> was so famous for his Prologues, that the players would act nothing without that decoration. His usual price till then had been four guineas: But when Southern came to him for the Prologue he had bespoke, Dryden told him he must have six guineas for it, 'which (said he) young man, is out of no disrespect to you, but the Players have had my goods too cheap'. (*Works of Alexander Pope*, 6.810)

A series of prologues for the King's Company on their summer tours to Oxford courted that audience by appealing to their superior critical faculties. 'How easy 'tis to passe any thing upon an University', Dryden remarked to Rochester, 'and how grosse flattery the learned will endure' (*Letters*, 10).

Others were less easily courted, including Rochester himself. Dryden had dedicated *Marriage à-la-mode* to the earl in 1673, but in 'An Allusion to Horace' (circulated in manuscript *c*.1675) Rochester mixed crude spite with some shrewd criticism of Dryden's willingness to pander to an audience. Dryden's reply was in studiously general terms, though with unmistakable reference to Rochester, in the 'Preface' to *All for Love* (1678), where he comments on the affectation of some courtiers who aspire to be poets and judges of poetry but do not have the talent, and merely make fools of themselves. The duke of Buckingham used Dryden as the principal model for the playwright satirized as Mr Bayes in his play *The Rehearsal* (staged 1671), while a series of pamphlets in 1673 mounted an extended criticism of Dryden's plays and poems, deriding his style. Public attacks dogged Dryden throughout his career. The altercations with Shadwell rumbled on; his political interventions on the king's side in the exclusion crisis brought many versified rejoinders; and his conversion to Catholicism in 1685 prompted further abuse and satire. There are several hundred contemporary works in prose and verse, both manuscript and print, which praise or vilify him on literary, political, or religious grounds. Very rarely did Dryden respond in kind, though the provocation was extreme. His career was supported by powerful (but not always loyal) patrons, as can be seen from the dedications which he attached to his plays: Mulgrave aided him for a while; Dorset was a more consistent patron, whose support became invaluable after the revolution in 1689.

The new Theatre Royal opened in Drury Lane in 1674, and it was partly to take advantage of the improved facilities that Dryden composed a rhymed dramatic adaptation of *Paradise Lost*, which he called *The State of Innocence: an Opera*. He had visited Milton to obtain the blind poet's permission, and according to Aubrey 'Milton recieved him civilly, & told him he would give him leave to tagge his Verses' (French, 5.46). (Tags were metal ornaments attached to the ends of ribbons.) The opera focuses on the choices made by Adam and Eve, exploring their decisions in a vocabulary influenced by libertine philosophy. But even the new house did not have the financial resources for the spectacular scenery and effects required, and the play was never staged. It did, however, have an extensive circulation in manuscript, and once it reached print in 1677 it went through nine editions by 1700, easily outselling Milton's own poem. Dryden's interest in his erstwhile colleague did not end there: over the years his poetry engaged extensively with Milton's verse, and particularly with *Paradise Lost*. Miltonic echoes shape the quasi-heroic satire of *Mac Flecknoe* and *Absalom and Achitophel*, while many of Dryden's original poems and translations deploy Miltonic phrasing, especially when addressing topics of love and freedom. Only Virgil is a more pervasive imaginative presence.

July 1676 saw the publication of Shadwell's play *The Virtuoso*, with a 'Dedication' which implicitly attacked Dryden. This seems to have been the last straw, the final insult which stirred Dryden into what was for him a novel form, the verse lampoon. *Mac Flecknoe* derides Shadwell's claim to be the legitimate successor to Ben Jonson by casting him instead as the heir of the prolifically dull poet and dramatist Richard Flecknoe, master of trivia and of self-importance, who

> In Prose and Verse, was own'd, without dispute
> Through all the Realms of *Non-sense*, absolute.
> (ll. 5–6)

Flecknoe, on the verge of retirement, hands over his kingdom of dullness to the only fitting successor, Shadwell. Witty, richly allusive to contemporary drama, and magnificently imaginative in its mock enthronement of this new king of dullness, the poem had a lasting impact on Shadwell's image. At first confined to manuscript circulation for a privileged readership, it appeared in a pirated printed edition in 1682, and in an authorized (though anonymous) text in the Dryden–Tonson *Miscellany Poems* of 1684. Dryden did not acknowledge his authorship publicly until 1692; by then Shadwell's reputation as a serious dramatist had been permanently damaged.

Dryden's own career as a writer of heroic plays was drawing to a close: the form was becoming dated, though in *Aureng-Zebe* (staged 17 November 1675, printed 1676) he achieved his most powerful play to date, one which combined the dilemmas of love and honour with philosophical reflections informed by Dryden's study of Epicurean thought, in particular of Lucretius. In one especially powerful speech, Aureng-Zebe reflects on man's capacity for self-deception:

> When I consider Life, 'tis all a cheat;
> Yet, fool'd with hope, men favour the deceit;
> Trust on, and think to morrow will repay;
> To morrow's falser than the former day;
> Lies worse; and while it says, We shall be blest
> With some new joys, cuts off what we possess.
> (IV.i.33–8)

It was his final, and finest, rhymed play, though in the 'Dedication' to the earl of Mulgrave he voiced a weariness with the form, and with the theatre itself: 'I desire to be no longer the *Sisyphus* of the Stage ... I never thought my self very fit for an Employment, where many of my Predecessors have excell'd me in all kinds', and he expressed a wish to 'make the world some part of amends, for many ill Playes, by an Heroique Poem' (*Works*, 12.154). But the epic never materialized, and the theatre still provided both an income and an artistic challenge. In *All for Love, or, The World Well Lost* (staged December 1677, printed 1678) he turned to blank verse, conscious that he was testing himself against an earlier master in this neoclassical treatment of the Antony and Cleopatra story. Clearer in design than Shakespeare's play, it concentrates more sharply on the final dilemma of Antony, torn between Rome, martial and marital duties, and masculine friendship on the one hand, and his love for Cleopatra on the other. The relationship has apparently already ended when the play opens, and much of the mood is retrospective and elegiac:

> While within your arms I lay,
> The World fell mouldring from my hands each hour.
> (II.i.295–6)

It is unfairly criticized by comparison with Shakespeare's version, for in its own terms it is eminently eloquent, moving, and (as revivals repeatedly attest) dramatic.

Less edifying plays followed: a comedy called *The Kind Keeper, or, Mr Limberham* (premièred 11 March 1678) was stopped after three performances, apparently because its satire of contemporary sexual behaviour offended; it is possible that recognizable individuals were (or were thought to be) represented. Since the text was revised before its publication in 1679 (dated 1680) it is impossible to be certain what the problem was. It was followed by a turgid *Oedipus*, co-authored with Lee (staged autumn 1678, printed 1679), and a rewriting of Shakespeare's *Troilus and*

Cressida (staged and printed 1679), which made it into a more regular tragedy. Prefixed to *Troilus and Cressida* when it was printed was an important essay entitled 'The grounds of criticism in tragedy', which included critical reflections on Shakespeare's language.

It was on 18 December 1679 that hostility to Dryden took physical form when he was attacked and badly injured by thugs in Rose Alley, near Covent Garden. It was clearly an organized revenge, and was almost certainly prompted by the manuscript circulation of *An Essay upon Satire*, in which various prominent figures (including the king, his mistresses, Rochester, and Dorset) were crudely vilified. The poem was attributed by some contemporaries to Dryden, by others to Mulgrave; its authorship has never been convincingly established, though the stylistic banality of all but occasional lines makes an attribution to Dryden difficult to sustain; nor is it clear why a professional writer, and poet laureate, would risk his reputation and livelihood by outraging his patrons. If he did sharpen a few of Mulgrave's couplets, he soon found the blows returned with interest.

Though *Troilus and Cressida* was far from being Dryden's most important play, its publication in 1679 marked a turning point in his career, for it was the first of his works to be handled by the young bookseller Jacob Tonson. Previously most of Dryden's poems and plays had been issued by Herringman, but Tonson was ambitious to establish himself as the leading literary publisher, and the partnership which he forged with Dryden would take both their careers into new territory. Their relationship bore fruit in 1680 with the publication of *Ovid's Epistles*, a translation of the *Heroides* by several hands, to which Dryden contributed three epistles and an influential critical preface on the art of translation. This distinguished three modes of translation: metaphrase, or a word-for-word rendering, which may be literally faithful but loses the life of the original; imitation, in which the original provides only a template for a new poem, which often transplants the work into a modern setting; and a mid-way between these two extremes which Dryden himself thinks the most acceptable method, attending not only to the words but also to the distinctive voice and spirit of the original poet. Dryden and Tonson were to collaborate on the series of *Miscellany Poems* (1684 onwards), and on notable collected translations from the classics by various writers whom Dryden would often be instrumental in recruiting from among his Cambridge connections, and from young writers such as Addison, Congreve, Duke, and Garth, whose careers he aided.

Polemical writings and translations, 1681–1685 Dryden's career—like so much else in English life—was profoundly affected by the Popish Plot (1678–9) and exclusion crisis (1680–83). The development of *ad hoc* or *ad hominem* factions into political parties effected a polarization of the political landscape, and compelled men to declare allegiances. Though his comedy *The Spanish Fryar* (staged November 1680, printed 1681) was not overtly political, its

anti-Catholic satire appealed to the times. Dryden's prologues and epilogues became more partisan as he engaged himself on the king's side and against the whigs. In June 1681 he published *His Majesties Declaration Defended*, while in November 1681 there appeared *Absalom and Achitophel*, now his most famous poem. It was timed to coincide with the trial of the earl of Shaftesbury on a charge of treason, with the aim of affecting public opinion. This satire casts contemporary politicians as biblical figures, and in particular represents Charles as the sensual but godlike and potentially merciful David, Shaftesbury as the scheming Achitophel, and Monmouth as the errant but not yet doomed Absalom; Titus Oates appears as the physically grotesque and manipulative Corah. The poem captivated contemporaries by its vivid characters, epigrammatic wit, and heady mixture of biblical, Miltonic, and classical language. Among the most memorable passages is the characterization of Zimri (the duke of Buckingham) as

> A man so various, that he seem'd to be
> Not one, but all Mankinds Epitome.
> Stiff in opinions, always in the wrong;
> Was every thing by starts, and nothing long:
> But, in the course of one revolving Moon,
> Was Chymist, Fidler, States-Man, and Buffoon.
> (ll. 545–50)

While sharing some features with the rough and scurrilous lampoons which were the common currency of the coffee houses, this poem has a nobility of imagination and precision of language which transcended its original milieu and left its stamp on later literature. Though published anonymously, its authorship was quickly known, and Dryden became the target of many rejoinders. A second part, written mainly by Tate but with a long passage by Dryden (notably on Shadwell and Settle) appeared a year later. In March 1682 the comparatively generous-spirited satire of *Absalom and Achitophel* was followed by *The Medall*, a more personal and vituperative satire on Shaftesbury, which took its title from the medal struck to celebrate Shaftesbury's acquittal. This too brought replies, including a vicious piece of character assassination called *The Medal of John Bayes*, perhaps penned by Shadwell. Nor was this the end of Dryden's polemical writing: *The Duke of Guise*, a play written jointly with Lee, was ready for performance in July 1682, but was banned by the lord chamberlain because its presentation of French history was too palpably a parallel with contemporary events, particularly in its reflections on Monmouth. By 28 November the tide had turned sufficiently in favour of the king's party for the play to be staged. It would be his last play for seven years.

In November 1682 there appeared a poem which must have surprised contemporaries, for it marked a distinct departure in Dryden's career. Though his plays had often shown an informed interest in religious and philosophical questions, in *Religio laici* Dryden produced a versified theological argument, a statement of a 'layman's faith' which presented a plea for rational Anglicanism against various positions which threatened this *via media*: against deism, with its over-reliance upon reason; against the wilder excesses of nonconformity, with its irrational enthusiasm and exaltation of the private spirit; and against Catholicism, with its subordination of the private judgement to the unwarranted authority of popes and councils.

> Dim, as the borrow'd beams of Moon and Stars
> To *lonely, weary, wandring* travellers,
> Is *Reason* to the *Soul*

the poem begins. Reason has to give way to supernatural revelation, and the private judgement to tradition and legitimate authority, for '*Common quiet is Mankind's concern*' (l. 450). Carefully researched and lucidly argued, this poem made Dryden's claim to be a serious didactic poet, not just a journalist in verse, however witty.

It was in the early 1680s, after *Ovid's Epistles*, that Dryden's commitment to the art of translation became apparent. His office as historiographer royal was no empty title, for his interest in historiography was wide-ranging. His version of Maimbourg's *History of the League* (1684) no doubt developed in tandem with work on *The Duke of Guise*, and his 'Life of Plutarch' was prefixed to the first volume of Tonson's collaborative version of *Plutarchs Lives* (1683–6). More indicative of the centrality of translation to his later poetry and philosophy are his revision of *The Art of Poetry* (1683), Sir William Soame's translation of Boileau, his poem in praise of Roscommon's *An Essay on Translated Verse* (1684), and his memorial verses in John Oldham's *Remains* (1684), the last ranking among the finest elegies in the language. In these lines Dryden praises the vigour of Oldham's satire, excuses its roughness, and hails him as the Marcellus of English poetry, Augustus's designated heir snatched away by premature death. A wholly classical vision animates the poem's closing lines:

> Once more, hail and farewel; farewel thou young
> But ah too short, *Marcellus* of our Tongue;
> Thy brows with Ivy, and with Laurels bound;
> But Fate and gloomy Night encompass thee around.
> (ll. 22–5)

Here Dryden showed that he was thinking profoundly about how a Restoration poet might use classical allusion, adaptation, and translation to create a new classical poetry in English. It was in these years that he turned over in his mind a scheme for an epic poem (on either King Arthur or the Black Prince) which would be an extended compliment to the Stuart line. Charles II encouraged him, short of actually providing the money which would enable the poem to be written. As Dryden recalled in 1692, 'being encourag'd only with fair Words, by King *Charles* II, my little Sallary ill paid, and no prospect of a future Subsistance, I was then Discourag'd in the beginning of my Attempt' (*Works*, 4.23). Instead, Dryden's epic ambitions, and his hard, often pained thinking about empire and its loss, would be realized in his translation of the *Aeneid* in 1697.

Meanwhile, other aspects of Roman literature caught his imagination, and the inaugural volume of the Dryden–Tonson *Miscellany Poems* (1684) included his translations from Virgil's *Eclogues*, to be followed in 1685 by substantial contributions to the second miscellany, *Sylvae*.

These comprised selections from Virgil's *Aeneid*, including the poignant episode of the young friends Nisus and Euryalus, from Theocritus's *Idylls*, from Lucretius, and from Horace. Out of *De rerum natura* Dryden translated long passages on the disturbance caused to man's equanimity by the fear of death and the power of love, showing an imaginative engagement with Lucretius's Epicurean philosophy. From Horace he chose several odes urging self-possession in the face of Fortune, and *Epode* 2, which he rendered with an obvious relish for the country life which Horace praises. These are among his most eloquent works. A critical preface to the volume provided readers with a poetic and philosophical evaluation of these four writers, an example of the comparative criticism which increasingly featured in the prefatory essays to Dryden's translations.

Though he had abandoned the commercial theatre, Dryden had not ceased to be interested in new developments on the stage, and in 1684 he drafted an ambitious operatic project on the subject of King Arthur. Only its prologue was brought to fruition as the masque-like *Albion and Albanius*, performed before Charles II in late 1684, and revised after the king's death for public performance at the Dorset Garden Theatre on 3 June 1685 (printed the same year). The music by Louis Grabu was not well received, but this did not deter Dryden from collaborating subsequently with Henry Purcell.

Conversion to Catholicism, 1685–1688 When *Sylvae* was published in January 1685, a profound change was happening in Dryden's religious thinking. His serious reflections on mortality, and on the use of his time and talents, which in various ways animated 'To the Memory of Mr Oldham' and the translations from Lucretius and Horace, show a poet engaged with spiritual matters at a more intimate level than the reasoned polemic exhibited in *Religio laici*. Although Dryden's conversion to Catholicism cannot be dated precisely, it was in or just before 1685; on 19 January 1686 John Evelyn noted sourly in his *Diary* that '*Dryden* the famous play-poet & his two sonns, & Mrs. *Nelle* [Gwyn] (Misse to the late … [King]) were said to go to Masse; & such purchases were no great losse to the Church.' Evelyn's language suggests that he thought there was something frivolous ('play-poet') and even mercenary ('purchases') about Dryden's attitude to religion, and many contemporaries agreed, penning satires which denounced him as a renegade and time-server. His master Charles II had died on 6 February 1685, converting (or acknowledging an earlier secret conversion) to Catholicism on his deathbed, and had been succeeded by his openly Catholic brother James. In his pindaric ode *Threnodia Augustalis* (1685), Dryden mourned the king who had brought the nation a good measure of peace and healing, and looked to his successor to add martial success to his brother's achievements. (Prophecy was not Dryden's forte.) The motives for Dryden's conversion are unclear; the move certainly appeared expedient politically, but only if he thought that the new reign would be long-lasting and that Catholicism would flourish under James. In fact, Dryden was one of many Catholics who thought that the new king's rapid (and sometimes illegal) promotion of Catholics to public office was rash and counter-productive. Moreover, if Dryden were really just a turncoat, he could have shifted political and religious allegiances again in 1689, whereas his adherence to Catholicism and the Jacobite cause was maintained at considerable cost and some risk.

Dryden had been buying religious and philosophical works (including Catholic theology and polemic) at book auctions in the early 1680s, and whatever the spiritual and emotional causes of his conversion, intellectual reasons certainly played their part. His own writing soon showed his new commitment: *A Defence of the Papers* (1686) argued for the authenticity of papers on Catholicism attributed to Charles II and to Anne Hyde, late duchess of York. A translation of Bouhours's life of St Francis Xavier (1688) extolled the Jesuit missionary. In June 1688, just months before the revolution, Dryden celebrated the birth of the new Catholic heir in *Britannia rediviva*, heralding a new period of Catholic and Stuart governance. His poetry seems now to have been rededicated to more moral and spiritual ends. In his memorial verses for the poet and painter Anne Killigrew (1685) he exclaimed:

> O Gracious God! How far have we
> Prophan'd thy Heav'nly Gift of Poesy?
> Made prostitute and profligate the Muse,
> Debas'd to each obscene and impious use,
> Whose Harmony was first ordain'd Above
> For Tongues of Angels, and for Hymns of Love?
> (ll. 56–61)

Eleonora (1692), meanwhile, is an extended eulogy of practical piety and charity.

But Dryden's major Catholic work was *The Hind and the Panther* (1687), an allegorical poem in which the spotless white Hind (representing the Church of Rome) engages the beautiful but dangerous Panther (the Church of England) in theological discussion about the nature of the true church, the authority of tradition, and the need for individual reason to subordinate itself to pope and councils, thus reversing the position adopted in *Religio laici*. Shared with the earlier poem, however, is a decided distrust of protestant sects, described here under the symbolism of wolves, bears, boars, and other animals. The poem shows strong imaginative and ratiocinative powers, and a clear grasp of contemporary apologetics on both sides, along with a gift for dialogue and a willingness to include theological and political criticism of Catholicism. One passage reveals a rarely seen visionary side to Dryden:

> Thy throne is darkness in th' abyss of light,
> A blaze of glory that forbids the sight
> (pt 1, ll. 66–7)

and leads into autobiographical lines which present him as the repentant prodigal son:

> My thoughtless youth was wing'd with vain desires,
> My manhood, long misled by wandering fires,
> Follow'd false lights; and when their glimps was gone,
> My pride struck out new sparkles of her own.
> (pt 1, ll. 72–5)

The scepticism of Dryden's earlier works has given way to an embrace of Rome as the longed-for 'unerring Guide' (pt

1, l. 65). But the essential incongruity of the allegory prompted the derision of many contemporaries, and the rapid change of political events stranded the poem on the wrong side of what would soon become a decisive ideological and historical watershed.

Post-revolutionary writings, 1689–1700 After the flight of James II from England in December 1688, and the accession of William and Mary in the following month, Dryden found himself in difficulty, and even in danger. As a Catholic convert he risked, at worst, prosecution for treason; at best, double taxation and restrictions on his movement. Unable to take the oath of allegiance to the new sovereigns, he lost his offices as poet laureate and historiographer royal. Gallingly, he was succeeded by Shadwell, whose whig credentials appealed to the new regime. Though the laureateship had never brought in a steady income under Charles, James was a more regular paymaster, and the loss of this support brought severe financial problems for Dryden. His solution was to return to the theatre, for which he had last written in 1682. His first new play was the tragedy *Don Sebastian* (staged 4 December 1689, printed 1690), a powerful drama whose themes of friendship, loyalty, true kingship, and love thwarted by destiny carried contemporary resonances. Dryden was treading carefully, not concealing his opinions and principles, but working primarily through indirections and implications. In dedicating the printed play to the earl of Leicester, he reflected on how the truly happy man is he 'who centring on himself, remains immovable, and smiles at the madness of the dance about him' (*Works*, 15.60); but in associating himself in the same pages with Cicero, whose head and hands were nailed to the rostrum after a Roman revolution, he shows how difficult such equanimity was in the circumstances which now prevailed.

More outspoken was the prologue which Dryden provided in May 1689 for a revival of Beaumont and Fletcher's *The Prophetess*, which glanced sarcastically at William III's expedition to Ireland, and was immediately suppressed. It circulated widely in manuscript, however. Less controversial was his second play under the new order, the comedy *Amphitryon* (staged and printed October 1690). Then Dryden turned to refurbishing old material: *King Arthur* (staged May or June 1691, and immediately printed) had its origins in the end of Charles II's reign in the project which produced *Albion and Albanius*. Now he presented it as an opera with music by Purcell. The two men had a strong mutual regard: Purcell supplied music for revivals of several plays by Dryden, including *The Indian Queen*, and Dryden drafted a preface for Purcell when his music for *The Prophetess* was printed in 1691. When Purcell died in 1695 Dryden published an eloquent memorial ode. Dryden's interest in music is evident not only in his accomplished songs, but also in his two contributions to the St Cecilia's day festival, *A Song for St Cecilia's Day, 1687* and *Alexander's Feast, or, The Power of Musique* (1697), the latter being perhaps his single most admired poem through the eighteenth century.

In the 1690s Dryden's health was often indifferent

(though he still enjoyed visits to his relatives in North-amptonshire) and he had to enlist the help of Thomas Southerne to complete his play *Cleomenes* (staged April 1692, printed the following month). The association with Southerne was one of several professional friendships through which Dryden encouraged the work of younger writers. For Southerne he supplied commendatory verses to *The Wives' Excuse* (1692), while Southerne complimented Dryden in verses prefixed to Congreve's *The Double Dealer* (1693, dated 1694). Dryden also contributed a poem to the same volume, in which he hailed Congreve as his succes-sor, and in the 'Dedication' to *Examen poeticum* (1693) he specially commended Congreve's abilities as a translator of Homer. Congreve would act as an honest broker between Dryden and Tonson in negotiating the contract for the translation of Virgil, and would check Dryden's work on the *Aeneid* against the Latin. Other friendships marked in verse letters were those with Sir George Ether-ege and Sir Godfrey Kneller. Kneller would paint two por-traits of Dryden (now in the National Portrait Gallery and Trinity College, Cambridge), and Dryden's own interest in the visual arts is clear not only in the images from paint-ing and architecture in his poetry, but also in his transla-tion of Du Fresnoy's *De arte graphica* (1695). Presiding at Will's Coffee House, Dryden was the dominant figure in the London world of arts and letters.

If the drama was one means of continuing his career, translation was the other, and here the collaboration with Tonson bore fruit in remarkable ways. The two earlier vol-umes of miscellanies were followed by a third, *Examen poeticum*, to which Dryden contributed translations from Ovid's *Metamorphoses* and Homer's *Iliad*, and a preface which includes some outspoken (if generalized) com-ments on the corruption of governments. But important as these translations were in their own right, they were overshadowed by the more systematic projects which the two men also had in hand. In October 1692 Tonson pub-lished *The Satires of Decimus Junius Juvenalis … [and] Aulus Per-sius Flaccus* (dated 1693), which assembled a complete translation of Juvenal's satires by various hands (numbers 1, 3, 6, 10, and 16 being by Dryden himself, 7 by his son Charles, and 14 by his son John), a complete translation of Persius by Dryden alone, and a substantial preface, the 'Discourse concerning the original and progress of satire', in which Dryden presented a history of the genre, a cri-tique of its principal Latin practitioners, and reflections on its modern use. While these were translations rather than imitations, and generally preserved the original Roman allusions, there are a number of turns of phrase which reflect satirically on William III. Doubtless both the tragic pessimism of Juvenal's tenth satire, and Persius's Stoicism in the face of Neronian terror, had a contempor-ary resonance for him. No reader of Juvenal's third satire could avoid hearing the translator's voice in these lines:

> Since Noble Arts in *Rome* have no support,
> And ragged Virtue not a friend at Court,
> No Profit rises from th' ungrateful Stage,
> My Poverty encreasing with my Age,

> 'Tis time to give my just Disdain a vent,
> And, Cursing, leave so base a Government.
> (ll. 39–44)

The tragi-comedy *Love Triumphant* (staged January 1694, published March) was Dryden's final work for the stage: on 15 June that year he signed a contract with Tonson to translate the whole of the works of Virgil, and the task was to occupy him for more than three years. *The Works of Virgil* (1697) was in many respects a remarkable undertak-ing, especially for a man in indifferent health, conscious of his advancing age: he was reported to be suffering from brain cancer as he worked on it. Artistically, and in its sheer length, it was an extraordinary challenge, but it pro-vided Dryden with much attractive material, even if he eventually came to think Homer more congenial. The *Georgics*, with their technical discussions of agriculture and their vision of the rural cycle, appealed to Dryden the countryman: the precision of his vocabulary here, and the imaginative empathy which he brings to the farmer's life, are much underrated. And the *Aeneid* taxed him with its range of heroic incident, strong emotion, and vivid visual imagination. Though often raiding his predecessors for happy turns of phrase or useful interpretations, Dryden's translation is a masterpiece which rarely flags, and often rises to heights of eloquence and tragic reflection. Into this text Dryden poured his feelings about exile, the loss of empire and the cost of creating it anew, the wasting of young talent, and dreams of restoration, without making his translation simply a Jacobite allegory. Commercially, too, it was a bold venture, for Tonson developed the arrangement which he had pioneered successfully with his 1688 *Paradise Lost*, and published the work by subscrip-tion. Patrons who subscribed 5 guineas had their titles and arms engraved on one of the 101 plates reused from Ogilby's Virgil, while the 2 guinea subscribers were listed in the preliminaries. Though Dryden resisted Tonson's plan to dedicate the work to William III, it was truly a cross-section of the nation which lent its support, for the list reveals backing from people of various political per-suasions, professions, and social classes. Some gave sup-port in kind, by lending him books and providing hospi-tality in quiet country houses where he could write undis-turbed. The work was widely regarded (and not only in England) as a great cultural achievement; soon Dryden was making corrections for a second edition in 1698.

The financial arrangements for the Virgil were not with-out their problems, for neither Dryden nor Tonson thought that the other was delivering exactly what they had agreed. Feathers were ruffled on both sides. But the bond between poet and publisher survived: Dryden trans-lated book 1 of the *Annals* for Tonson's collaborative Taci-tus (1698); on 20 March 1699 he signed a contract for what would be his final work, the *Fables Ancient and Modern*; and in October he was seeking patronage for a complete trans-lation of Homer. *Dis aliter visum*: Dryden's health was fail-ing, and only the first book of the *Iliad* was completed, to be included in the *Fables* in 1700. This collection (prefaced with another example of Dryden's brilliant comparative criticism) assembled versions of Homer, Chaucer, Ovid, and Boccaccio, demonstrating his mastery of diverse voices and tones, his narrative and argumentative skills, his philosophical vision and psychological insight. The Homeric translation catches the brutality of war and rapacious rulers; Ovid and Boccaccio provide opportunities to explore the mind under the stress of passion; while the poems from Chaucer show a gift for gentler ironies. In 'Of the Pythagorean philosophy' (from Ovid's *Metamorphoses* 15) Dryden brings a precise and vivid imagination to this exploration of change in the natural world, and in Theseus's speech at the end of 'Palamon and Arcite' (from Chaucer's 'The Knight's Tale') he interpolates a vision of man's place in a troubled but divinely ordered universe:

> Parts of the Whole are we; but God the Whole;
> Who gives us Life, and animating Soul.
> For Nature cannot from a Part derive
> That Being, which the Whole can only give:
> He perfect, stable; but imperfect We,
> Subject to Change, and diff'rent in Degree ...
> What then remains, but after past Annoy,
> To take the good Vicissitude of Joy?
> To thank the gracious Gods for what they give,
> Possess our Souls, and while we live, to live?
> (pt 3, ll. 1042–7, 1111–14)

Dryden lived long enough to see the *Fables* praised by the town, but died of gangrene on 1 May 1700 (apparently intestate), and was buried the following day in St Anne's Church, Soho. Belatedly, friends and patrons rallied to arrange a more appropriate funeral, for on 13 May he was reburied in Chaucer's grave in Westminster Abbey. There were a few posthumous publications: A 'Secular Masque' for *The Pilgrim* (adapted from Beaumont and Fletcher, 1700), and contributions to more of Tonson's classical translations: *Ovid's Art of Love* (1709), *The Works of Lucian* (1711), and *Ovid's Metamorphoses* (1717). Two volumes of memorial verses, *Luctus Britannici* and *The Nine Muses* (both 1700), attested to his standing, and it is notable that the latter volume was entirely by women admirers.

Character, achievement, and reputation Dryden's œuvre was extraordinarily wide-ranging and varied: only the personal lyric voice was one which he eschewed. His greatest success lay in two areas. The one was topical satire, for *Mac Flecknoe* and *Absalom and Achitophel* effected a metamorphosis of contemporary characters into new guises from which, in the collective memory, they never wholly escaped. The other was the art of translation, to which he came rather late in life. Though he is capable of many tones, and delighted in finding modern voices for originals as diverse as Homer and Chaucer, there is a recurring philosophical thread in these translations, for it was in this medium that Dryden asked his most profound questions—about men and gods, about desire and honour, about fortune, and the mutability of life. He had a conspicuous talent for dialogue, often casting his arguments in the form of debates, whether on critical matters in the essay *Of Dramatick Poesie*, or theological ones in *The Hind and the Panther*. But, paradoxically, he was not a great dramatist, though he wrote some great scenes and some good plays. As a critic he pioneered comparative criticism, and a civilized, conversational prose style, reforming the

syntax of our prose at the same time as he was perfecting the rhyming couplet as the dominant form for English verse, fashioning it into an instrument for argument, giving it a rhythmical variety and tonal range which no one has matched.

After his early service of the protectorate, Dryden was a loyal supporter of the Stuarts, and a believer in the divine right of kings; but he was too intelligent not to see the comic disparity between man and office, and a sense of the absurdity of rulers runs through his work from *Tyrannick Love* to 'The first book of Homer's *Ilias*'. A thoughtful if not a zealous Christian, he was widely read, appreciated the theological complexities and contradictions of his age, and recognized the strength of the alternatives to his own position; indeed, in his translations of Lucretius and Ovid he suspends his own beliefs sufficiently to present his readers with a faithfully imaginative version of classical philosophies. Like his mentor Montaigne, he was both sincere in his convictions, and aware of the fragility of human reason and selfhood: 'As I am a Man, I must be changeable ... An ill dream, or a Cloudy day, has power to change this wretched Creature, who is so proud of a reasonable Soul, and make him think what he thought not yesterday' (*Works*, 12.157). Eventually he grounded his beliefs on the rock of Rome. Loyal in friendship, eager to promote young talent, slow to rise to continual vilification from lesser men, but capable of annihilating satire when roused, he attracted the admiration of spirits such as Congreve, who wrote a shrewd and affectionate memoir of him in 1717:

> He was of a Nature exceedingly Humane and Compassionate; easily forgiving Injuries, and capable of a prompt and sincere reconciliation with them who offended him ... His Friendship, where he profess'd it, went much beyond his Professions; and I have been told of strong and generous Instances of it, by the persons themselves who received them; Tho' his Hereditary Income was little more than a bare Competency. As his reading was very extensive, so was he very happy in a Memory tenacious of every thing that he had read. He was not more possess'd of Knowledge than he was Communicative of it ... He was of very easy, I may say of very pleasing Access: But something slow, and as it were diffident in his Advances to others. He had something in his Nature that abhorr'd Intrusion into any Society whatsoever ... one of the most Modest, and the most Easily to be discountenanc'd, in his Approaches, either to his Superiors, or his Equals ... His Parts did not decline with his Years: But ... he was an improving Writer to his last, even to near seventy Years of Age; improving even in Fire and Imagination, as well as in Judgement. (Kinsley and Kinsley, 264–5)

With some exceptions, Dryden's plays soon faded from the stage, but his poetry and criticism remained influential. His satirical poetry, his odes, and his translations were widely read, admired, and imitated in the eighteenth century, and his influence on Pope was profound and extensive. The first scholarly work on Dryden was Edmond Malone's biography and edition of the prose works (1800). The Romantic poets, especially Coleridge, Keats, and Byron, held him in high esteem, and Sir Walter Scott's magisterial edition of Dryden's works (1808), with a judicious life and learned historical notes, re-established

Dryden for the nineteenth-century public: Tennyson and Hopkins read him attentively. After T. S. Eliot's lukewarm (and perhaps damaging) advocacy, Dryden's standing declined in the twentieth century, since he was regarded principally as a conservative satirist circumscribed by his own historical period, uncongenial to modern critical and political fashions. But recent scholarship has revalued the thoughtfulness and imagination of his political and religious poetry, while the wit and philosophy of his translations are once more being enjoyed.

Charles Dryden (1666–1704), the poet's eldest son, was born on 27 August 1666 at Charlton, his grandfather's estate, and educated at Westminster School and Trinity College, Cambridge. He contributed commendatory Latin verses to Roscommon's *Essay on Translated Verse* (1684) alongside his father's, Latin verses in *Sylvae* (1685), a version of Juvenal's seventh satire to his father's translation (1693), and an English poem to the fourth *Annual Miscellany* (1694). He was in Rome in the 1690s as chamberlain to the pope, returning to England about 1697. He was drowned in the Thames in 1704, and buried at Windsor on 20 August.

John Dryden junior (1668–1701), the poet's second son, was educated at Westminster School and University College, Oxford, under its Catholic master Obadiah Walker. He went to Rome with his brother Charles in the 1690s. He contributed satire 14 to his father's translation of Juvenal, and wrote a comedy *The Husband his Own Cuckold* which was staged and printed in 1696, appearing with a preface and prologue by his father, and an epilogue by Congreve. An account of a tour of Italy and Malta with a Mr Cecil was published in 1776. He died in Rome on 28 January 1701.

Sir Erasmus-Henry Dryden, fifth baronet (1669–1710), the poet's youngest son, was born on 2 May 1669, educated at Charterhouse School and the English College at Douai, and entered the Dominican noviciate in 1692, being ordained priest in 1694. In 1697 he was in Rome, and in the same year was sent to Bornheim, where he was sub-prior of the convent of the Holy Cross until 1700. He then returned to England, where he lived at Canons Ashby, Northamptonshire, a family seat. He inherited a baronetcy on the death of a cousin in 1710, and died soon after, being buried at Canons Ashby on 4 December 1710.

PAUL HAMMOND

Sources The works of John Dryden, ed. E. N. Hooker, H. T. Swedenberg, and V. A. Dearing, 20 vols. (1956–2000) · The poems of John Dryden, ed. P. Hammond, 4 vols. (1995–2000) · The letters of John Dryden, ed. C. E. Ward (1942) · J. A. Winn, John Dryden and his world (1987) · H. Macdonald, John Dryden: a bibliography of early editions and of Drydeniana (1939) · P. Beal and others, Index of English literary manuscripts, ed. P. J. Croft and others, [4 vols. in 11 pts] (1980–), vol. 2, pt 1 · The critical and miscellaneous prose works of John Dryden, ed. E. Malone, 3 vols. (1800) [vol. 1] · S. Johnson, Lives of the English poets, ed. G. B. Hill, [new edn], 3 vols. (1905) · P. Hammond, 'Dryden and Trinity', Review of English Studies, new ser., 36 (1985), 35–57 · P. Hammond and D. Hopkins, eds., John Dryden: tercentenary essays (2000) [incl. contemporary comments] · J. Kinsley and H. Kinsley, eds., Dryden: the critical heritage (1972) · J. M. Osborn, John Dryden: some biographical facts and problems, 2nd edn (1965) · muniments, Trinity Cam. · The medal of John Bayes (1682) · Pepys, Diary · Evelyn, Diary · J. M. French, The life records of John Milton, 5 vols. (1949–58) · The works of Alexander Pope, ed. J. Warburton, 9 vols. (1751) · DNB

Archives BL, agreement with Jacob Tonson for translations for Virgil · Folger, papers · Northants. RO, letter, copy letters, papers | Trinity Cam., muniments

Likenesses oils, c.1662, Bodl. Oxf. · J. Riley, oils, c.1685, Traquair House · W. Faithorne, mezzotint, c.1690 (after J. Closterman), BM, NPG · G. Kneller, oils, 1693, NPG · J. Maubert, oils, c.1695, NPG · G. Kneller, oils, 1697, Trinity Cam. [see illus.] · P. Scheemakers, marble bust, 1731, Westminster Abbey · P. van Gunst, line engraving (after J. Riley, c.1685), BM, NPG; repro. in The works of Virgil, trans. J. Dryden, 3rd edn, 3 vols. (1709) · G. Kneller, oils, second version, NPG · F. Kyte, mezzotint (after J. Closterman), BM, NPG · line engraving (after G. Kneller, 1693), BM; repro. in Luctus Britannici, or, The tears of the British muses (1700)

Dryden, John, junior (1668–1701). *See under* Dryden, John (1631–1700).

Dryland, Alfred (1865–1946), civil engineer, was born at Aldington, near Hythe in Kent, on 2 March 1865, the son of William Dryland, a farmer, and his wife, Sarah, *née* Butcher. The family moved to Surrey, where Dryland was educated at Farnham grammar school. In 1880 he was articled as a civil engineer under Alexander William Conquest, borough surveyor of Folkestone. Dryland became borough surveyor of Deal in 1883. He was still only eighteen years of age and claimed to be the youngest borough surveyor ever appointed in the country. At Deal he carried out extensions to the drainage system and sewer outfalls and also built a sea wall. On 18 April 1885 Dryland married Edith Rose Constance (b. 1861/2), daughter of H. R. Clarke, a magistrate and collector in the Indian Civil Service. They had two sons and one daughter.

After the establishment of county councils Dryland was appointed, in 1890, a divisional surveyor to Kent county council. Allocated to the north-western division adjoining the metropolis, he had specific responsibility for 136 miles of main roads. In 1898 he became county surveyor of Herefordshire, succeeding Henry Titus Wakelam who had become surveyor of Middlesex. He was also engineer and architect to the board of the joint city and county asylum and, with the passing of the Education Act, Dryland was, from 1902, additionally architect to the education committee. He also acted in an advisory capacity to several of the local authorities in regard to their engineering works.

In 1906 Dryland was appointed county surveyor of Wiltshire, which again included the duties of architect to the education and asylum committees. He was chiefly responsible for reorganizing the system of roads and their maintenance, especially in restoring those damaged in the region of Salisbury Plain by the heavy vehicles associated with the large permanent military establishments in an area which had hitherto been primarily agricultural.

Dryland was appointed county surveyor of Surrey in 1908, again supervising the modernization of the system of highway maintenance. The county's roads had suffered quite badly from early motor traffic. In particular he was prominent in introducing a variety of new methods in the surface treatment of roads and developing tarmacadam and subsequently asphalt surfacing. He was the first

Alfred Dryland (1865–1946), by Elliott & Fry

county surveyor to establish his own asphalt plant. It was at this time that he became chairman of a committee set up to investigate routes for a number of arterial roads in the London area. Many existing radial and circular routes are largely due to his foresight and energetic planning.

On the death of H. T. Wakelam in 1920, Dryland was appointed county engineer of Middlesex. In charge of the county's highways department, in addition to the routine work of road maintenance, he also planned a large programme of arterial roads. He was responsible for the construction of the Great West, the Great Cambridge, and the North Circular roads, the Barnet and Watford bypass roads, and the Western Avenue, and many other roads and bridges in the county. The construction of the Great West Road from Chiswick to East Bedfont, which was formally opened by George V in June 1925, was a triumph of modern engineering skill in the face of formidable problems. He gave credit to Wakelam, its designer, in a paper, 'Some general notes on the Great West Road', in the *Journal of the Institution of Municipal and County Engineers* (51, 1924–5, 18–30). As county engineer he was also in charge of the departments dealing with river regulation and licensing. He was engineer to the joint committee of Middlesex and Surrey for new bridges over the Thames at Chiswick and Twickenham, designed by Sir Maxwell Ayrton and Sir Herbert Baker respectively. They, and the Hampton Court Bridge of Lutyens, were all formally opened by the prince

of Wales in July 1933. The west Middlesex main drainage scheme was the result of a report made by him.

In the field of road engineering Dryland was considered the greatest expert in Britain of his day and he was a pioneer in the planning and construction of motorways in this country. He had much experience as a witness, particularly in connection with parliamentary bills, and in legal and arbitration cases with regard to road questions. To study highway problems and traffic conditions elsewhere he visited the United States and Canada and several European countries, and he contributed numerous articles to professional bodies and the technical press on the subject. In road and town planning Dryland also played a prominent part as chairman of a technical committee for three regional schemes in Middlesex and also of a similar committee charged with dealing with the large area within the jurisdiction of the London traffic committee. He was also a member of the engineering advisory committee of the road board until it became merged into the Ministry of Transport in 1921. He was appointed CBE in 1930 and retired in 1932.

Dryland was elected an associate member of the Institution of Civil Engineers in 1891, transferring to full membership in 1911. He was president of the County Surveyors' Society in 1908–9, its honorary secretary and treasurer from 1920 to 1937, and one of its representatives on the County Councils Association. He was president of the Institution of Municipal and County Engineers in 1928–9, having been chairman of the south-eastern district and a long-standing council member. He was also a member of the council of the Institute of Transport and the independent chairman of the British Granite and Whinstone Federation.

In 1932 Dryland was elected a member of the council of the royal borough of Kingston upon Thames and served as mayor of the town for two years from 1935 to 1937. He was an active member of the town council up to the time of his death and served as chairman of its highways committee. In his spare time he enjoyed golf and shooting. Upon returning from London on 26 November 1946 Dryland collapsed outside 26 Wolverton Avenue, off Kingston Hill, Kingston upon Thames, but a short distance from his home in nearby Crescent Road. He died immediately.

ROBERT SHARP

Sources DNB · *Journal of the Institution of Civil Engineers*, 27 (1946–7), 497 · *The Times* (2 Nov 1946), 7e · *Journal of the Institution of Municipal and County Engineers*, 55 (1928), 1–2 · WWW · b. cert. · m. cert. · d. cert.
Likenesses Elliott & Fry, photograph, NPG [*see illus.*] · A. E. Wragge, portrait, priv. coll. · photograph, repro. in *Journal of the Institution of Municipal and County Engineers*, frontispiece
Wealth at death £18,050 5s.: probate, 25 Feb 1947, CGPLA Eng. & Wales

PICTURE CREDITS

DeWint, Peter (1784–1849)—Lincolnshire County Council, Usher Gallery

Dexter, John Henry (1925–1990)—© News International Newspapers Ltd

D'Eyncourt, Charles Tennyson- (1784–1861)—© National Portrait Gallery, London

Diana, princess of Wales (1961–1997)—© Mario Testino

Dibdin, Charles (bap. 1745, d. 1814)—© National Portrait Gallery, London

Dibdin, Thomas Frognall (1776–1847)—© Copyright The British Museum

Dibdin, Thomas John (1771–1841)—Copyright 2004 Museum of Fine Arts, Boston; Abbott Lawrence Fund

Dicey, Albert Venn (1835–1922)—The President and Fellows of Trinity College, Oxford

Dick, Thomas (1774–1857)—Scottish National Portrait Gallery

Dick, Sir William Reid (1879–1961)—© Estate of Sir William Reid Dick; collection National Portrait Gallery, London

Dickens, Charles John Huffam (1812–1870)—© National Portrait Gallery, London

Dickens, Monica Enid (1915–1992)—© Mark Gerson; collection National Portrait Gallery, London

Dickins, Frederick Victor (1838–1915)—Douglas Dickins FRPS

Dickinson, John (1732–1808)—courtesy of the Historical Society of Pennsylvania Collection, Atwater Kent Museum of Philadelphia

Dickinson, John (1815–1876)—© National Portrait Gallery, London

Dickinson, Lowes Cato (1819–1908)—© National Portrait Gallery, London

Dickinson, Thorold Barron (1903–1984)—© Estate of Russell Westwood / National Portrait Gallery, London

Dickinson, William (bap. 1756, d. 1822)—© National Portrait Gallery, London

Dickson, Sir Alexander (1777–1840)—© National Portrait Gallery, London

Diefenbaker, John George (1895–1979)—© National Portrait Gallery, London

Digby, George, second earl of Bristol (1612–1677)—by permission of the Trustees of Dulwich Picture Gallery

Digby, Jane Elizabeth (1807–1881)—© National Portrait Gallery, London

Digby, John, first earl of Bristol (1580–1653)—by courtesy of the National Gallery of Ireland

Digby, Sir Kenelm (1603–1665)—© National Portrait Gallery, London

Diggle, Joseph Robert (1849–1917)—© National Portrait Gallery, London

Dighton, Robert (1751–1814)—© National Portrait Gallery, London

Dilke, Sir Charles Wentworth, second baronet (1843–1911)—© National Portrait Gallery, London

Dilke, Emilia Francis, Lady Dilke (1840–1904)—© National Portrait Gallery, London

Dill, Sir John Greer (1881–1944)—© Karsh / Camera Press; collection National Portrait Gallery, London

Dillenius, Johann Jakob (1687–1747)—© National Portrait Gallery, London

Dillon, Emile Joseph (1854–1933)—National Gallery of Ireland

Dillon, John (1851–1927)—© National Portrait Gallery, London

Dillon, John Blake (1814–1866)—National Gallery of Ireland

Dillwyn, Lewis Llewelyn (1814–1892)—© National Portrait Gallery, London

Dimbleby, Richard Frederick (1913–1965)—© Estate of John Gay; collection National Portrait Gallery, London

Dimsdale, Thomas (1712–1800)—© National Portrait Gallery, London

Dineley, Sir John, fifth baronet (c.1729–1809)—© National Portrait Gallery, London

Dirac, Paul Adrien Maurice (1902–1984)—© National Portrait Gallery, London

Disney, John (1677–1730)—© National Portrait Gallery, London

Disney, John (1746–1816)—© National Portrait Gallery, London

Disraeli, Benjamin, earl of Beaconsfield (1804–1881)—© National Portrait Gallery, London

D'Israeli, Isaac (1766–1848)—National Trust Photographic Library; photograph National Portrait Gallery, London

Disraeli, Mary Anne, Viscountess Beaconsfield (1792–1872)—National Trust Photographic Library / John Hammond

Dixie, Florence Caroline, Lady Dixie (1857–1905)—© National Portrait Gallery, London

Dixon, George (1820–1898)—© National Portrait Gallery, London

Dixon, Joshua (bap. 1743, d. 1825)—reproduced by kind permission of Copeland Borough Council and The Beacon, Whitehaven

Dixon, Sir Owen (1886–1972)—© National Portrait Gallery, London

Dixon, Sir Pierson John (1904–1965)—© National Portrait Gallery, London

Dixon, Richard Watson (1833–1900)—© National Portrait Gallery, London

Dixon, Robert (1614/15–1688)—© National Portrait Gallery, London

Dobbie, Sir William George Shedden (1879–1964)—© National Portrait Gallery, London

Dobbs, Arthur (1689–1765)—Ashmolean Museum, Oxford

Dobell, Bertram (1842–1914)—© National Portrait Gallery, London

Dobell, Sydney Thompson (1824–1874)—© National Portrait Gallery, London

Dobree, Peter Paul (1782–1825)—© Crown copyright. NMR

Dobson, (Henry) Austin (1840–1921)—© National Portrait Gallery, London

Dobson, John (1787–1865)—Tyne and Wear Museums

Dobson, Sir Richard Portway (1914–1993)—© News International Newspapers Ltd

Dobson, Sir Roy Hardy (1891–1968)—© National Portrait Gallery, London

Dobson, William (bap. 1611, d. 1646)—private collection; photograph National Portrait Gallery, London

Dobson, William Charles Thomas (1817–1898)—© National Portrait Gallery, London

Docker, (Frank) Dudley (1862–1944)—© reserved; photograph National Portrait Gallery, London

Dod, Charlotte [Lottie] (1871–1960)—Wimbledon Lawn Tennis Museum (Alan Little)

Dodd, Catherine Isabella (1860–1932)—© National Portrait Gallery, London

Dodd, Francis Edgar (1874–1949)—© Fitzwilliam Museum, University of Cambridge

Dodd, William (1729–1777)—© National Portrait Gallery, London

Dodderidge, Sir John (1555–1628)—Society of Antiquaries of London

Doddridge, Philip (1702–1751)—© National Portrait Gallery, London

Dodds, Eric Robertson (1893–1979)—© National Portrait Gallery, London

Dodgson, Charles Lutwidge [Lewis Carroll] (1832–1898)—© National Portrait Gallery, London

Dodsley, Robert (1704–1764)—by permission of the Trustees of Dulwich Picture Gallery

Dodson, John George, first Baron Monk Bretton (1825–1897)—© National Portrait Gallery, London

Dodsworth, William (1798–1861)—© National Portrait Gallery, London

Dodwell, Henry (1641–1711)—© National Portrait Gallery, London

Doggett, Thomas (c.1670–1721)—Sherborne Castle Estates / Courtauld Institute

Dolben, John (1625–1686)—© National Portrait Gallery, London

Dolben, Sir John, second baronet (1684–1756)—© National Portrait Gallery, London

Dolby, Charlotte Helen Sainton- (1821–1885)—© National Portrait Gallery, London

Dolin, Sir Anton (1904–1983)—V&A Images, The Victoria and Albert Museum

Dollan, Sir Patrick Joseph (1885–1963)—© reserved; Glasgow Museums: Art Gallery & Museum, Kelvingrove

Dolmetsch, (Eugène) Arnold (1858–1940)—© Jenny Letton, administered by Composer Prints Ltd.; collection National Portrait Gallery, London

Domett, Alfred (1811–1887)—Alexander Turnbull Library, National Library of New Zealand, Te Puna Matauranga o Aotearoa

Don, Sir George (1754–1832)—© National Portrait Gallery, London

Donaldson, Arthur William (1901–1993)—courtesy of the Scottish National Party

Donaldson, Frederick Lewis (1860–1953)—© National Portrait Gallery, London

Donat, (Frederick) Robert (1905–1958)—© Estate of Frederick William Daniels; collection National Portrait Gallery, London

Donkin, Sir Rufane Shaw (1773–1841)—© National Portrait Gallery, London

Donne, Sir John (d. 1503)—© The National Gallery, London

Donne, John (1572–1631)—The Royal Collection © 2004 HM Queen Elizabeth II

Donnelly, Desmond Louis (1920–1974)—© National Portrait Gallery, London

Donoghue, Stephen (1884–1945)—© National Portrait Gallery, London

Doo, George Thomas (1800–1886)—© National Portrait Gallery, London

Doolittle, Thomas (1630/1633?–1707)—Ashmolean Museum, Oxford

Dorman, Sir Maurice Henry (1912–1993)—© Kenneth Hughes / National Portrait Gallery, London

Dorn, Marion V. (1896–1964)—© National Portrait Gallery, London

Dorrien, Sir Horace Lockwood Smith- (1858–1930)—© National Portrait Gallery, London

Dors, Diana (1931–1984)—Associated British-Pathe Ltd (courtesy Kobal)

D'Orsay, Gédéon Gaspard Alfred de Grimaud, styled Count D'Orsay (1801–1852)—© National Portrait Gallery, London

Doubleday, Henry (1808–1875)—courtesy of the Library Committee of the Religious Society of Friends in Britain

Douce, Francis (1757–1834)—© Bodleian Library, University of Oxford

Doughty, Charles Montagu (1843–1926)—© National Portrait Gallery, London

Douglas, Lord Alfred Bruce (1870–1945)—© National Portrait Gallery, London

Douglas, Archibald James Edward, first Baron Douglas (1748–1827)—in the collection of Lennoxlove House; photograph courtesy the Scottish National Portrait Gallery

Douglas, Aretas Akers-, first Viscount Chilston (1851–1926)—© National Portrait Gallery, London

Douglas, Charles, third duke of Queensberry and second duke of Dover (1698–1778)—private collection; photograph National Galleries of Scotland

Douglas, Frances, Lady Douglas (1750–1817)—in a private Scottish collection

Douglas, Sir Howard, third baronet (1776–1861)—© National Portrait Gallery, London

Douglas, James, fourth earl of Morton (c.1516–1581)—Scottish National Portrait Gallery

Douglas, James, second duke of Queensberry and first duke of Dover (1662–1711)—Chatsworth House. Photograph: Photographic Survey, Courtauld Institute of Art, London

Douglas, James, fourteenth earl of Morton (1702–1768)—Scottish National Portrait Gallery

Douglas, Lady Jane (1698–1753)—© reserved; private collection

Douglas, John (1721–1807)—reproduced by kind permission of His Grace the Archbishop of Canterbury and the Church Commissioners. Photograph: Photographic Survey, Courtauld Institute of Art, London

Douglas, John (1830–1911)—RIBA Library Photographs Collection

Douglas, John Sholto, ninth marquess of Queensberry (1844–1900)—Horsham Museum (Horsham District Council); photograph National Portrait Gallery, London

Douglas, Keith Castellain (1920–1944)—© reserved; Brotherton Collection, University of Leeds; © reserved in the photograph

Douglas, Lady Margaret, countess of Lennox (1515–1578)—The Royal Collection © 2004 HM Queen Elizabeth II

Douglas, (George) Norman (1868–1952)—© Cecil Beaton Archive, Sotheby's; collection National Portrait Gallery, London

Douglas, Robert (1747–1820)—photograph by courtesy Sotheby's Picture Library, London

Douglas, (William) Sholto, Baron Douglas of Kirtleside (1893–1969)—© National Portrait Gallery, London

Douglas, Sylvester, Baron Glenbervie (1743–1823)—private collection

Douglas, Thomas, fifth earl of Selkirk (1771–1820)—Glenbow Archives, Calgary, Alberta (NA 2247-1)

Douglas, William, seventh earl of Morton (1582–1648)—Scottish National Portrait Gallery

Doulton, Sir Henry (1820–1897)—private collection / National Portrait Gallery, London

Dove, Evelyn Mary (1902–1987)—Collection Stephen Bourne

Dove, Dame (Jane) Frances (1847–1942)—© National Portrait Gallery, London

Dove, Thomas (1555–1630)—reproduced by kind permission of the Bishop of Peterborough; photograph: The Paul Mellon Centre for Studies in British Art

Dowden, Edward (1843–1913)—National Gallery of Ireland

Dowding, Hugh Caswall Tremenheere, first Baron Dowding (1882–1970)—© National Portrait Gallery, London

Dower, Kenneth Cecil Gandar- (1908–1944)—Getty Images – Hulton Archive

Downes, William, first Baron Downes (1751–1826)—photograph by courtesy Sotheby's Picture Library, London

Downey, Richard Joseph (1881–1953)—© National Portrait Gallery, London

Downing, Sir George, third baronet (1685–1749)—The Master, Fellows, and Scholars of Downing College in the University of Cambridge

Dowty, Sir George Herbert (1901–1975)—Royal Aeronautical Society Library

Doyle, Sir Arthur Ignatius Conan (1859–1930)—by permission of the E. O. Hoppé Trust, Curatorial Assistance, Inc., Los Angeles

Doyle, Sir Charles Hastings (1804–1883)—Lawrence's; photograph National Portrait Gallery, London

Doyle, Sir Francis Hastings Charles, second baronet (1810–1888)—© National Portrait Gallery, London

Doyle, Sir John, baronet (1756–1834)—Edward Reeves, Lewes, Photographers

Doyle, John [H. B.] (1797–1868)—© National Portrait Gallery, London

Doyle, Richard [Dick Kitcat] (1824–1883)—© National Portrait Gallery, London

D'Oyly, Sir Charles, seventh baronet (1781–1845)—HSBC Holdings plc

Dragonetti, Domenico Carlo Maria (1763–1846)—© National Portrait Gallery, London

Drake, Sir Francis (1540–1596)—© Copyright The British Museum

Drake, Francis (bap. 1696, d. 1771)—York City Art Gallery

Drane, Augusta Theodosia (1823–1894)—English Dominican Congregation, Stone

Drayton, Michael (1563–1631)—© Copyright The British Museum

Drebbel, Cornelis (1572–1633)—© National Portrait Gallery, London

Drew, Mary (1847–1927)—© National Portrait Gallery, London

Dreyer, John Louis Emil (1852–1926)—Mary Lea Shane Archives of the Lick Observatory, University Library, University of California

Driberg, Thomas Edward Neil, Baron Bradwell (1905–1976)—© Estate of Ronald Franks; collection National Portrait Gallery, London

Drinkwater, John (1882–1937)—© Estate of Sir William Rothenstein / National Portrait Gallery, London

Druce, George Claridge (1850–1932)—The de László Foundation; © Bodleian Library, University of Oxford

Drummond, (James) Eric, seventh earl of Perth (1876–1951)—© National Portrait Gallery, London

Drummond, Flora McKinnon (1878–1949)—© Museum of London

Drummond, George (1687–1766)—Scottish National Portrait Gallery

Drummond, Henry (c.1730–1795)—Collection of the Duke of

Northumberland. Photograph: Photographic Survey, Courtauld Institute of Art, London

Drummond, Henry (1786–1860)—© National Portrait Gallery, London

Drummond, Henry (1851–1897)—© National Portrait Gallery, London

Drummond, James, fourth earl of Perth and Jacobite first duke of Perth (1648–1716)—private collection

Drummond, James, styled fifth earl of Perth and Jacobite second duke of Perth (1674–1720)—Scottish National Portrait Gallery

Drummond, James, styled sixth earl of Perth and Jacobite third duke of Perth (1713–1746)—© reserved

Drummond, John, styled first earl of Melfort and Jacobite first duke of Melfort (1649–1714)—Scottish National Portrait Gallery

Drummond, John, styled seventh earl of Perth and Jacobite fourth duke of Perth (c.1714–1747)—Scottish National Portrait Gallery

Drummond, Dame (Edith) Margaret (1917–1987)—© National Portrait Gallery, London

Drummond, Robert Hay (1711–1776)—York City Art Gallery

Drummond, Thomas (1797–1840)—National Gallery of Ireland

Drummond, William, of Hawthornden (1585–1649)—Scottish National Portrait Gallery

Drummond, William Abernethy (b. before 1720, d. 1809)—Scottish National Portrait Gallery

Drummond, William Hamilton (1778–1865)—by courtesy of the National Gallery of Ireland

Drury, Sir William (1527–1579)—private collection; photograph © National Portrait Gallery, London

Dryander, Jonas Carlsson (1748–1810)—© National Portrait Gallery, London

Dryden, John (1631–1700)—The Master and Fellows, Trinity College, Cambridge

Dryland, Alfred (1865–1946)—© National Portrait Gallery, London

Oxford dictionary of
national biography